LIFE-SPAN
DEVELOPMENT

Eighteenth Edition

LIFE-SPAN
DEVELOPMENT

Eighteenth Edition

JOHN W. SANTROCK
University of Texas at Dallas

LIFE-SPAN DEVELOPMENT, EIGHTEENTH EDITION

Published by McGraw-Hill LLC, 1325 Avenue of the Americas, New York, NY 10121. Copyright ©2021 by McGraw-Hill LLC. All rights reserved. Printed in the United States of America. Previous editions ©2019, 2017, and 2015. No part of this publication may be reproduced or distributed in any form or by any means, or stored in a database or retrieval system, without the prior written consent of McGraw-Hill LLC, including, but not limited to, in any network or other electronic storage or transmission, or broadcast for distance learning.

Some ancillaries, including electronic and print components, may not be available to customers outside the United States.

This book is printed on acid-free paper.

1 2 3 4 5 6 7 8 9 LWI 24 23 22 21 20

ISBN 978-1-260-24584-4 (bound edition)
MHID 1-260-24584-5 (bound edition)
ISBN 978-1-260-47196-0 (loose-leaf edition)
MHID 1-260-47196-9 (loose-leaf edition)

Senior Portfolio Manager: *Ryan Treat*
Product Development Manager: *Dawn Groundwater*
Senior Product Developer: *Lauren Finn*
Marketing Manager: *Olivia Kaiser*
Lead Content Project Managers: *Mary E. Powers, Jodi Banowetz*
Buyer: *Sandy Ludovissy*
Designer: *David W. Hash*
Content Licensing Specialists: *Carrie Burger*
Cover Images: (group): *Monkey Business Images/Shutterstock; (baby): pkproject/Shutterstock; (child): Africa Studio/Shutterstock; (teens): Asiseeit/E+/Getty Images*
Compositor: *Aptara®, Inc.*

All credits appearing on page or at the end of the book are considered to be an extension of the copyright page.

Library of Congress Cataloging-in-Publication Data

Names: Santrock, John W., author.
Title: Life-span development / John Santrock, University of Texas at
  Dallas.
Description: Eighteenth edition. | New York, NY : McGraw-Hill Education,
  [2021] | Includes index.
Identifiers: LCCN 2020017548 (print) | LCCN 2020017549 (ebook) | ISBN
  9781260245844 (hardcover) | ISBN 9781260471960 (spiral bound) | ISBN
  9781260471953 (ebook) | ISBN 9781260471984 (ebook other)
Subjects: LCSH: Developmental psychology.
Classification: LCC BF713 .S26 2021 (print) | LCC BF713 (ebook) | DDC
  155–dc23
LC record available at https://lccn.loc.gov/2020017548
LC ebook record available at https://lccn.loc.gov/2020017549

The Internet addresses listed in the text were accurate at the time of publication. The inclusion of a website does not indicate an endorsement by the authors or McGrawHill LLC, and McGrawHill LLC does not guarantee the accuracy of the information presented at these sites.

brief contents

McGraw-Hill Education Psychology's APA Documentation Style Guide

contents

SECTION 1 THE LIFE-SPAN PERSPECTIVE   1

Prostock-studio/Shutterstock

SECTION 2 BEGINNINGS   47

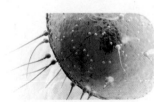
MedicalRF.com/Getty Images

SECTION 4 EARLY CHILDHOOD 197

Rawpixel.com/Shutterstock

BartCo/Getty Images

about the **author**

John W. Santrock

John Santrock received his Ph.D. from the University of Minnesota. He taught at the University of Charleston and the University of Georgia before joining the Program in Psychology at the University of Texas at Dallas, where he currently teaches a number of undergraduate courses and received the University's Effective Teaching Award. In 2010, he created the UT-Dallas Santrock undergraduate travel scholarship, an annual award that is given to outstanding undergraduate students majoring in developmental psychology to enable them to attend research conventions. In 2019, he created an endowment that will provide the travel awards for students at UT-Dallas for decades to come. Additionally, Dr. Santrock and his wife, Mary Jo, created a permanent endowment that will provide academic scholarships for six to ten undergraduate psychology students per year, with preference given to those majoring in developmental psychology.

John Santrock (back row middle) with recipients of the Santrock Travel Scholarship Award in developmental psychology. Created by Dr. Santrock, this annual award provides undergraduate students with the opportunity to attend a professional meeting. A number of the students shown here attended the meeting of the Society for Research in Child Development.
Jessica Serna

John has been a member of the editorial boards of *Child Development* and *Developmental Psychology*. His research on father custody is widely cited and used in expert witness testimony to promote flexibility and alternative considerations in custody disputes. John also has authored these exceptional McGraw-Hill texts: *Children* (14th edition), *Adolescence* (17th edition), *A Topical Approach to Life-Span Development* (10th edition), and *Educational Psychology* (6th edition).

For many years, John was involved in tennis as a player, teaching professional, and coach of professional tennis players. At the University of Miami (FL), the tennis team on which he played still holds the NCAA Division I record for most consecutive wins (137) in any sport. John has been married for four decades to his wife, Mary Jo, who created and directed the first middle school program for children with learning disabilities and behavioral disorders in the Clarke County Schools in Athens, Georgia. More recently, Mary Jo has worked as a Realtor. He has two daughters—Tracy, who worked for a number of years as a technology marketing specialist, and Jennifer, who has been a medical sales specialist. Both have followed in their mother's footsteps and are now Realtors. Jennifer was inducted into the SMU sports hall of fame, only the fifth female to ever have been given this award. He has one granddaughter, Jordan, age 27, who works for the accounting firm Ernst & Young, and two grandsons, Alex, age 15, and Luke, age 13. In the last two decades, John also has spent time painting divisionist and expressionist art.

Dedication:

With special appreciation to my mother, Ruth Santrock, and my father, John Santrock.

expert consultants

Life-span development has become an enormous, complex field, and no single author, or even several authors, can possibly keep up with all of the rapidly changing content in the many periods and different areas of life-span development. To solve this problem, author John Santrock has sought the input of leading experts about content in a number of areas of life-span development. These experts have provided detailed evaluations and recommendations in their area(s) of expertise.

The following individuals were among those who served as expert consultants for one or more of the previous editions of this text:

Urie Bronfenbrenner, *Cornell University*

K. Warner Schaie, *Pennsylvania State University*

Paul Baltes, *Max Planck Institute, Berlin*

Tiffany Field, *University of Miami*

James Birren, *University of Southern California*

Jean Berko Gleason, *Boston University*

Gilbert Gottlieb, *University of North Carolina–Chapel Hill*

Karen Adolph, *New York University*

Joseph Campos, *University of California–Berkeley*

George Rebok, *Johns Hopkins University*

Jean Mandler, *University of California–San Diego*

James Marcia, *Concordia University*

Andrew Meltzoff, *University of Washington*

Elizabeth Susman, *Pennsylvania State University*

David Almeida, *Pennsylvania State University*

John Schulenberg, *University of Michigan*

Margie Lachman, *Brandeis University*

Crystal Park, *University of Connecticut*

James Garbarino, *Cornell University*

Elena Grigorenko, *Yale University*

William Hoyer, *Syracuse University*

Ross Parke, *University of California–Riverside*

Ross Thompson, *University of California–Davis*

Phyllis Moen, *University of Minnesota*

Ravenna Helson, *University of California–Berkeley*

Patricia Reuter-Lorenz, *University of Michigan*

Toni Antonucci, *University of Michigan*

Scott Johnson, *University of California–Los Angeles*

Patricia Miller, *San Francisco State University*

Amanda Rose, *University of Missouri–Columbia*

Arthur Kramer, *University of Illinois*

Karen Fingerman, *Purdue University*

Cigdem Kagitcibasi, *Koc University*

Robert Kastenbaum, *Arizona State University*

Following are the expert consultants for the eighteenth edition, who (like those of previous editions) literally represent a *Who's Who* in the field of life-span development.

Charles Nelson Dr. Nelson is one of the world's leading neuroscientists in the field of child development. He is currently Professor of Pediatrics and Neuroscience and Professor of Psychology in the Department of Psychiatry at Harvard Medical School, and Professor of Education in the Harvard Graduate School of Education. Dr. Nelson also holds the Richard David Scott Chair in Pediatric Developmental Medicine Research at Boston Children's Hospital and serves as Director of Research in the Division of Developmental Medicine. His research interests center on a variety of problems in developmental cognitive neuroscience, including the development of social perception; developmental trajectories to autism; and the effects of early adversity on brain and behavioral development. Dr. Nelson chaired the John D. and Catherine T. MacArthur Foundation Research Network on Early Experience and Brain Development and served on the National Academy of Sciences (NAS) panels that wrote *From Neurons to Neighborhoods*, and more recently, *New Directions in Child Abuse and Neglect Research*. Among his many honors, he has received the Leon Eisenberg award from Harvard Medical School and an honorary Doctorate from Bucharest University (Romania), was a resident fellow at the Rockefeller Foundation Bellagio Center (Italy), has been elected to the American Academy of Arts and Sciences and the National Academy of Medicine, and has received the Ruane Prize for Child and Adolescent Psychiatric Research from the Brain & Behavior Research Foundation.

". . . I loved the book. It continues to be written in an engaging way. John's mastery of the literature is extraordinary and, honestly, there is very little that is missing from the book. In a word, if I still taught an introductory course in developmental psychology, I'm sure I would adopt this book." **–Charles Nelson, *Harvard University***

Laura Carstensen Dr. Carstensen is one of the world's leading experts on socioemotional development and aging. She currently is Professor of Psychology and the Fairleigh S. Dickinson Jr. Professor in Public Policy at Stanford University where she serves as founding director of the Stanford Center on Longevity. Dr. Carstensen's research has been supported continuously by the National Institute on Aging for more than 25 years and she is currently supported through a prestigious MERIT Award. In 2011, she authored the book, *A Long Bright Future: Happiness, Health, and Financial Security in an Age of Increased Longevity*. Dr. Carstensen has served on the National Advisory Council on Aging and the

MacArthur Foundation's Research Network on an Aging Society. In 2016, she was inducted into the National Academy of Medicine. Dr. Carstensen has won numerous awards, including the Kleemeier Award from the Gerontological Society of America, a Guggenheim fellowship, and the Master Mentor Award from the American Psychological Association. She also received a BS from the University of Rochester and Ph.D. in clinical psychology from West Virginia University.

"It's a great textbook." —**Laura Carstensen,** *Stanford University*

Photo courtesy of
Lauren H. Adams

James Graham Dr. Graham is a leading expert on the community aspects of ethnicity, culture, and development. He obtained his undergraduate degree from Miami University and received masters and doctoral degrees in developmental psychology from the University of Memphis. Dr. Graham's current position is Professor of Psychology, The College of New Jersey (TCNJ). His research addresses the social-cognitive aspects of relationships between group and dyadic levels across developmental periods in community-based settings. Three interdependent dimensions of his research program examine (1) populations that are typically understudied, conceptually limited, and methodologically constrained; (2) development of empathy and prosocial behavior with peer groups and friends; and (3) developmental science in the context of community-engaged research partnerships. Currently, he is Coordinator of the Developmental Specialization in Psychology at TCNJ. For a decade, Dr. Graham taught graduate courses in psychology and education in Johannesburg, South Africa, through TCNJ's Graduate Summer Global Program. He also is the co-author of *The African American Child: Development and Challenges* (2nd ed.) and *Children of Incarcerated Parents: Theoretical, Developmental, and Clinical Issues.* Dr. Graham has presented his work at a variety of international and national conferences and has published articles in a wide range of journals, including *Social Development, Child Study Journal, Behavior Modification, Journal of Multicultural Counseling and Development,* and *American Journal of Evaluation.*

"John Santrock seamlessly integrates the latest research on the physical, cognitive, and social processes of children in an ever-evolving multicultural society. . . . I am impressed with his sensitivity to the impact of culture, ethnicity, and socioeconomic status on child and adolescent development. . . .The text will help students learn to analyze, compare, and contrast alternative perspectives on children domestically and globally. . . . The text also will help students to understand the latest research regarding societal values about ethnicity, socioeconomic, and gender issues in child development, and how they influence individual growth as well as shape public policy."
—**James Graham,** *The College of New Jersey*

Photo courtesy of
Virginia Tech

Martha Ann Bell Dr. Bell is one of the world's leading experts on infants' and young children's cognitive development and socioemotional development. She obtained her Ph.D. from the University of Maryland and currently is Professor and College of Science Faculty Fellow at Virginia Tech University. Her research focuses on cognitive, emotional, and psychophysical processes associated with frontal lobe development in infants and children, with an emphasis on executive function, emotion regulation, and temperament. Her research is funded by the National Institutes of Health and published in leading developmental psychology journals such as *Child Development* and *Developmental Science.* Dr. Bell is an elected member of the Executive Board of the American Psychological Association (developmental division). She has been the Chief Editor of the journal *Infancy,* became an elected member of Executive Board of the International Society for Developmental Psychobiology, and was the recent chair of the *Cognition and Emotion* grant review panel at NIH. Dr. Bell is a fellow of the American Psychological Association (developmental and experimental/cognitive divisions) and of the Association for Psychological Science, as well as a recent recipient of the Senior Investigator Award from the International Society for Developmental Psychobiology.

"I have been a huge fan of this life-span text for many years. It is simply the best in the field because of its consistent high quality (especially its focus on the most important and timely research) from one edition to the next. It is a 'beautiful' textbook, meaning it is appealing and easy to read. The way it is organized makes you want to read it. And the little nudges throughout to go back and think about previous chapters is excellent." —**Martha Ann Bell,**
Virginia Tech University

Photo courtesy of
Robert Lickliter

David Moore Dr. Moore is a leading expert on infant perceptual and cognitive development, and on genetic and environmental influences on development. He obtained a Ph.D. in developmental and biological psychology from Harvard University. After completing a postdoctoral fellowship at the City University of New York, he joined the faculties of Pitzer College and Claremont Graduate University, where he currently is a professor of psychology. Dr. Moore's empirical research has produced numerous publications on the development of mental rotation in infancy, on the electrophysiological measurement of covert attention in infants, and on the emergence of infants' nascent "mathematical" competence. His theoretical writings have explored the contributions of genetic, environmental, and epigenetic factors to human development. His 2002 book, *The Dependent Gene,* was widely adopted for use in undergraduate education and was translated into Japanese. His 2015 book, *The Developing Genome: An Introduction to Behavioral Epigenetics,* won both the William James Book Award and the Eleanor Maccoby Book Award from the American Psychological Association (APA). Dr. Moore has served on the consulting editorial board of *Child Development Perspectives* and is currently a Member-at-Large of the Executive Committee of the APA's Developmental Psychology Division. From 2016 to 2018, he also served as the Director of the U.S. National Science Foundation's Developmental Sciences Program in Washington, D.C.

"I think this chapter (Biological Beginnings) will make an important contribution to the textbook. I think this book's primary strength is the clear, direct, and engaging way in which it has been written. I especially appreciate John Santrock's efforts to keep the book very up-to-date, both in terms of research-connected content and its supplementary materials. I also like the decision to find ways to encourage students to think about 'their own personal journey through life.'" —**David Moore,** *Pitzer College and Claremont University*

Connecting *research* and *results*

As a master teacher, John Santrock connects current research and real-world applications. Through an integrated, personalized digital learning program, students gain the insight they need to study smarter and improve performance.

McGraw-Hill Education's **Connect** is a digital assignment and assessment platform that strengthens the link between faculty, students, and coursework, helping everyone accomplish more in less time. *Connect Psychology* includes assignable and assessable videos, quizzes, exercises, and interactivities, all associated with learning objectives. Interactive assignments and videos allow students to experience and apply their understanding of psychology to the world with fun and stimulating activities.

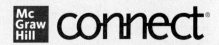

Apply Concepts and Theory in an Experiential Learning Environment

An engaging and innovative learning game, **Quest: Journey Through the Lifespan** provides students with opportunities to apply content from their human development curriculum to real-life scenarios. Students play unique characters who range in age and make decisions that apply key concepts and theories for each age as they negotiate events in an array of authentic environments. Additionally, as students analyze real-world behaviors and contexts, they are exposed to different cultures and intersecting biological, cognitive, and socioemotional processes. Each quest has layered replayability, allowing students to make new choices each time they play—or offering different students in the same class different experiences. Fresh possibilities and outcomes shine light on the complexity of and variations in real human development. This new experiential learning game includes follow-up questions, assignable in Connect and auto-graded, to reach a higher level of critical thinking.

Real People, Real World, Real Life

At the higher end of Bloom's taxonomy (analyze, evaluate, create), the McGraw-Hill Education **Milestones** video series is an observational tool that allows students to experience life as it unfolds, from infancy to late adulthood. This ground-breaking, longitudinal video series tracks the development of real children as they progress through the early stages of physical, social, and emotional development in their first few weeks, months, and years of life. Assignable and assessable within Connect Psychology, Milestones also includes interviews with adolescents and adults to reflect development throughout the entire life span. New to this edition, Milestones are available in a more engaging, WCAG-compliant format. Ask your McGraw-Hill representative about this new upgrade!

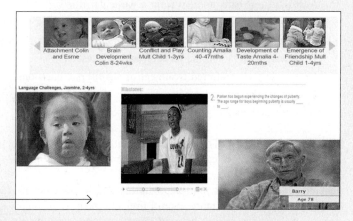

Develop Effective Responses

McGraw-Hill's new **Writing Assignment Plus** tool delivers a learning experience that improves students' written communication skills and conceptual understanding with every assignment. Assign, monitor, and provide feedback on writing more efficiently and grade assignments within McGraw-Hill Connect. Writing Assignment Plus gives you time-saving tools with a just-in-time basic writing and originality checker.

Prepare Students for Higher-Level Thinking

Also at the higher end of Bloom's taxonomy, **Power of Process** for Psychology helps students improve critical thinking skills and allows instructors to assess these skills efficiently and effectively in an online environment. Available through Connect, pre-loaded journal articles are available for instructors to assign. Using a scaffolded framework such as understanding, synthesizing, and analyzing, Power of Process moves students toward higher-level thinking and analysis.

Better Data, Smarter Revision, Improved Results

McGraw-Hill Education's **SmartBook** helps students distinguish the concepts they know from the concepts they don't, while pinpointing the concepts they are about to forget. SmartBook's real-time reports help both students and instructors identify the concepts that require more attention, making study sessions and class time more efficient.

SmartBook is optimized for mobile and tablet use and is accessible for students with disabilities. Content-wise, measurable and observable learning objectives help improve student outcomes. SmartBook personalizes learning to individual student needs, continually adapting to pinpoint knowledge gaps and focus learning on topics that need the most attention. Study time is more productive and, as a result, students are better prepared for class and coursework. For instructors, SmartBook tracks student progress and provides insights that can help guide teaching strategies.

Online Instructor Resources

The resources listed here accompany *Life-Span Development,* Eighteenth Edition. Please contact your McGraw-Hill representative for details concerning the availability of these and other valuable materials that can help you design and enhance your course.

Instructor's Manual   Broken down by chapter, this resource provides chapter outlines, suggested lecture topics, classroom activities and demonstrations, suggested student research projects, essay questions, and critical thinking questions.

Test Bank and Test Builder   This comprehensive Test Bank includes more than 1,500 multiple-choice, short answer, and essay questions. Organized by chapter, the questions are designed to test factual, applied, and conceptual knowledge. New to this edition and available within Connect, Test Builder is a cloud-based tool that enables instructors to format tests that can be printed and administered within a Learning Management System. Test Builder offers a modern, streamlined interface for easy content configuration that matches course needs without requiring a download. Test Builder enables instructors to:

- Access all test bank content from a particular title
- Easily pinpoint the most relevant content through robust filtering options
- Manipulate the order of questions or scramble questions and/or answers
- Pin questions to a specific location within a test
- Determine your preferred treatment of algorithmic questions
- Choose the layout and spacing
- Add instructions and configure default settings

PowerPoint Slides   The PowerPoint presentations, now WCAG compliant, highlight the key points of the chapter and include supporting visuals. All of the slides can be modified to meet individual needs.

Remote Proctoring   New remote proctoring and browser-locking capabilities are seamlessly integrated within Connect to offer more control over the integrity of online assessments. Instructors can enable security options that restrict browser activity, monitor student behavior, and verify the identity of each student. Instant and detailed reporting gives instructors an at-a-glance view of potential concerns, thereby avoiding personal bias and supporting evidence-based claims.

preface

Making Connections . . . From My Classroom to *Life-Span Development* to You

Having taught life-span development every semester for more than three decades, I'm always looking for ways to improve my course and *Life-Span Development*. Just as McGraw-Hill looks to those who teach the life-span development course for input, each year I ask the almost 200 students in my life-span development course to tell me what they like about the course and the text, and what they think could be improved. What have my students told me lately about my course and text? Students say that highlighting connections among the different aspects of life-span development helps them to better understand the concepts. They confirm that a *connections* theme provides a systematic, integrative approach to the course material. Thus, I have continued to use this theme to shape my current goals for my life-span development course, which, in turn, are incorporated into *Life-Span Development:*

1. **Connecting with today's students** To help students learn about life-span development more effectively.

2. **Connecting research to what we know about development** To provide students with the best and most recent theory and research in the world today about each of the periods of the human life span.

3. **Connecting developmental processes** To guide students in making developmental connections across different points in the human life span.

4. **Connecting development to the real world** To help students understand ways to apply content about the human life span to the real world and improve people's lives; and to motivate them to think deeply about their own personal journey through life and better understand who they were, are, and will be.

Connecting with Today's Students

In *Life-Span Development,* I recognize that today's students are as different in some ways from the learners of the last generation as today's discipline of life-span development is different from the field 30 years ago. Students now learn in multiple modalities; rather than sitting down and reading traditional printed chapters in linear fashion from beginning to end, their work preferences tend to be more visual and more interactive, and their reading and study often occur in short bursts. For many students, a traditionally formatted printed textbook is no longer enough when they have instant, 24/7 access to news and information from around the globe. Two features that specifically support today's students are the adaptive ebook, Smartbook (see xviii), and the learning goals system.

The Learning Goals System

My students often report that the life-span development course is challenging because of the amount of material covered. To help today's students focus on the key ideas, the Learning Goals System I developed for *Life-Span Development* provides extensive learning connections throughout the chapters. The learning system connects the chapter opening outline, learning goals for the chapter, mini-chapter maps that open each main section of the chapter, *Review,*

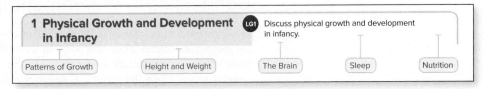

reach your learning goals

Physical Development in Infancy

1 Physical Growth and Development in Infancy **LG1** Discuss physical growth and development in infancy.

Patterns of Growth
- The cephalocaudal pattern is the sequence in which growth proceeds from top to bottom. The proximodistal pattern is the sequence in which growth starts at the center of the body and moves toward the extremities.

Height and Weight
- The average North American newborn is 20 inches long and weighs 7.6 pounds. Infants grow about 1 inch per month in the first year and nearly triple their weight by their first birthday. The rate of growth slows in the second year.

The Brain
- One of the most dramatic changes in the brain in the first two years of life is dendritic spreading, which increases the connections between neurons. Myelination, which speeds the conduction of nerve impulses, continues through infancy and even into adolescence.

- The cerebral cortex has two hemispheres (left and right). Lateralization refers to specialization of function in one hemisphere or the other. Early experiences play an important role in

Connect, and Reflect questions at the end of each main section, and the chapter summary at the end of each chapter.

The learning system keeps the key ideas in front of the student from the beginning to the end of the chapter. The main headings of each chapter correspond to the learning goals that are presented in the chapter-opening spread. Mini-chapter maps that link up with the learning goals are presented at the beginning of each major section in the chapter.

Then, at the end of each main section of a chapter, the learning goal is repeated in *Review, Connect, and Reflect,* which prompts students to review the key topics in the section, connect to existing knowledge, and relate what they learned to their own personal journey through life. *Reach Your Learning Goals,* at the end of the chapter, guides students through the bulleted chapter review, connecting with the chapter outline/learning goals at the beginning of the chapter and the *Review, Connect, and Reflect* questions at the end of major chapter sections.

connecting through research

How Does the Quality and Quantity of Child Care Affect Children?

In 1991, the National Institute of Child Health and Human Development (NICHD) began a comprehensive, longitudinal study of child-care experiences. Data were collected on a diverse sample of almost 1,400 children and their families at 10 locations across the United States over a period of seven years. Researchers used multiple methods (trained observers, interviews, questionnaires, and testing) and measured many facets of children's development, including physical health, cognitive development, and socioemotional development. Following are some of the results of what is now referred to as the NICHD Study of Early Child Care and Youth Development or NICHD SECCYD (NICHD Early Child Care Research Network, 2001, 2002, 2003, 2004, 2005, 2006, 2010).

- **Patterns of use.** Many families placed their infants in child care very soon after the child's birth, and there was considerable instability in the child-care arrangements. By 4 months of age, nearly three-fourths of the infants had entered some form of nonmaternal child care. Almost half of the infants were cared for by a relative when they first entered care; only 12 percent were enrolled in child-care centers.

  Socioeconomic factors were linked to the amount and type of care. For example, mothers with higher incomes and families that were more dependent on the mother's income placed their infants in child care at an earlier age. Mothers who believed that maternal employment has positive effects on children were more likely than other mothers to place their infant in nonmaternal care for more hours. Low-income families were more likely than more affluent families to use child care, but infants from low-income families who

What are some important findings from the national longitudinal study of child care conducted by the National Institute of Child Health and Human Development?
Reena Rose Sibayan/The Jersey Journal/Landov Images

linked with higher cognitive and social competence when children were 54 months of age. Using data collected as part of the NICHD early child care longitudinal study, a research analysis indicated that higher-quality early childhood care, especially at 27 months of age, was linked to children's higher vocabulary scores in the fifth grade (Belsky & others, 2007).

Higher-quality child care was also related to higher-quality mother-child interaction among the families that used nonmaternal care. Further, poor-quality care was related to higher rates of insecure attachment to the mother among infants who were 15 months of age, but only when the mother was low in sensitivity and responsiveness. However, child-care quality was not linked to attachment security at 36 months of age. In one study, higher-quality child care

Connecting Research to What We Know about Development

Over the years, it has been important for me to include the most up-to-date research available. I continue that tradition in this edition by looking closely at specific areas of research, involving experts in related fields, and updating research throughout. *Connecting Through Research* describes a study or program to illustrate how research in life-span development is conducted and how it influences our understanding of the discipline. Topics range from *How Can Newborns' Perception Be Studied?* to *Parenting and Children's Achievement: My Child Is My Report Card, Tiger Mothers,* and *Tiger Babies Strike Back* to *What Is the Relationship Between Fitness in Young Adults and Cardiovascular Health in Middle Age?* to *Does Engaging in Intellectually Challenging Activities Affect Quality of Life and Longevity?*

The tradition of obtaining detailed, extensive input from a number of leading experts in different areas of life-span development also continues in this edition. Biographies and photographs of the leading experts in the field of life-span development appear on pages xv to xvi, and the chapter-by-chapter highlights of new research content are listed on pages xxiii to xlvi. Finally, the research discussions have been updated in every period and topic. I expended every effort to make this edition of *Life-Span Development* as contemporary and up-to-date as possible. To that end, there are more than 1,500 citations from 2018 to 2021.

Connecting Developmental Processes

Development through the life span is a long journey, and too often we forget or fail to notice the many connections from one point in development to another. A significant number of these connections are made in the text narrative, and features are included to help students connect topics across the periods of development.

Developmental Connections, which appear multiple times in each chapter, point readers to where the topic is discussed in a previous or subsequent chapter. *Developmental Connections* highlight links across age periods of development *and* connections between biological, cognitive, and socioemotional processes. These key developmental processes are typically discussed in isolation from each other, and students often fail to see their connections. Included in the *Developmental Connection* is a brief description of the backward or forward connection. For example, consider the development of the brain. In recent editions, I have significantly expanded content on the changes in the brain through the life span, including new coverage of changes in the brain during prenatal development and an expanded discussion of the aging brain in older adults. The prenatal brain discussion appears in "Prenatal Development and Birth" and the aging brain is described in "Physical Development in Late Adulthood." An important brain topic that we discuss in these two chapters is neurogenesis, the production of new neurons. Connections between these topics in these two chapters are highlighted through *Developmental Connections.*

Topical Connections: Looking Back and *Looking Forward* begin and conclude each chapter by placing the chapter's coverage in the larger context of development. These sections remind the reader of what happened developmentally in previous periods of development and make connections to topics that will be discussed in more detail.

Finally, a *Connect* question appears in the section self-reviews—*Review, Connect, and Reflect*—so students can practice making connections between topics. For example, in "Physical and Cognitive Development in Middle and Late Childhood," students are asked to connect what they learned about attention in "Cognitive Development in Infancy" and "Cognitive Development in Early Childhood" with what they have just read about attention deficit hyperactivity disorder in the middle and late childhood chapter.

> developmental **connection**
>
> **Executive Function**
>
> In early childhood, executive function especially involves developmental advances in cognitive inhibition, cognitive flexibility, goal-setting, and delay of gratification. Connect to "Physical and Cognitive Development in Early Childhood."

> topical **connections** *looking **back***
>
> We have discussed that impressive advances occur in the development of the brain during infancy. Engaging in various physical, cognitive, and socioemotional activities strengthens the baby's neural connections. Motor and perceptual development also are key aspects of the infant's development. An important part of this development is the coupling of perceptions and actions. The nature-nurture issue continues to be debated with regard to the infant's perceptual development. In this chapter, you will expand your understanding of the infant's brain, motor, and perceptual development by further examining how infants develop their competencies, focusing on how advances in their cognitive development help them adapt to their world, and how the nature-nurture issue is a key aspect of the infant's cognitive and language development.

Connecting Development to the Real World

In addition to helping students make research and developmental connections, *Life-Span Development* shows the important connections between the concepts discussed and the real world. In recent years, students in my life-span development course have increasingly told me that they want more of this type of information. In this edition, real-life connections are explicitly made through the chapter opening vignette, *Connecting Development to Life,* the *Milestones* program that helps students watch life as it unfolds, and *Connecting with Careers.*

Each chapter begins with a story designed to increase students' interest and motivation to read the chapter. For example, "Cognitive Development in Late Adulthood" begins with a description of the remarkable Helen Small, who published her first book at age 91 and completed her undergraduate degree 70 years after she started college.

Connecting Development to Life describes the influence of development in a real-world context on topics including *From Waterbirth to Music Therapy, Increasing Children's Self-Esteem,* and *Health Care Providers and Older Adults.*

The *Milestones* program, described on page xvii, shows students what developmental concepts look like by letting them watch actual humans develop. Starting from infancy, students track several individuals, seeing them achieve major developmental milestones, both physically and cognitively. Clips continue through adolescence and adulthood, capturing attitudes toward issues such as family, sexuality, and death and dying.

> ### *connecting* development to life
>
> **Strategies for Parents and Their Young Adult Children**
>
> When adult children ask to return home to live, parents and their adult children should agree beforehand on the conditions and expectations. For example, they might discuss and agree on whether young adults will pay rent, wash their own clothes, cook their own meals, do any household chores, pay their phone bills, come and go as they please, be sexually active or drink alcohol at home, and so on. If these conditions aren't negotiated at the beginning, conflict often results because the expectations of parents and young adult children will likely be violated.
>
> Parents need to treat young adult children more like adults than children and to let go of much of their parenting role. Parents should interact with young adult children not as dependent children who need to be closely monitored and protected but rather as adults who are capable of responsible, mature behavior. Adult children have the right to choose how much they sleep and eat, how they dress, whom they choose as friends and lovers, what career they pursue, and how they spend
>
> *What are some strategies that can help parents and their young adult children get along better?*
> Fuse/Getty Images
>
> helicopter parenting was related to more negative emotional functioning, less competent decision making, and lower grades/poorer adjustment in college students (Luebbe & others, 2018).
>
> A new term that characterizes a number of parents today is "lawn mower parent"—a parent who goes to great lengths to prevent their child from experiencing adversity, stress, or failure. By "mowing down" obstacles and potential negative experiences for their children, these parents are not allowing their children to learn how to cope with such experiences themselves. After their children leave home, they are less likely to handle the pressure and challenges of life as well as they would have if their parents had provided them more space to make decisions and learn how to cope on their own.
>
> When they move back home, young adult children need to think about how they will need to change their behavior to make the living arrangement work. Elina Furman (2005) provides some good recommendations in *Boomerang*

Connecting with Careers profiles careers ranging from an educational psychologist to a toy designer to a marriage and family therapist to a research scientist at an educational center to a geriatric nurse—each of which requires knowledge about human development.

These career profiles include Gustavo Medrano, a clinical psychologist who works at the Family Institute at Northwestern University and provides therapy especially for Latino children; Dr. Faize Mustaf-Infante, a pediatrician who is passionate about preventing obesity in children; Dr. Melissa Jackson, a child and adolescent psychiatrist who provides therapy for children with a number of psychological disorders, including ADHD, anxiety, depression, and post-traumatic stress disorder; and Ahou Vaziri, a Teach for America Instructor and curriculum designer.

The careers highlighted extend from the Careers Appendix that provides a comprehensive overview of careers in life-span development to show students where knowledge of human development could lead them.

Part of applying development to the real world is understanding its impact on oneself. An important goal I have established for my life-span development course and this text is to motivate students to think deeply about their own journey of life. To further encourage students to make personal connections to content in the text, *Reflect: Your Own Personal Journey of Life* appears in the end-of-section review in each chapter. This feature involves a question that asks students to reflect on some aspect of the discussion in the section they have just read and connect it to their own life. For example, students are asked:

Do you think there is, was/will be a best age for you to be? If so, what is it? Why?

I always include this question in the first content lecture I give in life-span development, and it generates thoughtful and interesting class discussion. Early in the "Introduction" chapter is a research discussion on whether there is a best age to be, which includes recent research on the topic and a self-assessment that lets students evaluate their own life satisfaction. In addition, students are asked a number of personal connections questions in the photograph captions.

Content Revisions

A significant reason why *Life-Span Development* has been successfully used by instructors edition after edition is the painstaking effort and review that goes into making sure the text provides the latest research on all topic areas discussed in the classroom. This new edition is no exception, with more than 1,500 citations from 2018, 2019, 2020, and 2021.

New research and content that have especially been updated and expanded for this edition include health and well-being; development of the brain; culture and diversity; technology; and successful aging. Following is a sample of the many chapter-by-chapter changes that were made in this new edition of *Life-Span Development*.

Chapter 1: Introduction

- Revisions based on comments by leading diversity expert James Graham
- Update on life expectancy in the United States (Arias & Xu, 2019)
- New commentary that for the first time in history in the United States, in 2019 there were more individuals over 60 than under 18
- Greatly expanded discussion of high-interest topics related to health and well-being that are covered throughout this edition (Goode, 2020; Telljohann & others, 2020)
- Updated data on the percentage of U.S. children and adolescents 17 years and younger from different ethnic groups in 2017 and projected to 2050, with dramatic increases in Latino and Asian American children (ChildStats.gov, 2018)
- Updated data on the percentage of U.S. children and adolescents under age 18 living in poverty, including data reported separately for African American and Latino families, among whom the rates have declined since 2015 (Fontenot, Semega, & Kollar, 2018)
- Inclusion of a recent focus in the Ascend two-generation program on the importance of parents' education, economic stability, and overall health for their children's well-being (Ascend, 2019)
- New projections on the significant increase in older adults in the world, with predictions of a doubling of the population of individuals 60 and over and a tripling or quadrupling of those 80 and over by 2050 (United Nations, 2017)
- New commentary about how significant projected increases in the older population around the world make it necessary for countries to develop innovative policies and expanded services involving housing, employment, health care, and transportation
- Description of a recent research study that found older adults who were more conscientious and emotionally stable were less cognitively vulnerable (Duchek & others, 2020)
- Coverage of a recent study of cohort effects in which older adults report fewer constraints today than their counterparts 18 years ago, while younger adults report more constraints now than their counterparts 18 years ago (Drewelies & others, 2018)
- Inclusion of recent research across 150 countries indicating that health was a better predictor of life satisfaction in individuals 58 years and older than in younger age groups (Joshanloo & Jovanovic, 2019)
- Updated content on Bandura's (2018) social cognitive theory, in which he now emphasizes *forethought* as a key cognitive factor in the theory

- Updated content on cohort effects involving increased interest in a new generation, labeled generation Z and/or post-millennial, that is characterized by even greater technological immersion and sophistication, greater ethnic diversity, and higher educational attainment than the millennial generation (Dimock, 2019; Fry & Parker, 2018)

Chapter 2: Biological Beginnings

- Updates and revisions based on feedback from leading experts David Moore and Charles Nelson
- Expanded criticism of evolutionary psychology mentioning the difficulty of offering direct proof of an argument to support this view
- New criticism of the modularity of the human mind concept offered by evolutionary psychologists, pointing out that the human brain has extensive connections across different domains and does not function in nearly as compartmentalized a fashion as the modularity view proposes
- Updated data on the number of genes that humans have, now raised to 21,306 (Salzberg & others, 2018)
- Inclusion of loneliness as a factor that influences gene expression
- Updated and expanded research on how diet (Dasinger & others, 2020), tobacco use (Sugden & others, 2019), sleep (Lehtinen & others, 2019), obesity (Marousez, Lesage, & Eberle, 2020), and colorectal cancer (Alvizo-Rodriquez & others, 2020) can modify the expression of genes through the process of methylation
- Inclusion of recent research indicating that methylation may be involved in depression (Payne & others, 2020), breast cancer (Parashar & others, 2018), leukemia (Bewersdorf & others, 2019), and attention deficit hyperactivity disorder (Kim & others, 2018)
- New content on Prader-Willi syndrome that links mental health problems to genetic imprinting (Feieghan & others, 2020)
- Updated and expanded coverage of susceptibility genes, including those involved in arthritis (Reynard & Barter, 2020), cancer (Liu & Tan, 2019), and cardiovascular disease (Taylor & others, 2019)
- Updated and expanded research on gene-gene interaction to include immune system functioning (Kostel Bal & others, 2020), alcoholism (Chen & others, 2017), cancer (Lee & others, 2019), obesity (Wang & others, 2019), type 2 diabetes (Dominquez-Cruz & others, 2020), arthritis (Fathollahi & others, 2019), cardiovascular disease (Wang & others, 2020), and Alzheimer disease (Li & others, 2020)

- Coverage of a recent study that found XYY boys did not have more cognitive deficits than XY boys, but they did have more externalizing and internalizing problems (Operto & others, 2019)
- New content on the number of children born worldwide with sickle-cell anemia and how stem cell transplantation is being explored in the treatment of infants with sickle-cell anemia (Azar & Wong, 2017; Tanhehco & Bhatia, 2019)
- New content involving potential reduction or elimination of genetic diversity as genetic advances in prenatal testing allow pregnancy determination decisions to occur at earlier and earlier dates when termination is easier
- New coverage of cell-free fetal DNA in maternal blood and its testing as early as 10 weeks into the first trimester of pregnancy to test for such disorders as Down syndrome (Hui, 2019)
- Coverage of a recent study using non-invasive fetal diagnosis that determined fetal sex at 4.5 weeks (D'Aversa & others, 2018)
- Discussion of recent research indicating that a high level of oxidative stress is linked to male infertility and that a combination of oral antioxidants and lifestyle changes, such as reduced smoking and drinking, as well as increased exercise, may reduce male infertility (Barati, Nikzad, & Karimian, 2020)
- Description of the recent use of methylation to determine causes of infertility (Mohanty & others, 2020)
- Inclusion of a recent study that indicated birth fathers, who were often less likely to be included in open adoption, would like to be part of the open adoption triad (adoptee, birth family, and adoptive family) (Clutter, 2020)

Chapter 3: Prenatal Development and Birth

- New commentary about neurogenesis being largely complete by about the end of the fifth month of prenatal development (Borsani & others, 2019)
- Coverage of a recent study that confirmed a significant risk for suicidal behavior in adolescents with FASD (O'Connor & others, 2019)
- Inclusion of a recent study that revealed maternal alcohol use during pregnancy was associated with offsprings' anxiety, depression, and emotional problems, even at low to moderate levels of consumption (Easey & others, 2019)
- Discussion of a recent meta-analysis of 15 studies that concluded smoking during pregnancy increases offsprings' risk for ADHD and that the risk is greater if the mother is a heavy smoker (Huang & others, 2018)
- Description of a recent study that found a number of negative cognitive and behavioral outcomes for infants in the first year of life as a consequence of maternal cigarette smoking during pregnancy: negative affect, poorer attention, greater excitability, and more irritability (Froggatt, Covey, & Reissland, 2020)
- Coverage of a recent study in which higher maternal pregnancy-related stress was linked to more emotional symptoms, peer relationship problems, and overall child difficulties at 4 years of age (Acosta & others, 2019)

- New commentary that cessation of smoking by pregnant women by the third trimester is linked to improved birth outcomes (Crume, 2019)
- New coverage of a recent study in which chronic exposure to e-cigarette aerosols was linked to low birth weight in off-spring (Orzabal & others, 2019)
- Inclusion of a longitudinal study in which prenatal cocaine exposure was linked to early use of marijuana, arrest history, conduct disorder, and emotional regulation problems at 21 years of age (Richardson & others, 2019)
- Discussion of a recent study that found newborns born to mothers who had used marijuana during pregnancy were more likely to be born preterm or low birth weight (Petrangelo & others, 2019)
- Coverage of a recent study in which marijuana use during pregnancy was associated with an increased rate of chronic obstructive pulmonary disease in 4-year-old children (Villarreal & others, 2019)
- New section, "Synthetic Opioids and Opiate-Related Pain Killers," that discusses the increasing use of these substances by pregnant women and their possible harmful outcomes for pregnant women and their offspring (Clemens-Cope & others, 2019; Jantzie & others, 2020)
- Inclusion of a recent study that found that the offspring of mothers who had diabetes during pregnancy had an increased risk of developing early-onset cardiovascular disease in early adulthood (Yu & others, 2019)
- Discussion of evidence that being overweight and obese during pregnancy is linked to higher heart rate in the fetus (Mat Hustin & others, 2020)
- Discussion of a recent meta-analysis in which offspring of women who were overweight or obese had an increased risk of developing childhood diabetes and obesity (Hidayat, Zou, & Shi, 2019)
- Description of a recent study that found pregnant women 43 years and older were more likely to have infants who were stillborn (Wu & others, 2019)
- Inclusion of a recent, very large-scale study that indicated 40-year-old women had a twofold increased risk of having a stillborn baby, a risk that increased eightfold at 55 years of age (Mayo & others, 2019)
- New discussion of two recent studies that found advanced maternal age, especially 40 years and older, was linked to increased risk of offspring developing cancer in childhood (Contreras & others, 2017; Wang & others, 2017)
- Coverage of a recent study in which individuals whose mothers reported having higher levels of stress during pregnancy were at a higher risk of developing psychiatric disorders, such as mood disorders, later in life (Brannigan & others, 2019)
- Inclusion of a recent study that revealed prenatal maternal stress was associated with an increase in adolescent depressive symptoms (Davis & others, 2019)
- Discussion of a recent meta-analysis that concluded paternal smoking before and during pregnancy was linked to an increased risk of childhood leukemia (Cao, Lu, & Lu, 2020)

- Coverage of a recent study in which yoga was effective in reducing depressive symptoms in pregnant women (Ng & others, 2019)

- Inclusion of recent research indicating that pregnant women who exercised regularly in the second and third trimesters rated their quality of life higher (Krzepota, Sadowska, & Biernat, 2018)

- Description of a recent study that revealed regular exercise by pregnant women was linked to more advanced development in the neonatal brain (Laborte-Lemoyne, Currier, & Ellenberg, 2017)

- Updated data on the percentage of U.S. births attended by a midwife, which increased to 9.1 percent in 2017 (Center for Health Statistics, 2019)

- Coverage of a recent study in which one hour of traditional Thai massage decreased the duration of the first and second stage of labor (Sananpanichkul & others, 2019)

- Discussion of a recent large-scale study that found women who participated in CenteringPregnancy had offspring that were less likely to be born preterm or low birth weight (Cunningham & others, 2019)

- Inclusion of recent research that indicated women who participated in CenteringPregnancy used pain relief less during labor and were more likely to breast feed their infants (Rijnders & others, 2019)

- Coverage of a recent study of almost 27,000 births in the United States that found women giving birth in water had more favorable outcomes, including fewer prolonged first- and second-stage labors and less hemorrhaging (Snapp & others, 2020). Also in this study, newborns born in water were less likely to be transferred to a NICU, experience fetal heart rate abnormalities, or have respiratory complications.

- Update on cesarean delivery rates in the United States, which have declined from a high of 28.1 percent in 2009 to 25.9 percent in 2018 (Centers for Disease Control and Prevention, 2019)

- Updated data on the percentage of U.S. infants who are born preterm, including ethnic variations (March of Dimes, 2018)

- Updated weights for classification as a low birth weight baby, a very low birth weight baby, and an extremely low birth weight baby

- Coverage of a recent research review that concluded pregnant women's exercise was linked to a lower incidence of preterm birth (Matei & others, 2019)

- Coverage of a recent study that revealed a daily exercise program for 30 days improved the bone density and cortisol levels of very low birth weight preterm infants (Sezer Efe, Erdem, & Gunes, 2020)

- Updated data on the percentage of U.S. babies born at low birth weights, including ethnic variations (Centers for Disease Control and Prevention, 2018)

- Inclusion of a recent national study of 6- to 11-year-old children in which those born preterm had higher rates of developmental delay, intellectual disability, speech/language disorder, learning disability, and ADHD (Kelly & Li, 2019)

- Discussion of a recent study that revealed lower academic trajectories in elementary school for children born very preterm (Twilhaar & others, 2019)

- Description of recent research indicating that extremely preterm and low birth weight infants have lower executive function, especially in working memory and planning (Burnett & others, 2018)

- Coverage of a recent study that found kangaroo care promoted earlier initiation of breast feeding with preterm and low birth weight infants (Mekonnen, Yehualashet, & Bayleyegn, 2019)

- Inclusion of a recent large-scale experimental study in India in which low birth weight infants were randomly assigned to receive kangaroo care or standard care (Mazumder & others, 2019) and the kangaroo care infants had higher survival rates 30 days and 180 days after birth

- Description of a recent research review that concluded massage of preterm infants in the NICU was associated with shorter length of stay, reduced pain, improved weight gain, and better neurodevelopment (Pados & McGlothen-Bell, 2019). Also in this review, parents who massaged their preterm infants in the NICU reported experiencing less stress, anxiety, and depression.

- Discussion of a recent study in which parents trained in massage therapy conducted the therapy with their preterm infants, and their infants' weight, height, and head circumference increased faster than preterm infants who did not receive massage therapy (Zhang & Wang, 2019)

- Coverage of a recent meta-analysis that found 9 percent of fathers had postpartum depression within one month after birth, and 8 percent had it one to three months after birth (Rao & others, 2020)

- Inclusion of recent research in Japan indicating that 11.2 percent of fathers had postpartum depression one month after delivery (Nishigori & others, 2020)

- Description of a recent study that found fathers with postpartum depression had lower levels of responsiveness, mood, and sensitivity when interacting with their infants (Koch & others, 2019)

Chapter 4: Physical Development in Infancy

- Edits made based on comments by leading experts Charles Nelson and Martha Ann Bell

- Coverage of recent research documenting that attention (Bartolomeo & Seidel Malkinson, 2019) and emotion (Gainotti, 2019) are predominantly right-hemisphere activities

- New description of some of the aspects of brain activity that the brain imaging technique fNIRS can assess in infancy, including face processing, perception, attention, and memory (Emberson & others, 2019; Zhang & Roeyers, 2019)

- Coverage of a follow-up of children who were moved from an orphanage to stable foster care and showed improvement in brain functioning (Debnath & others, 2020)

- Discussion of World Health Organization (WHO) recommendations for the amount of quality sleep infants 0 to 3 months, 4 to 11 months, and 1 to 2 years should get daily (Willumsen & Bull, 2020)

- Inclusion of a recent study that found infants who were allowed to self-settle (that is, not nursed to sleep or rocked to sleep) showed increased duration of nighttime sleep during infancy (Hatch & others, 2019)

- Description of a recent research review that concluded the capacity to encode new memories is linked to sleep loss (Cousins & Fernandez, 2019)

- Discussion of a recent study that revealed persistent severe infant sleep problems were associated with prenatal and postnatal maternal depression (Cook & others, 2020)

- Coverage of a recent study in which a higher amount of screen time for infants was related to shorter sleep duration, with the link greater for those 6 months and under than for those 7 to 24 months in age (Chen & others, 2019)

- Inclusion of a recent study that found mothers who implemented a consistent bedtime routine had toddlers with longer sleep duration and fewer nighttime awakenings (Covington & others, 2019)

- Coverage of a recent study in which toddlers who experienced negative parenting but got adequate nighttime sleep had good self-regulation while those who encountered negative parenting and did not get adequate nighttime sleep had poor self-regulation (Julian & others, 2019)

- Discussion of a study of 732 cases of SIDS that found bed-sharing occurred prior to 53 percent of the deaths (Drake & others, 2019)

- Description of recent research indicating that preterm birth is linked to a higher incidence of SIDS (Elhaik, 2019)

- Coverage of a recent study in which shorter sleep duration in infancy was linked to lower cognitive and language development at 2 years of age (Smithson & others, 2019)

- Discussion of a longitudinal study that found shorter sleep duration at 3, 8, and 24 months was related to inattentive and hyperactive symptoms at 5 years of age (Huhdanpaa & others, 2019)

- Description of a recent research review that concluded the neurotransmitter serotonin plays an important role in SIDS (Cummings & Leiter, 2020)

- Inclusion of research indicating no advantage or even less effective reaching and grasping when infants wear sticky mittens (Corbetta, Wiener, & Thurman, 2018)

- Coverage of a research review that concluded breast milk contains immunomodulating components that benefit the development of the immune system and provide defenses for fighting off disease (Nolan, Parks, & Good, 2019)

- Inclusion of a recent study that revealed breast feeding was associated with lower rates of being overweight, lower blood pressure, and smaller waist circumference at 12 years of age (Pluymen & others, 2019)

- Discussion of a recent study that revealed breast fed infants were less likely to develop a fever in the first six months of their lives (Saeed, Haile, & Cherlok, 2020)

- Coverage of a recent meta-analysis in which breast feeding was linked to a higher level of cardiovascular fitness in children 4 to 18 years of age (Berlanga-Macias & others, 2020)

- Description of a recent study that found slightly higher intelligence in children who had been breast fed as infants (Strom & others, 2019)

- New discussion of a recent study that found breast feeding mothers had lower hospitalization rates for cardiovascular problems and diabetes (Bartick & others, 2019)

- Coverage of a recent study in which African American mothers who participated in WIC had lower diet quality than WIC participants from other ethnic groups (Parker & others, 2020)

- Inclusion of a recent study that found the percentage of preterm births was lower among expectant mothers covered by Medicaid who received WIC benefits during pregnancy than their counterparts who did not receive WIC benefits (Sneji & Beltan-Sanchez, 2019)

- Description of a recent study that found high-risk infants in a WIC program had higher cognitive scores on the Bayley Scales of Infant Development (Lakshmanan & others, 2020)

- Greatly expanded content on the latest dynamic systems theory's model of motor development emphasizing that motor development is (1) embodied, (2) embedded, (3) encultured, and (4) enabling (Adolph & Hoch, 2019)

- New content on a key aspect of motor development that involves behavioral flexibility to do what is necessary to accomplish life's everyday goals (Adolph & Hoch, 2019; Rachwani, Hoch, & Adolph, 2020). For example, infants' movements cannot be repeated in the same way across time and situations because their bodies, environments, and tasks change and require infants to engage in adaptive behavior.

- Updated and expanded content on eye tracking to include research on intermodal perception (Gergely & others, 2019), language (Comishen, Bialystok, & Adler, 2019), object categorization (LaTourrette & Waxman, 2019), and understanding of others' needs (Koster & others, 2019)

- Coverage of a recent study that found infants' looking times were highest for blue hues and lowest for yellow-green hues (Skelton & Franklin, 2020)

Chapter 5: Cognitive Development in Infancy

- Changes made based on comments by leading expert Martha Ann Bell

- Inclusion of a longitudinal study that found attention at 5 months was related to A-not-B performance at 10 months and also to executive function in early childhood and reading competence at 6 years of age (Blankenship & others, 2019)

- Added criticism of the core knowledge approach indicating that the modularity of the mind view does not adequately recognize the extensive connectivity of various regions of the brain

- Description of a recent study that found sustained attention in infancy was linked to better self-regulation in early childhood (Brandes-Aitken & others, 2019)

- Coverage of a recent study in which both joint attention and sustained attention at 9 months of age predicted vocabulary size at 12 and 15 months, but sustained attention was a better predictor of vocabulary size (Yu, Suanda, & Smith, 2019)

- Inclusion of a recent study that revealed initiation of joint attention is impaired at 12 months in children with autism spectrum disorder and language delay (Franchini & others, 2019)

- Coverage of a recent eye-tracking study that found 10- to 18-month-old infants who showed deficits in responding to others' joint attention bids and in initiating joint attention episodes were more likely to later be diagnosed with autism spectrum disorder (Nystrom & others, 2019)

- Description of a longitudinal study of participants from 1.5 to 16 years of age that revealed the age of first memory increased from 40 to 52 months as adolescents matured from 12 to 16 years of age (Reese & Robertson, 2019). In this study, individuals' differences in age of first memory were linked to the extent to which their mothers engaged in elaborative reminiscing.

- Discussion of a recent study in which infants at high risk for autism spectrum disorder used fewer gestures than their counterparts who were at low risk for autism spectrum disorders (Choi & others, 2019)

- Expanded content on Richard Aslin's conclusions that in addition to word segmentation, statistical learning has been documented as important in other domains such as musical tones, phonetic categories, sequences of visual shapes, sequences of motor responses, and combination of object parts in complex visual scenes

- Coverage of a recent study that revealed vocabulary comprehension at 23 months was linked to languages skills (morpheme knowledge and identification of correct sentences, for example) at 36 months of age (Friend & others, 2019)

- Description of a recent study in which learning new words at 21 months was associated with receptive vocabulary at 7 to 10 years of age (Rajan & others, 2019)

- Inclusion of a recent study that found parent coaching of 6- and 10-month-old infants involving the amount of child-directed speech, back and forth interactions, and parentese speech style improved the infants' language outcomes (more advanced babbling and greater word production) at 14 months of age (Ferjan Ramirez & others, 2019)

- Coverage of a recent study in which conversational turn counts at 18 to 24 months were linked to receptive and expressive vocabulary development 10 years later (Gilkerson & others, 2019)

- New discussion of English-speaking preschool children that revealed those from lower-income families had less advanced language-processing skills than children from middle- or high-income families, as well as a smaller vocabulary and syntax deficiencies (Levine & others, 2019)

- Discussion of a recent study that found children living in extreme poverty had much lower vocabulary and reading comprehension (Lervag & others, 2019)

- Description of a recent meta-analysis that concluded shared picture book reading was linked to children having better expressive and receptive language (Dowdall & others, 2020)

- Inclusion of a recent study that revealed higher rates of parent-child book reading interactions with 1- to 2.5-year-olds were linked to higher levels of receptive vocabulary, reading comprehension, and motivation to read in elementary school (Demir-Lira & others, 2019)

Chapter 6: Socioemotional Development in Infancy

- Revisions based on feedback from leading experts Martha Ann Bell and Pamela Cole

- New transition paragraph from the description of emotion in general to content on emotion regulation that emphasizes the positive, adaptive nature of emotion, which is reflected in our ability to regulate our emotions

- Discussion of a longitudinal study that revealed happiness at 1.5 years of age predicted intelligence in childhood (6 to 8 years of age) and educational attainment in adulthood (29 years of age) (Coffey, 2020)

- Description of recent research indicating that when fear was assessed at 6, 8, 10, and 12 months, it peaked at 10 months (Gartstein, Hancock, & Iverson, 2018)

- Coverage of a recent study that found children reported using more suppression and disengagement when experiencing early life stress, while adolescents used more engaging coping strategies when facing such stress (Johnson & others, 2019)

- Inclusion of a recent study in which maternal sensitivity was linked to better emotional self-regulation in 10-month-old infants (Frick & others, 2018)

- Coverage of a recent intervention study that involved training mothers to effectively use soothing techniques in the fourth week after birth, resulting in infants waking up less at night and crying less when assessed at 7, 11, and 23 weeks after birth (Ozturk Donmez & Temel, 2019)

- Description of a longitudinal study that found having a difficult temperament at 0 to 12 months of age predicted behavior problems at 36 months of age (Maltby & others, 2019)

- Inclusion of a recent meta-analysis that concluded secure attachment is linked to being more resilient (Darling Rasmussen & others, 2018)

- Discussion of a recent study that found an infant's secure attachment to its father was not enough to reduce the infant's stress reactivity when the mother-infant attachment was insecure (Kuo & others, 2019)

- Coverage of a recent study that indicated a higher level of testosterone in fathers in early infancy was linked to lower father-infant synchrony (Gordon & others, 2017). Also in this study, fathers with high testosterone levels had lower oxytocin levels and engaged in less touching of their infants than father with average or low levels of testosterone.

- Description of a recent study in which destructive marital conflict was linked to lower levels of coparenting alliance (Kopyslynska, Barnett, & Curran, 2020)

- Inclusion of a recent study revealing that higher levels of anxiety and depression symptoms in mothers during the last trimester of pregnancy was associated with increased rates of infants' externalizing problems at 2 years of age, and a higher level of these symptoms in fathers during the last trimester of pregnancy was related to higher levels of infants' internalizing and externalizing problems at 14 months of age (Hughes & others 2020)

- Coverage of a recent study involving the Bringing Home Baby project in which fathers who participated in the program felt more appreciated by their wives, and mothers were more satisfied with the division of labor when fathers were more involved in parenting (Shapiro, Gottman, & Fink, 2020)

Chapter 7: Physical and Cognitive Development in Early Childhood

- Coverage of a recent study in which the physical and socio-emotional health-related quality of life of children with growth hormone deficiency increased one year after they received growth hormone treatment (Quitmann & others, 2019)
- Description of a recent study that found maltreatment risk and home adversity in infancy were linked to cortical delays and brain immaturity at 8 years of age (Bick & others, 2019). However, children assigned to a biobehavioral catchup treatment showed improved brain functioning.
- Discussion of a recent research review that concluded advances in gross motor skills in early childhood are linked to better expressive and receptive language development (Gonzalez, Alvarez, & Nelson, 2019)
- Coverage of recent guidelines for 3- to 4-year-old children's sleep by the World Health Organization (WHO) recommending 10 to 13 hours of good quality sleep, including a nap, with consistent sleep and wake-up times (Willumsen & Bull, 2020)
- Inclusion of a recent study of 3-year-old children in which family irregularity was associated with shorter sleep duration and later sleep onset (Koopman-Verhoeff & others, 2019)
- Description of a recent study that found better-quality mother-child and father-child interactions were linked to preschool children's longer sleep duration (Dubois-Comptois & others, 2019)
- Discussion of a recent Chinese study that revealed sleep deprivation in early childhood was associated with ADHD in middle and late childhood (Tso & others, 2019)
- Coverage of a recent national study in which children's dietary quality decreased from 6 months to 4 years of age (Hamner & Moore, 2020)
- Inclusion of a recent study in which positive parenting that emphasized praise for healthy eating behavior improved young children's eating behavior and helped overweight children lose weight faster than negative comments by parents did (Rotman & others, 2020)
- Updated data on the percentage of U.S. 2- to 5-year-olds who are obese, which increased to 13.9 percent in 2015–2016 (Hales & others, 2017)
- Discussion of WHO's recommendation that 3- to 4-year-old children engage in no more than 1 hour of sedentary screen time daily (Willumsen & Bull, 2020)
- Inclusion of a recent study that revealed 3- to 4-year-old African American children and children who lived at or

below the poverty level were more likely than other young children to engage in more than 1 hour of screen time (Kracht, Webster, & Staiano, 2020)

- Coverage of a recent Chinese study in which longer TV viewing time was linked to an increase in 4- to 5-year-olds' overweight/obesity status (Hu & others, 2019)
- Description of the World Health Organization's recent guidelines for 3- to 4-year-olds' physical activity which recommend 3 hours per day of engaging in a variety of physical activities of any intensity, of which at least 60 minutes should be moderate- to vigorous-intensity physical activity, spread throughout the day (Willumsen & Bull, 2020)
- Update on changes in the leading causes of death in young children, with malignant neoplasms and homicides now the third and fourth leading causes of death and drowning and congenital malformation continuing to be the first and second leading causes, respectively (Centers for Disease Control and Prevention, 2019)
- Discussion of a recent national study that found children with a smoker in the home were 30 percent more likely to have an asthma diagnosis than children who did not have a smoker in the home (Xie & others, 2020)
- Coverage of a recent study in which young children exposed to environmental smoke were more likely to have hyperactivity and conduct problem symptoms than their counterparts who were not exposed to environmental smoke (Gatzke-Kopp & others, 2020)
- Discussion of a recent study that revealed mothers who engaged in sensitive parenting had children who used more private speech (Day & Smith, 2019)
- Description of a recent study in which executive attention was a good predictor of self-regulation (Tiego & others, 2020)
- Inclusion of recent research on 3- to 6-year-olds that found the volume of their autographical memories was linked to the volume of their self-knowledge (Ross, Hutchison, & Cunningham, 2020)
- Description of a recent research review that concluded interviewer support is linked to children's memory accuracy (Saywitz & others, 2019)
- Discussion of a recent study of preschool children in which conditions of socioeconomic disadvantage exerted a stressful influence on parent-child interactions and on young children's emergent executive function skills (Baker & Brooks-Gunn, 2020)
- Inclusion of a recent study of children in low-income families in Ghana that indicated executive function assessed at 5 years of age predicted higher subsequent literacy and math skills across the next two years (Wolf & McCoy, 2019)
- Coverage of a recent study in which higher parent education predicted children's superior executive function, whereas harsh parenting forecasted children's lower executive function (Halse & others, 2019)
- Description of a recent study of preschool children in which a lower level of executive function was associated with inattention and hyperactivity (Landis & others, 2020)

- Coverage of a recent study in which a lower level of executive function in preschool children was linked to onset and worsening of attention deficit hyperactivity disorder and depression at 6 to 12 years of age (Hawkey & others, 2019)

- Description of a recent study that found fathers' autonomy support improved young children's executive function (Meuwissen & Carlson, 2018)

- Discussion of a recent study that indicated teachers who conducted a 6-week small-group training program that focused on mindfulness and reflective thinking improved young children's executive function better than a business-as-usual condition, but a literacy training program was as effective in improving their executive function as the mindfulness and reflective thinking condition (Zelazo & others, 2018)

- Coverage of a recent cohort study that revealed young children in the 2000s are delaying gratification longer than their counterparts in the 1960s and 1980s, including content about why this might be happening (Carlson & others, 2018)

- Inclusion of a recent study of 3- to 5-year-old children that revealed earlier development of executive function predicted higher theory of mind performance, especially for false-belief tasks (Doenyas, Yavuz, & Selcuk, 2018)

- Coverage of an experimental study in which young children in high-poverty urban areas who were randomly assigned to participate in Montessori programs over a 3-year period fared better on academic achievement, social understanding, and mastery orientation than children who did not receive this intervention (Lillard & others, 2017)

- Inclusion of a recent study in which young children who attended Montessori schools displayed higher creativity than their counterparts in traditional schools (Denervaud & others, 2019)

- New description of an early-childhood intervention initiated by Jeff Bezos, CEO of Amazon, who recently provided 2 billion dollars to fund a new network of preschools in underserved communities that he says will be Montessori-inspired

- Discussion of an early childhood intervention designed to improve preschool children's developmental outcomes and to support the Head Start programs they attended in a high-violence, high-crime area of Chicago (Watts & others, 2018). The program was effective in improving the children's executive function and academic achievement but not their behavioral outcomes 10 to 11 years after the intervention.

- Coverage of a recent study of 3- to 4-, 5- to 6-, and 8- to 9-year-olds that found children in foster care who participated in Head Start programs had better cognitive, socioemotional, and health outcomes than their foster care counterparts who did not attend Head Start programs (Lee, 2020)

Chapter 8: Socioemotional Development in Early Childhood

- Coverage of a recent study that found by 5 years of age, children made both character and behavior judgments based on others' facial characteristics (Charlesworth & others, 2019). For example, they were more likely to give a gift to others with trustworthy and submissive facial expressions.

- Description of a recent study in which young children with higher emotion regulation were more popular with their peers (Nakamichi, 2020)

- Inclusion of a recent study that revealed low emotion regulation at age 5 was associated with emotional and school problems at age 10 (Perry & others, 2018a)

- New discussion of a longitudinal study in which a low level of emotion regulation in early childhood was linked to a higher level of externalizing problems in adolescence (Perry & others, 2018b)

- Coverage of a recent study that found emotion-dismissing mothers' parenting was linked to toddlers' lower emotional competence, while mothers' emotion-coaching parenting was associated with their toddlers' higher emotional competence (Ornaghi & others, 2019)

- Description of a recent study of 3- to 4-year-olds that indicated paternal emotion coaching predicted children's positive emotional expression one year later (Gerhardt & others, 2020)

- Description of a recent study in which 3-year-old boys with higher prenatal testosterone levels had shorter delay of gratification capabilities and more attention problems (Korner & others, 2019)

- Discussion of a recent study of 4- to 9-year-olds in which gender-nonconforming children were perceived more negatively than gender-conforming children (Kwan & others, 2020). Also in this study, gender-nonconforming boys were perceived more negatively than gender-nonconforming girls.

- Coverage of a recent study of 3- to 7-year-olds that revealed boys were more likely than girls to engage in gender stereotyping, especially with masculine stimuli such as toys, and to be sanctioned for not conforming to gender stereotypes (Skocajic & others, 2020)

- Description of a recent study in which authoritarian parenting was associated with being a bully perpetrator in adolescence (Krisnana & others, 2020)

- Inclusion of a recent study that found authoritarian parenting was linked to all forms of child maltreatment, while authoritative parenting was associated with a lower risk for all types of child maltreatment (Lo & others, 2019)

- Coverage of a recent study in which daughters were less likely than sons to be physically punished by both parents (Mehlhasen-Hassoen, 2019)

- Updates on the controversy about whether research adequately documents that physical punishment has detrimental effects on children's development (Gershoff & others, 2019; Larzelere & others, 2019)

- Discussion of recent research that revealed coparenting when children were 3 to 5 years of age was linked to less externalizing problems 8 to 10 years later (Parkes, Green, & Mitchell, 2019)

- Coverage of a recent study of low-income, unmarried couples that revealed cooperative coparenting at earlier stages of development resulted in fewer behavior problems later in childhood (Choi, Parra, & Jiang, 2019)

- Updated data on the extent of child maltreatment in the United States, including new data on specific types of abuse

- Inclusion of a recent large-scale Canadian study in which a history of child maltreatment involving either physical abuse or sexual abuse was linked to physical and mental health problems in adulthood (Cameranesi, Lix, & Piotrowski, 2019)

- Coverage of a recent study that found child maltreatment was associated with increased rates of psychiatric problems and substance abuse in adulthood (Wang & others, 2020)

- Discussion of a recent study in which child maltreatment was linked to increased emotion-focused coping and decreased problem-solving coping (VanMeter, Handley, & Cicchetti, 2020)

- Inclusion of a recent large-scale study in which social support and coping skills were linked to positive adult mental health outcomes for maltreated children (Su, D'Arcy, & Meng, 2020)

- Description of two recent national surveys focusing on various issues in working parent families (Career Builder, 2018; Livingston & Bialik, 2018)

- Coverage of research indicating that low SES in childhood was linked to lower cognitive function and greater cognitive decline in middle and late adulthood (Liu & Lachman, 2019). Also in this study, paternal discipline and high affection were positively associated with adult cognition function in children living in low-SES conditions, while paternal discipline was negatively related to adult cognition in children living in high-SES conditions.

- Inclusion of a recent study of preschool children in which frequent expressions of anger predicted lower social competence in peer relations one year later (Lindsey, 2019)

- Description of recommendations by the World Health Organization (WHO) that 3- to 4-year-old children engage in no more than 1 hour of screen time daily (Willumsen & Bull, 2020)

- Coverage of a recent study that revealed 3- to 4-year-old children and children who lived at or below the poverty line were more likely to engage in more than 1 hour of screen time compared with other children (Kracht, Webster, & Staiano, 2020)

- Inclusion of a recent study of 2- to 5-year-olds in which television/DVD/video viewing was negatively linked to young children's social skills, while outdoor play was positively associated with social skills (Hinkley & others, 2018)

- Discussion of a recent study of preschool children in which those who engaged in screen time 2 or more hours per day were much more likely to have inattention problems (including a higher risk of developing ADHD symptoms) and externalizing problems than children who engaged in screen time less than 30 minutes per day (Tamana & others, 2019)

- Description of a recent Australian study in which children and adolescents from lower-SES backgrounds were less likely to achieve a healthy level of physical fitness than their higher-SES counterparts (Peralta & others, 2019)

- New opening commentary in the section on Ethnicity focused on the importance of not using a deficit model in studying ethnic minority adolescents and of recognizing not just stressors in their lives but also positive aspects of their lives (Bornstein & Cote, 2019; Perreira & others, 2019)

- Updated data on the percentage of children 18 years of age or younger from different ethnic groups as well as predictions regarding when ethnic minority children will begin to outnumber non-Latino White children in the United States (U.S. Census Bureau, 2018)

- Coverage of a recent study in which immigrant children who had experienced separation from their parents had lower levels of literacy and higher levels of psychological problems than those who had migrated with their parents (Lu, He, & Brooks-Gunn, 2020). Also in this study, a protracted period of separation and prior undocumented status of parents further increased the children's disadvantages.

Chapter 9: Physical and Cognitive Development in Middle and Late Childhood

- Description of a recent study of 9- to 10-year-olds in which children with a high body mass index has less cortical thickness, which was linked to a lower level of executive function (Laurent & others, 2020)

- Coverage of recent research indicating that emerging cognitive control in children is mainly supported by the development of distributed neural networks in which the prefrontal cortex is central (Chevalier & others, 2019)

- Inclusion of a recent study in which reduced amygdala-prefrontal connectivity occurred in children with autism spectrum disorder (Ibrahim & others, 2019)

- Discussion of a recent study that examined children's physical activity in the transition from elementary to middle school (Pate & others, 2019). In this study, the following activities were associated with children's greater engagement of physical activity: parental encouragement and support of physical activity, time children spent outdoors, children's sports participation, and number of activity facilities near their home.

- Coverage of a recent study of 3- to 18-year-olds that found regular physical activity and higher levels of calcium intake improved their bone health (Yang & others, 2020)

- Description of a meta-analysis that concluded prolonged exercise interventions with 6- to 12-year-olds were effective in improving the children's executive function in general and their inhibitory control in particular (Xue, Yang, & Huang, 2019)

- Discussion of a recent research review of Chinese children that revealed lack of access to fruit and vegetable markets was linked to childhood obesity (Wang & others, 2020)

- Inclusion of a recent study in which high levels of screen time at 11 years of age was linked to increased body mass index 3 years later (Engberg & others, 2020)

- Updated data on the percentage of children who are obese, with continuing increases through 2015–2016 (Hales & others, 2017)

- Description of a recent Chinese study in which children and adolescents who were obese were more likely to have depression and anxiety symptoms than their non-obese counterparts (Wang & others, 2019)

- Coverage of a recent research review that concluded obesity is linked with low self-esteem in children (Moharei & others, 2018)

- Discussion of a recent study of Latino families in which parents who had a healthy weight were 3.7 times more likely to have a child who had a healthy weight (Coto & others, 2019)

- Inclusion of a recent study in which parental overweight and high blood pressure were linked to children's high blood pressure (Xu & others, 2019)

- Updated data on the percentage of children with a disability receiving special education services in different disability categories (National Center for Education Statistics, 2017)

- Updated content on links between ADHD and increased risk of school dropout, adolescent pregnancy, disordered eating, substance abuse, and antisocial behavior (Machado & others, 2019; Obsuth & others, 2020; Tistarelli & others, 2020; van der Burg & others, 2019)

- Coverage of a recent meta-analysis that found neurofeedback had moderate effects on improving children's attention and reducing their hyperactivity/impulsivity (Van Doren & others, 2019)

- Discussion of a research review that indicated physical exercise was effective in improving the attention of children with ADHD (Jeyanthi, Arumugam, & Parasher, 2019)

- Inclusion of a recent meta-analysis that found regular exercise was more effective than neurofeedback, cognitive training, and cognitive therapy in treating ADHD (Lambez & others, 2020)

- Description of a recent study that revealed children with ADHD were 21 percent less likely to engage in regular exercise than children not diagnosed with ADHD (Mercurio & others, 2020)

- Description of a recent review that concluded there are approximately 800 genes linked to autism (Gabrielli, Manzardo, & Butler, 2019)

- Discussion of a recent research summary that concluded key early warning signs for ASD are lack of social gestures at 12 months, using no meaningful words at 18 months, and having no interest in other children or no spontaneous two-word phrases at 24 months (Tsang & others, 2019)

- Inclusion of a recent study identifying different components of executive function, inhibition, and working memory that were associated with children's mindfulness (Geronimi, Arellano, & Woodruff-Borden, 2019)

- Coverage of a recent series of meta-analyses to discover which interventions are most likely to improve children's executive function; it was concluded that (a) for typically developing children, mindfulness training was effective, and (b) for non-typically developing children (including those with neurodevelopmental or behavioral problems), strategy teaching focused on self-regulation and biofeedback-enhanced relaxation were the most effective interventions (Takacs & Kassai, 2019)

- Discussion of a recent study in which mindful parenting was effective in improving children's social decision making (Wong & others, 2019)

- New coverage of how metacognition can significantly improve performance on many cognitive tasks (Morris, Savani, & Fincher, 2019; O'Leary & Sloutsky, 2019)

- Description of a recent study of 7- and 8-year-olds in which task-specific metacognitive monitoring skills in noticing one's own errors and learning from mistakes were linked to superior performance in arithmetic (Bellon, Fias, & DeSmelt, 2019)

- Inclusion of a recent study that revealed high-IQ adolescents engaged in a range of healthier behaviors such as exercise, better diet, and not smoking in middle adulthood (Wraw & others, 2018)

- Coverage of a recent study in which high IQ in adolescence was associated with having a younger subjective age 50 years later in late adulthood (Stephan & others, 2018)

- Description of a recent study that found genes were much more strongly linked to a person's scientific achievement than to his/or artistic achievement (de Manzano & Ullen, 2018)

- Inclusion of a recent study conducted in 22 countries in which intelligence varied across the countries, with the variations linked to income, educational attainment, health, and socioeconomic status (Lynn, Fuerst, & Kirkegaard, 2018)

- New content indicating that intelligence scores have decreased in several Scandinavian countries and suggesting possible reasons for this finding (Dutton & Lynn, 2013; Ronnlund & others, 2013)

- New content on how IQ gains continue to occur in the United States and developing countries (Flynn & Shayer, 2018), including a study that found IQ increased by 10 points from 2004 to 2016 in Khartoum, the capital of Sudan (Dutton & others, 2018)

- Inclusion of recent research with young children in which shared book reading at home and school in a second language improved their second-language learning; in addition, the perspective taking emphasized in the shared reading program increased their ability to shift perspectives and understand others' emotional states (Grover & others, 2020)

- Description of recent research that indicated 3-year-old bilingual children adapted to the needs of their communication partners better than their monolingual counterparts (Gampe, Wermelinger, & Daum, 2019)

- New discussion of a recent study of Chinese children indicating that bilingual children who were studying English as a foreign language outperformed monolingual Chinese children on an attention task and also had higher activation of the prefrontal cortex (Li & others, 2020)

Chapter 10: Socioemotional Development in Middle and Late Childhood

- Significant revisions and updates based on feedback from leading expert consultant Darcia Narváez

- Coverage of a recent study in which parental warmth, monitoring, low maternal depression, economic well-being, and father presence (versus father absence) were linked to higher self-esteem in children and adolescents (Krauss, Orth, & Robins, 2020)

- New content on the effects of the coronavirus (COVID-19) pandemic on children's stress and coping, including strategies parents can use to help children cope with uncertainty and disruption of normal routines
- Extensive updating and rewriting of Kohlberg's theory and criticisms of his view
- Discussion of a recent study in which children and adolescents said that changes in moral beliefs are more disruptive to identity than changes in social conventional beliefs (Lefebvre & Krettenaur, 2020). Also in this study, children and adolescents reported that changes in negative moral beliefs are more disruptive to identity than changes in positive moral beliefs.
- Coverage of a recent study in 12 countries that found sharing increased from 4 to 12 years of age in each of the countries (Samek & others, 2020)
- New Figure 1 that gives students an opportunity to evaluate the extent to which they have a moral identity
- Inclusion of a conclusion reached recently by Janet Shibley Hyde and her colleagues (2019), who stated that the distributions for males and females on different brain features overlap to such an extent that in most instances it is more accurate to characterize human brains as a mosaic of these features than as binary male-typical and female-typical brains
- Updated data on math and reading scores at the fourth- and eighth-grade levels in the National Assessment of Educational Progress (2017)
- Coverage of a recent large-scale study of seventh-grade girls that found girls' perceptions of teachers' gendered math expectations and how relevant and meaningful the math curriculum was for them were linked to their math beliefs and math achievement (McKellar & others, 2019)
- Update on Urban Prep Academy, the first all-male African American charter school, indicating that from 2010, its first year as a school, through 2018, 100 percent of the students in each graduating class enrolled in college
- Inclusion of a recent study that revealed females are better than males at facial emotion perception across the life span (Olderbak & others, 2019)
- Coverage of a recent study of adolescents that revealed those who observed relational aggression on television were more likely to engage in relational aggression when they were texting one year later (Coyne & others, 2019)
- Description of a recent study in which stepfathers' affinity-seeking (developing a friendship relation with stepchildren) was linked to less conflict with stepchildren, a better couple relationship, and closer stepfamily ties (Ganong & others, 2019)
- Discussion of recent research with third- and fourth-graders in which feeling related to peers at school was associated with the children's positive affectivity both at school and at home (Schmidt, Dirk, & Schiedek, 2019)
- Updated content on the negative outcomes of peer rejection to include antisocial behavior (Komienko, Ha, & Dishion, 2019)
- Inclusion of a recent study of adolescents in which peer rejection increased the likelihood that victims and bullies would engage in non-suicidal self-injury, such as cutting, burning, or hitting themselves (Esposito, Bacchini, & Affuso, 2019)

- Description of a recent analysis of bullying from 1998 to 2017 in the United States that indicated a significant increase in cyberbullying and face-to-face bullying in females (Kennedy, 2020)
- Coverage of a recent study of 12- to 15-year-olds in 48 countries worldwide that found being the victim of bullying was linked to an increased risk of suicide in 47 of the 48 countries (Koyanagi & others, 2019)
- Description of a recent study of 10- to 14-year-olds in which being a victim of a bully often led to a cascading effect of bullying perpetration that eventually produced disordered eating behavior (Lee & Vaillancourt, 2018)
- Discussion of a recent large-scale Norwegian study that concluded bullies, victims, and bully-victims are at increased risk of developing sleep problems, including shorter duration of sleep and higher prevalence of insomnia, as well as a lower grade point average (Hysing & others, 2020)
- Coverage of a recent study that revealed the most common behavioral reactions to cyberbullying were informing a friend, counterattacking, and ignoring the cyber incident (Heiman, Olenik-Shemesh, & Frank, 2019)
- Inclusion of a longitudinal study that involved implementation of the Child-Parent Center Program in high-poverty neighborhoods of Chicago, an intervention that provided school-based educational enrichment and comprehensive family services for children from 3 to 9 years of age (Reynolds, Ou, & Temple, 2018). Children who participated in the program had higher rates of postsecondary completion and increased likelihood of attaining an associate's degree or higher.
- New discussion exploring whether peer mindsets can influence a student's mindset (Sheffler & Chenug, 2020), including description of a recent study across most of a school year that found students who were around peers with a growth mindset for 7 months increased their growth mindset across that time frame (King, 2020)
- New content on a national experimental study conducted by David Yeager and his colleagues (Yeager, Dahl, & Dweck, 2018)—a brief, online, direct-to-student growth mindset intervention that increased the grade point averages of underachieving students and also improved the challenge-seeking mental activity of higher-achieving students. In other recent research, the positive outcomes of the U.S. online growth mindset intervention were replicated with students in Norway (Bettinger & others, 2018).

Chapter 11: Physical and Cognitive Development in Adolescence

- Description of a recent study of adolescent boys that indicated high levels of testosterone were linked to decreased ability to delay gratification (Laube, Lorenz, & van den Bos, 2019)
- Discussion of a recent study indicating that age at menarche has decreased recently in Portugal (Queiroga & others, 2020)
- Coverage of recent research that found a higher body mass index (BMI) (Deng & others, 2018) and obesity (Busch & others, 2020) were associated with earlier pubertal onset

- Inclusion of a recent study in which young adolescent girls had a more negative body image when they identified with an ideal social media portrayal (Rodgers & others, 2020)
- New discussion of research with seventh- to twelfth-graders in Thailand that revealed increased time spent on the Internet, especially when engaging in activities related to self-image and eating attitudes and behavior, was linked to increased body dissatisfaction (Kaewpradub & others, 2017)
- Inclusion of recent research in which higher social media use was linked to more negative body images for adolescents, more so for girls than boys (Kelly & others, 2019)
- Description of a recent Korean study of more than 30,000 girls that found early menarche was associated with increased risk-taking (Kim & others, 2019)
- Coverage of a recent study that found the fibers in the corpus callosum increased in adolescence (Genc & others, 2018)
- Discussion of recent research indicating that connectivity between the frontal cortex and hippocampus increased from adolescence to emerging and early adulthood, with this connectivity linked to improvement in higher-level cognition, especially in problem solving and planning (Calabro & others, 2020)
- Changes in the discussion of adolescent sexuality based on feedback from leading experts Bonnie Halpern-Felsher and Ritch Savin-Williams
- Discussion of a recent national study that focused on the percentage of U.S. middle and high school students who engage in sexting (Patcin & Hinduja, 2019)
- New emphasis on the similarities in sexual timing and developmental sequences in heterosexual and sexual minority adolescents, accompanied by acknowledgment that sexual minority adolescents have to cope with more stressful aspects of their sexual identity, including disclosure of this identity (Savin-Williams, 2019)
- Inclusion of a recent study of prime-time TV shows watched by U.S. adolescents and emerging adults in which sexual violence and abuse, casual sex, lack of contraception use, and no coverage of the negative consequences of risky sexual behavior were common (Kinsler & others, 2019)
- Updated data on the percentages of U.S. high school students who have ever had sexual intercourse, are currently sexually active, had sexual intercourse before 13 years of age, and engaged in sexual intercourse with 4 or more persons (Kann & others, 2018)
- Updated data on ethnic variations in percentages of adolescents who have ever had sexual intercourse (Kann & others, 2018)
- Coverage of the results of a recent national study of 7,000 15- to 24-year-olds' engagement in oral sex, including information on the low percentage of youth who use a condom when having oral sex (Holway & Hernandez, 2018)
- Description of a recent study of South African youth that found early sexual debut predicted a lower probability of graduating from high school (Bengesai, Khan, & Dube, 2018)
- Inclusion of a recent Australian study in which sex at age 15 or younger predicted higher rates of pregnancy in emerging adulthood, lifetime sexual partners, and sex without using a condom (Prendergrast & others, 2019)

- Coverage of a recent study of Korean adolescent girls in which early menarche was linked to earlier initiation of sexual intercourse (Kim & others, 2017)
- Description of a recent study of adolescents that indicated higher quality of experiences with parents were linked to decreased likelihood of engaging in vaginal sex, anal sex, oral sex, pornography viewing, and masturbation (Astle, Leonhardt, & Willoughby, 2020)
- New discussion of links between substance abuse and risky sexual practices, including a recent study in which the likelihood of initiating sexual intercourse before age 13 increased in those who engaged in substance abuse and had mental health problems (Okumu & others, 2019)
- Coverage of a recent study in which talk about sexual protection with extended family members was linked to adolescents having fewer sexual partners, while talk about sexual risks was associated with adolescents having more sexual partners (Grossman & others, 2019)
- New description of a recent study confirming that low self-control is linked to risky social behavior during adolescence (Magnusson, Crandall, & Evans, 2019)
- Inclusion of a new *Connecting with Careers* profile on Bonnie Halpern-Felsher, Professor in Pediatrics and Director of Community Efforts to Improve Adolescents' Health
- Updated data on the percentage of U.S. adolescents who used a contraceptive the last time they had sexual intercourse (Kann & others, 2018)
- Coverage of a recent national study that indicated adolescent use of long-acting reversible contraception (LARC) increased from 1.8 percent in 2013 to 5.3 percent in 2017 (Algne & others, 2020)
- Updated data on STIs in young people, with those 15 to 24 years of age accounting for almost half of the new STIs in the United States (Kann & others, 2018)
- Updated data on HIV in the United States, with individuals 13 to 24 years of age having 21 percent of all HIV diagnoses and, of these individuals, 81 percent being gay or bisexual males (Kann & others, 2018)
- Updated data on births to U.S. 15- to 19-year-olds which, in 2017, reached its lowest rate in history (Centers for Disease Control and Prevention, 2019). Especially noteworthy was the substantial decline in births to Latina and African American adolescent girls.
- Coverage of a recent Canadian study that found adolescents were much more likely than young adult mothers to live in low-SES neighborhoods, be depressed, and have higher rates of tobacco, marijuana, and alcohol use (Wong & others, 2020)
- Inclusion of a recent research review in which the following factors were associated with being an adolescent father: experiencing child maltreatment, serious family disruption, not living with either parent, and Latino ethnicity (Fasula & others, 2019)
- Update on Girls Inc. (2020), including recent research indicating that their adolescent pregnancy prevention program was effective in reducing pregnancy rates

- Update on the continuing government funding of pregnancy prevention programs through the Office of Adolescent Health (2020) and a description of the focus of several of the programs

- Description of 2017 data from the Youth Risk Survey documenting that 59.2 percent of U.S. high school students had not eaten vegetables one or more times in the last 7 days (Kann & others, 2018)

- Updated data from a recent national survey indicating that the percentage of adolescents who are obese has reached 20.6 percent (National Center for Health Statistics, 2017)

- Inclusion of recent research indicating that a higher level of parental monitoring was linked to adolescents' healthier diet intake and lower weight status (Kim & others, 2019)

- Coverage of a recent experimental study that found a 12-week jump rope exercise program was effective in improving obese adolescent girls' body composition, blood pressure, insulin level, and self-regulation (Kim & others, 2020)

- New content indicating that adolescents who engage in higher levels of screen time are more likely to be overweight or obese (Furthner & others, 2018)

- Updated data on the continuing dramatic gender difference in exercise during adolescence, with 56.9 percent of adolescent males exercising 5 or more days per week compared with only 38.8 percent of their female counterparts (Kann & others, 2018)

- Coverage of a recent meta-analysis that concluded supervised exercise, especially aerobic exercise, was linked to a reduction of abdominal fat in adolescents (Gonzalez-Ruis & others, 2017)

- Inclusion of research in which an after-school athletics program reduced the obesity risk of adolescents after one year of intervention (Glabaska & others, 2019)

- Updated research data indicating that adolescents are not getting nearly enough sleep (Kann & others, 2018)

- Coverage of a recent study in which adolescents with shorter or poorer-quality sleep in conjunction with less physical activity showed elevated rates of internalizing and externalizing problems (Gillis & El-Sheikh, 2019)

- Discussion of a recent study that revealed the highest level of internalizing and externalizing problems occurred for adolescents from lower-SES homes who had short sleep duration and poor-quality sleep (El-Sheikh & others, 2019)

- Discussion of a recent study of 13- to 19-year-olds in Singapore in which sleep duration of less than seven hours on school nights was associated with being overweight, having depression symptoms, being less motivated, not being able to concentrate adequately, having a higher level of anxiety, and engaging in self-harm/suicidal thoughts (Yeo & others, 2019)

- Inclusion of a recent study that found getting insufficient sleep was associated with alcohol and marijuana use among adolescents (Kwon & others, 2020)

- Discussion of research indicating that frequency of cordless phone calls, mobile phone dependency, and tablet use were linked to sleep problems in adolescence (Cabre-Riera & others, 2020)

- Coverage of a recent study in which spending multiple hours with portable electronic devices was linked to shorter sleep duration in adolescence, while time spent with non-portable electronic devices was not related to shorter sleep duration (Twenge, Hisler, & Rizan, 2019)

- Description of recent research in which the Seattle School District delayed the school start time for secondary school students by nearly one hour and it improved student sleep duration by an average of 34 minutes, increased student grade point averages, and improved school attendance (Dunster & others, 2018)

- Coverage of a recent study of college students in which shorter sleep duration was associated with increased suicide risk (Becker & others, 2018a)

- Inclusion of a recent study of college students in which 27 percent described their sleep as poor and 36 percent reported getting 7 hours or less of sleep on weeknights (Becker & others, 2018b)

- Description of a recent experimental study in which emerging adults who were given a brief sleep quality intervention reported that they experienced better sleep quality, stopped using electronic devices earlier, kept a more regular sleep schedule, and had earlier weekday rise times compared with a control group who did not receive the intervention (Hershner & O'Brien, 2018)

- Coverage of a longitudinal study that found binge drinking in the twelfth grade was linked to driving while impaired (DWI), riding with an impaired driver (RWI), blackouts, and riskier driving up to 4 years later (Vaca & others, 2020)

- Updated national data on the extent of illicit drug use among U.S. eighth-, tenth-, and twelfth-graders (Miech & others, 2019)

- Updated national data on the dramatically increased rates of U.S. adolescents who are vaping nicotine, while adolescent cigarette smoking continues to decline (Johnston & others, 2019)

- Inclusion of a recent study in which maternal and paternal knowledge of the adolescent's activities and whereabouts at age 13 was linked to lower rates of alcohol use at age 16 for boys and girls (Lindfor & others, 2019)

- Description of a recent study of 14- and 15-year-olds that found heavy episodic drinking by parents was a risk factor for adolescent drinking, with girls being especially vulnerable to their parents' episodic drinking (Homel & Warren, 2019)

- Inclusion of recent research indicating that increased use of e-cigarettes by adolescents may be a gateway for subsequent combustible cigarette smoking as well as marijuana use (Fadus, Smith, & Squeglia, 2019)

- Updated and revised definitions of anorexia nervosa and bulimia nervosa based on the DSM-V classification system

- Coverage of a recent meta-analysis that concluded both anorexics and bulimics engage in maladaptive perfectionism (Dahlenburg, Gleaves, & Hutchinson, 2019)

- Description of a recent national study that found anorexia nervosa and bulimia nervosa were associated with a higher incidence of major depressive disorder than any other disorder, followed by alcohol use disorder (Udo & Grilo, 2019)

- New coverage of the distinction between "hot" executive function and "cool" executive function (Koukari, Tserment-seli, & Monks, 2019; Semenov & Zelazo, 2018)
- Description of a recent study of 12- to 17-year-olds in which cool executive function increased with age while hot executive function peaked at 14 to 15 years of age and then declined (Poon, 2018)
- Discussion of a recent study of eighth-graders with high test anxiety in which an attention training intervention was effective in reducing their test anxiety, especially by reducing worry (Fergus & Limbers, 2019)
- Description of a recent study in which young adolescents showed a better understanding of metaphors if they were more cognitively flexible
- Inclusion of a recent Spanish study that documented middle school students had lower self-concepts in a number of areas (academic, social, family, and physical) than elementary school students (Onetti, Fernandez-Garcia, & Castillo-Rodriquez, 2019)
- Coverage of a recent study in which teacher warmth increased in the last 4 years of elementary school and then dropped during the middle school years (Hughes & Cao, 2018). The drop in teacher warmth was associated with lower student math scores.
- Discussion of a recent study that revealed increased rates of teacher-student conflict during the transitions from elementary school to middle school and middle school to high school were linked to increased externalizing symptoms during the students' first year at their new school (Longobardi & others, 2019)
- Update on work done by the "I Have a Dream" Foundation (2020) with students from low-income families, including data about participants' impressive college graduation rates compared with their low-income peers who did not participate in the program
- Description of a longitudinal study that found both breadth and intensity of extracurricular activities in the tenth grade were associated with higher educational attainment 8 years later (Haghighat & Knifsend, 2019)
- Inclusion of new information on the Bill and Melinda Gates Foundation's (2017, 2020) research indicating that many adolescents graduate from high school without the necessary academic skills to succeed in college or to meet the demands of the modern workplace
- Updated data on decreased school dropout rates in recent years, with the biggest percentage decline occurring among Latino adolescents (National Center for Education Statistics, 2019)

Chapter 12: Socioemotional Development in Adolescence

- Expanded and updated coverage of the importance of self-regulation in adolescence (Casey & others, 2019; Van Maderen & others, 2019)
- New description of a recent study that found a reciprocal relation between school engagement and self-regulation in adolescence (Stefansson & others, 2018)

- Coverage of a recent study of middle school students that revealed self-control was a key factor in developing good health habits (Kang & You, 2018)
- Discussion of a recent study of 13- to 16-year-olds in which females reported having a higher level of self-control and self-monitoring than their male counterparts did (Tetering & others, 2020)
- Inclusion of a recent study of Mexican American adolescents that indicated effortful control was linked to coping with stress more effectively (Taylor, Widman, & Robins, 2017)
- New discussion of a recent study of fifth- to eleventh-graders that found a bidirectional pattern between effortful control and school behavior problems (Atherton & others, 2019)
- New description of a recent meta-analysis of children up to 18 years of age that indicated those who were securely attached engaged in better effortful control (Pallini & others, 2018)
- Coverage of a recent study of Mexican-origin adolescents describing factors that were linked to different levels of effortful control (Atherton, Lawson, & Robins, 2020)
- New content on the recently created *dual cycle identity model* that separates identity development into two processes: (1) a formation cycle, and (2) a maintenance cycle (Luyckx & others, 2017; von Doeselaar & others, 2020)
- New section, "Identity Development and the Digital Environment," that explores how adolescents and emerging adults express their identity and get feedback about it from an expanding audience through their daily connections on social media such as Instagram, Snapchat, and Facebook (Davis & Weinstein, 2017)
- Updated content from a national study on the continuing decline in attendance at religious services by high school seniors (Stolzenberg & others, 2019)
- Coverage of a recent study in which religiosity was linked to a delayed initiation of alcohol use, more so for girls than for boys (Barry, Valdez, & Russell, 2020)
- Inclusion of a recent Slovakian study in which spirituality but not religiosity of adolescents was linked to better self-rated health, fewer health complaints, and higher life satisfaction (Dankulincova Veselska & others, 2019)
- Description of a recent study of young adolescents that found they got more sleep when their parents engaged in a higher level of parental monitoring of their activities (Gunn & others, 2019)
- Inclusion of a recent study in which parental active tracking measures during adolescence and college were associated with better health behavior in both developmental time frames (Abar & others, 2020)
- Discussion of a recent study that found adolescents who engaged in more problem behaviors were more secretive and revealed less information to their parents (Darling & Tilton-Weaver, 2019)
- Coverage of a recent study revealing that adolescents who had grown up in poverty engaged in less risk-taking if they had a history of secure attachments to caregivers (Delker, Bernstein, & Laurent, 2018)

- Inclusion of a recent analysis that found secure attachment to the mother and to the father was associated with fewer depressive symptoms in adolescents (Kerstis, Aslund, & Sonnby, 2018)

- Coverage of a recent study that revealed a parental profile involving high monitoring and high autonomy support was more positively linked to adolescent adjustment than low parental monitoring and high psychological control (Rodriquez-Meininhos & others, 2020)

- Description of a longitudinal study in which establishing positive expectations and the capacity to be assertive with peers at age 13, social competence at 15 and 16, and the ability to form and maintain strong close friendships at 16 to 18 predicted romantic life satisfaction at 27 to 30 years of age (Allen & others, 2020)

- Inclusion of a recent study that revealed peers' influence on adolescents' eating behavior is often negative and characterized by increased consumption of high-calorie foods with low nutritional value (Rageliene & Gronhoj, 2020)

- New discussion of five ways that social media have transformed peer and friendship interactions and relationships in adolescence (Nesi, Choukas-Bradley, & Prinstein, 2018)

- New description of a recent study revealing that for non-Latino White and Asian American young adolescents, higher academic achievement was associated with having same-ethnic friends, while for African American and Latino young adolescents, higher academic achievement was linked with having cross-ethnic friends (Chen, Saafir, & Graham, 2020)

- Inclusion of a recent study of eighth-graders that revealed peer pressure was associated with substance use (Jeisma & Varner, 2020)

- Discussion of a recent study that found the Hip Hop crowd and the alternative crowd were at increased risk for a number of negative behaviors (Jordan & others, 2019)

- New coverage of the influence of the coronavirus (COVID-19) on friendship and peer relations, including content on social distancing

- Description of recent research on 13- to 18-year-olds in the United States and the United Kingdom that found significant gender differences in the types of digital media they used (Twenge & Martin, 2020)

- Coverage of a recent study of 11- to 18-year-olds in Spain in which media multitasking during homework was linked to lower executive function, a lower level of working memory, and worse academic performance in language and math (Martin-Perona, Vinas Poch, & Malo Cerrato, 2019)

- Discussion of recent research indicating that parental monitoring of media exposure to violence was linked to lower levels of aggression in adolescents (Khurana & others, 2018)

- Description of two recent studies of adolescents that found higher levels of screen time were linked to lower academic achievement (Hunter & others, 2018; Poulan & others, 2018)

- Coverage of a longitudinal study that indicated low SES in childhood and adolescence was associated with lower cognitive function and more cognitive decline in middle and late adulthood (Liu & Lachman, 2019)

- New discussion of updated data (2017) on delinquency cases handled in juvenile court, including gender differences (Hockenberry & Puzzanchera, 2019)

- Inclusion of a recent research review that concluded lack of academic success and having a learning disability were linked to juvenile delinquency (Grigorenko & others, 2019)

- Description of a recent Australian study in which children and adolescents from lower-SES backgrounds were less likely to achieve a healthy level of physical fitness than their higher-SES counterparts (Peralta & others, 2019)

- Coverage of a recent study that found delinquency in adolescence was linked to a greater likelihood of being unemployed in adulthood (Carter, 2019)

- Discussion of a recent study that revealed an increase in the proportion of classmates who engage in delinquent behavior increased the likelihood that other classmates would also become delinquents (Kim & Fletcher, 2018)

- Inclusion of a recent study that indicated adolescent delinquents were high on affiliating with deviant peers and engaging in pseudomature behavior and low on peer popularity and school achievement (Gordon Simons & others, 2018)

- Description of a recent study that revealed having a best friend who was delinquent increased the probability that adolescents would become delinquent (Levey & others, 2019)

- Discussion of recent research indicating for populations with high risk profiles, as little as one teacher screen taken during kindergarten or the first grade predicted which males would have adult criminal convictions by age 25 (Kassing & others, 2019)

- Coverage of a recent study in which low self-esteem and negative emotion management were linked to adolescent depression (Fiorilli & others, 2019)

- Description of recent research in which interpersonal stress was linked to increased depression in adolescent girls (Slavich & others, 2020)

- Inclusion of a recent research review that concluded adolescents have difficulty recognizing signs of depression, are more likely to seek help from informal than from professional sources, and tend to attach stigma to depression (Singh, Zaki, & Farid, 2019)

- Description of a longitudinal study that found adolescents who had experienced a major depressive episode were more likely to experience a recurrence of depression 15 years later (Alaie & others, 2019). In addition, adolescent depression was associated with other mental health problems, low educational attainment, and problems in intimate relationships 15 years later.

- New content based on national data indicating that suicide has recently replaced homicide as the second leading cause of death in adolescence (National Center for Health Statistics, 2019)

- New discussion of cross-cultural suicide rates for 15- to 19-year-olds, with New Zealand and Iceland having the highest rates and Greece and Israel the lowest rates (OECD, 2017)

- Updated data on the percentages of U.S. adolescents who seriously consider suicide or attempt suicide each year, including gender and ethnicity statistics (Kann & others, 2018)
- Coverage of a recent study in which a sense of hopelessness predicted an increase in suicidal ideation in depressed adolescents (Wolfe & others, 2019)
- Discussion of a recent cross-cultural study of more than 130,000 12- to 15-year-olds indicating that in 47 of 48 countries, being a victim of bullying was associated with higher risk of attempting suicide (Kovanagi & others, 2019)
- Coverage of a recent study in which combined school difficulties (academic failure and inappropriate behavior) were associated with higher suicide risk (Ligier & others, 2020)
- Description of a recent analysis that revealed the main factor in adolescent suicidal deaths was the occurrence of recent stressful life events (Werbart Tomblom & others, 2020)
- Inclusion of recent research indicating that adolescents who had been victims of cyberbullying were 2.5 times more likely to attempt suicide and 2 times more likely to have suicidal thoughts than non-victims (John & others, 2018)

Chapter 13: Physical and Cognitive Development in Early Adulthood

- Coverage of a recent study of individuals 18 to 60 years of age in which the five characteristics used to describe emerging adulthood (identity exploration, self-focus, feeling in-between, instability, and possibilities/optimism) were more likely to be endorsed by 18- to 25-year-olds than older individuals (Arnett & Mitra, 2020)
- Updated content on American college freshmen's views on the relative importance of being well-off financially versus developing a meaningful philosophy of life (Stolzenberg & others, 2019)
- Inclusion of a recent study of college students in which sleep deprivation was linked to a lower grade point average and delayed college graduation (Chen & Chen, 2019)
- Discussion of a recent study that found poorer sleep quality was associated with smartphone dependence and less effective stress management (Wang & others, 2019)
- Inclusion of the National Sleep Foundation's (2019a) recommendation that 18- to 25-year-olds get 7 to 9 hours of sleep every night
- New description of the National Sleep Foundation's (2019b) explanation of why pulling an all-nighter to cram for an exam is not likely to be a good idea
- Updated data on the percentage of American college freshmen who felt overwhelmed with all they had to do, felt depressed, and felt anxious (Stolzenberg & others, 2019)
- Updated data on the percentage of obese adults in the United States, which continues to increase and is now just under 40 percent (Hales & others, 2017)
- Updated data on differences in obesity rates across gender and ethnicity groups in the United States (Hales, 2017)
- Updated content on countries with the highest and lowest obesity rates (OECD, 2017)

- Coverage of a recent study that found adult obesity in Mexico was associated with higher rates of screen time, lower rates of physical activity, and inadequate sleep (Kolovos & others, 2020)
- New commentary on research indicating that higher levels of physical activity, especially endurance training, are linked to weight loss maintenance (Petridou, Sippi, & Mouglos, 2019)
- Inclusion of a longitudinal study from adolescence through early adulthood that found three factors predicted maintenance of a healthy weight: having higher body satisfaction, avoiding unhealthy weight control behaviors, and dieting (Larson & others, 2018)
- New commentary from the World Health Organization underscoring that physical inactivity is a key factor in dying earlier (Han, Neufer, & Pilegaard, 2019)
- Coverage of a recent national poll conducted by the Centers for Disease Control and Prevention indicating that only 22 percent of U.S. adults 18 to 64 years of age met federal guidelines for aerobic and muscle-strengthening exercise (Blackwell & Clarke, 2018). In this poll, 27.2 percent of men and 18.7 percent of women met the exercise guidelines.
- Inclusion of a recent study of almost 18,000 adults in which engaging in both regular moderate-to-vigorous physical activity and muscle-strengthening exercise were linked with the lowest incidence of depressive symptoms (Bennie & others, 2019)
- Updated data on binge drinking in college students (Schulenberg & others, 2019)
- Updated data on when binge drinking peaks in the 18- to 30-year age range (Schulenberg & others, 2018)
- Updated data on the declining percentage of adults who smoke cigarettes in the United States (currently 14 percent); however, 34 million U.S. adults still smoke cigarettes (Centers for Disease Control and Prevention, 2019)
- New section on marijuana use, including data from the University of Michigan Monitoring the Future study indicating that in 2018, 19- to 22-year-old U.S. college students dramatically increased their use of marijuana (Schulenberg & others, 2019)
- Coverage of a recent study of first-year college students in six focus groups that found the following was a common theme in their discussion: "Sex is easier to get and love is harder to get" (Anders & others, 2020)
- Description of a recent study of emerging adults in which a higher percentage of women than men reported having sex, hooking up with an acquaintance, using partner characteristics as a reason to hook up, and expressing negative reactions to their most recent hookup (Olmstead, Noroan, & Anders, 2019). Also in this study, a higher percentage of men reported hooking up with a stranger, meeting at a bar/club, and hooking up at a party.
- Updated data on HIV statistics in the United States and worldwide (Centers for Disease Control and Prevention, 2018; UNAIDS, 2019)
- Inclusion of a recent study in which more than 87 percent of alcohol-involved sexual assaults on college campuses were

committed by serial perpetrators (Foubert & others, 2019). Also in this study, fraternity members and student athletes were more likely to commit alcohol-involved assaults than other men on campus.

- Coverage of a recent study that indicated women who had experienced sexual assault were more likely to subsequently have academic problems and engage in fewer serious romantic relationships while in college and 9 years later to have more symptoms of depression, anxiety, and post-traumatic stress (Rothman & others, 2020)

- New content on the recent movement toward *affirmative consent* for sexual activities on many college campuses (Goodcase, Spencer, & Toews, 2020)

- Description of a recent study of college students in which regularly eating breakfast was positively linked to grade point averages (GPAs) while regularly eating fast food was negatively related to GPAs (Reuter, Forster, & Brister, 2020)

- Major new section, "Achievement," added as the first part of the discussion of Achievement, Careers, and Work

- New coverage of motivation for success with a focus on intrinsic and extrinsic motivation (Ryan & Deci, 2019)

- New section on "Goal-Setting, Planning, and Self-Monitoring" (Schunk, 2020)

- New section, "Grit," including questions students can ask themselves to determine whether they have grit (Clark & Malecki, 2019)

- Updated information about the fastest-growing jobs anticipated through 2028 in the 2020–2021 *Occupational Outlook Handbook*

- Discussion of a recent study in which following a period of unemployment, recovery of a sense of well-being upon reemployment was fast and enduring even when individuals took less favorable jobs upon returning to work (Zhou & others, 2019)

- Update on the positive job outlook for 2020 U.S. college graduates, with a 5.8 percent increase in hiring of college graduates by employers (NACE, 2020)

- Update on the percentage of full-time and part-time students who are working while going to college (National Center for Education Statisics, 2018)

Chapter 14: Socioemotional Developent in Early Adulthood

- Inclusion of a recent longitudinal study in which insecurely attached infants had worse emotion-regulation strategies than their securely attached counterparts in relationship-challenging contexts 20 to 35 years later (Girme & others, 2020)

- Description of recent research indicating that insecure anxious and insecure avoidant individuals were more likely than securely attached individuals to engage in risky health behaviors, were more susceptible to physical illness, and had poorer disease outcomes (Pietromonaco & Beck, 2018)

- Discussion of a research review that revealed having an insecure attachment style increased the risk of engaging in suicidal thoughts (Zortea, Gray, & O'Connor, 2020)

- Inclusion of a recent study that indicated college students with an anxious attachment style were more likely to be addicted to social networking sites (Liu & Ma, 2019)

- Description of a recent research review that found maladaptive support behaviors were more likely to occur when one or both members of a romantic dyad had an insecure attachment (McLeod & others, 2019)

- Coverage of a recent meta-analysis that revealed adults with insecure attachment styles were more likely to engage in risky sexual behaviors (Kim & Miller, 2020)

- Inclusion of a recent study in which greater self-disclosure was associated with higher relationship intimacy offline but with lower relationship intimacy with romantic partners but not friends online (Lee, Gillath, & Miller, 2019)

- Coverage of a recent study that found being in a romantic relationship, interacting with a partner, and investing more time and effort in the relationship all predicted higher levels of well-being (Hudson, Lucas, & Donnellan, 2020). However, these effects were moderated by differences in relationship quality.

- Discussion of a recent study of emerging adults in which higher levels of optimism, self-esteem, and grit were associated with lower levels of depressive symptoms and rumination three months after a breakup (O'Sullivan & others, 2019)

- Updated data on the percentage of U.S. individuals 18 and older who are single (U.S.Census Bureau, 2018)

- Inclusion of a recent nationally representative survey of more than 35,000 U.S. single adults that found they are increasingly having uncommitted sexual encounters but taking far longer to make a formal commitment to a partner, a circumstance described as "fast sex and slow love" (Fisher & Garcia, 2019). Nonetheless, in this survey, today's singles show a strong interest in finding romantic love and a partner they can live with forever.

- Updated data on the increasing percentage of emerging and young adults who are cohabiting (U.S. Census Bureau, 2019)

- Coverage of a recent study that indicated early transitioning into a stepfamily home, especially for females, was linked to earlier entry into cohabitation (Johnston, Cavanagh, & Crosnoe, 2020)

- Discussion of recent research that confirms cohabitation is a risk factor for intimate partner violence in emerging adults (Manning,Longmore, & Giordano, 2018)

- Inclusion of a recent study in which cohabiting individuals were more likely to engage in risky sexual relationships and more likely to have unplanned pregnancies (Nugent & Daugherty, 2018)

- Description of a recent study that indicated cohabitation was associated with a risk for increased marijuana use among women but not men (Hoffman, 2018)

- Updated data on the percentage of U.S. adults 18 years and older who were married in 2019, which has declined to 48.2 percent (U.S. Census Bureau, 2019)

- Updated data on the age of first marriage in the United States, which in 2019 was 29.8 for men and 28 for women, higher than at any point in history (U.S. Census Bureau, 2019)

- Coverage of a recent study that found men had a higher level of marital satisfaction than women across a number of countries (Sorokowski, Kowal, & Sorokowska, 2019). In this study, marital satisfaction was similar among Muslims, Christians, and atheists.

- New comparison of age at first marriage in a number of developed countries, with individuals in Sweden getting married latest and those in Israel and Turkey earliest (OECD, 2019)

- Inclusion of a recent study that explored why individuals get married, with love (88 percent of the respondents) at the top of their list (Geiger & Livingston, 2019)

- Inclusion of a recent study in which couples high in neuroticism were less satisfied with their marriage than those high in conscientiousness (Sayehmiri & others, 2020)

- Coverage of a recent study of recently married low-income adults that revealed those who received premarital education were more likely to seek therapy when the marriage became distressed than those who had not received premarital therapy (Williamson & others, 2018)

- New Figure 5: Trends and Proposals for Improving Premarital Education in the Next Generation (Clyde, Hawkins, & Willoughby, 2020)

- Updated data indicating divorce rates in various countries, with Russia having the highest and Chile the lowest rate of divorce (OECD, 2019)

- Inclusion of a recent research review that concluded divorced adults have a higher rate of adverse cardiovascular events, including death due to cardiovascular disease, than their married counterparts (Dhindsa & others, 2020)

- Updated data on the average age at which U.S. mothers give birth, which is now the oldest age ever (26.9 years) (National Center for Health Statistics, 2019)

- Discussion of a recent study in which adults in same-sex relationships experienced similar levels of commitment, satisfaction, and emotional intimacy compared with their counterparts in different-sex relationships (Joyner, Manning, & Prince, 2019)

Chapter 15: Physical and Cognitive Development in Middle Adulthood

- Description of a recent study that found middle-aged adults 44 to 64 years of age perceived themselves to be younger than they actually were and wanting to be younger than their chronological age (Shinan-Altman & Werner, 2019). In this study, the beginning of old age was perceived to be 69 years.

- Inclusion of a recent study of individuals 19 to 77 years of age (mean age = 45) in which gain orientation decreased and maintenance orientation increased with age (Gong & Freund, 2020). Also in this study, perceived losses and accumulation of resources/assets increased with age.

- Coverage of a recent study of U.S. and Japanese adults in which younger adults in both countries perceived an improvement in their life satisfaction from the past to the present and expected further improvement in the future, but the improvement was more modest for middle-aged adults and

then shifted to a perceived decline in life satisfaction for older adults (Liu & Lachman, 2019)

- Updated data on the percentage of middle-aged adults who are obese compared with their younger adult counterparts (Hales, 2017)

- Updated content indicating that the highest obesity rate for women (44.7 percent) occurs during middle adulthood (Hales, 2017)

- New commentary that for individuals who are 30 percent or more overweight, the probability of dying in middle adulthood increases by 40 percent

- Discussion of a Chinese study that found men and women who gained an average of 22 pounds or more from 20 to 45–60 years of age had an increased risk of hypertension and high cholesterol levels, as well as elevated triglyceride levels in middle age (Zhou & others, 2018)

- Description of a recent large-scale study in which obesity was associated with earlier death and increased risk of death due to cardiovascular disease compared with normal-weight individuals (Khan & others, 2018)

- Inclusion of a recent study in which smoking and diabetes were risk factors for accelerated loss of muscle mass in middle-aged women (Lee & Choi, 2019)

- Discussion of a recent study of middle-aged adults that revealed difficulties reading the newspaper and recognizing known people on the street because of vision problems were linked to decreased life satisfaction, increased depressive symptoms, decreased self-esteem, and increased social isolation (Hajek & others, 2020)

- Coverage of a recent study of middle-aged adults that found higher cardiorespiratory fitness predicted lower cardiovascular disease risk (Swainson, Ingle, & Carroll, 2019)

- Inclusion of a recent global study that revealed from 1990 to 2017, cardiovascular mortality rates declined in high-income regions but only slightly decreased or even increased in most low- and middle-income regions of the world (Jagannathan & others, 2019). In this study, high blood pressure, unhealthy diet, high glucose levels, and high LDL accounted for most of the cardiovascular-linked deaths.

- Coverage of a recent study that found the triple combination of lower HDL, higher blood pressure, and larger waist circumference were linked to metabolic syndrome and cardiovascular disease (Mansourian & others, 2019)

- Description of a recent study in which sedentary behavior, especially moderate and high TV viewing time, was linked to metabolic syndrome (Lemes & others, 2019)

- Inclusion of a recent study that revealed lower body mass index, less exercise, frequent alcohol drinking, and a meat-based diet were risk factors for lung cancer in never-smoking women (Ko & others, 2020)

- Discussion of a recent research review of sleep in normal aging that concluded shortened nighttime sleep duration, increased nocturnal awakenings, and increased frequency of daytime naps are common changes in sleep patterns associated with aging (Li, Vitiello, & Gooneratne, 2018). Also in this review, it was concluded that these changes occur mainly between early and middle adulthood, then remain largely unchanged in healthy older adults.

- New description of a recent study of middle-aged adults that indicated lower sleep quality was linked to a lower level of executive function, lower processing speed, learning difficulty, and poorer memory recall (Kaur & others, 2019)

- New research indicating that obese middle-aged and older adults are more likely to have chronic diseases and earlier death than their normal-weight counterparts (Stenholm & others, 2017)

- Updated content on causes of death in middle age, with data indicating that in recent years cancer deaths have increased and cardiovascular diseases slightly decreased, with cancer and cardiovascular disease continuing to be the top two causes of death in middle age (Centers for Disease Control and Prevention, 2019)

- Coverage of a recent study of more than 300,000 women that found late menopause was associated with an increased risk of breast cancer (Gottschalk & others, 2020). Also in this study, the age of onset of menopause is increasing, as is the gap between menarche and menopause.

- Updated coverage of hormone replacement therapy and rewriting of section for greater clarity

- Description of a recent analysis of research that concluded mindfulness training is linked to improved psychological adjustment during the menopausal transition (Molefi-Youri, 2019)

- Revised conclusions about links between TRT and cardiovascular disease, with recent research being inconclusive about this association (Fode & others, 2019)

- Inclusion of a recent research review that concluded TRT is effective in improving sexual function but that evidence of its effects on other conditions, such as cardiovascular disease, is inconclusive (Corona, Torres, & Maggi, 2020)

- New discussion of the recently developed technique of using low-intensity shockwave therapy for treating ED (Kalyvianakis & others, 2020; Patel, Pastusak, & Hotaling, 2019)

- Coverage of a recent research review of low-intensity shockwave therapy that shows benefits after 6 months and continued but lesser effects at 1 year (Brunckhorst & others, 2019)

- Description of a recent study in which a combined treatment of low-intensity shockwave therapy and Cialis was more effective in reducing ED than Cialis alone (Verze & others, 2020)

- Inclusion of recent research on healthy middle-aged women indicating that interpersonal factors such as emotional support and relationship satisfaction, as well as the personality traits of optimism and self-esteem, were key predictors of quality of sexual functioning (Memone, Fiacco, & Ehlert, 2019)

- New description of a recent study of individuals 50 years and older that revealed a past-year decline in sexual desire or frequency of sexual activities was associated with an increase in depressive symptoms and lower quality of life (Jackson & others, 2019)

- Coverage of a recent study in which fluid intelligence decreased in individuals 65 years and older but not in individuals 45 to 60 years of age (Cornelis & others, 2019)

- New description of a study of middle-aged and older adults that indicated having a higher level of education and engaging in frequent physical exercise were linked to less decline in episodic memory (Liu & Lachman, 2019)

- Inclusion of a recent study of middle-aged and older adults that revealed a 12-week resistance exercise training program improved their delayed verbal memory performance (Marston & others, 2019)

- Updated data on the percentage of U.S. 45- to 64-year-olds in the workforce, including comparisons of 2019 to 2015 and 2000 (Mislinski, 2019)

- New description of a recent analysis of U.S. workers in which more than 50 percent of those 50 years and older are pushed out of longtime jobs before they choose to retire (Gosselin, 2019)

- New discussion of a recent study that found middle-aged and older adult women who engaged in a higher level of leisure-time physical activity were more likely to report experiencing positive affect (Holahan & others, 2020)

- Inclusion of recent research on middle-aged Europeans indicating that those who engaged in more physical activity during their leisure time were less likely to be depressed (Marques & others, 2020)

- Description of recent research in which individuals who engaged in more leisure-time physical activity experienced less work-related stress (du Prel, Siegrist, & Borchart, 2019)

- Coverage of a recent meta-analysis that concluded a higher level of meaning in life is linked to better physical health (Czekierda & others, 2017)

- Discussion of a recent U.S. study in which adults were asked what provides them with a sense of meaning in life. Sixty-nine percent said family, 34 percent said career, 23 percent said money, and 20 percent said spirituality and faith (Pew Research Center, 2018).

Chapter 16: Socioemotional Development in Middle Adulthood

- Inclusion of a recent study of middle-aged adults that revealed intrinsically rewarding work was associated with feelings of generativity (Chen & other, 2019)

- Description of recent research in which a 6-week generativity program with middle-aged and older adults produced positive outcomes involving an increase in perceived social support and a lower level of loneliness (Moieni & others, 2020)

- Coverage of a recent study in which openness to experience declined prior to death in older adults (Sharp & others, 2019)

- Inclusion of recent research indicating that adults high in conscientiousness are more satisfied with their marriage while those high in neuroticism are less satisfied with their marriage (Sayehmiri & others, 2020)

- Discussion of a recent study that revealed older adults characterized by high conscientiousness were more likely to experience optimal aging (Melendez & others, 2019) and less likely to develop dementia (Kaup, Hammell, & Yaffe, 2019)

- Description of recent research indicating that obese adults were characterized by low conscientiousness (Cheng & others, 2019)

- Discussion of research in which nursing professionals high in conscientiousness and low in neuroticism were characterized by lower work burnout rates (Perez-Fuentes & others, 2019)

- Coverage of a recent study that found older adults were more likely than younger adults to engage in proactive coping with minor hassles in their daily lives to manage these problems before they become more stressful (Neubauer, Smyth, & Sliwinski, 2019)

- Coverage of a recent study that found adults high in extraversion had a higher perceived level of well-being (Ortet & others, 2020)

- Inclusion of recent research indicating that individuals high in agreeableness were less likely to engage in physical activity (Hearon & Harrison, 2020)

- Discussion of recent research that revealed individuals characterized by high neuroticism avoided engaging in selfie-posting and selfie-editing, while those with high extraversion and agreeableness engaged in more selfie-posting and selfie-editing (Chaudhari & others, 2019)

- Coverage of a recent study that revealed regardless of growing up in disadvantaged circumstance as a child, being optimistic as an adult was linked to being a nonsmoker, having a healthy diet, and having a healthy body mass index (Non & others, 2020)

- Inclusion of a longitudinal study of middle-aged married adults that found negative behavior in their marriage decreased and positive behavior increased across 13 years during middle age (Verstaen & others, 2020)

- Revision and updating of the coverage of marriage and divorce in middle age to account for the recently increasing percentage of middle-aged adults who are getting divorced

- Discussion of a recent study in which high levels of parental control and helicopter parenting were detrimental to emerging adults' vocational identity development and perceived competence in transitioning to adulthood (Lindell, Campione-Barr, & Killoren, 2017)

- Coverage of a recent study that revealed helicopter parenting was related to more negative emotional functioning, less competent decision making, and lower grades/poorer adjustment in college students (Luebbe & others, 2018)

- New content on "lawnmower parents" who "mow down" obstacles, stressors, and potential failure for their children and adolescents rather than let them learn how to make decisions and develop coping strategies on their own

- Inclusion of a recent Korean study in which middle-aged individuals who were divorced were more likely to smoke, binge drink, get inadequate sleep, and be depressed than their married counterparts (Kim, Lee, & Park, 2018)

- Discussion of a recent study exploring the extent to which men and women repartner following a gray divorce (that is, when they are 50 years of age and older) (Brown & others, 2019). In this study, 22 percent of women and 37 percent of men repartnered following a gray divorce.

- Description of a recent cross-cultural study in which U.S. grandparents were characterized by higher parental efficacy, greater role satisfaction, better well-being, and more attachment than Chinese grandparents, who were characterized by more resilience and a higher level of authoritative parenting (Wang & others, 2019)

- Coverage of a recent study that found when children live with their grandparents, the arrangement especially benefitted low-income and single parents, who in this circumstance spent more money on their children's education and activities while saving on child care costs (Amorin, 2019)

- Discussion of a recent study that revealed middle-aged adults were happiest when they had harmonious relationships with their parents and their adult children (Kim & others, 2020)

Chapter 17: Physical Development in Late Adulthood

- Updated data on life expectancy in the United States (Xu & others, 2020)

- Updated data on life expectancy in 224 different countries in 2018, with Monaco having the highest (89.6 years), the United States in fifty-third place (78.6 years), and South Africa the lowest (50.6 years) (Geoba.se, 2019)

- In a recent (2020) list of the world's oldest living people, there were no males among the oldest 50 individuals

- Updated data on gender and ethnic differences in life expectancy in the United States (Murphy & others, 2018; Xu & others, 2020)

- New discussion of the "Latino Health Paradox," which refers to Latinos living 5.7 years longer than non-Latino Whites despite having lower incomes and less education, including explanations for why this higher longevity may occur (Brill, 2019)

- Coverage of a recent study that supported the "Latino Health Paradox," with older Latino adults reporting better health than their non-Latino White counterparts (Olsen, Basu Roy, & Tseng, 2019)

- Updated data on life expectancy for individuals 65 years of age (including gender differences) (Xu & others, 2020)

- Update on the oldest living person in the world in 2020 (Kane Tanakaa of Japan, 117 years old) and in the United States (Hester Ford, 114 years old, who lives in Charlotte, North Carolina)

- Coverage of a recent research review that concluded lifestyle interventions involving exercise and diet are linked to a slowing of telomere shortening (Fragkiadaki & others, 2020)

- Updated and expanded coverage of the diseases that are linked to mitochondrial dysfunction to include cardiovascular disease (Roushandeh, Kuwahara, & Roudkenar, 2019), Alzheimer disease (Li & others, 2020), Parkinson disease (Zhi & others, 2019), diabetic kidney disease (Forbes & Thorburn, 2018), and impaired liver functioning (Stevanovic & others, 2020)

- Updated and expanded discussion of links between sirtuins and diabetes, Alzheimer disease, and Parkinson disease

(Cacabelos & others, 2019; Liu & others, 2020; Shieh, Huang, & Lin, 2020)

- Update on the leading causes of death in older adults in the United States, with recent data indicating that beginning in the 65- to 74-year age range, cancer has replaced cardiovascular disease as the leading cause of death (Centers for Disease Control and Prevention, 2018)
- Coverage of a recent study that found declines in memory functioning were linked to lower volume of gray matter (which contains most of the brain's neuronal cell bodies) in the temporal lobe and hippocampus (Schneider & others, 2019)
- New discussion of research involving the Mankato Nun Study in which an analysis of essays written when the nuns were 18 to 32 years of age revealed that those whose essays reflected a higher level of self-reflection and parents' giving them more independence to make their own decisions lived longer (Weinstein & others, 2019)
- New research on middle-aged and older adults in which those who had limited mobility had lower cognitive functioning (Demnitz & others, 2018)
- New content indicating that the National Sleep Foundation (2020) recommends that older adults get 7 to 8 hours of sleep a night
- Coverage of a recent study that found older adults who slept 8 to 10 hours or more a night were more likely to have memory recall problems (Low & others, 2019)
- New description of a recent study of older adults in which an increase of 554 steps per day reduced physical limitations by 5.9 percent and improved quality of life by 3.2 percent (Kabiri & others, 2019)
- Inclusion of a recent study of older adult women that revealed a slowing of walking speed occurred on average at about 71 years of age (Noce Kirkwood & others, 2018)
- Inclusion of a recent study that found older adults who walk slowly are at increased risk for developing mild cognitive impairment (Rajtar-Zembaty & others, 2019)
- Coverage of a longitudinal study of individuals 60 years and older in which visual and hearing difficulties predicted cognitive difficulties 8 years later, with the greatest cognitive decline occurring in individuals who had both a visual and a hearing problem (de la Fuente & others, 2019)
- Description of a recent study that found declines in visual acuity, contrast sensitivity, and depth perception were associated with cognitive decline in older adults (Swenor & others, 2019)
- Inclusion of a recent study in which hearing impairment was associated with accelerated cognitive decline in older adults (Alattar & others, 2019)
- Discussion of a recent study of older adults in which implementation of hearing aid use was linked to stable or improved executive function (Sarant & others, 2020)
- Description of a recent study of older adults that indicated those with a dual sensory impairment involving vision and hearing had more depressive symptoms (Han & others, 2019)
- Coverage of a recent study of older adults that revealed an inability to smell some odors, especially peppermint, was linked to cognitive decline (Liang & others, 2020)

- Inclusion of a recent study of older adults in which high levels of pain were associated with memory impairment (van der Leeuw & others, 2018)
- Coverage of recent research in which older adults who engaged in sexual activity experienced greater enjoyment in life (Smith & others, 2019)
- Description of a recent study in which older adults were asked about their motivation for having sex (Gewirtz-Meydan & Avalon, 2019). In this study, five main reasons for having sex were to (1) maintain overall functioning, (2) feel young again, (3) feel attractive and desirable, (4) go from lust to love, and (5) change from "getting sex" to "giving sex."
- Inclusion of a recent Swiss study in which post-menopausal women consumed high amounts of vegetables but insufficient calcium and dairy products (Lanyan & others, 2020)
- Description of a recent meta-analysis confirming that physically active older adults have a greater likelihood of living longer (Cunningham & others, 2020)
- Discussion of a recent study that confirmed older adults who engage in regular exercise have a higher level of life satisfaction (Cho & Kim, 2020)
- Coverage of a recent large-scale study that found middle-aged and older adults, even those with cardiovascular disease and cancer, can gain considerable longevity benefits by engaging in a minimum of 150 minutes a week of moderate-intensity exercise (Mok & others, 2019)
- Inclusion of a study of middle-aged adults indicating that their estimated age based on exercise stress testing was a better predictor of how long they would live than their chronological age (Harb & others, 2020)
- Discussion of a recent meta-analysis that concluded moderate to vigorous physical exercise reduces depressive symptoms in older adults with an average age of 82 years (Klil-Drori & others, 2020)
- Updated data on the percentage of adults 60 years and older who are obese, which recently increased to 42.8 percent (Centers for Disease Control and Prevention, 2020)
- New content on the lack of exercise among many older adults, with one in three men and one in two women engaging in no physical exercise (Centers for Disease Control and Prevention, 2020)
- Description of a recent analysis in which it was concluded that antioxidant vitamins do not increase the life span and can even increase the incidence of some diseases (Milisav, Ribaric, & Poljsak, 2018)

Chapter 18: Cognitive Development in Late Adulthood

- Edits based on feedback from leading expert Laura Carstensen
- Inclusion of a recent study in which executive attention training improved the selective attention and divided attention of older adults (Yang & others, 2019)
- New description of a recent study in which age-related decline in episodic memory impaired access to specific autobiographical events and the details involved (Peters, Fan, & Sheldon, 2019)

- New discussion of the "reminiscence bump" in autobiographical memories in which older adults often remember more than would be expected from their second and third decades of life (Allen & others, 2018)

- Coverage of a recent study of 60- to 88-year-olds that revealed the first-time experience of a memory, how important the memory was, and the memory's emotional salience were associated with the reminiscence bump (Wolf & Zimprich, 2020)

- New content indicating that attention, as well as processing speed, likely play a role in declining working memory in older adults (Jariat, Portrat, & Hot, 2019)

- Inclusion of a recent study that revealed Latino older adults who were more acculturated in the United States had better working memory than their less acculturated counterparts (Mendoza & others, 2020)

- Deletion of a section on cognitive resources in the discussion of memory in late adulthood and addition of a new section head on working memory, which streamlines the discussion of processing speed

- Discussion of a recent study that indicated when older adults had good retrieval strategies they showed no deficits in source memory (Salhi & Bergstrom, 2020)

- Coverage of a recent study in which a cognitive training program that increased frontal and parietal lobe brain activity improved older adults' working memory (Gajewski & Falkenstein, 2018)

- Description of a recent study that found longer encoding time improved older adults' working memory (Bartsch, Loaiza, & Oberauer, 2019)

- Discussion of a recent study of older adults' source memory that found older adults with better source memory were characterized by healthy cardiovascular markers and psychological traits (higher achievement, less depression, for example) while lower source memory was predicted by relevant life experiences such as being retired and engaging in heavy drinking (Cansino & others, 2019)

- Inclusion of recent research indicating that prospective memory is impaired in individuals with mild Alzheimer disease (Lecouvey & others, 2019)

- Description of a recent study that found when older adults engaged in higher levels of physical activity their memory improved (de Lima & others, 2019)

- Discussion of a recent study in which highly educated older adults had better executive function than their less-educated counterparts, which was associated with slower age-related reduction in executive function (Chen & others, 2019)

- Inclusion of a recent study in which aerobic exercise improved older adults' executive function (McSween & others, 2019)

- Discussion of a recent study that revealed a combination of a Nordic Walking training program and vitamin D supplementation improved the processing speed, attention, and executive function of elderly women (Lipowski & others, 2019)

- Inclusion of a recent research review of 20 executive function training studies indicating that overall they promoted cognitive and neural plasticity in older adults (Nguyen, Murphy, & Andrews, 2019)

- Coverage of a recent study revealing that executive function in older adults increased their sense of control over obstacles that interfered with their ability to attain goals, which in turn was associated with higher life satisfaction (Toh, Yang, & Hartanto, 2020)

- Description of a recent study of older adults that revealed metacognitive monitoring benefitted their visual short-term memory (Mitchell, Cusack, & Cam-CAN, 2018)

- New description of recent research that found older adults perform worse on metacognition tasks, such as those involving beliefs, deception, and emotion recognition, than young adults (Caiso, Besnard, & Allain, 2019)

- New discussion of the decline in theory of mind abilities in late adulthood (Hughes & others, 2019)

- New discussion of a recent study of older adults in which mindfulness training increased their likelihood of engaging in physical exercise (Robin & others, 2020)

- Coverage of a number of recent studies focused on the developmental aspects of wisdom at different points in life (Ardelt & Jeste, 2018; Igareshi, Levenson, & Aldwin, 2018; Sternberg & Gluck, 2019)

- Inclusion of a recent study that found the personality trait of openness to experience in early adulthood predicted wisdom 60 years later (Ardelt, Gerlach, & Vaillant, 2018). Also in this study, wisdom in later adulthood could be traced to experiences and characteristics at different points in development: a supportive childhood, competence in adolescence, emotional stability in young adulthood, and generativity in middle adulthood.

- Coverage of a recent study that indicated wisdom peaked in midlife, with education especially linked to a higher level of wisdom (Ardelt, Pridgen, & Nutter-Pridgen, 2018)

- Inclusion of a recent study that found education had a strong effect on U.S. older adults' working memory (Salto & others, 2020)

- Discussion of a recent study of 50- to 75-year-old Chinese Americans that indicated a greater amount of education earlier in life was linked to a higher level of cognitive functioning in older adults (Zhang & others, 2019)

- Inclusion of a recent study of Puerto Rican older adults that revealed a higher level of cognitive complexity in work was associated with a lower risk of cognitive impairment (Andel & others, 2019)

- Inclusion of a recent study of older Latinos that found cardiovascular risk factors were linked to lower cognitive functioning (Tarraf & others, 2020)

- Discussion of a recent study of older adults that found depression was linked to lower executive attention, memory, and language performance (MacAulay & others, 2020)

- Description of a recent study of older adults in which moderate to intense physical activity modified the depression-cognition connection and preserved cognitive function (Hu & others, 2019)

- Coverage of a recent meta-analysis that concluded meditation, Tai Chi, and yoga interventions are effective in improving older adults' cognitive functioning (Chan & others, 2019)

- Description of research with two different samples of older adults in which a higher level of cognitive activity was linked to better cognitive functioning (Casaletto & others, 2020)

- Discussion of the Mayo Clinic Study of Aging, which found that engaging in a higher number of mentally stimulating activities (reading books, using a computer, participating in social activities, playing games, and doing craft activities) was associated with a decreased risk of mild cognitive impairment (Krell-Roesch & others, 2019)

- Inclusion of a recent research review that concluded low levels of social isolation characterized by high engagement in social activity and large social networks were linked to better cognition (memory and executive function, for example) in older adults (Evans & others, 2019)

- New commentary noting that cognitive gains based on cognitive training games are typically constrained to the specific task being assessed and do not generalize to broader cognitive function

- Description of a recent meta-analysis that indicated video game playing can have a small positive effect on older adults' memory but has no effect on other cognitive functions (Mansor, Chow, & Halaki, 2020)

- Coverage of a recent study of older adults in which an in-home exergame training program improved their executive function (Adcock & others, 2020)

- Discussion of a recent study that confirmed older adults have more difficulties in narrative discourse than younger age groups (Babaei & others, 2019)

- Coverage of a recent study of individuals with mild cognitive impairment in which those who were bilingual had better verbal memory than their monolingual counterparts (Rosselli & others, 2019)

- Description of a recent study of older adults that revealed a bilingual advantage in the alerting subcomponent of attention (Dash & others, 2019)

- Coverage of a recent study in which older adults participated in a 4-month-long second language program that improved their global cognition and connectivity across regions of the brain's frontal and parietal lobes (Bubbico & others, 2019)

- Updated data indicating that the percentage of individuals in the United States who expect to work after age 65 increased from 16 percent in 1991 to 48 percent in 2018 (Employee Benefit Research Center, 2018)

- Inclusion of a recent report indicating that 37 percent of individuals in the United States retire earlier than they had planned (Munnell, Rutledge, & Sanzenbacher, 2018)

- Discussion of a recent analysis in which older adults with better health, higher incomes, and greater educational attainment can work longer, while older adults without these assets tend to work in more physically demanding jobs, making it more difficult for them to continue working as older adults (United Income, 2019)

- Inclusion of recent findings indicating that older workers are more satisfied at work, take fewer sick days, and demonstrate stronger problem-solving skills than younger workers (Milken Institute and Stanford Center of Longevity, 2019)

- Discussion of a recent study that found all retirement pathways were associated with cognitive decline for workers in low-complexity jobs but were not linked to accelerated cognitive decline for those in high-complexity jobs (Carr & others, 2020). Also, after individuals retired and subsequently returned to work, a modest improvement in cognitive function occurred.

- Inclusion of a recent study that revealed retirement satisfaction was linked to capacity to fulfill retirement plans, resilience, social integration, adoption of new roles, and especially quality of family relationships (Principi & others, 2020)

- Description of a recent study in which a 12-week exercise program was effective in reducing depression in Mexican older adults (Borbon-Castro & others, 2020)

- Coverage of recent research indicating that two exercise therapies—Tai Chi and Qigong—were effective in reducing depression in older Chinese adults (Gill & others, 2020)

- Revised definition of dementia (Alzheimer's Association, 2020)

- Updated data on the percentage of older adults with Alzheimer disease and expanded facts about Alzheimer disease in 2019 (Alzheimer's Association, 2019)

- New data on African Americans and Latinos being more likely to have Alzheimer disease than non-Latino Whites

- New commentary that in the United States, 50 percent of the help provided by caregivers to older adults is given to individuals with Alzheimer disease (Alzheimer's Association, 2019)

- New coverage of the role of mitochondrial dysfunction as an early event in Alzheimer disease (Yang & others, 2020a)

- Discussion of a recent research review that concluded cognitive and physical interventions can improve the cognitive and physical function of individuals with mild cognitive impairment (Yang & others, 2020b)

- Inclusion of a recent research review that concluded deep brain stimulation (DBS) improves motor function in Parkinson patients for up to 10 years, but improvement tends to decline over time (Limousin & Foltynie, 2019)

Chapter 19: Socioemotional Development in Late Adulthood

- Updating, shortening, and rewriting of the section on attachment in late adulthood for greater clarity

- Inclusion of a number of changes based on feedback from leading expert Laura Carstensen

- Revised description of social selectivity theory

- Discussion of a recent research review of older adults' health that concluded ageism led to worse health outcomes, especially in less developed countries and among those who had less education (Chang & others, 2020)

- Inclusion of a longitudinal study of individuals from 13 to 72 years of age in which avoidant attachment declined across the life span, and being in a relationship predicted lower levels of anxious and avoidant attachment across adulthood (Chopik, Edelstein, & Grimm, 2019)

- Coverage of a recent study of older adult women that found avoidant attachment was linked to higher levels of social isolation (Spence, Jacobs, & Bifulco, 2019)
- Description of a recent study of older adults that revealed higher self-esteem was linked to better physical and psychological well-being (Ilkyas, Shahed, & Hussain, 2020)
- Inclusion of a recent study in which older adults who had a higher daily level of self-control perceived themselves to be younger (Bellingtier & Neurpert, 2019)
- Coverage of a recent study in which openness to experience declined in advance of death in older adults (Sharp & others, 2019)
- Description of recent research with older adults indicating that higher neuroticism and lower conscientiousness were linked to difficulties in perceived executive function (Bell, Hill, & Stavrinos, 2020)
- Discussion of a recent study that revealed older adults characterized by high conscientiousness were experiencing optimal aging (Melendez & others, 2019) and were less likely to develop dementia (Kaup, Hammell, & Yaffe, 2019)
- Reorganization and shortening of the section on "Older Adults and Society"
- Updated statistics on the percentage of older adults living in poverty, including gender and ethnic differences (U.S. Census Bureau, 2018). Especially noteworthy is the recent decrease in the percentage of Latino older adults living in poverty (17.4 percent in 2016, down from 20 percent in 2013).
- Updated data on the percentage of older adults who use the Internet, which increased to 90 percent in 2019 (Anderson & others, 2019)
- Inclusion of a recent U.S. national study that indicated a dramatic increase in the percentage of older adults who are using health technology (Hung, Lyons, & Wu, 2020)
- New data on the percentage of U.S. men 65 years and older (70 percent) and women in the same age range (46 percent) who were married in 2017 (U.S. Census Bureau, 2018)
- Updated data on the percentage of individuals 65 years and older who are divorced, which increased to 15 percent in 2017 (U.S. Census Bureau, 2018)
- Description of a recent study that indicated today's older adults are more accepting of divorce than their counterparts from two decades ago (Brown & Wright, 2019)
- Inclusion of a recent study of older adults in Great Britain that revealed those who were divorced were more likely to die earlier and have lower life satisfaction than their married counterparts (Bourassa, Ruiz, & Sbarra, 2019)
- Discussion of a recent study of middle-aged and older adults in which 22 percent of women and 37 percent of men repartnered within 10 years (Brown & others, 2019). Repartnering more often involved cohabitation than remarriage, especially for men.
- Description of a recent study of older adults that revealed those with secure attachment were competent in their daily lives, which in turn was related to psychological adjustment (Martin, Horn, & Allemand, 2020)
- Coverage of a recent study of older adults in which having a larger network of friend-confidants or closer connections with friend-confidants was linked to better marital quality for wives and husbands 5 years later (Zhaoyant & Martie, 2020)
- Inclusion of a recent study of older adults that revealed interactions with friends were more pleasant and were associated with fewer stressful discussions of experiences than interactions with partners or family members (Ng & others, 2020)
- Discussion of a recent study of older adults that revealed interactions involving a greater variety of social ties were linked to engaging in more physical activity and less sedentary behavior (Fingerman & others, 2020). Also in this study, greater involvement with diverse social ties was linked to more positive moods.

Chapter 20: Death, Dying, and Grieving

- Update on Physician Orders for Life-Sustaining Treatment (POLST), which in 2019 was available in 40 states
- Update on the number of states that allow assisted suicide, which recently increased to 8 states (with the addition of New Jersey in 2019 and Hawaii in 2018), plus Washington, DC
- Update on countries that allow assisted suicide and those that allow both assisted suicide and euthanasia
- New coverage on the shortage of individuals who have received training to work in hospices and as home health aides for dying individuals (Landes & Wang, 2019)
- Discussion of a recent study in which the Family Bereavement Program resulted in fewer mental health problems and less service use by bereaved young adults and their parents (Sandler & others, 2018)
- Description of a recent study of Mexican children aged 3.5 to 6.9 in which all of the children had a biological understanding of death, while older children were less likely than younger children to endorse the statement that all living things die (Gutierrez & others, 2019). Also in this study, older children reported that a child should feel sad following the death of a loved one.
- Coverage of a recent study in which females experienced a greater decline in mental health and socioemotional functioning than males did after the death of a close friend in adulthood (Liu, Forbat, & Anderson, 2019)
- Inclusion of a recent research review that revealed half of the studies involving heart failure patient interventions emphasizing meaning-making coping substantially improved the quality of life of the patients compared with less than one-third of the interventions not focusing on meaning-making coping (self-care or medical adherence, for example) (Sacco, Leahey, & Park, 2019)
- Coverage of a recent study in which finding meaning in life was negatively associated with depression but positively linked to grief in suicide survivors (Scharer & Hibberd, 2020)
- Discussion of a recent study that found individuals with complicated grief had a higher level of neuroticism (Goetter & others, 2019)

- Description of a recent research review that concluded the death of an only child and violent killings were most likely to be associated with prolonged grief disorder (Djelantik & others, 2020)
- Coverage of a recent study indicating that in the first two years of bereavement for family caregivers of terminally ill cancer patients, prolonged grief disorder preceded the onset of major depressive disorder (Tsai & others, 2020)
- New research indicating that cognitive behavior therapy reduced prolonged grief symptoms (Bartl & others, 2018; Lichtenthal & others, 2019)
- Inclusion of recent research using the dual-process model as a conceptual framework, including studies on parents' use of oscillating coping strategies following their infant's death (Currie & others, 2019) and the importance of restoration-oriented rather than loss-oriented coping both early and later in the bereavement process following a spouse's death (Lundorff & others, 2019)
- Discussion of a recent research review that concluded the dual-process model provides an accurate representation of the bereavement experience and is effective in describing how individuals cope (Fiore, 2020)
- Coverage of a recent research review of widowed Latinos that found risk factors for diminished well-being were being a male, financial strain, cultural stressors, having an undocumented legal status, experiencing widowhood at a younger age, and having poor physical health (Garcinia & others, 2020)
- Description of a recent meta-analysis of mental disorders in widows, with depressive disorders being the most prevalent, followed by anxiety disorders (Balnner Kristiansen & others, 2019)
- New commentary on how being a widow is especially difficult and stressful for individuals who have been happily married for decades
- Coverage of a recent study of widows' and widowers' mental health coping strategies in which widows were more likely to use positive reframing, active distraction, help-seeking, and turning to God for strength, while widowers were more likely to use avoidant strategies and to seek connection with their late spouse (Carr, 2020)
- Updated data on cremation indicating continuing increases in cremation in the United States and Canada (Cremation Association of North America, 2019)
- Updated data on the percentage of widowed women and men 65 years and older in the United States (Aministration on Aging, 2018)

acknowledgments

I very much appreciate the support and guidance provided to me by many people at McGraw-Hill Education. Ryan Treat, Senior Portfolio Manager for Psychology, has provided excellent guidance, vision, and direction for this book. Vicki Malinee provided considerable expertise in coordinating many aspects of the editorial process for this text. Janet Tilden again did an outstanding job as the book's copyeditor. Mary Powers did a terrific job in coordinating the book's production. Dawn Groundwater, Product Development Manager, did excellent work on various aspects of the book's development, technology, and learning systems. Thanks also to Olivia Kaiser for her extensive and outstanding work in marketing *Life-Span Development*. And Jennifer Blankenship provided me with excellent choices of new photographs for this edition.

I also want to thank my parents, John and Ruth Santrock, my wife, Mary Jo, our children, Tracy and Jennifer, and our grandchildren, Jordan, Alex, and Luke, for their wonderful contributions to my life and for helping me to better understand the marvels and mysteries of life-span development.

QUEST: JOURNEY THROUGH THE LIFESPAN BOARD OF ADVISORS AND SUBJECT MATTER EXPERTS

Admiration and appreciation to the following experts who have devoted a significant portion of their time and expertise to creating the first of its kind learning game for Developmental Psychology: Cheri Kittrell, *State College of Florida;* Brandy Young, *Cypress College;* Becky Howell, *Forsyth Technical College;* Gabby Principe, *College of Charleston;* Karen Schrier Shaenfield, *Marist College;* Steven Prunier, *Ivy Tech;* Amy Kolak, *College of Charleston;* Kathleen Hughes Stellmach, *Pasco-Hernando State College;* Lisa Fozio-Thielk, *Waubonsee Community College;* Tricia Wessel-Blaski, *University of Wisconsin-Milwaukee, Washington County;* Margot Underwood, *Joliet Junior College;* Claire Rubman, *Suffolk County Community College;* Alissa Knowles, *University of California-Irvine;* Cortney Simmons, *University of California-Irvine;* Kelli Dunlap, *Level Access-WCAG Accessibility Partners.*

EXPERT CONSULTANTS

As I develop a new edition of this text, I consult with leading experts in their respective areas of life-span development. Their invaluable feedback ensures that the latest research, knowledge, and perspectives are presented throughout the text. Their willingness to devote their time and expertise to this endeavor is greatly appreciated. The Expert Consultants who contributed to this edition, along with their biographies and commentary, can be found on pages xv-xvi.

REVIEWERS

I owe a special debt of gratitude to the reviewers who have provided detailed feedback on *Life-Span Development* over the years.

Patrick K. Ackles, *Michigan State University;* Berkeley Adams, *Jamestown Community College;* Jackie Adamson, *South Dakota School of Mines &* Technology; Judi Addelston, *Valencia College;* Pamela Adelmann, *Saint Paul Technical College;* Joanne M. Alegre, *Yavapai College;* Gary L. Allen, *University of South Carolina;* Kristy Allen, *Ozark Technical College;* Lilia Allen, *Charles County Community College;* Ryan Allen, *The Citadel;* Susan E. Allen, *Baylor University;* Paul Anderer Castillo, *SUNY Canton;* Doreen Arcus, *University of Massachusetts-Lowell;* Frank R. Ashbur, *Valdosta State College;* Leslie Ault, *Hostos Community College-CUNY;* Renee L. Babcock, *Central Michigan University;* John Bauer, *University of Dayton;* Diana Baumrind, *University of California-Berkeley;* Daniel R. Bellack, *Trident Technical College;* Helen E. Benedict, *Baylor University;* Alice D. Beyrent, *Hesser College;* John Biondo, *Community College of Allegheny County-Boyce Campus;* James A. Blackburn, *University of Wisconsin at Madison;* William Blackston, *Baltimore City Community College;* Stephanie Blecharczyk, *Keene State College;* Belinda Blevins-Knabe, *University of Arkansas-Little Rock;* Phaer Bonner, *Jefferson State Community College;* Marc H. Bornstein, *National Institute of Child Health & Development;* Karyn Mitchell Boutlin, *Massasoit Community College;* Donald Bowers, *Community College of Philadelphia;* Saundra Y. Boyd, *Houston Community College;* Michelle Boyer-Pennington, *Middle Tennessee State University;* Ann Brandt-Williams, *Glendale Community College;* Julia Braungart-Rieke, *University of Notre Dame;* Gregory Braswell, *Illinois State University;* Kathy Brown, *California State University-Fullerton;* Jack Busky, *Harrisburg Area Community College;* Marion Cahill, *Our Lady of the Lake College;* Joan B. Cannon, *University of Lowell;* Jeri Carter, *Glendale Community College;* Vincent Castranovo, *Community College of Philadelphia;* Ginny Chappeleau, *Muskingum Area Technical College;* Dominique Charlotteaux, *Broward Community College;* Rosalind Charlesworth, *Weber State University;* Yiwei Chen, *Bowling Green State University;* Bill Cheney, *Crichton College;* M.A. Christenberry, *Augusta College;* Saundra Ciccarelli, *Florida Gulf University;* Kevin Clark, *Indiana University-Kokomo;* Andrea Clements, *East Tennessee State University;* Meredith Cohen, *University of Pittsburgh;* Diane Cook, *Gainesville College;* Pamela Costa, *Tacoma Community College;* Molly Countermine, *Pennsylvania State University;* Ava Craig, *Sacramento City College;* Kathleen Crowley-Long, *College of Saint Rose;* Cynthia Crown, *Xavier University;* Jennifer Dale, *Community College of Aurora;* Dana Davidson, *University of Hawaii-Manoa;* Diane Davis, *Bowie State University;* Karen Davis, *Chippewa Valley Technical College;* Tom L. Day, *Weber State University;* Mehgen Delaney, *College of the Canyons;* Doreen DeSantio, *West Chester University;* Jill De Villiers, *Smith College;* Darryl M. Dietrich, *College of St. Scholastica;* Alisa Diop, *The Community College of Baltimore County;* Bailey Drechsler, *Cuesta College;* Joseph Durlack, *Loyola University;* Mary B. Eberly, *Oakland University;* Margaret Sutton Edmonds, *University of Massachusetts-Boston;* Glen Elder, *University of North Carolina-Chapel Hill;* Martha M. Ellis, *Collin County Community College;* Lena Eriksen, *Western Washington University;* Richard Ewy, *Pennsylvania State University;* Celeste Favela, *El Paso Community College;* Dan Fawaz, *Georgia Perimeter College;* Shirley Feldman, *Stanford University;* Roberta Ferra, *University of Kentucky;* Tiffany Field, *University of Miami;* Linda E. Flickinger, *St. Claire Community College;* Alan Fogel, *University of Utah;* Lynne Andreozzi Fontaine, *Community College of Rhode Island;* Angela Ford, *Jackson State Community College;* Lisa Fozio-Thielk,

Waubonsee Community College; **Tom Frangicetto**, *Northampton Community College;* **Kathleen Corrigan Fuhs**, *J. Sargeant Reynolds Community College;* **J. Steven Fulks**, *Utah State University;* **Cathy Furlong**, *Tulsa Junior College;* **Duwayne Furman**, *Western Illinois University;* **John Gat**, *Humboldt State University;* **Marvin Gelman**, *Montgomery County College;* **G.R. Germo**, *University of California–Irvine;* **Rebecca J. Glare**, *Weber State College;* **David Goldstein**, *Temple University;* **Arthur Gonchar**, *University of LaVerne;* **Judy Goodell**, *National University;* **Mary Ann Goodwyn**, *Northeast Louisiana University;* **Caroline Gould**, *Eastern Michigan University;* **Julia Graber**, *Columbia University;* **Peter C. Gram**, *Pensacola Junior College;* **Dan Grangaard**, *Austin Community College;* **Tom Gray**, *Laredo Community College;* **Michele Gregoire**, *University of Florida–Gainesville;* **Michael Green**, *University of North Carolina;* **Rea Gubler**, *Southern Utah University;* **Gary Gute**, *University of Northern Iowa;* **Laura Hanish**, *Arizona State University;* **Ester Hanson**, *Prince George's Community College;* **Marian S. Harris**, *University of Illinois–Chicago;* **Yvette R. Harris**, *Miami University of Ohio;* **Amanda W. Harrist**, *Oklahoma State University;* **Robert Heavilin**, *Greater Hartford Community College;* **Donna Henderson**, *Wake Forest University;* **Debra Hollister**, *Valencia Community College;* **Heather Holmes-Lonergan**, *Metropolitan State College of Denver;* **Ramona O. Hopkins**, *Brigham Young University;* **Donna Horbury**, *Appalachian State University;* **Susan Horton**, *Mesa Community College;* **Sharon C. Hott**, *Allegany College of Maryland;* **John Hotz**, *Saint Cloud State University;* **Tasha Howe**, *Humboldt State University;* **Kimberley Howe-Norris**, *Cape Fear Community College;* **Stephen Hoyer**, *Pittsburg State University;* **Charles H. Huber**, *New Mexico State University;* **Kathleen Day Hulbert**, *University of Massachusetts-Lowell;* **Derek Isaacowitz**, *Brandeis University;* **Kathryn French Iroz**, *Utah Valley State College;* **Terry Isbell**, *Northwestern State University of Louisiana;* **Erwin Janek**, *Henderson State University;* **Mark O. Jarvis**, *Salt Lake Community College;* **Jamia Jasper Jacobsen**, *Indiana University-Purdue University Indianapolis;* **Christina Jose-Kampfner**, *Eastern Michigan University;* **Ursula Joyce**, *St. Thomas Aquinas College;* **Barbara Kane**, *Indiana State University;* **Ulas Kaplan**, *Harvard University;* **Kevin Keating**, *Broward Community College;* **James L. Keeney**, *Middle Georgia College;* **Yuthika Kim**, *Oklahoma City Community College;* **Elinor Kinarthy**, *Rio Hondo College;* **Karen Kirkendall**, *Sangamon State University;* **A. Klingner**, *Northwest Community College;* **Steven J. Kohn**, *Nazareth College;* **Amanda Kowal**, *University of Missouri;* **Jane Krump**, *North Dakota State College of Science;* **Nadene L'Amoreaux**, *Indiana University of Pennsylvania;* **Gisela Labouvie-Vief**, *Wayne State University;* **Joseph C. LaVoie**, *University of Nebraska–Omaha;* **Juliet Lee**, *Cape Fear Community College;* **Kathy Lein**, *Community College of Denver;* **Jean Hill Macht**, *Montgomery County Community College;* **Salvador Macias**, *University of South Carolina–Sumter;* **Karen Macrae**, *University of South Carolina;* **Jennifer Maggs**, *Pennsylvania State University;* **Christine Malecki**, *Northern Illinois University;* **Kathy Manuel**, *Bossier Parish Community College;* **James Marcia**, *Simon Fraser University;* **Myra Marcus**, *Florida Gulf Coast University;* **Carrie Margolin**, *The Evergreen State College;* **Allan Mayotte**, *Riverland Community College;* **Susan McClure**, *Westmoreland Community College;* **Daniel McConnell**, *University of Central Florida;* **Michael J. McCoy**, *Cape Fear Community College;* **Dorothy H. McDonald**, *Sandhills Community College;* **Robert C. McGinnis**, *Ancilla College;* **Clara McKinney**, *Barstow College;* **Robert McLaren**, *California State University–Fullerton;* **Deborah H. McMurtrie**, *University of South Carolina–Aiken;* **Sharon McNeeley**, *Northeastern Illinois University;* **Daysi Mejia**, *Florida Gulf Coast University;* **Kathleen Mentink**, *Chippewa Valley Technical College;* **James Messina**, *University of Phoenix;* **Heather E. Metcalfe**, *University of Windsor;* **Karla Miley**, *Black Hawk College;* **Jessica Miller**, *Mesa State College;* **Scott Miller**, *University of Florida;* **Teri M. Miller-Schwartz**, *Milwaukee Area Technical College;* **David B. Mitchell**, *Loyola University;* **Joann Montepare**, *Emerson College;* **Gary T. Montgomery**, *University of Texas–Pan American;* **Martin D. Murphy**, *University of Akron;* **Malinda Muzi**, *Community College of Philadelphia;* **Gordon K. Nelson**, *Pennsylvania State University;* **Michael Newton**, *Sam Houston State University;* **Charisse Nixon**, *Pennsylvania State University–Erie;* **Beatrice Norrie**, *Mount Royal College;* **Jean O'Neil**, *Boston College;* **Laura Overstreet**, *Tarrant County College-Northeast;* **Karla Parise**, *The Community College of Baltimore County–Essex;* **Jennifer Parker**, *University of South Carolina;* **Barba Patton**, *University of Houston-Victoria;* **Lucinda Payne**, *Appalachian State University;* **Susan Perez**, *University of North Florida;* **Pete Peterson**, *Johnson County Community College;* **Richard Pierce**, *Pennsylvania State University-Altoona;* **David Pipes**, *Caldwell Community College;* **Leslee Pollina**, *Southeast Missouri State University;* **Robert Poresky**, *Kansas State University;* **Yvonne Valenzuela Portillo**, *Golden West College;* **Christopher Quarto**, *Middle Tennessee State University;* **Bob Rainey**, *Florida Community College;* **Nancy Rankin**, *University of New England;* **H. Ratner**, *Wayne State University;* **Cynthia Reed**, *Tarrant County College-Northeast;* **James Reid**, *Washington University;* **Amy Reesing**, *Arizona University;* **Russell Riley**, *Lord Fairfax Community College;* **Mark P. Rittman**, *Cuyahoga Community College;* **Cathie Robertson**, *Grossmont College;* **Clarence Romeno**, *Riverside Community College;* **Paul Roodin**, *SUNY-Oswego;* **Ron Rossac**, *University of North Florida;* **Peggy Russell**, *Indiana River State College;* **Julia Rux**, *Georgia Perimeter College;* **Carolyn Saarni**, *Sonoma State University;* **Karen Salekin**, *University of Alabama;* **Gayla Sanders**, *The Community College of Baltimore County-Essex;* **Toru Sato**, *Shippensburg University;* **Nancy Sauerman**, *Kirkwood Community College;* **Cynthia Scheibe**, *Ithaca College;* **Robert Schell**, *SUNY-Oswego;* **Derek Schorsch**, *Valencia College East;* **Rachel Schremp**, *Santa Fe Community College;* **Pamela Schuetze**, *Buffalo State College;* **Edythe Schwartz**, *California State University–Sacramento;* **Lisa Scott**, *University of Minnesota-Twin Cities;* **Owen Sharkey**, *University of Prince Edward Island;* **Elisabeth Shaw**, *Texarkana College;* **Susan Nakayama Siaw**, *California State Polytechnical University;* **Jessica Siebenbruner**, *Winona State College;* **Vicki Simmons**, *University of Victoria;* **Gregory Smith**, *University of Maryland;* **Jon Snodgrass**, *California State University-Los Angeles;* **Donald Stanley**, *North Dallas Community College;* **Jean A. Steitz**, *University of Memphis;* **Terre Sullivan**, *Chippewa Valley Technical College;* **Collier Summers**, *Florida Community College at Jacksonville;* **Samuel Taylor**, *Tacoma Community College;* **Barbara Thomas**, *National University;* **Stacy D. Thompson**, *Oklahoma State University;* **Debbie Tindell**, *Wilkes University;* **Stephen Truhon**, *Winston-Salem State University;* **James Turcott**, *Kalamazoo Valley Community College;* **Marian Underwood**, *University of Texas–Dallas;* **Dennis Valone**, *Pennsylvania State University–Erie;* **Gaby Vandergiessen**, *Fairmount State College;* **Elisa Velasquez**, *Sonoma State University;* **Ester Warren**, *Liberty University;* **Stephen Werba**, *The Community College of Baltimore County–Catonsville;* **B.D. Whetstone**, *Birmingham Southern College;* **Susan Whitbourne**, *University of Massachusetts–Amherst;* **Nancy C. White**, *Reynolds Community College;* **Lyn W. Wickelgren**, *Metropolitan State College;* **Ann M. Williams**, *Luzerne County Community College;* **Myron D. Williams**, *Great Lakes Bible College;* **Linda B. Wilson**, *Quincy College;* **Mark Winkel**, *University of Texas–Pan American;* **Mary Ann Wisniewski**, *Carroll College.*

All the world's a stage,
And all the men and women merely players.
They have their exits and their entrances;
And one man in his time plays many parts.

—WILLIAM SHAKESPEARE
English playwright, 17th century

The Life-Span Perspective

This book is about human development—its universal features, its individual variations, its nature. Every life is distinct, a new biography in the world. Examining the shape of life-span development allows us to understand it better. *Life-Span Development* is about the rhythm and meaning of people's lives, about turning mystery into understanding, and about weaving a portrait of who each of us was, is, and will be. In Section 1, you will read the "Introduction."

chapter 1

INTRODUCTION

chapter **outline**

① The Life-Span Perspective

Learning Goal 1 Discuss the distinctive features of a life-span perspective on development.

The Importance of Studying Life-Span Development
Characteristics of the Life-Span Perspective
Some Contemporary Concerns

② The Nature of Development

Learning Goal 2 Identify the most important processes, periods, and issues in development.

Biological, Cognitive, and Socioemotional Processes
Periods of Development
The Significance of Age
Developmental Issues

③ Theories of Development

Learning Goal 3 Describe the main theories of human development.

Psychoanalytic Theories
Cognitive Theories
Behavioral and Social Cognitive Theories
Ethological Theory
Ecological Theory
An Eclectic Theoretical Orientation

④ Research on Life-Span Development

Learning Goal 4 Explain how research on life-span development is conducted.

Methods for Collecting Data
Research Designs
Time Span of Research
Conducting Ethical Research
Minimizing Bias

Ariel Skelley/Getty Images

Ted Kaczynski sprinted through high school, not bothering with his junior year and making only passing efforts at social contact. Off to Harvard at age 16, Kaczynski was a loner during his college years.

One of his roommates at Harvard said that he avoided people by quickly shuffling by them and slamming the door behind him. After obtaining his Ph.D. in mathematics at the University of Michigan, Kaczynski became a professor at the University of California at Berkeley. His colleagues there remember him as hiding from social contact—no friends, no allies, no networking.

After several years at Berkeley, Kaczynski resigned and moved to a rural area of Montana where he lived as a hermit in a crude shack for 25 years. Town residents described him as a bearded eccentric. In 1996, he was arrested and charged as the notorious Unabomber, America's most-wanted killer. Over the course of 17 years, Kaczynski had sent 16 mail bombs that left 23 people wounded or maimed and 3 people dead. In 1998, he pleaded guilty to the offenses and was sentenced to life in prison.

A decade before Kaczynski mailed his first bomb, Alice Walker spent her days battling racism in Mississippi. She had recently won her first writing fellowship, but rather than use the money to follow her dream of moving to Senegal, Africa, she put herself into the heart and heat of the civil rights movement. Walker had grown up knowing the brutal effects of poverty and racism. Born in 1944, she was the eighth child of Georgia sharecroppers who earned $300 a year. When Walker was 8, her brother accidentally shot her in the left eye with a BB gun. By the time her parents got her to the hospital a week later (they had no car), she was blind in that eye, and it had developed a disfiguring layer of scar tissue. Despite the counts against her, Walker overcame pain and anger and went on to win a Pulitzer Prize for her book *The Color Purple*. She became not only a novelist but also an essayist, a poet, a short-story writer, and a social activist.

Ted Kaczynski, the convicted Unabomber, traced his difficulties to growing up as a genius in a kid's body and not fitting in when he was a child.
Seanna O'Sullivan

Ted Kaczynski, about age 15–16.
WBBM-TV/AFP/Getty Images

Alice Walker won the Pulitzer Prize for her book *The Color Purple*. Like the characters in her book, Walker overcame pain and anger to triumph and celebrate the human spirit.
Monica Morgan/WireImage/Getty Images

Alice Walker, about age 8.
Courtesy of Alice Walker

preview

What leads one individual, so full of promise, to commit brutal acts of violence and another to turn poverty and trauma into a rich literary harvest? If you have ever wondered why people turn out the way they do, you have asked yourself the central question we will be exploring. This text traces the journey of human development—your own and that of every other member of the human species. In this chapter, we will explore what it means to take a life-span perspective on development, examine the nature of development, and outline how science helps us to understand it.

1 The Life-Span Perspective

LG1 Discuss the distinctive features of a life-span perspective on development.

| The Importance of Studying Life-Span Development | Characteristics of the Life-Span Perspective | Some Contemporary Concerns |

> We reach backward to our parents and forward to our children, and through their children to a future we will never see, but about which we need to care.
>
> —CARL JUNG
> *Swiss psychiatrist, 20th century*

Each of us develops partly like all other individuals, partly like some other individuals, and partly like no other individual. Most of the time our attention is directed to each individual's uniqueness. But as humans, we have all traveled some common paths. Each of us—Leonardo da Vinci, Joan of Arc, George Washington, Martin Luther King, Jr., and you—walked at about 1 year, engaged in fantasy play as a young child, and became more independent as a youth. Each of us, if we live long enough, will experience hearing problems and the death of family members and friends. This is the general course of our **development,** the pattern of movement or change that begins at conception and continues through the human life span.

In this section, we will explore what is meant by the concept of development and why the study of life-span development is important. We will outline the main characteristics of the life-span perspective and discuss various sources of contextual influences. In addition, we will examine some contemporary concerns in life-span development.

THE IMPORTANCE OF STUDYING LIFE-SPAN DEVELOPMENT

How might people benefit from examining life-span development? Perhaps you are, or will be, a parent or teacher. If so, responsibility for children is, or will be, a part of your everyday life. The more you learn about them, the better you can deal with them. Perhaps you hope to gain some insight about your own history—as an infant, a child, an adolescent, or a young adult. Perhaps you want to know more about what your life will be like during your adult years—in middle age or old age, for example. Or perhaps you just stumbled onto this course, thinking that it sounded intriguing and that the study of the human life span might raise some provocative issues. Whatever your reasons for taking this course, you will discover that the study of life-span development is intriguing and filled with information about who we are, how we came to be this way, and where our future will take us.

Most development involves growth, but it also includes decline (as in dying). In exploring development, we will examine the life span from the point of conception until the time when life (or at least life as we know it) ends. You will see yourself as an infant, a child, and an adolescent, and be stimulated to think about how those years influenced the kind of individual you are today. And you will see yourself as a young adult, as a middle-aged adult, and as an adult in old age, and be motivated to think about how your experiences today will influence your development through the remainder of your adult years.

CHARACTERISTICS OF THE LIFE-SPAN PERSPECTIVE

Although growth and development are dramatic during the first two decades of life, development is not something that happens only to children and adolescents (Leipold, 2020). The traditional approach to the study of development emphasizes extensive change from birth to

development The pattern of change that begins at conception and continues through the life span. Most development involves growth, although it also includes decline brought on by aging and dying.

life-span perspective The perspective that development is lifelong, multidimensional, multidirectional, plastic, multidisciplinary, and contextual; involves growth, maintenance, and regulation; and is constructed through biological, sociocultural, and individual factors working together.

adolescence (especially during infancy), little or no change in adulthood, and decline in old age. But a great deal of change does occur in the five or six decades after adolescence. The life-span approach emphasizes developmental change throughout adulthood as well as childhood (Antonucci & Webster, 2019).

Life Expectancy   Recent increases in human life expectancy have contributed to the popularity of the life-span approach to development. The upper boundary of the human life span (based on the oldest age documented) is 122 years, as indicated in Figure 1; this maximum life span of humans has not changed since the beginning of recorded history. What has changed is life expectancy—the average number of years that a person born in a particular year can expect to live. In the twentieth century alone, life expectancy in the United States increased by 32 years, thanks to improvements in sanitation, nutrition, and medicine (see Figure 2). For individuals born in 2017 in the United States, their life expectancy is 78.6 years of age (Arias & Xu, 2019).

For the first time in U.S. history, in 2019 there were more people over 60 years of age than under 18 years of age. In less than a century, more years were added to human life expectancy than in all of the prior millennia.

Laura Carstensen (2015a, b, 2016, 2019a, b) recently has examined the challenges and opportunities presented by this dramatic increase in life expectancy. In her view, the remarkable increase in life span has happened so quickly that science, technology, and social expectations have not kept pace. She proposes that the challenge is to change from a world constructed mainly for young people to a world that is more compatible and supportive for the increasing number of people living to age 100 and beyond. Carstensen (2015b, p. 70) predicts that making this transformation will be no small feat:

> . . . parks, transportation systems, staircases, and even hospitals presume that the users have both strength and stamina; suburbs across the country are built for two parents and their young children, not single people, multiple generations or elderly people who are not able to drive. Our education system serves the needs of young children and young adults and offers little more than recreation for experienced people.

Indeed, the very conception of work as a full-time endeavor ending in the early sixties is ill suited for long lives (Carstensen, 2019a). Arguably the most troubling aspect of our view of aging is that we fret about ways the older people lack the qualities of younger people rather than exploit a growing new resource right before our eyes: citizens who have deep expertise, emotional balance, and the motivation to make a difference (Carstensen, 2019a).

Certainly some progress has been made recently in improving the lives of older adults. In our discussion of late adulthood, you will read about progress in understanding and influencing the aging process through interventions such as modifying the activity of genes related to aging, improving brain function in the elderly, and slowing or even reversing the effects of various chronic diseases. You'll also learn about ways to help people plan for a better life when they get old, become more cognitively sharp as they age, improve their physical fitness, and feel more satisfied with their lives as older adults. But much more remains to be accomplished (Rowe & others, 2019).

The Life-Span Perspective   The belief that development continues throughout life is central to the life-span perspective on human development, but this perspective has other characteristics as well. According to life-span development expert Paul Baltes (1939–2006), the **life-span perspective** views development as lifelong, multidimensional, multidirectional, plastic, multidisciplinary, and contextual, and as a process that involves growth, maintenance, and regulation of loss (Baltes, 1987, 2003; Baltes, Lindenberger, & Staudinger, 2006). In Baltes' view, it is important to understand that development is constructed through biological, sociocultural, and individual factors working together. Let's explore each of these components of the life-span perspective.

Development Is Lifelong   In the life-span perspective, early adulthood is not the endpoint of development; rather, no age period dominates development. Researchers increasingly study the experiences and psychological orientations of adults at different points in their lives. Later in this chapter, we will describe the age periods of development and their characteristics.

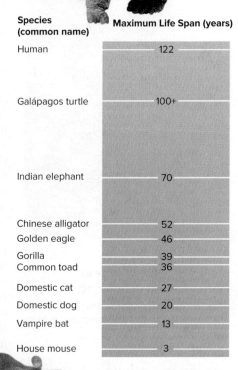

Species (common name)	Maximum Life Span (years)
Human	122
Galápagos turtle	100+
Indian elephant	70
Chinese alligator	52
Golden eagle	46
Gorilla	39
Common toad	36
Domestic cat	27
Domestic dog	20
Vampire bat	13
House mouse	3

FIGURE 1

MAXIMUM RECORDED LIFE SPAN FOR DIFFERENT SPECIES. Our only competitor for the maximum recorded life span is the Galápagos turtle.

(*Tortoise image on top*) Philip Coblentz/MedioImages/SuperStock; (*mouse image at bottom*) Redmond Durrell/Alamy Stock Photo

One-hundred-year-old Don Pellman from Santa Clara, California, keeps breaking world records in track for older adults, beating many contestants who are 20 and 30 years younger than he is.
Sandy Huffaker/The New York Times/Redux

Time Period	Average Life Expectancy (years)
2017, USA	79
1954, USA	70
1915, USA	54
1900, USA	47
19th century, England	41
1620, Massachusetts Bay Colony	35
Middle Ages, England	33
Ancient Greece	20
Prehistoric times	18

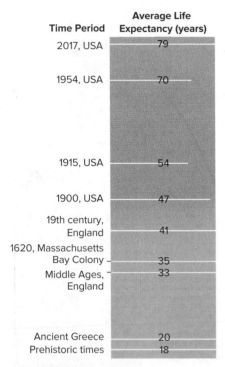

FIGURE 2

HUMAN LIFE EXPECTANCY AT BIRTH FROM PREHISTORIC TO CONTEMPORARY TIMES. It took 5,000 years to extend human life expectancy from 18 to 41 years of age.

Paul Baltes, a leading architect of the life-span perspective of development, converses with one of the long-time research participants in the Berlin Aging Study that he directs. She joined the study in the early 1990s and has participated six times in extensive physical, medical, psychological, and social assessments. In her professional life, she was a practicing medical doctor.
Margaret M. and Paul B. Baltes Foundation

normative age-graded influences Influences that are similar for individuals in a particular age group.

normative history-graded influences Influences that are common to people of a particular generation because of historical circumstances.

Development Is Multidimensional   No matter what your age might be, your body, mind, emotions, and relationships are changing and affecting each other. Consider the development of Ted Kaczynski, the Unabomber discussed at the beginning of this chapter. When he was 6 months old, he was hospitalized with a severe allergic reaction and his parents were rarely allowed to visit him. According to his mother, the previously happy baby was never the same after his hospitalization. He became withdrawn and unresponsive. As Ted grew up, he had periodic "shutdowns" accompanied by rage. In his mother's view, a biological event during infancy warped the development of her son's mind and emotions.

Development has biological, cognitive, and socioemotional dimensions. Even within a dimension, there are many components (Bermudez, 2020; Handing & others, 2019). For example, attention, memory, abstract thinking, speed of processing information, and social intelligence are just a few of the components of the cognitive dimension.

Development Is Multidirectional   Throughout life, some dimensions or components of a dimension expand and others shrink. For example, when one language (such as English) is acquired early in development, the capacity for acquiring second and third languages (such as Spanish and Chinese) decreases later in development, especially after early childhood (Levelt, 1989). During adolescence, as individuals establish romantic relationships, their time spent with friends may decrease. During late adulthood, older adults might become wiser because they have more experience than younger adults to draw upon to guide their decision making (Jeste & Lee, 2019), but they perform more poorly on tasks that require speed in processing information (Salthouse, 2019).

Development Is Plastic   Even at 10 years old, Ted Kaczynski was extraordinarily shy. Was he destined to remain forever uncomfortable with people? Developmentalists debate how much plasticity people have in various dimensions at different points in their development (Kinugawa, 2019; Thomas & Ansari, 2020). Plasticity means the capacity for change. For example, can you still improve your intellectual skills when you are in your seventies or eighties? Or might these intellectual skills be fixed by the time you are in your thirties so that further improvement is impossible? Researchers have found that the cognitive skills of older adults can be improved through training and acquisition of effective strategies (Calero, 2019; Dorrenbacher & others, 2020). However, possibly we possess less capacity for change as we grow older. Understanding plasticity and its constraints is a key element on the contemporary agenda for developmental research (Oakes & Rakison, 2020).

Developmental Science Is Multidisciplinary   Psychologists, sociologists, anthropologists, neuroscientists, and medical researchers all share an interest in unlocking the mysteries of development throughout the life span. How do your heredity and health limit your intelligence? Do intelligence and social relationships change with age in the same ways around the world? How do families and schools influence intellectual development? These are examples of research questions that cut across disciplines.

Development Is Contextual   All development occurs within a context, or setting. Contexts include families, schools, peer groups, churches, cities, neighborhoods, university laboratories, countries, and so on. Each of these settings is influenced by historical, economic, social, and cultural factors (Parke & Elder, 2020).

Contexts, like individuals, change (Levy & Wright, 2020; Marks, Woolverton, & Garcia Coll, 2020). Thus, individuals are changing beings in a changing world. As a result of these changes, contexts exert three types of influences (Baltes, 2003): (1) normative age-graded influences, (2) normative history-graded influences, and (3) nonnormative or highly individualized life events. Each type of influence can have a biological or environmental impact on development.

Normative age-graded influences are similar for individuals in a particular age group. These influences include biological processes such as puberty and menopause. They also include sociocultural factors and environmental processes such as beginning formal education (usually at about age 6 in most cultures) and retiring from the workforce (which takes place during the fifties and sixties in most cultures).

Normative history-graded influences are common to people of a particular generation because of historical circumstances (Elder & Cox, 2020). Examples of normative history-graded influences include economic, political, and social upheavals such as the Great Depression in the 1930s, World War II in the 1940s, the civil rights and women's rights movements of the 1960s and 1970s, the terrorist attacks of 9/11/2001, the integration of computers and cell phones into everyday life during the 1990s, and time spent on social media in the last decade (Pittinsky, 2019). Long-term changes in the genetic and cultural makeup of a population (due to immigration or changes in fertility rates) are also part of normative historical change.

Nonnormative life events are unusual occurrences that have a major impact on the lives of individual people. These events do not happen to everyone, and when they do occur they can influence people in different ways (Masten, Motti-Stefanidi, & Rahl-Brigman, 2020). Examples include the death of a parent when a child is young, pregnancy in early adolescence, a fire that destroys a home, winning the lottery, or getting an unexpected career opportunity.

Development Involves Growth, Maintenance, and Regulation of Loss   Baltes and his colleagues (2006) assert that the mastery of life often involves conflicts and competition among three goals of human development: growth, maintenance, and regulation of loss. As individuals age into middle and late adulthood, maintenance and regulation of loss in their capacities take center stage. Thus, a 75-year-old man might aim not to improve his memory or his golf swing but to maintain his independence and his ability to play golf at all. In the chapters on "Physical and Cognitive Development in Middle Adulthood" and "Socioemotional Development in Middle Adulthood" we will discuss maintenance and regulation of loss in greater depth.

Development Is a Co-construction of Biology, Culture, and the Individual   Development is a co-construction of biological, cultural, and individual factors working together (Baltes, Reuter-Lorenz, & Rösler, 2012). For example, the brain shapes culture, but it is also shaped by culture and the experiences that individuals have or pursue. In terms of individual factors, we can go beyond what our genetic inheritance and our environment give us. We can author a unique developmental path by actively choosing from the environment the things that optimize our lives (Rathunde & Csikszentmihalyi, 2006).

SOME CONTEMPORARY CONCERNS

Pick up a newspaper or magazine and you might see headlines like these: "Screen Time Linked to Children's Obesity," "Political Leanings May Be Written in the Genes," "FDA Warns About Long-Term Effects of ADHD Drug," "Heart Attack Deaths Higher in African American Patients," or "Test May Predict Alzheimer Disease." Researchers using the life-span perspective are examining these and many other topics of contemporary concern. The roles that health and well-being, parenting, education, sociocultural contexts, and technology play in life-span development, as well as how social policy is related to these issues, are a particular focus of this edition.

Health and Well-Being   Health professionals today recognize the powerful influences of lifestyles and psychological states on health and well-being (Graham, Holt/Hale, & Parker, 2020; Teague, Mackenzie, & Rosenthal, 2020). Does a pregnant woman endanger her fetus if she drinks a few beers per week? How does a poor diet affect a child's ability to learn? Are children getting less exercise today than in the past? What roles do parents and peers play in whether adolescents abuse drugs? What health-enhancing and health-compromising behaviors do college students engage in? What factors are causing the obesity epidemic in the United States and around the world? How can older adults cope with declining health? We will discuss many questions like these regarding health and well-being (Goode, 2020; Telljohann & others, 2020). In every chapter of *Life-Span Development*, issues of health and well-being are integrated into our discussions.

Clinical psychologists are among the health professionals who help people improve their well-being. Read about one clinical psychologist who helps adolescents and adults improve their developmental outcomes in *Connecting with Careers*.

What characterizes the life-span perspective on development?
Derek E. Rothchild/Photodisc/Getty Images

nonnormative life events Unusual occurrences that have a major impact on an individual's life.

developmental **connection**

Middle Age

Adults typically face more losses in middle age than earlier in life. Connect to "Physical and Cognitive Development in Middle Adulthood."

developmental **connection**

Exercise

What effect might exercise have on children's and older adults' ability to process information? Connect to "Physical and Cognitive Development in Middle and Late Childhood" and "Physical Development in Late Adulthood."

Nonnormative life events, such as Hurricane Maria in Puerto Rico in 2017, are unusual circumstances that can have a major influence on a person's development.
Mario Tama/Staff/Getty Images

Gustavo Medrano, Clinical Psychologist

Gustavo Medrano specializes in helping children, adolescents, and adults of all ages improve their lives when they have problems involving depression, anxiety, emotion regulation, chronic health conditions, and life transitions. He works individually with clients and provides therapy for couples and families. As a native Spanish speaker, he also provides bicultural and bilingual therapy for clients.

Dr. Medrano is a faculty member at the Family Institute at Northwestern University in Evanston, Illinois. He obtained his undergraduate degree in psychology at Northwestern and then became a high school teacher through Teach for America, a program where participants spend at least two years teaching in a high-poverty area. He received his master's and doctoral degrees in clinical psychology at the University of Wisconsin–Milwaukee. As a faculty member at Northwestern, in addition to doing clinical therapy with clients, he conducts research focusing on how family experiences, especially parenting, influence children's and adolescents' ability to cope with chronic pain and other challenges.

Gustavo Medrano, clinical psychologist, provides therapy to children, adolescents, and adults, especially using his bilingual background and skills to work with Latino clients.
©Avis Mandel Pictures

For more information about what clinical psychologists do, see the Careers in Life-Span Development appendix.

Children learn to love when they are loved

Robert Maust/Photo Agora

Parenting and Education Can two gay men raise a healthy family? Are children harmed if both parents work outside the home? Are U.S. schools failing to teach children how to read and write and calculate adequately? We hear many questions like these involving pressures on the contemporary family and conditions impairing the effectiveness of U.S. schools (Ellis, Riggs, & Peel, 2020; Gonzalez-Mena, 2020). In later chapters, we will analyze child care, the effects of divorce, parenting styles, child maltreatment, intergenerational relationships, early childhood education, links between childhood poverty and education, bilingual education, recent efforts to improve lifelong learning, and many other issues related to parenting and education (Crosnoe, 2020; Diaz-Rico, 2020).

Sociocultural Contexts and Diversity Health, parenting, and education—like development itself—are shaped by their sociocultural context (Marks, Woolverton, & Garcia-Coll, 2020; Walsh & Mortensen, 2020). To analyze this context, four concepts are especially useful: culture, ethnicity, socioeconomic status, and gender.

Culture encompasses the behavior patterns, beliefs, and all other products of a particular group of people that are passed on from generation to generation (Crosnoe, 2020; Li, 2020). Culture results from the interaction of people over many years (Schoon & Bynner, 2020). A cultural group can be as large as the United States or as small as an isolated Appalachian town. Whatever its size, the group's culture influences the behavior of its members (Leventhal, Anastasio, & Dupere, 2020).

Cross-cultural studies compare aspects of two or more cultures. The comparison provides information about the degree to which development is similar (or universal) across cultures,

culture The behavior patterns, beliefs, and all other products of a group that are passed on from generation to generation.

cross-cultural studies Comparison of one culture with one or more other cultures. These studies indicate the degree to which development is similar, or universal, across cultures, and the degree to which it is culture-specific.

or is instead culture-specific (Quashie & others, 2020). For example, in a recent study of 26 countries, individuals in Chile had the highest life satisfaction, while those in Bulgaria and Spain had the lowest (Jang & others, 2017).

Ethnicity (the word *ethnic* comes from the Greek word for "nation") is rooted in cultural heritage, nationality, race, religion, and language. African Americans, Latinos, Asian Americans, Native Americans, European Americans, and Arab Americans are a few examples of broad ethnic groups in the United States. Diversity exists within each ethnic group (Levy & Wright, 2020). In 2017, 50.5 percent of children 17 years and younger were non-Latino White; by 2050, this figure is projected to decrease to 38.8 percent (ChildStats.gov, 2018). In 2017 in the United States, 25.2 percent of children were Latino, but by 2050 that figure is projected to increase to 31.9 percent. Asian Americans are expected to be the fastest-growing ethnic group of children percentage-wise: In 2017, 5.1 percent were Asian American, and that figure is expected to grow to 7.4 percent in 2050. The percentage of African American children is expected to decrease slightly, from 13.6 percent in 2017 to 13.1 percent in 2050.

A special concern is the discrimination and prejudice experienced by ethnic minority children (Zeiders & others, 2020). Recent research indicates that pride in one's ethnic identity has positive outcomes (Umana-Taylor, 2018). For example, in a recent study, strong ethnic group affiliation and connection were associated with fewer psychiatric problems (Anglin & others, 2018).

Socioeconomic status (SES) refers to a person's position within society based on occupational, educational, and economic characteristics. Socioeconomic status implies certain inequalities (Cambron & others, 2020; Lervag & others, 2019). Differences in the ability to control resources and to participate in society's rewards produce unequal opportunities (Roos, Wall-Wieler, & Lee, 2020).

Gender refers to the characteristics of people as males and females. Few aspects of our development are more central to our identity and social relationships than gender (Best & Puzio, 2019; Helgeson, 2020).

Recently, considerable research interest has focused on a category of gender classification called *transgender,* a broad term that refers to individuals who adopt a gender identity that differs from the one assigned to them at birth (Ellis, Riggs, & Peel, 2020). A transgender identity of being born male but identifying with being a female is much more common than the reverse (Zucker, Lawrence, & Kreukels, 2016). We will have much more to say about gender and transgender later in the text.

In the United States, the sociocultural context has become increasingly diverse in recent years. The U.S. population includes a greater variety of cultures and ethnic groups than ever before. This changing demographic tapestry promises not only the richness that diversity brings but also difficult challenges in extending the American dream to all individuals (Parke, 2020). We will discuss sociocultural contexts and diversity in each chapter.

A special cross-cultural concern is the educational and psychological conditions of women around the world (UNICEF, 2018). Inadequate educational opportunities, violence, and mental health issues are among the problems faced by many women.

Considerable progress has been made in many parts of the world in girls' school attendance (UNICEF, 2020). However, in some regions, girls continue to receive less education. For example, in secondary schools in West and Central Africa, only 76 girls are enrolled for every 100 boys (UNICEF, 2015).

In this section, you have read about such important aspects of individuals as their cultural and socioeconomic backgrounds, ethnicity, and gender. As people go through the human life span, these categories intersect and can create systems of power and privilege as well as oppression and discrimination. For example, higher-socioeconomic-status, non-Latino White males have experienced considerably greater privilege and less discrimination than African American females. At various points in this text, we will further explore these category connections.

Social Policy **Social policy** is a government's course of action designed to promote the welfare of its citizens. Values, economics, and politics all shape a nation's social policy (Garbarino, Governale, & Kostelny, 2019). Out of concern that policy makers are doing too little to protect the well-being of children and older adults, life-span researchers are increasingly undertaking studies that they hope will lead to effective social policy (Bornstein & Lansford, 2019).

Statistics such as infant mortality rates, mortality among children under 5, and the percentage of children who are malnourished or living in poverty provide benchmarks for evaluating how well children are doing in a particular society (UNICEF, 2018). Marian Wright Edelman,

Asian American and Latino children are the fastest-growing immigrant groups in the United States. *How diverse are the students in your life-span development class? How are their experiences in growing up likely similar to or different from yours?*
Zuma Press Inc./Alamy Stock Photo

ethnicity A characteristic based on cultural heritage, nationality characteristics, race, religion, and language.

socioeconomic status (SES) Refers to the grouping of people with similar occupational, educational, and economic characteristics.

gender The characteristics of people as males or females.

social policy A national government's course of action designed to promote the welfare of its citizens.

Doly Akter, age 17, lives in a slum in Dhaka, Bangladesh, where sewers overflow, garbage rots in the streets, and children are undernourished. Nearly two-thirds of young women in Bangladesh marry before they are 18. Doly organized a club supported by UNICEF in which girls go door-to-door to monitor the hygiene habits of households in their neighborhood. The monitoring has led to improved hygiene and health in the families. Also, her group has managed to stop several child marriages by meeting with parents and convincing them that it is not in their daughters' best interests. When talking with parents in their neighborhoods, the girls in the club emphasize the importance of staying in school and how this will improve their daughters' future. Doly says that the girls in her UNICEF group are far more aware of their rights than their mothers ever were. (UNICEF, 2007).
Naser Siddique/UNICEF Bangladesh

Ann Masten (*far right*) with a homeless mother and her child who are participating in her research on resilience. Masten and her colleagues have found that good parenting skills and good cognitive skills (especially attention and self-control) improve the likelihood that children in challenging circumstances will do better when they enter elementary school.
Dawn Villella Photography

Marian Wright Edelman, president emerita and founder of the Children's Defense Fund (shown here advocating for health care), has been a tireless advocate of children's rights and has been instrumental in calling attention to the needs of children. *What are some of these needs?*
Courtesy of the Children's Defense Fund

a tireless advocate for children's rights, has pointed out that such indicators place the United States at or near the lowest rank for industrialized nations in the treatment of children.

Children who grow up in poverty represent a special concern (Barry & Overland, 2019). In 2017, 17.5 percent of U.S. children under 18 years of age were living in families with incomes below the poverty line (Jiang, Granja, & Koball, 2017). This is an increase from 2001 (16 percent) but a decrease from a peak of 23 percent in 1993 and also down from 19.7 percent in 2015 (Fontenot, Semega, & Kollar, 2018). However, the U.S. figure of 17.5 percent of children living in poverty is much higher than the rates in other developed countries. For example, Canada has a child poverty rate of 9 percent and Sweden has a rate of 2 percent (Fontenot, Semega, & Kollar, 2018).

Compared with non-Latino White children, ethnic minority children are more likely to experience persistent poverty over many years and live in isolated poor neighborhoods where social supports are minimal and threats to positive development are abundant (Leventhal, Anastasio, & Dupere, 2020). African American (33 percent, down from 36 percent in 2015) and Latino (26 percent down from 30 percent in 2015) families with children have especially high rates of poverty.

As indicated in Figure 3, one study found that a higher percentage of U.S. children in poor families than in middle-income families were exposed to family turmoil, separation from a parent, violence, crowding, excessive noise, and poor housing (Evans & English, 2002). One study also revealed that the more years children spent living in poverty, the higher were their physiological indices of stress (Evans & Kim, 2007).

Edelman says that parenting and nurturing the next generation of children is our society's most important function and that we need to take it more seriously than we have in the past. To read about efforts to improve the lives of children through social policies, see *Connecting Development to Life*.

Some children triumph over poverty or other adversities. They show *resilience* (Masten, 2017. 2019). Think back to the chapter-opening story about Alice Walker. In spite of racism, poverty, low socioeconomic status, and a disfiguring eye injury, she went on to become a successful author and champion for equality.

Are there certain characteristics that make children like Alice Walker resilient? Are there other characteristics that influence the development of children like Ted Kaczynski, who, despite his intelligence and education, became a killer? After analyzing research on this topic, Ann Masten and her colleagues (Masten, 2006, 2009, 2011, 2013, 2017, 2019; Masten, Burt, & Coatsworth, 2006) concluded that a number of individual factors, such as good intellectual functioning, influence resiliency. In addition, as Figure 4 shows, the families and extrafamilial contexts of resilient individuals

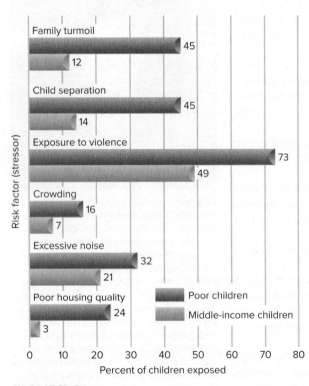

FIGURE 3

EXPOSURE TO SIX STRESSORS AMONG POOR AND MIDDLE-INCOME CHILDREN. One study analyzed exposure to six stressors among poor children and middle-income children (Evans & English, 2002). Poor children were much more likely to face each of these stressors.

Improving Family Policy

In the United States, the actions of the federal government, state governments, and city governments influence the well-being of children (Bojorquez & Fry-Bowers, 2019; Marks, Woolverton, & Garcia-Coll, 2020). When families seriously endanger a child's well-being, governments often step in to help. At the national and state levels, policy makers have debated for decades about whether helping poor parents ends up helping their children as well. Researchers are providing some answers by examining the effects of specific policies (Masten, Motti-Stefanidi, & Rahl-Brigman, 2020; Rose-Clarke & others, 2019).

A mother and her daughter who are participating in the Ascend two-generation education program. *What characterizes this program?*
Studio 1One/Shutterstock

For example, the Minnesota Family Investment Program (MFIP) was designed in the 1990s primarily to influence the behavior of adults—specifically, to move adults off the welfare rolls and into paid employment. A key element of the program was its guarantee that adults participating in the program would receive more income if they worked than if they did not. When the adults' income rose, how did that affect their children? A study of the effects of MFIP found that increased incomes of working poor parents were linked with benefits for their children (Gennetian & Miller, 2002). The children's achievement in school improved, and their behavior problems decreased.

There is increasing interest in developing two-generation educational interventions to improve the academic success of children living in poverty (Reichlin Cruse & others, 2019; Wladis, Hachey, &

Conway, 2018). For example, a recent large-scale effort to help children escape from poverty is the Ascend two-generation education intervention conducted by the Aspen Institute (2013, 2019). The intervention emphasizes education (increasing postsecondary education for mothers and improving the quality of their children's early childhood education), economic support (housing, transportation, financial education, health insurance, and food assistance), and social capital (peer support including friends and neighbors; participation in community and faith-based organizations; school and work contacts). In a recent report, the Ascend program emphasized the importance of parents' education, economic stability, and overall health for their children's well-being (Ascend, 2019).

Developmental psychologists and other researchers have examined the effects of many other government policies. They are seeking ways to help families living in poverty improve their well-being, and they have offered many suggestions for improving government policies (Leventhal, Anastasio, & Dupere, 2020).

Earlier, we learned that children who live in poverty experience higher levels of physiological stress. How might a child's stress level be affected by the implementation of MFIP?

---

tend to share certain features. For example, resilient children are likely to have a close relationship with a caring parent figure and bonds to caring adults outside the family.

At the other end of the life span, the well-being of older adults also creates policy issues (Chen & Cao, 2020; Vaughn & others, 2019). Key concerns are escalating health care costs and the access of older adults to adequate health care (Boulton & others, 2019). One study found that the U.S. health care system fails older adults in many areas (Wenger & others, 2003). For example, older adults received the recommended care for general medical conditions such as heart disease only 52 percent of the time; they received appropriate care for undernutrition and Alzheimer disease only 31 percent of the time.

These concerns about the well-being of older adults are heightened by two facts. First, the number of older adults in the United States is growing dramatically, as Figure 5 shows. Second, many of these older Americans are likely to need society's help (Polacsek, Boardman, & McCann, 2020).

Compared with adults in earlier decades, U.S. adults today are less likely to be married, more likely to be childless, and more likely to be living alone (Poey, Burr, & Roberts, 2017). As the older population continues to expand during the twenty-first century, an increasing number of older adults will be without a spouse or children—traditionally the main sources of support for older adults. These individuals will need social relationships, networks, and other forms of support (Antonucci & Webster, 2019).

Source	Characteristic
Individual	Good intellectual functioning
	Appealing, sociable, easygoing disposition
	Self-confidence, high self-esteem
	Talents
	Faith
Family	Close relationship to caring parent figure
	Authoritative parenting: warmth, structure, high expectations
	Socioeconomic advantages
	Connections to extended supportive family networks
Extrafamilial Context	Bonds to caring adults outside the family
	Connections to positive organizations
	Attending effective schools

FIGURE 4

CHARACTERISTICS OF RESILIENT CHILDREN AND THEIR CONTEXTS

FIGURE 5

THE AGING OF AMERICA. The number of Americans over age 65 has grown dramatically since 1900 and is projected to increase further from the present to the year 2040. A significant increase will also occur in the number of individuals in the 85-and-over group. Centenarians—persons 100 years of age or older—are the fastest-growing age group in the United States, and their numbers are expected to swell in the coming decades.

How might the infusion of technology into children's, adolescents', and adults' lives be changing the way they function and learn?
DaydreamsGirl/iStock/Getty Images

Not only is the population of older adults growing in the United States, but the world's population of people 60 years and older is projected to increase from 962 million in 2017 to 2.1 billion in 2050 (United Nations, 2017). The world's population 80 years of age and older is expected to triple or quadruple in this time frame. These significant increases in the world's older population have important implications for many sectors of society. As the percentage of a country's older population grows, governments must develop innovative policies and services that include improved housing, employment, health care, and transportation for older adults.

Technology   A final discussion in our exploration of contemporary topics is the recent dramatic, almost overwhelming increase in the use of technology at all points in human development (Gillain & others, 2019; Greenfield, 2020). From the introduction of television in the mid-1950s to the development of computers, the Internet, smartphones, social media, and robots, our way of life has been changed permanently by technological advances.

We will explore many technology topics in this edition. Later in this chapter you will read about the emerging field of developmental robotics in our discussion of information processing, and you will ponder the influence of technology on generations such as the millennials. Other topics we will consider include the potential effects of audiovisual media on language development in young children; indications that too much screen time reduces children's participation in physical activities and increases their risk for obesity and cardiovascular disease; the effects on learning when adolescents spend more time using various media than in school; the question of whether multitasking with various electronic devices is harmful or beneficial; as well as the degree to which older adults are adapting to the extensive role of technology in their lives.

Review *Connect* Reflect

 Discuss the distinctive features of a life-span perspective on development.

Review

- What is meant by the concept of development? Why is the study of life-span development important?
- What are the main characteristics of the life-span perspective? What are three sources of contextual influences?
- What are some contemporary concerns in life-span development?

Connect

- Give your own example (not found in this chapter) of how biology, culture, and individual experience interact to affect development.

Reflect *Your Own Personal Journey of Life*

- Imagine what your development would have been like in a culture that offered fewer or distinctly different choices. How might your development have been different if your family had been significantly richer or poorer?

| Biological, Cognitive, and Socioemotional Processes | Periods of Development | The Significance of Age | Developmental Issues |

In this section, we will explore what is meant by developmental processes and periods, as well as variations in the way age is conceptualized. We will examine key developmental issues and explore strategies for evaluating them.

If you wanted to describe how and why Alice Walker or Ted Kaczynski developed during their lifetimes, how would you go about it? A chronicle of the events in any person's life can quickly become a confusing and tedious array of details. Two concepts help provide a framework for describing and understanding an individual's development: developmental processes and periods.

BIOLOGICAL, COGNITIVE, AND SOCIOEMOTIONAL PROCESSES

At the beginning of this chapter, we defined development as the pattern of change that begins at conception and continues through the life span. The pattern is complex because it is the product of biological, cognitive, and socioemotional processes (see Figure 6).

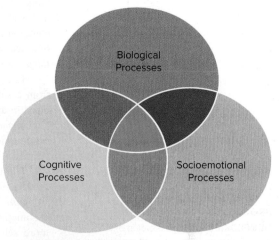

FIGURE 6

PROCESSES INVOLVED IN DEVELOPMENTAL CHANGES. Biological, cognitive, and socioemotional processes interact as individuals develop.

Biological Processes **Biological processes** produce changes in an individual's physical nature. Genes inherited from parents, brain development, height and weight gains, changes in motor skills, nutrition, exercise, the hormonal changes of puberty, and cardiovascular decline are all examples of biological processes that affect development. Especially in recent years with the advent of new techniques to study people's actual genetic makeup, there has been a substantial increase in studies that focus on the role of genes in development at different points in the life span. Likewise, with the invention of brain-imaging techniques such as magnetic resonance imaging, there has been an explosion of research on how the brain influences many aspects of development at different points in the life span.

Cognitive Processes **Cognitive processes** refer to changes in the individual's thought, intelligence, and language. Watching a colorful mobile swinging above the crib, putting together a two-word sentence, memorizing a poem, imagining what it would be like to be a movie star, and solving a crossword puzzle all involve cognitive processes.

Socioemotional Processes **Socioemotional processes** involve changes in the individual's relationships with other people, changes in emotions, and changes in personality. An infant's smile in response to a parent's touch, a toddler's aggressive attack on a playmate, a school-age child's development of assertiveness, an adolescent's joy at the senior prom, and the affection of an elderly couple all reflect the role of socioemotional processes in development.

Connecting Biological, Cognitive, and Socioemotional Processes Biological, cognitive, and socioemotional processes are inextricably intertwined (Diamond, 2013). Consider a baby smiling in response to a parent's touch. This response depends on biological processes (the physical nature of touch and responsiveness to it), cognitive processes (the ability to understand intentional acts), and socioemotional processes (the fact that smiling often reflects a positive emotional feeling and helps to connect us in positive ways with other human beings). Nowhere is the connection across biological, cognitive, and socioemotional processes more obvious than in two rapidly emerging fields:

- *developmental cognitive neuroscience*, which explores links between development, cognitive processes, and the brain (Dumonthiel & Mareschal, 2020; Kinugawa, 2019).
- *developmental social neuroscience*, which examines connections between socioemotional processes, development, and the brain (Gutchess, 2019; Hackman & Kraemer, 2020).

biological processes Changes in an individual's physical nature.

cognitive processes Changes in an individual's thought, intelligence, and language.

socioemotional processes Changes in an individual's interpersonal relationships, emotions, and personality.

In many instances, biological, cognitive, and socioemotional processes are bidirectional. For example, biological processes can influence cognitive processes and vice versa. Thus, although usually we will study the different processes of development (biological, cognitive, and socioemotional) separately, keep in mind that we are talking about the development of an integrated individual with a mind and body that are interdependent. In many places throughout the book, we will call attention to these connections.

PERIODS OF DEVELOPMENT

The interplay of biological, cognitive, and socioemotional processes produces the periods of the human life span (see Figure 7). A *developmental period* refers to a time frame in a person's life that is characterized by certain features. For the purposes of organization and understanding, we commonly describe development in terms of these periods. The most widely used classification of developmental periods involves the eight-period sequence shown in Figure 7. Approximate age ranges are listed for the periods to provide a general idea of when each period begins and ends.

The *prenatal period* is the time from conception to birth. It involves tremendous growth— from a single cell to an organism complete with brain and behavioral capabilities—and takes place in approximately a 9-month period.

Infancy is the developmental period from birth to 18 or 24 months. Infancy is a time of extreme dependence upon adults. During this period, many psychological activities—language, symbolic thought, sensorimotor coordination, and social learning, for example—are just beginning.

The term *toddler* is often used to describe a child from about 18 months to 3 years of age. Toddlers are in a transitional period between infancy and the next period, *early childhood*.

Early childhood is the developmental period from 3 through 5 years of age. This period is sometimes called the "preschool years." During this time, young children learn to become more self-sufficient and to care for themselves, develop school readiness skills (following instructions, identifying letters), and spend many hours playing with peers. First grade typically marks the end of early childhood.

Middle and late childhood is the developmental period from about 6 to 10 or 11 years of age, approximately corresponding to the elementary school years. During this period, children

Periods of Development

| Prenatal period (conception to birth) | Infancy (birth to 18–24 months) | Early childhood (3–5 years) | Middle and late childhood (6–10/11 years) | Adolescence (10–12 to 18–21 years) | Early adulthood (20s and 30s) | Middle adulthood (40s and 50s) | Late adulthood (60s–70s to death) |

Biological Processes

Cognitive Processes

Socioemotional Processes

Processes of Development

master the fundamental skills of reading, writing, and arithmetic, and they are formally exposed to the larger world and its culture. Achievement becomes a more central theme of the child's world, and self-control increases.

Adolescence is the developmental period of transition from childhood to early adulthood, entered at approximately 10 to 12 years of age and ending at 18 to 21 years of age. Adolescence begins with rapid physical changes—dramatic gains in height and weight, changes in body contour, and the development of sexual characteristics such as enlargement of the breasts, growth of pubic and facial hair, and deepening of the voice. At this point in development, the pursuit of independence and an identity are preeminent. Thought is more logical, abstract, and idealistic. More time is spent outside the family.

There has been a substantial increase in interest in the transition between adolescence and early adulthood, a transition that can be a long one as individuals develop more effective skills to become full members of society. Recently, the transition from adolescence to adulthood has been referred to as *emerging adulthood*, the period from approximately 18 to 25 years of age (Arnett, 2015a, b, 2016a, b). Experimentation and exploration characterize the emerging adult. At this point in their development, many individuals are still exploring which career path they want to follow, what they want their identity to be, and which lifestyle they want to adopt (for example, single, cohabiting, or married) (Schwartz & Petrova, 2019).

Early adulthood is the developmental period that begins in the early twenties and lasts through the thirties. It is a time of establishing personal and economic independence, advancing in a career, and for many, selecting a mate, learning to live with that person in an intimate way, starting a family, and rearing children.

Middle adulthood is the developmental period from approximately 40 to about 60 years of age. It is a time of expanding personal and social involvement and responsibility; of assisting the next generation in becoming competent, mature individuals; and of reaching and maintaining satisfaction in a career.

Late adulthood is the developmental period that begins during the sixties or seventies and lasts until death. It is a time of life review, retirement, and adjustment to new social roles and diminishing strength and health.

Late adulthood has the longest span of any period of development, and as noted earlier, the number of people in this age group has been increasing dramatically. As a result, life-span developmentalists have been paying more attention to late adulthood (Leipold, 2020). Paul Baltes and Jacqui Smith (2003) argue that a major change takes place in older adults' lives as they become the "oldest-old," on average at about 85 years of age. For example, the "young-old" (classified as 65 through 84 in this analysis) have substantial potential for physical and cognitive fitness, retain much of their cognitive capacity, and can develop strategies to cope with the gains and losses of aging. In contrast, the oldest-old (85 and older) show considerable loss in cognitive skills, experience an increase in chronic stress, and become more frail.

Thus, Baltes and Smith concluded that considerable plasticity and adaptability characterize adults from their sixties until their mid-eighties but that the oldest-old have reached the limits of their functional capacity, which makes interventions to improve their lives difficult. Nonetheless, as will be described in later chapters, considerable variation exists in the degree to which the oldest-old retain their capabilities (Cheng & others, 2019).

Four Ages   Life-span developmentalists who focus on adult development and aging increasingly describe life-span development in terms of four "ages" (Baltes, 2006; Willis & Schaie, 2006):

First age: Childhood and adolescence

Second age: Prime adulthood, ages 20 through 59

Third age: Approximately 60 to 79 years of age

Fourth age: Approximately 80 years and older

The major emphasis in this conceptualization is on the third and fourth ages, especially the increasing evidence that individuals in the third age are healthier and can lead more active, productive lives than their predecessors in earlier generations. However, when older adults reach their eighties (fourth age), especially 85 and over, health and well-being decline for many individuals.

One's children's children's children. Look back to us as we look to you; we are related by our imaginations. If we are able to touch, it is because we have imagined each other's existence, our dreams running back and forth along a cable from age to age.

—ROGER ROSENBLATT
Contemporary American writer

Three Developmental Patterns of Aging   K. Warner Schaie (2016a, b) recently described three different developmental patterns that provide a portrait of how aging can encompass individual variations:

- *Normal aging* characterizes most individuals, for whom psychological functioning often peaks in early middle age, remains relatively stable until the late fifties to early sixties, and then shows a modest decline through the early eighties. However, marked decline can occur as individuals approach death.
- *Pathological aging* characterizes individuals who show greater than average decline as they age through the adult years. In early old age, they may have mild cognitive impairment, develop Alzheimer disease later on, or have a chronic disease that impairs their daily functioning.
- *Successful aging* characterizes individuals whose positive physical, cognitive, and socioemotional development is maintained longer, declining later in old age than is the case for most people. For too long, only the declines that occur in late adulthood were highlighted, but recently there has been increased interest in the concept of successful aging.

Connections Across Periods of Development   A final important point needs to be made about the periods of the human life span. Just as there are many connections between biological, cognitive, and socioemotional processes, so are there many connections between the periods of the human life span. A key element in the study of life-span development is how development in one period is connected to development in another period. For example, when individuals reach adolescence, many developments and experiences have already taken place in their lives. If an adolescent girl becomes depressed, might her depression be linked to development early in her life, as well as recent and current development? Throughout this edition we will call attention to such connections across periods of development through *Developmental Connection* inserts that guide you to earlier or later connections with the material you are currently reading.

THE SIGNIFICANCE OF AGE

In our description of developmental periods, we linked an approximate age range with each period. But we also have noted that there are variations in the capabilities of individuals of the same age, and we have seen how age-related changes can be exaggerated. How important is age in understanding the characteristics of an individual?

Which of these individuals is likely to be the happiest and to report the highest level of psychological well-being?
Jetta Productions Inc./Getty Images

Age and Happiness   Is there a best age to be? An increasing number of studies indicate that U.S. adults are happier as they age. Consider also a U.S. study of approximately 28,000 individuals from 18 to 88 that revealed happiness increased with age (Yang, 2008). About 33 percent were very happy at 88 years of age, compared with only about 24 percent in their late teens and early twenties. Why might older people report being happier and more satisfied with their lives than younger people? Despite facing higher incidences of physical problems and losses, older adults are more content with their lives, have better relationships with the people who matter to them, are less pressured to achieve, have more time for leisurely pursuits, and have many years of experience resulting in wisdom that may help them adapt better to their circumstances than younger adults do (Carstensen, 2015a, b, 2019a, b; Kuntzmann, 2019; Sims, Hogan, & Carstensen, 2015). Because growing older is a certain outcome of staying alive, it is good to know that we are likely to be happier as older adults than we were when we were younger.

Not all studies, though, have found an increase in life satisfaction with age (Steptoe, Deaton, & Stone, 2015). Some studies indicate that the lowest levels of life satisfaction occur in middle age, especially from 45 to 54 years of age (OECD, 2014). Other studies have found that life satisfaction varies across some countries. For example, respondents in research studies conducted in the former Soviet Union and Eastern Europe, as well as in South American countries, reported a decrease in life satisfaction with advancing age (Deaton, 2008). Further, older adults in poor health, such as those with cardiovascular disease, chronic lung disease, and depression, tend to be less satisfied with their lives than older adults who are healthier (Lamont & others, 2017). Also, a recent study across 150 countries found that health was a better predictor of life satisfaction in individuals 58 years and older than in younger age groups (Joshanloo & Joyanovic, 2020).

Now that you have read about age variations in life satisfaction, think about how satisfied you are with your life. To help you answer this question, complete the items in Figure 8, which presents the most widely used measure in research on life satisfaction (Diener, 2020).

Conceptions of Age

According to some life-span experts, chronological age is not very relevant to understanding a person's psychological development (Botwinick, 1978). *Chronological age* is the number of years that have elapsed since birth. But time is a crude index of experience, and it does not cause anything. Chronological age, moreover, is not the only way to measure age (MacDonald & Stawski, 2016). Just as there are different domains of development, there are different ways of thinking about age.

Age has been conceptualized not just as chronological age but also as biological age, psychological age, and social age (Hoyer & Roodin, 2009). *Biological age* is a person's age in terms of biological health. Determining biological age involves knowing the functional capacities of a person's vital organs. One person's vital capacities may be better or worse than those of other people of comparable age (Richards & others, 2015). A study of 17-year survival rates in Korean adults 20 to 93 years of age found that when biological age was greater than chronological age, individuals were more likely to have died (Yoo & others, 2017). The younger the person's biological age, the longer the person is expected to live, regardless of chronological age.

Psychological age is an individual's adaptive capacities compared with those of other individuals of the same chronological age. Thus, older adults who continue to learn, are

Below are five statements that you may agree or disagree with. Using the 1–7 scale below, indicate your agreement with each item by placing the appropriate number on the line preceding that item. Please be open and honest in your responding.

Scale

7 Strongly agree
6 Agree
5 Slightly agree
4 Neither agree nor disagree
3 Slightly disagree
2 Disagree
1 Strongly disagree

Response	Statement
_____	In most ways my life is close to my ideal.
_____	The conditions of my life are excellent.
_____	I am satisfied with my life.
_____	So far I have gotten the important things I want in life.
_____	If I could live my life over, I would change almost nothing.
_____	Total score

Scoring

31–35 Extremely satisfied
26–30 Satisfied
21–25 Slightly satisfied
20 Neutral
15–19 Slightly dissatisfied
10–14 Dissatisfied
5–9 Extremely dissatisfied

FIGURE 8

HOW SATISFIED AM I WITH MY LIFE?
Source: E. Diener, R. A. Emmons, R. J. Larson, & S. Griffin. "The Satisfaction with Life Scale." *Journal of Personality Assessment, 48,* 1985, 71–75.

(*Left*): Seventy-four-year-old Barbara Jordan participating in the long-jump competition at a Senior Games in Maine; (*right*): a sedentary overweight middle-aged man. *Even though Barbara Jordan's chronological age is older, might her biological age be younger than the middle-aged man's?*
(*Left*) John Patriquin/Portland Press Herald/Getty Images; (*right*) Firehorse/E+/Getty Images

How old would you be if you didn't know how old you were?

—SATCHEL PAIGE

American baseball pitcher, 20th century

flexible, are motivated, have positive personality traits, control their emotions, and think clearly are engaging in more adaptive behaviors than their chronological age-mates who do not continue to learn, are rigid, are unmotivated, do not control their emotions, and do not think clearly (Thomas & Gutchess, 2020). A longitudinal study of more than 1,200 individuals across seven decades revealed that the personality trait of conscientiousness (being organized, careful, and disciplined, for example) predicted lower mortality (frequency of death) risk from childhood through late adulthood (Martin, Friedman, & Schwartz, 2007). And a recent study found that a higher level of conscientiousness and being more emotionally stable were protective of cognitive functioning in older adults (Duchek & others, 2020).

Social age refers to connectedness with others and the social roles individuals adopt. Individuals who have better social relationships with others are happier and more likely to live longer than individuals who are lonely (Carstensen, 2019a, b).

Life-span expert Bernice Neugarten (1988) argues that in U.S. society chronological age is becoming irrelevant. The 28-year-old mayor, the 35-year-old grandmother, the 65-year-old father of a preschooler, the 55-year-old widow who starts a business, and the 70-year-old student illustrate that old assumptions about the proper timing of life events no longer govern our lives. We still have some expectations for when certain life events—such as getting married, having children, and retiring—should occur. However, chronological age has become a less accurate predictor of these life events in our society. Moreover, issues such as how to deal with intimacy and how to cope with success and failure appear and reappear throughout the life span.

From a life-span perspective, an overall age profile of an individual involves not just chronological age but also biological age, psychological age, and social age. For example, a 70-year-old man (chronological age) might be in good physical health (biological age), be experiencing memory problems and not be coping well with the demands placed on him by his wife's recent hospitalization (psychological age), and have a number of friends with whom he regularly plays golf (social age).

developmental **connection**

Nature and Nurture

Can specific genes be linked to specific environmental experiences to influence development? Connect to "Biological Beginnings."

DEVELOPMENTAL ISSUES

Was Ted Kaczynski born a killer, or did his life turn him into one? Kaczynski himself thought that his childhood was the root of his troubles, saying that he grew up as a genius in a boy's body and never fit in with other children. Did his early experiences determine his later life? Is your own journey through life marked out ahead of time, or can your experiences change your path? Are the experiences you have early in your journey more important than later ones? Is your journey more like taking an elevator up a skyscraper with distinct stops along the way or more like a cruise down a river with smoother ebbs and flows? These questions point to three issues about the nature of development: the roles played by nature and nurture, stability and change, and continuity and discontinuity.

Nature and Nurture   The **nature-nurture issue** involves the extent to which development is influenced by nature and by nurture. Nature refers to an organism's biological inheritance, nurture to its environmental experiences.

According to those who emphasize the role of nature, just as a sunflower grows in an orderly way—unless flattened by an unfriendly environment—so too the human grows in an orderly way. An evolutionary and genetic foundation produces commonalities in growth and development (Brooker & others, 2020). We walk before we talk, speak one word before two words, grow rapidly in infancy and less so in early childhood, experience a rush of sex hormones in puberty, reach the peak of our physical strength in late adolescence and early adulthood, and then physically decline. Proponents of the importance of nature acknowledge that extreme environments—those that are psychologically barren or hostile—can depress development. However, they believe that basic growth tendencies are genetically programmed into humans (Willey, Sandman, & Wood, 2020).

By contrast, other psychologists emphasize the importance of nurture, or environmental experiences, in development (Parke & Elder, 2020). Experiences run the gamut from the

What are some key developmental issues?
Photodisc/Stockbyte/Getty Images

nature-nurture issue Debate about whether development is primarily influenced by nature or nurture. Nature refers to an organism's biological inheritance, nurture to its environmental experiences.

individual's biological environment (nutrition, medical care, drugs, and physical accidents) to the social environment (family, peers, schools, community, media, and culture).

There has been a dramatic increase in the number of studies that reflect the *epigenetic view,* which states that development reflects an ongoing, bidirectional interchange between genes and the environment. These studies involve specific DNA sequences (Ecker & Beck, 2019). The epigenetic mechanisms involve the actual molecular modification of the DNA strand as a result of environmental inputs in ways that alter gene functioning (Hein & others, 2019; Kresovich & others, 2020). In "Biological Beginnings" we will explore the epigenetic approach in greater depth.

Stability and Change

Is the shy child who hides behind the sofa when visitors arrive destined to become a wallflower at college dances, or might the child become a sociable, talkative individual? Is the fun-loving, carefree adolescent bound to have difficulty holding down a 9-to-5 job as an adult? These questions reflect the **stability-change issue,** which involves the degree to which early traits and characteristics persist through life or change.

Many developmentalists who emphasize stability in development argue that stability is the result of heredity and possibly early experiences in life. For example, many argue that if an individual is shy throughout life (as Ted Kaczynski was), this stability is due to heredity and possibly early experiences in which the infant or young child encountered considerable stress when interacting with people.

Developmentalists who emphasize change take the more optimistic view that later experiences can produce change. Recall that in the life-span perspective, plasticity, the potential for change, exists throughout the life span, although possibly to different degrees. Experts such as Paul Baltes (2003) argue that older adults often show less capacity for learning new things than younger adults do. However, many older adults continue to be good at practicing what they have learned earlier in life.

The roles of early and later experience are an aspect of the stability-change issue that has long been hotly debated (Farrell & others, 2019). Some argue that warm, nurturant caregiving during infancy and toddlerhood predicts optimal development later in life (Woodhouse & others, 2019). The later-experience advocates see children as malleable throughout development and believe later sensitive caregiving is just as important as earlier sensitive caregiving (De La Fuente, 2019; Thomas & Gutchess, 2020).

Continuity and Discontinuity

When developmental change occurs, is it gradual or abrupt? Think about your own development for a moment. Did you gradually become the person you are today? Or did you experience sudden, distinct changes as you matured? For the most part, developmentalists who emphasize nurture describe development as a gradual, continuous process. Those who emphasize nature often describe development as a series of distinct stages.

The **continuity-discontinuity issue** focuses on the degree to which development involves either gradual, cumulative change (continuity) or distinct stages (discontinuity). In terms of continuity, as the oak grows from seedling to giant oak, it becomes more of an oak—its development is continuous (see Figure 9). Similarly, a child's first word, though seemingly an abrupt, discontinuous event, is actually the result of weeks and months of growth and practice. Puberty might seem abrupt, but it is a gradual process that occurs over several years.

In terms of discontinuity, as an insect grows from a caterpillar to a chrysalis to a butterfly, it passes through a sequence of stages in which change is qualitatively rather than quantitatively different. Similarly, at some point a child moves from not being able to think abstractly about the world to being able to do so. This is a qualitative, discontinuous change in development rather than a quantitative, continuous change.

Evaluating the Developmental Issues

Most life-span developmentalists acknowledge that development is not all nature or all nurture, not all stability or all change, and not all continuity or all discontinuity. Nature and nurture, stability and change, continuity and discontinuity characterize development throughout the human life span.

Although most developmentalists do not take extreme positions on these three important issues, there is spirited debate regarding how strongly development is influenced by each of these factors (Bornstein, 2020; Oakes & Rakison, 2020).

developmental connection
Personality
How much does personality change as people go through the adult years? Connect to "Socioemotional Development in Middle Adulthood."

Continuity

Discontinuity

FIGURE 9

CONTINUITY AND DISCONTINUITY IN DEVELOPMENT. *Is our development like that of a seedling gradually growing into a giant oak? Or is it more like that of a caterpillar suddenly becoming a butterfly?*

stability-change issue Debate about whether we become older renditions of our early experience (stability) or whether we develop into someone different from who we were at an earlier point in development (change).

continuity-discontinuity issue Debate about the extent to which development involves gradual, cumulative change (continuity) or distinct stages (discontinuity).

Review *Connect* Reflect

LG2 Identify the most important processes, periods, and issues in development.

Review

- What are three key developmental processes?
- What are eight main developmental periods?
- How is age related to development?
- What are three main developmental issues?

Connect

- In the previous section, we discussed biological, cognitive, and socioemotional processes. What concepts do these processes have in common with the issue of nature versus nurture, which was also discussed in this section?

Reflect *Your Own Personal Journey of Life*

- Do you think there was/is/will be a best age for you to be? If so, what is it? Why?

3 Theories of Development

LG3 Describe the main theories of human development.

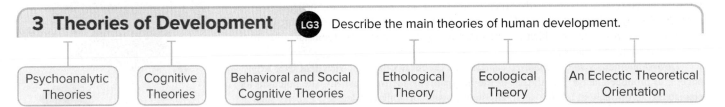

| Psychoanalytic Theories | Cognitive Theories | Behavioral and Social Cognitive Theories | Ethological Theory | Ecological Theory | An Eclectic Theoretical Orientation |

There is nothing quite so practical as a good theory.

—**KURT LEWIN**

American social psychologist, 20th century

scientific method An approach that can be used to obtain accurate information. It includes the following steps: (1) conceptualize the problem, (2) collect data, (3) draw conclusions, and (4) revise research conclusions and theory.

theory An interrelated, coherent set of ideas that helps to explain phenomena and facilitate predictions.

hypotheses Specific assumptions and predictions that can be tested to determine their accuracy.

psychoanalytic theories Theories that describe development as primarily unconscious and heavily colored by emotion. Behavior is merely a surface characteristic, and the symbolic workings of the mind have to be analyzed to understand behavior. Early experiences with parents are emphasized.

Erikson's theory Includes eight stages of human development. Each stage consists of a unique developmental task that confronts individuals with a crisis that must be resolved.

How can we answer questions about the roles of nature and nurture, stability and change, and continuity and discontinuity in development? How can we determine, for example, whether deterioration of memory in older adults can be prevented or whether special care can repair the harm inflicted by child neglect? The scientific method is the best tool we have to answer such questions (Smith & Davis, 2016).

The **scientific method** is essentially a four-step process: (1) conceptualize a process or problem to be studied, (2) collect research information (data), (3) analyze the data, and (4) draw conclusions.

In step 1, when researchers are formulating a problem to study, they often draw on theories and develop hypotheses. A **theory** is an interrelated, coherent set of ideas that helps to explain phenomena and facilitate predictions. It may suggest **hypotheses,** which are specific assertions and predictions that can be tested. For example, a theory on mentoring might state that sustained support and guidance from an adult makes a difference in the lives of children from impoverished backgrounds because the mentor gives the children opportunities to observe and imitate the behavior and strategies of the mentor.

This section outlines key aspects of five theoretical orientations to development: psychoanalytic, cognitive, behavioral and social cognitive, ethological, and ecological. Each contributes an important piece to the life-span development puzzle. Although the theories disagree about certain aspects of development, many of their ideas are complementary rather than contradictory. Together they let us see the total landscape of life-span development in all its richness.

PSYCHOANALYTIC THEORIES

Psychoanalytic theories describe development as primarily unconscious (beyond awareness) and heavily colored by emotion. Psychoanalytic theorists emphasize that behavior is merely a surface characteristic and that a true understanding of development requires analyzing the symbolic meanings of behavior and the deep inner workings of the mind. Psychoanalytic theorists also stress that early experiences with parents extensively shape development. These characteristics are highlighted in the main psychoanalytic theory, that of Sigmund Freud (1856–1939).

Freud's Theory   As Freud listened to, probed, and analyzed his patients, he became convinced that their problems were the result of experiences early in life. He thought that as children grow up, their focus of pleasure and sexual impulses shifts from the mouth to the

Oral Stage	Anal Stage	Phallic Stage	Latency Stage	Genital Stage
Infant's pleasure centers on the mouth.	Child's pleasure focuses on the anus.	Child's pleasure focuses on the genitals.	Child represses sexual interest and develops social and intellectual skills.	A time of sexual reawakening; source of sexual pleasure becomes someone outside the family.
Birth to 1½ Years	**1½ to 3 Years**	**3 to 6 Years**	**6 Years to Puberty**	**Puberty Onward**

FIGURE 10

FREUDIAN STAGES. Because Freud emphasized sexual motivation, his stages of development are known as psychosexual stages. In his view, if the need for pleasure at any stage is either undergratified or overgratified, an individual may become fixated, or locked in, at that stage of development.

anus and eventually to the genitals. As a result, we go through five stages of psychosexual development: oral, anal, phallic, latency, and genital (see Figure 10). Our adult personality, Freud (1917) claimed, is determined by the way we resolve conflicts between sources of pleasure at each stage and the demands of reality.

Freud's theory has been significantly revised by a number of psychoanalytic theorists. Many of today's psychoanalytic theorists maintain that Freud overemphasized sexual instincts; they argue that more emphasis should be placed on cultural experiences as determinants of an individual's development. Unconscious thought remains a central theme, but conscious thought plays a greater role than Freud envisioned. One of the most influential revisionists of Freud's ideas was Erik Erikson.

Sigmund Freud, the pioneering architect of psychoanalytic theory. *How did Freud portray the organization of an individual's personality?*
Bettmann/Getty Images

Erikson's Psychosocial Theory   Erik Erikson (1902–1994) recognized Freud's contributions but believed that Freud misjudged some important dimensions of human development. For one thing, Erikson (1950, 1968) said we develop in psychosocial stages, rather than in psychosexual stages as Freud maintained. According to Freud, the primary motivation for human behavior is sexual in nature; according to Erikson, it is social and reflects a desire to affiliate with other people. According to Freud, our basic personality is shaped during the first five years of life; according to Erikson, developmental change occurs throughout the life span. Thus, in terms of the early-versus-later-experience issue described earlier in the chapter, Freud viewed early experience as being far more important than later experiences, whereas Erikson emphasized the importance of both early and later experiences.

In **Erikson's theory,** eight stages of development unfold as we go through life (see Figure 11). At each stage, a unique developmental task confronts individuals with a crisis that must be resolved. According to Erikson, this crisis is not a catastrophe but a turning point marked by both increased vulnerability and enhanced potential. The more successfully an individual resolves each crisis, the healthier development will be.

Trust versus mistrust is Erikson's first psychosocial stage, which is experienced in the first year of life. The development of trust during infancy sets the stage for a lifelong expectation that the world will be a good and pleasant place to live.

Autonomy versus shame and doubt is Erikson's second stage. This stage occurs in late infancy and toddlerhood (1 to 3 years). After gaining trust in their caregivers, infants begin to discover that their behavior is their own. They start to assert their sense of independence or autonomy. They realize their will. If infants and toddlers are restrained too much or punished too harshly, they are likely to develop a sense of shame and doubt.

Initiative versus guilt, Erikson's third stage of development, occurs during the preschool years. As preschool children encounter a widening social world, they face new challenges that require active, purposeful, responsible behavior. Feelings of guilt may arise, though, if the child is irresponsible and is made to feel too anxious.

Industry versus inferiority is Erikson's fourth developmental stage, occurring approximately during the elementary school years. Children now need to direct their energy toward mastering knowledge and intellectual skills. The negative outcome is that the child may develop a sense of inferiority—feeling incompetent and unproductive.

During the adolescent years, individuals need to find out who they are, what they are all about, and where they are going in life. This is Erikson's fifth

Erik Erikson with his wife, Joan, an artist. Erikson generated one of the most important developmental theories of the twentieth century. *Which stage of Erikson's theory are you in? Does Erikson's description of this stage characterize you?*
Jon Erikson/Science Source

Erikson's Stages	Developmental Period
Integrity versus despair	Late adulthood (60s onward)
Generativity versus stagnation	Middle adulthood (40s, 50s)
Intimacy versus isolation	Early adulthood (20s, 30s)
Identity versus identity confusion	Adolescence (10 to 20 years)
Industry versus inferiority	Middle and late childhood (elementary school years, 6 years to puberty)
Initiative versus guilt	Early childhood (preschool years, 3 to 5 years)
Autonomy versus shame and doubt	Infancy (1 to 3 years)
Trust versus mistrust	Infancy (first year)

FIGURE 11

ERIKSON'S EIGHT LIFE-SPAN STAGES.
Like Freud, Erikson proposed that individuals go through distinct, universal stages of development. Thus, in terms of the continuity-discontinuity issue discussed in this chapter, both favor the discontinuity side of the debate. Notice that the timing of Erikson's first four stages is similar to that of Freud's stages. *What are the implications of saying that people go through stages of development?*

Piaget's theory Theory stating that children actively construct their understanding of the world and go through four stages of cognitive development.

developmental stage, *identity versus identity confusion*. If adolescents explore roles in a healthy manner and arrive at a positive path to follow in life, then they achieve a positive identity; if they do not, identity confusion reigns.

Intimacy versus isolation is Erikson's sixth developmental stage, which individuals experience during early adulthood. At this time, individuals face the developmental task of forming intimate relationships. If young adults form healthy friendships and an intimate relationship with another, intimacy will be achieved; if not, isolation will result.

Generativity versus stagnation, Erikson's seventh developmental stage, occurs during middle adulthood. By generativity Erikson means primarily a concern for helping the younger generation to develop and lead useful lives. The feeling of having done nothing to help the next generation is stagnation.

Integrity versus despair is Erikson's eighth and final stage of development, which individuals experience in late adulthood. During this stage, a person reflects on the past. If the person's life review reveals a life well spent, integrity will be achieved; if not, the retrospective glances likely will yield doubt or gloom—the despair Erikson described.

Evaluating Psychoanalytic Theories   Contributions of psychoanalytic theories include an emphasis on a developmental framework, family relationships, and unconscious aspects of the mind. Criticisms include a lack of scientific support, too much emphasis on sexual underpinnings, and an image of people that is too negative.

COGNITIVE THEORIES

Whereas psychoanalytic theories stress the importance of the unconscious, cognitive theories emphasize conscious thoughts. Three important cognitive theories are Jean Piaget's cognitive developmental theory, Lev Vygotsky's sociocultural cognitive theory, and the information-processing theory.

Piaget's Cognitive Developmental Theory   **Piaget's theory** states that children go through four stages of cognitive development as they actively construct their understanding of the world. Two processes underlie this cognitive construction of the world: organization and adaptation. To make sense of our world, we organize our experiences. For example, we separate important ideas from less important ideas, and we connect one idea to another. In addition to organizing our observations and experiences, we adapt, adjusting to new environmental demands (Miller, 2016).

Piaget (1954) identified four stages in understanding the world (see Figure 12). Each stage is age-related and consists of a distinct way of thinking, a different way of understanding the world. Thus, according to Piaget (1896–1980), the child's cognition is qualitatively different from one stage to another. What are Piaget's four stages of cognitive development?

- The *sensorimotor stage,* which lasts from birth to about 2 years of age, is the first Piagetian stage. In this stage, infants construct an understanding of the world by coordinating sensory experiences (such as seeing and hearing) with physical, motoric actions—hence the term *sensorimotor*.

- The *preoperational stage,* which lasts from approximately 2 to 7 years of age, is Piaget's second stage. In this stage, children begin to go beyond simply connecting sensory information with physical action and represent the world with words, images, and drawings. However, according to Piaget, preschool children still lack the ability to perform what he calls operations, which are internalized mental actions that allow children to do mentally what they previously could only do physically. For example, if you imagine putting two

Jean Piaget, the famous Swiss developmental psychologist, changed the way we think about the development of children's minds. *What are some key ideas in Piaget's theory?*
Yves de Braine/Black Star/Stock Photo

Sensorimotor Stage	Preoperational Stage	Concrete Operational Stage	Formal Operational Stage
The infant constructs an understanding of the world by coordinating sensory experiences with physical actions. An infant progresses from reflexive, instinctual action at birth to the beginning of symbolic thought toward the end of the stage.	The child begins to represent the world with words and images. These words and images reflect increased symbolic thinking and go beyond the connection of sensory information and physical action.	The child can now reason logically about concrete events and classify objects into different sets.	The adolescent reasons in more abstract, idealistic, and logical ways.
Birth to 2 Years of Age	**2 to 7 Years of Age**	**7 to 11 Years of Age**	**11 Years of Age Through Adulthood**

FIGURE 12

PIAGET'S FOUR STAGES OF COGNITIVE DEVELOPMENT. According to Piaget, how a child thinks—not how much the child knows—determines the child's stage of cognitive development.
(*Photo credit left to right*) Stockbyte/Getty Images; Jacobs Stock Photography/BananaStock/Getty Images; Fuse/image100/Corbis; Purestock/Getty Images

sticks together to see whether they would be as long as another stick, without actually moving the sticks, you are performing a concrete operation.

- The *concrete operational stage,* which lasts from approximately 7 to 11 years of age, is the third Piagetian stage. In this stage, children can perform operations that involve objects, and they can reason logically when the reasoning can be applied to specific or concrete examples. For instance, concrete operational thinkers cannot imagine the steps necessary to complete an algebraic equation, a task that is too abstract for individuals at this stage of development.

- The *formal operational stage,* which appears between the ages of 11 and 15 and continues through adulthood, is Piaget's fourth and final stage. In this stage, individuals move beyond concrete experiences and begin to think in abstract and more logical terms. As part of thinking more abstractly, adolescents develop images of ideal circumstances. They might think about what an ideal parent would be like and compare their parents to this ideal standard. They begin to entertain possibilities for the future and are fascinated with what they can be. In solving problems, they become more systematic, developing hypotheses about why something is happening the way it is and then testing these hypotheses. We will examine Piaget's cognitive developmental theory further in other chapters.

Vygotsky's Sociocultural Cognitive Theory Like Piaget, the Russian developmentalist Lev Vygotsky (1896–1934) argued that children actively construct their knowledge. However, Vygotsky (1962) gave social interaction and culture far more important roles in cognitive development than Piaget did. **Vygotsky's theory** is a sociocultural cognitive theory that emphasizes how culture and social interaction guide cognitive development.

Vygotsky portrayed the child's development as inseparable from social and cultural activities (Daniels, 2017). He maintained that cognitive development involves learning to use the inventions of society, such as language, mathematical systems, and memory strategies. Thus in one culture, children might learn to count with the help of a computer; in another, they might learn by using beads. According to Vygotsky, children's social interaction with more-skilled adults and peers is indispensable to their cognitive development. Through this interaction,

Lev Vygotsky was born the same year as Piaget, but he died much earlier, at the age of 37. There is considerable interest today in Vygotsky's sociocultural cognitive theory of child development. *What are some key characteristics of Vygotsky's theory?*
A.R. Lauria /Dr. Michael Cole, Laboratory of Human Cognition, University of California, San Diego

Vygotsky's theory A sociocultural cognitive theory that emphasizes how culture and social interaction guide cognitive development.

information-processing theory Emphasizes that individuals manipulate information, monitor it, and strategize about it. Central to this theory are the processes of memory and thinking.

they learn to use the tools that will help them adapt and be successful in their culture (Holzman, 2017). In later chapters, we will examine ideas about learning and teaching that are based on Vygotsky's theory.

The Information-Processing Theory **Information-processing theory** emphasizes that individuals manipulate information, monitor it, and strategize about it. Unlike Piaget's theory, but like Vygotsky's theory, information-processing theory does not describe development as stage-like. Instead, according to this theory, individuals develop a gradually increasing capacity for processing information, which allows them to acquire increasingly complex knowledge and skills (Goldstein, 2019; Gordon & others, 2020).

Robert Siegler (2006, 2017), a leading expert on children's information processing, states that thinking is information processing. In other words, when individuals perceive, encode, represent, store, and retrieve information, they are thinking. Siegler emphasizes that an important aspect of development is learning good strategies for processing information. For example, becoming a better reader might involve learning to monitor the key themes of the material being read.

Siegler (2006, 2017) also argues that the best way to understand how children learn is to observe them while they are learning. He emphasizes the importance of using the *microgenetic method* to obtain detailed information about processing mechanisms as they are occurring from moment to moment. Siegler concludes that most research methods indirectly assess cognitive change, being more like snapshots than movies. The microgenetic method seeks to discover not just what children know but the cognitive processes involved in how they acquired the knowledge. A typical microgenetic study will be conducted across a number of trials assessed at various times over weeks or months (Miller, 2016). A number of microgenetic studies have focused on a specific aspect of academic learning, such as how children learn whole number arithmetic, fractions, and other areas of math (Braithwaite & others, 2019). Microgenetic studies also have been used to discover how children learn a particular concept in science or master a key component of learning to read.

The information-processing approach often uses the computer as an analogy to help explain the connection between cognition and the brain (Goldstein, 2019). They describe the physical brain as the computer's hardware, and cognition as its software. In this analogy, the sensory and perceptual systems provide an "input channel," similar to the way data are entered into the computer (see Figure 13). As input (information) comes into the mind, mental processes, or operations, act on it, just as the computer's software acts on the data. The transformed input generates information that remains in memory in much the same way that a computer stores what it has worked on. Finally, the information is retrieved from memory and "printed out" or "displayed" (so to speak) as an observable response.

Computers provide a logical and concrete, but oversimplified, model of the mind's processing of information. Inanimate computers and human brains function quite differently in some respects. For example, most computers receive information from a human who has already coded the information and removed much of its ambiguity. In contrast, each brain cell, or neuron, can respond to ambiguous information transmitted through sensory receptors such as the eyes and ears.

Computers can do some things better than humans. For instance, computers can perform complex numerical calculations much more quickly and accurately than humans could ever hope to. Computers can also apply and follow rules more consistently and with fewer errors than humans and can process complex mathematical patterns better than humans.

Still, the brain's extraordinary capabilities will probably not be mimicked completely by computers at any time in the near future (Sternberg & Halpern, 2020). For example, although a computer can improve its ability to recognize patterns or use rules of thumb to make decisions, it does not have the means to develop new learning goals. Furthermore, the human mind is aware of itself; the computer is not. Indeed, no computer is likely to approach the richness of human consciousness.

Nonetheless, the computer's role in cognitive and developmental psychology continues to increase. An entire scientific field called *artificial intelligence (AI)* focuses on creating machines capable of performing activities that require intelligence when they are done by people. And a new field titled *developmental robotics* is emerging that examines various developmental topics and issues using robots, such as motor development, perceptual development, information processing, and language development (Vinanzi & others, 2019). The hope is to build robots that are as much like humans as possible in order to gain a better understanding of human development (Gordon, 2020).

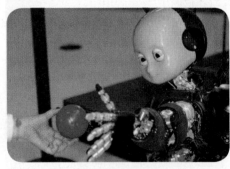

Above is the humanoid robot iCub created by the Italian Institute of Technology to study aspects of children's development such as perception, cognition, and motor development. In this situation, the robot, the size of a 3.5-year-old child, is catching a ball. This robot is being used by more than 20 laboratories worldwide and has 53 motors that move the head, arms and hands, waist, and legs. It also can see and hear, and has the sense of proprioception (body configuration) and movement (using gyroscopes).
Marco Destefanis/Pacific Press/Sipa USA/Newscom

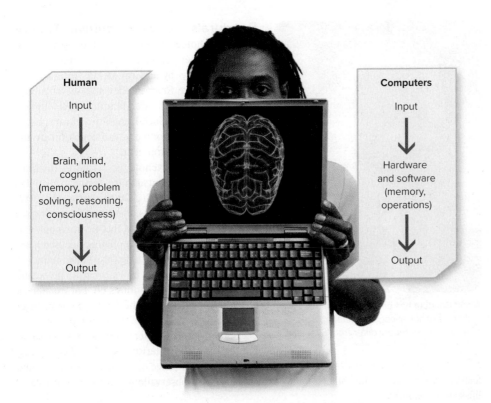

FIGURE **13**

COMPARING INFORMATION PROCESSING IN HUMANS AND COMPUTERS.
Psychologists who study cognition often use a computer analogy to explain how humans process information. The brain is analogous to the computer's hardware, and cognition is analogous to the computer's software.
Creatas/Getty Images

Evaluating Cognitive Theories   Contributions of cognitive theories include a positive view of development and an emphasis on the active construction of understanding. Criticisms include skepticism regarding the pureness of Piaget's stages and inadequate attention to individual variations.

BEHAVIORAL AND SOCIAL COGNITIVE THEORIES

Behaviorism essentially holds that we can study scientifically only what can be directly observed and measured. Out of the behavioral tradition grew the belief that development is observable behavior that can be learned through experience with the environment (Schunk, 2020). In terms of the continuity-discontinuity issue discussed earlier in this chapter, the behavioral and social cognitive theories emphasize continuity in development and argue that development does not occur in stage-like fashion. Let's explore two versions of behaviorism: Skinner's operant conditioning and Bandura's social cognitive theory.

Skinner's Operant Conditioning   According to B. F. Skinner (1904–1990), through operant conditioning the consequences of a behavior produce changes in the probability of the behavior's occurrence. A behavior followed by a rewarding stimulus is more likely to recur, whereas a behavior followed by a punishing stimulus is less likely to recur. For example, when an adult smiles at a child after the child has done something, the child is more likely to engage in that behavior again than if the adult gives the child a disapproving look.

In Skinner's (1938) view, such rewards and punishments shape development. For Skinner the key aspect of development is behavior, not thoughts and feelings. He emphasized that development consists of the pattern of behavioral changes that are brought about by rewards and punishments. For example, Skinner would say that shy people learned to be shy as a result of experiences they had while growing up. It follows that modifications in an environment can help a shy person become more socially oriented.

B. F. Skinner was a tinkerer who liked to make new gadgets. The younger of his two daughters, Deborah, spent much of her infancy in Skinner's enclosed Air-Crib, which he invented because he wanted to control her environment completely. The Air-Crib was sound-proofed and temperature controlled. Debbie, shown here as a child with her parents, is currently a successful artist, is married, and lives in London. *What do you think about Skinner's Air-Crib?*
AP Images

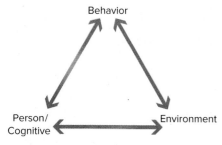

Behavior

Person/   Environment
Cognitive

FIGURE 14

BANDURA'S SOCIAL COGNITIVE MODEL.
The arrows illustrate how relations between
behavior, person/cognitive, and environment
are reciprocal rather than one-way. Person/
cognitive refers to cognitive processes (for
example, thinking and planning) and personal
characteristics (for example, believing that you
can control your experiences).

- - - - - - - - - - ➤

developmental **connection**

Achievement

Bandura emphasizes that self-
efficacy is a key person/cognitive factor in children's achievement. Connect
to "Socioemotional Development in
Middle and Late Childhood."

developmental **connection**

Attachment

Human babies go through a series of
phases in developing an attachment to
a caregiver. Connect to "Socioemotional
Development in Infancy."

◄ - - - - - - - - - ╝

social cognitive theory The view of
psychologists who emphasize behavior,
environment, and cognition as the key factors
in development.

ethology Stresses that behavior is strongly
influenced by biology, is tied to evolution, and
is characterized by critical or sensitive
periods.

Albert Bandura has been one of the leading
architects of social cognitive theory. *How
does Bandura's theory differ from Skinner's?*
Linda A Cicero/Stanford News Service

Bandura's Social Cognitive Theory

Some psychologists agree with the behaviorists'
notion that development is learned and is influenced strongly by environmental interactions.
However, unlike Skinner, they also see cognition
as important in understanding development
(Mischel, 2014). **Social cognitive theory** holds
that behavior, environment, and cognition are the
key factors in development.

American psychologist Albert Bandura
(1925–) is the leading architect of social cognitive
theory. Bandura (1986, 2004, 2010a, b, 2012,
2015, 2018) emphasizes that cognitive processes
have important links with the environment and
behavior. His early research program focused heavily on observational learning (also called imitation
or modeling), which is learning that occurs
through observing what others do. For example, a
young boy might observe his father yelling in anger
and treating other people with hostility; with his
peers, the young boy later is very aggressive, showing the same characteristics as his father's behav-
ior. Social cognitive theorists stress that people acquire a wide range of behaviors, thoughts, and
feelings through observing others' behavior and that these observations play a central role in
life-span development.

What is cognitive about observational learning in Bandura's view? He proposes that people
cognitively represent the behavior of others and then sometimes adopt this behavior themselves.

Bandura's (2004, 2015, 2018) most recent model of learning and development includes
three elements: behavior, the person/cognition, and the environment. An individual's confidence
in being able to control his or her success is an example of a person factor; strategies are an
example of a cognitive factor. Recently, Bandura (2018) described *forethought* as a key cognitive
factor in his social cognitive theory. When engaging in forethought, individuals guide and motivate themselves by creating action plans, formulating goals, and visualizing positive outcomes
of their actions. As shown in Figure 14, behavior, person/cognitive, and environmental factors
operate interactively.

Evaluating Behavioral and Social Cognitive Theories   Contributions of the
behavioral and social cognitive theories include an emphasis on scientific research and environmental determinants of behavior. Criticisms include too little emphasis on cognition in
Skinner's theory and inadequate attention paid to developmental changes.

ETHOLOGICAL THEORY

Ethology stresses that behavior is strongly influenced by biology, is tied to evolution, and is
characterized by critical or sensitive periods. These are specific time frames during which,
according to ethologists, the presence or absence of certain experiences has a long-lasting
influence on individuals (Bateson, 2015).

European zoologist Konrad Lorenz (1903–1989) helped bring ethology to prominence. In
his best-known research, Lorenz (1965) studied the behavior of greylag geese, which follow their
mothers as soon as they hatch. Lorenz separated the eggs laid by one goose into two groups.
One group he returned to the goose to be hatched by her. The other group was hatched in an
incubator. The goslings in the first group followed their mother as soon as they hatched. However, those in the second group, which saw Lorenz when they first hatched, followed him
everywhere, as though he were their mother. Lorenz marked the goslings and then placed both
groups under a box. Mother goose and "mother" Lorenz stood aside as the box was lifted. Each
group of goslings went directly to its "mother." Lorenz called this process imprinting—the rapid,
innate learning that involves attachment to the first moving object seen.

John Bowlby (1969, 1989) illustrated an important application of ethological theory to
human development. Bowlby stressed that attachment to a caregiver during the first year of life

Konrad Lorenz, a pioneering student of animal behavior, is followed through the water by three imprinted greylag geese. Describe Lorenz's experiment with the geese. *Do you think his experiment would have had the same results with human babies? Explain.*
Nina Leen/The LIFE Picture Collection/Getty Images

has important consequences throughout the life span. In his view, if this attachment is positive and secure, the individual will likely develop optimally in childhood and adulthood. If the attachment is negative and insecure, life-span development will likely not be optimal. We will explore the concept of infant attachment in much greater detail later in this edition.

In Lorenz's view, imprinting needs to take place at a certain, very early time in the life of the animal, or else it will not take place. This point in time is called a critical period. A related concept is that of a sensitive period, and an example of this is the time during infancy when, according to Bowlby, attachment should occur in order to promote optimal development of social relationships.

Another theory that emphasizes biological foundations of development—evolutionary psychology—will be presented in the chapter on "Biological Beginnings," along with views on the role of heredity in development (Buss & Schmidt, 2019; Hoye & others, 2020). In addition, we will examine a number of biological theories of aging in later chapters (Falandry, 2019).

Contributions of ethological theory include a focus on the biological and evolutionary basis of development, and the use of careful observations in naturalistic settings. Criticisms include too much emphasis on biological foundations and a belief that the concepts of critical and sensitive periods might be too rigid.

ECOLOGICAL THEORY

While ethological theory stresses biological factors, ecological theory emphasizes environmental factors. One ecological theory that has important implications for understanding life-span development was created by Urie Bronfenbrenner (1917–2005). **Bronfenbrenner's ecological theory** (Bronfenbrenner, 1986, 2004; Bronfenbrenner & Morris, 1998, 2006) holds that development reflects the influence of several environmental systems. The theory identifies five environmental systems: microsystem, mesosystem, exosystem, macrosystem, and chronosystem (see Figure 15).

The *microsystem* is the setting in which the individual lives. These contexts include the person's family, peers, school, and neighborhood. It is in the microsystem that the most direct interactions with social agents take place—with parents, peers, and teachers, for example. The individual is not a passive recipient of experiences in these settings, but someone who helps to construct the settings.

The *mesosystem* involves relations between microsystems or connections between contexts. Examples are the relation of family experiences to school experiences, school experiences to religious experiences, and family experiences to peer experiences. For example, children whose parents have rejected them may have difficulty developing positive relationships with teachers.

The *exosystem* consists of links between a social setting in which the individual does not have an active role and the individual's immediate context. For example, a husband's or child's experiences at home may be influenced by a mother's experiences at work. The mother might receive a promotion that requires more travel, which might increase conflict with the husband and change patterns of interaction with the child.

The *macrosystem* involves the culture in which individuals live. Remember from earlier in the chapter that culture refers to the behavior patterns, beliefs, and all other products of a group

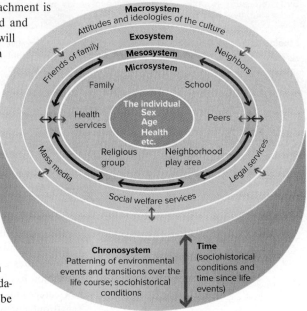

FIGURE **15**

BRONFENBRENNER'S ECOLOGICAL THEORY OF DEVELOPMENT. Bronfenbrenner's ecological theory consists of five environmental systems: microsystem, mesosystem, exosystem, macrosystem, and chronosystem.

developmental **connection**
Parenting
How are parent-child relationships and children's peer relations linked? Connect to "Socioemotional Development in Early Childhood."

Bronfenbrenner's ecological theory
Bronfenbrenner's environmental systems theory that focuses on five environmental systems: microsystem, mesosystem, exosystem, macrosystem, and chronosystem.

THEORY	ISSUES	
	Continuity/discontinuity, early versus later experiences	**Biological and environmental factors**
Psychoanalytic	Discontinuity between stages—continuity between early experiences and later development; early experiences very important; later changes in development emphasized in Erikson's theory	Freud's biological determination interacting with early family experiences; Erikson's more balanced biological-cultural interaction perspective
Cognitive	Discontinuity between stages in Piaget's theory; continuity between early experiences and later development in Piaget's and Vygotsky's theories; no stages in Vygotsky's theory or information-processing theory	Piaget's emphasis on interaction and adaptation; environment provides the setting for cognitive structures to develop; information-processing view has not addressed this issue extensively but mainly emphasizes biological-environmental interaction
Behavioral and social cognitive	Continuity (no stages); experience at all points of development important	Environment viewed as the cause of behavior in both views
Ethological	Discontinuity but no stages; critical or sensitive periods emphasized; early experiences very important	Strong biological view
Ecological	Little attention to continuity/discontinuity; change emphasized more than stability	Strong environmental view

FIGURE 16

A COMPARISON OF THEORIES AND ISSUES IN LIFE-SPAN DEVELOPMENT

eclectic theoretical orientation An orientation that does not follow any one theoretical approach but rather selects from each theory whatever is considered the best in it.

Urie Bronfenbrenner developed ecological theory, a perspective that is receiving increased attention today. His theory emphasizes the importance of both micro and macro dimensions of the environment in which the child lives.
Courtesy of Cornell University Photography

of people that are passed on from generation to generation. Remember also that cross-cultural studies—the comparison of one culture with one or more other cultures—provide information about the generality of development.

The *chronosystem* consists of the patterning of environmental events and transitions over the life course, as well as sociohistorical circumstances. For example, divorce is one transition. Researchers have found that the negative effects of divorce on children often peak during the first year after the divorce (Hetherington, 1993, 2006). By two years after the divorce, family interaction has become more stable. As an example of sociohistorical circumstances, consider how career opportunities for women have increased since the 1960s.

Bronfenbrenner (2004; Bronfenbrenner & Morris, 2006) subsequently added biological influences to his theory, describing it as a bioecological theory. Nonetheless, it is still dominated by ecological, environmental contexts.

Contributions of ecological theory include a systematic examination of macro and micro dimensions of environmental systems, and attention to connections between environmental systems. A further contribution of Bronfenbrenner's theory is an emphasis on a range of social contexts beyond the family, such as neighborhood, religion, school, and workplace, as influential in children's development (Shelton, 2018; Taliaferro & others, 2020). Criticisms include inadequate attention to biological factors, as well as too little emphasis on cognitive factors.

AN ECLECTIC THEORETICAL ORIENTATION

No single theory described in this chapter can explain entirely the rich complexity of life-span development, but each has contributed to our understanding of development. Psychoanalytic theory best explains the unconscious mind. Erikson's theory best describes the changes that occur during adult development. Piaget's, Vygotsky's, and the information-processing views provide the most complete description of cognitive development. The behavioral and social cognitive and ecological theories have been the most adept at examining the environmental determinants of development. The ethological theories have highlighted biology's role and the importance of sensitive periods in development.

In short, although theories are helpful guides, relying on a single theory to explain development is probably a mistake. This book instead takes an **eclectic theoretical orientation,** which does not follow any one theoretical approach but rather selects from each theory whatever is considered its best features. In this way, you can view the study of development as it actually exists—with different theorists making different assumptions, stressing different empirical problems, and using different strategies to discover information. Figure 16 compares the main theoretical perspectives in terms of how they view important issues in life-span development.

Review *Connect* Reflect

LG3 Describe the main theories of human development.

Review

- What are the four steps of the scientific method? How can theory and hypotheses be defined? What are two main psychoanalytic theories? What are some contributions and criticisms of the psychoanalytic theories?
- What are three main cognitive theories? What are some contributions and criticisms of the cognitive theories?
- What are two main behavioral and social cognitive theories? What are some contributions and criticisms of the behavioral and social cognitive theories?
- What is the nature of ethological theory? What are some contributions and criticisms of the theory?

- What characterizes ecological theory? What are some contributions and criticisms of the theory?
- What is an eclectic theoretical orientation?

Connect

- The beginning of this section started with a question about whether special care might be able to repair the harm inflicted by child neglect. How might this question be answered differently using the various theories outlined?

Reflect *Your Own Personal Journey of Life*

- Which of the life-span theories do you think best explains your own development? Why?

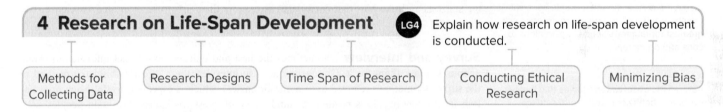

4 Research on Life-Span Development

LG4 Explain how research on life-span development is conducted.

Methods for Collecting Data   Research Designs   Time Span of Research   Conducting Ethical Research   Minimizing Bias

If they follow an eclectic orientation, how do scholars and researchers determine that one feature of a theory is somehow better than another? Through scientific research, the features of theories can be tested and refined (Pittinsky, 2019).

Generally, research on life-span development is designed to test hypotheses, which in some cases are derived from the theories just described. Through research, theories are modified to reflect new data, and occasionally new theories arise. How are data about life-span development collected? What types of research designs are used to study life-span development? And what are some ethical considerations in conducting research on life-span development?

> Science refines everyday thinking.
>
> —**Albert Einstein**
> *German-born American physicist, 20th century*

METHODS FOR COLLECTING DATA

Whether we are interested in studying attachment in infants, the cognitive skills of children, or social relationships in older adults, we can choose from several ways of collecting data (Gravetter & Forzano, 2019). Here we outline the measures most often used, beginning with observation.

Observation Scientific observation requires an important set of skills. For observations to be effective, they have to be systematic. We need to have some idea of what we are looking for. We have to know whom we are observing, when and where we will observe, how the observations will be made, and how they will be recorded.

Where should we make our observations? We have two choices: the laboratory and the everyday world.

When we observe scientifically, we often need to control certain factors that determine behavior but are not the focus of our inquiry (Stanovich, 2019). For this reason, some research on life-span development is conducted in a **laboratory**, a controlled setting where many of the complex factors of the "real world" are absent. For example, suppose you want to observe how children react when they see other people act aggressively. If you observe children in their

laboratory A controlled setting in which many of the complex factors of the "real world" are removed.

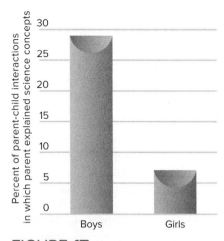

FIGURE **17**

PARENTS' EXPLANATIONS OF SCIENCE TO SONS AND DAUGHTERS AT A SCIENCE MUSEUM. In a naturalistic observation study at a children's science museum, parents were three times more likely to explain science to boys than to girls (Crowley & others, 2001). The gender difference occurred regardless of whether the father, the mother, or both parents were with the child, although the gender difference was greatest for fathers' science explanations to sons and daughters.

naturalistic observation Studies that involve observing behavior in real-world settings.

standardized test A test with uniform procedures for administration and scoring. Many standardized tests allow a person's performance to be compared with the performance of other individuals.

homes or schools, you have no control over how much aggression the children observe, what kind of aggression they see, which people they see acting aggressively, or how other people treat the children. In contrast, if you observe the children in a laboratory, you can control these and other factors and therefore have more confidence about how to interpret your observations.

Laboratory research does have some drawbacks, however, including the following:

1. It is almost impossible to conduct research without the participants knowing they are being studied.

2. The laboratory setting is unnatural and therefore can cause the participants to behave unnaturally.

3. People who are willing to come to a university laboratory may not accurately represent groups from diverse cultural backgrounds.

4. People who are unfamiliar with university settings and with the idea of "helping science" may be intimidated by the laboratory setting.

Naturalistic observation provides insights that sometimes cannot be attained in the laboratory (Neuman, 2020). **Naturalistic observation** means observing behavior in real-world settings, making no effort to manipulate or control the situation. Life-span researchers conduct naturalistic observations at sporting events, child-care centers, work settings, malls, and other places people live in and frequent.

Naturalistic observation was used in one study that focused on conversations in a children's science museum (Crowley & others, 2001). When visiting exhibits at the science museum, parents were far more likely to engage boys than girls in explanatory talk. This finding suggests a gender bias that encourages boys more than girls to be interested in science (see Figure 17).

Survey and Interview Sometimes the best and quickest way to get information about people is to ask them for it. One technique is to interview them directly. A related method is the survey (sometimes referred to as a questionnaire), which is especially useful when information from many people is needed. A standard set of questions is used to obtain peoples' self-reported attitudes or beliefs about a particular topic. In a good survey, the questions are clear and unbiased, allowing respondents to answer unambiguously.

Surveys and interviews can be used to study topics ranging from religious beliefs to sexual habits to attitudes about gun control to beliefs about how to improve schools. Surveys and interviews may be conducted in person, over the telephone, and over the Internet (Ary & others, 2019).

One problem with surveys and interviews is the tendency of participants to answer questions in a way that they think is socially acceptable or desirable rather than to say what they truly think or feel. For example, on a survey or in an interview some individuals might say that they do not take drugs even though they do.

Standardized Test A **standardized test** has uniform procedures for administration and scoring. Many standardized tests allow a person's performance to be compared with that of other individuals; thus they provide information about individual differences among people (Kaplan & Saccuzzo, 2018). One example is the Stanford-Binet intelligence test, which will be discussed in more detail later. Your score on the Stanford-Binet test tells you how your performance compares with that of thousands of other people who have taken the test.

One criticism of standardized tests is that they assume a person's behavior is consistent and stable, yet personality and intelligence—two primary targets of standardized testing—can vary with the situation. For

What are some important strategies in conducting observational research with children?
Charles Fox/Philadelphia Inquirer/MCT/Landov Images

example, a person may perform poorly on a standardized intelligence test in an office setting but score much higher at home, where he or she is less anxious.

Case Study   A **case study** is an in-depth look at a single individual. Case studies are performed mainly by mental health professionals when, for either practical or ethical reasons, the unique aspects of an individual's life cannot be duplicated and tested in other individuals. A case study provides information about one person's experiences; it may focus on nearly any aspect of the subject's life that helps the researcher understand the person's mind, behavior, or other attributes (Yin, 2012). A researcher may gather information for a case study from interviews and medical records. In later chapters, we discuss vivid case studies, such as that of Michael Rehbein, who had much of the left side of his brain removed at 7 years of age to end severe epileptic seizures.

A case study can provide a dramatic, in-depth portrayal of an individual's life, but we must be cautious when generalizing from this information. The subject of a case study is unique, with a genetic makeup and personal history that no one else shares. In addition, case studies involve judgments of unknown reliability. Researchers who conduct case studies rarely check to see if other professionals agree with their observations or findings.

Mahatma Gandhi was the spiritual leader of India in the middle of the twentieth century. Erik Erikson conducted an extensive case study of Gandhi's life to determine what contributed to his identity development. *What are some limitations of the case study approach?*
Bettmann/Getty Images

case study An in-depth look at a single individual.

Physiological Measures   Researchers are increasingly using physiological measures when they study development at different points in the life span (Kinugawa, 2019). Hormone levels are increasingly used in developmental research.

Cortisol is a hormone produced by the adrenal gland that is linked to the body's stress level and has been measured in studies of temperament, emotional reactivity, mood, and peer relations (Freberg, 2019; Jahangard & others, 2020). Also, as puberty unfolds, the blood levels of certain hormones increase. To determine the nature of these hormonal changes, researchers analyze blood samples from adolescent volunteers (Bae & others, 2020; Li & others, 2019).

Another physiological measure that is increasingly being used is neuroimaging, especially *functional magnetic resonance imaging* (fMRI), in which electromagnetic waves are used to construct images of a person's brain tissue and biochemical activity (Harrington, 2020). Figure 18

developmental **connection**
Cognitive Neuroscience and Aging
The cognitive neuroscience of aging involves the study of links between brain development in older adults and changes in their cognitive skills. Connect to "Cognitive Development in Late Adulthood."

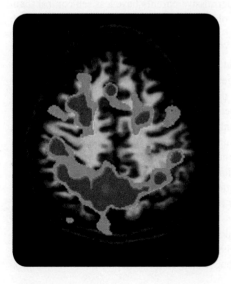
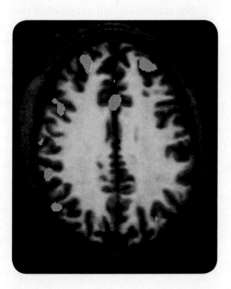

FIGURE **18**

BRAIN IMAGING OF 15-YEAR-OLD ADOLESCENTS. These two brain images indicate how alcohol can influence the functioning of an adolescent's brain. Notice the pink and red coloring (which indicates effective brain functioning involving memory) in the brain of the 15-year-old non-drinker (*left*) while engaging in a memory task, and compare it with the lack of those colors in the brain of the 15-year-old heavy drinker (*right*) under the influence of alcohol.
Dr. Susan F. Tapert, University of California, San Diego

compares the brain images of two adolescents—one a non-drinker and the other a heavy drinker—while they are engaged in a memory task.

Electroencephalography (EEG) is a physiological measure that has been used for many decades to monitor overall electrical activity in the brain (O'Toole & Boylan, 2019). Recent electroencephalograph research includes studies of infants' attention and memory (Bell & Cuevas, 2020). In many chapters of this edition, you will read about recent research on changes in the brain during prenatal development, infancy, childhood, adolescence, and aging.

Heart rate has been used as an indicator of infants' and children's development of perception, attention, and memory (Curtindale & others, 2019). Further, heart rate has served as an index of different aspects of emotional development, such as inhibition, stress, and anxiety (Liddell & Williams, 2019).

Researchers study eye movement to learn more about perceptual development and other developmental topics. Sophisticated eye-tracking equipment is especially being used to discover more detailed information about infants' perception (Gergely & others, 2019), attention (Wagner & others, 2020), autism (Harrison & Slane, 2020), and effects of preterm birth on language development (Imafuku & others, 2019).

Yet another dramatic change in physiological measures is the advancement in methods to assess the actual units of hereditary information—genes—in studies of biological influences on development (Falandry, 2019; Joshi & others, 2020). For example, recent advances in gene assessment have revealed several specific genes that are linked to childhood obesity (Costa-Urrulia & others, 2020). Also, in a later chapter you will read about the role of the ApoE4 gene in Alzheimer disease (Dumaz & others, 2019).

RESEARCH DESIGNS

When you are conducting research on life-span development, in addition to selecting a method for collecting data, you also need to choose a research design. There are three main types of research designs: descriptive, correlational, and experimental.

Descriptive Research   All of the data-collection methods that we have discussed can be used in **descriptive research,** which aims to observe and record behavior. For example, a researcher might observe the extent to which people are altruistic or aggressive toward each other. By itself, descriptive research cannot prove what causes some phenomenon, but it can reveal important information about people's behavior (Gravetter & Forzano, 2019).

Correlational Research   In contrast with descriptive research, correlational research goes beyond describing phenomena to provide information that will help us to predict how people will behave (Graziano & Raulin, 2020). In **correlational research,** the goal is to describe the strength of the relationship between two or more events or characteristics. The more strongly the two events are correlated (or related or associated), the more accurately we can predict one event from the other (Aron, Coups, & Aron, 2019).

For example, to find out whether children of permissive parents have less self-control than other children, you would need to carefully record observations of parents' permissiveness and their children's self-control. You might observe that the higher a parent was in permissiveness, the lower the child was in self-control. You would then analyze these data statistically to yield a numerical measure called a **correlation coefficient,** which is a number based on a statistical analysis that describes the degree of association between two variables. The correlation coefficient ranges from −1.00 to +1.00. A negative number means an inverse relation. In this example, you might find an inverse correlation between permissive parenting and children's self-control with a coefficient of, say, −.30. By contrast, you might find a positive correlation of +.30 between parental monitoring of children and children's self-control.

The higher the correlation coefficient (whether positive or negative), the stronger the association between the two variables. A correlation of 0 means that there is no association between the variables. A correlation of −.40 is stronger than a correlation of +.20 because we disregard whether the correlation is positive or negative in determining the strength of the correlation.

A caution is in order, however. Correlation does not equal causation. The correlational finding just mentioned does not mean that permissive parenting necessarily causes low self-control in children. It could have that meaning, but it also could indicate that a child's lack

developmental **connection**

Gene × Environment (G × E) Interaction

Increasingly, researchers are exploring how the interaction of a specific gene and a specific aspect of the environment affects development. Connect to "Biological Beginnings."

descriptive research Studies designed to observe and record behavior.

correlational research Research that attempts to determine the strength of the relationship between two or more events or characteristics.

correlation coefficient A number based on statistical analysis that is used to describe the degree of association between two variables.

Observed Correlation: As permissive parenting increases, children's self-control decreases.

Possible explanations for this observed correlation

Permissive parenting   **causes** ➡ Children's lack of self-control

Children's lack of self-control   **causes** ➡ Permissive parenting

A third factor such as genetic tendencies or poverty   **causes both** ➡ Permissive parenting and children's lack of self-control

An observed correlation between two events cannot be used to conclude that one event causes the second event. Other possibilities are that the second event causes the first event or that a third event causes the correlation between the first two events.

FIGURE 19
POSSIBLE EXPLANATIONS OF CORRELATIONAL DATA
JupiterImages/Getty Images

of self-control caused the parents to give up trying to control the child. It also could mean that other factors, such as heredity or poverty, caused the correlation between permissive parenting and low self-control in children. Figure 19 illustrates these possible interpretations of correlational data.

Experimental Research   To study causality, researchers turn to experimental research. An **experiment** is a carefully regulated procedure in which one or more factors believed to influence the behavior being studied are manipulated while all other factors are held constant. If the behavior under study changes when a factor is manipulated, we say that the manipulated factor has caused the behavior to change (Harrington, 2020). In other words, the experiment has demonstrated cause and effect. The cause is the factor that was manipulated. The effect is the behavior that changed because of the manipulation. Nonexperimental research methods (descriptive and correlational research) cannot establish cause and effect because they do not involve manipulating factors in a controlled way.

Independent and Dependent Variables   Experiments include two types of changeable factors, or variables: independent and dependent. An independent variable is a manipulated, influential, experimental factor. It is a potential cause. The label "independent" is used because this variable can be manipulated independently of other factors to determine its effect. An experiment may include one independent variable or several of them.

A dependent variable is a factor that can change in an experiment, in response to changes in the independent variable. As researchers manipulate the independent variable, they measure the dependent variable for any resulting effect (Christensen, Johnson, & Turner, 2020).

For example, suppose that you conducted a study to determine whether women could change the breathing and sleeping patterns of their newborn babies by meditating during pregnancy. You might require one group of pregnant women to engage in a certain amount and type of meditation each day while another group would not meditate; the meditation is thus the independent variable. When the infants are born, you would observe and measure their breathing and sleeping patterns. These patterns are the dependent variable, the factor that changes as the result of your manipulation.

Experimental and Control Groups   Experiments can involve one or more experimental groups and one or more control groups (Graziano & Raulin, 2020). An experimental group is a group whose experience is manipulated. A control group is a comparison group that is as similar to the experimental group as possible and that is treated in every way like the experimental group except for the manipulated factor (independent variable). The control group serves as a baseline against which the effects of the manipulated condition can be compared.

Random assignment is an important principle for deciding whether each participant will be placed in the experimental group or in the control group. Random assignment means that researchers assign participants to experimental and control groups by chance. It reduces the

experiment A carefully regulated procedure in which one or more of the factors believed to influence the behavior being studied are manipulated while all other factors are held constant.

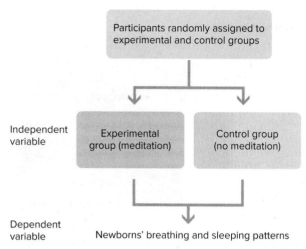

Participants randomly assigned to experimental and control groups

Independent variable

Experimental group (meditation) — Control group (no meditation)

Dependent variable — Newborns' breathing and sleeping patterns

FIGURE 20

PRINCIPLES OF EXPERIMENTAL RESEARCH. Imagine that you decide to conduct an experimental study of the effects of meditation by pregnant women on their newborns' breathing and sleeping patterns. You would randomly assign pregnant women to experimental and control groups. The experimental-group women would engage in meditation over a specified number of sessions and weeks. The control group would not. Then, when the infants are born, you would assess their breathing and sleeping patterns. If the breathing and sleeping patterns of newborns whose mothers were in the experimental group are more positive than those of the control group, you would conclude that meditation caused the positive effects.

developmental **connection**

Intelligence

Cohort effects help to explain differences in the intelligence of people born at different points in time. Connect to "Physical and Cognitive Development in Middle Adulthood."

cross-sectional approach A research strategy in which individuals of different ages are compared at one point in time.

longitudinal approach A research strategy in which the same individuals are studied over a period of time, usually several years or more.

cohort effects Characteristics determined by a person's time of birth, era, or generation rather than the person's actual age.

likelihood that the experiment's results will be due to any preexisting differences between groups. In the example involving the effects of meditation by pregnant women on the breathing and sleeping patterns of their newborns, you would randomly assign half of the pregnant women to engage in meditation over a period of weeks (the experimental group) and the other half to not meditate over the same number of weeks (the control group). Figure 20 illustrates the nature of experimental research.

TIME SPAN OF RESEARCH

Researchers in life-span development have a special concern with studies that focus on the relation of age to some other variable. We have two options: Researchers can study different individuals of varying ages and compare them, or they can study the same individuals as they age over time.

Cross-Sectional Approach   The **cross-sectional approach** is a research strategy that simultaneously compares individuals of different ages. A typical cross-sectional study might include three groups of children: 5-year-olds, 8-year-olds, and 11-year-olds. Another study might include groups of 15-year-olds, 25-year-olds, and 45-year-olds. The groups can be compared with respect to a variety of dependent variables: IQ, memory, peer relations, attachment to parents, hormonal changes, and so on. All of this can be accomplished in a short time. In some studies, data are collected in a single day. Even in large-scale cross-sectional studies with hundreds of subjects, data collection does not usually take longer than several months to complete.

The main advantage of the cross-sectional study is that the researcher does not have to wait for the individuals to grow up or become older. Despite its efficiency, though, the cross-sectional approach has its drawbacks. It gives no information about how individuals change or about the stability of their characteristics. It can obscure the increases and decreases of development—the hills and valleys of growth and development. For example, a cross-sectional study of life satisfaction might reveal average increases and decreases, but it would not show how the life satisfaction of individual adults waxed and waned over the years. It also would not tell us whether the same adults who had positive or negative perceptions of life satisfaction in early adulthood maintained their relative degree of life satisfaction as they became middle-aged or older adults.

Longitudinal Approach   The **longitudinal approach** is a research strategy in which the same individuals are studied over a period of time, usually several years or more (Kramer & Rodgers, 2020; Lichtenstein & others, 2020). For example, in a longitudinal study of life satisfaction, the same adults might be assessed periodically over a 70-year time span—at the ages of 20, 35, 45, 65, and 90, for example.

Longitudinal studies provide a wealth of information about vital issues such as stability and change in development and the influence of early experience on later development, but they do have drawbacks (Zhang & Liu, 2020). They are expensive and time-consuming. The longer the study lasts, the more participants drop out—they move, get sick, lose interest, and so forth. The participants who remain may be dissimilar to those who drop out, biasing the outcome of the study. Those individuals who remain in a longitudinal study over a number of years may be more responsible and conformity-oriented, for example, or they might lead more stable lives.

Cohort Effects   A *cohort* is a group of people who are born at a similar point in history and share similar experiences as a result, such as living through the Vietnam War or growing up in the same city around the same time. These shared experiences may produce a range of differences among cohorts (Hohls & others, 2019; Schaie, 2016a, b). For example, people who were teenagers during the Great Depression are likely to differ from people who were teenagers during the booming 1990s in regard to their educational opportunities and economic status, how they were raised, and their attitudes toward sex and religion. In life-span development research, **cohort effects** are due to a person's time of birth, era, or generation but not to actual age.

Cohort effects are important because they can powerfully affect the dependent measures in a study ostensibly concerned with age (Atkins & others, 2019). Researchers have shown

Cohort effects are due to a person's time of birth or generation but not actually to age. Think for a moment about growing up in (*left*) the Great Depression and (*right*) today. *How might your development differ depending on which of these time frames has dominated your life? your parents' lives? your grandparents' lives?*

(*Left*) Library of Congress Prints and Photographs Division [LC-USZ62-63966]; (*right*) Tom Grill/JGI/Blend Images LLC

that it is especially important to be aware of cohort effects when assessing adult intelligence (Schaie, 2016a, b). Individuals born at different points in time—such as 1920, 1940, and 1960—have had varying opportunities for education. Individuals born in earlier years had less access to education, and this fact may have a significant effect on how this cohort performs on intelligence tests. Further, in a recent study, older adults nowadays report fewer constraints on their lives than their counterparts 18 years ago, but younger adults report more constraints and lower mastery beliefs today than those 18 years ago (Drewelies & others, 2018). Another example of a cohort effect occurred in a study in which older adults assessed in 2013–2014 engaged in a higher level of abstract reasoning than their counterparts assessed two decades earlier in 1990–1993 (Gerstorf & others, 2015).

Cross-sectional studies can show how different cohorts respond, but they can confuse age changes and cohort effects. Longitudinal studies are effective in studying age changes, but only within one cohort.

Various generations have been given labels by the popular culture. Figure 21 describes the labels given to various generations, their historical periods, and the reasons for these labels. Consider the following description of the current generation of youth and think about how they differ from earlier youth generations:

> They are history's first "always connected" generation. Steeped in digital technology and social media, they treat their multi-tasking hand-held gadgets almost like a body part—for better or worse. More than 8 in 10 say they sleep with a cell phone glowing by the bed, poised to disgorge texts, phone calls, e-mails, songs, news, videos, games, and wake-up jingles. But sometimes convenience yields to temptation. Nearly two-thirds admit to texting while driving (Pew Research Center, 2010, p. 1).

Until recently, the latest generation was labeled "millennials" and described as being more technologically sophisticated and more ethnically diverse than earlier generations. However, the Pew Research Center, which has periodically assessed generational trends in recent decades, recently decided to define millennials as anyone born between 1981 and 1996, and anyone born in 1997 and later as part of a new generation (Dimock, 2019). Currently there is no consensus on what the name of this new generation should be, but two candidates are "generation Z" and "post-millennial." The oldest members of the new generation turn 23 in 2020 while the oldest millennials turn 40 in 2020. What characterizes this new Z/post-millennial generation? They are even more technologically sophisticated and ethnically diverse than millennials. Teenagers in this cohort have grown up with always-available/always-on technological devices, are immersed in social media, and communicate with others online and through mobile devices far more than in person. Also, generation Z/post-millennials are the best-educated generation yet, with more going to college and more living with a college-educated parent than millennials (Fry & Parker, 2018).

How are today's young people experiencing youth differently from earlier generations?
Mark Bowden/E+/Getty Images

FIGURE **21**
GENERATIONS, THEIR HISTORICAL
PERIODS, AND CHARACTERISTICS

Generation	Historical Period	Reasons for Label
Generation Z/ Post-Millennials	Individuals born in 1997 and later	More immersed in a technological world, especially social media, more ethnically diverse, and better educated than millennials.
Millennials	Individuals born between 1981 and 1996	First generation to come of age and enter emerging adulthood (18 to 25 years of age) in the twenty-first century (the new millennium). Two main characteristics: (1) connection to technology, and (2) ethnic diversity.
Generation X	Individuals born between 1965 and 1980	Described as lacking an identity and savvy loners.
Baby Boomers	Individuals born between 1946 and 1964	Label used because this generation represents the spike in the number of babies born after World War II; the largest generation ever to enter late adulthood in the United States.
Silent Generation	Individuals born between 1928 and 1945	Children of the Great Depression and World War II; described as conformists and civic minded.

CONDUCTING ETHICAL RESEARCH

Ethics in research may affect you personally if you ever serve as a participant in a study. In that event, you need to know your rights as a participant and the responsibilities of researchers to assure that these rights are safeguarded.

If you ever become a researcher in life-span development yourself, you will need an even deeper understanding of ethics (Parsons, 2020). Even if you only carry out experimental projects in psychology courses, you must consider the rights of the participants in those projects. A student might think, "I volunteer in a home for people with intellectual disabilities several hours per week. I can use the residents of the home in my study to see if a particular treatment helps improve their memory for everyday tasks." But without proper permissions, the most well-meaning, kind, and considerate studies still violate the rights of the participants (Neuman, 2020).

Today, proposed research at colleges and universities must pass the scrutiny of a research ethics committee before the research can be initiated (Graziano & Raulin, 2020). In addition, the American Psychological Association (APA) has developed ethics guidelines for its members. The code of ethics instructs psychologists to protect their participants from mental and physical harm. The participants' best interests need to be kept foremost in the researcher's mind. APA's guidelines address four important issues:

1. *Informed consent.* All participants must know what their research participation will involve and what risks might develop. Even after informed consent is given, participants must retain the right to withdraw from the study at any time and for any reason.

2. *Confidentiality.* Researchers are responsible for keeping all of the data they gather on individuals completely confidential and, when possible, completely anonymous.

3. *Debriefing.* After the study has been completed, participants should be informed of its purpose and the methods that were used. In most cases, the experimenter also can inform participants in a general manner beforehand about the purpose of the research without leading participants to behave in a way they think that the experimenter is expecting.

4. *Deception.* In some circumstances, telling the participants beforehand what the research study is about substantially alters the participants' behavior and invalidates the researcher's data. In all cases of deception, however, the psychologist must ensure that the deception will not harm the participants and that the participants will be debriefed (told the complete nature of the study) as soon as possible after the study is completed.

Pam Reid, Educational and Developmental Psychologist

When she was a child, Pam Reid liked to play with chemistry sets. Reid majored in chemistry during college and wanted to become a doctor. However, when some of her friends signed up for a psychology class as an elective, she decided to take the course. She was intrigued by learning about how people think, behave, and develop—so much so that she changed her major to psychology. Reid went on to obtain her Ph.D. in psychology (American Psychological Association, 2003, p. 16).

For a number of years, Reid was a professor of education and psychology at the University of Michigan, where she also was a research scientist at the Institute for Research on Women and Gender. Her main focus has been on how children and adolescents develop social skills, with a special interest in the development of African American girls (Reid & Zalk, 2001). She has been involved in numerous community activities, including the creation of a math and technology enrichment program for middle-school girls. In 2004, Reid became provost and executive vice-president at Roosevelt University in Chicago. From 2008

Pam Reid (center), with students at the University of Saint Joseph.
Courtesy of Dr. Pam Reid

to 2015, she was president of the University of Saint Joseph in Hartford, Connecticut, before retiring to pursue other interests.

For more information about what educational psychologists do, see the Careers in Life-Span Development appendix.

MINIMIZING BIAS

Studies of life-span development are most useful when they are conducted without bias or prejudice toward any particular group of people. Of special concern is bias based on gender and bias based on culture or ethnicity.

Gender Bias For most of its existence, our society has had a strong gender bias—a preconceived notion about the abilities of women and men that prevented individuals from pursuing their own interests and achieving their potential (Best & Puzio, 2019; Helgeson, 2020). Gender bias also has had a less obvious effect within the field of life-span development. For example, it is not unusual for conclusions to be drawn about females' attitudes and behaviors from research conducted with males as the only participants.

Furthermore, when researchers find gender differences, their reports sometimes magnify those differences (Denmark & others, 1988). For example, a researcher might report that 74 percent of the men in a study had high achievement expectations versus only 67 percent of the women and go on to talk about the differences in some detail. In reality, this might be a rather small difference. It also might disappear if the study were repeated, or the study might have methodological problems that don't allow such strong interpretations.

Pam Reid is a leading researcher who studies the effects of gender and ethnic bias on development. You can read about Dr. Reid's interests in *Connecting with Careers*.

Cultural and Ethnic Bias Today there is a growing realization that research on life-span development needs to include more people from diverse ethnic groups (Leventhal, Anastasio, & Dupere, 2020). Historically, people from ethnic minority groups (African American, Latino, Asian American, and Native American) were excluded from most research in the United States and simply thought of as variations from the norm or average. If minority individuals were included in samples and their scores didn't fit the norm, they were viewed as confounds or "noise" in data and discounted. Given the fact that individuals from diverse ethnic groups were excluded from research on life-span development for so long, we might reasonably conclude that people's real lives are perhaps more varied than research data have indicated in the past.

Look at these two photographs, one of all non-Latino White males, the other of a diverse group of females and males from different ethnic groups, including some non-Latino White males. Consider a topic in life-span development, such as parenting, love, or cultural values. *If you were conducting research on this topic, might the results of the study differ depending on whether the participants in your study were the individuals in the photograph on the left or on the right?*
(*Left*) Anthony Cassidy/The Image Bank/Getty Images; (*right*) Punchstock/Digital Vision

Researchers also have tended to overgeneralize about ethnic groups (Schaefer, 2019). **Ethnic gloss** involves using an ethnic label such as *African American* or *Latino* in a superficial way that portrays an ethnic group as being more homogeneous than it really is (Trimble, 1988). For example, a researcher might describe a research sample like this: "The participants were 60 Latinos." A more complete description of the group might be something like this: "The 60 Latino participants were Mexican Americans from low-income neighborhoods in the southwestern area of Los Angeles. Thirty-six were from homes in which Spanish is the dominant language spoken, 24 from homes in which English is the main language spoken. Thirty were born in the United States, 30 in Mexico. Twenty-eight described themselves as Mexican American, 14 as Mexican, 9 as American, 6 as Chicano, and 3 as Latino." Ethnic gloss can cause researchers to obtain samples of ethnic groups that are not representative of the group's diversity, which can lead to overgeneralization and stereotyping.

Ross Parke and Raymond Buriel (2006) described how research on ethnic minority children and their families has not been given adequate attention, especially in light of the significant rates of growth of these groups. Until recently, ethnic minority families were combined in the category "minority," which masks important differences among ethnic groups as well as diversity within an ethnic group. When research has been conducted on ethnic groups, most often they are compared to non-Latino Whites to identify group differences. An assumption in two-group studies is that ethnic minority children have not advanced far enough to be the same as non-Latino White children and that this developmental lag contributes to ethnic minority children's problems. Recently, some researchers have replaced two-group studies with more in-depth examination of variations within a single ethnic group. For example, a researcher might study how parents in an ethnic group adapt to the challenges they face as a minority in U.S. society and how these experiences contribute to the goals they have for their children.

The continued growth of minority families in the United States in approaching decades will mainly be due to the immigration of Latino and Asian families (Marks, Woolverton, & Garcia Coll, 2020). Researchers need "to take into account their acculturation level and generational status of parents and children," and consider how these factors might influence family processes and child outcomes (Parke & Buriel, 2006, p. 487). More attention also needs to be given to biculturalism because some children of color identify with two or more ethnic groups (Safa & others, 2019). And language development research needs to focus more on second-language acquisition (usually English) and bilingualism and how they are linked to school achievement (Diaz-Rico, 2020).

ethnic gloss Using an ethnic label such as African American or Latino in a superficial way that portrays an ethnic group as being more homogeneous than it really is.

Review *Connect* Reflect

 LG4 Explain how research on life-span development is conducted.

Review

- What methods do researchers use to collect data on life-span development?
- What research designs are used to study human development?
- How is research conducted on the time span of people's lives?
- What are researchers' ethical responsibilities to the people they study?
- How can gender, cultural, and ethnic bias affect the outcome of a research study?

Connect

- Earlier in the chapter, you read about normative age-graded influences, normative history-graded influences, and nonnormative life events. Describe how these influences relate to what you just read about cohort effects.

Reflect *Your Own Personal Journey of Life*

- You and your parents grew up in different time periods. Consider some ways that you are different from your parents. Do you think some of your differences might be due to cohort effects? Explain.

---

topical connections *looking* **forward**

In the chapter on "Biological Beginnings," you will continue to learn about theory and research as you explore the biological underpinnings of life-span development. The influence of human evolution on development will be covered, including a discussion of natural selection and adaptive behavior. You will examine how the human genome works, the collaborative nature of genes, and how DNA plays a role in creating the person each of us becomes. You also will explore the challenges and choices people encounter when deciding to reproduce, including infertility treatments and adoption. And you will read in greater depth about the many sides of the age-old nature-nurture debate, focusing on the way heredity and environment interact.

---

reach your **learning goals**

Introduction

1 The Life-Span Perspective

 LG1 Discuss the distinctive features of a life-span perspective on development.

The Importance of Studying Life-Span Development

Characteristics of the Life-Span Perspective

- Development is the pattern of change that begins at conception and continues through the human life span. It includes both growth and decline.

- Studying life-span development helps prepare us to take responsibility for children, gives us insight about our own lives, and gives us knowledge about what our lives will be like as we age.

- Life expectancy has increased dramatically in the last century, but life span has remained virtually the same.

- The life-span perspective includes these basic concepts: development is lifelong, multidimensional, multidirectional, and plastic; its study is multidisciplinary; it is contextual; it involves growth, maintenance, and regulation of loss; and it is a co-construction of biological, cultural, and individual factors.

- Three important sources of contextual influences are (1) normative age-graded influences, (2) normative history-graded influences, and (3) nonnormative life events.

- Health and well-being, parenting, education, sociocultural contexts and diversity, social policy, and technology are all areas of contemporary concern that are closely tied to life-span development.

- Important dimensions of the sociocultural context include culture, ethnicity, socioeconomic status, and gender.

- There is increasing interest in social policy issues related to children and to older adults.

- Recently there has been a dramatic infusion of technology in the lives of people of all ages, and the influence of technology on development is an important contemporary issue.

2 The Nature of Development

 LG2 Identify the most important processes, periods, and issues in development.

- Three key categories of developmental processes are biological, cognitive, and socioemotional. Throughout development, there are extensive connections between these types of processes.

- The life span is commonly divided into the following development periods: prenatal, infancy, early childhood, middle and late childhood, adolescence, early adulthood, middle adulthood, and late adulthood.

- Recently, life-span developmentalists have described the human life span in terms of four ages, with a special focus on the third and fourth ages, as well as a distinction between the young-old and oldest-old.

- An important aspect of life-span development involves connections across periods of development.

- According to some experts on life-span development, too much emphasis is placed on chronological age.

- In studies covering adolescence through late adulthood, older people report the highest level of happiness.

- We often think of age only in terms of chronological age, but a full evaluation of age requires consideration of chronological, biological, psychological, and social age. Neugarten emphasizes that we are moving toward a society in which chronological age is only a weak predictor of development in adulthood.

- The nature-nurture issue focuses on the extent to which development is mainly influenced by nature (biological inheritance) or nurture (experience).

- The stability-change issue focuses on the degree to which we become older renditions of our early experience or develop into someone different from who we were earlier in development. A special aspect of the stability-change issue is the extent to which development is determined by early versus later experiences.

- Developmentalists describe development as continuous (gradual, or cumulative change) or as discontinuous (abrupt, or a sequence of stages). Most developmentalists recognize that extreme positions on the nature-nurture, stability-change, and continuity-discontinuity issues are unwise. Despite this consensus, there is still spirited debate on these issues.

3 Theories of Development

 LG3 Describe the main theories of human development.

- The scientific method involves four main steps: (1) conceptualize a problem, (2) collect data, (3) analyze data, and (4) draw conclusions.

- Theory is often involved in conceptualizing a problem. A theory is a coherent set of interrelated ideas that helps to explain phenomena and to facilitate predictions. Hypotheses are specific, testable assertions and predictions, often derived from theory.

- According to psychoanalytic theories, development primarily depends on the unconscious mind and is heavily couched in emotion. Freud argued that individuals go through five psychosexual stages. Erikson's theory emphasizes eight psychosocial stages of development: trust versus mistrust, autonomy versus shame and doubt, initiative versus guilt, industry versus inferiority, identity versus identity confusion, intimacy versus isolation, generativity versus stagnation, and integrity versus despair.

- Contributions of psychoanalytic theories include an emphasis on a developmental framework, family relationships, and unconscious aspects of the mind. Criticisms include a lack of scientific support, too much emphasis on sexual underpinnings, and an image of people that is too negative.

Cognitive Theories

- Three main cognitive theories are Piaget's, Vygotsky's, and information-processing. Cognitive theories emphasize thinking, reasoning, language, and other cognitive processes. Piaget proposed a cognitive developmental theory in which children use their cognition to adapt to their world. In Piaget's theory, children go through four cognitive stages: sensorimotor, preoperational, concrete operational, and formal operational. Vygotsky's sociocultural cognitive theory emphasizes how culture and social interaction guide cognitive development. The information-processing approach emphasizes that individuals manipulate information, monitor it, and strategize about it.

- Contributions of cognitive theories include an emphasis on the active construction of understanding and a positive view of development. Criticisms include giving too little attention to individual variations and skepticism about the pureness of Piaget's stages.

Behavioral and Social Cognitive Theories

- Two main behavioral and social cognitive theories are Skinner's operant conditioning and Bandura's social cognitive theory. In Skinner's operant conditioning, the consequences of a behavior produce changes in the probability of the behavior's occurrence. In Bandura's social cognitive theory, observational learning is a key aspect of life-span development. Bandura emphasizes reciprocal interactions among person/cognition, behavior, and environment.

- Contributions of the behavioral and social cognitive theories include an emphasis on scientific research and a focus on environmental factors. Criticisms include inadequate attention to developmental changes and, in Skinner's theory, too little attention to cognition.

Ethological Theory

- Ethology stresses that behavior is strongly influenced by biology, is tied to evolution, and is characterized by critical or sensitive periods. Contributions of ethological theory include a focus on the biological and evolutionary basis of development. Criticisms include rigidity of the concepts of critical and sensitive periods.

Ecological Theory

- Ecological theory emphasizes environmental contexts. Bronfenbrenner's environmental systems view of development proposes five environmental systems: microsystem, mesosystem, exosystem, macrosystem, and chronosystem. Contributions of the theory include a systematic examination of macro and micro dimensions of environmental systems and attention to connections between them. Criticisms include inadequate attention to biological factors, as well as a lack of emphasis on cognitive factors.

An Eclectic Theoretical Orientation

- An eclectic theoretical orientation does not follow any one theoretical approach but rather selects from each theory whatever is considered the best in it.

4 Research on Life-Span Development

LG4 Explain how research on life-span development is conducted.

Methods for Collecting Data

- Methods for collecting data about life-span development include observation (in a laboratory or a naturalistic setting), survey (questionnaire) or interview, standardized test, case study, and physiological measures.

Research Designs

- Three main research designs are descriptive, correlational, and experimental. Descriptive research aims to observe and record behavior. In correlational research, the goal is to describe the strength of the relationship between two or more events or characteristics. Experimental research involves conducting an experiment, which can determine cause and effect. An independent variable is the manipulated factor. A dependent variable is a factor that can change in response to changes in the independent variable. Experiments can involve one or more experimental groups and control groups. In random assignment, researchers assign participants to experimental and control groups by chance.

Time Span of Research

Conducting Ethical Research

Minimizing Bias

- When researchers decide about the time span of their research, they can conduct cross-sectional or longitudinal studies. Life-span researchers are especially concerned about cohort effects.

- Researchers' ethical responsibilities include seeking participants' informed consent, ensuring their confidentiality, debriefing them about the purpose and potential personal consequences of participating, and avoiding unnecessary deception of participants.

- Researchers need to guard against gender, cultural, and ethnic bias in research. Every effort should be made to make research equitable for both females and males. Individuals from varied ethnic backgrounds need to be included as participants in life-span research, and overgeneralization about diverse members within a group must be avoided.

key **terms**

biological processes 13
Bronfenbrenner's ecological
    theory 27
case study 31
cognitive processes 13
cohort effects 34
continuity-discontinuity issue 19
correlation coefficient 32
correlational research 32
cross-cultural studies 8
cross-sectional approach 34

culture 8
descriptive research 32
development 4
eclectic theoretical orientation 28
Erikson's theory 20
ethnic gloss 38
ethnicity 9
ethology 26
experiment 33
gender 9
hypotheses 20

information-processing theory 24
laboratory 29
life-span perspective 4
longitudinal approach 34
naturalistic observation 30
nature-nurture issue 18
nonnormative life events 7
normative age-graded influences 6
normative history-graded
    influences 6
Piaget's theory 22

psychoanalytic theories 20
scientific method 20
social cognitive theory 26
social policy 9
socioeconomic status (SES) 9
socioemotional processes 13
stability-change issue 19
standardized test 30
theory 20
Vygotsky's theory 23

key **people**

Paul Baltes 5
Albert Bandura 26
John Bowlby 26
Urie Bronfenbrenner 27

Raymond Buriel 38
Laura Carstensen 5
Marian Wright Edelman 9
Erik Erikson 21

Konrad Lorenz 26
Bernice Neugarten 18
Ross Parke 38
Jean Piaget 22

Robert Siegler 24
B. F. Skinner 25
Lev Vygotsky 22

appendix

Careers in Life-Span Development

The field of life-span development offers an amazing breadth of careers that can provide extremely satisfying work. College and university professors teach courses in many areas of life-span development. Teachers impart knowledge, understanding, and skills to children and adolescents. Counselors, clinical psychologists, nurses, and physicians help people of different ages to cope more effectively with their lives and improve their well-being.

These and many other careers related to life-span development offer many rewards. By working in the field of life-span development, you can help people to improve their lives, understand yourself and others better, possibly advance the state of knowledge in the field, and have an enjoyable time while you are doing these things. Many careers in life-span development pay reasonably well. For example, psychologists earn well above the median salary in the United States.

If you are considering a career in life-span development, would you prefer to work with infants? children? adolescents? older adults? As you go through this term, try to spend some time with people of different ages. Observe their behavior. Talk with them about their lives. Think about whether you would like to work with people of this age in your life's work.

In addition, to find out about careers in life-span development you might talk with people who work in various jobs. For example, if you have some interest in becoming a school counselor, call a school, ask to speak with a counselor, and set up an appointment to discuss the counselor's career and work. If you have an interest in becoming a nurse, call the nursing department at a hospital and set up an appointment to speak with the nursing coordinator about a nursing career.

Another way of exploring careers in life-span development is to work in a related job while you are in college. Many colleges and universities offer internships or other work experiences for students who major in specific fields. Course credit or pay is given for some of these jobs. Take advantage of these opportunities. They can help you decide whether this is the right career for you, and they can help you get into graduate school, if you decide you want to go.

An advanced degree is not absolutely necessary for some careers in life-span development, but usually you can considerably expand your opportunities (and income) by obtaining a graduate degree. If you think you might want to go to graduate school, talk with one or more professors about your interests, maintain a high grade-point average, take appropriate courses, and realize that you likely will need to take the Graduate Record Examination at some point.

In the upcoming sections, we will profile a number of careers in four areas: education/research; clinical/counseling; medical/nursing/physical development; and families/relationships. These are not the only career options in life-span development, but the profiles should give you an idea of the range of opportunities available. For each career, we will describe the work and address the amount of education required and the nature of the training. We have provided chapter titles after some entries to help you find *Connecting with Careers,* the career profiles of people who hold some of these positions. The Web site for this book gives more detailed information about these careers in life-span development.

Education/Research

Numerous careers in life-span development involve education or research. The opportunities range from college professor to preschool teacher to school psychologist.

College/University Professor

Professors teach courses in life-span development at many types of institutions, including research universities with master's or Ph.D. programs in life-span development, four-year colleges with no graduate programs, and community colleges. The courses in life-span development are offered in many different programs and schools, including psychology, education, nursing, child and family studies, social work, and medicine. In addition to teaching at the undergraduate or graduate level (or both), professors may conduct research, advise students or direct their research, and serve on college or university committees. Research is part of a professor's job description at most universities with master's and Ph.D. programs, but some college professors do not conduct research and focus instead on teaching.

Teaching life-span development at a college or university almost always requires a Ph.D. or master's degree. Obtaining a Ph.D. usually takes four to six years of graduate work; a master's degree requires approximately two years. The training involves taking graduate courses, learning to conduct research, and attending and presenting papers at professional meetings. Many graduate students work as teaching or research assistants for professors in an apprenticeship relationship that helps them to become competent teachers and researchers. **Read the profiles of professors in the "Socioemotional Development in Middle Adulthood" and "Socioemotional Development in Late Adulthood" chapters.**

Researcher

Some individuals in the field of life-span development work in research positions. They might work for a university, a government agency such as the National Institute of Mental Health, or private industry. They generate research ideas, plan studies, carry out the research, and usually attempt to publish the research in a scientific journal. A researcher often works in collaboration with other researchers. One researcher might spend much of his or her time in a laboratory; another researcher might work in the field, such as in schools, hospitals, and so on. Most researchers in life-span development have either a master's or a Ph.D.

Elementary or Secondary School Teacher

Elementary and secondary school teachers teach one or more subject areas, preparing the curriculum, giving tests, assigning grades, monitoring students' progress, conducting parent-teacher conferences, and attending workshops. Becoming an elementary or secondary school teacher requires a minimum of an undergraduate degree. The training involves taking a wide range of courses with a major or concentration in education as well as completing supervised practice teaching.

Exceptional Children (Special Education) Teacher

Teachers of exceptional children spend concentrated time with children who have a disability such as ADHD, intellectual disabilities, or cerebral palsy, or with children who are gifted. Usually some of their work occurs outside of the students' regular classroom and some of it inside the students' regular classroom. A teacher of exceptional children works closely with each student's regular classroom teacher and parents to create the best educational program for that student. Teachers of exceptional children often continue their education after obtaining their undergraduate degree and attain a master's degree.

Early Childhood Educator

Early childhood educators work on college faculties and usually teach in community colleges that award an associate degree in early childhood education. They have a minimum of a master's degree in their field. In graduate school, they take courses in early childhood education and receive supervisory training in child-care or early childhood programs.

Preschool/Kindergarten Teacher

Preschool teachers teach mainly 4-year-old children, and kindergarten teachers primarily teach 5-year-old children. They usually have an undergraduate degree in education, specializing in early childhood education. State certification to become a preschool or kindergarten teacher usually is required.

Family and Consumer Science Educator

Family and consumer science educators may specialize in early childhood education or instruct middle and high school students about such matters as nutrition, interpersonal relationships, human sexuality, parenting, and human development. Hundreds of colleges and universities throughout the United States offer two- and four-year degree programs in family and consumer science. These programs usually require an internship. Additional education courses may be needed to obtain a teaching certificate. Some family and consumer science educators go on to graduate school for further training, which provides a background for possible jobs in college teaching or research. **Read a profile of a family and consumer science educator in the "Physical and Cognitive Development in Adolescence" chapter.**

Educational Psychologist

Educational psychologists most often teach in a college or university and conduct research in various areas of educational psychology such as learning, motivation, classroom management, and assessment. They help train students for positions in educational psychology, school psychology, and teaching. Most educational psychologists have a doctorate in education, which requires four to six years of graduate work. **Read a profile of an educational psychologist in the "Introduction" chapter.**

School Psychologist

School psychologists focus on improving the psychological and intellectual well-being of elementary, middle/junior, and high school students. They give psychological tests, interview students and their parents, consult with teachers, and may provide counseling to students and their families. They may work in a centralized office in a school district or in one or more schools.

School psychologists usually have a master's or doctoral degree in school psychology. In graduate school, they take courses in counseling, assessment, learning, and other areas of education and psychology.

Gerontologist

Gerontologists usually work in research in some branch of the federal or state government. They specialize in the study of aging with a particular focus on government programs for older adults, social policy, and delivery of services to older adults. In their research, gerontologists define problems to be studied, collect data, interpret the results, and make recommendations for social policy. Most gerontologists have a master's or doctoral degree and have taken a concentration of coursework in adult development and aging.

Clinical/Counseling

A wide variety of clinical and counseling jobs are linked with life-span development. These range from child clinical psychologist to adolescent drug counselor to geriatric psychiatrist.

Clinical Psychologist

Clinical psychologists seek to help people with psychological problems. They work in a variety of settings, including colleges and universities, clinics, medical schools, and private practice. Some clinical psychologists only conduct psychotherapy; others do psychological assessment and psychotherapy; some also do research. Clinical psychologists may specialize in a particular age group, such as children (child clinical psychologist) or older adults (often referred to as a geropsychologist).

Clinical psychologists have either a Ph.D. (which involves clinical and research training) or a Psy.D. degree (which only involves clinical training). This graduate training usually takes five to seven years and includes courses in clinical psychology and a one-year supervised internship in an accredited setting toward the end of the training. Many geropsychologists pursue a year or two of postdoctoral training. Most states require clinical psychologists to pass a test in order to become licensed in the state and to call themselves clinical psychologists. **Read a profile of a clinical psychologist in the "Prenatal Development and Birth" chapter.**

Psychiatrist

Psychiatrists obtain a medical degree and then do a residency in psychiatry. Medical school takes approximately four years and the psychiatry residency another three to four years. Unlike most psychologists (who do not go to medical school), psychiatrists can administer drugs to clients. (Recently, several states gave clinical psychologists the right to prescribe drugs.)

Like clinical psychologists, psychiatrists might specialize in working with children (child psychiatry) or with older adults (geriatric psychiatry). Psychiatrists might work in medical schools in teaching and research roles, in a medical clinic or hospital, or in private practice. In addition to

administering drugs to help improve the lives of people with psychological problems, psychiatrists also may conduct psychotherapy. **Read a profile of a child psychiatrist in the "Socioemotional Development in Middle and Late Childhood" chapter.**

Counseling Psychologist

Counseling psychologists work in the same settings as clinical psychologists and may do psychotherapy, teach, or conduct research. Many counseling psychologists do not do therapy with individuals who have severe mental disorders, such as schizophrenia.

Counseling psychologists go through much the same training as clinical psychologists, although in a graduate program in counseling rather than clinical psychology. Counseling psychologists have either a master's degree or a doctoral degree. They also must go through a licensing procedure. One type of master's degree in counseling leads to the designation of licensed professional counselor.

School Counselor

School counselors help students cope with adjustment problems, identify their abilities and interests, develop academic plans, and explore career options. The focus of the job depends on the age of the students. High school counselors advise students about vocational and technical training and admissions requirements for college, as well as about taking entrance exams, applying for financial aid, and choosing a major. Elementary school counselors mainly counsel students about social and personal problems. They may observe children in the classroom and at play as part of their work. School counselors may work with students individually, in small groups, or even in a classroom. They often consult with parents, teachers, and school administrators when trying to help students. School counselors usually have a master's degree in counseling.

Career Counselor

Career counselors help individuals to identify their best career options and guide them in applying for jobs. They may work in private industry or at a college or university. They usually interview individuals and give them vocational and/or psychological tests to identify appropriate careers that fit their interests and abilities. Sometimes they help individuals to create résumés or conduct mock interviews to help them feel comfortable in a job interview. They might arrange and promote job fairs or other recruiting events to help individuals obtain jobs.

Rehabilitation Counselor

Rehabilitation counselors work with individuals to identify career options, develop adjustment and coping skills to maximize independence, and resolve problems created by a disability. A master's degree in rehabilitation counseling or guidance or counseling psychology is generally considered the minimum educational requirement.

Social Worker

Many social workers are involved in helping people with social or economic problems. They may investigate, evaluate, and attempt to rectify reported cases of abuse, neglect, endangerment, or domestic disputes. They may intervene in families and provide counseling and referral services to individuals and families. Some social workers specialize in a certain area. For example, a medical social worker might coordinate support services to people with a long-term disability; family-care social workers often work with families with children or an older adult who needs support services. Social workers often work for publicly funded agencies at the city, state, or national level, although increasingly they work in the private sector in areas such as drug rehabilitation and family counseling.

Social workers have a minimum of an undergraduate degree from a school of social work that includes coursework in sociology and psychology. Some social workers also have a master's or doctoral degree. For example, medical social workers have a master's degree in social work (M.S.W.) and complete graduate coursework and supervised clinical experiences in medical settings.

Drug Counselor

Drug counselors provide counseling to individuals with drug-abuse problems. Some drug counselors specialize in working with adolescents or older adults. They may work on an individual basis with a substance abuser or conduct group therapy. They may work in private practice, with a state or federal government agency, for a company, or in a hospital.

At a minimum, drug counselors complete an associate's or certificate program. Many have an undergraduate degree in substance-abuse counseling, and some have master's and doctoral degrees. Most states provide a certification procedure for obtaining a license to practice drug counseling.

Medical/Nursing/Physical Development

This third main area of careers in life-span development includes a wide range of choices in the medical and nursing areas, as well as jobs that focus on improving some aspect of a person's physical development.

Obstetrician/Gynecologist

An obstetrician/gynecologist prescribes prenatal and postnatal care, performs deliveries in maternity cases, and treats diseases and injuries of the female reproductive system. Becoming an obstetrician/gynecologist requires a medical degree plus three to five years of residency in obstetrics/gynecology. Obstetricians may work in private practice, a medical clinic, a hospital, or a medical school.

Pediatrician

A pediatrician monitors infants' and children's health, works to prevent disease or injury, helps children attain optimal health, and treats children with health problems. Pediatricians have earned a medical degree and completed a three- to five-year residency in pediatrics.

Pediatricians may work in private practice or at a medical clinic, a hospital, or a medical school. Many pediatricians on the faculties of medical schools also teach and conduct research on children's health and diseases. **Read the profile of a pediatrician in the "Physical Development in Infancy" chapter.**

Geriatric Physician

Geriatric physicians diagnose medical problems of older adults, evaluate treatment options, and make recommendations for nursing care or other arrangements. They have a medical degree and a three- to five-year residency in geriatric medicine. Like other doctors, geriatric physicians may work in private practice or at a medical clinic, a hospital, or a medical school. Those in medical school settings may not only treat older adults but also teach future physicians and conduct research.

Neonatal Nurse

Neonatal nurses deliver care to newborn infants. They may work with infants born under normal circumstances or premature and critically ill neonates. A minimum of an undergraduate degree in nursing with a specialization in the newborn is required. This training involves coursework in nursing and the biological sciences, as well as supervised clinical experiences.

Nurse-Midwife

A nurse-midwife formulates and provides comprehensive care to expectant mothers as they prepare to give birth, guides them through the birth process, and cares for them after the birth. The nurse-midwife also may provide care to the newborn, counsel parents on the infant's development and parenting, and provide guidance about health practices. Becoming a nurse-midwife generally requires an undergraduate degree from a school of nursing. A nurse-midwife most often works in a hospital setting. **Read the profile of a perinatal nurse in the "Prenatal Development and Birth" chapter.**

Pediatric Nurse

Pediatric nurses monitor infants' and children's health, work to prevent disease or injury, and help children attain optimal health. They may work in hospitals, schools of nursing, or with pediatricians in private practice or at a medical clinic.

Pediatric nurses have a degree in nursing that takes two to five years to complete. They take courses in biological sciences, nursing care, and pediatrics, usually in a school of nursing. They also undergo supervised clinical experiences in medical settings. Some pediatric nurses go on to earn a master's or doctoral degree in pediatric nursing.

Geriatric Nurse

Geriatric nurses seek to prevent or intervene in the chronic or acute health problems of older adults. They may work in hospitals, nursing homes, schools of nursing, or with geriatric medical specialists or psychiatrists in a medical clinic or in private practice. Like pediatric nurses, geriatric nurses take courses in a school of nursing and obtain a degree in nursing, which takes from two to five years. They complete courses in biological sciences, nursing care, and mental health as well as supervised clinical training in geriatric settings. They also may obtain a master's or doctoral degree in their specialty. **Read a profile of a geriatric nurse in the "Physical Development in Late Adulthood" chapter.**

Physical Therapist

Physical therapists work with individuals who have a physical problem due to disease or injury to help them function as competently as possible. They may consult with other professionals and coordinate services for the individual. Many physical therapists work with people of all ages, although some specialize in working with a specific age group, such as children or older adults.

Physical therapists usually have an undergraduate degree in physical therapy and are licensed by a state. They take courses and undergo supervised training in physical therapy.

Occupational Therapist

Occupational therapists initiate the evaluation of clients with various impairments and manage their treatment. They help people regain, develop, and build skills that are important for independent functioning, health, well-being, security, and happiness. An "Occupational Therapist Registered" (OTR) must have a master's and/or doctoral degree with education ranging from two to six years. Training includes occupational therapy courses in a specialized program. National certification is required, and licensing/registration is required in some states.

Therapeutic/Recreation Therapist

Therapeutic/recreation therapists maintain or improve the quality of life for people with special needs through intervention, leisure education, and recreation. They work in hospitals, rehabilitation centers, local government agencies, at-risk youth programs, and other settings. Becoming a therapeutic/recreation therapist requires an undergraduate degree with coursework in leisure studies and a concentration in therapeutic recreation. National certification is usually required. Coursework in anatomy, special education, and psychology is beneficial.

Audiologist

Audiologists assess and identify the presence and severity of hearing loss, as well as problems in balance. They may work in a medical clinic, with a physician in private practice, in a hospital, or in a medical school.

An audiologist completes coursework and supervised training to earn a minimum of an undergraduate degree in hearing science. Some audiologists also obtain a master's or doctoral degree.

Speech Therapist

Speech therapists identify, assess, and treat speech and language problems. They may work with physicians, psychologists, social workers, and other health care professionals in a team approach to help individuals with physical or psychological problems that involve speech and language. Some speech therapists specialize in working with individuals of a particular age or people with a particular type of speech disorder. Speech therapists have a minimum of an undergraduate degree in speech and hearing science or in a specific type of communication disorder. They may work in private practice, hospitals and medical schools, and government agencies.

Genetic Counselor

Genetic counselors identify and counsel families at risk for genetic disorders. They work as members of a health care team, providing information and support to families with members who have genetic defects or disorders or are at risk for a variety of inherited conditions. They also serve as educators and resource people for other health care professionals and the public. Nearly half of genetic counselors work in university medical centers; one-fourth work in private hospital settings.

Genetic counselors have specialized graduate degrees and experience in medical genetics and counseling. Most enter the field after majoring in undergraduate school in such disciplines as biology, genetics, psychology, nursing, public health, or social work. **Read a profile of a genetic counselor in the "Biological Beginnings" chapter.**

Families/Relationships

A number of careers and jobs related to life-span development focus on working with families and addressing relationship problems. These range from home health aide to marriage and family therapist.

Home Health Aide

A home health aide provides services to older adults in the older adults' homes, helping them with basic self-care tasks. No higher education is required for this position. There is brief training by an agency.

Child Welfare Worker

Child protective services in each state employ child welfare workers. They protect children's rights, evaluate any maltreatment, and may have children removed from their homes if necessary. A child social worker has a minimum of an undergraduate degree in social work.

Child Life Specialist

Child life specialists work with children and their families when the child needs to be hospitalized. They monitor the child's activities, seek to reduce the child's stress, and help the child to cope and to enjoy the hospital experience as much as possible. Child life specialists may provide parent education and develop individualized treatment plans based on an assessment of the child's development, temperament, medical plan, and available social supports. Child life specialists have an undergraduate degree. They have taken courses in child development and education and usually completed additional courses in a child life program. **Read a profile of a child life specialist in the "Physical and Cognitive Development in Middle and Late Childhood" chapter.**

Marriage and Family Therapist

Marriage and family therapists work on the principle that many individuals who have psychological problems benefit when psychotherapy is provided in the context of a marital or family relationship. Marriage and family therapists may provide marital therapy, couple therapy to individuals in a relationship who are not married, and family therapy to two or more members of a family.

Marriage and family therapists have a master's or a doctoral degree. They complete a training program in graduate school similar to a clinical psychologist's but with a focus on marital and family relationships. In most states, it is necessary to go through a licensing procedure to practice marital and family therapy. **Read the profile of a marriage and family therapist in the "Socioemotional Development in Early Childhood" chapter.**

Further Careers

These are only a handful of careers that knowledge of developmental psychology can prepare you for. The *Connecting with Careers* profiles highlight additional careers, including an infant assessment specialist, child-care director, toy designer, health psychologist, college/career counselor, parent counselor, pastoral counselor, association director, and home hospice nurse. *What other careers can you think of that require a knowledge of human development?*

section two

There are one hundred and ninety-three living species of monkeys and apes. One hundred and ninety-two of them are covered with hair. The exception is the naked ape, self-named Homo sapiens.

—DESMOND MORRIS
British zoologist, 20th century

Beginnings

The rhythm and meaning of life involve beginnings. Questions are raised about how, from so simple a beginning, endless forms develop, grow, and mature. What was this organism, what is this organism, and what will this organism be? In this section, you will read two chapters: "Biological Beginnings" and "Prenatal Development and Birth."

chapter 2

BIOLOGICAL BEGINNINGS

Chapter **Outline**

① **The Evolutionary Perspective**

Learning Goal 1 Discuss the evolutionary perspective on life-span development.

Natural Selection and Adaptive Behavior

Evolutionary Psychology

② **Genetic Foundations of Development**

Learning Goal 2 Describe what genes are and how they influence human development.

The Collaborative Gene

Genes and Chromosomes

Genetic Principles

Chromosomal and Gene-Linked Abnormalities

③ **Reproductive Challenges and Choices**

Learning Goal 3 Identify some important reproductive challenges and choices.

Prenatal Diagnostic Tests

Infertility and Reproductive Technology

Adoption

④ **Heredity-Environment Interaction: The Nature-Nurture Debate**

Learning Goal 4 Explain some of the ways that heredity and environment interact to produce individual differences in development.

Behavior Genetics

Heredity-Environment Correlations

The Epigenetic View and Gene × Environment (G × E) Interaction

Conclusions About Heredity-Environment Interaction

China Tourism Press/The Image Bank/Getty Images

Jim Springer and Jim Lewis are identical twins. They were separated at 4 weeks of age and did not see each other again until they were 39 years old. Both worked as part-time deputy sheriffs, vacationed in Florida, drove Chevrolets, had dogs named Toy, and married and divorced women named Betty. One twin named his son James Allan, and the other named his son James Alan. Both liked math but not spelling, enjoyed carpentry and mechanical drawing, chewed their fingernails down to the nubs, had almost identical drinking and smoking habits, had hemorrhoids, put on 10 pounds at about the same point in development, first suffered headaches at the age of 18, and had similar sleep patterns.

The Jim and Jim twins
The Lima News

Jim and Jim do have some differences. One wears his hair over his forehead, the other slicks it back and has sideburns. One expresses himself best orally; the other is more proficient in writing. But, for the most part, their profiles are remarkably similar.

Another pair of identical twins, Daphne and Barbara, are called the "giggle sisters" because after being reunited they were always making each other laugh. A thorough search of their adoptive families' histories revealed no gigglers. The giggle sisters ignored stress, avoided conflict and controversy whenever possible, and showed no interest in politics.

Jim and Jim and the giggle sisters were part of the Minnesota Study of Twins Reared Apart, directed by Thomas Bouchard and his colleagues. The study brings identical twins (identical genetically because they come from the same fertilized egg) and fraternal twins (who come from different fertilized eggs) from all over the world to Minneapolis to investigate their lives. There the twins complete personality and intelligence tests, and they provide detailed medical histories, including information about diet and smoking, exercise habits, chest X-rays, heart stress tests, and EEGs. The twins are asked more than 15,000 questions about their family and childhood, personal interests, vocational orientation, values, and aesthetic judgments (Bouchard & others, 1990).

topical connections *looking **back***

The "Introduction" chapter introduced the field of life-span development, including discussion of three key categories of developmental processes: biological, cognitive, and socioemotional. In this chapter, we lay the foundation of the biological aspects of development. Biological processes, guided by genes, influence an individual's development in every period of the human life span. The forthcoming discussion of genetics and the previous discussion of theories (psychoanalytic, cognitive, behavioral and social cognitive, ethological, and ecological) provide a knowledge base from which to examine one of life-span development's major issues and debates—how strongly development is influenced by heredity (nature) and the environment (nurture).

When genetically identical twins who were separated as infants show such striking similarities in their tastes and habits and choices, can we conclude that their genes must have caused the development of those tastes and habits and choices? Other possible causes need to be considered. The twins shared not only the same genes but also some experiences. Some of the separated twins lived together for several months prior to their adoption; some of the twins had been reunited prior to testing (in some cases, many years earlier); adoption agencies often place twins in similar homes; and even strangers who spend several hours together and start comparing their lives are likely to come up with some coincidental similarities (Joseph, 2006). The Minnesota study of identical twins points to both the importance of the genetic basis of human development and the need for further research on genetic and environmental factors (Lykken, 2001). We will discuss twin studies in more detail in the section on behavior genetics later in this chapter.

preview

The examples of Jim and Jim and the giggle sisters stimulate us to think about our genetic heritage and the biological foundations of our existence. However, organisms are not like billiard balls, moved by simple external forces to predictable positions on life's table. Environmental experiences and biological foundations work together to make us who we are. Our coverage of life's biological beginnings focuses on evolution, genetic foundations, challenges and choices regarding reproduction, and the interaction of heredity and environment.

1 The Evolutionary Perspective

 LG1 Discuss the evolutionary perspective on life-span development.

Natural Selection and Adaptive Behavior

Evolutionary Psychology

In evolutionary time, humans are relative newcomers to Earth. As our earliest ancestors left the forest to feed on the savannahs and then to form hunting societies on the open plains, their minds and behaviors changed, and they eventually established humans as the dominant species on Earth. How did this evolution come about?

NATURAL SELECTION AND ADAPTIVE BEHAVIOR

How does the attachment of this Vietnamese baby to its mother reflect the evolutionary process of adaptive behavior?
Frans Lemmens/Lithium/age fotostock

Natural selection is the evolutionary process by which those individuals of a species that are best adapted are the ones that survive and leave the most fit offspring. To understand what this means, let's return to the middle of the nineteenth century, when British naturalist Charles Darwin was traveling around the world, observing many different species of animals in their natural surroundings. Darwin, who published his observations and thoughts in *On the Origin of Species* (1859), noted that most organisms reproduce at rates that would cause enormous increases in the population of most species and yet populations remain nearly constant. He reasoned that an intense, constant struggle for food, water, and resources must occur among the many young born in each generation, because many of the young do not survive. Those that do survive and reproduce pass on some of their characteristics to the next generation. Darwin argued that these survivors are better *adapted* to their world than are the nonsurvivors (Audesirk, Audesirk, & Byers, 2020). The best-adapted individuals survive to leave the most offspring. Over the course of many generations, organisms with the characteristics needed for survival make up an increasing percentage of the population. Over many, many generations, this could produce a gradual modification of the whole population. If environmental conditions change, however, other characteristics might become favored by natural selection, moving the species in a different direction (Mader & Windelspecht, 2020).

All organisms must adapt to particular places, climates, food sources, and ways of life (Simon, 2020). An eagle's claws are a physical adaptation that facilitates predation. *Adaptive behavior* is behavior that promotes an organism's survival in its natural habitat (Willey, Sandman, & Wood, 2020). For example, attachment between a caregiver and a baby ensures the infant's closeness to a caregiver for feeding and protection from danger, thus increasing the infant's chances of survival.

EVOLUTIONARY PSYCHOLOGY

Recently, Darwin's ideas have increasingly served as a foundation for explaining psychological aspects of human behavior. The field of **evolutionary psychology** emphasizes the importance of adaptation, reproduction, and "survival of the fittest" in shaping behavior (McDowell, 2019; Speakman, 2020). "Fit" in this sense refers to the ability to bear offspring that survive long enough to bear offspring of their own. In this view, natural selection favors behaviors that increase reproductive success—the ability to pass your genes to the next generation (Freeman & others, 2020).

David Buss (2008, 2012, 2015, 2018, 2019) has been especially influential in stimulating new interest in how evolution can explain human behavior. He reasons that just as evolution has contributed to our physical features such as body shape and height, it also influences psychological features such as how we make decisions, how aggressive we are, our fears, and our mating patterns. For example, assume that our ancestors were hunters and gatherers on the plains and that men did most of the hunting and women stayed close to home gathering seeds and plants for food. If you have to travel some distance from your home to find and slay a fleeing animal, you need certain physical traits along with the capacity for certain types of spatial thinking. Men with these traits would be more likely than men without them to survive, to bring home lots of food, and to be considered attractive mates—and thus to reproduce and pass on these characteristics to their children. In other words, if Buss' (2019) assumptions are correct, potentially these traits provide a reproductive advantage for males—over many generations, men with good spatial thinking skills might become more numerous in the population. Critics point out that these assumptions are not necessarily accurate and that this scenario might or might not have actually happened.

Evolutionary Developmental Psychology   Recently, interest has grown in using the concepts of evolutionary psychology to understand human development (Dantchev & Wolke, 2019; Knofe & others, 2019; Ko & others, 2020). Here we discuss some ideas proposed by evolutionary developmental psychologists (Bjorklund & Pellegrini, 2002).

An extended childhood period might have evolved because humans require time to develop a large brain and learn the complexity of human societies. Humans take longer to become reproductively mature than any other mammal (see Figure 1). During this extended childhood period, they develop a large brain and have the experiences needed to become competent adults in a complex society.

In the view of evolutionary psychologists, many of our evolved psychological mechanisms are domain-specific—they apply only to a specific aspect of a person's psychological makeup. Evolutionary psychologist also do not view the mind as a general-purpose device that can be applied equally to a vast array of problems. Instead, as our ancestors dealt with certain recurring problems such as hunting and finding shelter, specialized modules evolved to process information related to those problems. For example, such specialized modules might include a module for physical knowledge for tracking animals, a module for mathematical knowledge for trading, and a module for language.

The modularity of the mind view has sometimes been referred to as the *Swiss army knife theory* because much like a Swiss army knife, the human mind encompasses a number of independent domains or tools. This view has been increasingly criticized because it emphasizes

evolutionary psychology Emphasizes the importance of adaptation, reproduction, and "survival of the fittest" in shaping behavior.

What endless questions vex the thought, of whence and whither, when and how.

—Sir Richard Burton
British explorer, 19th century

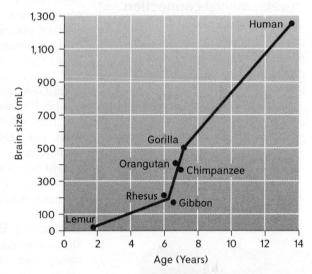

FIGURE **1**

THE BRAIN SIZES OF VARIOUS PRIMATES AND HUMANS IN RELATION TO THE LENGTH OF THE CHILDHOOD PERIOD. Compared with other primates, humans have both a larger brain and a longer childhood period. *What conclusions can you draw from the relationship indicated by this graph?*
Alan and Sandy Carey/Photodisc/Getty Images

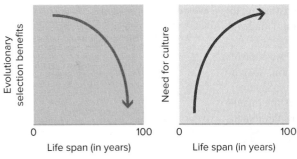

FIGURE 2

BALTES' VIEW OF EVOLUTION AND CULTURE ACROSS THE LIFE SPAN. Benefits derived from evolutionary selection decrease as we age, whereas the need for culture increases with age.

- - - - - - ->

developmental connection

Life-Span Perspective

Baltes described eight main characteristics of the life-span perspective. Connect to "Introduction."

<- - - - - - -

Children in all cultures are interested in the tools that adults in their culture use. For example, this young child is using a machete near the Ankgor Temples in Cambodia. *Might the child's behavior be evolutionary-based or reflect both biological and environmental conditions?*

Carol Adam/Moment Editorial/Getty Images

---

that the brain is extensively fragmented. Indeed, as you will see in our discussion of the brain at various points in this text, there is considerable connection between many areas of the brain and it is not exclusively compartmentalized as the modularity of the mind view proposes.

Further, evolved mechanisms are not always adaptive in contemporary society. Some behaviors that were adaptive for our prehistoric ancestors may not serve us well today. For example, the food-scarce environment of our ancestors likely led to humans' propensity to gorge when food is available and to crave high-caloric foods, a trait that might lead to an epidemic of obesity when food is plentiful.

Connecting Evolution and Life-Span Development   In evolutionary theory, what matters is that individuals live long enough to reproduce and pass on their characteristics (Urry & others, 2020). So why do humans live so long after reproduction? Perhaps evolution favored longevity because having older people around improves the survival rates of babies. Possibly having grandparents alive to care for the young while parents were out hunting and gathering food created an evolutionary advantage.

According to life-span developmentalist Paul Baltes (2003), the benefits conferred by evolutionary selection decrease with age. Natural selection has not weeded out many harmful conditions and nonadaptive characteristics that appear among older adults. Why? Natural selection operates primarily on characteristics that are tied to reproductive fitness, which extends through the earlier part of adulthood. Thus, says Baltes, selection primarily operates during the first half of life.

As an example, consider Alzheimer disease, an irreversible brain disorder characterized by gradual deterioration in thinking capacity. This disease typically does not appear until age 70 or later. If it struck 20-year-olds, perhaps natural selection would have eliminated it eons ago.

Thus, unaided by evolutionary pressures against nonadaptive conditions, we suffer the aches, pains, and infirmities of aging. And as the benefits of evolutionary selection decrease with age, argues Baltes, the need for culture increases (see Figure 2). That is, as older adults weaken biologically, they need culture-based resources such as cognitive skills, literacy, medical technology, and social support. For example, older adults may need help and training from other people to maintain their cognitive skills (Bisbe & others, 2020; Strandberg, 2019).

Evaluating Evolutionary Psychology   Although the popular press gives a lot of attention to the ideas of evolutionary psychology, it remains just one theoretical approach among many. Like the theories described earlier, it has limitations, weaknesses, and critics (Hyde & DeLamater, 2020). Among the criticisms of evolutionary psychology are that it is one-sided, not adequately valuing social/environmental factors; that it relies on after-the-fact explanations; and that it cannot be tested scientifically. Indeed, as with evolution, it is very difficult to offer direct proof of an argument to support evolutionary psychology

Albert Bandura (1998), whose social cognitive theory was described earlier, acknowledges the important influence of evolution on human adaptation. However, he rejects what he calls "one-sided evolutionism," which sees social behavior as strictly the product of evolved biology. An alternative is a bidirectional view in which environmental and biological conditions influence each other. In this view, evolutionary pressures created changes in biological structures that allowed the use of tools, which enabled our ancestors to manipulate their environment, constructing new environmental conditions. In turn, environmental innovations produced new selection pressures that led to the evolution of specialized biological systems for consciousness, thought, and language.

In other words, evolution does not dictate behavior. People have used their biological capacities to produce diverse cultures—aggressive and peace-loving, egalitarian and autocratic. As American scientist Stephen Jay Gould (1981) concluded, in most domains of human functioning, biology allows a broad range of cultural possibilities.

The "big picture" idea of natural selection leading to the development of human traits and behaviors is difficult to refute or test because evolution occurs on a time scale that does not lend itself to empirical study. Thus, studying specific genes in humans and other species—and their links to traits and behavior—may be the best approach for testing ideas coming out of evolutionary psychology.

Review *Connect* Reflect

 LG1 Discuss the evolutionary perspective on life-span development.

Review

- How can natural selection and adaptive behavior be defined?
- What is evolutionary psychology? What are some basic ideas about human development proposed by evolutionary psychologists? How might evolutionary influences have different effects at different points in the life span? How can evolutionary psychology be evaluated?

Connect

- In the section on ethological theory in the "Introduction" chapter, you learned about critical time periods. How does the concept of critical period relate to what you learned about older adults and aging in this section?

Reflect *Your Own Personal Journey of Life*

- Which do you think is more persuasive in explaining your development: the views of evolutionary psychologists or their critics? Why?

2 Genetic Foundations of Development

LG2 Describe what genes are and how they influence human development.

| The Collaborative Gene | Genes and Chromosomes | Genetic Principles | Chromosomal and Gene-Linked Abnormalities |

Genetic influences on behavior evolved over time and across many species. The many traits and characteristics that are genetically influenced have a long evolutionary history that is retained in our DNA (Brooker & others, 2020). Our DNA is not just inherited from our parents; it includes what we inherited as a species from other species that were our ancestors.

How are characteristics that suit a species for survival transmitted from one generation to the next? Darwin did not know the answer because genes and the principles of genetics had not yet been discovered. Each of us carries a "genetic code" that we inherited from our parents. Because a fertilized egg carries this human code, a fertilized human egg cannot grow into an egret, eagle, or elephant.

THE COLLABORATIVE GENE

Each of us began life as a single cell weighing about one twenty-millionth of an ounce! This tiny piece of matter housed our entire genetic code—information that helps us grow from that single cell to a person made of trillions of cells, each containing a replica of the original code. That code is carried by DNA, which includes our genes. What are genes and what do they do? For the answer, we need to look into our cells.

The nucleus of each human cell contains **chromosomes,** which are threadlike structures made up of deoxyribonucleic acid (DNA). **DNA** is a complex molecule that has a double helix shape, like a spiral staircase (shown in Figure 3) and contains genetic information. **Genes,** the units of hereditary information, are short segments of DNA. They help cells to reproduce themselves and to assemble proteins. Proteins, in turn, are the building blocks of cells as well as the regulators that direct the body's processes (Urry & others, 2020).

Each gene has its own location—its own designated place on a particular chromosome. Today, there is a great deal of enthusiasm about efforts to discover the specific locations of genes that are linked to certain functions and developmental outcomes (Klug & others, 2020). An important step in this direction is the Human Genome Project's efforts to map the human genome—the complete genetic content of our cells, which includes developmental information used for creating proteins that contribute to the making of a human organism (Freeman & others, 2020).

One of the big surprises of the Human Genome Project was an early report indicating that humans have only about 30,000 genes (U.S. Department of Energy, 2001). More recently,

> What is inherited is DNA. Everything else is developed.
>
> —James Tanner
> *British pediatrician, 20th century*

developmental connection

Biological Processes

A current biological theory of aging emphasizes that changes in the tips of chromosomes play a key role in aging. Connect to "Physical Development in Late Adulthood."

chromosomes Threadlike structures that come in 23 pairs, with one member of each pair coming from each parent. Chromosomes contain the genetic substance DNA.

DNA A complex molecule that contains genetic information.

genes Units of hereditary information composed of DNA. Genes help cells to reproduce themselves and help manufacture the proteins that maintain life.

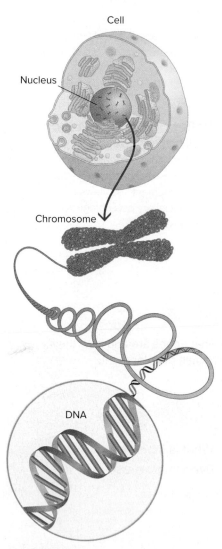

Cell

Nucleus

Chromosome

DNA

FIGURE 3

CELLS, CHROMOSOMES, DNA, AND GENES.

(*Top*) The body contains trillions of cells. Each cell contains a central structure, the nucleus. (*Middle*) Chromosomes are threadlike structures located in the nucleus of the cell. Chromosomes are composed of DNA. (*Bottom*) DNA has the structure of a spiral staircase. A gene is a segment of DNA.

mitosis Cellular reproduction in which the cell's nucleus duplicates itself with two new cells being formed, each containing the same DNA as the parent cell, arranged in the same 23 pairs of chromosomes.

meiosis A specialized form of cell division that occurs to form eggs and sperm (also known as gametes).

fertilization A stage in reproduction when an egg and a sperm fuse to create a single cell, called a zygote.

zygote A single cell formed through fertilization.

the number of human genes was revised further downward to approximately 20,700 (Ensembl Human, 2010; Flicek & others, 2013; Science Daily, 2008), then raised to 21,306 (Salzberg & others, 2018). Scientists had thought that humans had 100,000 or more genes. They had also maintained that each gene programmed just one protein. In fact, humans have far more proteins than they have genes, so there cannot be a one-to-one correspondence between genes and proteins (Commoner, 2002). Each gene is not translated, in automaton-like fashion, into a single protein (Moore, 2015, 2017). A gene does not act independently, as developmental psychologist David Moore (2001) emphasized by titling his book *The Dependent Gene*.

Rather than being a group of independent genes, the human genome consists of many genes that collaborate both with each other and with nongenetic factors inside and outside the body (Wang & others, 2019). The collaboration operates at many points. For example, the cellular machinery mixes, matches, and links small pieces of DNA to create the genes—and that machinery is influenced by what is going on around it.

Whether a gene is expressed—working to assemble proteins—is also a matter of collaboration. The activity of genes (genetic expression) is affected by their environment (Gottlieb, 2007; Moore, 2017). For example, hormones that circulate in the blood make their way into the cell where they can turn genes "on" and "off." And the flow of hormones can be affected by environmental conditions such as light, day length, nutrition, and behavior. Numerous studies have shown that external events outside of the original cell and the person, as well as events inside the cell, can excite or inhibit gene expression (Moore, 2017). Recent research has documented that factors such as stress, exercise, nutrition, respiration, radiation, temperature, loneliness, and sleep can influence gene expression (Cole, 2009; Cuevas-Sierra & others, 2019; Kesaniemi & others, 2019; Min & others, 2020; Wang, Lee, & Tian, 2019; Zimmerman & others, 2019). For example, one study revealed that an increase in the concentration of stress hormones such as cortisol produced a fivefold increase in DNA damage (Flint & others, 2007). Another study found that exposure to radiation changed the rate of DNA synthesis in cells (Lee & others, 2011). And research indicates that sleep deprivation can affect gene expression in negative ways such as increased inflammation, expression of stress-related genes, and impairment of protein functioning (da Costa Souza & Ribeiro, 2015).

Scientists have found that certain genes are turned on or off as a result of exercise mainly through a process called *methylation*, in which tiny molecules attached themselves to the outside of a gene (Ciuculete & others, 2020). This process makes the gene more or less capable of receiving and responding to biochemical signals from the body. In this way the behavior of the gene, but not its structure, is changed. Researchers also have found that diet (Dasinger & others, 2020), tobacco use (Sugden & others, 2019), and sleep (Lehtinen & others, 2019) may affect gene behavior through the process of methylation. Also, recent research indicates that methylation may be involved in depression (Payne & others, 2020), breast cancer (Parashar & others, 2018), lung cancer (Martinez-Ramirez & others, 2019), colorectal cancer (Alvizo-Rodriguez & others, 2020), leukemia (Bewersdorf & others, 2020), obesity (Marousez, Lesage, & Eberle, 2020), attention deficit hyperactivity disorder (Kim & others, 2020), and neurodevelopmental disorders (Wickramasekara & Stessman, 2019).

GENES AND CHROMOSOMES

Genes are not only collaborative, they are enduring. How do the genes manage to get passed from generation to generation and end up in all of the trillion cells in the body? Three processes are at the heart of the story: mitosis, meiosis, and fertilization.

Mitosis, Meiosis, and Fertilization   All of the cells in your body, except the sperm and egg, have 46 chromosomes arranged in 23 pairs. These cells reproduce through a process called **mitosis**. During mitosis, the cell's nucleus—including the chromosomes—duplicates itself and the cell divides. Two new cells are formed, each containing the same DNA as the original cell, arranged in the same 23 pairs of chromosomes.

However, a different type of cell division—**meiosis**—forms eggs and sperm (which also are called gametes). During meiosis, a cell of the testes (in men) or ovaries (in women) duplicates its chromosomes but then divides twice, thus forming four cells, each of which has only half of the genetic material of the parent cell. By the end of meiosis, each egg or sperm has 23 unpaired chromosomes.

During **fertilization,** an egg and a sperm fuse to create a single cell called a **zygote** (see Figure 4). In the zygote, the 23 unpaired chromosomes from the egg and the 23 unpaired chromosomes from the sperm combine to form one set of 23 paired chromosomes—one chromosome of each pair coming from the mother's egg and the other from the father's sperm. In this manner, each parent contributes half of the offspring's genetic material.

Figure 5 shows 23 paired chromosomes of a male and a female. The members of each pair of chromosomes are both similar and different: Each chromosome in the pair contains varying forms of the same genes, at the same location on the chromosome. A gene that influences hair color, for example, is located on both members of one pair of chromosomes, in the same location on each. However, one of those chromosomes might carry a gene associated with blond hair; the other chromosome in the pair might carry a gene associated with brown hair.

Do you notice any obvious differences between the chromosomes of the male and the chromosomes of the female in Figure 5? The difference lies in the 23rd pair. Ordinarily, in females this pair consists of two chromosomes called X chromosomes; in males, the 23rd pair consists of an X and a Y chromosome. The presence of a Y chromosome is one factor that makes a person male rather than female.

Sources of Variability Combining the genes of two parents in offspring increases genetic variability in the population, which is valuable for a species because it provides more characteristics for natural selection to operate on (Mader & Windelspecht, 2020). In fact, the human genetic process creates several important sources of *variability* (Klug & others, 2020).

First, the chromosomes in the zygote are not exact copies of those in the mother's ovaries or the father's testes. During the formation of the sperm and egg in meiosis, the members of each pair of chromosomes are separated, but which chromosome in the pair goes to the gamete is a matter of chance. In addition, before the pairs separate, pieces of the two chromosomes in each pair are exchanged, creating a new combination of genes on each chromosome (Audesirk, Audesirk, & Byers, 2020). Thus, when chromosomes from the mother's egg and the father's sperm are brought together in the zygote, the result is a truly unique combination of genes (Urry & others, 2020).

If each zygote is unique, how do identical twins like those discussed in the opening of the chapter exist? *Identical twins* (also called monozygotic twins) develop from a single zygote that splits into two genetically identical replicas, each of which becomes a person. *Fraternal twins* (called dizygotic twins) develop when two eggs are fertilized by different sperm, creating two zygotes that are genetically no more similar than ordinary siblings.

Another source of variability comes from DNA. Chance events, a mistake by cellular machinery, or damage from an environmental agent such as radiation may produce a *mutated gene*, which is a permanently altered segment of DNA (Freeman & others, 2020).

There is increasing interest in studying *susceptibility genes*, those that make the individual more vulnerable to accelerated aging and the development of specific diseases such as arthritis (Reynard & Barter, 2020), cancer (Liu & Tan, 2019) and cardiovascular disease (Taylor & others, 2019), and *longevity genes,* those that make the individual less vulnerable to certain diseases and more likely to live to an older age (Castillo-Morales & others, 2019; Pignolo, 2019; Romero-Ortuno, Kenny, & McManus, 2020). These are aspects of the individual's genotype.

In the search for longevity genes, Cynthia Kenyon (2010) has extensively studied *C. elegans,* a roundworm, the first animal to have its entire genome sequenced. In early research, she found that modifying a single gene, *daf-2,* which is linked to hormones, slows aging in the roundworm. She also discovered that another gene, *daf-16,* is necessary for the roundworm to live longer. *Daf-16* encodes a gene switch that turns on a number of genes related to stress resistance, immunity, and metabolism (Wang & others, 2019). These genes possibly can extend life by protecting and repairing body tissues (Xu & others, 2019). Other researchers have revealed that genetic variants in a human *daf-16* version labeled *FOX03A* are linked to greater longevity in a wide range of people, including Americans, Europeans, and Chinese (Link, 2019; Wang & others, 2020a). Further, *daf-2*-type mutations extend life and slow aging not only in roundworms but also in flies and mice, resulting in delayed onset and severity of many aging diseases, including cancer, cardiovascular disease, and Alzheimer disease (Kenyon, 2010). Cynthia Kenyon belongs to a think tank of scientists at Google's Calico (short for California Life Company) division who seek to understand the aging process and uncover ways to modify it. Kenyon

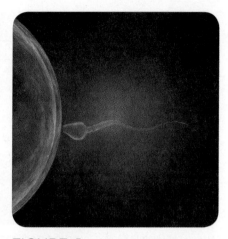

FIGURE **4**

A SINGLE SPERM PENETRATING AN EGG AT THE POINT OF FERTILIZATION
3Dalia/Shutterstock

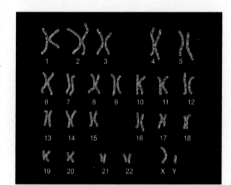

(a)

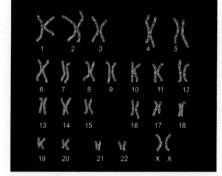

(b)

FIGURE **5**

THE GENETIC DIFFERENCE BETWEEN MALES AND FEMALES. Set (*a*) shows the chromosome structure of a male, and set (*b*) shows the chromosome structure of a female. The last pair of 23 pairs of chromosomes is in the bottom right box of each set. Notice that the Y chromosome of the male is smaller than the X chromosome of the female. To obtain this kind of chromosomal picture, a cell is removed from a person's body, usually from the inside of the mouth. The chromosomes are stained by chemical treatment, magnified extensively, and then photographed.
Kateryna Kon/Shutterstock

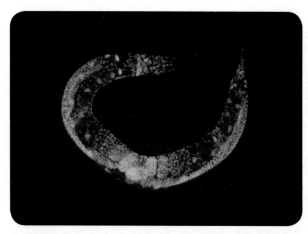

Researcher Cynthia Kenyon found that modifying a gene called *daf-16* slows the aging in *C. elegans* (*shown above*). This type of roundworm was the first animal to have its entire genome sequenced.

Washington University, St. Louis/KRT/Newscom

believes that interventions to extend the human life span might include drugs that mimic the action of gene mutations linked to greater longevity.

Even when their genes are identical, however, people vary. The difference between genotypes and phenotypes helps us to understand this source of variability. All of a person's genetic material makes up his or her **genotype.** However, our observed and measurable characteristics reflect more than just genetic material. A **phenotype** consists of observable characteristics. Phenotypes include physical characteristics (such as height, weight, and hair color) and psychological characteristics (such as personality and intelligence).

How does the process from genotype to phenotype work? It's highly complex, but at a very basic level in a cell, DNA information is transcribed to RNA (ribonucleic acid), which in turn is translated into amino acids that will become proteins (Freeman & others, 2020). Once proteins have been assembled, they become capable of contributing to the further development of phenotype traits and characteristics. Also, environments interact with genotypes to influence phenotypes.

Thus, for each genotype, a variety of phenotypes can be expressed, providing another source of variability (Klug & others, 2020). An individual can inherit the genetic potential to grow very large, for example, but environmental influences such as good nutrition are essential for achieving that potential.

GENETIC PRINCIPLES

What determines how a genotype is expressed to create a particular phenotype? Much is unknown about the answer to this question (Moore, 2017). However, a number of genetic principles have been discovered, among them those of dominant-recessive genes, sex-linked genes, genetic imprinting, and polygenically determined characteristics.

Dominant-Recessive Genes   In some cases, one gene of a pair always exerts its effects; it is *dominant* and overrides the potential influence of the other gene, called the recessive gene. This is the *dominant-recessive genes principle*. A recessive gene exerts its influence only if the two genes of a pair are both recessive. If you inherit a recessive gene for a trait from each of your parents, you will show the trait. If you inherit a recessive gene from only one parent, you may never know you carry the gene. Brown hair, farsightedness, and dimples are linked to dominant genes; blond hair, nearsightedness, and freckles are associated with recessive genes.

Can two brown-haired parents have a blond-haired child? Yes, they can. Suppose that each parent has a dominant gene for brown hair and a recessive gene for blond hair. Since dominant genes override recessive genes, the parents have brown hair, but both are carriers of genes that can contribute to blondness and pass on their recessive genes for producing blond hair. With no dominant gene to override them, the recessive genes can make the child's hair blond.

Sex-Linked Genes   Most mutated genes are recessive. When a mutated gene is carried on the X chromosome, the result is called *X-linked inheritance*. The implications for males may be very different from those for females (Schurz & others, 2019; Yang & Chen, 2019). Remember that males have only one X chromosome. Thus, if there is an absent or altered disease-relevant gene on the X chromosome, males have no "backup" copy to counter the harmful gene and therefore may develop an X-linked disease. However, females have a second X chromosome, which is likely to be unchanged. As a result, they are not likely to have the X-linked disease. Thus, most individuals who have X-linked diseases are males. Females who have one abnormal copy of the gene on the X chromosome are known as "carriers," and they usually do not show any signs of the X-linked disease. Hemophilia and fragile X syndrome, which we will discuss later in the chapter, are examples of X-linked inheritance diseases (Batty & Lillicrap, 2020).

Genetic Imprinting   Genetic imprinting occurs when the expression of a gene has different effects depending on whether the mother or the father passed on the gene (Liu & others, 2020; Singh, Sholma, & Belyakin, 2019). A chemical process "silences" one member of the gene pair. For example, as result of imprinting, only the maternally derived copy of the

genotype A person's genetic heritage; the actual genetic material.

phenotype The way an individual's genotype is expressed in observed and measurable characteristics.

expressed gene might be active, while the paternally derived copy of the same expressed gene is silenced—or vice versa (Lorgen-Ritchie & others, 2019). Only a small percentage of human genes appear to undergo imprinting, but it is a normal and important aspect of development. When imprinting goes awry, development is disturbed, as in the case of Beckwith-Wiedemann syndrome (a growth disorder) (Bachmann & others, 2017) and Prader-Willi syndrome (mental health problems) (Feighan & others, 2020).

Polygenic Inheritance   Genetic transmission is usually more complex than the simple examples we have examined thus far (Anderson & others, 2019; Bashor & others, 2019). Few characteristics reflect the influence of only a single gene or pair of genes. The term *polygenic inheritance* means that many different genes contribute to the development of a characteristic (La Starza &others, 2019; Patel & Bezzina, 2020). Even a simple characteristic such as height, for example, reflects the interaction of many genes as well as the influence of the environment. Most diseases, such as cancer and diabetes, develop as a consequence of complex gene interactions and environmental factors (Jia, Pei, & Zhao, 2019; Schubert & others, 2020).

The term *gene-gene interaction* is increasingly used to describe studies that focus on the interdependent process by which two or more genes influence characteristics, behavior, diseases, and development (Biczo & others, 2020; Tessler & others, 2019). For example, recent studies have documented gene-gene interaction in immune system functioning (Kostel Bal & others, 2020), obesity (D. X. Wang & others, 2019), type 2 diabetes (Dominguez-Cruz & others, 2020), alcoholism (Chen & others, 2017), cancer (Lee & others, 2019), cardiovascular disease (Wang & others, 2020b), arthritis (Fathollahi & others, 2019), and Alzheimer disease (Li & others, 2020).

These athletes, several of whom have Down syndrome, are participating in a Special Olympics competition. Notice the distinctive facial features of the individuals with Down syndrome, such as a round face and a flattened skull. *What causes Down syndrome?*
James Shaffer/PhotoEdit

CHROMOSOMAL AND GENE-LINKED ABNORMALITIES

Abnormalities characterize the genetic process in some individuals. Some of these abnormalities involve whole chromosomes that do not separate properly during meiosis. Other abnormalities are produced by harmful genes.

Chromosomal Abnormalities   Sometimes a gamete is formed in which the male's sperm and/or the female's ovum do not have their normal set of 23 chromosomes. The most notable examples involve Down syndrome and abnormalities of the sex chromosomes (see Figure 6).

Down Syndrome   **Down syndrome** is a form of intellectual disability caused by the presence of an extra copy of chromosome 21 (Popadin & others, 2018). It is not known why the extra chromosome is present, but the health of the male sperm or the female ovum

Down syndrome A form of intellectual disability that is caused by the presence of an extra copy of chromosome 21.

Name	Description	Treatment	Incidence
Down syndrome	An extra chromosome causes mild to severe intellectual disability and physical abnormalities.	Surgery, early intervention, infant stimulation, and special learning programs	1 in 1,900 births at age 20 1 in 300 births at age 35 1 in 30 births at age 45
Klinefelter syndrome (XXY)	An extra X chromosome causes physical abnormalities.	Hormone therapy can be effective	1 in 1,000 male births
Fragile X syndrome	An abnormality in the X chromosome can cause intellectual disability, learning disabilities, or short attention span.	Special education, speech and language therapy	More common in males than in females
Turner syndrome (XO)	A missing X chromosome in females can cause intellectual disability and sexual underdevelopment.	Hormone therapy in childhood and puberty	1 in 2,500 female births
XYY syndrome	An extra Y chromosome can cause above-average height.	No special treatment required	1 in 1,000 male births

FIGURE 6

SOME CHROMOSOMAL ABNORMALITIES. The treatments for these abnormalities do not necessarily erase the problem but may improve the individual's adaptive behavior and quality of life.

may be involved. An individual with Down syndrome has a round face, a flattened skull, an extra fold of skin over the eyelids, a protruding tongue, short limbs, and impaired motor and mental abilities.

Down syndrome appears approximately once in every 700 live births. Women between the ages of 16 and 34 are less likely to give birth to a child with Down syndrome than are younger or older women. African American children are rarely born with Down syndrome.

Sex-Linked Chromosomal Abnormalities Recall that a newborn normally has either an X and a Y chromosome, or two X chromosomes. Human embryos must possess at least one X chromosome to be viable. The most common sex-linked chromosomal abnormalities involve the presence of an extra chromosome (either an X or Y) or the absence of one X chromosome in females (Yang & Chen, 2019).

Klinefelter syndrome is a chromosomal disorder in which males have an extra X chromosome, making them XXY instead of XY (Vockel & others, 2020). Males with this disorder have undeveloped testes, and they usually have enlarged breasts and become tall (Flannigan & Schlegel, 2017). Klinefelter syndrome occurs approximately once in every 1,000 live male births. Only 10 percent of individuals with Klinefelter syndrome are diagnosed before puberty, with the majority not identified until adulthood (Aksglaede & others, 2013).

Fragile X syndrome (FXS) is a genetic disorder that results from an abnormality in the X chromosome, which becomes constricted and often breaks (Lee & others, 2020). An intellectual difficulty frequently is an outcome, and autism, a learning disability, or a short attention span also may be linked to the syndrome (McKechanie & others, 2020; Zafarullah & Tassone, 2019). This disorder occurs more frequently in males than in females, possibly because the second X chromosome in females negates the effects of the abnormal X chromosome (Mila & others, 2018). A recent study found that a higher level of maternal responsivity to the adaptive behavior of children with FXS had a positive effect on the children's communication skills (Warren & others, 2017).

Turner syndrome is a chromosomal disorder in females in which either an X chromosome is missing, making the person XO instead of XX, or part of one X chromosome is deleted (Bianchi, 2020). Females with Turner syndrome are short in stature and have a webbed neck (Kruszka & others, 2020). They might be infertile and have difficulty in mathematics, but their verbal ability is often quite good (Lleo & others, 2012). Turner syndrome occurs in approximately 1 of every 2,500 live female births (Culen & others, 2017).

XYY syndrome is a chromosomal disorder in which a male has an extra Y chromosome (Tartaglia & others, 2017). Early interest in this syndrome focused on the belief that the extra Y chromosome found in some males contributed to aggression and violence. However, researchers subsequently found that XYY males are no more likely to commit crimes than are normal XY males (Witkin & others, 1976). However, while a recent study did not find more cognitive deficits in XYY boys than in normal XY boys, they did have more externalizing and internalizing problems (Operto & others, 2019).

Gene-Linked Abnormalities
Abnormalities can be produced not only by an abnormal number of chromosomes but also by harmful genes. More than 7,000 such genetic disorders have been identified, although most of them are rare. Two widely studied *gene-linked abnormalities* are phenylketonuria and sickle-cell anemia.

Phenylketonuria (PKU) is a genetic disorder in which the individual cannot properly metabolize phenylalanine, an amino acid. It results from a recessive gene and occurs about once in every 10,000 to 20,000 live births. Today, phenylketonuria is easily detected during infancy, and it is treated by a diet that prevents an excess accumulation of phenylalanine (Weiss & others, 2020). If phenylketonuria is left untreated, however, excess phenylalanine builds up in the child, producing intellectual disability and hyperactivity (McBride & others, 2019). Phenylketonuria accounts for approximately 1 percent of institutionalized individuals with intellectual disabilities, and it occurs primarily in non-Latino Whites.

The story of phenylketonuria has important implications for the nature-nurture issue. Although phenylketonuria is often described as a genetic disorder (nature), how or whether a gene's influence in phenylketonuria is played out depends on environmental influences since the disorder can be treated (nurture) using an environmental manipulation (Wild & others, 2019). That is, the presence of a genetic defect does not inevitably lead to the development

Klinefelter syndrome A chromosomal disorder in which males have an extra X chromosome, making them XXY instead of XY.

fragile X syndrome A genetic disorder involving an abnormality in the X chromosome, which becomes constricted and often breaks.

Turner syndrome A chromosome disorder in females in which either an X chromosome is missing, making the person XO instead of XX, or the second X chromosome is partially deleted.

XYY syndrome A chromosomal disorder in which males have an extra Y chromosome.

phenylketonuria (PKU) A genetic disorder in which an individual cannot properly metabolize an amino acid called phenylalanine. PKU is now easily detected but, if left untreated, results in intellectual disability and hyperactivity.

Name	Description	Treatment	Incidence
Cystic fibrosis	Glandular dysfunction that interferes with mucus production; breathing and digestion are hampered, resulting in a shortened life span.	Physical and oxygen therapy, synthetic enzymes, and antibiotics; most individuals live to middle age.	1 in 2,000 births
Diabetes	Body does not produce enough insulin, which causes abnormal metabolism of sugar.	Early onset can be fatal unless treated with insulin.	1 in 2,500 births
Hemophilia	Delayed blood clotting causes internal and external bleeding.	Blood transfusions/injections can reduce or prevent damage due to internal bleeding.	1 in 10,000 males
Huntington's disease	Central nervous system deteriorates, producing problems in muscle coordination and mental deterioration.	Does not usually appear until age 35 or older; death likely 10 to 20 years after symptoms appear.	1 in 20,000 births
Phenylketonuria (PKU)	Metabolic disorder that, left untreated, causes intellectual disability and hyperactivity.	Special diet can result in average intelligence and normal life span.	1 in 10,000 to 1 in 20,000 births
Sickle-cell anemia	Blood disorder that limits the body's oxygen supply; it can cause joint swelling, as well as heart and kidney failure.	Penicillin, medication for pain, antibiotics, blood transfusions, and hydroxyurea.	1 in 400 African American children (lower among other groups)
Spina bifida	Neural tube disorder that causes brain and spine abnormalities.	Corrective surgery at birth, orthopedic devices, and physical/medical therapy.	2 in 1,000 births
Tay-Sachs disease	Deceleration of mental and physical development caused by an accumulation of lipids in the nervous system.	Medication and special diet are used, but death is likely by 5 years of age.	1 in 30 American Jews is a carrier.

FIGURE 7
SOME GENE-LINKED ABNORMALITIES

of the disorder if the individual develops in the right environment (one free of phenylalanine). This is one example of the important principle of heredity-environment interaction. Under one environmental condition (phenylalanine in the diet), intellectual disability results, but when other nutrients replace phenylalanine, intelligence develops in the normal range. The same genotype has different outcomes depending on the environment (in this case, the nutritional environment).

Sickle-cell anemia, which occurs most often in African Americans, is a genetic disorder that impairs the functioning of the body's red blood cells. More than 300,000 infants worldwide are born with sickle-cell anemia each year (Azar & Wong, 2017). Red blood cells carry oxygen to the body's other cells and are usually disk-shaped. In sickle-cell anemia, a recessive gene causes the red blood cell to become a hook-shaped "sickle" that cannot carry oxygen properly and dies quickly (Patterson & others, 2018). As a result, the body's cells do not receive adequate oxygen, causing anemia and early death (Fernandes, 2017). About 1 in 400 African American babies is affected by sickle-cell anemia. One in 10 African Americans is a carrier, as is 1 in 20 Latin Americans. Recent research strongly supports the use of hydroxyurea therapy for infants with sickle cell anemia, beginning at 9 months of age (Luzzatto & Makani, 2019). Stem cell transplantation also is being explored as a potential treatment for infants with sickle-cell anemia (Tanhehco & Bhatia, 2019).

Other diseases that result from genetic abnormalities include cystic fibrosis, some forms of diabetes, hemophilia, Huntington disease, spina bifida, and Tay-Sachs disease (Eno & others, 2020; Iacono & Feltis, 2019; Zhang & others, 2019). Figure 7 provides further information about these diseases. Someday scientists may be able to identify why these and other genetic abnormalities occur and discover how to cure them. The Human Genome Project has already linked specific DNA variations with increased risk of a number of diseases and conditions, including Huntington disease (in which the central nervous system deteriorates), some forms of cancer, asthma, diabetes, hypertension, and Alzheimer disease (Arjmand & others, 2020; Botti & others, 2019).

Dealing with Genetic Abnormalities Every individual carries DNA variations that might predispose the person to serious physical disease or mental disorder. But not

sickle-cell anemia A genetic disorder that affects the red blood cells and occurs most often in people of African descent.

Jennifer Leonhard, Genetic Counselor

Jennifer Leonhard is a genetic counselor at Sanford Bemidji Health Clinic in Bemidji, Minnesota. She obtained an undergraduate degree from Western Illinois University and a master's degree in genetic counseling from the University of Arkansas for Medical Sciences.

Genetic counselors like Leonhard work as members of a health care team, providing information and support to families with birth defects or genetic disorders. They identify families at risk by analyzing inheritance patterns and then explore options with the family. Some genetic counselors, like Leonhard, specialize in prenatal and pediatric genetics while others focus on cancer genetics or psychiatric genetic disorders.

Genetic counselors have specialized graduate degrees in medical genetics and counseling. They enter graduate school from undergraduate programs in a variety of disciplines, including biology, genetics, psychology, public health, and social work. There are approximately 30 graduate genetic counseling programs in the

Jennifer Leonard, shown here talking with a young couple about genetic influences on development, is a genetic counselor in Bemidji, Minnesota.
Courtesy of Jennifer Leonhard

United States. If you are interested in this profession, you can obtain further information from the National Society of Genetic Counselors at www.nsgc.org.

For more information about what genetic counselors do, see the Careers in Life-Span Development appendix.

all individuals who carry an abnormal genetic variation develop the disorder. Other genes or developmental events sometimes compensate for genetic abnormalities. For example, recall the earlier example of phenylketonuria: Even though individuals might carry the abnormal genetic variation associated with phenylketonuria, the abnormal phenotype does not develop when phenylalanine is replaced by other nutrients in their diet (Weiss & others, 2020).

Thus, genes are not destiny, but genes that are missing, nonfunctional, or mutated can contribute to disorders (Bertucci & others, 2019; Ivashko-Pachima & others, 2020). Identifying such genetic flaws could enable doctors to predict an individual's risks, recommend healthy practices, and prescribe the safest and most effective drugs (Arjmand & others, 2020). A decade or two from now, parents of a newborn baby may be able to leave the hospital with a full genome analysis of their offspring that identifies disease risks.

However, this knowledge might bring important costs as well as benefits. Who would have access to a person's genetic profile? An individual's ability to land and hold jobs or obtain insurance might be threatened if she or he is known to be at risk for some disease. For example, should an airline pilot or a neurosurgeon who is predisposed to develop a disorder that makes one's hands shake be required to leave that job early, before showing any symptoms of the disorder?

Further, given advances in prenatal genetic testing, it may someday be possible for a couple to learn in the first few weeks of pregnancy (when termination is easiest) that they are carrying an offspring with Down syndrome. What would it mean if all such pregnancies were terminated? What would the world look like with no genetic diversity in it? Who should decide how genetically "abnormal" an embryo can be before deciding whether to terminate a pregnancy?

Genetic counselors, usually physicians or biologists who are well-versed in the field of medical genetics, understand the kinds of problems just described, the odds of encountering them, and helpful strategies for offsetting some of their effects (Kim & others, 2020; Jamal, Schupmann, & Berkman 2020; Seiffert & others, 2019). To read about the career and work of a genetic counselor, see *Connecting with Careers*.

3 Reproductive Challenges and Choices

LG3 Identify some important reproductive challenges and choices.

Prenatal Diagnostic Tests | Infertility and Reproductive Technology | Adoption

The facts and principles we have discussed regarding meiosis, genetics, and genetic abnormalities are a small part of the recent explosion of knowledge about human biology. This knowledge not only helps us understand human development but also opens up many new choices to prospective parents—choices that can also raise ethical questions.

PRENATAL DIAGNOSTIC TESTS

One choice open to prospective mothers is the extent to which they will undergo prenatal testing. A number of tests can indicate whether a fetus is developing normally, including ultrasound sonography, fetal MRI, chorionic villus sampling, amniocentesis, and maternal blood screening.

Ultrasound Sonography An ultrasound test is often conducted seven weeks into a pregnancy and at various times later in pregnancy. *Ultrasound sonography* is a prenatal medical procedure in which high-frequency sound waves are directed into the pregnant woman's abdomen (Majeed & others, 2019; Pinto & others, 2020). The echo from the sounds is transformed into a visual representation of the fetus's inner structures. This technique can detect many abnormalities in the fetus, including microcephaly, in which an abnormally small brain can produce intellectual disability; it can also give clues to the baby's sex (Kaymak & others, 2020) and detect whether a woman is carrying more than one fetus. A research review concluded that many aspects of the developing prenatal brain can be detected by ultrasound in the first trimester and that about 50 percent of spina bifida cases can be identified at this time, most of these being severe cases (Engels & others, 2016). There is virtually no risk to the woman or fetus in using ultrasound.

Brain-Imaging Techniques The development of brain-imaging techniques has led to increasing use of *fetal MRI* to diagnose fetal malformations (Gilligan & others, 2020; Mervak & others, 2019; van der Knoop & others, 2020) (see Figure 8). MRI, which stands for magnetic resonance imaging, uses a powerful magnet and radio images to generate detailed images of the

A 6-month-old infant poses with the ultrasound sonography record taken four months into the baby's prenatal development. *What is ultrasound sonography?*
Jacques Pavlovsky/Sygma/Corbis/Getty Images

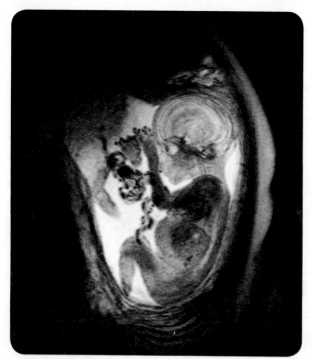

FIGURE **8**

A FETAL MRI, WHICH IS INCREASINGLY BEING USED IN PRENATAL DIAGNOSIS OF FETAL MALFORMATIONS

Du Cane Medical Imaging Ltd/Science Source

developmental **connection**

Biological Processes

Discover what the development of the fetus is like at the stages when chorionic villus sampling and amniocentesis can be used. Connect to "Prenatal Development and Birth."

body's organs and structures. Currently, ultrasound is still the first choice in fetal screening, but fetal MRI can provide more detailed images than ultrasound. In many instances, ultrasound will indicate a possible abnormality and then fetal MRI will be used to obtain a clearer, more detailed image (Griffiths & others, 2018). Among the malformations that fetal MRI may be able to detect better than ultrasound sonography are certain abnormalities of the central nervous system, chest, gastrointestinal tract, genital/urinary organs, and placenta (Marini & others, 2020; Pfeifer, 2019). In a research review, it was concluded that fetal MRI often does not provide good results in the first trimester of pregnancy because of small fetal structures and movement artifacts (Wataganara & others, 2016).

Chorionic Villus Sampling   At some point between the 10th and 12th weeks of pregnancy, chorionic villus sampling may be used to detect genetic defects and chromosomal abnormalities such as those discussed in the previous section. *Chorionic villus sampling (CVS)* is a prenatal medical procedure in which a small sample of the placenta (the vascular organ that links the fetus to the mother's uterus) is removed (Beksac & others, 2020; Gimovsky & others, 2020). Diagnosis takes about 10 days. There is a small risk of limb deformity when CVS is used.

Amniocentesis   Between the 15th and 18th weeks of pregnancy, amniocentesis may be performed. *Amniocentesis* is a prenatal medical procedure in which a sample of amniotic fluid is withdrawn by syringe and tested for chromosomal or metabolic disorders (Levy & Stosic, 2019; Xiang & others, 2020). The amniotic fluid is found within the amnion, a thin sac in which the embryo is suspended. Ultrasound sonography is often used during amniocentesis so that the syringe can be placed precisely. The later amniocentesis is performed, the better its diagnostic potential. The earlier it is performed, the more useful it is in deciding how to handle a pregnancy. It may take two weeks for enough cells to grow to allow amniocentesis test results to be obtained. Amniocentesis brings a small risk of miscarriage: About 1 woman in every 200 to 300 miscarries after amniocentesis.

Both amniocentesis and chorionic villus sampling provide valuable information about the presence of birth defects, but they also raise difficult issues for parents about whether an abortion should be obtained if birth defects are present. Chorionic villus sampling allows a decision to be made earlier, near the end of the first 12 weeks of pregnancy, when abortion is safer and less traumatic.

Maternal Blood Screening and Cell-Free DNA   During the 15th to 19th weeks of pregnancy, maternal blood screening may be performed. *Maternal blood screening* identifies pregnancies that have an elevated risk for birth defects such as spina bifida (a defect in the spinal cord) and Down syndrome (Seror & others, 2019). Recent research also indicates that maternal blood screening can be used to detect congenital heart disease risk in the fetus (Myoshi & others, 2019). A current blood test, the *triple screen*, measures three substances in the mother's blood in the second trimester of pregnancy. After an abnormal triple screen result, the next step is usually an ultrasound examination. If an ultrasound does not explain the abnormal triple screen results, amniocentesis is typically used.

Recent advances in molecular genetics and DNA sequencing allow accurate and noninvasive testing for some genetic abnormalities using cell-free fetal DNA in the mother's blood (Guseh, 2020; Hui, 2019). The cell-free DNA testing has especially improved the accuracy of prenatal testing for fetal abnormalities such as Down syndrome as early as 10 weeks of gestation.

Fetal Sex Determination   Chorionic villus sampling has often been used to determine the sex of the fetus at some point from 11 to 13 weeks of gestation. Also, in one study, ultrasound accurately identified the sex of the fetus at 11 to 13 weeks of gestation (Manzanares & others, 2016). Recently, though, some noninvasive techniques have been able to detect the sex of the fetus at an earlier point (Breveglieri & others, 2019; Kazachkova & others, 2020). Recently, non-invasive diagnosis of cell-free DNA in plasma was able to accurately determine fetal sex at 4.5 weeks (D'Aversa & others, 2018). Being able to detect an offspring's sex as well as the presence of various diseases and defects at such an early stage raises ethical concerns about couples' motivation to terminate a pregnancy (Bowman-Smart & others, 2020).

INFERTILITY AND REPRODUCTIVE TECHNOLOGY

Recent advances in biological knowledge have also opened up many choices for infertile individuals (Barati, Nikzad, & Karimian, 2020; Simoni & Santi, 2020). Approximately 10 to 15 percent of couples in the United States experience *infertility*, which is defined as the inability to conceive a child after 12 months of regular intercourse without contraception. The cause of infertility can rest with the woman or the man. The woman may not be ovulating (releasing eggs to be fertilized), she may be producing abnormal ova, her fallopian tubes through which ova normally reach the womb may be blocked, or she may have a disease that prevents implantation of the embryo into the uterus (Abrahami, Izhaki, & Younis, 2019). The man may produce too few sperm, the sperm may lack motility (the ability to move adequately), or he may have a blocked passageway (Tamrakar & Bastakoti, 2019). Also, recently a high level of oxidative stress has been linked to male infertility. A combination of oral antioxidants and lifestyle changes, such as reduced smoking and drinking, as well as increased exercise, may reduce male infertility (Barati, Nikzad, & Karimian, 2020). Further, methylation, which you read about earlier in the chapter, has been used to identify epigenetic factor that can be analyzed to predict infertility in men (Mohanty & others, 2020).

In the United States, more than 2 million couples seek help for infertility every year. In some cases of infertility, surgery may correct the cause; in others, hormone-based drugs may improve the probability of having a child. Of the 2 million couples who seek help for infertility every year, about 40,000 try high-tech assisted reproduction. By far the most common technique used is *in vitro fertilization (IVF)*, in which eggs and sperm are combined in a laboratory dish. If any eggs are successfully fertilized, one or more of the resulting zygotes is transferred into the woman's uterus. As indicated in Figure 9, the success rate of IVF depends on the mother's age.

The creation of families by means of the new reproductive technologies raises important questions about the physical and psychological consequences for children (Golombok, 2017). One result of fertility treatments is an increase in multiple births. Twenty-five to 30 percent of pregnancies achieved by fertility treatments—including in vitro fertilization—now result in multiple births. Any multiple birth increases the likelihood that the babies will have life-threatening and costly problems, such as extremely low birth weight (March of Dimes, 2020). However, research reviews conclude that children and adolescents conceived through new reproductive technologies—such as in vitro fertilization—are as well adjusted as their counterparts conceived by natural means (Golombok, 2011).

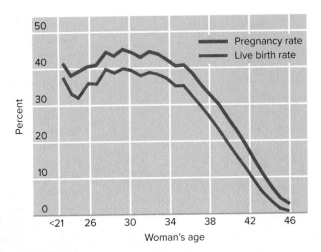

FIGURE 9

SUCCESS RATES OF IN VITRO FERTILIZATION VARY ACCORDING TO THE WOMAN'S AGE

ADOPTION

Although surgery and fertility drugs can sometimes solve infertility problems, another choice is to adopt a child (Farr & Grotevant, 2019; Pinderhughes & Brodzinsky, 2019). Adoption is a social and legal process that establishes a parent-child relationship between persons unrelated at birth.

The Increased Diversity of Adopted Children and Adoptive Parents

A number of changes have characterized adoptive children and adoptive parents during the last three to four decades (Brodzinsky & Pinderhughes, 2002; Farr & Grotevant, 2019). In the first half of the twentieth century, most U.S. adopted children were healthy, non-Latino White infants who were adopted at birth or soon after; however, in recent decades as abortion became legal and contraception increased, fewer of these infants became available for adoption. Increasingly, U.S. couples adopted a much wider diversity of children—from other countries, from other ethnic groups, children with physical and/or mental problems, and children who had been neglected or abused (Pinderhughes, Zhang, & Agerbak, 2015).

Changes also have characterized adoptive parents in the last three to four decades (Brodzinsky & Pinderhughes, 2002; Pinderhughes & Brodzinsky, 2019). In the first half of the twentieth century, most adoptive parents were from non-Latino White, middle or upper socioeconomic status backgrounds who were married and did not have any type of disability. However, in recent decades, increased diversity has characterized adoptive parents. Many adoption agencies today have no income requirements for adoptive parents and now allow adults from a wide range of backgrounds to adopt children, including single adults, gay and lesbian adults, and older adults (Farr & Vazquez, 2020; McConnachie & others, 2020). Further, many adoptions involve other family members (aunts/uncles/grandparents); currently, 30 percent of U.S. adoptions are made by relatives (Ledesma, 2012). And slightly more than 50 percent of U.S. adoptions occur through the foster care system; one survey found that more than 100,000 children in the U.S. foster care system were waiting for someone to adopt them (Ledesma, 2012).

Three pathways to adoption are (1) domestic adoption from the public welfare system, (2) domestic infant adoption through private agencies and intermediaries, and (3) international adoption (Grotevant & McDermott, 2014; Farr & Hrapczynski, 2020). In the next decade, the mix of U.S. adoptions is likely to include fewer domestic infant and international adoptions and more adoptions via the child welfare system (Farr & Grotevant, 2019).

Outcomes for Adopted Children   How well do adopted children fare in comparison with children who are raised by one or both of their birth parents? A research review concluded that adopted children are at higher risk for externalizing (aggression and conduct problems, for example), internalizing (anxiety and depression, for example), and attention problems (ADHD, for example) (Grotevant & McDermott, 2014). A more recent research review of internationally adopted adolescents found that although a majority were well adjusted, adoptees had higher rates of mental health problems than their non-adopted counterparts (Askeland & others, 2017). However, a majority of adopted children and adolescents (including those adopted at older ages, transracially, and across national borders) adjust effectively, and their parents report considerable satisfaction with their decision to adopt (Brodzinsky & Pinderhughes, 2002; Compton, 2016).

Adopted children fare much better than children raised in long-term foster care or in an institutional environment (Bernard & Dozier, 2008). A study of infants in China revealed that their cognitive development improved two to six months following their adoption from foster homes and institutions (van den Dries & others, 2010).

Children who are adopted very early in their lives are more likely to have positive outcomes than children adopted later in life (Bernard & Dozier, 2008; Julian, 2013). A Danish study indicated that being adopted was not a risk for juvenile delinquency if the individual was adopted at 12 months of age or earlier (Laubjerg & Petersson, 2011). However, those adopted after 12 months of age had a three to four times higher risk of becoming a juvenile delinquent than their nonadopted counterparts. Further, in a recent study, the adjustment of school-aged children who were adopted during infancy by gay, lesbian, and heterosexual parents showed no differences (Farr, 2017). Rather, children's behavior patterns and family functioning were predicted by earlier child adjustment issues and parental stress. Keep in mind that the changes in adoption practice over the last several decades make it difficult to generalize about the average adopted child or average adoptive parent.

An ongoing issue in adopting children is whether there should be any contact with the child's biological parents (Farr & Grotevant, 2019). Open adoption involves sharing identifying information and having contact with the biological parents; in contrast, closed adoption involves not having such sharing and contact. Most adoption agencies today offer adoptive parents the opportunity to have either an open or a closed adoption. A longitudinal study found that birth mothers, adoptive parents, and adopted children who had contact were more satisfied with their arrangements than those who did not have contact (Grotevant & others, 2013). Also, in this study, contact was linked to more optimal adjustment for adolescents and emerging adults. Birth fathers are often less likely to be included in open adoption, but a recent study indicated that they would like to be part of the open adoption triad (adoptee, birth family, and adoptive family) (Clutter, 2020). To read more about adoption, see *Connecting Development to Life,* in which we discuss effective parenting strategies with adopted children.

Parenting Adopted Children

Many of the keys to effectively parenting adopted children are no different from those for effectively parenting biological children: be supportive and caring, be involved and monitor the child's behavior and whereabouts, be a good communicator, and help the child learn to develop self-control. However, parents of adopted children face some unique circumstances (Grotevant & McDermott, 2014; Farr & others, 2018). They need to recognize the differences involved in adoptive family life, communicate about these differences, show respect for the birth family, and support the child's search for self and identity.

Following are some of the problems parents may face when their adopted children are at different points in development and some recommendations for handling these problems (Brodzinsky & Pinderhughes, 2002):

What are some strategies for parenting adopted children at different points in their development?
Don Mason/Blend Images/Getty Images

- **Infancy.** Researchers have found few differences in the attachments that adopted and nonadopted infants form with their parents. However, attachment can become problematic if parents have unresolved fertility issues or the child does not meet the parents' expectations. Counselors can help prospective adoptive parents develop realistic expectations.
- **Early childhood.** Because many children begin to ask where they came from when they are about 4 to 6 years old, this is a natural time to begin to talk in simple ways to children about their adoption status (Warshak, 2017). Some parents (although not as many as in the past) decide not to tell their children about the adoption. This secrecy may create psychological risks for the child if he or she later finds out about the adoption.
- **Middle and late childhood.** During the elementary school years, children begin to show more interest in their origins and may ask questions related to where they came from, what their birth parents looked like, and why their birth parents placed them for adoption. As they grow older, children may develop mixed feelings about being adopted and question their adoptive parents' explanations. It is important for adoptive parents to recognize that this ambivalence is normal. Also, problems may arise from the desire of adoptive parents to make life too perfect for the adoptive child and to present a perfect image of themselves to the child. The result too often is that adopted children feel that they cannot release any angry feelings or openly discuss problems.
- **Adolescence.** Adolescents are likely to develop more abstract and logical thinking, to focus their attention on their bodies, and to search for an identity. These characteristics provide the foundation for adopted adolescents to reflect on their adoption status in more complex ways, such as focusing on the fact that they look different from their adoptive parents. As they explore their identity, adopted adolescents may have difficulty incorporating their adopted status into their identity in positive ways. It is important for adoptive parents to understand the complexity of the adopted adolescent's identity exploration and be patient with the adolescent's lengthy identity search.

According to the information presented here and in the preceding discussion, how can mental health professionals help both adoptive parents and adopted children?

Review *Connect* Reflect

 Identify some important reproductive challenges and choices.

Review
- What are some common prenatal diagnostic tests?
- What are some techniques that help infertile people to have children?
- How does adoption affect children's development?

Connect
- The "Introduction" chapter discussed various methods of collecting data.

How would you characterize the methods used in prenatal diagnostic testing?

Reflect *Your Own Personal Journey of Life*
- If you were an adult who could not have children, would you want to adopt a child? Why or why not?

4 Heredity-Environment Interaction: The Nature-Nurture Debate

LG4 Explain some of the ways that heredity and environment interact to produce individual differences in development.

Behavior Genetics

Heredity-Environment Correlations

The Epigenetic View and Gene × Environment (G × E) Interaction

Conclusions About Heredity-Environment Interaction

Twin studies compare identical twins with fraternal twins. Identical twins develop from a single fertilized egg that splits into two genetically identical organisms. Fraternal twins develop from separate eggs, making them genetically no more similar than non-twin siblings. *What is the nature of the twin study method?*
Compassionate Eye Foundation/Stockbyte/Getty Images

Is it possible to untangle the influence of heredity from that of environment and discover the role of each in producing individual differences in development? When heredity and environment interact, how does heredity influence the environment and vice versa?

BEHAVIOR GENETICS

Behavior genetics is the field that seeks to discover the influence of heredity and environment on individual differences in human traits and development (Kendler & others, 2020; Riglin & others, 2020). Note that behavior genetics *does not* identify the extent to which genetics or the environment affects an individual's traits. Instead, behavior geneticists try to figure out what is responsible for the *differences* among people—that is, to what extent people vary because of differences in genes, environment, or a combination of these factors (Gasperi & others, 2019; Morneau-Vaillancourt & others, 2019). To study the influence of heredity on behavior, behavior geneticists often use either twins or adoption situations.

In the most common **twin study,** the behavioral similarity of identical twins (who are genetically identical) is compared with the behavioral similarity of fraternal twins. Recall that although fraternal twins share the same womb, they are no more genetically alike than non-twin siblings. Thus, by comparing groups of identical and fraternal twins, behavior geneticists capitalize on the basic knowledge that identical twins are more similar genetically than are fraternal twins (Inderkum & Tarokh, 2019; Wilson & others, 2020).

What are some of the thoughts and feelings people have about being a twin? In college freshman Colin Kunzweiler's (2007) view,

As a monozygotic individual, I am used to certain things. "Which one are you?" happens to be the most popular question I'm asked, which is almost always followed by "You're Colin. No, wait, you're Andy!" I have two names: one was given to me at birth, the other thrust on me in a random, haphazard way . . . My twin brother and I are as different from each other as caramel sauce is from gravy. We have different personalities, we enjoy different kinds of music, and I am even taller than he is (by a quarter of an inch). We are different; separate; individual. I have always been taught that I should maintain my own individuality; that I should be my own person. But if people keep constantly mistaking me for my twin, how can I be my own person with my own identity?

"Am I an 'I' or 'We'?" was the title of an article written by Lynn Perlman (2008) about the struggle twins have in developing a sense of being an individual. Of course, triplets have the same issue, possibly even more strongly so. One set of triplets entered a beauty contest as one person and won the contest!

Perlman, an identical twin herself, is a psychologist who works with twins (her identical twin also is a psychologist). She says that how twins move from a sense of "we" to "I" is a critical task for them as children and sometimes even as adults. For non-twins, separating oneself from a primary caregiver—mother and/or father—is an important developmental task in childhood, adolescence, and emerging adulthood. When a child has a twin, the separation process is likely to be more difficult because of the constant comparison with a twin. Because they are extremely similar in physical appearance, identical twins are likely to have more problems distinguishing themselves from their twin than are fraternal twins.

The twin separation process often accelerates in adolescence when one twin is likely to mature earlier than the other (Pearlman, 2013). However, for some twins it may not occur

behavior genetics The field that seeks to discover the influence of heredity and environment on individual differences in human traits and development.

twin study A study in which the behavioral similarity of identical twins is compared with the behavioral similarity of fraternal twins.

until emerging adulthood when they may go to different colleges and/or live apart for the first time. And for some twins, even separation during adulthood can be emotionally painful. One 28-year-old identical twin female got a new boyfriend, but the new relationship caused a great deal of stress and conflict with her twin sister (Friedman, 2013).

Several issues complicate interpretation of twin studies. For example, perhaps the environments of identical twins might be more similar than the environments of fraternal twins. Adults may stress the similarities of identical twins more than those of fraternal twins, and identical twins might perceive themselves as a "set" and play together more than fraternal twins do. If so, the influence of the environment on the observed similarities between identical and fraternal twins might be very significant.

In an **adoption study,** investigators seek to discover whether the behavior and psychological characteristics of adopted children are more like those of their adoptive parents, who have provided a home environment, or more like those of their biological parents, who have contributed their DNA (Leve & others, 2020). Another form of the adoption study compares adoptive and biological siblings (Kendler & others, 2016).

HEREDITY-ENVIRONMENT CORRELATIONS

The difficulties that researchers encounter when they interpret the results of twin studies and adoption studies reflect the complexities of heredity-environment interaction. Some of these interactions are heredity-environment correlations, which means that individuals' genes may be systematically related to the types of environments to which they are exposed. In a sense, individuals "inherit," seek out, or "construct" environments that may be related or linked to genetic "propensities." Behavior geneticist Sandra Scarr (1993) described three ways that heredity and environment can be correlated (see Figure 10):

- **Passive genotype-environment correlations** occur because biological parents, who are genetically related to the child, provide a rearing environment for the child. For example, the parents might be intelligent, skillful readers. And because they read well and enjoy reading, they provide their children with books to read. The likely outcome is that their children, because of both their own inherited genes and their book-filled environment, will become skilled readers.
- **Evocative genotype-environment correlations** occur because a child's genetically influenced characteristics elicit certain types of environments. For example, active, smiling children receive more social stimulation than passive, quiet children do. Cooperative, attentive children evoke more pleasant and instructional responses from the adults around them than uncooperative, distractible children do.
- **Active (niche-picking) genotype-environment correlations** occur when children seek out environments that they find compatible and stimulating. *Niche-picking* refers to finding a setting that is suited to one's genetically influenced abilities. Children select from their surrounding environment certain aspects that they respond to, learn about, or ignore.

adoption study A study in which investigators seek to discover whether, in behavior and psychological characteristics, adopted children are more like their adoptive parents, who provided a home environment, or more like their biological parents, who contributed their heredity. Another form of the adoption study compares adoptive and biological siblings.

passive genotype-environment correlations Correlations that exist when the natural parents, who are genetically related to the child, provide a rearing environment for the child.

evocative genotype-environment correlations Correlations that exist when the child's genetically influenced characteristics elicit certain types of environments.

active (niche-picking) genotype-environment correlations Correlations that exist when children seek out environments they find compatible and stimulating.

Heredity-Environment Correlation	Description	Examples
Passive	Children inherit genetic tendencies from their parents, and parents also provide an environment that matches their own genetic tendencies.	Musically inclined parents usually have musically inclined children, and they are likely to provide an environment rich in music for their children.
Evocative	The child's genetic tendencies elicit stimulation from the environment that supports a particular trait. Thus genes evoke environmental support.	A happy, outgoing child elicits smiles and friendly responses from others.
Active (niche-picking)	Children actively seek out "niches" in their environment that reflect their own interests and talents and are thus in accord with their genotype.	Libraries, sports fields, and a store with musical instruments are examples of environmental niches children might seek out if they have intellectual interests in books, talent in sports, or musical talents, respectively.

FIGURE **10**
EXPLORING HEREDITY-ENVIRONMENT CORRELATIONS

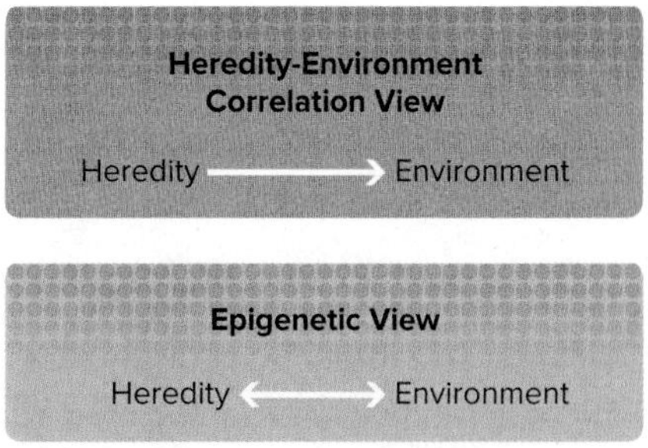

FIGURE **11**

COMPARISONS OF THE HEREDITY-
ENVIRONMENT CORRELATION AND
EPIGENETIC VIEWS OF DEVELOPMENT

Their active selections of environments are related to their particular genotype. For example, outgoing children tend to seek out social contexts in which to interact with people, whereas shy children don't. Children who are musically inclined are likely to select musical environments in which they can successfully perform their skills. How these "tendencies" come about will be discussed shortly under the topic of the epigenetic view.

Scarr observes that the relative importance of the three genotype-environment correlations changes as children develop from infancy through adolescence. In infancy, much of the environment that children experience is provided by adults. Thus, passive genotype-environment correlations are more common in the lives of infants and young children than they are in the lives of older children and adolescents who can extend their experiences beyond the family's influence and create or select their environments to a greater degree.

THE EPIGENETIC VIEW AND GENE × ENVIRONMENT (G × E) INTERACTION

Critics argue that the concept of heredity-environment correlation gives heredity too much of a one-sided influence in determining development because it does not consider the role of prior environmental influences in shaping the correlation itself (Gottlieb, 2007). Consistent with this view, earlier in the chapter we discussed how genes are collaborative, not determining an individual's traits independently but in conjunction with the environment.

The Epigenetic View   In line with the concept of a collaborative gene, Gilbert Gottlieb (2007) emphasizes the **epigenetic view,** which states that development reflects an ongoing, *bidirectional* interchange between heredity and the environment. Figure 11 compares the heredity-environment correlation and epigenetic views of development.

Let's look at an example that reflects the epigenetic view. A baby inherits genes from both parents at conception. During prenatal development, maternal environmental experiences such as toxins, nutrition, and stress can influence some genes to stop functioning while others become more active or less active. During infancy, environmental experiences such as exposure to toxins, nutrition, stress, learning, and encouragement continue to modify genetic activity and influence the activity of the nervous system that directly underlies behavior. Heredity and environment operate together—or collaborate—to produce a person's physical health, mental health, intelligence, temperament, height, weight, ability to pitch a baseball, ability to read, and so on (Allen & Dwivedi, 2020; Bleker & others, 2019; Pagiatakis & others, 2020; Schwartz, Wright, & Valgardson, 2019).

Gene × Environment (G × E) Interaction   An increasing number of studies are exploring how the interaction between heredity and environment influences development, including interactions that involve specific DNA sequences (Cunningham, Walker, & Nestler, 2020; Lindahl-Jacobsen & Christensen, 2019). The epigenetic mechanisms involve the actual molecular modification of the DNA strand as a result of environmental inputs in ways that alter gene functioning (Byrne & Drake, 2019; Kalashnikova, Goswami, & Burnham, 2018). One study found that individuals who have a short version of a gene labeled 5-HTTLPR (a gene involving the neurotransmitter serotonin) have an elevated risk of developing depression only if they *also* lead stressful lives (Caspi & others, 2003). Thus, the specific gene did not directly cause the development of depression; rather, the gene interacted with a stressful environment in a way that allowed the researchers to predict whether individuals would develop depression. A meta-analysis indicated that the short version of 5-HTTLPR was linked with higher cortisol stress reactivity (Miller & others, 2013). Researchers also have found support for the interaction between the 5-HTTLPR gene and stress levels in predicting depression in adolescents and older adults (Petersen & others, 2012; Zannas & others, 2012).

Other research on interactions between genes and environmental experiences has focused on attachment, parenting, and supportive child-rearing environments (Hoye & others, 2020). In one study, adults who experienced parental loss as young children were more likely to have unresolved attachment issues as adults only when they had the short version of the 5-HTTLPR gene (Caspers & others, 2009). The long version of the serotonin transporter gene apparently provided some protection and ability to cope better with parental loss. Other researchers have found that variations in dopamine-related genes interact with supportive or unsupportive rearing

developmental **connection**

Attachment

One study revealed links between infant attachment, responsive parenting, and the 5-HTTLPR gene. Connect to "Socioemotional Development in Infancy."

epigenetic view Emphasizes that development is the result of an ongoing, bidirectional interchange between heredity and environment.

environments to influence children's development (Bakermans-Kranenburg & van IJzendoorn, 2011). The type of research just described is referred to as studies of **gene × environment (G × E) interaction**—the interaction of a specific measured variation in DNA and a specific measured aspect of the environment (Hein & others, 2019).

Although there is considerable enthusiasm about the concept of gene × environment interaction (G × E), a research review concluded that the area is plagued by difficulties in replicating results, inflated claims, and other weaknesses (Manuck & McCaffery, 2014). The science of G × E interaction is very young, and over the next several decades it will likely produce more precise findings (Ecker & Beck, 2019; Tan, 2020).

gene × environment (G × E) interaction The interaction of a specific measured variation in the DNA and a specific measured aspect of the environment.

CONCLUSIONS ABOUT HEREDITY-ENVIRONMENT INTERACTION

If an attractive, popular, intelligent girl is elected president of her senior class in high school, is her success due to heredity or to environment? Of course, the answer is "both."

The relative contributions of heredity and environment are not additive. That is, we can't say that such-and-such a percentage of nature and such-and-such a percentage of experience make us who we are. Nor is it accurate to say that full genetic expression happens once, around conception or birth, after which we carry our genetic legacy into the world to see how far it takes us. Genes produce proteins throughout the life span, in many different environments. Or they don't produce these proteins, depending in part on how harsh or nourishing those environments are.

The emerging view is that complex behaviors are influenced by genes and environments in a way that gives people a propensity for a particular developmental trajectory (Ramos & others, 2019). The actual development requires both genes and an environment. And that environment is complex, just like the mixture of genes we inherit (Antonucci & Webster, 2019; Parke & Elder, 2020). Environmental influences range from the things we lump together under "nurture" (such as parenting, family dynamics, schooling, and neighborhood quality) to biological encounters (such as viruses, birth complications, and even biological events occurring at the cellular level).

In developmental psychologist David Moore's (2013, 2015, 2017) view, the biological systems that generate behaviors are extremely complex but too often these systems have been described in overly simplified ways that can be misleading. Thus, although genetic factors clearly contribute to behavior and psychological processes, they don't determine these phenotypes independently from the contexts in which they develop. From Moore's (2015, 2017) perspective, it is misleading to talk about "genes for" eye color, intelligence, personality, or other characteristics. Moore commented that in retrospect we should not have expected to be able to make the giant leap from DNA's molecules to a complete understanding of human behavior any more than we should anticipate being able to make the leap from understanding how sound waves move air molecules in a concert hall to a full-blown appreciation of a symphony's wondrous experience.

Imagine for a moment a cluster of genes somehow associated with youth violence (this example is hypothetical because we don't know of any such combination). The adolescent who carries this genetic mixture might experience a world of loving parents, regular nutritious meals, lots of books, and a series of masterful teachers. Or the adolescent's world might include parental neglect, a neighborhood in which gunshots and crime are everyday occurrences, and inadequate schooling. In which of these environments is the adolescent likely to become a criminal?

If heredity and environment interact to determine the course of development, is that all there is to answering the question of what causes development? Are humans completely at the mercy of their genes and environment as they develop through the life span? Our genetic heritage and environmental experiences are pervasive influences on development (Marks, Woolverton, & Garcia Coll, 2020; Simon, 2020). But in thinking about what causes development, recall from the "Introduction" chapter our discussion of development as the co-construction of biology, culture, *and* the individual. Not only are we the outcomes of our heredity and the environment we experience, but we also can author a unique developmental path by changing the environment. As one psychologist concluded:

> In reality, we are both the creatures and creators of our worlds. We are . . . the products of our genes and environments. Nevertheless, . . . the stream of causation that shapes the future runs through our present choices . . . Mind matters . . . Our hopes, goals, and expectations influence our future. (Myers, 2010, p. 168)

developmental **connection**

Nature Versus Nurture

The relative importance of nature and nurture is one of the main debates in the study of life-span development. Connect to "Introduction."

developmental **connection**

Life-Span Perspective

An important aspect of the life-span perspective is the co-construction of biology, environment, and the individual. Connect to "Introduction."

To what extent are this young girl's piano skills likely due to heredity, environment, or both?
Francisco Romero/E+/Getty Images

LG4 Explain some of the ways that heredity and environment interact to produce individual differences in development.

Review

- What is behavior genetics?
- What are three types of heredity-environment correlations?
- What is the epigenetic view of development? What characterizes gene × environment (G × E) interaction?
- What conclusions can be reached about heredity-environment interaction?

Connect

- Of passive, evocative, and active genotype-environment correlations, which is the best explanation for the similarities discovered between the twins discussed in the chapter-opening story?

Reflect *Your Own Personal Journey of Life*

- Someone tells you that she has analyzed your genetic background and environmental experiences and concluded that environment definitely has had little influence on your intelligence. What would you say about this analysis?

---

topical **connections** *looking **forward***

In the following chapters, we will continue to explore biological influences on development, especially in the chapters on physical development, but also in the chapters on cognitive and socioemotional development. For instance, biology's influence on infants' gross and fine motor skills may be obvious, but we will also discuss research questions such as "Is there a biological basis for sexual orientation?" In addition, we will examine reproduction when we look at adolescents and young adults who become parents. Finally, we will touch on the dual influence of nature and nurture in every period of life-span development.

---

reach your **learning goals**

Biological Beginnings

1 The Evolutionary Perspective

 LG1 Discuss the evolutionary perspective on life-span development.

Natural Selection and Adaptive Behavior

- Natural selection is the process by which those individuals of a species that are best adapted survive and reproduce. Darwin proposed that natural selection fuels evolution. In evolutionary theory, adaptive behavior is behavior that promotes the organism's survival in a natural habitat.

Evolutionary Psychology

- Evolutionary psychology holds that adaptation, reproduction, and "survival of the fittest" are important in shaping behavior. Ideas proposed by evolutionary developmental psychology include the view that an extended childhood period is needed to develop a large brain and learn the complexity of human social communities.

- According to Baltes, the benefits resulting from evolutionary selection decrease with age mainly because of a decline in reproductive fitness. At the same time, cultural needs increase.

- Like other theoretical approaches to development, evolutionary psychology has limitations. Bandura rejects "one-sided evolutionism" and argues for a bidirectional link between biology and environment. Biology allows for a broad range of cultural possibilities.

2 Genetic Foundations of Development

 LG2 Describe what genes are and how they influence human development.

The Collaborative Gene

- Short segments of DNA constitute genes, the units of hereditary information that help cells to reproduce and manufacture proteins. Genes act collaboratively, not independently.

Genes and Chromosomes

- Genes are passed on to new cells when chromosomes are duplicated during the processes of mitosis and meiosis, which are two ways in which new cells are formed. When an egg and a sperm unite in the fertilization process, the resulting zygote contains the genes from the chromosomes in the father's sperm and the mother's egg. Despite this transmission of genes from generation to generation, variability is created in several ways, including through the exchange of chromosomal segments during meiosis, through mutations, and through environmental influences.

Genetic Principles

- Genetic principles include those involving dominant-recessive genes, sex-linked genes, genetic imprinting, and polygenic inheritance.

Chromosomal and Gene-Linked Abnormalities

- Chromosomal abnormalities produce Down syndrome, which is caused by the presence of an extra copy of chromosome 21. Sex-linked conditions include Klinefelter syndrome, fragile X syndrome, Turner syndrome, and XYY syndrome. Gene-linked abnormalities involve harmful or absent genes. Gene-linked disorders include phenylketonuria (PKU) and sickle-cell anemia. Genetic counseling offers couples information about their risk of having a child with inherited abnormalities.

3 Reproductive Challenges and Choices

 LG3 Identify some important reproductive challenges and choices.

Prenatal Diagnostic Tests

- Ultrasound sonography, fetal MRI, chorionic villus sampling, amniocentesis, and maternal blood screening are used to determine whether a fetus is developing normally. Determination of the sex of the fetus is occurring earlier in prenatal development through noninvasive methods.

Infertility and Reproductive Technology

- Approximately 10 to 15 percent of U.S. couples have infertility problems, some of which can be corrected through surgery or fertility drugs. An additional option is in vitro fertilization.

Adoption

- A majority of adopted children adapt effectively. When adoption occurs very early in development, the outcomes for the child are improved. Because of the dramatic changes that have occurred in adoption in recent decades, it is difficult to generalize about the average adopted child or average adoptive family.

4 Heredity-Environment Interaction: The Nature-Nurture Debate

 LG4 Explain some of the ways that heredity and environment interact to produce individual differences in development.

Behavior Genetics

- Behavior genetics is the field concerned with the influence of heredity and environment on individual differences in human traits and development. Research methods used by behavior geneticists include twin studies and adoption studies.

Heredity-Environment Correlations

- In Scarr's heredity-environment correlations view, heredity directs the types of environments that children experience. She describes three genotype-environment correlations: passive, evocative, and active (niche-picking). Scarr argues that the relative importance of these three genotype-environment correlations changes as children develop.

The Epigenetic View and Gene × Environment (G × E) Interaction

- The epigenetic view emphasizes that development is the result of an ongoing, bidirectional interchange between heredity and environment. Gene × environment interaction involves the interaction of a specific measured variation in the DNA and a specific measured aspect of the environment. An increasing number of G × E studies are being conducted.

Conclusions About Heredity-Environment Interaction

- Behaviors are influenced by genes and environments in a way that gives people a propensity for a particular developmental trajectory. The actual development requires both genes and an environment, and that environment is complex. The interaction of heredity and environment is extensive. Much remains to be discovered about the specific ways that heredity and environment interact to influence development. Heredity and environment are pervasive influences on development, but humans can author a unique developmental path by changing their environments.

key **terms**

active (niche-picking) genotype-environment correlations 67
adoption study 67
behavior genetics 66
chromosomes 53
DNA 53
Down syndrome 57

epigenetic view 68
evocative genotype-environment correlations 67
evolutionary psychology 51
fertilization 54
fragile X syndrome 58
gene × environment (G × E) interaction 69

genes 53
genotype 56
Klinefelter syndrome 58
meiosis 54
mitosis 54
passive genotype-environment correlations 67
phenotype 56

phenylketonuria (PKU) 58
sickle-cell anemia 59
Turner syndrome 58
twin study 66
XYY syndrome 58
zygote 54

key **people**

Paul Baltes 52
Albert Bandura 52
Thomas Bouchard 49

David Buss 51
Charles Darwin 50
Gilbert Gottlieb 68

Stephen Jay Gould 52
Cynthia Kenyon 55

David Moore 69
Sandra Scarr 67

chapter 3

PRENATAL DEVELOPMENT AND BIRTH

chapter **outline**

① Prenatal Development

Learning Goal 1 Describe prenatal development.

The Course of Prenatal Development
Teratology and Hazards to Prenatal Development
Prenatal Care
Normal Prenatal Development

② Birth

Learning Goal 2 Describe the birth process.

The Birth Process
Assessing the Newborn
Preterm and Low Birth Weight Infants

③ The Postpartum Period

Learning Goal 3 Explain the changes that take place in the postpartum period.

Physical Adjustments
Emotional and Psychological Adjustments
Bonding

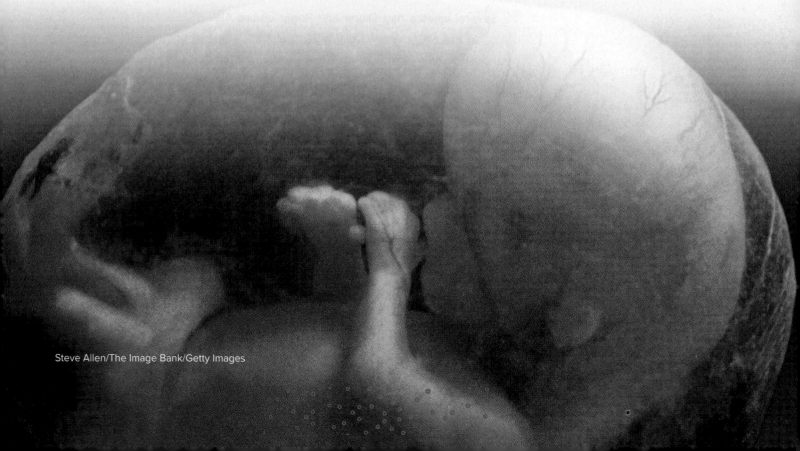

Steve Allen/The Image Bank/Getty Images

Diana and Roger married when he was 38 and she was 34. Both worked full-time and were excited when Diana became pregnant. Two months later, Diana began to have some unusual pains and bleeding. Just two months into her pregnancy she lost the baby. Although most early miscarriages are the result of embryonic defects, Diana thought deeply about why she had been unable to carry the baby to full term, and felt guilty that she might have done something "wrong."

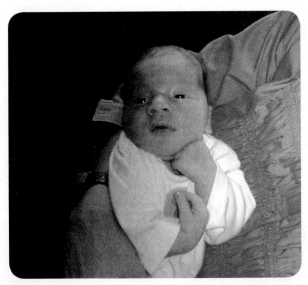

Alex, also known as "Mr. Littles."
Dr. John Santrock

Six months later, Diana became pregnant again. Because she was still worried about her prior loss, she made sure to follow every government recommendation such as getting enough folic acid, avoiding certain types of dairy products that might harbor bacteria, and letting someone else change their cat's litterbox to avoid toxoplasmosis. She and Roger read about pregnancy and signed up for birth preparation classes. Each Friday night for eight weeks they practiced techniques for dealing with contractions. They talked about what kind of parents they wanted to be and discussed what changes in their lives the baby would make. When they found out that their offspring was going to be a boy, they gave him a nickname: Mr. Littles.

This time, Diana's pregnancy went well, and Alex, also known as Mr. Littles, was born. During the birth, however, Diana's heart rate dropped precipitously, and she was given a stimulant to raise it. Apparently the stimulant also increased Alex's heart rate and breathing to a dangerous point, and he had to be placed in a neonatal intensive care unit (NICU).

Several times a day, Diana and Roger visited Alex in the NICU. A number of babies in the NICU with very low birth weights had been in intensive care for weeks, and some of the babies were not doing well. Fortunately, Alex was in better health. After he had spent several days in the NICU, his parents were permitted to take home a very healthy Alex.

topical **connections** *looking* **back**

Genes form the biological basis of our development. They are passed on through mitosis, meiosis, and, ultimately, fertilization. The impact of our genes involves the genetic principles of dominant-recessive genes, sex-linked genes, genetic imprinting, and polygenically determined characteristics. Approximately 10 to 15 percent of U.S. couples have problems with fertility. Some of these problems can be solved through surgery, drugs, or in vitro fertilization. Whether a pregnancy occurs naturally or with assistance, the resulting infant's development is shaped both by his or her genes (nature) and environment (nurture).

preview

This chapter chronicles the truly remarkable developments from conception through birth. Imagine . . . at one time you were an organism floating in a sea of fluid in your mother's womb. Let's now explore what your development was like from the time you were conceived through the time you were born. We will explore normal development in the prenatal period, as well as the period's hazards. We also will study the birth process and tests used to assess the newborn; discuss parents' adjustment during the postpartum period; and evaluate parent-infant bonding.

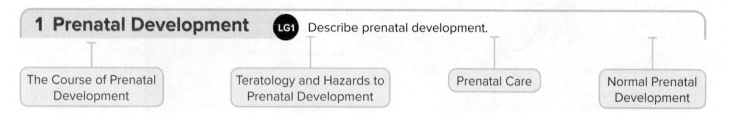

1 Prenatal Development **LG1** Describe prenatal development.

| The Course of Prenatal Development | Teratology and Hazards to Prenatal Development | Prenatal Care | Normal Prenatal Development |

Imagine how Alex ("Mr. Littles") came to be. Out of thousands of eggs and millions of sperm, one egg and one sperm united to produce him. Had the union of sperm and egg come a day or even an hour earlier or later, he might have been very different—maybe even of the opposite sex. Conception occurs when a single sperm cell from the male unites with an ovum (egg) in the female's fallopian tube in a process called fertilization. Over the next few months, the genetic code discussed in the "Biological Beginnings" chapter directs a series of changes in the fertilized egg, but many events and hazards will influence how that egg develops and becomes tiny Alex.

THE COURSE OF PRENATAL DEVELOPMENT

Typical prenatal development, which begins with fertilization and ends with birth, takes between 266 and 280 days (38 to 40 weeks). It can be divided into three periods: germinal, embryonic, and fetal.

The Germinal Period The **germinal period** is the period of prenatal development that takes place during the first two weeks after conception. It includes the creation of the fertilized egg, called a zygote; cell division; and the attachment of the zygote to the uterine wall.

Rapid cell division by the zygote continues throughout the germinal period (recall that this cell division occurs through a process called mitosis). *Differentiation*—specialization of cells to perform various tasks—starts to take place by approximately one week after conception. At this stage, the group of cells, now called the **blastocyst,** consists of an inner mass of cells that will eventually develop into the embryo, and the **trophoblast,** an outer layer of cells that later provides nutrition and support for the embryo. Implantation, the attachment of the zygote to the uterine wall, takes place about 11 to 15 days after conception. Figure 1 illustrates some of the most significant developments during the germinal period.

The Embryonic Period The **embryonic period** is the period of prenatal development that occurs from two to eight weeks after conception. During the embryonic period, the rate of cell differentiation intensifies, support systems for cells form, and organs appear.

This period begins as the blastocyst attaches to the uterine wall. The mass of cells is now called an *embryo*, and three layers of cells form. The embryo's *endoderm* is the inner layer of cells, which will develop into the digestive and respiratory systems. The *mesoderm* is the middle layer, which will become the circulatory system, bones, muscles, excretory system, and reproductive system. The *ectoderm* is the outermost layer, which will become the nervous system and brain, sensory receptors (ears, nose, and eyes, for example), and skin parts (hair

The history of man for the nine months preceding his birth would, probably, be far more interesting, and contain events of greater moment, than all the three score and ten years that follow it.

—Samuel Taylor Coleridge
English poet and essayist, 19th century

germinal period The period of prenatal development that takes place in the first two weeks after conception. It includes the creation of the zygote, continued cell division, and the attachment of the zygote to the uterine wall.

blastocyst The inner layer of cells that develops during the germinal period. These cells later develop into the embryo.

trophoblast The outer layer of cells that develops in the germinal period. These cells provide nutrition and support for the embryo.

embryonic period The period of prenatal development that occurs two to eight weeks after conception. During the embryonic period, the rate of cell differentiation intensifies, support systems for the cells form, and organs appear.

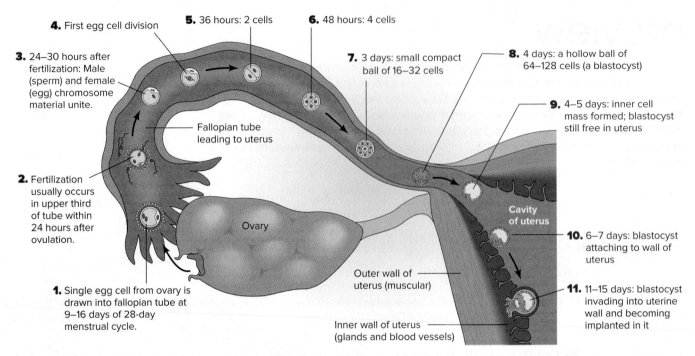

4. First egg cell division

5. 36 hours: 2 cells

6. 48 hours: 4 cells

3. 24–30 hours after fertilization: Male (sperm) and female (egg) chromosome material unite.

7. 3 days: small compact ball of 16–32 cells

8. 4 days: a hollow ball of 64–128 cells (a blastocyst)

9. 4–5 days: inner cell mass formed; blastocyst still free in uterus

Fallopian tube leading to uterus

2. Fertilization usually occurs in upper third of tube within 24 hours after ovulation.

Ovary

Cavity of uterus

10. 6–7 days: blastocyst attaching to wall of uterus

Outer wall of uterus (muscular)

11. 11–15 days: blastocyst invading into uterine wall and becoming implanted in it

1. Single egg cell from ovary is drawn into fallopian tube at 9–16 days of 28-day menstrual cycle.

Inner wall of uterus (glands and blood vessels)

FIGURE **1**

SIGNIFICANT DEVELOPMENTS IN THE GERMINAL PERIOD. Just one week after conception, cells of the blastocyst have already begun specializing. The germinal period ends when the blastocyst attaches to the uterine wall. *Which of the steps shown in the drawing occur in the laboratory when IVF is used?*

and nails, for example). Every body part eventually develops from these three layers. The endoderm primarily produces internal body parts, the mesoderm primarily produces parts that surround the internal areas, and the ectoderm primarily produces surface parts.

As the embryo's three layers form, life-support systems for the embryo develop rapidly. These life-support systems include the amnion, the umbilical cord (both of which develop from the fertilized egg, not the mother's body), and the placenta. The **amnion** is a sac (bag or envelope) that contains a clear fluid in which the developing embryo floats. The amniotic fluid provides an environment that is temperature and humidity controlled, as well as shockproof. The **umbilical cord** contains two arteries and one vein, and connects the baby to the placenta. The **placenta** consists of a disk-shaped group of tissues in which small blood vessels from the mother and the offspring intertwine but do not join.

Figure 2 illustrates the placenta, the umbilical cord, and the blood flow in the expectant mother and developing organism. Very small molecules—oxygen, water, salt, food from the mother's blood, as well as carbon dioxide and digestive wastes from the offspring's blood—pass back and forth between the mother and embryo or fetus (Cai & others, 2019). Virtually any drug or chemical substance the pregnant woman ingests can cross the placenta to some degree, unless it is metabolized or altered during passage, or the molecules are too large to pass through the placental wall (Jansson & others, 2020). Of special concern is the transfer through the placenta of drugs that can be harmful to the fetus, such as alcohol, nicotine, marijuana, and cocaine (de Araujo & others, 2020). For example, one study confirmed that ethanol crosses the human placenta and primarily reflects maternal alcohol use (Matlow & others, 2013). Another study revealed that cigarette smoke weakened and increased the oxidative stress of fetal membranes, from which the placenta develops (Menon & others, 2011). The stress hormone cortisol also can cross the placenta (Parrott & others, 2014). Large molecules that cannot pass through the placental wall include red blood cells and harmful substances, such as most bacteria, maternal wastes, and hormones. The complex mechanisms that govern the transfer of substances across the placental barrier are still not entirely understood (Hirchmugl & others, 2020; Malnou & others, 2019).

By the time most women know they are pregnant, the major organs have begun to form. **Organogenesis** is the name given to the process of organ formation during the first two months of prenatal development. While the embryo's organs are being formed, they are especially vulnerable to environmental changes (Bi, Ye, & Jin, 2020).

amnion The part of the prenatal life-support system that consists of a sac containing a clear fluid in which the developing embryo floats.

umbilical cord Part of the prenatal life-support system that contains two arteries and one vein that connect the baby to the placenta.

placenta A prenatal life-support system that consists of a disk-shaped group of tissues in which small blood vessels from the mother and offspring intertwine.

organogenesis Organ formation that takes place during the first two months of prenatal development.

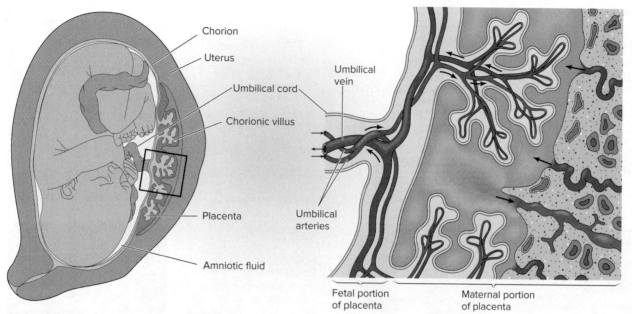

FIGURE 2

THE PLACENTA AND THE UMBILICAL CORD. The area bound by the square is enlarged in the right half of the illustration. Arrows indicate the direction of blood flow. Maternal blood flows through the uterine arteries to the spaces housing the placenta, and it returns through the uterine veins to the maternal circulation. Fetal blood flows through the umbilical arteries into the capillaries of the placenta and returns through the umbilical vein to the fetal circulation. The exchange of materials takes place across the layer separating the maternal and fetal blood supplies, so the bloods never come into contact. *What is known about how the placental barrier works and its importance?*

In the third week after conception, the neural tube that eventually becomes the spinal cord forms. At about 21 days, eyes begin to appear, and at 24 days the cells for the heart begin to differentiate. During the fourth week, the urogenital system becomes apparent, and arm and leg buds emerge. Four chambers of the heart take shape, and blood vessels appear. From the fifth to the eighth week, arms and legs differentiate further; at this time, the face starts to form but still is not very recognizable. The intestinal tract develops and the facial structures fuse. At eight weeks, the developing organism weighs about 1/30 ounce and is just over 1 inch long.

The Fetal Period   The **fetal period**, lasting about seven months, is the prenatal period between two months after conception and birth in typical pregnancies. Growth and development continue their dramatic course during this time.

Three months after conception (13 weeks), the fetus is about 3 inches long and weighs about four-fifths of an ounce. Its arms, legs, and head move randomly (or spontaneously), and its mouth opens and closes. The face, forehead, eyelids, nose, and chin are distinguishable, as are the upper arms, lower arms, hands, and lower limbs. In most cases, the genitals can be identified as male or female. By the end of the fourth month of pregnancy (17 weeks), the fetus has grown to about 5.5 inches in length and weighs about 5 ounces. At this time, a growth spurt occurs in the body's lower parts. For the first time, the mother can feel the fetus move.

By the end of the fifth month (22 weeks), the fetus is about 12 inches long and weighs close to a pound. Structures of the skin have formed—toenails and fingernails, for example. The fetus is more active, showing a preference for a particular position in the womb. By the end of the sixth month (26 weeks), the fetus is about 14 inches long and has gained another half-pound to a pound. The eyes and eyelids are completely formed, and a fine layer of hair covers the head. A grasping reflex is present and irregular breathing movements occur.

As early as six months of pregnancy (about 24 to 25 weeks after conception), the fetus for the first time has a chance of surviving outside the womb—that is, it is viable. Infants who are born early, or between 24 and 37 weeks of pregnancy, usually need help breathing because their lungs are not yet fully mature. By the end of the seventh month, the fetus is about 16 inches long and weighs about 3 pounds.

During the last two months of prenatal development, fatty tissues develop, and the functioning of various organ systems—heart and kidneys, for example—steps up. During the eighth

fetal period Lasting about seven months, the period between two months after conception and birth in typical pregnancies.

First trimester (first 3 months)

Conception to 4 weeks
- Is less than $1/10$ inch long
- Beginning development of spinal cord, nervous system, gastrointestinal system, heart, and lungs
- Amniotic sac envelops the preliminary tissues of entire body
- Is called a "zygote"

8 weeks
- Is about 0.6 inch long
- Face is forming with rudimentary eyes, ears, mouth, and tooth buds
- Arms and legs are moving
- Brain is forming
- Fetal heartbeat is detectable with ultrasound
- Is called an "embryo"

12 weeks
- Is about 2 inches long and weighs about 0.5 ounce
- Can move arms, legs, fingers, and toes
- Fingerprints are present
- Can smile, frown, suck, and swallow
- Sex is distinguishable
- Can urinate
- Is called a "fetus"

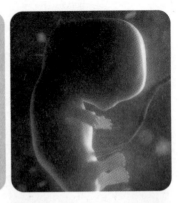

Second trimester (middle 3 months)

16 weeks
- Is about 5 inches long and weighs about 3.5 ounces
- Heartbeat is strong
- Skin is thin, transparent
- Downy hair (lanugo) covers body
- Fingernails and toenails are forming
- Has coordinated movements; is able to roll over in amniotic fluid

20 weeks
- Is about 6.5 inches long and weighs about 11 ounces
- Heartbeat is audible with ordinary stethoscope
- Sucks thumb
- Hiccups
- Hair, eyelashes, eyebrows are present

24 weeks
- Is about 12 inches long and weighs about 1.3 pounds
- Skin is wrinkled and covered with protective coating (vernix caseosa)
- Eyes are open
- Waste matter is collected in bowel
- Has strong grip

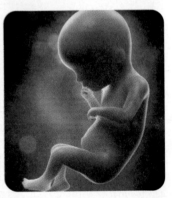

Third trimester (last 3 months)

28 weeks
- Is about 15 inches long and weighs about 2.3 pounds
- Is adding body fat
- Is very active
- Rudimentary breathing movements are present

32 weeks
- Is about 17 inches long and weighs about 4 pounds
- Has periods of sleep and wakefulness
- Responds to sounds
- May assume the birth position
- Bones of head are soft and flexible
- Iron is being stored in liver

36 to 38 weeks
- Is 19 to 20 inches long and weighs 6 to $7 1/2$ pounds
- Skin is less wrinkled
- Vernix caseosa is thick
- Lanugo is mostly gone
- Is less active
- Is gaining immunities from mother

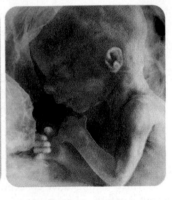

FIGURE 3

THE THREE TRIMESTERS OF PRENATAL DEVELOPMENT. Both the germinal and embryonic periods occur during the first trimester. The end of the first trimester as well as the second and third trimesters are part of the fetal period.
(Top to bottom): Konstantin Ermolaev/unlim3d/123RF; SCIEPRO/Science Photo Library/Getty Images; Steve Allen/Brand X Pictures/Getty Images

---

developmental connection

Brain Development

At birth, infants' brains weigh approximately 25 percent of what they will weigh in adulthood. Connect to "Physical Development in Infancy."

neurons Nerve cells that handle information processing at the cellular level in the brain.

and ninth months, the fetus grows longer and gains substantial weight—about another 4 pounds. At birth, the average American baby weighs 8 pounds and is about 20 inches long.

Figure 3 gives an overview of the main events during prenatal development. Notice that instead of describing development in terms of germinal, embryonic, and fetal periods, Figure 3 divides prenatal development into equal periods of three months, called trimesters. Remember that the three trimesters are not the same as the three prenatal periods we have discussed. The germinal and embryonic periods occur in the first trimester. The fetal period begins toward the end of the first trimester and continues through the second and third trimesters. Viability (the chances of surviving outside the womb) begins at the end of the second trimester.

Brain Development One of the most remarkable aspects of the prenatal period is the development of the brain (Turk & others, 2019). By the time babies are born, it has been estimated that they have as many as 20 to 100 billion **neurons,** or nerve cells, which handle information processing at the cellular level in the brain. During prenatal development, neurons spend time moving to the right locations and are starting to become connected. The basic architecture of the human brain is assembled during the first two trimesters of prenatal development. In typical development, the third trimester of prenatal development and the first two years of postnatal life are characterized by gradual increases in connectivity and functioning of neurons (Vasung & others, 2019).

Four important phases of the brain's development during the prenatal period involve: (1) the neural tube, (2) neurogenesis, (3) neuronal migration, and (4) neural connectivity.

Neural Tube As the human embryo develops inside its mother's womb, the nervous system begins forming as a long, hollow tube located on the embryo's back. This pear-shaped neural tube, which forms at about 18 to 24 days after conception, develops out of the ectoderm. The tube closes at the top and bottom ends at about 27 days after conception (Keunen, Counsell, & Bender, 2017). Figure 4 shows that the nervous system still has a tubular appearance six weeks after conception.

Two birth defects related to a failure of the neural tube to close are anencephaly and spina bifida. The highest regions of the brain fail to develop when fetuses have anencephaly or when the head end of the neural tube fails to close, and these fetuses die in the womb, during childbirth, or shortly after birth (Oakley, 2020). Spina bifida results in varying degrees of paralysis of the lower limbs (Savvidou & Jauniaux, 2019). Individuals with spina bifida usually need assistive devices such as crutches, braces, or wheelchairs. Both maternal diabetes and obesity place the fetus at risk for developing neural tube defects (Mowla & others, 2020). Also, one study found that maternal exposure to secondhand tobacco smoke was linked to neural tube defects (Suarez & others, 2011). A strategy that can help to prevent neural tube defects is for pregnant women to consume adequate amounts of the B vitamin folic acid (American Society for Reproductive Medicine & others, 2019; Li & others, 2020). A recent large-scale study in Brazil found that fortifying flour with folic acid significantly reduced the rate of neural tube defects (Santos & others, 2016).

Neurogenesis In a normal pregnancy, once the neural tube has closed, a massive proliferation of new immature neurons begins to take place at about the fifth prenatal week and continues throughout the remainder of the prenatal period. The generation of new neurons is called *neurogenesis,* a process that continues through the remainder of the prenatal period but is largely complete by the end of the fifth month after conception (Borsani & others, 2019). At the peak of neurogenesis, it is estimated that as many as 200,000 neurons are generated every minute.

Neuronal Migration At approximately 6 to 24 weeks after conception, *neuronal migration* occurs. This involves cells moving outward from their point of origin to their appropriate locations and creating the different levels, structures, and regions of the brain (Keunen, Counsell, & Benders, 2017). Once a cell has migrated to its target destination, it must mature and develop a more complex structure.

Neural Connectivity At about the 23rd prenatal week, connections between neurons begin to occur, a process that continues postnatally (Miller, Huppi, & Mallard, 2016). We will have much more to say about the structure of neurons, their connectivity, and the development of the infant brain in the chapter on "Physical Development in Infancy."

TERATOLOGY AND HAZARDS TO PRENATAL DEVELOPMENT

For Alex, the baby discussed at the opening of this chapter, the course of prenatal development went smoothly. His mother's womb protected him as he developed. Despite this protection, the environment can affect the embryo or fetus in many well-documented ways.

General Principles A **teratogen** is any agent that can potentially cause a birth defect or negatively alter cognitive and behavioral outcomes. (The word *teratogen* comes from the Greek word *tera,* meaning "monster.") So many teratogens exist that practically every fetus is exposed to at least some teratogens. For this reason, it is difficult to determine which teratogen causes which problem. In addition, it

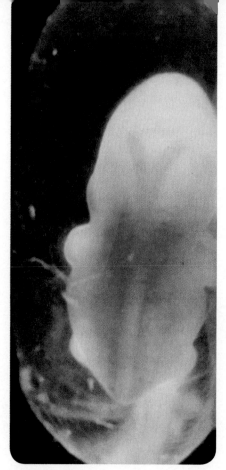

FIGURE 4

EARLY FORMATION OF THE NERVOUS SYSTEM. The photograph shows the primitive, tubular appearance of the nervous system at six weeks in the human embryo.
Claude Edelmann/Science Source

Yelyi Nordone, 12, of New York City, casts her line out into the pond during Camp Spifida at Camp Victory, near Millville, Pennsylvania. Camp Spifida is a week-long residential camp for children with spina bifida.
Bill Hughes/Bloomsburg Press Enterprise/AP Images

teratogen Any agent that causes a birth defect. The field of study that investigates the causes of birth defects is called teratology.

may take a long time for the effects of a teratogen to show up. Only about half of all potential effects are apparent at birth.

The field of study that investigates the causes of birth defects is called teratology (DeSesso, 2019). Some exposures to teratogens do not cause physical birth defects but can alter the developing brain and influence cognitive and behavioral functioning. These deficits in functioning are explored by researchers in the field of behavioral teratology.

The dose, genetic susceptibility, and the time of exposure to a particular teratogen influence both the severity of the damage to an embryo or fetus and the type of defect:

- *Dose.* The dose effect is rather obvious—the greater the dose of an agent, such as a drug, the greater the effect.
- *Genetic susceptibility.* The type or severity of abnormalities caused by a teratogen is linked to the genotype of the pregnant woman and the genotype of the embryo or fetus (Bianchi, 2020; Friedenson, 2020). For example, how a mother metabolizes a particular drug can influence the degree to which the drug's effects are transmitted to the embryo or fetus. Also, for unknown reasons, male fetuses are far more likely to be affected by teratogens than female fetuses.
- *Time of exposure.* Exposure to teratogens does more damage when it occurs at some points in development than at others (Cardoso-Moreira & others, 2019). Damage during the germinal period may even prevent implantation. In general, the embryonic period is more vulnerable than the fetal period.

Figure 5 summarizes additional information about the effects of time of exposure to a teratogen. The probability of a structural defect is greatest early in the *embryonic period*, when organs are being formed (Bi, Ye, & Jin, 2020). Each body structure has its own critical period of formation. Recall from earlier discussions that a critical period is a fixed time period very early in development during which certain experiences or events can have a

FIGURE 5

TERATOGENS AND THE TIMING OF THEIR EFFECTS ON PRENATAL DEVELOPMENT. The danger of structural defects caused by teratogens is greatest early in embryonic development. The period of organogenesis (red color) lasts for about six weeks. Later assaults by teratogens (blue-green color) mainly occur in the fetal period and instead of causing structural damage are more likely to stunt growth or cause problems involving organ function.

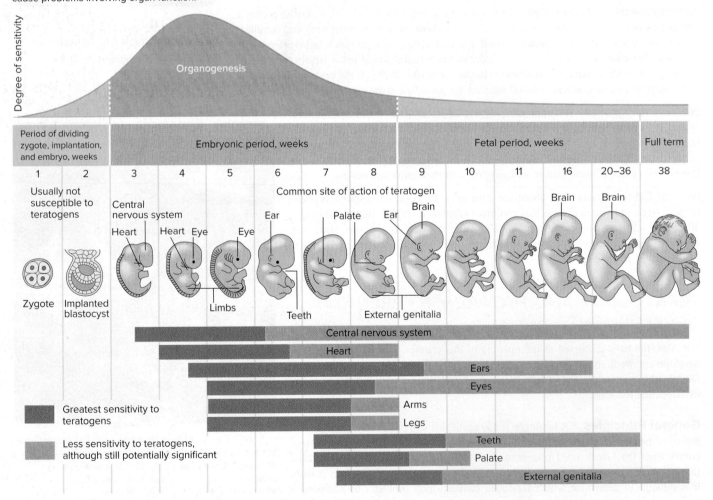

long-lasting effect on development. The critical period for the nervous system (week 3) is earlier than for arms and legs (weeks 4 and 5). Exposure to teratogens in the *fetal period* is more likely to cause problems in how organs function and may result in stunted growth rather than structural damage.

After organogenesis is complete, teratogens are less likely to cause anatomical defects. Instead, exposure during the fetal period is more likely to stunt growth or to create problems in the way organs function. This is especially true for the developing fetal brain, which continues to develop connections throughout pregnancy. To examine some key teratogens and their effects, let's begin with drugs.

Prescription and Nonprescription Drugs   Many U.S. women are given prescriptions for drugs while they are pregnant—especially antibiotics, analgesics, and asthma medications. Prescription as well as nonprescription drugs, however, may have effects on the embryo or fetus that the women never imagine.

Prescription drugs that can function as teratogens include antibiotics, such as streptomycin and tetracycline; some antidepressants; certain hormones, such as progestin and synthetic estrogen; and Accutane (the trade name for isotretinoin, a form of Vitamin A that is often used to treat acne) (Altintas Aykan & Ergun, 2020). Among the birth defects caused by Accutane are heart defects, eye and ear abnormalities, and brain malformation. In one study, isotretinoin was the fourth most common drug given to female adolescents who were seeking contraception advice from a physician (Stancil & others, 2016). However, physicians did not give the adolescent girls adequate information about the negative effects of isotretinoin on offspring if the girls were to become pregnant. In a research review of teratogens that should never be taken during the first trimester of pregnancy, isotretinoin was on the prohibited list (Eltonsy & others, 2016).

Psychoactive Drugs   *Psychoactive drugs* act on the nervous system to alter states of consciousness, modify perceptions, and change moods. Examples include caffeine, alcohol, and nicotine, as well as illicit drugs such as cocaine, marijuana, and heroin.

Caffeine   People often consume caffeine when they drink coffee, tea, or cola, or when they eat chocolate. Somewhat mixed results have been found for the extent to which maternal caffeine intake influences an offspring's development (Adams, Keisberg, & Safranek, 2016; de Medeiros & others, 2017). However, a large-scale study of almost 60,000 women revealed that maternal caffeine intake was linked to lower birth weight and babies being born small for gestational age (Sengpiel & others, 2013). Also, the influence of maternal consumption of highly caffeinated energy drinks on the development of offspring has not yet been studied. The U.S. Food and Drug Administration recommends that pregnant women either not consume caffeine or consume it only sparingly.

Alcohol   Heavy drinking by pregnant women can be devastating to their offspring (Baker & Stoler, 2020). **Fetal alcohol spectrum disorders (FASD)** are a cluster of abnormalities and problems that appear in the offspring of mothers who drink alcohol heavily during pregnancy (Carter, Jacobson, & Jacobson, 2020). The abnormalities include facial deformities and defects of the limbs and heart (Blanck-Lubarsch & others, 2020). Most children with FASD have learning problems and many are below average in intelligence, with some having an intellectual disability (Khoury & Milligan, 2016). Further, a research review concluded that FASD is linked to a lower level of executive function in children, especially in planning (Kingdon, Cardoso, & McGrath, 2016). And in a another study, FASD was associated with both externalized and internalized behavior problems in childhood (Tsang & others, 2016). Also, in a study in the United Kingdom, the life expectancy of individuals with FASD was only 34 years of age, about 42 percent of the average life expectancy in the general population (Thanh & Jonsson, 2016). In this study, the most common causes of death among individuals with FASD were suicide (15 percent), accidents (14 percent), and poisoning by illegal drugs or alcohol (7 percent). A recent study confirmed the significant risk of suicidal behavior in adolescents with FASD (O'Connor & others, 2019). Although many mothers of FASD infants are heavy drinkers, many mothers who are heavy drinkers do not have children with FASD or have one child with FASD and other children who do not have it.

What are some guidelines for alcohol use during pregnancy? Even drinking just one or two servings of beer or wine or one serving of hard liquor a few days a week can have negative

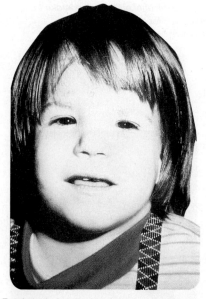

Fetal alcohol spectrum disorders (FASD) are characterized by a number of physical abnormalities and learning problems. Notice the wide-set eyes, flat cheekbones, and thin upper lip in this child with FASD.
Streissguth, AP, Landesman-Dwyer S, Martin, JC, & Smith, DW (1980). Teratogenic Effects of Alcohol in Humans and Laboratory Animals. *Science*, 209, 353–361.

fetal alcohol spectrum disorders (FASD) A cluster of abnormalities that appear in the offspring of some mothers who drink alcohol heavily during pregnancy.

What are some links between expectant mothers' alcohol and nicotine intake to outcomes for their offspring?
Altafulla/Shutterstock

effects on the fetus, although it is generally agreed that this level of alcohol use will not cause fetal alcohol syndrome (American Society for Reproductive Medicine & others, 2019). In a recent study, maternal alcohol use in pregnancy was associated with offspring mental health problems, such as anxiety, depression, and emotional problems, even at low to moderate levels of alcohol consumption (Easey & others, 2019). The U.S. Surgeon General recommends that no alcohol be consumed during pregnancy, as does the French Alcohol Society (Rolland & others, 2016). Despite such recommendations, a large-scale U.S. study found that 11.5 percent of adolescent and 8.7 percent of adult pregnant women reported using alcohol in the previous month (Oh & others, 2017).

However, in Great Britain, the National Institutes of Care and Health Excellence have concluded that it is safe to consume one to two drinks not more than twice a week during pregnancy (O'Keeffe, Greene, & Kearney, 2014). Nonetheless, some research suggests that it may not be wise to consume alcohol at the time of conception.

Nicotine Cigarette smoking by pregnant women can also adversely influence prenatal development, birth, and postnatal development (Moore & others, 2020). Preterm births and low birth weights, fetal and neonatal deaths, respiratory problems, and sudden infant death syndrome (SIDS, also known as crib death) are more common among the offspring of mothers who smoked during pregnancy (Zhang & others, 2017). Maternal smoking during pregnancy has been implicated in as many as 25 percent of infants being born with a low birth weight (Brown & Graves, 2013).

Maternal smoking during pregnancy also has been identified as a risk factor for the development of attention deficit hyperactivity disorder in offspring (Vogt, 2019). A recent meta-analysis of 15 studies concluded that smoking during pregnancy increased the risk that children would have ADHD, and the risk of ADHD was greater for children whose mothers were heavy smokers (Huang & others, 2018). A recent study also found a number of negative cognitive and behavioral outcomes in the infant's first year of life as a consequence of prenatal cigarette exposure: negative affect, poorer attention, greater excitability, and more irritability (Froggatt, Covey, & Reissland, 2020). And in another study, maternal cigarette smoking during pregnancy was linked to higher rates of cigarette smoking among offspring at 16 years of age (De Genna & others, 2016). Further, a recent study revealed that daughters whose mothers smoked during their pregnancy were more likely to smoke during their own pregnancy (Ncube & Mueller, 2017). Cessation of smoking by pregnant women by the third trimester is linked to improved birth outcomes (Crume, 2019).

Studies also indicate that environmental tobacco smoke is linked to impaired connectivity of the thalamus and prefrontal cortex in newborns (Salzwedel & others, 2016). Another study found that maternal exposure to environmental tobacco smoke during prenatal development increased the risk of stillbirth (Varner & others, 2014).

Despite the plethora of negative outcomes for maternal smoking during pregnancy, a large-scale U.S. study revealed that 23 percent of adolescent and 15 percent of adult pregnant women reported having used tobacco in the previous month (Oh & others, 2017). And a final point about nicotine use during pregnancy involves the recent dramatic increase in the use of e-cigarettes (Cooper & others, 2019). One study found that misconceptions about e-cigarettes were common among pregnant women (Mark & others, 2015). Women who were using e-cigarettes during pregnancy often stated that e-cigarettes were less harmful than regular cigarettes (74 percent) and helpful in easing smoking cessation (72 percent). And in a recent study, chronic exposure to e-cigarette aerosols was linked to low birth weight in offspring (Orzabal & others, 2019).

Cocaine Does cocaine use during pregnancy harm the developing embryo and fetus? A research review concluded that cocaine quickly crosses the placenta to reach the fetus (De Giovanni & Marchetti, 2012). The most consistent finding is that cocaine exposure during prenatal development is associated with reduced birth weight, length, and head circumference (Gouin & others, 2011). Also, in other studies, prenatal cocaine exposure has been linked to impaired connectivity of the thalamus and prefrontal cortex in newborns (Salzwedel & others, 2016); impaired motor development at 2 years of age and a slower rate of growth through 10 years of age (Richardson, Goldschmidt, & Willford, 2008); self-regulation problems at age 12 (Minnes & others, 2016); elevated blood pressure at 9 years of age (Shankaran & others, 2010); impaired language development and information processing (Beeghly & others, 2006), including attention deficits (especially impulsivity) (Accornero & others, 2006; Richardson &

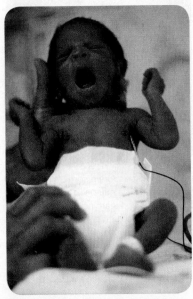

This baby was exposed to cocaine prenatally. *What are some of the possible developmental effects of prenatal exposure to cocaine?*
Chuck Nacke/Alamy Stock Photo

others, 2011); learning disabilities at age 7 (Morrow & others, 2006); increased likelihood of being in a special education program that involves supportive services (Levine & others, 2008); and increased behavioral problems, especially externalizing problems such as high rates of aggression and delinquency (Minnes & others, 2010; Richardson & others, 2011). Further, in a longitudinal study prenatal cocaine exposure was linked to early use of marijuana, arrest history, conduct disorder, and emotion regulation problems at 21 years of age (Richardson & others, 2019).

Some researchers argue that these findings should be interpreted cautiously (Accornero & others, 2006). Why? Because other factors in the lives of pregnant women who use cocaine (such as poverty, malnutrition, and other substance abuse) often cannot be ruled out as possible contributors to the problems found in their children (Hurt & others, 2005; Messiah & others, 2011). For example, cocaine users are more likely than nonusers to smoke cigarettes, use marijuana, drink alcohol, and take amphetamines.

Despite these cautions, the weight of research evidence indicates that children born to mothers who use cocaine are likely to have neurological, medical, and cognitive deficits (Baer & others, 2019; Parcianello & others, 2018; Richardson & others, 2019). Cocaine use by pregnant women is never recommended.

Marijuana An increasing number of studies find that marijuana use by pregnant women also has negative outcomes for offspring (Ruisch & others, 2018). For example, researchers found that prenatal marijuana exposure was related to lower intelligence in children (Goldschmidt & others, 2008). Research reviews concluded that marijuana use during pregnancy alters brain functioning in the fetus (Calvigioni & others, 2014; Jaques & others, 2014). In a recent meta-analysis, marijuana use during pregnancy was linked to offsprings' low birth weight and greater likelihood of being placed in a neonatal intensive care unit (Gunn & others, 2016). In another recent study, newborns born to mothers who used marijuana during pregnancy were more likely to be born preterm or low birth weight (Petrangelo & others, 2019). Also, a recent study found that marijuana use by pregnant women was associated with increased rates of chronic obstructive pulmonary disease in 4-year-old children (Villarreal & others, 2019). Further, another study indicated that prenatal exposure to marijuana was linked to marijuana use at 14 years of age (Day, Goldschmidt, & Thomas, 2006). In sum, marijuana use is not recommended for pregnant women.

Despite increasing evidence of negative outcomes, a recent survey found that marijuana use by pregnant women increased from 2.4 percent in 2002 to 3.85 percent in 2014 (Brown & others, 2016). And there is considerable concern that marijuana use by pregnant women may increase further given the growing number of states that have legalized marijuana (Hennessy, 2018).

Heroin It is well documented that infants whose mothers are addicted to heroin show several behavioral difficulties at birth (Carlier & others, 2020). The difficulties include withdrawal symptoms such as tremors, irritability, abnormal crying, disturbed sleep, and impaired motor control. Many still show behavioral problems at their first birthday, and attention deficits may appear later in development. The most common treatment for heroin addiction, methadone, is associated with very severe withdrawal symptoms in newborns (Lai & others, 2017).

Synthetic Opioids and Opiate-Related Pain Killers An increasing number of women are using synthetic opioids, such as fentanyl, and opiate-related pain relievers obtained legally by prescription (such as OxyContin and Vicodin) during their pregnancy (Clemens-Cope & others, 2019). Infants born to women using these substances during pregnancy are at increased risk for experiencing opioid withdrawal (Harter, 2019; Jantzie & others, 2020). Other possible outcomes for children exposed to these substances are just beginning to be studied (National Institute of Drug Abuse, 2019). Any prolonged use of synthetic opioids and opiate-related pain relievers is not recommended (U.S. Food and Drug Administration, 2019).

Environmental Hazards Many aspects of our modern industrial world can endanger the embryo or fetus. Some specific hazards to the embryo or fetus include radiation, toxic wastes, and other chemical pollutants (McCue & DeNicola, 2019).

X-ray radiation can affect the developing embryo or fetus, especially in the first several weeks after conception, when women do not yet know they are pregnant. Women and their

An explosion at the Chernobyl nuclear power plant in the Ukraine produced radioactive contamination that spread to surrounding areas. Thousands of infants were born with health problems and deformities as a result of the nuclear contamination, including this boy whose right arm did not form. *Other than radioactive contamination, what are some other types of environmental hazards to prenatal development?*
Sergey Guneev/RIA Novosti

physicians should weigh the risk of an X-ray when an actual or potential pregnancy is involved (Rajaraman & others, 2011). However, a routine diagnostic X-ray of a body area other than the abdomen, with the woman's abdomen protected by a lead apron, is generally considered safe (Brent, 2009, 2011).

Environmental pollutants and toxic wastes are also sources of danger to unborn children. Among the dangerous pollutants are carbon monoxide, mercury, and lead, as well as certain fertilizers and pesticides (Ko, Hwang, & Choi, 2019). Such pollutants can cross the placenta from mother to offspring (Piedimonte & Harford, 2020).

Maternal Diseases   Maternal diseases and infections can produce defects in offspring by crossing the placental barrier, or they can cause damage during birth (Koren & Ornoy, 2018). Rubella (German measles) is one disease that can cause prenatal defects. A recent study found that cardiac defects, pulmonary problems, and microcephaly (a condition in which the baby's head is significantly smaller and less developed than normal) were among the most common fetal and neonatal outcomes when pregnant women have rubella (Yazigi & others, 2017). Women who plan to have children should have a blood test before they become pregnant to determine whether they are immune to the disease.

Syphilis (a sexually transmitted infection) is more damaging later in prenatal development—four months or more after conception. Damage to offspring includes stillbirth, eye lesions (which can cause blindness), skin lesions, and congenital syphilis (Braccio, Sharland, & Ladhani, 2016). Penicillin is the only known treatment for syphilis during pregnancy (Moline & Smith, 2016).

Another infection that has received widespread attention is genital herpes. Newborns contract this virus when they are delivered through the birth canal of a mother with genital herpes. About one-third of babies delivered through an infected birth canal die; another one-fourth become brain damaged. If an active case of genital herpes is detected in a pregnant woman close to her delivery date, a cesarean section can be performed (in which the infant is delivered through an incision in the mother's abdomen) to keep the virus from infecting the newborn (Pinninti & Kimberlin, 2013).

AIDS is a sexually transmitted infection that is caused by the human immunodeficiency virus (HIV), which destroys the body's immune system. A mother can infect her offspring with HIV/AIDS in three ways: (1) during gestation across the placenta, (2) during delivery through contact with maternal blood or fluids, and (3) postpartum (after birth) through breast feeding. The transmission of AIDS through breast feeding is especially problematic in many developing countries (UNICEF, 2020). Babies born to HIV-infected mothers can be (1) infected and symptomatic (show HIV symptoms), (2) infected but asymptomatic (not show HIV symptoms), or (3) not infected at all. An infant who is infected and asymptomatic may still develop HIV symptoms through 15 months of age.

The more widespread disease of diabetes, characterized by high levels of sugar in the blood, also affects offspring (Briana & others, 2018). A research review indicated that newborns with physical defects are more likely to have diabetic mothers (Eriksson, 2009). Women who have gestational diabetes also may deliver very large infants (weighing 10 pounds or more), and the infants are at risk for diabetes (Alberico & others, 2014) and cardiovascular disease (Amrithraj & others, 2017). In a recent study, children of mothers who had diabetes during pregnancy were found to have increased rates of early-onset cardiovascular disease in early adulthood (Yu & others, 2019).

Other Parental Factors   So far we have discussed a number of drugs, environmental hazards, maternal diseases, and incompatible blood types that can harm the embryo or fetus. Here we will explore other characteristics of the mother and father that can affect prenatal and child development, including nutrition, age, and emotional states and stress.

Because the fetus depends entirely on its mother for nutrition, it is important for pregnant women to have good nutritional habits. In Kenya, this government clinic provides pregnant women with information about how their diet can influence the health of their fetus and offspring. *What might the information about diet be like?*
Delphine Bousquet/AFP/Getty Images

developmental **connection**

Conditions, Diseases, and Disorders

The greatest incidence of HIV/AIDS is in sub-Saharan Africa, where as many as 30 percent of mothers have HIV; many are unaware that they are infected with the virus. Connect to "Physical Development in Infancy."

Maternal Diet and Nutrition A developing embryo or fetus depends completely on its mother for nutrition, which comes from the mother's blood (Vander Wyst & others, 2020). The nutritional status of the embryo or fetus is determined by the mother's total caloric intake as well as her intake of proteins, vitamins, and minerals. Children born to malnourished mothers are more likely than other children to be malformed.

Maternal obesity adversely affects pregnancy outcomes through increased rates of hypertension, diabetes, respiratory complications, infections, and depression in the mother (Hu & others, 2019). Research indicates that maternal overweight and obesity during pregnancy are associated with increased risk of higher fetal heart rate (Mat Husin & others, 2020), preterm birth, extremely preterm delivery (Meghelli & others, 2020), stillbirth (Gardosi & others, 2013), and the newborn being placed in a neonatal intensive care unit (Minsart & others, 2013). Further, research indicates that maternal obesity during pregnancy is linked to cardiovascular disease and type 2 diabetes in the adolescent and adult offspring of these mothers (Agarwal & others, 2018). And in a recent meta-analysis, offspring of women who were overweight or obese were at increased risk of developing childhood onset diabetes and obesity (Hidayat, Zou, & Shi, 2019). Management of obesity that includes weight loss and increased exercise prior to pregnancy is likely to benefit the mother and the baby. Limiting gestational weight gain to 11 to 20 pounds among pregnant women is likely to improve outcomes for the mother and the child (Simmons, 2011).

One aspect of maternal nutrition that is important for normal prenatal development is folic acid, a B-complex vitamin (American Society for Reproductive Medicine & others, 2019). A study of more than 34,000 women showed that taking folic acid either alone or as part of a multivitamin for at least one year prior to conceiving was linked with a 70 percent lower risk of delivering between 20 and 28 weeks and a 50 percent lower risk of delivering between 28 and 32 weeks (Bukowski & others, 2008). Also, as indicated earlier in the chapter, a lack of folic acid is related to neural tube defects in offspring, such as spina bifida (a defect in the spinal cord) (Li & others, 2020). The U.S. Department of Health and Human Services (2019) recommends that pregnant women consume a minimum of 400 micrograms of folic acid per day (about twice the amount the average woman gets in one day). Orange juice and spinach are examples of foods rich in folic acid.

developmental **connection**
Conditions, Diseases, and Disorders
What are some key factors that influence whether individuals will become obese? Connect to "Physical and Cognitive Development in Early Adulthood."

Maternal Age When possible harmful effects on the fetus and infant are considered, two maternal age groups are of special interest: adolescents and women 35 years of age and older (Gockley & others, 2016; Kingsbury, Plotnikova, & Najman, 2018). The mortality rate of infants born to adolescent mothers is double that of infants born to mothers in their twenties. Adequate prenatal care decreases the probability that a child born to an adolescent girl will have physical problems. However, adolescents are the least likely of women in all age groups to obtain prenatal assistance from clinics and health services.

Advanced maternal age is also linked to risk for adverse pregnancy outcomes (Bergh, Pinborg, & Wennerholm, 2019). When a pregnant woman is older than 35, there is an increased risk that her child will have Down syndrome (Jaruratanasirikul & others, 2017). An individual with *Down syndrome* has distinctive facial characteristics, short limbs, intellectual disability, and motor difficulties. A baby with Down syndrome rarely is born to a mother 16 to 34 years of age. However, when the mother reaches 40 years of age, the probability is slightly over 1 in 100 that a baby born to her will have Down syndrome, and by age 50 it is almost 1 in 10. When mothers are 35 years and older, risks also increase for low birth weight, preterm delivery, and fetal death (Koo & others, 2012; Mbugua Gitau & others, 2009). Also, in a recent study, pregnant women aged 43 years and older were more likely to have infants who were stillborn (Wu & others, 2019). Further, a recent very large-scale U.S. study found that 40-year-old women had a two-fold increased risk of having a stillborn baby, a risk that increased to eight-fold at 55 years of age (Diaz & others, 2020). And in two studies, very advanced maternal age (40 years and older) was linked to adverse perinatal outcomes, including spontaneous abortion, preterm birth, stillbirth, and fetal growth restriction (Traisrisilp & Tongsong, 2015; Waldenstrom & others, 2015). In addition,

What are some of the risks for infants born to adolescent mothers?
Barbara Penoyar/Getty Images

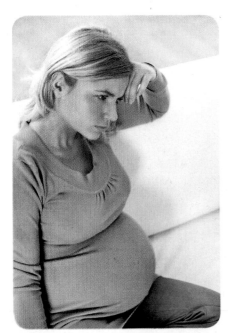

How do pregnant women's emotional states and stress levels affect prenatal development and birth?
Skynesher/E+/Getty Images

advanced maternal age, especially greater than 40 years of age, was linked to increased risk of offspring developing cancer in childhood in two recent studies (Contreras & others, 2017; Wang & others, 2017).

We still have much to learn about the influence of the mother's age on risks of adverse outcomes during pregnancy and childbirth (Bergh, Pinborg, & Wennerholm, 2019). As women remain active, exercise regularly, and are careful about their nutrition, their reproductive systems may remain healthier at older ages than was thought possible in the past.

Emotional States and Stress When a pregnant woman experiences intense fears, anxieties, and other emotions or negative mood states, physiological changes occur that may affect her fetus (Monk & others, 2020; Nazzari & Frigerio, 2020). A mother's stress may also influence the fetus indirectly by increasing the likelihood that the mother will engage in unhealthy behaviors such as taking drugs and receiving poor prenatal care.

High maternal anxiety and stress during pregnancy can have long-term consequences for the offspring (Murray & others, 2019). A research review indicated that pregnant women with high levels of stress are at increased risk for having a child with emotional or cognitive problems, attention deficit hyperactivity disorder (ADHD), and language delay (Taige & others, 2007). Maternal emotions and stress also can influence the fetus indirectly by increasing the likelihood that the mother will engage in unhealthy behaviors such as taking drugs and receiving inadequate prenatal care. Further, a recent research review concluded that regardless of the form of maternal prenatal stress or anxiety and the prenatal trimester in which the stress or anxiety occurred, during the first two years of life their offspring displayed lower levels of self-regulation (Korja & others, 2017). Also, a recent study indicated that higher maternal pregnancy-related anxiety was linked to increased rates of emotional symptoms, peer relationship problems, and overall child difficulties at 4 years of age (Acosta & others, 2019).

And a recent study found that individuals whose mothers reported a higher level of stress during pregnancy had an increased risk of developing psychological disorders, such as mood disorders, later in life (Brannigan & others, 2019).

Depression in expectant mothers can have an adverse effect on birth outcomes and children's development (Park & others, 2018). Maternal depression during pregnancy is linked to preterm birth (Mparmpakas & others, 2013), and to low birth weight in full-term offspring (Chang & others, 2014). Another study revealed that maternal depression during pregnancy was related to increased risk of depression in offspring at age 18 (Pearson & others, 2013). Also, a study found that taking antidepressants early in pregnancy was linked to an increased risk of miscarriage (Almeida & others, 2016). Further, another study revealed that taking antidepressants in the second or third trimesters of pregnancy was linked to an increased risk of autism spectrum disorders in children (Boukhris & others, 2016).

Paternal Factors So far, we have discussed how characteristics of the mother—such as drug use, disease, diet and nutrition, age, and emotional states—can influence prenatal development and the development of the child. Might there also be some paternal risk factors? Indeed, there are several (Mayo & others, 2019; Sigman, 2017). Men's exposure to lead, radiation, certain pesticides, and petrochemicals may cause abnormalities in sperm that lead to miscarriage or to diseases such as childhood cancer (Cordier, 2008). The father's smoking during the mother's pregnancy also can cause problems for the offspring. For example, a recent meta-analysis concluded that paternal smoking before and during pregnancy was linked to increased risk of childhood leukemia (Cao, Lu, & Lu, 2020). Also, a recent research review concluded that tobacco smoking is linked to impaired male fertility, as well as increased DNA damage, aneuploidy (abnormal number of chromosomes in a cell), and mutations in sperm (Beal, Yauk, & Marchetti, 2017). Further, in one study, heavy paternal smoking was associated with increased risk of early pregnancy loss (Venners & others, 2004). This negative outcome may be related to the effects of secondhand smoke. And in another study, paternal smoking around the time of the child's conception was linked to an increased risk of the child developing leukemia (Milne & others, 2012). Researchers have found that increasing paternal age decreases the success rate of in vitro fertilization and increases the risk of preterm birth (Sharma & others, 2015). In addition, a research review concluded that there is an increased risk of spontaneous abortion, autism, and schizophrenic disorders when the father is 40 years of age or older (Reproductive Endocrinology and Infertility Committee & others, 2012). A research study revealed that children born to fathers who were 40 years of age or older had increased risk of developing autism because of higher rates of random gene mutations in the older fathers (Kong & others, 2012). However, the age of the mother was not linked to development of autism in children.

Another way that the father can influence prenatal and birth outcomes is through his relationship with the mother (Braren & others, 2020). By being supportive, helping with chores, and having a positive attitude toward the pregnancy, the father can improve the physical and psychological well-being of the mother. Conversely, a conflictual relationship with the mother is likely to bring adverse outcomes (Molgora & others, 2019). For example, a study found that intimate partner violence increased the mother's stress level (Fonseca-Machado Mde & others, 2015).

In a study in China, the longer fathers smoked, the greater the risk that their children would develop cancer (Ji & others, 1997). *What are some other paternal factors that can influence the development of the fetus and the child?*
Ryan Pyle/Corbis/Getty Images

PRENATAL CARE

Although prenatal care varies enormously, it usually involves a defined schedule of visits for medical care, which typically includes screening for manageable conditions and treatable diseases that can affect the baby or the mother (Darling & others, 2019). In addition to medical care, prenatal programs often include comprehensive educational, social, and nutritional services.

An increasing number of studies are finding that exercise either benefits the mother's health and has positive neonatal outcomes or that there are no differences in outcomes (Mills & others, 2020; Nagpal & others, 2020). Exercise during pregnancy helps prevent constipation, conditions the body, reduces the likelihood of excessive weight gain, lowers the risk of developing hypertension, improves immune system functioning, and is associated with a more positive mental state, including reduced levels of stress and depression (Bacchi & others, 2018; D'Ascenzi & others, 2020). In a recent meta-analysis, yoga was effective in reducing depressive symptoms in pregnant women (Ng & others, 2019). Also, a recent study indicated that pregnant women who exercised regularly during the second and third trimesters gave their quality of life higher ratings than those who did not exercise (Krzepota, Sadowska, & Biernat, 2018).

Exercise during pregnancy can also have positive benefits for offspring. For example, a recent study revealed that regular exercise by pregnant women was linked to more advanced development of the neonatal brain (Laborte-Lemoyne, Currier, & Ellenberg, 2017).

Does prenatal care matter? Information about pregnancy, labor, delivery, and caring for the newborn can be especially valuable for first-time mothers (Liu & others, 2017). Prenatal care is also very important for women in poverty and immigrant women because it links them with other social services (Fabi, 2019; Fabi & Taylor, 2019).

An innovative program that is rapidly expanding in the United States is CenteringPregnancy (Saleh, 2019). This program is relationship-centered and provides complete prenatal care in a group setting. CenteringPregnancy replaces traditional 15-minute physician visits with 90-minute peer group support settings and self-examination led by a physician or certified nurse-midwife. Groups of up to 10 women (and often their partners) meet regularly beginning at 12 to 16 weeks of pregnancy. The sessions emphasize empowering women to play an active role in experiencing a positive pregnancy. Research increasingly shows positive outcomes of CenteringPregnancy for the fetus and child, as well as the mother (Darby-Stewart & Strickland, 2019; Tubay & others, 2019). A recent study large-scale study compared women who had participated in CenteringPregnancy programs with women who had received individual prenatal care at a university medical center (Cunningham & others, 2019). The offspring of women

How might a woman's exercise during pregnancy benefit her and her offspring?
Leszek Glasner/Shutterstock

The increasingly popular CenteringPregnancy program alters routine prenatal care by bringing women out of exam rooms and into relationship-oriented groups.
MBI/Alamy Stock Photo

who participated in CenteringPregnancy were less likely to be born preterm or low birth weight. In another recent study, women who participated in CenteringPregnancy used pain relief less during labor and were more likely to breast feed their infants (Rijnders & others, 2019).

NORMAL PRENATAL DEVELOPMENT

Much of our discussion so far in this chapter has focused on what can go wrong with prenatal development. Prospective parents should take steps to avoid the vulnerabilities to fetal development that we have described. But it is important to keep in mind that most of the time, prenatal development does not go awry, and development occurs along the positive path that we described at the beginning of the chapter.

Review Connect Reflect

 LG1 Describe prenatal development.

Review
- What is the course of prenatal development?
- What is teratology, and what are some of the main threats to prenatal development?
- What are some good prenatal care strategies?
- Why is it important to take a positive approach to prenatal development?

Connect
- We have discussed chromosomal and gene-linked abnormalities that can affect prenatal development. How are the symptoms of the related conditions or risks similar to or different from those caused by teratogens or other hazards?

Reflect *Your Own Personal Journey of Life*
- If you are a woman, imagine that you have just found out that you are pregnant. What health-enhancing strategies will you follow during the prenatal period? If you are not a woman, imagine that you are the partner of a woman who has just found out she is pregnant. What will be your role in increasing the likelihood that the prenatal period will go smoothly?

2 Birth **LG2** Describe the birth process.

| The Birth Process | Assessing the Newborn | Preterm and Low Birth Weight Infants |

Nature writes the basic script for how birth occurs, but parents make important choices about conditions surrounding birth. We look first at the sequence of physical stages that occur when a child is born.

> There was a star danced, and under that I was born.
>
> —**WILLIAM SHAKESPEARE**
> *English playwright, 17th century*

THE BIRTH PROCESS

The birth process occurs in stages, takes place in different contexts, and in most cases involves one or more attendants.

Stages of Birth   The birth process occurs in three stages. The first stage is the longest of the three. Uterine contractions are 15 to 20 minutes apart at the beginning and last up to a minute. These contractions cause the woman's cervix to stretch and open. As the first stage progresses, the contractions come closer together, appearing every two to five minutes. Their intensity increases. By the end of the first birth stage, contractions dilate the cervix to an opening of about 10 centimeters (4 inches), so that the baby can move from the uterus to the birth canal. For a woman having her first child, the first stage lasts an average of 6 to 12 hours; for subsequent children, this stage typically is much shorter.

The second birth stage begins when the baby's head starts to move through the cervix and the birth canal. It terminates when the baby completely emerges from the mother's body. With each contraction, the mother bears down hard to push the baby out of her body. By the time the baby's head is out of the mother's body, the contractions come almost every minute and last for about a minute. This stage typically lasts approximately 45 minutes to an hour.

Afterbirth is the third stage, at which time the placenta, umbilical cord, and other membranes are detached and expelled. This final stage is the shortest of the three birth stages, lasting only minutes.

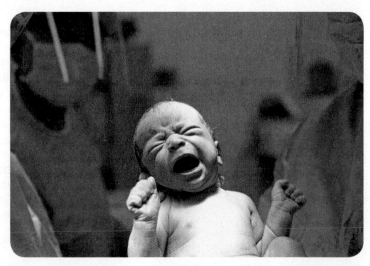

After the long journey of prenatal development, birth takes place. During birth the baby is on a threshold between two worlds. *What is the fetus/newborn transition like?*
ERproductions Ltd/Getty Images

Childbirth Setting and Attendants In 2015 in the United States, 98.5 percent of births took place in hospitals (Martin & others, 2017). Of the 1.5 percent of births occurring outside of a hospital, 63 percent took place in homes and almost 31 percent in free-standing birthing centers. The percentage of U.S. births at home is the highest since reporting of this context began in 1989. This increase in home births has occurred mainly among non-Latino White women, especially those who were older and married. For these non-Latino White women, two-thirds of their home births are attended by a midwife.

The people who help a mother during birth vary across cultures. In U.S. hospitals, it has become the norm for fathers or birth coaches to remain with the mother throughout labor and delivery. In the East African Nigoni culture, by contrast, men are completely excluded from the childbirth process. When a woman is ready to give birth, female relatives move into the woman's hut and the husband leaves, taking his belongings (clothes, tools, weapons, and so on) with him. He is not permitted to return until after the baby is born. In some cultures, childbirth is an open, community affair. For example, in the Pukapukan culture in the Pacific Islands, women give birth in a shelter that is open for villagers to observe.

Midwives *Midwifery* is a profession that provides health care to women during pregnancy, birth, and the postpartum period (Vogels-Broeke, de Vries, & Nieuwenhuijze, 2020). Midwives also may give women information about reproductive health and provide annual gynecological examinations. They may refer women to general practitioners or obstetricians if a pregnant woman needs medical care beyond a midwife's expertise and skill.

Midwifery is practiced in most countries throughout the world (Van Hecke & others, 2019). In Holland, more than 40 percent of babies are delivered by midwives rather than doctors. However, in the United States in 2017 only 9.1 percent of all births in the United States were attended by a midwife (National Center for Health Statistics, 2019). Nonetheless, the 9.1 percent figure represents a substantial increase from less than 1 percent in 1975. A research review concluded that for low-risk women, midwife-led care was characterized by a reduction in procedures during labor and increased satisfaction with care (Sutcliffe & others, 2012). Also, in this study no adverse outcomes were found for midwife-led care compared with physician-led care.

In India, a midwife checks on the size, position, and heartbeat of a fetus. Midwives deliver babies in many countries around the world. *What are some cultural variations in prenatal care?*
Viviane Moos/Corbis Historical/Getty Images

Doulas In some countries, a doula attends a childbearing woman. *Doula* is a Greek word that means "a woman who helps." A **doula** is a caregiver who provides continuous physical, emotional, and educational support for the mother before, during, and after childbirth (Lanning & others, 2019; O'Rourke & others, 2020). Doulas remain with the parents throughout labor, assessing and responding to the mother's needs. Researchers have found positive effects when a doula is present at the birth of a child (Wilson & others, 2017). One study found that

afterbirth The third stage of birth, when the placenta, umbilical cord, and other membranes are detached and expelled.

doula A caregiver who provides continuous physical, emotional, and educational support for the mother before, during, and after childbirth.

doula-assisted mothers were four times less likely to have a low birth weight baby and two times less likely to have experienced a birth complication involving themselves or their baby (Gruber, Cupito, & Dobson, 2013). Another study revealed that for Medicaid recipients the odds of having a cesarean delivery were 41 percent lower for doula-supported births in the United States (Kozhimmanil & others, 2013). Thus, increasing doula-supported births could substantially lower the cost of a birth by reducing cesarean rates.

In the United States, most doulas work as independent providers hired by the expectant parents. Doulas typically function as part of a "birthing team," serving as an adjunct to the midwife or the hospital's obstetrical staff.

Methods of Childbirth   U.S. hospitals often allow the mother and her obstetrician a range of options regarding the method of delivery (Hockenberry & Wilson, 2019). Key choices involve the use of medication, whether to use any of a number of nonmedicated techniques to reduce pain, and when to have a cesarean delivery.

Medication   Three basic kinds of drugs that are used for labor are analgesia, anesthesia, and oxytocin/Pitocin.

Analgesia is used to relieve pain. Analgesics include tranquilizers, barbiturates, and narcotics (such as Demerol).

Anesthesia is used in late first-stage labor and during delivery to block sensation in an area of the body or to block consciousness. There is a trend toward not using general anesthesia, which blocks consciousness, in normal births because general anesthesia can be transmitted through the placenta to the fetus (Edwards & Jackson, 2017). An *epidural block* is regional anesthesia that numbs the woman's body from the waist down. A research review concluded that epidural analgesia provides effective pain relief but increases the likelihood of having to use instruments during vaginal birth (Jones & others, 2012). Researchers are continuing to explore safer drug mixtures for use at lower doses to improve the effectiveness and safety of epidural anesthesia (Turner, Flatley, & Kumar, 2020).

Oxytocin is a hormone that promotes uterine contractions; a synthetic form called Pitocin® is widely used to decrease the duration of the first stage of labor. The relative benefits and risks of administering synthetic forms of oxytocin during childbirth continue to be debated (Carlson, Corwin, & Lowe, 2017).

Predicting how a drug will affect an individual woman and her fetus is difficult (Ansari & others, 2016). A particular drug might have only a minimal effect on one fetus yet have a much stronger effect on another. The drug's dosage also is a factor (Rankin, 2017). Stronger doses of tranquilizers and narcotics given to decrease the mother's pain potentially have a more negative effect on the fetus than mild doses. It is important for the mother to assess her level of pain and have a voice in deciding whether she receives medication.

Natural and Prepared Childbirth   For a brief time not long ago, the idea of avoiding all medication during childbirth gained favor in the United States. Instead, many women chose to reduce the pain of childbirth through techniques known as natural childbirth and prepared childbirth. Today, at least some medication is used in the typical childbirth, but elements of natural childbirth and prepared childbirth remain popular (Skowronski, 2015).

Natural childbirth is the method that aims to reduce the mother's pain by decreasing her fear by providing information about childbirth and teaching her and her partner to use breathing methods and relaxation techniques during delivery (Chen & Tan, 2019). One type of natural childbirth that is used today is the *Bradley Method,* which involves husbands as coaches, relaxation for easier birth, and prenatal nutrition and exercise.

French obstetrician Ferdinand Lamaze developed a method similar to natural childbirth that is known as **prepared childbirth,** or the Lamaze method. It includes a special breathing technique to control pushing in the final stages of labor, as well as more detailed education about anatomy and physiology. The Lamaze method has become very popular in the United States (Podgurski, 2016). The pregnant woman's partner usually serves as a coach who attends childbirth classes with her and helps with her breathing and relaxation during delivery.

natural childbirth This method of childbirth attempts to reduce the mother's pain by decreasing her fear through information about childbirth and instruction in relaxation techniques designed to reduce pain during delivery.

prepared childbirth Developed by French obstetrician Ferdinand Lamaze, this childbirth strategy is similar to natural childbirth but includes a special breathing technique to control pushing in the final stages of labor and a more detailed anatomy and physiology course.

An instructor conducts a Lamaze class. *What characterizes the Lamaze method?*
Stockbroker/MBI/Alamy Stock Photo

In sum, proponents of current natural and prepared childbirth methods conclude that when information and support are provided, women know how to give birth. To read about one nurse whose research focuses on fatigue during childbearing and breathing exercises during labor, see the *Connecting with Careers* profile. And to read about the wide variety of techniques now being used to reduce stress and control pain during labor, see *Connecting Development to Life*.

Cesarean Delivery   In a **cesarean delivery,** the baby is removed from the mother's uterus through an incision made in her abdomen. Cesarean deliveries are performed if the baby is lying crosswise in the uterus, if the baby's head is too large to pass through the mother's pelvis, if the baby develops complications, or if the mother is bleeding vaginally. Because of increased rates of respiratory complications, elective cesarean delivery is not recommended prior to 39 weeks of gestation unless there is an indication of fetal lung maturity (Greene, 2009).

The benefits and risks of cesarean deliveries continue to be debated in the United States and around the world (Bernitz & others, 2019; Visser & others, 2020). Some critics believe that too many babies are delivered by cesarean delivery in the United States (Blakey, 2011). The World Health Organization states that a country's delivery section rate should be 10 to 15 percent. The U.S. cesarean birth rate peaked at 28.1 percent of all births in 2009 and has since dropped to 25.9 in 2018 (Centers for Disease Control and Prevention, 2019).

What are some of the specific reasons why physicians do a cesarean delivery? The most common reasons are failure to progress through labor (hindered by epidurals, for example) and fetal distress. Normally, the baby's head comes through the vagina first. But if the baby is in a **breech position,** the baby's buttocks are the first part to emerge from the vagina. In 1 of every 25 deliveries, the baby's head is still in the uterus when the rest of the body is out. Breech births can cause respiratory problems. As a result, if the baby is in a breech position, a cesarean delivery is usually performed (Schmidt & others, 2019).

ASSESSING THE NEWBORN

Almost immediately after birth, after the baby and its parents have been introduced, a newborn is taken to be weighed, cleaned up, and tested for signs of developmental problems that might require urgent attention (Faranoff, 2020). The **Apgar Scale** is widely used to assess the health of newborns at *one* and *five* minutes after birth. The Apgar Scale evaluates an infant's heart rate, respiratory effort, muscle tone, body color, and reflex irritability. An obstetrician or a nurse does the evaluation and gives the newborn a score, or reading, of 0, 1, or 2 on each of these five health signs (see Figure 6). A total score of 7 to 10 indicates that the newborn's condition is good. A score of 5 indicates there may be developmental difficulties. A score of 3 or below signals an emergency and indicates that the baby might not survive.

cesarean delivery Surgical procedure in which the baby is removed from the mother's uterus through an incision made in her abdomen.

breech position The baby's position in the uterus that causes the buttocks to be the first part to emerge from the vagina.

Apgar Scale A widely used method of assessing the health of newborns at one and five minutes after birth. The Apgar Scale evaluates an infant's heart rate, respiratory effort, muscle tone, body color, and reflex irritability.

From Waterbirth to Music Therapy

The effort to reduce stress and control pain during labor has recently led to an increased use of older and newer nonmedicated techniques (Cooper, Warland, & McCutcheon, 2018; L. Lewis & others, 2018a, b). These include waterbirth, massage, acupuncture, hypnosis, and music therapy.

Waterbirth

Waterbirth involves giving birth in a tub of warm water. Some women go through labor in the water and get out for delivery; others remain in the water for delivery. The rationale for waterbirth is that the baby has been in an amniotic sac for many months and being delivered into a similar environment is likely to be less stressful for the baby and the mother (Kavosi & others, 2015). Mothers get into the warm water when contractions become closer together and more intense. Getting into the water too soon can cause labor to slow or stop. An increasing number of studies either show no differences in neonatal and maternal outcomes for waterbirth and non-waterbirth deliveries or positive outcomes for waterbirth (Davies & others, 2015; Hodgson, Comfort, & Albert, 2020; Taylor & others, 2016). For example, in a recent Swedish study, women who gave birth in water had a lower risk of vaginal tears, made quicker progress through the second stage of labor, needed fewer drugs for pain relief and interventions for medical problems, and rated their birth experience more positively than women who had conventional spontaneous vaginal births (Ulfsdottir, Saltvedt, & Georgsson, 2018). Waterbirth has been practiced more often in European countries such as Switzerland and Sweden in recent decades than in the United States but is increasingly being included in U.S. birth plans. Also, in a recent U.S. study of almost 27,000 births, women who gave birth in water had more favorable outcomes, including fewer prolonged first- and second-stage labors and less hemorrhaging (Snapp & others, 2020). In the same study, newborns born in water were less likely be admitted to a NICU, had fewer fetal heart rate abnormalities, and had lower rates of respiratory complications.

Massage

Massage is increasingly used prior to and during delivery (Withers, Kharazmi, & Lim, 2018). Researchers have found that massage therapy reduces pain during labor (Gallo & others, 2018). For example, a recent study found that lower back massage reduced women's labor pain and increased their satisfaction with the birth experience (Unalmis Erdogan, Yanikkerem, & Goker, 2017). In another recent study, one hour of Thai traditional massage decreased the duration of the first and second stages of labor (Sananpanichkul & others, 2019).

What characterizes the use of waterbirth in delivering a baby?
Courtesy of Dr. Holly Beckwith

Acupuncture

Acupuncture, the insertion of very fine needles into specific locations in the body, is used as a standard procedure to reduce the pain of childbirth in China, although it only recently has begun to be used in the United States for this purpose (Jo & Lee, 2018; Mollart & others, 2018). Recent research indicates that acupuncture can have positive effects on labor and delivery (Smith, Armour, & Ee, 2016). For example, in a recent study acupuncture was successful in reducing labor pain 30 minutes after the intervention (Allameh, Tehrani, & Ghasemi, 2015).

Hypnosis

Hypnosis, the induction of a psychological state of altered attention and awareness in which the individual is unusually responsive to suggestions, is also increasingly being used during childbirth (Mollart & others, 2018). Some studies have indicated positive effects of hypnosis for reducing pain during childbirth (Madden & others, 2016; McAllister & others, 2017).

Music Therapy

Music therapy during childbirth, which involves the use of music to reduce stress and manage pain, is becoming more common (Dehcheshmeh & Rafiel, 2015). More research is needed to determine its effectiveness (Azizmohammadi & Azizmohammadi, 2019).

What are some reasons that natural childbirth methods such as these might be chosen instead of medication?

Score	0	1	2
Heart rate	Absent	Slow—less than 100 beats per minute	Fast—100–140 beats per minute
Respiratory effort	No breathing for more than one minute	Irregular and slow	Good breathing with normal crying
Muscle tone	Limp and flaccid	Weak, inactive, but some flexion of extremities	Strong, active motion
Body color	Blue and pale	Body pink, but extremities blue	Entire body pink
Reflex irritability	No response	Grimace	Coughing, sneezing and crying

FIGURE 6

THE APGAR SCALE. A newborn's score on the Apgar Scale indicates whether the baby has urgent medical problems. *What are some trends in the Apgar scores of U.S. babies?*

The Apgar Scale is especially good at assessing the newborn's ability to cope with the stress of delivery and the demands of a new environment (Edwards & Coyne, 2020). It also identifies high-risk infants who need resuscitation. One study revealed that compared with children who have a high Apgar score (9 to 10), the risk of developing attention deficit hyperactivity disorder (ADHD) in childhood was 75 percent higher for newborns with a low Apgar score (1 to 4) and 63 percent higher for newborns with an Apgar score of 5 to 6 (Li & others, 2011). Recent studies have found that low Apgar scores are associated with long-term needs for additional support in education and decreased educational attainment (Tweed & others, 2016), increased risk of developmental vulnerability at 5 years of age (Razaz & others, 2016), and increased risk of developing ADHD (Hanc & others, 2018).

Another assessment of the newborn is the **Brazelton Neonatal Behavioral Assessment Scale (NBAS)**, named after American pediatrician T. Berry Brazelton (1918–2018). The NBAS typically is performed 24 to 36 hours after birth. It is also used as a sensitive index of *neurological competence* up to one month after birth for typical infants and as a measure in many studies of infant development (Barbosa & others, 2018). The NBAS assesses the newborn's neurological development, reflexes, and reactions to people and objects.

The NBAS is designed to assess normal, healthy, full-term infants. An "offspring" of the NBAS, the **Neonatal Intensive Care Unit Network Neurobehavioral Scale (NNNS)** provides another assessment of the newborn's behavior, neurological and stress responses, and regulatory capacities (Dorner & others, 2020; Hofheimer & others, 2020; Provenzi & others, 2019). The NBAS is especially designed to assess at-risk infants.

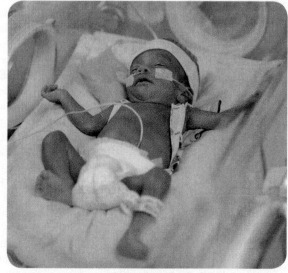

A "kilogram kid," weighing less than 2.3 pounds at birth. *What are some long-term outcomes for weighing so little at birth?*
Andresr/E+/Getty Images

Brazelton Neonatal Behavioral Assessment Scale (NBAS) A measure that is used in the first month of life to assess the newborn's neurological development, reflexes, and reactions to people and objects.

Neonatal Intensive Care Unit Network Neurobehavioral Scale (NNNS) An "offspring" of the NBAS, the NNNS provides an assessment of the newborn's behavior, neurological and stress responses, and regulatory capacities.

PRETERM AND LOW BIRTH WEIGHT INFANTS

Various conditions that pose threats for newborns have been given different labels. We will examine these conditions and discuss interventions for improving outcomes of preterm infants.

Preterm and Small for Date Infants Three related conditions pose threats to many newborns: low birth weight, being born preterm, and being small for date:

- **Low birth weight infants** weigh less than 5 pounds 8 ounces at birth. *Very low birth weight* newborns weigh less than 3 pounds 4 ounces, and *extremely low birth weight* newborns weigh less than 2 pounds 3 ounces.
- **Preterm infants** are those born three weeks or more before the pregnancy has reached its full term—in other words, 35 or fewer weeks after conception.
- **Small for date infants** (also called *small for gestational age infants*) are those whose birth weight is below normal when the length of the pregnancy is considered. They weigh less than 90 percent of all babies of the same gestational age. Small for date infants may be preterm or full term. One study found that small for date infants had more than a fourfold increased risk of death (Regev & others, 2003).

low birth weight infants Infants that weigh less than 5 pounds 8 ounces at birth.

preterm infants Those born before the completion of 37 weeks of gestation (the time between fertilization and birth).

small for date infants Also called small for gestational age infants, these infants' birth weights are below normal when the length of pregnancy is considered. Small for date infants may be preterm or full term.

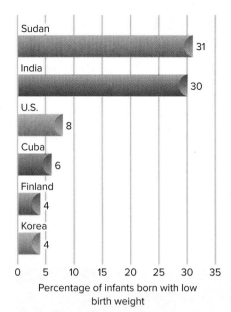

FIGURE 7

PERCENTAGE OF INFANTS BORN WITH LOW BIRTH WEIGHT IN SELECTED COUNTRIES

developmental **connection**

Poverty

Poverty continues to negatively affect development throughout childhood. Connect to "Socioemotional Development in Early Childhood" and "Socioemotional Development in Middle and Late Childhood."

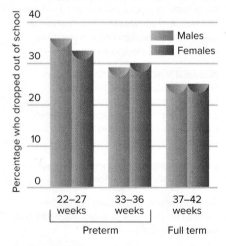

FIGURE 8

PERCENTAGE OF PRETERM AND FULL-TERM INFANTS WHO DROPPED OUT OF SCHOOL

In 2017, 9.9 percent of U.S. infants were born preterm—a significant increase since the 1980s (March of Dimes, 2018). The preterm birth rate was 9.1 percent for non-Latino White infants, down from 11.4 percent in 2011 (Centers for Disease Control and Prevention, 2018). In 2017, the preterm birth rate was 13.8 percent for African American infants (down from 16.7 percent in 2011) and 9.6 percent for Latino infants (down from 11.6 percent in 2011).

Recently, considerable attention has been directed to the role that progestin (a synthetic hormone similar to progesterone) might play in reducing preterm births (Mesiano & others, 2019). One study found that progestin treatment was associated with a decrease in preterm birth for women with a history of one or more spontaneous births (Markham & others, 2014). Increasing use of progestin and decreasing rates of smoking are among the factors that likely account for the recent decrease in preterm births (Schoen & others, 2015).

Might exercise during pregnancy reduce the likelihood of preterm birth? One study found that compared with sedentary pregnant women, women who engaged in light leisure-time physical activity had a 24 percent reduced likelihood of preterm delivery and those who participated in moderate to heavy leisure-time physical activity had a 66 percent reduced risk of preterm delivery (Hegaard & others, 2008). Also, a recent research review concluded that pregnant women's exercise was linked to a lower incidence of preterm birth (Matei & others, 2019). Further, a recent study revealed that a daily exercise program once a day for 30 days improved the bone density and cortisol levels of preterm infants with very low birth weights (Sezer Efe, Erdem, & Gunes, 2020).

The incidence of low birth weight varies considerably from country to country. In some countries, such as India and Sudan, where poverty is rampant and the health and nutrition of mothers are poor, the percentage of low birth weight babies reaches as high as 31 percent (see Figure 7). In the United States, there has been an increase in low birth weight infants in the last two decades, and the U.S. low birth weight rate of 8.3 percent in 2018 is considerably higher than that of many other developed countries (Centers for Disease Control and Prevention, 2018). For example, only 4 percent of the infants born in Sweden, Finland, Norway, and South Korea are low birth weight, and only 5 percent of those born in New Zealand, Australia, and France are low birth weight. As with preterm birth, ethnic variations characterize low birth weight, with 13.9 percent of African American babies born low birth weight compared to 7.4 percent of Latino infants and 7.0 percent of non-Latino White infants (Centers for Disease Control and Prevention, 2018).

In both developed and developing countries, adolescents who give birth when their bodies have not fully matured are at increased risk for having low birth weight babies (Bird & others, 2017). In the United States, the increased number of low birth weight infants in recent years is attributed to factors such as drug use, poor nutrition, multiple births, reproductive technologies, and improved technology and prenatal care that result in more high-risk babies surviving (National Center for Health Statistics, 2019). Poverty also continues to be a major factor in preterm births in the United States (Bublitz, Carpenter, & Bourjeily, 2020; Cubbin & others, 2020). Women living in poverty are more likely to be obese, have diabetes and hypertension, and to smoke cigarettes and use illicit drugs, and less likely to receive regular prenatal care (Timmermans & others, 2011).

Consequences of Preterm Birth and Low Birth Weight Although most preterm and low birth weight infants are healthy, as a group they have more health problems and developmental delays than normal birth weight infants (Cheong & others, 2020; Shaw, Herbers, & Cutuli, 2019). For preterm birth, the terms *extremely preterm* and *very preterm* are increasingly used (Ohlin & others, 2015). *Extremely preterm infants* are those born at less than 28 weeks gestation, and *very preterm infants* are those born at less than 33 weeks of gestational age. Figure 8 shows the results of a Norwegian study indicating that the earlier preterm infants are born, the more likely they are to drop out of school (Swamy, Ostbye, & Skjaerven, 2008).

The number and severity of health problems increase when infants are born very early and very small (Medina-Alva & others, 2019). Survival rates for these infants have risen, but with this improved survival rate have come an increased rate of severe brain damage (Rogers & Hintz, 2018); lower level of executive function, especially in working memory and planning (Burnett & others, 2018); and lower level of intelligence (Jaekel & others, 2019).

In a recent national study of 6- to 11-year-old U.S. children, those born preterm had higher rates of developmental delay, intellectual disability, speech/language disorder, learning disability, and ADHD (Kelly & Li, 2019). In another recent study, children who were born very preterm had lower achievement scores in math, reading, and spelling than their full-term counterparts in elementary school (Twilhaar & others, 2019). Approximately 50 percent of all low birth weight children are enrolled in special education programs.

Nurturing Low Birth Weight and Preterm Infants   Two increasingly used interventions in the neonatal intensive care unit (NICU) are kangaroo care and massage therapy. **Kangaroo care** involves skin-to-skin contact in which the baby, wearing only a diaper, is held upright against the parent's bare chest, much as a baby kangaroo is carried by its mother (Sohail & others, 2019). Kangaroo care is typically practiced for two to three hours per day, skin-to-skin over an extended time in early infancy.

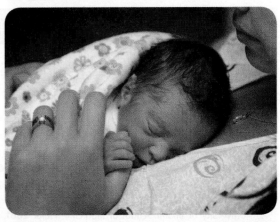

A new mother practices kangaroo care. *What is kangaroo care?*
Casenbina/iStockphoto

Why use kangaroo care with preterm infants? Preterm infants often have difficulty coordinating their breathing and heart rate, and the close physical contact with the parent provided by kangaroo care can help to stabilize the preterm infant's heartbeat, temperature, and breathing (El-Farrash & others, 2020). Preterm infants who experience kangaroo care gain more weight than their counterparts who are not given this care (Sharma, Murki, & Oleti, 2018). Recent research also revealed that kangaroo care decreased pain in newborns (Johnston & others, 2017) and promoted earlier breast feeding with preterm and low birth weight infants (Mekonnen, Yehualashet, & Bayleyegn, 2019). Also, a research study demonstrated positive long-term benefits of kangaroo care (Feldman, Rosenthal, & Eidelman, 2014). In this study, maternal-newborn kangaroo care with preterm infants was linked to better respiratory and cardiovascular functioning, sleep patterns, and cognitive functioning from 6 months to 10 years of age. And in a longitudinal study, the positive effects of kangaroo care with preterm and low birth weight infants that were initially found for intelligence and home environment at 1 year of age were still positive 20 years later in emerging adults' reduced school absenteeism, reduced hyperactivity, lower aggressiveness, and better social skills (Charpak & others, 2017). Further, in a large-scale experimental study in India, low birth weight infants were randomly assigned to receive kangaroo care or standard care (Mazumder & others, 2019). The low birth weight infants who receive kangaroo care had a higher survival rate in the first month of life as well as at 180 days after being born.

A survey conducted in the United States found that mothers were much more likely to have a positive view of kangaroo care and to believe it should be provided daily than were neonatal intensive care nurses (Hendricks-Munoz & others, 2013). There is concern that kangaroo care is not used as often as it could be used in neonatal intensive care units (NICUs) (Almazan & others, 2019; Stadd & others, 2020). Increasingly, kangaroo care is recommended as standard practice for all newborns (Maniago, Almazan, & Albougami, 2020).

Many adults will attest to the therapeutic effects of receiving a massage. In fact, many will pay a premium to receive one at a spa on a regular basis. But can massage play a role in improving the developmental outcomes of preterm infants? A study found that both kangaroo care and massage therapy were equally effective in improving body weight and reducing length of hospital stay for low birth weight infants (Rangey & Sheth, 2014). In another study, massage therapy improved the scores of HIV-exposed infants on both physical and mental scales, while also improving their hearing and speech (Perez & others, 2015). Also, just as with kangaroo care, there is concern that massage therapy is not being used nearly as often as it should be in the NICU. In a recent research review, infant massage of preterm infants in the NICU was associated with shorter length of stay, reduced pain, improved weight gain, and better weight gain (Pados & McGlothen-Bell, 2019). Also in this review, parents who performed massage on their preterm infants in the NICU reported experiencing less stress, anxiety, and depression. Most research studies in the area involve massage therapy provided by nurses, but a recent study also found that parents trained in massage therapy who then conducted the therapy for two weeks improved the weight, height, and head circumference of their preterm infants (Zhang & Wang, 2019). To read more about massage therapy, see *Connecting Through Research*.

developmental connection
Attachment
A classic study with surrogate cloth and wire monkeys demonstrated the important role that touch plays in infant attachment. Connect to "Socioemotional Development in Infancy."

kangaroo care Treatment for preterm infants that involves skin-to-skin contact.

How Does Massage Therapy Affect the Mood and Behavior of Babies?

Throughout history and in many cultures, caregivers have massaged infants. In Africa and Asia, infants are routinely massaged by parents or other family members for several months after birth. In the United States, interest in using touch and massage to improve the growth, health, and well-being of infants has been stimulated by the research of Tiffany Field, director of the Touch Research Institute at the University of Miami School of Medicine (Field, 2001, 2007, 2010b, 2017a, b, 2019; Diego, Field, & Hernandez-Reif, 2008, 2014; Field, Diego, & Hernandez-Reif, 2008, 2010; Field & others, 2006).

In one study, preterm infants in a neonatal intensive care unit (NICU) were randomly assigned to a massage therapy group or a control group (Hernandez-Reif, Diego, & Field, 2007). For five consecutive days, the preterm infants in the massage group were given three 15-minute moderate-pressure massages. Behavioral observations of the following stress behaviors were made on the first and last days of the study: crying, grimacing, yawning, sneezing, jerky arm and leg movements, startles, and finger flaring. The various stress behaviors were summarized in a composite stress behavior index. As indicated in Figure 9, massage had a stress-reducing effect on the preterm infants, which is especially important because they encounter numerous stressors while they are hospitalized.

In a research review of massage therapy with preterm infants, Field and her colleagues (Field, Hernandez-Reif, & Freedman, 2004) concluded that the most consistent findings involve two positive results: (1) increased weight gain and (2) discharge from the hospital three to six days earlier.

Infants are not the only ones who may benefit from massage therapy (Field, 2017b). In other studies, Field and her colleagues have demonstrated the benefits of massage therapy with women in reducing labor pain (Field, Hernandez-Reif, Taylor, & others, 1997), with children who have asthma (Field, Henteleff, & others, 1998), with autistic children's attentiveness (Field, Lasko, & others, 1997), and with adolescents who have attention deficit hyperactivity disorder (Field, Quintino, & others, 1998).

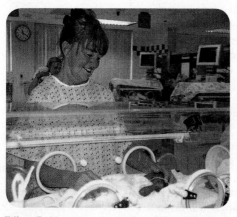

Tiffany Field massages a newborn infant. *What types of infants has massage therapy been shown to help?*
Courtesy of Dr. Tiffany Field

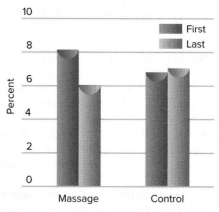

FIGURE 9

PRETERM INFANTS SHOW REDUCED STRESS BEHAVIORS AND ACTIVITY AFTER FIVE DAYS OF MASSAGE THERAPY
Source: M. Hernandez-Reif, M. Diego, & T. Field (2007). Preterm infants show reduced stress behaviors and activity after five days of massage therapy. *Infant Behavior and Development, 30,* 557–561.

Review *Connect* Reflect

 Describe the birth process.

Review
- What are the three main stages of birth? What are some examples of birth strategies? What is the transition from fetus to newborn like for infants?
- What are three measures of neonatal health and responsiveness?
- What are the outcomes for children if they are born preterm or at a low birth weight?

Connect
- What correlations have been found between birth weight and country of birth, and what might the causes be?

Reflect *Your Own Personal Journey of Life*
- If you are a female, which birth strategy do you prefer? Why? If you are a male, how involved would you want to be in helping your partner during the birth of your baby? Explain.

3 The Postpartum Period **LG3** Explain the changes that take place in the postpartum period.

Physical Adjustments   Emotional and Psychological Adjustments   Bonding

The weeks after childbirth present challenges for many new parents and their offspring. This is the **postpartum period,** the period after childbirth or delivery that lasts for about six weeks or until the mother's body has completed its adjustment and has returned to a nearly prepregnant state. It is a time when the woman adjusts, both physically and psychologically, to the process of childbearing.

The postpartum period involves a great deal of adjustment and adaptation (Zdolska-Wawrzkiewicz & others, 2019). The adjustments needed are physical, emotional, and psychological.

PHYSICAL ADJUSTMENTS

A woman's body makes numerous physical adjustments in the first days and weeks after childbirth (Tosun Guleroglu, Mucuk, & Ozgurluk, 2020). She may have a great deal of energy or feel exhausted and let down. Though these changes are normal, the fatigue can undermine the new mother's sense of well-being and confidence in her ability to cope with a new baby and a new family life (Henderson, Alderdice, & Redshaw, 2019).

A concern is the loss of sleep that the primary caregiver experiences in the postpartum period (Paul & Corwin, 2019). In the 2007 Sleep in America survey, a substantial percentage of women reported loss of sleep during pregnancy and in the postpartum period (National Sleep Foundation, 2007) (see Figure 10). The loss of sleep can contribute to stress, marital conflict, and impaired decision making (Meerlo, Sgoifo, & Suchecki, 2008). In a recent study, worsening or minimal improvement in sleep problems from 6 weeks to 7 months postpartum were associated with an increase in depressive symptoms (Lewis & others, 2018).

After delivery, a mother's body undergoes sudden and dramatic changes in hormone production. When the placenta is delivered, estrogen and progesterone levels drop steeply and remain low until the ovaries start producing hormones again.

EMOTIONAL AND PSYCHOLOGICAL ADJUSTMENTS

Emotional fluctuations are common for mothers in the postpartum period. For some women, emotional fluctuations decrease within several weeks after the delivery, but other women experience more long-lasting emotional swings (Wilson, Lee, & Bei, 2019).

As shown in Figure 11, about 70 percent of new mothers in the United States have what are called the postpartum blues. About two to three days after birth, they begin to feel depressed, anxious, and upset. These feelings may come and go for several months after the birth, often peaking about three to five days after birth. Even without treatment, these feelings usually go away after one or two weeks.

However, some women develop **postpartum depression,** which involves a major depressive episode that typically occurs about four weeks after delivery. Women with postpartum depression have such strong feelings of sadness, anxiety, or despair that for at least a two-week period they have trouble coping with their daily tasks (Holopainen & Hakulinen, 2019). Without treatment, postpartum depression may become worse and last for many months (Moustafa & others, 2020). And many women with postpartum depression don't seek help. For example, one study found that 15 percent of the women surveyed had postpartum depression symptoms but less than half had sought help (McGarry & others, 2009). Estimates indicate that 10 to 14 percent of new mothers experience postpartum depression.

A research review concluded that the following conditions are risk factors for developing postpartum depression: a history of depression, depression and anxiety during pregnancy, neuroticism, low self-esteem, postpartum blues, poor marital relationship, and a low level of social support (O'Hara & McCabe, 2013). And a recent study revealed that women who had

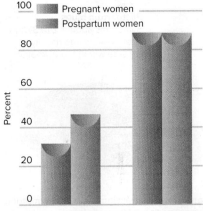

FIGURE **10**

SLEEP DEPRIVATION IN PREGNANT AND POSTPARTUM WOMEN

postpartum period The period after childbirth when the mother adjusts, both physically and psychologically, to the effects of childbirth. This period lasts for about six weeks or until her body has completed its adjustment and returned to a near prepregnant state.

postpartum depression A condition experienced by women who have such strong feelings of sadness, anxiety, or despair that they have trouble coping with daily tasks during the postpartum period.

Diane Sanford, Clinical Psychologist and Postpartum Expert

Diane Sanford has a doctorate in clinical psychology, and for many years she had a private practice that focused on marital and family relationships. But after she began collaborating with a psychiatrist whose clients included women with postpartum depression, Dr. Sanford, along with a women's health nurse, founded Women's Healthcare Partnership in St. Louis, Missouri, which specialized in women's adjustment during the postpartum period. Sanford (with Ann Dunnewold) authored *Life Will Never Be the Same: The Real Mom's Postpartum Survival Guide.* She also is a medical expert for BabyCenter.com.

Diane Sanford is a leading expert on postpartum depression.
Courtesy of Dr. Diane Sanford

For more information about what clinical psychologists do, see the Careers in Life-Span Development appendix.

Postpartum blues
Symptoms appear 2 to 3 days after delivery and usually subside within 1 to 2 weeks.

70%

10%   20%

Postpartum depression   **No symptoms**
Symptoms linger for weeks or months and interfere with daily functioning.

FIGURE 11

POSTPARTUM BLUES AND POSTPARTUM DEPRESSION AMONG U.S. WOMEN. Some health professionals refer to the postpartum period as the "fourth trimester." Though the time span of the postpartum period does not necessarily cover three months, the term "fourth trimester" suggests the continuity and the importance of the first several months after birth for the mother and baby.

a history of depression were 20 times more likely to develop postpartum depression than women who had no history of depression (Silverman & others, 2017).

Several antidepressant drugs are effective in treating postpartum depression and appear to be safe for breast-feeding women (Stewart & Vigod, 2019). Psychotherapy, especially cognitive therapy, is effective in easing postpartum depression for many women (Van Lieshout & others, 2020). Also, engaging in regular exercise may help in treating postpartum depression (Gobinath & others, 2018). For example, a recent meta-analysis concluded that physical exercise during the postpartum period is a safe strategy to reduce postpartum depressive symptoms (Poyatos-Leon & others, 2017).

A mother's postpartum depression can affect the way she interacts with her infant (Kleinman & Reizer, 2018). A research review concluded that the interaction difficulties of depressed mothers and their infants occur across cultures and socioeconomic status groups, and encompass less sensitivity of the mothers and less responsiveness on the part of their infants (Field, 2010a). Several caregiving activities also are compromised, including feeding (especially breast feeding), sleep routines, and safety practices. In a recent study, postpartum depression was associated with an increase in 4-month-old infants' unintentional injuries (Yamaoka, Fujiwara, & Tamiya, 2016). Further, a recent study revealed that mothers' postpartum depression, but not generalized anxiety, were linked to their children's emotional negativity and behavior problems at 2 years of age (Prenoveau & others, 2017). To read about one individual who specializes in women's adjustment during the postpartum period, see *Connecting with Careers.*

Fathers also undergo considerable adjustment in the postpartum period, even when they work away from home all day. When the mother develops postpartum depression, many fathers also experience feelings of depression (O'Brien, Chesla, & Humphreys, 2019). Many fathers feel that the baby comes first and gets all of the mother's attention; some feel that they have been replaced by the baby. In a recent meta-analysis, the prevalence of postpartum depression in fathers was 9 percent within the first month after birth and 8 percent 1 to 3 months after birth (Rao & others, 2020). Also, a recent Japanese study found that 11.2 percent of fathers had depressive symptoms at one month following delivery (Nishigori & others, 2020). In another recent study, fathers with postpartum depression had lower levels of responsiveness, mood, and sensitivity when interacting with their infants (Koch & others, 2019).

The father's support and caring can play a role in whether the mother develops postpartum depression (Kumar, Oliffe, & Kelly, 2018). One study revealed that higher support by fathers was related to a lower incidence of postpartum depression in women (Smith & Howard, 2008). Another study found that depressive symptoms in both the mother and father were associated with impaired bonding with their infant during the postpartum period (Kerstis & others, 2016).

BONDING

A special component of the parent-infant relationship is **bonding,** the formation of a connection, especially a physical bond between parents and the newborn in the period shortly after birth. Sometimes hospitals seem determined to deter bonding. Drugs given to the mother to make her delivery less painful can make the mother drowsy, interfering with her ability to respond to and stimulate the newborn. Mothers and newborns are often separated shortly after delivery, and preterm infants are isolated from their mothers even more than full-term infants.

Do these practices do any harm? Some physicians believe that during the period shortly after birth, the parents and newborn need to form an emotional attachment as a foundation for optimal development in years to come (Kennell, 2006; Kennell & McGrath, 1999). Is there evidence that close contact between mothers and babies in the first several days after birth is critical for optimal development later in life? Although some research supports this bonding hypothesis (Klaus & Kennell, 1976), a body of research challenges the significance of the first few days of life as a critical period (Bakeman & Brown, 1980; Rode & others, 1981). Indeed, the extreme form of the bonding hypothesis—that the newborn must have close contact with the mother in the first few days of life to develop optimally—simply is not true.

Nonetheless, the weakness of the bonding hypothesis should not be used as an excuse to keep motivated mothers from interacting with their newborns. Such contact brings pleasure to many mothers. In some mother-infant pairs—including preterm infants, adolescent mothers, and mothers from disadvantaged circumstances—early close contact may establish a climate for improved interaction after the mother and infant leave the hospital.

Many hospitals now offer a *rooming-in* arrangement, in which the baby remains in the mother's room most of the time during its hospital stay. However, if parents choose not to use this rooming-in arrangement, the weight of the research suggests that this decision will not harm the infant emotionally (Lamb, 1994).

The postpartum period is a time of considerable adjustment and adaptation for both the mother and the father. Fathers can provide an important support system for mothers, especially in helping mothers care for young infants. *What kinds of tasks might the father of a newborn do to support the mother?*
Howard Grey/Photodisc/Getty Images

developmental **connection**
Attachment
Konrad Lorenz demonstrated the importance of early bonding in greylag geese, but the first few days of life are unlikely to be a critical period for bonding in human infants. Connect to "Introduction."

Review Connect Reflect

 LG3 Explain the changes that take place in the postpartum period.

Review
- What does the postpartum period involve? What physical adjustments does the woman's body make during this period?
- What emotional and psychological adjustments characterize the postpartum period?
- Is bonding critical for optimal development?

Connect
- Compare and contrast what you learned about kangaroo care and breast feeding of preterm infants with what you learned about bonding and breast feeding when the mother is suffering from postpartum depression.

Reflect *Your Own Personal Journey of Life*
- If you are a female, what can you do to adjust effectively during the postpartum period? If you are a male, what can you do to help your partner during the postpartum period?

bonding The formation of a close connection, especially a physical bond, between parents and their newborn in the period shortly after birth.

```
topical connections looking forward
```

This chapter marks the beginning of our chronological look at the journey of life. In the next three chapters, we will follow the physical, cognitive, and socioemotional development of infants, including the theories, research, and milestones associated with the first 18 to 24 months of life. You will learn about the remarkable and complex physical development of infants' motor skills, such as learning to walk; trace the early development of infants' cognitive skills, such as the ability to form concepts; and explore infants' surprisingly sophisticated socioemotional capabilities, as reflected in the development of their motivation to share and to perceive others' actions as intentionally motivated.

reach your **learning goals**

Prenatal Development and Birth

1 Prenatal Development

 Describe prenatal development.

The Course of Prenatal Development

- Prenatal development is divided into three periods: germinal (conception until 10 to 14 days later), which ends when the zygote (a fertilized egg) attaches to the uterine wall; embryonic (two to eight weeks after conception), during which the embryo differentiates into three layers, life-support systems develop, and organ systems form (organogenesis); and fetal (from two months after conception until about nine months, or when the infant is born), a period when organ systems mature to the point at which life can be sustained outside the womb.

- The growth of the brain during prenatal development is nothing short of remarkable. By the time babies are born, they have approximately 100 billion neurons, or nerve cells. Neurogenesis is the term for the formation of new neurons. The nervous system begins with the formation of a neural tube at 18 to 24 days after conception. Proliferation and migration are two processes that characterize brain development in the prenatal period. The basic architecture of the brain is formed in the first two trimesters of prenatal development.

Teratology and Hazards to Prenatal Development

- Teratology is the field of study that investigates the causes of congenital (birth) defects. Any agent that causes birth defects is called a teratogen. The dose, genetic susceptibility, and time of exposure influence the severity of the damage to an unborn child and the type of defect that occurs.

- Prescription drugs that can be harmful include antibiotics. Nonprescription drugs that can be harmful include diet pills, aspirin, and caffeine. Legal psychoactive drugs that are potentially harmful to prenatal development include alcohol and nicotine.

- Fetal alcohol spectrum disorders are a cluster of abnormalities that appear in offspring of mothers who drink heavily during pregnancy. Even when pregnant women drink moderately (one to two drinks a few days a week), negative effects on their offspring have been found.

- Cigarette smoking by pregnant women has serious adverse effects on prenatal and child development, including low birth weight. Illegal psychoactive drugs that are potentially harmful to offspring include marijuana, cocaine, heroin, synthetic opioids, and opiate-related pain killers.

- Environmental hazards include radiation, environmental pollutants, and toxic wastes. Syphilis, rubella (German measles), genital herpes, and AIDS are infectious diseases that can harm the fetus.

- Other parental factors that affect prenatal development include maternal diet and nutrition, age, emotional states and stress, and paternal factors. A developing fetus depends entirely on its mother for nutrition. Maternal age can negatively affect the offspring's development if the mother is an adolescent or over 35. High stress in the mother is linked with less than optimal prenatal and birth outcomes. Paternal factors that can adversely affect prenatal development include exposure to lead, radiation, certain pesticides, and petrochemicals, as well as smoking.

Prenatal Care

- Prenatal care varies extensively but usually involves health maintenance services with a defined schedule of visits.

Normal Prenatal Development

- It is important to remember that, although things can go wrong during pregnancy, most of the time pregnancy and prenatal development go well.

2 Birth

LG2 Describe the birth process.

The Birth Process

- Childbirth occurs in three stages. The first stage, which lasts about 6 to 12 hours for a woman having her first child, is the longest stage. The cervix dilates to about 10 centimeters (4 inches) by the end of the first stage. The second stage begins when the baby's head starts to move through the cervix and ends with the baby's complete emergence. The third stage involves the delivery of the placenta after birth.

- Childbirth strategies involve the childbirth setting and attendants. In many countries, a doula attends a childbearing woman. Methods of delivery include medicated, natural or prepared, and cesarean.

Assessing the Newborn

- For many years, the Apgar Scale has been used to assess the newborn's health. The Brazelton Neonatal Behavioral Assessment Scale examines the newborn's neurological development, reflexes, and reactions to people. Recently, the Neonatal Intensive Care Unit Network Neurobehavioral Scale (NNNS) was created to assess at-risk infants.

Preterm and Low Birth Weight Infants

- Low birth weight infants weigh less than 5 pounds 8 ounces, and they may be preterm (born before the completion of 37 weeks of gestation) or small for date (also called small for gestational age, which refers to infants whose birth weight is below normal when the length of pregnancy is considered). Small for date infants may be preterm or full term. Although most low birth weight and preterm infants are normal and healthy, as a group they have more health problems and developmental delays than normal birth weight infants. Kangaroo care and massage therapy have been shown to have benefits for preterm infants.

3 The Postpartum Period

 Explain the changes that take place in the postpartum period.

Physical Adjustments

- The postpartum period is the name given to the period after childbirth or delivery. The period lasts for about six weeks or until the woman's body has completed its adjustment. Physical adjustments in the postpartum period include fatigue and hormonal changes.

Emotional and Psychological Adjustments

- Emotional fluctuations on the part of the mother are common in this period, and they can vary a great deal from one mother to the next. Postpartum depression characterizes women who have such strong feelings of sadness, anxiety, or despair that they have trouble coping with daily tasks in the postpartum period. Postpartum depression occurs in about 10 percent of new mothers. The father also goes through a postpartum adjustment.

Bonding

- Bonding is the formation of a close connection, especially a physical bond between parents and the newborn shortly after birth. Early bonding has not been found to be critical in the development of a competent infant.

key **terms**

key **people**

section three

Babies are such a nice way to start people.

—DON HEROLD
American writer, 20th century

Infancy

As newborns, we were not empty-headed organisms. We had some basic reflexes, among them crying, kicking, and coughing. We slept a lot, and occasionally we smiled, although the meaning of our first smiles was not entirely clear. We ate and we grew. We crawled and then we walked, a journey of a thousand miles beginning with a single step. Sometimes we conformed; sometimes others conformed to us. Our development was a continuous creation of more complex forms. We needed the meeting eyes of love. We juggled the necessity of curbing our will with becoming what we could will freely. This section contains three chapters: "Physical Development in Infancy," "Cognitive Development in Infancy," and "Socioemotional Development in Infancy."

chapter 4

PHYSICAL DEVELOPMENT IN INFANCY

chapter **outline**

① **Physical Growth and Development in Infancy**

Learning Goal 1 Discuss physical growth and development in infancy.

Patterns of Growth
Height and Weight
The Brain
Sleep
Nutrition

② **Motor Development**

Learning Goal 2 Describe infants' motor development.

The Dynamic Systems View
Reflexes
Gross Motor Skills
Fine Motor Skills

③ **Sensory and Perceptual Development**

Learning Goal 3 Summarize the course of sensory and perceptual development in infancy.

What Are Sensation and Perception?
The Ecological View
Visual Perception
Other Senses
Intermodal Perception
Nature, Nurture, and Perceptual Development
Perceptual-Motor Coupling

Image Source/Getty Images

Latonya is a newborn baby in Ghana. During her first days of life, she has been kept apart from her mother and bottle fed. Manufacturers of infant formula provide the hospital where she was born with free or subsidized milk powder. Her mother has been persuaded to bottle feed rather than breast feed her. When her mother bottle feeds Latonya, she overdilutes the milk formula with unclean water. Latonya's feeding bottles have not been sterilized. Latonya becomes very sick. She dies before her first birthday.

Ramona was born in a Nigerian hospital with a "baby-friendly" program. In this program, babies are not separated from their mothers when they are born, and the mothers are encouraged to breast feed them. The mothers are told of the perils that bottle feeding can bring because of unsafe water and unsterilized bottles. They also are informed about the advantages of breast milk, which include its nutritious and hygienic qualities, its ability to immunize babies against common illnesses, and the role of breast feeding in reducing the mother's risk of breast and ovarian cancer. Ramona's mother is breast feeding her. At 1 year of age, Ramona is very healthy.

For many years, maternity units in hospitals favored bottle feeding and did not give mothers adequate information about the benefits of breast feeding. In recent years, the World Health Organization and UNICEF have tried to reverse the trend toward bottle feeding of infants in many impoverished countries. They instituted "baby-friendly" programs in many countries (Grant, 1993). They also persuaded the International Association of Infant Formula Manufacturers to stop marketing their baby formulas to hospitals in countries where the governments support the baby-friendly initiatives (Grant, 1993). For the hospitals themselves, costs actually were reduced as infant formula, feeding bottles, and separate nurseries became unnecessary. For example, baby-friendly Jose Fabella Memorial Hospital in the Philippines reported saving 8 percent of its annual budget. Still, there are many places in the world where the baby-friendly initiatives have not been implemented.

The advantages of breast feeding in impoverished countries are substantial (UNICEF, 2019). However, these advantages must be balanced against the risk of passing the human immunodeficiency virus (HIV) to babies through breast milk if

(Top) An HIV-infected mother breast feeding her baby in Nairobi, Kenya. (Bottom) A Rwandan mother bottle feeding her baby. What are some concerns about breast versus bottle feeding in impoverished African countries?
(Top) Wendy Stone/Corbis Documentary/Getty Images; (bottom) Dave Bartruff/Corbis Documentary/Getty Images

topical connections *looking **back***

Previously, we followed the physical development that takes place from fertilization through the germinal, embryonic, and fetal periods of prenatal development. We learned that by the time the fetus has reached full gestational age (approximately 40 weeks), it has grown from a fertilized egg, barely visible to the human eye, to a fully formed human weighing approximately 8 pounds and measuring 20 inches in length. Also remarkable is the fact that by the end of the prenatal period the brain has developed approximately 100 billion neurons.

the mothers have the virus (Gross & others, 2019; Iliyasu & others, 2020; Remmart & others, 2020). In some areas of Africa, more than 30 percent of mothers have HIV, but the majority of these mothers don't know that they are infected (Mepham, Bland, & Newell, 2011). Later in this chapter, in the section on nutrition, we will look more closely at recent research on breast feeding in the United States, outlining the benefits for infants and mothers and discussing several life-threatening diseases that infants can contract as a result of malnutrition.

preview

It is very important for infants to get a healthy start. When they do, their first two years of life are likely to be a time of amazing development. In this chapter, we focus on the biological domain and the infant's physical development, exploring physical growth, motor development, and sensory and perceptual development.

1 Physical Growth and Development in Infancy **LG1** Discuss physical growth and development in infancy.

Patterns of Growth   Height and Weight   The Brain   Sleep   Nutrition

A baby is the most complicated object made by unskilled labor.

—Anonymous

Infants' physical development in the first two years of life is extensive. Newborns' heads are quite large in comparison with the rest of their bodies. Neck muscles are not yet strong enough to support the head, but newborns have some basic reflexes. In the span of 12 months, infants become capable of sitting, standing, stooping, climbing, and usually walking. During the second year, growth slows down but motor skills increase rapidly.

FIGURE 1

CHANGES IN PROPORTIONS OF THE HUMAN BODY DURING GROWTH. As individuals develop from infancy through adulthood, one of the most noticeable physical changes is that the head becomes smaller in relation to the rest of the body. The fractions listed refer to head size as a proportion of total body length at different ages.

PATTERNS OF GROWTH

An extraordinary proportion of the total body is occupied by the head during prenatal development and early infancy (see Figure 1). The **cephalocaudal pattern** is the sequence in which the earliest growth always occurs at the top—the head—with physical growth and differentiation of features gradually working their way down from top to bottom. This same pattern occurs

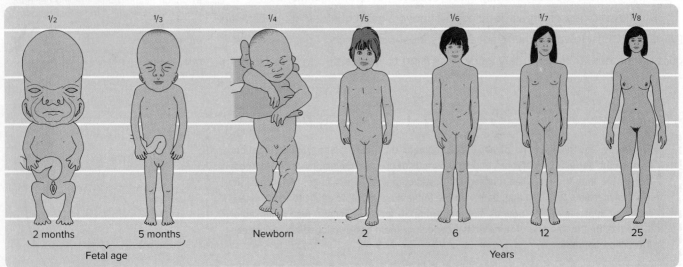

| 1/2 | 1/3 | | 1/4 | 1/5 | 1/6 | 1/7 | 1/8 |

2 months   5 months   Newborn   2   6   12   25

Fetal age   Years

in the head area, because the top parts of the head—the eyes and brain—grow faster than the lower parts such as the jaw.

Motor development generally proceeds according to the cephalocaudal principle. For example, infants see objects before they can control their torso, and they can use their hands long before they can crawl or walk. However, development does not follow a rigid blueprint. One study found that infants reached for toys with their feet prior to reaching with their hands (Galloway & Thelen, 2004). On average, infants first touched the toy with their feet when they were 12 weeks old and with their hands when they were 16 weeks old.

Growth also follows the **proximodistal pattern,** the sequence in which growth starts at the center of the body and moves toward the extremities. For example, infants control the muscles of their trunk and arms before they control their hands and fingers, and they use their whole hands before they can control individual fingers (Bindler & others, 2017).

HEIGHT AND WEIGHT

The average North American newborn is 20 inches long and weighs 7.6 pounds. Ninety-five percent of full-term newborns are 18 to 22 inches long and weigh between 5 and 10 pounds.

In the first several days of life, most newborns lose 5 to 7 percent of their body weight as they adjust to feeding by sucking, swallowing, and digesting. Then they grow rapidly, gaining an average of 5 to 6 ounces per week during the first month. They have doubled their birth weight by the age of 4 months and have nearly tripled it by their first birthday. Infants grow about 1 inch per month during the first year, approximately doubling their birth length by their first birthday.

Growth slows considerably in the second year of life (Hockenberry & Wilson, 2019). By 2 years of age, infants weigh approximately 26 to 32 pounds, having gained a quarter to half a pound per month during the second year to reach about one-fifth of their adult weight. At 2 years of age, infants average 32 to 35 inches in height, which is nearly half of their adult height.

An important point about growth is that it often is not smooth and continuous but rather is *episodic*, occurring in spurts (Rachwani, Hoch, & Adolph, 2020). In infancy, growth spurts may occur in a single day and alternate with long time frames characterized by little or no growth for days and weeks (Lampl & Johnson, 2011; Lampl & Schoen, 2018). In two analyses, infants grew seven-tenths of an inch in a single day (Lampl, 1993) and their head circumference increased by three-tenths of an inch (Caino & others, 2010).

THE BRAIN

We have described the amazing growth of the brain from conception to birth. By the time it is born, the infant that began as a single cell is estimated to have a brain that contains approximately 100 billion nerve cells, or neurons. Extensive brain development continues after birth, through infancy and later (Baum & others, 2020; Schneider & Ornstein, 2019). Because the brain is still developing so rapidly in infancy, the infant's head should be protected from falls or other injuries and the baby should never be shaken. *Shaken baby syndrome,* which includes brain swelling and hemorrhaging, affects hundreds of babies in the United States each year (Cohen, 2019; Thompson & others, 2020). One analysis found that fathers were the most frequent perpetrators of shaken baby syndrome, followed by child care providers and boyfriends of the victim's mother (National Center on Shaken Baby Syndrome, 2012).

Researchers have been successful in using the electroencephalogram (EEG), a measure of the brain's electrical activity, to learn about the brain's development in infancy (Cuevas & Bell, 2020; Xie, Mallin, & Richards, 2019) (see Figure 2). For example, one study found that higher-quality mother-infant interaction early in infancy predicted higher-quality frontal lobe functioning that was assessed with EEG later in infancy (Bernier, Calkins, & Bell, 2016).

Researchers also are increasingly using functional near-infrared spectroscopy (fNIRS), which uses very low levels of near-infrared light to monitor changes in blood oxygen, to study infants' brain activity related to face processing, perception, attention, and memory (Emberson & others, 2019; Perdue & others, 2019; Zhang & Roeyers, 2019) (see Figure 3). Unlike fMRI, which uses magnetic fields or electrical activity, fNIRS is portable and allows the infants to be assessed as they explore the world around them. Patricia Kuhl and her colleagues (Ferjan Ramirez & others, 2017) at the Institute for Learning and Brain Sciences at the University of Washington are using

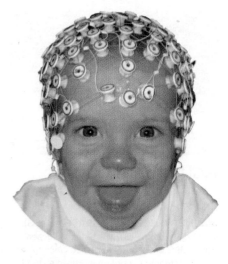

FIGURE 2

MEASURING THE ACTIVITY OF AN INFANT'S BRAIN WITH AN ELECTROENCEPHALOGRAM (EEG). By attaching up to 128 electrodes to a baby's scalp to measure the brain's activity, researchers have found that newborns produce distinctive brain waves that reveal they can distinguish their mother's voice from another woman's, even while they are asleep. *Why is it so difficult to measure infants' brain activity?*
Courtesy of Vanessa Vogel Farley

FIGURE 3

FUNCTIONAL NEAR-INFRARED SPECTROSCOPY (fNIRS) Functional near-infrared spectroscopy is increasingly being used to examine the brain activity of infants. fNIRS is non-invasive and can assess infants as they move and explore their environment.
Oli Scarff/Getty Images

cephalocaudal pattern Developmental sequence in which the earliest growth always occurs at the top—the head—with physical growth in size, weight, and feature differentiation gradually working from top to bottom.

proximodistal pattern Developmental sequence in which growth starts at the center of the body and moves toward the extremities.

FIGURE 4

MEASURING THE ACTIVITY OF AN INFANT'S BRAIN WITH MAGNETOENCEPHALOGRAPHY (MEG). This baby's brain activity is being assessed with a MEG brain-imaging device while the baby is listening to spoken words in a study at the Institute of Learning and Brain Sciences at the University of Washington. The infant sits under the machine and when he or she experiences a word, touch, sight, or emotion, the neurons working together in the infant's brain generate magnetic fields and MEG pinpoints the location of the fields in the brain.
Courtesy of Dr. Patricia Kuhl, Institute for Learning and Brain Sciences, University of Washington

developmental **connection**

Brain Development

How does the brain change from conception to birth? Connect to "Prenatal Development and Birth."

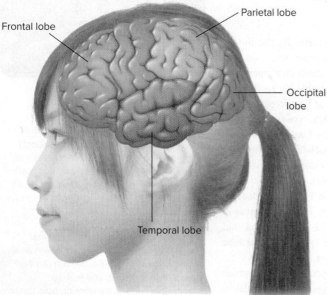

Frontal lobe

Parietal lobe

Occipital lobe

Temporal lobe

FIGURE 6

THE BRAIN'S FOUR LOBES. Shown here are the locations of the brain's four lobes: frontal, occipital, temporal, and parietal.
Takayuki/Shutterstock

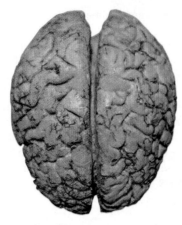

FIGURE 5

THE HUMAN BRAIN'S HEMISPHERES. The two hemispheres of the human brain are clearly seen in this photograph. It is a myth that the left hemisphere is the exclusive location of language and logical thinking and that the right hemisphere is the exclusive location of emotion and creative thinking.
IgorZD/Shutterstock

magnetoencephalography (MEG) brain-imaging machines to assess infants' brain activity. MEG maps brain activity by recording magnetic fields produced by electrical currents and is being used to assess such perceptual, motor, and cognitive activities as vision, hearing, and language in infants (Y. H. Chen & others, 2019; Gaetz & others, 2020) (see Figure 4).

Among the researchers who are making strides in finding out more about the brain's development in infancy are:

- Charles Nelson and his colleagues (Bick & Nelson, 2018; Debnath & others, 2020; Guyon-Harris & others, 2019; Kadlaskar & others, 2020; Lamm & others, 2018; Nelson, 2007, 2012, 2013a, b; Nelson, Fox, & Zeanah, 2014; Perdue & others, 2019; Wade & others, 2019, 2020; Wagner & others, 2020) who are exploring various aspects of memory development, face recognition and facial emotion, and the role of experience in influencing the course of brain development;

- Martha Ann Bell and her colleagues (Bell, 2015; Bell & Broomell, 2020; Bell & Cuevas, 2012, 2015; Bell, Diaz, & Liu, 2019; Bell & Garcia-Meza, 2020; Bell & others, 2018; Bell, Ross, & Patton, 2018; Broomell & others, 2020; Cuevas & Bell, 2020) who are studying brain-behavior links, emotion regulation, inhibitory control, and the integration of cognition and emotion;

- Mark Johnson and his colleagues (Johnson, Jones, & Gliga, 2015; Johnson, Senju, & Tomalski, 2015; Kolesnik & others, 2019; Milosavlijevic & others, 2017; Pijl & others, 2019; Saez de Urabain, Nuthmann, & Johnson, 2017), who are examining neuroconstructivist links between the brain, cognitive and perceptual processes, and environmental influences as well as studying the development of the prefrontal cortex and its functions, early identification of autism, face processing, and early social experiences;

- John Richards and his colleagues (Brito & others, 2019; Gao & others, 2019; Lunghi & others, 2019; Richards, 2009, 2010, 2013; Richards & others, 2015; Richards, Reynolds, & Courage, 2010; Richards & Xie, 2015; Xie, Mallin, & Richards, 2019; Xie & Richards, 2016, 2017) who are examining sustained attention, perception of TV programs, and eye movements.

The Brain's Development   At birth, the newborn's brain is about 25 percent of its adult weight. By the second birthday, the brain is about 75 percent of its adult weight. However, the brain's areas do not mature uniformly.

Mapping the Brain   Scientists analyze and categorize areas of the brain in numerous ways (Heilman, 2020; Houde, 2019). The portion farthest from the spinal cord is known as the forebrain. This region includes the cerebral cortex and several structures beneath it. The cerebral cortex covers the forebrain like a wrinkled cap. The brain has two halves, or hemispheres (see Figure 5). Based on ridges and valleys in the cortex, scientists distinguish four main areas, called lobes, in each hemisphere. Although the lobes usually work together through network connections, each has a somewhat different primary function (see Figure 6):

- *Frontal lobes* are involved in voluntary movement, thinking, personality, and intentionality or purpose.

- *Occipital lobes* function in vision.
- *Temporal lobes* have an active role in hearing, language processing, and memory.
- *Parietal lobes* play important roles involving spatial location, attention, and motor control.

To some extent, the type of information handled by neurons depends on whether they are in the left or right hemisphere of the cortex (Othman & others, 2020). Speech and grammar, for example, depend on activity in the left hemisphere in most people; humor and the use of metaphors depend on activity in the right hemisphere (Veronelli & others, 2020; Woodhead & others, 2019). Recent research also indicates that attention (Bartolomeo & Seidel Malkinson, 2019) and emotion (Gainotti, 2019) are predominantly right-hemisphere activities. This specialization of function in one hemisphere of the cerebral cortex or the other is called **lateralization.** However, most neuroscientists agree that complex functions such as reading or performing music involve both hemispheres. Labeling people as "left-brained" because they are logical thinkers or "right-brained" because they are creative thinkers does not correspond to the way the brain's hemispheres work. Complex thinking in normal people is the outcome of communication between both hemispheres of the brain (S. Wang & others, 2019).

At birth, the hemispheres of the cerebral cortex already have started to specialize: Newborns show greater electrical brain activity in the left hemisphere than the right hemisphere when they are listening to speech sounds (Telkemeyer & others, 2011). How are the areas of the brain different in the newborn and the infant from those in an adult, and why do the differences matter? Important differences have been documented at both the cellular and the structural levels.

Changes in Neurons Within the brain, nerve cells called neurons send electrical and chemical signals to communicate with each other. A *neuron* is a nerve cell that handles information processing (see Figure 7). Extending from the neuron's cell body are two types of fibers known as axons and dendrites. Generally, the axon carries signals away from the cell body and dendrites carry signals toward it. A *myelin sheath,* which is a layer of fat cells, encases many axons (see Figure 7). The myelin sheath insulates axons and helps electrical signals travel faster down the axon (McDougall & others, 2018). Myelination also is involved in providing energy to neurons and in communication (Shen & others, 2020). At the end of the axon are terminal buttons, which release chemicals called *neurotransmitters* into *synapses,* which are tiny gaps between neurons' fibers. Chemical interactions in synapses connect axons and dendrites, allowing information to pass from neuron to neuron (Ballintyn, Shlaer, & Miller, 2019). Think of the synapse as a river that blocks a road. A truck arrives at one bank of the river, crosses by ferry, and continues its journey. Similarly, a message in the brain is "ferried" across the synapse by a neurotransmitter, which pours out information contained in chemicals when it reaches the other side of the river.

Neurons change in two very significant ways during the first years of life. First, *myelination,* the process of encasing axons with fat cells, begins prenatally and continues into adolescence and emerging adulthood (Kwon & others, 2020). Second, connectivity among neurons increases, creating new neural pathways (van Duijvenvoorde & others, 2019). New dendrites grow, connections among dendrites increase, and synaptic connections between axons and dendrites proliferate. Whereas myelination speeds up neural transmissions, the expansion of dendritic connections facilitates the spreading of neural pathways in infant development.

How complex are these neural connections? In one analysis, it was estimated that each of the billions of neurons is connected to as many as 1,000 other neurons, producing neural networks with trillions of connections (de Haan, 2015). As we have discussed previously, most of these billions of neurons essentially have been created, have traveled to their correct locations, and are connected to other neurons by the time of full-term birth. Nonetheless, they undergo further differentiation, and neural connectivity patterns continue to change at least into emerging adulthood (Calabro & others, 2020).

Researchers have discovered an intriguing aspect of synaptic connections: nearly twice as many of these connections are made as will ever be used (Huttenlocher & Dabholkar, 1997). The connections that are used survive and become stronger, while the unused ones are replaced by other pathways or disappear. In the language of neuroscience, these connections are "pruned" (Dow-Edwards & others, 2019). For example, as babies engage in physical activity or use language, the corresponding synaptic pathways become stronger.

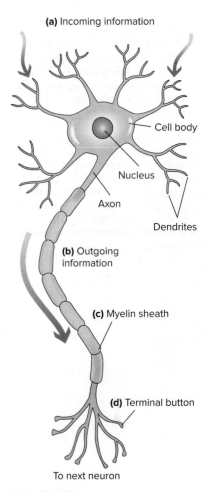

(a) Incoming information

Cell body

Nucleus

Axon

Dendrites

(b) Outgoing information

(c) Myelin sheath

(d) Terminal button

To next neuron

FIGURE 7

THE NEURON. (*a*) The dendrites of the cell body receive information from other neurons, muscles, or glands through the axon. (*b*) Axons transmit information away from the cell body. (*c*) A myelin sheath covers most axons and speeds information transmission. (*d*) As the axon ends, it branches out into terminal buttons.

developmental **connection**

Brain Development

Changes in the prefrontal cortex in adolescents and older adults have important implications for cognitive development. Connect to "Physical and Cognitive Development in Adolescence" and "Physical Development in Late Adulthood."

lateralization Specialization of function in one hemisphere of the cerebral cortex or the other.

FIGURE 8

EARLY DEPRIVATION AND BRAIN ACTIVITY. These two photographs are PET (positron emission tomography) scans, which use radioactive tracers to image and analyze blood flow and metabolic activity in the body's organs. These scans show the brains of (*a*) a typically developing child and (*b*) an institutionalized Romanian orphan who experienced substantial deprivation since birth. In PET scans, the highest to lowest brain activity is reflected in the colors of red, yellow, green, blue, and black, respectively. As can be seen, red and yellow show up to a much greater degree in the PET scan of the typically developing child than the deprived Romanian orphan.
Courtesy of Dr. Harry T. Chugani, Children's Hospital of Michigan

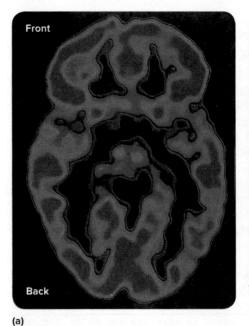

(a)

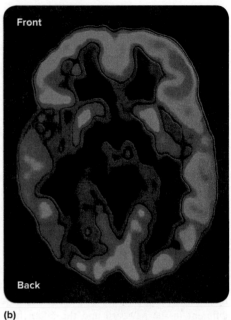

(b)

The age at which "blooming" and subsequent "pruning" of synapses occurs varies by brain region. For example, the peak of synaptic overproduction in the visual cortex occurs at about the fourth postnatal month, followed by a gradual retraction until the middle to end of the preschool years. In areas of the brain involved in hearing and language, a similar, though somewhat later, course is detected. However, in the prefrontal cortex, the area of the brain where higher-level thinking and self-regulation occur, the peak of overproduction takes place at about 1 year of age; it is not until emerging adulthood that adult density of synapses is attained. Both heredity and environment are thought to influence the timing and course of synaptic overproduction and subsequent retraction.

Early Experience and the Brain Children who grow up in a deprived environment may have depressed brain activity (Bick & Nelson, 2018; Nelson, Fox, & Zeanah, 2014; Wade & others, 2019, 2020). As shown in Figure 8, a child who grew up in the unresponsive and unstimulating environment of a Romanian orphanage showed considerably depressed brain activity compared with a child who grew up in a normal environment. In a recent follow-up assessment at 16 years of age, those who were placed in stable foster care showed improvement in brain functioning (Debnath & others, 2020).

Are the effects of deprived environments reversible? There is reason to think that for some individuals the answer is "yes" (Dennis & others, 2014). The brain demonstrates both flexibility and resilience. Consider 14-year-old Michael Rehbein. At age 7, he began to experience uncontrollable seizures—as many as 400 a day. Doctors said the only solution was to remove the left hemisphere of his brain where the seizures were occurring. Recovery was slow, but his right hemisphere began to reorganize and take over functions that normally occur in the brain's left hemisphere, including speech (see Figure 9).

Neuroscientists believe that what wires the brain—or rewires it, in the case of Michael Rehbein—is repeated experience. Each time a baby tries to touch an attractive object or gazes intently at a face, tiny bursts of electricity shoot through the brain, knitting together neurons into circuits. The results are some of the behavioral milestones we discuss in this chapter.

The Neuroconstructivist View Not long ago, scientists thought that our genes determined how our brains were "wired" and that the cells in the brain responsible for processing information just maturationally unfolded with little or no input from environmental experiences. Whatever brain your heredity had dealt you, you were essentially stuck with. This view, however, turned out to be wrong. Research reveals that the brain has plasticity and its development depends on context (Calabro & others, 2020; Pi & others, 2019).

developmental **connection**

Nature and Nurture

In the epigenetic view, development is an ongoing, bidirectional interchange between heredity and the environment. Connect to "Biological Beginnings."

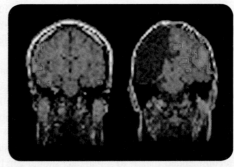

(b)

FIGURE 9

PLASTICITY IN THE BRAIN'S HEMISPHERES.
(*a*) Michael Rehbein at 14 years of age.
(*b*) Michael's right hemisphere (*right*) has reorganized to take over the language functions normally carried out by corresponding areas in the left hemisphere of an intact brain (*left*). However, the right hemisphere is not as efficient as the left, and more areas of the brain are recruited to process speech.
Courtesy of The Rehbein Family

(a)

The infant's brain depends on experiences to determine how connections are made. Before birth, it appears that genes mainly direct basic wiring patterns. Neurons grow and travel to distant places awaiting further instructions. After birth, the inflowing stream of sights, sounds, smells, touches, language, and eye contact help shape the brain's neural connections.

In the increasingly popular **neuroconstructivist view,** (a) biological processes (genes, for example) and environmental conditions (enriched or impoverished, for example) influence the brain's development; (b) the brain has plasticity and is context dependent; and (c) the child's cognitive development is closely linked to development of the brain. These factors constrain or advance the construction of cognitive skills (Borsani & others, 2019; Westermann, Thomas, & Karmiloff-Smith, 2011). The neuroconstructivist view emphasizes the importance of considering interactions between experience and gene expression in the brain's development, much as the epigenetic view proposes (Cinquina & others, 2020; Hanley, Burianova, & Tommerdahl, 2019; Ibanez & others, 2020).

SLEEP

Sleep restores, replenishes, and rebuilds our brains and bodies. What function does sleep have in people's lives? How do sleep patterns change in infancy?

Why Do We Sleep? A number of theories have been proposed about why we sleep. From an evolutionary perspective, all animals sleep and this sleep likely is necessary for survival. Thus, sleep may have developed because animals needed to protect themselves at night. A second perspective is that sleep replenishes and rebuilds the brain and body, which the day's waking activities can wear out. In support of this restorative function, many of the body's cells show increased production and reduced breakdowns of proteins during sleep (Ferrarelli & others, 2020). Further, a current emphasis is that sleep is essential to clearing out waste in neural tissues, such as metabolites and cerebrospinal fluid (Aguirre, 2016). A third perspective is that sleep is critical for brain plasticity (Maier & others, 2019). For example, neuroscientists recently have argued that sleep increases synaptic connections between neurons (Tononi & Cirelli, 2019). These increased synaptic connections have been linked to improved consolidation of memories (Gui & others, 2017). Sleep deprivation has a negative impact on many aspects of memory, especially the capacity to encode new memories (Cousins & Fernandez, 2019). Further, research indicates that not only can sleep improve memory, but losing a few hours of sleep a night is related to negative effects on attention, reasoning, and decision making (Diekelmann, 2014; Spruyt & others, 2019).

Sleep that knits up the ravelled sleave of care . . . Balm of hurt minds, nature's second course. Chief nourisher in life's feast.

—WILLIAM SHAKESPEARE
English playwright, 17th century

neuroconstructivist view A belief that biological processes and environmental conditions influence the brain's development; the brain has plasticity and is context dependent; and development of the brain and cognitive development are closely linked.

developmental **connection**

Sleep

Sleep patterns change in adolescence and are linked to changes in the brain. Connect to "Physical and Cognitive Development in Adolescence."

developmental **connection**

Sleep

What are some sleep problems that children encounter in early childhood? Connect to "Physical and Cognitive Development in Early Childhood."

In sum, sleep likely serves a number of functions, with no one theory accounting for all of these functions. Let's now turn our attention to sleep in infancy. In later chapters, we will explore sleep through the remainder of the life span.

Infant Sleep   When we were infants, sleep consumed more of our time than it does now (Goh & others, 2017). The typical newborn sleeps approximately 18 hours a day, but newborns vary greatly in how much they sleep (Dias & others, 2018). The range is from about 10 hours to about 21 hours a day. In a recent recommendation, the World Health Organization (WHO) stated that infants 0 to 3 months of age should get 14 to 17 hours of good-quality sleep daily and 4- to 12-month-olds 12 to 16 hours of good-quality sleep daily (Willumsen & Bull, 2020). WHO also recommended that 1- to 2-year-olds should get 11 to 14 hours of good-quality sleep daily.

A research review concluded that infants 0 to 2 years of age slept an average of 12.8 hours out of the 24, within a range of 9.7 to 15.9 hours (Galland & others, 2012). Another study revealed that by 6 months of age the majority of infants slept through the night, awakening their parents only once or twice a week (Weinraub & others, 2012).

Sleep problems have been estimated to affect 15 to 25 percent of infants. The most common infant sleep-related problem reported by parents is nighttime waking (Dias & others, 2018). Surveys indicate that 20 to 30 percent of infants have difficulty going to sleep at night and staying asleep until morning (Sadeh, 2008). Research indicates that (1) maternal depression during pregnancy, (2) early introduction of solid foods, (3) infant TV viewing, and (4) child care attendance are related to shorter duration of infant sleep (Nevarez & others, 2010). A recent study confirmed that persistent severe infant sleep problems were linked to prenatal and postnatal maternal depression (Cook & others, 2020). Also, a recent study indicated a higher amount of screen time for infants was related to shorter sleep duration (B. Chen & others, 2019). In this study, the link between greater screen time and less sleep was greater for infants 6 months and younger than for infants 7 to 24 months of age. In addition, a recent study revealed that later bedtime and less sleep across a 24-hour period were linked to infants having more separation distress, greater inhibition, and higher levels of anxiety and depression (Mindell & others, 2017).

Research also indicates that a number of parental factors are linked to infants' sleep patterns (Hatch & others, 2019). A recent study found that mothers who implemented a consistent bedtime routine had toddlers with longer sleep duration and fewer nighttime awakenings (Covington & others, 2019). And in a recent study of toddlers who experienced negative parenting, their self-regulation was good if they got adequate nighttime sleep but poorer if they received inadequate nighttime sleep (Julian & others, 2019). Further, a recent study found that infants who are allowed to self settle (that is, not nursed to sleep, not rocked to sleep) show increased nighttime sleep during infancy (Hatch & others, 2019).

Cultural variations influence infant sleeping patterns. For example, in the Kipsigis culture in Kenya, infants sleep with their mothers at night and are permitted to nurse on demand (Super & Harkness, 1997). During the day, they are strapped to their mothers' backs, accompanying them on daily rounds of chores and social activities. As a result, Kipsigis infants do not sleep through the night until much later than American infants do. During their first eight months, Kipsigis infants rarely sleep longer than three hours at a stretch, even at night. This sleep pattern contrasts with that of American infants, many of whom begin to sleep up to eight hours a night by 8 months of age.

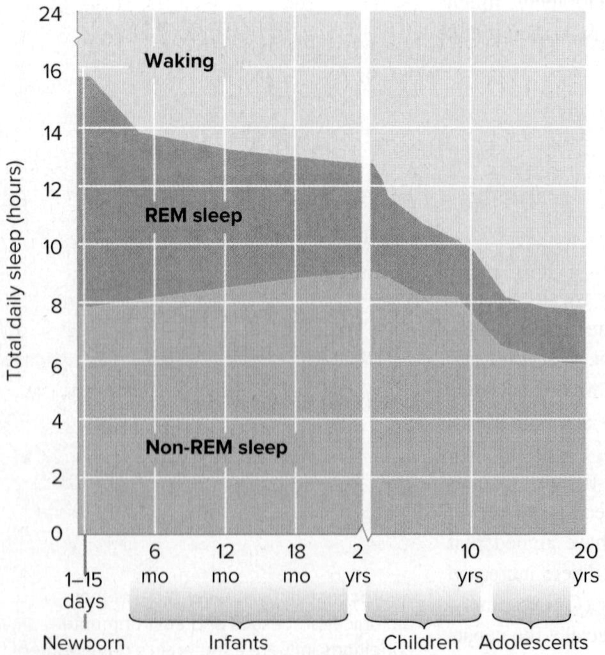

REM Sleep   In REM sleep, the eyes flutter beneath closed lids; in non-REM sleep, this type of eye movement does not occur and sleep is more quiet (Rodriguez, 2019). Figure 10 shows developmental changes in the average number of total hours spent in REM and non-REM sleep. By the time they reach adulthood, individuals spend about one-fifth of their night in REM sleep, and REM sleep usually appears about one hour after non-REM sleep. However, about half of an infant's sleep is REM sleep, and infants often begin their sleep cycle with REM sleep rather than non-REM sleep. A much greater amount of time is taken up by REM sleep in infancy than at any other point in the life span. By the time

FIGURE 10

DEVELOPMENTAL CHANGES IN REM AND NON-REM SLEEP

infants reach 3 months of age, the percentage of time they spend in REM sleep falls to about 40 percent, and REM sleep no longer begins their sleep cycle.

Why do infants spend so much time in REM sleep? Researchers are not certain. The large amount of REM sleep may provide infants with added self-stimulation, since they spend less time awake than do older children. REM sleep also might promote the brain's development in infancy (Del-Rio-Bermudez & Blumberg, 2018).

When adults are awakened during REM sleep, they frequently report that they have been dreaming, but when they are awakened during non-REM sleep, they are much less likely to report having been dreaming (Voss & Klimke, 2018). Since infants spend more time than adults in REM sleep, can we conclude that they dream a lot? We are unable to answer this question because infants cannot tell us about their dreams.

Shared Sleeping Sleeping arrangements for newborns vary from culture to culture. For example, sharing a bed with a mother is a common practice in many cultures, such as Guatemala and China, whereas in others, such as the United States and Great Britain, newborns usually sleep in a crib, either in the same room as the parents or in a separate room. In some cultures, infants sleep with their mother until they are weaned, after which they sleep with siblings until middle and late childhood (Walker, 2006). Whatever the sleeping arrangements, it is recommended that the infant's bedding provide firm support and that the crib or bed has side rails (Kreth & others, 2017).

In the United States, shared sleeping remains a controversial issue (Burnham, 2014). Some experts recommend it and others argue against it, although recently the recommendation trend has been to avoid infant-parent bed sharing, especially if the infant is younger than 6 months of age (Mitchell & others, 2017). In one study, infant-parent bed sharing was associated with more night waking for mothers as well as infants, and more marital distress (Teti & others, 2016). The American Academy of Pediatrics Task Force on Infant Positioning and SIDS (AAPTFIPS) (2000) recommends against shared sleeping. Its members argue that in some instances bed sharing might lead to sudden infant death syndrome (SIDS), as could be the case if a sleeping mother rolls over on her baby (Moon & others, 2017). Recent studies have found that bed sharing is linked with a higher incidence of SIDS, especially when parents smoke (Adams, Ward, & Garcia, 2015). Further, a recent large-scale study in six countries (including the United States) found that parents of 6- to 12-month-old infants reported earlier bedtimes, shorter time to fall asleep, fewer sleep interruptions, and more total sleep when the infants slept in a separate room than when infants slept in the same room or same bed with their parents (Mindell, Leichman, & Walters, 2019).

SIDS **Sudden infant death syndrome (SIDS)** is a condition that occurs when infants stop breathing, usually during the night, and die suddenly without any apparent reason. SIDS continues to be a leading cause of infant death in the United States, with more than 2,000 infant deaths annually attributed to SIDS (NICHD, 2019). Risk of SIDS is highest at 2 to 4 months of age.

Since 1992, the American Academy of Pediatrics (AAP) has recommended that infants be placed to sleep on their backs (supine position) to reduce the risk of SIDS, and the frequency of prone sleeping (on the stomach) among U.S. infants has dropped dramatically (AAPTFIPS, 2000). Researchers have found that SIDS is less likely when infants sleep on their backs rather than their stomachs or sides (Bombard & others, 2018; Horne, 2019). Why? Because sleeping on their backs increases their access to fresh air and reduces their chances of getting overheated.

In addition to sleeping in a prone position, researchers have found that the following factors are linked to SIDS:

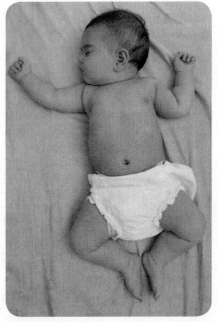

Is this a good sleep position for infants? Why or why not?
Maria Teijeiro/Cultura/Getty Images

sudden infant death syndrome (SIDS) A condition that occurs when an infant stops breathing, usually during the night, and suddenly dies without an apparent cause.

- SIDS occurs more often in infants with abnormal brain stem functioning involving the neurotransmitter serotonin (Kinney & Haynes, 2019). A recent review concluded that serotonin plays an important role in SIDS (Cummings & Leiter, 2020).

- Heart arrhythmias are estimated to occur in as many as 15 percent of SIDS cases, and two studies found that gene mutations were linked to the occurrence of these arrhythmias (Van Norstrand & others, 2012).

- Six percent of infants with sleep apnea die of SID (sleep apnea is a temporary cessation of breathing when the airway is completely blocked, usually for 10 seconds or longer) (Ednick & others, 2010).

- Breast feeding is linked to a lower incidence of SIDS (Bartick & others, 2020).
- Low birth weight infants are 5 to 10 times more likely to die of SIDS than are their normal-weight counterparts (Horne & others, 2002).
- SIDS is more likely to occur in infants who do not use a pacifier when they go to sleep than in those who do use a pacifier (Carlin & Moon, 2017).
- Infants whose siblings have died of SIDS are two to four times as likely to die of it (Lenoir, Mallet, & Calenda, 2000).
- African American and Eskimo infants are four to six times as likely as all others to die of SIDS (Moon & others, 2017).
- SIDS is more common in lower socioeconomic groups (Hogan, 2014).
- SIDS is more common in infants who are passively exposed to cigarette smoke (Horne, 2018).
- SIDS is more common when infants and parents share the same bed (Carlin & Moon, 2017). In a study of 732 cases of SIDS, bed-sharing occurred in 53 percent of the deaths (Drake & others, 2020).
- SIDS is more common if infants sleep in soft bedding (Erck Lambert & others, 2019).
- SIDS is less common when infants sleep in a bedroom with a fan. One study revealed that sleeping in a bedroom with a fan lowers the risk of SIDS by 70 percent (Coleman-Phox, Odouli, & Li, 2008).

It is generally accepted that the most critical factor in predicting whether an infant will develop SIDS is prone sleeping. As public awareness has grown regarding the importance of not letting infants sleep in a prone position, the number of infant deaths in the United States has decreased, although SIDS still is one of the leading causes of infant death (Bombard & others, 2018). A research review concluded that the two other factors that place infants at the highest risk for SIDS are (1) maternal smoking and (2) bed sharing (Mitchell & Krous, 2015).

One concern raised by critics of the "back to sleep movement" (ensuring that young infants sleep on their back rather than their stomach) is a decline in prone skills. To prevent this decline, many mothers provide their young infants with "tummy time" by periodically placing them on their stomach when they are awake.

Sleep and Cognitive Development   Might infant sleep be linked to children's cognitive development? A recent research review indicated that there is a positive link between infant sleep and cognitive functioning, including memory, language, and executive function (Tham, Schneider, & Broekman, 2017). A study also revealed that a lower quality of sleep at 1 year of age was linked to lower attention regulation and more behavior problems at 3 to 4 years of age (Sadeh & others, 2015). Further, a recent study found that infants with shorter sleep duration were characterized by a lower level of cognitive and language development at 2 years of age (Smithson & others, 2019). In addition, a recent study indicated that shorter sleep duration at 3, 8, and 24 months was linked to inattentiveness and hyperactivity symptoms at 5 years of age (Huhdanpaa & others, 2019). The link between infant sleep and children's cognitive functioning likely occurs because of sleep's role in brain maturation and memory consolidation, which may improve daytime alertness and learning.

NUTRITION

From birth to 1 year of age, human infants nearly triple their weight and increase their length by 50 percent. What type of fuel do they need to sustain this growth?

Nutritional Needs and Eating Behavior   Individual differences among infants in terms of their nutrient reserves, body composition, growth rates, and activity patterns make defining actual nutrient needs difficult (Blake, 2020). However, because parents need guidelines, nutritionists recommend that infants consume approximately 50 calories per day for each pound they weigh—more than twice an adult's caloric requirement per pound.

A number of developmental changes involving eating characterize the infant's first year (van der Veek & others, 2019). As infants' motor skills improve, they change from using suck-and-swallow movements with breast milk or formula to chew-and-swallow movements with semi-solid and then more complex foods. As their fine motor control improves in the first year, they transition from being fed by others toward self-feeding. "By the end of the first year of life, children can sit independently, can chew and swallow a range of textures, are learning to feed themselves, and are making the transition to the family diet and meal patterns" (Black & Hurley, 2007, p. 1). At this point, infants need to have a diet that includes a variety of foods—especially fruits and vegetables.

Caregivers play very important roles in infants' early development of eating patterns (Baye, Tariku, & Mouquet-Rivier, 2018; Brown, 2020). Caregivers who are not sensitive to developmental changes in infants' nutritional needs, caregivers who are negligent, and conditions of poverty can contribute to the development of eating problems in infants (Black & Hurley, 2017; Kavle & others, 2020). One study found that low maternal sensitivity when infants were 15 and 24 months of age was linked to a higher risk of obesity in adolescence (Anderson & others, 2012). And in a recent study, infants who were introduced to vegetables at 4 to 5 months of age showed less fussy eating behavior at 4 years of age than their counterparts who were introduced to vegetables after 6 months (de Barse & others, 2017).

A national study of more than 3,000 randomly selected 4- to 24-month-olds documented that many U.S. parents were feeding their babies too much junk food and not giving them enough fruits and vegetables (Fox & others, 2004). Up to one-third of the babies ate no vegetables and fruit but frequently ate French fries, and almost half of the 7- to 8-month-old babies were fed desserts, sweets, or sweetened drinks. By 15 months, French fries were the most common vegetable the babies ate.

Such poor dietary patterns early in development can result in more infants being overweight (Brown, 2020). In addition to consuming too many French fries, sweetened drinks, and desserts, are there other factors that might explain increased numbers of overweight U.S. infants? A mother's weight gain during pregnancy and a mother's own high weight before pregnancy may be factors (Dantas & da Silva, 2019). Also, an important factor likely is whether an infant is breast fed or bottle fed (Davie, Bick, & Chilcot, 2019). Breast-fed infants have lower rates of weight gain than bottle-fed infants in childhood and adolescence, and it is estimated that breast feeding reduces the risk of obesity by approximately 20 percent (Uwaezuoke, Eneh, & Ndu, 2017).

Breast versus Bottle Feeding   For the first four to six months of life, human milk or an alternative formula is the baby's source of nutrients and energy. For years, debate has focused on whether breast feeding is better for the infant than bottle feeding. The growing consensus is that breast feeding is better for the baby's health (Blake, 2020; Schiff, 2021). Since the 1970s, breast feeding by U.S. mothers has soared (see Figure 11). In 2016, 81 percent of U.S. mothers breast fed their newborns, and 52 percent breast fed their 6-month-olds (Centers for Disease Control and Prevention, 2016). The American Academy of Pediatrics Section on Breastfeeding (2012) reconfirmed its recommendation of exclusive breast feeding in the first six months followed by continued breast feeding as complementary foods are introduced, and further breast feeding for one year or longer as mutually desired by the mother and infant.

What are some of the benefits of breast feeding? The following conclusions have been supported by research.

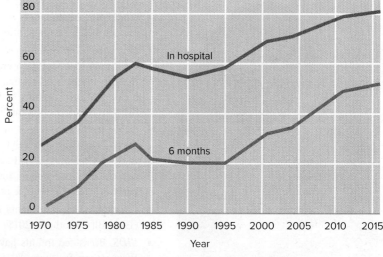

FIGURE **11**

TRENDS IN BREAST FEEDING IN THE UNITED STATES: 1970–2016

Outcomes for the Child

- *Gastrointestinal infections.* Breast-fed infants have fewer gastrointestinal infections (Bartick & others, 2017a, b).

- *Respiratory tract infections.* Breast-fed infants have fewer infections of the lower respiratory tract (Lee & Binns, 2019).

- *Allergies.* A recent research review found no support for breast feeding reducing the risk of allergies in young children (Heinrich, 2017).

- *Asthma.* Exclusive breast feeding for three months protects against wheezing in babies, but whether it prevents asthma in older children is unclear (Wang & others, 2017). However, a Japanese study found that breast feeding was linked to a lower incidence of asthma from 6 to 42 months of age (Yamakawa & others, 2015).

Human milk or an alternative formula is a baby's source of nutrients for the first four to six months. The growing consensus is that breast feeding is better for the baby's health, although controversy still swirls about the issue of breast feeding versus bottle feeding. *Why is breast feeding strongly recommended by pediatricians?*
JGI/Blend Images LLC

- *Immune system.* A recent research review concluded that breast milk contains immuno-modulating components that benefit the maturation of the infant's immune system and provide defenses for fighting off disease (Nolan, Parks, & Good, 2019).
- *Ear, throat, and sinus infections.* One study found that infants who had been breast fed for 9 months or longer were less likely to have developed ear, throat, and sinus infections in the past year when they were 6 years old than their counterparts who had been breast fed for 3 months or less (Li & others, 2014). Breast-fed infants also are less likely to develop otitis media, a middle ear infection (Pelton & Leibovitz, 2009).
- *Overweight and obesity.* Consistent evidence indicates that breast-fed infants are less likely to become overweight or obese in childhood, adolescence, and adulthood (Davie, Bick, & Chilcot, 2019). In a recent study, breast feeding was associated with a lower risk of being overweight, lower blood pressure, and a smaller waist circumference at 12 years of age (Pluymen & others, 2019).
- *Diabetes.* Breast-fed infants are less likely to develop type 1 diabetes in childhood (Lund-Blix & others, 2015) and type 2 diabetes in adulthood (Minniti & others, 2014).
- *SIDS.* Breast-fed infants have lower rates of SIDS (Bartick & others, 2017a, 2020; Wennergren & others, 2015).
- *Fever.* In a recent study, breast fed infants were less likely to develop a fever in their first six months of life (Saeed, Haile, & Chertok, 2020).
- *Cardiovascular fitness.* A recent meta-analysis found that breast feeding was linked to better cardiovascular fitness in children from 4 to 18 years of age (Berlanga-Macias & others, 2020).
- *Hospitalization.* A recent study of more than 500,000 Scottish children found that those who were breast fed exclusively at 6 to 8 weeks of age were less likely to have ever been hospitalized through early childhood than their formula-fed counterparts (Ajetunmobi & others, 2015). Other recent research has found that breast-fed infants had lower rates of hospitalization for a number of conditions, including gastrointestinal problems and lower respiratory tract infection, and breast-feeding mothers had lower rates of hospitalization for cardiovascular problems and diabetes (Bartick & others, 2017b).

In large-scale research reviews, no conclusive evidence for the benefits of breast feeding was found for children's cognitive development and cardiovascular health (Agency for Healthcare Research and Quality, 2007; Ip & others, 2009).

Outcomes for the Mother

- *Breast cancer.* Consistent evidence indicates a lower incidence of breast cancer in women who breast feed their infants (Bartick & others, 2017a; Mayor, 2015).
- *Ovarian cancer.* Evidence also reveals a reduction in ovarian cancer in women who breast feed their infants (Stuebe & Schwartz, 2010).
- *Type 2 diabetes.* Some evidence suggests that there is a reduction in type 2 diabetes in women who breast feed their infants (Bartick & others, 2017a).
- *Hospitalization.* Recent research found that breast feeding mothers had lower rates of hospitalization for cardiovascular problems and diabetes (Bartick & others, 2017b).

In large-scale research reviews, no conclusive evidence could be found for maternal benefits of breast feeding involving return to prepregnancy weight, reduced rates of osteoporosis, and decreased risk of postpartum depression (Agency for Healthcare Research and Quality, 2007; Ip & others, 2009). However, one study revealed that women who breast fed their infants had a lower incidence of metabolic syndrome (a disorder characterized by obesity, hypertension, and insulin resistance) in midlife (Ram & others, 2008).

Many health professionals have argued that breast feeding facilitates the development of an attachment bond between the mother and infant (Britton, Britton, & Gronwaldt, 2006; Wittig & Spatz, 2008). However, a research review found that the positive role of breast feeding on the mother-infant relationship is not supported by research (Jansen, de Weerth, & Riksen-Walraven, 2008). The review concluded that recommending breast feeding should not be based on its role in improving the mother-infant relationship but rather on its positive effects on infant and maternal health. Also, researchers have not consistently found links between breast feeding and higher intelligence in children, although in three studies, breast feeding was associated with a very small increase in children's intelligence (Bernard & others, 2017; Kanazawa, 2015; Strom & others, 2019).

Which women are least likely to breast feed? They include mothers who work full-time outside the home, are younger than 25, lack a high school diploma, are African American, and have a low income (Merewood & others, 2007). In one study of low-income mothers in Georgia, interventions (such as counseling focused on the benefits of breast feeding and the free loan of a breast pump) increased the incidence of breast feeding (Ahluwalia & others, 2000). Increasingly, mothers who return to work during the infant's first year of life use a breast pump to extract breast milk that can be stored for later feeding of the infant when the mother is not present.

As mentioned earlier, the American Academy of Pediatrics Section on Breastfeeding (2012) strongly endorses exclusive breast feeding for the first 6 months and further recommends breast feeding for another year. Are there circumstances when mothers should not breast feed? Yes, a mother should not breast feed (1) if she is infected with HIV or some other infectious disease that can be transmitted through her milk, (2) if she has active tuberculosis, or (3) if she is taking any drug that may not be safe for the infant (Iliyasu & others, 2020; Remmart & others, 2020).

Some women cannot breast feed their infants because of physical difficulties; others feel guilty if they terminate breast feeding early. Mothers may also worry that they are depriving their infants of important emotional and psychological benefits if they bottle feed rather than breast feed. Some researchers have found, however, that there are no psychological differences between breast-fed and bottle-fed infants (Ferguson, Harwood, & Shannon, 1987; Young, 1990).

A further issue in interpreting the benefits of breast feeding was underscored in large-scale research reviews (Agency for Healthcare Research and Quality, 2007; Ip & others, 2009). While highlighting a number of breast feeding benefits for children and mothers, the report issued a caution about breast feeding research: None of the findings imply causality. Breast versus bottle feeding studies are correlational rather than experimental, and women who breast feed tend to be wealthier, older, more educated, and likely more health-conscious than their bottle feeding counterparts, which could explain why breast-fed children are healthier.

developmental **connection**

Research Methods

How does a correlational study differ from an experimental study? Connect to "Introduction."

Malnutrition in Infancy   Many infants around the world are malnourished (UNICEF, 2020). Early weaning of infants from breast milk to inadequate sources of nutrients, such as unsuitable and unsanitary cow's milk formula, can cause protein deficiency and malnutrition in infants. However, as we saw in the discussion following the chapter opening story, a concern in developing countries is the increasing number of women who are HIV-positive and the fear that they will transmit this virus to their offspring (Remmart & others, 2020). Breast feeding is more optimal that formula feeding for mothers and infants in developing countries, except for mothers who have or are suspected of having HIV/AIDS.

A large-scale study that examined feeding practices in 28 developing countries found that the practices were far from optimal (Arabi & others, 2012). In this study, only 25 percent of infants 5 months of age and younger were breast fed.

Even if it is not fatal, severe and lengthy malnutrition is detrimental to physical, cognitive, and social development (Boyle, 2019; UNICEF, 2020). One study found that Asian Indian children who had a history of chronic malnutrition performed more poorly on tests of attention and memory than their counterparts who were not malnourished (Kar, Rao, & Chandramouli, 2008). And a longitudinal study revealed that Barbadians who had experienced moderate to severe protein/energy malnutrition during infancy had persisting attention deficits when they were 40 years old (Galler & others, 2012). Researchers also have found that interventions can benefit individuals who have experienced malnutrition in infancy. For example, in one study standard nutritional care combined with a psychosocial intervention (group meetings with mothers and play sessions with infants, as well as six months of home visits) reduced the negative effects of malnutrition on severely malnourished Bangladeshi 6- to 24-month-olds' cognitive development (Najar & others, 2008).

To read about programs designed to improve infants' and young children's nutrition, see *Connecting Development to Life.*

Adequate early nutrition is an important aspect of healthy development (Hill & others, 2020; Perez-Escamilla & Engmann, 2019). In addition to sound nutrition, children need a nurturing, supportive environment (Blake, 2020; Schiff, 2021). One individual who has stood out as an advocate of caring for children and who has been especially passionate about preventing child obesity is pediatrician Faize Mustafa-Infante, who is featured in *Connecting with Careers.*

Improving the Nutrition of Infants and Young Children Living in Low-Income Families

Poor nutrition is a special concern in the lives of infants from low-income families (Donatelle & Ketcham, 2020). To address this problem in the United States, the WIC (Women, Infants, and Children) program provides federal grants to states for healthy supplemental foods, health care referrals, and nutrition education for women from low-income families beginning in pregnancy, and to infants and young children up to 5 years of age who are at nutritional risk (Hamner & others, 2019; Lauer & others, 2019; Morrow, 2020; Schindler-Ruwisch & others, 2020). WIC serves approximately 7,500,000 participants in the United States. A recent study found that African American WIC women participants had lower-quality diets than their counterparts from other ethnic backgrounds (Parker & others, 2020).

However, overall, positive influences on women's infants', and young children's nutrition and health have been found for participants in WIC (Chaparro & others, 2019; Jung, Nobari, & Whaley, 2019). A recent study found that the percentage of preterm births was lower among expectant mothers covered by Medicaid who received WIC benefits during pregnancy than among their counterparts who did not receive WIC benefits (Soneji & Beltran-Sanchez, 2019). Another study revealed that a WIC program that introduced peer counseling services for pregnant women increased breast feeding initiation by 27 percent (Olson & others, 2010a, b). Also, a study found that entry to the WIC program during the first trimester of pregnancy reduced rates of maternal cigarette smoking (Brodsky, Viner-Brown, & Handler, 2009). Further, a multiple-year literacy intervention with Spanish-speaking families in the WIC program in Los Angeles increased literacy resources and activities at home, which in turn led to a higher level of

Participants in the WIC program. *What are some changes the WIC program is trying to implement?*
Source: USDA Food and Nutrition Service, Supplemental Nutrition Assistance Program

school readiness in children (Whaley & others, 2011). And recent longitudinal studies found that when mothers participated in WIC programs during pregnancy and beyond, their young children showed short-term cognitive benefits and longer-term reading and math benefits (Chen & others, 2018; Martinez-Brockman & others, 2018; McCoy & others, 2018). And in a recent study, high-risk infants in a WIC program had higher cognitive scores on the Bayley Scales of Infant Development (Lakshmanan & others, 2020).

Why would the WIC program provide lactation counseling as part of its services?

Faize Mustafa-Infante

Dr. Mustafa-Infante grew up in Colombia, South America. She began her career as an elementary school teacher in Colombia and then obtained her medical degree with a specialty in pediatrics. Once she finished her medical training, she moved to San Bernardino, California, to work as a health educator with a focus on preventing and treating childhood obesity in low-income communities. Dr. Mustafa-Infante currently works at Mission Pediatrics in Riverside, California, where she mainly treats infants. She continues her effort to prevent obesity in children and also serves as a volunteer for Ayacucho Mission, a nonprofit organization that provides culturally sensitive medical care for people living in poverty in Ayacucho, Peru. In regard to her cultural background, Dr. Mustafa-Infante describes herself as a Latino doctor with a Middle-Eastern name and a strong commitment to both heritages. Dr. Mustafa-Infante says that hard work and education have been the keys to her success and personal satisfaction.

For more information about what pediatricians do, see the Careers in Life-Span Development appendix.

Review *Connect* Reflect

LG1 Discuss physical growth and development in infancy.

Review
- What are cephalocaudal and proximodistal patterns?
- What changes in height and weight take place in infancy?
- What are some key features of the brain and its development in infancy?
- What changes occur in sleep during infancy?
- What are infants' nutritional needs?

Connect
- What types of brain research technology can be used to study infants that cannot be used to study them before they are born? Which techniques can be used on adults but not infants? How might these limitations affect our understanding of brain development across the life span?

Reflect *Your Own Personal Journey of Life*
- What sleep and nutrition guidelines would you follow to enhance the health and safety of your own infant?

2 Motor Development

LG2 Describe infants' motor development.

| The Dynamic Systems View | Reflexes | Gross Motor Skills | Fine Motor Skills |

As a newborn, Ramona, whom you read about in the chapter opening story, could suck, fling her arms, and tightly grip a finger placed in her tiny hand. Within just two years, she would be toddling around on her own, opening doors and jars as she explored her little world. Are her accomplishments inevitable? How do infants develop their motor skills, and which skills do they develop at specific ages?

THE DYNAMIC SYSTEMS VIEW

Developmentalist Arnold Gesell (1934) thought his painstaking observations had revealed how people develop their motor skills. He had discovered that infants and children develop rolling, sitting, standing, and other motor skills in a fixed order and within specific time frames. These observations, said Gesell, show that motor development comes about through the unfolding of a genetic plan, or *maturation.*

Later studies, however, demonstrated that the sequence of developmental milestones is not as fixed as Gesell indicated and not due as much to heredity as Gesell argued (Adolph, 2018, 2019; Hoch, Rachwani, & Adolph, 2020). Beginning in the 1980s, the study of motor development experienced a renaissance as psychologists developed new insights about *how* motor skills develop (Adolph, 2018). One increasingly influential perspective is dynamic systems theory, proposed by Esther Thelen (Thelen & Smith, 1998, 2006).

According to **dynamic systems theory,** infants assemble motor skills for perceiving and acting. Notice that perception and action are coupled, according to this theory. To develop motor skills, infants must perceive something in their environment that motivates them to act and use their perceptions to fine-tune their movements. Motor skills assist infants in reaching their goals (Heiman & others, 2019).

How is a motor skill developed, according to this theory? When infants are motivated to do something, they might create a new motor behavior. The new behavior is the result of many converging factors: the development of the nervous system, the body's physical properties and its possibilities for movement, the goal the child is motivated to reach, and availability of environmental support for the skill. For example, babies learn to walk only when maturation of the nervous system allows them to control certain leg muscles, when they want to move, when their legs are strong enough to support their weight, and when they have sufficient balance control to support their body on one leg.

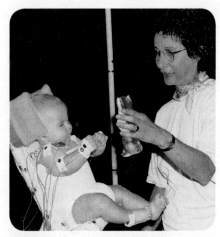

Esther Thelen is shown conducting an experiment to discover how infants learn to control their arm movements to reach and grasp for objects. A computer device is used to monitor the infant's arm movements and to track muscle patterns. Thelen's research is conducted from a dynamic systems perspective. *What is the nature of this perspective?*
Courtesy of Dr. David Thelen

dynamic systems theory The perspective on motor development that seeks to explain how motor behaviors are assembled for perceiving and acting.

How might dynamic systems theory explain the development of learning to walk?
Di Studio/Shutterstock

Mastering a motor skill requires the infant's active efforts to coordinate several components of the skill. Infants explore and select possible solutions to the demands of a new task; they assemble adaptive patterns by modifying their current movement patterns (Rachwani, Hoch, & Adolph, 2020). The first step occurs when the infant is motivated by a new challenge—such as the desire to cross a room—and gets into the "ballpark" of the task demands by taking a couple of stumbling steps. Then, the infant "tunes" these movements to make them smoother and more effective. The tuning is achieved through repeated cycles of action and perception of the consequences of that action. According to the dynamic systems view, even universal milestones, such as crawling, reaching, and walking, are learned through this process of adaptation: Infants modulate their movement patterns to fit a new task by exploring and selecting possible configurations (Hoch, O'Grady, & Adolph, 2019; Ossmy & others, 2020).

To see how dynamic systems theory explains motor behavior, imagine that you offer a new toy to a baby named Gabriel (Thelen & others, 1993). There is no exact program that can tell Gabriel ahead of time how to move his arm and hand and fingers to grasp the toy. Gabriel must adapt to his goal—grasping the toy—and the context. From his sitting position, he must make split-second adjustments to extend his arm, holding his body steady so that his arm and torso don't plow into the toy. Muscles in his arm and shoulder contract and stretch in a host of combinations, exerting a variety of forces. He improvises a way to reach out with one arm and wrap his fingers around the toy.

Recently, Karen Adolph and Justine Hoch (2019) described four key aspects that reflect the dynamic systems theory of motor development: (1) embodied, (2) embedded, (3) enculturated, and (4) enabling.

- *Motor Development Is Embodied.* Opportunities for motor behavior involve the current status of a child's body. Changes in infants' bodies modify the nature of their motor behavior. Walking is a good example of motor behavior being embodied. Over weeks and months of walking experiences, infants improve their walking skills. Initially, they walk very slowly in halting, inconsistent ways and have poor balance. With extensive experiences, they walk faster, their steps become more consistent, and they have much better balance. Their changing body interacts with experiences and opportunities to walk as they physically grow.

- *Motor Development Is Embedded.* Environmental circumstances can facilitate or restrict possibilities for motor behavior. Motor behavior occurs in a physical environment, and variations in the environment require infants to adapt. As they encounter steep slopes, narrow passageways, stairs, and many other circumstances, infants have to be flexible and modify how they move.

- *Motor Development Is Enculturated.* Social and cultural contexts influence motor behavior. Caregivers play important roles in infants' motor development. Caregivers often hold infants' hands and "walk" them around a room. And infants' first steps in learning to walk are likely in a social context as they go toward a caregiver's open arms. Cultures also vary in how much caregivers engage in behavior that stimulates and encourages infants' and children's motor development.

- *Motor Development Is Enabling.* Motor development is not isolated from other aspects of development, and it contributes to infants' and children's development in other domains. Before infants learn to crawl and walk, their exploration of the world depends on where their caregivers place them, but their expanding motor skills provide them with more independence in exploring and learning about the world that can improve their cognitive and socioemotional development.

Thus, according to dynamic systems theory, motor development is not a passive process in which genes dictate the unfolding of a sequence of skills over time. Rather, the infant actively puts together a skill to achieve a goal within the constraints set by the infant's body and environment. Nature and nurture, the infant and the environment, are all working together as part of an ever-changing system.

As we examine the course of motor development, we will describe how dynamic systems theory applies to specific skills. First, though, let's examine the beginning of motor development: the infant's reflexes.

reflexes Built-in reactions to stimuli that govern the newborn's movements, which are automatic and beyond the newborn's control.

rooting reflex A newborn's built-in reaction that occurs when the infant's cheek is stroked or the side of the mouth is touched. In response, the infant turns his or her head toward the side that was touched, in an apparent effort to find something to suck.

sucking reflex A newborn's built-in reaction to automatically suck an object placed in its mouth. The sucking reflex enables the infant to get nourishment before he or she has associated a nipple with food and also serves as a self-soothing or self-regulating mechanism.

Moro reflex A neonatal startle response in which the newborn arches its back, throws its head back, flings out its arms and legs, and then pulls its arms and legs close to the center of the body.

grasping reflex A neonatal reflex that occurs when something touches the infant's palms and the infant responds by grasping tightly.

gross motor skills Motor skills that involve large-muscle activities, such as walking.

REFLEXES

The newborn is not completely helpless. Among other things, it has some basic reflexes. For example, when submerged in water, the newborn automatically holds its breath and contracts its throat to keep water out.

Reflexes are built-in reactions to stimuli; they govern the newborn's movements, which are automatic and beyond the newborn's control. Reflexes are genetically carried survival mechanisms. They allow infants to respond adaptively to their environment before they have had the opportunity to learn. The rooting and sucking reflexes are important examples. Both have survival value for newborn mammals, who must find a mother's breast to obtain nourishment. The **rooting reflex** occurs when the infant's cheek is stroked or the side of the mouth is touched. In response, the infant turns its head toward the side that was touched in an apparent effort to find something to suck. The **sucking reflex** occurs when newborns automatically suck an object placed in their mouth. This reflex enables newborns to get nourishment before they have associated a nipple with food and also serves as a self-soothing or self-regulating mechanism.

Another example is the **Moro reflex,** which occurs in response to a sudden, intense noise or movement (see Figure 12). When startled, the newborn arches its back, throws back its head, and flings out its arms and legs. Then the newborn rapidly draws in its arms and legs. The Moro reflex is believed to be a way of grabbing for support while falling; it would have had survival value for our primate ancestors.

Some reflexes—coughing, sneezing, blinking, shivering, and yawning, for example—persist throughout life. They are as important for the adult as they are for the infant. Other reflexes, though, disappear several months following birth, as the infant's brain matures and voluntary control over many behaviors develops. The rooting and Moro reflexes, for example, tend to disappear when the infant is 3 to 4 months old.

The movements of some reflexes eventually become incorporated into more complex, voluntary actions. One important example is the **grasping reflex,** which occurs when something touches the infant's palms (see Figure 12). The infant responds by grasping tightly. By the end of the third month, the grasping reflex diminishes and the infant shows a more voluntary grasp. As its motor coordination becomes smoother, the infant will grasp objects, carefully manipulate them, and explore their qualities.

The old view of reflexes is that they were exclusively genetic, built-in mechanisms that governed the infant's movements. The new perspective on infant reflexes is that they are not automatic or completely beyond the infant's control. For example, infants can alternate the movement of their legs to make a mobile jiggle or change their sucking rate to listen to a recording (Adolph & Robinson, 2015).

GROSS MOTOR SKILLS

Ask any parents about their baby, and sooner or later you are likely to hear about one or more motor milestones, such as "Cassandra just learned to crawl," "Jesse is finally sitting alone," or "Angela took her first step last week." Parents proudly announce such milestones as their children transform themselves from babies unable to lift their heads to toddlers who grab things off the grocery store shelf, chase a cat, and participate actively in the family's social life (Thelen, 2000). These milestones are examples of **gross motor skills,** which involve large-muscle activities such as moving one's arms and walking.

The Development of Posture How do gross motor skills develop? As a foundation, these skills require postural control. For example, to track moving objects, you must be able to control the movement of your head in order to stabilize your gaze; before you can walk, you must be able to balance on one leg.

Posture is more than just holding still and straight. Posture is a dynamic process that is linked with sensory information in the skin, joints, and muscles, which tell us where we are in space; in vestibular organs in the inner ear that regulate balance and equilibrium; and in vision and hearing (Soska, Robinson, & Adolph, 2015).

Newborn infants cannot voluntarily control their posture. Within a few weeks, though, they can hold their heads erect, and soon they can lift their heads while prone. By 2 months

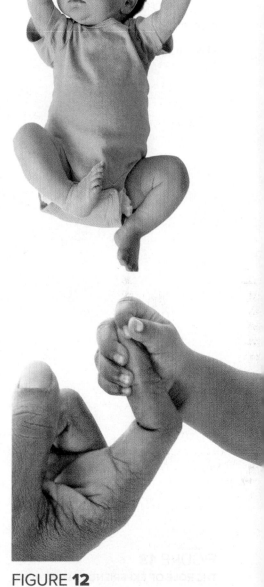

FIGURE **12**

NEWBORN REFLEXES. Young infants have several reflexes, including the Moro reflex (*top*) and grasping reflex (*bottom*).
(*Top*) Erik Isakson/Getty Images (*bottom*) Stockbyte/ Getty Images

of age, babies can sit while supported on a lap or an infant seat, but they cannot sit independently until they are 6 or 7 months of age. Standing also develops gradually during the first year of life. By about 8 to 9 months of age, infants usually learn to pull themselves up and hold on to a chair, and they often can stand alone by about 10 to 12 months of age.

Learning to Walk Even young infants can make the alternating leg movements that are needed for walking. The neural pathways that control leg alternation are in place from a very early age, even at birth or before. Indeed, researchers have found that alternating leg movements occur during the fetal period and at birth (Adolph & Robinson, 2015). Both alternating leg movements and forward stepping movements occur early in development and are precursors to walking.

If infants can produce forward stepping movements so early, why does it take them so long to learn to walk? The key skills in learning to walk appear to be stabilizing balance on one leg long enough to swing the other forward and shifting weight without falling. These are difficult biomechanical problems to solve, and it takes infants about a year to do it. Locomotion and postural control are closely linked, especially in walking upright (Kretch & Adolph, 2017).

In learning to locomote, infants learn what kinds of places and surfaces are safe for locomotion (Adolph, 2018, 2020; Adolph, Hoch, & Ossmy, 2020). Karen Adolph (1997) investigated how experienced and inexperienced crawling infants and walking infants go down steep slopes (see Figure 13). Newly crawling infants, who averaged about 8½ months in age, rather indiscriminately went down the steep slopes, often falling in the process (with their mothers next to the slope to catch them). After weeks of practice, the crawling babies became more adept at judging which slopes were too steep to crawl down and which ones they could navigate safely. New walkers also could not judge the safety of the slopes, but experienced walkers accurately matched their skills with the steepness of the slopes. They rarely fell downhill; instead, they either refused to go down the steep slopes or went down backward in a cautious manner. Experienced walkers perceptually assessed the situation—looking, swaying, touching, and thinking before they moved down the slope. With experience, both the crawlers and the walkers learned to avoid the risky slopes where they would fall, integrating perceptual information with the development of a new motor behavior. In this research, we again see the importance of perceptual-motor coupling and practice in the development of new motor skills (Adolph & Berger, 2015).

Practice is especially important in learning to walk (Adolph, 2018, 2020). "Thousands of daily walking steps, each step slightly different from the last because of variations in the terrain and the continually varying biomechanical constraints on the body, may help infants to identify the relevant" combination of strength and balance required to improve their walking skills (Adolph, Vereijken, & Shrout, 2003, p. 495). In one study, Adolph and her colleagues (2012) observed 12- to 19-month-olds during free play. Locomotor experience was extensive, with the infants averaging 2,368 steps and 17 falls per hour.

A recent study explored how infants plan and guide their locomotion in the challenging context of navigating a series of bridges varying in width (Kretch & Adolph, 2017). Infants' visual exploration (direction of their gaze) was assessed using a head-mounted eye-tracking device, and their locomotor actions were captured using video. The 14-month-olds engaged in

FIGURE **13**

THE ROLE OF EXPERIENCE IN CRAWLING AND WALKING INFANTS' JUDGMENTS OF WHETHER TO GO DOWN A SLOPE.
Karen Adolph (1997) found that locomotor experience rather than age was the primary predictor of adaptive responding on slopes of varying steepness. Newly crawling and walking infants could not judge the safety of the various slopes. With experience, they learned to avoid slopes where they would fall. When expert crawlers began to walk, they again made mistakes and fell, even though they had judged the same slope accurately when crawling. Adolph referred to this as the specificity of learning because it does not transfer across crawling and walking.
Dr. Karen Adolph, New York University

Newly crawling infant

Experienced walker

visual exploration from a distance as an initial assessment before they crossed almost every bridge. The visual information led to modifications in their gait when approaching narrow bridges, and they used haptic (touch) information at the edge of the bridges. As they gained more walking experience, their exploratory behaviors became more efficient and they became more adept at deciding which bridges were safe to walk across.

Might the development of walking be linked to advances in other aspects of development? Walking allows the infant to gain contact with objects that were previously out of reach and to initiate interaction with parents and other adults, thereby promoting language development (Adolph & Robinson, 2015; He, Walle, & Campos, 2015). Thus, just as with advances in postural skills, walking skills can produce a cascade of changes in the infant's development (Marrus & others, 2018).

The First Year: Motor Development Milestones and Variations Figure 14 summarizes the range of ages at which infants accomplish various gross motor skills during the first year, culminating in the ability to walk easily. After studying Figure 14, you should be able to order the milestones and describe the typical ages at which babies reach these milestones.

A recent study found a number of factors that are linked to motor development in the first year of life (Flensborg-Madsen & Mortensen, 2017). Twelve developmental milestones were assessed, including grasping, rolling, sitting, and crawling; standing and walking; and overall mean of milestones. A larger size at birth (such as birth weight, birth length, and head circumference) was the aspect of pregnancy and delivery that showed the strongest link to reaching motor milestones earlier. Mother's smoking in the last trimester of prenatal development was associated with reaching the motor milestones later. Also, increase in size (weight increase, length increase, and head increase) in the first year were related to reaching the motor milestones earlier. Breast feeding also was linked to reaching the milestones earlier.

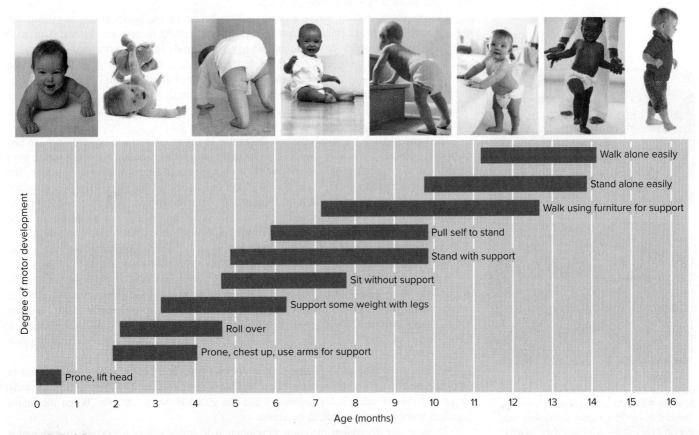

FIGURE 14

MILESTONES IN GROSS MOTOR DEVELOPMENT. The horizontal red bars indicate the range of ages at which most infants reach various milestones in gross motor development.

(*Photo credit left to right*) Barbara Penoyar/Photodisc/Getty Images; StephaneHachey/E+/Getty Images; Image Source/Alamy Stock Photo; Victoria Blackie/Photodisc/Getty Images; Cohen/Ostrow/Digital Vision/Getty Images; Fotosearch/Getty Images; Tom Grill/Fuse/Getty Images; Monika Wisniewska/Amaviael/123RF

However, the timing of these milestones, especially the later ones, may vary by as much as two to four months, and experiences can modify the onset of these accomplishments (Rachwani, Hoch, & Adolph, 2020). For example, since 1992, when pediatricians began recommending that parents place their babies on their backs to sleep, fewer babies crawled, and those who crawled did so later (Davis & others, 1998). Also, some infants do not follow the standard sequence of motor accomplishments. For example, many American infants never crawl on their belly or on their hands and knees. They may discover an idiosyncratic form of locomotion before walking, such as rolling or scooting, or they might never locomote until they are upright (Adolph & Robinson, 2015). In the African Mali tribe, most infants do not crawl (Bril, 1999). And in Jamaica, approximately one-fourth of babies skip crawling (Hopkins, 1991).

According to Karen Adolph and Sarah Berger (2005), "the old-fashioned view that growth and motor development reflect merely the age-related output of maturation is, at best, incomplete. Rather, infants acquire new skills with the help of their caregivers in a real-world environment of objects, surfaces, and planes."

Development in the Second Year The motor accomplishments of the first year bring increasing independence, allowing infants to explore their environment more extensively and to initiate interaction with others more readily. In the second year of life, toddlers become more motorically skilled and mobile. Motor activity during the second year is vital to the child's competent development, and few restrictions, except for safety, should be placed on their adventures.

By 13 to 18 months, toddlers can pull a toy attached to a string and use their hands and legs to climb a number of steps. By 18 to 24 months, toddlers can walk quickly or run stiffly for a short distance, balance on their feet in a squatting position while playing with objects on the floor, walk backward without losing their balance, stand and kick a ball without falling, stand and throw a ball, and jump in place.

Can parents give their babies a head start on becoming physically fit and physically talented through structured exercise classes? Most infancy experts recommend against structured exercise classes for babies. But there are other ways to guide infants' motor development.

Mothers in developing countries tend to stimulate their infants' motor skills more than mothers in more developed countries (Hopkins, 1991; Karasik & others, 2015). In many African, Indian, and Caribbean cultures, mothers massage and stretch their infants during daily baths (Adolph, Karasik, & Tamis-LeMonda, 2010). Mothers in the Gusii culture of Kenya also encourage vigorous movement in their babies.

Do these cultural variations make a difference in the infant's motor development? When caregivers provide babies with physical guidance by physically handling them in special ways (such as stroking, massaging, or stretching) or by giving them opportunities for exercise, the infants often reach motor milestones earlier than infants whose caregivers have not provided these activities (Adolph, 2018; Adolph, Karasik, & Tamis-LeMonda, 2010; Karasik & others, 2015). For example, Jamaican mothers expect their infants to sit and walk alone two to three months earlier than English mothers do (Hopkins & Westra, 1990). And in sub-Saharan Africa, traditional practices in many villages involve mothers and siblings engaging babies in exercises, such as frequent exercise for trunk and pelvic muscles (Super & Harkness, 1997).

Many forms of restricted movement—such as Chinese sandbags, orphanage restrictions, and failure of caregivers to encourage movement in Budapest—have been found to produce substantial delays in motor development (Adolph, Karasik, & Tamis-LeMonda, 2010). In some rural Chinese provinces, for example, babies are placed in a bag of fine sand, which acts as a diaper and is changed once a day. The baby is left alone, face up, and is visited only when being fed by the mother (Xie & Young, 1999).

Some studies of *swaddling* (wrapping an infant tightly in a blanket) show slight delays in motor development, but other studies show no delays. Cultures that do swaddle infants usually do so early in the infant's development when the infant is not yet mobile. When the infant becomes more mobile, swaddling decreases.

To close our discussion of motor development in infancy, it is important to highlight a key theme: infants' development of a skill, such as sitting, crawling or walking, requires considerable behavioral flexibility—the ability to do what is necessary to attain life's everyday goals (Adolph & Hoch, 2019; Rachwani, Hoch, & Adolph, 2020). Adaptive behavior involves finding an accurate solution to a current situation and challenge. The infant's movements cannot be

(*Top*) Some Native Americans sleep in a traditional cradle board, such as this baby from the Santa Clara Pueblo of New Mexico. (*Bottom*) In Jamaica, mothers massage and stretch their infants' arms and legs. *To what extent do cultural variations in the activity infants engage in influence the time at which they reach motor milestones?*
(*Top*) Danita Delimont/Alamy Stock Photo; (*bottom*) Pippa Hetherington/Earthstock/Newscom

repeated in the same way over time and in different situations because their bodies, the environments in which they behave, and the tasks they face change. Keep this theme in mind as you read about motor development in the remainder of the text because such behavioral flexibility continues to be required for finding successful solutions to changing bodies, contexts, and tasks as children continue to develop.

FINE MOTOR SKILLS

Whereas gross motor skills involve large muscle activity, **fine motor skills** involve finely tuned movements. Grasping a toy, using a spoon, buttoning a shirt, or any activity that requires finger dexterity demonstrates fine motor skills. Infants have hardly any control over fine motor skills at birth, but newborns do have many components of what will become finely coordinated arm, hand, and finger movements (McCormack, Hoerl, & Butterfill, 2012).

The onset of reaching and grasping marks a significant achievement in infants' ability to interact with their surroundings (Rachwani & others, 2015). During the first two years of life, infants refine how they reach and grasp (Chinn & others, 2019). Initially, infants reach by moving their shoulders and elbows crudely, swinging their arms toward an object. Later, when infants reach for an object they move their wrists, rotate their hands, and coordinate their thumb and forefinger. Infants do not have to see their own hands in order to reach for an object (Clifton & others, 1993). Cues from muscles, tendons, and joints, not sight of the limb, guide reaching by 4-month-old infants. Recent research studies found that short-term training involving practice of reaching movements increased both preterm and full-term infants' reaching for and touching objects (Cunha & others, 2016; Guimaraes & Tudella, 2015).

Infants refine their ability to grasp objects by developing two types of grasps. Initially, infants grip with the whole hand, which is called the *palmar grasp*. Later, toward the end of the first year, infants also grasp small objects with their thumb and forefinger, which is called the *pincer grip*. Their grasping system is very flexible. They vary their grip on an object depending on its size, shape, and texture, as well as the size of their own hands relative to the object's size. Infants grip small objects with their thumb and forefinger (and sometimes their middle finger too), but they grip large objects with all of the fingers of one hand or both hands.

Perceptual-motor coupling is necessary for the infant to coordinate grasping (Barrett, Traupman, & Needham, 2008). At different stages of development, infants use different perceptual systems to coordinate grasping. Four-month-old infants rely greatly on touch to determine how they will grip an object; 8-month-olds are more likely to use vision as a guide (Newell & others, 1989). This developmental change is efficient because vision lets infants preshape their hands as they reach for an object.

Experience plays a role in reaching and grasping. In a one study, 3-month-olds who were not yet engaging in reaching behavior were provided with reaching experiences. These experiences were linked to increased object exploration and attention focusing skills at 15 months of age (Libertus, Joh, & Needham, 2016). In another study, 3-month-old infants participated in play sessions wearing "sticky mittens . . . mittens with palms that stuck to the edges of toys and allowed the infants to pick up the toys" (Needham, Barrett, & Peterman, 2002, p. 279) (see Figure 15). Infants who participated in sessions with the mittens grasped and manipulated objects earlier in their development than a control group of infants who did not receive the "mitten" experience. The infants who had worn the sticky mittens looked at the objects longer, swatted at them more during visual contact, and were more likely to mouth the objects. In a later study, 5-month-old infants whose parents trained them to use the sticky mittens for 10 minutes a day over a two-week period showed advances in their reaching behavior at the end of the two weeks (Libertus & Needham, 2010). Also, in a recent study, 3-month-old infants participated in active motor training using sticky mittens that allowed them to pick up toys, and these infants engaged in more sophisticated object exploration at 5.5 months of age (Wiesen, Watkins, & Needham, 2016). However, other research found no advantage or even less effective reaching and grasping when infants wore sticky mittens (Corbetta, Wiener, & Thurman, 2018; Corbetta, Williams, & Haynes, 2016).

Just as infants need to exercise their gross motor skills, they also need to exercise their fine motor skills (Needham, 2009). Especially when they can manage a pincer grip, infants delight in picking up small objects. Many develop the pincer

A young girl uses a pincer grip to pick up puzzle pieces.
Newstockimages/SuperStock

fine motor skills Motor skills that involve more finely tuned movements, such as finger dexterity.

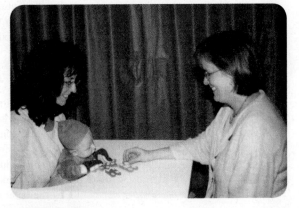

FIGURE 15

INFANTS' USE OF "STICKY MITTENS" TO EXPLORE OBJECTS. Amy Needham and her colleagues (2002) found that "sticky mittens" enhanced young infants' object exploration skills.
Courtesy of Amy Needham, Duke University

grip and begin to crawl at about the same time, and infants of this age pick up virtually everything in sight, especially on the floor, and put the objects in their mouth. Thus, parents need to be vigilant in regularly monitoring what objects are within the infant's reach (Keen, 2005).

Rachel Keen (2011; Keen, Lee, & Adolph, 2014) emphasizes that tool use is an excellent context for studying problem solving in infants because tool use provides information about how infants plan to reach a goal. Researchers in this area have studied infants' intentional actions, which range from picking up a spoon in different orientations to retrieving rakes from inside tubes. One study explored motor origins of tool use by assessing developmental changes in banging movements in 6- to 15-month-olds (Kahrs, Jung, & Lockman, 2013). In this study, younger infants were inefficient and variable when banging an object but by one year of age infants showed consistent straight up-and-down hand movements that resulted in precise aiming and consistent levels of force.

Review Connect Reflect

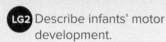 Describe infants' motor development.

Review
- What is the dynamic systems view?
- What are some reflexes that infants have?
- How do gross motor skills develop in infancy?
- How do fine motor skills develop in infancy?

Connect
- What are the differences between the grasping reflex present at birth and the fine motor grasping skills an infant develops between 4 and 12 months of age?

Reflect *Your Own Personal Journey of Life*
- Think of a motor skill that you perform. How would dynamic systems theory explain your motor skill performance?

---

3 Sensory and Perceptual Development

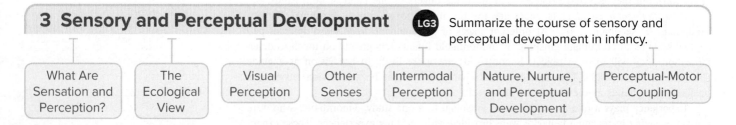

LG3 Summarize the course of sensory and perceptual development in infancy.

| What Are Sensation and Perception? | The Ecological View | Visual Perception | Other Senses | Intermodal Perception | Nature, Nurture, and Perceptual Development | Perceptual-Motor Coupling |

The experiences of the first three years of life are almost entirely lost to us, and when we attempt to enter into a small child's world, we come as foreigners who have forgotten the landscape and no longer speak the native tongue.

—Selma Fraiberg

Developmentalist and child advocate, 20th century

How do sensations and perceptions develop? Can a newborn see? If so, what can it perceive? What about the other senses—hearing, smell, taste, and touch? What are they like in the newborn, and how do they develop? Can an infant put together information from two modalities, such as sight and sound? These are among the intriguing questions that we will explore in this section.

WHAT ARE SENSATION AND PERCEPTION?

How does a newborn know that her mother's skin is soft rather than rough? How does a 5-year-old know what color his hair is? Infants and children "know" these things as a result of information that comes through the senses. Without vision, hearing, touch, taste, and smell, we would be isolated from the world; we would live in dark silence, a tasteless, colorless, feelingless void.

Sensation occurs when information interacts with sensory *receptors*—the eyes, ears, tongue, nostrils, and skin. The sensation of hearing occurs when waves of pulsating air are collected by the outer ear and transmitted through the bones of the inner ear to the auditory nerve. The sensation of vision occurs as rays of light contact the eyes, become focused on the retina, and are transmitted by the optic nerve to the visual centers of the brain.

Perception is the interpretation of what is sensed. The air waves that contact the ears might be interpreted as noise or as musical sounds, for example. The physical energy transmitted to the retina of the eye might be interpreted as a particular color, pattern, or shape, depending on how it is perceived.

THE ECOLOGICAL VIEW

For the past several decades, much of the research on perceptual development in infancy has been guided by the ecological view of Eleanor and James J. Gibson (E. J. Gibson, 1969, 1989, 2001; J. J. Gibson, 1966, 1979). They argue that we do not have to take bits and pieces of data from sensations and build up representations of the world in our minds. Instead, our perceptual system can select from the rich information that the environment itself provides.

According to the Gibsons' **ecological view,** we directly perceive information that exists in the world around us. This view is called *ecological* "because it connects perceptual capabilities to information available in the world of the perceiver" (Kellman & Arterberry, 2006, p. 112). Thus, perception brings us into contact with the environment so we can interact with and adapt to it (Kretch & Adolph, 2017). Perception is designed for action. Perception gives people information such as when to duck, when to turn their bodies as they move through a narrow passageway, and when to put their hands up to catch something.

In the Gibsons' view, objects have **affordances,** which are opportunities for interaction offered by objects that fit within our capabilities to perform activities. A pot may afford you something to cook with, and it may afford a toddler something to bang. Adults typically know when a chair is appropriate for sitting, when a surface is safe for walking, or when an object is within reach. An infant who runs down a steep slope or crawls across a narrow beam is determining the affordances of the slope or beam. We directly and accurately perceive these affordances by sensing information from the environment—the light or sound reflecting from the surfaces of the world—and from our own bodies through muscle receptors, joint receptors, and skin receptors, for example (Adolph, Hoch, & Ossmy, 2020).

An important developmental question is: What affordances can infants or children detect and use? In one study, for example, when babies who could walk were faced with a squishy waterbed, they stopped and explored it, then chose to crawl rather than walk across it (Gibson & others, 1987). They combined perception and action to adapt to the demands of the task.

Similarly, as we described earlier in the section on motor development, infants who were just learning to crawl or just learning to walk were less cautious when confronted with a steep slope than experienced crawlers or walkers were (Adolph, 1997). The more experienced crawlers and walkers perceived that a slope *affords* the possibility for not only faster locomotion but also for falling. Again, infants coupled perception and action to make a decision about what to do in their environment. Through perceptual development, children become more efficient at discovering and using affordances (Adolph, Hoch, & Ossmy, 2020).

Studying infants' perceptions has not been an easy task. For instance, if newborns have limited communication abilities and are unable to verbalize what they are seeing, hearing, smelling, and so on, how can we study their perception? *Connecting Through Research* describes some of the ingenious ways researchers study infants' perceptions.

How would you use the Gibsons' ecological theory of perception and the concept of affordance to explain the role that perception is playing in this baby's activity?
Ryan KC Wong/E+/Getty Images

VISUAL PERCEPTION

What do newborns see? How does visual perception develop in infancy?

Visual Acuity and Human Faces   Psychologist William James (1890/1950) called the newborn's perceptual world a "blooming, buzzing confusion." More than a century later, we can safely say that he was wrong (Johnson, 2020a, b). Even the newborn perceives a world with some order. That world, however, is far different from the one perceived by the toddler or the adult.

Just how well can infants see? At birth, the nerves and muscles and lens of the eye are still developing. As a result, newborns cannot see small things that are far away. The newborn's vision is estimated to be *20/240* on the well-known Snellen chart used for eye examinations, which means that a newborn can see at 20 feet what an adult with normal vision can see at 240 feet (Aslin & Lathrop, 2008). In other words, an object 20 feet away is only as clear to the newborn as it would be if it were 240 feet away from an adult with normal vision (20/20). By 6 months of age, though, on *average* vision is 20/40 (Aslin & Lathrop, 2008).

Faces are possibly the most important visual stimuli in children's social environment, and it is important that they extract key information from others' faces (Quinn, Lee, & Pascalis, 2019). Infants show an interest in human faces soon after birth (Johnson & Hannon, 2015). Research shows that within hours after infants are born, they prefer to look at faces rather than other objects and to look at attractive faces more than at unattractive ones (Lee & others, 2013).

sensation The product of the interaction between information and the sensory receptors—the eyes, ears, tongue, nostrils, and skin.

perception The interpretation of what is sensed.

ecological view The view that perception functions to bring organisms in contact with the environment and to increase adaptation.

affordances Opportunities for interaction offered by objects that fit within our capabilities to perform functional activities.

How Can Newborns' Perception Be Studied?

The creature has poor motor coordination and can move itself only with great difficulty. Although it cries when uncomfortable, it uses few other vocalizations. In fact, it sleeps most of the time, about 16 to 17 hours a day. You are curious about this creature and want to know more about what it can do. You think to yourself, "I wonder if it can see. How could I find out?"

You obviously have a communication problem with the creature. You must devise a way that will allow the creature to "tell" you that it can see. While examining the creature one day, you make an interesting discovery. When you move an object horizontally in front of the creature, its eyes follow the object's movement.

The creature's eye movement suggests that it has at least some vision. In case you haven't already guessed, the creature you have been reading about is the human infant, and the role you played is that of a researcher interested in devising techniques to learn about the infant's visual perception. After years of work, scientists have developed research methods and tools sophisticated enough to examine the subtle abilities of infants and to interpret their complex actions (Bendersky & Sullivan, 2007).

Following are six research techniques that are used to study sensory and perceptual development: (1) visual preference method, (2) habituation/dishabituation, (3) high-amplitude sucking, (4) orienting response, (5) eye tracking, and (6) equipment.

Visual Preference Method

Robert Fantz (1963) was a pioneer in this effort. Fantz made an important discovery that advanced the ability of researchers to investigate infants' visual perception: Infants look at different things for different lengths of time. Fantz placed an infant in a "looking chamber," which had two visual displays on the ceiling above the infant's head. An experimenter viewed the infant's eyes by looking through a peephole. If the infant was fixating on one of the displays, the experimenter could see the display's reflection in

visual preference method A method used to determine whether infants can distinguish one stimulus from another by measuring the length of time they attend to different stimuli.

habituation Decreased responsiveness to a stimulus after repeated presentations of the stimulus.

dishabituation Recovery of a habituated response after a change in stimulation.

the infant's eyes. This allowed the experimenter to determine how long the infant looked at each display. Fantz (1963) found that infants only 2 days old looked longer at patterned stimuli, such as faces and concentric circles, than at red, white, or yellow discs. Infants 2 to 3 weeks old also preferred to look at patterns—a face, a piece of printed matter, or a bull's-eye—longer than at red, yellow, or white discs (see Figure 16). Fantz's research method—studying whether infants can distinguish one stimulus from another by measuring the length of time they attend to different stimuli—is referred to as the **visual preference method**.

Habituation and Dishabituation

Another way that researchers have studied infant perception is to present a stimulus (such as a sight or a sound) a number of times. If the infant decreases its response to the stimulus after several presentations, it indicates that the infant is no longer interested in looking at the stimulus. If the researcher now presents a new stimulus, the infant's response will recover—indicating the infant can discriminate between the old and new stimulus (Messinger & others, 2017).

Habituation is the name given to decreased responsiveness to a stimulus after repeated presentations of the stimulus. **Dishabituation** is the recovery of a habituated response after a change in stimulation.

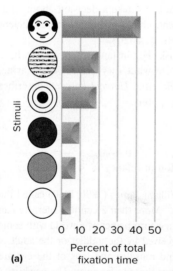

(a)

Stimuli

0 10 20 30 40 50
Percent of total fixation time

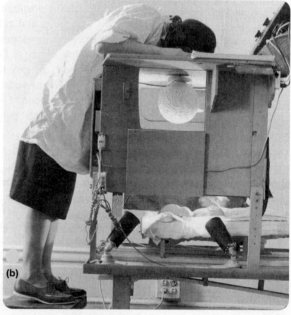

(b)

FIGURE 16

FANTZ'S EXPERIMENT ON INFANTS' VISUAL PERCEPTION. (*a*) Infants 2 to 3 weeks old preferred to look at some stimuli more than others. In Fantz's experiment, infants preferred to look at patterns rather than at color or brightness. For example, they looked longer at a face, a piece of printed matter, or a bull's-eye than at red, yellow, or white discs. (*b*) Fantz used a "looking chamber" to study infants' perception of stimuli.
David Linton, Courtesy of the Linton Family

(continued)

Habituation

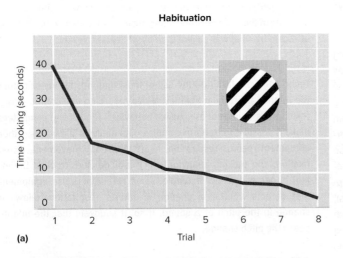

(a)

Dishabituation

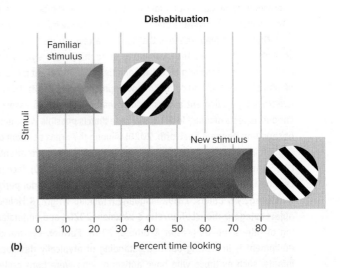

(b)

FIGURE 17

HABITUATION AND DISHABITUATION. In the first part of one study, (*a*) 7-hour-old newborns were shown a stimulus. As indicated, the newborns looked at it an average of 41 seconds when it was first presented to them (Slater, Morison, & Somers, 1988). Over seven more presentations of the stimulus, they looked at it less and less. In the second part of the study, (*b*) infants were presented with both the familiar stimulus to which they had just become habituated and a new stimulus (which was rotated 90 degrees). The newborns looked at the new stimulus three times as long as the familiar stimulus.

Newborn infants can habituate to repeated sights, sounds, smells, or touches (Rovee-Collier & Barr, 2010). Among the measures researchers use in habituation studies are sucking behavior (sucking stops when the young infant attends to a novel object), heart and respiration rates, and the length of time the infant looks at an object. Figure 17 shows the results of one study of habituation and dishabituation with newborns (Slater, Morison, & Somers, 1988).

High-Amplitude Sucking

To assess an infant's attention to sound, researchers often use a method called high-amplitude sucking. In this method, infants are given a nonnutritive nipple to suck, and the nipple is connected to a sound-generating system. The researcher computes a baseline high-amplitude sucking rate in a one-minute silent period. Following the baseline, presentation of a sound is made contingent on the rate of high-amplitude sucking. Initially babies suck frequently so the sound occurs often. Gradually they lose interest in hearing the

FIGURE 18

AN INFANT WEARING EYE-TRACKING HEADGEAR. Photo from Karen Adolph's laboratory at New York University.
Dr. Karen Adolph, New York University

same sound, so they begin to suck less often. Then the researcher changes the sound that is being presented. If the babies renew their vigorous sucking, the inference is that they have noticed the sound change and are sucking more because they want to hear the interesting new sound (Menn & Stoel-Gammon, 2009).

The Orienting Response and Eye-Tracking

A technique that can be used to determine whether an infant can see or hear is the orienting response, which involves turning one's head toward a sight or sound. However, the most important recent advance in measuring infant perception is the development of sophisticated eye-tracking equipment (Hoch, Rachwani, & Adolph, 2020). Eye tracking consists of measuring eye movements that follow (track) a moving object and can be used to evaluate an infant's early visual ability (Stone & Bosworth, 2020). Figure 18 shows an infant wearing an eye-tracking

(continued)

(continued)

headgear in a recent study on visually guided motor behavior and social interaction. Most studies of infant development use remote optics eye trackers that have a camera that is not attached to the infant's head.

One of the main reasons that infant perception researchers are so enthusiastic about the availability of sophisticated eye-tracking equipment is that looking time is among the most important measures of infant perceptual and cognitive development (Aslin, 2012). The new eye-tracking equipment allows much greater precision in assessing various aspects of infant looking and gaze than is possible with human observation (Stone & Bosworth, 2020). Among the areas of infant perception in which eye-tracking equipment is being used are attention (Yu, Suanda, & Smith, 2019), memory (Edgin & others, 2020), face processing (Bodenschatz, Kersting, & Suslow, 2019), intermodal perception (Gergely & others, 2019), language (Franklin, Wright, & Holmes), object categorization (LaTourrette & Waxman, 2020), and understanding of others' needs (Koster & others, 2019). Further, eye-tracking equipment is improving our understanding of atypically developing infants, such as those who have autism or who were born preterm (Avni & others, 2020; Imafuku & others, 2019).

One eye-tracking study shed light on the effectiveness of TV programs and DVDs that claim to educate infants (Kirkorian, Anderson, & Keen, 2012). In this study, 1-year-olds, 4-year-olds, and adults watched *Sesame Street* and the eye-tracking equipment recorded precisely what they looked at on the screen. The 1-year-olds were far less likely to consistently look at the same part of the screen than their older counterparts, suggesting that the 1-year-olds showed little understanding of the *Sesame Street* video but instead were more likely to be attracted by what was salient than by what was relevant.

Equipment

Technology can facilitate the use of most methods for investigating the infant's perceptual abilities. Video-recording equipment allows researchers to investigate elusive behaviors. High-speed computers make it possible to perform complex data analysis in minutes. Other equipment records respiration, heart rate, body movement, visual fixation, and sucking behavior, which provide clues to what the infant is perceiving. For example, some researchers use equipment that detects whether a change in infants' respiration follows a change in the pitch of a sound. If so, it suggests that the infants heard the pitch change.

Scientists have had to be very creative when assessing the development of infants, discovering ways to "interview" them even though they cannot yet talk. Other segments of the population, such as adults who have suffered from a stroke, have difficulty communicating verbally. What kinds of methods or equipment do you think researchers might use to evaluate their perceptual abilities?

Figure 19 shows a computer estimation of what a picture of a face looks like to an infant at different ages from a distance of about 6 inches. Infants spend more time looking at their mother's face than a stranger's face as early as 12 hours after being born (Bushnell, 2003). By 3 months of age, infants (1) match voices to faces, (2) distinguish between male and female faces, and (3) discriminate between faces of their own ethnic group and those of other ethnic groups (Fassbender & Lohaus, 2019; Kelly & others, 2005, 2007).

Experience plays an important role in face processing in infancy and later in development. One aspect of this experience involves the concept of *perceptual narrowing*, in which infants are more likely to distinguish between faces to which they have been exposed than faces that they have never seen before (Quinn & others, 2020).

FIGURE **19**

VISUAL ACUITY DURING THE FIRST MONTHS OF LIFE. The four photographs represent a computer estimation of what a picture of a face looks like to a 1-month-old, 2-month-old, 3-month-old, and 1-year-old (which approximates the visual acuity of an adult).
Kevin Peterson/Photodisc/Getty Images

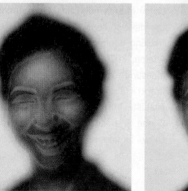   

Color Vision   The infant's color vision also improves. By 8 weeks, and possibly as early as 4 weeks, infants can discriminate between some colors (Kelly, Borchert, & Teller, 1997). By 4 months of age, they have color preferences that mirror adults' in some cases, preferring saturated colors such as royal blue over pale blue, for example (Bornstein, 1975). In recent research, infants' looking times were longest for blue hues and shortest for yellow-green hues (Skelton & Franklin, 2020). In part, the changes in vision described here reflect biological origins and maturation (Skelton & others, 2017). Experience, however, is also necessary for color vision to develop normally (Sugita, 2004).

Perceptual Constancy   Some perceptual accomplishments are especially intriguing because they indicate that the infant's perception goes beyond the information provided by the senses (Bremner & others, 2017; Johnson, 2019). This is the case in perceptual constancy, in which sensory stimulation is changing but perception of the physical world remains constant. If infants did not develop perceptual constancy, each time they saw an object at a different distance or in a different orientation, they would perceive it as a different object. Thus, the development of perceptual constancy allows infants to perceive their world as stable. Two types of perceptual constancy are size constancy and shape constancy.

Size constancy is the recognition that an object remains the same even though the retinal image of the object changes as you move toward or away from the object. The farther away from us an object is, the smaller its image is on our eyes. Thus, the size of an object on the retina is not sufficient to tell us its actual size. For example, you perceive a bicycle standing right in front of you as smaller than the car parked across the street, even though the bicycle casts a larger image on your eyes than the car does. When you move away from the bicycle, you do not perceive it to be shrinking even though its image on your retinas shrinks; you perceive its size as constant.

But what about babies? Do they have size constancy? Researchers have found that babies as young as 3 months of age show size constancy (Bower, 1966; Day & McKenzie, 1973). However, at 3 months of age, this ability is not full-blown. It continues to develop until 10 or 11 years of age (Kellman & Banks, 1998).

Shape constancy is the recognition that an object remains the same shape even though its orientation to us changes. Look around the room you are in right now. You likely see objects of varying shapes, such as tables and chairs. If you get up and walk around the room, you will see these objects from different sides and angles. Even though your retinal image of the objects changes as you walk and look, you will still perceive the objects as having the same shape.

Do babies have shape constancy? As with size constancy, researchers have found that babies as young as 3 months of age have shape constancy (Bower, 1966; Day & McKenzie, 1973). Three-month-old infants, however, do not have shape constancy for irregularly shaped objects such as tilted planes (Cook & Birch, 1984).

Perception of Occluded Objects   Look around where you are now. You likely see that some objects are partly occluded by other objects that are in front of them—possibly a desk behind a chair, some books behind a computer, or a car parked behind a tree. Do infants perceive an object as complete when it is occluded by an object in front of it?

In the first two months of postnatal development, infants don't perceive occluded objects as complete; instead, they perceive only what is visible (Johnson, 2019). Beginning at about 2 months of age, infants develop the ability to perceive that occluded objects are whole (Slater, Field, & Hernandez-Reif, 2007). How does perceptual completion develop? In Scott Johnson's research (2010, 2011, 2013, 2019, 2020a, b), learning, experience, and self-directed exploration via eye movements play key roles in the development of perceptual completion in young infants.

Many objects that are occluded appear and disappear behind closer objects, as when you are walking down the street and see cars appear and disappear behind buildings as they move or you move. Infants develop the ability to track briefly occluded moving objects at about 3 to 5 months of age (Bertenthal, 2008). One study explored the ability of 5- to 9-month-old infants to track moving objects that disappeared gradually behind an occluded partition, disappeared abruptly, or imploded (shrank quickly in size) (Bertenthal, Longo, & Kenny, 2007) (see Figure 20). In this study, the infants were more likely to accurately predict the reappearance of the moving object when it disappeared gradually than when it vanished abruptly or imploded.

Depth Perception   Might infants even perceive depth? To investigate this question, Eleanor Gibson and Richard Walk (1960) constructed a miniature cliff with a drop-off covered

size constancy The recognition that an object remains the same even though the retinal image of the object changes as the observer moves toward or away from the object.

shape constancy The recognition that an object's shape remains the same even though its orientation to the observer changes.

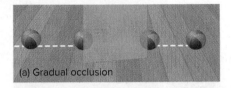
(a) Gradual occlusion

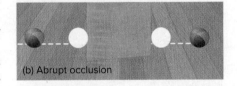
(b) Abrupt occlusion

(c) Implosion

FIGURE 20

INFANTS' PREDICTIVE TRACKING OF A BRIEFLY OCCLUDED MOVING BALL. The top picture shows the visual scene that infants experienced. At the beginning of each event, a multicolored ball bounced up and down with an accompanying bouncing sound, and then rolled across the floor until it disappeared behind the partition. The other three pictures show the three stimulus events that the 5- to 9-month-old infants experienced: (a) Gradual occlusion—the ball gradually disappears behind the right side of the occluding partition located in the center of the display. (b) Abrupt occlusion—the ball abruptly disappears when it reaches the location of the white circle and then abruptly reappears two seconds later at the location of the second white circle on the other side of the occluding partition. (c) Implosion—the rolling ball quickly decreases in size as it approaches the occluding partition and rapidly increases in size as it reappears on the other side of the occluding partition.

FIGURE 21

EXAMINING INFANTS' DEPTH PERCEPTION ON THE VISUAL CLIFF.
Eleanor Gibson and Richard Walk (1960) found that most infants would not crawl out on the glass, which, according to Gibson and Walk, indicated that they had depth perception. However, some critics point out that the visual cliff is a better indication of the infant's social referencing and fear of heights than of the infant's perception of depth.
Mark Richard/PhotoEdit

(a)

(b)

FIGURE 22

HEARING IN THE WOMB. (*a*) Pregnant mothers read *The Cat in the Hat* to their fetuses during the last few months of pregnancy. (*b*) When they were born, the babies preferred listening to a recording of their mothers reading *The Cat in the Hat*, as evidenced by their sucking on a nipple that produced this recording, rather than another story, *The King, the Mice and the Cheese.*
(*a*) Jill Braaten/McGraw-Hill; (*b*) Courtesy of Dr. Melanie J. Spence

by glass in their laboratory. They placed infants on the edge of this visual cliff and had their mothers coax them to crawl onto the glass (see Figure 21). Most infants would not crawl out on the glass, choosing instead to remain on the shallow side, an indication that they could perceive depth.

OTHER SENSES

Other sensory systems besides vision also develop during infancy. We will explore development in hearing, touch and pain, smell, and taste.

Hearing During the last two months of pregnancy, as the fetus nestles in its mother's womb, it can hear sounds such as the mother's voice, music, and so on (Das & others, 2020). Two psychologists wanted to find out if a fetus who heard Dr. Seuss' classic story *The Cat in the Hat* while still in the mother's womb would prefer hearing the story after birth (DeCasper & Spence, 1986). During the last months of pregnancy, 16 women read *The Cat in the Hat* to their fetuses. Then shortly after the babies were born, they listened to recordings of their mothers reading either *The Cat in the Hat* or a story with a different rhyme and pace, *The King, the Mice and the Cheese* (which was not read to them during prenatal development). The infants sucked on a nipple in a different way when they listened to the recordings of the two stories, suggesting that the infants recognized the pattern and tone of *The Cat in the Hat* (see Figure 22). This study illustrates not only that a fetus can hear but also that it has a remarkable ability to learn and remember even before birth. An fMRI study confirmed capacity of the fetus to hear at 33 to 34 weeks into the prenatal period by assessing fetal brain response to auditory stimuli (Jardri & others, 2012).

The fetus can also recognize the mother's voice, as one study demonstrated (Kisilevsky & others, 2003). Sixty term fetuses (mean gestational age, 38.4 weeks) were exposed to a tape recording either of their mother or of a female stranger reading a passage. The sounds of the tape were delivered through a loudspeaker held just above the mother's abdomen. Fetal heart rate increased in response to the mother's voice but decreased in response to the stranger's voice.

What kind of changes in hearing take place during infancy? They involve perception of a sound's loudness, pitch, and localization:

- *Loudness.* Immediately after birth, infants cannot hear soft sounds quite as well as adults can; a stimulus must be louder to be heard by a newborn than by an adult (Trehub & others, 1991). For example, an adult can hear a whisper from about 4 to 5 feet away, but a newborn requires that sounds be closer to a normal conversational level to be heard at that distance. By three months of age, infants' perception of sounds improves, although some aspects of loudness perception do not reach adult levels until 5 to 10 years of age (Trainor & He, 2013).

- *Pitch.* Infants are also less sensitive to the pitch of a sound than adults are. *Pitch* is the perception of the frequency of a sound. A soprano voice sounds high-pitched, a bass voice low-pitched. Infants are less sensitive to low-pitched sounds and are more likely to hear high-pitched sounds (Aslin, Jusczyk, & Pisoni, 1998). By 2 years of age, infants have considerably improved their ability to distinguish sounds of different pitch.

- *Localization.* Even newborns can determine the general location from which a sound is coming, but by 6 months of age, they are more proficient at *localizing* sounds or detecting their origins. Their ability to localize sounds continues to improve during the second year (Burnham & Mattock, 2010).

Although infants can process variations in sound loudness, pitch, and localization, these aspects of hearing continue to improve during the childhood years (Trainor & He, 2013).

Touch and Pain Do newborns respond to touch? Can they feel pain?

Newborns do respond to touch. A touch to the cheek produces a turning of the head; a touch to the lips produces sucking movements.

Regular gentle tactile stimulation prenatally may have positive developmental outcomes. For example, a recent study found that 3-month-olds who had regular gentle tactile stimulation as fetuses were more likely to have an easy temperament than their counterparts who had irregular gentle or no tactile stimulation as fetuses (Wang, Hua, & Xu, 2015).

Newborns can also feel pain (Ishak & others, 2019). If you have a son and consider whether he should be circumcised, the issue of an infant's pain perception probably will become important to you. Circumcision is usually performed on infant boys about the third day after birth. Will your son experience pain if he is circumcised when he is 3 days old? An investigation by Megan Gunnar and her colleagues (1987) found that newborn infant males cried intensely during circumcision. Circumcised infants also display amazing resiliency. Within several minutes after the surgery, they can nurse and interact in a normal manner with their mothers. And, if allowed to, the newly circumcised newborn drifts into a deep sleep, which seems to serve as a coping mechanism.

For many years, doctors performed operations on newborns without anesthesia. This practice was accepted because of the dangers of anesthesia and because of the supposition that newborns do not feel pain. As researchers demonstrated that newborns can feel pain, the practice of operating on newborns without anesthesia has been challenged. Anesthesia now is used in some circumcisions (Morris & others, 2012).

Neuroimaging studies indicate that newborn infants likely experience some aspects of pain similarly to adults (Ranger & Grunau, 2015). Magnetic resonance imaging (MRI) studies of adults have found that there is a complex brain activity network that underlies pain, which is called the "pain matrix." The pain matrix brain regions consist of areas located in the thalamus, somatosensory cortex, and amygdala (Denk, McMahon, & Tracey, 2014). In one study, researchers discovered that 18 of the 20 regions in the adult pain matrix also are present in the newborn's pain matrix (Goksan & others, 2015). However, a major brain region in the adult's pain matrix that was not present in the infant's was the amygdala, which involves emotional responses. Also in this study, the MRI information revealed that the pain threshold in newborns occurs at a lower level of stimulation than for adults, confirming newborns' heightened pain sensitivity that has been found in earlier behavioral studies. And in a recent study, kangaroo care was effective in reducing neonatal pain, especially indicated by the significantly lower level of crying when the care was instituted after the newborn's blood had been drawn by a heel stick (Seo, Lee, & Ahn, 2016).

Smell Newborns can differentiate odors (Doty & Shah, 2008). The expressions on their faces seem to indicate that they like the way vanilla and strawberries smell but do not like the way rotten eggs and fish smell (Steiner, 1979). In one investigation, 6-day-old infants who were breast fed showed a clear preference for smelling their mother's breast pad rather than a clean breast pad (MacFarlane, 1975) (see Figure 23). However, when they were 2 days old they did not show this preference, indicating that they require several days of experience to recognize this odor.

Taste Sensitivity to taste is present even before birth (Doty & Shah, 2008). Human newborns learn tastes prenatally through the amniotic fluid and in breast milk after birth (Beauchamp & Mennella, 2009). In one study, even at only 2 hours of age, babies made different facial expressions when they tasted sweet, sour, and bitter solutions (Rosenstein & Oster, 1988). At about 4 months of age, infants begin to prefer salty tastes, which as newborns they had found to be aversive (Doty & Shah, 2008).

INTERMODAL PERCEPTION

Imagine yourself playing basketball or tennis. You are experiencing many visual inputs: the ball coming and going, other players moving around, and so on. However, you are experiencing many auditory inputs as well: the sound of the ball bouncing or being hit, the grunts and groans of other players, and so on. There is good correspondence between much of the visual and auditory information: When you see the ball bounce, you hear a bouncing sound; when a player stretches to hit a ball, you hear a groan. When you look at and listen to what is going on, you do not experience just the sounds or just the sights—you put all these things together. You experience a unitary episode. This is **intermodal perception,** which involves integrating information from two or more sensory modalities, such as vision and hearing (Gergely & others, 2019). Most perception is intermodal (Bahrick, 2010).

developmental **connection**

Sensation and Perception

Kangaroo care and massage therapy are associated with many positive outcomes in preterm and low birth weight infants. Connect to "Prenatal Development and Birth."

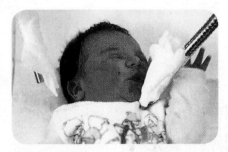

FIGURE 23

NEWBORNS' PREFERENCE FOR THE SMELL OF THEIR MOTHER'S BREAST PAD. In the experiment by MacFarlane (1975), 6-day-old infants preferred to smell their mother's breast pad rather than a clean one that had never been used, but 2-day-old infants did not show this preference, indicating that odor preference requires several days of experience to develop.
Jean Guichard

intermodal perception The ability to relate and integrate information from two or more sensory modalities, such as vision and hearing.

What is intermodal perception? Which two senses is this infant using to integrate information about the blocks?
Kaori Ando/Cultura/Getty Images

Early, exploratory forms of intermodal perception exist even in newborns (Bremner, 2017). For example, newborns turn their eyes and their head toward the sound of a voice or rattle when the sound is maintained for several seconds (Clifton & others, 1981), but the newborn can localize a sound and look at an object only in a crude way (Bechtold, Bushnell, & Salapatek, 1979). These early forms of intermodal perception become sharpened with experience in the first year of life (Bremner & Spence, 2017). In one study, infants as young as 3 months old looked longer at their parents when they also heard their voices (Spelke & Owsley, 1979). Thus, even young infants can coordinate visual-auditory information involving people.

Can young infants put vision and sound together as precisely as adults do? In the first six months, infants have difficulty connecting sensory input from different modes, but in the second half of the first year they show an increased ability to make this connection mentally (Hannon, Schachner, & Nave-Blodgett, 2017).

NATURE, NURTURE, AND PERCEPTUAL DEVELOPMENT

Now that we have discussed many aspects of perceptual development, let's explore one of developmental psychology's key issues in relation to perceptual development: the nature-nurture issue. There has been a longstanding interest in how strongly infants' perception is influenced by nature or nurture (Adolph, Hoch, & Ossmy, 2020; Bremner, 2017; Johnson, 2019, 2020a, b). In the field of perceptual development, nature proponents are referred to as *nativists* and those who emphasize learning and experience are called *empiricists.*

In the nativist view, the ability to perceive the world in a competent, organized way is inborn or innate. A completely nativist view of perceptual development no longer is accepted in developmental psychology.

The Gibsons argued that a key question in infant perception is what information is available in the environment and how infants learn to generate, differentiate, and discriminate the information—certainly not a nativist view. The Gibsons' ecological view also is quite different from Piaget's constructivist view. According to Piaget, much of perceptual development in infancy must await the development of a sequence of cognitive stages for infants to construct more complex perceptual tasks. Thus, in Piaget's view the ability to perceive size and shape constancy, a three-dimensional world, intermodal perception, and so on, develops later in infancy than the Gibsons envision.

The longitudinal research of Daphne Maurer and her colleagues (Maurer, 2016; Maurer & Lewis, 2013; Maurer & others, 1999) has focused on infants born with cataracts—a thickening of the lens of the eye that causes vision to become cloudy, opaque, and distorted and thus severely restricts infants' ability to experience their visual world. Studying infants whose cataracts were removed at different points in development, they discovered that those whose cataracts were removed and new lenses placed in their eyes in the first several months after birth showed a normal pattern of visual development. However, the longer the delay in removing the cataracts, the more their visual development was impaired. In their research, Maurer and her colleagues (2007) have found that experiencing patterned visual input early in infancy is important for holistic and detailed face processing after infancy. Maurer's (2016) research program illustrates how deprivation and experience influence visual development, revealing an early sensitive period when visual input is necessary for normal visual development.

Today, it is clear that just as an extreme nativist position on perceptual development is unwarranted, an extreme empiricist position also is unwarranted. Much of very early perception develops from innate (nature) foundations, and the basic foundation of many perceptual abilities can be detected in newborns (Bornstein, Arterberry, & Mash, 2015). However, as infants develop, environmental experiences (nurture) refine or calibrate many perceptual functions, and they may be the driving force behind some functions (Amso & Johnson, 2010). The accumulation of experience with and knowledge about their perceptual world contributes to infants' ability to process coherent perceptions of people and things (Johnson, 2019, 2020a, b). Thus, a full portrait of perceptual development includes the influence of nature, nurture, and a developing sensitivity to information (Johnson, 2019, 2020a, b).

What roles do nature and nurture play in the infant's perceptual development?
Boris Ryaposov/Shutterstock

PERCEPTUAL-MOTOR COUPLING

How are perception and action coupled in children's development?
Kevin Liu/Moment Open/Getty Images

As we come to the end of this chapter, we return to the important theme of perceptual-motor coupling. The distinction between perceiving and doing has been a time-honored tradition in psychology. However, a number of experts on perceptual and motor development question whether this distinction makes sense (Adolph, Hoch, & Ossmy, 2020; Vieira & others, 2019). The main thrust of research in Esther Thelen's dynamic systems approach is to explore how people assemble motor behaviors for perceiving and acting. The main theme of the ecological approach of Eleanor and James J. Gibson is to discover how perception guides action. Action can guide perception, and perception can guide action. Only by moving one's eyes, head, hands, and arms and by moving from one location to another can an individual fully experience his or her environment and learn how to adapt to it. Perception and action are coupled (Hoch, Rachwani, & Adolph, 2020).

Babies, for example, continually coordinate their movements with perceptual information to learn how to maintain balance, reach for objects in space, and move across various surfaces and terrains (Adolph, 2020; Heiman & others, 2019). They are motivated to move by what they perceive. Consider the sight of an attractive toy across the room. In this situation, infants must perceive the current state of their bodies and learn how to use their limbs to reach the toy. Although their movements at first are awkward and uncoordinated, babies soon learn to select patterns that are appropriate for reaching their goals.

Equally important is the other part of the perception-action coupling. That is, action educates perception (Adolph & Hoch, 2019). For example, watching an object while exploring it manually helps infants to determine its texture, size, and hardness. Locomoting in the environment teaches babies about how objects and people look from different perspectives, or whether various surfaces will support their weight.

How do infants develop new perceptual-motor couplings? Recall from our discussion earlier in this chapter that in the traditional view of Gesell, infants' perceptual-motor development is prescribed by a genetic plan to follow a fixed and sequential progression of stages in development. The genetic determination view has been replaced by the dynamic systems view that infants learn new perceptual-motor couplings by assembling skills for perceiving and acting. New perceptual-motor coupling is not passively accomplished; rather, the infant actively develops a skill to achieve a goal within the constraints set by the infant's body and the environment (Rachwani, Hoch, & Adolph, 2020).

Children perceive in order to move and move in order to perceive. Perceptual and motor development do not occur in isolation from each other but instead are coupled.

> The infant is by no means as helpless as it looks and is quite capable of some very complex and important actions.
>
> **—HERB PICK**
> *Developmental psychologist, University of Minnesota*

Review *Connect* Reflect

 LG3 Summarize the course of sensory and perceptual development in infancy.

Review
- What are sensation and perception?
- What is the ecological view of perception?
- How does visual perception develop in infancy?
- How do hearing, touch and pain, smell, and taste develop in infancy?
- What is intermodal perception?
- What roles do nature and nurture play in perceptual development?
- How is perceptual-motor development coupled?

Connect
- Perceptual-motor coupling was discussed in the previous section as well as in this section. Describe how this concept could be linked to the concept of nature versus nurture.

Reflect *Your Own Personal Journey of Life*
- How much sensory stimulation would you provide your own baby? A little? A lot? Could you overstimulate your baby? Explain.

topical connections *looking **forward***

In the next chapter, you will read about the remarkable cognitive changes that characterize infant development and how soon infants are able to competently process information about their world. Advances in infants' cognitive development—together with the development of the brain and perceptual-motor advances discussed in this chapter—allow infants to adapt more effectively to their environment. Later in this text, we will further explore physical development when we examine how children progress through early childhood (ages 3 to 5). Young children's physical development continues to change and to become more coordinated in early childhood, although gains in height and weight are not as dramatic in early childhood as in infancy.

reach your **learning goals**

Physical Development in Infancy

1 Physical Growth and Development in Infancy **LG1** Discuss physical growth and development in infancy.

Patterns of Growth

- The cephalocaudal pattern is the sequence in which growth proceeds from top to bottom. The proximodistal pattern is the sequence in which growth starts at the center of the body and moves toward the extremities.

Height and Weight

- The average North American newborn is 20 inches long and weighs 7.6 pounds. Infants grow about 1 inch per month in the first year and nearly triple their weight by their first birthday. The rate of growth slows in the second year.

The Brain

- One of the most dramatic changes in the brain in the first two years of life is dendritic spreading, which increases the connections between neurons. Myelination, which speeds the conduction of nerve impulses, continues through infancy and even into adolescence.

- The cerebral cortex has two hemispheres (left and right). Lateralization refers to specialization of function in one hemisphere or the other. Early experiences play an important role in brain development.

- Neural connections are formed early in an infant's life. Before birth, genes mainly direct neurons to different locations. After birth, the inflowing stream of sights, sounds, smells, touches, language, and eye contact helps to shape the brain's neural connections, as does stimulation from caregivers and others. The neuroconstructivist view, in which brain development is influenced by a person's environment and experiences, is an increasingly popular perspective.

Sleep

- Newborns usually sleep about 18 hours a day. By 6 months of age, many American infants approach adult-like sleeping patterns. REM sleep—during which dreaming occurs—is present more in early infancy than in childhood and adulthood.

- Sleeping arrangements for infants vary across cultures. In America, infants are more likely to sleep alone than in many other cultures. Some experts believe shared sleeping can lead to sudden infant death syndrome (SIDS), a condition that occurs when a sleeping infant suddenly stops breathing and dies without an apparent cause. However, it is generally accepted that the most critical factor in predicting whether an infant will develop SIDS is prone sleeping.

Nutrition

- Infants need to consume about 50 calories per day for each pound they weigh. The growing consensus is that in most instances breast feeding is superior to bottle feeding for both the infant and the mother, although the correlational nature of studies must be considered.

- Severe infant malnutrition is still prevalent in many parts of the world. A special concern in impoverished countries is early weaning from breast milk and the misuse and hygiene problems associated with bottle feeding in these countries. The Women, Infants, and Children (WIC) program has produced positive benefits in low-income families in the United States.

2 Motor Development

LG2 Describe infants' motor development.

The Dynamic Systems View

- Thelen's dynamic systems theory seeks to explain how motor behaviors are assembled for perceiving and acting. Perception and action are coupled. According to this theory, motor skills are the result of many converging factors, such as the development of the nervous system, the body's physical properties and its movement possibilities, the goal the child is motivated to reach, and environmental support for the skill. In the dynamic systems view, motor development is far more complex than the result of a genetic blueprint.

Reflexes

- Reflexes—automatic movements—govern the newborn's behavior. They include the sucking, rooting, and Moro reflexes. The rooting and Moro reflexes disappear after three to four months. Permanent reflexes include coughing and blinking. For infants, sucking is an especially important reflex because it provides a means of obtaining nutrition.

Gross Motor Skills

- Gross motor skills involve large-muscle activities. Key skills developed during infancy include control of posture and walking. Although infants usually learn to walk by their first birthday, the neural pathways that allow walking begin forming earlier. The age at which infants reach milestones in the development of gross motor skills may vary by as much as two to four months, especially for milestones in late infancy.

Fine Motor Skills

- Fine motor skills involve finely tuned movements. The onset of reaching and grasping marks a significant accomplishment, and this skill becomes more refined during the first two years of life.

3 Sensory and Perceptual Development

LG3 Summarize the course of sensory and perceptual development in infancy.

What Are Sensation and Perception?

The Ecological View

- Sensation occurs when information interacts with sensory receptors. Perception is the interpretation of sensation.

- Created by the Gibsons, the ecological view states that we directly perceive information that exists in the world around us. Perception brings people in contact with the environment to interact with and adapt to it. Affordances provide opportunities for interaction offered by objects that fit within our capabilities to perform activities.

Visual Perception

- Researchers have developed a number of methods to assess the infant's perception, including the visual preference method (which Fantz used to determine young infants' preference for looking at patterned over nonpatterned displays), habituation and dishabituation, and tracking.

- The infant's visual acuity increases dramatically in the first year of life. Infants' color vision improves as they develop. Young infants systematically scan human faces. As early as 3 months of age, infants show size and shape constancy. At approximately 2 months of age, infants develop the ability to perceive that occluded objects are complete. In Gibson and Walk's classic study, infants as young as 6 months of age indicated they could perceive depth.

Other Senses

- The fetus can hear during the last two months of pregnancy. Immediately after birth, newborns can hear, but their sensory threshold is higher than that of adults. Developmental changes in the perception of loudness, pitch, and localization of sound occur during infancy. Newborns can respond to touch and feel pain. Newborns can differentiate odors, and sensitivity to taste may be present before birth.

Intermodal Perception

- Early, exploratory forms of intermodal perception—the ability to relate and integrate information from two or more sensory modalities—are present in newborns and become sharper over the first year of life.

| Nature, Nurture, and Perceptual Development | • In describing the sources of perceptual development, nature advocates are referred to as nativists and nurture proponents are called empiricists. The Gibsons' ecological view that has guided much of perceptual development research leans toward a nativist approach but still allows for developmental changes in distinctive features. Piaget's constructivist view leans toward an empiricist approach, emphasizing that many perceptual accomplishments must await the development of cognitive stages in infancy. A strong empiricist approach is unwarranted. A full account of perceptual development includes the roles of nature, nurture, and the developing sensitivity to information. |

| Perceptual-Motor Coupling | • Perception and action are often not isolated but rather are coupled. Individuals perceive in order to move and move in order to perceive. |

key **terms**

affordances 127	grasping reflex 120	neuroconstructivist view 111	shape constancy 131
cephalocaudal pattern 107	gross motor skills 120	perception 127	size constancy 131
dishabituation 128	habituation 128	proximodistal pattern 107	sucking reflex 120
dynamic systems theory 119	intermodal perception 133	reflexes 120	sudden infant death
ecological view 127	lateralization 109	rooting reflex 120	syndrome (SIDS) 113
fine motor skills 125	Moro reflex 120	sensation 127	visual preference method 128

key **people**

Karen Adolph 120	James J. Gibson 127	Rachel Keen 126	John Richards 108
Martha Ann Bell 108	William James 127	Patricia Kuhl 107	Esther Thelen 119
Robert Fantz 128	Mark Johnson 108	Daphne Maurer 134	Richard Walk 131
Eleanor Gibson 131	Scott Johnson 131	Charles Nelson 108	

chapter 5

COGNITIVE DEVELOPMENT IN INFANCY

chapter outline

DreamPictures/Blend Images/Getty Images

Jean Piaget, the famous Swiss psychologist, was a meticulous observer of his three children—Laurent, Lucienne, and Jacqueline. His books on cognitive development are filled with these observations. Here are a few of Piaget's observations of his children in infancy (Piaget, 1952):

- At 21 days of age, "Laurent found his thumb after three attempts: prolonged sucking begins each time. But, once he has been placed on his back, he does not know how to coordinate the movement of the arms with that of the mouth and his hands draw back even when his lips are seeking them" (p. 27).

- During the third month, thumb sucking becomes less important to Laurent because of new visual and auditory interests. But when he cries, his thumb goes to the rescue.

- Toward the end of Lucienne's fourth month, while she is lying in her crib, Piaget hangs a doll above her feet. Lucienne thrusts her feet at the doll and makes it move. "Afterward, she looks at her motionless foot for a second, then recommences. There is no visual control of her foot, for the movements are the same when Lucienne only looks at the doll or when I place the doll over her head. On the other hand, the tactile control of the foot is apparent: after the first shakes, Lucienne makes slow foot movements as though to grasp and explore" (p. 159).

- At 11 months, "Jacqueline is seated and shakes a little bell. She then pauses abruptly in order to delicately place the bell in front of her right foot; then she kicks hard. Unable to recapture it, she grasps a ball which she then places at the same spot in order to give it another kick" (p. 225).

- At 1 year, 2 months, "Jacqueline holds in her hands an object which is new to her: a round, flat box which she turns all over, shakes, [and] rubs against the bassinet. . . . She lets it go and tries to pick it up. But she only succeeds in touching it with her index finger, without grasping it. She nevertheless makes an attempt and presses on the edge. The box then tilts up and falls again" (p. 273). Jacqueline shows an interest in this result and studies the fallen box.

For Piaget, these observations reflect important changes in the infant's cognitive development. Piaget maintained that infants go through a series of cognitive substages as they progress in less than two short years.

We have discussed that impressive advances occur in the development of the brain during infancy. Engaging in various physical, cognitive, and socioemotional activities strengthens the baby's neural connections. Motor and perceptual development also are key aspects of the infant's development. An important part of this development is the coupling of perceptions and actions. The nature-nurture issue continues to be debated with regard to the infant's perceptual development. In this chapter, you will expand your understanding of the infant's brain, motor, and perceptual development by further examining how infants develop their competencies, focusing on how advances in their cognitive development help them adapt to their world, and how the nature-nurture issue is a key aspect of the infant's cognitive and language development.

preview

Piaget's descriptions of infants are just the starting point for our exploration of cognitive development. Excitement and enthusiasm about the study of infant cognition have been fueled by an interest in what newborns and infants know, by continued fascination about innate and learned factors in the infant's cognitive development, and by controversies about whether infants construct their knowledge (Piaget's view) or know their world more directly. In this chapter, you will not only study Piaget's theory of infant development but also explore how infants learn, remember, and conceptualize; learn about some of their individual differences; and trace their language development.

1 Piaget's Theory of Infant Development

LG1 Summarize and evaluate Piaget's theory of infant development.

> Cognitive Processes · The Sensorimotor Stage · Evaluating Piaget's Sensorimotor Stage

Poet Nora Perry asks, "Who knows the thoughts of a child?" As much as anyone, Piaget knew. Through careful observations of his own three children—Laurent, Lucienne, and Jacqueline—and observations of and interviews with other children, Piaget changed perceptions of the way children think about the world.

Piaget's theory is a general, unifying story of how biology and experience sculpt cognitive development. Piaget thought that, just as our physical bodies have structures that enable us to adapt to the world, we build mental structures that help us adjust to new environmental demands. Piaget stressed that children actively construct their own cognitive worlds; information is not just poured into their minds from the environment. He sought to discover how children at different points in their development think about the world and how systematic changes in their thinking occur.

> We are born capable of learning.
>
> —**JEAN-JACQUES ROUSSEAU**
> *Swiss-born French philosopher, 18th century*

COGNITIVE PROCESSES

What processes do children use as they construct their knowledge of the world? Piaget developed several concepts to answer this question; especially important are schemes, assimilation, accommodation, organization, equilibrium, and equilibration.

Schemes   As the infant or child seeks to construct an understanding of the world, said Piaget (1954), the developing brain creates **schemes.** These are actions or mental representations that organize knowledge. In Piaget's theory, a baby's schemes are structured by simple actions that can be performed on objects, such as sucking, looking, and grasping. Older children have schemes that include strategies and plans for solving problems. For example, in the

schemes In Piaget's theory, actions or mental representations that organize knowledge.

In Piaget's view, what is a scheme? What schemes might this young infant be displaying?
Maya Kovacheva Photography/iStockphoto/Getty Images

developmental **connection**

Cognitive Theory

Recall the main characteristics of Piaget's four stages of cognitive development. Connect to "Introduction."

assimilation Piagetian concept of using existing schemes to deal with new information or experiences.

accommodation Piagetian concept of adjusting schemes to fit new information and experiences.

organization Piaget's concept of grouping isolated behaviors and thoughts into a higher-order, more smoothly functioning cognitive system.

equilibration A mechanism that Piaget proposed to explain how children shift from one stage of thought to the next.

sensorimotor stage The first of Piaget's stages, which lasts from birth to about 2 years of age; infants construct an understanding of the world by coordinating sensory experiences with motoric actions.

descriptions at the opening of this chapter, Laurent displayed a scheme for sucking. By the time we have reached adulthood, we have constructed an enormous number of diverse schemes, ranging from driving a car to balancing a budget to understanding the concept of fairness.

Assimilation and Accommodation   To explain how children use and adapt their schemes, Piaget offered two concepts: assimilation and accommodation. **Assimilation** occurs when children use their existing schemes to deal with new information or experiences. **Accommodation** occurs when children adjust their schemes to take new information and experiences into account.

Think about a toddler who has learned the word *car* to identify the family vehicle. The toddler might call all moving vehicles on roads "cars," including motorcycles and trucks; the child has assimilated these objects to his or her existing scheme. But the child soon learns that motorcycles and trucks are not cars and fine-tunes the category to exclude motorcycles and trucks, accommodating the scheme.

Assimilation and accommodation operate even in very young infants. Newborns reflexively suck everything that touches their lips; they assimilate all sorts of objects into their sucking scheme. By sucking different objects, they learn about their taste, texture, shape, and so on. After several months of experience, though, they construct their understanding of the world differently. Some objects, such as fingers and the mother's breast, can be sucked, and others, such as fuzzy blankets, should not be sucked. In other words, they accommodate their sucking scheme.

Organization   To make sense out of their world, said Piaget, children cognitively organize their experiences. **Organization** in Piaget's theory is the grouping of isolated behaviors and thoughts into a higher-order system. Continual refinement of this organization is an inherent part of development. A boy who has only a vague idea about how to use a hammer may also have a vague idea about how to use other tools. After learning how to use each one, he relates these uses, organizing his knowledge.

Equilibration and Stages of Development   Assimilation and accommodation always take the child to a higher ground, according to Piaget. In trying to understand the world, the child inevitably experiences cognitive conflict, or *disequilibrium*. That is, the child is constantly faced with counterexamples to his or her existing schemes and with inconsistencies. For example, if a child believes that pouring water from a short and wide container into a tall and narrow container changes the amount of water, then the child might be puzzled by where the "extra" water came from and whether there is actually more water to drink. The puzzle creates disequilibrium; for Piaget, an internal search for equilibrium creates motivation for change. The child assimilates and accommodates, adjusting old schemes, developing new schemes, and organizing and reorganizing the old and new schemes. Eventually, the new organization has become fundamentally different from the old organization; it is a new way of thinking.

In short, according to Piaget, children constantly assimilate and accommodate as they seek equilibrium. There is considerable movement between states of cognitive equilibrium and disequilibrium as assimilation and accommodation work in concert to produce cognitive change. **Equilibration** is the name Piaget gave to this mechanism by which children shift from one stage of thought to the next.

The result of these processes, according to Piaget, is that individuals go through four stages of development. A different way of understanding the world makes one stage more advanced than another. Cognition is *qualitatively* different in one stage compared with another. In other words, the way children reason at one stage is different from the way they reason at another stage. In this chapter we will focus on Piaget's stage of infant cognitive development. In later chapters we will explore Piaget's other three stages when we study cognitive development in early childhood, middle and late childhood, and adolescence.

THE SENSORIMOTOR STAGE

The **sensorimotor stage** lasts from birth to about 2 years of age. During this stage of cognitive development, infants construct an understanding of the world by coordinating sensory experiences (such as seeing and hearing) with physical, motoric actions—hence the term "sensorimotor." At the beginning of this stage, newborns have little more than reflexes with which

Substage	Age	Description	Example
1 Simple reflexes	Birth to 1 month	Coordination of sensation and action through reflexive behaviors.	Rooting, sucking, and grasping reflexes; newborns suck reflexively when their lips are touched.
2 First habits and primary circular reactions	1 to 4 months	Coordination of sensation and two types of schemes: habits (reflex) and primary circular reactions (reproduction of an event that initially occurred by chance). Main focus is still on the infant's body.	Repeating a body sensation first experienced by chance (sucking thumb, for example); then infants might accommodate actions by sucking their thumb differently from how they suck on a nipple.
3 Secondary circular reactions	4 to 8 months	Infants become more object-oriented, moving beyond self-preoccupation; repeat actions that bring interesting or pleasurable results.	An infant coos to make a person stay near; as the person starts to leave, the infant coos again.
4 Coordination of secondary circular reactions	8 to 12 months	Coordination of vision and touch—hand-eye coordination; coordination of schemes and intentionality.	Infant manipulates a stick in order to bring an attractive toy within reach.
5 Tertiary circular reactions, novelty, and curiosity	12 to 18 months	Infants become intrigued by the many properties of objects and by the many things they can make happen to objects; they experiment with new behavior.	A block can be made to fall, spin, hit another object, and slide across the ground.
6 Internalization of schemes	18 to 24 months	Infants develop the ability to use primitive symbols and form enduring mental representations.	An infant who has never thrown a temper tantrum before sees a playmate throw a tantrum; the infant retains a memory of the event, then throws one himself the next day.

FIGURE 1
PIAGET'S SIX SUBSTAGES OF SENSORIMOTOR DEVELOPMENT

to work. At the end of the sensorimotor stage, 2-year-olds can produce complex sensorimotor patterns and use primitive symbols. We will summarize Piaget's descriptions of how infants develop, then consider criticisms of his view.

Substages Piaget divided the sensorimotor stage into six substages: (1) simple reflexes; (2) first habits and primary circular reactions; (3) secondary circular reactions; (4) coordination of secondary circular reactions; (5) tertiary circular reactions, novelty, and curiosity; and (6) internalization of schemes (see Figure 1). Piaget argued that each substage builds on the previous one.

Simple reflexes, the first sensorimotor substage, corresponds to the first month after birth. In this substage, sensation and action are coordinated primarily through reflexive behaviors such as rooting and sucking. Soon the infant produces behaviors that resemble reflexes in the absence of the usual stimulus for the reflex. For example, a newborn will suck a nipple or bottle only when it is placed directly in the baby's mouth or touched to the lips. But soon the infant might suck when a bottle or nipple is only nearby. Even in the first month of life, the infant is initiating action and actively structuring experiences.

First habits and primary circular reactions is the second sensorimotor substage, which develops between 1 and 4 months of age. In this substage, the infant coordinates sensation and two types of schemes: habits and primary circular reactions. A *habit* is a scheme based on a reflex that has become completely separated from its eliciting stimulus. For example, infants in substage 1 suck when bottles are put to their lips or when they see a bottle. Infants in substage 2 might suck even when no bottle is present. A *circular reaction* is a repetitive action.

A **primary circular reaction** is a scheme based on the attempt to reproduce an event that initially occurred by chance. For example, suppose an infant accidentally sucks his fingers when they are placed near his mouth. Later, he searches for his fingers to suck them again, but the fingers do not cooperate because the infant cannot coordinate visual and manual actions.

Habits and circular reactions are stereotyped—that is, the infant repeats them the same way each time. During this substage, the infant's own body continues to be the center of attention. There is no outward pull by environmental events.

simple reflexes Piaget's first sensorimotor substage, which corresponds to the first month after birth. In this substage, sensation and action are coordinated primarily through reflexive behaviors.

first habits and primary circular reactions Piaget's second sensorimotor substage, which develops between 1 and 4 months of age. In this substage, the infant coordinates sensation and two types of schemes: habits and primary circular reactions.

primary circular reaction A scheme based on the attempt to reproduce an event that initially occurred by chance.

secondary circular reactions Piaget's third sensorimotor substage, which develops between 4 and 8 months of age. In this substage, the infant becomes more object-oriented, moving beyond preoccupation with the self.

This 7-month-old is in Piaget's substage of secondary circular reactions. *What might the infant do that suggests he is in this substage?*
Johnny Valley/Cultura/Getty Images

This 17-month-old is in Piaget's stage of tertiary circular reactions. *What might the infant do that suggests he is in this stage?*
Tom Grill/Corbis/Getty Images

Secondary circular reactions is the third sensorimotor substage, which develops between 4 and 8 months of age. In this substage, the infant becomes more object-oriented, moving beyond preoccupation with the self. The infant's schemes are not intentional or goal-directed, but they are repeated because of their consequences. By chance, an infant might shake a rattle. The infant repeats this action to produce the sound again. This is a *secondary circular reaction:* an action repeated because of its consequences. The infant also imitates some simple actions, such as the baby talk or burbling of adults, and some physical gestures. However, the baby imitates only actions that he or she is already able to produce.

Coordination of secondary circular reactions is Piaget's fourth sensorimotor substage, which develops between 8 and 12 months of age. To progress into this substage, the infant must coordinate vision and touch. Actions become more outwardly directed. Significant changes during this substage involve the coordination of schemes and intentionality. Infants readily combine and recombine previously learned schemes in a coordinated way. They might look at an object and grasp it simultaneously, or they might visually inspect a toy, such as a rattle, and finger it simultaneously. Related to this coordination is the second achievement—the presence of intentionality. For example, infants might manipulate a stick to bring a desired toy within reach, or they might knock over one block to reach and play with another one. Similarly, when 11-month-old Jacqueline, as described in the chapter opening, placed the ball in front of her and kicked it, she was demonstrating intentionality.

Tertiary circular reactions, novelty, and curiosity is Piaget's fifth sensorimotor substage, which develops between 12 and 18 months of age. In this substage, infants become intrigued by the many properties of objects and the many things they can do to objects. A block can be made to fall, spin, hit another object, and slide across the ground. *Tertiary circular reactions* are schemes in which the infant purposely explores new possibilities with objects, continually doing new things to them and exploring the results. Piaget says that this stage marks the starting point for human curiosity and interest in novelty.

Internalization of schemes is Piaget's sixth and final sensorimotor substage, which develops between 18 and 24 months of age. In this substage, the infant develops the ability to use primitive symbols. For Piaget, a *symbol* is an internalized sensory image or word that represents an event. Primitive symbols permit the infant to think about concrete events without directly acting them out or perceiving them. Moreover, symbols allow the infant to manipulate and transform the represented events in simple ways. In a favorite Piagetian example, Piaget's young daughter saw a matchbox being opened and closed. Later, she mimicked the event by opening and closing her mouth. This was an obvious expression of her image of the event.

Object Permanence

Imagine how chaotic and unpredictable your life would be if you could not distinguish between yourself and your world. This is what the life of a newborn must be like, according to Piaget. There is no differentiation between the self and world; objects have no separate, permanent existence.

By the end of the sensorimotor period, objects are both separate from the self and permanent. **Object permanence** is the understanding that objects continue to exist even when they cannot be seen, heard, or touched. Acquiring the sense of object permanence is one of the infant's most important accomplishments, according to Piaget.

-- -- -- -- -- →

developmental connection

Cognitive Theory

What are some changes in symbolic thought in young children? Connect to "Physical and Cognitive Development in Early Childhood."

← -- -- -- -- --

coordination of secondary circular reactions Piaget's fourth sensorimotor substage, which develops between 8 and 12 months of age. Actions become more outwardly directed, and infants coordinate schemes and act with intentionality.

tertiary circular reactions, novelty, and curiosity Piaget's fifth sensorimotor substage, which develops between 12 and 18 months of age. In this substage, infants become intrigued by the many properties of objects and by the many things they can do to objects.

internalization of schemes Piaget's sixth and final sensorimotor substage, which develops between 18 and 24 months of age. In this substage the infant develops the ability to use primitive symbols.

object permanence The Piagetian term for understanding that objects and events continue to exist even when they cannot directly be seen, heard, or touched.

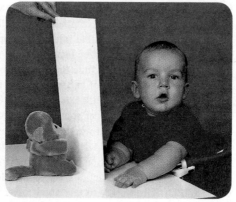

FIGURE **2**

OBJECT PERMANENCE. Piaget argued that object permanence is one of infancy's landmark cognitive accomplishments. For this 5-month-old boy, "out of sight" is literally out of mind. The infant looks at the toy monkey (*left*), but, when his view of the toy is blocked (*right*), he does not search for it. Several months later, he will search for the hidden toy monkey, an action reflecting the presence of object permanence.
Doug Goodman/Science Source

How could anyone know whether an infant had a sense of object permanence? The principal way to study object permanence is to watch an infant's reaction when an interesting object disappears (see Figure 2). If infants search for the object, it is assumed that they believe it continues to exist.

EVALUATING PIAGET'S SENSORIMOTOR STAGE

Piaget opened up a new way of looking at infants with his view that their main task is to coordinate their sensory impressions with their motor activity. However, the infant's cognitive world is not as neatly packaged as Piaget portrayed it, and some of Piaget's explanations of change are debated. In the past several decades, sophisticated experimental techniques have been devised to study infants, and a large number of research studies have focused on infant development. Much of the new research suggests that Piaget's view of sensorimotor development needs to be modified (Hoch, Rachwani, & Adolph, 2020; Johnson, 2019, 2020).

The A-not-B Error One modification concerns Piaget's claim that certain processes are crucial in transitions from one stage to the next. The data do not always support his explanations. For example, in Piaget's theory, an important feature in the progression into substage 4, *coordination of secondary circular reactions,* is an infant's inclination to search for a hidden object in a familiar location rather than to look for the object in a new location. If a toy is hidden twice—initially at location A and subsequently at location B—8- to 12-month-old infants search correctly at location A initially. But, when the toy is subsequently hidden at location B while the child watches, they make the mistake of continuing to search for it at location A. **A-not-B error** is the term used to describe this common mistake. Older infants are less likely to make the A-not-B error because their concept of object permanence is more complete.

Researchers have found, however, that the A-not-B error does not show up consistently (MacNeill & others, 2018; Sophian, 1985). The evidence indicates that A-not-B errors are sensitive to the delay between hiding the object at B and the infant's attempt to find it (Diamond, 1985). Thus, the A-not-B error might be due to a failure in memory. Another explanation is that infants tend to repeat a previous motor behavior (Clearfield & others, 2006). Further, research indicates that A-not-B performance also is linked to attention. For example, in one study, 5-month-olds' more focused attention on a separate task involving a puppet was linked to better performance on an A-not-B task that involved locating an object after it was hidden from view (Marcovitch & others, 2016). And in longitudinal research, attention at 5 months was related to A-not-B performance at 10 months, and also to executive function in early childhood and reading competence at 6 years of age (Blankenship & others, 2019).

Perceptual Development and Expectations A number of theorists, such as Eleanor Gibson (2001) and Elizabeth Spelke (1991, 2011, 2013), argue that infants' perceptual abilities are highly developed at a very early stage. Spelke concludes that young infants interpret the world as having predictable occurrences. For example, we have discussed research that demonstrated the presence of intermodal perception—the ability to coordinate information

developmental **connection**

Perceptual Development

Eleanor Gibson was a pioneer in crafting the ecological perception view of development. Connect to "Physical Development in Infancy."

A-not-B error Error that occurs when infants make the mistake of selecting the familiar hiding place (A) rather than the new hiding place (B) of an object.

from two or more sensory modalities, such as vision and hearing—by 3½ months of age, much earlier than Piaget would have predicted (Spelke & Owsley, 1979).

Research also suggests that infants develop the ability to understand how the world works at a very early age (Buyukozer Dawkins & others, 2019, 2021; Ruba, Meltzoff, & Repacholi, 2019). For example, by the time they are 3 months of age, infants develop expectations about future events. What kinds of expectations do infants form? Experiments by Elizabeth Spelke (Liu, Brooks, & Spelke, 2019; Spelke, 1991, 2000, 2016a, b) have addressed this question. In one study, she used a puppet stage to show babies a series of actions that are unexpected if you know how the physical world works—for example, one ball seemed to roll through a solid barrier, another seemed to leap between two platforms, and a third appeared to hang in midair (Spelke, 1979). Spelke measured and compared the babies' looking times for unexpected and expected actions. She concluded that by 4 months of age, even though infants do not yet have the ability to talk about objects, move around objects, manipulate objects, or even see objects with high resolution, they expect objects to be solid and continuous. However, at 4 months of age, infants do not expect an object to obey laws of gravity (Spelke & others, 1992). Similarly, research by Renee Baillargeon (1995, 2004, 2014, 2016) documents that infants as young as 3 to 4 months expect objects to be substantial (in the sense that other objects cannot move through them) and permanent (in the sense that objects continue to exist when they are hidden).

In sum, researchers conclude that infants see objects as bounded, unitary, solid, and separate from their background, possibly at birth or shortly thereafter, but definitely by 3 to 4 months of age—much earlier than Piaget envisioned. Young infants still have much to learn about objects, but they perceive their world as stable and orderly (Rachwani, Hoch, & Adolph, 2020).

By 6 to 8 months, infants have learned to perceive gravity and support—that an object hanging on the end of a table should fall, that ball bearings will travel farther when rolled down a longer rather than a shorter ramp, and that cup handles will not fall when attached to a cup (Slater, Field, & Hernandez-Reif, 2007). As infants develop, their experiences and actions on objects help them to understand physical laws (Soska & others, 2020).

The Nature-Nurture Issue   In considering the big issue of whether nature or nurture plays the more important role in infant development, Elizabeth Spelke (2003, 2011, 2013, 2016a, b) comes down clearly on the side of nature, a position often referred to as *nativist*. Spelke endorses a **core knowledge approach,** which states that infants are born with domain-specific innate knowledge systems. Among these domain-specific knowledge systems are those involving space, number sense, object permanence, and language (which we will discuss later in this chapter). Strongly influenced by evolution, the core knowledge domains are theorized to be prewired to allow infants to make sense of their world (Strickland & Chemla, 2018). After all, Spelke concludes, how could infants possibly grasp the complex world in which they live if they didn't come into the world equipped with core sets of knowledge? In this approach, the innate core knowledge domains form a foundation around which more mature cognitive functioning and learning develop (Baillargeon & DeJong, 2017). The core knowledge approach argues that Piaget greatly underestimated the cognitive abilities of infants, especially young infants (Liu, Brooks, & Spelke, 2019; Scott, Roby, & Baillargeon, 2021).

Some critics argue that the Spelke's research mainly demonstrates perceptual competencies or detection of regularities in the environment (Heyes, 2014; Ruffman, 2014). They stress that the infants in these studies reflect a very rudimentary understanding that likely differs greatly from the understanding of older children.

An intriguing domain of core knowledge that has been investigated in young infants is whether they have a sense of number. Spelke (2016a, b) concludes that they do (Spelke, 2016a, b). She has found that infants can distinguish between different numbers of objects, actions, and sounds (Spelke, 2016a, b). Of course, not everyone agrees with Spelke's conclusions about young infants' math skills (Cohen, 2002). One criticism is that infants in the number experiments are merely responding to changes in the display that violated their expectations.

Recently, researchers also have explored whether preverbal infants might have a built-in, innate sense of morality (Scott, Roby, & Baillargeon, 2021; Van de Vondervoort & Hamlin, 2016, 2018). In this research, infants as young as 4 months of age are more likely to make

developmental **connection**

Nature Versus Nurture

The nature-nurture debate is one of developmental psychology's main issues. Connect to "Introduction" and "Biological Beginnings."

core knowledge approach Theory that infants are born with domain-specific innate knowledge systems.

visually guided reaches toward a puppet who has acted as a helper (such as helping someone get up a hill, assisting in opening a box, or giving a ball back) rather than toward a puppet who has hindered others' efforts to achieve such goals (Hamlin, 2013, 2014). In a recent analysis, it was concluded that the following four sociomoral principles guide infants' actions toward others (Buyukozer Dawkins & others, 2021): fairness, harm avoidance, in-group support, and authority. However, the view that the emergence of morality in infancy is innate has been described as problematic (Carpendale & Hammond, 2016). Instead it is argued that morality may emerge through infants' early interactions with others and later be transformed through language and reflective thought.

In criticizing the core knowledge approach, British developmental psychologist Mark Johnson (2008) says that the infants studied by Spelke and other advocates of core knowledge already have accumulated hundreds, and in some cases even thousands, of hours of experience in grasping what the world is about, which gives considerable room for the environment's role in the development of infant cognition (Highfield, 2008). According to Johnson (2008), infants likely come into the world with "soft biases to perceive and attend to different aspects of the environment, and to learn about the world in particular ways." A major criticism is that nativists completely neglect the infant's social immersion in the world and instead focus only on what happens inside the infant's head, apart from the environment (de Haan & Johnson, 2016). And recall from "Biological Beginnings" that another major criticism is that the modularity of the mind view does not adequately recognize the extensive connectivity of various regions of the brain.

Aspects of infant cognitive development continue to be debated, yet most developmentalists agree that Piaget underestimated the early cognitive accomplishments of infants and that both nature and nurture are involved in infants' cognitive development (Tamis-Lemonda & Lockman, 2020).

What are some conclusions that can be reached about infant learning and cognition?
Baobao ou/Flickr/Getty Images

Conclusions   In sum, many researchers conclude that Piaget wasn't specific enough about how infants learn about their world and that infants, especially young infants, are more competent than Piaget thought (Adolph, Hoch, & Ossmy, 2020; Tichko & Large, 2019). As researchers have examined the specific ways that infants learn, the field of infant cognition has become very specialized. There are many researchers working on different questions, with no general theory emerging that can connect all of the different findings (Nelson, 1999). These theories often are local theories, focused on specific research questions, rather than grand theories like Piaget's (Kuhn, 1998). Among the unifying themes in the study of infant cognition are seeking to understand more precisely how developmental changes in cognition take place, to examine the big issue of nature and nurture, and to study the brain's role in cognitive development (Johnson, 2019; Scott, Roby, & Baillargeon, 2021). Recall that exploring connections between brain, cognition, and development involves the recently emerging field of *developmental cognitive neuroscience* (Bell & Broomell, 2021; Xie & others, 2019).

Review *Connect* Reflect

 LG1 Summarize and evaluate Piaget's theory of infant development.

Review
- What cognitive processes are important in Piaget's theory?
- What are some characteristics of Piaget's stage of sensorimotor development?
- What are some contributions and criticisms of Piaget's sensorimotor stage?

Connect
- You just read that by the age of 6 to 8 months infants have learned to perceive gravity and support. What physical developments occurring around this same time period might contribute to infants' exploration and understanding of these concepts?

Reflect *Your Own Personal Journey of Life*
- What are some implications of Piaget's theory for parenting your own baby?

LG2 Describe how infants learn, focus attention, remember, and conceptualize.

| Conditioning | Attention | Memory | Imitation | Concept Formation and Categorization |

developmental connection

Theories

The behavioral and social cognitive approaches emphasize continuity rather than discontinuity in development. Connect to "Introduction."

When Piaget hung a doll above 4-month-old Lucienne's feet, as described in the chapter opening, did she remember the doll? If Piaget had rewarded her for moving the doll with her foot, would that have affected Lucienne's behavior? If he had shown her how to shake the doll's hand, could she have imitated him? If he had shown her a different doll, could she have formed the concept of a "doll"?

Questions like these might be examined by researchers taking the behavioral and social cognitive or information-processing approaches introduced earlier. In contrast with Piaget's theory, these approaches do not describe infant development in terms of stages. Instead, they document gradual changes in the infant's ability to understand and process information about the world (Bell & Garcia Meza, 2020; Johnson, 2020). In this section, we explore what researchers using these approaches can tell us about how infants learn, remember, and conceptualize.

CONDITIONING

According to Skinner's theory of operant conditioning, the consequences of a behavior produce changes in the probability of the behavior's occurrence. For example, if an infant's behavior is followed by a rewarding stimulus, the behavior is likely to recur.

Carolyn Rovee-Collier (1987, 2009) has demonstrated how infants can retain information from the experience of being conditioned. In a characteristic experiment, she places a 2½-month-old baby in a crib under an elaborate mobile (see Figure 3). She then ties one end of a ribbon to the baby's ankle and the other end to the mobile. Subsequently, she observes that the baby kicks and makes the mobile move. The movement of the mobile is the reinforcing stimulus (which increases the baby's kicking behavior) in this experiment. Weeks later, the baby is returned to the crib, but its foot is not tied to the mobile. The baby kicks, which suggests it has retained the information that if it kicks a leg, the mobile will move.

ATTENTION

Attention, the focusing of mental resources on select information, improves cognitive processing on many tasks (Bell & Broomell, 2021; Kraybill, Kim-Spoon, & Bell, 2019). At any one time, though, people can pay attention to only a limited amount of information. Even newborns can detect a contour and fix their attention on it. Older infants scan patterns more thoroughly. By 4 months, infants can selectively attend to an object.

In adults, when individuals orient their attention to an object or event, the parietal lobes in the cerebral cortex are involved (Kulke, Atkinson, & Braddick, 2017). It is likely that the parietal lobes are active when infants orient their attention, although research has not yet documented this. (Figure 5 in the chapter on "Physical Development in Infancy" illustrates the location of the parietal lobes in the brain.)

Attention in the first year of life is dominated by an *orienting/investigative process* (Curtindale & others, 2019; Lunghi & others, 2019). This process involves directing attention to potentially important locations in the environment (that is, *where*) and recognizing objects and their features (such as color and form) (that is, *what*). From 3 to 9 months of age, infants can deploy their attention more flexibly and quickly. Another important type of attention is *sustained attention*. New stimuli typically elicit an orienting response followed by sustained attention. It is sustained attention that allows infants to learn about and remember characteristics of a stimulus as it becomes familiar. Researchers have found that infants as young as 3 months of age engage in 5 to 10 seconds of sustained attention. From this age through the second year, the length of sustained attention increases (Courage & Richards, 2008). In a recent study, sustained attention at 10 months of age was linked to better self-regulation at 18 months of age, even when infants had insensitive mothers

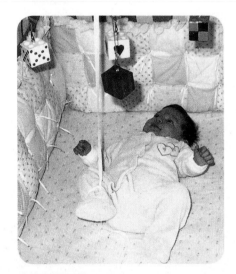

FIGURE 3

THE TECHNIQUE USED IN ROVEE-COLLIER'S INVESTIGATION OF INFANT MEMORY. In Rovee-Collier's experiment, operant conditioning was used to demonstrate that infants as young as 2½ months of age can retain information from the experience of being conditioned. *What did infants recall in Rovee-Collier's experiment?*
Courtesy of Dr. Carolyn Rovee-Collier

attention The focusing of mental resources on select information.

(Frick & others, 2018). And in another recent study, sustained attention in infancy was linked to better self-regulation in early childhood (Brandes-Aitken & others, 2019).

Habituation and Dishabituation   Closely linked with attention are the processes of habituation and dishabituation (de Paepe, de Williams, & Crombez, 2019). If you say the same word or show the same toy to a baby several times in a row, the baby usually pays less attention to it each time. This is *habituation*—decreased responsiveness to a stimulus after repeated presentations of the stimulus. *Dishabituation* is the increase in responsiveness after a change in stimulation. The chapter on "Physical Development in Infancy" described some of the measures that researchers use to study whether habituation is occurring, such as sucking behavior, heart rate, and the length of time the infant looks at an object.

This young infant's attention is riveted on the yellow toy duck that has just been placed in front of him. The young infant's attention to the toy will be strongly regulated by the processes of habituation and dishabituation. *What characterizes these processes?*
Sporrer/Rupp/Cultura/Getty Images

Infants' attention is strongly governed by novelty and habituation (Monroy & others, 2019). When an object becomes familiar, attention becomes shorter, and infants become more vulnerable to distraction.

Habituation provides a useful tool for assessing what infants can see, hear, smell, taste, and feel. When infants habituate to one object, and thus it becomes familiar, they will then tend to look at an unfamiliar object, which shows they can tell the objects apart.

Knowing about habituation and dishabituation can help parents interact effectively with infants. Infants respond to changes in stimulation. Wise parents sense when an infant shows an interest and realize that they may have to repeat something many times for the infant to process information. But if the stimulation is repeated often, the infant stops responding to the parent. In parent-infant interaction, it is important for parents to do novel things and to repeat them until the infant stops responding. The parent stops or changes behaviors when the infant redirects his or her attention (Rosenblith, 1992).

Joint Attention   Another type of attention that is an important aspect of infant development is **joint attention,** in which two or more individuals focus on the same object or event (Piazza & others, 2020; Suarez-Rivera, Smith, & Yu, 2019). Joint attention requires (1) an ability to track another's behavior, such as following the gaze of another person; (2) one person's directing another's attention; and (3) reciprocal interaction. Early in infancy, joint attention involves a caregiver pointing, turning the infant's head, snapping fingers, or using words to direct the infant's attention. Emerging forms of joint attention occur at about 7 to 8 months, but it is not until toward the end of the first year that joint attention skills are frequently observed (Niedzwiecka & Tomalski, 2015). In a study conducted by Andrew Meltzoff and Rechele Brooks (2006), at 10 to 11 months of age infants first began engaging in "gaze following," looking where another person has just looked (see Figure 4). And by their first birthday, infants have begun to direct adults' attention to objects that capture their interest (Heimann & others, 2006). One study found that problems in joint attention as early as 8 months of age were linked to the child being diagnosed with autism by 7 years of age (Veness & others, 2014). Further, a recent study indicated that initiation of joint attention is impaired from 12 months of age in children

joint attention Process that occurs when individuals focus on the same object and are able to track another's behavior, one individual directs another's attention, and reciprocal interaction takes place.

(a)

(b)

FIGURE 4

GAZE FOLLOWING IN INFANCY. Researcher Rechele Brooks shifts her eyes from the infant to a toy in the foreground (*a*). The infant then follows her eye movement to the toy (*b*). Brooks and colleague Andrew Meltzoff (2005) found that infants begin to engage in this kind of behavior, called "gaze following," at 10 to 11 months of age. *Why might gaze following be an important accomplishment for an infant?*
©2005 University of Washington, Institute for Learning & Brain Sciences

Age Group	Length of Delay
6-month-olds	24 hours
9-month-olds	1 month
10–11-month-olds	3 months
13–14-month-olds	4–6 months
20-month-olds	12 months

FIGURE 5

AGE-RELATED CHANGES IN THE LENGTH OF TIME OVER WHICH MEMORY OCCURS

A mother and her infant daughter engage in joint attention. *What about this photograph tells you that joint attention is occurring? Why is joint attention an important aspect of infant development?*
Tom Merton/OJO Images/Getty Images

with autism spectrum disorder as well as those with language delay (Franchini & others, 2019).

Joint attention plays important roles in many aspects of infant development and considerably increases infants' ability to learn from other people (McClure & others, 2018). Nowhere is this more apparent than in observations of interchanges between caregivers and infants as infants are learning language (Mason-Apps & others, 2018; Piazza & others, 2020). When caregivers and infants frequently engage in joint attention, infants say their first word earlier and develop a larger vocabulary (Mastin & Vogt, 2016). Later in this chapter in our discussion of language, we further discuss joint attention as an early predictor of language development in older infants and toddlers (Mastin & Vogt, 2016). In a recent study, both joint attention and sustained attention at 9 months predicted vocabulary size at 12 and 15 months, but sustained attention was a stronger predictor of vocabulary size (Yu, Suanda, & Smith, 2019). Researchers have found that joint attention is linked to memory (Kopp & Lindenberger, 2011), self-regulation (Van Hecke & others, 2012), and executive function (Gueron-Sela & others, 2018). Further, in a recent eye-tracking study, 10- to 18-month-olds who showed deficits in responding to others' joint attention bids and in initiating joint attention episodes were later diagnosed as having autism spectrum disorder (Nystrom & others, 2019).

MEMORY

Memory involves the retention of information over time. Attention plays an important role in memory as part of *encoding,* a process in which information is transferred to memory. What can infants remember, and when?

Some researchers, such as Carolyn Rovee-Collier (2009), have concluded that infants as young as 2 to 6 months of age can remember some experiences through 1½ to 2 years of age. However, critics such as Jean Mandler (2004), a leading expert on infant cognition, argue that the infants in Rovee-Collier's experiments were displaying only implicit memory. **Implicit memory** refers to memory without conscious recollection—memories of skills and routine procedures that are performed automatically. In contrast, **explicit memory** refers to conscious remembering of facts and experiences.

When people think about memory, they are usually referring to explicit memory. Most researchers find that babies do not show explicit memory until the second half of the first year (Bauer, 2018). Explicit memory improves substantially during the second year of life (Bauer, 2018). In one longitudinal study, infants were assessed several times during their second year (Bauer & others, 2000). Older infants showed more accurate memory and required fewer prompts to demonstrate their memory than younger infants did. Figure 5 summarizes the lengths of time that infants of different ages can remember information (Bauer, 2009a, b). As indicated in Figure 5, researchers have documented that 6-month-olds can retain information for 24 hours, but by 20 months of age infants can remember information they encountered 12 months earlier.

What changes in the brain are linked to infants' memory development? From about 6 to 12 months of age, the maturation of the hippocampus and the surrounding cerebral cortex, especially the frontal lobes, makes explicit memory possible (see Figure 6). Explicit memory continues to improve during the second year as these brain structures further mature and connections between them increase. Less is known about the areas of the brain involved in implicit memory in infancy.

Let's examine another aspect of memory. Do you remember your third birthday party? Probably not. Most adults can remember little if anything from their first three years of life. This is called *infantile* or *childhood amnesia.*

- - - - - - - ➤

developmental **connection**

Attention

In early childhood, children make significant advances in sustained attention. Connect to "Physical and Cognitive Development in Early Childhood."

◄ - - - - - - - -

memory A central feature of cognitive development, pertaining to all situations in which an individual retains information over time.

implicit memory Memory without conscious recollection; involves skills and routine procedures that are automatically performed.

explicit memory Memory of facts and experiences that individuals consciously know and can state.

Patricia Bauer and her colleagues (Bauer, 2018; Bauer & Larkina, 2016; Pathman, Doydum, & Bauer, 2013) have studied when infantile amnesia begins to occur. In one study, children's memory for events that occurred at 3 years of age was periodically assessed through age 9 (Bauer & Larkina, 2014). By 8 to 9 years of age, children's memory of events that occurred at 3 years of age began to fade away significantly. Also, in a longitudinal study of individuals from 1.5 years to 16 years of age, the age of first memory increased from 40 to 52 months as adolescents aged from 12 to 16 years of age (Reese & Robertson, 2019). In this study, individual differences in age of first memory were linked to the extent to which mothers engaged in elaborative reminiscing.

In Bauer's (2018) view, the processes that account for these developmental changes are early, gradual development of the ability to form, retain, and later retrieve memories of personally relevant past events followed by an accelerated rate of forgetting in childhood.

In sum, most of young infants' conscious memories appear to be rather fragile and short-lived, although their implicit memory of perceptual-motor actions can be substantial (Bauer, 2018; Mandler, 2004). By the end of the second year, long-term memory is more substantial and reliable (Hayne & Gross, 2017).

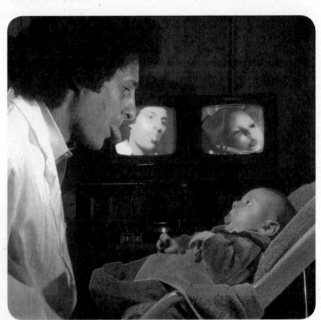

IMITATION

Can infants imitate someone else's emotional expressions? If an adult smiles, for example, will the baby respond with a smile? If an adult sticks out her tongue, wrinkles her forehead, and frowns, will the baby show a sad face?

Infant development researcher Andrew Meltzoff (Meltzoff, 2017; Meltzoff & Moore, 1999; Meltzoff & others, 2018a, b, 2019) has conducted numerous studies of infants' imitative abilities. He sees infants' imitative abilities as biologically based, because infants can imitate a facial expression within the first few days after birth. He also emphasizes that the infant's imitative abilities do not resemble a hardwired response but rather involve flexibility and adaptability. Meltzoff (2017) also emphasizes that infants' imitation informs us about their processing of social events and contributes to rapid social learning. In Meltzoff's observations of infants throughout their first 72 hours of life, the infants gradually displayed more complete imitation of an adult's facial expression, such as protruding the tongue or opening the mouth wide (see Figure 7).

Meltzoff (2007) concludes that infants don't blindly imitate everything they see and often make creative errors. He also argues that beginning at birth there is an interplay between learning by observing and learning by doing (Piaget emphasized learning by doing).

Meltzoff (2017) also has studied **deferred imitation,** which occurs after a time delay of hours or days. Piaget held that deferred imitation doesn't occur until about 18 months of age. Meltzoff's research suggested that it occurs much earlier. In one study, Meltzoff (1988) demonstrated that 9-month-old infants could imitate actions—such as pushing a recessed button in a box, which produced a beeping sound—that they had seen performed 24 hours earlier.

CONCEPT FORMATION AND CATEGORIZATION

Along with attention, memory, and imitation, concepts are key aspects of infants' cognitive development (Quinn, 2016, 2020). **Concepts** are cognitive groupings of similar objects, events, people, or ideas. Without concepts, you would see each object and event as unique; you would not be able to make any generalizations.

Do infants have concepts? Yes, they do, although we do not know precisely how early concept formation begins (Quinn & Bhatt, 2016).

FIGURE 6

KEY BRAIN STRUCTURES INVOLVED IN EXPLICIT MEMORY DEVELOPMENT IN INFANCY

FIGURE 7

INFANT IMITATION. Infant development researcher Andrew Meltzoff protrudes his tongue in an attempt to get the infant to imitate his behavior. *How do Meltzoff's findings about imitation compare with Piaget's descriptions of infants' abilities?*
Dr. Andrew Meltzoff

deferred imitation Imitation that occurs after a delay of hours or days.

concepts Cognitive groupings of similar objects, events, people, or ideas.

Using habituation experiments like those described earlier in the chapter, some researchers have found that infants as young as 3 to 4 months of age can group together objects with similar appearances, such as animals (Quinn, 2016, 2020). This research capitalizes on the knowledge that infants are more likely to look at a novel object than a familiar object. Jean Mandler (2004, 2009) argues that these early categorizations are best described as *perceptual categorization*. That is, the categorizations are based on similar perceptual features of objects, such as size, color, and movement, as well as parts of objects, such as legs for animals (Quinn & Bhatt, 2016). Mandler (2004) concludes that it is not until about 7 to 9 months of age that infants form *conceptual* categories rather than just making perceptual discriminations between different categories. In one study of 9- to 11-month-olds, infants classified birds as animals and airplanes as vehicles even though the objects were perceptually similar—airplanes and birds with their wings spread (Mandler & McDonough, 1993) (see Figure 8).

In addition to infants categorizing items on the basis of external, perceptual features such as shape, color, and parts, they also may categorize items on the basis of prototypes, or averages, that they extract from the structural regularities of items (Rakison & Lawson, 2013).

Further advances in categorization occur in the second year of life (Booth, 2006; Rakison & Lawson, 2013). Many infants' "first concepts are broad and global in nature, such as 'animal' or 'indoor thing.' Gradually, over the first two years these broad concepts become more differentiated into concepts such as 'land animal,' then 'dog,' or to 'furniture,' then 'chair'" (Mandler, 2009, p. 1). Also in the second year, infants often categorize objects on the basis of their shape (Landau, Smith, & Jones, 1998).

Learning to put things into the correct categories—what makes something one kind of thing rather than another kind of thing, such as what makes a bird a bird, or a fish a fish—is an important aspect of learning (Quinn, 2016). As infant development researcher Alison Gopnik (2010, p. 159) pointed out, "If you can sort the world into the right categories—put things in the right boxes—then you've got a big advance on understanding the world."

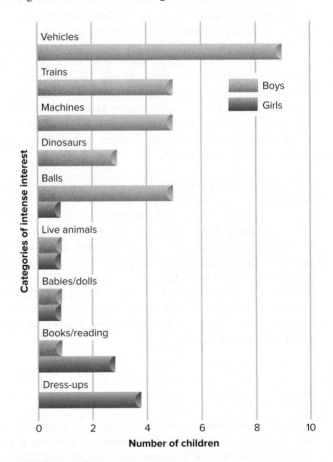

FIGURE **9**
CATEGORIZATION OF BOYS' AND GIRLS' INTENSE INTERESTS

FIGURE **8**
CATEGORIZATION IN 9- TO 11-MONTH-OLDS. These are the type of stimuli used in the study that indicated 9- to 11-month-old infants categorized birds as animals and airplanes as vehicles even though the objects were perceptually similar (Mandler & McDonough, 1993).

Do some very young children develop an intense, passionate interest in a particular category of objects or activities? One study confirmed that they do (DeLoache, Simcock, & Macari, 2007). A striking finding was the large gender difference in categories, with an intense interest in particular categories stronger for boys than girls. Categorization of boys' intense interests focused on vehicles, trains, machines, dinosaurs, and balls; girls' intense interests were more likely to involve dress-ups and books/reading (see Figure 9). When your author's grandson Alex was 18 to 24 months old, he already had developed an intense, passionate interest in the category of vehicles. For example, at this age, he categorized vehicles into such subcategories as cars, trucks, earth-moving equipment, and buses. In addition to common classifications of cars into police cars, jeeps, taxis, and such, and trucks into fire trucks, dump trucks, and the like, his categorical knowledge of earth-moving equipment included bulldozers and excavators, and he categorized buses into school buses, London buses, and funky Malta buses (retro buses on the island of Malta). Later, at 3 years of age, Alex developed an intense, passionate interest in categorizing dinosaurs.

The author's grandson Alex at 2 years of age showing his intense, passionate interest in the category of vehicles while playing with a London taxi and a funky Malta bus.
Dr. John Santrock

In sum, the infant's advances in processing information—through attention, memory, imitation, and concept formation—is much richer, more gradual and less stage-like, and occurs earlier than was envisioned by theorists such as Piaget (Bell & Broomell, 2021; Curtindale & others, 2019; Meltzoff & others, 2019; Quinn, Lee, & Pascalis, 2020). As leading infant researcher Jean Mandler (2004) concluded, "The human infant shows a remarkable degree of learning power and complexity in what is being learned and in the way it is represented" (p. 304).

Review Connect Reflect

 LG2 Describe how infants learn, focus attention, remember, and conceptualize.

Review

- How do infants learn through conditioning?
- What is attention? What characterizes attention in infants?
- To what extent can infants remember?
- How is imitation involved in infant learning?
- When do infants develop concepts, and how does concept formation change during infancy?

Connect

- In this section, we learned that explicit memory improves in the second year as the hippocampus and frontal lobes mature and as connections between them increase. What did you learn in the text associated with Figure 6 in the chapter on "Physical Development in Infancy" that might also contribute to improvements in a mental process such as memory during this same time frame?

Reflect Your Own Personal Journey of Life

- If a friend told you that she remembers being abused by her parents when she was 2 years old, would you believe her? Explain your answer.

3 Language Development

LG3 Describe the nature of language and how it develops in infancy.

| Defining Language | Language's Rule Systems | How Language Develops | Biological and Environmental Influences | An Interactionist View |

In 1799, a nude boy was observed running through the woods in France. The boy was captured when he was 11 years old. He was called the Wild Boy of Aveyron and was believed to have lived in the woods alone for six years (Lane, 1976). When found, he made no effort to communicate. He never learned to communicate effectively. Sadly, a modern-day wild child named Genie was discovered in Los Angeles in 1970. Despite intensive intervention, Genie has never acquired more than a primitive form of language. Both cases—the Wild Boy of Aveyron and Genie—raise questions about the biological and environmental determinants of language, topics that we also will examine later in this chapter. First, though, we need to define language.

DEFINING LANGUAGE

Language is a form of communication—whether spoken, written, or signed—that is based on a system of symbols. Language consists of the words used by a community and the rules for varying and combining them.

Think how important language is in our everyday lives. We need language to speak with others, listen to others, read, and write. Our language enables us to describe past events in detail and to plan for the future. Language lets us pass down information from one generation to the next and create a rich cultural heritage. Language learning involves comprehending a sound system (or sign system for individuals who are deaf), the world of objects, actions, and events, and how units such as words and grammar connect sound and world (Israel, 2019; López, 2020; Mithun, 2019; Vilma, 2020).

All human languages have some common characteristics (Abraham, 2020; Genetti, 2019). These include infinite generativity and organizational rules. **Infinite generativity** is the ability to produce and comprehend an endless number of meaningful sentences using a finite set of words and rules. Rules describe the way language works. Let's explore what these rules involve.

LANGUAGE'S RULE SYSTEMS

When nineteenth-century American writer Ralph Waldo Emerson said, "The world was built in order, and the atoms march in tune," he must have had language in mind. Language is highly ordered and organized (White, 2019). The organization involves five systems of rules: phonology, morphology, syntax, semantics, and pragmatics.

Phonology Every language is made up of basic sounds. **Phonology** is the sound system of the language, including the sounds that are used and how they may be combined. For example, English has the initial consonant cluster *spr* as in *spring,* but no words begin with the cluster *rsp.*

Phonology provides a basis for constructing a large and expandable set of words out of two or three dozen phonemes (Greenberg & Christiansen, 2019; Vihman, 2020). A *phoneme* is the basic unit of sound in a language; it is the smallest unit of sound that affects meaning. For example, in English the sound represented by the letter *p,* as in the words *pot* and *spot,* is a phoneme. The /p/ sound is slightly different in the two words, but this variation is not distinguished in English, and therefore the /p/ sound is a single phoneme. In some languages, such as Hindi, the variations of the /p/ sound represent separate phonemes.

Morphology **Morphology** refers to the units of meaning involved in word formation. A *morpheme* is a minimal unit of meaning; it is a word or a part of a word that cannot be broken into smaller meaningful parts (Mithun, 2019). Every word in the English language is made up of one or more morphemes. Some words consist of a single morpheme (for example, *help*), whereas others are made up of more than one morpheme (for example, *helper* has two morphemes, *help* and *er,* with the morpheme *-er* meaning "one who"—in this case, "one who helps"). Thus, not all morphemes are words by themselves; for example, *pre-, -tion,* and *-ing* are morphemes.

Just as the rules that govern phonology describe the sound sequences that can occur in a language, the rules of morphology describe the way meaningful units (morphemes) can be combined in words (Mithun, 2019). Morphemes have many jobs in grammar, such as marking tense (for example, "she walks" versus "she walked") and number ("she walks" versus "they walk").

Syntax **Syntax** involves the way words are combined to form acceptable phrases and sentences (Indefrey, 2019; Lopez, 2020; Meteyard & Vigliocco, 2019). If someone says to you, "Bob slugged Tom" or "Bob was slugged by Tom," you know who did the slugging and who was slugged in each case because you have a syntactic understanding of these sentence structures. You also understand that the sentence, "You didn't stay, did you?" is a grammatical sentence, but that "You didn't stay, didn't you?" is unacceptable and ambiguous.

If you learn another language, English syntax will not get you very far. For example, in English an adjective usually precedes a noun (as in *blue sky*), whereas in Spanish the adjective usually follows the noun (*cielo azul*). Despite the differences in their syntactic structures,

Language allows us to communicate with others. *What are some important characteristics of language?*
LiandStudio/Shutterstock

language A form of communication, whether spoken, written, or signed, that is based on a system of symbols. Language consists of the words used by a community and the rules for varying and combining them.

infinite generativity The ability to produce and comprehend an endless number of meaningful sentences using a finite set of words and rules.

phonology The sound system of the language, including the sounds that are used and how they may be combined.

morphology Units of meaning involved in word formation.

syntax The ways words are combined to form acceptable phrases and sentences.

Rule System	Description	Examples
Phonology	The sound system of a language. A phoneme is the smallest sound unit in a language.	The word *chat* has three phonemes or sounds: /ch/ /ã/ /t/. An example of phonological rule in the English language is while the phoneme /r/ can follow the phonemes /t/ or /d/ in an English consonant cluster (such as *track* or *drab*), the phoneme /l/ cannot follow these letters.
Morphology	The system of meaningful units involved in word formation.	The smallest sound units that have a meaning are called morphemes, or meaning units. The word *girl* is one morpheme, or meaning unit; it cannot be broken down any further and still have meaning. When the suffix *s* is added, the word becomes *girls* and has two morphemes because the *s* changed the meaning of the word, indicating that there is more than one girl.
Syntax	The system that involves the way words are combined to form acceptable phrases and sentences.	Word order is very important in determining meaning in the English language. For example, the sentence "Sebastian pushed the bike" has a different meaning than "The bike pushed Sebastian."
Semantics	The system that involves the meaning of words and sentences.	Knowing the meaning of individual words—that is, vocabulary. For example, semantics includes knowing the meaning of such words as *orange*, *transportation*, and *intelligent*.
Pragmatics	The system of using appropriate conversation and knowledge of how to effectively use language in context.	An example is using polite language in appropriate situations, such as being mannerly when talking with one's teacher. Taking turns in a conversation involves pragmatics.

FIGURE 10
THE RULE SYSTEMS OF LANGUAGE

however, syntactic systems in all of the world's languages have some common ground (Ringe, 2019). For example, no language we know of permits sentences like the following one:

The mouse the cat the farmer chased killed ate the cheese.

It appears that language users cannot process subjects and objects arranged in too complex a fashion in a sentence.

Semantics   **Semantics** refers to the meaning of words and sentences. Every word has a set of semantic features, which are required attributes related to meaning (Abraham, 2020; Israel, 2019). *Girl* and *woman*, for example, share many semantic features, but they differ semantically in regard to age.

Words have semantic restrictions on how they can be used in sentences (MacDonald & Hsiao, 2019). The sentence *The bicycle talked the boy into buying a candy bar* is syntactically correct but semantically incorrect. The sentence violates our semantic knowledge that bicycles don't talk.

Pragmatics   A final set of language rules involves **pragmatics,** the appropriate use of language in different contexts. Pragmatics covers a lot of territory (Abraham, 2020; Demuth, 2019; Garnham, 2019). When you take turns speaking in a discussion or use a question to convey a command ("Why is it so noisy in here? What is this, Grand Central Station?"), you are demonstrating knowledge of pragmatics. You also apply the pragmatics of English when you use polite language in appropriate situations (for example, when talking to your teacher) or tell stories that are interesting, jokes that are funny, and lies that convince. In each of these cases, you are demonstrating that you understand the rules of your culture for adjusting language to suit the context.

At this point, we have discussed five important rule systems involved in language. An overview of these rule systems is presented in Figure 10.

HOW LANGUAGE DEVELOPS

According to an ancient historian, in the thirteenth century the emperor of Germany, Frederick II, had a cruel idea. He wanted to know what language children would speak if no one talked to them. He selected several newborns and threatened their caregivers with death if they ever talked to the infants. Frederick never found out what language the children spoke because they all died. Today, we are still curious about infants' development of language, although our experiments and observations are, to say the least, far more humane than the evil Frederick's.

Whatever language they learn, infants all over the world follow a similar path in language development. What are some key milestones in this development?

semantics The meaning of words and sentences.

pragmatics The appropriate use of language in different contexts.

FIGURE **11**

FROM UNIVERSAL LINGUIST TO LANGUAGE-SPECIFIC LISTENER.
In Patricia Kuhl's research laboratory babies listen to tape-recorded voices that repeat syllables. When the sounds of the syllables change, the babies quickly learn to look at the bear. Using this technique, Kuhl has demonstrated that babies are universal linguists until about 6 months of age, but in their next six months they become language-specific listeners. *Does Kuhl's research give support to the view that either "nature" or "nurture" is the source of language acquisition?*
Courtesy of Dr. Patricia Kuhl, Institute for Learning and Brain Sciences, University of Washington

Recognizing Language Sounds   Long before they begin to learn words, infants can make fine distinctions among the sounds of the language. In Patricia Kuhl's (1993, 2009, 2015) research, phonemes from languages all over the world are piped through a speaker for infants to hear (see Figure 11). A box with a toy bear in it is placed where the infant can see it. A string of identical syllables is played; then the syllables are changed (for example, *ba ba ba ba*, and then *pa pa pa pa*). If the infant turns its head when the syllables change, the box lights up and the bear dances and drums, rewarding the infant for noticing the change.

Kuhl's (2015) research has demonstrated that from birth up to about 6 months of age, infants are "citizens of the world": They recognize when sounds change most of the time, no matter what language the syllables come from. But over the next six months, infants get even better at perceiving the changes in sounds from their "own" language (the one their parents speak) and gradually lose the ability to recognize differences in sounds that are not important in their own language (Kuhl, 2015). Kuhl (2015) has found that a baby's brain becomes most open to learning the sounds of a native language at 6 months for vowels and at 9 months for consonants.

Also, in the second half of the first year, infants begin to segment the continuous stream of speech they encounter into words (Ota & Skarabela, 2018). Initially, they likely rely on statistical information such as the co-occurrence patterns of phonemes and syllables, which allows them to extract potential word forms (Amon, 2019; Lany & Shoaib, 2020; Levine & others, 2019b; Saffran & Kirkham, 2018). For example, discovering that the sequence *br* occurs more often at the beginning of words while *nt* is more common at the end of words helps infants detect word boundaries. And as infants extract an increasing number of potential word forms from the speech stream they hear, they begin to associate these with concrete, perceptually available objects in their world (Saffran & Kirkham, 2018). For example, infants might detect that the spoken word "monkey" has a reliable statistical regularity of occurring in the visual presence of an observed monkey but not in the presence of other animals, such as bears (Pace & others, 2016). Thus, statistical learning involves extracting information from the world to learn about the environment (Lany & Shoaib, 2020).

Richard Aslin (2017) recently emphasized that statistical learning—which involves no instruction, reinforcement, or feedback—is a powerful learning mechanism in infant development. In statistical learning, infants soak up statistical regularities in the world merely through exposure to them (Levine & others, 2019a; Saffran & Kirkham, 2018). Aslin (2019) concludes that in addition to word segmentation from fluent speech, statistical learning has been documented in other domains, such as musical tones, phonetic categories, sequences of visual shapes, sequences of motor responses, and combination of object parts in complex visual scenes.

Babbling and Other Vocalizations   Long before infants speak recognizable words, they produce a number of vocalizations. The functions of these early vocalizations are to practice making sounds, to communicate, and to attract attention (Choi & others, 2019; Hirai & Kanakogi, 2019). Babies' sounds go through the following sequence during the first year:

- *Crying.* Babies cry even at birth. Crying can signal distress, but, as we will discuss in the chapter on "Socioemotional Development in Infancy," different types of cries signal different things.

- *Cooing.* Babies first coo at about 2 to 4 months (Menn & Stoel-Gammon, 2009). These are gurgling sounds that are made in the back of the throat and usually express pleasure during interaction with the caregiver.

- *Babbling.* In the middle of the first year, babies babble—that is, they produce strings of consonant-vowel combinations, such as "ba, ba, ba, ba." Infants' babbling influences the behavior of their caregivers, creating social interaction that facilitates their own communicative development (Albert, Schwade, & Goldstein, 2019; Casillas, Brown, & Levinson, 2020). In a recent study, babbling onset predicted when infants would say their first words (McGillion & others, 2017).

Gestures Infants start using gestures, such as showing and pointing, at about 7 to 15 months of age with a mean age of approximately 11 to 12 months. They may wave bye-bye, nod to mean "yes," show an empty cup to ask for more milk, and point to a dog to draw attention to it. Some early gestures are symbolic, as when an infant smacks her lips to indicate food or drink. Pointing is regarded by language experts as an important index of the *social aspects of language,* and it follows this developmental sequence: from pointing without checking on adult gaze to pointing while looking back and forth between an object and the adult (Goldin-Meadow, 2017a, b). Lack of pointing is a significant indicator of problems in the infant's communication system (Fenlon & others, 2019). For example, failure to engage in pointing characterizes many autistic children. In a recent study, infants at high risk for autism spectrum disorder used fewer gestures than their low-risk counterparts (Choi & others, 2020). Use of the pointing gesture becomes more effective in the second year of life alongside advances in other aspects of language communication.

Why might gestures such as pointing promote further language development? Infants' gestures advance their language development since caregivers often talk to them about what they are pointing to. Also, babies' first words often are for things they have previously pointed to.

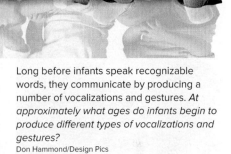

Long before infants speak recognizable words, they communicate by producing a number of vocalizations and gestures. *At approximately what ages do infants begin to produce different types of vocalizations and gestures?*
Don Hammond/Design Pics

First Words Infants understand their first words earlier than they speak them. As early as 5 months of age, infants recognize their name when someone says it. On average, infants understand about 50 words at about 13 months, but they can't say this many words until about 18 months (Menyuk, Liebergott, & Schultz, 1995). Thus, in infancy *receptive vocabulary* (words the child understands) considerably exceeds *spoken* (or *expressive*) *vocabulary* (words the child uses) (Vihman, 2019).

A child's first words include those that name important people (*dada*), familiar animals (*kitty*), vehicles (*car*), toys (*ball*), food (*milk*), body parts (*eye*), clothes (*hat*), household items (*clock*), and greeting terms (*bye*). These were the first words of babies 50 years ago, and they are the first words of babies today. Children often express various intentions with their single words, so that "cookie" might mean, "That's a cookie" or "I want a cookie." Nouns are easier to learn because the majority of words in this class are more perceptually accessible than words not in this class (Parish-Morris, Golinkoff, & Hirsh-Pasek, 2013). Think how the noun "car" is so much more concrete and imaginable than the verb "goes," making the word "car" much easier to acquire than the word "goes."

The infant's spoken vocabulary rapidly increases after the first word is spoken (Chow & others, 2019). The average 18-month-old can speak about 50 words, but most 2-year-olds can speak about 200 words. This rapid increase in vocabulary that begins at approximately 18 months is called the *vocabulary spurt* (Bloom, Lifter, & Broughton, 1985).

Like the timing of a child's first word, the timing of the vocabulary spurt varies (Lieven, 2008). Figure 12 shows the range for these two language milestones in 14 children. On average, these children said their first word at 13 months and had a vocabulary spurt at 19 months. However, the ages for the first spoken word of individual children varied from 10 to 17 months and for their vocabulary spurt from 13 to 25 months. Also, the spurt actually involves the

What characterizes the infant's early word learning?
JGI/Jamie Grill/Blend Images LLC

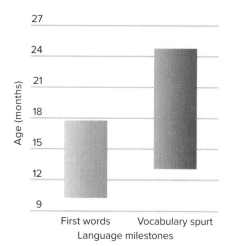

FIGURE **12**

VARIATION IN LANGUAGE MILESTONES.
What are some possible explanations for variations in the timing of language milestones?

increase in the rate at which words are learned. That is, early on, a few words are learned every few days, then later on, a few words are learned each day, and eventually many words each day.

Does early vocabulary development predict later language development? One study found that infant vocabulary development at 16 to 24 months of age was linked to vocabulary, phonological awareness, reading accuracy, and reading comprehension five years later (Duff & others, 2015). Also, in a recent study, vocabulary comprehension at 23 months was linked to language skills (morpheme knowledge and identification of correct sentences, for example) at 36 months (Friend & others, 2019). And in another recent study, learning new words at 21 months of age was associated with receptive vocabulary at 7 to 10 years of age (Rajan & others, 2019).

Cross-linguistic differences occur in word learning (Abraham, 2020; Waxman & others, 2013). Children learning Mandarin Chinese, Korean, and Japanese acquire more verbs earlier in their development than do children learning English. This cross-linguistic difference reflects the greater use of verbs in the language input to children in these Asian languages. Indeed, the language of Korean children is often described as verb friendly and the language of English as noun friendly (Waxman & others, 2013).

Children sometimes overextend or underextend the meanings of the words they use (Woodward & Markman, 1998). *Overextension* is the tendency to apply a word to objects that are inappropriate for the word's meaning by going beyond the set of referents an adult would use. For example, children at first may say "dada" not only for "father" but also for other men, strangers, or boys. Another example of overextension is calling any animal with four legs a "dog." With time, overextensions decrease and eventually disappear. *Underextension* is the tendency to apply a word too narrowly; it occurs when children fail to use a word to name a relevant event or object. For example, a child might use the word *boy* to describe a 5-year-old neighbor but not apply the word to a male infant or to a 9-year-old male.

Two-Word Utterances By the time children are 18 to 24 months of age, they usually speak in two-word utterances. To convey meaning with just two words, the child relies heavily on gesture, tone, and context. The wealth of meaning children can communicate with a two-word utterance includes the following (Slobin, 1972):

- Identification: "See doggie."
- Location: "Book there."
- Repetition: "More milk."
- Negation: "Not wolf."
- Possession: "My candy."
- Attribution: "Big car."
- Agent-action: "Mama walk."
- Action-direct object: "Hit you."
- Action-indirect object: "Give Papa."
- Action-instrument: "Cut knife."
- Question: "Where ball?"

These are examples from children whose first language is English, German, Russian, Finnish, Turkish, or Samoan.

Notice that the two-word utterances omit many parts of speech and are remarkably succinct. In fact, in every language, a child's first combinations of words have this economical quality; they are telegraphic. **Telegraphic speech** is the use of short and precise words without grammatical markers such as articles, auxiliary verbs, and other connectives. Telegraphic speech is not limited to two words. "Mommy give ice cream" and "Mommy give Tommy ice cream" also are examples of telegraphic speech.

We have discussed a number of language milestones in infancy; Figure 13 summarizes the approximate ages at which infants typically reach these milestones.

BIOLOGICAL AND ENVIRONMENTAL INFLUENCES

What makes it possible for infants to reach the milestones of language development described in Figure 13? Everyone who uses language in some way "knows" its rules and has the ability to create an infinite number of words and sentences. Where does this knowledge come from? Is it the product of biology? Is language learned and influenced by experiences?

Around the world, most young children learn to speak in two-word utterances at about 18 to 24 months of age. *What are some examples of these two-word utterances?*
McPhoto/age fotostock

telegraphic speech The use of short and precise words without grammatical markers such as articles, auxiliary verbs, and other connectives.

Biological Influences The ability to speak and understand language requires a specific vocal apparatus as well as a nervous system with certain capabilities. The nervous system and vocal apparatus of humanity's predecessors changed over hundreds of thousands or millions of years. With advances in the nervous system and vocal structures, *Homo sapiens* went beyond the grunting and shrieking of other animals to develop speech (de Boer & Verhoef, 2019; Bretas, Yamazaki, & Iriki, 2020; O'Grady & Smith, 2019; Prieur & others, 2020). Although estimates vary, many experts believe that humans acquired language about 100,000 years ago, which in evolutionary time represents a very recent acquisition. It gave humans an enormous edge over other animals and increased the chances of human survival (Prieur & others, 2020).

Some language scholars view the remarkable similarities in how children acquire language all over the world as strong evidence that language has a biological basis. There is evidence that particular regions of the brain are predisposed to be used for language. Two regions involved in language were first discovered in studies of brain-damaged individuals: **Broca's area,** an area in the left frontal lobe of the brain involved in producing words (Sakreida & others, 2019), and **Wernicke's area,** a region of the brain's left hemisphere involved in language comprehension (see Figure 14) (Blagovechtchenski & others, 2020). Damage to either of these areas produces types of **aphasia,** which is a loss or impairment of language processing. Individuals with damage to Broca's area have difficulty producing words correctly; individuals with damage to Wernicke's area have poor comprehension and often produce fluent but incomprehensible speech.

Linguist Noam Chomsky (1957) proposed that humans are biologically prewired to learn language at a certain time and in a certain way. He said that children are born into the world with a **language acquisition device (LAD),** a biological endowment that enables the child to detect certain features and rules of language, including phonology, syntax, and semantics. Children are equipped by nature with the ability to detect the sounds of language, for example, and to follow rules such as how to form plurals and ask questions.

Chomsky's LAD is a theoretical construct, not a physical part of the brain. Is there evidence for the existence of a LAD? Supporters of the LAD concept cite the uniformity of language milestones across languages and cultures, evidence that children create language even in the absence of well-formed input, and biological substrates of language. But, as we will see, critics argue that even if infants have something like a LAD, it cannot explain the whole story of language acquisition.

Typical Age	Language Milestones
Birth	Crying
2 to 4 months	Cooing begins
5 months	Understands first word
6 months	Babbling begins
6 to 12 months	Change from universal linguist to language-specific listener
8 to 12 months	Uses gestures, such as showing and pointing Comprehension of words appears
13 months	First word spoken
18 months	Vocabulary spurt starts
18 to 24 months	Uses two-word utterances Rapid expansion of understanding of words

FIGURE 13

SOME LANGUAGE MILESTONES IN INFANCY. Despite considerable variations in the language input received by infants, around the world they follow a similar path in learning to speak.

developmental **connection**

Language

Much of language is processed in the brain's left hemisphere. Connect to "Physical Development in Infancy."

Broca's area An area in the brain's left frontal lobe that is involved in speech production.

Wernicke's area An area in the brain's left hemisphere that is involved in language comprehension.

aphasia A loss or impairment of language ability caused by brain damage.

language acquisition device (LAD) Chomsky's term that describes a biological endowment enabling the child to detect the features and rules of language, including phonology, syntax, and semantics.

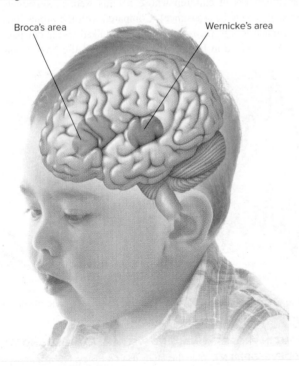

Broca's area Wernicke's area

FIGURE 14

BROCA'S AREA AND WERNICKE'S AREA. Broca's area is located in the frontal lobe of the brain's left hemisphere, and it is involved in the control of speech. Wernicke's area is a portion of the left hemisphere's temporal lobe that is involved in understanding language. *How does the role of these areas of the brain relate to lateralization?*
Photo: Swissmacky/Shutterstock

FIGURE 15

SOCIAL INTERACTION AND BABBLING.
One study focused on two groups of mothers and their 8-month-old infants (Goldstein, King, & West, 2003). One group of mothers was instructed to smile and touch their infants immediately after the babies cooed and babbled; the other group was also told to smile and touch their infants but in a random manner, unconnected to sounds the infants made. The infants whose mothers immediately responded in positive ways to their babbling subsequently made more complex, speechlike sounds, such as "da" and "gu," underscoring the importance of caregivers in language acquisition. The research setting for this study is shown here.
Courtesy of Dr. Michael Goldstein

Environmental Influences Our coverage of environmental influences on language development in infancy focuses on the important role of social interaction as well as child-directed speech and caregiver strategies.

The Role of Social Interaction Language is not learned in a social vacuum. Most children are bathed in language from a very early age, unlike the Wild Boy of Aveyron, who never learned to communicate effectively, having lived in social isolation for years. Thus, social cues play an important role in infant language learning (Ahun & others, 2018).

The support and involvement of caregivers and teachers greatly facilitate a child's language learning (Bredekamp, 2020; Gunning, 2020; Tompkins & Rodgers, 2020). In one study, both full-term and preterm infants who heard more caregiver talk based on all-day recordings at 16 months of age had better language skills (receptive and expressive language, language comprehension) at 18 months of age (Adams & others, 2018). Also, in a recent study, conversational turn counts at 18 to 24 months were linked to receptive and expressive vocabulary development 10 years later (Gilkerson & others, 2018). And in another study, when mothers immediately smiled and touched their 8-month-old infants after they babbled, the infants subsequently made more complex speech-like sounds than when mothers responded to their infants in a random manner (Goldstein, King, & West, 2003) (see Figure 15).

Michael Tomasello (2006, 2014) stresses that young children are intensely interested in their social world and that early in their development they can understand the intentions of other people. His *interaction view* of language emphasizes that children learn language in specific contexts. For example, when a toddler and a father are jointly focused on a book, the father might say, "See the birdie." In this case, even a toddler understands that the father intends to name something and knows to look in the direction of the pointing. Through this kind of joint attention, early in their development children are able to use their social skills to acquire language (Piazza & others, 2020).

Researchers have also found that the child's vocabulary development is linked to the family's socioeconomic status and the type of talk that parents direct to their children. In a recent study, children living in extreme poverty had much lower levels of vocabulary and reading comprehension (Lervag & others, 2019). In other research, Betty Hart and Todd Risley (1995) observed the language environments of children whose parents were professionals and children whose parents were on welfare (public assistance). Compared with the professional parents, the parents on welfare talked much less to their young children, talked less about past events, and provided less elaboration. As indicated in Figure 16, the children of the professional parents had a much

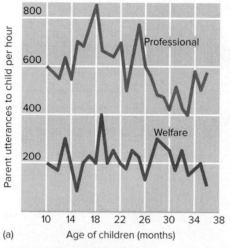

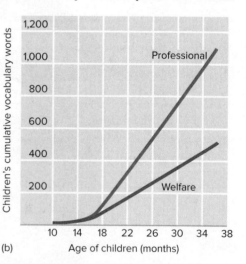

FIGURE 16

LANGUAGE INPUT IN PROFESSIONAL AND WELFARE FAMILIES AND YOUNG CHILDREN'S VOCABULARY DEVELOPMENT. (*a*) In this study (Hart & Risley, 1995), parents from professional families talked with their young children more than parents from welfare families. (*b*) All of the children learned to talk, but children from professional families developed vocabularies that were twice as large as those of children from welfare families. Thus, by the time children go to preschool, they already have experienced considerable differences in language input in their families and developed different levels of vocabulary that are linked to their socioeconomic context. *Does this study indicate that poverty caused deficiencies in vocabulary development?*

larger vocabulary at 36 months of age than the children of the welfare parents. One study also found that at 18 to 24 months of age, infants in low-SES families already had a smaller vocabulary and less efficient language processing than their infant counterparts in middle-SES families (Fernald, Marchman, & Weisleder, 2013). Further, in a recent study of English-speaking preschool children, those from lower-income families had less advanced language-processing skills, as well a smaller vocabulary and syntax deficiencies (Levine & others, 2019).

Other research has linked how much mothers speak to their infants with the size of the infants' vocabularies. For example, in one study by Janellen Huttenlocher and her colleagues (1991), infants whose mothers spoke more often to them had markedly larger vocabularies. By the second birthday, vocabulary differences were substantial.

However, a study of 1- to 3-year-old children living in low-income families found that the sheer amount of maternal talk was not the best predictor of a child's vocabulary growth (Pan & others, 2005). Rather, it was maternal language and literacy skills and mothers' diversity of vocabulary that best predicted children's vocabulary development. Also, mothers who frequently used pointing gestures had children with a greater vocabulary. Pointing usually occurs in concert with speech, and it may enhance the meaning of mothers' verbal input to their children. These research studies and others (NICHD Early Child Care Research Network, 2005; Perkins, Finegood, & Swain, 2013) demonstrate the important effects that early speech input and poverty can have on the development of a child's language skills.

Given that social interaction is critical for infants to learn language effectively, might they also be able to learn language effectively through television and videos? Researchers have found that infants and young children cannot effectively learn language (phonology or words) from television or videos (Zosh & others, 2017). A study of toddlers found that frequent viewing of television increased the risk of delayed language development (Lin & others, 2015). Thus, just hearing language is not enough even when infants seemingly are fully engaged in the experience. However, one study revealed that Skype provides some improvement in child language learning over videos and TV (Roseberry, Hirsh-Pasek, & Golinkoff, 2014), and older children can use information provided from television in their language development.

Also, recently the American Academy of Pediatrics (AAP) (2016) concluded that for infants from 15 months to 2 years of age, evidence indicates that if parents co-watch educational videos with their infant and communicate with the infant about the information conveyed, this shared activity can benefit the infant's development. These findings suggest that when parents treat an educational video or app like a picture book, infants can benefit from it. However, the AAP still recommends that children under 18 months of age not watch videos alone.

Child-Directed Speech and Other Caregiver Strategies   One intriguing component of the young child's linguistic environment is **child-directed speech** (also referred to as "parentese"), which is language spoken with a higher-than-normal pitch, slower tempo, and exaggerated intonation, with simple words and sentences (Antonijevic, Muckley, & Muller, 2020; Quick, Erickson, & McCright, 2019). It is hard to use child-directed speech when not in the presence of a baby, but parents shift into it when they start talking to a baby. Much of this is automatic and something most parents are not aware they are doing. Child-directed speech serves the important functions of capturing the infant's attention, maintaining communication and social interaction between infants and caregivers, and providing infants with information about their native language by heightening differences between speech directed to children and adults (Golinkoff & others, 2015). In a recent study, parent coaching of 6- and 10-month-old infants that involved the amount of child-directed speech, back and forth interactions, and parentese speech style improved the infants' language outcomes (more advanced babbling and greater word production) at 14 months of age (Ferjan Ramirez & others, 2019).

Even 4-year-olds speak in simpler ways to 2-year-olds than to their 4-year-old friends. In recent research, child-directed speech in a one-to-one social context at 11 to 14 months of age was related to productive vocabulary at 2 years of age for Spanish-English bilingual infants across languages and in each individual language (Ramirez-Esparza, Garcia-Sierra, & Kuhl, 2017). Most research on child-directed speech has involved mothers, but a recent study in several North American urban areas and a small society on the island of Tanna in the South Pacific Ocean found that fathers in both types of contexts engaged in child-directed speech with their infants (Broesch & Bryant, 2018).

A father using child-directed speech on the island of Tanna in the South Pacific Ocean.
Nick Perry/AP Images

child-directed speech Language spoken in a higher pitch and slower speed than normal, with simple words and sentences.

Adults often use strategies other than child-directed speech to enhance the child's acquisition of language, including recasting, expanding, and labeling:

- *Recasting* is rephrasing something the child has said that might lack the appropriate morphology or contain some other error. The adult restates the child's immature utterance in the form of a fully grammatical sentence. For example, if a 2-year-old says, "dog bark," the adult can respond by saying, "Oh, you heard the dog barking!" The adult sentence provides an acknowledgement that the child was heard and then adds the morphology (*/ing/*) and the article (*the*) that the child's utterance lacked.
- *Expanding* is adding information to a child's incomplete utterance. For example, a child says, "Doggie eat," and the parent replies, "Yes, the dog is eating his food out of his special dish."
- *Labeling* is naming objects that children seem interested in. Young children are forever being asked to identify the names of objects. Roger Brown (1968) called this "the original word game." Children want more than the names of objects, though; they often want information about the object too.

Parents use these strategies naturally and in meaningful conversations. Parents do not need to use a particular method to teach their children to talk, even for children who are slow in learning language. Children usually benefit when parents follow the child's lead, talking about things the child is interested in at the moment, and when parents provide information that children can process. If children are not ready to take in some information, they are likely to let you know (perhaps by turning away). Thus, giving the child more information is not always better.

Remember that encouragement of language development during parents' interaction with their children, not drill and practice, is the key. Language development is not a simple matter of imitation and reinforcement.

Infants, toddlers, and young children benefit when adults read books to and with them (shared reading) (Thompson, 2020). Storybook reading especially benefits children when parents extend the meaning of the text by discussing it with children and encouraging them to ask and answer questions (Harris, Golinkoff, & Hirsh-Pasek, 2011). In one study, reading daily to children 14 to 24 months of age was positively related to the children's language and cognitive development at 36 months of age (Raikes & others, 2006). Further, a recent meta-analysis concluded that shared picture book reading was linked to children having better expressive and receptive language (Dowdall & others, 2020). And in another recent study, the more parents engaged in parent-child book reading interactions from 1 to 2.5 years of age, the better their children's language development was in terms of receptive vocabulary, reading comprehension, and motivation to read in elementary school (Demir-Lira & others, 2019). To read further about ways that parents can facilitate children's language development, see *Connecting Development to Life*.

What characterizes shared reading in the lives of infants, toddlers, and young children?
Elyse Lewin/Brand X Pictures/Getty Images

AN INTERACTIONIST VIEW

If language acquisition depended only on biology, then the Wild Boy of Aveyron and Genie (discussed earlier in the chapter) should have talked without difficulty. A child's experiences influence language acquisition (Levine & others, 2020; Morrow, 2020; Smith & others, 2019). But we have seen that language does have strong biological foundations (Prieur & others, 2020). No matter how much you converse with a dog, it won't learn to talk. In contrast, children are biologically prepared to learn language. Children all over the world acquire language milestones at about the same time and in about the same order. However, there are cultural variations in the type of support given to children's language development. For example, caregivers in the Kaluli culture prompt young children to use a loud voice, to call out particular morphemes that direct the speech act the child is performing, and to refer to names, kinship relations, and places where there has been a shared past experience that indicates a closeness to the person being addressed (Ochs & Schieffelin, 2008; Schieffelin, 2005).

Environmental influences are also very important in developing competence in language (Morrison, 2020; Tompkins & Rodgers, 2020). Children whose parents provide them with

How Parents Can Facilitate Infants' and Toddlers' Language Development

Linguist Naomi Baron (1992) in *Growing Up with Language,* developmental psychologists Roberta Golinkoff and Kathy Hirsh-Pasek (2000) in *How Babies Talk,* and more recently Ellen Galinsky (2010) in *Mind in the Making* have provided ideas to help parents facilitate their infants' and toddlers' language development. Following is a summary of their suggestions:

- Be an active conversational partner. Talk to your baby from the time it is born. Initiate conversation with the baby. If the baby is in an all-day child-care program, ensure that he or she receives adequate language stimulation from adults.

- Narrate your daily activities to the baby as you do them. For example, talk about how you will put the baby in a high chair for lunch and ask what she would like to eat, and so on.

- Talk in a slowed-down pace and don't worry about how you sound to other adults when you talk to your baby. Talking slowly will help your baby detect words in the sea of sounds they experience. Babies enjoy and attend to the high-pitched sound of child-directed speech.

- Use parent-look and parent-gesture, and name what you are looking at. When you want your child to pay attention to something, look at it and point to it. Then name it—for example, you might say, "Look, Alex, there's an airplane."

- When you talk with infants and toddlers, be simple, concrete, and repetitive. Don't try to talk to them in abstract, high-level ways and think you have to say something new or different all of the time. Using familiar words often will help them remember the words.

- Play games. Use word games like peek-a-boo and pat-a-cake to help infants learn words.

- Remember to listen. Since toddlers' speech is often slow and laborious, parents are often tempted to supply words and thoughts for them. Be patient and let toddlers express themselves, no matter how painstaking the process is or how great a hurry you are in.

- Expand and elaborate language abilities and horizons with infants and toddlers. Ask questions that encourage answers other than "yes" or "no." Actively repeat, expand, and recast the utterances. Your toddler might say, "Dada." You could follow with, "Where's Dada?" and then you might continue, "Let's go find him."

It is a good idea for parents to begin talking to their babies at the start. The best language teaching occurs when the talking begins before the infant becomes capable of intelligible speech. What are some other guidelines for parents to follow in helping their infants and toddlers develop their language skills?
Camille Tokerud/Getty Images

- Adjust to your child's idiosyncrasies instead of working against them. Many toddlers have difficulty pronouncing words and making themselves understood. Whenever possible, make toddlers feel that they are understood.

- Resist making normative comparisons. Be aware of the ages at which your child reaches specific milestones (such as the first word, first 50 words), but do not measure this development rigidly against that of other children. Such comparisons can bring about unnecessary anxiety.

The first suggestion above to parents of infants is to "be an active conversational partner." What did you learn earlier in the chapter about the amount of conversation mothers have with their infants? Does the amount of conversation or the mother's literacy skills and vocabulary diversity have more of a positive effect on infants' vocabulary?

a rich verbal environment show many positive benefits (Gilkerson & others, 2018). Parents who pay attention to what their children are trying to say, expand their children's utterances, read to them, and label things in the environment, are providing valuable benefits for them (Morrow, 2020).

An *interactionist view* emphasizes that both *biology* and *experience* contribute to language development (Feeney, Moravcik, & Nolte, 2019; Sakreida & others, 2019). How much of language acquisition is biologically determined and how much depends on interaction with others is a subject of debate among linguists and psychologists. However, all agree that both biological capacity and relevant experience are necessary (Thompson, 2020).

LG3 Describe the nature of language and how it develops in infancy.

Review
- What is language?
- What are language's rule systems?
- How does language develop in infancy?
- What are some biological and environmental influences on language?
- To what extent do biological and environmental influences interact to produce language development?

Connect
- The more years children spend living in poverty, the higher are their physiological indices of stress. In this chapter, you learned about the effects of SES on children's language acquisition and vocabulary building. How might these effects influence children's school performance?

Reflect *Your Own Personal Journey of Life*
- Would it be a good idea for you as a parent to hold large flash cards of words in front of your baby for several hours each day to help the baby learn language and to raise the baby's intelligence? Why or why not? What do you think Piaget would say about this activity?

---

topical **connections** *looking* **forward**

Advances in infants' cognitive development are linked to their socioemotional development. In subsequent chapters, you will learn about the infant's developing social orientation and understanding, which involve perceiving people as engaging in intentional and goal-directed behavior, joint attention, and cooperation. You will read about two major theorists—Piaget and Vygotsky—and compare their views of how young children's thinking advances. You will see how young children become more capable of sustaining their attention; learn about the astonishing rate at which preschool children's vocabulary expands; and explore variations in early childhood education.

---

reach your **learning goals**

Cognitive Development in Infancy

1 Piaget's Theory of Infant Development

 LG1 Summarize and evaluate Piaget's theory of infant development.

Cognitive Processes

- In Piaget's theory, children actively construct their own cognitive worlds, building mental structures to adapt to their world. Schemes are actions or mental representations that organize knowledge. Behavioral schemes (physical activities) characterize infancy, whereas mental schemes (cognitive activities) develop in childhood. Assimilation occurs when children use their existing schemes to deal with new information; accommodation refers to children's adjustment of their schemes in the face of new information. Through organization, children group isolated behaviors into a higher-order, more smoothly functioning cognitive system.

- Equilibration is a mechanism Piaget proposed to explain how children shift from one cognitive stage to the next. As children experience cognitive conflict in trying to understand the world, they use assimilation and accommodation to attain equilibrium. The result is a new stage of thought.

- According to Piaget, there are four qualitatively different stages of thought. The first of these, the sensorimotor stage, is described in this chapter. The other three stages are discussed in subsequent chapters.

| The Sensorimotor Stage | • In sensorimotor thought, the first of Piaget's four stages, the infant organizes and coordinates sensations with physical movements. The stage lasts from birth to about 2 years of age. |

- Sensorimotor thought has six substages: simple reflexes; first habits and primary circular reactions; secondary circular reactions; coordination of secondary circular reactions; tertiary circular reactions, novelty, and curiosity; and internalization of schemes. One key accomplishment of this stage is object permanence, the ability to understand that objects continue to exist even when the infant is no longer observing them. Another aspect involves infants' understanding of cause and effect.

| Evaluating Piaget's Sensorimotor Stage | • Piaget opened up a whole new way of looking at infant development in terms of coordinating sensory input with motoric actions. In recent decades, revisions of Piaget's view have been proposed based on research. For example, researchers have found that a stable and differentiated perceptual world is established earlier than Piaget envisioned, and infants begin to develop concepts earlier as well. |

- The nature-nurture issue in regard to infant cognitive development continues to be debated. Spelke endorses a core knowledge approach which states that infants are born with domain-specific innate knowledge systems. Critics argue that Spelke has not given adequate attention to infants' early experiences.

2 Learning, Attention, Remembering, and Conceptualizing

LG2 Describe how infants learn, focus attention, remember, and conceptualize.

| Conditioning | • Operant conditioning techniques have been especially useful to researchers in demonstrating infants' perception and retention of information about perceptual-motor actions. |

| Attention | • Attention is the focusing of mental resources on select information, and in infancy attention is closely linked with habituation. In the first year, much of attention is of the orienting/investigative type, but sustained attention also becomes important. |

- Habituation is the repeated presentation of the same stimulus, causing reduced attention to the stimulus. If a different stimulus is presented and the infant pays increased attention to it, dishabituation is occurring.

- Joint attention plays an important role in infant development, especially in the infant's acquisition of language.

| Memory | • Memory is the retention of information over time. Infants as young as 2 to 6 months of age can retain information about perceptual-motor actions. However, many experts argue that what we commonly think of as memory (consciously remembering the past) does not occur until the second half of the first year of life. By the end of the second year, long-term memory is more substantial and reliable. |

- The hippocampus and frontal lobes of the brain are involved in development of explicit memory in infancy. The phenomenon of not being able to remember events that occurred before the age of 3—known as infantile or childhood amnesia—may be due to the immaturity of the prefrontal lobes of the brain at that age.

| Imitation | • Meltzoff has shown that newborns can match their behaviors (such as protruding their tongue) to those of a model. His research also shows that deferred imitation occurs as early as 9 months of age. |

| Concept Formation and Categorization | • Mandler argues that it is not until about 7 to 9 months of age that infants form conceptual categories, although we do not know precisely when concept formation begins. Infants' first concepts are broad. Over the first two years of life, these broad concepts gradually become more differentiated. |

3 Language Development

 LG3 Describe the nature of language and how it develops in infancy.

| Defining Language | • Language is a form of communication, whether spontaneous, written, or signed, that is based on a system of symbols. Language consists of the words used by a community and the rules for varying and combining them. Language is characterized by infinite generativity. |

Language's Rule Systems

How Language Develops

Biological and
Environmental Influences

An Interactionist View

- Phonology is the sound system of a language, including the sounds that are used and how they may be combined. Morphology refers to the units of meaning involved in word formation. Syntax is the way words are combined to form acceptable phrases and sentences. Semantics involves the meaning of words and sentences. Pragmatics is the appropriate use of language in different contexts.

- Among the milestones in infant language development are crying (birth), cooing (1 to 2 months), babbling (6 months), making the transition from universal linguist to language-specific listener (6 to 12 months), using gestures (8 to 12 months), comprehending words (8 to 12 months), speaking one's first word (13 months), undergoing a vocabulary spurt (19 months), rapidly expanding one's understanding of words (18 to 24 months), and producing two-word utterances (18 to 24 months).

- In evolution, language clearly gave humans an enormous advantage over other animals and increased their chances of survival. Broca's area and Wernicke's area are important locations for language processing in the brain's left hemisphere.

- Chomsky argues that children are born with the ability to detect basic features and rules of language. In other words, they are biologically equipped to learn language with a prewired language acquisition device (LAD). Adults help children acquire language by engaging in child-directed speech, recasting, expanding, and labeling.

- Environmental influences are demonstrated by differences in the language development of children as a consequence of being exposed to different language environments in the home. Parents should talk extensively with an infant, especially about what the baby is attending to.

- Today, most language researchers believe that children everywhere arrive in the world with special social and linguistic capacities that make language acquisition not just likely but inevitable for virtually all children. How much of the language is biologically determined, and how much depends on interaction with others, is a subject of debate among linguists and psychologists. However, all agree that both biological capacity and relevant experience are necessary.

key terms

A-not-B error 145
accommodation 142
aphasia 159
assimilation 142
attention 148
Broca's area 159
child-directed speech 161
concepts 151
coordination of secondary circular reactions 144

core knowledge approach 146
deferred imitation 151
equilibration 142
explicit memory 150
first habits and primary circular reactions 143
implicit memory 150
infinite generativity 154
internalization of schemes 144
joint attention 149

language 154
language acquisition device (LAD) 159
memory 150
morphology 154
object permanence 144
organization 142
phonology 154
pragmatics 155
primary circular reaction 143

schemes 141
secondary circular reactions 143
semantics 155
sensorimotor stage 142
simple reflexes 143
syntax 154
telegraphic speech 158
tertiary circular reactions, novelty, and curiosity 144
Wernicke's area 159

key people

Renee Baillargeon 146
Naomi Baron 163
Patricia Bauer 151
Roger Brown 162
Noam Chomsky 159

Ellen Galinsky 163
Eleanor Gibson 145
Roberta Golinkoff 163
Betty Hart 160
Kathy Hirsh-Pasek 163

Janellen Huttenlocher 161
Patricia Kuhl 156
Jean Mandler 150
Andrew Meltzoff 151
Jean Piaget 140

Todd Risley 160
Carolyn Rovee-Collier 148
Elizabeth Spelke 146
Michael Tomasello 160

chapter 6

SOCIOEMOTIONAL DEVELOPMENT IN INFANCY

chapter **outline**

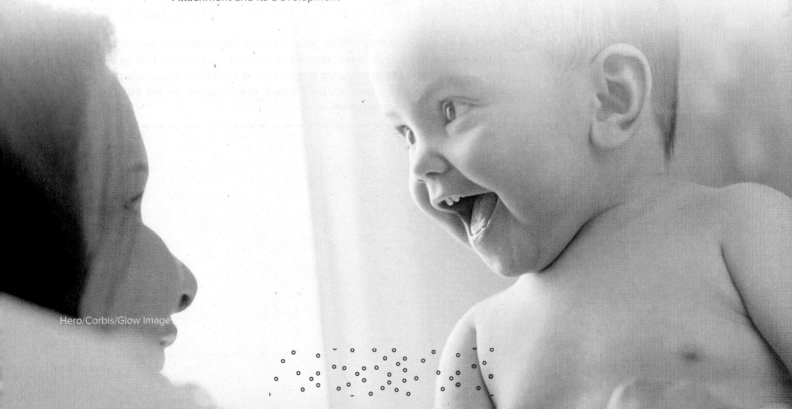

An increasing number of fathers are staying home to care for their children (Parke, Roisman, & Rose, 2019). Recent data indicate that 7 percent of fathers work from home and 24 percent of those fathers care for their children at home (Livingston, 2018).

Many fathers are spending more time with their infants today than in the past.
Tetra Images/Getty Images

And researchers are finding improved outcomes when fathers are positively engaged with their infants (Cabrera, 2020; Cowan & others, 2019a, b; Fagan, 2020). Consider 17-month-old Darius. On weekdays, Darius' father, a writer, cares for him during the day while his mother works full-time as a landscape architect. Darius' father is doing a great job of caring for him. He keeps Darius nearby while he is writing and spends lots of time talking to him and playing with him. From their interactions, it is clear that they genuinely enjoy each other.

Last month, Darius began spending one day a week at a child-care center. His parents carefully selected the center after observing a number of centers and interviewing teachers and center directors. His parents placed him in the center one day a week because they wanted to help Darius get some experience with peers and to give his father some time out from his caregiving.

Darius' father looks to the future and imagines the Little League games Darius will play in and the many other activities he can enjoy with Darius. Remembering how little time his own father spent with him, he is dedicated to making sure that Darius has an involved, nurturing experience with his father.

When Darius' mother comes home in the evenings, she spends considerable time with him. Darius has a secure attachment with both his mother and his father.

topical connections *looking **back***

Until now, we have only discussed the social situations and emotions of parents before and after the arrival of their infants, focusing on such topics as parents' feelings of joy, anticipation, anxiety, and stress during pregnancy; and parents' emotional and psychological adjustments during the postpartum period. In this chapter, we will explore the infant's socioemotional development.

preview

You have read about how the infant perceives, learns, and remembers. Infants also are socioemotional beings, capable of displaying emotions and initiating social interaction with people close to them. The main topics that we will explore in this chapter are emotional and personality development, social understanding and attachment, and the social contexts of the family and child care.

1 Emotional and Personality Development

LG1 Discuss the development of emotions and personality in infancy.

Emotional Development · Temperament · Personality Development

Anyone who has been around infants for even a brief time detects that they are emotional beings. Not only do infants express emotions, but they also vary in their temperaments. Some are shy and others are outgoing. Some are active and others much less so. In this section, we will explore these and other aspects of emotional and personality development in infants.

EMOTIONAL DEVELOPMENT

Imagine your life without emotion. Emotion is the color and music of life, as well as the tie that binds people together. How do psychologists define and classify emotions, and why are they important to development? How do emotions develop during the first two years of life?

What Are Emotions? For our purposes, we will define **emotion** as feeling, or affect, that occurs when a person is in a state or an interaction that is important to him or her, especially to his or her well-being. Especially in infancy, emotions play important roles in (1) communication with others, and (2) behavioral organization (Dollar & Calkins, 2019; Perry & Calkins, 2018). Through emotions, infants communicate important aspects of their lives such as joy, sadness, interest, and fear (Cataldo & Nelson, 2019). In terms of behavioral organization, emotions influence infants' social responses and adaptive behavior as they interact with others in their world (Denham & Bassett, 2019; Repacholi & Meltzoff, 2019).

Psychologists classify the broad range of emotions in many ways, but almost all classifications designate an emotion as either positive or negative (Tye, 2019). Positive emotions include enthusiasm, joy, and love. Negative emotions include anxiety, anger, guilt, and sadness.

Biological, Cognitive, and Environmental Influences Emotions are influenced by biological foundations, cognitive processes, and a person's experiences (Goldsmith, 2019; Kaywork, 2020; Lang & Bradley, 2019; Okun-Singer & others, 2019). Biology's importance to emotion is apparent in the changes in a baby's emotional capacities (Cataldo & Nelson, 2019). Certain regions of the brain that develop early in life (such as the brain stem, hippocampus, and amygdala) play a role in distress, excitement, and rage, and even infants display these emotions (Berridge, 2019). But, as we discuss later in the chapter, infants only gradually develop the ability to regulate their emotions, and this ability seems tied to the gradual maturation of the frontal regions of the cerebral cortex that can exert control over other areas of the brain (Bell & Broomell, 2020).

Cognitive processes, both in immediate "in the moment" contexts and throughout childhood, influence infants' and children's emotional development (Liu & others, 2019). Attention toward or away from an experience can influence infants' and children's emotional responses. For example, children who can distract themselves from a stressful encounter show a lower level of negative affect in the context and less anxiety over time (Crockenberg & Leerkes, 2006). Also, as children become older, they develop cognitive strategies for controlling their emotions and become more adept at modulating their emotional arousal (Nook & others, 2020). In a recent study, children reported using more suppression and disengagement when experiencing early life stress, while adolescents used more engagement coping strategies when facing such stress (Johnson & others, 2019).

Blossoms are scattered by the wind
And the wind cares nothing, but
The blossoms of the heart
No wind can touch.

—YOSHIDA KENKO
Buddhist monk, 14th century

How do biological, cognitive, and environmental factors influence the infant's emotional development?
Lawren/Moment/Getty Images

emotion Feeling, or affect, that occurs when a person is in a state or interaction that is important to him or her. Emotion is characterized by behavior that reflects (expresses) the pleasantness or unpleasantness of the state a person is in or the transactions being experienced.

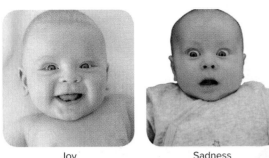

Joy   Sadness

Fear   Surprise

FIGURE 1

EXPRESSION OF DIFFERENT EMOTIONS IN INFANTS
(*Top left*) Kozak_O_O/Shutterstock (*top right*); Stanislav/Shutterstock;
(*bottom left*) Jill Braaten/McGraw-Hill; (*bottom right*) Photodisc Collection/
EyeWire/Getty Images

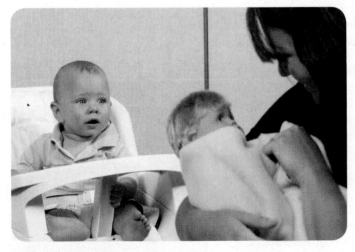

FIGURE 2

IS THIS THE EARLY EXPRESSION OF JEALOUSY? In the study by Hart
and Carrington (2002), the researchers concluded that the 6-month-old
infants who observed their mothers giving attention to a baby doll
displayed negative emotions—such as anger and sadness—which may
indicate the early appearance of jealousy. However, experts on emotional
development, such as Michael Lewis (2007) and Jerome Kagan (2010),
argue that it is unlikely emotions such as jealousy appear in the first year.
Why do they conclude that it is unlikely jealousy occurs in the first year?
Kenny Braun/Braun Photography

primary emotions Emotions that are present
in humans and other animals and emerge
early in life; examples are joy, anger, sadness,
fear, and disgust.

self-conscious emotions Emotions that require
self-awareness, especially consciousness and
a sense of "me"; examples include jealousy,
empathy, and embarrassment.

Biological evolution has endowed human beings to be *emotional,* but embeddedness in relationships and culture with others provides diversity in emotional experiences (Thompson, 2019). Infants' emotional development and how infants eventually learn to cope with stress is influenced by whether caregivers have maltreated or neglected children and whether children's caregivers are depressed or not (Cicchetti & Handley, 2019). When infants become stressed, they show better biological recovery from the stressors when their caregivers engage in sensitive caregiving with them (Sullivan & Wilson, 2018).

Social relationships provide the setting for the development of a rich variety of emotions (Eisenberg & Hernandez, 2019; Kaywork, 2020; Leerkes & Augustine, 2019; Leerkes, Bailes, & Augustine, 2020). When toddlers hear their parents quarreling, they often react with distress and inhibit their play. Well-functioning families make each other laugh and may develop a light mood to defuse conflicts.

Cultural differences occur in emotional experiences (Liddell & Williams, 2019). For example, researchers have found that East Asian infants display less frequent and less intense positive and negative emotions than non-Latino White infants (Cole & Tan, 2015). Further, Japanese parents try to prevent their children from experiencing negative emotions, whereas non-Latino White mothers are more likely to respond after their children become distressed and then help them cope (Cole & Tan, 2015).

Early Emotions A leading expert on infant emotional development, Michael Lewis (2007, 2008, 2010, 2015, 2018) distinguishes between primary emotions and self-conscious emotions. **Primary emotions** are present in humans and other animals; these emotions appear in the first 6 months of the human infant's development. Primary emotions include surprise, interest, joy, anger, sadness, fear, and disgust (see Figure 1 for infants' facial expressions of some of these early emotions). In Lewis' classification, **self-conscious emotions** require self-awareness that involves consciousness and a sense of "me." Self-conscious emotions include jealousy, empathy, embarrassment, pride, shame, and guilt, most of these occurring for the first time during the second half of the first year or within the second year. Some experts on emotion call self-conscious emotions such as embarrassment, shame, guilt, and pride *other-conscious emotions* because they involve the emotional reactions of others when they are generated (Saarni & others, 2006). For example, approval from parents is linked to toddlers' beginning to show pride when they successfully complete a task.

Researchers such as Joseph Campos (2005) and Michael Lewis (2018) debate how early in the infant and toddler years the emotions that we have described first appear and in what sequence. As an indication of the controversy regarding when certain emotions first are displayed by infants, consider jealousy. Some researchers argue that jealousy does not emerge until approximately 15 to 18 months of age (Lewis, 2018), whereas others assert that it is displayed as early as 9 months (Hart, 2018).

Consider the results of two research studies. In the first one, 9-month-old infants engaged in more approach-style, jealousy-related behaviors when their mothers gave attention to a social rival (a lifelike doll) than to a non-social rival (a book) (Mize & others, 2014). Further, in this study, the infants showed EEG activity during the social-rival condition that is associated with jealousy.

In a second study, 6-month-old infants observed their mothers in situations similar to the first study: either giving attention to a lifelike baby doll (hugging or gently rocking it, for example) or to a book (Hart & Carrington, 2002). When mothers directed their attention to the doll, the infants were more likely to display negative emotions, such as anger and sadness, which may have indicated their jealousy (see Figure 2). On the other hand, their expressions of anger and sadness may have reflected frustration in not being able to have the novel doll to play with.

Debate about the onset of an emotion such as jealousy illustrates the complexity and difficulty of indexing early emotions. That said, some experts on infant socioemotional development, such as Jerome Kagan (2010), conclude that the structural immaturity of the infant brain makes it unlikely that emotions which require thought—such as guilt, pride, despair, shame, empathy, and jealousy—can be experienced during the first year. Nonetheless, some leading researchers have argued that research now indicates empathy can be expressed before the infant's first birthday (Davidov & others, 2013).

Emotional Expression and Social Relationships Emotional expressions are involved in infants' first relationships. The ability of infants to communicate emotions permits coordinated interactions with their caregivers and the beginning of an emotional bond between them (Leerkes & Augustine, 2019; Leerkes, Bailes, & Augustine, 2020). Not only do parents change their emotional expressions in response to infants' emotional expressions, but infants also modify their emotional expressions in response to those of their parents (Johnson, 2018). Because of this coordination, the interactions are described as reciprocal, or synchronous, when all is going well. Sensitive, responsive parents help their infants grow emotionally, whether the infants respond in distressed or happy ways (Cicchetti & Handley, 2019; Ribeiro-Accioly & others, 2020). A recent observational study of mother-infant interaction found that maternal sensitivity was linked to a lower level of infant fear (Gartstein, Hancock, & Iverson, 2018). Another study revealed that parents' elicitation of talk about emotion with toddlers was associated with the toddlers' sharing and helping (Brownell & others, 2013).

One study documented that babies react to their mothers' stress (Waters, West, & Mendes, 2014). In this study, mothers were separated from their babies and asked to give a 5-minute speech, on which half of the mothers received a positive evaluation, the other half a negative evaluation. Mothers who received negative feedback reported an increase in negative emotion and cardiac stress, while those who were given positive feedback reported an increase in positive emotion. The babies quickly detected and responded to their mothers' stress, as reflected in an increased heart rate when reunited with them. And the greater the mother's stress response, the more her baby's heart rate increased.

Cries and smiles are two emotional expressions that infants display when interacting with parents. These are babies' first forms of emotional communication.

Crying Crying is the most important mechanism newborns have for communicating with their world. The first cry verifies that the baby's lungs have filled with air. Cries also may provide information about the health of the newborn's central nervous system. A recent study found that excessive infant crying in 3-month-olds doubled the risk of behavioral, hyperactive, and mood problems at 5 to 6 years of age (Smarius & others, 2017).

Babies have at least three types of cries:

What are some different types of cries?
Andy Cox/The Image Bank/Getty Images

- **Basic cry.** A rhythmic pattern that usually consists of a cry, followed by a briefer silence, then a shorter whistle that is somewhat higher in pitch than the main cry, then another brief rest before the next cry. Some infancy experts believe that hunger is one of the conditions that incites the basic cry.

- **Anger cry.** A variation of the basic cry in which more excess air is forced through the vocal cords.

- **Pain cry.** A sudden long, initial loud cry followed by breath holding; no preliminary moaning is present. The pain cry is stimulated by an intensely negative experience.

Most adults can determine whether an infant's cries signify anger or pain (Zeskind, Klein, & Marshall, 1992). Parents can interpret the cries of their own baby better than those of another baby.

Smiling Smiling is a key social signal and a very important aspect of positive social interaction (Martin & Messinger, 2018). Researchers have found that smiling and laughter at 7 months of age are associated with self-regulation at 7 years of age (Posner & others, 2014). Also, in a longitudinal study, positive affect, but not negative affect, at 1.5 years of age predicted higher childhood IQ (6 to 8 years of age) and higher educational attainment in adulthood (29 years of age)

basic cry A rhythmic pattern usually consisting of a cry, a briefer silence, a shorter inspiratory whistle that is higher pitched than the main cry, and then a brief rest before the next cry.

anger cry A variation of the basic cry, with more excess air forced through the vocal cords.

pain cry A sudden appearance of a long, initial loud cry without preliminary moaning, followed by breath holding.

He who binds himself to joy
Does the winged life destroy;
But he who kisses the joy as
it flies
Lives in eternity's sun rise.

—WILLIAM BLAKE
English poet, 19th century

(Coffey, 2020). The power of the infant's smiles was appropriately captured by British theorist John Bowlby (1969): "Can we doubt that the more and better an infant smiles the better he is loved and cared for? It is fortunate for their survival that babies are so designed by nature that they beguile and enslave mothers." Two types of smiling can be distinguished in infants:

- **Reflexive smile.** A smile that does not occur in response to external stimuli and appears during the first month after birth, usually during sleep.
- **Social smile.** A smile that occurs in response to an external stimulus, typically a face in the case of the young infant. Social smiling occurs as early as 2 months of age.

The infant's social smile can have a powerful impact on caregivers (Martin & Messinger, 2018). Following weeks of seemingly endless demands, fatigue, and little reinforcement, an infant starts smiling at them and all of the caregivers' efforts are rewarded. One study found that higher maternal effortful control and positive emotionality predicted more initial infant smiling and laughter, while a higher level of parenting stress predicted a lower trajectory of infant smiling and laughter (Bridgett & others, 2013).

Fear   One of a baby's earliest emotions is fear. Recent research indicated that when infants were assessed at 6, 8, 10, and 12 months, expressions of fear peaked at 10 months (Gartstein, Hancock, & Iverson, 2018). Fear typically first appears at about 6 months of age, but abused and neglected infants can show fear as early as 3 months (Witherington & others, 2010). Researchers have found that infant fear is linked to guilt, empathy, and low aggression at 6 to 7 years of age (Rothbart, 2007).

The most frequent expression of an infant's fear involves **stranger anxiety,** in which an infant shows a fear and wariness of strangers (Van Hulle & others, 2017). Stranger anxiety usually emerges gradually. It first appears at about 6 months of age in the form of wary reactions. By age 9 months, the fear of strangers is often more intense, reaching a peak toward the end of the first year of life and then decreasing thereafter (Scher & Harel, 2008).

Not all infants show distress when they encounter a stranger. Besides individual variations, whether an infant shows stranger anxiety also depends on the social context and the characteristics of the stranger.

Infants show less stranger anxiety when they are in familiar settings. For example, in one study 10-month-olds showed little stranger anxiety when they met a stranger in their own home but much greater fear when they encountered a stranger in a research laboratory (Sroufe, Waters, & Matas, 1974). Thus, it appears that when infants feel secure, they are less likely to show stranger anxiety.

Who the stranger is and how the stranger behaves also influence stranger anxiety in infants. Infants are less fearful of child strangers than adult strangers. They also are less fearful of friendly, outgoing, smiling strangers than of passive, unsmiling strangers (Bretherton, Stolberg, & Kreye, 1981).

In addition to stranger anxiety, infants experience fear of being separated from their caregivers. The result is **separation protest**—crying when the caregiver leaves. Separation protest is initially displayed by infants at approximately 7 to 8 months and peaks at about 15 months among U.S. infants (Kagan, 2008). In fact, one study found that separation protest peaked at about 13 to 15 months in four different cultures (Kagan, Kearsley, & Zelazo, 1978). Although the percentage of infants who engaged in separation protest varied across cultures, the infants reached a peak of protest at about the same age—just before the middle of the second year of life.

Emotion Regulation and Coping   Too often when people think about emotion they think about it negative ways, such as having emotional problems. However, emotion can be adaptive and help individuals live more competent, enriching lives. In terms of emotions being adaptive, consider that infants communicate via emotion even before they understand language and their emotions are critical to their survival and thus their adaptation. As we see next, emotion regulation plays a key role in emotion's adaptiveness, especially so they don't interfere with our daily functioning and relationships.

During the first year of life, the infant gradually develops an ability to inhibit, or minimize, the intensity and duration of emotional reactions (Ekas, Braungart-Ricker, & Messinger, 2018). From early in infancy, babies put their thumbs in their mouths to soothe themselves. But at first, infants mainly depend on caregivers to help them soothe their emotions, as when a caregiver rocks an infant to sleep, sings lullabyes to the infant, gently strokes the infant, and

reflexive smile A smile that does not occur in response to external stimuli. It happens during the first month after birth, usually during sleep.

social smile A smile in response to an external stimulus, which early in development is typically a face.

stranger anxiety An infant's fear and wariness of strangers; it tends to appear during the second half of the first year of life.

separation protest An infant's distressed crying when the caregiver leaves.

so on. Another recent study also linked maternal sensitivity to better emotion regulation in 10-month-old infants (Frick & others, 2018).

Later in infancy, when they become aroused, infants sometimes redirect their attention or distract themselves in order to reduce their arousal. By 2 years of age, toddlers can use language to define their feeling states and the context that is upsetting them. A toddler might say, "Doggy scary." This type of communication may help caregivers to assist the child in regulating emotion.

Contexts can influence emotion regulation (Dollar & Calkins, 2019; Thompson, 2019). Infants are often affected by fatigue, hunger, time of day, which people are around them, and where they are. Infants must learn to adapt to different contexts that require emotion regulation. Further, new demands appear as the infant becomes older and parents modify their expectations. For example, a parent may take it in stride if a 6-month-old infant screams in a restaurant but may react very differently if a 6-year-old starts screaming.

To soothe or not to soothe—should a crying baby be given attention and soothed, or does this spoil the infant? Many years ago, the behaviorist John Watson (1928) argued that parents spend too much time responding to infant crying. As a consequence, he said, parents reward crying and increase its incidence. Also, behaviorist Jacob Gewirtz (1977) found that a caregiver's quick, soothing response to crying increased crying. In contrast, infancy experts Mary Ainsworth (1979) and John Bowlby (1989) stress that it is not possible to respond too much to infant crying in the first year of life. They believe that a quick, comforting response to the infant's cries is an important ingredient in developing a strong bond between the infant and caregiver. In one of Ainsworth's studies, infants whose mothers responded quickly when they cried at 3 months of age cried less later in the first year of life (Bell & Ainsworth, 1972). Another study found that mothers were more likely than fathers to use soothing techniques to reduce infant crying (Dayton & others, 2015). Further, a recent study revealed that depressed mothers rocked and touched their crying infants less than non-depressed mothers (Esposito & others, 2017). Also, a recent study discovered that an intervention involving training of mothers to effectively use soothing techniques in the fourth week after birth resulted in infants' waking up less at night and crying less in assessments at 7, 11, and 23 weeks after birth (Ozturk Donmez & Bayik Temel, 2019).

Controversy still surrounds the question of whether or how parents should respond to an infant's cries (Zeifman & St. James-Roberts, 2017). However, developmentalists increasingly argue that infants cannot be spoiled in the first year of life, which suggests that parents should soothe a crying infant. This response should help infants develop a sense of trust and secure attachment to the caregiver. One study revealed that mothers' negative emotional reactions (anger and anxiety) to crying increased the risk of subsequent attachment insecurity (Leerkes, Parade, & Gudmundson, 2011). Another study found that problems in infant soothability at 6 months of age were linked to insecure attachment at 12 months of age (Mills-Koonce, Propper, & Barnett, 2012).

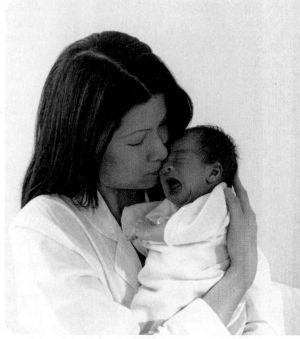

How should parents react when their infant is crying?
Larry Williams & Associates/Getty Images

TEMPERAMENT

Do you become upset often? Does it take much to get you angry, or to make you laugh? Even at birth, babies seem to have different emotional styles. One infant is cheerful and happy much of the time; another baby seems to cry constantly. These tendencies reflect **temperament,** which involves individual differences in behavioral styles, emotions, and characteristic ways of responding. With regard to its link to emotion, temperament refers to individual differences in how quickly the emotion is shown, how strong it is, how long it lasts, and how quickly it fades away.

Another way to describe temperament is in terms of predispositions toward emotional reactivity and self-regulation (Bates, McQuillan, & Hoyniak, 2019; Bowman & Fox, 2019). *Reactivity* involves variations in the speed and intensity with which an individual responds to situations with positive or negative emotions. *Self-regulation* involves variations in the extent or effectiveness of an individual's ability to control his or her emotions.

Describing and Classifying Temperament   How would you describe your temperament or the temperament of a friend? Researchers have described and classified the temperaments of individuals in different ways (Bates, McQuillan, & Hoyniak, 2019; Gartstein, & Hancock, 2019; Urbano Blackford & Zald, 2019). Here we will examine three of those ways.

temperament Involves individual differences in behavioral styles, emotions, and characteristic ways of responding.

What are some characteristics of an inhibited temperament?
Heide Benser/Corbis/Getty Images

easy child A child who is generally in a positive mood, quickly establishes regular routines in infancy, and adapts easily to new experiences.

difficult child A child who tends to react negatively and cry frequently, engages in irregular daily routines, and is slow to accept change.

slow-to-warm-up child A child who has a low activity level, is somewhat negative, and displays a low intensity of mood.

Chess and Thomas' Classification Psychiatrists Alexander Chess and Stella Thomas (Chess & Thomas, 1977; Thomas & Chess, 1991) identified three basic types, or clusters, of temperament:

- An **easy child** is generally in a positive mood, quickly establishes regular routines in infancy, and adapts easily to new experiences.
- A **difficult child** reacts negatively and cries frequently, engages in irregular daily routines, and is slow to accept change.
- A **slow-to-warm-up child** has a low activity level, is somewhat negative, and displays a low intensity of mood.

In their longitudinal investigation, Chess and Thomas found that 40 percent of the children they studied could be classified as easy, 10 percent as difficult, and 15 percent as slow to warm up. Notice that 35 percent did not fit any of the three patterns. Researchers have found that these three basic clusters of temperament are moderately stable across the childhood years. In a recent study of low-income families, having a difficult temperament at 0 to 12 months of age predicted behavior problems at 36 months of age (Maltby & others, 2019).

Kagan's Behavioral Inhibition Another way of classifying temperament focuses on the differences between a shy, subdued, timid child and a sociable, extraverted, bold child. Jerome Kagan (2002, 2008, 2010, 2013, 2019) regards shyness with strangers (peers or adults) as one feature of a broad temperament category called inhibition to the unfamiliar. Inhibited children react to many aspects of unfamiliarity with initial avoidance, distress, or subdued affect, beginning at about 7 to 9 months of age.

Kagan has found that inhibition shows considerable stability from infancy through early childhood. One study classified toddlers into extremely inhibited, extremely uninhibited, and intermediate groups (Pfeifer & others, 2002). Follow-up assessments were conducted at 4 and 7 years of age. Continuity was demonstrated for both inhibition and lack of inhibition, although a substantial number of the inhibited children had moved into the intermediate groups by 7 years of age. Researchers found that having an inhibited temperament at 2 to 3 years of age was related to having social phobia symptoms at 7 years of age (Lahat & others, 2014). Further, research findings also indicate that infants and young children who have an inhibited temperament are at risk for developing social anxiety disorder in adolescence and adulthood (Perez-Edgar & Guyer, 2014; Rapee, 2014).

Rothbart and Bates' Classification New classifications of temperament continue to be forged. Mary Rothbart and John Bates (2006) argue that prior classifications of temperament have not included a key temperament

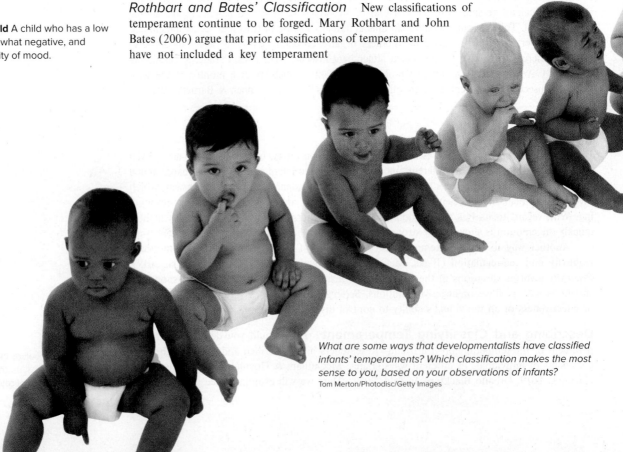

What are some ways that developmentalists have classified infants' temperaments? Which classification makes the most sense to you, based on your observations of infants?
Tom Merton/Photodisc/Getty Images

style: effortful control (self-regulation). They conclude that the following three broad dimensions best represent what researchers have found to characterize the structure of temperament: extraversion/surgency, negative affectivity, and effortful control (self-regulation):

- *Extraversion/surgency* includes approach, pleasure, activity, smiling, and laughter. Kagan's uninhibited children fit into this category

- *Negative affectivity* includes "fear, frustration, sadness, and discomfort" (Rothbart, 2004, p. 495). These children are easily distressed; they may fret and cry often. Kagan's inhibited children fit this category.

- *Effortful control (self-regulation)* includes "attentional focusing and shifting, inhibitory control, perceptual sensitivity, and low-intensity pleasure" (Rothbart, 2004, p. 495). Infants who are high on effortful control show an ability to keep their arousal from getting too high and have strategies for soothing themselves. By contrast, children low on effortful control are often unable to control their arousal; they become easily agitated and intensely emotional.

A number of studies have supported the view that effortful control is an important influence on children's development. For example, one study found that young children higher in effortful control were more likely to wait longer to express anger and were more likely to use a self-regulatory strategy, distraction (Tan, Armstrong, & Cole, 2013). Also, a study revealed that effortful control was a strong predictor of academic success skills (including school readiness, math skills, and reading skills) in kindergarten children from low-income families (Morris & others, 2013). And in another study, children with a lower level of effort control at 3 years of age were more likely to have ADHD symptoms at 13 years of age (Einziger & others, 2018).

In Rothbart's (2004, p. 497) view, "early theoretical models of temperament stressed the way we are moved by our positive and negative emotions or level of arousal, with our actions driven by these tendencies." The more recent focus on effortful control, however, emphasizes that individuals can engage in a more cognitive, flexible approach to stressful circumstances. It is Rothbart and Bates' addition of effortful control (self-regulation) that is their most important contribution to our understanding of temperament.

An important point about temperament classifications such as those of Chess and Thomas or Rothbart and Bates is that children should not be pigeonholed as having only one temperament dimension, such as "difficult" or "negative affectivity." A good strategy when attempting to classify a child's temperament is to think of temperament as consisting of multiple dimensions (Bates, 2012a, b). For example, a child might be extraverted, show little negative affectivity, and have good self-regulation. Another child might be introverted, show little negative affectivity, and have a low level of self-regulation.

The development of temperament capabilities such as effortful control allows individual differences to emerge (Bates & Pettit, 2015). For example, although maturation of the brain's prefrontal lobes must occur for any child's attention to improve and the child to achieve effortful control, some children develop effortful control while others do not. And it is these individual differences in children that are at the heart of what temperament is (Bates, McQuillan, & Hoyniak, 2019).

Biological Foundations and Experience   How does a child acquire a certain temperament? Kagan (2002, 2010, 2013, 2019) argues that children inherit a *physiology* that biases them to have a particular type of temperament (van Wijk & others, 2019). However, through experience they may learn to modify their temperament to some degree. Thus, Kagan stresses that temperament has both a physiological and experiential basis. For example, children may inherit a physiology that biases them to be fearful and inhibited, but they can learn to reduce their fear and inhibition to some degree.

Biological Influences   Physiological characteristics have been linked with different temperaments (Bates & Pettit, 2015). In particular, an inhibited temperament is associated with a unique physiological pattern that includes high and stable heart rate, high level of the hormone *cortisol*, and high activity in the right frontal lobe of the brain (Kagan, 2008, 2010). This pattern may be tied to the excitability of the amygdala, a structure of the brain that plays an important role in fear and inhibition.

What is heredity's role in the biological foundations of temperament? Twin and adoption studies suggest that heredity has a moderate influence on differences in temperament within a group of people (Plomin & others, 2009). The *contemporary view* is that temperament is a biologically based but evolving aspect of behavior; it evolves as the child's experiences are incorporated into a network of self-perceptions and behavioral preferences that characterize the child's personality (Thompson & Goodvin, 2016; van Wijk & others, 2019).

Too often the biological foundations of temperament are interpreted to mean that temperament cannot develop or change. However, important self-regulatory dimensions of temperament such as adaptability, soothability, and persistence look very different in a 1-year-old and a 5-year-old (Thompson, 2015). These temperament dimensions develop and change with the growth of the neurobiological foundations of self-regulation (Calkins & Perry, 2016).

Gender, Culture, and Temperament   Gender may be an important factor shaping the environmental context that influences temperament (Jenzer & others, 2019). Parents might react differently to an infant's temperament depending on whether the baby is a boy or a girl. For example, in one study, mothers were more responsive to the crying of irritable girls than to the crying of irritable boys (Crockenberg, 1986).

Similarly, the caregiver's reaction to an infant's temperament may depend in part on culture (Matsumoto & Juang, 2020). For example, behavioral inhibition is more highly valued in China than in North America, and researchers have found that Chinese children are more inhibited than Canadian infants are (Chen & others, 1998). The cultural differences in temperament were linked to parental attitudes and behaviors. Canadian mothers of inhibited 2-year-olds were less accepting of their infants' inhibited temperament, whereas Chinese mothers were more accepting.

In short, many aspects of a child's environment can encourage or discourage the persistence of temperament characteristics (Bates, McQuillan, & Hoyniak, 2019). For example, researchers found that fathers' internalizing problems (anxiety and depression, for example) were linked to a higher level of negative affectivity in 6-month-olds (Potapova, Gartstein, & Bridgett, 2014). And another study revealed that maternal negativity and child problem behavior were most strongly linked for children who were low in effortful control and living in chaotic homes (Chen, Deater-Deckard, & Bell, 2014). One useful way of thinking about temperament-environment connections involves the concept of goodness of fit, which we examine next.

Goodness of Fit and Parenting   **Goodness of fit** refers to the match between a child's temperament and the environmental demands the child must cope with. Suppose Jason is an active toddler who is made to sit still for long periods of time, and Jack is a slow-to-warm-up toddler who is abruptly pushed into new situations on a regular basis. Both Jason and Jack face a lack of fit between their temperament and environmental demands. Lack of fit can produce adjustment problems (Wagers & Kiel, 2019).

Some temperament characteristics pose more parenting challenges than others, at least in modern Western societies (Bates, McQuillan, & Hoyniak, 2018). When children are prone to distress, as exhibited by frequent crying and irritability, their parents may eventually respond

- - - - - - - - ➤

developmental connection

Community and Culture

Cross-cultural studies seek to determine culture-universal and culture-specific aspects of development. Connect to "Introduction."

◄- - - - - - - - -

An infant's temperament can vary across cultures. *What do parents need to know about a child's temperament?*
JGI/Blend Images LLC

goodness of fit Refers to the match between a child's temperament and the environmental demands with which the child must cope.

Parenting and the Child's Temperament

What are the implications of temperamental variations for parenting? Although answers to this question necessarily are speculative, temperament experts Ann Sanson and Mary Rothbart (1995) offer the following suggestions:

- *Pay attention to the child's individual characteristics.* A goal might be accomplished in one way with one child and in another way with a child of a different temperament.
- *Structure the child's environment.* Crowded, noisy environments can pose greater problems for some children than others. We might also expect that a fearful, withdrawing child would benefit from slower entry into new contexts.
- *Avoid labeling a child as "difficult."* Programs for parents often focus on dealing with children who have "difficult" temperaments. In some cases, "difficult child" refers to Thomas and Chess' description of a child who reacts negatively, cries frequently, engages in irregular daily routines, and is slow to accept change. In others, a "difficult child" might be one who is irritable, displays anger frequently, or has trouble following directions. Acknowledging that some children are harder to parent than other children is often helpful, and advice on how to handle specific characteristics can be useful. However, whether a particular characteristic is difficult depends on its fit with the environment. Labeling a child "difficult" can create a self-fulfilling prophecy. If a child is identified as "difficult," people may treat the child in a way that actually elicits "difficult" behavior.

What are some good strategies for parents to adopt when responding to their infant's temperament?
Ariel Skelley/Blend Images LLC

Too often, we pigeonhole children into categories without considering the context (Bates, 2012a, b; Rothbart, 2011). A more effective approach is to take children's temperament into account.

How does the advice to "structure the child's environment" relate to what you learned about the concept of "goodness of fit"?

---

by ignoring the child's distress or trying to force the child to "behave." In one research study, though, extra support and training for mothers of distress-prone infants improved the quality of mother-infant interaction (van den Boom, 1989). The training led the mothers to alter their demands on the child, improving the fit between the child and the environment. Researchers also have found that decreases in infants' negative emotionality are linked to higher levels of parental sensitivity, involvement, and responsiveness (Gartstein, Hancock, & Iverson, 2018; Parade & others, 2018). To read further about some positive strategies for parenting that take into account the child's temperament, see the *Connecting Development to Life* interlude.

A final comment about temperament is that recently the *differential susceptibility model* and the *biological sensitivity to context model* have been proposed and studied (Belsky & Pluess, 2016; Belsky & van IJzendoorn, 2017; Jolicoeur-Martineau & others, 2020). These models emphasize that certain characteristics that make children more vulnerable to setbacks in adverse contexts also make them more susceptible to optimal growth in very supportive conditions. These models put "negative" temperament characteristics in a new light.

PERSONALITY DEVELOPMENT

Emotions and temperament form key aspects of *personality*, the enduring personal characteristics of individuals. Let's now examine characteristics that often are thought of as central to personality development during infancy: trust and the development of self and independence.

Trust According to Erik Erikson (1968), the first year of life is characterized by the *trust-versus-mistrust* stage of development. Following a life of regularity, warmth, and protection in the

> **developmental connection**
> **Personality**
> Erikson proposed that individuals go through eight stages in the course of human development. Connect to "Introduction."

mother's womb, the infant faces a world that is less secure. Erikson proposed that infants learn trust when they are cared for in a consistent, warm manner. If the infant is not well fed and kept warm on a consistent basis, a sense of mistrust is likely to develop.

The issue of trust versus mistrust is not resolved once and for all in the first year of life. It arises again at each successive stage of development and can have positive or negative outcomes. For example, children who leave infancy with a sense of trust can still have their sense of mistrust activated at a later stage, perhaps if their parents are separated or divorced under conflictual circumstances.

The Developing Sense of Self   When does the individual begin to sense a separate existence from others? Studying the development of a sense of self in infancy is difficult mainly because infants cannot verbally express their thoughts and impressions. They also cannot understand complex instructions from researchers.

One ingenious strategy to test infants' visual self-recognition is the use of a mirror technique in which an infant's mother first puts a dot of rouge on the infant's nose. Then an observer watches to see how often the infant touches its nose. Next, the infant is placed in front of a mirror, and observers detect whether nose touching increases. Why does this matter? The idea is that increased nose touching indicates that the infant recognizes the self in the mirror and is trying to touch or rub off the rouge because the rouge violates the infant's view of the self. Increased touching indicates that the infant realizes that it is the self in the mirror but that something is not right since the real self does not have a dot of rouge on it.

Figure 3 displays the results of two investigations that used the mirror technique. The researchers found that infants younger than 1 year old did not recognize themselves in the mirror (Amsterdam, 1968; Lewis & Brooks-Gunn, 1979). Signs of self-recognition began to appear among some infants at 15 to 18 months. By the time they were 2 years old, most children recognized themselves in the mirror. In sum, infants begin to develop a self-understanding called self-recognition at approximately 18 months of age (Hart & Karmel, 1996; Lewis, 2005).

However, mirrors are not familiar to infants in all cultures (Rogoff, 2003). Thus, physical self-recognition may be a more important marker of self-recognition in Western than non-Western cultures (Thompson & Virmani, 2010). Supporting this cultural variation view, one study revealed that 18- to 20-month-old toddlers from urban middle-SES German families were more likely to recognize their mirror images than were toddlers from rural Cameroon farming families (Keller & others, 2005).

Late in the second year and early in the third year, toddlers show other emerging forms of self-awareness that reflect a sense of "me" (Thompson, Winer, & Goodvin, 2011). For example, they refer to themselves by making statements such as "me big"; they label their internal experiences such as emotions; they monitor themselves, as when a toddler says, "do it myself"; and they declare that things are theirs (Bates, 1990; Fasig, 2000).

developmental **connection**

Personality

Two key points in development when there is a strong push for independence are the second year of life and early adolescence. Connect to "Socioemotional Development in Adolescence."

FIGURE **3**

THE DEVELOPMENT OF SELF-RECOGNITION IN INFANCY. The graph shows the findings of two studies in which infants younger than 1 year of age did not recognize themselves in a mirror. A slight increase in the percentage of infant self-recognition occurred around 15 to 18 months of age. By 2 years of age, most children recognized themselves. *Why do researchers study whether infants recognize themselves in a mirror?*
Digital Vision/Getty Images

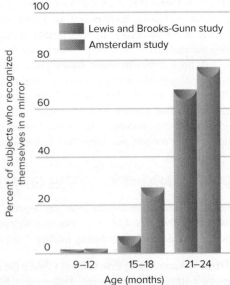

Also, researchers have found that infants begin developing an understanding of others (McDonald & Perdue, 2018). Research indicates that as early as 13 months of age, infants seem to consider another's perspective when predicting their actions (Choi & Luo, 2015).

Independence   Erik Erikson (1968) stressed that independence is an important issue in the second year of life. Erikson describes the second stage of development as the stage of *autonomy versus shame and doubt*. Autonomy builds as the infant's mental and motor abilities develop. At this point in development, not only can infants walk, but they can also climb, open and close, drop, push and pull, and hold and let go. Infants feel pride in these new accomplishments and want to do everything themselves, whether the activity is flushing a toilet, pulling the wrapping off a package, or deciding what to eat. It is important for parents to recognize the motivation of toddlers to do what they are capable of doing at their own pace. Then they can learn to control their muscles and their impulses themselves. But when caregivers are impatient and do for toddlers what they are capable of doing themselves, shame and doubt develop. Every parent has rushed a child from time to time. It is only when parents consistently overprotect toddlers or criticize accidents (wetting, soiling, spilling, or breaking, for example) that children develop an excessive sense of shame and doubt about their ability to control themselves and their world. As we discuss in later chapters, Erikson emphasized that the stage of autonomy versus shame and doubt has important implications for the individual's future development.

Erikson argued that autonomy versus shame and doubt is the key developmental theme of the toddler years. *What are some good strategies for parents to use with their toddlers?*
Marvin Fox/Moment/Getty Images

Review Connect Reflect

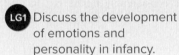

LG1 Discuss the development of emotions and personality in infancy.

Review
- What are emotions? What is the nature of an infant's emotions and how do they change?
- What is temperament, and how does it develop in infancy?
- What are some important aspects of personality in infancy, and how do they develop?

Connect
- In this section, you read that twin and adoption studies have been used to sort out the influences of heredity and environment on temperament. Earlier you learned how twin and adoption studies are conducted. Discuss the characteristics of twin and adoption studies.

Reflect *Your Own Personal Journey of Life*
- How would you describe your temperament? Does it fit one of Chess and Thomas' three styles—easy, slow to warm up, or difficult? If you have siblings, is your temperament similar to or different from theirs?

2 Social Orientation/Understanding and Attachment

LG2 Describe social orientation/understanding and the development of attachment in infancy.

| Social Orientation/ Understanding | Attachment and Its Development | Individual Differences in Attachment | Caregiving Styles and Attachment | Developmental Social Neuroscience and Attachment |

So far, we have discussed how emotions and emotional competence change as children develop. We have also examined the role of emotional style; in effect, we have seen how emotions set the tone of our experiences in life. But emotions also write the lyrics because they are at the core of our relationships with others.

SOCIAL ORIENTATION/UNDERSTANDING

In Ross Thompson's (2006, 2015, 2016) view, infants are socioemotional beings who show a strong interest in their social world and are motivated to orient to it and understand it. In previous chapters, we described many of the biological and cognitive foundations that

developmental **connection**

Life-Span Perspective

Biological, cognitive, and socioemotional processes are often linked as individuals go through the life span. Connect to "Introduction."

contribute to the infant's development of social orientation and understanding. In this section, we will call attention to relevant biological and cognitive factors as we explore social orientation; locomotion; intention and goal-directed behavior; social referencing; and social sophistication and insight. Discussing biological, cognitive, and social processes together reminds us of an important aspect of development: These processes are intricately intertwined (Dollar & Calkins, 2019; Perry & Calkins, 2018).

Social Orientation   From early in their development, infants are captivated by the social world. As we discussed in our coverage of infant perception, young infants stare intently at faces and are attuned to the sounds of human voices, especially the voices of their caregivers (Quinn, Lee, & Pascalis, 2019). Later, they become adept at interpreting the meaning of facial expressions and voices (Jessen & Grossman, 2020).

A mother and her baby engaging in face-to-face play. *At what age does face-to-face play usually begin, and when does it typically start decreasing in frequency?*
SelectStock/Getty Images

Face-to-face play often begins to characterize caregiver-infant interactions when the infant is about 2 to 3 months of age. The focused social interaction of face-to-face play may include vocalizations, touch, and gestures (Quinn & others, 2020). Such play illustrates many mothers' motivation to create a positive emotional state in their infants (Laible, Thompson, & Froimson, 2015).

In part because of such positive social interchanges between caregivers and infants, by 2 to 3 months of age infants respond in different ways to people and objects, showing more positive emotion to people than to inanimate objects such as puppets (Legerstee, 1997). At this age, most infants expect people to react positively when the infants initiate a behavior, such as a smile or a vocalization.

Even though infants as young as 6 months of age show an interest in each other, their interaction with peers increases considerably in the last half of the second year. Between 18 and 24 months of age, children markedly increase their imitative and reciprocal play, such as imitating nonverbal actions like jumping and running (Eckerman & Whitehead, 1999). One study involved presenting 1- and 2-year-olds with a simple cooperative task that consisted of pulling a lever to get an attractive toy (Brownell, Ramani, & Zerwas, 2006) (see Figure 4). Any coordinated actions of the 1-year-olds appeared to be coincidental rather than cooperative, whereas the 2-year-olds' behavior was characterized by active cooperation to reach a goal.

Locomotion   Recall from earlier in the chapter the growing importance of independence for infants, especially during the second year of life. As infants develop the ability to crawl, walk, and run, they are able to explore and expand their social world. These newly developed, self-produced locomotion skills allow the infant to independently initiate social interchanges on a more frequent basis (Laible, Thompson, & Froimson, 2015). The development of these gross motor skills results from factors such as the development of the nervous system, the goal the infant is motivated to reach, and environmental support for the skill (Hoch, Rachwani, & Adolph, 2020; Rachwani, Hoch, & Adolph, 2020).

The infant's and toddler's push for independence also is likely paced by the development of locomotion skills. Of further importance is locomotion's motivational implications. Once infants have the ability to move in goal-directed pursuits, the rewards from these pursuits lead to further efforts to explore and develop skills.

Intention, Goal-Directed Behavior, and Meaningful Interactions with Others   Perceiving people as engaging in intentional and goal-directed behavior is an important social cognitive accomplishment that initially occurs toward the end of the first year (Thompson, 2015). Another important aspect of infant development is engaging in meaningful interactions with others.

Joint attention and gaze-following help the infant to understand that other people have intentions (Piazza & others, 2020; Suarez-Rivera, Smith, & Yu, 2019). *Joint attention* occurs when the caregiver and infant focus on the same object or event. We indicated that emerging aspects of joint attention occur at about 7 to 8 months, but at about 10 to 11 months of age joint attention intensifies and infants begin to follow the caregiver's gaze. By their

FIGURE 4

THE COOPERATION TASK. The cooperation task consisted of two handles on a box, atop which was an animated musical toy, surreptitiously activated by remote control when both handles were pulled. The handles were placed far enough apart that one child could not pull both handles. The experimenter demonstrated the task, saying, "Watch! If you pull the handles, the doggie will sing." (Brownell, Ramani, & Zerwas, 2006).
Courtesy of Celia A. Brownell, University of Pittsburgh

first birthday, infants have begun to direct the caregiver's attention to objects that capture their interest (Marsh & Legerstee, 2017).

Amanda Woodward and her colleagues (Krogh-Jespersen & Woodward, 2016, 2018; Shneidman & others, 2016) argue that infants' ability to understand and respond to others' meaningful intentions is a critical cognitive foundation for effectively engaging in the social world. They especially emphasize that an important aspect of this ability is the capacity to grasp social knowledge quickly in order to make an appropriate social response. Although processing speed is an important contributor to social engagement, other factors are involved such as infants' motivation to interact with someone, the infant's social interactive history with the individual, the interactive partner's social membership, and culturally specific aspects of interaction (Krogh-Jespersen & Woodward, 2016, 2018; Liberman, Woodward, & Kinzler, 2017).

Social Referencing   Another important social cognitive accomplishment in infancy is developing the ability to "read" the emotions of other people. **Social referencing** is the term used to describe "reading" emotional cues in others to help determine how to act in a particular situation. The development of social referencing helps infants to interpret ambiguous situations more accurately, as when they encounter a stranger and need to know whether to fear the person (Stenberg, 2017). By the end of the first year, a mother's facial expression—either smiling or fearful—influences whether an infant will explore an unfamiliar environment.

Infants become better at social referencing in the second year of life. At this age, they tend to "check" with their mother before they act; they look at her to see if she is happy, angry, or fearful. For example, in one study 14- to 22-month-old infants were more likely to look at their mother's face to get information about how to act in a situation than were 6- to 9-month-old infants (Walden, 1991).

Infants' Social Sophistication and Insight   In sum, researchers are discovering that infants are more socially sophisticated and insightful at younger ages than was previously envisioned (Buyukozer Dawkins & others, 2021; Steckler & others, 2018; Thompson & Goodvin, 2016). This sophistication and insight are reflected in infants' perceptions of others' actions as intentionally motivated and goal-directed and their motivation to share and participate in that intentionality by their first birthday. The more advanced social cognitive skills of infants likely influence their understanding and awareness of attachment to a caregiver.

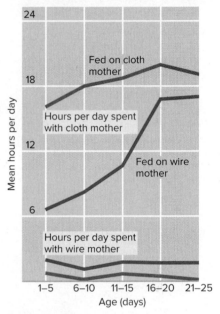

ATTACHMENT AND ITS DEVELOPMENT

Attachment is a close emotional bond between two people. There is no shortage of theories about infant attachment. Three theorists discussed earlier—Freud, Erikson, and Bowlby—proposed influential views.

Freud emphasized that infants become attached to the person or object that provides oral satisfaction. For most infants, this is the mother, since she is most likely to feed the infant. Is feeding as important as Freud thought? A classic study by Harry Harlow (1958) reveals that the answer is no (see Figure 5).

Harlow removed infant monkeys from their mothers at birth; for six months they were reared by surrogate (substitute) "mothers." One surrogate mother was made of wire, the other of cloth. Half of the infant monkeys were fed by the wire mother, half by the cloth mother. Periodically, the amount of time the infant monkeys spent with either the wire or the cloth mother was computed. Regardless of which mother fed them, the infant monkeys spent far more time with the cloth mother. Even if the wire mother, but not the cloth mother, provided nourishment, the infant monkeys spent more time with the cloth mother. And when Harlow frightened the monkeys, those "raised" by the cloth mother ran to the mother and clung to it; those raised by the wire mother did not. Whether the mother provided comfort seemed to determine whether the monkeys associated the mother with security. This study clearly demonstrated that feeding is not the crucial element in the attachment process and that contact comfort is important.

Physical comfort also plays a role in Erik Erikson's (1968) view of the infant's development. Recall Erikson's proposal that the first year of life represents the stage of trust versus mistrust. Physical comfort and sensitive care, according to Erikson (1968), are key to establishing a basic

FIGURE 5

CONTACT TIME WITH WIRE AND CLOTH SURROGATE MOTHERS. Regardless of whether the infant monkeys were fed by a wire or a cloth mother, they overwhelmingly preferred to spend contact time with the cloth mother. *How do these results compare with what Freud's theory and Erikson's theory would predict about human infants?*
Martin Rogers/The Image Bank/Getty Images

social referencing "Reading" emotional cues in others to help determine how to act in a particular situation.

attachment A close emotional bond between two people.

sense of trust in infants. The infant's sense of trust, in turn, is the foundation for attachment and sets the stage for a lifelong expectation that the world will be a good and pleasant place.

The ethological perspective of British psychiatrist John Bowlby (1969, 1989) also stresses the importance of attachment in the first year of life and the responsiveness of the caregiver. Bowlby maintains that both infants and their primary caregivers are biologically predisposed to form attachments. He argues that the newborn is biologically equipped to elicit attachment behavior. The baby cries, clings, coos, and smiles. Later, the infant crawls, walks, and follows the mother. The immediate result is to keep the primary caregiver nearby; the long-term effect is to increase the infant's chances of survival.

Attachment does not emerge suddenly but rather develops in a series of phases, moving from a baby's general preference for human beings to a partnership with primary caregivers. Following are four such phases based on Bowlby's conceptualization of attachment (Schaffer, 1996):

- *Phase 1: From birth to 2 months.* Infants instinctively direct their attachment to human figures. Strangers, siblings, and parents are equally likely to elicit smiling or crying from the infant.
- *Phase 2: From 2 to 7 months.* Attachment becomes focused on one figure, usually the primary caregiver, as the baby gradually learns to distinguish familiar from unfamiliar people.
- *Phase 3: From 7 to 24 months.* Specific attachments develop. With increased locomotor skills, babies actively seek contact with regular caregivers, such as the mother or father.
- *Phase 4: From 24 months on.* Children become aware of others' feelings, goals, and plans and begin to take these into account in forming their own actions.

Bowlby argued that infants develop an *internal working model* of attachment, a simple mental model of the caregiver, their relationship, and the self as deserving of nurturant care. The infant's internal working model of attachment with the caregiver influences the infant's and later the child's subsequent responses to other people (Dozier & Bernard, 2019; Dozier, Bernard, & Roben, 2019; Granqvist, 2020). The internal model of attachment also has played a pivotal role in the discovery of links between attachment and subsequent emotional understanding, conscience development, and self-concept (Psouni, 2019; Woodhouse & others, 2019).

INDIVIDUAL DIFFERENCES IN ATTACHMENT

Although attachment to a caregiver intensifies midway through the first year, isn't it likely that the quality of babies' attachment experiences varies? Mary Ainsworth (1979) thought so. Ainsworth created the **Strange Situation,** an observational measure of infant attachment that takes about 20 minutes in which the infant experiences a series of introductions, separations, and reunions with the caregiver and an adult stranger in a prescribed order. In using the Strange Situation, researchers hope that their observations will provide information about the infant's motivation to be near the caregiver and the degree to which the caregiver's presence provides the infant with security and confidence (Brown & Cox, 2020; Kohlhoff & others, 2020).

Based on how babies respond in the Strange Situation, they are described as being securely attached or insecurely attached (in one of three ways) to the caregiver:

- **Securely attached babies** use the caregiver as a secure base from which to explore the environment. When they are in the presence of their caregiver, securely attached infants explore the room and examine toys that have been placed in it. When the caregiver departs, securely attached infants might protest mildly, and when the caregiver returns these infants reestablish positive interaction with her, perhaps by smiling or climbing onto her lap. Subsequently, they often resume playing with the toys in the room.
- **Insecure avoidant babies** show insecurity by avoiding the caregiver. In the Strange Situation, these babies engage in little interaction with the caregiver, are not distressed when she leaves the room, usually do not reestablish contact when she returns, and may even turn their back on her. If contact is established, the infant usually leans away or looks away.

Strange Situation An observational measure of infant attachment that requires the infant to move through a series of introductions, separations, and reunions with the caregiver and an adult stranger in a prescribed order.

securely attached babies Babies who use the caregiver as a secure base from which to explore the environment.

insecure avoidant babies Babies who show insecurity by avoiding the caregiver.

- **Insecure resistant babies** often cling to the caregiver and then resist her by fighting against the closeness, perhaps by kicking or pushing away. In the Strange Situation, these babies often cling anxiously to the caregiver and don't explore the playroom. When the caregiver leaves, they often cry loudly and then push away if she tries to comfort them on her return.
- **Insecure disorganized babies** appear disoriented. In the Strange Situation, these babies might seem dazed, confused, and fearful. To be classified as disorganized, babies must show strong patterns of avoidance and resistance or display certain specified behaviors, such as extreme fearfulness around the caregiver.

Evaluating the Strange Situation
Does the Strange Situation capture important differences among infants? As a measure of attachment, it may be culturally biased (Gernhardt, Keller, & Rubeling, 2016). For example, German and Japanese babies often show patterns of attachment different from those of American infants. As illustrated in Figure 6, German infants are more likely to show an avoidant attachment pattern and Japanese infants are less likely to display this pattern than U.S. infants (van IJzendoorn & Kroonenberg, 1988). The avoidant pattern in German babies likely occurs because their caregivers encourage them to be independent (Grossmann & others, 1985). Also as shown in Figure 6, Japanese babies are more likely than American babies to be categorized as resistant. This may have more to do with the Strange Situation as a measure of attachment than with attachment insecurity itself. Japanese mothers rarely let anyone unfamiliar with their babies care for them. Thus, the Strange Situation might create considerably more stress for Japanese infants than for American infants, who are more accustomed to separation from their mothers (Miyake, Chen, & Campos, 1985). Even though there are cultural variations in attachment classification, the most frequent classification in every culture studied so far is secure attachment (Mooya, Sichimba, & Bakermans-Kranenburg, 2016; Mesman, van IJzendoorn, & Sagi-Schwartz, 2016).

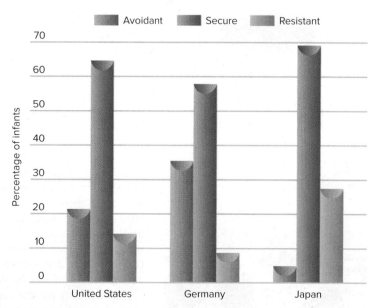

FIGURE **6**

CROSS-CULTURAL COMPARISON OF ATTACHMENT. In one study, infant attachment in three countries—the United States, Germany, and Japan—was measured in the Ainsworth Strange Situation (van IJzendoorn & Kroonenberg, 1988). The dominant attachment pattern in all three countries was secure attachment. However, German infants were more avoidant and Japanese infants were less avoidant and more resistant than U.S. infants. *What are some explanations for differences in how German, Japanese, and American infants respond to the Strange Situation?*

Interpreting Differences in Attachment
Do individual differences in attachment matter? Ainsworth argues that secure attachment in the first year of life provides an important foundation for psychological development later in life. The securely attached infant moves freely away from the mother but keeps track of where she is through periodic glances. The securely attached infant responds positively to being picked up by others, and when put back down, freely moves away to play. An insecurely attached infant, by contrast, avoids the mother or is ambivalent toward her, fears strangers, and is upset by minor, everyday separations.

If early attachment to a caregiver is important, it should be linked to a child's social behavior later in development. For some children, early attachments seem to foreshadow later functioning (Dozier, Bernard, & Roben, 2019; Sroufe, 2016; Woodhouse & others, 2019). In the extensive longitudinal study conducted by Alan Sroufe and his colleagues (2005), early secure attachment (assessed by the Strange Situation at 12 and 18 months) was linked with positive emotional health, high self-esteem, self-confidence, and socially competent interaction with peers, teachers, camp counselors, and romantic partners through adolescence. Also, a meta-analysis concluded that secure attachment in infancy was related to social competence with peers in early childhood (Groh & others, 2014). Another study revealed that attachment security at 2 years of age was linked to lower rates of peer conflict at 3 years of age (Raikes & others, 2013). Further, researchers have found that infant attachment insecurity (especially insecure resistant attachment) and early childhood behavioral inhibition predict adolescent social anxiety symptoms (Lewis-Morrarty & others, 2015). And a recent research meta-analysis concluded that secure attachment was linked to better resilience (Darling Rasmussen & others, 2019).

What is the nature of secure and insecure attachment?
Corbis/age fotostock

insecure resistant babies Babies who often cling to the caregiver, then resist the caregiver by fighting against the closeness, perhaps by kicking or pushing away.

insecure disorganized babies Babies who show insecurity by being disorganized and disoriented.

To what extent might this adolescent girl's development be linked to how securely or insecurely attached she was during infancy? (Top) Westend61/Getty Images (bottom) Andrew Rich/Signature/iStockphoto.com

developmental **connection**

Attachment

How might secure and insecure attachment be reflected in the relationships of young adults and older adults? Connect to "Socioemotional Development in Early Adulthood" and "Socioemotional Development in Late Adulthood."

developmental **connection**

Nature Versus Nurture

What is involved in gene × environment (G × E) interaction? Connect to "Biological Beginnings."

developmental cascade model Involves connections across domains over time that influence developmental pathways and outcomes.

Few studies have assessed infants' attachment security to the mother and the father separately (Ahnert & Schoppe-Sullivan, 2020; Walter & others, 2019). However, one study revealed that infants who were insecurely attached to their mother and father ("double-insecure") at 15 months of age had more externalizing problems (out-of-control behavior, for example) during their elementary school years than their counterparts who were securely attached to at least one parent (Kochanska & Kim, 2013). Also, a recent study found that an infant's secure attachment to the father was not enough to reduce the infant's stress reactions when the mother-infant attachment was insecure (Kuo & others, 2019).

An important issue regarding attachment is whether infancy is a critical or sensitive period for development. The studies just described show continuity, with secure attachment in infancy predicting subsequent positive development in childhood and adolescence. For some children, though, there is little continuity. Many studies show infant attachment as a very positive influence on children's development (Farrell & others, 2019; Steele & Steele, 2019; Teufl & others, 2020). However, not all research reveals the power of infant attachment to predict subsequent development (Lamb & Lewis, 2015; Roisman & Groh, 2011). In one longitudinal study, attachment classification in infancy did not predict attachment classification at 18 years of age (Lewis, Feiring, & Rosenthal, 2000). In this study, the best predictor of an insecure attachment classification at 18 was the occurrence of parental divorce in the intervening years.

Consistently positive caregiving over a number of years is likely an important factor in connecting early attachment with the child's functioning later in development (Cowan & others, 2019b; O'Connor & others, 2019). Indeed, researchers have found that early secure attachment and subsequent experiences, especially maternal care and life stresses, are linked with children's later behavior and adjustment (Roisman & Cicchetti, 2017; Thompson, 2015, 2016). For example, a longitudinal study revealed that changes in attachment security/insecurity from infancy to adulthood were linked to stresses and supports in socioemotional contexts (Van Ryzin, Carlson, & Sroufe, 2011). These results suggest that attachment continuity may reflect stable social contexts as much as early working models. The study just described (Van Ryzin, Carlson, & Sroufe, 2011) reflects an increasingly accepted view of the development of attachment and its influence on development. That is, it is important to recognize that attachment security in infancy does not always by itself produce long-term positive outcomes, but rather is linked to later outcomes through connections with the way children and adolescents subsequently experience various social contexts as they develop.

The Van Ryzin, Carlson, and Sroufe (2011) study reflects a **developmental cascade model,** which involves connections across domains over time that influence developmental pathways and outcomes (Cicchetti & Handley, 2019; St. George & others, 2020). Developmental cascades can include connections between a wide range of biological, cognitive, and socioemotional processes (attachment, for example), and also can involve social contexts such as families, peers, schools, and culture. Further, links can produce positive or negative outcomes at different points in development, such as infancy, early childhood, middle and late childhood, adolescence, and adulthood.

In addition to challenging the assumption that infancy is a critical or sensitive period for creating a secure attachment with a caregiver, some developmentalists argue that the secure attachment concept does not adequately consider certain biological factors in development, such as genes and temperament (Belsky & van IJzendoorn, 2017). For example, Jerome Kagan (1987, 2002) points out that infants are highly resilient and adaptive; he argues that they are evolutionarily equipped to stay on a positive developmental course even in the face of wide variations in parenting. Kagan and others stress that genetic characteristics and temperament play more important roles in a child's social competence than the attachment theorists, such as Bowlby and Ainsworth, are willing to acknowledge (Bakermans-Kranenburg & van IJzendoorn, 2011). For example, if some infants inherit a low tolerance for stress, this characteristic, rather than an insecure attachment bond, may be responsible for an inability to get along with peers. One study found links between disorganized attachment in infancy, a specific gene, and levels of maternal responsiveness (Spangler & others, 2009). In this study, infants with the short version of the serotonin transporter gene, 5-HTTLPR, developed a disorganized attachment style only when mothers were slow in responding to them. Other researchers have not always found support for genetic influences on infant-mother attachment (Leerkes & others, 2017) or for gene-environment interactions related to infant attachment (Fraley & others, 2013).

A third criticism of attachment theory (in addition to the critical/sensitive period issue and inadequate attention to biological-based factors) is that it ignores the diversity of socializing agents and contexts that exists in an infant's world. A culture's value system can influence the nature of attachment (Granqvist, 2020). In some contexts and cultures, infants show attachments to many people (Howes & Spieker, 2016). Among the Hausa (who live in Nigeria), grandmothers and siblings provide a significant amount of care for infants (Harkness & Super, 1995). Infants in agricultural societies tend to form attachments to older siblings, who are assigned a major responsibility for younger siblings' care. In a recent study in Zambia where siblings were substantially involved in caregiving activities, infants showed strong attachments to both their mothers and their sibling caregivers (Mooya, Sichimba, & Bakermans-Kranenburg, 2016). In this study, secure attachment was the most frequent attachment classification for both mother-infant and sibling-infant relationships.

Researchers recognize the influence of competent, nurturant caregivers on an infant's development (Parke, Roisman, & Rose, 2019; Raby & others, 2019). At issue, though, is whether or not secure attachment, especially to a single caregiver, is critical (Euler, 2020; Thompson, 2016; Verschueren, 2020).

Despite such questions, however, there is ample evidence that secure attachment is important in development (Dozier & Bernard, 2019; Martin & others, 2019; Nelson & others, 2020; Woodhouse & others, 2019). Is secure attachment the sole predictor of positive developmental outcomes for infants? No, and neither is any other single factor. Nonetheless, secure attachment in infancy is important because it reflects a positive parent-infant relationship and provides a foundation that supports healthy socioemotional development in the years that follow.

CAREGIVING STYLES AND ATTACHMENT

Is the style of caregiving linked with the quality of the infant's attachment? Securely attached babies have caregivers who are sensitive to their signals and are consistently available to respond to their infants' needs (Baradon & others, 2019; Davies & Troy, 2020; Dozier, Bernard, & Roben, 2019; Lieberman & others, 2020). These caregivers often let their babies have an active part in determining the onset and pacing of interaction in the first year of life. A recent study revealed that maternal sensitivity and a better home environment in infancy predicted higher self-regulation at 4 years of age (Birmingham, Bub, & Vaughn, 2017). Further, recent research indicates that providing parents who engage in inadequate and problematic caregiving with practice and feedback focused on interacting sensitively with infants enhances parent-infant attachment security (Dozier & Bernard, 2019; Dozier, Bernard, & Roben, 2019; Slade & others, 2019; Woodhouse & others, 2019).

In the Hausa culture, siblings and grandmothers provide a significant amount of care for infants. *How might these variations in care affect attachment?*
Penny Tweedie/The Image Bank/Getty Images

How do the caregivers of insecurely attached babies interact with them? Caregivers of avoidant babies tend to be unavailable or rejecting (Posada & Kaloustian, 2010). They often don't respond to their babies' signals and have little physical contact with them. When they do interact with their babies, they may behave in an angry and irritable way. Caregivers of resistant babies tend to be inconsistent; sometimes they respond to their babies' needs and sometimes they don't. In general, they tend not to be very affectionate with their babies and show little synchrony when interacting with them. Caregivers of disorganized babies often neglect or physically abuse them (Cicchetti & Handley, 2019). In some cases, these caregivers are depressed.

DEVELOPMENTAL SOCIAL NEUROSCIENCE AND ATTACHMENT

The emerging field of developmental social neuroscience examines connections between socioemotional processes, development, and the brain (Iyengar & others, 2019: Laurita, Hazan, & Spreng, 2019; Storey, Alloway, & Walsh, 2020). Attachment has been a major focus of theory and research on developmental social neuroscience. The connections between attachment and the brain involve the neuroanatomy of the brain, neurotransmitters, and hormones.

Theory and research on the role of the brain's regions in mother-infant attachment is just emerging (Storey, Alloway, & Walsh, 2020). One theoretical view proposed that the prefrontal cortex likely has an important role in maternal attachment behavior, as do the subcortical (areas of the brain lower than the cortex) regions of the amygdala (which is strongly involved in emotion) and the hypothalamus (Gonzalez, Atkinson, & Fleming, 2009).

Research on the role of hormones and neurotransmitters in attachment has emphasized the importance of the neuropeptide hormone *oxytocin* and the neurotransmitter *dopamine* in the formation of the maternal-infant bond (Feldman, 2019). Oxytocin, a mammalian

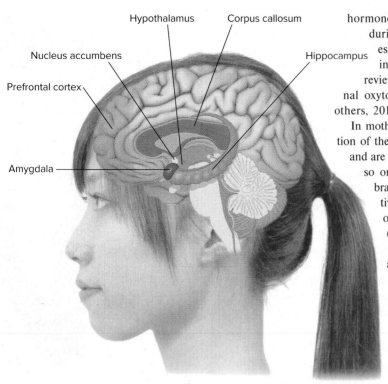

Hypothalamus
Corpus callosum
Nucleus accumbens
Hippocampus
Prefrontal cortex
Amygdala

FIGURE **7**

REGIONS OF THE BRAIN PROPOSED AS LIKELY TO BE IMPORTANT IN INFANT-MOTHER ATTACHMENT

Takayuki/Shutterstock

hormone that also acts as a neurotransmitter in the brain, is released during breast feeding and by contact and warmth. Oxytocin is especially thought to be a likely candidate in the formation of infant-mother attachment (Toepfer & others, 2019). A research review indicated strong links between levels or patterns of maternal oxytocin and aspects of mother-infant attachment (Galbally & others, 2011).

In mothers, the experience of pleasure and reward is linked to activation of the brain's dopamine circuits when mothers care for their infant and are exposed to their infants' cues, such as eye contact, smiling, and so on (Kim, Strathearn, & Swain, 2016). These experiences and brain changes likely promote mother-infant attachment and sensitive parenting (Kohlhoff & others, 2017). Also, the influence of oxytocin on dopamine in the mother's nucleus accumbens (a collection of neurons in the forebrain that are involved in pleasure) likely is important in motivating the mother's approach to the baby (de Haan & Gunnar, 2009).

In sum, it is likely that a number of brain regions, neurotransmitters, and hormones are involved in the development of infant-mother attachment (Feldman, 2019; Sullivan & Wilson, 2018). Key candidates for influencing this attachment are connections between the prefrontal cortex, amygdala, and hypothalamus; the neuropeptide oxytocin and the activity of the neurotransmitter dopamine in the nucleus accumbens. Figure 7 shows the regions of the brain we have described that are likely to play important roles in infant-mother attachment.

Although oxytocin release is stimulated by birth and lactation in mothers, might it also be released in fathers? Oxytocin is secreted in males, and one research study found that at both 6 weeks and 6 months after birth, when fathers engaged in more stimulation contact with babies, encouraged their exploration, and directed their attention to objects, the fathers' oxytocin levels increased (Gordon & others, 2010). In this study, mothers' behaviors that increased their oxytocin levels involved more affectionate parenting, such as gazing at their babies, expressing positive affect toward them, and touching them. Another study found that fathers with lower testosterone levels engaged in more optimal parenting with their infants (Weisman, Zagoory-Sharon, & Feldman, 2014). Also in this study, when fathers were administered oxytocin, their parenting behavior improved, as evidenced in increased positive affect, social gaze, touch, and vocal synchrony when interacting with their infants.

Testosterone levels are higher in males than in females. Might males' testosterone levels be linked to their behavior with infants? A recent study found that a high level of testosterone in fathers in early infancy was linked to lower father-infant synchrony (Gordon & others, 2017). Also in this study, only when fathers' level of testosterone was high did a negative link between their level of oxytocin and infant touch emerge.

Review *Connect* Reflect

 LG2 Describe social orientation/ understanding and the development of attachment in infancy.

Review

- How do infants orient to the social world?
- What is attachment, and how is it conceptualized?
- What are some individual variations in attachment? What are some criticisms of attachment theory?
- How are caregiving styles related to attachment?

Connect

- Do the different theories of attachment complement or contradict each other? Describe how the concept of nature versus nurture is involved.

Reflect *Your Own Personal Journey of Life*

- What can you do as a parent to improve the likelihood that your baby will form a secure attachment with you?

3 Social Contexts LG3 Explain how social contexts influence the infant's development.

The Family   Child Care

Now that we have explored the infant's emotional and personality development and attachment to caregivers, let's examine the social contexts in which these processes occur. We will begin by studying a number of aspects of the family and then turn to a social context in which infants increasingly spend time—child care.

THE FAMILY

The family can be thought of as a constellation of subsystems—a complex whole made up of interrelated, interacting parts—defined in terms of generation, gender, and role (Kerig, 2019). Each family member participates in several subsystems (McHale, Negrini, & Sirotkin, 2019). The father and child represent one subsystem, the mother and father another, the mother-father-child yet another, and so on.

These subsystems have reciprocal influences on each other (Gao & others, 2019). For example, Jay Belsky (1981) emphasizes that the marital relationship, parenting, and infant behavior and development can have both direct and indirect effects on each other (see Figure 8). An example of a direct effect is the influence of the parents' behavior on the child. An indirect effect is how the relationship between the spouses mediates the way a parent acts toward the child (Dubow & others, 2017). For example, marital conflict might reduce the efficiency of parenting, in which case marital conflict would indirectly affect the child's behavior. In a recent study, destructive marital conflict was linked to lower levels of coparenting alliance (Kopyslynska, Barnett, & Curran, 2020).

The Transition to Parenthood When people become parents through pregnancy, adoption, or stepparenting, they face disequilibrium and must adapt (Pinto & others, 2020; Ryan & Padilla, 2019). Parents want to develop a strong attachment with their infant, but they also want to maintain strong attachments to their spouse and friends, and possibly continue their careers. Parents ask themselves how the presence of this new individual will change their lives. A baby places new restrictions on partners; no longer will they be able to rush out to a movie on a moment's notice, and money may not be readily available for vacations and other luxuries. Dual-career parents ask, "Will it harm our baby if we place her in child care? Will we be able to find responsible babysitters?"

In a longitudinal investigation that tracked couples from late pregnancy until 3½ years after their baby was born, couples enjoyed more positive marital relations before the baby was born than after (Cowan & Cowan, 2000; Cowan & others, 2005). Still, almost one-third reported an increase in marital satisfaction. Some couples said that the baby had both brought them closer together and moved them farther apart; being parents enhanced their sense of themselves and also gave them a new, more stable identity as a couple. Babies opened men up to a concern with intimate relationships, and the demands of juggling work and family roles stimulated women to manage family tasks more efficiently and to pay attention to their own personal growth.

Other studies have explored the transition to parenthood (Kuersten-Hogan, 2017; Olsavsky & others, 2020; Ryan & Padilla, 2019). One study indicated that women and less avoidantly attached new parents adapted to the introduction of child care tasks better than most men, especially men who were avoidantly attached (Fillo & others, 2015). In another study, mothers experienced unmet expectations in the transition to parenting, with fathers doing less than their partners had anticipated (Biehle & Mickelson, 2012). Also, in a study of dual-earner couples, a gender division of labor across the transition to parenthood occurred (Yavorsky, Dush, & Schoppe-Sullivan, 2015). In this study, a gender gap was not present prior to the transition to parenthood, but after a child was born, women did more than 2 hours of additional work per day compared with an additional 40 minutes for men. Further, a recent study revealed that higher levels of anxiety and depression symptoms in mothers in the last trimester of pregnancy were associated with infants' externalizing problems at 2 years of age, and higher levels of these symptoms in fathers in the third trimester of pregnancy were related to higher levels of infants' internalizing and externalizing problems at 14 months of age (Hughes & others, 2020).

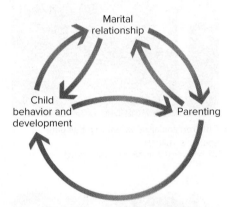

FIGURE 8
INTERACTION BETWEEN CHILDREN AND THEIR PARENTS: DIRECT AND INDIRECT EFFECTS

What characterizes the transition to parenting?
Chris Ryan/OJO Images/Getty Images

developmental **connection**
Cognitive Theory
A version of scaffolding is an important aspect of Lev Vygotsky's sociocultural cognitive theory of development. Connect to "Physical and Cognitive Development in Early Childhood."

Children socialize parents, just as parents socialize children.
SW Productions/BrandXPictures/Getty Images

Caregivers often play games such as peek-a-boo and pat-a-cake. *How is scaffolding involved in these games?*
(*Top*) BrandXPictures/Getty Images;
(*bottom*) monkeybusinessimages/Getty Images

reciprocal socialization Socialization that is bidirectional; children socialize parents, just as parents socialize children.

scaffolding Practice in which parents time interactions so that infants take turns with the parents; these interactions allow infants to be more skillful than they would be if they had to rely only on their own abilities.

The Bringing Home Baby project is a workshop that helps new parents to strengthen their relationship, understand and become acquainted with their baby, resolve conflict, and develop parenting skills (Gottman, 2018). Evaluations of the project revealed that participants improved their ability to work together as parents; fathers became more involved with their baby and sensitive to the baby's behavior; mothers had a lower incidence of postpartum depression symptoms; and babies showed better overall development than infants whose parents were part of a control group (Gottman, Shapiro, & Parthemer, 2004; Shapiro & Gottman, 2005). More recent research involving the Bringing Home Baby Project found that fathers who participated in the program felt more appreciated by their wives, and mothers were more satisfied with the division of labor when fathers were more involved in parenting (Shapiro, Gottman, & Fink, 2020).

Reciprocal Socialization   The mutual influence that parents and children exert on each other goes beyond specific interactions in games such as peek-a-boo; it extends to the whole process of socialization (Klein & others, 2018). Socialization between parents and children is not a one-way process (D'Angelo & others, 2019); instead, it is reciprocal. **Reciprocal socialization** is bidirectional: children socialize parents just as parents socialize children. These reciprocal interchanges and mutual influence processes are sometimes referred to as *transactional* (Dora & Baydar, 2020; Nelemans & others, 2020).

When reciprocal socialization has been studied in infancy, mutual gaze or eye contact plays an important role in early social interaction (Stern, 2010). In one investigation, the mother and infant engaged in a variety of behaviors while they looked at each other (Stern & others, 1977). By contrast, when they looked away from each other, the rate of such behaviors dropped considerably. The types of behaviors involved in reciprocal socialization in infancy are temporally connected, mutually contingent behaviors such as one partner imitating the sound of another or the mother responding with a vocalization to the baby's arm movements.

An important form of reciprocal socialization is **scaffolding,** in which parents time interactions in such a way that the infant takes turns with the parents. Scaffolding involves parental behavior that supports children's efforts, allowing them to be more skillful than they would be if they had to rely only on their own abilities (Norona & Baker, 2017). In using scaffolding, caregivers provide a positive, reciprocal framework in which they and their children interact (Graneist & Habermas, 2019). For example, in the game peek-a-boo, the mother initially covers the baby. Then she removes the cover and registers "surprise" at the infant's reappearance. As infants become more skilled at peek-a-boo, pat-a-cake, and so on, caregivers initiate other games that exemplify scaffolding and turn-taking sequences. Turn taking and games like peek-a-boo reflect the development of joint attention by the caregiver and infant (Melzi, Schick, & Kennedy, 2011).

Research supports the importance of scaffolding in infant development. For example, a recent study found that when adults used explicit scaffolding (encouragement and praise) with 13- and 14-month-old infants, the infants were twice as likely to engage in helping behavior as were their counterparts who did not receive the scaffolding (Dahl & others, 2017). Another study of disadvantaged families revealed that an intervention designed to enhance maternal scaffolding with infants was linked to improved cognitive skills when the children were 4 years old (Obradovic & others, 2016).

Increasingly, genetic and epigenetic factors are being studied to discover not only parental influences on children but also children's influence on parents (Hoye & others, 2020; Jylhava & others, 2019). The *epigenetic view* emphasizes that development is the result of an ongoing, bidirectional interchange between heredity and the environment (Ecker & Beck, 2019; Hein & others, 2019; Thaler & others, 2020). For example, harsh, hostile parenting is associated with negative outcomes for children, such as being defiant and oppositional (Deater-Deckard, 2013; Thompson & others, 2017). This likely reflects bidirectional influences rather than a unidirectional parenting effect. That is, the parents' harsh, hostile parenting and the children's defiant, oppositional behavior may influence each other. In this bidirectional influence, the parents' and children's behavior may have genetic linkages as well as experiential connections.

Managing and Guiding Infants' Behavior   In addition to sensitive parenting that involves warmth and caring that can help babies become securely attached to their parents, other important aspects of parenting infants involve managing and guiding their behavior in an attempt to reduce or eliminate undesirable behaviors (Holden, Vittrup, & Rosen, 2011). This management process includes (1) being proactive and childproofing the environment so infants won't encounter potentially dangerous objects or situations, and (2) engaging in corrective methods when infants engage in undesirable behaviors such as excessive fussing and crying, throwing objects, and so on.

One study assessed results of disciplinary and corrective methods that parents had used by the time infants were 12 and 24 months old (Vittrup, Holden, & Buck, 2006). As indicated in Figure 9, the main method parents used by the time infants were 12 months old was diverting the infants' attention, followed by reasoning, ignoring, and negotiating. Also note in Figure 9 that more than one-third of parents had yelled at their infant, about one-fifth had slapped the infant's hands or threatened the infant, and approximately one-sixth had spanked the infant before his or her first birthday.

As infants move into the second year of life and become more mobile and capable of exploring a wider range of environments, parental management of the toddler's behavior often triggers even more corrective feedback and discipline (Holden, Vittrup, & Rosen, 2011). As indicated in Figure 9, in the study just described, yelling increased from 36 percent at 1 year of age to 81 percent at 2 years of age, slapping the infant's hands increased from 21 percent at 1 year to 31 percent at age 2, and spanking increased from 14 percent at 1 year to 45 percent at age 2 (Vittrup, Holden, & Buck, 2006).

An important aspect of understanding why parents might increase their disciplinary corrective feedback in the second year involves their expectations for their toddlers' behavior. A national poll of parents who had children 3 years of age and younger found that parents have stronger expectations for their toddlers' ability to control their behavior than is warranted based on the maturation of the prefrontal cortex (Newton & Thompson, 2010). Thus, some of parents' corrective feedback likely arises because parents anticipate that toddlers and young children should be exercising greater self-control over their emotions and impulses than they are capable of achieving.

A special concern is that such corrective discipline tactics not become abusive (Cicchetti & Handley, 2019). Too often what starts out as mild to moderately intense discipline on the part of parents can move into highly intense anger. Later you will read more extensively about the use of punishment with children and child abuse.

Maternal and Paternal Caregiving As mentioned at the beginning of this chapter, an increasing number of U.S. fathers stay home full-time with their children (Bartel & others, 2018). As indicated at the beginning of this chapter, 7 percent of fathers do not work outside the home and 24 percent of those fathers care for their children at home (Livingston, 2018).

Many of these full-time fathers have career-focused wives who provide most of the family income. One study revealed that the stay-at-home fathers were as satisfied with their marriage as traditional parents, although they indicated that they missed their daily life in the workplace (Rochlen & others, 2008). In this study, the stay-at-home fathers reported that they tended to be ostracized when they took their children to playgrounds and often were excluded from parent groups.

Can fathers take care of infants as competently as mothers can? Observations of fathers and their infants suggest that fathers have the ability to act as sensitively and responsively as mothers with their infants (Cabrera, 2020; Fagan, 2020; Parke & Crookston, 2019; Parke, Roisman, & Rose, 2019). Consider the Aka pygmy culture in Africa where fathers spend as much time interacting with their infants as do their mothers (Hewlett, 1991, 2000; Hewlett & MacFarlan, 2010). Further, researchers found that infants who showed a higher level of externalizing, disruptive problems at 1 year of age had fathers who displayed a low level of engagement with them as early as the third month of life (Ramchandani & others, 2013). And in a recent study, children whose fathers' behavior was more withdrawn and depressed at 3 months had a lower level of cognitive development at 24 months of age (Sethna & others, 2018). Also in this study, children whose fathers were more engaged and sensitive, as well as less controlling, showed a higher level of cognitive development at 24 months of age. Further, a recent study revealed that both fathers' and mothers' sensitivity, assessed when infants were 10 to 12 months old, were linked to children's cognitive development at 18 months and language development at 36 months (Malmberg & others, 2016). Other recent studies indicate that when fathers are positively engaged with their children, improved developmental outcomes occur (Alexander & others, 2017).

Remember, however, that although fathers can be active, nurturing, involved caregivers with their infants, as Aka pygmy fathers are, in many cultures men have

developmental **connection**
Parenting
Psychologists give a number of reasons why harsh physical punishment can be harmful to children's development. Connect to "Socioemotional Development in Early Childhood."

Method	12 Months	24 Months
Spank with hand	14	45
Slap infant's hand	21	31
Yell in anger	36	81
Threaten	19	63
Withdraw privileges	18	52
Time-out	12	60
Reason	85	100
Divert attention	100	100
Negotiate	50	90
Ignore	64	90

FIGURE 9

PARENTS' METHODS FOR MANAGING AND CORRECTING INFANTS' UNDESIRABLE BEHAVIOR.
Shown here are the percentages of parents who had used various corrective methods by the time the infants were 12 and 24 months old.
Source: Vittrup, B., Holden, G. W., & Buck, M. "Attitudes Predict the Use of Physical Punishment: A Prospective Study of the Emergence of Disciplinary Practices," *Pediatrics, 117,* 2006, 2055–2064.

An Aka pygmy father with his infant son. In the Aka culture, fathers were observed to be holding or near their infants 47 percent of the time (Hewlett, 1991).
Nick Greaves/Alamy Stock Photo

not chosen to follow this pattern (Parkinson, 2010). Also, if fathers have mental health problems, they may not interact as effectively with their infants.

Do fathers and mothers interact with their infants in different ways? Maternal interactions usually center on child-care activities such as feeding, changing diapers, or bathing. Paternal interactions are more likely to include play (Lamb & Lewis, 2015). Fathers engage in more rough-and-tumble play than mothers do. Nonetheless, mothers engage in play with their children three times as often as fathers do and mothers and fathers play differently with their children (Cabrera & Roggman, 2017). Fathers tend to bounce infants, throw them up in the air, tickle them, and so on. Mothers do play with infants, but their play is less physical, less arousing, and more predictable than that of fathers (Lamb & Lewis, 2015; Parke, Roisman, & Rose, 2019). In a recent study of low-income families, fathers' playfulness with 2-year-olds was associated with more advanced vocabulary skills at 4 years of age, while mothers' playfulness with 2-year-olds was linked to a higher level of emotion regulation at 4 years of age (Cabrera & others, 2017).

CHILD CARE

Many U.S. children today experience multiple caregivers. Most do not have a parent staying home to care for them; instead, the children have some type of care provided by others—"child care." Many parents worry that child care will reduce their infants' emotional attachment to them, harm the infants' cognitive development, fail to teach them how to control anger, and allow them to become unduly influenced by their peers. How extensively is child care used by families? Are the worries of these parents justified?

Parental Leave Today far more young children are in child care than at any other time in history. About 2 million children in the United States currently receive formal, licensed child care, and uncounted millions of children are cared for by unlicensed babysitters. In part, these numbers reflect the fact that U.S. adults do not receive paid leave from their jobs to care for their young children.

Child-care policies around the world vary (Raikes & others, 2019; Sanders & Guerra, 2016). Europe led the way in creating new standards of parental leave: The European Union (EU) mandated a paid 14-week maternity leave in 1992. In most European countries today, working parents on leave receive from 70 to 100 percent of their prior wage, and paid leave averages about 16 weeks (Tolani & Brooks-Gunn, 2008). The United States currently grants up to 12 weeks of unpaid leave to workers caring for a newborn.

Most countries provide parental benefits only to women who have been employed for a minimum time prior to childbirth. In Denmark, however, even unemployed mothers are eligible for extended parental leave related to childbirth. In Germany, child-rearing leave is available to almost all parents. The Nordic countries (Denmark, Norway, and Sweden) have extensive gender-equity family leave policies for childbirth that emphasize the contributions of both women and men (O'Brien & Moss, 2010; Tolani & Brooks-Gunn, 2008). For example, in Sweden, parents can take an 18-month job-protected parental leave with benefits that can be shared by parents and applied to full-time or part-time work.

Variations in Child Care
Because the United States does not have a policy of paid leave for new parents, child care in the United States has become a major national concern (Shivers & Farago, 2016). Many factors influence the effects of child care, including the age of the child, the type of child care, and the quality of the program.

In the United States, approximately 15 percent of children 5 years of age and younger attend more than one child-care arrangement. One study of 2- and 3-year-old children

How do most fathers and mothers interact differently with infants?
Polka Dot Images/Photolibrary

How are child-care policies in many European countries, such as Sweden, different from those in the United States?
Matilda Lindeblad/Getty Images

Wanda Mitchell, Child-Care Director

Wanda Mitchell is the child-care director at the Hattie Daniels Day Care Center in Wilson, North Carolina. Her responsibilities include directing the operation of the center, which involves creating and maintaining an environment in which young children can learn effectively, and ensuring that the center meets state licensing requirements. Wanda obtained her undergraduate degree from North Carolina A & T University, majoring in Child Development. Prior to her current position, she was an education coordinator for Head Start and an instructor at Wilson Technical Community College. Describing her work, Wanda says, "I really enjoy working in my field. This is my passion. After graduating from college, my goal was to advance in my field."

For more information about what early childhood educators do, see the Careers in Life-Span Development appendix.

Wanda Mitchell, child-care director, works with some of the children at her center.
Courtesy of Wanda Mitchell

revealed that an increase in the number of child-care arrangements the children experienced was linked to an increase in behavioral problems and a decrease in prosocial behavior (Morrissey, 2009).

The type of child care varies extensively (Hasbrouck & Pianta, 2016). Child care is provided in large centers with elaborate facilities and in private homes. Some child-care centers are commercial operations; others are nonprofit centers run by churches, civic groups, and employers. Some child-care providers are professionals; others are mothers who want to earn extra money. Infants and toddlers are more likely to be found in family child care and informal care settings, while older children are more likely to be in child care centers and preschool and early education programs. Figure 10 presents the primary care arrangements for children under 5 years of age with employed mothers (Clarke-Stewart & Miner, 2008).

Child-care quality makes a difference (Howes, 2016; Vu, 2016). What constitutes a high-quality child-care program for infants? In high-quality child care (Clarke-Stewart & Miner, 2008, p. 273):

> Caregivers encourage the children to be actively engaged in a variety of activities, have frequent, positive interactions that include smiling, touching, holding, and speaking at the child's eye level, respond properly to the child's questions or requests, and encourage children to talk about their experiences, feelings, and ideas.

Children are more likely to experience poor-quality child care if they come from families with few resources (psychological, social, and economic). Many researchers have examined the role of poverty in the quality of child care (Howes, 2016; Shivers & Farago, 2016). One study found that extensive child care was harmful to low-income children only when the care was of low quality (Votruba-Drzal, Coley, & Chase-Lansdale, 2004). Another study revealed that children from low-income families benefited in terms of school readiness and language development when their parents selected higher-quality child care (McCartney & others, 2007).

High-quality child care also involves providing children with a safe environment, access to age-appropriate toys and participation in age-appropriate activities, and a low caregiver-to-child ratio that allows caregivers to spend considerable time with children on an individual basis. An Australian study revealed that higher-quality child care that included positive child-caregiver relationships at 2 to 3 years of age was linked to children's better self-regulation of attention and emotion at 4 to 5 and 6 to 7 years of age (Gialamas & others, 2014). Quality of child care matters in children's development, and according to UNICEF, the United States meets or exceeds only 3 of 10 child care quality benchmarks.

To read about one individual who provides quality child care to individuals from impoverished backgrounds, see *Connecting with Careers*. Do children in low-income families usually get quality child care? To answer that question and to learn more about the effects of child care, read *Connecting Through Research*.

> We have all the knowledge necessary to provide absolutely first-rate child care in the United States. What is missing is the commitment and the will.
>
> —EDWARD ZIGLER
> *Contemporary developmental psychologist, Yale University*

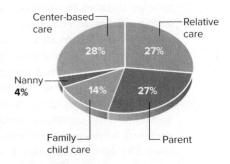

FIGURE 10

PRIMARY CARE ARRANGEMENTS IN THE UNITED STATES FOR CHILDREN UNDER 5 YEARS OF AGE WITH EMPLOYED MOTHERS

connecting through research

How Does the Quality and Quantity of Child Care Affect Children?

In 1991, the National Institute of Child Health and Human Development (NICHD) began a comprehensive, longitudinal study of child-care experiences. Data were collected on a diverse sample of almost 1,400 children and their families at 10 locations across the United States over a period of seven years. Researchers used multiple methods (trained observers, interviews, questionnaires, and testing) and measured many facets of children's development, including physical health, cognitive development, and socioemotional development. Following are some of the results of what is now referred to as the NICHD Study of Early Child Care and Youth Development or NICHD SECCYD (NICHD Early Child Care Research Network, 2001, 2002, 2003, 2004, 2005, 2006, 2010).

What are some important findings from the national longitudinal study of child care conducted by the National Institute of Child Health and Human Development?
Reena Rose Sibayan/The Jersey Journal/Landov Images

- **Patterns of use.** Many families placed their infants in child care very soon after the child's birth, and there was considerable instability in the child-care arrangements. By 4 months of age, nearly three-fourths of the infants had entered some form of nonmaternal child care. Almost half of the infants were cared for by a relative when they first entered care; only 12 percent were enrolled in child-care centers.

  Socioeconomic factors were linked to the amount and type of care. For example, mothers with higher incomes and families that were more dependent on the mother's income placed their infants in child care at an earlier age. Mothers who believed that maternal employment has positive effects on children were more likely than other mothers to place their infant in nonmaternal care for more hours. Low-income families were more likely than more affluent families to use child care, but infants from low-income families who were in child care averaged as many hours as other income groups. In the preschool years, mothers who were single, those with more education, and families with higher incomes used more hours of center care than other families. Minority families and mothers with less education used more hours of care by relatives.

- **Quality of care.** Evaluations of quality of care were based on characteristics such as group size, child-adult ratio, physical environment, caregiver characteristics (such as formal education, specialized training, and child-care experience), and caregiver behavior (such as sensitivity to children). An alarming conclusion is that a majority of the child care in the first three years of life was of unacceptably low quality. Positive caregiving by nonparents in child-care settings was infrequent—only 12 percent of the children studied had experienced positive nonparental child care (such as positive talk, lack of detachment and flat affect, and language stimulation). Further, infants from low-income families experienced lower-quality child care than did infants from higher-income families. When quality of caregivers' care was high, children performed better on cognitive and language tasks, were more cooperative with their mothers during play, showed more positive and skilled interaction with peers, and had fewer behavior problems. Caregiver training and good child-staff ratios were

linked with higher cognitive and social competence when children were 54 months of age. Using data collected as part of the NICHD early child care longitudinal study, a research analysis indicated that higher-quality early childhood care, especially at 27 months of age, was linked to children's higher vocabulary scores in the fifth grade (Belsky & others, 2007).

  Higher-quality child care was also related to higher-quality mother-child interaction among the families that used nonmaternal care. Further, poor-quality care was related to higher rates of insecure attachment to the mother among infants who were 15 months of age, but only when the mother was low in sensitivity and responsiveness. However, child-care quality was not linked to attachment security at 36 months of age. In one study, higher-quality child care from birth to 4½ years of age was linked to higher cognitive-academic achievement at 15 years of age (Vandell & others, 2010). In this study, early high-quality care also was related to youth reports of less externalizing behavior (lower rates of delinquency, for example). In another study, high-quality infant-toddler child care was linked to better memory skills at the end of the preschool years (Li & others, 2013).

- **Amount of child care.** In general, when children spent 30 hours or more per week in child care, their development was less than optimal (Ramey, 2005). In one study, more time spent in early nonrelative child care was related to higher levels of risk taking and impulsivity at 15 years of age (Vandell & others, 2010).

- **Family and parenting influences.** The influence of families and parenting was not weakened by extensive child care. Parents played a significant role in helping children to regulate their emotions. Especially important parenting influences were being sensitive to children's needs, being involved with children, and cognitively stimulating them. Indeed, parental sensitivity has been the most consistent predictor of a secure attachment, with child-care experiences being relevant in many cases only when mothers engage in insensitive parenting (Friedman, Melhuish, & Hill, 2010).

An important point about the extensive **NICHD** research is that findings show that family factors are considerably stronger and more consistent predictors of a wide variety of child outcomes than are child-care experiences (such as quality, quantity, type). The worst outcomes for children occur when both home and child-care settings are of poor quality. For example, a study involving the **NICHD SECCYD** data revealed that worse socioemotional outcomes (more problem behavior, lower levels of prosocial behavior) for children occurred when they experienced both home and child-care environments that conferred risk (Watamura & others, 2011).

This study reinforces the conclusion reached by other researchers cited earlier in this section of the chapter—it is not the quantity as much as the quality of child care a child receives that is important. What is also significant to note is the emphasis on the positive effect families and parents can have on children's child-care experiences.

What are some strategies parents can follow in regard to child care? Child-care expert Kathleen McCartney (2003, p. 4) offered this advice:

- *Recognize that the quality of your parenting is a key factor in your child's development.*
- *Monitor your child's development.* "Parents should observe for themselves whether their children seem to be having behavior problems." They need to talk with their child-care providers and pediatricians about their child's behavior.
- *Take some time to find the best child care.* Observe different child-care facilities and be certain that you like what you see. "Quality child care costs money, and not all parents can afford the child care they want. However, state subsidies, and other programs like Head Start, are available for families in need."

Review *Connect* Reflect

 LG3 Explain how social contexts influence the infant's development.

Review
- What are some important family processes in infant development?
- How does child care influence infant development?

Connect
- Earlier you learned about a fine motor skills experiment involving 3-month-olds and grasping. What concept in this section of the chapter is related to the use of "sticky mittens" in the experiment?

Reflect *Your Own Personal Journey of Life*
- Imagine that a friend of yours is getting ready to put her baby in child care. What advice would you give her? Do you think she should stay home with the baby? Why or why not? What type of child care would you recommend?

topical **connections** *looking* **forward**

In another chapter we will discuss socioemotional development in early childhood. Babies no more, young children make considerable progress in the development of their self, their emotions, and their social interactions. In early childhood, they show increased self-understanding and understanding of others, as well as an increased capacity to regulate their emotions. Many of the advances in young children's socioemotional development become possible because of the remarkable changes in their brain and cognitive development. In early childhood, relationships and interactions with parents and peers expand their knowledge of and connections with the social world. Additionally, play becomes something they not only enjoy doing on a daily basis but also a wonderful context for advancing both their socioemotional and cognitive development.

Socioemotional Development in Infancy

1 Emotional and Personality Development

 Discuss the development of emotions and personality in infancy.

Emotional Development

- Emotion is feeling, or affect, that occurs when a person is in a state or an interaction that is important to him or her. The broad range of emotions includes enthusiasm, joy, and love (positive emotions) and anxiety, anger, and sadness (negative emotions). Psychologists stress that emotions, especially facial expressions of emotions, have a biological foundation. Biological evolution endowed humans to be emotional, but embeddedness in culture and relationships provides diversity in emotional experiences.

- Emotions are the first language with which parents and infants communicate, and emotions play key roles in parent-child relationships. Infants display a number of emotions early in their development, although researchers debate the onset and sequence of these emotions. Lewis distinguishes between primary emotions and self-conscious emotions.

- Crying is the most important mechanism newborns have for communicating with the people in their world. Babies have at least three types of cries—basic, anger, and pain cries. Controversy swirls about whether babies should be soothed when they cry, although increasingly experts recommend immediately responding in a caring way during the first year. Social smiling occurs as early as 2 months of age. Two fears that infants develop are stranger anxiety and separation from a caregiver (which is reflected in separation protest). As infants develop, it is important for them to engage in emotion regulation.

Temperament

- Temperament involves individual differences in behavioral styles, emotions, and characteristic ways of responding. Chess and Thomas classified infants as (1) easy, (2) difficult, or (3) slow to warm up. Kagan proposed that inhibition to the unfamiliar is an important temperament category. Rothbart and Bates' view of temperament emphasizes this classification: (1) extraversion/surgency, (2) negative affectivity, and (3) effortful control (self-regulation).

- Physiological characteristics are associated with different temperaments. Children inherit a physiology that biases them to have a particular type of temperament, but through experience they learn to modify their temperament style to some degree.

- Goodness of fit refers to the match between a child's temperament and the environmental demands the child must cope with. Goodness of fit can be an important aspect of a child's adjustment. Although research evidence is sketchy at this point, some general recommendations are that caregivers should (1) be sensitive to the individual characteristics of the child, (2) be flexible in responding to these characteristics, and (3) avoid negatively labeling the child.

Personality Development

- Erikson argued that an infant's first year is characterized by the stage of trust versus mistrust. The infant begins to develop a self-understanding called self-recognition at about 18 months of age. Independence becomes a central theme in the second year of life. Erikson stressed that the second year of life is characterized by the stage of autonomy versus shame and doubt.

2 Social Orientation/Understanding and Attachment

 Describe social orientation/understanding and the development of attachment in infancy.

Social Orientation/ Understanding

- Infants show a strong interest in their social world and are motivated to understand it. Infants orient to the social world early in their development. Face-to-face play with a caregiver begins to occur at about 2 to 3 months of age. Newly developed self-produced locomotion skills significantly expand the infant's ability to initiate social interchanges and explore their social world more independently.

Attachment and Its Development	• Perceiving people as engaging in intentional and goal-directed behavior is an important social cognitive accomplishment that occurs toward the end of the first year. Also, engaging in meaningful interactions is an important aspect of infant development. Social referencing increases during the second year of life.
	• Attachment is a close emotional bond between two people. In infancy, contact comfort and trust are important in the development of attachment. Bowlby's ethological theory stresses that the caregiver and the infant are biologically predisposed to form an attachment. Attachment develops in four phases during infancy.
Individual Differences in Attachment	• Securely attached babies use the caregiver, usually the mother, as a secure base from which to explore the environment. Three types of insecure attachment are avoidant, resistant, and disorganized.
	• Ainsworth created the Strange Situation, an observational measure of attachment. Ainsworth points out that secure attachment in the first year of life provides an important foundation for psychological development later in life. The strength of the link found between early attachment and later development has varied somewhat across studies.
	• Three criticisms of the emphasis on secure attachment in infancy are (1) there is insufficient support for the assertion that infancy serves as a critical/sensitive period for later development; (2) biologically based factors such as genes and temperament have not been given adequate consideration; and (3) diversity of social agents and contexts have received insufficient attention. A current trend in attachment research reflects the developmental cascade model by considering not only attachment but also stability and change in stresses and social contexts as children and adolescents develop. Despite these criticisms, there is ample evidence that attachment is an important aspect of human development. Cultural variations in attachment have been found, but in all cultures secure attachment is the most common classification.
Caregiving Styles and Attachment	• Caregivers of securely attached babies are sensitive to the babies' signals and are consistently available to meet their needs. Caregivers of insecure avoidant babies tend to be unavailable or rejecting. Caregivers of insecure resistant babies tend to be inconsistently available to their babies and usually are not very affectionate. Caregivers of insecure disorganized babies often neglect or physically abuse their babies.
Developmental Social Neuroscience and Attachment	• Increased interest has been directed toward the role of the brain in the development of attachment. The hormone oxytocin is a key candidate for influencing the development of maternal-infant attachment.

3 Social Contexts

 LG3 Explain how social contexts influence the infant's development.

The Family	• The transition to parenthood requires considerable adaptation and adjustment on the part of parents. Children socialize parents, just as parents socialize children. Parent-infant synchrony and scaffolding are important aspects of reciprocal socialization. Belsky's model describes direct and indirect effects of marital relations, parenting, and infant behavior. Parents use a wide range of methods to manage and guide infants' behavior. The mother's primary role when interacting with the infant usually is caregiving; the father's is playful interaction.
Child Care	• More U.S. children are in child care now than at any earlier point in history. The quality of child care is uneven, and child care remains a controversial topic. Quality child care can be achieved and seems to have few adverse effects on children. In the NICHD child-care study, infants from low-income families were more likely to receive the lowest quality of care. Also, higher-quality child care was linked with fewer problems in children.

key **terms**

anger cry 171
attachment 181
basic cry 171
developmental cascade model 184
difficult child 174
easy child 174
emotion 169

goodness of fit 176
insecure avoidant babies 182
insecure disorganized babies 183
insecure resistant babies 183
pain cry 171
primary emotions 170
reciprocal socialization 188

reflexive smile 172
scaffolding 188
securely attached babies 182
self-conscious emotions 170
separation protest 172
slow-to-warm-up child 174
social referencing 181

social smile 172
Strange Situation 182
stranger anxiety 172
temperament 173

key **people**

Mary Ainsworth 173
John Bates 174
Jay Belsky 187
John Bowlby 172
Joseph Campos 170

Alexander Chess 174
Erik Erikson 177
Jacob Gewirtz 173
Harry Harlow 181
Jerome Kagan 170

Michael Lewis 170
Kathleen McCartney 193
Mary Rothbart 174
Stella Thomas 174
Ross Thompson 179

John Watson 173
Amanda Woodward 181

You are troubled at seeing him spend his early years doing nothing. What! Is it nothing to be happy? Is it nothing to skip, to play, to run about all day long? Never in his life will he be so busy as now.

—JEAN JACQUES ROUSSEAU
Swiss-born French philosopher, 18th century

Early Childhood

In early childhood, our greatest untold poem was being only 4 years old. We skipped and ran and played all the sun long, never in our lives so busy, busy being something we had not quite grasped yet. Who knew our thoughts, which we worked up into small mythologies all our own? Our thoughts and images and drawings took wings. The blossoms of our heart, no wind could touch. Our small world widened as we discovered new refuges and new people. When we said "I," we meant something totally unique, not to be confused with any other. This section consists of two chapters: "Physical and Cognitive Development in Early Childhood" and "Socioemotional Development in Early Childhood."

PHYSICAL AND COGNITIVE DEVELOPMENT IN EARLY CHILDHOOD

chapter outline

① Physical Changes

Learning Goal 1 Identify physical changes in early childhood.

Body Growth and Change
Motor and Perceptual Development
Sleep
Nutrition and Exercise
Illness and Death

② Cognitive Changes

Learning Goal 2 Describe three views of the cognitive changes that occur in early childhood.

Piaget's Preoperational Stage
Vygotsky's Theory
Information Processing

③ Language Development

Learning Goal 3 Summarize how language develops in early childhood.

Understanding Phonology and Morphology
Changes in Syntax and Semantics
Advances in Pragmatics
Young Children's Literacy

④ Early Childhood Education

Learning Goal 4 Evaluate different approaches to early childhood education.

Variations in Early Childhood Education
Education for Young Children Who Are Disadvantaged
Controversies in Early Childhood Education

Ariel Skelley/Blend Images/Getty Images

The Reggio Emilia approach is an educational program for young children that was developed in the northern Italian city of Reggio Emilia. Children of single parents and children with disabilities have priority in admission; other children are admitted according to a scale of needs. Parents pay on a sliding scale based on income.

The children are encouraged to learn by investigating and exploring topics that interest them (Bredekamp, 2020; Follari, 2019). A wide range of stimulating media and materials is available for children to use as they learn music, movement, drawing, painting, sculpting, collages, puppets and disguises, and photography, for example (Dev & others, 2019).

In this program, children often explore topics in a group, which fosters a sense of community, respect for diversity, and a collaborative approach to problem solving. Two co-teachers are present to serve as guides for children. The Reggio Emilia teachers treat each project as an adventure that may be sparked by an adult's suggestion, a child's idea, or an event such as a snowfall or something else unexpected. The teachers allow children enough time to think about a topic and craft a project.

A Reggio Emilia classroom in which young children explore topics that interest them.
Ruby Washington/The New York Times/Redux Pictures

At the core of the Reggio Emilia approach is the image of children who are competent and have rights, especially the right to receive outstanding care and education (Balfour & Vittoria, 2018). Parent participation is considered essential, and cooperation is a major theme in the schools. Many early childhood education experts believe the Reggio Emilia approach provides a supportive, stimulating context in which children are motivated to explore their world in a competent and confident manner (Feeney, Moravcik, & Nolte, 2019; Morrison, 2020).

topical connections looking *back*

Physical growth in infancy is dramatic. Even though physical growth in early childhood slows, it is not difficult to distinguish young children from infants when you look at them. Most young children lose their "baby fat," and their legs and trunks become longer. In addition to what you can see with the naked eye, much development also continues below the surface in the brain. In infancy, myelination of axons in the brain paved the way for development of such functions as full visual capacity. Continued myelination in early childhood provides children with much better hand-eye coordination. In terms of cognitive development, you learned that infants make amazing progress in their attentional, memory, concept formation, and language skills. In this chapter, you will discover that these information-processing skills continue to show remarkable advances in early childhood.

preview

Parents and educators who clearly understand how young children develop can play an active role in creating programs that foster their natural interest in learning, rather than stifling it. In this chapter we will explore the physical, cognitive, and language changes that typically occur as the toddler develops into the preschooler, and then examine different approaches to early childhood education.

1 Physical Changes   **LG1**   Identify physical changes in early childhood.

| Body Growth and Change | Motor and Perceptual Development | Sleep | Nutrition and Exercise | Illness and Death |

Recall that an infant's growth in the first year is rapid and follows cephalocaudal and proximodistal patterns. Improvement in fine motor skills—such as being able to turn the pages of a book one at a time—also contributes to the infant's sense of mastery in the second year. The growth rate continues to slow down in early childhood. If it did not, we would be a species of giants.

BODY GROWTH AND CHANGE

Growth in height and weight is the obvious physical change that characterizes early childhood. Unseen changes in the brain and nervous system are no less significant, however, in preparing children for advances in cognition and language.

Height and Weight The average child grows 2½ inches in height and gains 5 to 10 pounds a year during early childhood. As the preschool child grows older, the percentage of increase in height and weight decreases with each additional year (Hockenberry, Wilson, & Rodgers, 2019). Girls are only slightly smaller and lighter than boys during these years, a difference that continues until puberty. During the preschool years, both boys and girls slim down as the trunks of their bodies lengthen. Although their heads are still somewhat large for their bodies, by the end of the preschool years most children have lost their top-heavy look. Body fat also shows a slow, steady decline during the preschool years. The chubby baby often looks much leaner by the end of early childhood. Girls have more fatty tissue than boys; boys have more muscle tissue.

Growth patterns vary individually (Kliegman & others, 2019). Think back to your preschool years. This was probably the first time you noticed that some children were taller than you, some shorter; some were fatter, some thinner; some were stronger, some weaker. Much of the variation was due to heredity, but environmental experiences were also involved (Edwards & Coyne, 2020). A review of the height and weight of children around the world concluded that the two most important contributors to height differences are ethnic origin and nutrition (Meredith, 1978). Urban, middle-socioeconomic-status, and firstborn children were taller than rural, lower-socioeconomic-status, and later-born children. In the United States, African American children are taller than non-Latino White children.

Why are some children unusually short? The primary contributing influences are congenital factors (genetic or prenatal problems), growth hormone deficiency, a physical problem that develops in childhood, maternal smoking during pregnancy, or an emotional difficulty (Edwards & Coyne, 2020; Xu & others, 2019).

Growth hormone deficiency is the absence or deficiency of growth hormone produced by the pituitary gland to stimulate the body to grow (Butler & others, 2019; Canete & others, 2019). Growth hormone deficiency may be diagnosed during infancy or later in childhood (Rhie & others, 2019), and it affects as many as 10,000 to 15,000 U.S. children (Stanford University Medical Center, 2012). Without treatment, most children with growth hormone

The bodies of 5-year-olds and 2-year-olds are different. Notice that the 5-year-old not only is taller and weighs more, but also has a longer trunk and legs than the 2-year-old. *Can you think of some other physical differences between 2- and 5-year-olds?*
Michael Hitoshi/Digital Vision/Getty Images

growth hormone deficiency Absence or deficiency of growth hormone produced by the pituitary gland to stimulate the body to grow.

deficiency will not reach a height of five feet. Twice as many boys as girls are treated with growth hormone, likely because there is a greater stigma attached to boys being short. Also, in a recent study, the physical and socioemotional health-related quality of life of children with growth hormone deficiency increased one year after they received growth hormone treatment (Quitmann & others, 2019).

The Brain One of the most important physical changes during early childhood is the continuing development of the brain and nervous system (Schneider & Ornstein, 2019). Although the brain continues to grow in early childhood, it does not grow as rapidly as it did in infancy. By the time children reach 3 years of age, the brain is three-quarters of its adult size. By age 6, the brain has reached about 95 percent of its adult size (Lenroot & Giedd, 2006). Thus, the brain of a 5-year-old is nearly the size it will be when the child reaches adulthood, but as we will see in later chapters, development inside the brain continues through the remaining years of childhood and adolescence (Calabro & others, 2020; Icenogle & others, 2019).

Some of the brain's interior changes involve increases in dendritic connections as well as **myelination,** in which nerve cells are covered and insulated with a layer of fat cells (see Figure 1). Myelination increases the speed and efficiency with which information travels through the nervous system. Myelination is important in the development of a number of abilities during childhood (Kwon & others, 2020). For example, myelination in the areas of the brain related to hand-eye coordination is not complete until about 4 years of age. In a recent study, young children with higher cognitive ability showed increased myelination by 3 years of age (Deoni & others, 2016).

Researchers also have discovered that children's brains undergo dramatic anatomical changes between the ages of 3 and 15 (Dow-Edwards & others, 2019; Price & others, 2018). In comparing periodic brain scans of the same children for up to four years, they have found that children's brains undergo rapid, distinct spurts of growth. The amount of brain material in some areas can nearly double within as little as a year, followed by a drastic loss of tissue as unneeded cells are purged and the brain continues to reorganize itself. Scientists have discovered that the overall size of the brain does not show dramatic growth in the 3- to 15-year age range. However, dramatic changes occur in local patterns within the brain. Researchers have found that in children from 3 to 6 years of age the most rapid growth takes place in the frontal lobe areas involved in planning and organizing new actions, and in maintaining attention to tasks (Carlson, Zelazo, & Faja, 2013).

Recently, researchers have found that contextual factors such as poverty and parenting quality are linked to the development of the brain (Kim & others, 2019; Marshall & others, 2018; Merz & others, 2019). In one study, children from the poorest homes had significant maturational lags in their frontal and temporal lobes at 4 years of age, and these lags were associated with lower attainment of school readiness skills (Hair & others, 2015). In another study, higher levels of maternal sensitivity in early childhood were associated with higher total brain volume (Kok & others, 2015). Further, a recent study indicated that maltreatment risk and home adversity in infancy were linked to cortical delays and brain immaturity at 8 years of age (Bick & others, 2019). However, children assigned to an attachment and biobehavioral catchup intervention showed improved brain functioning.

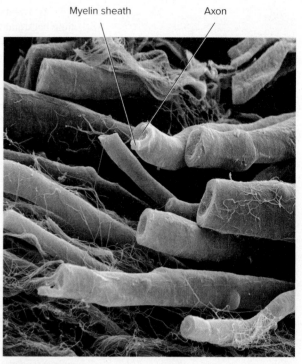

Myelin sheath   Axon

FIGURE **1**

A MYELINATED NERVE FIBER. A myelin sheath, shown in gray, encases the axons (shown in pink). *What roles does myelination play in the brain's development and children's cognition?*
Steve Gschmeissner/Science Photo Library/Getty Images

---

developmental **connection**

Brain Development

In middle and late childhood, cortical thickening occurs in the frontal lobes, which may be linked to improvements in language abilities such as reading. Connect to "Physical and Cognitive Development in Middle and Late Childhood."

MOTOR AND PERCEPTUAL DEVELOPMENT

Most preschool children are more active than they will ever be at any later period in life. Let's explore changes in physical activity as well as perceptual skills in young children.

Gross Motor Skills The preschool child no longer has to make an effort simply to stay upright and to move around. As children move their legs with more confidence and carry themselves more purposefully, moving around in the environment becomes more automatic (Perry & others, 2018). However, there are large individual differences in young children's gross motor skills (Kliegman & others, 2019).

myelination The process by which the nerve cells are covered and insulated with a layer of fat cells, which increases the speed at which information travels through the nervous system.

At 3 years of age, children enjoy simple movements, such as hopping, jumping, and running back and forth. They take considerable pride in showing how they can run across a room and jump all of 6 inches.

At 4 years of age, children are still enjoying the same kind of activities, but they have become more adventurous. They scramble over low jungle gyms as they display their athletic prowess.

At 5 years of age, children are even more adventuresome than they were at age 4. It is not unusual for self-assured 5-year-olds to perform hair-raising stunts on playground equipment. Five-year-olds run hard and enjoy races with each other and their parents.

How can early childhood educators support young children's motor development? Young children need to practice skills in order to learn them, so instruction should be followed with ample time for practice (Follari, 2019; Morrison, 2020). A recent study of 4-year-old girls found that a nine-week motor skills intervention improved the girls' ball skills (Veldman & others, 2017).

There can be long-term negative effects for children who fail to develop basic motor skills (Gorgon, 2018). These children will not be as able to join in group games or participate in sports during their school years and in adulthood. In one study, children with a low level of motor competence had a lower motivation for sports participation and had lower global self-worth than their counterparts with a high level of motor competence (Bardid & others, 2016). Another recent study found that higher motor proficiency in preschool was linked to higher levels of physical activity in adolescence (Venetsanou & Kambas, 2017).

Might gross motor skills in early childhood be linked to language development? Advances in gross motor skills provide children with new learning opportunities to interact with objects, their environment, and people. In a recent research review, both gross and fine motor skills were associated with better expressive and receptive language development in early childhood (Gonzalez, Alvarez, & Nelson, 2019).

Fine Motor Skills   At 3 years of age, although children have had the ability to pick up the tiniest objects between their thumb and forefinger for some time, they are still somewhat clumsy at it. Three-year-olds can build surprisingly high block towers, placing each block with intense concentration but often not in a completely straight line. When 3-year-olds play with a simple jigsaw puzzle, they are rather rough in placing the pieces. Even when they recognize the hole a piece fits into, they are not very precise in positioning the piece. They often try to force the piece into the hole or pat it vigorously.

By 4 years of age, children's fine motor coordination has improved substantially and become much more precise. Sometimes 4-year-old children have trouble building high towers with blocks because, in their attempts to place each of the blocks perfectly, they may knock over the existing stack. By age 5, children's fine motor coordination has improved further. Hand, arm, and body all move together under better command of the eye.

Perceptual Development   Changes in children's perceptual development continue in childhood (Bank & others, 2015). When children are about 4 or 5 years old, their eye muscles usually are developed enough that they can move their eyes efficiently across a series of letters. Many preschool children are farsighted, unable to see close up as well as they can see far away. By the time they enter first grade, though, most children can focus their eyes and sustain their attention effectively on close-up objects.

What are the signs of vision problems in children? They include rubbing the eyes, blinking or squinting excessively, appearing irritable when playing games that require good distance vision, shutting or covering one eye, and tilting the head or thrusting it forward when looking at something. A child who shows any of these behaviors should be examined by an ophthalmologist.

SLEEP

Getting a good night's sleep is important for children's development (Matricciani & others, 2019; Mi & others, 2019). Recently, the World Health Organization (WHO) concluded that 3- to 4-year-old children should have 10 to 13 hours of good-quality sleep, which may include a nap, with consistent sleep and wake times (Willumsen & Bull, 2020)

Sometimes, though, it is difficult to get young children to go to sleep as they drag out their bedtime routine. Studies often report that young children don't get adequate sleep (Palermo, 2014). A recent study of 3-year-old children discovered that family irregularity (irregular

What characterizes young children's sleep problems?
Imagemore/Glow Images

sleep onset and inconsistent mealtimes, for example) was associated with shorter sleep duration and later sleep onset (Koopman-Verhoeff & others, 2019). Also, in a recent observational study, better-quality interactions with parents (higher on harmonious and reciprocal, lower on indifferent and conflictual) were linked to preschool children's longer sleep duration (Dubois-Comtois & others, 2019).

Children can experience a number of sleep problems (Huhdanpaa & others, 2018). These include narcolepsy (extreme daytime sleepiness) (Sirkanta & Kumar, 2019), insomnia (difficulty getting to sleep or staying asleep) (Dewald-Kaufmann, de Bruin, & Michael, 2019), and nightmares (Nielsen & others, 2019). It is estimated that more than 40 percent of children experience a sleep problem at some point (Boyle & Cropley, 2004). The following research studies indicate links between children's sleep problems and negative developmental outcomes:

╭─ ─ ─ ─ ─ ─ ─ ─ →
developmental **connection**
Sleep
What sleep disorder in infancy leads to the most infant deaths, and at what age is the infant at highest risk for this disorder? Connect to "Physical Development in Infancy."
←─ ─ ─ ─ ─ ─ ─ ─ ─ ╯

- Sleep problems in early childhood were associated with subsequent attention problems that in some cases persisted into early adolescence (O'Callaghan & others, 2010).

- In a Chinese study, preschool children who slept seven hours per day or less had a worse school readiness profile (including language/cognitive deficits and emotional immaturity) (Tso & others, 2016).

- Preschool children with longer sleep duration were more likely to have better peer acceptance, social skills, and receptive vocabulary (Vaughn & others, 2015).

- Short sleep duration in children was linked with being overweight (Hart, Cairns, & Jelalian, 2011).

- In 2- to 5-year-old children, each additional hour of daily screen time was associated with a decrease in sleep time, less likelihood of sleeping 10 hours or more per night, and later bedtime (Xu & others, 2016).

- Recent research indicates that sleep deprivation in childhood is linked to attention deficit hyperactivity disorder (ADHD) (Arns & Vollebregt, 2019; Becker & others, 2019). For example, in a recent Chinese study, sleep deprivation in early childhood was associated with a higher incidence of ADHD in middle and late childhood (Tso & others, 2019).

To improve children's sleep, Mona El-Sheikh (2013) recommends making sure that the bedroom is cool, dark, and comfortable; maintaining consistent bedtimes and wake times; and building positive family relationships. Also, helping the child slow down before bedtime often contributes to less resistance to going to bed. Reading the child a story, playing quietly with the child in the bath, and letting the child sit on the caregiver's lap while listening to music are calming activities.

NUTRITION AND EXERCISE

Eating habits are important aspects of development during early childhood (Blake, Munoz, & Volpe, 2019; Donatelle & Ketcham, 2020). What children eat affects their skeletal growth, body shape, and susceptibility to disease. In a recent national study, dietary quality of U.S. children decreased from 6 months of age to 4 years of age (Hamner & Moore, 2020). Exercise and physical activity also are very important aspects of young children's lives (Hoeger & others, 2019; Lumpkin, 2021; Rink, 2020).

Overweight Young Children Being overweight has become a serious health problem in early childhood (Insel & Roth, 2020; Schiff, 2021). A national study revealed that 45 percent of children's meals exceed recommendations for saturated and trans fats, which can raise cholesterol levels and increase the risk of heart disease (Center for Science in the Public Interest, 2008). The same study found that one-third of children's daily caloric intake comes from restaurants—twice the percentage consumed away from home in the 1980s. Further, 93 percent of almost 1,500 possible choices at 13 major fast-food chains exceeded 430 calories—one-third of what the National Institute of Medicine recommends that 4- to 8-year-old children consume in a day. One study of U.S. 2- and 3-year-olds found that French fries and other fried potatoes were the vegetable they were most likely to consume (Fox & others, 2010).

Young children's eating behavior is strongly influenced by their caregivers' behavior (Souto-Gallardo & others, 2020). Young children's eating behavior improves when caregivers

What are some trends in the eating habits and weight of young children?
Jodie Griggs/Getty Images

eat with children on a predictable schedule, model choosing nutritious food, make mealtimes pleasant occasions, and engage in certain feeding styles. Distractions from television, family arguments, and competing activities should be minimized so that children can focus on eating. A sensitive/responsive caregiver feeding style, in which the caregiver is nurturant, provides clear information about what is expected, and appropriately responds to children's cues, is recommended (Black & Hurley, 2017). Forceful and restrictive caregiver behaviors are not recommended (Tylka, Lumeng, & Eneli, 2015). A recent study found that parental praise for healthy eating behavior was more effective than negative parental comments in improving young children's eating behavior (increasing their vegetable intake, for example) and helping overweight children lose weight (Rotman & others, 2020).

The Centers for Disease Control and Prevention (2020) has established categories for obesity, overweight, and at risk of being overweight. These categories are determined by body mass index (BMI), which is computed using a formula that takes into account height and weight. Children and adolescents at or above the 97th percentile are classified as obese, those at the 95th or 96th percentile as overweight, and those from the 85th to the 94th percentile as at risk of being overweight.

The percentages of young children who are overweight or at risk of being overweight in the United States have increased dramatically in recent decades (Insel & Roth, 2020). In 2009–2010, 12.1 percent of U.S. 2- to 5-year-olds were classified as obese, compared with 5 percent in 1976–1980 and 10.4 percent in 2007–2008 (Ogden & others, 2012). In 2015–2016, 13.9 percent of 2- to 5-year-olds were obese (Hales & others, 2017).

The risk that overweight children will continue to be overweight when they are older was underscored by a U.S. study of nearly 8,000 children (Cunningham, Kramer, & Narayan, 2014). In this study, overweight 5-year-olds were four times more likely to be obese at 14 years of age than their 5-year-old counterparts who began kindergarten at a normal weight. Also, in other research, preschool children who were obese were five times more likely to be overweight or obese as adults (Ogden & others, 2014).

One comparison of 34 countries revealed that the United States had the second highest rate of childhood obesity (Janssen & others, 2005). Obesity contributes to a number of health problems in young children (Insel & Roth, 2020). For example, physicians are now seeing type 2 (adult-onset) diabetes (a condition directly linked with obesity and a low level of fitness) and hypertension in children as young as 5 years of age (Chaturvedi & others, 2014).

Many aspects of children's lives can contribute to becoming overweight or obese (Meeks, Heit, & Page, 2020; Thompson, Manore, & Vaughan, 2020). Recently, the following 5-2-1-0 obesity prevention guidelines have been issued for young children: 5 or more servings of fruits and vegetables, 2 hours or less of screen time, minimum of 1 hour of physical activity, and 0 sugar-sweetened beverages daily (Khalsa & others, 2017). Strategies for preventing obesity in childhood include helping children, parents, and teachers see food as a way to satisfy hunger and meet nutritional needs, not as proof of love or as a reward for good behavior (Smith & Collene, 2019). Snack foods should be low in fat, simple sugars, and salt, as well as high in fiber (Schiff, 2021). Young children also should be encouraged to engage in exercise and other active daily activities on a daily basis (Meeks, Heit, & Page, 2020). Further, parents need to monitor young children's screen time (Venetsanou & others, 2019). A recent Chinese study revealed that longer TV viewing time was linked to an increase in 4- to 5-year-olds' overweight/obesity status (Hu & others, 2019). Recently, the World Health Organization (WHO) recommended that 3- to 4-year-olds should engage in no more than 1 hour of sedentary screen time daily (Willumsen & Bull, 2020). In a recent study, 3- to 4-year-old African American children and children who lived at or below the poverty level were more likely than other children to engage in more than 1 hour of screen time daily (Kracht, Webster, & Staiano, 2020).

Prevention and intervention studies are being conducted to increase overweight and obese young children's diet quality and physical activity level (Sanyaolu & others, 2020). For example, an intervention study with children attending Head Start programs found that getting parents involved in such activities as nutrition counseling, becoming more aware of their child's weight status, and developing healthy lifestyles was effective in lowering children's rate of obesity, increasing children's physical activity, reducing children's TV viewing, and improving children's eating habits (Davison & others, 2013). Other researchers also are finding that interventions with parents can reduce children's likelihood of being overweight or obese (Byrne & others, 2018; Sadeghi & others, 2019). And a research review concluded

How much physical activity should preschool children engage in per day?
RubberBall Productions/Getty Images

that family-based interventions were often effective in helping obese children lose weight (Kothandan, 2014).

Malnutrition in Young Children from Low-Income Families Malnutrition is a problem for many U.S. children, with approximately 11 million preschool children experiencing malnutrition that places their health at risk. Poverty is an especially strong risk factor for malnutrition in young children (Schiff, 2021). One of the most common nutritional problems in early childhood is iron deficiency anemia, which results in chronic fatigue. This problem results from the failure to eat adequate amounts of quality meats and dark green vegetables. Young children from low-income families are the most likely to develop iron deficiency anemia (Petry & others, 2017).

Exercise Routine physical activity should be a daily occurrence for young children (Graham, Holt/Hale, & Parker, 2020; Rink, 2020; Teague, Mackenzie, & Rosenthal, 2019). Too often children are not getting adequate exercise (Lumpkin, 2021; Ndabi, Nevill, & Sandercock, 2019; Tomkinson & Wong, 2019). The World Health Organization recently recommended that 3- to 4-year-olds engage in 3 hours of physical activity per day, of which at least 60 minutes should be of moderate to vigorous intensity (Willumsen & Bull, 2020). These guidelines reflect an increase from earlier guidelines (National Association for Sport and Physical Education, 2002). The child's life should center around activities, not meals (Meeks, Heit, & Page, 2020).

ILLNESS AND DEATH

What are the greatest risks to the health of young children in the United States? How pervasive is death among young children around the world?

The United States Young children's active and exploratory nature, coupled with their unawareness of danger in many instances, often puts them in situations in which they are at risk for injuries. In 2017 in the United States, accidents (unintentional injuries) were the leading cause of death in young children, followed by congenital malformations, malignant neoplasms, and homicide (Centers for Disease Control and Prevention, 2019). Drowning was the most common cause of accidental death in young children, followed by motor vehicles, homicide, and suffocation.

Children's Safety Children's safety is influenced not only by their own skills and safety behaviors but also by aspects of their family and home, school and peers, and community (Bauer & others, 2019; Telljohann & others, 2020). Figure 2 describes steps that can be taken in each of these contexts to enhance children's safety and prevent injury (Sleet & Mercy, 2003).

developmental **connection**
Health
As boys and girls reach and progress through adolescence, they tend to get less exercise. Connect to "Physical and Cognitive Development in Adolescence."

FIGURE 2

CHARACTERISTICS THAT ENHANCE YOUNG CHILDREN'S SAFETY. In each context of a child's life, steps can be taken to create conditions that improve the child's safety and reduce the likelihood of injury. *How are the contexts listed in the figure related to Bronfenbrenner's theory (described in the "Introduction" chapter)?*

Children in poverty have higher rates of accidents, death, and asthma than do children from higher-income families (Kelleher, Reece, & Sandel, 2018).

Environmental Tobacco Smoke Estimates indicate that approximately 22 percent of children and adolescents in the United States are exposed to tobacco smoke in the home. An increasing number of studies reach the conclusion that children are at risk for health problems when they live in homes in which a parent smokes (Gatzke-Kopp & others, 2020). Children exposed to tobacco smoke in the home are more likely to develop wheezing symptoms and asthma than are children in nonsmoking families (Hatoun & others, 2018). For example, a recent national study found that children with a smoker in the home were 30 percent more likely to have an asthma diagnosis than children with no smokers in their home (Xie & others, 2020). One study found that parental smoking was a risk factor for higher blood pressure in children (Simonetti & others, 2011). Also, a study revealed that maternal cigarette smoking and alcohol consumption when children were 5 years of age were linked to onset of smoking in early adolescence (Hayatbakhsh & others, 2013). Further, a recent study revealed that children living in low-income families are more likely to be exposed to environmental tobacco smoke than their counterparts in middle-income families (Kit & others, 2013). And a recent study found that young children exposed to environmental smoke were more likely to have hyperactivity and conduct problem symptoms than their counterparts who were not exposed to environmental smoke (Gatzke-Kopp & others, 2020).

The State of Illness and Health of the World's Children Devastating effects on the health of young children occur in countries where poverty rates are high (UNICEF, 2020). The poor are the majority in nearly one out of every five nations in the world. They often experience hunger, malnutrition, illness, inadequate access to health care, unsafe water, and a lack of protection from harm (Black & others, 2017).

In the last decade, there has been a dramatic increase in the number of young children who have died because HIV/AIDS was transmitted to them by their parents (UNICEF, 2019). Deaths of young children due to HIV/AIDS especially occur in countries with high rates of poverty and low levels of education (Tomlinson & others, 2016). Many of the deaths of young children could be prevented by reductions in poverty and improvements in nutrition, sanitation, education, and health services (Black & others, 2017; UNICEF, 2020).

Many children in impoverished countries die before reaching the age of 5 from dehydration and malnutrition brought about by diarrhea. *What are some of the other main causes of death in young children around the world?*
Kent Page/AP Images

Review *Connect* Reflect

Review

- How does the body grow and change during early childhood?
- What changes take place in motor and perceptual development during early childhood?
- What are some problems associated with sleep in young children?
- What roles do nutrition and exercise play in early childhood?
- What are some major causes of illness and death among young children in the United States and around the world?

Connect

- In this section you learned that experts recommend that children get 11 to 13 hours of sleep per night during early childhood. How does that compare with what you learned earlier about the sleep patterns of infants?

Reflect *Your Own Personal Journey of Life*

- What were your eating habits like when you were a young child? In what ways are they similar or different from your current eating habits? Did your early eating habits predict whether or not you have weight problems today?

---

2 Cognitive Changes

LG2 Describe three views of the cognitive changes that occur in early childhood.

Piaget's Preoperational Stage	Vygotsky's Theory	Information Processing

The cognitive world of the preschool child is creative, free, and fanciful. Preschool children's imaginations work overtime, and their mental grasp of the world improves. Our coverage of cognitive development in early childhood focuses on three theories: Piaget's, Vygotsky's, and information processing.

PIAGET'S PREOPERATIONAL STAGE

Recall that during Piaget's first stage of development, the sensorimotor stage, the infant progresses in the ability to organize and coordinate sensations and perceptions with physical movements and actions. The **preoperational stage,** which lasts from approximately 2 to 7 years of age, is the second Piagetian stage. In this stage, children begin to represent the world with words, images, and drawings. They form stable concepts and begin to reason. At the same time, the young child's cognitive world is dominated by egocentrism and magical beliefs.

Because Piaget called this stage "preoperational," it might sound like an unimportant waiting period. Not so. Instead, the label *preoperational* emphasizes that the child does not yet perform **operations,** which are reversible mental actions that allow children to do mentally what before they could do only physically. Adding and subtracting numbers mentally are examples of operations. *Preoperational thought* is the beginning of the ability to reconstruct in thought what has been established in behavior. This developmental stage can be divided into two substages: the symbolic function substage and the intuitive thought substage.

The Symbolic Function Substage The **symbolic function substage** is the first substage of preoperational thought, occurring roughly between the ages of 2 and 4. During this substage, the young child gains the ability to mentally represent an object that is not present. This ability vastly expands the child's mental world (Callaghan & Corbit, 2015). Young children use scribble designs to represent people, houses, cars, clouds, and so on; they begin to use language and engage in pretend play. However, although young children make distinct progress during this substage, their thought still has important limitations, two of which are egocentrism and animism.

Egocentrism is the inability to distinguish between one's own perspective and someone else's perspective. Piaget and Barbel Inhelder (1969) initially studied young children's egocentrism by

developmental **connection**

Cognitive Theory

Object permanence is an important accomplishment in the sensorimotor stage. Connect to "Cognitive Development in Infancy."

preoperational stage Piaget's second stage, lasting from about 2 to 7 years of age, during which children begin to represent the world with words, images, and drawings, and symbolic thought goes beyond simple connections of sensory information and physical action; stable concepts are formed, mental reasoning emerges, egocentrism is present, and magical beliefs are constructed.

operations In Piaget's theory, these are reversible mental actions that allow children to do mentally what they formerly did physically.

symbolic function substage Piaget's first substage of preoperational thought, in which the child gains the ability to mentally represent an object that is not present (between about 2 and 4 years of age).

egocentrism The inability to distinguish between one's own perspective and someone else's (salient feature of the first substage of preoperational thought).

Model of Mountains

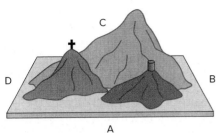

Child seated here

Photo 1
(View from A)

Photo 2
(View from B)

Photo 3
(View from C)

Photo 4
(View from D)

FIGURE 3

THE THREE MOUNTAINS TASK. View 1 shows the child's perspective from where he or she is sitting. View 2 is an example of one of the photographs the child would be shown, along with other photographs taken from different perspectives. It shows what the mountains look like to a person sitting at spot B. When asked what a view of the mountains looks like from position B, the preoperational child selects a photograph taken from location A, the child's view at the time. A child who thinks in a preoperational way cannot take the perspective of a person sitting at another spot.

devising the three mountains task (see Figure 3). The child walks around the model of the mountains and becomes familiar with what the mountains look like from different perspectives, and she can see that there are different objects on the mountains. The child is then seated on one side of the table on which the mountains are placed. The experimenter moves a doll to different locations around the table, at each location asking the child to select from a series of photos the one photo that most accurately reflects the view that the doll is seeing. Children in the preoperational stage often pick their own view rather than the doll's view. Preschool children frequently show the ability to take another's perspective on some tasks but not others.

Animism, another limitation of preoperational thought, is the belief that inanimate objects have lifelike qualities and are capable of action. A young child might show animism by saying, "That tree pushed the leaf off, and it fell down," or "The sidewalk made me mad; it made me fall down." A young child who uses animism fails to distinguish the appropriate occasions for using human and nonhuman perspectives (Opfer & Gelman, 2011).

Possibly because young children are not very concerned about reality, their drawings are fanciful and inventive. Suns are blue, skies are yellow, and cars float on clouds in their symbolic, imaginative world. One 3½-year-old looked at a scribble he had just drawn and described it as a pelican kissing a seal (see Figure 4a). The symbolism is simple but strong, like abstractions found in some modern art. Twentieth-century Spanish artist Pablo Picasso commented,

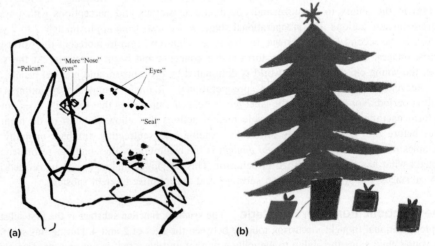

(a)

(b)

FIGURE 4

THE SYMBOLIC DRAWINGS OF YOUNG CHILDREN. (*a*) A 3½-year-old's symbolic drawing. Halfway into his drawing, the 3½-year-old artist said it was a "pelican kissing a seal." (*b*) This 11-year-old's drawing is neater and more realistic but also less inventive.

Wolf, D., and Nove, J. "The Symbolic Drawings of Young Children," Courtesy of D. Wolf and J. Nove. Copyright Dennie Palmer Wolf, Annenberg Institute, Brown University. All rights reserved. Used with permission.

animism The belief that inanimate objects have lifelike qualities and are capable of action.

"I used to draw like Raphael but it has taken me a lifetime to draw like young children." During the elementary school years, a child's drawings become more realistic, neat, and precise (see Figure 4b) (Winner, 1986).

The Intuitive Thought Substage   The **intuitive thought substage** is the second substage of preoperational thought, occurring between approximately 4 and 7 years of age. In this substage, children begin to use primitive reasoning and want to know the answers to all sorts of questions. Consider 4-year-old Tommy, who is at the beginning of the intuitive thought substage. Although he is starting to develop his own ideas about the world he lives in, his ideas are still simple, and he is not very good at thinking things out. He has difficulty understanding events that he knows are taking place but that he cannot see. His fantasized thoughts bear little resemblance to reality. He cannot yet answer the question "What if?" in any reliable way. For example, he has only a vague idea of what would happen if a car were to hit him. He also has difficulty negotiating traffic because he cannot do the mental calculations necessary to estimate whether an approaching car will hit him when he crosses the road.

By the age of 5, children have just about exhausted the adults around them with "why" questions. The child's questions signal the emergence of interest in reasoning and in figuring out why things are the way they are. Following are some samples of the questions children ask during the questioning period of 4 to 6 years of age (Elkind, 1976): "What makes you grow up?" "Who was the mother when everybody was a baby?" "Why do leaves fall?" "Why does the sun shine?" Piaget called this substage intuitive because young children seem so sure about their knowledge and understanding yet are unaware of how they know what they know. That is, they know something but know it without the use of rational thinking.

Centration and the Limits of Preoperational Thought   One limitation of preoperational thought is **centration,** a centering of attention on one characteristic to the exclusion of all others. Centration is most clearly evidenced in young children's lack of **conservation,** the awareness that altering an object's or a substance's appearance does not change its basic properties. For example, to adults, it is obvious that a certain amount of liquid stays the same, regardless of a container's shape. But this is not at all obvious to young children. Instead, they are struck by the height of the liquid in the container; they focus on that characteristic to the exclusion of others.

The situation that Piaget devised to study conservation is his most famous task. In the conservation task, children are presented with two identical beakers, each filled to the same level with liquid (see Figure 5). They are asked if these beakers have the same amount of liquid, and they usually say yes. Then the liquid from one beaker is poured into a third beaker, which is taller and thinner than the first two. The children are then asked if the amount of liquid in the tall, thin beaker is equal to that which remains in one of the original beakers. Children who are less than 7 or 8 years old usually say no and justify their answers in terms of the differing

intuitive thought substage Piaget's second substage of preoperational thought, in which children begin to use primitive reasoning and want to know the answers to all sorts of questions (between 4 and 7 years of age).

centration Focusing attention on one characteristic to the exclusion of all others.

conservation In Piaget's theory, awareness that altering an object's or a substance's appearance does not change its basic properties.

FIGURE 5

PIAGET'S CONSERVATION TASK. The beaker test is a well-known Piagetian test to determine whether a child can think operationally—that is, can mentally reverse actions and show conservation of the substance. (a) Two identical beakers are presented to the child. Then the experimenter pours the liquid from B into C, which is taller and thinner than A or B. (b) The child is asked if these beakers (A and C) have the same amount of liquid. The preoperational child says "no." When asked to point to the beaker that has more liquid, the preoperational child points to the tall, thin beaker.
Tony Freeman/PhotoEdit

height or width of the beakers. Older children usually answer yes and justify their answers appropriately ("If you poured the water back, the amount would still be the same").

In Piaget's theory, failing the conservation-of-liquid task is a sign that children are at the preoperational stage of cognitive development. The failure demonstrates not only centration but also an inability to mentally reverse actions. For example, in the conservation of matter example shown in Figure 6, preoperational children say that the longer shape has more clay because they assume that "longer is more." Preoperational children cannot mentally reverse the clay-rolling process to see that the amount of clay is the same in both the shorter ball shape and the longer stick shape.

In addition to failing to conserve volume, preoperational children also fail to conserve number, matter, length, and area. However, children often vary in their performance on different conservation tasks. Thus, a child might be able to conserve volume but not number. A recent fMRI brain-imaging study of conservation of number revealed that advances in a network in the parietal and frontal lobes were linked to 9- and 10-year-olds' conservation success in comparison with non-conserving 5- and 6-year-olds (Houde & others, 2011).

Some developmentalists disagree with Piaget's estimate of when children's conservation skills emerge. For example, Rochel Gelman (1969) showed that when the child's attention to relevant aspects of the conservation task is improved, the child is more likely to conserve. Gelman has also demonstrated that attentional training on one dimension, such as number, improves the preschool child's performance on another dimension, such as mass. Thus, Gelman argues that conservation appears earlier than Piaget thought and that attention is especially important in explaining conservation.

VYGOTSKY'S THEORY

Piaget's theory is a major developmental theory. Another developmental theory that focuses on children's cognition is Vygotsky's theory. Like Piaget, Vygotsky (1962) emphasized that children actively construct their knowledge and understanding. In Piaget's theory, children develop ways of thinking and understanding by their actions and interactions with the physical world. In Vygotsky's theory, children are more often described as social creatures than in Piaget's theory (Moura da Costa & Tuleski, 2017; Yu & Hu, 2017). They develop their ways of thinking and understanding primarily through social interaction (Clara, 2017). Their cognitive development depends on the tools provided by society, and their minds are shaped by the cultural context in which they live (Daniels, 2017; Gauvain, 2016; Holzman, 2017; Lewis, 2019).

zone of proximal development (ZPD)
Vygotsky's term for tasks that are too difficult for children to master alone but can be mastered with the assistance of adults or more-skilled children.

The Zone of Proximal Development Vygotsky's belief in the role of social influences, especially instruction, in children's cognitive development is reflected in his concept of the zone of proximal development. **Zone of proximal development (ZPD)** is Vygotsky's term for

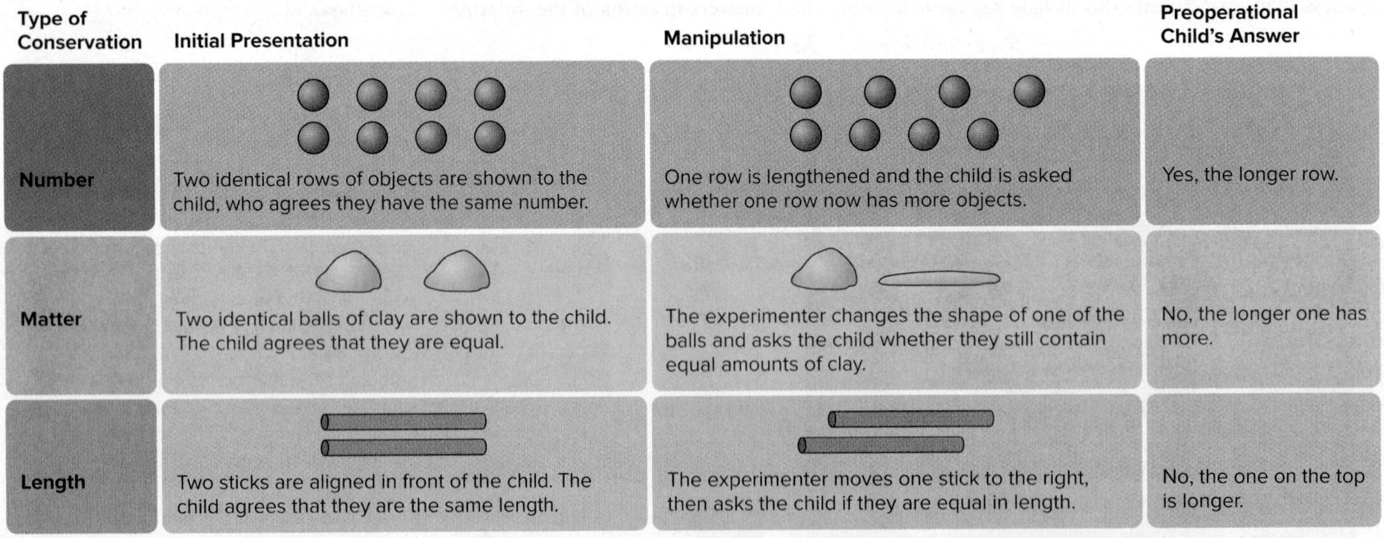

Type of Conservation	Initial Presentation	Manipulation	Preoperational Child's Answer
Number	Two identical rows of objects are shown to the child, who agrees they have the same number.	One row is lengthened and the child is asked whether one row now has more objects.	Yes, the longer row.
Matter	Two identical balls of clay are shown to the child. The child agrees that they are equal.	The experimenter changes the shape of one of the balls and asks the child whether they still contain equal amounts of clay.	No, the longer one has more.
Length	Two sticks are aligned in front of the child. The child agrees that they are the same length.	The experimenter moves one stick to the right, then asks the child if they are equal in length.	No, the one on the top is longer.

FIGURE **6**

SOME DIMENSIONS OF CONSERVATION: NUMBER, MATTER, AND LENGTH. *What characteristics of preoperational thought do children demonstrate when they fail these conservation tasks?*

the range of tasks that are too difficult for the child to master alone but can be learned with guidance and assistance from adults or more-skilled children. Thus, the lower limit of the ZPD is the level of skill reached by the child working independently. The upper limit is the level of additional responsibility the child can accept with the assistance of an able instructor (see Figure 7). The ZPD captures the child's cognitive skills that are in the process of maturing and can be accomplished only with the assistance of a more-skilled person (Clara, 2017; Holzman, 2017). Vygotsky (1962) called these the "buds" or "flowers" of development, to distinguish them from the "fruits" of development, which the child already can accomplish independently.

What are some factors that can influence the effectiveness of the ZPD in children's learning and development? Researchers have found that the following factors can enhance the ZPD's effectiveness (Gauvain & Perez, 2015): better emotion regulation, secure attachment, absence of maternal depression, and child compliance.

Scaffolding Closely linked to the idea of the ZPD is the concept of scaffolding. *Scaffolding* means changing the level of support. Over the course of a teaching session, a more-skilled person (a teacher or advanced peer) adjusts the amount of guidance to fit the child's current performance (Daniels, 2017). When the student is learning a new task, the skilled person may use direct instruction. As the student's competence increases, less guidance is given. A recent study found that scaffolding techniques that heighten engagement, direct exploration, and facilitate "sense-making," such as guided play, improved 4- to 5-year-old children's acquisition of geometric knowledge (Fisher & others, 2013).

Language and Thought The use of dialogue as a tool for scaffolding is only one example of the important role of language in a child's development. According to Lev Vygotsky, children use speech not only to communicate socially but also to help them solve tasks (van der Veer & Zavershneva, 2018). Vygotsky (1962) further believed that young children use language to plan, guide, and monitor their behavior. This use of language for self-regulation is called *private speech* (Lantolf, 2017). For Piaget, private speech is egocentric and immature, but for Vygotsky it is an important tool of thought during the early childhood years.

Vygotsky said that language and thought initially develop independently of each other and then merge. He emphasized that all mental functions have external, or social, origins. Children must use language to communicate with others before they can focus inward on their own thoughts. Children also must communicate externally and use language for a long period of time before they can make the transition from external to internal speech. This transition period occurs between 3 and 7 years of age and involves talking to oneself. After a while, the self-talk becomes second nature to children, and they can act without verbalizing. When they gain this skill, children have internalized their egocentric speech in the form of *inner speech,* which becomes their thoughts.

Vygotsky reasoned that children who use a lot of private speech are more socially competent than those who don't. He argued that private speech represents an early transition in becoming more socially communicative. In Vygotsky's view, when young children talk to themselves they are using language to govern their behavior and guide themselves. For example, a child working on a puzzle might say to herself, "Which pieces should I put together first? I'll try those green ones first. Now I need some blue ones. No, that blue one doesn't fit there. I'll try it over here."

Piaget maintained that self-talk is egocentric and reflects immaturity. However, researchers have found support for Vygotsky's view that private speech plays a positive

Upper limit

Level of additional responsibility child can accept with assistance of an able instructor

Zone of proximal development (ZPD)

Lower limit

Level of problem solving reached on these tasks by child working alone

FIGURE **7**

VYGOTSKY'S ZONE OF PROXIMAL DEVELOPMENT. Vygotsky's zone of proximal development has a lower limit and an upper limit. Tasks in the ZPD are too difficult for the child to perform alone. They require assistance from an adult or a more-skilled child. As children experience the verbal instruction or demonstration, they organize the information in their existing mental structures so that they can eventually perform the skill or task alone. Ariel Skelley/Blend Images LLC

> ## developmental **connection**
> ### Parenting
> Scaffolding also is an effective strategy for parents to adopt in interacting with their infants. Connect to "Socioemotional Development in Infancy."

Lev Vygotsky (1896–1934), shown here with his daughter, reasoned that children's cognitive development is advanced through social interaction with more-skilled individuals embedded in a sociocultural backdrop. *How is Vygotsky's theory different from Piaget's?*
Courtesy of James V. Wertsch, Washington University

role in children's development (Winsler, Carlton, & Barry, 2000). In one study, children's private speech was linked to increased emotion regulation (Day & Smith, 2013). Also, a recent study indicated that mothers who engage in sensitive parenting have children who use more private speech (Day & Smith, 2019).

Teaching Strategies   Vygotsky's theory has been embraced by many teachers and has been successfully applied to education (Clara, 2017; Holzman, 2017; Lewis, 2019). Here are some ways Vygotsky's theory can be incorporated in classrooms:

1. *Assess the child's ZPD.* Like Piaget, Vygotsky did not recommend formal, standardized tests as the best way to assess children's learning. Rather, Vygotsky argued that assessment should focus on determining the child's zone of proximal development. The skilled helper presents the child with tasks of varying difficulty to determine the best level at which to begin instruction.

2. *Use the child's ZPD in teaching.* Teaching should begin toward the zone's upper limit, so that the child can reach the goal with help and move to a higher level of skill and knowledge. Offer just enough assistance. You might ask, "What can I do to help you?" Or simply observe the child's intentions and attempts and provide support when it is needed. When the child hesitates, offer encouragement. And encourage the child to practice the skill. You may watch and appreciate the child's practice or offer support when the child forgets what to do.

3. *Use more-skilled peers as teachers.* Remember that it is not just adults who are important in helping children learn. Children also benefit from the support and guidance of more-skilled children.

4. *Place instruction in a meaningful context.* Educators today are moving away from abstract presentations of material; instead, they provide students with opportunities to experience learning in real-world settings. For example, rather than just memorizing math formulas, students work on math problems with real-world implications.

5. *Transform the classroom with Vygotskian ideas.* What does a Vygotskian classroom look like? The Kamehameha Elementary Education Program (KEEP) in Hawaii is based on Vygotsky's theory (Tharp, 1994). The ZPD is the key element of instruction in this program. Children might read a story and then interpret its meaning. Many of the learning activities take place in small groups. All children spend at least 20 minutes each morning in a setting called "Center One." In this context, scaffolding is used to improve children's literacy skills. The instructor asks questions, responds to students' queries, and builds on the ideas that students generate.

Connecting Development to Life further explores the implications of Vygotsky's theory for children's education.

Evaluating Vygotsky's Theory   Even though their theories were proposed at about the same time, most of the world learned about Vygotsky's theory later than they learned about Piaget's theory. Thus, Vygotsky's theory has not yet been evaluated as thoroughly. However, Vygotsky's view of the importance of sociocultural influences on children's development fits with the current belief that it is important to evaluate the contextual factors in learning (Gauvain, 2016; Holzman, 2017).

We already have compared several aspects of Vygotsky's and Piaget's theories, such as Vygotsky's emphasis on the importance of private speech in development and Piaget's view that such speech is immature. Although both theories are constructivist, Vygotsky's theory takes a **social constructivist approach,** which emphasizes the social contexts of learning and the construction of knowledge through social interaction (Gauvain, 2016; Holzman, 2017; Yu & Hu, 2017).

In moving from Piaget to Vygotsky, the conceptual shift is from the individual to collaboration, social interaction, and sociocultural activity (Daniels, 2017). The endpoint of cognitive development for Piaget is formal operational thought. For Vygotsky, the endpoint can differ depending on which skills are considered to be the most important in a particular culture. In Piaget's theory, children construct knowledge by transforming, organizing, and reorganizing previous knowledge. From Vygotsky's perspective, children construct knowledge through social interaction. The implication of Piaget's theory for teaching is that children need support to

social constructivist approach An approach that emphasizes the social contexts of learning and asserts that knowledge is mutually built and constructed. Vygotsky's theory reflects this approach.

connecting development to life

Tools of the Mind

Tools of the Mind is an early childhood education curriculum that emphasizes children's development of self-regulation and the cognitive foundations of literacy. The curriculum was created by Elena Bodrova and Deborah Leong (2007, 2015a, b) and has been implemented in more than 200 classrooms. Most of the children in the Tools of the Mind programs are at risk because of their living circumstances, which in many instances involve poverty and other difficult conditions such as being homeless and having parents with drug problems.

Tools of the Mind is grounded in Vygotsky's (1962) theory, with special attention given to cultural tools, development of self-regulation, use of the zone of proximal development, scaffolding, private speech, shared activity, and play as important activity. In a Tools of the Mind classroom, dramatic play has a central role. Teachers guide children in creating themes that are based on the children's interests, such as treasure hunt, store, hospital, and restaurant. Teachers also incorporate field trips, visitor presentations, videos, and books in the development of children's play. They help children develop a play plan, which increases the maturity of their play. Play plans describe what the children expect to do in the play period, including the imaginary context, roles, and props to be used. The play plans increase the quality of their play and self-regulation.

Scaffolding writing is another important theme in the Tools of the Mind classroom. Teachers guide children in planning their own message by drawing a line to stand for each word the child says. Children then repeat the message, pointing to each line as they say the word. Then, the child writes on the lines, trying to represent each word with some letters or symbols. Figure 8 shows how the scaffolding writing process improved a 5-year-old child's writing over the course of two months.

Research assessments of children's writing in Tools of the Mind classrooms revealed that they have more advanced writing skills than children in other early childhood programs (Bodrova & Leong, 2007) (see Figure 8). For example, they write more complex messages, use more words, spell more accurately, show better letter recognition, and have a better understanding of the concept of a sentence.

Also, the effectiveness of the Tools of the Mind approach was examined in 29 schools, 79 classrooms, and 759 schools (Blair & Raver, 2014). Positive effects of the Tools of the Mind program were found for the cognitive processes of executive function (improved self-regulation, for example) and attention control. Further, the Tools of the Mind program improved children's reading, vocabulary, and mathematics performance at the end of kindergarten and into the first grade. The most significant improvements occurred in high-poverty schools.

How does the Reggio Emilia approach to education that you read about in the story that opened this chapter compare with the Tools of the Mind approach described here?

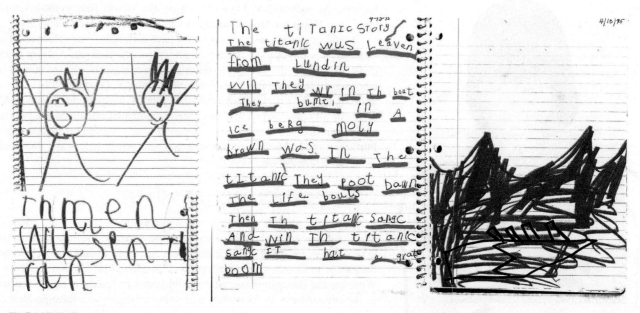

FIGURE 8

WRITING PROGRESS OF A 5-YEAR-OLD BOY OVER TWO MONTHS USING THE SCAFFOLDING WRITING PROCESS IN TOOLS OF THE MIND. (*a*) Five-year-old Aaron's independent journal writing prior to using the scaffolded writing technique. (*b*) Aaron's journal two months after beginning to use the scaffolded writing technique.
Bodrova, Elena and Leong, Deborah J. "Tools of the Mind: A Case Study of Implementing the Vygotskian Approach in American Early Childhood and Primary Classrooms," Geneva, Switzerland: International Bureau of Education, 2001, 36-38.

	Vygotsky		**Piaget**	
Sociocultural Context	Strong emphasis		Little emphasis	
Constructivism	Social constructivist		Cognitive constructivist	
Stages	No general stages of development proposed		Strong emphasis on stages (sensorimotor, preoperational, concrete operational, and formal operational)	
Key Processes	Zone of proximal development, language, dialogue, tools of the culture		Schema, assimilation, accommodation, operations, conservation, classification	
Role of Language	A major role; language plays a powerful role in shaping thought		Language has a minimal role; cognition primarily directs language	
View on Education	Education plays a central role, helping children learn the tools of the culture		Education merely refines the child's cognitive skills that have already emerged	
Teaching Implications	Teacher is a facilitator and guide, not a director; establish many opportunities for children to learn with the teacher and more-skilled peers		Also views teacher as a facilitator and guide, not a director; provide support for children to explore their world and discover knowledge	

FIGURE **9**

COMPARISON OF VYGOTSKY'S AND PIAGET'S THEORIES

(*Left*) A.R. Lauria /Dr. Michael Cole, Laboratory of Human Cognition, University of California, San Diego; (*right*) Bettmann/Getty Images

explore their world and discover knowledge. The main implication of Vygotsky's theory for teaching is that students need many opportunities to learn with the teacher and more-skilled peers. In both Piaget's and Vygotsky's theories, teachers serve as facilitators and guides, rather than as directors and molders of learning. Figure 9 compares Vygotsky's and Piaget's theories. As indicated in Figure 9, among the factors that Vygotsky emphasized more than Piaget are the sociocultural context, education, and language.

Criticisms of Vygotsky's theory also have surfaced. Some critics point out that Vygotsky was not specific enough about age-related changes. Another criticism is that Vygotsky did not adequately describe how changes in socioemotional capabilities contribute to cognitive development (Goncu & Gauvain, 2012). Yet another criticism is that he overemphasized the role of language in thinking. Also, his emphasis on collaboration and guidance has potential pitfalls. Might facilitators be too helpful in some cases, as when a parent becomes overbearing and controlling? Further, some children might become lazy and expect help when they could have done something on their own.

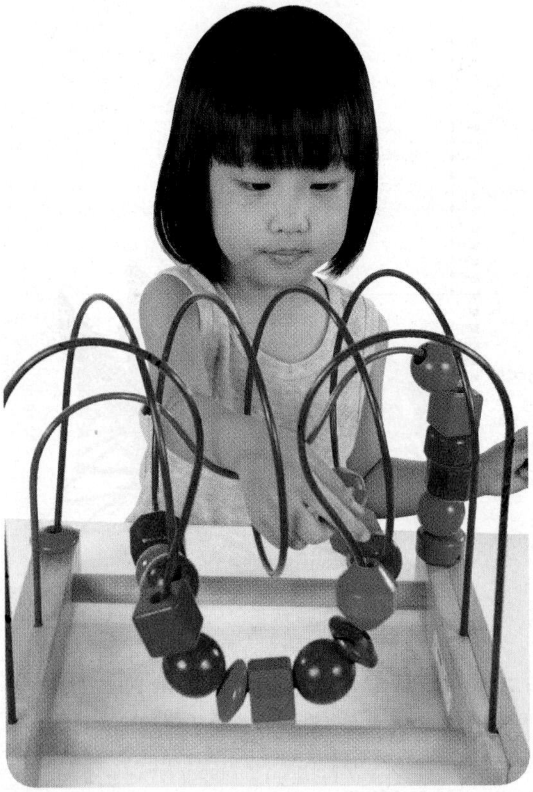

INFORMATION PROCESSING

Piaget's and Vygotsky's theories provided important ideas about how young children think and how their thinking changes. More recently, the information-processing approach has generated research that illuminates how children process information during the preschool years (Braithwaite & Siegler, 2018; Gordon & others, 2020). What are the limitations and advances in young children's ability to pay attention to the environment, to remember, to develop strategies and solve problems, and to understand their own mental processes and those of others?

Attention   Recall that *attention* is defined as the focusing of mental resources on select information. The child's ability to pay attention improves significantly during the preschool years (Posner, 2018; Wu & Scerif, 2018). Toddlers wander around, shift attention from one activity to another, and seem to spend little time focusing on any one object or event. By comparison, the preschool child might be observed watching television for a half hour or longer.

What are some advances in children's attention in early childhood?

Kiankhoon/iStock/Getty Images

Young children especially make advances in two aspects of attention—executive attention and sustained attention (Rothbart & Posner, 2015). **Executive attention** involves action planning, allocating attention to goals, error detection and compensation, monitoring progress on tasks, and dealing with novel or difficult circumstances (McClelland & others, 2017). In a recent study, children's executive attention was a good predictor of their self-regulation (Tiego & others, 2020). **Sustained attention** is focused and extended engagement with an object, task, event, or other aspect of the environment (Kamza & others, 2019; Xie, Mallin, & Richards, 2018, 2019). Sustained attention also is called *vigilance* (Benitez & others, 2017). Research indicates that although older children and adolescents show increases in vigilance, it is during the preschool years that individuals show the greatest increase in vigilance (Rothbart & Posner, 2015).

Mary Rothbart and Maria Gartstein (2008, p. 332) explained why advances in executive and sustained attention are so important in early childhood:

> The development of the . . . executive attention system supports the rapid increases in effortful control in the toddler and preschool years. Increases in attention are due, in part, to advances in comprehension and language development. As children are better able to understand their environment, this increased appreciation of their surroundings helps them to sustain attention for longer periods of time.

In at least two ways, however, the preschool child's control of attention is still deficient:

- *Salient versus relevant dimensions.* Preschool children are likely to pay attention to stimuli that stand out, or are *salient,* even when those stimuli are not relevant to solving a problem or performing a task. For example, if a flashy, attractive clown presents the directions for solving a problem, preschool children are likely to pay more attention to the clown than to the directions. After the age of 6 or 7, children attend more efficiently to the dimensions of the task that are relevant, such as the directions for solving a problem. This change reflects a shift to cognitive control of attention, so that children behave less impulsively and reflect more.

- *Planfulness.* When experimenters ask children to judge whether two complex pictures are the same, preschool children tend to use a haphazard comparison strategy, not examining all of the details before making a judgment. By comparison, elementary-school-age children are more likely to systematically compare the details across the pictures, one detail at a time (Vurpillot, 1968) (see Figure 10).

In Central European countries such as Hungary, kindergarten children participate in exercises designed to improve their attention (Mills & Mills, 2000; Posner & Rothbart, 2007). For example, in one eye-contact exercise, the teacher sits in the center of a circle of children and each child is required to catch the teacher's eye before being permitted to leave the group. In other exercises created to improve attention, teachers have children participate in stop-go activities during which they have to listen for a specific signal, such as a drumbeat or an exact number of rhythmic beats, before stopping the activity.

Computer exercises recently have been developed to improve children's attention (Jaeggi, Berman, & Jonides, 2009; Rothbart & Posner, 2015). For example, one study revealed that five days of computer exercises that involved learning how to use a joystick, working memory, and conflict resolution skills improved the attention of 4- to 6-year-old children (Rueda, Posner, & Rothbart, 2005). Although not commercially available, further information about computer exercises for improving children's attention can be found at www.teach-the-brain.org/learn/attention/index.

The ability of preschool children to control and sustain their attention is related to a number of positive academic outcomes. For example, a study of more than 1,000 children revealed that their ability to sustain their attention at 54 months of age was linked to their school readiness (which included achievement and language skills) (NICHD Early Child Care Research Network, 2005). In another study, the ability to focus attention better at age 5 was linked to a higher level of school achievement at age 9 (Razza, Martin, & Brooks-Gunn, 2012). Also, a study found that preschoolers' sustained attention was linked to a greater likelihood of completing college by 25 years of age (McClelland & others, 2013).

Memory   *Memory*—the retention of information over time—is a central process in children's cognitive development. Most of a young infant's memories are fragile and, for the most part,

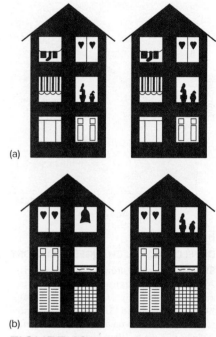

(a)

(b)

FIGURE **10**

THE PLANFULNESS OF ATTENTION. In one study, children were given pairs of houses to examine, like the ones shown here (Vurpillot, 1968). For three pairs of houses, what was in the windows was identical (*a*). For the other three pairs, the windows had different items in them (*b*). By filming the reflection in the children's eyes, researchers could determine what they were looking at, how long they looked, and the sequence of their eye movements. Children under 6 examined only a fragmentary portion of each display and made their judgments on the basis of insufficient information. By contrast, older children scanned the windows in more detailed ways and were more accurate in their judgments of which windows were identical.

executive attention Involves action planning, allocating attention to goals, error detection and compensation, monitoring progress on tasks, and dealing with novel or difficult circumstances.

sustained attention Focused and extended engagement with an object, task, event, or other aspect of the environment.

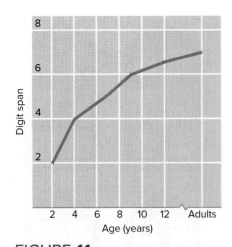

FIGURE 11

DEVELOPMENTAL CHANGES IN MEMORY SPAN. In one study, from 2 years of age to 7 years of age children's memory span increased from 2 digits to 5 digits (Dempster, 1981). Between 7 and 13 years of age, memory span had increased on average only another 2 digits, to 7 digits. *What factors might contribute to the increase in memory span during childhood?*

short-term memory The memory component in which individuals retain information for up to 30 seconds, assuming there is no rehearsal of the information.

short-lived—except for the memory of perceptual-motor actions, which can be substantial (Bauer, 2018). Thus, we saw that to understand the infant's capacity to remember, we need to distinguish *implicit memory* from *explicit memory*. Explicit memory itself, however, comes in many forms (Radvansky, 2018). One distinction involves relatively permanent or long-term memory versus short-term memory.

Short-Term Memory   In **short-term memory**, individuals retain information for up to 30 seconds if there is no rehearsal of the information. Using rehearsal (repeating information after it has been presented), we can keep information in short-term memory for a much longer period. One method of assessing short-term memory is the memory-span task. You hear a short list of stimuli—usually digits—presented at a rapid pace (one per second, for example). Then you are asked to repeat the digits.

Research with the memory-span task suggests that short-term memory increases during early childhood. For example, in one investigation memory span increased from about 2 digits in 2- to 3-year-old children to about 5 digits in 7-year-old children, yet between 7 and 13 years of age memory span increased by only 2 more digits (Dempster, 1981) (see Figure 11). Keep in mind, though, that memory span varies from one individual to another.

Why does memory span change with age? Rehearsal of information is important; older children rehearse the digits more than younger children do. Speed—especially the speed with which memory items can be identified—and efficiency of processing information are important, too (Schneider, 2011).

The speed-of-processing explanation highlights a key point in the information-processing perspective: The speed with which a child processes information is an important aspect of the child's cognitive abilities, and there is abundant evidence that the speed with which many cognitive tasks are completed improves dramatically across the childhood years (Rose, Feldman, & Jankowski, 2015). A recent study found that myelination (the process by which the sheath that encases axons helps electrical signals travel faster down the axon) in a number of brain areas was linked to young children's processing speed (Chevalier & others, 2015).

How Accurate Are Young Children's Long-Term Memories?   While toddlers' short-term memory span increases during the early childhood years, their memory also becomes more accurate. In contrast with short-term memory, *long-term memory* is a relatively permanent type of memory that stores huge amounts of information for a long time. Young children can remember a great deal of information over a long period of time if they are given appropriate cues and prompts (Bruck & Ceci, 2012). Increasingly, young children are even being allowed to testify in court, especially if they are the sole witnesses to abuse, a crime, and so forth (Andrews, Ahern, & Lamb, 2017; Brown & Lamb, 2020). Several factors can influence the accuracy of a young child's memory (Bruck & Ceci, 1999):

- *There are age differences in children's susceptibility to suggestion.* Preschoolers are more suggestible to suggestion than are older children and adults (Lehman & others, 2010). For example, preschool children are more susceptible to believing misleading or incorrect information given after an event (Ghetti & Alexander, 2004). Despite these differences among various age groups, there is still concern about the reaction of older children when they are subjected to suggestive interviews (Ahern, Kowalski, & Lamb, 2018; Peixoto & others, 2017).

- *There are individual differences in susceptibility.* Some preschoolers are highly resistant to interviewers' suggestions, whereas others immediately succumb to the slightest suggestion (Ceci, Hritz, & Royer, 2016).

- *Interviewing techniques can produce substantial distortions in children's reports about highly salient events.* Children are suggestible not just about peripheral details but also about the central aspects of an event (Andrews & Lamb, 2020). In some cases, children's false reports can be tinged with sexual connotations. In laboratory studies, young children have made false claims about "silly events" that involved body contact (such as "Did the nurse lick your knee?" or "Did she blow in your ear?"). A significant number of preschool children have falsely reported that someone touched their private parts, kissed them, and hugged them, when these events clearly did not happen in the research. Nonetheless, young children are capable of recalling much that is relevant about an event (Lamb & others, 2015). Young children are more likely to accurately recall information about an event if the interviewer has a neutral tone, there is limited use of misleading questions, and there is no motivation for the child to make a false report (Principe, Greenhoot, & Ceci, 2014). Also, a recent research review concluded that interviewer support increases children's memory accuracy (Saywitz & others, 2019).

In sum, whether a young child's eyewitness testimony is accurate or not may depend on a number of factors such as the type, number, and intensity of the suggestive techniques the child has experienced (Lamb & others, 2015). It appears that the reliability of young children's reports has as much to do with the skills and motivation of the interviewer as with any natural limitations on young children's memory (Ahern, VanMeter, & Lamb, 2018; Andrews & Lamb, 2017; Ceci, Hritz, & Royer, 2016).

Autobiographical Memory   Another aspect of long-term memory that has been extensively studied in research on children's development is autobiographical memory (Bauer, 2018; Bauer & others, 2017; de la Mata & others, 2019). *Autobiographical memory* involves memory of significant events and experiences in one's life. You are engaging in autobiographical memory when you answer questions such as: Who was your first-grade teacher and what was s/he like? What is the most traumatic event that happened to you as a child?

During the preschool years, young children's memories increasingly take on more autobiographical characteristics (Bauer, 2018; Bauer & Larkina, 2016). In some areas, such as remembering a story, a movie, a song, or an interesting event or experience, young children have been shown to have reasonably good memories. From 3 to 5 years of age, they (1) increasingly remember events as occurring at a specific time and location, such as "on my birthday at Chuck E. Cheese's last year" and (2) include more elements that are rich in detail in their narratives (Bauer, 2013). In one study, children went from including four descriptive items per event at 3½ years of age to 12 such items at 6 years of age (Fivush & Haden, 1997). Also, a recent study of 3- to 6-year-olds found that the volume of their autobiographical memories was linked to the volume of their self-knowledge (Ross, Hutchison, & Cunningham, 2020).

Executive Function
Recently, increasing attention has been given to the development of children's **executive function,** an umbrella-like concept that consists of a number of higher-level cognitive processes linked to the development of the brain's prefrontal cortex (Albert & others, 2020; McCoy, 2019). Executive function involves managing one's thoughts to engage in goal-directed behavior and self-control (Bell & Garcia Meza, 2020; Distefano & others, 2018; McClelland, Cameron, & Alonso, 2020). Earlier in this chapter, we described the recent interest in *executive attention*, which comes under the umbrella of executive function.

In early childhood, executive function especially involves developmental advances in cognitive inhibition (such as inhibiting a strong tendency that is incorrect), cognitive flexibility (such as shifting attention to another item or topic), goal-setting (such as sharing a toy or mastering a skill like catching a ball), and delay of gratification (waiting longer to get a more attractive reward, for example) (McClelland, Cameron, & Alonso, 2020). During early childhood, the relatively stimulus-driven toddler is transformed into a child capable of flexible, goal-directed problem solving that characterizes executive function (Zelazo & Muller, 2011). In a recent study of preschool children, conditions of socioeconomic disadvantage exerted a stressful influence on parent-child interactions and in turn on young children's emergent executive function skills (Baker & Brooks-Gunn, 2020).

Researchers have found that advances in executive function during the preschool years are linked with math skills, language development, school readiness, and attention (Blair, 2017; Blankenship & others, 2019; Hawes & others, 2019; Liu & others, 2018). A recent study revealed that executive function skills predicted mathematical gains in kindergarten (Fuhs & others, 2014). In another study of low-income families in Ghana, children's executive function assessed at 5 years of age predicted higher literacy and math skills across the next two years (Wolf & McCoy, 2019). Further, a recent study found that young children who showed delayed development of executive function had a lower level of school readiness (Willoughby & others, 2017). Also, a recent study of preschool children indicated that a lower level of executive function was associated with inattention and hyperactivity (Landis & others, 2020). And another recent study revealed that a lower level of executive function in preschool children was linked to the new onset and worsening of attention deficit hyperactivity disorder and depression at 6 to 12 years of age (Hawkey & others, 2018).

executive function An umbrella-like concept that consists of a number of higher-level cognitive processes linked to the development of the brain's prefrontal cortex. Executive function involves managing one's thoughts to engage in goal-directed behavior and to exercise self-control.

How did Walter Mischel and his colleagues study young children's delay of gratification? In their research, what later developmental outcomes were linked to the preschoolers' ability to delay gratification?
Amy Kiley Photography

Walter Mischel and his colleagues (Berman & others, 2013; Mischel, 2014; Mischel, Cantor, & Feldman, 1996; Mischel & Moore, 1980; Mischel & others, 2011; Schlam & others, 2013; Zayas, Mischel, & Pandey, 2014) have conducted a number of studies involving delay of gratification among young children. One way they assess delay of gratification is to place a young child alone in a room with an alluring marshmallow that is within reach. The children are told that they can either ring a bell at any time and eat the marshmallow or wait until the experimenter returns and then get two marshmallows. Among the young children who were able to wait for the experimenter to return, what did they do to help them wait? They engaged in a number of strategies to distract their attention from the marshmallows, including singing songs, picking their noses, or doing other things to keep from looking at the marshmallows. Mischel and his colleagues labeled these strategies "cool thoughts" (that is, doing non-marshmallow-related thoughts and activities), whereas they said that young children who looked at the marshmallow were engaging in "hot thoughts." The young children who engaged in cool thoughts were more likely to eat the marshmallow later or wait until the experimenter returned to the room.

In longitudinal research, Mischel and his colleagues have found that the preschool children who were able to delay gratification became more academically successful, had higher SAT scores and higher grade point averages at the end of college, and coped more effectively with stress as adolescents and emerging adults (Mischel, 2014). And as adults, they made more money in their career, were more law-abiding, were likely to have a lower body mass index, and were happier than individuals who were unable to delay gratification as preschoolers (Mischel, 2014; Moffitt, 2012; Moffitt & others, 2011; Schlam & others, 2013). Although the ability to delay gratification in preschool was linked to academic success and coping in adolescence and competence in adulthood, Mischel (2014) emphasizes that adolescents and adults can improve their ability to delay gratification.

Are young children less likely to delay gratification in the twenty-first century than in the twentieth century? Recent research examined this question about possible cohort effects (Carlson & others, 2018). In this research, the data from the original study in the 1960s as well as data from the 1980s and 2000s were analyzed. Young children in the 2000s waited an average of 2 minutes longer than their counterparts in the 1960s and 1 minute longer than those in the 1980s. This increase in delay of gratification in recent years likely is due to increases in symbolic thought, technological advances, more widely attended early childhood education programs, and public attention to the importance of children developing higher-level skills such as self-control.

What are some predictors of young children's executive function? Parenting and teaching practices are linked to children's development of executive function (Bernier & others, 2015; Cheng & others, 2018). For example, several studies have linked greater use of verbal scaffolding by parents (providing age-appropriate support during cognitive tasks) to children's more advanced executive function (Bibok, Carpendale, & Muller, 2009; Hammond & others, 2012). Also, a study revealed that secure attachment to mothers during the toddler years was linked to a higher level of executive function at 5 to 6 years of age (Bernier & others, 2015). In another study, higher parental education predicted superior executive function in children, whereas harsh parenting forecast lower executive function in children (Halse & others, 2019). Also, researchers have discovered that fathers' autonomy support improved young children's executive function (Meuwissen & Carlson, 2018). And a recent study indicated that teachers who conducted a six-week small-group training program focusing on mindfulness and reflection improved young children's executive function more than no intervention, but a literacy training program was as effective as the mindfulness/reflection program in improving their executive function (Zelazo & others, 2018).

Other predictors of better executive function include higher socioeconomic status (Last & others, 2019); some aspects of language, including vocabulary size, verbal labeling, and bilingualism (Anton, Carreiras, & Dunabeitia, 2019; Bell, Wolfe, & Adkins, 2007; Nesbitt, Farran, & Fuhs, 2015); imagination (generating novel ideas, for example) (White & Carlson, 2016); cultural background (Asian children, especially urban Chinese and Korean children, show better executive function than U.S. children) (Lan & others, 2011; Sabbagh & others, 2006); and fewer sleep problems (Friedman & others, 2009).

Some developmental psychologists use their training in areas such as cognitive development to pursue careers in applied areas. To read about the work of Helen Hadani, an individual who has followed this path, see the *Connecting with Careers* profile.

Helen Hadani, Ph.D., Developmental Psychologist, Toy Designer, and Associate Director of Research for the Center for Childhood Creativity

Helen Hadani obtained a Ph.D. in developmental psychology from Stanford University. As a graduate student at Stanford, she worked part-time for Hasbro Toys and Apple testing children's software and other computer products for young children. Her first job after graduate school was with Zowie Intertainment, which was subsequently bought by LEGO. In her work as a toy designer there, Helen conducted experiments and focus groups at different stages of a toy's development, and she also studied the age-effectiveness of each toy. In Helen's words, "Even in a toy's most primitive stage of development . . . you see children's creativity in responding to challenges, their satisfaction when a problem is solved or simply their delight in having fun" (Schlegel, 2000, p. 50).

More recently, she began working with the Bay Area Discovery Museum's Center for Childhood Creativity (CCC) in Sausalito, California, an education-focused think tank that pioneers new research, thought-leadership, and teacher training programs that advance creative thinking in all children. Helen is currently the Associate Director of Research for the CCC.

Helen Hadani has worked as a toy designer and currently holds a museum position that involves thinking of ways to increase children's creative thinking.
Courtesy of Helen Hadani

The Child's Theory of Mind Even young children are curious about the nature of the human mind (Bass & others, 2019; Devine & Hughes, 2019; Oktay-Gur, Schultz, & Rakoczy, 2018; Wellman, 2011, 2015). They have a **theory of mind,** which refers to awareness of one's own mental processes and the mental processes of others. Studies of theory of mind view the child as "a thinker who is trying to explain, predict, and understand people's thoughts, feelings, and utterances" (Harris, 2006, p. 847).

Developmental Changes Children's theory of mind changes as they develop through childhood (Wellman, 2015). Although whether infants have a theory of mind continues to be questioned by some (Rakoczy, 2012), the consensus is that some changes occur quite early in development, as we will see next (Scott & Baillargeon, 2017).

From 18 months to 3 years of age, children begin to understand three mental states:

- *Perceptions.* By 2 years of age, a child recognizes that another person will see what's in front of her own eyes instead of what's in front of the child's eyes (Lempers, Flavell, & Flavell, 1977), and by 3 years of age, the child realizes that looking leads to knowing what's inside a container (Pratt & Bryant, 1990).

- *Emotions.* The child can distinguish between positive (for example, happy) and negative (for example, sad) emotions. A child might say, "Tommy feels bad."

- *Desires.* All humans have some sort of desires. But when do children begin to recognize that someone else's desires may differ from their own? Toddlers recognize that if people want something, they will try to get it. For instance, a child might say, "I want my mommy."

Two- to three-year-olds understand the way that desires are related to actions and to simple emotions. For example, they understand that people will search for what they want and that if they obtain it, they are likely to feel happy, but if they don't, they will keep searching for it and are likely to feel sad or angry (Wellman & Woolley, 1990). Children also refer to desires earlier and more frequently than they refer to cognitive states such as thinking and knowing (Bartsch & Wellman, 1995; Wellman, 2015).

One of the landmark developments in understanding others' desires is recognizing that someone else may have different desires from one's own (Doherty, 2008; Wellman, 2015).

theory of mind Awareness of one's own mental processes and the mental processes of others.

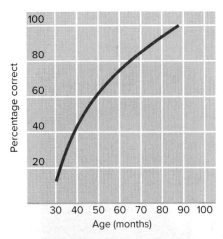

FIGURE 12

DEVELOPMENTAL CHANGES IN FALSE-BELIEF PERFORMANCE. False-belief performance—the child's understanding that a person may have a false belief that contradicts reality—dramatically increases from 2½ years of age through the middle of the elementary school years. In a summary of the results of many studies, 2½-year-olds gave incorrect responses about 80 percent of the time (Wellman, Cross, & Watson, 2001). At 3 years, 8 months, they were correct about 50 percent of the time, and after that, they gave increasingly correct responses.

Eighteen-month-olds understand that their own food preferences may not match the preferences of others—they will give an adult the food to which she says "Yummy!" even if the food is something that the infants detest (Repacholi & Gopnik, 1997). As they get older, they can verbalize that they themselves do not like something but an adult might (Flavell & others, 1992).

Between the ages of 3 and 5, children come to understand that the mind can represent objects and events accurately or inaccurately (Rhodes & Brandone, 2014; Tompkins & others, 2017). The realization that people can have *false beliefs*—beliefs that are not true—develops in a majority of children by the time they are 5 years old (Wellman, Cross, & Watson, 2001) (see Figure 12). This point is often described as a pivotal one in understanding the mind—recognizing that beliefs are not just mapped directly into the mind from the surrounding world, but that different people can also have different, and sometimes incorrect, beliefs (Gelman, 2009; Grosso & others, 2019; Tompkins, Farrar, & Montgomery, 2019). In a classic false-belief task, young children were shown a Band-Aids box and asked what was inside (Jenkins & Astington, 1996). To the children's surprise, the box actually contained pencils. When asked what a child who had never seen the box would think was inside, 3-year-olds typically responded, "Pencils." However, the 4- and 5-year-olds, grinning in anticipation of the false beliefs of other children who had not seen what was inside the box, were more likely to say "Band-Aids."

In a similar task, children are told a story about Sally and Anne: Sally places a toy in a basket and then leaves the room (see Figure 13). In her absence, Anne takes the toy from the basket and places it in a box. Children are asked where Sally will look for the toy when she returns. The major finding is that 3-year-olds tend to fail false-belief tasks, saying that Sally will look in the box (even though Sally could not have known that the toy had been moved to this new location). Four-year-olds and older children tend to perform the task correctly, saying that Sally will have a "false belief"—she will think the object is in the basket, even though that belief is now false. The conclusion from these studies is that children younger than 4 years old do not understand that it is possible to have a false belief.

It is only beyond the preschool years—at approximately 5 to 7 years of age—that children have a deepening appreciation of the mind itself rather than just an understanding of mental states (Lagattuta & others, 2015). For example, they begin to recognize that people's behaviors do not necessarily reflect their thoughts and feelings (Flavell, Green, & Flavell, 1993). Not until middle and late childhood do children see the mind as an active constructor of knowledge or a processing center (Flavell, Green, & Flavell, 1998) and move from understanding that beliefs can be false to realizing that the same event can be open to multiple interpretations (Carpendale & Chandler, 1996). For example, in one study, children saw an ambiguous line drawing (for example, a drawing that could be seen as either a duck or a rabbit); one puppet told the child she believed the drawing was a duck while another puppet told the child he believed the drawing was a rabbit (see Figure 14). Before the age of 7, children said that there was one right answer and that it was not okay for the two puppets to have different opinions.

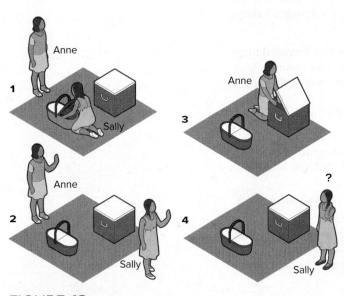

FIGURE 13

THE SALLY AND ANNE FALSE-BELIEF TASK. In the false-belief task, the skit above in which Sally has a basket and Anne has a box is shown to children. Sally places a toy in her basket and then leaves. While Sally is gone and can't watch, Anne removes the toy from Sally's basket and places it in her box. Sally then comes back and the children are asked where they think Sally will look for her toy. Children are said to "pass" the false-belief task if they understand that Sally looks in her basket first before realizing the toy isn't there.

Individual Differences and Factors that Influence Theory of Mind As in other developmental research, there are individual differences in the ages when children reach certain milestones in their theory of mind (Devine & Hughes, 2018). For example, *executive function,* which describes several functions discussed earlier in this chapter, such as planning and inhibition, that are important for flexible, future-oriented behavior, also is connected to theory of mind development (Benson & Sabbagh, 2017). Children who perform better at such executive function tasks show a better understanding of theory of mind (Benson & Sabbagh, 2017). For example, in one study of 3- to 5-year-old children, earlier development of executive function predicted theory of mind performance, especially on false belief tasks (Doenyas, Yavuz, & Selcuk, 2018).

Language development also likely plays a prominent role in the increasingly reflective nature of theory of mind as children go through early, middle, and late childhood (Meins & others, 2013). Researchers have found that differences in children's language skills predict performance on theory of mind tasks (Hughes & Devine, 2015).

Among other factors that influence children's theory of mind development are advances in prefrontal cortex functioning (Powers, Chavez, & Heatherton, 2016), engaging in make-believe play (Kavanaugh, 2006), and various aspects of social interaction (Hughes, Devine, & Wang, 2018). Among the social interaction factors that advance children's theory of mind are being securely attached to parents who engage children in mental state talk ("That's a good thought you have" or "Can you tell what he's thinking?") (Laranjo & others, 2010), having older siblings and friends who engage in mental state talk (Hughes & others, 2010), and living in a higher-socioeconomic-status family (Devine & Hughes, 2018). A recent study also found that parental mental state talk advanced preschool children's theory of mind (Devine & Hughes, 2019). Further, researchers have found that children who have an advanced theory of mind are more popular with their peers and have better social skills in peer relations (Peterson & others, 2016; Slaughter & others, 2014).

Another individual difference in understanding the mind involves autism (Jones & others, 2018). Researchers have found that children with autism have difficulty developing a theory of mind, especially in relation to understanding others' beliefs and emotions (Berenguer & others, 2018; Garon, Smith, & Bryson, 2018). A recent study found that theory of mind predicted the severity of autism in children (Hoogenhout & Malcolm-Smith, 2017). Thus, it is not surprising that autistic children have difficulty in interactions with others.

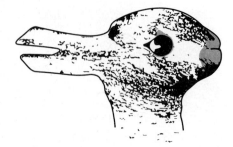

FIGURE 14
AMBIGUOUS LINE DRAWING

Review Connect Reflect

 Describe three views of the cognitive changes that occur in early childhood.

Review

- What characterizes Piaget's stage of preoperational thought?
- What does Vygotsky's theory suggest about how preschool children construct knowledge?
- What are some important ways in which information processing changes during early childhood? What characterizes children's theory of mind?

Connect

- In this section, you learned that children who frequently engage in pretend play perform better on theory of mind tasks. During which substage of Piaget's preoperational stage do children begin to engage in pretend play? What mental ability does it signify?

Reflect *Your Own Personal Journey of Life*

- If you were the parent of a 4-year-old child, would you try to train the child to develop conservation skills? Explain.

3 Language Development

LG3 Summarize how language develops in early childhood.

| Understanding Phonology and Morphology | Changes in Syntax and Semantics | Advances in Pragmatics | Young Children's Literacy |

Toddlers move rather quickly from producing two-word utterances to creating three-, four-, and five-word combinations. Between 2 and 3 years of age, they begin the transition from saying simple sentences that express a single proposition to saying complex sentences.

As young children learn the special features of their own language, there are extensive regularities in how they acquire that particular language (Genetti, 2019). For example, all children learn the prepositions *on* and *in* before other prepositions. Children learning other languages, such as Russian or Chinese, also acquire the particular features of those languages in a consistent order.

The greatest poem ever known
Is one all poets have outgrown;
The poetry, innate, untold,
Of being only four years old.

—CHRISTOPHER MORLEY
American novelist, 20th century

UNDERSTANDING PHONOLOGY AND MORPHOLOGY

During the preschool years, most children gradually become more sensitive to the sounds of spoken words and become increasingly capable of producing all the sounds of their language (Kelly & others, 2019). By the time children are 3 years of age, they can produce all the vowel

This is a wug.

Now there is another one. There are two of them. There are two _____.

FIGURE **15**

STIMULI IN BERKO'S STUDY OF YOUNG CHILDREN'S UNDERSTANDING OF MORPHOLOGICAL RULES. In Jean Berko's (1958) study, young children were presented cards, such as this one with a "wug" on it. Then the children were asked to supply the missing word; in supplying the missing word, they had to say it correctly, too. "Wugs" is the correct response here.
Gleason, Jean Berko. "The Child's Learning of English Morphology," *Word* 14, 1958, 154. Copyright 1958 by Jean Berko Gleason. All rights reserved. Used with permission.

> **developmental connection**
> Language
> The average 2-year-old can speak about 200 words. Connect to "Cognitive Development in Infancy."

fast mapping A process that helps to explain how young children learn the connection between a word and its referent so quickly.

sounds and most of the consonant sounds (Menn & Stoel-Gammon, 2009). They recognize the sounds in word combinations such as "Merry go round" before they can produce them.

As children move beyond two-word utterances, they demonstrate a knowledge of morphology rules (Mithun, 2019). Children begin using the plural and possessive forms of nouns (such as *dogs* and *dog's*). They put appropriate endings on verbs (such as *-s* when the subject is third-person singular and *-ed* for the past tense). They use prepositions (such as *in* and *on*), articles (such as *a* and *the*), and various forms of the verb *to be* (such as "I *was* going to the store"). Some of the best evidence for changes in children's use of morphological rules occurs in their overgeneralization of the rules, as when a preschool child says "foots" instead of "feet," or "goed" instead of "went."

In a classic experiment that was designed to study children's knowledge of morphological rules, such as how to make a plural, Jean Berko (1958) presented preschool children and first-grade children with cards such as the one shown in Figure 15. Children were asked to look at the card while the experimenter read aloud the words on the card. Then the children were asked to supply the missing word. This task might sound easy, but Berko was interested in the children's ability to apply the appropriate morphological rule—in this case to say "wugs" with the *z* sound that indicates the plural.

Although the children's answers were not perfect, they were much better than chance. What makes Berko's study impressive is that most of the words were made up for the experiment. Thus, the children could not base their responses on remembering past instances of hearing the words. That they could make the plurals or past tenses of words they had never heard before was proof that they knew the morphological rules.

CHANGES IN SYNTAX AND SEMANTICS

Preschool children also learn and apply rules of syntax (Tieu & others, 2018). They show a growing mastery of complex rules for how words should be ordered. Consider *wh-* questions, such as "Where is Daddy going?" or "What is that boy doing?" To ask these questions properly, the child must know two important differences between *wh-* questions and affirmative statements (for instance, "Daddy is going to work" and "That boy is waiting for the school bus"). First, a *wh-* word must be added at the beginning of the sentence. Second, the auxiliary verb must be inverted—that is, exchanged with the subject of the sentence. Young children learn quite early where to put the *wh-* word, but they take much longer to learn the auxiliary-inversion rule. Thus, preschool children might ask, "Where Daddy is going?" and "What that boy is doing?"

Gains in semantics also characterize early childhood (Indefrey, 2019). Vocabulary development is dramatic (Thornton, 2017). Some experts have concluded that between 18 months and 6 years of age, young children learn approximately one new word every waking hour (Gelman & Kalish, 2006). By the time they enter first grade, it is estimated that children know about 14,000 words (Clark, 1993).

Why can children learn so many new words so quickly? One possibility is **fast mapping,** which involves children's ability to make an initial connection between a word and its referent after only limited exposure to the word (Jackson & others, 2019). Researchers have found that exposure to words on multiple occasions over several days results in more successful word learning than the same number of exposures in a single day (Childers & Tomasello, 2002). Recent research using eye-tracking found that even 15-month-old infants fast map words (Puccini & Liszkowski, 2012). Also, fast mapping promotes deeper understanding of word meaning, such as learning where the word can apply and its nuances.

What are some important aspects of how word learning optimally occurs? Following are six key principles in young children's vocabulary development (Harris, Golinkoff, & Hirsh-Pasek, 2011):

1. *Children learn the words they hear most often.* They learn the words that they encounter when interacting with parents, teachers, siblings, and peers, as well as words that they hear when books are read aloud to them. They especially benefit from encountering words that they do not know.

2. *Children learn words for things and events that interest them.* Parents and teachers can direct young children to experience words in contexts that interest the children; playful peer interactions are especially helpful in this regard.

3. *Children learn words better in responsive and interactive contexts than in passive contexts.* Children who experience turn-taking opportunities, joint focusing experiences, and positive,

sensitive socializing contexts with adults encounter the scaffolding necessary for optimal word learning. They learn words less effectively when they are passive learners.

4. *Children learn words best in contexts that are meaningful.* Young children learn new words more effectively when new words are encountered in integrated contexts rather than as isolated facts.

5. *Children learn words best when they access clear information about word meaning.* Children whose parents and teachers are sensitive to words the children might not understand and provide support and elaboration with hints about word meaning learn words better than those whose parents and teachers quickly state a new word and don't monitor whether children understand its meaning.

6. *Children learn words best when grammar and vocabulary are considered.* Children who experience a large number of words and diversity in verbal stimulation develop a richer vocabulary and better understanding of grammar. In many cases, vocabulary and grammar development are connected.

What are some strategies parents can adopt to increase their young children's vocabulary development?
Thanasis Zovoilis/Moment/Getty Images

ADVANCES IN PRAGMATICS

Changes in pragmatics, the appropriate use of language in different contexts, also characterize young children's language development (Demuth, 2019; Garnham, 2019). A 6-year-old is simply a much better conversationalist than a 2-year-old is. What are some of the improvements in pragmatics during the preschool years?

Young children begin to engage in extended discourse (Akhtar & Herold, 2008). For example, they learn culturally specific rules of conversation and politeness and become sensitive to the need to adapt their speech in different settings. Their developing linguistic skills and increasing ability to take the perspective of others contribute to their generation of more competent narratives.

As children get older, they become increasingly able to talk about things that are not here (Grandma's house, for example) and not now (what happened to them yesterday or might happen tomorrow, for example). A preschool child can tell you what she wants for lunch tomorrow, something that would not have been possible at the two-word stage of language development.

Around 4 to 5 years of age, children learn to change their speech style to suit the situation. For example, even 4-year-old children speak to a 2-year-old differently from the way they speak to a same-aged peer; they use shorter sentences with the 2-year-old. They also speak differently to an adult and to a same-aged peer, using more polite and formal language with the adult (Shatz & Gelman, 1973).

YOUNG CHILDREN'S LITERACY

Concern about variations in U.S. children's ability to read and write has led to a careful examination of preschool and kindergarten children's experiences, with the hope that a positive orientation toward reading and writing can be developed early in life (Bredekamp, 2020; Tompkins, 2019). Parents and teachers need to provide young children with a supportive environment for developing literacy skills (Vukelich & others, 2020). Children should be active participants and be immersed in a wide range of interesting situations involving listening, talking, writing, and reading (Morrow, 2020; Reutzel & Cooter, 2019; Tompkins & Rodgers, 2020). One study revealed that children whose mothers had more education acquired more advanced emergent literacy levels than children whose mothers had less education (Korat, 2009). Another study found that literacy experiences (such as how often the child was read to), the quality of the mother's engagement with her child (such as attempts to cognitively stimulate the child), and provision of learning materials (such as age-appropriate books) were important home literacy experiences in low-income families that were linked to the children's language development in positive ways (Rodriguez & others, 2009). Instruction should be built on what children already know about oral language, reading, and writing. Further, early precursors of literacy and academic success include language skills, phonological and syntactic knowledge,

What are positive strategies for improving young children's literacy?
Ariel Skelley/Blend Images LLC

letter identification, and conceptual knowledge about print and its conventions and functions (Jalongo, 2014). Also, a recent study found that 60 minutes of physical activity per day in preschool academic contexts improved early literacy (Kirk & Kirk, 2016).

Books can be valuable in enhancing children's communication skills (Reutzel & Cooter, 2019). What are some strategies for using books effectively with preschool children? Ellen Galinsky (2010) suggests the following strategies:

- *Use books to initiate conversation with young children.* Ask them to put themselves in the book characters' places and imagine what they might be thinking or feeling.
- *Use what and why questions.* Ask young children what they think is going to happen next in a story and then to see if it occurs.
- *Encourage children to ask questions about stories.*
- *Choose some books that play with language.* Creative books on the alphabet, including those with rhymes, often interest young children.

The advances in language that take place in early childhood lay the foundation for further development in the elementary school years, as we will discuss in more detail later.

Review *Connect* Reflect

 LG3 Summarize how language develops in early childhood.

Review

- How do phonology and morphology change during early childhood?
- What characterizes young children's understanding of syntax and semantics in early childhood?
- What advances in pragmatics occur in early childhood?
- What are some effective ways to guide young children's literacy?

Connect

- In this section, you learned that children can sometimes

overgeneralize the rules for morphology. How is this different from or similar to the concept of overextension as it relates to infants' speech?

Reflect *Your Own Personal Journey of Life*

- As a parent, what could you do to improve the likelihood that your child would enter first grade with excellent literacy skills?

4 Early Childhood Education

 LG4 Evaluate different approaches to early childhood education.

Variations in Early Childhood Education

Education for Young Children Who Are Disadvantaged

Controversies in Early Childhood Education

To the teachers in a Reggio Emilia program (described in the chapter opening), preschool children are active learners who are engaged in exploring the world with their peers, constructing their knowledge of the world in collaboration with their community, and aided but not directed by their teachers. In many ways, the Reggio Emilia approach applies ideas consistent with the views of Piaget and Vygotsky that were discussed earlier in this chapter. Our exploration of early childhood education focuses on variations in programs, education for young children who are disadvantaged, and some controversies in early childhood education.

VARIATIONS IN EARLY CHILDHOOD EDUCATION

Attending preschool is rapidly becoming the norm for U.S. children. There are many variations in the way young children are educated (Bredekamp, 2020; Feeney, Moravcik, & Nolte, 2019). The foundation of early childhood education has been the child-centered kindergarten.

The Child-Centered Kindergarten Nurturing is a key aspect of the **child-centered kindergarten,** which emphasizes the education of the whole child and concern for his or her physical, cognitive, and socioemotional development (Morrison, 2020). Instruction is organized around the child's needs, interests, and learning styles. Emphasis is on the process of learning, rather than what is learned (Follari, 2019). The child-centered kindergarten honors three principles: (1) each child follows a unique developmental pattern; (2) young children learn best through firsthand experiences with people and materials; and (3) play is extremely important in the child's total development. *Experimenting, exploring, discovering, trying out, restructuring, speaking,* and *listening* are frequent activities in excellent kindergarten programs. Such programs are closely attuned to the developmental status of 4- and 5-year-old children.

The Montessori Approach Montessori schools are patterned after the educational philosophy of Maria Montessori (1870–1952), an Italian physician-turned-educator who at the beginning of the twentieth century crafted a revolutionary approach to young children's education. The **Montessori approach** is a philosophy of education in which children are given considerable freedom and spontaneity in choosing activities. They are allowed to move from one activity to another as they desire. The teacher acts as a facilitator rather than a director. The teacher shows the child how to perform intellectual activities, demonstrates interesting ways to explore curriculum materials, and offers help when the child requests it (Bahmaee, Saadatmand, & Yarmohammadian, 2016). "By encouraging children to make decisions from an early age, Montessori programs seek to develop self-regulated problem solvers who can make choices and manage their time effectively" (Hyson, Copple, & Jones, 2006, p. 14). The number of Montessori schools in the United States has expanded dramatically in recent years, from 1 school in 1959 to 355 schools in 1970 and more than 4,000 today. A study found that Latino children in low-income communities who began the school year having at-risk pre-academic and behavioral skills benefited from a Montessori public school pre-K program, ending the year scoring above national averages for school readiness (Ansari & Winsler, 2014). Also, an experimental study with young children living in high-poverty urban areas found that over a 3-year period children who were randomly assigned to Montessori programs fared better on academic achievement, social understanding, and mastery orientation than those who attended other schools (Lillard & others, 2017). And a recent study discovered that young children who attended Montessori schools displayed more creativity skills than their counterparts in traditional schools (Denervaud & others, 2019).

Some developmentalists favor the Montessori approach, but others believe that it neglects children's socioemotional development. For example, although Montessori fosters independence and the development of cognitive skills, it deemphasizes verbal interaction between the teacher and child and between peers. Montessori's critics also argue that it restricts imaginative play and that its heavy reliance on self-corrective materials may not adequately allow for creativity and for a variety of learning styles.

Developmentally Appropriate and Inappropriate Education Many educators and psychologists conclude that preschool and young elementary school children learn best through active, hands-on teaching methods such as games and dramatic play. They know that children develop at varying rates and that schools need to allow for these individual differences (Follari, 2019). They also argue that schools should focus on supporting children's socioemotional development as well as their cognitive development. Educators refer to this type of schooling as **developmentally appropriate practice (DAP),** which is based on knowledge of the typical development of children within an age span (age-appropriateness), as well as the uniqueness of the child (individual-appropriateness). DAP emphasizes the importance of creating settings that encourage active learning and reflect children's interests and capabilities (Bredekamp, 2020; Feeney, Moravcik, & Nolte, 2019). Desired outcomes for DAP include thinking critically, working cooperatively, solving problems, developing self-regulatory skills, and enjoying learning. The emphasis in DAP is on the process of learning rather than its content (Bredekamp, 2020).

Do developmentally appropriate educational practices improve young children's development? Some researchers have found that young children in developmentally appropriate classrooms are likely to have less stress, be more motivated, be more skilled socially, have better work habits, be more creative, have better language skills, and demonstrate better math skills than children in developmentally inappropriate classrooms (Hart & others, 2003). However,

Larry Page and Sergey Brin, founders of the highly successful Internet search engine Google, said that their early years at Montessori schools were a major factor in their success (International Montessori Council, 2006). During an interview with Barbara Walters, they said they learned how to be self-directed and self-starters at Montessori (ABC News, 2005). Montessori experiences encouraged them to think for themselves and allowed them the freedom to develop their own interests.
James Leynse/Corbis Historical/Getty Images

child-centered kindergarten Education that involves the whole child by considering both the child's physical, cognitive, and socioemotional development and the child's needs, interests, and learning styles.

Montessori approach An educational philosophy in which children are given considerable freedom and spontaneity in choosing activities and are allowed to move from one activity to another as they desire.

developmentally appropriate practice (DAP) Education that focuses on the typical developmental patterns of children (age-appropriateness) and the uniqueness of each child (individual-appropriateness).

(*Top*) Jeff Bezos, the CEO of Amazon who became the world's richest person in 2018, recently provided $2 billion to fund a new network of Montessori-inspired preschools in underserved communities. (*Bottom*) Shown here is a preschool program for homeless children in Washington, DC, funded by Bezos. (*Top*) Chip Somodevilla/Getty Images; (*Bottom*) Sarah L. Voisin/The Washington Post/Getty Images

What are some differences in developmentally appropriate and inappropriate practice?
Ariel Skelley/Blend Images/Getty Images

Project Head Start A government-funded program that is designed to provide children from low-income families with the opportunity to acquire the skills and experiences important for school success.

not all studies show significant positive benefits for developmentally appropriate education (Hyson, Copple, & Jones, 2006). Among the reasons it is difficult to generalize about research on developmentally appropriate education is that individual programs often vary, and developmentally appropriate education is an evolving concept. Recent changes in the concept have given more attention to sociocultural factors, to the teacher's active involvement and implementation of systematic intentions, and to the degree to which academic skills should be emphasized and how they should be taught.

EDUCATION FOR YOUNG CHILDREN WHO ARE DISADVANTAGED

For many years, U.S. children from low-income families did not receive any education before they entered first grade. Often, they began first grade already several steps behind their classmates in their readiness to learn. In the summer of 1965, the federal government began an effort to break the cycle of poverty and substandard education for young children in the United States through **Project Head Start.** It is a compensatory program designed to provide children from low-income families the opportunity to acquire the skills and experiences important for success in school (Lee, 2019; Paschall & Mastergeorge, 2018). After almost half a century, Head Start continues to be the largest federally funded program for U.S. children, with almost 1 million U.S. children enrolled annually (Hagen & Lamb-Parker, 2008). In 2007, 3 percent of Head Start children were 5 years old, 51 percent were 4 years old, 36 percent were 3 years old, and 10 percent were under 3 years of age (Administration for Children & Families, 2008).

Early Head Start was established in 1995 to serve children from birth to 3 years of age. In 2007, half of all new funds appropriated for Head Start programs were used for the expansion of Early Head Start (Burgette & others, 2017). Researchers have found positive effects for Early Head Start (Hoffman & Ewen, 2007). A recent study revealed that Early Head Start had a protective effect on risks young children might experience related to parenting stress, language development, and self-control (Ayoub, Vallotton, & Mastergeorge, 2011). Another recent study revealed language benefits for Early Head Start children (Love & others, 2013).

Head Start programs are not all created equal. One estimate is that 40 percent of the 1,400 Head Start programs are of questionable quality (Zigler & Styfco, 1994). More attention needs to be given to developing consistently high-quality Head Start programs (Lee, 2019). One individual who is strongly motivated to make Head Start a valuable learning experience for young children from disadvantaged backgrounds is Yolanda Garcia. To read about her work, see *Connecting with Careers.*

Evaluations support the positive influence of quality early childhood programs on both the cognitive and social worlds of disadvantaged young children (Chor, 2018; McCoy & others, 2016). A national evaluation of Head Start revealed that the program had a positive influence on the language and cognitive development of 3- and 4-year-olds (Puma & others, 2010). However, by the end of first grade, there were few lasting outcomes. One exception was a larger vocabulary for those who went to Head Start as 4-year-olds and better oral comprehension for those who went to Head Start as 3-year-olds. Further, in a recent study of 3-4-, 5-6-, and 8-9-year-olds, foster children who participated in Head Start programs had better cognitive, socioemotional, and health outcomes than foster children who did not participate in Head Start programs, with the positive outcomes stronger in 8-9-year-olds (Lee, 2020).

And two recent studies found that improved parenting engagement and skills were linked to the success of children in Head Start programs (Ansari & Gershoff, 2016; Roggman & others, 2016).

One-fourth of Head Start children have mothers who also participated in Head Start. In a multigenerational study, a positive influence on cognitive and socioemotional development (assessed in third grade) occurred for Head Start children whose mothers had also attended Head Start programs (when compared with Head Start children whose mothers were not in Head Start) (Chor, 2018). This result likely occurred because of improved family resources and home learning environments.

One high-quality early childhood education program (although not a Head Start program) was the Perry Preschool Project in Ypsilanti, Michigan, a two-year preschool program from 1962 to 1967 that included weekly home visits from program personnel. In analyses of the

Yolanda Garcia, Head Start Director and College Dean

Yolanda Garcia is the Director of WestEd's E3 Institute—Excellence in Early Education, a project for the Center for Child and Family Studies. She previously directed the Children's Services Department, Santa Clara County Office of Education. Her training includes two master's degrees, one in public policy and child welfare from the University of Chicago and another in education administration from San Jose State University.

Garcia has served on many national advisory committees that have resulted in improvements in the staffing of Head Start programs. Most notably, she served on the Head Start Quality Committee that recommended the development of Early Head Start and revised performance standards for Head Start programs.

Yolanda augmented her education by obtaining a doctorate from the University of San Francisco in 2011 in Leadership and Organizational Development. Currently, she is Dean of Child Development and Teacher Education for the Sonoma County College District in northern California.

Yolanda Garcia, Director of WestEd's E3 Institute, works with a child.
Courtesy of Yolanda Garcia

long-term effects of the program, adults who had been in the Perry Preschool program were compared with a control group of adults from the same background who had not received the enriched early childhood education (Schweinhart & others, 2005; Weikert, 1993). Those who had been in the Perry Preschool program had fewer teen pregnancies and higher rates of high school graduation, and at age 40 the former preschool students were more likely to be employed, own a home, and have a savings account, and less likely to have been arrested than adults in the control group.

Also, in an early childhood intervention designed to improve developmental outcomes and enhance the quality of Head Start programs in high-violence, high-crime areas of Chicago, initial assessments at the end of preschool indicated that the children involved in the intervention showed fewer behavior problems and had gains in executive function and academic achievement (Raver & others, 2008). In a recent analysis, 10 to 11 years after the intervention was finished, the children had long-term positive effects for executive function and grades but there was no evidence of long-term effects on behavioral problems (Watts & others, 2018).

CONTROVERSIES IN EARLY CHILDHOOD EDUCATION

Two current controversies in early childhood education involve (1) what the curriculum for early childhood education should be and (2) whether preschool education should be universal in the United States.

Curriculum Controversy A current controversy in early childhood education involves what the curriculum for early childhood education should be (Bredekamp, 2020; Follari, 2019; Morrison, 2020). On one side are those who advocate a child-centered, constructivist approach much like that emphasized by the National Association for the Education of Young Children (NAEYC), along the lines of developmentally appropriate practice. On the other side are those who advocate an academic, direct-instruction approach.

In practice, many high-quality early childhood education programs include both academic and constructivist approaches. Many education experts like Lilian Katz (1999), though, worry about academic approaches that place too much pressure on young children to achieve and don't provide any opportunities to actively construct knowledge. Competent

What is the curriculum controversy in early childhood education?
Ronnie Kaufman/Corbis/Getty Images

early childhood programs also should focus on cognitive development *and* socioemotional development, not exclusively on cognitive development (Feeney, Moravcik, & Nolte, 2019; Morrison, 2020).

Universal Preschool Education   Another early childhood education controversy focuses on whether preschool education should be instituted for all U.S. 4-year-old children. Publicly funded preschool programs now are present in 42 states and the District of Columbia (National Institute for Early Education Research, 2016).

Edward Zigler and his colleagues (2011) have argued that the United States should have universal preschool education. They emphasize that quality preschools prepare children for school readiness and academic success. Zigler and his colleagues (2006) cite research that shows quality preschool programs decrease the likelihood that once children go to elementary and secondary school they will be retained in a grade or drop out of school. They also point to analyses indicating that universal preschool would bring cost savings on the order of billions of dollars because of a diminished need for remedial and justice services (Karoly & Bigelow, 2005).

Critics of universal preschool education argue that the gains attributed to preschool and kindergarten education are often overstated. They especially stress that research has not proven that nondisadvantaged children benefit from attending a preschool. Thus, the critics say it is more important to improve preschool education for young children who are disadvantaged than to fund preschool education for all 4-year-old children. Some critics, especially home-schooling advocates, emphasize that young children should be educated by their parents, not by schools. Thus, controversy continues to surround questions about whether universal preschool education should be implemented.

Review *Connect* Reflect

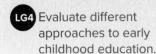 **LG4** Evaluate different approaches to early childhood education.

Review
- What are some variations in early childhood education?
- What are the main efforts to educate young children who are disadvantaged?
- What are two controversies about early childhood education?

Connect
- Earlier we discussed cross-sectional and longitudinal research designs.

Which type of research design was the Perry Preschool program?

Reflect *Your Own Personal Journey of Life*
- What type of early childhood education program would you want your child to attend? Why?

---

topical connections *looking forward*

In the next chapter, you will read about the many advances that take place during the socioemotional development of young children. The cognitive advances we discussed in this chapter, combined with the socioemotional experiences young children have in interacting with others, pave the way for social cognitive advances in understanding the self and others. Next, you will read about the continuing changes in children's physical and cognitive development in middle and late childhood. In terms of physical development, their motor skills become smoother and more coordinated. The development of their brain—especially the prefrontal cortex—provides the foundation for a number of cognitive advances, including the development of learning strategies and reading skills.

Physical and Cognitive Development in Early Childhood

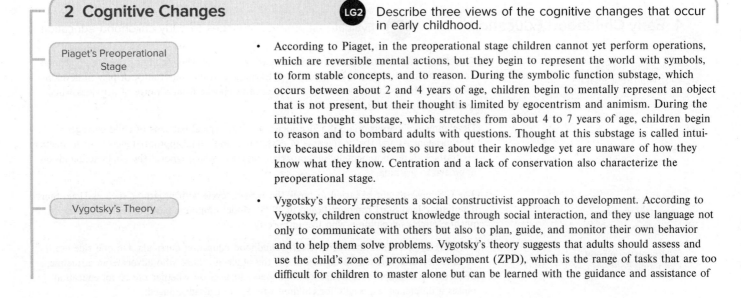

1 Physical Changes

LG1 Identify physical changes in early childhood.

Body Growth and Change

Motor and Perceptual Development

Sleep

Nutrition and Exercise

Illness and Death

- The average child grows 2½ inches in height and gains 5 to 10 pounds a year during early childhood. Growth patterns vary individually, though. Some of the brain's interior changes in early childhood are due to myelination. From 3 to 6 years of age, the most rapid growth in the brain occurs in the frontal lobes.

- Gross motor skills increase dramatically during early childhood. Children become increasingly adventuresome as their gross motor skills improve. Fine motor skills also improve substantially during early childhood. Young children also make advances in perceptual development.

- Experts recommend that young children get 11 to 13 hours of sleep each night. Most young children sleep through the night and have one daytime nap. Helping the young child slow down before bedtime often leads to less resistance in going to bed. Sleep problems in young children are linked to other problems, such as being overweight and being depressed. Disruptions in sleep in early childhood are related to less optimal adjustment in preschool.

- Too many young children in the United States are being raised on diets that are too high in fat. The child's life should be centered on activities, not meals. Other nutritional concerns include malnutrition in early childhood and the inadequate diets of many children living in poverty. Young children are not getting as much exercise as they need.

- In recent decades, vaccines have virtually eradicated many diseases that once resulted in the deaths of many young children. The disorders still most likely to be fatal for young children in the United States are cancer and cardiovascular disease, but accidents are the leading cause of death in young children. A special concern is the poor health status of many young children in low-income families. There has been a dramatic increase in deaths due to HIV/AIDS in young children in developing countries in the last decade.

2 Cognitive Changes

LG2 Describe three views of the cognitive changes that occur in early childhood.

Piaget's Preoperational Stage

Vygotsky's Theory

- According to Piaget, in the preoperational stage children cannot yet perform operations, which are reversible mental actions, but they begin to represent the world with symbols, to form stable concepts, and to reason. During the symbolic function substage, which occurs between about 2 and 4 years of age, children begin to mentally represent an object that is not present, but their thought is limited by egocentrism and animism. During the intuitive thought substage, which stretches from about 4 to 7 years of age, children begin to reason and to bombard adults with questions. Thought at this substage is called intuitive because children seem so sure about their knowledge yet are unaware of how they know what they know. Centration and a lack of conservation also characterize the preoperational stage.

- Vygotsky's theory represents a social constructivist approach to development. According to Vygotsky, children construct knowledge through social interaction, and they use language not only to communicate with others but also to plan, guide, and monitor their own behavior and to help them solve problems. Vygotsky's theory suggests that adults should assess and use the child's zone of proximal development (ZPD), which is the range of tasks that are too difficult for children to master alone but can be learned with the guidance and assistance of adults or more-skilled children. The theory also suggests that adults and peers should teach through scaffolding, which involves changing the level of support over the course of a teaching session, with the more-skilled person adjusting guidance to fit the student's current performance level.

Information Processing

- The child's ability to attend to stimuli dramatically improves during early childhood. Advances in executive attention and sustained attention are especially important in early childhood, but young children still attend to the salient rather than the relevant features of a task.

- Significant improvement in short-term memory occurs during early childhood. With good prompts, young children's long-term memories can be accurate, although young children can be led into developing false memories.

- Advances in executive function, an umbrella-like concept that consists of a number of higher-level cognitive processes linked to the development of the prefrontal cortex, occur in early childhood. Executive function involves managing one's thoughts to engage in goal-directed behavior and to exercise self-control.

- Young children express curiosity about the human mind, and this has been studied under the topic of theory of mind. A number of developmental changes characterize children's theory of mind, including their growing awareness that it is possible for people to hold false beliefs. Individual variations also are involved in theory of mind. For example, autistic children have difficulty developing such a theory.

3 Language Development

 LG3 Summarize how language develops in early childhood.

Understanding Phonology and Morphology

Changes in Syntax and Semantics

Advances in Pragmatics

Young Children's Literacy

- Young children increase their grasp of language's rule systems. In terms of phonology, most young children become more sensitive to the sounds of spoken language. Berko's classic experiment demonstrated that young children understand morphological rules.

- Preschool children learn and apply rules of syntax and of how words should be ordered. In terms of semantics, vocabulary development increases dramatically during early childhood.

- Young children's conversational skills improve, they increase their sensitivity to the needs of others in conversation, and they learn to change their speech style to suit the situation.

- Parents and teachers need to provide young children with a supportive environment in which to develop literacy skills. Children should be active participants and be immersed in a wide range of interesting experiences that involve listening, talking, writing, and reading.

4 Early Childhood Education

 LG4 Evaluate different approaches to early childhood education.

Variations in Early Childhood Education

- The child-centered kindergarten emphasizes educating the whole child, with particular attention to individual variation, the process of learning, and the importance of play in development. The Montessori approach allows children to choose from a range of activities while teachers serve as facilitators.

- Developmentally appropriate practice focuses on the typical patterns of children (age-appropriateness) and the uniqueness of each child (individual-appropriateness). Such practice contrasts with developmentally inappropriate practice, which ignores the concrete, hands-on approach to learning.

Education for Young Children Who Are Disadvantaged

- The U.S. government has tried to break the poverty cycle with programs such as Head Start. The Early Head Start program began in 1995. Model programs have been shown to have positive effects on children who live in poverty.

Controversies in Early Childhood Education

- Controversy surrounds the topic of early childhood education curricula. On one side are the child-centered, constructivist advocates; on the other are those who advocate an academic, direct-instruction approach. Another controversy focuses on whether preschool education makes a difference, especially for children who are not disadvantaged.

key terms

animism 208
centration 209
child-centered kindergarten 225
conservation 209
developmentally appropriate
   practice (DAP) 225
egocentrism 207
executive attention 215
executive function 217
fast mapping 222
growth hormone deficiency 200
intuitive thought substage 209
Montessori approach 225
myelination 201
operations 207
preoperational stage 207
Project Head Start 226
short-term memory 216
social constructivist approach 212
sustained attention 215
symbolic function substage 207
theory of mind 219
zone of proximal development
   (ZPD) 210

key people

Jean Berko 222
Mona El-Sheikh 203
Ellen Galinsky 224
Maria Gartstein 215
Rochel Gelman 210
Barbel Inhelder 207
Walter Mischel 218
Maria Montessori 225
Jean Piaget 207
Mary Rothbart 215
Lev Vygotsky 207

chapter 8

SOCIOEMOTIONAL DEVELOPMENT IN EARLY CHILDHOOD

chapter **outline**

① Emotional and Personality Development

Learning Goal 1 Discuss emotional and personality development in early childhood.

The Self
Emotional Development
Moral Development
Gender

② Families

Learning Goal 2 Explain how families can influence young children's development.

Parenting
Child Maltreatment
Sibling Relationships and Birth Order
The Changing Family in a Changing Society

③ Peer Relations, Play, and Media/Screen Time

Learning Goal 3 Describe the roles of peers, play, and media/screen time in young children's development.

Peer Relations
Play
Media/Screen Time

David Ewing/INSADCO Photography/Alamy Stock Photo

Like many children, Sarah Newland loves animals.

During a trip to the zoo when she was 4 years old, Sarah learned about an animal that was a member of an endangered species and became motivated to help. With her mother's guidance, she baked lots of cakes and cookies, then sold them on the sidewalk outside her home. She was excited about making $35 from the cake and cookie sales, and she donated it to the World Wildlife Fund. Several weeks later, the fund wrote back to Sarah requesting more money. Sarah was devastated because she thought she had taken care of the animal problem. Her mother consoled her and told her that the endangered animal problem and many others are so big that it takes ongoing help from many people to solve them. Her mother's guidance when Sarah was a young child must have worked, because by the end of elementary school, Sarah had begun helping out at a child care center and working with her mother to provide meals to the homeless.

As Sarah's mother did, sensitive parents can make a difference in encouraging young children's sense of morality. Just as parents support and guide their children to become good readers, musicians, or athletes, they also play key roles in young children's socioemotional development (Source: Kantrowitz, 1991).

topical connections *looking **back***

During infancy, children's socioemotional development makes considerable progress as their caregivers (especially their parents) socialize them and they develop more sophisticated ways of initiating social interactions with others. Development of a secure attachment is a key aspect of infant development, and the development of autonomy in the second year of life also signals an important accomplishment. As children move through infancy, it is important for caregivers to guide them in regulating their emotions. Temperament also is a central characteristic of the infant's profile, and some temperament styles are more adaptive than others. The use of child care has become increasingly common in recent years, and the quality of this care varies considerably. Parents continue to play key roles in children's development in early childhood, but peers begin to play more important roles as well.

preview

In early childhood, children's emotional lives and personalities develop in significant ways, and their small worlds widen. In addition to the continuing influence of family relationships, peers take on a more significant role in children's development, and play as well as media and screen time fill the days of many young children's lives.

1 Emotional and Personality Development

LG1 Discuss emotional and personality development in early childhood.

The Self | Emotional Development | Moral Development | Gender

Many changes characterize young children's socioemotional development in early childhood. Their developing minds and social experiences produce remarkable advances in the development of their self, emotional maturity, moral understanding, and gender awareness.

THE SELF

During the second year of life, children make considerable progress in self-recognition. In early childhood, young children develop in ways that enhance their self-understanding.

Initiative Versus Guilt   You have read about Erik Erikson's (1968) eight developmental stages during certain periods in the life span. Erikson's first two stages—trust versus mistrust, and autonomy versus shame and doubt—describe what he considers to be the main developmental tasks of infancy. Erikson's psychosocial stage associated with early childhood is initiative versus guilt. By now, children have become convinced that they are persons in their own right; during early childhood, they begin to discover what kind of person they will become. They identify intensely with their parents, who most of the time appear to them to be powerful and beautiful, although often unreasonable, disagreeable, and sometimes even dangerous. During early childhood, children use their perceptual, motor, cognitive, and language skills to make things happen. They have a surplus of energy that permits them to forget failures quickly and to approach new areas that seem desirable—even if dangerous—with undiminished zest and often an increased sense of direction. On their own initiative, then, children at this stage exuberantly move out into a wider social world.

The great governor of initiative is conscience. Young children's initiative and enthusiasm may bring them not only rewards but also guilt, which lowers self-esteem.

Self-Understanding and Understanding Others   Research studies have revealed that young children are more psychologically aware—of themselves and others—than used to be thought (Thompson, 2015). This psychological awareness reflects expanding psychological sophistication.

Self-Understanding   In Erikson's portrait of early childhood, the young child clearly has begun to develop **self-understanding,** which is the representation of self, the substance and content of self-conceptions (Harter, 2012, 2016). Mainly through interviews, researchers have probed many aspects of children's self-understanding.

Early self-understanding involves self-recognition. In early childhood, young children think that the self can be described by material characteristics such as size, shape, and color. They distinguish themselves from others through physical and material attributes. Says 4-year-old Sandra, "I'm different from Jennifer because I have brown hair and she has blond hair." Says 4-year-old Ralph, "I am different from Hank because I am taller, and I am different from my sister because I have a bicycle." Physical activities are also a central component of the self in early childhood (Keller, Ford, & Meacham, 1978). For example, preschool children often describe themselves in terms of activities such as play. In sum, during early childhood, children often provide self-descriptions that involve bodily attributes, material possessions, and physical activities.

What characterizes young children's self-understanding?
Asia Images/Getty Images

self-understanding The child's cognitive representation of self, the substance and content of the child's self-conceptions.

Although young children mainly describe themselves in terms of concrete, observable features and action tendencies, at about 4 to 5 years of age as they hear others use words describing psychological traits and emotions, they begin to include these in their own self-descriptions (Marsh, Ellis, & Craven, 2002). Thus, in a self-description, a 4-year-old might say, "I'm not scared. I'm always happy." Young children's self-descriptions are typically unrealistically positive, as reflected in the comment of a 4-year-old who says he is always happy, which he is not (Harter, 2012). They express this optimism because they don't yet distinguish between their desired competence and their actual competence, tend to confuse ability and effort (thinking that differences in ability can be changed as easily as can differences in effort), don't engage in spontaneous social comparison of their abilities with those of others, and tend to compare their present abilities with what they could do at an earlier age (which usually makes their abilities look quite good). This overestimation of their attributes helps to protect young children from negative self-evaluations.

Young children are more psychologically aware of themselves and others than used to be thought. Some children are better than others at understanding people's feelings and desires—and, to some degree, these individual differences are influenced by conversations caregivers have with young children about feelings and desires.
Don Hammond/DesignPics

However, as in virtually all areas of human development, there are individual variations in young children's self-conceptions, and there is increasing evidence that some children are vulnerable to negative self-attributions (Thompson, 2015). For example, one study revealed that insecurely attached preschool children whose mothers reported a high level of parenting stress and depressive symptoms had a lower self-concept than other young children in more positive family circumstances (Goodvin & others, 2008). This research indicates that young children's generally optimistic self-ascriptions do not buffer them from adverse, stressful family conditions (Thompson, 2011).

Understanding Others   Young children also make advances in their understanding of others and their capacity to learn from others (Koenig, Tiberius, & Hamlin, 2019; Stack & Romero-Rivas, 2020). Young children's theory of mind includes understanding that other people have emotions and desires (Devine & Hughes, 2018; Lin & others, 2020). And, at about 4 to 5 years, children not only start describing themselves in terms of psychological traits, but they also begin to perceive others in terms of psychological traits. Thus, a 4-year-old might say, "My teacher is nice."

As they mature, young children need to develop an understanding that people don't always give accurate reports of their beliefs (Mills & Elashi, 2014). Researchers have found that even 4-year-olds understand that people may make statements that aren't true to obtain what they want or to avoid trouble (Lee & others, 2002). For example, one study revealed that 4- and 5-year-olds were increasingly skeptical of another child's claim to be sick when the children were informed that the child wanted to avoid having to go to camp (Gee & Heyman, 2007).

Another important aspect of understanding others involves understanding joint commitments. As children approach their third birthday, their collaborative interactions with others increasingly involve obligations to the partner (Tomasello & Hamann, 2012).

Young children also learn extensively through observing others' behavior. For example, a recent study found that young children who observed a peer being rewarded for confessing to cheating on a task were more likely to be honest in the future (Ma & others, 2018). And in a recent study, by 5 years of age, children made both character and behavior judgments from others' facial characteristics (Charlesworth & others, 2019). For example, they were more likely to give gifts to others with trustworthy and submissive-looking faces.

Both the extensive theory of mind research and the recent research on young children's social understanding underscore that young children are not as egocentric as Jean Piaget envisioned (Dahl & Brownell, 2019). Piaget's concept of egocentrism has become so ingrained in people's thinking about young children that too often the current research on social awareness in infancy and early childhood has been overlooked. Research increasingly shows that young children are more socially sensitive and perceptive than was previously envisioned, suggesting that parents and teachers can influence children's development by interacting with them in ways that help them to better understand and navigate the social world (Thompson 2015, 2016). If young children are seeking to better understand various mental and emotional states (intentions, goals, feelings, desires) that underlie people's actions, then talking with them about these internal states can improve young children's understanding (Thompson, 2015, 2016).

However, debate continues to surround the question of whether young children are socially sensitive or basically egocentric (Birch & others, 2017). Ross Thompson (2015, 2016) comes down on the side of viewing young children as socially sensitive, while Susan Harter (2012, 2013, 2016) argues that there is still evidence to support the conclusion that young children are essentially egocentric.

EMOTIONAL DEVELOPMENT

The young child's growing awareness of self is linked to the ability to feel an expanding range of emotions. Young children, like adults, experience many emotions during the course of a day. Their emotional development in early childhood allows them to try to make sense of other people's emotional reactions and to begin to control their own emotions (Dollar & Calkins, 2019; Frydenberg, Deans, & Liang, 2020).

Expressing Emotions   Recall that even young infants experience emotions such as joy and fear, but to experience *self-conscious emotions* children must be able to refer to themselves and be aware of themselves as distinct from others (Lewis, 2018). Pride, shame, embarrassment, and guilt are examples of self-conscious emotions. Self-conscious emotions do not appear to develop until self-awareness occurs at approximately 15 to 18 months of age.

During early childhood, emotions such as pride and guilt become more common. They are especially influenced by parents' responses to children's behavior. For example, a young child may experience shame when a parent says, "You should feel bad about biting your sister."

A young child expressing the emotion of shame, which occurs when a child evaluates his or her actions as not living up to standards. A child experiencing shame wishes to hide or disappear. *Why is shame called a self-conscious emotion?*
James Woodson/Digital Vision/Getty Images

Understanding Emotions   One of the most important advances in emotional development in early childhood is an increased understanding of emotion (Denham & Bassett, 2019). During early childhood, young children increasingly understand that certain situations are likely to evoke particular emotions, facial expressions indicate specific emotions, emotions affect behavior, and emotions can be used to influence others' emotions (Cole & others, 2009).

Between 2 and 4 years of age, children considerably increase the number of terms they use to describe emotions. During this time, they are also learning about the causes and consequences of feelings (Denham & others, 2011).

When they are 4 to 5 years of age, children show an increased ability to reflect on emotions. They also begin to understand that the same event can elicit different feelings in different people. Moreover, they show a growing awareness that they need to manage their emotions to meet social standards.

Regulating Emotions   Emotion regulation is an important aspect of development. Emotion regulation especially plays a key role in children's ability to manage the demands and conflicts they face in interacting with others (Cole, Ram, & English, 2019).

Many researchers consider the growth of emotion regulation in children as fundamental to becoming socially competent (Pollak, Camras, & Cole, 2019). In a recent study, a low level of emotion regulation at age 5 was associated with emotional and school problems at age 10 (Perry & others, 2018a). In another recent study, a low level of emotion regulation in early childhood predicted a higher level of externalizing problems in adolescence (Perry & others, 2018b).

Emotion regulation also can be conceptualized as an important component of self-regulation or executive function. Recall that executive function is increasingly thought to be a key concept in describing young children's higher-level cognitive functioning (Bell & Garcia Meza, 2020; McClelland, Cameron, & Alonso, 2020).

Cybele Raver and her colleagues (Blair & Raver, 2012, 2015; Blair, Raver, & Finegood, 2016; Raver & others, 2011, 2012, 2013) have conducted a number of studies that explore the role of emotion regulation in young children's development. They use various interventions, such as increasing caregiver emotional expressiveness, to improve young children's emotion regulation and reduce behavior problems in children growing up in poverty conditions. To read in greater detail about one of Cybele Raver's studies, see *Connecting Through Research.*

developmental **connection**

Executive Function

In early childhood, executive function especially involves developmental advances in cognitive inhibition, cognitive flexibility, goal-setting, and delay of gratification. Connect to "Physical and Cognitive Development in Early Childhood."

Caregivers' Emotional Expressiveness, Children's Emotion Regulation, and Behavior Problems in Head Start Children

A study by Dana McCoy and Cybele Raver (2011) explored links between caregivers' reports of their positive and negative emotional expressiveness, observations of young children's emotion regulation, and teachers' reports of the children's internalizing and externalizing behavior problems. The participants were 97 mostly African American and Latino children whose mean age was 4 years and 3 months, along with their primary caregivers (90 mothers, 5 fathers, and 2 grandmothers).

To assess caregiver expressiveness, caregivers were asked to provide ratings from 1 (never/rarely) to 9 (very frequently) on seven items that reflect caregiver expressiveness, such as "telling family members how happy you are" and "expressing anger at someone's carelessness." Children's emotion regulation was assessed with (a) the emotion regulation part of the PSRA (preschool self-regulation assessment) in which observers rated young children's behavior on 4 delay tasks, 3 executive function tasks, and 3 compliance tasks; (b) an assessment report on children's emotion and emotion regulation; and (c) observations of the children's real-time emotion regulation related to positive emotion (expressions of happiness, for example) and negative emotion (expressions of anger or irritability, for example). Children's internalizing and externalizing behaviors were rated by their teachers on the extent to which the children had shown such behavioral problems in the last 3 months.

The researchers found that a higher level of caregiver negativity and a lower level of children's emotion regulation independently were

How might young children's emotion regulation be linked to caregivers' expressiveness?
Najlah Feanny/Corbis

linked to more internalizing behavior problems in the young Head Start children. Also, caregivers' reports of their positive emotional expressiveness were associated with a lower level of young children's externalizing behavior problems. The findings demonstrate the importance of family emotional climate and young children's emotion regulation in the development of young children.

The study you just read about was correlational in nature. If you were interested in conducting an experimental study of the effects of caregivers' emotional expressiveness and children's emotion regulation on children's problem behaviors, how would you conduct the study differently?

Emotion-Coaching and Emotion-Dismissing Parents   Parents can play an important role in helping young children regulate their emotions (Zimmer-Gembeck & others, 2019). Depending on how they talk with their children about emotion, parents can be described as taking an *emotion-coaching* or an *emotion-dismissing* approach (Gottman, 2020). The distinction between these approaches is most evident in the way the parent deals with the child's negative emotions (anger, frustration, sadness, and so on). *Emotion-coaching parents* monitor their children's emotions, view their children's negative emotions as opportunities for teaching, assist them in labeling emotions, and coach them in how to deal effectively with emotions. In contrast, *emotion-dismissing parents* view their role as to deny, ignore, or change negative emotions. Emotion-coaching parents interact with their children in a less rejecting manner, use more scaffolding and praise, and are more nurturant than are emotion-dismissing parents. Moreover, the children of emotion-coaching parents are better at soothing themselves when they get upset, more effective in regulating their negative affect, focus their attention better, and have fewer behavior problems than the children of emotion-dismissing parents (Gottman, 2020). In a recent study, emotion-dismissing mothers' parenting was linked to toddlers' lower emotional competence, while mothers' emotion-coaching parenting was associated with toddlers' higher emotional competence (Korner & others, 2019). Researchers also have found that fathers' emotion coaching is related to children's social competence (Baker, Fenning, & Crnic, 2011). For example, a recent study of 3- to 4-year-olds indicated that paternal emotion coaching predicted children's positive expression of emotion one year later (Gerhardt & others, 2020).

An emotion-coaching parent. *What are some differences in emotion-coaching and emotion-dismissing parents?*
Jamie Grill/Tetra images/Getty Images

Parents' knowledge of their children's emotional world can help them guide their children's emotional development and teach their children how to cope effectively with problems (Gottman, 2020). One study found that mothers' knowledge about what distresses and comforts their children predicted the children's coping, empathy, and prosocial behavior (Vinik, Almas, & Grusec, 2011).

A challenge parents face is that young children typically don't want to talk about difficult emotional topics, such as being distressed or engaging in negative behaviors. Among the strategies young children use to avoid these conversations is to not talk at all, change the topic, push away, or run away. In one study, young children were more likely to openly discuss difficult emotional circumstances when they were securely attached to their mother and when their mother conversed with them in a way that validated and accepted the child's views (Thompson & others, 2009).

Emotion Regulation and Peer Relations   Emotions play a strong role in determining the success of a child's peer relationships (Smetana & Ball, 2018). Specifically, the ability to modulate one's emotions is an important skill that benefits children in their relationships with peers. Moody and emotionally negative children are more likely to experience rejection by their peers, whereas emotionally positive children are more popular. A recent study found that young children with higher emotion regulation were more popular with their peers (Nakamichi, 2020). Also, in another recent study of preschool children, frequent expression of anger predicted lower social competence in peer relations one year later (Lindsey, 2019).

MORAL DEVELOPMENT

Moral development involves thoughts, feelings, and behaviors regarding rules and conventions about what people should do in their interactions with other people. Major developmental theories have focused on different aspects of moral development (Jambon & Smetana, 2020; Laible & others, 2020a; Miller, Wice, & Goyal, 2020; Narváez, 2019, 2020; Spinrad & Eisenberg, 2020).

Moral Feelings   Feelings of anxiety and guilt are central to the account of moral development provided by Sigmund Freud's psychoanalytic theory. According to Freud, children attempt to reduce anxiety, avoid punishment, and maintain parental affection by identifying with parents and internalizing their standards of right and wrong, thus forming the superego—the moral element of personality.

Freud's ideas are not backed by research, but guilt certainly can motivate moral behavior. Other emotions, however, also contribute to the child's moral development, including positive feelings. One important example is empathy, which involves responding to another person's feelings with an emotion that echoes the other's feelings (Boele & others, 2019).

Infants have the capacity for some purely empathic responses, but empathy often requires the ability to discern another's inner psychological states, which is also known as perspective taking (Aslan & Kosal Akyol, 2020). Learning how to identify a wide range of emotional states in others and to anticipate what kinds of action will improve another person's emotional state helps to advance children's moral development (Thompson, 2015).

Today, many child developmentalists believe that both positive feelings—such as empathy, sympathy, admiration, and self-esteem—and negative feelings—such as anger, outrage, shame, and guilt—contribute to children's moral development (Spinrad & Eisenberg, 2020). When these emotions are strongly experienced, they influence children to act in accord with standards of right and wrong. *Sympathy*—an other-oriented emotional response in which an observer experiences emotions that are similar or identical to what the other person is feeling—often motivates prosocial behavior (Eisenberg, Spinrad, & Knafo-Noam, 2015). In one study, young children's sympathy predicted whether they would share with others (Ongley & Malti, 2014).

Connections between emotions can occur, and these connections may influence children's development. For example, in a recent study, participants' guilt proneness combined with their empathy predicted an increase in prosocial behavior (Torstveit, Sutterlin, & Lugo, 2016).

Moral Reasoning   Interest in how children think about moral issues was stimulated by Piaget (1932), who extensively observed and interviewed children between the ages of 4 and 12. Piaget watched children play marbles to learn how they applied and thought about the game's rules. He also asked children about ethical issues—theft, lies, punishment, and justice, for

- - - - - - - →

developmental **connection**

Theories

Freud theorized that individuals go through five psychosexual stages. Connect to "Introduction."

← - - - - - - - - -

moral development Development that involves thoughts, feelings, and behaviors regarding rules and conventions about what people should do in their interactions with other people.

example. Piaget concluded that children go through two distinct stages in how they think about morality.

- From about 4 to 7 years of age, children display **heteronomous morality,** the first stage of moral development in Piaget's theory. Children think of justice and rules as unchangeable properties of the world, removed from the control of people.
- From 7 to 10 years of age, children are in a transition showing some features of the first stage of moral reasoning and some stages of the second stage, autonomous morality.
- At about 10 years of age and older, children show **autonomous morality.** They become aware that rules and laws are created by people, and in judging an action they consider the actor's intentions as well as the consequences.

How will this child's moral thinking about stealing a cookie differ depending on whether he is in Piaget's heteronomous or autonomous stage?
Fuse/Getty Images

Because young children are heteronomous moralists, they judge the rightness or goodness of behavior by considering its consequences, not the intentions of the actor. For example, to the heteronomous moralist, breaking 12 cups accidentally is worse than breaking one cup intentionally. As children develop into moral autonomists, intentions become more important than consequences.

The heteronomous thinker also believes that rules are unchangeable and are handed down by all-powerful authorities. When Piaget suggested to young children that they use new rules in a game of marbles, they resisted. By contrast, older children—moral autonomists—accept change and recognize that rules are merely convenient conventions, subject to change.

The heteronomous thinker also believes in **immanent justice,** the concept that if a rule is broken, punishment will be meted out immediately. The young child believes that a violation is connected automatically to its punishment. Immanent justice also implies that if something unfortunate happens to someone, the person must have transgressed earlier. Older children, who are moral autonomists, recognize that punishment occurs only if someone witnesses the wrongdoing and that even then, punishment is not inevitable.

How do these changes in moral reasoning occur? Piaget concluded that the changes come about through the mutual give-and-take of peer relations. In the peer group, where others have power and status similar to the child's, plans are negotiated and coordinated, and disagreements are reasoned about and eventually settled. Parent-child relations, in which parents have power and children do not, are less likely to advance moral reasoning, because rules are often handed down in an authoritarian way.

Moral Behavior The behavioral and social cognitive approaches initially described early in this edition focus on moral behavior rather than moral reasoning. Advocates of these perspectives hold that the processes of reinforcement, punishment, and imitation explain the development of moral behavior. When children are rewarded for behavior that is consistent with laws and social conventions, they are likely to repeat that behavior. When models who behave morally are provided, children are likely to adopt their actions. And, when children are punished for immoral behavior, those behaviors are likely to be reduced or eliminated. However, because punishment may have adverse side effects, as discussed later in this chapter, it should be used judiciously and cautiously.

In the moral behavior view, the situation also influences behavior. More than a half century ago, a comprehensive study of thousands of children in many situations—at home, at school, and at church, for example—found that the totally honest child was virtually nonexistent; so was the child who cheated in all situations (Hartshorne & May, 1928-1930). Behavioral and social cognitive researchers emphasize that what children do in one situation is often only weakly related to what they do in other situations. A child might cheat in class but not in a game; a child might steal a piece of candy when alone but not steal it when others are present.

And when children observe people behaving morally, they are likely to imitate their actions (Ma & others, 2018). In one study, 2-year-olds watched a video of an adult engaging in prosocial behavior in response to another person's distress (Williamson, Donohue, & Tully, 2013). Children who saw the prosocial video were more likely than children who did not see it to imitate the prosocial behavior in response to their own parents' distress.

Social cognitive theorists also stress that the ability to resist temptation is closely tied to the development of self-control. To achieve this self-control, children must learn to delay gratification. According to social cognitive theorists, cognitive factors are important in the child's development of self-control (Bandura, 2009, 2010a, b, 2012, 2015).

→ developmental **connection**

Development

Kohlberg's theory, like Piaget's, emphasizes that peers play more important roles in children's moral development than parents do. Connect to "Socioemotional Development in Middle and Late Childhood."

developmental **connection**

Theories

What are the main themes of Bandura's social cognitive theory? Connect to the "Introduction" chapter.

heteronomous morality The first stage of moral development in Piaget's theory, occurring from approximately 4 to 7 years of age. Justice and rules are conceived of as unchangeable properties of the world, removed from the control of people.

autonomous morality In Piaget's theory, older children (about 10 years of age and older) become aware that rules and laws are created by people and that in judging an action one should consider the actor's intentions as well as the consequences.

immanent justice The concept that if a rule is broken, punishment will be meted out immediately.

Conscience   Conscience refers to an internal regulation of standards of right and wrong that involves an integration of all three components of moral development we have described so far—moral thought, feeling, and behavior (Kochanska & others, 2010). Reflecting the presence of a conscience in young children, researchers have found that young children are aware of right and wrong, have the capacity to show empathy toward others, experience guilt, indicate discomfort following a transgression, and are sensitive to violating rules (Kochanska & Aksan, 2007; Kochanska & others, 2009).

Recent research focuses on the role of guilt in young children's cooperation. For example, researchers have found that experiencing guilt motivates reparative behavior as early as 2 to 3 years of age and transgressors' displays of guilt motivate cooperative behavior in 4- to 5-year-olds (Vaish, 2018; Vaish, Carpenter, & Tomasello, 2016).

A major research interest involving young children's conscience focuses on children's relationships with their caregivers. Especially important in this regard is the emergence of young children's willingness to embrace the values of their parents, an orientation that flows from a positive, close relationship (Kochanska & Aksan, 2007). For example, children who are securely attached are more likely to internalize their parents' values and rules (Kim & Kochanska, 2017).

Parenting and Young Children's Moral Development   In Ross Thompson's (2006, 2009, 2012) view, young children are moral apprentices, striving to understand what is moral. Among the most important aspects of the relationship between parents and children that contribute to children's moral development are relational quality, parental discipline, proactive strategies, and conversational dialogue.

Parent-child relationships introduce children to the mutual obligations of close relationships (Kochanska, Boldt, & Goffin, 2019). Parents' obligations include engaging in positive caregiving and guiding children to become competent human beings. Children's obligations include responding appropriately to parents' initiatives and maintaining a positive relationship with parents.

An important parenting strategy involves proactively averting potential misbehavior by children before it takes place (Thompson, 2009). With younger children, being proactive means using diversion, such as distracting their attention or moving them to alternative activities. With older children, being proactive may involve talking with them about values that the parents deem important.

Conversations related to moral development can benefit children, regardless of whether they occur as part of a discipline encounter or outside the encounter in the everyday stream of parent-child interaction (Laible & others, 2020b; Thompson & Newton, 2013). The conversations can be planned or spontaneous and can focus on topics such as past events (for example, a child's prior misbehavior or positive moral conduct), shared future events (for example, going somewhere that may involve a temptation and will require positive moral behavior), and immediate events (for example, talking with the child about a sibling's tantrums).

What are some aspects of relationships between parents and children that contribute to children's moral development?
Tanya Constantine/Blend Images/Getty Images

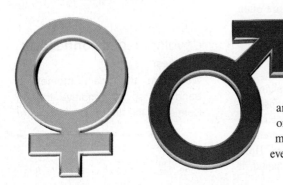

conscience An internal regulation of standards of right and wrong that involves integrating moral thought, feeling, and behavior.

gender The characteristics of people as males and females.

gender identity The sense of being male or female, which most children acquire by the time they are 3 years old.

gender role A set of expectations that prescribes how females or males should think, act, and feel.

gender typing Acquisition of a traditional masculine or feminine role.

GENDER

Gender refers to the characteristics of people as males and females. **Gender identity** involves a sense of one's own gender, including knowledge, understanding, and acceptance of being male or female (Best & Puzio, 2019; Erickson-Schroth & Davis, 2021). One aspect of gender identity involves knowing whether you are a girl or boy, an awareness that most children develop by about 2½ years of age (Blakemore, Berenbaum, & Liben, 2009). **Gender roles** are sets of expectations that prescribe how females or males should think, act, and feel. During the preschool years, most children increasingly act in ways that match their culture's gender roles. **Gender typing** refers to acquisition of a traditional masculine or feminine role. For example, fighting is more characteristic of a traditional masculine role and crying is more characteristic of a traditional feminine role (Helgeson, 2020).

Biological Influences   Biology clearly plays a role in gender development (Euler, 2020). Among the possible biological influences are chromosomes, hormones, and evolution (Pascual-Sagastizabal & others, 2019).

Chromosomes and Hormones   Biologists have learned a great deal about how sex differences develop. Recall that humans normally have 46 chromosomes arranged in pairs. The 23rd pair consists of a combination of X and Y chromosomes, usually two X chromosomes in a female and an X and a Y in a male. In the first few weeks of gestation, however, female and male embryos look alike.

Males start to differ from females when genes on the Y chromosome in the male embryo trigger the development of testes rather than ovaries; the testes secrete copious amounts of the class of hormones known as androgens. Low levels of androgens in the female embryo allow the normal development of female sex organs.

Thus, hormones play a key role in the development of sex differences (Hyde & Mezulis, 2020; Kruger & others, 2019). The two main classes of sex hormones, estrogens and androgens, are secreted by the *gonads* (ovaries in females, testes in males). *Estrogens,* such as estradiol, influence the development of female physical sex characteristics. *Androgens,* such as testosterone, promote the development of male physical sex characteristics. Sex hormones also can influence children's socioemotional development. For example, in a recent study, 3-year-old boys with higher prenatal testosterone levels had shorter delay of gratification times and more attention problems (Korner & others, 2019).

The Evolutionary Psychology View   How might physical differences between the sexes give rise to psychological differences between males and females? Evolutionary psychology offers one answer. According to evolutionary psychology, adaptation during human evolution produced psychological differences between males and females (Buss, 2015, 2019). Because of their differing roles in reproduction, males and females faced differing pressures when the human species was evolving. In particular, because having multiple sexual liaisons improves the likelihood that males will pass on their genes, natural selection favored males who adopted short-term mating strategies (Grebe & others, 2019). These are strategies that allow a male to win the competition with other males for sexual access to females. Therefore, say evolutionary psychologists, males evolved dispositions that favor violence, competition, and risk taking.

In contrast, according to evolutionary psychologists, females' contributions to the gene pool were improved when they secured resources that ensured that their offspring would survive. As a consequence, natural selection favored females who devoted effort to parenting and chose successful, ambitious mates who could provide their offspring with resources and protection.

Critics of evolutionary psychology argue that its hypotheses are backed by speculations about prehistory, not evidence, and that in any event people are not locked into behavior that was adaptive in the evolutionary past. Critics also claim that the evolutionary view pays little attention to cultural and individual variations in gender differences (Hyde & DeLamater, 2020).

Social Influences   Many social scientists do not locate the cause of psychological gender differences in biological dispositions. Rather, they argue that these differences reflect social experiences (Erickson-Schroth & Davis, 2020; MacPhee & Prendergast, 2019). Explanations for how gender differences come about through experience include both social and cognitive theories.

Social Theories of Gender   Three main social theories of gender have been proposed—social role theory, psychoanalytic theory, and social cognitive theory. Alice Eagly (2012, 2018) proposed **social role theory,** which states that gender differences result from the contrasting roles of women and men. In most cultures around the world, women have less power and status than men, and they control fewer resources (UNICEF, 2020). Compared with men, women perform more domestic work, spend fewer hours in paid employment, receive lower pay, and are more thinly represented in the highest levels of organizations (Helgeson, 2020). In Eagly's view, as women adapted to roles with less power and less status in society, they showed more cooperative, less dominant profiles than men. Thus, the social hierarchy and division of labor are important causes of gender differences in power, assertiveness, and nurturing (Eagly & Wood, 2017).

The **psychoanalytic theory of gender** stems from Freud's view that the preschool child develops a sexual attraction to the opposite-sex parent. This is the process known as the Oedipus (for boys) or Electra (for girls) complex. At 5 or 6 years of age, the child renounces this attraction because of anxious feelings. Subsequently, the child identifies with the same-sex parent, unconsciously adopting the same-sex parent's characteristics. However, developmentalists have observed that gender development does not proceed as Freud proposed. Children become gender-typed much earlier than 5 or 6 years of age, and they become masculine or feminine even when the same-sex parent is not present in the family.

social role theory A theory that gender differences result from the contrasting roles of men and women.

psychoanalytic theory of gender A theory deriving from Freud's view that the preschool child develops a sexual attraction to the opposite-sex parent, by approximately 5 or 6 years of age renounces this attraction because of anxious feelings, and subsequently identifies with the same-sex parent, unconsciously adopting the same-sex parent's characteristics.

First imagine that this is a photograph of a baby girl. *What expectations would you have of her?* Then imagine that this is a photograph of a baby boy. *What expectations would you have of him?*
Dmitry Lobanov/Shutterstock

social cognitive theory of gender A theory emphasizing that children's gender development occurs through the observation and imitation of gender behavior and through the rewards and punishments children experience for gender-appropriate and gender-inappropriate behavior.

The social cognitive approach provides an alternative explanation of how children develop gender-typed behavior. According to the **social cognitive theory of gender,** children's gender development occurs through observing and imitating what other people say and do, and through being rewarded and punished for gender-appropriate and gender-inappropriate behavior (Bussey & Bandura, 1999). From birth onward, males and females are treated differently from one another. When infants and toddlers show gender-appropriate behavior, adults tend to reward them. Parents often use rewards and punishments to teach their daughters to be feminine ("Karen, you are being a good girl when you play gently with your doll") and their sons to be masculine ("Keith, a boy as big as you is not supposed to cry"). Parents, however, are only one of many sources through which children learn gender roles (Brown & Stone, 2018). Culture, schools, peers, the media, and other family members also provide gender role models (Chen, Lee, & Chen, 2018). For example, children also learn about gender by observing the behavior of other adults in the neighborhood and on television. As children get older, peers become increasingly important. Let's take a closer look at the influences of parents and peers.

Parental Influences   Parents, by action and by example, influence their children's gender development. Both mothers and fathers are psychologically important to their children's gender development (Leaper, 2015). Cultures around the world, however, tend to give mothers and fathers different roles (Chen, Lee, & Chen, 2018). A research review yielded the following conclusions (Bronstein, 2006):

- *Mothers' socialization strategies.* In many cultures, mothers socialize their daughters to be more obedient and responsible than their sons. They also place more restrictions on daughters' autonomy.

- *Fathers' socialization strategies.* Fathers show more attention to sons than to daughters, engage in more activities with sons, and put forth more effort to promote sons' intellectual development.

Thus, according to Bronstein (2006, pp. 269–270), "Despite an increased awareness in the United States and other Western cultures of the detrimental effects of gender stereotyping, many parents continue to foster behaviors and perceptions that are consonant with traditional gender role norms."

Peer Influences   Parents provide the earliest discrimination of gender roles, but peers soon join the process of responding to and modeling masculine and feminine behavior (Rose & Smith, 2018). In fact, peers become so important to gender development that the playground has been called "gender school" (Luria & Herzog, 1985).

Peers extensively reward and punish gender behavior (Leaper & Bigler, 2018). For example, when children play in ways that the culture says are sex-appropriate, their peers tend to reward them. But peers often reject children who act in a manner that is considered more characteristic of the other gender (Xiao & others, 2019). A little girl who brings a doll to the park may find herself surrounded by new friends; a little boy who does the same thing might be jeered at. However, there is greater pressure for boys to conform to a traditional male role than for girls to conform to a traditional female role (Fagot, Rogers, & Leinbach, 2000). For example, a pre-school girl who wants to wear boys' clothing receives considerably more approval than a boy who wants to wear a dress. The very term "tomboy" implies broad social acceptance of girls' adopting traditional male behaviors. In a recent study of 4- to 9-year-olds, gender-nonconforming

What role does gender play in children's peer relations?
(*Left*) Eric Audras/Getty Images; (*right*) Alistair Berg/Getty Images

children were perceived less positively than gender-conforming children (Kwan & others, 2020). Also in this study, children expressed more negative perceptions of gender-nonconforming boys than gender-nonconforming girls. Further, in another recent study of 9- to 10-year-olds in Great Britain, gender-nonconforming boys were at the highest risk for peer rejection (Braun & Davidson, 2017). In addition, a recent study of 3- to 4- and 6- to 7-year-olds found that boys were more likely to engage in gender stereotyping, especially with masculine stimuli such as toys, and to be sanctioned for not conforming to gender stereotypes (Skocajic & others, 2020). In addition, gender stereotyping was more prevalent in the 6- to 7-year-olds than the 3- to 4-year-olds.

Gender molds important aspects of peer relations (Rose & Smith, 2018). It influences the composition of children's groups, the size of groups, and interactions within a group (Maccoby, 1998, 2002):

- *Gender composition of children's groups.* Around the age of 3, children already prefer to spend time with same-sex playmates. From 4 to 12 years of age, this preference for playing in same-sex groups increases, and during the elementary school years children spend a large majority of their free time with children of their own sex (see Figure 1). One study found that when preschool children select a playmate, both the sex of the playmate and the playmate's level of gender-typed activity are important, but sex of the playmate is more important (Martin & others, 2013).

- *Group size.* From about 5 years of age onward, boys are more likely to associate in larger clusters than girls are. Boys are also more likely to participate in organized group games than girls are. In one study, same-sex groups of six children were permitted to use play materials in any way they wished (Benenson, Apostolaris, & Parnass, 1997). Girls were more likely than boys to play in dyads or triads, while boys were more likely to interact in larger groups and seek to attain a group goal.

- *Interaction in same-sex groups.* Boys are more likely than girls to engage in rough-and-tumble play, competition, conflict, ego displays, risk taking, and quests for dominance. By contrast, girls are more likely to engage in "collaborative discourse," in which they talk and act in a more reciprocal manner.

Cognitive Influences

One influential cognitive theory is **gender schema theory,** which states that gender typing emerges as children gradually develop gender schemas of what is gender-appropriate and gender-inappropriate in their culture (Martin, Fabes, & Hanish, 2018). A *schema* is a cognitive structure, a network of associations that guides an individual's perceptions. A *gender schema* organizes the world in terms of female and male. Children are internally motivated to perceive the world and to act in accordance with their developing schemas. Bit by bit, children pick up what is gender-appropriate and gender-inappropriate in their culture, and develop gender schemas that shape how they perceive the world and what they remember (Liben, 2017). Children are motivated to act in ways that conform to these gender schemas. Thus, gender schemas fuel gender typing.

gender schema theory The theory that gender typing emerges as children develop gender schemas of their culture's gender-appropriate and gender-inappropriate behavior.

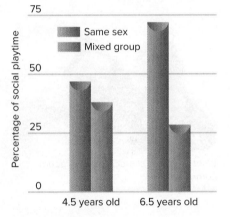

FIGURE 1

DEVELOPMENTAL CHANGES IN PERCENTAGE OF TIME SPENT IN SAME-SEX AND MIXED GROUP SETTINGS. Observations of children show that they are more likely to play in same-sex than mixed-sex groups. This tendency increases between 4 and 6 years of age.

Review Connect Reflect

 LG1 Discuss emotional and personality development in early childhood.

Review

- What changes in the self occur during early childhood?
- What changes take place in emotional development in early childhood?
- What are some key aspects of moral development in young children?
- How does gender develop in young children?

Connect

- In the previous section, you read about the influence of parents on children's gender development. How does this compare with what you learned about parental influences on children's temperament?

Reflect *Your Own Personal Journey of Life*

- Imagine that you are the parent of a 4-year-old child. What strategies would you use to increase your child's understanding of others?

2 Families

LG2 Explain how families can influence young children's development.

Parenting   Child Maltreatment   Sibling Relationships and Birth Order   The Changing Family in a Changing Society

Parenting is a very important profession, but no test of fitness for it is ever imposed in the interest of children.

—GEORGE BERNARD SHAW
Irish playwright, 20th century

What are some characteristics of good parenting?
Andres Rodriguez/Hemera/Getty Images

Attachment to a caregiver is a key social relationship during infancy; however, some experts maintain that secure attachment and other aspects of the infant years have been overdramatized as determinants of life-span development. Social and emotional development is also shaped by other relationships and by temperament, contexts, and social experiences during early childhood and later. In this section, we will discuss social relationships in early childhood beyond attachment. We will explore different types of parenting, sibling relationships, and variations in family structures.

PARENTING

Media accounts sometimes portray parents as unhappy, feeling little joy in caring for their children. However, one study found that parents were more satisfied with their lives than were nonparents, felt relatively better on a daily basis than did nonparents, and had more positive feelings related to caring for their children than toward doing other daily activities (Nelson & others, 2013).

Juggling work and child care can be challenging for families with young children. A survey of American parents found that approximately half of fathers and one-fourth of mothers reported feeling that they weren't spending enough time with their children (Pew Research, 2013). Nonetheless, this survey found that both mothers and fathers were spending more time with their children than parents did a generation earlier.

Good parenting takes time and effort (Grusec, 2020; Thompson & Baumrind, 2019). You can't do it in a minute here and a minute there. Of course, it's not just the quantity of time parents spend with children that is important for children's development—the quality of the parenting is clearly important (Grolnick, Caruso, & Levitt, 2019; Laible & others, 2020a). To understand variations in parenting, let's consider the styles parents use when they interact with their children, how they discipline their children, and the dynamics of coparenting.

Baumrind's Parenting Styles   Diana Baumrind (1971, 2012) argues that parents should be neither punitive nor aloof. Rather, they should develop rules for their children and be affectionate with them. She has described four types of parenting styles:

- **Authoritarian parenting** is a restrictive, punitive style in which parents exhort the child to follow their directions and respect their work and effort. The authoritarian parent places firm limits and controls on the child and allows little verbal exchange. For example, an authoritarian parent might say, "You will do it my way or else." Authoritarian parents also might spank the child frequently, enforce rules rigidly but not explain them, and show rage toward the child. Children of authoritarian parents are often unhappy, fearful, and anxious about comparing themselves with others, fail to initiate activity, and have weak communication skills. A recent research review of a large number of studies concluded that authoritarian parenting is linked to a higher level of externalizing problems (acting out, high levels of aggression, for example) (Pinquart, 2017). In addition, a recent study revealed that the authoritarian parenting style was associated with being a bully perpetrator (Krisnana & others, 2020). And in another recent study, authoritarian parenting was associated with all types of child maltreatment (Lo & others, 2019).
- **Authoritative parenting** encourages children to be independent but still places limits and controls on their actions. Extensive verbal give-and-take is allowed, and parents are warm and nurturing toward the child. An authoritative parent might put his arm around the child in a comforting way and say, "You know you should not have done that. Let's talk about how you can handle the situation better next time." Authoritative

authoritarian parenting A restrictive, punitive style in which parents exhort the child to follow their directions and to respect their work and effort. The authoritarian parent places firm limits and controls on the child and allows little verbal exchange. Authoritarian parenting is associated with children's social incompetence.

authoritative parenting A parenting style in which parents encourage their children to be independent but still place limits and controls on their actions. Extensive verbal give-and-take is allowed, and parents are warm and nurturing toward the child. Authoritative parenting is associated with children's social competence.

parents show pleasure and support in response to children's constructive behavior. They also expect mature, independent, and age-appropriate behavior from their children. Children whose parents are authoritative are often cheerful, self-controlled and self-reliant, and achievement-oriented; they tend to maintain friendly relations with peers, cooperate with adults, and cope well with stress. As was just indicated, authoritative parents do exercise some direction and control over their children. The children of authoritative parents who engage in behavioral or psychological control without being coercive or punitive often show positive developmental outcomes (Baumrind, Larzelere, & Owens, 2010). In a recent study, children of authoritative parents engaged in more prosocial behavior than their counterparts whose parents used the other parenting styles described in this section (Carlo & others, 2018). Further, in a recent study, authoritative parenting was associated with a lower risk of all types of child maltreatment (Lo & others, 2019).

- **Neglectful parenting** is a style in which the parent is uninvolved in the child's life. Children whose parents are neglectful develop the sense that other aspects of the parents' lives are more important than they are. These children tend to be socially incompetent. Many have poor self-control and don't handle independence well. They frequently have low self-esteem, are immature, and may be alienated from the family. In adolescence, they may show patterns of truancy and delinquency. In the recent research review cited in our description of authoritarian parenting, the review also found that neglectful parenting was associated with a higher level of externalizing problems (Pinquart, 2017).

- **Indulgent parenting** is a style in which parents are highly involved with their children but place few demands or controls on them. Such parents let their children do what they want. As a result, the children never learn to control their own behavior and always expect to get their way. Some parents deliberately rear their children in this way because they believe the combination of warm involvement and few restraints will produce a creative, confident child. However, children whose parents are indulgent rarely learn respect for others and have difficulty controlling their behavior. They might be domineering, egocentric, and noncompliant, and have difficulties in peer relations.

These four classifications of parenting involve combinations of acceptance and responsiveness on the one hand and demand and control on the other (Maccoby & Martin, 1983). How these dimensions combine to produce authoritarian, authoritative, neglectful, and indulgent parenting is shown in Figure 2.

	Accepting, responsive	Rejecting, unresponsive
Demanding, controlling	Authoritative	Authoritarian
Undemanding, uncontrolling	Indulgent	Neglectful

FIGURE 2

CLASSIFICATION OF PARENTING STYLES. The four types of parenting styles (authoritative, authoritarian, indulgent, and neglectful) involve the dimensions of acceptance and responsiveness, on the one hand, and demand and control on the other. For example, authoritative parenting involves being both accepting/responsive and demanding/controlling.
Steve Debenport/E+/Getty Images

Parenting Styles in Context Do the benefits of authoritative parenting transcend the boundaries of ethnicity, socioeconomic status (SES), and household composition? Although occasional exceptions have been found, evidence linking authoritative parenting with competence on the part of the child occurs in research across a wide range of ethnic groups, social strata, cultures, and family structures (Garcia, Lopez-Fernandez, & Serra, 2020; Steinberg, 2014).

Nonetheless, researchers have found that in some ethnic groups, aspects of the authoritarian style may be associated with more positive child outcomes than Baumrind predicts (Parke, Roisman, & Rose, 2019; Pinquart & Kauser, 2018). Elements of the authoritarian style may take on different meanings and have different effects depending on the context. For example, Asian American parents often continue aspects of traditional Asian child-rearing practices that have sometimes been described as authoritarian. The parents exert considerable control over their children's lives. However, Ruth Chao (2001, 2005, 2007) argues that the style of parenting used by many Asian American parents is distinct from the domineering control of the authoritarian style. Instead, Chao argues, this type of parental control reflects concern and involvement in their children's lives and is best conceptualized as a type of training. The high academic achievement of Asian American children may reflect the involvement of their "training" parents (Stevenson & Zusho, 2002).

neglectful parenting A style of parenting in which the parent is uninvolved in the child's life; this style is associated with children's social incompetence, especially a lack of self-control.

indulgent parenting A style of parenting in which parents are highly involved with their children but place few demands or controls on them. Indulgent parenting is associated with children's social incompetence, especially a lack of self-control.

According to Ruth Chao, which type of parenting style do many Asian American parents use?
somethingway/Getty Images

- - - - - - - - →

developmental **connection**

Family

Two recent books examine disciplinary tactics used by Chinese and Chinese American parents—*Battle Hymn of the Tiger Mom* and *Tiger Babies Strike Back*—and researchers have studied parenting in Chinese and Chinese American families. Connect to "Socioemotional Development in Middle and Late Childhood."

← - - - - - - - -

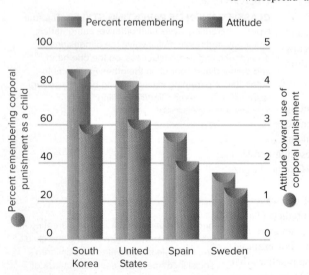

FIGURE 3

CORPORAL PUNISHMENT IN DIFFERENT COUNTRIES. A five-point scale was used to assess attitudes toward corporal punishment, with scores closer to 1 indicating an attitude against its use and scores closer to 5 suggesting an attitude favoring its use. *Why are studies of corporal punishment correlational studies, and how does that affect their usefulness?*

An emphasis on requiring respect and obedience is also associated with the authoritarian style, but in Latino child rearing this focus may be positive rather than punitive. Rather than suppressing the child's development, it may encourage the development of a self and an identity that are embedded in the family and require respect and obedience (Dixon, Graber, & Brooks-Gunn, 2008). In these circumstances, emphasizing respect and obedience may be part of maintaining a harmonious family and important in shaping the child's identity (Umana-Taylor & others, 2014).

Further Thoughts on Parenting Styles   Several caveats about parenting styles are in order. First, the parenting styles do not capture the important themes of reciprocal socialization and synchrony. Keep in mind that children socialize parents, just as parents socialize children (D'Angelo & others, 2019; Klein & others, 2018).

Second, many parents use a combination of techniques rather than a single technique, although one technique may be dominant. Although consistent parenting is usually recommended, the wise parent may sense the importance of being more permissive in certain situations, more authoritarian in others, and more authoritative in yet other circumstances. In addition, parenting styles often are talked about as if both parents have the same style, although this may not be the case.

Third, some critics argue that the concept of parenting style is too broad and that more research needs to be conducted to "unpack" parenting styles by studying various components that compose the styles (Grusec, 2017, 2020). For example, is parental monitoring more important than warmth in predicting child and adolescent outcomes?

Fourth, much of the parenting style research has involved mothers, not fathers. In many families, mothers will use one style, fathers another style. Especially in traditional cultures, fathers have an authoritarian style and mothers a more permissive, indulgent style. It has often been said that it is beneficial for parents to engage in a consistent parenting style; however, if fathers are authoritarian and aren't willing to change, children benefit when mothers use an authoritative style.

Punishment   For centuries, corporal (physical) punishment, such as spanking, has been considered a necessary and even desirable method of disciplining children. Use of corporal punishment is legal in every state in America. A study of more than 11,000 U.S. parents indicated that 80 percent of the parents reported spanking their children by the time they reached kindergarten (Gershoff & others, 2012). A recent research review concluded that there is widespread approval of corporal punishment by U.S. parents (Chiocca, 2017). A cross-cultural comparison found that individuals in the United States were among those with the most favorable attitudes toward corporal punishment and were the most likely to remember it being used by their parents (Curran & others, 2001) (see Figure 3). Physical punishment is outlawed in 41 countries, with an increasing number of countries banning physical punishment to protect children from abuse and exploitation (Committee on the Rights of the Child, 2014). Also, in a recent study, interviews with college students indicated that daughters were less likely than sons to report experiencing physical punishment as children and the daughters also said that they were less likely to be physically punished by both parents (Mehlhausen-Hassoen, 2019).

What are some reasons for avoiding spanking or similar harsh punishments? The reasons include the following:

- When adults punish a child by yelling, screaming, or spanking, they are presenting children with out-of-control models for handling stressful situations. Children may imitate this aggressive, out-of-control behavior.

- Punishment can instill fear, rage, or avoidance. For example, spanking the child may cause the child to avoid being around the parent and to fear the parent.

- Punishment tells children what not to do rather than what to do. Children should be given feedback, such as "Why don't you try this?"

- Punishment can be abusive. Parents might unintentionally become so angry when they are punishing the child that they injure the child physically or emotionally (Knox, 2010).

Most child psychologists recommend handling misbehavior by reasoning with the child, especially explaining the consequences of the child's actions for others. Time out, in which the child is removed from a setting that offers positive reinforcement, can also be effective. For example, when the child has misbehaved, a parent might take away TV viewing for a specified time.

Debate about the effects of punishment on children's development continues (Ferguson, 2013; Gershoff & others, 2018, 2019; Laible, Thompson, & Froimson, 2015; Lansford, 2019a, 2020; Larzelere & others, 2019; Rohner & Melendez-Rhodes, 2019). Several longitudinal studies have found that physical punishment of young children is associated with higher levels of aggression later in childhood and adolescence (Gershoff & others, 2012; Lansford & others, 2014; Thompson & others, 2017). In one longitudinal study, harsh physical punishment in childhood was linked to a higher incidence of intimate partner violence in adulthood (Afifi & others, 2017b).

However, a meta-analysis that focused on longitudinal studies revealed that the negative outcomes of punishment on children's internalizing and externalizing problems were minimal (Ferguson, 2013). A research review of 26 studies also concluded that only severe or predominant use of spanking, not mild spanking, compared unfavorably with alternative discipline practices (Larzelere & Kuhn, 2005). Nonetheless, in a recent meta-analysis, when physical punishment was not abusive it still was linked to detrimental child outcomes (Gershoff & Grogan-Kaylor, 2016).

Some experts (including Diana Baumrind) argue that much of the evidence for the negative effects of physical punishment is based on studies in which parents acted in an abusive manner (Baumrind, Larzelere, & Cowan, 2002). She concludes from her research that when parents use punishment in a calm, reasoned manner (which she says characterized most of the authoritative parents in her studies), children's development benefits. In sum, she emphasizes that physical punishment does not need to present children with an out-of-control adult who is yelling and screaming, as well as spanking.

Thus, in the view of some experts, it is still difficult to determine whether the effects of physical punishment are harmful to children's development, although such a view might be distasteful to some individuals (Ferguson, 2013; Grusec & others, 2013; Larzelere & others, 2019). And as with other research on parenting, research on punishment is correlational in nature, making it difficult to discover causal factors (Larzelere & others, 2019). Also, consider the concept of reciprocal socialization, discussed in the chapter on "Socioemotional Development in Infancy," which emphasizes bidirectional child and parent influences (Lansford & others, 2018). Researchers have found links between children's early behavioral problems and parents' greater use of physical punishment over time (Laible, Thompson, & Froimson, 2015; Sheehan & Watson, 2015).

In one research review, Elizabeth Gershoff (2013) concluded that the defenders of spanking have not produced any evidence that spanking produces positive outcomes for children, and she noted that negative outcomes of spanking have been replicated in many studies. Also, one thing that is clear regarding research on punishment of children is that if physical punishment is used, it needs to be mild, infrequent, age-appropriate, and used in the context of a positive parent-child relationship (Grusec, 2011). It is also clear that when physical punishment involves abuse, it can be very harmful to children's development (Cicchetti & Handley, 2019). And an increasing majority of leading experts on parenting conclude that physical punishment has harmful effects on children and should not be used (Afifi & others, 2017a; Gershoff & others, 2018, 2019).

Coparenting The support that parents provide one another in jointly raising a child is called **coparenting.** Poor coordination between parents, undermining of the other parent, lack of cooperation and warmth, and disconnection by one parent are conditions that place children at risk for problems (Le & others, 2019; McHale, Negrini, & Sirotkin, 2019; McHale & Sirotkin, 2019). For example, one study revealed that coparenting influenced young children's effortful control above and beyond maternal and paternal parenting by themselves (Karreman & others, 2008). Further, a recent study revealed that coparenting involving couple supportiveness, especially when their children were 3 to 5 years of age, was linked to reduced levels of externalizing problems 8 to 10 years later (Parkes, Green, & Mitchell, 2019). Researchers also have found that unmarried African American parents who were instructed in coparenting techniques during the prenatal period and also one month after the baby was born had higher levels of rapport, communication, and problem-solving skills when the baby was 3 months old (McHale, Salman-Engin, & Coovert, 2015). And a recent study of low-income, unmarried

What characterizes coparenting?
ESB Professional/Shutterstock

coparenting Support parents provide to each other in jointly raising their children.

Darla Botkin, Marriage and Family Therapist

Darla Botkin is a marriage and family therapist who teaches, conducts research, and engages in marriage and family therapy. She is on the faculty of the University of Kentucky. Botkin obtained a bachelor's degree in elementary education with a concentration in special education and then went on to receive a master's degree in early childhood education. She spent the next six years working with children and their families in a variety of settings, including child care, elementary school, and Head Start. These experiences led Botkin to recognize the interdependence of the developmental settings that children and their parents experience (such as home, school, and work). She returned to graduate school and obtained a Ph.D. in family studies from the University of Tennessee. She then became a faculty member in the Family Studies program at the University of Kentucky. Completing further coursework and clinical training in marriage and family therapy, she became certified as a marriage and family therapist.

Botkin's current interests include working with young children in family therapy, addressing gender and ethnic issues in family therapy, and exploring the role of spirituality in family wellness.

Darla Botkin (*left*) conducts a family therapy session.
Courtesy of Dr. Darla Botkin

For more information about what marriage and family therapists do, see the Careers in Life-Span Development appendix.

families revealed that cooperative coparenting at earlier points in time results in fewer child behavior problems later on (Choi, Parra, & Jiang, 2019).

Parents who do not spend enough time with their children or who have problems in child rearing can benefit from counseling and therapy. To read about the work of marriage and family counselor Darla Botkin, see *Connecting with Careers.*

CHILD MALTREATMENT

Unfortunately, punishment sometimes leads to the abuse of infants and children (Cicchetti & Handley, 2019; Ni & Hesketh, 2020). In 2017, approximately 674,000 U.S. children were found to be victims of child abuse at least once during that year (U.S. Department of Health and Human Services, 2017). In 2017, 1,720 U.S. children died of child maltreatment. Ninety-one percent of children were abused by a parent or both parents. Laws now require physicians and teachers to report suspected cases of child abuse, yet many cases go unreported, especially those involving battered infants (Nouman & others, 2020).

Whereas the public and many professionals use the term *child abuse* to refer to both abuse and neglect, developmentalists increasingly use the term *child maltreatment* (Cicchetti & Handley, 2019; Stacks & others, 2020; Sturge-Apple & others, 2019). This term does not have quite the emotional impact of the term *abuse* and acknowledges that maltreatment includes diverse conditions.

Types of Child Maltreatment   The four main types of child maltreatment are physical abuse, child neglect, sexual abuse, and emotional abuse (National Clearinghouse on Child Abuse and Neglect, 2019):

- *Physical abuse* is characterized by the infliction of physical injury as a result of punching, beating, kicking, biting, burning, shaking, or otherwise harming a child. The parent or other person may not have intended to hurt the child; the injury may have resulted

> Child maltreatment involves grossly inadequate and destructive aspects of parenting.
>
> —DANTE CICCHETTI
> *Contemporary developmental psychologist, University of Minnesota*

from excessive physical punishment (Lakhdir & others, 2020; Portnoy & others, 2020). In 2017, 18.3 percent of maltreated children were physically abused (U.S. Department of Health and Human Services, 2017).

- *Child neglect* is characterized by failure to provide for the child's basic needs (Font & Maguire-Jack, 2020; Maguire-Jack & others, 2019). Child neglect is extensive—in 2017, 74.9 percent of maltreated children were neglected (U.S. Department of Health and Human Services, 2017). Neglect can be physical (abandonment, for example), educational (allowing chronic truancy, for example), or emotional (marked inattention to the child's needs, for example). Child neglect is by far the most common form of child maltreatment.

- *Sexual abuse* includes fondling a child's genitals, intercourse, incest, rape, sodomy, exhibitionism, and commercial exploitation through prostitution or the production of pornographic materials (Ogunjimi & others, 2020; Tener, Katz, & Kaufmann, 2020). In 2017, 8.6 percent of maltreated children in the United States were sexually abused (U.S. Department of Health and Human Services, 2017).

- *Emotional abuse (psychological/verbal abuse/mental injury)* includes acts or omissions by parents or other caregivers that have caused, or could cause, serious behavioral, cognitive, or emotional problems (Ross, Kaminski, & Herrington, 2019).

Although any of these forms of child maltreatment may be found separately, they often occur in combination. Emotional abuse is almost always present when other forms are identified.

The Contexts of Abuse

No single factor causes child maltreatment (Cicchetti & Handley, 2019). A combination of factors, including the culture, family, and developmental characteristics of the child, likely contribute to child maltreatment.

The extensive violence that takes place in American culture, including TV violence, is reflected in the occurrence of violence in the family (Leppakoski, Flinck, & Paavilainen, 2015). The family itself is obviously a key part of the context of abuse (McCarroll & others, 2017). Among the family and family-associated characteristics that may contribute to child maltreatment are parenting stress, substance abuse, social isolation, single parenting, and socioeconomic difficulties (especially poverty) (Doyle & Cicchetti, 2018). The interactions of all family members need to be considered, regardless of who performs the violent acts against the child. For example, even though the father may be the one who physically abuses the child, the behavior of the mother, the child, and siblings also should be evaluated.

Were parents who abuse children abused by their own parents? A 30-year longitudinal study found that offspring of parents who engaged in child maltreatment and neglect are at risk for engaging in child neglect and sexual maltreatment themselves (Widom, Czaja, & DuMont, 2015). It is estimated that about one-third of parents who were abused themselves when they were young go on to abuse their own children (Cicchetti & Toth, 2006). Thus, some, but not a majority, of parents are involved in an intergenerational transmission of abuse.

Developmental Consequences of Abuse

Among the consequences of child maltreatment in childhood and adolescence are poor emotion regulation, attachment problems, problems in peer relations, difficulty in adapting to school, and other psychological problems such as depression, delinquency, and substance abuse (DePasquale, Handley, & Cicchetti, 2019). As shown in Figure 4, maltreated young children in foster care were more likely to show abnormal stress hormone levels than middle-SES young children living with their birth family (Gunnar, Fisher, & The Early Experience, Stress, and Prevention Network, 2006). In this study, the abnormal stress hormone levels were mainly present in the foster children who were neglected, best described as "institutional neglect" (Fisher, 2005). Abuse also may have this effect on young children (Gunnar & others, 2006). A recent study also found that physical abuse was linked to lower levels of cognitive development and school engagement in children (Font & Cage, 2018). In addition, adolescents who experienced abuse or neglect as children are at increased risk of engaging in violent romantic relationships, delinquency, sexual risk taking, and substance abuse (Trickett, Negriff, & Peckins, 2011). And a recent study found

Eight-year-old Donnique Hein lovingly holds her younger sister, 6-month-old Maria Paschel, after a meal at Laura's Home, a crisis shelter in Ohio.
Joshua Gunter/The Plain Dealer/Landov Images

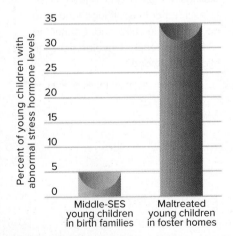

FIGURE 4

ABNORMAL STRESS HORMONE LEVELS IN YOUNG CHILDREN IN DIFFERENT TYPES OF REARING CONDITIONS

that exposure to either physical or sexual abuse in childhood and adolescence was linked to an increase in 13- to 18-year-olds' suicidal ideation, plans, and attempts (Gomez & others, 2017).

Later, during the adult years, individuals who were maltreated as children are more likely to experience physical ailments, mental problems, and sexual problems (Lacelle & others, 2012). In a recent large-scale Canadian study, a history of child maltreatment involving either physical abuse or sexual abuse was linked to having physical and mental health problems as adults (Cameranesi, Lix, & Piotrowski, 2019). Also, in a longitudinal study, people who had experienced abuse and neglect in the first five years of life had higher rates of interpersonal problems and lower academic achievement from childhood through their thirties (Raby & others, 2010). Among these interpersonal problems, people who were maltreated as children often have difficulty establishing and maintaining healthy intimate relationships (Dozier, Stovall-McClough, & Albus, 2009). As adults, maltreated children are also at higher risk for violent behavior toward other adults—especially dating partners and marital partners—as well as substance abuse, anxiety, and depression (Miller-Perrin, Perrin, & Kocur, 2009). And in a recent study, child maltreatment was associated with an increase in psychiatric disorders and substance abuse in adulthood (Wang & others, 2020).

An important research agenda is to discover how to prevent child maltreatment or to intervene in children's lives when they have been maltreated (DePasquale, Handley, & Cicchetti, 2019; Kim, 2019; Weiler & Taussig, 2019). In one study of maltreating mothers and their 1-year-olds, two treatments were effective in reducing child maltreatment: (1) home visitation that emphasized improved parenting, coping with stress, and increased support for the mother; and (2) parent-infant psychotherapy that focused on improving maternal-infant attachment (Cicchetti, Toth, & Rogosch, 2005). Further, a recent study found that child maltreatment was associated with increased emotion-focused coping (crying, verbal aggression, for example) and decreased problem-focused coping (seeking help from an adult, for example (VanMeter, Handley, & Cicchetti, 2020). Thus, clinicians may want to integrate reducing emotion-focused coping into their intervention strategies with maltreated children. And a recent large-scale study indicated that social support and coping skills were linked to positive adult mental health outcomes for maltreated children (Su, D'Arcy, & Meng, 2020).

SIBLING RELATIONSHIPS AND BIRTH ORDER

How do developmentalists characterize sibling relationships? How extensively does birth order influence behavior?

Sibling Relationships Approximately 80 percent of American children have one or more siblings—that is, sisters and brothers (Fouts & Bader, 2017). If you grew up with siblings, you probably have abundant memories of aggressive, hostile interchanges. Siblings in the presence of each other when they are 2 to 4 years of age, on average, have a conflict once every 10 minutes and then the conflicts go down somewhat at 5 to 7 years of age (Kramer, 2006). What do parents do when they encounter siblings having a verbal or physical confrontation? One study revealed that they do one of three things: (1) intervene and try to help their children resolve the conflict, (2) admonish or threaten them, or (3) do nothing at all (Kramer & Perozynski, 1999). Of interest is that in families with two siblings 2 to 5 years of age, the most frequent parental reaction is to do nothing at all.

Laurie Kramer (2006), who has conducted a number of research studies on siblings, says that not intervening and letting sibling conflict escalate are not good strategies. She developed a program titled "More Fun with Sisters and Brothers" that teaches 4- to 8-year-old siblings social skills for developing positive interactions (Kramer & Radey, 1997). Among the social skills taught in the program are how to appropriately initiate play, how to accept and refuse invitations to play, how to take another person's perspective, how to deal with angry feelings, and how to manage conflict.

However, conflict is only one of the many dimensions of sibling relations (Pike & Oliver, 2017). Sibling relations also include helping, sharing, teaching, and playing, and siblings can act as emotional supports and communication partners as well as rivals for parental attention (Kramer & Hamilton, 2019).

Do parents usually favor one sibling over others—and if so, does it make a difference in a child's development? One study of 384 sibling pairs revealed that 65 percent of their mothers and 70 percent of their fathers showed favoritism toward one sibling (Shebloski, Conger,

developmental **connection**

Family

Siblings who are psychologically close to each other in adulthood tended to be that way in childhood. Connect to "Socioemotional Development in Middle Adulthood."

& Widaman, 2005). When favoritism of one sibling occurred, it was linked to lower self-esteem and sadness in the less-favored sibling. Indeed, equality and fairness are major concerns of siblings' relationships with each other and how they are treated by their parents (Kramer & Hamilton, 2019).

Judy Dunn (2015), a leading expert on sibling relationships, recently described three important characteristics of sibling relationships:

- *Emotional quality of the relationship.* Intense positive and negative emotions are often expressed by siblings toward each other. Many children and adolescents have mixed feelings toward their siblings.

- *Familiarity and intimacy of the relationship.* Siblings typically know each other very well, and this intimacy suggests that they can either provide support or tease and undermine each other, depending on the situation.

- *Variation in sibling relationships.* Some siblings describe their relationships more positively than others. Thus, there is considerable variation in sibling relationships. We just discussed that many siblings have mixed feelings about each other, but some children and adolescents mainly describe their siblings in warm, affectionate ways, whereas others primarily talk about how irritating and mean a sibling is. Research indicates that a high level of sibling conflict is linked to negative developmental outcomes (Fosco & others, 2012).

Birth Order Whether a child has older or younger siblings has been linked to development of certain personality characteristics. For example, one research review concluded that "firstborns are the most intelligent, achieving, and conscientious, while later-borns are the most rebellious, liberal, and agreeable" (Paulhus, 2008, p. 210). Compared with later-born children, firstborn children have also been described as more adult-oriented, helpful, conforming, and self-controlled. However, when such birth-order differences are reported, they often are small.

What accounts for differences related to birth order? Proposed explanations usually point to variations in interactions with parents and siblings associated with being in a particular position in the family (Feinberg, McHale, & Whiteman, 2019). In one study, mothers became more negative, coercive, and restraining and played less with the firstborn following the birth of a second child (Dunn & Kendrick, 1982).

What is the only child like? The popular conception is that the only child is a "spoiled brat" with such undesirable characteristics as dependency, lack of self-control, and self-centered behavior. But researchers present a more positive portrayal of the only child. Only children often are achievement-oriented and display a desirable personality, especially in comparison with later-borns and children from large families (Falbo & Poston, 1993; Jiao, Ji, & Jing, 1996).

So far, our discussion suggests that birth order might be a strong predictor of behavior. However, an increasing number of family researchers stress that when all of the factors that influence behavior are considered, birth order by itself shows limited accuracy in predicting behavior. Think about some of the other important factors beyond birth order in children's lives that influence their behavior. They include heredity, models of competency or incompetency that parents present to children on a daily basis, peer influences, school influences, socioeconomic factors, sociohistorical factors, and cultural variations. When someone says firstborns are always like this but last-borns are always like that, the person is making overly simplistic statements that do not adequately take into account the complexity of influences on a child's development.

What characterizes children's sibling relationships?
(*Top*) RubberBall Productions/Getty Images; (*bottom*) RubberBall Productions/Photodisc/Getty Images

THE CHANGING FAMILY IN A CHANGING SOCIETY

Beyond variations in the number of siblings, the families that children experience differ in many important ways (Bernard & others, 2019; Pinderhughes & Brodzinsky, 2019). The number of children growing up in single-parent families is staggering. As shown in Figure 5, the United States has one of the highest percentages of single-parent families in the world. Among two-parent families, there are those in which both parents work outside the home, one or both parents had a previous marriage that ended in divorce, or the parents are gay or lesbian. Differences in culture and socioeconomic status (SES) also influence families. How do these variations in families affect children?

A one-child policy has been in place for a number of decades in China. However, in 2016, the Chinese government began allowing two children per family without a financial penalty. *In general, though, what have researchers found the only child to be like?*
Image Source/Getty Images

FIGURE 5

SINGLE-PARENT FAMILIES IN DIFFERENT COUNTRIES

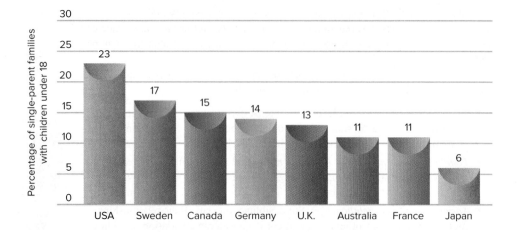

Percentage of single-parent families with children under 18

| USA | Sweden | Canada | Germany | U.K. | Australia | France | Japan |
| 23 | 17 | 15 | 14 | 13 | 11 | 11 | 6 |

How does work affect parenting?
Keith Brofsky/Photodisc/Getty Images

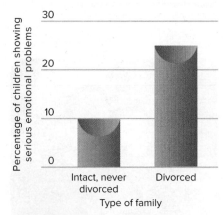

Percentage of children showing serious emotional problems

Intact, never divorced — Divorced

Type of family

FIGURE 6

DIVORCE AND CHILDREN'S EMOTIONAL PROBLEMS. In Hetherington's research, 25 percent of children from divorced families showed serious emotional problems compared with only 10 percent of children from intact, never-divorced families. However, keep in mind that a substantial majority (75 percent) of the children from divorced families did not show serious emotional problems.

Working Parents   More than one of every two U.S. mothers with a child under the age of 5 is in the labor force; more than two of every three with a child from 6 to 17 years of age is employed. Maternal employment is a part of modern life, but its effects continue to be debated.

In a recent national survey, working mothers (60 percent) were more likely than fathers (52 percent) to report that balancing work and family is difficult (Livingston & Bialik, 2018). Also in this survey, slightly more than half (54 percent) indicate that mothers do more than fathers when children's schedules and activities are involved. In another recent national survey, nearly one-fourth (24 percent) of working parents said that their children have asked them to work less, and a similar percentage (23 percent) report that work is negatively impacting their relationship with their children (Career Builder, 2018).

Most research on parental work has focused on the role of maternal employment on young children's development (Han, Hetzner, & Brooks-Gunn, 2019). However, the effects of working parents involve the father as well as the mother when such matters as work schedules, work-family stress, and unemployment are considered (Parke, Roisman, & Rose, 2019). For example, a study of almost 3,000 adolescents found a negative association between the father's, but not the mother's, unemployment and the adolescents' health (Bacikova-Sleskova, Benka, & Orosova, 2015).

Researchers have found that the nature of parents' work has more influence on children's development than whether a parent works outside the home (Han, Hetzner, & Brooks-Gunn, 2019). And work can produce both positive and negative effects on parenting (Crouter & McHale, 2005). Ann Crouter (2006) described how parents bring their experiences at work into their homes. She concluded that parents who face poor working conditions such as long hours, overtime work, stressful work, and lack of autonomy on the job are likely to be more irritable at home and to engage in less effective parenting than their counterparts with better working conditions. A consistent finding is that children (especially girls) of working mothers engage in less gender stereotyping and have more egalitarian views of gender than children whose mothers are not employed outside the home (Goldberg & Lucas-Thompson, 2008).

Children in Divorced Families   It is estimated that 40 percent of children born to married parents in the United States will experience their parents' divorce (Hetherington & Stanley-Hagan, 2002). Let's examine some important questions about children in divorced families.

Are children better adjusted in intact, never-divorced families than in divorced families? Most researchers agree that children from divorced families show poorer adjustment than their counterparts in nondivorced families (Hetherington, 2006; Kravdal & Grundy, 2019; Lansford, 2019b; Meland, Breidablik, & Theun, 2020) (see Figure 6). Those who have experienced multiple divorces are at greater risk. Children in divorced families are more likely than children in nondivorced families to have academic problems, to show externalized problems (such as acting out and delinquency) and internalized problems (such as anxiety and depression), to be less socially responsible, to have less competent intimate relationships, to drop out of school, to become sexually active at an early age, to take drugs, to associate with antisocial peers, to have low self-esteem, and to be less securely attached as young adults (Lansford, 2013, 2019b). A recent meta-analysis of 54 studies and 506,299 participants concluded that children who experience parental divorce are at risk for depression, anxiety, suicide attempts, distress, alcohol abuse, drugs, and smoking (Auersperg & others 2019). Nonetheless, keep in mind that a majority of children in divorced families do not have significant adjustment problems (Ahrons, 2007). One study found that 20 years after their parents had divorced when they were children, approximately 80 percent of adults concluded that their parents' decision to divorce had been a wise one (Ahrons, 2004).

Should parents stay together for the sake of the children? Whether parents should stay in an unhappy marriage for the sake of their children is one of the most commonly asked questions about divorce (Hetherington, 2006; Morrison, Fife, & Hertlein, 2017). If the stresses and disruptions in family relationships associated with an unhappy, conflictual marriage that erode the well-being of children are reduced by the move to a divorced, single-parent family, divorce can be advantageous. However, if the diminished resources and increased risks associated with divorce also are accompanied by inept parenting and sustained or increased conflict, not only within the divorced couple but also among the parents, children, and siblings, the best choice for the children would be for an unhappy marriage to be retained (Hetherington & Stanley-Hagan, 2002). It is difficult to determine how these "ifs" will play out when parents either remain together in an acrimonious marriage or become divorced.

Note that marital conflict may have negative consequences for children in the context of marriage or divorce (Gao & others, 2019). And many of the problems that children from divorced homes experience begin during the predivorce period, a time when parents are often in active conflict with each other. Thus, when children from divorced homes show problems, the problems may be due not only to the divorce but also to the marital conflict that led to it.

E. Mark Cummings and his colleagues (Cummings & others, 2017; Davies, Martin, & Cummings, 2018) have proposed *emotion security theory*, which has its roots in attachment theory and states that children appraise marital conflict in terms of their sense of security and safety in the family. These experts make a distinction between marital conflict that is negative for children (such as hostile emotional displays and destructive conflict tactics) and marital conflict that can be positive for children (such as marital disagreement that involves calmly discussing each person's perspective and then working together to reach a solution). In one study, interparental hostility was a stronger predictor of children's insecurity and externalizing problems than interparental disengagement and low levels of interparental cooperation (Davies & others, 2016). In another recent study, maladaptive marital conflict (destructive strategies, severity of arguments) when children were 2 years old was associated with an increase in internalizing problems eight years later due to an undermining of attachment security for girls, while negative emotional aftermath of conflict (unresolved, lingering tension) increased both boys' and girls' internalizing problems (Brock & Kochanska, 2016).

How much do family processes matter in divorced families? Family processes matter a great deal (Ganong, Coleman, & Sanner, 2019; Lansford, 2019b). For example, when divorced parents' relationship with each other is harmonious and when they use authoritative parenting, the adjustment of children improves (Hetherington, 2006). When the divorced parents can agree on child-rearing strategies and can maintain a cordial relationship with each other, frequent visits by the noncustodial parent usually benefit the child (Fabricius & others, 2010). Following a divorce, father involvement with children drops off more than mother involvement, especially if the children are girls. In one study, children were more likely to have behavior problems if their post-divorce home environment was less supportive and stimulating, their mother was less sensitive and more depressed, and if their household income was lower (Weaver & Schofield, 2015). Also, a study of divorced families revealed that an intervention focused on improving the mother-child relationship was linked to improvements in relationship quality that increased children's coping skills over the short term (6 months) and long term (6 years) (Velez & others, 2011). And a longitudinal study revealed that parental divorce experienced before age 7 was linked to a lower level of health through 50 years of age (Thomas & Hognas, 2015). Further, a recent study of noncustodial fathers in divorced families indicated that high father-child involvement and low interparental conflict were linked to positive child outcomes (Flam & others, 2016). Also, a recent research review concluded that coparenting (coparental support, cooperation, and agreement) following divorce was associated with positive child outcomes such as reduced anxiety and depression, as well as higher levels of self-esteem and academic performance (Lamela & Figueiredo, 2016).

> As marriage has become a more optional, less permanent institution in contemporary America, children and adolescents are encountering stresses and adaptive challenges associated with their parents' marital transitions.
>
> —E. MAVIS HETHERINGTON
> *Contemporary psychologist, University of Virginia*

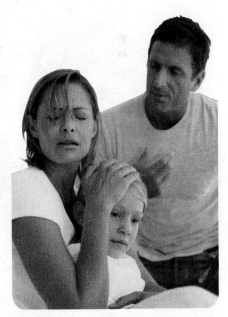

What concerns are involved in whether parents should stay together for the sake of the children or become divorced?
Zoey/Image Source/Getty Images

What factors influence an individual child's vulnerability to suffering negative consequences from living in a divorced family? Among the factors involved in the child's risk and vulnerability is the child's adjustment prior to the divorce, as well as the child's personality and temperament, gender, and custody situation (Hetherington, 2006). Children whose parents later divorce often show poor adjustment before the breakup (Amato & Booth, 1996). Children who are socially mature and responsible, who show few behavioral problems, and who have an easy temperament are better able to cope with their parents' divorce. Children with a difficult temperament often have problems coping with their parents' divorce (Hetherington, 2000).

Earlier studies reported gender differences in response to divorce, with divorce being more negative for boys than girls in mother-custody families. However, more recent studies have shown that gender differences are less pronounced and consistent than was previously believed. Some of the inconsistency may be due to the increase in father custody, joint custody, and increased involvement of noncustodial fathers, especially in their sons' lives (Ziol-Guest, 2009).

Research on whether different types of custodial arrangements are better for children in divorced families has yielded inconsistent results (Parke, 2013). An analysis of studies found that children in joint-custody families were better adjusted than children in sole-custody families (Bauserman, 2002). However, joint custody works best for children when the parents can get along with each other (Steinbach, 2019).

What role does socioeconomic status play in the lives of children in divorced families? Custodial mothers experience the loss of about one-fourth to one-half of their predivorce income, in comparison with a loss of only one-tenth by custodial fathers. This income loss for divorced mothers is accompanied by increased workloads, high rates of job instability, and residential moves to less desirable neighborhoods with inferior schools (Braver & Lamb, 2013). One study found that children from families with higher incomes before the separation/divorce had fewer internalizing problems (Weaver & Schofield, 2015).

In sum, many factors are involved in determining how divorce influences a child's development (Lansford, 2019b). To read about some strategies for helping children cope with the divorce of their parents, see *Connecting Development to Life.*

Gay and Lesbian Parents
Increasingly, gay and lesbian couples are creating families that include children (Farr & Vasquez, 2020; Farr, Vasquez, & Patterson, 2020; Patterson, 2019). Data indicate that approximately 20 percent of same-sex couples are raising children under the age of 18 in the United States (Gates, 2013).

Like heterosexual couples, gay and lesbian parents vary greatly. They may be single or they may have same-gender partners. Many lesbian mothers and gay fathers are noncustodial parents because they lost custody of their children to heterosexual spouses after a divorce. In addition, gays and lesbians are increasingly choosing parenthood through donor insemination or adoption (Carone & others, 2018). Researchers have found that the children conceived through new reproductive technologies—such as in vitro fertilization—are as well adjusted as their counterparts conceived by natural means (Golombok, 2011a, b).

Parenthood among lesbians and gays is controversial. Opponents claim that being raised by gay or lesbian parents harms the child's development. But researchers have found few differences between children growing up with lesbian mothers or gay fathers on the one hand, and children growing up with heterosexual parents on the other (Farr & Vasquez, 2020; Farr, Vasquez, & Patterson, 2020; Patterson, 2019). For example, children growing up with gay or lesbian parents are just as popular with their peers, and no differences are found in the adjustment and mental health of children in these families compared with children living with heterosexual parents (Hyde & DeLamater, 2020). For example, in a recent study, the adjustment of school-aged children adopted during infancy by gay, lesbian, and heterosexual parents showed no differences (Farr, 2017). Rather, children's behavior patterns and family functioning were predicted by earlier child adjustment issues and parental stress. In another recent study of lesbian and gay adoptive parents, 98 percent of the adoptive parents reported that their children had adjusted well to school (Farr, Oakley, & Ollen, 2016). Another study revealed more positive parenting in adoptive gay father families and fewer child externalizing problems in these families than in heterosexual families (Golombok & others, 2014). Contrary to the once-popular expectation that being raised by a gay or lesbian parent would result in the child growing up to be gay or lesbian, in reality the overwhelming

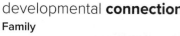

developmental **connection**

Family

Early marriage, low educational level, low income, not having a religious affiliation, having parents who are divorced, and having a baby before marriage are factors linked to an increased probability of divorce. Connect to "Socioemotional Development in Early Adulthood."

What are the research findings regarding the development and psychological well-being of children raised by gay and lesbian couples?
Creatas/Getty Images

Communicating with Children About Divorce

Ellen Galinsky and Judy David (1988) developed a number of guidelines for communicating with children about divorce.

- **Explain the separation.** As soon as daily activities in the home make it obvious that one parent is leaving, tell the children. If possible, both parents should be present when children are told about the separation to come. The reasons for the separation are very difficult for young children to understand. No matter what parents tell children, children can find reasons to argue against the separation. It is extremely important for parents to tell the children who will take care of them and to describe the specific arrangements for seeing the other parent.

- **Explain that the separation is not the child's fault.** Young children often believe their parents' separation or divorce is their own fault. Therefore, it is important to tell children that they are not the cause of the separation. Parents need to repeat this statement a number of times.

- **Explain that it may take time to feel better.** Tell young children that it's normal to not feel good about what is happening and that many other children feel this way when their parents become separated. It is also okay for divorced parents to share some of their emotions with children by saying something like "I'm having a hard time since the separation just like you, but I know it's going to get better after a while." Such statements are best kept brief and should not criticize the other parent.

- **Keep the door open for further discussion.** Tell your children to come to you anytime they want to talk about the separation. It is healthy for children to express their pent-up emotions in discussions with their parents and to learn that the parents are willing to listen to their feelings and fears.

- **Provide as much continuity as possible.** The less children's worlds are disrupted by the separation, the easier their transition to a single-parent family will be. Thus, parents should maintain the rules already in place as much as possible. Children need parents who care enough not only to give them warmth and nurturance but also to set reasonable limits.

- **Provide support for your children and yourself.** After a divorce or separation, parents are as important to children as before the divorce or separation. Divorced parents need to provide children with as much support as possible. Parents function best when other people are available to give them support as adults and as parents. Divorced parents can find people who provide practical help and encourage them to talk about their problems.

How does the third guideline above ("Explain that it may take time to feel better") relate to what you learned earlier in this chapter about emotion coaching?

majority of children from gay or lesbian families have a heterosexual orientation (Golombok & Tasker, 2010; Tasker & Golombok, 1997).

Researchers have compared the incidence of coparenting in adoptive heterosexual, lesbian, and gay couples with preschool-aged children (Patterson, 2019). Both self-reports and observations found that lesbian and gay couples shared child care more than heterosexual couples, with lesbian couples being more supportive than gay couples.

Cultural, Ethnic, and Socioeconomic Variations Parenting can be influenced by culture, ethnicity, and socioeconomic status (Fisher, 2020; Halgunseth, 2019; McLoyd, Hardaway, & Jocson, 2019; Sobo, 2020). Recall from Bronfenbrenner's ecological theory (see the "Introduction" chapter) that a number of social contexts influence the child's development. In Bronfenbrenner's theory, culture, ethnicity, and socioeconomic status are classified as part of the macrosystem because they represent broader, societal contexts.

Cross-Cultural Studies Different cultures often give different answers to basic questions such as what the father's role in the family should be, what support systems are available to families, and how children should be disciplined (Gaskins, 2016). There are important cross-cultural variations in parenting and the value placed on children (Matsumoto & Juang, 2020). In some cultures, such as rural areas of many countries, authoritarian parenting is widespread (Smetana & Ball, 2018).

Cultural change, brought about by factors such as increasingly frequent international travel, access to the Internet and electronic communications, and economic globalization, is coming to families in many countries around the world. There are trends toward greater family mobility, migration to urban areas, separation as some family members work in cities or countries far from their homes, smaller families, fewer extended-family households, and

What are some characteristics of families within different ethnic groups?
FatCamera/Getty Images

increased maternal employment (Brown & Larson, 2002). These trends can change the resources that are available to children. For example, when several generations no longer live near each other, children may lose support and guidance from grandparents, aunts, and uncles. On the positive side, smaller families may produce more openness and communication between parents and children.

Ethnicity   Families within different ethnic groups in the United States differ in their typical size, structure, composition, reliance on kinship networks, and levels of income and education (Banks, 2020; Ng & Wang, 2019). In 2016, 51 percent of children 18 years and younger were non-Latino White; by 2060, this figure is projected to decrease to 36 percent (U.S. Census Bureau, 2018). The ethnic minority U.S. population age 18 and younger is predicted to outnumber its non-Latino White counterpart in 2020. In 2016, among individuals age 18 and younger in the United States, 25 percent were Latino, 14 percent were African American, and 5 percent were Asian American. Large and extended families are more common among minority groups than among the non-Latino White majority. For example, 19 percent of Latino families have three or more children, compared with 14 percent of African American and 10 percent of White families. African American and Latino children interact more with grandparents, aunts, uncles, cousins, and more distant relatives than do White children.

Single-parent families are more common among African Americans and Latinos than among non-Latino White Americans. In comparison with two-parent households, single parents often have more limited resources of time, money, and energy (Weinraub & Kaufman, 2019). Ethnic minority parents also are less educated and more likely to live in low-income circumstances than their non-Latino White counterparts. Still, many impoverished ethnic minority families manage to find ways to raise competent children (Magnuson & Duncan, 2019; McLoyd, Hardaway, & Jocson, 2019).

A special point needs to be made as we explore various aspects of ethnicity, in this and other chapters in the text. For too long, the prevailing perspective on ethnic differences was deficit-based and assumed that children and adolescents in ethnic minority groups were inherently challenged and overwhelmed by stressors, especially in the case of immigrant ethnic minority adolescents (Bornstein & Cote, 2019; Weissmark, 2020). Countering this perspective is research indicating that ethnic minority adolescents, including those who are immigrants, fare better than expected (Perreira & others, 2019). Adolescents in immigrant families often assume higher levels of responsibility than non-immigrant adolescents and help their parents adapt to their new society (Halgunseth, 2019).

A major change in families in the last several decades has been the dramatic increase in the immigration of Latino and Asian families into the United States (McNeely & others, 2020; Ng & Wang, 2019). Immigrant families often experience stressors uncommon to or less prominent among longtime residents, such as language barriers, dislocations and separations from support networks, the dual struggle to preserve identity and to acculturate, changes in SES status, and health (Hill & others, 2019; Valenzuela-Araujo & others, 2020). In a recent study, immigrant children who were once separated from their parents had a lower level of literacy and a higher level of psychological problems than those who had migrated with parents (Lu, He, & Brooks-Gunn, 2020). Also in this study, a protracted period of separation and prior undocumented status of parents further increased children's disadvantages.

Further, an increasing number of children are growing up in transnational families, who move back and forth between the United States and countries and regions such as Mexico, Latin America, and China (Penas & others, 2020). In some cases these children are left behind in their home country, and in other cases (especially in China), they are sent back to China to be raised by grandparents during their early childhood years. Such children might benefit from economic remittances but suffer emotionally from prolonged separation from their parents (Mazzucato, 2015).

Of course, individual families vary, and how ethnic minority families deal with stress depends on many factors (Amuedo-Durantes & Arenas-Arroyo, 2019). Whether the parents are native-born or immigrants, how long the family has been in the United States, and their socioeconomic status and national origin all make a difference (Hoff & Laursen, 2019). The characteristics of the family's social context also influence its adaptation. What are the attitudes toward the family's ethnic group within its neighborhood or city? Can the family's children attend good schools? Are there community groups that welcome people from the family's ethnic group? Do members of the family's ethnic group form community groups of their own?

Ethnic minority/immigrant children and their parents are expected to move beyond their own cultural background and identify with aspects of the dominant culture. They undergo varying degrees of acculturation, which refers to cultural changes that occur when one culture comes in contact with another. Asian American parents, for example, may feel pressed to modify the traditional training style of parental control discussed earlier as they encounter the more permissive parenting typical of the dominant culture.

What are some of the stressors immigrant families experience when they come to the United States?
Alison Wright/Getty Images

Researchers have found that many members of families that have recently immigrated to the United States adopt a bicultural orientation, selecting characteristics of the U.S. culture that help them to survive and advance, while retaining some aspects of their culture of origin (Tikhonov & others, 2019). In adopting characteristics of the U.S. culture, Latino families are increasingly embracing its emphasis on education (Halgunseth, 2019). Although their school dropout rates have remained higher than those of other ethnic groups, during the second decade of the twenty-first century they declined considerably (National Center for Education Statistics, 2019). However, while many ethnic/immigrant families adopt a bicultural orientation, parenting in many ethnic minority families also focuses on issues associated with promoting children's ethnic pride, knowledge of their ethnic group, and awareness of discrimination (Stein & others, 2019).

Socioeconomic Status   Low-income families have less access to resources than higher-income families do (Hoff & Laursen, 2019). This reduced access to resources encompasses nutrition, health care, protection from danger, and enriching educational and socialization opportunities such as tutoring and lessons in various activities (Tian & others, 2019; Xuan & others, 2019). These differences are compounded in low-income families characterized by long-term poverty (Magnuson & Duncan, 2019). One study found that persistent economic hardship and very early poverty were linked to lower cognitive functioning in children at 5 years of age (Schoon & others, 2012). Also in another study, poverty-related adversity in family and school contexts in early childhood was linked to less effective executive function in second- and third-graders (Raver & others, 2013). A longitudinal study found that a multicomponent (school-based educational enrichment and comprehensive family services) preschool-to-third-grade intervention with low-income minority children in Chicago was effective in increasing their rates of high school graduation as well as their success in earning undergraduate and graduate degrees (Reynolds, Qu, & Temple, 2018). Further, a recent Australian study revealed that children and adolescents from lower-SES backgrounds were less likely achieve a healthy physical fitness level than their higher-SES counterparts (Peralta & others, 2019). And in a recent analysis, low SES in childhood was linked to lower cognitive function and greater cognitive decline in middle and late adulthood (Liu & Lachman 2019). Also in this study, paternal discipline and high affection were positively associated with adult cognitive function for children living in low-SES conditions, while paternal discipline was negatively related to adult cognition in children living in high-SES conditions.

In the United States and most Western cultures, differences have been found in child rearing among families with different socioeconomic statuses (SES) (Hoff, Laursen, & Tardif, 2002, p. 246):

- "Lower-SES parents (1) are more concerned that their children conform to society's expectations, (2) create a home atmosphere in which it is clear that parents have authority over children," (3) use physical punishment more in disciplining their children, and (4) are more directive and less conversational with their children.

- "Higher-SES parents (1) are more concerned with developing children's initiative" and delay of gratification, "(2) create a home atmosphere in which children are more nearly equal participants and in which rules are discussed as opposed to being laid down" in an authoritarian manner, (3) are less likely to use physical punishment, and (4) "are less directive and more conversational" with their children.

How might socioeconomic status and poverty be linked to parenting and young children's development?
Jens Kalaene/picture-alliance/dpa/AP Images

Review Connect Reflect

LG2 Explain how families can influence young children's development.

Review

- What are the four main parenting styles, and what aspects of parenting are linked with young children's development?
- What are the types and consequences of child maltreatment?
- How are sibling relationships and birth order related to young children's development?
- How is young children's development affected by having two wage-earning parents, having divorced parents, having gay or lesbian parents, and being part of a particular cultural, ethnic, and socioeconomic group?

Connect

- Fathers are most often the perpetrators in shaken baby syndrome. Given what you learned in this chapter, which family interactions would a researcher or marriage and family therapist be likely to explore in such a case of child maltreatment?

Reflect *Your Own Personal Journey of Life*

- Which style or styles of parenting did your mother and father use in rearing you? What effects do you think their parenting styles have had on your development?

---

3 Peer Relations, Play, and Media/Screen Time

LG3 Describe the roles of peers, play, and media/screen time in young children's development.

| Peer Relations | Play | Media/Screen Time |

The family is a very important social context for children's development. However, children's development also is strongly influenced by what goes on in other social contexts, such as in peer groups and when children are playing or spending time with media, computers, and other electronic devices (Ettekal & Ladd, 2020; Reaney, 2020; Smaldino & others, 2019; Willumsen & Bull, 2020).

PEER RELATIONS

As children grow older, they spend an increasing amount of time with their *peers*—children of about the same age or maturity level.

Peer Group Functions What are the functions of a child's peer group? One of its most important functions is to provide a source of information and comparison about the world outside the family. Children receive feedback about their abilities from their peer group. Children evaluate what they do in terms of whether it is better than, as good as, or worse than what other children do. It is hard to make these judgments at home because siblings are usually older or younger.

Good peer relations promote normal socioemotional development (Chen, Saafir, & Graham, 2020; Demirtas-Zorbaz & Ergene, 2019). Special concerns in peer relations focus on children who are withdrawn or aggressive (Coplan & others, 2018; Miller & Johnston, 2019). Withdrawn children who are rejected by peers or are victimized and feel lonely are at risk for depression (Rubin & others, 2018). Children who are aggressive with their peers are at risk for a number of problems, including delinquency and dropping out of school (Vitaro, Boivin, & Poulin, 2018).

Developmental Changes Recall from our discussion of gender that, by about the age of 3, children already prefer to spend time with same-sex rather than opposite-sex playmates, and this preference increases in early childhood. During these same years the frequency of peer interaction, both positive and negative, picks up considerably (Cillessen & Bukowski, 2018).

What are some characteristics of peer relations in early childhood?
Ariel Skelley/Blend Images LLC

Many preschool children spend considerable time in peer interaction conversing with playmates about such matters as "negotiating roles and rules in play, arguing, and agreeing" (Rubin, Bukowski, & Parker, 2006). And during early childhood children's interactions with peers become more coordinated and involve longer turns and sequences (Coplan & Arbeau, 2009).

Friends   In early childhood, children distinguish between friends and nonfriends (Howes, 2009). For most young children, a friend is someone to play with. Young preschool children are more likely than older children to have friends who are of a different gender and ethnicity (Howes, 2009).

The Connected Worlds of Parent-Child and Peer Relations   Parents may influence their children's peer relations in many ways, both directly and indirectly (Krisnana & others, 2020; Malti & others, 2019). Parents affect such relations through their interactions with their children, how they manage their children's lives, and the opportunities they provide to their children (Hastings & others, 2019; Ladd & Kochenderfer-Ladd, 2019). For example, one study found that when mothers coached their preschool daughters about the negative aspects of peer conflicts involving relational aggression (harming someone by manipulating a relationship), the daughters engaged in lower rates of relational aggression (Werner & others, 2014).

Basic lifestyle decisions by parents—their choices of neighborhoods, churches, schools, and their own friends—largely determine the pool from which their children select possible friends. These choices in turn affect which children their children meet, their purpose in interacting, and eventually which children become their friends.

Researchers also have found that children's peer relations are linked to attachment security and parents' marital quality (Booth-LaForce & Groh, 2018). Early attachments to caregivers provide a connection to children's peer relations not only by creating a secure base from which children can explore social relationships beyond the family but also by conveying a working model of relationships (Hartup, 2009).

Do these results indicate that children's peer relations always are wedded to parent-child relationships? Although parent-child relationships influence children's subsequent peer relations, children also learn other modes of relating through their relationships with peers. For example, rough-and-tumble play occurs mainly with other children, not in parent-child interaction. In times of stress, children often turn to parents rather than peers for support. In parent-child relationships, children learn how to relate to authority figures. With their peers, children are likely to interact on a much more equal basis and to learn a mode of relating based on mutual influence. We will have much more to say about peer relations later.

developmental **connection**
Peers
Children's peer relations have been classified in terms of five peer statuses. Connect to "Socioemotional Development in Middle and Late Childhood."

How are parent-child and peer relationships connected?
(*Top*) Monkeybusinessimages/iStockphoto/Getty Images; (*bottom*) Kali9/Getty Images

PLAY

An extensive amount of peer interaction during childhood involves play, but social play is only one type of play. Play is a pleasurable activity in which children engage for its own sake, and its functions and forms vary (Yogman & others, 2018).

Play's Functions   Play is an important aspect of children's development (Reaney, 2020; Tamis-LeMonda & others, 2019). Theorists have focused on different aspects of play and highlighted a long list of functions.

According to Freud and Erikson, play helps children master anxieties and conflicts (Demanchick, 2015). Because tensions are relieved in play, children can cope more effectively with life's problems. Play permits children to work off excess physical energy and to release pent-up tensions. Therapists use *play therapy* both to allow children to work off frustrations and to analyze children's conflicts and ways of coping with them. Children may feel less threatened and be more likely to express their true feelings in the context of play.

Play also is an important context for cognitive development (Taggart, Eisen, & Lillard, 2018). Both Jean Piaget and Lev Vygotsky concluded that play is a child's work. Piaget (1962) maintained that play advances children's cognitive development. At the same time, he said, children's cognitive development *constrains* the way they play. Play permits children to practice their competencies and acquired skills in a relaxed, pleasurable way (Hirsh-Pasek & Golinkoff, 2014). Piaget thought that cognitive structures need to be exercised, and play provides the perfect setting for this exercise (DeLisi, 2015).

Let us play, for it is yet day
And we cannot go to sleep;
Besides, in the sky the little birds fly
And the hills are all covered with sheep.

—**WILLIAM BLAKE**
English poet, 19th century

developmental **connection**

Sociocultural Cognitive Theory

Vygotsky emphasized that children develop their ways of thinking and understanding mainly through social interaction. Connect to "Physical and Cognitive Development in Early Childhood."

A preschool "superhero" at play.
Michelle D. Milliman/Shutterstock

sensorimotor play Behavior engaged in by infants that lets them derive pleasure from exercising their existing sensorimotor schemas.

practice play Play that involves repetition of behavior when new skills are being learned or when physical or mental mastery and coordination of skills are required for games or sports.

pretense/symbolic play Play in which the child transforms the physical environment into a symbol.

social play Play that involves social interactions with peers.

Vygotsky (1962) also considered play to be an excellent setting for cognitive development. He was especially interested in the symbolic and make-believe aspects of play, as when a child substitutes a stick for a horse and rides the stick as if it were a horse. For young children, the imaginary situation is real (Bodrova & Leong, 2015a, b). Parents should encourage such imaginary play, because it advances the child's cognitive development, especially creative thought (Tamis-LeMonda & others, 2019).

Daniel Berlyne (1960) described play as exciting and pleasurable in itself because it satisfies our exploratory drive. This drive involves curiosity and a desire for information about something new or unusual. Play encourages exploratory behavior by offering children the possibilities of novelty, complexity, uncertainty, surprise, and incongruity.

More recently, play has been described as an important context for the development of language and communication skills (Taggart, Eisen, & Lillard, 2018). Language and communication skills may be enhanced through discussions and negotiations regarding roles and rules in play as young children practice various words and phrases. These types of social interactions during play can benefit young children's literacy skills (Bredekamp, 2020). Play is a central focus of the child-centered kindergarten and is thought to be an essential aspect of early childhood education (Morrison, 2020).

Types of Play   The contemporary perspective on play emphasizes both the cognitive and the social aspects of play (Reaney, 2020). Among the most widely studied types of children's play today are sensorimotor and practice play, pretense/symbolic play, social play, constructive play, and games.

Sensorimotor and Practice Play   **Sensorimotor play** is behavior by infants that lets them derive pleasure from exercising their sensorimotor schemes. The development of sensorimotor play follows Piaget's description of sensorimotor thought. Infants initially engage in exploratory and playful visual and motor transactions in the second quarter of the first year of life. At about 9 months of age, infants begin to select novel objects for exploration and play, especially responsive objects such as toys that make noise or bounce.

Practice play involves the repetition of behavior when new skills are being learned or when physical or mental mastery and coordination of skills are required for games or sports. Sensorimotor play, which often involves practice play, is primarily confined to infancy, whereas practice play can be engaged in throughout life. During the preschool years, children often engage in practice play.

Pretense/Symbolic Play   **Pretense/symbolic play** occurs when the child transforms the physical environment into a symbol (Taggart, Eisen, & Lillard, 2018). Between 9 and 30 months of age, children increase their use of objects in symbolic play. They learn to transform objects—substituting them for other objects and acting toward them as if they were those other objects. For example, a preschool child treats a table as if it were a car and says, "I'm fixing the car," as he grabs a leg of the table.

Many experts on play consider the preschool years the "golden age" of symbolic/pretense play that is dramatic or sociodramatic in nature. This type of make-believe play often appears at about 18 months of age and reaches a peak at 4 to 5 years of age, then gradually declines.

Some child psychologists conclude that pretend play is an important aspect of young children's development and often reflects advances in their cognitive development, especially as an indication of symbolic understanding (Taggart, Eisen, & Lillard, 2018). For example, Catherine Garvey (2000) and Angeline Lillard (2006) emphasize that hidden in young children's pretend play narratives are remarkable capacities for role-taking, balancing of social roles, metacognition (thinking about thinking), testing of the reality-pretense distinction, and numerous nonegocentric capacities that reveal the remarkable cognitive skills of young children. A major accomplishment in early childhood is the development of children's ability to share their pretend play with peers (Coplan & Arbeau, 2009). And researchers have found that pretend play contributes to young children's self-regulation, mainly because of the self-monitoring and social sensitivity that is required in creating and enacting a sociodramatic narrative in cooperation with other children (Diamond & others, 2007).

Social Play   **Social play** involves interaction with peers. Social play increases dramatically during the preschool years. For many children, social play is the main context for young children's social interactions with peers (Solovieva & Quintanar, 2017).

What characterizes social play?
Fotostorm/E+/Getty Images

Constructive Play   **Constructive play** combines sensorimotor/practice play with symbolic representation. It occurs when children engage in the self-regulated creation of a product or a solution. Constructive play increases in the preschool years as symbolic play increases and sensorimotor play decreases. It also becomes a frequent form of play in the elementary school years, both within and outside the classroom.

Games   **Games** are activities that children engage in for pleasure and that have rules (Reaney, 2020). Often they involve competition. Preschool children may begin to participate in social games that involve simple rules of reciprocity and turn taking. However, games take on a much stronger role in the lives of elementary school children. In one study, the highest incidence of game playing occurred between 10 and 12 years of age (Eiferman, 1971). After age 12, games decline in popularity (Bergen, 1988).

Trends in Play   Kathy Hirsh-Pasek, Roberta Golinkoff, and Dorothy Singer (Hirsh-Pasek & others, 2009; Singer, Golinkoff, & Hirsh-Pasek, 2006) are concerned about the small amount of time for free play that young children have today, reporting that it has declined considerably in recent decades. They especially are worried about young children's playtime being restricted at home and school so they can spend more time on academic subjects. They also point out that many schools have eliminated recess. And it is not just the declining time for free play that bothers them. They underscore that learning in playful contexts captivates children's minds in ways that enhance their cognitive and socioemotional development—Singer, Golinkoff, and Hirsh-Pasek's (2006) first book on play was titled *Play = Learning*. Among the cognitive benefits of play they described are skills in the following areas: creativity; abstract thinking; imagination; attention, concentration, and persistence; problem-solving; social cognition, empathy, and perspective taking; language; and mastery of new concepts. Among the socioemotional experiences and development they believe play promotes are enjoyment, relaxation, and self-expression; cooperation, sharing, and turn-taking; anxiety reduction; and self-confidence. With so many positive cognitive and socioemotional outcomes of play, clearly it is important that we find more time for play in young children's lives (Taggart, Eisen, & Lillard, 2018; Yogman & others, 2019).

What are some of the benefits of play for children, according to Hirsh-Pasek and her colleagues?
ONOKY - Photononstop/Alamy Stock Photo

MEDIA/SCREEN TIME

Few developments in society in the second half of the twentieth century had a greater impact on children than television (Maloy & others, 2021; Roblyer & Hughes, 2019). Television continues to have a strong influence on children's development, but children's use of other media

constructive play Play that combines sensorimotor and repetitive activity with symbolic representation of ideas. Constructive play occurs when children engage in self-regulated creation or construction of a product or a solution.

games Activities engaged in for pleasure that include rules and often involve competition with one or more individuals.

What are some concerns about the increase in children's media and screen time?
Miguel Sanz/Moment/Getty Images

and information/communication devices has led to the use of the term *screen time* to describe the amount of time individuals spend with television, DVDs, computers, video games, and hand-held electronic devices such as smartphones (Vandendriessche & others, 2019). As we discussed in "Physical and Cognitive Development in Early Childhood," recently the World Health Organization (WHO) recommended that 3- to 4-year-olds should engage in no more than 1 hour of sedentary screen time daily (Willumsen & Bull, 2020). In a recent study, 3- to 4-year-old African American children and children who lived at or below the poverty level were more likely than other children to engage in more than 1 hour of screen time daily (Kracht, Webster, & Staiano, 2020).

Despite the move to mobile devices, young children still watch a lot of television. Compared with their counterparts in other developed countries, children in the United States watch television for longer periods. The American Academy of Pediatrics (2016) recommends that 2- to 5-year olds watch no more than one hour of TV a day. The Academy also recommends that they should watch only high-quality programs such as *Sesame Street* and other PBS shows for young children.

Some types of TV shows are linked to positive outcomes for children. For example, a meta-analysis of studies in 14 countries found that watching the TV show *Sesame Street* produced positive outcomes in three areas: cognitive skills, learning about the world, and social reasoning and attitudes toward outgroups (Mares & Pan, 2013).

However, too much screen time can have a negative influence on children by making them passive learners, distracting them from doing homework, teaching them stereotypes, providing them with violent models of aggression, and presenting them with unrealistic views of the world (Picherot & others, 2018). Among other concerns about young children having so much screen time are decreased time spent in play, less time interacting with peers, higher rates of aggression, decreased physical activity, lower cognitive development, poor sleep habits, and increased risk of being overweight or obese (Berglind & others, 2018). One research review concluded that greater amounts of screen time (mostly involving TV viewing) were associated with a lower level of cognitive development in early childhood (Carson & others, 2015). Also, in a recent study of preschool children, compared with children with less than 30 minutes of screen time a day, those with two hours or more a day were much more likely to have inattention problems (including a higher risk of developing ADHD symptoms) and externalizing problems (Tamana & others, 2019). And in another recent study of 2- to 5-year-olds, time spent in television/DVD/video viewing was negatively associated with their social skills while time spent in outdoor play was positively linked to their social skills (Hinkley & others, 2018). Further, a study of preschool children found that each additional hour of screen time was linked to less nightly sleep, later bedtimes, and reduced likelihood of sleeping 10 or more hours per night (Xu & others, 2016). And researchers have found that a high level of TV viewing is linked to a greater incidence of obesity in children and adolescents (Berglind & others, 2018). Indeed, viewing as little as one hour of television daily was associated with an increase in body mass index (BMI) between kindergarten and the first grade (Peck & others, 2015).

A higher degree of parental monitoring of children's media use was linked to a number of positive outcomes in children's lives (more sleep, better school performance, less aggressive behavior, and more prosocial behavior) (Gentile & others, 2014). Researchers also have found that parental reductions in their own screen time were associated with decreased screen time for their children (Barr, 2019; Sanders, Parent, & Forehand, 2018).

Effects of Television on Children's Aggression

The extent to which children are exposed to violence and aggression on television raises special concerns (Khurana & others, 2019). For example, Saturday morning cartoon shows average more than 25 violent acts per hour. One study revealed that spending increased time viewing TV violence, video game violence, and music video violence was independently associated with a higher level of physical aggression in children (Coker & others, 2015). Also, in one experiment, preschool children were randomly assigned to one of two groups: One group watched television shows taken directly from violent Saturday morning cartoons on 11 days; the second group watched television cartoon shows with all of the violence removed (Steur, Applefield, & Smith, 1971). The children were then observed during play at their preschool. The preschool children who had seen the TV cartoon shows with violence kicked, choked, and pushed their playmates more than did the preschool children who had watched nonviolent TV cartoon shows. Because the children were randomly assigned to the two conditions (TV cartoons with violence versus nonviolent TV cartoons), we can conclude that exposure to TV violence caused the increased aggression in the children in this investigation.

In addition to television violence, there is increased concern about children who play violent video games, especially those that are highly realistic (Coyne & others, 2018). Research reviews have concluded that playing violent video games is linked to aggression in both males and females (Gentile, 2011).

Effects of Television on Children's Prosocial Behavior   Television can have a positive influence on children's development by presenting motivating educational programs, providing information about the world beyond their immediate environment, and displaying models of prosocial behavior (Roblyer & Hughes, 2019). A recent meta-analysis found that children's exposure to prosocial media is linked to higher levels of prosocial behavior and empathetic concern (Coyne & others, 2018). For example, researchers have found that when children watch positive social interchanges on the TV show *Sesame Street,* they subsequently are likely to imitate these positive social behaviors (Truglio & Kotler, 2014).

Review *Connect* Reflect

 LG3 Describe the roles of peers, play, and media/ screen time in young children's development.

Review
- How do peers affect young children's development?
- What are some theories and types of play?
- How does television influence young children's development?

Connect
- Earlier in this chapter, you learned about Laurie Kramer's program for teaching siblings social skills to develop positive interactions. Do you think her recommendations would be relevant or irrelevant to peer relationships? Why?

Reflect *Your Own Personal Journey of Life*
- What guidelines would you adopt for your own children's television viewing?

topical connections *looking forward*

The middle and late childhood years bring further changes in children's socioemotional development. Development of self-understanding and understanding of others becomes more sophisticated, emotional understanding improves, and moral reasoning advances. Children now spend less time with parents, but parents continue to play very important roles in children's lives, especially in guiding their academic achievement and managing their opportunities. Peer status and friendship become more important in children's peer relations, and school takes on a stronger academic focus.

reach your **learning goals**

Socioemotional Development in Early Childhood

1 Emotional and Personality Development

LG1 Discuss emotional and personality development in early childhood.

The Self

- In Erikson's theory, early childhood is a period when development involves resolving the conflict of initiative versus guilt. The toddler's rudimentary self-understanding develops into the preschooler's representation of the self in terms of body parts, material possessions, and physical activities. At about 4 to 5 years of age, children also begin to use trait-like self-descriptions. Young children display more sophisticated self-understanding and understanding of others than was previously thought.

Emotional Development

- Advances in young children's emotional development involve expressing emotions, understanding emotions, and regulating emotions. Young children's range of emotions expands during early childhood as they increasingly experience self-conscious emotions such as pride, shame, and guilt. Between 2 and 4 years old, children use an increasing number of terms to describe emotion and learn more about the causes and consequences of feelings. At 4 to 5 years of age, children show an increased ability to reflect on emotions and understand that a single event can elicit different emotions in different people. They also show a growing awareness of the need to manage emotions to meet social standards.

- Emotion-coaching parents have children who engage in more effective self-regulation of their emotions than do emotion-dismissing parents. Emotion regulation plays an important role in successful peer relations.

Moral Development

- Moral development involves thoughts, feelings, and behaviors regarding rules and conventions about what people should do in their interactions with others. Freud's psychoanalytic theory emphasizes the importance of feelings in the development of the superego, the moral branch of personality. Positive emotions, such as empathy, also contribute to the child's moral development.

- Piaget analyzed moral reasoning and concluded that children from about 4 to 7 years of age display heteronomous morality, judging behavior by its consequences; then, at about 10 years of age and older, they develop autonomous morality.

- According to behavioral and social cognitive theorists, moral behavior develops as a result of reinforcement, punishment, and imitation, and there is considerable situational variability in moral behavior. Conscience refers to an internal regulation of standards of right and wrong that involves an integration of moral thought, feeling, and behavior.

- Young children's conscience emerges out of relationships with parents. Parents influence young children's moral development through the quality of parent-child relationships, by being proactive in helping children avert misbehavior, and by engaging children in conversational dialogue about moral issues.

Gender

- Gender refers to the social and psychological dimensions of being male or female. Gender identity is acquired by 2½ years of age for most children. A gender role is a set of expectations that prescribes how females or males should think, act, and feel. Gender typing refers to the acquisition of a traditional masculine or feminine role.

- Biological influences on gender development include chromosomes and hormones. However, biology does not completely dictate destiny in gender development; children's socialization experiences matter a great deal. Social role theory, psychoanalytic theory, and social cognitive theory emphasize various aspects of social experiences in the development of gender characteristics. Parents influence children's gender development, and peers are especially adept at rewarding gender-appropriate behavior. Gender schema theory emphasizes the role of cognition in gender development.

2 Families

 Explain how families can influence young children's development.

Parenting

- Authoritarian, authoritative, neglectful, and indulgent are four main parenting styles. Authoritative parenting is the most widely used style around the world and is the style most often associated with children's social competence. However, ethnic variations in parenting styles suggest that in Asian American families, some aspects of control may benefit children.

- Physical punishment is widely used by U.S. parents, but some experts conclude that there are a number of reasons it should not be used with children. However, there currently is controversy about the effects of physical punishment on children, with few studies making a distinction between abusive and mild physical punishment.

- Coparenting has positive effects on children's development.

Child Maltreatment

- Child maltreatment may take the form of physical abuse, child neglect, sexual abuse, and emotional abuse. Child maltreatment places the child at risk for academic, emotional, and social problems. Adults who suffered child maltreatment are also vulnerable to a range of problems.

Sibling Relationships and Birth Order

- Siblings interact with each other in positive and negative ways. Birth order is related in certain ways to personality characteristics—for example, firstborns are more adult-oriented and self-controlled than later-born children. Only children often are achievement-oriented. By itself, however, birth order is not a good predictor of behavior.

The Changing Family in a Changing Society

- In general, having both parents employed full-time outside the home has not been shown to have negative effects on children. However, the nature of parents' work can affect their parenting quality.

- Divorce can have negative effects on children's adjustment, but so can an acrimonious relationship between parents who stay together for their children's sake. If divorced parents develop a harmonious relationship and practice authoritative parenting, children's adjustment improves.

- Researchers have found few differences between children growing up in gay or lesbian families and children growing up in heterosexual families.

- Cultures vary on a number of issues regarding families. African American and Latino children are more likely than White American children to live in single-parent families and larger families and to have extended family connections.

- Low-income families have less access to resources than higher-income families do. Lower-SES parents create a home atmosphere with more parental authority and greater use of physical punishment, while higher-SES parents are more concerned about developing children's initiative and ability to delay gratification.

3 Peer Relations, Play, and Media/Screen Time

LG3 Describe the roles of peers, play, and media/screen time in young children's development.

Peer Relations

- Peers are powerful socialization agents. Peers provide a source of information and comparison about the world outside the family. In early childhood, children distinguish between friends and nonfriends, with a friend often described as someone to play with.

- Parent-child and peer relationships are often connected. Parents influence their children's peer relations by how they manage children's lives and the opportunities they provide for interacting with peers. Rough-and-tumble play is more likely to occur in peer relations, whereas in times of stress children often turn to parents rather than peers for support.

Play

- Play's functions include affiliation with peers, tension release, advances in cognitive development, exploration, and provision of a safe haven. The contemporary perspective on play emphasizes both the cognitive and the social aspects of play.

- Among the most widely studied types of children's play are sensorimotor play, practice play, pretense/symbolic play, social play, constructive play, and games.

- There is concern about the decreasing number of hours children spend in free play and in recess at school. Because play is a powerful positive context for the development of children's cognitive and socioemotional skills, it is important that we find more time for play in children's lives.

Media/Screen Time

- Young children watch 2 to 4 hours of TV per day on average, but experts recommend that they watch 1 hour or less. Young children increasingly are spending time with other media and information/communication devices such as computers, DVDs, video games, and smartphones, which has given rise to the term *screen time*. Screen time can have both negative influences (such as turning children into passive learners, presenting them with aggressive models, and decreasing time spent with peers and in play and physical activity) and positive influences (such as providing models of prosocial behavior) on children's development. Both watching TV violence and playing violent video games have been linked to children's aggressive behavior. Watching prosocial behavior on TV can teach children positive social skills.

key **terms**

key **people**

section five

Ariel Skelley/Digital Vision/Getty Images

Each forward step we take we leave some phantom of ourselves behind.

—JOHN LANCASTER SPALDING
American educator, 19th century

Middle and Late Childhood

In middle and late childhood, children are on a different plane, belonging to a generation and feeling all their own. It is the wisdom of the human life span that at no time are children more ready to learn than during the period of expansive imagination at the end of early childhood. Children develop a sense of wanting to make things—and not just to make them, but to make them well and even perfectly. They seek to know and to understand. They are remarkable for their intelligence and for their curiosity. Their parents continue to be important influences in their lives, but their growth also is shaped by peers and friends. They don't think much about the future or about the past, but they enjoy the present moment. This section consists of two chapters: "Physical and Cognitive Development in Middle and Late Childhood" and "Socioemotional Development in Middle and Late Childhood."

chapter 9

PHYSICAL AND COGNITIVE DEVELOPMENT IN MIDDLE AND LATE CHILDHOOD

chapter outline

① Physical Changes and Health

Learning Goal 1 Describe physical changes and health in middle and late childhood.

Body Growth and Change

The Brain

Motor Development

Exercise

Health, Illness, and Disease

② Children with Disabilities

Learning Goal 2 Identify children with different types of disabilities and discuss issues in educating them.

The Scope of Disabilities

Educational Issues

③ Cognitive Changes

Learning Goal 3 Explain cognitive changes in middle and late childhood.

Piaget's Cognitive Developmental Theory

Information Processing

Intelligence

Extremes of Intelligence

④ Language Development

Learning Goal 4 Discuss language development in middle and late childhood.

Vocabulary, Grammar, and Metalinguistic Awareness

Reading

Writing

Second-Language Learning and Bilingual Education

Hero Images/Getty Images

The following comments were made by Angie, an elementary-school-aged girl:

When I was 8 years old, I weighed 125 pounds. My clothes were the size that large teenage girls wear. I hated my body, and my classmates teased me all the time. I was so overweight and out of shape that when I took a P.E. class my face would get red and I had trouble breathing. I was jealous of the kids who played sports and weren't overweight like I was.

I'm 9 years old now and I've lost 30 pounds. I'm much happier and proud of myself. How did I lose the weight? My mom said she had finally decided enough was enough. She took me to a pediatrician who specializes in helping children lose weight and keep it off. The pediatrician counseled my mom about my eating and exercise habits, then had us join a group that he had created for overweight children and their parents. My mom and I go to the group once a week and we've now been participating in the program for 6 months. I no longer eat fast food meals and my mom is cooking more healthy meals. Now that I've lost weight, exercise is not as hard for me and I don't get teased by the kids at school. My mom's pretty happy too because she's lost 15 pounds herself since we've been in the counseling program.

Not all overweight children are as successful as Angie at reducing their weight. Indeed, being overweight or obese in childhood has become a major national concern in the United States. Later in this chapter, we will further explore being overweight and obese in childhood, including obesity's causes and outcomes.

topical connections *looking **back***

Children grow more slowly in early childhood than in infancy, but they still grow an average of 2.5 inches and gain 4 to 7 pounds a year. In early childhood, the most rapid growth in the brain occurs in the prefrontal cortex. The gross and fine motor skills of children also become smoother and more coordinated. In terms of cognitive development, early childhood is a period in which young children increasingly engage in symbolic thought. Young children's information-processing skills also improve considerably—executive and sustained attention advance, short-term memory gets better, executive function increases, and their understanding of the human mind makes considerable progress. Young children also increase their knowledge of language's rule systems, and their literacy benefits from active participation in a wide range of language experiences. Most young children attend an early childhood education program, and there are many variations in these programs.

preview

During the middle and late childhood years, children grow taller, heavier, and stronger. They become more adept at using their physical skills, and they develop new cognitive skills. This chapter is about physical and cognitive development in middle and late childhood. To begin, we will explore aspects of physical development.

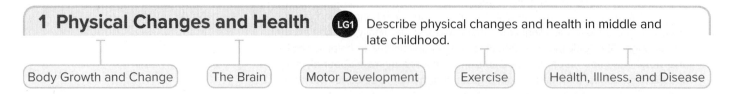

1 Physical Changes and Health **LG1** Describe physical changes and health in middle and late childhood.

| Body Growth and Change | The Brain | Motor Development | Exercise | Health, Illness, and Disease |

Continued change characterizes children's bodies during middle and late childhood, and their motor skills improve. As children move through the elementary school years, they gain greater control over their bodies and can sit and keep their attention focused for longer periods of time. Regular exercise is one key to making these years a time of healthy growth and development.

BODY GROWTH AND CHANGE

The period of middle and late childhood involves slow, consistent growth (Edwards & Coyne, 2020). This is a period of calm before the rapid growth spurt of adolescence. During the elementary school years, children grow an average of 2 to 3 inches a year until, at the age of 11, the average girl is 4 feet, 10 inches tall, and the average boy is 4 feet, 9 inches tall. During middle and late childhood, children gain about 5 to 7 pounds a year. The weight increase is due mainly to growth of the skeletal and muscular systems as well as some body organs.

Proportional changes are among the most pronounced physical changes in middle and late childhood. Head circumference and waist circumference decrease in relation to body height (Kliegman & others, 2019). A less noticeable physical change is that bones continue to ossify during middle and late childhood but yield to pressure and pull more than mature bones.

THE BRAIN

The development of brain-imaging techniques such as magnetic resonance imaging (MRI) has led to increased research on changes in the brain during middle and late childhood and links between these brain changes and cognitive development (Schneider & Ornstein, 2019). Total brain volume stabilizes by the end of late childhood, but significant changes in various structures and regions of the brain continue to occur (Torres-Ramos & others, 2020). In particular, the brain pathways and circuitry involving the prefrontal cortex, the highest level in the brain, continue to develop during middle and late childhood (see Figure 1). These advances in the prefrontal cortex are linked to children's improved attention, reasoning, and cognitive control (Aben & others, 2019).

Leading developmental neuroscientist Mark Johnson and his colleagues (2009) proposed that the prefrontal cortex likely orchestrates the functions of many other brain regions during development. As part of this neural leadership role, the prefrontal cortex may provide an advantage to neural networks and connections that include the prefrontal cortex. In their view, the prefrontal cortex coordinates the best neural connections for solving a problem at hand. Also, recent research indicates that emerging cognitive control during childhood is mainly supported by the development of distributed neural networks in which the prefrontal cortex is central (Chevalier & others, 2019).

Changes also occur in the thickness of the cerebral cortex (cortical thickness) in middle and late childhood (Thomason & Thompson, 2011). One study used brain scans to assess cortical thickness in 5- to 11-year-old children (Sowell & others, 2004). Cortical thickening across a two-year time period was observed in the temporal and frontal lobe areas that function in language, which may reflect improvements in language abilities such as reading. Figure 6 in "Physical Development in Infancy" shows the locations of the temporal and frontal lobes in the brain. Also, in a recent study of 9- to 10-year-olds, children with a high body mass index had less cortical thickness, which was linked to a lower level of executive function (Laurent & others, 2020).

developmental connection

Brain Development

Synaptic pruning is an important aspect of the brain's development, and the pruning varies by brain region across children's development. Connect to "Physical Development in Infancy."

What characterizes children's physical growth in middle and late childhood?
Chris Windsor/Digital Vision/Getty Images

As children develop, some brain areas become more active while others become less so (Kwon & others, 2020). One shift in activation that occurs as children develop is from diffuse, larger areas to more focal, smaller areas (Turkeltaub & others, 2003). This shift is characterized by synaptic pruning, a process in which areas of the brain that are not being used lose synaptic connections and areas that are used show increased connections. In one study, researchers found less diffusion and more focal activation in the prefrontal cortex from 7 to 30 years of age (Durston & others, 2006).

Increases in connectivity between brain regions also occurs as children develop (Twait & Horowitz-Kraus, 2019). In a longitudinal study of individuals from 6 to 22 years of age, connectivity between the prefrontal and parietal lobes in childhood was linked to better reasoning ability later in development (Wendelken & others, 2017). And in another recent study, reduced amygdala-prefrontal connectivity occurred in children with autism spectrum disorder (Ibrahim & others, 2019).

MOTOR DEVELOPMENT

During middle and late childhood, children's motor skills become much smoother and more coordinated than they were in early childhood (Hockenberry & Wilson, 2019). For example, only one child in a thousand can hit a tennis ball over the net at the age of 3, yet by the age of 10 or 11 most children can learn to play the sport. Running, climbing, skipping rope, swimming, bicycle riding, and skating are just a few of the many physical skills elementary school children can master. In gross motor skills involving large muscle activity, boys usually outperform girls.

Increased myelination of the central nervous system is reflected in the improvement of fine motor skills during middle and late childhood. Children can more adroitly use their hands as tools. Six-year-olds can hammer, paste, tie shoes, and fasten clothes. By 7 years of age, children's hands have become steadier. At this age, children prefer a pencil to a crayon for printing, and reversal of letters is less common. Printing becomes smaller. At 8 to 10 years of age, the hands can be used independently with more ease and precision. Fine motor coordination develops to the point at which children can write rather than print words. Cursive letter size becomes smaller and more even. At 10 to 12 years of age, children begin to show manipulative skills similar to the abilities of adults. They can master the complex, intricate, and rapid movements needed to produce fine-quality crafts or to play a difficult piece on a musical instrument. Girls usually outperform boys in their use of fine motor skills.

EXERCISE

America's children are not getting enough exercise (Graham, Holt/Hale, & Parker, 2020). Increasing children's exercise levels has a number of positive outcomes (Lumpkin, 2021; Rink, 2020). A recent study examined children's physical activity as they made the transition from elementary to middle school (Pate & others, 2019). In this study, the following activities were associated with children's greater physical activity: parents' encouragement of physical activity, parents' support of physical activity, time children spent outdoors, children's sports participation, and number of physical activity facilities near their home.

An increasing number of studies document the importance of exercise in children's physical development (Meeks, Heit, & Page, 2020; Teague, Mackenzie, & Rosenthal, 2019). One study of more than 6,000 elementary school children revealed that 55 minutes or more of moderate-to-vigorous physical activity daily was associated with a lower incidence of obesity (Nemet, 2016). Further, a research review concluded that exercise programs with a frequency of three weekly sessions lasting longer than 60 minutes were effective in lowering both systolic and diastolic blood pressure (Garcia-Hermoso, Saavedra, & Escalante, 2013). And a recent study indicated that regular physical activity combined with a high level of calcium intake increased the bone health of 3- to 18-year-olds (X. Yang & others, 2020).

Aerobic exercise also is linked to children's cognitive skills (Martin & others, 2018). Researchers have found that aerobic exercise benefits children's processing speed, attention, memory, effortful and goal-directed thinking and behavior, and creativity (Lind & others, 2018; Ludyga & others, 2017; Pan & others, 2017). A recent meta-analysis concluded that sustained physical activity programs were linked to improvements in children's attention, executive function, and academic achievement (de Greeff & others, 2018). Another recent meta-analysis concluded that prolonged exercise interventions with 6- to 12-year-olds that consisted of multiple exercise activities per week for more than 6 weeks improved the children's executive

Prefrontal cortex

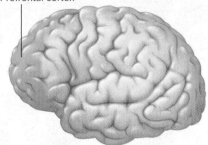

FIGURE 1

THE PREFRONTAL CORTEX. The brain pathways and circuitry involving the prefrontal cortex (shaded in purple) show significant advances in development during middle and late childhood. *What cognitive processes are linked to these changes in the prefrontal cortex?*

> developmental **connection**
> **Exercise**
> Experts recommend that preschool children engage in two hours of physical activity per day. Connect to "Socioemotional Development in Early Childhood."

What are some good strategies for increasing children's exercise?
Robert Kneschke/Shutterstock

function in general and their inhibitory control in particular (Xue, Yang, & Huang, 2019).

Parents and schools play important roles in determining children's exercise levels (Lumpkin, 2021; Pate & others, 2019). Growing up with parents who exercise regularly provides positive models of exercise for children (Crawford & others, 2010). In addition, a research review found that school-based physical activity was successful in improving children's fitness and lowering their fat levels (Kriemler & others, 2011).

Screen time also is linked with low activity, obesity, and worse sleep patterns in children (Vandendriessche & others, 2019). A recent research review found that a higher level of screen time increased the risk of obesity for low- and high-activity children (Lane, Harrison, & Murphy, 2014). Also, a recent study of 8- to 12-year-olds found that screen time was associated with lower connectivity between brain regions, as well as lower levels of language skills and cognitive control (Horowitz-Kraus & Hutton, 2018). In this study, time spent reading was linked to higher levels of functioning in these areas. And a recent study indicated that heavy screen time at 11 years of age was linked to an increase in body mass index 3 years later (Engberg & others, 2020).

Here are some ways to encourage children to exercise more:

- Offer more physical activity programs run by volunteers at school facilities.
- Improve physical fitness activities in schools.
- Have children plan community and school activities that interest them.
- Encourage families to focus more on physical activity, and encourage parents to exercise more.

HEALTH, ILLNESS, AND DISEASE

For the most part, middle and late childhood is a time of excellent health. Disease and death are less prevalent at this time than during other periods in childhood or adolescence. However, many children in middle and late childhood face health problems that harm their development.

Accidents and Injuries   Injuries are the leading cause of death during middle and late childhood, and the most common cause of severe injury and death in this period is motor vehicle accidents, either as a pedestrian or as a passenger (Centers for Disease Control and Prevention, 2020a). For this reason, safety advocates recommend the use of safety-belt restraints and child booster seats in vehicles because they can greatly reduce the severity of motor vehicle injuries (Shimony-Kanat & others, 2018). For example, one study found that child booster seats reduced the risk for serious injury by 45 percent for 4- to 8-year-old children (Sauber-Schatz & others, 2014). Other serious injuries involve bicycles, skateboards, roller skates, and other sports equipment (Perry & others, 2018).

Overweight Children   Being overweight is an increasingly prevalent health problem in children (Blake, 2020; Schiff, 2021). Recall that being overweight is defined in terms of body mass index (BMI), which is computed by a formula that takes into account height and weight—children at or above the 97th percentile are included in the obesity category, at or above the 95th percentile in the overweight category, and children at or above the 85th percentile are described as at risk for being overweight (Centers for Disease Control and Prevention, 2020b). Over the last three decades, the percentage of U.S. children who are at risk for being overweight has increased dramatically. In 2015-2016, 18.4 percent of 6- to 11-year-old U.S. children were classified as obese, an increase of one percent since 2009-2010 (Hales & others, 2017). Also, more children are overweight in middle and late childhood than in early childhood, which in 2015-2016 was 13.9 percent of 2- to 5-year-olds.

It is not just in the United States that children are becoming more overweight (Thompson, Manore, & Vaughan, 2020). For example, a study found that general and abdominal obesity in Chinese children increased significantly from 1993 to 2009 (Liang & others, 2012). Another Chinese study revealed that high blood pressure in 23 percent of boys and 15 percent of girls could be attributed to being overweight or obese (Dong & others, 2015).

Causes of Children Being Overweight   Heredity and environmental contexts are related to being overweight in childhood (Insel & Roth, 2020). Genetic analysis indicates that heredity is an important factor in children becoming overweight (Donatelle, 2019). Overweight

developmental **connection**

Conditions, Diseases, and Disorders

Metabolic syndrome has increased in middle-aged adults in recent years and is linked to early death. Connect to "Physical and Cognitive Development in Middle Adulthood."

parents tend to have overweight children (Pufal & others, 2012). For example, one study found that the greatest risk factor for being overweight at 9 years of age was having an overweight parent (Agras & others, 2004). Parents and their children often have similar body types, height, body fat composition, and metabolism (Pereira-Lancha, Campos-Ferraz, & Junior, 2012). In a 14-year longitudinal study, parental weight change predicted children's weight change (Andriani, Liao, & Kuo, 2015).

Environmental factors that influence whether children become overweight include availability of food (especially food high in fat content), use of energy-saving devices, declining physical activity, parents' eating habits and monitoring of children's eating habits, the context in which a child eats, and heavy screen time (Ren & others, 2017). Also, in a recent study of Latino families, parents with a healthy weight were 3.7 times more likely to have a child with a healthy weight (Coto & others, 2019). Further, a recent study found that children were less likely to be

What are some concerns about the increase in overweight and obese children?
Image Source/Getty Images

obese or overweight when they attended schools in states that had a strong policy emphasis on healthy foods and beverages (Datar & Nicosia, 2017). In addition, a recent research review of Chinese children revealed that lack of access to fruit and vegetable markets was linked to childhood obesity (S. Yang & others, 2020). And a behavior modification study of overweight and obese children made watching TV contingent on their engagement in exercise (Goldfield, 2012). The intervention markedly increased their exercise and reduced their TV viewing time.

Consequences of Being Overweight The high percentage of overweight children in recent decades is cause for great concern because being overweight raises the risk for many medical and psychological problems (Schiff, 2021). Diabetes, hypertension (high blood pressure), elevated blood cholesterol levels, and sleep problems are common in children who are overweight (Andersen, Holm, & Homoe, 2019). Further, a recent Chinese study found that children and adolescents who were obese were more likely to have depression and anxiety symptoms than non-obese children and adolescents (S. Wang & others, 2019). And a recent research review concluded that obesity is linked with low self-esteem in children (Moharei & others, 2018).

Intervention Programs A combination of diet, exercise, and behavior modification is often recommended to help children lose weight (Graham, Holt/Hale, & Parker, 2020). Intervention programs that emphasize getting parents to engage in healthier lifestyles themselves, as well as to feed their children healthier food and get them to exercise more, can produce weight reduction in overweight and obese children (Parsons, Rukowski, & Turel, 2019). For example, one study found that a combination of a child-centered activity program and a parent-centered dietary modification program helped overweight children lose pounds over a two-year period (Collins & others, 2011).

Cardiovascular Disease Cardiovascular disease is uncommon in children. Nonetheless, environmental experiences and behavior during childhood can sow the seeds for cardiovascular disease in adulthood (Neuhauser, Adler, & Sarganas, 2019). Many elementary-school-aged children already possess one or more of the risk factors for cardiovascular disease, such as hypertension (high blood pressure) and obesity (Kaplinski & others, 2020; Sivasankaran, 2019). In one study, the combination of a larger waist circumference and a higher body mass index (BMI) placed children at higher risk for developing cardiovascular disease (de Koning & others, 2015). Also in a longitudinal study, high levels of body fat and elevated blood pressure beginning in childhood were linked to premature death from coronary heart disease in adulthood (Berenson & others, 2016). Further, one study found that high blood pressure went undiagnosed in 75 percent of children with the disease (Hansen, Gunn, & Kaelber, 2007). And a recent study revealed that parental overweight and high blood pressure were linked to children's high blood pressure (Xu & others, 2019).

Cancer Cancer is the second leading cause of death in U.S. children 5 to 14 years of age. One in every 330 children in the United States develops cancer before the age of 19. The incidence of cancer in children has increased slightly in recent years (National Cancer Institute, 2020).

Childhood cancers mainly attack the white blood cells, brain, bone, lymph system, muscles, kidneys, and nervous system. All types of cancer are characterized by an uncontrolled proliferation of abnormal cells (Nagarajan & others, 2019). As indicated in Figure 2, the most

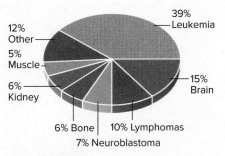

FIGURE 2
TYPES OF CANCER IN CHILDREN.
Cancers in children have a different profile from adult cancers, which attack mainly the lungs, colon, breast, prostate, and pancreas.

Sharon McLeod, Child Life Specialist

Sharon McLeod is a child life specialist who is senior clinical director in the Division of Child Life and Division of Integrative Care at the Children's Hospital Medical Center in Cincinnati.

Under McLeod's direction, the goals of her department are to promote children's optimal growth and development, reduce the stress of health care experiences, and provide support to child patients and their families. These goals are accomplished by facilitating therapeutic play and developmentally appropriate activities, educating and psychologically preparing children for medical procedures, and serving as a resource for parents and other professionals regarding children's development and health care issues.

McLeod says that human growth and development provides the foundation for her profession as a child life specialist. She also says her best times as a student were when she conducted fieldwork, had an internship, and experienced hands-on applications of the theories and concepts that she learned in her courses.

Sharon McLeod, child life specialist, works with a child at Children's Hospital Medical Center in Cincinnati.
Courtesy of Sharon McLeod

For more information about what child life specialists do, see the Careers in Life-Span Development appendix.

common cancer in children is leukemia, a cancer in which bone marrow manufactures an abundance of abnormal white blood cells that crowd out normal cells, making the child highly susceptible to bruising and infection (Grunnan & Rosthoj, 2019; Walker & others, 2020).

Because of advancements in cancer treatment, children with cancer are surviving longer than in the past (National Cancer Institute, 2020). For example, approximately 80 percent of children with acute lymphoblastic leukemia are cured with current chemotherapy treatment.

Child life specialists are among the health professionals who work to make the lives of children with diseases less stressful. To read about the work of child life specialist Sharon McLeod, see *Connecting with Careers*.

Review *Connect* Reflect

 LG1 Describe physical changes and health in middle and late childhood.

Review

- What are some changes in body growth and proportions in middle and late childhood?
- What characterizes the development of the brain in middle and late childhood?
- How do children's motor skills develop in middle and late childhood?
- What role does exercise play in children's lives?
- What are some characteristics of health, illness, and disease in middle and late childhood?

Connect

- In this section, you learned that increased myelination of the central nervous system is reflected in the improvement of fine motor skills during middle and late childhood. What developmental advances were connected with increased myelination in infancy and early childhood?

Reflect *Your Own Personal Journey of Life*

- One way that children get exercise is to play a sport. If you played a sport as a child, was it a positive or negative experience? Do you think that playing a sport as a child influenced whether you have continued to exercise on a regular basis? Explain. If you did not play a sport, do you wish you had? Explain.

The Scope of Disabilities   Educational Issues

THE SCOPE OF DISABILITIES

Of all children in the United States, 12.9 percent from 3 to 21 years of age received special education or related services in 2015-2016, an increase of 3 percent since 1980-1981 (National Center for Education Statistics, 2017). Figure 3 shows the five largest groups of students with a disability who were served by federal programs during the 2015-2016 school year (National Center for Education Statistics, 2017).

As indicated in Figure 3, students with a learning disability were by far the largest group of students with a disability who were enrolled in special education, followed by children with speech or hearing impairments, autism, intellectual disability, and emotional disturbance. Note that the U.S. Department of Education includes both students with a learning disability and students with ADHD in the category of learning disability.

Learning Disabilities   The U.S. government created a definition of learning disabilities in 1997 and then reauthorized the definition with a few minor changes in 2004. Following is a summary of the government's definition of the characteristics that determine whether a child should be classified as having a learning disability. A child with a **learning disability** has difficulty in learning that involves understanding or using spoken or written language, and the difficulty can appear in listening, thinking, reading, writing, and spelling. A learning disability also may involve difficulty in doing mathematics (Turnbull & others, 2020). To be classified as a learning disability, the learning problem is not primarily the result of visual, hearing, or motor disabilities; intellectual disability; emotional disorders; or environmental, cultural, or economic disadvantage.

About three times as many boys as girls are classified as having a learning disability. Among the explanations for this gender difference are a greater biological vulnerability among boys and *referral bias.* That is, boys are more likely to be referred by teachers for treatment because of troublesome behavior.

Approximately 80 percent of children with a learning disability have a reading problem (Shaywitz & Shaywitz, 2017). Three types of learning disabilities are dyslexia, dysgraphia, and dyscalculia:

- **Dyslexia** is a category reserved for individuals who have a severe impairment in their ability to read and spell (Kershner, 2019; Peter & others, 2020).

- **Dysgraphia** is a learning disability that involves difficulty in handwriting (Johnson, Ross, & Kiran, 2019). Children with dysgraphia may write very slowly, their writing products may be virtually illegible, and they may make numerous spelling errors because of their inability to match sounds and letters.

- **Dyscalculia,** also known as developmental arithmetic disorder, is a learning disability that involves difficulty in math computation (Moreau & others, 2019).

The precise causes of learning disabilities have not yet been determined. Researchers have used brain-imaging techniques, such as magnetic resonance imaging, to explore whether specific regions of the brain might be involved in learning disabilities (Ramus & others, 2018; Shaywitz, Lyon, & Shaywitz, 2006) (see Figure 4). This research indicates that it is unlikely learning disabilities reside in a single, specific brain location. More likely, learning disabilities involve difficulty integrating information from multiple brain regions or subtle impairments in brain structures and functions (Banker & others, 2020).

Interventions with children who have a learning disability often focus on improving reading ability (Gunning, 2020). Intensive instruction over a period of time by a competent teacher can help many children (Dewitz & others, 2020).

Disability	Percentage of Children with a Disability
Specific learning impairment	34.6
Speech or language impairment	19.5
Other health impairment	14.4
Autism	10.2
Developmental delay	6.6
Intellectual disability	6.3
Emotional disturbance	5.1

FIGURE 3

U.S. CHILDREN WITH A DISABILITY WHO RECEIVE SPECIAL EDUCATION SERVICES. Figures are for the 2017–2018 school year and represent the seven categories with the highest numbers and percentages of children (National Center for Education Statistics, 2019). Both learning disability and attention deficit hyperactivity disorder are combined in the specific learning disability category. The most dramatic increase in a disability has occurred for autism. The first time autism was included in this assessment was 2000–2001, with only 0.1 percent of children with a disability classified as autistic. This figure increased to 6.5 percent in 2010–2011 and to 10.2 percent in 2017–2018.

learning disability Difficulty in understanding or using spoken or written language or in doing mathematics. To be classified as a learning disability, the learning problem is not primarily the result of visual, hearing, or motor disabilities; intellectual disability; emotional disorders; or environmental, cultural, or economic disadvantage.

dyslexia A category of learning disabilities involving a severe impairment in the ability to read and spell.

dysgraphia A learning disability that involves difficulty in handwriting.

dyscalculia Also known as developmental arithmetic disorder; a learning disability that involves difficulty in math computation.

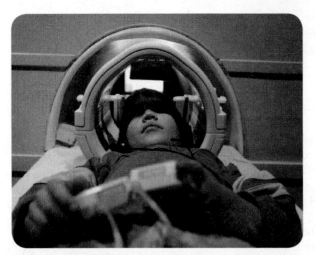

FIGURE 4

BRAIN SCANS AND LEARNING DISABILITIES. An increasing number of studies are using MRI brain scans to examine the brain pathways involved in learning disabilities. Shown here is 9-year-old Patrick Price, who has dyslexia. Patrick is going through an MRI scanner disguised by drapes to look like a child-friendly castle. Inside the scanner, children must lie virtually motionless as words and symbols flash on a screen, and they are asked to identify them by clicking different buttons.
Manuel Balce Ceneta/AP Images

attention deficit hyperactivity disorder (ADHD) A disability in which children consistently show one or more of the following characteristics: (1) inattention, (2) hyperactivity, and (3) impulsivity.

Attention Deficit Hyperactivity Disorder (ADHD) Attention deficit hyperactivity disorder (ADHD) is a disability in which children consistently show one or more of the following characteristics over a period of time: (1) inattention, (2) hyperactivity, and (3) impulsivity. Children who are inattentive have such difficulty focusing on any one thing that they may get bored with a task after only a few minutes—or even seconds. Children who are hyperactive show high levels of physical activity, seeming to be almost constantly in motion. Children who are impulsive have difficulty curbing their reactions; they do not do a good job of thinking before they act. Depending on the characteristics that children with ADHD display, they can be diagnosed as having (1) ADHD with predominantly inattention, (2) ADHD with predominantly hyperactivity/impulsivity, or (3) ADHD with both inattention and hyperactivity/impulsivity.

The number of children diagnosed and treated for ADHD has increased substantially in recent decades, by some estimates doubling in the 1990s. The American Psychiatric Association (2013) reported in the DSM-V that 5 percent of children have ADHD, although estimates are higher in community samples. For example, the Centers for Disease Control and Prevention (2016) estimates that ADHD has continued to increase in 4- to 17-year-old children from 8 percent in 2003 to 9.5 percent in 2007 and to 11 percent in 2016. According to the Centers for Disease Control and Prevention, 13.2 percent of U.S. boys and 5.6 of U.S. girls have ever been diagnosed with ADHD.

There is controversy, however, about the reasons for the increased diagnosis of ADHD (Hallahan, Kauffman, & Pullen, 2019). Some experts attribute the increase mainly to heightened awareness of the disorder; others are concerned that many children are being incorrectly diagnosed (Watson & others, 2014).

Adjustment and optimal development are difficult for children who have ADHD, so it is important that the diagnosis be accurate (Turnbull & others, 2020). Children diagnosed with ADHD have an increased risk of lower academic achievement, problematic peer relations, school dropout, disordered eating, adolescent pregnancy, substance use problems, and antisocial behavior (Obsuth & others, 2020; Tistarelli & others, 2020; van der Burg & others, 2019). For example, a recent study found that childhood ADHD was associated with long-term underachievement in math and reading (Voigt & others, 2017). Also, a research review concluded that in comparison with typically developing girls, girls with ADHD had more problems in friendship, peer interaction, social skills, and peer victimization (Kok & others, 2016). Further, a research review concluded that ADHD in childhood was linked to the following long-term outcomes: failure to complete high school, other mental and substance use disorders, criminal activity, and unemployment (Erskine & others, 2016). And a recent study revealed that individuals with ADHD were more likely to become parents at 12 to 16 years of age (Ostergaard & others, 2017).

Definitive causes of ADHD have not been found (Mash & Wolfe, 2019). However, a number of possible causes have been proposed (Hallahan, Kauffman, & Pullen, 2019). Some children likely inherit a tendency to develop ADHD from their parents (van Dongen & others, 2019; Tistarelli & others, 2020). Other children likely develop ADHD because of damage to their brain during prenatal or postnatal development (Wang & others, 2020). Among early possible contributors to ADHD are cigarette and alcohol exposure during prenatal development, as well as a high level of maternal stress during prenatal development and low birth weight (Sourander & others, 2019; Tole & others, 2019).

As with learning disabilities, advances in brain-imaging technology are facilitating a better understanding of ADHD (Kibby & others, 2020; Shephard & others, 2019; Wang & others, 2020). One study revealed that peak thickness of the cerebral cortex occurred three years later (at 10.5 years of age) in children with ADHD than in children without ADHD (7.5 years) (Shaw & others, 2007). The delay was more prominent in the prefrontal regions of the brain that are particularly important in attention and planning (see Figure 5). Researchers also are exploring the roles that various neurotransmitters, such as serotonin and dopamine, might play in ADHD (Halvorsen & others, 2019; Shang, Lin, & Gau, 2020).

Many children with ADHD show impulsive behavior, such as this boy reaching to pull a girl's hair. *How would you handle this situation if you were a teacher and this were to happen in your classroom?*
Nicole Hill/Rubberball/Getty Images

The delays in brain development just described are in areas linked to executive function (Yasumura & others, 2019). An increasing focus of interest in the study of children with ADHD is their difficulty with tasks involving executive function, such as behavioral inhibition when necessary, use of working memory, and effective planning (Groves & others, 2020). Researchers also have found deficits in theory of mind in children with ADHD (Maoz & others, 2019).

Stimulant medication such as Ritalin or Adderall (which has fewer side effects than Ritalin) is effective in improving the attention of many children with ADHD, but it usually does not improve their attention to the levels seen in children who do not have ADHD (Wong & Stevens, 2012). A recent research review also concluded that stimulant medications are effective in treating ADHD during the short term but that longer-term benefits of stimulant medications are not clear (Rajeh & others, 2017). A meta-analysis concluded that behavior management treatments are useful in reducing the effects of ADHD (Fabiano & others, 2009). Researchers have often found that a combination of medication (such as Ritalin) and behavior management improves the behavior of some but not all children with ADHD better than medication alone or behavior management alone (Parens & Johnston, 2009).

The sheer number of ADHD diagnoses has prompted speculation that psychiatrists, parents, and teachers are in fact labeling normal childhood behavior as psychopathology (Mash & Wolfe, 2019). One reason for concern about overdiagnosing ADHD is that the form of treatment in well over 80 percent of cases is psychoactive drugs, including stimulants such as Ritalin and Adderall (Garfield & others, 2012). Further, there is increasing concern that children who are given stimulant drugs such as Ritalin or Adderall are at risk for developing substance abuse problems, although evidence supporting this concern so far has been mixed (van der Burg & others, 2019).

Recently, researchers have been exploring the possibility that neurofeedback might improve the attention of children with ADHD (Bijlenga & others, 2019; Cueli & others, 2019). Neurofeedback trains individuals to become more aware of their physiological responses so they can attain better control over their brain's prefrontal cortex, where executive control primarily occurs. Individuals with ADHD have higher levels of electroencephalogram (EEG) abnormalities, and neurofeedback produces audiovisual profiles of these abnormal brain waves so that individuals can learn how to achieve normal EEG functioning (Riesco-Matias & others, 2019). In one study, 7- to 14-year-olds with ADHD were randomly assigned to either receive a neurofeedback treatment that consisted of 40 sessions or to take Ritalin (Meisel & others, 2013). Both groups showed a lower level of ADHD symptoms 6 months after the treatment, but only the neurofeedback group performed better academically. And a recent meta-analysis found that neurofeedback had moderate effects on improving children's attention and reducing their hyperactivity/impulsivity for at least 6 months after treatment (Van Doren & others, 2019).

Recently, mindfulness training also has been given to children and adolescents with ADHD (Siebelink & others, 2019). A meta-analysis concluded that mindfulness training significantly improved the attention of children with ADHD (Cairncross & Miller, 2016).

Exercise also is being investigated as a possible treatment for children with ADHD (Pan & others, 2019; Villa-Gonzalez & others, 2020). A meta-analysis concluded that physical exercise is effective in reducing cognitive symptoms of ADHD in individuals 3 to 25 years of age (Tan, Pooley, & Speelman, 2016). Also, a research review recently concluded that physical exercise was effective in improving the attention of children with ADHD (Jeyanthi, Arumugam, & Parasher, 2019). Further, a recent meta-analysis concluded that regular exercise was more effective than neurofeedback, cognitive training, or cognitive therapy in improving cognitive difficulties (attention, inhibition, and working memory deficiencies, for example) in treating ADHD (Lambez & others, 2020). And in a recent study, children with ADHD were 21 percent less likely to engage in regular exercise than children not diagnosed with ADHD (Mercurio & others, 2020). Among the reasons that exercise might reduce ADHD symptoms in children are (1) better allocation of attention resources, (2) positive influence on prefrontal cortex functioning, and (3) exercise-induced dopamine release (Chang & others, 2012).

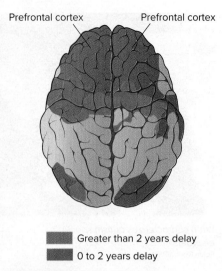

Prefrontal cortex   Prefrontal cortex

■ Greater than 2 years delay
■ 0 to 2 years delay

FIGURE 5

REGIONS OF THE BRAIN IN WHICH CHILDREN WITH ADHD HAD A DELAYED PEAK IN THE THICKNESS OF THE CEREBRAL CORTEX.

Note: The greatest delays occurred in the prefrontal cortex.

developmental **connection**

Cognitive Processes

Mindfulness training is being used to improve students' executive function. Connect to "Socioemotional Development in Adolescence."

How can neurofeedback reduce the symptoms of ADHD in children?

Jerilee Bennett/KRT/Newscom

What characterizes autism spectrum disorders?
Robin Nelson/PhotoEdit

developmental **connection**

Conditions, Diseases, and Disorders
Autistic children have difficulty in developing a theory of mind, especially in understanding others' beliefs and emotions. Connect to "Physical and Cognitive Development in Early Childhood."

emotional and behavioral disorders Serious, persistent problems that involve relationships, aggression, depression, fears associated with personal or school matters, as well as other inappropriate socioemotional characteristics.

autism spectrum disorders (ASD) Conditions ranging from the severe disorder labeled autistic disorder to the milder disorder called Asperger syndrome. Children with these disorders are characterized by problems in social interaction, verbal and nonverbal communication, and repetitive behaviors.

autistic disorder A severe autism spectrum disorder that has its onset in the first three years of life and includes deficiencies in social relationships, abnormalities in communication, and restricted, repetitive, and stereotyped patterns of behavior.

Asperger syndrome A relatively mild autism spectrum disorder in which the child has relatively good verbal language skills, milder nonverbal language problems, and a restricted range of interests and relationships.

Despite the encouraging results of recent studies involving the use of neurofeedback, mindfulness training, and exercise to improve the attention of children with ADHD, it still remains to be determined whether these non-drug therapies are as effective as stimulant drugs and/or whether they benefit children as add-ons to stimulant drugs to provide a combination treatment (Den Heijer & others, 2017; Riesco-Matias & others, 2019).

Emotional and Behavioral Disorders   Most children have minor emotional difficulties at some point during their school years. However, some children have problems so serious and persistent that they are classified as having an emotional or behavioral disorder (Mash & Wolfe, 2019). These problems may include internalized disorders such as depression or externalized disorders such as aggression.

Emotional and behavioral disorders consist of serious, persistent problems that involve relationships, aggression, depression, and fears associated with personal or school matters, as well as other inappropriate socioemotional characteristics (Meque & others, 2019; Sim & others, 2019). Approximately 8 percent of children who have a disability and require an individualized education plan fall into this classification. Boys are three times as likely as girls to have these disorders.

Autism Spectrum Disorders   **Autism spectrum disorders (ASD)** range from the severe disorder labeled autistic disorder to the milder disorder called Asperger syndrome. Autism spectrum disorders are characterized by problems in social interaction, problems in verbal and nonverbal communication, and repetitive behaviors (Lord & others, 2020; Watkins & others, 2019). Children with these disorders may also show atypical responses to sensory experiences (National Institute of Mental Health, 2020).

Recent estimates of autism spectrum disorders indicate dramatic increases in occurrence (or detection). Once thought to affect only 1 in 2,500 children decades ago, they were estimated to be present in about 1 in 150 children in 2002 (Centers for Disease Control and Prevention, 2007). However, in the most recent survey, the estimated percentage of 8-year-old children with autism spectrum disorders had increased to 1 in 68 (Christensen & others, 2016). In the recent surveys, autism spectrum disorders were identified five times more often in boys than in girls, and 8 percent of individuals aged 3 to 21 with these disorders were receiving special education services (Centers for Disease Control and Prevention, 2017).

Also, in recent surveys, only a minority of parents reported that their child's autistic spectrum disorder was identified prior to 3 years of age, and one-third to one-half of the cases were identified after 6 years of age (Sheldrick, Maye, & Carter, 2017). However, researchers are conducting studies that seek to identify earlier determinants of autism spectrum disorders (M. Wang & others, 2020). In a recent research summary, early warning signs for ASD were lack of social gestures at 12 months, using no meaningful words at 18 months, and having no interest in other children or no spontaneous two-word phrases at 24 months (Tsang & others, 2019).

Autistic disorder is a severe developmental autism spectrum disorder that has its onset during the first three years of life and includes deficiencies in social relationships, abnormalities in communication, and restricted, repetitive, and stereotyped patterns of behavior.

Asperger syndrome is a relatively mild autism spectrum disorder in which the child has relatively good verbal language skills, milder nonverbal language problems, and a restricted range of interests and relationships (Saisanen & others, 2019). Children with Asperger syndrome often engage in obsessive, repetitive routines and preoccupations with a particular subject. For example, a child may be obsessed with baseball scores or specific videos on YouTube.

Children with autism have deficits in cognitive processing of information (Lord & others, 2020; Valeri & others, 2020). For example, a recent study found that a lower level of working memory was the executive function most strongly associated with autism spectrum disorders (Ziermans & others, 2017). Children with these disorders may also show atypical responses to sensory experiences (National Institute of Mental Health, 2020). Intellectual disability is present in some children with autism; others show average or above-average intelligence (Bernier & Dawson, 2016).

In 2013, the American Psychiatric Association published the new edition (DSM-V) of its psychiatric classification of disorders. In the new classification, autistic disorder, Asperger's syndrome, and several other autistic variations were consolidated in the overarching category of autism spectrum disorder (Autism Research Institute, 2013). Distinctions are made in terms of the severity of problems based on amount of support needed due to challenges involving social communication, restricted interests, and repetitive behaviors. Critics argue that the umbrella category proposed for autism spectrum disorder masks the heterogeneity that characterizes the subgroups of autism (Lai & others, 2013).

What causes autism spectrum disorders? The current consensus is that autism is a brain dysfunction characterized by abnormalities in brain structure and neurotransmitters (Webster & others, 2020). Recent interest has focused on brain networks and a lack of connectivity between brain regions as a key factor in autism (Frega & others, 2020).

Genetic factors also are likely to play a role in the development of autism spectrum disorders (Koytun & others, 2020). In a recent review, it was concluded that there are approximately 800 genes linked to autism (Gabrielli, Manzardo, & Butler, 2019). There is no evidence that family socialization causes autism.

Children with autism benefit from a well-structured classroom, individualized teaching, and small-group instruction (Turnbull & others, 2020). Behavior modification techniques are sometimes effective in helping autistic children learn (Hall, 2018).

EDUCATIONAL ISSUES

Until the 1970s most U.S. public schools either refused enrollment to children with disabilities or inadequately served them. This changed in 1975 when Public Law 94-142, the Education for All Handicapped Children Act, required that all students with disabilities be given a free, appropriate public education. In 1990, Public Law 94-142 was recast as the Individuals with Disabilities Education Act (IDEA). IDEA was amended in 1997 and then reauthorized in 2004 and renamed the Individuals with Disabilities Education Improvement Act.

IDEA spells out broad mandates for services to children with disabilities of all kinds (Turnbull & others, 2020). These services include evaluation and eligibility determination, appropriate education and an individualized education plan (IEP), and education in the least restrictive environment (LRE).

An **individualized education plan (IEP)** is a written statement that spells out a program that is specifically tailored for the student with a disability. The **least restrictive environment (LRE)** is a setting that is as similar as possible to the one in which children who do not have a disability are educated. This provision of the IDEA has given a legal basis to efforts to educate children with a disability in the regular classroom. The term **inclusion** describes educating a child with special educational needs full-time in the regular classroom (Friend & Bursuck, 2019). In a recent school year (2014), 61 percent of U.S. students with a disability spent more than 80 percent of their school day in a general classroom (compared with only 33 percent in 1990) (Condition of Education, 2015).

The outcomes of many legal changes regarding children with disabilities have been extremely positive (Hallahan, Kauffman, & Pullen, 2019). Compared with several decades ago, far more children today are receiving competent, specialized services. For many children, inclusion in the regular classroom, with modifications or supplemental services, is appropriate (Friend & Bursuck, 2019). However, some leading experts on special education argue that in some cases the effort to educate children with disabilities in the regular classroom has become too extreme. For example, James Kauffman and his colleagues (Kauffman, McGee, & Brigham, 2004) state that inclusion too often has meant making accommodations in the regular classroom that do not always benefit children with disabilities. They advocate a more individualized approach that does not always involve full inclusion but allows options such as special education outside the regular classroom. Kauffman and his colleagues (2004, p. 620) acknowledge that children with disabilities "*do* need the services of specially trained professionals" and "*do* sometimes need altered curricula or adaptations to make their learning possible." However, they believe "we sell students with disabilities short when we pretend that they are not different from typical students. We make the same error when we pretend that they must *not* be expected to put forth extra effort if they are to learn to do some things—or learn to do something in a different way." Like general education, special education should challenge students with disabilities "to become all they can be."

IDEA mandates free, appropriate education for all children. *What services does IDEA mandate for children with disabilities?*
Ariel Skelley/Photodisc/Getty Images

individualized education plan (IEP) A written statement that spells out a program specifically tailored to a child with a disability.

least restrictive environment (LRE) A setting that is as similar as possible to the one in which children who do not have a disability are educated.

inclusion Educating a child with special requirements full-time in the regular classroom.

Review *Connect* Reflect

 LG2 Identify children with different types of disabilities and discuss issues in educating them.

Review

- Who are children with disabilities? What are some different types of disabilities and what characterizes these disabilities?
- What are some issues in educating children with disabilities?

Connect

- Earlier you learned about the development of attention in infancy and early childhood. How might ADHD be linked to earlier attention difficulties in infancy and early childhood?

Reflect *Your Own Personal Journey of Life*

- Think about your own schooling and how children with learning disabilities or ADHD either were or were not diagnosed. Were you aware of such individuals in your classes? Were they helped by specialists? You may know one or more individuals with a learning disability or ADHD. Ask them about their educational experiences and whether they think schools could have done a better job of helping them.

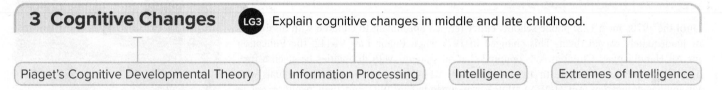

3 Cognitive Changes   **LG3**   Explain cognitive changes in middle and late childhood.

Piaget's Cognitive Developmental Theory   Information Processing   Intelligence   Extremes of Intelligence

Do children enter a new stage of cognitive development in middle and late childhood? How do children process information during this age period? What is the nature of children's intelligence? Let's explore some answers to these questions.

PIAGET'S COGNITIVE DEVELOPMENTAL THEORY

According to Jean Piaget (1952), the preschool child's thought is preoperational. Preschool children can form stable concepts, and they have begun to reason, but their thinking is flawed by egocentrism and magical belief systems. As we discussed earlier, however, Piaget may have underestimated the cognitive skills of preschool children. Some researchers argue that under the right conditions, young children may display abilities that are characteristic of Piaget's next stage of cognitive development, the stage of concrete operational thought (Gelman, 1969). Here we will cover the characteristics of concrete operational thought and evaluate Piaget's portrait of this stage.

The Concrete Operational Stage   Piaget proposed that the *concrete operational stage* lasts from approximately 7 to 11 years of age. In this stage, children can perform concrete operations, and they can reason logically as long as reasoning can be applied to specific or concrete examples. Remember that *operations* are mental actions that are reversible, and *concrete operations* are operations that are applied to real, concrete objects.

The conservation tasks described earlier indicate whether children are capable of concrete operations. For example, recall that in one task involving conservation of matter, the child is presented with two identical balls of clay. The experimenter rolls one ball into a long, thin shape; the other remains in its original ball shape. The child is then asked if there is more clay in the ball or in the long, thin piece of clay. By the time children reach the age of 7 or 8, most answer that the amount of clay is the same. To answer this problem correctly, children have to imagine the clay rolling back into a ball. This type of imagination involves a reversible mental action applied to a real, concrete object. Concrete operations allow the child to consider several characteristics rather than focusing on a single property of an object. In the clay example, the preoperational child is likely to focus on height *or* width. The concrete operational child coordinates information about both dimensions.

---

developmental connection

Centration

Centration, a centering of attention on one characteristic to the exclusion of all others, is present in young children's lack of conservation. Connect to "Physical and Cognitive Development in Early Childhood."

What other abilities are characteristic of children who have reached the concrete operational stage? One important skill is the ability to classify or divide things into different sets or subsets and to consider their interrelationships. Consider the family tree of four generations that is shown in Figure 6 (Furth & Wachs, 1975). This family tree suggests that the grandfather (A) has three children (B, C, and D), each of whom has two children (E through J), and that one of these children (J) has three children (K, L, and M). A child who comprehends the classification system can move up and down a level, across a level, and up and down and across within the system. The concrete operational child understands that person J can at the same time be father, brother, and grandson, for example.

Children who have reached the concrete operational stage are also capable of **seriation,** which is the ability to order stimuli along a quantitative dimension (such as length). To see if students can serialize, a teacher might haphazardly place eight sticks of different lengths on a table. The teacher then asks the students to order the sticks by length. Many young children end up with two or three small groups of "big" sticks or "little" sticks, rather than a correct ordering of all eight sticks. Another mistaken strategy they use is to evenly line up the tops of the sticks but ignore the bottoms. The concrete operational thinker simultaneously understands that each stick must be longer than the one that precedes it and shorter than the one that follows it.

Another aspect of reasoning about the relations between classes is **transitivity,** which is the ability to logically combine relations to understand certain conclusions. In this case, consider three sticks (A, B, and C) of differing lengths. A is the longest, B is intermediate in length, and C is the shortest. Does the child understand that if A is longer than B and B is longer than C, then A is longer than C? In Piaget's theory, concrete operational thinkers do, while preoperational thinkers do not.

Evaluating Piaget's Concrete Operational Stage

Has Piaget's portrait of the concrete operational child withstood the test of research? According to Piaget, various aspects of a stage should emerge at the same time. In fact, however, some concrete operational abilities do not appear in synchrony. For example, children do not learn to conserve at the same time they learn to cross-classify.

Furthermore, education and culture exert stronger influences on children's development than Piaget reasoned (Bredekamp, 2020; Morrison, 2020). Some preoperational children can be trained to reason at a concrete operational stage. And the age at which children acquire conservation skills is related to how much practice their culture provides in these skills.

Thus, although Piaget was a giant in the field of developmental psychology, his conclusions about the concrete operational stage have been challenged. Later, after examining the final stage in his theory of cognitive development, we will further evaluate Piaget's contributions and examine various criticisms of his theory.

Neo-Piagetians argue that Piaget got some things right but that his theory needs considerable revision. They give more emphasis to how children use attention, memory, and strategies to process information (Case & Mueller, 2001). They especially believe that a more accurate portrayal of children's thinking requires attention to children's strategies, the speed at which children process information, the particular task involved, and the division of problem solving into smaller, more precise steps (Morra & others, 2008). These issues are addressed by the information-processing approach, and we discuss some of them later in this chapter.

INFORMATION PROCESSING

If instead of describing children's stages of thinking we were to examine how they process information during middle and late childhood, what would we find? During these years, most children dramatically improve their ability to sustain and control attention (Posner & Rothbart, 2018). They pay more attention to task-relevant stimuli than to salient stimuli. Other changes in information processing during middle and late childhood involve memory, thinking, metacognition, and executive function (Gordon & others, 2020; Pennequin & others, 2020).

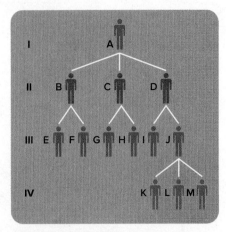

FIGURE 6

CLASSIFICATION: AN IMPORTANT ABILITY IN CONCRETE OPERATIONAL THOUGHT. A family tree of four generations (I to IV): The preoperational child has trouble classifying the members of the four generations, while the concrete operational child can classify the members vertically, horizontally, and obliquely (up and down and across). For example, the concrete operational child understands that a family member can be a son, a brother, and a father, all at the same time.

An outstanding teacher and instruction in the logic of science and mathematics are important cultural experiences that promote the development of operational thought. *Might Piaget have underestimated the roles of culture and schooling in children's cognitive development?*
Majority World/Universal Images Group Editorial/Getty Images

seriation The concrete operation that involves ordering stimuli along a quantitative dimension (such as length).

transitivity The ability to logically combine relations to understand certain conclusions.

neo-Piagetians Developmentalists who argue that Piaget got some things right but that his theory needs considerable revision. They have elaborated on Piaget's theory, giving more emphasis to information processing, strategies, and precise cognitive steps.

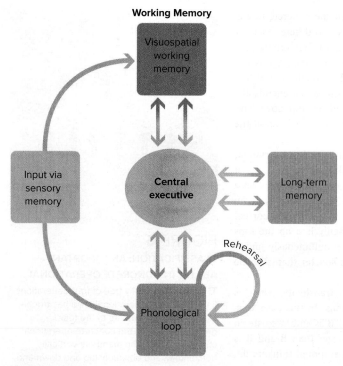

Working Memory

Visuospatial working memory

Input via sensory memory

Central executive

Long-term memory

Rehearsal

Phonological loop

FIGURE 7

WORKING MEMORY. In Baddeley's working memory model, working memory is like a mental workbench where a great deal of information processing is carried out. Working memory consists of three main components, with the phonological loop and visuospatial working memory helping the central executive do its work. Input from sensory memory goes to the phonological loop, where information about speech is stored and rehearsal takes place, and visuospatial working memory, where visual and spatial information, including imagery, are stored. Working memory is a limited-capacity system, and information is stored there for only a brief time. Working memory interacts with long-term memory, using information from long-term memory in its work and transmitting information to long-term memory for longer storage.

long-term memory A relatively permanent type of memory that holds huge amounts of information for a long period of time.

working memory A mental "workbench" where individuals manipulate and assemble information when making decisions, solving problems, and comprehending written and spoken language.

Memory   Earlier we concluded that short-term memory increases considerably during early childhood but after the age of 7 does not show as much increase. **Long-term memory,** a relatively permanent and unlimited type of memory, increases with age during middle and late childhood. In part, improvements in memory reflect children's increased knowledge and their increased use of strategies. Keep in mind that it is important not to view memory in terms of how children add something to it but rather to underscore how children actively construct their memory (Schacter, 2019).

Working Memory   Short-term memory is like a passive store-house with shelves to store information until it is moved to long-term memory. Alan Baddeley (1990, 2007, 2012, 2017, 2018, 2020) defines **working memory** as a kind of mental "workbench" where individuals manipulate and assemble information when they make decisions, solve problems, and comprehend written and spoken language (see Figure 7). Working memory is described as being more active and powerful in modifying information than short-term memory (Baddeley, 2020). Working memory involves bringing information to mind and mentally working with or updating it, as when you link one idea to another and relate what you are reading now to something you read earlier.

Note in Figure 7 that a key component of working memory is the *central executive,* which supervises and controls the flow of information. The central executive is especially involved in selective attention and inhibition, planning and decision making, and troubleshooting. Recall the description of *executive function* as an umbrella-like concept that encompasses a number of higher-level cognitive processes. One of those cognitive processes is working memory, especially its central executive dimension.

Working memory develops slowly. Even by 8 years of age, children can only hold in memory half the items that adults can remember (Kharitonova, Winter, & Sheridan, 2015).

Working memory is linked to many aspects of children's development (Vernucci & others, 2020). For example, children who have better working memory are more advanced in language comprehension, math skills, problem solving, and reasoning than their counterparts with less effective working memory (Ding & others, 2019; Simms, Frausel, & Richland, 2018). In a recent study, children's verbal working memory was linked to these aspects of both first and second language learners: morphology, syntax, and grammar (Verhagen & Leseman, 2016).

Knowledge and Expertise   Much of the research on the role of knowledge in memory has compared experts and novices. Experts have acquired extensive knowledge about a particular content area; this knowledge influences what they notice and how they organize, represent, and interpret information (Ericsson & others, 2018). These aspects in turn affect their ability to remember, reason, and solve problems. When individuals have expertise about a particular subject, their memory also tends to be good regarding material related to that subject (Brod & Shing, 2019).

For example, one study found that 10- and 11-year-olds who were experienced chess players ("experts") were able to remember more information about the location of chess pieces on a chess board than college students who were not chess players ("novices") (Chi, 1978) (see Figure 8). In contrast, when the college students were presented with other stimuli, they were able to remember them better than the children were. Thus, the children's expertise in chess gave them superior memories, but only in chess. A key reason the child chess experts did better at this activity was their ability to organize (chunk) the chess pieces into meaningful subgroups based on their understanding of chess.

There are developmental changes in expertise (Ericsson & others, 2018). Older children usually have more expertise about a subject than younger children do, which can contribute to their better memory for the subject.

Autobiographical Memory   In an earlier chapter we discussed *autobiographical memory,* which involves memory of significant events and experiences in one's life. You are engaging in autobiographical memory when you answer questions such as: Who was your first-grade teacher and what was s/he like? What is the most traumatic event that happened to you as a child?

As children go through middle and late childhood, and through adolescence, their autobiographical narratives become more complete (Bauer, 2018). Researchers have found that children develop more detailed, coherent, and evaluative autobiographical memories when their mothers reminisce with them in elaborated and evaluative ways (Bauer & Fivush, 2014; Wu & Jobson, 2019).

Culture influences children's autobiographical memories (Qi & Roberts, 2019). American children, especially American girls, produce autobiographical narratives that are longer, more detailed, more specific, and more personal than narratives by children from China and Korea (Bauer, 2013, 2015). In their conversations about past events, American mothers and their children are more elaborative and more focused on themes related to being independent while Korean mothers and their children less often engage in detailed conversations about the past. Possibly the more elaborated content of American children's narratives contributes to the earlier first memories researchers have found in American adults (Han, Leichtman, & Wang, 1998).

Strategies   If we know anything at all about long-term memory, it is that long-term memory depends on the learning activities individuals engage in when they are learning and remembering information. A key learning activity involves **strategies,** which consist of deliberate mental activities to improve the processing of information (Graham, 2020a, b; Graham & others, 2020). For example, organizing is a strategy that older children, adolescents, and adults use to remember more effectively. Strategies do not occur automatically; they require effort and work.

Following are some effective strategies for adults to use when attempting to improve children's memory skills:

- *Advise children to elaborate on what is to be remembered.* **Elaboration** is an important strategy that involves engaging in more extensive processing of information. When individuals engage in elaboration, their memory benefits (Schneider & Ornstein, 2019). Thinking of examples and relating information to one's own self and experiences are good ways to elaborate information. Forming personal associations with information makes the information more meaningful and helps children to remember it. For example, if the word *win* is on a list of words a child is asked to remember, the child might think of the last time he won a bicycle race with a friend.

- *Encourage children to engage in mental imagery.* Mental imagery can help even young schoolchildren to remember pictures. However, for remembering verbal information, mental imagery works better for older children than for younger children.

- *Motivate children to remember material by understanding it rather than by memorizing it.* Children will remember information better over the long term if they understand the information rather than just rehearse and memorize it. Rehearsal works well for encoding information into short-term memory, but when children need to retrieve the information from long-term memory, it is much less efficient. For most information, encourage children to understand it, give it meaning, elaborate it, and personalize it. Give children concepts and ideas to remember and then ask them how they can relate the concepts and ideas to their own personal experiences and meanings. Give them practice on elaborating a concept so they will process the information more deeply.

- *Repeat with variation on the instructional information and link early and often.* Variations on a lesson theme increase the number of associations in memory storage, while linking expands the network of associations in memory storage; both strategies expand the routes for retrieving information from storage.

- *Embed memory-relevant language when instructing children.* Teachers vary considerably in how much they use memory-relevant language that encourages students to remember information. In research that involved extensive observations of a number of first-grade teachers in the classroom, Peter Ornstein and his colleagues (Ornstein, Coffman, & Grammer, 2007, 2009; Ornstein & others, 2010) found that during the time segments observed, the teachers rarely used strategy suggestions or metacognitive (thinking about

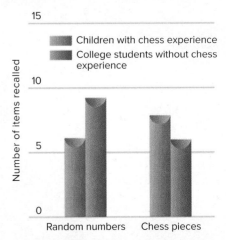

FIGURE 8

THE ROLE OF EXPERTISE IN MEMORY.
Notice that when 10- to 11-year-old children and college students were asked to remember a string of random numbers that had been presented to them, the college students fared better. However, the 10- to 11-year-olds who had experience playing chess ("experts") had better memory for the location of chess pieces on a chess board than college students with no chess experience ("novices") (Chi, 1978).

Anthony Harvie/Getty Images

strategies Deliberate mental activities that improve the processing of information.

elaboration An important strategy for remembering that involves engaging in more extensive processing of information.

thinking) questions. In this research, when lower-achieving students were placed in classrooms in which teachers were categorized as "high-mnemonic teachers" who frequently embedded memory-relevant information in their teaching, the students' achievement increased (Ornstein, Coffman, & Grammer, 2007).

Fuzzy Trace Theory   Might something other than knowledge and strategies be responsible for improvement in memory during the elementary school years? Charles Brainerd and Valerie Reyna (1993, 2014; Reyna, 2004; Reyna & others, 2016) argue that fuzzy traces account for much of this improvement. Their **fuzzy trace theory** states that memory is best understood by considering two types of memory representations: (1) verbatim memory trace, and (2) gist. The *verbatim memory trace* consists of the precise details of the information, whereas *gist* refers to the central idea of the information. When gist is used, fuzzy traces are built up. Although individuals of all ages extract gist, young children tend to store and retrieve verbatim traces. At some point during the early elementary school years, children begin to use gist more and, according to the theory, this contributes to the improved memory and reasoning of older children because fuzzy traces are more enduring and less likely to be forgotten than verbatim traces.

Thinking   Three important aspects of thinking are executive function, critical thinking, and creative thinking.

What are some key dimensions of executive function that are linked to children's cognitive development and school success?
Sigrid Olsson/PhotoAlto/Getty Images

Executive Function   In the chapter on "Physical and Cognitive Development in Early Childhood," you read about executive function and its characteristics in early childhood. Some of the cognitive topics we discuss in this chapter—working memory, critical thinking, creative thinking, and metacognition—can be considered under the umbrella of executive function and linked to the development of the brain's prefrontal cortex (McClelland, Cameron, & Alonso, 2019; Willoughby, Wylie, & Little, 2019). Also, earlier in this chapter in the coverage of brain development in middle and late childhood, you read about the increase in cognitive control, which involves flexible and effective control in a number of areas such as focusing attention, reducing interfering thoughts, inhibiting motor actions, and exercising flexibility in deciding between competing choices. In a recent study that examined different components of executive function, inhibition and working memory were linked to children's mindfulness (Geronimi, Arellano, & Woodruff-Borden, 2019).

Adele Diamond and Kathleen Lee (2011) highlighted the following dimensions of executive function that they conclude are the most important for 4- to 11-year-old children's cognitive development and school success:

- *Self-control/inhibition.* Children need to develop self-control that will allow them to concentrate and persist on learning tasks, to inhibit their tendencies to repeat incorrect responses, and to resist the impulse to do something now that they would regret later.

- *Working memory.* Children need an effective working memory to mentally work with the masses of information they will encounter as they go through school and beyond.

- *Flexibility.* Children need to be flexible in their thinking to consider different strategies and perspectives.

Researchers have found that executive function is a better predictor of school readiness than general IQ (Blair & Razza, 2007). A number of diverse activities and factors have been found to increase children's executive function, such as aerobic exercise (Kvalo & others, 2017); scaffolding of self-regulation (the Tools of the Mind program discussed in the chapter on "Physical and Cognitive Development in Early Childhood" is an example) (Bodrova & Leong, 2015a, b); mindfulness training (Gallant, 2016); and some types of school curricula (the Montessori curriculum, for example) (Diamond & Lee, 2011). In a recent series of meta-analyses to discover which interventions are most likely to increase children's executive function, it was concluded that (a) for typically developing children, mindfulness training was effective; (b) for non-typically developing children (including those with neurodevelopmental or behavioral problems), strategy teaching involving self-regulation and biofeedback-enhanced relaxation was more effective than mindfulness training (Takacs & Kassai, 2019).

Ann Masten and her colleagues (Masten, 2013, 2019; Masten & Palmer, 2019; Merrick & others, 2020; Monn & others, 2017) have found that executive function and parenting skills

developmental **connection**

Cognitive Processes

In early childhood, executive function especially involves advances in cognitive inhibition, cognitive flexibility, and goal-setting. Connect to "Physical and Cognitive Development in Early Childhood."

fuzzy trace theory States that memory is best understood by considering two types of memory representations: (1) verbatim memory trace, and (2) gist. In this theory, older children's better memory is attributed to the fuzzy traces created by extracting the gist of information.

are linked to homeless children's success in school. Masten believes that executive function and good parenting skills are related. In her words, "When we see kids with good executive function, we often see adults around them that are good self-regulators. . . . Parents model, they support, and they scaffold these skills" (Masten, 2012, p. 11).

How might mindfulness training be implemented in schools?
Ariel Skelley/Vetta/Blend Images/Getty Images

Critical Thinking   Currently, there is considerable interest among psychologists and educators regarding aspects of critical thinking (Baron, 2020; Sternberg & Halpern, 2020). **Critical thinking** involves thinking reflectively and productively and evaluating evidence. In this text, the second and third parts of the *Review, Connect, Reflect* sections of each chapter challenge you to think critically about a topic or an issue related to the discussion.

According to Ellen Langer (2005), **mindfulness**—being alert, mentally present, and cognitively flexible while going through life's everyday activities and tasks—is an important aspect of thinking critically. Mindful children and adults maintain an active awareness of the circumstances in their life and are motivated to find the best solutions to tasks. Mindful individuals create new ideas, are open to new information, and explore multiple strategies and perspectives. By contrast, mindless individuals are entrapped in old ideas, engage in automatic behavior, and often use a single strategy or adopt a single perspective.

Jacqueline and Martin Brooks (2001) lament that few schools really teach students to think critically and develop a deep understanding of concepts. Deep understanding occurs when students are stimulated to rethink previously held ideas. In Brooks and Brooks' view, schools spend too much time getting students to give a single correct answer in an imitative way, rather than encouraging them to expand their thinking by coming up with new ideas and rethinking earlier conclusions. They observe that too often teachers ask students to recite, define, describe, state, and list, rather than to analyze, infer, connect, synthesize, criticize, create, evaluate, think, and rethink. Many successful students complete their assignments, do well on tests and get good grades, yet they don't ever learn to think critically and deeply. They think superficially, staying on the surface of problems rather than stretching their minds and becoming deeply engaged in meaningful thinking.

Recently, Robert Roeser and his colleagues (Roeser & Eccles, 2015; Roeser & others, 2014; Roeser & Zelazo, 2012) have emphasized that mindfulness is an important mental process that children can engage in to improve a number of cognitive and socioemotional skills, such as executive function, focused attention, emotion regulation, and empathy. They have proposed that mindfulness training could be implemented in schools through practices such as using age-appropriate activities that increase children's reflection on moment-to-moment experiences, resulting in improved self-regulation.

In addition to mindfulness training, activities such as yoga, meditation, and tai chi recently have been suggested as candidates for improving children's cognitive and socioemotional development (Bostic & others, 2015; Roeser & Pinela, 2014). Together these activities are grouped under the topic of *contemplative science*, a cross-disciplinary term that involves the study of how various types of mental and physical training might enhance children's development (Roeser & Eccles, 2015; Roeser & Zelazo, 2012). In a recent study, a social and emotional learning program that focused on mindfulness and caring for others was effective in improving fourth- and fifth-graders' cognitive control, mindfulness, emotional control, optimism, and peer relations, and in reducing depressive symptoms (Schonert-Reichl & others, 2015). In other recent research, mindfulness training has been found to improve children's attention and self-regulation (Poehlmann-Tynan & others, 2016), as well as coping strategies in stressful situations (Dariotis & others, 2016). In a recent study, mindfulness training improved children's attention and self-regulation (Felver & others, 2017). Also, in two recent studies, mindfulness-based interventions reduced public school teachers' stress, produced a better mood at school and at home, and resulted in better sleep (Crain, Schonert-Reichl, & Roeser, 2017; Taylor & others, 2016). And in another recent study, mindful parenting was effective in improving children's social decision making (Wong & others, 2019).

Creative Thinking   Cognitively competent children engage in both critical and creating thinking (Glaveanu & others, 2020; Runco & Acar, 2019; Sternberg, 2020c). **Creative thinking** is the ability to think in novel and unusual ways and to come up with unique solutions to problems. Thus, intelligence and creativity are not the same thing. This difference was recognized by J. P. Guilford (1967), who distinguished between **convergent thinking,** which produces one correct answer and characterizes the kind of thinking that is required on conventional tests of intelligence, and **divergent thinking,** which produces many different answers to the same

critical thinking Thinking reflectively and productively, as well as evaluating evidence.

mindfulness Being alert, mentally present, and cognitively flexible while going through life's everyday activities and tasks.

creative thinking The ability to think in novel and unusual ways and to come up with unique solutions to problems.

convergent thinking Thinking that produces one correct answer and is characteristic of the kind of thinking tested by standardized intelligence tests.

divergent thinking Thinking that produces many answers to the same question and is characteristic of creativity.

developmental **connection**

Creativity

How can you cultivate your curiosity and interest to live a more creative life? Connect to "Physical and Cognitive Development in Early Adulthood."

developmental **connection**

Cognitive Theory

Theory of mind—awareness of one's own mental processes and the mental processes of others—involves metacognition. Connect to "Physical and Cognitive Development in Early Childhood."

question and characterizes creativity. For example, a typical item on a conventional intelligence test is "How many quarters will you get in return for 60 dimes?" In contrast, the following question has many possible answers: "What image comes to mind when you hear the phrase 'sitting alone in a dark room' or 'some unique uses for a paper clip'?"

A special concern is that children's creative thinking appears to be declining. A study of approximately 300,000 U.S. children and adults found that creativity scores rose until 1990 and then began steadily declining (Kim, 2010). Among the likely causes of declining creativity are the number of hours U.S. children spend watching TV and playing video games instead of engaging in creative activities, as well as the lack of emphasis on creative thinking skills in schools (Beghetto, 2019). Some countries, though, are placing increased emphasis on creative thinking in schools. For example, historically, creative thinking has been discouraged in Chinese schools. However, Chinese educators are now encouraging teachers to spend more classroom time on creative activities (Plucker, 2010).

It is important to recognize that children will show more creativity in some domains than others (Sternberg, 2019c, 2020c). A child who shows creative thinking skills in mathematics may not exhibit these skills in art, for example. An important goal is to help children become more creative. The *Connecting Development to Life* interlude offers some recommended ways to accomplish this goal.

Metacognition   **Metacognition** is cognition about cognition, or knowing about knowing (Flavell, 2004). Metacognition can take many forms, including thinking about and knowing when and where to use particular strategies for learning or solving problems (O'Leary & Sloutsky, 2019; Pennequin & others, 2020). Conceptualization of metacognition consists of several dimensions of executive function, such as planning (deciding how much time to spend focusing on a task, for example) and self-regulation (modifying strategies as work on a task progresses, for example) (Fergus & Bardeen, 2019).

Metacognition helps people to perform many cognitive tasks more effectively (Morris, Savani, & Fincher, 2019; O'Leary & Sloutsky, 2019). A study of young children found that their metacognitive ability in the numerical domain predicted their school-based math knowledge (Vo & others, 2014). Also, in a recent study of 7- and 8-year-olds, task-specific metacognitive monitoring skills in noticing one's own errors and learning from mistakes were linked to superior performance in arithmetic (Bellon, Fias, & De Smedt, 2019). And another study found that metacognition played an important role in adolescents' ability to generate effective hypotheses about solving problems (Kim & Pedersen, 2010).

Many early studies classified as "metacognitive" focused on *metamemory,* or knowledge about memory. This includes general knowledge about memory, such as knowing that recognition tests are easier than recall tests. It also encompasses knowledge about one's own memory, such as a student's ability to monitor whether she has studied enough for an upcoming test or a child's confidence in eyewitness judgments (Buratti, Allwood, & Johansson, 2014).

Young children do have some general knowledge about memory (Lukowski & Bauer, 2014). By 5 or 6 years of age, children usually know that familiar items are easier to learn than unfamiliar ones, that short lists are easier to memorize than long ones, that recognition is easier than recall, and that forgetting is more likely to occur over time (Lyon & Flavell, 1993). However, in other ways young children's metamemory is limited. They don't understand that related items are easier to remember than unrelated ones and that remembering the gist of a story is easier than remembering information verbatim (Kreutzer, Leonard, & Flavell, 1975). By the fifth grade, students understand that gist recall is easier than verbatim recall.

Cognitive developmentalist John Flavell is a pioneer in providing insights about children's thinking. Among his many contributions are establishing the field of metacognition and conducting numerous studies in this area, including metamemory and theory of mind studies.
Courtesy of Dr. John Flavell

Young children also have only limited knowledge about their own memory. They have an inflated opinion of their memory abilities. For example, in one study a majority of young children predicted that they would be able to recall all 10 items on a list of 10 items. When tested, none of the young children managed this feat (Flavell, Friedrichs, & Hoyt, 1970). As they move through the elementary school years, children give more realistic evaluations of their memory skills.

metacognition Cognition about cognition, or knowing about knowing.

Strategies for Increasing Children's Creative Thinking

Following are some strategies for increasing children's creative thinking.

Encourage Brainstorming

Brainstorming is a technique in which people are encouraged to come up with creative ideas in a group, play off each other's ideas, and say practically whatever comes to mind that seems relevant to a particular issue (Sawyer, 2019). Facilitators usually tell participants to hold off from criticizing others' ideas at least until the end of the brainstorming session.

Provide Environments That Stimulate Creativity

Some environments nourish creativity, while others inhibit it. Parents and teachers who encourage creativity often rely on children's natural curiosity. They provide exercises and activities that stimulate children to find insightful solutions to problems, rather than ask a lot of questions that require rote answers (Beghetto, 2019). Teachers also encourage creativity by taking students on field trips to locations where creativity is valued. Science, discovery, and children's museums offer rich opportunities to stimulate creativity.

Don't Overcontrol

Teresa Amabile (1993, 2018) says that telling children exactly how to do things leaves them feeling that originality is a mistake and exploration is a waste of time. Instead of dictating which activities they should engage in, teachers and parents can encourage creativity by allowing children to follow their interests (Hennessey, 2019).

Encourage Internal Motivation

Parents and teachers should avoid excessive use of prizes, such as gold stars, money, or toys, which can stifle creativity by undermining the intrinsic pleasure students derive from creative activities (Hennessey, 2019). Creative children's motivation is the satisfaction generated by the work itself.

Build Children's Confidence

To expand children's creativity, teachers and parents should encourage children to believe in their own ability to create something innovative and worthwhile. Building children's confidence in their creative skills aligns with Bandura's (2012) concept of self-efficacy, the belief that one can master a situation and produce positive outcomes.

What are some good strategies for guiding children in thinking more creatively?
Fuse/Corbis/Getty Images

Guide Children to Be Persistent and Delay Gratification

Parents and teachers need to be patient and understand that most highly successful creative products take years to develop (Sternberg, Kaufman, & Roberts, 2019). Most creative individuals work on ideas and projects for months and years without being rewarded for their efforts.

Encourage Children to Take Intellectual Risks

Parents and teachers should encourage children to take intellectual risks. Creative individuals take intellectual risks and seek to discover or invent something never before discovered or invented. Creative people are not afraid of failing or getting something wrong (Sternberg, 2019c).

Introduce Children to Creative People

Teachers can invite creative people to their classrooms and ask them to describe what helps them become creative or to demonstrate their creative skills. A writer, poet, musician, scientist, and many others can bring their props and productions to the classroom, turning it into a forum for stimulating students' creativity.

You learned that it is important to recognize that children will show more creativity in some domains than others. Choose one of the strategies mentioned above and describe how you would implement it differently to encourage creativity in writing, science, math, and art in children in middle and late childhood.

In addition to metamemory, metacognition includes knowledge about strategies (Graham, 2020a, b; Graham & others, 2020). In the view of Michael Pressley (2003), the key to education is helping students learn a rich repertoire of strategies that produce solutions to problems. Good thinkers routinely use strategies and effective planning to solve problems. Good thinkers also know when and where to use strategies. Understanding when and where to use strategies often results from monitoring the learning situation (Serra & Metcalfe, 2010).

Alfred Binet constructed the first intelligence test after being asked to create a measure to determine which children could benefit from instruction in France's schools and which could not.
Bettmann/Getty Images

developmental **connection**

Intelligence

Does intelligence decrease when individuals become middle-aged? Connect to "Physical and Cognitive Development in Middle Adulthood."

intelligence Problem-solving skills and the ability to learn from and adapt to the experiences of everyday life.

individual differences The stable, consistent ways in which people differ from each other.

mental age (MA) Binet's measure of an individual's level of mental development compared with that of others.

intelligence quotient (IQ) A person's mental age divided by chronological age, multiplied by 100.

Pressley and his colleagues (Pressley & others, 2003, 2004, 2007) spent considerable time in recent years observing strategy instruction by teachers and strategy use by students in elementary and secondary school classrooms. They conclude that strategy instruction is far less complete and intense than what students need to receive in order to learn how to use strategies effectively. They argue that education ought to be restructured so that students are provided with more opportunities to become competent strategic learners.

INTELLIGENCE

How can intelligence be defined? **Intelligence** is the ability to solve problems and to adapt and learn from experiences. Interest in intelligence has often focused on individual differences and assessment (Sternberg, 2020e). **Individual differences** are the stable, consistent ways in which people differ from each other (Elkana & others, 2020; Kaufman, Schneider, & Kaufman, 2019). We can talk about individual differences in personality or any other domain, but it is in the domain of intelligence that the most attention has been directed at individual differences (Richler & others, 2019). For example, an intelligence test purports to inform us about whether a student can reason better than others who have taken the test (Deckert & others, 2020). Let's go back in history and see what the first intelligence test was like.

The Binet Tests In 1904, the French Ministry of Education asked psychologist Alfred Binet to devise a method of identifying children who were unable to learn in school. School officials wanted to reduce crowding by placing students who did not benefit from regular classroom teaching in special schools. Binet and his student Theophile Simon developed an intelligence test to meet this request. The test is called the 1905 Scale. It consisted of 30 questions on topics ranging from the ability to touch one's ear to the ability to draw designs from memory and define abstract concepts.

Binet developed the concept of **mental age (MA)**, an individual's level of mental development relative to others. Not much later, in 1912, William Stern created the concept of **intelligence quotient (IQ)**, a person's mental age divided by chronological age (CA), multiplied by 100; that is, IQ = MA/CA × 100. If mental age is the same as chronological age, then the person's IQ is 100. If mental age is above chronological age, then IQ is more than 100. If mental age is below chronological age, then IQ is less than 100.

The Binet test has been revised many times to incorporate advances in the understanding of intelligence and intelligence tests. These revisions are called the *Stanford-Binet tests* (Stanford University is where the revisions have been done). In 2004, the test—now called the Stanford-Binet 5—was revised to analyze an individual's response in five content areas: fluid reasoning, knowledge, quantitative reasoning, visual-spatial reasoning, and working memory. A general composite score also is still obtained.

By administering the test to large numbers of people of different ages (preschool through late adulthood) with different backgrounds, researchers have found that scores on the Stanford-Binet approximate a normal distribution (see Figure 9). A **normal distribution** is symmetrical, with a majority of the scores falling in the middle of the possible range of scores and much fewer scores appearing toward the extremes of the range.

FIGURE **9**

THE NORMAL CURVE AND STANFORD-BINET IQ SCORES. The distribution of IQ scores approximates a normal curve. Most of the population falls in the middle range of scores. Notice that extremely high and extremely low scores are very rare. Slightly more than two-thirds of the scores fall between 85 and 115. Only about 1 in 50 individuals has an IQ higher than 130, and only about 1 in 50 individuals has an IQ lower than 70.

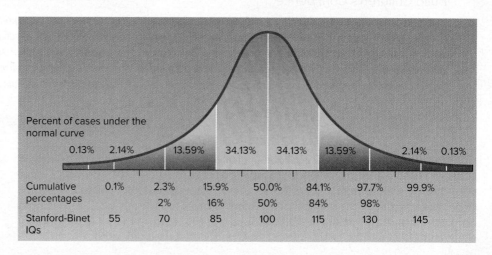

Percent of cases under the normal curve	0.13%	2.14%	13.59%	34.13%	34.13%	13.59%	2.14%	0.13%
Cumulative percentages	0.1%	2.3%	15.9%	50.0%	84.1%	97.7%	99.9%	
		2%	16%	50%	84%	98%		
Stanford-Binet IQs	55	70	85	100	115	130	145	

The Wechsler Scales Another set of widely used tests to assess students' intelligence is called the Wechsler scales, developed by psychologist David Wechsler (Elkana & others, 2020; MacAllister & others, 2019). They include the Wechsler Preschool and Primary Scale of Intelligence–Fourth Edition (WPPSI-IV) to test children from 2.5 years to 7.25 years of age; the Wechsler Intelligence Scale for Children–Fifth Edition (WISC-V) for children and adolescents 6 to 16 years of age; and the Wechsler Adult Intelligence Scale–Fourth Edition (WAIS-IV).

The WISC-V not only provides an overall IQ score but also yields five composite scores (Verbal Comprehension, Working Memory, Processing Speed, Fluid Reasoning, and Visual Spatial). These scores allow the examiner to quickly see whether the individual is strong or weak in different areas of intelligence (Canivez & others, 2020). The Wechsler scales also include 16 verbal and non-verbal subscales. Three of the Wechsler subscales are shown in Figure 10.

Types of Intelligence Is it more appropriate to think of a child's intelligence as a general ability or as a number of specific abilities? Robert Sternberg and Howard Gardner have proposed influential theories oriented to this second viewpoint.

Sternberg's Triarchic Theory Robert J. Sternberg (1986, 2004, 2010, 2014, 2016, 2017, 2018, 2019a, b, 2020a, b, c, d, e) developed the **triarchic theory of intelligence,** which states that intelligence comes in three forms: (1) *analytical intelligence,* which refers to the ability to analyze, judge, evaluate, compare, and contrast; (2) *creative intelligence,* which consists of the ability to create, design, invent, originate, and imagine; and (3) *practical intelligence,* which involves the ability to use, apply, implement, and put ideas into practice.

Sternberg (2019a, b, 2020a, b, c, d) says that children with different triarchic patterns "look different" in school. Students with high analytic ability tend to be favored in conventional schooling. They often do well under direct instruction, in which the teacher lectures and gives students objective tests. They often are considered to be "smart" students who get good grades, show up in high-level tracks, do well on traditional tests of intelligence and the SAT, and later get admitted to competitive colleges.

In contrast, children who are high in creative intelligence often are not on the top rung of their class (Sternberg, 2020c). Many teachers have specific expectations about how assignments should be done, and creatively intelligent students may not conform to those expectations. Instead of giving conformist answers, they give unique answers, for which they might get reprimanded or marked down. No teacher wants to discourage creativity, but Sternberg stresses that too often a teacher's desire to increase students' knowledge suppresses creative thinking.

Like children high in creative intelligence, children with predominantly practical intelligence often do not relate well to the demands of school. However, many of these children do well outside the classroom's walls. They may have excellent social skills and good common sense. As adults, some become successful managers, entrepreneurs, or politicians in spite of having undistinguished school records.

Gardner's Eight Frames of Mind Howard Gardner (1983, 1993, 2002, 2016) suggests there are eight types of intelligence, or "frames of mind." These are described here, with examples of the types of vocations in which they are regarded as strengths (Campbell, Campbell, & Dickinson, 2004):

Verbal: The ability to think in words and use language to express meaning. Occupations: authors, journalists, speakers.

Mathematical: The ability to carry out mathematical operations. Occupations: scientists, engineers, accountants.

Spatial: The ability to think three-dimensionally. Occupations: architects, artists, sailors.

Bodily-kinesthetic: The ability to manipulate objects and be physically adept. Occupations: surgeons, craftspeople, dancers, athletes.

Verbal Subscales

Similarities

A child must think logically and abstractly to answer a number of questions about how things might be similar.

Example: "In what way are a lion and a tiger alike?"

Comprehension

This subscale is designed to measure an individual's judgment and common sense.

Example: "What is the advantage of keeping money in a bank?"

Nonverbal Subscales

Block Design

A child must assemble a set of multicolored blocks to match designs that the examiner shows.
Visual-motor coordination, perceptual organization, and the ability to visualize spatially are assessed.

Example: "Use the four blocks on the left to make the pattern on the right."

FIGURE **10**

SAMPLE SUBSCALES OF THE WECHSLER INTELLIGENCE SCALE FOR CHILDREN—FIFTH EDITION (WISC-V). The Wechsler includes 16 subscales. Three of the subscales are shown here.
Source: Wechsler Intelligence Scale for Children®, Fifth Edition (WISC-V), Upper Saddle River, NJ: Pearson Education, Inc., 2014.

Robert J. Sternberg developed the triarchic theory of intelligence.
Courtesy of Dr. Robert Sternberg

normal distribution A symmetrical distribution with most scores falling in the middle of the possible range of scores and a few scores appearing toward the extremes of the range.

triarchic theory of intelligence Sternberg's theory that intelligence consists of analytical intelligence, creative intelligence, and practical intelligence.

Howard Gardner, here working with a young child, developed the view that intelligence comes in the forms of eight kinds of skills: verbal, mathematical, spatial, bodily-kinesthetic, musical, intrapersonal, interpersonal, and naturalist.
Courtesy of Dr. Howard Gardner and Jay Gardner

Musical: A sensitivity to pitch, melody, rhythm, and tone. Occupations: composers and musicians.

Interpersonal: The ability to understand and interact effectively with others. Occupations: successful teachers, mental health professionals.

Intrapersonal: The ability to understand oneself. Occupations: theologians, psychologists.

Naturalist: The ability to observe patterns in nature and understand natural and human-made systems. Occupations: farmers, botanists, ecologists, landscapers.

According to Gardner, everyone has all of these intelligences to varying degrees. As a result, we prefer to learn and process information in different ways. People learn best when they can do so in a way that uses their stronger intelligences.

Evaluating the Multiple-Intelligence Approaches   Sternberg's and Gardner's approaches have much to offer. They have stimulated teachers to think more broadly about what makes up children's competencies (Gardner, 2016; Gardner, Kornhaber, & Chen, 2018; Sternberg, 2019a, b, 2020a, b, c), and they have motivated educators to develop programs that instruct students in multiple domains. These approaches have also contributed to interest in assessing intelligence and classroom learning in innovative ways, such as by evaluating student portfolios (Moran & Gardner, 2006, 2007).

However, doubts about multiple-intelligence approaches persist and many psychologists endorse the general intelligence approach (Cox & others, 2019; Pesta & others, 2019). A number of psychologists think that the multiple-intelligence views have taken the concept of specific intelligences too far (Reeve & Charles, 2008). Some argue that a research base to support the three intelligences of Sternberg or the eight intelligences of Gardner has not yet emerged. One expert on intelligence, Nathan Brody (2007), observes that people who excel at one type of intellectual task are likely to excel in others. Thus, individuals who do well at memorizing lists of digits are also likely to be good at solving verbal problems and spatial layout problems. Other critics suggest that if musical skill reflects a distinct type of intelligence, why not label the skills of outstanding chess players, prizefighters, painters, and poets as types of intelligence?

Advocates of the concept of general intelligence point to its accuracy in predicting school and job success. For example, scores on tests of general intelligence are substantially correlated with school grades and achievement test performance, both at the time of the test and years later (Cucina & others, 2016; Strenze, 2007). For example, a meta-analysis of 240 independent samples and more than 100,000 individuals found a correlation of +.54 between intelligence and school grades (Roth & others, 2015). Also, a recent study found a significant link between children's general intelligence and their self-control (Meldrum & others, 2017). Another recent study revealed that adolescents with high IQs were more likely than other adolescents to engage in a range of health-promoting behaviors such as exercise, better diet, and not smoking in middle adulthood (Wraw & others, 2018). And in a recent study, higher IQ in adolescence also was associated with having a younger subjective age 50 years later in late adulthood (Stephan & others, 2018).

The argument between those who support the concept of general intelligence and those who advocate the multiple-intelligence view is ongoing (Gardner, Kornhaber, & Chen, 2018). Sternberg (2019a, b, 2020a) acknowledges the existence of a general intelligence for the kinds of analytical tasks that traditional IQ tests assess but thinks that the range of tasks those tests measure is far too narrow.

Interpreting Differences in IQ Scores   The IQ scores that result from tests such as the Stanford-Binet and Wechsler scales provide information about children's mental abilities. However, interpreting what performance on an intelligence test means is a subject of debate among researchers (Deary, 2012; Sternberg, 2019a, b, 2020a).

The Influence of Genetics   An area of considerable debate in the study of intelligence centers on the extent to which intelligence is influenced by genetics (nature) or environment (nurture) (Sternberg, 2020a; Tan & Grigorenko, 2019). It is difficult to tease apart these influences, but psychologists keep trying to unravel them.

Have scientists been able to pinpoint specific genes that are linked to intelligence? A research review concluded that there may be more than 1,000 genes that affect intelligence, each possibly having a small influence on an individual's intelligence (Davies & others, 2011).

Thus, some scientists argue that there is a strong genetic component to intelligence (Hill & others, 2019). One strategy for examining the role of heredity in intelligence is to compare the IQs of identical and fraternal twins. Recall that identical twins have exactly the same genetic makeup but fraternal twins do not. If intelligence is genetically determined, say some investigators, the IQs of identical twins should be more similar than the IQs of fraternal twins. A research review of many studies found that the difference between the average correlation of IQs of identical and fraternal twins was .15, a relatively small difference (Grigorenko, 2000) (see Figure 11). And genetic influences may be more influential in some aspects of life than others. For example, in a recent study genes were much more strongly linked to a person's scientific achievement than to his/her artistic achievement (de Manzano & Ullen, 2018).

Today, most researchers agree that genetics and environment interact to influence intelligence. For most people, this means that modifications in environment can change their IQ scores considerably. Although genetic endowment may always influence a person's intellectual ability, the environmental influences and opportunities available to children and adults do make a difference (Sternberg, 2019a, b, 2020a, b).

Environmental Influences　In the chapter on "Cognitive Development in Infancy" we described a study that demonstrated the influence of parental communication patterns on children's cognitive abilities. Researchers went into homes and observed how extensively parents from welfare (public assistance recipients) and middle-income professional families communicated with their young children (Hart & Risley, 1995). They found that the middle-income professional parents were much more likely to communicate with their young children than the welfare parents were. How much the parents communicated with their children in the first three years of their lives was correlated with the children's Stanford-Binet IQ scores at age 3. The more parents communicated with their children, the higher the children's IQs were.

The environment's role in intelligence also is reflected in the 12- to 18-point increase in IQ that occurs when children are adopted from lower-SES to middle-SES families (Nisbett & others, 2012). Environmental influences on intelligence also involve schooling (Gustafsson, 2007). The biggest effects have been found when large groups of children have been deprived of formal education for an extended period, resulting in lower intelligence (Ceci & Gilstrap, 2000).

Recent research indicates that intelligence varies across countries and is linked to a number of characteristics of individuals (Flynn & Sternberg, 2019). For example, in a recent study of 22 countries (including Argentina, China, France, India, Peru, Turkey, and the United States), variations in intelligence across countries were linked to these factors: income, educational attainment, health, and socioeconomic status (Lynn, Fuerst, & Kirkegaard, 2018).

Another possible effect of environmental influences and education can be seen in rapidly increasing IQ test scores around the world (Flynn, 2007, 2013, 2018). IQ scores have been increasing so quickly that a high percentage of people regarded as having average intelligence at the turn of the century would be considered below average in intelligence today (see Figure 12). If a representative sample of people today took the Stanford-Binet test version used in 1932, about 25 percent would be defined as having very superior intelligence, a label usually

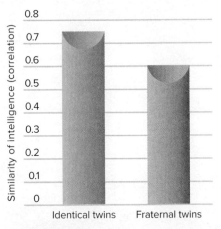

FIGURE **11**

CORRELATION BETWEEN INTELLIGENCE TEST SCORES AND TWIN STATUS. The graph represents a summary of research findings that have compared the intelligence test scores of identical and fraternal twins. An approximate .15 difference in correlation has been found, with a higher correlation for identical twins (.75) and a lower correlation for fraternal twins (.60).

developmental **connection**

Intelligence

Polygenic inheritance is the term used to describe the effects of multiple genes on a particular characteristic. Connect to "Biological Beginnings."

FIGURE **12**

INCREASING IQ SCORES FROM 1932 TO 1997. As measured by the Stanford-Binet intelligence test, American children seem to be getting smarter. Scores of a group tested in 1932 fell along a bell-shaped curve with half below 100 and half above. Studies show that if children took that same test today, half would score above 120 on the 1932 scale. Very few of them would score in the "intellectually deficient" end on the left side, and about one-fourth would rank in the "very superior" range on the right side.
Ulric Neisser. From *The Increase in IQ Scores from 1932 to 1997.* Copyright by the executors to the estate of Urlic Neisser. All rights reserved. Used with permission.

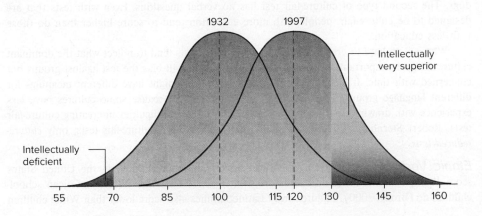

accorded to fewer than 3 percent of the population. Because the increase has taken place in a relatively short time, it can't be due to heredity, but rather may be due to increasing levels of education attained by a much greater percentage of the world's population, or to other environmental factors such as the explosion of information to which people are exposed (Flynn & Sternberg, 2019). The worldwide increase in intelligence test scores that has occurred over a short time frame has been called the *Flynn effect* after the researcher who discovered it, James Flynn.

Although rising intelligence test scores have been found in most countries in which cohort effects on intelligence have been assessed, a decrease in intelligence test scores has been found in Scandinavian countries (Finland, Denmark, and Norway) beginning about 1995 (Dutton & Lynn, 2013; Ronnlund & others, 2013). Explanations of the IQ decline focus on technological advances, such as television, smartphones, and social media, as well as weakening education systems. However, IQ gains continue to occur in the United States and most developing countries (Flynn & Shayer, 2018; Flynn & Sternberg, 2019). For example, in a recent study in the Sudanese capital of Khartoum in Africa, IQ scores increased by 10 points from 2004 to 2016 (Dutton & others, 2018).

Researchers are increasingly concerned about finding ways to improve the early environment of children who are at risk for impoverished intelligence and poor developmental outcomes (Bradley, 2019; Brody & others, 2020; Shuey & Leventhal, 2019). For various reasons, many low-income parents have difficulty providing an intellectually stimulating environment for their children. Programs that educate parents to be more sensitive caregivers and better teachers, as well as provision of support services such as quality child care and early childhood education programs, can make a difference in a child's intellectual development (Bredekamp, 2020; Morrison, 2020). Thus, the efforts to counteract a deprived early environment's effect on intelligence emphasize prevention rather than remediation. In a two-year intervention study with families living in poverty, maternal scaffolding and positive home stimulation improved young children's intellectual functioning (Obradovic & others, 2016).

In sum, there is a consensus among psychologists that both heredity and environment influence intelligence (Sternberg, 2020a). This consensus reflects the nature-nurture issue, which focuses on the extent to which development is influenced by nature (heredity) and nurture (environment). Although psychologists agree that intelligence is the product of both nature and nurture, there is still disagreement about how strongly each influences intelligence (Flynn & Sternberg, 2019; Haier, 2019).

Culture and Culture-Fair Tests Differing conceptions of intelligence occur not only among psychologists but also among cultures (Sternberg, 2020b). What is viewed as intelligent in one culture may not be thought of as intelligent in another. For example, people in Western cultures tend to view intelligence in terms of reasoning and thinking skills, whereas people in Eastern cultures see intelligence as a way for members of a community to engage successfully in social roles (Nisbett, 2003).

Culture-fair tests are tests of intelligence that are intended to be free of cultural bias. Two types of culture-fair tests have been devised. The first type includes items that are familiar to children from all socioeconomic and ethnic backgrounds, or items that at least are familiar to the children taking the test. For example, a child might be asked how a bird and a dog are different, on the assumption that all children have been exposed to birds and dogs. The second type of culture-fair test has no verbal questions. Even with tests that are designed to be culture-fair, people with more education tend to score higher than do those with less education.

Why is it so hard to create culture-fair tests? Most tests tend to reflect what the dominant culture thinks is important. If tests have time limits, that will bias the test against groups not concerned with time. If languages differ, the same words might have different meanings for different language groups. Even pictures can produce bias because some cultures have less experience with drawings and photographs. Because of such difficulties in creating culture-fair tests, Robert Sternberg (2020d) concludes that there are no culture-fair tests, only *culture-reduced tests*.

Ethnic Variations On average, African American schoolchildren in the United States score 10 to 15 points lower on standardized intelligence tests than White American schoolchildren do (Brody, 2000). Children from Latino families also score lower than White children

developmental **connection**

Nature Versus Nurture

The epigenetic view emphasizes that development is an ongoing, bidirectional interchange between heredity and environment. Connect to "Biological Beginnings."

culture-fair tests Tests of intelligence that are designed to be free of cultural bias.

do. These are average scores, however, and there is significant overlap in the distribution of scores. About 15 to 25 percent of African American schoolchildren score higher than half of White schoolchildren do, and many White schoolchildren score lower than most African American schoolchildren.

As African Americans have gained social, economic, and educational opportunities, the gap between African Americans and non-Latino Whites on standardized intelligence tests is shrinking (Daley & Onwuegbuzi, 2020). A research review concluded that the IQ gap between African Americans and non-Latino Whites has been reduced considerably in recent years (Nisbett & others, 2012). This gap especially narrows in college, where African American and non-Latino White students often experience more similar environments than during the elementary and high school years (Myerson & others, 1998). Further, a recent study using the Stanford Binet Intelligence Scales found no differences in overall intellectual ability between non-Latino White and African American preschool children when the children were matched on age, gender, and parental education level (Dale & others, 2014).

One potential influence on intelligence test performance is **stereotype threat,** the anxiety that one's behavior might confirm a negative stereotype about one's group (DeSombre & others, 2019; Laurin, 2020; Williams & others, 2019). For example, when African Americans take an intelligence test, they may experience anxiety about confirming the old stereotype that Blacks are "intellectually inferior." Research studies have confirmed the existence of stereotype threat (Laurin, 2020). Also, African American students do more poorly on standardized tests if they perceive that they are being evaluated. If they think the test doesn't count, they perform as well as White students (Aronson, 2002). However, some critics argue that the extent to which stereotype threat explains the testing gap has been exaggerated (Sackett, Borneman, & Connelly, 2009).

Using Intelligence Tests   Here are some cautions about IQ that can help you avoid the pitfalls of using information about a child's intelligence in negative ways:

- *Avoid stereotyping and expectations.* A special concern is that the scores on an IQ test easily can lead to stereotypes and expectations about students. Sweeping generalizations are too often made on the basis of an IQ score. An IQ test should always be considered a measure of current performance. It is not a measure of fixed potential. Maturational changes and enriched environmental experiences can increase a student's IQ score.

- *Know that IQ is not a sole indicator of competence.* Another concern about IQ tests involves their use as the main or sole assessment of competence. A high IQ is not the ultimate human value. As we have seen in this chapter, it is important to consider not only students' intellectual competence in such areas as verbal skills but also their creative and practical skills.

- *Use caution in interpreting an overall IQ score.* In evaluating a child's intelligence, it is wiser to think of intelligence as consisting of a number of domains. Keep in mind the different types of intelligence described by Sternberg and Gardner. Remember that by considering the different domains of intelligence you can find that every child has at least one area of strength.

EXTREMES OF INTELLIGENCE

Intelligence tests have been used to discover indications of intellectual disability or intellectual giftedness, the extremes of intelligence. At times, intelligence tests have been misused for this purpose. Keeping in mind the theme that an intelligence test should not be used as the sole indicator of intellectual disability or giftedness, we will explore the nature of these intellectual extremes.

Intellectual Disability   The most distinctive feature of intellectual disability (formerly called mental retardation) is inadequate intellectual functioning (Elliott & Resing, 2019). Long before formal tests were developed to assess intelligence, individuals with an intellectual disability were identified by a lack of age-appropriate skills in learning and caring for themselves. Once intelligence tests were developed, they were used to identify the degree of intellectual disability. However, even individuals with an intellectual disability who have the same low IQ

developmental **connection**
Conditions, Diseases, and Disorders
Down syndrome is caused by the presence of an extra copy of chromosome 21. Connect to "Biological Beginnings."

A child with Down syndrome. *What causes a child to develop Down syndrome? In which major classification of intellectual disability does the condition fall?*
George Doyle/Stockbyte/Getty Images

stereotype threat The anxiety that one's behavior might confirm a negative stereotype about one's group.

At age 2, art prodigy Alexandra Nechita (shown here as a teenager) colored in coloring books for hours and also took up pen and ink. She had no interest in dolls or friends. By age 5 she was using watercolors. Once she started school, she would start painting as soon as she got home. At the age of 8, in 1994, she saw the first public exhibit of her work. In succeeding years, working quickly and impulsively on canvases as large as 5 feet by 9 feet, she has completed hundreds of paintings, some of which sell for close to $100,000 apiece. As an adult, she continues to paint—relentlessly and passionately. It is, she says, what she loves to do. *What are some characteristics of children who are gifted?*
Koichi Kamoshida/Newsmakers/Hulton Archive/Getty Images

intellectual disability A condition of limited mental ability in which the individual (1) has a low IQ, usually below 70 on a traditional intelligence test; (2) has difficulty adapting to the demands of everyday life; and (3) first exhibits these characteristics by age 18.

organic intellectual disability A genetic disorder or condition involving brain damage that is linked to a low level of intellectual functioning.

cultural-familial intellectual disability Condition in which there is no evidence of organic brain damage but the individual's IQ is between 50 and 70.

gifted Having above-average intelligence (an IQ of 130 or higher) and/or superior talent for something.

may have very different levels of functioning (Fidler & others, 2020). One might be married, employed, and involved in the community and the other might require constant supervision in an institution. Such differences in social competence led psychologists to include deficits in adaptive behavior in their definition of intellectual disability.

Intellectual disability is a condition of limited mental ability in which the individual (1) has a low IQ, usually below 70 on a traditional intelligence test; (2) has difficulty adapting to the demands of everyday life; and (3) first exhibits these characteristics by age 18 (Hallahan, Kauffman, & Pullen, 2019; Turnbull & others, 2020). The age limit is included in the definition of intellectual disability because, for example, we don't usually think of a college student who suffers massive brain damage in a car accident, resulting in an IQ of 60, as having an "intellectual disability." The low IQ and low adaptiveness should be evident in childhood, not after normal functioning is interrupted by damage of some form (Burack & others, 2016). About 5 million Americans fit this definition of intellectual disability.

Some cases of intellectual disability have an organic cause. **Organic intellectual disability** describes a genetic disorder or a lower level of intellectual functioning caused by brain damage (Mir & Kuchay, 2019). Down syndrome is one form of organic intellectual disability, and it occurs when an extra chromosome is present. Other causes of organic intellectual disability include fragile X syndrome, an abnormality in the X chromosome that was discussed in "Biological Beginnings"; prenatal malformation; metabolic disorders; and diseases that affect the brain. Most people who suffer from organic intellectual disability have IQs between 0 and 50.

When no evidence of organic brain damage can be found, cases are labeled **cultural-familial intellectual disability**. Individuals with this type of disability have IQs between 55 and 70. Psychologists suspect that this type of disability often results from growing up in a below-average intellectual environment. Children with this type of disability can be identified in schools, where they often fail, need tangible rewards (candy rather than praise), and are highly sensitive to what others expect of them. However, as adults, they are usually not noticeable, perhaps because adult settings don't tax their cognitive skills as much. It may also be that their intelligence increases as they move toward adulthood.

Giftedness There have always been people whose abilities and accomplishments outshine those of others—the whiz kid in class, the star athlete, the natural musician. People who are **gifted** have above-average intelligence (an IQ of 130 or higher) and/or superior talent for something. When it comes to programs for gifted students, most school systems select children who have intellectual superiority and academic aptitude, whereas children who are talented in the visual and performing arts (art, drama, dance), who demonstrate skill in athletics, or who have other special aptitudes tend to be overlooked (Elliott & Resing, 2020; Reis & Renzulli, 2020). There also are increasing calls to further widen the criteria for giftedness to include such factors as creativity and commitment (Beghetto, 2019; Sternberg, Kaufman, & Roberts, 2019).

Estimates vary but indicate that approximately 6 to 10 percent of U.S. students are classified as gifted (National Association for Gifted Children, 2017). This percentage is likely conservative because it focuses on children who are gifted intellectually and academically, often failing to include those who are gifted in creative thinking or the visual and performing arts (Ford, 2016).

Characteristics   What are the characteristics of children who are gifted? Despite speculation that giftedness is linked with having a mental disorder, no relation between giftedness and mental disorder has been found. Similarly, the idea that gifted children are maladjusted is a myth, as Lewis Terman (1925) found when he conducted an extensive study of 1,500 children whose Stanford-Binet IQs averaged 150. The children in Terman's study were socially well adjusted, and many went on to become successful doctors, lawyers, professors, and scientists. Studies support the conclusion that gifted people tend to be more mature than others, have fewer emotional problems than average, and grow up in a positive family climate (Davidson, 2000). For example, a recent study revealed that parents and teachers identified elementary school children who are not gifted as having more emotional and behavioral risks than children who are gifted (Eklund & others, 2015). In this study, when children who are gifted did have problems, they were more likely to be internalized problems, such as anxiety and depression, than externalized problems such as acting out and high levels of aggression.

Ellen Winner (1996) described three criteria that characterize gifted children, whether in art, music, or academic domains:

1. *Precocity.* Gifted children are precocious. They begin to master an area earlier than their peers. Learning in their domain is more effortless for them than for ordinary children. In most instances, these gifted children are precocious because they have an inborn high ability in a particular domain or domains.

2. *Marching to their own drummer.* Gifted children learn in a qualitatively different way from ordinary children. One way that they march to a different drummer is that they need minimal help, or scaffolding, from adults to learn. In many instances, they resist any kind of explicit instruction. They often make discoveries on their own and solve problems in unique ways.

3. *A passion to master.* Gifted children are driven to understand the domain in which they have high ability. They display an intense, obsessive interest and an ability to focus. They motivate themselves, says Winner, and do not need to be "pushed" by their parents.

Also, researchers have found that children who are gifted learn at a faster pace, process information more rapidly, are better at reasoning, use superior strategies, and monitor their understanding better than their nongifted counterparts (Sternberg & Kaufman, 2018a).

Nature-Nurture   Is giftedness a product of heredity or environment? Likely both (2020a, b). Individuals who are gifted recall that they had signs of high ability in a particular area at a very young age, prior to or at the beginning of formal training. This suggests the importance of innate ability in giftedness. However, researchers have also found that individuals with world-class status in the arts, mathematics, science, and sports all report strong family support and years of training and practice (Bloom, 1985). Deliberate practice is an important characteristic of individuals who become experts in a particular domain. For example, in one study the best musicians engaged in twice as much deliberate practice over their lives as did the least successful ones (Ericsson, Krampe, & Tesch-Romer, 1993).

Domain-Specific Giftedness and Development   Individuals who are highly gifted are typically not gifted in many domains, and research on giftedness is increasingly focused on domain-specific developmental trajectories (Sternberg, 2019c; Winner, 2014). During the childhood years, the domain in which individuals are gifted usually emerges. Thus, at some point in childhood the individual who will become a gifted artist or a gifted mathematician begins to show expertise in that domain. Regarding domain-specific giftedness, software genius Bill Gates (1998), the founder of Microsoft and one of the world's richest persons, commented that when you are good at something you have to resist the urge to think that you will be good at everything. Gates says that because he has been so successful at software development, people expect him to be brilliant in other domains where he is far from being a genius.

Identifying an individual's domain-specific talent and providing individually appropriate and optional educational opportunities need to be accomplished at the very latest by adolescence (Keating, 2009). During adolescence, individuals who are talented become less reliant on parental support and increasingly pursue their own interests.

Education of Children Who Are Gifted   An increasing number of experts argue that the education of children who are gifted in the United States requires a significant overhaul (Beghetto, 2019; Reis & Renzulli, 2020). Ellen Winner (1996, 2009, 2014) argues that too often children who are gifted are socially isolated and underchallenged in the classroom. It is not unusual for them to be ostracized and labeled "nerds" or "geeks." Many eminent adults report that school was a negative experience for them, that they were bored and sometimes knew more than their teachers (Bloom, 1985). Winner argues that American education will benefit when standards are raised for all children. When some children are still underchallenged, she recommends that they be allowed to attend advanced classes in their domain of exceptional ability. Some especially precocious middle school students may benefit from taking college classes in their area of expertise. For example, Bill Gates took college math classes at 13; Yo-Yo Ma, a famous cellist, graduated from high school at 15 and attended Juilliard School of Music in New York City.

A final concern is that African American, Latino, and Native American children are underrepresented in gifted programs (Ford, 2016). Much of the underrepresentation involves the lower test scores for these children compared with non-Latino White and Asian American children, which may reflect test bias and fewer opportunities to develop language skills such as vocabulary and comprehension (Ford, 2016).

Bill Gates is the founder of Microsoft and one of the world's richest people. Like many highly gifted students, Gates was not especially fond of school. He hacked a computer security system when he was 13, and as a high school student he was allowed to take some college math classes. He dropped out of Harvard University and began developing a plan for what was to become Microsoft Corporation. *What are some ways that schools can enrich the education of such highly talented students as Gates to make it a more challenging, interesting, and meaningful experience?*
Joe McNally/Hulton Archive/Getty Images

Review *Connect* Reflect

 LG3 Explain cognitive changes in middle and late childhood.

Review

- What characterizes Piaget's stage of concrete operational thought? What are some contributions and criticisms of Piaget?
- How do children process information in middle and late childhood?
- What is intelligence, and how is it assessed? What characterizes links between neuroscience and intelligence? What determines individual and group differences in IQ scores?
- What are the key characteristics of intellectual disability and giftedness?

Connect

- In discussing memory, thinking, and intelligence, the topic of recommended educational strategies often came up. Compare these recommendations with those you learned earlier.

Reflect *Your Own Personal Journey of Life*

- There are many online programs that let parents test their child's IQ and identify how well the child is performing in relation to his or her grade in school. Would you want to personally test your own child's IQ? What might be some problems with parents giving their children an IQ test?

---

4 Language Development

 LG4 Discuss language development in middle and late childhood.

Vocabulary, Grammar, and Metalinguistic Awareness

Reading

Writing

Second-Language Learning and Bilingual Education

How do vocabulary, grammar, and metalinguistic awareness change in middle and late childhood?
Richard Howard Photography

Children gain new skills as they enter school that make it possible for them to learn to read and write (Bear & others, 2020; Graham & Harris, 2020; Gunning, 2020). These skills include increased use of language to talk about things that are not physically present, learning what a word is, and learning how to recognize and talk about sounds. Children also learn the *alphabetic principle*—that the letters of the alphabet represent sounds of the language.

VOCABULARY, GRAMMAR, AND METALINGUISTIC AWARENESS

During middle and late childhood, changes occur in the way children's mental vocabulary is organized. When asked to say the first word that comes to mind when they hear a word, preschool children typically provide a word that often follows the word in a sentence. For example, when asked to respond to *dog,* the young child may say "barks," or to the word *eat* respond with "lunch." At about 7 years of age, children begin to respond with a word that is the same part of speech as the stimulus word. For example, a child may now respond to the word *dog* with "cat" or "horse." To *eat,* they now might say "drink." This is evidence that children now have begun to categorize their vocabulary by parts of speech.

The process of categorizing becomes easier as children increase their vocabulary (Clark, 2017). Children's vocabulary increases from an average of about 14,000 words at age 6 to an average of about 40,000 words by age 11.

Children make similar advances in grammar (Clark, 2017). During the elementary school years, children's improvement in logical reasoning and analytical skills helps them understand such constructions as the appropriate use of comparatives (*shorter, deeper*) and subjunctives ("If you were president . . ."). During the elementary school years, children become increasingly able to understand and use complex grammar, such as the following sentence: *The boy who kissed his mother wore a hat.* They also learn to use language in a more connected way, producing connected discourse. They become able to relate sentences to one another to produce descriptions, definitions, and narratives that make sense. Children must be able to do these things orally before they can be expected to deal with them in written assignments.

These advances in vocabulary and grammar during the elementary school years are accompanied by the development of **metalinguistic awareness,** which is knowledge about language, such as understanding what a preposition is or being able to discuss the sounds of a language (Altman, Goldstein, & Armon-Lotem, 2018). Metalinguistic awareness allows children "to think about their language, understand what words are, and even define them" (Berko Gleason, 2009, p. 4). It improves considerably during the elementary school years (Pan & Uccelli, 2009). Defining words becomes a regular part of classroom discourse, and children increase their knowledge of syntax as they study and talk about the components of sentences such as subjects and verbs (Crain, 2012). And reading also feeds into metalinguistic awareness as children try to comprehend written text.

Children also make progress in understanding how to use language in culturally appropriate ways—a process called *pragmatics* (Gentilleau-Lambin & others, 2019). By the time they enter adolescence, most children know the rules for using language in everyday contexts—that is, what is appropriate and inappropriate to say.

READING

Before learning to read, children learn to use language to talk about things that are not present; they learn what a word is; and they learn how to recognize sounds and talk about them. Children who begin elementary school with a robust vocabulary have an advantage when it comes to learning to read. Vocabulary development plays an important role in reading comprehension (Gunning, 2020).

How should children be taught to read? For many years debate has focused on the whole-language approach versus the phonics approach (Dewitz & others, 2020; Reutzel & Cooter, 2019).

The **whole-language approach** stresses that reading instruction should parallel children's natural language learning. In some whole-language classes, beginning readers are taught to recognize whole words or even entire sentences, and to use the context of what they are reading to guess at the meaning of words. Reading materials that support the whole-language approach are whole and meaningful—that is, children are given material in its complete form, such as stories and poems, so that they learn to understand language's communicative function. Reading is connected with listening and writing skills. Although there are variations in whole-language programs, most share the premise that reading should be integrated with other skills and subjects, such as science and social studies, and that it should focus on real-world material. Thus, a class might read newspapers, magazines, or books, and then write about and discuss what they have learned.

This teacher is helping a student sound out words. Researchers have found that phonics instruction is a key aspect of teaching students to read, especially beginning readers and students with weak reading skills.
KatarzynaBialasiewicz/Getty Images

In contrast, the **phonics approach** emphasizes that reading instruction should teach basic rules for translating written symbols into sounds. Early phonics-centered reading instruction should involve simplified materials. Only after children have learned correspondence rules that relate spoken phonemes to the alphabet letters that are used to represent them should they be given complex reading materials, such as books and poems (Bear & others, 2020).

Which approach is better? Research suggests that children can benefit from both approaches, but instruction in phonics needs to be emphasized (Tompkins & Rogers, 2020). An increasing number of experts in the field of reading now conclude that direct instruction in phonics is a key aspect of learning to read (Bear & others, 2020; Morrow, 2020).

Beyond the phonics/whole language issue in learning to read, becoming a good reader includes learning to read fluently (Gunning, 2020). Many beginning or poor readers do not recognize words automatically. Their processing capacity is consumed by the demands of word recognition, so they have less capacity to devote to comprehension of groupings of words as phrases or sentences. As their processing of words and passages becomes more automatic, it is said that their reading becomes more *fluent* (Dewitz & others, 2020). Also, children's vocabulary development plays an important role in their reading comprehension (Morrow, 2020). And metacognitive strategies, such as learning to monitor one's reading progress, getting the gist of what is being read, and summarizing also are important in becoming a good reader (Connor & others, 2019).

metalinguistic awareness Knowledge about language, such as understanding what a preposition is or being able to discuss the sounds of a language.

whole-language approach An approach to reading instruction based on the idea that instruction should parallel children's natural language learning. Reading materials should be whole and meaningful.

phonics approach The idea that reading instruction should teach the basic rules for translating written symbols into sounds.

WRITING

As they begin to write, children often invent spellings. Parents and teachers should encourage children's early writing but not be overly concerned about the formation of letters or spelling. Corrections of spelling and printing should be selective and made in positive ways that do not discourage the child's writing and spontaneity.

Like becoming a good reader, becoming a good writer takes many years and lots of practice (Graham & Harris, 2020; Morrow, 2020; Tompkins & Rogers, 2020). Children should be given many writing opportunities. As their language and cognitive skills improve with good instruction, so will their writing skills. For example, developing a more sophisticated understanding of syntax and grammar serves as an underpinning for better writing. So do cognitive skills such as organization and logical reasoning. Through the course of the school years, students develop increasingly sophisticated methods of organizing their ideas.

The metacognitive strategies involved in being a competent writer are linked with those required to be a competent reader because the writing process involves competent reading and rereading during composition and revision (Graham, 2020a, b; Graham & others, 2020). Further, researchers have found that strategy instruction involving planning, drafting, revising, and editing improves older elementary school children's metacognitive awareness and writing competence.

Monitoring one's writing progress is especially important in becoming a good writer (Graham & Harris, 2019). This includes being receptive to feedback and applying what one learns in writing one paper to making the next paper better.

Major concerns about students' writing competence are increasingly being voiced (Tompkins & Rogers, 2020). One study revealed that 70 to 75 percent of U.S. students in grades 4 through 12 are low-achieving writers (Persky, Dane, & Jin, 2003). College instructors report that 50 percent of high school graduates are not prepared for college-level writing (Achieve, Inc., 2005).

SECOND-LANGUAGE LEARNING AND BILINGUAL EDUCATION

Are there sensitive periods in learning a second language? That is, if individuals want to learn a second language, how important is the age at which they begin to learn it? What is the best way to teach children who come from homes in which English is not the primary language?

Second-Language Learning For many years, it was claimed that if individuals did not learn a second language prior to puberty they would never reach native-language learners' proficiency in the second language (Johnson & Newport, 1991). However, recent research indicates a more complex conclusion: Sensitive periods likely vary across different language systems (Thomas & Johnson, 2008). Thus, for late language learners, such as adolescents and adults, new vocabulary is easier to learn than new sounds or new grammar (Neville, 2006). For example, children's ability to pronounce words with a native-like accent in a second language typically decreases with age, with an especially sharp drop occurring after the age of about 10 to 12. Also, adults tend to learn a second language faster than children, but their final level of second-language attainment is not as high as children's. And the way children and adults learn a second language differs somewhat. Compared with adults, children are less sensitive to feedback, less likely to use explicit strategies, and more likely to learn a second language from large amounts of input (Thomas & Johnson, 2008).

Students in the United States are far behind their counterparts in many developed countries in learning a second language. For example, in Russia, schools have 10 grades, called forms, which roughly correspond to the 12 grades in American schools. Russian children begin school at age 7 and begin learning English in the third form. Because of this emphasis on teaching English, most Russian citizens under the age of 40 today are able to speak at least some English. The United States is the only technologically advanced Western nation that does not have a national foreign language requirement at the high school level, even for students in rigorous academic programs.

Some aspects of children's ability to learn a second language transfer to success in other areas (Hernandez, Fernandez, & Aznar-Bese, 2019). Children who are fluent in two languages perform better than their single-language counterparts on tests of control of attention, concept formation, analytical reasoning, inhibition, cognitive flexibility, cognitive complexity, and cognitive monitoring (Białystok, 2011, 2015, 2017). Recent research has also documented that bilingual children are better at theory of mind tasks (Rubio-Fernandez, 2017). They also are more conscious of the structure of spoken and written language and better at noticing errors of grammar and meaning, skills that benefit their reading ability (Bialystok, 1997; Kuo & Anderson, 2012). Also, a recent study of 6- to 10-year-olds found that early bilingual exposure was a key factor in bilingual children outperforming monolingual children on phonological awareness and word learning (Jasinska & Petitto, 2018). Further, a recent study indicated that 3-year-old bilingual children adapted to the needs of their communication partners better than their monolingual counterparts did (Gampe, Wermelinger, & Daum, 2019). In addition, a recent study of 3-year-olds found that shared book reading at home and school in a second language not only improved their second-language learning but also the perspective taking emphasized in the shared reading program increased their ability to shift perspectives and understand others' emotional states (Grover & others, 2020). And a recent study of Chinese children found that bilingual children for whom English was a foreign language outperformed monolingual Chinese children on an attention task and also had higher activation of their prefrontal cortex (Li & others, 2020).

Thus, overall, bilingualism is linked to positive outcomes for children's language and cognitive development (Antovich & Graf Estes, 2018; Branzi, Calabria, & Costa, 2019; Hardy & others, 2020). An especially important developmental question that many parents of infants and young children have asked is whether they should teach them two languages simultaneously, or whether this might confuse them. The answer is that teaching infants and young children two languages simultaneously (as when a mother's native language is English and her husband's is Spanish) has numerous benefits and few drawbacks (Bialystok, 2015, 2017).

A first- and second-grade bilingual English-Cantonese teacher instructing students in Chinese in Oakland, California. *What have researchers found about the effectiveness of bilingual education?*
Elizabeth Crews

Bilingual Education A current controversy related to bilingualism involves the millions of U.S. children who come from homes in which English is not the primary language and then must learn English in school (Diaz-Rico, 2020; Herrell & Jordan, 2020). What is the best way to teach these English language learners (ELLs), many of whom in the United States are from immigrant families living in poverty?

ELLs have been taught in one of two main ways: (1) instruction in English only, or (2) a *dual-language* (formerly called *bilingual*) approach that combines instruction in their home language and English (Diaz-Rico, 2020; Herrell & Jordan, 2020). In a dual-language approach, instruction is given in both the ELL child's home language and English for varying amounts of time at certain grade levels. One of the arguments for the dual-language approach is the research discussed earlier demonstrating that bilingual children have more advanced information-processing skills than monolingual children (Genesee & Lindholm-Leary, 2012).

If a dual-language instructional strategy is used, too often it has been thought that immigrant children need only one or two years of this type of instruction. However, in general it takes immigrant children approximately three to five years to develop speaking proficiency and seven years to develop reading proficiency in English (Hakuta, Butler, & Witt, 2000). Also, immigrant children vary in their ability to learn English (Diaz-Rico, 2020). Children from lower socioeconomic backgrounds have more difficulty than those from higher socioeconomic backgrounds (Hakuta, 2001; Hoff & Place, 2013). Thus, especially for immigrant children from lower socioeconomic backgrounds, more years of dual-language instruction may be needed than they currently are receiving.

What have researchers found regarding outcomes of ELL programs? Drawing conclusions about the effectiveness of ELL programs is difficult because of variations across programs in the number of years they are in effect, type of instruction, quality of schooling other than ELL instruction, teachers, children, and other factors. Further, no effective experiments have been conducted that compare bilingual education with English-only education in the United States (Snow & Kang, 2006). Some experts have concluded that the quality of instruction is more important in determining outcomes than the language in which it is delivered (Lesaux & Siegel, 2003).

Nonetheless, other experts, such as Kenji Hakuta (2001, 2005), support the combined home language and English approach because (1) children have difficulty learning a subject when it is taught in a language they do not understand; and (2) when both languages are integrated in the classroom, children learn the second language more readily and participate more actively. In support of Hakuta's view, most large-scale studies have found that the academic achievement of ELLs is higher in dual-language programs than English-only programs (Genesee & Lindholm-Leary, 2012). To read about the work of one dual-language teacher, see *Connecting with Careers*.

Salvador Tamayo, Teacher of English Language Learners

Salvador Tamayo is an ELL fifth-grade teacher at Turner Elementary School in West Chicago. He recently was given a National Educator Award by the Milken Family Foundation for his work in educating ELLs. Tamayo is especially adept at integrating technology into his ELL classes. He and his students have created several award-winning Web sites about the West Chicago City Museum, the local Latino community, and the history of West Chicago. His students also developed an "I Want to Be an American Citizen" Web site to assist family and community members in preparing for the U.S. Citizenship Test. Tamayo also teaches an ELL class at Wheaton College.

Salvador Tamayo works with bilingual education students.
Courtesy of Salvador Tamayo

For more information about what elementary school teachers do, see the Careers in Life-Span Development appendix.

Review Connect Reflect

 LG4 Discuss language development in middle and late childhood.

Review

- What are some changes in vocabulary and grammar in middle and late childhood?
- What controversy characterizes how to teach children to read?
- What characterizes children's writing skills and their development?
- What is dual-language instruction? What issues are involved in this approach? What characterizes bilingual education?

Connect

- Earlier in the chapter you learned about metacognition. Compare that concept with metalinguistic awareness.

Reflect Your Own Personal Journey of Life

- Did you learn a second language as a child? If you did, do you think it was beneficial to you? If so, in what ways? If you did not learn a second language as a child, do you wish you had? Why or why not?

topical connections *looking forward*

The slow physical growth of middle and late childhood gives way to the dramatic changes of puberty in early adolescence. Significant changes also occur in the adolescent's brain in which earlier maturation of the amygdala (emotion processing) and later maturation of the prefrontal cortex (decision making, self-regulation) are likely linked to increases in risk-taking and sensation seeking. Sexual development is a normal aspect of adolescence, but having sexual intercourse early in adolescence is associated with a number of problems. Adolescence is a critical juncture in health because many poor health habits begin in adolescence. Despite recent declines, the United States has one of the highest rates of illicit drug use of any developed nation. Adolescent thought is more abstract, idealistic, and logical than children's. The transition from elementary school to middle school or junior high is difficult for many individuals because it coincides with so many physical, cognitive, and socioemotional changes in development.

Physical and Cognitive Development in Middle and Late Childhood

1 Physical Changes and Health

 Discuss physical changes and health in middle and late childhood.

Body Growth and Change

- The period of middle and late childhood involves slow, consistent growth. During this period, children grow an average of 2 to 3 inches a year. Muscle mass and strength gradually increase. Among the most pronounced changes in body growth and proportion are decreases in head circumference and waist circumference in relation to body height.

The Brain

- Changes in the brain in middle and late childhood include advances in functioning in the prefrontal cortex, which are reflected in improved attention, reasoning, and cognitive control. During middle and late childhood, less diffusion and more focal activation occurs in the prefrontal cortex, a change that is associated with increased cognitive control.

Motor Development

- During middle and late childhood, motor development becomes much smoother and more coordinated. Children gain greater control over their bodies and can sit and pay attention for longer periods of time. However, their lives should include abundant physical activity.

- Increased myelination of the central nervous system is reflected in improved motor skills. Improved fine motor skills appear in the form of handwriting development. Boys are usually better at gross motor skills, girls at fine motor skills.

Exercise

- Most American children do not get nearly enough exercise. Parents play an especially important role in guiding children to increase their exercise. Heavy television viewing and computer use are linked to lower activity levels in children.

Health, Illness, and Disease

- For the most part, middle and late childhood is a time of excellent health. The most common cause of severe injury and death in childhood is motor vehicle accidents. Being overweight or obese is an increasingly prevalent child health problem, raising the risk for many medical and psychological problems. Cardiovascular disease is uncommon in children, but the precursors to adult cardiovascular disease are often already apparent during childhood. Cancer is the second leading cause of death in children (after accidents). Leukemia is the most common childhood cancer.

2 Children with Disabilities

 Identify children with different types of disabilities and discuss issues in educating them.

The Scope of Disabilities

- Approximately 13 percent of U.S. children from 3 to 21 years of age receive special education or related services. A child with a learning disability has difficulty in learning that involves understanding or using spoken or written language, and the difficulty can appear in listening, thinking, reading, writing, and spelling. A learning disability also may involve difficulty in doing mathematics. To be classified as a learning disability, the learning problem is not primarily the result of visual, hearing, or motor disabilities; intellectual disabilities; emotional disorders; or environmental, cultural, or economic disadvantage.

- Dyslexia is a category of learning disabilities that involves a severe impairment in the ability to read and spell. Dysgraphia is a learning disability that involves difficulty in handwriting. Dyscalculia is a learning disability that involves difficulties in math computation.

- Attention deficit hyperactivity disorder (ADHD) is a disability in which individuals consistently show problems in one or more of these areas: (1) inattention, (2) hyperactivity, and (3) impulsivity. ADHD has been increasingly diagnosed. Emotional and behavioral disorders consist of serious, persistent problems that involve relationships, aggression, depression, fears associated with personal or school matters, as well as other inappropriate socioemotional characteristics.

- Autism spectrum disorders (ASD) range from autistic disorder, a severe developmental disorder, to Asperger syndrome, a relatively mild autism spectrum disorder. The current consensus is that autism is a brain dysfunction involving abnormalities in brain structure and neurotransmitters. Children with autism spectrum disorders are characterized by problems in social interaction, verbal and nonverbal communication, and repetitive behaviors.

Educational Issues

- In 1975, Public Law 94-142, the Education for All Handicapped Children Act, required that all children with disabilities be given a free, appropriate public education. This law was renamed the Individuals with Disabilities Education Act (IDEA) in 1990 and updated in 2004. IDEA includes requirements that children with disabilities receive an individualized education plan (IEP), which is a written plan that spells out a program tailored to the child and requires that they be educated in the least restrictive environment (LRE), which is a setting that is as similar as possible to the one in which children without disabilities are educated. The term *inclusion* means educating children with disabilities full-time in the regular classroom.

3 Cognitive Changes

 Explain cognitive changes in middle and late childhood.

Piaget's Cognitive Developmental Theory

- Piaget said that the stage of concrete operational thought characterizes children from about 7 to 11 years of age. During this stage, children are capable of concrete operations, conservation, classification, seriation, and transitivity. Critics argue that some abilities emerge earlier than Piaget thought, that elements of a stage do not appear at the same time, and that education and culture have more influence on development than Piaget predicted. Neo-Piagetians place more emphasis on how children process information, their use of strategies, speed of information processing, and division of cognitive problems into more precise steps.

Information Processing

- Long-term memory increases in middle and late childhood. Working memory is an important memory process. Knowledge and expertise influence memory. Changes in autobiographical memory occur in middle and late childhood. Strategies can be used by children to improve their memory, and it is important for adults who instruct children to encourage children's strategy use. Fuzzy trace theory has been proposed to explain developmental changes in memory.

- Among the key dimensions of executive function that are important in cognitive development and school success are self-control/inhibition, working memory, and flexibility.

- Critical thinking involves thinking reflectively and productively, as well as evaluating available evidence. Mindfulness is an important aspect of critical thinking. A special concern is the lack of emphasis on critical thinking in many schools.

- Creative thinking is the ability to think in novel and unusual ways and to come up with unique solutions to problems. Guilford distinguished between convergent and divergent thinking. A number of strategies can be used to encourage children's creative thinking, including brainstorming.

- Metacognition is knowing about knowing. Many metacognitive studies have focused on metamemory. Pressley views the key to education as helping students learn a rich repertoire of strategies for problem solving.

Intelligence

- Intelligence consists of problem-solving skills and the ability to adapt to and learn from life's everyday experiences. Interest in intelligence often focuses on individual differences and assessment. Widely used intelligence tests today include the Stanford-Binet tests and Wechsler scales. Results on these tests may be reported in terms of an overall IQ or in terms of performance on specific areas of the tests.

- Sternberg proposed that intelligence comes in three main forms: analytical, creative, and practical. Gardner proposes that there are eight types of intelligence: verbal, mathematical, spatial, bodily-kinesthetic, interpersonal, intrapersonal, musical, and naturalist. The multiple-intelligence approaches have expanded our conception of intelligence, but critics argue that the research base for these approaches is not well established.

- IQ scores are influenced by both genetics and characteristics of the environment. Parents, home environments, schools, and intervention programs can influence these scores. Intelligence test scores have risen considerably around the world in recent decades. This phenomenon is called the Flynn effect, and it supports the role of environment in intelligence. Group differences in IQ scores may reflect many influences, including cultural bias. Tests may be biased against certain groups that are not familiar with a standard form of English, with the content tested, or with the testing situation. Tests are likely to reflect the values and experience of the dominant culture.

Extremes of Intelligence

- Intellectual disability involves a low level of intellectual functioning as well as difficulty adapting to the demands of everyday life, with these characteristics occurring prior to age 18. One classification of intellectual disability distinguishes between organic and cultural-familial types.

- Individuals who are gifted have above-average intelligence (IQ of 130 or higher) and/or superior talent for something. Three characteristics of gifted children are precocity, marching to their own drummer, and a passion to master their domain. Giftedness is likely a consequence of both heredity and environment. Developmental changes characterize giftedness, and increasingly the domain-specific aspect of giftedness is emphasized. Concerns exist about the education of children who are gifted.

4 Language Development

 Discuss language development in middle and late childhood.

Vocabulary, Grammar, and Metalinguistic Awareness

- Children gradually become more analytical and logical in their approach to words and grammar. In terms of grammar, children now better understand comparatives and subjunctives. They become increasingly able to use complex grammar and produce narratives that make sense. Improvements in metalinguistic awareness—knowledge about language—are evident during the elementary school years as children increasingly define words, expand their knowledge of syntax, and understand better how to use language in culturally appropriate ways.

Reading

- A current debate in reading focuses on the phonics approach versus the whole-language approach. The phonics approach advocates phonetics instruction and giving children simplified materials. The whole-language approach stresses that reading instruction should parallel children's natural language learning and that children should be given whole-language materials such as books and poems. Three key processes in learning to read a printed word are being aware of sound units in words, decoding words, and accessing word meaning.

Writing

- Advances in children's language and cognitive development provide the underpinnings for improved writing. Major concerns are increasingly being voiced about deficits in children's writing competence. Teachers play a key role in improving children's writing skills.

Second-Language Learning and Bilingual Education

- Recent research indicates the complexity of determining whether there are sensitive periods in learning a second language. The dual-language approach (formerly called "bilingual") aims to teach academic subjects to immigrant children in their native languages while gradually adding English instruction. Researchers have found that the dual-language approach does not interfere with performance in either language.

key **terms**

key **people**

chapter 10

SOCIOEMOTIONAL DEVELOPMENT IN MIDDLE AND LATE CHILDHOOD

chapter outline

① Emotional and Personality Development

Learning Goal 1 Discuss emotional and personality development in middle and late childhood.

The Self
Emotional Development
Moral Development
Gender

② Families

Learning Goal 2 Describe developmental changes in parent-child relationships, parents as managers, attachment in families, and stepfamilies.

Developmental Changes in Parent-Child Relationships
Parents as Managers
Attachment in Families
Stepfamilies

③ Peers

Learning Goal 3 Identify changes in peer relationships in middle and late childhood.

Developmental Changes
Peer Status
Social Cognition
Bullying
Friends

④ Schools

Learning Goal 4 Characterize aspects of schooling in children's development in middle and late childhood.

Contemporary Approaches to Student Learning
Socioeconomic Status, Ethnicity, and Culture

FatCamera/Getty Images

In *The Shame of the Nation*, Jonathan Kozol (2005) described his visits to 60 U.S. schools in urban low-income areas in 11 states. He saw many schools in which minorities totaled 80 to 90 percent of the student population. Kozol observed numerous inequities—unkempt classrooms, hallways, and restrooms; inadequate textbooks and supplies; and lack of resources. He also saw teachers mainly instructing students to memorize material by rote, especially as preparation for mandated tests, rather than stimulating them to engage in higher-level thinking. Kozol also frequently observed teachers using threatening disciplinary tactics to control the classroom.

However, some teachers Kozol observed were effective in educating children in these undesirable conditions. At P.S. 30 in the South Bronx, Mr. Bedrock teaches fifth grade. One student in his class, Serafina, recently lost her mother to AIDS. When author Jonathan Kozol visited the class, he was told that two other children had taken the role of "allies in the child's struggle for emotional survival" (Kozol, 2005, p. 291). Textbooks are in short supply for the class, and the social studies text is so out of date it claims that Ronald Reagan is the country's president. But Mr. Bedrock told Kozol that it's a "wonderful" class this year. About their teacher, 56-year-old Mr. Bedrock, one student said, "'He's getting old, . . . but we love him anyway'" (p. 292). Kozol observed the students in Mr. Bedrock's class to be orderly, interested, and engaged.

What are some of the challenges faced by children growing up in the South Bronx?
Andy Levin/Science Source

topical connections *looking **back***

In early childhood, according to Erikson, young children are in the stage of initiative versus guilt. Parents continue to play an important role in their development, and an authoritative parenting style is most likely to have positive outcomes for children. In early childhood, peer relations begin to take on a more significant role as children's social worlds widen. Play has a special place in young children's lives and is an important context for both cognitive and socioemotional development.

preview

The years of middle and late childhood bring many changes to children's social and emotional lives. Transformations in their relationships with parents and peers occur, and schooling takes on a more academic flavor. The development of their self-conceptions, moral reasoning, and moral behavior is also significant.

1 Emotional and Personality Development **LG1** Discuss emotional and personality development in middle and late childhood.

| The Self | Emotional Development | Moral Development | Gender |

In this section, we will explore how the self continues to develop during middle and late childhood and consider the emotional changes that take place during these years. We will also discuss children's moral development and many aspects of the role that gender plays in their development in middle and late childhood.

THE SELF

What is the nature of the child's self-understanding, understanding of others, and self-esteem during the elementary school years? What roles do self-efficacy and self-regulation play in children's achievement?

The Development of Self-Understanding   Self-understanding becomes more complex in middle and late childhood (Carpendale & Lewis, 2015). From 8 to 11 years of age, children increasingly describe themselves in terms of psychological characteristics and traits, in contrast with the more concrete self-descriptions of younger children. For example, older children are more likely to describe themselves using adjectives such as "*popular, nice, helpful, mean, smart,* and *dumb*" (Harter, 2006, p. 526).

In addition, during the elementary school years, children become more likely to recognize social aspects of the self (Harter, 2012, 2016). They include references to social groups in their self-descriptions, such as referring to themselves as a Girl Scout, a Catholic, or someone who has two close friends (Lively & Bromley, 1973).

Children's self-understanding in the elementary school years also includes increasing reference to social comparison (Harter, 2013). At this point in development, children are more likely to distinguish themselves from others in comparative rather than in absolute terms. That is, elementary-school-age children are no longer as likely to think about what they do or do not do, but are more likely to think about what they can do in comparison with others.

Consider a series of studies in which Diane Ruble (1983) investigated children's use of social comparison in their self-evaluations. Children were given a difficult task and then offered feedback on their performance, as well as information about the performances of other children their age. The children were then asked for self-evaluations. Children younger than 7 made virtually no reference to the information about other children's performances. However, many children older than 7 included socially comparative information in their self-descriptions.

In sum, in middle and late childhood, self-description increasingly involves psychological and social characteristics, including social comparison.

Understanding Others   Earlier we described the advances and limitations of young children's social understanding. In middle and late childhood, **perspective taking**, the social cognitive process involved in assuming the perspective of others and understanding their thoughts and feelings, improves. Executive function is at work in perspective taking (Galinsky, 2010). Among the executive functions called on when children engage in perspective taking are cognitive inhibition (controlling one's own thoughts to consider the perspective of others) and cognitive flexibility (seeing situations in different ways). Recent research indicates that

Children are busy becoming something they have not quite grasped yet, something which keeps changing.

—Alastair Reid
American poet, 20th century

> developmental **connection**
>
> **Identity**
>
> In adolescence, individuals become more introspective and reflective in their self-understanding as they search for an identity. Connect to "Socioemotional Development in Adolescence."

perspective taking The social cognitive process involved in assuming the perspective of others and understanding their thoughts and feelings.

What are some changes in children's understanding of others in middle and late childhood?
Asiseeit/E+/Getty Images

children and adolescents who do not have good perspective taking skills are more likely to have difficulty in peer relations and engage in more aggressive and oppositional behavior (Morosan & others, 2017).

In Robert Selman's (1980) view, at about 6 to 8 years of age, children begin to understand that others may have a different perspective because some people have more access to information. Then, he says, in the next several years, children begin to realize that each individual is aware of the other's perspective and that putting oneself in the other's place is a way of judging the other person's intentions, purposes, and actions.

Perspective taking is thought to be especially important in determining whether children develop prosocial or antisocial attitudes and behavior. In terms of prosocial behavior, taking another's perspective improves children's likelihood of understanding and sympathizing with others when they are distressed or in need.

In middle and late childhood, children also become more skeptical of others' claims (Heyman, Fu, & Lee, 2013). In a study of 6- to 9-year-old children, older children were less trusting and better at explaining the reasons to doubt sources that might distort claims than were younger children (Mills & Elashi, 2014). Also, more intelligent children and children with better social cognitive skills were more likely to detect and explain distorted claims.

Self-Esteem and Self-Concept High self-esteem and a positive self-concept are important characteristics of children's well-being (Cloninger, 2019; Twenge & Campbell, 2020). Investigators sometimes use the terms *self-esteem* and *self-concept* interchangeably or do not precisely define them, but there is a meaningful difference between them (Harter, 2016). **Self-esteem** refers to global evaluations of the self; it is also called *self-worth* or *self-image*. For example, a child may perceive that she is not merely a person but a *good* person. **Self-concept** refers to domain-specific evaluations of the self (Ramirez-Granizo & others, 2020). Children can make self-evaluations in many domains of their lives—academic, athletic, appearance, and so on (Ehm, Hasselhorn, & Schmiedek, 2019). In sum, *self-esteem* refers to global self-evaluations, *self-concept* to domain-specific evaluations.

The foundations of self-esteem and self-concept emerge from the quality of parent-child interaction (Aremu, John-Akinola, & Desmennu, 2019). Thus, if children and adolescents have low self-esteem, they may have experienced neglect or abuse in relationships with their parents earlier in development. Children with high self-esteem are more likely to be securely attached to parents and have parents who engage in sensitive caregiving (Verschueren, 2020). Also, in a recent study, parental warmth, monitoring, low maternal depression, economic well-being, and father presence (versus absence) were linked to higher self-esteem in children and adolescents (Krauss, Orth, & Robins, 2020).

Self-esteem reflects perceptions that do not always match reality (Cramer, 2017). A child's self-esteem might reflect a belief about whether he or she is intelligent and attractive, for example, but that belief is not necessarily accurate. Thus, high self-esteem may refer to accurate, justified perceptions of one's worth as a person and one's successes and accomplishments, but it can also refer to an arrogant, grandiose, unwarranted sense of superiority over others (Derry, Ohan, & Bayliss, 2020). In the same manner, low self-esteem may reflect either an accurate perception of one's shortcomings or a distorted, even pathological insecurity and inferiority.

What are the consequences of low self-esteem? Low self-esteem has been implicated in overweight and obesity, anxiety, depression, suicide, and delinquency (Cruz-Saez & others, 2020; Gardner & Lambert, 2019; Levey & others, 2019). One study revealed that youths with low self-esteem had lower life satisfaction at 30 years of age (Birkeland & others, 2012). Another study found that low and decreasing self-esteem in adolescence was linked to adult depression two decades later (Steiger & others, 2014).

Although variations in self-esteem have been linked with many aspects of children's development, much of the research is *correlational* rather than *experimental*. Recall that correlation does not equal causation. Thus, if a correlational study finds an association between children's low self-esteem and low academic achievement, low academic achievement could cause the low self-esteem as much as low self-esteem causes low academic achievement. A longitudinal study explored whether self-esteem is a cause or consequence

self-esteem The global evaluative dimension of the self. Self-esteem is also referred to as self-worth or self-image.

self-concept Domain-specific evaluations of the self.

Increasing Children's Self-Esteem

Ways to improve children's self-esteem include identifying the causes of low self-esteem, providing emotional support and social approval, helping children achieve, and helping children cope (Bednar, Wells, & Peterson, 1995; Harter, 2006, 2012).

- *Identify the causes of low self-esteem.* Intervention should target the causes of low self-esteem. Children have the highest self-esteem when they perform competently in domains that are important to them. Therefore, children should be encouraged to identify and value areas of competence. These areas might include academic skills, athletic skills, physical attractiveness, and social acceptance.

- *Provide emotional support and social approval.* Some children with low self-esteem come from conflicted families or conditions in which they experienced abuse or neglect—situations in which support was not available. In some cases, alternative sources of support can be arranged either informally through the encouragement of a teacher, a coach,

How can parents help children develop higher self-esteem?
Ariel Skelley/DigitalVision/Getty Images

or another significant adult, or more formally through programs such as Big Brothers and Big Sisters.

- *Help children achieve.* Achievement also can improve children's self-esteem. For example, the straightforward teaching of real skills to children often results in increased achievement and, thus, in enhanced self-esteem. Children develop higher self-esteem because they know how to carry out the important tasks that will achieve their goals, and they have performed them or similar behaviors in the past.

- *Help children cope.* Self-esteem often increases when children face a problem and try to cope with it, rather than avoid it. If coping rather than avoidance prevails, children face problems realistically, honestly, and nondefensively. This produces favorable self-evaluative thoughts, which lead to the self-generated approval that raises self-esteem.

Which parenting approach might help accomplish the last goal mentioned here? How?

of social support in youth (Marshall & others, 2014). In this study, self-esteem predicted subsequent changes in social support, but social support did not predict subsequent changes in self-esteem.

In fact, there are only moderate correlations between school performance and self-esteem, and these correlations do not suggest that high self-esteem produces better school performance (Baumeister, 2013). Efforts to increase students' self-esteem have not always led to improved school performance (Davies & Brember, 1999).

Children with high self-esteem have greater initiative, but this can produce positive or negative outcomes (Baumeister & others, 2003). Children with high self-esteem are prone to both prosocial and antisocial actions (Krueger, Vohs, & Baumeister, 2008).

In addition, a current concern is that too many of today's children grow up receiving praise for mediocre or even poor performance and as a consequence have inflated self-esteem (Graham, 2005; Stipek, 2005). They may have difficulty handling competition and criticism. This theme is vividly captured by the title of a book, *Dumbing Down Our Kids: Why American Children Feel Good About Themselves But Can't Read, Write, or Add* (Sykes, 1995). A similar theme—the promise of high self-esteem for students in education, especially those who are impoverished or marginalized—characterized a more recent book, *Challenging the Cult of Self-Esteem in Education* (Bergeron, 2018). In a series of studies, researchers found that inflated praise, although well intended, may cause children with low self-esteem to avoid important learning experiences, such as tackling challenging tasks (Brummelman & others, 2014).

What are some good strategies for effectively increasing children's self-esteem? See the *Connecting Development to Life* interlude for some answers to this question.

Self-Efficacy   The belief that one can master a situation and produce favorable outcomes is called **self-efficacy**. Albert Bandura (2001, 2008, 2012) states that self-efficacy is a critical factor in whether or not students achieve. Self-efficacy is the belief that "I can"; helplessness is the belief that "I cannot." Students with high self-efficacy endorse such statements as "I know that I will be able to learn the material in this class" and "I expect to be able to do well at this activity."

Dale Schunk (2020) has applied the concept of self-efficacy to many aspects of students' achievement. In his view, self-efficacy influences a student's choice of activities. Students with low self-efficacy for learning may avoid many learning tasks, especially those that are challenging. By contrast, their counterparts with high self-efficacy eagerly work at learning tasks (Schunk, 2020). Students with high self-efficacy are more likely to expend effort and persist longer at a learning task than students with low self-efficacy.

Self-Regulation   One of the most important aspects of the self in middle and late childhood is an increased capacity for self-regulation (McClelland, Cameron, & Alonso, 2019; Miller & others, 2020). This increased capacity is characterized by deliberate efforts to manage one's behavior, emotions, and thoughts, leading to increased social competence and achievement (Schunk, 2020). One study found that self-control increased from 4 years to 10 years of age and that high self-control was linked to lower levels of deviant behavior (Vazsonyi & Huang, 2010). In this study, parenting characterized by warmth and positive affect predicted the developmental increase in self-control. Also, a study of almost 17,000 3- to 7-year-old children revealed that self-regulation was a protective factor for children growing up in low-socioeconomic-status (SES) conditions (Flouri, Midouhas, & Joshi, 2014). In this study, 7-year-old children with low self-regulation living in low-SES conditions had more emotional problems than their 3-year-old counterparts with higher self-regulation. Thus, low self-regulation was linked to a widening gap in low-SES children's emotional problems over time. Another study revealed that children from low-income families who had a higher level of self-regulation earned better grades in school than their counterparts who had a lower level of self-regulation (Buckner, Mezzacappa, & Beardslee, 2009).

The increased capacity for self-regulation is linked to developmental advances in the brain's prefrontal cortex (Palacios-Barrios & Hanson, 2019). Recall our earlier discussion of the increased focal activation in the prefrontal cortex that is linked to improved cognitive control, which includes self-regulation (Diamond, 2013).

Some researchers emphasize the early development of self-regulation in childhood and adolescence as a key contributor to adult health and even longevity (Miller & others, 2020). For example, Nancy Eisenberg and her colleagues (2014) concluded that research indicates self-regulation fosters conscientiousness later in life, both directly and through its link to academic motivation/success and internalized compliance with norms. Further, a longitudinal study found that a higher level of self-control in childhood was linked to a slower pace of aging (assessed with 18 biomarkers—cardiovascular and immune system, for example) at 26, 32, and 38 years of age (Belsky & others, 2017). An app for iPads has been developed to help children improve their self-regulation (for more information, go to www.selfregulation-station.com/sr-ipad-app/).

What characterizes Erikson's stage of industry versus inferiority?
LWA/Dann Tardif/Blend Images/Getty Images

Industry Versus Inferiority   Recall Erik Erikson's (1968) eight stages of human development. His fourth stage, industry versus inferiority, appears during middle and late childhood. The term *industry* expresses a dominant theme of this period: Children become interested in how things are made and how they work. When children are encouraged in their efforts to make, build, and work—whether building a model airplane, constructing a tree house, fixing a bicycle, solving an addition problem, or cooking—their sense of industry increases. However, parents who view their children's efforts to make things as "mischief" or "making a mess" can cause children to develop a sense of inferiority.

Children's social worlds beyond their families also contribute to a sense of industry. School becomes especially important in this regard. Consider children who are slightly below average

developmental **connection**

Erikson's Theory

Initiative versus guilt is Erikson's early childhood stage, and identity versus identity confusion is his adolescence stage. Connect to "Introduction."

in intelligence. They are too bright to be in special classes but not bright enough to be in gifted classes. They fail frequently in their academic efforts, developing a sense of inferiority. By contrast, consider children whose sense of industry is discouraged by their parents. A series of sensitive and committed teachers may revitalize their sense of industry (Elkind, 1970).

EMOTIONAL DEVELOPMENT

Preschoolers become more adept at talking about their own and others' emotions. They also show a growing awareness of the need to control and manage their emotions to meet social standards. In middle and late childhood, children further develop their understanding and self-regulation of emotion (Cole, Ram, & English, 2019; Dollar & Calkins, 2019).

Developmental Changes   Developmental changes in emotions during the middle and late childhood years include the following (Calkins & Perry, 2016; Cole, Ram, & English, 2019; Kuebli, 1994):

- *Improved emotional understanding.* For example, children in elementary school develop an increased ability to understand such complex emotions as pride and shame. These emotions become less tied to the reactions of other people; they become more self-generated and integrated with a sense of personal responsibility. Also, during middle and late childhood as part of their understanding of emotions, children can engage in "mental time travel," in which they anticipate and recall the cognitive and emotional aspects of events (Kramer & Lagattuta, 2018).

- *Increased understanding that more than one emotion can be experienced in a particular situation.* A third-grader, for example, may realize that achieving something might involve both anxiety and joy.

- *Increased tendency to be aware of the events leading to emotional reactions.* A fourth-grader may become aware that her sadness today is influenced by her friend moving to another town last week.

- *Ability to suppress or conceal negative emotional reactions.* A fifth-grader has learned to tone down his anger better than he used to when one of his classmates irritates him.

- *The use of self-initiated strategies for redirecting feelings.* In the elementary school years, children become more reflective about their emotional lives and increasingly use strategies to control their emotions. They become more effective at cognitively managing their emotions, such as soothing themselves after an upset.

- *A capacity for genuine empathy.* For example, a fourth-grader feels sympathy for a distressed person and experiences vicariously the sadness the distressed person is feeling.

What are some developmental changes in emotion during middle and late childhood?
Rawpixel.com/Shutterstock

Social-Emotional Education Programs   An increasing number of social-emotional educational programs have been developed to improve many aspects of children's and adolescents' lives (England-Mason & Gonzalez, 2020; Hoffman & others, 2020). Two such programs are the Second Step program created by the Committee for Children (2020) and the Collaborative for Academic, Social, and Emotional Learning (CASEL, 2020). Many social-emotional education programs only target young children, but Second Step can be implemented in pre-K through eighth grade and CASEL can used with pre-K through twelfth-grade students.

- *Second Step* focuses on the following aspects of social-emotional learning in students from pre-K through eighth grade: (1) pre-K: self-regulation and executive function skills that improve their attention and help them control their behavior; (2) K through grade 5: making friends, self-regulation of emotion, and solving problems; and (3) grades 6–8: communication skills, coping with stress, and decision making to avoid engaging in problem behaviors.

Children in a Second Step program. *How does this program work to improve children's social and emotional skills?*
Elizabeth D. Herman/The New York Times/Redux

- *CASEL* targets five core social and emotional learning domains: (1) self-awareness (recognizing one's emotions and how they affect behavior, for example); (2) self-management (self-control, coping with stress, and impulse control, for example); (3) social awareness (perspective taking and empathy, for example); (4) relationship skills (developing positive relationships and communicating effectively with individuals from diverse backgrounds, for example); and (5) responsible decision making (engaging in ethical behavior and understanding the consequences of one's actions, for example).

developmental **connection**

Biological Processes

In older adults, stress hormones stay elevated in the bloodstream longer, which can accelerate aging and harm immune system functioning. Connect to "Physical Development in Late Adulthood."

What are some effective strategies to help children cope with traumatic events such as the mass shooting in December 2012 at Sandy Hook Elementary School in Connecticut?
Stephanie Keith/Polaris/Newscom

developmental **connection**

Peer and Friendship Relations

The recent coronavirus pandemic has caused many children, adolescents, and adults to engage in "social distancing." Connect to "Socioemotional Development in Adolescence."

Coping with Stress　An important aspect of children's emotional lives is learning how to cope with stress (Doom & Cicchetti, 2020; Mash & Wolfe, 2019; Thompson, 2019; McLaughlin, 2020). As children get older, they are able to more accurately appraise a stressful situation and determine how much control they have over it. Older children generate more coping alternatives for stressful conditions and use more cognitive coping strategies (Saarni & others, 2006). They are better than younger children at intentionally shifting their thoughts to something that is less stressful and at reframing, or changing their perception of a stressful situation. For example, younger children may be very disappointed that their teacher did not say hello to them when they arrived at school. Older children may reframe this type of situation and think, "She may have been busy with other things and just forgot to say hello."

By 10 years of age, most children are able to use cognitive strategies to cope with stress (Saarni, 1999). However, in families that have not been supportive and are characterized by turmoil or trauma, children may be so overwhelmed by stress that they do not use such strategies.

Disasters can especially harm children's development and produce adjustment problems (Masten & Palmer, 2019). Among the outcomes for children who experience disasters are acute stress reactions, depression, panic disorder, and post-traumatic stress disorder (Narayan & Masten, 2019). The likelihood that a child will face these problems following a disaster depends on factors such as the nature and severity of the disaster and the type of support available to the child.

In research on disasters/trauma, the term *dose-response effects* is often used. A widely supported finding in this research area is that the more severe the disaster/trauma (dose), the worse the adaptation and adjustment (response) following the disaster/trauma (Masten & Palmer, 2019; Narayan & Masten, 2019).

The terrorist attacks on the World Trade Center in New York City and the Pentagon in Washington, D.C., on September 11, 2001, and hurricanes Katrina and Rita in September 2005 raised special concerns about how to help children cope with such stressful events. In 2020, the abrupt emergence of the worldwide spread of the new coronavirus, COVID-19, took everyone by surprise and increased the stress and anxiety levels of many adults and children. This pandemic caused a majority of schools to close and many adults to work from home. In such stressful circumstances, it is important for parents to stay calm, educate themselves about the ongoing issues (in this case, the virus), and communicate accurate information to their children. It is especially important for children to understand that such disruptions are not permanent and eventually their lives will return to normal, although with possible adaptations.

Children who have developed a number of coping techniques have the best chance of adapting and functioning competently in the face of disasters and traumas (Doom & Cicchetti, 2020; Mash & Wolfe, 2019). Researchers have offered the following recommendations for parents, teachers, and other adults caring for children after a disaster (Gurwitch & others, 2001, pp. 4–11):

- Reassure children (numerous times, if necessary) of their safety and security.
- Allow children to retell events and be patient in listening to them.
- Encourage children to talk about any disturbing or confusing feelings, reassuring them that such feelings are normal after a stressful event.
- Protect children from re-exposure to frightening situations and reminders of the trauma—for example, by limiting discussion of the event in front of the children.
- Help children make sense of what happened, keeping in mind that children may misunderstand what took place. For example, young children "may blame themselves, believe things happened that did not happen, believe that terrorists are in the school, etc. Gently help children develop a realistic understanding of the event" (p. 10).

Child and adolescent psychiatrists are among the mental health professionals who help youth cope with stress, including traumatic experiences. To read about a child psychiatrist who treats children and adolescents, see *Connecting with Careers.*

Traumatic events may cause individuals to think about the moral aspects of life. Hopelessness and despair may short-circuit moral development when a child is confronted by the violence of war zones and impoverished inner cities (Nader, 2001). Let's further explore children's moral development.

MORAL DEVELOPMENT

Recall our description of Piaget's view of moral development. Piaget proposed that younger children are characterized by heteronomous morality, but that by 10 years of age they have moved into a higher stage called autonomous morality. According to Piaget, older children consider the intentions of the individual, believe that rules are subject to change, and are aware that punishment does not always follow wrongdoing.

A second major perspective on moral development was proposed by Lawrence Kohlberg (1958, 1986). Piaget's cognitive stages of development serve as the underpinnings for Kohlberg's theory, but Kohlberg suggested that there are three levels of moral development. These levels, he argued, are universal. Development from one level to another, said Kohlberg, is fostered by opportunities to take the perspective of others and to experience conflict between one's current level of moral thinking and the reasoning of someone at a higher level.

Kohlberg arrived at his view after 20 years of using a unique interview with children. In the interview, children are presented with a series of stories in which characters face moral dilemmas. The following is the most popular Kohlberg dilemma:

> In Europe a woman was near death from a special kind of cancer. There was one drug that the doctors thought might save her. It was a form of radium that a druggist in the same town had recently discovered. The drug was expensive to make, but the druggist was charging ten times what the drug cost him to make. He paid $200 for the radium and charged $2,000 for a small dose of the drug. The sick woman's husband, Heinz, went to everyone he knew to borrow the money, but he could only get together $1,000, which is half of what it cost. He told the druggist that his wife was dying and asked him to sell it cheaper or let him pay later. But the druggist said, "No, I discovered the drug, and I am going to make money from it." So Heinz got desperate and broke into the man's store to steal the drug for his wife. (Kohlberg, 1969, p. 379)

This story is one of eleven that Kohlberg devised to investigate the nature of moral thought. After reading the story, the interviewee answers a series of questions about the moral dilemma. Should Heinz have stolen the drug? Was stealing it right or wrong? Why? Is it a husband's duty to steal the drug for his wife if he can get it no other way? Would a good husband steal? Did the druggist have the right to charge that much when there was no law setting a limit on the price? Why or why not?

Lawrence Kohlberg, the architect of a provocative cognitive developmental theory of moral development. *What is the nature of his theory?*
Harvard University Archives, UAV 605.295.8, Box 7, Kohlberg

The Kohlberg Levels   Based on the answers interviewees gave for this and other moral dilemmas, Kohlberg described three levels of moral thinking. A key concept in understanding progression through the levels is that the person's morality gradually becomes more internal or mature. That is, their reasons for moral decisions or values begin to go beyond the external or superficial reasons they gave when they were younger. Let's further examine Kohlberg's levels.

Kohlberg's Level 1: Preconventional Reasoning   **Preconventional reasoning** is the lowest level of moral reasoning in Kohlberg's theory. At this level, children interpret good and bad in terms of external rewards or punishments. For example, children and adolescents obey adults because they are afraid they will be punished. Or they decide to be obedient to get something out of it, such as a cookie. This earliest level has sometimes been described as "What's in it for me?"

Kohlberg's Level 2: Conventional Reasoning   **Conventional reasoning** is the second, or intermediate, level in Kohlberg's theory of moral development. In conventional reasoning, individuals develop expectations about social roles. Individuals abide by certain standards (internal), but they are the standards of others, such as parents or the laws of society.

Kohlberg's Level 3: Postconventional Reasoning   **Postconventional reasoning** is the third and highest level in Kohlberg's theory. At this level, morality involves flexible thinking and is more internalized. Also, in postconventional reasoning, individuals engage in deliberate checks on their reasoning to ensure that it meets high ethical standards.

Kohlberg maintained that these levels occur in a sequence and are age-related: Before age 9, most children use level 1, preconventional reasoning based on external rewards and punishments, when they consider moral choices. By early adolescence, their moral reasoning is increasingly based on the application of standards set by others, reflecting conventional reasoning. By early adulthood, a small number of individuals reason in postconventional ways.

Influences on the Kohlberg Levels   What factors influence movement through Kohlberg's levels? Although moral reasoning at each level presupposes a certain level of cognitive development, Kohlberg argued that advances in maturation did not ensure advances in moral reasoning. Instead, the development of moral reasoning requires children's experiences dealing with moral questions and moral conflict.

Kohlberg emphasized that peer interaction and perspective taking are critical aspects of the social stimulation that challenges children to change their moral reasoning. Whereas adults characteristically impose rules and regulations on children, the give-and-take among peers gives children an opportunity to take the perspective of another person and to generate rules democratically.

Kohlberg's Critics   Kohlberg's theory has provoked debate, research, and criticism (Jambon & Smetana, 2020; Miller, Wice, & Goyal, 2020; Narváez, 2019, 2020; Spinrad & Eisenberg, 2020). Key criticisms involve the link between moral thought and moral behavior, whether moral reasoning is conscious/deliberative or unconscious/automatic, the role of emotion, the importance of gender, as well as the roles of culture and the family in moral development.

Moral Thought and Moral Behavior   Kohlberg's theory has been criticized for placing too much emphasis on moral thought and not enough emphasis on moral behavior (Walker, 2004). Moral reasons can sometimes be a shelter for immoral behavior. Corrupt CEOs and politicians endorse the loftiest of moral virtues in public before their own behavior is exposed. Whatever the latest public scandal, you will probably find that the culprits displayed virtuous thoughts but engaged in immoral behavior. No one wants a nation of cheaters and thieves who can reason at the postconventional level. The cheaters and thieves may know what is right yet still do what is wrong. Heinous actions can be cloaked in a mantle of moral virtue.

Conscious/Deliberate Versus Unconscious/Automatic   Social psychologist Jonathan Haidt (2006, 2013, 2018) argues that Kohlberg's theory places too much emphasis on individuals deliberating and contemplating in their reasoning before they decide on a moral stance. Haidt believes that moral thinking is more often an intuitive gut reaction, with deliberative moral reasoning serving as an after-the-fact justification. Thus, in his view, much of morality begins with rapid evaluative judgments of others rather than with strategic reasoning about moral circumstances.

---

developmental connection

Peers

Piaget argued that the mutual give-and-take of peer relations is more important than parenting in enhancing children's moral reasoning. Connect to "Socioemotional Development in Early Childhood."

developmental connection

Moral Development

Positive and negative emotions play important roles in moral development. Connect to "Socioemotional Development in Early Childhood."

preconventional reasoning The lowest level in Kohlberg's theory of moral development. The individual's moral reasoning is controlled primarily by external rewards and punishment.

conventional reasoning The second, or intermediate, level in Kohlberg's theory of moral development. At this level, individuals abide by certain standards, but these are standards set by others such as parents or society.

postconventional reasoning The highest level in Kohlberg's theory of moral development. At this level, the individual recognizes alternative moral courses, explores the options, and then decides on a personal moral code.

The Role of Emotion   Kohlberg argued that emotion has negative effects on moral reasoning. However, increasing evidence indicates that emotions play an important role in moral thinking (Malti, Peplak, & Acland, 2020; Spinrad & Eisenberg, 2020). Research with healthy individuals indicates that the moral decisions individuals make are linked to the intensity and activation of emotion in the prefrontal cortex and the amygdala (Shenhav & Greene, 2014).

Gender and the Care Perspective   The most publicized criticism of Kohlberg's theory has come from Carol Gilligan (1982, 1992, 1996), who argues that Kohlberg's theory reflects a gender bias. According to Gilligan, Kohlberg's theory is based on a male norm that puts abstract principles above relationships and concern for others and sees the individual as standing alone and independently making moral decisions. It puts justice at the heart of morality. In contrast with Kohlberg's **justice perspective,** Gilligan argues for a **care perspective,** which is a moral perspective that views people in terms of their connectedness with others and emphasizes interpersonal communication, relationships with others, and concern for others. According to Gilligan, girls display much more sensitivity to others and Kohlberg greatly underplayed the care perspective, perhaps because he was a male, because most of his research was with males rather than females, and because he used male responses as a model for his theory.

However, questions have been raised about Gilligan's gender conclusions (Walker & Frimer, 2009). For example, a meta-analysis (a statistical analysis that combines the results of many different studies) casts doubt on Gilligan's claim of substantial gender differences in moral judgment (Jaffee & Hyde, 2000). And a research review concluded that girls' moral orientations are "somewhat more likely to focus on care for others than on abstract principles of justice, but they can use both moral orientations when needed (as can boys . . .)" (Blakemore, Berenbaum, & Liben, 2009, p. 132).

Culture and Moral Reasoning   Kohlberg emphasized that his levels of moral reasoning are universal, but some critics claim his theory is culturally biased (Miller, Wice, & Goyal, 2020). Both Kohlberg and his critics may be partially correct. In one study, individuals in diverse cultures developed through the first two levels in sequence as Kohlberg predicted. Level three thinking, however, has not been found in all cultures (Gibbs, 2019).

Darcia Narváez and Tracy Gleason (2013) have described cohort effects regarding moral reasoning. In recent decades, postconventional moral reasoning has been declining in college students, not down to the next level (conventional), but to the lowest level (personal interests) (Thoma & Bebeau, 2008). Narváez and Gleason (2013) also argue that declines in prosocial behavior have occurred in recent years and that humans, especially those living in Western cultures, are "on a fast train to demise." They emphasize that the path to improving people's moral lives involves better child-rearing strategies and social supports for families and children. In more recent commentary, Narváez and her colleagues (Christen, Narváez, & Gutzwiller, 2017) stress that economic and technical progress are not linked to moral advances when contemporary societies are compared with earlier sustainable ones that were more in tune with community and planetary well-being.

In sum, although Kohlberg's approach does capture much of the moral reasoning voiced in various cultures around the world, his approach misses or misconstrues some important moral concepts in specific cultures (Gibbs, 2019; Miller, Wice, & Goyal, 2020).

Families and Moral Development   Kohlberg argued that family processes are essentially unimportant in children's moral development. Like Piaget, he argued that parent-child relationships usually provide children with little opportunity for give-and-take or perspective taking because of power relationships. Rather, Kohlberg said that such opportunities are more likely to be provided by children's peer relationships. However, most experts on children's moral development conclude that parents' moral values and actions influence children's development of moral reasoning (Laible & others, 2020; Narváez, 2020; Padilla-Walker & Memmott-Elison, 2020). They stress that parents' responsiveness, communication, disciplinary techniques, and many other aspects of parent-child relationships influence children's moral development (Lansford, 2020; Thompson, 2020). Nonetheless, most developmentalists agree with Kohlberg and Piaget that peers play an important role in the development of moral reasoning.

In sum, Kohlberg's theory was a very important pioneering effort in describing and understanding the development of moral reasoning and to some degree still somewhat relevant in understanding the development of moral reasoning. However, as indicated by criticisms of the theory, the theory is no longer as influential as it once was. Let's now examine other views on moral development.

Carol Gilligan. *What is Gilligan's view of moral development?*
Courtesy of Dr. Carol Gilligan

This 14-year-old boy in Nepal is thought to be the sixth-holiest Buddhist in the world. In one study of 20 adolescent male Buddhist monks in Nepal, the issue of justice, a basic theme in Kohlberg's theory, was not a central focus in the monks' moral views (Huebner & Garrod, 1993). Also, the monks' concerns about prevention of suffering and the importance of compassion are not captured in Kohlberg's theory.
Thierry Falise/LightRocket/Getty Images

justice perspective A moral perspective that focuses on the rights of the individual and in which individuals independently make moral decisions.

care perspective The moral perspective of Carol Gilligan, which views people in terms of their connectedness with others and emphasizes interpersonal communication, relationships with others, and concern for others.

Domain Theory: Moral, Social Conventional, and Personal Reasoning The **domain theory of moral development** states that there are different domains of social knowledge and reasoning, including moral, social conventional, and personal domains. In domain theory, children's and adolescents' moral, social conventional, and personal knowledge and reasoning emerge from their attempts to understand and deal with different forms of social experience (Jambon & Smetana, 2020; Smetana, 2013; Turiel, 2018).

Some theorists and researchers argue that Kohlberg did not adequately distinguish between moral reasoning and social conventional reasoning (Jambon & Smetana, 2020). **Social conventional reasoning** focuses on conventional rules that have been established by social consensus in order to control behavior and maintain the social system. The rules themselves are arbitrary, such as raising your hand in class before speaking, using one staircase at school to go up and the other to go down, not cutting in front of someone standing in line to buy movie tickets, and stopping at a stop sign when driving. There are sanctions if we violate these conventions, although they can be changed by consensus.

In contrast, moral reasoning focuses on ethical issues and rules of morality. Unlike conventional rules, moral rules are not arbitrary. They are obligatory, widely accepted, and somewhat impersonal (Turiel, 2018). Rules pertaining to lying, cheating, stealing, and physically harming another person are moral rules because violation of these rules affronts ethical standards that exist apart from social consensus and convention. Moral judgments involve concepts of justice, whereas social conventional judgments are concepts of social organization. Violating moral rules is usually more serious than violating conventional rules.

The social conventional approach is a serious challenge to Kohlberg's approach because Kohlberg argued that social conventions are mixed in with moral concerns at the conventional level, a developmental stop-over on the road to higher moral sophistication, post-conventional reasoning, where they are separated. For social conventional reasoning advocates, social conventional reasoning is not lower than postconventional reasoning but rather something that needs to be disentangled from the moral thread (Smetana, 2013). However, in a recent study, children and adolescents said that changes in moral beliefs are more disruptive to one's identity than changes in social-conventional beliefs are (Lefebvre & Krettenaur, 2020). Also in this study, the children and adolescents reported that changes in negative moral beliefs are more disruptive to one's identity than changes in positive moral beliefs are.

Recently, a distinction also has been made between moral and conventional issues, which are viewed as legitimately subject to adult social regulation, and personal issues, which are subject to the child's or adolescent's independent decision making and personal discretion (Jambon & Smetana, 2020). Personal issues include control over one's body, privacy, and choice of friends and activities. Thus, some actions belong to a *personal* domain and are not governed by moral reasoning or social norms.

Prosocial Behavior

Whereas Kohlberg's and Gilligan's theories have focused primarily on the development of moral reasoning, the study of prosocial moral behavior has placed more emphasis on the behavioral aspects of moral development (Carlo & Conejo, 2020; Carlo & Pierotti, 2020; Spinrad & Eisenberg, 2020). Children engage in immoral, antisocial acts such as lying and cheating and also display prosocial moral behavior such as showing empathy or acting altruistically. Even during the preschool years, children may care for others or comfort others in distress (Spinrad & Eisenberg, 2020).

William Damon (1988) described how sharing develops. During their first years, when children share, it is usually not for reasons of empathy but for the fun of the social play ritual or out of imitation. Then, at about 4 years of age, a combination of empathic awareness and adult encouragement produces a sense of obligation on the part of the child to share with others. Most 4-year-olds are not selfless saints, however. Children believe they have an obligation to share but do not necessarily think they should be as generous to others as they are to themselves.

Children's sharing begins to reflect a more complex sense of what is just and right during middle and late childhood. By the start of the elementary school years, children begin to express objective ideas about fairness. It is common to hear 6-year-old children use the word *fair* as synonymous with *equal* or *same*. By the mid- to late elementary school years, children believe that equity can sometimes mean that people with special merit or special needs deserve special treatment. In a recent study in 12 countries, sharing increased considerably from 4 to 12 years of age in every country (Samek & others, 2020).

How does children's sharing change from the preschool to the elementary school years?
Ariel Skelley/Blend Images/age fotostock

domain theory of moral development Theory that identifies different domains of social knowledge and reasoning, including moral, social conventional, and personal domains. These domains arise from children's and adolescents' attempts to understand and deal with different forms of social experience.

social conventional reasoning Thoughts about social consensus and convention, in contrast with moral reasoning, which stresses ethical issues.

Moral Personality Beyond the development of moral reasoning and specific moral feelings and prosocial behaviors, do children also develop a pattern of moral characteristics that is distinctively their own? In other words, do children develop a *moral personality*, and if so, what are its components? Researchers have focused attention on three possible components: (1) moral identity, (2) moral character, and (3) moral exemplars.

Moral Identity Individuals have a moral identity when moral notions and moral commitments are central to their lives (Hardy, Krettenauer, & Hunt, 2020; Lefebvre & Krettenauer, 2020; Strohminger, 2018). They construct the self with reference to moral categories. Violating their moral commitment would place the integrity of their self at risk (Lapsley, Reilly, & Narváez, 2020). A study of 15- to 18-year-olds found that a higher level of moral identity could possibly reduce the negative effects of moral disengagement and low self-regulation (Hardy, Bean, & Olsen, 2015). To evaluate the extent to which you have a moral identity, see Figure 1.

Moral Character A person with moral character has the willpower, desire, and integrity to stand up to pressure, overcome distractions and disappointments, and behave morally. A person of good moral character displays moral virtues such as "honesty, truthfulness, and trustworthiness, as well as those of care, compassion, thoughtfulness, and considerateness. Other salient traits revolve around virtues of dependability, loyalty, and conscientiousness" (Walker, 2002, p. 74).

Moral Exemplars Moral exemplars are people who have lived exemplary moral lives. Their moral personality, identity, character, and set of virtues reflect moral excellence and commitment (Walker, 2016). The point of studying and conducting research on moral exemplars is to be able to characterize the ideal endpoint of moral development and understand how people got there.

In sum, moral development is a multifaceted, complex concept. Included in this complexity are an individual's thoughts, feelings, behaviors, and personality.

GENDER

Gilligan's claim that Kohlberg's theory of moral development reflects gender bias reminds us of the pervasive influence of gender on development. Long before elementary school, boys and girls show preferences for different toys and activities (Leaper & Bigler, 2018). Preschool children display a gender identity and gender-typed behavior that reflects biological, cognitive, and social influences. Here we will examine gender stereotypes as well as gender similarities and differences.

Gender Stereotypes According to the old ditty, boys are made of "frogs and snails" and girls are made of "sugar and spice and all that is nice." In the past, a well-adjusted boy was supposed to be independent, aggressive, and powerful, while a well-adjusted girl was supposed to be dependent, nurturing, and uninterested in power. These notions reflect **gender stereotypes**, which are broad categories that reflect general impressions and beliefs about females and males (Erikson-Schroth & Davis, 2021; Helgeson, 2020).

Recent research has found that gender stereotypes are, to a great extent, still present in today's world, in the lives of both children and adults (Best & Puzio, 2019; Erikson-Schroth, 2021; Helgeson, 2020; Hyde & others, 2019). Gender stereotyping continues to change during middle and late childhood and adolescence (Brannon, 2017). By the time children enter elementary school, they have considerable knowledge about which activities are linked with being male or female. Until about 7 to 8 years of age, gender stereotyping is extensive because young children don't recognize individual variations in masculinity and femininity. By 5 years of age, both boys and girls stereotype boys as powerful and in more negative terms, such as mean, and girls in more positive terms, such as nice (Martin & Ruble, 2010). Across the elementary school years, children become more flexible in their gender attitudes (Trautner & others, 2005).

A study of 3- to 10-year-old U.S. children revealed that girls and older children used a higher percentage of gender stereotypes (Miller & others, 2009). In this study, appearance stereotypes were more prevalent among girls while activity (sports, for example) and trait (aggressive, for example) stereotyping was more common among boys. Another study of 6- to 10-year-olds found that both boys and girls indicated math is for boys (Cvencek, Meltzoff, & Greenwald, 2011). Researchers also have found that boys' gender stereotypes are more rigid than girls' (Blakemore, Berenbaum, & Liben, 2009).

Moral Traits

The person with these characteristics could be you, or it could be someone else. For a moment, visualize in your mind the kind of person who has these characteristics. Imagine how the individual would think, feel, and act. When you have a clear image of what this person would be like, then answer the questions that follow.

Caring	Helpful
Compassionate	Honest
Fair	Kind
Generous	

Questions

- Is having these characteristics an important part of who you are?
- Are you actively involved in activities that indicate to others you have these characteristics?
- Would it make you feel good to have these characteristics?

FIGURE **1**

DO YOU HAVE A MORAL IDENTITY?
A moral identity questionnaire has been developed that has a number of moral traits and asks individuals about the extent to which these traits characterize them (Acquino & Reed, 2002).

What are little boys made of?
Frogs and snails
And puppy-dogs' tails.
What are little girls made of?
Sugar and spice
And all that is nice.

—J. O. HALLIWELL
English author, 19th century

gender stereotypes Broad categories that reflect our impressions and beliefs about females and males.

Gender Similarities and Differences What is the reality behind gender stereotypes? Let's examine some of the similarities and differences between the sexes, keeping in mind that (1) the differences are averages—not all females versus all males; (2) even when differences are reported, there is considerable overlap between the sexes; and (3) the differences may be due primarily to biological factors, sociocultural factors, or both. First, we will examine physical similarities and differences, and then we will turn to cognitive and socioemotional similarities and differences.

Physical Development Women have about twice the body fat of men, most of it concentrated around their breasts and hips. In males, fat is more likely to go to the abdomen. On average, males grow to be 10 percent taller than females. Other physical differences are less obvious. From conception on, females have a longer life expectancy than males, and females are less likely than males to develop physical or mental disorders. The risk of coronary disease in males is two times that of females.

Does gender matter when it comes to brain structure and function? Human brains are much alike, whether the brain belongs to a male or a female (Halpern & others, 2007). However, researchers have found some differences in the brains of males and females (Hofer & others, 2007). Female brains are approximately 10 percent smaller than male brains (Giedd, 2012). However, female brains have more folds; the larger folds (called convolutions) allow more surface brain tissue within the skulls of females than males (Luders & others, 2004). An area of the parietal lobe that functions in visuospatial skills is larger in males than females (Frederikse & others, 2000). And the areas of the brain involved in emotional expression show more metabolic activity in females than males (Gur & others, 1995).

Although some differences in brain structure and function have been found, many of these differences are small or ambiguous in regard to research results (Hyde & others, 2019). In fact, the distributions for males and females on different brain features overlap so much that Janet Shibley Hyde and her colleagues (2019) recently concluded that in most instances it is more accurate to describe these features as a mosaic rather than as male-typical and female-typical brains. Also, when sex differences in the brain are indicated, in many cases they have not been directly linked to psychological differences (Blakemore, Berenbaum, & Liben, 2009). Although research on sex differences in the brain is still in its infancy, it is likely that there are far more similarities than differences in the brains of females and males. A further point is worth noting: Anatomical sex differences in the brain may be due to the biological origins of these differences, behavioral experiences (which underscores the brain's continuing plasticity), or a combination of these factors (Hyde & others, 2019).

Cognitive Development No gender differences in general intelligence have been revealed, but gender differences have been found in some cognitive areas (Ganley, Vasilyeva, & Dulaney, 2014). Research has shown that girls and women tend to have slightly better verbal skills than boys and men, although in some areas of verbal skill the differences are substantial (Blakemore, Berenbaum, & Liben, 2009).

Are there gender differences in math skills? A very large-scale study of more than 7 million U.S. students in grades 2 through 11 revealed no differences in math test scores for boys and girls (Hyde & others, 2008). Further, in the National Assessment of Educational Progress (2017) there were virtually no gender differences in math scores at the fourth- and eighth-grade levels, with boys scoring only 2 points higher in the fourth grade and 1 point higher in the eighth grade on a 500-point scale. And a meta-analysis found no gender differences in math skills for adolescents (Lindberg & others, 2010). A research review concluded that girls have more negative math attitudes and that parents' and teachers' expectancies for children's math competence are often gender-biased in favor of boys (Gunderson & others, 2012).

One area of math that has been examined for possible gender differences is visuospatial skills, which include being able to rotate objects mentally and to determine what they would look like when rotated (Halpern, 2012). These types of skills are important in courses such as plane and solid geometry and geography. A research review revealed that boys have better visuospatial skills than girls (Halpern & others, 2007). For example, despite equal participation in the National Geography Bee, in most years all 10 finalists are boys (Liben, 1995). A research review found that having a stronger masculine gender role was linked to better spatial ability in males and females (Reilly & Neumann, 2013). However, some experts argue that the gender difference in visuospatial skills is small (Hyde, 2014; Hyde, 2017) (see Figure 2).

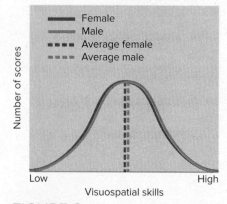

Female
Male
Average female
Average male

Number of scores

Low · Visuospatial skills · High

FIGURE 2

VISUOSPATIAL SKILLS OF MALES AND FEMALES. Notice that although an average male's visuospatial skills are higher than an average female's, the scores for the two sexes almost entirely overlap. Not all males have better visuospatial skills than all females—the overlap indicates that although the average male score is higher, many females outperform most males on such tasks.

Are there gender differences in reading and writing skills? There is strong evidence that females outperform males in reading and writing. In the National Assessment of Educational Progress (2017), girls had higher reading achievement than boys in both fourth- and eighth-grade assessments, with girls 6 points higher in fourth grade and 10 points higher in eighth grade. Also, an international study in 65 countries found that girls had higher reading achievement than did boys in every country (Reilly, 2012). In this study, the gender difference in reading was greater in countries with less gender equity and lower economic prosperity. In the United States, girls also consistently have outperformed boys in writing skills in the National Assessment of Educational Progress in fourth-, eighth-, and twelfth-grade assessments.

Are there gender differences in academic achievement? Girls earn better grades and complete high school at a higher rate, and they are less likely to drop out of school than boys are (Halpern, 2012). Males are more likely than females to be assigned to special/ remedial education classes. Girls are more likely than boys to be engaged with academic material, be attentive in class, put forth more academic effort, and participate more in class (DeZolt & Hull, 2001).

Keep in mind that measures of achievement in school or scores on standardized tests may reflect many factors besides cognitive ability. For example, performance in school may in part reflect attempts to conform to gender roles or differences in motivation, self-regulation, or other socioemotional characteristics (Becker & McElvany, 2018). For example, a recent large-scale study of seventh-graders found that girls' perception that teachers had gendered expectations favoring boys over girls was linked to girls having more negative math beliefs and lower math achievement (McKellar & others, 2019). Also, in this study, when girls perceived that the math curriculum was personally meaningful and relevant for them, they had more positive math beliefs and higher math achievement.

Might single-sex education be better for children than coeducation? The argument for single-sex education is that it eliminates distraction from the other sex and reduces sexual harassment. Single-sex public education has increased dramatically in recent years. In 2002, only 12 public schools in the United States provided single-sex education; during the 2011–2012 school year, 116 public schools were single-sex and an additional 390 provided such experiences (NASSPE, 2012).

What are some recent changes in single-sex education in the United States? What does research say about whether single-sex education is beneficial?
Jim Weber/ZUMAPRESS/Newscom

The increase in single-sex education has especially been fueled by its inclusion in the No Child Left Behind legislation as a means of improving the educational experiences and academic achievement of low-income students of color. It appears that many of the public schools offering single-sex education have a high percentage of such youth (Klein, 2012). However, two research reviews concluded that there have been no documented benefits of single-sex education for low-income students of color (Goodkind, 2013; Halpern & others, 2011). One review, titled "The Pseudoscience of Single-Sex Schooling," by Diane Halpern and her colleagues (2011) concluded that single-sex education is highly misguided, misconstrued, and unsupported by any valid scientific evidence. They emphasize that among the many arguments against single-sex education, the strongest is its reduction in the opportunities for boys and girls to work together in a supervised, purposeful environment.

There has been a special call for single-sex public education for one group of adolescents— African American boys—because of their historically poor academic achievement and high dropout rate from school (Mitchell & Stewart, 2013). In 2010, Urban Prep Academy for Young Men became the first all-male, all African American public charter school. One hundred percent of its first graduates enrolled in college, despite the school's location in a section of Chicago where poverty, gangs, and crime predominate. And continuing each year since through 2018, 100 percent of Urban Prep's graduates have gone on to college. Because so few public schools focus solely on educating African American boys, it is too early to tell whether this type of single-sex education can be effective across a wide range of participants.

Socioemotional Development   Three areas of socioemotional development in which gender similarities and differences have been studied extensively are aggression, emotion, and prosocial behavior.

One of the most consistent gender differences found is that boys are more physically aggressive than girls are (Hyde, 2017). The difference occurs in all cultures and appears very early in children's development (Dayton & Malone, 2017). The difference in physical aggression is especially pronounced when children are provoked. Both biological and environmental

What gender differences characterize aggression?
Fuse/Corbis RF/Getty Images

developmental **connection**

Gender

The nature and extent of gender differences in communication in relationships is controversial. Connect to "Socioemotional Development in Early Adulthood."

developmental **connection**

Community and Culture

Bronfenbrenner's ecological theory emphasizes the importance of contexts; in his theory the macrosystem includes cross-cultural comparisons. Connect to "Introduction."

factors have been proposed to account for gender differences in aggression. Biological factors include heredity and hormones. Environmental factors include cultural expectations, adult and peer models, and social agents that reward aggression in boys and punish aggression in girls.

Although boys are consistently more physically aggressive than girls, might girls show levels of verbal aggression, such as yelling, that equal or exceed the levels shown by boys? When verbal aggression is considered, gender differences often disappear, although sometimes verbal aggression is more pronounced in girls (Eagly & Steffen, 1986).

Recently, increased attention has been directed to *relational aggression*, which involves harming someone by manipulating a relationship. Relational aggression includes such behaviors as spreading malicious rumors about someone in order to make others dislike that person (Chen & Cheng, 2020; Padmanabha-nunni & Gerhardt, 2019; Reardon & others, 2020). Relational aggression increases in middle and late childhood (Dishion & Piehler, 2009). Mixed findings have characterized research on whether girls show more relational aggression than boys, but one consistent finding is that relational aggression comprises a greater percentage of girls' overall aggression than is the case for boys (Putallaz & others, 2007). And a research review revealed that girls engage in more relational aggression than boys in adolescence but not in childhood (Smith, Rose, & Schwartz-Mette, 2010). Also, in a recent study of adolescents, those who observed relational aggression on television were more likely to engage in relational aggression when they were texting one year later (Coyne & others, 2019).

Gender differences occur in some aspects of emotion (Brody, Hall, & Stokes, 2018; Connolly & others, 2019). Females express emotion more than males do, are better at decoding emotion, smile more, cry more, and are happier (Gross, Fredrickson, & Levenson, 1994; LaFrance, Hecht, & Paluck, 2003). Males report experiencing and expressing more anger than females do (Kring, 2000). A meta-analysis found that females are better than males at recognizing nonverbal displays of emotion (Thompson & Voyer, 2014). Another meta-analysis found that girls showed more positive emotions (sympathy, for example) and more internalized emotions (sadness and anxiety, for example); however, in this meta-analysis, overall gender differences in children's emotional expression were small (Chaplin & Aldao, 2013). The gender difference in positive emotions became more pronounced with age as girls more strongly expressed positive emotions than boys in middle and late childhood and in adolescence. Also, a recent study revealed that females are better than males at facial emotion perception across the life span (Olderbak & others, 2019).

An important skill is to be able to regulate and control one's emotions and behavior (Denham & Bassett, 2019; Miller & others, 2020). Boys usually show less self-regulation than girls do (Berke, Reidy, & Zeichner, 2018). This low self-control can translate into behavior problems.

Are there gender differences in prosocial behavior? Females view themselves as more prosocial and empathic than males (Eisenberg & Spinrad, 2016). Across childhood and adolescence, females engage in more prosocial behavior than males do (Hastings, Miller, & Troxel, 2015). The biggest gender difference occurs for kind and considerate behavior, with a smaller difference in sharing.

Gender in Context Gender stereotypes describe people in terms of personality traits such as "aggressive" or "caring." However, the traits people display may vary with the situation (Levy & others, 2020; Liben, 2017). Thus, the nature and extent of gender differences may depend on the context.

Consider helping behavior. The stereotype is that females are better than males at helping. But it depends on the situation. Females are more likely than males to volunteer their time to

What gender differences characterize children's prosocial behavior?
Fuse/Corbis/Getty Images

help children with personal problems and to engage in caregiving behavior. However, in situations in which males feel a sense of competence and in circumstances that involve danger, males are more likely than females to help (Eagly & Crowley, 1986). For example, a male is more likely than a female to stop and help a person stranded by the roadside with a flat tire. Indeed, one study documented that males are more likely to help when the context is masculine in nature (MacGeorge, 2003).

The importance of considering gender in context is nowhere more apparent than when examining what is culturally prescribed behavior for females and males in different countries around the world (Hyde & Else-Quest, 2013; UNICEF, 2020). Although there has been greater acceptance of androgyny and similarities in male and female behavior in the United States in recent years, in many countries gender roles have remained gender-specific. For example, in many Middle Eastern countries, the division of labor between males and females is dramatic. Males are socialized and schooled to work in the public sphere, females in the private world of home and child rearing. Also, in Iran the dominant view is that the man's duty is to provide for his family and the woman's is to care for her family and household. China also has been a male-dominant culture. Although women have made some strides in China, especially in urban areas, the male role is still dominant. Most males in China do not accept androgynous behavior or gender equity.

In a study of eighth-grade students in 36 countries, in every country girls had more egalitarian attitudes about gender roles than boys had (Dotti Sani & Quaranta, 2015). In this study, girls had more egalitarian gender attitudes in countries with higher levels of societal gender equality. In another recent study of 15- to 19-year-olds in the country of Qatar, males had more negative views of gender equality than females had (Al-Ghanim & Badahdah, 2017).

In China, females and males are usually socialized to behave, feel, and think differently. The old patriarchal traditions of male supremacy have not been completely uprooted. Chinese women still make considerably less money than Chinese men do, and in rural China (such as here in the Lixian Village of Sichuan) male supremacy still governs many women's lives.
Diego Azubel/EPA/Newscom

Review *Connect* Reflect

 LG1 Discuss emotional and personality development in middle and late childhood.

Review

- What changes take place in the self during middle and late childhood?
- How does emotional expression change during middle and late childhood?
- What characterizes moral development in middle and late childhood? What are gender stereotypes, and what are some important gender differences?

Connect

- Recall the concept of joint attention. How is joint attention similar to or different from the concept of perspective taking you learned about here?

Reflect *Your Own Personal Journey of Life*

- A young man who had been sentenced to serve 10 years for selling a small amount of marijuana escaped from prison six months after he was sent there. He is now in his fifties and has been a model citizen. Should he be sent back to prison? Why or why not? At which Kohlberg level should your response be placed? Do you think the level at which you placed your response accurately captures the level of your moral thinking? Explain.

---

2 Families   **LG2** Describe developmental changes in parent-child relationships, parents as managers, attachment in families, and stepfamilies.

| Developmental Changes in Parent-Child Relationships | Parents as Managers | Attachment in Families | Stepfamilies |

This section focuses on how parent-child interactions typically change in middle and late childhood, the importance of parents being effective managers of children's lives, the role of attachment in family relationships, and how children are affected by living with stepparents.

DEVELOPMENTAL CHANGES IN PARENT-CHILD RELATIONSHIPS

What are some changes in the focus of parent-child relationships in middle and late childhood?

Radius Images/Getty Images

As children move into the middle and late childhood years, parents spend considerably less time with them (Collins & Madsen, 2019; Grusec & Davidov, 2019). In one study, parents spent less than half as much time with their children aged 5 to 12 in caregiving, instruction, reading, talking, and playing as they did when the children were younger (Hill & Stafford, 1980). However, parents continue to be extremely important in their children's lives. One analysis concluded: "Parents serve as gatekeepers and provide scaffolding as children assume more responsibility for themselves and . . . regulate their own lives" (Huston & Ripke, 2006, p. 422).

Parents especially play an important role in supporting and stimulating children's academic achievement in middle and late childhood (Gottfried, 2019; Sternberg, Williams, & Sternberg, 2019). The value parents place on education can determine whether children do well in school. Parents not only influence children's in-school achievement, but they also make decisions about children's out-of-school activities. Whether children participate in sports, music, and other activities is heavily influenced by the extent to which parents sign up children for such activities and encourage their participation (Simpkins, Fredricks, & Eccles, 2015).

Elementary school children tend to receive less physical discipline than preschoolers do. Instead of spanking or coercive holding, their parents are more likely to use deprivation of privileges, appeals to the child's self-esteem, comments designed to increase the child's sense of guilt, and statements that the child is responsible for his or her actions. During middle and late childhood, some control is transferred from parent to child. A gradual process, it produces coregulation rather than control by either the child or the parent alone. Parents continue to exercise general supervision and control, while children are allowed to engage in moment-to-moment self-regulation. The major shift to autonomy does not occur until about the age of 12 or later. A key developmental task as children move toward autonomy is learning to relate to adults outside the family on a regular basis—adults such as teachers who interact with children much differently from their parents.

PARENTS AS MANAGERS

Parents can play important roles as managers of children's opportunities, as monitors of their behavior, and as social initiators and arrangers (Parke, Roisman, & Rose, 2019; Soenens, Vansteenkiste, & Beyers, 2019). Mothers are more likely than fathers to engage in a managerial role in parenting.

Family management practices are positively related to students' grades and self-responsibility, and negatively to school-related problems (Eccles, 2007). Among the most important are maintaining a structured and organized family environment, such as establishing routines for homework, chores, bedtime, and so on, and effectively monitoring the child's behavior. A research review of the role of family functioning in determining African American students' academic achievement found that when parents monitored their son's academic achievement by ensuring that homework was completed, by restricting time spent on nonproductive distractions (such as video games and TV), and by participating in a consistent, positive dialogue with teachers and school officials, their son's academic achievement benefited (Mandara, 2006).

ATTACHMENT IN FAMILIES

You have read about the importance of secure attachment in infancy and the role of sensitive parenting in attachment (Dozier, Bernard, & Ruben, 2019; Ahnert & Schoppe-Sullivan, 2020). In middle and late childhood, attachment becomes more sophisticated, and as children's social worlds expand to include peers, teachers, and others, they typically spend less time with parents (Verhees & others, 2020). Kathryn Kerns and her colleagues (Kerns & Brumariu, 2016; Kerns & Seibert, 2016; Movahed Abtahi & Kerns, 2017) have studied links between attachment to parents and various child outcomes in the middle and late childhood years and found that secure attachment is associated with lower levels of internalized symptoms of anxiety and depression in children (Kerns & Brumariu, 2016).

STEPFAMILIES

Not only has divorce become commonplace in the United States, so has remarriage (Ganong, Coleman, & Sanner, 2019; Jensen, 2020). It takes time to marry, have children, get divorced, and then remarry. Consequently, stepfamilies include far more elementary and secondary school children than infants or preschool children. The number of remarriages involving children has grown steadily in recent years. Also, the divorce rate is 10 percent higher in remarriages than in first marriages (Cherlin & Furstenberg, 1994). About half of all children whose parents divorce will have a stepparent within four years of the separation.

Remarried parents face unique tasks (Ganong & others, 2019, 2020; Papernow, 2018). The couple must define and strengthen their marriage while renegotiating the biological parent-child relationships and establishing step-parent-stepchild and stepsibling relationships. The complex histories and multiple relationships make adjustment difficult (Dodson & Davies, 2014). Only one-third of stepfamily couples stay remarried.

Most stepfamilies are preceded by divorce rather than the death of a spouse (Pasley & Moorefield, 2004). Three common types of stepfamily structure are (1) stepfather, (2) stepmother, and (3) blended or complex. In stepfather families, the mother typically had custody of the children and remarried, introducing a stepfather into her children's lives. In step-mother families, the father usually had custody and remarried, introducing a stepmother into his children's lives. In a blended or complex stepfamily, both parents bring children from previous marriages. In E. Mavis Hetherington's (2006) longi-tudinal analyses, children and adolescents who had been in a simple stepfamily (stepfather or stepmother) for a number of years were adjusting better than in the early years of the remarried family and were functioning well in comparison with children and adolescents in conflictual nondivorced families and children and adolescents in complex (blended) stepfamilies. Hether-ington (2006) concluded that in long-established simple stepfamilies adolescents seem to eventu-ally benefit from the presence of a stepparent and the resources provided by the stepparent.

How does living in a stepfamily influence a child's development?
Todd Wright/Blend Images/Getty Images

Children often have better relationships with their custodial parents (mothers in stepfather families, fathers in stepmother families) than with stepparents (Antfolk & others, 2017; Santrock, Sitterle, & Warshak, 1988). Nonetheless, recent research indicated that stepfathers' affinity-seeking (developing friendly relationships with their stepchildren) was linked to less conflict with stepchildren, a better couple relationship, and closer stepfamily ties (Ganong & others, 2019). And another recent study found that when children have a better parent-child affective relationship with their stepparent, the children have fewer internalizing and externalizing prob-lems (Jensen & others, 2018). Also, children in simple stepfamilies (stepmother, stepfather) often show better adjustment than their counterparts in complex (blended) families (Hethering-ton & Kelly, 2002). As in divorced families, children in stepfamilies show more adjustment problems than children in nondivorced families do—academic problems and lower self-esteem, for example (Anderson & others, 1999; Hetherington & Kelly, 2002). However, the majority of children in stepfamilies do not have such problems. In one analysis, 25 percent of children from stepfamilies showed adjustment problems, compared with 10 percent in intact, never-divorced families (Hetherington & Kelly, 2002). Adolescence is an especially difficult time for the forma-tion of a stepfamily (Gosselin, 2010). This difficulty may occur because becoming part of a stepfamily exacerbates normal adolescent concerns about identity, sexuality, and autonomy.

developmental connection

Family

Approximately 50 percent of remar-ried women bear children within their newly formed union. Connect to "Socioemotional Development in Early Adulthood."

Review Connect Reflect

 LG2 Describe developmental changes in parent-child relationships, parents as managers, attachment in families, and stepfamilies.

Review

- What changes characterize parent-child relationships in middle and late childhood?
- How can parents be effective managers of their children's lives?
- How is attachment linked to children's development in middle and late childhood?
- How does being in a stepfamily influence children's development?

Connect

- In this section you learned how being part of a stepfamily affects the development of children. What did you learn earlier about children in divorced families, parenting style, and children's adjustment?

Reflect *Your Own Personal Journey of Life*

- What was your relationship with your parents like when you were in elementary school? How do you think it influenced your development?

3 Peers

LG3 Identify changes in peer relationships in middle and late childhood.

Developmental Changes | Peer Status | Social Cognition | Bullying | Friends

Having positive relationships with peers is especially important in middle and late childhood (Demirtas-Zorbaz & Ergene, 2019; Ettekal & Ladd, 2019; Sebastian-Enesco, Guerrero, & Enesco, 2020). Engaging in positive interactions with peers, resolving conflicts in nonaggressive ways, and maintaining quality friendships produce positive outcomes at this time in children's lives (Vitaro, Boivin, & Poulin, 2018; Wang & Hawk, 2019). In recent research with third- and fourth-graders, feeling related to peers at school was associated with the children's positive affectivity both at school and at home (Schmidt, Dirk, & Schmiedek, 2019).

Positive peer relations in childhood also are linked to more positive relationships in adolescence and adulthood. For example, in a longitudinal study, being popular with peers and engaging in low levels of aggression at 8 years of age were related to higher levels of occupational status at 48 years of age (Huesmann & others, 2006). Further, a study found that peer competence (a composite measure that included social contact with peers, popularity with peers, friendship, and social skills) in middle and late childhood was linked to having better relationships with coworkers in early adulthood (Collins & van Dulmen, 2006). And another study indicated that low peer status in childhood (low acceptance/likeability) was linked to increased probability of being unemployed and having mental health problems in adulthood (Almquist & Brannstrom, 2014).

DEVELOPMENTAL CHANGES

As children enter the elementary school years, reciprocity becomes especially important in peer interchanges. Researchers estimate that the percentage of time spent in social interaction with peers increases from approximately 10 percent at 2 years of age to more than 30 percent in middle and late childhood (Rubin, Bukowski, & Parker, 2006). In an early classic study, a typical day in elementary school included approximately 300 episodes with peers (Barker & Wright, 1951). As children move through middle and late childhood, the size of their peer group increases, and peer interaction is less closely supervised by adults. Until about 12 years of age, children's preference for same-sex peer groups increases.

PEER STATUS

Which children are likely to be popular with their peers, and which ones tend to be disliked? Developmentalists address this and similar questions by examining *sociometric status,* a term that describes the extent to which children are liked or disliked by their peer group (Chen, Saafir, & Graham, 2020; Cillessen & Bukowski, 2018; Wang & Hawk, 2020). Sociometric status is typically assessed by asking children to rate how much they like or dislike each of their classmates. Or it may be assessed by asking children to name the children they like the most and those they like the least.

Developmentalists have distinguished five peer statuses (Wentzel & Asher, 1995):

- **Popular children** are frequently nominated as a best friend and are rarely disliked by their peers.
- **Average children** receive an average number of both positive and negative nominations from their peers.
- **Neglected children** are infrequently nominated as a best friend but are not disliked by their peers.
- **Rejected children** are infrequently nominated as someone's best friend and are actively disliked by their peers.
- **Controversial children** are frequently nominated both as someone's best friend and as being disliked.

Popular children have many social skills that contribute to their being well liked (Ferguson & Ryan, 2019; McDonald & Asher, 2018). They give out reinforcements, listen carefully, maintain

What are some statuses that children have with their peers?
BananaStock/Getty Images

popular children Children who are frequently nominated as a best friend and are rarely disliked by their peers.

average children Children who receive an average number of both positive and negative nominations from peers.

neglected children Children who are infrequently nominated as a best friend but are not disliked by their peers.

rejected children Children who are infrequently nominated as a best friend and are actively disliked by their peers.

controversial children Children who are frequently nominated both as a best friend and as being disliked by their peers.

open lines of communication with peers, are happy, control their negative emotions, show enthusiasm and concern for others, and are self-confident without being conceited (Hartup, 1983; Rubin, Bukowski, & Bowker, 2015). Rejected children often have serious adjustment problems (Hooijsma & others, 2020; Prinstein & others, 2018). Peer rejection is consistently linked to the development and maintenance of conduct problems and antisocial behavior (Kornienko, Ha, & Dishion, 2020; Prinstein & others, 2018). In a recent study of young adolescents, peer rejection predicted increases in aggressive and rule-breaking behavior (Janssens & others, 2017). And in another recent study of adolescents, peer rejection increased the likelihood that victims and bullies would engage in non-suicidal self-injury, such as cutting, burning, or hitting oneself (Esposito, Bacchini, & Affuso, 2019).

John Coie (2004, pp. 252–253) provided three reasons why aggressive, peer-rejected boys have problems in social relationships:

- "First, the rejected, aggressive boys are more impulsive and have problems sustaining attention. As a result, they are more likely to be disruptive of ongoing activities in the classroom and in focused group play.
- Second, rejected, aggressive boys are more emotionally reactive. They are aroused to anger more easily and probably have more difficulty calming down once aroused. Because of this they are more prone to become angry at peers and attack them verbally and physically. . . .
- Third, rejected children have fewer social skills in making friends and maintaining positive relationships with peers."

Not all rejected children are aggressive (Rubin, Bukowski, & Bowker, 2015). Although aggression and its related characteristics of impulsiveness and disruptiveness underlie rejection about half the time, approximately 10 to 20 percent of rejected children are shy.

Rejected children can be taught to more accurately assess whether the intentions of their peers are negative (Bierman & Powers, 2009). They can engage in role playing or discuss hypothetical situations involving negative encounters with peers, such as when a peer cuts into a line ahead of them. In some programs, children watch videotapes of appropriate peer interaction and are asked to draw lessons from what they have seen (Ladd, Buhs, & Troop, 2004).

SOCIAL COGNITION

A boy accidentally trips and knocks another boy's soft drink out of his hand. That boy misinterprets the encounter as hostile, which leads him to retaliate aggressively against the boy who tripped. Through repeated encounters of this kind, the aggressive boy's classmates come to perceive him as habitually acting in inappropriate ways. This encounter demonstrates the importance of *social cognition*—thoughts about social matters, such as the aggressive boy's interpretation of an encounter as hostile and his classmates' perception of his behavior as inappropriate (Fiske, 2018).

Children's social cognition about their peers becomes increasingly important for understanding peer relationships in middle and late childhood. Of special interest are the ways in which children process information about peer relations and their social knowledge (Dodge, 2011a, b). Kenneth Dodge (1983, 2011a, b) argues that children go through six steps in processing information about their social world. They (1) selectively attend to social cues, (2) attribute intent by interpreting social cues, (3) establish social goals, (4) access behavioral scripts from memory and generate problem-solving strategies, (5) evaluate the likely effectiveness of strategies and make decisions, and (6) enact behavior. Subsequently, children may evaluate the effectiveness of their response. Boys are less likely to spontaneously engage in this kind of self-evaluation of the outcomes of their behavior, and thus more likely than girls to engage in impulsive and aggressive behavior. Aggressive boys are more likely to perceive another child's actions as hostile when the child's intention is ambiguous. And when aggressive boys search for cues to determine a peer's intention, they respond more rapidly, less efficiently, and less reflectively than do nonaggressive children. These are among the social cognitive factors believed to be involved in children's conflicts.

Social knowledge also is involved in children's ability to get along with peers (Carpendale & Lewis, 2015). They need to know what goals to pursue in poorly defined or ambiguous situations, how to initiate and maintain a social bond, and what scripts to follow to get other

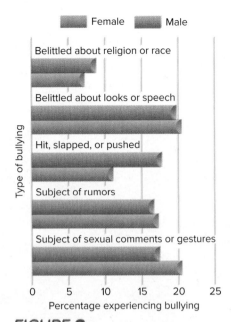

Female ▮ Male ▮

Type of bullying

Belittled about religion or race

Belittled about looks or speech

Hit, slapped, or pushed

Subject of rumors

Subject of sexual comments or gestures

0   5   10   15   20   25
Percentage experiencing bullying

FIGURE 3

BULLYING BEHAVIORS AMONG U.S. YOUTH. This graph shows the types of bullying most often experienced by U.S. youth. The percentages reflect the extent to which bullied students said that they had experienced a particular type of bullying. In terms of gender, note that when they were bullied, boys were more likely to be hit, slapped, or pushed than girls were.

Who is likely to be bullied? What are some outcomes of bullying?
Photodisc/Getty Images

children to be their friends. For example, as part of the script for getting friends, it helps to know that saying nice things, regardless of what the peer does or says, will make the peer like the child more.

BULLYING

Significant numbers of students are victimized by bullies (Mutiso & others, 2019; Juhnke, Granello, & Granello, 2020; Tas & others, 2020; Thornberg & others, 2020). In a survey of 15,000 sixth- through tenth-grade students, nearly one-third said that they had experienced occasional or frequent involvement as a victim or perpetrator in bullying (Nansel & others, 2001). Bullying was defined as verbal or physical behavior intended to disturb someone less powerful. Being belittled about looks or speech was the most frequent type of bullying (see Figure 3). Boys are more likely to be bullies than girls, but gender differences regarding victims of bullies are less clear (Salmivalli & Peets, 2018). In the study boys and younger middle school students were most likely to be bullied (Nansel & others, 2001). Bullied children reported more loneliness and difficulty in making friends, while those who did the bullying were more likely to have low grades and to smoke cigarettes and drink alcohol. And in a recent analysis of bullying in the United States, a significant increase in cyberbullying occurred from 1998 to 2017 (Kennedy, 2020). Also in this analysis, an increase in face-to-face bullying occurred for females.

Anxious, socially withdrawn, and aggressive children are often the victims of bullying (Chu & others, 2019; Coplan & others, 2018). Anxious and socially withdrawn children may be victimized because they are nonthreatening and unlikely to retaliate if bullied, whereas aggressive children may be the targets of bullying because their behavior is irritating to bullies.

Social contexts such as poverty, family, school, and peer groups can influence bullying (Bjarehed & others, 2020; Foody, Samara, & O'Higgins Norman, 2020). A meta-analysis indicated that positive parenting behavior (including having good communication, a warm relationship, being involved, and engaging in supervision of their children) was associated with reduced likelihood of children becoming either bully/victims or victims at school, while negative parenting behavior (including child maltreatment—physical abuse and neglect) was related to a greater likelihood of children becoming either bully/victims or victims at school (Lereya, Samara, & Wolke, 2013).

The social context of the peer group also plays an important role in bullying (Bjarehed & others, 2020). Seventy to 80 percent of victims and their bullies are in the same classroom (Salmivalli & Peets, 2018). Classmates are often aware of bullying incidents (Barhight & others, 2017). Bullies often torment victims to gain higher status in the peer group and need others to witness their power displays. Many bullies are not rejected by the peer group.

Peer victimization in the fifth grade has been associated with worse physical and mental health in the tenth grade (Bogart & others, 2014). Children who are bullied are more likely to experience depression, engage in suicidal ideation, and attempt suicide than their counterparts who have not been the victims of bullying (Lear & others, 2020; Naveed & others, 2019). One study also indicated that peer victimization during the elementary school years was a leading indicator of internalizing problems (depression, for example) in adolescence (Schwartz & others, 2015). Further, in a recent study of 12- to 15-year-olds in 48 countries worldwide, being a victim of bullying was a risk factor for attempting suicide in 47 of the 48 countries (Koyanagi & others, 2019). And a longitudinal study found that children who were bullied at 6 years of age were more likely to have excess weight gain when they were 12 to 13 years of age (Sutin & others, 2016). In addition, a recent study of 10- to 14-year-olds indicated that being a victim of a bully often led to a cascading effect of bullying perpetration that eventually produced disordered eating behavior (Lee & Vaillancourt, 2018). Also, a recent large-scale Norwegian study concluded that bullies, victims, and bully-victims all are at risk for developing sleep problems, including shorter sleep duration and a higher prevalence of insomnia, as well as a lower grade point average (Hysing & others, 2020). And a research analysis concluded that bullying can have long-term effects, including difficulty in forming lasting relationships and problems in the workplace (Wolke & Lereya, 2015).

An increasing concern is peer bullying and harassment on the Internet (called *cyberbullying*) (Barlett, 2019; Kennedy, 2020). A study involving third- to sixth-graders revealed that engaging in cyber aggression was related to loneliness, lower self-esteem, fewer mutual friendships, and lower peer popularity (Schoffstall & Cohen, 2011). A meta-analysis concluded that being the victim of cyberbullying was linked to stress and suicidal ideation (Kowalski & others,

2014), and another study found it was more strongly associated with suicidal ideation than traditional bullying was (van Geel, Vedder, & Tanilon, 2014). One meta-analysis revealed that cyberbullying occurred twice as much as traditional bullying and that those who engaged in cyberbullying were likely to also have engaged in traditional bullying (Modecki & others, 2014). Further, a longitudinal study found that adolescents experiencing social and emotional difficulties were more likely to be both cyberbullied and traditionally bullied than to be traditionally bullied only (Cross, Lester, & Barnes, 2015). Adolescents targeted in both ways stayed away from school more than their counterparts who were traditionally bullied only. And a recent study revealed that adolescents who were bullied both in a direct way and through cyberbullying had more behavioral problems and lower self-esteem than adolescents who were only bullied in one of these two ways (Wolke, Lee, & Guy, 2017). Also, a recent study found that the most common behavioral reactions to cyberbullying were informing a friend, counterattacking, and ignoring the cyber incident (Heiman, Olenik-Shemesh, & Frank, 2019). In this study, victims of cyberbullying were less likely than non-victims to use problem-focused coping strategies and more likely to use emotion-focused coping strategies.

Information about preventing cyberbullying can be found at www.stopcyberbullying.org/. Also, an excellent book on the topic is *Bullying Beyond the Schoolyard: Preventing and Responding to Cyberbullying* (Hinduja & Patchin, 2015).

Increasing interest is being directed to finding ways to prevent and treat bullying and victimization (Acosta & others, 2019; Cunningham & others, 2020; Juhnke, Granello, & Granello, 2020; Nickerson & others, 2019; Thornberg & others, 2020). School-based interventions vary greatly, ranging from involving the whole school in an antibullying campaign to providing individualized social skills training (Alsaker & Valanover, 2012). One of the most promising bullying intervention programs has been created by Dan Olweus (2003, 2013). This program focuses on 6- to 15-year-olds with the goal of decreasing opportunities and rewards for bullying. School staff are instructed in ways to improve peer relations and make schools safer. When properly implemented, the program reduces bullying by 30 to 70 percent (Ericson, 2001; Olweus, 2003). Information on how to implement the program can be obtained from the Center for the Prevention of Violence at the University of Colorado (www.blueprintsprograms.com). A research review concluded that interventions focused on the whole school, such as Olweus', are more effective than interventions involving classroom curricula or social skills training (Cantone & others, 2015).

What are some characteristics of children's friendships?
Don Hammond/Design Pics

FRIENDS

Friendship is an important aspect of children's development (Bagwell & Bukowski, 2018). Like adult friendships, children's friendships are typically characterized by similarity (Prinstein & Giletta, 2016). Throughout childhood, friends are more similar than dissimilar in terms of age, sex, race, and many other factors. Friends often have similar attitudes toward school, similar educational aspirations, and closely aligned achievement orientations.

Willard Hartup (1983, 1996, 2009) has studied peer relations and friendship for more than three decades. He concludes that friends provide cognitive and emotional resources from childhood through old age, such as fostering self-esteem and a sense of well-being. More specifically, children's friendships can serve six functions (Gottman & Parker, 1987):

- *Companionship.* Friendship provides children with a familiar partner and playmate, someone who is willing to spend time with them and join in collaborative activities.
- *Stimulation.* Friendship provides children with interesting information, excitement, and amusement.
- *Physical support.* Friendship provides resources and assistance.
- *Ego support.* Friendship provides the expectation of support, encouragement, and feedback, which helps children maintain an impression of themselves as competent, attractive, and worthwhile individuals.
- *Social comparison.* Friendship provides information about where the child stands vis-à-vis others and whether the child is doing okay.
- *Affection and intimacy.* Friendship provides children with a warm, close, trusting relationship with another individual. **Intimacy in friendships** is characterized by self-disclosure and the sharing of private thoughts. Research suggests that intimate friendships may not appear until early adolescence (Berndt & Perry, 1990).

developmental **connection**
Peers

Beginning in early adolescence, teenagers typically prefer to have a smaller number of friendships that are more intense and intimate. Connect to "Socioemotional Development in Adolescence."

intimacy in friendships Self-disclosure and the sharing of private thoughts.

Although having friends can be a developmental advantage, friendships are not all alike (Bagwell & Bukowski, 2018). People differ in the company they keep—that is, who their friends are. Developmental advantages occur when children have friends who are socially skilled and supportive (Laursen, 2018). However, it is not developmentally advantageous to have coercive and conflict-ridden friendships (Clayton & others, 2020). One study found that students who engaged in classroom aggressive-disruptive behavior were more likely to have aggressive friends (Powers & Bierman, 2013).

Friendship also plays an important role in children's emotional well-being and academic success (Ryan & Shin, 2018). Students with friends who are academically oriented are more likely to achieve success in school themselves (Wentzel & Ramani, 2016).

Review *Connect* Reflect

 LG3 Identify changes in peer relationships in middle and late childhood.

Review

- What developmental changes characterize peer relations in middle and late childhood?
- How does children's peer status influence their development?
- How is social cognition involved in children's peer relations?
- What is the nature of bullying?
- What are children's friendships like?

Connect

- Most developmentalists agree that peers play an important role in the development of moral reasoning. Of the five peer status groups, in which group do you think children would have the least opportunity to fully develop their moral reasoning capacities and why?

Reflect *Your Own Personal Journey of Life*

- Which of the five peer statuses characterized you as a child? Did your peer status change in adolescence? How did your peer status as a child influence your development?

4 Schools **LG4** Characterize aspects of schooling in children's development in middle and late childhood.

Contemporary Approaches to Student Learning   Socioeconomic Status, Ethnicity, and Culture

For most children, entering the first grade signals new obligations. They develop new relationships and adopt new standards by which to judge themselves. School provides children with a rich source of new ideas to shape their sense of self. They will spend many years in schools as members of small societies in which there are tasks to be accomplished, people to socialize with and be socialized by, and rules that define and limit behavior, feelings, and attitudes. By the time students graduate from high school, they have spent 12,000 hours in the classroom.

CONTEMPORARY APPROACHES TO STUDENT LEARNING

Controversy swirls about the best way to teach children and how to hold schools and teachers accountable for whether children are learning (Kauchak & Eggen, 2021; Morrison, 2020; Powell, 2019).

Constructivist and Direct Instruction Approaches   The **constructivist approach** to instruction is a learner-centered approach that emphasizes the importance of individuals actively constructing their knowledge and understanding with guidance from the teacher. In the constructivist view, teachers should not attempt to simply pour information into children's minds. Rather, children should be encouraged to explore their world, discover knowledge, reflect, and think critically with careful monitoring and meaningful guidance

constructivist approach A learner-centered educational approach that emphasizes the importance of individuals actively constructing their knowledge and understanding with guidance from the teacher.

from the teacher (Bredekamp, 2020; Burden & Byrd, 2020). Constructivists believe that for too long in American education children have been required to sit still, be passive learners, and rotely memorize irrelevant as well as relevant information (Parkay, 2020).

Constructivism may include an emphasis on collaboration—children working with each other in their efforts to know and understand (Johnson & others 2018). A teacher with a constructivist instructional philosophy would not have children memorize information rotely but would give them opportunities to meaningfully construct their knowledge and understand the material while guiding their learning (Brookhart & Nitko, 2019). By contrast, the **direct instruction approach** is a structured, teacher-centered approach that is characterized by teacher direction and control, high teacher expectations for students' progress, maximum time spent by students on academic tasks, and efforts by the teacher to keep negative affect to a minimum. An important goal in the direct instruction approach is maximizing student learning time (Burden & Byrd, 2020).

Is this classroom more likely constructivist or direct instruction? Explain.
Elizabeth Crews

Advocates of the constructivist approach argue that the direct instruction approach turns children into passive learners and does not adequately challenge them to think in critical and creative ways. Direct instruction enthusiasts say that the constructivist approaches do not give enough attention to the content of a discipline, such as history or science. They also believe that the constructivist approaches are too relativistic and vague.

Some experts believe that many effective teachers use both a constructivist *and* a direct instruction approach rather than relying exclusively on one or the other (Parkay, 2020). Some circumstances may call for a constructivist approach, others for direct instruction. For example, experts increasingly recommend an explicit, intellectually engaging direct instruction approach when teaching students who have a reading or a writing disability (Tompkins & Rodgers, 2020).

Accountability   Since the 1990s, the U.S. public and governments at every level have demanded increased accountability from schools. One result was the spread of state-mandated testing to measure what students had or had not learned (Brookhart & Nitko, 2019; Chappuis, 2020). Many states identified objectives for students in their state and created tests to measure whether students were meeting those objectives (Popham, 2020). This approach became national policy in 2002 when the No Child Left Behind (NCLB) legislation was signed into law.

No Child Left Behind (NCLB)   Advocates argue that statewide standardized testing will have a number of positive effects. These include improved student performance; more time spent teaching the subjects that are tested; high expectations for all students; identification of poorly performing schools, teachers, and administrators; and improved confidence in schools as test scores rise.

Critics argue that the NCLB legislation is doing more harm than good (Brookhart & Nitko, 2019). One criticism stresses that using a single test as the sole indicator of students' progress and competence presents a very narrow view of students' skills (Bland & Gareis, 2018). This criticism is similar to the one leveled at IQ tests. Many psychologists and educators emphasize that a number of measures should be used to assess student progress and achievement, including tests, quizzes, projects, portfolios, classroom observation, and so on. Also, the tests used as part of NCLB don't measure creativity, motivation, persistence, flexible thinking, or social skills. Teachers may end up spending far too much class time "teaching to the test" by drilling students and having them memorize isolated facts rather than focusing on the development of thinking skills needed for success in life (Flitcroft & Woods, 2018). Also, some individuals are concerned that gifted students are neglected in the effort to raise the achievement level of students who are not doing well.

Each state is allowed to establish its own criteria for what constitutes passing or failing grades on tests designated for NCLB inclusion. An analysis of NCLB data indicated that almost every fourth-grade student in Mississippi knows how to read but only half of Massachusetts' students do (Birman & others, 2007). Because state standards vary greatly, state-by-state comparisons of success on NCLB tests are likely to be unreliable. Many states

direct instruction approach A structured, teacher-centered educational approach that is characterized by teacher direction and control, mastery of academic skills, high expectations for students' progress, maximum time spent on learning tasks, and efforts to keep negative affect to a minimum.

have taken the safe route and kept the standard for passing low. Thus, while one of NCLB's goals is to raise standards for achievement in U.S. schools, apparently allowing states to set their own standards has lowered achievement standards.

Common Core   In 2009, the Common Core State Standards Initiative was endorsed by the National Governors Association in an effort to implement more rigorous state guidelines for educating students. The Common Core Standards specify what students should know and the skills they should develop at each grade level in various content areas (Common Core State Standards Initiative, 2016). A large majority of states have agreed to implement the Standards, but they have generated considerable controversy. Some critics argue that they are simply a further effort by the federal government to control education and that they emphasize a "one size fits all" approach that pays little attention to individual variations in students (Cizek, 2019). Supporters say that the Standards provide much-needed detailed guidelines and important milestones for students to achieve (McMillen, Graves-Demario, & Kieliszek, 2018).

Every Student Succeeds Act (ESSA)   The most recent initiative for accountability in education is the *Every Student Succeeds Act (ESSA),* which was passed into law in December 2015 and was supposed to be fully implemented during the 2017-2018 school year. However, in 2019 implementation was continuing but ESSA was still a work in progress (Klein, 2019). The law replaced *No Child Left Behind,* modifying but not completely eliminating standardized testing. ESSA retains annual testing for reading and writing in grades 3 to 8, then once more in high school. The new law also allows states to scale back the role of tests in holding schools accountable for student achievement. And schools must use at least one nonacademic factor— such as student engagement—in tracking success. Other aspects of the new law include continuing to require states and districts to improve their lowest-performing schools and to ensure that they improve their work with historically underperforming students, such as English-language learners, ethnic minority students, and students with a disability. States and districts are required to implement challenging academic standards, although they can opt out of state standards involving Common Core.

SOCIOECONOMIC STATUS, ETHNICITY, AND CULTURE

Children from low-income, ethnic minority backgrounds have more difficulties in school than do their middle-socioeconomic-status, White counterparts. Why? Critics argue that schools have not done a good job of educating low-income, ethnic minority students to overcome barriers to their achievement (Banks, 2019, 2020; McLoyd, Hardaway, & Jocson, 2019).

In *The Shame of a Nation*, Jonathan Kozol (2005) criticized the inadequate quality and lack of resources in many U.S. schools, especially those in the poverty areas of inner cities that have high concentrations of ethnic minority children. Kozol praises teachers like Angela Lively (above), who keeps a box of shoes in her Indianapolis classroom for students in need.
Michael Conroy/AP Images

The Education of Students from Low-Income Backgrounds
Many children living in poverty face problems that present barriers to their learning (Hoff & Laursen, 2019). They might have parents who don't set high educational standards for them, who are incapable of reading to them, or who can't afford educational materials and experiences such as books and trips to zoos and museums. They may be malnourished or live in areas with high rates of crime and violence (Bradley, 2019). One study revealed that the longer children experienced poverty, the more detrimental the poverty was to their cognitive development (Najman & others, 2009).

Schools in low-income areas are likely to have more students with low achievement test scores, lower graduation rates, and smaller percentages of students going to college; they are more likely to have young teachers with less experience; and they are more likely to encourage rote learning (Parillo, 2019). Many of the schools' buildings and classrooms are old and crumbling. These are the types of undesirable conditions Jonathan Kozol (2005) observed in many inner-city schools. Far too many schools in low-income neighborhoods provide students with environments that are not conducive to effective

connecting with careers

Ahou Vaziri, Teach for America Instructor

Ahou Vaziri was a top student in author John Santrock's educational psychology course at the University of Texas at Dallas, where she majored in Psychology and Child Development. The following year she served as a teaching intern for the educational psychology course, then submitted an application to join Teach for America and was accepted. Ahou was assigned to work in a low-income area of Tulsa, Oklahoma, where she taught English to seventh- and eighth-graders. In her words, "The years I spent in the classroom for Teach for America were among the most rewarding experiences I have had thus far in my career. I was able to go home every night after work knowing that I truly made a difference in the lives of my students."

Upon completion of her two-year teaching experience with Teach for America, Ahou continued working for the organization by recruiting college students to serve as Teach for America instructors. Subsequently, she moved into a role that involved developing curricula for Teach for America. Recently Ahou earned a graduate degree in counseling from Southern Methodist University, and in 2019 she entered a doctoral program in counseling at the University of North Texas.

Ahou Vaziri with her students in the Teach for America program. *What is Teach for America?*
Courtesy of Ahou Vaziri

learning. In a recent research review, it was concluded that increases in family income for children in poverty were associated with increased achievement in middle school as well as greater educational attainment in adolescence and emerging adulthood (Duncan, Magnuson, & Votruba-Drzal, 2017).

Schools and school programs are the focus of some poverty interventions (Abrahamse, Jonkman, & Harting, 2018; Dragoset & others, 2017). In a recent intervention with first-generation immigrant children attending high-poverty schools, the City Connects program was successful in improving children's math and reading achievement by the end of elementary school (Dearing & others, 2016). The program is directed by a full-time school counselor or social worker in each school. Annual reviews of children's needs are conducted during the first several months of the school year. Then site coordinators and teachers collaborate to develop a student support plan that might include an after-school program, tutoring, mentoring, or family counselling. For children identified as having intense needs (about 8 to 10 percent), a wider team of professionals becomes involved, possibly including school psychologists, principals, nurses, and/or community agency staff, to create additional supports. Also, a recent longitudinal study focused on outcomes of the Child-Parent Center Program in high-poverty Chicago neighborhoods, an intervention that provided school-based educational enrichment and comprehensive family services for children from 3 to 9 years of age (Reynolds, Ou, & Temple, 2018). Children who participated in the program had higher rates of post-secondary completion, including more years of education and attainment of undergraduate and postgraduate degrees.

Another important effort to improve the education of children who are growing up in low-income conditions is Teach for America (2020), a nonprofit organization that recruits and selects college graduates from universities to serve as teachers for two years in public schools in low-income communities. Since the program's inception in 1990, more than 42,000 individuals have taught more than 50,000 students for Teach for America. These teachers can be, but are not required to be, education majors. During the summer before beginning to teach, they attend an intensive training program. To read about one individual who became a Teach for America instructor, see *Connecting with Careers.*

Ethnicity in Schools   More than one-third of African American and almost one-third of Latino students attend schools in the 47 largest city school districts, compared with only 5 percent of White and 22 percent of Asian American students. Many of these inner-city schools continue to be racially segregated, are grossly underfunded, and do not provide adequate opportunities for children to learn effectively. Thus, the effects of low SES and of ethnicity are often intertwined (Banks, 2020; Bennett, 2019; Parillo, 2019).

The school experiences of students from different ethnic groups vary considerably (Banks, 2020; Chen, Fu, & Yu, 2019; Gollnick & Chinn, 2021; Koppelman, 2020). African American and Latino students are much less likely than non-Latino White or Asian American students to be enrolled in college preparatory programs and more likely to be enrolled in remedial and special education programs. Asian American students are far more likely to take advanced math and science courses. African American students are twice as likely as Latinos, Native Americans, or non-Latino Whites to be suspended from school. The comparisons just described do not address the reasons for the educational disparities. For the ethnic minority students, such as African American and Latino students, many have grown up in poverty conditions, less well-funded schools, and experienced discrimination, bias, and prejudice (U.S. Department of Education, Office of Civil Rights, 2018). For example, in regard to African American students being suspended from school more than other ethnic groups, a recent study found that African American students are more likely to be perceived as troublemakers and be given more severe punishment than non-Latino White students (Jarvis & Okonofua, 2020).

However, diversity characterizes every ethnic group (Banks, 2019, 2020; Gollnick & Chinn, 2021). For example, the higher percentage of Asian American students in advanced classes is mainly true for students with Chinese, Taiwanese, Japanese, Korean, and East Indian cultural backgrounds; students with Hmong and Vietnamese cultural backgrounds have had less academic success. Following are some strategies for improving relationships among ethnically diverse students:

- *Turn the class into a jigsaw classroom.* When Eliot Aronson was a professor at the University of Texas at Austin, the school system contacted him for ideas on how to reduce the increasing racial tension in classrooms. Aronson (1986) developed the concept of a "jigsaw classroom" in which students from different cultural backgrounds are placed in a cooperative group in which they have to construct different parts of a project to reach a common goal. Aronson used the term *jigsaw* because he saw the technique as much like a group of students cooperating to put different pieces together to complete a jigsaw puzzle. How might this work? Team sports, drama productions, and musical performances are examples of contexts in which students participate cooperatively to reach a common goal; however, the jigsaw technique also lends itself to group science projects, history reports, and other learning experiences with a variety of subject matter.

- *Encourage students to have positive personal contact with diverse other students.* Mere contact does not do the job of improving relationships with diverse others. For example, busing ethnic minority students to predominantly White schools, or vice versa, has not reduced prejudice or improved interethnic relations. What matters is what happens after children get to school. Especially beneficial in improving interethnic relations is sharing one's worries, successes, failures, coping strategies, interests, and other personal information with people of other ethnicities. When this happens, people tend to look at others as individuals rather than as members of a homogeneous group.

- *Reduce bias.* Teachers can reduce bias by displaying images of children from diverse ethnic and cultural groups, selecting play materials and classroom activities that encourage cultural understanding, helping students resist stereotyping, and working with parents to reduce children's exposure to bias and prejudice at home.

- *View the school and community as a team.* James Comer (1988, 2004, 2006, 2010) advocates a community-based, team approach as the best way to educate children. Three important aspects of the Comer Project for Change are (1) a governance and management team that develops a comprehensive school plan, assessment strategy, and staff development plan; (2) a mental health or school support team; and (3) a parents' program. Comer believes that the entire school community should have a cooperative rather than an adversarial attitude. The Comer program is currently operating in more than 600 schools in 26 states.

James Comer is shown with some of the inner-city children who attend a school that became a better learning environment because of Comer's intervention.
Chris Volpe Photography

- *Be a competent cultural mediator.* Teachers can play a powerful role as cultural mediators by being sensitive to biased content in materials and classroom interactions, learning more about different ethnic groups, being aware of children's ethnic attitudes, viewing students of color positively, and thinking of positive ways to get parents of color more involved as partners with teachers in educating children.

Cross-Cultural Comparisons International assessments indicate that the United States has not fared well in comparisons with many other countries in the areas of math and science (Desilver, 2017). In 2015 comparisons of 15-year-olds on the Program for International Student Assessment (PISA), the United States placed 38th out of 71 countries in math and 24th in science (PISA, 2015). In another assessment of fourth- and eighth-grade students on the Trends in International Mathematics and Science Study (TIMSS), U.S. students fared somewhat better, placing 11th out of 48 countries in fourth-grade math and 8th in fourth-grade science (TIMSS, 2015). Also in the TIMSS, U.S. students placed 8th in math and 8th in science in the 37 countries studied. The top five spots in the international assessments mainly go to East Asian countries, especially Singapore, China, and Japan. The only two countries to crack the top five in recent years for math and science are Finland and Estonia.

How do U.S. students fare against Asian students in math and science achievement? What were some findings in Stevenson's research that might explain the results of those international comparisons?
ViewStock/Getty Images

Despite the recent gains by U.S. elementary school students, it is disconcerting that the rankings for U.S. students in reading, math, and science compared with students in other countries tend to decline as they go from elementary school to high school. Also, U.S. students' achievement scores in math and science continue to be far below those of students in many East Asian countries.

Harold Stevenson's (1995, 2000; Stevenson, Hofer, & Randel, 1999; Stevenson & others, 1990) research explores possible reasons for the poor performance of American students compared with students in selected Asian countries. Stevenson and his colleagues have completed five cross-cultural comparisons of students in the United States, China, Taiwan, and Japan. In these studies, Asian students consistently outperform American students. And, the longer the students are in school, the wider the gap becomes between Asian and American students—the lowest difference is in the first grade, the highest in the eleventh grade (the highest grade studied). Stevenson and his colleagues spent thousands of hours observing in classrooms, as well as interviewing and surveying teachers, students, and parents. They found that the Asian teachers spent more of their time teaching math than did the American teachers. More than one-fourth of total classroom time in the first grade was spent on math instruction in Japan, compared with only one-tenth of the time in U.S. first-grade classrooms. Also, the Asian students were in school an average of 240 days a year, compared with 178 days in the United States.

Differences were also found between the Asian and American parents. The American parents had much lower expectations for their children's education and achievement than did the Asian parents. Also, the American parents were more likely to believe that their children's math achievement was due to innate ability, while the Asian parents were more likely to say that their children's math achievement was the consequence of effort and training (see Figure 4). The Asian students were more likely to do math homework than were the American students, and the Asian parents were far more likely to help their children with their math homework than were the American parents (Chen & Stevenson, 1989). *Connecting Through Research* explores why parenting practices may be an important aspect of the lower achievement of U.S. children compared with East Asian children.

Related to the differences between Asian and U.S. parents in explaining the roles of effort and ability, Carol Dweck (2006, 2012, 2016, 2019) described the importance of children's **mindset,** which she defines as the cognitive view individuals develop for themselves. She concludes that each individual has one of two mindsets: (1) a *fixed mindset,* in which they believe that their qualities cannot change; or (2) a *growth mindset,* in which they believe their qualities can change and improve through their own effort. Dweck (2006, 2012, 2016, 2019) argued that individuals' mindsets influence whether they will be optimistic or pessimistic, what their goals will be and how hard they will strive to reach those goals, and what they will achieve. Dweck says that mindsets begin to be shaped in childhood

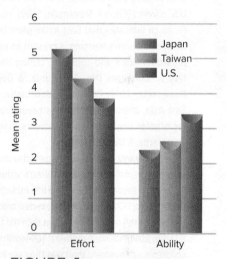

FIGURE 4

MOTHERS' BELIEFS ABOUT THE FACTORS RESPONSIBLE FOR CHILDREN'S MATH ACHIEVEMENT IN THREE COUNTRIES. In one study, mothers in Japan and Taiwan were more likely to believe that their children's math achievement was due to effort rather than innate ability, while U.S. mothers were more likely to believe their children's math achievement was due to innate ability (Stevenson, Lee, & Stigler, 1986). If parents believe that their children's math achievement is due to innate ability and their children are not doing well in math, the implication is that they are less likely to think their children will benefit from putting forth more effort.

mindset The cognitive view, either fixed or growth, that individuals develop for themselves.

connecting through research

Parenting and Children's Achievement: My Child Is My Report Card, Tiger Mothers, and Tiger Babies Strike Back

There is rising concern that U.S. children are not reaching their full academic potential, which ultimately will reduce the capacity of the United States to compete globally (Ng & others, 2019; Pomerantz, 2019). Interested in identifying how parents can maximize their children's motivation and achievement in school while also maintaining positive emotional adjustment, Eva Pomerantz and her colleagues are conducting research with children and their parents in the United States and in China, where children often attain higher levels of achievement than their U.S. counterparts (Pomerantz, 2019; Pomerantz & Grolnick, 2017; Qu, Pomerantz, & Deng, 2016).

East Asian parents spend considerably more time helping their children with homework than do U.S. parents (Chen & Stevenson, 1989). Pomerantz's research indicates that East Asian parental involvement in children's learning is present as early as the preschool years and continues during the elementary school years (Ng, Pomerantz, & Deng, 2014; Pomerantz, 2019; Pomerantz & Grolnick, 2017). In East Asia, children's learning is considered to be a far greater responsibility of parents than in the United States (Ng, Pomerantz, & Deng, 2014).

Pomerantz and her colleagues also are conducting research on the role of parental control in children's achievement (Cheung & others, 2016). In a research study whose title included the phrase "My Child Is My Report Card," Chinese mothers exerted more control (especially psychological control) over their children than did U.S. mothers (Ng, Pomerantz, & Deng, 2014). Chinese mothers' self-worth was more contingent on their children's achievement than was the case for U.S. mothers.

Pomerantz's research reflects the term "training parents," a variation of authoritarian parenting in which the parenting strategy of many Asian parents is to train their children to achieve high levels of academic success. Amy Chua's 2011 book, *Battle Hymn of the Tiger Mother,* sparked considerable interest in the role of parenting in children's achievement. Chua uses the term Tiger Mother to mean a mother who engages in strict disciplinary practices. In another book, *Tiger Babies Strike Back,* Kim Wong Keltner (2013) argues that the Tiger Mother parenting style can be so demanding and confining that being an Asian American child is like being in an "emotional jail." She says that the Tiger Mother authoritarian style does provide some advantages for children, such as learning to go for what you want and not to take no for an answer, but that too often the results are not worth the emotional costs.

Researchers studying Chinese American immigrant families with first- and second-grade children have found that the children with authoritarian (highly controlling) parents are more aggressive, are more depressed, have a higher anxiety level, and show poorer social skills

Qing Zhou, who has recently conducted research on authoritarian parenting of immigrant children, with her children. *What are the results of her research?*
Courtesy of Qing Zhou

than children whose parents have non-authoritarian styles (Zhou & others, 2012). Qing Zhou (2013), lead author on the study just described and the director of the University of California's Culture and Family Laboratory, is conducting workshops to teach Chinese mothers positive parenting strategies such as listening skills, praising their children for good behavior, and spending more time with their children in fun activities. Also, in a recent study in China, young adolescents with authoritative parents showed better adjustment than their counterparts with authoritarian parents (Zhang & others, 2017). In sum, while an authoritarian, psychologically controlling style of parenting may be associated with higher levels of achievement, especially in Asian children, there are concerns that authoritarian parenting also may produce more emotional difficulties in children (Pomerantz, 2019; Pomerantz & Grolnick, 2017).

Eva Pomerantz (2019) offers the following recommendations for parents who want to increase the motivation of their children and adolescents to do well in school:

- *Realize that ability is not fixed and can change.* Although it is difficult and takes a lot of patience, understand that children's and adolescents' abilities can improve.
- *Be involved.* One of the most important things parents can do is to become involved in their children's and adolescents' academic life and talk often with them about what they are learning.
- *Support autonomy and self-initiative.* An important aspect of children's and adolescents' motivation to do well in school is whether they believe they are responsible for their learning and are self-motivated.
- *Be positive.* Schoolwork and homework can be frustrating for children and adolescents. Interact with them in positive ways and let them know that life is often tough but that you know they can do well and overcome difficulties.
- *Understand that every child and adolescent is different.* Get to know your child or adolescent—don't let them be a psychological stranger to you. Be sensitive to their unique characteristics and know that sometimes you may need to adapt to such idiosyncrasies.

What are the best parenting strategies for rearing children to reach high levels of achievement and be emotionally healthy?

as children interact with parents, teachers, and coaches, who themselves have either a fixed mindset or a growth mindset. However, recent research indicates that many parents and teachers with growth mindsets don't always instill them in children and adolescents (Haimovitz & Dweck, 2016, 2017). The following approach has been found to increase adolescents' growth mindset: teach for understanding, provide feedback that improves understanding, give students opportunities to revise their work, communicate how effort and struggling are involved in learning, and function as a partner with children and adolescents in the learning process (Dweck & Yeager, 2020; Haimovitz & Dweck, 2017; Hooper & others, 2016; Sun, 2015).

In recent research by Dweck and her colleagues, students from lower-income families were less likely to have a growth mindset than their counterparts from wealthier families (Claro, Paunesku, & Dweck, 2016). However, the achievement of students from lower-income families who did have a growth mindset was more likely to be protected from the negative effects of poverty.

Dweck and her colleagues (Dweck, 2012, 2016, 2019; Dweck & Master, 2009; Dweck & Yeager, 2019, 2020; Yeager, Dahl, & Dweck, 2018) have incorporated information about the brain's plasticity into their efforts to improve students' motivation to achieve and succeed. In one study, they assigned two groups of students to eight sessions of either (1) study skills instruction or (2) study skills instruction plus information about the importance of developing a growth mindset (called incremental theory in the research) (Blackwell, Trzesniewski, & Dweck, 2007). One of the exercises in the growth mindset group was titled "You Can Grow Your Brain" and emphasized that the brain is like a muscle that can change and grow as it is exercised and develops new connections. Students were informed that the more you challenge your brain to learn, the more your brain cells grow. Both groups had a pattern of declining math scores prior to the intervention. Following the intervention, the math scores of the group who only received the study skills instruction continued to decline, but the group that received the combination of study skills instruction plus the growth mindset emphasis reversed the downward trend and improved their math achievement. In a recent study conducted by Dweck and her colleagues (Paunesku & others, 2015), underachieving high school students read online modules about how the brain changes when you learn and study hard. Following the online exposure about the brain and learning, the underachieving students improved their grade point averages.

Dweck created a computer-based workshop, "Brainology," to teach students that their intelligence can change (Dweck, 2012, 2016). Students experience six modules about how the brain works and how they can make their brain perform better (see Figure 5). After the program was tested in 20 New York City schools, students strongly endorsed the value of the modules. Said one student, "I will try harder because I know that the more you try the more your brain knows" (Dweck & Master, 2009, p. 137).

Recently, researchers have explored whether peer mindsets can influence a child's mindset (Sheffler & Cheung, 2020). In a recent study, the mindset of a student's classmates at time 1 (2 months into the school year) was linked to the student's mindset at time 2 (7 months later, near the end of the school year) (King, 2020).

Also, although some interventions have not been successful in improving students' growth mindset (Boulay & others, 2018), David Yeager and his colleagues (2018) conducted a national intervention study that involved a brief, online, direct-to-student growth mindset intervention that increased the grade point average of underachieving students and improved the challenge-seeking mental activity of higher achievers. In other recent research, the positive outcomes of the U.S. online growth mindset intervention were replicated with students in Norway (Bettinger & others, 2018).

Carol Dweck, who created the concept of mindset
Courtesy of Dr.Carol Dweck

Keep the growth mindset in your thoughts. Then, when you bump up against obstacles, you can turn to it . . . showing you a path into the future.

—CAROL DWECK
Contemporary psychologist, Stanford University

FIGURE 5

CAROL DWECK'S BRAINOLOGY PROGRAM IS DESIGNED TO CULTIVATE CHILDREN'S GROWTH MINDSETS
Courtesy of Dr. Carol S. Dweck

LG4 Characterize aspects of schooling in children's development in middle and late childhood.

Review
- What are two major contemporary issues in educating children?
- How do socioeconomic status, ethnicity, and culture influence schooling?

Connect
- One of Carol Dweck's exercises in the growth-mindset group was titled "You Can Grow Your Brain." Can you

actually grow your brain? What physical changes, if any, are still occurring in the brain in middle and late childhood?

Reflect *Your Own Personal Journey of Life*
- How would you rate the quality of your teachers in elementary school? Were their expectations for your achievement too low or too high?

topical **connections** *looking* **forward**

In adolescence, children begin spending more time thinking about their identity—who they are, what they are all about, and where they are going in life. Time spent with peers increases in adolescence, and friendships become more intense and intimate. Dating and romantic relationships also become more central to the lives of most adolescents. Parents continue to have an important influence on adolescent development. Having good relationships with parents provides support for adolescents as they seek more autonomy and explore a widening social world. Problems that adolescents can develop include juvenile delinquency and depression.

reach your **learning goals**

Socioemotional Development in Middle and Late Childhood

1 Emotional and Personality Development

 LG1 Discuss emotional and personality development in middle and late childhood.

The Self

- In middle and late childhood, self-understanding increasingly involves social and psychological characteristics, including social comparison. Children increase their perspective taking in middle and late childhood, and their social understanding shows increasing psychological sophistication as well.

- Self-concept refers to domain-specific evaluations of the self. Self-esteem refers to global evaluations of the self and is also referred to as self-worth or self-image. Self-esteem is only moderately related to school performance but is more strongly linked to initiative. Four ways to increase self-esteem are to (1) identify the causes of low self-esteem, (2) provide emotional support and social approval, (3) help children achieve, and (4) help children cope.

- Self-efficacy is the belief that one can master a situation and produce positive outcomes. Bandura believes that self-efficacy is a critical factor in whether students will achieve. Schunk argues that self-efficacy influences a student's choice of tasks, with low-efficacy students avoiding many learning tasks.

- The development of self-regulation is an important aspect of children's development. Erikson's fourth stage of development, industry versus inferiority, characterizes middle and late childhood.

Emotional Development	• Developmental changes in emotion include increased understanding of complex emotions such as pride and shame, detecting that more than one emotion can be experienced in a particular situation, taking into account the circumstances that led to an emotional reaction, improvements in the ability to suppress and conceal negative emotions, and the use of self-initiated strategies to redirect feelings. As children get older, they use a greater variety of coping strategies and more cognitive strategies.
Moral Development	• Kohlberg developed an influential theory of moral reasoning. He documented three levels in the development of moral reasoning—preconventional, conventional, and postconventional. Research subsequently documented that these levels were not only related to age but also to diverse social experiences. Influences on the development of moral reasoning include cognitive maturation, cognitive conflict, peer relations, and perspective taking.
	• Criticisms of Kohlberg's theory have been made, especially by Gilligan, who advocates a stronger care perspective. Other criticisms focus on the inadequacy of moral reasoning to predict moral behavior, the intuitiveness of moral thought, and the roles of emotion, culture, and family influences.
	• The domain theory of moral development states that there are different domains of social knowledge and reasoning, including moral, social conventional, and personal.
	• Prosocial behavior involves positive moral behaviors such as sharing. Most sharing in the first three years is not motivated by empathy, but at about 4 years of age empathy contributes to sharing. By the start of the elementary school years, children express objective ideas about fairness. By the mid- to late elementary school years, children believe equity can mean that others with special needs/merit deserve special treatment. Recently, there has been a surge of interest in moral personality.
Gender	• Gender stereotypes are prevalent around the world. A number of physical differences exist between males and females. Some experts argue that cognitive differences between males and females have been exaggerated. In terms of socioemotional differences, males are more physically aggressive than females, whereas females regulate their emotions better and engage in more prosocial behavior than males do. When thinking about gender it is important to consider the social context involved.

2 Families

LG2 Describe developmental changes in parent-child relationships, parents as managers, attachment in families, and stepfamilies.

Developmental Changes in Parent-Child Relationships	• Parents spend less time with children during middle and late childhood than in early childhood. Parents especially play an important role in supporting and stimulating children's academic achievement. Discipline changes, and control becomes more coregulatory.
Parents as Managers	• Parents have important roles as managers of children's opportunities, as monitors of their behavior, and as social initiators and arrangers. Mothers are more likely to function in these parental management roles than fathers are.
Attachment in Families	• Secure attachment to parents is linked to a lower level of internalized symptoms, anxiety, and depression in children during middle and late childhood. Also in middle and late childhood, attachment becomes more complex as children's social worlds expand.
Stepfamilies	• As in divorced families, children living in stepparent families face more adjustment problems than their counterparts in nondivorced families. However, a majority of children in stepfamilies do not have adjustment problems. Children in complex (blended) stepfamilies have more problems than children in simple stepfamilies or nondivorced families.

3 Peers

LG3 Identify changes in peer relationships in middle and late childhood.

Developmental Changes	• Among the developmental changes in peer relations in middle and late childhood are increased preference for same-sex groups, increased time spent in peer relations, and less supervision of the peer group by adults.
Peer Status	• Popular children are frequently named as a best friend and are rarely disliked by their peers. Average children receive an average number of both positive and negative nominations from their peers. Neglected children are infrequently named as a best friend but are not disliked by

their peers. Rejected children are infrequently named as a best friend and are actively disliked by their peers. Controversial children are frequently named both as a best friend and as being disliked by peers. Rejected children are especially at risk for a number of problems.

- Social information-processing skills and social knowledge are two important dimensions of social cognition in peer relations.

- Significant numbers of children are bullied, and this can result in short-term and long-term negative effects for both the victims and bullies.

- Like adult friends, children who are friends tend to be similar to each other. Children's friendships serve six functions: companionship, stimulation, physical support, ego support, social comparison, and intimacy/affection.

4 Schools

LG4 Characterize aspects of schooling in children's development in middle and late childhood.

Contemporary Approaches to Student Learning

- Two contemporary issues involve whether it is better to educate students by using a constructivist approach (a learner-centered approach) or a direct instruction approach (a teacher-centered approach) and how to hold teachers accountable for whether children are learning.

- In the United States, standardized testing of elementary school students has been mandated by many state governments and by the No Child Left Behind federal legislation. Numerous criticisms of NCLB have been made. Common Core standards, which attempt to provide more specific recommendations for what students need to know at different grade levels, have recently been proposed by the U.S. Department of Education. And the most recent educational legislation, the Every Student Succeeds Act (ESSA), was passed into law in December 2015 to replace NCLB. ESSA reduces the number of state-mandated tests and advocates multiple measures of school success.

Socioeconomic Status, Ethnicity, and Culture

- Children in poverty face many barriers to learning at school as well as at home. The effects of SES and ethnicity on school performance are intertwined, and many U.S. schools are segregated. Low expectations for ethnic minority children represent one of the barriers to their learning.

- American children are more achievement-oriented than children in many countries but are less achievement-oriented than many children in Asian countries such as China, Taiwan, and Japan.

- Mindset is the cognitive view, either fixed or growth, that individuals develop for themselves. Dweck argues that a key aspect of supporting children's development is to guide them in developing a growth mindset. Pomerantz emphasizes that parental involvement is a key aspect of children's achievement.

key **terms**

key **people**

Monkeybusinessimages/iStock/Getty Images

In no order of things is adolescence the simple time of life.

—JEAN ERSKINE STEWART
American writer, 20th century

Adolescence

Adolescents try on one face after another, seeking to find a face of their own. Their generation of young people is the fragile cable by which the best and the worst of their parents' generation is transmitted to the present. In the end, there are only two lasting bequests parents can leave youth— one is roots, the other wings. This section contains two chapters: "Physical and Cognitive Development in Adolescence" and "Socioemotional Development in Adolescence."

chapter 11

PHYSICAL AND COGNITIVE DEVELOPMENT IN ADOLESCENCE

chapter outline

① The Nature of Adolescence

Learning Goal 1 Discuss the nature of adolescence.

② Physical Changes

Learning Goal 2 Describe the changes involved in puberty, as well as changes in the brain and sexuality during adolescence.

Puberty
The Brain
Adolescent Sexuality

③ Issues in Adolescent Health

Learning Goal 3 Identify adolescent problems related to health, substance use and abuse, and eating disorders.

Adolescent Health
Substance Use and Abuse
Eating Disorders

④ Adolescent Cognition

Learning Goal 4 Explain cognitive changes in adolescence.

Piaget's Theory
Adolescent Egocentrism
Information Processing

⑤ Schools

Learning Goal 5 Summarize some key aspects of how schools influence adolescent development.

The Transition to Middle or Junior High School
Effective Schools for Young Adolescents
High School
Extracurricular Activities
Service Learning

Monkey Business Images/Shutterstock

Fifteen-year-old Latisha developed a drinking problem, and she was kicked off the cheerleading squad for missing too many practice sessions—but that didn't make her stop drinking. She and her friends began skipping school regularly so they could drink.

Fourteen-year-old Arnie is a juvenile delinquent. Last week he stole a TV set, struck his mother and bloodied her face, broke some streetlights in the neighborhood, and threatened a boy with a wrench and hammer.

Twelve-year-old Katie, more than just about anything else, wanted a playground in her town. She knew that the other kids also wanted one, so she put together a group that generated funding ideas for the playground. They presented their ideas to the town council. Her group attracted more youth, and they raised money by selling candy and sandwiches door-to-door. The playground became a reality, a place where, as Katie says, "People have picnics and make friends." Katie's advice: "You won't get anywhere if you don't try."

Adolescents like Latisha and Arnie are the ones we hear about the most. But there are many adolescents like Katie who contribute in positive ways to their communities and competently make the transition through adolescence. Indeed, for most young people, adolescence is not a time of rebellion, crisis, pathology, and deviance. A far more accurate vision of adolescence is that it is a time of evaluation, decision making, commitment, and carving out a place in the world. Most of the problems of today's youth are not with the youth themselves, but with needs that go unmet. To reach their full potential, adolescents need a range of legitimate opportunities as well as long-term support from adults who care deeply about them (Connor, 2020; Ogden & Hagen, 2019).

Katie Bell (*front*) and some of her volunteers.
Ronald Cortes

topical connections *looking **back***

In middle and late childhood, physical growth continues but at a slower pace than in infancy and early childhood. Gross motor skills become much smoother and more coordinated, and fine motor skills also improve. Significant advances in the development of the prefrontal cortex occur. Cognitive and language skills also improve considerably. In terms of cognitive development, most children become concrete operational thinkers, long-term memory increases, and metacognitive skills improve, especially if children learn a rich repertoire of strategies. In terms of language development, children's understanding of grammar and syntax increases, and learning to read becomes an important achievement.

preview

Adolescence is a transitional period in the human life span, linking childhood and adulthood. We begin the chapter by examining some general characteristics of adolescence and then explore the major physical changes and health issues of adolescence. Next, we consider the significant cognitive changes that characterize adolescence and conclude the chapter by describing various aspects of schools for adolescents.

1 The Nature of Adolescence LG1 Discuss the nature of adolescence.

As in development during childhood, genetic/biological and environmental/social factors influence adolescent development. During their childhood years, adolescents experienced thousands of hours of interactions with parents, peers, and teachers, but now they face dramatic biological changes, new experiences, and new developmental tasks. Relationships with parents take a different form, moments with peers become more intimate, and dating occurs for the first time, as do sexual exploration and possibly intercourse. The adolescent's thoughts become more abstract and idealistic. Biological changes trigger a heightened interest in body image. Adolescence has both continuity and discontinuity with childhood.

There is a long history of worrying about how adolescents will "turn out." In 1904, G. Stanley Hall proposed the "storm-and-stress" view that adolescence is a turbulent time charged with conflict and mood swings. However, when Daniel Offer and his colleagues (1988) studied the self-images of adolescents in the United States, Australia, Bangladesh, Hungary, Israel, Italy, Japan, Taiwan, Turkey, and West Germany, at least 73 percent of the adolescents displayed a healthy self-image. Although there were differences among them, the adolescents were happy most of the time, they enjoyed life, they perceived themselves as able to exercise self-control, they valued work and school, they felt confident about their sexual selves, they expressed positive feelings toward their families, and they felt they had the capability to cope with life's stresses—not exactly a storm-and-stress portrayal of adolescence.

Public attitudes about adolescence emerge from a combination of personal experience and media portrayals, neither of which produces an objective picture of how normal adolescents develop (Feldman & Elliott, 1990). Some of the readiness to assume the worst about adolescents likely involves the short memories of adults. Many adults measure their current perceptions of adolescents by their memories of their own adolescence. Adults may portray today's adolescents as more troubled, less respectful, more self-centered, more assertive, and more adventurous than they were.

However, in matters of taste and manners, the young people of every generation have seemed unnervingly radical and different from adults—different in how they look, in how they behave, in the music they enjoy, in their hairstyles, and in the clothing they choose. It would be an enormous error, though, to confuse adolescents' enthusiasm for trying on new identities and enjoying moderate amounts of outrageous behavior with hostility toward parental and societal standards. Acting out and boundary testing are time-honored ways in which adolescents move toward accepting, rather than rejecting, parental values.

Negative stereotyping of adolescence has been extensive (Jiang & others, 2018). However, much of the negative stereotyping has been fueled by the media's focus on a visible minority of adolescents. In the last decade there has been a call for adults to have a more positive attitude toward youth and emphasize their positive development. Indeed, researchers have found that a majority of adolescents are making the transition from childhood through adolescence to adulthood in a positive way (Lerner & others, 2019). For example, a recent study of non-Latino White and African American 12- to 20-year-olds in the United States found that they were characterized much more by positive than problematic development, even in their most vulnerable times (Gutman & others, 2017). Their engagement in healthy behaviors, supportive relationships with parents and friends, and positive self-perceptions were much stronger than their angry and depressed feelings.

Growing up has never been easy. However, adolescence is not best viewed as a time of rebellion, crisis, pathology, and deviance. A far more accurate vision of adolescence describes it as a time of evaluation, of decision making, of commitment, and of carving out a place in the world. Most of the problems of today's youth are not with the youth themselves. What adolescents need is access to a range of legitimate opportunities and to long-term support from adults who care deeply about them. *What might be some examples of such support and caring?*
Thomas Barwick/Getty Images

Although most adolescents negotiate the lengthy path to adult maturity successfully, too large a group does not. Ethnic, cultural, gender, socioeconomic, age, and lifestyle differences influence the actual life trajectory of each adolescent (Ferrer-Wreder & Kroger, 2020; Magnuson & Duncan, 2019). Different portrayals of adolescence emerge, depending on the particular group of adolescents being described. Today's adolescents are exposed to a complex menu of lifestyle options through the media, and many face the temptations of drug use and sexual activity at increasingly young ages (D'Amico & others, 2020; Okumu & others, 2019). Too many adolescents are not provided with adequate opportunities and support to become competent adults (Bill & Melinda Gates Foundation, 2020; Terrell & others, 2021).

Recall that *social policy* is the course of action designed by the national government to influence the welfare of its citizens. Currently, many researchers in adolescent development are designing studies that they hope will lead to wise and effective social policy decision making (Bojorquez & Fry-Bowers, 2019; Garbarino, Governale, & Kostelny, 2019).

Research indicates that youth benefit enormously when they have caring adults in their lives in addition to parents or guardians (Frydenberg, 2019; Larson, Walker, & McGovern, 2020). Caring adults—such as coaches, neighbors, teachers, mentors, and after-school leaders—can serve as role models, confidants, advocates, and resources. Relationships with caring adults are powerful when youth know they are respected, that they matter to the adult, and that the adult wants to be a resource in their lives. However, in a survey, only 20 percent of U.S. 15-year-olds reported having meaningful relationships with adults outside their family who were helping them to succeed in life (Search Institute, 2010).

RubberBall Productions/Getty Images

---

2 Physical Changes

LG2 Describe the changes involved in puberty, as well as changes in the brain and sexuality during adolescence.

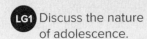

| Puberty | The Brain | Adolescent Sexuality |

One father remarked that the problem with his teenage son was not that he grew, but that he did not know when to stop growing. As we will see, there is considerable variation in the timing of the adolescent growth spurt. In addition to describing pubertal changes, we will also explore changes in sexuality and the brain.

PUBERTY

Puberty is not the same as adolescence. For most of us, puberty ends long before adolescence does, although puberty is the most important marker of the beginning of adolescence.

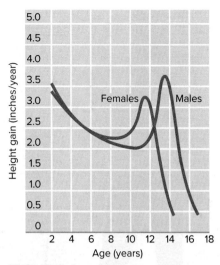

FIGURE 1

PUBERTAL GROWTH SPURT. On average, the peak of the growth spurt during puberty occurs two years earlier for girls (11½) than for boys (13½). *How are hormones related to the growth spurt and to the difference between the average heights of adolescent boys and girls?*

puberty A period of rapid physical maturation, occurring primarily in early adolescence, that involves hormonal and bodily changes.

menarche A girl's first menstruation.

hormones Powerful chemical substances secreted by the endocrine glands and carried through the body by the bloodstream.

Puberty is a brain-neuroendocrine process occurring primarily in early adolescence that provides stimulation for the rapid physical changes that take place during this period of development (Nguyen, 2018; Sanfilippo & others, 2020). Puberty is not a single, sudden event. We know whether a young boy or girl is going through puberty, but pinpointing puberty's beginning and end is difficult. Among the most noticeable changes are signs of sexual maturation and increases in height and weight.

Sexual Maturation, Height, and Weight   Think back to the onset of your puberty. Of the striking changes that were taking place in your body, what was the first to occur? Researchers have found that male pubertal characteristics typically develop in this order: increase in penis and testicle size, appearance of straight pubic hair, minor voice change, first ejaculation (which usually occurs through masturbation or a wet dream), appearance of kinky pubic hair, onset of maximum growth in height and weight, growth of hair in armpits, more detectable voice changes, and, finally, growth of facial hair.

What is the order of appearance of physical changes in females? First, either the breasts enlarge or pubic hair appears. Later, hair appears in the armpits. As these changes occur, the female grows in height and her hips become wider than her shoulders. **Menarche**—a girl's first menstruation—comes rather late in the pubertal cycle. Initially, her menstrual cycles may be highly irregular. For the first several years, she may not ovulate every menstrual cycle; some girls do not ovulate at all until a year or two after menstruation begins. No voice changes comparable to those in pubertal males occur in pubertal females. By the end of puberty, the female's breasts have become more fully rounded.

Marked weight gains coincide with the onset of puberty. During early adolescence, girls tend to outweigh boys, but by about age 14 boys begin to surpass girls. Similarly, in early adolescence girls tend to be as tall as or taller than boys of their age, but by the end of the middle school years most boys have caught up or surpassed girls in height.

As indicated in Figure 1, the growth spurt occurs approximately two years earlier for girls than for boys. The mean age at the beginning of the growth spurt in girls is 9; for boys, it is 11. The peak rate of pubertal change occurs at 11½ years for girls and 13½ years for boys. During their growth spurt, girls increase in height about 3½ inches per year, boys about 4 inches. Boys and girls who are shorter or taller than their peers before adolescence are likely to remain so during adolescence; however, as much as 30 percent of an individual's height in late adolescence is unexplained by his or her height in the elementary school years.

Is age of pubertal onset linked to how tall boys and girls will be toward the end of adolescence? One study found that for girls, earlier onset of menarche, breast development, and growth spurt were linked to being shorter at 18 years of age; however, for boys, earlier age of growth spurt and slower progression through puberty were associated with being taller at 18 years of age (Yousefi & others, 2013).

Hormonal Changes   Behind the first whisker in boys and the widening of hips in girls is a flood of **hormones,** powerful chemical substances secreted by the endocrine glands and carried through the body by the bloodstream.

The concentrations of certain hormones increase dramatically during adolescence (Bhattacharya & others, 2019; Frederiksen & others, 2020). *Testosterone* is a hormone associated in boys with genital development, increased height, and deepening of the voice. *Estradiol* is a type of estrogen that in girls is associated with breast, uterine, and skeletal development. In one study, testosterone levels increased eighteenfold in boys but only twofold in girls during puberty; estradiol increased eightfold in girls but only twofold in boys (Nottelmann & others, 1987). Thus, both testosterone and estradiol are present in the hormonal makeup of both boys and girls, but testosterone dominates in male pubertal development, estradiol in female pubertal development (Balzer & others, 2019). A study of 9- to 17-year-old boys found that testosterone levels peaked at 17 years of age (Khairullah & others, 2014).

The same influx of hormones that grows hair on a male's chest and increases the fatty tissue in a female's breasts may also contribute to psychological development in adolescence. In one study of boys and girls ranging in age from 9 to 14, a higher concentration of testosterone was present in boys who rated themselves as more socially competent (Nottelmann & others, 1987). Also, in a recent study of adolescent boys, higher testosterone levels were linked to lower capacity for delay of gratification (Laube, Lorenz, & van den Bos, 2019). However, a research review concluded that there is insufficient quality research to confirm that changing testosterone levels during puberty are linked to mood and behavior in adolescent males (Duke, Balzer, & Steinbeck, 2014). And hormonal effects by themselves do not account for adolescent development (Cicek & others, 2018). For example, in one study, social factors were much better predictors of young adolescent girls' depression and anger than hormonal factors (Brooks-Gunn & Warren, 1989). Behavior and moods also can affect hormones (DeRose & Brooks-Gunn, 2008). Stress, eating patterns, exercise, sexual activity, tension, and depression can activate or suppress various aspects of the hormonal system (Marceau, Dorn, & Susman, 2012). In sum, the hormone-behavior link is complex.

Timing and Variations in Puberty In the United States—where children mature up to a year earlier than children in European countries—the average age of menarche has declined significantly since the mid-nineteenth century (see Figure 2). Also, recent studies in Korea and Japan (Cole & Mori, 2017), China (Song & others, 2017), Saudi Arabia (Al Alwan & others, 2017), and Portugal (Queiroga & others, 2020) found that pubertal onset has been occurring earlier in recent years. Fortunately, however, we are unlikely to see pubescent toddlers, since what has happened in the past century is likely the result of improved nutrition and health.

Why do the changes of puberty occur when they do, and how can variations in their timing be explained? The basic genetic program for puberty is wired into the species (Lardone & others, 2020; Toro, Aylwin, & Lomniczi, 2018). Weight also is linked to pubertal onset. Recent research revealed that a higher BMI (Deng & others, 2018) and obesity (Busch & others, 2020) were associated with earlier pubertal onset.

Experiences that are linked to earlier pubertal onset include nutrition, an urban environment, low socioeconomic status, adoption, father absence, family conflict, maternal harshness, child maltreatment, and early substance use (Bratke & others, 2017). For example, a recent study found that child sexual abuse was linked to earlier pubertal onset (Noll & others, 2017). In many cases, puberty comes months earlier in these situations, and this earlier onset of puberty is likely explained by high rates of conflict and stress in these social contexts.

For most boys, the pubertal sequence may begin as early as age 10 or as late as 13½, and it may end as early as age 13 or as late as 17. Thus, the normal range is wide enough that, given two boys of the same chronological age, one might complete the pubertal sequence before the other one has begun it. For girls, menarche is considered within the normal range if it appears between the ages of 9 and 15. An increasing number of U.S. girls are beginning puberty at 8 and 9 years of age, with African American girls developing earlier than non-Latino White girls (Selkie, 2019).

Body Image One psychological aspect of physical change in puberty is universal: Adolescents are preoccupied with their bodies and develop images of what their bodies are like (Jankauskiene & others, 2019; McCullough, Pieloch, & Marks, 2020). Preoccupation with body image is strong throughout adolescence but is especially acute during early adolescence, a time when adolescents are more dissatisfied with their bodies than in late adolescence.

The recent dramatic increase in Internet and social media use has raised concerns about its impact on adolescents' body images. For example, a recent study of U.S. 12- to 14-year-olds found that heavier social media use was associated with body dissatisfaction (Burnette, Kwitowski, & Mazzeo, 2017). Also, a recent study of young adolescents indicated that girls had a more negative body image when they identified with an ideal social media portrayal (for example, stating that they want their body to look like the models they see on social media) (Rodgers & others, 2020). Further, a recent study of seventh- to twelfth-graders in Thailand found that increased time spent on the Internet, especially in activities related to self-image and eating attitudes and behavior, was linked to increased body dissatisfaction

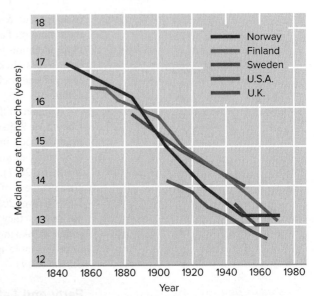

FIGURE 2

AGE AT MENARCHE IN NORTHERN EUROPEAN COUNTRIES AND THE UNITED STATES IN THE NINETEENTH AND TWENTIETH CENTURIES. Notice the steep decline in the age at which girls experienced menarche in four northern European countries and the United States from 1845 to 1969. Recently the age at which girls experience menarche has been leveling off.

What are some of the differences in the ways girls and boys experience pubertal growth?
Fuse/Corbis/Getty Images

(Kaewpradub & others, 2017). In addition, in a recent study of U.S. college women, spending more time on Facebook was related to more frequent weight comparisons with other women, more attention to the physical appearance of others, and more negative feelings about their own bodies (Eckler, Kalyango, & Paasch, 2017), In sum, various aspects of exposure to the Internet and social media are increasing the body dissatisfaction of adolescents and emerging adults, especially females.

Gender differences characterize adolescents' perceptions of their bodies (Pullmer, Coelho, & Zaitsoff, 2019). In general, girls are less happy with their bodies and have more negative body images than boys throughout puberty (Griffiths & others, 2017). In a recent U.S. study of young adolescents, boys had a more positive body image than girls (Morin & others, 2017). Girls' more negative body images may be due to media portrayals of the attractiveness of being thin and the increase in body fat in girls during puberty (Calugi & Dalle Grave, 2019). One study found that both boys' and girls' body images became more positive as they moved from the beginning to the end of adolescence (Holsen, Carlson Jones, & Skogbrott Birkeland, 2012). Also, in a recent study, higher social media use was linked to more negative body images for adolescents, more so for girls than boys (Kelly & others, 2019).

Early and Late Maturation   You may have entered puberty earlier or later than average, or perhaps you were right on schedule. Adolescents who mature earlier or later than their peers perceive themselves differently (Khan, 2019; Selkie, 2018). In the Berkeley Longitudinal Study some years ago, early-maturing boys perceived themselves more positively and had more successful peer relations than did their late-maturing counterparts (Jones, 1965). When the late-maturing boys were in their thirties, however, they had developed a stronger sense of identity than the early-maturing boys had (Peskin, 1967). This identity development may have occurred because the late-maturing boys had more time to explore life's options, or because the early-maturing boys continued to focus on their advantageous physical status instead of on career development and achievement. More recent research confirms, though, that at least during adolescence it is advantageous to be an early-maturing rather than a late-maturing boy (Graber, Brooks-Gunn, & Warren, 2006).

Early and late maturation have been linked with body image. In one study, in the sixth grade, early-maturing girls showed greater satisfaction with their figures than did late-maturing girls, but by the tenth grade late-maturing girls were more satisfied (Simmons & Blyth, 1987) (see Figure 3). A possible reason for this is that in late adolescence early-maturing girls are shorter and stockier, whereas late-maturing girls are taller and thinner. Thus, late-maturing girls in late adolescence have bodies that more closely approximate the current American ideal of feminine beauty—tall and thin. Also, one study found that in the early high school years, late-maturing boys had a more negative body image than early-maturing boys (de Guzman & Nishina, 2014).

An increasing number of researchers have found that early maturation increases girls' vulnerability to a number of problems (Selkie, 2019). Early-maturing girls are more likely to smoke, drink, be depressed, have an eating disorder, engage in delinquency, struggle for earlier independence from their parents, and have older friends; and their bodies are likely to elicit responses from males that lead to earlier dating and earlier sexual experiences (Mendle, Ryan, & McKone, 2019). One study found that early maturation predicted a stable higher level of depression for adolescent girls (Rudolph & others, 2014). More recently, researchers found that early-maturing girls had higher rates of depression and antisocial behavior as middle-aged adults, mainly because their difficulties began in adolescence and did not lessen over time (Mendle & others, 2019). Further, early-maturing girls tend to have sexual intercourse earlier and to have more unstable sexual relationships, and they are more at risk for physical and verbal abuse in dating (Chen, Rothman, & Jaffee, 2017; Moore, Harden, & Mendle, 2014). In addition, a recent Korean study of more than 30,000 girls found that early menarche was associated with increased risk-taking (Kim & others, 2017). And early-maturing girls are less likely to graduate from high school and tend to cohabit and marry earlier (Cavanagh, 2009). Apparently as a result of their social and cognitive immaturity combined with early physical development, early-maturing girls are easily lured into problem behaviors, not recognizing the possible long-term negative effects on their development.

In sum, early maturation often has more favorable outcomes in adolescence for boys, especially in early adolescence. However, late maturation may be more favorable for boys,

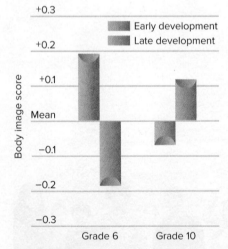

FIGURE 3

EARLY- AND LATE-MATURING ADOLESCENT GIRLS' PERCEPTIONS OF BODY IMAGE IN EARLY AND LATE ADOLESCENCE. The sixth-grade girls in this study had positive body image scores if they were early maturers but negative body image scores if they were late maturers (Simmons & Blyth, 1987). Positive body image scores indicated satisfaction with their figures. By the tenth grade, however, it was the late maturers who had positive body image scores.

especially in terms of identity and career development. Research increasingly has found that early-maturing girls are vulnerable to a number of problems.

THE BRAIN

Along with the rest of the body, the brain changes during adolescence, but the study of adolescent brain development is still in its infancy. As advances in technology take place, significant strides are also likely to be made in charting developmental changes in the adolescent brain (Jadhav & Boutrel, 2019; Volkow & others, 2020). What do we know now?

The dogma of the unchanging brain has been discarded, and researchers are mainly focused on context-induced plasticity of the brain over time (Ladouceur & others, 2019). The development of the brain mainly changes in a bottom-up, top-down sequence with sensory, appetitive (eating, drinking), sexual, sensation-seeking, and risk-taking brain linkages maturing first and higher-level brain linkages such as self-control, planning, and reasoning maturing later (Zelazo, 2013).

Using fMRI brain scans, scientists have recently discovered that adolescents' brains undergo significant structural changes (Fuhrmann & others, 2019; Vasa & others, 2020). The **corpus callosum,** where fibers connect the brain's left and right hemispheres, thickens in adolescence, and this improves adolescents' ability to process information (Chavarria & others, 2014). For example, a recent study found that the density of fibers in the corpus callosum increased in adolescence (Genc & others, 2018).

We have described advances in the development of the prefrontal cortex—the highest level of the frontal lobes involved in reasoning, decision making, and self-control. However, the prefrontal cortex doesn't finish maturing until emerging adulthood (approximately 18 to 25 years of age) or later (Brown & Wisco, 2019).

At a lower, subcortical level, the **limbic system,** which is the seat of emotions and where rewards are experienced, matures much earlier than the prefrontal cortex and is almost completely developed in early adolescence (Brown & Wisco, 2019). The limbic system structure that is especially involved in emotion is the **amygdala.** Figure 4 shows the locations of the corpus callosum, prefrontal cortex, and limbic system.

With the onset of puberty, the levels of neurotransmitters change (Casey & others, 2019). For example, an increase in the neurotransmitter dopamine occurs in both the prefrontal cortex and the limbic system during adolescence (Cohen & Casey, 2017). Increases in dopamine have been linked to increased risk taking and the use of addictive drugs (Webber & others, 2017). Researchers also have found that dopamine plays an important role in reward seeking during adolescence (Dubol & others, 2018).

Earlier we described the increased focal activation that is linked to synaptic pruning in a specific region, such as the prefrontal cortex. In middle and late childhood, while there is increased focal activation within a specific brain region such as the prefrontal cortex, there are limited connections across distant brain regions. As adolescents develop, they have more connections across brain areas (Tooley & others, 2020; Vasa & others, 2020). The increased connectedness (referred to as brain networks) is especially prevalent across more distant brain regions. Thus, as children develop, greater efficiency and focal activation occurs in close-by areas of the brain, and simultaneously there is an increase in brain networks connecting more distant brain regions. In a recent study, reduced connectivity between the brain's frontal lobes and amygdala during adolescence was linked to increased depression (Scheuer & others, 2017). And in another recent study, connectivity between the prefrontal cortex and hippocampus increased from adolescence to emerging and early adulthood, with this connectivity linked to improvement in higher-level cognition, especially in problem solving and future planning (Calabro & others, 2020).

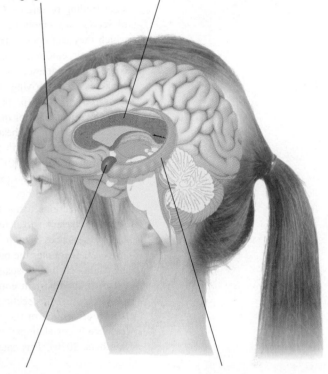

Prefrontal cortex
This "judgment" region reins in intense emotions but doesn't finish developing until at least emerging adulthood.

Corpus callosum
These nerve fibers connect the brain's two hemispheres; they thicken in adolescence to process information more effectively.

Amygdala
Limbic system structure especially involved in emotion.

Limbic system
A lower, subcortical system in the brain that is the seat of emotions and experience of rewards. This system is almost completely developed in early adolescence.

FIGURE 4

THE CHANGING ADOLESCENT BRAIN: PREFRONTAL CORTEX, LIMBIC SYSTEM, AND CORPUS CALLOSUM
Takayuki/Shutterstock

developmental **connection**
Brain Development
Although the prefrontal cortex shows considerable development in childhood, it is still not fully mature even in adolescence. Connect to "Physical and Cognitive Development in Middle and Late Childhood."

corpus callosum The location where fibers connect the brain's left and right hemispheres.

limbic system The part of the brain where emotions and rewards are processed.

amygdala The region of the brain that is the seat of emotions.

Many of the changes in the adolescent brain that have been described here involve the rapidly emerging fields of *developmental cognitive neuroscience* and *developmental social neuroscience,* in which researchers explore connections between development, the brain, and cognitive or socioemotional processes (Albaugh & others, 2019; Li & others, 2019). For example, consider leading researcher Charles Nelson's (2003) view that, although adolescents are capable of very strong emotions, their prefrontal cortex hasn't adequately developed to the point at which they can control these passions. It is as if their brain doesn't have the brakes to slow down their emotions. Or consider this interpretation of the development of emotion and cognition in adolescents: "early activation of strong 'turbo-charged' feelings with a relatively unskilled set of 'driving skills' or cognitive abilities to modulate strong emotions and motivations" (Dahl, 2004, p. 18).

Of course, a major question is which comes first, biological changes in the brain or experiences that stimulate these changes (Brody & others, 2019). In a longitudinal study, 11- to 18-year-olds who lived in poverty conditions had diminished brain functioning at 25 years of age (Brody & others, 2017). However, the adolescents from poverty backgrounds whose families participated in a supportive parenting intervention did not show this diminished brain functioning in adulthood. Another study found that the prefrontal cortex thickened and more brain connections formed when adolescents resisted peer pressure (Paus & others, 2007). Scientists have yet to determine whether the brain changes come first or whether they result from experiences with peers, parents, and others (Lauharatanahirun & others, 2018). Once again, we encounter the nature-nurture issue that is so prominent in an examination of development through the life span. Nonetheless, there is adequate evidence that environmental experiences make important contributions to the brain's development (Duell & Steinberg, 2019).

In closing this section on the development of the brain in adolescence, a further caution is in order. Much of the research on neuroscience and the development of the brain in adolescence is correlational in nature, and thus causal statements need to be scrutinized (Volkow & others, 2020). This caution, of course, applies to any period in the human life span.

ADOLESCENT SEXUALITY

Not only is adolescence characterized by substantial changes in physical growth and the development of the brain, but adolescence also is a bridge between the asexual child and the sexual adult (Diamond, 2019; Hyde & DeLamater, 2020). Adolescence is a time of sexual exploration and experimentation, of sexual fantasies and realities, of incorporating sexuality into one's identity. Adolescents have an almost insatiable curiosity about sexuality. They are concerned about whether they are sexually attractive, how to have sex, and what the future holds for their sexual lives. Although most adolescents experience times of vulnerability and confusion, the majority will eventually develop a mature sexual identity.

In the United States, the sexual culture is widely available to adolescents (Herdt & Polen-Petit, 2021). In addition to any advice adolescents get from parents, they learn a great deal about sex from television, videos, magazines, the lyrics of popular music, and the Internet (Naezer & Ringrose, 2019; Ward, Moorman, & Grower, 2019). A recent study of the prime-time television shows viewed by U.S. adolescents and emerging adults found that sexual violence and abuse, casual sex, lack of contraception use, and no coverage of the consequences of risky sexual behavior were common (Kinsler & others, 2019). Also, adolescent engagement in *sexting,* which involves sending sexually explicit images, videos, or text messages via electronic communication, has become increasingly common (Bianchi & others, 2020; Steinberg & others, 2019). For example, in a recent national study of U.S. middle and high school students, 13 percent reported they had sent a sext, and 18.5 percent indicated they had received a sext (Patchin & Hinduja, 2019). And in another study of 13- to 21-year-old Latinos, engaging in sexting was linked to engaging in penetrative sex (oral, vaginal, or anal sex) (Romo & others, 2017).

Developing a Sexual Identity Mastering emerging sexual feelings and forming a sense of sexual identity are multifaceted and lengthy processes (DeLamater, 2019; Diamond, 2019; Savin-Williams, 2019). They involve learning to manage sexual feelings (such as sexual arousal and attraction), developing new forms of intimacy, and learning how to regulate sexual behavior to avoid undesirable consequences.

An adolescent's sexual identity involves activities, interests, styles of behavior, and an indication of sexual orientation (whether an individual has same-sex or other-sex

Sexual arousal emerges as a new phenomenon in adolescence and it is important to view sexuality as a normal aspect of adolescent development.

—SHIRLEY FELDMAN
Contemporary psychologist, Stanford University

attractions, or both) (Taggart & others, 2019). For example, some adolescents have a high anxiety level about sex, others a low level. Some adolescents are strongly aroused sexually, others less so. Some adolescents are very active sexually, others not at all (Hyde & DeLamater, 2020). Some adolescents are sexually inactive in response to their strong religious upbringing; others go to church regularly and yet their religious training does not inhibit their sexual activity.

It is commonly thought that most gays and lesbians quietly struggle with same-sex attractions in childhood, do not engage in heterosexual dating, and gradually recognize that they are gay or lesbian in mid- to late adolescence. Many youth do follow this developmental pathway, but others do not (Diamond, 2019; Savin-Williams, 2019). For example, many youth have no recollection of early same-sex attractions and experience a more abrupt sense of their same-sex attraction in late adolescence. The majority of adolescents with same-sex attractions also experience some degree of other-sex attractions (Carroll, 2019). Even though some adolescents who are attracted to individuals of their same sex fall in love with these individuals, others claim that their same-sex attractions are purely physical (Diamond, 2019; Savin-Williams, 2019). In the timing and sequence of sexual developmental milestones, there are few individual differences between heterosexual and sexual minority adolescents except that sexual minority adolescents have to cope with their sexual identity in more stressful ways, including disclosing their sexual identity to family members (Savin-Williams, 2019).

Further, the majority of sexual minority (gay, lesbian, and bisexual) adolescents have competent and successful paths of development through adolescence and become healthy and productive adults. However, in a recent large-scale study, sexual minority adolescents did engage in a higher prevalence of health-risk behaviors (greater drug use and sexual risk taking, for example) compared with heterosexual adolescents (Kann & others, 2016).

The Timing of Adolescent Sexual Behaviors What is the current profile of sexual activity of adolescents? In a U.S. national survey conducted in 2017, 57.3 percent of twelfth-graders reported having experienced sexual intercourse, compared with 30 percent of ninth-graders (Kann & others, 2018). By age 20, 77 percent of U.S. youth report having engaged in sexual intercourse (Dworkin & Santelli, 2007). Nationally, 44.3 percent of twelfth-graders, 35.3 percent of eleventh-graders, 24.9 percent of tenth-graders, and 12.9 percent of ninth-graders recently reported that they were currently sexually active (Kann & others, 2018).

What trends in adolescent sexual activity have occurred in recent decades? From 1991 to 2017, fewer adolescents reported any of the following: ever having had sexual intercourse, currently being sexually active, having had sexual intercourse before the age of 13, and having had sexual intercourse with four or more persons during their lifetime (Kann & others, 2018) (see Figure 5).

Sexual initiation varies by ethnic group in the United States (Kann & others, 2018). African Americans are likely to engage in sexual behaviors earlier than other ethnic groups, whereas Asian Americans are likely to engage in them later (Feldman, Turner, & Araujo, 1999). In a U.S. survey of ninth- to twelfth-graders, 45.8 percent of African Americans, 37.9 percent of Latinos, and 38.6 percent of non-Latino Whites said they had experienced sexual intercourse (Kann & others, 2018). In this study, 7.5 percent of African Americans (compared with 4 percent of Latinos and 2.1 percent of non-Latino Whites) reported having had their first sexual experience before 13 years of age.

Research indicates that oral sex is common among U.S. adolescents (Fava & Bay-Cheng, 2012; Song & Halpern-Felsher, 2010). In a recent national survey of more than 7,000 15- to 24-year-olds, 58.6 percent of the females reported ever having performed oral sex and 60.4 percent said they had ever received oral sex (Holway & Hernandez, 2018). Researchers have also found that among female adolescents who reported having vaginal sex first, 31 percent reported having a teen pregnancy, whereas among those who initiated oral-genital sex first, only 8 percent reported having a teen pregnancy (Reese & others, 2013). Thus, how adolescents initiate their sex lives may have positive or negative consequences for their sexual health.

Risk Factors in Adolescent Sexual Behavior In a recent study of Korean adolescent girls, early menarche was linked to earlier initiation of

developmental **connection**

Sexuality

What characterizes the sexual activity of emerging adults (18 to 25 years of age)? Connect to "Physical and Cognitive Development in Early Adulthood."

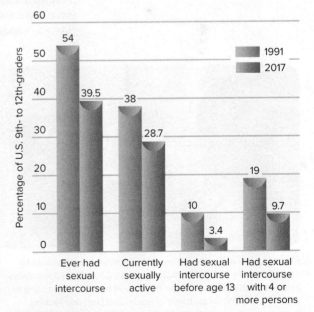

FIGURE 5

SEXUAL ACTIVITY OF U.S. ADOLESCENTS FROM 1991 TO 2017

What are some risks associated with early initiation of sexual intercourse?
Stockbyte/Punchstock/Getty Images

sexual intercourse (Kim & others, 2017). Many adolescents are not emotionally prepared to handle sexual experiences, especially in early adolescence (Leonardi & others, 2019). Early sexual activity is linked with risky behaviors such as drug use, delinquency, school-related problems, and mental health problems (Barragan & others, 2019; Okumu & others, 2019). A study of more than 3,000 Swedish adolescents revealed that sexual intercourse before age 14 was linked to risky behaviors such as an increased number of sexual partners, experience of oral and anal sex, negative health behaviors (smoking, drug and alcohol use), and antisocial behavior (being violent, stealing, running away from home) at 18 years of age (Kastbom & others, 2016). Further, a recent South African study found that early sexual debut predicted a lower probability of graduating from high school (Bengesai, Khan, & Dube, 2018). And in an Australian study, sex at age 15 or younger predicted higher rates of emerging adult (average age 21) pregnancy, lifetime sexual partners, and sex without using a condom (Prendergast & others, 2019). In this study, early sex also was associated with higher rates of emerging adult substance use and antisocial behavior.

Substance abuse, especially in early adolescence, is linked to sexual risk practices. For example, in a recent study, adolescents who initiated sexual intercourse before age 13 were more likely to engage in substance abuse and have mental health problems (Okumu & others, 2019).

In addition to having sex in early adolescence, other risk factors for sexual problems in adolescence include contextual factors such as socioeconomic status (SES) and poverty, immigration/ethnic minority status, family/parenting and peer factors, and school-related influences (Barragan & others, 2019). The percentage of sexually active young adolescents is higher in low-income areas of inner cities (Morrison-Beedy & others, 2013). One study revealed that neighborhood poverty concentrations predicted 15- to 17-year-old girls' and boys' sexual initiation (Cubbin & others, 2010).

A number of family factors are associated with sexual risk-taking (Ruiz-Casares & others, 2017; Verbeek & others, 2020). In a recent study of adolescents, quality time spent with parents was linked to a lower likelihood of engaging in vaginal sex, anal sex, oral sex, pornography use, and masturbation (Astle, Leonhardt, & Willoughby, 2020). Also, one study revealed that adolescents who in the eighth grade reported greater parental knowledge and more family rules about dating were less likely to initiate sex from the eighth to tenth grade (Ethier & others, 2016). Another study revealed that of a number of parenting practices the factor that best predicted a lower level of risky sexual behavior by adolescents was supportive parenting (Simons & others, 2016). Also, having older sexually active siblings or pregnant/parenting teenage sisters placed adolescent girls at higher risk for pregnancy (Miller, Benson, & Galbraith, 2001). Further, in a recent study of urban, predominantly Latino and African American adolescents, talk with extended family members about sexual protection was linked to adolescents having fewer sexual partners, while talk about sexual risks was associated with adolescents having more sexual partners (Grossman & others, 2019).

Peer, school, sport, and religious contexts provide further information about sexual risk taking in adolescents (Taggart & others, 2019). One study found that adolescents who associated with more deviant peers in early adolescence were likely to have more sexual partners at age 16 (Lansford & others, 2010). Also, a research review found that school connectedness was linked to positive sexuality outcomes (Markham & others, 2010). A study of middle school students revealed that better academic achievement was a protective factor in preventing boys and girls from engaging in early sexual intercourse (Laflin, Wang, & Barry, 2008). Also, one study found that adolescent males who play sports engage in a higher level of sexual risk taking, while adolescent females who play sports engage in a lower level of sexual risk taking (Lipowski & others, 2016). And a recent study of African American adolescent girls indicated that those who reported that religion was of low or moderate importance to them had a much earlier sexual debut that their counterparts who said that religion was very important or extremely important to them (George Dalmida & others, 2018).

Cognitive and personality factors are increasingly implicated in sexual risk taking in adolescence. Weak self-regulation (difficulty controlling one's emotions and behavior) and impulsiveness are two such factors. A longitudinal study found that weak self-regulation at 8 to 9 years of age and risk proneness (tendency to seek sensation and make poor decisions) at 12 to 13 years of age

Psychologists are exploring ways to encourage adolescents to make less risky sexual decisions. Here an adolescent participates in an interactive video session developed by Julie Downs and her colleagues at the Department of Social and Decision Making Sciences at Carnegie Mellon University. The videos help adolescents evaluate their responses and decisions in high-risk sexual contexts.
Michael Ray

Bonnie Halpern-Felsher, University Professor in Pediatrics and Director of Community Efforts to Improve Adolescents' Health

Dr. Halpern-Felsher recently became a professor in the Department of Pediatrics at Stanford University after holding this position for a number of years at the University of California–San Francisco. Her work exemplifies how some professors not only teach and conduct research in a single discipline, like psychology, but do research in multiple disciplines and also work outside their university in the community in an effort to improve the lives of youth. Dr. Halpern-Felsher is a developmental psychologist with additional training in adolescent health. She is especially interested in understanding why adolescents engage in risk-taking and in using this research to develop intervention programs for improving adolescents' lives.

In particular, Dr. Halpern-Felsher has studied adolescent sexual decision-making and reproductive health, including cognitive and socioemotional predictors of sexual behavior. Her research has included influences of parenting and peer relationships on adolescent sexual behavior. Dr. Halpern-Felsher also has served as a consultant for a number of community-based adolescent health promotion campaigns, and she has been involved in community-based efforts to reduce substance abuse in adolescence. For example, recently she worked with the state of California to implement new school-based tobacco prevention educational materials. As a further indication of her strong commitment to improving adolescents' lives, Dr. Halpern-Felsher

Dr. Bonnie Halpern-Felsher (*second from left*) with some of the students she is mentoring in the STEP-UP program.
Courtesy of Dr. Bonnie Halpern-Felsher

coordinates the STEP-UP program (Short-Term Research Experience for Underrepresented Persons) in which she has personally mentored and supervised 22 to 25 middle and high school students every year since 2007.

set the stage for sexual risk taking at 16 to 17 years of age (Crockett, Raffaelli, & Shen, 2006). Also, a recent study confirmed that low self-control is linked to risky sexual behavior in adolescence (Magnusson, Crandall, & Evans, 2019).

To read about an individual who has made a number of contributions to a better understanding of adolescent sexual behavior as well as other areas of adolescent development, especially adolescent health, see the *Connecting with Careers* profile.

Contraceptive Use   Too many sexually active adolescents still do not use contraceptives, use them inconsistently, or use contraceptive methods that are less effective than others (Summit & others, 2019; Turner, 2019). In a recent national survey of U.S. high school students, 53.8 percent reported that either they or their partner had used a contraceptive the last time they had sexual intercourse, compared with 46 percent in 1991 and 53.8 percent in 2011 (Kann & others, 2018). Researchers also have found that U.S. adolescents are less likely to use condoms than their European counterparts (Jorgensen & others, 2015).

Recently, a number of leading medical organizations and experts have recommended that adolescents use long-acting reversible contraception (LARC) (Summit & others, 2019; Turner, 2019). These include the Society for Adolescent Health and Medicine (2017), the American Academy of Pediatrics and American College of Obstetrics and Gynecology (Allen & Barlow, 2017), and the World Health Organization (2020). LARC consists of the use of intrauterine devices (IUDs) and contraceptive implants, which have a much lower failure rate and are more effective in preventing unwanted pregnancy than birth control pills and condoms (Brittain & others, 2020). LARC use is still low in the United States, but its use by adolescents increased from 1.8 percent in 2013 to 5.3 percent in 2017 (Aligne & others, 2020).

Sexually Transmitted Infections   Some forms of contraception, such as birth control pills or implants, do not protect against sexually transmitted infections, or STIs.

> **developmental connection**
> Conditions, Diseases, and Disorders
> What are some good strategies for protecting against HIV and other sexually transmitted infections? Connect to "Physical and Cognitive Development in Early Adulthood."

Sexually transmitted infections (STIs) are contracted primarily through sexual contact, including oral-genital and anal-genital contact. Nearly half of the 20 million new STI infections each year in the United States occur in 15- to 24-year-olds (Kann & others, 2018). Individuals 13 to 24 years of age accounted for 21 percent of new HIV diagnoses in the United States, and 81 percent of these young people were gay or bisexual males (Kann & others, 2018). Yet another very widespread STI is chlamydia. We will consider these and other sexually transmitted infections in more detail in "Physical and Cognitive Development in Early Adulthood."

Adolescent Pregnancy Adolescent pregnancy is another problematic outcome of sexuality in adolescence and requires major efforts to reduce its occurrence (Kudesia & Talib, 2019; Wong & others, 2020). In cross-cultural comparisons, the United States continues to have one of the highest rates of adolescent pregnancy and childbearing in the industrialized world, despite a considerable decline during the 1990s. Although U.S. adolescents are no more sexually active than their counterparts in the Netherlands, for example, their adolescent pregnancy rate is eight times as high as that of adolescents in the Netherlands. In the United States, 82 percent of pregnancies in adolescents 15 to 19 years of age are unintended (Koh, 2014). A cross-cultural comparison found that among 21 countries, the United States had the highest adolescent pregnancy rate among 15- to 19-year-olds and Switzerland the lowest (Sedgh & others, 2015).

Despite the negative comparisons of the United States with many other developed countries, there have been some encouraging trends in U.S. adolescent pregnancy rates. In 2018, the U.S. birth rate among 15- to 19-year-olds was 17.4 births per 1,000 females, the lowest rate ever recorded, which represents a dramatic decrease from the 61.8 births for the same age range in 1991 and even a 9 percent drop since 2014 (Centers for Disease Control and Prevention, 2019) (see Figure 6). There also has been a substantial decrease in adolescent pregnancies across ethnic groups in recent years. Reasons for the decline include school/community health classes, increased use of contraceptives, and fear of sexually transmitted infections such as AIDS.

Adolescent pregnancy creates health risks for both the baby and the mother (Devakumar & others, 2019; Mullick, 2019). Infants born to adolescent mothers are more likely to have low birth weights—a prominent factor in infant mortality—as well as neurological problems and childhood illness (Leftwich & Alves, 2017). One study assessed the reading and math achievement trajectories of children born to adolescent and non-adolescent mothers with different levels of education (Tang & others, 2016). In this study, higher levels of maternal education were linked to higher academic achievement through the eighth grade. Nonetheless, the achievement of children born to adolescent mothers never reached the levels of children born to adult mothers.

What are some of the problems that characterize adolescent mothers? In a recent Canadian study, 18 percent of adolescent mothers lived in low-SES neighborhoods (compared to 11 percent of mothers 20 to 34 years of age), and adolescent mothers had higher rates of depression during pregnancy as well as higher rates of tobacco, marijuana, and alcohol use than adult mothers (Wong & others, 2020). Adolescent mothers also are more likely to be depressed and to drop out of school than their peers are (Siegel & Brandon, 2014; Stoner & others, 2019). Although many adolescent mothers resume their education later in life, they generally never catch up economically with women who postpone childbearing until their twenties. Further, a study of African American urban youth found that at 32 years of age, women who had become mothers as teenagers were more likely than non-teen mothers to be unemployed, live in poverty, depend on welfare, and not have completed college (Assini-Meytin & Green, 2015). In this study, at 32 years of age, men who had become fathers as teenagers were more likely than non-teen fathers to be unemployed.

Most studies of adolescent pregnancy focus on adolescent girls, overlooking the factors associated with being an adolescent father. A recent research review found that problems associated with becoming an adolescent father included

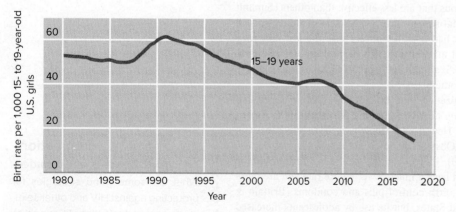

FIGURE 6

BIRTH RATES FOR U.S. 15- TO 19-YEAR-OLD GIRLS FROM 1980 TO 2018.
Source: National Center for Health Statistics (2019, July). *Births in the United States, 2018. NCIS Data Brief No. 346.* Atlanta: Centers for Disease Control and Prevention.

experiencing child maltreatment, serious family disruption, not living with either parent, and Latino ethnicity (Fasula & others, 2019).

A special concern is repeated adolescent pregnancy. In a recent national study, the percentage of teen births that were repeat births decreased from 2004 (21 percent) to 2015 (17 percent) (Dee & others, 2017). In a recent meta-analysis, use of effective contraception, especially LARC, and education-related factors (higher level of education and school continuation) resulted in a lower incidence of repeated teen pregnancy, while depression and a history of abortion were linked to a higher percentage of repeated teen pregnancy (Maravilla & others, 2017).

Researchers have found that adolescent mothers interact less effectively with their infants than do adult mothers (Leftwich & Alves, 2017). One study revealed that adolescent mothers spent more time negatively interacting and less time in play and positive interactions with their infants than did adult mothers (Riva Crugnola & others, 2014). However, an intervention called "My Baby and Me" that involved frequent, intensive home visitation coaching sessions with adolescent mothers across three years resulted in improved maternal behavior and child outcomes (Guttentag & others, 2014).

Although the consequences of America's high rate of adolescent pregnancy are cause for great concern, it often is not pregnancy alone that leads to negative consequences for an adolescent mother and her offspring. Adolescent mothers are more likely to come from low-SES backgrounds (Mollborn, 2017). Many adolescent mothers also were not good students before they became pregnant (Malamitsi-Puchner & Boutsikou, 2006). However, not every adolescent female who bears a child lives a life of poverty and low achievement. Thus, although adolescent pregnancy is a high-risk circumstance and adolescents who do not become pregnant generally fare better than those who do, some adolescent mothers do well in school and have positive outcomes (Schaffer & others, 2012).

Serious, extensive efforts are needed to help pregnant adolescents and young mothers enhance their educational and occupational opportunities (Carroll, 2019; Hyde & DeLamater, 2020). Adolescent mothers also need help obtaining competent child care and planning for the future.

Adolescents can benefit from age-appropriate family-life education (Harding & others, 2020). Family and consumer science educators teach life skills such as effective decision making to adolescents. To read about the work of one family and consumer science educator, see *Connecting with Careers*. And to learn more about ways to reduce adolescent pregnancy, see *Connecting Development to Life*.

What are some consequences of adolescent pregnancy?
Geoff Manasse/Photodisc/Getty Images

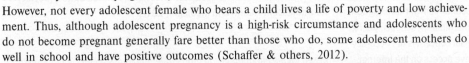

connecting with careers

Lynn Blankinship, Family and Consumer Science Educator

Lynn Blankinship is a family and consumer science educator with an undergraduate degree in this field from the University of Arizona. She has taught for more than 20 years, the last 14 at Tucson High Magnet School.

Blankinship has been honored as the Tucson Federation of Teachers Educator of the Year and the Arizona Teacher of the Year. Blankinship especially enjoys teaching life skills to adolescents. One of her favorite activities is having students care for an automated baby that imitates the needs of real babies. She says that this program has a profound impact on students because the baby must be cared for around the clock for the duration of the assignment. Blankinship also coordinates real-world work experiences and training for students in several child-care facilities in the Tucson area.

Lynn Blankinship (*center*) teaches life skills to students.
Lynn Blankinship

For more information about what family and consumer science educators do, see the Careers in Life-Span Development appendix.

Reducing Adolescent Pregnancy

Girls Inc (2020) has created programs that benefit adolescents at risk for problems. Their program focused on adolescent pregnancy provides girls with skills, motivation, and support to postpone sexual activity and use effective protection. In a recent analysis, girls who participated in the Girls Inc pregnancy prevention program were less likely to become pregnant (5.9 percent) than a matched control group of girls who did not participate in the program (12.3 percent) (Girls Inc, 2020).

In 2010, the U.S. government launched the Teen Pregnancy Prevention (TPP) program under the direction of the newly created Office of Adolescent Health. Currently, a number of studies are being funded by the program in an effort to find ways to reduce the rate of adolescent pregnancy (Office of Adolescent Health, 2020). These diverse programs focus on areas such as improving adolescent self-control, developing a positive relationship with a trusted adult, delaying sexual initiation, and planning for a future that includes positive opportunities and outcomes.

The sources and the accuracy of adolescents' sexual information are linked to adolescent pregnancy. Adolescents can get information about sex from many sources, including parents, siblings, schools, peers, magazines, television, and the Internet. A special concern is the accuracy of sexual information to which adolescents have access on the Internet.

Currently, a major controversy in sex education is whether schools should have an abstinence-only program or a program that emphasizes contraceptive knowledge (Kramer, 2019; Wiley & others, 2020). Recent research reviews have concluded that abstinence-only programs do not delay the initiation of sexual intercourse and do not reduce HIV risk behaviors (Denford & others, 2017; Santelli & others, 2017).

Despite the evidence that favors comprehensive sex education, there recently has been an increase in government funding for abstinence-only programs (Donovan, 2017). Also, in some states (Texas and Mississippi, for example), many students still receive either abstinence-only or no sex education at all (Campbell, 2016; Pollock, 2017).

Recently, there also has been an increased emphasis in abstinence-only-until-marriage (AOUM) policies and programs. However, a major problem with such policies and programs is that a very large majority of individuals engage in sexual intercourse at some point in adolescence or emerging adulthood while the age of marriage continues to go up (27 for females, 29 for males in the United States) (Society for Adolescent Health and Medicine, 2017).

Based on the information you read earlier about risk factors in adolescent sexual behavior, which segments of the adolescent population would benefit most from the types of sex education programs described here?

Review Connect Reflect

 Describe the changes involved in puberty, as well as changes in the brain and sexuality during adolescence.

Review

- What are some key aspects of puberty?
- What changes typically occur in the brain during adolescence?
- What are some important aspects of sexuality in adolescence?

Connect

- How might adolescent brain development be linked to adolescents' decisions to engage in sexual activity or to abstain from it?

Reflect *Your Own Personal Journey of Life*

- Did you experience puberty earlier or later than your peers? How did this timing affect your development?

---

3 Issues in Adolescent Health

 Identify adolescent problems related to health, substance use and abuse, and eating disorders.

| Adolescent Health | Substance Use and Abuse | Eating Disorders |

Many health experts argue that whether adolescents are healthy depends primarily on their own behavior. To improve adolescent health, adults should aim to (1) increase adolescents' *health-enhancing* behaviors, such as eating nutritious foods, exercising, wearing seat belts, and getting adequate sleep; and (2) reduce adolescents' *health-compromising* behaviors, such as drug abuse, violence, unprotected sexual intercourse, and dangerous driving.

ADOLESCENT HEALTH

Adolescence is a critical juncture in the adoption of behaviors that are relevant to health (Graham, Holt/Hale, & Parker 2020; Hales, 2019). Many of the behaviors that are linked to poor health habits and early death in adults begin during adolescence (Insel & Roth, 2020). Conversely, the early formation of healthy behavior patterns, such as regular exercise and a preference for foods low in fat and cholesterol, not only has immediate health benefits but helps in adulthood to delay or prevent disability and mortality from heart disease, stroke, diabetes, and cancer (Donatelle & Ketcham, 2020).

Thirteen/Shutterstock

Nutrition and Exercise Concerns are growing about adolescents' nutrition and exercise habits (Blake, 2020; Schiff, 2021). National data indicated that the percentage of U.S. 12- to 19-year-olds who were overweight increased from 11 percent in the early 1990s to nearly 20.6 percent in 2016 (National Center for Health Statistics, 2017).

A special concern in American culture is the amount of fat we consume. Many of today's adolescents virtually live on fast-food meals, which are high in fat. A comparison of adolescents in 28 countries found that U.S. and British adolescents were more likely to eat fried food and less likely to eat fruits and vegetables than adolescents in most other countries that were studied (World Health Organization, 2000). Also, the National Youth Risk Survey has found that U.S. high school students show a long-term linear decrease in their intake of fruits and vegetables, with 59.2 percent of high school students not eating vegetables one or more times in the last 7 days (Kann & others, 2018).

Being obese in adolescence predicts obesity in emerging adulthood. For example, a longitudinal study of more than 8,000 adolescents found that obese adolescents were more likely to develop severe obesity in emerging adulthood than were overweight or normal-weight adolescents (The & others, 2010). In another longitudinal study, the percentage of overweight individuals increased from 20 percent at 14 years of age to 33 percent at 24 years of age (Patton & others, 2011).

Researchers have found that individuals frequently become less active during adolescence (Chong & others, 2020). A national study of U.S. adolescents revealed that physical activity increased until 13 years of age in boys and girls but then declined through 18 years of age (Kahn & others, 2008). A recent national study also found that adolescent girls were much less likely to have engaged in 60 minutes or more of vigorous exercise per day in 5 of the last 7 days (56.9 percent) than were boys (36.8 percent) (Kann & others, 2018). Ethnic differences in exercise participation rates of U.S. adolescents also occur, and these rates vary by gender. In the national study just mentioned, non-Latino White boys exercised the most, African American girls the least (Kann & others, 2018).

Positive physical outcomes of exercise in adolescence include a lower rate of obesity, reduced triglyceride levels, lower blood pressure, and a lower incidence of type II diabetes (Meeks, Heit, & Page, 2020; Rink, 2020). Also, one study found that adolescents who were high in physical fitness had better connectivity between brain regions than adolescents who were low in physical fitness (Herting & others, 2014).

Exercise in adolescence also is linked to other positive outcomes. For example, higher levels of exercise are related to fewer depressive symptoms in adolescents (Hamer & others, 2020). Also, in other research, young adolescents who exercised regularly had higher academic achievement (Hashim, Freddy, & Rosmatunisah, 2012). And in a recent research review, among a number of cognitive factors, memory was the factor that most often was improved by exercise in adolescence (Li & others, 2017). Further, a recent meta-analysis concluded that supervised exercise, especially aerobic exercise, was linked to a reduction of abdominal fat in adolescents (Gonzalez-Ruis & others, 2017). In addition, a recent study found that a combination of regular exercise and a diet plan resulted in weight loss and enhanced executive function in adolescents (Xie & others, 2017). And an after-school athletics program reduced the obesity risk of adolescents after one year of intervention (Glabska & others, 2019).

Adolescents' exercise is increasingly being found to be associated with parenting and peer relationships (Baker & others, 2020). One study revealed that family meals during adolescence protected against becoming overweight or obese in adulthood (Berge & others, 2015). Another study revealed that female adolescents' physical activity was linked to their male and female friends' physical activity, while male adolescents' physical activity was associated with their female friends' physical activity (Sirard & others, 2013).

What are some characteristics of adolescents' exercise patterns?
Alistair Berg/Getty Images

Researchers have found that screen time is associated with a number of adolescent health problems, including a lower rate of exercise and a higher rate of sedentary behavior (Chong & others, 2020; Lizandra & others, 2019). In one research review, a higher level of screen-based sedentary behavior was associated with being overweight, having sleep problems, being depressed, and having lower levels of physical activity/fitness and psychological well-being (higher stress levels, for example) (Costigan & others, 2013). And a recent study revealed that adolescents who engage in higher levels of screen time are more likely to be overweight or obese (Furthner & others, 2018).

What types of interventions and activities have been successful in reducing overweight in adolescents and emerging adults? Research indicates that dietary changes and regular exercise are key components of weight reduction in adolescence and emerging adulthood (Donatelle & Ketcham, 2020; Graham, Holt-Hale, & Parker, 2020). For example, one study found that a combination of regular exercise and a diet plan resulted in weight loss and enhanced executive function in adolescents (Xie & others, 2017). Also in recent research, a higher level of parental monitoring was linked to adolescents having a healthier diet and lower weight status (Kim & others, 2019). And a recent experimental study of obese adolescent girls found that a 12-week jump rope exercise program was effective in improving their body composition, blood pressure, insulin level, and self-regulation (Kim & others, 2020).

Sleep   Like nutrition and exercise, sleep is an important influence on well-being. Might changing sleep patterns in adolescence contribute to adolescents' health-compromising behaviors? Recently there has been a surge of research interest in adolescent sleep patterns (Kracht & others, 2020; Rojo-Wissar & others, 2020; Yildiz & others, 2020). In a study of 13- to 19-year-olds in Singapore, short sleep duration (less than 7 hours) on school nights was associated with an increased risk of being overweight, having depression symptoms, being less motivated, not being able to concentrate adequately, having a high level of anxiety, and engaging in self-harm/suicidal thoughts (Yeo & others, 2019). Also, a longitudinal study in which adolescents completed a 24-hour diary every 14 days in ninth, tenth, and twelfth grades found that regardless of how much students studied each day, when the students sacrificed sleep time to study more than usual they had difficulty understanding what was taught in class and were more likely to struggle with class assignments the next day (Gillen-O'Neel, Huynh, & Fuligni, 2013). Further,, a recent experimental study indicated that when adolescents' sleep was restricted to five hours nightly for five nights, then returned to ten hours for two nights, their sustained attention was negatively affected (especially in the early morning) and did not return to baseline levels during recovery (Agostini & others, 2017). In addition, researchers have found that adolescents who get less than 7.7 hours of sleep per night on average have more emotional and peer-related problems, higher anxiety, and a higher level of suicidal ideation (Sarchiapone & others, 2014). And a recent study found that adolescents with shorter or poorer-quality sleep in conjunction with less physical activity showed higher levels of internalizing and externalizing problems (Gillis & El-Sheikh, 2019). In another study, the highest level of internalizing and externalizing problems occurred in adolescents from lower-SES homes who had short sleep duration and poor sleep quality (El-Sheikh & others, 2019). Further, a recent study of adolescents indicated that insufficient sleep was associated with alcohol and marijuana use (Kwon & others, 2020).

In a recent national survey of youth, only 25.4 percent of U.S. adolescents got eight or more hours of sleep on an average school night (Kann & others, 2018). In this study, the percentage of adolescents getting this much sleep on an average school night decreased as they got older (see Figure 7). Also, in other research with more than 270,000 U.S. adolescents from 1991 to 2012, adolescents were getting less sleep in recent years than in the past (Keyes & others, 2015).

The National Sleep Foundation (2006) conducted a U.S. survey of adolescent sleep patterns. Those who got inadequate sleep (eight hours or less) on school nights were more likely to feel tired or sleepy, to be cranky and irritable, to fall asleep in school, to be in a depressed mood, and to drink caffeinated beverages than their counterparts who got optimal sleep (nine or more hours). Also, a longitudinal study of more than 6,000 adolescents found that sleep problems were linked to subsequent suicidal thoughts and attempts in adolescence and early adulthood (Wong & Brower, 2012). Further, one study found that adolescents who got less than 7.7 hours of sleep per night on average had more emotional and peer-related problems, higher anxiety, and a higher level of suicidal ideation than their peers who got 7.7 hours of sleep or more (Sarchiapone & others, 2014).

Percentage of students who got 8 hours of sleep or more on an average school night

- 9th: 34.8
- 10th: 26.6
- 11th: 21.4
- 12th: 17.6

Grade

FIGURE 7

DEVELOPMENTAL CHANGES IN U.S. ADOLESCENTS' SLEEP PATTERNS ON AN AVERAGE SCHOOL NIGHT

Why are adolescents getting too little sleep? Among the reasons given are those involving electronic media, caffeine, and changes in the brain coupled with early school start times (Bartel, Scheeren, & Gradisar, 2019; Mireku & others, 2019). Recent research found that frequency of cordless telephone calls, mobile phone dependency, and tablet use were linked to sleep problems in adolescence (Cabre-Riera & others, 2020). Further, in a recent study, spending multiple hours on portable electronic devices was linked to shorter sleep duration in adolescence, while time spent on non-portable electronic devices was not related to sleep duration in adolescence (Twenge, Hisler, & Rizan, 2019).

Caffeine intake by adolescents appears to be related to inadequate sleep (Ruiz & Scherr, 2018). Greater caffeine intake as early as 12 years of age is linked to later sleep onset, shorter sleep duration, and increased daytime sleepiness (Carskadon & Tarokh, 2014). Further, researchers have yet to study the connection between adolescent sleep patterns and high levels of caffeine intake from energy drinks.

Mary Carskadon and her colleagues (2004, 2005, 2011a, b; Crowley & Carskadon, 2010; Tarokh & Carskadon, 2010) have conducted a number of research studies on adolescent sleep patterns. They found that when given the opportunity, adolescents will sleep an average of 9 hours and 25 minutes a night. Most get considerably less than nine hours of sleep, however, especially during the week. This shortfall creates a sleep deficit, which adolescents often attempt to make up on the weekend. The researchers also found that older adolescents tend to be sleepier during the day than younger adolescents. They theorized that this sleepiness was not due to academic work or social pressures. Rather, their research suggests that adolescents' biological clocks undergo a shift as they get older, delaying their period of sleepiness by about one hour. A delay in the nightly release of the sleep-inducing hormone melatonin, which is produced in the brain's pineal gland, seems to underlie this shift. Melatonin is secreted at about 9:30 p.m. in younger adolescents and approximately an hour later in older adolescents.

Carskadon concludes that early school starting times may cause grogginess, inattention in class, and poor performance on tests. Based on her research, school officials in Edina, Minnesota, decided to start classes at 8:30 a.m. rather than the usual 7:25 a.m. Since then there have been fewer referrals for discipline problems, and the number of students who report being ill or depressed has decreased. The school system reports that test scores have improved for high school students but not for middle school students. This finding supports Carskadon's suspicion that early start times are likely to be more stressful for older than for younger adolescents.

One study found that just a 30-minute delay in school start time was linked to improvements in adolescents' sleep, alertness, mood, and health (Owens, Belon, & Moss, 2010). In another study, early school start times were linked to a higher vehicle crash rate in adolescent drivers (Vorona & others, 2014). Further, in a recent study, the Seattle School District delayed the school start time for secondary school students and it resulted in a 34-minute average increase in sleep duration, a 4.5 percent increase in grades, and an improvement in school attendance (Dunster & others, 2018). The American Academy of Pediatrics recommends that schools institute start times between 8:30 and 9:30 a.m. to improve adolescents' academic performance and quality of life (Adolescent Sleep Working Group, AAP, 2014).

Do sleep patterns change in emerging adulthood? Research indicates that they do (Galambos, Howard, & Maggs, 2011). One study revealed that more than 60 percent of college students were categorized as poor-quality sleepers (Lund & others, 2010). In this study, the weekday bedtimes and rise times of first-year college students were approximately 1 hour and 15 minutes later than those of seniors in high school (Lund & others, 2010). However, the first-year college students had later bedtimes and rise times than third- and fourth-year college students, indicating that at about 20 to 22 years of age, a reverse in the timing of bedtimes and rise times occurs. In another study, consistently low sleep duration in college students was associated with less effective attention the next day (Whiting & Murdock, 2016). Also, in a study of college students, a higher level of text messaging (greater number of daily texts, awareness of nighttime cell phone notifications, and compulsion to check nighttime notifications) was linked to a lower level of sleep quality (Murdock, Horissian, & Crichlow-Ball, 2017).

In Mary Carskadon's sleep laboratory at Brown University, an adolescent girl's brain activity is being monitored. Carskadon (2005) says that in the morning, sleep-deprived adolescents' "brains are telling them it's night time . . . and the rest of the world is saying it's time to go to school" (p. 19).
Courtesy of Jim LoScalzo

Other recent research provides further insight into emerging adult sleep problems. A recent study of college students indicated that shorter sleep duration was associated with increased suicide risk (Becker & others, 2018a). In another recent study of college students, 27 percent described their sleep as poor and 36 percent reported getting 7 hours or less of sleep per night (Becker & others, 2018b). And in a recent experimental study, emerging adults (mean age: 21.9 years) who were given a brief sleep quality intervention reported improved sleep, stopped using electronic devices earlier, kept a more regular sleep schedule, and had an earlier weekday rise time than a control group who did not receive the intervention (Hershner & O'Brien, 2018).

Leading Causes of Death in Adolescence   The three leading causes of death in adolescence are unintentional injuries, suicide, and homicide (National Center for Health Statistics, 2020). Almost half of all deaths of individuals from 15 to 24 years of age are due to unintentional injuries, the majority of them involving motor vehicle accidents. Risky driving habits, such as speeding, tailgating, and driving under the influence of alcohol or other drugs, may be more important contributors to these accidents than lack of driving experience (White & others, 2018; Williams & others, 2018). In a recent study, binge drinking among twelfth-graders was linked to driving while impaired (DWI), riding with an impaired driver (RWI), blackouts, and riskier driving habits up to four years later (Vaca & others, 2020).

In about 50 percent of motor vehicle fatalities involving adolescents, the driver has a blood alcohol level of 0.10 percent—twice the level at which a driver is designated as "under the influence" in some states. Of growing concern is the increasingly common practice of mixing alcohol and energy drinks, which is linked to a higher rate of driving while intoxicated (Wilson & others, 2018). A high rate of intoxication is also found in adolescents who die as pedestrians or while using vehicles other than automobiles.

Suicide was the third leading cause of death in adolescence for many years but recently it replaced homicide as the second leading cause (National Center for Health Statistics, 2020). Homicide is especially high among African American male adolescents.

SUBSTANCE USE AND ABUSE

Each year since 1975, the Institute of Social Research at the University of Michigan has monitored the drug use of America's high school seniors in a wide range of public and private high schools. Since 1991, they also have surveyed drug use by eighth- and tenth-graders. In 2018, the study surveyed approximately 44,500 secondary school students in 392 public and private schools (Miech & others, 2019). In the University of Michigan study, overall drug use among U.S. secondary school students declined in the 1980s but began to increase in the early 1990s.

The overall decline in the use of illicit drugs by adolescents in the last several decades is approximately one-third for eighth-graders, one-fourth for tenth-graders, and one-eighth for twelfth-graders (Miech & others, 2019). The most notable declines in drug use by U.S. adolescents in the twenty-first century have occurred for LSD, cocaine, cigarettes, sedatives, tranquilizers, and Ecstasy. Marijuana is the illicit drug most widely used in the United States and Europe (Miech & others, 2019). Even with the recent decline in overall drug use by adolescents, the United States still has one of the highest rates of adolescent drug use of any developed nation. Also, because of the increased legalization of marijuana use for adults in a number of states, youth are likely to have increased access to the drug and it is expected that marijuana use by adolescents will increase in the future.

developmental **connection**

Substance Abuse

Does substance abuse increase or decrease in emerging adulthood? Connect to "Physical and Cognitive Development in Early Adulthood."

Alcohol   How extensive is alcohol use by U.S. adolescents? Sizable declines in adolescent alcohol use have occurred in recent years (Miech & others, 2019). The percentage of U.S. eighth-graders who reported having had any alcohol to drink in the past 30 days fell from a 1996 high of 26 percent to 8.2 percent in 2018. The 30-day prevalence fell among tenth-graders from 39 percent in 2001 to 18.6 percent in 2018 and among high school seniors from 72 percent in 1980 to 30.2 percent in 2018. Binge drinking (defined in the University of Michigan surveys as having five or more drinks in a row in the last two weeks) by high school seniors declined from 41 percent in 1980 to 17.5 percent in 2018. Binge drinking by eighth- and tenth-graders also has dropped significantly in recent years. A consistent gender difference occurs in binge drinking, with males engaging in this behavior more than females do (Miech & others, 2019).

A special concern is adolescents who drive while they are under the influence of alcohol or other substances (Vaca & others, 2020). In the University of Michigan Monitoring the Future Study, 30 percent of high school seniors said they had been in a vehicle with a drugged or drinking driver in the past two weeks (Johnston & others, 2008). And in a national study, one in four twelfth-graders reported that they had consumed alcohol mixed with energy drinks in the last 12 months, and this combination was linked to their unsafe driving (Martz, Patrick, & Schulenberg, 2015).

What are some trends in alcohol use by U.S. adolescents?
Image Source/123RF

Smoking Cigarette smoking (in which the active drug is nicotine) has been one of the most serious yet preventable health problems among adolescents and emerging adults (Sonnenberg, Bostic, & Halpern Felsher, 2020). Cigarette smoking among U.S. adolescents peaked in 1996 and has declined significantly since then (Miech & others, 2019). Following peak use in 1996, smoking rates for U.S. eighth-graders have fallen by 50 percent. In 2018, the percentage of twelfth-graders who reported having smoked cigarettes in the last 30 days was 7.6 percent, an 11 percent decrease from 2011, while the rate for tenth-graders was 4.2 percent and the rate for eighth-graders was 2.2 percent. Since the mid-1990s an increasing percentage of adolescents have reported that they perceive cigarette smoking as dangerous, that they disapprove of it, that they are less accepting of being around smokers, and that they prefer to date nonsmokers (Miech & others, 2019).

E-cigarettes—battery-powered devices with a heating element—produce a vapor that users inhale. In most cases the vapor contains nicotine, but the specific contents of "vape" formulas are not regulated (Fadus, Smith, & Squeglia, 2019). While adolescent cigarette use has decreased significantly in recent years, a substantial number of U.S. adolescents are now vaping nicotine. In the national study just described, in 2017 11.0 percent of twelfth-graders, 8.2 percent of tenth-graders, and 3.5 percent of eighth-graders had vaped nicotine in the last 30 days (Johnston & others, 2018). In 2018 these figures dramatically increased to 20.9 percent of twelfth-graders, 16.1 percent of tenth-graders, and 10.4 percent of eighth-graders vaping nicotine in the last 30 days (Miech & others, 2019). Thus, adolescents currently are vaping nicotine far more than they are smoking cigarettes. Also, in a recent meta-analysis of longitudinal studies, it was concluded that when adolescents use e-cigarettes they are at increased risk for subsequent combustible cigarette smoking (Soneji & others, 2018). Other research also suggests a gateway effect of e-cigarette use not only for future combustible cigarette smoking but marijuana use as well (Fadus, Smith, & Squeglia, 2019).

The Roles of Development, Parents, Peers, and Education

There are serious consequences when adolescents begin to use drugs early in adolescence or even in childhood (Donatelle & Ketcham, 2020; Goode, 2020). For example, a study revealed that the onset of alcohol use before age 11 was linked to a higher risk of alcohol dependence in early adulthood (Guttmannova & others, 2012). Another study found that early onset of drinking and a quick progression to drinking to intoxication were linked to drinking problems in high school (Morean & others, 2014).

Parents play an important role in preventing adolescent drug abuse (Marsiglia & others, 2019; Voce & Anderson, 2020). Positive relationships with parents and others can reduce adolescents' drug use (Eun & others, 2018), and researchers have found that parental monitoring is linked with a lower incidence of drug use by adolescents (Chan & others, 2017). Also, in a recent study, maternal and paternal knowledge of the adolescent's activities and whereabouts at age 13 was linked to lower alcohol use at age 16 for girls and boys (Lindfors & others, 2019). In addition, a recent study of 14- to 15-year-olds revealed that heavy episodic drinking by parents was a risk factor for adolescent drinking, with girls being especially vulnerable to their parents' heavy episodic drinking (Homel & Warren, 2019). And a research review concluded that the more frequently adolescents ate dinner with their families, the less likely they were to have substance abuse problems (Sen, 2010).

What are some of the ways that parents influence whether their adolescents take drugs?
Picturenet/Blend Images LLC

What Can Families Do to Reduce Drinking and Smoking by Young Adolescents?

Experimental studies have been conducted to determine whether family programs can reduce drinking and smoking by young adolescents. In one experimental study, 1,326 families with 12- to 14-year-old adolescents living in various parts of the United States were interviewed (Bauman & others, 2002). After the baseline interviews, participants were randomly assigned either to go through the Family Matters program (experimental group) or not to experience the program (control group) (Bauman & others, 2002).

The families assigned to the Family Matters program received four mailings of booklets. Each mailing was followed by a telephone call from a health educator to "encourage participation by all family members, answer any questions, and record information" (Bauman & others, 2002, pp. 36–37). The first booklet focused on the negative consequences of adolescent substance abuse to the family. The second emphasized "supervision, support, communication skills, attachment, time spent together, educational achievement, conflict reduction, and how well adolescence is understood." The third booklet asked parents to list things they do that might inadvertently encourage their child's use of tobacco or alcohol, identify rules that might influence the child's use, and consider ways to monitor use. Then adult family members and the child met "to agree upon rules and sanctions related to adolescent use." Booklet four dealt with "what the child can do to resist peer and media pressures for use."

Two follow-up interviews with the parents and adolescents were conducted three months and one year after the experimental group had completed the program. Adolescents in the Family Matters program reported lower alcohol and cigarette use at three months and at one year after the program had been completed. Figure 8 shows the results for alcohol.

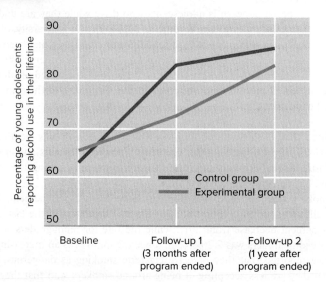

FIGURE 8

YOUNG ADOLESCENTS' REPORTS OF ALCOHOL USE IN THE FAMILY MATTERS PROGRAM. Note that at baseline (before the program started) the young adolescents in the Family Matters program (experimental group) and their counterparts who did not go through the program (control group) reported approximately the same lifetime use of alcohol (slightly higher use by the experimental group). However, three months after the program ended, the experimental group reported lower alcohol use, and this reduction was still present one year after the program had ended, although at a reduced level.

The topics covered in the second booklet underscore the importance of parental influence earlier in development. For instance, staying actively involved and establishing an authoritative, as opposed to a neglectful, parenting style early in children's lives will better ensure that children have a clear understanding of the parents' level of support and expectations when the children reach adolescence.

Along with parents, peers play a very important role in adolescent substance use (D'Amico & others, 2020; Hennenberger, Mushonga, & Preston, 2020). For example, a large-scale national study of adolescents indicated that friends' use of alcohol was a stronger influence on adolescent alcohol use than parental use (Deutsch, Wood, & Slutske, 2017).

Academic success is also a strong buffer for the emergence of drug problems in adolescence (Kendler & others, 2018). In one study, early educational achievement considerably reduced the likelihood that adolescents would develop drug problems (Bachman & others, 2008). But what can families do to educate themselves and their children and reduce adolescent drinking and smoking behavior? To find out, see *Connecting Through Research*.

EATING DISORDERS

Let's now examine two eating problems—anorexia nervosa and bulimia nervosa—that are far more common in adolescent girls than boys.

Anorexia Nervosa   Although most U.S. girls have been on a diet at some point, slightly less than 1 percent ever develop anorexia nervosa. **Anorexia nervosa** is an eating disorder that involves the relentless pursuit of thinness through starvation. It is a serious disorder that can lead to death (Farasat & others, 2020). According to the *DSM-5* psychiatric classification system, individuals have anorexia nervosa when the following factors are present: (1) restricted energy intake leading to significantly low body weight; (2) presence of intense fear of gaining weight or becoming fat or persistent behavior that interferes with gaining weight; and (3) disturbance in how body weight or shape is experienced or not recognizing the seriousness of the current low weight.

Obsessive thinking about weight and compulsive exercise also are linked to anorexia nervosa (Simpson & others, 2013). Even when they are extremely thin, they see themselves as too fat (Phillipou, Castle, & Rossell, 2019). They never think they are thin enough, especially in the abdomen, buttocks, and thighs. They usually weigh themselves frequently, often take their body measurements, and gaze critically at themselves in mirrors.

Anorexia nervosa typically begins in the early to middle adolescent years, often following an episode of dieting and some type of life stress (Fitzpatrick, 2012). It is about 10 times more likely to occur in females than males. When anorexia nervosa does occur in males, the symptoms and other characteristics (such as a distorted body image and family conflict) are usually similar to those reported by females who have the disorder (Ariceli & others, 2005).

Most anorexics are non-Latina White adolescent or young adult females from well-educated middle- and upper-income families and are competitive and high-achieving (Darcy, 2012). They set high standards, become stressed about not being able to reach the standards, and are intensely concerned about how others perceive them (Calugi & Dalle Grave, 2019). Unable to meet these high expectations, they turn to something they can control: their weight. Offspring of mothers with anorexia nervosa are at risk for becoming anorexic themselves (Machado & others, 2014). Problems in family functioning are increasingly being found to be linked to the appearance of anorexia nervosa in adolescent girls (Dimitropoulos & others, 2018), and research indicates that family therapy is often an effective treatment for adolescent and emerging adult girls with anorexia nervosa (Nyman-Carlsson & others, 2020).

Biology and culture are involved in anorexia nervosa (Kwok & others, 2020; Marks, 2019). Genes play an important role in this eating disorder (Ehrlich, King, & Boehm, 2019). Also, the physical effects of dieting may change neural networks and thus sustain the disordered pattern (Ehrlich, King, & Boehm, 2019). The thin fashion-model image in U.S. culture likely contributes to the incidence of anorexia nervosa (Cazzato & others, 2016). The media portray thin as beautiful in their choice of fashion models, whom many adolescent girls strive to emulate. Social media may also fuel the relentless pursuit of thinness by making it easier for anorexic adolescents to find each other online. A recent study found that having an increased number of Facebook friends across two years was linked to enhanced motivation to be thin (Tiggemann & Slater, 2017).

Bulimia Nervosa   Whereas anorexics control their weight by restricting food intake, most bulimics cannot. **Bulimia nervosa** is an eating disorder in which the individual consistently follows a binge-and-purge pattern. According to the DSM-V classification system, an individual with bulimia nervosa is characterized by: (1) eating in a specific amount of time (such as within a 2-hour time frame) an amount of food that is larger than what most people would eat in a similar period in similar circumstances, and (2) sense of a lack of control over eating during an episode (Gorrell & others, 2019). The bulimic goes on an eating binge and then purges by self-inducing vomiting or using a laxative. Although many people binge and purge occasionally and some experiment with it, a person is considered to have a serious bulimic disorder if the episodes occur at least twice a week for three months (Castillo & Weiselberg, 2017).

As with anorexics, most bulimics are preoccupied with food, have a strong fear of becoming overweight, are depressed or anxious, and have a distorted body image (Sattler, Eickmeyer, & Eisenkolb, 2020). One study found that bulimics have difficulty controlling their emotions (Lavender & others, 2014). Also, a recent meta-analysis concluded that anorexics and bulimics engage in maladaptive perfectionism (Dahlenburg, Gleaves, & Hutchinson, 2019). Like individuals who are anorexic, individuals with bulimia are highly perfectionistic (Lampard & others, 2012). Unlike anorexics, individuals who binge and purge typically fall within a normal weight range, which makes bulimia more difficult to detect.

Anorexia nervosa has become an increasing problem for adolescent girls and young adult women. *What are some possible causes of anorexia nervosa?*
PeopleImages/E+/Getty Images

anorexia nervosa An eating disorder that involves the relentless pursuit of thinness through starvation.

bulimia nervosa An eating disorder in which the individual consistently follows a binge-and-purge pattern.

Approximately 1 to 2 percent of U.S. women are estimated to develop bulimia nervosa, and about 90 percent of bulimics are women. Bulimia nervosa typically begins in late adolescence or early adulthood. Many women who develop bulimia nervosa were somewhat overweight before the onset of the disorder, and the binge eating often began during an episode of dieting. As with anorexia nervosa, about 70 percent of individuals who develop bulimia nervosa eventually recover from the disorder (Agras & others, 2004).

In a recent national study, both anorexia nervosa and bulimia nervosa were associated with a higher incidence of major depressive disorder more than any other disorder, followed by alcohol use disorder (Udo & Grilo, 2019). Drug therapy and psychotherapy have been effective in treating anorexia nervosa and bulimia nervosa (Himmerich & Treasure, 2018; Nyman-Carlsson & others, 2020). Cognitive behavioral therapy has especially been helpful in treating bulimia nervosa (Daglish & Waller, 2019; Hay, 2020).

Review *Connect* Reflect

 LG3 Identify adolescent problems related to health, substance use and abuse, and eating disorders.

Review
- What are key concerns about the health of adolescents?
- What are some characteristics of adolescents' substance use and abuse?
- What are the characteristics of the major eating disorders?

Connect
- In *Connecting Through Research,* you learned that attachment was one of the things that the Family Matters program emphasized as important in

reducing drinking and smoking behavior in adolescents. Do the research findings discussed in the chapter entitled "Socioemotional Development in Infancy" support or contradict this emphasis on early attachment's effect on development and behavior later in life?

Reflect *Your Own Personal Journey of Life*
- How health-enhancing and health-compromising were your patterns of behavior in adolescence? Explain.

4 Adolescent Cognition   **LG4** Explain cognitive changes in adolescence.

Piaget's Theory   Adolescent Egocentrism   Information Processing

Adolescents' developing power of thought opens up new cognitive and social horizons. Let's examine some explanations of how their power of thought develops, beginning with Piaget's theory (1952).

PIAGET'S THEORY

Jean Piaget proposed that around 7 years of age children enter the *concrete operational stage* of cognitive development. They can reason logically about concrete events and objects, and they make gains in their ability to classify objects and to reason about the relationships between classes of objects. Around age 11, according to Piaget, the fourth and final stage of cognitive development—the formal operational stage—begins.

The Formal Operational Stage What are the characteristics of the formal operational stage? Formal operational thought is more abstract than concrete operational thought. Adolescents are no longer limited to actual, concrete experiences as anchors for thought. They can conjure up make-believe situations, abstract propositions, and events that are purely hypothetical, and can try to reason logically about them.

The abstract quality of thinking during the formal operational stage is evident in the adolescent's verbal problem-solving ability. Whereas the concrete operational thinker needs to

----

developmental **connection**

Cognitive Theory

Is there a fifth, postformal stage of cognitive development that characterizes young adults? Connect to "Physical and Cognitive Development in Early Adulthood."

----

see the concrete elements A, B, and C to be able to make the logical inference that if A = B and B = C, then A = C, the formal operational thinker can solve this problem merely through verbal presentation.

Another indication of the abstract quality of adolescents' thought is their increased tendency to think about thought itself. One adolescent commented, "I began thinking about why I was thinking what I was. Then I began thinking about why I was thinking about what I was thinking about what I was." If this sounds abstract, it is, and it characterizes the adolescent's enhanced focus on thought and its abstract qualities.

Accompanying the abstract nature of formal operational thought is thought full of idealism and possibilities, especially during the beginning of the formal operational stage, when assimilation dominates. Adolescents engage in extended speculation about ideal characteristics—qualities they desire in themselves and in others. Such thoughts often lead adolescents to compare themselves with others in regard to such ideal standards. And their thoughts are often fantasy flights into future possibilities.

At the same time that adolescents think more abstractly and idealistically, they also think more logically. Children are likely to solve problems through trial and error; adolescents begin to think more as a scientist thinks, devising plans to solve problems and systematically testing solutions. This type of problem solving requires **hypothetical-deductive reasoning,** which involves creating a hypothesis and deducing its implications, steps that provide ways to test the hypothesis. Thus, formal operational thinkers develop hypotheses about ways to solve problems and then systematically deduce the best path to follow to solve the problem.

Might adolescents' ability to reason hypothetically and to evaluate what is ideal versus what is real lead them to engage in demonstrations such as this protest related to improving education? What other causes might be attractive to adolescents' newfound cognitive abilities of hypothetical-deductive reasoning and idealistic thinking?
Jim West/Alamy Stock Photo

Evaluating Piaget's Theory   Researchers have challenged some of Piaget's ideas about the formal operational stage (Reyna, 2019). Among their findings is that there is much more individual variation than Piaget envisioned: Only about one in three young adolescents is a formal operational thinker, and many American adults (and adults in other cultures) never become formal operational thinkers.

Furthermore, education in the logic of science and mathematics promotes the development of formal operational thinking. This point recalls a criticism of Piaget's theory that suggests culture and education exert stronger influences on cognitive development than Piaget maintained (Wagner, 2018).

Piaget's theory of cognitive development has been challenged on other points as well. Children's cognitive development is not as stage-like as Piaget envisioned (Kouklari, Tsermentseli, & Monks, 2019). Because some cognitive abilities have been found to emerge earlier than Piaget thought, and others later, children and adolescents do not appear to move neatly from one stage to another (Nolte & others, 2019). Other evidence casting doubt on the stage notion is that children often show more understanding on one task than on another, similar task.

Despite these challenges to Piaget's ideas, we owe him a tremendous debt (Miller, 2016). Piaget was the founder of the present field of cognitive development, and he developed a long list of masterful concepts of enduring power and fascination: assimilation, accommodation, object permanence, egocentrism, conservation, and others. Psychologists also owe him the current vision of children as active, constructive thinkers. And they are indebted to him for creating a theory that has generated a huge volume of research on children's cognitive development (Miller, 2016).

Piaget also was a genius when it came to observing children. His careful observations demonstrated inventive ways to discover how children act on and adapt to their world. He showed us how children need to make their experiences fit their schemes yet simultaneously adapt their schemes to accommodate their experiences. And Piaget revealed how cognitive change is likely to occur if the context is structured to allow gradual movement to the next higher level.

Many adolescent girls spend long hours in front of the mirror, depleting cans of hairspray, tubes of lipstick, and jars of cosmetics. *How might this behavior be related to changes in adolescent cognitive and physical development?*
Image Source/Getty Images

hypothetical-deductive reasoning Piaget's formal operational concept that adolescents have the cognitive ability to develop hypotheses, or best guesses, about ways to solve problems.

adolescent egocentrism The heightened self-consciousness of adolescents.

imaginary audience Adolescents' belief that others are as interested in them as they themselves are, as well as attention-getting behavior motivated by a desire to be noticed, visible, and "on stage."

ADOLESCENT EGOCENTRISM

Adolescent egocentrism is the heightened self-consciousness of adolescents. David Elkind (1976) points out that adolescent egocentrism has two key components—the imaginary audience and personal fable. The **imaginary audience** is reflected in adolescents' belief that others are as interested in them as they themselves are, as well as attention-getting behavior—attempts

Might frequent use of social media increase adolescents' egocentrism?
Andrey_Popov/Shutterstock

┌ ─ ─ ─ ─ ─ ─ ─ ─ ─ ─ ▸ ┐

developmental connection

Cognitive Theory

Piaget described a form of egocentrism that characterizes young children. Connect to "Physical and Cognitive Development in Early Childhood."

└ ◂ ─ ─ ─ ─ ─ ─ ─ ─ ─ ─ ┘

┌ ─ ─ ─ ─ ─ ─ ─ ─ ─ ─ ▸ ┐

developmental connection

The Brain

The prefrontal cortex is the location in the brain where much of executive function occurs. Connect to "Physical and Cognitive Development in Early Childhood."

└ ◂ ─ ─ ─ ─ ─ ─ ─ ─ ─ ─ ┘

personal fable The part of adolescent egocentrism that involves an adolescent's sense of uniqueness and invincibility (or invulnerability).

to be noticed, visible, and "on stage." For example, an eighth-grade boy might walk into a classroom and think that all eyes are riveted on his spotty complexion. Adolescents sense that they are "on stage" in early adolescence, believing they are the main actors and all others are the audience.

According to Elkind, the **personal fable** is the part of adolescent egocentrism involving a sense of uniqueness and invincibility (or invulnerability). For example, 13-year-old Adrienne says this about herself: "No one understands me, particularly my parents. They have no idea of what I am feeling." Adolescents' sense of personal uniqueness makes them believe that no one can understand how they really feel. As part of their effort to retain a sense of personal uniqueness, adolescents might craft a story about the self that is filled with fantasy, immersing themselves in a world that is far removed from reality. Personal fables frequently show up in adolescent diaries.

Adolescents often have been portrayed as having a sense of invincibility or invulnerability. For example, during a conversation with a girl who is the same age, 14-year-old Margaret says, "Are you kidding? I won't get pregnant." This sense of invincibility may lead adolescents to believe that they themselves are invulnerable to dangers and catastrophes (such as deadly car wrecks) that happen to other people. As a result, some adolescents engage in risky behaviors such as drag racing, drug use, suicide attempts, and having sexual intercourse without using contraceptives or barriers against STIs (Alberts, Elkind, & Ginsberg, 2007).

Might social media be an amplification tool for adolescent egocentrism? Earlier generations of adolescents did not have social media to connect with large numbers of people; instead, they connected with fewer people, either in person or via telephone. Might today's teens be drawn to social media and its virtually unlimited friend base to express their imaginary audience and sense of uniqueness? One analysis concluded that amassing a large number of friends (audience) may help to validate adolescents' perception that their life is on stage and everyone is watching them (Psychster Inc, 2010). A recent meta-analysis concluded that a greater use of social networking sites was linked to a higher level of narcissism (Gnambs & Appel, 2018).

What about having a sense of invulnerability—is that aspect of adolescent egocentrism as accurate as Elkind argues? An increasing number of research studies suggest that rather than perceiving themselves to be invulnerable, adolescents tend to portray themselves as vulnerable to experiencing a premature death (Reyna & Rivers, 2008). For example, in one study, 12- to 18-year-olds were asked about their chances of dying in the next year and prior to age 20 (Fischhoff & others, 2010). The adolescents greatly overestimated their chances of dying prematurely.

INFORMATION PROCESSING

Deanna Kuhn (2009) identified some important characteristics of adolescents' information processing and thinking. In her view, in the later years of childhood and continuing in adolescence, individuals approach cognitive levels that may or may not be achieved, in contrast to the largely universal cognitive levels that young children attain. By adolescence, considerable variation in cognitive functioning is present across individuals. This variability supports the argument that adolescents are producers of their own development to a greater extent than are children.

Kuhn (2009) further argues that the most important cognitive change in adolescence is improvement in *executive function*—an umbrella-like concept that consists of a number of higher-level cognitive processes linked to the development of the prefrontal cortex. Executive function involves managing one's thoughts to engage in goal-directed behavior and to exercise self-control. Our further coverage of executive function in adolescence focuses on cognitive control, decision making, and critical thinking.

Two categories of executive function are *cool executive function*, psychological processes involving conscious control driven by logical thinking and critical analysis; and *hot executive function*, psychological processes driven by emotion, with emotion regulation an especially important process (Kouklari, Tsermentseli, & Monks, 2019; Semenov & Zelazo, 2018). In a recent study of 12- to 17-year-olds, cool executive function increased with age, while hot executive function peaked at 14 to 15 years of age and then declined (Poon, 2018).

Cognitive Control A very important aspect of executive function in adolescence is cognitive control. Indeed, for most purposes, executive function and cognitive control can be thought of as synonyms. **Cognitive control** involves exercising effective control in a number of areas, including focusing attention, reducing interfering thoughts, and being cognitively flexible (Stewart & others, 2017). Cognitive control increases in adolescence and emerging adulthood (Calabro & others, 2020; Chevalier, Dauvier, & Blaye, 2018). Think about all the times adolescents need to engage in cognitive control, such as the following situations (Galinsky, 2010):

What are some different aspects of cognitive control that can benefit adolescents' development?
PeopleImages/Getty Images

- making a real effort to stick with a task, avoiding interfering thoughts or environmental events, and instead doing what is most effective;
- stopping and thinking before acting to avoid blurting out something that a minute or two later they wished they hadn't said;
- continuing to work on something that is important but boring when there is something a lot more fun to do, inhibiting their behavior and doing the boring but important task, saying to themselves, "I have to show the self-discipline to finish this."

Control Attention and Reduce Interfering Thoughts Controlling attention is a key aspect of learning and thinking in adolescence and emerging adulthood (Brooker & others, 2020). Distractions that can interfere with attention in adolescence and emerging adulthood come from the external environment (other students talking while the student is trying to listen to a lecture, or the student turning on a laptop or tablet PC during a lecture and looking at a new friend request on Facebook, for example) or intrusive distractions from competing thoughts in the individual's mind. Self-oriented thoughts, such as worrying, self-doubt, and intense emotionally laden thoughts may especially interfere with focusing attention on thinking tasks (Gillig & Sanders, 2011). In a recent study of eighth-graders with high test anxiety, an attention training intervention was effective in reducing their test anxiety, especially in regard to reduction in worrying (Fergus & Limbers, 2019).

Be Cognitively Flexible *Cognitive flexibility* involves being aware that options and alternatives are available and then adapting to the situation. Before adolescents and emerging adults adapt their behavior in a situation, they must be aware that they need to change their way of thinking and be motivated to do so (Calabro & others, 2020; Gopnik & others, 2017). Having confidence in their ability to adapt their thinking to a particular situation, an aspect of *self-efficacy,* also is important in being cognitively flexible (Bandura, 2012). In a recent study, young adolescents showed greater understanding of metaphors than children, and this understanding was linked to increased cognitive flexibility in the young adolescents (Willinger & others, 2019).

Decision Making Adolescence is a time of increased decision making—which friends to choose; which person to date; whether to have sex, buy a car, go to college, and so on (Reyna, 2018). How competent are adolescents at making decisions? Older adolescents are described as more competent than younger adolescents, who in turn are more competent than children (Keating, 1990). Compared with children, young adolescents are more likely to generate different options, examine a situation from a variety of perspectives, anticipate the consequences of decisions, and consider the credibility of sources.

Most people make better decisions when they are calm than when they are emotionally aroused. That may especially be true for adolescents, who have a tendency to be emotionally intense (Cohen & Casey, 2017). The same adolescent who makes a wise decision when calm may make an unwise decision when emotionally aroused. In the heat of the moment, emotions may overwhelm decision-making ability (Goddings & Mills, 2017).

The social context plays a key role in adolescent decision making (Sherman, Steinberg, & Chein, 2018). For example, adolescents' willingness to make risky decisions is more likely to occur in contexts where substances and other temptations are readily available (Helm & Reyna, 2018; Reyna, 2019; Reyna & Rivers, 2008). Research reveals that the presence of peers in risk-taking situations increases the likelihood that adolescents will make risky decisions (Silva & others, 2017; Steinberg, 2015a, b). In one study, adolescents took greater

cognitive control Exercising effective control in a number of areas, including focusing attention, reducing interfering thoughts, and being cognitively flexible.

How do emotions and social contexts influence adolescents' decision making?
Jodi Jacobson/E+/Getty Images

fuzzy-trace theory dual-process model
States that decision making is influenced by two systems—"verbatim" analytical (literal and precise) and gist-based intuition (simple bottom-line meaning)—which operate in parallel; in this model, gist-based intuition benefits adolescent decision making more than analytical thinking does.

risks and showed stronger preference for immediate rewards when they were with three same-aged peers than when they were alone (Silva, Chein, & Steinberg, 2016).

To better understand adolescent decision making, Valerie Reyna and her colleagues (Reyna, 2018; Reyna & others, 2017) have proposed the **fuzzy-trace theory dual-process model,** which states that decision making is influenced by two cognitive systems—"verbatim" analytical (literal and precise) and gist-based intuitional (simple bottom-line meaning)—which operate in parallel. Basing judgments and decisions on simple gist is viewed as more beneficial than analytical thinking to adolescents' decision making. In this view, adolescents don't benefit from engaging in reflective, detailed, higher-level cognitive analysis about a decision, especially in high-risk, real-world contexts where they would get bogged down in trivial detail. In such contexts, adolescents need to rely on their awareness that some circumstances are simply so dangerous that they must be avoided at all costs.

In risky situations it is important for an adolescent to quickly get the *gist,* or meaning, of what is happening and glean that the situation is a dangerous context, which can cue personal values that will protect the adolescent from making a risky decision (Reyna, 2018; Reyna & others, 2015). An experiment showed that encouraging gist-based thinking about risks (along with factual information) reduced self-reported risk taking up to one year after exposure to the curriculum (Reyna & Mills, 2014). However, some experts on adolescent cognition argue that in many cases adolescents benefit from both analytical and experiential systems (Kuhn, 2009).

Adolescents need more opportunities to practice and discuss realistic decision making. Many real-world decisions on matters such as sex, drugs, and daredevil driving occur in an atmosphere of stress that includes time constraints and emotional involvement. One strategy for improving adolescent decision making is to provide more opportunities for them to engage in role playing and peer group problem solving.

Critical Thinking   Adolescence is an important transitional period in the development of critical thinking (Keating, 1990). In one study of fifth-, eighth-, and eleventh-graders, critical thinking increased with age but still occurred in only 43 percent of even the eleventh-graders, and many adolescents showed self-serving biases in their reasoning.

If fundamental skills (such as literacy and math skills) are not developed during childhood, critical-thinking skills are unlikely to mature in adolescence. For the subset of adolescents who lack such fundamental skills, potential gains in adolescent thinking are unlikely. For other adolescents, however, cognitive changes that allow improved critical thinking in adolescence include the following: (1) increased speed, automaticity, and capacity of information processing, which free cognitive resources for other purposes; (2) more breadth of content knowledge in a variety of domains; (3) increased ability to construct new combinations of knowledge; and (4) a greater range and more spontaneous use of strategies or procedures for applying or obtaining knowledge, such as planning, considering alternatives, and cognitive monitoring.

Review Connect Reflect

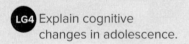

LG4 Explain cognitive changes in adolescence.

Review
- What is Piaget's theory of adolescent cognitive development?
- What is adolescent egocentrism?
- What are some important aspects of information processing in adolescence?

Connect
- Egocentrism was also mentioned earlier in the context of early childhood cognitive development. How is adolescent egocentrism

similar to or different from egocentrism in early childhood?

Reflect *Your Own Personal Journey of Life*
- Evaluate the level of your thinking as you made the transition to adolescence and through adolescence. Does Piaget's stage of formal operational thinking accurately describe the changes that occurred in your thinking? Explain.

The Transition to Middle or Junior High School | Effective Schools for Young Adolescents | High School | Extracurricular Activities | Service Learning

What is the transition from elementary to middle or junior high school like? What are the characteristics of effective schools for adolescents? How can adolescents benefit from service learning?

THE TRANSITION TO MIDDLE OR JUNIOR HIGH SCHOOL

The first year of middle school or junior high school can be difficult for many students (Bialecka-Pikul & others, 2019; Crosnoe & Ressler, 2019). For example, in one study of the transition from sixth grade in an elementary school to seventh grade in a junior high school, adolescents' perceptions of the quality of their school life plunged in the seventh grade (Hirsch & Rapkin, 1987). Compared with their earlier feelings as sixth-graders, the seventh-graders were less satisfied with school, were less committed to school, and liked their teachers less. The drop in school satisfaction occurred regardless of how academically successful the students were. The transition to middle or junior high school is less stressful when students have positive relationships with friends and go through the transition in team-oriented schools where 20 to 30 students take the same classes together (Hawkins & Berndt, 1985).

The transition to middle or junior high school takes place at a time when many changes—in the individual, in the family, and in school—are occurring simultaneously (Wigfield, Rosenzweig, & Eccles, 2017). These changes include puberty and related concerns about body image; the emergence of at least some aspects of formal operational thought and changes in social cognition; increased responsibility and decreased dependency on parents; change to a larger, more impersonal school structure; change from one teacher to many teachers and from a small, homogeneous set of peers to a larger, more heterogeneous set of peers; and an increased focus on achievement and performance. Moreover, when students make the transition to middle or junior high school, they experience the **top-dog phenomenon,** moving from being the oldest, biggest, and most powerful students in elementary school to being the youngest, smallest, and least powerful students in middle or junior high school. A recent Spanish study discovered that middle school students had a lower level of self-concept in a number of areas (academic, social, family, and physical) than elementary school students (Onetti, Fernandez-Garcia, & Castillo-Rodriguez, 2019). Further, a recent study found that teacher warmth was higher in the last four years of elementary school and then dropped in the middle school years (Hughes & Cao, 2018). The drop in teacher warmth was associated with lower student math scores.

The transition to middle or junior high school also can have positive aspects. Students are more likely to feel grown up, have more subjects from which to select, have more opportunities to spend time with peers and locate compatible friends, and enjoy increased independence from direct parental monitoring. They also may be more challenged intellectually by academic work.

The transition from elementary to middle or junior high school occurs at the same time as a number of other developmental changes. *What are some of these other developmental changes?*
Creatas Images/Punchstock/Getty Images

EFFECTIVE SCHOOLS FOR YOUNG ADOLESCENTS

Critics argue that middle and junior high schools should offer activities that reflect a wide range of individual differences in biological and psychological development among young adolescents. In 1989 the Carnegie Corporation issued an extremely negative evaluation of U.S. middle schools. It concluded that most young adolescents attended massive, impersonal schools; were taught from irrelevant curricula; trusted few adults in school; and lacked access to health care and counseling. It recommended that the nation develop smaller "communities" or "houses" to lessen the impersonal nature of large middle schools, have lower student-to-counselor ratios (10 to 1 instead of several hundred to 1), involve parents and community leaders in schools, develop new curricula, have teachers team teach in more flexibly designed curriculum blocks that integrate several disciplines, boost students' health and fitness with more in-school programs, and help students who need public health care to get it. Thirty years

top-dog phenomenon The circumstance of moving from the top position in elementary school to the lowest position in middle or junior high school.

Katherine McMillan Culp, Research Scientist at an Educational Center

Katherine McMillan Culp wanted mainly to live in New York City when she graduated from college and became a receptionist at a center that focused on children and technology. More than 20 years later she is leading research projects at the center (Center for Children and Technology). Not long after starting her receptionist job, she combined work at the center with graduate school at Columbia University. Culp became especially interested in how content and instruction can best be created to link with the developmental level of children and adolescents.

Today Culp holds the position of principal research scientist at Education Development Center, directing a number of projects. One of her main current interests is middle school students' science learning. In this area, she consults with game designers, teachers, and policy makers to help them understand how adolescents think and learn.

Her advice to anyone wanting to do this type of work outside of academia is to get the best education and training possible, then become connected with schools, work with teachers, and obtain experience related to practical problems involved with schools and learning (Culp, 2012).

later, experts are still finding that middle schools throughout the nation need a major redesign if they are to be effective in educating adolescents (Roeser, 2016; Wigfield & others, 2017).

To read about one individual whose main career focus is improving middle school students' learning and education, see *Connecting with Careers.*

HIGH SCHOOL

Just as there are concerns about U.S. middle school education, so are there concerns about U.S. high school education. A recent analysis indicated that only 25 percent of U.S. high school graduates have the academic skills required to succeed in college (Bill & Melinda Gates Foundation, 2017). Not only are many high school graduates poorly prepared for college, they also are poorly prepared for the demands of the modern, high-performance workplace (Bill & Melinda Gates Foundation, 2020).

Critics stress that in many high schools expectations for success and standards for learning are too low. Critics also argue that too often high schools foster passivity and that schools should create a variety of pathways for students to achieve an identity. Many students graduate from high school with inadequate reading, writing, and math skills—including many who go on to college and must enroll in remediation classes there. Other students drop out of high school and do not have skills that will allow them to obtain decent jobs, much less to be informed citizens.

The transition to high school can have problems just as the transition to middle school does. For example, high schools are often even larger, more bureaucratic, and more impersonal than middle schools are; there isn't much opportunity for students and teachers to get to know each other, which can lead to distrust; and teachers rarely make content relevant to students' interests (Eccles & Roeser, 2016). Such experiences likely undermine the motivation of students. In a recent study, increased teacher-student conflict during the transitions from elementary to middle school and from middle school to high school were linked to an increase in externalizing symptoms (fighting with others, for example) in the first year at the new school (Longobardi & others, 2019).

Robert Crosnoe's (2011) book, *Fitting In, Standing Out,* highlighted another major problem with U.S. high schools: how the negative social aspects of adolescents' lives undermine their academic achievement. In his view, adolescents become immersed in complex peer group cultures that demand conformity. High school is supposed to be about getting an education, but for many youth it is about navigating the social worlds of peer relations that may or may not value education and academic achievement. Adolescents who fail to fit in, especially those who are obese or gay, become stigmatized. Crosnoe recommends increased school counseling services, expanded extracurricular activities, and improved parental monitoring to reduce such problems (Crosnoe & Benner, 2015; Crosnoe & Ressler, 2019).

Dropout Rates Yet another concern about U.S. high schools involves students dropping out of school. In the last half of the twentieth century and the first decade of the twenty-first century, U.S. high school dropout rates declined (National Center for Education Statistics,

2019). In the 1940s, more than half of U.S. 16- to 24-year-olds had dropped out of school; by 2015, this figure had decreased to 5.9 percent. The dropout rate of Latino adolescents remains high, although it has been decreasing considerably in the twenty-first century (from 27.8 percent in 2000 to 8.6 percent in 2016). The lowest dropout rate in 2015 was for Asian American adolescents (1 percent), followed by non-Latino White adolescents (5.2 percent), African American adolescents 6.2 percent), and Latino adolescents (8.6 percent) (National Center for Education Statistics, 2019).

National data on Native American adolescents are inadequate because statistics have been collected sporadically and/or from small samples. However, there are indications that Native American adolescents have the highest school dropout rate (National Center for Education Statistics, 2019).

Gender differences have characterized U.S. dropout rates for many decades, but they have been narrowing in recent years. In 2015, the dropout rate for males was 7.1 percent and for females it was 5.1 percent (National Center for Education Statistics, 2019).

The average U.S. high school dropout rates just described mask some very high dropout rates in low-income areas of inner cities. For example, in cities such as Detroit, Cleveland, and Chicago, dropout rates are higher than 50 percent. Also, the percentages cited earlier are for 16- to 24-year-olds. When dropout rates are calculated in terms of students who do not graduate from high school within four years, the percentage of students who drop out is also much higher. Thus, in considering high school dropout rates, it is important to examine age, the number of years it takes to complete high school, and various contexts including ethnicity, gender, and school location.

Students drop out of school for many reasons (Bill and Melinda Gates Foundation, 2020). In one study, almost 50 percent of the dropouts cited school-related reasons for leaving school, such as not liking school or being expelled or suspended (Rumberger, 1983). Twenty percent of the dropouts (but 40 percent of the Latino students) cited economic reasons for leaving school. One-third of the female students dropped out for personal reasons such as pregnancy or marriage.

According to a research review, the most effective programs to discourage dropping out of high school provide early intervention for reading problems, tutoring, counseling, and mentoring (Lehr & others, 2003). Clearly, then, early detection of children's school-related difficulties and getting children engaged with school in positive ways are important strategies for reducing the dropout rate (Crosnoe, Bonazzo, & Wu, 2015).

One program that has been very effective in reducing school dropout rates is "I Have a Dream" (IHAD), an innovative, comprehensive, long-term dropout prevention program administered by the National "I Have a Dream" Foundation in New York ("I Have a Dream" Foundation, 2020). It has grown to encompass more than 200 projects in 64 cities and 28 states plus Washington, DC, and New Zealand, serving more than 18,000 children ("I Have a Dream" Foundation, 2020). Local IHAD projects around the country "adopt" entire grades (usually the third or fourth) from public elementary schools, or corresponding age cohorts from public housing developments. These children—"Dreamers"—are then provided with a program of academic, social, cultural, and recreational activities throughout their elementary, middle school, and high school years. Evaluations of IHAD programs have found improvements in grades, test scores, school attendance, college attendance, and graduating from college, as well as a reduction in behavioral problems among Dreamers ("I Have a Dream" Foundation, 2015, 2019). For example, most Dreamers are the first in their family to go to college and Dreamers are three times more likely to earn a college degree than their low-income peers ("I Have a Dream" Foundation, 2019).

EXTRACURRICULAR ACTIVITIES

Adolescents in U.S. schools usually can choose from a wide array of extracurricular activities in addition to their academic courses. These adult-sanctioned activities typically occur during the after-school hours and can be sponsored either by the school or by the community. They include such diverse activities as sports, academic clubs, band, drama, and math clubs. Researchers have

An important educational goal is to increase the high school graduation rate of Native youth. An excellent strategy to accomplish this goal is high quality early childhood educational programs such as this one at St. Bonaventure Indian School on the Navajo Nation in Thoreau, New Mexico.
Jim West/Alamy Stock Photo

These adolescents are participating in the "I Have a Dream" (IHAD) Program, a comprehensive, long-term dropout prevention program that has been very successful. *What are some other strategies for reducing high school dropout rates?*
Courtesy of "I Have a Dream" Foundation of Boulder County (www.ihadboulder.org)

found that participation in extracurricular activities is linked to higher grades, greater school engagement, less likelihood of dropping out of school, improved probability of going to college, higher self-esteem, and lower rates of depression, delinquency, and substance abuse (Denault & Guay, 2017; Oberle & others, 2019). One study revealed that immigrant adolescents who participated in extracurricular activities improved their academic achievement and increased their school engagement (Camacho & Fuligni, 2015). Adolescents gain more benefit from a breadth of extracurricular activities than from focusing on a single extracurricular activity. In a longitudinal study, both breadth and intensity of extracurricular activity involvement in the tenth grade were associated with higher educational attainment (Haghighat & Knifsend, 2019).

Of course, the quality of the extracurricular activities matters (Simpkins, Fredricks, & Eccles, 2015). High-quality extracurricular activities that are likely to promote positive adolescent development provide competent, supportive adult mentors; opportunities for increasing school connectedness; challenging and meaningful activities; and opportunities for improving skills.

SERVICE LEARNING

Service learning is a form of education that promotes social responsibility and service to the community. In service learning, adolescents engage in activities such as tutoring, helping older adults, working in a hospital, assisting at a child-care center, or cleaning up a vacant lot to make a play area. An important goal of service learning is that adolescents become less self-centered and more strongly motivated to help others (Hart, 2020; Hart & others, 2017). Service learning is often more effective when two conditions are met (Nucci, 2006): (1) giving students some degree of choice in the service activities in which they participate, and (2) providing students opportunities to reflect about their participation.

Researchers have found that service learning benefits adolescents in a number of ways (Hart, 2020; Santiago-Ortiz, 2019). Improvements in adolescent development related to service learning include higher grades in school, increased goal setting, higher self-esteem, and a greater sense of being able to make a difference for others (Hart, Goel, & Atkins, 2017; Jagla & Tice, 2019). Also, one study found that adolescents' volunteer activities provided opportunities to explore and reason about moral issues (van Goethem & others, 2012).

What are some of the positive effects of service learning?
Ariel Skelley/Blend Images LLC

service learning A form of education that promotes social responsibility and service to the community.

Review Connect Reflect

 LG5 Summarize some key aspects of how schools influence adolescent development.

Review
- What is the transition to middle or junior high school like?
- What are some characteristics of effective schools for young adolescents?
- What are some important things to know about high school dropouts and improving high schools?
- How does participation in extracurricular activities influence adolescent development?
- What is service learning, and how does it affect adolescent development?

Connect
- Compare the optimal school learning environments for adolescents described in this chapter with those described for younger children in previous chapters. Aside from age-appropriate curricula, what else is similar or different?

Reflect *Your Own Personal Journey of Life*
- What was your middle or junior high school like? How did it measure up to the Carnegie Corporation's recommendations?

---

topical connections *looking forward*

From 18 to 25 years of age, individuals make a transition from adolescence to adulthood. This transitional period, called emerging adulthood, is characterized by identity exploration, instability, and awareness of possibilities. Individuals often reach the peak of their physical skills between 19 and 26 years of age, followed by declining physical development during the early thirties. Cognitive development becomes more pragmatic and realistic, as well as more reflective and relativistic. Work becomes a more central aspect of individuals' lives.

reach your **learning goals**

Physical and Cognitive Development in Adolescence

1 The Nature of Adolescence

 Discuss the nature of adolescence.

- Many stereotypes of adolescents are too negative. Most adolescents today successfully negotiate the path from childhood to adulthood. However, too many of today's adolescents are not provided with adequate opportunities and support to become competent adults. It is important to view adolescents as a heterogeneous group because different portraits of adolescents emerge, depending on the particular set of adolescents being described.

- Social policy regarding adolescents too often has focused on health-compromising behaviors and not enough on strength-based approaches. Adolescents need more caring adults in their lives.

2 Physical Changes

 Describe the changes involved in puberty, as well as changes in the brain and sexuality during adolescence.

Puberty

- Puberty is a period of rapid physical maturation involving hormonal and bodily changes that occur primarily during early adolescence. Determinants of pubertal timing include nutrition, health, and heredity. The pubertal growth spurt begins at an average age of 9 years for girls and 11 for boys, reaching a peak at 11½ for girls and 13½ for boys. Individual variation in pubertal changes is substantial.

- Adolescents show considerable interest in their body image, with girls having more negative body images than boys do. For boys, early maturation brings benefits, at least during early adolescence. Early-maturing girls are vulnerable to a number of risks.

The Brain

- Changes in the brain during adolescence involve the thickening of the corpus callosum and a gap in maturation between the limbic system and the prefrontal cortex, which functions in reasoning and self-regulation.

Adolescent Sexuality

- Adolescence is a time of sexual exploration and sexual experimentation. Having sexual intercourse in early adolescence is associated with negative developmental outcomes.

- Contraceptive use by adolescents is increasing. About one in four sexually experienced adolescents acquires a sexually transmitted infection (STI). The adolescent pregnancy rate is higher in the United States than in other industrialized nations, but the U.S. rate of adolescent pregnancy has been decreasing in recent years.

3 Issues in Adolescent Health

 Identify adolescent problems related to health, substance use and abuse, and eating disorders.

Adolescent Health

- Adolescence is a critical juncture in health because many of the factors related to poor health habits and early death in the adult years begin during adolescence. Poor nutrition, lack of exercise, and inadequate sleep are concerns. The three leading causes of death in adolescence are unintentional injuries, homicide, and suicide.

Substance Use and Abuse

- Despite recent declines, the United States has one of the highest rates of adolescent illicit drug use of any industrialized nation. Alcohol abuse is a major adolescent problem, although its rate has been dropping in recent years, as has the rate of cigarette smoking. Parents, peers, social support, and educational success play important roles in determining whether adolescents take drugs.

Eating Disorders

- Eating disorders have increased in adolescence, along with the percentage of adolescents who are overweight. Two eating disorders that may emerge in adolescence are anorexia nervosa and bulimia nervosa. Anorexia nervosa typically starts in the early to middle adolescent years following a dieting episode and involves the relentless pursuit of thinness through starvation. Bulimia nervosa involves a binge-and-purge pattern, and bulimics (unlike anorexics) typically fall within a normal weight range.

4 Adolescent Cognition

 LG4 Explain cognitive changes in adolescence.

Piaget's Theory

- During the formal operational stage, Piaget's fourth stage of cognitive development, thinking becomes more abstract, idealistic, and logical than during the concrete operational stage. However, many adolescents are not formal operational thinkers but are consolidating their concrete operational thought.

Adolescent Egocentrism

- Elkind describes adolescent egocentrism as the heightened self-consciousness of adolescents that consists of two parts: the imaginary audience and the personal fable. Recent research questions whether adolescents perceive themselves to be invulnerable.

Information Processing

- Adolescence is characterized by a number of advances in executive function. Cognitive control involves effective control and flexible thinking in a number of areas, including controlling attention, reducing interfering thoughts, remaining cognitively flexible, making decisions, and thinking critically.

5 Schools

 LG5 Summarize some key aspects of how schools influence adolescent development.

The Transition to Middle or Junior High School

- The transition to middle or junior high school coincides with many social, familial, and individual changes in the adolescent's life, and this transition is often stressful. One source of stress is the move from the top-dog position to the lowest position in school.

Effective Schools for Young Adolescents

- Some critics argue that a major redesign of U.S. middle schools is needed. Critics say that U.S. high schools foster passivity and do not develop students' academic skills adequately. Characteristics of effective schools include lower student-to-counselor ratios, involvement of parents and community leaders in schools, team teaching, and efforts to boost students' health and fitness.

High School

- A number of strategies have been proposed for improving U.S. high schools, including raising expectations and providing better support. The overall high school dropout rate declined considerably in the last half of the twentieth century, but the dropout rates among Latino and Native American youth remain very high.

Extracurricular Activities

- Participation in extracurricular activities is associated with positive academic and psychological outcomes. Adolescents benefit from participating in a variety of extracurricular activities; the quality of the activities also matters.

Service Learning

- Service learning, a form of education that promotes social responsibility and service to the community, has been linked with positive benefits for adolescents such as higher grades, increased goal setting, and improved self-esteem.

key terms

adolescent egocentrism 363
amygdala 347
anorexia nervosa 361
bulimia nervosa 361
cognitive control 365
corpus callosum 347

fuzzy-trace theory
   dual-process model 366
hormones 344
hypothetical-deductive
   reasoning 363

imaginary audience 363
limbic system 347
menarche 344
personal fable 364
puberty 344

service learning 370
sexually transmitted
   infections (STIs) 352
top-dog phenomenon 367

key people

David Elkind 363

Deanna Kuhn 364

Jean Piaget 362

Valerie Reyna 366

Chapter 12

SOCIOEMOTIONAL DEVELOPMENT IN ADOLESCENCE

chapter outline

① The Self, Identity, and Religious/Spiritual Development

Learning Goal 1 Discuss self, identity, and religious/spiritual development in adolescence.

Self-Esteem
Self-Regulation
Identity
Religious/Spiritual Development

② Families

Learning Goal 2 Describe changes that take place in adolescents' relationships with their parents.

Parental Monitoring and Information Management
Autonomy and Attachment
Parent-Adolescent Conflict

③ Peers

Learning Goal 3 Characterize the changes that occur in peer relationships during adolescence.

Friendships
Peer Groups
Dating and Romantic Relationships

④ Culture and Adolescent Development

Learning Goal 4 Explain how culture influences adolescent development.

Cross-Cultural Comparisons
Socioeconomic Status and Poverty
Ethnicity
Media Use and Screen Time

⑤ Adolescent Problems

Learning Goal 5 Identify adolescent problems in socioemotional development and strategies for helping adolescents with problems.

Juvenile Delinquency
Depression and Suicide
The Interrelation of Problems and Successful Prevention/Intervention Programs

monkeybusinessimages/Getty Images

The mayor of the city says she is "everywhere." She persuaded the city's school committee to consider ending the practice of locking tardy students out of their classrooms. She also swayed a neighborhood group to support her proposal for a winter jobs program. According to one city councilman, "People are just impressed with the power of her arguments and the sophistication of the argument" (Silva, 2005, pp. B1, B4). Who is she? Jewel E. Cash, age 16.

Jewel was raised in one of Boston's housing projects by her mother, a single parent. As a high school student at Boston Latin Academy, she was a member of the Boston Student Advisory Council, mentored children, volunteered at a women's shelter, managed and danced in two troupes, and was a member of a neighborhood watch group—among other activities.

Jewel told an interviewer from the Boston Globe, "I see a problem and I say, 'How can I make a difference?' . . . I can't take on the world, even though I can try. . . . I'm moving forward but I want to make sure I'm bringing people with me" (Silva, 2005, pp. B1, B4). Jewel is far from typical, but her activities illustrate that cognitive and socioemotional development allows adolescents to be capable, effective individuals. As an adult, Jewel now works with a public consulting group and has continued helping others as a mentor and community organizer.

Jewel Cash, seated next to her mother, participates in a crime watch meeting at a community center.
Matthew J. Lee/The Boston Globe/Getty Images

topical connections *looking back*

In middle and late childhood, development of self-understanding and understanding others becomes more sophisticated, emotional understanding improves, and moral reasoning advances. In Erikson's view, children now are in the industry versus inferiority stage, with their industry expressed as an interest in building things and figuring out how things work. Children now spend more time with peers, but parents continue to play important roles in their development, especially in guiding their academic achievement and managing their opportunities. Peer status and friendship become more important in children's peer relations, and school takes on a stronger academic focus.

preview

Significant changes characterize socioemotional development in adolescence. These changes include increased efforts to understand themselves and to find their identity. Changes also take place in the social contexts of adolescents' lives, with transformations occurring in relationships with families and peers in cultural contexts. Adolescents also may develop socioemotional problems such as delinquency and depression.

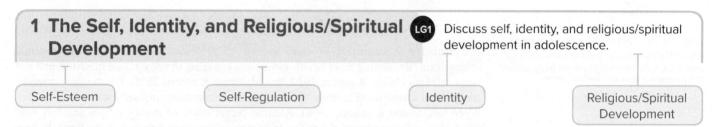

1 The Self, Identity, and Religious/Spiritual Development

LG1 Discuss self, identity, and religious/spiritual development in adolescence.

| Self-Esteem | Self-Regulation | Identity | Religious/Spiritual Development |

Jewel's confidence and positive identity sound at least as impressive as her activities. This section examines how adolescents develop characteristics like these. How well did you understand yourself during adolescence, and how did you acquire the stamp of your identity? Is your identity still developing?

SELF-ESTEEM

Recall that self-esteem is the overall way we evaluate ourselves. Controversy characterizes the extent to which self-esteem changes during adolescence and whether there are gender differences in adolescents' self-esteem (Harter, 2006, 2016). In one study, both boys and girls had particularly high self-esteem in childhood, but their self-esteem dropped considerably during adolescence (Robins & others, 2002). In this study, the self-esteem of girls declined more than the self-esteem of boys during adolescence.

Does self-esteem in adolescence foreshadow adjustment and competence in adulthood? A New Zealand longitudinal study assessed the self-esteem of adolescents at 11, 13, and 15 years of age and then assessed the adjustment and competence of the same individuals when they were 26 years old (Trzesniewski & others, 2006). The results revealed that adults with poorer mental and physical health, worse economic prospects, and higher levels of criminal behavior were more likely to have had low self-esteem in adolescence than their better-adjusted, more competent adult counterparts. Also, a recent study found that low self-esteem in early adolescence predicted depressive symptoms in late adolescence and emerging adulthood (Messelink, Van Roekel, & Oldehinkel, 2018).

Some critics argue that developmental changes and gender differences in self-esteem during adolescence have been exaggerated (Harter, 2006, 2016). Despite the differing results and interpretations, however, the self-esteem of girls is likely to decline at least somewhat during early adolescence.

Why would the self-esteem of girls decline during early adolescence? One explanation points to girls' negative body images during pubertal change. Another explanation involves the greater interest young adolescent girls take in social relationships and society's failure to reward that interest (Impett & others, 2008).

Self-esteem reflects perceptions that do not always match reality (Twenge & Campbell, 2020). An adolescent's self-esteem might indicate a perception about whether he or she is intelligent and attractive, for example, but that perception may not be accurate. Thus, high self-esteem may refer to accurate, justified perceptions of one's worth as a person and one's successes and accomplishments, but it can also indicate an arrogant, grandiose, unwarranted sense of superiority over others. In the same manner, low self-esteem may suggest either an accurate perception of one's shortcomings or a distorted, even pathological insecurity and inferiority.

Narcissism refers to a self-centered and self-concerned approach toward others. Typically, narcissists are unaware of their actual self and how others perceive them (Ackerman, 2021;

narcissism A self-centered and self-concerned approach toward others.

What characterizes narcissistic adolescents? Are today's adolescents more narcissistic than their counterparts in earlier generations?
CSP_karelnoppe/Fotosearch LBRF/age fotostock

Derry, Ohan, & Bayliss, 2020). This lack of awareness contributes to their adjustment problems. Narcissists are excessively self-centered and self-congratulatory, viewing their own needs and desires as paramount (Donnellan, Ackerman, & Wright, 2021).

Are today's adolescents and emerging adults more self-centered and narcissistic than their counterparts in earlier generations? Research by Jean Twenge and her colleagues (2008a, b) indicated in comparison with Baby Boomers who were surveyed in 1975, twelfth-graders surveyed in 2006 were more self-satisfied overall and far more confident that they would be very good employees, mates, and parents. However, other large-scale analyses have revealed no increase in high school and college students' narcissism from the 1980s through the first decade of the twenty-first century (Roberts, Edmonds, & Grijalva, 2010; Trzesniewski, Donnellan, & Robins, 2013).

SELF-REGULATION

Self-regulation is important in many aspects of adolescents' lives, including academic achievement, developing good health habits, not engaging in risky sexual behavior, and not binge drinking (Miller & others, 2020; Van Malderen & others, 2019). For example, a recent study found a reciprocal relation between school engagement and self-regulation in adolescence (Stefansson & others, 2018). Another recent study of middle school students indicated that self-control was a key factor in developing good health habits (Kang & You, 2018). And a recent study indicated that among 13- to 16-year-olds, females reported having a higher level of self-control and self-monitoring than did their male counterparts (Tetering & others, 2020).

A key component of self-regulation is engaging in *effortful control*, which involves inhibiting impulses and not engaging in destructive behavior, focusing and maintaining attention despite distractions, and initiating and completing tasks that have long-term value, even if they may seem unpleasant (Kim & Kim, 2019; Qi, 2019). One study found that effortful control at 17 years of age predicted academic persistence and educational attainment at 23 to 25 years of age (Veronneau & others, 2014). In this study, effortful control was just as strong a predictor of educational attainment as were past grade point averages and parents' educational levels. Also, a study of Mexican American adolescents revealed that effortful control was linked to coping with stress more effectively (Taylor, Widaman, & Robins, 2018). Further, a recent study found a bidirectional pattern between effortful control and school behavioral problems in fifth- to eleventh-graders; that is, low effortful control was associated with increases in school behavioral problems, and school behavioral problems were linked to decreases in effortful control (Atherton & others, 2019). In addition, a recent meta-analysis of children up to 18 years of age found that those who were securely attached to their parents had better effortful control (Pallini & others, 2018). And another recent study of Mexican-origin families revealed that adolescents who experienced more hostility from their parents, associated more with deviant peers, lived in more violent neighborhoods, and encountered more ethnic discrimination were characterized by a lower level of effortful control (Atherton, Lawson, & Robins, 2020). Also in this study, adolescents whose parents closely monitored their behavior and whereabouts showed a smaller decline in effortful control.

------- ▶

developmental **connection**

Information Processing

Cognitive control (inhibition and flexibility) increases from childhood through early adulthood. Connect to "Information Processing."

◀ - - - - - - - - - - - ┘

IDENTITY

Who am I? What am I all about? What am I going to do with my life? What is different about me? How can I make it on my own? These questions reflect the search for an identity. By far the most comprehensive and provocative theory of identity development is Erik Erikson's. In this section, we examine his views on identity. We also discuss contemporary research on how identity develops and how social contexts influence that development.

What Is Identity?   When identity has been conceptualized and researched, it typically is explored in a broad sense. However, identity is a self-portrait that is composed of many pieces and domains:

- The career and work path the person wants to follow (vocational/career identity)
- Whether the person is conservative, liberal, or middle-of-the-road (political identity)

- The person's spiritual beliefs (religious identity)
- Whether the person is single, married, divorced, and so on (relationship identity)
- The extent to which the person is motivated to achieve and is intellectually oriented (achievement, intellectual identity)
- Whether the person is heterosexual, homosexual, bisexual, or transgendered (sexual identity)
- Which part of the world or country a person is from and how intensely the person identifies with his or her cultural heritage (cultural/ethnic identity)
- The kinds of things a person likes to do, which can include sports, music, hobbies, and so on (interests)
- The individual's personality characteristics, such as being introverted or extroverted, anxious or calm, friendly or hostile, and so on (personality)
- The individual's body image (physical identity)

Currently, too little research attention has been given to developmental changes in specific domains of identity (Negru-Subtirica & Pop, 2018).

Synthesizing the identity components can be a long and drawn-out process, with many negations and affirmations of various roles and facets (Ferrer-Wreder & Kroger, 2020; Neblett, Roth, & Syed, 2019). Identity development takes place in bits and pieces. Decisions are not made once and for all, but have to be made again and again. Identity development does not happen neatly, and it does not happen cataclysmically (Palmeroni & others, 2020; Syed, Pasupathi, & McLean, 2020).

Erikson's View   It was Erik Erikson (1950, 1968) who first understood how central questions about identity are to understanding adolescent development. Recall that Erikson's fifth developmental stage, which individuals experience during adolescence, is *identity versus identity confusion*. During this time, said Erikson, adolescents are faced with deciding who they are, what they are all about, and where they are going in life.

The search for an identity during adolescence is aided by a *psychosocial moratorium*, which is Erikson's term for the gap between childhood security and adult autonomy. During this period, society leaves adolescents relatively free of responsibilities and able to try out different identities. Adolescents experiment with different roles and personalities. They may want to pursue one career one month (lawyer, for example) and another career the next month (doctor, actor, teacher, social worker, or astronaut, for example). They may dress neatly one day, sloppily the next. This experimentation is a deliberate effort on the part of adolescents to find out where they fit in the world. Most adolescents eventually discard undesirable roles.

Youth who successfully cope with conflicting identities emerge with a new sense of self that is both refreshing and acceptable. Adolescents who do not successfully resolve this identity crisis suffer what Erikson calls identity confusion. The confusion takes one of two courses: Individuals either withdraw, isolating themselves from peers and family, or they immerse themselves in the world of peers and lose their identity in the crowd.

Developmental Changes   Although questions about identity may be especially important during adolescence and emerging adulthood, identity formation neither begins nor ends during these years. What is important about identity development in late adolescence and emerging adulthood is that for the first time, physical development, cognitive development, and socioemotional development advance to the point at which the individual can sort through and synthesize childhood identities and identifications to construct a viable path toward adult maturity.

How do individual adolescents undergo the process of forming an identity? Eriksonian researcher James Marcia (1980, 1994) reasons that Erikson's theory of identity development contains four statuses of identity, or ways of resolving the identity crisis: identity diffusion, identity foreclosure, identity moratorium, and identity achievement. What determines an individual's identity status? Marcia classifies individuals based on the existence or extent of their crisis or commitment (see Figure 1). **Crisis** is defined as a period of identity development during which the individual is exploring alternatives. Most researchers use the term *exploration* rather than *crisis*. **Commitment** is personal investment in identity.

"Who are you?" said the Caterpillar. Alice replied, rather shyly, "I—I hardly know, Sir, just at present—at least I know who I was when I got up this morning, but I must have changed several times since then."

— LEWIS CARROLL
English writer, 19th century

What are some important dimensions of identity?
Digital Vision/Getty Images

developmental **connection**
Erikson's Theory
Erikson's stage for middle and late childhood is industry versus inferiority and for early adulthood is intimacy versus isolation. Connect to "Socioemotional Development in Middle and Late Childhood" and "Socioemotional Development in Early Adulthood."

crisis Marcia's term for a period of identity development during which the adolescent is exploring alternatives.

commitment Marcia's term for the part of identity development in which adolescents show a personal investment in identity.

FIGURE **1**

MARCIA'S FOUR STATUSES OF IDENTITY.

According to Marcia, an individual's status in developing an identity can be categorized as identity diffusion, identity foreclosure, identity moratorium, or identity achievement. The status depends on the presence or absence of (1) a crisis or exploration of alternatives and (2) a commitment to an identity. *What is the identity status of most young adolescents?*

	Identity Status			
Position on Occupation and Ideology	Identity Diffusion	Identity Foreclosure	Identity Moratorium	Identity Achievement
Crisis	Absent	Absent	Present	Present
Commitment	Absent	Present	Absent	Present

> Once formed, an identity furnishes individuals with a historical sense of who they have been, a meaningful sense of who they are now, and a sense of who they might become in the future.
>
> —JAMES MARCIA
>
> *Contemporary psychologist, Simon Fraser University*

identity diffusion Marcia's term for the status of individuals who have not yet experienced a crisis (explored meaningful alternatives) or made any commitments.

identity foreclosure Marcia's term for the status of individuals who have made a commitment but have not experienced a crisis.

identity moratorium Marcia's term for the status of individuals who are in the midst of a crisis, but their commitments are either absent or vaguely defined.

identity achievement Marcia's term for the status of individuals who have undergone a crisis and have made a commitment.

The four statuses of identity are described below:

- **Identity diffusion** is the status of individuals who have not yet experienced a crisis or made any commitments. Not only are they undecided about occupational and ideological choices, they are also likely to show little interest in such matters.
- **Identity foreclosure** is the status of individuals who have made a commitment but not experienced a crisis. This occurs most often when parents hand down commitments to their adolescents, usually in an authoritarian way, before adolescents have had a chance to explore different approaches, ideologies, and vocations on their own.
- **Identity moratorium** is the status of individuals who are in the midst of a crisis but whose commitments are either absent or are only vaguely defined.
- **Identity achievement** is the status of individuals who have undergone a crisis and made a commitment.

Some critics argue that the identity status approach does not provide a deep understanding of identity development (Vosylis, Erentaite, & Crocetti, 2018). The newer dual cycle identity model divides identity development into two separate processes: (1) a formation cycle that relies on exploration in breadth and identification with commitment; and (2) a maintenance cycle that involves exploration in depth as well as reconsideration of commitments (Luyckz & others, 2017; von Doeselaar & others, 2020).

One way that researchers are now examining identity changes in depth is to use a narrative approach. This involves asking individuals to tell their life stories and evaluate the extent to which their stories are meaningful and integrated (McLean & others, 2020; Wicks, Berger, & Camic, 2019). The term *narrative identity* "refers to the stories people construct and tell about themselves to define who they are for themselves and others. Beginning in adolescence and young adulthood, our narrative identities are the stories we live by" (McAdams, Josselson, & Lieblich, 2006, p. 4).

How does identity change in emerging adulthood?
Tom Grill/Corbis/Getty Images

Emerging Adulthood and Beyond There is a growing consensus that key changes in identity are more likely to take place in emerging adulthood (18 to 25 years of age) or later than during adolescence (Neblet, Roth, & Syed, 2019). College upperclassmen are more likely to be identity achieved than college freshmen or high school students. Many young adolescents, on the other hand, are identity diffused. One study found that as individuals matured from early adolescence to emerging adulthood, they increasingly pursued in-depth exploration of their identity (Klimstra & others, 2010).

Why might college produce some key changes in identity? Increased complexity in the reasoning skills of college students, combined with a wide range of new experiences that highlight contrasts between home and college and between themselves and others, stimulate them to reach a higher level of integrating various dimensions of their identity (Phinney, 2008). College contexts serve as a virtual "laboratory" for identity development through such experiences as diverse coursework and exposure to peers from diverse backgrounds. Also, one of emerging adulthood's key themes is not having many social commitments, which gives individuals considerable independence in developing a life path (Arnett, 2015a, b).

Resolution of the identity issue during adolescence and emerging adulthood does not mean that identity will be stable throughout the remainder of life (Feliciano & Rumbaut, 2019; Ferrer-Wreder & Kroger, 2020). Many individuals who develop positive identities follow what are called "MAMA" cycles; that is, their identity status changes from moratorium to achievement to moratorium to achievement (Marcia, 1994). These cycles may be repeated throughout life (Francis, Fraser, & Marcia, 1989). Marcia (2002) points out that the first identity is just that—it is not, and should not be expected to be, the final product.

Cultural and Ethnic Identity   Identity development is influenced by culture and ethnicity (Moffitt, Juang, & Syed, 2020; Wang & Yip, 2020). Most research on identity development has historically been based on data obtained from adolescents and emerging adults in the United States and Canada, especially those who are non-Latino Whites (Schwartz & others, 2012, 2015a, b). Many of these individuals have grown up in cultural contexts that value individual autonomy. However, in many countries around the world, adolescents and emerging adults have grown up influenced by a collectivist emphasis on fitting in with the group and connecting with others (Schwartz & others, 2015a, b). The collectivist emphasis is especially prevalent in East Asian countries such as China. Researchers have found that self-oriented identity exploration may not be the main process through which identity achievement is attained in East Asian countries (Schwartz & others, 2015a, b). Rather, East Asian adolescents and emerging adults may develop their identity through identification with and imitation of others in their cultural group (Bosma & Kunnen, 2001).

Identity development may take longer in some countries than in others (Schwartz & others, 2015a, b). For example, research indicates that Italian youth may postpone significant identity exploration beyond adolescence and emerging adulthood, not settling on an identity until their mid- to late twenties (Crocetti, Rabaglietti, & Sica, 2012). This delayed identity development is strongly influenced by many Italian youth living at home with their parents until 30 years of age and older.

Throughout the world, ethnic minority groups have struggled to maintain their ethnic identities while blending in with the dominant culture (Erikson, 1968). **Ethnic identity** is an enduring aspect of the self that includes a sense of membership in an ethnic group, along with the attitudes and feelings related to that membership (Umana-Taylor, 2019). Most adolescents from ethnic minority groups develop a *bicultural identity.* That is, they identify in some ways with their ethnic group and in other ways with the majority culture (Neblett, Roth, & Syed, 2019).

For ethnic minority individuals, adolescence and emerging adulthood are often special junctures in their development (Neblett, Roth, & Syed, 2019; Umana-Taylor & others, 2020). Although children are aware of some ethnic and cultural differences, individuals consciously confront their ethnicity for the first time in adolescence or emerging adulthood. Unlike children, adolescents and emerging adults have the ability to interpret ethnic and cultural information, to reflect on the past, and to speculate about the future. With their advancing cognitive skills of abstract thinking and self-reflection, adolescents (especially older adolescents) increasingly consider the meaning of their ethnicity and also have more ethnic-related experiences.

The indicators of identity change often differ for each succeeding generation (Vedder & Phinney, 2014). First-generation immigrants are likely to be secure in their identities and unlikely to change much; they may or may not develop a new identity. The degree to which they begin to feel "American" appears to be related to whether or not they learn English, develop social networks beyond their ethnic group, and become culturally competent in their new country. Second-generation immigrants are more likely to think of themselves as "American," possibly because citizenship is granted at birth. Their ethnic identity is likely to be linked to retention of their ethnic language and social networks. In the third and later generations, the issues become more complex. Historical, contextual, and political factors that are unrelated to acculturation may affect the extent to which members of this generation retain their ethnic identities. For non-European ethnic groups, racism and discrimination influence whether ethnic identity is retained.

Recent research indicates that pride in one's ethnic identity group has positive outcomes (Umana-Taylor, 2018; Umana-Taylor & Hill, 2020). In one recent study, strong ethnic group affiliation and connection served a protective function in reducing risk for psychiatric problems (Anglin & others, 2018).

One adolescent girl, 16-year-old Michelle Chin, made these comments about ethnic identity development: "My parents do not understand that teenagers need to find out who they are, which means a lot of experimenting, a lot of mood swings, a lot of emotions and awkwardness. Like any teenager, I am facing an identity crisis. I am still trying to figure out whether I am a Chinese American or an American with Asian eyes."
Red Chopsticks/Getty Images

ethnic identity An enduring, basic aspect of the self that includes a sense of membership in an ethnic group and the attitudes and feelings related to that membership.

Identity Development and the Digital Environment　For today's adolescents and emerging adults, the contexts involving the digital world, especially social media platforms such as Instagram, Snapchat, and Facebook, have introduced new ways for youth to express and explore their identity (Davis, 2020, 2021; Davis & others, 2020; Davis & Weinstein, 2017). Adolescents and emerging adults often cast themselves as positively as they can on their digital devices—posting their most attractive photos and describing themselves in idealistic ways, continually editing and reworking their online self-portraits to enhance them. Adolescents' and emerging adults' online world provides extensive opportunities for both expressing their identity and getting feedback about it. Of course, such feedback is not always positive, just as in their offline world.

RELIGIOUS/SPIRITUAL DEVELOPMENT

In the chapter on "Physical and Cognitive Development in Adolescence" we described the many benefits of service learning. A number of studies have found that adolescents who are involved in religious institutions are more likely to engage in service learning than their counterparts who don't participate in religious institutions (Hart, 2020; Lerner & others, 2015). Let's explore adolescents' religious and spiritual experiences.

Religious issues are important to many adolescents, but during the twenty-first century religious interest among adolescents has declined. In a 2017 national study of American college freshmen, 69.2 percent said they had attended religious services frequently or occasionally during their senior year in high school, down from a high of 85 percent in 1997 (Stolzenberg & others, 2019).

A developmental study revealed that religiousness declined from 14 to 20 years of age in the United States (Koenig, McGue, & Iacono, 2008) (see Figure 2). In this study, religiousness was assessed with items such as frequency of prayer, frequency of discussing religious teachings, frequency of deciding moral actions for religious reasons, and the overall importance of religion in everyday life. As indicated in Figure 2, more change in religiousness occurred from 14 to 18 years of age than from 20 to 24 years of age. Also in this study, attending religious services declined from 14 to 18 years of age and then began to increase at 20 years of age. And in a recent study, as adolescents got older, their religious service attendance declined and this decline was linked to such factors as becoming employed, leaving home, and engaging in sexual activity (Hardie, Pearce, & Denton, 2016). Also in this study, parents' religious affiliation and attendance provided some protection against decreasing attendance.

Researchers have found that adolescent girls are more religious than are adolescent boys (King & Boyatzis, 2015). One study of 13- to 17-year-olds revealed that girls are more likely to attend religious services frequently, to perceive that religion shapes their daily lives, to participate in religious youth groups, to pray alone, and to feel closer to God (Smith & Denton, 2005).

Analysis of the World Values Survey of 18- to 24-year-olds revealed that emerging adults in less developed countries were more likely to be religious than their counterparts in more developed countries (Lippman & Keith, 2006). For example, emerging adults' reports that religion was very important in their lives ranged from a low of 0 in Japan to 93 percent in Nigeria, and belief in God ranged from a low of 40 percent in Sweden to a high of 100 percent in Pakistan.

Religion and Identity Development　As we saw earlier in this chapter, identity development becomes a central focus during adolescence and emerging adulthood (Syed, Pasupathi, & McLean, 2020). As part of their search for identity, adolescents and emerging adults begin to grapple in more sophisticated, logical ways with such questions as "Why am I on this planet?" "Is there really a God or higher spiritual being, or have I just been believing what my parents and the church imprinted in my mind?" "What really are my religious views?"

Cognitive Development and Religion in Adolescence　Many of the cognitive changes thought to influence religious development involve Piaget's cognitive developmental theory. More so than in childhood, adolescents think abstractly, idealistically, and logically. The increase in abstract

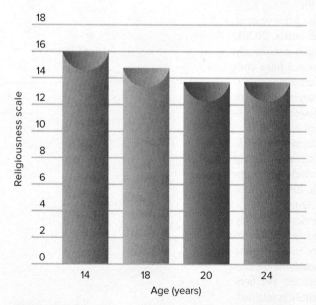

FIGURE **2**

DEVELOPMENTAL CHANGES IN RELIGIOUSNESS FROM 14 TO 24 YEARS OF AGE. *Note:* The religiousness scale ranged from 0 to 32, with higher scores indicating stronger religiousness.

Many children and adolescents show an interest in religion, and many religious institutions created by adults (such as this Muslim school in Malaysia) are designed to introduce them to religious benefits and ensure that they will carry on a religious tradition.
Grigvovan/Shutterstock

thinking lets adolescents consider various ideas about religious and spiritual concepts. For example, an adolescent might ask how a loving God can possibly exist given the extensive suffering of many people in the world (Good & Willoughby, 2008). Adolescents' increased idealistic thinking provides a foundation for thinking about whether religion provides the best route to a better world. And adolescents' increased capacity for logical reasoning gives them the ability to develop hypotheses and systematically sort through different answers to spiritual questions (Good & Willoughby, 2008).

The Positive Role of Religion in Adolescents' Lives   Researchers have found that various aspects of religion are linked with positive outcomes for adolescents (Hardy & King, 2019; King, Schnitker, & Houltberg, 2020). Religion plays a role in adolescents' health and has an influence on whether they engage in problem behaviors (Hardy & others, 2019; Sartor, Hipwell, & Chung, 2020). A recent study revealed that high school students who reported turning to spiritual beliefs when they were experiencing problems were less likely to engage in substance use (Debnam & others, 2018). Also, in a recent study, religiosity was linked to delayed onset of alcohol use, more so for adolescent girls than boys (Barry, Valdez, & Russell, 2020). Further, across three countries (England, Scotland, and Canada), adolescents who reported having a higher level of spirituality were more likely to have positive health outcomes (Brooks & others, 2018). And a recent Slovakian study of adolescents found that spirituality but not religiosity was linked to better self-reported health, fewer health complaints, and higher life satisfaction (Dankulincova Veselska & others, 2018).

Many religious adolescents also adopt their religion's message about caring and concern for people (Lerner & others, 2015). For example, in one survey religious youth were almost three times as likely to engage in community service as nonreligious youth (Youniss, McLellan, & Yates, 1999).

developmental **connection**

Religion

Religion plays an important role in the lives of many individuals in adulthood and is linked to their health and coping. Connect to "Physical and Cognitive Development in Middle Adulthood" and "Cognitive Development in Late Adulthood."

Review *Connect* Reflect

LG1 Discuss self, identity, and religious/spiritual development in adolescence.

Review

- What are some changes in self-esteem that take place during adolescence?
- What characterizes self-regulation in adolescence?
- How does identity develop in adolescence?
- What characterizes religious and spiritual development in adolescence?

Connect

- Compare what is said about inflated self-esteem in middle and late childhood in the chapter on "Socioemotional Development in Middle and Late Childhood" to what is said in this section about potential narcissism in adolescence. What are your conclusions?

Reflect *Your Own Personal Journey of Life*

- What role did religion/spiritual development play in your life during adolescence? Has your religious/spiritual thinking changed since you were an adolescent? If so, how?

---

2 Families

 LG2 Describe changes that take place in adolescents' relationships with their parents.

Parental Monitoring and Information Management	Autonomy and Attachment	Parent-Adolescent Conflict

Adolescence typically alters the relationship between parents and their children. Among the most important aspects of family relationships in adolescence are those that involve parental monitoring and information management, autonomy and attachment, and parent-adolescent conflict.

PARENTAL MONITORING AND INFORMATION MANAGEMENT

In "Socioemotional Development in Middle and Late Childhood," we discussed the importance of parents as managers of children's development. A key aspect of the managerial role of parenting is effective monitoring, which is especially important as children move into the adolescent years (Atheron, Lawson, & Robins, 2020; Soenens, Vansteeenkiste, & Beyers, 2019). Monitoring includes supervising adolescents' choice of social settings, activities, and friends, as well as their academic efforts. In a recent study of fifth- to eighth-graders, a higher level of parental monitoring was associated with students having higher grades (Top, Liew, & Luo, 2017). A meta-analysis also found that higher levels of parental monitoring and rule enforcement were linked to later initiation of sexual intercourse and increased use of condoms by adolescents (Dittus & others, 2015). Also, a recent study of young adolescents found that they got more sleep when their parents engaged in more parental monitoring of their waking activities (Gunn & others, 2019). And a recent study indicated that parental active tracking measures during adolescence and college were linked to better health behavior in both developmental time frames (Abar & others, 2020).

A current interest involving parental monitoring focuses on adolescents' management of their parents' access to information, especially strategies used in disclosing or concealing information about their activities (Campione-Barr & Smetana, 2019). When parents engage in positive parenting practices, adolescents are more likely to disclose information. A study of U.S. and Chinese young adolescents found that adolescents' disclosure to parents was linked with a higher level of academic competence (better learning strategies, autonomous motivation, and better grades) over time (Cheung, Pomerantz, & Dong, 2012). Researchers have found that adolescents' disclosure to parents about their whereabouts, activities, and friends is linked to positive adolescent adjustment (Cottrell & others, 2017; Smetana, Robinson, & Rote, 2015). Also, recent research indicated that adolescents who engaged in problem behavior were more secretive and disclosed less information to parents (Darling & Tilton-Weaver, 2019).

---

developmental **connection**

Parenting

In authoritative parenting, parents encourage children and adolescents to be independent but still place limits and controls on their actions. Extensive verbal give-and-take is allowed, and parents are warm and nurturant. Connect to "Socioemotional Development in Early Childhood."

AUTONOMY AND ATTACHMENT

With most adolescents, parents are likely to find themselves engaged in a delicate balancing act, weighing competing needs for autonomy and control, for independence and connection.

What role do parental monitoring and information management play in adolescent development?
Wavebreakmedia Ltd/Getty Images

Autonomy The typical adolescent's push for autonomy and responsibility puzzles and angers many parents. Most parents anticipate that their teenager will have some difficulty adjusting to the changes that adolescence brings, but few parents imagine and predict just how strong an adolescent's desires will be to spend time with peers or how intensely adolescents will want to show that it is they—not their parents—who are responsible for their successes and failures.

Adolescents' ability to attain autonomy and gain control over their behavior is acquired through appropriate adult reactions to their desire for control (Rodriguez-Meirinhos & others, 2020; Soenens, Vansteenkiste, & Beyers, 2019). At the onset of adolescence, the average individual does not have the knowledge to make appropriate or mature decisions in all areas of life. As the adolescent pushes for autonomy, the wise adult relinquishes control in those areas where the adolescent can make reasonable decisions, but continues to guide the adolescent to make reasonable decisions in areas where the adolescent's knowledge is more limited. Gradually, adolescents acquire the ability to make mature decisions on their own (Li & Hein, 2019). A recent study also found that from 16 to 20 years of age, adolescents perceived that they had increasing independence and improved relationships with their parents (Hadiwijaya & others, 2017).

Gender differences characterize autonomy-granting in adolescence. Boys are given more independence than girls. In one study, this was especially true in U.S. families with a traditional gender-role orientation (Bumpus, Crouter, & McHale, 2001).

Expectations about the appropriate timing of adolescent autonomy often vary across cultures, parents, and adolescents (Tran & Raffaelli, 2020). For example, expectations for early autonomy on the part of adolescents are more prevalent among non-Latino Whites, single parents, and adolescents themselves than they are among Asian Americans or Latinos, married parents, and parents themselves (Feldman & Rosenthal, 1999). Nonetheless, although Latino cultures may place a stronger emphasis on parental authority and restrict adolescent autonomy, one study revealed that regardless of where they were born, Mexican-origin adolescent girls living in the United States expected autonomy at an earlier age than their mothers preferred (Bamaca-Colbert & others, 2012).

The Role of Attachment Recall that one of the most widely discussed aspects of socioemotional development in infancy is secure attachment to caregivers (Granqvist, 2020; Woodhouse & others, 2019). In the past decade, researchers have explored whether secure attachment also might be an important aspect of adolescents' relationships with their parents (Khan & others, 2020; Shulman & others, 2019).

Researchers have found that insecurely attached adolescents are more likely than securely attached adolescents to have emotional difficulties and to engage in problem behaviors such as juvenile delinquency and drug abuse (Fairbairn & others, 2018; Hoeve & others, 2012). In a longitudinal study, Joseph Allen and his colleagues (2009) found that secure attachment at 14 years of age was linked to a number of positive outcomes at 21 years of age, including relationship competence, financial/career competence, and fewer problematic behaviors. In addition, a recent study revealed that when they had grown up in poverty, adolescents engaged in less risk-taking if they had a history of secure attachments to caregivers (Delker, Bernstein, & Laurent, 2018). Also, in another recent study, more secure attachment to the mother and to the father was associated with fewer depressive symptoms in adolescents (Kerstis, Aslund, & Sonnby, 2018). And in a research review, the most consistent outcomes of secure attachment in adolescence involved positive peer relations and development of the adolescent's capacity to regulate emotions (Allen & Miga, 2010).

Might secure attachment be linked to parenting styles in adolescence? A study of Chinese adolescents revealed that authoritative parenting positively predicted parent-adolescent attachment, which in turn was associated with a higher level of adolescent self-esteem and positive attachment to peers (Cai & others, 2013). And a longitudinal study revealed that secure attachment in adolescence and emerging adulthood was predicted by observations of maternal sensitivity across childhood and adolescence (Waters, Ruiz, & Roisman, 2017).

> **developmental connection**
> **Attachment**
> In secure attachment during infancy, babies use the caregiver as a secure base from which to explore the environment. Connect to "Socioemotional Development in Infancy."

According to one adolescent, Stacey Christensen, age 16: "I am lucky enough to have open communication with my parents. Whenever I am in need or just need to talk, my parents are there for me. My advice to parents is to let your teens grow at their own pace, be open with them so that you can be there for them. We need guidance; our parents need to help but not be too overwhelming."
Stockbyte/Getty Images

Balancing Freedom and Control We have seen that parents play very important roles in adolescent development (Herd, King-Casas, & Kim-Spoon, 2020). Although adolescents are moving toward independence, they still need to stay connected with their family (Calders & others, 2020). The National Longitudinal Study on Adolescent Health surveyed more than 12,000 adolescents and found that those who did not eat dinner with a parent five or more days a week had dramatically higher rates of smoking, drinking, using marijuana, getting into fights, and initiating sexual activity (Council of Economic Advisors, 2000). In another longitudinal study, parental psychological control (extent to which parents use guilt, anxiety, love withdrawal, and other psychologically controlling behaviors) was linked to decreases in adolescents' autonomy and relatedness with friends between 13 and 18 years of age and lower levels of autonomy and relatedness with romantic partners at 18 (Oudekerk & others, 2015). And a recent study found that a high monitoring, high autonomy support parenting profile was more positively linked to adolescent adjustment than a low monitoring, high psychological control parenting profile (Rodriguez-Meininhos & others, 2020).

PARENT-ADOLESCENT CONFLICT

Although parent-adolescent conflict increases in early adolescence, it does not reach the tumultuous proportions G. Stanley Hall envisioned at the beginning of the twentieth century (Bornstein, Jager, & Steinberg, 2013). Rather, much of the conflict involves the everyday events of family life, such as keeping a bedroom clean, dressing neatly, getting home by a certain time, and not talking endlessly on the phone. The conflicts rarely involve major dilemmas such as drugs or delinquency.

Conflict with parents often escalates during early adolescence and then lessens as the adolescent reaches 17 to 20 years of age. In a recent study of Chinese American families, parent-adolescent conflict increased in early adolescence, peaked at about 16 years of age, and then decreased through late adolescence and emerging adulthood (Juang & others, 2018). Parent-adolescent relationships become more positive if adolescents go away to college than if they attend college while living at home (Sullivan & Sullivan, 1980).

The everyday conflicts that characterize parent-adolescent relationships may actually serve a positive developmental function. These minor disputes and negotiations facilitate the adolescent's transition from being dependent on parents to becoming an autonomous individual. Recognizing that conflict and negotiation can serve a positive developmental function can reduce parental hostility.

The old model of parent-adolescent relationships suggested that as adolescents mature they detach themselves from parents and move into a world of autonomy apart from parents. The old model also suggested that parent-adolescent conflict is intense and stressful throughout adolescence. A newer model emphasizes that parents serve as important attachment figures and support systems while adolescents explore a wider, more complex social world. The newer model also emphasizes that in most families parent-adolescent conflict is moderate rather than severe and that the everyday negotiations and minor disputes not only are normal but also can serve the positive developmental function of helping the adolescent make the transition from childhood dependency to adult independence (see Figure 3).

Still, a high degree of conflict characterizes some parent-adolescent relationships (Brouillard & others, 2018; Liu, Wang, & Tiun, 2019; Nguyen & others, 2018). And this prolonged, intense conflict is associated with various adolescent problems: moving out of the home, juvenile delinquency, depression, school dropout, pregnancy and early marriage, membership in religious cults, and drug abuse (Akin & others, 2020; Delgado & others, 2019; Juang & others, 2018).

Cross-cultural studies reveal that parent-adolescent conflict is lower in some countries than in the United States. Two countries where parent-adolescent conflict is lower than in the United States are Japan and India.

When families emigrate to another country, adolescents typically acculturate more quickly to the norms and values of their new country than do their parents (Nguyen & others, 2018). This likely occurs because of immigrant adolescents' exposure in school to the language and culture of the host country. The norms and values immigrant adolescents experience are especially likely to diverge from those of their parents in areas such as autonomy and romantic relationships (Nair, Roche, & White, 2018). In a study of Chinese American families, parent-adolescent

Conflict with parents increases in early adolescence. *What is the nature of this conflict in a majority of American families?*
Wavebreak Media/age fotostock

Old Model
Autonomy, detachment from parents; parent and peer worlds are isolated
Intense, stressful conflict throughout adolescence; parent-adolescent relationships are filled with storm and stress on virtually a daily basis

New Model
Attachment and autonomy; parents are important support systems and attachment figures; adolescent-parent and adolescent-peer worlds have some important connections
Moderate parent-adolescent conflict is common and can serve a positive developmental function; conflict greater in early adolescence

FIGURE **3**

OLD AND NEW MODELS OF PARENT-ADOLESCENT RELATIONSHIPS
Martin Barraud/Caia Image/Glow Images

conflict was linked to a sense of alienation between parents and adolescents, which in turn was related to more depressive symptoms, delinquent behavior, and lower levels of academic achievement (Hou, Kim, & Wang, 2016).

Review *Connect* Reflect

 Describe changes that take place in adolescents' relationships with their parents.

Review

- What roles do parental managing and monitoring play in adolescent development?
- How do needs for autonomy and attachment develop in adolescence?
- What characterizes parent-adolescent conflict?

Connect

- Adolescence is identified as the second time in an individual's life when the quest for independence is especially strong. When is the other

time, and what characterizes that stage of development?

Reflect *Your Own Personal Journey of Life*

- How much autonomy did your parents give you in adolescence? Too much? Too little? How intense was your conflict with your parents during adolescence? What were the conflicts mainly about? Would you interact with your own adolescents differently from the way your parents did with you? If so, how?

3 Peers

LG3 Characterize the changes that occur in peer relationships during adolescence.

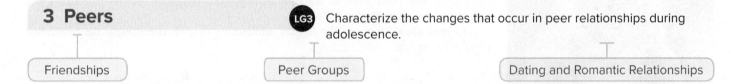

Friendships   Peer Groups   Dating and Romantic Relationships

Peers play powerful roles in the lives of adolescents (Esposito, Bacchini, & Affuso, 2020; Umana-Taylor & others, 2020). Peer relations undergo important changes in adolescence, including changes in friendships and in peer groups, as well as initiation into romantic relationships (Ferguson & Ryan, 2019). Peer and romantic relationships have some connections. For example, in a longitudinal study, establishing positive expectations and the capacity for assertiveness with peers at age 13, being socially competent at 15 and 16, and being able to form and maintain strong close friendships at 16 to 18 predicted romantic life satisfaction at 27 to 30 years of age (Allen & others, 2020).

FRIENDSHIPS

For most children, being popular with their peers is a strong motivator. Beginning in early adolescence, however, teenagers typically prefer to have a smaller number of friendships that are more intense and intimate than those of young children.

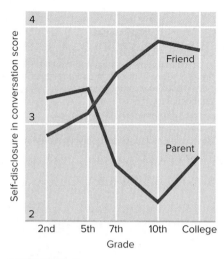

FIGURE 4

DEVELOPMENTAL CHANGES IN SELF-DISCLOSING CONVERSATIONS. Self-disclosing conversations with friends increased dramatically in adolescence while declining in an equally dramatic fashion with parents. However, self-disclosing conversations with parents began to pick up somewhat during the college years. The measure of self-disclosure involved a 5-point rating scale completed by the children and youth, with a higher score representing greater self-disclosure. The data shown represent the means for each age group.

How do characteristics of an adolescent's friends influence whether the friends have a positive or negative influence on the adolescent?

SW Productions/Brand X Pictures/Getty Images

Harry Stack Sullivan (1953) was the most influential theorist to discuss the importance of adolescent friendships. During adolescence, said Sullivan, friends become increasingly important in meeting social needs. In particular, Sullivan argued, the need for intimacy intensifies during early adolescence, motivating teenagers to seek out close friends. If adolescents fail to develop such close friendships, they experience loneliness and a reduced sense of self-worth.

Many of Sullivan's ideas have withstood the test of time. For example, adolescents report disclosing intimate and personal information to their friends more often than do younger children (Buhrmester, 1998) (see Figure 4). Adolescents also say they depend more on friends than on parents to satisfy their needs for companionship, reassurance of worth, and intimacy. The ups and downs of experiences with friends shape adolescents' well-being (Bagwell & Bukowski, 2018; Felton & others, 2019). Adolescent girls are more likely to disclose information about problems to a friend than are adolescent boys (Rose & Smith, 2018).

Although having friends can be a developmental advantage, not all friendships are alike and the quality of friendship matters (Bagwell & Bukowski, 2018; Felton & others, 2019). It is a developmental disadvantage to have coercive, conflict-ridden, and poor-quality friendships (Clayton & others, 2020). One study revealed that having friends who engage in delinquent behavior is associated with early onset and more persistent delinquency (Evans, Simons, & Simons, 2016). Another study found that adolescents adapted their smoking and drinking behavior to that of their best friends (Wang & others, 2016). Further, a recent study of adolescent girls revealed that friends' dieting predicted whether adolescent girls would engage in dieting or extreme dieting (Balantekin, Birch, & Savage, 2018). And a recent study indicated that peers' influence on adolescents' healthy eating is often negative and characterized by an increase in consumption of energy-dense and low-nutritional-value foods (Rageliene & Gronhoj, 2020).

Developmental advantages occur when adolescents have friends who are socially skilled, supportive, and oriented toward academic achievement (Ryan & Shin, 2018). Positive friendships in adolescence are associated with a host of beneficial outcomes, including lower rates of delinquency, substance abuse, risky sexual behavior, and bullying victimization, and higher levels of academic achievement (Kindermann & Gest, 2018; Laursen & Adams, 2018). In a recent study of young adolescents, for non-Latino White and Asian Americans, higher academic achievement was linked to having same-ethnicity friends, while for African-American and Latino adolescents, higher academic achievement was associated with having more cross-ethnicity friendships (Chen, Saafir, & Graham, 2020).

Although most adolescents develop friendships with individuals who are close to their own age, some adolescents become friends with younger or older individuals. Do older friends encourage adolescents to engage in delinquent behavior or early sexual behavior? Adolescents who interact with older youth do engage in more problem behaviors, such as delinquency and early sexual behavior (Poulin & Pedersen, 2007).

To read about strategies for helping adolescents develop friendships, see *Connecting Development to Life*.

PEER GROUPS

How have social media changed the way that peers and friends interact? How extensive is peer pressure in adolescence? What roles do cliques and crowds play in adolescents' lives? As we see next, researchers have found that the standards of peer groups and the influence of crowds and cliques become increasingly important during adolescence.

Social Media and Peer Relations Nowhere have changes in peer and friendship relations been more evident in recent years than the increased connections adolescents make with peers and friends through networked technologies (Glover & Fritsch, 2018; Maheux & others, 2020; Nesi & Prinstein, 2019). Compared with earlier decades when the vast majority of adolescent contacts with peers and friends were made in person, today adolescents also spend considerable time using social media to connect with peers and friends (Nesi & Prinstein, 2019). Text messaging has become the main way adolescents connect with friends, surpassing even face-to-face contact (Lenhart, 2015).

Effective and Ineffective Strategies for Making Friends

Here are some strategies for making friends that adults can recommend to adolescents (Wentzel, 1997):

- **Initiate interaction.** Learn about a friend: Ask for his or her name, age, favorite activities. Use these prosocial overtures: introduce yourself, start a conversation, and invite him or her to do things.
- **Be nice.** Show kindness, be considerate, and compliment the other person.
- **Engage in prosocial behavior.** Be honest and trustworthy: Tell the truth, keep promises. Be generous, share, and be cooperative.
- **Show respect for yourself and others.** Have good manners, be polite and courteous, and listen to what others have to say. Have a positive attitude and personality.
- **Provide social support.** Show you care.

And here are some inappropriate strategies for making friends that adults can recommend that adolescents avoid using (Wentzel, 1997):

- **Be psychologically aggressive.** Show disrespect and have bad manners. Use others, be uncooperative, don't share, ignore others, gossip, and spread rumors.
- **Present yourself negatively.** Be self-centered, snobby, conceited, and jealous; show off; care only about yourself. Be mean, have a bad attitude, be angry, throw temper tantrums, and start trouble.
- **Behave antisocially.** Be physically aggressive, yell at others, pick on them, make fun of them, be dishonest, tell secrets, and break promises.

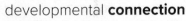

Based on what you read earlier in this chapter, what might you recommend to an adolescent about whom to approach as a potential friend?

A recent analysis described five ways in which social media transform adolescent peer relationships (Nesi, Choukas-Bradley, & Prinstein, 2018):

1. *Changing the frequency or immediacy of experiences* (potential for immediate, frequent social support, reassurance, negative feedback, and co-rumination)
2. *Amplifying experiences and demands* (heightened feedback seeking and expectations for relationship maintenance and access)
3. *Altering the qualitative aspects of interactions* (less rich social support, increased comfort in interactions)
4. *Facilitating new opportunities for compensatory behaviors* (possible exclusive online relationships and communication with geographically distant friends)
5. *Creating completely novel behaviors* (new opportunities to publicize "top friends" and relationships.

More information about peer relations and social media will be provided later in this chapter.

developmental connection

Peers

Five peer statuses can be used to categorize peer relationships. Connect to "Socioemotional Development in Early Childhood."

Peer Pressure Young adolescents conform more to peer standards than children do (Nesi & others, 2017). Around the eighth and ninth grades, conformity to peers—especially to their antisocial standards—peaks (Brown & Larson, 2009). At this point, adolescents are most likely to go along with a peer to steal hubcaps off a car, draw graffiti on a wall, or steal cosmetics from a store counter. One study found that U.S. adolescents are more likely than Japanese adolescents to put pressure on their peers to resist parental influence (Rothbaum & others, 2000). Also, a recent study found that boys were more likely to be influenced by peer pressure involving sexual behavior than were girls (Widman & others, 2016). And a recent study of eighth-graders revealed that peer pressure was associated with substance use (Jelsma & Varner, 2020).

Research indicates that found adolescents who feel uncertain about their social identity, which may be evident in low self-esteem and high social anxiety, are most likely to conform to peers (Prinstein & Giletta, 2016). This uncertainty often increases during times of transition, such as changing circumstances in school and family life. Also, adolescents are more likely to conform to peers whom they perceive to have higher status than they do.

What characterizes peer pressure in adolescence?
Christin Rose/Image Source/Getty Images

Cliques and Crowds   Cliques and crowds assume more important roles during adolescence than during childhood (Stalgatis & others, 2019). **Cliques** are small groups that range from 2 to about 12 individuals and average about 5 or 6 individuals. The clique members are usually of the same sex and about the same age.

Cliques can form because adolescents engage in similar activities, such as belonging to a club or playing on a sports team. Some cliques also form because of friendship. Several adolescents may form a clique because they have spent time with each other, share mutual interests, and enjoy each other's company.

Crowds are larger than cliques and less personal. Adolescents are usually members of a crowd based on reputation, and they may or may not spend much time together. Many crowds are defined by the activities adolescents engage in (such as "jocks" who are good at sports or "druggies" who take drugs) (Brown, 2011). In a recent study of adolescents, risky behavior was associated with two crowds—the Hip Hop crowd was especially linked with substance use and violence and the alternative crowd was associated with substance use, depression, suicide, bullying, physical inactivity, and obesity (Jordan & others, 2019). Also in this study, the mainstream and popular crowds were characterized by a lower level of risk taking for most behaviors.

So far, we have discussed many aspects of friendship and peer relations in adolescence. A final point about these very important socioemotional interactions of adolescents is how the abrupt appearance of the Coronavirus (COVID-19) in 2020 quickly affected the ways friendship and peer relations take place. One of the most widely recommended changes to respond to the virus outbreak emphasized *social distancing*, which involves maintaining a distance of 6 feet or more from others to prevent getting the virus or giving the virus to them. For some individuals, social distancing may increase feelings of social isolation and decrease connection with peers and friends, which is so important to adolescents. One benefit of the dramatic increase in social media use is that it allows adolescents to stay connected with friends and peers online. Although in these situations adolescents are going to press parents to let them congregate in person with peers and friends, given the potential damaging consequences of such viruses it is important for parents to set limits and not give into such demands, especially when they involve groups, and assure their children that eventually they will be able to go back to engaging in in-person friendship and peer interactions.

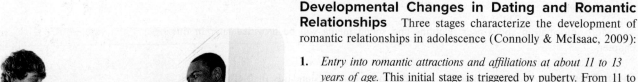

developmental **connection**

Emotional Development

The Coronavirus outbreak and other events like it can cause a great deal of anxiety and stress for children and youth. Parents can guide them in using a number of effective strategies to cope with such stressful circumstances. Connect with "Socioemotional Development in Middle and Late Childhood."

DATING AND ROMANTIC RELATIONSHIPS

Adolescents spend considerable time either dating or thinking about dating (Shulman & others, 2019, 2020). Dating can be a form of recreation, a source of status, or a setting for learning about close relationships, as well as a way of finding a mate.

What are some developmental changes in romantic relationships in adolescence?
Digital Vision/Getty Images

Developmental Changes in Dating and Romantic Relationships   Three stages characterize the development of romantic relationships in adolescence (Connolly & McIsaac, 2009):

1. *Entry into romantic attractions and affiliations at about 11 to 13 years of age.* This initial stage is triggered by puberty. From 11 to 13, adolescents become intensely interested in romance and it dominates many conversations with same-sex friends. Developing a crush on someone is common and the crush often is shared with a same-sex friend. Young adolescents may or may not interact with the individual who is the object of their infatuation. When dating occurs, it usually takes place in a group setting.

2. *Exploring romantic relationships at approximately 14 to 16 years of age.* At this point in adolescence, two types of romantic involvement occur: (a) Casual dating emerges between individuals who are mutually attracted. These dating experiences are often short-lived, lasting a few months at best, and usually endure for only a few weeks. (b) Dating in groups is common and reflects embeddedness in the peer context. Friends often act as third-party facilitators of a potential dating relationship by communicating their friend's romantic interest and determining whether this attraction is reciprocated.

3. *Consolidating dyadic romantic bonds at about 17 to 19 years of age.* At the end of the high school years, more serious romantic relationships develop. This is characterized by strong emotional bonds more closely resembling those in adult romantic relationships. These bonds often are more stable and enduring than earlier bonds, typically lasting one year or more.

Two variations on these stages in the development of romantic relationships in adolescence involve early and late bloomers (Connolly & McIsaac, 2009). *Early bloomers* include 15 to 20 percent of 11- to 13-year-olds who say that they currently are in a romantic relationship and 35 percent who indicate that they have had some prior experience in romantic relationships. One study found that early bloomers externalized problem behaviors through adolescence more than their on-time and late-bloomer counterparts (Connolly & others, 2013). *Late bloomers* comprise approximately 10 percent of 17- to 19-year-olds who say that they have had no experience with romantic relationships and another 15 percent who report that they have not engaged in any romantic relationships that lasted more than four months.

Dating in Gay and Lesbian Youth Recently, researchers have begun to study romantic relationships among gay and lesbian youth (Diamond, 2019; Savin-Williams, 2019). Many sexual minority youth date other-sex peers, which can help them to clarify their sexual orientation or disguise it from others (Savin-Williams, 2019). Most gay and lesbian youth have had some same-sex sexual experience, often with peers who are "experimenting." Some gay and lesbian youth continue to have a same-sex orientation, while others have a primarily heterosexual orientation (Savin-Williams, 2019).

Sociocultural Contexts and Dating The sociocultural context exerts a powerful influence on adolescents' dating patterns (Reid & others, 2019). This influence may be seen in differences in dating patterns among ethnic groups within the United States. For example, one study found that Asian American adolescents were less likely to have been involved in a romantic relationship in the past 18 months than African American or Latino adolescents were (Carver, Joyner, & Udry, 2003).

Values, religious beliefs, and traditions often dictate the age at which dating begins, how much freedom in dating is allowed, whether dates must be chaperoned by older siblings or parents, and the roles of males and females in dating. For example, Latino and Asian American cultures have more conservative standards regarding adolescent dating than does the Anglo-American culture. Dating may become a source of conflict within a family if the parents grew up in cultures where dating begins at a late age, little freedom in dating is allowed, dates are chaperoned, and dating by adolescent girls is especially restricted. When immigrant adolescents choose to adopt the ways of the dominant U.S. culture (such as unchaperoned dating), they often clash with parents and extended-family members who have more traditional values. Also, a recent study found that mother-daughter conflict in Mexican American families was linked to an increase in daughters' romantic involvement (Tyrell & others, 2016).

Dating and Adjustment Researchers have linked dating and romantic relationships with various measures of how well-adjusted adolescents are (Furman, 2018; Shulman & others, 2019, 2020). For example, a study of tenth-graders revealed that the greater the number of romantic encounters they had experienced, the more likely they were to report high levels of social acceptance, friendship competence, and romantic competence; however, having more romantic experience also was linked with a higher level of substance use, delinquency, and sexual behavior (Furman, Low, & Ho, 2009). In another study conducted among adolescent girls but not adolescent boys, having an older romantic partner was linked with an increase in depressive symptoms, largely influenced by an increase in substance use (Haydon & Halpern, 2010).

However, in some cases, romantic relationships in adolescence are linked with positive developmental changes. For example, in one study, having a supportive romantic relationship in adolescence was linked to positive outcomes for adolescents who had negative relationships with their mothers (Szwedo, Hessel, & Allen, 2017). And in a recent study, hostile conflict with a romantic partner at age 17 predicted an increase in internalizing behaviors (depression, for example) from 17 to 27 (Kansky & Allen, 2018). Also in this study, romantic partner support at age 17 predicted decreases in externalizing behaviors (high levels of aggression, for example) over time.

How are adolescent romantic relationships linked to adjustment?
Pascal Broze/Onoky/Getty Images/SuperStock

Dating and romantic relationships at an early age can be especially problematic (Furman, 2018). One study found that romantic activity was linked to depression in early adolescent girls (Starr & others, 2012). Researchers also have found that early dating and "going with" someone are linked with adolescent pregnancy and problems at home and school (Florsheim, Moore, & Edgington, 2003).

Review *Connect* Reflect

 LG3 Characterize the changes that occur in peer relationships during adolescence.

Review
- What changes take place in friendship during adolescence?
- What are adolescents' peer groups like?
- What is the nature of adolescent dating and romantic relationships?

Connect
- Relational aggression was discussed here and in the chapter on "Socioemotional Development in Middle and Late Childhood." In one of the studies described in that chapter, what connection was made between parents and the relational aggression of their children?

Reflect *Your Own Personal Journey of Life*
- What were your peer relationships like during adolescence? What peer groups were you involved in? How did they influence your development? What were your dating and romantic relationships like in adolescence? If you could change anything about the way you experienced peer relations in adolescence, what would it be?

4 Culture and Adolescent Development

 LG4 Explain how culture influences adolescent development.

Cross-Cultural Comparisons   Socioeconomic Status and Poverty   Ethnicity   Media Use and Screen Time

In this section, we will discuss cross-cultural variations in a number of aspects of adolescent development. We also will examine how ethnicity affects U.S. adolescents and influences their development. Further, we will consider the many challenges faced by adolescents who grow up in low-income and impoverished families. Finally, we will explore an important aspect of the cultural worlds of adolescents—the media.

CROSS-CULTURAL COMPARISONS

What traditions continue to influence the lives of adolescents around the globe? What circumstances are changing adolescents' lives? Depending on the culture, adolescence may involve many different experiences (Matsumoto & Hwang, 2019; Rowland & others, 2020).

Health   Adolescent health and well-being have improved in some respects but not in others. Overall, fewer adolescents around the world die from infectious diseases and malnutrition now than in the past (UNICEF, 2020). However, a number of adolescent health-compromising behaviors (especially illicit drug use and unprotected sex) are increasing in frequency. Extensive increases in the rates of HIV in adolescents have occurred in many sub-Saharan countries (UNICEF, 2020).

Gender   Around the world, the experiences of male and female adolescents continue to be quite different (Brown & Larson, 2002; Peitzmeier & others, 2016). Except in a few regions, such as Japan, the Philippines, and Western countries, males have far greater access to educational opportunities than females do (UNICEF, 2020). In many countries, adolescent females have less freedom than males to pursue a variety of careers and engage in various leisure activities. Gender differences in sexual expression are widespread, especially in India, Southeast Asia, Latin America, and Arab countries where far more restrictions are placed on the sexual activity of adolescent females than on that of males. These gender differences do appear to be narrowing over time, however. In some countries, educational and career opportunities for women are expanding, and control over adolescent girls' romantic and sexual relationships is weakening.

Muslim school in Middle East with boys only.
Alzuddin Saad/Shutterstock

Family   In some countries, adolescents grow up in closely knit families with extensive kin networks that retain a traditional way of life. For example, in Arab countries "adolescents are taught strict codes of conduct and loyalty" (Brown & Larson, 2002, p. 6). However, in Western countries such as the United States, parenting is less authoritarian than in the past, and much larger numbers of adolescents are growing up in divorced families and stepfamilies.

In many countries around the world, current trends "include greater family mobility, migration to urban areas, family members working in distant cities or countries, smaller families, fewer extended-family households, and increases in mothers' employment" (Brown & Larson, 2002, p. 7). Unfortunately, many of these changes may reduce the ability of parents to spend time with their adolescents.

Peers   Some cultures give peers a stronger role in adolescence than other cultures do (Brown & others, 2008). In most Western nations, peers figure prominently in adolescents' lives, in some cases taking on roles that in other cultures are assumed by parents. Among street youth in South America, the peer network serves as a surrogate family that supports survival in dangerous and stressful settings. In other regions of the world, such as in Arab countries, peer relations are restricted, especially for girls (Booth, 2002).

Time Allocation to Different Activities   Reed Larson and his colleagues (Larson, 2001; Larson, McGovern, & Orson, 2019; Larson, Walker, & McGovern, 2019) have examined how adolescents spend their time in work, play, and developmental activities such as school. U.S. adolescents spend about 60 percent as much time on schoolwork as East Asian adolescents do, which is mainly due to U.S. adolescents doing less homework (Larson & Verma, 1999).

U.S. adolescents have greater quantities of discretionary time than adolescents in other industrialized countries do (Larson, McGovern, & Orson, 2019; Larson, Walker, & McGovern, 2019). About 40 to 50 percent of U.S. adolescents' waking hours (not counting summer vacations) is spent in discretionary activities, compared with 25 to 35 percent in East Asia and 35 to 45 percent in Europe. Whether this additional discretionary time is a liability or an asset for U.S. adolescents, of course, depends on how they use it.

According to Larson (2001), U.S. adolescents may have too much unstructured time because when they are given a choice they typically engage in unchallenging activities such as hanging out and watching TV. Although relaxation and social interaction are important aspects of adolescence, it seems unlikely that spending large amounts of time in unchallenging activities would foster development. Structured voluntary activities may promote positive adolescent development more than unstructured time, especially if adults give responsibility to adolescents, challenge them, and provide competent guidance in these activities (Larson, Walker, & McGovern, 2019).

Rites of Passage   Another variation in the experiences of adolescents in different cultures is whether the adolescents undergo a rite of passage. Some societies have elaborate ceremonies that signal the adolescent's move to maturity and achievement of adult status (Ember & Ember, 2019). A **rite of passage** is a ceremony or ritual that marks an individual's transition from one status to another. Most rites of passage focus on the transition to adult status. In some traditional cultures, rites of passage are the avenue through which adolescents gain access to sacred adult practices, to knowledge, and to sexuality. These rites often involve dramatic practices intended to facilitate the adolescent's separation from the immediate family, especially the mother. The transformation is usually characterized by some form of ritual death and rebirth, or by means of contact with the spiritual world. Bonds are forged between the adolescent and the adult instructors through shared rituals, hazards, and secrets to allow the adolescent to enter the adult world. This kind of ritual provides a forceful and discontinuous entry into the adult world at a time when the adolescent is perceived to be ready for the change.

An especially rich tradition of rites of passage for adolescents has prevailed in African cultures, especially sub-Saharan Africa. Under the influence of Western industrialized culture, many of these rites are disappearing today, although they are still prevalent in locations where formal education is not readily available.

Do we have such rites of passage for American adolescents? We do not have universal formal ceremonies that mark the passage from adolescence to adulthood. Some religious and social groups do, however, have initiation ceremonies that indicate that an advance in maturity has been reached, such as the Jewish bar and bat mitzvah, the Catholic confirmation, and social debuts, for example. School graduation ceremonies come the closest to being

rite of passage A ceremony or ritual that marks an individual's transition from one status to another. Most rites of passage focus on the transition to adult status.

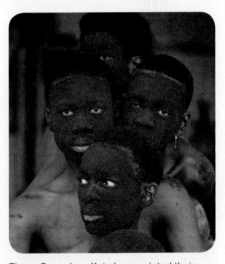

These Congolese Kota boys painted their faces as part of a rite of passage to adulthood. *What rites of passage do American adolescents have?*
Daniel Laine/Gamma Rapho

culture-wide rites of passage in the United States. The high school graduation ceremony has become nearly universal for middle-class adolescents and increasing numbers of adolescents from low-income backgrounds.

SOCIOECONOMIC STATUS AND POVERTY

In the chapter on "Socioemotional Development in Middle and Late Childhood" we described many aspects of the challenges faced by children who live in low-income and impoverished families. Here we focus on challenges that adolescents have to cope with under these circumstances.

Adolescents from low-SES backgrounds are at risk for experiencing low academic achievement and emotional problems, as well as lower occupational attainment in adulthood (Magnuson & Duncan, 2019; McLoyd, Hardaway, & Jocson, 2019). Psychological problems such as smoking, depression, and juvenile delinquency as well as physical illnesses are more prevalent among low-SES adolescents than among economically advantaged adolescents (American Psychological Association, 2019). For example, a recent study found that of 13 risk factors, low SES was most likely to be associated with smoking initiation in fifth-graders (Wellman & others, 2018). Further, in a U.S. longitudinal study, low SES in adolescence was linked to having a higher level of depressive symptoms at age 54 for females (Pino & others, 2018). In another longitudinal study, low SES in adolescence was a risk factor for having cardiovascular disease 30 years later (Doom & others, 2017). In this study, the following factors were found to be involved in the pathway to cardiovascular disease for low-SES individuals: health-compromising behaviors, financial stress, inadequate medical care, and lower educational attainment. In addition, a longitudinal study indicated that low SES in childhood was associated with lower cognitive function and more cognitive decline in middle and late adulthood (Liu & Lachman, 2019). Also, a recent Australian study revealed that children and adolescents from low-SES backgrounds were less likely to achieve a healthy physical fitness level than their high-SES counterparts (Peralta & others, 2019).

Are there psychological and social factors that predict higher achievement for some of the adolescents living in poverty? One study found that higher levels of the following four factors assessed at the beginning of the sixth grade were linked to higher grade point averages at the end of the seventh grade for children living in poverty: (1) academic commitment, (2) emotional control, (3) family involvement, and (4) school climate (Li, Allen, & Casillas, 2017).

When poverty is persistent and long-standing, it can have especially damaging effects on adolescents (Magnuson & Duncan, 2019). A recent study found that 12- to 19-year-olds' perceived well-being was lowest when they had lived in poverty from birth to 2 years of age (compared to ages 3 to 5, 6 to 8, and 9 to 11), and each additional year of living in poverty was associated with even lower perceived well-being (Gariepy & others, 2017).

ETHNICITY

Earlier in this chapter, we explored the identity development of ethnic minority adolescents. Here we will further examine immigration and the relationship between ethnicity and socioeconomic status.

Immigration   Relatively high rates of immigration are contributing to the growing proportion of ethnic minority adolescents and emerging adults in the United States (Banks, 2020; Bennett, 2019). Immigrant families are those in which at least one of the parents was born outside the country of residence. Variations in immigrant families involve whether one or both parents are foreign born, whether the child was born in the host country, and the ages at which immigration took place for both the parents and the children (Hill & others, 2019; Simha, 2019). Robert Crosnoe and Andrew Fuligni (2012, p. 1473) concluded:

> Some children from immigrant families are doing quite well, some less so, depending on the characteristics of migration itself (including the nation of origin) and their families' circumstances in their new country (including their position in socioeconomic and race-ethnic stratification systems).

What are some of the circumstances immigrants face that challenge their adjustment? Immigrants often experience stressors uncommon to or less prominent among long-time residents, such as language barriers, dislocations and separations from support networks, the dual struggle to preserve identity and to acculturate, and changes in socioeconomic status (Romero & others, 2020; White & others, 2019).

---

developmental connection

Poverty

Poverty is linked to family turmoil, separation from a parent, violence, crowding, excessive noise, and poor housing. Connect to "Introduction" and "Socioemotional Development in Middle and Late Childhood."

Many individuals in immigrant families are dealing with the problem of being undocumented (Amuedo-Durantes & Arenas-Arroyo, 2019). Living in an undocumented family can affect children's and adolescents' developmental outcomes through parents being unwilling to sign up for services for which they are eligible, through conditions linked to low-wage work and lack of benefits, through stress, and through a lack of cognitive stimulation in the home (Cobb & others, 2017). Consequently, when working with adolescents and their immigrant families, counselors need to adapt intervention programs to optimize cultural sensitivity (Bornstein & Cote, 2019).

The ways in which ethnic minority families deal with stress depend on many factors (Bucay-Harari & others, 2020; Lu, He, & Brooks-Gunn, 2020). Whether the parents are native-born or immigrants, how long the family has been in the United States, its socioeconomic status, family values, how competently parents rear their children and adolescents, and their national origin all make a difference (Hou & Kim, 2018; Zhang & others, 2020). A recent study of Mexican-origin youth found that when adolescents reported a higher level of familism (giving priority to one's family), they engaged in lower levels of risk taking (Wheeler & others, 2017). Another study revealed that parents' education before migrating was strongly linked to their children's academic achievement (Pong & Landale, 2012).

What are some cultural adaptations these Mexican American girls likely will have to make as immigrants to the United States?
Caroline Woodham/Getty Images

Ethnicity and Socioeconomic Status   Much of the research on ethnic minority adolescents has failed to distinguish between the influences of ethnicity and socioeconomic status. Ethnicity and socioeconomic status can interact in ways that exaggerate the influence of ethnicity because ethnic minority individuals are overrepresented in the lower socioeconomic levels of American society (Banks, 2020; Gollnick & Chinn, 2021). Consequently, researchers too often have given ethnic explanations for aspects of adolescent development that were largely attributable to socioeconomic status.

Not all ethnic minority families are poor. However, as we saw earlier in this chapter, poverty contributes to the stressful life experiences of many ethnic minority adolescents (McLoyd, Hardaway, & Jocson, 2019). Thus, many ethnic minority adolescents experience a double disadvantage: (1) prejudice, discrimination, and bias because of their ethnic minority status; and (2) the stressful effects of poverty (Chen & others, 2020). Although some ethnic minority youth have middle-income backgrounds, economic advantage does not entirely enable them to escape the prejudice, discrimination, and bias associated with being a member of an ethnic minority group (McDermott, Umana-Taylor, & Zeiders, 2019).

MEDIA USE AND SCREEN TIME

The culture adolescents experience involves not only cultural values, SES, and ethnicity, but also media and screen time influences (Maloy & others, 2021; Roblyer & Hughes, 2019). Television continues to have a strong influence on children's and adolescents' development, but children's use of other media and information/communication devices has led to the use of the term *screen time,* which includes how much time individuals spend watching television or DVDs, playing video games, and using computers or mobile media such as iPhones (Boers, Afzali, & Conrod, 2020; Vandendriessche & others, 2019). A recent study found that nighttime mobile phone use and poor sleep behavior increased from 13 to 16 years of age (Vernon, Modecki, & Barber, 2018). In this study, increased nighttime mobile phone use was linked to increased externalizing problems, as well as decreased self-esteem and coping.

Are there gender differences in digital media use? In recent research on 13- to 18-year-olds in the United States and the United Kingdom, adolescent girls spent more time on smartphones, social media, texting, general computer use, and being online while boys spent more time engaging in gaming and on electronic devices in general (Twenge & Martin, 2020). For both girls and boys, heavy users of digital media were twice as likely as low users to have low psychological well-being and mental health issues.

Prevalence of Media Use and Screen Time   If the amount of time spent in an activity is any indication of its importance, there is no doubt that media use and screen time play important roles in adolescents' lives (Rodgers & others, 2020; Zhang & others, 2019). To better understand various aspects of U.S. adolescents' media use and screen time, the Kaiser Family Foundation funded three national surveys in 1999, 2004, and 2009. The 2009 survey

Jason Leonard, age 15: "I want America to know that most of us black teens are not troubled people from broken homes and headed to jail. . . . In my relationships with my parents, we show respect for each other and we have values in our house. We have traditions we celebrate together, including Christmas and Kwanzaa."
Comstock/Getty Images

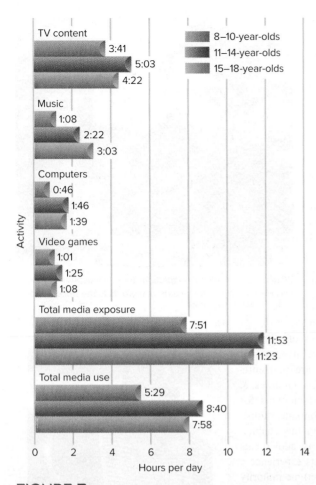

TV content
3:41
5:03
4:22

Music
1:08
2:22
3:03

Computers
0:46
1:46
1:39

Video games
1:01
1:25
1:08

Total media exposure
7:51
11:53
11:23

Total media use
5:29
8:40
7:58

■ 8–10-year-olds
■ 11–14-year-olds
■ 15–18-year-olds

Activity

Hours per day
0   2   4   6   8   10   12   14

FIGURE 5

DEVELOPMENTAL CHANGES IN THE AMOUNT OF TIME U.S. 8- TO 18-YEAR-OLDS SPEND WITH DIFFERENT TYPES OF MEDIA AND ELECTRONIC DEVICES

How much time do adolescents spend using different types of media?
Inti St Clair/Blend Images/Getty Images

included more than 2,000 8- to 18-year-olds and documented that adolescent media use and screen time had increased dramatically in the previous decade (Rideout, Foehr, & Roberts, 2010). In this survey, in 2009, 8- to 11-year-olds used media 5 hours and 29 minutes a day, 11- to 14-year-olds averaged 8 hours and 40 minutes a day, and 15- to 18-year-olds averaged 7 hours and 58 minutes a day (see Figure 5). Thus, media use jumped more than 3 hours in early adolescence! The largest increases in media use in early adolescence are for TV and video games. TV use by youth increasingly has involved watching TV on the Internet via a notebook computer or cell phone. As indicated in Figure 5, listening to music and using computers also increase considerably among 11- to 14-year-old adolescents. And based on the 2009 survey, adding up the daily media use figures to obtain weekly media use leads to the staggering levels of more than 60 hours a week of media use by 11- to 14-year-olds and almost 56 hours a week by 15- to 18-year-olds!

The more screen time adolescents have, the more their academic achievement suffers. For example, in a recent study of adolescents, increased screen time was associated with lower academic achievement in English and math (Hunter, Leatherdale, & Carson, 2018). Another recent study of adolescents confirmed that lower screen time was linked to higher math achievement (Poulain & others, 2018).

Higher levels of parental monitoring of children's and adolescents' media use have been linked to a number of positive outcomes, including more sleep, better school performance, less aggressive behavior, and more prosocial behavior (Barr, 2019). Further, a recent study indicated that parental monitoring of media violence exposure was linked to less aggressive behavior in adolescents (Khurana & others, 2019).

A major trend in the use of technology is the dramatic increase in media multitasking (Uncapher & Wagner, 2018). In the 2009 survey, when the amount of time spent multitasking was included in computing media use, 11- to 14-year-olds spent nearly 12 hours a day (compared with almost 9 hours a day when multitasking was not included) exposed to media (Rideout, Foehr, & Roberts, 2010)! In this survey, 39 percent of seventh- to twelfth-graders said "most of the time" they used two or more media concurrently, such as surfing the Web while listening to music.

In some cases, media multitasking—such as text messaging, listening to an iPod, and updating a YouTube site—is engaged in while doing homework. It is hard to imagine that this allows a student to do homework efficiently, although there is little research on media multitasking. A recent research review concluded that at a general level, digital technologies (surfing the Internet, texting someone) while engaging in a learning task (reading, listening to a lecture) distract learners and result in impaired performance on many tasks (Courage & others, 2015). The same research review also concluded that when driving subtasks such as various perceptual-motor activities (steering control, changing lanes, maneuvering through traffic, braking, and acceleration) and ongoing cognitive tasks (planning, decision making, or maintaining a conversation with a passenger) are combined with interactive in-vehicle devices (phones, navigation aids, portable music devices), the task of driving becomes more complex and the potential for distraction increases. Also, in a recent study, heavy multimedia multitaskers were less likely than light media multitaskers to delay gratification and more likely to endorse intuitive, but wrong, answers on a cognitive reflection task (Schutten, Stokes, & Arnell, 2017). Further, in a recent study of 11- to 18-year-olds in Spain, media multitasking during homework was linked to lower executive function, a lower level of working memory, and worse academic performance in language and math (Martin-Perpiña, Vinas Poch, & Malo Cerrato, 2019).

Technology and Digitally Mediated Communication Culture involves change, and nowhere is that change greater than in the technological revolution individuals are experiencing with increased use of computers and the Internet (Maloy & others, 2021; Smaldino & others, 2019). Mobile media, such as smartphones, are mainly driving the increased media use by adolescents (Foerster & others, 2019; O'Reilly, 2020). For example, in 2004, 39 percent of adolescents owned a cell phone, a figure that jumped to 66 percent in 2009 and then to 87 percent in 2016 with a prediction of 92 percent in 2019 (eMarketeer.com, 2016; Rideout, Foehr, & Roberts, 2010).

A national survey revealed dramatic increases in adolescents' use of social media and text messaging (Lenhart, 2015). In 2015, 92 percent of U.S. 13- to 17-year-olds reported using social networking sites daily. Twenty-four percent of the adolescents said they were online almost constantly. Much of this increase in going online has been fueled by smartphones and mobile devices. Facebook was the most popular and frequently used social networking site—71 percent reported using Facebook and half said they used Instagram. A recent study found that less screen time was linked to adolescents' better health-related quality of life (Wong & others, 2017). Another recent study indicated that a higher level of social media use was associated with a higher level of heavy drinking by adolescents (Brunborg, Andreas, & Kvaavik, 2017).

Text messaging has become the main way that adolescents connect with their friends, surpassing face-to-face contact, e-mail, instant messaging, and voice calling (Lenhart, 2015). In the national survey and a further update (Lenhart & others, 2015), daily text messaging increased from 38 percent who texted friends daily in 2008 to 55 percent in 2015. However, voice mail was the primary way that most adolescents preferred to connect with parents.

What characterizes the online social environment of adolescents and emerging adults?

Anne Ackermann/Digital Vision/Alamy Stock Photo

Review Connect Reflect

 Explain how culture influences adolescent development.

Review

- What are some comparisons of adolescents in different cultures? How do adolescents around the world spend their time? What is the purpose of rites of passage?
- How does ethnicity influence adolescent development?
- How do socioeconomic status and poverty influence adolescent development?
- What characterizes media use and screen time among adolescents?

Connect

- How might what you learned about school dropout rates and extracurricular activities be linked to the view of Reed Larson and his colleagues regarding adolescents' lack of adequate self-initiative?

Reflect *Your Own Personal Journey of Life*

- What is your ethnicity? Have you ever been stereotyped because of your ethnicity? How different is your identity from the mainstream culture?

---

5 Adolescent Problems

LG5 Identify adolescent problems in socioemotional development and strategies for helping adolescents with problems.

Juvenile Delinquency

Depression and Suicide

The Interrelation of Problems and Successful Prevention/Intervention Programs

Earlier we described several adolescent problems: substance abuse, sexually transmitted infections, and eating disorders. In this chapter, we will examine the problems of juvenile delinquency, depression, and suicide. We will also explore interrelationships among adolescent problems and describe how such problems can be prevented or remediated.

JUVENILE DELINQUENCY

The label **juvenile delinquent** is applied to an adolescent who breaks the law or engages in behavior that is considered illegal. Like other categories of disorders, juvenile delinquency is a broad concept, encompassing legal infractions that range from littering to murder (Mash & Wolfe, 2019).

juvenile delinquent An adolescent who breaks the law or engages in behavior that is considered illegal.

Delinquency Rates   Juvenile court delinquency caseloads in the United States increased dramatically from 1960 to 1996 but have decreased slightly since 1996 (Puzzanchera & Robson, 2014). Note that this figure reflects only adolescents who have been arrested and assigned to juvenile court delinquency caseloads and does not include those who were arrested but not assigned to the delinquency caseloads, nor does the figure include youth who committed offenses but were not apprehended. In 2017, there were 818,900 delinquency cases in which juveniles were charged with violating criminal laws—down from 1,400,000 in 2010 but up from 400,000 in 1960 (Hockenberry & Puzzanchera, 2019).

Males are more likely to engage in delinquency than are females. However, U.S. government statistics revealed that the percentage of delinquency cases involving females increased from 19 percent in 1985 to 27 percent in 2017 (Hockenberry & Puzzanchera, 2019).

Delinquency rates among minority groups and lower-socioeconomic-status youth are higher than the proportions of these groups within the general population. However, such groups have less influence over the judicial decision-making process in the United States and therefore may be judged delinquent more readily than their non-Latino White, middle-SES counterparts who have committed similar offenses.

Is delinquency in adolescence linked to adult outcomes? In a recent study, delinquency in adolescence was associated with a greater likelihood of being unemployed in adulthood (Carter, 2019).

A distinction is made between early-onset (before age 11) and late-onset (after age 11) antisocial behavior. Early-onset antisocial behavior is associated with more negative developmental outcomes than late-onset antisocial behavior (Schulenberg & Zarrett, 2006; Wiecko, 2014). Not only is early-onset antisocial behavior more likely to persist into emerging adulthood, but it is also associated with more mental health and relationship problems (Pechorro & others, 2014).

Causes of Delinquency   Although delinquency is less exclusively a phenomenon of lower socioeconomic status than it was in the past, some characteristics of lower-SES culture might promote delinquency (Thio, Taylor, & Schwartz, 2019). A recent study of more than 10,000 children and adolescents found that family environments characterized by poverty and child maltreatment were linked to entering the juvenile justice system in adolescence (Vidal & others, 2017). The norms of many lower-SES peer groups and gangs are antisocial, or counterproductive to the goals and norms of society at large. Getting into and staying out of trouble are prominent features of life for some adolescents in low-income neighborhoods. Being "tough" and "masculine" are high-status traits for lower-SES boys, and these traits are often measured by the adolescent's success in performing and getting away with delinquent acts. And adolescents in communities with high crime rates observe many models who engage in criminal activities. These communities may be characterized by poverty, unemployment, and feelings of alienation toward the middle class. Quality schooling, educational funding, and organized neighborhood activities often are lacking in these communities (Crosnoe & Benner, 2015). One study found that youth whose families had experienced repeated poverty were more than twice as likely to be delinquent at 14 and 21 years of age (Najman & others, 2010).

Certain characteristics of families are also associated with delinquency (Farrington & Hawkins, 2019). Parental monitoring of adolescents is especially important in determining whether an adolescent becomes a delinquent (Bendezu & others, 2018; Dishion & Patterson, 2016). Family discord and inconsistent and inappropriate discipline are also associated with delinquency (Bor, McGee, & Fagan, 2004). And one study found that low rates of delinquency from 14 to 23 years of age were associated with an authoritative parenting style (Murphy & others, 2012). An increasing number of studies have found that siblings can have a strong influence on delinquency (Laursen & others, 2017; Wallace, 2017). Recent research indicates that family therapy is often effective in reducing delinquency (Henderson, Hogue, & Dauber, 2019).

Having delinquent peers and friends increases the risk of becoming delinquent (Walters, 2020). In a recent study, classrooms in which higher rates of students were engaging in delinquency had an increased likelihood that other classmates would become delinquent (Kim & Fletcher, 2018). Also, another recent study found that having a best friend who was delinquent was linked a higher probability that adolescents themselves would become delinquent (Levey & others, 2019).

Lack of academic success is associated with delinquency (Gordon Simons & others, 2018). In a recent research review, lack of academic success and having a learning disability were linked to delinquency (Grigorenko & others, 2019). And a number of cognitive factors such as low self-control, low intelligence, and lack of sustained attention are linked to

What are some factors that are linked to whether adolescents engage in delinquent acts?
Fertnig/iStock/Getty Images

Rodney Hammond, Health Psychologist

Rodney Hammond described how his college experiences led to his career choice:

> "When I started as an undergraduate at the University of Illinois, Champaign-Urbana, I hadn't decided on my major. But to help finance my education, I took a part-time job in a child development research program sponsored by the psychology department. There, I observed inner-city children in settings designed to enhance their learning. I saw firsthand the contribution psychology can make, and I knew I wanted to be a psychologist" (American Psychological Association, 2003, p. 26).

Rodney Hammond went on to obtain a doctorate in school and community psychology with a focus on children's development. For a number of years, he trained clinical psychologists at Wright State University in Ohio and directed a program to reduce violence in ethnic minority youth. There, he and his associates taught at-risk youth how to use social skills to effectively manage conflict and to recognize situations that could lead to violence. Hammond became the first Director of Violence Prevention at the Centers for Disease Control and Prevention in Atlanta. Following his recent retirement from CDC, he is now Adjunct Professor of Human Development and Counseling at the University of Georgia.

Rodney Hammond counsels an adolescent girl about the risks of adolescence and how to effectively cope with them.
Courtesy of Dr. Rodney Hammond

delinquency (Muftic & Updegrove, 2018). Further, recent research indicates that having callous-unemotional personality traits predicts an increased risk of engaging in delinquency for adolescent males (Ray & others, 2017).

One individual whose goal is to help at-risk adolescents, such as juvenile delinquents, cope more effectively with their lives is Rodney Hammond. Read about his work in *Connecting with Careers*.

DEPRESSION AND SUICIDE

What is the nature of depression in adolescence? What causes adolescents to commit suicide?

Depression   How widespread is depression in adolescence? Rates of ever experiencing major depressive disorder range from 15 to 20 percent for adolescents (Graber & Sontag, 2009). Adolescents who are experiencing a high level of stress and/or a loss of some type are at increased risk for developing depression (Cohen & others, 2018). Also, one study found that adolescents who became depressed were characterized by a sense of hopelessness (Weersing & others, 2016). Another study revealed that low self-esteem and negative emotion management in adolescence was linked to depression (Fiorilli & others, 2019). Further, a recent study revealed that interpersonal stress was linked to increased depression in adolescent girls (Slavich & others, 2020). And a recent research review concluded that adolescents are very poor at recognizing depression, likely to seek help from informal rather than professional sources, and tend to attach stigma to depression (Singh, Zaki, & Farid, 2019).

Adolescent females are far more likely to develop depression than are their male counterparts. In a recent study, at 12 years of age, 5.2 percent of females compared to 2 percent of males had experienced first-onset depression (Breslau & others, 2017). In this study, the cumulative incidence of depression from 12 to 17 years of age was 36 percent for females and 14 percent for males. Among the reasons for this gender difference are that females tend to ruminate in their depressed mood and amplify it; females' self-images, especially their body images, are more negative than males'; females face more discrimination than males do; and puberty occurs earlier for girls than for boys (Bunge & others, 2017).

What are some characteristics of adolescents who become depressed?
Science Photo Library/age fotostock

```
- - - - - - - >
```

developmental **connection**

The Epigenetic Approach

The epigenetic approach states that development is an ongoing, bidirectional interaction between heredity and the environment. Connect to "Biological Beginnings."

developmental **connection**

Conditions, Diseases, and Disorders

What characterizes depression in older adults? Connect to "Cognitive Development in Late Adulthood."

```
< - - - - - - - -
```

Is adolescent depression linked to problems in emerging and early adulthood? In one study, researchers initially assessed U.S. adolescents when they were 16 to 17 years of age and then again every two years until they were 26 to 27 years of age (Naicker & others, 2013). In this study, significant effects that persisted after 10 years were depression recurrence, stronger depressive symptoms, migraine headaches, poor self-rated health, and low levels of social support. Also, a longitudinal study found that a majority of adolescents who had a major depressive episode were likely to experience a recurrence of depression 15 years later (Alaie & others, 2019). In addition, adolescent depression was associated with other mental health problems, low educational attainment, and problems in intimate relationships when assessed 15 years later. And in a recent study, having a persistent depressive disorder in adolescence was linked to requiring more health-care resources in middle adulthood (Ssegonia & others, 2020).

Genes are linked to adolescent depression (Brouillard & others, 2019; Hannigan, McAdams, & Eley, 2017). One study found that certain dopamine-related genes were associated with depressive symptoms in adolescents (Adkins & others, 2012). And another study revealed that the link between adolescent girls' perceived stress and depression occurred only when the girls had the short version of the serotonin-related gene 5HTTLPR (Beaver & others, 2012).

Certain family factors place adolescents at risk for developing depression (Griffith & others, 2019; Loechner & others, 2020). These include having a depressed parent, emotionally unavailable parents, parents who have high marital conflict, and parents with financial problems (Rasing & others, 2020). One study also revealed that mother-daughter co-rumination (extensively discussing, rehashing, and speculating about problems) was linked to increased rates of anxiety and depression in adolescent girls (Waller & Rose, 2010). Also, one study found that positive parenting characteristics such as emotional and educational support were associated with lower rates of depression in adolescents (Smokowski & others, 2015).

Poor peer relationships also are associated with adolescent depression (Costello & others, 2020). A recent study found that adolescents who were isolated from their peers and whose caregivers emotionally neglected them were at significant risk for developing depression (Christ, Kwak, & Lu, 2017). Not having a close relationship with a best friend, having less contact with friends, and being rejected by peers increase depressive tendencies in adolescents (Platt, Kadosh, & Lau, 2013). One study also found that relational aggression was linked to depression for girls (Spieker & others, 2012).

Friendship often provides social support. However, whether friendship is linked with a lower level of depression among girls and boys depends on the type of friendship. For example, in one study young adolescents with nondepressed friends were less likely to be depressed than young adolescents without friends, whereas young adolescents with depressed friends were more likely to be depressed (Brendgen & others, 2010). And a study of third- through ninth-graders revealed that girls' co-rumination predicted not only an increase in the positive quality of the friendship, but also an increase in further co-rumination and in depressive and anxiety symptoms (Rose, Carlson, & Waller, 2007). In another study, co-rumination with friends was linked to greater peer stress for adolescent girls (Rose & others, 2017). Further, problems in romantic relationships can produce adolescent depression (Furman, 2018).

A recent meta-analysis found that adolescent females who were obese were more likely to have depression (Quek & others, 2017). Being stressed about weight-related concerns is increasingly thought to contribute to the greater incidence of depression in adolescent girls than in adolescent boys (Herpertz-Dahlmann & others, 2015).

Some therapy treatments have been shown to reduce adolescent depression (Bernal & others, 2019). A research review concluded that drug therapy using SSRIs (selective serotonin reuptake inhibitors), cognitive behavioral therapy, and interpersonal therapy were effective in treating adolescent depression (Maalouf & Brent, 2012). However, in this review, the most effective treatment was a combination of drug therapy and cognitive behavioral therapy. Also, a research review concluded that Prozac and other SSRIs show clinical benefits for adolescents at risk for moderate and severe depression (Cousins & Goodyer, 2015). Other recent research indicates that family therapy also can be effective in reducing adolescent depression (Poole & others, 2018).

Suicide Suicidal behavior is rare in childhood but escalates in adolescence and then increases further in emerging adulthood (Park & others, 2006). Suicide is now the second-leading cause of death in 10- to 19-year-olds today in the United States (National Center for Health Statistics, 2019). Overall, suicide rates for adolescent males and females have declined in the last 40 years. However, in a study of more than 85,000 10- to 19-year-olds who committed suicide from 1975 to 2016, suicide rates had increased in males and females since 2007. Also, in one group of females—those 10 to 14 years old—there was a disproportionate, steeper increase in suicide.

There are cultural differences in suicide (Naghavi & others, 2019). Recent cross-cultural comparisons of 15- to 19-year-olds indicated that the highest suicide rates occurred in New Zealand, followed by Iceland, and that the lowest rates occurred in Greece and Israel (OECD, 2017).

Although a suicide threat should always be taken seriously, far more adolescents contemplate or attempt it unsuccessfully than actually commit it (Castellvi & others, 2017). As indicated in Figure 6, from 1991 to 2009 there was a considerable decline in the percentage of adolescents who seriously considered committing suicide, but from 2009 to 2017 there was an increase from 14 to 17 percent (Kann & others, 2018). In this national study, in 2017, 7.4 percent had attempted suicide one or more times in the last 12 months and 2.4 percent had engaged in suicide attempts that required medical attention.

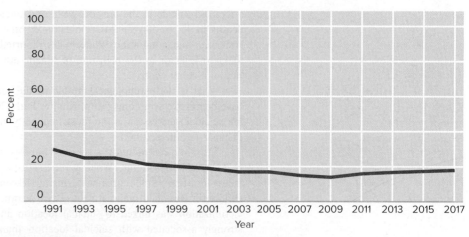

FIGURE 6

PERCENTAGE OF U.S. NINTH- TO TWELFTH-GRADE STUDENTS WHO SERIOUSLY CONSIDERED ATTEMPTING SUICIDE IN THE PREVIOUS 12 MONTHS FROM 1991 TO 2017

Females are more likely to attempt suicide than males, but males are more likely to succeed in committing suicide, although in recent years the gender gap has narrowed (Molina & Farley, 2019). Males use more lethal means, such as guns, in their suicide attempts, whereas adolescent females are more likely to cut their wrists or take an overdose of sleeping pills—methods less likely to result in death.

Just as genetic factors are associated with depression, they also are associated with suicide (Orri & others, 2020; Zai & others, 2019). The closer a person's genetic relationship to someone who has committed suicide, the more likely that person is to also commit suicide.

Both earlier and later experiences are linked to suicide attempts, and these can involve family relationships (Jimenez-Trevino & others, 2019). The adolescent may have a long-standing history of family instability and unhappiness (Wan & Leung, 2010). Just as a lack of affection and emotional support, high control, and parental pressure for achievement during childhood are related to adolescent depression, such combinations of family experiences also are likely to show up as distal factors in adolescents' suicide attempts. In two recent studies, maltreatment during childhood was linked with suicide attempts in adulthood (Park, 2017; Turner & others, 2017). Recent and current stressful circumstances, such as getting poor grades in school or experiencing the breakup of a romantic relationship, also may trigger suicide attempts (Im, Oh, & Suk, 2017). For example, in a recent study, combined school difficulties (academic failure and inappropriate behavior) were associated with higher suicide risk (Ligier & others, 2020). And in a recent research analysis, the main factor in adolescent suicide deaths was the occurrence of recent stressful life events (Tornblom & others, 2020).

Further, as discussed in the chapter on socioemotional development in middle and late childhood, being victimized by bullying is associated with suicide-related thoughts and behavior (Lear & others, 2020). In a recent cross-cultural study of more than 130,000 12- to 15-year-olds, in 47 of 48 countries being a victim of bullying was associated with a higher probability of attempting suicide (Koyanagi & others, 2019). And a recent meta-analysis revealed that adolescents who had been victims of cyberbullying were 2½ times more likely to attempt suicide and 2 times more likely to have suicidal thoughts than non-victims (John & others, 2018).

Adolescent suicide attempts also vary across ethnic groups in the United States (Erausquin & others, 2019). As indicated in Figure 7, more than 20 percent of American Indian/Alaska Native (AI/AN) female adolescents reported that they had

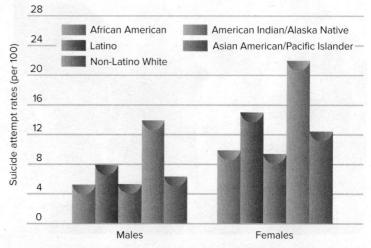

FIGURE 7

SUICIDE ATTEMPTS BY U.S. ADOLESCENTS FROM DIFFERENT ETHNIC GROUPS. Note: Data shown are for one-year rates of self-reported suicide attempts.

attempted suicide in the previous year, and suicide accounts for almost 20 percent of AI/AN deaths in 15- to 19-year-olds (Goldston & others, 2008). As indicated in Figure 7, African American and non-Latino White males reported the lowest incidence of suicide attempts. A major risk factor in the high rate of suicide attempts by AI/AN adolescents is their elevated rate of alcohol abuse.

What is the psychological profile of the suicidal adolescent? Suicidal adolescents often have depressive symptoms (Kim, Kim, & Park, 2020). Although not all depressed adolescents are suicidal, depression is the most frequently cited factor associated with adolescent suicide (Thapar & others, 2012).

Also, in a recent study, a sense of hopelessness predicted an increase in suicidal ideation in depressed adolescents (Wolfe & others, 2019). In another recent study, the most significant factor in a first suicide attempt during adolescence was a major depressive episode, while for children it was child maltreatment (Peyre & others, 2017). Further, one study found that peer victimization was linked to suicidal ideation and suicide attempts, with cyberbullying more strongly associated with suicidal ideation than traditional bullying (van Geel, Vedder, & Tanilon, 2014).

THE INTERRELATION OF PROBLEMS AND SUCCESSFUL PREVENTION/INTERVENTION PROGRAMS

We have described some of the major adolescent problems: substance abuse; juvenile delinquency; school-related problems such as dropping out of school; adolescent pregnancy and sexually transmitted infections; eating disorders; depression; and suicide.

The four problems that affect the most adolescents are (1) drug abuse, (2) juvenile delinquency, (3) sexual problems, and (4) school-related problems (Dryfoos, 1990; Dryfoos & Barkin, 2006). The adolescents most at risk have more than one of these problems. Researchers are increasingly finding that problem behaviors in adolescence are interrelated (Zijlmans & others, 2020). For example, heavy substance abuse is related to early sexual activity, lower grades, dropping out of school, and delinquency (Okumu & others, 2019). Early initiation of sexual activity and inadequate use of contraception is associated with the use of cigarettes and alcohol, the use of marijuana and other illicit drugs, lower grades, dropping out of school, and delinquency (Barragan & others, 2019). Delinquency is related to early sexual activity, early pregnancy, substance abuse, and dropping out of school (Stenbacks, Moberg, & Jokinen, 2019).

As many as 10 percent of adolescents in the United States have been estimated to engage in all four of these problem behaviors (for example, adolescents who have dropped out of school are behind in their grade level, are heavy users of drugs, regularly use cigarettes and marijuana, and are sexually active but do not use contraception). In 1990, it was estimated that another 15 percent of high-risk youth engaged in two or three of the four main problem behaviors (Dryfoos, 1990). Sixteen years later, this figure had increased to 20 percent of all U.S. adolescents (Dryfoos & Barkin, 2006).

A review of the programs that have been successful in preventing or reducing adolescent problems found these common components (Dryfoos, 1990; Dryfoos & Barkin, 2006):

1. *Intensive individualized attention.* In successful programs, high-risk adolescents are attached to a responsible adult who gives the adolescent attention and deals with the adolescent's specific needs (Plourde & others, 2017). This theme occurs in a number of programs. In a successful substance-abuse program, a student assistance counselor is available full-time for individual counseling and referral for treatment.

2. *Community-wide multiagency collaborative approaches.* The basic philosophy of community-wide programs is that a number of different programs and services have to be in

How are problems interrelated in adolescence? Which components of programs have been successful in preventing or reducing adolescent problems?
Paul Michael Hughes/Image Source/Alamy Stock Photo

Which Children Are Most Likely to Benefit from Early Intervention?

Fast Track is an intervention that attempts to lower the risk of juvenile delinquency and other problems (Conduct Problems Prevention Research Group, 2013, 2019; Dodge & others, 2015; Zheng & others, 2017). Schools in four areas (Durham, North Carolina; Nashville, Tennessee; Seattle, Washington; and rural central Pennsylvania) were identified as high-risk based on neighborhood crime and poverty data. Researchers screened more than 9,000 kindergarten children in the four schools and randomly assigned 891 of the highest-risk and moderate-risk children to intervention or control groups. The average age of the children when the intervention began was 6.5 years.

The 10-year intervention consisted of parent behavior management training, child social cognitive skills training, reading tutoring, home visitations, mentoring, and a revised classroom curriculum that was designed to increase socioemotional competence and decrease aggression. Outcomes were assessed in the third, sixth, and ninth grades for conduct disorder (multiple instances of behaviors such as truancy, running away, fire setting, cruelty to animals, breaking and entering, and excessive fighting across a 6-month period), oppositional defiant disorder (an ongoing pattern of disobedient, hostile, and defiant behavior toward authority figures), attention deficit hyperactivity disorder (described as having one or more of these characteristics over a period of time: inattention, hyperactivity, and impulsivity), any externalizing disorder (presence of any of the three disorders previously described), and self-reported antisocial behavior (a list of 34 behaviors, such as skipping school, stealing, and attacking someone with an intent to hurt them).

The extensive intervention was successful only for children and adolescents who were identified as having the highest risk in kindergarten, lowering their incidence of conduct disorder, attention deficit hyperactivity disorder, any externalized disorder, and antisocial behavior (Dodge & McCourt, 2010). Positive outcomes for the intervention occurred as early as the third grade and continued through the ninth grade. For example, in the ninth grade the intervention reduced the likelihood that the highest-risk kindergarten children would develop conduct disorder by 75 percent, attention deficit hyperactivity disorder by 53 percent, and any externalized disorder by 43 percent. Through age 19, the comprehensive Fast Track early intervention was successful in reducing youth arrest rates (Conduct Problems Prevention Research Group, 2013, 2019). And at age 25, the early intervention was effective in reducing violent and drug crimes as well as risky sexual behavior (Dodge & others, 2015). Also, at age 25 those who were given the early intervention had higher well-being scores. Further, one study found that the intervention's impact on adolescents' antisocial behavior was linked to three social cognitive processes: reducing hostile-attribution biases, improving responses to social problems, and devaluing aggression (Conduct Problems Prevention Research Group, 2013, 2019). In addition, in other research, approximately one-third of Fast Track's reduction in later crime outcomes in emerging adulthood was attributed to improvements in social and self-regulation skills, such as prosocial behavior, emotion regulation, and problem solving, at 6 to 11 years of age (Sorensen, Dodge, & Conduct Problems Prevention Research Group, 2016). And in a recent study, it was found that for populations with high risk rates, as little as one teacher screen taken during kindergarten or the first grade predicted whether males would have adult criminal convictions by age 25 (Kassing & others, 2019).

place (Trude & others, 2018). In one successful substance-abuse program, a community-wide health promotion campaign has been implemented that uses local media and community education, in concert with a substance-abuse curriculum in the schools.

3. *Early identification and intervention.* Reaching younger children and their families before children develop problems or at the onset of their problems is a successful strategy (Cicchetti & Handley, 2019). One preschool program provides an excellent model for preventing delinquency, pregnancy, substance abuse, and dropping out of school. Operated by the High/Scope Foundation in Ypsilanti, Michigan, from 1962 to 1967, the Perry Preschool had a long-term positive impact on its students. This enrichment program, directed by David Weikart, served disadvantaged African American children. They attended a high-quality two-year preschool program and received weekly home visits from program personnel. Based on official police records, by age 19, individuals who had attended the Perry Preschool program were less likely to have been arrested and reported fewer adult offenses than a control group did. The Perry Preschool students also were less likely to drop out of high school, and teachers rated their social behavior as more competent than that of a control group who had not received the enriched preschool experience (High/Scope Resource, 2005).

To read further about which children are most likely to benefit from early intervention, see *Connecting Through Research.*

What are some strategies for preventing and intervening in adolescent problems?
Purestock/Getty Images

LG5 Identify adolescent problems in socioemotional development and strategies for helping adolescents with problems.

Review
- What is juvenile delinquency? What causes it?
- What is the nature of depression and suicide in adolescence?
- How are adolescent problems interrelated? What are some components of successful prevention/ intervention programs for adolescents?

Connect
- What have you learned about the connection between bullying in middle and late childhood and problems in adolescence?

Reflect *Your Own Personal Journey of Life*
- When you were an adolescent, did you experience any of the problems that have been discussed, such as substance abuse, eating disorders, juvenile delinquency, depression, and attempted suicide? If you had one or more of the problems, why do you think you developed the problem? If you did not have one of the problems, why do you think you didn't develop one or more of them?

⌐- topical **connections** *looking* **forward** ¬

The transitional time frame between adolescence and adulthood that is labeled emerging adulthood occurs between approximately 18 and 25 years of age. Many emerging adults explore their identity and experience instability in different contexts with greater intensity than they did as adolescents. As adults, they benefit from a secure attachment style in close relationships. Love and possibly marriage become central aspects of many young adults' socioemotional development. Many young adults not only are marrying later or not at all but also are having children later than in past decades. Many young adults also cohabit with a romantic partner.

reach your **learning goals**

Socioemotional Development in Adolescence

1 The Self, Identity, and Religious/ Spiritual Development

 LG1 Discuss self, identity, and religious/spiritual development in adolescence.

> Self-Esteem

- Some researchers have found that self-esteem declines in early adolescence for both boys and girls, but the drop for girls is greater. Other researchers caution that these declines are often exaggerated and actually are small. Self-esteem reflects perceptions that do not always match reality. Thus, high self-esteem may be justified or it might reflect an arrogant, grandiose self-image that is not warranted. Controversy surrounds the question of whether today's adolescents and emerging adults are more narcissistic than their counterparts in earlier generations.

> Self-Regulation

- Self-regulation is important in many aspects of adolescents' lives, including academic achievement and developing good health habits. A key component of self-regulation is effortful control.

> Identity

- Identity development is complex and takes place in bits and pieces. Erikson argues that identity versus identity confusion is the fifth stage of the human life span, which individuals experience during adolescence.

- A psychosocial moratorium during adolescence allows the personality and role experimentation that are important aspects of identity development. James Marcia proposed four identity statuses—identity diffusion, foreclosure, moratorium, and achievement—that are based on crisis (exploration) and commitment. Increasingly, experts argue that the main changes in identity occur in emerging adulthood rather than adolescence. Individuals often follow moratorium-achievement-moratorium-achievement (MAMA) cycles in their lives. Throughout the world, ethnic minority groups have struggled to maintain their identities while blending into the majority culture.

Religious/Spiritual Development

- Many adolescents show an interest in religious and spiritual development. As part of their search for identity, many adolescents and emerging adults begin to grapple with more complex aspects of religion. Various aspects of religion are linked with positive outcomes in adolescent development.

2 Families

LG2 Describe changes that take place in adolescents' relationships with their parents.

Parental Monitoring and Information Management

- A key aspect of parenting an adolescent is effectively monitoring the adolescent's development. Monitoring includes supervising adolescents' choice of social settings, activities, friends, and academic efforts. Adolescents' management of information involves the extent to which adolescents disclose information to parents about their whereabouts. This disclosure, which is more likely when parents engage in positive parenting practices, is linked to positive adolescent adjustment.

Autonomy and Attachment

- Many parents have a difficult time handling the adolescent's push for autonomy, even though the push is one of the hallmarks of adolescence. Adolescents do not simply move into a world isolated from parents; attachment to parents increases the probability that an adolescent will be socially competent.

Parent-Adolescent Conflict

- Parent-adolescent conflict increases in adolescence. The conflict is usually moderate rather than severe, and the increased conflict may serve the positive developmental function of promoting autonomy and identity. A subset of adolescents experience high parent-adolescent conflict, which is linked with negative outcomes.

3 Peers

LG3 Characterize the changes that occur in peer relationships during adolescence.

Friendships

- Harry Stack Sullivan was the most influential theorist to discuss the importance of adolescent friendships. He argued that there is a dramatic increase in the psychological importance and intimacy of close friends in early adolescence. Friends become increasingly important in meeting social needs.

Peer Groups

- Nowhere have changes been more apparent in peer and friendship relations in recent years than in the way social media have transformed them. The pressure to conform to peers is strong during adolescence, especially during the eighth and ninth grades. Cliques and crowds assume more importance in the lives of adolescents than in the lives of children.

Dating and Romantic Relationships

- Dating can have many functions. Three stages characterize the development of romantic relationships in adolescence: (1) entry into romantic attractions and affiliations at about 11 to 13 years of age; (2) exploring romantic relationships at approximately 14 to 16 years of age; and (3) consolidating dyadic romantic bonds at about 17 to 19 years of age. Many gay and lesbian youth date other-sex peers, which can help them to clarify their sexual orientation or disguise it from others. Culture can exert a powerful influence on adolescent dating. Dating shows mixed connections with adjustment during adolescence. Early dating is linked with developmental problems.

4 Culture and Adolescent Development

LG4 Explain how culture influences adolescent development.

Cross-Cultural Comparisons

- There are similarities and differences in the lives of adolescents in different countries. In some countries, traditions are being continued in the socialization of adolescents, whereas in others, substantial changes in the experiences of adolescents are taking place. Adolescents fill their time with different activities, depending on the culture in which they live.

- A rite of passage is a ceremony or ritual that marks an individual's transition from one status to another, especially from childhood to adulthood. In primitive cultures, rites of passage are often well defined. In contemporary America, rites of passage to adulthood are ill-defined.

Socioeconomic Status and Poverty

- Low socioeconomic status and poverty can have extremely negative effects on adolescents' development, including lower academic achievement, lower occupational attainment, and more psychological problems.

Ethnicity

- Many of the families that have immigrated to the United States in recent decades come from collectivist cultures in which there is a strong sense of family obligation. Much of the research on ethnic minority adolescents has not distinguished between the influences of ethnicity and socioeconomic status. Because of this failure, too often researchers have given ethnic explanations for characteristics that were largely due to socioeconomic factors. Although not all ethnic minority families are poor, poverty contributes to the stress experienced by many ethnic minority adolescents.

Media Use and Screen Time

- In terms of media use and screen time, the average U.S. 8- to 18-year-old spends 6½ hours a day using electronic media. If media multitasking is taken into account, adolescents use electronic media 8 hours a day. Adolescents are rapidly increasing the time they spend online. Older adolescents reduce their TV viewing and video game playing and increase their music listening and computer use. Large numbers of adolescents engage in social networking.

5 Adolescent Problems

 Identify adolescent problems in socioemotional development and strategies for helping adolescents with problems.

Juvenile Delinquency

- A juvenile delinquent is an adolescent who breaks the law or engages in conduct that is considered illegal. Low socioeconomic status, negative family experiences (especially a low level of parental monitoring and having a sibling who is a delinquent), and negative peer influences have been linked to juvenile delinquency.

Depression and Suicide

- Adolescents and emerging adults have higher rates of depression than children do. Female adolescents and emerging adults are more likely to have mood and depressive disorders than their male counterparts. Suicide is the third-leading cause of death in U.S. adolescents.

The Interrelation of Problems and Successful Prevention/Intervention Programs

- Researchers are increasingly finding that problem behaviors in adolescence are interrelated, and at-risk adolescents have one or more of these problems: (1) drug abuse, (2) juvenile delinquency, (3) sexual problems, and (4) school-related problems. Dryfoos found a number of common components in successful programs designed to prevent or reduce adolescent problems: These programs provide individual attention to high-risk adolescents, they develop community-wide intervention strategies, and they include early identification and intervention.

key terms

clique 388
commitment 377
crisis 377

crowd 388
ethnic identity 379
identity achievement 378

identity diffusion 378
identity foreclosure 378
identity moratorium 378

juvenile delinquent 395
narcissism 375
rite of passage 391

key people

Erik Erikson 376

Andrew Fuligni 392

James Marcia 377

Harry Stack Sullivan 386

Relax. You will become an adult. You will figure out your career. You will find someone who loves you. You have a whole lifetime; time takes time. The only way to fail at life is to abstain.

—JOHANNA DE SILENTIO
Contemporary philosopher

Early Adulthood

Early adulthood is a time for work and a time for love, sometimes leaving little time for anything else. For some of us, finding our place in adult society and committing to a more stable life take longer than we imagine. We still ask ourselves who we are and wonder if it isn't enough just to be. Our dreams continue and our thoughts are bold, but at some point we become more pragmatic. Sex and love are powerful passions in our lives—at times angels of light, at others fiends of torment. And we possibly will never fully know the love of our parents until we become parents ourselves. This section contains two chapters: "Physical and Cognitive Development in Early Adulthood" and "Socioemotional Development in Early Adulthood."

chapter 13

PHYSICAL AND COGNITIVE DEVELOPMENT IN EARLY ADULTHOOD

chapter outline

① The Transition from Adolescence to Adulthood

Learning Goal 1 *Describe the transition from adolescence to adulthood.*

Becoming an Adult
The Transition from High School to College

② Physical Development

Learning Goal 2 *Identify the changes in physical development in young adults.*

Physical Performance and Development
Health
Eating and Weight
Regular Exercise
Substance Abuse

③ Sexuality

Learning Goal 3 *Discuss sexuality in young adults.*

Sexual Activity in Emerging Adulthood
Sexual Orientation and Behavior
Sexually Transmitted Infections
Forcible Sexual Behavior and Sexual Harassment

④ Cognitive Development

Learning Goal 4 *Characterize cognitive changes in early adulthood.*

Cognitive Stages
Creativity

⑤ Achievement, Careers, and Work

Learning Goal 5 *Explain the key dimensions of achievement, careers, and work in early adulthood.*

Achievement
Developmental Changes in Careers
Finding a Path to Purpose
Monitoring the Occupational Outlook
The Impact of Work

Tim Robbins/Mint Images/Getty Images

He was a senior in college when both of his parents died of cancer within five weeks of each other. What would he do? He and his 8-year-old brother left Chicago to live in California where their older sister was entering law school. Dave would take care of his younger brother, but he needed a job. That first summer, he took a class in furniture painting; then he worked for a geological surveying company, re-creating maps on a computer. Soon, though, he did something very different: with friends from high school, Dave Eggers started Might, a satirical magazine for twenty-somethings. It was an edgy, highly acclaimed publication, but not a moneymaker. After a few years, Eggers had to shut down the magazine, and he abandoned California for New York.

This does not sound like a promising start for a career. But within a decade after his parents died, Eggers had not only raised his younger brother but had also founded a quarterly journal and Web site, McSweeney's, and had written a best-selling book, *A Heartbreaking Work of Staggering Genius,* which received the National Book Critics Circle Award and was nominated for a Pulitzer Prize. It is a slightly fictionalized account of Eggers' life as he helped care for his dying mother, raised his brother, and searched for his own place in the world. Despite the pain of his losses and the responsibility for his brother, Eggers quickly built a record of achievement as a young adult.

Dave Eggers is a talented and insightful author.
Cosima Scavolini/LaPresse/Zumapress.com/Newscom

topical connections *looking* **back**

Early adolescence is a time of dramatic physical change as puberty unfolds. Pubertal change also brings considerable interest in one's body image. And pubertal change ushers in an intense interest in sexuality. Although most adolescents develop a positive sexual identity, many encounter sexual risk factors that can lead to negative developmental outcomes. Adolescence also is a critical time in the development of behaviors related to health, such as good nutrition and regular exercise, which are health enhancing, and drug abuse, which is health compromising. Significant changes occur in the adolescent's brain—the early development of the amygdala and the delayed development of the prefrontal cortex—that may contribute to risk taking and sensation seeking. Adolescent thinking becomes more abstract, idealistic, and logical—which Piaget described as the key aspects of formal operational thought. The brain's development and social contexts influence adolescents' decision making.

preview

In this chapter we will explore many aspects of physical and cognitive development in early adulthood. These include some of the areas that were so important in Dave Eggers' life, such as using his creative talents and pursuing a career. We also will examine changes in physical development, sexuality, and cognitive development. We will begin by addressing the transition from adolescence to adulthood, a time during which Dave Eggers displayed resilience in the face of intense stress.

1 The Transition from Adolescence to Adulthood

LG1 Describe the transition from adolescence to adulthood.

Becoming an Adult

The Transition from High School to College

When does an adolescent become an adult? We've discussed that it is not easy to tell when a girl or a boy enters adolescence. The task of determining when an individual becomes an adult is even more difficult.

BECOMING AN ADULT

For most individuals, becoming an adult involves a lengthy transition period (Hochberg & Konner, 2020). Recently, the transition from adolescence to adulthood has been referred to as **emerging adulthood,** which occurs from approximately 18 to 25 years of age (Arnett, 2006, 2007, 2010, 2012, 2015). Experimentation and exploration characterize the emerging adult. At this point in their development, many individuals are still exploring which career path they want to follow, what they want their identity to be, and which lifestyle they want to adopt (for example, single, cohabiting, or married).

Key Features   Jeffrey Arnett (2006) concluded that five key features characterize emerging adulthood:

- *Identity exploration, especially in love and work.* Emerging adulthood is a time during which key changes in identity take place for many individuals (Neblett, Roth, & Syed, 2019).
- *Instability.* Residential changes peak during early adulthood, a time during which instability also is common in love, work, and education.
- *Self-focused.* According to Arnett (2006, p. 10), emerging adults "are self-focused in the sense that they have little in the way of social obligations, little in the way of duties and commitments to others, which leaves them with a great deal of autonomy in running their own lives."
- *Feeling in-between.* Many emerging adults don't consider themselves adolescents or full-fledged adults.
- *The age of possibilities, a time when individuals have an opportunity to transform their lives.* Arnett (2006) describes two ways in which emerging adulthood is the age of possibilities: (1) many emerging adults are optimistic about their future; and (2) for emerging adults who have experienced difficult times while growing up, emerging adulthood presents an opportunity to chart their life course in a more positive direction.

Research indicates that these five aspects characterize not only individuals in the United States as they make the transition from adolescence to early adulthood, but also their counterparts in European countries and Australia (Arnett, 2012, 2015; Buhl & Lanz, 2007; Sirsch & others, 2009). Although emerging adulthood does not characterize development in all cultures, it does appear to occur in cultures that postpone assuming adult roles and responsibilities (Kins & Beyers, 2010). The concept of emerging adulthood has been criticized

emerging adulthood The transition from adolescence to adulthood (occurring from approximately 18 to 25 years of age), which is characterized by experimentation and exploration.

as applying mainly to privileged adolescents and not being a self-determined choice for many young people, especially those in limiting socioeconomic conditions (Cote & Bynner, 2008; Mitchell & Syed, 2015). One study revealed that U.S. at-risk youth entered emerging adulthood slightly earlier than the general population of youth (Lisha & others, 2014).

Increasingly, instead of describing emerging adulthood as occurring from 18 to 25 years of age, the range has been expanded to 18 to 29 years (Arnett, 2014). However, in a recent study of individuals 18 to 60 years of age, the five characteristics of emerging adulthood mentioned above (identity exploration, self-focus, feeling in-between, instability, and possibilities/optimism) were more likely to be endorsed by 18- to 25-year-olds than by older individuals (Arnett & Mitra, 2020).

In a recent analysis, Seth Schwartz (2016) described the two-sided coin of emerging adulthood. As indicated by Arnett, for emerging adults who have experienced troubled times while growing up, emerging adulthood represents a time when they can redirect their lives into a more positive developmental trajectory. Indeed, for many individuals, emerging adulthood brings a higher level of well-being than they had in adolescence. But for others, emerging adulthood is a time of increasing anxiety, depression, and problems, as well as considerable worry about one's future. As will be seen later in this chapter, emerging adulthood also is a time when many individuals engage in unhealthy behaviors. During this period binge drinking peaks, risky sexual behavior is more frequent than it will be in the late twenties, and poor sleep habits are common. However, as with any period of development, there are clusters of emerging adults who are engaging in health-enhancing behaviors while others are engaging in health-damaging behaviors (Schwartz & Petrova, 2019). In a national longitudinal study of emerging adults' health choices, three categories became apparent. The following categories reflected whether individuals smoked or not, engaged in binge drinking or not, were obese or not, and engaged in exercise regularly or were sedentary: (1) consistently healthy lifestyle, (2) consistently unhealthy lifestyle, and (3) shifting lifestyle over time (Daw, Margolis, & Wright, 2017).

What characterizes emerging adults?
Peter Cade/Photodisc/Getty Images

But as indicated earlier, an important aspect of emerging adulthood is the resilience that some individuals have shown in moving their life in a positive direction following a troubled adolescence (Masten, 2017, 2019; Masten, Motti-Stefanidi, & Rahl, 2020). A review and analysis of research on resilience during the transition to adulthood concluded that the increased freedom that is available to emerging adults in Western society places a premium on the capacity to plan ahead, delay gratification, and make positive choices (Burt & Paysnick, 2012). Also emphasized in resilient adaptation during emerging adulthood was the importance of forming positive close relationships—to some degree with parents, but more often with supportive romantic partners, close friends, and mentors.

The Changing Landscape of Emerging and Early Adulthood In earlier generations, individuals in their mid-twenties at the latest were expected to have finished college, obtained a full-time job, and established their own household, most often with a spouse and a child. However, individuals are now taking much longer to reach these developmental milestones, many of which they are not experiencing until their late twenties or even thirties (Vespa, 2017). It is not surprising that their parents recall having had a much earlier timetable for reaching these developmental milestones.

Consider that for the first time in the modern era, in 2014 living with parents was the most frequent living arrangement for 18- to 34-year-olds (Fry, 2016). Dating all the way back to 1880, living with a romantic partner, whether a spouse or a significant other, was the most common living arrangement for emerging and young adults. In 2014, 32.1 percent of 18- to 34-year-olds lived with their parents, followed by 31.6 percent who lived with a spouse or partner in their own home, while 14 percent lived alone. The remaining 22 percent lived in another family member's home, with a non-relative, or in group quarters (a college dorm, for example).

In terms of education, today's emerging and young adults are better educated than their counterparts in the 1970s (Vespa, 2017). For example, they are much more likely to have a college degree today. The biggest reason for this increased educational attainment since the 1970s, though, is a gender difference reversal. In 1975, more young men had college degrees, but today more young women than young men have a college degree.

In terms of work, more young adults are working today than in 1975 (Vespa, 2017). The main reason for this increase also involves a gender change—the significant rise of young

What are some strategies parents can adopt to help adolescents gain adult maturity sooner?

Jamie Grill/Wavebreak Media/Tetra images/Getty Images

developmental **connection**

Families

Secure attachment to parents increases the likelihood that adolescents will be socially competent. Connect to "Physical and Cognitive Development in Adolescence."

developmental **connection**

Community

Service learning is linked to many positive outcomes for adolescents. Connect to "Physical and Cognitive Development in Adolescence."

women in the workforce, which has increased from slightly below 50 percent to more than two-thirds of young women in the workforce today. In 1975, almost all of the women who were not in the workforce were taking care of their home and family. However, in 2016, less than 50 percent of the women who were not in the workforce were homemakers.

We will further discuss these lifestyle changes in the chapter on "Socioemotional Development in Early Adulthood."

Parents can play an important role in guiding and preparing adolescents for the changing landscape of emerging adulthood (Padilla-Walker & Nelson, 2019). Joseph and Claudia Allen (2009), authors of *Escaping the Endless Adolescence: How We Can Help Our Teenagers Grow Up Before They Grow Old,* opened their book with a chapter titled, "Is Twenty-Five the New Fifteen?" They argue that in recent decades adolescents have experienced a world that places more challenges on maturing into a competent adult. In their words (p. 17),

> Generations ago, fourteen-year-olds used to drive, seventeen-year-olds led armies, and even average teens contributed labor and income that helped keep their families afloat. While facing other problems, those teens displayed adult-like maturity far more quickly than today's, who are remarkably well kept, but cut off from most of the responsibility, challenge, and growth-producing feedback of the adult world. Parents of twenty-somethings used to lament, "They grow up so fast." But that seems to be replaced with, "Well, . . . Mary's living at home a bit while she sorts things out."

The Allens conclude that what is happening to the current generation of adolescents is that after adolescence, they are experiencing "more adolescence" instead of adequately being launched into the adult years. Even many adolescents who have gotten good grades and then as emerging adults continued to achieve academic success in college later find themselves in their mid-twenties not having a clue about how to find a meaningful job, manage their finances, or live independently. In a recent study, maturity fears among undergraduate students were assessed from 1982 to 2012 (Smith & others, 2017). Both male and female undergraduates' maturity fears increased across time. Thus, recent cohorts of emerging adults seem more reluctant to mature than earlier cohorts were.

The Allens offer the following suggestions for helping adolescents become more mature on their way to adulthood:

- *Provide them with opportunities to be contributors.* Help them move away from being consumers by creating more effective work experiences (quality work apprenticeships, for example), or service learning opportunities that allow adolescents to make meaningful contributions.

- *Give candid, quality feedback to adolescents.* Don't just shower praise and material things on them, but let them see how the real world works. Don't protect them from criticism, constructive or negative. Protecting them in this way only leaves them ill-equipped to deal with the ups and downs of the real world of adulthood.

- *Create positive adult connections with adolescents.* Many adolescents deny that they need parental support or attachment to parents, but to help them develop maturity on the way to adulthood, they do. Exploring a wider social world than in childhood, adolescents need to be connected to parents and other adults in positive ways to be able to handle autonomy maturely.

- *Challenge adolescents to become more competent.* Adults need to do fewer things for adolescents that they can accomplish for themselves. Providing adolescents with opportunities to engage in tasks that are just beyond their current level of ability stretches their minds and helps them to make progress along the road to maturity.

Markers of Becoming an Adult In the United States, the most widely recognized marker of entry into adulthood is holding a more or less permanent, full-time job, which usually happens when an individual finishes school—high school for some, college for others, graduate or professional school for still others. However, other criteria are far from clear. Economic independence is one marker of adult status, but achieving it is often a long process. College graduates are increasingly returning to live with their parents as they attempt to establish themselves economically. However, one study revealed that continued co-residence with parents during emerging adulthood slowed down the process of becoming a self-sufficient and independent adult (Kins & Beyers, 2010).

Other studies suggest that taking responsibility for oneself may be an important marker of adult status for many individuals (Smith & others, 2017). In one study, both parents and college students agreed that taking responsibility for one's actions and developing emotional control are important aspects of becoming an adult (Nelson & others, 2007). And in a study of Danish emerging adults, the most widely described markers of emerging adulthood were accepting self-responsibility, making independent decisions, and becoming financially independent (Arnett & Padilla-Walker, 2015). In this study the least-described markers were the traditional transition events of getting married and avoiding getting drunk. Also, a recent U.S. study of community college students found that they believed adulthood would mean being able to care for themselves and others (Katsiaficas, 2017).

What we have identified as markers of adult status mainly characterize individuals in developed countries, especially the United States. Are the criteria for adulthood the same in developing countries as they are in the United States? In developing countries, marriage is more often a significant marker for entry into adulthood, and this usually occurs much earlier than the adulthood markers in the United States (Arnett, 2004, 2015b). In one study, the majority of 18- to 26-year-olds in India felt that they had achieved adulthood (Seiter & Nelson, 2011).

The transition from high school to college often involves positive as well as negative features. In college, students are likely to feel grown up, be able to spend more time with peers, have more opportunities to explore different lifestyles and values, and enjoy greater freedom from parental monitoring. However, college involves a larger, more impersonal school structure and an increased focus on achievement and its assessment. *What was your transition to college like?*
Stockbyte/Stockdisc/Getty Images

THE TRANSITION FROM HIGH SCHOOL TO COLLEGE

For many individuals in developed countries, graduating from high school and going to college is an important aspect of the transition to adulthood (Stolzenberg & others, 2019). Just as the transition from elementary school to middle or junior high school involves change and possible stress, so does the transition from high school to college. The two transitions have many parallels. Going from being a senior in high school to being a freshman in college replays the top-dog phenomenon of transferring from the oldest and most powerful group of students to the youngest and least powerful group of students that occurred as adolescence began. For many students, the transition from high school to college involves movement to a larger, more impersonal school structure; interaction with peers from more diverse geographical and sometimes more diverse ethnic backgrounds; and increased focus on achievement and its assessment. And like the transition from elementary to middle or junior high school, the transition from high school to college can involve positive features. Students are more likely to feel grown up, have more subjects from which to select, have more time to spend with peers, have more opportunities to explore different lifestyles and values, enjoy greater independence from parental monitoring, and be challenged intellectually by academic work (Halonen & Santrock, 2013; Staley, 2019).

Over the past three decades, the Higher Education Research Institute at UCLA has surveyed first-year college students regarding their backgrounds, experiences, and views on a number of topics. In recent years, traditional-aged college students have shown increased concern for personal well-being and decreased concern for the well-being of others, especially for the disadvantaged (Stolzenberg & others, 2019). Today's college freshmen are more strongly motivated to be well-off financially and less motivated to develop a meaningful philosophy of life than were their counterparts of 40 years ago. In 2017, 82.5 percent of students (the highest percent ever in this survey) viewed becoming well-off financially as an "essential" or a "very important" objective compared with only 42 percent in 1971.

There are, however, some signs that U.S. college students are shifting toward a stronger interest in the welfare of society. In the survey just described, interest in developing a meaningful philosophy of life increased from 39 percent to 48.1 percent of U.S. college freshmen from 2001 through 2017 (Stolzenberg & others, 2019). In addition, 86.5 percent of college freshmen said that they had frequently or occasionally engaged in volunteer work in the past year.

An increasing number of first-year college students also report having higher levels of stress and depression. In the national survey just described, 38.7 percent of first-year college students said they frequently or occasionally felt overwhelmed with all they had to do, 12.2 percent indicated they were depressed, and 32.5 percent reported feeling anxious (Stolzenberg & others, 2019).

Most college campuses have a counseling center that provides access to mental health professionals who can help students learn effective ways to cope with stress. Counselors can provide good information about coping with stress and dealing with academic challenges. To read about the work of college counselor Grace Leaf, see *Connecting with Careers*.

Grace Leaf, College/Career Counselor

Grace Leaf is a counselor at Spokane Community College in Washington. She has a master's degree in educational leadership and is working toward a doctoral degree in educational leadership at Gonzaga University in Washington. Her job involves providing orientation sessions for international students, advising individuals and groups, and facilitating individual and group career planning. Leaf tries to connect students with their own goals and values and to help them design an educational program that fits their needs and visions. Following a long career as a counselor, she is now vice-president for instruction at Lower Columbia College in Washington.

For more information about what career counselors do, see the Careers in Life-Span Development appendix.

Grace Leaf counsels college students at Spokane Community College about careers.
Courtesy of Grace Leaf

Review *Connect* Reflect

 LG1 Describe the transition from adolescence to adulthood.

Review
- What is the nature of emerging adulthood? What are two main criteria for becoming an adult?
- What are some positive and negative aspects of the transition from high school to college?

Connect
- You have learned about a number of effective strategies for parenting adolescents. Which of those strategies might provide a foundation for individuals to experience a more successful adulthood?

Reflect *Your Own Personal Journey of Life*
- What do you think is the most important criterion for becoming an adult? Does it make sense to describe becoming an adult in terms of "emerging adulthood" over a period of years, or is there a specific age at which someone becomes an adult? Explain.

---

2 Physical Development   **LG2** Identify the changes in physical development in young adults.

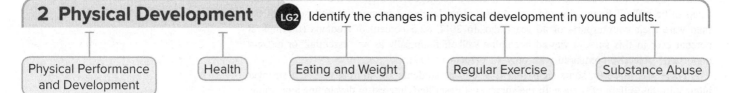

Physical Performance and Development   Health   Eating and Weight   Regular Exercise   Substance Abuse

As more information becomes available about healthy lifestyles and how they contribute to a longer life span, emerging and young adults are increasingly interested in learning about physical performance, health, nutrition, exercise, and addiction.

PHYSICAL PERFORMANCE AND DEVELOPMENT

Most of us reach our peak levels of physical performance before the age of 30, often between the ages of 19 and 26. This peak of physical performance occurs not only for the average young adult but for outstanding athletes as well. Different types of athletes, however, reach their peak performances at different ages. Most swimmers and gymnasts peak in their late teens. Golfers and marathon runners tend to peak in their late twenties. In other areas of athletics, peak performance often occurs in the early to mid-twenties. However, in recent years, some highly conditioned athletes—such as Dana Torres (Olympic swimming) and Tom Brady (football)—have stretched the upper age limits of award-winning performances.

Not only do we reach our peak in physical performance during early adulthood, but it is also during this age period that we begin to decline in physical performance. Muscle tone and strength usually begin to show signs of decline around the age of 30. Sagging chins and protruding abdomens also may begin to appear for the first time. The lessening of physical abilities is a common complaint among the just-turned thirties.

HEALTH

Emerging adults have more than twice the mortality rate of adolescents (Park & others, 2006). As indicated in Figure 1, males are mainly responsible for the higher mortality rate of emerging adults. Further, compared with adolescents, emerging adults engage in more health-compromising behaviors, have more chronic disorders, are more likely to be obese, and are more likely to have a mental disorder than are adolescents (Irwin, 2010). In a more recent analysis, most health care indicators had changed little across the previous decade for adolescents and emerging adults (Park & others, 2014).

Although most college students know what it takes to prevent illness and promote health, they don't fare very well when it comes to applying this information to themselves. In many cases, emerging adults are not as healthy as they seem. One study revealed that college students from low-SES backgrounds engaged in lower levels of physical activity, ate more fast food and fewer fruits/vegetables, and used more unhealthy weight control methods than their higher-SES counterparts did (VanKim & Laska, 2012).

A longitudinal study revealed that most bad health habits in adolescence increased during emerging adulthood (Harris & others, 2006). Inactivity, poor diet, obesity, substance abuse, inadequate reproductive health care, and use of health care facilities worsened in emerging adulthood. For example, when they were 12 to 18 years of age, only 5 percent of the study participants reported no weekly exercise, but when they became 19 to 26 years of age, 46 percent said they did not exercise during a typical week. Also, a more recent study found that rates of being overweight or obese increased from 25.6 percent for college freshmen to 32 percent for college seniors (Nicoteri & Miskovsky, 2014).

In emerging and early adulthood, few individuals consider how their current lifestyles will affect their health later on. As emerging adults, many of us develop a pattern of not eating breakfast, not eating regular meals, and relying on snacks as our main food source during the day, overeating to the point where we exceed the normal weight for our age, smoking moderately or excessively, drinking moderately or excessively, failing to exercise, getting by with only a few hours of sleep at night, and engaging in risky sexual behavior (Carpenter & others, 2019; Jansen & others, 2020). These lifestyles are associated with poor health, which in turn diminishes life satisfaction (Foulkes, McMillan, & Gregory, 2019). In the Berkeley Longitudinal Study—in which individuals were evaluated over a period of 40 years—physical health at age 30 predicted life satisfaction at age 70, more so for men than for women (Mussen, Honzik, & Eichorn, 1982).

One study explored links between health behavior and life satisfaction in more than 17,000 individuals 17 to 30 years of age in 21 countries (Grant, Wardle, & Steptoe, 2009). The young adults' life satisfaction was positively related to not smoking, exercising regularly, using sun protection, eating fruit, and limiting fat intake, but was not related to alcohol consumption and fiber intake.

The health profile of emerging and young adults can be improved by reducing the incidence of certain health-impairing lifestyles, such as overeating, and by engaging in health-improving lifestyles that include good eating habits, regular exercise, abstaining from drugs, and getting adequate sleep (Prichard, 2020). For example, a study of college students found that regularly engaging in moderate or vigorous physical activity was linked to adequate daily fruit and vegetable consumption, healthy body mass index, not smoking, being less depressed, having a lower incidence of binge drinking, being less likely to have multiple sex partners, and getting adequate sleep (Dinger, Brittain, & Hutchinson, 2014). And a recent study of college students revealed that regularly eating breakfast was positively linked to their grade point

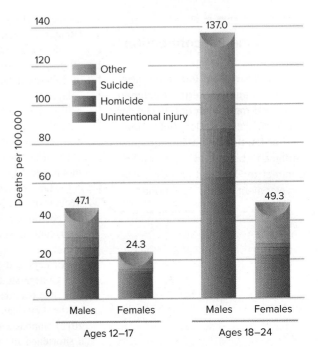

FIGURE 1

MORTALITY RATES OF U.S. ADOLESCENTS AND EMERGING ADULTS

Why might it be easy to develop bad health habits in emerging and early adulthood?
Igor-Kardasov/iStockphoto/Getty Images

developmental **connection**

Health

Recent research indicates that traditional-age college freshmen go to bed more than one hour later than high school seniors but by their third or fourth years of college, their bedtimes begin to get earlier. Connect to "Physical and Cognitive Development in Early Adulthood."

average (GPA), while regularly eating fast food was negatively associated with their GPA (Reuter, Forster, & Brister, 2020).

Research indicates that 70 percent of college students do not get adequate sleep and that 50 percent of them report daytime sleepiness (Hershner & Chervin, 2015). In a recent study of college students, sleep deprivation was linked to having a lower grade point average and delayed college graduation (Chen & Chen, 2019). Also, in another recent study of female college students, poorer sleep quality was associated with smartphone dependence and less effective stress management (Wang & others, 2019). Further, in another study, higher consumption of energy drinks was linked to more sleep problems in college students (Faris & others, 2017). The National Sleep Foundation (2019a) recently recommended that 18- to 25-year-olds should get 7 to 9 hours of sleep every night.

Many college students occasionally or often pull an all-nighter to cram for an exam. Recent, the National Sleep Foundation (2019b) described why this might not be a good idea and could harm your exam performance: It can distort your memory, cause thinking to be less clear, and impair concentration. Thus, your exam performance will likely be much better if you engage in effective planning and time management and spread your studying over a number of days and weeks.

College students are not the only ones who are getting inadequate sleep. Many adults in their late twenties and thirties don't get enough either (Mamun & others, 2020). A statement by the American Academy of Sleep Medicine and Sleep Research Society (Luyster & others, 2012) emphasized that chronic sleep deprivation may contribute to cardiovascular disease and a shortened life span, and also result in cognitive and motor impairment that increases the risk of motor vehicle crashes and work-related accidents.

The average American adult gets just under seven hours of sleep a night. How much sleep do adults need to function optimally the next day? An increasing number of experts note that eight hours of sleep or more per night are necessary for optimal performance the next day. These experts argue that many adults have become sleep deprived (Makarem & others, 2019). Work pressures, school pressures, family obligations, and social obligations often lead to long hours of wakefulness and irregular sleep/wake schedules (Haun & Oppenauer, 2019; Riemann, 2019).

Professional guidelines for adolescents and emerging adults recommend annual preventive medical visits with screening and guidance for health-related behaviors. One study examined the delivery of preventive health-care services to emerging adults 18 to 26 years of age (Lau & others, 2013). In this study, rates of preventive services utilized by emerging adults were generally low. Females were more likely to receive health care services than males were.

EATING AND WEIGHT

Earlier we discussed aspects of overweight children's lives and examined the eating disorders of anorexia nervosa and bulimia nervosa in adolescence. Now we will turn our attention to obesity and the extensive preoccupation that many young adults have with dieting.

Obesity Obesity is not only a problem for many children and adolescents but also a serious and pervasive problem for many adults (Blake, 2020; Schiff, 2021; Thompson, Manore, & Vaughan, 2020). In the United States, 39.8 percent of adults 20 years and older were classified as obese in 2016 (Hales & others, 2017). This represents a 9.1 percent increase since 2000 and a 4.7 percent increase since 2012. The prevalence of obesity in middle-aged adults (40.8 percent) was higher than in younger adults (35.7 percent). Women (41.1 percent) were more likely to be obese than men (37.9 percent). In terms of ethnic groups, Latinos and African American adults had the highest obesity rates (47 and 46.8 percent, respectively), followed by non-Latino White adults (37.6 percent). Asian American adults had the lowest rate of obesity by far (12.7 percent). The highest rate of obesity (combining gender and ethnicity) occurred for African American females (54.8 percent), the lowest for Asian American men (10.1 percent). In a recent international comparison of 33 countries, the United States had the highest adult obesity rate (38.2 percent) followed by Mexico (32.4 percent); Japan had the lowest rate (3.7 percent) followed by South Korea (5.3 percent) (OECD, 2017).

Being overweight or obese is linked to increased risk of hypertension, diabetes, and cardiovascular disease (Ali & others, 2019; Koehler & Drenowatz, 2019). Overweight and obesity also are associated with mental health problems, especially depression (Hong & Hong, 2019).

What factors determine whether a person becomes obese? Possible influences include both heredity and environmental conditions, and dieting.

Heredity Until recently, the genetic component of obesity was underestimated by scientists. Some individuals inherit a tendency to be overweight (Joseph & others, 2019). Researchers have documented that animals can be inbred to have a propensity for obesity (Kwitek, 2019). Further, identical human twins have similar weights, even when they are reared apart (Zhou & others, 2015). However, one study found that a high level of activity reduced the degree of genetic linkage for obesity in same-sex twins (Horn & others, 2015).

Environmental Factors Environmental factors play an important role in obesity (Schiff, 2021). The human genome has not changed markedly in the last century, yet obesity has noticeably increased. The obesity rate has doubled in the United States since 1900. This dramatic increase in obesity likely is due to greater availability of food (especially food high in fat), greater reliance on energy-saving devices, and declining physical activity. In a recent study, adult obesity in Mexico was associated with engaging in a greater amount of screen time, participating in a lower level of physical activity, and getting inadequate amounts of sleep (Kolovos & others, 2020).

Sociocultural factors are involved in obesity, which is six times more prevalent among women with low incomes than among women with high incomes. Americans also are more obese than Europeans and people in many other areas of the world.

Dieting With obesity on the rise, dieting has become an obsession with many Americans (Blake, 2020; Donatelle & Ketcham, 2020). Although many Americans regularly embark on a diet, few are successful in keeping weight off over the long term and many dieters risk becoming fatter (Thompson, Manore, & Vaughan, 2020). A research review of the long-term outcomes of calorie-restricting diets revealed that one-third to two-thirds of dieters regain more weight than they lost on their diets (Mann & others, 2007). However, some individuals do lose weight and maintain the loss (Benson & others, 2020; Stice & others, 2019). How often this occurs and whether some diet programs work better than others are still open questions.

What we *do* know about losing weight is that the most effective programs include exercise (Hynes, 2020; Petroni & others, 2019). Researchers have found that higher levels of physical activity, especially endurance training, are linked to weight loss maintenance (Petridou, Siopi, & Mougios, 2019). A research review concluded that adults who engaged in diet-plus-exercise programs lost more weight than those who relied on diet-only programs (Wu & others, 2009). A study of approximately 2,000 U.S. adults found that exercising 30 minutes a day, planning meals, and weighing themselves daily were the main strategies used by successful dieters as compared with unsuccessful dieters (Kruger, Blanck, & Gillespie, 2006) (see Figure 2). In addition, a longitudinal study from adolescence through early adulthood found that three factors especially predicted maintenance of a healthy weight: Having higher body satisfaction, avoiding unhealthy weight control behaviors (skipping meals, for example), and dieting (Larson & others, 2018). Also in this study, social support for healthy eating and physical activity were linked to healthy weight maintenance, while having close relationships with individuals who were dieting (parents and significant others, for example) reduced the likelihood of maintaining a healthy weight. Another study also revealed that daily weigh-ins were linked to maintaining weight loss (Wing & others, 2007).

Binge Eating Disorder (BED) In the chapter on "Physical and Cognitive Development in Adolescence," we discussed the eating problems of anorexia nervosa and bulimia. Here we discuss another eating problem, **binge eating disorder (BED),** which involves frequent binge eating without compensatory behavior like the purging that characterizes bulimics. Individuals with BED engage in recurrent episodes of eating large quantities of food, during which they feel a lack of control over eating (Goode & others, 2020). Because they don't purge, individuals with BED are frequently overweight. For the first time, binge eating disorder was included by the American Psychiatric Association in the fifth edition of its classification of psychiatric disorders in 2013. As with anorexia nervosa and bulimia disorder, BED is far more common in females than males.

binge eating disorder (BED) Involves frequent binge eating but without compensatory behavior like the purging that characterizes bulimics.

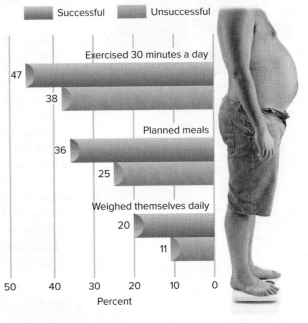

Successful   Unsuccessful

Exercised 30 minutes a day
47
38

Planned meals
36
25

Weighed themselves daily
20
11

50   40   30   20   10   0
Percent

FIGURE **2**

COMPARISON OF STRATEGIES USED BY SUCCESSFUL AND UNSUCCESSFUL DIETERS
Ljupco Smokovski/Essentials/iStockphoto.com

Researchers are examining the role of biological and psychological factors in BED (Atwood & Friedman, 2019; Grant & Chamberlain, 2020). Genes play a role, as does dopamine, the neurotransmitter related to reward pathways in the brain (Palmeira & others, 2019). Also, one study found that adolescents with BED were more likely to live in families with less effective family functioning, especially in the area of emotional involvement (Tetzlaff & others, 2016). Cognitive behavior therapy and pharmacological treatments have been successful with BED patients (Appolinario, Nardi, & McElroy, 2019; Hilbert & others, 2020).

REGULAR EXERCISE

One of the main reasons health experts want people to exercise is that it helps to prevent chronic disorders such as heart disease and diabetes (Insel & Roth, 2020). Many health experts recommend that young adults engage in 30 minutes or more of aerobic exercise daily. **Aerobic exercise** is sustained exercise—jogging, swimming, or cycling, for example—that stimulates heart and lung activity. Most health experts recommend raising your heart rate to at least 60 percent of your maximum heart rate. Only about one-fifth of adults, however, achieve these recommended levels of physical activity.

The World Health Organization recognizes physical inactivity as a key factor in dying earlier (Han, Neufer, & Pilegaard, 2019). A recent national U.S. poll conducted by the Centers for Disease Control and Prevention found that only 22.9 percent of U.S. adults 18 to 64 years of age met federal guidelines for aerobic and muscle-strengthening exercise (Blackwell & Clarke, 2018). In this poll, 27.2 percent of men and 18.7 percent of women met the exercise guidelines.

Researchers have found that exercise is linked not only to physical health, but mental health as well. In particular, exercise is associated with a higher self-concept, as well as lower anxiety and depression (Bennie & others, 2020; Elbe & others, 2019). For example, in a recent study of almost 18,000 adults, engaging in regular moderate-to-vigorous physical activity along with muscle-strengthening exercise was associated with the lowest incidence of depressive symptoms (Bennie & others, 2019). Further, data from a national survey revealed that individuals with higher levels of physical activity and cardiovascular fitness were less likely to have depressive symptoms (Loprinzi & others, 2017). And a recent research review concluded that studies in which individuals are randomly assigned to engage in exercise have found that exercise and pharmacological treatments are equally effective in treating depression (Netz, 2017). Here are some helpful strategies for making exercise part of your life:

- *Reduce your screen time.* Heavy screen viewing (TV, Internet, and so on) is linked to poor health and obesity (Kolovos & others, 2020). A recent study found that higher screen time by parents was linked to parents' and children's higher waist-to-height ratio (Dong & others, 2017). Another study revealed that compared with individuals who watch no TV, watching TV 6 hours a day reduces life expectancy by 4.8 years (Veerman & others, 2012). And yet another study indicated that mortality risk decreased when screen time was replaced by an increase in daily activity levels (Wijndaele & others, 2017). Replace some of your screen time with exercise.

- *Chart your progress.* Systematically recording your exercise workouts will help you to chart your progress. This strategy is especially helpful over the long term.

- *Get rid of excuses.* People make up all kinds of excuses for not exercising. A typical excuse is "I don't have enough time." You likely do have enough time to exercise 30 minutes per day.

- *Imagine the alternative.* Ask yourself whether you are too busy to take care of your own health. What will your life be like if you lose your health?

SUBSTANCE ABUSE

Earlier we explored substance abuse in adolescence. Fortunately, by the time individuals reach their late twenties, many have begun reducing their use of alcohol and drugs. That is the conclusion reached by John Schulenberg and his colleagues (2017, 2018, 2019), who have collected extensive data on individuals as they age from secondary school through early adulthood.

developmental **connection**

Health

Do adolescents exercise more or less than children do? Connect to "Physical and Cognitive Development in Adolescence."

What are your exercise goals? What are some strategies for incorporating exercise into your life?
Laura Doss/Fancy Collection/SuperStock

aerobic exercise Sustained exercise (such as jogging, swimming, or cycling) that stimulates heart and lung activity.

As in adolescence, male college students and young adults are more likely to take drugs than their female counterparts (Schulenberg & others, 2017, 2018, 2019). One study revealed that only 20 percent of college students reported abstaining from alcohol (Huang & others, 2009).

Let's take a closer look at alcohol consumption and nicotine use by young adults and consider how this activity may become an **addiction,** which is a behavior pattern characterized by an overwhelming involvement with a drug and a preoccupation with securing its supply.

addiction A pattern of behavior characterized by an overwhelming involvement with using a drug and a preoccupation with securing its supply.

Alcohol Two problems associated with excessive alcohol consumption are binge drinking and alcoholism.

Binge Drinking Heavy binge drinking often occurs in college, and it can take its toll on students (Creswell & others, 2020). Chronic binge drinking is more common among college men, especially those who live in fraternity houses (Schulenberg & others, 2019).

In 2018, 28 percent of U.S. college students reported having had five or more drinks in a row at least once in the last two weeks (Schulenberg & others, 2019). The term *extreme binge drinking* (also called high-intensity drinking) describes individuals who had 10 or more drinks in a row or 15 or more drinks in a row in the last two weeks (Schulenberg & Patrick, 2018). In 2017, 11.2 percent of college students reported having 10 or more drinks in a row in the last two weeks and 4 percent reported having 15 or more drinks in a row in the last two weeks (Schulenberg & others, 2018). While drinking rates among college students have remained high, overall levels of drinking, including binge drinking, in this age group have declined in recent years.

In a national survey of drinking patterns on 140 campuses, almost half of the binge drinkers reported problems that included absence from classes, physical injuries, troubles with police, and unprotected sex (Wechsler & others, 2002). For example, binge-drinking college students were 11 times as likely to fall behind in school, 10 times as likely to drive after drinking, and twice as likely to have unprotected sex as college students who did not engage in binge drinking. Further, in another study, college men who frequently engaged in binge drinking had vascular changes in blood flow that are a precursor for developing arteriosclerosis (hardening of the arteries) and other cardiovascular problems such as having a heart attack or a stroke (Goslawski & others, 2013). And a longitudinal study revealed that frequent binge drinking and marijuana use during the freshman year of college predicted delayed college graduation (White & others, 2017).

Getting generally intoxicated or drunk before going out and socializing or attending an event—called *pregaming*—has become a common practice among college students (Pedersen & others, 2020; Perrotte & others, 2019). One study revealed that almost two-thirds of students on one campus had pregamed at least once during a two-week period (DeJong, DeRicco, & Schneider, 2010). In a recent study, pregaming occurred more frequently when college women drank alcohol mixed with energy drinks (Linden-Carmichael & Lau-Barraco, 2017). Drinking games, in which the goal is to become intoxicated, also have become common on college campuses (Perrotte & others, 2019). Higher levels of alcohol use have been consistently linked to higher rates of sexual risk taking, such as engaging in casual sex, having sex without using contraception, and committing sexual assaults (Looby & others, 2019).

When does binge drinking peak during development? As shown in Figure 3, recent data from the *Monitoring the Future* study at the University of Michigan indicate that binge drinking

What kinds of problems are associated with binge drinking in college?
Sean Murphy/Getty Images

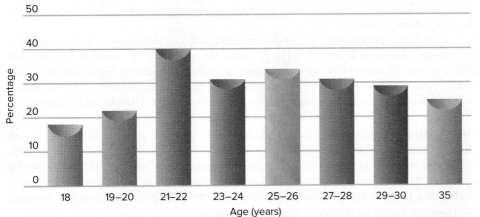

Age (years)

FIGURE 3

BINGE DRINKING IN THE ADOLESCENCE–EARLY ADULTHOOD TRANSITION. Note that the percentage of individuals engaging in binge drinking peaked at 21–22 years of age, remained high through the mid-twenties, then began to decline in the late twenties. Binge drinking was defined as having five or more alcoholic drinks in a row in the past two weeks (Schulenberg & others, 2018).

peaked at 21 to 22 years of age, with 40 percent in this age group reporting that they had engaged in binge drinking at least once in the last two weeks (Schulenberg & others, 2018).

Alcoholism *Alcoholism* is a disorder that involves long-term, repeated, uncontrolled, compulsive, and excessive use of alcoholic beverages and impairs the drinker's health and social relationships. A national study of more than 43,000 U.S. adults found that between 2001–2002 and 2012–2013, high-risk drinking and alcohol use disorder increased more in women, older adults, ethnic minorities, and individuals from low socioeconomic groups (Grant & others, 2017). One in nine individuals who drink will become an alcoholic. Those who do are disproportionately related to alcoholics (Gowin & others, 2017). Family studies consistently reveal a high frequency of alcoholism in the first-degree relatives of alcoholics (Lee & others, 2013).

Researchers have found a genetic influence on alcoholism (Palmer & others, 2019). An estimated 50 to 60 percent of individuals who become alcoholics are believed to have a genetic predisposition for it. Researchers also have documented that environmental factors play a role in alcoholism (Sun & others, 2016). For example, family studies indicate that many individuals who suffer from alcoholism do not have close relatives who are addicted to alcohol (McCutcheon & others, 2012). Large cultural variations in alcohol use also underscore the environment's role in alcoholism (Castro & others, 2015). For example, Orthodox Jews and Mormons have especially low rates of alcohol use and alcoholism.

About one-third of alcoholics recover, whether or not they are ever in a treatment program. This figure was found in a long-term study of 700 individuals over 50 years and has consistently been found by other researchers as well (Vaillant, 1992). There is a "one-third rule" for alcoholism: By age 65, one-third of alcoholics are dead or in terrible shape, one-third are abstinent or drinking socially, and one-third are still trying to beat their addiction.

Cigarette Smoking and Nicotine Converging evidence from a number of studies underscores the dangers of smoking or being around those who smoke (American Cancer Society, 2020). For example, smoking is linked to 30 percent of cancer deaths, 21 percent of heart disease deaths, and 82 percent of chronic pulmonary disease deaths. Secondhand smoke is implicated in as many as 9,000 lung cancer deaths a year. Children of smokers are at increased risk for a number of health problems, especially asthma (Gatzke-Kopp & others, 2019; Xie & others, 2020).

Fewer people smoke today than in the past, and almost half of all living adults who ever smoked have quit. In the United States, the prevalence of smoking in individuals 18 years of age and older dropped from 42 percent in 1965 to 18 percent in 2012, and then further to 13.7 percent (15.6 percent of males, 12.0 percent of females) in 2018 (Centers for Disease Control and Prevention, 2019). However, 34 million Americans still smoke cigarettes today. Cigarette smoking accounts for approximately 480,000 deaths, or 1 in 5 deaths, annually in the United States, including 41,000 deaths resulting from secondhand smoke exposure (Centers for Disease Control and Prevention, 2019). On average, smokers die 10 years earlier than nonsmokers.

Recently, just as there has been in adolescence, there has been a dramatic increase in use of e-cigarettes among individuals in emerging and early adulthood (Jankowski & others, 2019; Schulenberg, 2019). A recent study also found that emerging adults who used e-cigarettes were more likely to view emerging adulthood as a time of experimentation and were likely to experience such role transitions as loss of a job, dating someone new, and experiencing a romantic breakup (Allen & others, 2015).

Most adult smokers would like to quit, but their addiction to nicotine often makes quitting a challenge (Kinnunen & others, 2019). Nicotine, the active drug in cigarettes, is a stimulant that increases the smoker's energy and alertness, providing a pleasurable and reinforcing experience (Yong & others, 2018). Nicotine also stimulates neurotransmitters (especially dopamine) that have a calming or pain-reducing effect (Powers & others, 2020; Zarrindast & Khakpai, 2019).

Marijuana Marijuana use by college students has increased dramatically in recent years. In the University of Michigan *Monitoring the Future* Study (Schulenberg & others, 2019), marijuana use by 19- to 22-year-old college students doubled from 2017 to 2018, with 43 percent reporting that they had used marijuana at least once in the prior 12 months and 25 percent stating that they had used marijuana at least once in the prior 30 days. In addition, vaping of marijuana is rapidly increasing among college students.

developmental **connection**

Health

Many individuals who smoke in emerging adulthood and early adulthood began smoking during adolescence. Connect to "Physical and Cognitive Development in Adolescence."

Review *Connect* Reflect

LG2 Identify the changes in physical development in young adults.

Review

- When does physical performance peak and then slow down in adulthood?
- What characterizes health in emerging and early adulthood?
- What are some important things to know about eating and weight?
- What are the benefits of exercise?
- How extensive is substance abuse in young adults? What effects does it have on their lives?

Connect

- Problems with weight in adulthood are often preceded by problems with weight earlier in life. What are some of the influences on children's eating and exercise behavior in early childhood?

Reflect *Your Own Personal Journey of Life*

- What is (or was) your life like from age 18 to 25? Do Arnett's five characteristics of emerging adulthood accurately describe your own experience during this period?

3 Sexuality

LG3 Discuss sexuality in young adults.

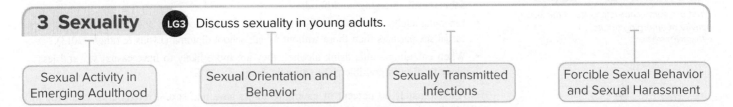

| Sexual Activity in Emerging Adulthood | Sexual Orientation and Behavior | Sexually Transmitted Infections | Forcible Sexual Behavior and Sexual Harassment |

We do not need sex for everyday survival the way we need food and water, but we do need it for the survival of the species. We have examined how adolescents develop a sexual identity and become sexually active. What happens to their sexuality in early adulthood? Let's explore the sexual activity of Americans and their sexual orientation, as well as some of the problems that can be associated with sexual activity.

SEXUAL ACTIVITY IN EMERGING ADULTHOOD

At the beginning of emerging adulthood (age 18), surveys indicate that slightly more than 60 percent of individuals have experienced sexual intercourse, but by the end of emerging adulthood (age 25), most individuals have had sexual intercourse (Lefkowitz & Gillen, 2006). Also, the U.S. average age for a first marriage has now climbed to 29.8 years for men and 28 years for women, higher than at any other point in history (U.S Census Bureau, 2019). Thus, emerging adulthood is a time frame during which most individuals are both sexually active and unmarried.

Uncertainty characterizes many emerging adults' sexual relationships (Wesche & Lefkowitz, 2020). Consider a study of emerging adult daters and cohabitors that found nearly half reported a reconciliation (a breakup followed by a reunion) (Halpern-Meekin & others, 2013). Also, one study of 18- to 26-year-olds revealed that perceived relationship commitment, though not formal relationship commitment (usually indexed by marriage), was linked to sexual enjoyment (Galinsky & Sonenstein, 2013).

Casual sex is more common in emerging adulthood than in the late twenties (Lefkowitz & others, 2019; Wesche & Lefkowitz, 2020). A recent trend has involved "hooking up" to have non-relationship sex (from kissing to intercourse) (Sutton, Simons, & Tyler, 2020). In a recent analysis of first-year college students in six focus groups, a common theme the students expressed was "Sex is easier to get and love is harder to find" (Anders & others, 2020). Also, one study revealed that 20 percent of first-year college women on one large university campus engaged in at least one hook-up over the course of the school year (Fielder & others, 2013). In this study, impulsivity, sensation seeking, and alcohol use were among the predictors of a higher likelihood of hooking up. Further, in a recent study, a greater percentage of emerging adult women than men reported having sex, hooking up with an acquaintance, using partner characteristics as a reason to hook up, and having negative reactions to their most recent hookup (Olmstead,

> **developmental connection**
> **Sexuality**
> Having intercourse in early adolescence is a risk factor in development. Connect to "Physical and Cognitive Development in Adolescence."

What are some characteristics of the sexual activity of emerging adults?
L. Mouton/PhotoAlto

Norona, & Anders, 2019). In this study, a greater percentage of emerging adult men than women reported hooking up with a stranger, meeting at a bar/club, and hooking up at a party.

In addition to hooking up, another type of casual sex that has recently increased in emerging adults is "friends with benefits (FWB)," which involves a relationship formed by the integration of friendship and sexual intimacy without an explicit commitment characteristic of an exclusive romantic relationship (Weger, Cole, & Akbulut, 2019). A recent study found that suicidal ideation was associated with entrance into a friends-with-benefits relationship as well as continuation of the FWB relationship (Dube & others, 2017). Another study indicated that 40 percent of 22-year-olds reporting having had a recent casual sexual partner (Lyons & others, 2015). And a study of more than 3,900 18- to 25-year-olds revealed that having casual sex was negatively linked to well-being and positively related to psychological distress (Bersamin & others, 2014).

What are some predictors of risky heterosexual behavior in emerging adults, such as engaging in casual and unprotected sexual intercourse? Research findings offer some answers (Lefkowitz & Gillen, 2006; Leftkowitz & others, 2019; Wesche & Leftkowitz, 2020):

- Sexual risk factors increase in emerging adulthood, with males engaging in more of these risk factors than females (Willie & others, 2018). For example, males have more casual sexual partners, while females report being more selective about their choice of a sexual partner.
- Individuals who become sexually active in adolescence engage in more risky sexual behaviors in emerging adulthood than do their counterparts who delay their sexual debuts until emerging adulthood.
- Emerging adults who are in college or who have graduated from college report having fewer casual sex partners than those without a high school diploma (Lyons & others, 2013).
- When emerging adults drink alcohol, they are more likely to have casual sex and less likely to discuss possible risks (Simons & others, 2018).

Approximately 60 percent of emerging adults have had sexual intercourse with only one individual in the past year, but compared with young adults in their late twenties and thirties, emerging adults are more likely to have had sexual intercourse with two or more individuals. Although emerging adults have sexual intercourse with more individuals than young adults do, they have sex less frequently. Approximately 25 percent of emerging adults report having sexual intercourse only a couple of times a year or not at all (Michael & others, 1994).

SEXUAL ORIENTATION AND BEHAVIOR

A national study of sexual behavior in the United States among adults 25 to 44 years of age found that 98 percent of the women and 97 percent of the men said that they had ever engaged in vaginal intercourse (Chandra & others, 2011). Also in this study, 89 percent of the women and 90 percent of the men reported that they had ever had oral sex with an opposite-sex partner, and 36 percent of the women and 44 percent of the men stated that they had ever had anal sex with an opposite-sex partner.

Detailed information about various aspects of sexual activity in adults of different ages comes from the 1994 Sex in America survey. In this study Robert Michael and his colleagues (1994) interviewed more than 3,000 people from 18 to 59 years of age who were randomly selected, in sharp contrast with earlier samples that were based on unrepresentative groups of volunteers.

Heterosexual Attitudes and Behavior   Here are some of the key findings from the 1994 Sex in America survey:

- Americans tend to fall into three categories: one-third have sex twice a week or more, one-third a few times a month, and one-third a few times a year or not at all.
- Married (and cohabiting) couples have sex more often than noncohabiting couples (see Figure 4).
- Most Americans do not engage in kinky sexual acts. When asked about their favorite sexual acts, the vast majority (96 percent) said that vaginal sex was "very" or "somewhat" appealing. Oral sex was in third place, after an activity that many have not labeled a sexual act—watching a partner undress.
- Adultery is clearly the exception rather than the rule. Nearly 75 percent of the married men and 85 percent of the married women indicated that they have never been unfaithful.

- Men think about sex far more often than women do—54 percent of the men said they think about it every day or several times a day, whereas 67 percent of the women said they think about it only a few times a week or a few times a month.

In sum, one of the most powerful messages in the 1994 survey was that Americans' sexual lives are more conservative than was previously believed. Although 17 percent of the men and 3 percent of the women reported having had sex with at least 21 partners, the overall impression from the survey was that sexual behavior is ruled by marriage and monogamy for most Americans.

How extensive are gender differences in sexuality? A meta-analysis revealed that men reported having slightly more sexual experience and more permissive attitudes than women for most aspects of sexuality (Petersen & Hyde, 2010). For the following factors, stronger differences were found: Men indicated that they engaged more in masturbation, pornography use, and casual sex, and they held more permissive attitudes about casual sex than their female counterparts did. A more recent analysis (Sprecher, Treger, & Sakaluk, 2013) of almost 8,000 emerging adults found that males had stronger permissive attitudes, especially about sex in casual relationships, than the "slightly more" permissive attitudes in the meta-analysis (Petersen & Hyde, 2010) just described. In the more recent study, African American males had more permissive sexual attitudes than non-Latino White, Latino, and Asian males, while there no ethnic differences were found among females (Sprecher, Treger, & Sakaluk, 2013).

Given all of the media and public attention to the negative aspects of sexuality—such as adolescent pregnancy, sexually transmitted infections, rape, and so on—it is important to underscore that research has strongly supported the role of sexual activity in well-being (Brody, 2010; King, 2019, 2020). For example, in a Swedish study, frequency of sexual intercourse was strongly related to life satisfaction for both men and women (Brody & Costa, 2009). And in a recent study, sexual activity in adults on day 1 was linked to greater well-being the next day (Kashdan & others, 2018). Also in this study, higher levels of reported sexual pleasure and intimacy predicted more positive affect and less negative affect the next day.

Sources of Sexual Orientation

In the Sex in America survey, 2.7 percent of the men and 1.3 percent of the women reported having had same-sex relations in the past year (Michael & others, 1994). However, in a recent national survey a higher percentage (3.8 percent) of U.S. adults reported that they were gay, lesbian, bisexual, or transsexual (Gallup, 2015).

Why are some individuals lesbian, gay, or bisexual (LGB) and others heterosexual? Speculation about this question has been extensive (Hyde & De Lamater, 2020; King & Regan, 2019). Until the end of the nineteenth century, it was generally believed that people were either heterosexual or homosexual. Today, sexual orientation is generally seen not as an either/or proposition but as a continuum ranging from exclusive male-female relations to exclusive same-sex relations (King, 2019, 2020). Some individuals are bisexual, being sexually attracted to people of both sexes.

People sometimes think that bisexuality is simply a stepping-stone to homosexuality, while others view it as a sexual orientation itself or as an indicator of sexual fluidity (King, 2019, 2020). Evidence supports the notion that bisexuality is a stable orientation that involves attraction to both sexes (Lippa, 2013).

Compared with men, women are more likely to change their sexual patterns and desires (Knight & Hope, 2012). Women are more likely than men to have sexual experiences with same- and opposite-sex partners, even if they identify themselves strongly as being heterosexual or lesbian (King, 2019, 2020). Also, women are more likely than men to identify themselves as bisexual (Gates, 2011).

All people, regardless of their sexual orientation, have similar physiological responses during sexual arousal and seem to be aroused by the same types of tactile stimulation. Investigators typically find no differences between LGBs and heterosexuals in a wide range of attitudes, behaviors, and adjustments (Fingerhut & Peplau, 2013).

Recently, researchers have explored the possible biological basis of same-sex relations. The results of hormone studies have been inconsistent. If gays are given male sex hormones (androgens), their sexual orientation doesn't change. Their sexual desire merely increases. A very early prenatal critical period might influence sexual orientation (Bogaert & Skorska, 2020; Mitsui & others, 2019). If this critical-period hypothesis turns out to be correct, it would explain why clinicians have found that sexual orientation is difficult, if not impossible, to modify.

An individual's sexual orientation—same-sex, heterosexual, or bisexual—is most likely determined by a combination of genetic, hormonal, cognitive, and environmental factors

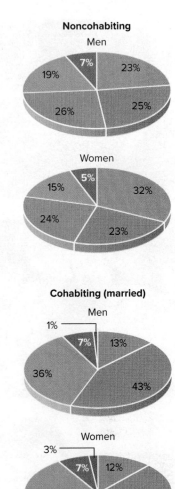

Noncohabiting
Men

Women

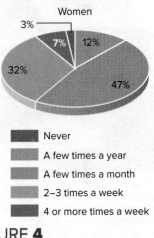

Cohabiting (married)
Men

Women

- Never
- A few times a year
- A few times a month
- 2–3 times a week
- 4 or more times a week

FIGURE 4

THE SEX IN AMERICA SURVEY. The percentages show noncohabiting and cohabiting (married) males' and females' responses to the survey question "How often have you had sex in the past year?" (Michael & others, 1994). *What was one feature of the Sex in America survey that made it superior to most surveys of sexual behavior?*

What likely determines an individual's sexual orientation?
(*Top to bottom*) Laurence Mouton/PhotoAlto/Getty Images; Creatas/Getty Images; Creatas/Getty Images

sexually transmitted infections (STIs)
Diseases that are contracted primarily through sexual activity.

(Hyde & DeLamater, 2020; King, 2019, 2020). Most experts on same-sex relations point out that no single factor alone causes sexual orientation and that the relative weight of each factor can vary from one individual to the next.

Researchers have examined the role of genes in sexual orientation by using twins to estimate the genetic and environmental contributions to sexual orientation. A Swedish study of almost 4,000 twins demonstrated that only about 35 percent of the variation in homosexual behavior in men and 19 percent in women were explained by genetic differences (Langstrom & others, 2010). This result indicates that although genes likely play a role in sexual orientation, their influence is not as strong in explaining sexuality as it is for other characteristics such as intelligence (King, 2019, 2020). That said, it has become clear that no matter whether people are heterosexual, gay, lesbian, or bisexual, they cannot be talked out of their sexual orientation (King, 2019, 2020).

Attitudes and Behavior of Lesbians and Gays   Many gender differences that appear in heterosexual relationships also occur in same-sex relationships (Diamond, 2019; Savin-Williams, 2019). For example, like heterosexual women, lesbians have fewer sexual partners than gay men, and lesbians have less permissive attitudes about casual sex outside a primary relationship than gay men do (Fingerhut & Peplau, 2013).

A special concern involving sexual minority individuals are the hate crimes and stigma-related experiences they encounter (Smith, Perrin, & Sutter, 2020). In one study, approximately 20 percent of sexual minority adults reported having experienced a person or property crime related to their sexual orientation, and about 50 percent said they had experienced verbal harassment (Herek, 2009).

SEXUALLY TRANSMITTED INFECTIONS

Sexually transmitted infections (STIs) are diseases that are primarily spread through sexual contact—intercourse as well as oral-genital and anal-genital sex. STIs affect about one in six U.S. adults (National Center for Health Statistics, 2019). Among the most prevalent STIs are bacterial infections (such as gonorrhea, syphilis, and chlamydia) and STIs caused by viruses—genital herpes, genital warts, and HIV, which can lead to AIDS. Figure 5 describes several sexually transmitted infections.

No single STI has had a greater impact on sexual behavior, or created more public fear in the last several decades, than infection with the human immunodeficiency virus (HIV). HIV is a sexually transmitted infection that destroys the body's immune system. Once a person is infected with HIV, the virus breaks down and overpowers the immune system, which leads to acquired immune deficiency syndrome (AIDS). An individual sick with AIDS has such a weakened immune system that a common cold can be life-threatening.

In 2017, approximately 1.1 million people in the United States were living with an HIV infection (Centers for Disease Control and Prevention, 2018). In 2017, male-male sexual contact continued to be the most frequent AIDS transmission category. In 2017, gay and bisexual men accounted for 66 percent of all HIV diagnoses (Centers for Disease Control and Prevention, 2018).

Because of education and the development of more effective drug treatments, deaths due to HIV/AIDS have begun to decline in the United States (National Center for Health Statistics, 2019). To read about the background and work of one individual who counsels HIV/AIDS patients, see *Connecting with Careers.*

Globally, the total number of individuals living with HIV was 37.9 million in 2018, with the majority of individuals with HIV living in sub-Saharan Africa (UNAIDS, 2019). Worldwide there were 1.7 million new cases of HIV in 2018. Currently, only about 60 percent of individuals with HIV know they have the disease (UNAIDS, 2019). Approximately half of all new HIV infections around the world occur in the 15- to 24-year-old age category. The good news is that global rates of HIV infection have fallen extensively since 2000 (UNAIDS, 2019).

What are some effective strategies for protecting against HIV and other sexually transmitted infections? They include the following:

- *Know your risk status and that of your partner.* Anyone who has had previous sexual activity with another person might have contracted an STI without being aware of it. Spend time getting to know a prospective partner before you have sex. Use this time to inform the other person of your STI status and inquire about your partner's. Remember that many people lie about their STI status.

- *Obtain medical examinations.* Many experts recommend that couples who want to begin a sexual relationship have a medical checkup to rule out STIs before they engage in sex. If cost is an issue, contact your campus health service or a public health clinic.

Pat Hawkins, Community Psychologist and Director of an HIV/AIDS Clinic

Pat Hawkins is the associate executive director for policy and external affairs of the Whitman-Walker Clinic in Washington, D.C., a facility that serves HIV and AIDS patients. She came to the clinic as a volunteer in 1983, just after HIV/AIDS exploded into an epidemic. Hawkins says that she would not do anything else but community work. "Nothing gets you engaged so fast as getting involved," she comments. "We often keep the academic world separate from the real world, and we desperately need psychologists' skills in the real world." Hawkins had a double major in psychology and sociology as an undergraduate and then went on to obtain her Ph.D. in community psychology.

Pat Hawkins counsels an AIDS patient.
Courtesy of Dr. Patricia D. Hawkins

- *Have protected, not unprotected, sex.* When used correctly, latex condoms help to prevent many STIs from being transmitted. Condoms are most effective in preventing gonorrhea, syphilis, chlamydia, and HIV. They are less effective against the spread of herpes.
- *Do not have sex with multiple partners.* One of the best predictors of getting an STI is having sex with multiple partners. Having more than one sex partner elevates the likelihood that you will encounter an infected partner.

FIGURE 5

SEXUALLY TRANSMITTED INFECTIONS

STI	Description/cause	Incidence	Treatment
Gonorrhea	Commonly called the "drip" or "clap." Caused by the bacterium *Neisseria gonorrhoeae*. Spread by contact between infected moist membranes (genital, oral-genital, or anal-genital) of two individuals. Characterized by discharge from penis or vagina and painful urination. Can lead to infertility.	500,000 cases annually in U.S.	Penicillin, other antibiotics
Syphilis	Caused by the bacterium *Treponema pallidum*. Characterized by the appearance of a sore where syphilis entered the body. The sore can be on the external genitals, vagina, or anus. Later, a skin rash breaks out on palms of hands and bottom of feet. If not treated, can eventually lead to paralysis or even death.	100,000 cases annually in U.S.	Penicillin
Chlamydia	A common STI named for the bacterium *Chlamydia trachomatis*, an organism that spreads by sexual contact and infects the genital organs of both sexes. A special concern is that females with chlamydia may become infertile. It is recommended that adolescent and young adult females have an annual screening for this STI.	About 3 million people in U.S. annually	Antibiotics
Genital herpes	Caused by a family of viruses with different strains. Involves an eruption of sores and blisters. Spread by sexual contact.	One of five U.S. adults	No known cure but antiviral medications can shorten outbreaks
AIDS	Caused by a virus, the human immunodeficiency virus (HIV), which destroys the body's immune system. Semen and blood are the main vehicles of transmission. Common symptoms include fevers, night sweats, weight loss, chronic fatigue, and swollen lymph nodes.	More than 300,000 cumulative cases of HIV virus in U.S. 25–34-year-olds; epidemic incidence in sub-Saharan countries	New treatments have slowed the progression from HIV to AIDS; no cure
Genital warts	Caused by the human papillomavirus (HPV), which does not always produce symptoms. Usually appear as small, hard painless bumps in the vaginal area, or around the anus. Very contagious. Certain high-risk types of this virus cause cervical cancer and other genital cancers. May recur despite treatment. A new HPV preventive vaccine, Gardasil, has been approved for girls and women 9–26 years of age.	About 5.5 million new cases annually; considered the most common STI in the U.S.	A topical drug, freezing, or surgery

FORCIBLE SEXUAL BEHAVIOR AND SEXUAL HARASSMENT

Too often, sex involves the exercise of power. Here, we will briefly look at two of the problems that may result: rape and sexual harassment.

rape Forcible sexual intercourse with a person who does not consent to it.

date or acquaintance rape Coercive sexual activity directed at someone with whom the perpetrator is at least casually acquainted.

Rape   **Rape** is forcible sexual intercourse with a person who does not give consent. Legal definitions of rape differ from state to state. For example, in some states husbands are not prohibited from forcing their wives to have intercourse, although this has been challenged in several of those states.

Because victims may be reluctant to suffer the consequences of reporting rape, the actual incidence is not easily determined (Littleton, Layh, & Rudolph, 2018). A meta-analysis found that 60 percent of rape victims do not acknowledge that they have been raped, with the percentage of unacknowledged rape especially high in college students (Wilson & Miller, 2016).

Nearly 200,000 rapes are reported each year in the United States. One study of college women who had been raped revealed that only 11.5 percent of them reported the rape to authorities, and of those for which the rape involved drugs and/or alcohol, only 2.7 percent of the rapes were reported (Wolitzky-Taylor & others, 2011).

Although most victims of rape are women, rape of men does occur (Anderson & others, 2020). Men in prisons are especially vulnerable to rape, usually by heterosexual males who use rape as a means of establishing their dominance and power.

Why does rape of women occur so often in the United States? Among the causes given are that males are socialized to be sexually aggressive, to regard women as inferior beings, and to view their own pleasure as the most important objective in sexual relations (Tarzia, 2020). Researchers have found that male rapists share the following characteristics: aggression enhances their sense of power or masculinity; they are angry at women in general; and they want to hurt and humiliate their victims (Bevens & Loughnan, 2019; Bock & Burkley, 2019). One study revealed that a higher level of men's sexual narcissism (assessed by these factors: sexual exploitation, sexual entitlement, low sexual empathy, and low sexual skill) was linked to a greater likelihood that they would engage in sexual aggression (Widman & McNulty, 2010). Rape is more likely to occur when one or both individuals are drinking alcohol (Brown, Horton, & Guillory, 2018). One study found that males and heavy drinkers are more likely to adhere to rape myths (such as women being held responsible for preventing the rape) than females or people who drink little or no alcohol (Hayes, Abbott, & Cook, 2016).

Rape is a traumatic experience for the victims and those close to them. As victims strive to get their lives back to normal, they may experience depression, fear, anxiety, posttraumatic stress disorder, increased substance use, and suicidal thoughts for months or years (Basile & others, 2020). Many rape victims also make changes in their lives, such as moving to a new apartment or refusing to go out at night. Recovery depends on the victim's coping abilities, psychological adjustment prior to the assault, and social support (Graham & others, 2020). Parents, a partner, and others close to the victim can provide important support for recovery, as can mental health professionals.

An increasing concern is **date or acquaintance rape,** which is coercive sexual activity directed at someone with whom the perpetrator is at least casually acquainted (Gravelin, Biernat, & Bucher, 2019). In one survey, two-thirds of female college freshmen reported having been date raped or having experienced an attempted date rape at least once (Watts & Zimmerman, 2002). About two-thirds of college men admit that they fondle women against their will, and half admit to forcing sexual activity. Also, in another recent study, more than 87 percent of alcohol-involved sexual assault on college campuses was committed by serial perpetrators (Foubert, Clark-Taylor, & Wall, 2020). In this study, fraternity men and student athletes were more likely to commit alcohol-involved sexual assault than other men on campus. And a recent study found that women who had experienced sexual assault in college were subsequently more likely to have a lower grade point average, miss more classes, and have fewer serious romantic relationships while in college (Rothman & others, 2020). Also in this study, nine years later, women who had experienced sexual assault in college were more likely to report having symptoms of depression, anxiety, and post-traumatic stress.

What are some characteristics of acquaintance rape in colleges and universities?
Juanmonino/E+/Getty Images

How Prevalent Are Sexual Assaults on College Campuses?

A major study that focused on campus sexual assault involved a phone survey of 4,446 women attending two- or four-year colleges (Fisher, Cullen, & Turner, 2000). Sexual victimization was measured in a two-stage process. First, a series of screening questions were asked to determine whether the respondent had experienced an act that might be a victimization. Second, if the respondent answered "yes," she was asked detailed questions about the incident, such as the type of unwanted contact and the means of coercion. In addition, respondents were asked about other aspects of their lives, including their lifestyles, routine activities, living arrangements, and prior sexual victimization.

Slightly less than 3 percent said that they had experienced either a rape or an attempted rape during the current academic year. About 1 in 10 college women said that they had experienced rape in their lifetime. Unwanted or uninvited sexual contacts were widespread, with more than one-third of the college women reporting these incidents. As shown in Figure 6, in this study, most women (about 9 out of 10) knew the person who had sexually victimized them. Most of the women attempted to take protective actions against their assailants but were reluctant to report the victimization to the police for a number of reasons (such as embarrassment, not clearly understanding the legal definition of rape, or not wanting to define someone they knew who had victimized them as a rapist). Several factors were associated with sexual victimization: living on campus, being unmarried, getting drunk frequently, and experiencing prior sexual victimization. The majority of rapes occurred in living quarters.

In addition, the researchers in this study examined a form of sexual victimization that has been studied infrequently: stalking. Thirteen percent of the female students said they had been stalked since the school year began. As with other sexual victimizations, 80 percent knew their stalkers, who most often were boyfriends (42 percent) or classmates (24 percent). Stalking incidents lasted an average of 60 days.

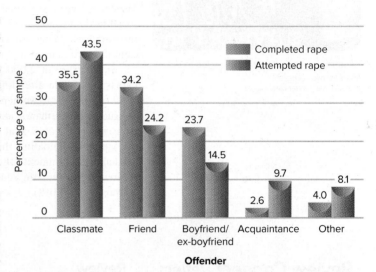

FIGURE 6

RELATIONSHIP BETWEEN VICTIM AND OFFENDER IN COMPLETED AND ATTEMPTED RAPES OF COLLEGE WOMEN. In a phone survey of college women, slightly less than 3 percent of the women said they had experienced a rape or attempted rape during the academic year (Fisher, Cullen, & Turner, 2000). The percentages shown here indicate the relationship between the victim and the offender. *What were some possible advantages and disadvantages of using a phone survey rather than face-to-face interviews to conduct this study?*

Given the prevalence of sexual assault on college campuses and the frequency with which those assaults involve perpetrators the victims know, it is clear that more research needs to be dedicated to identifying effective intervention strategies for young men and women. In the past, too often the responsibility of prevention was placed on the would-be victim's behavior. While those sorts of strategies are not unhelpful, prevention strategies that target the behavior of the would-be rapist might get closer to the root of the problem.

A number of colleges and universities have identified a "red zone" among female students—a period of time early in the first year of college when women are at especially high risk for unwanted sexual experiences. One study revealed that first-year women were at higher risk for unwanted sexual experiences, especially early in the fall term, than second-year women (Kimble & others, 2008). Exactly how prevalent are sexual assaults on college campuses? To find out, see *Connecting Through Research*.

The personal autonomy and rights of individuals to resist coercion in sexual experiences has recently produced a movement called *affirmative consent* on many college campuses (Goodcase, Spencer, & Toews, 2020). Affirmative consent means that instead of assuming that both partners are comfortable with sexual activity, each individual gives in words or actions an indication of willingness to participate in the sexual activity.

What are some factors that likely led to the Me Too Movement?
FS2/FayesVision/WENN/Newscom

Sexual Harassment   Sexual harassment is a manifestation of power of one person over another. It takes many forms, ranging from inappropriate sexual remarks and physical contact (patting, brushing against another person's body) to blatant propositions and sexual assaults. Millions of women experience sexual harassment each year in work and educational settings (Halper & Rios, 2019; Klein & Martin, 2020). Sexual harassment of men by women also occurs but to a far lesser extent than sexual harassment of women by men. In 2017, the Me Too Movement began to spread extensively with "Me Too" (or "#MeToo") used as a hashtag on social media to show the prevalence of sexual assault and harassment of women, especially in the workplace. Many women who previously had remained silent about being sexually harassed came forward and openly discussed their experiences.

In a survey of 2,000 college women, 62 percent reported having experienced sexual harassment while attending college (American Association of University Women, 2006). Most of the college women said that the sexual harassment involved noncontact forms such as crude jokes, remarks, and gestures. However, almost one-third said that the sexual harassment was physical. Sexual harassment can result in serious psychological consequences for the victim. Eliminating this type of exploitation requires the establishment of work and academic environments that provide women and men with equal opportunities to develop a career and obtain an education in a climate free of sexual harassment (Riddle, Dagenais, & Daigneault, 2019).

 Review Connect Reflect

LG3 Discuss sexuality in young adults.

Review
- What characterizes the sexual activity of emerging adults?
- What is the nature of heterosexuality and same-sex sexual orientation?
- What are sexually transmitted infections? What are some important things to know about AIDS?
- What is rape? What is date or acquaintance rape? What are the effects of forcible sexual behavior and sexual harassment?

Connect
- As you learned in this section, sexual assault is connected with aggression in males. In the chapter entitled "Socioemotional Development in Early Childhood," what was identified as one way in which children learn to behave aggressively?

Reflect *Your Own Personal Journey of Life*
- How would you describe your sexual experiences during emerging adulthood? How similar or dissimilar are they to the way sexuality in emerging adulthood was described in this section?

4 Cognitive Development

LG4 Characterize cognitive changes in early adulthood.

 Cognitive Stages

 Creativity

Are there changes in cognitive performance during early adulthood? To explore the nature of cognition during this period of development, we will focus on issues related to cognitive stages and creative thinking.

COGNITIVE STAGES

Are young adults more advanced in their thinking than adolescents are? Let's examine how Jean Piaget and others have answered this intriguing question.

Piaget's View   Piaget concluded that an adolescent and an adult think in the same way qualitatively. That is, Piaget argued that at approximately 11 to 15 years of age, adolescents enter the formal operational stage, which is characterized by more logical, abstract, and idealistic thinking than the concrete operational thinking of 7- to 11-year-olds. Piaget did stress that young adults are more quantitatively advanced in their thinking in the sense that they have more knowledge than adolescents. He also reasoned, as do information-processing psychologists, that adults especially increase their knowledge in a specific area, such as a physicist's understanding of physics or a financial analyst's knowledge of finance. According to Piaget, however, formal operational thought is the final stage in cognitive development, and it characterizes adults as well as adolescents.

Some developmentalists theorize it is not until adulthood that many individuals consolidate their formal operational thinking. That is, they may begin to plan and hypothesize about intellectual problems in adolescence, but they become more systematic and sophisticated at this process as young adults. Nonetheless, even many adults do not think in formal operational ways (Keating, 2004).

Is There a Fifth, Postformal Stage?   Some theorists have pieced together these descriptions of adult thinking and have proposed that young adults move into a new qualitative stage of cognitive development described as postformal thought (Sinnott, 2003). **Postformal thought** is:

- *Reflective, relativistic, and contextual.* As young adults engage in solving problems, they might think deeply about many aspects of work, politics, relationships, and other areas of life (Labouvie-Vief, 1986). They find that what might be the best solution to a problem at work (with a boss or co-worker) might not be the best solution at home (with a romantic partner). Thus, postformal thought holds that the correct solution to a problem requires reflective thinking and may vary from one situation to another. Some psychologists argue that reflective thinking continues to increase and becomes more internal and less contextual in middle age (Labouvie-Vief, Gruhn, & Studer, 2010; Mascalo & Fischer, 2010).
- *Provisional.* Many young adults also become more skeptical about the truth and seem unwilling to accept an answer as final. Thus, they come to see the search for truth as an ongoing and perhaps never-ending process.
- *Realistic.* Young adults understand that thinking can't always be abstract. In many instances, it must be realistic and pragmatic.
- *Recognized as being influenced by emotion.* Emerging and young adults are more likely than adolescents to understand that their thinking is influenced by emotions (Girgis & others, 2018; Labouvie-Vief, Gruhn, & Studer, 2010). However, too often negative emotions produce thinking that is distorted and self-serving at this point in development.

How strong is the evidence for a fifth, postformal stage of cognitive development? Researchers have found that young adults are more likely to engage in postformal thinking than adolescents are (Commons & Bresette, 2006). But critics argue that research has yet to document that postformal thought is a qualitatively more advanced stage than formal operational thought.

In addition to the characteristics just described for a possible fifth, postformal stage, a recent study explored wisdom and meaning as important developments in emerging adulthood (Webster & others, 2018). In this study, it was found that the search for and presence of meaning was linked to wisdom, which was assessed with five components: critical life experiences, reminiscence/reflectiveness, openness to experience, emotional regulation, and humor. We will further explore meaning in life in the chapter on "Socioemotional Development in Middle Adulthood" and wisdom in the chapter on "Cognitive Development in Late Adulthood."

CREATIVITY

At the age of 30, Thomas Edison invented the phonograph, Hans Christian Andersen wrote his first volume of fairy tales, and Mozart composed *The Marriage of Figaro.* One early study of creativity found that individuals' most creative products were generated in their thirties and that 80 percent of the most important creative contributions were completed by age 50 (Lehman, 1960).

What are some ways that young adults might think differently from adolescents?
wavebreakmedia/Shutterstock

developmental **connection**

Cognitive Theory

Adolescent cognition also includes adolescent egocentrism. Connect to "Physical and Cognitive Development in Adolescence."

developmental **connection**

Cognitive Theory

Links between cognition and emotion are increasingly being studied. Connect to "Introduction."

postformal thought Thinking that is reflective, relativistic, contextual, provisional, realistic, and influenced by emotions.

Flow and Other Strategies for Living a More Creative Life

Mihaly Csikszentmihalyi (pronounced **ME**-high **CHICK**-sent-me-high-ee) has studied the nature of creativity and recommends a number of strategies for becoming more creative (Csikszentmihalyi, 1995, 2014, 2018). In one project, Csikszentmihalyi (1995) interviewed 90 leading figures in art, business, government, education, and science to learn how creativity works. He discovered that creative people regularly experience a state he calls flow, a heightened state of pleasure experienced when we are engaged in mental and physical challenges that absorb us. Csikszentmihalyi (2000) points out that everyone is capable of achieving flow. Based on his interviews with some of the most creative people in the world, the first step toward a more creative life is cultivating your curiosity and interest. How can you do this? Here are some ideas:

- Try to be surprised by something every day. It may be something you see, hear, or read about. Become absorbed in a lecture or a book. Be open to what the world is telling you.
- Try to surprise at least one person every day. In a lot of things you do, you have to be predictable and patterned. Do something different for a change. Ask a question you normally would not ask. Invite someone to go to a show or a museum you never have visited.
- Write down each day what surprised you and how you surprised others. Most creative people keep a diary or notes to ensure that their experience is not fleeting or forgotten. Start with a specific task. Each evening record the most surprising event that occurred that day and your

Mihaly Csikszentmihalyi, in the setting where he gets his most creative ideas. *When and where do you get your most creative thoughts?*
Courtesy of Dr. Mihaly Csiksentmihalyi

most surprising action. After a few days, reread your notes and reflect on your past experiences. After a few weeks, you might see a pattern of interest emerging in your notes, one that might suggest an area you can explore in greater depth.

- When something sparks your interest, follow it. Usually when something captures your attention, it is short-lived—an idea, a song, a flower. Too often we are too busy to explore these further. Or we think these areas are none of our business because we are not experts about them. Yet the world is our business. We can't know which part of it is best suited to our interests until we make a serious effort to learn as much about as many aspects of it as possible.
- Wake up in the morning with a specific goal to look forward to. Creative people wake up eager to start the day, not necessarily because they are cheerful, enthusiastic types but because they know that there is something meaningful to accomplish each day, and they can't wait to get started.
- Spend time in settings that stimulate your creativity. In Csikszentmihalyi's (1995) research, he gave people an electronic pager and beeped them randomly at different times of the day. When he asked them how they felt, they reported the highest levels of creativity when walking, driving, or swimming. I (your author) do my most creative thinking when I'm jogging. These activities are semiautomatic in that they take a certain amount of attention while leaving some time free to make connections among ideas.

Can the strategies for stimulating creative thinking in children also be used by adults? How do the strategies discussed in the chapter entitled "Physical and Cognitive Development in Middle and Late Childhood" compare with those discussed here?

developmental **connection**

Creativity

What strategies are likely to enhance children's creative thinking? Connect to "Physical and Cognitive Development in Middle and Late Childhood."

More recently, researchers have found that creativity peaks in adulthood and then declines, but the peak often occurs in the forties. However, qualifying any conclusion about age and creative accomplishments are (1) questions about the magnitude of the decline in productivity, (2) contrasts across creative domains, and (3) individual differences in lifetime output (Simonton, 1996).

Even though a decline in creative contributions is often found in the fifties and later, the decline is not as great as is commonly thought. An impressive array of creative accomplishments can occur in late adulthood. One of the most remarkable examples of creative accomplishment in late adulthood is the life of Henri Chevreul. After a distinguished career as a physicist, Chevreul switched fields in his nineties to become a pioneer in gerontological research. He published his last research paper just a year prior to his death at the age of 103!

Any consideration of decline in creativity with age requires attention to the field of creativity involved (Kozbelt, 2014; McKay & Kaufman, 2014). In fields such as philosophy and history, older adults often show as much creativity as they did when they were in their thirties and forties. By contrast, in fields such as lyrical poetry, abstract math, and theoretical physics, the peak of creativity is often reached in the twenties or thirties.

There also is extensive individual variation in the lifetime output of creative individuals (Kandler & others, 2016). Typically, the most productive creators in any field are far more prolific than their least productive counterparts. The top 10 percent of creative producers often account for 50 percent of the creative output in a particular field. For instance, only 16 composers account for half of the music regularly performed in the classical repertoire.

Researchers have found that personality traits are linked to creativity (Feist, 2018; Kandler & others, 2016). In one recent study, the personality trait of openness to experience predicted creativity in the arts, while intellect predicted creativity in the sciences (Kaufman & others, 2016). See *Connecting Development to Life* for strategies for becoming more creative.

Review *Connect* Reflect

 LG4 Characterize cognitive changes in early adulthood.

Review
- What changes in cognitive development in young adults have been proposed?
- Does creativity decline in adulthood? How can people lead more creative lives?

Connect
- Postformal thought is characterized in part by an understanding that emotions and subjective factors influence thinking. Why are adolescents not typically capable of this kind of awareness?

Reflect *Your Own Personal Journey of Life*
- If you are in emerging adulthood, what do you think are the most important cognitive changes that have taken place so far in the transition period? If you are older, reflect on your emerging adult years and describe some of the cognitive changes that occurred during this time.

5 Achievement, Careers, and Work

 LG5 Explain the key dimensions of achievement, careers, and work in early adulthood.

| Achievement | Developmental Changes in Careers | Finding a Path to Purpose | Monitoring the Occupational Outlook | The Impact of Work |

Achieving success; choosing, establishing, and developing a career; and working are important themes of early adulthood. What are some of the factors that go into achieving success in life, having a rewarding career, and working effectively?

ACHIEVEMENT

In "Cognitive Development in Early Childhood" and "Socioemotional Development in Middle and Late Childhood," we described some important aspects of achievement in children's lives that continue to be important in adults' achievement. These include *self-efficacy,* the belief that one can master a situation and produce favorable outcomes (Bandura, 2012) and *mindset,* the cognitive view individuals develop for themselves (Dweck & Yeager, 2019). Recall that a *growth mindset,* in which people believe their qualities can change and improve through effort, is linked to success and achievement, whereas a *fixed mindset,* in which they believe their qualities are carved in stone and cannot change, is associated with lower achievement and less success. Also remember our discussion of *delay of gratification,* engaging in self-control by waiting until later to obtain something more valuable rather than immediately seeking satisfaction with something less valuable (Mischel, 2014). Here we explore other factors that are important in adults' success and achievement: motivation; goal-setting, planning, and self-monitoring; and grit.

Life is a gift . . . Accept it.
Life is a puzzle . . . Solve it.
Life is an adventure . . . Dare it.
Life is an opportunity . . . Take it.
Life is a mystery . . . Unfold it.
Life is a mission . . . Fulfill it.
Life is a struggle . . . Face it.
Life is a goal . . . Achieve it.

—Author Unknown

extrinsic motivation Doing something to obtain something else (the activity is a means to an end).

intrinsic motivation Doing something for its own sake; involves factors such as self-determination and opportunities to make choices.

grit Involves passion and persistence in achieving long-term goals.

How are goals, planning, and self-monitoring involved in achieving success?
Westend61/Getty Images

Meredith MacGregor, pictured here as a senior at Fairview High School in Boulder, Colorado, was one of Colorado's top high school long-distance runners and aspired to become a scientist. As a high school student, she was awarded the Intel Young Scientist Award. Meredith went on to obtain undergraduate, master's, and Ph.D. degrees in astronomy and astrophysics at Harvard University, followed by a post-doctoral degree in this area at Carnegie Mellon University. In 2020, she became a professor of Astrophysics and Planetary Sciences at the University of Colorado in Boulder. *What are some aspects of grit that likely characterize Meredith MacGregor?*
Kevin Moloney

Motivation   In thinking about a person's motivation, psychologists have examined whether it is advantageous to be extrinsically or intrinsically motivated. **Extrinsic motivation** involves doing something to obtain something else (the activity is a means to an end). Extrinsic motivation is often influenced by external incentives such as rewards and punishments (Thomas & Gullich, 2019). For example, an individual might work very hard at a job to earn money. **Intrinsic motivation** involves the internal motivation to do something for its own sake (the activity is an end in itself). For example, an individual might work very hard at a job because they are self-motivated (Reitz, 2019). A recent meta-analysis concluded that self-determination plays a central role in human motivation (Howard, Gagne, & Bureau, 2017).

An overwhelming conclusion of motivation research is that it is important to be intrinsically motivated (Ryan & Deci, 2019; von Egmond & others, 2020). That said, the real world includes both intrinsic and extrinsic motivation, and too often intrinsic and extrinsic motivation have been pitted against each other as polar opposites. In many aspects of students' lives, both intrinsic and extrinsic motivation are at work (Schunk, 2020). Further, intrinsic and extrinsic motivation can operate simultaneously. Thus, people might work hard at a job because they enjoy the work and like learning about it (intrinsic), and because they want to earn a good salary (extrinsic). Keep in mind, though, that many psychologists suggest that extrinsic motivation by itself is not a good strategy.

Goal-Setting, Planning, and Self-Monitoring   Setting goals, planning how to reach those goals, and engaging in self-regulation and monitoring of progress toward goals are important aspects of achievement (Schunk, 2020). Individuals should set both long-term and short-term goals. A long-term goal might be "I want to get an undergraduate degree in four years." A short-term goal might be "I want to get an A on the biology test on Monday."

Another good strategy is to set challenging goals. A challenging goal is a commitment to self-improvement. Challenging activities spark interest and involvement, while easily accomplished goals generate little interest or effort. However, goals should be optimally matched to the individual's skill level. If goals are unrealistically high, the result will be repeated failures that lower the individual's self-efficacy.

It is not enough just to set goals. In order to achieve, it also is important to plan how to reach those goals. Being a good planner means managing time effectively, setting priorities, and being organized. Individuals should not only plan their next week's activities but also monitor how well they are sticking to their plan. Once engaged in a task, they need to monitor their progress, judge how well they are doing on the task, and evaluate the outcomes to regulate what they do in the future.

Grit   Recently, as part of an ongoing effort to study key aspects of achievement, interest has been shown in the concept of **grit,** which involves passion and persistence in achieving long-term goals. Research indicates that grit is linked to academic engagement and achieving success, including obtaining a higher grade point average (Clark & Malecki, 2019). Recent research also suggests that antecedents of grit include life purpose commitment (Hill & others, 2016a), mindfulness (Raphiphatthana & others, 2018), and goal-commitment (Tang & others, 2019).

Among the questions to ask yourself to determine if you have grit are the following (Clark & Malecki, 2019):

Do I push myself do be my best?

Do I work hard to reach goals, no matter how long it takes to reach them?

Once I set a goal, do I strive to overcome any challenges I might encounter?

How passionate am I about the work I am doing?

Now that we have explored some key aspects of achieving success, let's turn our attention to developmental changes in careers and then examine various aspects of the world of work.

DEVELOPMENTAL CHANGES IN CAREERS

Many young children have idealistic fantasies about what they want to be when they grow up, such as superheroes, sports stars, or movie actors. In their high school years, they begin to think about careers from a somewhat less idealistic perspective. In their late teens and early twenties, their career decision making has usually turned more serious as they explore different career possibilities and zero in on the career they want to enter. In college, this often means choosing a major or specialization that is designed to lead to work in a particular field. By their early and mid-twenties, many individuals have completed their education or training and entered a full-time occupation. From the mid-twenties through the remainder of early adulthood, individuals often seek to establish their emerging career in a particular field, working hard to move up the career ladder and improve their financial standing.

Phyllis Moen (2009a) described the career mystique—an ingrained cultural belief that engaging in hard work for long hours through adulthood will lead to status, security, and happiness. That is, many individuals envision a career path that will enable them to fulfill the American dream of upward mobility by climbing occupational ladders. However, the lockstep career mystique has never been a reality for many individuals, especially ethnic minority individuals, women, and poorly educated adults. Further, the career mystique has increasingly become a myth for many individuals in middle-income occupations as global outsourcing of jobs, rapid technological change, and the long-term effects of the 2007–2009 recession have threatened the job security of millions of Americans.

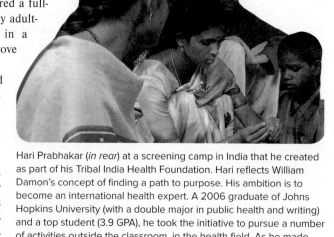

Hari Prabhakar (*in rear*) at a screening camp in India that he created as part of his Tribal India Health Foundation. Hari reflects William Damon's concept of finding a path to purpose. His ambition is to become an international health expert. A 2006 graduate of Johns Hopkins University (with a double major in public health and writing) and a top student (3.9 GPA), he took the initiative to pursue a number of activities outside the classroom, in the health field. As he made the transition from high school to college, Hari created the Tribal India Health Foundation (www.tihf.org), which provides assistance in bringing low-cost health care to rural areas in India. Juggling roles as a student and as the foundation's director, Hari spent about 15 hours a week leading Tribal India Health throughout his four undergraduate years. In describing his work, Hari said (Johns Hopkins University, 2006): "I have found it very challenging to coordinate the international operation. . . . It takes a lot of work, and there's not a lot of free time. But it's worth it when I visit our patients and see how they and the community are getting better."
Hari Prabhakar

FINDING A PATH TO PURPOSE

William Damon (2008) proposed in his book *The Path to Purpose: Helping Our Children Find Their Calling in Life* that purpose is a missing ingredient in many adolescents' and emerging adults' achievement and career development. Too many youth drift aimlessly through their high school and college years, Damon says, engaging in behavior that places them at risk for not fulfilling their potential and not finding a life pursuit that energizes them.

In interviews with 12- to 22-year-olds, Damon found that only about 20 percent had a clear vision of where they wanted to go in life, what they wanted to achieve, and why. The largest percentage—about 60 percent—had engaged in some potentially purposeful activities, such as service learning or fruitful discussions with a career counselor—but they still did not have a real commitment or any reasonable plans for reaching their goals. And slightly more than 20 percent expressed no aspirations and in some instances said they didn't see any reason to have aspirations.

Damon concludes that most teachers and parents communicate the importance of studying hard and getting good grades but rarely discuss the purpose of academic achievement. Damon emphasizes that too often students focus only on short-term goals and don't explore the big, long-term picture of what they want to do in life (Damon & Malin, 2020). The following interview questions that Damon (2008, p. 135) has used in his research are good springboards for helping individuals to reflect on their purpose:

- What's most important to you in your life?
- Why do you care about those things?
- Do you have any long-term goals?
- Why are these goals important to you?
- What does it mean to have a good life?
- What does it mean to be a good person?
- If you were looking back on your life now, how would you like to be remembered?

Recent research has provided support for the importance of purpose in people's lives (Chen & Cheng, 2020; Damon & Malin, 2020). In one study, purpose predicted emerging adults' well-being (Hill & others, 2016b). In another study, a high sense of purpose in life was associated with a lower incidence of cardiovascular disease and increased longevity (Cohen, Bavishi, & Rozanski, 2016).

MONITORING THE OCCUPATIONAL OUTLOOK

As you explore the type of work you are likely to enjoy and in which you can succeed, keep in mind that occupations may have many job openings one year but few in another year as economic conditions change. Thus, it is critical to keep up with the occupational outlook in various fields. An excellent resource for doing this is the U.S. government's *Occupational Outlook Handbook,* which is revised every two years. According to the 2020–2021 edition, solar power installers, wind turbine service technicians, home health aides, personal care aides, occupational therapy assistants, information security analysts, physician assistants, statisticians, nurse practitioners, speech-language pathologists, physical therapist assistants, and genetic counselors are the job categories that are projected to grow most rapidly through 2028 (*Occupational Outlook Handbook,* 2020–2021). Projected job growth varies widely by educational requirements. Most of the highest-paying occupations require a college degree. To read about the work of one individual who advises about careers, see the *Connecting with Careers* profile of Grace Leaf earlier in this chapter.

THE IMPACT OF WORK

Work defines people in fundamental ways (Ferrell, Hirt, & Ferrell, 2020). It influences their financial standing, housing, the way they spend their time, where they live, their friendships, and their health (Pride, Hughes, & Kapoor, 2019). Some people define their identity through their work. Work also creates a structure and rhythm to life that is often missed when individuals do not work for an extended period. Many individuals experience emotional distress and low self-esteem when they are unable to work.

Most individuals spend about one-third of their time at work. In one survey, U.S. individuals age 18 and older who were employed full-time were working an average of 47 hours per week, almost a full work day longer than the standard 9-to-5, Monday-through-Friday schedule (Saad, 2014). In this survey, half of all individuals working full-time reported that they work more than 40 hours a week and nearly 40 percent said they work 50 hours a week or more. Only 8 percent indicated they worked less than 40 hours per week.

The job outlook in 2020 for college graduates in the United States was very positive, with employers planning to increase college hiring by 5.8 percent compared with college hiring in 2019 (NACE, 2020).

A trend in the U.S. workforce is the disappearing long-term career for an increasing number of adults, especially men in private-sector jobs (Hollister, 2011). Among the reasons is the dramatic increase in technology and availability of cheaper labor in other countries. Many young and older adults are working at a series of jobs that often last for a short time (Greenhaus & Callanan, 2013). Early careers are especially unstable as some young workers move from "survival jobs" to "career jobs" while seeking a job that matches their personal interests and goals (Staff, Mont'Alvao, & Mortimer, 2015). A study of 1,100 individuals from 18 to 31 years of age revealed that maintaining a high level of aspiration and certainty over career goals better insulated individuals against unemployment in the severe economic recession that began in 2007 (Vuolo, Staff, & Mortimer, 2012).

An important consideration regarding work is how stressful it is (Lee & Jang, 2020). A national survey of U.S. adults revealed that 55 percent indicated that stress prevented them from being as productive as they wanted to be (American Psychological Association, 2007). In this study, 52 percent reported that they had considered or made a career decision, such as looking for a new job, declining a promotion, or quitting a job, because of stress in the workplace (American Psychological Association, 2007). In this survey, main sources of stress included low salaries (44 percent), lack of advancement opportunities (42 percent), uncertain job expectations (40 percent), and long hours (39 percent). One study revealed that stressors at work were linked to arterial hypertension in employees (Lamy & others, 2014). Another recent study indicated that an increase in job strain increased workers' insomnia, while a decrease in job strain reduced their insomnia (Halonen & others, 2017).

Many adults have changed their expectations about work, yet employers often aren't meeting their expectations (Hall & Mirvis, 2013). For example, current policies and practices were designed for male breadwinners and an industrial economy, making these policies and practices out of step with a workforce of women and men, and of single parents and dual earners. Many workers today want flexibility and greater control over their work schedules, yet most employers offer little flexibility, even though policies like flextime may be "on the books."

developmental **connection**

Work

The middle-aged worker faces a number of challenges in the twenty-first century. Connect to "Physical and Cognitive Development in Middle Adulthood."

What are some characteristics of work settings linked with employees' stress?
Creativa Images/Shutterstock

Work During College   The percentage of full-time U.S. college students who also held jobs increased from 34 percent in 1970 to 47 percent in 2008, then declined to 43 percent in 2017 (down from a peak of 52 percent in 2000) (National Center for Education Statistics, 2018). In 2017, 81 percent of part-time U.S. college students were employed, up from 74 percent in 2011 but slightly down from 81 percent in 2008.

Working can offset some of the costs of schooling, but it also can restrict learning opportunities. For those who identified themselves primarily as students, one study found that as the number of hours worked per week increased, their grades suffered (National Center for Education Statistics, 2002) (see Figure 7). Students need to examine whether the number of hours they work is having a negative impact on their college success.

Of course, jobs also can enhance your education. More than 1,000 colleges in the United States offer *cooperative (co-op) programs,* which are paid apprenticeships in a field that you are interested in pursuing. (You may not be permitted to participate in a co-op program until your junior year.) Other useful opportunities for working while going to college include internships and part-time or summer jobs relevant to your field of study. Participating in these work experiences can help you land the job you want after you graduate.

Unemployment   Unemployment produces stress regardless of whether the job loss is temporary, cyclical, or permanent (Alvaro & others, 2019). In a recent study, depression following job loss predicted increased risk of continued unemployment (Stolove, Galatzer-Levy, & Bonanno, 2017). Researchers have found that unemployment is related to physical problems (such as heart attack and stroke), substance abuse, emotional problems (such as depression and anxiety), marital difficulties, and homicide (Bui & Wijesekera, 2019; Yoo & others, 2016). A recent study found that following a period of unemployment, recovery of a sense of well-being upon reemployment was fast and enduring even when individuals took less favorable employment upon returning to work (Zhou & others, 2019).

Dual-Earner Couples   Dual-earner couples may face special challenges finding a balance between work and family life (Booth-LeDoux, Matthews, & Wayne, 2020; Carlson, Thompson, & Kacmar, 2019). If both partners are working, who takes care of the seemingly endless details involved in maintaining a home? If the couple has children, who is responsible for making sure that the children get to school, who fills out field trip forms, and who makes the dental appointments?

Although single-earner married families make up a sizeable minority of families, the proportion of two-earner couples has increased considerably. As more U.S. women took jobs outside the home, the division of responsibility for work and family changed in three ways: (1) men began taking more responsibility for maintaining the home; (2) women began taking more responsibility for breadwinning; (3) men began to show greater interest in their families and parenting.

Many jobs have been designed for single earners, usually male breadwinners, without regard to family responsibilities or the realities of people's lives (Richardson & Schaeffer, 2013). Consequently, many dual-earner couples engage in a range of adaptive strategies to coordinate their work and manage the family side of the work-family equation (Moen, 2009a, b; Sun & others, 2017). Researchers have found that even though couples may strive for gender equality in dual-earner families, gender inequalities persist (Cunningham, 2009). For example, women still do not earn as much as men in the same jobs, and this inequity leads to ongoing gender differences in how much time each partner spends in paid work, homemaking, and caring for children. Thus, dual-earner career decisions often are made in favor of men's greater earning power, with women spending more time than men taking care of the home and caring for children (Moen, 2009b). One study indicated that women reported more family interference from work than did men (Allen & Finkelstein, 2014). Another recent study found that partner coping, having a positive attitude toward multiple roles, using planning and management skills, and not having to cut back on professional responsibilities were linked to better relationships between dual earners (Matias & Fontaine, 2015).

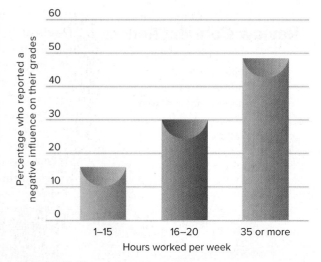

FIGURE 7

THE RELATION OF HOURS WORKED PER WEEK IN COLLEGE TO GRADES. Among students working to pay for school expenses, 16 percent of those working 1 to 15 hours per week reported that working negatively affected their grades (National Center for Education Statistics, 2002). Thirty percent of college students who worked 16 to 20 hours a week said the same, as did 48 percent who worked 35 hours or more per week.

How has the division of responsibility for work and family changed with the increase in dual-work couples?
Mareen Fischingerz/Westend61/Getty Images

Review *Connect* Reflect

LG5 Explain the key dimensions of achievement, careers, and work in early adulthood.

Review

- What are some key aspects of achieving success?
- What are some developmental changes in careers and work?
- What does Damon argue is missing in many individuals' career pursuits?
- Which occupational areas are likely to offer the greatest increase in jobs in the next decade?
- What are some important things to know about work?

Connect

- Relate what you have previously learned about gender to how gender might affect work opportunities and work environments.

Reflect *Your Own Personal Journey of Life*

- If you are an emerging adult, what careers do you want to pursue? How much education will they require? If you are older, how satisfied are you with your career choices? Explain.

topical connections *looking **forward***

At some point in middle age, more time stretches behind us than ahead of us. Midlife is changing—entered later and lasting longer—for many people. Middle adulthood is a time of declining physical skills and expanding responsibility, as well as balancing work and relationships. For many individuals, cognitive abilities peak in middle age, although some aspects of information processing, such as perceptual speed and memory, decline. Work continues to be central to people's lives in middle adulthood. Middle age also is when individuals become more interested in understanding the meaning of life.

reach your **learning goals**

Physical and Cognitive Development in Early Adulthood

1 The Transition from Adolescence to Adulthood

 Describe the transition from adolescence to adulthood.

Becoming an Adult

- Emerging adulthood is the term given to the transition from adolescence to adulthood. This period ranges from about 18 to 25 years of age, and it is characterized by experimentation and exploration. Today's emerging and young adults are experiencing emerging and early adulthood quite differently from their counterparts in earlier generations. There is both continuity and change in the transition from adolescence to adulthood. Two criteria for adult status are economic independence and taking responsibility for the consequences of one's actions.

The Transition from High School to College

- The transition from high school to college can have both positive and negative aspects. Although students may feel more grown up and be intellectually challenged by academic work, for many the transition involves a focus on the stressful move from being the oldest and most powerful group of students to being the youngest and least powerful. U.S. college students today report experiencing more stress and depression than college students in the past.

2 Physical Development

LG2 Identify the changes in physical development in young adults.

- Physical Performance and Development
- Health
- Eating and Weight
- Regular Exercise
- Substance Abuse

- Peak physical performance is often reached between 19 and 26 years of age. Toward the latter part of early adulthood, a detectable slowdown in physical performance is apparent for most individuals.

- Emerging adults have more than twice the mortality rate of adolescents, with males being mainly responsible for the increase. Despite their higher mortality rate, emerging adults in general have few chronic health problems. Many emerging adults develop bad health habits that can impair their health later in life.

- Obesity is a serious problem, with about 33 percent of Americans overweight enough to be at increased health risk. Hereditary and environmental factors are involved in obesity. Most diets don't work over the long term. For those that do, exercise is usually an important component. People with binge eating disorder (BED) frequently binge but do not purge and thus are often overweight.

- Both moderate and intense exercise programs lead to important physical and psychological gains.

- By the mid-twenties, a reduction in alcohol and drug use often takes place. Binge drinking among college students is still a major concern and can cause students to miss classes, have trouble with police, and engage in unprotected sex. Alcoholism is a disorder that impairs an individual's health and social relationships. Fewer young adults are smoking cigarettes now than in past decades, although the use of e-cigarettes is becoming more common. Most adult smokers would like to quit, but their addiction to nicotine makes quitting a challenge.

3 Sexuality

LG3 Discuss sexuality in young adults.

- Sexual Activity in Emerging Adulthood
- Sexual Orientation and Behavior
- Sexually Transmitted Infections
- Forcible Sexual Behavior and Sexual Harassment

- Emerging adulthood is a time during which most individuals are sexually active and may cohabit or get married. Emerging adults have sexual intercourse with more individuals than young adults, but they have sex less frequently. Also, casual sex is more common in emerging adulthood than early adulthood.

- In the 1994 Sex in America survey, American adults' sexual lives were portrayed as more conservative than was previously believed. An individual's sexual preference likely is the result of a combination of genetic, hormonal, cognitive, and environmental factors.

- Also called STIs, sexually transmitted infections are contracted primarily through sexual contact. The STI that has received the most attention in the last several decades is infection with HIV, which can lead to AIDS (acquired immune deficiency syndrome). A person with AIDS has such a weakened immune system that even a cold can be life-threatening.

- Rape is forcible sexual intercourse with a person who does not give consent. Date or acquaintance rape involves coercive sexual activity directed at someone with whom the perpetrator is at least casually acquainted. Sexual harassment occurs when one person uses his or her power over another individual in a sexual manner, which can result in serious psychological consequences for the victim.

4 Cognitive Development

LG4 Characterize cognitive changes in early adulthood.

- Cognitive Stages
- Creativity

- Formal operational thought is Piaget's final cognitive stage, beginning at about age 11 to 15. According to Piaget, although adults are quantitatively more knowledgeable than adolescents, adults do not enter a new, qualitatively different stage. However, some have proposed that young adults move into a qualitatively higher stage called postformal thought that is more reflective, relativistic, and contextual; provisional; realistic; and recognized as being influenced by emotion.

- Creativity peaks in adulthood, often during the forties, and then declines. However, there is extensive individual variation in lifetime creative output. Csikszentmihalyi proposed that the first step toward living a more creative life is to cultivate curiosity and interest.

5 Achievement, Careers, and Work Explain the key dimensions of achievement, careers, and work in early adulthood.

Achievement

- Among the key factors in achieving success are being highly motivated, especially in terms of intrinsic motivation, setting goals, planning, and self-monitoring, and having grit.

Developmental Changes in Careers

- Many young children have idealistic fantasies about a career. In the late teens and early twenties, their career thinking has usually turned more serious. By their early to mid-twenties, many individuals have completed their education or training and started in a career. In the remainder of early adulthood, they seek to establish their emerging career and start moving up the career ladder. Many individuals believe in the career mystique, but recently this has become a myth for increasing numbers of Americans.

Finding a Path to Purpose

- Damon argues that too many individuals have not found a path to purpose in their career development. He concludes that too often individuals focus on short-term goals and don't explore the big, long-term picture of what they want to do with their lives.

Monitoring the Occupational Outlook

- Jobs that require a college education are expected to be the fastest-growing and highest-paying occupational sector in the United States over the next decade. Education, health care, business, and professional services are projected to account for most of the new jobs.

The Impact of Work

- Work defines people in fundamental ways and is a key aspect of their identity. Most individuals spend about one-third of their adult life at work. Seventy-four percent of part-time U.S. college students work while going to college. Working during college can have positive or negative outcomes. Unemployment produces stress regardless of whether the job loss is temporary, cyclical, or permanent. The increasing number of women who work in careers outside the home has led to new work-related issues. Because of the growing number of dual-earner households, there has been a considerable increase in the time men spend in household work and child care.

key **terms**

addiction 417
aerobic exercise 416
binge eating disorder (BED) 415

date or acquaintance rape 424
emerging adulthood 408
extrinsic motivation 430

grit 430
intrinsic motivation 430
postformal thought 427

rape 424
sexually transmitted infections (STIs) 422

key **people**

Claudia Allen 410
Joseph Allen 410
Jeffrey Arnett 408

Mihaly Csikszentmihalyi 428
William Damon 431
Robert Michael 420

Phyllis Moen 431
Jean Piaget 426

John Schulenberg 416
Seth Schwartz 409

chapter 14

SOCIOEMOTIONAL DEVELOPMENT IN EARLY ADULTHOOD

chapter **outline**

Ariel Skelley/Blend Images/Corbis

Commitment is an important issue in a romantic **c**relationship for most individuals. Consider Gwenna, who decides that it is time to have a talk with Greg about his commitment to their relationship (Lerner, 1989, pp. 44–45):

She shared her perspective on both the strengths and weaknesses of their relationship and what her hopes were for the future. She asked Greg to do the same. Unlike earlier conversations, this one was conducted without her pursuing him, pressuring him, or diagnosing his problems with women. At the same time, she asked Greg some clear questions, which exposed his vagueness.

"How will you know when you are ready to make a commitment? What specifically would you need to change or be different than it is today?"

"I don't know," was Greg's response. When questioned further, the best he could come up with was that he'd just feel it.

"How much more time do you need to make a decision one way or another?"

"I'm not sure," Greg replied. "Maybe a couple of years, but I really can't answer a question like that. I can't predict my feelings."

And so it went.

Gwenna really loved this man, but two years (and maybe longer) was longer than she could comfortably wait. So, after much thought she told Greg that she would wait till fall (about ten months), and that she would move on if he couldn't commit himself to marriage by then. She was open about her wish to marry and have a family with him, but she was equally clear that her first priority was a mutually committed relationship. If Greg was not at that point by fall, then she would end the relationship—painful though it would be.

During the waiting period, Gwenna was able to not pursue him and not get distant or otherwise reactive to his expressions of ambivalence and doubt. In this way she gave Greg emotional space to struggle with his dilemma, and the relationship had its best chance of succeeding. Her bottom-line position ("a decision by fall") was not a threat or an attempt to rope Greg in, but rather a clear statement of what was acceptable to her.

When fall arrived, Greg told Gwenna he needed another six months to make up his mind. Gwenna deliberated a while and decided she could live with that. But when the six months were up, Greg was uncertain and asked for more time. It was then that Gwenna took the painful but ultimately empowering step of ending their relationship.

topical connections *looking **back***

A key aspect of socioemotional development in adolescence is an increased interest in identity; many of the key changes in identity, though, take place in emerging adulthood. Seeking autonomy in healthy ways while still being securely attached to parents are important aspects of parent-adolescent relationships. Adolescents also are motivated to spend more time with peers, friendships become more intimate, and romantic relationships begin to play a more important role in adolescents' lives.

preview

Love is of central importance in each of our lives, as it is in Gwenna and Greg's lives. Shortly, we will discuss the many faces of love, as well as marriage and the family, the diversity of adult lifestyles, and the role of gender in relationships. To begin, though, we will return to the issue of stability and change.

---

1 Stability and Change from Childhood to Adulthood

 LG1 Describe stability and change in temperament, and summarize adult attachment styles.

Temperament

Attachment

For adults, socioemotional development revolves around adaptively integrating our emotional experiences into enjoyable relationships with others. Young adults like Gwenna and Greg face choices and challenges in adopting lifestyles that will be emotionally satisfying, predictable, and manageable for them. They do not come to these tasks as blank slates, but do their decisions and actions simply reflect the persons they had become by the end of adolescence?

Current research shows that the first 20 years of life are not meaningless in predicting an adult's socioemotional well-being (VanMeter, Handley, & Cicchetti, 2020). And there is also every reason to believe that experiences in the early adult years are important in determining what the individual will be like later in adulthood (Fraley & Shaver, 2020). A common finding is that the smaller the time intervals over which we measure socioemotional characteristics, the more similar an individual will look from one measurement to the next. Thus, if we measure an individual's self-esteem at the age of 20 and then again at the age of 30, we will probably find more stability than if we measured the individual's self-esteem at the age of 10 and then again at the age of 30.

In trying to understand the young adult's socioemotional development, it would be misleading to look at an adult's life only in the present tense, ignoring the unfolding of social relationships and emotions (Dollar & Calkins, 2019). So, too, would it be a mistake to search only through a 30-year-old's first 5 to 10 years of life in trying to understand why he or she is having difficulty in a close relationship.

TEMPERAMENT

How stable is temperament? Recall that *temperament* is an individual's behavioral style and characteristic emotional responses. In early adulthood, most individuals show fewer emotional mood swings than they did in adolescence, and they become more responsible and engage in less risk-taking behavior (Charles & Luong, 2011). Along with these signs of a general change in temperament, researchers also find links between some dimensions of childhood temperament and adult personality (Shiner, 2019; Zorzetti & others, 2019). For example, in one longitudinal study, children who were highly active at age 4 were likely to be very outgoing at age 23 (Franz, 1996).

Are other aspects of temperament in childhood linked with adjustment in adulthood? Researchers have proposed various ways to describe and classify types and dimensions of personality. Research has linked several of these types and dimensions during childhood with characteristics of adult personality (Shiner, 2019; Zorzetti & others, 2019). For example:

- *Easy and difficult temperaments.* In one longitudinal study, children who had an easy temperament at 3 to 5 years of age were likely to be well adjusted as young adults (Chess & Thomas, 1987). In contrast, many children who had a difficult temperament at 3 to 5 years of age were not well adjusted as young adults.

- *Inhibition.* Individuals who had an inhibited temperament in childhood are less likely than other adults to be assertive or experience social support, and more likely to delay entering a stable job track (Lengua & Wachs, 2012). Further, one study found that

To what extent is temperament in childhood linked to temperament in adulthood?
(*Top*) Volodymyr Tverdokhlib/Shutterstock;
(*bottom*) Elenaleonova/E+/Getty Images

---

developmental connection

Temperament

Among the main temperament categories are Chess and Thomas' easy and difficult; Kagan's inhibition; and Rothbart and Bates' effortful control (self-regulation). Connect to "Socioemotional Development in Infancy."

	Child A	Child B
Intervening Context		
Caregivers	Caregivers (parents) who are sensitive and accepting, and let child set his or her own pace.	Caregivers who use inappropriate "low-level control" and attempt to force the child into new situations.
Physical Environment	Presence of "stimulus shelters" or "defensible spaces" that the children can retreat to when there is too much stimulation.	Child continually encounters noisy, chaotic environments that allow no escape from stimulation.
Peers	Peer groups with other inhibited children with common interests, so the child feels accepted.	Peer groups consist of athletic extroverts, so the child feels rejected.
Schools	School is "undermanned," so inhibited children are more likely to be tolerated and feel they can make a contribution.	School is "overmanned," so inhibited children are less likely to be tolerated and more likely to feel undervalued.
Personality Outcomes		
	As an adult, individual is closer to extraversion (outgoing, sociable) and is emotionally stable.	As an adult, individual is closer to introversion and has more emotional problems.

FIGURE 1

TEMPERAMENT IN CHILDHOOD, PERSONALITY IN ADULTHOOD, AND INTERVENING CONTEXTS. Varying experiences with caregivers, the physical environment, peers, and schools can modify links between temperament in childhood and personality in adulthood. The example given here is for inhibition.

disinhibition in the toddler years was linked to career stability in middle adulthood (Blatny & others, 2015). Also in this study, disinhibition in childhood predicted self-efficacy in adulthood. And in a longitudinal study tracing individuals from 8 to 35 years of age, an increasing trajectory of shyness was linked to social anxiety, mood disorders, and substance use in adulthood (Tang & others, 2017).

- *Ability to control one's emotions.* In one longitudinal study, when 3-year-old children showed good control of their emotions and were resilient in the face of stress, they were likely to continue to handle emotions effectively as adults (Block, 1993). By contrast, when 3-year-olds had low emotional control and were not very resilient, they were likely to show problems in these areas as young adults. Also, another study revealed a high level of emotionality at 6 years of age was associated with depression in emerging adulthood (Bould & others, 2015). And a longitudinal study found that emotion dysregulation in fifth-graders was linked to engaging in violent crime at 22 to 23 years of age (Kalvin & Bierman, 2017).

In sum, research reveals some continuity between certain aspects of temperament in childhood and adjustment in early adulthood (Atherton, Lawson, & Robins, 2020; Shiner, 2019). However, as Theodore Wachs (1994, 2000) has proposed, links between temperament in childhood and personality in adulthood might vary depending on the intervening contexts in individuals' experience. For example, Figure 1 describes contexts in which an infant who displayed an inhibited temperament might or might not develop a relatively sociable adult personality.

ATTACHMENT

Like temperament, attachment appears during infancy and plays an important part in socioemotional development (Woodhouse & others, 2020). We have discussed its role in infancy and adolescence. How do these earlier patterns of attachment and adults' attachment styles influence the lives of adults?

Although relationships with romantic partners differ from those with parents, romantic partners fulfill some of the same needs for adults as parents do for their children. Recall that *securely attached* infants are defined as those who use the caregiver as a secure base from which to explore the environment (Woodhouse & others, 2020). Similarly, adults may count on their romantic partners to be a secure base to which they can return and obtain comfort and security in stressful times (Fraley & Shaver, 2020).

> **developmental connection**
>
> **Attachment**
>
> Secure and insecure attachment have been proposed as important aspects of infants' and adolescents' socioemotional development. Connect to "Socioemotional Development in Infancy" and "Socioemotional Development in Adolescence."

How are attachment patterns in childhood linked to relationships in emerging and early adulthood?
(*Left*) itakayuki/Getty Images; (*right*) Jade/Blend Images/Getty Images

Do adult attachment patterns with partners reflect childhood and adolescent attachment patterns with parents? In a widely cited retrospective study, Cindy Hazan and Phillip Shaver (1987) revealed that young adults who were securely attached in their romantic relationships were more likely to describe their early relationship with their parents as securely attached. Also, in a longitudinal study, infants who were securely attached at 1 year of age were securely attached 20 years later in their adult romantic relationships (Steele & others, 1998). Further, a longitudinal study revealed that securely attached infants were in more stable romantic relationships in adulthood than their insecurely attached counterparts (Salvatore & others, 2011). A longitudinal study found that insecure avoidant attachment at 8 years of age was linked to a lower level of social initiative and prosocial behavior and a higher level of social anxiety and loneliness at 21 years of age (Fransson & others, 2016). Further, a recent study revealed that compared with stable secure infants at 12 and 18 months, their stable insecure infant counterparts had worse emotion-regulation strategies in relationship-challenging contexts 20 to 35 years later (Girme & others, 2020). And in a longitudinal study of individuals from 13 to 72 years of age, avoidant attachment declined across the life span and being in a relationship predicted lower levels of anxious and avoidant attachment across adulthood (Chopik, Edelstein, & Grimm, 2019). However, in another study the links between early attachment styles and later attachment styles were weakened by stressful and disruptive experiences such as the death of a parent or instability of caregiving (Lewis, Feiring, & Rosenthal, 2000).

Consistently positive caregiving over a number of years is likely an important factor in connecting early attachment with functioning later in development. A longitudinal study revealed that changes in attachment security/insecurity from infancy to adulthood were linked to stresses and supports in socioemotional contexts (Van Ryzin, Carlson, & Sroufe, 2011). The study just described (Van Ryzin, Carlson, & Sroufe, 2011) reflects an increasingly accepted view of the nature of attachment and its influence on development. That is, it is important to recognize that attachment security in infancy does not always by itself produce long-term positive outcomes, but rather is linked to later outcomes through connections with the way children, adolescents, and adults subsequently experience various social contexts as they develop (Khan & others, 2020; Simpson & Karantzas, 2019). Recall that the Van Ryzin, Carlson, and Sroufe (2011) study reflects a *developmental cascade model,* which involves connections across domains over time that influence developmental pathways and outcomes (VanMeter, Handley, & Cicchetti, 2020).

Following is a description of the widely used measure of adult attachment created by Hazan and Shaver (1987, p. 515):

Read each paragraph and then place a check mark next to the description that best describes you:

1. I find it relatively easy to get close to others and I am comfortable depending on them and having them depend on me. I don't worry about being abandoned or about someone getting too close to me.

2. I am somewhat uncomfortable being close to others. I find it difficult to trust them completely and to allow myself to depend on them. I get nervous when anyone gets too close to me and it bothers me when someone tries to be more intimate with me than I feel comfortable with.

3. I find that others are reluctant to get as close as I would like. I often worry that my partner doesn't really love me or won't want to stay with me. I want to get very close to my partner, and this sometimes scares people away.

These items correspond to three attachment styles: secure (option 1 above), insecure avoidant (option 2 above), and insecure anxious (option 3 above):

- **Secure attachment style.** Securely attached adults have positive views of relationships, find it easy to get close to others, and are not overly concerned with or stressed out about their romantic relationships. These adults tend to enjoy sexuality in the context of a committed relationship and are less likely than others to have one-night stands.

- **Avoidant attachment style.** Avoidant individuals are hesitant about getting involved in romantic relationships and once they are in a relationship tend to distance themselves from their partner.

- **Anxious attachment style.** These individuals demand closeness, are less trusting, and are more emotional, jealous, and possessive.

The majority of adults (about 60 to 80 percent) describe themselves as securely attached, and not surprisingly adults prefer having a securely attached partner (Zeifman & Hazan, 2008).

Researchers are studying links between adults' current attachment styles and many aspects of their lives (Fraley & Shaver, 2020; Mikulincer & Shaver, 2019; Rowe, Gold, & Carnelley, 2020). For example, securely attached adults are more satisfied with their close relationships than insecurely attached adults, and the relationships of securely attached adults are more likely to be characterized by trust, commitment, and longevity.

The following studies have confirmed the importance of adult attachment styles in people's lives:

- Insecure anxious individuals showed strong ambivalence toward a romantic partner (Mikulincer & others, 2010).

- Insecure anxious and insecure avoidant individuals were more likely than securely attached individuals to engage in risky health behaviors, were more susceptible to physical illness, and had worse disease outcomes (Pietromonaco & Beck, 2018).

- In a recent research review, having an insecure attachment style increased the risk of engaging in suicidal thoughts (Zortea, Gray, & O'Connor, 2020).

- College students with an anxious attachment style were more likely to be addicted to social networking sites (Liu & Ma, 2019).

- In a recent research review, maladaptive support behaviors were more likely to occur when one or both members of a romantic dyad had an insecure attachment style (McLeod & others, 2020). Also in this review, individuals with an anxious or avoidant attachment style were more likely to provide poor-quality support, and when receiving support from others, to interpret it in a negative manner.

- Adults with avoidant and anxious attachment styles had a lower level of sexual satisfaction than their securely attached counterparts (Brassard & others, 2012).

- In a recent meta-analysis, adults with insecure attachment styles were more likely to engage in risky sexual behaviors (Kim & Miller, 2020).

- In two longitudinal studies of newlywed marriages, spouses were more likely to engage in infidelity when either they or their partner had a highly anxious attachment style (Russell, Baker, & McNulty, 2013).

Leading experts Mario Mikulincer and Phillip Shaver (2016, 2019) reached the following conclusions about the benefits of secure attachment. Individuals who are securely attached have a well-integrated sense of self-acceptance, self-esteem, and self-efficacy. They are able to control their emotions, are optimistic, and are resilient. When they face stress and adversity, they are mindful of what is happening around them and choose effective coping strategies.

If you have an insecure attachment style, are you stuck with it and does it doom you to have problematic relationships? Attachment categories are somewhat stable in adulthood, but

What are some key dimensions of attachment in adulthood, and how are they related to relationship patterns and well-being?
Fuse/Corbis/Getty Images

secure attachment style An attachment style that describes adults who have positive views of relationships, find it easy to get close to others, and are not overly concerned or stressed out about their romantic relationships.

avoidant attachment style An attachment style that describes adults who are hesitant about getting involved in romantic relationships and once in a relationship tend to distance themselves from their partner.

anxious attachment style An attachment style that describes adults who demand closeness, are less trusting, and are more emotional, jealous, and possessive.

adults do have the capacity to change their attachment thinking and behavior (Mikulincer & Shaver, 2019). Although attachment insecurities are linked to relationship problems, attachment style makes only a moderate contribution to relationship functioning because other factors contribute to relationship satisfaction and success. Later in the chapter, we will discuss such factors in our coverage of marital relationships.

Review Connect Reflect

 LG1 Describe stability and change in temperament, and summarize adult attachment styles.

Review
- How stable is temperament from childhood to adulthood?
- What attachment styles characterize adults, and how are they linked to relationship outcomes?

Connect
- What behaviors have been linked to insecure attachment in adolescence?

Reflect *Your Own Personal Journey of Life*
- What is your attachment style? How do you think it affects your relationships?

2 Attraction, Love, and Close Relationships

 LG2 Identify some key aspects of attraction, love, and close relationships.

Attraction   The Faces of Love   Falling Out of Love

These are the themes of our exploration of close relationships: how these relationships get started, the faces of love, and falling out of love.

ATTRACTION

What attracts people like Gwenna and Greg to each other and motivates them to spend more time together? How important are first impressions, personality traits, and physical attraction in determining the relationships we form?

First Impressions   When we first meet someone, typically the new acquaintance quickly makes an impression (Alaei & others, 2020; King, 2020). That first impression can have lasting effects (South Palomares, Sutherland, & Young, 2018). How fast do we make these initial impressions of others? In one study, judgments made after just a 100-millisecond exposure time to unfamiliar faces were sufficient for individuals to form an impression (Willis & Todorov, 2006).

Are first impressions accurate? Numerous studies have found that immediate impressions can be accurate. Based on very little evidence, such as that provided by photographs, very brief interactions, or video clips, individuals can accurately detect a person's romantic interest in them (Place & others, 2012), their tendency to be violent (Stillman, Maner, & Baumeister, 2010), and their sexual orientation (Stern & others, 2013). However, in some cases first impressions can be misleading. In a recent study, individuals who encountered others with attractive faces were more likely to overestimate their intelligence (Talamas, Mavor, & Perrett, 2016).

Familiarity and Similarity   Although first impressions may contribute to whether a relationship will develop, much more is involved in whether a relationship will endure. Familiarity may breed contempt, as the old saying goes, but researchers have found that familiarity is an important condition for a close relationship to develop. For the most part, friends and lovers are people who have been around each other for a long time: they may have grown up together, gone to high school or college together, worked together, or gone to the same social events (Anderson & Sabatelli, 2011).

Another old saying, "Birds of a feather flock together," also helps to explain attraction. Overall, our friends and lovers are much more like us than unlike us (Guerrero, Andersen, & Afifi, 2011). Friends and lovers tend to have similar attitudes, values, lifestyles, and physical

(*Left*) Manti Te'o; (*Right*) Michelle Przybyksi and Andy Lalinde.
(*Left*) John Biever/Sports Illustrated/Getty Images; (*right*) Courtesy of Michelle and Andres Lalinde

attractiveness. For some characteristics, though, opposites may attract. An introvert may wish to be with an extravert, or someone with little money may wish to associate with someone who is wealthy, for example.

Why are people attracted to others who have similar attitudes, values, and lifestyles? **Consensual validation** is one reason. Our own attitudes and values are supported when someone else's attitudes and values are similar to ours—their attitudes and values validate ours. Another reason similarity matters is that people tend to shy away from the unknown. We often prefer to be around people whose attitudes and values we can predict. And similarity implies that we will enjoy doing things with another person who likes the same things and has similar attitudes.

This is DEFINITELY the LAST time I arrange a date over the internet!

Fran Orford, www.francartoons.com

Recently, attraction has not only taken place in person but also over the Internet (Jin, Ryu, & Mugaddam, 2020). In a recent U.S. survey, 10 percent of 18- to 24-year-olds, 22 percent of 25- to 34-year-olds, and 17 percent of 35- to 44-year-olds reported that they had used online dating sites or apps (Pew Research Center, 2015a). In their twenties, women have more online pursuers than men, but in their forties, men have more online pursuers. When online dating first began in 2005, it was viewed by most people as not being a good way to meet people, but in a recent national survey, a majority of Americans said that online dating is a good way to meet people (Pew Research Center, 2015a).

Is looking for love online likely to work out? It didn't work out so well in 2012 for Notre Dame linebacker Manti Te'o, whose online girlfriend turned out to be a "catfish," someone who fakes an identity online. Connecting online for love did turn out positively for two Columbia University graduate students, Michelle Przybyksi and Andy Lalinde (Steinberg, 2011). They lived only a few blocks away from each other, so soon after they communicated online through Datemyschool.com, an online dating site exclusively for college students, they met in person, really hit it off, applied for a marriage license 10 days later, and eventually got married.

However, an editorial by Samantha Nickalls (2012) in *The Tower*, the student newspaper at Arcadia University in Philadelphia, argued that online dating sites might be okay for people in their thirties and older but not for college students. She commented:

consensual validation An explanation of why individuals are attracted to people who are similar to them. Our own attitudes and behavior are supported and validated when someone else's attitudes and behavior are similar to ours.

The dating pool of our age is huge. Huge. After all, marriage is not on most people's minds when they're in college, but dating (or perhaps just hooking up) most certainly is. A college campus, in fact, is like living a dating service because the majority of people are looking for the same thing you are. As long as you put yourself out there, flirt a bit, and be friendly, chances are that people will notice.

Some critics argue that online romantic relationships lose the interpersonal connection, while others emphasize that the Internet may benefit shy or anxious individuals who find it difficult to meet potential partners in person (Holmes, Little, & Welsh, 2009). One problem with online matchmaking is that many individuals misrepresent their characteristics, such as how old they are, how attractive they are, and their occupation. Recent data indicate that men lie most about their age, height, and income; women lie most about their weight, physical build, and age (statisticbrain.com, 2017). Despite such dishonesty, some researchers have found that romantic relationships initiated on the Internet are more likely than relationships established in person to last for more than two years (Bargh & McKenna, 2004). And a national study of more than 19,000 individuals found that more than one-third of married people initially met their future spouse online (Cacioppo & others, 2013). Also in this study, marriages that began online were slightly less likely to break up and were characterized by slightly higher marital satisfaction than those that started in traditional offline contexts.

What do you think? Is searching online for romantic relationships a good idea? What are some cautions that should be taken if you pursue an online romantic relationship?

Physical Attractiveness As important as familiarity and similarity may be, they do not explain the spark that often ignites a romantic relationship: physical attractiveness. How important is physical attractiveness in relationships? Psychologists do not consider the link between physical beauty and attraction to be as clear-cut as many advertising agencies would like us to believe. For example, psychologists have determined that men and women differ on the importance of good looks when they seek an intimate partner. Women tend to rate as most important such traits as considerateness, honesty, dependability, kindness, understanding, and earning prospects; men prefer good looks, cooking skills, and frugality (Buss & Barnes, 1986; Eastwick & Finkel, 2008). And in one study, researchers found that partner physical attractiveness played a larger role in predicting husbands' marital satisfaction than in predicting wives' marital satisfaction (Meltzer & others, 2014).

Complicating research about the role of physical attraction are changing standards of what is deemed attractive. The criteria for beauty can differ not just across cultures but over time within cultures as well. In the 1950s, the ideal of female beauty in the United States was exemplified in the well-rounded figure of Marilyn Monroe. Today, Monroe's 135-pound, 5-foot, 5-inch physique might be regarded as a bit overweight. The current ideal physique for both men and women is neither pleasingly plump nor extremely slender.

The force of similarity also operates at a physical level. We usually seek a partner who shares our own level of attractiveness in physical characteristics as well as social attributes. Research validates the **matching hypothesis,** which states that although we may prefer a more attractive person in the abstract, in the real world we end up choosing someone who is close to our own level of attractiveness.

THE FACES OF LOVE

Once we are initially attracted to another person, other opportunities exist that may deepen the relationship to love. Love refers to a vast and complex territory of human behavior, spanning a range of relationships that includes friendship, romantic love, affectionate love, and consummate love (Felton & others, 2019; Murray & others, 2019). In most of these types of love, one recurring theme is intimacy (Sternberg & Sternberg, 2019).

Intimacy Self-disclosure and the sharing of private thoughts are hallmarks of intimacy. Adolescents have an increased need for intimacy. At the same time, they are engaged in the essential tasks of developing an identity and establishing their independence from their parents. Juggling the competing demands of intimacy, identity, and independence also becomes a central task of adulthood. In a recent study, greater self-disclosure was associated with higher relational intimacy offline but lower relational intimacy online in romantic relationships but not friendships (Lee, Gillath, & Miller, 2019).

Recall that Erik Erikson (1968) argues that identity versus identity confusion—pursuing who we are, what we are all about, and where we are going in life—is the most important issue to be negotiated in adolescence. In early adulthood, according to Erikson, after individuals are well on their way to establishing stable and successful identities, they enter the sixth developmental stage, which is intimacy versus isolation. Erikson describes intimacy as finding oneself while losing oneself in another person, and it requires a commitment to another person. If a person fails to develop an intimate relationship in early adulthood, according to Erikson, isolation results.

> We are what we love.
>
> —Erik Erikson
> *Danish-born American psychoanalyst and author, 20th century*

→ developmental **connection**

Erikson's Theory

Erikson's adolescence stage is identity versus identity confusion, and his middle adulthood stage is generativity versus stagnation. Connect to "Socioemotional Development in Adolescence" and "Socioemotional Development in Middle Adulthood."

matching hypothesis Theory that although we prefer a more attractive person in the abstract, in the real world we end up choosing someone who is close to our own level of attractiveness.

Why is intimacy an important aspect of early adulthood?
Lane Oatey/Blue Jean Images/Getty Images

Love is a canvas furnished by nature and embroidered by imagination.

—VOLTAIRE

French essayist, 18th century

romantic love Also called passionate love or *eros,* romantic love has strong sexual and infatuation components and often predominates early in a love relationship.

affectionate love In this type of love, also called companionate love, an individual desires to have the other person near and has a deep, caring affection for the other person.

Types of Love	Passion	Intimacy	Commitment
Infatuation	Present	Absent or low	Absent or low
Affectionate love	Absent or low	Present	Present
Fatuous love	Present	Absent or low	Present
Consummate love	Present	Present	Present

■ Present   ■ Absent or low

FIGURE 2

STERNBERG'S TRIANGLE OF LOVE. Sternberg identified three dimensions of love: passion, intimacy, and commitment. Various combinations of these dimensions result in infatuation, affectionate love, fatuous love, and consummate love.

One study confirmed Erikson's theory that identity development in adolescence is a precursor to intimacy in romantic relationships during emerging adulthood (Beyers & Seiffge-Krenke, 2010). And a meta-analysis revealed a positive link between identity development and intimacy, with the connection being stronger for men than for women (Arseth & others, 2009).

Friendship   Increasingly researchers are finding that friendship plays an important role in development throughout the life span (Allen & others, 2020). Most U.S. men and women have a best friend—92 percent of women and 88 percent of men have a best friend of the same sex (Blieszner, 2009). Many friendships are long-lasting, as 65 percent of U.S. adults have known their best friend for at least 10 years and only 15 percent have known their best friend for less than 5 years. Adulthood brings opportunities for new friendships as individuals move to new locations and may establish new friendships in their neighborhood or at work (Blieszner & Ogletree, 2017, 2018).

Romantic Love   Some friendships evolve into **romantic love,** which is also called passionate love or *eros.* Romantic love has strong components of sexuality and infatuation, and it often predominates in the early part of a love relationship (Berscheid, 2010; Hendrick & Hendrick, 2019). A meta-analysis found that males show higher avoidance and lower anxiety about romantic love than females do (Del Giudice, 2011).

A complex intermingling of different emotions goes into romantic love—including such emotions as passion, fear, anger, sexual desire, joy, and jealousy (Feybesse & Hatfield, 2019; Hendrick & Hendrick, 2019). Well-known love researcher Ellen Berscheid (1988) says that sexual desire is the most important ingredient of romantic love. Obviously, some of these emotions are a source of anguish, which can lead to other issues such as depression. Indeed, one study revealed that a heightened state of romantic love in young adults was linked to stronger depression and anxiety symptoms but better sleep quality (Bajoghli & others, 2014). And a recent study confirmed that declaring a relationship status on Facebook was associated with both romantic love and jealousy (Orosz & others, 2015).

How do romantic relationships change in emerging adulthood? In a recent study that spanned 10 years, short-term relationships were supported more as individuals moved into emerging adulthood (Lantagne, Furman, & Novak, 2017). Long-term adolescent relationships were both supportive and turbulent, characterized by elevated levels of support, negative interactions, higher control, and more jealousy. In emerging adulthood, long-term relationships continued to have high levels of support, but negative interactions, control, and jealousy decreased.

Affectionate Love   Love is more than just passion (Clark, Hirsch, & Monin, 2019; Langeslag & van Steenbergen, 2020; Surti & Langeslag, 2019). **Affectionate love,** also called *companionate love,* is the type of love that occurs when someone desires to have the other person near and has a deep, caring affection for the person. The early stages of love have more romantic love ingredients—but as love matures, passion tends to give way to affection (Sternberg & Sternberg, 2019).

Consummate Love   So far we have discussed two forms of love: romantic (or passionate) and affectionate (or companionate). According to Robert J. Sternberg (1988), these are not the only forms of love. Sternberg proposed a triarchic theory of love in which love can be thought of as a triangle with three main dimensions—passion, intimacy, and commitment. Passion, as described earlier in the romantic love section, is physical and sexual attraction to another. Intimacy relates to the emotional feelings of warmth, closeness, and sharing in a relationship. Commitment is the cognitive appraisal of the relationship and the intent to maintain the relationship even in the face of problems.

In Sternberg's theory, the strongest, fullest form of love is *consummate love,* which involves all three dimensions (see Figure 2). If passion is the only ingredient in a relationship (with intimacy and commitment low or absent), we are merely *infatuated.* An affair or a fling involving little intimacy and even less commitment is an example. A relationship marked by intimacy and commitment but low or lacking in passion is called *affectionate love,* a pattern often found among couples who have been married for many years. If passion and commitment are present but intimacy is not, Sternberg calls the relationship *fatuous love,* as when one person worships another from a distance. But if couples share all three dimensions—passion, intimacy, and commitment—they experience consummate love (Sternberg & Sternberg, 2019). In a recent study, being in a romantic relationship, spending more time interacting with a partner, and investing more time and effort in the relationship all predicted greater well-being (Hudson, Lucas, & Donnellan, 2020). However, these effects were moderated by relationship quality—being in a relatively neutral relationship was associated with lower well-being than being unpartnered.

Cross-Cultural Variations in Romantic Relationships   Culture has strong influences on many aspects of human development, including romantic relationships (Gao, 2016). In collectivist countries like China and Korea, intimacy is more diffused in love because of the strong group emphasis on connections outside of a romantic love relationship. By contrast, in individualistic countries such as the United States and most European countries, intimacy is often more intensified because an individual's social network is likely to be smaller and less group-oriented (Gao, 2016). Also, research indicates that greater passion characterizes U.S. romantic relationships than Chinese romantic relationships (Gao, 2001). And researchers have found that self-disclosure is more common in U.S. romantic relationships than Japanese romantic relationships (Kito, 2005). Feelings of commitment are stronger in Chinese romantic relationships than in U.S. romantic relationships (Dion & Dion, 1993).

What are some characteristics of romantic relationships in China?
Lane Oatey/Blue Jean Images/Getty Images

In a recent exploration of cross-cultural variations, romantic relationships were studied in three countries—Japan, France, and Argentina (Ansari, 2015). In Japan, the marriage rate is declining so rapidly that the Japanese government is very concerned that this could lead to a considerable drop in Japan's population. In 2013, 45 percent of Japanese women 16 to 24 years of age reported that they were not interested in or despised having sexual contact. Also, the percentage of Japanese men and women who aren't involved in any romantic relationship has increased significantly in recent years.

In Argentina, romantic interest is much stronger than in Japan (Ansari, 2015). Sexual and romantic flirtation is a way of life for many Argentinians. Online dating is not nearly as frequent as in the United States, apparently because men are so forward in their romantic pursuits in person.

In France, as in Argentina, interest in passionate love is strong. However, in the three-country comparison, one aspect of French interest in romantic relationships stood out—their affinity for having extramarital affairs. In one comparison, only 47 percent in France reported that having an extramarital affair is morally wrong, compared with 69 percent in Japan and 72 percent in Argentina (Wike, 2014). In this survey, 84 percent of people in the United States said it was morally wrong. In sum, there are striking cultural variations in many aspects of romantic relationships.

As part of this exploration of romantic relationships in different countries, the Middle Eastern country of Qatar also was studied (Ansari, 2015). In Qatar, casual dating is forbidden and public displays of affection can be punished with prison time. However, with the recent advent of smartphones, social media, and the Internet, young adults in Qatar are now contacting each other about co-ed parties in hotel rooms—a way to hang out while avoiding the monitoring of parents, neighbors, and government officials.

What are romantic relationships like in Argentina?
JAG IMAGES/Cultura RF/Getty Images

Relationship Education for Adolescents and Emerging Adults   Traditionally, programs in relationship education have focused on helping committed adult couples to strengthen their relationships. Recently, though, an increasing number of relationship education programs have been developed for adolescents and emerging adults (Hawkins, 2018). *Relationship education* consists of interventions to provide individuals and couples with information and skills that produce positive romantic relationships and marriages. These interventions are diverse and include offering classroom instruction in basic relationship knowledge and skills to young people, helping unmarried couples learn more about relationships in small-group settings, and providing premarital counseling to engaged couples.

A recent meta-analysis of 30 studies of relationship education for adolescents and emerging adults found a positive effect of the programs (Simpson, Leonhardt, & Hawkins, 2018). The skills most often assessed in these studies are interpersonal communication, problem-solving and conflict strategies, and self-regulation (Simpson, Lenohardt, & Hawkins, 2018). The positive effects of relationship education were stronger for emerging adults than for adolescents. They also were stronger for disadvantaged participants than for more advantaged participants.

FALLING OUT OF LOVE

The collapse of a close relationship may feel tragic. In the long run, however, as was the case for Gwenna, our happiness and personal development may benefit from ending a close relationship.

What Are the Positive Outcomes to the Breakup of a Romantic Relationship?

Studies of romantic breakups have mainly focused on their negative aspects (Kato, 2005; Moreau & others, 2011; Simon & Barrett, 2010). Few studies have explored the possibility that a romantic breakup might lead to positive changes.

One study assessed the personal growth that can follow the breakup of a romantic relationship (Tashiro & Frazier, 2003). The participants were 92 undergraduate students who had experienced a relationship breakup in the past nine months. They were asked to describe "what positive changes, if any, have happened as a result of your breakup that might serve to improve your future romantic relationships" (p. 118).

Self-reported positive growth was common following a romantic breakup. Changes were categorized as personal, relational, and environmental. The most commonly reported types of growth were personal changes, which included feeling stronger and more self-confident, more independent, and better off emotionally. Relational positive changes included gaining relational wisdom, and environmental positive changes included having better friendships because of the breakup. Figure 3 provides examples of these positive changes. Women were more likely to report positive growth than men were.

Of course, not all romantic relationships produce positive changes in the aftermath. In a recent large-scale study of more than 9,000 adults, experiencing a romantic breakup lowered individuals' self-esteem, but the effect disappeared one year after the breakup (Luciano & Orth, 2017).

Change category	Exemplars of frequently mentioned responses
Personal positives	1. "I am more self-confident." 2. "Through breaking up I found I could handle more on my own." 3. "I didn't always have to be the strong one, it's okay to cry or be upset without having to take care of him."
Relational positives	1. "Better communication." 2. "I learned many relationship skills that I can apply in the future (for example, the importance of saying you're sorry)." 3. "I know not to jump into a relationship too quickly."
Environmental positives	1. "I rely on my friends more. I forgot how important friends are when I was with him." 2. "Concentrate on school more: I can put so much more time and effort toward school." 3. "I believe friends' and family's opinions count—will seek them out in future relationships."

FIGURE 3

EXAMPLES OF POSITIVE CHANGES IN THE AFTERMATH OF A ROMANTIC BREAKUP

In particular, ending a relationship may be wise if you are obsessed with someone who repeatedly betrays your trust; if you are involved with someone who is draining you emotionally or financially or both; or if you are desperately in love with someone who does not return your feelings.

Being in love when love is not returned can lead to depression, obsessive thoughts, sexual dysfunction, health problems, inability to work effectively, difficulty in making new friends, and self-condemnation (Sbarra, 2012). Thinking clearly in such relationships is often difficult because our thoughts are so colored by arousing emotions (Guerrero, Andersen, & Afifi, 2011). A study of unmarried relationship dissolution in 18- to 35-year-olds revealed that experiencing a breakup was linked to an increase in psychological stress and a decrease in life satisfaction (Rhoades & others, 2011).

Studies of romantic breakups have mainly focused on their negative aspects (Verhallen & others, 2019). Few studies have explored the possibility that a romantic breakup might lead to positive change, although an increasing number of studies have focused on factors that can improve adjustment and produce positive outcomes following a romantic breakup. For example, in a recent study of emerging adults, higher optimism, self-esteem, and grit were associated with lower levels of depressive symptoms and rumination three months after a romantic breakup (O'Sullivan & others, 2019). To read in greater detail about a study of positive outcomes following a romantic breakup, see *Connecting Through Research*.

Review *Connect* Reflect

LG2 Identify some key aspects of attraction, love, and close relationships.

Review
- What attracts someone to another person?
- What are some different types of love?
- What characterizes falling out of love?

Connect
- Describe how dating in adolescence differs from dating in early adulthood.

Reflect *Your Own Personal Journey of Life*
- Think about your own experiences with love. Based on those experiences, what advice about love would you give to someone else?

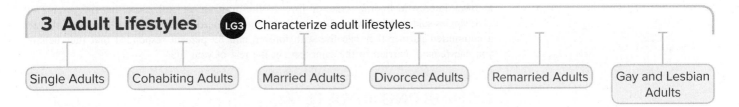

3 Adult Lifestyles **LG3** Characterize adult lifestyles.

Single Adults | Cohabiting Adults | Married Adults | Divorced Adults | Remarried Adults | Gay and Lesbian Adults

A striking social change in recent decades has been the decreased stigma attached to individuals who do not maintain what were long considered conventional families. Adults today choose many lifestyles and form many types of families (Seccombe, 2020). They live alone, cohabit, marry, divorce, and remarry partners of the same or opposite sex.

In his book, *The Marriage-Go-Round,* sociologist Andrew Cherlin (2009) concluded that the United States has more marriages and remarriages, more divorces, and more short-term cohabitation (living together) relationships than most countries. Combined, these lifestyles create more turnover and movement in and out of relationships in the United States than in virtually any other country. Let's explore these varying relationship lifestyles.

SINGLE ADULTS

Recent decades have seen a dramatic rise in the percentage of single (unmarried) adults. In 2017, 44.9 percent of U.S. adults 18 years of age and older had never been married (U.S. Census Bureau, 2018). The increasing number of single adults is the result of rising rates of cohabitation and a trend toward postponing marriage. The United States has a lower percentage of single adults than do many other countries such as Great Britain, Germany, and Japan. Also, the fastest growth in the number of people adopting a single adult lifestyle is occurring in rapidly developing countries such as China, India, and Brazil (Klinenberg, 2012, 2013).

Even when single adults enjoy their lifestyles and are highly competent individuals, they often are stereotyped (Schwartz & Scott, 2012). Stereotypes associated with being single range from the "swinging single" to the "desperately lonely, suicidal" single. Of course, most single adults are somewhere between these extremes.

Common challenges faced by single adults may include forming intimate relationships with other adults, confronting loneliness, and finding a niche in a society that is marriage-oriented. Bella DePaulo (2006, 2011) argues that society has a widespread bias against unmarried adults that is seen in everything from missed perks in jobs to deep social and financial prejudices.

Advantages of being single include having time to make decisions about one's life course, time to develop personal resources to meet goals, freedom to make autonomous decisions and pursue one's own schedule and interests, opportunities to explore new places and try out new things, and privacy. Compared with married adults, single adults are more likely to spend time with friends and neighbors, dine in restaurants, and attend art classes and lectures (Klinenberg, 2012, 2013). Once adults reach the age of 30, they may face increasing pressure to settle down and get married. This is when many single adults make a conscious decision to marry or to remain single.

A nationally representative U.S. survey of more than 5,000 single adults 21 years and older who were not in a committed relationship revealed that men had become more interested in love, marriage, and children than their counterparts were in earlier generations (Match.com, 2011). The same study found that women desired more independence in their relationships than their mothers did. Across every age group, more women than men reported wanting to pursue their own interests, have personal space, have their own bank account, have regular nights out with friends, and take vacations on their own. In a second national survey, many single adults reported that they were looking for love but not marriage (Match.com, 2012).

In recent nationally representative survey of more than 35,000 U.S. single adults, fast sex and slow love characterized their responses (Fisher & Garcia, 2019). In terms of fast sex, 66 percent of U.S. singles reported having had a one-night stand, 34 percent mentioned having had sex with someone before a first date, and 54 percent said they had engaged in an uncommitted, secretive friends-with-benefits relationship. However, in terms of slow love, today's singles are taking far longer than past generations to commit to love and marriage, wanting to know everything they can about a potential partner before they invest time, effort, and money in making a formal commitment to him or her (Fisher & Garcia, 2019). And even though uncommitted sexual experiences are much more common among today's singles, they still have a strong interest in finding romantic love. In the most recent poll, more than 54 percent of U.S. singles said they believe in "love at first sight," 86 percent reported that they want to find a committed partner they can live with forever, and 89 percent responded that they believe you can remain married to the same person the rest of your life.

COHABITING ADULTS

Cohabitation refers to living together in a sexual relationship without being married. Cohabitation has undergone considerable changes in recent years (Kamp Dush & others, 2019; Lamidi, Manning, & Brown, 2019). Cohabitation rates in the U.S. continue to rise (Lamidi, Manning, & Brown, 2019; Manning, Longmore, & Gordano, 2019). In a recent national poll, the number of cohabiting adults had increased 29 percent from 2007 to 2016, reaching a figure of 18 million adults in a cohabiting relationship (U.S. Census Bureau, 2016). In 2018, 15 percent of U.S. adults 25 to 34 and 9 percent who were 18 to 24 years old were cohabiting (U.S. Census Bureau, 2019). Also, a recent study indicated that transitioning into a stepfamily home in early childhood, especially for females, was linked to earlier entry into cohabitation in adulthood (Johnston, Cavanaugh, & Crosnoe, 2020).

Cohabitation rates are even higher in some countries—in Sweden, for example, cohabitation before marriage is virtually universal (Stokes & Raley, 2009). And from 2004 to 2014, the percentage of cohabiting couples grew by 30 percent in Great Britain (Office for National Statistics, 2015).

A national study of women in the United States found the following statistics regarding cohabitation based on interviews conducted between 2006 and 2010 (Copen & others, 2012):

- Length of cohabitation is increasing—an average of 22 months in 2010 compared with 13 months in 1995.

- After three years of cohabiting, 40 percent of women got married, 32 percent continued to live with their partner, and 27 percent had moved out of the cohabiting relationship.

- Education is linked to cohabitation rates—70 percent of women who did not have a high school diploma cohabited in their first union, compared with 47 percent of women who had a bachelor's degree or higher. For women who cohabited in their twenties to forties, among those with higher education the cohabitation was more likely to result in marriage (53 percent) than it was for their counterparts who had not graduated from high school (30 percent).

Some couples view their cohabitation not as a precursor to marriage but as an ongoing lifestyle (Klinenberg, 2013). These couples do not want the official aspects of marriage. One study revealed that young adults' main reasons for cohabiting are to spend time together, share expenses, and evaluate compatibility (Huang & others, 2011). In this study, gender differences emerged regarding perceived drawbacks of cohabiting: men were more concerned about their loss of freedom while women were more concerned about delays in getting married.

Couples who cohabit face certain problems (Kamp Dush & others, 2019). Disapproval by parents and other family members can place emotional strain on the cohabiting couple. Some cohabiting couples have difficulty purchasing and owning property jointly. Legal rights involving the dissolution of the relationship are less clear than in a divorce. Other recent research confirmed that cohabitation is a risk factor for intimate partner violence in emerging adults (Manning,

What are some potential advantages and disadvantages of cohabitation?
Chris Ryan/OJO Images/Getty Images

Longmore, & Gordano, 2018). Also, in a recent study, cohabiting individuals were more likely to have their first sexual relationship prior to age 18 and to have cohabited two or more times in the past than both married and unmarried non-cohabiting individuals, and they were more likely than married men and women to have had an unintended birth (Nugent & Daugherty, 2018). Further, a recent study revealed that cohabitation was associated with increased marijuana use among women but not men (Hoffman, 2018). Researchers also have found that cohabiting individuals are not as mentally and emotionally healthy as their counterparts in committed marital relationships (Braithwaite & Holt-Lunstad, 2017; Memitz, 2018).

If a couple lives together before they marry, does cohabiting help or harm their chances of having a stable and happy marriage? The majority of studies have found lower rates of marital satisfaction and higher rates of divorce in couples who lived together before getting married (Copen & others, 2012). However, research indicates that the link between premarital cohabitation and marital instability in first marriages has weakened in recent cohorts (Copen & others, 2012; Smock & Gupta, 2013).

What might explain the possibility that cohabiting is linked with divorce more than not cohabiting? The most frequently given explanation is that the less traditional lifestyle of cohabitation may attract less conventional individuals who are not great believers in marriage in the first place. An alternative explanation is that the experience of cohabiting changes people's attitudes and habits in ways that increase their likelihood of divorce.

Recent research has provided clarification of cohabitation outcomes (Willoughby & Belt, 2016). One meta-analysis found that the link between cohabitation and marital instability did not hold up when only cohabitation with the eventual marital partner was examined, indicating that these cohabitors may attach more long-term positive meaning to living together (Jose, O'Leary, & Moyer, 2010). Another study also revealed that for first marriages, cohabiting with the spouse without first being engaged was linked to more negative interaction and a higher probability of divorce than cohabiting after engagement (Stanley & others, 2006). In contrast, premarital cohabitation prior to a second marriage placed couples at risk for divorce regardless of whether they were engaged. Researchers have also found that the marriages of couples who had cohabited without being engaged were less likely to survive to the 10- to 15-year mark than the marriages of their counterparts who were engaged when they cohabited (Copen & others, 2012). Also, one analysis indicated that cohabiting does not have a negative effect on marriage if the couple did not have any previous live-in lovers and did not have children prior to the marriage (Cherlin, 2009). And another study concluded that the risk of marital dissolution between cohabitors was much smaller when they cohabited in their mid-twenties and later (Kuperberg, 2014).

MARRIED ADULTS

Until about 1930, stable marriage was widely accepted as the endpoint of adult development. In the last 70 to 80 years, however, personal fulfillment both inside and outside marriage has emerged as a goal that competes with marital stability. The changing norm of male-female equality in marriage and increasingly high expectations for what a marital relationship should be has produced marital relationships that are more fragile and intense than they were for earlier generations (Seccombe, 2020). A study of 502 newlyweds found that nearly all couples had optimistic forecasts of how their marriage would change over the next four years (Lavner, Karney, & Bradbury, 2013). Despite their optimistic forecasts, their marital satisfaction declined across this time frame. Wives with the most optimistic forecasts showed the steepest declines in marital satisfaction. Also, in a recent study across a number of countries and religions, men reported higher marital satisfaction than women did (Sorokowski, Kowal, & Sorokowska, 2019). In this study, levels of marital satisfaction was similar for Muslims, Christians, and atheists.

Some characteristics of marital partners predict whether the marriage will last longer (van Scheppingen & Leopold, 2020). Two such characteristics are education and ethnicity. In a study that involved interviews with more than 22,000 women, both women and men with a bachelor's degree were found to be more likely to delay marriage but also more likely to eventually get married and stay married for more than 20 years (Copen & others, 2012). Also in this study, Asian American women were the most likely of all ethnic groups to be in a first marriage that lasted at least 20 years—70 percent were in a first marriage that lasted this long, compared with 54 percent of non-Latino White women, 53 percent of Latino women, and 37 percent of African American women.

Luca Santilli/Shutterstock

When two people are under the influence of the most violent, most insane, most delusive, and most transient of passions, they are required to swear that they will remain in that excited, abnormal, and exhausting condition continuously until death do them part.

—GEORGE BERNARD SHAW
Irish playwright, 20th century

Marital Trends In 2019, 48.2 percent of adults in the United States were married, down from 72 percent in 1960 (U.S. Census Bureau, 2019). Also, in 2018, the U.S. average age for a first marriage had climbed to 29.8 years for men and 28 years for women, higher than at any other point in history (U.S. Census Bureau, 2019). In 1960, the average age for a first marriage in the United States was 23 years for men and 20 years for women. Also, a higher percentage of U.S. adults never marry—in 2019, record percentages of adults (35 percent of men, 23 percent of women) had never married. In addition, the increased cohabitation rate in the United States has contributed to the lower percentage of adults who are married (Wang & Parker, 2014). Although marriage rates are declining, the United States continues to be a marrying society, with 78.5 percent of U.S. adults 25 years and older having been married at some point in their lives in 2016.

The age at which individuals get married is going up not only in the United States but also in many countries around the world. Also, in recent analyses, first marriage occurs at older ages in most developed countries than in the United States (OECD, 2019). For example, in a comparison of 39 developed countries, average age at first marriage now is older in Sweden (33.8 for females and 36.6 for males) than in the other 38 countries. Earliest average age at first marriage in these developed countries is occurring in Israel and Turkey (25 for females and 27 for males). In most of the countries, individuals are getting married later than their counterparts in the United States, and in most countries marriage is occurring later than in previous decades.

While marriage rates are declining and the average age of marriage is going up, recent research with emerging and young adults indicates that they view marriage as a very important life pursuit. Indeed, young adults in one study predicted that marriage would be more important in their life than parenting, careers, or leisure activities (Willoughby, Hall, & Goff, 2015). In a recent book, *The Marriage Paradox* (Willoughby & James, 2017), the authors concluded that emerging and young adults may be motivated to build a better career and financial foundation before marrying in order to increase the likelihood that their marriage will be successful later. In this perspective, emerging and young adults may not be abandoning marriage because they don't like it or are not interested in it, but instead delaying marriage because they value marriage and want to position themselves in the best possible way for developing a healthy marital relationship.

A recent survey explored why individuals get married (Geiger & Livingston, 2019). At the top of the list was love (88 percent), followed by making a lifelong commitment (81 percent), companionship (76 percent), and having children (49 percent). Another study explored what U.S. never-married men and women are looking for in a potential spouse (Wang & Parker, 2014). Following are the percentages who reported that various factors would be very important for them:

Factor	Men	Women
Similar ideas about having and raising children	62	70
A steady job	46	78
Same moral and religious beliefs	31	38
At least as much education	26	28
Same racial or ethnic background	7	10

Thus, in this study, never-married men said that the most important factor for a potential spouse was similar ideas about having and raising children, but never-married women placed greater importance on having a steady job.

Is there a best age to get married? Marriages in adolescence are more likely to end in divorce than marriages in adulthood (Copen & others, 2012). However, researchers have not been able to pin down a specific age or age span for getting married in adulthood that is most likely to result in a successful marriage (Furstenberg, 2007).

How happy are people who do marry? The average duration of a marriage in the United States is currently just over nine years. As indicated in Figure 4, the percentage of married individuals in the United States who said their marriages were "very happy" declined from the 1970s through the early 1990s before approaching a plateau (Popenoe, 2009). Notice in Figure 4 that married men consistently reported being happier than married women.

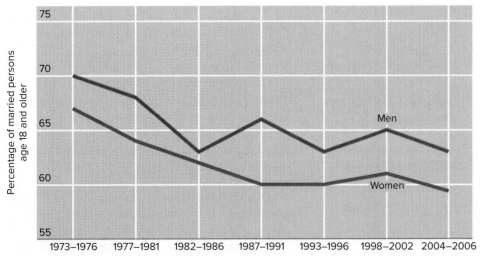

Percentage of married persons age 18 and older (y-axis)

75
70
65 — Men
60 — Women
55

1973–1976   1977–1981   1982–1986   1987–1991   1993–1996   1998–2002   2004–2006

FIGURE 4
PERCENTAGE OF MARRIED PERSONS AGE 18 AND OLDER WITH "VERY HAPPY" MARRIAGES

Cross-Cultural Comparisons   Earlier we described cross-cultural variations in romantic relationships and touched on some cultural variations in marriage. Here we further explore other aspects of marriage that vary across cultures (John & others, 2017). For example, as part of China's efforts to control population growth, a 1981 law sets the minimum age for marriage at 22 years for males and 20 for females.

The traits that people look for in a marriage partner vary around the world. In one large-scale study of 9,474 adults from 37 cultures on six continents and five islands, people varied most regarding how much they valued chastity—desiring a marital partner with no previous experience in sexual intercourse (Buss & others, 1990). Chastity was the most important characteristic in selecting a marital partner in China, India, Indonesia, Iran, Taiwan, and the Palestinian Arab culture. Adults from Ireland and Japan placed moderate importance on chastity. In contrast, adults in Sweden, Finland, Norway, the Netherlands, and Germany generally said that chastity was not important in selecting a marital partner.

Domesticity is also valued in some cultures and not in others. In this study, adults from the Zulu culture in South Africa, Estonia, and Colombia placed a high value on housekeeping skills in their marital preferences. By contrast, adults in the United States, Canada, and all western European countries except Spain said that housekeeping skill was not an important trait in their partner.

Religion plays an important role in marriage in many cultures (Sorokowsi, Kowal, & Sorokowska, 2019). For example, Islam stresses the honor of the male and the purity of the female. It also emphasizes the woman's role in childbearing, child rearing, educating children, and instilling the Islamic faith in their children. In India, a majority of marriages continue to be arranged. However, as more women have entered the workforce in India and moved from rural areas to cities, these Indian women increasingly resist an arranged marriage. In one study conducted in a small village in India, elopement (also called love marriages there) had become more common than arranged marriages (Allendorf, 2013).

Premarital Education   Earlier we discussed the positive influence of relationship education for adolescents and emerging adults. Here we further explore premarital education and examine whether it can improve the quality of a marriage and possibly reduce the chances that the marriage will end in divorce. Researchers have found that it can (Markman, Halford, & Hawkins, 2019; Simpson, Leonhardt, & Hawkins, 2018). For example, a survey of more than 3,000 adults revealed that premarital education was linked to a higher level of marital satisfaction and commitment to a spouse, a lower level of destructive marital conflict, and a 31 percent lower likelihood of divorce (Stanley & others, 2006). The premarital education programs in the study ranged from several hours to 20 hours, with a median of 8 hours. It is recommended that premarital education begin approximately six months to a year before the wedding. Researchers also found that the effectiveness of a premarital education program was enhanced when the couples had a better level of communication prior to the intervention (Markman & others, 2013).

(*a*) In Scandinavian countries, cohabitation is popular; only a small percentage of 20- to 24-year-olds are married. (*b*) Islam stresses male honor and female purity. (*c*) Japanese young adults live at home longer with their parents before marrying than young adults in most other countries.
(*Top to bottom*) Mats Widen/Johner Images/Getty Images; Image Source/Getty Images; BloomImage/Getty Images

FIGURE **5**

**TRENDS AND PROPOSALS FOR
IMPROVING PREMARITAL EDUCATION
IN THE NEXT GENERATION**
Source: After Clyde, Hawkins,
& Willoughby (2020)

Trend	Proposal
Individualism and Commitment Ambivalence	Premarital education needs to guide couples in transitioning from "me" to "we" and developing a strong commitment to their marriage.
Meaning of and Attitudes about Marriage	Premarital education should help individuals clarify for themselves and with their partner the meaning of marriage and their attitudes about it.
Premarital Relationship History and Experiences	Premarital education needs to focus on the complexities and challenges of marriage that many couples will experience as a result of considerable premarital experience, cohabitation, and premarital childbearing.
Effects of Media	Premarital education should help couples explore the effects of media use on marital attitudes and behavior.

Low-income couples are especially unlikely to engage in relationship interventions despite being at greater risk for relationship dissolution (Seccombe, 2020). One study of recently married low-income couples revealed that those who received premarital education were more likely to seek therapy to improve their relationship when the marriage became distressed than those who did not receive this education (Williamson & others, 2018).

In a recent analysis and review, research on contemporary trends that influence the next generation's ability to form and sustain a positive marriage was examined (Clyde, Hawkins, & Willoughby, 2020). Then, four proposals involving these trends were made to improve the effectiveness of premarital education. Figure 5 describes the trends and proposals.

The Benefits of a Good Marriage   Are there any benefits to having a good marriage? Yes. Individuals who are married live longer, healthier lives than those who are single, cohabiting, or divorced (Schwartz & Scott, 2018). In a recent research review, it was concluded that the experience of divorce or separation confers risk for poor health outcomes, including a 23 percent higher mortality rate (Sbarra, 2015). One study indicated that the longer women were married, the less likely they were to develop a chronic health condition and that the longer men were married, the lower their risk of developing a disease (Dupre & Meadows, 2007). Also, in a large-scale study conducted in the United States and six European countries, not being in the labor force was associated with higher mortality, but marriage attenuated the increased mortality risk linked to labor force inactivity (Van Hedel & others, 2015). And a recent research review of individuals who were married, divorced, widowed, and single found that married individuals had the best cardiovascular profile and single men the worst (Manfredini & others, 2017). Further, an unhappy marriage can shorten a person's life by an average of four years (Gove, Style, & Hughes, 1990). What are the reasons for the benefits of being married? Overall, people in marriages likely feel less physically and emotionally stressed, which puts less wear and tear on a person's body. Such wear and tear can lead to physical ailments such as high blood pressure and heart disease, as well as psychological problems such as anxiety, depression, and substance abuse.

developmental connection

Family and Peers

Children in divorced families have more adjustment problems than children in never-divorced, intact families, but a majority of children in divorced families do not have adjustment problems. Connect to "Socioemotional Development in Early Childhood."

DIVORCED ADULTS

Divorce has become an epidemic in the United States (Sbarra, Bourassa, & Manvellian, 2019). However, the divorce rate has declined in recent decades, peaking at 5.1 divorces per 1,000 people in 1981 and declining to 3.2 divorces per 1,000 people in 2016 (U.S. Census Bureau, 2017). The 2016 divorce rate of 3.2 compares with a marriage rate of 6.9 per 1,000 people in 2014. Although the U.S. divorce rate has dropped, it continues to be one of the highest in the world. Russia has the highest divorce rate of the countries surveyed (4.6 divorces per 1,000 people), Chile the lowest (0.2 divorces per 1,000 people) (OECD, 2019). In the United States, nearly half of first marriages will break up within 20 years (Copen & others, 2012).

Although U.S. divorce rates have increased in all socioeconomic groups, some groups have a higher incidence of divorce (Perelli-Harris & others, 2017). Youthful marriage, low educational level, low income, not having a religious affiliation, having parents who are divorced, and having a baby before marriage are associated with increased risk of divorce (Hoelter, 2009). And the following characteristics of one's partner increase the likelihood of divorce: alcoholism, psychological problems, domestic violence, infidelity, and inadequate division of household labor (Perelli-Harris & others, 2017).

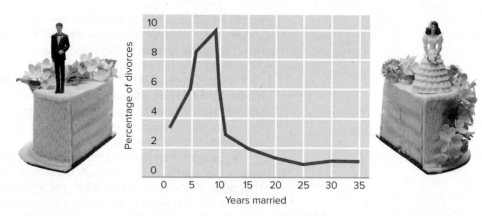

FIGURE 6

THE DIVORCE RATE IN RELATION TO NUMBER OF YEARS MARRIED. Shown here is the percentage of divorces as a function of how long couples have been married. Notice that most divorces occur in the early years of marriage, peaking in the fifth to tenth years of marriage.
Digital Vision/Getty Images

Earlier, we indicated that researchers have not been able to pin down a specific age that is the best time to marry so that the marriage will be unlikely to end in a divorce. However, if a divorce is going to occur, it is most likely to happen between the fifth and tenth years of marriage, according to U.S. data (National Center for Health Statistics, 2000) (see Figure 6). Similarly, one study found that divorce peaked in Finland at approximately five to seven years of marriage, after which the rate of divorce gradually declined (Kulu, 2014). This timing may reflect an effort by partners in troubled marriages to stay in the marriage and try to work things out. If after several years these efforts have not improved the relationship, the couple may then seek a divorce.

What causes people to get divorced? A recent study in Great Britain found no differences in the causes of breakdowns in marriage and cohabitation (Gravningen & others, 2017). In this study, the following reasons for breaking up were cited: "grew apart" (men, 39 percent; women, 36 percent), "arguments" (27 percent, 30 percent), "unfaithfulness/adultery" (18 percent, 24 percent), "lack of respect, appreciation" (17 percent, 25 percent), and "domestic violence" (4 percent, 16 percent).

Both partners experience challenges after a marriage dissolves (Sbarra, Hasselmo, & Bourassa, 2015). Divorced adults have higher rates of depression, anxiety, physical illnesses, suicide, motor vehicle accidents, alcoholism, and mortality (Axinn & others, 2020; Marcus & others, 2019). In a recent study, individuals who were divorced had a higher risk of alcohol use disorder (Kendler & others, 2017). Also, a recent research review concluded that divorced men and women are more likely to commit suicide than their married counterparts (Yip & others, 2015). Further, a recent research review concluded that divorced adults have a higher rate of adverse cardiovascular events, including death due to cardiovascular disease, than their married counterparts (Dhindsa & others, 2020). And both women and men complain of loneliness, diminished self-esteem, anxiety about the unknowns in their lives, and difficulty in forming satisfactory new intimate relationships after divorce (Hetherington, 2006).

There are gender differences in the process and outcomes of divorce (Daoulah & others, 2017a; Marcus & others, 2019). A recent study of couples who had been married from 1 to 16 years before divorce found that wives' increased tension over the course of a marriage was a factor that was consistently linked to an eventual divorce (Birditt & others, 2017). Women are more likely to sense that something is wrong with the marriage and are more likely to seek a divorce than are men. Women also show better emotional adjustment and are more likely to perceive divorce as a "second chance" to increase their happiness, improve their social lives, and pursue better work opportunities. However, divorce typically has a more negative economic impact on women than it does on men.

Despite all of these stresses and challenges, many people do cope effectively with divorce. Later in this chapter, we consider the varied paths people take after a divorce and suggested strategies for coping.

REMARRIED ADULTS

Men remarry after a divorce sooner than women do, and men with higher incomes are more likely to remarry than their counterparts with lower incomes. Remarriage occurs sooner for partners who initiate a divorce (especially in the first several years after divorce and for older women) than those who do not (Sweeney, 2009, 2010). Statistics indicate that the remarriage rate in the United States has declined in recent decades, going from 50 of every 1,000 divorced or widowed Americans in 1990 to 29 of every 1,000 in 2011 (U.S. Census Bureau, 2013). One reason for the decline is the dramatic increase in cohabitation in recent years. Men are more likely to remarry than women; in 2013, the remarriage rate was almost twice as high for men as women (40 per 1,000 for men and 21 per 1,000 for women in that year) (Livingston, 2017). Thus, men are either more eager or more able to find new spouses than are women.

Nonetheless, remarried adults often find it difficult to stay remarried. While the divorce rate in first marriages has declined, the divorce rate of remarriages continues to increase (DeLongis & Zwicker, 2017). Why? For one thing, many remarry not for love but for financial reasons, for help in rearing children, and to reduce loneliness. They also might carry into the stepfamily negative patterns that produced failure in an earlier marriage. Remarried couples also experience more stress in rearing children than parents in never-divorced families (Bray, 2019; Ganong & Coleman, 2018). And one study found that remarried adults had less frequent sex than those in their first marriage (Stroope, McFarland, & Uecker, 2015).

GAY AND LESBIAN ADULTS

developmental **connection**

Parenting

Researchers have found few differences between children who are being raised by gay and lesbian parents and children who are being raised by heterosexual parents. Connect to "Socioemotional Development in Early Childhood."

Until recently, the legal context of marriage created barriers to breaking up that did not exist for same-sex partners. However, the legalization of same-sex marriage in all 50 states in 2015 extended this barrier to same-sex couples (Colistra & Johnson, 2020). In many additional ways, researchers have found that gay and lesbian relationships are similar—in their satisfactions, loves, joys, and conflicts—to heterosexual relationships (Baker & Halford, 2020). For example, a recent study indicated that adults in same-sex relationships were experiencing levels of commitment, satisfaction, and emotional intimacy similar to those of adults in different-sex relationships (Joyner, Manning, & Prince, 2019).

Lesbian couples especially place a high priority on equality in their relationships (Fingerhut & Peplau, 2013). One study of couples revealed that over the course of 10 years of cohabitation, partners in gay and lesbian relationships showed a higher average level of relationship quality than heterosexual couples did (Kurdek, 2007). A survey found that a greater percentage of same-sex, dual-earner couples than different-sex couples said they share laundry (44 versus 31 percent), household repairs (33 versus 15 percent), and routine (74 versus 38 percent) and sick (62 versus 32 percent) child-care responsibilities (Matos, 2015).

It is estimated that of same-sex couples in the United States, lesbian couples are approximately five times more likely to be raising children than are gay couples (Miller & Price, 2013). An increasing number of same-sex couples are adopting children (Farr & Grotevant, 2019). The percentage of same-sex couples who have adopted children increased from 10 percent in 2000 to 19 percent in 2009 (DiBennardo & Gates, 2014; Gates, 2013). Recall that in one study lesbian and gay couples shared child care more than heterosexual couples, with lesbian couples being the most supportive and gay couples the least supportive (Farr & Patterson, 2013).

There are numerous misconceptions about gay and lesbian couples (Goldberg & Allen, 2020; Patterson, 2019). Contrary to stereotypes, one partner is masculine and the other feminine in only a small percentage of gay and lesbian couples. Only a small segment of the gay population has a large number of sexual partners, and this is uncommon among lesbians. Furthermore, researchers have found that gays and lesbians prefer long-term, committed relationships (Fingerhut & Peplau, 2013). About half of committed gay couples do have an open relationship that allows the possibility of sex (but not affectionate love) outside the relationship. Lesbian couples usually do not have this type of open relationship.

A special concern is the stigma, prejudice, and discrimination that lesbian, gay, and bisexual individuals experience because of widespread social devaluation of same-sex relationships (Conlin, Douglass, & Ouch, 2019; Vargas, Huey, & Miranda, 2020). However, one study indicated that many individuals in these relationships saw stigma as bringing them closer together and strengthening their relationship (Frost, 2011).

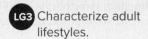
4 Marriage and the Family

LG4 Discuss making marriage work, parenting, and divorce.

Making Marriage Work   Becoming a Parent   Dealing with Divorce

Whatever lifestyles young adults choose, their choices will bring certain challenges. Because many choose the lifestyle of marriage, we'll consider some of the challenges in marriage and suggestions for making it work. We will also examine some challenges in parenting and trends in childbearing. Given the statistics about divorce rates in the previous section, we'll then consider how to deal with divorce.

MAKING MARRIAGE WORK

John Gottman (1994, 2006, 2011; Gottman & Silver, 1999, 2015) has been studying married couples' lives since the early 1970s. He uses many methods to analyze what makes marriages work. Gottman interviews couples about the history of their marriage, their philosophy about marriage, and how they view their parents' marriages. He videotapes them talking to each other about how their day went and evaluates what they say about the good and bad times in their marriages. Gottman also uses physiological measures to record their heart rate, blood flow, blood pressure, and immune functioning moment by moment. He checks back with the couples every year to see how their marriage is faring. Gottman's research represents the most extensive assessment of marital relationships available. Currently, he and his colleagues are following 700 couples in seven studies.

Gottman argues that it is important to realize that love is not something magical and that through knowledge and effort couples can improve their relationship. In his research, Gottman has identified seven main practices that help marriages succeed:

- *Establish love maps.* Individuals in successful marriages have personal insights and detailed maps of each other's life and world. They aren't psychological strangers. In good marriages, partners are willing to share their feelings with each other. They use these "love maps" to express not only their understanding of each other but also their fondness and admiration.
- *Nurture fondness and admiration.* In successful marriages, partners sing each other's praises. More than 90 percent of the time, when couples put a positive spin on their marriage's history, the marriage is likely to have a positive future.
- *Turn toward each other instead of away.* In good marriages, spouses are adept at turning toward each other regularly. They see each other as friends. This friendship doesn't keep arguments from occurring, but it can prevent differences from overwhelming the relationship. In these good marriages, spouses respect each other and appreciate each other's point of view despite disagreements.

John Gottman has conducted extensive research on what makes marriages work.
Courtesy of The Gottman Institute, www.gottman.com

Unlike most approaches to helping couples, mine is based on knowing what makes marriages succeed rather than fail.

—JOHN GOTTMAN
Contemporary psychologist, University of Washington

- *Let your partner influence you.* Bad marriages often involve one spouse who is unwilling to share power with the other. Although power-mongering is more common in husbands, some wives also show this trait. A willingness to share power and to respect the other person's view is a prerequisite to compromising. One study revealed that equality in decision making was one of the main factors that predicted positive marriage quality (Amato, 2007).

- *Solve solvable conflicts.* Two types of problems occur in marriage: (1) perpetual and (2) solvable. Perpetual problems are the type that do not go away and may include disagreements about whether to have children and how often to have sex. Solvable problems can be worked out and may include such things as not helping each other reduce daily stresses and not being verbally affectionate. Unfortunately, more than two-thirds of marital problems fall into the perpetual category. Fortunately, marital therapists have found that couples often don't have to solve their perpetual problems for the marriage to work. In his research, Gottman has found that to resolve conflicts, couples should start out with a soft rather than a harsh approach, try to make and receive "repair attempts," regulate their emotions, compromise, and be tolerant of each other's faults. Conflict resolution is not about one person making changes; it is about negotiating and accommodating each other.

- *Overcome gridlock.* One partner wants the other to attend church; the other is an atheist. One partner is a homebody; the other wants to go out and socialize a lot. Such problems often produce gridlock. Gottman believes the key to ending gridlock is not to solve the problem but to move from gridlock to dialogue and be patient.

- *Create shared meaning.* The more partners can speak candidly and respectfully with each other, the more likely it is that they will create shared meaning in their marriage. This also includes sharing goals with one's spouse and working together to achieve each other's goals.

What makes marriages work? What are the benefits of having a good marriage?
wavebreakmedia/Shutterstock

In addition to Gottman's view, other experts on marriage argue that such factors as forgiveness and commitment are important aspects of a successful marriage (Lavner & Bradbury, 2019). These factors function as self-repair processes in healthy relationships. For example, spouses may have a heated argument that has the potential to harm their relationship. After calming down, they may forgive each other and repair the damage.

Spouses with a strong commitment to each other may in times of conflict sacrifice their personal self-interest for the benefit of the marriage (Lavner & Bradbury, 2019). Commitment especially becomes important when a couple is not happily married and can help them get through hard times with the hope that the future will involve positive changes in the relationship. A couple's personality traits also may influence how satisfied individuals are with their marriage. For example, a recent study found that couples high in neuroticism were less satisfied with their marriage than couples high in conscientiousness (Sayehmiri & others, 2020).

How important is the sexual aspect of a relationship in the couple's marital satisfaction? A recent study in the second to fourteenth years of a marriage found that frequency of engaging in sexual intercourse was linked to a couple's marital satisfaction, but that a satisfying sex life and a warm interpersonal relationship were more important (Schoenfeld & others, 2017).

For remarried couples, strategies for coping with the stress of living in a remarried family include the following (Bray, 2008, 2019; Sierra, 2015; Visher & Visher, 1989):

- *Have realistic expectations.* Allow time for loving relationships to develop, and look at the complexity of the stepfamily as a challenge to overcome.

- *Develop new positive relationships within the family.* Create new traditions and ways of dealing with difficult circumstances. Allocation of time is especially important because so many people are involved. The remarried couple needs to allot time alone for each other.

- *Counter set relationship patterns or "ghosts."* In prior relationships, spouses learned certain interaction patterns and these patterns can continue into the remarriage. Sometimes they have been called "ghosts" because they continue to haunt the individual unless he or she works to change them. For example, the husband in the newly created remarried family may have difficulty trusting his new wife because his previous wife cheated on him.

BECOMING A PARENT

For many young adults, parental roles are well planned, coordinated with other roles in life, and developed with the parents' economic situation in mind. For others, the discovery that they are about to become parents is a startling surprise. In either case, the prospective parents may have mixed emotions and idealistic illusions about having a child (Perry-Jenkins & Schoppe-Sullivan, 2019).

Parenting Myths and Reality   The needs and expectations of parents have stimulated many myths about parenting. These parenting myths include the following:

- The birth of a child will save a failing marriage.
- As a possession or extension of the parent, the child will think, feel, and behave as the parent did in his or her childhood.
- Having a child gives the parents a "second chance" to achieve what they wish they had achieved.
- Parenting is instinctual and requires no training.

What are some parenting myths?
Ryan McVay/Photodisc/Getty Images

Parenting requires a number of interpersonal skills and imposes emotional demands (Compas & others, 2019; Padilla-Walker & Memmott-Elison, 2020). However, there is little in the way of formal education for this task. Most parents learn parenting practices from their own parents, accepting some and discarding others. Unfortunately, when methods of parents are passed on from one generation to the next, both desirable and undesirable practices are perpetuated. Adding to the challenges of the task of parenting, husbands and wives may bring different parenting practices to the marriage. The parents, then, may struggle with each other about who has a better way to interact with a child.

Parent educators seek to help individuals to become better parents. To read about the work of one parent educator, see *Connecting with Careers.*

Trends in Childbearing   As with marriage, the age at which people have children has been increasing (Blieszner, 2018). In 2016, for the first time ever, more U.S. women were giving birth in their thirties than in their twenties (Centers for Disease Control and Prevention, 2017). In 2018, the average age for women giving birth was the highest it has ever been: 26.9 years of age (National Center for Health Statistics, 2019). A national poll of 40- to 50-year-old U.S. women found that those with a master's degree or higher first became mothers at 30; in comparison, the average age for women with a high school diploma was just 24 (Pew Research Center, 2015b).

> We never know the love of our parents until we have become parents.
>
> **—HENRY WARD BEECHER**
> *American clergyman, 19th century*

developmental **connection**
Parenting

For most families, an authoritative parenting style is linked to more positive behavior on the part of children than authoritarian, indulgent, and neglectful styles. Connect to "Socioemotional Development in Early Childhood."

connecting with careers

Janis Keyser, Parent Educator

Janis Keyser is a parent educator who teaches in the Department of Early Childhood Education at Cabrillo College in California. In addition to teaching college classes and conducting parenting workshops, she also has coauthored a book with Laura Davis (1997) titled *Becoming the Parent You Want to Be: A Sourcebook of Strategies for the First Five Years.*

Keyser also writes about parenting topics on Internet sites and coauthored a nationally syndicated parenting column, "Growing Up, Growing Together." Keyser is a mother of three, stepmother of five, grandmother of twelve, and great-grandmother of six.

Janis Keyser (*right*) conducts a parenting workshop.
Courtesy of Janis Keyser

As the use of birth control has become common, many individuals consciously choose when they will have children and how many children they will rear. The number of one-child families is increasing, and U.S. women overall are having fewer children. These childbearing changes are creating several trends:

- By giving birth to fewer children and reducing the demands of child care, women free up a significant portion of their life spans for other endeavors.
- Men are apt to invest a greater amount of time in fathering.
- Parental care is often supplemented by institutional care (child care, for example).

As more women show an increased interest in developing a career, they are not only marrying later but also having fewer children and having them later in life. What are some of the advantages of having children early or late? Some of the advantages of having children early (in the twenties) are that the parents are likely to have more physical energy (for example, they can cope better with such matters as getting up in the middle of the night with infants and waiting up until adolescents come home at night); the mother is likely to have fewer medical problems with pregnancy and childbirth; and the parents may be less likely to build up expectations for their children, as do many couples who have waited many years to have children.

There are also advantages to having children later (in the thirties): The parents will have had more time to consider their goals in life, such as what they want from their family and career roles; the parents will be more mature and will be able to benefit from their life experiences to engage in more competent parenting; and the parents will be better established in their careers and have more income for child-rearing expenses.

DEALING WITH DIVORCE

If a marriage doesn't work, what happens after divorce? Psychologically, one of the most common characteristics of divorced adults is difficulty trusting a new partner in a romantic relationship (Perelli-Harris & others, 2017). Following a divorce, though, people's lives can take diverse turns (Sbarra, Bourassa, & Manvellian, 2019). In E. Mavis Hetherington's research, men and women took six common pathways after divorce (Hetherington & Kelly, 2002, pp. 98–108):

- *The enhancers.* Accounting for 20 percent of the divorced group, most were females who "grew more competent, well-adjusted, and self-fulfilled" following their divorce (p. 98). They were competent in multiple areas of life, showing a remarkable ability to bounce back from stressful circumstances and to create something meaningful out of problems.
- *The good-enoughs.* The largest group of divorced individuals, they were described as average people coping with divorce. They showed some strengths and some weaknesses, some successes and some failures. When they experienced a problem, they tried to solve it. Many of them attended night classes, found new friends, developed active social lives, and were motivated to get higher-paying jobs. However, they were not as good at planning and were less persistent than the enhancers. Good-enough women usually married men who educationally and economically were similar to their first husbands, often going into a new marriage that was not much of an improvement over the first one.
- *The seekers.* These individuals were motivated to find new mates as soon as possible. "At one year post-divorce, 40 percent of the men and 38 percent of the women had been classified as seekers. But as people found new partners or remarried, or became more secure or satisfied in their single life, this category shrank and came to be predominated by men" (p. 102).
- *The libertines.* People in this category often spent more time in singles bars and had more casual sex than their counterparts in the other divorce categories. However, by the end of the first year post-divorce, they often grew disillusioned with their sensation-seeking lifestyle and wanted a stable relationship.
- *The competent loners.* These individuals, who made up only about 10 percent of the divorced group, were "well-adjusted, self-sufficient, and socially skilled." They had a successful career, an active social life, and a wide range of interests. However, "unlike enhancers, competent loners had little interest in sharing their lives with anyone else" (p. 105).

Coping and Adapting in the Aftermath of Divorce

Hetherington recommends the following strategies for divorced adults (Hetherington & Kelly, 2002):

- Think of divorce as a chance to grow personally and to develop more positive relationships.
- Make decisions carefully. The consequences of your decisions regarding work, lovers, and children may last a lifetime.
- Focus more on the future than the past. Think about what is most important for you going forward in your life, set some challenging goals, and plan how to reach them.

- Use your strengths and resources to cope with difficulties.
- Don't expect to be successful and happy in everything you do. "The road to a more satisfying life is bumpy and will have many detours" (p. 109).
- Remember that "you are never trapped by one pathway. Most of those who were categorized as defeated immediately after divorce gradually moved on to a better life, but moving onward usually requires some effort" (p. 109).

- *The defeated.* Some of these individuals had problems before their divorce, and these problems increased after the breakup when "the added stress of a failed marriage was more than they could handle. Others had difficulty coping because divorce cost them a spouse who had supported them, or in the case of a drinking problem, restricted them" (p. 106).

To read about some guidelines for coping and adapting in the aftermath of divorce, see *Connecting Development to Life.*

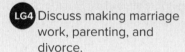

Review *Connect* Reflect

LG4 Discuss making marriage work, parenting, and divorce.

Review

- What makes a marriage work?
- What are some current trends in childbearing?
- What paths do people take after a divorce?

Connect

- In this section you read about some of the advantages of having children early or late in one's life. What did you learn about maternal age earlier in this text?

Reflect *Your Own Personal Journey of Life*

- What do you think would be the best age to have children? Why?

5 Gender and Communication Styles, Relationships, and Classification

LG5 Summarize the influence of gender on communication styles and relationships, and discuss gender classification.

Gender and Communication Styles

Gender and Relationships

Gender Classification

In our discussion of children's socioemotional development, we described many aspects of gender development. Gender continues to be a very important aspect of adults' lives and a strong influence on their development. Here we discuss the communication styles of males

How are women's and men's communication styles different?
Eric Audras/Onoky/SuperStock

and females, how males and females relate to others, and how gender is classified in different ways, including the recent interest in transgender.

GENDER AND COMMUNICATION STYLES

Stereotypes about differences in men's and women's attitudes toward communication and about differences in how they communicate with each other have spawned countless cartoons and jokes. Are the supposed differences real?

When Deborah Tannen (1990) analyzed the talk of women and men, she found that many wives complained about their husbands by saying that "He doesn't listen to me anymore" and "He doesn't talk to me anymore." Lack of communication, although high on women's lists of reasons for divorce, is mentioned much less often by men.

Communication problems between men and women may come in part from differences in their preferred ways of communicating. Tannen distinguishes *rapport talk* from *report talk*. **Rapport talk** is the language of conversation; it is a way of establishing connections and negotiating relationships. **Report talk** is talk that is designed to give information; this category of communication includes public speaking. According to Tannen, women enjoy rapport talk more than report talk, and men's lack of interest in rapport talk bothers many women. In contrast, men prefer to engage in report talk. Men hold center stage through verbal performances such as telling stories and jokes. They learn to use talk as a way to get and keep attention.

How extensive are gender differences in communication? Research has yielded somewhat mixed results. There is evidence of some gender differences (Anderson, 2006). One study of a sampling of students' e-mails found that people could guess the writer's gender two-thirds of the time (Thompson & Murachver, 2001). Another study revealed that women make 63 percent of phone calls and when talking to another woman stay on the phone longer (7.2 minutes) than men do when talking with other men (4.6 minutes) (Smoreda & Licoppe, 2000). However, meta-analyses suggest that overall gender differences in communication are small in both children and adults (Hyde, 2014; Leaper & Smith, 2004).

GENDER AND RELATIONSHIPS

Beyond communication skills, what characterizes women's relationships? What characterizes men's relationships? What role does gender play in friendship?

Women's Development Tannen's analysis of women's preference for rapport talk suggests that women place a high value on relationships and focus on nurturing their connections with others. This view echoes some ideas of Jean Baker Miller (1986), who has been an important advocate for examining psychological issues from a female perspective. Miller argues that when researchers examine what women have been doing in life, a large part of it involves active participation in the development of others. In Miller's view, women often try to interact with others in ways that will foster the other person's development along many dimensions—emotional, intellectual, and social.

Most experts stress that it is important for women not only to maintain their competency in relationships but to be self-motivated, too (Brabek & Brabek, 2006). As Harriet Lerner (1989) concludes in her book *The Dance of Intimacy,* it is important for women to bring to their relationships nothing less than a strong, assertive, independent, and authentic self. She emphasizes that competent relationships are those in which the separate "I-ness" of both persons can be appreciated and enhanced while the partners remain emotionally connected with each other.

In sum, Miller, Tannen, and other gender experts such as Carol Gilligan note that women are more relationship-oriented than men are—and that this relationship orientation should be valued more highly in our culture than it currently is. Critics of this view of gender differences in relationships contend that it is too stereotypical (Hyde & others, 2019). They argue that there is greater individual variation in the relationship styles of men and women than this view acknowledges.

In the field of the psychology of women, there is increased interest in women of color. To read about the work and views of one individual in this field, see the *Connecting with Careers* profile.

rapport talk The language of conversation; it is the way of establishing connections and negotiating relationships.

report talk Talk that is designed to give information; this category of communication includes public speaking.

Men's Development   The male of the species—what is he really like? What are his concerns? According to Joseph Pleck's (1995) role-strain view, male roles are contradictory and inconsistent. Men not only experience stress when they violate men's roles, they also are harmed when they act in accord with men's roles. Here are some of the areas where men's roles can cause considerable strain (Levant, 2001):

- *Health.* Men die 8 to 10 years earlier than women do. They have higher rates of stress-related disorders, alcoholism, car accidents, and suicide. Men are more likely than women to be the victims of homicide. In sum, the male role is hazardous to men's health.

- *Male-female relationships.* Too often, the male role involves expectations that men should be dominant, powerful, and aggressive and should control women. "Real men," according to many traditional definitions of masculinity, look at women in terms of their bodies, not their minds and feelings, have little interest in rapport talk and relationships, and do not consider women equal to men in work or many other aspects of life. Thus, the traditional view of the male role encourages men to disparage women, be violent toward women, and refuse to have equal relationships with women.

- *Male-male relationships.* Too many men have had too little interaction with their fathers, especially fathers who are positive role models. Nurturing and being sensitive to others have been considered aspects of the female role, not the male role. And the male role emphasizes competition rather than cooperation. All of these aspects of the male role have left men with inadequate positive, emotional connections with other males.

To reconstruct their masculinity in more positive ways, Ron Levant (2001) suggests that every man should (1) reexamine his beliefs about manhood, (2) separate out the valuable aspects of the male role, and (3) get rid of those parts of the masculine role that are destructive. All of these tasks involve becoming more "emotionally intelligent"—that is, becoming more emotionally self-aware, managing emotions more effectively, reading emotions better (one's own emotions and those of others), and being motivated to improve close relationships.

Gender's Role in Friendships   As in the childhood and adolescent years, there are gender differences in adult friendship (Blieszner & Ogletree, 2017). Compared with men, women have more close friends and their friendships involve more self-disclosure and exchange

How can men improve their relationships?
Hero/Corbis/Glow Images

How is adult friendship different among female friends, male friends, and cross-gender friends?
(*Top to bottom*) Stockbyte/Stockdisc/Getty Images; Loreanto/
Shutterstock; Ingram Publishing/age fotostock

androgyny The presence of positive masculine and feminine characteristics in the same person.

transgender A broad term that refers to individuals who adopt a gender identity that differs from the one assigned to them at birth.

of mutual support (Dow & Wood, 2006). Women are more likely to listen at length to what a friend has to say and be sympathetic, and women have been labeled as "talking companions" because talk is so central to their relationships (Gouldner & Strong, 1987). Women's friendships tend to be characterized not only by depth but also by breadth: Women share many aspects of their experiences, thoughts, and feelings (Blieszner, 2016). When female friends get together, they like to talk, but male friends are more likely to engage in activities, especially outdoors. Thus, the adult male pattern of friendship often involves keeping one's distance while sharing useful information. Men are less likely than women to talk about their weaknesses with their friends, and men seek practical solutions to their problems rather than sympathy (Tannen, 1990). Also, adult male friendships are more competitive than those of women (Helgeson, 2012).

What are some characteristics of female-male friendships? Cross-gender friendships are more common among adults than children but less common than same-gender friendships in adulthood (Blieszner & Ogletree, 2017). Cross-gender friendships can present both opportunities and problems (Helgeson, 2012). The opportunities involve learning more about common feelings and interests and shared characteristics, as well as acquiring knowledge and understanding of beliefs and activities that historically have been typical of the other gender.

Problems can arise in cross-gender friendships because of different expectations. One problem that can plague an adult cross-gender friendship is unclear sexual boundaries, which can produce tension and confusion (Hart, Adams, & Tullett, 2016).

GENDER CLASSIFICATION

Gender can be classified in multiple ways. In recent years, emphasis has been placed more on flexibility and equality in gender roles (Leaper, 2017).

Masculinity, Femininity, and Androgyny   In the mid-20th century, it was widely accepted that boys should grow up to be masculine (powerful, assertive, for example) and girls to be feminine (sensitive to others, caring, for example). In the 1970s, however, as both females and males became dissatisfied with the burdens imposed by their stereotypic roles, alternatives to femininity and masculinity were proposed. Instead of describing masculinity and femininity as a continuum in which more of one means less of the other, it was proposed that individuals could have both masculine and feminine traits.

This thinking led to the development of the concept of **androgyny,** the presence of positive masculine and feminine characteristics in the same person (Bem, 1977, 1993). The androgynous male might be assertive (masculine) and nurturing (feminine). The androgynous female might be powerful (masculine) and sensitive to others' feelings (feminine). Measures have been developed to assess androgyny, such as the Bem Sex Role Inventory (Bem, 1997).

Gender experts such as Sandra Bem (1977, 1993) argue that androgynous individuals are more flexible, competent, and mentally healthy than their masculine or feminine counterparts. A recent study found that androgynous children had high self-esteem and few internalizing problems (Pauletti & others, 2017). To some degree, though, which gender-role classification is best may depend on the context involved. For example, in close relationships, feminine and androgynous orientations might be more desirable. One study found that girls and individuals high in femininity showed a stronger interest in caring than did boys and individuals high in masculinity (Karniol, Grosz, & Schorr, 2003). However, masculine and androgynous orientations might be more desirable in traditional academic and work settings because of the achievement demands in these contexts.

Transgender   Recently, considerable interest has been directed toward a new category of gender classification, **transgender,** a broad term that refers to individuals who adopt a gender identity that differs from the one assigned to them at birth (Budge & others, 2018; Hyde & others, 2019; King, 2019, 2020). For example, an individual may have female body but identify more strongly with being masculine than being feminine, or have a male body but identify more strongly with being feminine than masculine (Sinclair-Palm, 2019). A transgender identity of being born male but identifying with being a female is much more common than the reverse (Zucker, Lawrence, & Kreukels, 2016). Transgender persons also may not want to be labeled "he" or "she" but prefer a more neutral label such as "they" or "ze" (Scelfo, 2015).

Because of the nuances and complexities involved in such gender categorizations, some experts have recently argued that a better overarching umbrella term might be *trans* to identify a variety of gender identities and expressions different from the gender identity they were assigned at birth (Sinclair-Palm, 2019). The variety of gender identities might include transgender, gender queer (also referred to as gender expansive, this broad gender identity category encompasses individuals who are not exclusively masculine or exclusively feminine), and gender nonconforming (individuals whose behavior/appearance does not conform to social expectations for what is appropriate for their gender). Another recently generated term, *cisgender,* can be used to describe individuals whose gender identity and expression match the gender identity assigned at birth (Hyde & others, 2019).

Transgender individuals can be straight, gay, lesbian, or bisexual. A recent research review concluded that transgender youth have higher rates of depression, suicide attempts, and eating disorders than their non-transgender peers (Connolly & others, 2016). Among the explanations for this higher rate of disorders are the distress of living in the wrong body and the discrimination and misunderstanding they experience as gender-minority individuals (Budge, Chin, & Minero, 2017).

Among individuals who identify themselves as transgender, the majority eventually adopt a gender identity in line with the body into which they were born (Byne & others, 2012; King, 2019, 2020). Some transgender individuals seek transsexual surgery to go from a male body to a female body or vice versa, but most do not. Some choose just to have hormonal treatments, such as biological females who use testosterone to enhance their masculine characteristics, or biological males who use estrogen to increase their feminine characteristics. Yet other transgender individuals opt for another, broader strategy that involves a non-binary lifestyle (rejecting the traditional practice of choosing between two opposing categories) (King, 2019, 2020; Savin-Williams, 2019). Because trans individuals experience considerable discrimination, it is important that society adopt a more welcoming and accepting attitude toward them (Vargas, Huey, & Miranda, 2020).

What characterizes transgender individuals?
Johnny Greig/E+/Getty Images

Review *Connect* Reflect

LG5 Summarize the influence of gender on communication styles and relationships, and discuss gender classification.

Review

- What are some differences in how women and men communicate?
- What are some important aspects of women's and men's roles in relationships?
- What are some different ways that gender can be classified?

Connect

- In this section you read about many aspects of gender classification. How do you think the development of sexuality that was discussed in "Physical and Cognitive Development in Adolescence" and "Physical and Cognitive Development in Early Adulthood" might influence an individual's gender classification?

Reflect *Your Own Personal Journey of Life*

- How would you classify your own gender? What do you think influenced you to have that particular gender classification?

---

topical connections *looking forward*

Middle adulthood is a time when individuals experience Erikson's seventh life-span stage, generativity versus stagnation. During this stage, it is important for middle-aged adults to contribute in meaningful ways to the next generation. In Levinson's theory, one of the key conflicts of middle age involves coping with the young-old polarity in life. Midlife crises are not as common as many people assume, but when they occur, negative life events usually are involved. A number of longitudinal studies of stability and change in adult development have been conducted, and recently it has been argued that stability peaks in middle adulthood. Affectionate love increases in middle age. Many middle-aged adults become grandparents. Middle-aged women especially play an important role in connecting generations.

Socioemotional Development in Early Adulthood

1 Stability and Change from Childhood to Adulthood

 LG1 Describe stability and change in temperament, and summarize adult attachment styles.

Temperament

- Links between childhood temperament and adult personality can vary, depending on contexts in an individual's experience. A high activity level in early childhood is linked with being an outgoing young adult. Young adults show fewer mood swings, are more responsible, and engage in less risk taking than adolescents. In some cases, certain dimensions of temperament in childhood are linked with adjustment problems in early adulthood.

Attachment

- Three adult attachment styles are secure attachment, avoidant attachment, and anxious attachment. Attachment styles in early adulthood are linked with a number of relationship patterns and developmental outcomes. For example, securely attached adults often show more positive relationship patterns than insecurely attached adults. Also, adults with avoidant and anxious attachment styles tend to be more depressed and to have more relationship problems than securely attached adults.

2 Attraction, Love, and Close Relationships

 LG2 Identify some key aspects of attraction, love, and close relationships.

Attraction

- First impressions can be enduring. Familiarity precedes a close relationship. We like to associate with people who are similar to us. The principles of consensual validation and matching can explain this. Similarity in personality attributes may be especially important to a relationship's success. The criteria for physical attractiveness vary across cultures and historical periods.

The Faces of Love

- The different types of love include friendship, romantic love, affectionate love, and consummate love. Friendship plays an important role in adult development, especially in providing emotional support. Romantic love, also called passionate love, includes passion, sexuality, and a mixture of emotions, not all of which are positive. Affectionate love, also called companionate love, usually becomes more important as relationships mature. Shaver proposed a developmental model of love and Sternberg a triarchic model of love (with dimensions of passion, intimacy, and commitment).

Falling Out of Love

- The collapse of a close relationship can be traumatic, but for some individuals it results in happiness and personal development. For most individuals, falling out of love is painful and emotionally intense.

3 Adult Lifestyles

 LG3 Characterize adult lifestyles.

Single Adults

- Being single has become an increasingly prominent lifestyle. Autonomy is one of its advantages. Intimacy, loneliness, and finding a positive identity in a marriage-oriented society are challenges faced by single adults.

Cohabiting Adults

- Cohabitation is an increasingly popular lifestyle, but researchers have found it is often linked to negative marital outcomes, although this link depends on the timing of cohabitation. Negative marital outcomes are more likely when cohabitation occurs prior to becoming engaged.

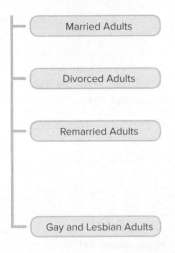

Married Adults

- The age at which individuals marry in the United States is increasing. Despite a decline in marriage rates, a large percentage of Americans still marry. The benefits of marriage include better physical and mental health and a longer life.

Divorced Adults

- The U.S. divorce rate increased dramatically in the middle of the twentieth century but began to decline in the 1980s. Divorce is complex and emotional. Both divorced men and women can experience loneliness, anxiety, and difficulty in forming new relationships.

Remarried Adults

- When adults remarry, they tend to do so rather quickly, with men remarrying sooner than women. Remarriage confers some benefits on adults but also some problems. Remarried families are less stable than families in first marriages, and remarried adults have a lower level of mental health than adults in first marriages, although remarriage improves adults' (especially women's) financial status. Stepfamilies come in many sizes and forms.

Gay and Lesbian Adults

- One of the most striking findings about gay and lesbian couples is how similar their relationships are to heterosexual couples' relationships.

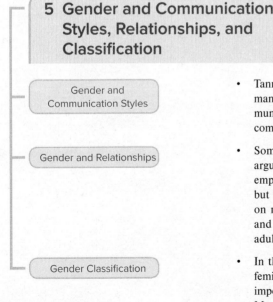

4 Marriage and the Family

 LG4 Discuss making marriage work, parenting, and divorce.

Making Marriage Work

- Gottman's research indicates that happily married couples establish love maps, nurture fondness and admiration, turn toward each other, accept the influence of the partner, resolve conflicts, overcome gridlock, and create shared meaning.

Becoming a Parent

- Families are becoming smaller, and many women are delaying childbirth until they are well established in a career. There are some advantages to having children earlier in adulthood and other advantages to having them later.

Dealing with Divorce

- Hetherington identified six pathways taken by people after divorce: enhancers, good-enoughs, seekers, libertines, competent loners, and the defeated. About 20 percent became better adjusted and more competent after the divorce.

---

5 Gender and Communication Styles, Relationships, and Classification

LG5 Summarize the influence of gender on communication styles and relationships, and discuss gender classification.

Gender and Communication Styles

- Tannen distinguishes between report talk, which many men prefer, and rapport talk, which many women prefer. Meta-analyses have found only small gender differences in overall communication, but recent research suggests some gender differences in specific aspects of gender communication, such as the way men and women use words.

Gender and Relationships

- Some gender experts argue that women are more relationship-oriented than men. Critics argue that there is considerable variation in gender relationships. Many experts emphasize that it is important for women to retain their competence in relationships but also be self-motivated. The traditional male role involves strain, which takes a toll on men's health. The role also tends to discourage both equal relationships with females and positive emotional connections with other men. Gender differences characterize adult friendships.

Gender Classification

- In the mid-20th century, gender was classified as an individual being either masculine or feminine. In the 1970s, the concept of androgyny became popular and emphasized the importance of both positive masculine and feminine characteristics in the same individual. More recently, considerable attention has focused on a new gender category, transgender, which characterizes individuals whose gender identity is different from the one assigned to them at birth.

key terms

affectionate love 445
androgyny 464
anxious attachment style 442

avoidant attachment style 442
consensual validation 444
matching hypothesis 445

rapport talk 462
report talk 462
romantic love 445

secure attachment style 442
transgender 464

key people

Sandra Bem 464
Ellen Berscheid 446
Andrew Cherlin 449
Bella DePaulo 449

Erik Erikson 445
John Gottman 457
Cindy Hazan 441
E. Mavis Hetherington 460

Harriet Lerner 462
Mario Mikulincer 442
Jean Baker Miller 462
Joseph Pleck 463

Phillip Shaver 441
Robert J. Sternberg 446
Deborah Tannen 462
Theodore Wachs 440

Tomas Rodriguez/Corbis/Getty Images

Generations will depend on the ability of every procreating individual to face his children.

—**Erik Erikson**
American psychologist, 20th century

Middle Adulthood

In middle adulthood, what we have been forms what we will be. For some of us, middle age is a foggy place, a time when we need to discover what we are running from and to and why. We compare our life with what we vowed to make it. In middle age, more time stretches behind us than before us, and some evaluations, however reluctant, have to be made. As the young-old polarity greets us with a special force, we need to join the daring of youth with the discipline of age in a way that does justice to both. As middle-aged adults, we come to sense that the generations of living things pass in a short while and, like runners, hand on the torch of life. This section consists of two chapters: "Physical and Cognitive Development in Middle Adulthood" and "Socioemotional Development in Middle Adulthood."

chapter 15

PHYSICAL AND COGNITIVE DEVELOPMENT IN MIDDLE ADULTHOOD

chapter outline

① The Nature of Middle Adulthood

Learning Goal 1 Explain how midlife is changing, and define middle adulthood.

Changing Midlife
Defining Middle Adulthood

② Physical Development

Learning Goal 2 Discuss physical changes in middle adulthood.

Physical Changes
Chronic Disorders
Mortality Rates
Sexuality

③ Cognitive Development

Learning Goal 3 Identify cognitive changes in middle adulthood.

Intelligence
Information Processing

④ Careers, Work, and Leisure

Learning Goal 4 Characterize career development, work, and leisure in middle adulthood.

Work in Midlife
Career Challenges and Changes
Leisure

⑤ Religion, Spirituality, and Meaning in Life

Learning Goal 5 Explain the roles of religion, spirituality, and meaning in life during middle adulthood.

Religion, Spirituality, and Adult Lives
Religion, Spirituality, and Health
Meaning in Life

Digital Vision/Getty Images

Our perception of time depends on where we are in the life span. We are more concerned about time at some points in life than others. The rock group Pink Floyd, in their song "Time," described how when we are young life seems longer and time passes more slowly, but when we get older, time seems to fly by so quickly.

In middle adulthood as well as late adulthood, individuals increasingly think about time-left-to-live instead of time-since-birth (Li & Siu, 2020; Rohr & others, 2017). Middle-aged adults begin to look back to where they have been, reflecting on what they have done with the time they have had. They look toward the future in terms of how much time remains to accomplish what they hope to do with their lives. Older adults look backward even more than middle-aged adults, not surprising given the shorter future in the life that they have. Also not surprisingly, given the many years they still have to live, emerging adults and young adults are more likely to look forward in time than backward in time.

A recent research review examined subjective time in middle and late adulthood, including such components as future time perspective, personal goals, and autobiographical memories (Gabrian, Dutt, & Wahl, 2017). The review concluded that positive subjective time perceptions (such as an expanded view of the future, a focus on positive past and future life content, and favorable time-related evaluations) were linked to better health and well-being, while negative subjective time perceptions were associated with lower levels of health and well-being.

Another aspect of time perception in middle age is the observation that time seems to speed by much faster as we get older. Talk to just about any middle-aged person and he or she will tell you that time does indeed fly by much faster than it did earlier in life. Why might this be?

One view is that for 10-year-olds, one year makes up 10 percent of their life so far and for 20-year-olds, it makes up 5 percent of their life. However, for 50-year-olds, one year represents just one-fiftieth of their life, and thus the one year seems to fly by more quickly since it makes up a much smaller portion of the time they have lived.

A second view is that as middle age sets in, we begin to think more about the diminishing time we have left to live. Because of the fewer years we have left, we wish time would slow down. Because that can't happen, we perceive time to be flying by even faster. A common comment by someone who has reached 60 is, "Where did my fifties go? It seems like only yesterday I was 50 and now I'm 60."

A third view is that new experiences slow down our perception of time, while repeated experiences make time seem to go faster. Younger people are more likely to have new experiences, and all of these new experiences slow down their perception of time. By contrast, when we reach middle age, more of our experiences are ones we already have had and thus we perceive time to be speeding by.

preview

When young adults look forward in time to what their lives might be like as middle-aged adults, too often they anticipate that things will go downhill. However, like all periods of the human life span, middle age usually holds both positive and negative features. In this first chapter on middle adulthood, we will discuss physical changes; cognitive changes; changes in careers, work, and leisure; as well as the importance of religion and meaning in life during middle adulthood. To begin, though, we will explore how middle age is changing.

1 The Nature of Middle Adulthood

LG1 Explain how midlife is changing, and define middle adulthood.

Changing Midlife

Defining Middle Adulthood

Is midlife experienced the same way today as it was 100 years ago? Is it different from what it was like just 25 years ago? How can middle adulthood be defined, and what are some of its main characteristics?

CHANGING MIDLIFE

Many of today's 50-year-olds are in better shape, more alert, and more productive than their 40-year-old counterparts from a generation or two earlier. As more people lead healthier lifestyles and medical discoveries help to slow down the aging process, the boundaries of middle age are being pushed upward. It looks like middle age is starting later and lasting longer for increasing numbers of active, healthy, and productive people. A current saying is "60 is the new 40," implying that many 60-year-olds today are living a life that is as active, productive, and healthy as earlier generations did in their forties.

Questions such as, "To which age group do you belong?" and "How old do you feel?" reflect the concept of age identity. A consistent finding is that as adults become older their age identity is younger than their chronological age (Setterson & Trauten, 2009; Westerhof, 2009). For example, a recent study found that adults 44 to 64 years of age reported feeling younger than they actually were and wanting to be younger than their chronological age (Shinan-Altman & Werner, 2019). For the participants in this study, the perceived beginning of old age was 69 years. Another study discovered a similar pattern: Half of the 60- to 75-year-olds viewed themselves as being middle-aged (Lachman, Maier, & Budner, 2000). And a British survey of people over 50 years of age revealed that they perceived middle age to begin at 53 (Beneden Health, 2013). In this study, respondents said that being middle-aged is characterized by enjoying afternoon naps, groaning when you bend down, and preferring a quiet night in rather than a night out. Also, some individuals consider the upper boundary of midlife as the age at which they make the transition from work to retirement.

When Carl Jung studied midlife transitions early in the twentieth century, he referred to midlife as the afternoon of life (Jung, 1933). Midlife serves as an important preparation for

How is midlife changing?
Color/Blend Images/Getty Images

late adulthood, "the evening of life" (Lachman, 2004, p. 306). But "midlife" came much earlier in Jung's time. In 1900 the average life expectancy was only 47 years of age; only 3 percent of the population lived past 65. Today, the average life expectancy is 79, and 15 percent of the U.S. population is older than 65 (U.S. Census Bureau, 2019). As a much greater percentage of the population lives to an older age, the midpoint of life and what constitutes middle age or middle adulthood are getting harder to pin down (Cohen, 2012).

In her book titled *In Our Prime: The Invention of Middle Age,* Patricia Cohen (2012) describes how middle age wasn't thought of as a separate developmental period until the mid-1800s and the term *midlife* wasn't in a dictionary until 1895. In Cohen's analysis, advances in health and more people living to older ages especially fueled the emergence of thinking about middle age. People today take longer to grow up and longer to age than in past centuries.

Compared with previous decades and centuries, an increasing percentage of the population is made up of middle-aged and older adults. In the past, the age structure of the population could be represented by a pyramid, with the largest percentage of the population in the childhood years. Today, the percentages of people at different ages in the life span are more similar, creating what is called the "rectangularization" of the age distribution (a vertical rectangle) (Tannenbaum & Boyle, 2019). The rectangularization has been created by health advances that promote longevity, low fertility rates, and the aging of the baby-boom cohort (Moen, 2007).

Compared with late adulthood, far less research attention has been devoted to middle adulthood (Hamm & others, 2019; Liu & Lachman, 2019). In a U.S. Census Bureau (2012) assessment, more than 102,713,000 people in the U.S. were 40 to 64 years of age, which accounts for 33.2 percent of the U.S. population. Given the large percentage of people in middle adulthood and the key roles that individuals in midlife play in families, the workplace, and the community, researchers need to pay more attention to this age period.

The portrait of midlife described so far here suggests that for too long the negative aspects of this developmental period have been overemphasized. Indeed, in a recent study, undergraduate college students were shown a computer-generated graphic of a person identified as a younger adult, middle-aged adult, or older adult (Kelley, Soboroff, & Lovaglia, 2017). When asked which person they would choose for a work-related task, they selected the middle-aged adult most often. However, as will be seen in the following sections, it is important not to go too far in describing midlife positively. Many physical aspects decline in middle adulthood, and increased rates of health problems such as obesity and cardiovascular disease need to be considered in taking a balanced perspective on this age period (Kanesarajah & others, 2018). Further, a recent study of U.S. and Japanese adults found that in both countries younger adults perceived that their life satisfaction improved from the past to the present and from the present to the future, but the improvement was perceived as more modest by middle-aged adults, and then shifted to a perceived decline in life satisfaction among older adults (Hong & others, 2019).

DEFINING MIDDLE ADULTHOOD

Although the age boundaries are not set in stone, we will consider **middle adulthood** to be the developmental period that begins at approximately 40 to 45 years of age and extends to about 60 to 65 years of age. For many people, middle adulthood is a time of declining physical skills and expanding responsibility; a period in which people become more conscious of the young-old polarity and the shrinking amount of time left in life; a point when individuals seek to transmit something meaningful to the next generation; and a time when people reach and maintain satisfaction in their careers. In sum, middle adulthood involves "balancing work and relationship responsibilities in the midst of the physical and psychological changes associated with aging" (Lachman, 2004, p. 305).

In midlife, as in other age periods, individuals make choices—selecting what to do, deciding how to invest time and resources, and evaluating what aspects of their lives they need to change (Hahn & Lachman, 2015). In midlife, "a serious accident, loss, or illness" may be a "wake-up call" and produce "a major restructuring of time and a reassessment" of life's priorities (Lachman, 2004, p. 310). And with an absence of seniority protections, many middle-aged adults experience unexpected job loss or are strongly encouraged to take early retirement packages.

The concept of gains (growth) and losses (decline) is an important one in life-span development (Robinson & Lachman, 2017). Middle adulthood is the age period in which gains and losses as well as biological and sociocultural factors balance each other (Baltes, Lindenberger, & Staudinger, 2006). Although biological functioning declines in middle adulthood, sociocultural

developmental **connection**

Life-Span Perspective

There are four types of age: chronological, biological, psychological, and social. Connect to "Introduction."

middle adulthood The developmental period that begins at approximately 40 to 45 years of age and extends to about 60 to 65 years of age.

supports such as education, career, and relationships may peak in middle adulthood (Willis & Schaie, 2005). For example, neurobiological decline involves slow, gradual age-related decline in middle age, yet there are usually little or no negative consequences for effective functioning at work and completing the tasks of everyday living. Indeed, middle-aged adults may sense an urgency that now is the time to accomplish and do their best work. Also, in a recent study, gain orientation decreased and maintenance orientation increased with age (Gong & Freund, 2020). Also in this study, both perceived losses and accumulation of resources and assets increased with age.

Margie Lachman and her colleagues (2015) have described middle age as a pivotal period because it is a time of balancing growth and decline, linking earlier and later periods of development, and connecting younger and older generations.

Remember from our discussion in the "Introduction" chapter that individuals have not only a chronological age but also biological, psychological, and social ages. Some experts conclude that compared with earlier and later periods, middle age is influenced more heavily by sociocultural factors (Willis & Martin, 2005).

For many healthy adults, middle age is lasting longer than it did for previous generations. Indeed, an increasing number of experts on middle adulthood describe the age period of 55 to 65 as *late midlife* (Deeg, 2005). Compared with earlier midlife, late midlife is more likely to be characterized by "the death of a parent, the last child leaving the parental home, becoming a grandparent, the preparation for retirement, and in most cases actual retirement. Many people in this age range experience their first confrontation with health problems" (Deeg, 2005). Overall, then, although gains and losses may balance each other in early midlife, losses may begin to outnumber gains for many individuals in late midlife (Baltes, Lindenberger, & Staudinger, 2006).

Keep in mind, though, that midlife is characterized by individual variations (Lachman, Agrigoroaei, & Hahn, 2016). As life-span expert Gilbert Brim (1992) commented, middle adulthood is full of changes, twists, and turns; the path is not fixed. People move in and out of states of success and failure.

Review Connect Reflect

LG1 Explain how midlife is changing, and define middle adulthood.

Review

- How is middle age today different from the way it was for past generations?
- How is middle adulthood defined, and what are some of its characteristics?

Connect

- In this section you read about the "rectangularization" of age distribution in our current times being influenced

by, among other things, increasing longevity. What did you learn earlier about the history of human longevity?

Reflect *Your Own Personal Journey of Life*

- How do you think you will experience (are experiencing or have experienced) middle age differently from your parents or grandparents?

---

2 Physical Development

LG2 Discuss physical changes in middle adulthood.

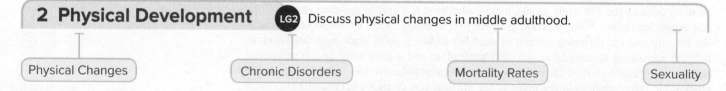

Physical Changes | Chronic Disorders | Mortality Rates | Sexuality

What physical changes characterize middle adulthood? How healthy are middle-aged adults? What are the main causes of death in middle age? How sexually active are individuals in middle adulthood?

Middle age is a mix of new opportunities and expanding resources accompanied by declines in physical abilities.

—LOIS VERBRUGGE

Research professor, Institute of Gerontology, University of Michigan

PHYSICAL CHANGES

Unlike the rather dramatic physical changes that occur in early adolescence and the sometimes abrupt decline in old age, midlife physical changes are usually more gradual. Although everyone experiences some downward physical change due to aging in middle adulthood, the rates of this aging vary considerably from one individual to another. Genetic makeup and lifestyle factors play important roles in determining whether chronic disease will appear and when (Santacreu, Rodriguez, & Molina, 2019; Wang & others, 2020). Middle age is a window through which we can glimpse later life while there is still time to engage in prevention and to influence some aspects of aging (Lachman & others, 2018). Recent research has shown that a combination of multiple adaptive factors, such as positive health behaviors (physical exercise and sleep), a sense of control, social support and social connections, and emotion regulation help to buffer declines in physical health and cognitive functioning in middle age (Liu & Lachman, 2020).

Let's now explore some of the physical changes of middle age.

Visible Signs   The most visible signs of physical changes in middle adulthood involve physical appearance. The first outwardly noticeable signs of aging usually are apparent by the forties or fifties. The skin begins to wrinkle and sag because of a loss of fat and collagen in underlying tissues (Sifaki & others, 2020). Small, localized areas of pigmentation in the skin produce age spots, especially in areas that are exposed to sunlight, such as the hands and face. Hair becomes thinner and grayer due to a lower replacement rate and a decline in melanin production. Fingernails and toenails develop ridges and become thicker and more brittle.

Since a youthful appearance is valued in many cultures, individuals whose hair is graying, whose skin is wrinkling, whose bodies are sagging, and whose teeth are yellowing may strive to make themselves look younger. Undergoing cosmetic surgery, dyeing hair, purchasing wigs, enrolling in weight reduction programs, participating in exercise regimens, and taking heavy doses of vitamins are common in middle age. Baby boomers have shown a strong interest in plastic surgery and Botox, which may reflect their desire to slow down the aging process (Abelsson & Willman, 2020; Casabona & others, 2019).

Height and Weight   Individuals lose height in middle age, and many gain weight (Blake, 2020). On average, men from 30 to 50 years of age lose about one inch in height, then may lose another inch from 50 to 70 years of age (Hoyer & Roodin, 2009). The height loss for women can be as much as 2 inches from 25 to 75 years of age. Note that there are large variations in the extent to which individuals become shorter with aging. The decrease in height is due to bone loss in the vertebrae. On average, body fat accounts for about 10 percent of body weight in adolescence; it makes up 20 percent or more in middle age.

Obesity increases from early to middle adulthood. In 2016, the prevalence of obesity in middle-aged adults (40.8 percent) was higher than in younger adults (35.7 percent). No significant differences in obesity were found between adults 60 years and older (41 percent) and younger age groups (Hales & others, 2017). Women had a higher rate of obesity than men in middle age (44.7 percent versus 40.8), and the 44.7 percent rate for women was higher than for women in early (41.1 percent) and late adulthood (43.1 percent).

Being overweight or obese is a critical health problem in middle adulthood (Itoh & others, 2020; Syme & others, 2019). For example, overweight and obesity are linked to increased risk of earlier death, hypertension, diabetes, and cardiovascular disease (Blake, 2020). For individuals who are 30 percent overweight, the probability of dying in middle adulthood increases by about 40 percent. Also, in a recent large-scale study, obesity was associated with shorter longevity and increased risk of death due to cardiovascular disease compared with normal-weight individuals (Khan & others, 2018). Further, in another recent study, obese middle-aged and older adults were more likely to have chronic diseases and experience an earlier death than their normal-weight counterparts (Stenholm & others, 2017). And in a Chinese study, men and women who gained an average of 22 pounds from 20 to 45–60 years of age had an increased risk of hypertension and cholesterol, as well as elevated triglyceride levels in middle age (Zhou & others, 2018).

Famous actor Sean Connery as a young adult in his twenties (*top*) and as a middle-aged adult in his fifties (*bottom*). *What are some of the most outwardly noticeable signs of aging in middle adulthood?*
(*Top*) Bettmann/Getty Images; (*bottom*) Life Picture Collection/ Getty Images

Strength, Joints, and Bones   Maximum physical strength often is attained during the twenties. The term *sarcopenia* is given to age-related loss of muscle mass and strength (Clark, 2019; Ebner, Anker, & von Haehling, 2020). Muscle loss with age occurs at a rate of approximately 1 to 2 percent per year after age 50 (Marcell, 2003). A loss of strength especially occurs in the back and legs. Researchers are seeking to identify genes and proteins that are linked to the development of sarcopenia (Kapitansky & Gozes, 2019). Also, a recent study found that smoking and diabetes were risk factors for accelerated loss of muscle mass in middle-aged women (Lee & Choi, 2019).

> Middle age is when your age starts to show around your middle.
>
> **—Bob Hope**
> *American comedian, 20th century*

Obesity also is a significant risk factor for sarcopenia (Rubio-Ruiz & others, 2019). Recently, researchers have increasingly used the term "sarcopenic obesity" to describe individuals who have sarcopenia and are obese (El Bizri & Batsis, 2020). One study found that sarcopenic obesity was linked to hypertension (Park & others, 2013). In one study sarcopenic obesity was associated with a 24 percent increase in risk for all-cause mortality, with a higher risk for men than for women (Tian & Xu, 2016). And a research review concluded that weight management and resistance training were the best strategies to slow down the decline of muscle mass and muscle strength (Rolland & others, 2011).

Peak functioning of the body's joints usually occurs in the twenties. The cushions for the movement of bones (such as tendons and ligaments) become less efficient in middle adulthood, a time when many individuals experience joint stiffness and more difficulty in movement.

Maximum bone density occurs by the mid- to late thirties, after which there is a progressive loss of bone. The rate of this bone loss begins slowly but accelerates with further aging (Locquet & others, 2018). Women lose bone mass twice as fast as men do. By the end of midlife, bones break more easily and heal more slowly (de Villiers, 2018). A recent study found that greater intake of fruits and vegetables was linked to increased bone density in middle-aged and older adults (Qiu & others, 2017).

Vision and Hearing

Accommodation of the eye—the ability to focus and maintain an image on the retina—experiences its sharpest decline between 40 and 59 years of age. In particular, middle-aged individuals begin to have difficulty viewing close objects.

The eye's blood supply also diminishes, although usually not until the fifties or sixties. The reduced blood supply may decrease the visual field's size and account for an increase in the eye's blind spot. At 60 years of age, the retina receives only one-third as much light as it did at 20 years of age, mostly because of the reduced size of the pupil (Scialfa & Kline, 2007). A recent study of middle-aged adults found that vision problems—especially difficulty reading the newspaper and recognizing people on the street—were linked to decreased life satisfaction, decreased self-esteem, increased depressive symptoms, and increased social isolation (Hajek & others, 2020).

Hearing also can start to decline by age 40. Auditory assessments indicate that hearing loss occurs in up to 50 percent of individuals 50 years and older (Fowler & Leigh-Paffenroth, 2007). Sensitivity to high pitches usually declines first; the ability to hear low-pitched sounds does not seem to decline much in middle adulthood. Men usually lose their sensitivity to high-pitched sounds sooner than women do. However, this gender difference might be due to men's greater exposure to noise in occupations such as mining, automobile work, and so on.

Researchers are identifying new possibilities for improving the vision and hearing of people as they age (Nkyekyer & others, 2019). One strategy involves better control of glare or background noise (Richter & others, 2018). Laser surgery and implantation of intraocular lenses have become routine procedures for correcting vision in middle-aged adults (Oshika & others, 2020; Wallerstein & others, 2019). In addition, recent advances in hearing aids have dramatically improved hearing for many individuals (Edwards, 2020; Willink, Reed, & Lin, 2019). However, even with the advent of technologically sophisticated hearing devices, many people don't always wear them, or they wear them incorrectly.

Cardiovascular System

Midlife is a time when high blood pressure and high cholesterol often take adults by surprise. Cardiovascular disease increases considerably in middle age (Masson & others, 2019; Mosley & others, 2020), as indicated in Figure 1.

The level of cholesterol in the blood increases during the adult years and in midlife begins to accumulate on the artery walls, increasing the risk of cardiovascular disease (Rosenson,

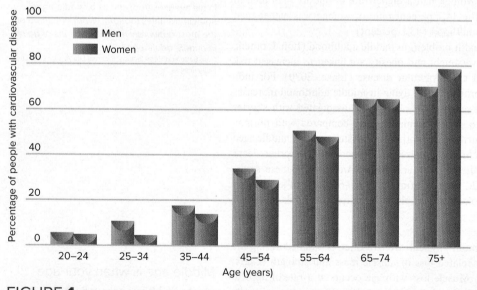

FIGURE 1

THE RELATION OF AGE AND GENDER TO CARDIOVASCULAR DISEASE. Notice the sharp increase in cardiovascular disease in middle age.

Hegele, & Koenig, 2019; Zhou & others, 2020). The type of cholesterol in the blood, however, influences its effect (Pencina & others, 2019). Cholesterol comes in two forms: LDL (low-density lipoprotein) and HDL (high-density lipoprotein). LDL is often referred to as "bad" cholesterol because when the level of LDL is too high, it sticks to the lining of blood vessels, which can lead to arteriosclerosis (hardening of the arteries) (Wang, Wilcox, & Lal, 2020). HDL is often referred to as "good" cholesterol because when it is high and LDL is low, the risk of cardiovascular disease is lower.

High blood pressure (hypertension), too, often begins to appear for many individuals in their forties and fifties (Syme & others, 2019). At menopause, a woman's blood pressure rises sharply and usually remains above that of a man through life's later years (Di Giosia & others, 2018). One study found that uncontrolled hypertension can damage the brain's structure and function as early as the late thirties and early forties (Maillard & others, 2012). In this study, structural damage to the brain's white matter (axons) and decreased volume of gray matter (cell bodies and dendrites) occurred for individuals who had hypertension (systolic number above 140 and diastolic number above 90). Another study revealed that hypertension in middle age was linked to risk of cognitive impairment in late adulthood (23 years later) (Virta & others, 2013).

Exercise, weight control, and a diet rich in fruits, vegetables, and whole grains can often help to stave off many cardiovascular problems in middle age (Quindry & others, 2019). In a recent study of middle-aged adults, higher cardiorespiratory fitness predicted lower cardiovascular disease risk (Swainson, Ingle, & Carroll, 2019). Also, although cholesterol levels are influenced by heredity, LDL can be reduced and HDL increased by eating food that is low in saturated fat and cholesterol and by exercising regularly (Schiff, 2021).

The good news is that deaths due to cardiovascular disease have been decreasing in the United States since the 1970s. Why is this so? Advances in medications to lower blood pressure and cholesterol in high-risk individuals have been major factors in reducing deaths due to cardiovascular disease (Rosensen, Hegele, & Koenig, 2019). Regular exercise and healthy eating habits also have considerable benefits in preventing cardiovascular disease (D'Alessandro, Lampignano, & De Pergola, 2019; Marin-Jimenez & others, 2020). A recent Chinese study revealed that men and women who gained an average of 22 pounds or more from 20 to 60 years of age had an increased risk of hypertension and cholesterol, as well as elevated triglyceride levels in middle age (Zhou & others, 2018). And risk factors for cardiovascular disease in middle adulthood can show up even earlier in development. For example, a recent study indicated that a healthy diet in adolescence was linked to a lower risk of cardiovascular disease in middle-aged women (Dahm & others, 2018). Socioeconomic status (SES) factors also play a role in cardiovascular disease in middle adulthood. A 32-year study found that middle-aged individuals who continued to have a lower SES through early adulthood and into middle adulthood were more likely to have a lower level of cardiovascular health than their counterparts who experienced an improvement in their SES status across the study years (Savelieva & others, 2017). And in a recent global study, from 1990 to 2017, a decline in cardiovascular mortality rates occurred in high-income regions but only slightly decreased or even increased in most low- and middle-income regions of the world (Jagannathan & others, 2019). In this study, high blood pressure, unhealthy diet, high glucose levels, and high LDL accounted for most of the cardiovascular-related deaths.

As reflected in the research we have just described, the American Heart Association has proposed Life's Simple 7—a list of things people can do to improve their cardiovascular health: (1) manage blood pressure, (2) control cholesterol, (3) reduce blood sugar, (4) get active, (5) eat better, (6) lose weight, and (7) quit smoking. In a recent study, optimal Life's Simple 7 at middle age was linked to better cardiovascular health recovery following a heart attack later in life (Mok & others, 2018).

An increasing problem in middle and late adulthood is **metabolic syndrome,** a condition characterized by hypertension, obesity, and insulin resistance (Gharipour & others, 2019). Researchers have found that chronic stress exposure is linked to metabolic syndrome (Alves Freire Ribeiro & others, 2020). Metabolic syndrome often leads to the development of diabetes and cardiovascular disease (Savadatti & others, 2019). In a recent study, the triple combination of low HDL, high blood pressure, and larger waist circumference was linked to the connection between metabolic syndrome and cardiovascular disease (Mansourian & others, 2019). Weight loss and exercise are strongly recommended as part of the treatment of metabolic syndrome (Paydar & Johnson, 2020; Siopi & others, 2019; Y. Wang & others, 2020). Also, a recent study found that sedentary behavior, especially moderate and high TV viewing time, was linked to metabolic syndrome (Lemes & others, 2019).

Members of the Masai tribe in Kenya, Africa, can stay on a treadmill for a long time because of their active lives. The extremely low incidence of heart disease in the Masai tribe is likely linked to their energetic lifestyle.
The Family of Dr. George T. Mann

What characterizes metabolic syndrome?
Ryan McVay/Photodisc/Getty Images

metabolic syndrome A condition characterized by hypertension, obesity, and insulin resistance. Metabolic syndrome often leads to the onset of diabetes and cardiovascular disease.

Lungs There is little change in lung capacity through most of middle adulthood for many individuals. However, at about age 55, the proteins in lung tissue become less elastic. This change, combined with a gradual stiffening of the chest wall, decreases the lungs' capacity to shuttle oxygen from the air people breathe to the blood in their veins. The lung capacity of individuals who are smokers drops precipitously in middle age, but if the individuals quit smoking, their lung capacity improves, although not to the level of individuals who have never smoked.

Exercise is linked to better lung functioning and a lower risk of developing lung cancer (Veldhuizen & others, 2019). In one study, more than 17,000 men were given a cardiovascular fitness assessment at 50 years of age (Lakoski & others, 2013). In this study, subsequent analysis of Medicare claims and deaths found that the risk of being diagnosed with lung cancer was reduced by 68 percent for men who were the most fit compared with those who were the least fit. A longitudinal study also found that increased cardiorespiratory fitness from early adulthood to middle adulthood was linked to less decline in lung health over time (Benck & others, 2017). And in a recent study, lower body mass index, less exercise, frequent alcohol drinking, and a meat-based diet were risk factors for lung cancer among never-smoking women (Ko & others, 2020).

Sleep The average American adult gets just under seven hours of sleep a night. How much sleep do adults need to function optimally the next day? An increasing number of experts note that eight hours of sleep or more per night are necessary for optimal performance the next day. These experts argue that many adults have become sleep deprived (McKenna & others, 2013). Work pressures, school pressures, family obligations, and social obligations often lead to long hours of wakefulness and irregular sleep/wake schedules (Soderstrom & others, 2012). The National Sleep Foundation (2019) recommends that 26- to 64-year-olds should get 7 to 9 hours of sleep per night.

Habitual sleep deprivation is linked to morbidity, especially among people with cardiovascular disease (Grandner & others, 2013). A recent Korean study found that the following factors were linked to sleep problems in middle age: unemployment, being unmarried, currently being a smoker, lack of exercise, having irregular meals, and frequently experiencing stressful events (Yoon & others, 2015). In a recent study of young and middle-aged adults, females had more severe sleep problems than males did (Rossler & others, 2017). However, in this study the good news is that a majority of individuals (72 percent) reported no sleep disturbances (Rossler & others, 2017). And a recent research review of sleep in normal aging concluded that shortened nighttime sleep duration, increased nocturnal awakenings, and increased frequency of daytime naps are common changes in sleep patterns associated with aging (Li, Vitiello, & Gooneratne, 2018). Also in this review, it was concluded that sleep patterns change mainly between early and middle adulthood and then remain stable in healthy older adults.

Some aspects of sleep become more problematic in middle age (Baker & others, 2018). Beginning in the forties, wakeful periods are more frequent and there is less of the deepest type of sleep. The amount of time spent lying awake in bed at night begins to increase in middle age, and this can produce a feeling of being less rested in the morning. Sleep-disordered breathing and restless legs syndrome become more prevalent in middle age (Arnold & Guilleminault, 2019). Further, a recent study revealed that poor sleep quality in middle adulthood was linked to a lower level of executive function, slower processing speed, increased learning difficulties, and poorer memory recall (Kaur & others, 2019). Sleep problems in midlife are more common among individuals who use a higher number of prescription and nonprescription drugs, are obese, have cardiovascular disease, or are depressed (Muller & others, 2017).

CHRONIC DISORDERS

In middle adulthood, the frequency of accidents declines and individuals are less susceptible to colds and allergies than in childhood, adolescence, or early adulthood. Indeed, many individuals live through middle adulthood without having a disease or persistent health problem. However, disease and persistent health problems become more common in middle adulthood for some individuals (Koyanagi & others, 2018).

Chronic disorders are characterized by a slow onset and a long duration. Chronic disorders are rare in early adulthood, increase in middle adulthood, and become common in late adulthood. Chronic disorders account for 86 percent of total health care spending in the United States (Qin & others, 2015). Overall, arthritis is the leading chronic disorder in middle age,

chronic disorders Disorders that are characterized by slow onset and long duration. They are rare in early adulthood, increase during middle adulthood, and become common in late adulthood.

followed by hypertension, but the frequency of chronic disorders in middle age varies by gender. Men have a higher incidence of fatal chronic conditions (such as coronary heart disease, cancer, and stroke); women have a higher incidence of nonfatal ones (such as arthritis, varicose veins, and bursitis).

About 50 percent of U.S. adults have one chronic health condition, and the prevalence of multiple (two or more) chronic health conditions increased from 21.8 percent in 2001 to 25.5 percent in 2012 (Qin & others, 2015). In one analysis, adults with arthritis as one of their multiple chronic conditions had more adverse outcomes (restricted social participation, serious psychological distress, and work limitations) than their counterparts who had multiple chronic conditions but did not have arthritis (Qin & others, 2015).

MORTALITY RATES

Infectious disease was the main cause of death until the middle of the twentieth century. As infectious disease rates declined and more individuals lived through middle age, rates of chronic disorders increased. Chronic diseases are now the main causes of death for individuals in middle adulthood.

In middle age, many deaths are caused by a single, readily identifiable condition, whereas in old age, death is more likely to result from the combined effects of several chronic conditions (Pizza & others, 2011). For many years heart disease was the leading cause of death in middle adulthood, followed by cancer; however, since 2005 more individuals 45 to 64 years of age in the United States died of cancer, followed by cardiovascular disease (Centers for Disease Control and Prevention, 2015). However, between 2011 and 2017 the rate of deaths in middle age due to cardiovascular disease increased 4 percent, likely linked to increased obesity (Centers for Disease Control and Prevention, 2019). Deaths due to cancer in middle age have been declining recently, but cancer continues to be the number one cause of death in middle age, followed by cardiovascular disease. Men have higher mortality rates than women for all of the leading causes of death (Centers for Disease Control and Prevention, 2019).

SEXUALITY

What kinds of changes characterize the sexuality of women and men as they go through middle age? **Climacteric** is a term that is used to describe the midlife transition in which fertility declines. Let's explore the substantial differences in the climacteric experienced by women and men.

climacteric The midlife transition during which fertility declines.

menopause Cessation of a woman's menstrual periods, usually during the late forties or early fifties.

Menopause **Menopause** is the time in middle age, usually during the late forties or early fifties, when a woman's menstrual periods cease. The average age at which U.S. women have their last period is 51 (Mayo Clinic, 2020a). However, there is a large variation in the age at which menopause occurs—from 39 to 59 years of age. A recent Norwegian study of more than 300,000 women found that late menopause was associated with an increased risk of breast cancer (Gottschalk & others, 2020).

The timing of menarche, a girl's first menstruation, has significantly decreased since the mid-nineteenth century, occurring as much as four years earlier in some countries (Susman & Dorn, 2013). Has there been an earlier or later onset in the occurrence of menopause? In the study just mentioned above, the mean age of menopause increased 2½ years in recent decades to 52.7 years (Gottschalk & others, 2020). Also in this study, the number of years between menarche and menopause increased from 36.5 to 40 years.

Perimenopause is the transitional period from normal menstrual periods to no menstrual periods at all, which often takes up to 10 years. Perimenopause usually occurs during the forties but can occur in the thirties (Raglan, Schulkin, & Micks, 2020). One study of 30- to 50-year-old women found that depressed feelings, headaches, moodiness, and heart palpitations were the perimenopausal symptoms that these women most frequently discussed with health-care providers (Lyndaker & Hulton, 2004). Lifestyle factors such as whether women are overweight, smoke, drink heavily, feel depressed, or exercise regularly during perimenopause influence aspects of their future health such as whether they develop cardiovascular disease or chronic illnesses (Honour, 2018; Shorey, Ang, & Lau, 2020). A recent study found that the more minutes per week that women exercised during the menopausal transition, the lower their perceived stress was (Guerin & others, 2019).

Mosuo women, who live in a matriarchal tribe in southern China, have fewer negative menopausal symptoms than women in many cultures.
Patrick Aventurier/Gamma-Rapho/Getty Images

In menopause, production of estrogen by the ovaries declines dramatically, and this decline produces uncomfortable symptoms in some women—"hot flashes," nausea, fatigue, and rapid heartbeat, for example (Hachul & Tufik, 2019). However, cross-cultural studies reveal variations in the menopause experience (Rathnayake & others, 2018). For example, hot flashes are uncommon in Mayan women (Beyene, 1986). Asian women report fewer hot flashes than women in Western societies (Payer, 1991). In a recent study in China, Mosuo women (Mosuo is a matriarchal tribe in southern China where women have the dominant role in society, don't marry, and can take on as many lovers as they desire) had fewer negative menopausal symptoms, higher self-esteem, and better family support than Han Chinese women (the majority ethnic group in China) (Zhang & others, 2016). It is difficult to determine the extent to which these cross-cultural variations are due to genetic, dietary, reproductive, or cultural factors.

For most women, menopause overall is not the highly negative experience it was once thought to be (Brown & others, 2018). Few women have severe physical or psychological problems related to menopause. In fact, a research review concluded that there is no clear evidence that depressive disorders occur more often during menopause than at other times in a woman's reproductive life (Judd, Hickey, & Bryant, 2012).

However, the loss of fertility is an important marker for women—it means that they have to make final decisions about having children. Women in their thirties who have never had children sometimes speak about being "up against the biological clock" because they cannot postpone choices about having children much longer.

Until recently, hormone replacement therapy was often prescribed as treatment for unpleasant side effects of menopause. *Hormone replacement therapy (HRT)* augments the declining levels of reproductive hormone production by the ovaries (Andersson, Borgquist, & Jirstrom, 2018). HRT can consist of various forms of estrogen, usually in combination with a progestin.

The National Institutes of Health recommends that women who have not had a hysterectomy and who are currently taking hormones consult with their doctor to determine whether they should continue the treatment. If they are taking HRT for short-term relief of menopausal symptoms, the benefits may outweigh the risks. HRT also lowers the risk of bone loss and bone fractures in post-menopausal women (de Villiers & others, 2016). Also, research indicates that if women take HRT within 10 years following menopause, it is associated with reduced risk of coronary heart disease (Langer, 2017). However, research indicates that hormone replacement therapy is linked to a slightly higher risk of breast cancer and the longer HRT is taken, the greater the risk of breast cancer (American Cancer Society, 2020; Breastcancer.org, 2020). The current consensus is that HRT increases the risk of breast cancer in women (Breastcancer.org, 2020).

Many middle-aged women are seeking alternatives to HRT such as regular exercise, mindfulness training, dietary supplements, herbal remedies, relaxation therapy, acupuncture, hypnosis, and nonsteroidal medications (Lund & others, 2020; Morardpour & others, 2019). One study revealed that in sedentary women, aerobic training for six months decreased menopausal symptoms, especially night sweats, mood swings, and irritability (Moilanen & others, 2012). Another study found that yoga improved the quality of life of menopausal women (Reed & others, 2014). And in a recent analysis of research it was concluded that mindfulness training is linked to improved psychological adjustment during the menopause transition (Molefi-Youri, 2019).

Hormonal Changes in Middle-Aged Men

Do men go through anything like the menopause that women experience? In other words, is there a male menopause? During middle adulthood, most men do not lose their capacity to father children, although there usually is a modest decline in their sexual hormone level and activity (Abootalebi & others, 2020; Kaufman & others, 2019). They experience hormonal changes in their fifties and sixties, but nothing like the dramatic drop in estrogen that women experience. Testosterone production begins to decline about 1 percent a year during middle adulthood, and sperm count usually declines slowly, but men do not lose their fertility in middle age. The term *male hypogonadism* is used to describe a condition in which the body does not produce enough testosterone (Mayo Clinic, 2020b).

Recently, there has been a dramatic surge of interest in *testosterone replacement therapy* *(TRT)* (Barbonetti, D'Andrea, & Francavilla, 2020; Moon & Park, 2019). For many decades, it was thought that TRT increased the risk of prostate cancer; however, recent studies and research reviews indicate that this is not the case (Corona, Torres, & Maggi, 2020). Recent research indicates that TRT can improve sexual functioning, muscle strength, and bone health (Mayo Clinic, 2020b). One study also found that TRT was associated with increased longevity in men with a low level of testosterone (Comhaire, 2016). Another recent study indicated that TRT-related benefits in quality of life and sexual function were maintained for 36 months after initial treatment (Rosen & others, 2017). And two studies found that TRT improved older men's sexual function as well as their mood (Miner & others, 2013; Okada & others, 2014). Also, some research studies have revealed that testosterone replacement therapy is associated with a lower incidence of having a heart attack or a stroke, as well as a reduction in all-cause mortality (Cheetham & others, 2017; Jones & Kelly, 2018). However, other researchers have not reached these conclusions, and some studies have shown an increase in stroke among men undergoing TRT (Fode & others, 2019).

Erectile dysfunction (ED) (difficulty attaining or maintaining penile erection) affects approximately 50 percent of men 40 to 70 years of age and 75 percent of men over 70 years of age (Mola, 2015). Low testosterone levels can contribute to erectile dysfunction (Huang & others, 2019). Smoking, diabetes, hypertension, elevated cholesterol levels, obesity, depression, and lack of exercise also are associated with erectile problems in middle-aged men (Azab & others, 2020). The main treatment for men with erectile dysfunction has not focused on TRT but on Viagra and similar drugs such as Levitra and Cialis (Krishnappa & others, 2019). Viagra works by allowing increased blood flow into the penis, which produces an erection. Its success rate is in the 60 to 85 percent range (Claes & others, 2010). Low-intensity shockwave therapy, which also has been used in wound healing and musculoskeletal disorders, has recently been used for treating ED (Kalyvianakis & others, 2020; Patel, Pastuszak, & Hotaling, 2019). A recent research review concluded that low-intensity shockwave therapy shows benefits in reducing ED after 6 months of treatment and ongoing but lesser benefits at 1 year, with results weaker overall for older adults (Brunckhorst & others, 2019). In addition, a recent study found that a combined treatment of low-intensity shockwave therapy and Cialis was superior to Cialis alone in reducing ED (Verze & others, 2020). However, too few studies of the efficacy of this therapy have been conducted to draw conclusions at this time about its effectiveness.

erectile dysfunction (ED) The inability to adequately achieve and maintain an erection to attain satisfactory sexual performance.

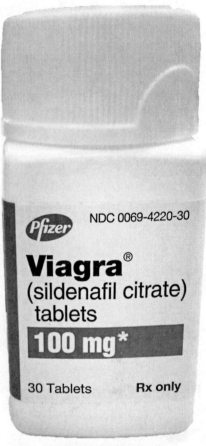

PureRadiancePhoto/Shutterstock

Sexual Attitudes and Behavior Although the ability of men and women to function sexually shows little biological decline in middle adulthood, sexual activity usually occurs less frequently in midlife than in early adulthood (Rees & others, 2018). Figure 2 shows the age trends in frequency of sex from the Sex in America survey. The frequency of having sex was greatest for individuals aged 25 to 29 years old (47 percent had sex twice a week or more) and dropped off for individuals in their fifties (23 percent of 50- to 59-year-old males said they had sex twice a week or more, and only 14 percent of the females in this age group reported this frequency) (Michael & others, 1994). Note, though, that the Sex in America survey may underestimate the frequency of sexual activity of middle-aged adults because the data were collected prior to the widespread use of erectile dysfunction drugs such as Viagra. Other research indicates that middle-aged men want sex more, think about it more, and masturbate more often than middle-aged women (Stones & Stones, 2007). For many other forms of sexual behavior, such as kissing and hugging, sexual touching, and oral sex, male and female middle-aged adults report similar frequency of engagement (Stones & Stones, 2007).

		Percentage Engaging in Sex			
Age Groups	**Not at all**	**A few times per year**	**A few times per month**	**2–3 times a week**	**4 or more times a week**
Men					
18–24	15	21	24	28	12
25–29	7	15	31	36	11
30–39	8	15	37	23	6
40–49	9	18	40	27	6
50–59	11	22	43	20	3
Women					
18–24	11	16	2	9	12
25–29	5	10	38	37	10
30–39	9	16	6	33	6
40–49	15	16	44	20	5
50–59	30	22	35	12	2

FIGURE 2

THE SEX IN AMERICA SURVEY: FREQUENCY OF SEX AT DIFFERENT POINTS IN ADULT DEVELOPMENT. *Why do you think the frequency of sex declines as men and women get older?*

If middle-aged adults have sex less frequently than they did in early adulthood, does it mean they are less satisfied with their sex lives? In a Canadian study of 40- to 64-year-olds, only 30 percent reported that their sexual life was less satisfying than it had been when they were in their twenties (Wright, 2006). In a recent study, middle-aged and older adults who had sex more frequently also had better overall cognitive functioning, especially working memory and executive function (Wright, Jenks, & Demeyere, 2019). Further, in a recent study of individuals 50 years and older, a past-year decline in sexual desire or frequency of sexual activities was associated with an increase in depressive symptoms and lower quality of life (Jackson & others, 2019).

Living with a spouse or partner makes all the difference in whether people engage in sexual activity, especially for women over 40 years of age. In one study conducted as part of the Midlife in the United States Study (MIDUS), 95 percent of women in their forties with partners said that they had been sexually active in the last six months, compared with only 53 percent of those without partners (Brim, 1999). By their fifties, 88 percent of women living with a partner have been sexually active in the last six months, but only 37 percent of those who are neither married nor living with someone say they have had sex in the last six months.

A large-scale study of U.S. adults 40 to 80 years of age found that premature ejaculation (26 percent) and erectile difficulties (22 percent) were the most common sexual problems of older men, while lack of sexual interest (33 percent) and lubrication difficulties (21 percent) were the most common sexual problems of older women (Laumann & others, 2009).

A person's health in middle age is a key factor in sexual activity (Rees & others, 2018). For example, a study of aging adults 55 years and older revealed that their level of sexual activity was associated with their physical and mental health (Bach & others, 2013). Social and relationship factors also are important in middle age sexual functioning. For example, in a recent study of healthy middle-aged women, interpersonal aspects such as emotional support and relationship satisfaction, as well the personality traits of optimism and self-esteem, were key predictors of the quality of sexual functioning (Memone, Fiacco, & Ehlert, 2019).

Review Connect Reflect

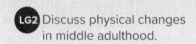 **LG2** Discuss physical changes in middle adulthood.

Review

- What are some key physical changes in middle adulthood?
- What characterizes the nature of chronic disorders?
- What are the main causes of death in middle age?
- What are the sexual lives of middle-aged adults like?

Connect

- In this section, you read that the production of estrogen by the ovaries declines dramatically in menopause. What have you learned about estrogen's role in puberty?

Reflect *Your Own Personal Journey of Life*

- If you are a young or middle-aged adult, what can you do at this point in your life to optimize your health in middle age? If you are an older adult, what could you have done differently to optimize your health in middle age?

3 Cognitive Development   **LG3** Identify cognitive changes in middle adulthood.

Intelligence   Information Processing

We have seen that middle-aged adults may not see as well, run as fast, or be as healthy as they were in their twenties and thirties. But what about their cognitive skills? Do these skills decline as we enter and move through middle adulthood? To answer this question, we will explore the possibility of age-related cognitive changes in intelligence and information processing.

INTELLIGENCE

Our exploration of possible changes in intelligence in middle adulthood focuses on the concepts of fluid and crystallized intelligence, the Seattle Longitudinal Study, and cohort effects.

Fluid and Crystallized Intelligence   John Horn argues that some abilities begin to decline in middle age while others increase (Horn & Donaldson, 1980). Horn maintains that **crystallized intelligence,** an individual's accumulated information and verbal skills, continues to increase in middle adulthood, whereas **fluid intelligence,** one's ability to reason abstractly, begins to decline in middle adulthood (see Figure 3). However, in a recent large-scale study, fluid intelligence declined in individuals 65 years of age and older but not in those who were 45 to 60 years old (Cornelis & others, 2019).

Horn's data were collected in a cross-sectional manner. Remember that a cross-sectional study assesses individuals of different ages at the same point in time. For example, a cross-sectional study might assess the intelligence of different groups of 40-, 50-, and 60-year-olds in a single evaluation, such as in 1980. The 40-year-olds in the study would have been born in 1940 and the 60-year-olds in 1920—different eras that offered different economic and educational opportunities. The 60-year-olds likely had fewer educational opportunities as they grew up. Thus, if we find differences between 40- and 60-year-olds on intelligence tests when they are assessed cross-sectionally, these differences might be due to cohort effects related to educational differences rather than to age.

By contrast, in a longitudinal study, the same individuals are studied over a period of time. Thus, a longitudinal study of intelligence in middle adulthood might consist of giving the same intelligence test to the same individuals when they are 40, 50, and 60 years of age. As we see next, whether data on intelligence are collected cross-sectionally or longitudinally can make a difference in what is found about changes in crystallized and fluid intelligence and about intellectual decline (Schaie, 2011a, b, 2013).

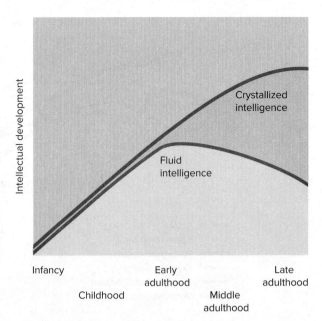

FIGURE 3

FLUID AND CRYSTALLIZED INTELLECTUAL DEVELOPMENT ACROSS THE LIFE SPAN. According to Horn, crystallized intelligence (based on cumulative learning experiences) increases throughout the life span, but fluid intelligence (the ability to perceive and manipulate information) steadily declines from middle adulthood onward.

The Seattle Longitudinal Study   The Seattle Longitudinal Study that involves extensive evaluation of intellectual abilities during adulthood was initiated by K. Warner Schaie (1994, 1996, 2005, 2010, 2011a, b, 2013). Participants have been assessed at seven-year intervals between 1956 and 2012. Five hundred individuals initially were tested in 1956, and new waves of participants are added periodically. The main focus in the Seattle Longitudinal Study has been on individual change and stability in intelligence, and the study is regarded as one of the most thorough examinations of how people develop and change as they go through adulthood.

The main cognitive abilities tested in this study are:

- *Verbal comprehension* (ability to understand ideas expressed in words)
- *Verbal memory* (ability to encode and recall meaningful language units, such as a list of words)
- *Numeric facility* (ability to perform simple mathematical computations such as addition, subtraction, and multiplication)
- *Spatial orientation* (ability to visualize and mentally rotate stimuli in two- and three-dimensional space)
- *Inductive reasoning* (ability to recognize and understand patterns and relationships in a problem and to use this understanding to solve other instances of the problem)
- *Perceptual speed* (ability to quickly and accurately make simple discriminations in visual stimuli)

As shown in Figure 4, the highest level of functioning for four of the six intellectual abilities occurred in middle adulthood (Schaie, 2013). For both women and men, peak performance on verbal ability, verbal memory, inductive reasoning, and spatial orientation was attained in middle age. Only two of the six abilities—numeric facility and perceptual speed—declined during middle age. Perceptual speed showed the earliest decline, actually beginning

┌ ─ ─ ─ ─ ─ ─ ─ ─ ─ ─ ➤
¦ developmental **connection**
¦ **Cognitive Theory**
¦ A fifth, postformal stage of cognitive
¦ development has been proposed to
¦ describe cognitive advances in early
¦ adulthood. Connect to "Physical and
¦ Cognitive Development in Early
¦ Adulthood."
◄ ─ ─ ─ ─ ─ ─ ─ ─ ─ ─ ─ ┘

crystallized intelligence Accumulated information and verbal skills, which increase in middle adulthood, according to Horn.

fluid intelligence The ability to reason abstractly, which begins to decline from middle adulthood onward, according to Horn.

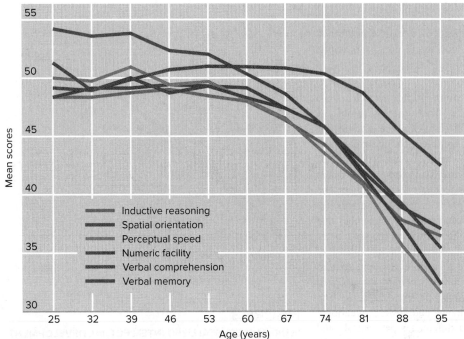

FIGURE 4

LONGITUDINAL CHANGES IN SIX INTELLECTUAL ABILITIES FROM AGE 25 TO AGE 95.
Source: K. W. Schaie: "Longitudinal Changes in Six Intellectual Abilities from Age 25 to Age 95"
Figure 5.7a, in *Developmental Influences on Intelligence: The Seattle Longitudinal Study* (2nd ed.),
2013, p. 162.

in early adulthood. Interestingly, in terms of John Horn's ideas that were discussed earlier, for the participants in the Seattle Longitudinal Study, middle age was a time of peak performance for some aspects of both crystallized intelligence (verbal ability) and fluid intelligence (spatial orientation and inductive reasoning).

When Schaie (1994) assessed intellectual abilities both cross-sectionally and longitudinally, he found declines to be more likely in the cross-sectional than in the longitudinal assessments. For example, as shown in Figure 5, when assessed cross-sectionally, inductive reasoning showed a consistent decline during middle adulthood. In contrast, when assessed longitudinally, inductive reasoning increased until the end of middle adulthood when it began to show a slight decline. In Schaie's (2008, 2009, 2010, 2011a, b, 2013, 2016a, b) view, it is in middle adulthood, not early adulthood, that people reach a peak in many intellectual skills. Some researchers have found that cross-sectional studies indicate that more than 90 percent of cognitive decline in aging is due to a slowing of processing speed, whereas longitudinal studies reveal that 20 percent or less of cognitive decline is due to slowing of processing speed (MacDonald & others, 2003; MacDonald & Stawski, 2015, 2016; Stawski, Sliwinski, & Hofer, 2013).

In further analysis, Schaie (2007) examined generational differences in parents and their children over a seven-year time frame from 60 to 67 years of age. That is, parents were assessed when they were 60 to 67 years of age; and when their children reached 60 to 67 years of age, they also were assessed. Higher levels of cognitive functioning occurred for the second generation in inductive reasoning, verbal memory, and spatial orientation, whereas the first generation scored higher on numeric ability. Noteworthy was the finding that the parent generation showed cognitive decline from 60 to 67 years of age, but their offspring showed stability or modest increases in cognitive functioning across the same age range.

Such differences across generations involve cohort effects. In one analysis, Schaie (2011b) concluded that the advances in cognitive functioning in middle age that have occurred in recent decades are likely due to factors such as educational attainment, occupational structures (increasing numbers of workers in professional occupations involving complex work), health care and lifestyles, immigration, and social interventions in poverty. The impressive gains in cognitive functioning in recent cohorts have been documented more clearly for fluid intelligence than for crystallized intelligence (Schaie, 2011b).

The results from Schaie's study that have been described so far focus on average cognitive stability or change for all participants across middle adulthood. Schaie and Sherry Willis (Schaie, 2005; Willis & Schaie, 2005) examined individual differences for the participants in the Seattle study and found substantial individual variations. They classified participants as "decliners," "stable," or "gainers" for three categories—numeric ability, delayed recall (a verbal memory task), and word fluency—from 46 to 60 years of age. The largest percentage of decline (31 percent) or gain (16 percent) occurred for delayed recall; the largest percentage of stable scores (79 percent) occurred for numeric ability. Word fluency declined in 20 percent of the individuals from 46 to 60 years of age.

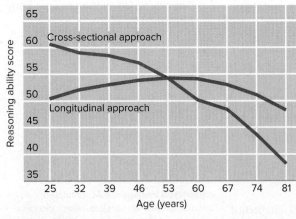

FIGURE 5

CROSS-SECTIONAL AND LONGITUDINAL COMPARISONS OF INTELLECTUAL CHANGE IN MIDDLE ADULTHOOD. *Why do you think reasoning ability peaks during middle adulthood?*

Might the individual variations in cognitive trajectories in midlife be linked to cognitive impairment in late adulthood? In Willis and Schaie's analysis, cognitively normal and impaired older adults did not differ on measures of vocabulary, spatial orientation, and numeric ability in middle adulthood. However, declines in memory (immediate recall and delayed recall), word fluency, and perceptual speed in middle adulthood were linked to neuropsychologists' ratings of the individuals' cognitive impairment in late adulthood.

Some researchers disagree with Schaie that middle adulthood is a time when the level of functioning in a number of cognitive domains is maintained or even increases (Finch, 2009). For example, Timothy Salthouse (2009, 2012, 2014, 2016, 2017, 2018, 2019) recently has argued that cross-sectional research on aging and cognitive functioning should not be dismissed and that this research indicates reasoning, memory, spatial visualization, and processing speed begin declining in early adulthood and show further decline in the fifties. Salthouse (2009, 2012) agrees that cognitive functioning involving accumulated knowledge, such as vocabulary and general information, does not show early age-related decline but rather continues to increase at least until 60 years of age. Salthouse (2014, 2016) recently has argued that a main reason for different trends in longitudinal and cross-sectional comparisons of cognitive functioning is that prior experience with tests increases scores the next time a test is taken.

K. Warner Schaie (*right*) is one of the leading pioneers in the field of life-span development. He is shown here with two older adults who are actively using their cognitive skills. Schaie's research represents one of the most thorough examinations of how individuals develop and change as they go through the adult years.
Courtesy of Dr. K. Warner Schaie

Salthouse (2009, 2012, 2018, 2019) has emphasized that a lower level of cognitive functioning in early and middle adulthood is likely due to age-related neurobiological decline. Cross-sectional studies have shown that the following neurobiological factors decline during the twenties and thirties, then continue to decline in middle adulthood: regional brain volume, cortical thickness, synaptic density, some aspects of myelination, the functioning of some aspects of neurotransmitters such as dopamine and serotonin, blood flow in the cerebral cortex, and the accumulation of tangles in neurons (Del Tredici & Braak, 2008; Finch, 2009; Hsu & others, 2008; Pieperhoff & others, 2008).

Schaie (2009, 2010, 2011a, b, 2013) continues to emphasize that longitudinal studies hold the key to determining age-related changes in cognitive functioning and that middle age is the time when many cognitive skills actually peak. In the next decade, expanding research on age-related neurobiological changes and their possible links to cognitive skills should further refine our knowledge about age-related cognitive functioning in the adult years (Kinugawa, 2019; Strandberg, 2019).

INFORMATION PROCESSING

As we saw in our discussion of theories of cognitive development from infancy through adolescence, the information-processing approach provides another way to examine cognitive abilities (Braithwaite, Tian, & Siegler, 2018). Among the information-processing changes that take place in middle adulthood are those involved in speed of processing information, memory, expertise, and practical problem-solving skills.

Speed of Information Processing As we saw in Schaie's (1994, 1996, 2011a, b, 2013) Seattle Longitudinal Study, perceptual speed begins declining in early adulthood and continues to decline in middle adulthood. A common way to assess speed of information processing is through a reaction-time task, in which individuals simply press a button as soon as they see a light appear. Middle-aged adults are slower to push the button when the light appears than young adults are. However, keep in mind that the decline is not dramatic—under 1 second in most investigations.

A current research interest focuses on possible causes for declining speed of processing information in adults (Siedlecki & others, 2020; Tucker-Drob, Brandmaier, & Lindenberger, 2019). This research may involve different levels of analysis, such as cognitive ("maintaining goals, switching between tasks, or preserving internal representations despite distraction"), neuroanatomical ("changes in specific brain regions, such as the prefrontal cortex"), and neurochemical ("changes in neurotransmitter systems" such as dopamine) (Hartley, 2006, p. 201).

Memory In Schaie's (1994, 1996, 2013) Seattle Longitudinal Study, verbal memory peaked during the fifties. However, in some other studies verbal memory has shown a decline

developmental **connection**

Memory

Some types of memory decline more than others in older adults. Connect to "Cognitive Development in Late Adulthood."

developmental **connection**

Memory

Working memory plays an important role in many aspects of children's cognitive and language development. Connect to "Physical and Cognitive Development in Middle and Late Childhood."

developmental **connection**

Information Processing

One study found that 10- and 11-year-old children who were experienced chess players ("experts") remembered more about chess pieces than college students who were not chess players ("novices"). Connect to "Physical and Cognitive Development in Middle and Late Childhood."

in middle age, especially when assessed in cross-sectional studies (Salthouse, 2018, 2019). For example, when people were asked to remember lists of words, numbers, or meaningful prose, younger adults outperformed middle-aged adults (Salthouse & Skovronek, 1992). Although there still is some controversy about whether memory declines during middle adulthood, most experts conclude that it does decline at some point during this period of adult development (Davis & others, 2017; Salthouse, 2019). However, some experts argue that studies indicating a decline in memory during middle age often have compared young adults in their twenties with older middle-aged adults in their late fifties and even have included some individuals in their sixties (Schaie, 2000). In this view, memory decline is either nonexistent or minimal in the early part of middle age but does occur in the latter part of middle age or in late adulthood.

Cognitive aging expert Denise Park (2001) argues that starting in late middle age, more time is needed to learn new information. The slowdown in learning new information has been linked to changes in *working memory*, the mental "workbench" where individuals manipulate and assemble information when making decisions, solving problems, and comprehending written and spoken language (Baddeley, 2020). In this view, in late middle age working memory capacity becomes more limited (Baddeley, Hitch, & Allen, 2019). Think of this situation as an overcrowded desk with many items in disarray. As a result of the overcrowding and disarray, long-term memory becomes less reliable, more time is needed to enter new information into long-term storage, and more time is required to retrieve the information. Thus, Park concludes that much of the blame for declining memory in late middle age is a result of information overload that builds up as we go through the adult years.

Memory decline is more likely to occur when individuals don't use effective memory strategies, such as organization and imagery (Hertzog & others, 2019). By organizing lists of phone numbers into different categories, or imagining the phone numbers as representing different objects around the house, many individuals can improve their memory in middle adulthood. Further, in recent research, having a higher level of education and engaging in frequent physical exercise were linked to less decline in middle-aged and older adults' episodic memory (retention of information about the details of life's happenings) (Liu & Lachman, 2019). And a recent study of middle-aged and older adults found that a 12-week resistance exercise training program improved their delayed verbal memory performance (Marston & others, 2019).

Expertise   Because it takes so long to attain, expertise often shows up more in middle adulthood than in early adulthood (Charness & Krampe, 2008). Recall that expertise involves having extensive, highly organized knowledge and understanding of a particular domain. Developing expertise and becoming an "expert" in a field usually requires many years of experience, learning, and effort (Ericsson, 2020).

Strategies that distinguish experts from novices include these:

- Experts are more likely to rely on their accumulated experience to solve problems.
- Experts often process information automatically and analyze it more efficiently when solving a problem in their domain than novices do.
- Experts have better strategies and shortcuts for solving problems in their domain than novices do.
- Experts are more creative and flexible in solving problems in their domain than novices are.

Practical Problem Solving   Everyday problem solving is another important aspect of cognition (Chen & others, 2018). Nancy Denney (1986, 1990) observed circumstances such as how young and middle-aged adults handled a landlord who would not fix their stove and what they did if a bank failed to deposit a check. She found that the ability to solve such practical problems improved through the forties and fifties as individuals accumulated practical experience.

However, since Denney's research other studies have been conducted on everyday problem-solving and decision-making effectiveness across the adult years (Cheek, Piercy, & Kohlenberg, 2015). In a recent study of individuals from 24 to 93 years of age, everyday problem solving showed an increase in performance from early adulthood to middle adulthood, with performance then beginning to decrease at about 50 years of age (Chen, Hertzog, & Park, 2017). Also in this study, fluid intelligence predicted performance on everyday problem solving in young adults but with increasing age, crystallized intelligence became a better predictor.

4 Careers, Work, and Leisure

 LG4 Characterize career development, work, and leisure in middle adulthood.

Work in Midlife   Career Challenges and Changes   Leisure

What are some issues that workers face in midlife? What role does leisure play in the lives of middle-aged adults?

WORK IN MIDLIFE

The role of work, whether one works in a full-time career, in a part-time job, as a volunteer, or as a homemaker, is central during middle adulthood (Cahill, Giandrea, & Quinn, 2016). Many middle-aged adults reach their peak in position and earnings. However, they may also be saddled with multiple financial burdens including rent or mortgage, child care, medical bills, home repairs, college tuition, loans to family members, or bills from nursing homes.

In 2019 in the United States, 81.1 percent of 45- to 54-year-olds were in the workforce (a decrease of 1.8 percent since 2000 but an increase of 1.7 percent since 2015) and 65.2 percent of 55- to 64-year-olds were in the workforce (an increase of 9.8 percent since 2000 and an increase of 1.1 percent since 2015) (Mislinski, 2019). Later in the text, we will describe various aspects of workforce participation of individuals 65 and over in the United States, which has increased a remarkable 59.9 percent since 2000 and 9.9 percent since 2015 (Mislinski, 2019).

Do middle-aged workers perform their work as competently as younger adults? Age-related declines occur in some occupations, such as air traffic controllers and professional athletes, but for most jobs, no differences have been found in the work performance of young adults and middle-aged adults (Salthouse, 2012; Sturman, 2003).

However, leading Finnish researcher Clas-Hakan Nygard (2013) concludes from his longitudinal research that the ability to work effectively peaks during middle age because of increased motivation, work experience, employer loyalty, and better strategic thinking. Nygard also has found that the quality of work done by employees in middle age is linked to how much their work is appreciated and how well they get along with their immediate supervisors. And Nygard and his colleagues discovered that work ability in middle age was linked to mortality and disability 28 years later (von Bonsdorff & others, 2011, 2012).

developmental **connection**

Work

Work defines people in fundamental ways, influencing their financial standing, housing, the way they spend their time, where they live, their friendships, and their health. Connect to "Physical and Cognitive Development in Early Adulthood."

What characterizes work in middle adulthood?
Ariel Skelley/Blend Images/Getty Images

For many people, midlife is a time of evaluation, assessment, and reflection in terms of the work they are doing now and what they want to do in the future (Cahill, Giandrea, & Quinn, 2015). Among the work issues that some people face in midlife are recognizing limitations in career progress, deciding whether to change jobs or careers, determining how and when to rebalance family and work, and planning for retirement (Sterns & Huyck, 2001).

Couples increasingly have both spouses in the workforce who are expecting to retire. Historically retirement has been a male transition, but today far more couples are planning two retirements—his and hers (Moen, 2009b; Moen, Kelly, & Magennis, 2008).

Economic downturns and recessions in the United States have forced some middle-aged individuals into premature retirement because of job loss and fear of not being able to reenter the work force (Cahill, Giandrea, & Quinn, 2016). Such premature retirement also may result in accumulating insufficient financial resources to cover an increasingly long retirement period (de Wind & others, 2014).

CAREER CHALLENGES AND CHANGES

Middle-aged workers face several important challenges in the twenty-first century (Brand, 2014). These include the globalization of work, rapid developments in information technologies, downsizing of organizations, early retirement, and concerns about pensions and health care.

Globalization has replaced what was once a primarily White male workforce with employees of different ethnic and national backgrounds (Cahill, Giandrea, & Quinn, 2016; Short, 2015a). To improve profits, many companies are restructuring, downsizing, and outsourcing jobs. One of the outcomes of these changes is to offer incentives to middle-aged employees to retire early—in their fifties, or in some cases even forties, rather than their sixties.

The decline in defined-benefit pensions and increased uncertainty about the fate of health insurance are decreasing the sense of personal control among middle-aged workers. As a consequence, many are delaying retirement.

Some midlife career changes are self-motivated; others are the consequence of losing one's job (Brand, 2014). A recent analysis found that for many U.S. workers 50 years of age and older, the decision to leave a job won't be theirs (Gosselin, 2019). In this study, more than 50 percent of these workers are pushed out of longtime jobs before they choose to retire, suffering considerable financial damage. Also, only 10 percent of these workers ever again earn as much as they did before they were forced to leave their longtime jobs.

However, some individuals in middle age decide that they don't want to spend the rest of their lives doing the same kind of work they have been doing (Hoyer & Roodin, 2009). One aspect of middle adulthood involves adjusting idealistic hopes to accommodate realistic possibilities in light of how much time individuals have before they retire and how fast they are reaching their occupational goals (Levinson, 1978). If individuals perceive that they are behind schedule, if their goals are unrealistic, they don't like the work they are doing, or their job has become too stressful, they could become motivated to change jobs.

A final point to make about career development in middle adulthood is that cognitive factors earlier in development are linked to occupational attainment in middle age. In one study, task persistence at 13 years of age was related to occupational success in middle age (Andersson & Bergman, 2011).

LEISURE

As adults, not only must we learn how to work well, but we also need to learn how to relax and enjoy leisure (Byambasukh, Sneider, & Corpeleijn, 2020; Finkel, Andel, & Pedersen, 2018). **Leisure** refers to the pleasant times after work when individuals are free to pursue activities and interests of their own choosing—hobbies, sports, or reading, for example. In one analysis of research on what U.S. adults regret the most, not engaging in more leisure was one of the top six regrets (Roese & Summerville, 2005).

Leisure can be an especially important aspect of middle adulthood (Nicolaisen, Thorsen, & Eriksen, 2012). By middle adulthood, more money is available to many individuals, and there may be more free time and paid vacations. In short, midlife changes may produce expanded opportunities for leisure.

Sigmund Freud once commented that the two things adults need to do well to adapt to society's demands are to work and to love. To his list we add "to play." In our fast-paced society, it is all too easy to get caught up in the frenzied, hectic pace of our achievement-oriented work world and ignore leisure and play. Imagine your life as a middle-aged adult. *What would be the ideal mix of work and leisure? What leisure activities do you want to enjoy as a middle-aged adult?*
Compassionate Eye Foundation/Colorblind Images/Digital Vision/Getty Images

leisure The pleasant times after work when individuals are free to pursue activities and interests of their own choosing.

In one study, 12,338 men 35 to 57 years of age were assessed each year for five years regarding whether or not they took vacations (Gump & Matthews, 2000). Then the researchers examined the medical and death records over nine years for men who lived for at least a year after the last vacation survey. Compared with those who never took vacations, men who went on annual vacations were 21 percent less likely to die over the nine years and 32 percent less likely to die of coronary heart disease. And a Finnish study found that engaging in less leisure-time activity in middle age was linked to increased risk of cognitive impairment in late adulthood (23 years later) (Virta & others, 2013).

Adults at midlife need to begin preparing psychologically for retirement. Constructive and fulfilling leisure activities in middle adulthood are an important part of this preparation. If an adult develops leisure activities that can be continued into retirement, the transition from work to retirement can be less stressful.

Also, the type of leisure activity may be linked to different outcomes (Hagnas & others, 2018; Kelley & Kelley, 2019). A recent study found that engaging in higher complexity of work before retirement was associated with a smaller decline in cognitive performance in retirement (Andel, Finkel, & Pedersen, 2016). However, when those who had worked in occupations with fewer cognitive challenges prior to retirement engaged in physical (sports, walking) and cognitive (reading books, doing puzzles, and playing chess) leisure activities during retirement, they showed less cognitive decline. Also, a Danish longitudinal study of 20- to 93-year-olds found that those who engaged in a light level of leisure-time physical activity lived 2.8 years longer, those who engaged in a moderate level of leisure-time physical activity lived 4.5 years longer, and those who engaged in high level of leisure-time physical activity lived 5.5 years longer (Schnohr & others, 2017).

Further, a study revealed that when middle-aged adults engaged in active leisure pursuits they had a higher level of cognitive performance in late adulthood (Ihle & others, 2015). In another study, individuals who engaged in a greater amount of sedentary screen-based leisure-time activity (TV, video games, computer use) had shorter telomere length (telomeres cover the end of chromosomes, and as people age their telomeres become shorter and this shorter telomere length is linked to mortality) (Loprinzi, 2015). Further, a recent study found that middle-aged and older adult women who engaged in a higher level of leisure-time physical activity were more likely to report experiencing positive affect (Holahan & others, 2020). And a recent European study of middle-aged adults revealed that the more they engaged in physical activity during their leisure time, the less likely they were to be depressed (Marques & others, 2020).

Research also has highlighted links between stress and leisure time (Qian, Yamal, & Almeida, 2014a, b, c). In one study, after individuals experienced daily stressful events, if they engaged in more leisure time than usual on those days, the leisure time served as a positive coping strategy in improving their moods. Also, a recent study indicated that the more individuals engaged in leisure-time physical activity, the less work-related stress they had (Du Prel, Siegrist, & Borchart, 2019).

Review Connect Reflect

 LG4 Characterize career development, work, and leisure in middle adulthood.

Review

- What are some issues that workers face in midlife?
- What career challenges and changes might people experience in middle adulthood?
- What characterizes leisure in middle age?

Connect

- In this section you learned about the leisure time of adults in middle age.

What have you learned about cultural differences and leisure time in adolescence?

Reflect *Your Own Personal Journey of Life*

- What do you want your work life and leisure to be like in middle age? If you are middle-aged, what are your work life and leisure activities like now? If you are an older adult, what were these activities like for you in middle age?

LG5 Explain the roles of religion, spirituality, and meaning in life during middle adulthood.

Religion, Spirituality, and Adult Lives

Religion, Spirituality, and Health

Meaning in Life

What roles do religion and spirituality play in our development as adults? Is the meaning of life an important theme for many middle-aged adults?

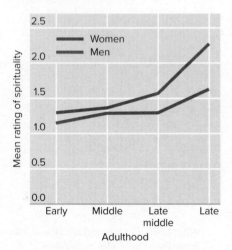

What roles do religion and spirituality play in the lives of middle-aged adults?
A katz/Shutterstock

FIGURE 6

LEVEL OF SPIRITUALITY IN FOUR ADULT AGE PERIODS. In a longitudinal study, the spirituality of individuals in four different adult age periods—early (thirties), middle (forties), late middle (mid-fifties/early sixties), and late (late sixties/early seventies) adulthood—was assessed (Wink & Dillon, 2002). Based on responses to open-ended questions in interviews, the spirituality of the individuals was coded on a 5-point scale with 5 being the highest level of spirituality and 1 the lowest.

RELIGION, SPIRITUALITY, AND ADULT LIVES

Can religion be distinguished from spirituality? Pamela King and her colleagues (2011) provide the following distinctions:

- **Religion** is an organized set of beliefs, practices, rituals, and symbols that increases an individual's connection to a sacred or transcendent other (God, higher power, or ultimate truth).

- **Religiousness** refers to the degree of affiliation with an organized religion, participation in its prescribed rituals and practices, connection with its beliefs, and involvement in a community of believers.

- **Spirituality** involves experiencing something beyond oneself in a transcendent manner and living in a way that benefits others and society.

In thinking about religion, spirituality, and adult development, it is important to consider the role of individual differences. Religion and spirituality are powerful influences for some adults but hold little or no significance for others (Krause & Hayward, 2016; McCullough & others, 2005). In a recent national poll, 92 percent of U.S. adults said that they believe in God and 50 percent reported that religion is very important to them (Pew Research Center, 2015). Further, the influence of religion and spirituality in people's lives may change as they develop (Sapp, 2010). In John Clausen's (1993) longitudinal investigation, some individuals who had been strongly religious in their early adult years became less so in middle age, while others became more religious in middle age.

In the MacArthur Foundation Study of Midlife Development, more than 70 percent of U.S. middle-aged adults described themselves as religious and said that spirituality was a major part of their lives (Brim, 1999). In a longitudinal study of individuals from their early thirties through their early seventies, a significant increase in spirituality occurred between late middle adulthood (mid-fifties/early sixties) and late adulthood (Wink & Dillon, 2002) (see Figure 6). Another survey found that 77 percent of 30- to 49-year-olds and 84 percent of 50- to 64-year-olds reported having a religious affiliation, compared with 67 percent of 18- to 29-year-olds and 90 percent of adults age 90 and over (Pew Research Center, 2012).

Women have consistently shown a stronger interest in religion and spirituality than men have. In the longitudinal study just described, the spirituality of women increased more than that of men in the second half of life (Wink & Dillon, 2002). And in a recent national U.S. study, 60 percent of women compared with 47 percent of men said that religion is very important in their lives (Pew Research Center, 2016).

RELIGION, SPIRITUALITY, AND HEALTH

How might religion influence physical health? Some cults and religious sects encourage behaviors that can be damaging to health, such as ignoring sound medical advice (Manca, 2013). For individuals in the religious mainstream, researchers increasingly are finding that

Religion, Spirituality, and Coping

What is the connection between religion, spirituality, and the ability to cope with stress? Researchers are increasingly finding that religion and spirituality are related to well-being (Krause, 2019; Milner & others, 2019). One study revealed that highly religious individuals were less likely than their moderately religious, somewhat religious, and non-religious counterparts to be psychologically distressed (Park, 2013). Also, in a study of 850 medically ill patients admitted to an acute-care hospital, religious coping was related to lower rates of depression (Koenig & others, 1992).

Religious coping is often beneficial during times of high stress (Carney & Park, 2018). For example, in one study individuals were divided into those who were experiencing high stress and those with low stress (Manton, 1989). In the high-stress group, spiritual support was significantly related to low rates of depression and high levels of self-esteem. No such links were found in the low-stress group. One study revealed that when religion was an important aspect of people's lives, they frequently prayed, had positive religious core beliefs, worried less, were less anxious, and had a lower level of depressive symptoms (Rosmarin, Krumrei, & Andersson, 2009).

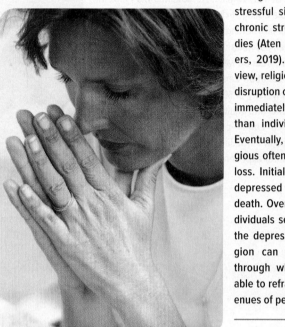

How is religion linked to the ability to cope with stress?
Image Source/Alamy Stock Photo

A recent interest in linking religion and coping focuses on **meaning-making coping**, which involves drawing on beliefs, values, and goals to change the meaning of a stressful situation, especially in times of chronic stress such as when a loved one dies (Aten & others, 2019; Rabelais & others, 2019). In Crystal Park's (2007, 2013) view, religious individuals experience more disruption of their beliefs, values, and goals immediately after the death of a loved one than individuals who are not religious. Eventually, though, individuals who are religious often show better adjustment to the loss. Initially, religion is linked with more depressed feelings about a loved one's death. Over time, however, as religious individuals search for meaning in their loss, the depressed feelings lessen. Thus, religion can serve as a meaning system through which bereaved individuals are able to reframe their loss and even find avenues of personal growth.

If religion is linked to the ability to cope with stress better and if stress is linked to disease (as indicated earlier in the chapter), what can be concluded about a possible indirect link between religion and disease?

spirituality/religion is positively linked to health (Krause, 2019). In a recent study, spiritual well-being predicted which heart failure patients would still be alive five years later (Park & others, 2016). In another study, adults who did volunteer work had lower resting pulse rates, and their resting pulse rates improved if they were more deeply committed to religion (Krause, Ironson, & Hill, 2017). And in one study of middle-aged adults, those who attended church had a lower level of allostatic load (a wearing down of one's body because of constant stress) than their counterparts who did not attend church (Bruce & others, 2017). In an analysis of a number of studies, adults with a higher level of spirituality/religion had an 18 percent reduction in mortality (Lucchetti, Lucchetti, & Koenig, 2011). In this analysis, a high level of spirituality/religion had a stronger link to longevity than 60 percent of 25 other health interventions (such as eating fruits and vegetables and taking statin drugs for cardiovascular disease). In *Connecting Development to Life,* we explore links between religion, spirituality, and coping.

In sum, various dimensions of religion and coping can help some individuals cope more effectively with challenges in their lives (Krause, 2019; Milner & others, 2019). Religious counselors often advise people about mental health and coping. To read about the work of one religious counselor, see *Connecting with Careers.*

religion An organized set of beliefs, practices, rituals, and symbols that increases an individual's connection to a sacred or transcendent other (God, higher power, or higher truth).

religiousness The degree to which an individual is affiliated with an organized religion, participates in prescribed rituals and practices, feels a sense of connection with its beliefs, and is involved in a community of believers.

spirituality Experiencing something beyond oneself in a transcendent manner and living in a way that benefits others and society.

meaning-making coping Drawing on beliefs, values, and goals to change the meaning of a stressful situation, especially in times of chronic stress such as when a loved one dies.

Gabriel Dy-Liacco, University Professor and Pastoral Counselor

Gabriel Dy-Liacco is a professor in religious and pastoral counseling at Regent University in Virginia Beach, Virginia. He obtained his Ph.D. in pastoral counseling from Loyola College in Maryland and has worked as a psychotherapist in mental health settings such as a substance-abuse program, military family center, psychiatric clinic, and community mental health center. Earlier in his career he was a pastoral counselor at the Pastoral Counseling and Consultation Centers of Greater Washington, D.C., and taught at Loyola University in Maryland. As a pastoral counselor, he works with adolescents and adults in the aspects of their lives that they show the most concern about—psychological, spiritual, or the interface of both. Having lived in Peru, Japan, and the Philippines, he brings considerable multicultural experience to teaching and counseling settings.

Gabriel Dy-Liacco, university professor and pastoral counselor.
Courtesy of Dr. Gabriel Dy-Liacco

---

developmental connection

Religion

Religion and spirituality play important roles in the lives of many older adults. Connect to "Cognitive Development in Late Adulthood."

MEANING IN LIFE

Austrian psychiatrist Viktor Frankl's mother, father, brother, and wife died in the concentration camps and gas chambers in Auschwitz, Poland. Frankl survived the concentration camp and went on to write about meaning in life. In his book *Man's Search for Meaning*, Frankl (1984) emphasized each person's uniqueness and the finiteness of life. He argued that examining the finiteness of our existence and the certainty of death adds meaning to life. If life were not finite, said Frankl, we could spend our life doing just about anything we pleased because time would continue forever.

Frankl said that the three most distinct human qualities are spirituality, freedom, and responsibility. Spirituality, in his view, does not have a religious underpinning. Rather, it refers to a human being's uniqueness of spirit, philosophy, and mind. Frankl proposed that people need to ask themselves questions such as why they exist, what they want from life, and what the meaning of their life might be. Also, in a recent U.S. study, when participants were asked to describe what provides them with a sense of meaning in life, 69 percent said family, 34 percent said career, and 20 percent said spirituality and faith (Pew Research Center, 2018).

It is in middle adulthood that individuals begin to be faced with death more often, especially the deaths of parents and other older relatives. Also, when facing less time ahead of them than behind them, many individuals in middle age begin to ask and evaluate the questions that Frankl proposed (Cohen, 2009). And, as indicated in *Connecting Development to Life*, meaning-making coping is especially helpful in times of chronic stress and loss.

Having a sense of meaning in life can lead to clearer guidelines for living one's life and enhanced motivation to take care of oneself and reach goals (Ju, 2017). Also, a recent meta-analysis concluded that a higher level of meaning in life is linked to better physical health (Czekierda & others, 2017). Roy Baumeister and Kathleen Vohs (2002, pp. 610-611) argue that this quest can be understood in terms of four main needs for meaning that guide how people try to make sense of their lives:

- *Need for purpose.* "Present events draw meaning from their connection with future events." Purposes can be divided into (1) goals and (2) fulfillments. Life can be oriented toward a future anticipated state, such as living happily ever after or being in love.

- *Need for values.* This "can lend a sense of goodness or positive characterization of life and justify certain courses of action. Values enable people to decide whether certain acts are right or wrong." Frankl's (1984) view of meaning in life emphasized values as the main form of meaning that people need.

- *Need for a sense of efficacy.* This involves the "belief that one can make a difference. A life that had purposes and values but no efficacy would be tragic. The person might know what is desirable but could not do anything with that knowledge." With a sense of efficacy, people believe that they can control their environment, which has positive physical and mental health benefits (Bandura, 2012).

- *Need for self-worth.* Most individuals want to be "good, worthy persons. Self-worth can be pursued individually."

Researchers are increasingly studying the factors involved in a person's exploration of meaning in life and whether developing a sense of meaning in life is linked to positive developmental outcomes. Many individuals state that religion played an important role in increasing their exploration of meaning in life (Krause, 2008, 2009, 2019). Studies also suggest that individuals who have found a sense of meaning in life are physically healthier, happier, and less depressed than their counterparts who report that they have not discovered meaning in life (Krause & Hayward, 2016).

What characterizes the search for meaning in life?
Eric Audras/Onoky/Getty Images

When more time stretches behind than stretches before one, some assessments, however reluctantly and incompletely, begin to be made.

—JAMES BALDWIN
American novelist, 20th century

Review Connect Reflect

LG5 Explain the roles of religion, spirituality, and meaning in life during middle adulthood.

Review
- What are some characteristics of religion and spirituality in middle-aged individuals?
- How are religion and spirituality linked to physical and mental health?
- What role does meaning in life play in middle adulthood?

Connect
- In this section, you read about religion and spirituality in middle adulthood.

What have you learned about the role of religion in adolescents' lives?

Reflect *Your Own Personal Journey of Life*
- How important is finding a meaning in life to you at this point in your development? What do you think the most important aspects of meaning in life are?

topical connections *looking forward*

Later you will read about biological views on why people age and what people can do to possibly slow down the aging process. You also will learn about the factors that influence life expectancy and what the lives of centenarians—people who live to be 100 or older—are like. The many physical changes that occur in late adulthood, including those involving the brain, also will be described. You will also learn about numerous cognitive changes in older adults, as well as the influences of work and retirement, mental health, and religion in their lives.

Physical and Cognitive Development in Middle Adulthood

1 The Nature of Middle Adulthood

LG1 Explain how midlife is changing, and define middle adulthood.

Changing Midlife

- As more people live to older ages, the life stage that we think of as middle age seems to be occurring later. A major reason developmentalists are beginning to study middle age is the dramatic increase in the number of individuals entering this period of the life span.

Defining Middle Adulthood

- Middle age involves extensive individual variation. With this variation in mind, we will consider middle adulthood to be entered at about 40 to 45 years of age and exited at approximately 60 to 65 years of age. Middle adulthood is the age period in which gains and losses as well as biological and sociocultural factors balance each other. Some experts conclude that sociocultural factors influence development in midlife more than biological factors do.

2 Physical Development

LG2 Discuss physical changes in middle adulthood.

Physical Changes

- The physical changes of midlife are usually gradual. Genetic and lifestyle factors play important roles in whether chronic diseases will appear and when. Among the physical changes of middle adulthood are changes in physical appearance (wrinkles, age spots); height (decrease) and weight (increase); strength, joints, and bones; vision and hearing; cardiovascular system; lungs; and sleep.

Chronic Disorders

- In middle age, the frequency of accidents declines and individuals are less susceptible to colds and allergies. Chronic disorders appear rarely in early adulthood, increase in middle adulthood, and become more common in late adulthood. Arthritis is the leading chronic disorder in middle age, followed by hypertension. Men have more fatal chronic disorders, women more nonfatal ones in middle age. Immune system functioning declines with age.

Mortality Rates

- In middle adulthood, chronic diseases are the main causes of death. Until recently, cardiovascular disease was the leading cause of death in middle age, but now cancer is the leading cause of death in this age group.

Sexuality

- Climacteric is the midlife transition in which fertility declines. The vast majority of women do not have serious physical or psychological problems related to menopause, which usually takes place in the late forties or early fifties, but menopause is an important marker because it signals the end of childbearing capability. Hormone replacement therapy (HRT) augments the declining levels of reproductive hormone production by the ovaries. HRT consists of various forms of estrogen, usually combined with progestin. Recent evidence of risks associated with HRT suggests that its long-term use should be seriously evaluated.

- Men do not experience an inability to father children in middle age, although their testosterone levels decline. Men do not experience a male menopause similar to the dramatic decline in estrogen in middle-aged women.

- Sexual activity occurs less frequently in middle adulthood than in early adulthood. Nonetheless, a majority of middle-aged adults show a moderate or strong interest in sex.

3 Cognitive Development

 Identify cognitive changes in middle adulthood.

Intelligence

- Horn argued that crystallized intelligence (accumulated information and verbal skills) continues to increase in middle adulthood, whereas fluid intelligence (ability to reason abstractly) begins to decline. Schaie and Willis found that longitudinal assessments of intellectual abilities are less likely than cross-sectional assessments to find declines in middle adulthood and are more likely to find improvements. The highest level of four intellectual abilities (vocabulary, verbal memory, inductive reasoning, and spatial orientation) occurred in middle age.

- Recent analysis shows considerable individual variation in intellectual abilities across middle adulthood and indicates that variations in some abilities are more predictive of cognitive impairment in late adulthood than others. Salthouse argues that decline in a number of cognitive functions begins in early adulthood and continues through the fifties. Declines have recently been identified in some aspects of neurobiological functioning that may be linked to age-related changes in cognitive functioning.

Information Processing

- Speed of information processing, often assessed through reaction time, continues to decline in middle adulthood. Although Schaie found that verbal memory increased in middle age, some researchers have found that memory declines in middle age. Working memory declines in late middle age. Memory is more likely to decline in middle age when individuals don't use effective strategies.

- Expertise involves having an extensive, highly organized knowledge and an understanding of a particular domain. Expertise often increases in middle adulthood. Practical problem-solving ability remains stable in early and middle adulthood but declines in late adulthood.

4 Careers, Work, and Leisure

 Characterize career development, work, and leisure in middle adulthood.

Work in Midlife

- For many people, midlife is a time of reflection, assessment, and evaluation of their current work and what they plan to do in the future. One important issue is whether individuals will continue to do the type of work they currently do or change jobs or careers.

Career Challenges and Changes

- Today's middle-aged workers face challenges such as the globalization of work, rapid developments in information technologies, downsizing of organizations, pressure to take early retirement, and concerns about pensions and health care. Midlife job or career changes can be self-motivated or forced on individuals.

Leisure

- We not only need to learn to work well, but we also need to learn to enjoy leisure. Midlife may be an especially important time for leisure because of the physical changes that occur and because of a desire to prepare for an active retirement.

5 Religion, Spirituality, and Meaning in Life

 Explain the roles of religion, spirituality, and meaning in life during middle adulthood.

Religion, Spirituality, and Adult Lives

- Religion and spirituality are important dimensions of many Americans' lives. Women show a stronger interest in religion and spirituality than men do. It is important to consider individual differences in religious and spiritual interest.

Religion, Spirituality, and Health

- In some cases, religion and spirituality can be negatively linked to physical health, as when cults or religious sects discourage individuals from obtaining medical care. In mainstream religions, researchers are increasingly finding that religion is positively related to health. Religion and spirituality can enhance coping for some individuals.

Meaning in Life

- Viktor Frankl argued that examining the finiteness of our existence leads to exploration of meaning in life. Faced with the death of older relatives and less time ahead of them than behind them, many middle-aged individuals increasingly examine life's meaning. Baumeister and Vohs argue that a quest for a meaningful life involves fulfilling four main needs: purpose, values, efficacy, and self-worth.

key **terms**

chronic disorders 478
climacteric 479
crystallized intelligence 483
erectile dysfunction (ED) 481

fluid intelligence 483
leisure 488
meaning-making coping 491

menopause 479
metabolic syndrome 477
middle adulthood 473

religion 491
religiousness 491
spirituality 491

key **people**

Roy Baumeister 492
Gilbert Brim 474
John Clausen 490
Nancy Denney 486

Viktor Frankl 492
John Horn 483
Pamela King 490
Margie Lachman 474

Clas-Hakan Nygard 487
Crystal Park 491
Denise Park 486
Timothy Salthouse 485

K. Warner Schaie 483
Kathleen Vohs 492
Sherry Willis 484

chapter **16**

SOCIOEMOTIONAL DEVELOPMENT IN MIDDLE ADULTHOOD

chapter **outline**

① Personality Theories and Adult Development

Learning Goal 1 Describe personality theories and socioemotional development in middle adulthood.

Stages of Adulthood

The Life-Events Approach

Stress and Personal Control in Midlife

Contexts of Midlife Development

② Stability and Change

Learning Goal 2 Discuss stability and change in development during middle adulthood, as reflected in longitudinal studies.

Longitudinal Studies

Conclusions

③ Close Relationships

Learning Goal 3 Identify some important aspects of close relationships in middle adulthood.

Love, Marriage, and Divorce at Midlife

The Empty Nest and Its Refilling

Sibling Relationships and Friendships

Grandparenting

Intergenerational Relationships

monkeybusinessimages/Getty Images

Forty-five-year-old Sarah feels tired, depressed, and angry when she looks back on the way her life has gone. She became pregnant when she was 17 and married Ben, the baby's father. They stayed together for three years after their son was born, and then Ben left her for another woman. Sarah went to work as a salesclerk to make ends meet. Eight years later, she married Alan, who had two children from a previous marriage. Sarah stopped working for several years to care for the children. Then, like Ben, Alan started seeing someone else. Sarah found out about it from a friend. Nevertheless, Sarah stayed with Alan for another year. Finally, he was gone so much that she could not take it anymore and decided to divorce him. Sarah went back to work again as a salesclerk; she has been in the same position for 16 years now. During those 16 years, she dated a number of men, but the relationships never seemed to work out. Her son never finished high school and has drug problems. Her father died last year, and Sarah is trying to help her mother financially, although she can barely pay her own bills. Sarah looks in the mirror and does not like what she sees. She sees her past as a shambles and holds little hope for a better future.

Forty-five-year-old Wanda feels energetic, happy, and satisfied. As a young woman, she graduated from college and worked for three years as a high school math teacher. She married Andy, who had just finished law school. One year later, they had their first child, Josh. Wanda stayed home with Josh for two years and then returned to her job as a math teacher. Even during her pregnancy, Wanda stayed active and exercised regularly, playing tennis almost every day. After her pregnancy, she kept up her exercise habits. Wanda and Andy had another child, Wendy. Now, as they move into their middle-age years, their children are both off at college, and Wanda and Andy are enjoying spending more time with each other. Last weekend, they visited Josh at his college, and the weekend before that they visited Wendy at hers. Wanda continued working as a high school math teacher until six years ago. She had developed computer skills as part of her job and had taken some computer courses at a nearby college. She resigned her math teaching job and took a job with a computer company, where she has already worked her way into management. Wanda looks in the mirror and likes what she sees. She sees her past as enjoyable, although not without hills and valleys, and she looks toward the future with enthusiasm.

topical connections *looking back*

Emerging adulthood, which occurs from approximately 18 to 25 years of age, is a transitional period between adolescence and early adulthood—a time when individuals intensely explore their identity and experience instability in different contexts. A secure attachment style benefits young adults. Love and possibly marriage become central aspects of many young adults' socioemotional development. Searching for a balance between the need for independence and freedom and the need for intimacy and commitment characterizes the lives of many young adults. Many young adults not only are marrying later or not at all but are having children later than in past decades, and many choose to cohabit with a romantic partner.

preview

As with Sarah and Wanda, there are individual variations in the way people experience middle age. To begin the chapter, we will examine personality theories and development in middle age, including ideas about individual variation. Then we will turn our attention to the ways in which individuals change or stay the same as they go through the adult years. Finally, we will explore a number of aspects of close relationships during middle adulthood.

1 Personality Theories and Adult Development

LG1 Describe personality theories and socioemotional development in middle adulthood.

| Stages of Adulthood | The Life-Events Approach | Stress and Personal Control in Midlife | Contexts of Midlife Development |

What is the best way to conceptualize middle age? Is it a stage or a crisis? How extensively is middle age influenced by life events? Do middle-aged adults experience stress and personal control differently from adults at other life stages? Is personality linked with contexts such as the point in history when individuals go through midlife, their culture, and their gender?

STAGES OF ADULTHOOD

Adult stage theories have been plentiful, and they have contributed to the view that midlife brings a crisis in development. Two prominent theories that define stages of adult development are Erik Erikson's life-span view and Daniel Levinson's seasons of a man's life.

Erikson's Stage of Generativity Versus Stagnation Erikson (1968) proposed that middle-aged adults face a significant issue—generativity versus stagnation, which is the name Erikson gave to the seventh stage in his life-span theory. Generativity encompasses adults' desire to leave legacies of themselves to the next generation (Moieni & others, 2020). Through these legacies adults achieve a kind of immortality. By contrast, stagnation (sometimes called "self-absorption") develops when individuals sense that they have done nothing for the next generation.

Middle-aged adults can develop generativity in a number of ways (Kotre, 1984). Through biological generativity, adults have offspring. Through parental generativity, adults nurture and guide children. Through work generativity, adults develop skills that are passed down to others. And through cultural generativity, adults create, renovate, or conserve some aspect of culture that ultimately survives (Lewis & Allen, 2017).

Adults promote and guide the next generation by parenting, teaching, leading, and doing things that benefit the community (Russo-Netzer & Moran, 2018). One of the participants in a study of aging said, "From twenty to thirty I learned how to get along with my wife. From thirty to forty I learned how to be a success at my job, and at forty to fifty I worried less about myself and more about the children" (Vaillant, 2002, p. 114). Generative adults commit themselves to the continuation and improvement of society as a whole through their connection to the next generation. Generative adults develop a positive legacy of the self and then offer it as a gift to the next generation.

Does research support Erikson's theory that generativity is an important dimension of middle age? Yes, it does (Stewart & Deaux, 2019). In George Vaillant's (2002) longitudinal studies of aging, generativity (defined in this study as "taking care of the next generation") in middle age was more strongly related than intimacy to whether individuals would have an enduring and happy marriage at 75 to 80 years of age.

Other research also supports Erikson's (1968) emphasis on the importance of generativity in middle adulthood. In one study, Carol Ryff (1984) examined the views of women and men at different ages and found that middle-aged adults especially were concerned about generativity. In a longitudinal study of Smith College women, the desire for generativity increased as the participants aged from their thirties to their fifties (Stewart, Ostrove, & Helson, 2001) (see Figure 1). In another study, participating in an intergenerational civic engagement program

> The generations of living things pass in a short time, and like runners, hand on the torch of life.
>
> —LUCRETIUS
> *Roman poet, 1st century B.C.*

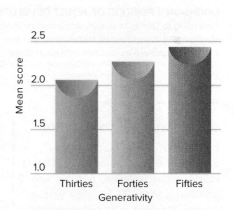

FIGURE 1

CHANGES IN GENERATIVITY FROM THE THIRTIES THROUGH THE FIFTIES. Generativity increased in Smith College women as they aged from their thirties through their fifties (Stewart, Ostrove, & Helson, 2001). The women rated themselves on a 3-point scale indicating the extent to which they thought the statements about generativity were descriptive of their lives. Higher scores reflect greater generativity.

Era of late adulthood:
60 to ?

Late adult transition: Age 60 to 65

Culminating life structure
for middle adulthood:
55 to 60

Age 50 transition:
50 to 55

Entry life structure for
middle adulthood:
45 to 50

Middle adult transition: Age 40 to 45

Culminating life structure
for early adulthood:
33 to 40

Age 30 transition:
28 to 33

Entry life structure for early
adulthood:
22 to 28

Early adult transition: Age 17 to 22

FIGURE 2

LEVINSON'S PERIODS OF ADULT DEVELOPMENT.
According to Daniel Levinson, adulthood for men has three main stages that are surrounded by transition periods. Specific tasks and challenges are associated with each stage.
(*Top to bottom*) Amos Morgan/Photodisc/Getty Images; Corbis/VCG/Getty Images; Thomas Northcut/Digital Vision/Getty Images

developmental **connection**

Personality

Erikson's early adulthood stage is intimacy versus isolation, and his late adulthood stage is integrity versus despair. Connect to "Socioemotional Development in Early Adulthood" and "Socioemotional Development in Late Adulthood."

Midlife crises are greatly
exaggerated in America.

—GEORGE VAILLANT
Contemporary psychologist, Harvard University

enhanced older adults' perceptions of generativity (Gruenewald & others, 2016). In a more recent study, a higher level of generativity in midlife was linked to greater wisdom in late adulthood (Ardelt, Gerlach, & Vaillant, 2018). In a recent study of middle-aged adults, intrinsically rewarding work was positively associated with feelings of generativity (Chen & others, 2019). In another recent study, older women were randomly assigned to either a 6-week generativity condition in which they wrote about life experiences and shared advice with other participants or a control condition in which they wrote about neutral topics (Moieni & others, 2020). The participants in the generativity condition who held more positive expectations for mental health during the aging process reported greater perceived social support and lower levels of loneliness.

Levinson's Seasons of a Man's Life In *The Seasons of a Man's Life* (1978), clinical psychologist Daniel Levinson reported the results of extensive interviews with 40 middle-aged men. The interviews were conducted with hourly workers, business executives, academic biologists, and novelists. Levinson bolstered his conclusions with information from the biographies of famous men and the development of memorable characters in literature. Although Levinson's major interest focused on midlife change, he described a number of stages and transitions during the period from 17 to 65 years of age, as shown in Figure 2. Levinson emphasizes that developmental tasks must be mastered at each stage.

At the end of one's teens, according to Levinson, a transition from dependence to independence should occur. This transition is marked by the formation of a dream—an image of the kind of life the youth wants to have, especially in terms of a career and marriage. Levinson sees the twenties as a novice phase of adult development. It is a time of reasonably free experimentation and of testing the dream in the real world. In early adulthood, the two major tasks to be mastered are exploring the possibilities for adult living and developing a stable life structure.

From about the ages of 28 to 33, a man goes through a transition period in which he must face the more serious question of determining his goals. During his thirties, he usually focuses on family and career development. In the later years of this period, he enters a phase of Becoming One's Own Man (or BOOM, as Levinson calls it). By age 40, he has reached a stable point in his career, has outgrown his earlier, more tenuous attempts at learning to become an adult, and now must look forward to the kind of life he will lead as a middle-aged adult.

According to Levinson, the transition to middle adulthood lasts about five years (ages 40 to 45) and requires the adult male to come to grips with four major conflicts that have existed in his life since adolescence: (1) being young versus being old, (2) being destructive versus being constructive, (3) being masculine versus being feminine, and (4) being attached to others versus being separated from them. Seventy to 80 percent of the men Levinson interviewed found the midlife transition tumultuous and psychologically painful, as many aspects of their lives came into question. According to Levinson, the success of the midlife transition rests on how effectively the individual reduces the polarities and accepts each of them as an integral part of his being.

Because Levinson interviewed middle-aged men, we can consider the data about middle adulthood more valid than the data about early adulthood. When individuals are asked to remember information about earlier parts of their lives, they may distort and forget things. The original Levinson data included no women, although Levinson (1996) reported that his stages, transitions, and the crisis of middle age hold for women as well as men. Levinson's work included no statistical analysis. However, the quality and quantity of the Levinson biographies make them outstanding examples of the clinical tradition.

How Pervasive Are Midlife Crises? Levinson (1978) views midlife as a crisis, arguing that the middle-aged adult is suspended between the past and the future, trying to cope with this gap that threatens life's continuity. George Vaillant (1977) has a different view. Vaillant's study—called the "Grant Study"—involved Harvard University men in their early thirties and in their late forties who initially had been interviewed as undergraduates. He concludes that just as adolescence is a time for detecting parental flaws and discovering the truth about childhood, the forties are a decade of reassessing and recording the truth about one's adolescence and adulthood. However, whereas Levinson sees midlife as a crisis, Vaillant maintains that only a minority of adults experience a midlife crisis:

> Just as pop psychologists have reveled in the not-so-common high drama of adolescent turmoil, just so the popular press, sensing good copy, has made all too much of the midlife crisis. The term *midlife crisis* brings to mind some variation of the renegade minister who leaves behind four children and the congregation that loved him in order to drive off in a magenta Porsche with a 25-year-old striptease artiste. . . . As with adolescent turmoil, midlife crises are much rarer in community samples than in clinical samples. (pp. 222–223)

Thus, for most people midlife is not a crisis (Lachman, Teshale, & Agrigoroaei, 2015). Many cognitive skills, such as vocabulary, verbal memory, and inductive reasoning, peak in midlife, and many individuals reach the height of their career success in midlife (Schaie, 2016). Further, happiness and positive affect have an upward trajectory from early adulthood to late adulthood (Carstensen, 2015a, b). A longitudinal study of more than 2,000 individuals found few midlife crises (McCrae & Costa, 1990; Siegler & Costa, 1999). In this study, the emotional instability of individuals did not significantly increase during their middle-aged years (see Figure 3).

Adult development experts are virtually unanimous in their belief that midlife crises have been exaggerated (Lachman, Teshale, & Agrigoroaei, 2015). In sum:

- The stage theories place too much emphasis on crises in development, especially midlife crises.
- There often is considerable individual variation in the way people experience the stages, a topic that we will turn to next.

Individual Variations Stage theories focus on the universals of adult personality development as they try to pin down stages that all individuals go through in their adult lives. These theories do not adequately address individual variations in adult development. One extensive study of a random sample of 500 men at midlife, for example, found considerable individual variation among men (Farrell & Rosenberg, 1981). In the individual variations view, middle-aged adults interpret, shape, alter, and give meaning to their lives.

Some individuals may experience a midlife crisis in some contexts of their lives but not others (Lachman, 2004). For example, turmoil and stress may characterize a person's life at work even while things are going smoothly at home.

Researchers have found that in one-third of the cases in which individuals have reported going through a midlife crisis, the "crisis is triggered by life events such as a job loss, financial problems, or illness" (Lachman, 2004, p. 315). Let's now explore the role of life events in midlife development.

THE LIFE-EVENTS APPROACH

Age-related stages represent one major way to examine adult personality development. A second major way to conceptualize adult personality development is to focus on life events (Marselle, Warber, & Irvine, 2019; Munro & others, 2019). In the early version of the life-events approach, life events were viewed as taxing circumstances for individuals, forcing them to change their personality (Holmes & Rahe, 1967). Events such as the death of a spouse, divorce, marriage, and so on were believed to involve varying degrees of stress, and therefore likely to influence the individual's development. One study found that stressful life events were associated with cardiovascular disease in middle-aged women (Kershaw & others, 2014). And a meta-analysis found an association between stressful life events and autoimmune diseases, such as arthritis and psoriasis (Porcelli & others, 2016).

Today's life-events approach is more sophisticated (Mo & others, 2019). In the **contemporary life-events approach,** how life events influence the individual's development depends not only on the life event itself but also on mediating factors (such as physical health and family supports), the individual's adaptation to the life event (such as appraisal of the threat and coping strategies), the life-stage context, and the sociohistorical context (see Figure 4). For example, if individuals are in poor health and have little family support, life events are likely to be more

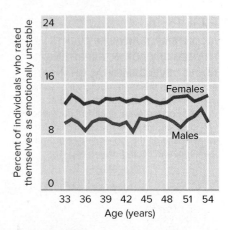

FIGURE 3

EMOTIONAL INSTABILITY AND AGE. In one longitudinal study, the emotional instability of individuals was assessed from age 33 to age 54 (McCrae & Costa, 1990). No significant increase in emotional instability occurred during the middle-aged years.

contemporary life-events approach
Approach emphasizing that how a life event influences the individual's development depends not only on the life event but also on mediating factors, the individual's adaptation to the life event, the life-stage context, and the sociohistorical context.

FIGURE 4

A CONTEMPORARY LIFE-EVENTS FRAMEWORK FOR INTERPRETING ADULT DEVELOPMENTAL CHANGE.
According to the contemporary life-events approach, the influence of a life event depends on the event itself, on mediating variables, on the life-stage and sociohistorical context, and on the individual's appraisal of the event and coping strategies.

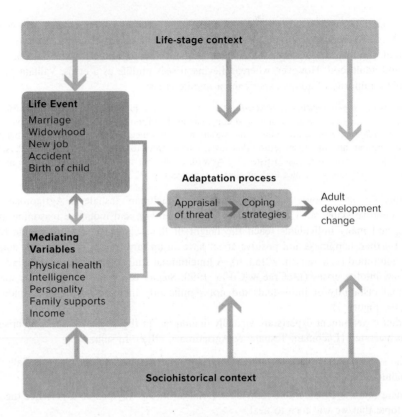

stressful. And a divorce may be more stressful after many years of marriage when adults are in their fifties than when they have been married just a few years and are in their twenties, a finding indicating that the life-stage context of an event makes a difference. The sociohistorical context also makes a difference. For example, adults may be able to cope more effectively with divorce today than in the 1950s because divorce has become more commonplace and accepted in today's society. Whatever the context or mediating variables, however, one individual may perceive a life event as highly stressful, whereas another individual may perceive the same event as an interesting challenge.

Although the life-events approach offers valuable insights for understanding adult development, it has its drawbacks. One drawback is that the life-events approach places too much emphasis on change. It does not adequately recognize the stability that, at least to some degree, characterizes adult development.

Another drawback is the possibility that life's major events may not be as stressful as the cumulative effects of our daily experiences (Stensvehagen & others, 2019). Enduring a boring but tense job or living in poverty does not show up on scales of major life events. Yet the everyday pounding from these conditions can add up to a highly stressful life and eventually lead to illness. Greater insight into the source of life's stresses might come from focusing on daily hassles and daily uplifts (Parker & others, 2020; Zawadzki & others, 2019). Researchers have found that young and middle-aged adults experience a greater daily frequency of stressors than older adults do (Almeida & Horn, 2004). Researchers have also found that stressful daily hassles are linked to increased anxiety and lower physical well-being (Falconier & others, 2015). And a recent study revealed that older adults are more likely than younger adults to use proactive strategies to deal with minor daily hassles before they become more stressful (Neubauer, Smyth, & Sliwinski, 2019).

One study found that the daily hassles most frequently reported by college students were wasting time, concerns about meeting high standards, and feeling lonely (Kanner & others, 1981). Among the uplifts reported most frequently by college students were entertainment, getting along well with friends, and completing a task. In this same study, the daily hassles reported most often by middle-aged adults were concerns about weight and the health of a family member, while their most frequently reported daily uplifts involved relating well with a spouse, lover, or friend (see Figure 5). And the middle-aged adults were more likely than the college students to report that their daily hassles involved economic concerns (rising prices and taxes, for example).

Critics of the daily hassles approach argue that some of the same problems involved with life-events scales occur when daily hassles are assessed. For example, knowing about an adult's daily hassles tells us nothing about physical changes, about how the individual copes with hassles, or about how the individual perceives hassles.

STRESS AND PERSONAL CONTROL IN MIDLIFE

As we have seen, there is conclusive evidence that midlife is not a time when a majority of adults experience a tumultuous crisis, but if they do experience a midlife crisis it is often linked to stressful life events. Do middle-aged adults experience stress differently from young adults and older adults?

Stress, Personal Control, and Age Margie Lachman and her colleagues (2016) have explored how personal control changes when individuals move into middle age. In their view, middle age is a time when a person's sense of control is frequently challenged by many demands and responsibilities, as well as physical and cognitive aging. By contrast, young people are more likely to have a sense of invulnerability, to be unrealistic about their personal control, and to be unaware of the aging process. Many young people focus primarily on self-pursuits and don't worry much about responsibilities for others. But in middle age, less attention is given to self-pursuits and more to responsibility for others, including people who are younger and older than they are. According to Lachman and her colleagues (2016), how the midlife years play out is largely in one's own hands, which can be stressful as individuals are faced with taking on and juggling responsibilities in different areas of their lives.

One study using daily diaries over a one-week period found that both young and middle-aged adults had more days that were stressful and that were characterized by multiple stresses than older adults did (Almeida & Horn, 2004). In this study, although young adults experienced daily stressors more frequently than middle-aged adults, middle-aged adults experienced more "overload" stressors that involved juggling too many activities at once. Another study also revealed that middle-aged and older adults showed a smaller increase in psychological distress to interpersonal stressors than did younger adults, and middle-aged adults were less physically reactive to work stressors than were younger adults (Neupert, Almeida, & Charles, 2007).

To what extent do middle-aged adults perceive that they can control what happens to them? Researchers have found that on average a sense of personal control peaks in midlife and then declines (Robinson & Lachman, 2017). In one study, approximately 80 percent of the young adults (25 to 39 years of age), 71 percent of the middle-aged adults (40 to 59 years of age), and 62 percent of the older adults (60 to 75 years of age) reported that they were often in control of their lives (Lachman & Firth, 2004). However, some aspects of personal control increase with age while others decrease (Lachman, Neupert, & Agrigoroaei, 2011). For example, middle-aged adults feel a greater sense of control over their finances, work, and marriage than younger adults but less control over their sex life and their children (Lachman & Firth, 2004).

Stress and Gender Women and men differ in the way they experience and respond to stressors (Taylor, 2018; Taylor & Stanton, 2021). Women are more vulnerable to social stressors such as those involving romance, family, and work. For example, women experience higher levels of stress than men do when things go wrong in romantic and marital relationships. Women also are more likely than men to become depressed when they encounter stressful life events such as divorce or the death of a friend. A recent study found that in coping with stress, women were more likely than men to seek psychotherapy, talk to friends about the stress, read

Daily Hassles	Percentage of Times Checked
Concerns about weight	52.4
Health of family member	48.1
Rising prices of common goods	43.7
Home maintenance	42.8
Too many things to do	38.6
Misplacing or losing things	38.1
Yardwork/outside home maintenance	38.1
Property, investment, or taxes	37.6
Crime	37.1
Physical appearance	35.9

Daily Uplifts	
Relating well with your spouse or lover	76.3
Relating well with friends	74.4
Completing a task	73.3
Feeling healthy	72.7
Getting enough sleep	69.7
Eating out	68.4
Meeting your responsibilities	68.1
Visiting, phoning, or writing someone	67.7
Spending time with family	66.7
Home (inside) pleasing to you	65.5

FIGURE 5

THE TEN MOST FREQUENT DAILY HASSLES AND UPLIFTS OF MIDDLE-AGED ADULTS OVER A NINE-MONTH PERIOD. *How do these hassles and uplifts compare with your own?*

developmental **connection**

Stress

Adolescence has been characterized too negatively, dating from Hall's storm and stress view of adolescents. Connect to "Physical and Cognitive Development in Adolescence."

How do women and men differ in the way they experience and respond to stressors?
moodboard/Getty Images

developmental **connection**

Research Methods

Cohort effects have also been described as normative, history-graded influences. Connect to "Introduction."

fight-or-flight The view that when men experience stress, they are more likely to engage in a fight-or-flight pattern, as reflected in being aggressive, withdrawing from social contact, or drinking alcohol.

tend-and-befriend Taylor's view that when women experience stress, they are likely to engage in a tend-and-befriend pattern, seeking social alliances with others, especially female friends.

social clock The timetable according to which individuals are expected to accomplish life's tasks, such as getting married, having children, or establishing themselves in a career.

Critics say the stage theories of adult development reflect a male bias by emphasizing career choice and achievement, and that they do not adequately address women's concerns about relationships, interdependence, and caring. The stage theories assume a normative sequence of development, but as women's roles have become more varied and complex, determining what is normative is difficult. *What kinds of changes have taken place in middle-aged women's lives in recent years?*
Corbis/VCG/Getty Images

a self-help book, take prescription medication, and engage in comfort eating (Liddon, Kingerlee, & Barry, 2017). In this study, in coping with stress men were more likely than women to attend a support group meeting, have sex or use pornography, try to fix problems themselves, and not admit to having problems.

When men face stress, they are more likely to respond in a **fight-or-flight** manner—to become aggressive, withdraw from social contact, or drink alcohol. By contrast, according to Shelley Taylor and her colleagues (2011, 2018), when women experience stress, they are more likely to engage in a **tend-and-befriend** pattern, seeking social alliances with others, especially friends. Taylor argues that when women experience stress, their bodies produce heightened levels of the hormone *oxytocin,* which is linked to nurturing in animals.

CONTEXTS OF MIDLIFE DEVELOPMENT

Both Sarah and Wanda, whose stories appeared at the beginning of this chapter, are working mothers. In almost every other way, however, their lives could scarcely be more different. Why? Part of the answer might lie in the different contexts of their lives. The contemporary life-events approach (like Bronfenbrenner's theory) highlights the importance of the complex settings of our lives, exploring everything from our income and family supports to our sociohistorical circumstances. Let's examine how three aspects of the contexts of life influence development during middle adulthood: historical contexts (cohort effects), gender, and culture.

Historical Contexts (Cohort Effects)   Some developmentalists conclude that changing historical times and different social expectations influence how different cohorts—groups of individuals born in the same year or time period—move through the life span (Schaie, 2016). Bernice Neugarten (1986) argues that our values, attitudes, expectations, and behaviors are influenced by the period in which we live. For example, individuals born during the difficult times of the Great Depression may have a different outlook on life from those born during the optimistic 1950s, says Neugarten.

Neugarten (1986) holds that the social environment of a particular age group can alter its **social clock**—the timetable on which individuals are expected to accomplish life's tasks, such as getting married, having children, or establishing themselves in a career. Social clocks provide guidance for our lives; individuals whose lives are not synchronized with these social clocks find life to be more stressful than those who are on schedule, says Neugarten. For example, the fact that Sarah's pregnancy occurred when she was a teenager probably increased the stressfulness of that pregnancy. Neugarten argues that today there is much less agreement than in the past on the right age or sequence for the occurrence of major life events such as having children or retiring. Indeed, one study found that between the late 1950s and the late 1970s, there was a dramatic decline in adults' beliefs that there is a "best age" for major life events and achievements (Passuth, Maines, & Neugarten, 1984) (see Figure 6).

Gender Contexts   Critics say that the stage theories of adult development have a male bias. For example, the central focus of stage theories is on career choice and work achievement, which historically have dominated men's life choices and life chances more than women's. The stage theories do not adequately address women's concerns about relationships, interdependence, and caring (Gilligan, 1982). The adult stage theories have also placed little importance on childbearing and child rearing. Women's family roles are complex and often have a higher salience in their lives than in men's lives. The role demands that women experience in balancing career and family are usually not experienced as intensely by men.

Should midlife and the years beyond be feared by women as a time of declining youth and opportunity? Or is middle adulthood a new prime of life, a time for renewal, for shedding preoccupations with a youthful appearance and body, and for seeking new challenges, valuing maturity, and enjoying change?

In one study, the early fifties were indeed a new prime of life for many women (Mitchell & Helson, 1990). In this sample of 700 women aged 26 to 80, women in their early fifties most often described their lives as "first-rate." Conditions

Activity/event	Appropriate age range	Percent who agree (late '50s study)		Percent who agree (late '70s study)	
		Men	Women	Men	Women
Best age for a man to marry	20–25	80	90	42	42
Best age for a woman to marry	19–24	85	90	44	36
When most people should become grandparents	45–50	84	79	64	57
Best age for most people to finish school and go to work	20–22	86	82	36	38
When most men should be settled on a career	24–26	74	64	24	26
When most men hold their top jobs	45–50	71	58	38	31
When most people should be ready to retire	60–65	83	86	66	41
When a man has the most responsibilities	35–50	79	75	49	50
When a man accomplishes most	40–50	82	71	46	41
The prime of life for a man	35–50	86	80	59	66
When a woman has the most responsibilities	25–40	93	91	59	53
When a woman accomplishes the most	30–45	94	92	57	48

FIGURE 6

INDIVIDUALS' CONCEPTIONS OF THE BEST AGE FOR MAJOR LIFE EVENTS AND ACHIEVEMENTS: LATE 1950S AND LATE 1970S. *What do you think is the best age to experience each of these major life events and accomplishments?*
(*Top*) George Marks/Retrofile/Getty Images; (*bottom*) H. Armstrong Roberts/Retrofile/Getty Images

that distinguished the lives of women in their early fifties from those of women in other age periods included more "empty nests," better health, higher income, and more concern for parents. Women in their early fifties showed confidence, involvement, security, and breadth of personality.

In sum, the view that midlife is a negative age period for women is stereotypical, as so many perceptions of age periods are. Midlife is a diversified, heterogeneous period for women, just as it is for men.

Cultural Contexts   In many cultures, especially nonindustrialized cultures, the concept of middle age is not very clear, or in some cases is absent. It is common in nonindustrialized societies to describe individuals as young or old but not as middle-aged (Grambs, 1989). Some cultures have no words for "adolescent," "young adult," or "middle-aged adult."

Consider the Gusii culture, located in the African country of Kenya. The Gusii divide the life course differently for females and males (LeVine, 1979): females: (1) infant, (2) uncircumcised girl, (3) circumcised girl, (4) married woman, and (5) female elder; males: (1) infant, (2) uncircumcised boy, (3) circumcised boy warrior, and (4) male elder. Thus, movement from one status to the next is due primarily to life events, not age, in the Gusii culture.

Although the Gusii do not have a clearly labeled midlife transition, some of the Gusii adults do reassess their lives around the age of 40. At this time, these Gusii adults examine their current status and the limited time they have remaining in their lives. Their physical strength is decreasing, and they know they cannot farm their land forever, so they seek spiritual powers by becoming ritual practitioners or healers. As in the American culture, however, a midlife crisis in the Gusii culture is the exception rather than the rule.

Gusii dancers perform on habitat day in Nairobi, Kenya. Movement from one status to another in the Gusii culture is due primarily to life events, not age. The Gusii do not have a clearly labeled midlife transition.
Betty Press

Review *Connect* Reflect

LG1 Describe personality theories and socioemotional development in middle adulthood.

Review

- What are some theories of adult stages of development?
- What is the life-events approach?
- How do middle-aged adults experience stress and personal control differently from young and older adults?
- How do contexts influence midlife development?

Connect

- In this section, you read that some researchers criticize the stage theories

of adult development as having a male bias. What have you learned about gender bias in research?

Reflect *Your Own Personal Journey of Life*

- Which approach makes more sense—adult stage or life events—in explaining your own development as you go through adulthood? Or do you think both approaches should be considered in understanding your development as an adult? Explain your answer.

---

2 Stability and Change

LG2 Discuss stability and change in development during middle adulthood, as reflected in longitudinal studies.

Longitudinal Studies   Conclusions

Sarah's adult life, described in the chapter opening, has followed a painful path. Were her sorrows an inevitable result of how she learned to cope with problems earlier in life? Is it possible for her, in middle age, to change her coping strategies or how she relates to other people?

LONGITUDINAL STUDIES

developmental connection

Life-Span Perspective

The extent to which development is characterized by stability and/or change is one of the key issues in the study of life-span development. Connect to "Introduction."

A number of longitudinal studies have assessed stability and change in the personalities of individuals at different points in their lives (Nye & Roberts, 2020; Roberts & Nickel, 2020; Senia & Donellan, 2019; Stewart & Deaux, 2019). We will examine four longitudinal studies that can help us understand the extent to which there is stability or change during adult development: Costa and McCrae's Baltimore Study, the Berkeley Longitudinal Studies, Helson's Mills College Study, and Vaillant's studies.

Costa and McCrae's Baltimore Study   A major, ongoing study of adult personality development is being conducted by Paul Costa and Robert McCrae (1998, 2013; McCrae & Costa, 2003, 2006). They focus on what are called the **Big Five factors of personality,** which are openness to experience, conscientiousness, extraversion, agreeableness, and neuroticism (emotional stability); these personality factors are described in Figure 7. (Notice that if you create an acronym from these factor names, you will get the word OCEAN.) A number of research studies point toward these factors as important dimensions of personality (Jackson & Hill, 2019; Shiner, 2019).

Big Five factors of personality Openness to experience, conscientiousness, extraversion, agreeableness, and neuroticism (emotional stability).

Openness	**C**onscientiousness	**E**xtraversion	**A**greeableness	**N**euroticism (emotional stability)
• Imaginative or practical	• Organized or disorganized	• Sociable or retiring	• Softhearted or ruthless	• Calm or anxious
• Interested in variety or routine	• Careful or careless	• Fun-loving or somber	• Trusting or suspicious	• Secure or insecure
• Independent or conforming	• Disciplined or impulsive	• Affectionate or reserved	• Helpful or uncooperative	• Self-satisfied or self-pitying

FIGURE 7

THE BIG FIVE FACTORS OF PERSONALITY. Each of the broad supertraits encompasses more narrow traits and characteristics. Use the acronym OCEAN to remember the Big Five personality factors: openness, conscientiousness, extraversion, agreeableness, and neuroticism.

Using their five-factor personality test, Costa and McCrae (1995, 2000) studied approximately 1,000 college-educated men and women ages 20 to 96, assessing the same individuals over many years. Data collection began in the 1950s and is ongoing. Costa and McCrae concluded that considerable stability occurs in the five personality factors—emotional stability, extraversion, openness, agreeableness, and conscientiousness. However, more recent research indicates greater developmental changes in the five personality factors in adulthood (Hampson, 2019; Roberts & Nickel, 2020). For example, one study found that emotional stability, extraversion, openness, and agreeableness were lower in early adulthood, peaked between 40 and 60 years of age, and decreased in late adulthood, while conscientiousness showed a continuous increase from early adulthood to late adulthood (Specht, Egloff, & Schukle, 2011). Most research studies indicate that the greatest change occurs in early adulthood (Roberts & Nickel, 2020; Senia & Donnellan, 2019).

Further evidence for the importance of the Big Five factors indicates that they are related to such important aspects of a person's life as health, intelligence and cognitive functioning, achievement and work, and relationships (Chapman & others, 2020; Hampson, 2019; Senia & Donnellan, 2019). The following research supports these links:

- *Openness to experience.* Individuals high on openness to experience are more likely to have better health and well-being (Strickhouser, Zell, & Krizan, 2017); be tolerant (McCrae & Sutin, 2009); have superior cognitive functioning, achievement, and IQ across the life span (Briley, Domiteaux, & Tucker-Drob, 2014); show creative achievement in the arts (Kaufman & others, 2016); experience less negative affect to stressors (Leger & others, 2016); have greater success as entrepreneurs (Zhao, Seibert, & Lumpkin, 2010); eat more fruits and vegetables (Conner & others, 2017); and as older adults they show declining openness as they approach death (Sharp & others, 2019)

- *Conscientiousness.* Individuals high in conscientiousness often do well in a variety of life domains (Boyce, Wood, & Ferguson, 2016; Mike & others, 2015; Roberts & Damian, 2018; Roberts & Hill, 2017). For example, they are more likely to live longer (Graham & others, 2017); experience optimal aging, including positive affect, life satisfaction, and positive psychological well-being (Melendez & others, 2019); have a lower risk of dementia in African and non-Latino White older adults (Kaup, Harmell, & Yaffe, 2019); have better health and less stress (Strickhouser, Zell, & Krizan, 2017); engage in superior problem-focused coping (Sesker & others, 2016); have a higher level of marital satisfaction (Sayehmiri & others, 2020); maintain better-quality friendships (Jensen-Campbell & Malcolm, 2007); achieve higher grade point averages in college (McAbee & Oswald, 2013); be more successful academically in medical school (Sobowale & others, 2018); be more successful at accomplishing goals (McCabe & Fleeson, 2016); engage in less substance abuse (Walton & Roberts, 2004); experience less negative affect to stressors (Leger & others, 2016); and gamble less (Hwang & others, 2012). They also are less likely to have an alcohol addiction (Raketic & others, 2017); be obese (Cheng & others, 2020); experience cognitive decline in aging (Luchetti & others, 2016); develop Internet addiction (Kircaburun & Griffiths, 2018); and if they are nursing professionals they tend to have lower work burnout rates (Perez-Fuentes & others, 2019).

- *Extraversion.* Individuals high in *extraversion* are more likely than others to live longer (Graham & others, 2017); engage in social activities (Emmons & Diener, 1986); be more satisfied in relationships (Toy, Nai, & Lee, 2016); have fewer sleep problems (Hintsanen & others, 2014); show less negative affect to stressors (Leger & others, 2016); and have a higher level of perceived well-being (Ortet & others, 2020).

- *Agreeableness.* People who are high in agreeableness are more likely to live longer (Graham & others, 2017); be generous and altruistic (Caprara & others, 2010); have more satisfying romantic relationships (Donnellan, Larsen-Rife, & Conger, 2005); view other people positively (Wood, Harms, & Vazire, 2010); show more positive affect to stressors (Leger & others, 2016); lie less about themselves in online dating profiles (Hall & others, 2010); are less likely to engage in physical activity (Hearon & Harrison, 2020); and have a lower risk of dementia (Terracciano & others, 2017).

- *Neuroticism.* People high in neuroticism are more likely to die at a younger age (Graham & others, 2017); have worse health and report having more health complaints (Strickhouser, Zell, & Krizan, 2017); feel more negative emotion than positive emotion in daily life; experience more lingering negative states and have more stressor-related

developmental **connection**

Life-Span Perspective

The extent to which development is characterized by stability and/or change is one of the key issues in the study of life-span development. Connect to "Introduction."

developmental **connection**

Personality

The Big Five factors are linked to longevity. Connect to "Socioemotional Development in Late Adulthood."

negative affect (Leger & others, 2016; Widiger, 2009); have a lower level of marital satisfaction (Sayehmiri & others, 2020); develop coronary heart disease (Lee & others, 2014); have a lower sense of well-being 40 years later (Gale & others, 2013); develop dementia (Terracciano & others, 2017); become drug dependent (Raketic & others, 2017); and if they are nursing professionals, they tend to have higher work burnout rates (Perez-Fuentes & others, 2019). Also, research indicates that a combination of a higher level of conscientiousness and a lower level of neuroticism is linked to better health (Turiano & others, 2013). And a recent study found that individuals characterized by high neuroticism avoided engaging in selfie-posting and selfie-editing, while those with high extraversion and agreeableness engaged in more selfie-posting and selfie-editing (Chaudhari & others, 2019).

Another important personality characteristic is *optimism,* which involves having a positive outlook on the future and minimizing problems. Optimism is often referred to as a style of thinking. Researchers increasingly are finding that optimism is linked to better adjustment, improved health, and increased longevity (Ait-Hadad & others, 2020; Felt & others, 2020; Kolokotroni, Anagnostopoulos, & Hantzi, 2018). A study involving adults 50 years of age and older revealed that being optimistic and having an optimistic spouse were both associated with better health and physical functioning (Kim, Chopik, & Smith, 2014). Further, another study of married couples found that the worst health outcomes occurred when both spouses decreased in optimism across a four-year time frame (Chopik, Kim, & Smith, 2018). In another study, a higher level of optimism following an acute coronary event was linked to engaging in more physical activity and experiencing fewer cardiac readmissions (Huffman & others, 2016). Also, in a recent study, lonely individuals who were optimistic had a lower suicide risk than their counterparts who were more pessimistic (Chang & others, 2018). Further, a research review concluded that the influence of optimism on positive outcomes for people who have chronic diseases (such as cancer, cardiovascular disease, and respiratory disease) may involve (a) a possible direct effect on the neuroendocrine system and on immune system function, and/or (b) an indirect effect on health outcomes by increasing protective health behaviors, adaptive coping strategies, and positive mood (Avvenuti, Baiardini, & Giardini, 2016). And a recent study revealed that regardless of growing up in disadvantaged circumstances as a child, being optimistic as an adult was linked to not smoking, having a healthy diet, and maintaining a healthy body mass index (Non & others, 2020).

Berkeley Longitudinal Studies   In the Berkeley Longitudinal Studies, more than 500 children and their parents were initially studied in the late 1920s and early 1930s. The book *Present and Past in Middle Life* (Eichorn & others, 1981) profiles these individuals as they became middle-aged. The results from early adolescence through a portion of midlife did not support either extreme in the debate over whether personality is characterized by stability or change. Some characteristics were more stable than others, however. The most stable characteristics were the degree to which individuals were intellectually oriented, self-confident, and open to new experiences. The characteristics that changed the most included the extent to which the individuals were nurturant or hostile and whether or not they had good self-control.

John Clausen (1993), one of the researchers in the Berkeley Longitudinal Studies, stresses that too much attention has been given to discontinuities for all members of the human species, as exemplified in the adult stage theories. He points out that some people experience recurrent crises and undergo substantial changes over the life course, whereas others have more stable lives entailing very little change.

Helson's Mills College Study   Another longitudinal investigation of adult personality development was conducted by Ravenna Helson and her colleagues (George, Helson, & John, 2011; Helson, 1997; Helson & Wink, 1992; Stewart, Ostrove, & Helson, 2001). They initially studied 132 women who were seniors at Mills College in California in the late 1950s and then studied them again when they were in their thirties, forties, and fifties. Helson and her colleagues distinguished three main groups among the Mills women: family-oriented, career-oriented (whether or not they also wanted families), and those who followed neither path (women without children who pursued only low-level work).

During their early forties, many of the women shared the concerns that stage theorists such as Levinson found in men: concern for young and old, introspectiveness, interest in roots, and awareness of limitations and death. However, the researchers in the Mills College

Based on their study of middle-aged women, Ravenna Helson and her colleagues described the women as experiencing a midlife consciousness rather than a midlife crisis. *What were some other findings in the Mills College study?*
kupicoo/Getty Images

Study concluded that rather than being in a midlife crisis, the women were experiencing *midlife consciousness.* The researchers also discovered that commitment to the tasks of early adulthood—whether to a career or family (or both)—helped women learn to control their impulses, develop interpersonal skills, become independent, and work hard to achieve goals. Women who did not commit themselves to one of these lifestyle patterns faced fewer challenges and did not develop as fully as the other women did (Rosenfeld & Stark, 1987).

In the Mills College Study, some women moved toward becoming "pillars of society" in their early forties to early fifties. Menopause, caring for aging parents, and having an empty nest were not associated with an increase in responsibility and self-control (Helson & Wink, 1992).

George Vaillant's Studies Longitudinal studies by George Vaillant help us explore a question that differs somewhat from the topics examined by the studies described so far: Does personality at middle age predict what a person's life will be like in late adulthood? Vaillant (2002) has conducted three longitudinal studies of adult development and aging: (1) a sample of 268 socially advantaged Harvard graduates born in about 1920 (called the "Grant Study"); (2) a sample of 456 socially disadvantaged inner-city men born in about 1930; and (3) a sample of 90 middle-SES, intellectually gifted women born in about 1910. These individuals have been assessed numerous times (in most cases, every two years), beginning in 1938 and continuing today for those who are still living. The main assessments involve extensive interviews with the participants, their parents, and teachers.

Vaillant categorized 75- to 80-year-olds as "happy-well," "sad-sick," or "dead." He used data collected from these individuals when they were 50 years of age to predict which categories they were likely to end up in at 75 to 80 years of age. Alcohol abuse and smoking at age 50 were the best predictors of which individuals would be dead at 75 to 80 years of age. Factors at age 50 that were linked with being in the "happy-well" category at 75 to 80 years of age included getting regular exercise, avoiding being overweight, being well educated, having a stable marriage, being future-oriented, being thankful and forgiving, empathizing with others, being active with other people, and having good coping skills.

In Vaillant's longitudinal research, which characteristics at age 50 predicted better health and well-being at 75 to 80?
Ariel Skelly/Blend Images/Getty Images

Wealth and income at age 50 were not linked with being in the "happy-well" category at 75 to 80 years of age. Generativity in middle age (defined as "taking care of the next generation") was more strongly related than intimacy to whether individuals would have an enduring and happy marriage at 75 to 80 years of age (Vaillant, 2002).

The results for one of Vaillant's studies, the Grant Study of Harvard men, indicate that when individuals at 50 years of age were not heavy smokers, did not abuse alcohol, had a stable marriage, exercised, maintained a normal weight, and had good coping skills, they were more likely to be alive and happy at 75 to 80 years of age.

CONCLUSIONS

What can be concluded about stability and change in regard to personality development during the adult years? There is increasing evidence that personality traits continue to change during the adult years, even into late adulthood. However, in a meta-analysis of 92 longitudinal studies, the greatest change in personality traits occurred in early adulthood—from about 20 to 40 years of age (Roberts, Walton, & Viechtbauer, 2006).

Thus, people show more stability in their personality when they reach midlife than they did when they were younger adults (Roberts & Nickel, 2020; Senia & Donnellan, 2019). These findings support what is called a *cumulative personality model of personality development,* which states that with time and age people become more adept at interacting with their environment in ways that promote increased stability of personality (Caspi & Roberts, 2001; Hill & Roberts, 2016; Nye & Roberts, 2020).

This does not mean that change is absent throughout middle and late adulthood. Ample evidence shows that social contexts, new experiences, and sociohistorical changes can affect

At age 55, actor Jack Nicholson said, "I feel exactly the same as I've always felt: a slightly reined-in voracious beast." Nicholson felt his personality had not changed much. Some others might think they have changed more. *How much does personality change and how much does it stay the same through adulthood?*
Noel Vasquez/Stringer/Getty Images

personality development, but the changes in middle and late adulthood are usually not as great as those in early adulthood (Roberts & Nickel, 2020; Senia & Donnellan, 2019). In a recent research review, the personality trait that changed the most as a result of psychotherapy intervention was emotional stability, followed by extraversion (Roberts & others, 2017). In this review, the personality traits of individuals with anxiety disorders changed the most and those with substance use disorders the least.

In general, changes in personality traits across adulthood also occur in a positive direction. Over time, "people become more confident, warm, responsible, and calm" (Roberts & Mroczek, 2008, p. 33). Such positive changes equate with becoming more socially mature.

In sum, recent research contradicts the old view that stability of personality begins to set in at about 30 years of age (Jackson & Hill, 2019; Roberts & Nickel, 2020). Although there are some consistent developmental changes in the personality traits of large numbers of people, at the individual level people can show unique patterns of personality traits—and these patterns often reflect life experiences related to themes of their particular developmental period (Roberts & Mroczek, 2008). For example, researchers have found that individuals who are in a stable marriage and a solid career track become more socially dominant, conscientious, and emotionally stable as they go through early adulthood (Roberts & Wood, 2006). And for some of these individuals there is greater change in their personality traits than for other individuals (Roberts & Nickel, 2020).

Review Connect Reflect

 LG2 Discuss stability and change in development during middle adulthood, as reflected in longitudinal studies.

Review
- Identify four longitudinal studies and describe their results.
- What conclusions can be reached about stability and change in development during middle adulthood?

Connect
- This section discussed four different longitudinal studies. What are the pros and cons of using a longitudinal study to collect data?

Reflect *Your Own Personal Journey of Life*
- How much stability and change have characterized your life so far? How much stability and change do you predict will characterize your future development as an adult? Explain.

3 Close Relationships

LG3 Identify some important aspects of close relationships in middle adulthood.

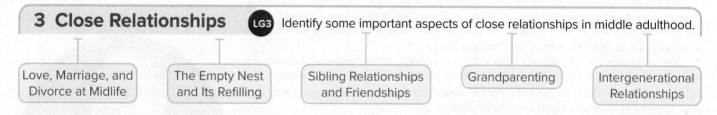

| Love, Marriage, and Divorce at Midlife | The Empty Nest and Its Refilling | Sibling Relationships and Friendships | Grandparenting | Intergenerational Relationships |

There is a consensus among middle-aged Americans that a major component of well-being involves positive relationships with others, especially parents, spouse, and offspring (Blieszner & Roberto, 2012a, b; Markus & others, 2004). To begin our examination of midlife relationships, let's explore love, marriage, and divorce in middle-aged adults.

LOVE, MARRIAGE, AND DIVORCE AT MIDLIFE

Two major forms of love are romantic love and affectionate love. The fires of romantic love are strong in early adulthood. Affectionate, or companionate, love increases during middle adulthood. That is, physical attraction, romance, and passion are more important in new relationships, especially in early adulthood. Security, loyalty, and mutual emotional interest become more important as relationships mature, especially in middle adulthood (Crowley, 2019).

Marriage   Middle-aged partners are more likely to view their marriage as positive if they engage in mutual activities. Also, a study found that middle-aged married individuals had a lower likelihood of work-related health limitations (Lo, Cheng, & Simpson, 2016). Further, a study of middle-aged adults revealed that positive marital quality was linked to better health for both spouses (Choi, Yorgason, & Johnson, 2016). And, in a 13-year longitudinal study, married couples who were 40–50 years old and had been married for at least 15 years were periodically observed while they engaged in 15-minute unrehearsed conversations about an area of disagreement in their marriage (Verstaen & others, 2020). For both husbands and wives, negative emotional behavior (primarily belligerence, defensiveness, fear/tension, and whining) decreased and positive emotional behavior (primarily humor, enthusiasm, and validation) increased with age.

What characterizes marriage in middle adulthood?
Absolut/Shutterstock

Divorce   What trends characterize divorce in U.S. middle-aged adults? In a recent analysis that compared divorce rates for different age groups in 1990 to 2015, the divorce rate decreased for young adults but increased for middle-aged and older adults (Stepler, 2017):

25 to 39 years	40 to 49 years	50+ years
−21 percent	+14 percent	+109 percent

This recent increase in divorce among middle-aged adults has led to divorce in middle adulthood being labeled "gray divorce" when it occurs after 50 years of age (Crowley, 2018; Lin & others, 2018). What accounts for the increase? One explanation is the changing view of women, who initiate approximately 60 percent of the divorces after 40 years of age. Compared with earlier decades, divorce has less stigma for women and they are more likely to leave an unhappy marriage. Also compared with earlier decades, more women are employed and are less dependent on their husband's income. Another explanation involves the increase in remarriages, in which the divorce rate is 2½ times as high as it is for couples in first marriages.

A survey by AARP (2004) of 1,148 people between the ages of 40 and 79 who were divorced at least once in their forties, fifties, or sixties found that staying married because of their children was by far the main reason many people postponed divorce. Despite the worry and stress involved in going through a divorce, three out of four of the divorcees said they had made the right decision to dissolve their marriage and reported a positive outlook on life. Sixty-six percent of the divorced women said they had initiated the divorce, compared with only 41 percent of the divorced men. The divorced women were much more afraid of having financial problems (44 percent) than were the divorced men (11 percent). Following are the main reasons the middle-aged and older adult women cited for their divorce: (1) verbal, physical, or emotional abuse (23 percent); (2) alcohol or drug abuse (18 percent); and (3) cheating (17 percent). The main reasons the middle-aged and older men cited for their divorce were (1) no obvious problems, just fell out of love (17 percent); (2) cheating (14 percent); and (3) different values, lifestyles (14 percent).

In recent research on the antecedents of "gray divorce," factors traditionally associated with divorce in young adults also were reflected in the divorces of adults 50 years and older (Crowley, 2019; Lin & others, 2018). Divorce was more likely to occur in these older adults when they had been married fewer years, their marriage was of lower quality (less marital satisfaction, for example), they did not own a home, and they had financial problems. Factors that were not linked to divorce in these older adults were the onset of an empty nest, the wife's or husband's retirement, and whether the wife or husband had a chronic health condition. Also, as with younger adults, middle-aged adults who are divorced have more physical and mental health problems than those who are married. In a recent Korean study of middle-aged adults, those who were divorced were more likely to smoke, binge drink, get inadequate sleep, and be depressed than their married counterparts (Kim, Lee, & Park, 2018). Further, in a Swiss study of middle-aged adults, single divorcees were more lonely and less resilient than their married and remarried counterparts (Knopfli & others, 2016). In the same study, single divorcees had the lowest self-rated health.

After they get divorced, how likely are middle-aged adults to repartner? In a recent study, approximately 22 percent of women and 37 percent of men repartnered within 10 years after a gray divorce (that is, divorce at 50 years of age and older) (Brown & others, 2019). Also in this study, repartnering occurred more through cohabitation than remarriage, especially for men.

What are some ways that divorce might be more positive or more negative in middle adulthood than in early adulthood?
kurhan/Shutterstock

empty nest syndrome A decrease in marital satisfaction that occurs after children leave home, because parents derive considerable satisfaction from their children.

THE EMPTY NEST AND ITS REFILLING

An important event in a family is the launching of a child into adult life. Parents undergo adjustments as a result of the child's absence. College students usually think that their parents suffer from their absence. In fact, parents who live vicariously through their children might experience the **empty nest syndrome,** which includes a decline in marital satisfaction after children leave the home. For most parents, however, marital satisfaction does not decline after children have left home but rather increases during the years after child rearing (Fingerman & Baker, 2006). With their children gone, marital partners have time to pursue career interests and to spend with each other. One study revealed that the transition to an empty nest increased marital satisfaction due to an increase in the quality of time—but not the quantity of time—spent with partners (Gorchoff, John, & Helson, 2008).

In today's uncertain economic climate, the refilling of the empty nest is becoming a common occurrence as adult children return home after several years of college, after graduating from college, or to save money after taking a full-time job (Merrill, 2009). Young adults also may move in with their parents after an unsuccessful career or a divorce. And some individuals don't leave home at all until their middle to late twenties because they cannot support themselves financially. Numerous labels have been applied to young adults who return to their parents' homes to live, including "boomerang kids" and "B2B" (or Back-to-Bedroom) (Furman, 2005).

The middle generation has always provided support for the younger generation, even after the nest is bare. Through loans and monetary gifts for education, and through emotional support, the middle generation has helped the younger generation. Adult children appreciate the financial and emotional support their parents provide them at a time when they often feel considerable stress about their career, work, and lifestyle. And parents feel good that they can provide this support. A study of 40- to 60-year-old parents revealed that they provided financial, practical, and emotional support on average every few weeks to each of their children over 18 years of age (Fingerman & others, 2009).

However, as with most family living arrangements, there are both pluses and minuses when adult children return home. A common complaint voiced by both adult children and their parents is a loss of privacy. The adult children complain that their parents restrict their independence, cramp their sex lives, reduce their music listening, and treat them as children rather than adults. Parents often complain that their quiet home has become noisy, that they stay up late wondering when their adult children will come home, that meals are difficult to plan because of conflicting schedules, that their relationship as a married couple has been invaded, and that they have to shoulder too much responsibility for their adult children. In sum, when adult children return home to live, there is a disequilibrium in family life that requires considerable adaptation by parents and their adult children. To read about strategies that young adults and their parents can use to get along better, see *Connecting Development to Life.*

SIBLING RELATIONSHIPS AND FRIENDSHIPS

Sibling relationships persist over the entire life span for most adults (Whiteman, McHale, & Soli, 2011). Eighty-five percent of today's adults have at least one living sibling. Sibling relationships in adulthood may be extremely close, apathetic, or highly rivalrous (Bedford, 2009). The majority of sibling relationships in adulthood are close (Cicirelli, 2009). Those siblings who are psychologically close to each other in adulthood tended to be that way in childhood. It is rare for sibling closeness to develop for the first time in adulthood (Dunn, 1984, 2007). One study revealed that adult siblings often provide practical and emotional support to each other (Voorpostel & Blieszner, 2008). Another study revealed that men who had poor sibling relationships in childhood were more likely to develop depression by age 50 than men who had more positive sibling relationships as children (Waldinger, Vaillant, & Orav, 2007).

Friendships are as important in middle adulthood as they were in early adulthood (Blieszner & Roberto, 2012b). It takes time to develop intimate friendships, so friendships that have endured over the adult years are often deeper than those that are newly formed in middle adulthood.

developmental **connection**

Family and Peers

Many siblings have mixed feelings about each other. Connect to "Socioemotional Development in Early Childhood."

connecting development to life

Strategies for Parents and Their Young Adult Children

When adult children ask to return home to live, parents and their adult children should agree beforehand on the conditions and expectations. For example, they might discuss and agree on whether young adults will pay rent, wash their own clothes, cook their own meals, do any household chores, pay their phone bills, come and go as they please, be sexually active or drink alcohol at home, and so on. If these conditions aren't negotiated at the beginning, conflict often results because the expectations of parents and young adult children will likely be violated.

Parents need to treat young adult children more like adults than children and to let go of much of their parenting role. Parents should interact with young adult children not as dependent children who need to be closely monitored and protected but rather as adults who are capable of responsible, mature behavior. Adult children have the right to choose how much they sleep and eat, how they dress, whom they choose as friends and lovers, what career they pursue, and how they spend their money. However, if the young adult children act in ways that interfere with their parents' lifestyles, parents need to say so. The discussion should focus not on the young adult children's choices but on how their activities are unacceptable while living together in the same home.

Some parents don't let go of their young adult children when they should. They engage in "permaparenting," which can impede not only their adult children's movement toward independence and responsibility but also their own postparenting lives. "Helicopter parents" is another label that describes parents who hover too closely in their effort to ensure that their children succeed in college and adult life (Weitkamp & Seiffge-Krenke, 2019). Although well intentioned, this intrusiveness by parents can slow the process by which their children become responsible adults. In a recent study, high levels of parental control and helicopter parenting were detrimental to emerging adults' vocational identity development and perceived competence in transitioning to adulthood (Lindell, Campione-Barr, & Killoren, 2017). And in another recent study,

What are some strategies that can help parents and their young adult children get along better?
Fuse/Getty Images

helicopter parenting was related to more negative emotional functioning, less competent decision making, and lower grades/poorer adjustment in college students (Luebbe & others, 2018).

A new term that characterizes a number of parents today is "lawn mower parent"—a parent who goes to great lengths to prevent their child from experiencing adversity, stress, or failure. By "mowing down" obstacles and potential negative experiences for their children, these parents are not allowing their children to learn how to cope with such experiences themselves. After their children leave home, they are less likely to handle the pressure and challenges of life as well as they would have if their parents had provided them more space to make decisions and learn how to cope on their own.

When they move back home, young adult children need to think about how they will need to change their behavior to make the living arrangement work. Elina Furman (2005) provides some good recommendations in *Boomerang Nation: How to Survive Living with Your Parents . . . the Second Time Around.* She recommends that when young adult children move back home they expect to make adjustments. And as recommended earlier, she urges young adults to sit down with their parents and negotiate the ground rules for living at home before they actually move back. Furman also recommends that young adults set a deadline for how long they will live at home and then stay focused on their goals (whether they want to save enough money to pay off their debts, save enough to start a business or buy their own home, finish graduate school, and so on). Too often young adults spend the money they save by moving home on luxuries such as shopping binges, nights on the town, expensive clothes, and unnecessary travel, further delaying their ability to move out of their parents' home.

Children who leave college and return to live at home with their parents are on the cusp of young adulthood, a time called emerging adulthood. What characterizes individuals' identity development during this time?

GRANDPARENTING

The increase in longevity is influencing the nature of grandparenting (Dolbin, 2019; Hayslip, Fruhaf, & Dolbin-MacNab, 2019; Huo & Fingerman, 2018; Smith & Wild, 2019). In 1900, only 4 percent of 10-year-old children had four living grandparents, but in 2000 that figure had risen to more than 40 percent. And in 1990 only about 20 percent of people who were 30 years of age had living grandparents, a figure that is projected to increase to 80 percent in 2020 (Hagestad & Uhlenberg, 2007). Further increases in longevity are likely to support this trend in the future, although the current trend in delayed childbearing is likely to undermine it (Szinovacz, 2009).

How might U.S. grandparents compare with their counterparts in other countries? In a recent cross-cultural comparison, U.S. grandparents were characterized by higher parental efficacy, more role satisfaction, better well-being, and more attachment than Chinese grandparents, who were characterized by better resilience and more authoritative parenting (Wang & others, 2019).

Grandparents play important roles in the lives of many grandchildren (Condon, Luszcz, & McKee, 2020; Hayslip, Fruhauf, & Dolbin-MacNab, 2019). Grandparents especially play important roles in grandchildren's lives when family crises such as divorce, death, illness, abandonment, or poverty occur (Dolbin-MacNab & Yancura, 2018). In many countries around the world, grandparents facilitate women's participation in the labor force by providing child care. Some estimates suggest that worldwide more than 160 million grandparents are raising grandchildren (Leinaweaver, 2014).

Many adults become grandparents for the first time during middle age. Researchers have consistently found that grandmothers have more contact with grandchildren than grandfathers do (Watson, Randolph, & Lyons, 2005). Perhaps women tend to define their role as grandmothers as part of their responsibility for maintaining ties between family members across generations. Men may have fewer expectations about the grandfather role and see it as more voluntary.

Most research on grandparents has focused on grandchildren as children or adolescents. A recent study focused on grandparents and their adult grandchildren (Huo & others, 2018). In this study, grandparents' contact with their adult grandchildren involved frequent listening, emotional support, and companionship. Also in this study, grandparents provided more frequent emotional support to their adult grandchildren when parents were having life problems and more frequent financial support when parents were unemployed.

Grandparent Roles and Styles   What is the meaning of the grandparent role? Three prominent meanings are attached to being a grandparent (Neugarten & Weinstein, 1964). For some older adults, being a grandparent brings a sense of biological reward and continuity. For others, being a grandparent is a source of emotional self-fulfillment, generating feelings of companionship and satisfaction that may have been missing in earlier adult-child relationships. And for yet others, being a grandparent is a remote role. One study revealed that grandparenting can provide a sense of purpose and a feeling of being valued during middle and late adulthood when generative needs are strong (Thiele & Whelan, 2008).

The grandparent role may have different functions in different families, in different ethnic groups and cultures, and in different situations (Hayslip, Fruhauf, & Dolbin-MacNab, 2019). For example, in one study of White, African American, and Mexican American grandparents and grandchildren, the Mexican American grandparents saw their grandchildren most frequently, provided the most support for the grandchildren and their parents, and had the most satisfying relationships with their grandchildren (Bengtson, 1985). And in a study of three generations of families in Chicago, grandmothers had closer relationships with their children and grandchildren and gave more personal advice than grandfathers did (Hagestad, 1985).

What are some grandparents' roles and styles?
JGI/Jamie Grill/Blend Images/Getty Images

The Changing Profile of Grandparents   In 2014, 10 percent (7.4 million) of children in the United States lived with at least one grandparent, a dramatic increase since 1981 when 4.7 million children were living with at least one grandparent (U.S. Census Bureau, 2015). Divorce, adolescent pregnancies, and drug use by parents are the main reasons that grandparents are thrust back into the "parenting" role they thought they had shed. One study revealed that grandparent involvement was linked with better adjustment in single-parent and stepparent families than in two-parent biological families (Attar-Schwartz & others, 2009).

Less than 20 percent of grandparents whose grandchildren move in with them are 65 years old or older. Almost half of the grandchildren who move in with grandparents are raised by a single grandmother. These families are mainly African American (53 percent). When both grandparents are raising grandchildren, the families are overwhelmingly non-Latino White.

Grandparents who are full-time caregivers for grandchildren are at elevated risk for health problems, depression, and stress (Hayslip, Fruhauf, & Dolbin-MacNab, 2019). One research review concluded that grandparents raising grandchildren are especially at risk for developing depression (Hadfield, 2014). Caring for grandchildren is linked with these problems in part because full-time grandparent caregivers are often characterized by low-income, minority status and by not being married (Minkler & Fuller-Thompson, 2005). However, a recent study found that when children live with grandparents this arrangement especially benefits low-income and single parents, who in this circumstance invested more money on their children's education and activities, as well as saving on child care costs (Amorim, 2019).

Grandparents who are part-time caregivers are less likely to have the negative health status that full-time grandparent caregivers have. In a study of part-time grandparent caregivers, few negative effects on grandparents were found (Hughes & others, 2007).

As divorce and remarriage have become more common, a special concern of grandparents is visitation privileges with their grandchildren (Kivnik & Sinclair, 2007). In the last two decades, more states have passed laws giving grandparents the right to petition a court for visitation privileges with their grandchildren, even if a parent objects. Whether such forced visitation rights for grandparents are in the child's best interest is still being debated.

INTERGENERATIONAL RELATIONSHIPS

Family is important to most people (Chai, Zarit, & Fingerman, 2020; Steinbach & others, 2020). When 21,000 adults aged 40 to 79 in 21 countries were asked, "When you think of who you are, you think mainly of _____," 63 percent said "family," 9 percent said "religion," and 8 percent said "work" (HSBC Insurance, 2007). In this study, in all 21 countries, middle-aged and older adults expressed a strong feeling of responsibility between generations in their family, with the strongest intergenerational ties indicated in Saudi Arabia, India, and Turkey. More than 80 percent of the middle-aged and older adults reported that adults have a duty to care for their parents (and parents-in-law) in time of need later in life.

Middle-aged and older adults around the world show a strong sense of family responsibility. A study of middle-aged and older adults in 21 countries revealed the strongest intergenerational ties in Saudi Arabia.
OlegD/Shutterstock

Adults in midlife play important roles in the lives of the young and the old (Fingerman, Zarit, & Birditt, 2019; Wang & others, 2020). Middle-aged adults share their experience and transmit values to the younger generation. They may be launching children and experiencing the empty nest, adjusting to having grown children return home, or becoming grandparents. They also may be giving or receiving financial assistance, caring for a widowed or sick parent, or adapting to being the oldest generation after both parents have died. A recent study indicated that middle-aged adults are happiest when they have harmonious relationships with their parents and their grown children (Kim & others, 2020).

Middle-aged adults have been described as the "sandwich," "squeezed," or "overload" generation because of the responsibilities they have for their adolescent and young adult children as well as their aging parents (Etaugh & Bridges, 2010). However, an alternative view is that in the United States, a "sandwich" generation, in which the middle generation cares for both grown children and aging parents simultaneously, occurs less often than a "pivot" generation, in which the middle generation alternates attention between the demands of grown children and aging parents (Fingerman, Zarit, & Birditt, 2019).

Many middle-aged adults experience considerable stress when their parents become very ill and die. One survey found that when adults enter midlife, 41 percent have both parents alive, but that 77 percent leave midlife with no parents alive (Bumpass & Aquilino, 1994). By middle age, more than 40 percent of adult children (most of them daughters) provide care for aging parents or parents-in-law (Blieszner & Roberto, 2012a; National

What is the nature of intergenerational relationships?
Todd Wright/Getty Images

Alliance for Caregiving, 2009). However, two studies revealed that middle-aged parents are more likely to provide support to their grown children than to their parents (Fingerman & others, 2011a, 2012). When middle-aged adults have a parent with a disability, their support for that parent increases (Fingerman & others, 2011b). This support might involve locating a nursing home and monitoring its quality, procuring medical services, arranging public service assistance, and handling finances. In some cases, adult children provide direct assistance with daily living, including such activities as eating, bathing, and dressing. Even less severely impaired older adults may need help with shopping, housework, transportation, home maintenance, and bill paying.

Some researchers have found that relationships between aging parents and their children are usually characterized by ambivalence (Fingerman, Zarit, & Birditt, 2019). Perceptions include love, reciprocal help, and shared values on the positive side and isolation, family conflicts and problems, abuse, neglect, and caregiver stress on the negative side. One study found that middle-aged adults positively supported family responsibility to emerging adult children but were more ambivalent about providing care for aging parents, viewing it as both a joy and a burden (Igarashi & others, 2013). However, a study in the Netherlands revealed that affection and support, reflecting solidarity, were more prevalent than ambivalence in intergenerational relationships (Hogerbrugge & Komter, 2012).

With each new generation, personality characteristics, attitudes, and values are replicated or changed (Fingerman, Zarit, & Birditt, 2019). As older family members die, their biological, intellectual, emotional, and personal legacies are carried on in the next generation. Their children become the oldest generation and their grandchildren the second generation. As adult children become middle-aged, they often develop more positive perceptions of their parents (Field, 1999). Both similarity and dissimilarity across generations are found. For example, similarity between parents and an adult child is most noticeable in religion and politics, least in gender roles, lifestyle, and work orientation.

Gender differences also characterize intergenerational relationships (Pei, Cong, & Wu, 2020). Women play an especially important role in maintaining family relationships across generations. Women's relationships across generations are typically closer than other family bonds (Merrill, 2009). In one study, mothers and their daughters had much closer relationships during their adult years than mothers and sons, fathers and daughters, and fathers and sons (Rossi, 1989). Also in this study, married men were more involved with their wives' kin than with their own. One study revealed that mothers' intergenerational ties were more influential for grandparent-grandchild relationships than fathers' (Monserud, 2008).

When adults immigrate into another country, intergenerational stress may increase (Lin & others, 2014). In the last several decades, increasing numbers of Mexicans have immigrated into the United States, and their numbers are expected to increase. The pattern of immigration usually involves separation from the extended family (Parra-Cardona & others, 2006). It may also involve separation of immediate family members, with the husband coming first and then later bringing his wife and children. Those who were initially isolated, especially the wife, experience considerable stress due to relocation and the absence of family and friends. Within several years, a social network is usually established in the ethnic neighborhood.

As soon as some stability in their lives is achieved, Mexican families may sponsor the immigration of extended family members, such as a maternal or paternal sister or mother who provides child care and enables the mother to go to work. In some cases, the older generation remains behind and then joins their grown children in old age. The accessibility of Mexico facilitates visits to and from the village for vacations or at a time of crisis, such as when an adolescent runs away from home.

The discrepancies between acculturation levels can give rise to conflicting expectations within Mexican American families (Simpkins, Vest, & Price, 2011). The immigrant parents' model of child rearing may be out of phase with the dominant culture's model, which may cause reverberations through the family's generations, as discussed in earlier chapters. For example, parents and grandparents may be especially resistant to the demands for autonomy and dating made by adolescent daughters (Wilkinson-Lee & others, 2006). And in recent years an increasing number of female youth have left their Mexican American homes to further their education, an event that is often stressful for families with strong ties to Mexican values.

Karen Fingerman has conducted research on intergenerational relations and development in midlife. To read about her work, see the *Connecting with Careers* profile.

What are some different levels of acculturation that characterize many Mexican American families?
aldomurillo/Getty Images

How Do Mothers' and Daughters' Descriptions of Enjoyable Visits Differ at Different Points in Adult Development?

Dr. Karen Fingerman is a leading expert on aging, families, and socio-emotional development. She currently is a professor in the Department of Human Development and Family Sciences within the School of Human Ecology at the University of Texas at Austin. Prior to coming to UT-Austin, she was the Berner Hanley Professor of Gerontology at Purdue University. Dr. Fingerman obtained her Ph.D. from the University of Michigan and did post-doctoral work at Stanford University. She has published numerous articles on the positive and negative aspects of relationships involving mothers and daughters, grandparents and grandchildren, friends, and acquaintances, and on peripheral social ties. The National Institute of Aging, the Brookdale Foundation, and the MacArthur Transitions to Adulthood group have funded her research. Dr. Fingerman has received the Springer Award for Early Career Achievement in Research on Adult Development and Aging from the American Psychological Association, as well as the Margaret Baltes Award for Early Career Achievement in Behavioral and Social Gerontology from the Gerontological Association of America.

Dr. Karen Fingerman is a leading expert on aging, families, and socioemotional development. *For more information on what professors and researchers do, see the Careers in Life-Span Development Appendix.*
Courtesy of Dr. Karen Fingerman

Review *Connect* Reflect

 LG3 Identify some important aspects of close relationships in middle adulthood.

Review

- How can love, marriage, and divorce at midlife be characterized?
- What is the empty nest? How has it been refilling?
- What are sibling relationships and friendships like in middle adulthood?
- What is the nature of grandparenting?
- What are relationships across generations like?

Connect

- In this section, you read about divorce in middle adulthood. Based on what you learned earlier, what is one of the most common characteristics of divorced adults?

Reflect *Your Own Personal Journey of Life*

- What was or is the nature of your relationship with your grandparents? What are intergenerational relationships like in your family?

topical connections *looking forward*

Erikson's eighth and final stage of development—integrity versus despair—occurs in late adulthood. In this stage, individuals engage in a life review. Being active is linked with life satisfaction in late adulthood. Older adults become more selective about their social networks and choose to spend more time with emotionally rewarding relationships and less time with peripheral relationships. Older adults also experience more positive emotions and fewer negative emotions than younger adults. The personality traits of conscientiousness and agreeableness also increase in late adulthood. Because of losses (declines in physical or cognitive skills, for example), older adults often have to use accommodative strategies to reach their goals.

Socioemotional Development in Middle Adulthood

1 Personality Theories and Adult Development

 Describe personality theories and socioemotional development in middle adulthood.

Stages of Adulthood

- Erikson says that the seventh stage of the human life span, generativity versus stagnation, occurs in middle adulthood. Four types of generativity are biological, parental, work, and cultural.

- In Levinson's theory, developmental tasks must be mastered at different points in development, and changes in middle age focus on four conflicts: being young versus being old, being destructive versus being constructive, being masculine versus being feminine, and being attached to others versus being separated from them. Levinson asserted that a majority of Americans, especially men, experience a midlife crisis. Research, however, indicates that midlife crises are not pervasive. There is considerable individual variation in development during middle adulthood.

The Life-Events Approach

- According to the early version of the life-events approach, life events produce taxing circumstances that create stress. In the contemporary version of the life-events approach, the developmental effects of life events depend not only on the event itself but also on mediating factors, adaptation to the event, the life-stage context, and the sociohistorical context.

Stress and Personal Control in Midlife

- Researchers have found that young and middle-aged adults experience more stressful days and more multiple stressors than do older adults. On average, a sense of personal control decreases as adults become older—however, some aspects of personal control increase. Women and men differ in the way they experience and respond to stressors. Women are more likely to respond to stress in a tend-and-befriend manner, men in a fight-or-flight manner.

Contexts of Midlife Development

- Neugarten argues that the social environment of a particular cohort can alter its social clock—the timetable on which individuals are expected to accomplish life's tasks. Critics say that the adult stage theories are male-biased because they place too much emphasis on achievement and careers and do not adequately address women's concerns about relationships. Midlife varies for women, as it does for men. For some women, midlife is the prime of their lives. Many cultures do not have a clear concept of middle age. In many nonindustrialized societies, a woman's status improves in middle age.

2 Stability and Change

 Discuss stability and change in development during middle adulthood, as reflected in longitudinal studies.

Longitudinal Studies

- In Costa and McCrae's Baltimore Study, the Big Five personality factors—openness to experience, conscientiousness, extraversion, agreeableness, and neuroticism—showed considerable stability. However, researchers recently have found that the greatest change in personality occurs in early adulthood, with positive aspects of the factors peaking in middle age. The Big Five factors are linked to important aspects of a person's life, such as health and work.

- In the Berkeley Longitudinal Studies, extremes in the stability-change argument were not supported. The most stable characteristics were intellectual orientation, self-confidence, and openness to new experiences. The characteristics that changed the most were nurturance, hostility, and self-control.

- Helson's Mills College Study of women distinguished family-oriented and career-oriented women, as well as those who followed neither path. In their early forties, women experienced many of the concerns that Levinson described for men. However, rather than a midlife crisis, women experienced midlife consciousness.

- George Vaillant's research revealed links between a number of characteristics at age 50 and health and well-being at 75 to 80 years of age.

Conclusions

- The cumulative personality model states that with time and age personality becomes more stable. Changes in personality traits occur more in early adulthood than middle and late adulthood, but a number of aspects of personality do continue to change after early adulthood. Personality changes usually occur in a positive direction, reflecting social maturity. At the individual level, changes in personality are often linked to life experiences related to a particular developmental period. Some people change more than others.

3 Close Relationships

 LG3 Identify some important aspects of close relationships in middle adulthood.

Love, Marriage, and Divorce at Midlife

- Affectionate love increases in midlife, especially in marriages that have endured for many years. Marriage is more positive in middle adulthood when partners engage in activities together, and at midlife married couples have fewer health-related work problems than single people. Also, when couples have been married for at least 15 years, as they get older in middle age they show more positive characteristics. Although divorce has recently been decreasing in early adulthood, it has been increasing in middle adulthood.

The Empty Nest and Its Refilling

- Rather than decreasing marital satisfaction as once thought, the empty nest increases it for most parents. Following an unsuccessful career or a divorce, an increasing number of young adults are returning home to live with their parents. Some young adults do not leave home until their middle to late twenties because they are unable to support themselves financially.

Sibling Relationships and Friendships

- Sibling relationships continue throughout life. Some are close; others are distant. Friendships continue to be important in middle age.

Grandparenting

- There are different grandparent roles and styles. Grandmothers spend more time with grandchildren than grandfathers do, and the grandmother role involves greater expectations for maintaining ties across generations than the grandfather role. The profile of grandparents is changing because of factors such as divorce and remarriage. An increasing number of U.S. grandchildren live with their grandparents.

Intergenerational Relationships

- Family members usually maintain contact across generations. Mothers and daughters have the closest relationships. The middle-aged generation, which has been called the "sandwich" or "squeezed" generation, plays an important role in linking generations.

key **terms**

Big Five factors of
    personality 506
contemporary life-events
    approach 501

empty nest syndrome 512
fight-or-flight 504

social clock 504

tend-and-befriend 504

key **people**

John Clausen 508
Paul Costa 506
Erik Erikson 499

Karen Fingerman 516
Ravenna Helson 508
Daniel Levinson 499

Robert McCrae 506
Bernice Neugarten 504
Carol Ryff 499

Shelley Taylor 504
George Vaillant 499

section nine

To be seventy years young is sometimes far more cheerful and hopeful than to be forty years old.

—OLIVER WENDELL HOLMES, SR.
American physician, 19th century

Late Adulthood

The rhythm and meaning of human development eventually wend their way to late adulthood, when each of us stands alone at the heart of the earth and suddenly it is evening. We shed the leaves of youth and are stripped by the winds of time down to the truth. We learn that life is lived forward but understood backward. We trace the connection between the end and the beginning of life and try to figure out what this whole show is about before it is out. Ultimately, we come to know that we are what survives of us. This section contains three chapters: "Physical Development in Late Adulthood," "Cognitive Development in Late Adulthood," and "Socioemotional Development in Late Adulthood."

chapter 17

PHYSICAL DEVELOPMENT IN LATE ADULTHOOD

chapter **outline**

Jonathan Swift said, "No wise man ever wished to be younger." Without a doubt, a 70-year-old body does not work as well as it once did. It is also true that an individual's fear of aging is often greater than need be. As more individuals live to a ripe and active old age, our image of aging is changing. Although on average a 75-year-old's joints should be stiffening, people can practice not to be average. For example, a 75-year-old man might choose to train for and run a marathon; an 80-year-old woman whose capacity for work is undiminished might choose to make and sell children's toys.

Consider Mary "May" Segal, who was diagnosed with cardio-vascular problems about the time she retired at the age of 65. Her heart complications spurred her to begin an exercise program that involved climbing the steps at Duke University's football stadium in Durham, North Carolina. May turned 100 years of age in 2013 and maintained a regular exercise regimen for more than 35 years. When May was 78, she began exercising at the newly opened Duke University Health and Fitness Center. At 100, she was still going to the Center regularly, starting just after 9 a.m. May's exercise regimen included a swim, four laps walking around a track, and a 30-minute workout on a NuStep machine that combined leg exercise akin to climbing stairs with arm exercise similar to cross-country skiing. May's exercise speed was slower at age 100 than it had been when she was younger, and she was using a walker for her four laps around the track. In addition, she had reduced her workout regimen to three days per week.

May's motivation, resilience, and persistence is evident in her response to an unexpected injury. When she was 94 she fell and broke her hip, which for elderly adults can be a difficult setback with a prolonged recovery period. Her doctor told her she would never walk again, but May recovered and resumed her regular exercise program. After living a very long and fulfilling life, May passed away in December 2015.

May Segal engages in her exercise routine on her 100th birthday at the Duke University Health and Fitness Center.
Jill Knight/The News & Observer/AP Images

topical connections *looking back*

As more individuals are living healthier lives and medical discoveries are slowing down the aging process, middle age appears to be starting later and lasting longer. Increasingly, early middle age (40–54) is distinguished from late middle age (55–65). However, middle age is a time of declining physical skills—such as loss of height, impaired vision and hearing, and reduced cardiovascular functioning. Sleep also becomes more problematic. Sexual changes occur as women enter menopause, many middle-aged men begin to experience erectile dysfunction, and couples engage less frequently in sexual intercourse.

preview

The story of May Segal's physical development and well-being raises some truly fascinating questions about life-span development, which we will explore in this chapter. They include: Why do we age, and what, if anything, can we do to slow down the process? How long can we live? What chance do we have of living to be 100? How does the body change in old age? Can certain eating habits and exercise patterns help us live longer? How can we enhance older adults' quality of life?

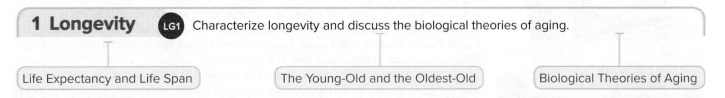

1 Longevity LG1 Characterize longevity and discuss the biological theories of aging.

| Life Expectancy and Life Span | The Young-Old and the Oldest-Old | Biological Theories of Aging |

In his eighties, Nobel-winning chemist Linus Pauling argued that vitamin C slows the aging process. Aging researcher Roy Walford fasted two days a week because he believed calorie restriction slowed the aging process. What do we really know about longevity?

LIFE EXPECTANCY AND LIFE SPAN

We are no longer a youthful society. The proportion of individuals at different ages has become increasingly similar. Since the beginning of recorded history, **life span,** the maximum number of years an individual can live, has continued to be approximately 120 to 125 years of age. But since 1900, improvements in medicine, nutrition, exercise, and lifestyle have increased our life expectancy by an average of 30 years. Keep in mind that it is not just improvements in the health and well-being of adults that have contributed to increased longevity but also the substantial reduction in infant deaths in recent decades.

Recall that **life expectancy** is the number of years that the average person born in a particular year will probably live. The average life expectancy of individuals born in 2018 in the United States was 78.6 years (Xu & others, 2020). Sixty-five-year-olds in the United States today can expect to live an average of 19.5 more years (20.7 for females, 18.1 for males) (Xu & others, 2020).

Life Expectancy How does the United States fare in life expectancy, compared with other countries around the world? We do considerably better than some and somewhat worse than others. In 2018, Monaco had the highest estimated life expectancy at birth (89.4 years), followed by Japan, Singapore, and Macau (a region of China near Hong Kong) (85 years) (Central Intelligence Agency, 2015). Of 224 countries surveyed, the United States ranked 53rd at 78.6 years. The lowest estimated life expectancy in 2015 occurred in the African countries of South Africa (50.6 years), Chad (51), and Namibia (51). Differences in life expectancies across countries reflect factors such as health conditions and medical care throughout the life span.

In a recent analysis, projections of life expectancy in 2030 were made for 35 developed countries (Kontis & others, 2017). Life expectancy in the United States is predicted to increase to 83.3 years for women and 79.5 years for men by 2030. However, the United States, although expected to increase in life expectancy, has one of the lowest growth rates in life expectancy among all the countries in the study. South Korea is projected to have the highest life expectancy in 2030, with South Korean women predicted to have an average life expectancy of 90.8, the first nation to break the 90-year life expectancy barrier. Why is life expectancy for the United States predicted to increase so much more slowly than South Korea? The United States has the highest child and maternal mortality rates, homicide rate, and body-mass index of high-income countries in the world. In South Korea, delayed onset of chronic diseases is occurring and children's nutrition is improving. South Korea also has a low rate of obesity, and blood pressure is not as high as it is in most countries.

Life expectancy also differs for various ethnic groups within the United States and for men and women. For example, in 2017 the life expectancy of African Americans (75.3) in the

> To me old age is always fifteen years older than I am.
>
> —**Bernard Baruch**
> *American statesman, 20th century*

> Each of us stands alone at the heart of the earth, pierced through by a ray of sunshine: And suddenly it is evening.
>
> —**Salvatore Quasimodo**
> *Italian poet, 20th century*

life span The maximum number of years an individual can live. The life span of human beings is about 120 to 125 years of age.

life expectancy The number of years that will probably be lived by the average person born in a particular year.

(a)

(b)

(c)

(*a*) People in Monaco, a very wealthy country with virtually no poverty and superb health care, have the highest life expectancy in the world (89.4 years); (*b*) Life expectancy in Russia is only 66 years of age, likely due to high rates of alcohol consumption and tobacco use; and (*c*) South Africa, a country with high rates of poverty where many newborns have a low birth weight, has a life expectancy of 50.3.

(*a*) Christophe Ena/AP Images; (*b*) Sergei Supinsky/AFP/Getty Images; (*c*) Conrad Bornman/Gallo Images/Getty Images

United States was 6.5 years lower than the life expectancy for Latinos (81.8) and 3.2 years lower than for non-Latino Whites (78.5) (Murphy & others, 2018). Latino women had a life expectancy of 84.3 and non-Latino White women had a life expectancy of 81.2, followed by African American women (78.5), non-Latino White men (76.4 years), and African American men (71.9 years) (Murphy & others, 2018).

The fact that Latinos live 3.3 years longer than non-Latino Whites despite having lower educational attainment and income levels is called the "Latino Health Paradox" (Atiemo & others, 2019). Why does this discrepancy occur? Among the proposed reasons are migration patterns, extended family connections, and rates of smoking. In terms of migration patterns, Latino immigrants who stay in the United States tend to be healthier than average, while those who return to their countries of origin tend to be older and less healthy. In terms of extended family connections, Latinos provide more support and interaction to their relatives, resulting in less loneliness for Latinos than for non-Latino Whites (Brill, 2019). And in terms of smoking, Latinos are less likely to smoke than non-Latino Whites. In a recent study supporting the Latino Health Paradox, older adult Latinos reported being healthier than their non-Latino White counterparts (Olsen, Basu Roy, & Tseng, 2019).

In 2018, the overall life expectancy for U.S. women was 81.2 years of age, and for men it was 76.2 years of age (Xu & others, 2020). Beginning in their mid-thirties, women outnumber men; this gap widens during the remainder of the adult years. By the time adults are 75 years of age, more than 61 percent of the population is female; for those 85 and over, the figure is almost 70 percent female. Why can women expect to live longer than men? Social factors such as health attitudes, habits, lifestyles, and occupation are probably important. Men are more likely than women to die from most of the leading causes of death in the United States, including cancer of the respiratory system, motor vehicle accidents, cirrhosis of the liver, emphysema, and heart disease (Alfredsson & others, 2018). These causes of death are associated with lifestyle. For example, the sex difference in deaths due to lung cancer and emphysema occurs because men are heavier smokers than women. However, women are more likely than men to die from some disorders such as Alzheimer disease and some aspects of cardiovascular disease, such as hypertension-related problems (Ostan & others, 2016).

The sex difference in longevity also is influenced by biological factors (Nusselder & others, 2019: Sampathkumar & others, 2020). In virtually all species, females outlive males. Women have more resistance to infections and degenerative diseases (Pan & Chang, 2012). For example, the female's estrogen production helps to protect her from arteriosclerosis (hardening of the arteries) (Valera & others, 2015). And the additional X chromosome that women carry in comparison with men may be associated with the production of more antibodies to fight off disease. The sex difference in mortality is still present but less pronounced than in the past. In 1979, the sex difference in longevity favored women by 7.8 years, but in 2017 the difference was down to 5.0 years (Xu & others, 2020).

Among various groups, the longest average longevity in the United States belongs to Seventh Day Adventists, who have a life expectancy of 88 years. One reason for their longevity is that their religious practices include positive lifestyle choices such as a vegetarian diet.

What about your own life expectancy? What is the likelihood that you will live to be 100? To evaluate this possibility, see Figure 1.

Centenarians In developed countries, the number of centenarians (individuals 100 years and older) is increasing at a rate of approximately 7 percent each year (Perls, 2007). In the United States, there were only 15,000 centenarians in 1980, but that number rose to 50,000 in 2000 and to 82,000 in 2016 (Statista, 2020). The number of U.S. centenarians is projected to reach 589,000 by 2060. The United States has the most centenarians, followed by Japan, China, and England/Wales (Goodman, 2019). The label *supercentenarian* is now being applied to individuals who live to be 110. Statistics are somewhat sketchy about how many people are currently alive at 110 years and older in the United States and in the world, although it is agreed that it is a small number and also that the number has been increasing in the last decade. One estimate is that there are about 60 supercentenarians alive in a given year in the United States and about 300 in the world (Perls, 2015).

Three major studies of centenarians are the New England Centenarian Study, the Georgia Centenarian Study, and the Chinese Longitudinal Healthy Longevity Survey. The New England Centenarian Study (NECS) began in 1994 under the direction of Thomas Perls and his colleagues (Fagan & others, 2017; Perls, 2007, 2009). Many people expect that "the older you get, the sicker

Life Expectancy

Decide how each item applies to you and add or subtract the appropriate number of years from your basic life expectancy.

1. Family history
____ Add five years if two or more of your grandparents lived to 80 or beyond.
____ Subtract four years if any parent, grandparent, sister, or brother died of a heart attack or stroke before 50.
____ Subtract two years if anyone died from these diseases before 60.
____ Subtract three years for each case of diabetes, thyroid disorder, breast cancer, cancer of the digestive system, asthma, or chronic bronchitis among parents or grandparents.

2. Marital status
____ If you are married, add four years.
____ If you are over 25 and not married, subtract one year for every unmarried decade.

3. Economic status
____ Add two years if your family income is over $60,000 per year.
____ Subtract three years if you have been poor for the greater part of your life.

4. Physique
____ Subtract one year for every 10 pounds you are overweight.
____ For each inch your girth measurement exceeds your chest measurement deduct two years.
____ Add three years if you are over 40 and not overweight.

5. Exercise
____ Add three years if you exercise regularly and moderately (jogging three times a week).
____ Add five years if you exercise regularly and vigorously (long-distance running three times a week).
____ Subtract three years if your job is sedentary.
____ Add three years if your job is active.

6. Alcohol
____ Add two years if you are a light drinker (one to three drinks a day).
____ Subtract five to ten years if you are a heavy drinker (more than four drinks per day).
____ Subtract one year if you are a teetotaler.

7. Smoking
____ Subtract eight years if you smoke two or more packs of cigarettes per day.
____ Subtract two years if you smoke one to two packs per day.
____ Subtract two years if you smoke less than one pack.
____ Subtract two years if you regularly smoke a pipe or cigars.

8. Disposition
____ Add two years if you are a reasoned, practical person.
____ Subtract two years if you are aggressive, intense, and competitive.
____ Add one to five years if you are basically happy and content with life.
____ Subtract one to five years if you are often unhappy, worried, and often feel guilty.

9. Education
____ Subtract two years if you have less than a high school education.
____ Add one year if you attended four years of school beyond high school.
____ Add three years if you attended five or more years beyond high school.

10. Environment
____ Add four years if you have lived most of your life in a rural environment.
____ Subtract two years if you have lived most of your life in an urban environment.

11. Sleep
____ Subtract five years if you sleep more than nine hours a day.

12. Temperature
____ Add two years if your home's thermostat is set at no more than 68° F.

13. Health care
____ Add three years if you have regular medical checkups and regular dental care.
____ Subtract two years if you are frequently ill.

____ **Your Life Expectancy Total**

FIGURE 1

CAN YOU LIVE TO BE 100? This test gives you a rough guide for predicting your longevity. The basic life expectancy for men is 75 years, and for women it is 81. Write down your basic life expectancy. If you are in your fifties or sixties, you should add ten years to the basic figure because you have already proved yourself to be a durable individual. If you are over age 60 and active, you can add another two years.

you get." However, according to the NECS, this is not true for a majority of centenarians. The researchers have found that chronic high-mortality diseases are markedly delayed for many years in centenarians, with many not experiencing disability until near the end of their lives (Sebastiani & Perls, 2012). A NECS study of centenarians from 100 to 119 years of age found that the older the age group (110 to 119—referred to as *supercentenarians*—compared with 100 to 104, for example), the later the onset of diseases such as cancer and cardiovascular disease, as well as functional decline (Andersen & others, 2012). Perls refers to this process of staving off high-mortality chronic diseases until much later ages than usual as the *compression of morbidity*.

Among the factors in the NECS that are associated with living to be 100 are longevity genes and the ability to cope effectively with stress. The researchers also have discovered a strong genetic component of living to be 100 that consists of many genetic links that each have modest effects but as a group can have a strong influence (Sebastiani & Perls, 2012). For example, a meta-analysis of five studies in the United States, Europe, and Japan concluded that when their influence is combined, approximately 130 genes "do a relatively good job" of differentiating centenarians from non-centenarians (Sebastiani & others, 2013). These genes play roles in Alzheimer disease, diabetes, cardiovascular disease, cancer, and various biological processes. Other characteristics of centenarians in the New England Centenarian Study include

Three participants in the New England Centenarian Study: (*Top*) Agnes Fenton, a resident of Englewood, New Jersey, celebrated her 110th birthday in 2015. She still cooked her own meals and said that believing in God was a key factor in her longevity. (*Middle*) Louis Charpentier, age 104, lived near Boston and his main hobby was carving wooden figures in his basement shop. Louis said his memory was still very good. (*Bottom*) Edythe Kirchmaier, from the New York City area, was Facebook's oldest user at 105 years of age with more than 51,000 followers. She volunteered every week at her favorite charity, still drove her car, and used the Internet to look up information and facts. (*Top*) Carmine Galasso/The Record/MCT/Newscom; (*middle*) Courtesy of the New England Centenarian Study, Boston University; (*bottom*) Isaac Hernandez

the following: few of the centenarians are obese, habitual smoking is rare, and only a small percentage (less than 15 percent) have had significant changes in their thinking skills (disproving the belief that most centenarians are likely to develop Alzheimer disease).

In addition to the New England Centenarian Study, another major ongoing study is the Georgia Centenarian Study conducted by Leonard Poon and his colleagues (Cho & others, 2020; Nakagawa & others, 2018; Poon & others, 2010, 2012; Tanprasertsuk & others, 2020). In a review, Poon and his colleagues (2010) concluded that social dynamics involving life events (experiencing a higher number of negative life events is linked to lower self-rated health), personality (conscientiousness is positively associated with higher levels of physical and mental health), cognition (cognitive measures are better predictors of mental health than physical health), and socioeconomic resources and support systems (social, economic, and personal resources are related to mental and physical health) contribute to the health and quality of life of older adults, including centenarians. And in a recent study of U.S. and Japanese centenarians, in both countries, health resources (better cognitive function, fewer hearing problems, and positive activities in daily living) were linked to a higher level of well-being (Nakagawa & others, 2019).

Yet another major study is the Chinese Longitudinal Healthy Longevity Survey, which includes older adults, some of whom are centenarians (An & others, 2019; Hu & others, 2019; Kuang & others, 2020; X. Li & others, 2020a; Xiao, Wu, & Zeng, 2019; Xu & others, 2019; Yang, 2020). In one investigation involving this sample, Chinese centenarians showed better coping and adjustment (greater personal tenacity, optimism, coping with negative moods, secure relationships, and personal control) than their Chinese counterparts in their nineties, eighties, or seventies (Zeng & Shen, 2010). In this study, 94- to 98-year-olds with better resilience had a 43 percent higher likelihood of becoming a centenarian than their same-aged counterparts who were less resilient. In a Chinese Longitudinal Healthy Longevity survey, a higher level of education was linked to greater longevity (Luo, Zhang, & Gu, 2015). And in a recent study with this sample, severe loneliness at prior assessment points predicted poorer cognitive function in subsequent assessments (Zhong & others, 2017).

How do centenarians view their lives? What are their opinions about why they have been able to live so long?

- Elza Wynn concludes that he has been able to live so long because he has made up his mind to do so. He says he was thinking about dying when he was 77, but decided to wait a while (Segerberg, 1982).

- Ruth Climer was a physical education teacher for many years and later competed in the Senior Olympics. To live to be 100, she says, it is important to stay focused on what is good now and not give in to negative thoughts. Ruth also believes that staying busy and always moving forward are keys to longevity (O'Dell, 2013).

- Billy Red Fox thinks that being active and not worrying are important keys to living to be 100. At 95, he switched jobs to become a public relations representative. Even at 100, he travels 11 months of the year making public appearances and talking with older adults (Segerberg, 1982).

- Simo Radulovich thinks that living to an old age requires having a sense of humor, living moderately, and sleeping well. He continues to engage in exercise games with his friends every day and says he has never been afraid of anything but always had confidence that he could get through the tough times (O'Dell, 2013).

- Mary Butler says that finding something to laugh about every day has helped her live longer. She thinks a good laugh is better than a dose of medicine anytime (Segerberg, 1982).

- Duran Baez remarried at 50 and went on to have 15 more children. At 100 years of age, he was asked if he had any ambitions he had not yet realized. Duran replied, "No" (Segerberg, 1982).

- Jeanne Louise Calment, the world's longest-living person who died at 122, attributed her longevity to a number of things: Don't worry about things you can't do anything about. Enjoy an occasional glass of port wine and a diet rich in olive oil. Laugh often. Regarding her ability to live so long, she once said that God must have forgotten about her. On her 120th birthday, an interviewer asked her what kind of future she anticipated. Jeanne Louise replied, "A very short one." Becoming accustomed to the media attention she got, at 117 she stated, "I wait for death . . . and journalists." She walked, biked, and exercised regularly. Jeanne Louise began taking fencing lessons at 85 and rode a bicycle until she was 100.

(a)

(b)

(a) Frenchwoman Jeanne Louise Calment, shown here celebrating her 117th birthday, was the oldest documented living person. She lived to be 122 years of age. (b) Simo Radulovich, 103 years of age in 2013, says that the best thing about living past 100 is being able to enjoy family and friends. He and his wife have been married more than 60 years.
(a) Jean-Pierre Fizet/Sygma/Getty Images; (b) Courtesy of The Radulovich Family

As of March 1, 2020, the oldest living person in the world was 117-year-old Kane Tanakaa of Japan. The oldest living person in the United States was 114-year-old Hester Ford of Charlotte, North Carolina.

What chance do you have of living to be 100? Genes play an important role in surviving to an extreme old age (Toupance & Benetos, 2019; Yuan & others, 2020). As we saw in the chapter on "Biological Beginnings," the search for longevity genes has recently intensified (Romero-Ortuno, Kenny, & McManus, 2020; Tan & others, 2020). But there are additional factors at work, such as family history, health (weight, diet, smoking, and exercise), education, personality, stress, and lifestyle (Belenguer-Varea & others, 2020; Diekmann & Bauer, 2019). Recall that in the epigenetic approach, there is an increased focus on identifying gene × environment (G × E) interactions that influence development (Lindahl-Jacobsen & Christensen, 2019). For example, a Chinese study found that a combination of particular FOXO genotypes and drinking tea was associated with the prevention of cognitive decline in the oldest-old, aged 92+ (Zeng & others, 2016).

To further examine the factors that are involved in living to a very old age, let's journey to the island of Okinawa in the East China Sea where individuals live longer than anywhere else in the world. In Okinawa, there are 34.7 centenarians for every 100,000 inhabitants, the highest ratio in the world. In comparison, the United States has about 10 centenarians for every 100,000 residents. The life expectancy in Okinawa is 81.2 years (86 for women, 78 for men), also one of the highest in the world.

What is responsible for such longevity in Okinawa? Some possible explanations include the following (Nishihara & others, 2016; Willcox & Willcox, 2014; Willcox, Willcox, & Suzuki, 2017; Willcox & others, 2007, 2008):

- *Diet.* Okinawans eat very healthy food, heavy on grains, fish, and vegetables, light on meat, eggs, and dairy products. This diet actually produces mild caloric restriction (10 to 15 percent) (Willcox & Willcox, 2014). The risk of dying from cancer is far lower among Okinawans than among Japanese and Americans (see Figure 2). About 100,000 Okinawans moved to Brazil during the mid-twentieth century and quickly adopted the eating patterns of their new home, which rely heavily on red meat. The result: The life expectancy of the Brazilian Okinawans is now 17 years lower than Okinawa's 81 years!
- *Low-stress lifestyle.* The easygoing lifestyle in Okinawa more closely resembles that of a laid-back South Sea island than that of the high-stress Japanese mainland.
- *Caring community.* Okinawans look out for each other and do not isolate or ignore their older adults. If older adults need help, they don't

developmental **connection**

Heredity

Scientists are increasing their search for genes that are linked to how long people are likely to live. Connect to "Biological Beginnings."

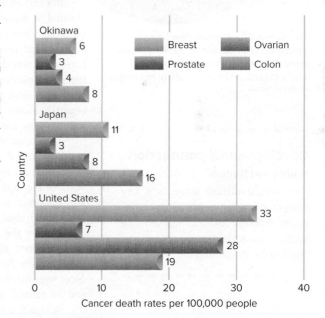

FIGURE **2**

RISKS OF DYING FROM CANCER IN OKINAWA, JAPAN, AND THE UNITED STATES. The risk of dying from different forms of cancer is lower in Okinawa than in the United States and Japan (Willcox, Willcox, & Suzuki, 2002). Okinawans eat lots of tofu and soy products, which are rich in flavonoids (substances that are believed to lower the risk of breast and prostate cancer). They also consume large amounts of fish, especially tuna, mackerel, and salmon, which reduces the risk of breast cancer.

hesitate to ask a neighbor. Such support and caring is likely responsible for Okinawa having the lowest suicide rate among older women in East Asia, a region noted for its high suicide rate among older women.

- *Activity.* Many older adults in Okinawa are physically vigorous, engaging in activities such as taking walks and working in their gardens. Many older Okinawans also continue working at their jobs.

- *Spirituality.* Many older adults in Okinawa find a sense of purpose in spiritual practice. Prayer is commonplace and believed to ease the mind of stress and problems.

THE YOUNG-OLD AND THE OLDEST-OLD

Teru Kingjo, 88, continues to work as a weaver on Okinawa Island, Japan. She, like many Okinawans, believes that having a sense of purpose helps people to live longer.
Ana Nance/Redux

Do you want to live to be 100, or 90? These ages are part of late adulthood, which begins in the sixties and extends to approximately 120 to 125 years of age. This is the longest span of any period of human development—50 to 60 years. Increasingly, a distinction is being made between the *young-old* (65 to 84 years of age) and *oldest-old* (85 years and older). An increased interest in successful aging is producing a portrayal of the oldest-old that is more optimistic than past stereotypes (Kinugawa, 2019; Teater & Chonody, 2020). Interventions such as cataract surgery and a variety of rehabilitation strategies are improving the functioning of the oldest-old (Stringa & others, 2020). And there is cause for optimism in the development of new regimens of prevention and intervention, such as engaging in regular exercise (Garcia-Hermoso & others, 2020).

Many experts on aging prefer to talk about the categories of young-old and oldest-old in terms of *function* rather than age. Recall that we have described age not only in terms of chronological age but also in terms of biological age, psychological age, and social age. Thus, in terms of *functional age*—the person's actual ability to function—an 85-year-old might well be more biologically and psychologically fit than a 65-year-old.

Still, there are some significant differences between adults in their sixties or seventies and adults who are 85 and older. Paul Baltes and his colleagues (Baltes, 2003; Scheibe, Freund, & Baltes, 2007) argue that the oldest-old (85 and over) face a number of problems, including sizable losses in cognitive potential and ability to learn; an increase in chronic stress; a substantial prevalence of physical and mental disabilities; high levels of frailty; increased loneliness; and the difficulty of dying with dignity at older ages. He contrasts the problems of the oldest-old with the increase in successful aging of adults in their sixties and seventies. Compared with the oldest-old, the young-old have a substantial potential for physical and cognitive fitness, higher levels of emotional well-being, and more effective strategies for mastering the gains and losses of old age.

The oldest-old today are mostly female, and the majority of these women are widowed and live alone if they are not institutionalized. A recent list (2020) of the world's oldest living people had no men in the top 50. The majority also are hospitalized at some time in the last years of life, and the majority die alone in a hospital or institution. Their needs, capacities, and resources are often different from those of older adults in their sixties and seventies (Scheibe, Freund, & Baltes, 2007).

Despite the negative portrait of the oldest-old by Baltes and his colleagues, they are a heterogeneous, diversified group (Lindahl-Jacobsen & Christensen, 2019; Ribeiro & Araujo, 2019). In the New England Centenarian Study, 15 percent of the individuals 100 years and older were living independently at home, 35 percent with family members or in assisted living, and 50 percent in nursing homes (Perls, 2007).

A significant number of the oldest-old have cognitive impairments, but many do not (Nikitin & Freund, 2019). Almost one-fourth of the oldest-old are institutionalized, and many report some limitation of activity or difficulties in caring for themselves. However, more than three-fourths are not institutionalized. The majority of older adults aged 80 and over continue to live in the community. More than one-third of people who are 80-plus and live in the community report that their health is excellent or good; 40 percent say that they have no activity limitations (Suzman & others, 1992). A substantial subgroup of the oldest-old are robust and active. The oldest-old who have aged successfully have often been unnoticed and unstudied.

---

developmental connection

Nature and Nurture

The nature-nurture issue is a key aspect of understanding development throughout the human life span. Connect to "Introduction" and "Biological Beginnings."

BIOLOGICAL THEORIES OF AGING

Even if we stay remarkably healthy, we begin to age at some point. In fact, some life-span experts argue that biological aging begins at birth (Schaie, 2000). What are the biological explanations of aging? Intriguing explanations of why we age are provided by three categories of biological theories: evolutionary theory, genetic/cellular process theories, and hormonal stress theory.

Evolutionary Theory of Aging   Recall from "Biological Beginnings" the view that the benefits conferred by evolutionary selection decrease with age (Baltes, 2003). In the **evolutionary theory of aging,** natural selection has not eliminated many harmful conditions and nonadaptive characteristics in older adults (Laisk & others, 2019). Why? Because natural selection is linked to reproductive fitness, which is present only in the earlier part of adulthood (Buss, 2019). For example, consider Alzheimer disease, an irreversible brain disorder that does not appear until late middle adulthood or late adulthood. In evolutionary theory, if Alzheimer disease occurred earlier in development, it might have been eliminated many centuries ago. Evolutionary theory, however, has its critics (Cohen, 2015). One criticism is that the "big picture" idea of natural selection leading to the development of human traits and behaviors is difficult to refute or test because evolution occurs on a time scale that does not lend itself to empirical study. Another criticism is the failure of evolutionary theory to account for cultural influences (Sueur & others, 2019).

Genetic/Cellular Process Theories   Some experts believe that aging is best explained by cellular maintenance requirements and evolutionary constraints (Vanhaelen, 2015). In recent decades, there has been a significant increase in research on genetic and cellular processes involved in aging (Entringer & Epel, 2020). Five such advances involve telomeres, free radicals, mitochondria, sirtuins, and the mTOR pathway.

Cellular Clock/Telomere Theory   **Cellular clock theory** is Leonard Hayflick's (1977) theory that cells can divide a maximum of about 75 to 80 times, and that as we age our cells become less capable of dividing. Hayflick found that cells extracted from adults in their fifties to seventies divided fewer than 75 to 80 times. Based on the ways cells divide, Hayflick places the upper limit of the human life-span potential at about 120 to 125 years of age.

In the last decade, scientists have tried to fill a gap in cellular clock theory (Toubiana & Selig, 2020; Toupance & Benetos, 2019): Hayflick did not know why cells die. The answer may lie at the tips of chromosomes, at telomeres, which are DNA sequences that cap chromosomes (Fani & others, 2020; Shay & Wright, 2019).

Each time a cell divides, the telomeres become shorter (Fragkiadaki & others, 2020) (see Figure 3). After about 70 or 80 replications, the telomeres are dramatically shortened, and the cell no longer can reproduce. Research indicates that telomere shortening does play a role in aging (Toupance & Benetos, 2019). For example, one study revealed that healthy centenarians had longer telomeres than unhealthy centenarians (Terry & others, 2008). Further, a recent study confirmed that shorter telomere length was linked to Alzheimer disease (Scarabino & others, 2017). And a recent research review concluded that lifestyle modifications involving exercise and diet show encouraging results for delaying telomere shortening (Qiao, Jiang, & Li, 2020).

Injecting the enzyme telomerase into human cells grown in the laboratory has been found to substantially extend the life of the cells beyond the approximately 70 to 80 normal cell divisions (Harrison, 2012). However, telomerase is present in approximately 85 to 90 percent of cancerous cells and thus may not promote healthy life extension of cells (Cleal, Norris, & Baird, 2018). To capitalize on the high presence of telomerase in cancerous cells, researchers currently are investigating telomerase-related gene therapies that inhibit telomerase and lead to the death of cancerous cells while keeping healthy cells alive (Shay & Wright, 2019; Wu & others, 2020). A recent focus of these gene therapies is on stem cells and their renewal (Bonafe, Sabbatinelli, & Olivieri, 2020; Ye, Yang, & Lei, 2019). Telomeres and telomerase are increasingly thought to be key components of the stem cell regeneration process, providing a possible avenue to restrain cancer and delay aging (Ullah & Sun, 2019).

Free-Radical Theory   A second microbiological theory of aging is **free-radical theory,** which states that people age because when cells metabolize energy, the by-products include unstable oxygen molecules known as *free radicals*. The free radicals ricochet around the cells, damaging DNA and other cellular structures (Kowalska & others, 2020). The damage can lead to a range of disorders, including cancer (Purohit, Simeone, & Lyssiotis, 2019) and arthritis (Mateen &

developmental **connection**
Genes
Scientists are conducting research on specific longevity and susceptibility genes. Connect to "Biological Beginnings."

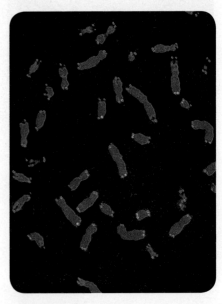

FIGURE 3
TELOMERES AND AGING. The photograph shows actual telomeres lighting up the tips of chromosomes.
Courtesy of Dr. Jerry Shay

evolutionary theory of aging This theory states that natural selection has not eliminated many harmful conditions and nonadaptive characteristics in older adults; thus, the benefits conferred by evolution decline with age because natural selection is linked to reproductive fitness.

cellular clock theory Leonard Hayflick's theory that the maximum number of times that human cells can divide is about 75 to 80. As we age, our cells have less capacity to divide.

free-radical theory A microbiological theory stating that people age because normal metabolic processes within their cells produce unstable oxygen molecules known as free radicals. These molecules ricochet around inside cells, damaging DNA and other cellular structures.

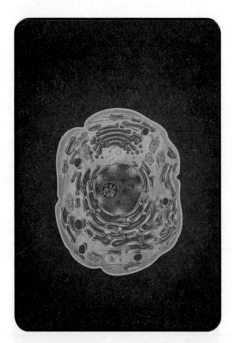

FIGURE 4

MITOCHONDRIA. This color-coded illustration of a typical cell shows mitochondria in green. The illustration also includes the nucleus (pink) with its DNA (brown). *In what ways might changes in mitochondria be involved in aging?*
J. Bavosi/Science Source

mitochondrial theory The theory that aging is caused by the decay of mitochondria, tiny cellular bodies that supply energy for function, growth, and repair.

sirtuins A family of proteins that have been proposed as having important influences on longevity, mitochondria functioning in energy, calorie restriction benefits, stress resistance, and cardiovascular functioning.

mTOR pathway A cellular pathway involving the regulation of growth and metabolism that has been proposed as a key aspect of longevity

hormonal stress theory The theory that aging in the body's hormonal system can decrease resistance to stress and increase the likelihood of disease.

others, 2019). Overeating is linked with an increase in free radicals, and researchers recently found that calorie restriction—a diet restricted in calories but adequate in proteins, vitamins, and minerals—reduces the oxidative damage created by free radicals (Wei & Ji, 2018). In a recent study of 57- to 83-year-olds, a healthy body weight was linked to reduced oxidative stress (Anusruti & others, 2020). In addition to looking at diet, researchers also are exploring the role that exercise might play in reducing oxidative damage in cells (Kruk, Kotarska, & Aboul-Enein, 2020).

Mitochondrial Theory   There is increasing interest in the role that *mitochondria*—tiny bodies within cells that supply essential energy for function, growth, and repair—might play in aging (Ahmadi, Golalipour, & Samaei, 2019) (see Figure 4). **Mitochondrial theory** states that aging is due to the decay of mitochondria. Mitochondrial theory emphasizes that this decay is primarily caused by oxidative damage and loss of critical micronutrients supplied by the cell (Gollihue & Norris, 2020; Son & Lee, 2019).

Defects in mitochondria are linked with cardiovascular disease (Roushandeh, Kuwahara, & Roudkenar, 2019); neurodegenerative diseases such as Alzheimer disease (X. Li & others, 2020b) and Parkinson disease (Zhi & others, 2019); diabetic kidney disease (Forbes & Thorburn, 2018); and impaired liver functioning (Stevanovic & others, 2020). Mitochondria also likely play important roles in neuronal plasticity (Lees, Johnson, & Ashby, 2020). However, it is not known whether the defects in mitochondria cause aging or are merely accompaniments of the aging process (Brand, 2011).

Sirtuin Theory   **Sirtuins** are a family of proteins that have been linked to longevity, regulation of mitochondria functioning in energy, possible benefits of calorie restriction, stress resistance, and lower rates of diabetes, Alzheimer disease, Parkinson disease, cardiovascular disease, and cancer (Cacabelos & others, 2019; Fang, Tang, & Li, 2019; Y. Liu & others, 2020; Shieh, Huang, & Lin, 2020). Later in the chapter, we will discuss one of the sirtuins, SIRT 1, that has been connected to DNA repair and aging.

mTOR Pathway Theory   The **mTOR pathway** is a cellular pathway that involves the regulation of growth and metabolism. TOR stands for "target of rapamycin," and in mammals it is called mTOR. Rapamycin is a naturally derived antibiotic and immune system suppressant/modulator that was discovered in the 1960s on Easter Island. It has been commonly used and is FDA approved for preventing rejection of transplanted organs and bone marrow. Recently, proposals have been made that the mTOR pathway plays a central role in the life of cells, acting as a cellular router for growth, protein production/metabolism, and stem cell functioning (Jin & others, 2019; Lee & others, 2020). Some scientists also argue that the pathway is linked to longevity, the successful outcomes of calorie restriction, and reducing cognitive decline, and that it plays a role in a number of diseases, including cancer, cardiovascular disease, and Alzheimer disease (Dimri & Satyanarayana, 2020; Rostamzadeh & others, 2019). The rapamycin drug has not been approved as an anti-aging drug and has some serious side effects, including increased risk of infection and lymphoma, a deadly cancer.

Some critics argue that scientific support has not been found for the role of sirtuins and the mTOR pathway in the aging process in humans and that research has not adequately documented the capacity of drugs such as rapamycin to slow the aging process or extend the human life span (Ehninger, Neff, & Xie, 2014).

Hormonal Stress Theory   Cellular clock, free-radical, mitochondrial, sirtuin, and mTOR pathway theories attempt to explain aging at genetic and cellular levels. In contrast, **hormonal stress theory** argues that aging in the body's hormonal system can lower resistance to stress and increase the likelihood of disease (Finch & Seeman, 1999).

When faced with external challenges such as stressful situations, the human body adapts by altering internal physiological processes (van Deurzen & Vanhoutte, 2019). This process of adaptation and adjustment is referred to as *allostasis*. Allostasis is adaptive in the short term; however, continuous accommodation of physiological systems in response to stressors may result in *allostatic load*, a wearing down of body systems due to constant activity (Bourdon & others, 2020; Piazza, Stawski, & Sheffler, 2019).

Normally, when people experience stressors, the body responds by releasing certain hormones. As people age, the hormones stimulated by stress remain at elevated levels longer than they did when people were younger (Gekle, 2017). These prolonged, elevated levels of stress-related hormones are associated with increased risks for many diseases, including cardiovascular disease, cancer, diabetes, and hypertension (J. Li & others, 2020). Researchers are exploring stress-buffering strategies, including exercise, in an effort to find ways to attenuate some of the negative effects of stress on the aging process (Venkatesh & others, 2020).

Recently, a variation of hormonal stress theory has emphasized the role of declining immune system functioning in aging (de la Fuente, 2019; Fulop & others, 2019). In a recent study, the percentage of T cells (a type of white blood cell essential for immunity) decreased in older adults in their seventies, eighties, and nineties (Song & others, 2018). Aging contributes to immune system deficits that give rise to infectious diseases in older adults (Salminen, 2020). The extended duration of stress and diminished restorative processes in older adults may accelerate the effects of aging on immunity.

Conclusions Which of these biological theories best explains aging? That question has yet to be answered. It likely will turn out that more than one—or perhaps all—of these biological processes contribute to aging. In one analysis, it was concluded that aging is a very complex process involving multiple degenerative factors, including interacting cell- and organ-level communications (de Magalhaes & Tacutu, 2016). Although there are some individual aging triggers such as telomere shortening, a full understanding of biological aging encompasses multiple processes operating at different biological levels.

Review *Connect* Reflect

LG1 Characterize longevity and discuss the biological theories of aging.

Review
- What is the difference between life span and life expectancy? What characterizes centenarians? What sex differences exist in longevity?
- How can the differences between the young-old and oldest-old be summarized?
- What are the five main biological theories of aging?

Connect
- Go back to Figure 1 and see if you can link any of the items listed with

research or theories you read about in this section or in earlier chapters (for example, item 2 states "If you are married, add four years," and earlier we read that "Individuals who are happily married live longer, healthier lives than either divorced individuals or those who are unhappily married").

Reflect *Your Own Personal Journey of Life*
- To what age do you think you will live? Why? To what age would you like to live?

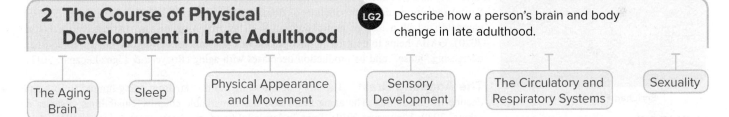

2 The Course of Physical Development in Late Adulthood

LG2 Describe how a person's brain and body change in late adulthood.

The Aging Brain | Sleep | Physical Appearance and Movement | Sensory Development | The Circulatory and Respiratory Systems | Sexuality

The physical decline that accompanies aging usually occurs slowly, and sometimes lost function can even be restored. We'll examine the main physical changes behind the losses of late adulthood and describe ways that older adults can age successfully.

THE AGING BRAIN

How does the brain change during late adulthood? Does it retain plasticity?

The Shrinking, Slowing Brain On average, the brain loses 5 to 10 percent of its weight between the ages of 20 and 90. Brain volume also decreases (Taubert & others, 2020; Zhao & others, 2019). One study found a decrease in total brain volume and volume in key brain structures such as the frontal lobes and hippocampus from 22 to 88 years of age (Sherwood & others, 2011). Another study found that the volume of the brain was 15 percent

developmental **connection**

Brain Development

Substantial growth in the prefrontal cortex occurs throughout infancy, childhood, and adolescence. Connect to "Physical Development in Infancy"; "Physical and Cognitive Development in Early Childhood"; "Physical and Cognitive Development in Middle and Late Childhood"; and "Physical and Cognitive Development in Adolescence."

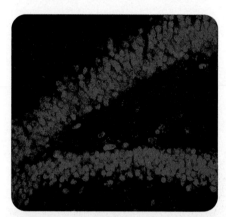

Exercise

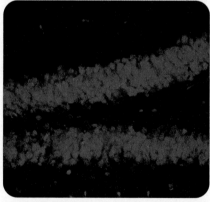

Enriched Environment

FIGURE **5**

GENERATING NEW NERVE CELLS IN ADULT MICE. Researchers have found that exercise (running) and an enriched environment (a larger cage and many toys) can cause brain cells in adult mice to divide and form new brain cells (Kempermann, van Praag, & Gage, 2000). Cells were labeled with a chemical marker that becomes integrated into the DNA of dividing cells (red). Four weeks later, they were also labeled to mark neurons (nerve cells). As shown here, both the running mice and the mice in an enriched environment had many cells that were still dividing (red) and others that had differentiated into new nerve cells (orange). Courtesy of Dr. Fred Gage, The Salk Institute for Biological Studies

less in older adults than in younger adults (Shan & others, 2005). Recent analyses concluded that in healthy aging the decrease in brain volume is due mainly to shrinkage of neurons, lower numbers of synapses, reduced length and complexity of axons, and reduced tree-like branching in dendrites, but only to a minor extent attributable to neuron loss (Penazzi, Bakota, & Brandt, 2016; Skaper & others, 2017). Also, a recent study of older adults revealed that declines in memory functioning were linked to lower gray matter volume (which contains most of the brain's neuronal cell bodies) in the temporal lobe and hippocampus (Schneider & others, 2019). Of course, brain volume loss occurs in individuals with disorders such as Alzheimer disease (Adduru & others, 2020; Krashia, Nobili, & D'Amelio, 2019). Further, one study found that global brain volume predicted mortality in a large population of stroke-free community-dwelling adults (Van Elderen & others, 2016).

Some areas of the brain shrink more than others. The prefrontal cortex is one area that shrinks the most with aging, and recent research has linked this shrinkage with decreased working memory and slower motor behavior in older adults (Hoyer, 2015). The sensory regions of the brain—such as the primary visual cortex, primary motor cortex, and somatosensory cortex—are less vulnerable to the aging process (Rodrique & Kennedy, 2011).

A general slowing of function in the brain and spinal cord begins in middle adulthood and accelerates in late adulthood (Cohen, Marsiske, & Smith, 2019; Salthouse, 2017). Both physical coordination and intellectual performance are affected. For example, after age 70 many adults no longer show a knee jerk reflex, and by age 90 most reflexes are much slower (Spence, 1989). The slowing of the brain can impair the performance of older adults on intelligence tests and various cognitive tasks, especially those that are timed (Lu & others, 2011). For example, a neuroimaging study revealed that older adults were more likely to be characterized by slower processing in the prefrontal cortex during retrieval of information on a cognitive task than were younger adults (Rypma, Eldreth, & Rebbechi, 2007).

Historically, as in the research just discussed, much of the focus on links between brain functioning and aging has been on volume of brain structures and regions. Today, increased emphasis is being given to changes in myelination and neural networks (Amoroso & others, 2019; Wen & others, 2020). Recent research indicates that demyelination (a deterioration in the myelin sheath that encases the axons and is associated with information processing) of the brain occurs with aging in older adults (Cercignani & others, 2017).

Aging has also been linked to reduced synaptic functioning and decreased production of some neurotransmitters, including acetylcholine, dopamine, and gamma-aminobutyric acid (GABA) (Robinson, Barat, & Mellott, 2019). Reductions in acetylcholine have been linked to small declines in memory functioning and to the severe memory loss associated with Alzheimer disease, which will be further discussed in the chapter on "Cognitive Development in Late Adulthood" (Benfante & others, 2020; Utkin, 2019). Normal age-related reductions in dopamine may cause problems in planning and carrying out motor activities (Latt & others, 2019). Severe reductions in the production of dopamine have been linked with age-related diseases characterized by a loss of motor control, such as Parkinson disease (Armstrong & Okun, 2020). GABA helps to control the preciseness of the signal sent from one neuron to another, decreasing "noise," and its production decreases with aging (Rozycka & Liguz-Lecznar, 2017).

The Adapting Brain   The story of the aging brain is far from being limited to loss and decline in functioning. The aging brain also has remarkable adaptive capabilities (Esteves & others, 2020; Kinugawa, 2019). Even in late adulthood, the brain loses only a portion of its ability to function, and the activities older adults engage in can influence the brain's development (Ji & others, 2019). For example, in one fMRI study, higher levels of aerobic fitness were linked with greater volume in the hippocampus, which translates to better memory (Erickson & others, 2009). Also, a recent study found that a higher level of aerobic fitness embedded in a health promotion program for older adults was associated with higher cortical and hippocampal volumes (Carlson & others, 2015).

Three topics reflect the adaptiveness of the human brain in older adults: (1) the possibility that the brain might be able to generate new neurons; (2) the role of dendritic growth; and (3) the adaptive potential of delateralization.

Can the brains of adults, even aging adults, generate new neurons? Researchers have found that **neurogenesis,** the generation of new neurons, does occur in lower mammalian species, such as mice (Jain & others, 2019). Also, research indicates that exercise and an enriched, complex environment can generate new brain cells in rats and mice, and that stress reduces the survival rate of these new cells (Kempermann, 2019) (see Figure 5). For example, in one study, mice in an enriched environment learned more flexibly because of adult hippocampal neurogenesis (Garthe, Roeder, & Kempermann, 2016). An earlier study revealed that coping with stress stimulated hippocampal neurogenesis in adult monkeys (Lyons & others, 2010). Researchers also have discovered that if rats are cognitively challenged to learn something, new brain cells survive longer (Shors, 2009).

It also is now accepted that neurogenesis can occur in human adults (Berdugo-Vega & others, 2020). However, researchers have documented neurogenesis in only two brain regions: the hippocampus (Snyder & Drew, 2020) and the olfactory bulb (Durante & others, 2020), which is involved in smell. Researchers currently are studying factors that might inhibit or promote neurogenesis, including various drugs, stress, and exercise (Kempermann, 2019). They also are exploring whether grafting of neural stem cells to various regions of the brain, such as the hippocampus, might increase neurogenesis (Tsutsui, 2020). Research attention also is being directed to the possible role neurogenesis might play in slowing the impairment caused by neurodegenerative diseases such as Alzheimer disease, Parkinson disease, and Huntington disease (Bobkova & others, 2020).

Dendritic growth can occur in human adults, possibly even in older adults (Eliasieh, Liets, & Chalupa, 2007). Recall that dendrites are the receiving portion of the neuron. One study compared the brains of adults at various ages (Coleman, 1986). From the forties through the seventies, the growth of dendrites increased. However, among people in their nineties dendritic growth no longer occurred. This dendritic growth might compensate for the possible loss of neurons through the seventies but not during the nineties. Lack of dendritic growth in older adults could be due to a lack of environmental stimulation and activity. Further research is needed to clarify precisely how dendrites change during aging.

Changes in lateralization may provide one type of adaptation in aging adults (Hong & others, 2015). Recall that lateralization is the specialization of function in one hemisphere of the brain or the other. Using neuroimaging techniques, researchers found that brain activity in the prefrontal cortex is lateralized less in older adults than in younger adults when they are engaging in cognitive tasks (Cabeza, 2002; Esteves & others, 2020). For example, Figure 6 shows that when younger adults are given the task of recognizing words they have previously seen, they process the information primarily in the right hemisphere; in contrast, older adults are more likely to use both hemispheres (Madden & others, 1999). The decrease in lateralization in older adults likely plays a compensatory role in the aging brain (Duda & others, 2019). That is, using both hemispheres may improve the cognitive functioning of older adults.

Of course, there are individual differences in how the brain changes in older adults (Kinugawa, 2019). Consider highly successful business executive T. Boone Pickens, who continued to lead a very active lifestyle at age 85, regularly exercising and engaging in cognitively complex work. Pickens underwent an fMRI in cognitive neuroscientist Denise Park's laboratory, during which he was presented with various cognitive tasks. Instead of both hemispheres being active, his left hemisphere was dominant, just as it is for most younger adults (Helman, 2008). On tough questions—such as "Are 'zombies' and 'unicorns' living or nonliving?"—Pickens was relying mainly on the left hemisphere of his brain to make a decision. Indeed, as the cognitive tasks became more complex, Pickens was more likely to use the left hemisphere of his brain.

Does staying intellectually challenged affect one's quality of life and longevity? To read further about aging and the brain, see *Connecting Through Research*.

SLEEP

How much sleep should older adults get? The National Sleep Foundation (2020) recommends that they get 7 to 8 hours a night. However, 5 percent or more of older adults complain of having difficulty sleeping, which can have detrimental effects on their lives (Farajinia & others, 2014). In an analysis of sleep patterns from 20 to 90 years of age, total sleep decreased about 8 minutes per decade for males and about 10 minutes per decade for females as they got older (Dorffner, Vitr, & Anderer, 2015). Also in this study, as individuals aged, they engaged in more light sleep and less deep sleep. Researchers also have found that older adults' sleep is more easily disrupted than that of younger adults (it takes longer for older adults to fall asleep initially, they wake up more often during the night, and they have greater difficulty going back to sleep) (McRae & others, 2016). Further, the significant reduction in deep sleep in older adults is more likely to occur in men than women (Redline & others, 2004). And in a recent study, older adults who slept 6 hours or less per day were more likely to have fair or poor health (Lauderdale & others, 2016).

developmental **connection**

Brain Development

At the peak of neurogenesis in prenatal development, it is estimated that as many as 200,000 neurons are being generated every minute. Connect to "Prenatal Development and Birth."

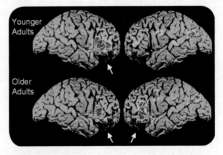

FIGURE 6

THE DECREASE IN BRAIN LATERALIZATION IN OLDER ADULTS. Younger adults primarily used the right prefrontal region of the brain (*top left image*) during a recall memory task, whereas older adults used both the left and right prefrontal regions (*bottom two images*).
Courtesy of Dr. Roberto Cabeza

developmental **connection**

Language

Speech and grammar are highly lateralized functions, strongly depending on activity in the left hemisphere. Connect to "Physical Development in Infancy."

neurogenesis The generation of new neurons.

Does Engaging in Intellectually Challenging Activities Affect Quality of Life and Longevity?

The Nun Study, directed by David Snowdon, is an intriguing ongoing investigation of aging in 678 nuns, many of whom live in a convent in Mankato, Minnesota (Hack & others, 2019; Latimer & others, 2017; Snowdon, 2003). All of the 678 nuns agreed to participate in annual assessments of their cognitive and physical functioning. They also agreed to donate their brains for scientific research when they die, and they are the largest group of brain donors in the world. Examination of the nuns' donated brains, as well as brains donated by others, has led neuroscientists to believe that the brain has a remarkable capacity to change and grow, even in old age. The Sisters of Notre Dame in Mankato lead intellectually challenging lives, and brain researchers believe this contributes to their quality of life as older adults and possibly increases their longevity.

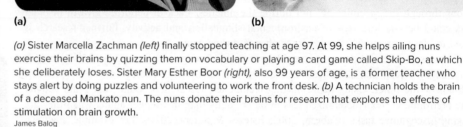

(a) **(b)**

(a) Sister Marcella Zachman *(left)* finally stopped teaching at age 97. At 99, she helps ailing nuns exercise their brains by quizzing them on vocabulary or playing a card game called Skip-Bo, at which she deliberately loses. Sister Mary Esther Boor *(right),* also 99 years of age, is a former teacher who stays alert by doing puzzles and volunteering to work the front desk. *(b)* A technician holds the brain of a deceased Mankato nun. The nuns donate their brains for research that explores the effects of stimulation on brain growth.
James Balog

Findings from the Nun Study so far include the following:

- Higher levels of idea density, a measure of linguistic ability assessed through autobiographies written in early adulthood (at age 22), were linked with higher brain weight, fewer incidences of mild cognitive impairment, and fewer characteristics of Alzheimer disease in 75- to 95-year-old nuns (Riley & others, 2005).
- Positive emotions early in adulthood were linked to longevity (Danner, Snowdon, & Friesen, 2001). Handwritten autobiographies from 180 nuns, composed when they were 22 years of age, were scored for emotional content. The nuns whose early writings had higher scores for positive emotional content were more likely to still be alive at 75 to 95 years of age than their counterparts whose early writings were characterized by negative emotional content.
- Sisters who had taught for most of their lives showed more moderate declines in intellectual skills than those who had spent most of

their lives doing service-based tasks, which supports the notion that stimulating the brain with intellectual activity keeps neurons healthy and alive (Snowdon, 2002).

- An analysis of essays written when the nuns were 18 to 32 years of age found that those whose essays reflected a higher level of self-reflection and parental encouragement of independence lived longer (Weinstein & others, 2019).

This study and other research provides hope that scientists will discover ways to tap into the brain's capacity to adapt in order to prevent and treat brain diseases (Cattaneo & others, 2020). For example, scientists might learn more effective ways to improve older adults' cognitive functioning, reduce Alzheimer disease, improve motor functioning, and help older adults recover from strokes (Pahor & others, 2020; Zhao & others, 2020). Even when areas of the brain are permanently damaged by stroke, new message routes can be created to get around the blockage or to resume the function of that area, indicating that the brain does adapt.

Sleep factors are linked to many aspects of older adults' lives (Bernstein, DeVito, & Calamia, 2019; Kaur & others, 2020). Poor sleep is a risk factor for falls, obesity, a lower level of cognitive functioning, and earlier death (Kohn & others, 2020; J. H. Liu & others, 2020; Winer & others, 2019). Research indicates that improving older adults' sleep through behavioral and pharmaceutical treatments may enhance their cognitive skills (Dzierzewski, Dautovich, & Ravyts, 2018). Further, one study found poor quality of sleep in individuals with mild cognitive impairment, which in some cases is a precursor for Alzheimer disease (Hita-Yanez, Atienza, & Cantero, 2013). In another study, sleep duration of more than seven hours per night in older adults was linked to longer telomere length, which was similar to the telomere length of middle-aged adults

(Cribbet & others, 2014). And one study revealed that even just one night of partial sleep deprivation activated DNA damage characteristic of biological aging (Carroll & others, 2015).

However, excessively long sleep duration also is often an indicator of less effective physical and cognitive functioning (Nutakor & others, 2020). In a recent study, long sleep duration predicted an increase in all-cause mortality in individuals 65 years and older (Beydoun & others, 2017). Research indicates that older adults who slept 10 or more hours a day were more likely to have cardiovascular disease and diabetes (Han & others, 2016; Yang & others, 2016). And in a recent study, older adults who slept 8 to 10 hours or more a night were more likely to have memory recall problems (Low, Wu, & Spira, 2019). In general, it now appears that when older adults sleep less than 7 hours or more than 9 hours a night, their cognitive functioning is harmed (Lo & others, 2016).

Many of the sleep problems of older adults are associated with health problems (Campanini & others, 2019). Strategies to help older adults sleep better at night include avoiding caffeine, avoiding over-the-counter sleep remedies, staying physically active during the day, staying mentally active, and limiting naps (Vanderlinden, Boen, & van Uffelen, 2020). In addition, one study of older adults indicated that walking at or above the internationally recommended level of 150 minutes per week predicted a lower likelihood of problems with sleep onset or sleep maintenance four years later (Hartescu, Morgan, & Stevinson, 2016). And a recent Chinese study revealed that older adults who engaged in a higher level of overall physical activity, leisure-time exercise, and household activity were less likely to have sleep problems (Li & others, 2018).

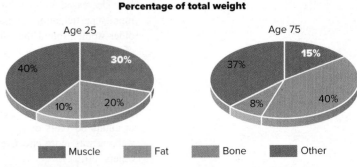

Percentage of total weight

FIGURE 7

CHANGES IN BODY COMPOSITION OF BONE, MUSCLE, AND FAT FROM 25 TO 75 YEARS OF AGE. Notice the decrease in bone and muscle and the increase in fat from 25 to 75 years of age.

PHYSICAL APPEARANCE AND MOVEMENT

In late adulthood, the changes in physical appearance that began occurring during middle age become more pronounced. Wrinkles and age spots are the most noticeable changes.

We also become shorter as we get older. Both men and women become shorter in late adulthood because of bone loss in their vertebrae (Hoyer & Roodin, 2009).

Our weight usually drops after we reach 60 years of age. This likely occurs because of muscle loss, which also gives our bodies a "sagging" look (Evans, 2010). Figure 7 shows the declining percentage of muscle and bone from age 25 to age 75, and the corresponding increase in the percentage of fat. One study found that long-term aerobic exercise was linked with greater muscle strength in 65- to 86-year-olds (Crane, Macneil, & Tarnopolsky, 2013). In another study, at-risk overweight and obese older adults lost significant weight and improved their mobility considerably by participating in a community-based weight reduction program (Rejeski & others, 2017).

Older adults move more slowly than young adults, and this slowing occurs for movements with a wide range of difficulty (Davis & others, 2013) (see Figure 8). Adequate mobility is an important aspect of maintaining an independent and active lifestyle in late adulthood (Patel & others, 2019). Recent research indicates that obesity contributes to mobility limitations in older adults (Adair, Duazo, & Borja, 2018). The good news is that regular walking decreases the onset of physical disability and reduces functional limitations in older adults (Mullen & others, 2012). For example, a recent study of older adults found that walking a dog regularly was associated with better physical health (Curl, Bibbo, & Johnson, 2017). Exercise also benefitted frail elderly adults in another study (Danilovich, Conroy, & Hornby, 2018). In this study, high-intensity walking regimens reduced the older adults' frailty, increased their walking speed, and improved their balance. Further, in another recent study, a 10-week exercise program improved the physical capabilities (aerobic endurance, agility, and mobility) and cognitive function (selective attention and planning) of elderly nursing home residents (Pereira & others, 2018). Another study revealed that middle-aged and older adults who had limited mobility also had lower cognitive functioning (Demnitz & others, 2017). And a recent large-scale study of older adults indicated that a 554-step-per-day increase in mobility reduced physical function limitations by 5.9 percent and improved quality of life by 3.2 percent (Kabiri & others, 2018).

developmental **connection**

Biological Processes

On average, men lose 1 to 2 inches in height from 30 to 70 years of age and women can lose as much as 2 inches in height from age 25 to 75. Connect to "Physical and Cognitive Development in Middle Adulthood."

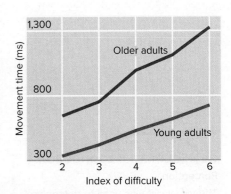

FIGURE 8

MOVEMENT AND AGING. Older adults take longer to move than young adults, and this change occurs across a range of movement difficulty (Ketcham & Stelmach, 2001).

Decreased walking speed in older adults is associated with limited mobility, less community participation, greater cognitive decline, and increased risk of falls. A recent study of older women found that on average a reduction in walking speed occurred at about 71 years of age (Noce Kirkwood & others, 2018). Another recent study also found that older adults who walked slowly were more likely to have mild cognitive impairment (Rajtar-Zembaty & others, 2019).

The risk of falling in older adults also increases with age and is greater for women than for men (Granbom & others, 2019). A research meta-analysis found that exercise reduces falls in adults 60 years of age and older (Stubbs, Brefka, & Denkinger, 2015). And in one study, walking was more effective than balance training in reducing falls in older adults (Okubo & others, 2016).

SENSORY DEVELOPMENT

Seeing, hearing, and other aspects of sensory functioning are linked with our ability to perform everyday activities. This link was documented in a study of more than 500 adults, 70 to 102 years of age, in which sensory acuity, especially visual capacity, was related to whether and how well older adults bathed and groomed themselves, completed household chores, engaged in intellectual activities, and watched TV (Marsiske, Klumb, & Baltes, 1997). How do vision, hearing, taste, smell, touch, and sensitivity to pain change in late adulthood?

Vision Recently, researchers have found that visual decline in late adulthood is linked to (a) cognitive decline (Monge & Madden, 2016), and (b) having fewer social contacts and engaging in less challenging social/leisure activities (Cimarolli & others, 2017). For example, in a longitudinal study of individuals 60 years and older, visual and hearing difficulties predicted cognitive difficulties in verbal fluency, processing speed, and memory 8 years later (de la Fuente & others, 2019). In this study, cognitive decline was steepest in individuals with both visual and hearing problems. Also, declining visual acuity, color vision, and depth perception are associated with aging. Several diseases of the eye may emerge in aging adults.

Visual Acuity In late adulthood, the decline in vision that began for most adults in early or middle adulthood becomes more pronounced (Moreno-Cugnon & others, 2018). Visual processing of information declines in older adults (Ebaid & Crewther, 2019). Night driving is especially difficult, to some extent because of diminishing sensitivity to contrasts and reduced tolerance for glare (Allen, Beck, & Zanjani, 2019). Dark adaptation is slower—that is, older individuals take longer to recover their vision when going from a well-lighted room to semidarkness. The area of the visual field becomes smaller, a change suggesting that the intensity of a stimulus in the peripheral area of the visual field needs to be increased if the stimulus is to be seen. Events taking place away from the center of the visual field might not be detected (West & others, 2010).

This visual decline often can be traced to a reduction in the quality or intensity of light reaching the retina (Nag & Wadhwa, 2012). At 60 years of age, the retina receives only about one-third as much light as it did at 20 years of age (Scialfa & Kline, 2007). In extreme old age, these changes might be accompanied by degenerative changes in the retina, causing severe difficulty in seeing. Large-print books and magnifiers might be needed in such cases.

Recent research has shown that sensory decline in older adults is linked to a decline in cognitive functioning (Ji, Peng, & Mao, 2019). In a recent study, declines in visual acuity, contrast sensitivity, and depth perception were associated with cognitive decline in older adults (Swenor & others, 2019). Also, one study of individuals in their seventies revealed that visual decline was related to slower speed of processing information, which in turn was associated with greater cognitive decline (Clay & others, 2009).

Color Vision Color vision also may decline with age in older adults as a result of the yellowing of the lens of the eye (Scialfa & Kline, 2007). This decline is most likely to occur in the green-blue-violet part of the color spectrum. As a result, older adults may have trouble accurately distinguishing between objects of closely related colors, such as navy blue socks and black socks.

Depth Perception As with many types of perception, depth perception changes little after infancy until adults become older. Depth perception typically declines in late adulthood,

developmental **connection**

Perception

The visual cliff was used to determine whether infants have depth perception. Connect to "Physical Development in Infancy."

which can make it difficult for an older adult to determine how close or far away or how high or low something is (Bian & Anderson, 2008). A decline in depth perception can make steps or street curbs difficult to manage.

Diseases of the Eye   Three diseases that can impair the vision of older adults are cataracts, glaucoma, and macular degeneration:

- **Cataracts** involve a thickening of the lens of the eye that causes vision to become cloudy and distorted (Zheng & others, 2020). By age 70, approximately 30 percent of individuals experience a partial loss of vision due to cataracts. Initially, cataracts can be treated by glasses; if they worsen, the cloudy lens should be surgically removed and replaced with an artificial one (Jackson, Edmiston, & Bedi, 2020). A recent Japanese study found that older adults (mean age: 76 years) who had undergone cataract surgery were less likely to develop mild cognitive impairment than their counterparts who had not had the surgery (Miyata & others, 2018). Also, diabetes is a risk factor for the development of cataracts (Becker & others, 2018).

- **Glaucoma** involves damage to the optic nerve because of the pressure created by a buildup of fluid in the eye (Serbin & others, 2020). Approximately 1 percent of individuals in their seventies and 10 percent of those in their nineties have glaucoma, which can be treated with eye drops. If left untreated, glaucoma can ultimately destroy a person's vision.

- **Macular degeneration** involves deterioration of the macula of the retina, which corresponds to the focal center of the visual field. Individuals with macular degeneration may have relatively normal peripheral vision but be unable to see clearly what is right in front of them (Heesterbeek & others, 2020) (see Figure 9). This condition affects 1 in 25 individuals from 66 to 74 years of age and 1 in 6 of those 75 years old and older. One study revealed that cigarette smoking contributes to macular degeneration (Schmidt & others, 2006). If the disease is detected early, it can be treated with laser surgery (Hernandez-Zimbron & others, 2017). However, macular degeneration is difficult to treat and thus is a leading cause of blindness in older adults (Zhu & others, 2019). Also, there is increased interest in using stem-cell-based therapy for macular degeneration (Ludwig, Freeman, & Janot, 2019; Munoz-Ramon, Hernandez Martinez, & Munoz-Negrete, 2020).

Hearing   For hearing as for vision, the age of older adults is important in determining the degree of decline (see Figure 10). The decline in vision and hearing is much greater in individuals 75 years and older than in individuals 65 to 74 years of age (Charness & Bosman, 1992).

Hearing impairment usually does not become much of an impediment until late adulthood (Moore, Mariathasan, & Sek, 2020). Only 19 percent of individuals from 45 to 54 years of age experience some type of hearing problem (Harris, 1975). By contrast, a national survey revealed that 63 percent of adults 70 years and older had a hearing loss defined as an inability to hear sounds at frequencies higher than 25 dB with their better ear (Lin & others, 2011). In this study, hearing aids were used by 40 percent of those with moderate hearing loss. Also, a recent study of 80- to 106-year-olds found a substantial increase in hearing loss in the ninth and tenth decades of life (Wattamwar & others, 2017).

cataracts A thickening of the lens of the eye that causes vision to become cloudy, opaque, and distorted.

glaucoma Damage to the optic nerve because of the pressure created by a buildup of fluid in the eye.

macular degeneration A disease that involves deterioration of the macula of the retina, which corresponds to the focal center of the visual field.

FIGURE 9

MACULAR DEGENERATION. This simulation of the effect of macular degeneration shows how individuals with this eye disease can see their peripheral field of vision but can't clearly see what is in their central visual field.
Cordelia Molloy/Science Source

Perceptual System	65 to 74 years	75 years and older
Vision	There is a loss of acuity even with corrective lenses. Less transmission of light occurs through the retina (half as much as in young adults). Greater susceptibility to glare occurs. Color discrimination ability decreases.	There is a significant loss of visual acuity and color discrimination, and a decrease in the size of the perceived visual field. In late old age, people are at significant risk for visual dysfunction from cataracts and glaucoma.
Hearing	There is a significant loss of hearing at high frequencies and some loss at middle frequencies. These losses can be helped by a hearing aid. There is greater susceptibility to masking of what is heard by noise.	There is a significant loss at high and middle frequencies. A hearing aid is more likely to be needed than in young-old age.

FIGURE 10
VISION AND HEARING DECLINE IN LATE ADULTHOOD

Older adults often don't recognize that they have a hearing problem, deny that they have one, or accept it as a part of growing old. Also, a study that spanned 10 years found that poor nutrition and a lifetime of smoking were linked to more rapid onset of hearing difficulties in older adults (Heine & others, 2013).

Hearing loss in older adults is linked to declining performance in activities of daily living, cognitive functioning, and language (Armstrong & others, 2020; Huber & others, 2020). Recent research has found that older adults' hearing problems are linked to impaired activities of daily living (Lazzarotto & others, 2019), less time spent out of home and in leisure activities (Mikkola & others, 2016), increased falls (Jindal & others, 2019), reduced cognitive functioning (Bowl & Dawson, 2019), and loneliness (Mick & others, 2018). For example, in a recent study, hearing impairment was associated with accelerated cognitive decline in older adults (Alattar & others, 2019). In addition, a recent study found that initiation of hearing aid use in older adults was linked to either stable or improved executive function 18 months later (Sarant & others, 2020). And in another study, older adults' hearing aid use was associated with less loneliness (Weinstein, Sirow, & Moser, 2016).

What outcomes occur when older adults have dual sensory loss in vision and hearing? In a recent study of 65- to 85-year-olds, dual sensory loss in vision and hearing was linked to reduced social participation and less social support, as well as increased loneliness (Mick & others, 2018). In another recent study, this type of dual sensory loss in older adults (mean age of 82 years) involved greater functional limitations, increased loneliness, cognitive decline, and communication problems (Davidson & Guthrie, 2019). And in another recent study, older adults who had a dual sensory impairment involving vision and hearing had more depressive symptoms (Han & others, 2019).

Smell and Taste   Most older adults lose some of their sense of taste or smell, or both (Churnin & others, 2019). A recent national study of community-dwelling older adults revealed that 74 percent had impaired taste and 22 percent had impaired smell (Correia & others, 2016). These losses often begin around 60 years of age (Hawkes, 2006). A majority of individuals age 80 and older experience a significant reduction in smell (Lafreniere & Mann, 2009). Researchers have found that older adults show a greater decline in their sense of smell than in their sense of taste (Schiffman, 2007). Smell and taste decline less in healthy older adults than in their less healthy counterparts. A recent study found that a poorer sense of smell in older adults was associated with increased feelings of depression and loneliness (Sivam & others, 2016). And a recent study of older adults revealed that an inability to smell some odors, especially peppermint, was linked to cognitive decline (Liang & others, 2020).

Touch and Pain   Changes in touch and pain sensitivity are also associated with aging (Garcia & others, 2019). A recent national study of community-dwelling older adults revealed that 70 percent of older adults had impaired touch (Correia & others, 2016). One study found that with aging, individuals could detect touch less in the lower extremities (ankles, knees, and so on) than in the upper extremities (wrists, shoulders, and so on) (Corso, 1977). For most older adults, a decline in touch sensitivity is not problematic (Hoyer & Roodin, 2009). And one study revealed that older adults who are blind retain a high level of touch sensitivity, which likely is linked to their use of active touch in their daily lives (Legge & others, 2008).

An estimated 60 to 75 percent of older adults report at least some persistent pain (Molton & Terrill, 2014). The most frequent pain complaints of older adults are back pain (40 percent), peripheral neuropathic pain (35 percent), and chronic joint pain (15 to 25 percent) (Denard & others, 2010). The presence of pain increases with age in older adults, and women are more likely to report having pain than are men (Tsang & others, 2008). In a recent research review, it was concluded that older adults have lower pain sensitivity but only for lower pain intensities (Lautenbacher & others, 2017). Older adults also are less sensitive to pain than are younger adults (Harkins, Price, & Martinelli, 1986). Although decreased sensitivity to pain can help older adults cope with disease and injury, it can also mask injuries and illnesses that need to be treated. Also, a recent study found that high levels of pain were linked to memory impairment in older adults (van der Leeuw & others, 2018).

Perceptual Motor Coupling   Perception and action are coupled throughout the life span. Driving a car illustrates the coupling of perceptual and motor skills. The decline in perceptual-motor skills in late adulthood makes driving a car difficult for many older adults

(Allen, Beck, & Zanjani, 2019; Chen & others, 2020). Drivers over the age of 65 are involved in more traffic accidents than middle-aged adults because of mistakes such as improper turns, not yielding the right of way, and not obeying traffic signs; their younger counterparts are more likely to have accidents because they are speeding (Lavalliere & others, 2011; Sterns, Barrett, & Alexander, 1985). Older adults can compensate for declines in perceptual-motor skills by driving shorter distances, choosing less congested routes, and driving only in daylight.

An extensive research review evaluated the effectiveness of two types of interventions in improving older adults' driving: cognitive training and education (Ross, Schmidt, & Ball, 2013):

- *Cognitive training.* Cognitive training programs have shown some success in older adults, including improving their driving safety and making driving less difficult. In one study conducted by Karlene Ball and her colleagues (2010), training designed to enhance speed of processing produced more than a 40 percent reduction in at-fault crashes over a six-year period.
- *Education.* Results are mixed regarding the effectiveness of educational interventions that seek to improve older adults' driving ability and to reduce their involvement in traffic accidents (Gaines & others, 2011).

THE CIRCULATORY AND RESPIRATORY SYSTEMS

Cardiovascular disorders increase in late adulthood (Macek & others, 2020; van Bussel & others, 2019). In older adults, 64 percent of men and 69 percent of women 65 to 74 years of age have hypertension (high blood pressure) (Centers for Disease Control and Prevention, 2018). More than 70 percent of older adults who have a heart attack or stroke have preexisting hypertension.

Today, most experts on aging recommend that consistent blood pressures above 120/80 should be treated to reduce the risk of heart attack, stroke, or kidney disease. A rise in blood pressure with age can be linked to illness, obesity, stiffening of blood vessels, stress, or lack of exercise (Cheng & others, 2017). The longer any of these factors persist, the higher the individual's blood pressure gets.

Various drugs, a healthy diet, and exercise can reduce the risk of cardiovascular disease in many older adults (Jefferson, Demasi, & Doshi, 2020; Quindry & others, 2019). In one study of older adults, a faster exercise walking pace, not smoking, modest alcohol intake, and avoiding obesity were associated with a lower risk of heart failure (Del Gobbo & others, 2015). Another study revealed that diminished exercise capacity and lack of walking were the best predictors of earlier death in older adults with heart problems (Reibis & others, 2010). And in a recent study of adults 65 and older, a Mediterranean diet lowered their risk of cardiovascular problems (Nowson & others, 2018).

In the respiratory system, lung capacity drops 40 percent between the ages of 20 and 80, even when disease is not present (Fozard, 1992). Lungs lose elasticity, the chest shrinks, and the diaphragm weakens (Lalley, 2013). The good news, though, is that older adults can improve lung functioning with diaphragm-strengthening exercises. Severe impairments in lung functioning and death can result from smoking (Kraen & others, 2017).

SEXUALITY

In the absence of two circumstances—disease and the belief that old people are or should be asexual—sexuality can be lifelong (Hyde & DeLamater, 2020). Aging, however, does induce some changes in human sexual performance, more so in males than in females (Herdt & Polen-Petit, 2021).

Orgasm becomes less frequent in males with age, occurring in every second to third attempt rather than every time. More direct stimulation usually is needed to produce an erection. From 65 to 80 years of age, approximately one out of four men have serious problems getting and/or keeping erections, and after 80 years of age the percentage rises to one out of two men (Butler & Lewis, 2002). However, with recent advances in erectile dysfunction medications such as Viagra, an increasing number of older men, especially the young-old, are able to have an erection. Also, recent research suggests that declining levels of serum testosterone, which is linked to erectile dysfunction, can be treated with testosterone replacement therapy to improve sexual functioning in males (Mayo Clinic, 2020). However, the benefit-risk ratio of testosterone replacement therapy is uncertain for older males (Isidori & others, 2014).

developmental **connection**

Sexuality

Older adults may express their sexuality differently from younger adults, focusing on touching and caressing in their sexual relationship when sexual intercourse becomes difficult. Connect to "Socioemotional Development in Late Adulthood."

What are some characteristics of sexuality in older adults? How does sexuality change during late adulthood?
Image Source/Getty Images

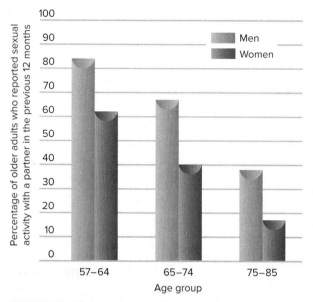

FIGURE 11

SEXUAL ACTIVITY IN OLDER ADULTS WITH A PARTNER

A considerable proportion of older adults remain sexually active (Sinkovic & Towler, 2019; Wright, Jenks, & Demeyere, 2019). An interview study of more than 3,000 adults 57 to 85 years of age revealed that many older adults continue to be sexually active as long as they are healthy (Lindau & others, 2007). Sexual activity does decline through the later years of life: 73 percent of people 57 to 64 years old, 53 percent of people 65 to 74 years old, and 26 percent of adults 75 to 85 years old reported that they were sexually active. Even in the sexually active oldest group (75 to 85), more than 50 percent said they still have sex at least two to three times a month. Fifty-eight percent of sexually active 65- to 74-year-olds and 31 percent of 75- to 85-year-olds said they engage in oral sex. As with middle-aged and younger adults, older adults who did not have a partner were far less likely to be sexually active than those who had a partner. For older adults with a partner who reported not having sex, the main reason was poor health, especially the male partner's physical health. Also, older adults are increasingly using online dating sites. A recent study of 4,000 dating profiles online found that older adults were more likely to use first-person plural pronouns (we, our), not be self-enhancing, focus more on connectedness and relationships with others, describe positive emotions, and use words associated with health than were younger adults when seeking a romantic partnership (Davis & Fingerman, 2016).

A large-scale study of individuals from 57 to 85 years of age revealed that sexual activity, a good-quality sexual life, and interest in sex were positively related to health in middle and late adulthood (Lindau & Gavrilova, 2010). Also in this study, these aspects of sexuality were higher for aging men than aging women, and this gap widened with age. Further, sexually active life expectancy was longer for men than women, but men lost more years of sexually active life due to poor health than women did.

As indicated in Figure 11, sexual activity with a partner declined from the last part of middle adulthood through late adulthood, with a lower rate of sexual activity with a partner for women than men. Indeed, a challenge for a sexually interested older woman is finding a partner. At 70 years of age, approximately 70 percent of women don't have a partner compared with only about 35 percent of men. Many older women's husbands have died, and many older men are in relationships with younger women.

In other research on sexual behavior in older adults, engaging in sexual activity was linked to greater enjoyment of life (Smith & others, 2019). Also, in another study, older adults were asked about their motivation for having sex (Gewirtz-Meydan & Ayalon, 2019). In this study, five main reasons for having sex were: (1) to maintain their functioning; (2) to feel young again; (3) to feel attractive and desirable; (4) to go from lust to love; and (5) to change from "getting sex" to "giving sex."

Review Connect Reflect

 LG2 Describe how a person's brain and body change in late adulthood.

Review

- How much plasticity and adaptability does the aging brain have?
- What characterizes older adults' sleep?
- What changes in physical appearance and movement characterize late adulthood?
- How do vision, hearing, smell and taste, touch, and sensitivity to pain change in older adults?
- How do the circulatory and respiratory systems change in older adults?
- What is the nature of sexuality in late adulthood?

Connect

- Many of the declines in the functioning of individuals in late adulthood start occurring in middle adulthood. Which declines in functioning occur mainly in late adulthood?

Reflect *Your Own Personal Journey of Life*

- If you could interview the Mankato nuns, what questions would you want to ask them to help you improve your understanding of successful aging?

3 Health LG3 Identify health problems in older adults and describe how they can be treated.

| Health Problems | Substance Use and Abuse | Exercise, Nutrition, and Weight | Health Treatment |

How healthy are older adults? What types of health problems do they have, and what can be done to maintain or improve their health and ability to function in everyday life?

HEALTH PROBLEMS

As we age, we become more susceptible to disease or illness (Benetos & others, 2019; Vaish, Patra, & Chhabra, 2020). The majority of adults who are still alive at 80 years of age or older are likely to have some type of impairment. Chronic diseases (those with a slow onset and a long duration) are rare in early adulthood, increase in middle adulthood, and become more common in late adulthood (Hirsch & Sirois, 2016). As indicated in Figure 12, 84 percent of U.S. adults 65 years of age and older have one or more chronic conditions, and 62 percent have two or more chronic conditions (Partnership for Solutions, 2002).

As shown in Figure 13, arthritis is the most common chronic disorder in late adulthood, followed by hypertension. Older women have a higher incidence of arthritis and hypertension and are more likely to have visual problems, but are less likely to have hearing problems, than older men are.

Although adults over the age of 65 often have a physical impairment, many of them can still carry on their everyday activities or work. Chronic conditions associated with the greatest limitations on work are heart conditions (52 percent), diabetes (34 percent), asthma (27 percent), and arthritis (27 percent). Low income is strongly related to health problems in late adulthood (Elfassy & others, 2019). Approximately three times as many poor as non-poor older adults report that their activities are limited by chronic disorders. Recent research documents links between low socioeconomic status and health problems (Boylan, Cundiff, & Matthews, 2018).

Causes of Death in Older Adults Nearly 60 percent of deaths among U.S. adults 65 to 74 years are caused by cancer or cardiovascular disease. Cancer recently replaced cardiovascular disease as the leading cause of death in U.S. middle-aged adults. The decline in cardiovascular disease in middle-aged adults has been attributed to improved drugs, decreased rates of smoking, improved diets, and increased exercise (Jefferson, Demasi, & Doshi, 2020; Quindry & others, 2019). The same realignment of causes of death recently occurred in 65- to 74-year-olds, with cancer now the leading cause of death in this age group (U.S. Census Bureau, 2019). However, in the 75-to-84 and 85-and-over age groups, cardiovascular disease is the leading cause of death (U.S. Census Bureau, 2019). As individuals age through the late adult years, the older they are the more likely they are to die of cardiovascular disease rather than cancer.

Ethnicity is linked with the death rates of older adults (U.S. Census Bureau, 2019). Among ethnic groups in the United States, African Americans have high death rates for stroke, heart disease, lung cancer, and female breast cancer. Asian Americans and Latinos have low death rates for these diseases. In the last decade, death rates for most diseases in African Americans, Latinos, and Asian Americans have decreased. However, death rates for most diseases remain high for African Americans (U.S. Census Bureau, 2019).

Arthritis Arthritis is an inflammation of the joints accompanied by pain, stiffness, and movement problems. Arthritis is especially common in older adults (Subedi & others, 2020). This disorder can affect hips, knees, ankles, fingers, and vertebrae. Individuals with arthritis often experience pain and stiffness, as well as problems in moving about and performing

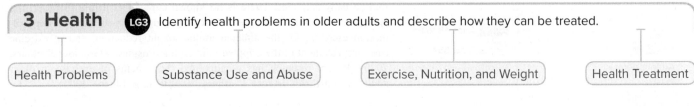

FIGURE 12

PERCENT OF U.S. POPULATION WITH CHRONIC CONDITIONS ACROSS AGE GROUPS

How many of us older persons have really been prepared for the second half of life, for old age, and eternity?

—CARL JUNG
Swiss psychoanalyst, 20th century

arthritis Inflammation of the joints accompanied by pain, stiffness, and movement problems; this disease is especially common in older adults.

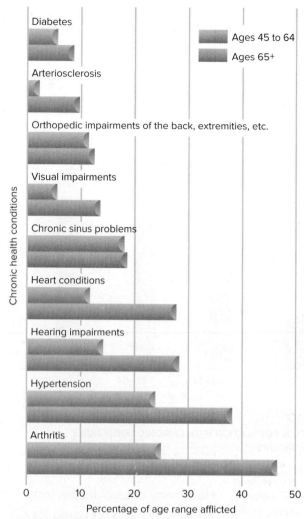

FIGURE 13
THE MOST PREVALENT CHRONIC CONDITIONS IN MIDDLE AND LATE ADULTHOOD

Age Group	Percent	Drinks Per Occasion	Frequency
18–24	28	9	4.2
25–34	28	8	4.2
35–44	19	8	4.1
45–64	13	7	4.7
65 & over	4	5	5.5

FIGURE 14
BINGE DRINKING THROUGH THE LIFE SPAN. *Note:* Percent refers to percent of individuals in a particular age group who engaged in binge drinking on an occasion in the past 30 days (4 or more drinks for women, 5 or more for men). Drinks per occasion reflects the intensity of the binge drinking. Frequency indicates the number of occasions in which binge drinking occurred in the past 30 days.
Source: After data presented by the Centers for Disease Control and Prevention, 2012, Table 1.

osteoporosis A chronic condition that involves an extensive loss of bone tissue and is the main reason many older adults walk with a marked stoop.

routine daily activities. There is no known cure for arthritis. However, the symptoms of arthritis can be reduced by drugs such as aspirin, range-of-motion exercises for the afflicted joints, weight reduction, and in extreme cases, replacement of the crippled joint with a prosthesis (Gomides & others, 2020). Recent research has documented the benefits of exercise in older adults with arthritis (Azeez & others, 2020; Kim & others, 2020).

Osteoporosis   Normal aging brings some loss of bone tissue, but in some instances loss of bone tissue can become severe (Fougere & Cesari, 2019). **Osteoporosis** involves an extensive loss of bone tissue. Osteoporosis is the main reason many older adults walk with a marked stoop. Women are especially vulnerable to osteoporosis, which is the leading cause of broken bones in women (Madrasi & others, 2018). Approximately 80 percent of osteoporosis cases in the United States occur in females, and almost two-thirds of all women over the age of 60 are affected by osteoporosis. It is more common in non-Latina White, thin, and small-framed women.

Osteoporosis is related to deficiencies in calcium, vitamin D, and estrogen, and to lack of exercise (Kataoka & others, 2020). To prevent osteoporosis, young and middle-aged women should eat foods rich in calcium (such as dairy products, broccoli, turnip greens, and kale), exercise regularly, and avoid smoking (Garcia-Gomariz & others, 2018). However, a recent Swiss study indicated that postmenopausal women consume high amounts of vegetables but insufficient amounts of calcium-rich foods such as dairy products (Lanyan & others, 2020). Drugs such as Fosamax can be used to reduce the risk of osteoporosis (Curtis & others, 2020). Aging women should also get bone density checks.

Accidents   Unintended injuries are the eighth leading cause of death among older adults (Centers for Disease Control and Prevention, 2020). Injuries resulting from a fall at home or a traffic accident in which an older adult is a driver or an older pedestrian is hit by a vehicle are common. Falls are the leading cause of injury deaths among adults who are 65 years and older (Centers for Disease Control and Prevention, 2019). Each year, approximately 200,000 adults over the age of 65 (most of them women) fracture a hip in a fall. Half of these older adults die within 12 months, frequently from pneumonia. Two-thirds of older adults who experience a fall are likely to fall again in the next six months.

SUBSTANCE USE AND ABUSE

In many cases, older adults are taking multiple medications, which can increase the risks associated with consuming alcohol or other drugs. For example, when combined with tranquilizers or sedatives, alcohol use can impair breathing, produce excessive sedation, and be fatal. Optimization of drug use, especially not overdosing, is a key factor in successful aging (Marien & Spinewine, 2019).

How extensive is substance abuse in older adults? A national survey found that in 2010 the percentage of individuals who engaged in binge drinking (defined as four or more drinks for women and five or more drinks for men on one occasion in the past 30 days) declined considerably in middle and late adulthood (Centers for Disease Control and Prevention, 2012) (see Figure 14). However, the frequency of binge drinking in the past 30 days was highest among older adults (5.5 episodes).

Despite the decline in the percentage of individuals who engage in binge drinking in late adulthood, the Substance Abuse and Mental Health Services Administration (2003) has identified substance abuse among older adults as an "invisible epidemic" in the United States. The belief is that substance abuse often goes undetected in older adults, and there is concern about older adults who abuse not only illicit drugs but prescription drugs as well (Petrovic & others, 2019). Too often, screening questionnaires are not appropriate for older adults, and the consequences of alcohol abuse—such as depression, inadequate nutrition, congestive heart failure, and frequent falls—may erroneously be attributed to other medical or psychological conditions (Hoyer & Roodin, 2009). Because of the dramatic increase in the number of older adults anticipated over the twenty-first century, substance abuse is likely to characterize an increasing number of older adults.

Late-onset alcoholism is the label used to describe the onset of alcoholism after the age of 65. Late-onset alcoholism is often related to loneliness, loss of a spouse, or a disabling condition.

Researchers have found a protective effect of moderate alcohol use in older adults (O'Keefe & others, 2014). One study revealed better physical and mental health as well as increased longevity in older adults who drank moderately compared with those who drank heavily or did not drink at all (Rozzini, Ranhoff, & Trabucchi, 2007). Benefits of moderate drinking include better physical well-being and mental performance, greater openness to social contacts, and increased ability to assert mastery over one's life. A recent study of older adults found that moderate alcohol consumption was linked to greater volume in the brain's hippocampus (Downer & others, 2015). Another recent study revealed that moderate drinkers were more likely to be alive and not have a cognitive impairment at 85 years of age (Richards & others, 2018). And a study of aging adults indicated that moderate wine consumption was associated with lower inflammatory risk factors related to cardiovascular disease across an 8-year period (Janssen & others, 2014).

Researchers have especially found that moderate drinking of red wine is linked to better health and increased longevity (Li & others, 2019). Explanations of the benefits of red wine center on its role in lowering stress and reducing the risk of heart disease (Li, Li, & Lin, 2018). Evidence is increasing that a chemical in the skin of red wine grapes—resveratrol—plays a key role in red wine's health benefits (Cheng & others, 2020; Wu & others, 2019). One study found that red wine, but not white, killed several lines of cancer cells (Wallenborg & others, 2009). Scientists are exploring how resveratrol, as well as calorie restriction, increases SIRT 1, an enzyme that is involved in DNA repair and aging (Lee & others, 2019; Yoon & others, 2019). Some critics argue that there is inconsistent evidence that resveratrol and SIRT 1 are linked to longevity (Tang & others, 2014).

EXERCISE, NUTRITION, AND WEIGHT

Can exercise slow the aging process? Can eating a nutritious but calorie-reduced diet increase longevity? Let's examine how exercise, nutrition, and weight control might influence how healthily we age.

Exercise Although we may be in the evening of our lives in late adulthood, we are not meant to live out our remaining years passively. Everything we know about older adults suggests that the more active they are, the healthier and happier they are likely to be (Strandberg, 2019). For example, a recent study confirmed that older adults who engage in regular exercise have a higher level of life satisfaction (Cho & Kim, 2020).

In one study, exercise literally made the difference between life and death for middle-aged and older adults. More than 10,000 men and women were divided into categories of low fitness, medium fitness, and high fitness (Blair & others, 1989). Then they were studied over a period of eight years. Sedentary participants (low fitness) were more than twice as likely to die during the eight-year time span of the study than those who were moderately fit and more than three times as likely to die as those who were highly fit. The positive effects of being physically fit occurred for both men and women in this study. Further, one study revealed that 60-year-old and older adults who were in the lowest fifth in terms of physical fitness as determined by a treadmill test were four times more likely to die over a 12-year period than their counterparts who were in the top fifth of physical fitness (Sui & others, 2007). A longitudinal study found that men who exercised regularly at 72 years of age had a 30 percent higher

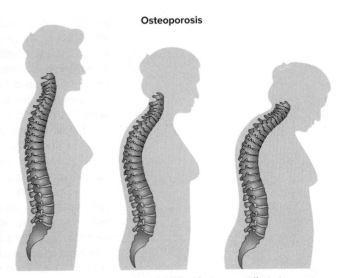

Osteoporosis

What characterizes osteoporosis? What factors contribute to osteoporosis?

What might explain the finding that drinking red wine in moderation is linked to better health and increased longevity?
LightFieldStudios/iStockphoto/Getty Images

developmental **connection**

Health

Being physically fit and cognitively fit are key aspects of successful aging. Connect to "Socioemotional Development in Late Adulthood."

probability of still being alive at 90 years of age than their sedentary counterparts (Yates & others, 2008). And a study of more than 11,000 women found that low cardiorespiratory fitness was a significant predictor of death (Farrell & others, 2010). Also, a study of joggers in Copenhagen, Denmark, revealed that engaging in light or moderate jogging on a regular basis was linked to increased longevity (Schnohr & others, 2015). In another study, individuals who increased their fitness level from low to intermediate or high were at a lower risk for all-cause mortality (Brawner & others, 2017).

Setting exercise goals and then carrying out an exercise plan are important not only in young adults but older adults as well. For example, a study of elderly women revealed that those who had set exercise-related personal goals were four times more likely to report high exercise activity eight years later (Saajanaho & others, 2014).

Gerontologists increasingly recommend strength training in addition to aerobic activity and stretching for older adults (Naczk, Marszalek, & Naczk, 2020). The average person's lean body mass declines with age—about 6.6 pounds of lean muscle are lost each decade during the adult years. The rate of loss accelerates after age 45. Resistance exercises can preserve and possibly increase muscle mass in older adults (van Dongen & others, 2020). A recent study of older adults found that resistance training improved their physical function, psychological well-being, and quality of life (Pedersen & others, 2017).

Exercise is an excellent way to maintain health and live longer (Strandberg, 2019). The current recommendations for older adults' physical activity are 2 hours and 30 minutes of moderate-intensity aerobic activity (brisk walking, for example) per week and muscle-strengthening activities on two or more days per week (Centers for Disease Control and Prevention, 2019). In the recent recommendations, even greater benefits can be attained with 5 hours of moderate-intensity aerobic activity per week.

Researchers continue to document the positive effects of exercise in older adults (Borbon-Castro & others, 2020). Exercise helps people to live independent lives with dignity in late adulthood (Morgan & others, 2019). At 80, 90, and even 100 years of age, exercise can help prevent older adults from falling down or even being institutionalized (Kaushal & others, 2019). Being physically fit means being able to do the things you want to do, whether you are young or old. More about research on exercise's positive benefits for health is shown in Figure 15.

Researchers who study exercise and aging have made the following discoveries:

FIGURE 15

THE JOGGING HOG EXPERIMENT. Jogging hogs reveal the dramatic effects of exercise on health. In one investigation, a group of hogs was trained to run approximately 100 miles per week (Bloor & White, 1983). Then the researchers narrowed the arteries that supplied blood to the hogs' hearts. The hearts of the jogging hogs developed extensive alternate pathways for blood supply, and 42 percent of the threatened heart tissue was salvaged, compared with only 17 percent in a control group of non-jogging hogs.
Courtesy of Maxine Bloor

- *Exercise is linked to increased longevity.* A recent meta-analysis confirmed that physically active older adults have an increased likelihood of living longer (Cunningham & others, 2020). A recent large-scale study found that middle-aged and older adults, including those with cardiovascular disease and cancer, can gain considerable longevity benefits by becoming more physically active and engaging in at least 150 minutes a week of moderate-intensity physical exercise (Mok & others, 2019). Also, another recent study of middle-aged adults revealed that their estimated age based on exercise stress testing was a better predictor of how long they would live than their chronological age (Harb & others, 2020). And in one analysis, energy expenditure by older adults during exercise that burns up at least 1,000 calories a week was estimated to increase life expectancy by about 30 percent, while burning up 2,000 calories a week in exercise was estimated to increase life expectancy by about 50 percent (Lee & Skerrett, 2001).

- *Exercise is related to prevention of common chronic diseases.* Exercise can reduce the risk of developing arthritis, cardiovascular disease, type 2 diabetes, osteoporosis, stroke, and breast cancer (Choi & others, 2020). For example, a study of older adults found that a higher lifetime physical activity level reduced age-related decline in cardiovascular and respiratory functions (Bailey & others, 2013).

- *Exercise is associated with increased effectiveness of treatment for many diseases.* When exercise is used as part of the treatment, individuals with these diseases show improvement in symptoms: arthritis, pulmonary disease, congestive heart failure, coronary artery disease, hypertension, type 2 diabetes, obesity, and Alzheimer disease (Kokkinos & others, 2019; Ricci & Cunha, 2020).

- *Exercise improves older adults' cellular functioning.* Researchers increasingly are finding that exercise improves cellular functioning in older adults (Qiao, Jiang, & Li, 2020; Srivastava & Veech, 2019). For example, researchers recently have discovered that aerobic exercise is linked to greater telomere length in older adults (Denham, O'Brien, & Charchar, 2016).

- *Exercise improves immune system functioning in older adults* (Duggal & others, 2019).

- *Exercise can optimize body composition and reduce the decline in motor skills as aging occurs.* Exercise can increase muscle mass and bone mass, improve balance and reduce falls, as well as decrease bone fragility (Fougere & Cesari, 2019; O'Connell, Coppinger, & McCarthy, 2020).

- *Exercise reduces the likelihood that older adults will develop mental health problems and can be effective in the treatment of mental health problems* (Sexton & Taylor, 2019). For example, a recent meta-analysis concluded that moderate to vigorous physical exercise was effective in reducing depressive symptoms in older adults with a mean age of 82 years (Klil-Drori & others, 2020).

- *Exercise is linked to improved brain, cognitive, and affective functioning in older adults.* Older adults who exercise regularly not only show better brain functioning but also process information more effectively than older adults who are more sedentary (Tsai & Chang, 2019; Wang & Guo, 2020).

Despite the extensive research documenting the power of exercise to improve older adults' health and quality of life, many older adults do not engage in any exercise. In the United States, physical inactivity increases with age. By age 75, about one in three men and one in two women engage in no physical exercise (Centers for Disease Control and Prevention, 2020). Possible explanations of older adults' reduction in exercise compared with middle-aged adults focus on such factors as chronic illnesses and life crises (a spouse's death, for example), that disrupt exercise schedules, embarrassment at being around others who are in better shape (especially if they haven't exercised much earlier in life), and the "why bother?" factor (not believing that exercise will improve their lives much). But as we have seen, it is never too late to begin exercising, and older adults can significantly benefit from regular exercise (Bouaziz & others, 2020; Strandberg, 2019).

Nutrition and Weight Four aspects of nutrition are especially important in older adults: (1) getting adequate nutrition, (2) avoiding overweight and obesity, (3) deciding whether to restrict calorie intake to improve health and extend life, and (4) determining whether to take specific vitamin supplements to slow the aging process.

Healthy Nutrition Eating a healthy, balanced diet and taking appropriate vitamins help older adults maintain their health (Diekmann & Bauer, 2019; Schiff, 2021). One change in eating behavior that can occur in older adults is a decrease in snacking between meals, which contributes to harmful weight loss, especially in women. Among the strategies for increasing weight gain in these women are the use of taste enhancers and calorie supplements between meals.

Overweight and Obesity A national survey found that 42.8 percent of U.S. adults 60 years of age and older were obese in 2017–2018 (Centers for Disease Control and Prevention, 2020). This figure is lower than the 44.8 percent of individuals 40 to 59 years of age who were obese. In this survey, 42.2 percent of men and 43.3 percent of women 60 years of age and older were obese. A large-scale study found a substantial link between being overweight/obese and having a higher mortality risk (Masters & others, 2013). However, some studies have reported that overweight adults live longer than normal-weight adults or that being overweight is not a risk factor for earlier death, especially in older adults (Chang & others, 2012). In a meta-analysis, being overweight was associated with lower all-cause mortality but being obese was associated with higher all-cause mortality (Flegal & others, 2013).

A magazine article even suggested that "chubby might be the new healthy" (Kolata, 2007). It's not clear why a few extra pounds that place someone in the overweight category might be linked to longevity. Possibly for some older adults, such as those recovering from surgery or those who develop pneumonia, the extra pounds may be protective. Some researchers argue that research evidence revealing a link between being overweight and living longer is likely due to inclusion of participants who have preexisting diseases (sometimes labeled "reverse causality") or sarcopenia (loss of lean body mass) (Greenberg, 2006).

Despite the several studies that have found a link between being overweight and living longer, the majority of studies have revealed that being overweight is a risk factor for an earlier death (Sun & others, 2019; Zhang & others, 2019). For example, in a recent large-scale study, obesity was associated with shorter longevity and increased risk of death due to cardiovascular

Johnny Kelley, finishing one of the many Boston Marathons he ran as an older adult. In 1991, he ran his sixtieth Boston Marathon and, in 2000, was named "Runner of the Century" by *Runner's World* magazine. At 70 years of age, Kelley was still running 50 miles a week. At that point in his life, Kelley said, "I'm afraid to stop running. I feel so good. I want to stay alive." He lived 27 more years and died at age 97 in 2004.
Charles Krupa/AP Images

What characterizes the current controversy about longevity and being overweight?
Curtoicurto/iStockphoto/Getty Images

disease compared with normal-weight individuals (Khan & others, 2018). In another recent large-scale study, obesity, as well as high body mass index (BMI) and waist circumference, were linked to earlier death (Batsis & others, 2017).

Obesity also is linked to the acceleration of diseases in many older adults (Katsiki & others, 2019; Noale, Limongi, & Maggi, 2020). However, although the link between obesity and disease is present in older adults, the link is weaker than it is for young and middle-aged adults (Kalish, 2016). Researchers also consistently find that when individuals are overweight and fit, they have a much better health profile and greater longevity than those who are overweight and not fit (Sardinha & others, 2016). Some researchers now conclude that inactivity and low cardiorespiratory fitness are greater threats to health and longevity than being overweight (McAuley & Blair, 2011).

Calorie Restriction Some studies have shown that calorie restriction in laboratory animals (such as rats and roundworms) can increase the animals' longevity (Someya & others, 2017). Research indicates that calorie restriction slows RNA decline during the aging process (Yamada & others, 2020). And researchers have found that chronic problems with the cardiovascular system, kidneys, and liver appear at a later age when calories are restricted (Hegab & others, 2019). In addition, research indicates that calorie restriction may provide neuroprotection for an aging central nervous system (White & others, 2017). One study found that calorie restriction maintained more youthful functioning in the hippocampus, which is an important brain structure for memory (Schafer & others, 2015).

No one knows for certain how calorie restriction works to increase the life span of animals. Some scientists suggest that it might lower the level of free radicals and reduce oxidative stress in cells (Tanajak & others, 2017). For example, one study found that calorie restriction slowed the age-related increase in oxidative stress (Ward & others, 2005). Other experts argue that calorie restriction might trigger stress and a state of emergency called "survival mode" in which the body eliminates all unnecessary functions to focus only on staying alive (Moatt & others, 2019). This survival mode likely is the result of evolution in which calorie restriction allowed animals to survive periods of famine, and thus the genes remain in the genomes of animal and human species today (Chen & Guarente, 2007).

Do underweight women and men live longer? One study revealed that women who were 20 pounds or more underweight lived longer even after controlling for smoking, hypertension, alcohol intake, and other factors (Wandell, Carlsson, & Theobald, 2009). In this study, underweight men did not live longer when various factors were controlled.

The research findings on the effects of calorie restriction in humans are mixed (Dorling, Martin, & Redman, 2020; Locher & others, 2014). Thus, an appropriate conclusion at this time is that further research is needed to definitively determine whether calorie restriction increases longevity, especially in humans.

The Controversy Over Vitamins and Aging For years, most experts on aging and health argued that a balanced diet was all that was needed for successful aging; vitamin supplements were not recommended. However, there have been some proposals that certain vitamin supplements—mainly a group called "antioxidants," which includes vitamin C, vitamin E, and beta-carotene—might help to slow the aging process and improve the health of older adults (Yeung & others, 2019).

The theory is that antioxidants counteract the cell damage caused by free radicals, which are produced both by the body's own metabolism and by environmental factors such as smoking, pollution, and harmful chemicals in the diet (Jabeen & others, 2018; Jeremic & others, 2018; Tonnies & Trushina, 2017). When free radicals cause damage (oxidation) in one cell, a chain reaction of damage follows. Antioxidants are theorized to act much like a fire extinguisher, helping to neutralize free-radical activity and reduce oxidative stress (Da Costa, Badawi, & El-Sohemy, 2012).

What have research studies found about the role of antioxidants in health? In two studies, no link was found between antioxidant vitamin intake and mortality (Henriquez-Sanchez & others, 2016; Stepaniak & others, 2016). Additionally, research reviews have not supported the belief that antioxidant vitamin supplements can reduce the incidence of cancer and cardiovascular disease (Khodaeian & others, 2015; Paganini-Hill, Kawas, & Corrada, 2015). And in a recent analysis, it was concluded that antioxidant supplements do not increase the life span and even can increase the incidence of diseases (Milisav, Ribaric, & Poljsak, 2018). However, a meta-analysis of seven studies concluded that dietary intakes (not vitamin supplements) of vitamins E, C, and beta-carotene were linked to a reduced risk of Alzheimer disease (Li, Shen, & Ji, 2012).

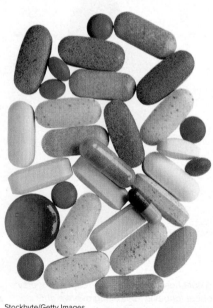

Stockbyte/Getty Images

Sarah Kagan, Geriatric Nurse

Sarah Kagan is a professor of nursing at the University of Pennsylvania School of Nursing. She provides nursing consultation to patients, their families, nurses, and physicians regarding the complex needs of older adults related to their hospitalization. She also consults on research and the management of patients who have head and neck cancers. Kagan teaches in the undergraduate nursing program, where she directs a course on "Nursing Care in the Older Adult." In 2003, she was awarded a MacArthur Fellowship for her work in the field of nursing.

Kagan says her work has allowed her the privilege of being with patients at the best and worst times of their lives. In the United States, older adults comprise close to half of all hospital stays, a quarter of ambulatory visits, and more than 70 percent of home health services. Many hospitals now employ emergency room staff who specialize in geriatric health care, and some offer separate geriatric emergency departments focused on treating older adults and reducing repeat admissions. The number of elders in developing countries is also expected to rise, from 400 million in 2000 to 1.7 billion by 2050—making geriatric health care a global issue.

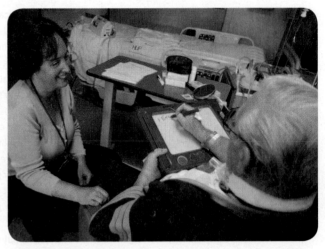

Sarah Kagan with a patient.
Jacqueline Larma/AP Images

For more information about what geriatric nurses do, see the Careers in Life-Span Development appendix.

HEALTH TREATMENT

The increase in the aging population is predicted to dramatically escalate health-care costs over the foreseeable future. As older adults live longer, disease management programs will need to be expanded to handle the chronic disorders of older adults. The increasing demand for health services among the expanding population of older adults is likely to bring shortages of many types of health professionals, including geriatric nurses, doctors, and health-care aides.

What is the quality of health treatment that older adults in the United States receive? A study of older adults with health problems revealed that they receive the recommended medical care they need only half the time (Wenger & others, 2003). The researchers examined the medical records of 372 frail older adults who had been treated by two managed-care organizations over the course of one year. Then they documented the medical care each patient received and judged it using standard indicators of quality. For example, many older adults with an unsteady gait didn't get the help they needed, such as physical therapy to improve their walking ability. Clearly, the quality of health treatment provided to older adults needs to be significantly improved (Ryskina, Lam, & Jung, 2019).

Geriatric nurses can be especially helpful in treating the health-care problems of older adults. To read about the work of one geriatric nurse, see *Connecting with Careers.*

The development of alternative home and community-based care has decreased the percentage of older adults who live in nursing homes (Walters & others, 2017). Still, as older adults age, their probability of being in a nursing home increases (see Figure 16). The quality of nursing homes and other extended-care facilities for older adults varies enormously and is a source of ongoing concern (Marshall & Hale, 2018). More than one-third of these facilities are seriously deficient. They fail federally mandated inspections because they do not meet the minimum standards for physicians, pharmacists, and various rehabilitation specialists (occupational and physical therapists). Further

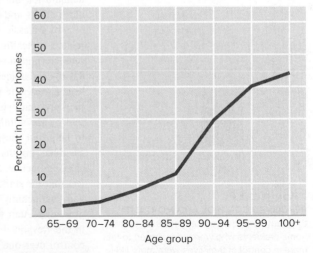

FIGURE 16

PERCENTAGE OF U.S. OLDER ADULTS OF DIFFERENT AGES IN NURSING HOMES

connecting development to life

Health-Care Providers and Older Adults

The demand for home-care aides is predicted to increase dramatically in the next several decades because of the likely doubling of the 65-and-older population and older adults' preference for remaining out of nursing homes (Moos, 2007). The attitudes of both the health-care provider and the older adult are important aspects of the older adult's health care (Cagle & others, 2016). Unfortunately, health-care providers too often share society's stereotypes and negative attitudes toward older adults (Eymard & Douglas, 2012). In a health-care setting, these attitudes can take the form of avoidance, dislike, and begrudged tolerance rather than positive, hopeful treatment. Health-care personnel are more likely to be interested in treating younger persons, who more often have acute problems with a higher prognosis for successful recovery. They often are less motivated to treat older persons, who are more likely to have chronic problems with a lower prognosis for successful recovery.

Not only are physicians less responsive to older patients, but older patients often take a less active role in medical encounters with health-care personnel than do younger patients. Older adults should be encouraged to take a more active role in their own health care.

Not only is it important to increase the number of health-care professionals available to treat older adults, but it is also very important that they show positive attitudes toward them.
Jonya/E+/Getty Images

concerns focus on the patient's right to privacy, access to medical information, safety, and lifestyle freedom within the individual's range of mental and physical capabilities (Weech-Maldonado & others, 2020).

Because of the inadequate quality of many nursing homes and the escalating costs for nursing home care, many specialists in the health problems of the aged stress that home health care, elder-care centers, and preventive medicine clinics are good alternatives (Nordstrom & Wangmo, 2018). They are potentially less expensive than hospitals and nursing homes (Rotenberg & others, 2018). They also are less likely to engender the feelings of depersonalization and dependency that occur so often in residents of institutions. Currently, there is an increased demand for, but shortage of, home-care workers because of the increase in the population of older adults and their preference to stay out of nursing homes (Barooah & others, 2019).

In a classic study, Judith Rodin and Ellen Langer (1977) found that an important factor related to health, and even survival, in a nursing home is the patient's feelings of control and self-determination. A group of elderly nursing home residents were encouraged to make more day-to-day choices and thus feel they had more responsibility for control over their lives. They began to decide such matters as what they ate, when their visitors could come, what movies they saw, and who could come to their rooms. A similar group in the same nursing home was told by the administrator how caring the nursing home was and how much the staff wanted to help, but these residents were given no opportunity to take more control over their lives. Eighteen months later, the residents who had been given responsibility and control were more alert and active, and said they were happier, than the residents who were only encouraged to feel that the staff would try to satisfy their needs. And the "responsible" or "self-control" group had significantly better improvement in their health than did the "dependent" group. Even more important was the finding that after 18 months only half as many nursing home residents in the "responsibility" group had died as in the "dependent" group (see Figure 17). Perceived control over one's environment, then, can literally be a matter of life or death.

Rodin's research shows that simply giving nursing home residents options for control can change their behavior and improve their health. To read further about health-care providers and older adults, see *Connecting Development to Life.*

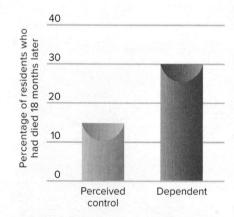

FIGURE 17

PERCEIVED CONTROL AND MORTALITY. In the study by Rodin and Langer (1977), nursing home residents who were encouraged to feel more in control of their lives were more likely to be alive 18 months later than those who were treated as being more dependent on the nursing home staff.

Review

- What are some common health problems in older adults? What are the main causes of death in older adults?
- What characterizes substance abuse in late adulthood?
- How do exercise, nutrition, and weight influence development?
- What are some options and issues in the health treatment of older adults?

Connect

- Older adults fare better when they are given more responsibility and control

in various aspects of their lives. At what other age stages is giving individuals more responsibility and control particularly important for their development?

Reflect *Your Own Personal Journey of Life*

- What changes in your lifestyle now might help you age more successfully when you become an older adult?

---

topical connections *looking forward*

In the next chapter, you will read about the benefits of engaging in challenging cognitive activities and staying cognitively fit in late adulthood. Links between the development of the brain and cognitive functioning will be examined. Aspects of work and retirement issues also will be explored. Mental health problems, including the dramatic increase in Alzheimer disease, will be discussed. And the roles of religion and spirituality in older adults' lives will be described.

---

reach your **learning goals**

Physical Development in Late Adulthood

1 Longevity

Life Expectancy and Life Span

The Young-Old and the Oldest-Old

Biological Theories of Aging

LG1 Characterize longevity and discuss the biological theories of aging.

- Life expectancy refers to the number of years that will probably be lived by an average person born in a particular year. Life span is the maximum number of years an individual can live. Life expectancy has dramatically increased; life span has not.

- An increasing number of individuals live to be 100 or older. Genetics, health, and coping well with stress can contribute to becoming a centenarian. On average, females live about six years longer than males do. The sex difference is likely due to biological and social factors.

- In terms of chronological age, the young-old have been described as being 65 to 84 years of age and the oldest-old as 85 years and older. Many experts on aging prefer to describe the young-old, old-old, and oldest-old in terms of functional age rather than chronological age. This view accounts for the fact that some 85-year-olds are more biologically and psychologically fit than some 65-year-olds. However, those 85 and older face significant problems, whereas those in their sixties and seventies are increasingly likely to experience successful aging.

- The evolutionary theory of aging proposes that natural selection has not eliminated many harmful conditions and nonadaptive characteristics in older adults; thus, the benefits conferred by evolution decline with age because natural selection is linked to reproductive fitness.

- One recent view is that aging is caused by a combination of cellular maintenance requirements and evolutionary constraints. Among the key genetic and cellular processes that have been proposed to explain aging are those involving telomeres, free radicals, mitochondria, sirtuins, and the mTOR pathway. According to hormonal stress theory, aging in the body's hormonal system can lower resilience and increase the likelihood of disease.

2 The Course of Physical Development in Late Adulthood

 Describe how a person's brain and body change in late adulthood.

The Aging Brain

- The brain loses weight and volume with age, and there is a general slowing of function in the central nervous system that begins in middle adulthood and increases in late adulthood. However, researchers have recently found that older adults can generate new neurons, and at least through the seventies, new dendrites.

- The aging brain retains considerable plasticity and adaptiveness. For example, it may compensate for losses in some regions of the brain by shifting responsibilities to other regions. A decrease in lateralization may reflect this kind of compensation, or it may reflect an age-related decline in the specialization of function.

Sleep

- Approximately 50 percent of older adults complain of having difficulty sleeping. Poor sleep can result in earlier death and lower cognitive functioning. Many sleep problems among older adults are linked to health conditions.

Physical Appearance and Movement

- The most obvious signs of aging are wrinkled skin and age spots on the skin. People get shorter as they age, and their weight often decreases after age 60 because of loss of muscle. The movement of older adults slows across a wide range of movement tasks.

Sensory Development

- Declines in visual acuity, color vision, and depth perception usually occur with age, especially after age 75. The yellowing of the eye's lens with age reduces color differentiation. The ability to see the periphery of a visual field also declines in older adults. Significant declines in visual functioning related to glare characterize adults 75 years and older and are prevalent among those 85 and older. Three diseases that can impair the vision of older adults are cataracts, glaucoma, and macular degeneration.

- Hearing decline can begin in middle age but usually does not become much of an impediment until late adulthood. Smell and taste can decline, although the decline is minimal in healthy older adults.

- Changes in touch sensitivity are associated with aging, although this does not present a problem for most older adults. Sensitivity to pain decreases in late adulthood. Declines in perceptual motor coupling characterize older adults; driving a vehicle is an example of this coupling.

The Circulatory and Respiratory Systems

- Cardiovascular disorders increase in late adulthood. Consistently high blood pressure should be treated to reduce the risk of stroke, heart attack, and kidney disease. Lung capacity decreases with age, but older adults can improve lung functioning with diaphragm-strengthening exercises.

Sexuality

- Aging in late adulthood brings some changes in sexual performance, more so for males than females. Nonetheless, there are no known age limits to sexual activity.

3 Health

Identify health problems in older adults and describe how they can be treated.

Health Problems

- As we age, our probability of disease or illness increases. Chronic disorders are rare in early adulthood, increase in middle adulthood, and become more common in late adulthood. The most common chronic disorder in late adulthood is arthritis. Nearly three-fourths of older adults die of cancer, heart disease, or stroke.

- Osteoporosis is the main reason many older adults walk with a stoop; women are especially vulnerable to this condition. Accidents are usually more debilitating to older adults than to younger adults.

Substance Use and Abuse

- The percentage of older adults who engage in binge drinking is smaller than in early and middle adulthood, but moderate drinking of red wine can bring health benefits. Abuse of illicit and prescription drugs is a growing problem in the United States, although substance addiction is more difficult to detect in older adults than in younger adults.

- The physical benefits of exercise have been demonstrated in older adults. Aerobic exercise and weight lifting are recommended for people who are physically capable of them. It is important for older adults to eat healthy foods and take appropriate vitamins.

- Being overweight is linked to health problems, and being obese predicts earlier death. Calorie restriction in animals can increase the animals' life span, but whether this works with humans is not known. In humans, there has been recent controversy about whether being overweight is associated with increased or reduced mortality rates in older adults.

- Most nutritional experts recommend a well-balanced, low-fat diet for older adults but do not recommend an extremely low-calorie diet. Controversy surrounds the question of whether vitamin supplements—especially the antioxidants vitamin C, vitamin E, and beta-carotene—can slow the aging process and improve older adults' health. Recent research reviews concluded that taking antioxidant vitamin supplements does not reduce the risk of cancer and cardiovascular disease.

- Although only 3 percent of adults over 65 reside in nursing homes, 23 percent of adults 85 and older do. The quality of nursing homes varies enormously, and alternatives to nursing home care are being proposed. Simply giving nursing home residents options for control can change their behavior and improve their health. The attitudes of both the health-care provider and the older adult patient are important aspects of the older adult's health care. Too often health-care personnel share society's negative view of older adults.

key **terms**

arthritis 541	free-radical theory 529	life span 523	neurogenesis 533
cataracts 537	glaucoma 537	macular degeneration 537	osteoporosis 542
cellular clock theory 529	hormonal stress theory 530	mitochondrial theory 530	sirtuins 530
evolutionary theory of aging 529	life expectancy 523	mTOR pathway 530	

key **people**

Leonard Hayflick 529	Ellen Langer 548	Judith Rodin 548

chapter 18

COGNITIVE DEVELOPMENT IN LATE ADULTHOOD

chapter **outline**

① Cognitive Functioning in Older Adults

Learning Goal 1 Describe the cognitive functioning of older adults.

Multidimensionality and Multidirectionality
Education, Work, and Health
Use It or Lose It
Training Cognitive Skills
Cognitive Neuroscience and Aging

② Language Development

Learning Goal 2 Characterize changes in language skills in older adults.

③ Work and Retirement

Learning Goal 3 Discuss aging and adaptation to work and retirement.

Work
Retirement in the United States and in Other Countries
Adjustment to Retirement

④ Mental Health

Learning Goal 4 Describe mental health problems in older adults.

Depression
Dementia, Alzheimer Disease, and Other Afflictions

⑤ Religion and Spirituality

Learning Goal 5 Explain the role of religion and spirituality in the lives of older adults.

Jonathan Kirn/Getty Images

In 2010, 90-year-old Helen Small completed her master's degree at the University of Texas at Dallas (UT-Dallas). The topic of her master's degree research project was romantic relationships in older adults. Helen said she had interviewed only one individual who was older than she was at the time—a 92-year-old man.

I (your author, John Santrock) first met Helen when she took my undergraduate course in life-span development in 2006. After the first test, Helen stopped showing up and I wondered what had happened to her. It turned out that she had broken her shoulder when she tripped over a curb while hurrying to class. The next semester, she took my class again and did a great job in it, even though for the first several months she had to take notes with her left hand (she's right-handed) because of her lingering shoulder problem.

Helen grew up during the Great Depression and first went to college in 1938 at the University of Akron but attended for only one year. She got married and her marriage lasted 62 years. After her husband's death, Helen went back to college in 2002, first at Brookhaven Community College and then at UT-Dallas. When I interviewed her several years ago, she told me that she had promised her mother that she would finish college. Her most important advice for college students was this: "Finish college and be persistent. When you make a commitment, always see it through. Don't quit. Go after what you want in life."

Helen not only was a cognitively fit older adult, she also was physically fit. She regularly worked out three times a week for about an hour each time—aerobically on a treadmill for about 30 minutes and then on six different weight machines.

What struck me most about Helen when she took my undergraduate course in life-span development was how appreciative she was of the opportunity to learn and how tenaciously she pursued studying and doing well in the course. Helen was quite popular with the younger students and was a terrific role model for them.

Helen Small with the author of your text, John Santrock, in his undergraduate course on life-span development at the University of Texas at Dallas in spring 2012. Helen returned each semester to talk with students in the class about cognitive aging.
Dr. John Santrock

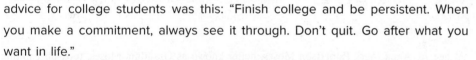

topical connections *looking back*

Most individuals reach the peak of their cognitive functioning in middle adulthood. However, some cognitive processes increase while others decline in middle age. For example, vocabulary peaks and speed of processing decreases in middle age. Expertise also typically increases during this age period. For many people, midlife is a time when individuals reflect and evaluate their current work and what they plan to do in the future. Many middle-aged adults increasingly examine life's meaning.

Helen Small published her first book, *Why Not? My Seventy Year Plan for a College Degree*, in 2011 at the age of 91.
Courtesy of Helen Small

After her graduation, I asked her what she planned to do during the next few years and she responded, "I've got to figure out what I'm going to do with the rest of my life." Helen came each semester to my course in life-span development when we were discussing cognitive aging. She wowed the class and was an inspiration to all who came in contact with her.

What did Helen do to stay cognitively fit? She worked as a public ambassador both for Dr. Denise Park's Center for Vital Longevity at UT-Dallas and the Perot Science Museum. And Helen was active in delivering meals through the Meals on Wheels organization that seeks to reduce hunger and social isolation in older adults. She also wrote a book titled *Why Not? My Seventy Year Plan for a College Degree* (Small, 2011). It's a wonderful, motivating invitation to live your life fully and reach your potential no matter what your age. After living an amazing, fulfilling life, Helen Small passed away in 2017 at the age of 97.

preview

Helen Small led a very active cognitive life as an older adult. Just how well older adults can and do function cognitively is an important question we will explore in this chapter. We also will examine aspects of language development, work and retirement, mental health, and religion.

1 Cognitive Functioning in Older Adults LG1 Describe the cognitive functioning of older adults.

| Multidimensionality and Multidirectionality | Education, Work, and Health | Use It or Lose it | Training Cognitive Skills | Cognitive Neuroscience and Aging |

At age 76, Anna Mary Robertson Moses, better known as Grandma Moses, took up painting and became internationally famous, staging 15 one-woman shows throughout Europe. At age 89, Arthur Rubinstein gave one of his best performances at New York's Carnegie Hall. When Pablo Casals was 95, a reporter asked him, "Mr. Casals, you are the greatest cellist who ever lived. Why do you still practice six hours a day?" Mr. Casals replied, "Because I feel like I am making progress" (Canfield & Hansen, 1995).

developmental **connection**

Intelligence

Fluid intelligence is the ability to reason abstractly; crystallized intelligence is an individual's accumulated information and verbal skills. Connect to "Physical and Cognitive Development in Middle Adulthood."

cognitive mechanics The "hardware" of the mind, reflecting the neurophysiological architecture of the brain. Cognitive mechanics involve the speed and accuracy of the processes involving sensory input, visual and motor memory, discrimination, comparison, and categorization.

MULTIDIMENSIONALITY AND MULTIDIRECTIONALITY

In thinking about the nature of cognitive change in adulthood, it is important to keep in mind that cognition is a multidimensional concept (Brathen & others, 2020; Kinugawa, 2019). It is also important to realize that although some dimensions of cognition might decline as we age, others might remain stable or even improve.

Cognitive Mechanics and Cognitive Pragmatics Paul Baltes (2003; Baltes, Lindenberger, & Staudinger, 2006) clarified the distinction between those aspects of the aging mind that show decline and those that remain stable or even improve:

- **Cognitive mechanics** are the "hardware" of the mind and reflect the neurophysiological architecture of the brain that was developed through evolution. Cognitive mechanics consist of these components: speed and accuracy of the processes involved in sensory input, attention, visual and motor memory, discrimination, comparison, and categorization. Because of the strong influence of biology, heredity, and health on cognitive mechanics, this aspect of thinking is likely to decline with age. Some researchers conclude that the decline in cognitive mechanics may begin as soon as early midlife (Salthouse, 2013a, b).

- **Cognitive pragmatics** are the culture-based "software programs" of the mind. Cognitive pragmatics include reading and writing skills, language comprehension, educational qualifications, professional skills, and also the self-understanding and life skills that help us to master or cope with challenges. Because of the strong influence of culture on cognitive pragmatics, it is possible for them to continue improving into old age. Thus, although cognitive mechanics may decline in old age, cognitive pragmatics may actually improve, at least until individuals become very old (see Figure 1).

The distinction between cognitive mechanics and cognitive pragmatics is similar to the one between fluid (mechanics) and crystallized (pragmatics) intelligence. Indeed, the similarity is so strong that some experts now describe cognitive aging patterns in terms of *fluid mechanics* and *crystallized pragmatics* (Lovden & Lindenberger, 2007).

What factors are most likely to contribute to the decline in fluid mechanics in late adulthood? Among the most likely candidates are declines in processing speed and working memory capacity, and reduced effectiveness in suppressing irrelevant information (inhibition) (Lovden & Lindenberger, 2007).

Now that we have examined the distinction between fluid mechanics and crystallized pragmatics, let's explore some of the more specific cognitive processes that reflect these two general domains, beginning with speed of processing.

Speed of Processing

It is now well accepted that the speed of processing information declines in late adulthood (Salthouse, 2018, 2019). Figure 2 illustrates this decline through the results of a study that measured reaction times in adults. A meta-analysis confirmed that processing speed increases through the childhood and adolescent years, begins to decline at some point during the latter part of early adulthood, and then continues to decline through the remainder of the adult years (Verhaeghen, 2013).

Although speed of processing information slows down in late adulthood, there is considerable individual variation in this ability. These variations in thinking speed appear to be correlated with physical aspects of aging. A recent study found that slow processing speed predicted an increase in older adults' falls one year later (Davis & others, 2017). Accumulated knowledge may compensate to some degree for slower processing speed in older adults.

Researchers have found that a slowing of processing speed is linked to the emergence of dementia over the next six years (Welmer & others, 2014). And in a large-scale study of middle-aged and older adults, out of 65 mortality risk factors, processing speed and health status were among the best predictors of living longer (Aichele, Rabbitt, & Ghisletta, 2016).

The decline in processing speed in older adults is likely due to a decline in functioning of the brain and central nervous system (Tsapanou & others, 2019). In a research meta-analysis, age-related losses in processing speed were explained by declining neural connectivity, changes in dopamine levels, or both (Verhaeghen, 2013).

Research suggests that processing speed is an important indicator of the ability of older adults to continue to safely drive a vehicle (Ross & others, 2016). For example, one study indicated that impaired visual processing speed predicted an increase in vehicle crashes in older adults (Huisingh & others, 2017).

Recent research has included an effort to improve older adults' processing speed through exercise interventions (Eckardt, Braun, & Kibele, 2020). For example, an experimental study found that high-intensity aerobic training was more effective than moderate-intensity aerobic training or resistance training in improving older adults' processing speed (Coetsee & Terblanche, 2017). And in a study of older adults, playing processing speed games for five sessions a week over four weeks improved their processing speed (Nouchi & others, 2016).

Attention

Changes in attention are important aspects of cognitive aging (Loaiza & Souza, 2019; Nemy & others, 2020). In many contexts older adults may not be able to focus on relevant information as effectively as younger adults can. In a recent study, less effective attention and processing speed were linked to declining memory in older adults (Jariat, Portrat, & Hot, 2019).

Researchers have found that older adults are less able to ignore distracting information than younger adults, and this distractibility becomes more pronounced as attentional demands increase (Ziegler, Janowich, & Gazzaley, 2018). Research indicates that the greater distractibility of older adults is associated with less effective functioning in neural networks running

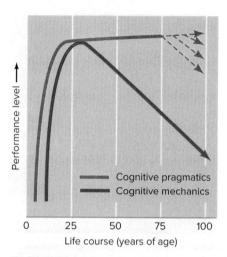

FIGURE 1

THEORIZED AGE CHANGES IN COGNITIVE MECHANICS AND COGNITIVE PRAGMATICS. Baltes argues that cognitive mechanics decline during aging, whereas cognitive pragmatics do not decline for many people until they become very old. Cognitive mechanics have a biological/genetic foundation; cognitive pragmatics have an experiential/cultural foundation. The broken lines from 75 to 100 years of age indicate possible individual variations in cognitive pragmatics.

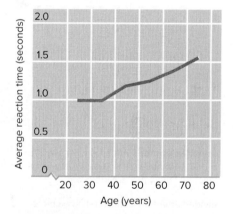

FIGURE 2

THE RELATION OF AGE TO REACTION TIME. In one study, the average reaction time began to slow in the forties, and this decline accelerated in the sixties and seventies (Salthouse, 1994). The task used to assess reaction time required individuals to match numbers with symbols on a computer screen.

cognitive pragmatics The culture-based "software programs" of the mind. Cognitive pragmatics include reading and writing skills, language comprehension, educational qualifications, professional skills, and also knowledge about the self and life skills that help us to master or cope with life.

What are some developmental changes in attention in late adulthood?
Manchan/Digital Vision/Getty Images

developmental **connection**

Attention

Young children make progress in many aspects of attention, including sustained attention and executive attention. Connect to "Physical and Cognitive Development in Early Childhood."

selective attention Focusing on a specific aspect of experience that is relevant while ignoring others that are irrelevant.

divided attention Concentrating on more than one activity at the same time.

sustained attention Focused and extended engagement with an object, task, event, or other aspect of the environment.

executive attention Aspects of thinking that include planning actions, allocating attention to goals, detecting and compensating for errors, monitoring progress on tasks, and dealing with novel or difficult circumstances.

explicit memory Memory of facts and experiences that individuals consciously know and can state.

implicit memory Memory without conscious recollection; involves skills and routine procedures that are automatically performed.

through the frontal and parietal lobes of the brain, which are involved in cognitive control (Campbell & others, 2012). Also, a research review concluded that more active and physically fit older adults are better able to allocate attention when interacting with the environment (Gomez-Pinilla & Hillman, 2013). And another study found that when older adults regularly engaged in mindfulness meditation, their goal-directed attention improved (Malinowski & others, 2017).

The chapter on "Physical and Cognitive Development in Early Childhood" described two types of attention—sustained and executive. Here we will discuss those two types of attention in older adults as well as two other types of attention: selective and divided attention.

- **Selective attention** involves focusing on a specific aspect of experience that is relevant while ignoring others that are irrelevant. An example of selective attention is the ability to focus on one voice among many in a crowded room or a noisy restaurant. Another is making a decision about which stimuli to attend to when making a left turn at an intersection. Generally, older adults are less adept at selective attention than younger adults are (Fernandez & others, 2019). Also, in one study, 10 weeks of training in speed of processing improved the selective attention of older adults (O'Brien & others, 2013).

- **Divided attention** involves concentrating on more than one activity at the same time. When the two competing tasks are reasonably easy, age differences among adults are minimal or nonexistent. However, the more difficult the competing tasks are, the less effectively older adults divide attention compared with younger adults (Bucur & Madden, 2007).

- **Sustained attention** is focused and extended engagement with an object, task, event, or some other aspect of the environment. Sometimes sustained attention is referred to as *vigilance*. On tests of simple vigilance and sustained attention, older adults usually perform as well as younger adults. However, on complex vigilance tasks, older adults' performance usually drops (Bucur & Madden, 2007). And a study of older adults found that the greater the variability in their sustained attention (vigilance), the more likely they were to experience falls (O'Halloran & others, 2011). It is possible, however, that older adults' experience and wisdom might offset some of their declines in vigilance. For example, consider how frequently young people focus intently on their smartphone rather than looking at traffic when crossing a dangerous intersection.

- **Executive attention** involves planning actions, allocating attention to goals, detecting and compensating for errors, monitoring progress on tasks, and dealing with novel or difficult circumstances. One study found that older adults had deficiencies in executive attention (Mahoney & others, 2010). In this study, a lower level of executive attention in older adults was linked to low blood pressure, which likely is related to reduced blood flow to the brain's frontal lobes. Also, in a recent study, executive attention training improved the selective attention and divided attention of older adults (Yang & others, 2019).

Memory   The main dimensions of memory and aging that have been studied include explicit and implicit memory, episodic memory, semantic memory, working memory, source memory, and prospective memory.

Explicit and Implicit Memory   Researchers have found that aging is linked with a decline in explicit memory (Reuter-Lorenz & Lustig, 2017). **Explicit memory** is memory of facts and experiences that individuals consciously know and can state. Explicit memory also is sometimes called declarative memory. Examples of explicit memory include being at a grocery store and remembering what you wanted to buy, being able to name the capital of Illinois, or recounting the events in a movie you have seen. **Implicit memory** is memory without conscious recollection; it involves skills and routine procedures that are performed automatically. Examples of implicit memory include driving a car, swinging a golf club, or typing on a computer keyboard without having to consciously think about how to perform these tasks.

Implicit memory is less likely to be adversely affected by aging than explicit memory is (Ward, 2018). Thus, older adults are more likely to forget what items they wanted to buy at a grocery store (unless they write them down on a list and take it with them) than they are to forget how to drive a car. Their perceptual speed might be slower in driving a car, but they remember how to do it.

Episodic Memory and Semantic Memory   Episodic and semantic memory are viewed as forms of explicit memory. **Episodic memory** is the retention of information about the details of life's happenings. For example, what was the color of the walls in your bedroom when you were a child, what was your first date like, what were you doing when you heard that airplanes had struck the World Trade Center, and what did you eat for breakfast this morning?

Younger adults have better episodic memory than older adults have, both for real and imagined events (Greene & Naveh-Benjamin, 2020; James, Rajah, & Duarte, 2019). A study of 18- to 94-year-olds revealed that increased age was linked to increased difficulty in retrieving episodic information, facts, and events (Siedlecki, 2007). Also, older adults think that they can remember older events better than more recent events, typically reporting that they can remember what happened to them years ago but can't remember what they did yesterday. However, researchers consistently have found that, contrary to such self-reports, in older adults the older the memory, the less accurate it is. This has been documented in studies of memory for high school classmates, foreign languages learned in school over the life span, names of grade school teachers, and autobiographical facts kept in diaries (Smith, 1996).

Autobiographical memories are stored as episodic memories (Allen & others, 2018). A recent study found that age-related decline in episodic memory impairs access to specific autobiographical events and the details involved (Peters, Fan, & Sheldon, 2019). Although in many cases older adults remember more about recent events than events that occurred long ago, a robust finding in autobiographical memory is called the *reminiscence bump,* in which adults remember more events from the second and third decades of their lives than from other decades (Munawar, Kuhn, & Hague, 2018). The "bump" is found more for positive than negative life events. Also, a recent study of 60- to 88-year-olds revealed that the first-time experience of a memory, the importance of the memory, and the emotional salience of the memory were associated with the reminiscence bump (Wolf & Zimprich, 2020).

Semantic memory is a person's knowledge about the world. It includes a person's fields of expertise, such as knowledge of chess for a skilled chess player; general academic knowledge of the sort learned in school, such as knowledge of geometry; and "everyday knowledge" about the meanings of words, the names of famous individuals, the significance of important places, and common things such as what day is Valentine's Day. Semantic memory appears to be independent of an individual's personal identity with the past. For example, you can access a fact—such as "Lima is the capital of Peru"—without having the foggiest idea of when and where you learned it.

Does semantic memory decline with age? Among the tasks that researchers often use to assess semantic memory are those involving vocabulary, general knowledge, and word identification. Older adults often take longer to retrieve semantic information, but usually they can ultimately retrieve it. However, the ability to retrieve very specific information (such as names) usually declines in older adults (Hoffman & Morcom, 2018). For the most part, episodic memory declines more than semantic memory in older adults (Jarjat & others, 2020).

Although many aspects of semantic memory are reasonably well preserved in late adulthood, a common memory problem for older adults is the *tip-of-the-tongue (TOT) phenomenon,* in which individuals can't quite retrieve familiar information but have the feeling that they should be able to retrieve it (Schmank & James, 2020). Researchers have found that older adults are more likely to experience TOT states than younger adults are (Huijbers & others, 2017). A study of older adults found that the most commonly reported errors in memory over the last 24 hours were those involving tip-of-the-tongue (Ossher, Flegal, & Lustig, 2013).

Working Memory   Recall that *working memory* is closely linked to short-term memory but places more emphasis on memory as a place for mental work. Working memory is like a mental "workbench" that allows children and adults to manipulate and assemble information when making decisions, solving problems, and comprehending written and spoken language (Baddeley, 2012, 2015, 2017, 2018, 2020). Researchers have found declines in working memory during late adulthood (Rhodes & others, 2019). One study revealed that working memory continued to decline from 65 to 89 years of age (Elliott & others, 2011).

Explanations of the decline in working memory in older adults often focus on their less efficient inhibition (preventing irrelevant information from entering working memory) and their increased distractibility (Lopez-Higes & others, 2018). Is there plasticity in the working memory of older adults? Researchers have found that older adults' working memory can be improved

episodic memory The retention of information about the details of life's happenings.

semantic memory A person's knowledge about the world—including one's fields of expertise, general academic knowledge of the sort learned in school, and "everyday knowledge."

This older woman has forgotten where she put the keys to her car. *What type of memory is involved in this situation?*
triffitt/Getty Images

Prospective memory involves remembering to do something in the future. This woman is keeping track of what she plans to buy when she goes to a grocery store the next day.
DAJ/Amana images/Getty Images

source memory The ability to remember where one learned something.

prospective memory Remembering to do something in the future.

through training (Brum & others, 2020). Further, in a recent study, aerobic endurance was linked to better working memory in older adults (Zettel-Watson & others, 2017). However, a recent study of young, middle-aged, and older adults found that all age groups' working memory improved with working memory training, but there was less improvement in older adults than in younger adults (Rhodes & Katz, 2017). Also, a recent study revealed that Latino older adults who were more acculturated (better adjusted to their new culture in the United States, for example) had better working memory than their less acculturated counterparts (Mendoza & others, 2020).

Source Memory **Source memory** is the ability to remember where one learned something (Ward, 2018). Failures of source memory increase with age in the adult years and they can create awkward situations, as when an older adult forgets who told a joke and retells it to the source (Meusel & others, 2017). One study revealed that self-referenced encoding improved the source memory of older adults (Leshikar & Duarte, 2014). Further, a recent study found that older adults with better source memory were characterized by healthy cardiovascular markers and psychological traits (higher achievement, less depression, for example) while lower source memory was predicted by relevant life experiences such as being retired and drinking heavily (Cansino & others, 2019). And a recent study indicated that older adults with good retrieval strategies had no deficits in source memory (Salhi & Bergstrom, 2020).

Lynn Hasher (2003, p. 1301) argues that age differences in performance are substantial in many tests of memory, such as source memory, when individuals are asked "for a piece of information that just doesn't matter much. But if you ask for information that is important, old people do every bit as well as young adults . . . young people have mental resources to burn. As people get older, they get more selective in how they use their resources."

Prospective Memory **Prospective memory** involves remembering to do something in the future, such as remembering to take your medicine or remembering to do an errand (Bozdemir & Cinan, 2020; Monti & others, 2020). Also, prospective memory has been referred to as remembering to remember (Kliegel & others, 2016). In one study, prospective memory played an important role in older adults' successful management of the medications they needed to take (Woods & others, 2014). Some researchers have found a decline in prospective memory with age (Kennedy & others, 2015; Smith & Hunt, 2014). However, a number of studies show that whether there is a decline depends on factors such as the nature of the task, what is being assessed, and the context of the assessment (Mullet & others, 2013; Scullin, Bugg, & McDaniel, 2012). For example, age-related deficits occur more often in prospective memory tasks that are time-based (such as remembering to call someone next Friday) than in those that are event-based (remembering to tell your friend to read a particular book the next time you see her). In addition, recent research indicates that prospective memory is impaired in individuals with mild Alzheimer disease (Lecouvey & others, 2019).

Further, declines in prospective memory occur more often in laboratories than in real-life settings (Bozdemir & Cinan, 2020). Indeed, in some real-life settings, such as keeping appointments, older adults' prospective memory is better than younger adults' (Luo & Craik, 2008). And a recent study found that planning strategies were associated with older adults' prospective memory (Wolff & others, 2016).

Conclusions About Memory and Aging Most, but not all, aspects of memory decline during late adulthood (Reuter-Lorenz & Lustig, 2017). The decline occurs primarily in explicit, episodic, and working memory, not in semantic memory or implicit memory (Zheng & others, 2019). A decline in perceptual speed is associated with memory decline (Salthouse, 2018, 2019). Successful aging does not mean eliminating memory decline altogether, but it does mean reducing the decline and adapting to it.

Older adults can use certain strategies to reduce memory decline (Chevalere, Lemaire, & Camos, 2020; Hertzog & others, 2019). Research indicates that strategies involving elaboration and self-referential processing are effective in improving the memory of older adults, actually helping older adults' memory more than younger adults' memory (Trelle, Henson, & Simons, 2015). However, one analysis concluded that older adults are slower than younger adults in shifting from an initial effortful strategy to using a faster and easier memory-based strategy (Touron, 2015). In a recent study, using compensation strategies (for example, managing appointments by routinely writing them on a calendar) was associated with higher levels of independence in everyday function in cognitively normal older adults and older adults with mild cognitive impairment (Tomaszewski Farias & others, 2018). Also, a recent study confirmed that when older adults engaged in higher levels of physical activity their memory improved (de Lima & others, 2019).

Executive Function   Recall that *executive function* is an umbrella-like concept that consists of a number of higher-level cognitive processes linked to the development of the brain's prefrontal cortex. Executive function involves managing one's thoughts to engage in goal-directed behavior and to exercise self-control.

How does executive function change in late adulthood? The prefrontal cortex is one area of the brain that especially shrinks with aging, and recent research has linked this shrinkage with a decrease in working memory and other cognitive activities in older adults (Lamballais & others, 2020; Reuter-Lorenz & Lustig, 2017).

Executive function skills decline in older adults (Gaillardin & Baudry, 2018). Aspects of working memory that especially decline in older adults involve (1) updating memory representations that are relevant for the task at hand and (2) replacing old, no longer relevant information (Friedman & others, 2008). Older adults also are less effective at engaging in cognitive control than when they were younger (Zammit & others, 2018). For example, in terms of cognitive flexibility, older adults don't perform as well as younger adults at switching back and forth between tasks or mental sets (Chiu & others, 2018). And in terms of cognitive inhibition, older adults are less effective than younger adults at inhibiting dominant or automatic responses (Lopez-Higes & others, 2018).

Although aspects of executive function tend to decline in late adulthood, there is considerable variability in executive function among older adults (Maldonado & others, 2020). For example, some older adults have a better working memory and are more cognitively flexible than other older adults (Kayama & others, 2014). In a recent study, highly educated older adults had better executive function than their less educated counterparts, which was associated with slower aged-related reduction in executive function (Chen & others, 2019). Further, there is increasing research evidence that aerobic exercise improves executive function in older adults (Eggenberger & others, 2015). For example, a recent study of older adults revealed that across a 10-year period physically active women experienced less decline in executive function than sedentary women (Hamer, Muniz Terrera, & Demakakos, 2018). Also, in a recent study, engaging in aerobic exercise improved older adults' executive function (McSween & others, 2019). In addition, in another recent study a combination of a Nordic Walking training program and vitamin D supplementation improved the processing speed, attention, and executive function of elderly women (Lipowski & others, 2019). And a recent research review of 20 executive function training studies found that overall they promoted cognitive and neural plasticity in older adults (Nguyen, Murphy, & Andrews. 2019).

Executive function increasingly is thought to be involved not only in cognitive performance but also in health, emotion regulation, adaptation to life's challenges, motivation, and social functioning (Forte & others, 2013). In one study, deficits in executive function but not memory predicted a higher risk of coronary heart disease and stroke three years later in older adults (Rostamian & others, 2015). And a recent study found that executive function in older adults increased their sense of control over obstacles that interfered with attaining goals, which in turn was associated with higher life satisfaction and positive affect (Toh, Yang, & Hartanto, 2020).

Metacognition   By middle age, adults have accumulated a great deal of metacognitive knowledge. They can draw on this metacognitive knowledge to help them combat a decline in memory skills. For example, they are likely to understand that they need to have good organizational skills and reminders to help combat the decline in memory skills they face.

Researchers have recently begun to study older adults' metacognition (Guerrero Sastoque & others, 2019; Siegel & Castel, 2019). For example, a recent study found that when older adults engaged in metacognitive monitoring of their performance, their visual short-term memory benefitted (Mitchell, Cusack, & Cam-CAN, 2018). In another recent study, older adults performed worse on metacognition tasks, including those involve false beliefs, deception, and emotion recognition, than young adults (Caiso, Besnard, & Allain, 2019). However, this deterioration in metacognition was linked to older adults' life satisfaction.

Recall from "Cognitive Development in Early Childhood" that theory of mind refers to awareness of one's own mental processes and the mental processes of others. Research indicates that theory of mind abilities decline in older adults (Hughes & others, 2019). This decline

developmental **connection**

Cognitive Processes

Executive function is increasingly recognized as an important facet of cognitive development. Connect to "Physical and Cognitive Development in Early Childhood," "Physical and Cognitive Development in Middle and Late Adulthood," and "Physical and Cognitive Development in Adolescence."

is likely due to declines in other cognitive skills, such as executive function, as well as declines in the brain's prefrontal cortex functioning (Duval & others, 2011).

Mindfulness   Recall that *mindfulness* involves being alert, mentally present, and cognitively flexible while going through life's everyday activities and tasks. Recently, there has been growing interest in mindfulness training with older adults, which has mainly focused on meditation. Some, but not all, studies have shown that mindfulness training improves older adults' cognitive functioning (Kovach & others, 2018; Mahio & Windsor, 2020). In one study, a mindfulness-based stress reduction program involving meditation improved older adults' memory and inhibitory control (Lenze & others, 2014). Further, a recent mindfulness training program increased older adults' aerobic physical activity duration (Robin & others, 2020).

Wisdom   Does wisdom, like good wine, improve with age? What is this thing we call "wisdom"? A research review found 24 definitions of wisdom, although there was significant overlap in the definitions (Bangen, Meeks, & Jeste, 2013). In this review, the following subcomponents of wisdom were commonly cited: knowledge of life, prosocial values, self-understanding, acknowledgment of uncertainty, emotional balance, tolerance, openness, spirituality, and sense of humor.

Thus, while there is still some disagreement regarding how wisdom should be defined, the following definition of wisdom has been used by leading expert Paul Baltes and his colleagues (Baltes & Kunzmann, 2007; Baltes & Smith, 2008): **Wisdom** is expert knowledge about the practical aspects of life that permits excellent judgment about important matters. This practical knowledge involves exceptional insight into human development and life matters, good judgment, and an understanding of how to cope with difficult life problems.

In regard to wisdom, research by Baltes and his colleagues (Baltes & Kunzmann, 2007; Baltes & Smith, 2008) yielded the following findings:

- High levels of wisdom are rare. Few people, including older adults, attain a high level of wisdom. That only a small percentage of adults show wisdom supports the contention that it requires experience, practice, or complex skills.

- The time frame of late adolescence and early adulthood is the main age window for wisdom to emerge (Staudinger & Dorner, 2007; Staudinger & Gluck, 2011). No further advances in wisdom have been found for middle-aged and older adults beyond the level they attained as young adults.

- Factors other than age are critical for wisdom to develop to a high level. For example, certain life experiences, such as being trained and working in a field concerned with difficult life problems and having wisdom-enhancing mentors, contribute to higher levels of wisdom. Also, people higher in wisdom have values that are more likely to consider the welfare of others than to focus solely on their own happiness.

- Personality-related factors, such as openness to experience, generativity, and creativity, are better predictors of wisdom than cognitive factors such as intelligence.

An increasing number of research studies have focused on the developmental aspects of wisdom at different points in life (Kunzmann, 2019; Sternberg & Gluck, 2019). One study found that self-reflective exploratory processing of difficult life experiences (meaning-making and personal growth) was linked to a higher level of wisdom (Westrate & Gluck, 2017). Another recent study found that the personality trait of openness to experience in early adulthood predicted wisdom 60 years later (Ardelt, Gerlach, & Vaillant, 2018). Also in this study, wisdom in late adulthood could be traced back to experiences and characteristics at different points in development: a supportive childhood, adolescent competence, emotional stability in young adults, and generativity in middle adulthood. And a recent study indicated that wisdom peaked in midlife, with education especially linked to a higher level of wisdom (Ardelt, Pridgen, & Nutter-Pridgen, 2018).

EDUCATION, WORK, AND HEALTH

Education, work, and health are three important influences on the cognitive functioning of older adults (Calero, 2019; Walker, 2019). They are also three of the most important factors involved in understanding why cohort effects need to be taken into account in studying the cognitive functioning of older adults. Indeed, cohort effects are very important considerations in the study of cognitive aging (Schaie, 2013, 2016). For example, one study found that older

Older adults might not be as quick with their thoughts or behavior as younger people, but wisdom may be an entirely different matter. This older woman shares the wisdom of her experience with a classroom of children. *How is wisdom described by life-span developmentalists?*
Elizabeth Crews

wisdom Expert knowledge about the practical aspects of life that permits excellent judgment about important matters.

adults assessed in 2013–2014 engaged in a higher level of abstract reasoning than their counterparts who had been assessed two decades earlier (Gerstorf & others, 2015). And a recent study of older adults in 10 European countries revealed improved memory between 2004 and 2013, with the changes more positive for older adults who had lower levels of cardiovascular disease and higher levels of exercise and educational achievement (Hessel & others, 2018).

Education Successive generations in America's twentieth century were better educated, and this trend continues in the twenty-first century (Schaie, 2013, 2016). Not only were today's older adults more likely to go to college when they were young adults than were their parents or grandparents, but more older adults are returning to college today to further their education than in past generations. Educational experiences are positively correlated with scores on intelligence tests and information-processing tasks, such as memory exercises. For example, a recent study indicated that higher educational attainment is strongly associated with older adults' working memory (Saito & others, 2020). Also, another study revealed that older adults with less education had lower cognitive abilities than those with more education (Lachman & others, 2010). However, for older adults with less education, frequently engaging in cognitive activities improved their episodic memory. And a recent study of 50- to 75-year-old Chinese Americans indicated that having a greater amount of schooling earlier in life was linked to a higher level of cognitive functioning in a number of areas, including processing speed, working memory, and episodic memory (Zhang & others, 2019). In this study, greater engagement in cognitive activity mediated the link between education and cognition functioning.

Work Successive generations have also had work experiences that included a stronger emphasis on cognitively oriented labor. Our great-grandfathers and grandfathers were more likely to be manual laborers than were our fathers, who are more likely to be involved in cognitively oriented occupations. As the industrial society continues to be replaced by the information society, younger generations will have more experience in jobs that require considerable cognitive investment. The increased emphasis on complex information processing in jobs likely enhances an individual's intellectual abilities (Sorman & others, 2020).

Researchers have found that when older adults engage in complex working tasks and challenging daily work activities, their cognitive functioning shows less age-related decrease (Fujishiro & others, 2019; Lovden, Backman, & Lindenberger, 2017). For example, in a recent study of Puerto Rican older adults, a higher complexity of work was associated with a reduced risk of cognitive impairment (Andel & others, 2019).

Health Successive generations have also been healthier in late adulthood as better treatments for a variety of illnesses (such as hypertension) have been developed. Many of these illnesses, such as stroke, heart disease, and diabetes, have a negative impact on intellectual performance (Callisaya & others, 2019). For example, researchers have found that cardiovascular disease is associated with cognitive decline in older adults (Lai & others, 2020). For example, a recent study of older Latinos revealed that cardiovascular risk factors were linked to lower cognitive functioning (Tarraf & others, 2020). And, as we will see later in this chapter, Alzheimer disease has a devastating effect on older adults' physical and cognitive functioning. Researchers also have found age-related cognitive decline in adults with mood disorders such as depression (Wei & others, 2019). For example, a recent study of older adults indicated that depression was linked to lower executive attention, memory, and language performance (MacAulay & others, 2020). Thus, some of the decline in intellectual performance found in older adults is likely due to health-related factors rather than to age per se (Mantri & others, 2019).

A number of research studies have found that exercise is linked to improved cognitive functioning in older adults (Redwine & others, 2020; Walker, 2019). Walking or any other aerobic exercise appears to get blood and oxygen pumping to the brain, which can help people think more clearly. For example, a recent study of older adults revealed that moderate to intense physical activity modified the depression-cognition connection and preserved cognitive function (Hu & others, 2019). And a recent meta-analysis concluded that meditation, tai chi, and yoga interventions are effective in improving older adults' cognitive functioning (Chan & others, 2019).

Dietary patterns also are linked to cognitive functioning in older adults (Perkisas & Vandewoude, 2019). For example, a recent research review concluded that multinutrient approaches using the Mediterranean diet are linked to a lower risk of cognitive impairment (Abbatecola, Russo, & Barbieri, 2018).

How are education, work, and health linked to cognitive functioning in older adults?
(Top) Silverstock/Digital Vision/Getty Images; (middle) Kurt Paulus/Cultura/Getty Images; (bottom) Tom Grill/Corbis/Getty Images

developmental **connection**

Health

Exercise is linked to increased longevity and the prevention of common chronic diseases. Connect to "Physical Development in Late Adulthood."

A final aspect of health that is related to cognitive functioning in older adults is *terminal decline*. This concept emphasizes that changes in cognitive functioning may be linked more to distance from death or cognition-related pathology than to distance from birth (Wilson & others, 2018). In one study, on average, a faster rate of cognitive decline occurred about 7.7 years prior to death and varied across individuals (Muniz-Terrera & others, 2013). Also, in a recent Swedish study, time to death was a good predictor of cognitive decline over time (Bendayan & others, 2017).

USE IT OR LOSE IT

Changes in cognitive activity patterns might result in disuse and consequent atrophy of cognitive skills (Kunzmann, 2019). This concept is captured by the phrase "use it or lose it." Mental activities that likely benefit the maintenance of cognitive skills in older adults include reading books, doing crossword puzzles, and going to lectures and concerts. "Use it or lose it" also is a significant component of the engagement model of cognitive optimization that emphasizes how intellectual and social engagement can buffer age-related declines in intellectual development (Kurita & others, 2020; Sharifian & others, 2019).

The following studies support the "use it or lose it" concept and the engagement model of cognitive optimization:

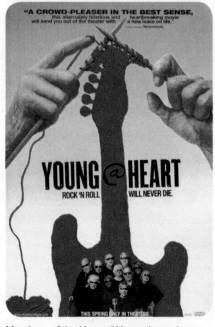

Members of the Young@Heart chorus have an average age of 80. Young@Heart became a hit documentary in 2008. The documentary displays the singing talents, energy, and optimism of a remarkable group of older adults, who clearly are on the "use it" side of "use it or lose it."
Everett Collection, Inc./Alamy Stock Photo

- In two different samples of older adults, a higher level of cognitive activity (reading newspapers, magazines, and books; writing letters; and playing games) was linked to better cognitive functioning (executive function, processing speed, and semantic processing) (Casaletto & others, 2020).

- In the Mayo Clinic Study of Aging, engaging in a higher number of mentally stimulating activities (reading books, using a computer, participating in social activities, playing games, and engaging in craft activities) was associated with a decreased risk of mild cognitive impairment, a condition that we will discuss later in the chapter in terms of its possible connection to Alzheimer disease (Krell-Roesch & others, 2019).

- In the Victoria Longitudinal Study, participation in intellectually engaging activities buffered middle-aged and older adults against cognitive decline (Hultsch & others, 1999). Further analyses of the participants in this study revealed that engagement in cognitively complex activities was linked to faster and more consistent processing speed (Bielak & others, 2007). And in another analysis of these older adults over a 12-year period, those who reduced their cognitive lifestyle activities (such as using a computer, playing bridge) subsequently showed decline in cognitive functioning in verbal speed, episodic memory, and semantic memory (Small & others, 2012).

- In the Baltimore Experience Corps program, an activities engagement–health promotion for older adults that involved their volunteerism in underserved urban elementary schools–improved older adults' cognitive and brain functioning (Carlson & others, 2015; Parisi & others, 2012, 2014, 2015).

- In a longitudinal study of 801 Catholic priests 65 years and older, those who regularly read books, did crossword puzzles, or otherwise exercised their minds were 47 percent less likely to develop Alzheimer disease than priests who rarely engaged in these activities (Wilson & others, 2002).

- Reading daily was linked to increased longevity for men in their seventies (Jacobs & others, 2008).

- At the beginning of a longitudinal study, 75- to 85-year-olds indicated how often they participated in six activities: reading, writing, doing crossword puzzles, playing card games or board games, having group discussions, and playing music (Hall & others, 2009). Across the five years of the study, the point at which memory loss accelerated was assessed and it was found that for each additional activity the older adult engaged in, the onset of rapid memory loss was delayed by 0.18 years. For older adults who participated in 11 activities per week compared with their counterparts who engaged in only 4 activities per week, the point at which accelerated memory decline occurred was delayed by 1.29 years.

- A recent research review concluded that low levels of social isolation characterized by high engagement in social activity and large social networks were linked to better cognition (memory and executive function, for example) in older adults (Evans & others, 2019).

TRAINING COGNITIVE SKILLS

If older adults are losing cognitive skills, can they be retrained? An increasing number of research studies indicate that cognitive retraining is possible to some degree (Calero, 2019; Kinugawa, 2019). Two key conclusions can be derived from research in this area: (1) training can improve the cognitive skills of many older adults, but (2) there is some loss in plasticity in late adulthood, especially in those who are 85 years and older (Baltes, Lindenberger, & Staudinger, 2006). Let's now examine the results of several cognitive training studies involving older adults.

A study of 60- to 90-year-olds found that sustained engagement in cognitively demanding, novel activities improved the older adults' episodic memory (Park & others, 2014). To produce this result, the older adults spent an average of 16.5 hours a week for three months learning how to quilt or how to use digital photography. Consider also a recent study of 60- to 90-year-olds in which iPad training 15 hours a week for 3 months improved their episodic memory and processing speed relative to engaging in social or non-challenging activities (Chan & others, 2016).

Researchers are also finding that improving the physical fitness of older adults can enhance their cognitive functioning (Bangsbo & others, 2019; Wang & Guo, 2020). A research review revealed that aerobic fitness training in older adults improved their performance in the areas of planning, scheduling, working memory, resistance to distraction, and handling multiple tasks (Colcombe & Kramer, 2003). In another research review, engaging in mild or moderate exercise was linked to improved cognitive functioning in older adults with chronic diseases (Cai & others, 2017). Also, in a recent study, engagement in physical activity in late adulthood was linked to less cognitive decline (Gow, Pattie, & Deary, 2017). And a recent study of older adults indicated that an in-home exergame training program improved their executive function (Adcock & others, 2020).

Meta-examinations of four longitudinal observational studies (Long Beach Longitudinal Study; Origins of Variance in the Oldest-old [Octo-Twin] Study in Sweden; Seattle Longitudinal Study; and Victoria Longitudinal Study in Canada) of older adults' naturalistic cognitive activities found that changes in cognitive activity predicted cognitive outcomes as long as two decades later (Brown & others, 2012; Lindwall & others, 2012; Mitchell & others, 2012). However, the studies provided no support for the concept that engaging in cognitive activity at an earlier point in development improved older adults' ability to later withstand cognitive decline. On a positive note, when older adults continued to increase their engagement in cognitive and physical activities, they were better able to maintain their cognitive functioning in late adulthood.

The Stanford Center for Longevity (2011) and the Stanford Center for Longevity in partnership with the Max Planck Institute for Human Development (2014) reported information based on the views of leading scientists in the field of aging. One of their concerns is the misinformation given to the public touting products to improve the functioning of the mind for which there is no scientific evidence. Nutritional supplements, brain games, and software products have all been advertised as "magic bullets" to slow the decline of mental functioning and improve the mental ability of older adults. Some of the claims are reasonable but not scientifically tested, while others are unrealistic and implausible (Willis & Belleville, 2016). A research review of dietary supplements and cognitive aging did indicate that ginkgo biloba was linked with improvements in some aspects of attention in older adults and that consuming omega-3 polyunsaturated fatty acids (fish oil) was related to reduced risk of age-related cognitive decline (Gorby, Brownawell, & Falk, 2010). In this research review, there was no evidence of cognitive improvements in aging adults who took supplements containing ginseng and glucose. Also, an experimental study with 50- to 75-year-old females found that those who took fish oil for 26 weeks had improved executive function and beneficial effects on a number of areas of brain functioning compared with their female counterparts who took a placebo pill (Witte & others, 2014). In other studies, fish oil supplement use was linked to higher cognitive scores and less atrophy in one or more brain regions (Daiello & others, 2015) and improvements in the working memory of older adults (Boespflug & others, 2016). Overall, though, most research has not provided consistent plausible evidence that dietary supplements can accomplish major cognitive goals in aging adults over a number of years.

However, some software-based cognitive training games have been found to improve older adults' cognitive functioning, but the gains typically occur only for the specific cognitive task

It is always in season for the old to learn.

—AESCHYLUS
Greek playwright, 5th century B.C.

To what extent can training improve cognitive functioning of older adults?
Stewart Cohen/Pam Ostrow/Blend Images/Alamy Stock Photo

assessed and do not generalize to broad effects on cognitive performance (Belchior & others, 2019; Sosa & Lagana, 2019). In a study of 60- to 85-year-olds found that a multitasking video game that simulates day-to-day driving experiences (NeuroRacer) improved cognitive control skills, such as sustained attention and working memory, after training on the video game and six months later (Anguera & others, 2013). In a research meta-analysis, computerized cognitive training resulted in modest improvement in some cognitive processes (nonverbal memory, verbal memory, working memory, processing speed, and visuospatial skills) but did not improve executive function and attention (Lampit, Hallock, & Valenzuela, 2014). Further, in a recent meta-analysis it was concluded that video games have small training effects on improving older adults' memory but no positive outcomes for other cognitive functions (Mansor, Chow, & Halaki, 2020). Nonetheless, it is possible that the training games may improve cognitive skills in a laboratory setting but not generalize to gains in the real world.

After examining research findings, the Stanford Center for Longevity and the Max Planck Institute for Human Development (2014) concluded that the effectiveness of brain games has often been exaggerated and the research evidence for many success claims is often weak or unfounded. They also concluded that there is little evidence that playing brain games in late adulthood improves underlying broad cognitive abilities or that the games help older adults to function more competently in everyday life.

In sum, some improvements in the cognitive vitality of older adults can be accomplished through some types of cognitive, physical activity, and nutritional interventions (Casaletto & others, 2020; Gillain & others, 2019). However, benefits have not been observed in all studies (Salthouse, 2017). Further research is needed to determine more precisely which cognitive improvements occur in older adults as a result of training (Salthouse, 2019).

----------->

developmental **connection**

Brain Development

The activities older adults engage in can influence the brain's development. Connect to "Physical Development in Late Adulthood."

<-----------

COGNITIVE NEUROSCIENCE AND AGING

We have seen that certain regions of the brain are involved in links between aging and cognitive functioning. In this section, we further explore the substantial increase in interest in the brain's role in aging and cognitive functioning. The field of *cognitive neuroscience* has emerged as the major discipline that explores the links between brain activity and cognitive functioning (Chen & others, 2020; Nyberg & Pudas, 2019). This field especially relies on brain-imaging techniques such as fMRI, PET, and DTI (diffusion tensor imaging) to reveal the areas of the brain that are activated when individuals engage in certain cognitive activities (Duda & others, 2019; Lizuka & others, 2020). For example, as an older adult is asked to encode and then retrieve verbal materials or images of scenes, the older adult's brain activity will be monitored by an fMRI brain scan.

Changes in the brain can influence cognitive functioning, and changes in cognitive functioning can influence the brain (Kinugawa, 2019; Schnellbacher & others, 2020). For example, aging of the brain's prefrontal cortex may produce a decline in working memory (Reuter-Lorenz & Lustig, 2017). And when older adults do not regularly use their working memory (recall the section titled "Use It or Lose It"), neural connections in the prefrontal lobe may atrophy. Further, cognitive interventions that activate older adults' working memory may increase these neural connections.

Despite being in its infancy as a field, the cognitive neuroscience of aging is beginning to uncover some important links between aging, the brain, and cognitive functioning (Filip & others, 2019; Rakesh, Fernando, & Mansour, 2020). These include the following:

- Neural circuits in specific regions of the brain's prefrontal cortex decline, and this decline is linked to poorer performance by older adults on tasks involving complex reasoning, cognitive inhibition, working memory, and episodic memory (Park & Festini, 2018; Reuter-Lorenz & Lustig, 2017) (see Figure 3).
- Older adults are more likely than younger adults to use both hemispheres of the brain to compensate for declines in attention, memory, executive function, and language that occur with age (Davis & others, 2012; Dennis & Cabeza, 2008; Esteves & others, 2020). For example, two neuroimaging studies found that older adults showed better memory performance when both hemispheres of the brain were active in processing information (Angel & others, 2011; Manenti, Cotelli, & Miniussi, 2011).

- Functioning of the hippocampus declines to a lesser degree than the functioning of the frontal lobes in older adults (Antonenko & Floel, 2014). In K. Warner Schaie's (2013) research, individuals whose memory and executive function declined in middle age had more hippocampal atrophy in late adulthood, but those whose memory and executive function improved in middle age did not show a decline in hippocampal functioning in late adulthood.
- Patterns of neural decline with aging are more dramatic for retrieval than for encoding (Gutchess & others, 2005).
- Compared with younger adults, older adults often show greater activity in the frontal and parietal lobes of the brain on simple tasks but as attentional demands increase, older adults display less effective functioning in areas of the frontal and parietal lobes of the brain that are involved in cognitive control (Campbell & others, 2012).
- Cortical thickness in the frontoparietal network predicts executive function in older adults (Schmidt & others, 2016).
- Younger adults have better connectivity between brain regions than older adults do (Damoiseaux, 2017). For example, one study revealed that younger adults had more connections between brain activations in frontal, occipital, and hippocampal regions than older adults during a difficult encoding task (Leshikar & others, 2010).
- An increasing number of cognitive and physical fitness training studies are using brain-imaging techniques such as fMRI to assess the results of such training on brain function (Kinugawa, 2019; Walker, 2019). In one study, older adults who walked one hour a day three days a week for six months showed increased volume in the frontal and temporal lobes of the brain (Colcombe & others, 2006).

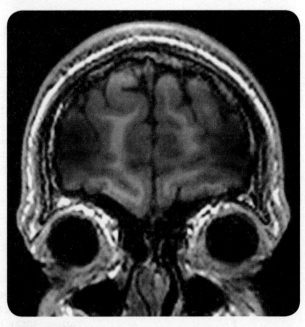

FIGURE 3

THE PREFRONTAL CORTEX. Advances in neuroimaging are allowing researchers to make significant progress in connecting changes in the brain with cognitive development. Shown here is an fMRI of the brain's prefrontal cortex. *What links have been found between the prefrontal cortex, aging, and cognitive development?*
Courtesy of Dr. Sam Gilbert, Institute of Cognitive Neuroscience, UK

Denise Park and Patricia Reuter-Lorenz (2009) proposed a neurocognitive scaffolding view of connections between the aging brain and cognition. In this view, increased activation in the prefrontal cortex with aging reflects an adaptive brain that is compensating for declining neural structures and function and declines in various aspects of cognition, including working memory and long-term memory. Scaffolding involves the use of complementary neural circuits to protect cognitive functioning in an aging brain. Among the factors that can strengthen brain scaffolding are cognitive engagement and exercise.

Review *Connect* Reflect

 Describe the cognitive functioning of older adults.

Review
- How is cognition multidimensional and multidirectional in older adults? What changes in cognitive processing take place in aging adults?
- How do education, work, and health affect cognition in aging adults?
- What is the concept of "use it or lose it"?
- To what extent can older adults' cognitive skills be retrained?
- What characterizes the cognitive neuroscience of aging?

Connect
- The term *scaffolding* was used in this section to describe the use of complementary neural circuits to protect cognitive functioning in an aging brain. How has the term *scaffolding* been used elsewhere in the text?

Reflect *Your Own Personal Journey of Life*
- Can you think of older adults who have made significant contributions in late adulthood, other than those we mentioned in the chapter? Spend some time reading about these individuals and evaluate how their intellectual interests contributed to their life satisfaction as older adults. What did you learn from their lives that might benefit your cognitive development and life satisfaction as an older adult?

Most research on language development has focused on infancy and childhood. It is generally thought that for most of adulthood individuals maintain their language skills (Wingfield & Lash, 2016). The vocabulary of individuals often continues to increase throughout most of the adult years, at least until late adulthood (Schaie, 2013). Many older adults maintain or improve their word knowledge and word meaning (Burke & Shafto, 2004).

In late adulthood, however, some decrements in language skills may appear (Payne & Federmeier, 2018; Valech & others, 2018). Among the most common language-related complaints reported by older adults are difficulty in retrieving words to use in conversation and problems understanding spoken language in certain contexts (Clark-Cotton & others, 2007). This often involves the *tip-of-the-tongue phenomenon* mentioned earlier, in which individuals are confident that they know something but can't quite seem to retrieve it from memory (James & others, 2018). Older adults also report that in less than ideal listening conditions they can have difficulty understanding speech. This difficulty is most likely to occur when speech is rapid, competing stimuli are present (a noisy room, for example), and when they can't see their conversation partner (in a telephone conversation, for example). The difficulty in understanding speech may be due to hearing loss as well as cognitive impairment (Benichov & others, 2012). In general, though, most language skills decline little among older adults if they are healthy (Wingfield & Lash, 2016).

Some aspects of the phonological skills of older adults are different from those of younger adults (Robert & Mathey, 2018). Older adults' speech is typically lower in volume, slower, less precisely articulated, and less fluent (more pauses, fillers, repetition, and corrections). Despite these age differences, most older adults' speech skills are adequate for everyday communication.

Researchers have found conflicting information about changes in *discourse* (extended verbal expression in speech or writing) with aging. "Some (researchers) have reported increased elaborateness, while others have reported less varied and less complex syntax" (Obler, 2009, p. 459). One aspect of discourse where age differences have been found involves retelling a story or giving instructions for completing a task. When engaging in this type of discourse, older adults are more likely than younger adults to omit key elements, creating discourse that is less fluent and more difficult to follow (Clark-Cotton & others, 2007). One study found that when retelling a story, older adults were more likely than younger adults to compress discourse and less likely to improve the cohesiveness of their narratives (Saling, Laroo, & Saling, 2012). Also, a recent study of 19- to 75-year-olds confirmed that older adults were more likely to have difficulties in narrative discourse than younger age groups (Babaei & others, 2019).

Nonlanguage factors may be responsible for some of the declines in language skills that do occur in older adults (Obler, 2009). Slower information-processing speed and a decline in working memory, especially in being able to keep information in mind while processing, likely contribute to decreased language efficiency in older adults (Salthouse, 2017). For example, a recent study found that the lower working memory capacity of older adults compared with younger adults impaired their comprehension of sentences (Sung & others, 2017).

Language skills decline among individuals with Alzheimer disease, as we will discuss later in the chapter (Resende & others, 2020; Valech & others, 2018). Difficulties in finding and generating words are one of the earliest symptoms of Alzheimer disease (Haugrud, Crossley, & Vrbancic, 2011). Individuals with Alzheimer disease especially have difficulty on tests of semantic verbal fluency, in which they have to say as many words as possible in a category (fruits or animals, for example) in a given time, typically one minute (Weakley & Schmitter-Edgecombe, 2014). Most individuals with the disease do retain much of their ability to produce well-formed sentences until the late stages of the disease. Nonetheless, they do make more grammatical errors than older adults without the disease (Huang, Meyer, & Federmeier, 2012). In a recent study, individuals with Alzheimer disease were less likely to use syntactic components in their language than those who did not have Alzheimer disease (Orimaye & others, 2017).

Recently, interest has been generated by the possibility that bilingualism may delay the onset of Alzheimer disease (Borsa & others, 2018; Kim & others, 2019). One study found that the onset of Alzheimer disease occurred 4.5 years later in bilingual older adults than in their counterparts who were not bilingual (Alladi & others, 2013). Another study revealed that the onset of symptoms and the first office visit for Alzheimer disease occurred several years later for bilingual than for monolingual older adults (Bialystok & others, 2014). These results led Ellen Bialystok and her colleagues (2016) to recently conclude that being bilingual may be one of the best ways to delay the onset of Alzheimer disease by as much as four to five years. Also, in a recent study of individuals with mild cognitive impairment, those who were bilingual had better verbal memory than monolingual individuals (Rosselli & others, 2019). In addition, a recent study indicated a bilingual advantage for the alerting subcomponent of attention (Dash & others, 2019). With these results in mind, might learning a second language as an older adult be beneficial? In a recent study of 59- to 79-year-olds, a 4-month-long second language program produced improvements in global cognitive functioning and connectivity among different regions of the brain's frontal and parietal lobes (Bubbico & others, 2019).

Review Connect Reflect

 LG2 Characterize changes in language skills in older adults.

Review
- What are the main changes in language skills in older adults?

Connect
- In this section, we learned that some aspects of the phonological skills of older adults are different from those of younger adults. By what age are

children typically capable of producing all the vowel sounds and most of the consonant sounds of their language?

Reflect *Your Own Personal Journey of Life*
- What might you be able to do as an older adult to preserve or even enhance your language skills?

---

3 Work and Retirement

 LG3 Discuss aging and adaptation to work and retirement.

| Work | Retirement in the United States and in Other Countries | Adjustment to Retirement |

What percentage of older adults continue to work? How productive are they? Who adjusts best to retirement? What is the changing pattern of retirement in the United States and around the world? Let's look at the answers to these and other questions.

WORK

In 2000, 23 percent of U.S. 65- to 69-year-olds were in the workforce; in 2017, this percentage had jumped to 32 percent (Mislinksi, 2018). Among 70- to 74-year-olds, 13 percent were in the workforce in 2000, but this percentage had increased to 19 percent in 2015. The increased percentage of older adults who continue to work has occurred more for women than men. For example, the labor force participation for 75-and-over women has risen 87 percent since 2000, while participation in the work force for 75-and-over men has increased by 45 percent (Mislinski, 2018). These increases likely are mainly driven by the need to have adequate money to meet living expenses in old age (Cahill, Giandrea, & Quinn, 2016).

The proportion of workers who expect to work past age 65 increased from 16 percent in 1991 to 48 percent in 2018 (Employee Benefit Research Institute, 2018). One study found that older workers who continued working beyond retirement age were motivated by factors involving financial status, health, knowledge, and purpose in life (Sewdas & others, 2017). A recent analysis concluded that healthier, better-educated, and higher-earning older adults can work longer (United Income, 2019). Lower-income older adults are more likely to work in more physically demanding jobs, making it more difficult for them to continue working when they get old.

developmental **connection**

Work

In the United States, approximately 80 percent of individuals 40 to 59 years of age are employed. Connect to "Physical and Cognitive Development in Middle Adulthood."

The night hath not yet come:
We are not quite cut off from labor by the failing of light; some work remains for us to do and dare.

—HENRY WADSWORTH LONGFELLOW
American poet, 19th century

Ninety-two-year-old Russell "Bob" Harrell (right) puts in 12-hour days at Sieco Consulting Engineers in Columbus, Indiana. A highway and bridge engineer, he designs and plans roads. James Rice (age 48), a vice president of client services at Sieco, says that Bob wants to learn something new every day and that he has learned many life lessons from being around him. Harrell says he is not planning to retire. *What are some variations in work and retirement in older adults?*
Greg Sailor

Research suggests that U.S. workers are reasonably satisfied with their jobs and that older U.S. workers are the most satisfied of all age groups (AP-NORC Center for Public Affairs Research, 2013). However, there are significant individual variations in worker satisfaction at all adult ages (Antonucci & others, 2016). Further, recent research indicates that older workers not only are more satisfied at work than their younger colleagues, but also take fewer sick days and demonstrate stronger problem-solving skills (Milken Institute and Stanford Center on Longevity, 2019).

Cognitive ability is one of the best predictors of job performance in older adults (Fisher & others, 2017; Lovden, Backman, & Lindenberger, 2017). And older workers have lower rates of absenteeism, fewer accidents, and higher job satisfaction than their younger counterparts (Warr, 2004). Thus, the older worker can be of considerable value to a company, above and beyond the older worker's cognitive competence. Changes in federal law now allow individuals over the age of 65 to continue working (Shore & Goldberg, 2005). Also, remember from our discussion earlier in this chapter that substantively complex work is linked with a higher level of intellectual functioning (Schooler, 2007; Wang & Shi, 2016). Further, researchers have found that working in an occupation with a high level of mental demands is linked to higher levels of cognitive functioning before retirement and a slower rate of cognitive decline after retirement (Fisher & others, 2014). In sum, a cognitively stimulating work context promotes successful aging (Fisher & others, 2017).

Several studies also have found that older adults who work have better physical and cognitive profiles that those who retire. For example, one study found that physical functioning declined faster in retirement than in full-time work for individuals 65 years of age and older, with the difference not explained by absence of chronic diseases and lifestyle risks (Stenholm & others, 2014). Another study revealed that retirement increased the risk of having a heart attack in older adults (Olesen & others, 2014). Further, a recent study found that individuals who retired for health reasons had lower verbal memory and verbal fluency than their counterparts who retired voluntarily or for family reasons (Denier & others, 2017). In addition, in another recent study of older adults, those who continued to work in paid jobs had better physical and cognitive functioning than retirees (Tan & others, 2017). And a recent study found that all retirement pathways were associated with accelerated cognitive decline for workers in low-complexity jobs but were not linked to accelerated cognitive decline for workers in high-complexity jobs (Carr & others, 2020). Also, after retiring and subsequently returning to work, a modest improvement in cognitive functioning occurred.

In sum, age affects many aspects of work (Lovden, Backman, & Lindenberger, 2017). Nonetheless, many studies of work and aging—such as evaluation of hiring and performance—have yielded inconsistent results. Contextual factors such as age composition of departments or applicant pools, occupations, and jobs all affect decisions about older workers. It also is important to recognize that ageist stereotypes of workers and of tasks can limit older workers' career opportunities and can encourage early retirement or other forms of downsizing that adversely affect older workers (Finkelstein & Farrell, 2007). A study of older workers found that accurately self-evaluating one's skills and values, being positive about change, and participating in a supportive work environment were linked to adaptive competence on the job (Unson & Richardson, 2013).

RETIREMENT IN THE UNITED STATES AND IN OTHER COUNTRIES

At what age do most people retire in the United States? Do many people return to the workforce at some point after they have retired? What is retirement like in other countries?

Retirement in the United States   The option to retire is a late-twentieth-century phenomenon in the United States (Coe & others, 2012). It exists largely because of the 1935 implementation of the Social Security system, which gives benefits to older workers when they retire. On average, today's workers will spend 10 to 15 percent of their lives in retirement. A survey revealed that as baby boomers move into their sixties, they expect to retire later than their parents or their grandparents did (Frey, 2007). In 2017, in the United States, the average age of retirement was 64 for men and 62 for women (Anspach, 2017). The labor force participation for women is now very close to that of men, especially among workers over 65 years of age (Munnell, 2015). The average number of years spent in retirement by Americans is 18 years. A recent study found that baby boomers expect to continue working to older ages than their predecessors in prior generations did (Dong & others, 2017).

Of course, some individuals do retire early. A recent report concluded that 37 percent of U.S. workers retire earlier than they planned (Munnell, Rutledge, & Sanzenbacher, 2018). Also, a recent analysis indicated that a variety of factors could force people to retire early although health problems like play the most important role, both because those in poor initial health overestimate how long they can work or because their health worsens before the age at which they planned to retire (Munnell, Rutledge, & Sanzenbacher, 2018).

In the past, when most people reached an accepted retirement age, such as some point in their sixties, retirement meant a one-way exit from full-time work to full-time leisure. Increasingly, individuals are delaying retirement and moving into and out of work as the traditional lock-step transition from full-time work to full-time retirement occurs less often (Cahill & others, 2019). Currently, there is no single dominant pattern of retirement but rather a diverse mix of pathways involving occupational identities, finances, health, and expectations and perceptions of retirement. Leading expert Phyllis Moen (2007) noted that when people reach their sixties, the life path they follow has become less clear:

- Some individuals don't retire, continuing in their career jobs.
- Some retire from their career work and then take up a new and different job.
- Some retire from career jobs but do volunteer work.
- Some retire from a post-retirement job and go on to yet another job.
- Some move in and out of the workforce, so they never really have a "career" job from which they retire.
- Some individuals who are in poor health move to a disability status and eventually into retirement.
- Some who are laid off define it as "retirement."

Approximately 7 million retired Americans return to work after they have retired (Putnam Investments, 2006). When retired adults return to the labor force, it occurs on average four years after retirement (Hardy, 2006). In many instances, the jobs pay much less than their pre-retirement jobs. In one study of older adults who returned to work, approximately two-thirds said they were happy they had done so, while about one-third indicated they were forced to go back to work to meet financial needs (Putnam Investments, 2006).

Just as individuals may follow different life paths after reaching retirement age, they also may have different reasons for working. For example, some older adults who reach retirement age work for financial reasons, others to stay busy, and yet others to "give back" (Moen, 2007).

Work and Retirement in Other Countries   What characterizes work and retirement in other countries? One analysis concluded that France has the earliest average retirement age: 60 for men and 61 for women (OECD, 2017). In this analysis, Korea had the oldest average retirement age: 72 for men and 73 for women.

A large-scale study of 21,000 individuals aged 40 to 79 in 21 countries examined patterns of work and retirement (HSBC Insurance, 2007). On average, 33 percent of individuals in their sixties and 11 percent in their seventies were still in some kind of paid employment. In this study, 19 percent of those in their seventies in the United States were still working. A substantial percentage of individuals expect to continue working as long as possible before retiring (HSBC Insurance, 2007).

In the study of work and retirement in 21 countries, Japanese retirees missed the work slightly more than they expected and the money considerably less than they expected (HSBC Insurance, 2007). U.S. retirees missed both the work and the money slightly less than they expected. German retirees were the least likely to miss the work, Turkish and Chinese retirees the most likely to miss it. Regarding money, Japanese and Chinese retirees were the least likely to miss it, Turkish retirees the most likely to miss it.

Early retirement policies were introduced by many companies in the 1970s and 1980s with the intention of making room for younger workers (Coe & others, 2012). A recent research review found that workplace organizational pressures, financial security, and poor physical and mental health were antecedents of early retirement (Topa, Depolo, & Alcover,

In the study of work and retirement in 21 countries, what were some variations across countries regarding the extent to which retirees missed work and money?
Ronnie Kaufman/Blend Images LLC

2018). However, an increasing number of adults are beginning to reject the early retirement option as they hear about people who retired and then regretted it. In a 21-country study, on average only 12 percent of individuals in their forties and fifties expected to take early retirement, while 16 percent in their sixties and seventies had taken early retirement (Coe & others, 2012). Only in Germany, South Korea, and Hong Kong did a higher percentage of individuals expect to take early retirement than in the past.

ADJUSTMENT TO RETIREMENT

What are some keys to adjusting effectively in retirement?
Bronwyn Kidd/Photodisc/Getty Images

Retirement is a process, not just an event. Older adults who adjust best to retirement are healthy, have adequate income, are active, are better educated, have an extended social network including both friends and family, and usually were satisfied with their lives before they retired (Ilmakunnas & Ilmakunnas, 2018; Miller, 2018). Older adults with inadequate income and poor health, and those who must adjust to other stress that occurs at the same time as retirement, such as the death of a spouse, have the most difficult time adjusting to retirement (Reichstadt & others, 2007). In a recent study, retirement satisfaction was linked to realizing retirement plans, resilience, social integration, adopting new roles, and especially quality of family relationships (Principi & others, 2020).

As mentioned earlier, the U.S. retirement system is in transition (Fox, 2020; Kintzel, 2020). A 2017 survey indicated that only 18 percent of American workers feel very confident that they will have enough money to have a comfortable retirement (Greenwald, Copeland, & VanDerhei, 2017). However, 60 percent said they feel somewhat or very confident they will have enough money to live comfortably in retirement. In this survey, 30 percent of American workers reported that preparing for retirement made them feel mentally or emotionally distressed. In regard to retirement income, the two main worries of individuals as they approach retirement are: (1) having to draw retirement income from savings, and (2) paying for health-care expenses (Yakoboski, 2011).

Flexibility is also a key factor in whether individuals adjust well to retirement (Mossburg, 2018). When people retire, they no longer have the structured environment they had when they were working, so they need to be flexible and discover and pursue their own interests. Cultivating interests and friends unrelated to work improves adaptation to retirement.

Planning ahead and then successfully carrying out the plan are important aspects of adjusting well in retirement (Eismann, Verbeij, & Henkens, 2019; Harlow, Brown, & Jenks, 2020). A special concern in retirement planning involves the recognition that women are likely to live longer than men, more likely to live alone, and to have lower retirement income (because they are less likely to remarry and more likely to be widowed) (Prickett & Angel, 2011).

It is important not only to plan financially for retirement but also to consider other aspects of life (Henning & others, 2020). In addition to planning their financial future, individuals need to ask questions about retirement such as these: What am I going to do with my leisure time? How am I going to stay physically fit? What am I going to do socially? What will I do to keep my mind active?

Review Connect Reflect

 LG3 Discuss aging and adaptation to work and retirement.

Review
- What characterizes the work of older adults?
- Compare retirement in the United States with retirement in other countries.
- How can individuals adjust effectively to retirement?

Connect
- U.S. adolescents spend much more time in unstructured leisure activities

than East Asian adolescents do. How might establishing challenging lifelong leisure activities as an adolescent benefit an individual at retirement age?

Reflect *Your Own Personal Journey of Life*
- At what age would you like to retire? Or would you prefer to continue working as an older adult as long as you are healthy?

Depression   Dementia, Alzheimer Disease, and Other Afflictions

Although a substantial portion of the population can now look forward to a longer life, that life may unfortunately be hampered by having a mental disorder in old age (Laheij-Rooijakkers & others, 2020). This prospect is both troubling to the individual and costly to society. Mental disorders make individuals increasingly dependent on the help and care of others. The cost of caring for older adults with mental health disorders is estimated to be more than $40 billion per year in the United States. More important than the loss in dollars, though, is the loss of human potential and the suffering involved for individuals and their families (Quach & Burr, 2020). Although mental disorders in older adults are a major concern, it is important to understand that older adults do not have a higher incidence of mental disorders than younger adults do (Busse & Blazer, 1996).

DEPRESSION

Major depression is a mood disorder in which the individual is deeply unhappy, demoralized, self-derogatory, and bored. The person does not feel well, loses stamina easily, has a poor appetite, and is listless and unmotivated. Major depression has been called the "common cold" of mental disorders. A recent research review conducted over the last two decades concluded that depression is not more common in older adults than in younger adults and is not more often caused by psychological factors in older adults (Haigh & others, 2018). Also, compared with middle-aged adults, depression in older adults is more likely to be chronic (that is, to have a higher rate of relapse), which is likely linked to higher rates of medical problems in older adults (Haigh & others, 2018).

One study found that the lower frequency of depressive symptoms in older adults compared with middle-aged adults was linked to fewer economic hardships, fewer negative social interchanges, and increased religiosity (Schieman, van Gundy, & Taylor, 2004). Depressive symptoms increase among the oldest-old (85 years and older), and this increase is associated with a higher percentage of women in the group, more physical disability, greater cognitive impairment, and lower socioeconomic status (Hybels & Blazer, 2004).

In childhood, adolescence, and early adulthood, females have higher rates of depression than males do (Nolen-Hoeksema, 2011). Does this gender difference hold for middle-aged and older adults? For most of late adulthood, women have higher rates of depression and more severe depression than males, with the differences narrowing only among the oldest-old (Barry & Byers, 2016). These gender differences in depression among older adults likely reflect factors such as women having lower incomes and having one or more chronic illnesses.

Among the most common predictors of depression in older adults are earlier depressive symptoms, poor health, disability, losses such as the death of a spouse, low social support, and social isolation (Cheng & others, 2020; Taylor & others, 2018). In a recent study, suicidal ideation was strongly associated with depression severity in older adults (Rossom & others, 2019). In this study, older adults who had moderate to severe depression were 48 times more likely to engage in suicidal ideation than their counterparts who had minimal to mild depressive symptoms. Insomnia is often overlooked as a risk factor for depression in older adults (Fiske, Wetherell, & Gatz, 2009). Curtailment of daily activities also is a common pathway to late-life depression (Fiske, Wetherell, & Gatz, 2009). Often accompanying this curtailment of activity is an increase in self-critical thinking that exacerbates depression. A meta-analysis found that the following living arrangements were linked to increased risk for depression in older adults: living alone, in a nursing home, or in an institutionalized setting (Xiu-Ying & others, 2012). Also, in a recent study of community-dwelling older adults, engaging in light physical exercise, taking lessons, using a computer, and participating in community events predicted a lower level of depressive symptoms (Uemura & others, 2018).

Depression is a treatable condition, not only in young adults but in older adults as well (Perez-Sousa & others, 2020). Unfortunately, depressed older adults are less likely to receive treatment for their depression than younger adults are (Sanglier & others, 2015), and up to

---

developmental **connection**

Gender

One reason females have higher rates of depression is that they ruminate more in their depressed mood and amplify it more than males do. Connect to "Socioemotional Development in Adolescence."

---

major depression A mood disorder in which the individual is deeply unhappy, demoralized, self-derogatory, and bored. The person does not feel well, loses stamina easily, has poor appetite, and is listless and unmotivated. Major depression is so widespread that it has been called the "common cold" of mental disorders.

What characterizes depression in older adults?
Science Photo Library/Getty Images

80 percent of older adults with depressive symptoms receive no treatment at all. Combinations of medications and psychotherapy produce significant improvement in almost four out of five older adults with depression (Koenig & Blazer, 1996). In a recent research review it was concluded that depressed older adults respond to psychological treatments as well as younger adults do (Haigh & others, 2018). However, this review found that antidepressants are less effective with older adults than younger adults. Researchers have discovered that electroconvulsive treatment (ECT) is more effective in treating older adults' depression than antidepressants (Dols & others, 2017). Further, exercise can reduce depression in older adults (Perez-Sousa & others, 2020). In a Taiwanese study, consistent exercise of moderate intensity for at least 15 minutes three times a week was associated with a lower risk of developing depressive symptoms (Chang & others, 2017). In another study, a 12-week exercise program was effective in reducing depression in Mexican older adults (Borbon-Castro & others, 2020). Also, a recent meta-analysis of older Chinese adults concluded that two exercise therapies—Tai Chi and Qigong—were effective in reducing depression (Gill & others, 2020). Further, engagement in valued activities and religious/spiritual involvement can reduce depressive symptoms (Krause & Hayward, 2016). Life review/reminiscence therapy, which we will discuss further in the chapter on "Socioemotional Development in Late Adulthood," is linked to a reduction in depressive symptoms and is underutilized in the treatment of depression in older adults (Gill & others, 2020).

Major depression can result not only in sadness but also in suicidal tendencies (Yeh, Ng, & Wu, 2020). Recent national statistics indicate that the highest suicide rate occurs among 45- to 64-year-olds (19.6 per 100,000 individuals), followed by individuals 85 years or older (19.4 per 100,000 individuals) (Centers for Disease Control and Prevention, 2015). For older adults aged 65 to 84, the suicide rate per 100,000 individuals was 16.1, similar to the rate for individuals 20 to 34 (15.5).

The older adult most likely to commit suicide is a male who lives alone, has lost his spouse, and is experiencing failing health (Balasubramaniam, 2018). A recent study further explored the influencing and protective factors involving suicidal ideation in older adults (Huang & others, 2017). In this study, the triggers for suicidal ideation included physical discomfort, loss of respect and/or support from family, impulsive emotions due to conflicts with others, and painful memories. Psychological factors contributing to suicidal ideation included feelings of loneliness, sense of helplessness, and low self-worth. Protective factors that were linked to lower levels of suicidal ideation included support from family and friends, emotional control, and comfort from religion. Further, a recent study found that declines in socioeconomic status were linked to increased suicide attempts in older adults (Dombrovski & others, 2018).

DEMENTIA, ALZHEIMER DISEASE, AND OTHER AFFLICTIONS

Among the most debilitating of mental disorders in older adults are the dementias (Brown & Wolf, 2018). In recent years, extensive attention has been focused on the most common dementia, Alzheimer disease.

Dementia   **Dementia** is a global term for several neurological disorders involving an irreversible decline in mental function severe enough to interfere with daily life (Alzheimer's Association, 2020). Alzheimer disease accounts for 60 to 80 percent of dementias, with the second most frequent dementia being vascular dementia. In a recent Chinese study, medium to high levels of physical activity were linked with lower rates of dementia in 60- to 65-year-olds (Wu & others, 2020).

Alzheimer Disease   **Alzheimer disease** is a progressive, irreversible brain disorder that is characterized by a gradual deterioration of memory, reasoning, language, and eventually, physical function. Following are some recent facts about Alzheimer disease in the United States (Alzheimer's Association, 2020):

- Alzheimer disease is now the sixth leading cause of death in the United States.
- Between 2000 and 2017, deaths from cardiovascular disease decreased 9 percent while deaths from Alzheimer disease increased 145 percent.

dementia A global term for several neurological disorders involving an irreversible decline in mental function severe enough to interfere with daily living.

Alzheimer disease A progressive, irreversible brain disorder characterized by a gradual deterioration of memory, reasoning, language, and eventually, physical function.

- In 2019, 5.8 million Americans were living with Alzheimer disease, and this figure is projected to rise to nearly 14 million by 2050.
- One in 10 individuals 65 and older has Alzheimer disease.
- Compared with non-Latino whites, twice as many older African Americans and one and one-half times as many Latinos have Alzheimer disease.
- Two-thirds of those with Alzheimer disease in the United States are women.

The percentage of individuals with Alzheimer disease increases dramatically with age: 3 percent from 65 to 74, 17 percent from 75 to 84, and 32 percent 85 and older. It is estimated that Alzheimer disease triples the health-care costs of Americans 65 years of age and older (Alzheimer's Association, 2020). Because of the increasing prevalence of Alzheimer disease, researchers have stepped up their efforts to discover the causes of the disease and to find more effective ways to treat it (Elangovan & Holsinger, 2020; Falandry, 2019; Hodler, Kubik-Huch, & von Schulthess, 2020).

Former president Ronald Reagan was diagnosed with Alzheimer disease at age 83.
Bettmann/Getty Images

Causes Alzheimer disease involves a deficiency in the brain messenger chemical called acetylcholine, which plays an important role in memory (Guest, 2019). Also, as Alzheimer disease progresses, the brain shrinks and deteriorates (see Figure 4). This deterioration is characterized by the formation of *amyloid plaques* (dense deposits of protein that accumulate in the blood vessels) (Lin & others, 2020) and *neurofibrillary tangles* (twisted fibers that build up in neurons) (Sharma & others, 2020). Neurofibrillary tangles consist mainly of a protein called *tau* (Kim & Park, 2020). Currently, there is considerable research interest in the roles that amyloid and tau play in Alzheimer disease (Gonzalez-Escamilla & others, 2020).

Until recently, neuroimaging of plaques and tangles had not been developed. However, recently new neuroimaging techniques have been developed that can detect these key indicators of Alzheimer disease in the brain (Lauretti & Pratico, 2020). This imaging breakthrough is providing scientists with an improved opportunity to identify the transition from healthy cognitive functioning to the earliest indication of Alzheimer disease (Vernooij & van Buchem, 2020).

There also is increasing interest in the role that oxidative stress and mitochondria might play in Alzheimer disease (Mi & others, 2020; Yeung & others, 2019). Oxidative stress occurs when the body's antioxidant defenses don't cope with free radical attacks and oxidation in the body (Jurcau & Simon, 2020). Recall that free radical theory is a major theory of aging. Further, mitochondrial dysfunction is an early event in Alzheimer disease (P. Yang & others, 2020).

Although scientists are not certain what causes Alzheimer disease, age is an important risk factor and genes also are likely to play an important role (Sims, Hill, & Williams, 2020). The percentage of individuals with Alzheimer disease doubles every five years after the age of 65. A gene called *apolipoprotein E* (*ApoE*) is linked to increased presence of plaques and tangles in the brain (Minta & others, 2020). Researchers are paying special attention to an allele (an alternative form of a gene) labeled ApoE4, an allele that is a strong risk factor for Alzheimer disease (Akhter & Bekris, 2019; Montagne, Nation, & Ziokovic, 2020). More than 60 percent of individuals with Alzheimer disease have at least one ApoE4 allele, and females are more likely than males to have this allele (Dubal & Rogine, 2017). Indeed, the ApoE4 gene is the strongest genetic predictor of late-onset (65 years and older) Alzheimer disease (Carmona, Hardy, & Guerreiro, 2018). APP, PSEN1, and PSEN2 gene mutations are linked to early-onset Alzheimer disease (Carmona, Hardy, & Guerreiro, 2018; Lin & others, 2020).

Although individuals with a family history of Alzheimer disease are at greater risk, the disease is complex and likely caused by a number of factors (Ettcheto & others, 2020). Recently, researchers have shown increasing interest in exploring how epigenetics may improve understanding of Alzheimer disease (Mahajan & others, 2020). This interest especially has focused on DNA methylation, which we discussed in "Biological Beginnings" (Sharma, Mehta, & Singh, 2020). Recall that DNA methylation involves tiny atoms attaching themselves to the outside of a gene, a process that is increased through exercise and healthy diet but reduced by tobacco use (Dasinger & others, 2020). Thus, lifestyles likely interact with genes to influence Alzheimer disease (Ferretti & others, 2020). For example, older adults with Alzheimer disease are more likely to have cardiovascular disease than are individuals

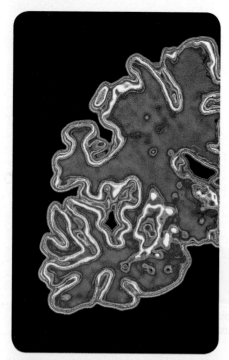

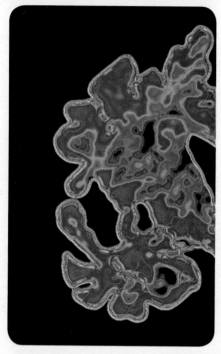

FIGURE 4

TWO BRAINS: NORMAL AGING AND ALZHEIMER DISEASE. The photograph on the top shows a slice of a normal aging brain and the photograph on the bottom shows a slice of a brain ravaged by Alzheimer disease. Notice the deterioration and shrinking in the brain with Alzheimer disease.
Alfred Pasieka/Science Source

who do not have Alzheimer disease (Zhou & others, 2020). Recently, a number of cardiac risk factors have been implicated in Alzheimer disease—obesity, smoking, atherosclerosis, hypertension, high cholesterol, lipids, and permanent atrial fibrillation (Jiang & others, 2020). One of the best strategies for intervening in the lives of people who are at risk for Alzheimer disease is to improve their cardiac functioning through diet, drugs, and exercise (Serrano-Poso & Growdon, 2019). One study of older adults found that those who exercised three or more times a week were less likely to develop Alzheimer disease over a six-year period than those who exercised less (Larson & others, 2006).

A meta-analysis of modifiable risk factors in Alzheimer disease found that some medical exposures (estrogen, statins, and nonsteroidal anti-inflammatory drugs) and some dietary factors (folate, vitamins E and C, and coffee) were linked to a reduced incidence of Alzheimer disease (Xu & others, 2015). Also in this meta-analysis, some preexisting diseases (atherosclerosis and hypertension) as well as depression increased the risk of developing Alzheimer disease. Further, increased cognitive activity and low-to-moderate alcohol use decreased the risk of developing Alzheimer disease.

Early Detection   *Mild cognitive impairment* (*MCI*) represents a potential transitional state between the cognitive changes of normal aging and very early stages of Alzheimer disease and other dementias. MCI is increasingly recognized as a risk factor for Alzheimer disease (Blanken & others, 2020; Venneri & others, 2019). Estimates indicate that as many as 10 to 20 percent of individuals 65 years of age and older have MCI (Alzheimer's Association, 2020). Many individuals with MCI do not go on to develop Alzheimer disease, but MCI is a risk factor for Alzheimer disease (Cui & others, 2019). Distinguishing between individuals who merely have age-associated declines in memory and those with MCI is difficult, as is predicting which individuals with MCI will subsequently develop Alzheimer disease (Lee & others, 2019; Xu & others, 2020). One study revealed that individuals with mild cognitive impairment who developed Alzheimer disease had at least one copy of the ApoE4 gene (Alegret & others, 2014). In this study, the extent of memory impairment was the key factor linked to the speed of decline from mild cognitive impairment to Alzheimer disease. Also, a recent research review concluded that combined cognitive and physical interventions can improve cognitive (executive function and memory, for example) and physical function (mobility and balance, for example) in individuals with mild cognitive impairment (C. Yang & others, 2020).

Drug Treatment of Alzheimer Disease   Five drugs have been approved by the U.S. Food and Drug Administration (FDA) for the treatment of Alzheimer disease (Almeida, 2018). Three of the medications, Aricept (donepezil), Razadyne (galantamine), and Exelon (rivastigmine), are cholinesterase inhibitors designed to improve memory and other cognitive functions by increasing levels of acetylcholine in the brain (Gareri & others, 2017). A fourth drug, Namenda (memantine), regulates the activity of glutamate, which is involved in processing information. Namzatric, a combination of memantine and donepezil, is the fifth approved medicine to treat Alzheimer disease; this medicine is designed to improve cognition and overall mental ability (Almeida, 2018). A research review concluded that cholinesterase inhibitors do not reduce progression to dementia from mild cognitive impairment (Masoodi, 2013). Also, keep in mind that the current drugs used to treat Alzheimer disease only slow the downward progression of the disease; they do not address its cause (Rajeshwari & others, 2019). Also, no drugs have yet been approved by the Food and Drug Administration (FDA) for the treatment of MCI (Alzheimer's Association, 2020).

Caring for Individuals with Alzheimer Disease   A special concern is caring for Alzheimer patients (Alzheimer's Association, 2020). Health-care professionals emphasize that the family can be an important support system for the Alzheimer patient, but this support can have costs for family members who become emotionally and physically drained by the extensive care required by a person with Alzheimer disease (White & others, 2018). In 2019, 83 percent of the help provided to older adults in the United States came from family members, friends, or unpaid caregivers, and nearly half of these individuals were caring for someone with Alzheimer disease (Alzheimer's Association, 2020). A recent study confirmed that family caregivers' health-related quality of life in the first three years after they began caring for a family member with Alzheimer disease deteriorated more than their same-age and same-gender counterparts who were not caring for an Alzheimer patient (Valimaki & others, 2016). Another

Jan Weaver, Director of the Alzheimer's Association of Dallas

Dr. Weaver joined the Alzheimer's Association, Greater Dallas Chapter, as director of services and education in 1999. Prior to that time, she served as associate director of education for the Texas Institute for Research and Education on Aging and director of the National Academy for Teaching and Learning About Aging at the University of North Texas. As a gerontologist, Weaver plans and develops services and educational programs that address patterns of human development related to aging. Among the services that Weaver supervises at the Alzheimer's Association are a resource center and helpline, a family assistance program, a care program, support groups, referrals and information, educational conferences, and community seminars.

Weaver recognizes that people of all ages should have an informed and balanced view of older adults that helps them perceive aging as a process of growth and fulfillment rather than a process of decline and dependency. Weaver earned her Ph. D. in sociology, with an emphasis in gerontology, from the University of Texas.

Jan Weaver gives a lecture on Alzheimer disease.
Courtesy of Jan DeCrescenzo

study compared family members' perception of caring for someone with Alzheimer disease, cancer, or schizophrenia (Papastavrou & others, 2012). In this study, the highest perceived burden was reported for Alzheimer disease.

Respite care (services that provide temporary relief for those who are caring for individuals with disabilities, individuals with illnesses, or the elderly) has been developed to help people who have to meet the day-to-day needs of Alzheimer patients. This type of care provides an important break from the burden of providing chronic care (Riekkola & others, 2019).

There are many career opportunities that involve working with individuals who have Alzheimer disease. To read about the work of a director of an Alzheimer association, see *Connecting with Careers.*

Parkinson Disease   Another type of dementia is **Parkinson disease,** a chronic, progressive disease characterized by muscle tremors, slowing of movement, and partial facial paralysis. Parkinson disease is triggered by degeneration of dopamine-producing neurons in the brain (Foley, 2019). Dopamine is a neurotransmitter that is necessary for normal brain functioning. Why these neurons degenerate is not known.

The main treatment for Parkinson disease involves administering drugs that enhance the effect of dopamine (dopamine agonists) in the disease's earlier stages and later administering the drug L-dopa, which is converted by the brain into dopamine (Chu, 2020; Trujillo & others, 2019).

Another treatment for advanced Parkinson disease is deep brain stimulation (DBS), which involves implantation of electrodes within the brain (Boon & others, 2020). The electrodes are then stimulated by a pacemaker-like device. Recent studies indicated that deep brain stimulation may provide benefits for individuals with Parkinson disease (Little & Brown, 2020). A recent research review concluded that DBS improves motor function for up to 10 years in Parkinson patients but improvement tends to decline over time (Limousin & Foltynie, 2019). Stem cell transplantation and gene therapy also offer hope for treating the disease (Sadatpoor & others, 2020).

Older adults who are depressed, have a dementia, or have another mental disorder, may need mental health treatment (Reynolds, Lenze, & Mulsant, 2019). To read about this topic, see *Connecting Development to Life.*

Muhammad Ali, considered one of the world's most influential sports figures, had Parkinson disease.
AP Images

Parkinson disease A chronic, progressive disease characterized by muscle tremors, slowing of movement, and partial facial paralysis.

Meeting the Mental Health Needs of Older Adults

Older adults receive disproportionately fewer mental health services than young or middle-aged adults (Sanglier & others, 2015). One estimate is that only 2.7 percent of all clinical services provided by psychologists go to older adults, although individuals aged 65 and over make up more than 11 percent of the population.

Psychotherapy can be expensive. Although reduced fees and sometimes no fee can be arranged in public hospitals for older adults from low-income backgrounds, many older adults who need psychotherapy do not get it (Brown & Menec, 2019).

It has been said that psychotherapists like to work with young, attractive, verbal, intelligent, and successful clients (called YAVISes) rather than those who are quiet, ugly, old, institutionalized, and different (called QUOIDs). Psychotherapists have been accused of not working with older adults because they perceive that older adults have a poor prognosis for therapy success; they do not feel they have adequate training to treat older adults, who may have special problems requiring special treatment; and they may have stereotypes that label older adults as low-status and unworthy recipients of treatment (Virnig & others, 2004). Also, many older adults do not seek mental health treatment because of a fear that they will be stigmatized or because of a lack of understanding about the nature of mental health treatment and care.

How can we better meet the mental health needs of older adults? First, mental health professionals must be encouraged to include greater numbers of older adults in their client lists, and older adults must be convinced that they can benefit from therapy (Olfson & others, 2018). Second, we must make mental health care affordable. For example, Medicare continues to fall short of providing many mental health services for older adults, especially for those in need of long-term care (Travers & others, 2020).

Margaret Gatz (*right*) has been a crusader for better mental health treatment of older adults. She believes that mental health professionals need to be encouraged to include greater numbers of older adults in their client lists and that we need to better educate the elderly about how they can benefit from therapy. *What are some common mechanisms of change that can be used to improve the mental health of older adults?*
Courtesy of Dr. Margaret Gatz

Review Connect Reflect

 LG4 Describe mental health problems in older adults.

Review
- What is the nature of depression in older adults?
- What are dementia, Alzheimer disease, and Parkinson disease like in older adults?

Connect
- What are some differences in how depression is characterized in adolescence as opposed to late adulthood?

Reflect *Your Own Personal Journey of Life*
- Have any of your relatives experienced mental health problems as older adults? If so, what were these mental health problems? If they have experienced mental health problems, what were the likely causes of the problems?

5 Religion and Spirituality

LG5 Explain the role of religion and spirituality in the lives of older adults.

Earlier we discussed religion, spirituality, and meaning in life with a special focus on middle age, including links between religion/spirituality and health. Here we will continue our exploration of religion and spirituality by considering their importance in the lives of many older adults.

In many societies around the world, older adults are the spiritual leaders in their churches and communities. For example, in the Catholic Church more popes have been elected in their eighties than in any other 10-year period of the human life span.

The religious patterns of older adults have increasingly been studied (Krause & Hayward, 2016). A longitudinal study found that religious service attendance was stable in middle adulthood, increased in late adulthood, then declined later in the older adult years (Hayward & Krause, 2013b). A research review concluded that individuals with a stronger spiritual/religious orientation were more likely to live longer (Lucchetti, Lucchetti, & Koenig, 2011). Also, in a recent study of older adults, those who regularly attended religious services lived longer than their counterparts who did not attend these services (Idler & others, 2017).

Individuals over 65 years of age are more likely than younger people to say that religious faith is the most significant influence in their lives, that they try to put religious faith into practice, and that they attend religious services (Gallup & Bezilla, 1992). A study of more than 500 African Americans 55 to 105 years of age revealed that they had a strong identification with religious institutions and high levels of attendance and participation in religious activities (Williams, Keigher, & Williams, 2012). And a Pew poll found that belief in God was higher in older adulthood than in any other age period (Pew Forum on Religion and Public Life, 2008). Further, a recent study revealed that older women had higher levels of spirituality than did older men (Bailly & others, 2018).

Is religion related to a sense of well-being and life satisfaction in old age? In a recent study of older adults, secure attachment to God was linked to increased optimism and self-esteem (Kent, Bradshaw, & Uecker, 2018). In another study, older adults who derived a sense of meaning in life from religion had higher levels of life satisfaction, self-esteem, and optimism (Krause, 2003). Further, a recent study of older adults revealed that religious service attendance was associated with a higher level of resilience in life and lower levels of depression (Manning & Miles, 2018). And in a recent study of Korean older adults, higher levels of religious/spiritual coping were linked to lower levels of depressive symptoms (Lee & others, 2017). Further, a recent study of Latinos found that lack of religiosity was associated with elevated anxiety and depressive symptoms in older adults but not in young and middle-aged adults (Leman & others, 2018).

Religion and spirituality can meet some important psychological needs in older adults, helping them to face impending death, to find and maintain a sense of meaning in life, and to accept the inevitable losses of old age (Krause & Hayward, 2016; Park & others, 2016). Socially, the religious community can serve many functions for older adults by providing social activities, social support, and the opportunity to assume teaching and leadership roles (Krause, 2012). One study revealed that over a period of seven years, older adults who attended church regularly increased the amount of emotional support they gave and received but decreased the amount of tangible support they gave and received (Hayward & Krause, 2013a).

During late adulthood, many individuals increasingly engage in prayer. *How might this be linked with longevity?*
Ozgurdonmaz/Vetta/Getty Images

> **developmental connection**
>
> **Religion and Spirituality**
>
> Meaning-making coping involves drawing on beliefs, values, and goals to change the meaning of a stressful situation, especially in times of chronic stress such as when a loved one dies. Connect to "Physical and Cognitive Development in Middle Adulthood."

Review Connect Reflect

LG5 Explain the role of religion and spirituality in the lives of older adults.

Review
- What are some characteristics of religion and spirituality in older adults?

Connect
- Prayer and meditation may reduce stress and reduce the body's production of stress hormones. Why is this especially important in the aging process?

Reflect *Your Own Personal Journey of Life*
- Do you think you will become more or less religious as an older adult than you are now? Explain.

topical connections *looking **forward***

In the next chapter, you will read about a number of theories that seek to explain older adults' socioemotional development, including Erikson's final stage (integrity versus despair). Older adults become more selective than middle-aged adults about the people they want to spend time with. There is considerable diversity in older adults' lifestyles, and an increasing number of older adults cohabit. Social support is especially important in older adults' lives and is linked to their physical and mental health. An important aspect of late adulthood is not dwelling too extensively on the negative aspects of aging but rather pursuing the key dimensions of successful aging.

reach your **learning goals**

Cognitive Development in Late Adulthood

1 Cognitive Functioning in Older Adults

 Describe the cognitive functioning of older adults.

Multidimensionality and Multidirectionality

- Cognitive mechanics (the neurophysiological architecture, including the brain) are more likely to decline in older adults than are cognitive pragmatics (the culture-based software of the mind). Speed of processing declines in older adults. Older adults' attention declines more on complex than simple tasks.

- Regarding memory, in late adulthood explicit memory declines more than implicit memory; episodic memory declines more than semantic memory; working memory also declines. Components of executive function—such as cognitive control and working memory—decline in late adulthood. Declines also occur in metacognition and theory of mind in older adults.

- Wisdom is expert knowledge about the practical aspects of life that permits excellent judgment about important matters. Baltes and his colleagues have found that high levels of wisdom are rare, the time frame of late adolescence and early adulthood is the main window for wisdom to emerge, factors other than age are critical for wisdom to develop, and personality-related factors are better predictors of wisdom than cognitive factors such as intelligence.

Education, Work, and Health

- Successive generations of Americans have been better educated. Education is positively correlated with scores on intelligence tests. Older adults may return to college for a number of reasons.

- Recent generations have had work experiences that include a stronger emphasis on cognitively oriented labor. The increased emphasis on information processing in jobs likely enhances an individual's intellectual abilities.

- Poor health is related to decreased performance on intelligence tests by older adults. Exercise is linked to higher cognitive functioning in older adults.

Use It or Lose It

- Researchers are finding that older adults who engage in cognitive activities, especially challenging ones, have higher cognitive functioning than those who don't use their cognitive skills.

Training Cognitive Skills

- Two main conclusions can be derived from research on training cognitive skills in older adults: (1) training can improve the cognitive skills of many older adults, but often only on a specific task and not for broad effects on cognitive performance, and (2) there is some loss in plasticity in late adulthood.

| Cognitive Neuroscience and Aging | • There has been considerable recent interest in the cognitive neuroscience of aging that focuses on links among aging, the brain, and cognitive functioning. This field especially relies on fMRI and PET scans to assess brain functioning while individuals are engaging in cognitive tasks. One of the most consistent findings in this field is a decline in the functioning of specific regions in the prefrontal cortex in older adults and links between this decline and poorer performance on tasks involving complex reasoning, working memory, and episodic memory. |

2 Language Development

 LG2 Characterize changes in language skills in older adults.

- For many individuals, knowledge of words and word meanings continues unchanged or may even improve in late adulthood. However, some decline in language skills may occur in retrieval of words for use in conversation, comprehension of speech, phonological skills, and some aspects of discourse. These changes in language skills in older adults likely occur as a consequence of declines in hearing or memory, a reduced speed of processing information, or disease.

3 Work and Retirement

 LG3 Discuss aging and adaptation to work and retirement.

Work

- An increasing number of older adults are continuing to work past 65 years of age, compared with their counterparts in past decades. An important change in older adults' work patterns is the increase in part-time work. Some individuals continue a life of strong work productivity throughout late adulthood.

Retirement in the United States and in Other Countries

- A retirement option for older workers is a late-twentieth-century phenomenon in the United States. Americans are more likely to continue working in their seventies than are workers in other countries.

Adjustment to Retirement

- The pathways individuals follow when they reach retirement age today are less clear than in the past. Those who adjust best to retirement are individuals who are healthy, have adequate income, are active, are better educated, have an extended social network of friends and family, and are satisfied with their lives before they retire.

4 Mental Health

 LG4 Describe mental health problems in older adults.

Depression

- Depression has been called the "common cold" of mental disorders. However, a majority of older adults with depressive symptoms never receive mental health treatment.

Dementia, Alzheimer Disease, and Other Afflictions

- Dementia is a global term for several neurological disorders involving an irreversible decline in mental function that interferes with daily life.

- Alzheimer disease is by far the most common dementia. This progressive, irreversible disorder is characterized by gradual deterioration of memory, reasoning, language, and eventually physical functioning. Special efforts are being made to discover the causes of Alzheimer disease and effective treatments for it. The increase in amyloid plaques and neurofibrillary tangles in Alzheimer patients may hold important keys to improving our understanding of the disease. Alzheimer disease is characterized by a deficiency in acetylcholine, a brain chemical that affects memory. Also, in Alzheimer disease the brain shrinks and deteriorates as plaques and tangles form. Important concerns are the financial implications of caring for Alzheimer patients and the burdens placed on caregivers.

- In addition to Alzheimer disease, another type of dementia is Parkinson disease.

5 Religion and Spirituality

LG5 Explain the role of religion and spirituality in the lives of older adults.

- Many older adults are spiritual leaders in their church and community. Religious interest increases in old age and is related to a sense of well-being in the elderly.

key **terms**

key **people**

SOCIOEMOTIONAL DEVELOPMENT IN LATE ADULTHOOD

chapter **outline**

① Theories of Socioemotional Development

Learning Goal 1 Discuss four theories of socioemotional development and aging.

Erikson's Theory

Activity Theory

Socioemotional Selectivity Theory

Selective Optimization with Compensation Theory

② Personality, the Self, and Society

Learning Goal 2 Describe links between personality and mortality, and identify changes in the self and society in late adulthood.

Personality

The Self and Society

Older Adults in Society

③ Families and Social Relationships

Learning Goal 3 Characterize the families and social relationships of aging adults.

Lifestyle Diversity

Attachment

Older Adult Parents and Their Adult Children

Great-Grandparenting

Friendship

Social Support and Social Integration

Altruism and Volunteering

④ Ethnicity, Gender, and Culture

Learning Goal 4 Summarize how ethnicity, gender, and culture are linked with aging.

Ethnicity

Gender

Culture

⑤ Successful Aging

Learning Goal 5 Explain how to age successfully.

George Shelley/Getty Images

Bob Cousy was a star player on Boston Celtics teams that won numerous National Basketball Association championships. In recognition of his athletic accomplishments, Cousy was honored by ESPN as one of the top 100 athletes of the twentieth century. After he retired from basketball, he coached college basketball and was a broadcaster for Boston Celtics basketball games into his late seventies. Cousy has retired from broadcasting but continues to play golf and tennis on a regular basis. He has positive social relationships with family members and many friends. When his wife developed dementia, he cared for her in their home as she slowly succumbed to the deterioration of her mind and body. In 2013, after 63 years of marriage, Cousy's wife died. Since her death, when he goes to bed each night, he tells her he loves her (Williamson, 2013).

As is the case with many famous people, Cousy's awards reveal little about his personal life and contributions. In addition to his extensive provision of care for his wife in her last years, two other examples illustrate his humanitarian efforts to help others (McClellan, 2004). First, when Cousy played for the Boston Celtics, his African American teammate, Chuck Cooper, was refused a room on a road trip because of his race. Cousy expressed anger to his coach about the situation and then accompanied an appreciative Cooper on a train back to Boston. Second, the Bob Cousy Humanitarian Fund "honors individuals who have given their lives to using the game of basketball as a medium to help others" (p. 4). The Humanitarian Fund reflects Cousy's motivation to care for others, be appreciative and give something back, and make the world less self-centered.

Bob Cousy as a Boston Celtics star when he was a young adult (*left*) and as an older adult (*right*). *What are some changes he has made in his life as an older adult?*
(*Left*) Hulton Archive/Getty Images; (*right*) Charles Krupa/AP Images

topical connections *looking back*

Middle adulthood is a time when individuals become more conscious of the young-old polarity in life and the shrinking amount of time left in their lives. And it is a time when individuals seek to transmit something meaningful to the next generation. The concept of midlife crisis has been exaggerated; when people do experience this crisis, it often is linked to negative life events. Stability of personality peaks in middle adulthood, and marital satisfaction often increases at this time. Many middle-aged adults become grandparents, and the middle-aged generation plays a key role in intergenerational relationships, with middle-aged women especially connecting generations.

preview

Bob Cousy's life as an older adult reflects some of the themes of socioemotional development in older adults that we will discuss in this chapter. These include the important role that being active plays in life satisfaction, the need to adapt to changing skills, and the ways in which close relationships with friends and family contribute to an emotionally fulfilling life.

1 Theories of Socioemotional Development

LG1 Discuss four theories of socioemotional development and aging.

Erikson's Theory | Activity Theory | Socioemotional Selectivity Theory | Selective Optimization with Compensation Theory

We will explore four main theories that focus on socioemotional development in late adulthood: Erikson's theory, activity theory, socioemotional selectivity theory, and selective optimization with compensation theory.

ERIKSON'S THEORY

We initially discussed Erik Erikson's (1968) eight stages of the human life span in the "Introduction" chapter. In other chapters we examined Erikson's stages in greater detail as we explored different periods of development. Here we will discuss his final stage.

Integrity Versus Despair   **Integrity versus despair** is Erikson's eighth and final stage of development, which individuals experience during late adulthood. This stage involves reflecting on the past and either piecing together a positive review or concluding that one's life has not been well spent. Through many different routes, the older adult may have developed a positive outlook in each of the preceding periods. If so, retrospective glances and reminiscences will reveal a picture of a life well spent, and the older adult will be satisfied (integrity). But if the older adult resolved one or more of the earlier stages in a negative way (being socially isolated in early adulthood or stagnating in middle adulthood, for example), retrospective evaluations of the total worth of his or her life might be negative (despair). Figure 1 portrays how positive resolutions of Erikson's eight stages can culminate in wisdom and integrity for older adults.

Life Review   Life review is prominent in Erikson's final stage of integrity versus despair. Life review involves looking back at one's life experiences, evaluating them, interpreting them, and often reinterpreting them (Rubin, Parrish, & Miyawaki, 2019). A leading expert on aging, Robert Butler, provided this perspective on life review: ". . . there are chances for pain, anger, guilt, and grief, but there are also opportunities for resolution and celebration, for affirmation and hope, for reconciliation and personal growth" (Butler, 2007, p. 72).

> ### developmental **connection**
> **Erikson's Theory**
> Erikson's other two adult stages are intimacy versus isolation (early adulthood) and generativity versus stagnation (middle adulthood). Connect to "Socioemotional Development in Early Adulthood" and "Socioemotional Development in Middle Adulthood."

integrity versus despair Erikson's eighth and final stage of development, which occurs in late adulthood. This stage involves reflecting on the past and either piecing together a positive review or concluding that one's life has not been well spent.

FIGURE 1

ERIKSON'S VIEW OF HOW POSITIVE RESOLUTION OF THE EIGHT STAGES OF THE HUMAN LIFE SPAN CAN CULMINATE IN WISDOM AND INTEGRITY IN OLD AGE. In Erikson's view, each stage of life is associated with a particular psychosocial conflict and a particular resolution. In this chart, Erikson describes how the issue from each of the earlier stages can mature into the many facets of integrity and wisdom in old age.

Conflict and Resolution	Culmination in Old Age
Old age Integrity vs. despair: wisdom	Existential identity; a sense of integrity strong enough to withstand physical disintegration.
Middle adulthood Generativity vs. stagnation: care	Caring for others, and empathy and concern.
Early adulthood Intimacy vs. isolation: love	Sense of complexity of relationships; value of tenderness and loving freely.
Adolescence Identity vs. confusion: fidelity	Sense of complexity of life; merger of sensory, logical, and aesthetic perception.
School age Industry vs. inferiority: competence	Humility; acceptance of the course of one's life and unfulfilled hopes.
Early childhood Initiative vs. guilt: purpose	Humor; empathy; resilience.
Toddlerhood Autonomy vs. shame: will	Acceptance of the cycle of life, from integration to disintegration.
Infancy Basic trust vs. mistrust: hope	Appreciation of interdependence and relatedness.

What characterizes a life review in late adulthood?
PeopleImages/DigitalVision/Getty Images

Butler (2007) states that the life review is set in motion by looking forward to death. Sometimes the life review proceeds quietly; at other times it is intense, requiring considerable work to achieve some sense of personality integration. The life review may be observed initially in stray and insignificant thoughts about oneself and one's life history. These thoughts may continue to emerge in brief intermittent spurts or become essentially continuous. One 76-year-old man commented, "My life is in the back of my mind. It can't be any other way. Thoughts of the past play on me. Sometimes I play with them, encouraging and savoring them; at other times I dismiss them."

Life reviews can include sociocultural dimensions, such as culture, ethnicity, and gender. Life reviews also can include interpersonal, relationship dimensions, including sharing and intimacy with family members or friends (Korte & others, 2014). And life reviews can include personal dimensions, which might involve the creation and discovery of meaning and coherence. These personal dimensions might unfold in such a way that the pieces do or don't make sense to the older adult. The life review might result in increased meaning in life and mastery, but it also might revive bitterness and negative thoughts (Korte, Westerhof, & Bohlmeijer, 2012). In the final analysis, each person's life review is to some degree unique.

One aspect of life review involves identifying and reflecting on both positive and negative aspects of one's experiences as a means of developing wisdom and self-understanding (Choi & Jun, 2009). The hope is that by examining not only the positive aspects of one's life but also what one has regretted doing (or not doing), a more accurate vision of the complexity of one's life and possibly increased life satisfaction will be attained (King & Hicks, 2007).

When working with older clients, some clinicians use *reminiscence therapy,* which involves discussing past activities and experiences with another individual or group (Ching-Teng & others, 2020; Ingersoll-Dayton & others, 2019). The therapy may include the use of photographs, familiar items, and video/audio recordings. Researchers have found that reminiscence therapy promotes a positive outlook and enhances quality of life for older adults, including those with dementia (Cuevas & others, 2020; Yen & Lin, 2018). A meta-analysis of 128 studies found that through reminiscence therapy clients attained a higher sense of integrity (based on Erikson's concept of integrity versus despair) (Pinquart & Forstmeier, 2012). Further, a variation of reminiscence therapy, *instrumental* reminiscence therapy (recalling the times one coped with stressful circumstances and analyzing what it took to adapt in those contexts), improved the adaptive ability and resilience of older adults in coping with adverse situations (Satorres & others, 2018). In another version of reminiscence therapy, *attachment-focused* reminiscence therapy reduced depressive symptoms, perceived stress, and emergency room visits in older African Americans (Sabir & others, 2016).

ACTIVITY THEORY

Activity theory states that the more active and involved older adults are, the more likely they are to be satisfied with their lives. Researchers have found strong support for activity theory, beginning in the 1960s and continuing into the twenty-first century (Antonucci & Webster, 2019; Neugarten, Havighurst, & Tobin, 1968; Strandberg, 2019). These researchers have found that when older adults are active, energetic, and productive, they age more successfully and are happier than if they disengage from society (Walker, 2019). Activity theory suggests that many individuals will achieve greater life satisfaction if they continue their middle-adulthood roles into late adulthood. If these roles are stripped from them (as in early retirement), it is important for them to find substitute roles that keep them active and involved.

Should adults stay active or become more disengaged as they become older? Explain.
Chuck Savage/Getty Images

SOCIOEMOTIONAL SELECTIVITY THEORY

Socioemotional selectivity theory states that motivation changes in response to narrowing time horizons. When time horizons are limited, there is a shift to priorities that favor emotional meaning and satisfaction. Older adults become more selective about their social networks. Because they place a high value on emotional satisfaction, older adults spend more time with familiar individuals with whom they have had rewarding relationships. Developed by Laura Carstensen (1998, 2006, 2011, 2016, 2019), this theory states that older adults actively withdraw from social contacts with individuals who are peripheral to their lives while maintaining or increasing contact with close friends and family members with whom they have had enjoyable relationships. This selective narrowing of social interaction maximizes positive emotional experiences and minimizes emotional risks as individuals become older. The fact that older adults have a decreasing number of years to live likely influences them to place more emphasis on prioritizing meaningful relationships (Moss & Wilson, 2018; Segerstrom & others, 2016). The priority placed on meaning is associated with greater selectivity about their social networks as they grow older.

Socioemotional selectivity theory challenges the stereotype that the smaller networks of older adults are related to emotional despair (Carstensen, 2011, 2014, 2016, 2019). Rather, carefully chosen and meaningful social networks lead them to spend most of their time engaged in emotionally rewarding moments with friends and family. That is, they systematically refine their social networks so that available social partners satisfy their emotional needs (Carstensen, 2019; Sims, Hogan, & Carstensen, 2015).

Laura Carstensen (*right*), in a caring relationship with an older woman. Her theory of socioemotional selectivity is gaining recognition as an important perspective on aging.
Courtesy of Dr. Laura Carstensen

Is there research evidence to support life-span differences in the composition of social networks? Researchers have found that older adults have far smaller social networks than younger adults do (Wrzus & others, 2013). In a study of individuals from 18 to 94 years of age, older adults had fewer peripheral social contacts but retained close relationships with people who provided them with emotional support (English & Carstensen, 2014a).

However, social networks can get too small. In the Sightlines Project, a large-scale examination of healthy living in different age groups conducted by the Stanford Center on Longevity, social engagement with individuals and communities appeared to be weaker than it had been 15 years earlier for 55- to 64-year-olds (Parker, 2016). Many of these individuals, who were about to reach retirement age, had weaker relationships with spouses, partners, family, friends, and neighbors than did their counterparts of 15 years ago. The Sightlines Project (2016) recommended the following interventions to increase the social engagement of older adults: employer wellness programs that strengthen support networks, environmental design that improves neighborhood and community life, technologies that improve personal relationships, and opportunities for volunteerism.

Socioemotional selectivity theory also focuses on the types of goals that individuals are motivated to achieve (Sims, Hogan, & Carstensen, 2015). It states that two important classes of goals are (1) knowledge-related and (2) emotional. This theory emphasizes that the trajectory of motivation for knowledge-related goals starts relatively high in the early years of life, peaks in adolescence and early adulthood, and then declines during middle and late adulthood (see Figure 2). By contrast, the trajectory of motivation for emotional goals is high during infancy and early childhood, declines from middle childhood through early adulthood, and increases in middle and late adulthood. Laura Carstensen (2016) noted that when older adults focus on emotionally meaningful goals, they are more satisfied with their lives, feel better, and experience fewer negative emotions.

activity theory The theory that the more active and involved older adults are, the more likely they are to be satisfied with their lives.

socioemotional selectivity theory The theory that motivation changes as a function of time horizons. When time horizons are limited, there is a shift toward prioritizing emotional meaning and satisfaction. Older adults become more selective about their social networks. Because they place a high value on emotional satisfaction, older adults often spend more time with familiar individuals with whom they have had rewarding relationships.

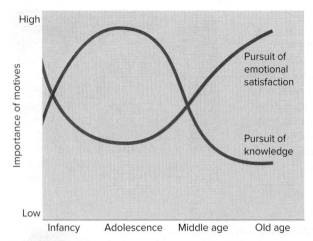

High

Importance of motives

Pursuit of emotional satisfaction

Pursuit of knowledge

Low

Infancy   Adolescence   Middle age   Old age

FIGURE 2

IDEALIZED MODEL OF SOCIOEMOTIONAL SELECTIVITY THROUGH THE LIFE SPAN. In Carstensen's theory of socioemotional selectivity, the motivation to reach knowledge-related and emotion-related goals changes across the life span.

One of the main reasons given for these changing trajectories in knowledge-related and emotion-related goals involves the perception of time (Carstensen, 2019). When time is perceived as open-ended, as it is when individuals are younger, people are more strongly motivated to pursue information, even at the cost of emotional satisfaction. But as older adults perceive that they have less time left in their lives, they are motivated to spend more time pursuing emotional satisfaction (Paul, 2019).

Are older adults more emotionally satisfied than younger adults? In a meta-analysis of 72 studies of more than 19,000 individuals in 19 countries, it was concluded that emotional experiences are more positive in the lives of older adults than in the lives of younger adults (Laureiro-Martinez, Trujillo, & Unda, 2017). Also, in this review, it was concluded that older adults focus less on negative events in their past than younger adults do. Compared with younger adults, older adults react less strongly to negative circumstances, are better at ignoring irrelevant negative information, and remember more positive than negative information (Mather, 2012). Also, compared with younger adults, older adults' emotional lives are on a more even keel, with fewer highs and lows. Thus, the emotional life of older adults is more positive and less negative than stereotypes suggest (Carstensen, 2019).

SELECTIVE OPTIMIZATION WITH COMPENSATION THEORY

Selective optimization with compensation theory states that successful aging depends on three main factors: selection, optimization, and compensation (SOC). The theory describes how people can produce new resources and allocate them effectively to the tasks they want to master (Nikitin & Freund, 2019). *Selection* is based on the concept that older adults have a reduced capacity and loss of functioning, which require a reduction in performance in most life domains. *Optimization* suggests that it is possible to maintain performance in some areas through continued practice and the use of new technologies. *Compensation* becomes relevant when life tasks require a level of capacity beyond the current level of the older adult's performance potential. Older adults especially need to compensate in circumstances involving high mental or physical demands, such as when thinking about and memorizing new material in a very short period of time, reacting quickly when driving a car, or moving quickly. When older adults develop an illness, the need for compensation is obvious.

Selective optimization with compensation theory was proposed by Paul Baltes and his colleagues (Baltes, 2003; Baltes, Lindenberger, & Staudinger, 2006). They describe the life of the late Arthur Rubinstein to illustrate their theory. When he was interviewed at 80 years of age, Rubinstein said that three factors were responsible for his ability to maintain his status as an admired concert pianist into old age. First, he mastered the weakness of old age by reducing the scope of his performances and playing fewer pieces (which reflects selection). Second, he spent more time practicing than earlier in his life (which reflects optimization). Third, he used special strategies, such as slowing down before fast segments, thus creating a perception of faster playing (which reflects compensation).

Theoretically, the processes of selective optimization with compensation contribute to successful outcomes (Nikitin & Freund, 2019). In a recent study of individuals from 22 to 94 years of age, on days when middle-aged and older adults, as well as individuals who were less healthy, used more strategies related to selective optimization with compensation, they reported higher levels of happiness (Teshale & Lachman, 2016).

SOC is attractive to researchers who study aging because it offers a conceptual framework about the ways that individuals can manage and adapt to losses (Nikitin & Freund, 2019). By engaging in SOC strategies, older adults can continue to lead satisfying lives, although in a more restricted manner (Nimrod, 2020). In a study of 22- to 94-year-olds, middle-aged adults had the highest daily use of SOC, although older adults also showed high SOC use if they had a high level of cognitive resources (Robinson, Rickenbach, & Lachman, 2016).

Loss is a common dimension of old age, although there are wide variations in the nature of the losses involved. Because of these individual variations, the specific form of selection,

selective optimization with compensation theory The theory that successful aging is related to three main factors: selection, optimization, and compensation.

Strategies for Effectively Engaging in Selective Optimization with Compensation

What are some good strategies that aging adults can engage in to attain selective optimization with compensation? According to Paul Baltes and his colleagues (Baltes, Lindenberger, & Staudinger, 2006), the following strategies are likely to be effective.

Selection Strategies

- Focus on the most important goal at a particular time.
- Think about what you want in life and commit yourself to one or two major goals.
- Realize that to reach a particular goal, you may need to abandon other goals.

Optimization Strategies

- Keep working on what you have planned until you are successful.
- Persevere until you reach your goal.

- When you want to achieve something, realize that you may need to be patient until the right moment arrives.

Compensation Strategies

- When things don't go the way they used to, search for other ways to achieve what you want.
- If things don't go well for you, be willing to let others help you.
- When things don't go as well as in the past, keep trying other ways until you can achieve results that are similar to what you accomplished earlier in your life.

How might you revise these guidelines to include the use of new technologies?

optimization, and compensation will likely vary, depending on the person's life history, pattern of interests, values, health, skills, and resources (Nimrod, 2020). To read about some strategies for effectively engaging in selective optimization with compensation, see *Connecting Development to Life*.

In Baltes' view (2003; Baltes, Lindenberger, & Staudinger, 2006), the selection of domains and life priorities is an important aspect of development. Life goals and priorities likely vary across the life course for most people. For many individuals, it is not just the sheer attainment of goals, but rather the attainment of *meaningful* goals, that makes life satisfying.

A cross-sectional study by Ursula Staudinger (1996) assessed the personal life investments of 25- to 105-year-olds (see Figure 3). From 25 to 34 years of age, participants said that they personally invested more time in work, friends, family, and independence, in that order. From 35 to 54 and 55 to 65 years of age, family became more important than friends in terms of their personal investment. Little changed in the rank ordering of persons 70 to 84 years old, but for participants 85 to 105 years old, health became their most important personal investment. Thinking about life showed up for the first time on the most important list for those who were 85 to 105 years old.

FIGURE 3

DEGREE OF PERSONAL LIFE INVESTMENT AT DIFFERENT POINTS IN LIFE. Shown here are the top four domains of personal life investment at different points in life. The highest degree of investment is listed at the top (for example, work was the highest personal investment from 25 to 34 years of age, family from 35 to 84, and health from 85 to 105). *(Left to right)* Diane Macdonald/Eyewire/Getty Images; Ryan McVay/Photodisc/Getty Images; Purestock/SuperStock; Hoby Finn/Photodisc/Getty Images; PointImages/iStock/Getty Images

25 to 34 Years	35 to 54 Years	55 to 65 Years	70 to 84 Years	85 to 105 Years
Work	Family	Family	Family	Health
Friends	Work	Health	Health	Family
Family	Friends	Friends	Cognitive fitness	Thinking about life
Independence	Cognitive fitness	Cognitive fitness	Friends	Cognitive fitness

One point to note about the study just described is the demarcation of late adulthood into the subcategories of 70 to 84 and 85 to 105 years of age. This fits with our comments on a number of occasions in this book that researchers increasingly recognize the importance of comparing older adults of different ages rather than studying them as one age group.

Review *Connect* Reflect

 Discuss four theories of socioemotional development and aging.

Review

- What is Erikson's theory of late adulthood?
- What is activity theory?
- What is socioemotional selectivity theory?
- What is selective optimization with compensation theory?

Connect

- How does the life reflection of older adults differ from the life reflection of individuals in middle adulthood who are approaching retirement age?

Reflect *Your Own Personal Journey of Life*

- Which of the four theories best describes the lives of older adults you know? Explain.

2 Personality, the Self, and Society

 Describe links between personality and mortality, and identify changes in the self and society in late adulthood.

Personality   The Self and Society   Older Adults in Society

Do some personality traits change in late adulthood? Is personality linked to mortality in older adults? Do self-perceptions and self-control change in late adulthood? How are older adults perceived and treated by society? We will explore these and other topics next.

PERSONALITY

Recall the Big Five factors of personality. Researchers have found that several of the Big Five factors of personality continue to change in late adulthood (Nye & Roberts, 2019; Roberts & Nickel, 2020). For example, in one study conscientiousness continued to increase in late adulthood (Roberts, Walton, & Bogg, 2005) and in another study older adults were more conscientious and agreeable than middle-aged and younger adults (Allemand, Zimprich, & Hendriks, 2008).

Might certain personality traits be related to how long older adults live? Researchers have found that some personality traits are associated with the mortality of older adults (Roberts & Nickel, 2020). A longitudinal study of more than 1,200 individuals across seven decades revealed that a higher score on the Big Five personality factor of conscientiousness predicted a lower risk of earlier death from childhood through late adulthood (Martin, Friedman, & Schwartz, 2007). A higher level of conscientiousness has been linked to living a longer life than the other four factors (Roberts & Damian, 2018). Also, individuals who are extraverted live longer, as do individuals who are low on neuroticism (Graham & others, 2017).

Following are the results of other studies of the influence of the Big Five personality factors in the lives of older adults:

- Older adults higher in conscientiousness experienced optimal aging, including positive affect, life satisfaction, and positive psychological well-being (Melendez & others, 2019).
- Older adults with a higher level of conscientiousness experience less cognitive decline as they age (Luchetti & others, 2016).
- Older adults with higher neuroticism and lower conscientiousness had more difficulty in perceived executive function (perceived cognitive control of processes for goal-directed behavior) (Bell, Hill, & Stavrinos, 2020)
- African American and non-Latino White older adults higher in conscientiousness had a lower risk of dementia (Kaup, Harmell, & Yaffe, 2019).

---

developmental connection

Personality

The Big Five factors of personality are openness, conscientiousness, extraversion, agreeableness, and neuroticism. Connect to "Socioemotional Development in Middle Adulthood."

- In older adults, higher levels of neuroticism predicted higher frailty, as did lower levels of openness and agreeableness (Stephan & others, 2017).
- More severe depression in older adults was associated with higher neuroticism and lower extraversion and conscientiousness (Koorevaar & others, 2013).
- In older adults, higher levels of conscientiousness, openness to experience, agreeableness, and extraversion were linked to positive emotions, while neuroticism was associated with negative emotions (Kahlbaugh & Huffman, 2017).
- Openness to experience declined prior to death in older adults (Sharp & others, 2019).

Affect (emotion) and outlook on life are also linked to mortality in older adults (Carstensen, 2014). Older adults characterized by negative affect don't live as long as those who display more positive affect, and optimistic older adults who have a positive outlook on life live longer than their counterparts who are more pessimistic and have a negative outlook on life (Kolokotroni, Anagnostopoulos, & Hantzi, 2018).

THE SELF AND SOCIETY

Our exploration of the self focuses on self-esteem and self-control. We have described how self-esteem drops in adolescence, especially for girls. How does self-esteem change during the adult years?

Self-Esteem In a cross-sectional study of self-esteem, researchers studied a very large, diverse sample of more than 300,000 individuals from 9 to 90 years of age (Robins & others, 2002). About two-thirds of the participants were from the United States. The individuals were asked to respond to the item "I have high self-esteem" on the following five-point scale:

1	2	3	4	5
Strongly Disagree				**Strongly Agree**

Self-esteem increased in the twenties, leveled off in the thirties and forties, rose considerably in the fifties and sixties, and then dropped significantly in the seventies and eighties (see Figure 4). Throughout most of the adult years, the self-esteem of males was higher than the self-esteem of females. However, in the seventies and eighties, the self-esteem of males and females converged.

Why might self-esteem decline in older adults? Explanations include deteriorating physical health and negative societal attitudes toward older adults, although these factors were not examined in the large-scale study just described.

A recent 13-year German longitudinal study found a somewhat more positive portrait of self-esteem in older adults than the study by Robins and others (2002). In the German study of older adults from 70 to 103 years of age, on average self-esteem declined in very

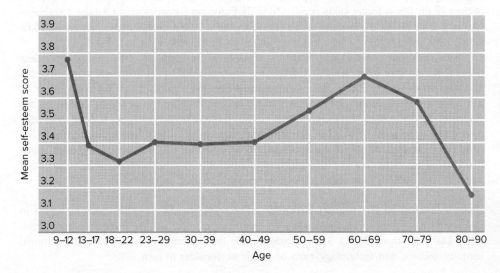

FIGURE 4

SELF-ESTEEM ACROSS THE LIFE SPAN. One cross-sectional study found that self-esteem was high in childhood, dropped in adolescence, increased through early and middle adulthood, then dropped in the seventies and eighties (Robins & others, 2002). More than 300,000 individuals were asked to rate the extent to which they have high self-esteem on a five-point scale, with 5 being "Strongly Agree" and 1 being "Strongly Disagree."

old age and when individuals were close to death, but the amount of the decline was small (Wagner & others, 2015). In this study, health problems and disabilities as well as higher levels of loneliness and lower levels of control beliefs were linked to lower self-esteem in late life. In other research on older adults, being widowed, institutionalized, or physically impaired, having a low religious commitment, and experiencing a decline in health are linked to low self-esteem (Giarrusso & Bengtson, 2007). Also, in one study, older adults with varied interests had a higher level of self-esteem (Krause & Hayward, 2014). In addition, in a recent study, emotionally unstable individuals' self-esteem declined the most in the second half of life (von Soest & others, 2018). In this study, not having a cohabiting partner, being unemployed, and having a disability each were associated with having a lower level of self-esteem and a steeper decline in self-esteem over a five-year period. And in a recent study of older adults, higher self-esteem was linked to better physical and psychological well-being (Ilyas, Shahed, & Hussain, 2020).

Self-Control   Although older adults are aware of age-related losses, most still effectively maintain a sense of self-control. Recent research indicates that self-control plays an important role in older adults' quality of life, with high levels of self-control linked to lower levels of depression and obesity (Bercovitz, Ngnoumen, & Langer, 2019). Also, recent research indicates that having a high sense of control over outcomes in life is linked to better cognitive performance, especially in older adults (Dixon & Lachman, 2019; Robinson & Lachman, 2017).

Self-control plays an important role in older adults' engagement in health-promoting activities (Bercovitz, Ngnoumen, & Langer, 2019). A study of 65- to 92-year-olds found that self-control was linked to better outcomes for well-being and depression following a six-week program of yoga (Bonura & Tenenbaum, 2014). Another study revealed that self-control was a key factor in older adults' physical activity levels (Franke & others, 2013).

Researchers also have studied how people self-regulate their behavior in specific areas of their lives (Dixon & Lachman, 2020). One study examined individuals from 13 to 90 years of age. For the oldest group (60 to 90 years of age), control was lowest in the physical domain; for the youngest group (13 to 18 years of age), it was lowest in the social domain (Bradley & Webb, 1976)

OLDER ADULTS IN SOCIETY

Does society negatively stereotype older adults? What are some social policy issues in an aging society?

Stereotyping Older Adults   Social participation by older adults is often discouraged by **ageism,** which is prejudice against others because of their age, especially prejudice against older adults (Airth & Oelke, 2020; Lytle, Levy, & Meeks, 2019). Older adults are often perceived as incapable of thinking clearly, learning new things, enjoying sex, contributing to the community, or holding responsible jobs. Many older adults face painful discrimination and might be too polite or timid to attack it. Because of their age, older adults might not be hired for new jobs or might be eased out of old ones; they might be shunned socially; and they might be edged out of their family life. A recent study conducted in 29 European countries examined age discrimination in individuals 15 to 115 years of age (Bratt & others, 2018). In this study, younger individuals showed more age discrimination toward older adults than did older individuals.

Ageism is widespread (Lytle, Nowacek, & Levy, 2020; Yunus & Hairi, 2020). One study found that men were more likely to negatively stereotype older adults than were women (Rupp, Vodanovich, & Crede, 2005). Research indicates that the most frequent form of ageism is disrespect for older adults, followed by assumptions about ailments or frailty caused by age (Palmore, 2004). A recent research review on the health of older adults in 45 countries concluded that ageism led to worse health outcomes, especially in less-developed countries where people were less educated (Chang & others, 2020). However, the increasing number of adults living to older ages has led to active efforts to improve society's image of older adults, to obtain better living conditions for older adults, and to increase their political clout.

Policy Issues in an Aging Society   The aging society and older persons' status in this society raise policy issues related to the well-being of older adults (Fernandez-Ballesteros, 2019; Leslie & others, 2020). These issues include the provision of health care, generational inequity, income, and technology, each of which we consider in turn.

ageism Prejudice against others because of their age, especially prejudice against older adults.

Health Care   An aging society also brings with it various problems involving health care (Lipsitz, 2020). Escalating health-care costs are currently the focus of considerable concern (Gorges, Sanghavi, & Konetzka, 2019). One factor that contributes to rising health care costs is the increasing proportion of older adults in the population. Older adults have more illnesses, especially chronic diseases, than younger adults do (Straatmann & others, 2020). Older adults see doctors more often, are hospitalized more often, and have longer hospital stays (Quesnel-Vallée, Willson, & Reiter-Campeau, 2016). Approximately one-third of the total health bill of the United States is for the care of adults 65 and over, who comprise only 12 percent of the population. The health care needs of older adults in the United States are reflected in Medicare and Medicaid (Kobayashi & others, 2019). A special concern is the increasing cost of Alzheimer disease, especially for women, who are far more likely than men to develop Alzheimer disease (Alzheimer's Association, 2020). Of interest is the fact that until the Affordable Care Act was recently enacted, the United States was the only developed country that did not have a national health-care system. Older adults themselves still pay about one-third of their total health-care costs. Thus, older adults as well as younger adults are adversely affected by rising medical costs (Findling & others, 2020).

A special concern is that while many of the health problems of older adults are chronic rather than acute, the medical system is still based on a "cure" rather than a "care" model. Chronic illness is long-term, often lifelong, and requires long-term, if not lifelong, management (Van Ness & others, 2019). Chronic illness often follows a pattern of an acute period that may require hospitalization, followed by a longer period of remission, and then repetitions of this pattern. The patient's home, rather than the hospital, often becomes the location for managing the patient's chronic illness. In a home-based system, a new type of cooperative relationship between doctors, nurses, patients, family members, and other service providers needs to be developed. Health-care personnel need to be trained and be available to provide services in patients' homes (Sterling & others, 2020).

Generational Inequity   Yet another policy issue that involves aging is **generational inequity,** the view that our aging society is being unfair to its younger members because older adults pile up advantages by receiving an inequitably large allocation of resources (Kershaw, 2018). Some authors have argued that generational inequity produces intergenerational conflict and divisiveness in the society at large (Longman, 1987). The generational equity issue raises questions about whether the young should be required to pay for the old (Jones & Roy, 2017). This concern has especially increased with the enactment of the U.S. government's Affordable Care Act in which healthy younger adults, who use the health-care system far less than older adults, nonetheless are required to sign up for the health-care program or pay a penalty (Hero, Zaslavsky, & Blendon, 2017).

Income   Economic security is clearly one of the most important aspects of older adults' well-being. Many older adults are understandably concerned about the adequacy of their income (Topa, Lunceford, & Boyatzis, 2018). Of special concern are older adults who are poor. Researchers have found that poverty in late adulthood is linked to increased physical and mental health problems (Elfassy & others, 2019). Poverty also is linked to lower levels of physical and cognitive fitness in older adults (Johnson & others, 2011). Research studies reveal that low SES is linked to increased risk of earlier death in older adults (Domenech-Abella & others, 2018).

Census data suggest that the overall number of older people living in poverty has declined since the 1960s, but 9.3 percent of older adults in the United States were living in poverty in 2016, down from 10 percent in 2014 (U.S. Census Bureau, 2018). In 2016, U.S. women 65 years and older were more likely to live in poverty (10.6 percent) than their male counterparts were (7.6 percent) (U.S. Census Bureau, 2018). There is a special concern about poverty among older women and considerable discussion about the role of Social Security in providing a broad economic safety net for them (Christ & Gronniger, 2018).

Poverty rates among older adults who belong to ethnic minorities are much higher than the rate for non-Latino Whites. In 2016, 18.7 percent of African American older adults lived in poverty, compared with 17.4 percent of Latino older adults, 11.8 percent of Asian American older adults, and 7.1 percent of non-Latino White older adults (U.S. Census Bureau, 2018). The poverty rate of 17.4 percent for Latino older adults reflects a significant decline from 20 percent in 2013, while the African American rate had remained essentially unchanged since 2013.

What are some concerns about health care for older adults?
Fuse/Getty Images

generational inequity The view that our aging society is being unfair to its younger members because older adults receive inequitably large allocations of resources.

Are older adults keeping up with changes in technology?
Image Source/Getty Images

Technology   The Internet plays an increasingly important role in providing access to information and communication for older adults as well as younger adults and youth (Fields & others, 2020; Gillain & others, 2019). A longitudinal study revealed that Internet use by older adults reduced their likelihood of being depressed by one-third (Cotten & others, 2014). And in a recent study of older adults, having an iPad strengthened their family ties and brought a greater sense of overall connection to society (Delello & McWhorter, 2017).

How well are older adults keeping up with changes in technology? Older adults are less likely to have a computer in their home and less likely to use the Internet than younger adults are, but older adults are the fastest-growing segment of Internet users. In 2019, 73 percent of U.S. adults 65 years of age and over were using the Internet, up from 59 percent in 2013 and 14 percent in 2000 (Anderson & others, 2019). In the general U.S. population, 90 percent are Internet users. Younger seniors use the Internet more than older seniors do (82 percent of 65- to 69-year-olds, compared with 44 percent of adults age 80 and older in 2016) (Anderson, 2017). Also, in a recent national U.S. survey, older adults' health information technology use increased from 9.3 million in 2009 to 22.3 million users in 2018 (Hung, Lyons, & Wu, 2020).

Increasing numbers of older adults use e-mail and smartphones to communicate, especially with friends and relatives (Gillain & others, 2019). In 2016, approximately 40 percent of U.S. adults 65 years of age and older were smartphone users, up 24 percent from 2013 (Anderson, 2017). In this survey, 59 percent of 65- to 69-year-olds but only 17 percent of adults age 80 and older used smartphones. For both Internet and smartphone use, lower-SES older adults use these communication tools much less than middle- and upper-SES older adults.

Older adults also are using social media more than in the past. In 2016, 34 percent of U.S. adults 65 and over reported using social networking sites like Facebook and Twitter, compared with 27 percent in 2013 (Anderson, 2017).

A recent study in Hong Kong found that adults 75 and older who used smartphones and the Internet to connect with family, friends, and neighbors had a higher level of psychological well-being than their counterparts who did not use this information and communicative technology (Fang & others, 2018). As with children and younger adults, cautions about verifying the accuracy of information—especially on topics involving health care—on the Internet should always be kept in mind (Miller & Bell, 2012).

Although computers and the Internet are playing more important roles in the lives of people of all ages, people continue to spend a great deal of time watching television, especially in late adulthood. In a 2016 Nielsen survey, adults age 65 and older watched television an average of 51 hours, 32 minutes per week (Recode, 2016). That 51+ hours per week is far more than any other adult age group: 18 to 24 years (16 hrs, 18 min), 25 to 34 years (23 hrs, 26 min), 35 to 49 years (32 hrs, 7 min), and 50 to 64 years (44 hrs, 6 min). The staggering number of hours older adults spend watching television each week raises concerns about the fact that spending so much time in sedentary behavior reduces the amount of time available for physical exercise and social activities, which are linked to healthy physical and socioemotional development.

Review *Connect* Reflect

 LG2 Describe links between personality and mortality, and identify changes in the self and society in late adulthood.

Review

- How are personality traits related to mortality in older adults?
- How does self-esteem change in late adulthood? What characterizes self-control in older adults?
- How are older adults perceived and treated by society?

Connect

- In "Socioemotional Development in Middle Adulthood," we described stability and change in personality development. What aspects of that discussion also pertain to stability and change in personality development in late adulthood?

Reflect *Your Own Personal Journey of Life*

- What do you envision your life will be like as an older adult?

| Lifestyle Diversity | Attachment | Older Adult Parents and Their Adult Children | Great-Grandparenting | Friendship | Social Support and Social Integration | Altruism and Volunteering |

Are the close relationships of older adults different from those of younger adults? What are some of the lifestyles of older adults? What characterizes the relationships of older adult parents and their adult children? Is the role of great-grandparents different from the role of grandparents? What do friendships and social networks contribute to the lives of older adults? What types of social support do older adults need and want? How might older adults' altruism and volunteerism contribute to positive outcomes?

LIFESTYLE DIVERSITY

The lifestyles of older adults are changing. Formerly, the later years of life were likely to consist of marriage for men and widowhood for women. With demographic shifts toward marital dissolution characterized by divorce, one-third of adults can now expect to marry, divorce, and remarry during their lifetime. Let's now explore some of the diverse lifestyles of older adults, beginning with those who are married or partnered.

Married Older Adults   In 2017, 57.8 percent of U.S. adults over 65 years of age were married (U.S. Census Bureau, 2018). There was a huge gender difference, with 70 percent of men but only 46 percent of women still married at age 65 and older.

The time from retirement until death is sometimes referred to as the "final stage in the marriage process." The portrait of marriage in the lives of older adults is a positive one for most couples (Blieszner, 2018). Individuals who are in a marriage or a partnership in late adulthood usually are happier, are less distressed, and live longer than those who are single (Roberto & Weaver, 2019).

Retirement alters a couple's lifestyle, requiring adaptation (Suitor, Gilligan, & Pillemer, 2016). Retirement demands the greatest adaptation when one partner has been a homemaker and the other has been working. Though historically, this was a common occurrence for middle-income families where the husband was employed while the wife managed the household, it no longer is typical of most American families. In such cases, however, husbands may not know what to do with their time and wives may feel uneasy having to share the household. Both partners may need to move toward more egalitarian roles. The husband must adjust from being the provider outside of the home to being a helper around the house; the wife must change from being the only homemaker to being a partner who shares and delegates household duties. Marital happiness of older adults is also affected by each partner's ability to deal with personal challenges, including aging, illness, and the prospect of widowhood. Overall, though, there is little evidence that retirement has negative effects on marriage.

In late adulthood, married individuals are more likely to find themselves having to care for a sick partner with a limiting health condition (Ornstein & others, 2019). The stress of caring for a spouse who has a chronic disease can place demands on intimacy (Polenick & DePasquale, 2019).

How might marriage affect the health and well-being of LGBT older adults? In a recent study of LGBT individuals 50 years and older, 24 percent were legally married, 26 percent unmarried and partnered, and 50 percent single (Goldsen & others, 2017). In this study, those who were legally married reported having a better quality of life and more economic and social resources than their unmarried and partnered counterparts. And those who were single reported having poorer health and fewer resources than those who were legally married or unmarried and partnered.

Divorced and Remarried Older Adults   An increasing number of older adults are divorced (Lin & others, 2018; Suitor, Gilligan, & Pillemer, 2016). In 1980, 3 percent of women 65 years and older were divorced, but that rate had increased to 15 percent by 2017. In 1980, 4 percent of men 65 and older were divorced, but that rate had increased to 11 percent in 2015 (U.S. Census Bureau, 2018). Many of these individuals were divorced or separated before entering late adulthood. The majority of divorced older adults are women due to their greater

I am the family face;
Flesh perishes,
I live on,
Projecting trait and trace
Through time to times anon,
And leaping from place to
   place
Over oblivion.

—Thomas Hardy
English novelist and poet, 19th century

> ---→
> **developmental connection**
> **Marriage**
> The benefits of a happy marriage include less physical and emotional stress, which puts less wear and tear on the body. Connect to "Socioemotional Development in Early Adulthood."
> ←---

What are some adaptations that many married older adults need to make?
Thinkstock/Stockbyte/Getty Images

- - - - - - - →

developmental **connection**

Widows

Women 65 years and older are far more likely to be widowed than to be divorced. Connect to "Death, Dying, and Grieving."

← - - - - - - - -

longevity. Men are more likely than women to remarry, thus removing themselves from the pool of divorced older adults (Peek, 2009). Divorce is far less common among older adults than younger adults, likely reflecting cohort effects rather than age effects since divorce was somewhat rare when current cohorts of older adults were young (Peek, 2009). In a recent study, many of the same factors traditionally associated with divorce in younger adults were also likely to occur in older adults (Lin & others, 2018). Older adults who had been married for many years, who had better marital quality, who owned a home, and who were wealthy were less likely than other older couples to get divorced.

There are social, financial, and physical consequences of divorce for older adults (Suitor, Gilligan, & Pillemer, 2016). Divorce can weaken kinship ties when it occurs in later life, especially in the case of older men. Divorced older women are less likely to have adequate financial resources than married older women, and older adults who are divorced have more health problems than those who are married (Bennett, 2006). Further, a recent study of older adults in Great Britain (average age: 63) found that those were divorced were more likely to die earlier and have lower life satisfaction than their married counterparts (Bourassa, Ruiz, & Sbarra, 2019). And a recent study indicated that today's older adults are more accepting of divorce than their counterparts from two decades ago (Brown & Wright, 2019).

Rising divorce rates, increased longevity, and better health have led to increased rates of remarriage among older adults (Papernow, 2018). A recent study of middle-aged and older adults found that 22 percent of women and 37 percent of men repartnered within 10 years following divorce (Brown & others, 2019). Repartnering occurred more through cohabitation than remarriage, especially for men. What happens when an older adult who is divorced or widowed wants to remarry or does remarry? Some older adults perceive negative social pressure about their decision to remarry. These negative sanctions range from raised eyebrows to rejection by adult children (Ganong & Coleman, 2018). However, the majority of adult children support the decision of their older adult parents to remarry. A research analysis revealed that divorce rates were 2.5 times higher for middle-aged and older adults who had remarried than for those in first marriages (Brown & Lin, 2012).

Researchers have found that remarried parents and stepparents provide less support to adult stepchildren than parents in first marriages provide to their adult children (Ganong, Coleman, & Sanner, 2018). One study revealed relatively weak ties between older adults and their stepchildren (Noel-Miller, 2013). In this study, older stepparents' social contact with their stepchildren was mainly linked to the stepparent continuing to be married to the stepchildren's biological parent. When divorce occurred in an older adult stepfamily, the divorced stepparent's frequency of contact with stepchildren dropped abruptly.

Cohabiting Older Adults An increasing number of older adults cohabit (Wright, 2020). In 1960, hardly any older adults cohabited (Chevan, 1996). The number of cohabiting adults 50 years and older rose rapidly in recent years, increasing from 2.3 million in 2007 to 4 million in 2016 (Stepler, 2017). The number of cohabiting older adults is expected to increase further as the large cohort of baby boomers continues to move through late adulthood, bringing their historically more nontraditional attitudes regarding love, sex, and relationships with them. In many cases, older adult couples cohabit more for companionship than for love. In some cases, such as when one partner faces the potential for expensive care, a couple may decide to maintain their assets separately and thus not marry. One study found that older adults who cohabited had a more positive, stable relationship than younger adults who cohabited, although older adults were less likely to have plans to marry their partner (King & Scott, 2005).

Does cohabiting affect an individual's health and psychological well-being? In a recent national study of older adults, the psychological well-being (lower levels of depression, stress, and loneliness) of men who cohabited was similar to that of married men and better than that of daters and unpartnered men (Wright & Brown, 2017). In contrast, there were few differences in the psychological well-being of women who were married, cohabiting, or single.

ATTACHMENT

There has been far less research on how attachment influences the lives of aging adults than on the effects of attachment in children, adolescents, and young adults (Fraley, 2019; Homan, 2018). One large-scale study examined attachment anxiety and avoidance in individuals from 18 to 70 years of age (Chopik, Edelstein, & Fraley, 2013). In this study, attachment anxiety was highest among adults in their mid-twenties and lowest among middle-aged and older adults. Developmental changes in avoidant attachment were not as strong as in anxious attachment, although anxious attachment was highest for middle-aged adults and lowest for young adults and older adults. And in related longitudinal data for individuals from 13 to 72 years of age, avoidant attachment declined across the life span and being in a relationship predicted lower levels of anxious and avoidant attachment across adulthood (Chopik, Edelstein, & Grimm, 2019). Further, a recent study of older adult women found that avoidant attachment was linked to higher levels of social isolation (Spence, Jacobs, & Bifulco, 2019). And a recent study of older adults indicated that attachment security was linked to competence in daily life, which in turn was related to psychological adjustment (Martin, Horn, & Allemand, 2020).

OLDER ADULT PARENTS AND THEIR ADULT CHILDREN

Parent-child relationships in later life differ from those earlier in the life span (Antonucci & Webster, 2019; Birditt & others, 2019; Kim & others, 2020). These relationships are influenced by a lengthy joint history and extensive shared experiences and memories.

Approximately 80 percent of older adults have living children, many of whom are middle-aged. About 10 percent of older adults have children who are 65 or older. Adult children are an important part of the aging parent's social network. Researchers have found that older adults with children have more contacts with relatives than those without children (Johnson & Troll, 1992).

The lifestyles of older adult parents and their adult children have become increasingly diverse. Divorce, remarriage, cohabitation, and nonmarital childbearing are more common in the history of older adults today than in the past (Papernow, 2018).

Gender plays an important role in relationships involving older adult parents and their children (Antonucci & Webster, 2019). Adult daughters are more likely than adult sons to be involved in the lives of their aging parents. For example, adult daughters are three times more likely than are adult sons to give parents assistance with daily living activities (Dwyer & Coward, 1991).

Middle-aged adults are more likely to provide support if their parents have a disability (Huo & others, 2019). A valuable service that adult children can perform is to coordinate and monitor services for an aging parent who becomes disabled (Jones & others, 2011). Even less severely impaired older adults may need help with shopping, housework, transportation, home maintenance, and bill paying.

Some researchers have found that relationships between aging parents and their children are usually characterized by ambivalence (Fingerman, Huo, & Birditt, 2020; Fingerman & others, 2018). Perceptions include love, reciprocal help, and shared values on the positive side and isolation, family conflicts and problems, abuse, neglect, and caregiver stress on the negative side. A study of adult children's relationships with their older adult parents revealed that ambivalence was likely to be present when relationships involved in-laws, those in poor health, and adult children with poor parental relationships in early life (Wilson, Shuey, & Elder, 2003). Another study, though, revealed that affection and support, reflecting solidarity, were more prevalent than ambivalence in intergenerational relationships (Hogerbrugge & Komter, 2012). Researchers also have found that middle-aged adults feel more positive about providing support for their children than for their aging parents (Birditt & others, 2019).

GREAT-GRANDPARENTING

Because of increased longevity, more grandparents today than in the past are also great-grandparents. At the turn of the twentieth century, the three-generation family was common, but today the four-generation family is common. One contribution of great-grandparents is to transmit family history by telling their children, grandchildren, and great-grandchildren where the family came from, what their members achieved, what they endured, and how their lives changed over the years (Harris, 2002).

There has been little research on great-grandparenting. One study examined the relationship between young adults and their grandparents and great-grandparents (Roberto & Skoglund, 1996). The young adults interacted with, and participated in more activities with, their grandparents than their great-grandparents. They also perceived their grandparents as having a more defined role and being more influential in their lives than their great-grandparents were.

At the beginning of the twentieth century, the three-generation family was common, but now the four-generation family is common as well. Thus, an increasing number of grandparents are also great-grandparents. The four-generation family shown here is the Jordans—author John Santrock's mother-in-law, daughter, granddaughter, and wife.
Courtesy of Dr. John Santrock

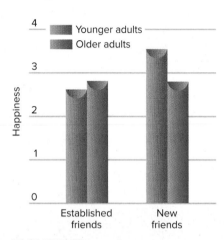

developmental connection

Family and Peers

It takes time to develop intimate friendships, so friendships that have endured over the adult years are often deeper than those that were formed in middle adulthood. Connect to "Socioemotional Development in Middle Adulthood."

FIGURE 5

HAPPINESS OF YOUNGER ADULTS AND OLDER ADULTS WITH NEW AND ESTABLISHED FRIENDS. Note: The happiness scale ranged from 0 to 6, with participants rating how intensely they experienced happiness (0 = not at all, 6 = extremely intense). Older adults' mean age was 71; younger adults' mean age was 23.

What are some contributions of social integration to successful aging?
Terry Vine/Blend Images/Getty Images

convoy model of social relations Model in which individuals go through life embedded in a personal network of individuals to whom they give and from whom they receive support.

FRIENDSHIP

In early adulthood, friendship networks expand as new social connections are made away from home. In late adulthood, new friendships are less likely to be forged but close friendships are maintained, although some older adults do seek out new friendships, especially following the death of a spouse (Blieszner & Ogletree, 2018).

A recent study found that compared with younger adults, older adults reported fewer problems with friends, fewer negative friendship qualities, less frequent contact with friends, and more positive friendship qualities with a specific friend (Schlosnagle & Strough, 2017). In another study, adults who had close ties with friends were less likely to die across a seven-year age span (Rasulo, Christensen, & Tomassini, 2005). These findings were stronger for women than for men. Further, in a recent study of older couples, having a larger friend confidant network or closer connections with friend confidants was linked to better marital quality for wives and husbands 5 years later (Zhaoyang & Martire, 2020). And in another recent study of older adults, interactions with friends were more pleasant and were associated with fewer discussions about stressful experiences than were interactions with partners or family members (Ng & others, 2020).

Aging expert Laura Carstensen and her colleagues (2009; Sims, Hogan, & Carstensen, 2015) have concluded that people choose close friends over new friends as they grow older. And as long as they have several close people in their network, they seem content, says Carstensen. Supporting Carstensen's view, researchers found that in comparison with younger adults, older adults said they tended to experience less intense positive emotions with new friends and equal levels of positive emotions with established friends (Charles & Piazza, 2007) (see Figure 5). Carstensen also states that it is important to remember that older adults are less lonely and more happy than young adults.

SOCIAL SUPPORT AND SOCIAL INTEGRATION

Social support and social integration play important roles in the physical and mental health of older adults (Antonucci & Webster, 2019).

Social Support   In the **convoy model of social relations,** individuals go through life embedded in a personal network of individuals to whom they give and from whom they receive social support (Antonucci & others, 2016; Antonucci & Webster, 2019). For older adults, social support is related to their physical health, mental health, and life satisfaction (Bui, 2020). It is linked with a reduction in symptoms of disease, with the ability to meet one's own health-care needs, and increased longevity (Kong & others, 2019; Smith & others, 2018). Further, one study revealed that older adults who experienced a higher level of social support showed later cognitive decline than their counterparts with a lower level of social support (Dickinson & others, 2011).

Social support for older adults can be provided by different adults (Antonucci & others, 2016; Antonucci & Webster, 2019). Older adults who are married are less likely to need formal social supports, such as home nursing care, adult day care, and home-delivered meals, than are nonmarried older adults. Families play important roles in social support for older adults, but friends also can provide invaluable resources for social support (Blieszner & Ogletree, 2018). Recent analyses, though, indicate that 80 percent of supportive care for older adults with some form of limitation is provided by family members or other informal caregivers, which places an enormous burden on the caregiver (Antonucci & others, 2016; Antonucci & Webster, 2019; Shi & others, 2020). Also, social support for older adults may vary across cultures. For example, in the United States, the focal support person for an older adult is most likely to be a daughter, whereas in Japan it is most likely to be a daughter-in-law.

Social Integration   Social integration—the extent to which individuals are involved in social exchanges with others, whether it is with family members, social networks, or in their communities, and feel a sense of belonging in these social contexts—also plays an important role in the lives of many older adults (Antonucci & Webster, 2019; Hawkley & Kocherginsky, 2018). One study found that older adults with higher levels of social integration were less depressed (Ivan Santini & others, 2015). And a recent study of older adults found that interactions with a greater variety of social ties was associated with engaging in more physical activity and less sedentary time (Fingerman & others, 2020). Also in this study, greater involvement with diverse social ties was linked to having more positive mood.

Remember from our earlier discussion of socioemotional selectivity theory that many older adults choose to have fewer peripheral social contacts and more emotionally positive contacts with friends and family (Carstensen, 2015, 2016, 2019). Researchers have found that older adults tend to report being less lonely than younger adults and less lonely than would be expected based on their circumstances (Schnittker, 2007), likely because of their selective social networks and greater acceptance of solitude in their lives (Antonucci & others, 2016; Antonucci & Webster, 2019). In a recent study, only 18 percent of older adults stated that they were often or frequently lonely (Due, Sandholdt, & Waldorff, 2017). In this study, the most important predictors of feeling lonely were anxiety and depression, living alone, and low social participation. Also, in a national longitudinal study, loneliness was linked with earlier death (Luo & others, 2012).

ALTRUISM AND VOLUNTEERING

Are older adults more altruistic than younger adults? In a series of studies, older adults were more likely to behave in altruistic ways and to value contributions to the public good than younger adults were (Freund & Blanchard-Fields, 2014). For example, in two of the studies, older adults were more likely than younger adults to donate money for a good cause.

A common perception is that older adults are receivers of help rather than providers of help to others. This perception is contradicted by results of a national survey indicating that 24.1 percent of U.S. adults 65 years and older engaged in volunteering in 2013 (U.S. Bureau of Labor Statistics, 2013). In this survey, the highest percentage of volunteering occurred between 35 and 44 years of age (30.6 percent); however, older adults are more likely than any other age group to volunteer more than 100 hours annually (Burr, 2009). Almost 50 percent of the volunteering efforts of older adults are for services provided by religious organizations (Burr, 2009).

Might volunteering improve the well-being and life-satisfaction of older adults? Volunteering is associated with a number of positive outcomes for aging adults (Carr, 2018; Guiney & Machado, 2018; Jongenelis & others, 2020). Recent studies have found that when aging adults volunteer, they have better health (Burr & others, 2018; Carr, Kail, & Rowe, 2018), have better cognitive functioning (Proulx, Curl, & Ermer, 2018), and are less lonely (Carr & others, 2018). Among the reasons for the positive outcomes of volunteering are its provision of constructive activities and productive roles, social integration, and enhanced meaningfulness (Tan & others, 2007).

Might providing help to others even be linked to longevity in late adulthood? In a recent study, of four indices (volunteering, informally helping others through a modest time commitment, attending religious services, and going to social group meetings), the strongest predictor of longevity and lower risk for cardiovascular disease was volunteering (S. H. Han & others, 2017). Also, a recent study revealed that older adults who volunteered regularly had a lower risk of cognitive impairment (Infurna, Okun, & Grimm, 2016). And in a research meta-analysis, older adults who engaged in organizational volunteering had a lower mortality risk than those who did not (Okun, Yeung, & Brown, 2013).

developmental **connection**
Community and Culture
Service learning is linked with numerous positive outcomes in youth. Connect to "Physical and Cognitive Development in Adolescence."

Ninety-eight-year-old volunteer Iva Broadus plays cards with 10-year-old DeAngela Williams in Dallas, Texas. Iva was recognized as the oldest volunteer in the Big Sisters program in the United States. Iva says that card-playing helps to keep her memory and thinking skills sharp and can help DeAngela's as well.
Jim Mahoney/Dallas Morning News

Review Connect Reflect

 LG3 Characterize the families and social relationships of aging adults.

Review
- How would you profile the diversity of adult lifestyles?
- How does attachment change in older adults?
- What characterizes the relationships of older adult parents and their adult children?
- Is the role of great-grandparents different from the role of grandparents?
- What are friendships of older adults like?
- What roles do social support and social integration play in late adulthood?
- How are altruism and volunteerism linked to positive outcomes in older adults?

Connect
- In this section, you read that a low level of social integration is linked with coronary heart disease in older adults. What have you already learned about heart disease and stress in middle adulthood?

Reflect *Your Own Personal Journey of Life*
- If you are an emerging or young adult, what is the nature of the relationship of your parents with their parents and grandparents (if they are alive)? If you are a middle-aged adult, how would you characterize your relationship with your parents (if they are still alive)?

4 Ethnicity, Gender, and Culture LG4 Summarize how ethnicity, gender, and culture are linked with aging.

Ethnicity   Gender   Culture

How is ethnicity linked with aging? Do gender roles change in late adulthood? What are the social aspects of aging in different cultures?

ETHNICITY

Of special concern are ethnic minority older adults, especially African Americans and Latinos, who are overrepresented in poverty statistics (U.S. Census Bureau, 2018). Consider Harry, a 72-year-old African American who lives in a rundown hotel in Los Angeles. He suffers from arthritis and uses a walker. He has not been able to work for years, and government payments are barely enough to meet his needs.

Comparative information about African Americans, Latinos, and Whites indicates a possible double jeopardy for elderly ethnic minority individuals. They face problems related to both ageism and racism (McCluney & others, 2018). Both the wealth and the health of ethnic minority older adults decrease more rapidly than for elderly non-Latino Whites (Angel, Mudrazija, & Benson, 2016). Older ethnic minority individuals are more likely to become ill but less likely to receive treatment (Nguyen & others, 2018). They also are more likely to have a history of less education, higher levels of unemployment, worse housing conditions, and shorter life expectancies than their non-Latino White counterparts (Treas & Gubernskaya, 2016). Also, too many ethnic minority workers never enjoy the Social Security and Medicare benefits to which their earnings contribute, because they die before reaching the age of eligibility for benefits. And non-Latino White men and women with 16 years or more of schooling have been found to have a life expectancy 14 years higher than African Americans with fewer than 12 years of education (Antonucci & others, 2016).

Despite the stress and discrimination older ethnic minority individuals face, many of these older adults have developed coping mechanisms that allow them to survive in the dominant non-Latino White world. Extended family networks help older minority-group individuals cope with the bare essentials of living and give them a sense of being loved (Antonucci & Webster, 2019). Churches in African American and Latino communities provide avenues for meaningful social participation, feelings of power, and a sense of internal satisfaction (Hill & others, 2006). And residential concentrations of ethnic minority groups give their older members a sense of belonging. Thus, it always is important to consider individual variations in the lives of aging minorities.

Further, a recent study found that the life satisfaction of Latino older adults was higher than for African American and non-Latino White older adults (Zhang, Braun, & Wu, 2017). And in another recent study, older adult immigrants had higher levels of life satisfaction than native-born older adult U.S. residents did (Calvo, Carr, & Matz-Costa, 2017). In this study, Latino immigrants had the highest life satisfaction of all the groups studied. These findings have recently been called a "happiness paradox" because older Latino immigrants have been found to have greater life satisfaction than non-immigrant Latinos and non-Latino Whites in the United States, despite experiencing the greatest financial disadvantages and limitations (Calvo, Carr, & Matz-Costa, 2017, 2019).

To read about one individual who is providing help for aging minorities, see *Connecting with Careers*.

GENDER

Do our gender roles change when we become older adults? Some developmentalists conclude that femininity decreases in women and that masculinity decreases in men when they

Norma Thomas, Social Work Professor and Administrator

Dr. Norma Thomas has worked for more than three decades in the field of aging. She obtained her undergraduate degree in social work from Pennsylvania State University and her doctoral degree in social work from the University of Pennsylvania. Thomas' activities are varied. Earlier in her career, she was a social work practitioner who provided services to older adults of color in an effort to improve their lives. She currently is a professor and academic administrator at Widener University in Chester, Pennsylvania, a fellow of the Institute of Aging at the University of Pennsylvania, and the chief executive officer and cofounder of the Center on Ethnic and Minority Aging (CEMA). CEMA was formed to provide research, consultation, training, and services to benefit aging individuals of color, their families, and their communities. Thomas has created numerous community service events that benefit older adults of color, especially African Americans and Latinos. She has also served as a consultant to various national, regional, and state agencies in her effort to improve the lives of aging adults of color.

For more information about what professors and social workers do, see the Careers in Life-Span Development appendix.

Norma Thomas.
Courtesy of Dr. Norma Thomas

reach late adulthood (Gutmann, 1975). The evidence suggests that older men do become more feminine—nurturant, sensitive, and so on—but it appears that older women do not necessarily become more masculine—assertive, dominant, and so on (Turner, 1982). In a more recent cross-sectional study of individuals from 12 to 80 years and older, men in their seventies were more likely than adolescents and younger men to endorse androgynous traits (Strough & others, 2007). Also in this study, women in their eighties and older were less likely than younger and middle-aged women to endorse masculine and androgynous traits. And in an even more recent study, among older adult men, those who were married were more likely to endorse stereotypically masculine traits but also to have higher androgyny scores than unmarried older men (Lemaster, Delany, & Strough, 2017). However, these studies of age differences were cross-sectional and may reflect cohort effects. Keep in mind that cohort effects are especially important to consider in areas such as gender roles. As sociohistorical changes take place and are assessed more frequently in life-span investigations, what were once perceived to be age effects may turn out to be cohort effects (George & Ferraro, 2016).

A possible double jeopardy also faces many women—the burden of both ageism and sexism (Angel, Mudrazija, & Benson, 2016). Not only is it important to be concerned about older women's double jeopardy of ageism and sexism, but special attention also needs to be devoted to female ethnic minority older adults (Jackson, Govia, & Sellers, 2011). They face what could be described as triple jeopardy—ageism, sexism, and racism (Hinze, Lin, & Andersson, 2012). Older women in ethnic minority groups have faced considerable stress in their lives. In dealing with this stress, they have shown remarkable adaptability, resilience, responsibility, and coping skills.

CULTURE

Culture plays an important role in aging (Yeo & Yoshikawa, 2019). What promotes a good old age in most cultures? One analysis indicated that three factors are important in living the "good life" as an older adult: health, security, and kinship/support (Fry, 2007).

A special concern is the stress faced by older African American women, many of whom view religion as a source of strength to help them cope. *What are some other characteristics of being female, a member of an ethnic minority, and old?*
Matt Gray/Radius Images/Getty Images

Cultures vary in the prestige they give to older adults. In the Navajo culture, older adults are especially treated with respect because of their wisdom and extensive life experiences. *What are some other factors that are linked with respect for older adults in a culture?*
Alison Wright/Getty Images

Another important question is this: What factors are associated with whether older adults are accorded a position of high status in a culture? In one view, seven cultural factors are most likely to predict high status for older adults (Sangree, 1989):

- Older persons have valuable knowledge.
- Older persons control key family/community resources.
- Older persons are permitted to engage in useful and valued functions as long as possible.
- There is role continuity throughout the life span.
- Age-related role changes involve greater responsibility, authority, and advisory capacity.
- The extended family is a common family arrangement in the culture, and the older person is integrated into the extended family.
- In general, respect for older adults is greater in collectivistic cultures (such as China and Japan) than in individualistic cultures (such as the United States). However, some researchers are finding that this collectivistic/individualistic difference in respect for older adults is not as strong as it used to be, and that in some cases older adults in individualistic cultures receive considerable respect (Antonucci, Vandewater, & Lansford, 2000).

Review *Connect* Reflect

 LG4 Summarize how ethnicity, gender, and culture are linked with aging.

Review
- How does ethnicity modify the experience of aging?
- Do gender roles change in late adulthood? Explain.
- How is aging experienced in different cultures?

Connect
- In this section, you read that ethnic minorities face additional challenges in aging. What have you learned about ethnicity and life expectancy?

Reflect *Your Own Personal Journey of Life*
- How would you describe the experiences of the older adults in your family that have been influenced by their ethnicity, gender, and culture?

5 Successful Aging   **LG5** Explain how to age successfully.

As we have discussed various aspects of late adulthood, it should be apparent that there are large individual differences in the patterns of change experienced by older adults. The most common pattern is *normal aging*, which characterizes most individuals (Schaie, 2016b). Their psychological functioning often peaks in early midlife, plateaus until the late fifties to early sixties, then modestly declines through the early eighties, although marked decline often occurs prior to death. Another pattern involves *pathological aging*, which characterizes individuals who in late adulthood show greater than average decline. These individuals may have mild cognitive impairment in early old age, develop Alzheimer disease later, or have chronic disease that impairs their daily functioning. A third pattern of change in old age is *successful aging*, which characterizes individuals whose physical, cognitive, and socioemotional development is maintained longer than for most individuals and declines later than for most people.

For too long successful aging has been ignored (Fernandez-Ballesteros, 2019; Henning-Smith, 2020). Throughout this edition, we have called attention to the positive aspects of aging. There are many robust, healthy older adults. With a proper diet, an active lifestyle, mental stimulation and flexibility, positive coping skills, good social relationships and support, and the absence of disease, many abilities can be maintained or in some cases even improved as we get older (Antonucci & Webster, 2019; Fingerman & others, 2020). Even when individuals develop a disease, improvements in medicine and lifestyle modifications mean that increasing numbers of older adults can continue to lead active, constructive lives (Santacreu, Rodriguez, & Molina, 2019). A Canadian study found that the self-rated probability of aging successfully was 41 percent for those 65 to 74, 33 percent for those 75 to 84, and 22 percent for those 85+ years of age

(Meng & D'Arcy, 2014). In this study, being younger, married, a regular drinker, in better health (self-perceived), and satisfied with life were associated with successful aging. Presence of disease was linked to a significant decline in predictions of successful aging. In another recent study, the following four factors emerged as best characterizing successful aging: proactive engagement, wellness resources, positive spirit, and valued relationships (Lee, Kahana, & Kahana, 2017).

Being active and socially engaged are especially important for successful aging (Lee & others, 2020; Walker, 2019). Older adults who exercise regularly, attend meetings, participate in church activities, and go on trips are more satisfied with their lives than their counterparts who disengage from society (Strandberg, 2019). Older adults who engage in challenging cognitive activities are more likely to retain their cognitive skills for a longer period of time (Calero, 2019). Older adults who are emotionally selective, optimize their choices, and compensate effectively for losses increase their chances of aging successfully (Nikitin & Freund, 2019). Also, a recent study of 90- to 91-year-olds found that living circumstances, especially owning one's own home and living there as long as possible; independence in various aspects of life; good health; and a good death were described as important themes of successful aging (Nosraty & others, 2015). In this study, social and cognitive aspects were thought to be more important than physical health.

Successful aging also involves perceived control over the environment (Dixon & Lachman, 2020). We have described how perceived control over the environment had a positive effect on nursing home residents' health and longevity. In recent years, the term *self-efficacy* has often been used to describe perceived control over the environment and confidence in one's ability to produce positive outcomes (Bandura, 2010a, 2012, 2015). Researchers have found that many older adults maintain a sense of control and have a positive view of themselves (Bercoviz, Ngnoumen, & Langer, 2019). Examining the positive aspects of aging is an important trend in life-span development that is likely to benefit future generations of older adults (Robine, 2019). And a very important agenda is to continue to improve our understanding of how people can live longer, healthier, more productive, and satisfying lives (Henning-Smith, 2020; Santacreu, Rodriguez, & Molina, 2019).

In the "Introduction" chapter we described Laura Carstensen's (2015) perspective on the challenges and opportunities presented by the dramatic increase in life expectancy that has been occurring and continues to occur. In her view, the recent increase in longevity has taken place so rapidly that science, technology, and behavioral adaptations have not kept pace. She proposes that the challenge is to change a world constructed mainly for young people to a world that is more compatible and supportive for the increasing number of people living to 100 and older.

In further commentary, Carstensen (2015, p. 70) remarked that making this change would be no small feat:

> . . . parks, transportation systems, staircases, and even hospitals presume that the users have both strength and stamina; suburbs across the country are built for two parents and their young children, not single people, multiple generations or elderly people who are not able to drive. Our education system serves the needs of young children and young adults and offers little more than recreation for experienced people.

Indeed, the very conception of work as a full-time endeavor ending in the early sixties is ill suited for long lives. Arguably the most troubling fact is that we fret about ways that older people lack the qualities of younger people rather than exploit a growing new resource right before our eyes: citizens who have deep expertise, emotional balance, and the motivation to make a difference.

developmental **connection**

Health

Regular exercise is linked to increased longevity and prevention of many chronic diseases. Connect to "Physical Development in Late Adulthood."

Warren Buffett, one of the world's wealthiest persons (net worth in 2018: $82 billion), is now in his early nineties and continues to stay very active, especially making high-level decisions in his company. Buffett also is one of the world's most generous philanthropists, giving more than $30 billion to charities.
Alex Wong/Staff/Getty Images

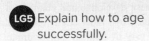

Review *Connect* Reflect

LG5 Explain how to age successfully.

Review

- What factors are linked with aging successfully?

Connect

- In this section, you read that self-efficacy and an optimistic attitude are linked to the happiness of centenarians. What factors play important roles in helping people survive to extreme old age?

Reflect *Your Own Personal Journey of Life*

- How might your ability to age successfully as an older adult be related to what you are doing in your life now?

topical connections looking *forward*

As people approach death, dying individuals and those close to them experience intense emotions. The dying individual doesn't go through a set sequence of stages, but at various points may show denial, anger, or acceptance. It is important for family and friends to communicate effectively with a dying person. In coping with the death of another person, grief may be experienced as emotional numbness, separation anxiety, despair, sadness, or loneliness. In some cases, grief may last for years. Among the most difficult losses are the death of a child or a spouse. Social support benefits widows and widowers.

reach your **learning goals**

Socioemotional Development in Late Adulthood

1 Theories of Socioemotional Development

LG1 Discuss four theories of socioemotional development and aging.

Erikson's Theory

- Erikson's eighth and final stage of development, which individuals experience in late adulthood, involves reflecting on the past and either integrating it positively or concluding that one's life has not been well spent. Life review is an important theme in Erikson's stage of integrity versus despair.

Activity Theory

- Activity theory states that the more active and involved older adults are, the more likely they are to be satisfied with their lives. This theory has been strongly supported by research.

Socioemotional Selectivity Theory

- Socioemotional selectivity theory states that motivation changes as a function of time horizons. When time horizons are limited, there is a shift toward prioritizing emotional meaning and satisfaction. Older adults become more selective about their social networks. Because they place a high value on emotional satisfaction, they are motivated to spend more time with familiar individuals with whom they have formed rewarding relationships. Knowledge-related and emotion-related goals change across the life span, with emotion-related goals becoming more important as individuals get older.

Selective Optimization with Compensation Theory

- Selective optimization with compensation theory states that successful aging is linked with three main factors: (1) selection of performance domains, (2) optimization of existing capacities, and (3) compensation for deficits. This theory is especially likely to be relevant when loss occurs.

2 Personality, the Self, and Society

LG2 Describe links between personality and mortality, and identify changes in the self and society in late adulthood.

Personality

- The personality traits of conscientiousness and agreeableness increase in late adulthood. Lower levels of conscientiousness, extraversion, and openness to experience, a higher level of neuroticism, negative affect, pessimism, and a negative outlook on life are related to earlier death in late adulthood.

The Self and Society

- In one large-scale study, self-esteem increased through most of adulthood but declined in the seventies and eighties. Further research is needed to verify these developmental changes in self-esteem. The stability of self-esteem declines in older adults. Most older adults effectively maintain a sense of self-control, although self-regulation may vary by domain. For example, older adults often show less self-regulation in the physical domain than younger adults do.

Older Adults in Society

- Ageism is prejudice against others because of their age. Too many negative stereotypes of older adults continue to exist.

- Social policy issues in an aging society include the provision of health care, generational inequity, income, and technology.

3 Families and Social Relationships Characterize the families and social relationships of aging adults.

Lifestyle Diversity

- Older adult men are more likely to be married than older adult women. Retirement alters a couple's lifestyle and requires adaptation. Married older adults are often happier than single older adults. There are social, financial, and physical consequences of divorce for older adults. Greater numbers of divorced older adults, increased longevity, and better health have led to increased remarriage by older adults. Some older adults perceive negative pressure about their decision to remarry after becoming widowed or divorced, although the majority of adult children support the decision of their older adult parents to remarry. An increasing number of older adults cohabit.

Attachment

- Older adults have fewer attachment relationships than younger adults; attachment anxiety decreases with increasing age; attachment security is linked to psychological and physical well-being in older adults; and insecure attachment is associated with a greater perceived negative caregiving burden in caring for people with Alzheimer disease.

Older Adult Parents and Their Adult Children

- Approximately 80 percent of older adults have living children, many of whom are middle-aged. Increasingly, diversity characterizes the relationships of older parents and their adult children. Adult daughters are more likely than adult sons to be involved in the lives of aging parents. An important task that adult children can perform is to coordinate and monitor services for an aging parent who becomes disabled. Ambivalence can characterize the relationships of adult children with their aging parents.

Great-Grandparenting

- Because of increased longevity, more grandparents today are also great-grandparents. One contribution of great-grandparents is knowledge of family history. One research study found that young adults have closer relationships with grandparents than with great-grandparents.

Friendship

- There is more continuity than change in friendship for older adults.

Social Support and Social Integration

- Social support is linked with improved physical and mental health in older adults. Older adults who participate in more organizations live longer than their counterparts who have low participation rates. Older adults often have fewer peripheral social ties but a strong motivation to spend time in emotionally rewarding relationships with close friends and family members.

Altruism and Volunteering

- Altruism is linked to having a longer life. Volunteering is associated with higher life satisfaction, less depression and anxiety, better physical health, and more positive emotions.

4 Ethnicity, Gender, and Culture Summarize how ethnicity, gender, and culture are linked with aging.

Ethnicity

- Aging minorities cope with the double burden of ageism and racism. Nonetheless, there is considerable variation in the lives of aging minorities.

Gender

- There is stronger evidence that men become more feminine (nurturant, sensitive) as older adults than there is that women become more masculine (assertive). Older women face a double jeopardy of ageism and sexism.

Culture

- Historically, respect for older adults in China and Japan was high, but today their status is more variable. Factors that predict high status for the elderly across cultures range from their valuable knowledge to integration into the extended family.

5 Successful Aging Explain how to age successfully.

- Three patterns of aging are normal, pathological, and successful. Increasingly, the positive aspects of older adulthood are being studied. Factors that are linked with successful aging include an active lifestyle, positive coping skills, good social relationships and support, and the absence of disease.

key **terms**

activity theory 585
ageism 590
convoy model of social
   relations 596

generational inequity 591
integrity versus despair 583

selective optimization with
   compensation theory 586

socioemotional selectivity
   theory 585

key **people**

Paul Baltes 586
Robert Butler 583

Laura Carstensen 585
Erik Erikson 583

Ursula Staudinger 587

section ten

Years following years steal something every day;
At last they steal us from ourselves away.

—Alexander Pope
English Poet, 18th Century

Endings

Our life ultimately ends—when we approach life's grave sustained and soothed with unfaltering trust or rave at the close of day; when at last years steal us from ourselves; and when we are linked to our children's children's children by an invisible cable that runs from age to age. This final section contains one chapter: "Death, Dying, and Grieving."

chapter 20

DEATH, DYING, AND GRIEVING

chapter **outline**

Fuse/Getty Images

Paige Farley-Hackel and her best friend Ruth McCourt teamed up to take McCourt's 4-year-old daughter, Juliana, to Disneyland. They were originally booked on the same flight from Boston to Los Angeles, but McCourt decided to use her frequent flyer miles and go on a different airplane. Both their flights exploded 17 minutes apart after terrorists hijacked them, then rammed them into the twin towers of the World Trade Center in New York City on 9/11/2001.

Forty-five-year-old Ruth McCourt was a homemaker from New London, Connecticut, who had met Farley-Hackel at a day spa she used to own in Boston. McCourt gave up the business when she married, but the friendship between the two women lasted. They often traveled together and shared their passion for reading, cooking, and learning.

Forty-six-year-old Farley-Hackel was a writer, motivational speaker, and spiritual counselor who lived in Newton, Massachusetts. She was looking forward to the airing of the first few episodes of her new radio program, "Spiritually Speaking," and wanted to eventually be on The Oprah Winfrey Show, said her husband, Allan Hackel. Following 9/11, Oprah provided a memorial tribute to Farley-Hackel, McCourt, and Juliana.

topical connections *looking **back***

In the United States, the leading cause of death in infancy is sudden infant death syndrome (SIDS). In early childhood, motor vehicle accidents are the leading cause of death, followed by cancer and cardiovascular disease. Injuries are the leading cause of death during middle and late childhood, and the most common cause of severe injury and death in this period is motor vehicle accidents, either as a pedestrian or as a passenger. The three leading causes of death in adolescence are accidents, suicide, and homicide. Emerging adults have more than twice the mortality rate of adolescents. For many years, heart disease was the leading cause of death in middle adulthood, followed by cancer; however, since 2005 more individuals 45 to 64 years of age in the United States die of cancer, followed by cardiovascular disease. Men have higher mortality rates than women for all of the leading causes of death. Nearly 60 percent of deaths among 65- to 74-year-old U.S. adults are caused by cancer or cardiovascular disease, with cancer now the leading cause of death. However, in the age groups of 75 to 84 and 85 and over, cardiovascular disease is the leading cause of death.

preview

In this final chapter, we will explore many aspects of death and dying. Among the questions that we will ask are these: What characterizes the death system, and what are its cultural and historical contexts? How can death be defined? What are some links between development and death? How do people face their own death? How do individuals cope with the death of someone they love?

1 The Death System and Cultural Contexts

LG1 Describe the death system and its cultural and historical contexts.

The Death System and Its Cultural Variations

Changing Historical Circumstances

Today in the United States, deaths of older adults account for approximately two-thirds of the 2 million deaths that occur each year. Thus, what we know about death, dying, and grieving mainly is based on information about older adults. Youthful death is far less common. What has changed historically in the United States is when, where, and how people die. And how we deal with death is part of our culture. Every culture has a death system, and variations in this death system occur across cultures.

THE DEATH SYSTEM AND ITS CULTURAL VARIATIONS

Robert Kastenbaum (1932–2013) emphasizes that the *death system* in any culture comprises the following components (Kastenbaum, 2009, 2012):

- *People.* Because death is inevitable, everyone is involved with death at some point, either their own death or the death of others. Some individuals have a more systematic role with death, such as those who work in the funeral industry and the clergy, as well as people who work in life-threatening contexts such as firefighters and police officers.

- *Places or contexts.* These include hospitals, funeral homes, cemeteries, hospices, battlefields, and memorials (such as the Vietnam Veterans Memorial wall in Washington, DC).

- *Times.* Death involves times or occasions, such as Memorial Day in the United States and the Day of the Dead in Mexico, which are times to honor those who have died. Also, anniversaries of disasters such as D-Day in World War II, 9/11/2001, and Hurricane Sandy in 2012, as well as the 2004 tsunami in Southeast Asia that took approximately 100,000 lives, are times when those who died are remembered in special ways such as ceremonies.

- *Objects.* Many objects in a culture are associated with death, including caskets and clothes, armbands, and hearses in specific colors. In the United States black is associated with death, but in China white is linked to death.

- *Symbols.* Symbols such as a skull and crossbones, as well as last rites in the Catholic religion and various religious ceremonies, are connected to death.

Cultural variations characterize death and dying (Dierickx & others, 2019; Guilbeau, 2018). To live a full life and die with glory was the prevailing goal of the ancient Greeks. Individuals are more conscious of death in times of war, famine, and plague. Whereas Americans are conditioned from early in life to live as though they were immortal, in much of the world this fiction cannot be maintained. Death crowds the streets of Mumbai in daily overdisplay, as it does in the impoverished towns of Bangladesh. By contrast, in the

In 2017, Hurricane Harvey wreaked havoc on Houston, Texas, causing 125 billion dollars in damages. At least 88 people died as a result of the devastating hurricane.
Steve Gonzales/Houston Chronicle/AP Images

United States it is not uncommon to reach adulthood without having talked about death or experienced the death of someone close.

Most societies throughout history have had philosophical or religious beliefs about death, and most societies have a ritual that deals with death (Ahluwalia & Mohabir, 2019; Kaldahl, 2019). Death may be seen as a punishment for one's sins, an act of atonement, or a judgment from a just God. For some, death means loneliness; for others, death is a quest for happiness. For still others, death represents redemption, a relief from the trials and tribulations of the earthly world. Some embrace death and welcome it; others abhor and fear it. For those who welcome it, death may be seen as the fitting end to a fulfilled life. From this perspective, how we depart from Earth is influenced by how we have lived.

In most societies, death is not viewed as the end of existence—after the biological body has died, the spiritual body is believed to live on (Hamilton & others, 2018; Tiso, 2019). This religious perspective is favored by most Americans as well (Gowan, 2003). Cultural variations in attitudes toward death include belief in reincarnation, which is an important aspect of the Hindu and Buddhist religions. In the Gond culture of India, death is believed to be caused by magic and demons. The members of the Gond culture react angrily to death. In the Tanala culture of Madagascar, death is believed to be caused by natural forces. The members of the Tanala culture show a much more peaceful reaction to death than members of the Gond culture. Figure 1 shows a ritual associated with death in South Korea.

In many ways, we in the United States are death avoiders and death deniers (Norouzieh, 2005). This denial can take many forms, including our persistent search for a fountain of youth through diet, surgery, and other means, as well as the tendency of the funeral industry to gloss over death and fashion lifelike qualities in the dead.

FIGURE 1

A RITUAL ASSOCIATED WITH DEATH. Family memorial day at the national cemetery in Seoul, South Korea.
Ahn Young-joon/AP Images

CHANGING HISTORICAL CIRCUMSTANCES

One historical change involves the age group in which death most often occurs. Two hundred years ago, almost one of every two children died before the age of 10, and one parent died before children grew up. Today, death occurs most often among older adults (Carr, 2009). Life expectancy has increased from 47 years for a person born in 1900 to 79 years for someone born today (U.S. Census Bureau, 2019). Today, the life expectancy in the U.S. for women is 81, for men 76. In 1900, most people died at home, cared for by their family. As our population has aged and become more mobile, greater numbers of older adults die apart from their families (Carr, 2009). In the United States today, more than 80 percent of all deaths occur in institutions or hospitals. The care of a dying older person has shifted away from the family and minimized our exposure to death and its painful surroundings (Gold, 2011).

developmental **connection**

Life Expectancy

The upper boundary of the human life span is 122 years of age (based on the oldest age documented). Connect to "Introduction."

Review *Connect* Reflect

 Describe the death system and its cultural and historical contexts.

Review

- What characterizes the death system in a culture? What are some cultural variations in the death system?
- What are some changing sociohistorical circumstances regarding death?

Connect

- You just read about how changes in life expectancy over time have affected our experience of death. In earlier chapters, what did you learn about life expectancy and the age span that encompasses older adulthood?

Reflect *Your Own Personal Journey of Life*

- How extensively have death and dying been discussed in your family? Explain.

2 Defining Death and Life/Death Issues

 LG2 Evaluate issues in determining death and decisions regarding death.

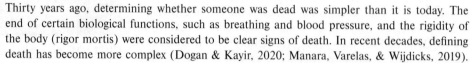

Issues in Determining Death   Decisions Regarding Life. Death, and Health Care

Is there one point in the process of dying that is the point at which death takes place, or is there a gradual transition between life and death? What are some decisions individuals can make about life, death, and health care?

ISSUES IN DETERMINING DEATH

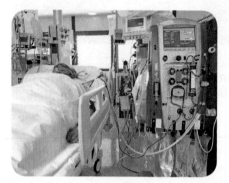

What are some issues in determining death?
Paolo_Toffanin/Getty Images

Thirty years ago, determining whether someone was dead was simpler than it is today. The end of certain biological functions, such as breathing and blood pressure, and the rigidity of the body (rigor mortis) were considered to be clear signs of death. In recent decades, defining death has become more complex (Dogan & Kayir, 2020; Manara, Varelas, & Wijdicks, 2019).

Brain death is a neurological definition of death which states that a person is brain dead when all electrical activity of the brain has ceased for a specified period of time. A flat EEG (electroencephalogram) reading for a specified period of time is one criterion of brain death. The higher portions of the brain often die sooner than the lower portions. Because the brain's lower portions monitor heartbeat and respiration, individuals whose higher brain areas have died may continue to breathe and have a heartbeat (MacDougall & others, 2014). The definition of brain death currently followed by most physicians includes the death of both the higher cortical functions and the lower brain stem functions (Koenig & Kaplan, 2019).

Some medical experts argue that the criteria for death should include only higher cortical functioning. If the cortical death definition were adopted, then physicians could declare that a person is dead when there is no cortical functioning in that person, even though the lower brain stem is functioning. Supporters of the cortical death policy argue that the functions we associate with being human, such as intelligence and personality, are located in the higher cortical part of the brain. They believe that when these functions are lost, the "human being" is no longer alive.

DECISIONS REGARDING LIFE, DEATH, AND HEALTH CARE

In cases of catastrophic illness or accidents, patients might not be able to respond adequately to participate in decisions about their medical care. To prepare for this situation, some individuals make choices earlier.

Advance Care Planning *Advance care planning* refers to the process of patients thinking about and communicating their preferences about end-of-life care (Baran & Sanders, 2019; Freytag & others, 2020). For many patients in a coma, it is not clear what their wishes regarding termination of treatment might be if they still were conscious (Abu Snineh, Camicioli, & Miyasaki, 2017). One study found that advance care planning decreased life-sustaining treatment, increased hospice use, and decreased hospital use (Brinkman-Stoppelenburg, Rietjens, & van der Heide, 2014). Another recent study revealed that completion of an advance directive was associated with a lower probability of receiving life-sustaining treatments (Yen & others, 2017). Recognizing that some terminally ill patients might prefer to die rather than linger in a painful or vegetative state, the organization "Choice in Dying" created the *living will,* a legal document that reflects the patient's advance care planning. A study of older adults found that advance care planning was associated with improved quality of care at the end of life, including less in-hospital death and greater use of hospice care (Bischoff & others, 2013).

Physicians' concerns over malpractice suits and the efforts of people who support the living will concept have produced natural death legislation (Chessa & Moreno, 2019). Laws in all 50 states now accept an *advance directive* such as a living will. An advance directive must be signed while the individual still is able to think clearly (Cattagni Kleiner & others, 2019; Kosar & others, 2020). A study of end-of-life planning revealed that only 15 percent of patients

brain death A neurological definition of death. A person is brain dead when all electrical activity of the brain has ceased for a specified period of time. A flat EEG recording is one criterion of brain death.

18 years of age and older had a living will (Clements, 2009). A research review concluded that physicians have a positive attitude toward advance directives (Coleman, 2013).

Recently, Physician Orders for Life-Sustaining Treatment (POLST), a document that is more specific than previous advance directives, was created (Hickman & others, 2019; Lee & others, 2020). POLST translates treatment preferences into medical orders such as those involving cardiopulmonary resuscitation, extent of treatment, and artificial nutrition via a tube (Mack & Dosa, 2020; Vranas & others, 2020). POLST involves the health-care professional and the patient or surrogate conferring to determine and state the wishes of the patient. In 2019, POLST was available in 40 states.

Euthanasia   Euthanasia ("easy death") is the act of painlessly ending the lives of individuals who are suffering from an incurable disease or severe disability (Van den Eynde, 2020). Sometimes euthanasia is called "mercy killing." Euthanasia also involves the physician or a third party administering the lethal medication. Euthanasia is legal in Belgium, Colombia, the Netherlands, and Luxembourg, but is not legal in the United States. Distinctions are made between two types of euthanasia: passive and active.

- **Passive euthanasia** occurs when a person is allowed to die by withholding available treatment, such as withdrawing a life-sustaining device. For example, this might involve turning off a respirator or a heart-lung machine.
- **Active euthanasia** occurs when death is deliberately induced, as when a lethal dose of a drug is injected.

Technological advances in life-support devices raise the issue of quality of life (Latorre, Schmidt, & Greer, 2020). Nowhere was this more apparent than in the highly publicized case of Terri Schiavo, who suffered severe brain damage related to cardiac arrest and a lack of oxygen to the brain. She went into a coma and spent 15 years in a vegetative state. Across the 15 years, the question of whether passive euthanasia should be implemented or whether she should be kept in the vegetative state with the hope that her condition might change for the better was debated between family members and eventually at a number of levels in the judicial system. At one point toward the end of her life in the early spring of 2005, a court ordered that her feeding tube be removed. However, subsequent appeals led to its reinsertion twice. The feeding tube was removed a third and final time on March 18, 2005, and she died 13 days later.

Should individuals like Terri Schiavo be kept alive in a vegetative state? The trend is toward acceptance of passive euthanasia in the case of terminally ill patients (Barnett, Cantu, & Galvez, 2020).

The inflammatory argument that once equated this practice with suicide rarely is heard today. However, experts do not yet entirely agree on the precise boundaries or the exact mechanisms by which treatment decisions should be implemented (Liao, 2019; Razmetaeva & Sydorenko, 2020). Can a comatose patient's life-support systems be disconnected when the patient has left no written instructions to that effect? Does the family of a comatose patient have the right to overrule the attending physician's decision to continue life-support systems? These questions have no simple or universally agreed-upon answers.

Assisted suicide requires the patient to self-administer the lethal medication and to determine when and where to do this, whereas active euthanasia involves the physician or a third party administering the lethal medication (Dierickx & others, 2020; Friesen, 2020). The most widely publicized assisted suicides were carried out by Jack Kevorkian, a Michigan physician who assisted a number of terminally ill patients in ending their lives. After a series of trials, Kevorkian was convicted of second-degree murder and given a 10- to 15-year sentence. He was released from prison at age 79 for good behavior in June 2007 and promised not to participate in any further assisted suicides. Kevorkian died in 2011 at the age of 83.

Assisted suicide continued to be legal in Belgium, Canada, Finland, Luxembourg, the Netherlands, and Switzerland, as well as just becoming legal in the Australian state of Victoria in 2019. Belgium, Canada, Colombia, and Luxembourg also allow both euthanasia and assisted suicide, although assisted suicide is allowed in Colombia only if the individual has a terminal illness. The United States government has no official policy on assisted suicide and leaves the decision up to each of the states. An increasing number of states now allow

Terri Schiavo (*right*) shown with her mother. *What issues did the Terri Schiavo case raise?*
Stringer/Getty Images

euthanasia The act of painlessly ending the lives of persons who are suffering from incurable diseases or severe disabilities; sometimes called "mercy killing." In euthanasia, the physician or a third party administers the lethal medication (active euthanasia) or withholds life-sustaining treatments.

passive euthanasia Withholding available treatments, such as life-sustaining devices, in order to allow a person to die.

active euthanasia Death induced deliberately, as by injecting a lethal dose of a drug.

assisted suicide Requires the patient to self-administer the lethal medication and to decide when and where to do this.

assisted suicide: California, Colorado, Hawaii, Maine, New Jersey, Oregon, Vermont, and Washington, as well as Washington, DC. Two of these states—New Jersey (2019) and Hawaii (2018)—only recently approved assisted suicide. Assisted suicide involves the physician giving the patient an overdose of muscle relaxants or sedatives to take, which causes a coma and then death. In states where assisted suicide is illegal, the crime is typically considered manslaughter or a felony.

Even in places where assisted suicide is legal, it is not a common practice. A research review revealed that the percentage of physician-assisted deaths ranged from 0.1 to 0.2 percent in the United States and Luxembourg to 1.8 to 2.9 percent in the Netherlands (Steck & others, 2013). In this review, the percentage of assisted suicide cases reported to authorities has increased in recent years, and the individuals who die through assisted suicide are most likely to be males from 60 to 75 years of age.

To what extent do people in the United States think euthanasia and assisted suicide should be legal? A recent Gallup poll found that 69 percent of U.S. adults said euthanasia should be legal, 51 percent said they would consider ending their own lives if faced with a terminal illness, and 50 percent reported that physician-assisted suicide is morally acceptable (Swift, 2016).

Why is euthanasia so controversial? Those in favor of euthanasia argue that death should be calm and dignified, not full of agony, pain, and prolonged suffering. Those against euthanasia stress that it is a criminal act of murder in most states in the United States and in most other countries. Many religious individuals, especially Christians, say that taking a life for any reason is against God's will and is an act of murder.

Needed: Better Care for Dying Individuals

In the United States, the process of dying is often lonely, prolonged, and painful. Dying individuals often get too little or too much care. Scientific advances sometimes have made dying harder by delaying the inevitable. And even though effective painkillers are available, too many people experience severe pain during their last days and months of life (Merchant & others, 2019). One study found that 61 percent of dying patients were in pain in the last year of life and that nearly one-third had symptoms of depression and confusion prior to death (Singer & others, 2015).

Many health-care professionals have not been trained to provide adequate end-of-life care or to understand its importance. One study revealed that in many cases doctors don't give dying patients adequate information about how long they are likely to live or how various treatments will affect their lives (Harrington & Smith, 2008). For example, in this study of patients with advanced cancer, only 37 percent of doctors told patients how long they were likely to live.

Care providers are increasingly interested in helping individuals experience a "good death" (Cain & McCleskey, 2019; Koksvik, 2020). One view is that a good death involves physical comfort, support from loved ones, acceptance, and appropriate medical care (Krishnan, 2017). For some individuals, a good death involves accepting one's impending death and not feeling like a burden to others (Carr, 2009). In a recent review, the three most frequent themes described in articles on a good death involved (1) preference for dying process (94 percent of reports); (2) pain-free status (81 percent); and (3) emotional well-being (64 percent) (Meier & others, 2016).

Recent criticisms of the "good death" concept emphasize that death itself has shifted from being an event at a single point in time to a process that takes place over years and even decades (Pollock & Seymour, 2018). Thus, say the critics, we need to move away from the concept of a "good death" as a specific event for an individual person to a larger vision of a world that not only meets the needs of individuals at their moment of death but also focuses on making their lives better during their final years and decades.

Hospice is a program committed to making the end of life as free from pain, anxiety, and depression as possible (Anchang Price & others, 2020). Traditionally, a hospital's goals have been to cure illness and prolong life (Koksvik, 2020). By contrast, hospice care emphasizes **palliative care,** which involves reducing pain and suffering and helping individuals die with dignity (Norris, Minkowitz, & Scharbach, 2019; Pettis & de Lima, 2020). However, U.S. hospitals recently have rapidly expanded their provision of palliative care. One study found that more than 85 percent of mid- to large-size U.S. hospitals have a palliative care team (Morrison, 2013). Hospice-care professionals work together to treat the dying person's symptoms, make the individual as comfortable as possible, show interest in the patient and his or her family, and help everyone involved cope with death (Mechler & Liantonio, 2019).

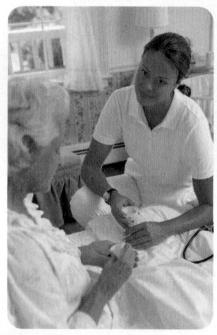

What characterizes hospice care?
Comstock Images/Getty Images

hospice A program committed to making the end of life as free from pain, anxiety, and depression as possible. The goals of hospice contrast with those of a hospital, which are to cure disease and prolong life.

palliative care The type of care emphasized in a hospice, which involves reducing pain and suffering and helping individuals die with dignity.

Kathy McLaughlin, Home Hospice Nurse

Kathy McLaughlin is a home hospice nurse in Alexandria, Virginia. She provides care for individuals with terminal cancer, Alzheimer disease, and other diseases. There currently is a shortage of home hospice nurses in the United States.

McLaughlin says that she has seen too many people dying in pain, away from home, hooked up to needless machines. Reflecting on her work as a home hospice nurse, she comments,

> "I know I'm making a difference. I just feel privileged to get the chance to meet this person who is not going to be around much longer. I want to enjoy the moment with this person. And I want them to enjoy the moment. They have great stories. They are better than novels." (McLaughlin, 2003, p. 1)

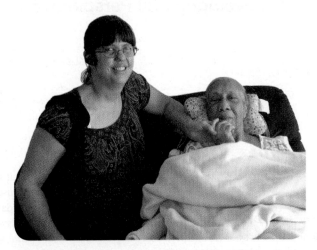

Kathy McLaughlin with her hospice patient Mary Monteiro.
Courtesy of the Family of Mary Monteiro

A primary hospice goal is to bring pain under control and to help dying patients face death in a psychologically healthy way (Flieger, Chui, & Koch-Weser, 2020). The hospice also makes every effort to include the dying individual's family; it is believed that this strategy benefits not only the dying individual but family members as well, probably diminishing their guilt after the death.

The hospice movement has grown rapidly in the United States. More than 1,500 community groups are involved nationally in establishing hospice programs. Hospices are more likely to serve people with terminal cancer than those with other life-threatening conditions (Kastenbaum, 2012). Hospice advocates emphasize the advantages of controlling pain for dying individuals and creating an environment for the patient that is superior to that found in most hospitals (Lazris, 2019). For hospice services to be covered by Medicare, a patient must be deemed by a physician to have six months or fewer to live. Also, some hospice providers will provide care only if the patient has a family caregiver living in the home (or nearby).

Approximately 90 percent of hospice care is provided in patients' homes (Hayslip & Hansson, 2007). In some cases, home-based care is provided by community-based health-care professionals or volunteers; in other cases, home-based care is provided by home health-care agencies or Visiting Nurse Associations (Abrahamson, Davila, & Hountz, 2018). There is a rapidly growing need for competent home health aides in hospice and palliative care (Feldman & others, 2019; Landes & Weng, 2020). Also, some hospice care is provided in free-standing, full-service hospice facilities and in hospice units in hospitals. To read about the work of a home hospice nurse, see *Connecting with Careers*.

Review *Connect* Reflect

 Evaluate issues in determining death and decisions regarding death.

Review
- What are some issues regarding the determination of death?
- What are some decisions to be made regarding life, death, and health care?

Connect
- In this section, you learned that hospices try to provide dying patients with adequate pain relief. What did you learn earlier about older adults that might help them deal with pain better than younger adults?

Reflect *Your Own Personal Journey of Life*
- Have you signed an advance directive (living will)? Why or why not?

3 A Developmental Perspective on Death

LG3 Discuss death and attitudes about it at different points in development.

| Causes of Death | Attitudes Toward Death at Different Points in the Life Span |

Do the causes of death vary across the life span? Do we have different expectations and attitudes about death at different stages of our development?

CAUSES OF DEATH

Death can occur at any point in the human life span. Death can occur during prenatal development through miscarriages or stillborn births. Death can also occur during the birth process or in the first few days after birth, which usually happens because of a birth defect or because infants have not developed adequately to sustain life outside the uterus. Earlier we described *sudden infant death syndrome (SIDS)*, in which infants stop breathing, usually during the night, and die without apparent cause (Horne, 2019). SIDS currently is the leading cause of infant death in the United States, with the risk highest at 2 to 4 months of age (NICHD, 2019).

In childhood, death occurs most often because of accidents or illness. Accidental death in childhood can be the consequence of events such as an automobile accident, drowning, poisoning, fire, or a fall from a high place. Major illnesses that cause death in children are heart disease, cancer, and birth defects.

Compared with childhood, death in adolescence is more likely to occur because of motor vehicle accidents, suicide, and homicide. Many motor vehicle accidents that cause death in adolescence are alcohol-related. We will examine suicide in greater depth shortly.

Older adults are more likely to die from chronic ailments such as heart disease and cancer, whereas younger adults are more likely to die from accidents. Older adults' diseases often incapacitate before they kill, which produces a course of dying that slowly leads to death. Of course, many young and middle-aged adults also die of heart disease, cancer, and other diseases.

ATTITUDES TOWARD DEATH AT DIFFERENT POINTS IN THE LIFE SPAN

The ages of children and adults influence the way they experience and think about death. A mature, adult-like conception of death includes an understanding that death is final and irreversible, that death represents the end of life, and that all living things die. Most researchers have found that as children grow, they develop a more mature approach to death (Yang & Park, 2017).

Childhood Researchers have found that children's conception of death changes as they develop but that even young children begin to develop views of death that are more cognitively advanced than was previously thought (Rosengren, Gutierrez, & Schein, 2014a, b) For example, a recent study found that as early as 4 to 5 years of age, many young children understand the irreversibility of death and that it involves the cessation of mental and physical functioning (Panagiotaki & others, 2018). At some point during middle and late childhood, many children develop more realistic and accurate perceptions of death, such as increasingly viewing its cause as biological in nature (Panagiotaki & others, 2018).

Children's views of death and their experiences with death vary with the contexts and cultures in which they grow up. As we indicated earlier in this chapter, U.S. children are not exposed to death nearly as much as children in some other cultures. In one study, researchers found that higher-SES non-Latino White parents were likely to shield their children from death, while immigrant Mexican American parents thought it was important for their children to learn about death and talk about it (Gutierrez, Rosengren, & Miller, 2014). Further, in a recent study of Mexican children 3.5 to 6.9 years of age, all of the children had a biological understanding of death, while older children were less likely than younger children to endorse that all living things die (Gutierrez & others, 2020). In this study, older children also reported that a child should feel sad following the death of a loved one.

The death of a parent is especially difficult for children (Fearnley & Boland, 2019). When a child's parent dies, the child's school performance and peer relationships often suffer. For some

---

developmental connection

Conditions, Diseases, and Disorders

Nearly 3,000 deaths of infants per year in the United States are attributed to SIDS. Connect to "Physical Development in Infancy."

---

children as well as adults, a parent's death can be devastating and result in a hypersensitivity about death, including a fear of losing others close to the individual. In some cases, loss of a sibling can result in similar negative outcomes (Sood & others, 2006). However, a number of factors, such as relationship quality and cause of death (whether due to an accident, long-standing illness, suicide, or murder, for example), can influence the individual's trajectory following the death of a person close to the individual.

Most psychologists emphasize that honesty is the best strategy in discussing death with children. Treating the concept as unmentionable is thought to be an inappropriate strategy, yet most of us have grown up in a society where death is rarely discussed.

In addition to honesty, the best response to a child's query about death might depend on the child's maturity level (Sheehan & others, 2019). For example, a preschool child requires a less elaborate explanation than an older child. Death can be explained to preschool children in simple physical and biological terms. Actually, what young children need more than elaborate explanations of death is reassurance that they are loved and will not be abandoned. Regardless of children's ages, adults should be sensitive and sympathetic, encouraging them to express their own feelings and ideas.

Also, support programs for parentally bereaved children and their caregivers can be beneficial. In a recent research review, it was concluded that relatively brief interventions can prevent children from developing severe problems such as traumatic grief and mental disorders (Bergman, Axberg, & Hanson, 2017). One of the most successful interventions is the Family Bereavement Program, a 12-session program designed to promote effective parenting and teach coping skills following the death of a parent or caregiver. In a recent experimental study, children and adolescents who participated in the program showed better adjustment up to 6 years following the program (Sandler & others, 2017). In addition, bereaved parents who participated in the program had lower levels of depression, were less likely to have prolonged grief disorders, less likely to have alcohol problems, and more likely to have better coping skills up to 6 years after participating in the program. And in another recent study, the Family Bereavement Program resulted in fewer mental health problems and less service use by bereaved young adults and their parents compared with a control group who did not participate in the program (Sandler & others, 2018).

Adolescence   Deaths of peers, friends, siblings, parents, grandparents, or great-grandparents bring death to the forefront of adolescents' lives. Adolescents develop more abstract conceptions of death than children do. For example, adolescents describe death in terms of darkness, light, transition, or nothingness (Wenestam & Wass, 1987). They also develop religious and philosophical views about the nature of death and whether there is life after death.

Adulthood   A recent study of young adults and middle-aged adults found that women had more difficulty than men in adjusting to the death of a parent and also that women had a more intense grief response to a parent's death (Hayslip, Pruett, & Caballero, 2015). Also, in a recent study of death of a close friend in adulthood, females experienced a greater decline in mental health and impaired socioemotional functioning than males as long as 4 years following the death (Liu, Forbat, & Anderson, 2019).

There is no evidence that a special orientation toward death develops in early adulthood. An increase in consciousness about death accompanies individuals' awareness that they are aging, which usually intensifies in middle adulthood. In our discussion of middle adulthood, we indicated that midlife is a time when adults begin to think more about how much time is left in their lives. Researchers have found that middle-aged adults actually fear death more than do young adults or older adults (Kalish & Reynolds, 1976). Older adults, though, think about death more and talk about it more in conversation with others than do middle-aged and young adults. They also have more direct experience with death as their friends and relatives become ill and die. Older adults are forced to examine the meanings of life and death more frequently than are younger adults.

In old age, one's own death may take on an appropriateness it lacked in earlier years. Increased thinking and conversing about death, and an increased sense of integrity resulting from a positive life review, may help older adults accept death. Older adults are less likely to have unfinished business than are younger adults. They usually do not have children who need to be guided to maturity, their spouses are more likely to be dead, and they are less likely to have work-related projects that require completion. Lacking such anticipations, death may be less emotionally painful to them than to young or middle-aged adults. Even among older adults, however, attitudes toward death vary (Whitbourne & Meeks, 2011).

Three- to nine-year-old children with their mother visiting their father's grave in Kenya. *What are some developmental changes in children's conceptions of death?*
Per-Anders Pettersson/Getty Images

We keep on thinking and rethinking death after we have passed through childhood's hour.

—Robert Kastenbaum
Leading expert on death, dying, and grieving, 20th–21st century

How might older adults' attitudes about death differ from those of younger adults?
Fuse/Corbis/Getty Images

Review *Connect* Reflect

Review
- What are some developmental differences in the causes of death?
- What are some attitudes about death at different points in development?

Connect
- In "Socioemotional Development in Adolescence," you read about adolescent suicide. What aspects of that discussion have helped you understand causes of death and attitudes about death in adolescence?

Reflect *Your Own Personal Journey of Life*
- What is your current attitude about death? Has it changed since you were an adolescent? If so, how?

4 Facing One's Own Death

 LG4 Explain the psychological aspects involved in facing one's own death and the contexts in which people die.

| Kübler-Ross' Stages of Dying | Perceived Control and Denial | The Context in Which People Die |

Sustained and soothed by an
unfaltering trust, approach
thy grave,
Like one who wraps the
drapery of his couch
About him, and lies down to
pleasant dreams.

—WILLIAM CULLEN BRYANT
American poet, 19th century

Knowledge of death's inevitability permits us to establish priorities and structure our time accordingly. As we age, these priorities and structurings change in recognition of diminishing future time. Values concerning the most important uses of time also change. For example, when asked how they would spend the rest of their life if they had only 6 months to live, younger adults described such activities as traveling and accomplishing things they previously had not done; older adults described more inner-focused activities—contemplation and meditation, for example (Kalish & Reynolds, 1976).

Most dying individuals want an opportunity to make some decisions regarding their own life and death (Kastenbaum, 2012). Some individuals want to complete unfinished business; they want time to resolve problems and conflicts and to put their affairs in order.

KÜBLER-ROSS' STAGES OF DYING

We are all born to die, and our lives prepare us for that finality. Dealing with our own death usually becomes the focal point in our life only when we are nearing death, but we live with an awareness of death throughout our lives. However, as indicated earlier in the chapter, people (especially in the United States) often try to avoid thinking about death in any way.

Might there be a sequence of stages we go through as we face death? Elisabeth Kübler-Ross (1969) divided the behavior and thinking of dying persons into five stages: denial and isolation, anger, bargaining, depression, and acceptance.

Denial and isolation is Kübler-Ross' first stage of dying, in which the person denies that death is really going to take place. The person may say, "No, this can't be happening to me. It's not possible." This is a common reaction to a diagnosis of terminal illness. However, denial is usually only a temporary defense. It is eventually replaced with increased awareness when the person is confronted with such matters as financial considerations, unfinished business, and worry about the well-being of surviving family members.

Anger is Kübler-Ross' second stage of dying, in which the dying person recognizes that denial can no longer be maintained. Denial often gives way to anger, resentment, rage, and envy. The dying person's question becomes "Why me?" At this point, the person becomes increasingly difficult to care for as anger may become displaced and projected onto physicians, nurses, family members, and even God. The realization of loss is great, and those who symbolize life, energy, and competent functioning are especially salient targets of the dying person's resentment and jealousy.

denial and isolation Kübler-Ross' first stage of dying, in which the dying person denies that she or he is really going to die.

anger Kübler-Ross' second stage of dying, in which the dying person's denial gives way to anger, resentment, rage, and envy.

bargaining Kübler-Ross' third stage of dying, in which the dying person develops the hope that death can somehow be postponed.

depression Kübler-Ross' fourth stage of dying, in which the dying person comes to accept the certainty of her or his death. A period of depression or preparatory grief may appear.

acceptance Kübler-Ross' fifth stage of dying, in which the dying person develops a sense of peace, an acceptance of her or his fate, and in many cases, a desire to be left alone.

Bargaining is Kübler-Ross' third stage of dying, in which the person develops the hope that death can somehow be postponed or delayed. Some persons enter into a bargaining or negotiation—often with God—as they try to delay their death. Psychologically, the person is saying, "Yes, me, but . . ." In exchange for a few more days, weeks, or months of life, the person promises to lead a reformed life dedicated to worshipping God or serving others.

Depression is Kübler-Ross' fourth stage of dying, in which the dying person comes to accept the certainty of death. At this point, a period of depression or preparatory grief may appear. Dying persons may become silent, refuse visitors, and spend much of their time crying or grieving. This behavior is normal and is an effort to disconnect the self from love objects. Attempts to cheer up the dying person at this stage should be discouraged, says Kübler-Ross, because the dying person has a need to contemplate impending death.

Acceptance is Kübler-Ross' fifth stage of dying, in which the person develops a sense of peace, an acceptance of his or her fate, and in many cases, a desire to be left alone. In this stage, feelings and physical pain may be virtually absent. Kübler-Ross describes this fifth stage as the end of the dying struggle, the final resting stage before death. A summary of Kübler-Ross' dying stages is presented in Figure 2.

What is the current evaluation of Kübler-Ross' theory? According to Robert Kastenbaum (2009, 2012), there are some problems with Kübler-Ross' approach:

- The existence of the five-stage sequence has not been demonstrated by either Kübler-Ross or independent research.
- The five-stage interpretation neglected to consider variations in patients' situations, including degrees of relationship support, specific effects of illness, family obligations, and institutional climate in which they were interviewed.

Despite these shortcomings, however, Kübler-Ross' pioneering efforts were important in calling attention to the needs of people who are attempting to cope with life-threatening illnesses. She did much to encourage attention to the quality of life for dying persons and their families.

Because of the criticisms of Kübler-Ross' stages, some psychologists prefer to describe them not as stages but as potential reactions to dying. At any given moment, a number of emotions may wax and wane. Hope, disbelief, bewilderment, anger, and acceptance may come and go as individuals try to make sense of what is happening to them (Renz & others, 2013).

In facing their own death, some individuals struggle until the end, desperately trying to hang on to their lives. Acceptance of death never comes for them. Some psychologists believe that the harder individuals fight to avoid the inevitable death they face and the more they deny it, the more difficulty they will have in dying peacefully and in a dignified way; other psychologists argue that not confronting death until the end may be adaptive for some individuals (Lifton, 1977).

The extent to which people have found meaning and purpose in their lives is linked with how they approach death (Balon & Morreale, 2016; Kalanithi, 2016). One study revealed that individuals with a chronic, life-threatening illness—congestive heart failure—were trying to find meaning in life (Park & others, 2008). In another study, individuals with less than 3 months to live who had found purpose and meaning in their lives felt the least despair in their final weeks, whereas dying individuals who saw no reason for living were the most distressed and wanted to hasten death (McClain, Rosenfeld, & Breitbart, 2003). In this and other studies, spirituality helped to buffer dying individuals from severe depression (Park, 2012a, b). Researchers also have found that critically ill patients gradually become more religious as they get closer to death (Park, 2010). Further, a recent research review found that interventions that focused on meaning-making coping substantially improved the quality of life for half of the heart failure patients who participated, compared with less than one-third of patients participating in interventions that did not focus on meaning-making coping (Sacco, Leahey, & Park, 2019).

PERCEIVED CONTROL AND DENIAL

Perceived control may work as an adaptive strategy for some older adults who face death. When individuals are led to believe they can influence and control events—such as prolonging their lives—they may become more alert and cheerful. Giving nursing home residents options for control improved their attitudes and increased their longevity (Rodin & Langer, 1977).

Denial also may be a fruitful way for some individuals to approach death. It can be adaptive or maladaptive (Cottrell & Duggleby, 2016). Denial can be used to avoid the destructive impact

FIGURE 2

KÜBLER-ROSS' STAGES OF DYING.
According to Elisabeth Kübler-Ross, we go through five stages of dying: denial and isolation, anger, bargaining, depression, and acceptance. *Does everyone go through these stages, and do we go through them in the same order? Explain.*
Science Photo Library/Getty Images

developmental **connection**

Religion

Religion can fulfill some important psychological needs in older adults, helping them face impending death and accept the inevitable losses that accompany old age. Connect to "Cognitive Development in Late Adulthood."

Man is the only animal that finds his own existence a problem he has to solve and from which he cannot escape. In the same sense man is the only animal who knows he must die.

—Erich Fromm
American psychotherapist, 20th century

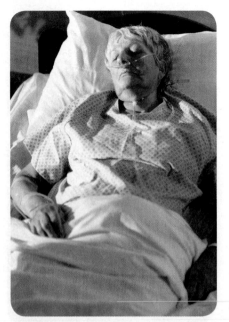

What are some positive and negative aspects of dying at home compared with dying in a hospital?
Photodisc/Getty Images

of shock by delaying the necessity of dealing with one's death. Denial can insulate the individual from having to cope with intense feelings of anger and hurt; however, if denial keeps us from undergoing a life-saving operation, it clearly is maladaptive. Denial is neither good nor bad; its adaptive qualities need to be evaluated on an individual basis.

THE CONTEXTS IN WHICH PEOPLE DIE

For dying individuals, the context in which they die is important. More than 50 percent of Americans die in hospitals and nearly 20 percent die in nursing homes. Some people, though, spend their final days in isolation and fear. An increasing number of people choose to die in the humane atmosphere of hospice care (Roth & Canedo, 2019). A Canadian study found that 71 percent of adults preferred to be at home if they were near death, 15 percent preferred to be in a hospice/palliative care facility, 7 percent preferred to be in a hospital, and only 2 percent preferred to be in a nursing home (Wilson & others, 2013).

Hospitals offer several important advantages to the dying individual; for example, professional staff members are readily available, and the medical technology present may prolong life. But a hospital may not be the best place for many people to die. Most individuals say they would rather die at home (Bannon & others, 2018). Others feel, however, that they will be a burden at home, that space is inadequate there, and that dying at home may alter relationships. Individuals who are facing death also worry about the competency of caregivers and availability of emergency medical treatment if they remain at home.

Review *Connect* Reflect

LG4 Explain the psychological aspects involved in facing one's own death and the contexts in which people die.

Review

- What are Kübler-Ross' five stages of dying? What conclusions can be reached about them?
- What roles do perceived control and denial play in facing one's own death?
- What are the contexts in which people die?

Connect

- In this section, you learned that the extent to which people have found meaning and purpose in their lives is linked with how they approach death. What did Roy Baumeister and Kathleen Vohs say are the four main needs for meaning that guide how people try to make sense of their lives?

Reflect *Your Own Personal Journey of Life*

- How do you think you will psychologically handle facing your own death?

5 Coping with the Death of Someone Else

LG5 Identify ways to cope with the death of another person.

| Communicating with a Dying Person | Grieving | Making Sense of the World | Losing a Life Partner | Forms of Mourning |

Loss can come in many forms in our lives—divorce, a pet's death, being fired from a job—but no loss is greater than that which comes through the death of someone we love and care for, such as a parent, sibling, spouse, relative, or friend. In the ratings of life's stresses that require the most adjustment, death of a spouse is given the highest number. How should we communicate with a dying individual? How can we cope with the death of someone we love?

COMMUNICATING WITH A DYING PERSON

Most psychologists argue that it is best for dying individuals to know that they are dying and for significant others to know they are dying so they can interact and communicate with each

Effective Strategies for Communicating with a Dying Person

Effective strategies for communicating with a dying person include the following suggestions:

- Establish your presence, be at the same eye level; don't be afraid to touch the dying person—dying individuals are often starved for human touch.
- Eliminate distraction—for example, ask if it is okay to turn off the TV. Realize that excessive small talk can be a distraction.
- Dying individuals who are very frail often have little energy. If the dying person you are visiting is very frail, you may not want to visit for very long.
- Don't insist that the dying person feel acceptance about death if the dying person wants to deny the reality of the situation; on the other hand, don't insist on denial if the dying individual indicates acceptance.
- Allow the dying person to express guilt or anger; encourage the expression of feelings.
- Don't be afraid to ask the person about the expected outcome of his or her illness. Discuss alternatives and unfinished business.
- Sometimes dying individuals don't have access to other people. Ask the dying person if there is anyone he or she would like to see that you can contact.
- Encourage the dying individual to reminisce, especially if you have memories in common.

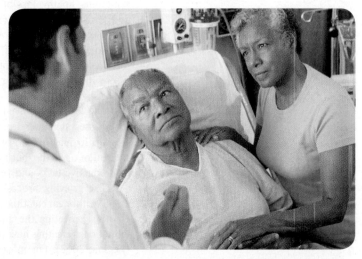

What are some good strategies for communicating with a dying person?
Monkey Business Images/Getty Images

- Talk with the individual when she or he wishes to talk. If this is impossible, make an appointment and keep it.
- Express your regard for the dying individual. Don't be afraid to express love, and don't be afraid to say good-bye.

other on the basis of this mutual knowledge (Banja, 2005). What are some of the advantages of this open awareness for the dying individual? First, dying individuals can close their lives in accord with their own ideas about proper dying. Second, they may be able to complete some plans and projects, to make arrangements for survivors, and to participate in decisions about a funeral and burial. Third, dying individuals have the opportunity to reminisce and to converse with people who have been important to them. And fourth, individuals who know they are dying have more understanding of what is happening within their bodies and what the medical staff is doing for them (Kalish, 1981).

In addition to keeping communication open, some experts reason that conversation should not focus on mental pathology or preparation for death but should focus on strengths of the individual and preparation for the remainder of life. Since external accomplishments are no longer possible at this stage, communication should be directed toward internal growth. Keep in mind also that important support for a dying individual may come not only from mental health professionals but also from nurses, physicians, a spouse, or intimate friends. In *Connecting Development to Life,* you can read further about effective ways to communicate with a dying person.

GRIEVING

Our exploration of grief focuses on dimensions of grieving, the dual-process model of coping with bereavement, and cultural diversity in healthy grieving.

Dimensions of Grieving **Grief** is the emotional numbness, disbelief, separation anxiety, despair, sadness, and loneliness that accompany the loss of someone we love. Grief is not a simple emotional state but rather a complex, evolving process with multiple dimensions (Bonanno & Malgaroli, 2020). In this view, pining for the lost person is one important dimension. Pining

grief The emotional numbness, disbelief, separation anxiety, despair, sadness, and loneliness that accompany the loss of someone we love.

What characterizes prolonged grief disorder?
Lisay/Getty Images

prolonged grief disorder Grief that involves
enduring despair and remains unresolved
over an extended period of time.

or yearning reflects an intermittent, recurrent wish or need to recover the lost person. Another important dimension of grief is separation anxiety, which not only includes pining and preoccupation with thoughts of the deceased person but also focuses on places and things associated with the deceased, as well as crying or sighing (Schiele & others, 2018). Grief may also involve despair and sadness, which include a sense of hopelessness and defeat, depressive symptoms, apathy, loss of meaning for activities that used to involve the person who is gone, and growing desolation (Strada, 2019). Further, another study found that college students who had lost someone close to them in campus shootings and had severe posttraumatic stress symptoms four months after the shootings were more likely to have severe grief one year after the shootings (Smith & others, 2015). And in a recent study, meaning was negatively associated with depression but positively associated with grief in suicide survivors (Scharer & Hibberd, 2020).

The feelings involved in grief occur repeatedly shortly after a loss (Shear, 2012a, b). As time passes, pining and protest over the loss tend to diminish, although episodes of depression and apathy may remain or increase. The sense of separation anxiety and loss may continue to the end of one's life, but most of us emerge from grief's tears, turning our attention once again to productive tasks and regaining a more positive view of life (Mendes, 2016).

The grieving process is more like a roller-coaster ride than an orderly progression of stages with clear-cut time frames. The ups and downs of grief often involve rapidly changing emotions, meeting the challenges of learning new skills, detecting personal weaknesses and limitations, creating new patterns of behavior, and forming new friendships and relationships (Feldon, 2003). For most individuals, grief becomes more manageable over time, with fewer abrupt highs and lows. But many grieving spouses report that even though time has brought some healing, they have never gotten over their loss. They have just learned to live with it. One study found that individuals in the early stages of spousal bereavement are at increased risk for distress in situations with special significance for the couple, such as the late spouse's birthday or a wedding anniversary (Carr & others, 2014).

Long-term grief is sometimes masked and can predispose individuals to become depressed and even suicidal (Miller, 2012). Good family communication can help reduce the incidence of depression and suicidal thoughts. An estimated 80 to 90 percent of survivors experience normal or uncomplicated grief reactions that include sadness and even disbelief or considerable anguish. By 6 months after their loss, they accept it as a reality, are more optimistic about the future, and function competently in their everyday lives.

However, even 6 months after their loss, some individuals have difficulty moving on with their lives and continue feeling numb or detached, believing their life is empty without the deceased, and feeling that the future has no meaning. This type of grief reaction has been referred to as *prolonged or complicated grief* (Ghesquiere & others, 2020; Zhang & others, 2020). It is estimated that approximately 7 to 10 percent of bereaved individuals have this type of grief (Shear, Ghesquiere, & Glickman, 2013). Prolonged grief, in which feelings of despair remain unresolved over an extended period of time, is described as *complicated grief* or **prolonged grief disorder** (Maciejewski & Prigerson, 2017). Prolonged grief usually has negative consequences for physical and mental health (Maccallum & Bryant, 2020). A person who loses someone on whom he or she was emotionally dependent is often at greatest risk for developing prolonged grief (Rodriguez Villar & others, 2012). A recent research review concluded that prolonged grief disorder is more prevalent after the loss of an only child or a death caused by violence (Djelantik & others, 2020).

Recently, there has been a substantial amount of research on complicated or prolonged grief (O'Connor, 2019; Pan, 2020; Stelzer & others, 2020). In a recent meta-analysis, 9.8 percent of adult bereavement cases were classified as characterized by prolonged grief disorder (Lundorff & others, 2017). In this study, the older individuals were, the more likely prolonged grief disorder was present. In another study, prolonged grief was more likely to occur when individuals had lost their spouse, lost a loved one unexpectedly, or spent time with the deceased every day in the last week of the person's life (Fujisawa & others, 2010). Also, a recent 7-year longitudinal study of older adults found that those who were experiencing prolonged grief had greater cognitive decline than their counterparts with normal grief (Perez & others, 2018). Another recent study found that during the first two years of bereavement for family caregivers of terminally ill cancer patients, prolonged grief disorder preceded the onset of major depressive disorder (Tsai & others, 2020). Further, another recent study revealed that individuals with complicated grief had a higher level of the personality trait neuroticism (Goetter & others, 2019). And recent research indicated that cognitive-behavioral therapy reduced prolonged grief symptoms (Bartl & others, 2018; Lichtenthal & others, 2019).

Complicated grief or prolonged grief disorder was considered for possible inclusion in DSM-V, the psychiatric classification system for mental health disorders (Bonanno & Malgaroli, 2020; Bryant, 2012, 2013). Although it ended up not being included as a psychiatric disorder, it was described in an Appendix (American Psychiatric Association, 2013). The argument for not including complicated grief or prolonged grief as a psychiatric disorder was based on concerns that normal grieving would be viewed as a medical condition (Breen & others, 2015).

Another type of grief is *disenfranchised grief,* which describes an individual's grief over a deceased person that is a socially ambiguous loss and can't be openly mourned or supported (Baker, Norris, & Cherneva, 2020; Garcini & others, 2020a). Examples of disenfranchised grief include a relationship that isn't socially recognized such as an ex-spouse, a hidden loss such as an abortion, and circumstances of the death that are stigmatized such as death because of AIDS. Disenfranchised grief may intensify an individual's grief because the feelings cannot be publicly acknowledged. This type of grief may be hidden or repressed for many years, only to be reawakened by later deaths.

A death can sometimes bring out the best in people as they provide support and caring for the grieving person, but in other cases a death can bring out the worst in people (Lightner & Hathaway, 1990). When death brings out the best, mourners feel recognized and consoled, touched by others' sympathy, and shored up by their kindness. Consider Jennifer Block's experience. After her husband died, her best friend encouraged her to get out and do things. The friend called Jennifer every day and took her out for ice cream, on walks, and to community events. Jennifer says that she will never forget her friend's support and caring.

Sometimes, however, friends may say and do the wrong things when someone dies (Lightner & Hathaway, 1990). Their grieving friend may feel slighted, insulted, disappointed, and alone when this happens. Perhaps a friend disappears from sight or makes an inappropriate or cruel remark, such as "I thought you two were not getting along that well anyway." Consider Martha Cooper's experience. When her husband died, her friend told her to forget that part of her life because it was over. Martha was terribly disappointed at her friend's lack of empathy. As Martha remarked, you can't just forget about someone who was a part of your life for 45 years.

Dual-Process Model of Coping with Bereavement

The **dual-process model** of coping with bereavement has two main dimensions: (1) loss-oriented stressors, and (2) restoration-oriented stressors (Stroebe & others, 2017a, b; Stroebe & Schut, 2015, 2017). Loss-oriented stressors focus on the deceased individual and can include grief work and both positive and negative reappraisals of the loss. A positive reappraisal of the loss might include acknowledging that death brought relief at the end of suffering, whereas a negative reappraisal might involve yearning for the loved one and ruminating about the death. Restoration-oriented stressors involve the secondary stressors that emerge as indirect outcomes of bereavement (Mulligan & Karel, 2018). They can include a changing identity (such as from "wife" to "widow") and mastering specific skills (such as dealing with finances). Restoration rebuilds "shattered assumptions about the world and one's own place in it."

In the dual-process model, effective coping with bereavement often involves an oscillation between coping with loss and coping with restoration (Cantwell-Bartl, 2018; Stroebe & others, 2017a, b). Earlier models often emphasized a sequence of coping with loss through such strategies as grief work as an initial phase, followed by restoration efforts. However, in the dual-process model, coping with loss and engaging in restoration can be carried out concurrently (Richardson, 2007). According to this model, the person coping with death might be involved in grief group therapy while settling the affairs of the loved one. Oscillation might occur in the short term during a particular day as well as across weeks, months, and even years. Although loss and restoration coping can occur concurrently, over time there often is an initial emphasis on coping with loss followed by greater emphasis on restoration (Milberg & others, 2008).

Recently, a variation of the dual-process model has been developed for families (Stroebe & Schut, 2015, 2017; Stroebe & others, 2017a, b). The original model focused mainly on the bereaved individual, while the revised model recognizes that many people do not grieve in isolation—most do so with immediate family members and relatives who also are bereaved by the loss. This recent extension of the dual-process model also focuses on such matters as

dual-process model A model of coping with bereavement that emphasizes oscillation between two dimensions: (1) loss-oriented stressors, and (2) restoration-oriented stressors.

reduced finances, legal consequences, and changed family relationships that must be dealt with, and seeks to integrate intrapersonal and interpersonal coping.

The dual-process model has been used as a conceptual framework in a number of studies involving grief and bereavement (Lundberg & others, 2018; Ross & others, 2018). In one recent study, parents' lives following their infant's death involved oscillating among various coping strategies (Currie & others, 2019). In another recent study following spousal bereavement, individuals who engaged more in restoration-oriented coping were better adjusted both early and later in the bereavement process than those who relied more on loss-oriented coping (Lundorff & others, 2019). And a recent research review concluded that the dual-process model accurately represents the bereavement experience and is effective in describing how individuals cope (Fiore, 2020).

Coping and Type of Death
The impact of death on surviving individuals is strongly influenced by the circumstances under which the death occurred (Liu, Forbat, & Anderson, 2019). Deaths that are sudden, untimely, violent, or traumatic are likely to have more intense and prolonged effects on surviving individuals and make the coping process more difficult for them (Currie & others, 2019). Such deaths often are accompanied by post-traumatic stress disorder (PTSD) symptoms, such as intrusive thoughts, flashbacks, nightmares, sleep disturbance, problems in concentrating, and other difficulties (Lubens & Silver, 2019). The death of a child can be especially devastating and extremely difficult for parents to cope with (Wang & others, 2019).

How might grieving vary across individuals and cultures?
Xinhua/eyevine/Redux

Cultural Diversity in Healthy Grieving
Some approaches to grieving emphasize the importance of breaking bonds with the deceased and returning to autonomous lifestyles. People who persist in holding on to the deceased are believed to be in need of therapy. However, doubt has been cast on whether this recommendation to break bonds is always the best therapeutic advice (Reisman, 2001).

Analyses of non-Western cultures suggest that beliefs about maintaining bonds with the deceased vary extensively. Maintenance of ties with the deceased is accepted and sustained in the religious rituals of Japan. Among the Hopi of Arizona, the deceased are forgotten as quickly as possible and life is carried on as usual. Their funeral ritual concludes with a break-off between mortals and spirits. The diversity of grieving is nowhere more clear than in two Muslim societies—one in Egypt, the other in Bali. In Egypt, the bereaved are encouraged to dwell at length on their grief, surrounded by others who relate similarly tragic accounts and express their own sorrow. By contrast, in Bali, the bereaved are encouraged to laugh and be joyful.

In sum, people grieve in a variety of ways. The diverse grieving patterns are culturally embedded practices. Thus, there is no one correct, ideal way to grieve. There are many different ways to feel about a deceased person and no set series of stages that the bereaved must pass through to become well adjusted. The stoic widower may need to cry out over his loss at times. The weeping widow may need to put her husband's wishes aside as she becomes the financial manager of her estate. Healthy coping with the death of a loved one involves growth, flexibility, and appropriateness within a cultural context.

MAKING SENSE OF THE WORLD

Not only do many individuals who face death search for meaning in life, so do many bereaved individuals (Bottomley & others, 2019; Breen & others, 2018). One beneficial aspect of grieving is that it can stimulate people to try to make sense of their world (Yang & Lee, 2020). After a death, bereaved persons often go over again and again all of the events that led up to the death. In the days and weeks after the death, the closest family members share experiences with each other, sometimes reminiscing over family experiences. In one study, women who became widowed in midlife were challenged by the crisis of their husband's death to examine meaningful directions for their lives (Danforth & Glass, 2001). Another study found that mourners who expressed positive themes of hope showed better adjustment than those who focused on negative themes of pain and suffering (Gamino & Sewell, 2004). And one study revealed that finding meaning in the death of a spouse was linked to a lower level of anger during bereavement (Kim, 2009). One study examined meaning-making following a child's death (Meert & others, 2015). From 8 to 20 weeks following the child's death, the child's intensive care physician conducted a bereavement meeting with 53 parents of 35 children who had died. One meeting was held with each family. Four meaning-making processes were identified in the meetings: (1) sense making (seeking biomedical explanations for the death, revisiting parents' prior decisions and roles, and assigning blame); (2) benefit finding (exploring possible positive consequences of the death, such as ways to help others; providing feedback to the hospital; and making donations); (3) continuing bonds (reminiscing about the child, sharing photographs, and participating in community events to honor the child); and (4) identity reconstruction (changes in the parents' sense of self, including changes in relationships, work, and home).

When a death is caused by an accident or a disaster, the effort to make sense of it is pursued more vigorously (Davis & others, 2019; Park, 2016). As added pieces of news come trickling in, they are integrated into the puzzle. The bereaved want to put the death into a perspective that they can understand—divine intervention, a curse from a neighboring tribe, a logical sequence of cause and effect, or whatever it may be. A study of more than 1,000 college students found that making sense was an important factor in their grieving of a violent loss by accident, homicide, or suicide (Currier, Holland, & Neimeyer, 2006).

These restaurant workers, who lost their jobs on 9/11/01, made a bittersweet return by establishing a New York restaurant they call their own. Colors, named for the many nationalities and ethnic groups among its owners, is believed to be the city's first cooperative restaurant. World-famous restaurant Windows on the World was destroyed and 73 workers killed when the Twin Towers were destroyed by terrorists. The former Windows survivors at the new venture planned to split 60 percent of the profits between themselves and to donate the rest to a fund to open other cooperative restaurants.
Thomas Hinton/Splash News/Newscom

LOSING A LIFE PARTNER

In 2017, 33 percent of U.S. women 65 years and older were widowed, compared with only 11 percent of their male counterparts (Administration on Aging, 2018). Thus, approximately three times as many women as men are widowed. Those left behind after the death of an intimate partner often suffer profound grief, die earlier than expected, and may endure financial loss, loneliness, increased physical illness, and psychological disorders, including depression (Holm, Berland, & Severinsson, 2019). In a recent cross-cultural study conducted in the United States, England, Europe, Korea, and China, depression peaked in the first year of widowhood for men and women (Jadhav & Weir, 2018). In this study, widowed women recovered to levels similar to married individuals in all countries, but widowed men continued to have high levels of depression 6 to 10 years post-bereavement everywhere except in Europe. Also, a recent research review of widowed Latinos found that risk factors for diminished well-being were being a male, financial strain, cultural stressors, having an undocumented legal status, experiencing widowhood at a younger age, and having poor physical health (Garcini & others, 2020b).

In a recent meta-analysis of mental disorders in widows, it was concluded that the two most prevalent conditions were depressive disorders and anxiety disorders (Blanner Kristiansen & others, 2019). In another study, becoming widowed was associated with a 48 percent higher risk of mortality (Sullivan & Fenelon, 2014). If the spouse's death was unexpected, the mortality risk for the surviving spouse is higher for men but not for women.

Surviving spouses seek to cope with the loss of their spouse in various ways (Yopp & others, 2019; Yu & others, 2020). In one study, widowed individuals were more likely to intensify their religious and spiritual beliefs following the death of a spouse, and this increase was linked with a lower level of grief (Brown & others, 2004). In another study, widows were more likely to use positive reframing, active distraction, help-seeking, and turning to God for strength, while widowers were more likely to use avoidant strategies and seek connection with their late spouse (Carr, 2020). Another study revealed that finding meaning in the death of a spouse was linked to a lower level of anger during bereavement (Kim, 2009). And researchers have found that widowed persons who did not expect to be reunited with their loved ones in the afterlife reported more depression, anger, and intrusive thoughts at 6 and 18 months after their loss (Carr & Sharp, 2014). The poorer and less educated they are, the lonelier they tend to be. The bereaved are also at increased risk for many physical illnesses (Jadhav & Weir, 2018).

Becoming widowed is likely to be especially difficult for individuals who have been happily married for a number of decades. In such circumstances, losing their spouse, who may also

developmental **connection**
Stress
Meaning-making coping involves drawing on beliefs, values, and goals to change the meaning of a stressful situation, especially in times of chronic stress such as when a loved one dies. Connect to "Physical and Cognitive Development in Middle Adulthood."

developmental **connection**
Religion
Religious participation is positively linked to health and longevity. Connect to "Physical and Cognitive Development in Middle Adulthood."

A widow holds the photo of her husband who was killed in Afghanistan. *What are some factors that are related to the adjustment of a widow after the death of her husband?*
Peter Power/Toronto Star/Getty Images

developmental **connection**

Community and Culture

For older adults, social support is linked with a reduction in the symptoms of disease and increased longevity. Connect to "Socioemotional Development in Late Adulthood."

have been their best friend and the person with whom they lived a deeply connected life, can be an extremely emotional event that is difficult to cope with.

Optimal adjustment after a death depends on several factors (Chen, Chow, & Tang, 2020; Yang, 2020). For example, researchers have found that religiosity and coping skills are related to well-being following the loss of a spouse in late adulthood (Jones & others, 2019).

Also, for both widows and widowers, social support helps them adjust to the death of a spouse (Holm, Berland, & Severinsson, 2019; King, Carr, & Taylor, 2020). The Widow-to-Widow program, begun in the 1960s, provides support for newly widowed women. Volunteer widows reach out to other widows, introducing them to others who may have similar problems, leading group discussions, and organizing social activities. The program has been adopted by the AARP and disseminated throughout the United States as the Widowed Persons Service. The model has since been adopted by numerous community organizations to provide support for people who are going through a difficult transition. Other widow support groups also are often beneficial in reducing depression in bereaved spouses (Collins, 2018; Recksiedler & others, 2018).

FORMS OF MOURNING

One decision facing the bereaved is what to do with the body. In the United States in 2018, 53.1 percent of deaths were followed by cremation—a significant increase from a cremation rate of 14 percent in 1985 and 27 percent in 2000 (Cremation Association of North America, 2019). In 2018, in Canada 72.1 percent of deaths were followed by cremation. Projections indicate that in 2023, 59.4 percent of U.S. deaths will be followed by cremation while the rate in Canada will increase to 76.9 percent. Cremation is more popular in the Pacific region of the United States and less popular in the South. Cremation also is more popular in Canada than in the United States and most popular of all in Japan and many other Asian countries.

The funeral is an important aspect of mourning in many cultures. In the United States, the trend is away from public funerals and displaying the body in an open casket and toward private funerals followed by a memorial ceremony (Beard & Burger, 2017, 2018).

The funeral industry in the United States has been a focus of controversy in recent years (Beard & Burger, 2017, 2018). Funeral directors and their supporters argue that the funeral provides a form of closure to the relationship with the deceased, especially when there is an open casket. Their critics claim that funeral directors are just trying to make money and that embalming is grotesque. One way to avoid being exploited during bereavement is to purchase funeral arrangements in advance, but many people are reluctant to do this.

In some cultures, a ceremonial meal is shared after a death; in others, a black armband is worn by bereaved family members for one year following a death. Cultures vary in how they practice mourning. Two of those cultures are the Amish and traditional Judaism (Worthington, 1989).

How significantly has the frequency of cremation changed in recent years in the United States and Canada?
Anze Furlan/psgtproductions/Getty Images

(*Left*) A widow leading a funeral procession in the United States. (*Right*) A crowd gathered at a cremation ceremony in Bali, Indonesia, balancing decorative containers on their heads.
(*Left*) Russell Underwood/Corbis/Getty Images; (*right*) Paul Almasy/Corbis/VCG/Getty Images

The Amish are a conservative Christian group with approximately 80,000 members in the United States, Ontario, and several small settlements in South and Central America. The Amish live in a family-oriented society in which family and community support are essential for survival. Today, they live at the same unhurried pace as that of their ancestors, using horses instead of cars and facing death with the same steadfast faith as their forebears. At the time of death, close neighbors assume the responsibility of notifying others of the death. The Amish community handles virtually all aspects of the funeral.

The funeral service is held in a barn in the warmer months and in a house during colder months. Calm acceptance of death, influenced by a deep religious faith, is an integral part of the Amish culture. Following the funeral, a high level of support is given to the bereaved family for at least a year. Visits to the family, special scrapbooks and handmade items for family members, new work projects started for the widow, and quilting days that combine fellowship and productivity are among the supports given to the bereaved family. A profound example of the Amish culture's religious faith and acceptance of death occurred after Charles Roberts shot and killed five Amish schoolgirls and then apparently took his own life in October 2006 in Bart Township, Pennsylvania. Soon after the murders and suicide, members of the Amish community visited his widow and offered their support and forgiveness.

The family and community also have specific and important roles in mourning in traditional Judaism. The program of mourning is divided into graduated time periods, each with its appropriate practices. The observance of these practices is required of the spouse and the immediate blood relatives of the deceased. The first period is *aninut,* the period between death and burial. The next two periods make up *avelut,* or mourning proper. The first of these is *shivah,* a period of seven days, which commences with the burial. It is followed by *sheloshim,* the 30-day period following the burial, including shivah. At the end of *sheloshim,* the mourning process is considered over for all but one's parents. For parents, mourning continues for 11 months, although observances are minimal.

The seven-day period of the shivah is especially important in traditional Judaism. The mourners, sitting together as a group through an extended period, have an opportunity to project their feelings to the group as a whole. Visits from others during shivah may help the mourners deal with feelings of guilt. After shivah, the mourners are encouraged to resume normal social interaction. In fact, it is customary for the mourners to walk together a short distance as a symbol of their return to society. In its entirety, the elaborate mourning system of traditional Judaism is designed to promote personal growth and to reintegrate bereaved individuals into the community.

(*Top*) A funeral procession of horse-drawn buggies on their way to the burial of five young Amish girls who were murdered in October 2006. A remarkable aspect of their mourning involved the outpouring of support and forgiveness they gave to the widow of the murderer. (*Bottom*) Meeting in a Jewish graveyard.
(*Top*) Glenn Fawcett/Baltimore Sun; (*bottom*) Robert Mulder/Corbis/ Getty Images

Review *Connect* Reflect

 LG5 Identify ways to cope with the death of another person.

Review

- What are some strategies for communicating with a dying person?
- What is the nature of grieving?
- How is making sense of the world a beneficial outcome of grieving?
- What are some characteristics and outcomes of losing a life partner?
- What are some forms of mourning? What is the nature of a funeral?

Connect

- In this section, we learned that one advantage of knowing you are dying is that you have the opportunity to reminisce. Which of Erikson's stages of development involves reflecting on the past and either piecing together a positive review or concluding that one's life has not been well spent?

Reflect *Your Own Personal Journey of Life*

- What are considered appropriate forms of mourning in the culture in which you live?

reach your **learning goals**

Death, Dying, and Grieving

1 The Death System and Cultural Contexts

 Describe the death system and its cultural and historical contexts.

The Death System and Its Cultural Variations

Changing Historical Circumstances

- In Kastenbaum's view, every culture has a death system that involves these components: people, places, times, objects, and symbols. Most cultures do not view death as the end of existence—spiritual life is thought to continue. Most societies throughout history have had philosophical or religious beliefs about death, and most societies have rituals that deal with death. The United States has been described as more of a death-denying and death-avoiding culture than most cultures.

- When, where, and why people die have changed historically. Today, death occurs most often among older adults. More than 80 percent of all deaths in the United States now occur in a hospital or other institution; our exposure to death in the family has been minimized.

2 Defining Death and Life/ Death Issues

 Evaluate issues in determining death and decisions regarding death.

Issues in Determining Death

Decisions Regarding Life, Death, and Health Care

- Twenty-five years ago, determining whether someone was dead was simpler than it is today. Brain death is a neurological definition of death which states that a person is brain dead when all electrical activity of the brain has ceased for a specified period of time. Medical experts debate whether this cessation should include the higher and lower brain functions or just the higher cortical functions. Currently, most physicians define brain death as the death of both the higher cortical functions and the lower brain stem functions.

- Decisions regarding life, death, and health care can involve creating a living will, considering the possibility of euthanasia, and arranging for hospice care. Living wills and advance directives are increasingly used.

- Euthanasia ("mercy killing") is the act of painlessly ending the life of a person who is suffering from an incurable disease or disability. Distinctions are made between active and passive euthanasia. Assisted suicide involves the patient self-administering the lethal medication. Hospice care emphasizes reducing pain and suffering rather than prolonging life.

3 A Developmental Perspective on Death

 Discuss death and attitudes about it at different points in development.

Causes of Death

Attitudes Toward Death at Different Points in the Life Span

- Although death is more likely to occur in late adulthood, death can come at any point in development. In children and younger adults, death is more likely to occur because of accidents or illness; in older adults, death is more likely to occur because of chronic illnesses such as heart disease or cancer.

- Infants do not have a concept of death. Preschool children also have little concept of death. Preschool children sometimes blame themselves for a person's death.

- In the elementary school years, children develop a more realistic orientation toward death. Most psychologists argue that honesty is the best strategy for helping children cope with death.

- Death may be glossed over in adolescence. Adolescents have more abstract, philosophical views of death than children do.

- There is no evidence that a special orientation toward death emerges in early adulthood. Middle adulthood is a time when adults show a heightened consciousness about death and death anxiety. Older adults often show less death anxiety than middle-aged adults, but older adults are more likely to experience bereavement and tend to converse about death more. Attitudes about death may vary considerably among adults of any age.

4 Facing One's Own Death

 Explain the psychological aspects involved in facing one's own death and the contexts in which people die.

Kübler-Ross' Stages of Dying

Perceived Control and Denial

The Contexts in Which People Die

- Kübler-Ross proposed five stages of dying: denial and isolation, anger, bargaining, depression, and acceptance. Not all individuals go through the same sequence.

- Perceived control and denial may work together as an adaptive orientation for the dying individual. Denial can be adaptive or maladaptive, depending on the circumstances.

- The fact that most deaths in the United States occur in hospitals has advantages and disadvantages. Most individuals say they would rather die at home, but they are concerned that they will be a burden to family members and they worry about the lack of medical care at home.

5 Coping with the Death of Someone Else

 Identify ways to cope with the death of another person.

Communicating with a Dying Person

Grieving

Making Sense of the World

- Most psychologists recommend open communication with the dying. Communication should not dwell on mental pathology or preparation for death but should emphasize the dying person's strengths.

- Grief is the emotional numbness, disbelief, separation anxiety, despair, sadness, and loneliness that accompany the loss of someone we love. Grief is multidimensional and in some cases may last for years. Prolonged grief involves enduring despair that is still unresolved after an extended period of time.

- In the dual-process model of coping with bereavement, oscillation occurs between two dimensions: (1) loss-oriented stressors and (2) restoration-oriented stressors. Grief and coping vary with the type of death. There are cultural variations in grieving.

- The grieving process may stimulate individuals to strive to make sense of their world. When a death is caused by an accident or disaster, the effort to make sense of it is pursued more vigorously.

- The death of an intimate partner often leads to profound grief. The bereaved are at risk for many health problems, although there are variations in the distress experienced by a surviving spouse. Social support benefits widows and widowers.

- Forms of mourning vary across cultures. In the United States and many other countries today, cremation is chosen more often than burial. An important aspect of mourning in many cultures is the funeral. In recent years, the funeral industry has been the focus of controversy. In some cultures, a ceremonial meal is shared by mourners after a death.

key **terms**

acceptance 616	bargaining 616	dual-process model 621	palliative care 612
active euthanasia 611	brain death 610	euthanasia 611	passive euthanasia 611
anger 616	denial and isolation 616	grief 619	prolonged grief disorder 620
assisted suicide 611	depression 616	hospice 612	

key **people**

Robert Kastenbaum 608   Elisabeth Kübler-Ross 616

glossary

A

A-not-B error Error that occurs when infants make the mistake of selecting the familiar hiding place (A) rather than the new hiding place (B) of an object.

acceptance Kübler-Ross' fifth stage of dying, in which the dying person develops a sense of peace, an acceptance of her or his fate, and in many cases, a desire to be left alone.

accommodation Piagetian concept of adjusting schemes to fit new information and experiences.

active euthanasia Death induced deliberately, as by injecting a lethal dose of a drug.

active (niche-picking) genotype-environment correlations Correlations that exist when children seek out environments they find compatible and stimulating.

activity theory The theory that the more active and involved older adults are, the more likely they are to be satisfied with their lives.

addiction A pattern of behavior characterized by an overwhelming involvement with using a drug and a preoccupation with securing its supply.

adolescent egocentrism The heightened self-consciousness of adolescents.

adoption study A study in which investigators seek to discover whether, in behavior and psychological characteristics, adopted children are more like their adoptive parents, who provided a home environment, or more like their biological parents, who contributed their heredity. Another form of the adoption study compares adoptive and biological siblings.

aerobic exercise Sustained exercise (such as jogging, swimming, or cycling) that stimulates heart and lung activity.

affectionate love In this type of love, also called companionate love, an individual desires to have the other person near and has a deep, caring affection for the other person.

affordances Opportunities for interaction offered by objects that fit within our capabilities to perform functional activities.

afterbirth The third stage of birth, when the placenta, umbilical cord, and other membranes are detached and expelled.

ageism Prejudice against others because of their age, especially prejudice against older adults.

Alzheimer disease A progressive, irreversible brain disorder characterized by a gradual deterioration of memory, reasoning, language, and eventually, physical function.

amnion The part of the prenatal life-support system that consists of a sac containing a clear fluid in which the developing embryo floats.

amygdala The region of the brain that is the seat of emotions.

androgyny The presence of positive masculine and feminine characteristics in the same person.

anger Kübler-Ross' second stage of dying, in which the dying person's denial gives way to anger, resentment, rage, and envy.

anger cry A variation of the basic cry, with more excess air forced through the vocal cords.

animism The belief that inanimate objects have lifelike qualities and are capable of action.

anorexia nervosa An eating disorder that involves the relentless pursuit of thinness through starvation.

anxious attachment style An attachment style that describes adults who demand closeness, are less trusting, and are more emotional, jealous, and possessive.

Apgar Scale A widely used method of assessing the health of newborns at one and five minutes after birth. The Apgar Scale evaluates an infant's heart rate, respiratory effort, muscle tone, body color, and reflex irritability.

aphasia A loss or impairment of language ability caused by brain damage.

arthritis Inflammation of the joints accompanied by pain, stiffness, and movement problems; this disease is especially common in older adults.

Asperger syndrome A relatively mild autism spectrum disorder in which the child has relatively good verbal language skills, milder nonverbal language problems, and a restricted range of interests and relationships.

assimilation Piagetian concept of using existing schemes to deal with new information or experiences.

assisted suicide Requires the patient to self-administer the lethal medication and to decide when and where to do this.

attachment A close emotional bond between two people.

attention The focusing of mental resources on select information.

attention deficit hyperactivity disorder (ADHD) A disability in which children consistently show one or more of the following characteristics: (1) inattention, (2) hyperactivity, and (3) impulsivity.

authoritarian parenting A restrictive, punitive style in which parents exhort the child to follow their directions and to respect their work and effort. The authoritarian parent places firm limits and controls on the child and allows little verbal exchange. Authoritarian parenting is associated with children's social incompetence.

authoritative parenting A parenting style in which parents encourage their children to be independent but still place limits and controls on their actions. Extensive verbal give-and-take is allowed, and parents are warm and nurturing toward the child. Authoritative parenting is associated with children's social competence.

autism spectrum disorders (ASD) Conditions ranging from the severe disorder labeled autistic disorder to the milder disorder called Asperger syndrome. Children with these disorders are characterized by problems in social interaction, verbal and nonverbal communication, and repetitive behaviors.

autistic disorder A severe autism spectrum disorder that has its onset in the first three years of life and includes deficiencies in social relationships, abnormalities in communication, and restricted, repetitive, and stereotyped patterns of behavior.

autonomous morality In Piaget's theory, older children (about 10 years of age and older) become aware that rules and laws are created by people and that in judging an action one should consider the actor's intentions as well as the consequences.

average children Children who receive an average number of both positive and negative nominations from peers.

avoidant attachment style An attachment style that describes adults who are hesitant about getting involved in romantic relationships and once in a relationship tend to distance themselves from their partner.

B

bargaining Kübler-Ross' third stage of dying, in which the dying person develops the hope that death can somehow be postponed.

basic cry A rhythmic pattern usually consisting of a cry, a briefer silence, a shorter inspiratory whistle that is higher pitched than the main cry, and then a brief rest before the next cry.

behavior genetics The field that seeks to discover the influence of heredity and environment on individual differences in human traits and development.

Big Five factors of personality Openness to experience, conscientiousness, extraversion, agreeableness, and neuroticism (emotional stability).

binge eating disorder (BED) Involves frequent binge eating but without compensatory behavior like the purging that characterizes bulimics.

biological processes Changes in an individual's physical nature.

blastocyst The inner layer of cells that develops during the germinal period. These cells later develop into the embryo.

bonding The formation of a close connection, especially a physical bond, between parents and their newborn in the period shortly after birth.

brain death A neurological definition of death. A person is brain dead when all electrical activity of the brain has ceased for a specified period of time. A flat EEG recording is one criterion of brain death.

Brazelton Neonatal Behavioral Assessment Scale (NBAS) A measure that is used in the first month of life to assess the newborn's neurological development, reflexes, and reactions to people and objects.

breech position The baby's position in the uterus that causes the buttocks to be the first part to emerge from the vagina.

Broca's area An area in the brain's left frontal lobe that is involved in speech production.

Bronfenbrenner's ecological theory Bronfenbrenner's environmental systems theory that focuses on five environmental systems: microsystem, mesosystem, exosystem, macrosystem, and chronosystem.

bulimia nervosa An eating disorder in which the individual consistently follows a binge-and-purge pattern.

C

care perspective The moral perspective of Carol Gilligan, which views people in terms of their connectedness with others and emphasizes interpersonal communication, relationships with others, and concern for others.

case study An in-depth look at a single individual.

cataracts A thickening of the lens of the eye that causes vision to become cloudy, opaque, and distorted.

cellular clock theory Leonard Hayflick's theory that the maximum number of times that human cells can divide is about 75 to 80. As we age, our cells have less capacity to divide.

centration Focusing attention on one characteristic to the exclusion of all others.

cephalocaudal pattern Developmental sequence in which the earliest growth always occurs at the top—the head—with physical growth in size, weight, and feature differentiation gradually working from top to bottom.

cesarean delivery Surgical procedure in which the baby is removed from the mother's uterus through an incision made in her abdomen.

child-centered kindergarten Education that involves the whole child by considering both the child's physical, cognitive, and socioemotional development and the child's needs, interests, and learning styles.

child-directed speech Language spoken in a higher pitch and slower speed than normal, with simple words and sentences.

chromosomes Threadlike structures that come in 23 pairs, with one member of each pair coming from each parent. Chromosomes contain the genetic substance DNA.

chronic disorders Disorders that are characterized by slow onset and long duration. They are rare in early adulthood, increase during middle adulthood, and become common in late adulthood.

climacteric The midlife transition during which fertility declines.

clique A small group of about five or six individuals that may form among adolescents who engage in similar activities.

cognitive control Exercising effective control in a number of areas, including focusing attention, reducing interfering thoughts, and being cognitively flexible.

cognitive mechanics The "hardware" of the mind, reflecting the neurophysiological architecture of the brain. Cognitive mechanics involve the speed and accuracy of the processes involving sensory input, visual and motor memory, discrimination, comparison, and categorization.

cognitive pragmatics The culture-based "software programs" of the mind. Cognitive pragmatics include reading and writing skills, language comprehension, educational qualifications, professional skills, and also knowledge about the self and life skills that help us to master or cope with life.

cognitive processes Changes in an individual's thought, intelligence, and language.

cohort effects Characteristics determined by a person's time of birth, era, or generation rather than the person's actual age.

commitment Marcia's term for the part of identity development in which adolescents show a personal investment in identity.

concepts Cognitive groupings of similar objects, events, people, or ideas.

conscience An internal regulation of standards of right and wrong that involves integrating moral thought, feeling, and behavior.

consensual validation An explanation of why individuals are attracted to people who are similar to them. Our own attitudes and behavior are supported and validated when someone else's attitudes and behavior are similar to ours.

conservation In Piaget's theory, awareness that altering an object's or a substance's appearance does not change its basic properties.

constructive play Play that combines sensorimotor and repetitive activity with symbolic representation of ideas. Constructive play occurs when children engage in self-regulated creation or construction of a product or a solution.

constructivist approach A learner-centered educational approach that emphasizes the importance of individuals actively constructing their knowledge and understanding with guidance from the teacher.

contemporary life-events approach Approach emphasizing that how a life event influences the individual's development depends not only on the life event but also on mediating factors, the individual's adaptation to the life event, the life-stage context, and the sociohistorical context.

continuity-discontinuity issue Debate about the extent to which development involves gradual, cumulative change (continuity) or distinct stages (discontinuity).

controversial children Children who are frequently nominated both as a best friend and as being disliked by their peers.

conventional reasoning The second, or intermediate, level in Kohlberg's theory of moral development. At this level, individuals abide by certain standards, but these are standards set by others such as parents or society.

convergent thinking Thinking that produces one correct answer and is characteristic of the kind of thinking tested by standardized intelligence tests.

convoy model of social relations Model in which individuals go through life embedded in a personal network of individuals to whom they give and from whom they receive support.

coordination of secondary circular reactions Piaget's fourth sensorimotor substage, which develops between 8 and 12 months of age. Actions become more outwardly directed, and infants coordinate schemes and act with intentionality.

coparenting Support parents provide to each other in jointly raising their children.

core knowledge approach Theory that infants are born with domain-specific innate knowledge systems.

corpus callosum The location where fibers connect the brain's left and right hemispheres.

correlation coefficient A number based on statistical analysis that is used to describe the degree of association between two variables.

correlational research Research that attempts to determine the strength of the relationship between two or more events or characteristics.

creative thinking The ability to think in novel and unusual ways and to come up with unique solutions to problems.

crisis Marcia's term for a period of identity development during which the adolescent is exploring alternatives.

critical thinking Thinking reflectively and productively, as well as evaluating evidence.

cross-cultural studies Comparison of one culture with one or more other cultures. These studies indicate the degree to which development is similar, or universal, across cultures, and the degree to which it is culture-specific.

cross-sectional approach A research strategy in which individuals of different ages are compared at one point in time.

crowd A larger group structure than a clique that is usually based on reputation; members may or may not spend much time together.

crystallized intelligence Accumulated information and verbal skills, which increase in middle adulthood, according to Horn.

cultural-familial intellectual disability Condition in which there is no evidence of organic brain damage but the individual's IQ is between 50 and 70.

culture The behavior patterns, beliefs, and all other products of a group that are passed on from generation to generation.

culture-fair tests Tests of intelligence that are designed to be free of cultural bias.

D

date or acquaintance rape   Coercive sexual activity directed at someone with whom the perpetrator is at least casually acquainted.

deferred imitation   Imitation that occurs after a delay of hours or days.

dementia   A global term for several neurological disorders involving an irreversible decline in mental function severe enough to interfere with daily living.

denial and isolation   Kübler-Ross' first stage of dying, in which the dying person denies that she or he is really going to die.

depression   Kübler-Ross' fourth stage of dying, in which the dying person comes to accept the certainty of her or his death. A period of depression or preparatory grief may appear.

descriptive research   Studies designed to observe and record behavior.

development   The pattern of change that begins at conception and continues through the life span. Most development involves growth, although it also includes decline brought on by aging and dying.

developmental cascade model   Involves connections across domains over time that influence developmental pathways and outcomes.

developmentally appropriate practice (DAP)   Education that focuses on the typical developmental patterns of children (age-appropriateness) and the uniqueness of each child (individual-appropriateness).

difficult child   A child who tends to react negatively and cry frequently, engages in irregular daily routines, and is slow to accept change.

direct instruction approach   A structured, teacher-centered educational approach that is characterized by teacher direction and control, mastery of academic skills, high expectations for students' progress, maximum time spent on learning tasks, and efforts to keep negative affect to a minimum.

dishabituation   Recovery of a habituated response after a change in stimulation.

divergent thinking   Thinking that produces many answers to the same question and is characteristic of creativity.

divided attention   Concentrating on more than one activity at the same time.

DNA   A complex molecule that contains genetic information.

domain theory of moral development   Theory that identifies different domains of social knowledge and reasoning, including moral, social conventional, and personal domains. These domains arise from children's and adolescents' attempts to understand and deal with different forms of social experience.

doula   A caregiver who provides continuous physical, emotional, and educational support for the mother before, during, and after childbirth.

Down syndrome   A form of intellectual disability that is caused by the presence of an extra copy of chromosome 21.

dual-process model   A model of coping with bereavement that emphasizes oscillation between two dimensions: (1) loss-oriented stressors, and (2) restoration-oriented stressors.

dynamic systems theory   The perspective on motor development that seeks to explain how motor behaviors are assembled for perceiving and acting.

dyscalculia   Also known as developmental arithmetic disorder; a learning disability that involves difficulty in math computation.

dysgraphia   A learning disability that involves difficulty in handwriting.

dyslexia   A category of learning disabilities involving a severe impairment in the ability to read and spell.

E

easy child   A child who is generally in a positive mood, quickly establishes regular routines in infancy, and adapts easily to new experiences.

eclectic theoretical orientation   An orientation that does not follow any one theoretical approach but rather selects from each theory whatever is considered the best in it.

ecological view   The view that perception functions to bring organisms in contact with the environment and to increase adaptation.

egocentrism   The inability to distinguish between one's own perspective and someone else's (salient feature of the first substage of preoperational thought).

elaboration   An important strategy for remembering that involves engaging in more extensive processing of information.

embryonic period   The period of prenatal development that occurs two to eight weeks after conception. During the embryonic period, the rate of cell differentiation intensifies, support systems for the cells form, and organs appear.

emerging adulthood   The transition from adolescence to adulthood (occurring from approximately 18 to 25 years of age), which is characterized by experimentation and exploration.

emotion   Feeling, or affect, that occurs when a person is in a state or interaction that is important to him or her. Emotion is characterized by behavior that reflects (expresses) the pleasantness or unpleasantness of the state a person is in or the transactions being experienced.

emotional and behavioral disorders   Serious, persistent problems that involve relationships, aggression, depression, fears associated with personal or school matters, as well as other inappropriate socioemotional characteristics.

empty nest syndrome   A decrease in marital satisfaction that occurs after children leave home, because parents derive considerable satisfaction from their children.

epigenetic view   Emphasizes that development is the result of an ongoing, bidirectional interchange between heredity and environment.

episodic memory   The retention of information about the details of life's happenings.

equilibration   A mechanism that Piaget proposed to explain how children shift from one stage of thought to the next.

erectile dysfunction (ED)   The inability to adequately achieve and maintain an erection to attain satisfactory sexual performance.

Erikson's theory   Includes eight stages of human development. Each stage consists of a unique developmental task that confronts individuals with a crisis that must be resolved.

ethnic gloss   Using an ethnic label such as African American or Latino in a superficial way that portrays an ethnic group as being more homogeneous than it really is.

ethnic identity   An enduring, basic aspect of the self that includes a sense of membership in an ethnic group and the attitudes and feelings related to that membership.

ethnicity   A characteristic based on cultural heritage, nationality characteristics, race, religion, and language.

ethology   Stresses that behavior is strongly influenced by biology, is tied to evolution, and is characterized by critical or sensitive periods.

euthanasia   The act of painlessly ending the lives of persons who are suffering from incurable diseases or severe disabilities; sometimes called "mercy killing." In euthanasia, the physician or a third party administers the lethal medication (active euthanasia) or withholds life-sustaining treatments.

evocative genotype-environment correlations   Correlations that exist when the child's genetically influenced characteristics elicit certain types of environments.

evolutionary psychology   Emphasizes the importance of adaptation, reproduction, and "survival of the fittest" in shaping behavior.

evolutionary theory of aging   This theory states that natural selection has not eliminated many harmful conditions and nonadaptive characteristics in older adults; thus, the benefits conferred by evolution decline with age because natural selection is linked to reproductive fitness.

executive attention   Aspects of thinking that include planning actions, allocating attention to goals, detecting and compensating for errors, monitoring progress on tasks, and dealing with novel or difficult circumstances.

executive function   An umbrella-like concept that consists of a number of higher-level cognitive processes linked to the development of the brain's prefrontal cortex. Executive function involves managing one's thoughts to engage in goal-directed behavior and to exercise self-control.

experiment   A carefully regulated procedure in which one or more of the factors believed to influence the behavior being studied are manipulated while all other factors are held constant.

explicit memory   Memory of facts and experiences that individuals consciously know and can state.

extrinsic motivation   Doing something to obtain something else (the activity is a means to an end).

F

fast mapping   A process that helps to explain how young children learn the connection between a word and its referent so quickly.

fertilization   A stage in reproduction when an egg and a sperm fuse to create a single cell, called a zygote.

fetal alcohol spectrum disorders (FASD)   A cluster of abnormalities that appear in the offspring of some mothers who drink alcohol heavily during pregnancy.

fetal period   Lasting about seven months, the period between two months after conception and birth in typical pregnancies.

fight-or-flight   The view that when men experience stress, they are more likely to engage in a fight-or-flight pattern, as reflected in being aggressive, withdrawing from social contact, or drinking alcohol.

fine motor skills   Motor skills that involve more finely tuned movements, such as finger dexterity.

first habits and primary circular reactions   Piaget's second sensorimotor substage, which develops between 1 and 4 months of age. In this substage, the infant coordinates sensation and two types of schemes: habits and primary circular reactions.

fluid intelligence   The ability to reason abstractly, which begins to decline from middle adulthood onward, according to Horn.

fragile X syndrome   A genetic disorder involving an abnormality in the X chromosome, which becomes constricted and often breaks.

free-radical theory   A microbiological theory stating that people age because normal metabolic processes within their cells produce unstable oxygen molecules known as free radicals. These molecules ricochet around inside cells, damaging DNA and other cellular structures.

fuzzy trace theory   States that memory is best understood by considering two types of memory representations: (1) verbatim memory trace, and (2) gist. In this theory, older children's better memory is attributed to the fuzzy traces created by extracting the gist of information.

fuzzy-trace theory dual-process model   States that decision making is influenced by two systems—"verbatim" analytical (literal and precise) and gist-based intuition (simple bottom-line meaning)—which operate in parallel; in this model, gist-based intuition benefits adolescent decision making more than analytical thinking does.

G

games   Activities engaged in for pleasure that include rules and often involve competition with one or more individuals.

gender   The characteristics of people as males and females.

gender identity   The sense of being male or female, which most children acquire by the time they are 3 years old.

gender role   A set of expectations that prescribes how females or males should think, act, and feel.

gender schema theory   The theory that gender typing emerges as children develop gender schemas of their culture's gender-appropriate and gender-inappropriate behavior.

gender stereotypes   Broad categories that reflect our impressions and beliefs about females and males.

gender typing   Acquisition of a traditional masculine or feminine role.

gene × environment (G × E) interaction   The interaction of a specific measured variation in the DNA and a specific measured aspect of the environment.

generational inequity   The view that our aging society is being unfair to its younger members because older adults receive inequitably large allocations of resources.

genes   Units of hereditary information composed of DNA. Genes help cells to reproduce themselves and help manufacture the proteins that maintain life.

genotype   A person's genetic heritage; the actual genetic material.

germinal period   The period of prenatal development that takes place in the first two weeks after conception. It includes the creation of the zygote, continued cell division, and the attachment of the zygote to the uterine wall.

gifted   Having above-average intelligence (an IQ of 130 or higher) and/or superior talent for something.

glaucoma   Damage to the optic nerve because of the pressure created by a buildup of fluid in the eye.

goodness of fit   Refers to the match between a child's temperament and the environmental demands with which the child must cope.

grasping reflex   A neonatal reflex that occurs when something touches the infant's palms and the infant responds by grasping tightly.

grief   The emotional numbness, disbelief, separation anxiety, despair, sadness, and loneliness that accompany the loss of someone we love.

grit   Involves passion and persistence in achieving long-term goals.

gross motor skills   Motor skills that involve large-muscle activities, such as walking.

growth hormone deficiency   Absence or deficiency of growth hormone produced by the pituitary gland to stimulate the body to grow.

H

habituation   Decreased responsiveness to a stimulus after repeated presentations of the stimulus.

heteronomous morality   The first stage of moral development in Piaget's theory, occurring from approximately 4 to 7 years of age. Justice and rules are conceived of as unchangeable properties of the world, removed from the control of people.

hormonal stress theory   The theory that aging in the body's hormonal system can decrease resistance to stress and increase the likelihood of disease.

hormones   Powerful chemical substances secreted by the endocrine glands and carried through the body by the bloodstream.

hospice   A program committed to making the end of life as free from pain, anxiety, and depression as possible. The goals of hospice contrast with those of a hospital, which are to cure disease and prolong life.

hypotheses   Specific assumptions and predictions that can be tested to determine their accuracy.

hypothetical-deductive reasoning   Piaget's formal operational concept that adolescents have the cognitive ability to develop hypotheses, or best guesses, about ways to solve problems.

I

identity achievement   Marcia's term for the status of individuals who have undergone a crisis and have made a commitment.

identity diffusion   Marcia's term for the status of individuals who have not yet experienced a crisis (explored meaningful alternatives) or made any commitments.

identity foreclosure   Marcia's term for the status of individuals who have made a commitment but have not experienced a crisis.

identity moratorium   Marcia's term for the status of individuals who are in the midst of a crisis, but their commitments are either absent or vaguely defined.

imaginary audience   Adolescents' belief that others are as interested in them as they themselves are, as well as attention-getting behavior motivated by a desire to be noticed, visible, and "on stage."

immanent justice   The concept that if a rule is broken, punishment will be meted out immediately.

implicit memory   Memory without conscious recollection; involves skills and routine procedures that are automatically performed.

inclusion   Educating a child with special requirements full-time in the regular classroom.

individual differences   The stable, consistent ways in which people differ from each other.

individualized education plan (IEP)   A written statement that spells out a program specifically tailored to a child with a disability.

indulgent parenting   A style of parenting in which parents are highly involved with their children but place few demands or controls on them. Indulgent parenting is associated with children's social incompetence, especially a lack of self-control.

infinite generativity   The ability to produce and comprehend an endless number of meaningful sentences using a finite set of words and rules.

information-processing theory   Emphasizes that individuals manipulate information, monitor it, and strategize about it. Central to this theory are the processes of memory and thinking.

insecure avoidant babies Babies who show insecurity by avoiding the caregiver.

insecure disorganized babies Babies who show insecurity by being disorganized and disoriented.

insecure resistant babies Babies who often cling to the caregiver, then resist the caregiver by fighting against the closeness, perhaps by kicking or pushing away.

integrity versus despair Erikson's eighth and final stage of development, which occurs in late adulthood. This stage involves reflecting on the past and either piecing together a positive review or concluding that one's life has not been well spent.

intellectual disability A condition of limited mental ability in which the individual (1) has a low IQ, usually below 70 on a traditional intelligence test; (2) has difficulty adapting to the demands of everyday life; and (3) first exhibits these characteristics by age 18.

intelligence Problem-solving skills and the ability to learn from and adapt to the experiences of everyday life.

intelligence quotient (IQ) A person's mental age divided by chronological age, multiplied by 100.

intermodal perception The ability to relate and integrate information from two or more sensory modalities, such as vision and hearing.

internalization of schemes Piaget's sixth and final sensorimotor substage, which develops between 18 and 24 months of age. In this substage the infant develops the ability to use primitive symbols.

intimacy in friendships Self-disclosure and the sharing of private thoughts.

intrinsic motivation Doing something for its own sake; involves factors such as self-determination and opportunities to make choices.

intuitive thought substage Piaget's second substage of preoperational thought, in which children begin to use primitive reasoning and want to know the answers to all sorts of questions (between 4 and 7 years of age).

J

joint attention Process that occurs when individuals focus on the same object and are able to track another's behavior, one individual directs another's attention, and reciprocal interaction takes place.

justice perspective A moral perspective that focuses on the rights of the individual and in which individuals independently make moral decisions.

juvenile delinquent An adolescent who breaks the law or engages in behavior that is considered illegal.

K

kangaroo care Treatment for preterm infants that involves skin-to-skin contact.

Klinefelter syndrome A chromosomal disorder in which males have an extra X chromosome, making them XXY instead of XY.

L

laboratory A controlled setting in which many of the complex factors of the "real world" are removed.

language A form of communication, whether spoken, written, or signed, that is based on a system of symbols. Language consists of the words used by a community and the rules for varying and combining them.

language acquisition device (LAD) Chomsky's term that describes a biological endowment enabling the child to detect the features and rules of language, including phonology, syntax, and semantics.

lateralization Specialization of function in one hemisphere of the cerebral cortex or the other.

learning disability Difficulty in understanding or using spoken or written language or in doing mathematics. To be classified as a learning disability, the learning problem is not primarily the result of visual, hearing, or motor disabilities; intellectual disability; emotional disorders; or environmental, cultural, or economic disadvantage.

least restrictive environment (LRE) A setting that is as similar as possible to the one in which children who do not have a disability are educated.

leisure The pleasant times after work when individuals are free to pursue activities and interests of their own choosing.

life expectancy The number of years that will probably be lived by the average person born in a particular year.

life span The maximum number of years an individual can live. The life span of human beings is about 120 to 125 years of age.

life-span perspective The perspective that development is lifelong, multidimensional, multidirectional, plastic, multidisciplinary, and contextual; involves growth, maintenance, and regulation; and is constructed through biological, sociocultural, and individual factors working together.

limbic system The part of the brain where emotions and rewards are processed.

long-term memory A relatively permanent type of memory that holds huge amounts of information for a long period of time.

longitudinal approach A research strategy in which the same individuals are studied over a period of time, usually several years or more.

low birth weight infants Infants that weigh less than 5 pounds 8 ounces at birth.

M

macular degeneration A disease that involves deterioration of the macula of the retina, which corresponds to the focal center of the visual field.

major depression A mood disorder in which the individual is deeply unhappy, demoralized, self-derogatory, and bored. The person does not feel well, loses stamina easily, has poor appetite, and is listless and unmotivated. Major depression is so widespread that it has been called the "common cold" of mental disorders.

matching hypothesis Theory that although we prefer a more attractive person in the abstract, in the real world we end up choosing someone who is close to our own level of attractiveness.

meaning-making coping Drawing on beliefs, values, and goals to change the meaning of a stressful situation, especially in times of chronic stress such as when a loved one dies.

meiosis A specialized form of cell division that occurs to form eggs and sperm (also known as gametes).

memory A central feature of cognitive development, pertaining to all situations in which an individual retains information over time.

menarche A girl's first menstruation.

menopause Cessation of a woman's menstrual periods, usually during the late forties or early fifties.

mental age (MA) Binet's measure of an individual's level of mental development compared with that of others.

metabolic syndrome A condition characterized by hypertension, obesity, and insulin resistance. Metabolic syndrome often leads to the onset of diabetes and cardiovascular disease.

metacognition Cognition about cognition, or knowing about knowing.

metalinguistic awareness Knowledge about language, such as understanding what a preposition is or being able to discuss the sounds of a language.

middle adulthood The developmental period that begins at approximately 40 to 45 years of age and extends to about 60 to 65 years of age.

mindfulness Being alert, mentally present, and cognitively flexible while going through life's everyday activities and tasks.

mindset The cognitive view, either fixed or growth, that individuals develop for themselves.

mitochondrial theory The theory that aging is caused by the decay of mitochondria, tiny cellular bodies that supply energy for function, growth, and repair.

mitosis Cellular reproduction in which the cell's nucleus duplicates itself with two new cells being formed, each containing the same DNA as the parent cell, arranged in the same 23 pairs of chromosomes.

Montessori approach An educational philosophy in which children are given considerable freedom and spontaneity in choosing activities and are allowed to move from one activity to another as they desire.

moral development Development that involves thoughts, feelings, and behaviors regarding rules and conventions about what people should do in their interactions with other people.

Moro reflex A neonatal startle response in which the newborn arches its back, throws its head back, flings out its arms and legs, and then pulls its arms and legs close to the center of the body.

morphology Units of meaning involved in word formation.

mTOR pathway   A cellular pathway involving the regulation of growth and metabolism that has been proposed as a key aspect of longevity.

myelination   The process by which the nerve cells are covered and insulated with a layer of fat cells, which increases the speed at which information travels through the nervous system.

N

narcissism   A self-centered and self-concerned approach toward others.

natural childbirth   This method of childbirth attempts to reduce the mother's pain by decreasing her fear through information about childbirth and instruction in relaxation techniques designed to reduce pain during delivery.

naturalistic observation   Studies that involve observing behavior in real-world settings.

nature-nurture issue   Debate about whether development is primarily influenced by nature or nurture. Nature refers to an organism's biological inheritance, nurture to its environmental experiences.

neglected children   Children who are infrequently nominated as a best friend but are not disliked by their peers.

neglectful parenting   A style of parenting in which the parent is uninvolved in the child's life; this style is associated with children's social incompetence, especially a lack of self-control.

neo-Piagetians   Developmentalists who argue that Piaget got some things right but that his theory needs considerable revision. They have elaborated on Piaget's theory, giving more emphasis to information processing, strategies, and precise cognitive steps.

Neonatal Intensive Care Unit Network Neurobehavioral Scale (NNNS)   An "offspring" of the NBAS, the NNNS provides an assessment of the newborn's behavior, neurological and stress responses, and regulatory capacities.

neuroconstructivist view   A belief that biological processes and environmental conditions influence the brain's development; the brain has plasticity and is context dependent; and development of the brain and cognitive development are closely linked.

neurogenesis   The generation of new neurons.

neurons   Nerve cells that handle information processing at the cellular level in the brain.

nonnormative life events   Unusual occurrences that have a major impact on an individual's life.

normal distribution   A symmetrical distribution with most scores falling in the middle of the possible range of scores and a few scores appearing toward the extremes of the range.

normative age-graded influences   Influences that are similar for individuals in a particular age group.

normative history-graded influences   Influences that are common to people of a particular generation because of historical circumstances.

O

object permanence   The Piagetian term for understanding that objects and events continue to exist even when they cannot directly be seen, heard, or touched.

operations   In Piaget's theory, these are reversible mental actions that allow children to do mentally what they formerly did physically.

organic intellectual disability   A genetic disorder or condition involving brain damage that is linked to a low level of intellectual functioning.

organization   Piaget's concept of grouping isolated behaviors and thoughts into a higher-order, more smoothly functioning cognitive system.

organogenesis   Organ formation that takes place during the first two months of prenatal development.

osteoporosis   A chronic condition that involves an extensive loss of bone tissue and is the main reason many older adults walk with a marked stoop.

P

pain cry   A sudden appearance of a long, initial loud cry without preliminary moaning, followed by breath holding.

palliative care   The type of care emphasized in a hospice, which involves reducing pain and suffering and helping individuals die with dignity.

Parkinson disease   A chronic, progressive disease characterized by muscle tremors, slowing of movement, and partial facial paralysis.

passive euthanasia   Withholding available treatments, such as life-sustaining devices, in order to allow a person to die.

passive genotype-environment correlations   Correlations that exist when the natural parents, who are genetically related to the child, provide a rearing environment for the child.

perception   The interpretation of what is sensed.

personal fable   The part of adolescent egocentrism that involves an adolescent's sense of uniqueness and invincibility (or invulnerability).

perspective taking   The social cognitive process involved in assuming the perspective of others and understanding their thoughts and feelings.

phenotype   The way an individual's genotype is expressed in observed and measurable characteristics.

phenylketonuria (PKU)   A genetic disorder in which an individual cannot properly metabolize an amino acid called phenylalanine. PKU is now easily detected but, if left untreated, results in intellectual disability and hyperactivity.

phonics approach   The idea that reading instruction should teach the basic rules for translating written symbols into sounds.

phonology   The sound system of the language, including the sounds that are used and how they may be combined.

Piaget's theory   Theory stating that children actively construct their understanding of the world and go through four stages of cognitive development.

placenta   A prenatal life-support system that consists of a disk-shaped group of tissues in which small blood vessels from the mother and offspring intertwine.

popular children   Children who are frequently nominated as a best friend and are rarely disliked by their peers.

postconventional reasoning   The highest level in Kohlberg's theory of moral development. At this level, the individual recognizes alternative moral courses, explores the options, and then decides on a personal moral code.

postformal thought   Thinking that is reflective, relativistic, contextual, provisional, realistic, and influenced by emotions.

postpartum depression   A condition experienced by women who have such strong feelings of sadness, anxiety, or despair that they have trouble coping with daily tasks during the postpartum period.

postpartum period   The period after childbirth when the mother adjusts, both physically and psychologically, to the effects of childbirth. This period lasts for about six weeks or until her body has completed its adjustment and returned to a near prepregnant state.

practice play   Play that involves repetition of behavior when new skills are being learned or when physical or mental mastery and coordination of skills are required for games or sports.

pragmatics   The appropriate use of language in different contexts.

preconventional reasoning   The lowest level in Kohlberg's theory of moral development. The individual's moral reasoning is controlled primarily by external rewards and punishment.

preoperational stage   Piaget's second stage, lasting from about 2 to 7 years of age, during which children begin to represent the world with words, images, and drawings, and symbolic thought goes beyond simple connections of sensory information and physical action; stable concepts are formed, mental reasoning emerges, egocentrism is present, and magical beliefs are constructed.

prepared childbirth   Developed by French obstetrician Ferdinand Lamaze, this childbirth strategy is similar to natural childbirth but includes a special breathing technique to control pushing in the final stages of labor and a more detailed anatomy and physiology course.

pretense/symbolic play   Play in which the child transforms the physical environment into a symbol.

preterm infants   Those born before the completion of 37 weeks of gestation (the time between fertilization and birth).

primary circular reaction   A scheme based on the attempt to reproduce an event that initially occurred by chance.

primary emotions   Emotions that are present in humans and other animals and emerge early in life; examples are joy, anger, sadness, fear, and disgust.

Project Head Start A government-funded program that is designed to provide children from low-income families with the opportunity to acquire the skills and experiences important for school success.

prolonged grief disorder Grief that involves enduring despair and remains unresolved over an extended period of time.

prospective memory Remembering to do something in the future.

proximodistal pattern Developmental sequence in which growth starts at the center of the body and moves toward the extremities.

psychoanalytic theories Theories that describe development as primarily unconscious and heavily colored by emotion. Behavior is merely a surface characteristic, and the symbolic workings of the mind have to be analyzed to understand behavior. Early experiences with parents are emphasized.

psychoanalytic theory of gender A theory deriving from Freud's view that the preschool child develops a sexual attraction to the opposite-sex parent, by approximately 5 or 6 years of age renounces this attraction because of anxious feelings, and subsequently identifies with the same-sex parent, unconsciously adopting the same-sex parent's characteristics.

puberty A period of rapid physical maturation, occurring primarily in early adolescence, that involves hormonal and bodily changes.

R

rape Forcible sexual intercourse with a person who does not consent to it.

rapport talk The language of conversation; it is the way of establishing connections and negotiating relationships.

reciprocal socialization Socialization that is bidirectional; children socialize parents, just as parents socialize children.

reflexes Built-in reactions to stimuli that govern the newborn's movements, which are automatic and beyond the newborn's control.

reflexive smile A smile that does not occur in response to external stimuli. It happens during the first month after birth, usually during sleep.

rejected children Children who are infrequently nominated as a best friend and are actively disliked by their peers.

religion An organized set of beliefs, practices, rituals, and symbols that increases an individual's connection to a sacred or transcendent other (God, higher power, or higher truth).

religiousness The degree to which an individual is affiliated with an organized religion, participates in prescribed rituals and practices, feels a sense of connection with its beliefs, and is involved in a community of believers.

report talk Talk that is designed to give information; this category of communication includes public speaking.

rite of passage A ceremony or ritual that marks an individual's transition from one status to another. Most rites of passage focus on the transition to adult status.

romantic love Also called passionate love or eros, romantic love has strong sexual and infatuation components and often predominates early in a love relationship.

rooting reflex A newborn's built-in reaction that occurs when the infant's cheek is stroked or the side of the mouth is touched. In response, the infant turns his or her head toward the side that was touched, in an apparent effort to find something to suck.

S

scaffolding Practice in which parents time interactions so that infants take turns with the parents; these interactions allow infants to be more skillful than they would be if they had to rely only on their own abilities.

schemes In Piaget's theory, actions or mental representations that organize knowledge.

scientific method An approach that can be used to obtain accurate information. It includes the following steps: (1) conceptualize the problem, (2) collect data, (3) draw conclusions, and (4) revise research conclusions and theory.

secondary circular reactions Piaget's third sensorimotor substage, which develops between 4 and 8 months of age. In this substage, the infant becomes more object-oriented, moving beyond preoccupation with the self.

secure attachment style An attachment style that describes adults who have positive views of relationships, find it easy to get close to others, and are not overly concerned or stressed out about their romantic relationships.

securely attached babies Babies who use the caregiver as a secure base from which to explore the environment.

selective attention Focusing on a specific aspect of experience that is relevant while ignoring others that are irrelevant.

selective optimization with compensation theory The theory that successful aging is related to three main factors: selection, optimization, and compensation.

self-concept Domain-specific evaluations of the self.

self-conscious emotions Emotions that require self-awareness, especially consciousness and a sense of "me"; examples include jealousy, empathy, and embarrassment.

self-efficacy The belief that one can master a situation and produce favorable outcomes.

self-esteem The global evaluative dimension of the self. Self-esteem is also referred to as self-worth or self-image.

self-understanding The child's cognitive representation of self, the substance and content of the child's self-conceptions.

semantic memory A person's knowledge about the world—including one's fields of expertise, general academic knowledge of the sort learned in school, and "everyday knowledge."

semantics The meaning of words and sentences.

sensation The product of the interaction between information and the sensory receptors—the eyes, ears, tongue, nostrils, and skin.

sensorimotor play Behavior engaged in by infants that lets them derive pleasure from exercising their existing sensorimotor schemas.

sensorimotor stage The first of Piaget's stages, which lasts from birth to about 2 years of age; infants construct an understanding of the world by coordinating sensory experiences with motoric actions.

separation protest An infant's distressed crying when the caregiver leaves.

seriation The concrete operation that involves ordering stimuli along a quantitative dimension (such as length).

service learning A form of education that promotes social responsibility and service to the community.

sexually transmitted infections (STIs) Infections that are contracted primarily through sexual contact, including oral-genital and anal-genital contact.

shape constancy The recognition that an object's shape remains the same even though its orientation to the observer changes.

short-term memory The memory component in which individuals retain information for up to 30 seconds, assuming there is no rehearsal of the information.

sickle-cell anemia A genetic disorder that affects the red blood cells and occurs most often in people of African descent.

simple reflexes Piaget's first sensorimotor substage, which corresponds to the first month after birth. In this substage, sensation and action are coordinated primarily through reflexive behaviors.

sirtuins A family of proteins that have been proposed as having important influences on longevity, mitochondria functioning in energy, calorie restriction benefits, stress resistance, and cardiovascular functioning.

size constancy The recognition that an object remains the same even though the retinal image of the object changes as the observer moves toward or away from the object.

slow-to-warm-up child A child who has a low activity level, is somewhat negative, and displays a low intensity of mood.

small for date infants Also called small for gestational age infants, these infants' birth weights are below normal when the length of pregnancy is considered. Small for date infants may be preterm or full term.

social clock The timetable according to which individuals are expected to accomplish life's tasks, such as getting married, having children, or establishing themselves in a career.

social cognitive theory   The view of psychologists who emphasize behavior, environment, and cognition as the key factors in development.

social cognitive theory of gender   A theory emphasizing that children's gender development occurs through the observation and imitation of gender behavior and through the rewards and punishments children experience for gender-appropriate and gender-inappropriate behavior.

social constructivist approach   An approach that emphasizes the social contexts of learning and asserts that knowledge is mutually built and constructed. Vygotsky's theory reflects this approach.

social conventional reasoning   Thoughts about social consensus and convention, in contrast with moral reasoning, which stresses ethical issues.

social play   Play that involves social interactions with peers.

social policy   A national government's course of action designed to promote the welfare of its citizens.

social referencing   "Reading" emotional cues in others to help determine how to act in a particular situation.

social role theory   A theory that gender differences result from the contrasting roles of men and women.

social smile   A smile in response to an external stimulus, which early in development is typically a face.

socioeconomic status (SES)   Refers to the grouping of people with similar occupational, educational, and economic characteristics.

socioemotional processes   Changes in an individual's interpersonal relationships, emotions, and personality.

socioemotional selectivity theory   The theory that motivation changes as a function of time horizons. When time horizons are limited, there is a shift toward prioritizing emotional meaning and satisfaction. Older adults become more selective about their social networks. Because they place a high value on emotional satisfaction, older adults often spend more time with familiar individuals with whom they have had rewarding relationships.

source memory   The ability to remember where one learned something.

spirituality   Experiencing something beyond oneself in a transcendent manner and living in a way that benefits others and society.

stability-change issue   Debate about whether we become older renditions of our early experience (stability) or whether we develop into someone different from who we were at an earlier point in development (change).

standardized test   A test with uniform procedures for administration and scoring. Many standardized tests allow a person's performance to be compared with the performance of other individuals.

stereotype threat   The anxiety that one's behavior might confirm a negative stereotype about one's group.

Strange Situation   An observational measure of infant attachment that requires the infant to move through a series of introductions, separations, and reunions with the caregiver and an adult stranger in a prescribed order.

stranger anxiety   An infant's fear and wariness of strangers; it tends to appear during the second half of the first year of life.

strategies   Deliberate mental activities that improve the processing of information.

sucking reflex   A newborn's built-in reaction to automatically suck an object placed in its mouth. The sucking reflex enables the infant to get nourishment before he or she has associated a nipple with food and also serves as a self-soothing or self-regulating mechanism.

sudden infant death syndrome (SIDS)   A condition that occurs when an infant stops breathing, usually during the night, and suddenly dies without an apparent cause.

sustained attention   Focused and extended engagement with an object, task, event, or other aspect of the environment.

symbolic function substage   Piaget's first substage of preoperational thought, in which the child gains the ability to mentally represent an object that is not present (between about 2 and 4 years of age).

syntax   The ways words are combined to form acceptable phrases and sentences.

T

telegraphic speech   The use of short and precise words without grammatical markers such as articles, auxiliary verbs, and other connectives.

temperament   Involves individual differences in behavioral styles, emotions, and characteristic ways of responding.

tend-and-befriend   Taylor's view that when women experience stress, they are likely to engage in a tend-and-befriend pattern, seeking social alliances with others, especially female friends.

teratogen   Any agent that causes a birth defect. The field of study that investigates the causes of birth defects is called teratology.

tertiary circular reactions, novelty, and curiosity   Piaget's fifth sensorimotor substage, which develops between 12 and 18 months of age. In this substage, infants become intrigued by the many properties of objects and by the many things they can do to objects.

theory   An interrelated, coherent set of ideas that helps to explain phenomena and facilitate predictions.

theory of mind   Awareness of one's own mental processes and the mental processes of others.

top-dog phenomenon   The circumstance of moving from the top position in elementary school to the lowest position in middle or junior high school.

transgender   A broad term that refers to individuals who adopt a gender identity that differs from the one assigned to them at birth.

transitivity   The ability to logically combine relations to understand certain conclusions.

triarchic theory of intelligence   Sternberg's theory that intelligence consists of analytical intelligence, creative intelligence, and practical intelligence.

trophoblast   The outer layer of cells that develops in the germinal period. These cells provide nutrition and support for the embryo.

Turner syndrome   A chromosome disorder in females in which either an X chromosome is missing, making the person XO instead of XX, or the second X chromosome is partially deleted.

twin study   A study in which the behavioral similarity of identical twins is compared with the behavioral similarity of fraternal twins.

U

umbilical cord   Part of the prenatal life-support system that contains two arteries and one vein that connect the baby to the placenta.

V

visual preference method   A method used to determine whether infants can distinguish one stimulus from another by measuring the length of time they attend to different stimuli.

Vygotsky's theory   A sociocultural cognitive theory that emphasizes how culture and social interaction guide cognitive development.

W

Wernicke's area   An area in the brain's left hemisphere that is involved in language comprehension.

whole-language approach   An approach to reading instruction based on the idea that instruction should parallel children's natural language learning. Reading materials should be whole and meaningful.

wisdom   Expert knowledge about the practical aspects of life that permits excellent judgment about important matters.

working memory   A mental "workbench" where individuals manipulate and assemble information when making decisions, solving problems, and comprehending written and spoken language.

X

XYY syndrome   A chromosomal disorder in which males have an extra Y chromosome.

Z

zone of proximal development (ZPD)   Vygotsky's term for tasks that are too difficult for children to master alone but can be mastered with the assistance of adults or more-skilled children.

zygote   A single cell formed through fertilization.

references

A

AARP (2004). *The divorce experience: A study of divorce at midlife and beyond.* Washington, DC: AARP.

Abar, C.C., & others (2020, in press). Parental active tracking measures and health behaviors during high school and college. *Journal of American College Health.*

Abbatecola, A.M., Russo, M., & Barbieri, M. (2018). Dietary patterns and cognition in older persons. *Current Opinion in Clinical Nutrition and Metabolic Care, 21,* 10–13.

ABC News (2005, December 12). Larry Page and Sergey Brin. Retrieved September 16, 2007, from http://abcnews.go.com?Entertainment/12/8/05

Abelsson, A., & Willman, A. (2020, in press). Ethics and aesthetics in injection treatments with Botox and filler. *Journal of Women's Aging.*

Aben, B., & others (2019). Context-dependent modulation of cognitive control involves different temporal profiles of fronto-parietal activity. *Neuroimage, 189,* 755–762.

Abootalebi, M., & others (2020, in press). Effect of education about andropause health on the level of the knowledge and attitude of men referring to the education and training retirement center of Shiraz. *Aging Male.*

Abraham, W. (2020). *Modality in syntax, semantics, and pragmatics.* New York: Cambridge University Press.

Abrahami, N., Izhaki, I., & Younis, J.S. (2019). Do young women with unexplained infertility show manifestations of decreased ovarian reserve? *Journal of Assisted Reproduction and Genetics, 36,* 1143–1152.

Abrahamse, M.E., Jonkman, C.S., & Harting, J. (2018). A school-based interdisciplinary approach to promote health and academic achievement among children in a deprived neighborhood: Study protocol for a mixed-methods evaluation. *BMC Public Health, 18,* 465.

Abrahamson, K., Davila, H., & Hountz, D. (2018). Involving nursing assistants in nursing home QI. *American Journal of Nursing, 118*(2), 11.

Abu Snineh, M., Camicioli, R., & Miyasaki, J.M. (2017). Decisional capacity for advanced care directives in Parkinson's disease with cognitive concerns. *Parkinsonism and Related Diseases. 39,* 77–79.

Accornero, V.H., Anthony, J.C., Morrow, C.E., Xue, L., & Bandstra, E.S. (2006). Prenatal cocaine exposure: An examination of childhood externalizing and internalizing behavior problems at age 7 years. *Epidemiology, Psychiatry, and Society, 15,* 20–29.

Achieve, Inc. (2005). *An action agenda for improving America's high schools.* Washington, DC: Author.

Ackerman, R.A. (2021). Narcissistic Personality Inventory. In V. Ziegler-Hill & T.K. Shackelford

(Eds.). *Encyclopedia of personality and individual differences.* New York: Springer.

Acosta, H., & others (2019). Maternal pregnancy-related anxiety is associated with sexually dimorphic alterations in amygdala volume in 4-year-old children. *Frontiers in Behavioral Neuroscience, 13,* 175.

Acosta, J., & others (2019). Evaluation of a whole-school change intervention: Findings from a two-year cluster-randomized trial of restorative practices intervention. *Journal of Youth and Adolescence, 48,* 876–890.

Acquino, K., & Reed, A. (2002). The self-importance of moral identity. *Journal of Personality and Social Psychology, 83,* 1423–1440.

Adair, L.S., Duazo, P., & Borja, J.B. (2018). How overweight and obesity relate to the development of functional limitations in Filipino women. *Geriatrics, 3*(4). doi:10.3390/geriatrics3040063

Adams, K.A., & others (2018). Caregiver talk and medical risk as predictors of language outcomes in full term and preterm toddlers. *Child Development, 89*(5), 1674–1690.

Adams, S.M., Ward, C.E., & Garcia, K.L. (2015). Sudden infant death syndrome. *American Family Physician, 91,* 778–783.

Adams, T., Keisberg, G., & Safranek, S. (2016). Clinical inquiry: Does caffeine intake during pregnancy affect birth weight? *Journal of Family Practice, 65,* 205–213.

Adcock, M., & others (2020). Effects of an in-home multicomponent exergame training on physical functions, cognition, and brain volume of older adults: A randomized controlled trial. *Frontiers in Medicine, 28*(6), 321.

Adduru, V., & others (2020). A method to estimate brain volume from head CT images and application to detect brain atrophy in Alzheimer disease. *AJNR American Journal of Neuroradiology, 41,* 224–230.

Adkins, D.E., Daw, J.K., McClay, J.L., & van den Oord, E.J. (2012). The influence of five monoamine genes on trajectories of depressive symptoms across adolescence and young adulthood. *Development and Psychopathology, 24,* 267–285.

Administration for Children and Families (2008). *Statistical Fact Sheet Fiscal Year 2008.* Washington, DC: Author.

Administration on Aging (2018). *A profile of older Americans: 2017.* Washington, DC: U.S. Department of Health and Human Services.

Adolescent Sleep Working Group, AAP (2014). School start times for adolescents. *Pediatrics, 134,* 642–649.

Adolph, K.E. (1997). Learning in the development of infant locomotion. *Monographs of the Society for Research in Child Development, 62*(3), Serial No. 251.

Adolph, K.E. (2018). Motor development. In M.H. Bornstein (Ed.), *SAGE encyclopedia of lifespan human development.* Thousand Oaks, CA: Sage.

Adolph, K.E. (2019). An ecological approach to learning in (not and) development. *Human Development, 63.* 180–201.

Adolph, K.E., & Berger, S.E. (2005). Physical and motor development. In M.H. Bornstein & M.E. Lamb (Eds.), *Developmental psychology* (5th ed.). Mahwah, NJ: Erlbaum.

Adolph, K.E., & Berger, S.E. (2015). Physical and motor development. In M.H. Bornstein & M.E. Lamb (Eds.), *Developmental science* (7th ed.). New York: Psychology Press.

Adolph, K.E., & Hoch, J.E. (2019). Motor development: Embodied, embedded, enculturated, and enabling. *Annual Review of Psychology* (Vol. 70). Palo Alto, CA: Annual Reviews.

Adolph, K.E., Hoch, J.E., & Ossmy, O. (2020). James Gibson's ecological approach to locomotion and manipulation: Development and changing affordances. In J. Wagman & J. Blau (Eds.). *Perception as information detection: Reflections on Gibson's ecological approach to visual perception.* New York: Elsevier.

Adolph, K.E., Karasik, L.B., & Tamis-LeMonda, C.S. (2010). Moving between cultures: Cross-cultural research on motor development. In M. Bornstein & L.R. Cote (Eds.), *Handbook of cross-cultural developmental science: Vol. 1. Domains of development across cultures.* Clifton, NJ: Psychology Press.

Adolph, K.E., & Robinson, S.R. (2015). Motor development. In R. Lerner (Ed.), *Handbook of child psychology and developmental science* (7th ed.). New York: Wiley.

Adolph, K.E., Vereijken, B., & Shrout, P.E. (2003). What changes in infant walking and why? *Child Development, 74,* 475–497.

Adolph, K.E., & others (2012). How do you learn to walk? Thousands of steps and dozens of falls per day. *Psychological Science, 23*(11), 1387–1394.

Afifi, T.O., & others (2017a). Spanking and adult mental health impairment: The case for the designation of spanking as an adverse childhood experience. *Child Abuse and Neglect, 71,* 24–31.

Afifi, T.O., & others (2017b). The relationships between harsh physical punishment and child maltreatment in childhood and intimate partner violence in adulthood. *BMC Public Health, 17*(1), 493.

Agarwal, P., & others (2018). Maternal obesity, diabetes during pregnancy and epigenetic mechanisms that influence the developmental origins of cardiometabolic disease in the offspring. *Critical Reviews in Clinical Laboratory Sciences, 55,* 71–101.

Agency for Healthcare Research and Quality (2007). *Evidence report/Technology assessment Number 153: Breastfeeding and maternal and health outcomes in developed countries.* Rockville, MD: U.S. Department of Health and Human Services.

Agostini, A., & others (2017). An experimental study of adolescent sleep restriction during a simulated school week: Changes in phase, sleep staging, performance, and sleepiness. *Journal of Sleep Research, 26,* 227-235.

Agras, W.S., Hammer, L.D., McNicholas, F., & Karemer, H.C. (2004). Risk factors for childhood overweight: A prospective study from birth to 9.5 years. *Journal of Pediatrics, 145,* 20-25.

Aguirre, C.C. (2016). Sleep deprivation: A mind-body approach. *Current Opinion in Pulmonary Medicine, 22,* 583-588.

Ahern, E., Kowalski, M., & Lamb, M.E. (2018). A case study perspective: The experiences of young persons testifying to child sexual exploitation in British Criminal Court. *Journal of Child Sexual Abuse, 27,* 321-334.

Ahern, E., VanMeter, F., & Lamb, M.E. (2018). A macro-coding perspective: Interviewer support and child comfort in investigative interviews with young alleged victims of sexual abuse. *Children and Youth Services Review, 95,* 361-367.

Ahluwalia, I.B., Tessaro, I., Grumer-Strawn, L.M., MacGowan, C., & Benton-Davis, S. (2000). Georgia's breastfeeding promotion program for low-income women. *Pediatrics, 105,* E-85-E-87.

Ahluwalia, M.K., & Mohabir, R.K. (2019). Turning to Waheguru: Religious and cultural coping mechanism of bereaved Sikhs. *Omega, 78,* 302-313.

Ahmadi, M., Golalipour, M., & Samaei, N.M. (2019). Mitochondrial common deletion in blood: New insight into the effects of age and body mass index. *Current Aging Science, 11,* 250-254.

Ahnert, L., & Schoppe-Sullivan, S.J. (2020). Fathers from an attachment perspective. *Attachment and Human Development, 22,* 1-3.

Ahrons, C. (2004). *We're still family.* New York: HarperCollins.

Ahrons, C. (2007). Family ties after divorce: Long-term implications for children. *Family Process, 46,* 53-65.

Ahun, M.N., & others (2018). Child development in rural Ghana between cognitive/language milestones and indicators of nutrition and stimulation of children under two years of age. *Canadian Journal of Public Health, 108,* e578-e585.

Aichele, S., Rabbitt, P., & Ghisletta, P. (2016). Think fast, feel fine: A 29-year study of cognition, health, and survival in middle-aged and older adults. *Psychological Science, 27,* 518-529.

Ainsworth, M.D.S. (1979). Infant-mother attachment. *American Psychologist, 34,* 932-937.

Airth, L., & Oelke, N.D. (2020, in press). How neoliberalism, ageism, and stigma drive the lack of policy for older adults' mental health. *Journal of Psychiatric and Mental Health Nursing.*

Ait-Hadad, W., & others (2020, in press). Optimism is associated with diet quality, food group consumption, and snacking behavior in a general population. *Nutrition Journal.*

Ajetunmobi, O.M., & others (2015). Breastfeeding is associated with reduced childhood hospitalization: Evidence from a Scottish birth cohort (1997-2009). *Journal of Pediatrics, 166,* 620-625.

Akhtar, N., & Herold, K. (2008). Pragmatic development. In M.M. Haith & J.B. Benson (Eds.), *Encyclopedia of infant and early childhood development.* Oxford, UK: Elsevier.

Akhter, R., & Bekris, L.M. (2019). Potential role of miRNA-140 in Alzheimer's disease. *Aging, 11,* 1087-1088.

Akin, R.I., & others (2020). Parent-adolescent relationship quality as a predictor of leaving home. *Journal of Adolescence, 79,* 81-90.

Aksglaede, L., & others (2013). 47, XXY Klinefelter syndrome: Clinical characteristics and age-specific recommendations for medical management. *American Journal of Medical Genetics C: Seminars in Medical Genetics, 163,* 55-63.

Al Alwan, I.A., & others (2017). Decline in menarcheal age among Saudi girls. *Saudi Medical Journal, 36,* 1324-1328.

Alaei, R., & others (2020, in press). Accuracy and bias in first impressions of attachment style from faces. *Journal of Personality.*

Alaie, I., & others (2019). Uppsala Longitudinal Adolescent Depression Study (ULADS). *BMJ Open, 9*(3), e024939.

Alattar, A.A., & others (2019). Hearing impairment and cognitive decline in older, community-dwelling adults. *Journals of Gerontology A: Biological Sciences and Medical Sciences, 75,* 567-573.

Albaugh, M.D., & others (2019). Amygdalar reactivity is associated with prefrontal cortical thickness in a large population-based sample of adolescents. *PLoS One, 14*(5), e0216152.

Alberico, S., & others (2014). The role of gestational diabetes, pre-pregnancy body mass index, and gestational weight gain on the risk of newborn macrosoma: Results from a prospective multicenter study. *BMC Pregnancy and Childbirth, 14*(1), 23.

Albert, R.R., Schwade, J.A., & Goldstein, M.H. (2019). The social functions of babbling: Acoustic and contextual characteristics that facilitate maternal responsiveness. *Developmental Science, 5,* e12641.

Albert, W.D., & others (2020). Individual differences in executive function partially explain the socioeconomic gradient in middle-school academic achievement. *Developmental Science, 8,* e12937.

Alberts, E., Elkind, D., & Ginsberg, S. (2007). The personal fable and risk taking in early adolescence. *Journal of Youth and Adolescence, 36,* 71-76.

Alegret, M., & others (2014). Cognitive, genetic, and brain perfusion factors associated with four-year incidence of Alzheimer's disease from mild cognitive impairment. *Journal of Alzheimer's Disease, 41,* 739-748.

Alexander, C.P., & others (2017). Fathers make a difference: Positive relationships with mother and baby in relation to infant colic. *Child Care, Health, and Development, 43,* 687-696.

Alfredsson, J., & others (2018). Sex differences in management and outcomes of patients with type 2 diabetes and cardiovascular disease: A report from TECOS. *Diabetes, Obesity, and Metabolism, 20,* 2379-2388.

Al-Ghanim, K.A., & Badahdah, A.M. (2017). Gender roles in the Arab world: Development and psychometric properties of the Arab Adolescents Gender Roles Attitude Scale. *Sex Roles, 77,* 165-177.

Ali, S., & others (2019). Primary and secondary prevention of cardiovascular disease in patients with chronic kidney disease. *Current Atherosclerosis Reports, 21*(9), 32.

Aligne, C.A., & others (2020, in press). Impact of the Rochester LARC initiative on adolescents' utilization of long-acting reversible contraception. *American Journal of Obstetrics and Gynecology.*

Alladi, S., & others (2013). Bilingualism delays age of onset of dementia, independent of education and immigration status. *Neurology, 81,* 1938-1944.

Allameh, Z., Tehrani, H.G., & Ghasemi, M. (2015). Comparing the impact of acupuncture and pethidine on reducing labor pain. *Advanced Biomedical Research, 4,* 46.

Allemand, M., Zimprich, D., & Hendriks, A.A.J. (2008). Age differences in five personality domains across the life span. *Developmental Psychology, 44,* 758-770.

Allen, A.P., & others (2018). Autobiographical memory, the aging brain, and mechanisms of psychological interventions. *Aging Research Reviews, 42,* 100-111.

Allen, H.K., Beck, K.H., & Zanjani, F. (2019). Driving concerns among older adults: Associations with driving skill, behaviors, and experiences. *Traffic Injury Prevention, 20,* 45-51.

Allen, J., & Allen, C. (2009). *Escaping the endless adolescence.* New York: Ballantine.

Allen, J.P., Forster, M., Neiberger, A., & Unger, J.B. (2015). Characteristics of emerging adulthood and e-cigarette use: Findings from a pilot study. *Addictive Behaviors, 50,* 40-44.

Allen, J.P., & Miga, E.M. (2010). Attachment in adolescence: A move to the level of emotion regulation. *Journal of Social and Personal Relationships, 27,* 226-234.

Allen, J.P., & others (2009, April). *Portrait of the secure teen as an adult.* Paper presented at the meeting of the Society for Research in Child Development, Denver.

Allen, J.P., & others (2020). Adolescent peer relationship qualities as predictors of long-term romantic life satisfaction. *Child Development. 91,* 327-340.

Allen, L., & Dwivedi, U. (2020, in press). MicroRNA mediators of early life stress vulnerability to depression and suicidal behavior. *Molecular Psychiatry.*

Allen, S., & Barlow, E. (2017). Long-acting reversible contraception: An essential guide for pediatric primary care. *Pediatric Clinics of North America, 64,* 359-369.

Allen, T.D., & Finkelstein, L.M. (2014). Work-family conflict among members of full-time dual-earner couples: An examination of family life stage, gender, and age. *Journal of Occupational Health Psychology, 19,* 376-384.

Allendorf, K. (2013). Schemas of marital change: From arranged marriages to eloping for love. *Journal of Marriage and the Family, 75,* 453-469.

Almazan, J.U., & others (2019). Maternity-ward nurses' kangaroo mother care attitudes and practices: Implications and future challenges. *Scandinavian Journal of Caring Science, 33,* 848-856.

Almeida, D.M., & Horn, M.C. (2004). Is daily life more stressful during middle adulthood? In C.D. Ryff & R.C. Kessler (Eds.), *A portrait of midlife in the United States.* Chicago: University of Chicago Press.

Almeida, M.J. (2018). *Approved drugs for Alzheimer's disease.* Retrieved March 1, 2018, from https://alzheimersnewstoday.com/alzheimers-disease-treatment/approved-drugs/

Almeida, N.D., & others (2016). Risk of miscarriage in women receiving antidepressants in early pregnancy, correcting for induced abortions. *Epidemiology, 27,* 538-546.

Almquist, Y.B., & Brannstrom, L. (2014). Childhood peer status and the clustering of social, economic, and health-related circumstances in adulthood. *Social Science & Medicine, 105,* 67-75.

Alsaker, F.D., & Valanover, S. (2012). The Bernese Program Against Victimization in Kindergarten and Elementary School. *New Directions in Youth Development, 133,* 15-28.

Altintas Aykan, D., & Ergun, Y. (2020, in press). Isoretretinoin: Still the cause of anxiety for teratogenicity. *Dermatologic Therapy.*

Altman, C., Goldstein, T., & Armon-Lotem, S. (2018). Vocabulary, metalinguistic awareness, and language dominance among bilingual preschool children. *Frontiers in Psychology, 9,* 1953.

Alvaro, J.L., & others (2019). Unemployment, self-esteem, and depression: Differences between men and women. *Spanish Journal of Psychology, 22,* E1.

Alves Freire Ribeiro, A.C., & others (2020, in press). Metabolic syndrome accentuates post-traumatic stress disorder-like symptoms and glial activation. *Behavioral Brain Research.*

Alvizo-Rodriguez, C.R., & others (2020, in press). Methylation analysis of MIR200 family in Mexican patients with colorectal cancer. *Journal of Investigative Medicine.*

Alzheimer's Association (2020). *2020 Alzheimer's disease facts and figures.* Chicago: Alzheimer's Association.

Amabile, T.M. (1993). Commentary. In D. Goleman, P. Kaufman, & M. Ray, *The creative spirit.* New York: Plume.

Amabile, T.M. (2018). Creativity and the labor of love. In R.J. Sternberg & J.C. Kaufman (Eds.), *The nature of human creativity.* New York: Cambridge University Press.

Amato, P.R. (2007). Transformative processes in marriage: Some thoughts from a sociologist. *Journal of Marriage and the Family, 69,* 305-309.

Amato, P.R., & Booth, A. (1996). A prospective study of divorce and parent-child relationships, *Journal of Marriage and the Family, 58,* 356-365.

American Academy of Pediatrics (2016). *American Academy of Pediatrics announces new recommendations for children's media use.* Elk Grove Village, IL: AAP.

American Academy of Pediatrics Section on Breastfeeding (2012). Breastfeeding and the use of human milk. *Pediatrics, 129,* e827-e841.

American Academy of Pediatrics Task Force on Infant Positioning and SIDS (AAPTFIPS) (2000). Changing concepts of sudden infant death syndrome. *Pediatrics, 105,* 650-656.

American Association of University Women (2006). *Drawing the line: Sexual harassment on campus.* Washington, DC: American Association of University Women.

American Cancer Society (2020). *Information and resources for cancer.* Retrieved February 11, 2020, from http:www.cancer.org

American Cancer Society (2020). *Menopausal hormone therapy and cancer risk.* Retrieved February 21, 2020, from www.cancer.org

American Psychiatric Association (2013). *Diagnostic and statistical manual of mental disorders* (5th ed.) (DSM-V). Washington, DC: Author.

American Psychological Association (2003). *Psychology: Scientific problem solvers.* Washington, DC: Author.

American Psychological Association (2007). *Stress in America.* Washington, DC: Author.

American Psychological Association (2019). *Education and socioeconomic status.* Retrieved April 19, 2019, from www.apa.org/pi/ses/resources/publications/education

American Society for Reproductive Medicine & others (2019). Prepregnancy counseling: Committee opinion No. 762. *Fertility and Sterility, 111,* 32-42.

Amon, I. (2019). Statistical learning, implicit learning, and first language acquisition: A critical evaluation of two developmental predictions. *Topics in Cognitive Science, 11,* 504-519.

Amorim, M. (2019). Are grandparents a blessing or a burden? Multigenerational coresidence and child-related spending. *Social Science Research, 80,* 132-144.

Amoroso, N., & others (2019). Deep learning and multiplex networks for accurate modeling of brain age. *Frontiers in Aging Neuroscience, 11,* 115.

Amrithraj, A.I., & others (2017). Gestational diabetes alters functions in offspring's umbilical cord cells with implications for cardiovascular health, *158,* 2102-2112.

Amso, D., & Johnson, S.P. (2010). Building object knowledge from perceptual input. In B. Hood & L. Santos (Eds.), *The origins of object knowledge.* New York: Oxford University Press.

Amsterdam, B.K. (1968). *Mirror behavior in children under two years of age.* Unpublished doctoral dissertation. University of North Carolina, Chapel Hill.

Amuedo-Durantes, C., & Arenas-Arroyo, E. (2019). Immigration enforcement and children's living arrangements. *Journal of Policy Analysis and Management, 38,* 11-40.

An, R., & others (2019). Dietary habits and cognitive impairment risk among-oldest-old Chinese. *Journals of Gerontology B: Psychological Sciences and Social Sciences, 74,* 474-483.

Anchang Price, R., & others (2020, in press). Characteristics of hospices providing high-quality care. *Journal of Palliative Medicine.*

Andel, R., Finkel, D., & Pedersen, N.L. (2016). Effects of preretirement work complexity and postretirement leisure activity on cognitive aging. *Journals of Gerontology B: Psychological Sciences and Social Sciences, 71,* 849-856.

Andel, R., & others (2019). Complexity of work and incident impairment in Puerto Rican older adults. *Journals of Gerontology B: Psychological Sciences and Social Sciences, 74,* 785-795.

Anders, K.M., & others (2020). "Sex is easier to get and love is harder to find": Costs and rewards of hooking up among first-year college students. *Journal of Sex Research, 57,* 247-259.

Andersen, I.G., Holm, J.C., & Homoe, P. (2019). Obstructive sleep apnea in children and adolescents with and without obesity. *European Archives of Otorhinolaryngology, 276,* 871-878.

Andersen, S.L., Sebastiani, P., Dworkis, D.A., Feldman, L., & Perls, T.T. (2012). Health span approximates life span among many supercentenarians: Compression of morbidity at the approximate limit of life span. *Journals of Gerontology A: Biological Sciences and Medical Sciences, 67A,* 395-405.

Anderson, E., Greene, S.M., Hetherington, E.M., & Clingempeel, W.G. (1999). The dynamics of parental remarriage. In E.M. Hetherington (Ed.), *Coping with divorce, single parenting, and remarriage.* Mahwah, NJ: Erlbaum.

Anderson, E.M., & others (2019). It is a complex issue: Emerging connections between epigenetic regulators in drug addiction. *European Journal of Neuroscience, 50,* 2477-2491.

Anderson, M.A. (2017, May 17). *Technology use among seniors.* Washington, DC: Pew Research Center.

Anderson, M.A., & others (2019, April 22). 10 percent of Americans don't use the Internet: Who are they? Washington, DC: Pew Research Center.

Anderson, P.A. (2006). The evolution of biological sex differences in communication. In K. Dindia & D.J. Canary (Eds.), *Sex differences and similarities in communication.* Mahwah, NJ: Erlbaum.

Anderson, R.E., & others (2020, in press). The frequency of sexual perpetration in college men: A systematic review of reported prevalence rates from 2000 to 2017. *Trauma, Violence, and Abuse.*

Anderson, S.A., & Sabatelli, R.M. (2011). *Family interaction* (5th ed.). Upper Saddle River, NJ: Pearson.

Anderson, S.E., Gooze, R.A., Lemeshow, S., & Whitaker, R.C. (2012). Quality of early maternal-child relationship and risk of adolescent obesity. *Pediatrics, 129,* 132-140.

Andersson, G., Borgquist, S., & Jirstrom, K. (2018). Hormonal factors and pancreatic cancer risk in women: The Malmo Diet and Cancer Study. *International Journal of Cancer, 143,* 52-62.

Andersson, H., & Bergman, L.R. (2011). The role of task persistence in young adolescence for successful educational and occupational attainment in middle adulthood. *Developmental Psychology, 47*, 950–960.

Andrews, S.J., Ahern, E.C., & Lamb, M.E. (2017). Children's uncertain responses when testifying about alleged sexual abuse in Scottish courts. *Behavioral Sciences and the Law, 35*, 204–224.

Andrews, S.J., & Lamb, M.E. (2017). Lawyers' question repetition and children's responses in Scottish courts. *Journal of Interpersonal Violence, 62*, 182–193.

Andrews, S.J., & Lamb, M.E. (2020, in press). Lawyers' question content and children's responses in Scottish criminal courts. *Psychology, Crime, and Law.*

Andriani, H., Liao, C.Y., & Kuo, H.W. (2015). Parental weight changes as key predictors of child weight changes. *BMC Public Health, 15*, 645.

Angel, J.L., Mudrazija, S., & Benson, R. (2016). In L.K. George & K.F. Ferraro (Eds.), *Handbook of aging and the social sciences* (8th ed.). New York: Elsevier.

Angel, L., Fay, S., Bouazzaoui, B., & Isingrini, M. (2011). Two hemispheres for better memory in old age: Role of executive functioning. *Journal of Cognitive Neuroscience, 23*(12), 3767–3777.

Anglin, D.M., & others (2018). Ethnic identity, racial discrimination, and attenuated psychotic symptoms in an urban population of emerging adults. *Early Intervention in Psychiatry, 12*(3), 380–390.

Anguera, J.A., & others (2013). Video game training enhances cognitive control in older adults. *Nature, 501*, 97–101.

Ansari, A. (2015). *Modern romance.* New York: Penguin.

Ansari, A., & Gershoff, E. (2016). Parent involvement in Head Start and children's development: Indirect effects through parenting. *Journal of Marriage and the Family, 78*, 562–579.

Ansari, A., & Winsler, A. (2014). Montessori public school pre-K programs and the school readiness of low-income Black and Latino children. *Journal of Educational Psychology, 106*, 1066–1079.

Ansari, J., Carvalho, B., Shafer, S.L., & Flood, P. (2016). Pharmacokinetics and pharmacodynamics of drugs commonly used in pregnancy and parturition. *Anesthesia and Analgesia, 122*, 786–804.

Anspach, D. (2017). *Average retirement age in the United States.* Retrieved March 30, 2017, from www.thebalance.com

Antfolk, J., & others (2017). Willingness to invest in children: Psychological kinship estimates and emotional closeness. *Evolutionary Psychology, 15*(2), 1474704917705730.

Anton, E., Carreiras, M., & Dunabeitia, J.A. (2019). The impact of bilingualism on executive functions and working memory in young adults. *PLoS One, 14*(2), e0206770.

Antonenko, D., & Floel, A. (2014). Healthy aging by staying selectively connected: A mini-review. *Gerontology, 60*(1), 3–9.

Antonijevic, S., Muckley, S.A., & Muller, N. (2020, in press). The role of consistency in use of morphosyntactic forms in child-directed speech in the acquisition of Irish, a minority language undergoing rapid language change. *Journal of Child Language.*

Antonucci, T.C., Vandewater, E.A., & Lansford, J.E. (2000). Adulthood and aging: Social processes and development. In A. Kazdin (Ed.), *Encyclopedia of psychology.* Washington, DC, & New York: American Psychological Association and Oxford University Press.

Antonucci, T.C., & Webster, N.J. (2019). Involvement with life and social networks: A pathway for successful aging. In R. Fernandez-Ballesteros & others (Eds.), *Cambridge handbook of successful aging.* New York: Cambridge University Press.

Antonucci, T.C., & others (2016). Society and the individual at the dawn of the twenty-first century. In K.W. Schaie & S.L. Willis (Eds.), *Handbook of the psychology of aging* (8th ed.). New York: Elsevier.

Antovich, D.M., & Graf Estes, K. (2018). Learning across languages: Bilingual experience supports dual language statistical word segmentation. *Developmental Science, 21*, 2.

Anusruti. A., & others (2020). Longitudinal associations of body mass index, waist circumference, and waist-to-hip ratio with biomarkers of oxidative stress in older adults: Results of a large cohort study. *Obesity Facts, 13*, 66–76.

AP-NORC Center for Public Affairs Research (2013). Working longer: Older Americans' attitudes on work and retirement. Retrieved March 1, 2018, from http://apnorc.org/PDFs/Working%20Longer/ AP-NORC%20Center_Working%20Longer%20 Report-FINAL.pdf

Appolinario, J.C., Nardi, A.E., & McElroy, S.L. (2019). Investigational drugs for the treatment of binge eating disorder (BED): An update. *Expert Opinion on Investigational Drugs, 28*, 1081–1094.

Arabi, M., Frongillo, E.A., Avula, R., & Mangasaryan, N. (2012). Infant and young child feeding in developing countries. *Child Development, 83*, 32–45.

Ardelt, M., Gerlach, K.R., & Vaillant, G.E. (2018). Early and midlife predictors of wisdom and subjective well-being in old age. *Journals of Gerontology B: Psychological Sciences and Social Sciences, 73*, 1514–1525.

Ardelt, M., Pridgen, S., & Nutter-Pridgen, K.L. (2018). The relation between age and three-dimensional wisdom: Variations by wisdom dimensions and education. *Journals of Gerontology B: Psychological Sciences and Social Sciences, 73*, 1339–1349.

Aremu, T.A., John-Akinola, Y.O., & Desmennu, A.T. (2019). Relationship between parenting styles and adolescents' self-esteem. *International Quarterly of Community Health Education, 39*, 91–99.

Arias, E., & Xu, J. (2019). United States life tables, 2017. *National Vital Statistics Reports, 68*(7), 1–66.

Ariceli, G., Castro, J., Cesena, J., & Toro, J. (2005). Anorexia nervosa in male adolescents: Body image, eating attitudes, and psychological traits. *Journal of Adolescent Health, 36*, 221–226.

Arjmand, B., & others (2020, in press). The horizon of gene therapy in modern medicine: Advances and challenges. *Advances in Experimental Medicine and Biology.*

Armstrong, M.J., & Okun, M.S. (2020). Diagnosis and treatment of Parkinson disease: A review. *JAMA, 323*, 548–560.

Armstrong, N.M., & others (2020). Temporal sequence of hearing impairment and cognition in the Baltimore Longitudinal Study of Aging. *Journals of Gerontology A: Biological Sciences and Medical Sciences, 75*, 574–580.

Arnett, J.J. (2004). *Emerging adulthood.* New York: Oxford University Press.

Arnett, J.J. (2006). Emerging adulthood: Understanding the new way of coming of age. In J.J. Arnett & J.L. Tanner (Eds.), *Emerging adults in America.* Washington, DC: American Psychological Association.

Arnett, J.J. (2007). Socialization in emerging adulthood. In J.E. Grusec & P.D. Hastings (Eds.), *Handbook of socialization.* New York: Guilford.

Arnett, J.J. (2010). Oh, grow up! Generational grumbling and the new life stage of emerging adulthood—Commentary on Trzesniewski & Donnellan (2010). *Perspectives on Psychological Science, 5*, 89–92.

Arnett, J.J. (Ed.) (2012). *Adolescent psychology around the world.* New York: Psychology Press.

Arnett, J.J. (2015a). *Emerging adulthood* (2nd ed.). New York: Oxford University Press.

Arnett, J.J. (2015b). Identity development from adolescence to emerging adulthood: What we know and (especially) don't know. In K.C. McLean & M. Syed (Eds.), *Oxford handbook of identity development.* New York: Oxford University Press.

Arnett, J.J. (2016a). Does emerging adulthood theory apply across social classes? National data on a persistent question. *Emerging Adulthood, 4*, 227–235.

Arnett, J.J. (2016b). Emerging adulthood and social class: Rejoinder to Furstenberg, Silva, and du Bois-Reymond. *Emerging Adulthood, 4*, 244–247.

Arnett, J.J., & Mitra, D. (2020, in press). Are the features of emerging adulthood developmentally distinctive? A comparison of ages 18–60 in the United States. *Emerging Adulthood.*

Arnett, J.J., & Padilla-Walker, L.M. (2015). Brief report: Danish emerging adults' conceptions of adulthood. *Journal of Adolescence, 38*, 39–44.

Arnold, W.C., & Guilleminault, C. (2019). Upper airway resistance syndrome 2018: Non-hypoxic sleep-disordered breathing. *Expert Review in Respiratory Medicine, 13*, 317–326.

Arns, M., & Vollebregt, M.A. (2019). Editorial: Time to wake up: Appreciating the role of sleep in ADHD. *Journal of the American Academy of Child and Adolescent Psychiatry, 58*(4), 398–400.

Aron, A., Coups, E.J., & Aron, E.N. (2019). *Statistics for psychology, brief course* (6th ed.). Upper Saddle River, NJ: Pearson.

Aronson, E. (1986, August). *Teaching students things they think they already know about: The case of prejudice and desegregation.* Paper presented at the meeting of the American Psychological Association, Washington, DC.

Aronson, J. (2002). Stereotype threat: Contending and coping with unnerving expectations. *Improving academic achievement.* San Diego: Academic Press.

Arseth, A., Kroger, J., Martinussen, M., & Marcia, J.E. (2009). Meta-analytic studies of identity status and the relational issues of attachment and intimacy. *Identity, 9,* 1–32.

Ary, D., & others (2019). *Introduction to research in education* (10th ed.). Boston: Cengage.

Ascend (2019). *Accelerating postsecondary success for parents: Identifying and addressing mental health needs.* Aspen, CO: The Aspen Institute.

Askeland, K.G., & others (2017). Mental health in internationally adopted adolescents: A meta-analysis. *Journal of the American Academy of Child and Adolescent Psychiatry, 56,* 202–213.

Aslan, D., & Koksal Akyol, A. (2020, in press). Impact of an empathy training program on children's perspective-taking abilities. *Psychological Reports.*

Aslin, R.N. (2012). Infant eyes: A window on cognitive development. *Infancy, 17,* 126–140.

Aslin, R.N. (2017). Statistical learning: A powerful mechanism that operates by mere exposure. *Wiley Interdisciplinary Reviews: Cognitive Science, 8,* 1–2.

Aslin, R. (2019). *Research overview.* Retrieved August 8, 2019, from haskinslabs.org/people/Richard-aslin

Aslin, R.N., Jusczyk, P.W., & Pisoni, D.B. (1998). Speech and auditory processing during infancy: Constraints on and precursors to language. In W. Damon (Ed.), *Handbook of child psychology* (5th ed., Vol. 2). New York: Wiley.

Aslin, R.N., & Lathrop, A.L. (2008). Visual perception. In M. Haith & J. Benson (Eds.), *Handbook of infant and early childhood development.* London: Elsevier.

Aspen Institute (2013). *Two generations, one future.* Washington, DC: Aspen Institute.

Aspen Institute (2019). *Making tomorrow better together.* Washington, DC: Aspen Institute.

Assini-Meytin, L.C., & Green, K.M. (2015). Long-term consequences of adolescent parenthood among African-American youth: A propensity score matching approach. *Journal of Adolescent Health, 56,* 529–535.

Astle, S., Leonhardt, N., & Willoughby, B. (2020, in press). Home base: Family of origin factors and the debut of vaginal sex, anal sex, oral sex, masturbation, and pornography use in a national sample of adolescents. *Journal of Sex Research.*

Aten, J.D., & others (2019). The psychological study of religion and spirituality in a disaster context: A systematic review. *Psychological Trauma, 11,* 597–613.

Atherton, O.E., Lawson, K.M., & Robins, R.W. (2020, in press). The development of effortful control from late childhood to young adulthood. *Journal of Personality and Social Psychology.*

Atherton, O.E., & others (2019). The codevelopment of effortful control and school behavioral problems. *Journal of Personality and Social Psychology, 117,* 659–673.

Atiemo, K., & others (2019). The Hispanic paradox in patients with liver cirrhosis: Current evidence from a large regional retrospective cohort study. *Transplantation, 103*(12), 2531–2538.

Atkins, J.L., & others (2019). Impact of low cardiovascular risk profiles on geriatric outcomes: Evidence from 421,000 participants in two cohorts. *Journals of Gerontology A: Biological Sciences and Medical Sciences, 74,* 350–357.

Attar-Schwartz, S., Tan, J.P., Buchanan, A., Flouri, E., & Griggs, J. (2009). Grandparenting and adolescent development in two-parent biological, lone-parent, and step-families. *Journal of Family Psychology, 23,* 67–75.

Atwood, M.E., & Friedman, A. (2020, in press). A systematic review of enhanced cognitive behavioral therapy (CBT-E) for eating disorders. *International Journal of Eating Disorders.*

Audesirk, G., Audesirk, T., & Byers, B.E. (2020). *Biology* (12th ed.). Upper Saddle River, NJ: Pearson.

Auersperg, F., & others (2019). Long-term effects of parental divorce on mental health—A meta-analysis. *Journal of Psychiatric Research, 119,* 107–115.

Autism Research Institute (2013). DSM-V: What changes may mean. Retrieved May 7, 2013, from www.autism.com/index.php/news_dsmV

Avni, I., & others (2020, in press). Children with autism observe social interactions in an idiosyncratic manner. *Autism Research.*

Avvenuti, G., Baiardini, I., & Giardini, A. (2016). Optimism's explicative role for chronic diseases. *Frontiers in Psychology, 7,* 295.

Axinn, W.G., & others (2020). The association between transitions and the onset of major depressive disorder in a South Asian general population. *Journal of Affective Disorders, 266,* 165–172.

Ayoub, C., Vallotton, C.D., & Mastergeorge, A.M. (2011). Developmental pathways to integrated social skills: The role of parenting and early intervention. *Child Development, 82,* 583–600.

Azab, S.S., & others (2020, in press). Penile hemodynamics study in erectile dysfunction men: The influence of smoking obesity on the parameters of penile duplex. *International Urology and Nephrology.*

Azar, S., & Wong, T.E. (2017). Sickle cell disease: A brief update. *Medical Clinics of North America, 101,* 375–393.

Azeez, M., & others (2020, in press). Benefits of exercise in patients with rheumatoid arthritis: A randomized controlled trial of a patient-specific exercise program. *Clinical Rheumatology.*

Azizmohammadi, S., & Azizmohammadi, S. (2019). Hypnotherapy in management of delivery pain: A review. *European Journal of Translational Myology, 29*(3), 8365.

B

Babaei, Z., Ghayoumi-Anaraki, Z., & Mahmoodi-Bakhtiari, B. (2019). Discourse in aging: Narrative and persuasive. *Dementia and Neuropsychologia, 13*(4), 444–449.

Bacchi, M., & others (2018). Aquatic activities during pregnancy prevent excessive maternal weight gain and preserve birthweight. *American Journal of Health Promotion, 32,* 729–735.

Bach, L.E., Mortimer, J.A., Vandeweerd, C., & Corvin, J. (2013). The association of physical and mental health with sexual activity in older adults in a retirement community. *Journal of Sexual Medicine, 10*(11), 2671–2678.

Bachman, J.G., & others (2008). *The education-drug use connection.* Clifton, NJ: Psychology Press.

Bachmann, N., & others (2017). Novel deletion in 11p15.5 imprinting center region 1 in a patient with Beckwith-Wiedemann syndrome provides insight into distal enhancer regulation and tumorigenesis. *Pediatric Blood & Cancer, 64,* 3.

Bacikova-Sleskova, M., Benka, J., & Orosova, O. (2015). Parental employment status and adolescents' health: The role of financial situation, parent-adolescent relationship, and adolescents' resilience. *Psychology and Health, 30,* 400–422.

Baddeley, A.D. (1990). *Human memory: Theory and practice.* Boston: Allyn & Bacon.

Baddeley, A.D. (2007). *Working memory, thought, and action.* New York: Oxford University Press.

Baddeley, A.D. (2012). Working memory: Theories, models, and controversies. *Annual Review of Psychology* (Vol. 63). Palo Alto, CA: Annual Reviews.

Baddeley, A.D. (2015). Origins of the multicomponent working memory model. In M. Eysenck & D. Groome (Eds.), *Cognitive psychology.* London: Sage.

Baddeley, A.D. (2017). *Working memories.* New York: Routledge.

Baddeley, A.D. (2018). *Exploring working memory: Selected works of Alan Baddeley.* New York: Routledge.

Baddeley, A.D. (2020, in press). When and where is cognitive psychology useful? The case of working memory. *Psychology in Practice.*

Baddeley, A.D., Hitch, G.J., & Allen, R.J. (2019). From short-term store to multicomponent working memory: The role of the modal model. *Memory and Cognition, 47,* 575–588.

Bae, Y.J., & others (2020, in press). Reference intervals of nine steroid hormones over the life-span analyzed by LC-MSD/MS: Effect of age, gender, puberty, and oral contraceptives. *Journal of Steroid Biochemistry and Molecular Biology.*

Baer, R.J., & others (2019). Risk of preterm and early term birth by maternal drug use. *Journal of Perinatology, 39,* 286–294.

Bagwell, C.L., & Bukowki, W.M. (2018). Friendship in childhood and adolescence. In W. M. Bukowski & others (Eds.), *Handbook of peer interactions, relationships, and groups* (2nd ed.). New York: Guilford.

Bahmaee, A.B., Saadatmand, Z., & Yarmohammadian, M.H. (2016). Principle elements of curriculum in the preschool pattern of Montessori. *International Education Studies, 9,* 148–153.

Bahrick, L.E. (2010). Intermodal perception and selective attention to intersensory redundancy: Implications for social development and autism. In

J.G. Bremner & T.D. Wachs (Eds.), *Wiley-Blackwell handbook of infant development* (2nd ed.). New York: Wiley.

Bailey, D.M., & others (2013). Elevated aerobic fitness sustained throughout the adult lifespan is associated with improved cerebral hemodynamics. *Stroke, 44*(11), 3235-3238.

Baillargeon, R. (1995). The object concept revisited: New directions in the investigation of infants' physical knowledge. In C.E. Granrud (Ed.), *Visual perception and cognition in infancy*. Hillsdale, NJ: Erlbaum.

Baillargeon, R. (2004). The acquisition of physical knowledge in infancy: A summary in eight lessons. In U. Goswami (Ed.), *Blackwell handbook of childhood cognitive development*. Malden, MA: Blackwell.

Baillargeon, R. (2014). Cognitive development in infancy. *Annual Review of Psychology* (Vol. 65). Palo Alto, CA: Annual Reviews.

Baillargeon, R. (2016). Cognitive development in infancy. *Annual Review of Psychology* (Vol. 67). Palo Alto, CA: Annual Reviews.

Baillargeon, R., & DeJong, G.F. (2017). Explanation-based reasoning in infancy. *Psychonomic Bulletin and Review, 24,* 1511-1526.

Bailly, N., & others (2018). Spirituality, social support, and flexibility among older adults: A five-year longitudinal study. *International Psychogeriatrics, 30,* 1745-1752.

Bajoghli, H., & others (2014). "I love you more than I can stand!"—Romantic love, symptoms of depression and anxiety, and sleep complaints are related among young adults. *International Journal of Psychiatry in Clinical Practice, 18,* 169-174.

Bakeman, R., & Brown, J.V. (1980). Early interaction: Consequences for social and mental development at three years. *Child Development, 51,* 437-447.

Baker, C.E., & Brooks-Gunn, J. (2020, in press). Early parenting and the intergenerational transmission of self-regulation and behavioral problems in African American Head Start families. *Child Psychiatry and Human Development.*

Baker, D., Norris, D., & Cherneva, V. (2020, in press). Disenfranchised grief and families' experiences of death after police contact in the United States. *Omega.*

Baker, F.C., & others (2018). Sleep problems during the menopausal transition: Prevalence, impact, and management implications. *Nature and the Science of Sleep, 10,* 73-95.

Baker, J.J., & Stoler, J.M. (2020). Recent developments in fetal alcohol spectrum disorder. *Current Opinion in Endocrinology, Diabetes, and Obesity, 27,* 77-81.

Baker, J.K., Fenning, R.M., & Crnic, K.A. (2011). Emotion socialization by mothers and fathers: Coherence among behaviors and associations with parent attitudes and children's competence. *Social Development, 20,* 412-430.

Baker, K.M., & others (2020, in press). Adolescent weight and health behaviors and their associations with individual, social, and parental factors. *Journal of Physical Activity and Health.*

Baker, N.A., & Halford, W.K. (2020, in press). Assessment of couple relationships standards in same-sex attracted adults. *Family Process.*

Bakermans-Kranenburg, M.J., & van IJzendoorn, M.H. (2011). Differential susceptibility to rearing environment depending on dopamine-related genes: New evidence and a meta-analysis. *Development and Psychopathology, 23,* 39-52.

Balantekin, K.N., Birch, L.L., & Savage, J.S. (2018). Family, friend, and media factors are associated with patterns of weight-control behavior among adolescent girls. *Eating and Weight Disorders, 23,* 215-223.

Balasubramaniam, M. (2018). Rational suicide in elderly adults: A clinician's perspective. *Journal of the American Geriatrics Society, 66,* 998-1001.

Balfour, B., & Vittoria, J. (2018). 'Wounded memory', post-war gender conflict, and narrative identity: Reinterpreting Reggio Emilia schools' origin stories. *History of Education, 47,* 727-740.

Ball, K., Edwards, J.D., Ross, L.A., & McGwin, G. (2010). Effects of cognitive training interventions with older adults: A randomized controlled trial. *Journal of the American Geriatrics Society, 55,* 1-10.

Ballintyn, B., Shlaer, B., & Miller, P. (2019). Spatiotemporal discrimination in attractor networks with short-term synaptic plasticity. *Journal of Computational Neuroscience, 46,* 279-297.

Balon, R., & Morreale, M.K. (2016). In search of meaning: What makes life worth living in the face of death. *Academic Psychiatry, 40,* 634.

Baltes, P.B. (1987). Theoretical propositions of life-span developmental psychology: On the dynamics between growth and decline. *Developmental Psychology, 23,* 611-626.

Baltes, P.B. (2003). On the incomplete architecture of human ontogeny: Selection, optimization, and compensation as foundation for developmental theory. In U.M. Staudinger & U. Lindenberger (Eds.), *Understanding human development*. Boston: Kluwer.

Baltes, P.B. (2006). *Facing our limits: The very old and the future of aging*. Unpublished manuscript, Max Planck Institute, Berlin.

Baltes, P.B., & Kunzmann, U. (2007). Wisdom and aging: The road toward excellence in mind and character. In D.C. Park & N. Schwarz (Eds.), *Cognitive aging: A primer* (2nd ed.). Philadelphia: Psychology Press.

Baltes, P.B., Lindenberger, U., & Staudinger, U. (2006). Life-span theory in developmental psychology. In W. Damon & R. Lerner (Eds.), *Handbook of child psychology* (6th ed.), New York: Wiley.

Baltes, P.B., Reuter-Lorenz, P., & Rösler, F. (Eds.) (2012). *Lifespan development and the brain*. New York: Cambridge University Press.

Baltes, P.B., & Smith, J. (2003). New frontiers in the future of aging: From successful aging of the young old to the dilemmas of the fourth age. *Gerontology, 49,* 123-135.

Baltes, P.B., & Smith, J. (2008). The fascination of wisdom: Its nature, ontogeny, and function. *Perspectives in Psychological Sciences, 3,* 56-64.

Balzer, B.W.R., & others (2019). Self-rated Tanner stage and subjective measures of puberty are associated with longitudinal gonadal hormone changes. *Journal of Pediatric Endocrinology and Metabolism.*

Bamaca-Colbert, M., Umana-Taylor, A.J., Espinosa-Hernandez, G., & Brown, A.M. (2012). Behavioral autonomy expectations among Mexican-origin mother-daughter dyads: An examination of within-group variability. *Journal of Adolescence, 35,* 691-700.

Bandura, A. (1986). *Social foundations of thought and action: A social cognitive theory*. Englewood Cliffs, NJ: Prentice Hall.

Bandura, A. (1998, August). *Swimming against the mainstream: Accentuating the positive aspects of humanity*. Paper presented at the meeting of the American Psychological Association, San Francisco.

Bandura, A. (2001). Social cognitive theory. *Annual Review of Psychology* (Vol. 52). Palo Alto, CA: Annual Reviews.

Bandura, A. (2004, May). *Toward a psychology of human agency*. Paper presented at the meeting of the American Psychological Society, Chicago.

Bandura, A. (2008). Reconstrual of free will from the agentic perspective of social cognitive theory. In J. Baer, J.C. Kaufman, & R.F. Baumeister (Eds.), *Are we free? Psychology and free will*. Oxford, UK: Oxford University Press.

Bandura, A. (2009). Social and policy impact of social cognitive theory. In M. Mark, S. Donaldson, & B. Campbell (Eds.), *Social psychology and program/policy evaluation*. New York: Guilford.

Bandura, A. (2010a). Self-efficacy. In D. Matsumoto (Ed.), *Cambridge dictionary of psychology*. New York: Cambridge University Press.

Bandura, A. (2010b). Vicarious learning. In D. Matsumoto (Ed.), *Cambridge dictionary of psychology*. New York: Cambridge University Press.

Bandura, A. (2012). Social cognitive theory. *Annual Review of Clinical Psychology* (Vol. 8). Palo Alto, CA: Annual Reviews.

Bandura, A. (2015). *Moral disengagement*. New York: Worth.

Bandura, A. (2018). Toward a psychology of human agency: Pathways and reflections. *Perspectives on Psychological Science, 13,* 130-136.

Bangen, K.J., Meeks, T.W., & Jeste, D.V. (2013). Defining and assessing wisdom: A review of the literature. *American Journal of Geriatric Psychiatry, 21,* 1254-1266.

Bangsbo, J., & others (2019). Copenhagen consensus statement 2019: Physical activity and aging. *British Journal of Sports Medicine, 53,* 856-858.

Banja, J. (2005). Talking to the dying. *Case Manager, 16,* 37-39.

Bank, S., Rhodes, G., Read, A., & Jeffery, L. (2015). Face and body recognition show similar improvement during childhood. *Journal of Experimental Child Psychology, 137*(1), 1-11.

Banker, S.M., & others (2020). Spatial network connectivity and spatial reasoning ability in children with nonverbal learning disability. *Scientific Reports, 10*(1), 561.

Banks, J.A. (2019). *Multicultural education* (6th ed.). Upper Saddle River, NJ: Pearson.

Banks, J.A. (2020). *Diversity, transformative knowledge, and civic education.* New York: Routledge.

Bannon, F., & others (2018). Insights into the factors associated with achieving the preference of home death in terminal cancer: A national population-based study. *Palliative and Supportive Care, 16,* 749–755.

Baradon, T., & others (2019). New beginnings: A time-limited group intervention for high-risk infants and mothers. In H. Steele & M. Steele (Eds.), *Handbook of attachment-based interventions.* New York: Guilford.

Baran, C.N., & Sanders, J.J. (2019). Communication skills: Delivering bad news, conducting a goals of care family meeting, and advance care planning. *Primary Care, 46,* 353–372.

Barati, E., Nikzad, H., & Karimian, M. (2020, in press). Oxidative stress and male infertility: Current knowledge of pathophysiology and role of antioxidant therapy in disease management. *Cellular and Molecular Life Sciences.*

Barbonetti, A., D'Andrea, S., & Francavilla, S. (2020, in press). Testosterone replacement therapy. *Andrology.*

Barbosa, M., & others (2018). Neonatal Behavioral Assessment Scale (NBAS): Confirmatory factor analysis of the six behavioral clusters. *Early Human Development, 124,* 1–6.

Bardid, F., & others (2016). Configurations of actual and perceived motor competence among children: Associations with motivation for sports and global self-worth. *Human Movement Science. 50,* 1–9.

Bargh, J.A., & McKenna, K.Y.A. (2004). The Internet and social life. *Annual Review of Psychology* (Vol. 55). Palo Alto, CA: Annual Reviews.

Barhight, L.R., Hubbard, J.A., Grassetti, S.N., & Morrow, M.T. (2017). Relations between actual group norms, perceived peer behavior, and bystander children's intervention to bullying. *Journal of Clinical Child and Adolescent Psychology, 46,* 394–400.

Barker, R., & Wright, H.F. (1951). *One boy's day.* New York: Harper & Row.

Barlett, C. (2019). *Predicting cyberbullying.* New York: Elsevier.

Barnett, M.D., Cantu, C., & Galvez, A.M. (2020). Attitudes toward euthanasia among hospice nurses: Political ideology or religious commitment. *Death Studies, 44,* 195–200.

Baron, J. (2020). Why science succeeds, and sometimes doesn't. In R.J. Sternberg & D.F. Halpern (Eds.), *Critical thinking in psychology* (2nd ed.). New York: Cambridge University Press.

Baron, N.S. (1992). *Growing up with language.* Reading, MA: Addison-Wesley.

Barooah, A., & others (2019). Immediate aftermath of a client's death: The experience of home health aides. *Home Health Care Services Quarterly, 38,* 14–28.

Barr, R. (2019). Parenting in the digital age. In M.H. Bornstein (Ed.), *Handbook of parenting* (3rd ed.). New York: Elsevier.

Barragan, V., & others (2019). Factors associated with sexual debut in Mexican adolescents: Results of the National Survey on Drug Use among Students in 2014. *Journal of Sexual Medicine, 16,* 418–426.

Barrett, T.M., Traupman, E., & Needham, A. (2008). Infants' visual anticipation of object structure in grasp planning. *Infant Behavior and Development, 31,* 1–9.

Barry, A.E., Valdez, D., & Russell, A.M. (2020). Does religiosity delay adolescent alcohol initiation? A long-term analysis (2008–2015) of nationally representative sample of 12th-graders. *Substance Use and Misuse, 55,* 503–511.

Barry, C., & Overland, G. (2019). *Responding to global poverty.* New York: Cambridge University Press.

Barry, L.C., & Byers, A.L. (2016). Risk factors and prevention: Strategies for late-life mood and anxiety disorders. In K.W. Schaie & S.L. Willis (Eds.), *Handbook of the psychology of aging* (8th ed.). New York: Elsevier.

Bartel, A.P., & others (2018). Paid family leave, fathers' leave taking, and leave-sharing in dual-family households. *Journal of Policy Analysis and Management, 37,* 10–37.

Bartel, K., Scheeren, R., & Gradisar, M. (2019). Altering adolescents' pre-bedtime phone use to achieve better sleep health. *Health Communication, 34,* 456–462.

Bartick, M.C., & others (2017a). Disparities in breastfeeding: Impact of maternal and child health outcomes and costs. *Journal of Pediatrics, 181,* 49–55.

Bartick, M.C., & others (2017b). Suboptimal breastfeeding in the United States: Maternal and pediatric health outcomes and costs. *Maternal and Child Nutrition.* doi: 10.1111/mcn.12366

Bartick, M.C., & others (2020, in press). Trends in breastfeeding interventions, skin-to-skin contact, and sudden infant death in the first 6 days after birth. *Journal of Pediatrics.*

Bartl, H., & others (2018). Does prolonged grief treatment foster posttraumatic growth? Secondary results from a treatment study with long-term follow-up and mediation analysis. *Psychology and Psychotherapy, 91,* 27–41.

Bartolomeo, P., & Seidel Malkinson, T. (2019). Hemispheric lateralization of attention processes in the human brain. *Current Opinion in Psychology, 29,* 90–96.

Bartsch, K., & Wellman, H.M. (1995). *Children talk about the mind.* New York: Oxford University Press.

Bashor, C.J., & others (2019). Complex signal processing in synthetic gene circuits using cooperative regulatory assemblies. *Science, 364,* 593–597.

Basile, K.C., & others (2020, in press). Chronic diseases, health conditions, and other impacts associated with rape victimization of U.S. women. *Journal of Interpersonal Violence.*

Bass, L., & others (2019). Children's developing theory of mind and pedagogical evidence selection. *Developmental Psychology, 55,* 286–302.

Bates, E. (1990). Language about me and you: Pronominal reference and the emerging concept of self. In D. Cicchetti & M. Beeghly (Eds.), *The self in transition: Infancy to childhood.* Chicago: University of Chicago Press.

Bates, J.E. (2012a). Behavioral regulation as a product of temperament and environment. In S.L. Olson & A.J. Sameroff (Eds.), *Biopsychosocial regulatory processes in the development of childhood behavioral problems.* New York: Cambridge University Press.

Bates, J.E. (2012b). Temperament as a tool in promoting early childhood development. In S.L. Odom, E.P. Pungello, & N. Gardner-Neblett (Eds.), *Infants, toddlers, and families in poverty.* New York: Guilford.

Bates, J.E., McQuillan, M.E., & Hoyniak, C.P. (2019). Parenting and temperament. In M.H. Bornstein (Ed.), *Handbook of parenting* (3rd ed.). New York: Elsevier.

Bates, J.E., & Pettit, G.S. (2015). Temperament, parenting, and social development. In J.E. Grusec & P.D. Hastings (Eds.), *Handbook of socialization* (2nd ed.). New York: Guilford.

Bateson, P. (2015). Human evolution and development: An ethological perspective. In R.M. Lerner (Ed.), *Handbook of child psychology and developmental science* (7th ed.). New York: Wiley.

Batsis, J.A., & others (2018). Association of adiposity, telomere length, and mortality: Data from the NHANES 1999–2002. *International Journal of Obesity, 42,* 198–204.

Batty, P., & Lillicrap, D. (2020, in press). Advances and challenges for hemophilia gene therapy. *Human Molecular Genetics.*

Bauer, K.W., & others (2019). Maternal executive function and the family food environment. *Appetite, 137,* 21–26.

Bauer, P.J. (2009a). Learning and memory: Like a horse and carriage. In A. Woodward & A. Needham (Eds.), *Learning and the infant mind.* New York: Oxford University Press.

Bauer, P.J. (2009b). Neurodevelopmental changes in infancy and beyond: Implications for learning and memory. In O.A. Barbarin & B.H. Wasik (Eds.), *Handbook of child development and early education.* New York: Guilford.

Bauer, P.J. (2013). Memory. In P.D. Zelazo (Ed.), *Oxford handbook of developmental psychology.* New York: Oxford University Press.

Bauer, P.J. (2015). A complementary processes account of the development of childhood amnesia and a personal past. *Psychological Review, 122,* 204–231.

Bauer, P.J. (2018). Memory development. In J. Rubenstein & P. Rakic (Eds.), *Neural circuit development and function in the healthy and diseased brain* (2nd ed.). New York: Elsevier.

Bauer, P.J., & Fivush, R. (Eds.) (2014). *Wiley-Blackwell handbook of children's memory.* New York: Wiley.

Bauer, P.J., & Larkina, M. (2014). The onset of childhood amnesia in childhood: A prospective investigation of the course and determinants of forgetting of early-life events. *Memory, 22,* 907–924.

Bauer, P.J., & Larkina, M. (2016). Predicting remembering and forgetting of autobiographical memories in children and adults: A 4-year prospective study. *Memory, 24,* 1345-1368.

Bauer, P.J., Wenner, J.A., Dropik, P.I., & Wewerka, S.S. (2000). Parameters of remembering and forgetting in the transition from infancy to early childhood. *Monographs of the Society for Research in Child Development, 65*(4), Serial No. 263.

Bauer, P.J., & others (2017). Neural correlates of autobiographical memory retrieval in children and adults. *Memory, 25,* 450-466.

Baum, G.L. & others (2020, in press). Development of structure-function coupling in human brain networks during youth. *Proceedings of the National Academy of Sciences U.S.A.*

Bauman, K.E., & others (2002). Influence of a family program on adolescent smoking and drinking prevalence. *Prevention Science, 3,* 35-42.

Baumeister, R.F. (2013). Self-esteem. In E. Anderson (Ed.), *Psychology of classroom learning: An encyclopedia.* Detroit: Macmillan.

Baumeister, R.F., Campbell, J.D., Krueger, J.I., & Vohs, K.D. (2003). Does high self-esteem cause better performance, interpersonal success, happiness, or healthier lifestyles? *Psychological Science in the Public Interest, 4*(1), 1-44.

Baumeister, R.F., & Vohs, K.D. (2002). The pursuit of meaningfulness in life. In C.R. Snyder & S.J. Lopez (Eds.), *Handbook of positive psychology.* New York: Oxford University Press.

Baumrind, D. (1971). Current patterns of parental authority. *Developmental Psychology Monographs, 4*(1, Pt. 2).

Baumrind, D. (2012). Authoritative parenting revisited: History and current status. In R. Larzelere, A.S. Morris, & A.W. Harist (Eds.), *Authoritative parenting.* Washington, DC: American Psychological Association.

Baumrind, D., Larzelere, R.E., & Cowan, P.A. (2002). Ordinary physical punishment: Is it harmful? Comment on Gershoff. *Psychological Bulletin, 128,* 590-595.

Baumrind, D., Larzelere, R.E., & Owens, E.B. (2010). Effects of preschool parents' power assertive patterns and practices on adolescent development. *Parenting, 10,* 157-201.

Bauserman, R. (2002). Child adjustment in joint-custody versus sole-custody arrangements: A meta-analytical review. *Journal of Family Psychology, 16,* 91-102.

Baye, K., Tariku, A., & Mouquet-Rivier, C. (2018). Caregiver-infant's feeding behaviors are associated with energy intake of 9-11-month-old infants in rural Ethiopia. *Maternal and Child Nutrition, 14,* 1.

Beal, M.A., Yauk, C.L., & Marchetti, F. (2017). From sperm to offspring: Assessing the heritable genetic consequences of paternal smoking and potential public health impacts. *Mutation, 773,* 26-50.

Bear, D.R., & others (2020). *Words their way* (7th ed.). Upper Saddle River, NJ: Pearson.

Beard, V.R., & Burger, W.C. (2017). Change and innovation in the funeral industry. *Omega, 75,* 47-68.

Beard, V.R., & Burger, W.C. (2020). Selling in a dying business: An analysis of trends during a period of major market transition in the funeral industry. *Omega. 80*(4), 544-567.

Beauchamp, G., & Mennella, J.A. (2009). Early flavor learning and its impact on later feeding behavior. *Journal of Pediatric Gastroenterology and Nutrition, 48*(1, Suppl.), S25-S30.

Beaver, K.M., Vaughn, M.G., Wright, J.P., & Delisi, M. (2012). An interaction between perceived stress and 5HTTLPR genotype in the prediction of stable depressive symptomatology. *American Journal of Orthopsychiatry, 82,* 260-266.

Bechtold, A.G., Bushnell, E.W., & Salapatek, P. (1979, April). *Infants' visual localization of visual and auditory targets.* Paper presented at the meeting of the Society for Research in Child Development, San Francisco.

Becker, C., & others (2018). Cataract in patients with diabetes mellitus—Incidence rates in the UK and risk factors. *Eye, 32,* 1028-1035.

Becker, M., & McElvany, N. (2018). The interplay of gender and social background: A longitudinal study of interaction effects in reading attitudes and behavior. *British Journal of Educational Psychology, 88,* 529-549.

Becker, S.P., & others (2018a). Sleep problems and suicidal behaviors in college students. *Journal of Psychiatric Research, 99,* 122-128.

Becker, S.P., & others (2018b). Sleep in a large, multi-university sample of college students: Sleep problem prevalence, sex differences, and mental health correlates. *Sleep Health, 4,* 174-181.

Becker, S.P., & others (2019). Shortened sleep duration causes sleepiness, inattention, and oppositionality in adolescents with ADHD: Findings from a crossover sleep restriction/extension study. *JAACAP, 58,* 433-442.

Bedford, V.H. (2009). Sibling relationships: Adulthood. In D. Carr (Ed.), *Encyclopedia of the life course and human development.* Boston: Gale Cengage.

Bednar, R.L., Wells, M.G., & Peterson, S.R. (1995). *Self-esteem* (2nd ed.). Washington, DC: American Psychological Association.

Beeghly, M., & others (2006). Prenatal cocaine exposure and children's language functioning at 6 and 9.5 years: Moderating effects of child age, birthweight, and gender. *Journal of Pediatric Psychology, 31,* 98-115.

Beghetto, R.A. (2019). Creativity in classrooms. In J.C. Kaufman & R.J. Sternberg (Eds.), *Cambridge handbook of creativity* (2nd ed.). New York: Cambridge University Press.

Beksac, M.S., & others (2020, in press). Chorionic villus sampling experience of a reference perinatal medicine center. *Annals of Human Genetics.*

Belchior, P., & others (2019). Computer and videogame interventions for older adults' cognitive and everyday functioning. *Games for Health Journal, 8,* 129-143.

Belenguer-Varea, A., & others (2020). Oxidative stress and exceptional human longevity: Systematic review. *Free Radical Biology and Medicine, 149,* 51-63.

Bell, M.A. (2015). Bringing the field of infant cognition and perception toward a biopsychosocial perspective. In S.D. Calkins (Ed.), *Handbook of infant development.* New York: Guilford.

Bell, M.A., & Broomell, A.P.R. (2020). Development of inhibitory control from infancy to early childhood. In O. Houde & G. Borst (Eds.), *Cambridge handbook of cognitive development.* New York: Cambridge University Press.

Bell, M.A., & Cuevas, K. (2012). Using EEG to study cognitive development: Issues and practices. *Journal of Cognition and Development, 13,* 281-294.

Bell, M.A., & Cuevas, K. (2015). Psychobiology of executive function in early development. In J.A. Griffin, L.S. Freund, & P. McCardle (Eds.), *Executive function in preschool-age children.* Washington, DC: American Psychological Association.

Bell, M.A., & Cuevas, K. (2020). EEG frequency development across infancy and childhood. In P. Gable & others (Eds.), *Oxford handbook of human EEG frequency analysis.* New York: Oxford University Press.

Bell, M.A., Diaz, A., & Liu, R. (2018). Cognition-emotion interactions. In V. LaBue & others (Eds.), *Handbook of emotional development.* New York: Springer.

Bell, M.A., & Garcia Meza, T. (2020). Executive function. In J.B. Benson (Ed.), *Encyclopedia of infant and early child development.* New York: Elsevier.

Bell, M.A., Ross, A.P., & Patton, L.K. (2018). Emotion regulation. In M.H. Bornstein (Ed.), *SAGE encyclopedia of lifespan human development.* Thousand Oaks, CA: Sage.

Bell, M.A., Wolfe, C.D., & Adkins, D.R. (2007). Frontal lobe development during infancy and childhood. In D.J. Coch, K.W. Fischer, & G. Dawson (Eds.), *Human behavior, learning, and the developing brain.* New York: Guilford.

Bell, M.A., & others (2018). Brain development. In M.H. Bornstein (Ed.), *SAGE encyclopedia of lifespan human development.* Thousand Oaks, CA: Sage.

Bell, S.M., & Ainsworth, M.D.S. (1972). Infant crying and maternal responsiveness. *Child Development, 43,* 1171-1190.

Bell, T., Hill, N., & Stavrinos, D. (2020, in press). Personality determinants of subjective executive function in older adults. *Aging and Mental Health.*

Bellon, E., Fias, W., & De Smedt, B. (2019). More than number sense: The additional role of executive functions and metacognition in arithmetic. *Journal of Experimental Child Psychology, 182,* 38-60.

Belsky, D.W., & others (2017). Impact of early personal-history characteristics on the pace of aging: Implications for clinical trials of therapies to slow aging and extend healthspan. *Aging Cell, 16,* 644-651.

Belsky, J. (1981). Early human experience: A family perspective. *Developmental Psychology, 17,* 3-23.

Belsky, J., & Pluess, M. (2016). Differential susceptibility to context: Implications for developmental psychopathology. In D. Cicchetti (Ed.), *Developmental psychopathology* (3rd ed.). New York: Wiley.

Belsky, J., & van IJzendoorn, M.H. (2017). Genetic differential susceptibility to the effects of parenting. *Current Opinion in Psychology, 15,* 125-130.

Belsky, J., & others (2007). Are there long-term effects of early child care? *Child Development, 78,* 681-701.

Bem, S.L. (1977). On the utility of alternative procedures for assessing psychological androgyny. *Journal of Consulting and Clinical Psychology, 45,* 196-205.

Bem, S.L. (1993). *The lenses of gender.* New Haven, CT: Yale University Press.

Benck, L.R., & others (2017). Association between cardiorespiratory fitness and lung health from young adulthood to middle age. *American Journal of Respiratory and Critical Care Medicine, 195,* 1236-1243.

Bendayan, R., & others (2017). Decline in memory, visuospatial ability, and crystallized cognitive abilities in older adults: Normative aging or terminal decline? *Journal of Aging Research, 2017,* 6210105.

Bendersky, M., & Sullivan, M.W. (2007). Basic methods in infant research. In A. Slater & M. Lewis (Eds.), *Introduction to infant development* (2nd ed.). New York: Oxford University Press.

Bendezu, J.J., & others (2018). Child language and parenting antecedents and externalizing outcomes of emotion regulation pathways across early childhood: A person-centered approach. *Development and Psychopathology, 30,* 1253-1268.

Beneden Health (2013). *Middle age survey.* Unpublished data, Beneden Health, York, England.

Benenson, J.F., Apostolaris, N.H., & Parnass, J. (1997). Age and sex differences in dyadic and group interaction. *Developmental Psychology, 33,* 538-543.

Benetos, A., & others (2019). Arterial stiffness and blood pressure during the aging process. In R. Fernandez-Ballesteros & others (Eds.), *Cambridge handbook of successful aging.* New York: Cambridge University Press.

Benfante, R., & others (2020, in press). Acetylcholinesterase inhibitors targeting the cholinergic anti-inflammatory pathway: A new therapeutic perspective in aging-related disorders. *Aging: Clinical and Experimental Research.*

Bengesai, A.V., Khan, H.T.A., & Dube, R. (2018). Effect of early sexual debut on high completion in South Africa. *Journal of Biological Science, 50,* 124-143.

Bengtson, V.L. (1985). Diversity and symbolism in grandparental roles. In V.L. Bengtson & J. Robertson (Eds.), *Grandparenthood.* Newbury Park, CA: Sage.

Benichov, J., Cox, L.C., Tun, P.A., & Wingfield, A. (2012). Word recognition within a linguistic context: Effects of age, hearing acuity, verbal ability, and cognitive function. *Ear and Hearing, 33,* 250-256.

Benitez, V.L., & others (2017). Sustained selective attention predicts flexible switching in preschoolers. *Journal of Experimental Child Psychology, 156,* 29-42.

Bennett, C. (2019). *Comprehensive multicultural education* (9th ed.). Upper Saddle River, NJ: Pearson.

Bennett, K.M. (2006). Does marital status and marital status change predict physical health in older adults? *Psychological Medicine, 36,* 1313-1320.

Bennie, J.A., & others (2019). Associations between aerobic and muscle-strengthening exercise with depressive symptom severity among 17,839 U.S. adults. *Preventive Medicine, 121,* 121-127.

Bennie, J.A., & others (2020). Joint and dose-dependent associations between aerobic and muscle-strengthening activity with depression: A cross-sectional study of 1.48 million adults between 2011 and 2017. *Depression and Anxiety, 37,* 166-178.

Benson, J.E., & Sabbagh, M.A. (2017). Executive function helps children think about and learn about others' mental states. In M.J. Hoskyns & others (Eds.), *Executive functions in children's everyday lives.* New York: Oxford University Press.

Benson, L., & others (2020, in press). Weight variability during self-monitored weight loss predicts future weight loss outcome. *International Journal of Obesity.*

Bercovitz, K.E., Ngnoumen, C., & Langer, E.J. (2019). Personal control and aging. In R. Fernandez-Ballesteros & others (Eds.), *Cambridge handbook of successful aging.* New York: Cambridge University Press.

Berdugo-Vega, G., & others (2020). Increasing neurogenesis refines hippocampal activity, rejuvenating navigational learning strategies and contextual memory throughout life. *Nature Communication, 11*(1), 135.

Berenguer, C., & others (2018). Contribution of theory of mind, executive functioning, and pragmatics to socialization behaviors of children with high-functioning autism. *Journal of Autism and Developmental Disorders, 48,* 430-441.

Berenson, G.S., Srinivasan, S.R., Xu, J.H., & Chen, W. (2016). Adiposity and cardiovascular risk factor variables in childhood are associated with premature death from coronary heart disease in adults: The Bogalusa Heart Study. *American Journal of Medical Science, 352,* 448-454.

Berge, J.M., & others (2015). The protective role of family dinners for youth obesity: 10-year longitudinal associations. *Journal of Pediatrics, 166,* 296-301.

Bergen, D. (1988). Stages of play development. In D. Bergen (Ed.), *Play as a medium for learning and development.* Portsmouth, NH: Heinemann.

Bergeron, K.E. (2018). *Challenging the cult of self-esteem in education.* New York: Routledge.

Bergh, C., Pinborg, A., & Wennerholm, U-B. (2019). Parental age and child outcomes. *Fertility and Sterility, 111,* 1036-1046.

Berglind, D., & others (2018). Cross-sectional and prospective associations of meeting 24-h movement guidelines with overweight and obesity in preschool children. *Pediatric Obesity, 13,* 442-449.

Bergman, A.S., Axberg, U., & Hanson, E. (2017). When a parent dies—A systematic review of the effects of support programs for parentally bereaved children and their caregivers. *BMC Palliative Care, 16,* 39.

Berke, D.S., Reidy, D., & Zeichner, A. (2018). Masculinity, emotion regulation, and psychopathology: A critical review and integrated model. *Clinical Psychology Review, 66,* 106-116.

Berko, J. (1958). The child's learning of English morphology. *Word, 14,* 150-177.

Berko Gleason, J. (2009). The development of language: An overview. In J. Berko Gleason & N.B. Ratner (Eds.), *The development of language* (7th ed.). Boston: Allyn & Bacon.

Berlanga-Macias, C., & others (2020, in press). Relationship between exclusive breastfeeding and cardiorespiratory fitness in children and adolescents: A meta-analysis. *Scandinavian Journal of Medicine and Science in Sports.*

Berlyne, D.E. (1960). *Conflict, arousal, and curiosity.* New York: McGraw-Hill.

Berman, M.G., & others (2013). Dimensionality of brain networks linked to lifelong individual differences in self-control. *Nature Communications, 4,* 1373.

Bermudez, J.L. (2020). *Cognitive science.* New York: Cambridge University Press.

Bernal, G., & others (2019). Can cognitive-behavioral therapy be optimized with parent psychoeducation? A randomized effectiveness trial of adolescents with major depression in Puerto Rico. *Family Process, 58,* 832-854.

Bernard, J.Y., & others (2017). Breastfeeding, polyunsaturated fatty acid levels in colostrum and child intelligent quotient at age 5-6 years. *Journal of Pediatrics, 183,* 43-50.

Bernard, K., & Dozier, M. (2008). Adoption and foster placement. In M.M. Haith & J.B. Benson (Eds.), *Encyclopedia of infant and early childhood development.* Oxford, UK: Elsevier.

Bernard, K., & others (2019). Foster parenting. In M.H. Bornstein (Ed.), *Handbook of parenting* (3rd ed.). New York: Elsevier.

Berndt, T.J., & Perry, T.B. (1990). Distinctive features and effects of early adolescent friendships. In R. Montemayor (Ed.), *Advances in adolescent research.* Greenwich, CT: JAI Press.

Bernier, A., Beauchamp, M.H., Carlson, S.M., & Lalonde, G. (2015). A secure base from which to regulate: Attachment security in toddlerhood is a predictor of executive functioning at school entry. *Developmental Psychology, 51,* 1177-1189.

Bernier, A., Calkins, S.D., & Bell, M.A. (2016). Longitudinal associations between the quality of mother-infant interactions and brain development across infancy. *Child Development, 87,* 1159-1174.

Bernier, R., & Dawson, G. (2016). Autism spectrum disorders. In D. Cicchetti (Ed.), *Developmental psychopathology* (3rd ed.). New York: Wiley.

Bernitz, S., & others (2019). The frequency of intrapartum cesarean section use with the WHO partograph versus Zhang's guideline in the Labor Progression Study (LaPS): A multicenter, cluster-randomized controlled trial. *Lancet, 393,* 340-348.

Bernstein, J.P.K., DeVito, A., & Calamia, M. (2019). Subjectively and objectively measured sleep predict differing aspects of cognitive functioning in adults. *Archives of Clinical Neuropsychology, 34,* 1127-1137.

Berridge, K.C. (2019). Brain limbic systems as flexible generators of emotion. In A.S. Fox & others (Eds.), *The nature of emotion* (2nd ed.). New York: Oxford University Press.

Bersamin, M.M., & others (2014). Risky business: Is there an association between casual sex and mental health among emerging adults? *Journal of Sex Research, 51,* 43–51.

Berscheid, E. (1988). Some comments on love's anatomy: Or, whatever happened to old-fashioned lust? In R.J. Sternberg (Ed.), *Anatomy of love.* New Haven, CT: Yale University Press.

Berscheid, E. (2010). Love in the fourth dimension. *Annual Review of Psychology* (Vol. 61). Palo Alto, CA: Annual Reviews.

Bertenthal, B.I. (2008). Perception and action. In M.M. Haith & J.B. Benson (Eds.), *Encyclopedia of infant and early childhood development.* Oxford, UK: Elsevier.

Bertenthal, B.I., Longo, M.R., & Kenny, S. (2007). Phenomenal permanence and the development of predictive tracking in infancy. *Child Development, 78,* 350–363.

Bertucci, F., & others (2019). Genomic characterization of metastatic breast cancers. *Nature, 569,* 580–584.

Best, D.L., & Puzio, A.R. (2019). Gender and culture. In D. Matsumoto & H.C. Hwang (Eds.), *Handbook of culture and psychology.* New York: Oxford University Press.

Bettinger, E.P., & others (2018). Increasing perseverance in math. Evidence from a field experiment in Norway. *Journal of Economic Behavior and Organization, 146,* 1–15.

Bevens, C.L., & Loughnan, S. (2019). Insights into men's sexual aggression toward women: Dehumanization and objectification. *Sex Roles, 81,* 713–730.

Bewersdorf, J.P., & others (2020, in press). Epigenetic therapy combinations in acute myeloid leukemia: What are the options? *Therapeutic Advances in Hematology.*

Beydoun, H.A., & others (2017). Sex and age differences in the associations between sleep behaviors and all-cause mortality in older adults: Results from the National Health and Nutrition Examination Surveys. *Sleep Medicine, 36,* 141–151.

Beyene, Y. (1986). Cultural significance and physiological manifestations of menopause: A biocultural analysis. *Culture, Medicine and Psychiatry, 10,* 47–71.

Beyers, E., & Seiffge-Krenke, I. (2010). Does identity precede intimacy? Testing Erikson's theory on romantic development in emerging adults of the 21st century. *Journal of Adolescent Research, 25,* 387–415.

Bhattacharya, I., & others (2019). Testosterone augments FSH signaling by upregulating the expression and activity of FSH-receptor in pubertal primate sertoli cells. *Molecular and Cellular Endocrinology, 482,* 70–80.

Bi, H., Ye, K., & Jin, S. (2020, in press). Proteomic analysis of decellularized pancreatic matrix identifies collagen V as a critical regulator for islet organogenesis from human pluripotent stem cells. *Biomaterials.*

Bialecka-Pikul, M., & others (2019). Change and consistency of self-esteem in early and middle adolescence in the context of school transition. *Journal of Youth and Adolescence, 48,* 1605–1618.

Bialystok, E. (1997). Effects of bilingualism and biliteracy on children's emerging concepts of print. *Developmental Psychology, 33,* 429–440.

Bialystok, E. (2011, April). *Becoming bilingual: Emergence of cognitive outcomes of bilingualism in immersion education.* Paper presented at the meeting of the Society for Research in Child Development, Montreal.

Bialystok, E. (2015). The impact of bilingualism on cognition. In R. Scott & S. Kosslyn (Eds.), *Emerging trends in the social and behavioral sciences.* New York: Wiley.

Bialystok, E. (2017). The bilingual adaptation: How minds accommodate experience. *Psychological Bulletin, 143,* 233–262.

Bialystok, E., Craik, F.I., Binns, M.A., Ossher, L., & Freedman, M. (2014). Effects of bilingualism on the age of onset and progression of MCI and AD: Evidence from executive function tests. *Neuropsychology, 28,* 290–304.

Bialystok, E., & others (2016). Aging in two languages: Implications for public health. *Aging Research Reviews, 27,* 56–60.

Bian, Z., & Anderson, G.J. (2008). Aging and the perceptual organization of 3-D scenes. *Psychology and Aging, 23,* 342–352.

Bianchi, D., & others (2020, in press). A bad romance: Sexting motivations and teen dating violence. *Journal of Interpersonal Violence.*

Bianchi, D.W. (2020, in press). Turner syndrome: New insights from prenatal genomics and transcriptomics. *American Journal of Medical Genetics C: Seminars in Medical Genetics.*

Bibok, M.B., Carpendale, J.I., & Muller, U. (2009). Parental scaffolding and the development of executive function. *New Directions in Child and Adolescent Development, 123,* 17–24.

Bick, J., & Nelson, C.A. (2018). Early experience and brain development. *Wiley Interdisciplinary Review of Cognitive Science, 8,* 1–2.

Bick, J., & others (2019). Early parenting intervention and adverse family environments affect neural function in middle childhood. *Biological Psychiatry, 85,* 326–335.

Biczo, A., & others (2020, in press). Association of vitamin D receptor gene polymorphisms with disc degeneration. *European Spine Research.*

Biehle, S.N., & Mickelson, K.D. (2012). First-time parents' expectations about the division of childcare and play. *Journal of Family Psychology, 26,* 36–45.

Bielak, A.A.M., Hughes, T.F., Small, B.J., & Dixon, R.A. (2007). It's never too late to engage in lifestyle activities: Significant concurrent but not change relationships between lifestyle activities and cognitive speed. *Journals of Gerontology B: Psychological Sciences and Social Sciences, 62B,* P331–P339.

Bierman, K.L., & Powers, C.J. (2009). Social skills training to improve peer relations. In K.H. Rubin, W.M. Bukowski, & B. Laursen (Eds.), *Handbook of peer interactions, relationships, and groups.* New York: Guilford.

Bijlenga, D., & others (2019). The role of the circadian system in the etiology and pathophysiology of ADHD: Time to redefine ADHD? *Attention Deficit and Hyperactivity Disorders, 11,* 5–19.

Bill and Melinda Gates Foundation (2017). *K-12 education.* Retrieved March 28, 2017, from www.gatesfoundation.org/What-We-Do/US-Program/K-12-Education

Bill and Melinda Gates Foundation (2020). *All lives have equal value.* Retrieved January 23, 2020, from www.gatesfoundation.org

Bindler, R.C., & others (2017). *Clinical manual for maternity and pediatric nursing* (5th ed.). Upper Saddle River, NJ: Pearson.

Birch, S.A., & others (2017). Perspectives on perspective taking: How children think about the minds of others. *Advances in Child Development and Behavior, 52,* 185–226.

Bird, A.L., & others (2017). Maternal health in pregnancy and associations with adverse birth outcomes: Evidence from Growing Up in New Zealand. *Australia and New Zealand Obstetrics and Gynecology, 57,* 16–24.

Birditt, K.S., & others (2017). The development of marital tension: Implications for divorce among married couples. *Developmental Psychology, 53,* 1995–2006.

Birditt, K.S., & others (2019). Conflict strategies in the parent-adult child tie: Generation differences and implications for well-being. *Journals of Gerontology B: Psychological Sciences and Social Sciences, 74,* 232–241.

Birkeland, M.S., Melkevick, O., Holsen, I., & Wold, B. (2012). Trajectories of global self-esteem development during adolescence. *Journal of Adolescence, 35,* 43–54.

Birman, B.F., & others (2007). *State and local implementation of the "No Child Left Behind" act. Volume II–Teacher quality under "NCLB": Interim report.* Jessup, MD: U.S. Department of Education.

Birmingham, R.S., Bub, K.L., & Vaughn, B.E. (2017). Parenting in infancy and self-regulation in preschool: An investigation of the role of attachment history. *Attachment and Human Development, 19,* 107–129.

Bisbe, M., & others (2020, in press). Comparing cognitive effects of choreographed exercise and multimodal physical therapy in older adults with amnestic mild cognitive impairment: Randomized clinical trial. *Journal of Alzheimer's Disease.*

Bischoff, K.E., Sudore, R., Miao, Y., Boscardin, W.J., & Smith, A.K. (2013). Advance care planning and the quality of end-of-life care in older adults. *Journal of the American Geriatrics Society, 61,* 209–214.

Bjarehed, M., & others (2020, in press). Individual moral disengagement and bullying among Swedish fifth graders: The role of collective moral disengagement and pro-bullying behavior within classrooms. *Journal of Interpersonal Violence.*

Bjorklund, D.F., & Pellegrini, A.D. (2002). *The origins of human nature.* New York: Oxford University Press.

Black, M.M., & Hurley, K.M. (2007). Helping children develop healthy eating habits. In R.E. Tremblay, R.G. Barr, R.D. Peters, & M. Boivin (Eds.), *Encyclopedia on early childhood development*. Retrieved March 19, 2008, from http://www.child-encyclopedia.com/documents/Black-HurleyANGxp_rev-Eating.pdf

Black, M.M., & Hurley, K.M. (2017). Responsive feeding: Strategies to promote healthy mealtime interactions. *Nestle Nutrition Institute Workshop Series, 87*, 153-165.

Black, M.M., & others (2017). Early childhood development coming of age: Science through the life course. *Lancet, 389*(10064), 77-90.

Blackwell, D.L., & Clarke, T.C. (2018, June 28). State variation in meeting the 2008 federal guidelines for both aerobic and muscle-strengthening activities through leisure-time physical activity among adults aged 18-64: United States 2010-2015. *National Health Statistics Reports, 112*, 1-21.

Blackwell, L.S., Trzesniewski, K.H., & Dweck, C.S. (2007). Implicit theories of intelligence predict achievement across an adolescent transition: A longitudinal study and an intervention. *Child Development, 78*, 246-263.

Blagovechtchenski, E., & others (2020, in press). Transcranial direct current stimulation (tDCS) of Wernicke's and Broca's areas in studies of language learning and word acquisition. *Journal of Visualized Experiments*.

Blair, C. (2017). Educating executive function. *Wiley Interdisciplinary Reviews: Cognitive Science, 8*, e1403.

Blair, C., & Raver, C.C. (2012). Child development in the context of poverty: Experiential canalization of brain and behavior. *American Psychologist, 67*, 309-318.

Blair, C., & Raver, C.C. (2014). Closing the achievement gap through modification of neurocognitive and neuroendocrine function: Results from a cluster randomized controlled trial of an innovative approach to the education of children in kindergarten. *PLoS One, 9*(11), e112393.

Blair, C., & Raver, C.C. (2015). School readiness and self-regulation: A developmental psychobiological approach. *Annual Review of Psychology* (Vol. 66). Palo Alto, CA: Annual Reviews.

Blair, C., Raver, C.C., & Finegood, E.D. (2016). Self-regulation and developmental psychopathology: Experiential canalization of brain and behavior. In D. Cicchetti (Ed.), *Developmental psychopathology* (3rd ed.). New York: Wiley.

Blair, C., & Razza, R.P. (2007). Relating effortful control, executive functioning, and false belief understanding to emerging math and literacy ability in kindergarten. *Child Development, 78*, 647-663.

Blair, S.N., & others (1989). Physical fitness and all-cause mortality: A prospective study of healthy men and women. *Journal of the American Medical Association, 262*, 2395-2401.

Blake, J.S. (2020). *Nutrition and you* (5th ed.). Upper Saddle River, NJ: Pearson.

Blake, J.S., Munoz, K.D., & Volpe, S. (2019). *Nutrition* (4th ed.). Upper Saddle River, NJ: Pearson.

Blakemore, J.E.O., Berenbaum, S.A., & Liben, L.S. (2009). *Gender development*. Clifton, NJ: Psychology Press.

Blakey, J. (2011). Normal births or spontaneous vertex delivery? *Practicing Midwife, 14*, 12-13.

Blanck-Lubarsch, M., & others (2020, in press). 3D-analysis of mouth, nose, and eye parameters in children with fetal alcohol syndrome (FAS). *International Journal of Environmental Research and Public Health*.

Bland, L.M., & Gareis, C.R. (2018). Performance assessments: A review of definitions, quality characteristics, and outcomes associated with their use in K-12 schools. *Teacher Educators' Journal, 11*, 52-69.

Blanken, A.E., & others (2020). Distilling heterogeneity of mild cognitive impairment in the National Alzheimer Coordinating Center Database using latent profile analysis. *JAMA New Open, 3*(3), e200413.

Blankenship, T.L., & others (2019). Attention and executive function in infancy: Links to childhood executive function and reading achievement. *Developmental Science, 22*, e12824. doi:10.1111/desc.12824

Blanner Kristiansen, C., & others (2019). Prevalence of common mental disorders in widowhood: A systematic review and meta-analysis. *Journal of Affective Disorders, 245*, 1016-1023.

Blatny, M., Millova, K., Jelinek, M., & Osecka, T. (2015). Personality predictors of successful development: Toddler temperament and adolescent personality traits predict well-being and career stability in middle adulthood. *PLoS One, 10*(94), e0126032.

Bleker, L.S., & others (2019). Exploring the effect of antenatal depression treatment on children's epigenetic profiles: Findings from a pilot randomized controlled trial. *Clinical Epigenetics, 11*(1), 18.

Blieszner, R. (2009). Friendship, adulthood. In D. Carr (Ed.), *Encyclopedia of the life course and human development*. Boston: Gale Cengage.

Blieszner, R. (2016). Friendships. In S.K. Whitbourne (Ed.), *Encyclopedia of adulthood and aging* (Vol. 2). New York: Wiley.

Blieszner, R.A. (2018). Family life cycle. In M.H. Bornstein (Ed.), *SAGE encyclopedia of lifespan human development*. Thousand Oaks, CA: Sage.

Blieszner, R.A., & Ogletree, A.M. (2017). We get by with a little help from our friends. *Generations, 41*, 55-62.

Blieszner, R.A., & Ogletree, A.M. (2018). Relationships in middle and late adulthood. In D.A. Vangelisti & D. Perlman (Eds.), *Cambridge handbook of personal relationships* (2nd ed.). New York: Cambridge University Press.

Blieszner, R.A., & Roberto, K.A. (2012a). Intergenerational relationships and aging. In S.K. Whitbourne & M. Sliwinski (Eds.), *Wiley-Blackwell handbook of adult development and aging*. New York: Wiley.

Blieszner, R.A., & Roberto, K.A. (2012b). Partner and friend relationships in adulthood. In S.K. Whitbourne & M. Sliwinski (Eds.), *Wiley-Blackwell handbook of adult development and aging*. New York: Wiley.

Block, J. (1993). Studying personality the long way. In D. Funder, R.D. Parke, C. Tomlinson-Keasey, & K. Widaman (Eds.), *Studying lives through time*. Washington, DC: American Psychological Association.

Bloom, B. (1985). *Developing talent in young people*. New York: Ballantine.

Bloom, L., Lifter, K., & Broughton, J. (1985). The convergence of early cognition and language in the second year of life. Problems in conceptualization and measurement. In M. Barren (Ed.), *Single word speech*. London: Wiley.

Bloor, C., & White, F. (1983). *Unpublished manuscript*. La Jolla, CA: University of California at San Diego.

Bobkova, N.V., & others (2020). Neuroregeneration: Regulation in neurodegenerative diseases and aging. *Biochemistry, 85*(Suppl. 1), S108-S130.

Bock, J., & Burkley, M. (2019). On the prowl: Examining the impact of men-as-predators and women-as-prey metaphors on attitudes that perpetuate sexual violence. *Sex Roles, 5-6*, 262-276.

Bodenschatz, C.M., Kersting, A., & Suslow, T. (2019). Effects of briefly presented masked emotional facial expressions on gaze behavior: An eye-tracking study. *Psychological Reports, 122*(4), 1432-1448.

Bodrova, E., & Leong, D.J. (2007). *Tools of the mind* (2nd ed.). Geneva, Switzerland: International Bureau of Education, UNESCO.

Bodrova, E., & Leong, D.J. (2015a). Standing 'A head taller than himself': Vygotskian and post-Vygotskian views on children's play. In J.E. Johnson & others (Eds.), *Handbook of the study of play*. Blue Ridge Summit, PA: Rowman & Littlefield.

Bodrova, E., & Leong, D.J. (2015b). Vygotskian and post-Vygotskian views of children's play. *American Journal of Play, 7*, 371-388.

Boele, S., & others (2019). Linking parent-child and peer relationship quality to empathy in adolescence: A multi-level meta-analysis. *Journal of Youth and Adolescence, 48*, 1033-1055.

Boers, E., Afzali, M.H., & Conrod, P. (2020). A longitudinal study on the relationship between screen time and adolescent alcohol use: The mediating role of social norms. *Preventive Medicine, 132*, 105992.

Boespflug, E.L., & others (2016). Fish oil supplementation increases event-related posterior cingulate activation in older adults with subjective memory impairment. *Journal of Nutritional Health and Aging, 20*, 161-169.

Bogaert, A.F., & Skorska, M.N. (2020). A short review of biological research on the development of sexual orientation. *Human Behavior, 119*, 104659.

Bogart, L.M., & others (2014). Peer victimization in the fifth grade and health in the tenth grade. *Pediatrics, 133*, 440-447.

Bojorquez, G.R., & Fry-Bowers, E.K. (2019). Beyond eligibility: Access to federal public benefit programs for immigrant families in the United States. *Journal of Pediatric Health Care, 33*, 210-213.

Bombard, J.M., & others (2018). Vital signs: Trends and disparities in infant safe sleep practices–United States, 2009-2015. *MMWR: Morbidity and Mortality Weekly Report, 67*(1), 39-46.

Bonafe, M., Sabbatinelli, J., & Olivieri, F. (2020). Exploiting the telomere machinery to put the brakes on inflamm-aging. *Aging Research Reviews, 59,* 101027.

Bonanno, G.A., & Malgaroli, M. (2020). Trajectories of grief: Comparing symptoms from the DSM-5 and ICD-11 diagnoses. *Depression and Anxiety, 37,* 17-25.

Bonura, K.B., & Tenenbaum, G. (2014). Effects of yoga on psychological health in older adults. *Journal of Physical Activity and Health, 11,* 1334-1341.

Boon, L.I., & others (2020). Motor effects of deep brain stimulation correlate with increased functional connectivity in Parkinson's disease: An MEG study. *Neuoroimage.Clinical, 26,* 102225.

Booth, A. (2006). Object function and categorization in infancy: Two mechanisms of facilitation. *Infancy, 10,* 145-169.

Booth, M. (2002). Arab adolescents facing the future: Enduring ideals and pressures to change. In B.B. Brown, R.W. Larson, & T.S. Saraswathi (Eds.), *The world's youth.* New York: Cambridge University Press.

Booth-Laforce, C., & Groh, A.M. (2018). Parent-child attachment and peer relations. In W.M. Bukowski & others (Eds.), *Handbook of peer interaction, relationships, and groups.* New York: Guilford.

Booth-LeDoux, S.M., Mathews, R.A., & Wayne, J.H. (2020, in press). Testing a resource-based spillover-crossover-spillover model: Transmission of social support in dual-earner couples. *Journal of Applied Psychology.*

Bor, W., McGee, T.R., & Fagan, A.A. (2004). Early risk factors for adolescent antisocial behavior: An Australian longitudinal study. *Australian and New Zealand Journal of Psychiatry, 38,* 365-372.

Borbon-Castro, N.A., & others (2020). The effects of a multidimensional exercise program on health behavior and biopsychological factors in Mexican older adults. *Frontiers in Psychology, 10,* 2668.

Bornstein, M.H. (1975). Qualities of color vision in infancy. *Journal of Experimental Child Psychology, 19,* 401-409.

Bornstein, M.H. (2020). A developmentalist's viewpoint: "It's about time!" Ecological systems, transaction, and specificity as key developmental principles in children's changing worlds. In R.D. Parke & G.H. Elder (Eds.), *Children in changing worlds.* New York: Cambridge University Press.

Bornstein, M.H., Arterberry, M.E., & Mash, C. (2015). Perceptual development. In M.H. Bornstein & M.E. Lamb (Eds.), *Developmental psychology: An advanced textbook* (7th ed.). New York: Psychology Press.

Bornstein, M.H., & Cote, L.R. (2019). Immigrant parenthood. In M.H. Bornstein (Ed.), *Handbook of parenting* (3rd ed.). New York: Routledge.

Bornstein, M.H., Jager, J., & Steinberg, L. (2013). Adolescents, parents/friends/peers: A relationship model. In I. Weiner & others (Eds.), *Handbook of psychology* (2nd ed., Vol. 6). New York: Wiley.

Bornstein, M.H., & Lansford, J.E. (2019). Culture and family functioning. In *APA handbook of contemporary family psychology.* Washington, DC: APA Books.

Borsa, V.M., & others (2018). Bilingualism and healthy aging: Aging effects and neural maintenance. *Neuropsychologia, 111,* 51-61.

Borsani, E., & others (2019). Correlation between human nervous system development and acquisition of fetal skills: An overview. *Brain Development, 41,* 225-233.

Bosma, H.A., & Kunnen, E.S. (2001). Determinants and mechanisms in ego identity development: A review and synthesis. *Developmental Review, 21,* 39-66.

Bostic, J.Q., & others (2015). Being present at school: Implementing mindfulness in schools. *Child and Adolescent Psychiatric Clinics of North America, 24,* 245-259.

Botti, G., & others (2019). Paralogous HOX13 genes in human cancer. *Cancers, 11,* 5.

Bottomley, J.S., & others (2019). Distinguishing the meaning making processes of survivors of suicide loss: An expansion of the meaning of loss codebook. *Death Studies, 43,* 92-102.

Botwinick, J. (1978). *Aging and behavior* (2nd ed.). New York: Springer.

Bouaziz, W., & others (2020, in press). Effect of high-intensity interval training and continuous endurance training on peak oxygen uptake among seniors aged 65 and older: A meta-analysis of randomized controlled trials. *International Journal of Clinical Practice.*

Bouchard, T.J., Lykken, D.T., McGue, M., Segal, N.L., & Tellegen, A. (1990). Source of human psychological differences. The Minnesota Study of Twins Reared Apart. *Science, 250,* 223-228.

Boukhris, T., Sheehy, O., Mottron, L., & Berard, A. (2016). Antidepressant use during pregnancy and the risk of autism spectrum disorder in children. *JAMA Pediatrics, 170,* 117-124.

Boulay, B., & others (2018). *The Investing in Innovation Fund. Summary of 67 evaluations (NCEE No. 2018-4013).* Washington, DC: National Center for Education Evaluation and Regional Assistance, Institute of Education Sciences. U.S. Department of Education.

Bould, H., & others (2015). Association between early temperament and depression at 18 years. *Depression and Anxiety, 31,* 729-736.

Boulton, E., & others (2019). Implementing behavior change theory and techniques to increase physical activity and prevent functional decline among adults aged 61-70: The PreventIT Project. *Progress in Cardiovascular Diseases, 62,* 147-156.

Bourassa, K.J., Ruiz, J.M., & Sbarra, D.A. (2019). Smoking and physical activity explain the increased mortality risk following marital separation and divorce: Evidence from the English Longitudinal Study of Aging. *Annals of Behavioral Medicine, 53,* 255-266.

Bourdon, O., & others (2020). A time to be chronically stressed? Maladaptive time perspectives are associated with allostatic load. *Biological Psychology, 152,* 107671.

Bower, T.G.R. (1966). Slant perception and shape constancy in infants. *Science, 151,* 832-834.

Bowl, M.R., & Dawson, S.J. (2019). Age-related hearing loss. *Cold Springs Harbor Perspectives in Medicine. 9,* 8.

Bowlby, J. (1969). *Attachment and loss* (Vol. 1). London: Hogarth Press.

Bowlby, J. (1989). *Secure and insecure attachment.* New York: Basic Books.

Bowman, L.C., & Fox, N.A. (2019). Distinction between temperament and emotion: Examining reactivity, regulation, and social understanding. In A.S. Fox & others (Eds.), *The nature of emotion* (2nd ed.). New York: Oxford University Press.

Bowman-Smart, H., & others (2020, in press). Sex selection and non-invasive prenatal testing: A review of current practices, evidence, and ethical issues. *Prenatal Design.*

Boyce, C.J., Wood, A.M., & Ferguson, E. (2016). Individual differences in loss aversion: Conscientiousness predicts how life satisfaction responds to losses versus gains in income. *Personality and Social Psychology Bulletin, 42,* 471-484.

Boylan, J.M., Cundiff, J.M., & Matthews, K.A. (2018). Socioeconomic status and cardiovascular responses to standardized stressors: A systematic review and meta-analysis. *Psychosomatic Medicine, 80,* 278-293.

Boyle, J., & Cropley, M. (2004). Children's sleep: Problems and solutions. *Journal of Family Health Care, 14,* 61-63.

Boyle, M.A. (2019). *Personal nutrition* (10th ed.). Boston: Cengage.

Bozdemir, M., & Cinan, S. (2020, in press). Age-related differences in intentional forgetting of prospective memory. *International Journal of Aging and Human Development.*

Brabek, M.M., & Brabek, K.M. (2006). Women and relationships. In J. Worell & C.D. Goodheart (Eds.), *Handbook of girls' and women's psychological health.* New York: Oxford University Press.

Braccio, S., Sharland, M., & Ladhani, S.N. (2016). Prevention and treatment of mother-to-child syphilis. *Current Opinion on Infectious Diseases, 29,* 268-274.

Bradley, R.E., & Webb, R. (1976). Age-related differences in locus of control orientation in three behavior domains. *Human Development, 19,* 49-55.

Bradley, R.H. (2019). Environment and parenting. In M.H. Bornstein (Ed.), *Handbook of parenting* (3rd ed.) (Vol. 2). New York: Routledge.

Brainerd, C.J., & Reyna, V.E. (1993). Domains of fuzzy-trace theory. In M.L. Howe & R. Pasnak (Eds.), *Emerging themes in cognitive development.* New York: Springer.

Brainerd, C.J., & Reyna, V.E. (2014). Dual processes in memory development: Fuzzy-trace theory. In P. Bauer & R. Fivush (Eds.), *Wiley-Blackwell handbook of children's memory.* New York: Wiley.

Braithwaite, D.W., & Siegler, R.S. (2018). Developmental changes in whole number bias. *Developmental Science, 21,* 2.

Braithwaite, D.W., Tian, J., & Siegler, R.S. (2018). Do children understand fraction addition? *Developmental Science, 21*(4), e12601.

Braithwaite, D.W., & others (2019). Individual differences in fraction arithmetic learning. *Cognitive Psychology, 112,* 81-98.

Braithwaite, S., & Holt-Lunstad, J. (2017). Romantic relationships and mental health. *Current Opinion in Psychology, 13,* 120-125.

Brand, J. (2014). Social consequences of job loss and unemployment. *Annual Review of Sociology* (Vol. 40). Palo Alto, CA: Annual Reviews.

Brand, M. (2011). Mitochondrial functioning and aging. In E. Masoro & S. Austad (Eds.), *Handbook of the biology of aging* (7th ed.). New York: Elsevier.

Brandes-Aitken, A., & others (2019). Sustained attention in infancy: A foundation for the developmental of multiple aspects of self-regulation for children in poverty. *Journal of Experimental Child Psychology, 184,* 192-209.

Brannigan, R., & others (2019). The association between subjective maternal stress during pregnancy and offspring clinically diagnosed psychiatric disorders. *Acta Psychiatrica Scandinavica, 139,* 304-310.

Brannon, L. (2017). *Gender.* New York: Routledge.

Branzi, F.M., Calabria, M., & Costa, A. (2019). Cross-linguistic/bilingual language production.In S-A. Rueschemeyer & M. Gareth Gaskell (Eds.), *Oxford handbook of psycholinguistics* (2nd ed.). New York: Oxford University Press.

Braren, S.H., & others (2020). Maternal psychological stress moderates diurnal cortisol linkage in expectant fathers and mothers during late pregnancy. *Psychoneuroendocrinology, 11,* 104474.

Brassard, A., & others (2012). Romantic attachment insecurity predicts sexual dissatisfaction in couples seeking marital therapy. *Journal of Sexual and Marital Therapy, 38,* 245-262.

Brathen, A.C.S., & others (2020, in press). Risk and protective factors for memory plasticity in aging. *Neuropsychology, Development, and Cognition B: Aging, Neuropsychology, and Cognition.*

Bratke, H., & others (2017). Timing of menarche in Norwegian girls: Associations with body mass, waist circumference, and skinfold thickness. *BMC Pediatrics, 17,* 138.

Bratt, C., & others (2018). Perceived age discrimination across age in Europe: From an aging society to a society for all ages. *Developmental Psychology, 54,* 167-180.

Braun, S.S., & Davidson, A.J. (2017). Gender (non) conformity in middle childhood: A mixed methods approach to understanding gender-typed behavior, friendship, and peer preference. *Sex Roles, 77,* 16-29.

Braver, S.L., & Lamb, M.E. (2013). Marital dissolution. In G.W. Peterson & K.R. Bush (Eds.), *Handbook of marriage and the family* (3rd ed.). New York: Springer.

Brawner, C.A., & others (2017). Change in maximal exercise capacity is associated with survival in men and women. *Mayo Clinic Proceedings, 92,* 383-390.

Bray, J.H. (2008). Couple therapy with remarried partners. In A.S. Gurman (Ed.), *Clinical handbook of couple therapy* (4th ed.). New York: Guilford.

Bray, J.H. (2019). Remarriage and stepfamilies. In B.H. Friese (Ed.), *APA handbook of contemporary family psychology.* Washington, DC: APA Books.

Breastcancer.org (2020). Using HRT (hormone replacement therapy). Retrieved February 21, 2020, from www.breastcancer.org/risk/factors/hrt

Bredekamp, S. (2020). *Effective practices in early childhood education* (4th ed.). Upper Saddle River, NJ: Pearson.

Breen, L.J., Penman, E.L., Prigerson, H.G., & Hewitt, L.Y. (2015). Can grief be a mental disorder? *Journal of Nervous and Mental Disease, 203,* 569-573.

Breen, L.J., & others (2018). Differences in meanings made according to prolonged grief symptomatology. *Death Studies, 42,* 69-78.

Bremner, A.J. (2017). Multisensory development: Calibrating a coherent sensory milieu in early life. *Current Biology, 27,* R305-R307.

Bremner, A.J., & Spence, C. (2017). The development of tactile perception. *Advances in Child Development and Behavior, 52,* 227-268.

Bremner, J.G., & others (2017). Limits of object persistence: Young infants perceive continuity of vertical and horizontal trajectories but not 45-degree oblique trajectories. *Infancy, 22,* 303-322.

Brendgen, M., Lamarche, V., Wanner, B., & Vitaro, F. (2010). Links between friendship relations and early adolescents' trajectories of depressed mood. *Developmental Psychology, 46,* 491-501.

Brent, R.L. (2009). Saving lives and changing family histories: Appropriate counseling of pregnant women and men and women of reproductive age concerning the risk of diagnostic radiation exposure during and before pregnancy. *American Journal of Obstetrics and Gynecology, 200,* 4-24.

Brent, R.L. (2011). The pulmonologist's role in caring for pregnant women with regard to reproductive risks of diagnostic radiological studies or radiation therapy. *Clinics in Chest Medicine, 32*(1), 33-42.

Breslau, J., & others (2017). Sex differences in recent first-onset depression in an epidemiological sample of adolescents. *Translational Psychiatry, 7*(5), e1139.

Bretas, R.V., Yamazaki, Y., & Iriki, A. (2020, in press). Phase transitions of brain evolution that produced human language and beyond. *Neuroscience Research.*

Bretherton, I., Stolberg, U., & Kreye, M. (1981). Engaging strangers in proximal interaction: Infants' social initiative. *Developmental Psychology, 17,* 746-755.

Breveglieri, G., & others (2019). Non-invasive prenatal testing using fetal DNA. *Molecular Diagnosis and Therapy, 23,* 291-299.

Briana, D.D., & others (2018). Differential expression of cord blood neurotrophins in gestational diabetes: The impact of fetal growth abnormalities. *Journal of Maternal-Fetal and Neonatal Medicine, 31,* 278-283.

Bridgett, D.J., Laake, L.M., Gartstein, M.A., & Dorn, D. (2013). Development of infant positive emotionality: The contribution of maternal characteristics and effects on subsequent parenting. *Infant and Child Development, 22*(4), 362-382.

Bril, B. (1999). Dires sur l'enfant selon les cultures: Etat des lieux et perspectives. In B. Brill, P.R. Dasen, C. Sabatier, & B. Krewer (Eds.), *Propos sur l'enfant et l'adolescent. Quels enfants pour quelles cultures?* Paris: L'Harmattan.

Briley, D.A., Domiteaux, M., & Tucker-Drob, E.M. (2014). Achievement-relevant personality: Relations with the Big Five and validation of an efficient instrument. *Learning and Individual Differences, 32,* 26-39.

Brill, H. (2019, January 11). Why Hispanics live longer than non-Hispanic Whites. *The Berkeley Daily Planet.* Retrieved February 26, 2020, from berkeleydailyplanet.com/issue/2019-01-11/article/47300

Brim, G. (1992, December 7). Commentary. *Newsweek,* p. 52.

Brim, O. (1999). *The MacArthur Foundation study of midlife development.* Vero Beach, FL: MacArthur Foundation.

Brinkman-Stoppelenburg, A., Rietjens, J.A., & van der Heide, A. (2014). The effects of advance care planning on end-of-life care: A systematic review. *Palliative Medicine, 28,* 1000-1025.

Brito, N.H., & others (2019). Beyond the Bayley: Neurocognitive assessments of development during infancy and toddlerhood. *Developmental Neuropsychology, 49,* 220-247.

Brittain, A.W., & others (2020, in press). The Teen Access and Quality Initiative: Improving adolescent reproductive health best practices in publicly funded health centers. *Journal of Community Health.*

Britton, J.R., Britton, H.L., & Gronwaldt, V. (2006). Breastfeeding, sensitivity, and attachment. *Pediatrics, 118,* e1436-e1443.

Brock, R.L., & Kochanska, G. (2016). Interparental conflict, children's security with parents, and long-term risk of internalizing problems: A longitudinal study from ages 2 to 10. *Development and Psychopathology, 28,* 45-54.

Brod, G., & Shing, Y.L. (2019). A boon and a bane: Comparing the effects of prior knowledge on memory across the lifespan. *Developmental Psychology, 55,* 1326-1337.

Brodsky, J.L., Viner-Brown, S., & Handler, A.S. (2009). Changes in maternal cigarette smoking among pregnant WIC participants in Rhode Island. *Maternal and Child Health Journal, 13*(6), 822-831.

Brody, G.H., & others (2017). Protective prevention effects on the association of poverty with brain development. *JAMA Pediatrics, 17,* 46-52.

Brody, G.H., & others (2019). The protective effects of supportive parenting on the relationship between adolescent poverty and resting-state functional brain connectivity in adulthood. *Psychological Science, 30,* 1040-1049.

Brody, G.H., & others (2020, in press). A family-centered prevention ameliorates the associations of low self-control during childhood with employment income and poverty status in young African American adults. *Journal of Child Psychology and Psychiatry.*

Brody, L.R., Hall, J.A., & Stokes, L.R. (2018). Gender and emotion: Theory, findings, and content.

In L.F. Barrett & others (Eds.), *Handbook of emotion* (4th ed.). New York: Guilford.

Brody, N. (2000). Intelligence. In A. Kazdin (Ed.), *Encyclopedia of psychology*. Washington, DC, & New York: American Psychological Association and Oxford University Press.

Brody, N. (2007). Does education influence intelligence? In P.C. Kyllonen, R.D. Roberts, & L. Stankov (Eds.), *Extending intelligence*. Mahwah, NJ: Erlbaum.

Brody, R.M., & Costa, R.M. (2009). Satisfaction (sexual, life, relationship, and mental health) is associated directly with penile-vaginal intercourse, but inversely related to other sexual behavior frequencies. *Journal of Sexual Medicine, 6,* 1947-1954.

Brody, S. (2010). The relative health benefits of different sexual activities. *Journal of Sexual Medicine, 7,* 1336-1361.

Brodzinsky, D.M., & Pinderhughes, E. (2002). Parenting and child development in adoptive families. In M.H. Bornstein (Ed.), *Handbook of parenting* (Vol. 1). Mahwah, NJ: Erlbaum.

Broesch, T., & Bryant, G.A. (2018). Fathers' infant-directed speech in a small-scale society. *Child Development, 89,* e29-e41.

Bronfenbrenner, U. (1986). Ecology of the family as a context for human development research perspectives. *Developmental Psychology, 22,* 723-742.

Bronfenbrenner, U. (2004). *Making human beings human*. Thousand Oaks, CA: Sage.

Bronfenbrenner, U., & Morris, P. (1998). The ecology of developmental processes. In W. Damon (Ed.), *Handbook of child psychology* (5th ed., Vol. 1). New York: Wiley.

Bronfenbrenner, U., & Morris, P.A. (2006). The ecology of human development. In W. Damon & R. Lerner (Eds.), *Handbook of child psychology* (6th ed.). New York: Wiley.

Bronstein, P. (2006). The family environment: Where gender role socialization begins. In J. Worell & C.D. Goodheart (Eds.), *Handbook of girls' and women's psychological health*. New York: Oxford University Press.

Brooker, R. & others (2020). *Biology* (5th ed.). New York: McGraw-Hill.

Brooker, R.J., & others (2020, in press). Attentional control explains covariation between symptoms of attention-deficit/hyperactivity disorder and anxiety during adolescence. *Journal of Research on Adolescence*.

Brookhart, S.M., & Nitko, A.J. (2019). *Educational assessment of students* (8th ed.). Upper Saddle River, NJ: Pearson.

Brooks, F., & others (2018). Spirituality as a protective health asset for young people: An international comparative analysis from three countries. *International Journal of Public Health, 63,* 232-238.

Brooks, J.G., & Brooks, M.G. (2001). *The case for constructivist classrooms* (2nd ed.). Upper Saddle River, NJ: Erlbaum.

Brooks-Gunn, J., & Warren, M.P. (1989). The psychological significance of secondary sexual characteristics in 9- to 11-year-old girls. *Child Development 59,* 161-169.

Broomell, A.P.R., & others (2020, in press). Context of maternal intrusiveness during infancy and associations with preschool executive function. *Infant and Child Development*.

Brouillard, C., & others (2018). Links between mother-adolescent and father-adolescent relationships and adolescent depression: A genetically informed study. *Journal of Clinical Child and Adolescent Psychiatry, 47*(Suppl. 1), S397-S408.

Brouillard, C., & others (2019). Predictive links between genetic vulnerability to depression and trajectories of warmth and conflict in mother-adolescent and father-adolescent relationships. *Developmental Psychology, 55,* 1743-1757.

Brown, A.L., Horton, J., & Guillory, A. (2018). The impact of victim alcohol consumption and perpetrator use of force on perceptions in an acquaintance rape vignette. *Violence and Victims, 33,* 40-52.

Brown, B.B. (2011). Popularity in peer group perspective: The role of status in adolescent peer systems. In A.H.N. Cillessen, D. Schwartz, & L. Mayeux (Eds.), *Popularity in the peer system*. New York: Guilford.

Brown, B.B., Bakken, J.P., Ameringer, S.W., & Mahon, S.D. (2008). A comprehensive conceptualization of the peer influence process in adolescence. In M.J. Prinstein & K.A. Dodge (Eds.), *Understanding peer influence in children and adolescents*. New York: Guilford.

Brown, B.B., & Larson, J. (2009). Peer relationships in adolescence. In R.M. Lerner & L. Steinberg (Eds.), *Handbook of adolescent development* (3rd ed.). New York: Wiley.

Brown, B.B., & Larson, R.W. (2002). The kaleidoscope of adolescence: Experiences of the world's youth at the beginning of the 21st century. In B.B. Brown, R.W. Larson, & T.S. Saraswathi (Eds.), *The world's youth*. New York: Cambridge University Press.

Brown, C.L., & Menec, V. (2019). Health, social, and functional characteristics of older adults with continuing care needs: Implications for integrated care. *Journal of Aging and Health, 31,* 1085-1105.

Brown, C.L., & others (2012). Social activity and cognitive functioning over time: A coordinated analysis of four longitudinal studies. *Journal of Aging Research, 2012,* 287438.

Brown, C.S., & Stone, E.A. (2018). Environmental and social contributions to children's gender-typed toy play: The role of family, peers, and the media. In E.S. Weisgram & L.M. Dinella (Eds.), *Gender typing of children's play*. Washington, DC: APA Books.

Brown, D., & Lamb, M.E. (2020, in press). Forks in the road, routes chosen, and journeys that beckon: A selective review of scholarship on children's testimony. *Applied Cognitive Psychology*.

Brown, G.L., & Cox, M.J. (2020). Pleasure in parenting and father-child attachment security. *Attachment and Human Development, 22,* 51-65.

Brown, H.L., & Graves, C.R. (2013). Smoking and marijuana in pregnancy. *Clinical Obstetrics and Gynecology, 56,* 107-113.

Brown, J.A., & Wisco, J.J. (2019). The components of the adolescent brain and its unique sensitivity to sexually explicit material. *Journal of Adolescence, 72,* 10-13.

Brown, J.E. (2020). *Nutrition through the life cycle* (7th ed.). Boston: Cengage.

Brown, L., & others (2018). It's not as bad as you think: Menopausal representations are more positive in postmenopausal women. *Journal of Psychosomatic Obstetrics and Gynecology, 39,* 281-288.

Brown, M.T., & Wolf, D.A. (2018). Estimating the prevalence of serious mental illness and dementia diagnoses among Medicare beneficiaries in the Health and Retirement Study. *Research on Aging, 40*(7), 668-686.

Brown, Q.L., & others (2016). Trends in marijuana use among pregnant and non-pregnant reproductive-aged women, 2002-2014. *JAMA, 317,* 207-209.

Brown, R. (1968). *Words and things*. Glencoe, IL: Free Press.

Brown, S.L., & Lin, I-F. (2012). The gray divorce revolution: Rising divorce among middle-aged and older adults: 1990-2010. *Journals of Gerontology B: Psychological Sciences and Social Sciences, 67,* 731-741.

Brown, S.L., Nesse, R.M., House, J.S., & Utz, R.L. (2004). Religion and emotional compensation: Results from a prospective study of widowhood. *Personality and Social Psychology Bulletin, 30,* 1165-1174.

Brown, S.L., & Wright, M.R. (2019). Divorce attitudes among older adults: Two decades of change. *Journal of Family Issues, 40,* 1018-1037.

Brown, S.L., & others (2019). Repartnering following gray divorce: The roles of resources and constraints for women and men. *Demography, 56,* 503-523.

Brownell, C.A., Ramani, G.B., & Zerwas, S. (2006). Becoming a social partner with peers: Cooperation and social understanding in one- and two-year-olds. *Child Development, 77,* 803-821.

Brownell, C.A., Svetlova, M., Anderson, R., Nichols, S.R., & Drummond, J. (2013). Socialization of early prosocial behavior: Parents' talk about emotions is associated with sharing and helping in toddlers. *Infancy, 18,* 91-119.

Bruce, M.A., & others (2017). Church attendance, allostatic load, and mortality in middle-aged adults. *PLoS One, 12*(5), e0177618.

Bruck, M., & Ceci, S.J. (1999). The suggestibility of children's memory. *Annual Review of Psychology, 50,* 419-439.

Bruck, M., & Ceci, S.J. (2012). Forensic developmental psychology in the courtroom. In D. Faust & M. Ziskin (Eds.), *Coping with psychiatric and psychological testimony*. New York: Cambridge University Press.

Brum, P.S., & others (2020). Verbal working memory training in older adults: An investigation of dose response. *Aging and Mental Health, 24,* 81-91.

Brummelman, J.E., & others (2014). "That's not beautiful—That's incredibly beautiful!" The adverse impact of inflated praise on children with low self-esteem. *Psychological Science, 25,* 728-735.

Brunborg, G.S., Andeas, J.B., & Kvaavik, E. (2017). Social media use and episodic heavy drinking among adolescents. *Psychological Reports, 120,* 475–490.

Brunckhorst, O., & others (2019). A systematic review of the long-term efficacy of low-intensity shockwave therapy for vasculogenic erectile dysfunction. *International Journal of Urology and Nephrology, 51,* 773–781.

Bryant, R.A. (2012). Grief as a psychiatric disorder. *British Journal of Psychiatry, 201,* 9–10.

Bryant, R.A. (2013). Is pathological grief lasting more than 12 months grief or depression? *Current Opinion in Psychiatry, 26,* 41–46.

Bubbico, G., & others (2019). Effects of second language learning on the plastic aging brain: Functional connectivity, cognitive decline, and reorganization. *Frontiers in Neuroscience, 13,* 423.

Bublitz, M., Carpenter, M., & Bourjeily, G. (2020, in press). Preterm birth disparities between states in the United States: An opportunity for public health interventions. *Journal of Psychosomatic Obstetrics and Gynecology.*

Bucay-Harari, L., & others (2020, in press). Mental health needs of an emerging Latino community. *Journal of Behavioral Health Services and Research.*

Buckner, J.C., Mezzacappa, E., & Beardslee, M.R. (2009). Self-regulation and its relations to adaptive functioning in low-income youths. *American Journal of Orthopsychiatry, 79,* 19–30.

Bucur, B., & Madden, D.J. (2007). Information processing/cognition. In J.E. Birren (Ed.), *Encyclopedia of gerontology* (2nd ed.). San Diego: Academic Press.

Budge, S.L., Chin, M.Y., & Minero, L.P. (2017). Trans individuals' facilitative coping: An analysis of internal and external processes. *Journal of Counseling Psychology, 64,* 12–25.

Budge, S.L., & others (2018). The relationship between conformity to gender norms, sexual orientation, and gender identity for sexual minorities. *Counseling Psychology Quarterly, 64,* 12–25.

Buhl, H.M., & Lanz, M. (2007). Emerging adulthood in Europe: Common traits and variability across five European countries. *Journal of Adolescent Research, 22,* 439–443.

Buhrmester, D. (1998). Need fulfillment, interpersonal competence, and the developmental contexts of early adolescent friendship. In W.M. Bukowski & A.F. Newcomb (Eds.), *The company they keep: Friendship in childhood and adolescence.* New York: Cambridge University Press.

Bui, B.K.H. (2020, in press). The relationship between social network characteristics and depressive symptoms among older adults in the United States: Differentiating between network structure and network function. *Psychogeriatrics.*

Bui, T.A., & Wijesekera, N. (2019). Unemployment and the rate of psychoactive-substance-related psychiatric hospital admission in regional Queensland: An observational, longitudinal study. *Australas Psychiatry, 27,* 388–391.

Bukowski, R., & others (2008, January). *Folic acid and preterm birth.* Paper presented at the meeting of the Society for Maternal-Fetal Medicine, Dallas.

Bumpass, L., & Aquilino, W. (1994). *A social map of midlife: Family and work over the middle life course.* Center for Demography and Ecology, University of Wisconsin, Madison, WI.

Bumpus, M.F., Crouter, A.C., & McHale, S.M. (2001). Parental autonomy granting during adolescence: Gender differences in context. *Developmental Psychology, 37,* 163–173.

Bunge, E.L., & others (2017). *CBT strategies for anxious and depressed children and adolescents.* New York: Guilford.

Burack, J.A., & others (2016). Developments in the developmental approach to intellectual disability. In D. Cicchetti (Ed.), *Developmental psychopathology* (3rd ed.). New York: Wiley.

Buratti, S., Allwood, C.M., & Johansson, M. (2014). Stability in the metamemory realism of eyewitness confidence judgments. *Cognitive Processing, 15,* 39–53.

Burden, P.R., & Byrd, D.M. (2020). *Foundations of teaching education: A practical perspective.* Upper Saddle River, NJ: Pearson.

Burgette, J.M., & others (2017). Impact of Early Head Start in North Carolina on dental care use among children younger than 3 years. *American Journal of Public Health, 107,* 614–620.

Burke, D.M., & Shafto, M.A. (2004). Aging and language production. *Current Directions in Psychological Science, 13,* 21–24.

Burnett, A.C., & others (2018). Trends in executive functioning in extremely preterm children across 3 birth eras. Pediatrics, 141(1), e20171958.

Burnette, C.B., Kwitowski, M.A., & Mazzeo, S.E. (2017). "I don't need people to tell me I'm pretty on social media": A qualitative study of social media and body image in early adolescent girls. *Body Image, 23,* 114–125.

Burnham, D., & Mattock, K. (2010). Auditory development. In J.G. Bremner & T.D. Wachs (Eds.), *Wiley-Blackwell handbook of infant development* (2nd ed.). New York: Wiley.

Burnham, M.M. (2014). Co-sleeping and self-soothing during infancy. In A.R. Wolfson & H.E. Montgomery-Downs (Eds.), *Oxford handbook of infant, child, and adolescent sleep and behavior.* New York: Oxford University Press.

Burr, J. (2009). Volunteering, later life. In D. Carr (Ed.), *Encyclopedia of the life course and human development.* Boston: Gale Cengage.

Burr, J.A., & others (2018). Health benefits associated with three helping behaviors: Evidence for incident cardiovascular disease. *Journals of Gerontology B: Psychological Sciences and Social Sciences, 73,* 492–500.

Burt, K.B., & Paysnick, A.A. (2012). Resilience in the transition to adulthood. *Development and Psychopathology, 24,* 493–505.

Busch, A.S., & others (2020, in press). Obesity is associated with earlier puberty in boys. *Journal of Clinical Endocrinology and Metabolism.*

Bushnell, I.W.R. (2003). Newborn face recognition. In O. Pascalis & A. Slater (Eds.), *The development of face processing in infancy and early childhood.* New York: NOVA Science.

Buss, D.M. (2008). *Evolutionary psychology* (3rd ed.). Boston: Allyn & Bacon.

Buss, D.M. (2012). *Evolutionary psychology* (4th ed.). Boston: Allyn & Bacon.

Buss, D.M. (2015). *Evolutionary psychology* (5th ed.). Upper Saddle River, NJ: Pearson.

Buss, D.M. (2018). Sexual and emotional infidelity: Evolved gender differences in jealousy prove robust and reliable. *Perspectives on Psychological Science, 13,* 155–160.

Buss, D.M. (2019). *Evolutionary psychology* (6th ed.). New York: Routledge.

Buss, D.M., & Barnes, M. (1986). Preferences in human mate selection. *Journal of Personality and Social Psychology, 50,* 559–570.

Buss, D.M., & Schmitt, D.P. (2019). Mate preferences and their behavioral manifestations. *Annual Review of Psychology, 70,* 77–110. Palo Alto, CA: Annual Reviews.

Buss, D.M., & others (1990). International preferences in selecting mates: A study of 37 cultures. *Journal of Cross-Cultural Psychology, 21,* 5–47.

Busse, E.W., & Blazer, D.G. (1996). *The American Psychiatric Press textbook of geriatric psychiatry* (2nd ed.). Washington, DC: American Psychiatric Press.

Bussey, K., & Bandura, A. (1999). Social cognitive theory of gender development and differentiation. *Psychological Review, 106,* 676–713.

Butler, G., & others (2019). Growth hormone treatment and health-related quality of life in children and adolescents: A national, prospective, one-year controlled study. *Clinical Endocrinology, 91,* 304–313.

Butler, R.N. (2007). Life review. In J.E. Birren (Ed.), *Encyclopedia of gerontology* (2nd ed.). San Diego: Academic Press.

Butler, R.N., & Lewis, M. (2002). *The new love and sex after 60.* New York: Ballantine.

Buyukozer Dawkins, M., & others (2019). Do infants in the first year of life expect equal resource allocations? *Frontiers in Psychology, 10,* 116.

Buyukozer Dawkins, M., & others (2021, in press). Early moral development: A principle-based approach. In D. Poeppel & others (Eds.), *The cognitive neurosciences* (6th ed.). Cambridge, MA: MIT Press.

Byambasukh, O., Snieder, H., & Corpeleijn, E. (2020). Relation between leisure time, commuting, and occupational physical activity with blood pressure in 125,402 adults: The Lifelines cohort. *Journal of the American Heart Association, 9,* e014313.

Byne, W., & others (2012). Report of the American Psychiatric Association Task Force on the treatment of gender identity disorder. *Archives of Sexual Behavior, 41,* 759–796.

Byrne, J.L., & others (2018). A brief eHealth tool delivered in primary care to help parents prevent childhood obesity: A randomized controlled trial. *Pediatric Obesity, 13,* 659–667.

Byrne, L., & Drake, A.J. (2019). Pediatrician's guide to epigenetics. *Archives of Disease in Childhood, 104,* 297–301.

C

Cabeza, R. (2002). Hemispheric asymmetry reduction in older adults: The HAROLD model. *Psychology and Aging, 17,* 85-100.

Cabrera, N.J. (2020). Father involvement, father-child relationship, and attachment: The early years. *Attachment and Human Development, 22,* 134-138.

Cabrera, N.J., & Roggman, L. (2017). Father play: Is it special? *Infant Mental Health, 38,* 706-708.

Cabrera, N.J., & others (2017). The magic of play: Low-income mothers' and fathers' playfulness and children's emotion regulation and vocabulary skills. *Infant Mental Health Journal, 38,* 757-771.

Cabre-Riera, A., & others (2019). Telecommunication devices use, screen time, and sleep in adolescents. *Environmental Research, 171,* 341-347.

Cacabelos, R., & others (2019). Sirtuins in Alzheimer's disease: SIRT2-related genophenotypes and implications for pharmacoepigenetics. *International Journal of Molecular Science, 20,* 5.

Cacioppo, J.T., Cacioppo, S., Gonzaga, G.C., Ogburn, E.L., & VanderWheele, T.J. (2013). Marital satisfaction and break-ups differ across on-line and off-line meeting venues. *Proceedings of the National Academy of Sciences, 110*(25), 10135-10140.

Cagle, J.G., & others (2016). Predictors of preference for hospice care among diverse older adults. *American Journal of Hospice and Palliative Care, 33,* 574-584.

Cahill, K.E., Giandrea, M.D., & Quinn, J.F. (2015). Retirement patterns and the macroeconomy, 1992-2010: The prevalence and determinants of bridge jobs, retirement, and reentry among three recent cohorts of older Americans. *Gerontologist, 55,* 384-403.

Cahill, K.E., Giandrea, M.D., & Quinn, J.F. (2016). Evolving patterns of work and retirement. In L.K. George & K.F. Ferraro (Eds.), *Handbook of aging and the social sciences* (8th ed.). New York: Elsevier.

Cahill, M., & others (2019). The transition to retirement experiences of academics in "higher education": A meta-ethnography. *Gerontologist, 59,* e177-e195.

Cai, D., & others (2019). High trans-placental transfer of perfluoroalkyl substances alternatives in the matched maternal-cord blood serum: Evidence from a birth cohort study. *The Science of the Total Environment, 705,* 135885.

Cai, H., & others (2017). Effect of exercise on cognitive function in chronic disease patients: A meta-analysis and systematic review of randomized controlled trials. *Clinical Interventions in Aging. 12,* 773-783.

Cai, M., & others (2013). Adolescent-parent attachment as a mediator of relationships between parenting and adolescent social behavior and wellbeing in China. *International Journal of Psychology, 48,* 1185-1190.

Cain, C.L., & McCleskey, S. (2019). Expanded definitions of the 'good death'? Race, ethnicity, and medical aid in dying. *Sociology of Health and Illness, 41,* 1175-1191.

Caino, S., & others (2010). Short-term growth in head circumference and its relationship with supine length in healthy infants. *Annals of Human Biology, 37,* 108-116.

Cairncross, M., & Miller, C.J. (2016). The effectiveness of mindfulness-based therapies for ADHD: A meta-analytic review. *Journal of Attention Disorders, 2,* 2.

Caiso, C., Besnard, J., & Allain, P. (2019). Frontal lobe functions in normal aging: Metacognition, autonomy, and quality of life. *Experimental Aging Research, 45,* 10-27.

Calabro, F.J., & others (2020, in press). Development of hippocampal-prefrontal cortex interactions through adolescence. *Cerebral Cortex.*

Calders, F., & others (2020, in press). Investigating the interplay between parenting dimensions and styles, and the association with adolescent outcomes. *European Child and Adolescent Psychiatry.*

Calero, M.D. (2019). Effects of environmental enrichment and training across the life span in cognition. In R. Fernandez-Ballesteros & others (Eds.), *Cambridge handbook of successful aging.* New York: Cambridge University Press.

Calkins, S.D., & Perry, N.B. (2016). The development of emotion regulation. In D. Cicchetti (Ed.), *Developmental psychopathology* (3rd ed.). New York: Wiley.

Callaghan, T., & Corbit, J. (2015). The development of symbolic representation. In R.M. Lerner (Ed.), *Handbook of child psychology and developmental science* (7th ed.). New York: Wiley.

Callisaya, M.L., & others (2019). Type 2 diabetes mellitus, brain atrophy, and cognitive decline in older people: A longitudinal study. *Diabetologia, 62,* 448-458.

Calugi, S., & Dalle Grave, R. (2019). Body image concern and treatment outcomes in adolescents with anorexia nervosa. *International Journal of Eating Disorders, 52,* 582-585.

Calvigioni, D., Hurd, Y.L., Harkany, T., & Keimpema, E. (2014). Neuronal substrates and functional consequences of prenatal cannabis exposures. *European Child and Adolescent Psychiatry, 23,* 931-941.

Calvo, R., Carr, D.C., & Matz-Costa, C. (2017). Another paradox? The life satisfaction of older Hispanic immigrants in the United States. *Journal of Aging and Health, 29,* 3-24.

Calvo, R., Carr, D.C., & Matz-Costa, C. (2019). Expanding the happiness paradox: Ethnoracial disparities in life satisfaction among older immigrants in the United States. *Journal of Aging and Health, 3,* 231-245.

Camacho, D.E., & Fuligni, A.J. (2015). Extracurricular participation among adolescents from immigrant families. *Journal of Youth and Adolescence, 44,* 1251-1262.

Cambron, C., & others (2020, in press). Neighborhood structural factors and proximal risk for youth substance abuse. *Prevention Science.*

Cameranesi, M., Lix, L.M., & Piotrowski, C.C. (2019). Linking a history of child abuse to adult health among Canadians: A structural equation modeling analysis. *International Journal of Environmental Research and Public Health, 16,* 11.

Campanini, M.Z., & others (2019). Duration and quality of sleep and risk of physical function impairment and disability in older adults: Results from the ENRICA and ELSA cohorts. *Aging and Disease, 10,* 557-569.

Campbell, K.L., Grady, C.L., Ng, C., & Hasher, L. (2012). Age differences in the frontoparietal cognitive control network: Implications for distractibility. *Neuropsychologia, 50*(9), 2212-2223.

Campbell, L. (2016, March 29). Mississippi extends abstinence-based sex-ed. *Mississippi Today.* Retrieved from http://mississippitoday.org/2016/3/29

Campbell, L., Campbell, B., & Dickinson, D. (2004). *Teaching and learning through multiple intelligences* (3rd ed.). Boston Allyn & Bacon.

Campione-Barr, N., & Smetana, J.G. (2019). Families with adolescents. In B.H. Friese (Ed.), *APA handbook of contemporary family psychology.* Washington, DC: APA Books.

Campos, J.J. (2005). Unpublished review of J.W. Santrock's *Life-span development* (10th ed.). New York: McGraw-Hill.

Canete, M.D., & others (2019). Effects of growth hormone therapy on metabolic parameters, adipokine, and endothelial dysfunction in prepubertal children. *Acta Pediatrica, 108,* 2027-2033.

Canfield, J., & Hansen, M.V. (1995). *A second helping of chicken soup for the soul.* Deerfield Beach, FL: Health Communications.

Canivez, G.L., & others (2020, in press). Construct validity of the WISC-V in clinical cases: Exploratory and confirmatory factor analyses of the 10 primary subtests. *Assessment.*

Cansino, S., & others (2019). Predictors of source memory success and failure in older adults. *Frontiers in Aging Neuroscience, 11,* 17.

Cantone, E., & others (2015). Interventions on bullying and cyberbullying in schools: A systematic review. *Clinical Practice and Epidemiology in Mental Health, 11*(Suppl. 1), S58-S76.

Cantwell-Bartl, A. (2018). Grief and coping of parents whose child has a constant life-threatening disability, hypoplastic left heart syndrome, with reference to the dual process model. *Death Studies, 42*(9), 569-578.

Cao, Y., Lu, J., & Lu, J. (2020). Paternal smoking before conception and during pregnancy is associated with an increased risk of childhood acute lymphoblastic leukemia: A systematic review and meta-analysis of 17 case-control studies. *Journal of Pediatric Hematology/Oncology, 42,* 32-40.

Caprara, G.V., & others (2010). The contributions of agreeableness and self-efficacy beliefs to prosociality. *European Journal of Personality, 24,* 36-55.

Cardoso-Moreira, M., & others (2019). Gene expression across mammalian organ development. *Nature, 571,* 505-509.

Career Builder (2018). *Working parents.* Chicago: Career Builder.

Carlier, J., & others (2020, in press). Testing unconventional matrices to monitor for prenatal exposure to heroin, cocaine, amphetamines, synthetic cahinones, and synthetic opioids. *Therapeutic Drug Monitoring.*

Carlin, R.E., & Moon, R.Y. (2017). Risk factors, protective factors, and current recommendations to reduce sudden infant death syndrome: A review. *JAMA Pediatrics, 17,* 175-180.

Carlo, G., & Conejo, L.D. (2020). Traditional and culture-specific parenting of prosociality in U.S. Latino/as. In D.J. Laible & others (Eds.), *Oxford handbook of parenting and moral development.* New York: Oxford University Press.

Carlo, G., & Pierotti, S.L. (2020). The development of prosocial motives. In L.A. Jensen (Ed.), *Oxford handbook of moral development.* New York: Oxford University Press.

Carlo, G., & others (2018). Longitudinal relations among parenting styles, prosocial behaviors, and academic outcomes in U.S. Mexican adolescents. *Child Development, 89,* 577-592.

Carlson, D.S., Thompson, M.J., & Kacmar, K.M. (2019). Double crossed: The spillover effects of work demands on work outcomes throughout the family. *Journal of Applied Psychology, 104,* 214-228.

Carlson, M.C., & others (2015). Impact of the Baltimore Experience Corps Trial on cortical and hippocampal volumes. *Alzheimer's and Dementia, 11,* 1340-1348.

Carlson, N.S., Corwin, E.J., & Lowe, N.K. (2017). Oxytocin augmentation in spontaneously laboring, nulliparous women. *Biological Research in Nursing, 19,* 382-392.

Carlson, S.M., Zelazo, P.D., & Faja, S. (2013). Executive function. In P.D. Zelazo (Ed.), *Oxford handbook of developmental psychology.* New York: Oxford University Press.

Carlson, S.M., & others (2018). Cohort effects in children's delay of gratification. *Developmental Psychology, 54,* 1395-1407.

Carmona, S., Hardy, J., & Guerreiro, R. (2018). The genetic landscape of Alzheimer's disease. *Handbook of Clinical Neurology, 148,* 395-408.

Carney, L.M., & Park, C. (2018). Cancer survivors' understanding of the cause and cure of their illness: Religious and secular appraisals. *Psycho-Oncology, 27,* 1553-1558.

Carone, N., & others (2018). Italian gay father families formed by surrogacy: Parenting, stigmatization, and children's psychological adjustment. *Developmental Psychology, 54,* 1904-1916.

Carpendale, J.I., & Chandler, M.J. (1996). On the distinction between false belief in understanding and subscribing to an interpretive theory of mind. *Child Development, 67,* 1686-1706.

Carpendale, J.I., & Hammond, S.I. (2016). The development of moral sense and moral thinking. *Current Opinion in Pediatrics, 28,* 743-747.

Carpendale, J.I.M., & Lewis, C. (2015). The development of social understanding. In R.M. Lerner (Ed.), *Handbook of child psychology and developmental science* (7th ed.). New York: Wiley.

Carpenter, R.W., & others (2019). Rate of alcohol consumption in the daily life of adolescents and emerging adults. *Psychopharmacology, 236,* 3111-3124.

Carr, D. (2009). Death and dying. In D. Carr (Ed.), *Encyclopedia of the life course and human development.* Boston: Gale Cengage.

Carr, D. (2018). Volunteering among older adults: Life course correlates and consequences. *Journals of Gerontology B: Psychological Sciences and Social Sciences, 73,* 479-481.

Carr, D. (2020). Mental health of older widows and widowers: Which coping strategies are most protective? *Aging and Mental Health, 24,* 291-299.

Carr, D., Kail, B.L., & Rowe, J.W. (2018). The relation of volunteering and subsequent changes in physical disability in older adults. *Journals of Gerontology B: Psychological Sciences and Social Sciences, 73,* 511-521.

Carr, D., & Sharp, S. (2014). Do afterlife beliefs affect psychological adjustment to late-life spousal loss? *Journals of Gerontology B: Psychological Sciences and Social Sciences, 69B*(1), 103-112.

Carr, D., Sonnega, J., Nesse, R.M., & House, J.S. (2014). Do special occasions trigger psychological distress among older bereaved spouses? An empirical assessment of clinical wisdom. *Journals of Gerontology B: Psychological Sciences and Social Sciences, 69B,* 113-122.

Carr, D., & others (2018). Does becoming a volunteer attenuate loneliness among recently widowed older adults? *Journals of Gerontology B: Psychological Sciences and Social Sciences, 73,* 501-510.

Carr, D.C., & others (2020, in press). Alternative retirement paths and cognitive performance: Exploring the role of preretirement complexity. *Gerontologist.*

Carroll, J.E., & others (2015). Partial sleep deprivation activates DNA damage response (DDR) and the senescence-associated secretory phenotype (SASP) in aged humans. *Brain, Behavior, and Immunity, 38,* 205-211.

Carroll, J.L. (2019). *Sexuality now* (6th ed.). Boston: Cengage.

Carskadon, M.A. (2004). Sleep difficulties in young people. *Archives of Pediatric and Adolescent Medicine, 158,* 597-598.

Carskadon, M.A. (2005). Sleep and circadian rhythms in children and adolescents: Relevance for athletic performance of young people. *Clinical Sports Medicine, 24,* 319-328.

Carskadon, M.A. (2011a). Sleep in adolescents: The perfect storm. *Pediatric Clinics of North America, 58,* 637-647.

Carskadon, M.A. (2011b). Sleep's effects on cognition and learning in adolescence. *Progress in Brain Research, 190,* 137-143.

Carskadon, M.A., & Tarokh, L. (2014). Developmental changes in sleep biology and potential effects on adolescent behavior and caffeine use. *Nutrition Review, 72*(Suppl. 1), S60-S64.

Carson, V., & others (2015). Systematic review of sedentary behavior and cognitive development in early childhood. *Preventive Medicine, 78,* 15-22.

Carstensen, L.L. (1998). A life-span approach to social motivation. In J. Heckhausen & C. Dweck (Eds.), *Motivation and self-regulation across the life span.* New York: Cambridge University Press.

Carstensen, L.L. (2006). The influence of a sense of time on human development. *Science, 312,* 1913-1915.

Carstensen, L.L. (2009). *A long bright future.* New York: Random House.

Carstensen, L.L. (2011). *A long bright future: Happiness, health, and financial health in an age of increased longevity.* New York: Public Affairs.

Carstensen, L.L. (2014). Our aging population may just save us all. In P. Irving (Ed.), *The upside of aging.* New York: Wiley.

Carstensen, L.L. (2015a). How we'll be fit and happy at 100. *The technology of us.* Retrieved March 5, 2018, from http://technologyofus.com/carstensen-fit-and-happy/

Carstensen, L.L. (2015b, February). The new age of much older age. *Time, 185*(6), 68-70.

Carstensen, L.L. (2016, February). The new age of aging. *Time, 187*(6-7), 60-62.

Carstensen, L.L. (2019a, November 29). We need a major redesign of life. Retrieved December 20, 2019, from www.washingtonpost.com/opinions/2019/11/29

Carstensen, L.L. (2019b). Integrating cognitive and emotion paradigms to address the paradox of aging. *Cognition and Emotion, 33,* 119-125.

Carter, A. (2019). The consequences of adolescent delinquent behavior for adult employment outcomes. *Journal of Youth and Adolescence, 48,* 17-29.

Carter, R.C., Jacobson, J.L., & Jacobson, S.W. (2020). Early detection of fetal alcohol spectrum disorders: An elusive but critical goal. *Pediatrics, 144*(6), e20193080.

Carver, K., Joyner, K., & Udry, J.R. (2003). National estimates of romantic relationships. *Annual Review of Psychology* (Vol. 54). Palo Alto, CA: Annual Reviews.

Casabona, G., & others (2019). Six years of experience using an advanced algorithm for botulinum toxin application. *Journal of Cosmetic Dermatology, 18,* 21-35.

Casaletto, K.B., & others (2020, in press). Late-life physical and cognitive activities independently contribute to brain and cognitive resilience. *Journal of Alzheimer's Disease.*

Case, R., & Mueller, M.R. (2001). Differentiation, integration, and covariance mapping as fundamental processes in cognitive and neurological growth. In J.L. McClelland & R.S. Siegler (Eds.), *Mechanisms of cognitive development.* Mahwah, NJ: Erlbaum.

CASEL (2020). *Collaborative for Academic, Social, and Emotional Learning.* Retrieved January 24, 2020, from www.casel.org

Casey, B.J., & others (2019). Development of the emotional brain. *Neuroscience Letters, 693,* 29-34.

Caspers, K.M., & others (2009). Association between the serotonin transporter polymorphism (5-HTTLPR) and adult unresolved attachment. *Developmental Psychology, 45,* 64-76.

Caspi, A., & Roberts, B.W. (2001). Personality development across the life course: The argument for change and continuity. *Psychological Inquiry, 12*, 49-66.

Caspi, A., & others (2003). Influence of life stress on depression: Moderation by a polymorphism in the 5-HTT gene. *Science, 301*, 386-389.

Cassilas, M., Brown, P., & Levinson, S.C. (2020, in press). Early language experience in a Tseltal Mayan village. *Child Development.*

Castellvi, P., & others (2017). Longitudinal association between self-injurious thoughts and behaviors and suicidal behavior in adolescents and young adults: A systematic review and meta-analysis. *Journal of Affective Disorders, 215*, 37-48.

Castillo, M., & Weiselberg, E. (2017). Bulimia nervosa/purging disorder. *Current Problems in Pediatric and Adolescent Health Care, 47*, 85-94.

Castillo-Morales, A., & others (2019). Postmitotic cell longevity-associated genes: A transcriptional signature of postmitotic maintenance in neural tissues. *Neurobiology of Aging, 74*, 147-160.

Castro, F.G., Barrera, M., Mena, L.A., & Aguirre, K.M. (2015). Culture and alcohol use: Historical and sociocultural themes from 75 years of alcohol research. *Journal of Studies on Alcohol and Drugs, 75*(Suppl. 17), S36-S49.

Cataldo, J., & Nelson, C.A. (2019). The recognition of emotion during the first years of life. In A.S. Fox & others (Eds.), *The nature of emotion* (2nd ed.). New York: Oxford University Press.

Cattagni Kleiner, A., & others (2019). Advance care planning dispositions: The relationship between knowledge and perception. *BMC Geriatrics, 19*(1), 118.

Cattaneo, G., & others (2020). The Barcelona Brain Health Initiative: Cohort description and first follow-up. *PLoS One, 15*(2), e0228754.

Cavanagh, S.E. (2009). Puberty. In D. Carr (Ed.), *Encyclopedia of the life course and human development*. Boston: Gale Cengage.

Cazzato, V., & others (2016). The effects of body exposure on self-body image and esthetic appreciation in anorexia nervosa. *Experimental Brain Research, 234*, 695-709.

Ceci, S.J., & Gilstrap, L.L. (2000). Determinants of intelligence: Schooling and intelligence. In A. Kazdin (Ed.), *Encyclopedia of psychology*. Washington, DC, & New York: American Psychological Association and Oxford University Press.

Ceci, S.J., Hritz, A., & Royer, C.E. (2016). Understanding suggestibility. In W. O'Donohue & M. Fanetti (Eds.), *A guide to evidence-based practice*. New York: Springer.

Center for Science in the Public Interest (2008). Obesity on the kids' menu at top chains. Retrieved October 2, 2008, from http://cspinet.org/new/200808041.html

Centers for Disease Control and Prevention (2007). *Autism and developmental disabilities monitoring (ADDM) network*. Atlanta: Author.

Centers for Disease Control and Prevention (2012). *By the numbers full year 2011: Health measures from the National Health Interview Study, January-December 2011.* Atlanta: Author.

Centers for Disease Control and Prevention (2015). *Depression*. Atlanta: Author.

Centers for Disease Control and Prevention (2015). *National Health Interview Survey 2014*. Atlanta: Author.

Centers for Disease Control and Prevention (2016). *ADHD*. Retrieved January 12, 2016, from www.cdc.gov/ncbddd/adhd/data.html

Centers for Disease Control and Prevention (2016). *Breastfeeding rates continue to rise in the U.S.* Atlanta: Author.

Centers for Disease Control and Prevention (2017). *Autism spectrum disorders*. Atlanta: Author.

Centers for Disease Control and Prevention (2017). *Births, marriages, divorces, and deaths*. Atlanta: Author.

Centers for Disease Control and Prevention (2018). *High blood pressure facts*. Atlanta; Author.

Centers for Disease Control and Prevention (2018). *HIV/AIDS*. Atlanta: Author.

Centers for Disease Control and Prevention (2018). *Preterm birth and low birth rate*. Atlanta: Author.

Centers for Disease Control and Prevention (2019). *Cesarean section rates 2018*. Atlanta: Author.

Centers for Disease Control and Prevention (2019). *Child health*. Atlanta: Author.

Centers for Disease Control and Prevention (2019). *Current cigarette smoking among adults in the United States*. Atlanta: Author.

Centers for Disease Control and Prevention (2019). *How much physical activity do older adults need?* Atlanta: Author.

Centers for Disease Control and Prevention (2019). *National Health Interview Survey 2018*. Atlanta: Author.

Centers for Disease Control and Prevention (2019, January 10). *Reproductive health: Teen pregnancy*. Retrieved March 29, 2019, from www.cdc.gov/teenpregnancy/

Centers for Disease Control and Prevention (2020). *Causes of death*. Atlanta: Author.

Centers for Disease Control and Prevention (2020). *Physical activity and health: Older adults*. Atlanta: Author.

Centers for Disease Control and Prevention (2020a). *Births, marriages, divorces, and deaths*. Atlanta: Author.

Centers for Disease Control and Prevention (2020b). *Body mass index for children and teens*. Atlanta: Author.

Central Intelligence Agency (2015). *The world factbook: Life expectancy at birth*. Washington, DC: CIA.

Cercignani, M., & others (2017). Characterizing axonal myelination within the healthy population: A tract-by-tract mapping of effects of age and gender on the fiber-g ratio. *Neurobiology of Aging, 49*, 109-118.

Chai, H.W., Zarit, S.H., & Fingerman, K.L. (2020, in press). Revisiting intergenerational contact and relationship quality in later life: Parental characteristics matter. *Research on Aging.*

Chan, G.C., & others (2017). Peer drug use and adolescent polysubstance use: Do parenting and school factors moderate this association? *Addictive Behaviors, 64*, 78-81.

Chan, J.S.Y., & others (2019). Effects of meditation and mind-body exercises on older adults' cognitive performance: A meta-analysis. *Gerontologist, 59*, e782-e790.

Chan, M.Y., Haber, S., Drew, L.M., & Park, D.C. (2016). Training older adults to use tablet computers: Does it enhance cognitive function? *Gerontologist, 56*, 475-484.

Chandra, A., Mosher, W.D., Copen, C., & Sionean, C. (2011, March 3). Sexual behavior, sexual attraction, and sexual identity in the United States: Data from the 2006-2008 National Survey of Family Growth. *National Health Statistics Reports, 36*, 1-28.

Chang, E.C., & others (2018). Does optimism weaken the negative effects of being lonely on suicide risk? *Death Studies, 42*, 63-68.

Chang, E.S., & others (2020). Global reach of ageism on older persons' health: A systematic review. *PLoS One, 15*(1), e0220857.

Chang, H.Y., & others (2014). Prenatal maternal depression is associated with low birth weight through shorter gestational age in term infants in Korea. *Early Human Development, 90*, 15-20.

Chang, S.H., Beason, T.S., Hunleth, J.M., & Colditz, G.A. (2012). A systematic review of body fat distribution and mortality in older people. *Maturitas, 72*, 175-191.

Chang, Y.C., & others (2017). Effects of different amounts of exercise on preventing depressive symptoms in community-dwelling older adults: A prospective study in Taiwan. *BMJ Open, 7*(4), 014256.

Chang, Y.K., Liu, S., Yu, H.H., & Lee, Y.H. (2012). Effect of acute exercise on executive function in children with attention deficit hyperactivity disorder. *Archives of Clinical Neuropsychology, 27*, 225-237.

Chao, R.K. (2001). Extending research on the consequences of parenting style for Chinese Americans and European Americans. *Child Development, 72*, 1832-1843.

Chao, R.K. (2005, April). *The importance of Guan in describing control of immigrant Chinese*. Paper presented at the meeting of the Society for Research in Child Development, Atlanta.

Chao, R.K. (2007, March). *Research with Asian Americans: Looking back and moving forward*. Paper presented at the meeting of the Society for Research in Child Development, Boston.

Chaparro, M.P., & others (2019). The 2009 Special Supplementation Nutrition Program for Women, Infants, and Children (WIC) food package change and children's growth trajectories and obesity in Los Angeles County. *American Journal of Nutrition, 109*, 1414-1421.

Chaplin, T.M., & Aldao, A. (2013). Gender differences in emotion expression in children: A meta-analytic review. *Psychological Bulletin, 139*(4), 735-765.

Chapman, B.P., & others (2020). Mortality risk associated with personality facets of the Big Five and interpersonal circumplex across three aging cohorts. *Psychosomatic Medicine, 82,* 64–73.

Chappuis, J. (2020). *Classroom assessment for student learning* (3rd ed.). Upper Saddle River, NJ: Pearson.

Charles, S.T., & Luong, G. (2011). Emotional experience across the life span. In K.L. Fingerman, C.A. Berg, J. Smith, & T.C. Antonucci (Eds.), *Handbook of life-span development.* New York: Springer.

Charles, S.T., & Piazza, J.R. (2007). Memories of social interactions: Age differences in emotion intensity. *Psychology and Aging, 22,* 300–309.

Charlesworth, T.E.S., & others (2019). Children use targets' facial appearance to guide and predict social behavior. *Developmental Psychology, 55,* 1400–1413.

Charness, N., & Bosman, E.A. (1992). Human factors and aging. In F.I.M. Craik & T.A. Salthouse (Eds.), *The handbook of aging and cognition.* Hillsdale, NJ: Erlbaum.

Charness, N., & Krampe, R.T. (2008). Expertise and knowledge. In D.F. Alwin & S.M. Hofer (Eds.), *Handbook on cognitive aging.* Thousand Oaks, CA: Sage.

Charpak, N., & others (2017). Twenty-year follow-up of kangaroo mother care versus traditional care. *Pediatrics, 139,* 1.

Chaturvedi, S., & others (2014). Pharmacological interventions for hypertension in children. *Cochrane Database of Systematic Reviews, 2,* CD008117.

Chaudhari, B.L., & others (2019). Correlation of motivations for selfie-posting behavior with personality traits. *Indian Psychiatry Journal, 28,* 123–129.

Chavarria, M.C., & others (2014). Puberty in the corpus callosum. *Neuroscience, 265,* 1–8.

Cheek, C., Piercy, K.W., & Kohlenberg, M. (2015). Have I ever done anything like this before? Older adults solving ill-defined problems in intensive volunteering. *International Journal of Aging and Human Development, 80,* 184–207.

Cheetham, T.C., & others (2017). Association of testosterone replacement with cardiovascular outcomes among men with androgen deficiency. *JAMA Internal Medicine, 177,* 491–499.

Chen, B., & others (2018). The effects of cognitive training on cognitive abilities and everyday function: A 10-week randomized controlled trial. *International Journal of Aging and Human Development, 86,* 69–81.

Chen, B., & others (2019). Screen viewing behavior and sleep duration among children aged 2 and below. *BMC Public Health, 19*(1), 59.

Chen, C., & Stevenson, H.W. (1989). Homework: A cross-cultural comparison. *Child Development, 60,* 551–561.

Chen, C., Chow, A.Y.M., & Tang, S. (2020, in press). Trajectories of depressive symptoms in Chinese elderly during widowhood: A secondary analysis. *Aging and Mental Health.*

Chen, D., & Guarente, L. (2007). SIR2: A potential target for calorie restriction mimetics. *Trends in Molecular Medicine, 13,* 64–71.

Chen, F.R., Rothman, E.F., & Jaffee, S.R. (2019). Early puberty, friendship, group characteristics, and dating abuse in U.S. girls. *Pediatrics, 139,* 6.

Chen, F.Y., & others (2020). Fluid intelligence is associated with cortical volume and white matter tract integrity within multiple-demand system across adult lifespan. *Neuorimage, 212,* 116576.

Chen, G., & others (2017). An association study revealed substantial effects of dominance, epistasis, and substance dependence co-morbidity on alcohol dependence symptom count. *Addiction Biology, 22,* 1475–1485.

Chen, H., & Cheng, C.L. (2020, in press). Parental psychological control and children's relational aggression: Examining the roles of gender and normative beliefs about relational aggression. *Journal of Psychology.*

Chen, H., & Tan, D. (2019). Cesarean section or natural childbirth? Cesarean birth may damage your health. *Frontiers in Psychology, 10,* 351.

Chen, H.Y., & Cheng, C.L. (2020). Developmental trajectory of purpose identification during adolescence: Links to life satisfaction and depressive symptoms. *Journal of Adolescence, 80,* 10–18.

Chen, J., & others (2019). Wanting to be remembered: Intrinsically rewarding work and generativity in early midlife. *Canadian Review of Sociology, 56,* 30–46.

Chen, L., & Cao, Q. (2020, in press). Poverty increases the risk of independent cognitive impairment among older adults: A longitudinal study in China. *Aging and Mental Health.*

Chen, L.W., & others (2018). Measuring the cost and value of quality improvement initiatives for local health departments. *Journal of Public Health Management and Practice, 24,* 164–171.

Chen, N., Deater-Deckard, K., & Bell, M.A. (2014). The role of temperament by family interactions in child maladjustment. *Journal of Abnormal Child Psychology, 42,* 1251–1262.

Chen, S., & others (2020). Discrimination, language brokering efficacy, and academic competence among adolescent language brokers. *Journal of Adolescence, 59,* 247–257.

Chen, W.L., & Chen, J.H. (2019). Consequences of inadequate sleep during the college years: Sleep deprivation, grade point average, and college graduation. *Preventive Medicine, 124,* 23–28.

Chen, X., Fu, R., & Yu, Y.V. (2019). Culture and parenting. In M.H. Bornstein (Ed.), *Handbook of parenting* (3rd ed.). New York: Elsevier.

Chen, X., Lee, J., & Chen, L. (2018). Culture and peer relationships. In W.M. Bukowski & others (Eds.), *Handbook of peer interactions, relationships, and groups* (2nd ed.). New York: Guilford.

Chen, X., Saafir, A., & Graham, S. (2020, in press). An association study revealed substantial effects of dominance, epistasis, and substance dependence co-morbidity on alcohol dependence symptom count. *Journal of Youth and Adolescence.*

Chen, X., & others (1998). Childrearing attitudes and behavioral inhibition in Chinese and Canadian toddlers: A cross-cultural study. *Developmental Psychology, 34,* 677–686.

Chen, X.I., Hertzog, C., & Park, D.C. (2017). Cognitive predictors of everyday problem solving across the lifespan. *Gerontology, 63,* 372–384.

Chen, Y., & others (2019). The positive effects of early-life education on cognition, leisure activity, and brain structure in healthy aging. *Aging, 11*(14), 4923–4942.

Chen, Y., & others (2020, in press). Personal and clinical factors associated with older drivers' self-awareness of driving performance. *Canadian Journal of Aging.*

Chen, Y.H., & others (2019). Magnetoencephalography and the infant brain. *Neuroimage, 189,* 445–458.

Cheng, A., & others (2019). The psychological health of 207 near-centenarians (95–99) and centenarians from the Sydney Centenarian Study. *Australian and New Zealand Journal of Psychiatry, 53,* 976–988.

Cheng, C.K., & others (2020, in press). Pharmacological basis and new insights of resveratrol action in the cardiovascular system. *British Journal of Pharmacology.*

Cheng, G.H., & others (2020, in press). Productive engagement patterns and their association with depressive symptomatology, loneliness, and cognitive function among older adults. *Aging and Mental Health.*

Cheng, H., & others (2020, in press). Biomedical, psychological, environmental, and behavioral factors associated with adult obesity in a nationally representative sample. *Journal of Public Health.*

Cheng, H.M., & others (2017). Vascular aging and hypertension: Implications for the clinical application of central blood pressure. *International Journal of Cardiology, 230,* 209–213.

Cheng, N., & others (2018). Quality of maternal parenting of 9-month-old infants predicts executive function performance at 2 and 3 years of age. *Frontiers in Psychology, 8,* 2293.

Cheong, J.L.Y., & others (2020, in press). Early environment and long-term outcomes of preterm infants. *Journal of Neural Transmission.*

Cherlin, A.J. (2009). *The marriage-go-round.* New York: Random House.

Cherlin, A.J., & Furstenberg, F.F. (1994). Stepfamilies in the United States: A reconsideration. In J. Blake & J. Hagen (Eds.), *Annual Review of Sociology* (Vol. 20). Palo Alto, CA: Annual Reviews.

Chess, S., & Thomas, A. (1977). Temperamental individuality from childhood to adolescence. *Journal of Child Psychiatry, 16,* 218–226.

Chess, S., & Thomas, A. (1987). *Origins and evolution of behavior disorders.* Cambridge, MA: Harvard University Press.

Chessa, F., & Moreno, F. (2019). Ethical and legal considerations in end-of-life care. *Primary Care, 46,* 387–398.

Cheung, C., & others (2016). Controlling and autonomy-supportive parenting in the United States and China: Beyond children's reports. *Child Development, 87,* 1992–2007.

Cheung, C.S., Pomerantz, E.M., & Dong, W. (2012). Does adolescents' disclosure to their parents matter for their academic adjustment? *Child Development, 84*(2), 693–710.

Chevalere, J., Lemaire, P., & Camos, V. (2020). Age-related changes in verbal working memory strategies. *Experimental Aging Research, 46,* 93–127.

Chevalier, N., Dauvier, B., & Blaye, A. (2018). From prioritizing objects to prioritizing cues: A developmental shift for cognitive control. *Developmental Science. 21,* 2.

Chevalier, N., & others (2015). Myelination is associated with processing speed in early childhood: Preliminary insights. *PLoS One, 10,* e0139897.

Chevalier, N., & others (2019). Differentiation in prefrontal cortex recruitment during childhood: Evidence from cognitive control demands and social contexts. *Developmental Cognitive Neuroscience, 36,* 100629.

Chevan, A. (1996). As cheaply as one: Cohabitation in the older population. *Journal of Marriage and the Family, 58*(August), 656–667.

Chi, M.T. (1978). Knowledge structures and memory development. In R.S. Siegler (Ed.), *Children's thinking: What develops?* Hillsdale, NJ: Erlbaum.

Childers, J.B., & Tomasello, M. (2002). Two-year-olds learn novel nouns, verbs, and conventional actions from massed or distributed exposures. *Developmental Psychology, 38,* 967–978.

ChildStats.gov (2018). *POP3 Race and Hispanic origin composition.* Washington, DC: Author.

Ching-Teng, Y., & others (2020). Effect of group reminiscence therapy on depression and perceived meaning of life of veterans diagnosed with dementia at veteran homes. *Social Work in Health Care, 59,* 75–90.

Chinn, L.K., & others (2019). Development of infant reaching strategies to tactile targets on the face. *Frontiers in Psychology, 10,* 9.

Chiocca, E.M. (2017). American parents' attitudes and beliefs about corporal punishment: An integrative literature review. *Journal of Pediatric Health Care, 31,* 372–383.

Chiu, H.L., & others (2018). Effectiveness of executive function training on mental set shifting, working memory, and inhibition in healthy older adults: A double-blind randomized controlled trial. *Journal of Advanced Nursing, 74,* 1099–1113.

Cho, D., & Kim, S.H. (2020, in press). Health capability and psychological effects of regular exercise on adults: Middle-aged and older. *International Journal of Aging and Human Development.*

Cho, J., & others (2020, in press). Caregiving centenarians: Cross-national comparison in caregiver burden between the United States and Japan. *Aging and Mental Health.*

Choi, B., & others (2020, in press). Gesture development, caregiver responsiveness, and language, and diagnostic outcomes in infants at high and low risk for autism. *Journal of Autism and Developmental Disorders.*

Choi, H., Yorgason, J.B., & Johnson, D.R. (2016). Marital quality and health in middle and later adulthood: Dyadic associations. *Journals of Gerontology B: Psychological Sciences and Social Sciences, 7,* 154–164.

Choi, J.K., Parra, G., & Jiang, Q. (2019). The longitudinal and bidirectional relationships between cooperative coparenting and child behavior problems in low-income, unmarried families. *Journal of Family Psychology, 33,* 203–214.

Choi, N.G., & Jun, J. (2009). Life regrets and pride among low-income older adults: Relationships with depressive symptoms, current life stressors, and coping resources. *Aging and Mental Health, 13,* 213–225.

Choi, N.G., & others (2020, in press). Physical activity frequency among older adults with diabetes or prediabetes: Associations with sociodemographics, comorbidity, and medical advice. *Journal of Aging and Physical Activity.*

Choi, Y.J., & Luo, Y. (2015). 13-month-olds' understanding of social interaction. *Psychological Science, 26,* 274–283.

Chomsky, N. (1957). *Syntactic structures.* The Hague: Mouton.

Chong, K.H., & others (2020, in press). Changes in physical activity, sedentary behavior, and sleep across the transition from primary to secondary school: A systematic review. *Journal of Science and Medicine in Sport.*

Chopik, W.J., Edelstein, R.S., & Fraley, R.C. (2013). From the cradle to the grave: Age differences in attachment from early adulthood to old age. *Journal of Personality, 81,* 171–183.

Chopik, W.J., Edelstein, R.S., & Grimm, K.J. (2019). Longitudinal changes in attachment orientation over a 59-year period. *Journal of Personality and Social Psychology, 116,* 598–611.

Chopik, W.J., Kim, E.S., & Smith, J. (2018). An examination of dyadic changes in optimism and physical health over time. *Health Psychology, 37,* 42–50.

Chor, E. (2018). Multigenerational Head Start participation: An unexpected marker of progress. *Child Development, 89,* 264–279.

Chow, J., & others (2019), The vocabulary spurt predicts the emergence of backward semantic inhibition in 18-month-old toddlers. *Developmental Science, 22*(2), e12754.

Christ, A., & Gronniger, T. (2018). *Older women in poverty.* Washington, DC: Justice in Aging, U.S. Department of Health and Human Services.

Christ, S.L., Kwak, Y.Y., & Lu, T. (2017). The joint impact of parental psychological neglect and peer isolation on adolescents' depression. *Child Abuse and Neglect, 69,* 151–162.

Christen, M., Narváez, D., & Gutzwiller, E. (2017). Comparing and integrating biological and cultural moral progress. *Ethical Theory and Moral Practice, 20,* 53–73.

Christensen, D.L., & others (2016). *Prevalence and characteristics of autism spectrum disorder among children aged 8 years–Autism and Developmental Disabilities Monitoring Network, 11 sites, United States 2012.* Atlanta: Centers for Disease Control and Prevention.

Christensen, L.B., Johnson, R.B., & Turner, L.A. (2020). *Research methods, design, and analysis* (13th ed., loose leaf). Upper Saddle River, NJ: Pearson.

Chu, H.Y. (2020, in press). Synaptic and cellular plasticity in Parkinson's disease. *Acta Pharmacologica Sinica.*

Chu, X.W., & others (2019). Does bullying victimization really influence adolescents' psychosocial problems? A three-wave longitudinal study in China. *Journal of Affective Disorders, 246,* 603–610.

Chua, A. (2011). *Battle hymn of the tiger mother.* New York: Penguin.

Churnin, I., & others (2019). Association between olfactory and gustatory dysfunction and cognition in older adults. *American Journal of Rhinology and Allergy, 33,* 170–177.

Cicchetti, D., & Handley, E.D. (2019). Child maltreatment and the development of substance use and disorder. *Neurobiology of Stress, 20,* 100144.

Cicchetti, D., & Toth, S.L. (2006). Developmental psychopathology and preventive intervention. In W. Damon & R. Lerner (Eds.), *Handbook of child psychology* (6th ed.). New York: Wiley.

Cicchetti, D., Toth, S.L., & Rogosch, F.A. (2005). *A prevention program for child maltreatment.* Unpublished manuscript, University of Rochester, Rochester, NY.

Cicek, D., & others (2018). Clinical follow-up data and the rate of development of precocious and rapidly progressive puberty in patients with premature thelarche. *Journal of Pediatric Endocrinology and Metabolism, 31,* 305–312.

Cicirelli, V. (2009). Sibling relationships, later life. In D. Carr (Ed.), *Encyclopedia of the life course and human development.* Boston: Gale Cengage.

Cillessen, A.H.N., & Bukowski, W.M. (2018). Sociometric perspectives. In W.M. Bukowski & others (Eds.), *Handbook of peer interactions, relationships, and groups* (2nd ed.). New York: Guilford.

Cimarolli, V.R., & others (2017). A population study of correlates of social participation in older adults with age-related vision loss. *Clinical Rehabilitation, 31,* 115–125.

Cinquina, V., & others (2020). Life-long epigenetic programming of cortical architecture by maternal "Western" diet during pregnancy. *Molecular Psychiatry.*

Ciuculete, D.M., & others (2020, in press). Longitudinal DNA methylation changes at MET may alter HGF/c-MET signaling in adolescents at risk for depression. *Epigenetics.*

Cizek, G.J. (2019). Common Core-ruption: The gulf between large-scale and classroom assessment. *Education Week, 38*(29), 24.

Claes, H.I., & others (2010). Understanding the effects of sildenafil treatment on erection maintenance and erection hardness. *Journal of Sexual Medicine, 7*(6), 2184–2191.

Clara, M. (2017). How instruction influences conceptual development: Vygotsky's theory revisited. *Educational Psychologist, 52,* 50–62.

Clark, B.C. (2019). Neuromuscular changes with aging and sarcopenia. *Journal of Frailty and Aging, 8,* 7–9.

Clark, E.V. (1993). *The lexicon in acquisition.* New York: Cambridge University Press.

Clark, E.V. (2017). *Language in children.* New York: Psychology Press.

Clark, K.N., & Malecki, C.K. (2019). Academic Grit Scale: Psychometric properties and associations with achievement and life satisfaction. *Journal of School Psychology, 72,* 49–66.

Clark, M.S., Hirsch, J.L., & Monin, J.K. (2019). Love conceptualized as mutual communal responsiveness. In R.J. Sternberg & K. Sternberg (Eds.), *The new psychology of love* (2nd ed.). New York: Cambridge University Press.

Clark-Cotton, M.R., Williams, R.K., Goral, M., & Obler, L.K. (2007). Language and communication in aging. In J.E. Birren (Ed.), *Encyclopedia of gerontology* (2nd ed.). San Diego: Academic Press.

Clarke-Stewart, A.K., & Miner, J.L. (2008). Child and day care, effects of. In M.M. Haith & J.B. Benson (Eds.), *Encyclopedia of infant and early childhood development.* Oxford, UK: Elsevier.

Claro, S., Paunesku, D., & Dweck, C.S. (2016). Growth mindset tempers the effect of poverty on academic achievement. *Proceedings of the National Academy of Sciences USA, 113,* 8664–8868.

Clausen, J.A. (1993). *American lives.* New York: Free Press.

Clay, O.J., & others (2009). Visual function and cognitive speed of processing mediate age-related decline in memory span and fluid intelligence. *Journal of Aging and Health, 21,* 547–566.

Clayton, M.G., & others (2020, in press). Determinants of excessive reassurance-seeking: Adolescents' internalized distress, friendship conflict, and behavioral inhibition as prospective predictors. *Journal of Clinical Child and Adolescent Psychology.*

Cleal, K., Norris, K., & Baird, D. (2018). Telomere length dynamics and the evolution of cancer genome architecture. *International Journal of Molecular Sciences, 19,* 2.

Clearfield, M.W., Diedrich, F.J., Smith, L.B., & Thelen, E. (2006). Young infants reach correctly in A-not-B tasks: On the development of stability and perseveration. *Infant Behavior and Development, 29,* 435–444.

Clemens-Cope, L., & others (2019). Pregnant women with opioid use disorder and their infants in three state Medicaid programs in 2013–2016. *Drug and Alcohol Dependence, 195,* 156–163.

Clements, J.M. (2009). Patient perceptions on the use of advance directives and life prolonging technology. *American Journal of Hospice and Palliative Care, 26,* 270–276.

Clifton, R.K., Morrongiello, B.A., Kulig, J.W., & Dowd, J.M. (1981). Developmental changes in auditory localization in infancy. In R.N. Aslin, J.R. Alberts, & M.R. Petersen (Eds.), *Development of perception* (Vol. 1). Orlando, FL: Academic Press.

Clifton, R.K., Muir, D.W., Ashmead, D.H., & Clarkson, M.G. (1993). Is visually guided reaching in early infancy a myth? *Child Development, 64,* 1099–1110.

Cloninger, S. (2019). *Theories of personality* (7th ed.). Upper Saddle River, NJ: Pearson.

Clutter, L.B. (2020). Perceptions of birth fathers about their open adoption. *MCN American Journal of Maternal Child Nursing, 45,* 26–32.

Clyde, T.L., Hawkins, A.J., & Willoughby, B.J. (2020). Revisiting premarital relationship interventions for the next generation. *Journal of Marital and Family Therapy, 46,* 149–164.

Cobb, C.L., & others (2017). Perceptions of legal status: Associations with psychosocial experiences among undocumented Latino/a immigrants. *Journal of Counseling Psychology, 64,* 167–178.

Coe, N.B., von Gaudecker, H.M., Lindeboom, M., & Maurer, J. (2012). The effect of retirement on cognitive functioning. *Health Economics, 21,* 913–927.

Coetsee, C., & Terblanche, E. (2017). The effect of three different exercise training modalities on cognitive and physical function in a healthy older population. *European Review of Aging and Physical Activity, 14,* 13.

Coffey, J.K. (2020, in press). Cascades of infant happiness: Infant positive affect predicts childhood IQ and adult educational attainment. *Emotion.*

Cohen, A.A. (2015). Physiological and comparative evidence fails to confirm an adaptive role for aging in evolution. *Current Aging Science, 8,* 14–23.

Cohen, A.O., & Casey, B.J. (2017). The neurobiology of adolescent self-control. In T. Egner (Ed.), *Wiley handbook of cognitive control.* New York: Wiley.

Cohen, G.D. (2009). Creativity, later life. In D. Carr (Ed.), *Encyclopedia of the life course and human development.* Boston: Gale Cengage.

Cohen, J.R., & others (2018). Anxiety and depression during childhood and adolescence: Testing theoretical models of continuity and discontinuity. *Journal of Abnormal Child Psychology, 46,* 1295–1308.

Cohen, L.B. (2002, April). *Can infants really add and subtract?* Paper presented at the meeting of the International Conference on Infant Studies, Toronto.

Cohen, M.C. (2019). The Swedish shaken baby syndrome report and review: What does the latest knowledge tell us? *Acta Pediatrica, 108*(2).

Cohen, P. (2012). *In our prime: The invention of middle age.* New York: Scribner.

Cohen, R., Bavishi, C., & Rozanski, A. (2016). Purpose in life and its relationship to all-cause mortality and cardiovascular events: A meta-analysis. *Psychosomatic Medicine, 78,* 122–133.

Cohen, R.A., Marsiske, M.M., & Smith, G.E. (2019). Neuropsychology of aging. *Handbook of Clinical Neurology, 167,* 149–180.

Coie, J. (2004). The impact of negative social experiences on the development of antisocial behavior. In J.B. Kupersmidt & K.A. Dodge (Eds.), *Children's peer relations: From development to intervention.* Washington, DC: American Psychological Association.

Coker, T.R., & others (2015). Media violence exposure and physical aggression in fifth-grade children. *Academic Pediatrics, 15,* 82–88.

Colcombe, S., & Kramer, A.F. (2003). Fitness effects on the cognitive function of older adults: A meta-analytic study. *Psychological Science, 14,* 125–130.

Colcombe, S.J., & others (2006). Aerobic exercise training increases brain volume in aging humans. *Journals of Gerontology: Medical Sciences, 61A,* 1166–1170.

Cole, P.M., Dennis, T.A., Smith-Simon, K.E., & Cohen, L.H. (2009). Preschoolers' emotion regulation strategy understanding: Relations with maternal socialization and child behavior. *Social Development, 18*(2), 324–352.

Cole, P.M., Ram, N., & English, M.S. (2019). Toward a unifying model of self-regulation: A developmental approach. *Child Development Perspectives, 13,* 91–96.

Cole, P.M., & Tan, P.Z. (2015). Emotion socialization from a cultural perspective. In J.E. Grusec & P.D. Hastings (Eds.), *Handbook of socialization* (2nd ed.). New York: Guilford.

Cole, S.W. (2009). Social regulation of human gene expression. *Current Directions in Psychological Science, 18,* 132–137.

Cole, T.J., & Mori, H. (2017). Fifty years of child height and weight in Japan and South Korea: Contrasting secular trend patterns analyzed by SITAR. *American Journal of Human Biology, 30,* e23054.

Coleman, A.M. (2013). Physicians' attitudes toward advance directives: A literature review of variables impacting on physicians' attitude toward advance directives. *American Journal of Hospice and Palliative Care, 30,* 696–706.

Coleman, P.D. (1986, August). *Regulation of dendritic extent: Human aging brain and Alzheimer's disease.* Paper presented at the meeting of the American Psychological Association, Washington, DC.

Coleman-Phox, K., Odouli, R., & Li, D.K. (2008). Use of a fan during sleep and the risk of sudden infant death syndrome. *Archives of Pediatric and Adolescent Medicine, 162,* 963–968.

Colistra, R., & Johnson, C.B. (2020, in press). Framing the legalization of marriage for same-sex couples: An examination of news coverage surrounding the U.S. Supreme Court's landmark decision. *Journal of Homosexuality.*

Collins, C.E., & others (2011). Parent diet modification, child activity, or both in obese children: An RCT. *Pediatrics, 127,* 619–627.

Collins, T. (2018). The personal communities of men experiencing later life widowed. *Health and Social Care in the Community, 26*(3), e422–e430.

Collins, W.A., & Madsen, M. (2019). Parenting during middle childhood. In M.H. Bornstein (Ed.), *Handbook of parenting* (3rd ed.). New York: Elsevier.

Collins, W.A., & van Dulmen, M. (2006). The significance of middle childhood peer competence for work and relationships in early childhood. In A.C. Huston & M.N. Ripke (Eds.), *Developmental contexts in middle childhood.* New York: Cambridge University Press.

Comer, J. (1988). Educating poor minority children. *Scientific American, 259,* 42–48.

Comer, J. (2004). *Leave no child behind.* New Haven, CT: Yale University Press.

Comer, J. (2006). Child development: The under-weighted aspect of intelligence. In P.C. Kyllonen, R.D. Roberts, & L. Stankov (Eds.), *Extending intelligence*. Mahwah, NJ: Erlbaum.

Comer, J. (2010). Comer School Development Program. In J. Meece & J. Eccles (Eds.), *Handbook of research on schools, schooling, and human development*. New York: Routledge.

Comhaire, F. (2016). Hormone replacement therapy and longevity. *Andrologia, 48*, 65-68.

Committee for Children (2020). *Second Step*. Retrieved January 24, 2020, from www.cfchildren.org/second-step

Committee on the Rights of the Child (2014). *The Convention on the Rights of the Child and Its Treaty body—The Committee on the Rights of the Child*. Retrieved April 14, 2015, from http://endcorporalpunishment.org/pages/hrlaw/crc_session.html

Common Core State Standards Initiative (2016). *Common Core*. Retrieved July 15, 2016, from www.corestandards.org/

Commoner, B. (2002). Unravelling the DNA myth: The spurious foundation of genetic engineering. *Harper's Magazine, 304*, 39-47.

Commons, M.L., & Bresette, L.M. (2006). Illuminating major creative scientific innovators with postformal stages. In C. Hoare (Ed.), *Handbook of adult development and learning*. New York: Oxford University Press.

Compas, B.E., & others (2019). Stress and coping in families. In B.H. Friese (Ed.), *APA handbook of contemporary family psychology*. Washington, DC: APA Books.

Compton, R.J. (2016). *Adoption beyond borders*. New York: Oxford University Press.

Condition of Education (2015). *Participation in education*. Washington, DC: U.S. Office of Education.

Condon, J., Luszcz, M., & McKee, I. (2020, in press). First-time grandparents' role satisfaction and its determinants. *International Journal of Aging and Human Developmnt*.

Conduct Problems Prevention Research Group (2013). Assessing findings from the Fast Track Study. *Journal of Experimental Criminology, 9*, 119-126.

Conduct Problems Prevention Research Group (2019). *The Fast Track Program for children at risk: Preventing antisocial behavior*. New York: Guilford.

Conlin, S.E., Douglass, & Ouch, S. (2019). Discrimination, subjective wellbeing, and the role of gender: A mediation model of LGB minority stress. *Journal of Homosexuality, 66*, 238-259.

Conner, T.S., & others (2017). The role of personality traits in young adult fruit and vegetable consumption. *Frontiers in Psychology, 8*, 119.

Connolly, H.L., & others (2019). Sex differences in emotion recognition: Evidence for a small overall female superiority on facial disgust. *Emotion, 19*, 455-464.

Connolly, J.A., & McIsaac, C. (2009). Romantic relationships in adolescence. In R.M. Lerner & L. Steinberg (Eds.), *Handbook of adolescent psychology* (3rd ed.), New York: Wiley.

Connolly, J.A., Nguyen, H.N., Pepler, D., Craig, W., & Jiang, D. (2013). Developmental trajectories of romantic stages and associations with problem behaviors during adolescence. *Journal of Adolescence, 36*(6), 1013-1024.

Connolly, M.D., & others (2016). The mental health of transgender youth: Advances in understanding. *Journal of Adolescent Health, 59*, 489-495.

Connor, C.M., & others (2019). Building word knowledge, learning strategies, and metacognition with the Word-Knowledge E-Book. *Computers and Education, 128*, 284-311.

Connor, J. (2020). *Reflective practice in child and adolescent psychotherapy*. New York: Routledge.

Contreras, Z.A., & others (2017). Parental age and childhood cancer risk: A Danish population-based registry study. *Cancer Epidemiology, 49*, 202-215.

Cook, F., & others (2020, in press). Profiles and predictors of infant sleep problems across the first year. *Journal of Developmental and Behavioral Pediatrics*.

Cook, M., & Birch, R. (1984). Infant perception of the shapes of tilted plane forms. *Infant Behavior and Development, 7*, 389-402.

Cooper, M., Warland, J., & McCutcheon, H. (2018). Australian midwives' views and experiences of practice and politics related to water immersion for labor and birth: A web based survey. *Women and Birth, 31*, 184-193.

Cooper, S., & others (2019). Attitudes to E-cigarettes and cessation support for pregnant women from English Stop Smoking Services: A mixed methods approach. *International Journal of Environmental Research and Public Health, 16*, 1.

Copen, C.E., Daniels, K., Vespa, J., & Mosher, W.D. (2012). First marriages in the United States: Data from the 2006-2010 National Survey of Family Growth. *National Health Statistics Report, 49*, 1-22.

Coplan, R.J., & Arbeau, K.A. (2009). Peer interactions and play in early childhood. In K.H. Rubin, W.M. Bukowski, & B. Laursen (Eds.), *Handbook of peer interactions, relationships, and groups*. New York: Guilford.

Coplan, R.J., & others (2018). Peer-based interventions with behaviorally inhibited, withdrawn, and socially anxious children. In W.M. Bukowski & others (Eds.), *Handbook of peer interactions, relationships, and groups* (2nd ed.). New York: Guilford.

Corbetta, D., Wiener, R.F., & Thurman, S.L. (2018). Learning to reach in infancy. In D. Corbetta & M. Santello (Eds.), *Reach-to-grasp behavior: Brain, behavior, and modeling across the lifespan*. New York: Taylor & Francis.

Corbetta, D., Williams, J.L., & Haynes, J.M. (2016). Bare fingers, but no obvious influence of "prickly" Velcro! In the absence of parents' encouragement, it is not clear that "sticky mittens" provide an advantage in the process of learning to reach. *Infant Behavior and Development, 42*, 168-178.

Cordier, S. (2008). Evidence for a role of paternal exposure in developmental toxicity. *Basic and Clinical Pharmacology and Toxicology, 102*, 176-181.

Cornelis, M.C., & others (2019). Age and cognitive decline in the UK Biobank. *PLoS One, 14*(3), e0213948.

Corona, G., Torres, L.O., & Maggi, M. (2020, in press). Testosterone therapy: What we have learned from trials. *Journal of Sexual Medicine*.

Correia, C., & others (2016). Global sensory impairment in older adults in the United States. *Journal of the American Geriatrics Society, 64*, 306-313.

Corso, J.F. (1977). Auditory perception and communication. In J.E. Birren & K.W. Schaie (Eds.), *Handbook of the psychology of aging* (2nd ed.). New York: Van Nostrand Reinhold.

Costa, P.T., & McCrae, R.R. (1995). Solid ground on the wetlands of personality. A reply to Black. *Psychological Bulletin, 117*, 216-220.

Costa, P.T., & McCrae, R.R. (1998). Personality assessment. In H.S. Friedman (Ed.), *Encyclopedia of mental health* (Vol. 3). San Diego: Academic Press.

Costa, P.T., & McCrae, R.R. (2000). Contemporary personality psychology. In C.E. Coffey and J.L. Cummings (Eds.), *Textbook of geriatric neuropsychiatry*. Washington, DC: American Psychiatric Press.

Costa, P.T., & McCrae, R.R. (2013). A theoretical context for adult temperament. In T.D. Wachs & others (Eds.), *Temperament in context*. New York: Psychology Press.

Costa-Urrulia, P., & others (2020, in press). Genome-wide association study of body mass index and body fat in Mexican-Mestizo children. *Genes*.

Costello, M.A., & others (2020, in press). The intensity effect in adolescent close relationships. *Journal of Research on Adolescence*.

Costigan, S.A., Barnett, L., Plotnikoff, R.C., & Lubans, D.R. (2013). The health indicators associated with screen-based sedentary behavior among adolescent girls: A systematic review. *Journal of Adolescent Health, 52*(4), 382-392.

Cote, J., & Bynner, J.M. (2008). Changes in the transition to adulthood in the UK and Canada: The role of structure and aging in emerging adulthood. *Journal of Youth Studies, 11*, 251-258.

Coto, J., & others (2019). Parents as role models: Associations between parent and young children's weight, dietary intake, and physical activity in a minority sample. *Maternal and Child Health Journal, 23*, 943-950.

Cotten, S.R., Ford, G., Ford, S., & Hale, T.M. (2014). Internet use and depression among retired older adults in the United States: A longitudinal analysis. *Journals of Gerontology B: Psychological Sciences and Social Sciences, 69*, 763-771.

Cottrell, L., & Duggleby, W. (2016). The "good death": An integrative literature review. *Palliative and Supportive Care, 14*, 686-712.

Cottrell, L.A., & others (2017). Constructing tailored parental monitoring strategy profiles to predict adolescent disclosure and risk involvement. *Preventive Medicine Reports, 7*, 147-151.

Council of Economic Advisors (2000). *Teens and their parents in the 21st century: An examination of trends in teen behavior and the role of parent involvement*. Washington, DC: Author.

Courage, M.L., Bakhtiar, A., Fitzpatrick, C., Kenny, S., & Brandeau, K. (2015). Growing up multitasking: The costs and benefits for cognitive development. *Developmental Review, 35,* 5-41.

Courage, M.L., & Richards, J.E. (2008). Attention. In M.M. Haith & J.B. Benson (Eds.), *Encyclopedia of infant and early childhood development.* Oxford, UK: Elsevier.

Cousins, J.N., & Fernandez, G. (2019). The impact of sleep deprivation on declarative memory. *Progress in Brain Research, 246,* 27-53.

Cousins, L., & Goodyer, I.M. (2015). Antidepressants and the adolescent brain. *Journal of Psychopharmacology, 29,* 545-555.

Covington, L.B., & others (2019). Toddler bedtime routines and associations with nighttime sleep duration and maternal and household factors. *Journal of Clinical Sleep Medicine, 15,* 805-811.

Cowan, C.P., & Cowan, P.A. (2000). *When partners become parents.* Mahwah, NJ: Erlbaum.

Cowan, P.A., Cowan, C., Ablow, J., Johnson, V.K., & Measelle, J. (2005). *The family context of parenting in children's adaptation to elementary school.* Mahwah, NJ: Lawrence Erlbaum Associates.

Cowan, P.A., & others (2019a). Supporting father involvement: A father-inclusive couples group approach to parenting interventions. In H. Steele & M. Steele (Eds.), *Handbook of attachment interventions.* New York: Guilford.

Cowan, P.A., & others (2019b). Fathers' and mothers' attachment styles, couple conflict, parenting quality, and children's behavior problems: An intervention test of mediation. *Attachment and Human Development, 21,* 532-550.

Cox, S.R., & others (2019). Structural brain imaging correlates of general intelligence in UK biobank. *Intelligence, 76,* 101376.

Coyne, S.M., & others (2018). A meta-analysis of prosocial media on prosocial behavior, aggression, and empathetic concern: A multidimensional approach. *Developmental Psychology, 54,* 331-347.

Coyne, S.M., & others (2019). "We're not gonna be friends anymore": Associations between viewing relational aggression on television and relational aggression in text messaging during adolescence. *Aggressive Behavior, 45,* 1319-1326.

Crain, S. (2012). Sentence scope. In E.L. Bavin (Ed.), *Cambridge handbook of child language.* New York: Cambridge University Press.

Crain, T.L., Schonert-Reichl, K.A., & Roeser, R.W. (2017). Cultivating teacher mindfulness: Effects of a randomized controlled trial on work, home, and sleep outcomes. *Journal of Occupational Health Psychology, 22,* 138-152.

Cramer, P. (2017). Childhood precursors of the narcissistic personality. *Journal of Nervous and Mental Diseases, 205,* 679-684.

Crane, J.D., Macneil, L.G., & Tarnopolsky, M.A. (2013). Long-term aerobic exercise is associated with greater muscle strength throughout the life span. *Journals of Gerontology A: Biological Sciences and Medical Sciences, 68,* 631-638.

Crawford, D., & others (2010). The longitudinal influence of home and neighborhood environments on children's body mass index and physical activity over five years: The CLAN study. *International Journal of Obesity, 34,* 1177-1187.

Cremation Association of North America (2019). *Industry statistical information.* Wheeling, IL: Author.

Creswell, K.G., & others (2020, in press). Drinking beyond the binge threshold in a clinical sample of adolescents. *Addiction.*

Cribbet, M.R., & others (2014). Cellular aging and restorative processes: Subjective sleep quality and duration moderate the association between age and telomere length in a sample of middle-aged and older adults. *Sleep, 37,* 65-70.

Crocetti, E., Rabaglietti. E., & Sica, L.S. (2012). Personal identity in Italy. *New Directions in Child and Adolescent Development, 138,* 87-102.

Crockenberg, S.B. (1986). Are temperamental differences in babies associated with predictable differences in caregiving? In J.V. Lerner & R.M. Lerner (Eds.), *Temperament and social interaction during infancy and childhood.* San Francisco: Jossey-Bass.

Crockenberg, S.B., & Leerkes, E.M. (2006). Infant and maternal behaviors moderate reactivity to novelty to predict anxious behavior at 2.5 years. *Development and Psychopathology, 18,* 17-24.

Crockett, L.J., Raffaelli, M., & Shen, Y-L. (2006). Linking self-regulation and risk proneness to risky sexual behavior: Pathways through peer pressure and early substance use. *Journal of Research on Adolescence, 16,* 503-525.

Crosnoe, R. (2011). *Fitting in, standing out.* New York: Cambridge University Press.

Crosnoe, R. (2020). Education in historical and cultural perspective. In R.D. Parke & G.H. Elder (Eds.), *Children in changing worlds.* New York: Cambridge University Press.

Crosnoe, R., & Benner, A.D. (2015). Children at school. In R.M. Lerner (Ed.), *Handbook of child psychology and developmental science* (7th ed.). New York: Wiley.

Crosnoe, R., Bonazzo, C., & Wu, N. (2015). *Healthy learners: A whole child approach to disparities in early education.* New York: Teachers College Press.

Crosnoe, R., & Fuligni, A.J. (2012). Children from immigrant families: Introduction to the special section. *Child Development, 83,* 1471-1476.

Crosnoe, R., & Ressler, R.W. (2019). Parenting the child in school. In M.H. Bornstein (Ed.), *Handbook of parenting* (3rd ed.). New York: Routledge.

Cross, D., Lester, L., & Barnes, A. (2015). A longitudinal study of the social and emotional predictors and consequences of cyber and traditional bullying victimization. *International Journal of Public Health, 60,* 207-217.

Crouter, A.C. (2006). Mothers and fathers at work. In A. Clarke-Stewart & J. Dunn (Eds.), *Families count.* New York: Cambridge University Press.

Crouter, A.C., & McHale, S. (2005). The long arm of the job revisited: Parenting in dual-earner families. In T. Luster & L. Okasagi (Eds.), *Parenting.* Mahwah, NJ: Erlbaum.

Crowley, J.E. (2019). Gray divorce: Explaining midlife marital splits. *Journal of Women and Aging, 31,* 49-72.

Crowley, K., Callahan, M.A., Tenenbaum, H.R., & Allen, E. (2001). Parents explain more to boys than to girls during shared scientific thinking. *Psychological Science, 12,* 258-261.

Crowley, S.J., & Carskadon, M.A. (2010). Modifications to weekend recovery sleep delay circadian phase in older adolescents. *Chronobiology International, 27,* 1469-1492.

Crume, T. (2019). Tobacco use during pregnancy. *Clinical Obstetrics and Gynecology, 62,* 128-141.

Cruz-Saez, S., & others (2020, in press). The effect of body satisfaction on disordered eating: The mediating role of self-esteem and negative affect in male and female adolescents. *Journal of Health Psychology.*

Csikszentmihalyi, M. (1995). *Creativity.* New York: HarperCollins.

Csikszentmihalyi, M. (2000). Creativity: An overview. In A. Kazdin (Ed.), *Encyclopedia of psychology.* Washington, DC, & New York: American Psychological Association and Oxford University Press.

Csikszentmihalyi, M. (2014). The systems model of creativity and its applications. In D.K. Simonton (Ed.), *Wiley-Blackwell handbook of genius.* New York: Wiley.

Csikszentmihalyi, M. (2018). Society, culture, and person: A systems view. In R.J. Sternberg (Ed.), *The nature of creativity.* New York: Cambridge University Press.

Cubbin, C., Brindis, C.D., Jain, S., Santelli, J., & Braveman, P. (2010). Neighborhood poverty, aspirations and expectations, and initiation of sex. *Journal of Adolescent Health, 47,* 399-406.

Cubbin, C., & others (2020). Longitudinal measures of neighborhood poverty and income inequality are associated with adverse birth outcomes in Texas. *Social Science and Medicine, 245,* 112665.

Cucina, J.M., Peyton, S.T., Su, C., & Byle, K.A. (2016). Role of mental abilities and mental tests in explaining school grades. *Intelligence, 54,* 90-104.

Cueli, M., & others (2019). Differential efficacy of neurofeedback in children with ADHD presentations. *Journal of Clinical Medicine, 8,* 2.

Cuevas, K., & Bell, M.A. (2020, in press). EEG frequency development across infancy and childhood. In P. Gable & others (Eds.), *Oxford handbook of human EEG frequency analysis.* New York: Oxford University Press.

Cuevas, P.E.Q., & others (2020, in press). Reminiscence therapy for older adults with Alzheimer's disease: A literature review. *International Journal of Mental Health Nursing.*

Cuevas-Sierra, A., & others (2019). Diet, gut microbiota, and obesity: Links with host genetics and epigenetics and potential applications. *Advances in Nutrition, 10*(Suppl. 1), S17-S30.

Cui, R., & others (2019). RNN-based longitudinal analysis of diagnosis of Alzheimer's disease. *Computational Medical Imaging and Graphics, 73,* 1-10.

Culen, C., & others (2017). Care of girls and women with Turner syndrome: Beyond growth and hormones. *Endocrine Connections, 6,* R39-R51.

Culp, K.M. (2012). *An interesting career in psychological science: Research scientist at an education research organization.* Retrieved July 30, 2013, from www.apa.org/science/about/psa/2012/10/education-research.aspx

Cummings, E.M., & others (2017). Emotional insecurity about the community: A dynamic, within-person mediator of child adjustment in contexts of political violence. *Development and Psychopathology, 29,* 27-36.

Cummings, K.J., & Leiter, J.C. (2020, in press). Take a deep breath and wake up: The protean role of serotonin in preventing sudden infant death. *Experimental Neurology.*

Cunha, A.B., & others (2016). Effect of short-term training on reaching behavior in infants: A randomized controlled trial. *Journal of Motor Behavior, 48,* 132-142.

Cunningham, A.M., Walker, D.M., & Nestler, E.J. (2020, in press). Paternal transgenerational epigenetic mechanisms mediating stress phenotypes of offspring. *European Journal of Neuroscience.*

Cunningham, C., & others (2020, in press). Consequences of physical inactivity in older adults: A systematic review of reviews and meta-analyses. *Scandinavian Journal of Medicine and Science in Sports.*

Cunningham, C.E., & others (2020, in press). What antibullying program designs motivate student intervention in grades 5 to 8? *Journal of Clinical Child and Adolescent Psychology.*

Cunningham, M. (2009). Housework. In D. Carr (Ed.), *Encyclopedia of the life course and human development.* Boston: Gale Cengage.

Cunningham, S.A., Kramer, M.R., & Narayan, K.M. (2014). Incidence of childhood obesity in the United States. *New England Journal of Medicine, 370,* 403-411.

Cunningham, S.D., & others (2019). Group prenatal care reduces risk of preterm birth and low birth weight: A matched cohort study. *Journal of Women's Health, 28,* 17-22.

Curl, A.L., Bibbo, J., & Johnson, R.A. (2017). Dog walking, the human-animal bond, and older adults' physical health. *Gerontologist, 57,* 930-939.

Curran, K., DuCette, J., Eisenstein, J., & Hyman, I.A. (2001, August). *Statistical analysis of the cross-cultural data: The third year.* Paper presented at the meeting of the American Psychological Association, San Francisco, CA.

Currie, E.R., & others (2019). Life after loss: Parent bereavement and coping experiences after infant death in the neonatal intensive care unit. *Death Studies, 43,* 333-342.

Currier, J.M., Holland, J.M., & Neimeyer, R.A. (2006). Sense-making, grief, and the experience of violent loss: Toward a mediational model. *Death Studies, 30,* 403-428.

Curtindale, L.M., & others (2019). Effects of multimodal synchrony on infant attention and heart rate during events with social and nonsocial stimuli. *Journal of Experimental Child Psychology, 178,* 283-294.

Curtis, E.M., & others (2020, in press). General and specific considerations as to why osteoporosis-related care is suboptimal. *Current Osteoporosis Reports.*

Cvencek, D., Meltzoff, A.N., & Greenwald, A.G. (2011). Math-gender stereotypes in elementary school children. *Child Development, 82,* 766-779.

Czekierda, K., & others (2017). Meaning in life and physical health: Systematic review and meta-analysis. *Health Psychology Review, 11,* 387-414.

D

D'Alessandro, A., Lampignano, L., & De Pergola, G. (2019). Mediterranean diet pyramid: A proposal for Italian people: A systematic review of prospective studies to derive serving sizes. *Nutrients, 11,* 6.

D'Amico, E.J., & others (2020, in press). Early and late adolescent factors that predict co-use of cannabis with alcohol and tobacco in young adulthood. *Prevention Science.*

D'Angelo, C.M., & others (2019). Coping, attributions, and health functioning among adolescents with chronic illness and their parents: Reciprocal relations over time. *Journal of Clinical Psychology in Medical Settings, 26,* 495-506.

D'Ascenzi, F., & others (2020, in press). When should cardiovascular prevention begin? The importance of antenatal, perinatal, and primordial prevention. *European Journal of Preventive Cardiology.*

D'Aversa, E., & others (2018). Non-invasive fetal sex diagnosis in plasma of early weeks pregnants using droplet digital PCR. *Molecular Medicine, 24*(1), 14.

Da Costa, L.A., Badawi, A., & El-Sohemy, A. (2012). Nutrigenetics and modulation of oxidative stress. *Annals of Nutrition and Metabolism* (3, Suppl.), S27-S36.

da Costa Souza, A., & Ribeiro, S. (2015). Sleep deprivation and gene expression. *Current Topics in Behavioral Neurosciences, 25,* 65-90.

Daglish, A., & Waller, G. (2019). Clinician and patient characteristics and cognitions that influence weighing practice in cognitive-behavioral therapy for eating disorders. *International Journal of Eating Disorders, 52,* 977-986.

Dahl, A., & Brownell, C.A. (2019). The social origins of human prosociality. *Current Directions in Psychological Science, 28,* 274-279.

Dahl, A., & others (2017). Explicit scaffolding increases simple helping in younger infants. *Developmental Psychology, 53,* 407-416.

Dahl, R.E. (2004). Adolescent brain development: A period of vulnerability and opportunity. *Annals of the New York Academy of Sciences, 1021,* 1-122.

Dahlenburg, S.C., Gleaves, D.H., & Hutchinson, A.D. (2019). Anorexia and perfectionism: A meta-analysis. *International Journal of Eating Disorders, 52,* 219-229.

Dahm, C.C., & others (2018). Adolescent diet quality and cardiovascular disease risk factors and incident cardiovascular disease in middle-aged women. *Journal of the American Heart Association, 5,* 12.

Daiello, L.A., & others (2015). Association of fish oil supplement use with preservation of brain volume and cognitive function. *Alzheimer's and Dementia, 11,* 226-235.

Dale, B., & others (2014). Utility of the Stanford-Binet Intelligence Scales, Fifth Edition, with ethnically diverse preschoolers. *Psychology in the Schools, 51,* 581-590.

Daley, C.E., & Onwuegbuzi, A.J. (2020). It's not a Black and White issue. In R.J. Sternberg (Ed.), *Cambridge handbook of intelligence.* New York: Cambridge University Press.

Damoiseaux, J.S. (2017). Effects of aging on functional and structural brain connectivity. *NeuroImage, 160,* 32-40.

Damon, W. (1988). *The moral child.* New York: Free Press.

Damon, W. (2008). *The path to purpose.* New York: Free Press.

Damon, W., & Malin, H. (2020). The development of purpose: An international perspective. In L.A. Jensen (Ed.), *Oxford handbook of moral development.* New York: Oxford University Press.

Danforth, M.M., & Glass, J.C. (2001). Listen to my words, give meaning to my sorrow: A study in cognitive constructs in middle-aged bereaved widows. *Death Studies, 25,* 513-548.

Daniels, H. (Ed.) (2017). *Introduction to Vygotsky* (3rd ed.). New York: Routledge.

Danilovich, M.K., Conroy, D.E., & Hornby, T.G. (2018), Feasibility and impact of high-intensity walking training in frail older adults. *Physical Therapy and Movement Sciences, 25,* 533-538.

Dankulincova Veselska, Z., & others (2018). Spirituality but not religiosity is associated with better health and higher life satisfaction among adolescents. *International Journal of Environmental Research and Public Health, 15,* 12.

Danner, D., Snowdon, D., & Friesen, W. (2001). Positive emotions in early life and longevity: Findings from the Nun Study. *Journal of Personality and Social Psychology, 80*(5), 804-813.

Dantas, R.R., & da Silva, G.AP. (2019). The role of the obesogenic environment and parental lifestyles in infant feeding behavior. *Revista Paulista de Pediatria, 37*(3), 363-371.

Dantchev, S., & Wolke, D. (2019). Trouble in the nest: Antecedents of sibling bullying victimization and perpetration. *Developmental Psychology, 55,* 1059-1071.

Daoulah, A., & others (2017a). Divorce and severity of coronary heart disease: A multicenter study. *Cardiology Research and Practice, 2017,* 4751249.

Darby-Stewart, A., & Strickland, C. (2019). Group prenatal care to reduce preterm labor and improve outcomes. *American Family Physician, 99,* 141-142.

Darcy, E. (2012). Gender issues in child and adolescent eating disorders. In J. Lock (Ed.), *Oxford handbook of child and adolescent eating disorders: Developmental perspectives.* New York: Oxford University Press.

Dariotis, J.K., & others (2016). A qualitative evaluation of student learning and skills use in a school-based mindfulness and yoga program. *Mindfulness, 7,* 76-89.

Darling, E.K., & others (2019). Access to midwifery care for people of low socio-economic status: A qualitative descriptive study. *BMC Pregnancy and Childbirth, 19*(1), 416.

Darling, N., & Tilton-Weaver, L. (2019). All in the family: Within-family differences in parental monitoring and adolescent information management. *Developmental Psychology, 55,* 390-402.

Darling Rasmussen, P., & others (2019). Attachment as a core feature of resilience: A systematic review and meta-analysis. *Psychological Reports, 122,* 1259-1296.

Darwin, C. (1859). *On the origin of species.* London: John Murray.

Das, R., & others (2020, in press). Ultrasound assessment of fetal hearing response to vibroacoustic stimulation. *Journal of Maternal-Fetal and Neonatal Medicine.*

Dash, T., & others (2019). Alerting, orienting, and executive control: The effect of bilingualism and age on subcomponents of attention. *Frontiers in Neurology, 10,* 1122.

Dasinger, J.H., & others (2020, in press). Epigenetic modifications in T cells: The role of DNA methylation in salt-sensitive hypertension. *Hypertension.*

Datar, A., & Nicosia, N. (2017). The effect of state competitive food and beverage regulations on childhood overweight and obesity. *Journal of Adolescent Health, 60,* 520-527.

Davidov, M., Zhan-Waxler, C., Roth-Hanania, C., & Knafo, A. (2013). Concern for others in the first year of life: Theory, evidence, and avenues of research. *Child Development Perspectives, 7,* 126-131.

Davidson, J. (2000). Giftedness. In A. Kazdin (Ed.), *Encyclopedia of psychology.* Washington, DC, & New York: American Psychological Association and Oxford University Press.

Davidson, J.G.S., & Guthrie, D.M. (2019). Older adults with a combination of vision and hearing impairment experience higher rates of cognitive impairment, functional dependence, and worse outcomes across a set of quality indicators. *Journal of Aging and Health, 31,* 85-108.

Davie, P., Bick, D., & Chilcot, J. (2019). To what extent does maternal body mass index (BMI) predict intentions, attitudes, or practices of early infant feeding? *Maternal Child Nutrition, 15*(4), e12837.

Davies, D., & Troy, M.F. (2020). *Child development* (4th ed.). New York: Guilford.

Davies, G., & others (2011). Genome-wide association studies establish that human intelligence is highly heritable and polygenic. *Molecular Psychiatry, 16,* 996-1005.

Davies, J., & Brember, I. (1999). Reading and mathematics attainments and self-esteem in years 2 and 6—An eight-year cross-sectional study. *Educational Studies, 25,* 145-157.

Davies, P.T., Martin, M.J., & Cummings, E.M. (2018). Interparental conflict and children's social problems: Insecurity and friendship affiliation as cascading mediators. *Developmental Psychology, 54,* 83-97.

Davies, P.T., & others (2016). Transactional cascades of destructive interparental conflict,

children's emotional insecurity, and psychological problems across childhood and adolescence. *Development and Psychopathology, 27,* 653-671.

Davies, R., Davis, D., Pearce, M., & Wong, N. (2015). The effect of waterbirth on neonatal mortality and morbidity: A systematic review and meta-analysis. *JBI Database of Systematic Reviews and Implementation Reports, 13,* 180-231.

Davis, B.E., Moon, R.Y., Sachs, M.C., & Ottolini, M.C. (1998). Effects of sleep position on infant motor development. *Pediatrics, 102,* 1135-1140.

Davis, D., & others (2017). Decline in search speed and verbal memory over 26 years of midlife in a British birth cohort. *Neuroendocrinology, 49,* 121-128.

Davis, E.B., & others (2019). Religious meaning making and attachment in a disaster context: A longitudinal qualitative study of flood survivors. *Journal of Positive Psychology, 14,* 659-671.

Davis, E.M., & Fingerman, K.L. (2016). Digital dating: Online profile content of older and younger adults. *Journals of Gerontology B: Psychological Sciences and Social Sciences, 71,* 959-967.

Davis, J.C., & others (2017). Slow processing speed predicts falls in older adults with a falls history: 1-year prospective cohort study. *Journal of the American Geriatrics Society, 65,* 916-923.

Davis, K. (2020, April). *Youth agency in a digital age.* Paper presented at the annual meeting of the American Educational Research Association, San Francisco.

Davis, K. (2021, in press). *Beyond the screen.* Cambridge, MA: Harvard University Press.

Davis, K., & Weinstein, E. (2017). Identity development in the digital age: An Eriksonian perspective. In M.F. Wright (Ed.), *Identity, sexuality, and relationships in the digital age.* Hershey, PA: IGI Global.

Davis, K., & others (2020, April). *So you've earned a badge, now what?* Paper presented at annual meeting of the American Educational Research Association, San Francisco.

Davis, L., & Keyser, J. (1997). *Becoming the parent you want to be: A sourcebook of strategies for the first five years.* New York: Broadway.

Davis, M.C., Burke, H.M., Zautra, A.J., & Stark, S. (2013). Arthritis and musculoskeletal conditions. In I.B. Weiner & others (Eds.), *Handbook of psychology* (2nd ed., Vol. 9). New York: Wiley.

Davis, S.W., Kragel, J.E., Madden, D.J., & Cabeza, R. (2012). The architecture of cross-hemispheric communication in the aging brain: Linking behavior to functional and structural connectivity. *Cerebral Cortex, 22,* 232-242.

Davison, S.M., & others (2013). CHILE: An evidence-based preschool intervention for obesity prevention in Head Start. *Journal of School Health, 83,* 223-229.

Daw, J., Margolis, R., & Wright, L. (2017). Emerging adult, emergent adult lifestyles: Sociodemographic determinants of trajectories of smoking, binge drinking, obesity, and sedentary behavior. *Journal of Health and Social Behavior, 58,* 181-197.

Day, K.I., & Smith, C.I. (2013). Understanding the role of private speech in children's emotion regulation. *Early Childhood Research Quarterly, 28,* 405-414.

Day, K.I., & Smith, C.I. (2019). Maternal behaviors in toddlerhood as predictors of children's private speech in preschool. *Journal of Experimental Child Psychology, 177,* 132-140.

Day, N.L., Goldschmidt, L., & Thomas, C.A. (2006). Prenatal marijuana exposure contributes to the prediction of marijuana use at age 14. *Addiction, 101,* 1313-1322.

Day, R.H., & McKenzie, B.E. (1973). Perceptual shape constancy in early infancy. *Perception, 2,* 315-320.

Dayton, C.J., & Malone, J.C. (2017). Development and socialization of physical aggression in very young boys. *Infant Mental Health, 38,* 150-165.

Dayton, C.J., Walsh, T.B., Oh, W., & Volling, B. (2015). Hush now baby: Mothers' and fathers' strategies for soothing their infants and associated parenting outcomes. *Journal of Pediatric Health Care, 29,* 145-155.

de Araujo, T.E., & others (2020, in press). Experimental models of maternal-fetal interface and their potential for nanotechnology applications. *Cell Science International.*

de Barse, L.M., & others (2017). Infant feeding and child fussy eating: The Generation R Study. *Appetite, 114,* 374-381.

de Boer, B., & Verhoef, T. (2019). Evolution of speech. In S-A. Rueschemeyer & M. Gareth Gaskell (Eds.), *Oxford handbook of psycholinguistics* (2nd ed.). New York: Oxford University Press.

De Genna, N.M., Goldschmidt, L., Day, N.L., & Cornelius, M.D. (2016). Prenatal and postnatal maternal trajectories of cigarette use predict adolescent cigarette use. *Nicotine and Tobacco Research, 18,* 988-992.

De Giovanni, N., & Marchetti, D. (2012). Cocaine and its metabolites in the placenta: A systematic review of the literature. *Reproductive Toxicology, 33,* 1-14.

de Greeff, J.W., & others (2018). Effects of physical activity on executive functions, attention, and academic performance in preadolescent children: A meta-analytic review. *Journal of Science and Medicine in Sport, 21,* 501-507.

de Guzman, N.S., & Nishina, A. (2014). A longitudinal study of body dissatisfaction and pubertal timing in an ethnically diverse adolescent sample. *Body Image, 11,* 68-71.

de Haan, M. (2015). Neuroscientific methods with children. In R.M. Lerner (Ed.), *Handbook of child psychology and developmental science* (7th ed.). New York: Wiley.

de Haan, M., & Gunnar, M.R. (Eds.) (2009). *Handbook of developmental social neuroscience.* New York: Guilford.

de Haan, M., & Johnson, M.H. (2016). Typical and atypical human functional brain development. In D. Cicchetti (Ed.), *Developmental psychopathology* (3rd ed.). New York: Wiley.

de Koning, L., Denhoff, E., Kellogg, M.D., & de Ferranti, S.D. (2015). Associations of total and abdominal adiposity with risk marker patterns in children at high risk for cardiovascular disease. *BMC Obesity, 2,* 15.

de la Fuente, J., & others (2019). Longitudinal associations of sensory and cognitive functioning: A structural equation modeling approach. *Journals of Gerontology B: Psychological Sciences and Social Sciences, 74,* 1308-1316.

De La Fuente, M. (2019). Biopsychosocial bridge: The psychoneuroimmune system in successful aging. In R. Fernandez-Ballesteros & others (Eds.), *Cambridge handbook of successful aging.* New York: Cambridge University Press.

de la Mata, M.L., & others (2019). The relationship between social factors and autobiographical memories from childhood: The role of formal schooling. *Memory, 27,* 103-114.

De Lamater, J. (2019). The diversity of adolescent male sexuality. In S. Lamb & J. Gilbert (Eds.), *Cambridge handbook of sexual development.* New York: Cambridge University Press.

de Lima, D.B., & others (2019). Episodic memory boosting in older adults: Exploring the association of encoding strategies and physical activity. *Aging and Mental Health, 23,* 1218-1226.

de Magalhaes, J.P., & Tacutu, R. (2016). Integrative genomics and aging. In M.R. Kaeberlein & G.M. Martin (Eds.), *Handbook of the biology of aging* (8th ed.). New York: Elsevier.

de Manzano, O., & Ullen, F. (2018). Genetic and environmental influences on the phenotypic associations between intelligence, personality, and creative achievement in the arts and sciences. *Intelligence, 69,* 123-133.

de Medeiros, T.S., & others (2017). Caffeine intake during pregnancy in different intrauterine environments and its association with infant anthropometric measurements at 3 and 6 months of age. *Maternal and Child Health Journal, 19,* 382-392.

De Paepe, A., de Williams, A.C., & Crombez, G. (2019). Habituation to pain: A motivational-ethological perspective. *Pain, 160,* 1693-1697.

de Villiers, T.J. (2018). Should women be screened for osteoporosis at midlife? *Climacteric, 21,* 239-242.

de Villiers, T.J., & others (2016). Revised global consensus statement on menopausal hormone therapy. *Climacteric, 19,* 313-315.

de Wind, A.W., & others (2014). Health, job characteristics, skills, and social and financial factors in relation to early retirement—Results from a longitudinal study in the Netherlands. *Scandinavian Journal of Work, Environment, and Health, 40,* 186-194.

Dearing, E., & others (2016). Can community and school-based supports improve the achievement of first-generation immigrant children attending high-poverty schools? *Child Development, 87,* 883-897.

Deary, I.J. (2012). Intelligence. *Annual Review of Intelligence* (Vol. 63). Palo Alto, CA: Annual Reviews.

Deater-Deckard, K. (2013). The social environment and the development of psychopathology. In P.D. Zelazo (Ed.), *Handbook of developmental psychology.* New York: Oxford University Press.

Deaton, A. (2008). Income, health, and well-being around the world: Evidence from the Gallup World Poll. *Journal of Economic Perspectives, 22,* 53-72.

Debnam, K.J., & others (2018). The moderating role of spirituality in the association between stress and substance use among adolescents: Differences by gender. *Journal of Youth and Adolescence, 47,* 818-828.

Debnath, R., & others (2020). The long-term effects of institutional rearing, foster care intervention, and disruptions in care on brain electrical activity in adolescence. *Developmental Science, 23*(1), e12872.

DeCasper, A.J., & Spence, M.J. (1986). Prenatal maternal speech influences newborns' perception of speech sounds. *Infant Behavior and Development, 9,* 133-150.

Deckert, M., & others (2020, in press). Metaphor processing in middle childhood and at the transition to early adolescence: The role of chronological age, mental age, and verbal intelligence. *Journal of Child Language.*

Dee, D.L., & others (2017). Trends in repeat births and use of postpartum contraception among teens—United States 2004-2015. *MMWR: Morbidity and Mortality Weekly Reports, 66,* 422-426.

Deeg, D.J.H. (2005). The development of physical and mental health from late midlife to early old age. In S.L. Willis & M. Martin (Eds.), *Middle adulthood.* Thousand Oaks, CA: Sage.

Dehcheshmeh, F.S., & Rafiel, H. (2015). Complementary and alternative therapies to relieve labor pain: A comparative study between music therapy and Hoku point ice massage. *Complementary Therapies in Clinical Practice, 21,* 229-232.

DeJong, W., DeRicco, B., & Schneider, S.K. (2010). Pregaming: An exploratory study of strategic drinking by college students in Pennsylvania. *Journal of American College Health, 58,* 307-316.

Del Giudice, M. (2011). Sex differences in romantic attachment: A meta-analysis. *Personality and Social Psychology Bulletin, 37,* 193-214.

Del Gobbo, L.C., & others (2015). Contribution of major lifestyle risk factors for incident heart failure in older adults: The Cardiovascular Health Study. *JACC Heart Failure, 3,* 520-528.

Del Rio-Bermudez, C., & Blumberg, M.S. (2018). Active sleep promotes functional connectivity in developing sensorimotor networks. *Bioessays, 40*(4), e1700234.

Del Tredici, K., & Braak, H. (2008). Neurofibrillary changes of the Alzheimer type in very elderly individuals: Neither inevitable nor benign. Commentary on no disease in the brain of a 115-year-old woman. *Neurobiology of Aging, 29,* 1133-1136.

Delello, J.A., & McWhorter, R.R. (2017). Reducing the digital divide: Connecting older adults to iPad technology. *Journal of Applied Gerontology, 36,* 3-28.

Delgado, M.Y., & others (2019). Discrimination, parent-adolescent conflict, and peer intimacy: Examining risk and resilience in Mexican-origin youths' adjustment trajectories. *Child Development, 90,* 894-910.

DeLisi, R. (2015). Piaget's sympathetic but unromantic account of children's play. In J.E. Johnson & others (Eds.), *Handbook of the study of play.* Blue Ridge Summit, PA: Rowman & Littlefield.

Delker, B.C., Bernstein, R.E., & Laurent, H.K. (2018). Out of harm's way: Secure versus insecure-disorganized attachment predicts less adolescent risk taking related to childhood poverty. *Development and Psychopathology, 30,* 283-296.

DeLoache, J.S., Simcock, G., & Macari, S. (2007). Planes, trains, and automobiles—and tea sets: Extremely intense interests in very young children. *Developmental Psychology, 43,* 1579-1586.

DeLongis, A., & Zwicker, A. (2017). Marital satisfaction and divorce in couples in stepfamilies. *Current Opinion in Psychology, 13,* 158-161.

Demanchick, S.P. (2015). The interpretation of play: Psychoanalysis and beyond. In J.E. Johnson & others (Eds.), *Handbook of the study of play.* Blue Ridge Summit, PA: Rowman & Littlefield.

Demir-Lira, E., & others (2019). Parents' early book reading to children: Relation to children's later language and literacy outcomes controlling for other parent language input. *Developmental Science, 22*(3), e12764.

Demirtas-Zorbaz, S., & Ergene, T. (2019). School adjustment of first-grade primary school students: Effects of family involvement, externalizing behavior, teacher, and peer relations. *Child and Youth Services Review, 101,* 307-316.

Demnitz, N., & others (2017). Associations between mobility, cognition, and brain structure in healthy older adults. *Frontiers in Aging Neuroscience, 9,* 155.

Dempster, F.N. (1981). Memory span: Sources of individual and developmental differences. *Psychological Bulletin, 80,* 63-100.

Demuth, K. (2019). Development of prosodic pragmatics. In S-A. Rueschemeyer & M. Gareth Gaskell (Eds.), *Oxford handbook of psycholinguistics* (2nd ed.). New York: Oxford University Press.

Den Heijer, A.E., & others (2017). Sweat it out? The effects of physical exercise on cognition and behavior in children and adults with ADHD: A systematic literature review. *Journal of Neural Transmission, 124*(Suppl. 1), S3-S26.

Denard, P.J., & others (2010). Back pain, neurogenic symptoms, and physical function in relation to spondylolisthesis among elderly men. *Spine Journal, 10,* 865-887.

Denault, A.S., & Guay, F. (2017). Motivation towards extracurricular activities and motivation at school: A test of the generalization effect hypothesis. *Journal of Adolescence, 54,* 94-103.

Denervaud, S., & others (2019). Beyond executive functions, creativity skills benefit academic outcomes: Insights from Montessori education. *PLoS One, 14*(1), e025319.

Denford, S., & others (2017). A comprehensive review of reviews of school-based intervention to improve sexual health. *Health Psychology Review, 11,* 33-52.

Deng, Y., & others (2018). Timing of spermarche and menarche among urban students in Guangzhou, China: Trends from 2005 to 2012 and association with obesity. *Scientific Reports, 8*(1), 263.

Denham, J., O'Brien, B.J., & Charchar, F.J. (2016). Telomere length maintenance and cardio-metabolic disease prevention through exercise training. *Sports Medicine, 46,* 1213-1237.

Denham, S., & others (2011). Emotions and social development in childhood. In P.K. Smith & C.H. Hart (Eds.), *Wiley-Blackwell handbook of childhood social development* (2nd ed.). New York: Wiley.

Denham, S.A., & Bassett, H.H. (2019). Implications of preschoolers' emotional competence in the classroom. In K. Keefer & others (Eds.), *Handbook of emotional intelligence in education.* New York: Springer.

Denier, N., & others (2017). Retirement and cognition: A life course view. *Advances in Life Course Research, 31,* 11-21.

Denk, F., McMahon, S.B., & Tracey, I. (2014). Pain vulnerability: A neurobiological perspective. *Nature Neuroscience, 17,* 192-200.

Denmark, F.L., Russo, N.F., Frieze, I.H., & Eschuzur, J. (1988). Guidelines for avoiding sexism in psychological research: A report of the ad hoc committee on nonsexist research. *American Psychologist. 43,* 582-585.

Denney, N.W. (1986, August). *Practical problem solving.* Paper presented at the meeting of the American Psychological Association, Washington, DC.

Denney, N.W. (1990). Adult age differences in traditional and practical problem solving. *Advances in Psychology, 72,* 329-349.

Dennis, M., & others (2014). Functional plasticity in childhood brain disorders: When, what, how, and whom to assess. *Neuropsychology Review, 24*(4), 389-408.

Dennis, N.A., & Cabeza, R. (2008). Neuroimaging of healthy cognitive aging. In F.I.M. Craik & T.A. Salthouse (Eds.), *Handbook of aging and cognition* (3rd ed.). Mahwah, NJ: Erlbaum.

Deoni, S.C., & others (2016). White matter maturation profiles through early childhood predict general cognitive ability. *Brain Structure and Function, 22,* 1189-1203.

DePasquale, C.E., Handley, E.D., & Cicchetti, D. (2019). Investigating multilevel pathways of developmental consequences of maltreatment. *Development and Psychopathology, 31,* 1227-1236.

DePaulo, B. (2006). *Singled out.* New York: St. Martin's Press.

DePaulo, B. (2011). Living single: Lightening up those dark, dopey myths. In W.R. Cupach & B.H. Spitzberg (Eds.), *The dark side of close relationships.* New York: Routledge.

DeRose, L., & Brooks-Gunn, J. (2008). Pubertal development in early adolescence: Implications for affective processes. In N.B. Allen & L. Sheeber (Eds.), *Adolescent emotional development and the emergence of depressive disorders.* New York: Cambridge University Press.

Derry, K.L., Ohan, J.L., & Bayliss, D.M. (2020, in press). Fearing failure: Grandiose narcissism, vulnerable narcissism, and emotional reactivity in children. *Child Development.*

DeSesso, M. (2019). The arrogance of teratology: A brief chronology of attitudes throughout history. *Birth Defects Research, 111,* 123-141.

Desilver, D. (2017). *U.S. students' academic achievement still lags that of their peers in many other countries.* Washington, DC: Pew Research Center.

Desombre, C., & others (2019). The distinct effect of multiple sources of stereotype threat. *Journal of Social Psychology, 159,* 628-641.

Deutsch, A.R., Wood, P.K., & Slutske, W.S. (2017). Developmental etiologies of alcohol use and their relations to parent and peer influences over adolescence and young adulthood: A genetically informed approach. *Alcoholism: Clinical and Experimental Research, 41,* 2151-2162.

Dev, D., & others (2019). An innovative, cross-disciplinary approach to promoting child health: The Reggio Emilia approach and the ecological approach to family style dining program. *Childhood Education, 95,* 57-63.

Devakumar, D., & others (2019). *Oxford textbook of global health of women, newborns, children, and adolescents.* New York: Oxford University Press.

Devine, R.T., & Hughes, C. (2018). Family correlates of false belief understanding in early childhood: A meta-analysis. *Child Development, 89,* 971-987.

Devine, R.T., & Hughes, C. (2019). Let's talk: Parents' mental talk (not mind-mindedness or mindreading capacity) predicts children's false belief understanding. *Child Development, 90,* 1236-1253.

Dewald-Kaufmann, J., de Bruin, E., & Michael, G. (2019). Cognitive behavioral therapy for insomnia (CBT-i) in school-aged children and adolescents. *Sleep Medicine Clinics, 14,* 155-165.

Dewtiz, P.F., & others (2020). *Teaching reading in the 21st century* (6th ed.). Upper Saddle River, NJ: Pearson.

DeZolt, D.M., & Hull, S.H. (2001). Classroom and school climate. In J. Worell (Ed.), *Encyclopedia of women and gender.* San Diego: Academic Press.

Dhindsa, D.S., & others (2020, in press). Marital status and outcomes in patients with cardiovascular disease: A review. *Trends in Cardiovascular Medicine.*

Di Giosia, P., & others (2018). Gender differences in epidemiology, pathophysiology, and treatment of hypertension. *Current Atherosclerosis Reports, 20*(3), 13.

Diamond, A.D. (1985). Development of the ability to use recall to guide action, as indicated by infants' performance on A not B. *Child Development, 56,* 868-883.

Diamond, A.D. (2013). Executive functions. *Annual Review of Psychology* (Vol. 64). Palo Alto, CA: Annual Reviews.

Diamond, A.D., Barnett, W.S., Thomas, J., & Munro, S. (2007). Preschool program improves cognitive control. *Science, 318,* 1387-1388.

Diamond, A.D., & Lee, K. (2011). Interventions shown to aid executive function development in children 4 to 12 years old. *Science, 333,* 959-964.

Diamond, L.M. (2019). The dynamic expression of sexual-minority and gender-minority experience during childhood and adolescence. In S. Lamb & J.

Gilbert (Eds.), *Cambridge handbook of sexual development.* New York: Cambridge University Press.

Dias, C.C., & others (2018). Reference values and changes in infant sleep-wake behavior during the first 12 months of life: A systematic review. *Journal of Sleep Research, 5,* e12654.

Diaz, E.C., & others (2020, in press). Parental adiposity differentially associates with newborn body composition. *Pediatric Obesity.*

Diaz-Rico, L.T. (2020). *A course for teaching English Language Learners* (3rd ed.). Upper Saddle River, NJ: Pearson.

DiBennardo, R., & Gates, G.J. (2014). Research note: U.S. Census same-sex couple data: Adjustments to reduce measurement error and empirical implications. *Population Research and Policy Review, 33,* 603-614.

Dickinson, W.J., & others (2011). Change in stress and social support as predictors of cognitive decline in older adults with and without depression. *International Journal of Geriatric Psychiatry, 26,* 1267-1274.

Diego, M.A., Field, T., & Hernandez-Reif, M. (2008). Temperature increases in preterm infants during massage therapy. *Infant Behavior and Development, 31,* 149-152.

Diego, M.A., Field, T., & Hernandez-Reif, M. (2014). Preterm infant weight gain is increased by massage therapy and exercise via different underlying mechanisms. *Early Human Development, 90,* 137-140.

Diekelmann, S. (2014). Sleep for cognitive enhancement. *Frontiers in Systems Neuroscience, 8,* 46.

Diekmann, R., & Bauer, J.M. (2019). Nutrition, muscle function, and mobility in older people. In R. Fernandez-Ballesteros & others (Eds.), *Cambridge handbook of successful aging.* New York: Cambridge University Press.

Diener, E. (2020). *Subjective well-being.* Retrieved January 4, 2019, from labspsychologyllinois.edu/~ediener/SWLS.html

Dierickx, S., & others (2020). Commonalities and differences in legal euthanasia and physician-assisted suicide in three countries: A population-level comparison. *International Journal of Public Health, 65,* 65-73.

Dimitropoulos, G., & others (2018). Open trial of family-based treatment of anorexia nervosa for transition age of youth. *Journal of the Canadian Academy of Child and Adolescent Psychiatry, 27,* 50-61.

Dimock, M. (2019, January 17). *Defining generations: Where millennials end and generation Z begins.* Washington, DC: Pew Research Center.

Dimri, M., & Satyanarayana, A. (2020) Molecular signaling pathways and therapeutic targets in hepatocellular carcinoma. *Cancers, 12,* 2.

Ding, Y., & others (2019). Effects of working memory, strategy use, and single-step mental addition on multi-step mental addition in Chinese elementary students. *Frontiers in Psychology, 10,* 148.

Dinger, M.K., Brittain, D.R., & Hutchinson, S.R. (2014). Associations between physical activity and health-related factors in a national sample of college students. *Journal of American College Health, 62,* 67-74.

Dion, K.L., & Dion, K.K. (1993). Individualistic and collectivistic perspectives on gender and the cultural context of love and intimacy. *Journal of Social Issues, 49,* 53-69.

Dishion, T.J., & Patterson, G.R. (2016). The development and ecology of antisocial behavior. In D. Cicchetti (Ed.), *Developmental psychopathology* (3rd ed.). New York: Wiley.

Dishion, T.J., & Piehler, T.F. (2009). Deviant by design: Peer contagion in development, interventions, and schools. In K.H. Rubin, W.M. Bukowski, & B. Laursen (Eds.), *Handbook of peer interactions, relationships, and groups.* New York: Guilford.

Distefano, R., & others (2018). Autonomy-supportive parenting and associations with child and parent executive function. *Applied Developmental Psychology, 58,* 77-85.

Dittus, P.J., & others (2015). Parental monitoring and its associations with adolescent sexual risk behavior: A meta-analysis. *Pediatrics, 136,* e1587-e1599.

Dixon, R.A., & Lachman, M.E. (2020, in press). Risk and protective factors in cognitive aging: Advances in the assessment, prevention, and promotion of alternative pathways. In E.G. Samanez-Larkin (Ed.), *The aging brain.* Washington, DC: American Psychological Association.

Dixon, S.V., Graber, J.A., & Brooks-Gunn, J. (2008). The roles of respect for parental authority and parenting practices in parent-child conflict among African American, Latino, and European American families. *Journal of Family Psychology, 22,* 1-10.

Djelantik, A.A.A.M.J., & others (2020). The prevalence of prolonged grief disorder in bereaved individuals following unnatural losses: Systematic review and meta regression analysis. *Journal of Affective Disorders, 265,* 146-156.

Dodge, K.A. (1983). Behavioral antecedents of peer social status. *Child Development, 54,* 1386-1399.

Dodge, K.A. (2011a). Context matters in child and family policy. *Child Development, 82,* 433-442.

Dodge, K.A. (2011b). Social information processing models of aggressive behavior. In M. Mikulincer & P.R. Shaver (Eds.), *Understanding and reducing aggression, violence, and their consequences.* Washington, DC: American Psychological Association.

Dodge, K.A., & McCourt, S.N. (2010). Translating models of antisocial behavioral development into efficacious intervention policy to prevent adolescent violence. *Developmental Psychobiology, 52,* 277-285.

Dodge, K.A., & others (2015). Impact of early intervention on psychopathology, crime, and well-being at age 25. *American Journal of Psychiatry, 172,* 59-70.

Dodson, L.J., & Davies, A.P.C. (2014). Different challenges, different well-being: A comparison of psychological well-being across stepmothers and biological mothers and across four categories of stepmothers. *Journal of Divorce & Remarriage, 55,* 49-63.

Doenyas, C., Yavuz, H.M., & Selcuk, B. (2018). Not just a sum of its parts: How tasks of theory of mind scale relate to executive function across time. *Journal of Experimental Child Psychology, 166,* 485-501.

Dogan, G., & Kayir, S. (2020). Global scientific outputs of brain death publications and evaluation according to religions of countries. *Journal of Religion and Health, 59*(1), 96-112.

Doherty, M. (2008). *Theory of mind.* Philadelphia: Psychology Press.

Dolbin, M.L. (2019). Grandparenthood. In B.H. Friese (Ed.), *APA handbook of contemporary family psychology.* Washington, DC: APA Books.

Dolbin-MacNab, M.L., & Yancura, L.A. (2018). International perspectives on grandparents raising grandchildren. *International Journal of Aging and Human Development, 86,* 3-33.

Dollar, J., & Calkins, S.D. (2019). Developmental psychology. In T. Ollendick & others (Eds.), *Oxford handbook of clinical child and adolescent psychology.* New York: Oxford University Press.

Dols, A., & others (2017). Early- and late-onset depression in late life: A prospective study on clinical and structural brain characteristics and response to electroconvulsive therapy. *American Journal of Geriatric Psychiatry, 25,* 175-189.

Dombrovski, A.Y., & others (2018). Losing the battle: Perceived status loss and contemplated or attempted suicide in older adults. *International Journal of Geriatric Psychiatry, 33,* 907-914.

Domenech-Abella, J., & others (2018). The impact of socioeconomic status on the association between biomedical well-being and all-cause mortality in older Spanish adults. *Social Psychiatry and Psychiatric Epidemiology, 53,* 259-268.

Dominguez-Cruz, M.G., & others (2020, in press). Maya gene variants related to the risk of type 2 diabetes in a family-based association study. *Gene.*

Donatelle, R.J. (2019). *Health* (13th ed.). Upper Saddle River, NJ: Pearson.

Donatelle, R.J., & Ketcham, P. (2020). *Access to health* (16th ed.). Upper Saddle River, NJ: Pearson.

Dong, B., Wang, Z., Wang, H.J., & Ma, J. (2015). Population attributable risk of overweight and obesity for high blood pressure in Chinese children. *Blood Pressure, 24,* 230-236.

Dong, F., & others (2017). Longitudinal associations of away-from-home eating, snacking, screen time, and physical activity behaviors with cardiometabolic risk factors among Chinese children and their parents. *American Journal of Clinical Nutrition, 106,* 168-178.

Dong, X.S., & others (2017). Baby boomers in the United States: Factors associated with working longer and delaying retirement. *American Journal of Industrial Medicine, 60,* 315-328.

Donnellan, M.B., Ackerman, R.A., & Wright, A.G.C. (2020, in press). Narcissism in contemporary personality psychology. In O.P. John & R.W. Robins (Eds.), *Handbook of personality: Theory and research* (4th ed.). New York: Guilford.

Donnellan, M.B., Larsen-Rife, D., & Conger, R.D. (2005). Personality, family history, and competence in early adult romantic relationships. *Journal of Personality and Social Psychology, 88,* 562-576.

Donovan, M.K. (2017). The looming threat to sex education: A resurgence of federal funding for abstinence-only programs? *Guttmacher Policy Review, 20,* 44-47.

Doom, J., & Cicchetti, D. (2020). The developmental psychopathology of stress exposure in childhood. In K.L. Harkness & E.P. Hayden (Eds.), *Oxford handbook of stress and mental health.* New York: Oxford University Press.

Doom, J.R., & others (2017). Pathways between childhood/adolescent adversity, adolescent socioeconomic status, and long-term cardiovascular disease risk in young adulthood. *Social Science & Medicine, 188,* 166-175.

Dora, B., & Baydar, N. (2020, in press). Transactional associations of maternal depressive symptoms with child externalizing behaviors are small after age 3. *Development and Psychopathology.*

Dorffner, G., Vitr, M., & Anderer, P. (2015). The effects of aging on sleep architecture in healthy subjects. *Advances in Experimental Medicine and Biology, 821,* 93-100.

Dorling, J.L., Martin, C.K., & Redman, L.M. (2020, in press). Calorie restriction for enhanced longevity: The role of novel dietary strategies in the present obesogenic environment. *Aging Research Reviews.*

Dorner, R.A., & others (2020, in press). Early neurodevelopmental outcome in preterm posthemorrhagic ventricular dilation and hydrocephalus: Neonatal ICU Network Neurobehavioral Scale and imaging predict 3-6 month motor quotients and Capute scales. *Journal of Neurosurgery, Pediatrics.*

Dorrenbacher, S., & others (2020, in press). Plasticity in brain activity dynamics after task-shifting training in older adults. *Neuropsychologia.*

Dotti Sani, G.M., & Quaranta, M. (2015). The best is yet to come? Attitudes toward gender roles among adolescents in 36 countries. *Sex Roles, 65,* 80-99.

Doty, R.L., & Shah, M. (2008). Taste and smell. In M.M. Haith & J.B. Benson (Eds.), *Encyclopedia of infant and early childhood development.* Oxford, UK: Elsevier.

Dow, B.J., & Wood, J. (Eds.) (2006). *The SAGE handbook of gender and communication.* Thousand Oaks, CA: Sage.

Dowdall, N., & others (2020, in press). Shared picture book reading interventions for child language development: A systematic review and meta-analysis. *Child Development.*

Dow-Edwards, D., & others (2019). Experience during adolescence shapes brain development: From synapses and networks to normal and pathological behavior. *Neurotoxicology and Toxicology.* doi:10.1016/j.ntt.2019.106834

Downer, B., Jiang, Y., Zanjani, F., & Fardo, D. (2015). Effects of alcohol consumption on cognition and regional brain volumes among older adults. *American Journal of Alzheimer's Disease and Other Dementias, 30,* 364-374.

Doyle, C., & Cicchetti, D. (2018). Child maltreatment. In M.H. Bornstein (Ed.), *SAGE encyclopedia of lifespan human development.* Thousand Oaks, CA: Sage.

Dozier, M., & Bernard, K. (2019). *Coaching parents of vulnerable infants.* New York: Guilford.

Dozier, M., Bernard, K., & Roben, C.K.P. (2019). Attachment and biobehavioral catch-up. In H. Steele & M. Steele (Eds.), *Handbook of attachment-based interventions.* New York: Guilford.

Dozier, M., Stovall-McClough, K.C., & Albus, K.E. (2009). Attachment and psychopathology in adulthood. In J. Cassidy & P.R. Shaver (Eds.), *Handbook of attachment* (2nd ed.). New York: Guilford.

Dragoset, L., & others (2017). School improvement grants: Implementation and effectiveness. NCEE 2017-4013. *ERIC,* ED572215.

Drake, S.A., & others (2020, in press). A descriptive and geospatial analysis of environmental factors attributing to sudden unexpected infant death. *American Journal of Forensic Medicine and Pathology.*

Drewelies, J., & others (2018). Age variations in cohort differences in the United States: Older adults report fewer constraints nowadays than those 18 years ago, but mastery beliefs are diminished among younger adults. *Developmental Psychology, 54,* 1408-1425.

Dryfoos, J., & Barkin, C. (2006). *Growing up in America today.* New York: Oxford University Press.

Dryfoos, J.G. (1990). *Adolescents at risk: Prevalence or prevention.* New York: Oxford University Press.

Du Prel, J.B., Siegrist, J., & Bochart, D. (2019). The role of leisure-time physical activity in the change of work-related stress (ERI) over time. *International Journal of Environmental Research and Public Health, 16,* 23.

Dubal, D.B., & Rogine, C. (2017). Apolipoprotein E4 and risk factors for Alzheimer disease—Let's talk about sex. *JAMA Neurology, 74,* 1167-1168.

Dube, S., & others (2017). Psychological well-being as a predictor of casual sex relationships and experiences among adolescents: A short-term prospective study. *Archives of Sexual Behavior, 46,* 1807-1818.

Dubois-Comtois, K., & others (2019). Family environment and preschoolers' sleep: The complementary role of both parents. *Sleep Medicine, 58,* 114-122.

Dubol, M., & others (2018). Dopamine transporter and reward anticipation in a dimensional perspective: A multimodal brain imaging study. *Neuropsychopharmacology, 43,* 820-837.

Dubow, E.F., & others (2017). Conducting longitudinal, process-oriented research with conflict-affected youth: Solving the inevitable challenges. *Development and Psychopathology, 29,* 85-92.

Duchek, J.M., & others (2020, in press). The relation between personality and biomarkers in sensitivity and conversion to Alzheimer-type dementia. *Journal of the International Neuropsychological Society.*

Duda, B.M., & others (2019). Neurocompensatory effects on the default network in older adults. *Frontiers in Aging Neuroscience, 11,* 111.

Due, T.D., Sandholdt, H., & Waldorff, F.B. (2017). Social relations and loneliness among older patients consulting a general practitioner. *Danish Medical Journal, 64,* 3.

Duell, N., & Steinberg, L. (2019). Positive risk-taking in adolescence. *Child Development Perspectives, 13,* 48-52.

Duff, F.J., Reen, G., Plunkett, K., & Nation, K. (2015). Do infant vocabulary skills predict school-age language and literacy outcomes? *Journal of Child Psychology and Psychiatry, 56,* 848-856.

Duggal, N.A., & others (2019). Major features of immunosenescence, including reduced thymic output, are ameliorated by high levels of physical activity in adulthood. *Aging Cell, 17*(2). doi:10.1111/acel.12750

Duke, S.A., Balzer, B.W., & Steinbeck, K.S. (2014). Testosterone and its effects on human male adolescent mood and behavior: A systematic review. *Journal of Adolescent Health, 55,* 315-322.

Dumaz, A., & others (2019). Genetic factors associated with the predisposition to late onset Alzheimer's disease. *Gene, 707,* 212-215.

Dumontheil, I., & Mareschal, D. (2020). An introduction to brain and cognitive development—The key concepts you need to know. In M. Thomas, D. Mareschal, & I. Dumontheil (Eds.), *Educational neuroscience.* New York: Routledge.

Duncan, G.J., Magnuson, K., & Votruba-Drzal, E. (2017). Moving beyond correlations in assessing the consequences of poverty. *Annual Review of Psychology* (Vol. 68). Palo Alto, CA: Annual Reviews.

Dunn, J. (1984). Sibling studies and the developmental impact of critical incidents. In P.B. Baltes & O.G. Brim (Eds.), *Life-span development and behavior* (Vol. 6). Orlando, FL: Academic Press.

Dunn, J. (2007). Siblings and socialization. In J.E. Grusec & P.D. Hastings (Eds.), *Handbook of socialization.* New York: Guilford.

Dunn, J. (2015). Siblings. In J.E. Grusec & P.D. Hastings (Eds.), *Handbook of socialization* (2nd ed.). New York: Guilford.

Dunn, J., & Kendrick, C. (1982). *Siblings.* Cambridge, MA: Harvard University Press.

Dunster, G.P., & others (2018). Sleepmore in Seattle: Later school start times are associated with more sleep and better performance in high school students. *Science Advances, 4*(12), eaau6200.

Dupre, M.E., & Meadows, S.O. (2007). Disaggregating the effects of marital trajectories on health. *Journal of Family Issues, 28,* 623-652.

Durante, M.A., & others (2020, in press). Single-cell analysis of olfactory neurogenesis and differentiation in adult humans. *Nature Neuroscience.*

Durston, S., & others (2006). A shift from diffuse to focal cortical activity with development. *Developmental Science, 9,* 1-8.

Dutton, E., & Lynn, R. (2013). A negative Flynn effect in Finland, 1997-2009. *Intelligence, 41,* 817-820.

Dutton, E., & others (2018). A Flynn effect in Khartoum, the Sudanese capital, 2004-2016. *Intelligence, 68,* 82-86.

Duval, C., & others (2011). Age effects on different components of theory of mind. *Consciousness and Cognition, 20,* 627-642.

Dweck, C.S. (2006). *Mindset.* New York: Random House.

Dweck, C.S. (2012). Mindsets and social nature: Promoting change in the Middle East, the schoolyard, the racial divide, and willpower. *American Psychologist, 67,* 614-622.

Dweck, C.S. (2016, March 11). *Growth mindset, revisited.* Invited address at Leaders to Learn From. Washington, DC: Education Week.

Dweck, C.S. (2019). The choice to make a difference. *Perspectives on Psychological Science, 14*(1), 21-25.

Dweck, C.S., & Master, A. (2009). Self-theories and motivation: Students' beliefs about intelligence. In K.R. Wentzel & A. Wigfield (Eds.), *Handbook of motivation at school.* New York: Routledge.

Dweck, C.S., & Yeager, D.S. (2019). Mindsets: A view from two eras. *Perspectives on Psychological Science, 14,* 481-496.

Dweck, C.S., & Yeager, D.S. (2020, in press). The growth mindset of intelligence intervention. In G. Walton & A. Crum (Eds.), *Handbook of wise interventions.* New York: Guilford.

Dworkin, S.L., & Santelli, J. (2007). Do abstinence-plus interventions reduce sexual risk behavior among youth? *PLoS Medicine, 4,* 1437-1439.

Dwyer, J.W., & Coward, R.T. (1991). A multivariate comparison of the involvement of adult sons versus daughters in the care of impaired parents. *Journals of Gerontology B: Psychological Sciences and Social Sciences, 46,* S259-S269.

Dzierzewski, J.M., Dautovich, N., & Ravyts, S. (2018). Sleep and cognition in older adults. *Sleep Medicine Clinics, 13,* 93-106.

E

Eagly, A.H. (2012). Women as leaders: Paths through the labyrinth. In M.C. Bligh & R. Riggio (Eds.), *When near is far and far is near: Exploring distance in leader-follower relationships.* New York: Wiley Blackwell.

Eagly, A.H. (2018). Making a difference: Feminist scholarship. In C.B. Gravis & J.W. White (Eds.), *Handbook of the psychology of women.* Washington, DC: APA Books.

Eagly, A.H., & Crowley, M. (1986). Gender and helping: A meta-analytic review of the social psychological literature. *Psychological Bulletin, 108,* 233-256.

Eagly, A.H., & Steffen, V.J. (1986). Gender and aggressive behavior: A meta-analytic review of the social psychological literature. *Psychological Bulletin, 100,* 309-330.

Eagly, A.H., & Wood, W. (2017). Gender identity: Nature and nurture working together. *Evolutionary Studies in Imaginative Culture, 1,* 59-62.

Easey, K.E., & others (2019). Prenatal alcohol exposure and offspring mental health: A systematic review. *Drug and Alcohol Dependence, 197,* 344-353.

Eastwick, P.W., & Finkel, E.J. (2008). Sex differences in mate preferences revisited: Do people know what they initially desire in a romantic partner? *Journal of Personality and Social Psychology, 94,* 245-264.

Ebaid, D., & Crewther, S.G. (2019). Visual information processing in young and older adults. *Frontiers in Aging Neuroscience, 11,* 116.

Ebner, N., Anker, S.D., & von Haehling, S. (2020). Recent developments in the field of cachexia, sarcopenia, and muscle wasting: Highlights from the 12 Cachexia Conference. *Journal of Cachexia, Sarcopenia, and Muscle, 11,* 274–285.

Eccles, J.S. (2007). Families, schools, and developing achievement-related motivations and engagement. In J.E. Grusec & P.D. Hastings (Eds.), *Handbook of socialization.* New York: Guilford.

Eccles, J.S., & Roeser, R.W. (2016). School and community influences on human development. In M.H. Bornstein & M.E. Lamb (Eds.), *Developmental science* (7th ed.). New York: Psychology Press.

Eckardt, N., Braun, C., & Kibele, A. (2020). Instability resistance training improves working memory, processing speed, and response inhibition in healthy older adults: A double-blinded, randomized controlled trial. *Scientific Reports, 10*(1), 2056.

Ecker, S., & Beck, S. (2019). The epigenetic clock: A molecular crystal ball for human aging? *Aging, 11,* 833–835.

Eckerman, C., & Whitehead, H. (1999). How toddler peers generate coordinated action: A cross-cultural exploration. *Early Education & Development, 10,* 241–266.

Eckler, P., Kalyango, Y., & Paasch, E. (2017). Facebook use and negative body image among U.S. college women. *Women and Health, 57,* 249–267.

Edgin, J.O., & others (2020, in press). The "eyes have it," but when in development? The importance of a developmental perspective in our understanding of behavioral memory formation and the hippocampus. *Hippocampus.*

Ednick, M., & others (2010). Sleep-related respiratory abnormalities and arousal pattern in achondroplasia during early infancy. *Journal of Pediatrics, 155,* 510–515.

Edwards, B. (2020). Emerging technologies, market segments, and markeTrak 10 insights in hearing health technology. *Seminars in Hearing, 41,* 37–54.

Edwards, M.L., & Jackson, A.D. (2017). The historical development of obstetric anesthesia and its contributions to perinatology. *American Journal of Perinatology, 34,* 211–216.

Edwards, S.L., & Coyne, I. (2020). *A nurse's survival guide to children's nursing* (updated 1st ed.). New York: Elsevier.

Eggenberger, P., & others (2015). Does multicomponent physical exercise with simultaneous cognitive training boost cognitive performance in older adults? A 6-month randomized controlled trial with a 1-year follow-up. *Clinical Interventions in Aging, 10,* 1335–1349.

Ehm, J.H., Hasselhorn, M., & Schmiedek, F. (2019). Analyzing the developmental relation of academic self-concept and achievement in elementary school children: Alternative models point to different results. *Developmental Psychology, 55,* 2336–2351.

Ehninger, D., Neff, F., & Xie, K. (2014). Longevity, aging, and rapamycin. *Cellular and Molecular Life Sciences, 71,* 4325–4346.

Ehrlich, S., King, J.A., & Boehm, I. (2019). Editorial: Connecting the nodes of altered brain network organization in eating disorders. *Journal of the American Academy of Child and Adolescent Psychiatry, 58,* 156–158.

Eichorn, D.H., Clausen, J.A., Haan, N., Honzik, M.P., & Mussen, P.H. (Eds.) (1981). *Present and past in middle life.* New York: Academic Press.

Eiferman, R.R. (1971). Social play in childhood. In R. Herron & B. Sutton-Smith (Eds.), *Child's play.* New York: Wiley.

Einziger, T., & others (2018). Predicting ADHD symptoms in adolescence from early childhood temperament traits. *Journal of Abnormal Child Psychology, 46,* 265–276.

Eisenberg, N., Duckworth, A., Spinrad, L., & Valiente, C. (2014). Conscientiousness and healthy aging. *Developmental Psychology, 50,* 1331–1349.

Eisenberg, N., & Hernandez, M.M. (2019). Connections between emotions and the social world: Numerous and complex. In A.S. Fox & others (Eds.), *The nature of emotion* (2nd ed.). New York: Oxford University Press.

Eisenberg, N., & Spinrad, T.L. (2016). Multidimensionality of prosocial behavior: Rethinking the conceptualization and development of prosocial behavior. In L. Padilla-Walker & G. Carlo (Eds.), *Prosocial behavior.* New York: Oxford University Press.

Eisenberg, N., Spinrad, T.L., & Knafo-Noam, A. (2015). Prosocial development. In R.M. Lerner (Ed.), *Handbook of child psychology and developmental science* (7th ed.). New York: Wiley.

Eismann, M., Verbeij, T., & Henkens, K. (2019). Older workers' plans for activities in retirement: The role of opportunities, spousal support, and time perception. *Psychology and Aging, 34,* 738–749.

Ekas, N.A., Braungart-Rieker, J.M., & Messinger, D.S. (2018). The development of infant emotion regulation: Time is of the essence. In P.M. Cole & T. Hollenstein (Eds.), *Emotion regulation.* New York: Routledge.

Eklund, K., Tanner, N., Stoll, K., & Anway, L. (2015). Identifying emotional and behavioral risk among gifted and nongifted children: A multi-gate, multi-informant approach. *School Psychology Quarterly, 30,* 197–211.

El Bizri, I., & Batsis, J.A. (2020, in press). Linking epidemiology and molecular mechanisms in sarcopenic obesity in populations. *Proceedings of the Nutrition Society.*

Elangovan, S., & Holsinger, R.M.D. (2020). Cyclical amyloid beat-astrocyte activity induces oxidative stress in Alzheimer's disease. *Biochimie, 171,* 38–42.

Elbe, A-M., & others (2019). Is regular physical activity a key to mental health? Commentary. *Journal of Sport and Health Science, 8,* 6–7.

Elder, G.H., & Cox, M.J. (2020). When social events occur in lives, developmental linkages, and turning points. In R.D. Parke & G.H. Elder (Eds.), *Children in changing worlds.* New York: Cambridge University Press.

El-Farrash, R.A., & others (2020, in press). Longer duration of kangaroo care improves neurobehavioral performance and feeding in preterm infants: A randomized controlled trial. *Pediatric Research.*

Elfassy, T., & others (2019). Sociodemographic disparities in long-term mortality among stroke survivors in the United States. *Stroke, 50,* 805–812.

Eliasieh, K., Liets, L.C., & Chalupa, L.M. (2007). Cellular reorganization in the human retina during normal aging. *Investigative Ophthalmology and Visual Science, 48,* 2824–2830.

Elkana, O., & others (2020, in press). WAIS Information Subtest as an indicator of crystallized cognitive abilities and brain reserve among highly educated older adults: A three-year longitudinal study. *Applied Neuropsychology, Adult.*

Elkind, D. (1970, April 5). Erik Erikson's eight ages of man. *New York Times Magazine.*

Elkind, D. (1976). *Child development and education: A Piagetian perspective.* New York: Oxford University Press.

Elliott, E.M., & others (2011). Working memory in the oldest-old: Evidence from output serial position curves. *Memory and Cognition, 39*(8), 1423–1434.

Elliott, J.G., & Resing, W.C. (2019). Extremes of intelligence. In R.J. Sternberg (Ed.), *Human intelligence.* New York: Cambridge University Press.

Ellis, S.D., Riggs, D.W., & Peel, E. (2020). *Lesbian, gay, bisexual, trans, intersex, and queer psychology* (2nd ed.). New York: Cambridge University Press.

El-Sheikh, M. (2013). *Auburn University Child Sleep, Health, and Development Center.* Auburn, AL: Auburn University. *Society, 67,* 82–90.

El-Sheikh, M., & others (2019). Interactions between sleep duration and quality as predictors of adolescents' adjustment. *Sleep Health, 5,* 180–186.

Eltonsy, S., Martin, B., Ferreira, E., & Blais, L. (2016). Systematic procedure for the classification of proven and potential teratogens for use in research. *Birth Defects Research A: Clinical and Molecular Teratology, 106,* 285–297.

eMarketeer.com (2016). *Trends in social media use.* Retrieved November 15, 2016, from eMarketing.com.

Ember, C.R., & Ember, M. (2019). *Cultural anthropology* (15th ed.). Upper Saddle River, NJ: Pearson.

Emberson, L.L., & others (2019). Expectation affects neural repetition suppression in infancy. *Developmental Cognitive Neuroscience, 37,* 10097.

Emmons, R.A., & Diener, E. (1986). Situation selection as a moderator of response consistency and stability. *Journal of Personality and Social Psychology, 51,* 1013–1019.

Employee Benefit Research Institute (2018). *Expectations about retirement.* Washington, D.C.: Author.

Engberg, E., & others (2020, in press). Heavy screen use on weekends in childhood predicts increased body mass index in adolescence: A three-year follow-up study. *Journal of Adolescent Health.*

Engels, A.C., & others (2016). Sonographic detection of central nervous system in the first trimester of pregnancy. *Prenatal Diagnosis, 36,* 266–273.

England-Mason, G., & Gonzalez, A. (2020). Intervening to shape children's emotion regulation: A review of emotion socialization programs for young children. *Emotion, 20,* 98–104.

English, T., & Carstensen, L.L. (2014a). Selective narrowing of social networks across adulthood is associated with improved emotional experience in life. *International Journal of Behavioral Development, 38*, 195-202.

Eno, C.C., & others (2020, in press). Confidential genetic testing and health records: A survey of current practices among Huntington disease testing centers. *Molecular Genetics and Genomic Medicine.*

Ensembl Human (2010). Explore the *Homo sapiens* genome. Retrieved March 17, 2010, from www.ensembl.org/Homo_sapiens/index.html

Entringer, S., & Epel, E.S. (2020, in press). The stress field ages: A close look into cellular aging processes. *Psychoneuroendocrinology.*

Erausquin, J.T., & others (2019). Trajectories of suicide ideation and attempts from early adolescence to mid-adulthood: Associations with race/ethnicity. *Journal of Youth and Adolescence, 48*, 1796-1805.

Erck Lambert, A.B., & others (2019). Sleep-related infant suffocation deaths attributable to soft bedding, overlay, and wedging. *Pediatrics, 143*, 5.

Erickson, K.I., & others (2009). Aerobic fitness is associated with hippocampal volume in elderly humans. *Hippocampus, 19*, 1030-1039.

Erickson-Schroth, L., & Davis, B. (2021). *Gender.* New York: Oxford University Press.

Ericson, N. (2001, June). *Addressing the problem of juvenile bullying.* Washington, DC: Office of Juvenile Justice and Delinquency Prevention, Office of Justice Programs, U.S. Department of Justice.

Ericsson, K.A. (2020). Toward a science of the acquisition of expert performance in sports: Clarifying the differences between deliberate practice and other types of practice. *Journal of Sports Science, 38*, 159-176.

Ericsson, K.A., Krampe, R., & Tesch-Romer, C. (1993). The role of deliberate practice in the acquisition of expert performance. *Psychological Review, 100*, 363-406.

Ericsson, K.A., & others (Eds.) (2018). *Cambridge handbook of expertise and expert performance* (2nd ed.). New York: Cambridge University Press.

Erikson, E.H. (1950). *Childhood and society.* New York: W.W. Norton.

Erikson, E.H. (1968). *Identity: Youth and crisis.* New York: W.W. Norton.

Erikson-Schroth, L., & Davis, B. (2021). *Gender.* New York: Oxford University Press.

Eriksson, U.J. (2009). Congenital anomalies in diabetic pregnancy. *Seminars in Fetal and Neonatal Medicine, 14*, 85-93.

Erskine, H.E., & others (2016). Long-term outcomes of attention-deficit/hyperactivity disorder and conduct disorder: A systematic review and meta-analysis. *Journal of the American Academy of Child and Adolescent Psychiatry, 55*, 841-850.

Esposito, C., Bacchini, D., & Affuso, G. (2019). Adolescent non-suicidal self-injury and its relationship with school bullying and peer rejection. *Psychiatry Research, 274*, 1-6.

Esposito, G., & others (2017). Response to infant cry in clinically depressed and non-depressed mothers. *PLoS One, 12*(1), e0169066.

Esteves, M., & others (2020, in press). Asymmetrical brain plasticity: Physiology and pathology. *Neuroscience.*

Etaugh, C., & Bridges, J.S. (2010). *Women's lives* (2nd ed.). Boston: Allyn & Bacon.

Ethier, K.A., Harper, C.R., Hoo, E., & Ditts, P.J. (2016). The longitudinal impact of perceptions of parental monitoring on adolescent initiation of sexual activity. *Journal of Adolescent Health, 59*, 570-576.

Ettcheto, M., & others (2020, in press). Chronological review of potential disease modifying therapeutic strategies for Alzheimer's disease. *Current Pharmaceutical Design.*

Ettekal, I., & Ladd, G.W. (2019). Development of aggressive-victims from childhood through adolescence: Associations with emotion dysregulation, withdrawn behaviors, moral disengagement, peer rejection, and friendships. *Development and Psychopathology, 32*, 271-291.

Euler, H.A. (2020). Gender differences in attachment from an evolutionary perspective: What is good for the goose may not be good for the gander. *Attachment and Human Development, 22*, 4-8.

Eun, J.D., & others (2018). Parenting style and mental disorders in a nationally representative sample of U.S. adolescents. *Social Psychiatry and Psychiatric Epidemiology, 53*, 11-20.

Evans, G.W., & English, G.W. (2002). The environment of poverty. *Child Development, 73*, 1238-1248.

Evans, G.W., & Kim, P. (2007). Childhood poverty and health: Cumulative risk exposure and stress dysregulation. *Psychological Science, 18*, 953-957.

Evans, I.E.M., & others (2019). Social isolation and cognitive function in later life: A systematic review and meta-analysis. *Journal of Alzheimer's Disease, 23*, 1691-1700.

Evans, S.Z., Simons, L.G., & Simons, R.L. (2016). Factors that influence trajectories of delinquency throughout adolescence. *Journal of Youth and Adolescence, 45*, 156-171.

Evans, W.J. (2010). Skeletal muscle loss: Cachexia, sarcopenia, and inactivity. *American Journal of Clinical Nutrition, 91*, S1123-S1127.

Eymard, A.S., & Douglas, D.H. (2012). Ageism among health care providers and interventions to improve their attitudes toward older adults: An integrative review. *Journal of Gerontological Nursing, 38*, 26-35.

F

Fabi, R.E. (2019). Why physicians should advocate for undocumented immigrants' unimpeded access to prenatal care. *AMA Journal of Ethics, 21*, E93-E99.

Fabi, R.E., & Taylor, H.A. (2019). Prenatal care for undocumented immigrants: Professional norms, ethical tensions, and practical workarounds. *Journal of Law and Medical Ethics, 47*, 398-408.

Fabiano, G.A., & others (2009). A meta-analysis of behavioral treatments for attention deficit/hyperactivity disorder. *Clinical Psychology Review, 29*, 129-140.

Fabricius, W.V., Braver, S.L., Diaz, P., & Schenck, C. (2010). Custody and parenting time: Links to family relationships and well-being after divorce. In M.E. Lamb (Ed.), *The role of the father in child development* (5th ed.). New York: Wiley.

Fadus, M.C., Smith, T.T., & Squeglia, L.M. (2019). The rise of e-cigarettes, pod mod devices, and JUUL among youth: Factors influencing use, health implications, and downstream effects. *Drug and Alcohol Dependence, 201*, 85-93.

Fagan, E., & others (2017). Telomere length is longer in women with late maternal age. *Menopause, 24*, 497-501.

Fagan, J. (2020). Broadening the scope of father-child attachment research to include the family context. *Attachment and Human Development, 22*, 139-142.

Fagot, B.I., Rogers, C.S., & Leinbach, M.D. (2000). Theories of gender socialization. In T. Eckes & H.M. Trautner (Eds.), *The developmental social psychology of gender.* Mahwah, NJ: Erlbaum.

Fairbairn, C.E., & others (2018). A meta-analysis of longitudinal associations between substance use and interpersonal attachment security. *Psychological Bulletin, 144*, 532-555.

Falandry, C. (2019). The connection between cellular senescence and age-related diseases. In R. Fernandez-Ballesteros & others (Eds.), *Cambridge handbook of successful aging.* New York: Cambridge University Press.

Falbo, T., & Poston, D.L. (1993). The academic, personality, and physical outcomes of only children in China. *Child Development, 64*, 18-35.

Falconier, M.K., & others (2015). Stress from daily hassles in couples: Its effects on intradyadic relationship satisfaction and physical and psychological well-being. *Journal of Marital and Family Therapy, 41*, 221-235.

Fang, Y., Tang, S., & Li, X. (2019). Sirtuins in metabolic and epigenetic regulation of stem cells. *Trends in Endocrinology and Metabolism, 30*, 177-188.

Fang, Y., & others (2018). Information and communicative technology use enhances psychological well-being of older adults: The roles of age, social connectedness, and frailty status. *Aging and Mental Health, 22*, 519-525.

Fani, L., & others (2020). Telomere length and the risk of Alzheimer's disease: The Rotterdam study. *Journal of Alzheimer's Disease, 73*, 707-714.

Fantz, R.L. (1963). Pattern vision in newborn infants. *Science, 140*, 286-297.

Farajinia, S., & others (2014). Aging of the suprachiasmatic clock. *Neuroscientist, 21*, 44-55.

Faranoff, A.A. (2020). *Care of the high-risk neonate* (7th ed.). New York: Elsevier.

Farasat, M., & others (2020). Long-term cardiac arrhythmia and chronotropic evaluation in patients with severe anorexia nervosa (LACE-AN): A pilot study. *Journal of Cardiovascular Electrophysiology, 31*(2), 432-439.

Faris, M.A.E., & others (2017). Energy drink consumption is associated with reduced sleep quality among college students: A cross-sectional study. *Nutrition and Dietetics, 74*, 268-274.

Farr, R.H. (2017). Does parental sexual orientation matter? A longitudinal follow-up of adoptive families with a school-age child. *Developmental Psychology, 53*, 252–264.

Farr, R.H., & Grotevant, H.D. (2019). Adoption. In B.H. Friese (Ed.), *APA handbook of contemporary family psychology.* Washington, DC: APA Books.

Farr, R.H., & Hrapczynski, K.M. (2020, in press). Transracial adoption: Psychology, law, and policy. In M. Stevenson & others (Eds.), *Children and race: Psychology, law, and public policy.* New York: Oxford University Press.

Farr, R.H., Oakley, M.K., & Ollen, E.W. (2016). School experiences of young children and their lesbian and gay adoptive parents. *Psychology of Sexual Orientation and Gender Diversity, 3*, 442–447.

Farr, R.H., & Patterson, C.J. (2013). Coparenting among lesbian, gay, and heterosexual couples: Associations with adopted children's outcomes. *Child Development, 84*, 1226–1240.

Farr, R.H., & Vasquez, C.P. (2020, in press). Adoptive families headed by LGBTQ parents. In E. Helder & others (Eds.), *Handbook of adoption.* New York: Routledge.

Farr, R.H., Vasquez, C.P., & Patterson, C.J. (2020, in press). LGBTQ adoptive parents and their children. In A.E. Goldberg & K.R. Allen (Eds.), *LGBTQ adoptive parent families* (2nd ed.). New York: Springer.

Farr, R.H., & others (2018). Children's gender-typed behavior from early to middle childhood in adoptive families with lesbian, gay, and heterosexual parents. *Sex Roles, 78*, 528–541.

Farrell, A.K., & others (2019). Early maternal sensitivity, attachment security in young adulthood, and cardiovascular risk at midlife. *Attachment and Human Development, 21*, 70–86.

Farrell, M.P., & Rosenberg, S.D. (1981). *Men at mid-life.* Boston: Auburn House.

Farrell, S.W., Fitzgerald, S.J., McAuley, P., & Barlow, C.E. (2010). Cardiorespiratory fitness, adiposity, and all-cause mortality in women. *Medicine and Science in Sports and Exercise, 42*(11), 2006–2012.

Farrington, D., & Hawkins, J.D. (2019). The need for long-term follow-ups of delinquency prevention experiments. *JAMA Network Open, 21*(3), e190780.

Fasig, L. (2000). Toddlers' understanding of ownership: Implications for self-concept development. *Social Development, 9*, 370382.

Fassbender, I., & Lohaus, A. (2019). Fixations and fixation shifts in own-race and other-face pairs at three, six, and nine months. *Infant Behavior and Development, 57*, 101328.

Fasula, A.M., & others (2019). Socioecological risk factors associated with teen pregnancy or birth for young men: A scoping review. *Journal of Adolescence, 74*, 130–145.

Fathollahi, A., & others (2019). Epigenetics in osteoarthritis: Novel spotlight. *Journal of Cellular Physiology, 234*, 12309–12324.

Fava, N.M., & Bay-Cheng, L.Y. (2012). Young women's adolescent experiences of oral sex: Relation of age of initiation to sexual motivation, sexual coercion, and psychological functioning. *Journal of Adolescence. 35*(5), 1191–1201.

Fearnley, R., & Boland, J.W. (2019). Parental life-limiting illness: What do we tell the children? *Healthcare, 7*, 1.

Feeney, S., Moravcik, E., & Nolte, S. (2019). *Who am I in the lives of children?* (11th ed.). Upper Saddle River, NJ: Pearson.

Feighan, S.M., & others (2020, in press). A profile of mental health and behavior in Prader-Willi syndrome. *Journal of Intellectual Disability Research.*

Feinberg, M.E., McHale, S.M., & Whiteman, S.D. (2019). Parenting siblings. In M.H. Bornstein (Ed.), *Handbook of parenting* (3rd ed.). New York: Routledge.

Feist, G.J. (2018). In search of the creative personality. In R.J. Sternberg & J.C. Kaufman (Eds.), *The nature of human creativity.* New York: Cambridge University Press.

Feldman, P.H., & others (2019). The Homecare Aide Workforce Initiative: Implementation and outcomes. *Journal of Applied Gerontology, 38*, 253–276.

Feldman, R. (2019). The social neuroendocrinology of human parenting. In M.H. Bornstein (Ed.), *Handbook of parenting* (3rd ed.). New York: Routledge.

Feldman, R., Rosenthal, Z., & Eidelman, A.I. (2014). Maternal-preterm skin-to-skin contact enhances child physiologic organization and cognitive control across the first 10 years of life. *Biological Psychiatry, 75*, 56–64.

Feldman, S.S., & Elliott, G.R. (1990). Progress and promise of research on normal adolescent development. In S.S. Feldman & G. Elliott (Eds.), *At the threshold: The developing adolescent.* Cambridge, MA: Harvard University Press.

Feldman, S.S., & Rosenthal, D.A. (1999). *Factors influencing parents' and adolescents' evaluations of parents as sex communicators.* Unpublished manuscript. Stanford Center on Adolescence, Stanford University.

Feldman, S.S., Turner, R., & Araujo, K. (1999). Interpersonal context as an influence on sexual timetables of youths: Gender and ethnic effects. *Journal of Research on Adolescence, 9*, 25–52.

Feldon, J.M. (2003). Grief as a transformative experience: Weaving through different life worlds after a loved one has committed suicide. *International Journal of Mental Health Nursing, 12*, 74–85.

Feliciano, C., & Rumbaut, R.G. (2019). The evolution of ethnic identity from adolescence to middle adulthood: The case of the immigrant second generation. *Emerging Adulthood, 7*, 85–96.

Felt, J.M., & others (2020, in press). A multimethod approach examining the relative contributions of optimism and pessimism to cardiovascular disease risk markers. *Journal of Behavioral Medicine.*

Felton, J.W., & others (2019). Talking together, thinking alone: Relations among co-rumination, peer relationships, and rumination. *Journal of Youth and Adolescence, 48*, 731–743.

Felver, J.C., & others (2017). The effects of mindfulness-based intervention on children's attention regulation. *Journal of Attention Disorders, 21*, 872–881.

Fenlon, J., & others (2019). Comparing sign language and gesture: Insights and pointing. *Glossa: A Journal of General Linguistics, 1*, 2.

Fergus, T.A., & Bardeen, J.R. (2019). The metacognitions questionnaire-30. *Assessment, 26*, 223–234.

Fergus, T.A., & Limbers, C.A. (2019). Reducing test anxiety in school settings: A controlled pilot study examining a group format delivery of the attention training technique among adolescent students. *Behavior Therapy, 50*, 803–816.

Ferguson, C.J. (2013). Spanking, corporal punishment, and negative long-term outcomes: A meta-analytic review of longitudinal studies. *Clinical Psychology Review, 33*, 196–208.

Ferguson, D.M., Harwood, L.J., & Shannon, F.T. (1987). Breastfeeding and subsequent social adjustment in 6- to 8-year-old children. *Journal of Child Psychology and Psychiatry, 28*, 378–386.

Ferguson, S.M., & Ryan, A.M. (2019). It's lonely at the top: Adolescent students' perceived popularity and self-perceived social contentment. *Journal of Youth and Adolescence, 48*, 341–358.

Ferjan Ramirez, N., & others (2017). Speech discrimination in 11-month-old bilingual and monolingual infants: A magnetoencephalography study. *Developmental Science, 20*, e12427.

Ferjan Ramirez, N., & others (2019). Parent coaching at 6 and 10 months improves language outcomes at 14 months: A randomized controlled trial. *Developmental Science, 23*, e12762.

Fernald, A., Marchman, V.A., & Weisleder, A. (2013). SES differences in language processing skill and vocabulary are evident at 18 months. *Developmental Science, 16*, 234–248.

Fernandes, Q. (2017). Therapeutic strategies in sickle cell anemia: The past, present, and future. *Life Sciences, 178*, 100–108.

Fernandez, N.B., & others (2019). Age-related changes in attention control and their relationship with gait performance in older adults with high risk for falls. *NeuroImage, 189*, 551–559.

Fernandez-Ballesteros, R. (2019). The concept of successful aging and related terms. In R. Fernandez-Ballesteros & others (Eds.), *Cambridge handbook of successful aging.* New York: Cambridge University Press.

Ferrarelli, F. & others (2020, in press). An increase in sleep slow waves predicts better working memory performance in healthy individuals. *Neuroimage.*

Ferrell, S.C., Hirt, G., & Ferrell, L. (2020). *Business foundations* (12th ed.). New York: McGraw-Hill.

Ferrer-Wreder, L., & Kroger, J. (2020). *Identity in adolescence* (4th ed.). New York: Routledge.

Ferretti, M.T., & others (2020, in press). Sex and gender differences in Alzheimer's disease: Current challenges and implications for clinical practice. *European Journal of Neurology.*

Feybesse, C., & Hatfield, E. (2019). Passionate love. In R.J. Sternberg & K. Sternberg (Eds.), *The new psychology of love* (2nd ed.). New York: Cambridge University Press.

Fidler, D.J., & others (2020). Intellectual disability. In R.J. Sternberg (Ed.), *Cambridge handbook of intelligence*. New York: Cambridge University Press.

Field, D. (1999). A cross-cultural perspective on continuity and change in social relations in old age: Introduction to a special issue. *International Journal of Aging and Human Development, 48,* 257-262.

Field, T.M. (2001). Massage therapy facilitates weight gain in preterm infants. *Current Directions in Psychological Science, 10,* 51-55.

Field, T.M. (2007). *The amazing infant.* Malden, MA: Blackwell.

Field, T.M. (2010a). Postpartum depression effects on early interactions, parenting, and safety practices: A review. *Infant Behavior and Development, 33,* 1-6.

Field, T.M. (2010b). Pregnancy and labor massage. *European Review of Obstetrics and Gynecology, 5,* 177-181.

Field, T.M. (2017a). Infant sleep problems and interventions: A review. *Infant Behavior and Development, 47,* 40-53.

Field, T.M. (2017b). Preterm newborn pain research review. *Infant Behavior and Development, 49,* 141-150.

Field, T.M. (2019). Pediatric massage therapy research: A narrative review. *Children, 6,* 6.

Field, T.M., Diego, M., & Hernandez-Reif, M. (2008). Prematurity and potential predictors. *International Journal of Neuroscience, 118,* 277-289.

Field, T.M., Diego, M., & Hernandez-Reif, M. (2010). Preterm infant massage therapy research: A review. *Infant Behavior and Development, 33,* 115-124.

Field, T.M., Henteleff, T., & others (1998). Children with asthma have improved pulmonary functions after massage therapy. *Journal of Pediatrics, 132,* 854-858.

Field, T.M., Hernandez-Reif, M., Feijo, L., & Freedman, J. (2006). Prenatal, perinatal, and neonatal stimulation. *Infant Behavior & Development, 29,* 24-31.

Field, T.M., Hernandez-Reif, M., & Freedman, J. (2004, Fall). Stimulation programs for preterm infants. *SRCD Social Policy Reports, 28*(1), 1-20.

Field, T.M., Hernandez-Reif, M., Taylor, S., Quintino, O., & Burman, I. (1997). Labor pain is reduced by massage therapy. *Journal of Psychosomatic Obstetrics and Gynecology, 18,* 286-291.

Field, T.M., Lasko, D., & others (1997). Brief report: Autistic children's attentiveness and responsivity improve after touch therapy. *Journal of Autism and Developmental Disorders, 27,* 333-338.

Field, T.M., Quintino, O., Hernandez-Reif, M., & Koslosky, G. (1998). Adolescents with attention deficit hyperactivity disorder benefit from massage therapy. *Adolescence, 33,* 103-108.

Fielder, R.L., Walsh, J.L., Carey, K.B., & Carey, M.P. (2013). Predictors of sexual hookups: A theory-based, prospective study of first-year college women. *Archives of Sexual Behavior, 42,* 1425-1441.

Fields, J., & others (2020, in press). In-home technology training among socially isolated older adults: Findings from the tech allies program. *Journal of Applied Gerontology.*

Filip, P., & others (2019). Neural scaffolding as the foundation for stable performance of aging cerebellum. *Cerebellum, 18,* 500-510.

Fillo, J., Simpson, J.A., Rholes, W.S., & Kohn, J.L. (2015). Dads doing diapers: Individual and relational outcomes associated with the division of childcare across the transition to parenthood. *Journal of Personality and Social Psychology, 108,* 298-316.

Finch, C.E. (2009). The neurobiology of middle age has arrived. *Neurobiology of Aging, 30,* 515-520.

Finch, C.E., & Seeman, T.E. (1999). Stress theories of aging. In V.L. Bengtson & K.W. Schaie (Eds.), *Handbook of theories of aging.* New York: Springer.

Findling, M.G., & others (2020). Views of rural U.S. adults about health and economic concerns. *JAMA New Open, 3*(1), e1918745.

Fingerhut, A.W., & Peplau, L.A. (2013). Same-sex romantic relationships. In C.J. Patterson & A.R. D'Augelli (Eds.), *Handbook of psychology and sexual orientation.* New York: Oxford University Press.

Fingerman, K.L., & Baker, B. (2006). Socioemotional aspects of aging. In J. Wilmouth & K. Ferraro (Eds.), *Perspectives in gerontology* (3rd ed.). New York: Springer.

Fingerman, K.L., Cheng, Y.P., Tighe, L., Birditt, K.S., & Zarit, S. (2011b). Parent-child relationships in young adulthood. In A. Booth & others (Eds.), *Early adulthood in a family context.* New York: Springer.

Fingerman, K.L., Huo, M., & Birditt, K.S. (2020, in press). A decade of research on intergenerational ties: Technological, economic, political, and demographic changes. *Journal of Marriage and the Family.*

Fingerman, K.L., Miller, L., Birditt, K., &. Zarit, S. (2009). Giving to the good and needy: Parental support of grown children. *Journal of Marriage and the Family, 71,* 1220-1233.

Fingerman, K.L., Pillemer, K.A., Silverstein, M., & Suitor, J.J. (2012). The Baby Boomers' intergenerational relationships. *Gerontologist, 52,* 199-209.

Fingerman, K.L., Zarit, S.H., & Birditt, K.S. (2019). Parent-child relationships in adulthood and old age. In M.H. Bornstein (Ed.), *Handbook of parenting* (3rd ed.). New York: Routledge.

Fingerman, K.L., & others (2011a). Who gets what and why: Help middle-aged adults provide to parents and grown children. *Journals of Gerontology B: Psychological Sciences and Social Sciences, 66,* 87-98.

Fingerman, K.L., & others (2018). A family affair: Family typologies of life problems and midlife well-being. *Gerontologist, 58,* 654-664.

Fingerman, K.L., & others (2020). Variety is the spice of life: Social integration and daily activity. *Journals of Gerontology B: Psychological Sciences and Social Sciences, 75,* 377-388.

Finkel, D., Andel, R., & Pedersen, N.L. (2018). Gender differences in longitudinal trajectories of change in physical, social, and cognitive/sedentary leisure activities. *Journals of Gerontology B: Psychological Sciences and Social Sciences, 73,* 1491-1500.

Finkelstein, L.M., & Farrell, S.K. (2007). An expanded view of age bias in the workplace. In K.S. Shultz & G.A. Adams (Eds.), *Aging and work in the 21st century.* Mahwah, NJ: Erlbaum.

Fiore, J. (2020, in press). A systematic review of the dual process model of coping with bereavement. *Omega.*

Fiorilli, C., & others (2019). Predicting adolescent depression: The interrelated roles of self-esteem and interpersonal stressors. *Frontiers in Psychology, 10,* 565.

Fischhoff, B., de Bruin, W., Parker, A.M., Millstein, S.G., & Halpern-Felsher, B.L. (2010). Adolescents' perceived risk of dying. *Journal of Adolescent Health, 46,* 265-269.

Fisher, B.S., Cullen, F.T., & Turner, M.G. (2000). *The sexual victimization of college women.* Washington, DC: National Institute of Justice.

Fisher, G.G., & others (2014). Mental work demands, retirement, and longitudinal trajectories of cognitive functioning. *Journal of Occupational Health Psychology, 19,* 231-242.

Fisher, G.G., & others (2017). Cognitive functioning, aging, and work: A review and recommendations for research and practice. *Journal of Occupational Health Psychology, 22,* 314-336.

Fisher, H. (2020). Poverty and homelessness. In C. Grauf-Grounds & others (Eds.), *A practice beyond cultural humility,* New York: Routledge.

Fisher, H., & Garcia, J.R. (2019). SLOW LOVE: Courtship in the digital age. In R.J. Sternberg & K. Sternberg (Eds.), *The new psychology of love* (2nd ed.). New York: Cambridge University Press.

Fisher, K.R., Hirsh-Pasek, K., Newcombe, N., & Golinkoff, R.M. (2013). Taking shape: Supporting preschoolers' acquisition of geometric knowledge through guided play. *Child Development, 84*(6), 1872-1878.

Fisher, P.A. (2005, April). *Translational research on underlying mechanisms of risk among foster children: Implications for prevention science.* Paper presented at the meeting of the Society for Research in Child Development, Washington, DC.

Fiske, A., Wetherell, J.L., & Gatz, M. (2009). Depression in older adults. *Annual Review of Clinical Psychology* (Vol. 5). Palo Alto, CA: Annual Reviews.

Fiske, S. (2018). *Social cognition.* New York: Psychology Press.

Fitzpatrick, K.K. (2012). Developmental considerations when treating anorexia nervosa in adolescents and young adults. In J. Lock (Ed.), *Oxford handbook of child and adolescent eating disorders: Developmental perspectives.* New York: Oxford University Press.

Fivush, R., & Haden, C.A. (1997). Narrating and representing experience: Preschoolers' developing autobiographical accounts. In P. van den Broek, P.J. Bauer, & T. Bourg (Eds.), *Developmental spans in event representations and comprehension: Bridging fictional and actual events.* Mahwah, NJ: Erlbaum.

Flam, K.K., Sandler, I., Wolchik, S., & Tein, J.Y. (2016). Non-residential father-child involvement, interparental conflict, and mental health of children following divorce: A person-focused approach. *Journal of Youth and Adolescence, 45,* 581-593.

Flannigan, R., & Schlegel, P.N. (2017). Genetic diagnostics of male infertility in clinical practice. *Best Practice and Research: Clinical Obstetrics and Gynecology, 44,* 26-37.

Flavell, J.H. (2004). Theory-of-mind development: Retrospect and prospect. *Merrill-Palmer Quarterly, 50,* 274–290.

Flavell, J.H., Friedrichs, A., & Hoyt, J. (1970). Developmental changes in memorization processes. *Cognitive Psychology, 1,* 324–340.

Flavell, J.H., Green, F.L., & Flavell, E.R. (1993). Children's understanding of the stream of consciousness. *Child Development, 64,* 95–120.

Flavell, J.H., Green, F.L., & Flavell, E.R. (1998). The mind has a mind of its own: Developing knowledge about mental uncontrollability. *Cognitive Development, 13,* 127–138.

Flavell, J.H., Mumme, D., Green, F., and Flavell, E. (1992). Young children's understanding of different types of beliefs. *Child Development, 63,* 960–977.

Flegal, K.M., Kit, B.K., Orpana, H., & Graubard, B.I. (2013). Association of all-cause mortality with overweight and obesity using standard body mass index categories. *JAMA, 309,* 71–82.

Flensborg-Madsen, T., & Mortensen, E.L. (2017). Predictors of motor developmental milestones during the first year. *European Journal of Pediatrics, 176,* 109–119.

Flicek, P., & others (2013). Ensembl 2013. *Nucleic Acids Research, 41,* D48–D55.

Flieger, S.P., Chui, K., & Koch-Weser, S. (2020, in press). Lack of awareness and common misperceptions about palliative care among adults: Insights from a national survey. *Journal of General Internal Medicine.*

Flint, M.S., Baum, A., Chambers, W.H., & Jenkins, F.J. (2007). Induction of DNA damage, alteration of DNA repair, and transcriptional activation by stress hormones. *Psychoneuroendocrinology, 32,* 470–479.

Flitcroft, D., & Woods, K. (2018). What does research tell us about student motivation for test performance? *Pastoral Care in Education, 36,* 112–125.

Florsheim, P., Moore, D., & Edgington, C. (2003). Romantic relationships among pregnant and parenting adolescents. In P. Florsheim (Ed.), *Adolescent romantic relations and sexual behavior.* Mahwah, NJ: Erlbaum.

Flouri, E., Midouhas, E., & Joshi, H. (2014). Family poverty and trajectories of children's emotional and behavioral problems: The moderating role of self-regulation and verbal cognitive ability. *Journal of Abnormal Child Psychology, 42,* 1043–1056.

Flynn, J.R. (2007). The history of the American mind in the 20th century: A scenario to explain IQ gains over time and a case for the relevance of g. In P.C. Kyllonen, R.D. Roberts, & L. Stankov (Eds.), *Extending intelligence.* Mahwah, NJ: Erlbaum.

Flynn, J.R. (2013). *Are we getting smarter?* New York: Cambridge University Press.

Flynn, J.R. (2018). Reflections about intelligence over 40 years. *Intelligence, 70,* 73–83.

Flynn, J.R., & Shayer, M. (2018). IQ decline and Piaget: Does the rot start at the top? *Intelligence, 66,* 112–121.

Flynn, J.R., & Sternberg, R.J. (2019). Environment and intelligence. In R.J. Sternberg (Ed.), *Human intelligence.* New York: Cambridge University Press.

Fode, M., & others (2019). Late-onset hypogonadism and testosterone therapy—A summary of guidelines from the American Urological Association and the European Association of Urology. *European Urology Focus, 5,* 537–544.

Foerster, M., Henneke, A., Chetty-Mhlanga, S., & Röösli, M. (2019). Impact of adolescents' screen time and nocturnal mobile phone-related awakenings on sleep and general health symptoms: A prospective cohort study. *International Journal of Environmental Research and Public Health, 16,* 3.

Foley, P.B. (2019). Dopamine in psychiatry: A historical perspective. *Journal of Neural Transmission, 126,* 413–419.

Follari, L. (2019). *Foundations and best practices in early childhood education* (4th ed.). Upper Saddle River, NJ: Pearson.

Fonseca-Machado Mde, O., & others (2015). Depressive disorder in Latin women: Does intimate partner violence matter? *Journal of Clinical Nursing, 24,* 1289–1299.

Font, S.A., & Cage, J. (2018). Dimensions of physical punishment and their associations with children's cognitive performance and school adjustment. *Child Abuse and Neglect, 75,* 29–40.

Font, S.A., & Maguire-Jack, K. (2020). It's not "just poverty": Educational, social, and economic functioning among young adults exposed to childhood neglect, abuse, and poverty. *Child Abuse and Neglect, 101,* 104356.

Fontenot, K., Semega, J., & Kollar, M. (2018, September 18). *Income and poverty in the United States: 2017.* Washington, DC: U.S. Census Bureau.

Foody, M., Samara, M., & O'Higgins Norman, J. (2020, in press). Bullying by siblings and peers: Poly-setting victimization and the association with problem behaviors and depression. *British Journal of Educational Psychology.*

Forbes, J.M., & Thorburn, D.R. (2018). Mitochondrial dysfunction in diabetic kidney disease. *Nature Reviews. Nephrology, 14,* 291–312.

Ford, D.Y. (2016). Black and Hispanic students. In L. Corno & E.M. Anderman (Eds.), *Handbook of educational psychology* (3rd ed.). New York: Routledge.

Forte, R., & others (2013). Executive function moderates the role of muscular fitness in determining functional mobility in older adults. *Aging: Clinical and Experimental Research, 25,* 291–298.

Fosco, G.M., Stormshak, E.A., Dishion, T.J., & Winter, C. (2012). Family relationships and parental monitoring during middle school as predictors of early adolescent problem behavior. *Journal of Clinical Child and Adolescent Psychology, 41,* 202213.

Foubert, J.D., Clark-Taylor, A., & Wall, A.F. (2020). Is campus rape primarily a serial or one-time problem? Evidence from a multicampus study. *Violence Against Women, 26*(3–4), 296–311.

Fougere, B., & Cesari, M. (2019). Prevention of frailty. In R. Fernandez-Ballesteros & others (Eds.), *Cambridge handbook of successful aging.* New York: Cambridge University Press.

Foulkes, L., McMillan, D., & Gregory, A.M. (2019). A bad night's sleep on campus: An interview study of first-year university students with poor sleep quality. *Sleep Health, 5*(3), 280–287.

Fouts, H.N., & Bader, L.R. (2017). Transitions in siblinghood: Integrating developments, cultural, and evolutionary perspectives. In D. Narváez & others (Eds.), *Contexts for young child flourishing.* New York: Oxford University Press.

Fowler, C.G., & Leigh-Paffenroth, W.B. (2007). Hearing. In J.E. Birren (Ed.), *Encyclopedia of gerontology* (2nd ed.). San Diego: Academic Press.

Fox, M.K., Pac, S., Devancy, B., & Jankowski, L. (2004). Feeding infants and toddlers study: What foods are infants and toddlers eating? *American Dietetic Association Journal, 104*(Suppl.), S22–S30.

Fox, M.K., & others (2010). Food consumption patterns of young preschoolers: Are they starting off on the right path? *Journal of the American Dietetic Association, 110*(Suppl. 12), S52–S59.

Fox, S. (2020). Linking metrics to objectives: retirement saving, spending, and active management. *Journal of Retirement, 7*(3), 6–29.

Fozard, J.L. (1992, December 6). Commentary in "We can age successfully." *Parade Magazine,* pp. 14–15.

Fragkiadaki, P., & others (2020). Telomere length and telomerase activity in osteoporosis and osteoarthritis. *Experimental and Therapeutic Medicine, 19,* 1626–1632.

Fraley, R.C. (2019). Attachment in adulthood: Recent developments, emerging debates, and future directions. *Annual Review of Psychology* (Vol. 70). Palo Alto, CA: Annual Reviews.

Fraley, R.C., Roisman, G.I., Booth-LaForce, C., Owen, M.T., & Holland, A.S. (2013). Interpersonal and genetic origins of adult attachment styles: A longitudinal study from infancy to early adulthood. *Journal of Personality and Social Psychology, 104,* 817–838.

Fraley, R.C., & Shaver, P.R. (2020, in press). Attachment theory and its place in contemporary personality theory and research. In R.W. Robins & O. John (Eds.), *Handbook of personality: theory and research* (4th ed.). New York: Guilford.

Franchini, M., & others (2019). Infants at risk for autism spectrum disorder: Frequency, quality, and variety of joint attention behaviors. *Journal of Abnormal Child Psychology, 47,* 907–920.

Francis, J., Fraser, G., & Marcia, J.E. (1989). *Cognitive and experimental factors in moratorium-achievement-moratorium-achievement (MAMA) cycles.* Unpublished manuscript, Department of Psychology, Simon Fraser University, Burnaby, British Columbia.

Franke, T., & others (2013). The secrets of highly active older adults. *Journal of Aging Studies, 27,* 398–409.

Frankl, V. (1984). *Man's search for meaning.* New York: Basic Books.

Franklin, Z.C., Wright, D.J., & Holmes, P.S. (2020, in press). Using action-congruent language facilitates the motor responses during action observation: A combined transcranial magnetic stimulation and eye-tracking study. *Journal of Cognitive Neuroscience.*

Fransson, M., & others (2016). Is middle childhood attachment related to social functioning in young adulthood? *Scandinavian Journal of Psychology, 57,* 108–116.

Franz, C.E. (1996). The implications of preschool tempo and motoric activity level for personality decades later. Reported in A. Caspi, *Personality development across the life course.* In W. Damon (Ed.), *Handbook of child psychology* (Vol. 3). New York: Wiley.

Freberg, L.A. (2019). *Discovering behavioral neuroscience* (4th ed.). Boston: Cengage.

Frederikse, M., & others (2000). Sex differences in inferior lobule volume in schizophrenia. *American Journal of Psychiatry, 157,* 422–427.

Frederiksen, H., & others (2020, in press). Sex-specific estrogen levels and reference intervals from infancy to late adulthood determined by LC-MS/MS. *Journal of Endocrinology and Metabolism.*

Freeman, S., & others (2020). *Biological science* (7th ed.). Upper Saddle River, NJ: Pearson.

Frega, M., & others (2020). Distinct pathogenic genes causing intellectual disability and autism exhibit a common neuronal network hyperactivity phenotype. *Cell Reports, 30,* 173–186.

Freud, S. (1917). *A general introduction to psychoanalysis.* New York: Washington Square Press.

Freund, A.M., & Blanchard-Fields, F. (2014). Age-related differences in altruism across adulthood: Making personal financial gain versus contributing to the public good. *Developmental Psychology, 50*(4), 1125–1136.

Frey, W.H. (2007). *Mapping the growth of older America: Seniors and boomers in the early 21st century.* Washington, DC: The Brookings Institution.

Freytag, J., & others (2020, in press). Empowering older adults to discuss advance care planning during clinical visits: The PREPARE randomized trial. *Journal of the American Geriatrics Society.*

Frick, M.A., & others (2018). The role of sustained attention, maternal sensitivity, and infant temperament in the development of early self-regulation. *British Journal of Psychology, 109,* 277–298.

Friedenson, B. (2020, in press). A genome model to explain major features of neurodevelopmental disorders in newborns. *Biomedical Informatics Insights.*

Friedman, D., Nessler, D., Johnson, R., Ritter, W., & Bersick, M. (2008). Age-related changes in executive function: An event-related potential (ERP) investigation of task-switching. *Aging, Neuropsychology, and Cognition, 15,* 95–128.

Friedman, J. (2013). *Twin separation.* Retrieved February 14, 2013, from http://christinabaglivitinglof.com/twin-pregnancy/six-twin-experts-tell-all

Friedman, N.P., & others (2009). Individual differences in childhood sleep problems predict later cognitive control. *Sleep, 32,* 323–333.

Friedman, S.L., Melhuish, E., & Hill, C. (2010). Childcare research at the dawn of a new millennium: An update. In G. Bremner & T. Wachs (Eds.), *Wiley-Blackwell handbook of infant development* (2nd ed.). Oxford, UK: Wiley-Blackwell.

Friend, M., & Bursuck, W.D. (2019). *Including students with special needs* (8th ed.). Upper Saddle River, NJ: Pearson.

Friend, M., & others (2019). Language status at age 3: Group and individual prediction from vocabulary comprehension in the second year. *Developmental Psychology, 55,* 9–22.

Friesen, P. (2020). Medically assisted dying and suicide: How are they different, and how are they similar? *Hastings Center Report, 50,* 32–43.

Froggatt, S., Covey, J., & Reissland, N. (2020, in press). Infant neurobehavioral consequences of prenatal cigarette exposure: A systematic review and meta-analysis. *Acta Pediatrica.*

Frost, D.M. (2011). Stigma and intimacy in same-sex relationships: A narrative approach. *Journal of Family Psychology, 25,* 1–10.

Fry, C.L. (2007). Comparative and cross-cultural studies. In J.E. Birren (Ed.), *Encyclopedia of gerontology* (2nd ed.). San Diego: Academic Press.

Fry, R. (2016, May 14). *For first time in modern era, living with parents edges out other living arrangements for 18- to 34-year-olds.* Washington, DC: Pew Research Center.

Fry, R., & Parker, K. (2018, November 15). *Early benchmarks show 'post-millennials' on track to be most diverse, best-educated generation yet.* Washington, DC: Pew Research Center.

Frydenberg, E. (2019). *Adolescent coping* (3rd ed.). New York: Routledge.

Frydenberg, E., Deans, J., & Liang, R. (2020). *Promoting well-being in the pre-school years.* New York: Routledge.

Fuhrmann, D., & others (2019). The neurocognitive correlates of academic diligence in adolescent girls. *Cognitive Neuroscience, 10,* 88–89.

Fuhs, M.W., Nesbitt, K.T., Farran, D.C., & Dong, N. (2014). Longitudinal associations between executive functioning and academic skills across content areas. *Developmental Psychology, 50,* 1698–1709.

Fujisawa, D., & others (2010). Prevalence and determinants of complicated grief in general population. *Journal of Affective Disorders, 127,* 352–358.

Fujishiro, K., & others (2019). The role of occupation in explaining cognitive functioning in later life: Education and occupational complexity in a U.S. national sample of Black and White men and women. *Journals of Gerontology B: Psychological Sciences and Social Sciences, 74,* 1189–1199.

Fulop, T., & others (2019). From inflammaging to immunosenescence. In R. Fernandez-Ballesteros & others (Eds.), *Cambridge handbook of successful aging.* New York: Cambridge University Press.

Furman, E. (2005). *Boomerang nation.* New York: Fireside.

Furman, W. (2018). The romantic relationships of youth. In W.M. Bukowski & others (Eds.), *Handbook of peer interactions, relationships, and groups* (2nd ed.). New York: Guilford.

Furman, W., Low, S., & Ho, M.J. (2009). Romantic experience and psychosocial adjustment in middle adolescence. *Journal of Clinical Child and Adolescent Psychology, 38,* 75–90.

Furstenberg, F.F. (2007). The future of marriage. In A.S. Skolnick & J.H. Skolnick (Eds.), *Family in transition* (14th ed.). Boston: Allyn & Bacon.

Furth, H.G., & Wachs, H. (1975). *Thinking goes to school.* New York: Oxford University Press.

Furthner, D., & others (2018). Education, school type, and screen time were associated with overweight and obesity in 2,930 adolescents. *Acta Pediatrica, 107,* 517–522.

G

Gabrian, M., Dutt, A.J., & Wahl, H.W. (2017). Subjective time perceptions and aging well: A review of concepts and empirical research-A mini-review. *Gerontology, 63,* 350–358.

Gabrielli, A.P., Manzardo, A.M., & Butler, M.G. (2019). GeneAnalytics pathways and profiling of shared autism and cancer genes. *International Journal of Molecular Sciences, 20,* 5.

Gaetz, W., & others (2020, in press). Evaluating motor cortical oscillations and age-related changes in autism spectrum disorder. *NeuroImage.*

Gaillardin, F., & Baudry, S. (2018). Influence on working memory and executive function on stair ascent and descent in young and older adults. *Experimental Gerontology, 106,* 74–79.

Gaines, J.M., Burke, K.L., Marx, K.A., Wagner, M., & Parrish, J.M. (2011). Enhancing older driver safety: A driving survey and evaluation of the CarFit program. *Journal of Safety Research, 42,* 351–358.

Gainotti, G. (2019). A historical review of investigations on laterality of emotions in the human brain. *Journal of the History of the Neurosciences, 28,* 23–41.

Galambos, N.L., Howard, A.L., & Maggs, J.L. (2011). Rise and fall of sleep quality with student experiences across the first year of the university. *Journal of Research on Adolescence, 21,* 342–349.

Galbally, M., Lewis, A.J., IJzendoorn, M., & Permezel, M. (2011). The role of oxytocin in mother-infant relations: A systematic review of human studies. *Harvard Review of Psychiatry, 19,* 1–14.

Gale, C.R., Booth, T., Mottus, R., Kuh, D., & Deary, J.J. (2013). Neuroticism and extraversion in youth predict mental well-being and life satisfaction 40 years later. *Journal of Research in Personality, 47,* 687–697.

Galinsky, A.M., & Sonenstein, F.L. (2013). Relationship commitment, perceived equity, and sexual enjoyment among young adults in the United States. *Archives of Sexual Behavior, 42,* 93–104.

Galinsky, E. (2010). *Mind in the making.* New York: Harper Collins.

Galinsky, E., & David, J. (1988). *The preschool years: Family strategies that work—from experts and parents.* New York: Times Books.

Galland, B.C., Taylor, B.J., Edler, D.E., & Herbison, P. (2012). Normal sleep patterns in infants and children: A systematic review of observational studies. *Sleep Medicine Review, 16,* 213–222.

Gallant, S.N. (2016). Mindfulness meditation practice and executive functioning: Breaking down the benefit. *Consciousness and Cognition, 40,* 116–130.

Galler, J.R., & others (2012). Infant malnutrition is associated with persisting attention deficits in middle childhood. *Journal of Nutrition, 142,* 788-794.

Gallo, R.B.S., & others (2018). Sequential application of non-pharmacological interventions reduces the severity of labor pain, delays use of pharmacological analgesia, and improves some obstetrics outcomes: A randomized trial. *Journal of Physiotherapy, 64,* 33-40.

Galloway, J.C., & Thelen, E. (2004). Feet first: Object exploration in young infants. *Infant Behavior & Development, 27,* 107-112.

Gallup (2015, May 21). *Americans greatly overstate percent gay, lesbian in U.S.* Washington, DC: Gallup.

Gallup, G.W., & Bezilla, R. (1992). *The religious life of young Americans.* Princeton, NJ: Gallup Institute.

Gamino, L.A., & Sewell, K.W. (2004). Meaning constructs as predictors of bereavement adjustment: A report from the Scott & White grief study. *Death Studies, 28,* 397-421.

Gampe, A., Wermelinger, S., & Daum, M.M. (2019). Bilingual children adapt to the needs of their communication partners, monolinguals do not. *Child Development, 90,* 98-107.

Ganley, C.M., Vasilyeva, M., & Dulaney, A. (2014). Spatial ability mediates the gender difference in middle school students' science performance. *Child Development, 85,* 1419-1432.

Ganong, L., & Coleman, M. (2018). Studying stepfamilies: Four eras of scholarship. *Family Process, 57,* 7-24.

Ganong, L., Coleman, M., & Sanner, C. (2018). Stepfamilies. In M.H. Bornstein (Ed.), *SAGE encyclopedia of lifespan human development.* Thousand Oaks, CA: Sage.

Ganong, L., Coleman, M., & Sanner, C. (2019). Divorced and remarried parenting. In M.H. Bornstein (Ed.), *Handbook of parenting* (3rd ed.). New York: Routledge.

Ganong, L., & others (2019). Stepfathers' affinity-seeking with stepchildren, stepfather-stepchild relationship quality, marital quality, and stepfamily cohesion among stepfathers and mothers. *Journal of Family Psychology, 33,* 521-531.

Ganong, L., & others (2020, in press). Stepparents' attachment orientation, parental gatekeeping, and stepparents' affinity-seeking with stepchildren. *Family Process.*

Gao, C., & others (2019). The neural sources of N170: Understanding timing of activation in face-selective areas. *Psychophysiology, 58*(6), e13336.

Gao, G. (2001). Intimacy, passion, and commitment in Chinese and U.S. American romantic relationships. *International Journal of Intercultural Relations, 25,* 329-342.

Gao, G. (2016). Cross-cultural romantic relationships. *Oxford research encyclopedia of romantic relationships.* New York: Oxford University Press.

Gao, M.M., & others (2019). Marital conflict behaviors and parenting: Dyadic links over time. *Family Relations, 68,* 135-149.

Garbarino, J., Governale, A., & Kostelny, K. (2019). Parenting and public policy. In M.H. Bornstein (Ed.), *Handbook of parenting.* New York: Routledge.

Garcia, O.F., Lopez-Fernandez, O., & Serra, E. (2020, in press). Raising Spanish children with an antisocial tendency: Do we know what the optimal parenting style is? *Journal of Interpersonal Violence.*

Garcia, W.J., & others (2019). Exercise and low back pain in the older adult: Current recommendations. *Journal of Allied Health, 48,* 302-307.

Garcia-Gomariz, C., & others (2018). Effects of 2 years of endurance and high-impact training on preventing osteoporosis in postmenopausal women: Randomized clinical trial. *Menopause, 25,* 301-306.

Garcia-Hermoso, A., Saavedra, J.M., & Escalante, Y. (2013). Effects of exercise on resting blood pressure in obese children: A meta-analysis of randomized controlled trials. *Obesity Reviews, 14*(11), 919-928.

Garcini, L.M., & others (2020a). Miles over mind: Transnational death and its association with psychological distress among undocumented Mexican immigrants. *Death Studies, 44,* 35-75.

Garcini, L.M., & others (2020b, in press). Bereavement among widowed Latinos in the United States: A systematic review of methodology and findings. *Death Studies.*

Gardner, A.A., & Lambert, C.A. (2019). Examining the interplay of self-esteem, trait-emotional intelligence, and age with depression across adolescence. *Journal of Adolescence, 71,* 162-166.

Gardner, H. (1983). *Frames of mind.* New York: Basic Books.

Gardner, H. (1993). *Multiple intelligences.* New York: Basic Books.

Gardner, H. (2002). The pursuit of excellence through education. In M. Ferrari (Ed.), *Learning from extraordinary minds.* Mahwah, NJ: Erlbaum.

Gardner, H. (2016). Multiple intelligences: Prelude, theory, and aftermath. In R.J. Sternberg, S.T. Fiske, & J. Foss (Eds.), *Scientists making a difference.* New York: Cambridge University Press.

Gardner, H., Kornhaber, W., & Chen, J-Q. (2018). The theory of multiple intelligences: Psychological and educational perspectives. In R.J. Sternberg (Ed.), *The nature of human intelligence.* New York: Cambridge University Press.

Gardosi, J., & others (2013). Maternal and fetal risk factors for stillbirth: Population-based study. *British Medical Journal, 346,* f108.

Gareri, P., & others (2017). The Citicholinage study: Citicoline plus cholinesterase inhibitors in aged patients affected with Alzheimer's disease study. *Journal of Alzheimer's Disease, 56,* 557-565.

Garfield, C.F., & others (2012). Trends in attention deficit hyperactivity disorder ambulatory diagnosis and medical treatment in the United States, 2000-2010. *Academic Pediatrics, 12,* 110-116.

Gariepy, G., & others (2017). Early-life family income and subjective well-being in adolescents. *PLoS One, 12*(7), e0179380.

Garnham, A. (2019). Pragmatics and inference. In S-A. Rueschemeyer & M. Gareth Gaskell (Eds.), *Oxford handbook of psycholinguistics* (2nd ed.). New York: Oxford University Press.

Garon, N., Smith, I.M., & Bryson, S.E. (2018). Early executive dysfunction in ASD: Simple versus complex skills. *Autism Research, 11,* 318-330.

Garthe, A., Roeder, I., & Kempermann, G. (2016). Mice in an enriched environment learn more flexibly because of adult hippocampal neurogenesis, *26,* 261-271.

Gartstein, M.A., & Hancock, G.R. (2019). Temperamental growth in infancy: Demographic, maternal symptom, and stress contributions to overarching and fine-grained dimensions. *Merrill-Palmer Quarterly, 65*(2), 1.

Gartstein, M.A., Hancock, G.R., & Iverson, S.L. (2018). Positive affectivity and fear trajectories in infancy: Contributions of mother-child interaction factors. *Child Development, 89*(5), 1519-1534.

Garvey, C. (2000). *Play* (enlarged ed.). Cambridge, MA: Harvard University Press.

Gaskins, S. (2016). Childhood practices across cultures: Play and household work. In L.J. Arnett (Ed.), *Oxford handbook of human development and culture.* New York: Oxford University Press.

Gasperi, M., & others (2019). Genetic and environmental influences on urinary conditions in men: A classical twin study. *Urology, 129,* 54-59.

Gates, C.J. (2011). *How many people are lesbian, gay, bisexual, and transgender?* Los Angeles: Williams Institute, UCLA.

Gates, G.J. (2013, February). *LGBT parenting in the United States.* Los Angeles: The Williams Institute, UCLA.

Gates, W. (1998, July 20). Charity begins when I'm ready (interview). *Fortune.*

Gatzke-Kopp, L.M., & others (2019). Magnitude and chronicity of environmental smoke exposure across infancy and early childhood in a sample of low-income children. *Nicotine and Tobacco Research, 21,* 1665-1672.

Gauvain, M. (2016). Peer contributions to cognitive development. In K. Wentzel & G.B. Ramani (Eds.), *Handbook of social influences in school contexts.* New York: Routledge.

Gauvain, M., & Perez, S. (2015). Cognitive development in the context of culture. In R.M. Lerner (Ed.), *Handbook of child psychology and developmental science* (7th ed.). New York: Wiley.

Gee, C.L., & Heyman, G.D. (2007). Children's evaluations of other people's self-descriptions. *Social Development, 16,* 800-818.

Geiger, A.W., & Livingston, G. (2019). *8 facts about love and marriage in America.* Washington, DC: Pew Research.

Gekle, M. (2017). Kidney and aging—A narrative review. *Experimental Gerontology, 87*(Pt. B), 153-155.

Gelman, R. (1969). Conservation acquisition: A problem of learning to attend to relevant attributes. *Journal of Experimental Child Psychology, 7,* 67-87.

Gelman, S.A. (2009). Learning from others: Children's construction of concepts. *Annual Review of Psychology, 60,* 115-140.

Gelman, S.A., & Kalish, C.W. (2006). Conceptual development. In W. Damon & R. Lerner (Eds.), *Handbook of child psychology* (6th ed.). New York: Wiley.

Genc, S., & others (2018). Age, sex, and puberty related development of the corpus callosum: A multi-technique diffusion MRI study. *Brain Structure and Function, 223,* 2753-2765.

Genesee, F., & Lindholm-Leary, K. (2012). The education of English language learners. In K. Harris, S. Graham, & T. Urdan (Eds.), *APA educational psychology handbook.* Washington, DC: American Psychological Association.

Genetti, C. (Ed.) (2019). *How languages work* (2nd ed.). New York: Cambridge University Press.

Gennetian, L.A., & Miller, C. (2002). Children and welfare reform: A view from an experimental welfare reform program in Minnesota. *Child Development, 73,* 601-620.

Gentile, D.A. (2011). The multiple dimensions of video game effects. *Child Development Perspectives, 5,* 75-81.

Gentile, D.A., & others (2014). Protective effects of parental monitoring of children's media use: A prospective study. *JAMA Pediatrics, 168,* 479-484.

Gentilleau-Lambin, P., & others (2019). Assessment of conversational pragmatics: A screening tool for pragmatic language impairment in a control population of children aged 6-12 years. *Archives de Pediatrie, 26,* 214-219.

George, L.G., Helson, R., & John, O.P. (2011). The "CEO" of women's work lives: How Big Five conscientiousness, extraversion, and openness predict 50 years of work experiences in a changing sociocultural context. *Journal of Personality and Social Psychology, 101,* 812-830.

George, L.K., & Ferraro, K.F. (2016). Aging and the social sciences: Progress and prospects. In L.K. George & K.F. Ferraro (Eds.), *Handbook of aging and the social sciences* (8th ed.). New York: Elsevier.

George Dalmida, S., & others (2018). Sexual risk behaviors of African American adolescent females: The role of cognitive and religious factors. *Journal of Transcultural Nursing, 29,* 74-83.

Gergely, A., & others (2019). Auditory-visual matching of conspecifics and non-conspecifics by dogs and human infants. *Animals, 9*(1), E17.

Gerhardt, M., & others (2020, in press). A naturalistic study of parental emotion socialization: Unique contribution of fathers. *Journal of Family Psychology.*

Gernhardt, A., Keller, H., & Rubeling, H. (2016). Children's family drawings as expressions of attachment representations across cultures: Possibilities and limitations. *Child Development, 87,* 1069-1078.

Geronimi, E.M.C., Arellano, B., & Woodruff-Borden, J. (2019). Relating mindfulness and executive function in children. *Clinical Child Psychology and Psychiatry.* doi:10.1177/1359104519833737.

Gershoff, E.T. (2013). Spanking and development: We know enough now to stop hitting our children. *Child Development Perspectives, 7,* 133-137.

Gershoff, E.T., & Grogan-Kaylor, A. (2016). Spanking and child outcomes: Old controversies and new meta-analyses. *Journal of Family Psychology, 30,* 453-469.

Gershoff, E.T., & others. (2012). Longitudinal links between spanking and children's externalizing behaviors in a national sample of White, Black, Hispanic, and Asian American families. *Child Development, 83,* 838-843.

Gershoff, E.T., & others (2018). The strength of the causal evidence against physical punishment of children and its implications for parents, psychologists, and policymakers. *American Psychologist, 73,* 628-638.

Gershoff, E.T., & others (2019). There is still no evidence that physical punishment is effective or beneficial: Reply to Larzelere, Gunnoe, Ferguson, and Robers (2019) and Rohner and Melendez-Rhodes (2019). *American Psychologist, 74,* 503-505.

Gerstorf, D., & others (2015). Secular changes in late-life cognition and well-being: Towards a long bright future with a short brisk ending. *Psychology and Aging, 30,* 301-310.

Gesell, A.L. (1934). *Infancy and human growth.* New York: Macmillan.

Gewirtz, J. (1977). Maternal responding and the conditioning of infant crying: Directions of influence within the attachment-acquisition process. In B.C. Etzel, J.M. LeBlanc, & D.M. Baer (Eds.), *New developments in behavioral research.* Hillsdale, NJ: Erlbaum.

Gewirtz-Meydan, A., & Ayalon, L. (2019). Why do older adults have sex? Approach and avoidance sexual motives among older women and men. *Journal of Sexual Research, 56*(7), 870-881.

Gharipour, M., & others (2019). Cardiovascular disease risk assessment: Triglyceride/high-density lipoprotein versus metabolic syndrome criteria. *Journal of Research in Health Sciences, 19,* e00442.

Ghesquiere, A., & others (2020, in press). Investigating associations between pain and complicated grief symptoms in Japanese older adults. *Aging and Mental Health.*

Ghetti, S., & Alexander, K.W. (2004). "If it happened, I would remember it": Strategic use of event memorability in the rejection of false autobiographical events. *Child Development, 75,* 542-561.

Gialamas, A., & others (2014). Quality of childcare influences children's attentiveness and emotional regulation at school entry. *Journal of Pediatrics, 165,* 813-819.

Giarrusso, R., & Bengtson, V.L. (2007). Self-esteem. In J.E. Birren (ed.), *Encyclopedia of gerontology* (2nd ed.). San Diego: Academic Press.

Gibbs, J.C. (2019). *Moral development and reality: Beyond the theories of Kohlberg, Hoffman, & Haidt.* New York: Oxford University Press.

Gibson, E.J. (1969). *Principles of perceptual learning and development.* New York: Appleton-Century-Crofts.

Gibson, E.J. (1989). Exploratory behavior in the development of perceiving, acting, and the acquiring of knowledge. *Annual Review of Psychology* (Vol. 39). Palo Alto, CA: Annual Reviews.

Gibson, E.J. (2001). *Perceiving the affordances.* Mahwah, NJ: Erlbaum.

Gibson, E.J., & Walk, R.D. (1960). The "visual cliff." *Scientific American, 202,* 64-71.

Gibson, E.J., & others (1987). Detection of the traversability of surfaces by crawling and walking infants. *Journal of Experimental Psychology: Human Perception and Performance, 13,* 533-544.

Gibson, J.J. (1966). *The senses considered as perceptual systems.* Boston: Houghton Mifflin.

Gibson, J.J. (1979). *The ecological approach to visual perception.* Boston: Houghton Mifflin.

Giedd, J.N. (2012). The digital revolution and the adolescent brain. *Journal of Adolescent Health, 51,* 101-105.

Gilkerson, J., & others (2018). Language experience in the second year of life and language outcomes in late childhood. *Pediatrics, 142*(4), e20174276.

Gill, B.K., & others (2020). Non-pharmacological depression therapies for older Chinese adults: A systematic review and meta-analysis. *Acta Gerontology and Geriatrics, 88,* 104537.

Gillain, D., & others (2019). Gerontechnologies and successful aging. In R. Fernandez-Ballesteros & others (Eds.), *Cambridge handbook of successful aging.* New York: Cambridge University Press.

Gillen-O'Neel, C., Huynh, V.W., & Fuligni, A.J. (2013). To study or to sleep? The academic costs of extra studying at the expense of sleep. *Child Development, 84*(1), 133-142.

Gillig, P.M., & Sanders, R.D. (2011). Higher cortical functions: Attention and vigilance. *Innovations in Clinical Neuroscience, 8,* 43-46.

Gilligan, C. (1982). *In a different voice.* Cambridge, MA: Harvard University Press.

Gilligan, C. (1992, May). *Joining the resistance: Girls' development in adolescence.* Paper presented at the symposium on development and vulnerability in close relationships, Montreal, Quebec.

Gilligan, C. (1996). The centrality of relationships in psychological development: A puzzle, some evidence, and a theory. In G.G. Noam & K.W. Fischer (Eds.), *Development and vulnerability in close relationships.* Hillsdale, NJ: Erlbaum.

Gilligan, L.A., & others (2020, in press). Fetal magnetic resonance imaging of skeletal dysplasias. *Pediatric Radiology.*

Gillis, B.T., & El-Sheikh, M. (2019). Sleep and adjustment in adolescence: Physical activity as a moderator of risk. *Sleep Health, 5,* 266-272.

Gimovsky, A.C., & others (2020, in press). Genetic abnormalities seen on CVS in early pregnancy failure. *Journal of Maternal-Fetal and Neonatal Medicine.*

Girgis, F., & others (2018). Toward a neuroscience of adult cognitive development. *Frontiers of Neuroscience, 12,* 4.

Girls Inc (2020). *Preventing adolescent pregnancy.* New York: Girls Inc.

Girme, Y.U., & others (2020, in press). Infants' attachment insecurity predicts attachment-relevant emotion regulation strategies in adulthood. *Emotion.*

Glabska, D., & others (2019). The National After-School Athletics Program participation as a tool to reduce the risk of obesity in adolescents after one year of intervention: A nationwide study. *International Journal of Environmental Research and Public Health, 16,* 3.

Glaveanu, V.P., & others (2020, in press). Advancing creativity theory and research: A sociocultural manifesto. *Journal of Creative Behavior.*

Glover, J., & Fritsch, S.L. (2018). #KidsAnxiety and social media; A review. *Child and Adolescent Psychiatry Clinics of North America, 27,* 171–182.

Gnambs, T., & Appel, M. (2018). Narcissism and social networking behavior: A meta-analysis. *Journal of Personality, 86,* 200–212.

Gobinath, A.R., & others (2018). Voluntary running influences the efficacy of fluoxetine in a model of postpartum depression. *Neuropharmacology, 128,* 106–128.

Gockley, A.A., & others (2016). The effect of adolescence and advanced maternal age on the incidence of partial molar pregnancy. *Gynecology and Oncology, 140,* 470–473.

Goddings, A-L., & Mills, K. (2017). *Adolescence and the brain.* New York: Psychology Press.

Goetter, E., & others (2019). The five-factor model in bereaved adults with and without complicated grief. *Death Studies, 43,* 204–209.

Goh, S.K.Y., & others (2017). Infant night sleep trajectory from age 3–24 months: Evidence from the Singapore GUSTO study. *Sleep Medicine, 33,* 82–84.

Goksan, S., & others (2015). fMRI reveals neural activity overlap between adult and infant pain. *eLife, 4,* e06356.

Gold, D. (2011). Death and dying. In R.H. Binstock & L.K. George (Eds.), *Handbook of aging and the social sciences* (7th ed.). New York: Elsevier.

Goldberg, A.E., & Allen, K.R. (Eds.) (2020). *LGBTQ-parent families: Possibilities for new research and implications for practice* (2nd ed.). New York: Springer.

Goldberg, W.A., & Lucas-Thompson, R. (2008). Maternal and paternal employment, effects of. In M.M. Haith & J.B. Benson (Eds.), *Encyclopedia of infant and early childhood development.* Oxford, UK: Elsevier.

Goldfield, G.S. (2012). Making access to TV contingent on physical activity: Effects on liking and relative reinforcing value of TV and physical activity in overweight and obese children. *Journal of Behavioral Medicine, 35,* 1–7.

Goldin-Meadow, S. (2017a). Using our hands to change our minds. *Wiley Interdisciplinary Reviews. Cognitive Science, 8,* 1–2.

Goldin-Meadow, S. (2017b). What the hands can tell us about language emergence. *Psychonomic Bulletin & Review, 24,* 213–218.

Goldschmidt, L., Richardson, G.A., Willford, J., & Day, N.L. (2008). Prenatal marijuana exposure and intelligence test performance at age 6. *Journal of the American Academy of Child and Adolescent Psychiatry, 47,* 254–263.

Goldsen, J., & others (2017). Who says I do: The changing context of marriage and health and quality of life for LGBT older adults. *Gerontologist, 57*(Suppl. 1), S50–S62.

Goldsmith, H.H. (2019). Everything develops during emotional development. In A.S. Fox & others (Eds.), *The nature of emotion* (2nd ed.). New York: Oxford University Press.

Goldstein, E.B. (2019). *Cognitive psychology* (5th ed.). Boston: Cengage.

Goldstein, M.H., King, A.P., & West, M.J. (2003). Social interaction shapes babbling: Testing parallels between birdsong and speech. *Proceedings of the National Academy of Sciences, 100*(13), 8030–8035.

Goldston, D.B., & others (2008). Cultural considerations in adolescent suicide prevention and psychosocial treatment. *American Psychologist, 63,* 14–31.

Golinkoff, R.M., Can, D.D., Soderstrom, M., & Hirsh-Pasek, K. (2015). (Baby) talk to me: The social context of infant-directed speech and its effect on early language acquisition. *Current Directions in Psychological Science, 24,* 339–344.

Golinkoff, R.M., & Hirsh-Pasek, K.H. (2000). *How babies talk.* New York: Plume.

Gollihue, J.L., & Norris, C.M. (2020, in press). Astrocyte mitochondria: Central players and potential therapeutic targets for neurodegenerative diseases and injury. *Aging Research Reviews.*

Gollnick, D.M., & Chinn, P.C. (2021). *Multicultural education in a pluralistic society* (11th ed.). New York: Pearson.

Golombok, S. (2011a). Children in new family forms. In R. Gross (Ed.), *Psychology* (6th ed.). London: Hodder Education.

Golombok, S. (2011b). Why I study lesbian families. In S. Ellis, V. Clarke, E. Peel, & D. Riggs (Eds.), *LGBTQ psychologies.* New York: Cambridge University Press.

Golombok, S. (2017). Disclosure and donor-conceived children. *Human Reproduction, 32,* 1532–1536.

Golombok, S., & Tasker, F. (2010). Gay fathers. In M.E. Lamb (Ed.), *The role of the father in child development* (5th ed.). New York: Wiley.

Golombok, S., & others (2014). Adoptive gay father families: Parent-child relationships and children's psychological adjustment. *Child Development, 85,* 456–468.

Gomez, S.H., & others (2017). Are there sensitive periods when child maltreatment substantially elevates suicide risk? Results from a nationally representative sample of adolescents. *Depression and Anxiety, 34,* 734–741.

Gomez-Pinilla, F., & Hillman, C. (2013). The influence of exercise on cognitive abilities. *Comprehensive Physiology, 3,* 403–428.

Gomides, A.P.M., & others (2020). Rheumatoid arthritis treatment in Brazil: Data from a large real-life multicenter study. *Advances in Rheumatology, 60*(1), 16.

Goncu, A., & Gauvain, M. (2012). Sociocultural approaches in educational psychology. In K.H. Harris, S. Graham, & T. Urdan (Eds.), *APA educational psychology handbook.* Washington, DC: American Psychological Association.

Gong, X., & Freund, A.M. (2020, in press). It is what you have, not what you lose: Effects of perceived gains and losses on goal orientation across adulthood. *Journals of Gerontology B: Psychological Sciences and Social Sciences.*

Gonzales-Ruis, K., & others (2017). The effects of exercise on abdominal fat and liver enzymes in pediatric obesity: A systematic review and meta-analysis. *Child Obesity, 13,* 272–282.

Gonzalez, A., Atkinson, L., & Fleming, A.S. (2009). Attachment and the comparative psychobiology of mothering. In M. de Haan & M.R. Gunnar (Eds.), *Developmental social neuroscience.* New York: Guilford.

Gonzalez, S.L., Alvarez, V., & Nelson, E.L. (2019). Do gross and fine motor skills differentially contribute to language outcomes? A systematic review. *Frontiers in Psychology, 10,* 2670.

Gonzalez-Escamilla, G., & others (2020, in press). Metabolic and amyloid PET network reorganization in Alzheimer's disease: Differential patterns and partial volume effects. *Brain Imaging and Behavior.*

Gonzalez-Mena, J. (2020). *Foundations of early childhood education* (7th ed.). New York: McGraw-Hill.

Good, M., & Willoughby, T. (2008). Adolescence as a sensitive period for spiritual development. *Child Development Perspectives, 2,* 32–37.

Goodcase, E.T., Spencer, C.M., & Toews, M.L. (2020, in press). Who understands consent? A latent profile analysis of college students' attitudes toward consent. *Journal of Interpersonal Violence.*

Goode, E. (2020). *Drugs in American society* (10th ed.). New York: McGraw-Hill.

Goode, R.W., & others (2020, in press). Binge eating and binge-eating disorder in Black women: A systematic review. *International Journal of Eating Disorders.*

Goodkind, S. (2013). Single-sex public education for low-income youth of color: A critical theoretical review. *Sex Roles, 69,* 393–402.

Goodman, S. (2019, January 14). *How many people live to be 100 across the globe?* Retrieved February 20, 2019, from www.thecentenarian.co.uk

Goodvin, R., Meyer, S., Thompson, R.A., & Hayes, R. (2008). Self-understanding in early childhood: Associations with child attachment security and maternal negative affect. *Attachment and Human Development, 10,* 433–450.

Gopnik, A. (2010). Commentary in E. Galinsky (2010), *Mind in the making.* New York: Harper Collins.

Gopnik, A., & others (2017). Changes in cognitive flexibility and hypothesis search across human life history from childhood to adolescence to adulthood. *Proceedings of the National Academy of Sciences U.S.A., 114*(30), 7092–7099.

Gorby, H.E., Brownawell, A.M., & Falk, M.C. (2010). Do specific dietary constituents and supplements affect mental energy? Review of the evidence. *Nutrition Reviews, 68,* 697–718.

Gorchoff, S.M., John, O.P., & Helson, R. (2008). Contextualizing change in marital satisfaction during middle age: An 18-year longitudinal study. *Psychological Science, 19,* 1194–1200.

Gordon Simons, L., & others (2018). The cost of being cool: How adolescents' pseudomature behavior maps onto adult adjustment. *Journal of Youth and Adolescence, 47,* 1007–1021.

Gordon, I., & others (2010). Oxytocin and the development of parenting in humans. *Biological Psychiatry, 68,* 377–382.

Gordon, I., & others (2017). Testosterone, oxytocin, and the development of human parental care. *Hormones and Behavior. 93*, 184–192.

Gordon, J.S. (2020, in press). Building moral robots: Ethical pitfalls and challenges. *Science and Engineering Ethics.*

Gordon, R., & others (2020, in press). Working memory and high-level cognition in children: An analysis of timing and accuracy in complex span tasks. *Journal of Experimental Child Psychology.*

Gorges, R.J., Sanghavi, P., & Konetzka, R.T. (2019). A national examination of long-term care setting, outcomes, and disparities among elderly dual eligible. *Health Affairs, 38,* 1110–1118.

Gorgon, E.J.R. (2018). Caregiver-provided physical therapy home programs for children with motor delay: A scoping review. *Physical Therapy, 98,* 480–493.

Gorrell, S., & others (2019). A test of the DSM-5 severity specifier for bulimia nervosa in adolescents: Can we anticipate clinical treatment outcomes? *International Journal of Eating Disorders. 52,* 586–590.

Goslawski, M., & others (2013). Binge drinking impairs vascular function in young adults. *Journal of the American College of Cardiology, 62,* 201–207.

Gosmann, N.P., & others (2015). Association between internalizing disorders and day-to-day activities of low energetic expenditure. *Child Psychiatry and Human Development, 46,* 67–74.

Gosselin, J. (2010). Individual and family factors related to psychosocial adjustment in stepmother families with adolescents. *Journal of Divorce and Remarriage, 51,* 108–123.

Gosselin, P. (2019, January 4). *If you're over 50, chances are the decision to leave a job won't be yours.* Retrieved July 20, 2019, from www.propublica.org

Gottfried, A.E. (2019). Parenting and children's academic motivation. In M.H. Bornstein (Ed.), *Handbook of parenting* (3rd ed.). New York: Elsevier.

Gottlieb, G. (2007). Probabilistic epigenesis. *Developmental Science, 10,* 1–11.

Gottman, J.M. (1994). *What predicts divorce?* Mahwah, NJ: Erlbaum.

Gottman, J.M. (2006, April 29). Secrets of long-term love. *New Scientist, 2549,* 40.

Gottman, J.M. (2011). *The science of trust.* New York: Norton.

Gottman, J.M. (2018). *Bringing baby home.* Retrieved March 26, 2018, from https://www.gottman.com/professionals/training/bringing-baby-home/

Gottman, J.M. (2020). *Emotion coaching.* Retrieved January 14, 2020, from www.gottman.com/parenting

Gottman, J.M., & Parker, J.G. (Eds.) (1987). *Conversations of friends.* New York: Cambridge University Press.

Gottman, J.M., Shapiro, A.F., & Parthemer, J. (2004). Bringing baby home: A preventative intervention program for expectant couples. *International Journal of Childbirth Education, 19,* 28–30.

Gottman, J.M., & Silver, N. (1999). *The seven principles for making marriages work.* New York: Crown.

Gottman, J.M., & Silver, N. (2015). *The seven principles for making marriages work* (rev. ed.). New York: Crown.

Gottschalk, M.S., & others (2020, in press). Temporal trends in age at menarche and age at menopause: A population study of 313,656 women in Norway. *Human Reproduction.*

Gouin, K., & others (2011). Effects of cocaine use during pregnancy on low birthweight and preterm birth: Systematic review and metaanalyses. *American Journal of Obstetrics and Gynecology, 204*(4), 340. e1–340.e12.

Gould, S.J. (1981). *The mismeasure of man.* New York: W.W. Norton.

Gouldner, H., & Strong, M.M. (1987). *Speaking of friendship.* New York: Greenwood Press.

Gove, W.R., Style, C.B., & Hughes, M. (1990). The effect of marriage on the well-being of adults. *Journal of Marriage and the Family, 11,* 4–35.

Gow, A.J., Pattie, A., & Deary, I.J. (2017). Lifecourse activity participation from early, mid, and later adulthood as determinants of cognitive aging: The Lothian Birth Cohort 1921. *Journals of Gerontology B: Psychological Sciences and Social Sciences, 72,* 25–37.

Gowan, D.E. (2003). Christian beliefs concerning death and life after death. In C.D. Bryant (Ed.), *Handbook of death and dying.* Thousand Oaks, CA: Sage.

Gowin, J.L., & others (2017). Vulnerability for alcohol use disorder and rate of alcohol consumption. *American Journal of Psychiatry, 174,* 1094–1101.

Graber, J.A., Brooks-Gunn, J., & Warren, M.P. (2006). Pubertal effects on adjustment in girls: Moving from demonstrating effects to identifying pathways. *Journal of Youth and Adolescence, 35,* 391–401.

Graber, J.A., & Sontag, L.M. (2009). Internalizing problems during adolescence. In R.M. Lerner & L. Steinberg (Eds.), *Handbook of adolescent psychology* (3rd ed.). New York: Wiley.

Graham, A.C., & others (2020, in press). Sexual assault, campus resource use, and psychological distress in undergraduate women. *Journal of Interpersonal Violence.*

Graham, E.K., & others (2017). Personality and mortality risk: An integrative data analysis of 15 international longitudinal studies. *Journal of Research on Personality, 70,* 174–186.

Graham, G., Holt/Hale, A., & Parker, M. (2020). *Children moving* (10th ed.). New York: McGraw-Hill.

Graham, S. (2005, February 16). Commentary in *USA TODAY,* p. 20.

Graham, S. (2020a). Teaching writing in the digital age. In G. Noblit (Ed.), *Oxford research encyclopedia (Curriculum and pedagogy, languages and literacy).* New York: Oxford University Press.

Graham, S. (2020b). Reading and writing connections: A commentary. In R. Alves & others (Eds.), *Reading-writing connections.* New York: Springer.

Graham, S., & Harris, K.R. (2019). Designing an effective writing program. In S. Graham & others (Eds.), *Best practices in writing instruction* (3rd ed.). New York: Guilford.

Graham, S., & Harris, K.R. (2020). Writing and students with learning disabilities. In A. Martin & others (Eds.), *Handbook of educational psychology and students with special needs.* New York: Routledge.

Graham, S., & others (2020). Writing strategy interventions. In D. Dinsmore & others (Eds.), *Handbook of strategies and strategic processing.* New York: Routledge.

Grambs, J.D. (1989). *Women over forty* (rev. ed.). New York: Springer.

Granbom, M., & others (2019). Preventing falls among older fallers: Study protocol for a two-phase pilot study of the multicomponent LIVE LIFE program. *Trials, 20*(1), 2.

Grandner, M.A., Sands-Lincoln, M.R., Pak, V.M., & Garland, S.N. (2013). Sleep duration, cardiovascular disease, and proinflammatory biomarkers. *Nature Science: Sleep, 5,* 93–107.

Graneist, A., & Habermas, T. (2019). Beyond the text given: Studying the scaffolding of narrative emotion regulation as a contribution to Bruner and Feldman's cultural cognitive developmental psychology. *Integrated Psychology and Behavioral Science, 53,* 644–660.

Granqvist, P. (2020, in press). Attachment, culture, and gene-culture co-evolution: Expanding the evolutionary toolbox of attachment theory. *Attachment and Human Development.*

Grant, B.F., & others (2017). Prevalence of 12-month alcohol use, high-risk drinking, and DSM-IV alcohol use disorder in the United States, 2001–2002 to 2012–2013: Results from the National Epidemiologic Survey on Alcohol and Related Conditions. *JAMA Psychiatry, 74,* 911–923.

Grant, J. (1993). *The state of the world's children.* New York: UNICEF and Oxford University Press.

Grant, J.E., & Chamberlain, S.R. (2020, in press). Neurocognitive findings in young adults with binge eating disorder. *International Journal of Psychiatry in Clinical Practice.*

Grant, N., Wardle, J., & Steptoe, A. (2009). The relationship between life satisfaction and health behavior: A cross-cultural analysis of young adults. *International Journal of Behavioral Medicine, 16,* 259–268.

Gravelin, C.R., Biernat, M., & Bucher, C.E. (2019). Blaming the victim of acquaintance rape: Individual, situational, and sociocultural factors. *Frontiers in Psychology, 9,* 2422.

Gravetter, F.J., & Forzano, L.B. (2019). *Research methods for the behavioral sciences* (6th ed.). Boston: Cengage.

Gravningen, K., & others (2017). Reported reasons for breakdown of marriage and cohabitation in Britain: Findings from the Third National Survey of Sexual Attitudes and Lifestyles (Natsal-3). *PLoS One, 12*(3), e0174129.

Graziano, A., & Raulin, M. (2020). *Research methods* (9th ed., loose leaf). Upper Saddle River, NJ: Pearson.

Grebe, N.M., & others (2019). Pair-bonding, fatherhood, and the role of testosterone:

A meta-analytic review. *Neuroscience and Biobehavioral Reviews, 98,* 221–233.

Greenberg, J.A. (2006). Correcting biases in estimates of mortality attributable to obesity. *Obesity, 14,* 2071–2079.

Greenberg, S., & Christiansen, T.U. (2019). The perceptual flow of phonetic information. *Attention, Perception, and Psychophysics, 81,* 884–896.

Greene, M.F. (2009). Making small risks even smaller. *New England Journal of Medicine, 360,* 183–184.

Greene, N.R., & Naveh-Benjamin, M. (2020, in press). A specificity principle of memory: Evidence from aging and associative memory. *Psychological Science.*

Greenfield, P.M. (2020). Communication technologies and social transformation: Their impact on human development. In R.D. Parke & G.H. Elder (Eds.), *Children in changing worlds.* New York: Cambridge University Press,

Greenhaus, J., & Callanan, G.A. (2013). Career dynamics. In I.B. Weiner & others (Eds.), *Handbook of psychology* (2nd ed., Vol. 12). New York: Wiley.

Greenwald, L., Copeland, C., & VanDerhei, J. (2017, March 21). *The 2017 retirement confidence survey.* Retrieved March 27, 2017, from www.ebri.org

Griffith, J.M., & others (2019). Parenting and youth onset of depression across three years: Examining the influence of observed parenting on child and adolescent depressive outcomes. *Journal of Abnormal Child Psychology, 47,* 1969–1980.

Griffiths, P.D., & others (2018). Should we perform in utero MRI on a fetus at increased risk of a brain abnormality if ultrasonography is normal or shows non-specific findings? *Clinical Radiology, 73,* 123–134.

Griffiths, S., & others (2017). Sex differences in quality of life impairment associated with body dissatisfaction in adolescents. *Journal of Adolescent Health, 61,* 77–82.

Grigorenko, E.R. (2000). Heritability and intelligence. In R.J. Sternberg (Ed.), *Handbook of intelligence.* New York: Cambridge University Press.

Grigorenko, E.L., & others (2019). Improved educational achievement as a path to desistance. *New Directions in Child and Adolescent Development, 165,* 111–135.

Groh, A.M., & others (2014). The significance of attachment security for children's social competence with peers: A meta-analytic study. *Attachment and Human Development, 16,* 103–136.

Grolnick, W.S., Caruso, A., & Levitt, M. (2019). Parenting and children's self-regulation. In M.H. Bornstein (Ed.), *Handbook of parenting* (3rd ed.). New York: Routledge.

Gross, J.J., Fredrickson, B.L., & Levenson, R.W. (1994). The psychophysiology of crying. *Psychophysiology, 31,* 460–468.

Gross, M.S., & others (2019). Breastfeeding with HIV: An evidence-based case for new policy. *Journal of Law, Medicine, and Ethics, 47*(1), 152–160.

Grossman, J.M., & others (2019). Extended-family talk about sex and teen sexual behavior. *International Journal of Environmental Research and Public Health, 16,* 3.

Grossmann, K., Grossmann, K.E., Spangler, G., Suess, G., & Unzner, L. (1985). Maternal sensitivity and newborns' orientation responses as related to quality of attachment in northern Germany. In L. Bretherton & E. Waters (Eds.), Growing points of attachment theory and research. *Monographs of the Society for Research in Child Development, 50*(1–2, Serial No. 209).

Grosso, S.S., & others (2019). 33-month-old children succeed in false belief task with reduced processing demands: A replication of Setoh et al. (2016). *Infant Behavior and Development, 54,* 151–155.

Grotevant, H.D., & McDermott, J.M. (2014). Adoption: Biological and social processes linked to adaptation. *Annual Review of Psychology* (Vol. 65). Palo Alto, CA: Annual Reviews.

Grotevant, H.D., McRoy, R.G., Wrobel, G.M., & Ayers-Lopez, S. (2013). Contact between adoptive and birth families: Perspectives from the Minnesota/Texas Adoption Research Project. *Child Development Perspectives, 7*(3), 193–198.

Grover, V., & others (2020, in press). Shared book reading in preschool supports bilingual children's second-language learning: A cluster-randomized trial. *Child Development.*

Groves, N.B., & others (2020, in press). An examination of relations among working memory, ADHD symptoms, and emotion regulation. *Journal of Abnormal Child Psychology.*

Gruber, K.J., Cupito, S.H., & Dobson, C.F. (2013). Impact of doulas on healthy birth outcomes. *Journal of Perinatal Education, 22,* 49–58.

Gruenewald, T.L., & others (2016). The Baltimore Experience Corps trial: Enhancing generativity via intergenerational activity engagement in later life. *Journals of Gerontology B: Psychological Sciences and Social Sciences, 71,* 661–670.

Grunnan, J.D., & Rosthoj, S. (2019). Time course of peripheral blood count recovery during induction chemotherapy for childhood acute lymphoblastic leukemia. *Hematology, 24,* 467–472.

Grusec, J.E. (2011). Socialization processes in the family: Social and emotional development. *Annual Review of Psychology* (Vol. 62). Palo Alto, CA: Annual Reviews.

Grusec, J.E. (2017). A domains-of-socialization perspective on children's social development. In N. Budwig, E. Turiel, & P.D. Zelazo (Eds.), *New perspectives on human development.* New York: Cambridge University Press.

Grusec, J.E. (2020). Domains of socialization: Implications for parenting and the development of children's moral behavior and cognitions. In D.J. Laible & others (Eds.), *Oxford handbook of parenting and moral development.* New York: Oxford University Press.

Grusec, J.E., Chaparro, M.P., Johnston, M., & Sherman, A. (2013). Social development and social relationships in middle childhood. In I.B. Weiner & others (Eds.), *Handbook of psychology* (2nd ed., Vol. 6). New York: Wiley.

Grusec, J.E., & Davidov, M. (2019). Parent socialization and children's values. In M.H. Bornstein (Ed.), *Handbook of parenting* (3rd ed.). New York: Routledge.

Guerin, E., & others (2019). Physical activity and perceptions of stress during the menopause transition: A longitudinal study. *Journal of Health Psychology, 24,* 799–811.

Gueron-Sela, N., & others (2018). Maternal depressive symptoms, mother-child interactions, and children's executive function. *Developmental Psychology, 54,* 71–82.

Guerrero, L.K., Andersen, P.A., & Afifi, W.A. (2011). *Close encounters: Communication in relationships* (3rd ed.). Thousand Oaks, CA: Sage.

Guerrero Sastoque, L., & others (2019). Optimizing memory strategy use in young and older adults: The role of metamemory and internal strategy use. *Acta Psychologica, 192,* 73–86.

Guest, F.L. (2019). Early detection and treatment of patients with Alzheimer's disease: Future perspectives. *Advances in Experimental Medicine and Biology, 1118,* 295–317.

Gui, W.J., & others (2017). Age-related differences in sleep-based memory consolidation: A meta-analysis. *Neuropsychologia, 97,* 46–55.

Guilbeau, C. (2018). End-of-life care in the Western world: Where are we now and how did we get here? *BMJ Supportive and Palliative Care, 8,* 136–144.

Guilford, J.P. (1967). *The structure of intellect.* New York: McGraw-Hill.

Guimaraes, E.L., & Tudella, E. (2015). Immediate effect of training at the onset of reaching in preterm infants: Randomized clinical trial. *Journal of Motor Behavior, 47,* 535–549.

Guiney, H., & Machado, L. (2018). Volunteering in the community: Potential benefits for cognitive aging. *Journals of Gerontology B: Psychological Sciences and Social Sciences, 73,* 399–408.

Gump, B., & Matthews, K. (2000, March). *Annual vacations, health, and death.* Paper presented at the meeting of American Psychosomatic Society, Savannah, GA.

Gunderson, E.A., Ramirez, G., Beilock, S.L., & Levine, S.C. (2012). The role of parents and teachers in the development of gender-related attitudes. *Sex Roles, 66,* 153–166.

Gunn, H.E., & others (2019). Young adolescent sleep is associated with parental monitoring. *Sleep Health, 5,* 58–63.

Gunn, J.K., & others (2016). Prenatal exposure to cannabis and maternal and child health outcomes: A systematic review and meta-analysis. *BMJ Open, 6*(4), e009986.

Gunnar, M.R., Fisher, P.A., & The Early Experience, Stress, and Prevention Network (2006). Bringing basic research on early experience and stress neurobiology to bear on preventive interventions for neglected and maltreated children. *Development and Psychopathology, 18,* 651–677.

Gunnar, M.R., Malone, S., & Fisch, R.O. (1987). The psychobiology of stress and coping in the human neonate: Studies of the adrenocortical activity in response to stress in the first week of life. In T. Field, P. McCabe, & N. Scheiderman (Eds.), *Stress and coping.* Hillsdale, NJ: Erlbaum.

Gunning, T.G. (2020). *Creating literacy for all students* (10th ed.). Upper Saddle River, NJ: Pearson.

Gur, R.C., & others (1995). Sex differences in regional cerebral glucose metabolism during a resting state. *Science, 267,* 528–531.

Gurwitch, R.H., Silovsky, J.F., Schultz, S., Kees, M., & Burlingame, S. (2001). *Reactions and guidelines for children following trauma/disaster.* Norman, OK: Department of Pediatrics, University of Oklahoma Health Sciences Center.

Guseh, S.H. (2020, in press). Noninvasive prenatal testing: From aneuploidy to single genes. *Human Genetics.*

Gustafsson, J-E. (2007). Schooling and intelligence. Effects of track of study on level and profile of cognitive abilities. In P.C. Kyllonen, R.D. Roberts, & L. Stankov (Eds.), *Extending intelligence.* Mahwah, NJ: Erlbaum.

Gutchess, A. (2019). *Cognitive and social neuroscience of aging.* New York: Cambridge University Press.

Gutchess, A.H., & others (2005). Aging and the neural correlates of successful picture encoding: Frontal activations compensate for decreased medial-temporal activity. *Journal of Cognitive Neuroscience, 17,* 84–96.

Gutierrez, I.T., Rosengren, K.S., & Miller, P. (2014). Mexican American immigration in the Centerville region: Teachers, children, and parents. In K.S. Rosengren & others (Eds.), Children's understanding of death: Toward a contextualized and integrated account. *Monographs of the Society for Research on Child Development, 79*(1), 97–112.

Gutierrez, I.T., & others (2020). Embracing death: Mexican parent and child perspectives on death. *Child Development, 91,* e491–e511.

Gutman, L.M., & others (2017). Moving through adolescence: Developmental trajectories of African American and European American youth. *Monographs of the Society for Research in Child Development, 82*(4), 1–196.

Gutmann, D.L. (1975). Parenthood: A key to the comparative study of the life cycle. In N. Datan & L. Ginsberg (Eds.), *Life-span developmental psychology: Normative life crises.* New York: Academic Press.

Guttentag, C.L., & others (2014). "My Baby and Me": Effects of an early, comprehensive parenting intervention on at-risk mothers and their children. *Developmental Psychology, 50,* 1482–1496.

Guttmannova, K., & others (2012). Examining explanatory mechanisms of the effects of early alcohol use on young adult alcohol competence. *Journal of Studies of Alcohol and Drugs, 73,* 379–390.

Guyon-Harris, K.L., Humphreys, K.L., Degnan, K., Fox, N.A., Nelson, C.A., & Zeanah, C.H. (2019). A prospective longitudinal study of reactive attachment disorder following early institutional care: Considering variable- and person-centered approaches. *Attachment and Human Development, 21,* 95–110.

H

Hachul, H., & Tufik, S. (2019). Hot flashes: Treating the mind, body, and soul. *Menopause, 26,* 461–462.

Hackman, D.A., & Kraemer, J.M. (2020). Socioeconomic disparities in achievement: Insights on neurocognitive development and educational interventions. In M. Thomas, D. Mareschal, & I. Dumontheil (Eds.), *Educational neuroscience.* New York: Routledge.

Hadfield, J.C. (2014). The health of grandparents raising grandchildren: A literature review. *Journal of Gerontological Nursing, 40,* 37–40.

Hadiwijaya, H., & others (2017). On the development of harmony, turbulence, and independence in parent-adolescent relationships: A five-wave longitudinal study. *Journal of Youth and Adolescence, 46,* 1772–1788.

Hagen, J.W., & Lamb-Parker, F.G. (2008). Head Start. In M.M. Haith & J.B. Benson (Eds.), *Encyclopedia of infant and early childhood development.* Oxford, UK: Elsevier.

Hagestad, G.O. (1985). Continuity and connectedness. In V.L. Bengston & J. Robertson (Eds.), *Grandparenthood.* Newbury Park, CA: Sage.

Hagestad, G.O., & Uhlenberg, P. (2007). The impact of demographic changes on relations between age groups and generations: A comparative perspective. In K.W. Schaie & P. Uhlenberg (Eds.), *Demographic changes and the well-being of older persons.* New York: Springer.

Haghighat, M.D., & Knifsend, C.A. (2019). The longitudinal influence of 10th grade extracurricular activity involvement: Implications for 12th grade academic practices and future educational achievement. *Journal of Youth and Adolescence, 48,* 609–619.

Hagnas, M.J., & others (2018). High leisure-time physical activity is associated with reduced risk of sudden cardiac death among men with low cardiorespiratory fitness. *Canadian Journal of Cardiology, 34,* 288–294.

Hahn, E.A., & Lachman, M.E. (2015). Everyday experience of memory problems and control: The adaptive role of selective optimization with compensation in the context of memory decline. *Aging, Neuropsychology, and Cognition, 22,* 25–41.

Haidt, J. (2006). *The happiness hypothesis.* New York: Basic Books.

Haidt, J. (2013). *The righteous mind.* New York: Random House.

Haidt, J. (2018). *Three stories about capitalism.* New York: Pantheon.

Haier, R.J. (2019). Biological approaches to intelligence. In R.J. Sternberg (Ed.), *Human intelligence.* New York: Cambridge University Press.

Haigh, E.A.P., & others (2018). Depression among older adults: A 20-year update on five common myths and misconceptions. *American Journal of Geriatric Psychiatry, 26,* 107–122.

Haimovitz, K., & Dweck, C.S. (2016). What predicts children's fixed and growth mindsets? Not their parents' views of intelligence but their parents' views of failure. *Psychological Science, 27,* 859–869.

Haimovitz, K., & Dweck, C.S. (2017). The origins of children's growth and fixed mindsets: New research and a new proposal. *Child Development, 88,* 1849–1859.

Hair, N.L., Hanson, J.L., Wolfe, B.L., & Pollack, S.D. (2015). Association of poverty, brain development, and academic achievement. *JAMA Pediatrics, 169,* 822–829.

Hajek, A., & others (2020, in press). Association of vision problems with psychosocial factors among middle-aged and older individuals: Findings from a nationally representative study. *Aging and Mental Health.*

Hakuta, K. (2001, April). *Key policy milestones and directions in the education of English language learners.* Paper prepared for the Rockefeller Symposium on educational equity, Washington, DC.

Hakuta, K. (2005, April). *Bilingualism at the intersection of research and public policy.* Paper presented at the meeting of the Society for Research in Child Development, Atlanta.

Hakuta, K., Butler, Y.G., & Witt, D. (2000). *How long does it take English learners to attain proficiency?* Berkeley, CA: The University of California Linguistic Minority Research Institute Policy Report 2000-1.

Hales, C.M., & others (2017, October). Prevalence of obesity among adults and youth: United States, 2015–2016. *NCHS Data Brief,* No. 288, pp. 1–8.

Hales, D. (2019). *An invitation to health* (18th ed.). Boston: Cengage.

Halgunseth, L.C. (2019). Latino and Latin American parenting. In M.H. Bornstein (Ed.), *Handbook of parenting* (3rd ed.). New York: Elsevier.

Hall, C.B., & others (2009). Cognitive activities delay onset of memory decline in persons who develop dementia. *Neurology, 73,* 356–361.

Hall, D.T., & Mirvis, P.H. (2013). Redefining work, work identity, and career success. In D.L. Blustein (Ed.), *Oxford handbook of the psychology of working.* New York: Oxford University Press.

Hall, G.S. (1904). *Adolescence* (Vols. 1 & 2). Englewood Cliffs, NJ: Prentice Hall.

Hall, J.A., Park, N., Song, H., & Cody, M.J. (2010). Strategic misrepresentation in online dating: The effects of gender, self-monitoring, and personality traits. *Journal of Social and Personal Relationships, 27,* 117–135.

Hall, L.J. (2018). *Autism spectrum disorders* (3rd ed.). Upper Saddle River, NJ: Pearson.

Hallahan, D.P., Kauffman, J.M., & Pullen, P.C. (2019). *Exceptional learners* (14th ed.). Upper Saddle River, NJ: Pearson.

Halonen, J., & Santrock, J.W. (2013). *Your guide to college success* (7th ed.). Boston: Cengage.

Halonen, J.I., & others (2017). Change in job strain as a predictor of insomnia symptoms: Analyzing observational data as a non-randomized pseudo-trial. *Sleep, 40,* 1.

Halper, L.R., & Rios, K. (2019). Feeling powerful but incompetent: Fear of negative evaluation predicts men's sexual harassment of subordinates. *Sex Roles, 80,* 247–261.

Halpern, D.F. (2012). *Sex differences in cognitive abilities* (2nd ed.). New York: Psychology Press.

Halpern, D.F., & others (2007). The science of sex differences in science and mathematics. *Psychological Science in the Public Interest, 8,* 1–51.

Halpern, D.F., & others (2011). The pseudoscience of single-sex schooling. *Science, 333,* 1706–1717.

Halpern-Meekin, S., Manning, W., Giordano, P.C., & Longmore, M.A. (2013). Relationship churning in emerging adulthood: On/off relationships and sex with an ex. *Journal of Adolescent Research, 28,* 166–188.

Halse, M., & others (2019). Parental predictors of children's executive functioning from ages 6 to 10. *British Journal of Developmental Psychology, 37,* 410–426.

Halvorsen, A., & others (2019). In utero exposure to selective serotonin reuptake inhibitors and development of mental disorders: A systematic review and meta-analysis. *Acta Psychiatrica Scandinavica, 139,* 493–507.

Hamer, M., Muniz Terrera, G., & Demakakos, P. (2018). Physical activity and trajectories of cognitive function: English Longitudinal Study of Aging. *Journal of Epidemiology and Community Health, 72,* 477–483.

Hamer, M., & others (2020, in press). Change in device-measured physical activity assessed in childhood and adolescence in relation to depressive symptoms: A general population-based cohort study. *Journal of Epidemiology and Community Health.*

Hamilton, J.B., & others (2018). Making sense of loss through spirituality: Perspectives of African American family members who have experienced the death of a close family member to cancer. *Palliative and Supportive Care, 16,* 662–688.

Hamlin, J.K. (2013). Moral judgment and action in preverbal infants and toddlers: Evidence for an innate moral core. *Current Directions in Psychological Science, 22,* 186–193.

Hamlin, J.K. (2014). The origins of human morality: Complex socio-moral evaluations by preverbal infants. In J. Decety & Y. Christen (Eds.), *New frontiers in social neuroscience.* New York: Springer.

Hamm, J.M., & others (2019). Engagement with six major life domains during the transition to retirement: Stability and change for better or worse. *Psychology and Aging, 34,* 441–456.

Hammond, S.I., & others (2012). The effects of parental scaffolding on preschoolers' executive function. *Developmental Psychology, 48,* 271–281.

Hamner, H.C., & Moore, V. (2020). Dietary quality among children from 6 months to 4 years, NHANES 2011–2016. *American Journal of Clinical Nutrition, 111,* 61–69.

Hamner, H.C., & others (2019). Food and beverage intake from 12 to 23 months by WIC status. *Pediatrics, 143,* 3.

Hampson, S.E. (2019). Personality development and health. In D.P. McAdams & others (Eds.), *Handbook of personality development.* New York: Guilford.

Han, J., Neufer, D., & Pilegaard, H. (2019). Exercise physiology: Future opportunities and challenges. *Pflugers Archive–European Journal of Physiology, 47,* 381.

Han, J.H., & others (2019). Effects of self-reported hearing or vision impairment on depressive symptoms: A population-based longitudinal study. *Epidemiology and Psychiatric Sciences, 28,* 343–355.

Han, J.J., Leichtman, M.D., & Wang, Q. (1998). Autobiographical memory in Korean, Chinese, and American children. *Developmental Psychology, 34,* 701–713.

Han, S.H., & others (2017). Social activities, incident cardiovascular disease, and mortality: Health behaviors mediation. *Journal of Aging and Health, 29,* 268–288.

Han, W-J., Hetzner, N.P., & Brooks-Gunn, J. (2019). Employment and parenting. In M.H. Bornstein (Ed.), *Handbook of parenting* (3rd ed.). New York: Routledge.

Han, X., & others (2016). Long sleep duration and afternoon napping are associated with higher risk of incident diabetes in middle-aged and older Chinese: The Dongfeng-Tongji cohort study. *Annals of Medicine, 48,* 216–223.

Hanc, T., & others (2018). Perinatal risk factors and ADHD in children and adolescents: A hierarchical structure of disorder predictors. *Journal of Attention Disorders, 22,* 855–863.

Handing, E.P., & others (2019). Cognitive function as a predictor of major mobile disability in older adults: Results from the LIFE study. *Innovations in Aging, 3,* 2.

Hanley, C.J., Burianova, H., & Tommerdahl, M. (2019). Towards establishing age-related cortical plasticity on the basis of somatosensation. *Neuroscience, 143,* 3.

Hannigan, L.J., McAdams, T.A., & Eley, T.C. (2017). Development change in the association between adolescent depressive symptoms and the home environment: Results from a longitudinal, genetically informative investigation. *Journal of Child Psychology and Psychiatry, 58,* 787–797.

Hannon, E.E., Schachner, A., & Nave-Blodgett, J.E. (2017). Babies know bad dancing when they see it: Older but not younger infants discriminate between synchronous and asynchronous audiovisual musical displays. *Journal of Experimental Child Psychology, 159,* 159–174.

Hansen, M.L., Gunn, P.W., & Kaelber, D.C. (2007). Underdiagnosis of hypertension in children and adolescents. *JAMA, 298,* 874–879.

Harb, S.C., & others (2020, in press). Estimated age based on exercise stress testing performance outperforms chronological age in predicting mortality. *European Journal of Preventive Cardiology.*

Hardie, J.H., Pearce, L.D., & Denton, M.L. (2016). The dynamics and correlates of religious service attendance in adolescence. *Youth & Society, 48,* 151–175.

Harding, J.F., & others (2020, in press). A systematic review of programs to promote aspects of teen parents' self-sufficiency: Supporting educational outcomes and healthy birth spacing. *Maternal and Child Health Journal.*

Hardy, L.M., & others (2020, in press). Bilingualism may be protective against executive functioning and visual processing deficits among children with attention problems. *Journal of Attention Disorders.*

Hardy, M. (2006). Older workers. In R.H. Binstock & L.K. George (Eds.), *Handbook of aging and the social sciences* (6th ed.). San Diego: Academic Press.

Hardy, S.A., Bean, D.S., & Olsen, J.A. (2015). Moral identity and adolescent prosocial and antisocial behaviors: Interactions with moral disengagement and self-regulation. *Journal of Youth and Adolescence, 44,* 1542–1554.

Hardy, S.A., & King, P.E. (2019). Processes of religious and spiritual influence in adolescence: Introduction to special section. *Journal of Research on Adolescence, 29,* 244–253.

Hardy, S.A., Krettenauer, T., & Hunt, N. (2020). Moral identitiy development. In L.A. Jensen (Ed.), *Oxford handbook of moral development.* New York: Oxford University Press.

Hardy, S.A., & others (2019). Processes of religious and spiritual influence in adolescence: A systematic review of 30 years of research. *Journal of Research on Adolescence, 29,* 254–275.

Harkins, S.W., Price, D.D., & Martinelli, M. (1986). Effects of age on pain perception. *Journal of Gerontology, 41,* 58–63.

Harkness, S., & Super, E.M. (1995). Culture and parenting. In M.H. Bornstein (Ed.), *Handbook of parenting* (Vol. 3). Hillsdale, NJ: Erlbaum.

Harlow, H.F. (1958). The nature of love. *American Psychologist, 13,* 673–685.

Harlow, W.V., Brown, K.C., & Jenks, S.E. (2020). The use and value of financial advice for retirement planning. *Journal of Retirement, 7*(3), 46–79.

Harrington, M. (2020). *The design of experiments in neuroscience.* New York: Cambridge University Press.

Harrington, S.E., & Smith, T.J. (2008). The role of chemotherapy at the end of life: "When is enough, enough?" *JAMA, 299,* 2667–2678.

Harris, G. (2002). *Grandparenting: How to meet its responsibilities.* Los Angeles: The Americas Group.

Harris, J., Golinkoff, R.M., & Hirsh-Pasek, K. (2011). Lessons from the crib for the classroom: How children really learn vocabulary. In S.B. Neuman & D.K. Dickinson (Eds.), *Handbook of early literacy research* (Vol. 3). New York: Guilford.

Harris, K.M., Gorden-Larsen, P., Chantala, K., & Udry, J.R. (2006). Longitudinal trends in race/ethnic disparities in leading health indicators from adolescence to young adulthood. *Archives of Pediatrics and Adolescent Medicine, 160,* 74–81.

Harris, L. (1975). *The myth and reality of aging in America.* Washington, DC: National Council on Aging.

Harris, P.L. (2006). Social cognition. In W. Damon & R. Lerner (Eds.), *Handbook of child psychology* (6th ed.). New York: Wiley.

Harrison, A.J., & Slane, M.M. (2020, in press). Examining how types of object distractors distinctly compete for facial attention in autism spectrum disorder using eye tracking. *Journal of Autism and Developmental Disorders.*

Harrison, C. (2012). Aging: Telomerase gene therapy increases longevity. *Nature Reviews. Drug Discovery, 11,* 518.

Hart, B., & Risley, T.R. (1995). *Meaningful differences in the everyday experience of young Americans.* Baltimore: Paul H. Brookes.

Hart, C.H., Yang, C., Charlesworth, R., & Burts, D.C. (2003, April). *Early childhood teachers' curriculum beliefs, classroom practices, and children's* outcomes: *What are the connections?* Paper presented at the biennial meeting of the Society for Research in Child Development, Tampa, FL.

Hart, C.N., Cairns, A., & Jelalian, E. (2011). Sleep and obesity in children and adolescents. *Pediatric Clinics of North America, 58,* 15–33.

Hart, D. (2020). Moral development in civic and political contexts. In L.A. Jensen (Ed.), *Oxford handbook of moral development.* New York: Oxford University Press.

Hart, D., Goel, N., & Atkins, R. (2017). Prosocial tendencies, antisocial behavior, and moral development in childhood. In A. Slater & G. Bremner (Eds.), *Introduction to developmental psychology* (3rd ed.). New York: Wiley.

Hart, D., & Karmel, M.P. (1996). Self-awareness and self-knowledge in humans, great apes, and monkeys. In A. Russori, K. Bard, & S. Parker (Eds.), *Reaching into thought.* New York: Cambridge University Press.

Hart, D., & others (2017). Morality and mental health. In C. Markey (Ed.), *Encyclopedia of mental health.* New York: Elsevier.

Hart, S. (2018). Jealousy and attachment: Adaptations to threat posed by the birth of a sibling. *Evolutionary Behavioral Sciences, 12,* 263–275.

Hart, S., & Carrington, H. (2002). Jealousy in 6-month-old infants. *Infancy, 3,* 395–402.

Hart, W., Adams, J., & Tullett, A. (2016). "It's complicated"—Sex differences in perceptions of cross-aged friendships. *Journal of Social Psychology, 156,* 190–201.

Harter, K. (2019). Opioid use disorder during pregnancy. *Mental Health Clinics, 9,* 359–372.

Harter, S. (2006). The self. In W. Damon & R. Lerner (Eds.), *Handbook of child psychology* (6th ed.). New York: Wiley.

Harter, S. (2012). *The construction of the self* (2nd ed.). New York: Wiley.

Harter, S. (2013). The development of self-esteem. In M.H. Kernis (Ed.), *Self-esteem issues and answers.* New York: Psychology Press.

Harter, S. (2016). I-self and me-self processes affecting developmental psychopathology and mental health. In D. Cicchetti (Ed.), *Developmental psychopathology* (3rd ed.). New York: Wiley.

Hartescu, I., Morgan, K., & Stevinson, C.D. (2016). Sleep quality and recommended levels of physical activity in older adults. *Journal of Aging and Physical Activity, 24,* 201–206.

Hartley, A. (2006). Changing role of the speed of processing construct in the cognitive psychology of human aging. In J.E. Birren & K.W. Schaie (Eds.), *Handbook of the psychology of aging* (6th ed.). San Diego: Academic Press.

Hartshorne, H., & May, M.S. (1928–1930). *Moral studies in the nature of character: Studies in the nature of character.* New York: Macmillan.

Hartup, W.W. (1983). The peer system. In P.H. Mussen (Ed.), *Handbook of child psychology* (4th ed., Vol. 4). New York: Wiley.

Hartup, W.W. (1996). The company they keep: Friendships and their developmental significance. *Child Development, 67,* 1–13.

Hartup, W.W. (2009). Critical issues and theoretical viewpoints. In K.H. Rubin, W.M. Bukowski, & B. Laursen (Eds.), *Handbook of peer interactions, relationships, and groups.* New York: Guilford.

Hasbrouck, S.L., & Pianta, R. (2016). Understanding child care quality and implications for dual language learners. In K.E. Sanders & A.W. Guerra (Eds.), *The culture of child care.* New York: Oxford University Press.

Hasher, L. (2003, February 28). Commentary in "The wisdom of the wizened." *Science, 299,* 1300–1302.

Hashim, H.A., Freddy, G., & Rosmatunisah, A. (2012). Relationships between negative affect and academic achievement among secondary school students: The mediating effects of habituated exercise. *Journal of Physical Activity and Health, 9,* 1012–1019.

Hastings, P.D., Miller, J.G., & Troxel, N.R. (2015). Making good: The socialization of children's prosocial development. In J.E. Grusec & P.D. Hastings (Eds.), *Handbook of socialization* (2nd ed.). New York: Guilford.

Hastings, P.D., & others (2019). Parenting behaviorally inhibited and socially withdrawn children. In M.H. Bornstein (Ed.), *Handbook of parenting* (3rd ed.). New York: Routledge.

Hatch, B., & others (2019). Consistent use of bedtime parenting strategies mediates the effects of sleep education on child sleep: Secondary findings from an early-life randomized controlled trial. *Sleep Health, 5,* 433–443.

Hatoun, J., & others (2018). Tobacco control laws and pediatric asthma. *Pediatrics, 141*(Suppl. 1), S130–S136.

Haugrud, N., Crossley, M., & Vrbancic, M. (2011). Clustering and switching strategies during verbal fluency performance differentiate Alzheimer's disease and healthy aging. *Journal of the International Alzheimer's Society, 17,* 1153–1157.

Haun, V.C., & Oppenauer, V. (2019). The role of job demands and negative work reflection in employees' trajectory of sleep quality over the workweek. *Journal of Occupational Health Psychology, 24*(6), 675–688.

Hawes, Z., & others (2019). Relations between numerical, spatial, and executive function skills and mathematics achievement: A latent-variable approach. *Cognitive Psychology, 109,* 68–90.

Hawkes, C. (2006). Olfaction in neurodegenerative disorder. *Advances in Otorhinolaryngology, 63,* 133–151.

Hawkey, E.J., & others (2018). Preschool executive function predicts childhood resting-state functional connectivity and attention-deficit/hyperactivity disorder and depression. *Biological Psychiatry. Cognitive Neuroscience and Neuroimaging, 3,* 927–936.

Hawkins, A.J. (2018). Shifting the relationship education field to prioritize youth relationship education. *Journal of Couple and Relationship Therapy, 17,* 165–180.

Hawkins, J.A., & Berndt, T.J. (1985, April). *Adjustment following the transition to junior high school.* Paper presented at the biennial meeting of the Society for Research in Child Development, Toronto.

Hawkley, L.C., & Kocherginsky, M. (2018). Transitions in loneliness among older adults: A 5-year follow-up in the National Social Life, Health, and Aging Project. *Research on Aging, 40,* 365–387.

Hay, P. (2020). Current approach to eating disorders: A clinical update. *Internal Medicine Journal, 50,* 24–29.

Hayatbakhsh, R., & others (2013). Early childhood predictors of early onset of smoking: A birth prospective study. *Addictive Behaviors, 38,* 2513–2519.

Haydon, A., & Halpern, G.T. (2010). Older romantic partners and depressive symptoms during adolescence. *Journal of Youth and Adolescence, 39,* 1240–1251.

Hayes, R.M., Abbott, R.L., & Cook, S. (2016). It's her fault: Student acceptance of rape myths on two college campuses. *Violence Against Women, 22,* 1540–1555.

Hayflick, L. (1977). The cellular basis for biological aging. In C.E. Finch & L. Hayflick (Eds.), *Handbook of the biology of aging.* New York: Van Nostrand.

Hayne, H., & Gross, J. (2017). Memory by association: Integrating memories prolongs retention by two-year-olds. *Infant Behavior and Development, 46,* 7–13.

Hayslip, B., Fruhauf, C.A., & Dolbin-MacNab, M.L. (2019). Grandparents raising grandchildren: What have we learned over the past decade? *Gerontologist, 59,* e152–e163.

Hayslip, B., & Hansson, R.O. (2007). Hospice. In J.E. Birren (Ed.), *Encyclopedia of gerontology* (2nd ed.). San Diego: Academic Press.

Hayslip, B., Pruett, J.H., & Caballero, D.M. (2015). The "how" and "when" of parental loss in adulthood: Effects on grief and adjustment. *Omega, 71,* 3–18.

Hayward, R.D., & Krause, N. (2013a). Changes in church-based social support relationships during older adulthood. *Journals of Gerontology B: Psychological Sciences and Social Sciences, 68,* 85–96.

Hayward, R.D., & Krause, N. (2013b). Patterns of change in religious service attendance across the life course: Evidence from a 34-year longitudinal study. *Social Science Research, 42,* 1480–1489.

Hazan, C., & Shaver, P.R. (1987). Romantic love conceptualized as an attachment process. *Journal of Personality and Social Psychology, 52,* 522–524.

He, M., Walle, E.A., & Campos, J.J. (2015). A cross-national investigation between infant walking and language development. *Infancy, 20,* 283–305.

Hearon, B.A., & Harrison, T.J. (2020, in press). Not the exercise type? Personality traits and anxiety sensitivity as predictors of objectively measured physical activity and sedentary time. *Journal of Health Psychology.*

Heesterbeek, T.J., & others (2020, in press). Risk factors for progression of age-related macular degeneration. *Ophthalmic & Physiological Optics.*

Hegaard, H.K., & others (2008). Leisure time physical activity is associated with a reduced risk of preterm delivery. *American Journal of Obstetrics and Gynecology, 198,* e1–e5.

Hegab, A.E., & others (2019). Calorie restriction enhances adult mouse lung stem cells function and reverses several aging-induced changes. *Journal of Tissue Engineering and Regenerative Medicine, 13,* 295–308.

Heilman, K.M. (Ed.) (2020). *Cognitive changes in the aging brain.* New York: Cambridge University Press.

Heiman, C.M., & others (2019). Object interaction and walking: Integration of old and new skills in infant development. *Infancy, 24,* 547–569.

Heiman, T., Olenik-Shemesh, D., & Frank, G. (2019). Patterns of coping with cyberbullying: Emotional, behavioral, and strategic coping reactions among middle school students. *Violence and Victimization, 34,* 28–45.

Heimann, M., & others (2006). Exploring the relation between memory, gestural communication, and the emergence of language in infancy: A longitudinal study. *Infant and Child Development, 15,* 233–249.

Hein, S., & others (2019). Negative parenting modulates the association between mother's DNA methylation profiles and adult offspring depression. *Developmental Psychobiology, 61,* 304–310.

Heine, C., Browning, C., Cowlishaw, S., & Kendig, H. (2013). Trajectories of older adults' hearing difficulties: Examining the influence of health behaviors and social activity over ten years. *Geriatrics and Gerontology International, 13,* 911–918.

Heinrich, J. (2017). Modulation of allergy risk by breast feeding. *Current Opinion in Clinical Nutrition and Metabolic Care, 20,* 217–221.

Helgeson, V.S. (2012). *Psychology of gender* (4th ed.). Upper Saddle River, NJ: Pearson.

Helgeson, V.S. (2020). *Psychology of gender* (6th ed.). New York: Routledge.

Helm, R.K., & Reyna, V.F. (2018). Cognitive and neurobiological aspects of risk. In M. Raue & others (Eds.), *Psychological aspects of risk and risk analysis.* New York: Springer.

Helman, C. (2008). Inside T. Boone Pickens' brain. *Forbes.* Retrieved June 15, 2008, from http://www.forbes.com/billionaires/forbes/2008/0630/076.html

Helson, R. (1997, August). *Personality change: When is it adult development?* Paper presented at the meeting of the American Psychological Association, Chicago.

Helson, R., & Wink, P. (1992). Personality change in women from the early 40s to early 50s. *Psychology and Aging, 7,* 46–55.

Henderson, C.E., Hogue, A., & Dauber, S. (2019). Family therapy techniques and one-year clinical outcomes among adolescents in usual care for behavior problems. *Journal of Consulting and Clinical Psychology, 87,* 308–312.

Henderson, J., Alerdice, E., & Redshaw, M. (2019). Factors associated with maternal postpartum fatigue: An observational study. *BMJ Open, 9*(7), e025927.

Hendrick, C., & Hendrick, S.S. (2019). Styles of romantic love. In R.J. Sternberg & K. Sternberg (Eds.), *The new psychology of love* (2nd ed.). New York: Cambridge University Press.

Hendricks-Munoz, K.D., & others (2013). Maternal and neonatal nurse perceived value of kangaroo mother care and maternal care partnership in the neonatal intensive care unit. *American Journal of Perinatology, 30,* 875–880.

Hennenberger, A.K., Mushonga, D.R., & Preston, A.M. (2020, in press). Peer influence and adolescent substance use: A systematic review of dynamic social network research. *Adolescent Research Review.*

Hennessey, B. (2019). Motivation and creativity. In J.C. Kaufman & R.J. Sternberg (Eds.), *Cambridge handbook of creativity* (2nd ed.). New York: Cambridge University Press.

Hennessy, G. (2018). Marijuana and pregnancy. *American Journal of Addiction, 27,* 44–45.

Henning, G., & others (2020, in press). Towards an active and happy retirement? Changes in leisure activity and depressive symptoms during the retirement transition. *Aging and Mental Health.*

Henning-Smith, C. (2020). Strategies for promoting successful aging and well-being. *Journal of Applied Gerontology, 39,* 231–232.

Henriquez-Sanchez, P., & others (2016). Dietary total antioxidant capacity and mortality in the PREDIMED study. *European Journal of Nutrition, 55,* 227–236.

Herd, T., King-Casas, B., & Kim-Spoon, J. (2020, in press). Developmental changes in emotion regulation during adolescence: Associations with socioeconomic risk and family emotional context. *Journal of Youth and Adolescence.*

Herdt, G., & Polen-Petit, N. (2021). *Human sexuality* (2nd ed.). New York McGraw-Hill.

Herek, G.M. (2009). Hate crimes and stigma-related experiences among sexual minority adults in the United States: Prevalence estimates from a national probability sample. *Journal of Interpersonal Violence, 24,* 54–74.

Hernandez, A.E., Fernandez, E.M., & Aznar-Bese, N. (2019). Bilingual sentence processing. In S.A. Rueschemeyer & M. Gereth Gaskell (Eds.), *Oxford handbook of psycholinguistics* (2nd ed.). New York: Oxford University Press.

Hernandez-Reif, M., Diego, M., & Field, T. (2007). Preterm infants show reduced stress behaviors and activity after 5 days of massage therapy. *Infant Behavior and Development, 30,* 557–561.

Hernandez-Zimbron, L.F., & others (2017). Age-related macular degeneration: New paradigms for treatment and management of AMD. *Oxidative Medicine and Cell Longevity, 2017,* 1295132.

Hero, J.O., Zaslavsky, A.M., & Blendon, R.J. (2017). The United States leads other nations in differences by income in perceptions of health and health care. *Health Affairs, 36,* 1032–1040.

Herpertz-Dahlmann, B., & others (2015). Eating disorder symptoms do not just disappear: The implications of adolescent eating-disordered behavior for body weight and mental health in young adulthood. *European Child and Adolescent Psychiatry, 24,* 177–196.

Herrell, A.L., & Jordan, M. (2020). *50 strategies for teaching English Language Learners* (6th ed.). Upper Saddle River, NJ: Pearson.

Hershner, S.D., & Chervin, R.D. (2015). Causes and consequences of sleepiness among college students. *Nature and Science of Sleep, 6,* 73–84.

Hershner, S.D., & O'Brien, L.M. (2018). The impact of randomized sleep education intervention for college students. *Journal of Clinical Sleep Medicine, 14,* 337–347.

Herting, M.M., Colby, J.B., Sowell, E.R., & Nagel, B.J. (2014). White matter connectivity and aerobic fitness in male adolescents. *Developmental Cognitive Neuroscience, 7,* 65–75.

Hertzog, C., & others (2019). Behaviors and strategies supporting everyday memory in older adults. *Gerontology, 65,* 419–429.

Hessel, P., & others (2018). Trends and determinants of the Flynn effect in cognitive functioning among older individuals in 10 European countries. *Journal of Epidemiology and Community Health, 72,* 383–389.

Hetherington, E.M. (1993). An overview of the Virginia Longitudinal Study of Divorce and Remarriage with a focus on early adolescence. *Journal of Family Psychology, 7,* 39–56.

Hetherington, E.M. (2000). Divorce. In A. Kazdin (Ed.), *Encyclopedia of psychology.* Washington, DC, & New York: American Psychological Association and Oxford University Press.

Hetherington, E.M. (2006). The influence of conflict, marital problem solving, and parenting on children's adjustment in nondivorced, divorced, and remarried families. In A. Clarke-Stewart & J. Dunn (Eds.), *Families count.* New York: Oxford University Press.

Hetherington, E.M., & Kelly, J. (2002). *For better or for worse: Divorce reconsidered.* New York: Norton.

Hetherington, E.M., & Stanley-Hagan, M. (2002). Parenting in divorced and remarried families. In M.H. Bornstein (Ed.), *Handbook of parenting* (2nd ed., Vol. 3). Mahwah, NJ: Erlbaum.

Hewlett, B.S. (1991). *Intimate fathers: The nature and context of Aka Pygmy.* Ann Arbor, MI: University of Michigan Press.

Hewlett, B.S. (2000). Culture, history, and sex: Anthropological perspectives on father involvement. *Marriage and Family Review, 29,* 324–340.

Hewlett, B.S., & MacFarlan, S.J. (2010). Fathers, roles in hunter-gatherer and other small-scale cultures. In M.E. Lamb (Ed.), *The role of the father in child development* (5th ed.). New York: Wiley.

Heyes, C. (2014). Rich interpretations of infant behavior are popular, but are they valid? A reply to Scott and Baillargeon. *Developmental Science, 17,* 665–666.

Heyman, G.D., Fu, G., & Lee, K. (2013). Selective skepticism: American and Chinese children's reasoning about evaluative feedback. *Developmental Psychology, 49,* 543–553.

Hickman, S.E., & others (2019). A tool to assess patient and surrogate knowledge about the POLST (Physician Orders for Life-Sustaining Treatment) program. *Journal of Pain and Symptom Management, 57,* 1143–1150.

Hidayat, K., Zou, S.Y., & Shi, B.M. (2019). The influence of body mass index, maternal diabetes mellitus, and maternal smoking during pregnancy on the risk of childhood-onset type 1 diabetes mellitus in the offspring: Systematic review and meta-analysis of observational studies. *Obesity Reviews, 20,* 1106–1120.

High/Scope Resource. (2005, Spring). The High/Scope Perry Preschool Study and the man who began it. *High/Scope Resource 9.* Ypsilanti, MI: High/Scope Press.

Highfield, R. (2008, April 30). Harvard's baby brain research lab. Retrieved January 24, 2009, from www.telegraph.co.uk/scienceandtechnology/science/sciencenews/3341166/Harvards-baby-brain-research-lab.html

Hilbert, A., & others (2020). Cognitive-behavioral therapy for adolescents with an age-adapted diagnosis of binge-eating disorder: A randomized clinical trial. *Psychotherapy and Psychosomatics, 89,* 51–53.

Hill, A.M., & others (2020, in press). Racial/ethnic differences in diet quality and eating habits among WIC pregnant women: Implications for policy and practice. *American Journal of Health Promotion.*

Hill, C.R., & Stafford, E.P. (1980). Parental care of children: Time diary estimate of quantity, predictability, and variety. *Journal of Human Resources, 15,* 219–239.

Hill, D.J., & others (2019). Depressive symptoms in Latina mothers in an emerging immigrant community. *Cultural Diversity and Ethnic Minority Psychology, 25,* 397–402.

Hill, P.I., & others (2016a). Persevering with positivity and purpose: An examination of purpose commitment and positive affect as predictors of grit. *Journal of Happiness Studies, 17,* 257–269.

Hill, P.I., & others (2016b). Purpose in life in emerging adulthood: Development and validation of a new brief measure. *Journal of Positive Psychology, 11,* 237–245.

Hill, P.L., & Roberts, B.W. (2016). Personality and health: Reviewing recent research and setting a directive for the future. In K.W. Schaie & S. Willis (Eds.), *Handbook of the psychology of aging* (8th ed.). New York: Elsevier.

Hill, T.D., Burdette, A.M., Angel, J.L., & Angel, R.J. (2006). Religious attendance and cognitive functioning among older Mexican Americans. *Journals of Gerontology B: Psychological Sciences and Social Sciences, 61,* P3–P9.

Hill, W.D., & others (2019). A combined analysis of genetically correlated traits identifies 187 loci and a role for neurogenesis and myelination in intelligence. *Molecular Psychiatry, 24,* 169–181.

Himmerich, H., & Treasure, J. (2018). Psychopharmacological advances in eating disorders. *Expert Review of Clinical Pharmacology, 11,* 95–106.

Hinduja, S., & Patchin, J.W. (2015). *Bullying beyond the schoolyard: Preventing and responding to cyberbullying* (2nd ed.). Thousand Oaks, CA: Corwin Press.

Hinkley, T., & others (2018). Cross sectional associations of screen time and outdoor play with social skills in preschool children. *PLoS One, 13*(4), 0193700.

Hintsanen, M., & others (2014). Five-factor personality traits and sleep: Evidence from two population-based cohort studies. *Health Psychology, 33,* 214–233.

Hinze, S.W., Lin, J., & Andersson, T.E. (2012). Can we capture the intersections? Older black women, education, and health. *Women's Health Issues, 22,* e91–e98.

Hirai, M., & Kanakogi, Y. (2019). Communicative hand-waving gestures facilitate object learning in preverbal infants. *Developmental Science, 22*(4), e12787.

Hirsch, B.J., & Rapkin, B.D. (1987). The transition to junior high school: A longitudinal study of self-esteem, psychological symptomatology, school life, and social support. *Child Development, 58,* 1235–1243.

Hirsch, J.K., & Sirois, F.M. (2016). Hope and fatigue in chronic illness: The role of perceived stress. *Journal of Health Psychology, 21,* 451–456.

Hirschmugl, B., & others (2020, in press). Evidence of human milk oligosaccharides in cord blood and maternal-to-fetal transport across the placenta. *Nutrients.*

Hirsh-Pasek, K., & Golinkoff, R.M. (2014). Early language and literacy: Six principles. In S. Gilford (Ed.), *Head Start teacher's guide.* New York: Teacher's College Press.

Hirsh-Pasek, K., Golinkoff, R.M., Singer, D., & Berk, L. (2009). *A mandate for playful learning in preschool: Presenting the evidence.* New York: Oxford University Press.

Hita-Yanez, E., Atienza, M., & Cantero, J.L. (2013). Polysomnographic and subjective sleep markers of mild cognitive impairment. *Sleep, 36,* 1327–1334.

Hoch, J.E., O'Grady, S., & Adolph, K.E. (2019). It's the journey, not the destination: Locomotor exploration in infants. *Developmental Science. 22*(2), e12740.

Hoch, J.E., Rachwani, J., & Adolph, K.E. (2020, in press). Looking and locomotion: Real-time dynamics of locomotor exploration in crawling and walking infants. *Child Development.*

Hochberg, Z.E., & Konner, M. (2020). Emerging adulthood: A pre-adult life-history stage. *Frontiers in Endocrinology, 10,* 918.

Hockenberry, M.J., & Wilson, D. (2019). *Wong's nursing care of infants and children* (11th ed.). New York: Elsevier.

Hockenberry, M.J., Wilson, D., & Rodgers, C.C. (2019). *Wong's essentials of pediatric nursing* (11th ed.). Maryland Heights, MO: Mosby.

Hockenberry, S., & Puzzanchera, C. (2019). *Juvenile court statistics 2017.* Pittsburgh: National Center for Juvenile Justice.

Hodgson, Z.G., Comfort, L.R., & Albert, A.A.Y. (2020, in press). Water birth and perinatal outcomes in British Columbia: A retrospective cohort study. *Journal of Obstetrics and Gynecology Canada.*

Hodler, J., Kubik-Huch, R.A., & von Schulthess, G.K. (Eds.) (2020). *Diseases of the brain, head, and neck.* New York: Springer.

Hoeger, W.W.K., & others (2019). *Fitness and wellness* (13th ed.). Boston: Cengage.

Hoelter, L. (2009). Divorce and separation. In D. Carr (Ed.), *Encyclopedia of the life course and human development.* Boston: Gale Cengage.

Hoeve, M., & others (2012). A meta-analysis of attachment to parents and delinquency. *Journal of Abnormal Child and Adolescent Psychology, 40*(5), 771–785.

Hofer, A., & others (2007). Sex differences in brain activation patterns during processing of positively and negatively balanced emotional stimuli. *Psychological Medicine, 37,* 109–119.

Hoff, E., & Laursen, B. (2019). Socioeconomic status and parenting. In M.H. Bornstein (Ed.), *Handbook of parenting* (3rd ed.). New York: Elsevier.

Hoff, E., Laursen, B., & Tardif, T. (2002). Socioeconomic status and parenting. In M.H. Bornstein (Ed.), *Handbook of parenting* (2nd ed.). Mahwah, NJ: Erlbaum.

Hoff, E., & Place, S. (2013). Bilingual language learners. In S.L. Odom, E. Pungello, & N. Gardner-Neblett (Eds.), *Re-visioning the beginning: Developmental and health science contributions to infant/toddler programs for children and families living in poverty.* New York: Guilford.

Hoffman, E., & Ewen, D. (2007). Supporting families, nurturing young children. *CLASP Policy Brief No. 9,* 1–11.

Hoffman, J.D., & others (2020). Teaching emotion regulation in schools: Translating research into practice with the RULER approach to social and emotional learning. *Emotion, 20,* 105–109.

Hoffman, J.P. (2018). Cohabitation, marijuana use, and heavy alcohol use in young adulthood. *Substance Use and Abuse, 3,* 2394–2404.

Hoffman, P., & Morcom, A.M. (2018). Age-related changes in the neural networks supporting semantic cognition: A meta-analysis of 47 functional neuroimaging studies. *Neuroscience and Biobehavioral Reviews, 84,* 134–150.

Hofheimer, J.A., & others (2020, in press). Psychosocial and medical adversity associated with neonatal neurobehavior in infants born before 30 weeks gestation. *Pediatric Research.*

Hogan, C. (2014). Socioeconomic factors affecting infant sleep-related deaths in St. Louis. *Public Health Nursing, 31,* 10–18.

Hogerbrugge, M.J., & Komter, A.E. (2012). Solidarity and ambivalence: Comparing two perspectives on intergenerational relations using longitudinal panel data. *Journals of Gerontology B: Psychological Sciences and Social Sciences, 67,* 372–383.

Hohls, J.K., & others (2019). Association of generalized anxiety symptoms and panic with health care costs in older age—Results from the ESTHER cohort study. *Journal of Affective Disorders, 245,* 978–986.

Holahan, C.K., & others (2020, in press). Leisure-time physical activity and affective experience in middle-aged and older women. *Journal of Women and Aging.*

Holden, G.W., Vittrup, B., & Rosen, L.H. (2011). Families, parenting, and discipline. In M.K. Underwood & L.H. Rosen (Eds.), *Social development.* New York: Guilford.

Hollister, M. (2011). Employment stability in the U.S. labor market: Rhetoric versus reality. *Annual*

Review of Sociology (Vol. 37). Palo Alto, CA: Annual Reviews.

Holm, A.L., Berland, A.K., & Severinsson, E. (2019). Factors that influence the health of older widows and widowers—A systematic review of quantitative research. *Nursing Open, 26,* 591–611.

Holmes, R.M., Little, K.C., & Welsh, D. (2009). Dating and romantic relationships, adulthood. In D. Carr (Ed.), *Encyclopedia of the life course and human development.* Boston: Gale Cengage.

Holmes, T.H., & Rahe, R.H. (1967). The social readjustment rating scale. *Journal of Psychosomatic Research, 11,* 213–218.

Holopainen, A., & Hakulinen, T. (2019). New parents' experiences of postpartum depression: A systematic review of qualitative evidence. *JBI Database of Systematic Reviews and Implementation Reports, 17,* 1731–1769.

Holsen, I., Carlson Jones, D., & Skogbrott Birkeland, M. (2012). Body image satisfaction among Norwegian adolescents and young adults: A longitudinal study of the influence of interpersonal relationships and BMI. *Body Image, 9,* 201–208.

Holway, G.V., & Hernandez, S.M. (2018). Oral sex and condom use in a US national sample of adolescents and young adults. *Journal of Adolescent Health, 62,* 402–410.

Holzman, L. (2017). *Vygotsky at work and play* (2nd ed.). New York: Routledge.

Homan, K.J. (2018). Secure attachment and eudaimonic well-being in late adulthood: The mediating role of self-compassion. *Aging and Mental Health 22,* 363–370.

Homel, J., & Warren, D. (2019). The relationship between parent drinking and adolescent drinking: Differences for mothers and fathers and boys and girls. *Substance Use and Misuse, 54,* 661–669.

Hong, G.W., & Hong, S.M. (2019). Relationships among body mass index, body image, and depression in Korean adults: Korea National Health and Nutrition Examination Survey 2014 and 2016. *Journal of Obesity and Metabolic Syndrome, 28,* 61–68.

Hong, J.H., & others (2019). Perceived changes in life satisfaction from the past, present, and to the future: A comparison of U.S. and Japan. *Psychology and Aging, 34,* 317–329.

Hong, X., & others (2015). Normal aging selectivity diminishes alpha lateralization in visual spatial attention. *Neuroimage, 106,* 353–363.

Honour, J.W. (2018). Biochemistry of the menopause. *Annals of Clinical Biochemistry, 55,* 18–33.

Hoogenhout, M., & Malcolm-Smith, S. (2017). Theory of mind predicts severity level in autism. *Autism, 21,* 242–252.

Hooijsma, M., & others (2020, in press). Being friends with or rejected by classmates: Aggression toward same- and cross-ethnic peers. *Journal of Youth and Adolescence.*

Hooper, S.Y. & others (2016). *Creating a classroom—Incremental theory matters, but it is not as straightforward as you might think: Evidence from a multi-level analysis at ten high schools.* Poster presented at the biennial meeting of the Society for Research on Adolescence, Baltimore.

Hopkins, B. (1991). Facilitating early motor development: An intracultural study of West Indian mothers and their infants living in Britain. In J.K. Nugent, B.M. Lester, & T.B. Brazelton (Eds.), *The cultural context of infancy, Vol. 2: Multicultural and interdisciplinary approaches to parent relations.* New York: Ablex.

Hopkins, B., & Westra, T. (1990). Motor development, maternal expectations, and the role of handling. *Infant Behavior and Development, 13,* 117–122.

Horn, E.E., Turkheimer, E., Strachan, E., & Duncan, G.E. (2015). Behavioral and environmental modification of the genetic influence on body mass index: A twin study. *Behavior Genetics, 45,* 409–426.

Horn, J.L., & Donaldson, G. (1980). Cognitive development II: Adulthood development of human abilities. In O.G. Brim & J. Kagan (Eds.), *Constancy and change in human development.* Cambridge, MA: Harvard University Press.

Horne, R.S., Franco, P., Adamson, T.M., Groswasser, J., & Kahn, A. (2002). Effects of body position on sleep and arousal characteristics in infants. *Early Human Development, 69,* 25–33.

Horne, R.S.C. (2018). Cardiovascular autonomic dysfunction in sudden infant death syndrome. *Clinical Automatic Research, 28,* 535–543.

Horne, R.S.C. (2019). Sudden infant death syndrome: Current perspectives. *Internal Medicine Journal, 49,* 433–438.

Horowitz-Kraus, T., & Hutton, J.S. (2018). Brain connectivity in children is increased by the time they spend reading books and decreased by the length of exposure to screen-based media. *Acta Pediatrica, 107,* 685–693.

Hou, Y., & Kim, S.Y. (2018). Acculturation-related stressors and individual adjustment in Asian American families. In S.S. Chuang & C. Costigan (Eds.), *An international approach to parenting and parent-child families in immigrant families.* New York: Routledge.

Hou, Y., Kim, S.Y., & Wang, Y. (2016). Parental acculturative stressors and adolescent adjustment through interparental and parent-child relationships in Chinese American families. *Journal of Youth and Adolescence, 45,* 1466–1481.

Houde, B. (2019). *3-system theory of the cognitive brain.* New York: Routledge.

Houde, O., & others (2011). Functional magnetic resonance imaging study of Piaget's conservation-of-number task in preschool and school-age children: A neo-Piagetian approach. *Journal of Experimental Child Psychology, 110*(3), 332–346.

Howard, J.L., Gagne, M., & Bureau, J.S. (2017). Testing a continuum structure of self-determined motivation: A meta-analysis. *Psychological Bulletin, 143,* 1346–1377.

Howes, C. (2009). Friendship in early childhood. In K.H. Rubin, W.M. Bukowski, & B. Laursen (Eds.), *Handbook of peer interactions, relationships, and groups.* New York: Guilford.

Howes, C. (2016). Children and child care: A theory of relationships within cultural communities. In K. Sanders & A.W. Guerra (Eds.), *The culture of child care.* New York: Oxford University Press.

Howes, C., & Spieker, S. (2016). Attachment relationships in the context of multiple caregivers. In J. Cassidy & P.R. Shaver (Eds.), *Handbook of attachment* (3rd ed.). New York: Guilford.

Hoye, J.R., & others (2020, in press). Preliminary indications that attachment and biobehavioral catch-up intervention alters DNA methylation in maltreated children. *Development and Psychopathology.*

Hoyer, W.J. (2015). Brain aging: Behavioral, cognitive, and personality consequences. In J.D. Wright (Ed.), *International encyclopedia of the social and behavioral sciences* (2nd ed.). New York: Elsevier.

Hoyer, W.J., & Roodin, P.A. (2009). *Adult development and aging* (6th ed.). New York: McGraw-Hill.

HSBC Insurance (2007). *The future of retirement: The new old age—Global report.* London: HSBC.

Hsu, J.L., & others (2008). Gender differences and age-related white matter changes of the human brain: A diffusion tensor imaging study. *Neuroimage, 39,* 566–577.

Hu, J., & others (2019). Association between television viewing and early childhood overweight and obesity: A pair-matched case-control study in China. *BMC Pediatrics, 19*(1), 184.

Hu, L., & others (2019). Physical activity modifies the association between depression and cognitive function in older adults. *Journal of Affective Disorders, 246,* 800–805.

Hu, X., & others (2019). Cognitive aging trajectories and mortality of Chinese oldest-old. *Archives of Gerontology and Geriatrics, 82,* 81–87.

Hu, Z., & others (2019). Maternal metabolic factors during pregnancy predict early childhood growth trajectories and obesity risk: The CANDLE study. *International Journal of Obesity, 43,* 1914–1922.

Huang, H.W., Meyer, A.M., & Federmeier, K.D. (2012). A "concrete view" of aging: Event-related potentials reveal age-related changes in basic integrated processes in language. *Neuropsychologia, 50,* 26–35.

Huang, J-H., DeJong, W., Towvim, L.G., & Schneider, S.K. (2009). Sociodemographic and psychobehavioral characteristics of U.S. college students who abstain from alcohol. *Journal of American College Health, 57,* 395–410.

Huang, L., & others (2018). Maternal smoking and attention-deficit/hyperactivity disorder in offspring: A meta-analysis. *Pediatrics, 141,* 1.

Huang, L., & others (2018). The mediating role of placenta in the relationship between maternal exercise during pregnancy and full-term low birth weight. *Journal of Maternal-Fetal and Neonatal Medicine, 3* (12), 1561–1567.

Huang, L.B., & others (2017). Influencing and protective factors of suicide ideation among older adults. *International Journal of Mental Health Nursing, 26,* 191–199.

Huang, P.M., Smock, P.J., Manning, W.D., & Bergstrom-Lynch, C.A. (2011). He says, she says:

Gender and cohabitation. *Journal of Family Issues, 32,* 876–905.

Huang, Y.P., & others (2019). Free testosterone correlated with erectile dysfunction severity among young men with normal total testosterone. *International Journal of Impotence, 31,* 132–138.

Huber, M., & others (2020, in press). Cognition in older adults with severe to profound sensorineural hearing loss compared to peers with normal hearing for age. *International Journal of Audiology.*

Hudson, N.W., Lucas, R.E., & Donnellan, M.B. (2020, in press). The highs and lows of love: Romantic relationship quality moderates whether spending time with one's partner predicts gains or losses in well-being. *Personality and Social Psychology Bulletin.*

Huebner, A.M., & Garrod, A.C. (1993). Moral reasoning among Tibetan monks: A study of Buddhist adolescents and young adults in Nepal. *Journal of Cross-Cultural Psychology, 24,* 167–185.

Huesmann, L.R., Dubow, E.F., Eron, L.D., & Boxer, P. (2006). Middle childhood family-contextual and personal factors as predictors of adult outcomes. In A.G. Huston & M.N. Ripke (Eds.), *Developmental contexts in middle childhood: Bridges to adolescence and adulthood.* New York: Cambridge University Press.

Huffman, J.C., & others (2016). Effects of optimism and gratitude on physical activity, biomarkers, and readmissions after an acute coronary syndrome: The Gratitude Research in Acute Coronary Events Study. *Circulation: Cardiovascular Quality and Outcomes, 9,* 55–63.

Hughes, C., & Devine, R.T. (2015). Individual differences in theory of mind: A social perspective. In R.M. Lerner (Ed.), *Handbook of child psychology and developmental science* (7th ed.). New York: Wiley.

Hughes, C., Devine, R.T., & Wang, Z. (2018). Does parental mind-mindedness account for cross-cultural differences in preschoolers' theory of mind? *Child Development, 89*(4), 1296–1310.

Hughes, C., Marks, A., Ensor, R., & Lecce, S. (2010). A longitudinal study of conflict and inner state talk in children's conversations with mothers and younger siblings. *Social Development, 19,* 822–837.

Hughes, C., & others (2019). Age differences in specific neural connections within the default mode network underlie theory of mind. *NeuroImage, 191,* 269–277.

Hughes, C., & others (2020, in press). Parental well-being, couple relationship quality, and children's behavioral problems in the first 2 years of life. *Development and Psychopathology.*

Hughes, J.N., & Cao, Q. (2018).Trajectories of teacher-student warmth and conflict at the transition to middle school: Effects on academic engagement and achievement. *Journal of School Psychology, 67,* 148–162.

Hughes, M.E., Waite, L.J., LaPierre, T.A., & Luo, Y. (2007). All in the family: The impact of caring for grandchildren on grandparents' health. *Journals of Gerontology B: Psychological Sciences and Social Sciences, 62,* S108–S119.

Huhdanpaa, H., & others (2018). Sleep and psychiatric symptoms in young child psychiatric outpatients. *Clinical Child Psychology and Psychiatry, 23,* 77–95.

Huhdanpaa, H., & others (2019). Sleep difficulties in infancy are associated with symptoms of inattention and hyperactivity at the age of 5 years: A longitudinal study. *Journal of Developmental and Behavioral Pediatrics, 40,* 432–440.

Hui, L. (2019). Noninvasive approaches to prenatal diagnosis: Historical perspective and future directions. *Methods in Molecular Biology, 1885,* 45–58.

Huijbers, W., & others (2017). Age-related increases in tip-of-the-tongue are distinct from decreases in remembering names: A functional MRI study. *Cerebral Cortex, 27,* 4339–4349.

Huisingh, C., & others (2017). Visual sensory and visual-cognitive function and rate of crash and near-crash involvement among older drivers using naturalistic driving data. *Investigative Ophthalmology and Visual Science, 58,* 2959–2967.

Hultsch, D.F., Hertzog, C., Small, B.J., & Dixon, R.A. (1999). Use it or lose it: Engaged lifestyle as a buffer of cognitive decline in aging? *Psychology and Aging, 14,* 245–263.

Hung, L.Y., Lyons, J.G., & Wu, C.H. (2020, in press). Health information technology use among older adults in the United States, 2009–2018. *Current Medical Research and Opinion.*

Hunter, S., Leatherdale, S.T., & Carson, V. (2018). The 3-year longitudinal impact of sedentary behavior on the academic achievement of secondary school students. *Journal of School Health, 88,* 660–668.

Huo, M., & Fingerman, K.L. (2018). Grandparents. In M.H. Bornstein (Ed.), *SAGE encyclopedia of lifespan human development.* Thousand Oaks, CA: Sage.

Huo, M., & others (2018). Support grandparents give to their adult grandchildren. *Journals of Gerontology B: Psychological Sciences and Social Sciences, 58,* 872–882.

Huo, M., & others (2019). Aging parents' daily support exchanges with adult children suffering problems. *Journals of Gerontology B: Psychological Sciences and Social Sciences, 74,* 449–459.

Hurt, H., Brodsky, N.L., Roth, H., Malmud, F., & Giannetta, J.M. (2005). School performance of children with gestational cocaine exposure. *Neurotoxicology and Teratology, 27,* 203–211.

Huston, A.C., & Ripke, N.N. (2006). Experiences in middle and late childhood and children's development. In A.C. Huston & M.N. Ripke (Eds.), *Developmental contexts in middle childhood.* New York: Cambridge University Press.

Huttenlocher, J., Haight, W., Bruk, A., Seltzer, M., & Lyons, T. (1991). Early vocabulary growth: Relation to language input and gender. *Developmental Psychology, 27,* 236–248.

Huttenlocher, P.R., & Dabholkar, A.S. (1997). Regional differences in synaptogenesis in human cerebral cortex. *Journal of Comparative Neurology, 37*(2), 167–178.

Hwang, J.Y., & others (2012). Multidimensional comparison of personality characteristics of the Big Five model, impulsiveness, and affect in pathological gambling and obsessive-compulsive disorder. *Journal of Gambling Studies, 28,* 351–362.

Hybels, C.F., & Blazer, D.G. (2004). Epidemiology of the late-life mental disorders. *Clinical Geriatric Medicine, 19,* 663–696.

Hyde, J.S. (2014). Gender similarities and differences. *Annual Review of Psychology* (Vol. 66). Palo Alto, CA: Annual Reviews.

Hyde, J.S. (2017). Gender similarities. In C.B. Travis & J.W. White (Eds.), *APA handbook of the psychology of women.* Washington, DC: American Psychological Association.

Hyde, J.S., & DeLamater, J.D. (2020). *Understanding human sexuality* (14th ed.). New York: McGraw-Hill.

Hyde, J.S., & Else-Quest, N. (2013). *Half the human experience* (8th ed.). Boston: Cengage.

Hyde, J.S., & Mezulis, A.H. (2020). Gender differences in depression: Biological, affective, cognitive, and sociocultural factors. *Harvard Review of Psychiatry, 28,* 4–13.

Hyde, J.S., & others (2008). Gender similarities characterize math performance. *Science, 321,* 494–495.

Hyde, J.S., & others (2019). The future of sex and gender in psychology: Five challenges to the gender binary. *American Psychology, 74,* 171–193.

Hynes, M. (2020). 10 proven strategies to help patients maintain weight loss. *Journal of Family Practice, 69,* 20–25.

Hysing, M., & others (2020, in press). Bullying involvement in adolescence: Implications for sleep, mental health, and academic outcomes. *Journal of Interpersonal Violence.*

Hyson, M.C., Copple, C., & Jones, J. (2006). Early childhood development and education. In W. Damon & R. Lerner (Eds.), *Handbook of child psychology* (6th ed.). New York: Wiley.

I

"I Have a Dream" Foundation (2015). *Research on "I Have a Dream."* Retrieved July 15, 2017, from www.ihad.org

"I Have a Dream" Foundation (2020). *About us.* Retrieved February 1, 2020, from www.ihad.org

Iacono, D., & Feltis, G.C. (2019). Impact of Apolipoprotein E gene polymorphism during normal and pathological conditions of the brain across the lifespan. *Aging, 11*(2), 787–816.

Ibanez, J., & others (2020, in press). Plasticity induced by pairing brain stimulation with motor-related states only targets a subset of cortical neurons. *Brain Stimulation.*

Ibrahim, K., & others (2019). Reduced amygdala-prefrontal functional connectivity in children with autism spectrum disorder and co-occurring disruptive behavior. *Biological Psychiatry. Cognitive Neuroscience and Neuroimaging, 4,* 1031–1041.

Icenogle, G., & others (2019). Adolescents' cognitive capacity reaches adult levels prior to their psychosocial maturity: Evidence for a "maturity gap" in multinational, cross-sectional sample. *Law and Human Behavior, 43,* 69–85.

Idler, E., & others (2017). Religion, a social determinant of mortality? A 10-year follow-up of the Health and Retirement Study. *PLoS One, 12*(12), e0189134.

Igarashi, H., Hooker, K., Coehlo, D.P., & Manoogian, M.M. (2013). "My nest is full": Intergenerational relationships at midlife. *Journal of Aging Studies, 27*, 102–112.

Ihle, A., & others (2015). The association of leisure activities in middle adulthood with cognitive performance in old age: The moderating role of educational level. *Gerontology, 61*, 543–550.

Iliyasu, Z., & others (2020, in press). Healthcare workers' knowledge of HIV-exposed infant feeding options and infant feeding counseling practice in northern Nigeria. *Current HIV Research.*

Ilmakunnas, P., & Ilmakunnas, S. (2018). Health and retirement age: Comparison of expectations and actual retirement. *Scandinavian Journal of Public Health, 46*(Suppl. 19), S18–S31.

Ilyas, Z., Shahed, S., & Hussain, S. (2020, in press). An impact of perceived social support on old age well-being mediated by spirituality, self-esteem, and ego integrity. *Journal of Religion and Health.*

Im, Y., Oh, W.O., & Suk, M. (2017). Risk factors for suicide ideation among adolescents: Five-year national data analysis. *Archives of Psychiatric Nursing, 31*, 282–286.

Imafuku, M., & others (2019). Audiovisual speech perception and language acquisition in preterm infants: A longitudinal study. *Early Human Development, 128*, 93–100.

Impett, E.A., Schoolder, D., Tolman, L., Sorsoli, L., & Henson, J.M. (2008). Girls' relationship authenticity and self-esteem across adolescence, *Developmental Psychology, 44*, 722–733.

Indefrey, P. (2019). The relationship between semantic production and comprehension. In S-A. Rueschemeyer & M. Gareth Gaskell (Eds.), *Oxford handbook of psycholinguistics* (2nd ed.). New York: Oxford University Press.

Inderkum, A.P., & Tarokh, L. (2018). High heritability of adolescent sleep-wake behavior on free, but not school days: A long-term twin study. *Sleep, 41*(3). doi:10.1093/sleep/zsy004

Infurna, F.J., Okun, M.A., & Grimm, K.J. (2016). Volunteering is associated with lower risk of cognitive impairment. *Journal of the American Geriatrics Society, 64*, 2263–2269.

Ingersoll-Dayton, B., & others (2019). A systematic review of dyadic approaches to reminiscence and life review among older adults. *Aging and Mental Health, 23*, 1074–1085.

Insel, P., & Roth, W. (2020). *Core concepts in health* (16th ed.). New York: McGraw-Hill.

Ip, S., Chung, M., Raman, G., Trikalinos, T.A., & Lau, J. (2009). A summary of the Agency for Healthcare Research and Quality's evidence report on breastfeeding in developed countries. *Breastfeeding Medicine, 4*(1, Suppl.), S17–S30.

Irwin, C.E. (2010). Young adults are worse off than adolescents. *Journal of Adolescent Health, 46*, 405–406.

Ishak, S., & others (2019). Neonatal pain: Knowledge and perception among pediatric doctors in Malaysia. *Pediatrics International, 61*, 67–72.

Isidori, A.M., & others (2014). A critical analysis of the role of testosterone in erectile function: From pathophysiology to treatment—A systematic analysis. *European Urology, 65*(1), 99–112.

Israel, M. (2019). Semantics. In C. Genetti (Ed.), *How languages work* (2nd ed.). New York: Cambridge University Press.

Itoh, H., & others (2020). Associations between changes in body weight and fat weight in middle age general population. *International Heart Journal, 61*, 15–20.

Ivan Santini, Z., Koyanagi, A., Tyrovolas, S., & Haro, J.M. (2015). The association of relationship quality and social networks with depression, anxiety, and suicidal ideation among older married adults: Findings from a cross-sectional analysis of The Irish Longitudinal Study on Aging (TILDA). *Journal of Affective Disorders, 179*, 134–141.

Ivashko-Pachima, Y., & others (2020, in press). Discovery of autism/intellectual disability somatic mutations in Alzheimer's brains: Mutated ADNP cytoskeletal impairments and repairs as a case study. *Molecular Psychiatry.*

Iyengar, U., & others (2019). Unresolved trauma and reorganization in mothers: Attachment and neuroscience perspectives. *Frontiers in Psychology, 10*, 110.

J

Jabeen, H., & others (2018). Investigating the scavenging of reactive oxygen species by antioxidants via theoretical and experimental methods. *Journal of Photochemistry and Photobiology B, 180*, 268–275.

Jackson, E., & others (2019). Fast mapping short and long words: Examining the influence of phonological short-term memory and receptive vocabulary in children with developmental language disorder. *Journal of Communication Disorders, 79*, 11–23.

Jackson, J.J., & Hill, P. (2019). Lifespan development of conscientiousness. In D.P. McAdams & others (Eds.), *Handbook of personality development*. New York: Guilford.

Jackson, J.S., Govia, I.O., & Sellers, S.L. (2011). Racial and ethnic influences over the life course. In R.H. Binstock & L.K. George (Eds.), *Handbook of aging and the social sciences* (7th ed.). New York: Elsevier.

Jackson, M.A., Edmiston, A.M., & Bedi, R. (2020). Optimum refractive target in patients with bilateral implantation of extended depth of focus intraocular lenses. *Clinical Ophthalmology, 14*, 455–462.

Jackson, S.E., & others (2019). Decline in sexuality and wellbeing in older adults: A population-based study. *Journal of Affective Disorders, 245*, 912–917.

Jacobs, J.M., Hammerman-Rozenberg, R., Cohen, A., & Stressman, J. (2008). Reading daily predicts reduced mortality among men from a cohort of community dwelling 70-year-olds. *Journals of Gerontology B: Psychological Sciences and Social Sciences, 63*, S73–S80.

Jadhav, A., & Weir, D. (2018). Widowhood and depression in a cross-national perspective: Evidence from the United States, Europe, Korea, and China. *Journals of Gerontology B: Psychological Sciences and Social Sciences, 73*(8), e143–e153.

Jadhav, K.S., & Boutrel, B. (2019). Prefrontal cortex development and emergence of self-regulatory competence: The two cardinal features of adolescence disrupted in context of alcohol abuse. *European Journal of Neuroscience, 50*(3), 2274–2281.

Jaeggi, S.M., Berman, M.G., & Jonides, J. (2009). Training attentional processes. *Trends in Cognitive Science, 37*, 644–654.

Jaekel, J., & others (2019). Head growth and intelligence from birth to adulthood in very preterm and term born individuals. *Journal of the International Neuropsychology Association, 25*, 48–56.

Jaffee, S., & Hyde, J.S. (2000). Gender differences in moral orientation: A meta-analysis. *Psychological Bulletin, 126*, 703–726.

Jagannathan, R., & others (2019). Global updates on cardiovascular disease mortality trends and attribution of traditional risk factors. *Current Diabetes Reports, 19*(7), 44.

Jagla, V.M., & Tice, K.C. (Eds.) (2019). *Educating teachers and tomorrow's students through service-learning pedagogy. Advances in service-learning research.* Charlotte, NC: Information Age Publishing.

Jahangard, L., & others (2020, in press). Prenatal and postnatal hair steroid levels predict post-partum depression 12 weeks after delivery. *Journal of Clinical Medicine.*

Jain, S., & others (2019). Adult neurogenesis in the mouse dendate gyrus protects the hippocampus from neuronal injury following severe seizures. *Hippocampus, 29*, 683–709.

Jalongo, M.R. (2014). *Early childhood language arts* (6th ed.). Upper Saddle River, NJ: Pearson.

Jamal, L., Schupmann, W., & Berkman, B.E. (2020, in press). An ethical framework for genetic counseling in the genomic era. *Journal of Genetic Counseling.*

Jambon, M., & Smetana, J.G. (2020). Socialization of moral judgments and reasoning. In D.J. Laible & others (Eds.), *Oxford handbook of parenting and moral development.* New York: Oxford University Press.

James, L.E., & others (2018). Tip of the tongue states increase under evaluative observation. *Journal of Psycholinguistic Research.*

James, T., Rajah, M.N., & Duarte, A. (2019). Multielement episodic encoding in young and older adults. *Journal of Cognitive Neuroscience, 6*, 837–854.

James, W. (1890/1950). *The principles of psychology.* New York: Dover.

Jang, S., & others (2017). Measurement invariance of the Satisfaction with Life Scale across 26 countries. *Journal of Cross-Cultural Psychology, 48*, 560–576.

Jankauskiene, R., & others (2019). Are adolescent body image concerns associated with health-compromising physical activity behaviors?

International Journal of Environmental Research and Public Health, 16, 7.

Jankowski, M., & others (2019). E-cigarettes are more addictive than traditional cigarettes—A study in highly educated young people. *International Journal of Environmental Research and Public Policy, 16*, 13.

Jansen, E.C., & others (2020, in press). Sleep duration and quality in relation to fruit and vegetable intake of U.S. adults: A secondary analysis. *International Journal of Behavioral Medicine.*

Jansen, J., de Weerth, C., & Riksen-Walraven, J.M. (2008). Breastfeeding and the mother-infant relationship—A review. *Developmental Review, 28*, 503–521.

Janssen, I., Landay, A.L., Ruppert, K., & Powerll, L.H. (2014). Moderate wine consumption is associated with lower hemostatic and inflammatory risk factors over 8 years: The study of women's health across the nation (SWAN). *Nutrition and Aging, 2*, 91–99.

Janssen, I., & others (2005). Comparison of overweight and obesity prevalence in school-aged youth from 34 countries and their relationships with physical activity and dietary patterns. *Obesity Reviews, 6*, 123–132.

Janssens, A., & others (2017). Adolescent externalizing behavior, psychological control, and rejection: Transactional links and dopaminergic moderation. *British Journal of Developmental Psychology, 35*, 420–438.

Jansson, T., & others (2020, in press). Down regulation of placental Cdc42 and Rac1 links mTORC2 inhibition to decreased trophoblast amino acid transport in human intrauterine growth restriction. *Clinical Science.*

Jantzie, L.L., & others (2020, in press). Prenatal opioid exposure: The next neonatal neuroinflammatory disease. *Brain, Behavior, and Immunity.*

Jaques, S.C., & others (2014). Cannabis, the pregnant woman, and her child: Weeding out the myths. *Journal of Perinatology, 34*, 417–424.

Jardri, R., & others (2012). Assessing fetal response to maternal speech using a noninvasive functional brain imaging technique. *International Journal of Developmental Neuroscience, 30*, 159–161.

Jariat, G., Portrat, S., & Hot, P. (2019). Aging influences the efficiency of attentional maintenance in verbal working memory. *Journals of Gerontology B: Psychological Sciences and Social Sciences, 74*, 600–608.

Jariat, G., & others (2020, in press). Distinguishing the impact of age on semantic and nonsemantic associations of episodic memory. *Journals of Gerontology B: Psychological and Social Sciences.*

Jaruratanasirikul, S., & others (2017). A population-based study of Down syndrome in Southern Thailand. *World Journal of Pediatrics, 13*, 63–69.

Jarvis, S.N., & Okonofua, J.A. (2020). School deferred: When bias affects school leaders. *Social Psychological and Personality Science, 11*, 492–498.

Jasinska, K.K., & Petitto, L-A. (2018). Age of bilingual exposure is related to the contribution of phonological and semantic knowledge to successful reading development. *Child Development, 89*, 310–331.

Jefferson, T., Demasi, M., & Doshi, P. (2020, in press). Statins for primary prevention: What is the regulator's role? *BMJ Evidence Based Medicine.*

Jelsma, E., & Varner, F. (2020). African American adolescent substance use: The roles of racial discrimination and peer pressure. *Addictive Behaviors, 101*, 106154.

Jenkins, J.M., & Astington, J.W. (1996). Cognitive factors and family structure associated with theory of mind development in young children. *Developmental Psychology, 32*, 70–78.

Jensen, T.M. (2020, in press). Stepfamily processes and youth adjustment: The role of perceived neighborhood collective efficacy. *Journal of Research on Adolescence.*

Jensen-Campbell, L.A., & Malcolm, K.T. (2007). The importance of conscientiousness in adolescent interpersonal relationships. *Personality and Social Psychology Bulletin, 33*, 368–383.

Jenzer, T., & others (2019). Coping trajectories in emerging adulthood: The influence of temperament and gender. *Journal of Personality, 87*, 607–619.

Jeremic, S., & others (2018). Selected anthraquinones as potential free radical scavengers and P-glycoprotein inhibitors. *Organic and Biomedical Chemistry, 16*(11), 1890–1902.

Jessen, S., & Grossman, T. (2020, in press). Neural evidence for the impact of facial trustworthiness on object processing in a gaze-cueing task in 7-month-old infants. *Social Neuroscience.*

Jeste, D.V., & Lee, E.E. (2019). The emerging empirical science of wisdom: Definition, measurement, neurobiology, longevity, and interventions. *Harvard Review of Psychiatry, 27*, 127–140.

Jeyanthi, S.J., Arumugam, N., & Parasher, R.K. (2019). Effect of physical exercises on attention, motor skills, and physical fitness in children with attention deficit hyperactivity disorder: A systematic review. *Attention Deficit Hyperactivity Disorder, 11*, 125–137.

Ji, B.T., & others (1997). Paternal cigarette smoking and the risk of childhood cancer among offspring of nonsmoking mothers. *Journal of the National Cancer Institute, 89*, 238–244.

Ji, L., Peng, H., & Mao, X. (2019). The role of sensory function in processing speed and working memory aging. *Experimental Aging Research, 45*, 234–251.

Ji, N., & others (2019). Aerobic exercise promotes the expression of ERCC1 to prolong lifespan: A new possible mechanism. *Medical Hypotheses, 122*, 22–25.

Jia, P., Pei, G., & Zhao, Z. (2019, in press). CNet: A multi-omics approach to detecting clinically associated, combinatory genomic signatures. *Bioinformatics.*

Jiang, X., & others (2018). Hope and adolescent mental health. In M.W. Gallagher & S.J. Lopez (Eds.), *Oxford handbook of hope.* New York: Oxford University Press.

Jiang, Y., Granja, M.R., & Koball, H. (2017). *Basic facts about low-income children.* New York: National Center for Children in Poverty, Columbia University.

Jiang, Y., & others (2020). Temporal trends in the mortality rate of Alzheimer's disease and other dementias attributable to smoking, 1990–2017. *Environmental Research 184*, 109183.

Jiao, S., Ji, G., & Jing, Q. (1996). Cognitive development of Chinese urban only children and children with siblings. *Child Development, 67*, 387–395.

Jimenez-Trevino, L., & others (2019). 5-HTTLPR-brain-derived neurotrophic factor (BDNF) gene interactions and early adverse life events effect on impulsivity in suicide attempters. *World Journal of Biological Psychiatry, 20*, 137–149.

Jin, M.M., & others (2019). A critical role of autophagy in regulating microglia polarization in neurodegeneration. *Frontiers in Aging Neuroscience, 10*, 378.

Jin, S.V., Ryu, E., & Mugaddam, A. (2020, in press). Romance 2.0 on Instagram! "What type of girlfriend would you date?" *Evolutionary Psychology.*

Jindal, H.A., & others (2019). Mental health and environmental factors associated with falls in the elderly in North India: A naturalistic community study. *Asian Journal of Psychiatry, 39*, 17–21.

Jo, J., & Lee, Y.J. (2018). Effectiveness of acupuncture in women with polycystic ovarian syndrome undergoing in vitro fertilization or intracytoplasmic sperm injection: A systematic review and meta-analysis. *Acupuncture, 35*, 162–170.

John, A., & others (2018). Self-harm, suicidal behaviors, and cyberbullying in children and young people: Systematic review. *Journal of Medical Internet Research, 20*, e129.

John, N.A., & others (2017). Understanding the meaning of marital relationship quality among couples in peri-urban Ethiopia. *Culture, Health, and Sexuality, 19*, 267–278.

Johns Hopkins University (2006, February 17). *Undergraduate honored for launching health programs in India.* Baltimore: Johns Hopkins University News Releases.

Johnson, A.E., & others (2019). Cognitive-affective strategies and cortisol stress reactivity in children and adolescents: Normative development and effects of early life stress. *Developmental Psychobiology, 61*, 999–1013.

Johnson, C.L., & Troll, L.E. (1992). Family functioning in late life. *Journals of Gerontology, 47*, S66–S72.

Johnson, J.A., & others (2018). *Foundations of American education* (17th ed.). Upper Saddle River, NJ: Pearson.

Johnson, J.P., Ross, K., & Kiran, S. (2019). Multi-step treatment for acquired dyslexia and agraphia (Part 1): Efficacy, generalization, and identification of beneficial treatment steps. *Neuropsychological Rehabilitation, 29*, 534–564.

Johnson, J.S., & Newport, E.L. (1991). Critical period effects on universal properties of language: The status of subjacency in the acquisition of a second language. *Cognition, 39*, 215–258.

Johnson, M. (2008, April 30). Commentary in R. Highfield, Harvard's baby brain research lab. Retrieved January 24, 2008, from www.telegraph.co.

uk/scienceandtechnology/science/sciencenews/
3341166/Harvards-baby-brain-research-lab.html

Johnson, M.H., Grossmann, T., & Cohen-Kadosh, K. (2009). Mapping functional brain development: Building a social brain through interactive specialization. *Developmental Psychology, 45,* 151–159.

Johnson, M.H., Jones, E., & Gliga, T. (2015). Brain adaptation and alternative developmental trajectories. *Development and Psychopathology, 27,* 425–442.

Johnson, M.H., Senju, A., & Tomalski, P. (2015). The two-process theory of face processing: Modifications based on two decades of data from infants and adults. *Neuroscience and Biobehavioral Reviews, 50,* 169–179.

Johnson, P. (2018). *The emotional needs of young children.* New York: Routledge.

Johnson, S.P. (2010). Perceptual completion in infancy. In S.P. Johnson (Ed.), *Neoconstructivism: The new science of cognitive development* (pp. 45–60). New York: Oxford University Press.

Johnson, S.P. (2011). A constructivist view of object perception in infancy. In L.M. Oakes, C.H. Cashon, M. Casasola, & D.H. Rakison (Eds.), *Infant perception and cognition.* New York: Oxford University Press.

Johnson, S.P. (2013). Object perception. In P.D. Zelazo (Ed.), *Handbook of developmental psychology.* New York: Oxford University Press.

Johnson, S.P. (2019). Object perception. In O. Braddick (Ed.), *Oxford research encyclopedia of psychology.* New York: Oxford University Press.

Johnson, S.P. (2020a, in press). Development of the visual system. In J. Rubenstein (Ed.), *Comprehensive developmental neuroscience.* New York: Elsevier.

Johnson, S.P. (2020b, in press). Development of visual-spatial attention. In T. Hodgson (Ed.), *Comprehensive topics in behavioral neurosciences.* New York: Elsevier.

Johnson, S.P., & Hannon, E.E. (2015). Perceptual development. In R.M. Lerner (Ed.), *Handbook of child psychology and developmental science* (7th ed.). New York: Wiley.

Johnson, W., Corley, J., Starr, J.M., & Deary, I.J. (2011). Psychological and physical health at age 70 in the Lothian Birth Cohort 1936: Links with early life IQ, SES, and current cognitive function and neighborhood environment. *Health Psychology, 30,* 1–11.

Johnston, C., & others (2017). Skin-to-skin care for procedural pain in neonates. *Cochrane Database of Systematic Reviews, 2,* CD008435.

Johnston, C.A., Cavanaugh, S.E., & Crosnoe, R. (2020). Family structure patterns from childhood through adolescence and the timing of cohabitation among diverse groups of young adult women and men. *Developmental Psychology, 58,* 165–179.

Johnston, L.D., O'Malley, P.M., Bachman, J.G., & Schulenberg, J.E. (2008). *Monitoring the Future national survey results on drug use, 1975–2007, Volume 1: Secondary school students* (NIH Publication No. 08-6418A). Bethesda, MD: National Institute on Drug Abuse.

Johnston, L.D., & others (2018). *Monitoring the future: National survey results on drug use, 1975–2017.* Ann Arbor, MI: Institute for Social Research, University of Michigan.

Jolicoeur-Martineau, A., & others (2020, in press). Distinguishing differential susceptibility, diathesis-stress, and vantage sensitivity: Beyond the single gene and environment model. *Development and Psychopathology.*

Jones, C.R.G., & others (2018). The association between theory of mind, executive function, and the symptoms of autism spectrum disorder. *Autism Research, 11,* 95–109.

Jones, E., & others (2019). Lived experience of young widowed individuals: A qualitative study. *Death Studies, 43,* 183–192.

Jones, L., & others (2012). Pain management for women in labor: An overview of systematic reviews. *Cochrane Database of Systematic Reviews, 14*(3), CD009234.

Jones, M.C. (1965). Psychological correlates of somatic development. *Child Development, 36,* 899–911.

Jones, M.M., & Roy, K. (2017). Placing health trajectories in family and historical context: A proposed enrichment of the Life Course Health and Developmental Model. *Maternal and Child Health Journal, 21,* 1853–1860.

Jones, P.S., & others (2011). Development of a caregiver empowerment model to promote positive outcomes. *Journal of Family Nursing, 17,* 11–28.

Jones, T.H., & Kelly, D.M. (2018). Randomized controlled trials—Mechanistic studies of testosterone and the cardiovascular system. *Asian Journal of Andrology, 20,* 120–130.

Jongenelis, M.I., & others (2020). Improving attitudes to volunteering among older adults: A randomized trial approach. *Research on Aging, 42,* 51–61.

Jordan, J.W., & others (2019). Peer crowd identification and adolescent health behaviors: Results from a statewide representative study. *Heath Education and Behavior, 46,* 40–52.

Jorgensen, M.J., & others (2015). Sexual behavior among young Danes aged 15–29 years: A cross-sectional study of core indicators. *Sexually Transmitted Infections, 91,* 171–177.

Jose, A., O'Leary, K.D., & Moyer, A. (2010). Does premarital cohabitation predict subsequent marital stability and marital quality? A meta-analysis. *Journal of Marriage and the Family, 72,* 105–116.

Joseph, J. (2006). *The missing gene.* New York: Algora.

Joseph, P.V., & others (2019). Comprehensive and systematic analysis of gene expression patterns associated with body mass index. *Scientific Reports, 9*(1), 7447.

Joshanloo, M., & Jovanovic, V. (2020, in press). Similarities and differences in predictors of life satisfaction across age groups: A 150-country study. *Journal of Health Psychology.*

Joshi, A., & others (2020, in press). Gestational diabetes and maternal obesity are associated with sex-specific changes in miRNA and target gene expression in the fetus. *International Journal of Obesity.*

Joyner, K., Manning, W., & Prince, B. (2019). The qualities of same-sex and different-sex couples in young adulthood. *Journal of Marriage and the Family, 81,* 487–505.

Ju, H. (2017). The relationship between physical activity, meaning in life, and subjective vitality in community-dwelling older adults. *Archives of Gerontology and Geriatrics, 73,* 120–124.

Juang, L.P., & others (2018). Time-varying associations of parent-adolescent cultural conflict and youth adjustment among Chinese American families. *Developmental Psychology, 30,* 1661–1668.

Judd, F.K., Hickey, M., & Bryant, C. (2012). Depression and midlife: Are we overpathologising the menopause? *Journal of Affective Disorders, 136,* 199–211.

Juhnke, G.A., Granello, H., & Granello, P. (2020). *School bullying and violence.* New York: Oxford University Press.

Julian, M.M. (2013). Age at adoption from institutional care as a window into the lasting effects of early experience. *Clinical Child and Family Psychology Review, 16*(2), 101–145.

Julian, M.M., & others (2019). Parenting and toddler self-regulation in low-income families: What does sleep have to do with it? *Infant Mental Health, 40,* 479–495.

Jung, C. (1933). *Modern man in search of a soul.* New York: Harcourt Brace.

Jung, S., Nobari, T.Z., & Whaley, S.E. (2019). Breastfeeding outcomes among WIC-participating infants and their relationships to baby-friendly hospital practices. *Breastfeeding Medicine. 40,* 424–431.

Juraska, J.M., & Willing, J. (2017). Pubertal onset as a critical transition for neural development and cognition. *Brain Research, 1654*(Pt. B), 87–94.

Jurcau, A., & Simon, A. (2020, in press). Oxidative stress in the pathogenesis of Alzheimer's disease and cerebrovascular disease with therapeutic implications. *CNS & Neurological Disorders Drug Targets.*

Jylhava, J., & others (2019). Longitudinal changes in the genetic and environmental influences on the epigenetic clocks across old age: Evidence from two twin cohorts. *EBioMedicine, 40,* 710–716.

K

Kabiri, M., & others (2018). Long-term health and economic value of improved mobility among older adults in the United States. *Value in Health, 21,* 792–798.

Kadlaskar, G., & others (2020, in press). Caregiver touch-speech communication and infant responses in 12-month-olds at high risk for autism spectrum disorder. *Journal of Autism and Developmental Disorders.*

Kaewpradub, N., & others (2017). Association among Internet usage, body image, and eating behaviors among secondary school students. *Shanghai Archives of Psychiatry, 29,* 208–217.

Kagan, J. (1987). Perspectives on infancy. In J.D. Osofsky (Ed.), *Handbook on infant development* (2nd ed.). New York: Wiley.

Kagan, J. (2002). Behavioral inhibition as a temperamental category. In R.J. Davidson, K.R. Scherer, & H.H. Goldsmith (Eds.), *Handbook of affective sciences.* New York: Oxford University Press.

Kagan, J. (2008). Fear and wariness. In M.M. Haith & J.B. Benson (Eds.), *Encyclopedia of infant and early childhood development.* Oxford, UK: Elsevier.

Kagan, J. (2010). Emotions and temperament. In M.H. Bornstein (Ed.), *Handbook of cultural developmental science.* New York: Psychology Press.

Kagan, J. (2013). Temperamental contributions to inhibited and uninhibited profiles. In P.D. Zelazo (Ed.), *Oxford handbook of developmental psychology.* New York: Oxford University Press.

Kagan, J. (2019). Distinction between moods and temperament. In A.S. Fox & others (Eds.), *The nature of emotion* (2nd ed.). New York: Oxford University Press.

Kagan, J.J., Kearsley, R.B., & Zelazo, P.R. (1978). *Infancy: Its place in human development.* Cambridge, MA: Harvard University Press.

Kahlbaugh, P., & Huffman, L. (2017). Personality, emotional qualities of leisure, and subjective well-being in the elderly. *International Journal of Aging and Human Development, 85,* 164–184.

Kahn, J.A., & others (2008). Patterns and determinants of physical activity in U.S. adolescents. *Journal of Adolescent Health, 42,* 369–377.

Kahrs, B.A., Jung, W.P., & Lockman, J.J. (2013). Motor origins of tool use. *Child Development, 84*(3), 810–818.

Kalanithi, P. (2016). *When breath becomes air.* New York: Random House.

Kalashnikova, M., Goswami, U., & Burnham, D. (2018). Mothers speak differently to infants at-risk for dyslexia. *Developmental Science, 21,* 1.

Kaldahl, J. (2019). On life after death: A chaplain's view on the process of dying. *Journal of Pastoral Care and Counseling, 73,* 49–51.

Kalish, R.A. (1981). *Death, grief, and caring relationships,* Monterey, CA: Brooks/Cole.

Kalish, R.A., & Reynolds, D.K. (1976). *An overview of death and ethnicity.* Farmingdale, NY: Baywood.

Kalish, V.B. (2016). Obesity in older adults. *Primary Care, 43,* 137–144.

Kalvin, C.B., & Bierman, K.L. (2017). Child and adolescent risk factors that differentially predict violent versus nonviolent crime. *Aggressive Behavior, 43,* 568–577.

Kalyvianakis, D., & others (2020, in press). Low-intensity shockwave therapy (LIST) for erectile dysfunction: A randomized clinical trial assessing the impact of energy flux density (EF) and frequency of sessions. *International Journal of Impotence Research.*

Kamp Dush, C.M., & others (2019). Cohabitation and single mothering in the United States: A review and call for psychological research. In B.H. Friese (Ed.), *APA handbook of contemporary family psychology.* Washington, DC: APA Books.

Kamza, A., & others (2019). Can sustained attention adapt to prior cognitive effort? An evidence from experimental study. *Acta Psychologica, 192,* 181–193.

Kanazawa, S. (2015). Breastfeeding is positively associated with child intelligence even net of parental IQ. *Developmental Psychology, 51,* 1683–1689.

Kandler, C., & others (2016). The nature of creativity: The roles of genetic factors, personality traits, cognitive abilities, and environmental sources. *Journal of Personality and Social Psychology, 111,* 230–249.

Kanesarajah, J., & others (2018). Multimorbidity and quality of life at mid-life: A systematic review of general population studies. *Maturitas, 109,* 53–62.

Kang, N.G., & You, M.A. (2018). Association of perceived stress and self-control with health-promoting behaviors in adolescents: A cross-sectional study. *Medicine, 97*(34), e11880.

Kann, L., & others (2016, August 12). Sexual identity, sex of sexual contacts, and health-related behaviors among students in grades 9–12—United States and selected sites, 2015. *MMWR Surveillance Summary, 65*(9), 1–202.

Kann, L., & others (2018). *Youth Risk Behavior Surveillance United States 2017.* Atlanta: Centers for Disease Control and Prevention.

Kanner, A.D., Coyne, J.C., Schaefer, C., & Lazarus, R.S. (1981). Comparison of two modes of stress measurement: Daily hassles and uplifts versus major life events. *Journal of Behavioral Medicine, 4,* 1–39.

Kansky, J., & Allen, J.P. (2018). Long-term risks and possible benefits associated with late adolescent romantic relationship quality. *Journal of Youth and Adolescence, 6,* 172–190.

Kantrowitz, B. (1991, Summer). The good, the bad, and the difference. *Newsweek,* pp. 48–50.

Kapitansky, O., & Gozes, I. (2019). ADNP differentially interact with genes/proteins in correlation with aging: A novel marker of muscle aging. *Geroscience, 41,* 321–340.

Kaplan, R.M., & Saccuzzo, D.P. (2018). *Psychological testing* (9th ed.). Boston: Cengage.

Kaplinski, M., & others (2020, in press). Clinical innovation: A multidisciplinary program for the diagnosis and treatment of systematic hypertension in children and adolescents. *Clinical Pediatrics.*

Kar, B.R., Rao, S.L., & Chandramouli, B.A. (2008). Cognitive development in children with chronic energy malnutrition. *Behavioral and Brain Functions, 4,* 31.

Karasik, L.B., Tamis-LeMonda, C.S., Adolph, K.E., & Bornstein, M.H. (2015). Places and postures: A cross-cultural comparison of sitting in 5-month-olds. *Journal of Cross-Cultural Psychology, 46,* 1023–1038.

Karniol, R., Grosz, E., & Schorr, I. (2003). Caring, gender-role orientation, and volunteering. *Sex Roles, 49,* 11–19.

Karoly, L.A., & Bigelow, J.H. (2005). *The economics of investing in universal preschool education in California.* Santa Monica, CA: RAND Corporation.

Karreman, A., van Tuijl, C., van Aken, M.A., & Dekovic, M. (2008). Parenting, coparenting, and effortful control in preschoolers. *Journal of Family Psychology, 22,* 30–40.

Kashdan, T.B., & others (2018). Sexuality leads to boosts in mood and meaning in life with no evidence for the reverse direction: A daily diary investigation. *Emotion, 18,* 563–576.

Kassing, F., & others (2019). Using early childhood behavior problems to predict adult convictions. *Journal of Abnormal Child Psychology, 47,* 765–778.

Kastbom, A.A., & others (2016). Differences in sexual behavior, health, and history of child abuse among school students who had and had not engaged in sexual activity by the age of 18 years: A cross-sectional study. *Adolescent Health, Medicine, and Therapeutics, 7,* 1–11.

Kastenbaum, R.J. (2009). *Death, society, and human experience* (10th ed.). Boston: Allyn & Bacon.

Kastenbaum, R.J. (2012). *Death, society, and human experience* (11th ed.). Boston: Allyn & Bacon.

Kataoka, Y., & others (2020). Cumulative network meta-analyses, practice guidelines, and actual prescriptions for postmenopausal osteoporosis: A meta-epidemiological study. *Archives of Osteoporosis, 15*(1), 21.

Kato, T. (2005). The relationship between coping with stress due to romantic break-ups and mental health. *Japanese Journal of Social Psychology, 20,* 171–180.

Katsiaficas, D. (2017). "I know I'm an adult when . . . I can care for myself and others." *Emerging Adulthood, 5,* 392–405.

Katsiki, N., & others (2019). Obesity, metabolic syndrome, and the risk of microvascular complications in patients with diabetes mellitus. *Current Pharmaceutical Design, 25,* 2051–2059.

Katz, L. (1999). Curriculum disputes in early childhood education. *ERIC Clearinghouse on Elementary and Early Childhood Education,* Document EDO-PS-99-13.

Kauchak, D., & Eggen, P. (2021). *Introduction to teaching* (7th ed.). Upper Saddle River, NJ: Pearson.

Kauffman, J.M., McGee, K., & Brigham, M. (2004). Enabling or disabling? Observations on changes in special education. *Phi Delta Kappan, 85,* 613–620.

Kaufman, A.S., Schneider, W.J., & Kaufman, J.C. (2019). Psychometric approaches to intelligence. In R.J. Sternberg (Ed.), *Human intelligence.* New York: Cambridge University Press.

Kaufman, J.M., & others (2019). Aging and the male reproductive system. *Endocrine Reviews, 40,* 906–972.

Kaufman, S.B., & others (2016). Openness to experience and intellect differentially predict creative achievement in the arts and sciences. *Journal of Personality, 84,* 248–258.

Kaup, A.R., Harmell, A.L., & Yaffe, K. (2019). Conscientiousness is associated with lower risk of dementia among Black and older adults. *Neuroepidemiology, 52,* 86–92.

Kaur, S., & others (2019). Sleep quality mediates the relationship between frailty and cognitive dysfunction in non-demented middle aged to older adults. *International Psychogeriatrics, 31,* 779–788.

Kaushal, N., & others (2019). Investigating dose-response effects of multimodal exercise programs on health-related quality of life in older adults. *Clinical Interventions in Aging, 14,* 209-217.

Kavanaugh, R.D. (2006). Pretend play and theory of mind. In L.L. Balter & C.S. Tamis-LeMonda (Eds.), *Child psychology* (2nd ed.). New York: Psychology Press.

Kavle, J.A., & others (2020, in press). Baby-friendly community initiative–From national guidelines to implementation: A multisectoral platform for improving infant and young child feeding practices and integrated health services. *Maternal and Child Nutrition.*

Kavosi, Z., & others (2015). A comparison of mothers' quality of life after normal vaginal, cesarean, and water birth deliveries. *International Journal of Community Based Nursing and Midwifery, 3,* 198-204.

Kayama, H., & others (2014). Effects of a Kinect-based exercise game on improving executive cognitive performance in community-dwelling elderly: Case control study. *Journal of Medical Internet Research, 16,* e61.

Kaymak, D., & others (2020, in press). Prenatal diagnosis of 5p deletion syndrome with brain abnormalities by ultrasonography and fetal magnetic resonance imaging: A case report. *Fetal and Pediatric Pathology.*

Kaywork, J. (2020). *An educator's guide to infant and toddler development.* New York: Routledge.

Kazachkova, N., & others (2020, in press). Successful early fetal sex determination using cell-free fetal DNA isolated from maternal capillary blood: A pilot study. *European Journal of Obstetrics & Gynecology and Reproductive Biology X.*

Keating, D.P. (1990). Adolescent thinking. In S.S. Feldman & G.R. Elliott (Eds.), *At the threshold: The developing adolescent.* Cambridge, MA: Harvard University Press.

Keating, D.P. (2004). Cognitive and brain development. In R. Lerner & L. Steinberg (Ed.), *Handbook of adolescent psychology.* New York: Wiley.

Keating, D.P. (2009). Developmental science and giftedness: An integrated life-span framework. In F.D. Horowitz, R.F. Subotnik, & D.J. Matthews (Eds.), *The development of giftedness and talent across the life span.* Washington, DC: American Psychological Association.

Keen, R. (2005). Unpublished review of Santrock's *Topical approach to life-span development,* 3rd ed. New York: McGraw-Hill.

Keen, R. (2011). The development of problem solving in young children: A critical cognitive skill. *Annual Review of Psychology* (Vol. 62). Palo Alto, CA: Annual Reviews.

Keen, R., Lee, M-H., & Adolph, K.E. (2014). Planning an action: A developmental progression in tool use. *Ecological Psychology, 26*(1-2), 98-108.

Kelleher, K., Reece, J., & Sandel, M. (2018). The Healthy Neighborhood, Healthy Families Initiative. *Pediatrics, 142,* 3.

Keller, A., Ford, L., & Meacham, J. (1978). Dimensions of self-concept in preschool children. *Developmental Psychology, 14,* 485-489.

Keller, H., Kartner, J., Borke, J., Yvosi, R., & Kleis, A. (2005). Parenting styles and the development of the categorical self: A longitudinal study on mirror self-recognition in Cameroonian Nso and German families. *International Journal of Behavioral Development, 29,* 496-504.

Kelley, C.P., Soboroff, S.D., & Lovaglia, M.J. (2017). The status value of age. *Social Science Research, 66,* 22-31.

Kelley, G.A., & Kelley, K.S. (2019). Leisure time physical activity reduces the risk of stroke in adults: A reanalysis of a meta-analysis using the inverse-heterogeneity model. *Stroke Research and Treatment, 2019,* 8264502.

Kellman, P.J., & Arterberry, M.E. (2006). Infant visual perception. In W. Damon & R. Lerner (Eds.), *Handbook of child psychology* (6th ed.). New York: Wiley.

Kellman, P.J., & Banks, M.S. (1998). Infant visual perception. In W. Damon (Ed.), *Handbook of child psychology* (5th ed., Vol. 2). New York: Wiley.

Kelly, C., & others (2019). The effectiveness of a classroom-based phonological awareness program for 4-5-year-olds. *International Journal of Speech-Language Pathology, 21,* 101-113.

Kelly, D.J., & others (2005). Three-month-olds, but not newborns, prefer own-race faces. *Developmental Science, 8,* F31-F36.

Kelly, D.J., & others (2007). Cross-race preferences for same-race faces extend beyond the African versus Caucasian contrast in 3-month-old infants. *Infancy, 11,* 87-95.

Kelly, J.P., Borchert, J., & Teller, D.Y. (1997). The development of chromatic and achromatic sensitivity in infancy as tested with the sweep VEP. *Vision Research, 37,* 2057-2072.

Kelly, M.M., & Li, K. (2019). Poverty, toxic stress, and education in children born preterm. *Nursing Research, 68,* 275-284.

Kelly, Y., & others (2019). Social media use and adolescent mental health: Findings from the UK Millennium Cohort Study. *EClinicalMedicine, 6,* 59-68.

Keltner, K.W. (2013). *Tiger babies strike back.* New York: William Morrow.

Kempermann, G. (2019). Environmental enrichment, new neurons, and the neurobiology of individuality. *Nature Reviews. Neuroscience, 20,* 235-245.

Kempermann, G., van Praag, H., & Gage, F.H. (2000). Activity-dependent regulation of neuronal plasticity and self-repair. *Progress in Brain Research 127,* 35-48.

Kendler, K.S., Ohlsson, H., Sundquist, K., & Sundquist, J. (2016). The rearing environment and risk for drug use: A Swedish national high-risk adopted and not adopted co-sibling control study. *Psychological Medicine, 46,* 1359-1366.

Kendler, K.S., & others (2017). Divorce and the onset of alcohol use disorder: A Swedish population-based longitudinal cohort and co-relative study. *American Journal of Psychiatry, 174,* 45-58.

Kendler, K.S., & others (2018). Prediction of drug abuse recurrence: A Swedish national study. *Psychological Medicine, 48,* 1367-1374.

Kendler, K.S., & others (2020, in press). The nature of the shared environment. *Behavior Genetics.*

Kennedy, K.M., & others (2015). BDNF val66met polymorphism affects aging of multiple types of memory. *Brain Research, 1612,* 104-117.

Kennedy, R.S. (2020, in press). Bullying trends in the United States: A meta-regression. *Trauma, Violence, and Abuse.*

Kennell, J.H. (2006). Randomized controlled trial of skin-to-skin contact from birth versus conventional incubator for physiological stabilization in 1200 g to 2199 g newborns. *Acta Paediatica (Sweden), 95,* 15-16.

Kennell, J.H., & McGrath, S.K. (1999). Commentary: Practical and humanistic lessons from the Third World for perinatal caregivers everywhere. *Birth, 26,* 9-10.

Kent, B.V., Bradshaw, M., & Uecker, J.E. (2018). Forgiveness, attachment to God, and mental health outcomes in older U.S. adults: A longitudinal study. *Research on Aging, 40,* 456-479.

Kenyon, C. (2010). A pathway that links reproductive status to lifespan in *Caenorhabditis elegans. Annals of the New York Academy of Sciences, 1204,* 156-162.

Kerig, P.K. (2019). Parenting and family systems. In M.H. Bornstein (Ed.), *Handbook of parenting* (3rd ed.). New York: Routledge.

Kerns, K.A., & Brumariu, L.E. (2016). Attachment in middle childhood. In J. Cassidy & P. Shaver (Eds.), *Handbook of attachment* (3rd ed.). New York: Guilford.

Kerns, K.A., & Seibert, A.C. (2016). Finding your way through the thicket: Promising approaches to assessing attachment in middle childhood. In E. Waters, B. Vaughn, & H. Waters (Eds.), *Measuring attachment.* New York: Guilford.

Kershaw, K.N., & others (2014). Associations of stressful life events and social strain with incident cardiovascular disease in the Women's Health Initiative. *Journal of the American Heart Association, 3*(3), e000687.

Kershaw, P. (2018). The need for health in all policies in Canada. *Canadian Medical Association Journal, 190*(3), E64-E65.

Kershner, J.R. (2019). Neurobiological systems in dyslexia. *Trends in Neuroscience and Education, 14,* 11-24.

Kerstis, B., Aslund, C., & Sonnby, K. (2018). More secure attachment to the father and the mother is associated with fewer depressive symptoms in adolescence. *Upsala Journal of Medical Sciences, 123,* 62-67.

Kerstis, B., & others (2016). Association between parental depressive symptoms and impaired bonding with the infant. *Archives of Women's Mental Health, 19,* 87-94.

Kesaniemi, J., & others (2019). Exposure to environmental radionuclides associates with tissue-specific impacts on telomerase expression and telomere length. *Scientific Reports, 9*(1), 850.

Ketcham, C.J., & Stelmach, G.E. (2001). Age-related declines in motor control. In J.E. Birren & K.W. Schaie (Eds.), *Handbook of the psychology of aging* (5th ed.). San Diego: Academic Press.

Keunen, K., Counsell, & Benders, M.J. (2017). The emergence of functional architecture during early brain development. *NeuroImage, 160*, 2-14.

Keyes, K.M., Maslowsky, J., Hamilton, A., & Schulenberg, J. (2015). The great sleep recession: Changes in sleep duration among U.S. adolescents, 1991-2012. *Pediatrics, 135*, 460-468.

Khairullah, A., & others (2014). Testosterone trajectories and reference ranges in a large longitudinal sample of adolescent males. *PLoS One, 9*(9), e108838.

Khalsa, A.S., & others (2017). Attainment of '5-2-1-0' obesity recommendations in preschool-aged children. *Preventive Medicine Reports, 8*, 79-87.

Khan, F., & others (2020, in press). Development and change in attachment: A multi-wave assessment of attachment and its correlates across childhood and adolescence. *Journal of Personality and Social Psychology.*

Khan, L. (2019). Puberty: Onset and progression. *Pediatric Annals, 48*, e141-e145.

Khan, S.S., & others (2018). Association of body mass index with lifetime risk of cardiovascular disease and compression of morbidity. *JAMA Cardiology, 3*(4), 280-287.

Kharitonova, M., Winter, W., & Sheridan, M.A. (2015). As working memory grows: A developmental account of neural bases of working memory capacity in 5- to 8-year-old children and adults. *Journal of Cognitive Neuroscience, 27*, 1775-1788.

Khodaeian, M., & others (2015). Effects of vitamins C and E on insulin resistance in diabetes: A meta-analysis study. *European Journal of Clinical Investigation, 45*, 1161-1174.

Khoury, J.E., & Milligan, K. (2016). Comparing executive functioning in children and adolescents with fetal alcohol spectrum disorders and ADHD: A meta-analysis. *Journal of Attention Disorders, 20*(1), 1-15.

Khurana, A., & others (2019). Media violence exposure and aggression in adolescents: A risk and resilience perspective. *Aggressive Behavior, 45*, 70-81.

Kibby, M.Y., & others (2020). Frontal volume as a potential source of the comorbidity between attention-deficit/hyperactivity disorder and reading disorders. *Behavioral and Brain Research.*

Kim, A., Lee, J.A., & Park, H.S. (2018). Health behaviors and illness according to marital status in middle-aged Koreans. *Journal of Public Health, 40*, e99-e106.

Kim, D.J., & others (2019). Childhood poverty and the organization of the structural brain connectome. *Neuroimage, 184*, 409-416.

Kim, E.M., Kim, H., & Park, E. (2020, in press). How are depression and suicide ideation associated with multiple health risk behaviors among adolescents? A secondary data analysis using the 2016 Korea Youth Risk Behavior web-based survey. *Journal of Psychiatric and Mental Health Nursing.*

Kim, E.S., Chopik, W.J., & Smith, J. (2014). Are people healthier if their partners are more optimistic? The dyadic effect of optimism on health among older adults. *Journal of Psychosomatic Research, 76*, 447-453.

Kim, G.J., & others (2020). Effects of resistance exercise using the elastic band on the pain and function of patients with degenerative knee arthritis. *Journal of Physical Therapy Science, 32*, 52-54.

Kim, H. (2019). To prevent child maltreatment, home visiting programs are one part of a complete response. *American Journal of Public Health, 109*, 653-655.

Kim, H.J., & Pedersen, S. (2010). Young adolescents' metacognition and domain knowledge as predictors of hypothesis-development performance in a computer-supported context. *Educational Psychology, 30*, 565-582.

Kim, H.M., & Miller, H.C. (2020). Are insecure attachment styles related to risky behavior? A meta-analysis. *Health Psychology, 39*, 48-57.

Kim, J., & Fletcher, J.M. (2018). The influence of classmates on adolescent criminal activities in the United States. *Deviant Behavior, 39*, 275-292.

Kim, J., & Kim, H.K. (2019). Intergenerational transmission of effortful control in families with school-age children in Korea. *Journal of Family Psychology, 33*, 88-97.

Kim, J., & others (2020). The effects of a 12-week jump rope exercise program on body composition, insulin sensitivity, and academic self-efficacy in obese adolescent girls. *Journal of Pediatric Endocrinology and Metabolism, 33*, 129-137.

Kim, J., & others (2020, in press). Genetic counseling status and perspectives based on a 2018 professional survey in Korea. *Annals of Laboratory Medicine.*

Kim, J.I., & others (2020, in press). Interaction of DRD4 methylation and phthalate metabolites affects continuous performance test performance in ADHD. *Journal of Attention Disorders.*

Kim, K., & others (2020, in press). Typology of parent-child ties within families: Associations with psychological well-being. *Journal of Family Psychology.*

Kim, K., & Park, C.B. (2020). Femtomolar sensing of Alzheimer's tau proteins by water oxidation-coupled photoelectrochemical platform. *Biosensors and Bioelectronics, 154*, 112075.

Kim, K.H. (2010, May). Unpublished data. School of Education, College of William & Mary, Williamsburg, VA.

Kim, K.W., & others (2019). Associations of parental general monitoring with adolescent weight-related behaviors and weight status. *Obesity, 27*, 280-287.

Kim, P., Strathearn, L., & Swain, J.E. (2016). The maternal brain and its plasticity in humans. *Hormones and Behavior, 77*, 113-123.

Kim, S., & Kochanska, G. (2017). Relational antecedents and social implications of the emotion of empathy: Evidence from three studies. *Emotion*, 981-992.

Kim, S., & others (2019). Bilingualism for dementia: Neurological mechanisms associated with functional and structural changes in the brain. *Frontiers in Neuroscience, 13*, 1224.

Kim, S.H. (2009). The influence of finding meaning and worldview of accepting death on anger among bereaved older spouses. *Aging and Mental Health, 13*, 38-45.

Kim, S.H., & others (2017). Early menarche and risk-taking behavior in Korean adolescent students. *Asia Pacific-Psychiatry, 9*, 3.

Kimble, M., Neacsiu, A.D., Flack, W.F., & Horner, J. (2008). Risk of unwanted sex for college women: Evidence for a red zone. *Journal of American College Health, 57*, 331-338.

Kindermann, T.A., & Gest, S.D. (2018). The peer group: Linking conceptualizations, theories, and methods. In W.M. Bukowski & others (Eds.), *Handbook of peer interactions, relationships, and groups* (2nd ed.). New York: Guilford.

King, B.M., Carr, D.C., & Taylor, M.G. (2020, in press). Loneliness following widowhood: The role of the military and social support. *Journals of Gerontology B: Psychological Sciences and Social Sciences.*

King, B.M., & Regan, P. (2019). *Human sexuality* (9th ed.). Upper Saddle River, NJ: Pearson.

King, L.A. (2019). *Psychology: An appreciative experience* (4th ed.). New York: McGraw-Hill.

King, L.A. (2020). *Science of psychology* (5th ed.). New York: McGraw-Hill.

King, L.A., & Hicks, J.A. (2007). Whatever happened to "What might have been?": Regrets, happiness, and maturity. *American Psychologist, 62*, 625-636.

King, P.E., & Boyatzis, C.J. (2015). The nature and functions of religious and spiritual development in childhood and adolescence. In R.M. Lerner (Ed.), *Handbook of child psychology and developmental science* (7th ed.). New York: Oxford University Press.

King, P.E., Carr, A., & Boiter, C. (2011). Spirituality, religiosity, and youth thriving. In R.M. Lerner, J.V. Lerner, & J.B. Benson (Eds.), *Advances in child development and behavior: Positive youth development.* New York: Elsevier.

King, P.E., Schnitker, S.A.,& Houltberg, B.J. (2020). Religious groups and institutions as a context for moral development. In L.A. Jensen (Ed.), *Oxford handbook of moral development.* New York: Oxford University Press.

King, R.B. (2020, in press). Mindsets are contagious: The social contagion of implicit theories of intelligence among classmates. *British Journal of Educational Psychology.*

King, V., & Scott, M.E. (2005). A comparison of cohabiting relationships among older and younger adults. *Journal of Marriage and the Family, 67*, 271-285.

Kingdon, D., Cardoso, C., & McGrath, J.J. (2016). Research review: Executive function deficits in fetal alcohol spectrum disorders and attention-deficit/hyperactivity disorder—A meta-analysis. *Journal of Child Psychology and Psychiatry, 57*, 116-131.

Kingsbury, A.M., Plotnikova, M., & Najman, J.M. (2018). Commonly occurring adverse birth outcomes and maternal depression: A longitudinal study. *Public Health, 155*, 45-54.

Kinney, H.C., & Haynes, R.L. (2019). The serotonin brainstem hypothesis for sudden infant death syndrome. *Journal of Neuropathology and Experimental Neurology, 78*, 665-779.

Kinnunen, J.M., & others (2019). Nicotine matters in predicting subsequent smoking after e-cigarette experimentation: A longitudinal study among Finnish adolescents. *Drug and Alcohol Dependence, 201,* 182–187.

Kins, E., & Beyers, W. (2010). Failure to launch, failure to achieve criteria for adulthood? *Journal of Adolescent Research, 25,* 743–777.

Kinsler, J.J., & others (2019). A content analysis of how sexual behavior and reproductive health are being portrayed on primetime television shows being watched by teens and young adults. *Health Communication, 34,* 644–651.

Kintzel, D. (2020). Income sustainability in retirement: A case study of the life-cycle account. *Journal of Retirement, 7*(3), 31–45.

Kinugawa, K. (2019). Plasticity of the brain and cognition in older adults. In R. Fernandez-Ballesteros & others (Eds.), *Cambridge handbook of successful aging.* New York: Cambridge University Press.

Kircaburun, K., & Griffiths, M.D. (2018). Instagram addiction and the Big Five of personality: The mediating role of self-liking. *Journal of Behavioral Addictions, 7,* 158–170.

Kirk, S.M., & Kirk, E.P. (2016). Sixty minutes of physical activity per day included within preschool academic lessons improves early literacy. *Journal of School Health, 86,* 155–163.

Kirkorian, H.L., Anderson, D.R., & Keen, R. (2012). Age differences in online processing of video: An eye movement study. *Child Development, 83,* 497–507.

Kisilevsky, B.S., & others (2003). Effects of experience on fetal voice recognition. *Psychological Science, 14,* 220–224.

Kit, B.K., Simon, A.E., Brody, D.J., & Akinbami, L.J. (2013). U.S. prevalence and trends in tobacco smoke exposure among children and adolescents with asthma. *Pediatrics, 131,* 407–414.

Kito, M. (2005). Self-disclosure in romantic relationships and friendships among American and Japanese college students. *Journal of Social Psychology, 145,* 127–140.

Kivnik, H.Q., & Sinclair, H.M. (2007). Grandparenthood. In J.E. Birren (Ed.), *Encyclopedia of gerontology* (2nd ed.). San Diego: Academic Press.

Klaus, M., & Kennell, H.H. (1976). *Maternal-infant bonding.* St. Louis: Mosby.

Klein, A.C. (2019). Q & A: Answering your ESSA questions. *Education Week, 38*(27), 20–21.

Klein, L.B., & Martin, S.L. (2020, in press). Sexual harassment of college and university students: A systematic review. *Trauma, Violence, and Abuse.*

Klein, M.R., & others (2018). Bidirectional relations between temperament and parenting predicting preschool-age children's adjustment. *Journal of Clinical Child and Adolescent Psychology, 47*(Suppl. 1), S113–S126.

Klein, S. (2012). *State of public school segregation in the United States, 2007–2010.* Washington, DC: Feminist Majority Foundation.

Kleinman, C., & Reizer, A. (2018). Negative caregiving representations and postpartum depression: The mediating roles of parenting efficacy and relationship

satisfaction. *Health for Women International, 39,* 79–84.

Kliegel, M., & others (2016). Prospective memory in older adults: Where we are now and what is next. *Gerontology, 62,* 459–466.

Kliegman, R.M., & others (2019). *Nelson textbook of pediatrics* (21st ed.). New York: Elsevier.

Klil-Drori, S., & others (2020). Exercise intervention for late-life depression: A meta-analysis. *Journal of Clinical Psychiatry, 81,* 1.

Klimstra, T.A., & others (2017). Daily dynamics of adolescent mood and identity. *Journal of Research on Adolescence, 28,* 459–473.

Klinenberg, E. (2012, February 4). Sunday Review: One's a crowd. *The New York Times.* Retrieved from http://www.nytimes.com/2012/02/05/opinion/sunday/living-alone-means-being-social.html?_r0

Klinenberg, E. (2013). *Going solo: The extraordinary rise and surprising appeal of living alone.* New York: Penguin.

Klug, W.S., & others (2020). *Essentials of genetics* (10th ed.). Upper Saddle River, NJ: Pearson.

Knight, L.F., & Hope, D.A.M. (2012). Correlates of same-sex attractions and behaviors among self-identified heterosexual university students. *Archives of Sexual Behavior, 41,* 1199–1208.

Knofe, H., & others (2019). Chimpanzees monopolize and children take turns in a limited resource problem. *Scientific Reports, 9*(1), 7597.

Knopfli, B., & others (2016). Marital breakup in later adulthood and self-rated health: A cross-sectional survey in Switzerland. *International Journal of Public Health, 61,* 357–366.

Knox, M. (2010). On hitting children: A review of corporal punishment in the United States. *Journal of Pediatric Health Care, 24,* 103–107.

Ko, A., & others (2020, in press). Family matters: Rethinking the psychology of human social motivation. *Perspectives on Psychological Science.*

Ko, E.B., Hwang, K.A., & Choi, K.C. (2019). Prenatal toxicity of the environmental pollutants on neuronal and cardiac development derived from embryonic stem cells. *Reproductive Toxicity, 90,* 15–23.

Ko, Y.H., & others (2020, in press). Risk factors for primary lung cancer among never-smoking women in South Korea: A retrospective nationwide population-based cohort study. *Korean Journal of Internal Medicine.*

Kobayashi, L.C., & others (2019). Effects of the Affordable Care Act Medicaid expansion on subjective well-being in the U.S. adult population, 2010–2016. *American Journal of Public Health, 109,* 1236–1242.

Koch, S., & others (2019). Effects of male postpartum depression on father-infant interactions: The mediating role of face processing. *Infant Mental Health Journal, 40,* 263–276.

Kochanska, G., & Aksan, N. (2007). Conscience in childhood: Past, present, and future. *Merrill-Palmer Quarterly, 50,* 299–310.

Kochanska, G., Barry, R.A., Jimenez, N.B., Hollatz, A.L., & Woodard, J. (2009). Guilt and effortful control: Two mechanisms that prevent disruptive

developmental trajectories. *Journal of Personality and Social Psychology, 97,* 322–333.

Kochanska, G., Boldt, L.J., & Goffin, K.C. (2019). Early relational experience: A foundation for the unfolding dynamics of parent-child socialization. *Child Development Perspectives, 13,* 41–47.

Kochanska, G., & Kim, S. (2013). Early attachment organization with both parents and future behavior problems: From infancy to middle childhood. *Child Development, 84*(1), 283–296.

Kochanska, G., Koenig, J.L., Barry, R.A., Kim, S., & Yoon, J.E. (2010). Children's conscience during toddler and preschool years, moral self, and a competent, adaptive developmental trajectory. *Developmental Psychology, 46,* 1320–1322.

Koehler, K., & Drenowatz, C. (2019). Integrated role of nutrition and physical activity for lifelong health. *Nutrients, 16*(11), 7.

Koenig, H.G., & Blazer, D.G. (1996). Depression. In J.E. Birren (Ed.), *Encyclopedia of gerontology* (Vol. 1). San Diego: Academic Press.

Koenig, H.G., & others (1992). Religious coping and depression in elderly hospitalized medically ill men. *American Journal of Psychiatry, 149,* 1693–1700.

Koenig, L.B., McGue, M., & Iacono, W.G. (2008). Stability and change in religiousness during emerging adulthood. *Developmental Psychology, 44,* 523–543.

Koenig, M.A., & Kaplan, P.W. (2019). Brain death. *Handbook of Clinical Neurology, 161,* 89–102.

Koenig, M.A., Tiberius, V., & Hamlin, J.K. (2019). Children's judgments of epistemic and moral agents: From situations to intentions. *Perspectives on Psychological Science, 14,* 344–360.

Koh, H. (2014). The Teen Pregnancy Prevention Program: An evidence-based public health program model. *Journal of Adolescent Health, 54*(1, Suppl.), S1–S2.

Kohlberg, L. (1958). *The development of modes of moral thinking and choice in the years 10 to 16.* Unpublished doctoral dissertation, University of Chicago.

Kohlberg, L. (1969). Stage and sequence: The cognitive-developmental approach to socialization. In D.A. Goslin (Ed.), *Handbook of socialization theory and research.* Chicago: Rand McNally.

Kohlberg, L. (1986). A current statement of some theoretical issues. In S. Modgil & C. Modgil (Eds.), *Lawrence Kohlberg.* Philadelphia: Falmer.

Kohlhoff, J., & others (2017). Oxytocin in the postnatal period: Associations with attachment and maternal caregiving. *Comprehensive Psychiatry, 76,* 56–68.

Kohlhoff, J., & others (2020, in press). Callous-unemotional traits and disorganized attachment: Links with disruptive behaviors in toddlers. *Child Psychiatry and Human Development.*

Kohn, J.N., & others (2020, in press). Self-reported sleep disturbances are associated with poorer cognitive performance in older adults with hypertension: A multi-parameter risk factor investigation. *International Psychogeriatrics.*

Kok, F.M., Groen, Y., Fuermaier, A.B., & Tucha, O. (2016). Problematic peer functioning in girls with

ADHD: A systematic literature review. *PLoS One, 11,* e0165118.

Kok, R., & others (2015). Normal variation in early parental sensitivity predicts child structural brain development. *Journal of the American Academy of Child and Adolescent Psychiatry, 54,* 824–831.

Kokkinos, P., & others (2019). Cardiorespiratory fitness, body mass index, and heart failure. *European Journal of Heart Failure, 21,* 435–444.

Koksvik, G.H. (2020, in press). Medically timed death as an enactment of good death: An ethnographic study of three European intensive care units. *Omega.* doi:10.1177/0030222818756555

Kolata, G. (2007, Nov. 11). Chubby gets a second look. *New York Times,* p. D4.

Kolesnik, A., & others (2019). Increased cortical reactivity to repeated tones at 8 months in infants with later ASD. *Translational Psychiatry, 9*(1), 46.

Kolokotroni, P., Anagnostopoulos, F., & Hantzi, A. (2018). The role of optimism, social constraints, coping, and cognitive processing in psychosocial adjustment among breast cancer survivors. *Journal of Clinical Psychology in Medical Settings, 25,* 452–462.

Kolovos, S., & others (2020, in press). Association of sleep, screen time, and physical activity with overweight and obesity in Mexico. *Eating and Weight Disorders.*

Kong, A., & others (2012). Rate of *de novo* mutations and the importance of the father's age to disease risk. *Nature, 488,* 471–475.

Kong, L.N., & others (2019). Relationships among social support, coping strategy, and depressive symptoms in older adults with diabetes. *Journal of Gerontological Nursing, 45,* 40–46.

Kontis, V., & others (2017). Future life expectancy in 35 industrialized countries: Projections with a Bayesian model ensemble. *Lancet, 389*(10076), 1323–1335.

Koo, Y.J., & others (2012). Pregnancy outcomes according to increasing maternal age. *Taiwan Journal of Obstetrics and Gynecology, 51,* 60–65.

Koopman-Verhoeff, M.E., & others (2019). Preschool irregularity and the development of sleep problems in childhood: A longitudinal study. *Journal of Child Psychology and Psychiatry, 60,* 857–865.

Koorevaar, A.M., & others (2013). Big Five personality factors and depression diagnosis, severity, and age of onset in older adults. *Journal of Affective Disorders, 151,* 178–185.

Kopp, F., & Lindenberger, U. (2011). Effects of joint attention on long-term memory in 9-month-old infants: An event-related potentials study. *Developmental Science, 14,* 660–672.

Koppelman, K.L. (2020). *Understanding human differences* (6th ed.). Upper Saddle River, NJ: Pearson.

Kopyslynska, O., Barnett, M.A., & Curran, M.A. (2020, in press). Constructive and destructive marital conflict, parenting, and coparenting alliance. *Journal of Family Psychology.*

Korat, O. (2009). The effect of maternal teaching talk on children's emergent literacy as a function of type of activity and maternal education level. *Journal of Applied Developmental Psychology, 30,* 34–42.

Korja, R., & others (2017). The relations between maternal prenatal anxiety or stress and the child's early negative reactivity or self-regulation: A systematic review. *Child Psychiatry and Human Development, 48,* 851–859.

Korner, L.M., & others (2019). Prenatal testosterone exposure is associated with delay of gratification and attention problems/overactive behavior in 3-year-old boys. *Psychoneuroimmunology, 104,* 49–54.

Kornienko, O., Ha, T., & Dishion, T.J. (2020). Dynamic pathways between rejection and antisocial behavior in peer networks: Update and test of confluence model. *Development and Psychopathology, 32,* 175–188.

Korte, J., Dorssaert, C.H., Westerhof, G.J., & Bohlmeijer, E.T. (2014). Life review in groups? An explorative analysis of social processes that facilitate or hinder the effectiveness of life review. *Aging and Mental Health, 18,* 376–384.

Korte, J., Westerhof, G.J., & Bohlmeijer, E.T. (2012). Mediating processes in an effective life-review intervention. *Psychology and Aging, 27,* 1172–1181.

Kosar, I., & others (2020, in press). Assessment of knowledge and preferences regarding advance directives among patients in university family medicine outpatient clinics. *Gerontology and Geriatric Medicine.*

Kostel Bal, S., & others (2020, in press). Rheumatological manifestations in inborn errors of immunity. *Pediatric Research.*

Koster, M., & others (2019). From understanding others' needs to prosocial action: Motor and social abilities promote infants' helping. *Developmental Science, 22*(6), e12804.

Kothandan, S.K. (2014). School based interventions versus family based interventions in the treatment of childhood obesity—A systematic review. *Archives of Public Health, 73*(1), 3.

Kotre, J. (1984). *Outliving the self: Generativity and the interpretation of lives.* Baltimore: Johns Hopkins University Press.

Kouklari, E.C., Tsermentseli, S., & Monks, C.P. (2019). Developmental trends of hot and cool executive function in school-aged children with and without autism spectrum disorder: Links with theory of mind. *Development and Psychopathology, 31,* 541–556.

Kovach, C.R., & others (2018). Feasibility and pilot testing of a mindfulness intervention for frail older adults and individuals with dementia. *Research in Gerontological Nursing, 11,* 137–150.

Kowalska, M., & others (2020, in press). Genetic variants and oxidative stress in Alzheimer's disease. *Current Alzheimer Research.*

Kowalski, R.M., Giumetti, G.W., Schroeder, A.N., & Lattanner, M.R. (2014). Bullying in the digital age: A critical review and meta-analysis of cyberbullying research on youth. *Psychological Bulletin, 140,* 1073–1137.

Koyanagi, A., & others (2018). Chronic physical conditions, multimorbidity, and mild cognitive impairment in low- and middle-income countries. *Journal of the American Geriatric Society, 66,* 721–727.

Koyanagi, A., & others (2019). Bullying victimization and suicide attempt among adolescents aged 12–15 years from 48 countries. *Journal of the American Academy of Child and Adolescent Psychiatry, 58,* 907–918.

Koytun, A.S., & others (2020, in press). Antibiotic resistance genes in gut microbiota of children with autism spectrum disorder as possible predictors of the disease. *Microbial Drug Resistance.*

Kozbelt, A. (2014). Musical creativity over the lifespan. In D.K. Simonton (Ed.), *Wiley-Blackwell handbook of genius.* New York: Wiley.

Kozhimmanil, K.B., & others (2013). Doula care, birth outcomes, and costs among Medicaid beneficiaries. *American Journal of Public Health, 103*(4), e113–e121.

Kozol, J. (2005). *The shame of the nation.* New York: Crown.

Kracht, C.L., Webster, E.K., & Staiano, A.E. (2020, in press). Sociodemographic differences in young children meeting 24-hour movement guidelines. *Journal of Physical Activity and Health.*

Kracht, C.L., & others (2020, in press). Association between meeting physical activity, sleep, and dietary guidelines and cardiometabolic risk factors and adiposity in adolescents. *Journal of Adolescent Health.*

Kraen, M., & others (2017). Ethnocardiographic consequences of smoking status in middle-aged subjects. *Echocardiography, 34,* 14–19.

Kramer, A.S. (2019). Framing the debate: The status of U.S. sex education policy and the dual narratives of abstinence-only versus comprehensive sex education policy. *American Journal of Sexuality Education, 14,* 490–513.

Kramer, H.J., & Lagattuta, K.H. (2018). Social categorization. In M.H. Bornstein (Ed.), *SAGE handbook of lifespan human development.* Thousand Oaks, CA: Sage.

Kramer, L. (2006, July 10). Commentary in "How your siblings make you who you are" by J. Kluger, *Time,* pp. 46–55.

Kramer, L., & Hamilton, T. (2019). Parenting siblings. In M.H. Bornstein (Ed.), *Handbook of parenting* (3rd ed.). New York: Routledge.

Kramer, L., & Perozynski, L. (1999). Parental beliefs about managing sibling conflict. *Developmental Psychology, 35,* 489–499.

Kramer, L., & Radey, C. (1997). Improving sibling relationships among young children: A social skills training model. *Family Relations, 46,* 237–246.

Kramer, M.D., & Rodgers, J.L. (2020, in press). The impact of having children on domain-specific life-satisfaction: A quasi-experimental longitudinal investigation using the Socio-Economic Panel (SOEP) data. *Journal of Personality and Social Psychology.*

Krashia, P., Nobili, A., & D'Amelio, M. (2019). Unifying hypothesis of dopamine neuron loss in neurodegenerative diseases: Focusing on Alzheimer's disease. *Frontiers in Molecular Neuroscience, 12,* 123.

Krause, N. (2003). Religious meaning and subjective well-being in late life. *Journals of Gerontology B: Psychological and Social Sciences, 58,* S160–S170.

Krause, N. (2008). The social foundations of religious meaning in life. *Research on Aging, 30*(4), 395–427.

Krause, N. (2009). Deriving a sense of meaning in late life. In V.L. Bengtson, D. Gans, N.M. Putney, & M. Silverstein (Eds.), *Handbook of theories of aging.* New York: Springer.

Krause, N. (2012). Valuing the life experience of old adults and change in depressive symptoms: Exploring an overlooked benefit of involvement in religion. *Journal of Aging Health, 24,* 227–247.

Krause, N. (2019). Assessing the relationships among stress, god-mediated control, and psychological distress/well-being: Does the level of education matter? *Journal of Social Psychology, 159,* 2–14.

Krause, N., & Hayward, R.D. (2014). Religion, finding interests in life, and change in self-esteem during late life. *Research on Aging, 36,* 364–381.

Krause, N., & Hayward, R.D. (2016). Religion, health, and aging. In L.K. George & K.F. Ferraro (Eds.), *Handbook of aging and the social sciences* (8th ed.). New York: Elsevier.

Krause, N., Ironson, G., & Hill, P.C. (2017). Volunteer work, religious commitment, and resting pulse rates. *Journal of Religion and Health, 56,* 591–603.

Krauss, S., Orth, U., & Robins, R.W. (2020, in press). Family environment and self-esteem development: A longitudinal study from 10 to 16. *Journal of Personality and Social Psychology.*

Kravdal, O., & Grundy, E. (2019). Children's age at parental divorce and depression in early and mid-adulthood. *Population Studies, 73,* 37–56.

Kraybill, J.H., Kim-Spoon, J., & Bell, M.A. (2019). Infant attention and age 3 executive function. *Yale Journal of Biology and Medicine, 92,* 3–11.

Krell-Roesch, J., & others (2019). Quantity and quality of mental activities and the risk of incident mild cognitive impairment. *Neurology, 93*(6), e548–e58.

Kresovich, K., & others (2020, in press). Epigenetic mortality predictors and incidence of breast cancer. *Aging.*

Kretch, K.S., & Adolph, K.E. (2017). The organization of exploratory behaviors in infant locomotor planning. *Developmental Science, 20*(4).

Kreth, M., & others (2017). Safe sleep guideline adherence in a nationwide marketing of infant cribs and products. *Pediatrics, 139*(1), e20161729.

Kreutzer, M., Leonard, C., & Flavell, J.H. (1975). An interview study of children's knowledge about memory. *Monographs of the Society for Research in Child Development, 40*(1), Serial No. 159.

Kriemler, S., & others (2011). Effect of school-based interventions on activity and fitness in children and adolescents: A review of reviews and systematic update. *British Journal of Sports Medicine, 45,* 923–930.

Kring, A.M. (2000). Gender and anger. In A.H. Fischer (Ed.), *Gender and emotion: Social psychological perspectives.* New York: Cambridge University Press.

Krishnan, P. (2017). Concept analysis of good death in long term care residents. *International Journal of Palliative Nursing, 23,* 29–34.

Krishnappa, P., & others (2019). Sildenafil/Viagra in the treatment of premature ejaculation. *International Journal of Impotence Research 31,* 65–70.

Krisnana, I., & others (2020, in press). Adolescent characteristics and parenting style as the determinant of bullying in Indonesia: A cross-sectional study. *International Journal of Adolescent Medicine and Health.*

Krogh-Jespersen, S., & Woodward, A.L. (2016). Infant origins of social cognition. In L. Balter & C. Tamis-LeMonda (Eds.), *Child psychology* (3rd ed.). New York: Psychology Press.

Krogh-Jespersen, S., & Woodward, A.L. (2018). Reaching the goal: Active experience facilitates 8-month-old infants' prospective analysis of goal-based actions. *Journal of Experimental Psychology, 171,* 31–45.

Krueger, J.I., Vohs, K.D., & Baumeister, R.F. (2008). Is the allure of self-esteem a mirage after all? *American Psychologist, 63,* 64.

Kruger, J., Blanck, H.M., & Gillespie, C. (2006). Dietary and physical activity behaviors among adults successful at weight loss management. *International Journal of Behavioral Nutrition and Physical Activity, 3,* 17.

Kruger, T.H.C., & others (2019). Child sexual offenders show prenatal and epigenetic alterations of the androgen system. *Translational Psychiatry, 9*(1), 28.

Kruk, J., Kotarska, K., & Aboul-Enein, B.H. (2020, in press). Physical exercise and catecholamines response: Benefits and health risk: Possible mechanisms. *Free Radical Research.*

Kruszka, P., & others (2020, in press). Turner syndrome in diverse populations. *American Journal of Medical Genetics A.*

Krzepota, J., Sadowska, D., & Biernat, E. (2018). Relationships between physical activity and quality of life in pregnant women in the second and third trimester. *International Journal of Environmental Research and Public Health, 15*(12), E2745.

Kuang, W., & others (2020, in press). Trends in the prevalence of cognitive impairment in Chinese older adults: Based on the Chinese Longitudinal Healthy Longevity Survey cohorts from 1988 to 2014. *International Health.*

Kübler-Ross, E. (1969). *On death and dying.* New York: Macmillan.

Kudesia, R., & Talib, H.J. (2019). Fertility counseling for adolescents. *Pediatric Annals, 48,* e86–e91.

Kuebli, J. (1994, March). Young children's understanding of everyday emotions. *Young Children, 49*(3), 36–47.

Kuersten-Hogan, R. (2017). Bridging the gap across the transition to coparenthood: Triadic interactions and coparenting representations from pregnancy through 12 months postpartum. *Frontiers in Psychology, 8,* 475.

Kuhl, P.K. (1993). Infant speech perception: A window on psycholinguistic development. *International Journal of Psycholinguistics, 9,* 33–56.

Kuhl, P.K. (2009). Linking infant speech perception to language acquisition: Phonetic learning predicts language growth. In J. Colombo, P. McCardle, & L. Freund (Eds.), *Infant pathways to language.* New York: Psychology Press.

Kuhl, P.K. (2015). Baby talk. *Scientific American, 313,* 64–69.

Kuhn, D. (1998). Afterword to Volume 2: Cognition, perception, and language. In W. Damon (Ed.), *Handbook of child psychology* (5th ed., Vol. 2). New York: Wiley.

Kuhn, D. (2009). Adolescent thinking. In R.M. Lerner & L. Steinberg (Eds.), *Handbook of adolescent psychology* (3rd ed.). New York: Wiley.

Kulke, L., Atkinson, J., & Braddick, O. (2017). Neural mechanisms of attention become more specialized during infancy: Insights from combined eye tracking and EEG. *Developmental Psychobiology, 59,* 250–260.

Kulu, H. (2014). Marriage duration and divorce: The seven-year itch or a lifelong itch? *Demography, 51,* 881–893.

Kumar, S.V., Oliffe, J.L., & Kelly, M.T. (2018). Promoting postpartum mental health in fathers: Recommendations for nurse practitioners. *American Journal of Men's Health, 12,* 221–228.

Kunzmann, U. (2019). Wisdom: The royal road to personality growth. In R. Fernandez-Ballesteros & others (Eds.), *Cambridge handbook of successful aging.* New York: Cambridge University Press.

Kunzweiler, C. (2007). Twin individuality. *Fresh ink: Essays from Boston College's first-year writing seminar, 9*(1), 2–3.

Kuo, L.J., & Anderson, R.C. (2012). Effects of early bilingualism on learning phonological regularities in a new language. *Journal of Experimental Child Psychology, 111,* 455–467.

Kuo, P.X., & others (2019). Is one secure attachment enough? Infant cortisol reactivity and the security of infant-mother and infant-father attachments at the end of the first year. *Attachment and Human Development, 26,* 426–444.

Kuperberg, A. (2014). Age at coresidence, premarital cohabitation, and marriage dissolution: 1985–2009. *Journal of Marriage and Family, 76,* 352–369.

Kurdek, L.A. (2007). The allocation of household labor between partners in gay and lesbian couples. *Journal of Family Issues, 28,* 132–148.

Kurita, S., & others (2020). Association of physical and/or cognitive activity with cognitive impairment in older adults. *Geriatrics and Gerontology International, 20,* 31–35.

Kvalo, S.E., & others (2017). Does increased physical activity in school affect children's executive function and aerobic fitness? *Scandinavian Journal of Medicine and Science in Sports, 27,* 1833–1841.

Kwan, K.M.W., & others (2020, in press). Children's appraisals of gender nonconformity: Developmental pattern and intervention. *Child Development.*

Kwitek, A.E. (2019). Rate models of metabolic syndrome. *Methods in Molecular Biology, 2019,* 269–285.

Kwok, C., & others (2020, in press). Clinical and socio-demographic features in childhood versus adolescent-onset anorexia nervosa in an Asian population. *Eating and Weight Disorders.*

Kwon, D., & others (2020, in press). Regional growth trajectories of cortical myelination in adolescents and young adults: Longitudinal validation and functional correlates. *Brain Imaging and Behavior.*

Kwon, M., & others (2020, in press). Association between substance use and insufficient sleep in U.S. high school students. *Journal of School Nursing.*

L

La Starza, S., & others (2019). Genome-wide multiple sclerosis association data and coagulation. *Frontiers in Neurology, 10*, 95.

Laborte-Lemoyne, E., Currier, D., & Ellenberg, D. (2017). Exercise during pregnancy enhances cerebral maturation in the newborn: A randomized controlled trial. *Journal of Clinical and Experimental Neuropsychology, 39*, 347-354.

Labouvie-Vief, G. (1986, August). *Modes of knowing and life-span cognition.* Paper presented at the meeting of the American Psychological Association, Washington, DC.

Labouvie-Vief, G., Gruhn, D., & Studer, J. (2010). Dynamic integration of emotion and cognition: Equilibrium regulation in development and aging. In M.E. Lamb, A. Freund, & R.M. Lerner (Eds.), *Handbook of life-span development* (Vol. 2). New York: Wiley.

Lacelle, C., Hebert, M., Lavoie, F., Vitaro, F., & Tremblay, R.E. (2012). Sexual health in women reporting a history of child sexual abuse. *Child Abuse and Neglect, 36*, 247-259.

Lachman, M.E. (2004). Development in midlife. *Annual Review of Psychology* (Vol. 55). Palo Alto, CA: Annual Reviews.

Lachman, M.E., Agrigoroaei, S., & Hahn, E.A. (2016). Making sense of control: Change and consequences. In R. Scott & S. Kosslyn (Eds.), *Emerging trends in the social and behavioral sciences.* New York: Wiley.

Lachman, M.E., Agrigoroaei, S., Murphy, C., & Tun, P.A. (2010). Frequent cognitive activity compensates for education differences in episodic memory. *American Journal of Geriatric Psychiatry, 18*, 4-10.

Lachman, M.E., & Firth, K.M.P. (2004). The adaptive value of feeling in control during midlife. In O.G. Brim, C.D. Ruff, & R.C. Kessler (Eds.), *How healthy are we?* Chicago: University of Chicago Press.

Lachman, M.E., Maier, H., & Budner, R. (2000). *A portrait of midlife.* Unpublished manuscript, Brandeis University, Waltham, MA.

Lachman, M.E., Neupert, S.D., & Agrigoroaei, S. (2011). The relevance of control beliefs for health and aging. In K.W. Schaie & S.L. Willis (Eds.), *Handbook of the psychology of aging* (7th ed.). New York: Elsevier.

Lachman, M.E., Teshale, S., & Agrigoroaei, S. (2015). Midlife as a pivotal period in the life course balancing growth and decline at the crossroads of youth and old age. *International Journal of Behavioral Development, 39*, 20-31.

Lachman, M.E., & others (2018). When adults don't exercise: Behavioral strategies to increase physical activity in sedentary middle-aged and older adults. *Innovation in Aging, 2*, 1-12.

Ladd, G., Buhs, E., & Troop, W. (2004). School adjustment and social skills training. In P.K. Smith & C.H. Hart (Eds.), *Blackwell handbook of childhood social development.* Malden, MA: Blackwell.

Ladd, G.W., & Kochenderfer-Ladd, B. (2019). Parents and children's peer relationships. In M.H. Bornstein (Ed.), *Handbook of parenting* (3rd ed.). New York: Routledge.

Ladouceur, C.D., & others (2019). Neural systems underlying reward cue processing in early adolescence: The role of puberty and puberty hormones. *Psychoneuroendocrinology, 102*, 281-291.

Laflin, M.T., Wang, J., & Barry, M. (2008). A longitudinal study of adolescent transition from virgin to nonvirgin status. *Journal of Adolescent Health, 42*, 228-236.

LaFrance, M., Hecht, M.A., & Paluck, E.L. (2003). The contingent smile: A meta-analysis of sex differences in smiling. *Psychological Bulletin, 129*, 305-334.

Lafreniere, D., & Mann, N. (2009). Anosmia: Loss of smell in the elderly. *Otolaryngologic Clinics of North America, 42*, 123-131.

Lagattuta, K.H., & others (2015). Beyond Sally's missing marble: Further development in children's understanding of mind and emotion in middle childhood. *Advances in Child Development and Behavior, 48*, 185-217.

Lahat, A., & others (2014). Early behavioral inhibition and increased error monitoring predict later social phobia symptoms in childhood. *Journal of the American Academy of Child and Adolescent Psychiatry, 53*, 447-455.

Laheij-Rooijakkers, LA.E., & others (2020, in press). Development of a tool to detect older adults with severe personality disorders for highly specialized care. *International Psychogeriatrics.*

Lai, A., & others (2017). An outpatient methadone weaning program by a neonatal intensive care unit for neonatal abstinence syndrome. *Population Health Management, 20*, 397-401.

Lai, M.M.Y., & others (2020, in press). Relationship of established cardiovascular risk factors and peripheral biomarkers on cognitive function in adults at risk of cognitive deterioration. *Journal of Alzheimer's Disease.*

Lai, M-C., Lombardo, M.V., Chakrabarti, B., & Baron-Cohen, S. (2013). Subgrouping the autism "spectrum": Reflections on DSM-5. *PLoS Biology, 11*(4), e1001544.

Laible, D., Thompson, R.A., & Froimson, J. (2015). Early socialization: The influence of close relationships. In J.E. Grusec & P.D. Hastings (Eds.), *Handbook of socialization* (2nd ed.). New York: Guilford.

Laible, D.J., & others (Eds.) (2020a). *Oxford handbook of parenting and moral development.* New York: Oxford University Press.

Laible, D.J., & others (2020b). The socialization of children's moral understanding in the context of everyday discourse. In D.J. Laible & others (Eds.), *Oxford handbook of parenting and moral development.* New York: Oxford University Press.

Laisk, T., & others (2019). Demographic and evolutionary trends in ovarian functioning and aging. *Human Reproduction Update, 2*, 31-50.

Lakhdir, M.P.A., & others (2020, in press). Physical maltreatment and its associated factors among adolescents in Karachi, Pakistan. *Journal of Interpersonal Violence.*

Lakoski, S., & others (2013, June 2). *Exercise lowers cancer risk in middle-aged men.* Paper presented at the American Society of Clinical Oncology meeting, Chicago, IL.

Lakshmanan, A., & others (2020). Association of WIC participation and growth and developmental outcomes in high-risk infants. *Clinical Pediatrics, 59*, 53-61.

Lalley, P.M. (2013). The aging respiratory system— Pulmonary structure, function, and neural control. *Respiratory Physiology and Neurology, 187*, 199-210.

Lamb, M.E. (1994). Infant care practices and the application of knowledge. In C.B. Fisher & R.M. Lerner (Eds.), *Applied developmental psychology.* New York: McGraw-Hill.

Lamb, M.E., & Lewis, C. (2015). The role of parent-child relationships in child development. In M.H. Bornstein & M.E. Lamb (Eds.), *Developmental science* (7th ed.). New York: Psychology Press.

Lamb, M.E., Malloy, L.C., Hershkowitz, I., & La Rooy, D. (2015). Children and the law. In R.E. Lerner (Ed.), *Handbook of child psychology and developmental science* (7th ed.). New York: Wiley.

Lamballais, S., & others (2020). Cortical gyrification in relation to age and cognition in older adults. *Neuroimage, 212*, 1166357.

Lambez, B., & others (2020). Non-pharmacological interventions for cognitive difficulties in ADHD: A systematic review and meta-analysis. *Journal of Psychiatry Research, 120*, 40-55.

Lamela, D., & Figueiredo, B. (2016). Co-parenting after marital dissolution and children's mental health: A systematic review. *Journal de Pediatria (Rio), 92*, 331-342.

Lamidi, E.O., Manning, W.D., & Brown, S.L. (2019). Change in the stability of first premarital cohabitation among women in the United States, 1983-2013. *Demography, 56*(2), 427-450.

Lamm, C., & others (2018). Impact of early institutionalization on attention mechanisms underlying the inhibition of planned action. *Neuropsychologia, 117*, 339-346.

Lamont, R.A., Nelis, S.M., Quinn, C., & Clare, L. (2017). Social support and attitudes to aging in later life. *International Journal of Aging and Human Development, 84*, 109-125.

Lampard, A.M., Byrne, S.M., McLean, N., & Fursland, A. (2012). The Eating Disorder Inventory-2 perfectionism scale: Factor structure and associations with dietary restraint and weight and shape concern in eating disorders. *Eating Behaviors, 13*, 49-53.

Lampit, A., Hallock, H., & Valenzuela, M. (2014). Computerized cognitive training in cognitively healthy older adults: A systematic review and meta-analysis of effect modifiers. *PLoS Medicine, 11,* e1001756.

Lampl, M. (1993). Evidence of saltatory growth in infancy. *American Journal of Human Biology, 5,* 641-652.

Lampl, M., & Johnson, M.L. (2011). Infant growth in length follows prolonged sleep and increased naps. *Sleep, 34,* 641-650.

Lampl, M., & Schoen, M. (2018). How long bones grow children: Mechanistic paths to variation in human height growth. *American Journal of Human Biology, 29,* 2.

Lamy, S., & others (2014). Psychosocial and organizational work factors and incidence of arterial hypertension among female healthcare workers: Results of the Organisation des soins et santÈ des soignants cohort. *Journal of Hypertension, 32,* 1229-1236.

Lan, X., & others (2011). Investigating the links between the subcomponents of executive function and academic achievement: A cross-cultural analysis of Chinese and American preschoolers. *Journal of Experimental Child Psychology, 108,* 677-692.

Landau, B., Smith, L., & Jones, S. (1998). Object perception and object naming in early development. *Trends in Cognitive Science, 2,* 19-24.

Landes, S.D., & Weng, S.S. (2020, in press). Racial-ethnic differences in turnover intent among home health aides. *Journal of Applied Gerontology.*

Landis, T.D., & others (2020, in press). Differentiating symptoms of ADHD in preschoolers: The role of emotion regulation and executive function. *Journal of Attention Disorders.*

Lane, A., Harrison, M., & Murphy, N. (2014). Screen time increases risk of overweight and obesity in active and inactive 9-year-old Irish children: A cross sectional analysis. *Journal of Physical Activity and Health, 11,* 985-991.

Lane, H. (1976). *The wild boy of Aveyron.* Cambridge, MA: Harvard University Press.

Lang, P.J., & Bradley, M.N. (2019). What is emotion? A natural science perspective. In A.S. Fox & others (Eds.), *The nature of emotion* (2nd ed.). New York: Oxford University Press.

Langer, E. (2005). *On becoming an artist.* New York: Ballantine.

Langer, R.D. (2017). The evidence base for HRT: What can we believe? *Climacteric, 20,* 91-98.

Langeslag, S.J.E., & van Steenbergen, H. (2020, in press). Cognitive control in romantic love: The roles of infatuation and attachment in interference and adaptive cognitive control. *Cognition and Emotion.*

Langstrom, N., Rahman, Q., Carlstrom, E., & Lichtenstein, P. (2010). Genetic and environmental effects on same-sex sexual behavior: A population study of twins in Sweden. *Archives of Sexual Behavior, 39,* 75-80.

Lanning, R.K., & others (2019). Doulas in the operating room: An innovative approach to supporting skin-to-skin care during Cesarean birth. *Journal of Midwifery and Women's Health, 64,* 112-117.

Lansford, J.E. (2013). Single- and two-parent families. In J. Hattie & E. Anderman (Eds.), *International guide to student achievement.* New York: Routledge.

Lansford, J.E. (2019a). Parenting and child discipline. In M.H. Bornstein (Ed.), *Handbook of parenting* (3rd ed.). New York: Routledge.

Lansford, J.E. (2019b). Single- and two-parent families. In J. Hattie & E. Anderman (Eds.), *International handbook of student achievement.* New York: Routledge.

Lansford, J.E. (2020). Parental discipline practices associated with preventing children's aggressive and immoral behavior. In D.J. Laible & others (Eds.), *Oxford handbook of parenting and moral development.* New York: Oxford University Press.

Lansford, J.E., & others (2010). Developmental precursors of number of sexual partners from ages 16 to 22. *Journal of Research on Adolescence, 20,* 651-677.

Lansford, J.E., & others (2014). Pathways of peer relationships from childhood to young adulthood. *Journal of Applied Developmental Psychology, 35,* 111-117.

Lansford, J.E., & others (2018). Bidirectional relations between parenting and behavior problems from age 8 to 13 in nine countries. *Journal of Research on Adolescence, 28,* 571-590.

Lantagne, A., Furman, W., & Novak, J. (2017). "Stay or leave": Predictors of relationship dissolution in emerging adulthood. *Emerging Adulthood, 5,* 241-250.

Lantolf, J. (2017). Materialist dialectics in Vygotsky's methodological approach: Implications for second language education research. In C. Ratner & D. Silva (Eds.), *Vygotsky and Marx.* New York: Routledge.

Lany, J., & Shoaib, A. (2020, in press). Individual differences in non-adjacent statistical dependency learning in infants. *Journal of Child Language.*

Lanyan, A., & others (2020, in press). Postmenopausal women with osteoporosis consume high amounts of vegetables but insufficient dairy products and calcium to benefit from their virtues: The CoLaus/OsteoLaus cohort. *Osteoporosis International.*

Lapsley, D., Reilly, T., & Narváez, D. (2020). Moral self-identity and character development. In L.A. Jensen (Ed.), *Oxford handbook of moral development.* New York: Oxford University Press.

Laranjo, J., Bernier, A., Meins, E., & Carlson, S.M. (2010). Early manifestations of theory of mind: The roles of maternal mind-mindedness and infant security of attachment. *Infancy, 15,* 300-323.

Lardone, M.C., & others (2020, in press). A polygenic risk score suggests shared genetic architecture of voice break with early markers of pubertal onset in boys. *Journal of Clinical Endocrinology and Metabolism.*

Larson, F.B., & others (2006). Exercise is associated with reduced risk for incident dementia among persons 65 years of age and older. *Annals of Internal Medicine, 144,* 73-81.

Larson, N., & others (2018). Personal, behavioral, and environmental predictors of healthy weight maintenance during the transition to adulthood. *Preventive Medicine, 113,* 80-90.

Larson, R.W. (2001). How U.S. children and adolescents spend their time: What it does (and doesn't) tell us about their development. *Current Directions in Psychological Science, 10,* 160-164.

Larson, R.W., McGovern, G., & Orson, C. (2019). How adolescents develop self-motivation in complex learning environments: Processes and practices in afterschool programs. In A. Renninger & S. Hidi (Eds.), *Cambridge handbook of motivation and learning.* New York: Cambridge University Press.

Larson, R.W., & Verma, S. (1999). How children and adolescents spend time across the world: Work, play, and developmental opportunities. *Psychological Bulletin, 125,* 701-736.

Larson, R.W., Walker, K.C., & McGovern, G. (2020). Youth programs as contexts for development of ethical judgment and action. In L.A. Jensen (Ed.), *Oxford handbook of moral development.* New York: Oxford University Press.

Larzelere, R.E., & Kuhn, B.R. (2005). Comparing child outcomes of physical punishment and alternative disciplinary tactics: A meta-analysis. *Clinical Child and Family Psychology Review, 8,* 1-37.

Larzelere, R.E., & others (2019). The insufficiency of the evidence to categorically oppose spanking and its implications for families and psychological science: Comment on Gershoff et al. (2018). *American Psychologist, 74,* 497-499.

Last, B.S., & others (2019). Childhood socioeconomic status and executive function in childhood and beyond. *PLoS One, 13*(8), 0202964.

Latimer, C.S., & others (2017). Resistance to Alzheimer's disease neuropathologic changes and apparent cognitive resilience in the Nun and Honolulu-Asia aging studies. *Journal of Neuropathology and Experimental Neurology, 76,* 458-466.

Latorre, J.G.S., Schmidt, E.B., & Greer, D.M. (2020, in press). Another pitfall in brain death diagnosis: Return of cerebral function after determination of brain death by both clinical and radionuclide cerebral perfusion imaging. *Neocritical Care.*

LaTourrette, A., & Waxman, S.R. (2020, in press). Defining the role of language in infants' object categorization with eye-tracking paradigms. *Journal of Visualized Experiments.*

Latt, M.D., & others (2019). Factors to consider in the selection of dopamine agonists for older persons with Parkinson's disease. *Drugs and Aging, 36,* 189-202.

Lau, J.S., Adams, S.H., Irwin, C.E., & Ozer, E.M. (2013). Receipt of preventive health services in young adults. *Journal of Adolescent Health, 52,* 42-49.

Laube, C., Lorenz, R., & van den Bos, W. (2019). Pubertal testosterone correlates with impatience and dorsal striatal activity. *Developmental Cognitive Neuroscience, 42,* 100749.

Laubjerg, M., & Petersson, B. (2011). Juvenile delinquency and psychiatric contact among adoptees compared to non-adoptees in Denmark: A nationwide register-based comparative study. *Nordic Journal of Psychiatry, 65,* 365-372.

Lauderdale, D.S., & others (2016). Sleep duration and health among older adults: Associations vary by how sleep is measured. *Journal of Epidemiology and Community Health, 70,* 361–366.

Lauer, E.A., & others (2019). Identifying barriers and supports to breastfeeding in the workplace experienced by mothers in the New Hampshire supplemental nutrition program for women, infants, and children utilizing the total worker health framework. *International Journal of Environmental Research and Public Health, 16,* 4.

Lauharatanahirun, N., & others (2018). Neural correlates of risk processing among adolescents: Influences of parental monitoring and household chaos. *Child Development, 89,* 784–796.

Laumann, E.O., Glasser, D.B., Neves, R.C., & Moreira, E.D. (2009). A population-based survey of sexual activity, sexual problems, and associated help-seeking behavior patterns in mature adults in the United States of America. *International Journal of Impotence Research, 21,* 171–178.

Laureiro-Martinez, D., Trujillo, C.A., & Unda, J. (2017). Time perspective and age: A review of age-associated differences. *Frontiers in Psychology, 8,* 101.

Laurent, J.S., & others (2020, in press). Associations among body mass, cortical thickness, and executive function in children. *JAMA Pediatrics.*

Lauretti, E., & Pratico, D. (2020, in press). Alzheimer's disease: Phenotypic approaches using disease models and the targeting of tau protein. *Expert Opinion on Therapeutic Targets.*

Laurin, R. (2020, in press). An investigation of the roles of group identification, perceived ability, and evaluative conditions in stereotype threat experiences. *Psychological Reports.*

Laurita, A.C., Hazan, C., & Spreng, R.N. (2019). An attachment theoretical perspective for the neural representation of close others. *Social Cognitive and Affective Neuroscience, 14,* 237–251.

Laursen, B. (2018). Peer influence. In W.M. Bukowski & others (Eds.), *Handbook of peer interactions, relationships, and groups* (2nd ed.). New York: Guilford.

Laursen, B., & Adams, R. (2018). Conflict between peers. In W.M. Bukowski & others (Eds.), *Handbook of peer interactions, relationships, and groups* (2nd ed.). New York: Guilford.

Laursen, B., & others (2017). The spread of substance use and delinquency between adolescent twins. *Developmental Psychology, 53,* 329–339.

Lautenbacher, S., & others (2017). Age changes in pain perception: A systematic-review and meta-analysis of age effects on pain and tolerance thresholds. *Neuroscience and Biobehavioral Reviews, 75,* 104–113.

Lavalliere, M., & others (2011). Changing lanes in a simulator: Effects of aging on the control of the vehicle and visual inspection of mirrors and the blind spot. *Traffic Injury Prevention, 12,* 191–200.

Lavender, J.M., & others (2014). Dimensions of emotion dysregulation in bulimia nervosa. *European Eating Disorders Review, 22,* 212–216.

Lavner, J.A., & Bradbury, T.N. (2019). Marriage and committed relationships. In B.H. Friese (Ed.), *APA handbook of contemporary family psychology.* Washington, DC: APA Books.

Lavner, J.A., Karney, B.R., & Bradbury, T.N. (2013). Newlyweds' optimistic forecasts of their marriage: For better or for worse? *Journal of Family Psychology, 27,* 531–540.

Lazris, A. (2019). Geriatric palliative care. *Primary Care, 46,* 447–459.

Lazzarotto, S., & others (2019). Coping with age-related hearing loss: Patient-caregiver dyad effects on quality of life. *Health Quality and Life Outcomes, 17*(1), 86.

Le, Y., & others (2019). Cross-day influences between couple closeness and coparenting support among new parents. *Journal of Family Psychology, 33,* 360–369.

Leaper, C. (2015). Gender development from a social-cognitive perspective. In R.M. Lerner (Ed.), *Handbook of child psychology and developmental science* (7th ed.). New York: Wiley.

Leaper, C. (2017). Further reflections on Sandra Lipsitz Bem's impact. *Sex Roles, 76,* 759–765.

Leaper, C., & Bigler, R.S. (2018). Societal causes and consequences of gender typing on children's toys. In E.S. Weisgram & L.M. Dinella (Eds.), *Gender typing of children's play.* Washington, DC: APA Books.

Leaper, C., & Smith, T.E. (2004). A meta-analytic review of gender variations in children's language use: Talkativeness, affiliative speech, and assertive speech. *Developmental Psychology, 40,* 993–1027.

Lear, M.K., & others (2020). Differential suicide risk factors in rural middle and high school students. *Psychiatry Research, 284,* 112773.

Lecouvey, G., & others (2019). An impairment of prospective memory in mild Alzheimer's disease: A ride in a virtual town. *Frontiers in Psychology, 10,* 241.

Ledesma, K. (2012). A place to call home. *Adoptive Families.* Retrieved from www.adoptivefamilies.com/articles.php?aid52129

Lee, A., & others (2019). BOADICEA: A comprehensive breast cancer risk prediction model incorporating genetic and nongenetic risk factors. *Genetics in Medicine, 21,* 1708–1718.

Lee, E., & Jang, I. (2020). Nurses' fatigue, job stress, organizational culture, and turnover intention: A culture-work-health model. *Western Journal of Nursing, 42,* 108–116.

Lee, G., & others (2019). Predicting Alzheimer's disease progression using multi-modal deep learning approach. *Scientific Reports, 9*(1), 1952.

Lee, I.M., & Skerrett, P.J. (2001). Physical activity and all-cause mortality: What is the dose-response relation? *Medical Science and Sports Exercise, 33*(6, Suppl.), S459–S471.

Lee, J., Gillath, O., & Miller, A. (2019). Effects of self- and partner's online disclosure on relationship intimacy and satisfaction. *PLoS One, 14,* e0212186.

Lee, J.E., Kahana, B., & Kahana, E. (2017). Successful aging from the viewpoint of older adults: Development of a brief Successful Aging Inventory (SAI). *Gerontology, 63,* 359–371.

Lee, J.H., & others (2014). Five-factor model personality traits as predictors of incident coronary heart disease in the community. *Psychosomatics, 55,* 352–361.

Lee, K. (2019). Impact of Head Start quality on children's developmental outcomes. *Social Work in Public Health, 34,* 239–250.

Lee, K. (2020). Long-term Head Start impact on developmental outcomes for children in foster care. *Child Abuse and Neglect, 201,* 104329.

Lee, K., Cameron, C.A., Doucette, J., & Talwar, V. (2002). Phantoms and fabrications: Young children's detection of implausible lies. *Child Development, 73,* 1688–1702.

Lee, K.S., & Vaillancort, T. (2018). Longitudinal associations among bullying by peers, disordered eating behavior, and symptoms of depression during adolescence. *JAMA Psychiatry, 75,* 605–612.

Lee, K.Y., & others (2011). Effects of combined radiofrequency radiation exposure on the cell cycle and its regulatory proteins. *Bioelectromagnetics, 32,* 169–178.

Lee, M.K., & Binns, C. (2019). Breastfeeding and the risk of infant illness in Asia: A review. *International Journal of Environmental Research and Public Health, 17,* 1.

Lee, N., & Choi, C.J. (2019). Smoking and diabetes as predictive factors of accelerated loss of muscle mass in middle-aged and older women: A six-year retrospective cohort study. *Journal of Women's Health, 28,* 1391–1398.

Lee, R.Y., & others (2020, in press). Association of Physician Orders for Life-Sustaining Treatment with ICU admission among patients hospitalized near the end of life. *JAMA.*

Lee, S., & others (2020, in press). Validation of fragile X screening in the newborn population using a fit-for-purpose fMRI PCR assay system. *Journal of Molecular Diagnosis.*

Lee, S.H., Lee, B.C., Kim, J.W., Yi, J.S., & Choi, I.G. (2013). Association between alcoholism family history and alcohol screening scores among alcohol-dependent patients. *Clinical Psychopharmacology and Neuroscience, 11,* 89–95.

Lee, S.H., & others (2019). Sirtuin signaling in cellular senescence and aging. *BMB Reports, 52,* 24–34.

Lee, S.H., & others (2020). CXCR2 ligands and mTOR activation enhance reprogramming of human somatic cells to pluripotent stem cells. *Stem Cells and Development, 29,* 119–132.

Lee, W.J., & others (2020). Determinants and indicators of successful aging associated with mortality: A 4-year population-based study. *Aging, 12,* 2670–2679.

Lee, Y.S., & others (2017). The role of religiousness/spirituality and social networks in predicting depressive symptoms among older Korean Americans. *Journal of Cross-Cultural Psychology, 32,* 239–254.

Leerkes, E.M., & Augustine, M.E. (2019). Parenting and emotions. In M.H. Bornstein (Ed.)., *Handbook of parenting* (3rd ed.) (Vol. 3). New York: Routledge.

Leerkes, E.M., Bailes, L.G., & Augustine, M. (2020, in press). The intergenerational transmission of emotion socialization. *Developmental Psychology.*

Leerkes, E.M., Parade, S.H., & Gudmundson, J.A. (2011). Mothers' emotional reactions to crying pose risk for subsequent attachment insecurity. *Journal of Family Psychology, 25,* 635-643.

Leerkes, E.M., & others (2017). Further evidence of the limited role of candidate genes in relation to mother-infant attachment. *Attachment and Human Development, 19,* 76-105.

Lees, R.M., Johnson, J.D., & Ashby, M.C. (2020). Presynaptic buttons that contain mitochondria are more stable. *Frontiers in Synaptic Neuroscience, 11,* 37.

Lefebvre, J.P., & Krettenaur, T. (2020). Is the true self truly moral? Identity intuitions across domains of sociomoral reasoning and age. *Journal of Experimental Child Psychology, 192,* 104769.

Lefkowitz, E.S., & Gillen, M.M. (2006). "Sex is just a normal part of life": Sexuality in emerging adulthood. In J.J. Arnett & J.L. Tanner (Eds.), *Emerging adults in America.* Washington, DC: American Psychological Association.

Lefkowitz, E.S., & others (2019). Changes in diverse sexual and contraceptive behaviors across college. *Journal of Sex Research, 56,* 965-976.

Leftwich, H., & Alves, M.V. (2017). Adolescent pregnancy. *Pediatric Clinics of North America, 64,* 381-388.

Leger, K.A., & others (2016). Personality and stressor-related affect. *Journal of Personality and Social Psychology, 111,* 917-928.

Legerstee, M. (1997). Contingency effects of people and objects on subsequent cognitive functioning in 3-month-old infants. *Social Development, 6,* 307-321.

Legge, G.E., Madison, C., Vaughn, B.N., Cheong, A.M., & Miller, J.C. (2008). Retention of high tactile acuity throughout the lifespan in blindness. *Perception and Psychophysics, 70,* 1471-1488.

Lehman, E.B., & others (2010). Long-term stability of young children's eyewitness accuracy, suggestibility, and resistance to misinformation. *Journal of Applied Developmental Psychology, 31,* 145-154.

Lehman, H.C. (1960). The age decrement in outstanding scientific creativity. *American Psychologist, 15,* 128-134.

Lehr, C.A., Hanson, A., Sinclair, M.F., & Christenson, S.I. (2003). Moving beyond dropout prevention towards school completion. *School Psychology Review, 32,* 342-364.

Lehtinen, A., & others (2019). A distinctive DNA methylation pattern in insufficient sleep. *Scientific Reports, 9*(1), 1193.

Leinaweaver, J. (2014). Informal kinship-based fostering around the world: Anthropological findings. *Child Development Perspectives, 8,* 131-136.

Leipold, B. (2020). *Intentional self-development and positive aging.* New York: Routledge.

Leman, S., & others (2018). Religiosity preference and its association with depression and anxiety symptoms among Hispanic/Latino adults. *PLoS One, 13*(2), e0185661.

Lemaster, P., Delaney, R., & Strough, J.N. (2017). Crossover, degendering, or . . . ? A multidimensional approach to lifespan gender development. *Sex Roles, 76,* 669-681.

Lemes, I.R., & others (2019). Association of sedentary behavior and metabolic syndrome. *Public Health, 167,* 96-102.

Lempers, J.D., Flavell, E.R., & Flavell, J.H. (1977). The development in very young children of tacit knowledge concerning visual perception. *Genetic Psychology Monographs, 95,* 3-53.

Lengua, L., & Wachs, T.D. (2012). Temperament and risk: Resilient and vulnerable responses to adversity. In M. Zentner & R. Shiner (Eds.), *Handbook of temperament.* New York: Guilford.

Lenhart, A. (2015, April 9). *Teens, social media, and technology overview 2015.* Washington, DC: Pew Research Center.

Lenhart, A., Smith, A., Anderson, M., Duggan, M., & Perrin, A. (2015, August 6). *Teens, technology, and friendships.* Washington, DC: Pew Research Center.

Lenoir, C.P., Mallet, E., & Calenda, E. (2000). Siblings of sudden infant death syndrome and near miss in about 30 families: Is there a genetic link? *Medical Hypotheses, 54,* 408-411.

Lenroot, R.K., & Giedd, J.N. (2006). Brain development in children and adolescents: Insights from anatomical magnetic resonance imaging. *Neuroscience and Biobehavioral Reviews, 30,* 718-729.

Lenze, E.J., & others (2014). Mindfulness-based stress reduction for older adults with worry symptoms and co-occurring cognitive dysfunction. *International Journal of Geriatric Psychiatry, 29,* 991-1000.

Leonardi, M., & others (2019). Reproductive health considerations in sexual and/or gender minority adolescents. *Journal of Pediatric and Adolescent Gynecology, 32,* 15-20.

Leppakoski, T.H., Flinck, A., & Paavilainen, E. (2015). Greater commitment to the domestic violence training is required. *Journal of Interprofessional Care, 29,* 281-289.

Lereya, S.T., Samara, M., & Wolke, D. (2013). Parenting behavior and the risk of becoming a victim and a bully/victim: A meta-analysis study. *Child Abuse and Neglect, 37*(12), 1091-1098.

Lerner, H.G. (1989). *The dance of intimacy.* New York: Harper & Row.

Lerner, R.M., Lerner, J.V., Bowers, E., & Geldhof, G.J. (2015). Positive youth development: A relational developmental systems model. In R.M. Lerner (Ed.), *Handbook of child psychology and developmental science* (7th ed.). New York: Wiley.

Lerner, R.M., & others (2019). The end of the beginning: Evidence and absences in studying PYD in a global context. *Adolescent Research Review, 4,* 1-14.

Lervag, A., & others (2019). Socioeconomic background, nonverbal IQ, and school absence affects the development of vocabulary and reading comprehension in children living in severe poverty. *Developmental Science, 22*(5), e12858.

Lesaux, N.K., & Siegel, L.S. (2003). The development of reading in children who speak English as a second language. *Developmental Psychology, 39,* 1005-1019.

Leshikar, E.D., & Duarte, A. (2014). Medial prefrontal cortex supports source memory for self-referenced materials in young and older adults. *Cognitive, Affective, and Behavioral Neuroscience, 14,* 236-252.

Leshikar, E.D., Gutchess, A.H., Hebrank, A.C., Sutton, B.P., & Park, D.C. (2010). The impact of increased relational encoding demands in frontal and hippocampal function in older adults. *Cortex, 46,* 507-521.

Leslie, M., & others (2020). The care capacity goals of family carers and the role of technology in achieving them. *BMC Geriatrics, 20*(1), 52.

Levant, R.F. (2001). Men and masculinity. In J. Worell (Ed.), *Encyclopedia of women and gender.* San Diego: Academic Press.

Leve, L.D., & others (2020, in press). The Early Growth and Development Study: A dual-family adoption study from birth through adolescence. *Twin Research and Human Genetics.*

Levelt, W.J.M. (1989). *Speaking: From intention to articulation.* Cambridge, MA: MIT Press.

Leventhal, T., Anastasio, J., & Dupere, V. (2020). The urban world of minority and majority children. In R.D. Parke & G.H. Elder (Eds.), *Children in changing worlds.* New York: Cambridge University Press.

Levey, E.K.V., & others (2019). The longitudinal role of self-concept clarity and best friend delinquency in adolescent delinquency behavior. *Journal of Youth and Adolescence, 48,* 1068-1081.

Levine, D., & others (2019). Finding events in a continuous world: A developmental account. *Developmental Psychology, 61,* 376-389.

Levine, D., & others (2020). Evaluating socioeconomic gaps in preschoolers' vocabulary, syntax, and language process skills with the Quick Interactive Language Screener (QUILS). *Early Childhood Research Quarterly, 50,* 114-128.

LeVine, S. (1979). *Mothers and wives: Gusii women of East Africa.* Chicago: University of Chicago Press.

Levine, T.P., & others (2008). Effects of prenatal cocaine exposure on special education in school-aged children. *Pediatrics, 122,* e83-e91.

Levinson, D.J. (1978). *The seasons of a man's life.* New York: Knopf.

Levinson, D.J. (1996). *The seasons of a woman's life.* New York: Knopf.

Levy, B., & Stosic, M. (2019). Traditional prenatal diagnosis: Past to present. *Methods in Molecular Biology, 1885,* 3-22.

Levy, J.K., & others (2020). Characteristics of successful programs targeting gender inequality and restrictive gender norms for the health and wellbeing of children, adolescents, and young adults: A systematic review. *Lancet. Global Health, 8*(2), e225-e236.

Levy, M., & Wright, M. (2020). *Immigration and American ethos.* New York: Cambridge University Press.

Lewis, B.A., & others (2018). The effect of sleep pattern changes on postpartum depressive symptoms. *BMC Women's Health, 18*(1), 12.

Lewis, C.J. (2019). Vygotsky and moral education: A response to and expansion of Tappan. *Educational Philosophy and Theory, 51,* 41-50.

Lewis, J.P., & Allen, J. (2017). Alaska native elders in recovery: Linkages between indigenous cultural generativity and sobriety to promote successful aging. *Journal of Cross-Cultural Psychology, 32,* 209-222.

Lewis, L., & others (2018a). The perceptions and experiences of women who achieved and did not achieve waterbirth. *BMC Pregnancy and Childbirth, 18*(1), 23.

Lewis, L., & others (2018b). Obstetric and neonatal outcomes for women intending to use immersion in water for labor and birth in Western Australia (2015-2016): A retrospective audit of clinical outcomes. *Australian and New Zealand Journal of Obstetrics and Gynecology, 58,* 539-547.

Lewis, M. (2005). Selfhood. In B. Hopkins (Ed.), *The Cambridge encyclopedia of child development.* Cambridge, UK: Cambridge University Press.

Lewis, M. (2007). Early emotional development. In A. Slater & M. Lewis (Eds.), *Introduction to infant development.* Malden, MA: Blackwell.

Lewis, M. (2008). The emergence of human emotions. In M. Lewis, J.M. Haviland Jones, & L. Feldman Barrett (Eds.), *Handbook of emotions* (3rd ed.). New York: Guilford.

Lewis, M. (2010). The emergence of consciousness and its role in human development. In W.F. Overton & R.M. Lerner (Eds.), *Handbook of life-span development* (2nd ed.). New York: Wiley.

Lewis, M. (2015). Emotional development and consciousness. In R.M. Lerner (Ed.), *Handbook of child psychology and developmental science* (7th ed.). New York: Wiley.

Lewis, M. (2018). The emergence of human emotions. In L.F. Barrett & others (Eds.), *Handbook of emotion* (4th ed.). New York: Guilford.

Lewis, M., & Brooks-Gunn, J. (1979). Social cognition and the acquisition of the self. New York: Plenum.

Lewis, M., Feiring, C., & Rosenthal, S. (2000). Attachment over time. *Child Development, 71,* 707-720.

Lewis-Morrarty, E., & others (2015). Infant attachment security and early childhood behavioral inhibition interact to predict adolescent social anxiety symptoms. *Child Development, 86,* 598-613.

Li, C., & others (2019). Effect of English learning experience on young children's prefrontal cortex functioning for attentional control: An fNIRS study. *Conference Proceedings. Annual International Conference of the IEEE Engineering in Medicine and Biology Society, 2019,* 4832-4835.

Li, C.P., & others (2019). A novel fluorescence assay for resveratrol determination in red wine based on competitive host-guest recognition. *Food Chemistry, 283,* 191-198.

Li, F.J., Shen, L., & Ji, H.F. (2012). Dietary intakes of vitamin E, vitamin C, and b-carotene, and risk of Alzheimer's disease: A meta-analysis. *Journal of Alzheimer's Disease, 31,* 753-758.

Li, H., & others (2020). Low folate acid concentration impacts mismatch repair deficiency in neural tube defects. *Ergogenomics, 12,* 5-18.

Li, J. (2020). The cultural framing of development. In. M.F. Mascolo & T.R. Bidell (Eds.), *Handbook of integrative developmental science.* New York: Routledge.

Li, J., Olsen, J., Vestergaard, M., & Obel, C. (2011). Low Apgar scores and risk of childhood attention deficit hyperactivity disorder. *Journal of Pediatrics, 158,* 775-779.

Li, J., Vitiello, M.V., & Gooneratne, N.S. (2018). Sleep in normal aging. *Sleep Medicine Clinics, 13*(1), 1-11.

Li, J., & others (2018). Physical activity in relation to sleep among community-dwelling older adults in China. *Journal of Aging and Physical Activity, 26,* 647-654.

Li, J., & others (2020). Glucose-induced oxidative stress and accelerated aging in endothelial cells are mediated by the depletion of mitochondrial SIRTs. *Physiological Reports, 8*(3), e14331.

Li, J., & others (2020, in press). Genome-wide network-assisted association and enrichment study of amyloid imaging phenotype in Alzheimer's disease. *Current Alzheimer Research.*

Li, J.W., & others (2017). The effect of acute and chronic exercise on cognitive function and academic performance in adolescents: A systematic review. *Journal of Science and Medicine in Sport, 20,* 841-848.

Li, M., & others (2019). Longitudinal link between trait motivation and risk-taking behaviors via neural risk processing. *Developmental Cognitive Neuroscience, 40,* 100725.

Li, N., & Hein, S. (2019). Parenting, autonomy in learning, and development during adolescence in China. *New Directions in Child and Adolescent Development, 163,* 67-80.

Li, R., & others (2014). Breastfeeding and risk of infections at 6 years. *Pediatrics, 134*(Suppl. 1), S13-S20.

Li, T., & Siu, P.M. (2020, in press). Unraveling the direct and indirect effects between future time perspective and subjective well-being across adulthood. *Aging and Mental Health.*

Li, T., & others (2019). The associations between left-hand digit ration (2D:4D) and puberty characteristics in Chinese girls. *Early Human Development, 130,* 22-26.

Li, W., Farkas, G., Duncan, G.J., Burchinal, M.R., & Vandell, D.L. (2013). Timing of high-quality child care and cognitive, language, and preacademic development. *Developmental Psychology, 49,* 1440-1451.

Li, X., & others (2020a). The influence of disabilities in activities of daily living on successful aging: The role of well-being and residence location. *Frontiers in Public Health, 7,* 417.

Li, X., & others (2020b). OCIAD1 contributes to neurodegeneration in Alzheimer's disease by inducing mitochondria dysfunction, neuronal vulnerability, and synaptic damages. *EBioMedicine, 51,* 102569.

Li, Y., Allen, J., & Casillas, A. (2017). Relating psychological and social factors to academic performance: A longitudinal investigation of high-poverty middle school students. *Journal of Adolescence, 56,* 179-189.

Li, Y.R., Li, S., & Lin, C.C. (2018). Effect of resveratrol and pterostilbene on aging and longevity. *Biofactors, 44,* 69-82.

Liang, X., & others (2020, in press). Inability to smell peppermint is related to cognitive decline: A prospective community-based study. *Neuroepidemiology.*

Liang, Y.J., Xi, B., Song, A.Q., Liu, J.X., & Mi, J. (2012). Trends in general and abdominal obesity among Chinese children and adolescents, 1993-2009. *Pediatric Obesity, 7,* 355-364.

Liao, Y.W. (2019). Should physician-assisted suicide be accepted in the practice of medicine? A literature review. *Future Healthcare, 6* (Suppl. 1), 37.

Liben, L.S. (1995). Psychology meets geography: Exploring the gender gap on the national geography bee. *Psychological Science Agenda, 8,* 8-9.

Liben, L.S. (2017). Gender development: A constructivist-ecological perspective. In N. Budwig, E. Turiel, & P.D. Zelazo (Eds.), *New perspectives on human development.* New York: Cambridge University Press.

Liberman, Z., Woodward, A.L., & Kinzler, K.D. (2017). The origins of social categorization. *Trends in Cognitive Science, 21,* 551-568.

Libertus, K., Joh, A.S., & Needham, A.W. (2016). Motor training at 3 months affects object exploration 12 months later. *Developmental Science, 19,* 1058-1066.

Libertus, K., & Needham, A. (2010). Teach to reach: The effects of active versus passive reaching experiences on action and perception. *Vision Research, 50,* 2750-2757.

Lichtenstein, P., & others (2020, in press). Associations between conduct problems in childhood and adverse outcomes in emerging adulthood: A longitudinal Swedish nationwide twin cohort. *Journal of Child Psychology and Psychiatry.*

Lichtenthal, W.G., & others (2019). An open trial of meaning-centered grief therapy: Rationale and preliminary evaluation. *Palliative Support and Care, 17,* 2-12.

Liddell, B.J., & Williams, E.N. (2019). Cultural differences in interpersonal emotion regulation. *Frontiers in Psychology, 10,* 999.

Liddon, L., Kingerlee, R., & Barry, J.A. (2018). Gender differences in preference for psychological treatment, coping strategies, and triggers to help-seeking. *British Journal of Clinical Psychology, 57,* 42-58.

Lieberman, A.F., & others (2020). *Make room for baby.* New York: Guilford.

Lieven, E. (2008). Language development: Overview. In M.M. Haith & J.B. Benson (Eds.), *Encyclopedia of infant and early childhood development.* Oxford, UK: Elsevier.

Lifton, R.J. (1977). The sense of immortality: On death and the continuity of life. In H. Feifel (Ed.), *New meanings of death.* New York: McGraw-Hill.

Lightner, C., & Hathaway, N. (1990). *Giving sorrow words*. New York: Warner.

Ligier, F., & others (2020). Are school difficulties an early sign for mental disorder diagnosis and suicide prevention? A comparative study of individuals who died by suicide and control group. *Child and Adolescent Psychiatry and Mental Health, 14*, 1.

Lillard, A. (2006). Pretend play in toddlers. In C.A. Brownell & C.B. Kopp (Eds.), *Socioemotional development in the toddler year*. New York: Oxford University Press.

Lillard, A.S., & others (2017). Montessori elevates and equalizes child outcomes: A longitudinal study. *Frontiers in Psychology, 8*, 1783.

Limousin, P., & Foltynie, T. (2019). Long-term outcomes of deep brain stimulation in Parkinson disease. *Nature Reviews. Neurology, 142*, 2417–2431.

Lin, F.R., Thorpe, R., Gordon-Salant, S., & Ferrucci, L. (2011). Hearing loss prevalence and risk factors among older adults in the United States. *Journals of Gerontology A: Biological Sciences and Medical Sciences, 66A*(5), 582–590.

Lin, I.F., & others (2018). Antecedents of gray divorce: A life course perspective. *Journals of Gerontology B: Psychological Sciences and Social Sciences, 73*, 1022–1031.

Lin, L.Y., & others (2015). Effects of television exposure on developmental skills of young children. *Infant Behavior and Development, 38*, 20–26.

Lin, Q., & others (2020). Relationship between Chinese children's imaginary companions and their understanding of second-order false beliefs and emotions. *International Journal of Psychology, 55*, 98–105.

Lin, X., Bryant, C., Boldero, J., & Dow, B. (2014). Older Chinese immigrants' relationships with their children: A literature review from a solidarity-conflict perspective. *Gerontologist, 55*, 990–1005.

Lin, X., & others (2020). Contributions of DNA damage to Alzheimer's disease. *International Journal of Molecular Science, 21*, 5.

Lind, R.R., & others (2018). Improved cognitive performance in preadolescent Danish children after the school-based physical activity program "FIFA 11 for Health" for Europe—A cluster-randomized controlled trial. *European Journal of Sport Science, 18*, 130–139.

Lindahl-Jacobsen, R., & Christensen, K. (2019). Gene-lifestyle interactions in longevity. In R. Fernandez-Ballesteros & others (Eds.), *Cambridge handbook of successful aging*. New York: Cambridge University Press.

Lindau, S.T., & Gavrilova, N. (2010). Sex, health, and years of sexually active life gained due to good health: Evidence from two U.S. population based cross sectional surveys of aging. *British Medical Journal, 340*, c810.

Lindau, S.T., & others (2007). A study of sexuality and health among older adults in the United States. *New England Journal of Medicine, 357*, 762–774.

Lindberg, S.M., Hyde, J.S., Petersen, J.L., & Lin, M.C. (2010). New trends in gender and mathematics performance: A meta-analysis. *Psychological Bulletin, 136*, 1123–1135.

Lindell, A.K., Campione-Barr, N., & Killoren, S.E. (2017). Implications of parent-child relationships for emerging adults' feelings about adulthood. *Journal of Family Psychology, 31*, 810–820.

Linden-Carmichael, A.N., & Lau-Barraco, C. (2017). Alcohol mixed with energy drinks: Daily context of use. *Alcoholism: Clinical and Experimental Research, 41*, 863–869.

Lindfors, P., & others (2019). Do maternal knowledge and paternal knowledge of children's whereabouts buffer differently against alcohol use? A longitudinal study among Finnish boys and girls. *Drug and Alcohol Dependency, 194*, 351–357.

Lindsey, E.W. (2019). Frequency and intensity of emotional expressiveness and preschool children's peer competence. *Journal of Genetic Psychology, 180*, 45–61.

Lindwall, M., & others (2012). Dynamic associations of change in physical activity and change in cognitive function: Coordinated analyses across four studies with up to 21 years of longitudinal data. *Journal of Aging Research*. doi:10.1155/2012/493598

Link, W. (2019). Introduction to FOXO biology. *Methods in Molecular Biology, 1890*, 1–9.

Lipowski, M., Lipowska, M., Jochimek, M., & Krokosz, D. (2016). Resilience as a factor protecting youths from risky behavior: Moderating effects of gender and sport. *European Journal of Sport Science, 16*, 246–255.

Lipowski, M., & others (2019). Improvement of attention, executive functions, and processing speed in elderly women as a result of involvement in the Nordic Walking Training program and vitamin D supplementation. *Nutrients, 11*, 6.

Lippa, R.A. (2013). Men and women with bisexual identities show bisexual patterns of sexual attraction to male and female "swimsuit models." *Archives of Sexual Behavior, 42*, 187–196.

Lippman, L.A., & Keith, J.D. (2006). The demographics of spirituality among youth: International perspectives. In E. Roehlkepartain, P.E. King, L. Wagener, & P.L. Benson (Eds.), *The handbook of spirituality in childhood and adolescence*. Thousand Oaks, CA: Sage.

Lipsitz, L.A. (2020, in press). When I'm 84: What should life look like in old age? *Journal of the American Geriatrics Society*.

Lisha, N.E., & others (2014). Evaluation of the psychometric properties of the Revised Inventory of the Dimensions of Emerging Adulthood (IDEA-R) in a sample of continuation high school students. *Evaluation and the Health Professions, 37*, 158–177.

Little, S., & Brown, P. (2020, in press). Debugging adaptive deep brain stimulation for Parkinson's disease. *Movement Disorders*.

Littleton, H., Layh, M., & Rudolph, K. (2018). Unacknowledged rape in the community: Rape characteristics and adjustment. *Violence and Victims, 33*, 142–156.

Liu, C., & Ma, J.L. (2019). Adult attachment style, emotion regulation, and social networking sites addiction. *Frontiers in Psychology, 10*, 2352.

Liu, J.H., & others (2020, in press). Depressive symptoms as a mediator of the influence of self-reported sleep quality on falls: A mediation analysis. *Aging and Mental Health*.

Liu, L., Wang, N., & Tian, L. (2019). The parent-adolescent relationship and risk-taking behaviors among Chinese adolescents: The moderating role of self-control. *Frontiers in Psychology, 10*, 542.

Liu, L.Y., Brooks, N.B., & Spelke, E.S. (2019). Origins of the concepts cause, cost, and goal in prereaching infants. *Proceedings of the National Academy of Sciences U.S.A., 116*(36), 17747–17752.

Liu, Q., & Tan, Y.Q. (2019). Advances in the identification of susceptibility gene defects of hereditary colorectal cancer. *Journal of Cancer, 10*, 643–653.

Liu, R., & others (2017). Does CenteringPregnancy group prenatal care affect the birth experience of underserved women? A mixed methods analysis. *Journal of Immigration and Minority Health, 19*, 415–422.

Liu, W., & others (2019). Cognitive reappraisal in children: Neuropsychological evidence of up-regulating positive emotion from an ERP study. *Frontiers in Psychology, 10*, 147.

Liu, W., & others (2020, in press). X-chromosome genetic association test incorporating X-chromosome inactivation and imprinting effects. *Journal of Genetics*.

Liu, W.M., Forbat, L., & Anderson, K. (2019). Death of a close friend: Short and long-term impacts on physical, psychological, and social well-being. *PLoS One, 14*(4), e0214838.

Liu, Y., & Lachman, M.E. (2019). Socioeconomic status and parenting style in childhood: Long-term effects on cognitive function in middle and later adulthood. *Journals of Gerontology B: Psychological Sciences and Social Sciences, 74*(6), e13–e24.

Liu, Y., & Lachman, M.E. (2020, in press). Education and cognition in middle age and later life: The mediating role of physical and cognitive activity. *Journals of Gerontology B: Psychological Sciences and Social Sciences*.

Liu, Y., & others (2018). The unique role of executive function skills in predicting Hong Kong kindergarteners' reading comprehension. *British Journal of Educational Psychology, 88*, 628–644.

Liu, Y., & others (2020). Emerging role of sirtuin 2 in Parkinson disease. *Frontiers in Aging Neuroscience, 11*, 372.

Lively, W., & Bromley, D. (1973). *Person perception in childhood and adolescence*. New York: Wiley.

Livingston, G. (2017). *5 facts on love and marriage in America*. Washington, DC: Pew Research Center.

Livingston, G. (2018, September 24). *Stay-at-home moms and dads account for about one-in-five U.S. parents*. Washington, DC: Pew Research.

Livingston, G., & Bialik, K. (2018, May 10). *7 facts about U.S. moms*. Washington, DC: Pew Research Center.

Lizandra, J., & others (2019). Screen time and moderate-to-vigorous physical activity changes and displacement in adolescence: A prospective cohort study. *European Journal of Sport Science, 19,* 686–695.

Lizuka, A., & others (2020, in press). Neural substrate of a cognitive intervention program using Go game: A positron emission tomography study. *Aging: Clinical and Experimental Research.*

Lleo, A., Moroni, L., Caliari, L., & Invernizzi, P. (2012). Autoimmunity and Turner's syndrome. *Autoimmunity Reviews, 11,* A538–543.

Lo, C.C., Cheng, T.C., & Simpson, G.M. (2016). Marital status and work-related health limitation: A longitudinal study of young adult and middle-aged Americans. *International Journal of Public Health, 61,* 91–100.

Lo, C.K., & others (2019). Prevalence of child maltreatment and its association with parenting style: A population study in Hong Kong. *International Journal of Environmental Research and Public Health, 16,* 9.

Lo, J.C., & others (2016). Self-reported sleep duration and cognitive performance in older adults: A systematic review and meta-analysis. *Sleep Medicine, 17,* 87–98.

Loaiza, V.M., & Souza, A.S. (2019). An age-related deficit in preserving the benefits of attention in working memory. *Psychology and Aging, 34,* 282–293.

Locher, J.L., & others (2014). Caloric restriction in overweight older adults: Do benefits exceed potential risks? *Experimental Gerontology, 33,* 376–400.

Locquet, M., & others (2018). Bone health assessment in older people with or without muscle health impairment. *Osteoporosis International, 29,* 1057–1067.

Loechner, J., & others (2020, in press). Risk of depression in the offspring of parents with depression: The role of emotion regulation, cognitive style, parenting, and life events. *Child Psychiatry and Human Development.*

Londono, P. (2017). *Human rights and violence against women.* New York: Oxford University Press.

Longman, P. (1987). *Born to pay: The new politics of aging in America.* Boston: Houghton Mifflin.

Longobardi, C., & others (2019). Students' psychological adjustment in normative school transitions from kindergarten to high school: Investigating the role of teacher-student relationship quality. *Frontiers in Psychology, 10,* 1238.

Looby, A., & others (2019). Alcohol-related protective behavioral strategies as a mediator of the relationship between drinking motives and risky sexual behaviors. *Addictive Behaviors, 93,* 1–8.

Lopez, L. (2020). *Bilingual grammar.* New York: Cambridge University Press.

Lopez-Higes, R., & others (2018). Efficacy of cognitive training in older adults with and without subjective cognitive decline is associated with inhibition efficiency and working memory span, not cognitive reserve. *Frontiers in Aging Neuroscience, 10,* 23.

Loprinzi, P.D. (2015). Leisure-time screen-based sedentary behavior and leukocyte telomere length: Implications for a new leisure-time screen-based sedentary behavior mechanism. *Mayo Clinic Proceedings, 90,* 786–790.

Loprinzi, P.D., & others (2017). Cross-sectional association of exercise, strengthening activities, and cardiorespiratory fitness on generalized anxiety, panic, and depressive symptoms. *Postgraduate Medicine, 129,* 676–685.

Lord, C., & others (2020). Autism spectrum disorder. *Nature Reviews. Disease Primers, 6*(1), 5.

Lorenz, K.Z. (1965). *Evolution and the modification of behavior.* Chicago: University of Chicago Press.

Lorgen-Ritchie, M., & others (2019). Imprinting methylation in SNRPN and MEST1 in adult blood predicts cognitive ability. *PLoS One, 14*(2), e0211799.

Lovden, M., Backman, L., & Lindenberger, U. (2017). The link of intellectual engagement to cognitive and brain aging. In R. Cabeza, L. Nyberg, and D. Park (Eds.), *Cognitive neuroscience of aging* (2nd ed.). New York: Oxford University Press.

Lovden, M., & Lindenberger, U. (2007). Intelligence. In J.E. Birren (Ed.), *Encyclopedia of gerontology* (2nd ed.). San Diego: Academic Press.

Love, J.M., Chazan-Cohen, R., Raikes, H., & Brooks-Gunn, J. (2013). What makes a difference: Early Head Start evaluation findings in a developmental context. *Monographs of the Society for Research in Child Development, 78,* 1–173.

Low, D.V., Wu, M.N., & Spira, A.P. (2019). Sleep duration and cognition in a nationally representative sample of U.S. older adults. *American Journal of Geriatric Psychiatry, 27,* 1386–1396.

Lu, P.H., & others (2011). Age-related slowing in cognitive processing speed is associated with myelin integrity in a very healthy elderly sample. *Journal of Clinical and Experimental Neuropsychology, 33,* 1059–1068.

Lu, Y., He, Q., & Brooks-Gunn, J. (2020). Diverse experience of immigrant children: How do separation and reunification shape their development? *Child Development. 91*(1), e146–e163.

Lubens, P., & Silver, R.C. (2019). U.S. combat veterans' responses to suicide and combat deaths: A mixed-methods study. *Social Science and Medicine, 236,* 112341.

Lucchetti, G., Lucchetti, A.L., & Koenig, H.G. (2011). Impact of spirituality/religiosity on mortality: Comparison with other health interventions. *Explore, 7,* 234–238.

Luchetti, M., Terracciano, A., Stephan, Y., & Sutin, A.R. (2016). Personality and cognitive decline in older adults: Data from a longitudinal sample and meta-analysis. *Journals of Gerontology B: Psychological Sciences and Social Sciences, 71,* 591–601.

Luciano, E.C., & Orth, U. (2017). Transitions in romantic relationships and development of self-esteem. *Journal of Personality and Social Psychology, 112,* 307–328.

Luders, E., & others (2004). Gender differences in cortical complexity. *Nature, 7*(8), 799–800.

Ludwig, P.E., Freeman, S.C., & Janot, A.C. (2019). Novel stem cell and gene therapy in diabetic retinopathy, age related macular degeneration, and retinitis pigmentosa. *International Journal of Retina Vitreous, 5,* 7.

Ludyga, S., & others (2017). An event-related potential investigation of the acute effects of aerobic and coordinative exercise on inhibitory control in children with ADHD. *Developmental Cognitive Neuroscience, 28,* 21–28.

Luebbe, A.M., & others (2018). Dimensionality of helicopter parenting and relations to emotional, decision-making, and academic functioning in emerging adults. *Assessment, 25,* 841–857.

Lukowski, A.F., & Bauer, P.J. (2014). Long-term memory in infancy and early childhood. In P.J. Bauer & R. Fivush (Eds.), *Wiley-Blackwell handbook of children's memory.* New York: Wiley.

Lumpkin, A. (2021). *Introduction to physical education, exercise science, and sports* (11th ed.). New York: McGraw-Hill.

Lund, H.G., Reider, B.D., Whiting, A.B., & Prichard, J.R. (2010). Sleep patterns and predictors of disturbed sleep in a large population of college students. *Journal of Adolescent Health, 46,* 124–132.

Lund, K.S., & others (2019). Efficacy of a standardized acupuncture approach for women with bothersome menopausal symptoms: A pragmatic randomized study in primary care (the ACOM study). *BMJ Open, 9*(1), e023637.

Lundberg, T., & others (2018). Bereavement stressors and psychological well-being of young adults following the loss of a parent—A cross-sectional survey. *European Journal of Oncology Nursing, 35,* 33–38.

Lund-Blix, N.A., & others (2015). Infant feeding in relation to islet autoimmunity and type 1 diabetes in genetically susceptible children: The MIDIA Study. *Diabetes Care, 39,* 258–263.

Lundorff, M., & others (2017). Prevalence of prolonged grief disorder in adult bereavement: A systematic review and meta-analysis. *Journal of Affective Disorders, 212,* 138–149.

Lundorff, M., & others (2019). How do loss- and restoration-oriented coping change across time? A prospective study on adjustment following spousal bereavement. *Anxiety, Stress, and Coping, 32,* 270–285.

Lunghi, M., & others (2019). The neural correlates of orienting to walking direction in 6-month-old infants: An ERP study. *Developmental Science, 22*(6), e12811.

Luo, L., & Craik, F.I.M. (2008). Aging and memory: A cognitive approach. *Canadian Journal of Psychology, 53,* 346–353.

Luo, Y., Hawkley, L.C., Waite, L.J., & Cacioppo, J.T. (2012). Loneliness, health, and mortality in old age: A national longitudinal study. *Social Science and Medicine, 74,* 907–914.

Luo, Y., Zhang, Z., & Gu, D. (2015). Education and mortality among older adults in China. *Social Science and Medicine, 137,* 134–142.

Luria, A., & Herzog, E. (1985, April). *Gender segregation across and within settings.* Paper presented at the biennial meeting of the Society for Research in Child Development, Toronto.

Luyckz, K., & others (2017). Identity processes and intrinsic and extrinsic goal pursuits: Directionality of effects in college students. *Journal of Youth and Adolescence, 46,* 1758–1771.

Luyster, F.S., & others (2012). Sleep: A health imperative. *Sleep, 35,* 727–734.

Luzzatto, L., & Makani, J. (2019). Hydroxyurea–An essential medicine for sickle cell disease in Africa. *New England Journal of Medicine, 380*(2), 187–189.

Lykken, D. (2001). *Happiness: What studies on twins show us about nature, nurture, and the happiness set point.* New York: Golden Books.

Lyndaker, C., & Hulton, L. (2004). The influence of age on symptoms of perimenopause. *Journal of Obstetric, Gynecological, and Neonatal Nursing, 33,* 340–347.

Lynn, R., Fuerst, J., & Kirkegaard, E.O.W. (2018). Regional differences in intelligence in 22 countries and their economic, social, and demographic correlates: A review. *Intelligence, 69,* 24–36.

Lyon, T.D., & Flavell, J.H. (1993). Young children's understanding of forgetting over time. *Child Development, 64,* 789–800.

Lyons, D.M., & others (2010). Stress coping stimulates hippocampal neurogenesis in adult monkeys. *Proceedings of the National Academy of Sciences U.S.A., 107,* 14823–14827.

Lyons, H., Manning, W., Giordano, P., & Longmore, M. (2013). Predictors of heterosexual casual sex among young adults. *Archives of Sexual Behavior, 42,* 585–593.

Lyons, H., Manning, W.D., Longmore, M.A., & Giordano, P.C. (2015). Gender and casual sexual activity from adolescence to emerging adulthood: Social and life course correlates. *Journal of Sex Research, 52,* 543–557.

Lytle, A., Levy, S.R., & Meeks, S. (2019). Reducing ageism: Education about aging and extended contact with older adults. *Gerontologist, 59,* 580–588.

Lytle, A., Nowacek, N., & Levy, S.R. (2020, in press). Instapals: Reducing ageism by facilitating intergenerational contact and providing aging education. *Gerontology and Geriatrics Education.*

M

Ma, F., & others (2018). Promoting honesty in young children through observational learning. *Journal of Experimental Child Psychology, 167,* 234–245.

Maalouf, F.T., & Brent, D.A. (2012). Child and adolescent depression intervention overview: What works for whom and how well? *Child and Adolescent Psychiatry Clinics of North America, 21,* 299–312.

MacAllister, W.S., & others (2019). The WISC-V in children and adolescents with epilepsy. *Child Neuropsychology. 25,* 992–1002.

MacAulay, P.K., & others (2020, in press). Predictors of heterogeneity in cognitive function: APOE-e4, sex, education, depression, and vascular risk. *Archives of Clinical Neuropsychology.*

Maccallum, F., & Bryant, R.A. (2020, in press). A network approach to understanding quality of life impairments in prolonged grief disorder. *Journal of Traumatic Stress.*

Maccoby, E.E. (1998). *The two sexes: Growing up apart, coming together.* Cambridge, MA: Harvard University Press.

Maccoby, E.E. (2002). Gender and group processes. *Current Directions in Psychological Science, 11,* 54–58.

Maccoby, E.E., & Martin, J.A. (1983). Socialization in the context of the family: Parent-child interaction. In P.H. Mussen (Ed.), *Handbook of child psychology* (4th ed., Vol. 4). New York: Wiley.

MacDonald, M.C., & Hsiao, Y. (2019). Sentence comprehension. In S-A. Rueschemeyer & M. Gareth Gaskell (Eds.), *Oxford handbook of psycholinguistics* (2nd ed.). New York: Oxford University Press.

MacDonald, S.W.S., Hultch, D., Strauss, E., & Dixon, R. (2003). Age-related slowing of digit symbol substitution revisited: What do longitudinal age changes reflect? *Journals of Gerontology B: Psychological Sciences and Social Sciences, 58B,* P187–P194.

MacDonald, S.W.S., & Stawski, R.S. (2015). Intraindividual variability–An indicator of vulnerability or resilience in adult development and aging? In M. Diehl, I. Hooker, & M. Sliwinski (Eds.), *Handbook of intraindividual variability across the life span.* New York: Routledge.

MacDonald, S.W.S., & Stawski, R.S. (2016). Methodological considerations for the study of adult development and aging. In K.W. Schaie & S.L. Willis (Eds.), *Handbook of the psychology of aging* (8th ed.). New York: Elsevier.

MacDougall, B.J., Robinson, J.D., Kappus, L., Sudikoff, S.N., & Greer, D.M. (2014). Simulation-based training in brain death determination. *Neurocritical Care, 21,* 383–391.

Macek, P., & others (2020). Age-dependent disparities in the prevalence of single and clustering cardiovascular risk factors: A cross-sectional cohort study in middle-aged and older adults. *Clinical Interventions in Aging, 15,* 161–169.

MacFarlane, J.A. (1975). Olfaction in the development of social preferences in the human neonate. In *Parent-infant interaction.* Ciba Foundation Symposium No. 33. Amsterdam: Elsevier.

MacGeorge, E.L. (2003). Gender differences in attributions and emotions in helping contexts. *Sex Roles, 48,* 175–182.

Machado, B., & others (2014). Risk factors and antecedent life events in the development of anorexia nervosa: A Portuguese case-control study. *European Eating Disorders Review, 22,* 243–251.

Maciejewski, P.K., & Prigerson, H.G. (2017). Prolonged, but not complicated, grief is a mental disorder. *British Journal of Psychology, 211,* 189–191.

Mack, D.S., & Dosa, D. (2020). Improving advance care planning through Physician Orders for Life-Sustaining Treatment (POLST) expansion across the United States: Lessons learned from state-based developments. *American Journal of Palliative Care, 37,* 19–26.

MacNeill, L., & others (2018). Trajectories of infants' biobehavioral development: Timing and rate of A-not-B performance gains and EEG maturation. *Child Development, 89,* 711–724.

MacPhee, D., & Prendergast, S. (2019). Room for improvement: Girls' and boys' home environments are still gendered. *Sex Roles, 80*(5–6), 332–346.

Madden, D.J., & others (1999). Aging and recognition memory: Changes in regional cerebral blood flow associated with components of reaction time distributions. *Journal of Cognitive Neuroscience, II,* 511–520.

Madden, K., & others (2016). Hypnosis for pain management during labor and childbirth. *Cochrane Database of Systematic Reviews, 5,* CD009356.

Mader, S., & Windelspecht, M. (2020). *Human biology* (16th ed.). New York: McGraw-Hill.

Madrasi, K., & others (2018). Regulatory perspectives in pharmacometric models of osteoporosis. *Journal of Clinical Pharmacology, 58,* 572–585.

Magnuson, K.A., & Duncan, G.J. (2019). Parents in poverty. In M.H. Bornstein (Ed.), *Handbook of parenting* (3rd ed.). New York: Routledge.

Magnusson, B.M., Crandall, A., & Evans, K. (2019). Early sexual debut and risky sex in young adults: The role of low self-control. *BMC Public Health, 19*(1), 1483.

Maguire-Jack, K., & others (2019). Preventive benefits of U.S. childcare subsidies in supervisory child neglect. *Children and society, 32,* 185–194.

Mahajan, U.V., & others (2020). Dysregulation of multiple metabolic networks related to brain transmethylation and polyamine pathways in Alzheimer disease: A targeted metabolomics and transcriptomic study. *PLoS Medicine, 17*(1), e1003012.

Maheux, A.J., & others (2020). Popular peer norms and adolescent sexting behavior. *Journal of Adolescence, 78,* 62–66.

Mahio, L., & Windsor, T.D. (2020, in press). Older and more mindful: Age differences in mindfulness components and well-being. *Aging and Mental Health.*

Mahoney, J.R., Verghese, J., Goldin, Y., Lipton, R., & Holtzer, R. (2010). Altering orienting and executive attention in older adults. *Journal of the International Neuropsychological Society, 16*(5), 877–889.

Maier, J.G., & others (2019). Sleep orchestrates indices of local plasticity and global network stability in the human cortex. *Sleep, 42,* 4.

Maillard, P., & others (2012). Effects of systolic blood pressure on white-matter integrity in young adults in the Framington Heart Study: A cross-sectional study. *Lancet Neurology, 11,* 1039–1047.

Majeed, A., & others (2019). Can ultrasound in early gestation improve visualization of fetal cardiac structures in obese pregnant women? *Journal of Ultrasound Medicine, 38,* 2057–2063.

Makarem, N., & others (2019). Sleep duration and blood pressure: Recent advances and future directions. *Current Hypertension Research, 21*(5), 33.

Malamitsi-Puchner, A., & Boutsikou, T. (2006). Adolescent pregnancy and perinatal outcome. *Pediatric Endocrinology Review, 3*(1, Suppl.), S170–S171.

Maldonado, T., & others (2020, in press). Age difference in the subcomponents of executive functioning. *Journals of Gerontology B: Psychological Sciences and Social Sciences.*

Malinowski, P., & others (2017). Mindful aging: The effects of regular brief mindfulness practice on electrophysiological markers of cognitive and affective processing in older adults. *Mindfulness, 8,* 78–84.

Malmberg, L.E., & others (2016). The influence of mothers' and fathers' sensitivity in the first year of life on children's cognitive outcomes at 18 and 36 months. *Child Care, Health, and Development, 42,* 1–7.

Malnou, E.C., & others (2019). Imprinted microRNA gene clusters in the evolution, development, and functions of mammalian placenta. *Frontiers in Genetics, 9,* 706.

Maloy, R.W., & others (2021). *Transforming learning with new technologies* (4th ed.). Upper Saddle River, NJ: Pearson.

Maltby, L.E., & others (2019). Infant temperament and behavioral problems: Analysis of high-risk infants in child welfare. *Journal of Public Child Welfare, 13,* 512–528.

Malti, T., Peplak, J., & Acland, E. (2020). Emotion experiences in moral context: Developmental perspectives. In L.A. Jensen (Ed.), *Oxford handbook of moral development.* New York: Oxford University Press.

Malti, T., & others (2019). Parenting aggressive children. In M.H. Bornstein (Ed.), *Handbook of parenting* (3rd ed.). New York: Routledge.

Mamun, A.A., & others (2020, in press). Generational changes in young adults' sleep duration: A prospective analysis of mother-offspring dyads. *Sleep Health.*

Manara, A., Varelas, P., & Wijdicks, E.F. (2019). Brain death in patients with "isolated" brainstem lesions: A case against controversy. *Journal of Neurosurgical Anesthesiology, 31,* 171–173.

Manca, T. (2013). Medicine and spiritual healing within a region of Canada: Preliminary findings concerning Christian Scientists' healthcare practices. *Journal of Religion and Health, 52,* 789–803.

Mandara, J. (2006). The impact of family functioning on African American males' academic achievement: A review and clarification of the empirical literature. *Teachers College Record, 108,* 206–233.

Mandler, J.M. (2004). *The foundations of the mind: Origins of conceptual thought.* New York: Oxford University Press.

Mandler, J.M. (2009). Conceptual categorization. In D.H. Rakison & L.M. Oakes (Eds.), *Early category and concept development.* New York: Oxford University Press.

Mandler, J.M., & McDonough, L. (1993). Concept formation in infancy. *Cognitive Development, 8,* 291–318.

Manenti, R., Cotelli, M., & Miniussi, C. (2011). Successful physiological aging and episodic memory: A brain stimulation study. *Behavioral Brain Research, 216,* 153–158.

Manfredini, R., & others (2017). Marital status, cardiovascular diseases, and cardiovascular risk factors: A review of the evidence. *Journal of Women's Health, 26,* 624–632.

Maniago, J.D., Almazan, J.U., & Albougami, A.S. (2020, in press). Nurses' kangaroo mother care practice implementation and future challenges: An integrative review. *Scandinavian Journal of Caring Science.*

Mann, T., & others (2007). Medicare's search for effective obesity treatments. *American Psychologist, 62,* 220–233.

Manning, L.K., & Miles, A. (2018). Examining the effects of religious attendance on resilience for older adults. *Journal of Religion and Health, 57,* 191–208.

Manning, W.D., Longmore, M.A., & Gordano, P.C. (2018). Cohabitation and intimate partner violence during emerging adulthood: High constraints and low commitment. *Journal of Family Issues, 39,* 1030–1055.

Mansor, N.S., Chow, C.M., & Halaki, M. (2020, in press). Cognitive effects of videogames in older adults and their moderators: A systematic review with meta-analysis and meta-regression. *Aging and Mental Health.*

Mansourian, M., & others (2019). Metabolic syndrome components and long-term incidence of cardiovascular disease in Eastern Mediterranean region: A 13-year population-based cohort. *Metabolic Syndrome and Related Disorders, 17,* 362–366.

Manton, K.I. (1989). The stress buffering role of spiritual support: Cross-sectional and prospective investigations. *Journal for the Scientific Study of Religion, 28,* 310–323.

Mantri, S., & others (2019). Quality of education impacts late-life cognition. *International Journal of Geriatric Psychiatry, 34,* 855–862.

Manuck, S.B., & McCaffery, J.M. (2014). Gene-environment interaction. *Annual Review of Psychology* (Vol. 65). Palo Alto, CA: Annual Reviews.

Manzanares, S., & others (2016). Accuracy of fetal sex determination on ultrasound examination in the first trimester of pregnancy. *Journal of Clinical Ultrasound, 44,* 272–277.

Maoz, H., & others (2019). Theory of mind and empathy in children with ADHD. *Journal of Attention Disorders, 23,* 1331–1338.

Maravilla, J.C., & others (2017). Factors influencing repeated adolescent pregnancy: A review and meta-analysis. *American Journal of Obstetrics and Gynecology, 217,* 527–545.

Marceau, K., Dorn, L.D., & Susman, E.J. (2012). Stress and puberty-related hormone reactivity, negative emotionality, and parent-adolescent relationships. *Psychoneuroimmunology, 37*(8), 1286–1298.

Marcell, J.J. (2003). Sarcopenia: Causes, consequences, and preventions. *Journals of Gerontology A: Biological and Medical Sciences,* M911–M916.

March of Dimes (2018). *Premature birth report card.* White Plains, NY: Author.

March of Dimes (2020). *Multiple pregnancy and birth: Considering fertility treatments.* White Plains, NY: Author.

Marcia, J.E. (1980). Ego identity development. In J. Adelson (Ed.), *Handbook of adolescent psychology.* New York: Wiley.

Marcia, J.E. (1994). The empirical study of ego identity. In H.A. Bosma, T.L.G. Graafsma, H.D. Grotevant, & D.J. De Levita (Eds.), *Identity and development.* Newbury Park, CA: Sage.

Marcia, J.E. (2002). Identity and psychosocial development in adulthood. *Identity: An International Journal of Theory and Research, 2,* 7–28.

Marcovitch, S., & others (2016). Attentional predictors of 5-month-olds' performance on a looking A-not-B task. *Infant and Child Development, 25,* 233–246.

Marcus, G., & others (2019). Impact of marital status on the outcome of acute coronary syndrome: Results from the Acute Coronary Syndrome Israeli Survey. *Journal of the American Heart Association, 8*(14), e011664.

Mares, M-L., & Pan, Z. (2013). Effects of *Sesame Street*: A meta-analysis of children's learning in 15 countries. *Journal of Applied Developmental Psychology, 34,* 140–151.

Marien, S., & Spinewine, A. (2019). Optimization of drug use in older people: A key factor in successful aging. In R. Fernandez-Ballesteros & others (Eds.), *Cambridge handbook of successful aging.* New York: Cambridge University Press.

Marini, D., & others (2020, in press). Current and future role of fetal cardiovascular MRI in the setting of fetal cardiac interventions. *Prenatal Diagnosis.*

Marin-Jimenez, N., & others (2020, in press). Association of objectively measured sedentary behavior and physical activity levels with health-related quality of life in middle-aged women: The FLAMENCO Project. *Menopause.*

Mark, K.S., & others (2015). Knowledge, attitudes, and practice of electronic cigarette use among pregnant women. *Journal of Addiction Medicine, 9,* 266–272.

Markham, C.M., & others (2010). Connectedness as a predictor of sexual and reproductive health outcomes for youth. *Journal of Adolescent Health, 46*(3, Suppl.), S23–S41.

Markham, K.B., Walker, H., Lynch, C.D., & Iams, J.D. (2014). Preterm birth rates in a prematurity prevention clinic after adoption of progestin prophylaxis. *Obstetrics and Gynecology, 123,* 34–39.

Markman, H.J., Halford, W.K., & Hawkins, A.J. (2019). Couple and relationship education. In B.H. Fiese (Ed.), *APA handbook of contemporary family psychology.* Washington, DC: APA Books.

Markman, H.J., & others (2013). A randomized clinical trial of the effectiveness of premarital intervention: Moderators of divorce outcomes. *Journal of Family Psychology, 27,* 165–172.

Marks, A. (2019). The evolution of our understanding and treatment of eating disorders over the past 50 years. *Journal of Clinical Psychology, 75,* 1380–1391.

Marks, A.K., Woolverton, G.A., & Garcia Coll, C. (2020). Children's migratory paths between cultures: The effects of migration experiences on the adjustment of children and families. In R.D. Parke & G.H. Elder (Eds.), *Children in changing worlds.* New York: Cambridge University Press.

Markus, H.R., Ryff, C.D., Curhan, K., & Palmersheim, K. (2004). In their own words: Well-being among high school and college-educated adults. In G. Brim, C.D. Ryff, & R. Kessler (Eds.), *How healthy we are: A national study of well-being in midlife.* Chicago: University of Chicago Press.

Marousez, L., Lesage, J., & Eberle, D. (2020, in press). Epigenetics: Linking early postnatal nutrition to obesity programming. *Nutrients.*

Marques, A., & others (2020, in press). Leisure-time physical activity is negatively associated with depression symptoms independently of the socioeconomic status. *European Journal of Sport Science.*

Marrus, N., & others (2018). Walking, gross motor development, and brain functional connectivity in infants and toddlers. *Cerebral Cortex, 28,* 750–763.

Marselle, M.R., Warber, S.L., & Irvine, K.N. (2019). Growing resilience through interaction with nature: Can group walks in nature buffer the effects of stressful life events on mental health? *International Journal of Environmental Research and Public Health, 26,* 6.

Marsh, H., Ellis, L., & Craven, R. (2002). How do preschool children feel about themselves? Unraveling measurement and multidimensional self-concept structure. *Developmental Psychology, 38,* 376–393.

Marsh, H.L., & Legerstee, M. (2017). Awareness of goal-directed behavior during infancy and early childhood, in human- and non-human primates. *Infant Behavior and Development, 48,* 30–37.

Marshall, K.A., & Hale, D. (2018). Elder abuse. *Home Healthcare Now, 36,* 51–52.

Marshall, N.A., & others (2018). Socio-economic disadvantage and altered corticostriatal circuitry in urban youth. *Human Brain Mapping, 39,* 1982–1994.

Marshall, S.L., Parker, P.D., Ciarrochi, J., & Heaven, P.C.L. (2014). Is self-esteem a cause or consequence of social support? A 4-year longitudinal study. *Child Development, 85,* 1275–1291.

Marsiglia, F.F., & others (2019). The role of culture of origin on the effectiveness of parents-involved intervention to prevent substance use among Latino middle school youth: Results from a cluster randomized controlled trial. *Prevention Science, 20,* 643–654.

Marsiske, M., Klumb, P.L., & Baltes, M.M. (1997). Everyday activity patterns and sensory functioning in old age. *Psychology and Aging, 12,* 444–457.

Marston, K.J., & others (2019). Resistance training enhances delayed memory in healthy middle-aged and older adults: A randomized controlled trial. *Journal of Science and Medicine in Sport, 22,* 1226–1231.

Martin, A., & others (2018). Physical activity, diet, and other behavioral interventions for improving cognition and school achievement in children and adolescents with obesity or overweight. *Cochrane Database of Systematic Reviews, 1,* CD009728.

Martin, A.A., Horn, A.B., & Allemand, M. (2020, in press). Within-person association between attachment security, need satisfaction, and psychological adjustment in daily life of older adults. *Journals of Gerontology B: Psychological Sciences and Social Sciences.*

Martin, C.L., Fabes, R.A., & Hanish, L. (2018). Differences and similarities: The dynamics of same-and other-sex peer relationships. In W. Bukowski, B. Laursen, & K. Rubin (Eds.), *Handbook of peer interactions, relationships, and groups* (2nd ed.). New York: Guilford.

Martin, C.L., & Ruble, D.N. (2010). Patterns of gender development. *Annual Review of Psychology* (Vol. 61). Palo Alto, CA: Annual Reviews.

Martin, C.L., & others (2013). The role of sex of peers and gender-typed activities in young children's peer affiliative networks: A longitudinal analysis of selection and influence. *Child Development, 84,* 921–937.

Martin, J., & others (2018). Maternal sensitivity in the first 3½ years of life predicts electrophysiological responding to and cognitive appraisals of infant crying at midlife. *Developmental Psychology, 54,* 1917–1927.

Martin, J.A., & others (2017). Births: Final data for 2015. *National Vital Statistics Reports, 66*(1), 1.

Martin, K.B., & Messinger, D.B. (2018). Smile. In M.H. Bornstein (Ed.), *SAGE encyclopedia of lifespan human development.* Thousand Oaks, CA: Sage.

Martin, L.R., Friedman, H.S., & Schwartz, J.E. (2007). Personality and mortality risk across the life span: The importance of conscientiousness as a biopsychosocial attribute. *Health Psychology, 26,* 428–436.

Martinez-Brockman, J.L., & others (2018). Impact of Lactation Advice through Texting Can Help (LATCH) trial on time to first contact and exclusive breastfeeding among WIC participants. *Journal of Nutrition Education and Behavior, 50,* 33–42.

Martinez-Ramirez, O.C., & others (2019). Association of the promoter methylation and the rs12917 polymorphism of MGMT with formation of DNA bulky adducts and the risk of lung cancer in Mexican Mestizo population. *DNA and Cell Biology, 38,* 307–313.

Martin-Perpiña, M.M., Vinas Poch, F., & Malo Cerrato, S. (2019). Media multitasking impact in homework, executive function, and academic performance in Spanish students. *Psicothema, 31,* 81–87.

Martz, M.E., Patrick, M.E., & Schulenberg, J.E. (2015). Alcohol mixed with energy drink use among U.S. 12th grade students: Prevalence, correlates, and associations with safe driving. *Journal of Adolescent Health, 56,* 557–563.

Mascalo, M.F., & Fischer, K.W. (2010). The dynamic development of thinking, feeling, and acting over the life span. In W.F. Overton & R.M. Lerner (Eds.), *Handbook of life-span development* (Vol. 1). New York: Wiley.

Mash, E.J., & Wolfe, D.A. (2019). *Abnormal child psychology* (7th ed.). Boston: Cengage.

Mason-Apps, E., & others (2018). Longitudinal predictors of early language in infants with Down syndrome: A preliminary study. *Research in Developmental Disabilities, 81,* 37–51.

Masoodi, N. (2013). Review: Cholinesterase inhibitors do not reduce progression to dementia from mild cognitive impairment. *Annals of Internal Medicine, 158,* JC2–JC3.

Masson, W., & others (2019). Association between non-HDL-C ratio and carotid atherosclerosis in postmenopausal middle-aged women. *Climacteric, 22,* 518–522.

Masten, A.S. (2006). Developmental psychopathology: Pathways to the future. *International Journal of Behavioral Development, 31,* 46–53.

Masten, A.S. (2009). Ordinary magic: Lessons from research on resilience in human development. *Education Canada, 49*(3), 28–32.

Masten, A.S. (2011). Resilience in children threatened by extreme adversity: Frameworks for research, practice, and translational synergy. *Development and Psychopathology, 23,* 141–153.

Masten, A.S. (2012). Faculty profile: Ann Masten. *The Institute of Child Development further developments.* Minneapolis: School of Education.

Masten, A.S. (2013). Risk and resilience in development. In P.D. Zelazo (Ed.), *Oxford handbook of developmental psychology.* New York: Oxford University Press.

Masten, A.S. (2017). Building a translational science on children and youth affected by political violence and armed conflict: A commentary. *Development and Psychopathology, 29,* 79–84.

Masten, A.S. (2019). Resilience from a developmental systems perspective. *World Psychiatry, 18,* 101–102.

Masten, A.S., Burt, K., & Coatsworth, J.D. (2006). Competence and psychopathology in development. In D. Cicchetti & D. Cohen (Eds.), *Developmental psychopathology: Risk, disorder, and psychopathology* (2nd ed., Vol. 3). New York: Wiley.

Masten, A.S., Motti-Stefanidi, F., & Rahl-Brigman, H.A. (2020). Developmental risk and resilience in the context of devastation and forced migration. In R.D. Parke & G.H. Elder (Eds.), *Children in changing worlds.* New York: Cambridge University Press.

Masten, A.S., & Palmer, A. (2019). Parenting to promote resilience in children. In M.H. Bornstein (Ed.), *Handbook of parenting* (3rd ed.). New York: Elsevier.

Masters, R.K., & others (2013). The impact of obesity on U.S. mortality levels: The importance of age and cohort factors in population estimates. *American Journal of Public Health, 103,* 1895–1901.

Mastin, J.D., & Vogt, P. (2016). Infant engagement and early vocabulary development: A naturalistic observation study of Mozambican infants from 1:1 to 2:1. *Journal of Child Language, 43,* 235–264.

Mat Husin, H., & others (2020, in press). Maternal weight, weight gain, and metabolism are associated with changes in fetal heart rate and variability. *Obesity.*

Match.com (2011). *The Match.com Singles in America Study.* Retrieved February 7, 2011, from http://blog.match.com/singles-study

Match.com (2012). *Singles in America 2012.* Retrieved June 10, 2012, from http://blog.match.com/singles-in-america

Mateen, S., & others (2019). Cinnamaldehyede and eugenol attenuates collagen induced arthritis via reduction of free radicals and pro-inflammatory cytokines. *Phytomedicine.*

Matei, A., Saccone, G., Vogel, J.P., & Armson, A.B. (2019). Primary and secondary prevention of preterm birth: A review of systematic reviews and ongoing randomized controlled trials. *European Journal of Obstetrics, Gynecology, and Reproductive Biology, 236,* 224–239.

Mather, M. (2012). The emotion paradox in the human brain. *Annals of the New York Academy of Sciences, 1251,* 33–49.

Matias, M., & Fontaine, M. (2015). Coping with work and family: How do dual-earners interact? *Scandinavian Journal of Psychology, 56,* 212–222.

Matlow, J.N., Jubetsky, A., Aleksa, K., Berger, H., & Koren, G. (2013). The transfer of ethyl glucuronide across the dually perfused human placenta. *Placenta, 34*(4), 369–373.

Matos, K. (2015). *Modern families: Same- and different-sex couples negotiating at home.* New York: Families and Work Institute.

Matricciani, L., & others (2019). Children's sleep and health: A meta-review. *Sleep Medicine Reviews, 46,* 136–150.

Matsumoto, D., & Hwang, H.C. (Eds.) (2019). *Handbook of culture and psychology* (2nd ed.). New York: Oxford University Press.

Matsumoto, D., & Juang, L. (2020). *Culture and psychology* (7th ed.). Boston: Cengage.

Maurer, D. (2016). How the baby learns to see: Donald O. Hebb Award lecture, Canadian Society for Brain, Behavior, and Cognitive Science, Ottawa, June 2015. *Canadian Journal of Experimental Psychology, 70,* 195–200.

Maurer, D., & Lewis, T.L. (2013). Sensitive periods in visual development. In P.D. Zelazo (Ed.), *Oxford handbook of developmental psychology.* New York: Oxford University Press.

Maurer, D., Lewis, T.L., Brent, H.P., & Levin, A.V. (1999). Rapid improvement in the acuity of infants after visual input. *Science, 286,* 108–110.

Maurer, D., Mondloch, C.J., & Leis, T.L. (2007). Effects of early visual deprivation on perceptual and cognitive development. In C. von Hofsten & K. Rosander (Eds.), *Progress in Brain Research, 164,* 87–104.

Mayo Clinic (2020a). *Menopause.* Rochester, MN: Mayo Clinic.

Mayo Clinic (2020b). *Male hypogonadism.* Rochester, MN: Mayo Clinic.

Mayo, J.A., & others (2019). Parental age and stillbirth: A population-based cohort study of nearly 10 million California deliveries from 1991 to 2011. *Annals of Epidemiology, 31,* 32–37.

Mayor, S. (2015). Breast feeding reduces risk of breast cancer recurrence, study finds. *BMJ, 350,* h2325.

Mazumder, S., & others (2019). Effect of community-initiated kangaroo mother care on survival of infants with low birthweight: A randomized controlled trial. *Lancet, 394*(10210), 1724–1736.

Mazzucato, V. (2015). Transnational families and the well-being of children and caregivers who stay in origin countries. *Social Science & Medicine, 132,* 208–214.

Mbugua Gitau, G., & others (2009). The influence of maternal age on the outcomes of pregnancy complicated by bleeding at less than 12 weeks. *Acta Obstetricia et Gynecologica Scandinavica, 88,* 116–118.

McAbee, S.T., & Oswald, F.L. (2013). The criterion-related validity of personality measures for predicting GPA: A meta-analytic validity comparison. *Psychological Assessment, 25*(2), 532–544.

McAdams, D.P., Josselson, R., & Lieblich, A. (2006). *Identity and story: Creating self in narrative.* Washington, DC: American Psychological Association.

McAllister, S., & others (2017). Healthcare professionals' attitudes, knowledge, and self-efficacy levels regarding the use of self-hypnosis in childbirth: A prospective questionnaire survey. *Midwifery, 47,* 8–14.

McAuley, P.A., & Blair, S.N. (2011). Obesity paradoxes. *Journal of Sports Sciences, 29,* 773–782.

McBride, K.L., & others (2019). Phenylalanine and tyrosine measurements across gestation by tandem mass spectrometer on dried blood spot cards from normal pregnant women. *Genetics in Medicine, 21,* 1821–1826.

McCabe, K.O., & Fleeson, W. (2016). Are traits useful? Explaining trait manifestations as tools in the pursuit of goals. *Journal of Personality and Social Psychology, 110,* 287–301.

McCarroll, J.E., & others (2017). Characteristics, classification, and prevention of child maltreatment fatalities. *Military Medicine, 182,* e1551–e1557.

McCartney, K. (2003, July 16). Interview with Kathleen McCartney in A. Bucuvalas, "Child care and behavior," *HGSE News,* pp. 1–4. Cambridge, MA: Harvard Graduate School of Education.

McCartney, K., Dearing, E., Taylor, B.A., & Bub, K.L. (2007). Quality child care supports the achievement of low-income children: Direct and indirect pathways through caregiving and the home environment. *Journal of Applied Developmental Psychology, 28,* 411–426.

McClain, C.S., Rosenfeld, B., & Breitbart, W.S. (2003, March). *The influence of spirituality on end-of-life despair in cancer patients close to death.* Paper presented at the meeting of American Psychosomatic Society, Phoenix.

McClellan, M.D. (2004, February 9). Captain Fantastic: The interview. *Celtic Nation,* pp. 1–9.

McClelland, M.M., Acock, A.C., Piccinin, A., Rhea, S.A., & Stallings, M.C. (2013). Relations between preschool attention span persistence and age 25 educational outcomes. *Early Childhood Research Quarterly, 28,* 314–324.

McClelland, M.M., Cameron, C.E., & Alonso, J. (2019). The development of self-regulation in young children. In D. Whitebread (Ed.), *Handbook of developmental psychology and early childhood education.* Thousand Oaks, CA: Sage.

McClelland, M.M., & others (2017). Self-regulation. In N. Halfon & others (Eds.), *Handbook of life course health development.* New York: Springer.

McCluney, C.L., & others (2018). Structural racism in the workplace: Does perception matter for health inequalities? *Social Science and Medicine, 199,* 106–144.

McClure, E.R., & others (2018). Look at that! Video chat and joint visual attention development among babies and toddlers. *Child Development, 89,* 27–36.

McConnachie, A.L., & others (2020, in press). Father-child attachment in adoptive gay father families. *Attachment and Human Development.*

McCormack, T., Hoerl, C., & Butterfill, C. (2012). *Tool use and causal cognition.* New York: Oxford University Press.

McCoy, D.C. (2019). Measuring young children's executive function and self-regulation in classrooms and other real-world settings. *Clinical Child and Family Psychology Review, 22,* 63–74.

McCoy, D.C., & Raver, C.C. (2011). Caregiver emotional expressiveness, child emotion regulation, and child behavior problems among Head Start families. *Social Development, 20,* 741–761.

McCoy, D.C., & others (2016). Differential effectiveness of Head Start in urban and rural communities. *Journal of Applied Developmental Psychology, 43,* 29–42.

McCoy, M.B., & others (2018). Associations between peer counseling and breastfeeding initiation and duration: An analysis of Minnesota participants in the Special Supplemental Nutrition Program for Women, Infants, and Children (WIC). *Maternal and Child Health Journal, 22,* 71–81.

McCrae, R.R., & Costa, P.T. (1990). *Personality in adulthood.* New York: Guilford.

McCrae, R.R., & Costa, P.T. (2003). *Personality in adulthood* (2nd ed.). New York: Guilford.

McCrae, R.R., & Costa, P.T. (2006). Cross-cultural perspectives on adult personality trait development. In D.K. Mroczek & T.D. Little (Eds.), *Handbook of personality development.* Mahwah, NJ: Erlbaum.

McCrae, R.R., & Sutin, A.R. (2009). Openness to experience. In M.R. Leary & R.H. Hoyle (Eds.), *Handbook of individual differences in social behavior.* New York: Guilford.

McCue, K., & DeNicola, N. (2019). Environmental exposures in reproductive health. *Obstetric and Gynecological Clinics of North America, 46,* 455–468.

McCullough, M.B., Pieloch, K.A., & Marks, A.K. (2020, in press). Body image, assimilation, and weight of immigrant adolescents in the United States: A person-centered analysis. *Journal of Immigrant Mental Health.*

McCullough, M.E., Enders, C.K., Brion, S.L., & Jain, A.R. (2005). The varieties of religious development in adulthood: A longitudinal investigation of religion and rational choice. *Journal of Personality and Social Psychology, 89,* 78–89.

McCutcheon, V.V., & others (2012). Environmental influences predominate in remission from alcohol use disorder in young adult twins. *Psychological Medicine, 42*(11), 2421–2431.

McDermott, E.R., Umana-Taylor, A.J., & Zeiders, K.H. (2019). Profiles of coping with ethnic-racial discrimination and Latina/o adolescents' adjustment. *Journal of Youth and Adolescence, 48,* 908–923.

McDonald, K.L., & Asher, S.R. (2018). Peer acceptance, peer rejection, and popularity: Social cognitive and behavioral perspectives. In W.M. Bukowski & others (Eds.), *Handbook of peer interactions, relationships, and groups* (2nd ed.). New York: Guilford.

McDonald, N.M., & Perdue, K.L. (2018). The infant brain in the social world: Moving toward interactive social neuroscience with functional near-infrared spectroscopy. *Neuroscience and Biobehavioral Reviews, 87,* 38-49.

McDougall, S., & others (2018). Myelination of axons corresponds with faster transmission speed in the prefrontal cortex of developing male rats. *eNeuro, 5,* 4.

McDowell, J.J. (2019). On the current state of the evolutionary theory of behavior dynamics. *Journal of the Experimental Analysis of Behavior, 111,* 130-145.

McGarry, J., Kim, H., Sheng, X., Egger, M., & Baksh, L. (2009). Postpartum depression and help seeking behavior. *Journal of Midwifery and Women's Health, 54,* 50-56.

McGillion, M., & others (2017). What paves the way to conventional language? The predictive value of babble, pointing, and socioeconomic status. *Child Development, 88,* 156-166.

McHale, J.P., Negrini, L., & Sirotkin, Y. (2019). Coparenting. In B.H. Friese (Ed.), *APA handbook of contemporary family psychology.* Washington, DC: APA Books.

McHale, J.P., & Sirotkin, Y. (2019). Coparenting in diverse family systems. In M.H. Bornstein (Ed.), *Handbook of parenting* (3rd ed.). New York: Routledge.

McHale, S.M., Salman-Engin, S., & Coovert, M.D. (2015). Improvements in unmarried African American parents' rapport, communication, and problem-solving following a prenatal parenting intervention. *Family Process, 54,* 619-629.

McKay, A.S., & Kaufman, J.C. (2014). Literary geniuses: Their life, work, and death. In D.K. Simonton (Ed.), *Wiley-Blackwell handbook of genius.* New York: Wiley.

McKechanie, A.G., & others (2020, in press). Autism in fragile X syndrome: A functional MRI study of facial emotion-processing. *Genes.*

McKellar, S.E., & others (2019). Threats and supports to female students' math beliefs and achievement. *Journal of Research on Adolescence, 29,* 449-465.

McKenna, L., Kodner, I.J., Healy, G.G., & Keune, J.D. (2013). Sleep deprivation: A call for institutional rules. *Surgery, 154,* 118-122.

McLaughlin, K. (2003, December 30). Commentary in K. Painter, "Nurse dispenses dignity for dying." *USA Today,* Section D, pp. 1-2.

McLaughlin, K.A. (2020). Early life stress and psychopathology. In K.L. Harkness & E.P. Hayden (Eds.), *Oxford handbook of stress and mental health.* New York: Oxford University Press.

McLean, K.C., & others (2020, in press). The empirical structure of narrative identity: The big three. *Journal of Personality and Social Psychology.*

McLeod, S., & others (2020). Attachment and social support in romantic dyads: A systematic review. *Journal of Clinical Psychology, 76,* 59-101.

McLoyd, V.C., Hardaway, C., & Jocson, R.M. (2019). African American parenting. In M.H. Bornstein (Ed.), *Handbook of parenting* (3rd ed.). New York: Elsevier.

McMillen, C.M., Graves-Demario, A., & Kieliszek, D. (2018). Tackling literacy: A collaborative approach to developing materials for assessing science literacy skills in content classrooms through a STEM perspective. *Language and Literacy Spectrum, 28,* 2.

McNeely, C.A., & others (2020). Identifying essential components of school-linked mental health services for refugee and immigrant children: A comparative case study. *Journal of School Health, 90,* 3-14.

McRae, C.S., Petrov, M.E., Dautovich, N., & Lichstein, K.L. (2016). Late-life sleep and sleep disorders. In K.W. Schaie & S. Willis (Eds.), *Handbook of the psychology of aging* (8th ed.). New York: Elsevier.

McSween, M.P., & others (2019). The immediate effects of acute aerobic exercise on cognition in healthy older adults: A systematic review. *Sports Medicine, 49,* 67-82.

Mechler, K., & Liantonio, J. (2019). Palliative care approach to chronic diseases: End stages of heart failure, chronic obstructive pulmonary disease, liver failure, and renal failure. *Primary Care, 46,* 415-432.

Medina-Alva, P., & others (2019). Combined predictors of neurodevelopment in very low birth weight preterm infants. *Early Human Development, 130,* 109-115.

Meeks, L., Heit, P., & Page, R. (2020). *Comprehensive school health education* (9th ed.). New York: McGraw-Hill.

Meerlo, P., Sgoifo, A., & Suchecki, D. (2008). Restricted and disrupted sleep: Effects on autonomic function, neuroendocrine stress systems, and stress responsivity. *Medicine Review, 12,* 197-210.

Meert, K.L., & others (2015). Meaning making during parent-physician bereavement meetings after a child's death. *Health Psychology, 34,* 453-461.

Meghelli, L., & others (2020, in press). Complications of pregnancy in morbidly obese patients: What is the impact of gestational diabetes mellitus? *Journal of Gynecology, Obstetrics, and Human Reproduction.*

Mehlhausen-Hassoen, D. (2019). Gender-specific differences in corporal punishment and children's perceptions of their mothers' and fathers' parenting. *Journal of Interpersonal Violence.* doi:10.1177/0886260519842172

Meier, E.A., & others (2016). Defining a good death (successful dying): Literature review and a call for research and public dialogue. *American Journal of Geriatric Psychiatry, 24,* 261-271.

Meins, E., & others (2013). Mind-mindedness and theory of mind: Mediating processes of language and perspectival symbolic play. *Child Development, 84,* 1777-1790.

Meisel, V., Servera, M., Garcia-Banda, G., Cardo, E., & Moreno, I. (2013). Neurofeedback and standard pharmacological intervention in ADHD: A randomized controlled trial with six-month follow-up. *Biological Psychology, 94,* 12-21.

Mekonnen, A.G., Yehualashet, S.S., & Bayleyegn, A.D. (2019). The effects of kangaroo mother care on the time to breastfeeding initiation among preterm and LBW infants: A meta-analysis of published studies. *International Breastfeeding Journal, 14,* 12.

Meland, E., Breidablik, H.J., & Theun, F. (2020, in press). Divorce and conversational difficulties with parents: Impact on adolescent health and self-esteem. *Scandinavian Journal of Public Health.*

Meldrum, R.C., & others (2017). Reassessing the relationship between general intelligence and self-control in childhood. *Intelligence, 60,* 1-9.

Melendez, J.C., & others (2019). Big Five and psychological and subjective well-being in Colombian older adults. *Archives of Gerontology and Geriatrics, 82,* 88-93.

Meltzer, A., McNulty, J.K., Jackson, G.L., & Karney, B.R. (2014). Sex differences in the implications of partner physical attractiveness for the trajectory of marital satisfaction. *Journal of Personality and Social Psychology, 106,* 418-428.

Meltzoff, A.N. (1988). Infant imitation and memory: Nine-month-old infants in immediate and deferred tests. *Child Development, 59,* 217-225.

Meltzoff, A.N. (2005). Imitation. In B. Hopkins (Ed.), *Cambridge encyclopedia of child development.* Cambridge: Cambridge University Press.

Meltzoff, A.N. (2007). Infants' causal learning. In A. Gopnik & L. Schulz (Eds.), *Causal learning.* New York: Oxford University Press.

Meltzoff, A.N. (2017). Elements of a comprehensive theory of infant imitation. *Behavioral and Brain Sciences, 40,* e396.

Meltzoff, A.N., & Brooks, R. (2006). Eyes wide shut: The importance of eyes in infant gaze following and understanding of other minds. In R. Flom, K. Lee, & D. Muir (Eds.), *Gaze following: Its development and significance.* Mahwah, NJ: Erlbaum.

Meltzoff, A.N., & Moore, M.K. (1999). A new foundation for cognitive development in infancy: The birth of the representational infant. In E.K. Skolnick, K. Nelson, S.A. Gelman, & P.H. Miller (Eds.), *Conceptual development.* Mahwah, NJ: Erlbaum.

Meltzoff, A.N., & others (2018a). Infant brain responses to felt and observed touch of hands and feet: An MEG study. *Developmental Science, 21,* e12651.

Meltzoff, A.N., & others (2018b). Re-examination of Oostenbroek et al. (2016): Evidence for neonatal imitation of tongue protrusion. *Developmental Science, 21,* e12609.

Meltzoff, A.N., & others (2019). Eliciting imitation in early infancy. *Developmental Science, 22*(2), e12738.

Melzi, G., Schick, A.R., & Kennedy, J.L. (2011). Narrative elaboration and participation: Two dimensions of maternal elicitation style. *Child Development, 82,* 1282-1296.

Memitz, S.A. (2018). The mental health implications of emerging adult long-term cohabitation. *Emerging Adulthood, 6,* 312–326.

Memone, L., Fiacco, S., & Ehlert, U. (2019). Psychobiological factors in sexual functioning in aging women–Findings from the Women 40+ Healthy Aging Study. *Frontiers in Psychology, 10,* 546.

Mendes, A. (2016). Nursing care to facilitate and support 'good' grieving. *British Journal of Nursing, 24,* 95.

Mendle, J., Ryan, R.M., & McKone, K.M.P. (2019). Age at menarche, depression, and antisocial behavior in adulthood. *Pediatrics, 65,* 599–606.

Mendoza, L., & others (2020, in press). The effect of acculturation on cognitive performance among older Hispanics in the United States. *Applied Neuropsychology. Adult.*

Meng, X., & D'Arcy, C. (2014). Successful aging in Canada: Prevalence and predictors from a population-based sample of older adults. *Gerontology, 60,* 65–72.

Menn, L., & Stoel-Gammon, C. (2009). Phonological development: Learning sounds and sound patterns. In J. Berko Gleason (Ed.), *The development of language* (7th ed.). Boston: Allyn & Bacon.

Menon, R., & others (2011). Cigarette smoking induces oxidative stress and apoptosis in normal fetal membranes. *Placenta, 32,* 317–322.

Menyuk, P., Liebergott, J., & Schultz, M. (1995). *Early language development in full-term and premature infants.* Hillsdale, NJ: Erlbaum.

Mepham, S.O., Bland, R.M., & Newell, M.L. (2011). Prevention of mother-to-child transmission of HIV in resource-rich and poor settings. *BJOG, 118,* 202–218.

Meque, I., & others (2019). Externalizing and internalizing symptoms in childhood and adolescence and the risk of alcohol use disorders in young adulthood: A meta-analysis of longitudinal studies. *Australian and New Zealand Journal of Psychiatry, 53,* 965–975.

Merchant, S.J., & others (2019). Palliative care and symptom burden in the last year of life: A population-based study of patients with gastrointestinal cancer. *Annals of Surgical Oncology, 26,* 2336–2345.

Mercurio, L.Y., & others (2020, in press). Children with ADHD engage in less physical activity. *Journal of Attention Disorders.*

Meredith, N.V. (1978). Research between 1960 and 1970 on the standing height of young children in different parts of the world. In H.W. Reece & L.P. Lipsitt (Eds.), *Advances in child development and behavior* (Vol. 12). New York: Academic Press.

Merewood, A., & others (2007). Breastfeeding duration rates and factors affecting continued breastfeeding among infants born at an inner-city U.S. baby-friendly hospital. *Journal of Human Lactation, 23,* 157–164.

Merrick, J.S., & others (2020, in press). Benevolent childhood experiences (BCEs) in homeless parents: A validation and replication study. *Journal of Family Psychology.*

Merrill, D.M. (2009). Parent-child relationships: Later-life. In D. Carr (Ed.), *Encyclopedia of the life course and human development.* Boston: Gale.

Mervak, B.M., & others (2019). MRI in pregnancy: Indications and practical considerations. *Journal of Magnetic Resonance Imaging, 49,* 621–631.

Merz, E.C., & others (2019). Socioeconomic disparities in chronic physiologic stress are associated with brain structure in children. *Biological Psychiatry, 88,* 921–929.

Mesiano, S.A., & others (2019). Progestin therapy to prevent preterm birth: History and effectiveness of current strategies and development of novel approaches. *Placenta, 79,* 46–52.

Mesman, J., van IJzendoorn, M.H., & Sagi-Schwartz, A. (2016). Cross-cultural patterns of attachment: Universal and contextual dimensions. In J. Cassidy & P.R. Shaver (Eds.), *Handbook of attachment* (3rd ed.). New York: Guilford.

Messelink, M., Van Roekel, E., & Oldehinkel, A.J. (2018). Self-esteem in early adolescence as predictor of depressive symptoms in late adolescence and early adulthood: The mediating role of motivational and social factors. *Journal of Youth and Adolescence, 47,* 932–946.

Messiah, S.E., Miller, T.L., Lipshultz, S.E., & Bandstra, E.S. (2011). Potential latent effects of prenatal cocaine exposure on growth and the risk of cardiovascular and metabolic disease in childhood. *Progress in Pediatric Cardiology, 31,* 59–65.

Messinger, D.S., & others (2017). Temporal dependency and the structure of early looking. *PLoS One, 12,* e0169458.

Meteyard, L., & Vigliocco, G. (2019). Lexico-semantics. In S. A. Rueschemeer & M. Gareth Gaskell (Eds.), *Oxford handbook of psycholinguistics* (2nd ed.). New York: Oxford University Press.

Meusel, L.A., & others (2017). Brain-behavior relationships in source memory: Effects of age and memory ability. *Cortex, 91,* 221–233.

Meuwissen, A.S., & Carlson, S.M. (2018). The role of father parenting in children's school readiness: A longitudinal follow-up. *Journal of Family Psychology, 32,* 588–599.

Mi, S.J., & others (2019). Association of sleep patterns with metabolic syndrome indices, body composition, and energy intake in children and adolescents. *Pediatric Obesity, 14*(6), e12507.

Mi, Y., & others (2020, in press). Mitochondria targeted therapeutics for Alzheimer's disease: The good. The bad. The potential. *Antioxidants and Redox Signaling.*

Michael, R.T., Gagnon, J.H., Laumann, E.O., & Kolata, G. (1994). *Sex in America.* Boston: Little, Brown.

Mick, P., & others (2018). Associations between sensory loss and social networks, participation, support, and loneliness: Analysis of the Canadian Longitudinal Study of Aging. *Canadian Family Physician, 64,* e33–e41.

Miech, R.A., & others (2019). *Monitoring the Future: National survey results on drug use, 1975–2018. Vol. 1: Secondary school students.* Ann Arbor, MI: University of Michigan Institute for Social Research.

Mike, A., Harris, K., Roberts, B.W., & Jackson, J.J. (2015). Conscientiousness: Lower-order structure, life course consequences, and development. In J. Wright (Ed.), *International encyclopedia of social and behavioral sciences* (2nd ed.). New York: Elsevier.

Mikkola, T.M., & others (2016). Self-reported hearing is associated with time spent out-of-home and withdrawal from leisure activities in older community-dwelling adults. *Aging: Clinical and Experimental Research, 28,* 297–302.

Mikulincer, M., & Shaver, P.R. (2016). *Attachment in adulthood* (2nd ed.). New York: Guilford.

Mikulincer, M., & Shaver, P.R. (2019). Attachment theory expanded: A behavioral systems approach to personality. In K. Deaux & M. Snyder (Eds.), *Oxford handbook of personality and social psychology.* New York: Oxford University Press.

Mikulincer, M., Shaver, P.R., Bar-On, N., & Ein-Dor, T. (2010). The pushes and pulls of close relationships: Attachment insecurities and relational ambivalence. *Journal of Personality and Social Psychology, 98,* 450–468.

Mila, M., & others (2018). Fragile X syndrome: An overview and update of the FMR1 gene, *93,* 197–205.

Milberg, A., Olsson, E.C., Jakobsson, M., Olsson, M., & Friedrichsen, M. (2008). Family members' perceived needs for bereavement follow-up. *Journal of Pain and Symptom Management, 35,* 58–69.

Milisav, L., Ribaric, S., & Poljsak, B. (2018). Antioxidant vitamins and aging. *Biochemistry and Cell Biology of Aging. Part I: Biomedical Science, 90,* 1–23.

Milken Institute and Stanford Center on Longevity (2019). *Future of aging.* Santa Monica, CA, and Palo Alto, CA: Authors.

Miller, A.L., & others (2020, in press). Developmentally informed behavior change techniques to enhance self-regulation in a health promotion context: A conceptual review. *Health Psychology Review.*

Miller, B.C., Benson, B., & Galbraith, K.A. (2001). Family relationships and adolescent pregnancy risk: A research synthesis. *Developmental Review, 21,* 1–38.

Miller, C., & Price, J. (2013). *The number of children being raised by gay or lesbian parents.* Unpublished manuscript, Department of Economics, Brigham Young University, Provo, UT.

Miller, C.F., Lurye, L.E., Zusuls, K.M., & Ruble, D.N. (2009). Accessibility of gender stereotype domains: Developmental and gender differences in children. *Sex Roles, 60,* 870–881.

Miller, J.B. (1986). *Toward a new psychology of women* (2nd ed.). Boston: Beacon Press.

Miller, J.G., Wice, M., & Goyal, N. (2020). Culture, parenting practices, and moral development. In D.J. Laible & others (Eds.), *Oxford handbook of moral development.* New York: Oxford University Press.

Miller, L.M., & Bell, R.A. (2012). Online health information seeking: The influence of age, information trustworthiness, and search challenges. *Journal of Aging and Health, 24,* 525–541.

Miller, M.D. (2012). Complicated grief in late life. *Dialogues in Clinical Neuroscience, 14,* 195–202.

Miller, M.S. (2018). Save for retirement. *Annals of Emergency Medicine, 71,* 252.

Miller, N.V., & Johnston, C. (2019). Social threat attentional bias in childhood: Relations to aggression and hostile intent attributions. *Aggressive Behavior, 45,* 245–254.

Miller, P.H. (2016). *Theories of developmental psychology* (6th ed.). New York: Worth.

Miller, R., Wankerl, M., Stalder, T., Kirschbaum, C., & Alexander, N. (2013). The serotonin transporter gene-linked polymorphic region (5-HTTLPR) and cortisol stress reactivity: A meta-analysis. *Molecular Psychiatry, 18,* 1018–1024.

Miller, S.L., Huppi, P.S., & Mallard, C. (2016). The consequences of fetal growth restriction on brain structure and neurodevelopmental outcome. *Journal of Physiology, 594,* 807–823.

Miller-Perrin, C.L., Perrin, R.D., & Kocur, J.L. (2009). Parental, physical, and psychological aggression: Psychological symptoms in young adults. *Child Abuse and Neglect, 33,* 1–11.

Mills, C.M., & Elashi, F.B. (2014). Children's skepticism: Developmental and individual differences in children's ability to detect and explain distorted claims. *Journal of Experimental Child Psychology, 12,* 1–17.

Mills, D., & Mills, C. (2000). *Hungarian kindergarten curriculum translation.* London: Mills Production.

Mills, H., & others (2020, in press). Bump start needed: Linking guidelines, policy, and practice in promoting physical activity during and beyond pregnancy. *British Journal of Sports Medicine.*

Mills-Koonce, W.R., Propper, C.B., & Barnett, M. (2012). Poor infant soothability and later insecure-ambivalent attachment: Developmental change in phenotypic markers of risk or two measures of the same construct? *Infant Behavior and Development, 35,* 215–235.

Milne, E., & others (2012). Parental prenatal smoking and risk of childhood acute lymphoblastic leukemia. *American Journal of Epidemiology, 175,* 43–53.

Milner, K., & others (2019). The experiences of spirituality among adults with mental health difficulties: A qualitative systematic review. *Epidemiology and Psychiatric Sciences, 29,* e34.

Milosavljevic, B., & others (2017). Anxiety and attentional bias to threat in children at increased familial risk for autism spectrum disorder. *Journal of Autism and Developmental Disorders, 47,* 3714–3727.

Min, S.Y., & others (2020, in press). Exercise rescues gene pathways involved in vascular expansion and promotes functional angiogenesis in subcutaneous white adipose tissue. *International Journal of Molecular Science.*

Mindell, J.A., Leichman, E.S., & Walters, R.M. (2017). Sleep location and parent-perceived sleep outcomes in older infants. *Sleep Medicine, 39,* 1–7.

Mindell, L.A., & others (2017). Sleep and socio-emotional development in infants and toddlers.

Miner, M.M., Bhattacharya, R.K., Blick, G., Kushner, H., & Khera, M. (2013). 12-month observation of testosterone replacement effectiveness in a general population of men. *Postgraduate Medicine, 125,* 8–18.

Minkler, M., & Fuller-Thompson, E. (2005). African American grandparents raising grandchildren: A national study using the Census 2000 American Community Survey. *Journals of Gerontology B: Psychological Sciences and Social Sciences, 60,* S82–S92.

Minnes, S., & others (2010). The effects of prenatal cocaine exposure on problem behavior in children 4–10 years. *Neurotoxicology and Teratology, 32,* 443–451.

Minnes, S., & others (2016). Executive function in children with prenatal cocaine exposure (12–15 years). *Neurotoxicology and Teratology, 57,* 79–86.

Minniti, F., & others (2014). Breast-milk characteristics protecting against allergy. *Endocrine, Metabolic, and Immune Disorders Drug Targets, 14,* 9–15.

Minsart, A.F., Buekens, P., Spiegelaere, M., & Englert, Y. (2013). Neonatal outcomes in obese mothers: A population-based analysis. *BMC Pregnancy and Childbirth, 13,* 36.

Minta, K., & others (2020). Quantification of total apolipoprotein E and its isoforms in cerebrospinal fluid from patients with neurodegenerative diseases. *Alzheimer's Research and Therapy, 12*(1), 19.

Mir, Y.R., & Kuchay, R.A.H. (2019). Advances in identification of genes involved in autosomal recessive intellectual disability: A brief review. *Journal of Medical Genetics, 56,* 567–573.

Mireku, M.O., & others (2019). Night-time screen-based media device use and adolescents' sleep and health-related quality of life. *Environmental Intervention, 124,* 66–78.

Mischel, W. (2014). *The marshmallow test: Mastering self-control.* New York: Little Brown.

Mischel, W., Cantor, N., & Feldman, S. (1996). Principles of self-regulation: The nature of will power and self-control. In E.T. Higgins & A.W. Kruglanski (Eds.), *Social psychology.* New York: Guilford.

Mischel, W., & Moore, B.S. (1980). The role of ideation in voluntary delay for symbolically presented rewards. *Cognitive Therapy and Research, 4,* 211–221.

Mischel, W., & others (2011). 'Willpower' over the life span: Decomposing self-regulation. *Social Cognitive and Affective Neuroscience, 6,* 252–256.

Mislinksi, J. (2018). *Demographic trends for the 50-and-older work force.* Retrieved March 2, 2018, from https://seekingalpha.com/article/4136795-demographic-trends-50-older-workforce

Mislinksi, J. (2019, July 19). *Long-term trends in employment by age group.* Retrieved July 25, 2019, from www.advisorperspectives.com/

Mitchell, A.B., & Stewart, J.B. (2013). The efficacy of all-male academies: Insights from critical race theory (CRT). *Sex Roles, 69,* 382.

Mitchell, D.J., Cusack, R., & Cam-CAN (2018). Visual short-term memory through the lifespan: Preserved benefits of context and metacognition. *Psychology of Aging, 33,* 841–854.

Mitchell, E.A., & Krous, H.F. (2015). Sudden unexpected death in infancy: A historical perspective. *Journal of Pediatrics and Child Health, 5,* 108–112.

Mitchell, E.A., & others (2017). The combination of bed sharing and maternal smoking leads to a greatly increased risk of sudden unexpected death in infancy: The new Zealand SUDI Nationwide Case Control. *New Zealand Medicine, 130,* 52–64.

Mitchell, L.L., & Syed, M. (2015). Does college matter for emerging adulthood? Comparing developmental trajectories of educational groups. *Journal of Youth and Adolescence, 44,* 2012–2017.

Mitchell, M.B., & others (2012). Cognitively stimulating activities: Effects on cognition across four studies with up to 21 years of longitudinal data. *Journal of Aging Research.* doi:10.1155/2012/461592

Mitchell, V., & Helson, R. (1990). Women's prime of life: Is it the 50s? *Psychology of Women Quarterly, 14,* 451–470.

Mithun, M. (2019). Morphology: What's in a word. In C. Genetti (Ed.), *How languages work* (2nd ed.). New York: Cambridge University Press.

Mitsui, T., & others (2019). Effects of prenatal sex hormones on behavioral sexual dimorphism. *Pediatric International, 61,* 140–146.

Miyake, K., Chen, S., & Campos, J. (1985). Infants' temperament, mothers' mode of interaction and attachment in Japan: An interim report. In I. Bretherton & F. Waters (Eds.), Growing points of attachment theory and research, *Monographs of the Society for Research in Child Development, 50* (1–2, Serial No. 109), 276–297.

Miyata, K., & others (2018). Effects of cataract surgery on cognitive function in elderly: Results of Fujiwara-kyo Eye Study. *PLoS One, 13*(2), e0192677.

Mize, K.D., Pineda, M., Blau, A.K., Marsh, K., & Jones, N.A. (2014). Infant physiological and behavioral responses to a jealousy provoking condition. *Infancy, 19,* 338–348.

Mo, J., & others (2019). The relationship between impulsivity and self-injury in Chinese undergraduates: The chain mediating role of stressful life events and negative affect. *Journal of Affective Disorders, 256,* 259–266.

Moatt, J.P., & others (2019). Reconciling nutritional geometry with classical dietary restriction: Effects of nutrient intake, not calories, on survival and reproduction. *Aging Cell, 18*(1), e12868.

Modecki, K.L., & others (2014). Bullying prevalence across contexts: A meta-analysis measuring cyber and traditional bullying. *Journal of Adolescent Health, 55,* 602–611.

Moen, P. (2007). Unpublished review of J.W. Santrock's *Life-span development* (12th ed.). New York: McGraw-Hill.

Moen, P. (2009a). Careers. In D. Carr (Ed.), *Encyclopedia of the life course and human development.* Boston: Gale Cengage.

Moen, P. (2009b). Dual-career couples. In D. Carr (Ed.), *Encyclopedia of the life course and human development*. Boston: Gale Cengage.

Moen, P., Kelly, E., and Magennis, R. (2008). Gender strategies: Social and institutional convoys, mystiques, and cycles of control. In M.C. Smith & T.G. Reio (Eds.), *Handbook of research on adult development and learning*. Mahwah: Erlbaum.

Moffitt, T.E. (2012). *Childhood self-control predicts adult health, wealth, and crime*. Paper presented at the Symposium on Symptom Improvement in Well-Being, Copenhagen.

Moffitt, T.E., & others (2011). A gradient of childhood self-control predicts health, wealth, and public safety. *Proceedings of the National Academy of Sciences U.S.A., 108*, 2693-2698.

Moffitt, U., Juang, L.P., & Syed, M. (2020, in press). Intersectionality and youth identity development research in Europe. *Frontiers in Psychology*.

Mohanty, S.K., & others (2020, in press). Increased DNA methylation in the spermatogenesis associated (SPATA) genes correlates with infertility. *Andrology*.

Moharei, F., & others (2018). Evaluating of psychiatric behavior in obese children and adolescents. *Iranian Journal of Child Neurology, 12*, 26-36.

Moieni, M., & others (2020, in press). Generativity and social well-being in older women: Expectations regarding aging matter. *Journals of Gerontology B: Psychological Sciences and Social Sciences*.

Moilanen, J.M., & others (2012). Effect of aerobic training on menopausal symptoms—A randomized controlled trial. *Menopause, 19*, 691-696.

Mok, A., & others (2019). Physical activity trajectories and mortality: Population based cohort study. *BMJ, 365*, l2323.

Mok, Y., & others (2018). American Heart Association's Life's Simple 7 at middle age and prognosis after myocardial infarction in later life. *Journal of the American Heart Association, 7*, 4.

Mola, J.R. (2015). Erectile dysfunction in the older adult male. *Urological Nursing, 35*, 87-93.

Molefi-Youri, W. (2019). Is there a role for mindfulness-based interventions (here defined as MBCT and MBSR) in facilitating optimal psychological adjustment in the menopause? *Post Reproductive Health, 25*, 143-149.

Molgora, S., & others (2019). Dyadic coping and marital adjustment during pregnancy: A cross-sectional study of Italian couples expecting their first child. *International Journal of Psychology, 54*, 271-285.

Molina, D.K., & Farley, N.J. (2019). A 25-year review of pediatric suicides: Distinguishing features and risk factors. *American Journal of Forensic Medicine and Pathology, 40*, 220-226.

Moline, H.R., & Smith, J.F. (2016). The continuing threat of syphilis in pregnancy. *Current Opinion in Obstetrics and Gynecology, 28*, 101-104.

Mollart, L., & others (2018). Midwives' personal use of complementary and alternative medicine (CAM) influences their recommendations to women experiencing a post-date pregnancy. *Women and Birth, 31*(1), 44-51.

Mollborn, S. (2017). Teenage mothers today: What we know and how it matters. *Child Development Perspectives, 11*, 63-69.

Molton, I.R., & Terrill, A.L. (2014). Overview of persistent pain in older adults. *American Psychologist, 69*, 197-207.

Monge, Z.A., & Madden, D.J. (2016). Linking cognitive and visual perceptual decline in healthy aging: The information degradation hypothesis. *Neuroscience and Biobehavioral Reviews, 69*, 166-173.

Monk, C., & others (2020, in press). Associations of perceived prenatal stress and adverse pregnancy outcomes with perceived stress after delivery. *Archives of Women's Mental Health*.

Monn, A.R., & others (2017). Executive function and parenting in the context of homelessness. *Journal of Family Psychology, 31*, 61-70.

Monroy, C. & others (2019). Visual habituation in deaf and hearing infants. *PLoS One, 14*(2), e0209265.

Monserud, M.A. (2008). Intergenerational relationships and affectual solidarity between grandparents and young adults. *Journal of Marriage and the Family, 70*, 182-195.

Montagne, A., Nation, D.A., & Ziokovic, B.V. (2020). APOE4 accelerates development of dementia after stroke: Is there a role for cerebrovascular dysfunction? *Stroke, 51*, 699-700.

Monti, C., & others (2020, in press). Prospective memories and working memories: Shared resources or distinct mechanisms? *Applied Neuropsychology. Adult*.

Moon, D.G., & Park, H.J. (2019). The ideal goal of testosterone replacement therapy: Maintaining testosterone levels or managing symptoms? *Journal of Clinical Medicine, 8*, 3.

Moon, R.Y., & others (2017). Impact of a randomized controlled trial to reduce bedsharing on breastfeeding rates and duration for African American infants. *Journal of Community Health, 42*, 707-715.

Moore, B.C.J., Mariathasan, S., & Sek, A.P. (2020, in press). Effects of age and hearing loss on the discrimination of amplitude and frequency modulation for 2- and 10-Hz rates. *Trends in Hearing*.

Moore, B.F., & others (2020, in press). Prenatal exposure to tobacco and offspring neurocognitive development in the Healthy Start Study. *Journal of Pediatrics*.

Moore, D.S. (2001). *The dependent gene*. New York: W.H. Freeman.

Moore, D.S. (2013). Behavioral genetics, genetics, and epigenetics. In P.D. Zelazo (Ed.), *Handbook of developmental psychology*. New York: Oxford University Press.

Moore, D.S. (2015). *The developing genome*. New York: Oxford University Press.

Moore, D.S. (2017). Behavioral epigenetics. *Wiley Interdisciplinary Reviews. Systems Biology and Medicine, 9*, 1.

Moore, S.R., Harden, K.P., & Mendle, J. (2014). Pubertal timing and adolescent sexual behavior in girls. *Developmental Psychology, 50*, 1734-1745.

Moos, B. (2007, July 4). Who'll care for aging boomers? *Dallas Morning News*, A1-A2.

Mooya, H., Sichimba, F., & Bakermans-Kranenburg, M. (2016). Infant-mother and infant-sibling attachment in Zambia. *Attachment and Human Development, 18*, 618-635.

Moran, S., & Gardner, H. (2006). Extraordinary achievements. In W. Damon & R. Lerner (Eds.), *Handbook of child psychology* (6th ed.). New York: Wiley.

Moran, S., & Gardner, H. (2007). Hill, skill, and will: Executive function from a multiple intelligences perspective. In L. Meltzer (Ed.), *Executive function in education*. New York: Guilford.

Morardpour, F., & others (2020). Association between physical activity, cardiorespiratory fitness, and body composition with menopausal symptoms in early postmenopausal women. *Menopause, 27*, 230-237.

Morean, M.E., & others (2014). First drink to first drunk: Age of onset and delay to intoxication are associated with adolescent alcohol use and binge drinking. *Alcoholism: Clinical and Experimental Research, 38*, 2615-2621.

Moreau, C., Beltzer, N., Bozon, M., Bajos, N., & The CSF Group (2011). Sexual risk taking following relationship break-ups. *European Journal of Contraception and Reproductive Health Care, 16*, 95-99.

Moreau, D., & others (2019). Volumetric and surface characteristics of gray matter in adult dyslexia and dyscalculia. *Neuropsychologia, 127*, 204-210.

Moreno-Cugnon, L., & others (2018). SOX2 haploinsufficiency promotes impaired vision at advanced age. *Oncotarget, 9*, 36684-36692.

Morgan, G.S., & others (2019). A life fulfilled: Positively influencing physical activity in older adults—A systematic review and meta-ethnography. *BMC Public Health, 19*(1), 362.

Morin, A.J.S., & others (2017). Adolescents' body image trajectories: A further test of the self-equilibrium hypothesis. *Developmental Psychology, 53*, 1501-1521.

Morneau-Vaillancourt, G., & others (2019). The genetic and environmental etiology of shyness through childhood. *Behavior Genetics, 49*, 376-385.

Morosan, L., & others (2017). Emotion recognition and perspective taking: A comparison between typical and incarcerated male adolescents. *PLoS One, 12*(1), e0170646.

Morra, S., Gobbo, C., Marini, Z., & Sheese, R. (2008). *Cognitive development: Neo-Piagetian perspectives*. Mahwah, NJ: Erlbaum.

Morris, A.S., & others (2013). Effortful control, behavior problems, and peer relations: What predicts academic adjustment in kindergartners from low-income families. *Early Education Development, 24*, 813-828.

Morris, B.J., & others (2012). A 'snip' in time: What is the best age to circumcise? *BMC Pediatrics, 12*, 20.

Morris, M.W., Savani, K., & Fincher, K. (2019). Metacognition fosters cultural learning: Evidence from individual differences and situational prompts. *Journal of Personality and Social Psychology, 116,* 46-68.

Morrison, G.S. (2020). *Early childhood education today* (15th ed.). Upper Saddle River, NJ: Pearson.

Morrison, R.S. (2013). Models of palliative care delivery in the United States. *Current Opinion in Supportive and Palliative Care, 7,* 201-206.

Morrison, S.C., Fife, T., & Hertlein, K.M. (2017). Mechanisms behind prolonged effects of parental divorce: A phenomenological study. *Journal of Divorce and Remarriage, 58,* 54-63.

Morrison-Beedy, D., & others (2013). Reducing sexual risk behavior in adolescent girls: Results from a randomized trial. *Journal of Adolescent Health, 52,* 314-322.

Morrissey, T.W. (2009). Multiple child-care arrangements and young children's behavioral outcomes. *Child Development, 80,* 59-76.

Morrow, C.B. (2020). Fifty years of WIC: Celebration and caution. *Journal of Public Health Management and Practice, 26,* 3-4.

Morrow, C.E., & others (2006). Learning disabilities and intellectual functioning in school-aged children with prenatal cocaine exposure. *Developmental Neuropsychology, 30,* 905-931.

Morrow, L.M. (2020). *Literacy development in the early years* (9th ed.). Upper Saddle River, NJ: Pearson.

Mosley, J.D., & others (2020). Predictive accuracy of a polygenic risk score compared with a clinical risk score for incident coronary heart disease. *JAMA, 323*(7), 627-635.

Moss, S.A., & Wilson, S.G. (2018). Why are older people often so responsible and considerate even when their future seems limited? A systematic review. *International Journal of Aging and Human Development, 86,* 82-108.

Mossburg, S.E. (2018). Baby boomer retirement: Are you up to the challenge? *Nursing Management, 49,* 13-14.

Moura da Costa, E., & Tuleski, S.C. (2017). Social constructivist interpretation of Vygotsky. In C. Ratner & D. Silva (Eds.), *Vygotsky and Marx.* New York: Routledge.

Moustafa, A.A., & others (2020, in press). Depression following major life transitions in women: A review and theory. *Psychological Reports.*

Movahed Abtahi, M., & Kerns, K.A. (2017). Attachment and emotion regulation in middle childhood: Changes in affect and vagal tone during a social stress task. *Attachment and Human Development, 19,* 221-242.

Mowla, S., & others (2020, in press). Association between maternal pregestational diabetes mellitus and spina bifida: A population-based case-control study, Finland, 2000-2014. *Birth Defects Research.*

Mparmpakas, D., & others (2013). Immune system function, stress, exercise, and nutrition profile can affect pregnancy outcome: Lessons from a Mediterranean cohort. *Experimental and Therapeutic Medicine, 5,* 411-418.

Muftic, L.R., & Updegrove, A.H. (2018). The mediating effect of self-control on parenting and delinquency: A gendered approach with a multinational sample. *International Journal of Offender Therapy and Comparative Criminology, 62,* 3058-3076.

Mullen, S.P., & others (2012). Physical activity and functional limitations in older adults: The influence of self-efficacy and functional performance. *Journals of Gerontology B: Psychological Sciences and Social Sciences, 67,* 354-361.

Muller, M.J., & others (2017). Sleep duration of inpatients with a depressive disorder: Associations with age, subjective sleep quality, and cognitive complaints. *Archives of Psychiatric Nursing, 31,* 77-82.

Mullet, H.G., & others (2013). Prospective memory and aging: Evidence for preserved spontaneous retrieval with exact but not related cues. *Psychology and Aging, 28,* 910-922.

Mullick, S. (2019). Adolescent sexual and reproductive health. In D. Devakumar & others (Eds.), *Oxford textbook of global health of women, infants, children, and adolescents.* New York: Oxford University Press.

Mulligan, E.A., & Karel, M.J. (2018). Development of a bereavement group in a geriatric mental health clinic for veterans. *Clinical Gerontology, 41,* 445-457.

Munawar, K., Kuhn, S.K., & Hague, S. (2018). Understanding the reminiscence bump: A systematic review. *PLoS One, 13*(12), e0208595.

Muniz-Terrera, G., & others (2013). Investigating terminal decline: Results from a UK population-based study of aging. *Psychology and Aging, 28,* 377-385.

Munnell, A.H. (2015, March). *The average retirement age–An update.* Boston: Center for Retirement Research at Boston College.

Munnell, A.H., Rutledge, M.S., & Sanzenbacher, G.T. (2018). What causes workers to retire before they plan? *Journal of Retirement, 6,* 35-51.

Munoz-Ramon, P.V., Hernandez Martinez, P., & Munoz-Negrete, F.J. (2020). New therapeutic targets in the treatment of age-related macular degeneration. *Archivos de la Sociedad Espanola de Oftalmologia, 95,* 75-83.

Munro, C.A., & others (2019). Stressful life events and cognitive decline: Sex differences in the Baltimore Epidemiologic Catchment Area Follow-Up Study. *International Journal of Geriatric Psychiatry. 34,* 1008-1017.

Murdock, K.K., Horissian, M., & Crichlow-Ball, C. (2017). Emerging adults' text message use and sleep characteristics: A multimethod, naturalistic study. *Behavioral Sleep Medicine, 15,* 228-241.

Murphy, D.A., Brecht, M.L., Huang, D., & Herbeck, D.M. (2012). Trajectories of delinquency from age 14 to 23 in the National Longitudinal Survey of Youth sample. *International Journal of Adolescence and Youth, 17,* 47-62.

Murphy, S.L., & others (2018). Mortality in the United States, 2017. *NCHS Data Brief, 328,* 1-8.

Murray, A.L., & others (2020, in press). The intergenerational effects of intimate partner violence in pregnancy: Mediating pathways and implications for prevention. *Trauma, Violence, and Abuse.*

Murray, D.R., & others (2019). Falling in love is associated with immune system gene regulation. *Psychoneuroimmunology, 100,* 120-126.

Mussen, P.H., Honzik, M., & Eichorn, D. (1982). Early adult antecedents of life satisfaction at age 70. *Journal of Gerontology, 37,* 316-322.

Mutiso, V.N., & others (2019). Relationship between bullying, substance use, psychiatric disorders, and social problems in a sample of Kenyan secondary schools. *Prevention Science, 20,* 544-554.

Myers, D.G. (2010). *Psychology* (9th ed.). New York: Worth.

Myerson, J., Rank, M.R., Raines, F.Q., & Schnitzler, M.A. (1998). Race and general cognitive ability: The myth of diminishing returns in education. *Psychology Science, 9.*

Myoshi, T., & others (2019). Maternal biomarkers for fetal heart failure in fetuses with congenital heart defects or arrhythmias. *American Journal of Obstetrics and Gynecology, 220,* e1-104, e15.

N

NACE (2020, February 12). *Employers plan to increase college hiring by 5.8 percent.* Retrieved February 12, 2020, from www.naceweb.org/job-market

Naczk, M., Marszalek, S., Naczk, A. (2020). Inertial training improves strength, balance, and gait speed in elderly nursing home residents. *Clinical Interventions in Aging, 15,* 177-184.

Nader, K. (2001). Treatment methods for childhood trauma. In J.P. Wilson, M.J. Friedman, & J. Lindy (Eds.), *Treating psychological trauma and PTSD.* New York: Guilford.

Naezer, M., & Ringrose, J. (2019). Adventure, intimacy, identity, and knowledge: Exploring how social media are shaping and transforming youth sexuality. In S. Lamb & J. Gilbert (Eds.), *Cambridge handbook of sexual development.* New York: Cambridge University Press.

Nag, T.C., & Wadhwa, S. (2012). Ultrastructure of the human retina in aging and various pathological states. *Micron, 43,* 759-781.

Nagarajan, R., & others (2019). Quality of life in pediatric acute myeloid leukemia: Report from the Children's Oncology Group. *Cancer Medicine, 8,* 4454-4464.

Naghavi, M., & others (2019). Global, regional, and national burden of suicide mortality, 1990 to 2016: Systematic analysis for the Global Burden of Disease Study, 2016. *BMJ, 364,* 194.

Nagpal, T.S., & others (2020, in press). Sequential introduction of exercise first followed by nutrition improves program adherence during pregnancy: A randomized controlled trial. *International Journal of Behavioral Medicine.*

Naicker, K., Galambos, N.L., Zeng, Y., Senthilselvan, A., & Colman, I. (2013). Social, demographic, and health outcomes in the 10 years following adolescent depression. *Journal of Adolescent Health, 52,* 533-538.

Nair, R.L., Roche, K.M., & White, R.M.B. (2018). Acculturation gap distress among Latino youth: Prospective links to family processes and youth depressive symptoms, alcohol use, and academic performance. *Journal of Youth and Adolescence, 47,* 105-120.

Najar, B., & others (2008). Effects of psychosocial stimulation on growth and development of severely malnourished children in a nutrition unit in Bangladesh. *European Journal of Clinical Nutrition, 63*(6), 725-731.

Najman, J.M., & others (2009). The impact of episodic and chronic poverty on child cognitive development. *Journal of Pediatrics, 154,* 284-289.

Najman, J.M., & others (2010). Timing and chronicity of family poverty and development of unhealthy behaviors in children: A longitudinal study. *Journal of Adolescent Health, 46,* 538-544.

Nakagawa, T., & others (2018). Subjective well-being in centenarians: A comparison of Japan and the United States. *Aging and Mental Health, 22,* 1313-1320.

Nakamichi, K. (2020, in press). Differences in young children's peer preference by inhibitory control and emotion regulation. *Psychological Reports.*

Nansel, T.R., & others (2001). Bullying behaviors among U.S. youth. *JAMA, 285,* 2094-2100.

Narayan, A.J., & Masten, A.S. (2019). Resilience in the context of violence and trauma: Promotive and protective processes of positive caregiving. In. J. Osofsky & B.M. Groves (Eds.), *Violence and trauma in the lives of children.* Santa Barbara, CA: Praeger.

Narváez, D. (2019). Moral development and moral values: Evolutionary and neurobiological influences. In D.P. McAdams & others (Eds.), *Handbook of personality.* New York: Guilford.

Narváez, D. (2020). Evolution and the parenting ecology of moral development. In D. Laible, L. Padilla-Walker, & G. Carlo (Ed.), *Handbook of parenting and moral development.* New York: Oxford University Press.

Narváez, D., & Gleason, T.R. (2013). Developmental optimism. In D. Narváez & others (2013). *Evolution, early experience, and human development.* New York: Oxford University Press.

NASSPE (2012). Single-sex schools and schools with single-sex classrooms: What's the difference? Retrieved from www.singlesexschools.org/schools-schools.com

National Alliance for Caregiving (2009). Caregiving in the United States 2009. Retrieved June 29, 2012, from www.caregiving.org/pdf/research/Caregiving

National Assessment of Educational Progress (2017). *Mathematics and reading, 4th and 8th grade.* Washington, DC: National Center for Education Statistics.

National Association for Gifted Children (2017). *Gifted children.* Washington, DC: Author.

National Association for Sport and Physical Education (2002). *Active start: A statement of physical activity guidelines for children from birth to five years.* Reston, VA: National Association for Sport and Physical Education Publications.

National Cancer Institute (2020). *Childhood cancer.* Rockville, MD: Author.

National Center for Education Statistics (2002). *Work during college.* Washington, DC: U.S. Office of Education.

National Center for Education Statistics (2018). *College student employment.* Washington, DC: U.S. Office of Education.

National Center for Education Statistics (2019). *The condition of education, 2019.* Washington, DC: U.S. Department of Education.

National Center for Education Statistics (2019). *Trends in high school dropout and completion rates in the United States: 2018.* Washington, DC: U.S. Department of Education.

National Center for Health Statistics (2000). *Health United States 2000, with adolescent health chartbook.* Bethesda, MD: U.S. Department of Health and Human Services.

National Center for Health Statistics (2017). *Prevalence of obesity among adults and youth: United States, 2015-2016.* Atlanta: Centers for Disease Control and Prevention.

National Center for Health Statistics (2019). *Accidents and deaths.* Atlanta: Centers for Disease Control and Prevention.

National Center for Health Statistics (2019. July). *Births in the United States, 2018. NCIS Data Brief No. 346.* Atlanta: Centers for Disease Control and Prevention.

National Center for Health Statistics (2019). *Childbirth.* Atlanta: Bethesda, MD: U.S. Department of Health and Human Services.

National Center for Health Statistics (2019). *Sexually transmitted diseases.* Atlanta: Centers for Disease Control and Prevention.

National Center for Health Statistics (2020). *Accidents and deaths.* Atlanta: Centers for Disease Control and Prevention.

National Center on Shaken Baby Syndrome (2012). *Shaken baby syndrome.* Retrieved April 20, 2012, from www.dontshake.org

National Clearinghouse on Child Abuse and Neglect (2019). *What is child abuse and neglect?* Washington, DC: U.S. Department of Health and Human Services.

National Institute for Early Education Research (2016). *Did state pre-K get back on track in 2015?* Retrieved November 29, 2016, from http://nieer.org

National Institute of Drug Abuse (2019). Treating opioid use disorder during pregnancy. Washington, DC: Author.

National Institute of Mental Health (2020). Autism spectrum disorders (pervasive developmental disorders). Retrieved January 21, 2020, from www.nimh.nih.gov/Publicat/autism.clm

National Sleep Foundation (2006). *2006 Sleep in America poll.* Washington, DC: Author.

National Sleep Foundation (2007). *2007 Sleep in America poll.* Washington, DC: Author.

National Sleep Foundation (2019a). *Sleep time recommendations: What's changed?* Washington, DC: National Sleep Foundation.

National Sleep Foundation (2019b). *Sleep topics: Why an all-nighter can be harmful to your health.* Washington, DC: National Sleep Foundation.

National Sleep Foundation (2020). *How much sleep do we really need?* Washington, DC: Author.

Naveed, S., & others (2019). Association of bullying experiences with depressive symptoms and psychosocial functioning among school going children and adolescents. *BMC Research Notes, 12*(1), 198.

Nazzari, S., & Frigerio, A. (2020, in press). The programming role of maternal antenatal inflammation on infants' early neurodevelopment: A review of human studies. *Journal of Affective Disorders.*

Ncube, C.N., & Mueller, B.A. (2017). Daughters of mothers who smoke: A population-based cohort study of maternal prenatal tobacco use and subsequent prenatal smoking in offspring. *Pediatric and Perinatal Epidemiology, 31,* 14-20.

Ndabi, J., Nevill, A.M., & Sandercock, G.R.H. (2019). Cross-cultural comparisons of aerobic and muscular fitness in Tanzanian and English youth: An allometric approach. *PLoS One, 14*(2), e0211414.

Neblett, E.W., Roth, W.D., & Syed, M. (2019). Ethnic and racial identity development from an interdisciplinary perspective: Introduction to the special issue. *Emerging Adulthood, 7,* 1-12.

Needham, A. (2009). Learning in infants' object perception, object-directed action, and tool use. In A. Needham & A. Woodward (Eds.), *Learning and the infant mind.* New York: Oxford University Press.

Needham, A., Barrett, T., & Peterman, K. (2002). A pick-me-up for infants' exploratory skills: Early simulated experiences reaching for objects using 'sticky mittens' enhances young infants' object exploration skills. *Infant Behavior and Development, 25,* 279-295.

Negru-Subtirica, O., & Pop, E.L. (2018). Reciprocal associations between educational identity and vocational identity in adolescence: A three-wave longitudinal investigation. *Journal of Youth and Adolescence, 47*(4), 703-716.

Nelemans, S.A., & others (2020, in press). Transactional links between social anxiety symptoms and parenting across adolescence: Between- and within-person associations. *Child Development.*

Nelson, B.W., & others (2020, in press). The quality of early infant-caregiver relational attachment and longitudinal changes in infant inflammation across 6 months. *Developmental Psychobiology.*

Nelson, C.A. (2003). Neural development and lifelong plasticity. In R.M. Lerner, F. Jacobs, & D. Wertlieb (Eds.), *Handbook of applied developmental science* (Vol. 1). Thousand Oaks, CA: Sage.

Nelson, C.A. (2007). A developmental cognitive neuroscience approach to the study of atypical development: A model system involving infants of diabetic mothers. In D. Coch, G. Dawson, & K.W. Fischer (Eds.), *Human behavior, learning, and the developing brain.* New York: Guilford.

Nelson, C.A. (2012). Brain development and behavior. In A.M. Rudolph, C. Rudolph, L. First, G. Lister, & A.A. Gersohon (Eds.), *Rudolph's pediatrics* (22nd ed.). New York: McGraw-Hill.

Nelson, C.A. (2013a). The effects of early psychosocial deprivation. In M. Woodhead & J. Oates (Eds.), *Early childhood in focus 7: Developing brains.* Great Britain: The Open University.

Nelson, C.A. (2013b). Some thoughts on the development and neural bases of face processing. In M. Banaji & S. Gelman (Eds.), *The development of social cognition*. New York: Oxford University Press.

Nelson, C.A., Fox, N.A., & Zeanah, C.H. (2014). *Romania's abandoned children*. Cambridge, MA: Harvard University Press.

Nelson, K. (1999). Levels and modes of representation: Issues for the theory of conceptual change and development. In E.K. Skolnick, K. Nelson, S.A. Gelman, & P.H. Miller (Eds.), *Conceptual development*. Mahwah, NJ: Erlbaum.

Nelson, L.J., & others (2007). "If you want me to treat you like an adult, start acting like one!" Comparing the criteria that emerging adults and their parents have for adulthood. *Journal of Family Psychology, 21,* 665-674.

Nelson, S.K., & others (2013). In defense of parenthood: Children associated with more joy than misery. *Psychological Science, 24,* 3-10.

Nemet, D. (2016). Childhood obesity, physical activity, and exercise. *Pediatric Exercise Science, 28,* 48-51.

Nemy, M., & others (2020). Cholinergic white matter pathways make a stronger contribution to attention and memory in normal aging than cerebrovascular health and nucleus basalis of Meynert. *Neuroimage, 211,* 116607.

Nesbitt, K.T., Farran, D.C., & Fuhs, M.W. (2015). Executive function skills and academic gains in prekindergarten: Contributions of learning-related behaviors. *Developmental Psychology, 51,* 865-878.

Nesi, J., Choukas-Bradley, S., & Prinstein, M.J. (2018). Transformation of adolescent peer relations in the social media context: Part 2—Application to peer group processes and future directions for research. *Clinical Child and Family Psychology Review, 21,* 295-319.

Nesi, J., & Prinstein, M.J. (2019). In search of likes: Longitudinal associations between adolescents' digital status seeking and health-seeking behaviors. *Journal of Clinical Child and Adolescent Psychology, 48,* 470-478.

Nesi, J., & others (2017). Friends' alcohol-related social networking site activity predicts escalations in adolescent drinking: Mediation by peer norms. *Journal of Adolescent Health, 60,* 641-647.

Netz, Y. (2017). Is the comparison between exercise and pharmacologic treatment of depression in the clinical practice guideline of the American College of Physicians evidence-based? *Frontiers in Pharmacology, 8,* 257.

Neubauer, A.B., Smyth, J.M., & Sliwinski, M.J. (2019). Age differences in proactive coping with minor hassles in daily life. *Journals of Gerontology B: Psychological Sciences and Social Sciences, 74*(1), 7-16.

Neugarten, B.L. (1986). The aging society. In A. Pifer & L. Bronte (Eds.), *Our aging society: Paradox and promise*. New York: W.W. Norton.

Neugarten, B.L. (1988, August). *Policy issues for an aging society*. Paper presented at the meeting of the American Psychological Association, Atlanta.

Neugarten, B.L., Havighurst, R.J., & Tobin, S.S. (1968). Personality and patterns of aging. In B.L.

Neugarten (Ed.), *Middle age and aging*. Chicago: University of Chicago Press.

Neugarten, B.L., & Weinstein, K.K. (1964). The changing American grandparent. *Journal of Marriage and the Family, 26,* 199-204.

Neuhauser, H., Adler, C., & Sarganas, G. (2019). Selective blood pressure screening in the young: Quantification of population wide underestimation of elevated blood pressure. *International Journal of Hypertension, 2019,* 2314029.

Neuman, W.L. (2020). *Social science research methods* (8th ed.). Upper Saddle River, NJ: Pearson.

Neupert, S.D., Almeida, D.M., & Charles, S.T. (2007). Age differences in reactivity to daily stressors: The role of personal control. *Journals of Gerontology: Psychological Sciences and Social Sciences, 62B,* P316-P225.

Nevarez, M.D., & others (2010). Associations of early life risk factors with infant sleep duration. *Academic Pediatrics, 10,* 187-193.

Neville, H.J. (2006). Different profiles of plasticity within human cognition. In Y. Munakata & M.H. Johnson (Eds.), *Attention and Performance XXI: Processes of change in brain and cognitive development*. Oxford, UK: Oxford University Press.

Newell, K., Scully, D.M., McDonald, P.V., & Baillargeon, R. (1989). Task constraints and infant grip configurations. *Developmental Psychobiology, 22,* 817-832.

Newton, E.K., & Thompson, R.A. (2010). Parents' views of early social and emotional development: More and less than meets the eye. *Zero to Three, 30*(4), 10-16.

Ng, F.F., Pomerantz, E.M., & Deng C. (2014). Why are Chinese parents more psychologically controlling than American parents? "My child is my report card." *Child Development, 85,* 355-369.

Ng, F.F., & others (2019). The role of mothers' child-based worth in their affective responses to children's performance. *Child Development, 90*(1), e165-e181.

Ng, F. F-Y., & Wang, Q. (2019). Asian and Asian-American parenting. In M.H. Bornstein (Ed.), *Handbook of parenting* (3rd ed.). New York: Elsevier.

Ng, Q.X., & others (2019). A meta-analysis of the effectiveness of yoga-based interventions for maternal depression during pregnancy. *Complementary Therapies in Clinical Practice, 34,* 8-12.

Ng, Y.T., & others (2020, in press). Friendships in old age: Daily encounters and emotional well-being. *Journals of Gerontology B: Psychological Sciences and Social Sciences.*

Nguyen, D.J., & others (2018). Prospective relations between parent-adolescent acculturation conflict and mental health symptoms among Vietnamese American adolescents. *Cultural Diversity and Ethnic Minority Psychology, 24,* 151-161.

Nguyen, L., Murphy, K., & Andrews, G. (2019). Cognitive and neural plasticity in old age: A systematic review of evidence from executive functions cognitive training. *Aging Research Reviews, 53,* 100912.

Nguyen, T.T., & others (2018). Trends for reported discrimination in health care in a national sample of older adults with chronic conditions. *Journal of General Internal Medicine, 33,* 291-297.

Nguyen, T.V. (2018). Developmental effects of androgens in the human brain. *Journal of Neuroendocrinology, 30,* 2.

Ni, Y., & Hasketh, T. (2020, in press). Childhood maltreatment: Experiences and perceptions among Chinese young people. *Journal of Interpersonal Violence.*

NICHD (2019). *SIDS facts*. Retrieved August 4, 2019, from http://www.nichd.nih/gov/sids

NICHD Early Child Care Research Network (2001). Nonmaternal care and family factors in early development: An overview of the NICHD study of Early Child Care. *Journal of Applied Developmental Psychology, 22,* 457-492.

NICHD Early Child Care Research Network (2002). Structure → Process → Outcome: Direct and indirect effects of child care quality on young children's development. *Psychological Science, 13,* 199-206.

NICHD Early Child Care Research Network (2003). Does amount of time spent in child care predict socioemotional adjustment during the transition to kindergarten? *Child Development, 74,* 976-1005.

NICHD Early Child Care Research Network (2004). Type of child care and children's development at 54 months. *Early Childhood Research Quarterly, 19,* 203-230.

NICHD Early Child Care Research Network (2005). Predicting individual differences in attention, memory, and planning in first graders from experiences at home, child care, and school. *Developmental Psychology, 41,* 99-114.

NICHD Early Child Care Research Network (2006). Infant-mother attachment classification: Risk and protection in relation to changing maternal caregiving quality. *Developmental Psychology, 42,* 38-58.

NICHD Early Child Care Research Network (2010). Testing a series of causal propositions relating time spent in child care to children's externalizing behavior. *Developmental Psychology, 46*(1), 1-17.

Nickalls, S. (2012, March 9). Why college students shouldn't online date. *The Tower*. Philadelphia: Arcadia University. Retrieved February 27, 2013, from http://tower.arcadia.edu/?p=754

Nickerson, A.B., & others (2019). Social emotional learning (SEL) practices in schools: Effects on perceptions of bullying victimization. *Journal of School Psychology, 73,* 74-88.

Nicolaisen, M., Thorsen, K., & Eriksen, S.H. (2012). Jump into the void? Factors related to a preferred retirement age: Gender, social interests, and leisure activities. *International Journal of Aging and Human Development, 75,* 239-271.

Nicoteri, J.A., & Miskovsky, M.J. (2014). Revisiting the freshman "15": Assessing body mass index in the first college year and beyond. *Journal of the American Association of Nurse Practitioners, 26,* 220-224.

Niedzwiecka, A., & Tomalski, P. (2015). Gaze-cueing effect depends on facial expression of emotion in 9- to 12-month-old infants. *Frontiers in Psychology, 6,* 122.

Nielsen, T., & others (2019). Early childhood adversity associations with nightmare severity and sleep spindles. *Sleep Medicine, 58,* 57-65.

Nikitin, J., & Freund, A.M. (2019). The adaptation process of aging. In R. Fernandez-Ballesteros & others (Eds.), *Cambridge handbook of successful aging.* New York: Cambridge University Press.

Nimrod, G. (2020, in press). Aging well in the digital age: Technology in processes of selective optimization with compensation. *Journals of Gerontology B: Psychological Sciences and Social Sciences.*

Nisbett, R.E. (2003). *The geography of thought.* New York: Free Press.

Nisbett, R.E., & others (2012). Intelligence: New findings and theoretical developments. *American Psychologist, 67*(2), 130-159.

Nishigori, H., & others (2020, in press). The prevalence and risk factors for postpartum depression symptoms of fathers at one and 6 months postpartum: Birth cohort study of an adjunct study of the Japan Environment & Children's Study. *Journal of Maternal-Fetal and Neonatal Medicine.*

Nishihira, J., & others (2016). Associations between serum omega-3 fatty acid levels and cognitive function among community-dwelling octogenarians in Okinawa, Japan: The KOCOA study. *Journal of Alzheimer's Association, 51,* 857-866.

Nkyekyer, J., & others (2019). The cognitive and psychological effects of auditory training and hearing aids in adults with hearing loss. *Clinical Interventions in Aging, 14,* 123-135.

Noale, M., Limongi, F., & Maggi, S. (2020). Epidemiology of cardiovascular disease in the elderly. *Advances in Experimental Medicine and Biology, 16,* 29-38.

Noce Kirkwood, R., & others (2018). The slowing down phenomenon: What is the age of major gait velocity decline? *Maturitas, 115,* 31-36.

Noel-Miller, C.M. (2013). Former stepparents' contact with their stepchildren after midlife. *Journals of Gerontology B: Psychological Sciences and Social Sciences, 68,* 409-419.

Nolan, L.S., Parks, O.B., & Good, M. (2019). A review of immunomodulating components of maternal breast milk and protection against necrotizing enterocolitis. *Nutrients, 12*(1), E14.

Nolen-Hoeksema, S. (2011). *Abnormal psychology* (5th ed.). New York: McGraw-Hill.

Noll, J.G., & others (2017). Childhood sexual abuse and early timing of puberty. *Journal of Adolescent Health, 60,* 65-71.

Nolte, J., & others (2019). Decision making. In R.J. Sternberg & J. Funke (Eds.), *Introduction to the psychology of thought.* Heidelberg, Germany: Heidelberg University Publishing.

Non, A.L., & others (2020, in press). Optimism and social support predict healthier adult behaviors despite socially disadvantaged childhoods. *International Journal of Behavioral Medicine.*

Nook, E.C., & others (2020, in press). Use of linguistic distancing and cognitive reappraisal strategies during emotion regulation in children, adolescents, and young adults. *Emotion.*

Nordstrom, K., & Wangmo, T. (2018). Caring for elder patients. *Nursing Ethics, 25,* 1004-1016.

Norona, A.N., & Baker, B.L. (2017). The effects of early positive parenting and developmental delay status on child emotion dysregulation. *Journal of Intellectual Disability Research, 61,* 130-143.

Norouzieh, K. (2005). Case management of the dying child. *Case Manager, 16,* 54-57.

Norris, S., Minkowitz, S., & Scharbach, K. (2019). Pediatric palliative care. *Primary Care, 46,* 461-473.

Nosraty, L., Jylha, M., Raittila, T., & Lumme-Sandt, K. (2015). Perceptions by the oldest old of successful aging, Vitality 901 Study. *Journal of Aging Studies, 32,* 50-58.

Nottelmann, E.D., & others (1987). Gonadal and adrenal hormone correlates of adjustment in early adolescence. In R.M. Lerner & T.T. Foch (Eds.), *Biological-psychological interactions in early adolescence.* Hillsdale, NJ: Erlbaum.

Nouchi, R., & others (2016). Small acute benefits of 4 weeks processing speed training games on processing speed and inhibition performance and depressive mood in healthy elderly people: Evidence from a randomized trial. *Frontiers in Aging Neuroscience, 8,* 302.

Nouman, H., & others (2020). Mandatory reporting between legal requirements and personal interpretations: Community healthcare professionals' reporting of child maltreatment. *Child Abuse and Neglect, 101,* 104261.

Nowson, C.A., & others (2018). The impact of dietary factors on indices of chronic disease in older people: A systematic review. *Journal of Nutrition, Health, and Aging, 22,* 282-296.

Nucci, L. (2006). Education for moral development. In M. Killen & J. Smetana (Eds.), *Handbook of moral development.* Mahwah, NJ: Erlbaum.

Nugent, C.N., & Daugherty, J. (2018, May). A demographic, attitudinal, and behavioral profile of cohabiting adults in the United States, 2011-2015. *National Health Statistics Reports, 111,* 1-11.

Nusselder, W.J., & others (2019). Women's excess unhealthy life years: Disentangling the unhealthy life years gap. *European Journal of Public Health, 29*(5), 914-919.

Nutakor, J.A., & others (2020, in press). Relationship between chronic diseases and sleep duration among older adults in Ghana. *Quality of Life Research.*

Nyberg, L., & Pudas, S. (2019). Successful memory aging. *Annual Review of Psychology* (Vol. 71). Palo Alto, CA: Annual Reviews.

Nye, C.D., & Roberts, B.W. (2020, in press). A neo-socioanalytic model of personality development. In B. Baltes (Ed.), *Work over the lifespan.* New York: Elsevier.

Nygard, C-H. (2013). The ability to work peaks in middle age. Interview. Retrieved September 15, 2013, from http://researchandstudy.uta.fi/2013/09/12/the-ability-to-work-peaks-in-middle-age/

Nyman-Carlsson, E., & others (2020, in press). Individual cognitive behavior therapy and combined family/individual therapy for young adults with anorexia nervosa: A randomized controlled trial. *Psychotherapy Research.*

Nystrom, P., & others (2019). Joint attention in infancy and the emergence of autism. *Biological Psychiatry, 86,* 631-638.

O

O'Brien, A.J., Chesla, C.A., & Humphreys, J.C. (2019). Couples' experiences of maternal postpartum depression. *Journal of Obstetric, Gynecologic, and Neonatal Nursing, 48,* 341-350.

O'Brien, J.L., & others (2013). Cognitive training and selective attention in the aging brain: An electrophysiological study. *Clinical Neurophysiology, 124,* 2198-2208.

O'Brien, M., & Moss, P. (2010). Fathers, work, and family policies in Europe. In M.E. Lamb (Ed.), *The father's role in child development* (5th ed.). New York: Wiley.

O'Callaghan, F.V., & others (2010). The link between sleep problems in infancy and early childhood and attention problems at 5 and 14 years: Evidence from a birth cohort study. *Early Human Development, 86,* 419-424.

O'Connell, M.L., Coppinger, T., & McCarthy, A.L. (2020, in press). The role of nutrition and physical activity in frailty: A review. *Clinical Nutrition ESPEN.*

O'Connor, M.F. (2019). Grief: A brief history of research on how body, mind, and brain adapt. *Psychosomatic Medicine, 81,* 731-738.

O'Connor, M.J., & others (2019). Suicide risk in adolescents with fetal alcohol spectrum disorders. *Birth Defects Research, 111,* 822-828.

O'Connor, T.G., & others (2019). Early caregiving predicts attachment representations in adolescence: Findings from two longitudinal studies. *Journal of Child Psychology and Psychiatry, 60,* 944-952.

O'Dell, C. (2013). *Centenarians' secrets: What you can learn from people who've lived 100-plus years.* Retrieved February 20, 2013, from www.caring.com/articles/centenarians-secrets

O'Grady, C., & Smith, K. (2019). Models of language evolution. In S-A. Rueschemeyer & M. Gareth Gaskell (Eds.), *Oxford handbook of psycholinguistics* (2nd ed.). New York: Oxford University Press.

O'Halloran, A.M., & others (2011). Falls and fall efficacy: The role of sustained attention in older adults. *BMC Geriatrics, 11,* 85.

O'Hara, M.W., & McCabe, F. (2013). Postpartum depression: Current status and future directions. *Annual Review of Clinical Psychology* (Vol. 9). Palo Alto, CA: Annual Reviews.

O'Keefe, J.H., Bhatti, S.K., Baiwa, A., Dinicolantonio, J.J., & Lavie, C.J. (2014). Alcohol and cardiovascular health: The dose does make the poison . . . or the remedy. *Mayo Clinic Proceedings, 89,* 382-393.

O'Keeffe, L.M., Greene, R.A., & Kearney, P.M. (2014). The effect of moderate gestational alcohol consumption during pregnancy on speech and language outcomes in children: A systematic review. *Systematic Reviews, 3.*

O'Leary, A.P., & Sloutsky, V.M. (2019). Components of metacognition can function independently across development. *Developmental Psychology, 55,* 315-328.

O'Reilly, M. (2020, in press). Social media and adolescent mental health: The good, the bad, and the ugly. *Journal of Mental Health.*

O'Rourke, K.M., & others (2020, in press). An Australian doula program for socially disadvantaged women: Developing realist evaluation theories. *Women and Birth.*

O'Sullivan, L.F., & others (2019). Plenty of fish in the ocean: How do traits reflecting resiliency moderate adjustment after experiencing a romantic breakup in emerging adulthood? *Journal of Youth and Adolescence, 48,* 949-962.

O'Toole, J.M., & Boylan, G.B. (2019). Quantitative preterm EEG analysis: The need for caution in using modern data science techniques. *Frontiers in Pediatrics, 7,* 174.

Oakes, L.M., & Rakison, D.M. (2020). *Developmental cascades.* New York: Oxford University Press.

Oakley, G.P. (2020, in press). Classifying by cause and preventing many causes of spina bifida and anencephaly. *Pediatric Research.*

Oberle, E., & others (2019). Benefits of extracurricular participation in early adolescence: Associations with peer belonging and mental health. *Journal of Youth and Adolescence, 48,* 2255-2270.

Obler, L.K. (2009). Development in the older years. In J. Berko Gleason (Ed.), *The development of language* (7th ed.). Boston: Allyn & Bacon.

Obradovic, J., Yousafzai, A.K., Finch, J.E., & Rasheed, M.A. (2016). Maternal scaffolding and home stimulation: Key mediators of early intervention effects on children's cognitive development. *Developmental Psychology, 52,* 1409-1421.

Obsuth, I., & others (2020). Patterns of homotypic and heterotypic continuity between ADHD symptoms, externalizing and internalizing problems from age 7 to 15. *Journal of Abnormal Child Psychology, 48,* 223-236.

Occupational Outlook Handbook (2020-2021). Washington, DC: U.S. Department of Labor, Bureau of Labor Statistics.

Ochs, E., & Schieffelin, B. (2008). Language socialization and language acquisition. In P.A. Duff & N.H. Hornberger (Eds.), *Encyclopedia of language and education.* New York: Springer.

OECD (2014). Life satisfaction. *Society at a glance 2014: OECD social indicators.* Paris, France: OECD Publishing.

OECD (2017). *OECD health statistics.* Paris: OECD.

OECD (2017). *Pensions at a glance 2017.* Paris: OECD.

OECD (2017). *Teenage suicide.* Paris: OECD.

OECD (2019). *Marriage and divorce rates.* Paris: OECD.

Offer, D., Ostrov, E., Howard, K.I., & Atkinson, R. (1988). *The teenage world: Adolescents' self-image in ten countries.* New York: Plenum.

Office for National Statistics (2015, January 28). *Families and households: 2014.* London: Author.

Office of Adolescent Health (2020). *Teen Pregnancy Prevention Program.* Washington, DC: U.S. Department of Health and Human Services.

Ogden, C.L., Carroll, M.D., Kit, B.K., & Flegal, K.M. (2012, January). Prevalence of obesity in the United States, 2009-2010. *NCHS Data Brief,* 1-9.

Ogden, C.L., Carroll, M.D., Kit, B.K., & Flegal, K.M. (2014). Prevalence of childhood and adult obesity in the United States, 2011-2012. *JAMA, 311,* 806-814.

Ogden, T., & Hagen, T. (2019). *Adolescent mental health* (2nd ed.). New York: Routledge.

Ogunjimi, A.I., & others (2020, in press). Experience-based perception of vulnerability factors to child sexual abuse by health care professionals in Nigeria: A qualitative approach. *Journal of Interpersonal Violence.*

Oh, S., & others (2017). Prevalence and correlates of alcohol and tobacco use among pregnant women in the United States: Evidence from the NSDUH 205-2014. *Preventive Medicine, 97,* 93-99.

Ohlin, A., & others (2015). Sepsis as a risk factor for neonatal morbidity in extremely preterm infants. *Acta Pediatrica, 104,* 1070-1076.

Okada, K., & others (2014). Comprehensive evaluation of androgen replacement therapy in aging Japanese men with late-onset hypogonadism. *Aging Male, 17,* 72-75.

Oktay-Gur, N., Schultz, A., & Rakoczy, H. (2018). Children exhibit different performance patterns in explicit and implicit theory of mind tasks. *Cognition.*

Okubo, Y., & others (2016). Walking can be more effective than balance in fall prevention among community-dwelling older adults. *Geriatrics and Gerontology International, 16,* 118-125.

Okumu, M., & others (2019). Psychosocial syndemics and sexual risk practices among U.S. adolescents: Findings from the 2017 U.S. Youth Behavioral Survey. *International Journal of Behavioral Medicine, 26,* 297-305.

Okun, M.A., Yeung, E.W., & Brown, S. (2013). Volunteering by older adults and risk of mortality: A meta-analysis. *Psychology and Aging, 28,* 564-577.

Okun-Singer, H., & others (2019). The interplay of emotion and cognition. In A.S. Fox & others (Eds.), *The nature of emotion* (2nd ed.). New York: Oxford University Press.

Olderbak, S., & others (2019). Sex differences in facial emotion perception ability across the lifespan. *Cognition and Emotion, 33,* 579-588.

Olesen, K., Rugulies, R., Rod, N.H., & Bonde, J.P. (2014). Does retirement reduce the risk of myocardial infarction? A prospective registry linkage study of 617,511 Danish workers. *International Journal of Epidemiology, 43,* 160-167.

Olfson, M., & others (2018). Prospective service use and health care costs of Medicaid beneficiaries with treatment-resistant depression. *Journal of Managed Care and Specialty Pharmacy, 24,* 226-236.

Olmstead, S.B., Norona, J.C., & Anders, K.M. (2019). How do college experience and gender differentiate the enactment of hookup scripts among emerging adults? *Archives of Sexual Behavior, 48,* 1769-1783.

Olsavsky, A.L., & others (2020, in press). New fathers' perceptions of dyadic adjustment: The roles of maternal gatekeeping and coparenting closeness. *Family Process.*

Olsen, R., Basu Roy, S., & Tseng, H.K. (2019). The Hispanic health paradox for older Americans: An empirical note. *International Journal of Health Economics and Management, 19,* 33-51.

Olson, B.H., Haider, S.J., Vangjel, L., Bolton, T.A., & Gold, J.G. (2010a). A quasi-experimental evaluation of a breastfeeding support program for low-income women in Michigan. *Maternal and Child Health Journal, 14*(1), 86-93.

Olson, B.H., Horodynski, M.A., Brophy-Herb, H., & Iwanski, K.C. (2010b). Health professionals' perspectives on the infant feeding practices of low-income mothers. *Maternal and Child Health Journal, 14*(1), 75-85.

Olweus, D. (2003). Prevalence estimation of school bullying with the Olweus bully/victim questionnaire. *Aggressive Behavior, 29*(3), 239-269.

Olweus, D. (2013). School bullying: Development and some important challenges. *Annual Review of Clinical Psychology* (Vol. 9). Palo Alto, CA: Annual Reviews.

Onetti, W., Fernandez-Garcia, J.C., & Castillo-Rodriguez, A. (2019). Transition to middle school: Self-concept changes. *PLoS One, 14*(2), e0212640.

Ongley, S.F., & Malti, T. (2014). The role of moral emotions in the development of children's sharing behavior. *Developmental Psychology, 50,* 1148-1159.

Operto, F.F., & others (2019). Cognitive profile, emotional-behavioral features, and parental stress in boys with 47, XYY syndrome. *Cognitive and Behavioral Neurology, 32,* 87-94.

Opfer, J.E., & Gelman, S.A. (2011). Development of the animate-inanimate distinction. In U. Goswami (Ed.), *Wiley-Blackwell handbook of childhood cognitive development* (2nd ed.). New York: Wiley.

Orimaye, S.O., & others (2017). Predicting probable Alzheimer's disease using linguistic deficits and biomarkers. *BMC Bioinformatics, 18*(1), 34.

Ornstein, K.A., & others (2019). Spousal caregivers are caregiving alone in the last years of life. *Health Affairs, 38,* 964-972.

Ornstein, P.A., Coffman, J.L., & Grammer, J.K. (2007, April). *Teachers' memory-relevant conversations and children's memory performance.* Paper presented at the biennial meeting of the Society for Research in Child Development, Boston.

Ornstein, P.A., Coffman, J.L., & Grammer, J.K. (2009). Learning to remember. In O.A. Barbarin & B.H. Wasik (Eds.), *Handbook of child development and early education.* New York: Guilford.

Ornstein, P.A., Coffman, J.L., Grammer, J.K., San Souci, P.P., & McCall, L.E. (2010). Linking the classroom context and the development of children's memory skills. In J. Meece & J. Eccles (Eds.), *Handbook of research on schools, schooling, and human development.* New York: Routledge.

Orosz, G., & others (2015). Elevated romantic love and jealousy if relationship is declared on Facebook. *Frontiers in Psychology, 6,* 214.

Orri, M., & others (2020, in press). Contributions of genes and environment to the longitudinal association between childhood impulsive-aggression and suicidality in adolescence. *Journal of Child Psychology and Psychiatry.*

Ortet, G., & others (2020). Personality and nonjudging make you happier: Contribution of the big-five factor model, mindfulness facets, and a mindfulness intervention to subjective well-being. *PLoS One, 15*(2), e0228655.

Orzabal, M.R., & others (2019). Chronic exposure to e-cig aerosols during early development causes vascular dysfunction and offspring growth deficits. *Translational Research, 14,* 14–20.

Oshika, T., & others (2020, in press). Mid- and long-term clinical assessment of a new single-piece hydrophobic acrylic intraocular lens with hydroxyethyl-methacrylate. *Journal of Cataract and Refractive Surgery.*

Ossher, L., Flegal, K.E., & Lustig, C. (2013). Everyday memory errors in older adults. *Neuropsychology, Development, and Cognition, B: Aging, Neuroscience, and Cognition, 20,* 220–244.

Ossmy, O., & others (2020, in press). Look before you fit: The real-time planning cascade in children and adults. *Journal of Experimental Child Psychology.*

Ostan, R., & others (2016). Gender, aging, and longevity in humans: An update of an intriguing/neglected scenario paving the way to a gender-specific medicine. *Clinical Science, 150,* 1711–1725.

Ostergaard, S.D., & others (2017). Teenage parenthood and birth rates for individuals with and without attention-deficit/hyperactivity disorder: A nationwide cohort study. *Journal of the American Academy of Child and Adolescent Psychiatry, 56,* 578–584.

Ota, M., & Skarabela, B. (2018). Reduplication facilitates early word segmentation. *Journal of Child Language, 45,* 204–218.

Othman, E.A., & others (2020, in press). Hemispheric lateralization of auditory working memory regions during stochastic resonance: An fMRI study. *Journal of Magnetic Resonance Imaging.*

Oudekerk, B.A., Allen, J.P., Hessel, E.T., & Molloy, L.E. (2015). The cascading development of autonomy and relatedness from adolescence to adulthood. *Child Development, 86,* 472–485.

Owens, J.A., Belon, K., & Moss, P. (2010). Impact of delaying school start time on adolescent sleep, mood, and behavior. *Archives of Pediatric and Adolescent Medicine, 164,* 608–614.

Ozturk Donmez, R., & Bayik Temel, A. (2019). Effect of soothing techniques on infants' self-regulation behaviors (sleeping, crying, feeding): A randomized controlled study. *Japanese Journal of Nursing Science, 16,* 407–419.

P

Pace, A., Levine, D.F., Morini, G., Hirsh-Pasek, K., & Golinkoff, R.M. (2016). Language acquisition: From words to world and back again. In L. Balter &

C.S. Tamis-LeMonda (Eds.), *Child psychology: A contemporary handbook* (3rd ed.). New York: Psychology Press.

Padilla-Walker, L.M., & Memmott-Elison, M.K. (2020). Family and moral development. In L.A. Jensen (Ed.), *Oxford handbook of moral development.* New York: Oxford University Press.

Padilla-Walker, L.M., & Nelson, L.J. (2019). Parenting emerging adults. In M.H. Bornstein (Ed.), *Handbook of parenting* (3rd ed.). New York: Elsevier.

Padmanabhanunni, A., & Gerhardt, M. (2019). Normative beliefs as predictors of physical, non-physical, and relational aggression among South African adolescents. *Journal of Child and Adolescent Mental Health, 31*(1), 1–11.

Pados, B.F., & McGlothen-Bell, K. (2019). Benefits of infant massage for infants and parents in the NICU. *Nursing for Women's Health, 23,* 265–271.

Paganini-Hill, A., Kawas, C.H., & Corrada, M.M. (2015). Antioxidant vitamin intake and mortality: The Leisure World Cohort Study. *American Journal of Epidemiology, 181,* 120–126.

Pagiatakis, C., & others (2020, in press). Epigenetics of aging and disease: A brief overview. *Aging: Clinical and Experimental Research.*

Pahor, M., & others (2020, in press). Impact and lessons from the Lifestyle Interventions and Independence for Elders (LIFE) Clinical Trials of Physical Activity to Prevent Mobility Disability. *Journal of the American Geriatrics Society.*

Palacios-Barrios, E.E., & Hanson, J.L. (2019). Poverty and self-regulation: Connecting psychosocial processes, neurobiology, and the risk for psychopathology. *Comprehensive Psychology, 90,* 52–64.

Palermo, T.M. (2014). A brief history of child and adolescent sleep research: Key contributions in psychology. In A.R. Wolfson & E. Montgomery-Downs (Eds.), *Oxford handbook of infant, child, and adolescent sleep and behavior.* New York: Oxford University Press.

Pallini, S., & others (2018). The relation of attachment security status to effortful self-regulation: A meta-analysis. *Psychological Bulletin, 144,* 501–531.

Palmeira, L., & others (2019). Association study of variants in genes FTO, SLC6A4, DRD2, BDNF, and GHRL with binge eating disorder (BED) in Portuguese women. *Psychiatry Research, 273,* 309–311.

Palmer, R.H.C., & others (2019). The etiology of DSM-5 alcohol use disorder: Evidence of shared and non-shared additive genetic effects. *Drug and Alcohol Dependence, 201,* 147–154.

Palmeroni, N., & others (2020, in press). Identity stress throughout adolescence and emerging adulthood: Age trends and associations with exploration and commitment processes. *Emerging Adulthood.*

Palmore, E.B. (2004). Research note: Ageism in Canada and the United States. *Journal of Cross Cultural Gerontology, 19,* 41–46.

Pan, B.A., Rowe, M.L., Singer, J.D., & Snow, C.E. (2005). Maternal correlates of growth in toddler vocabulary production in low-income families. *Child Development, 76,* 763–782.

Pan, B.A., & Uccelli, P. (2009). Semantic development. In J. Berko Gleason & N. Rather (Eds.), *The development of language* (7th ed.). Boston: Allyn & Bacon.

Pan, C.Y., & others (2019). Effects of physical exercise intervention on motor skills and executive functions in children with ADHD: A pilot study. *Journal of Attention Disorders, 23*(4), 384–397.

Pan, H. (2020). Deepening the understanding of complicated grief among Chinese older adults: A network approach. *Asian Journal of Psychotherapy, 50,* 101966.

Pan, Z., & Chang, C. (2012). Gender and the regulation of longevity: Implications for autoimmunity. *Autoimmunity Reviews, 11,* A393–A403.

Panagiotaki, G., & others (2018). Children's and adults' understanding of death: Cognitive, parental, and experiential influences. *Journal of Experimental Child Psychology, 166,* 96–115.

Papastavrou, E., Charlalambous, A., Tsangari, H., & Karayiannis, G. (2012). The burdensome and depressive experience of caring: What cancer, schizophrenia, and Alzheimer's disease caregivers have in common. *Cancer Nursing, 35,* 187–194.

Papernow, P.L. (2018). Clinical guidelines for working with stepfamilies: What family, couple, and child therapists need to know. *Family Process, 57,* 25–51.

Papernow, P.L. (2018). Recoupling in mid-life and beyond: From love at last to not so fast. *Family Process, 57,* 52–69.

Parade, S.H., & others (2018). Family context moderates the association of maternal postpartum depression and stability of infant attachment. *Child Development, 89,* 2118–2135.

Parashar, S., & others (2018). DNA methylation signatures of breast cancer in peripheral T-cells. *BMC Cancer, 18*(1), 574.

Parcianello, R.R., & others (2018). Increased cocaine and amphetamine-regulated transcript cord blood levels in the newborns exposed to crack cocaine in utero. *Psychopharmacology, 235,* 215–222.

Parens, E., & Johnston, J. (2009). Facts, values, and attention-deficit hyperactivity disorder (ADHD): An update on the controversies. *Child and Adolescent Psychiatry and Mental Health, 3,* 1.

Parillo, V.N. (2019). *Strangers to these shores* (12th ed.). Upper Saddle River, NJ: Pearson.

Parish-Morris, J., Golinkoff, R.M., & Hirsh-Pasek, K. (2013). From coo to code: A brief story of language development. In P.D. Zelazo (Ed.), *Oxford handbook of developmental psychology.* New York: Oxford University Press.

Parisi, J.M., & others (2012). The role of education and intellectual activity on cognition. *Journal of Aging Research, 2012,* 416132.

Parisi, J.M., & others (2014). The association between lifestyles and later-life depression. *Activities, Adaptation, and Aging, 38,* 1–10.

Parisi, J.M., & others (2015). Increases in lifestyle activity as a result of Experience Corps participation. *Journal of Urban Health, 92,* 55–66.

Park, C.L. (2007). Religiousness/spirituality and health: A meaning systems perspective. *Journal of Behavioral Medicine, 30,* 319-328.

Park, C.L. (2010). Making sense out of the meaning literature: An integrative review of meaning making and its effect on adjustment to stressful life events. *Psychological Bulletin, 136,* 257-301.

Park, C.L. (2012a). Meaning making in cancer survivorship. In P.T.P. Wong (Ed.), *Handbook of meaning* (2nd ed.). Thousand Oaks, CA: Sage.

Park, C.L. (2012b). Meaning, spirituality, and growth: Protective and resilience factors in health and illness. In A.S. Baum, T.A. Revenson, & J.E. Singer (Eds.), *Handbook of health psychology* (2nd ed.). New York: Sage.

Park, C.L. (2013). Religion and meaning. In R.F. Paloutzian & C.L. Park (Eds.), *Handbook of the psychology of religion* (2nd ed.). New York: Guilford.

Park, C.L. (2016). Meaning making in the context of disasters. *Journal of Clinical Psychology, 72,* 1234-1246.

Park, C.L., Malone, M.R., Suresh, D.P., Bliss, D., & Rosen, R.I. (2008). Coping, meaning in life, and the quality of life in congestive heart failure patients. *Quality of Life Research, 17,* 21-26.

Park, C.L., & others (2016). Spiritual peace predicts 5-year mortality in congestive heart failure patients. *Health Psychology, 35,* 203-210.

Park, D.C. (2001). Commentary in R. Restak, *The secret life of the brain.* Washington, DC: Joseph Henry Press.

Park, D.C., & Festini, S.B. (2018). Cognitive health. In M.H. Bornstein (Ed.), *SAGE encyclopedia of lifespan human development.* Thousand Oaks, CA: Sage.

Park, D.C., & Reuter-Lorenz, P. (2009). The adaptive brain: Aging and neurocognitive scaffolding. *Annual Review of Psychology* (Vol. 60). Palo Alto, CA: Annual Reviews.

Park, D.C., & others (2014). The impact of sustained engagement on cognitive function in older adults: The Synapse Project. *Psychological Science, 25,* 103-112.

Park, M., & others (2018). Maternal depression trajectories from pregnancy to 3 years postpartum are associated with children's behavior and executive functions at 3 and 6 years. *Archives of Women's Mental Health, 21,* 353-363.

Park, M.J., Mulye, T.P., Adams, S.H., Brindis, C.D., & Irwin, C.E. (2006). The health status of young adults in the United States. *Journal of Adolescent Health, 39,* 305-317.

Park, M.J., & others (2014). Adolescent and young adult health in the United States in the past decade: Little improvement and young adults remain worse than adolescents. *Journal of Adolescent Health, 55,* 3-16.

Park, S.H., & others (2013). Sarcopenic obesity as an independent risk factor of hypertension. *Journal of the American Society of Hypertension, 7*(6), 420-425.

Park, Y.M. (2017). Relationship between child maltreatment, suicidality, and bipolarity: A retrospective study. *Psychiatry Investigation, 14,* 136-140.

Parkay, F.W. (2020). *Becoming a teacher* (11th ed.). Upper Saddle River, NJ: Pearson.

Parke, R.D. (2013). *Future families: Diverse forms, rich possibilities.* New York: Wiley Blackwell.

Parke, R.D. (2020). Changing family forms: The implications for children's development. In R.D. Parke & G.H. Elder (Eds.), *Children in changing worlds.* New York: Cambridge University Press.

Parke, R.D., & Buriel, R. (2006). Socialization in the family: Ethnic and ecological perspectives. In W. Damon & R. Lerner (Eds.), *Handbook of child psychology* (6th ed.). New York: Wiley.

Parke, R.D., & Crookston, J.T. (2019). Fathers and families. In M.H. Bornstein (Ed.), *Handbook of parenting* (3rd ed.). New York: Elsevier.

Parke, R.D., & Elder, G.H. (Eds.) (2020). *Children in changing worlds.* New York: Cambridge University Press.

Parke, R.D., Roisman, G.I., & Rose, A.J. (2019). *Social development* (3rd ed.). New York: Wiley.

Parker, C.B. (2016, February 11, 2016). Stanford project suggests longer, healthier lives possible. *Stanford Report,* 1-4.

Parker, H.W., & others (2020, in press). Socio-economic and racial prenatal diet quality disparities in a national U.S. sample. *Public Health Nutrition.*

Parker, S.L., & others (2020, in press). Relaxation during the evening and next-morning energy: The role of hassles, uplifts, and heart rate variability during work. *Journal of Occupational Health Psychology.*

Parkes, A., Green, M., & Mitchell, K. (2019). Coparenting and parenting pathways from the couple relationship to children's behavior problems. *Journal of Family Psychology, 33,* 215-225.

Parkinson, P. (2010). Changing policies regarding separated fathers in Australia. In M.E. Lamb (Ed.), *The role of the father in child development* (5th ed.). New York: Wiley.

Parra-Cardona, J.R., Bulock, L.A., Imig, D.R., Villarruel, F.A., & Gold, S.J. (2006). "Trabajando duro todos los dias": Learning from the life experiences of Mexican-origin migrant families. *Family Relations, 55,* 361-375.

Parrott, A.C., & others (2014). MDMA and heightened cortisol: A neurohormonal perspective on the pregnancy outcomes of mothers who used 'Ecstasy' during pregnancy. *Human Psychopharmacology, 29,* 1-7.

Parsons, K., Rutkowski, E.M., & Turel, O. (2019). Health behavior knowledge among Hispanic California islanders: Evaluation of a parental educational intervention. *Journal for Specialists in Pediatric Nursing, 24*(1), e12235.

Parsons, T.D. (2020). *Ethical challenges in digital psychology and cyberpsychology.* New York: Cambridge University Press.

Partnership for Solutions (2002). *Multiple chronic conditions: Complications in care and treatment.* Baltimore: Johns Hopkins University.

Paschall, K.W., & Mastergeorge, A.M. (2018). A longitudinal, person-centered analysis of Head Start mothers' parenting. *Infant Mental Health, 39,* 70-84.

Pascual-Sagastizabal, E., & others (2019). Testosterone and cortisol modulate the effects of empathy and aggression in children. *Psychoneuroendocrinology, 103,* 118-124.

Pasley, K., & Moorefield, B.S. (2004). Step-families. In M. Coleman & L. Ganong (Eds.), *Handbook of contemporary families.* Thousand Oaks, CA: Sage.

Passuth, P.M., Maines, D.R., & Neugarten, B.L. (1984). *Age norms and age constraints twenty years later.* Paper presented at the annual meeting of the Midwest Sociological Society, Chicago.

Patchin, J.W., & Hinduja, S. (2019). The nature and extent of sexting among a national sample of middle and high school students in the U.S. *Archives of Sexual Behavior, 48,* 2333-2343.

Pate, R.R., & others (2019). Change in children's physical activity: Predictors in the transition from elementary to middle school. *American Journal of Preventive Medicine, 56*(3), e65-e73.

Patel, D.P., Pastuszak, A.W., & Hotaling, J.M. (2019). Emerging treatments for erectile dysfunction: A review of novel, non-surgical options. *Current Urology Reports, 20*(8), 44.

Patel, J., & Bezzina, C.R. (2020). Scientists on the spot: The complex inheritance of cardiac disorders. *Cardiovascular Research, 116*(1), e11.

Patel, K.V., & others (2019). Symptom burden among community-dwelling older adults in the United States. *Journal of the American Geriatrics Society, 67,* 223-231.

Pathman, T., Doydum, A., & Bauer, P.J. (2013). Bringing order to life events: Memory for the temporal order of autobiographical events over an extended period in school-aged children and adults. *Journal of Experimental Child Psychology, 115,* 309-325.

Patterson, C.J. (2019). Lesbian and gay parenthood. In M.H. Bornstein (Ed.), *Handbook of parenting* (3rd ed.). New York: Routledge.

Patterson, G.D., & others (2018). Recurrent acute chest syndrome in pediatric sickle cell disease: Clinical features and risk factors. *Journal of Pediatric Hematology/ Oncology, 40,* 51-55.

Patton, G.C., & others (2011). Overweight and obesity between adolescence and early adulthood: A 10-year prospective study. *Journal of Adolescent Health, 45,* 275-280.

Paul, C. (2019). Emotions and successful aging. In R. Fernandez-Ballesteros & others (Eds.), *Cambridge handbook of successful aging.* New York: Cambridge University Press.

Paul, S., & Corwin, E.J. (2019). Identifying clusters from multidimensional symptom trajectories in postpartum women. *Research in Nursing and Health, 42,* 119-127.

Pauletti, R.E., & others (2017). Psychological androgyny and children's mental health: A new look with new measures. *Sex Roles, 76,* 705-718.

Paulhus, D.L. (2008). Birth order. In M.M. Haith & J.B. Benson (Eds.), *Encyclopedia of infant and early childhood development.* Oxford, UK: Elsevier.

Paunesku, D., & others (2015). Mind-set interventions are a scaleable treatment for academic underachievement. *Psychological Science, 26,* 784-793.

Paus, T., & others (2007). Morphological properties of the action-observation cortical network in adolescents with low and high resistance to peer influence. *Social Neuroscience 3*(3), 303–316.

Paydar, M., & Johnson, A.A. (2020, in press). Dietary intake, physical activity, and metabolic syndrome in African Americans, Hispanics, and Whites. *Journal of the American Medical Association.*

Payer, L. (1991). The menopause in various cultures. In H. Burger & M. Boulet (Eds.), *A portrait of the menopause.* Park Ridge, NJ: Parthenon.

Payne, B.R., & Federmeier, K.D. (2018). Contextual constraints on lexico-semantic processing in aging: Evidence from single-word event-related brain potentials. *Brain Research, 1687,* 117–128.

Payne, J.L., & others (2020, in press). DNA methylation biomarkers prospectively predict both antenatal and postpartum depression. *Psychiatry Research.*

Pearlman, E. (2013). Twin psychological development. Retrieved February 14, 2013, from http://christinabaglivitinglof.com/twin-pregnancy/six-twin-experts-tell-all

Pearson, R.M., & others (2013). Maternal depression during pregnancy and the postnatal period: Risk and possible mechanisms for offspring depression at age 18 years. *JAMA Psychiatry, 70,* 1312–1319.

Pechorro, P., & others (2014). Age of crime onset and psychopathic traits in female juvenile delinquents. *International Journal of Offender Therapy and Comparative Criminology, 58,* 1101–1119.

Peck, T., Scharf, R.J., Conaway, M.R., & DeBoer, M.D. (2015). Viewing as little as 1 hour of TV daily is associated with higher change in BMI between kindergarten and first grade. *Obesity, 23,* 1680–1686.

Pedersen, E.R., & others (2020, in press). Development of a measure to assess protective behavioral strategies for pregaming among young adults. *Substance Use and Abuse.*

Pedersen, M.T., & others (2017). Effect of team sports and resistance training on physical function, quality of life, and motivation in older adults. *Scandinavian Journal of Medicine and Science in Sports, 27,* 852–864.

Peek, M.K. (2009). Marriage in later life. In D. Carr (Ed.), *Encyclopedia of the life course and human development.* Boston: Gale Cengage.

Pei, Y., Cong, Z., & Wu, B. (2020, in press). The impact of living alone and intergenerational support on depressive symptoms among older Mexican Americans: Does gender matter? *International Journal of Aging and Human Development.*

Peitzmeier, S.M., & others (2016). Intimate partner violence perpetration among adolescent males in disadvantaged neighborhoods globally. *Journal of Adolescent Health, 59,* 696–702.

Peixoto, C.E., & others (2017). Interviews of children in a Portuguese special judicial procedure. *Behavioral Sciences & the Law, 35,* 189–203.

Pelton, S.L., & Leibovitz, E. (2009). Recent advances in otitis media. *Pediatric Infectious Disease Journal, 28*(Suppl. 10), S133–S137.

Penas, S., & others (2020, in press). Transnational links and family functioning in reunited Latin American families: Premigration variables' impact. *Cultural Diversity and Ethnic Minority Psychology.*

Penazzi, L., Bakota, L., & Brandt, R. (2016). Microtubule dynamics in neuronal development, plasticity, and neurodegeneration. *International Review of Cell and Molecular Biology, 321,* 89–169.

Pencina, K.M., & others (2019). Trajectories of non-HDL cholesterol across midlife: Implications for cardiovascular protection. *Journal of the American College of Cardiology, 74,* 70–79.

Pennequin, V., & others (2020, in press). Metacognition and emotional regulation in children from 8 to 12 years old. *British Journal of Educational Psychology.*

Peralta, L.R., & others (2019). Influence of school-level socioeconomic status on children's physical activity, fitness, and fundamental movement skills. *Journal of School Health, 90,* 460–467.

Perdue, K.L., & others (2019). Using functional near-infrared spectroscopy to assess social information processing in poor urban Bangladeshi infants and toddlers. *Developmental Science, 22*(5), e12839.

Pereira, C., & others (2018). Effects of a 10-week multimodal exercise program on physical and cognitive function of nursing home residents: A psychomotor intervention pilot study. *Aging: Clinical and Experimental Research, 80,* 471–479.

Pereira-Lancha, L.L., Campos-Ferraz, P.L., & Junior, L.A.H. (2012). Obesity: Considerations about etiology, metabolism, and the use of experimental models. *Diabetes, Metabolic Syndrome, and Obesity, 5,* 75–87.

Perelli-Harris, B., & others (2017). The rise in divorce and cohabitation: Is there a link? *Population and Development Review, 43,* 303–329.

Perez, E.M., & others (2015). Massage therapy improves the development of HIV-exposed infants living in a low socioeconomic, peri-urban community of South Africa. *Infant Behavior and Development, 38,* 135–146.

Perez, H.C.S., & others (2018). Prolonged grief and cognitive decline: A prospective population-based study in middle-aged and older persons. *American Journal of Geriatric Psychiatry, 26,* 451–460.

Perez-Edgar, K.E., & Guyer, A.E. (2014). Behavioral inhibition: Temperament or prodrome? *Current Behavioral Neuroscience Reports, 1,* 182–190.

Perez-Escamilla, R., & Engmann, C. (2019). Integrating nutrition services into health care systems platforms: Where are we and where do we go from here. *Maternal and Child Nutrition, 15*(Suppl. 1), e12743.

Perez-Fuentes, M.D.C., & others (2019). Burnout and engagement: Personality profiles in nursing professionals. *Journal of Clinical Medicine, 8,* 3.

Perez-Sousa, M.A., & others (2020, in press). Effects of an exercise program linked to primary care on depression in the elderly: Fitness as mediator of the improvement. *Quality of Life Research.*

Perkins, S.C., Finegood, E.D., & Swain, J.E. (2013). Poverty and language development: Roles of parenting and stress. *Innovations in Clinical Neuroscience, 10,* 10–19.

Perkisas, S., & Vandewoude, M. (2019). Nutrition and cognition. In R. Fernandez-Ballesteros & others (Eds.), *Cambridge handbook of successful aging.* New York: Cambridge University Press.

Perlman, L. (2008, July 22). Am I an I or We? *Twins,* pp. 1–2.

Perls, T.T. (2007). Centenarians. In J.E. Birren (Ed.), *Encyclopedia of gerontology* (2nd ed.). San Diego: Academic Press.

Perls, T.T. (2009). Health and disease in 85-year-olds: Baseline findings from the Newcastle 851 cohort study. *British Medical Journal, 339,* b4904.

Perls, T.T. (2015, June 8). Commentary in interview with A.M. Miller, "The secret lives of supercentenarians." *U.S. News & World Report,* section on Health.

Perreira, K.M., & others (2019). Stress and resilience: Key correlates of mental health and substance use in the Hispanic Community Health Study of Latino Youth. *Journal of Immigrant and Minority Health, 21,* 4–13.

Perrotte, J.K., & others (2019). Pregaming among Latina/o emerging adults: Do acculturation and gender matter? *Journal of Ethnicity in Substance Abuse, 18,* 535–548.

Perry, N.B., & Calkins, S.D. (2018). Emotion regulation across childhood. In P.M. Cole & T. Hollenstein (Eds.), *Emotion regulation.* New York: Routledge.

Perry, N.B., & others (2018a). Childhood self-regulation as a mechanism through which early overcontrolling parenting is associated with adjustment in preadolescence. *Developmental Psychology, 54,* 1542–1554.

Perry, N.B., & others (2018b). Self-regulation as a predictor of patterns of change in externalizing behaviors from infancy to adolescence. *Development and Psychopathology, 30,* 497–510.

Perry, S.E., & others (2018). *Maternal child nursing care* (6th ed.). New York: Elsevier.

Perry-Jenkins, M., & Schoppe-Sullivan, S. (2019). The transition to parenthood in social context. In B.H. Friese (Ed.), *APA handbook of contemporary family psychology.* Washington, DC: APA Books.

Persky, H.R., Dane, M.C., & Jin, Y. (2003). *The nation's report card: Writing 2002.* Washington, DC: U.S. Department of Education.

Peskin, H. (1967). Pubertal onset and ego functioning. *Journal of Abnormal Psychology, 72,* 1–15.

Pesta, B.J., & others (2019). Does intelligence explain national score variance on graduate admission exams? *Intelligence, 73,* 8–15.

Peter, B., & others (2020, in press). Sequential and spatial letter reversals in adults with dyslexia during a word completion task: Demystifying the "was saw" and "db" myths. *Clinical Linguistics and Phonetics.*

Peters, S.L., Fan, C.L., & Sheldon, S. (2019). Episodic memory contributions to autobiographical memory and open-ended problem-solving specificity in younger and older adults. *Memory and Cognition 47,* 1592–1605.

Petersen, I.T., & others (2012). Interaction between serotonin transporter polymorphism (5-HTTLPR) and stressful life events in adolescents' trajectories of anxious/depressed symptoms. *Developmental Psychology, 48*(5), 1463–1475.

Petersen, J.L., & Hyde, J.S. (2010). A meta-analytic review of research on gender differences in sexuality, 1973–2007. *Psychological Bulletin, 136,* 21–38.

Peterson, C.C., & others (2016). Peer social skills and theory of mind in children with autism, deafness, or typical development. *Developmental Psychology, 52,* 46–57.

Petrangelo, A., & others (2019). Cannabis abuse or dependence during pregnancy: A population-based cohort study on 12 million births. *Journal of Obstetrics and Gynecology Canada.*

Petridou, A., Siopi, A., & Mougios, V. (2019). Exercise in the management of obesity. *Metabolism, 92,* 163–169.

Petroni, M.L., & others (2019). Prevention and treatment of sarcopenic obesity in women. *Nutrients, 11,* 6.

Petrovic, A., & others (2019). Optimization of drug use in older people: A key factor for successful aging. In R. Fernandez-Ballesteros & others (Eds.), *Cambridge handbook of successful aging.* New York: Cambridge University Press.

Petry, N., & others (2017). The proportion of anemia associated with iron deficiency in low, medium, and high human development index countries: A systematic analysis of national surveys. *Nutrients, 49,* 43–52.

Pettis, K.I., & de Lima, L. (2020, in press). Palliative care advocacy: Why does it matter? *Journal of Palliative Medicine.*

Pew Forum on Religion and Public Life (2008). *U.S. religious landscape study.* Washington, DC: Pew Research Center.

Pew Research Center (2010). *Millennials: Confident, connected, open to change.* Washington, DC: Pew Research Center.

Pew Research Center (2012). *Religion and Public Life Project.* Washington, DC: Pew Research.

Pew Research Center (2013). *Social and demographic trends.* Washington, DC: Pew Research Center.

Pew Research Center (2015). *U.S. public becoming less religious.* Washington, DC: Pew Research.

Pew Research Center (2015a, April 20). *Five facts about online dating.* Washington, DC: Author.

Pew Research Center (2015b). *For most highly educated women, motherhood doesn't start until the 30s.* Washington, DC: Pew Research Center.

Pew Research Center (2016). *The gender gap in religion around the world.* Washington, DC: Pew Research.

Pew Research Center (2018). *Where Americans find meaning in life.* Washington, DC: Pew Research.

Peyre, H., & others (2017). Contributing factors and mental health outcomes of first suicide attempt during childhood and adolescence: Results from a nationally representative study. *Journal of Clinical Psychiatry, 78,* e622–e630.

Pfeifer, C.M. (2019). Maternal-fetal medicine specialists should manage patients requiring fetal MRI of the central nervous system. *AJNR. American Journal of Neuroradiology, 40*(2), E6.

Pfeifer, M., Goldsmith, H.H., Davidson, R.J., & Rickman, M. (2002). Continuity and change in inhibited and uninhibited children. *Child Development, 73,* 1474–1485.

Phillipou, A., Castle, D.J., & Russell, S.L. (2019). Direct comparisons of anorexia nervosa and body dysmorphic disorder: A systematic review. *Psychiatry Research, 274,* 129–137.

Phinney, J.S. (2008). Bridging identities and disciplines: Advances and challenges in understanding multiple identities. *New Directions for Child and Adolescent Development, 120 (Special issue: The Intersections of Personal and Social Identities),* 97–109.

Pi, Y.L., & others (2019). Motor skill learning includes brain network plasticity: A diffusion-tensor imaging study. *PLoS One, 14*(2), e0210015.

Piaget, J. (1932). *The moral judgment of the child.* New York: Harcourt Brace Jovanovich.

Piaget, J. (1952). *The origins of intelligence in children* (M. Cook, Trans.). New York: International Universities Press.

Piaget, J. (1954). *The construction of reality in the child.* New York: Basic Books.

Piaget, J. (1962). *Play, dreams, and imitation.* New York: W.W. Norton.

Piaget, J., & Inhelder, B. (1969). *The child's conception of space* (F.J. Langdon & J.L. Lunger, Trans.). New York: W.W. Norton.

Piazza, E.A., & others (2020, in press). Infant and adult brains are coupled to the dynamics of natural communication. *Psychological Science.*

Piazza, J.R., Stawski, R.S., & Sheffler, J.L. (2019). Age, daily stress processes, and allostatic load: A longitudinal study. *Journal of Aging and Health, 31,* 1671–1691.

Picherot, G., & others (2018). Children and screens: Groupe de Pediatrie Generale guidelines for pediatricians and families. *Archives in Pediatrics, 35,* 170–174.

Piedimonte, G., & Harford, T.J. (2020, in press). Effects of maternal-fetal transmission of viruses and other environmental agents on lung development. *Pediatric Research.*

Pieperhoff, P., & others (2008). Deformation field morphometry reveals age-related structural differences between the brains of adults up to 51 years. *Journal of Neuroscience, 28,* 828–842.

Pietromonaco, P.R., & Beck, L.A. (2018). Adult attachment and physical health. *Current Opinion in Psychology, 25,* 115–120.

Pignolo, R.J. (2019). Exceptional human longevity. *Mayo Clinic Proceedings, 94,* 110–124.

Pijl, M.K.J., & others (2019). Temperament as an early risk marker for autism spectrum disorders? A longitudinal study of high-risk and low-risk infants. *Journal of Autism and Developmental Disorders, 49,* 1825–1836.

Pike, A., & Oliver, B.R. (2017). Child behavior and sibling relationship quality: A cross-lagged analysis. *Journal of Family Psychology, 31,* 250–255.

Pinderhughes, E.E., & Brodzinsky, D.M. (2019). Parenting in adoptive families. In M.H. Bornstein (Ed.), *Handbook of parenting* (3rd ed.). New York: Elsevier.

Pinderhughes, E.E., Zhang, X., & Agerbak, S. (2015). "American" or "multiethnic"? Family ethnic identity among transracial adoptive families, ethnic-racial socialization, and children's self-perception. *New Directions in Child and Adolescent Development, 150,* 5–18.

Pinninti, S.G., & Kimberlin, D.W. (2013). Neonatal herpes simplex virus infections. *Pediatric Clinics of North America, 60,* 351–365.

Pino, E.C., & others (2018). Adolescent socioeconomic status and depressive symptoms in later life: Evidence from structural equation models. *Journal of Affective Disorders, 225,* 702–708.

Pinquart, M. (2017). Associations of parenting dimensions and styles with externalizing problems of children and adolescents: An updated meta-analysis. *Developmental Psychology, 53,* 873–932.

Pinquart, M., & Forstmeier, S. (2012). Effects of reminiscence interventions on psychosocial outcomes: A meta-analysis. *Aging and Mental Health, 16,* 541–558.

Pinquart, M., & Kauser, R. (2018). Do the associations of parenting styles with behavior problems and academic achievement vary by culture? Results from a meta-analysis. *Cultural Diversity and Ethnic Minority Psychology, 24,* 75–100.

Pinto, N.M., & others (2020, in press). Physician barriers and facilitators for screening for congenital heart disease with routine obstetric ultrasound: A national United States survey. *Journal of Ultrasound Medicine.*

Pinto, T.M., & others (2020, in press). Depression and paternal adjustment and attitudes during the transition to parenthood. *Journal of Reproductive and Infant Psychology.*

PISA (2015). *PISA 2015: Results in focus.* Paris, France: OECD.

Pittinsky, T.L. (Ed.) (2019). *Science, technology, and society.* New York: Cambridge University Press.

Pizza, V., & others (2011). Neuroinflammatory and neurodegenerative diseases: An overview. *CNS & Neurological Disorders Drug Targets, 10,* 621–634.

Place, S.S., Todd, P.M., Zhuang, J., Penke, L., & Asendorf, J.B. (2012). Judging romantic interest of others from thin slices is a cross-cultural ability. *Evolution & Human Behavior, 335*(5), 547–550.

Platt, B., Kadosh, K.C., & Lau, J.Y. (2013). The role of peer rejection in adolescent depression. *Depression and Anxiety, 30,* 809–821.

Pleck, J.H. (1995). The gender-role strain paradigm. In R.F. Levant & W.S. Pollack (Eds.), *A new psychology of men.* New York: Basic Books.

Plomin, R., DeFries, J.C., McClearn, G.E., & McGuffin, P. (2009). *Behavioral genetics* (5th ed.). New York: W.H. Freeman.

Plourde, K.F., & others (2017). Mentoring interventions and the impact of protective assets on the reproductive health of adolescent girls and young women. *Journal of Adolescent Health, 61,* 131–139.

Plucker, J. (2010, July 19). Commentary in P. Bronson & A. Merryman, The creativity crisis. *Newsweek,* 45–46.

Pluymen, L.P.M., & others (2019). Breastfeeding and cardiovascular markers at age 12: A population-based birth cohort study. *International Journal of Obesity*, 15681.

Podgurski, M.J. (2016). Theorists and techniques: Connecting education theories to Lamaze teaching techniques. *Journal of Perinatal Education, 25*, 9–17.

Poehlmann-Tynan, J., & others (2016). A pilot study of contemplative practices with economically disadvantaged preschoolers: Children's empathic and self-regulatory behaviors. *Mindfulness, 7*, 146–158.

Poey, J.L., Burr, J.A., & Roberts, J.S. (2017). Social connectedness, perceived isolation, and dementia: Does the social environment moderate the relationship between genetic risk and cognitive well-being? *Gerontologist, 57*, 1031–1040.

Polacsek, M., Boardman, G.H., & McCann, T.V. (2020, in press). The influence of a successful wellness-illness transition on the experience of depression in older adults. *Issues in Mental Health Nursing*.

Polenick, C.A., & DePasquale, N. (2019). Predictors of secondary role strains among spousal caregivers of older adults with functional disability. *Gerontologist, 59*, 486–498.

Pollak, S.D., Camras, L.A., & Cole, P.M. (2019). Progress in understanding human emotion. *Developmental Psychology, 55*, 1801–1811.

Pollock, C. (2017, February 14). Study: A quarter of Texas public schools no longer teach sex ed. Retrieved March 27, 2018, from www.texastribune.org/2017/02/14

Pollock, K., & Seymour, J. (2018). Reappraising 'the good death' for populations in the age of aging. *Age and Aging, 47*, 328–330.

Pomerantz, E.M. (2019). *Center for Parent-Child Studies*. Retrieved June 20, 2019, from http://labs.psychology.illinois.edu/cpcs

Pomerantz, E.M., & Grolnick, W.S. (2017). The role of parenting in children's motivation and competence: What underlies facilitative parenting? In A.S. Elliott, C.S. Dweck, and D.S. Yeager (Eds.), *Handbook of competence and motivation* (2nd ed.). New York: Guilford.

Pong, S., & Landale, N.S. (2012). Academic achievement of legal immigrants' children: The roles of parents' pre- and post-immigration characteristics in origin-group differences. *Child Development, 83*, 1543–1559.

Poole, L.A., & others (2018). A randomized controlled trial of the impact of a family-based adolescent depression intervention on both youth and parent mental health outcomes. *Journal of Abnormal Child Psychology, 46*, 169–181.

Poon, K. (2018). Hot and cool executive functions in adolescence: Development and contributions to important developmental outcomes. *Frontiers in Psychology, 8*, 2311.

Poon, L.W., & others (2010). Understanding centenarians' psychosocial dynamics and their contributions to health and quality of life. *Current Gerontology and Geriatrics Research*. doi:10.1155/2010/680657

Poon, L.W., & others (2012). Understanding dementia prevalence among centenarians. *Journals of Gerontology A: Biological Sciences and Medical Sciences, 67*, 358–365.

Popadin, K., & others (2018). Slightly deleterious genomic variants and transcriptome perturbations in Down syndrome embryonic selection. *Genome Research, 28*(1), 1–10.

Popenoe, D. (2009). *The state of our unions 2008. Updates of social indicators: Tables and charts*. Piscataway, NJ: The National Marriage Project.

Popham, W.J. (2020). *Classroom assessment* (9th ed.). Upper Saddle River, NJ: Pearson.

Porcelli, B., & others (2016). Association between stressful life events and autoimmune diseases: A systematic review and meta-analysis of retrospective case-control studies. *Autoimmunity Reviews, 15*, 325–334.

Portnoy, J., & others (2020). Autonomic nervous system activity and callous-unemotional traits in physically maltreated youth. *Child Abuse and Neglect, 101*, 104308.

Posada, G., & Kaloustian, G. (2010). Parent-infant interaction. In J.G. Bremner & T.D. Wachs (Eds.), *Wiley-Blackwell handbook of infant development* (2nd ed.). New York: Wiley.

Posner, M.I. (2018). Developing attention and self-regulation in childhood. In K. Nobre & S. Kastner (Eds.), *Oxford handbook of attention*. New York: Oxford University Press.

Posner, M.I., & Rothbart, M.K. (2007). *Educating the human brain*. Washington, DC: American Psychological Association.

Posner, M.I., & Rothbart, M.K. (2018). Temperament and brain networks of attention. *Philosophical Transactions of the Royal Society of London. Series B: Biological Sciences, 373*, 1744.

Posner, M.I., Rothbart, M.K., Sheese, B.E., & Voelker, P. (2014). Developing attention: Behavioral and brain mechanisms. *Advances in Neuroscience, 2014*, 405094.

Potapova, N.V., Gartstein, M.A., & Bridgett, D.J. (2014). Paternal influences on infant temperament: Effects of father internalizing problems, parent-related stress, and temperament. *Infant Behavior and Development, 37*, 105–110.

Poulain, T., & others (2018). Cross-sectional and longitudinal associations of screen time and physical activity with school performance at different types of secondary school. *BMC Public Health, 18*(1), 563.

Poulin, F., & Pedersen, S. (2007). Developmental changes in gender composition of friendship networks in adolescent girls and boys. *Developmental Psychology, 43*, 1484–1496.

Powell, S.D. (2019). *Your introduction to education* (4th ed.). Upper Saddle River, NJ: Pearson.

Powers, C.J., & Bierman, K.L. (2013). The multifaceted impact of peer relations on aggressive-disruptive behavior in early elementary school. *Developmental Psychology, 49*(6), 1174–1186.

Powers, J.M., & others (2020, in press). Smokers with pain are more likely to report use of e-cigarettes and other nicotine products. *Experimental and Clinical Psychopharmacology*.

Powers, K.E., Chavez, R.S., & Heatherton, T.F. (2016). Individual differences in response of dorsomedial prefrontal cortex predict daily social behavior. *Social Cognitive and Affective Neuroscience, 11*, 121–126.

Poyatos-Leon, R., & others (2017). Effects of exercise-based interventions on post-partum depression: A meta-analysis of randomized controlled trials. *Birth, 44*, 200–208.

Pratt, C., & Bryant, P.E. (1990). Young children understand that looking leads to knowing (so long as they are looking in a single barrel). *Child Development, 61*, 973–982.

Prendergast, L.E., & others (2019). Outcomes of early adolescent sexual behavior in Australia: Longitudinal findings in young adulthood. *Journal of Adolescent Health, 64*, 516–522.

Prenoveau, J.M., & others (2017). Maternal postnatal depression and anxiety and their association with child emotional negativity and behavior problems at two years. *Developmental Psychology, 53*, 50–62.

Pressley, M. (2003). Psychology of literacy and literacy instruction. In I.B. Weiner (Ed.), *Handbook of psychology*. New York: Wiley.

Pressley, M., Mohan, L., Fingeret, L., Reffitt, K., & Raphael-Bogaert, L.R. (2007). Writing instruction in engaging and effective elementary settings. In S. Graham, C.A. MacArthur, & J. Fitzgerald (Eds.), *Best practices in writing instruction*. New York: Guilford.

Pressley, M., Raphael, L., Gallagher, D., & DiBella, J. (2004). Providence-St. Mel School: How a school that works for African-American students works. *Journal of Educational Psychology, 96*, 216–235.

Pressley, M., & others (2003). *Motivating primary-grades teachers*. New York: Guilford.

Price, D.J., & others (2018). *Building brains* (2nd ed.). New York: Wiley.

Prichard, J.R. (2020). Sleep predicts collegiate academic performance: Implications for equity in student retention and success. *Sleep Medicine Clinics, 15*, 59–69.

Prickett, K.C., & Angel, J.L. (2011). The new health care law: How will women near retirement fare? *Women's Health Issues, 21*, 331–337.

Pride, W.M., Hughes, R.J., & Kapoor, J.R. (2019). *Foundations of business* (6th ed.). Boston: Cengage.

Prieur, J., & others (2020, in press). The origins of gestures and language: History, current advances, and proposed theories. *Biological Reviews of the Cambridge Philosophical Society*.

Principe, G., Greenhoot, A.F., & Ceci, S.J. (2014). Young children's eyewitness memory. In D.S. Lindsay & T. Perfect (Eds.), *SAGE handbook of applied memory*. Thousand Oaks, CA: Sage.

Principi, A., & others (2020, in press). What happens to retirement plans, and does this affect retirement satisfaction? *International Journal of Aging and Human Development*,

Prinstein, M.J., & Giletta, M. (2016). Peer relations and developmental psychopathology. In D. Cicchetti (Ed.), *Developmental psychopathology* (3rd ed.). New York: Wiley.

Prinstein, M.J., & others (2018). Peer status and psychopathology. In W.M. Bukowski & others (Eds.), *Handbook of peer interactions, relationships, and groups* (2nd ed.). New York: Guilford.

Proulx, C.M., Curl, A.L., & Ermer, A.E. (2018). Longitudinal associations between formal volunteering and cognitive functioning. *Journals of Gerontology B: Psychological Sciences and Social Sciences, 73*, 522–531.

Provenzi, L., & others (2019). NICU Network Neurobehavioral Scale: 1-month normative data and variation from birth to 1 month. *Pediatric Research, 83*, 1104–1109.

Psouni, E. (2019). The influence of attachment representations and co-parents' scripted knowledge of attachment on fathers' and mothers' caregiving representations. *Attachment and Human Development, 21*, 485–509.

Psychster Inc. (2010). *Psychology of social media.* Retrieved February 21, 2013, from www.psychster.com

Puccini, D., & Liszkowski, U. (2012). 15-month-old infants fast map words but not representational gestures of multimodal labels. *Frontiers in Psychology, 3*, 101.

Pufal, M.A., & others (2012). Prevalence of overweight in children of obese patients: A dietary overview. *Obesity Surgery, 22*(8), 1220–1224.

Pullmer, R., Coelho, J.S., & Zaitsoff, S.L. (2019). Kindness begins with yourself: The role of self-compassion in adolescent body satisfaction and eating pathology. *International Journal of Eating Disorders, 52*, 809–816.

Puma, M., & others (2010). *Head Start impact study. Final report.* Washington, DC: Administration for Children & Families.

Purohit, V., Simeone, D.M., & Lyssiotis, C.A. (2019). Metabolic regulation of redox balance in cancer. *Cancers, 11*, 7.

Putallaz, M., & others (2007). Overt and relational aggression and victimization: Multiple perspectives within the school setting. *Journal of School Psychology, 45*, 523–547.

Putnam Investments (2006). *Survey of the working retired.* Franklin, MA: Putnam Investments.

Puzzanchera, C., & Robson, C. (2014, February). Delinquency cases in juvenile court, 2010. *Juvenile offenders and victims: National Report Series.* Washington, DC: U.S. Department of Justice.

Q

Qi, H., & Roberts, K.P. (2019). Cultural influences on children's memory and cognition. *Advances in Child Development and Behavior, 56*, 183–225.

Qian, X.L., Yamal, C.M., & Almeida, D.M. (2014a). Does leisure time as stress coping resource increase affective complexity? Applying the dynamic model of affect (DMA). *Journal of Leisure Research, 45*, 393–414.

Qian, X.L., Yamal, C.M., & Almeida, D.M. (2014b). Does leisure time moderate or mediate the effect of daily stress on positive affect? An examination using eight-day diary data. *Journal of Leisure Research, 46*, 106–124.

Qian, X.L., Yamal, C.M., & Almeida, D.M. (2014c). Using the dynamic model of affect (DMA) to examine leisure time as a stress coping resource: Taking into account stress severity and gender difference. *Journal of Leisure Research, 46*, 483–505.

Qiao, S., Jiang, Y., & Li, X. (2020, in press). The impact of health promotion interventions on telomere length: A systematic review. *American Journal of Health Promotion.*

Qin, J., & others (2015). Impact of arthritis and multiple chronic conditions on selected life domains—United States, 2013. *MMWR: Morbidity and Mortality Weekly Report, 64*, 578–582.

Qiu, R., & others (2017). Greater intake of fruits and vegetables is associated with greater bone density and lower osteoporosis risk in middle-aged and elderly adults. *PLoS One, 12*(1), e168906.

Qu, Y., Pomerantz, E.M., & Deng, C. (2016). American and Chinese parents' goals for their early adolescents: Content and transmission. *Journal of Research on Adolescence, 26*, 126–141.

Quach, L.T., & Burr, J.A. (2020, in press). Perceived social isolation, social disconnectedness, and falls: The mediating role of depression. *Aging and Mental Health.*

Quashie, N.T., & others (2020, in press). Childlessness and health among older adults: Variation across 5 outcomes and 20 countries. *Journals of Gerontology B: Psychological Sciences and Social Sciences.*

Queiroga, A.C., & others (2020, in press). Secular trend in age at menarche for women in Portugal born 1920 to 1992: Results from three population-based studies. *American Journal of Human Biology.*

Quek, Y.H., & others (2017). Exploring the association between childhood and adolescent obesity and depression: A meta-analysis. *Obesity Reviews, 18*, 742–754.

Quesnel-Vallée, A., Willson, A., & Reiter-Campeau, S. (2016). Health inequalities among older adults in developed countries: Reconciling theories and policy approaches. In L.K. George & K.F. Ferraro (Eds.), *Handbook of aging and the social sciences* (8th ed.). New York: Elsevier.

Quick, N., Erickson, K., & McCright, J. (2019). The most frequently used words: Comparing child-directed speech and young children's speech to inform vocabulary selection for aided input. *Augmentative and Alternative Communication, 35*, 120–131.

Quindry, J.C., & others (2019). Benefits and risks of high-intensity interval training in patients with coronary artery disease. *American Journal of Cardiology, 123*, 1370–1377.

Quinn, P.C. (2016). What do infants know about cats, dogs, and people? Development of a "like-people" representation for non-human animals. In L.L. Freund, S. McCune, L. Esposito, N. Gee, & P. McCardle (Eds.), *The social neuroscience of human-animal interaction.* Washington, DC: American Psychological Association.

Quinn, P.C. (2020, in press). Category formation in infancy. In S. Hupp & others (Eds.), *Encyclopedia of child and adolescent development.* New York: Wiley.

Quinn, P.C., & Bhatt, R.S. (2016). Development of perceptual organization in infancy. In J. Wagemans (Ed.), *Oxford handbook of perceptual organization.* New York: Oxford University Press.

Quinn, P.C., Lee, K., & Pascalis, O. (2019). Face processing in infancy and beyond: The case of social categories. *Annual Review of Psychology, 70.* Palo Alto, CA: Annual Reviews.

Quinn, P.C., Lee, K., & Pascalis, O. (2020, in press). Beyond perceptual development: Infant responding to social categories. In J.B. Benson (Ed.), *Advances in child development and behavior.* New York: Elsevier.

Quinn, P.C., & others (2020). Emotional expressions reinstate recognition of other-race faces in infants following perceptual narrowing. *Developmental Psychology, 56*, 15–27.

Quitmann, J., & others (2019). Quality of life of short-statured children born small for gestational age or idiopathic growth hormone deficiency within 1 year of growth hormone treatment. *Frontiers in Pediatrics, 7*, 164.

R

Rabelais, E., & others (2019). Meaning making and religious engagement among survivors of childhood brain tumors and their caregivers. *Oncology Nursing Forum, 46*, 170–184.

Raby, K.L., & others (2019). The legacy of early abuse and neglect for social and academic competence from childhood to adulthood. *Child Development, 90*(5), 1684–1701.

Rachwani, J., Hoch, J.E., & Adolph, K.E. (2020). Action in development: Variability, flexibility, and plasticity. In C.S. Tamis-LeMonda & J.J. Lochman (Eds.), *Handbook of infant development.* New York: Cambridge University Press.

Rachwani, J., Santamaria, V., Saavedra, S.L., & Woollacott, M.H. (2015). The development of trunk control and its relation to reaching in infancy: A longitudinal study. *Frontiers in Human Neuroscience, 9*, 94.

Radvansky, G.A. (2018). *Human memory.* New York: Elsevier.

Rageliene, T., & Granhoj, A. (2020). The influence of peers' and siblings' on children and adolescents' healthy eating behavior: A systematic literature review. *Appetite, 148*, 104592.

Raglan, G.B., Schulkin, J., & Micks, E. (2020). Depression during perimenopause: The role of the obstetrician-gynecologist. *Archives of Women's Mental Health, 23*(1), 1–10.

Raikes, H., & others (2006). Mother-child bookreading in low-income families: Correlates and outcomes during the first three years of life. *Child Development, 77*, 924–953.

Raikes, H.A., Virmani, E.A., Thompson, R.A., & Hatton, H. (2013). Declines in peer conflict from preschool through first grade: Influences from early attachment and social information processing. *Attachment and Human Development, 15*(1), 65–82.

Raikes, H.A., & others (2019). Non-parental caregiving. In M.H. Bornstein (Ed.). *Handbook of parenting* (3rd ed.). New York: Elsevier.

Rajan, V., & others (2019). Novel word learning at 21 months predicts receptive vocabulary outcomes in later childhood. *Journal of Child Language, 46,* 617–631.

Rajaraman, P., & others (2011). Early life exposure to diagnostic radiation and ultrasound scans and risk of childhood cancer: Case-control study. *British Medical Journal, 342,* d472.

Rajeh, A., & others (2017). Interventions in ADHD: A comparative review of stimulant medications and behavioral therapies. *Asian Journal of Psychiatry, 25,* 131–135.

Rajeshwari, R., & others (2019). New multitarget hybrids bearing tacrine and phenylbenzothiazole motifs as potential drug candidates for Alzheimer's disease. *Molecules, 24,* 3.

Rajtar-Zembaty, A., & others (2019). Slow gait as a motor marker of mild cognitive impairment? The relationships between functional mobility and mild cognitive impairment. *Neuropsychology, Development, and Cognition: Section B, Aging, Neuropsychology, and Cognition, 26,* 521–530.

Rakesh, D., Fernando, K.B., & Mansour, L.S. (2020, in press). Functional dedifferentiation of the brain during healthy aging. *Journal of Neurophysiology.*

Raketic, D., & others (2017). Five-factor model personality profiles: The differences between alcohol and opiate addiction among females. *Psychiatria Danubina, 29,* 74–80.

Rakison, D.H., & Lawson, C.A. (2013). Categorization. In P. Zelazo (Ed.), *Oxford handbook of developmental psychology.* New York: Oxford University Press.

Rakoczy, H. (2012). Do infants have a theory of mind? *British Journal of Developmental Psychology, 30,* 59–74.

Ram, K.T., & others (2008). Duration of lactation is associated with lower prevalence of the metabolic syndrome in midlife—SWAN, the study of women's health across the nation. *American Journal of Obstetrics and Gynecology, 198,* e1–e6.

Ramchandani, P.G., & others (2013). Do early father-infant interactions predict the onset of externalizing behaviors in young children? Findings from a longitudinal cohort study. *Journal of Child Psychology and Psychiatry, 54,* 56–64.

Ramey, S.L. (2005). Human developmental science serving children and families: Contributions of the NICHD study of early child care. In NICHD Early Child Care Research Network (Eds.), *Child care and development.* New York: Guilford.

Ramirez-Esparza, N., Garcia-Sierra, A., & Kuhl, P.K. (2017). The impact of early social interactions on later language development in Spanish-English bilingual infants. *Child Development, 85,* 1216–1234.

Ramirez-Granizo, I.A., & others (2020). Multidimensional self-concept depending on levels of resilience and the motivational climate directed toward sport in schoolchildren. *International Journal of Environmental Research and Public Health, 17,* 2.

Ramos, A.M., & others (2019). Did I inherit my moral compass? Examining socialization and evocative mechanisms for virtuous character development. *Behavior Genetics, 49,* 175–186.

Ramus, F., & others (2018). Neuroanatomy of developmental dyslexia: Pitfalls and promise. *Neuroscience and Biobehavioral Review, 84,* 434–452.

Ranger, M., & Grunau, R.E. (2015). How do babies feel pain? *eLife, 4,* e07552.

Rangey, P.S., & Sheth, M. (2014). Comparative effect of massage therapy versus kangaroo mother care on body weight and length of hospital stay in low birth weight infants. *International Journal of Pediatrics, 2014,* 434060.

Rankin, J. (2017). *Physiology in childbearing* (4th ed.). New York: Elsevier.

Rao, W.W., & others (2020, in press). Prevalence of prenatal and postpartum depression in fathers: A comprehensive meta-analysis of observational surveys. *Journal of Affective Disorders.*

Rapee, R.M. (2014). Preschool environment and temperament as predictors of social and nonsocial anxiety disorders in middle adolescence. *Journal of the American Academy of Child and Adolescent Psychiatry, 53,* 320–328.

Raphiphatthana, B., Jose, P., & Slamon, K. (2018). Does dispositional mindfulness predict the development of grit? *Journal of Individual Differences, 29,* 76–87.

Rasing, S.P.A., & others (2020, in press). Depression and anxiety symptoms in female adolescents: Relations with parental psychopathology and parenting behavior. *Journal of Research on Adolescence.*

Rasulo, D., Christensen, K., & Tomassini, C. (2005). The influence of social relations on mortality in later life: A study on elderly Danish twins. *Gerontologist, 45,* 601–608.

Rathnayake, N., & others (2018). Cross cultural adaptation and analysis of psychometric properties of Sinhala version on Menopause Rating Scale. *Health and Quality of Life Outcomes, 16*(1), 161.

Rathunde, K., & Csikszentmihalyi, M. (2006). The developing person: An experiential perspective. In W. Damon & R. Lerner (Eds.), *Handbook of child psychology* (6th ed.). New York: Wiley.

Raver, C.C., & others (2008). Improving preschool classroom processes: Preliminary findings from a randomized trial implemented in Head Start settings. *Early Childhood Research Quarterly, 23,* 10–26.

Raver, C.C., & others (2011). CSRP's impact on low-income preschoolers' preacademic skills: Self-regulation as a mediating mechanism. *Child Development, 82,* 362–378.

Raver, C.C., & others (2012). Testing models of children's self-regulation within educational contexts: Implications for measurement. *Advances in Child Development and Behavior, 42,* 245–270.

Raver, C.C., & others (2013). Predicting individual differences in low-income children's executive control from early to middle childhood. *Developmental Science, 16,* 394–408.

Ray, J., & others (2017). Callous-unemotional traits predict self-reported offending in adolescent boys: The mediating role of delinquent peers and the moderating role of parenting practices. *Developmental Psychology, 53,* 319–328.

Razaz, N., & others (2016). Five-minute Apgar score as a marker for developmental vulnerability at 5 years of age. *Archives of Disease in Childhood: Fetal and Neonatal Edition, 101,* F114–F120.

Razmetaeva, Y., & Sydorenko, O. (2020). Euthanasia in the digital age: Medical and legal issues and challenges. *Georgian Medical News, 298,* 175–180.

Razza, R.A., Martin, A., & Brooks-Gunn, J. (2012). The implications of early attentional regulation for school success among low-income children. *Journal of Applied Developmental Psychology, 33,* 311–319.

Reaney, M.J. (2020). *The place of play in education.* New York: Routledge.

Reardon, K.W., & others (2020, in press). Relational aggression and narcissistic traits: How youth personality pathology informs aggressive behavior. *Journal of Personality Disorders.*

Recksiedler, C., & others (2018). Social dimensions of personal growth following widowhood: A three-wave study. *Gerontology, 64,* 344–366.

Recode (2016, June 27). *You are still watching a staggering amount of TV every day.* Retrieved March 6, 2018, from https://www.recode.net/2016/6/27/12041028/tv-hours-per-week-nielsen

Redline, S., & others (2004). The effects of age, sex, ethnicity, and sleep-disordered breathing on sleep architecture. *Archives of Internal Medicine, 164,* 406–418.

Redwine, L.S., & others (2020). An exploratory randomized sub-study of light-to-moderate intensity exercises on cognitive function, depression symptoms, and inflammation in older adults with heart failure. *Journal of Psychosomatic Research, 128,* 109883.

Reed, A.E., & Carstensen, L.L. (2015). Age-related positivity effect and its implications for social and health gerontology. In N.A. Pachana (Ed.), *Encyclopedia of geropsychology.* New York: Springer.

Reed, S.D., & others (2014). Menopausal quality of life: RCT of yoga, exercise, and omega-3 supplements. *American Journal of Obstetrics and Gynecology, 210,* 244.e1–244.e14.

Rees, M., & others (2018). Joint opinion paper—"Aging and sexual health" by the European Board & College of Obstetrics and Gynecology (EBCOG) and the European Menopause and Andropause Society (EMAS). *European Journal of Obstetrics, Gynecology, and Reproductive Biology, 200,* P132–P134.

Reese, B.M., Haydon, A.A., Herring, A.H., & Halpern, C.T. (2013). The association between sequences of sexual initiation and the likelihood of teenage pregnancy. *Journal of Adolescent Health, 52,* 228–233.

Reese, E., & Robertson, S.J. (2019). Origins of adolescents' earliest memories. *Memory, 27,* 79–91.

Reeve, C.L., & Charles, J.E. (2008). Survey of opinions on the primacy of g and social consequences of ability testing: A comparison of expert and non-expert views. *Intelligence, 36,* 681–688.

Regev, R.H., & others (2003). Excess mortality and morbidity among small-for-gestational-age premature infants: A population-based study. *Journal of Pediatrics, 143,* 186–191.

Reibis, R.K., Treszi, A., Wegscheider, K., Ehrlich, B., Dissmann, R., & Voller, H. (2010). Exercise capacity is the most powerful predictor of 2-year mortality in patients with left ventricular systolic dysfunction. *Herz, 35,* 104–110.

Reichlin Cruse, L., & others (2019). *Parents in college: By the numbers.* Aspen, CO: Ascend at the Aspen Institute.

Reichstadt, J., Depp, C.A., Palinkas, L.A., Folsom, D.P., & Jeste, D.V. (2007). Building blocks of successful aging: A focus group study of older adults' perceived contributors to successful aging. *American Journal of Geriatric Psychiatry, 15,* 194–201.

Reid, A., & others (2019). Cultural values and romantic relationship satisfaction in Mexican adolescents: The moderating effect of parental psychological control and gender. *Journal of Adolescence, 77,* 118–128.

Reid, P.T., & Zalk, S.R. (2001). Academic environments: Gender and ethnicity in U.S. higher education. In J. Worell (Ed.), *Encyclopedia of women and gender.* San Diego: Academic Press.

Reilly, D. (2012). Gender, culture, and sex-typed cognitive abilities. *PLoS One, 7*(7), e39904.

Reilly, D., & Neumann, D.L. (2013). Gender-role differences in spatial ability: A meta-analytic review. *Sex Roles, 68,* 521–535.

Reis, S.M., & Renzulli, J.S. (2020). Intellectual giftedness. In R.J. Sternberg (Ed.), *Cambridge handbook of intelligence.* New York: Cambridge University Press.

Reisman, A.S. (2001). Death of a spouse: Basic assumptions and continuation of bonds. *Death Studies, 25,* 445–460.

Reitz, R. (2019). Creating a culture of intrinsic motivation. *Family Practice Management, 26*(2), 36.

Rejeski, W.J., & others (2017). Community weight loss to combat obesity and disability in at-risk older adults. *Journals of Gerontology A: Biological Sciences and Medical Sciences, 72,* 1547–1553.

Remmart. J.E., & others (2020, in press). Breastfeeding practices among women living with HIV in KwaZulu-Natal, South Africa: An observational study. *Maternal and Child Health Journal.*

Ren, H., & others (2017). Excessive homework, inadequate sleep, physical inactivity, and screen viewing time are major contributors to high pediatric obesity. *Acta Pediatrica, 106,* 120–127.

Renz, M., & others (2013). Dying is a transition. *American Journal of Hospice and Palliative Care, 30,* 283–290.

Repacholi, B.M., & Gopnik, A. (1997). Early reasoning about desires: Evidence from 14- and 18-month-olds. *Developmental Psychology, 33,* 12–21.

Repacholi, B.M., & Meltzoff, A.N. (2019). The web of emotion understanding in infants. In A.S. Fox & others (Eds.), *The nature of emotion* (2nd ed.). New York: Oxford University Press.

Reproductive Endocrinology and Infertility Committee & others (2012). Advanced reproductive age and fertility. *International Journal of Gynecology and Obstetrics, 117,* 95–102.

Resende, E.P.F., & others (2020, in press). Language and spatial dysfunction in Alzheimer disease with white matter thorn-shaped astrocytes: Astrocytic tau, cognitive function, and Alzheimer disease. *Neurology.*

Reuter, P.R., Forster, B.L., & Brister, S.R. (2020, in press). The influence of eating habits on the academic performance of university students. *Journal of American College Health.*

Reuter-Lorenz, P.A., & Lustig, C. (2017). Working memory and executive functions in the aging brain. In R. Cabeza, L. Nyberg, & D.C. Park (Eds.), *Cognitive neuroscience of aging* (2nd ed.). New York: Oxford University Press.

Reutzel, D.R., & Cooter, R.B. (2019). *Teaching children to read* (8th ed.). Upper Saddle River, NJ: Pearson.

Reyna, V.F. (2004). How people make decisions that involve risk: A dual-process approach. *Current Directions in Psychological Science, 13,* 60–66.

Reyna, V.F. (2018). Neurobiological models of risky decision-making and adolescent substance use. *Current Addiction Reports, 5,* 128–133.

Reyna, V.F., & Mills, B.A. (2014). Theoretically motivated interventions for reducing sexual risk taking in adolescence: A randomized controlled experiment applying fuzzy-trace theory. *Journal of Experimental Psychology: General, 143,* 1627–1648.

Reyna, V.F., & Rivers, S.E. (2008). Current theories of risk and rational decision making. *Developmental Review, 28,* 1–11.

Reyna, V.F., Wilhelms, E.A., McCormick, M.J., & Weldon, R.B. (2015). Development of risky decision making: Fuzzy-trace theory and neurobiological perspectives. *Child Development Perspectives, 9,* 122–127.

Reyna, V.F., & others (2016). How fuzzy-trace theory predicts true and false memories for words, sentences, and narratives. *Journal of Applied Research in Memory and Cognition, 5,* 1–9.

Reyna, V.F., & others (2017). The fuzzy-trace dual-process model. In W. De Neys (Ed.), *Dual process theory 2.0.* New York: Taylor & Francis.

Reynard, L.N., & Barter, M.J. (2020, in press). Osteoarthritis year in review 2019: Genetics, genomics, and epigenetics. *Osteoarthritis and Cartilage.*

Reynolds, A.J., Ou, S.R., & Temple, J.A. (2018). A multicomponent, preschool to third grade prevention intervention and educational attainment at 35 years of age. *JAMA Pediatrics, 17*(3), 247–256.

Reynolds, C.F., Lenze, E., & Mulsant, B.H. (2019). Assessment and treatment of major depression in older adults. *Handbook of Clinical Neurology, 167,* 429–435.

Rhie, Y.J., & others (2019). Long-term safety and effectiveness of growth hormone therapy in Korean children with growth disorders: 5-year results of LG Growth Study. *PLoS One, 14*(5), e0216927.

Rhoades, G.K., Kamp Dusch, C.M., Atkins, D.C., Stanley, S.M., & Markman, H.J. (2011). Breaking up is hard to do: The impact of unmarried relationship dissolution on mental health and life satisfaction. *Journal of Family Psychology 25,* 366–374.

Rhodes, M., & Brandone, A.C. (2014). Three-year-olds' theories of mind in actions and words. *Frontiers in Psychology, 5,* 263.

Rhodes, R.E., & Katz, B. (2017). Working memory plasticity and aging. *Psychology and Aging, 32,* 51–59.

Rhodes, S., & others (2019). Storage and processing in working memory: Assessing dual-task performance and task prioritization across the adult lifespan. *Journal of Experimental Psychology: General, 148,* 1204–1227.

Ribeiro, O., & Araujo, L. (2019). Defining "success" in exceptional longevity. In R. Fernandez-Ballesteros & others (Eds.), *Cambridge handbook of successful aging.* New York: Cambridge University Press.

Ribeiro-Accioly, A.C.L., & others (2020, in press). Maternal sensitivity in interactions with their 2-month-old infants in Rio de Janeiro, Brazil. *Attachment and Human Development.*

Ricci, N.A., & Cunha, A.I.L. (2020). Physical exercise for frailty and cardiovascular diseases. *Advances in Experimental Medicine and Biology, 16,* 115–129.

Richards, E.L., & others (2018). Alcohol intake and cognitively healthy longevity in community-dwelling adults: The Rancho Bernardo study. *Journal of Alzheimer's Disease, 59,* 803–814.

Richards, J., & others (2015). Don't worry, be happy: Cross-sectional associations between physical activity and happiness in 15 European countries. *BMC Public Health, 15*(1), 53.

Richards, J.E. (2009). Attention to the brain in infancy. In S. Johnson (Ed.), *Neuroconstructivism: The new science of cognitive development.* New York: Oxford University Press.

Richards, J.E. (2010). Infant attention, arousal, and the brain. In L.M. Oakes, C.H. Cashon, M. Casasola, & D.H. Rakison (Eds.), *Infant perception and cognition.* New York: Oxford University Press.

Richards, J.E. (2013). Cortical sources of ERP in the prosaccade and antisaccade task using realistic source models. *Frontiers in Systems Neuroscience, 7,* 27.

Richards, J.E., Boswell, C., Stevens, M., & Vendemia, J.M. (2015). Evaluating methods for constructing average high-density electrode positions. *Brain Topography, 28,* 70–86.

Richards, J.E., Reynolds, G.D., & Courage, M.I. (2010). The neural bases of infant attention. *Current Directions in Psychological Science, 19,* 41–46.

Richards, J.E., & Xie, W. (2015). Brains for all the ages: Structural neurodevelopment in infants and children from a life-span perspective. *Advances in Child Development and Behavior, 48,* 1–52.

Richardson, G.A., Goldschmidt, L., Leech, S., & Willford, J. (2011). Prenatal cocaine exposure: Effects on mother- and teacher-rated behavior problems and growth in school-aged children. *Neurotoxicology and Teratology, 33,* 69–77.

Richardson, G.A., Goldschmidt, L., & Willford, J. (2008). The effects of prenatal cocaine use on infant development. *Neurotoxicology and Teratology, 30,* 96–106.

Richardson, G.A., & others (2019). Prenatal cocaine exposure: Direct and indirect associations with

21-year-old offspring substance use and behavior problems. *Drug and Alcohol Dependence, 195,* 121–131.

Richardson, M.S., & Schaeffer, C. (2013). From work and family to a dual model of working. In D.L. Blustein (Ed.), *Oxford handbook of the psychology of working.* New York: Oxford University Press.

Richardson, V.E. (2007). A dual process model of grief counseling: Findings from the Changing Lives of Older Couples (CLOC) study. *Journal of Gerontological Social Work, 48,* 311–329.

Richler, J.J., & others (2019). Individual differences in object recognition. *Psychological Review, 126,* 226–251.

Richter, C.P., & others (2018). Fluvastatin protects cochleae from damage by high-level noise. *Scientific Reports, 8*(1), 3033.

Riddle, V., Dagenais, C., & Daigneault, I. (2019). It's time to address sexual violence in academic global health. *BMJ Global Health, 4*(2), e001616.

Rideout, V., Foehr, U.G., & Roberts, D.P. (2010). *Generation M: Media in the lives of 8- to 18-year-olds.* Menlo Park, CA: Kaiser Family Foundation.

Riekkola, J., & others (2019). Healthcare professionals' perspective on how to promote older couples' participation in everyday life when using respite care. *Scandinavian Journal of Caring Science, 33,* 427–435.

Riemann, D. (2019). Sleep deprivation/sleep restriction and shift work. *Sleep Health, 28*(3), e12879.

Riesco-Matias, P., & others (2019, January 15). What do meta-analyses have to say about the efficacy of neurofeedback applied to children with ADHD? Review of previous meta-analyses and a new meta-analysis. *Journal of Attention Disorders,* 1087054718821731.

Riglin, L., & others (2020, in press). Using genetics to examine a general liability to childhood psychopathology. *Behavior Genetics.*

Rijnders, M., & others (2019). Women-centered care: Implementation of CenteringPregnancy in the Netherlands. *Birth, 46,* 450–460.

Riley, K.P., Snowdon, D.A., Derosiers, M.F., & Markesbery, W.R. (2005). Early life linguistic ability, late life cognitive function, and neuropathology: Findings from the Nun Study. *Neurobiology of Aging, 26,* 341–347.

Ringe, D. (2019). *An introduction to grammar for language learners.* New York: Cambridge University Press.

Rink, J. (2020). *Teaching physical education for learning* (8th ed.). New York: McGraw-Hill.

Riva Crugnola, C., Ierardi, E., Gazzotti, S., & Albizzati, A. (2014). Motherhood in adolescent mothers: Maternal attachment, mother-infant styles of interaction, and emotion regulation at three months. *Infant Behavior and Development, 37,* 44–56.

Robert, C., & Mathey, S. (2018). The oral and written side of word production in young and older adults: Generation of lexical neighbors. *Neuropsychology, Development, and Cognition B: Aging, Neuropsychology, and Cognition, 25*(2), 231–243.

Roberto, K.A., & Skoglund, R.R. (1996). Interactions with grandparents and great grandparents: A comparison of activities, influences, and relationships. *International Journal of Aging and Human Development, 43,* 107–117.

Roberto, K.A., & Weaver, R.H. (2019). Late-life families. In B.H. Friese (Ed.), *APA handbook of contemporary family psychology.* Washington, DC: APA Books.

Roberts, B.W., & Damian, R.I. (2018). The principles of personality trait development and their relation to psychopathology. In D. Lynam & D. Samuel (Eds.), *Using basic personality research to inform the personality disorders.* New York: Oxford University Press.

Roberts, B.W., Edmonds, G., & Grijalva, E. (2010). It is developmental me, not generation me: Developmental changes are more important than generational changes in narcissism. Commentary on Trzesniewski & Donnellan (2010). *Perspectives on Psychological Science,* 97–102.

Roberts, B.W., & Hill, P.L. (2017). The sourdough bread model of conscientiousness. In J. Burrus & others (Eds.), *Building better students: Preparation for the workforce.* New York: Oxford University Press.

Roberts, B.W., & Mroczek, D. (2008). Personality trait change in adulthood. *Current Directions in Psychological Science, 17,* 31–35.

Roberts, B.W., & Nickel, L.B. (2020). Personality development across the life course: A neo-socioanalytic perspective. In O.P. John & R.W. Robins (Eds.), *Handbook of personality theory and research.* New York: Guilford.

Roberts, B.W., Walton, K.E., & Bogg, T. (2005). Conscientiousness and health across the life course. *Review of General Psychology, 9,* 156–168.

Roberts, B.W., Walton, K.E., & Viechtbauer, W. (2006). Patterns of mean-level change in personality traits across the life course. A meta-analysis of longitudinal studies. *Psychological Bulletin, 132,* 1–25.

Roberts, B.W., & Wood, D. (2006). Personality development in the context of the neo-socioanalytic model of personality. In D. Mroczek & T. Little (Eds.), *Handbook of personality development.* Mahwah, NJ: Erlbaum.

Roberts, B.W., & others (2017). A systematic review of personality trait change through intervention. *Psychological Bulletin, 143,* 117–141.

Robin, N., & others (2020, in press). Beneficial influence of mindfulness training promoted by text messages on self-reported aerobic physical activity in older adults: A randomized controlled study. *Journal of Aging and Physical Activity.*

Robine, J-M. (2019). Successful aging and the longevity revolution. In R. Fernandez-Ballesteros & others (Eds.), *Cambridge handbook of successful aging.* New York: Cambridge University Press.

Robins, R.W., Trzesniewski, K.H., Tracey, J.L., Potter, J., & Gosling, S.D. (2002). Age differences in self-esteem from age 9 to 90. *Psychology and Aging, 17,* 423–434.

Robinson, A., & Lachman, M.E. (2017). Perceived control and aging: A mini-review and directions for future research. *Gerontology, 63,* 435–442.

Robinson, L.C., Barat, O., & Mellott, J.G. (2019). GABAergic and glutamatergic cells in the inferior colliculus dynamically express the GABA ARγ1 subunit during aging. *Neurobiology of Aging, 80,* 99–110.

Robinson, S.A., & Lachman, M.E. (2017). Perceived control and aging: A mini-review and directions for future research. *Gerontology, 63,* 435–442.

Robinson, S.A., Rickenbach, E.H., & Lachman, M.E. (2016). Self-regulatory strategies in daily life: Selection, optimization, and compensation and everyday memory problems. *International Journal of Behavioral Development, 40,* 126–136.

Roblyer, M.D., & Hughes, J.E. (2019). *Integrating technology into teaching* (8th ed.). Upper Saddle River, NJ: Pearson.

Rochlen, A.B., McKelley, R.A., Suizzo, M-A., & Scaringi, V. (2008). Predictors of relationship satisfaction, psychological well-being, and life-satisfaction among stay-at-home fathers. *Psychology of Men and Masculinity, 9,* 17–28.

Rode, S.S., Chang, P., Fisch, R.O., & Sroufe, L.A. (1981). Attachment patterns of infants separated at birth. *Developmental Psychology, 17,* 188–191.

Rodgers, R.F., & others (2020). A biopsychosocial model of social media use and body image concerns, disordered eating, and muscle-building behaviors among adolescent boys and girls. *Journal of Youth and Adolescence, 49,* 399–409.

Rodin, J., & Langer, E.J. (1977). Long-term effects of a control-relevant intervention with the institutionalized aged. *Journal of Personality and Social Psychology, 35,* 397–402.

Rodriguez, E.T., & others (2009). The formative role of home literacy experiences across the first three years of life in children from low-income families. *Journal of Applied Developmental Psychology, 30*(6), 677–694.

Rodriguez, R.M.D. (2019). Rapid-eye-movement sleep behavior disorder: A book review. *Sleep Science, 12,* 122–123.

Rodriguez-Meirinhos, A., & others (2020). When is parental monitoring effective? A person-centered analysis of the role of autonomy-supportive and psychologically controlling parenting in referred and non-referred adolescents. *Journal of Youth and Adolescence, 49,* 352–368.

Rodriguez Villar, S., & others (2012). Prolonged grief disorder in the next of kin of adult patients who die during or after admission to intensive care. *Chest, 141,* 1635–1636.

Rodrique, K.M., & Kennedy, K.M. (2011). The cognitive consequences of structural changes to the aging brain. In K.W. Schaie & S.L. Willis (Eds.), *Handbook of the psychology of aging* (7th ed.). New York: Elsevier.

Roese, N.J., & Summerville, A. (2005). What we regret most . . . and why. *Personality and Social Psychology Bulletin, 31,* 1273–1285.

Roeser, R.W. (2016). Beyond all splits: Mindfulness in students' motivation, learning, and self-identity at school. In K.R. Wentzel & D.B. Miele (Eds.), *Handbook of motivation at school.* New York: Routledge.

Roeser, R.W., & Eccles. J.S. (2015). Mindfulness and compassion in human development: Introduction to the special section. *Developmental Psychology, 51,* 1–6.

Roeser, R.W., & Pinela, C. (2014). Mindfulness and compassion training in adolescence: A developmental contemplative science perspective. *New Directions in Youth Development, 142,* 9–30.

Roeser, R.W., & Zelazo, P.D. (2012). Contemplative science, education and child development. *Child Development Perspectives, 6,* 143–145.

Roeser, R.W., & others (2014). Contemplative education. In L. Nucci & others (Eds.), *Handbook of moral and character education.* New York: Routledge.

Rogers, E.E., & Hintz, S.R. (2016). Early neurodevelopmental outcomes of extremely preterm infants. *Seminars in Perinatology, 40,* 479–509.

Roggman, L.A., & others (2016). Home visit quality variations in two Early Head Start programs in relation to parenting and child vocabulary outcomes. *Infant Mental Health Journal, 37,* 193–207.

Rogoff, B. (2003). *The cultural nature of human development.* New York: Oxford University Press.

Rohner, R.P., & Melendez-Rhodes, T. (2019). Perceived acceptance-rejection mediates or moderates the relation between corporal punishment and psychological adjustment. Comment on Gershoff et al. (2018). *American Psychologist, 74,* 500–502.

Rohr, M.K., & others (2017). A three-component model of future time perspective across adulthood. *Psychology and Aging, 32,* 597–607.

Roisman, G.I., & Cicchetti, D. (2017). Attachment in the context of atypical caregiving: Harnessing insights from developmental psychopathology. *Development and Psychopathology, 29,* 331–335.

Roisman, G.I., & Groh, A.M. (2011). Attachment theory and research in developmental psychology: An overview and appreciative critique. In M.K. Underwood & L.H. Rosen (Eds.), *Social development.* New York: Wiley.

Rojo-Wissar, D.M., & others (2020, in press). Parent-child relationship quality and sleep among adolescents: Modification by race/ethnicity. *Sleep Health.*

Rolland, B., & others (2016). Pharmacotherapy for alcohol dependence: The 2015 recommendations of the French Alcohol Society, issued in partnership with the European Federation of Addiction Societies. *CNS Neuroscience and Therapeutics, 22,* 25–37.

Rolland, Y., & others (2011). Treatment strategies for sarcopenia and frailty. *Medical Clinics of North America, 95,* 427–438.

Romero, A., & others (2020). Disentangling relationships between bicultural stress and mental well-being among Latinx immigrant adolescents. *Journal of Consulting and Clinical Psychology, 88,* 149–159.

Romero-Ortuno, R., Kenny, R.A., & McManus, R. (2020). Collagens and elastin genetic variations and their potential role in aging-related diseases and longevity in humans. *Experimental Gerontology, 129,* 110781.

Romo, D.L., & others (2017). Social media use and its association with sexual risk and parental monitoring among a primarily Hispanic adolescent population. *Journal of Pediatric and Adolescent Gynecology, 30,* 466–473.

Ronnlund, M., & others (2013). Secular trends in cognitive test performance: Swedish conscript data, 1970–1993. *Intelligence, 41,* 19–24.

Roos, L.L., Wall-Wieler, E., & Lee, J.B. (2020, in press). Poverty and early childhood outcomes. *Pediatrics.*

Rose, A.J., Carlson, W., & Waller, E.M. (2007). Prospective associations of co-rumination with friendship and emotional adjustment: Considering the socioemotional trade-offs of co-rumination. *Developmental Psychology, 43,* 1019–1031.

Rose, A.J., & Smith, R.L. (2018). Gender and peer relationships. In W.M. Bukowski & others (Eds.), *Handbook of peer interactions, relationships, and groups* (2nd ed.). New York: Guilford.

Rose, A.J., & others (2017). Co-rumination exacerbates stress generation among adolescents with depressive symptoms. *Journal of Abnormal Child Psychology, 45,* 985–995.

Rose, S.A., Feldman, J.F., & Jankowski, J.J. (2015). Pathways from toddler information processing to adolescent lexical proficiency. *Child Development, 86,* 1935–1947.

Roseberry, S., Hirsh-Pasek, K., & Golinkoff, R. (2014). Skype me! Socially contingent interactions help toddlers learn language. *Child Development, 85,* 956–970.

Rose-Clarke, K., & others (2019). Peer-facilitated community-based interventions for adolescent health in low- and middle-income countries: A systematic review. *PLoS One, 14*(1), e-210468.

Rosen, R.C., & others (2017). Quality of life and sexual function benefits of long-term testosterone treatment: Longitudinal results from the Registry of Hypogonadism in Men (RHYME). *Journal of Sexual Medicine, 14,* 1104–1115.

Rosenblith, J.F. (1992). *In the beginning* (2nd ed.). Newbury Park, CA: Sage.

Rosenfeld, A., & Stark, E. (1987, May). The prime of our lives. *Psychology Today,* pp. 62–72.

Rosengren, K.S., Gutierrez, I.T., & Schein, S.S. (2014a). Cognitive dimensions of death in context. In K.S. Rosengren & others (Eds.), Children's understanding of death: Toward a contextualized and integrative account. *Monographs of the Society for Research in Child Development, 79*(1), 62–82.

Rosengren, K.S., Gutierrez, I.T., & Schein, S.S. (2014b). Cognitive models of death. In K.S. Rosengren & others (Eds.), Children's understanding of death: Toward a contextualized and integrative account. *Monographs of the Society for Research in Child Development, 79*(1), 83–96.

Rosenson, R.S., Hegele, R.A., & Koenig, W. (2019). Cholesterol-lowering agents. *Circulation Research, 124,* 364–385.

Rosenstein, D., & Oster, H. (1988). Differential facial responses to four basic tastes in newborns. *Child Development, 59,* 1555–1568.

Rosmarin, D.H., Krumrei, E.J., & Andersson, G. (2009). Religion as a predictor of psychological distress in two religious communities. *Cognitive Behavior Therapy, 38,* 54–64.

Ross, J., Hutchison, J., & Cunningham, S.J. (2020, in press). The me in memory: The role of the self in autobiographical memory development. *Child Development.*

Ross, L.A., Schmidt, E.L., & Ball, K. (2013). Interventions to maintain mobility: What works? *Accident Analysis and Prevention, 61,* 167–196.

Ross, L.A., & others (2016). The transfer of cognitive speed of process training to older adults' driving mobility across 5 years. *Journals of Gerontology B: Psychological Sciences and Social Sciences, 71,* 87–97.

Ross, N.D., Kaminski, P.L., & Herrington, R. (2019). From childhood emotional maltreatment to depressive symptoms in adulthood: The roles of self-compassion and shame. *Child Abuse and Neglect, 92,* 32–42.

Ross, V., & others (2018). Parents' experiences of suicide-bereavement: A qualitative study at 6 and 12 months after loss. *International Journal of Environmental Research and Public Health, 15,* 4.

Rosselli, M., & others (2019). Effects of bilingualism on verbal and nonverbal memory measures in mild cognitive impairment. *Journal of the International Neuropsychology Society, 25,* 15–26.

Rossi, A.S. (1989). A life-course approach to gender, aging, and intergenerational relations. In K.W. Schaie & C. Schooler (Eds.), *Social structure and aging.* Hillsdale, NJ: Erlbaum.

Rossler, W., & others (2017). Sleep disturbances in young and middle-aged adults—Empirical patterns and related factors from an epidemiological survey. *Comprehensive Psychiatry, 78,* 83–90.

Rossom, R.C., & others (2019). Are wishes for death or suicidal ideation symptoms of depression in older adults? *Aging and Mental Health, 23,* 912–918.

Rostamian, S., & others (2015). Executive function, but not memory, associates with incident coronary heart disease and stroke. *Neurology, 85,* 783–789.

Rostamzadeh, D., & others (2019). mTOR signaling pathway as a master regulator of memory CD81 T-cells, Th17, and NK cells development and their functional properties. *Journal of Cellular Physiology, 234,* 12353–12368.

Rotenberg, J., & others (2018). Home-based primary care: Beyond extension of the independence at home demonstration. *Journal of the American Geriatrics Society, 66,* 812–817.

Roth, A.R., & Canedo, A.R. (2019). Introduction to hospice and palliative care. *Primary Care, 46,* 287–302.

Roth, B., & others (2015). Intelligence and school grades: A meta-analysis. *Intelligence, 52,* 118–137.

Rothbart, M.K. (2004). Temperament and the pursuit of an integrated developmental psychology. *Merrill-Palmer Quarterly, 50,* 492–505.

Rothbart, M.K. (2007). Temperament, development, and personality. *Current Directions in Psychological Science, 16,* 207–212.

Rothbart, M.K. (2011). *Becoming who we are.* New York: Guilford.

Rothbart, M.K., & Bates, J.E. (2006). Temperament. In W. Damon & R. Lerner (Eds.), *Handbook of child psychology* (6th ed.). New York: Wiley.

Rothbart, M.K., & Gartstein, M.A. (2008). Temperament. In M.M. Haith & J.B. Benson (Eds.), *Encyclopedia of infant and early childhood development.* Oxford, UK: Elsevier.

Rothbart, M.K., & Posner, M. (2015). The developing brain in a multitasking world. *Developmental Review, 35,* 42–63.

Rothbaum, F., Poll, M., Azuma, H., Miyake, K., & Welsz, J. (2000). The development of close relationships in Japan and the United States: Paths of symbiotic harmony and generative tension. *Child Development, 71,* 1121–1142.

Rothman, K., & others (2020, in press). Sexual assault among women in college: Immediate and long-term associations with mental health, psychological functioning, and romantic relationships. *Journal of Interpersonal Violence.*

Rotman, S.A., & others (2020, in press). Family encouragement of healthy eating habits predicts child dietary intake and weight loss in family-based behavioral weight-loss treatment. *Childhood Obesity.*

Roushandeh, A.M., Kuwahara, Y., & Roudkenar, M.H. (2019). Mitochondrial transplantation as a potential and novel master key for treatment of various incurable diseases. *Cytotechnology, 71*(2), 647–663.

Rovee-Collier, C. (1987). Learning and memory in children. In J.D. Osofsky (Ed.), *Handbook of infant development* (2nd ed.). New York: Wiley.

Rovee-Collier, C. (2009). The development of infant memory. In N. Cowan & M. Courage (Eds.), *The development of memory in infancy and childhood* (2nd ed.). Hove, UK: Psychology Press.

Rovee-Collier, C., & Barr, R. (2010). Infant learning and memory. In U.J.G. Bremner & T.D. Wachs (Ed.), *Wiley-Blackwell handbook of infant development* (2nd ed.). New York: Wiley.

Rowe, A.C., Gold, E.R., & Carnelley, K.B. (2020, in press). The effectiveness of attachment security priming in improving positive affect and reducing negative affect: A systematic review. *International Journal of Environmental Research and Public Health.*

Rowe, J.W., & others (2019). Challenges for middle-income elders in a changing society. *Health Affairs, 38,* 1–5.

Rowland, B., & others (2020, in press). A cross-national comparison of the development of adolescent problem behavior: A 1-year longitudinal study in India, the Netherlands, the USA, and Australia. *Prevention Science.*

Rozycka, A., & Liguz-Lecznar, M. (2017). The space where aging acts: Focus on the GABAergic synapse. *Aging Cell, 16,* 634–643.

Rozzini, R., Ranhoff, A., & Trabucchi, M. (2007). Alcoholic beverage and long-term mortality in elderly people living at home. *Journals of Gerontology A: Biological Sciences and Medical Sciences, 62,* M1313–M1314.

Ruba, A.L., Melzoff, A.N., & Repacholi, B.R. (2019). How do you feel? Preverbal infants match negative emotions to events. *Developmental Psychology, 55,* 1138–1149.

Rubin, A., Parrish, D.E., & Miyawaki, C.E. (2019). Benchmarks for evaluating life review and reminiscence therapy in alleviating depression among older adults. *Social Work, 64,* 61–72.

Rubin, K.H., Bukowski, W.M., & Bowker, J. (2015). Children in peer groups. In R.M. Lerner (Ed.), *Handbook of child psychology and developmental science* (7th ed.). New York: McGraw-Hill.

Rubin, K.H., Bukowski, W.M., & Parker, J. (2006). Peer interactions, relationships, and groups. In W. Damon & R. Lerner (Eds.), *Handbook of child psychology* (6th ed.). New York: Wiley.

Rubin, K.H., & others (2018). Avoiding and withdrawing from the peer group. In W.M. Buksowski & others (Eds.), *Handbook of peer interaction, relationships, and groups.* New York: Guilford.

Rubio-Fernandez, P. (2017). Why are bilinguals better than monolinguals at false-belief tasks? *Psychonomic Bulletin and Review, 24,* 987–998.

Rubio-Ruiz, M.E., & others (2019). Mechanisms underlying syndrome-related sarcopenia and possible therapeutic measures. *International Journal of Molecular Science, 20,* 3.

Ruble, D. (1983). The development of social comparison processes and their role in achievement-related self-socialization. In E. Higgins, D. Ruble, & W. Hartup (Eds.), *Social cognitive development: A social-cultural perspective.* New York: Cambridge University Press.

Rudolph, K.D., Troop-Gordon, W., Lambert, S.F., & Natsuaki, M.N. (2014). Long-term consequences of pubertal timing for youth depression: Identifying personal and contextual pathways of risk. *Development and Psychopathology, 26,* 1423–1444.

Rueda, M.R., Posner, M.I., & Rothbart, M.K. (2005). The development of executive attention: Contributions to the emergence of self-regulation. *Developmental Neuropsychology, 28,* 573–594.

Ruffman, T. (2014). To belief or not belief: Children's theory of mind. *Developmental Review, 34,* 265–293.

Ruisch, I.H., & others (2018). Maternal substance use during pregnancy and offspring conduct problems: A meta-analysis. *Neuroscience and Biobehavioral Reviews, 84,* 325–336.

Ruiz, L.D., & Scherr, R.E. (2018). Risk of energy drink consumption to adolescent health. *American Journal of Lifestyle Medicine, 13,* 22–25.

Ruiz-Casares, M., & others (2017). Parenting for the promotion of adolescent mental health: A scoping review of programs targeting ethnoculturally diverse families. *Health & Social Care in the Community, 25,* 743–757.

Rumberger, R.W. (1983). Dropping out of high school: The influence of race, sex, and family background. *American Educational Research Journal, 20,* 194–220.

Runco, M.A., & Acar, S. (2019). Divergent thinking. In J.C. Kaufman & R.J. Sternberg (Eds.), *Cambridge handbook of creativity* (2nd ed.). New York: Cambridge University Press.

Rupp, D.E., Vodanovich, S.J., & Crede, M. (2005). The multidimensional nature of ageism: Construct validity and group differences. *Journal of Social Psychology, 145,* 335–362.

Russell, V.M., Baker, L.R., & McNulty, J.K. (2013). Attachment insecurity and infidelity in marriage: Do studies of dating relationships inform us about marriage? *Journal of Family Psychology, 27,* 242–251.

Russo-Netzer, P., & Moran, G. (2018). Positive growth from adversity and beyond: Insights gained from cross-examination of clinical and non-clinical samples. *American Journal of Orthopsychiatry, 88,* 59–68.

Ryan, A.M., & Shin, H. (2018). Peers, academics, and teachers. In W.M. Bukowski & others (Eds.), *Handbook of peer interactions, relationships, and groups* (2nd ed.). New York: Guilford.

Ryan, R.M., & Deci, E.L. (2019, May, 22). *Self-determination theory.* Plenary talk at the International Self-Determination Theory conference, Amsterdam.

Ryan, R.M., & Padilla, C.M. (2019). Transition to parenting. In M.H. Bornstein (Ed.), *Handbook of parenting* (3rd ed.). New York: Routledge.

Ryff, C.D. (1984). Personality development from the inside: The subjective experience of change in adulthood and aging. In P.B. Baltes & O.G. Brim (Eds.), *Life-span development and behavior.* New York: Academic Press.

Rypma, B., Eldreth, D.A., & Rebbechi, D. (2007). Age-related differences in activation-performance relations in delayed-response tasks: A multiple component analysis. *Cortex, 43,* 65–76.

Ryskina, K.L., Lam, C., & Jung, H.Y. (2019). Association between clinician specialization in nursing home care and nursing home clinical quality scores. *Journal of the American Medical Directors Association, 20,* 1007–1012.

S

Saad, L. (2014). The "40-hour" workweek is actually longer—by seven hours. Washington, DC: Gallup.

Saajanaho, M., & others (2014). Older women's personal goals and exercise activity: An eight-year follow-up. *Journal of Aging and Physical Activity, 22,* 386–392.

Saarni, C. (1999). *The development of emotional competence.* New York: Guilford.

Saarni, C., Campos, J., Camras, L.A., & Witherington, D. (2006). Emotional development. In W. Damon & R. Lerner (Eds.), *Handbook of child psychology* (6th ed.). New York: Wiley.

Sabbagh, M.A., Xu, F., Carlson, S.M., Moses, L.J., & Lee, K. (2006). The development of executive functioning and theory of mind: A comparison of Chinese and U.S. preschoolers. *Psychological Science, 17,* 74–81.

Sabir, M., Henderson, C.R., Kang, S.Y., & Pillemer, K. (2016). Attachment-focused integrative reminiscence with older African Americans: A randomized controlled intervention study. *Aging and Mental Health, 20,* 517–528.

Sacco, S.J., Leahey, T.M., & Park, C.L. (2019). Meaning-making and quality of life in heart failure interventions: A systematic review. *Quality of Life Research, 28*, 557–565.

Sackett, P.R., Borneman, M.J., & Connelly, B.S. (2009). Responses to issues raised about validity, bias, and fairness in high-stakes testing. *American Psychologist, 64*, 285–287.

Sadatpoor, S.O., & others (2020, in press). Manipulated mesenchymal stem cells applications in neurodegenerative diseases. *International Journal of Stem Cells.*

Sadeghi, B., & others (2019). A three-year multifaceted intervention to prevent obesity in children of Mexican-heritage. *BMC Public Health, 19*(1), 582.

Sadeh, A. (2008). Sleep. In M.M. Haith & J.B. Benson (Eds.), *Encyclopedia of infant and early childhood development*. Oxford, UK: Elsevier.

Sadeh, A., & others (2015). Infant sleep predicts attention regulation and behavior problems at 3–4 years of age. *Developmental Neuropsychology, 40*, 122–137.

Saeed, O.B., Haile, Z.T., & Chertok, I.A. (2020, in press). Association between exclusive breastfeeding and infant health outcomes in Pakistan. *Journal of Pediatric Nursing.*

Saez de Urabain, I.R., Nuthmann, A., & Johnson, M.H. (2017). Disentangling the mechanisms underlying infant fixation durations in scene perception: A computational account. *Vision Research, 134*, 43–59.

Safa, M.D., & others (2019). U.S. Mexican-origin adolescents' bicultural competence and mental health in context. *Cultural Diversity and Ethnic Minority Psychology, 25*, 299–310.

Saffran, J.R., & Kirkham, N.Z. (2018). Infant statistical learning. *Annual Review of Psychology* (Vol. 69). Palo Alto, CA: Annual Reviews.

Saisanen, L., & others (2019). Functional and structural symmetry in primary motor cortex in Asperger syndrome: A navigated TMS and imaging study. *Brain Topography, 32*, 504–518.

Saito, Y., & others (2020). Cognitive performance among older persons in Japan and the United States. *Journal of the American Geriatrics Society, 68*, 354–361.

Sakreida, K., & others (2019). Phonological picture-word interference in language mapping with transcranial magnetic stimulation: An objective approach for functional parcellation of Broca's area. *Brain, Structure, and Function, 224*, 2027–2044.

Saleh, L. (2019). Women's perceived quality of care and self-reported empowerment with CenteringPregnancy versus individual prenatal care. *Nursing for Women's Health, 23*, 234–244.

Salhi, L., & Bergstrom, Z.M. (2020, in press). Intact strategic retrieval processes in older adults: No evidence for age-related deficits in source-constrained retrieval. *Memory.*

Saling, L.L., Laroo, N., & Saling, M.M. (2012). When more is less: Failure to compress discourse with re-telling in normal aging. *Acta Psychologica, 139*, 220–224.

Salminen, A. (2020). Activation of immunosuppressive network in the aging process. *Aging Research Reviews, 57*, 100998.

Salmivalli, C., & Peets, K. (2018). Bullying and victimization. In W.M. Bukowski & others (Eds.), *Handbook of peer interactions, relationships, and groups* (2nd ed.). New York: Guilford.

Salthouse, T.A. (1994). The nature of influence of speed on adult age differences in cognition. *Developmental Psychology, 30*, 240–259.

Salthouse, T.A. (2009). When does age-related cognitive decline begin? *Neurobiology of Aging, 30*, 507–514.

Salthouse, T.A. (2012). Consequences of age-related cognitive declines. *Annual Review of Psychology* (Vol. 63). Palo Alto, CA: Annual Reviews.

Salthouse, T.A. (2013a). Executive functioning. In D.C. Park & N. Schwartz (Eds.), *Cognitive aging* (2nd ed.). New York: Psychology Press.

Salthouse, T.A. (2013b). Within-cohort age-related differences in cognitive functioning. *Psychological Science, 24*, 123–130.

Salthouse, T.A. (2014). Why are there different age relations in cross-sectional and longitudinal comparisons of cognitive functioning? *Current Directions in Psychological Science, 23*, 252–256.

Salthouse, T.A. (2016). Aging cognition unconfounded by prior test experiences. *Journals of Gerontology B: Psychological Sciences and Social Sciences, 71*, 49–58.

Salthouse, T.A. (2017). Neural correlates of age-related slowing. In R. Cabeza, L. Nyberg, & D.C. Park (Eds.), *Cognitive neuroscience of aging* (2nd ed.). New York: Oxford University Press.

Salthouse, T.A. (2017). Shared and unique influences on age-related cognitive change. *Neuropsychology, 31*, 11–19.

Salthouse, T.A. (2018). Why is cognitive change more negative with increased age? *Neuropsychology, 32*, 110–120.

Salthouse, T.A. (2019). Comparable consistency, coherence, and commonality of measures of cognitive functioning across adulthood. *Assessment, 26*, 726–736.

Salthouse, T.A., & Skovronek, E. (1992). Within-context assessment of working memory. *Journal of Gerontology, 47*, P110–P117.

Salvatore, J.E., Kuo, S.I., Steele, R.D., Simpson, J.A., & Collins, W.A. (2011). Recovering from conflict in romantic relationships: A developmental perspective. *Psychological Science, 22*, 376–383.

Salzberg, S.L., & others (2018). Open questions: How many genes do we have? *BMC Biology, 816*, 94.

Salzwedel, A.P., & others (2016). Thalamocortical functional connectivity and behavioral disruptions in neonates with prenatal cocaine exposure. *Neurotoxicology and Teratology, 56*, 16–25.

Samek, A., & others (2020). The development of social comparisons and sharing behavior across 12 countries. *Journal of Experimental Child Psychology, 192*, 104778.

Sampathkumar, N.K., & others (2020). Widespread sex dimorphism in aging and age-related diseases. *Human Genetics, 139*, 333–356.

Sananpanichkul, P., & others (2019). Possible role of court-type Thai traditional massage during parturition: A randomized controlled trial. *International Journal of Therapeutic Massage and Bodywork, 12*, 23–28.

Sanders, K.E., & Guerra, A.W. (Eds.) (2016). *The culture of child care*. New York: Oxford University Press.

Sanders, W., Parent, J., & Forehand, R. (2018). Parenting to reduce child screen time: A feasibility pilot study. *Journal of Developmental and Behavioral Pediatrics, 39*, 46–54.

Sandler, I., & others (2017). *Evidence-based programs: Family Bereavement Program.* Retrieved September 9, 2017, from https://reachinstitute.asu.edu/programs/family-bereavement

Sandler, L., & others (2018). Three perspectives on mental health problems of young adults and their parents at a 15-year follow-up of the family bereavement program. *Journal of Consulting and Clinical Psychology, 88*, 845–855.

Sanfilippo, J.S., & others (2020). *Sanfilippo's textbook of pediatric and adolescent gynecology* (2nd ed.). New York: Routledge.

Sanglier, T., Saragoussi, D., Milea, D., & Tournier, M. (2015). Depressed older adults may be less cared for than depressed younger ones. *Psychiatry Research, 229*, 905–912.

Sangree, W.H. (1989). Age and power: Life-course trajectories and age structuring of power relations in East and West Africa. In D.I. Kertzer & K.W. Schaie (Eds.), *Age structuring in comparative perspective*. Hillsdale, NJ: Erlbaum.

Sanson, A., & Rothbart, M.K. (1995). Child temperament and parenting. In M.H. Bornstein (Ed.), *Handbook of parenting* (Vol. 4). Hillsdale, NJ: Erlbaum.

Santacreu, M., Rodriguez, A., & Molina, M.A. (2019). Behavioral health. In R. Fernandez-Ballesteros & others (Eds.), *Cambridge handbook of successful aging*. New York: Cambridge University Press.

Santelli, J., & others (2017). Abstinence-only-until-marriage: An updated review of U.S. policies and programs for their impact. *Journal of Adolescent Health, 61*, 273–280.

Santiago-Ortiz, A. (2019). From critical to decolonizing service-learning: Limits and possibilities of social-justice based approaches to community service-learning. *Michigan Journal of Community Service Learning, 25*, 43–54.

Santrock, J.W., Sitterle, K.A., & Warshak, R.A. (1988). Parent-child relationships in stepfather families. In P. Bronstein & C.P. Cowan (Eds.), *Fatherhood today: Men's changing roles in the family*. New York: Wiley.

Sanyaolu, A., & others (2020, in press). Childhood and adolescent obesity in the United States: A public health concern. *Global Pediatric Health.*

Sapp, S. (2010). What have religion and spirituality to do with aging? Three approaches. *Gerontologist, 50*, 271–275.

Sarant, J., & others (2020). The effect of hearing aid use on cognition in older adults: Can we delay decline or even improve cognitive function? *Journal of Clinical Medicine, 9,* 1.

Sarchiapone, M., & others (2014). Hours of sleep in adolescents and its association with anxiety, emotional concerns, and suicidal ideation. *Sleep Medicine, 15,* 248-254.

Sardinha, L.B., & others (2016). Fitness but not weight status is associated with projected physical dependence in older adults. *Age, 38*(3), 54.

Sartor, C.E., Hipwell, A.E., & Chung, T. (2020, in press). Public and private religious involvement and initiation of alcohol, cigarette, and marijuana use in Black and White adolescent girls. *Social Psychiatry and Psychiatric Epidemiology.*

Satorres, E., & others (2018). Effectiveness of instrumental reminiscence intervention on improving coping in healthy older adults. *Stress and Health, 34,* 227-234.

Sattler, F.A., Eickmeyer, S., & Eisenkolb, J. (2020, in press). Body image disturbance in children and adolescents with anorexia nervosa and bulimia nervosa: A systematic review. *Eating and Weight Disorders.*

Sauber-Schatz, E.K., & others (2014). Vital signs: Restraint use and motor vehicle occupant death rates among children aged 0-12—United States, 2002-2011. *MMWR: Morbidity and Mortality Weekly Reports, 63*(5), 113-118.

Savadatti, S.S., & others (2019). Metabolic syndrome among Asian Indians in the United States. *Journal of Public Health Management and Practice, 25,* 45-52.

Savelieva, K., & others (2017). Intergenerational transmission of socioeconomic position and ideal cardiovascular health: 32-year follow-up study. *Health Psychology, 36*(3), 270-279.

Savin-Williams, R.C. (2019). Developmental trajectories and milestones of sexual-minority youth. In J. Gilbert & S. Lamb (Eds.), *Cambridge handbook of sexuality.* New York: Cambridge University Press.

Savvidou, M., & Jauniaux, E. (2019). Prenatal spina bifida: What has changed in diagnosis and management. *BJOG, 126*(3), 329.

Sawyer, R.K. (2019). Individual and group creativity. In J.C. Kaufman & R.J. Sternberg (Eds.), *Cambridge handbook of creativity* (2nd ed.). New York: Cambridge University Press.

Sayehmiri, K., & others (2020). The relationship between personality traits and marital satisfaction: A systematic review and meta-analysis. *BMC Psychology, 8*(1), 15.

Saywitz, K.J., & others (2019). Effects of interviewer support on children's memory and suggestibility: Systematic review and meta-analyses of experimental research. *Trauma, Violence, and Abuse, 20,* 22-39.

Sbarra, D.A. (2012). Marital dissolution and physical health outcomes: A review of mechanisms. *The science of the couple. The Ontario Symposium* (Vol. 12). New York: Psychology Press.

Sbarra, D.A. (2015). Divorce and health: Current trends and future directions. *Psychosomatic Medicine, 77,* 227-236.

Sbarra, D.A., Bourassa, K.J., & Manvellian, A. (2019). Marital separation and divorce: Correlates and consequences. In B.H. Friese (Ed.), *APA handbook of contemporary family psychology.* Washington, DC: APA Books.

Sbarra, D.A., Hasselmo, K., & Bourassa, K.J. (2015). Divorce and health: Beyond individual differences. *Current Directions in Psychological Science, 24,* 109-113.

Scarabino, D., & others (2017). Leukocyte telomere length in mild cognitive impairment and Alzheimer's disease patients. *Experimental Gerontology, 98,* 143-147.

Scarr, S. (1993). Biological and cultural diversity: The legacy of Darwin for development. *Child Development, 64,* 1333-1353.

Scelfo, J. (2015, February 3). A university recognizes a third gender: Neutral. *New York Times.* Retrieved December 20, 2016, from https://www.nytimes.com/2015/02/08/education/edlife/a-university- recognizes-a-third-gender-neutral.html

Schacter, D.L. (2019). Implicit memory, constructive memory, and imagining the future: A career perspective. *Perspectives on Psychological Science, 14,* 256-272.

Schaefer, R.T. (2019). *Racial and ethnic groups* (15th ed.). Upper Saddle River, NJ: Pearson.

Schafer, M.J., & others (2015). Calorie restriction suppresses age-dependent hippocampal transcriptional signatures. *PLoS One, 10*(7), e0133923.

Schaffer, H.R. (1996). *Social development.* Cambridge, MA: Blackwell.

Schaffer, M.A., Goodhue, A., Stennes, K., & Lanigan, C. (2012). Evaluation of a public health nurse visiting program for pregnant and parenting teens. *Public Health Nursing, 29,* 218-231.

Schaie, K.W. (1994). The life course of adult intellectual abilities. *American Psychologist, 49,* 304-313.

Schaie, K.W. (1996). *Intellectual development in adulthood: The Seattle Longitudinal Study.* New York: Cambridge University Press.

Schaie, K.W. (2000). Unpublished review of J.W. Santrock's *Life-span development,* 8th ed. New York: McGraw-Hill.

Schaie, K.W. (2005). *Developmental influences on adult intelligence: The Seattle Longitudinal Study.* New York: Oxford University Press.

Schaie, K.W. (2007). Generational differences: Age-period cohort. In J.E. Birren (Ed.), *Encyclopedia of gerontology* (2nd ed.). San Diego: Academic Press.

Schaie, K.W. (2008). Historical processes and patterns of cognitive aging. In S.M. Hofer & D.F. Alwin (Eds.), *Handbook on cognitive aging: An interdisciplinary perspective.* Thousand Oaks, CA: Sage.

Schaie, K.W. (2009). "When does age-related cognitive decline begin?" Salthouse again reifies the "cross-sectional fallacy." *Neurobiology of Aging, 30,* 528-529.

Schaie, K.W. (2010). Adult intellectual abilities. *Corsini encyclopedia of psychology.* New York: Wiley.

Schaie, K.W. (2011a). *Developmental influences on adult intellectual development.* New York: Oxford University Press.

Schaie, K.W. (2011b). Historical influences on aging and behavior. In K.W. Schaie & S.L. Willis (Eds.), *Handbook of the psychology of aging* (7th ed.). New York: Elsevier.

Schaie, K.W. (2013). *The Seattle Longitudinal Study: Developmental influences on adult intellectual development* (2nd ed.). New York: Oxford University Press.

Schaie, K.W. (2016a). Historical influences on aging and behavior. In K.W. Schaie & S.L. Willis (Eds.), *Handbook of the psychology of aging* (8th ed.). New York: Elsevier.

Schaie, K.W. (2016b). Theoretical perspectives for the psychology of aging in a lifespan context. In K.W. Schaie & S.L. Willis (Eds.), *Handbook of the psychology of aging* (8th ed.). New York: Elsevier.

Scharer, J.L., & Hibberd, R. (2020, in press). Meaning differentiates depression and grief among suicide survivors. *Death Studies.*

Scheibe, S., Freund, A.M., & Baltes, P.B. (2007). Toward a psychology of life-longings: The optimal (utopian) life. *Developmental Psychology, 43,* 778-795.

Scher, A., & Harel, J. (2008). Separation and stranger anxiety. In M.M. Haith & J.B. Benson (Eds.), *Encyclopedia of infant and early childhood development.* Oxford, UK: Elsevier.

Scheuer, H., & others (2017). Reduced fronto-amygdalar connectivity in adolescence is associated with increased depression symptoms over time. *Psychiatry Research, 266,* 35-41.

Schieffelin, B. (2005). *The give and take of everyday life.* Tucson, AZ: Fenestra.

Schiele, M.A., & others (2018). Oxytocin receptor gene variation, behavioral inhibition, and adult separation anxiety: Role in complicated grief. *World Journal of Biological Psychiatry, 19,* 471-479.

Schieman, S., van Gundy, K., & Taylor, J. (2004). The relationship between age and depressive symptoms: A test of competing explanatory and suppression influences. *Journal of Aging Health, 14,* 260-285.

Schiff, W.J. (2021). *Nutrition essentials* (3rd ed.). New York: McGraw-Hill.

Schiffman, S.S. (2007). Smell and taste. In J.E. Birren (ed.), *Encyclopedia of gerontology* (2nd ed.). San Diego: Academic Press.

Schindler-Ruwisch, J., & others (2020, in press). Limitations of workplace lactation support: The case for DC WIC recipients. *Journal of Human Lactation.*

Schlam, T.R., Wilson, N.L., Shoda, Y., Mischel, W., & Ayduk, O. (2013). Preschoolers' delay of gratification predicts their body mass 30 years later. *Journal of Pediatrics, 162,* 90-93.

Schlegel, M. (2000). All work and play. *Monitor on Psychology, 31*(11), 50-51.

Schlosnagle, L., & Strough, J. (2017). Understanding adult age differences in the frequency of problems with friends. *International Journal of Aging and Human Development, 84,* 159-179.

Schmank, C.J., & James, L.E. (2020, in press). Adults of all ages experience increased tip-of-the-tongue states under ostensible evaluative observation. *Neuropsychology, Development, and*

Cognition. Section B: Aging, Neuropsychology, and Cognition.

Schmidt, A., Dirk, J., & Schmiedek, F. (2019). The importance of peer relatedness at school for affective well-being in children: Between- and within-person associations. *Social Development, 28*(4), 873–892.

Schmidt, E.L., Burge, W., Visscher, K.M., & Ross, L.A. (2016). Cortical thickness in frontoparietal and cingulo-opercular networks predicts executive function performance in older adults. *Neuropsychology, 30,* 322–331.

Schmidt, S., & others (2006). Cigarette smoking strongly modifies the association of LOC387715 and age related macular degeneration. *American Journal of Human Genetics, 78,* 852–864.

Schmidt, S., & others (2019). Mode of delivery and morbidity for very preterm singleton infants in a breech position: A European cohort study. *European Journal of Obstetric, Gynecologic, and Reproductive Biology, 234,* 96–102.

Schneider, A.L.C., & Ornstein, P.A. (2019). Determinants of memory development in childhood and adolescence. *International Journal of Psychology, 54*(3), 307–315.

Schneider, A.L.C., & others (2019). Neural correlates of domain-specific cognitive decline: The ARIC-NCS study. *Neurology, 92,* e1051–1063.

Schneider, W. (2011). Memory development in childhood. In U. Goswami (Ed.), *Wiley-Blackwell handbook of childhood cognitive development* (2nd ed.). New York: Wiley-Blackwell.

Schneider, W., & Ornstein, P.A. (2019). Determinants of memory development in childhood and adolescence. *International Journal of Psychology, 54,* 307–315.

Schnellbacher, GJ., & others (2020). Functional characterization of atrophy patterns related to cognitive impairment. *Frontiers of Neurology, 11,* 18.

Schnittker, J. (2007). Look (closely) at all the lonely people: Age and social psychology of social support. *Journal of Aging and Health, 19,* 659–682.

Schnohr, P., & others (2015). Dose of jogging and long-term mortality: The Copenhagen City Heart Study. *Journal of the American College of Cardiology, 65,* 411–419.

Schnohr, P., & others (2017). Impact of persistence and non-persistence in leisure time physical activity on coronary heart disease and all-cause mortality: The Copenhagen City Heart Study. *European Journal of Cardiology, 24,* 1615–1623.

Schoen, C.N., & others (2015). Why the United States preterm birth rate is declining. *American Journal of Obstetrics and Gynecology, 213,* 175–180.

Schoenfeld, E.A., & others (2017). Does sex really matter? Examining the connections between spouses' nonsexual behaviors, sexual frequency, sexual satisfaction, and marital satisfaction. *Archives of Sexual Behavior, 46,* 489–501.

Schoffstall, C.L., & Cohen, R. (2011). Cyber aggression: The relation between online offenders and offline social competence. *Social Development, 20*(3), 587–604.

Schonert-Reichl, K.A., & others (2015). Enhancing cognitive and social-emotional development through a simple-to-administer mindfulness-based school program for elementary school children: A randomized controlled trial. *Developmental Psychology, 51,* 52–66.

Schooler, C. (2007). Use it—and keep it, longer, probably: A reply to Salthouse (2006). *Perspectives on Psychological Science, 2,* 24–29.

Schoon, I., & Bynner, J. (2020). Entering adulthood in the Great Depression: A tale of three countries. In R.D. Parke & G.H. Elder (Eds.), *Children in changing worlds.* New York: Cambridge University Press..

Schoon, I., Jones, E., Cheng, H., & Maughan, B. (2012). Family hardship, family instability, and cognitive development. *Journal of Epidemiology and Community Health, 66*(8), 716–722.

Schubert, S.A., & others (2020, in press). The missing heritability of familial colorectal cancer. *Mutagenesis.*

Schulenberg, J.E., & Patrick, J.E. (2018). Binge drinking. In M.H. Bornstein (Ed.), *SAGE encyclopedia of lifespan human development.* Thousand Oaks, CA: Sage.

Schulenberg, J.E., & Zarrett, N.R. (2006). Mental health during emerging adulthood: Continuity and discontinuity in courses, causes, and functions. In J.J. Arnett & J.L. Tanner (Eds.), *Emerging adults in America.* Washington, DC: American Psychological Association.

Schulenberg, J.E., & others (2017). *Monitoring the Future national survey results on drug use, 1975–2016: Vol. II, College students and adults ages 19–55.* Ann Arbor, MI: Institute for Social Research, University of Michigan.

Schulenberg, J.E., & others (2018). *Monitoring the Future national survey results on drug use, 1975–2017: Vol. II, College students and adults ages 19–55.* Ann Arbor, MI: Institute for Social Research, University of Michigan.

Schulenberg, J.E., & others (2019). *Monitoring the Future: National survey results on drug use, 1975–2018: Vol. II, College students and adults ages 19–60.* Washington, DC: National Institute on Drug Abuse.

Schunk, D.H. (2020). *Learning theories: An educational perspective* (8th ed.). Upper Saddle River, NJ: Prentice Hall.

Schurz, H., & others (2019). The X chromosome and sex-specific effects in infectious disease susceptibility. *Human Genomics, 13*(1), 2.

Schutten, D., Stokes, K.A., & Arnell, K.M. (2017). I want to media multitask and I want to do it now: Individual differences in media multitasking predict delay of gratification and system-1 thinking. *Cognitive Research: Principles and Implications, 2*(1), 8.

Schwartz, D., & others (2015). Peer victimization during middle childhood as a lead indicator of internalizing problems and diagnostic outcomes in late adolescence. *Journal of Clinical Child and Adolescent Psychology, 44,* 393–404.

Schwartz, J.A., Wright, E.M., & Valgardson, B.A. (2019). Adverse childhood experiences and deleterious outcomes in adulthood: A consideration of the simultaneous role of genetic and environmental influences in two independent samples from the United States. *Child Abuse and Neglect, 88,* 420–431.

Schwartz, M.A., & Scott, B.M. (2012). *Marriages and families, census update* (6th ed.). Upper Saddle River, NJ: Pearson.

Schwartz, M.A., & Scott, B.M. (2018). *Marriages and families* (8th ed.). Upper Saddle River, NJ: Pearson.

Schwartz, S.J. (2016). Turning point for a turning point: Advancing emerging adulthood theory and research. *Emerging Adulthood, 45,* 307–317.

Schwartz, S.J., & Petrova, M. (2019). Prevention science in emerging adulthood: A field coming of age. *Prevention Science, 20,* 305–309.

Schwartz, S.J., Zamboanga, B.L., Meca, A., & Ritchie, R.A. (2012). Identity around the world: An overview. *New Directions in Child and Adolescent Development, 138,* 1–18.

Schwartz, S.J., & others (2015a). The identity dynamics of acculturation and multiculturalism: Situating acculturation in context. In V. Benet-Martinez & Y.Y. Hong (Eds.), *Oxford handbook of multicultural identity.* New York: Oxford University Press.

Schwartz, S.J., & others (2015b). Personal, ethnic, and cultural identity in urban youth: Links with risk and resilience. In G. Creasey & P. Jarvis (Eds.), *Adolescent development and school achievement in urban communities.* New York: Routledge.

Schweinhart, L.J., & others (2005). *Lifetime effects: The High/Scope Perry Preschool study through age 40.* Ypsilanti, MI: High/Scope Press.

Scialfa, C.T., & Kline, D.W. (2007). Vision. In J.E. Birren (Ed.), *Encyclopedia of gerontology* (2nd ed.). San Diego: Academic Press.

Science Daily (2008, January 15). Human gene count tumbles again, p. 1.

Scott, R.M., & Baillargeon, R. (2017). Early false-belief understanding. *Trends in Cognitive Science, 21,* 237–249.

Scott, R.M., Roby, E., & Baillargeon, R. (2021, in press). How sophisticated is infants' theory of mind? In O. Houde & G. Borst (Eds.), *Cambridge handbook of cognitive development.* New York: Cambridge University Press.

Scullin, M.K., Bugg, J.M., & McDaniel, M.A. (2012). Whoops, I did it again: Commission errors in prospective memory. *Psychology of Aging, 27,* 46–53.

Search Institute (2010). *Teen voice.* Minneapolis: Search Institute.

Sebastian-Enesco, C., Guerrero, S., & Enesco, I. (2020, in press). What makes children defy their peers? Chinese and Spanish preschoolers' decisions to trust (or not) peer consensus. *Social Development.*

Sebastiani, P., & Perls, T.T. (2012). The genetics of extreme longevity: Lessons from the New England Centenarian study. *Frontiers in Genetics, 30*(3), 277.

Sebastiani, P., & others (2013). Meta-analysis of genetic variants associated with human exceptional longevity. *Aging, 5,* 653–661.

Seccombe, K.T. (2020). *Exploring families and their social worlds* (4th ed.). Upper Saddle River, NJ: Pearson.

Sedgh, G., & others (2015). Adolescent pregnancy, birth, and abortion rates across countries: Levels and recent trends. *Journal of Adolescent Health, 56,* 223-230.

Segerberg, O. (1982). *Living to be 100: 1,200 who did and how they did it.* New York: Charles Scribner's Sons.

Segerstrom, S.C., & others (2016). Time perspective and social preference in older and younger adults: Effects of self-regulatory fatigue. *Psychology and Aging, 31,* 594-604.

Seiffert, D.J., & others (2019). Beyond medical actionability: Public perceptions of important actions in response to hypothetical genetic testing results. *Journal of Genetic Counseling, 28,* 355-366.

Seiter, L.N., & Nelson, L.J. (2011). An examination of emerging adulthood in college students and nonstudents in India. *Journal of Adolescent Research, 26,* 506-536.

Selkie, E. (2018). When age-based guidance is not enough: The problem of early puberty. *Pediatrics, 14,* 1.

Selman, R.L. (1980). *The growth of interpersonal understanding.* New York: Academic Press.

Semenov, A.D., & Zelazo, P.D. (2018). The development of hot and cool executive function: A foundation for learning in the preschool years. In L. Melzer (Ed.), *Executive function in education.* New York: Guilford.

Sen, B. (2010). The relationship between frequency of family dinner and adolescent problem behaviors after adjusting for other characteristics. *Journal of Adolescence, 33,* 187-196.

Sengpiel, V., & others (2013). Maternal caffeine intake during pregnancy is associated with birth weight but not gestational length: Results from a large prospective observational cohort study. *BMC Medicine, 11,* 42.

Senia, J.M., & Donnellan, B. (2019). Personality, development, and relationships in adulthood. In D.P. McAdams & others (Eds.), *Handbook of personality development.* New York: Guilford.

Seo, Y.S., Lee, J., & Ahn, H.Y. (2016). Effects of kangaroo care on neonatal pain in South Korea. *Journal of Tropical Pediatrics, 62,* 246-249.

Serbin, M., & others (2020). Assessing health care burden in glaucoma patients with and without physical or mental comorbidities. *Journal of Managed Care Pharmacy, 26,* 325-331.

Seror, V., & others (2019). Women's attitudes toward invasive and noninvasive testing when facing a high risk of fetal Down syndrome. *JAMA Network Open, 2*(3), e191062.

Serra, M.J., & Metcalfe, J. (2010). Effective implementation of metacognition. In D.J. Hacker, J. Dunlosky, & A.C. Graesser (Eds.), *Handbook of metacognition and education.* New York: Psychology Press.

Serrano-Pozo, A., & Growdon, J.H. (2019). Is Alzheimer's disease risk modifiable? *Journal of Alzheimer's Disease, 67,* 795-819.

Sesker, A.A., Suilleabhain, P.O., Howard, S., & Hughes, B.M. (2016). Conscientiousness and mindfulness in midlife coping: An assessment based on MIDUS II. *Personality and Mental Health, 10,* 28-42.

Sethna, V., & others (2018). Father-child interactions at 3 months and 24 months: Contributions to children's cognitive development at 24 months. *Infant Mental Health Journal, 229,* 364-370.

Setterson, R.A., & Trauten, M.E. (2009). The new terrain of old age: Hallmarks, freedoms, and risks. In V.L. Bengtson, D. Gans, N.M. Putney, & M. Silverstein (Eds.), *Handbook of theories of aging.* New York: Springer.

Sewdas, R., & others (2017). Why older workers work beyond the retirement age: A qualitative study. *BMC Public Health, 17*(1), 672.

Sexton, B.P., & Taylor, N.F. (2019). To sit or not to sit? A systematic review and meta-analysis of seated exercise for older adults. *Australian Journal of Aging, 38,* 15-27.

Sezer Efe, Y., Erdem, E., & Gunes, T. (2020, in press). The effect of a daily exercise program on bone mineral density and cortisol level in preterm infants with very low birth weight: A randomized controlled trial. *Journal of Pediatric Nursing.*

Shan, Z.Y., Liu, J.Z., Sahgal, V., Wang, B., & Yue, G.H. (2005). Selective atrophy of left hemisphere and frontal lobe of the brain in older men. *Journals of Gerontology A: Biological Sciences and Medical Sciences, 60,* A165-A174.

Shang, C.Y., Lin, H.Y., & Gau, S.S. (2020, in press). Effects of the dopamine transporter gene on striatal functional connectivity in youths with attention-deficit/hyperactivity disorder. *Psychological Medicine.*

Shankaran, S., & others (2010). Prenatal cocaine exposure and BMI and blood pressure at 9 years of age. *Journal of Hypertension, 28,* 1166-1175.

Shapiro, A.F., & Gottman, J.M. (2005). Effects on marriage of a psycho-education intervention with couples undergoing the transition to parenthood, evaluation at 1 year post-intervention. *Journal of Family Communication, 5,* 1-24.

Shapiro, A.F., Gottman, J.M., & Fink, B.C. (2020, in press). Father's involvement when bringing baby home: Efficacy testing of a couple-focused transition to parenthood intervention for promoting father involvement. *Psychological Reports.*

Sharifian, N., Manly, J.J., Brickman, A.M., & Zahodne, L.B. (2019). Social network characteristics and cognitive functioning in ethnically diverse older adults: The role of network size and composition. *Neuropsychology, 33*(7), 956-963.

Sharma, P., & others (2020, in press). Biological signatures of Alzheimer disease. *Current Topics in Medicinal Chemistry.*

Sharma, R., Murki, S., & Oleti, T.P. (2018). Study comparing "kangaroo ward care" with "intermediate intensive care" for improving the growth outcome and cost effectiveness: Randomized control trial. *Journal of Maternal-Fetal and Neonatal Medicine, 31,* 2986-2993.

Sharma, R., & others (2015). Effects of increased paternal age on sperm quality, reproductive outcome, and associated epigenetic risks to offspring. *Reproductive Biology and Endocrinology, 13,* 35.

Sharma, V.K., Mehta, V., & Singh, T.G. (2020, in press). Alzheimer's disorder: Epigenetic connection and associated risk factors. *Current Neuropharmacology.*

Sharp, E.S., & others (2019). Openness declines in advance of death in late adulthood. *Psychology and Aging, 34,* 124-138.

Shatz, M., & Gelman, R. (1973). The development of communication skills: Modifications in the speech of young children as a function of the listener. *Monographs of the Society for Research in Child Development, 38* (Serial No. 152).

Shaw, P., & others (2007). Attention-deficit/hyperactivity disorder is characterized by a delay in cortical maturation. *Proceedings of the National Academy of Sciences, 104*(49), 19649-19654.

Shaw, S.H., Herbers, J.E., & Cutuli, J.J. (2019). Medical and psychosocial risk profiles for low birthweight and preterm birth. *Women's Health Issues, 29,* 400-406.

Shay, J.W., & Wright, W.E. (2019). Telomeres and telomerase: Three decades of progress. *Nature Reviews. Genetics, 20,* 299-309.

Shaywitz, B.A., Lyon, G.R., & Shaywitz, S.E. (2006). The role of functional magnetic resonance imaging in understanding reading and dyslexia. *Developmental Neuropsychology, 30,* 613-632.

Shaywitz, S.E., & Shaywitz, B.B. (2017). Dyslexia. In R. Schwartz (Ed.), *Handbook of child language disorders* (2nd ed.). New York: Routledge.

Shear, M.K. (2012a). Getting straight about grief. *Depression and Anxiety, 29,* 461-464.

Shear, M.K. (2012b). Grief and mourning gone awry: Pathway and course of complicated grief. *Dialogues in Clinical Neuroscience, 14,* 119-128.

Shear, M.K., Ghesquiere, A., & Glickman, K. (2013). Bereavement and complicated grief. *Current Psychiatric Reports, 15*(11), 406.

Shebloski, B., Conger, K.J., & Widaman, K.F. (2005). Reciprocal links among differential parenting, perceived partiality, and self-worth: A three-wave longitudinal study. *Journal of Family Psychology, 19,* 633-642.

Sheehan, D.K., & others (2019). Telling adolescents that a parent has died. *Journal of Hospice and Pediatric Nursing, 21,* 152-159.

Sheehan, M.J., & Watson, M.W. (2015). Reciprocal influences between maternal discipline and techniques and aggression in children and adolescents. *Aggressive Behavior, 34,* 245-255.

Sheffler, P.C., & Cheung, C.S. (2020, in press). The role of peer mindsets in students' learning: An experimental study. *British Journal of Educational Psychology.*

Sheldrick, R.C., Maye, M.P., & Carter, A.S. (2017). Age at first identification of autism spectrum disorder: An analysis of two U.S. surveys. *Journal of the American Academy of Child and Adolescent Psychiatry, 56,* 313-320.

Shelton, L. (2018). *The Bronfenbrenner primer: A guide to develecology.* New York: Routledge.

Shen, Y., & others (2020, in press). Evolutionary genomics analysis of human nucleus-encoded mitochondrial genes: Implications for the roles of energy production and metabolic pathways in the pathogenesis and pathophysiology of demyelinating diseases. *Neuroscience Letters.*

Shenhav, A., & Greene, J.D. (2014). Integrative moral judgment: Dissociating the roles of the amygdala and the ventromedial prefrontal cortex. *Journal of Neuroscience, 34,* 4741–4749.

Shephard, E., & others (2019). Oscillatory neural networks underlying resting-state, attentional control, and social cognition task conditions in children with ASD, ADHD and ASD1ADHD. *Cortex, 117,* 96–110.

Sherman, L., Steinberg, L., & Chein, J. (2018). Connecting brain responsivity and real-world risk taking: Strengths and weaknesses of current methodological approaches. *Developmental Cognitive Neuroscience, 33,* 27–41.

Sherwood, C.C., & others (2011). Aging of the cerebral cortex differs between humans and chimpanzees. *Proceedings of the National Academy of Sciences U.S.A., 108,* 13029–13034.

Shi, J., & others (2020, in press). Perceived stress and social support influence anxiety symptoms of Chinese family caregivers of community-dwelling older adults: A cross-sectional study. *Psychogeriatrics.*

Shieh, J.C., Huang, P.T., & Lin, Y.T. (2020, in press). Alzheimer's disease and diabetes: Insulin signaling as the bridge linking two pathologies. *Molecular Neurobiology.*

Shimony-Kanat, S., & others (2018). Do parental decision-making patterns predict compliance with use of child booster seats? *International Journal of Injury Control and Safety Promotion, 25,* 53–57.

Shinan-Altman, S., & Werner, P. (2019). Subjective age and its correlates among middle-aged and older adults. *International Journal of Aging and Human Development, 88,* 3–21.

Shiner, R.L. (2019). Negative emotionality and neuroticism from childhood through adulthood: A lifespan perspective. In D.P. McAdams (Ed.), *Handbook of personality development.* New York: Guilford.

Shivers, E., & Farago, F. (2016). Where the children are: Exploring quality, community, and support for family, friend, and neighbor care. In K.E. Sanders & A.W. Guerra (Eds.), *The culture of child care.* New York: Oxford University Press.

Shneidman, O., Gweon, H., Schultz, L., & Woodward, A.L. (2016). Learning from others and spontaneous exploration: A cross-cultural investigation. *Child Development, 87,* 1221–1232.

Shore, L.M., & Goldberg, C.B. (2005). Age discrimination in the work place. In R.L. Dipobye & A. Colella (Eds.), *Discrimination at work.* Mahwah, NJ: Erlbaum.

Shorey, S., Ang, L., & Lau, Y. (2020, in press). Efficacy of mind-body therapies and exercise-based interventions on menopausal-related outcomes among Asian perimenopause women: A systematic review, meta-analysis, and synthesis without a meta-analysis. *Journal of Advanced Nursing.*

Shors, T.J. (2009). Saving new brain cells. *Scientific American, 300,* 46–52.

Short, D. (2015a, August 11). *Another look at long-term trends in employment by age group.* Lexington, MA: Advisor Perspectives.

Shuey, E.A. & Leventhal, T. (2019). Neighborhoods and parenting. In M.H. Bornstein (Ed.), *Handbook of parenting* (3rd ed.) (Vol. 2). New York: Routledge.

Shulman, S., Scharf, M., Ziv, I., Norona, J., & Welsh, D.P. (2020). Adolescents' sexual encounters with either romantic or casual partners and the quality of their romantic relationships four years later. *Journal of Sex Research, 57*(2), 156–165.

Shulman, S., Seiffge-Krenke, I., Ziv, I., & Tuval-Mashiach, R. (2019). Patterns of romantic pathways among 23-year-olds and their adolescent antecedents. *Journal of Youth and Adolescence, 48*(7), 1390–1402.

Siebelink, N.M., & others (2019). Genetic and environmental etiologies of associations between dispositional mindfulness and ADHD traits: A population-based twin study. *European Child and Adolescent Psychiatry, 28,* 1241–1251.

Siedlecki, K.L. (2007). Investigating the structure and age invariance of episodic memory across the adult life span. *Psychology and Aging, 22,* 251–268.

Siedlecki, K.L., & others (2020). Examining processing speed as a predictor of subjective well-being across age and time in the German Aging Survey. *Neuropsychology, Development, and Cognition. Section B: Aging and Cognition, 27,* 66–82.

Siegel, A.L.M., & Castel, A.D. (2019). Age-related differences in metacognition for memory capacity and selectivity. *Memory, 27,* 1236–1249.

Siegel, R.S., & Brandon, A.R. (2014). Adolescents, pregnancy, and mental health. *Journal of Pediatric and Adolescent Gynecology, 27*(3), 138–150.

Siegler, I.C., & Costa, P.T. (1999, August). *Personality change and continuity in midlife: UNC Alumni Heart Study.* Paper presented at the meeting of the American Psychological Association, Boston.

Siegler, R.S. (2006). Microgenetic analysis of learning. In W. Damon & R. Lerner (Eds.), *Handbook of child psychology* (6th ed.). New York: Wiley.

Siegler, R.S. (2017). Foreword: Build it and they will come. In D.G. Geary & others (Eds.), *Acquisition of complex arithmetic skills and higher order mathematics concepts.* New York: Academic Press.

Sierra, T.A. (2015). *Working with remarried couples.* Unpublished manuscript, MMATE Center. Virginia Beach, VA: Regent University.

Sifaki, M., & others (2020). A novel approach regarding the anti-aging of facial skin through collagen reorganization. *Experimental Therapeutic Medicine, 19,* 717–721.

Sightlines Project (2016). *Seeing our way to living long, living well in 21st century America.* Palo Alto, CA: Stanford University.

Sigman, M. (2017). Introduction: What to do with older prospective fathers: The risks of advanced paternal age. *Fertility and Sterility, 107,* 299–300.

Silva, C. (2005, October 31). When teen dynamo talks, city listens. *Boston Globe,* pp. B1, B4.

Silva, K., Chein, J., & Steinberg, L. (2016). Adolescents in peer groups make more prudent decisions when a slightly older adult is present. *Psychological Science, 27,* 322–330.

Silva, K., & others (2017). Joint effects of peer presence and fatigue on risk and reward processing in late adolescence. *Journal of Youth and Adolescence, 46,* 1878–1890.

Silverman, M.E., & others (2017). The risk factors for postpartum depression. *Depression and Anxiety, 34,* 178–187.

Sim, W.H., & others (2019). Development and evaluation of the Parenting to Reduce Anxiety and Depression Scale (PaRCADS): Assessment of parental concordance with guidelines for the prevention of child anxiety and depression. *PeerJ, 7,* 36865.

Simha, S. (2019). The impact of family separation on immigrant and refugee families. *North Carolina Medical Journal, 80,* 95–96.

Simmons, D. (2011). Diabetes and obesity in pregnancy. *Best Practice and Research, Clinical Obstetrics and Gynecology, 25,* 25–36.

Simmons, R.G., & Blyth, D.A. (1987). *Moving into adolescence.* Hawthorne, NY: Aldine.

Simms, N.K., Frausel, R.R., & Richland, E.E. (2018). Working memory predicts children's analogical reasoning. *Journal of Experimental Child Psychology, 166,* 160–177.

Simon, E.J. (2020). *Biology* (3rd ed.). Upper Saddle River, NJ: Pearson.

Simon, R.W., & Barrett, A.E. (2010). Nonmarital romantic relationships and mental health in early adulthood: Does the association differ for women and men? *Journal of Health and Social Behavior, 51,* 168–182.

Simonetti, G.D., & others (2011). Determinants of blood pressure in preschool children: The role of parental smoking. *Circulation, 123,* 292–298.

Simoni, M., & Santi, D. (2020, in press). FSH treatment of male idiopathic infertility: Time for a paradigm change. *Andrology.*

Simons, J.S., & others (2018). Daily associations between alcohol and sexual behavior in young adults. *Experimental and Clinical Psychopharmacology, 26,* 36–48.

Simons, L.G., & others (2016). Mechanisms that link parenting practices to adolescents' risky sexual behavior: A test of six competing theories. *Journal of Youth and Adolescence, 45,* 255–270.

Simonton, D.K. (1996). Creativity. In J.E. Birren (Ed.), *Encyclopedia of aging.* San Diego: Academic Press.

Simpkins, S.D., Fredricks, J.A., & Eccles, J.S. (2015). Families, schools, and developing achievement-related motivations. In J.E. Grusec & P.D. Hastings (Eds.), *Handbook of socialization* (2nd ed.). New York: Guilford.

Simpkins, S.D., Vest, A.E., & Price, C.D. (2011). Intergenerational continuity and discontinuity in Mexican-origin youths' participation in organized activities: Insights from mixed-methods. *Journal of Family Psychology, 25,* 814–824.

Simpson, D.M., Leonhardt, N.D., & Hawkins, A.J. (2018). Learning about love: A meta-analytic study of individually-oriented relationship education programs for adolescents and emerging adults. *Journal of Youth and Adolescence, 417,* 477–489.

Simpson, H.B., & others (2013). Treatment of obsessive-compulsive disorder complicated by comorbid eating disorders. *Cognitive Behavior Therapy, 42,* 64–76.

Simpson, J.A., & Karantzas, G.C. (2019). Editorial overview: Attachment in adulthood: A dynamic field with a rich past and a bright future. *Current Opinion in Psychology, 25,* 177–181.

Sims, R., Hill, M., & Williams, J. (2020, in press). The multiplex model of the genetics of Alzheimer's disease. *Nature Neuroscience.*

Sims, T., Hogan, C., & Carstensen, L.L. (2015). Selectivity as an emotion regulation strategy: Lessons from older adults. *Current Opinion in Psychology, 3,* 80–84.

Sinclair-Palm, J. (2019). Conceptualizing sexuality in research about trans youth. In S. Lamb & J. Gilbert (Eds.), *Cambridge handbook of sexual development.* New York: Cambridge University Press.

Singer, A.E., & others (2015). Symptom trends in the last year of life from 1998 to 2010: A cohort study. *Annals of Internal Medicine, 162,* 175–183.

Singer, D., Golinkoff, R.M., & Hirsh-Pasek, K. (Eds.) (2006). *Play = learning: How play motivates and enhances children's cognitive and social-emotional growth.* New York: Oxford University Press.

Singh, P.B., Sholma, V.V., & Belyakin, S.N. (2019). Maternal regulation of chromosomal imprinting in animals. *Chromosoma, 128,* 69–80.

Singh, S., Zaki, R.A., & Farid, N.D.N. (2019). A systematic review of depression literacy: Knowledge, help-seeking, and stigmatizing among adolescents. *Journal of Adolescence, 74,* 154–172.

Sinkovic, M., & Towler, L. (2019). Sexual aging: A systematic review of qualitative research on the sexuality and sexual health of older adults. *Quality Health Research, 29,* 1231–1254.

Sinnott, J.D. (2003). Postformal thought and adult development: Living in balance. In J. Demick & C. Andreoletti (Eds.), *Handbook of adult development.* New York: Kluwer.

Siopi, A., & others (2019). Comparison of the serum metabolic fingerprint of different exercise models in men with and without metabolic syndrome. *Metabolites, 9,* 6.

Sirard, J.R., & others (2013). Physical activity and screen time in adolescents and their friends. *American Journal of Preventive Medicine, 44,* 48–55.

Sirkanta, J.T., & Kumar, K.M.C. (2019). Narcolepsy—A rare but under-recognized problem in children. *Indian Pediatrics, 56*(2), 147.

Sirsch, U., Dreher, E., Mayr, E., & Willinger, U. (2009). What does it take to be an adult in Australia? Views of adulthood in Australian adolescents, emerging adults and adults. *Journal of Adolescent Research, 24,* 275–292.

Sivam, A., & others (2016). Olfactory dysfunction in older adults is associated with feelings of depression and loneliness. *Chemical Senses, 41,* 293–299.

Sivasankaran, S. (2019). High blood pressure in children: The invisible dragon. *Annals of Pediatric Cardiology, 12,* 73–76.

Skaper, S.D., & others (2017). Synaptic plasticity, dementia, and Alzheimer disease. *CNS & Neurological Disorders Drug Targets, 16,* 220–233.

Skelton, A.E., & Franklin, A. (2020, in press). Infants look longer at colors that adults like when colors are highly saturated. *Psychological Bulletin and Review.*

Skelton, A.E., & others (2017). Biological origins of color categorization. *Proceedings of the National Academy of Sciences U.S.A., 114,* 5545–5550.

Skinner, B.F. (1938). *The behavior of organisms: An experimental analysis.* New York: Appleton-Century-Crofts.

Skocajic, M., & others (2020, in press). Boys just don't! Gender stereotyping and sanctioning of counter-stereotypical behavior in preschoolers. *Sex Roles.*

Skowronski, G.A. (2015). Pain relief in childbirth: Changing historical and feminist perspectives. *Anesthesia and Intensive Care, 43*(Suppl.), S25–S28.

Slade, A., & others (2019). Minding the baby: Complex trauma and attachment-based home intervention. In H. Steele & M. Steele (Eds.), *Handbook of attachment-based interventions.* New York: Guilford.

Slater, A., Field, T., & Hernandez-Reif, M. (2007). The development of the senses. In A. Slater & M. Lewis (Eds.), *Introduction to infant development* (2nd ed.). New York: Oxford University Press.

Slater, A.M., Morison, V., & Somers, M. (1988). Orientation discrimination and cortical function in the human newborn. *Perception, 17,* 597–602.

Slaughter, V., & others (2014). Meta-analysis of theory of mind and peer popularity in the preschool and early school years. *Child Development, 86,* 1159–1174.

Slavich, G.M., & others (2020). Interpersonal life stress, inflammation, and depression in adolescence: Testing social signal transduction theory of depression. *Depression and Anxiety, 37,* 179–193.

Sleet, D.A., & Mercy, J.A. (2003). Promotion of safety, security, and well-being. In M.H. Bornstein, L. Davidson, C.L.M. Keyes, & K.A. Moore (Eds.), *Well-being.* Mahwah, NJ: Erlbaum.

Slobin, D. (1972, July). Children and language: They learn the same way around the world. *Psychology Today,* 71–76.

Smaldino, S.E., & others (2019). *Instructional technology and media for learning* (12th ed.). Upper Saddle River, NJ: Pearson.

Small, B.J., Rawson, K.S., Eisel, S., & McEvoy, C.L. (2012). Memory and aging. In S.K. Whitbourne & M. Sliwinski (Eds.), *Wiley-Blackwell handbook of adulthood and aging.* New York: Wiley.

Small, H. (2011). *Why not? My seventy year plan for a college degree.* Franklin, TN: Carpenter's Son Publishing.

Smarius, L.J., & others (2017). Excessive infant crying doubles the risk of mood and behavioral problems at age 5: Evidence for mediation by maternal characteristics. *European Child and Adolescent Psychiatry, 26,* 293–302.

Smetana, J.G. (2013). Moral development: The social domain theory view. In P.D. Zelazo (Ed.), *Oxford handbook of developmental psychology.* New York: Oxford University Press.

Smetana, J.G., & Ball, C.L. (2018). Young children's moral judgments: justifications, and emotion attributions in peer relationship contexts. *Child Development, 89,* 2245–2263.

Smetana, J.G., Robinson, J., & Rote, W.M. (2015). Socialization in adolescence. In J.E. Grusec & P.D. Hastings (Eds.), *Handbook of socialization* (2nd ed.). New York: Guilford.

Smith, A., & Collene, A. (2019). *Wardlaw's contemporary nutrition* (11th ed.). New York: McGraw-Hill.

Smith, A.D. (1996). Memory. In J.E. Birren (Ed.), *Encyclopedia of gerontology* (Vol. 2). San Diego: Academic Press.

Smith, A.J., Abeyta, A.A., Hughes, M., & Jones, R.T. (2015). Persistent grief in the aftermath of mass violence: The predictive roles of posttraumatic stress symptoms, self-efficacy, and disrupted worldview. *Psychological Trauma, 7,* 179–186.

Smith, A.R., & others (2017). "I don't want to grow up, I'm a (Gen X, Y, Me) kid": Increasing maturity fears across the decades. *International Journal of Behavioral Development, 41,* 655–662.

Smith, C., & Denton, M. (2005). *Soul searching: The religious and spiritual lives of American teenagers.* New York: Oxford University Press.

Smith, C.A., Armour, M., & Ee, C. (2016). Complementary therapies and medicines and reproductive medicine. *Seminars in Reproductive Medicine, 34,* 67–73.

Smith, E.R., Perrin, P.B., & Sutter, M.E. (2020, in press). Factor analysis of the heterosexist harassment, rejection, and discrimination scale in lesbian, gay, bisexual, transgender, and queer people of color. *International Journal of Psychology.*

Smith, J., & others (2019). Associations between early maternal behaviors and child language at 36 months in a cohort experiencing adversity. *International Journal of Language and Communication Disorders, 54*(1), 110–122.

Smith, L., & others (2019). Sexual activity is associated with greater enjoyment of life in older adults. *Sexual Medicine, 7*(1), 11–18.

Smith, L.E., & Howard, K.S. (2008). Continuity of paternal social support and depressive symptoms among new mothers. *Journal of Family Psychology, 22,* 763–773.

Smith, P.K., & Wild, L.G. (2019). Grandparenting. In M.H. Bornstein (Ed.), *Handbook of parenting* (3rd ed.). New York: Routledge.

Smith, R.A., & Davis, S.F. (2016). *The psychologist as detective* (7th ed.). Upper Saddle River, NJ: Prentice Hall.

Smith, R.E., & Hunt, R.R. (2014). Prospective memory in young and older adults: The effects of task importance and ongoing task load. *Neuropsychology, Development, and Cognition B: Aging, Neuropsychology, and Cognition, 21,* 411–431.

Smith, R.L., Rose, A.J., & Schwartz-Mette, R.A. (2010). Relational and overt aggression in childhood and adolescence: Clarifying mean-level gender differences and associations with peer acceptance. *Social Development, 19,* 243-269.

Smith, S.G., & others (2018). Social isolation, health literacy, and mortality risk: Findings from the English Longitudinal Study of Aging. *Health Psychology, 37,* 160-169.

Smithson, L., & others (2019). Shorter sleep duration is associated with reduced cognitive development at two years of age. *Sleep Medicine, 48,* 131-139.

Smock, P.J., & Gupta, S. (2013). Cohabitation in contemporary North America. In A. Booth, A.C. Crouter, & N.S. Landale (Eds.), *Just living together.* New York: Psychology Press.

Smokowski, P.R., Bacallao, M.L., Cotter, K.L., & Evans, C.B. (2015). The effects of positive and negative parenting practices on adolescent mental health outcomes in a multicultural sample of rural youth. *Child Psychiatry and Human Development, 46,* 333-345.

Smoreda, Z., & Licoppe, C. (2000). Gender-specific use of the domestic telephone. *Social Psychology Quarterly, 63,* 238-252.

Snapp, C., & others (2020, in press). The experience of land and water birth within the American Association of Birth Centers perinatal birth registry, 2012-2017. *Journal of Perinatal and Neonatal Nursing.*

Snow, C.E., & Kang, J.Y. (2006). Becoming bilingual, biliterate, and bicultural. In W. Damon & R. Lerner (Eds.), *Handbook of child psychology* (6th ed.). New York: Wiley.

Snowdon, D.A. (2002). *Aging with grace: What the Nun Study teaches us about leading longer, healthier, and more meaningful lives.* New York: Bantam.

Snowdon, D.A. (2003). Healthy aging and dementia: Findings from the Nun Study. *Annals of Internal Medicine, 139,* 450-454.

Snyder, J.S., & Drew, M.R. (2020). Functional neurogenesis over the years. *Behavioral Brain Research, 382,* 112470.

Sobo, E.J. (2020). *Dynamics of human biocultural diversity.* New York: Routledge.

Sobowale, K., & others (2018). Personality traits are associated with academic achievement in medical school: A nationally representative study. *Academic Psychiatry. 42,* 338-345.

Society for Adolescent Health and Medicine (2017). Improving knowledge about, access to, and utilization of long-acting reversible contraception among adolescents and young adults. *Journal of Adolescent Health, 60,* 472-474.

Soderstrom, M., & others (2012). Insufficient sleep predicts clinical burnout. *Journal of Occupational Health Psychology, 17,* 175-183.

Soenens, B., Vansteenkiste, M., & Beyers, W. (2019). Parenting adolescents. In M.H. Bornstein (Ed.), *Handbook of parenting* (3rd ed.). New York: Routledge.

Sohail, R., & others (2019). Kangaroo care: Need of the day. *BMJ Case Report, 12,* 12.

Solovieva, Y., & Quintanar, L. (2017). Play with social roles as a method for psychological development in young children. In T. Bruce & others

(Eds.), *Routledge international handbook of early childhood play.* New York: Routledge.

Someya, S., & others (2017). Effects of calorie restriction on the lifespan and healthspan of POLG mitochondrial mutator mice. *PLoS One, 12*(2), e0171159.

Son, J.M., & Lee, C. (2019). Mitochondria: Multifaceted regulators of aging. *BMB Reports, 52,* 13-23.

Soneji, S., & Beltran-Sanchez, H. (2019). Association of Special Supplementation Nutrition Program for Women, Infants, and Children with preterm birth and infant mortality. *JAMA Network Open, 2*(12), e1916722.

Soneji, S., & others (2018). Association between initial use of e-cigarettes and subsequent cigarette smoking among adolescents and young adults: A systematic review and meta-analysis. *JAMA Pediatrics, 171,* 788-797.

Song, A.V., & Halpern-Felsher, B.L. (2010). Predictive relationship between adolescent oral and vaginal sex: Results from a prospective, longitudinal study. *Archives of Pediatric and Adolescent Medicine, 165,* 243-249.

Song, Y., & others (2017). Secular trends for age at spermarche among Chinese boys from 11 ethnic minorities, 1995-2010: A multiple cross-sectional study. *BMJ Open, 6*(2), e010518.

Song, Y., & others (2018). T-cell immunoglobin and ITIM domain contributes to CD8+ T-cell immunosenescence. *Aging Cell, 17,* 2.

Sonnenberg, J., Bostic, C., & Halpern-Felsher, B. (2020, in press). Support for aggressive tobacco control interventions among California adolescents and young adults. *Journal of Adolescent Health.*

Sood, A.B., Razdan, A., Weller, E.B., & Weller, R.A. (2006). Children's reactions to parental and sibling death. *Current Psychiatry Reports, 8,* 115-120.

Sophian, C. (1985). Perseveration and infants' search: A comparison of two- and three-location tasks. *Developmental Psychology, 21,* 187-194.

Sorensen, L.C., Dodge, K.A., & Conduct Problems Prevention Research Group (2016). How does the Fast Track intervention prevent adverse outcomes in young adulthood? *Child Development, 87,* 429-445.

Sorman, D.E., & others (2020). Complexity of primary lifetime occupation and cognitive processing. *Frontiers in Psychology, 10,* 1861.

Sorokowski, P., Kowal, M., & Sorokowska, A. (2019). Religious affiliation and marital satisfaction: Commonalities among Christians, Muslims, and atheists. *Frontiers in Psychology, 10,* 2798.

Sosa, G.W., & Lagana, L. (2019). The effects of video game training on the cognitive functioning of older adults: A community-based randomized controlled trial. *Archives of Gerontology and Geriatrics, 80,* 20-30.

Soska, K.C., Robinson, S.R., & Adolph, K.E. (2015). A new twist on old ideas: How sitting orients crawlers. *Developmental Science, 18,* 206-218.

Soska, K.C., & others (2020, in press). Infants plan prehension while pivoting. *Developmental Psychobiology.*

Sourander, A., & others (2019). Prenatal cotinine levels and ADHD among offspring. *Pediatrics, 143,* 3.

South Palomares, J.K., Sutherland, C.A.M., & Young, A.M. (2018). Facial first impressions and partner preference models: Comparable or distinct underlying structures. *British Journal of Psychology, 109,* 538-563.

Souto-Gallardo, M.C., & others (2020, in press). Association of food parenting practices on Child BMI z score and waist circumference in Mexican preschool children after 1 year of follow-up. *Journal of Nutrition and Physical Activity.*

Sowell, E.R., & others (2004). Longitudinal mapping of cortical thickness and brain growth in children. *Journal of Neuroscience, 24,* 8223-8231.

Spangler, G., Johann, M., Ronai, Z., & Zimmermann, P. (2009). Genetic and environmental influence on attachment disorganization. *Journal of Child Psychology and Psychiatry, 50,* 952-961.

Speakman, J.R. (2020). An evolutionary perspective on sedentary behavior. *Bioessays, 42*(1), e1900156.

Specht, J., Egloff, B., & Schukle, S.C. (2011). Stability and change of personality across the life course: The impact of age and major life events on mean-level and rank-order stability of the Big Five. *Journal of Personality and Social Psychology, 101,* 862-882.

Spele, E.S. (2000). Core knowledge. *American Psychologist, 55,* 1233-1244.

Spelke, E.S. (1979). Perceiving bimodally specified events in infancy. *Developmental Psychology, 5,* 626-636.

Spelke, E.S. (1991). Physical knowledge in infancy: Reflections on Piaget's theory. In S. Carey & R. Gelman (Eds.), *The epigenesis of mind: Essays on biology and cognition.* Hillsdale, NJ: Erlbaum.

Spelke, E.S. (2003). Developing knowledge of space: Core systems and new combinations. In S.M. Kosslyn & A. Galaburda (Eds.), *Languages of the brain.* Cambridge, MA: Harvard University Press.

Spelke, E.S. (2011). Natural number and natural geometry. In E. Brannon & S. Dehaene (Eds.), *Space, time, and number in the brain.* New York: Oxford University Press.

Spelke, E.S. (2013). Developmental sources of social divisions. *Neurosciences and the human person: New perspectives on human activities.* Unpublished manuscript, Department of Psychology, Harvard University, Cambridge, MA.

Spelke, E.S. (2016a). Core knowledge and conceptual change: A perspective on social cognition. In D. Barner & A.S. Baron (Eds.), *Core knowledge and conceptual change.* New York: Oxford University Press.

Spelke, E.S. (2016b). Cognitive abilities of infants. In R.J. Sternberg, S.T. Fiske, & J. Foss (Eds.), *Scientists making a difference.* New York: Cambridge University Press.

Spelke, E.S., Breinlinger, K., Macomber, J., & Jacobson, K. (1992). Origins of knowledge. *Psychological Review, 99,* 605-632.

Spelke, E.S., & Owsley, C.J. (1979). Intermodal exploration and knowledge in infancy. *Infant Behavior and Development, 2,* 13-28.

Spence, A.P. (1989). *Biology of human aging.* Englewood Cliffs, NJ: Prentice Hall.

Spence, R., Jacobs, C., & Bifulco, A. (2019, in press). Attachment style, loneliness, and depression in older women. *Aging and Mental Health.*

Spieker, S.J., & others (2012). Relational aggression in middle childhood: Predictors and adolescent outcomes. *Social Development, 21,* 354–375.

Spinrad, T.L., & Eisenberg, N. (2020). Socialization of moral emotions and behavior. In D.J. Laible & others (Eds.), *Oxford handbook of parenting and moral development.* New York: Oxford University Press.

Sprecher, S., Treger, S., & Sakaluk, J.K. (2013). Premarital sexual standards and sociosexuality: Gender, ethnicity, and cohort differences. *Archives of Sexual Behavior, 42,* 1395–1405.

Spruyt, K., & others (2019). Mind-wandering, or the allocation of attentional resources, is sleep-driven across childhood. *Scientific Reports, 9*(1), 1269.

Srivastava, S., & Veech, R.L. (2019). Brown and brite: The fat soldiers in the anti-obesity fight. *Frontiers in Physiology, 10,* 38.

Sroufe, L.A. (2016). The place of attachment in development. In J. Cassidy & P.R. Shaver (Eds.), *Handbook of attachment* (3rd ed.). New York: Guilford.

Sroufe, L.A., Egeland, B., Carlson, E., & Collins, W.A. (2005). The place of early attachment in developmental context. In K.E. Grossman, K. Grossman, & E. Waters (Eds.), *The power of longitudinal attachment research. From infancy and childhood to adulthood.* New York: Guilford.

Sroufe, L.A., Waters, E., & Matas, L. (1974). Contextual determinants of infant affectional response. In M. Lewis & L. Rosenblum (Eds.), *Origins of fear.* New York: Wiley.

Ssegonia, R., & others (2019). Depressive disorders in adolescence, recurrence in early adulthood, and healthcare usage in mid-adulthood: A longitudinal cost-of-illness study. *Journal of Affective Disorders, 258,* 33–41.

St. George, S.M., & others (2020, in press). A developmental cascade perspective of pediatric obesity: A systematic review of preventive interventions from infancy through late adolescence. *Obesity Reviews.*

Stack, J., & Romero-Rivas, C. (2020). Merit overrules theory of mind when children share resources with others. *PLoS One, 15*(1), e-0227375.

Stacks, A.M., & others (2020). Permanency and well-being outcomes for maltreated infants: Pilot results from an infant-toddler court team. *Child Abuse and Neglect, 101,* 104332.

Stadd, K., & others (2020, in press). A kangaroo care pathway for NICU staff and families: The proof is in the pouch. *Advanced Neonatal Care.*

Staff, J., Mont'Alvao, A., & Mortimer, J.T. (2015). Children at work. In R.M. Lerner (Ed.), *Handbook of child psychology and developmental psychology* (7th ed.). New York: Wiley.

Staley, C. (2019). *College success and study skills.* Boston: Cengage.

Stalgaitis, C.A., & others (2019). Understanding adversity and peer crowds to prevent youth health risks. *American Journal of Health Behavior, 43,* 767–780.

Stancil, S.L., & others (2016). Contraceptive provision to adolescent females prescribed teratogenic medicines. *Pediatrics, 137,* 1–8.

Stanford Center for Longevity (2011). Experts' consensus on brain health. Retrieved April 30, 2011, from http://longevity.stanford.edu/mymind/cognitiveagingstatement

Stanford Center for Longevity and Max Planck Institute for Human Development (2014). A consensus on the brain training industry from the scientific community. Retrieved September 16, 2015, from http://longevity3.stanford.edu.blog/2014/10/15

Stanford University Medical Center (2012). *Growth hormone deficiency.* Palo Alto, CA: Author.

Stanley, S.M., Amato, P.R., Johnson, C.A., & Markman, H.J. (2006). Premarital education, marital quality, and marital stability: Findings from a large, household survey. *Journal of Family Psychology, 20,* 117–126.

Stanovich, K.E. (2019). *How to think straight about psychology* (11th ed.). Upper Saddle River, NJ: Pearson.

Starr, L.R., & others (2012). Love hurts (in more ways than one): Specificity of psychological symptoms as predictors and consequences of romantic activity among early adolescent girls. *Journal of Clinical Psychology, 68*(4), 373–381.

statisticbrain (2017). *Online dating statistics.* Retrieved November 4, 2017, from www.statisticbrain.com/online-dating-statistics

Staudinger, U.M. (1996). Psychologische Produktivität und Selbstentfaltung im Alter. In M.M. Baltes & L. Montada (Eds.), *Produktives leben im alter.* Frankfurt: Campus.

Staudinger, U.M., & Dorner, J. (2007). Wisdom. In J.E. Birren (Ed.), *Encyclopedia of gerontology* (2nd ed.). San Diego: Academic Press.

Staudinger, U.M., & Gluck, J. (2011). Psychological wisdom research. *Annual Review of Psychology* (Vol. 62). Palo Alto, CA: Annual Reviews.

Stawski, R.S., Sliwinski, M.J., & Hofer, S.M. (2013). Between-person and within-person associations among processing speed, attention switching, and working memory in younger and older adults. *Experimental Aging Research, 39,* 194–214.

Steck, N., & others (2013). Euthanasia and assisted suicide in selected European countries and U.S. states: Systematic literature review. *Medical Care, 51,* 938–944.

Steckler, C.M., & others (2018). Feeling out a link between feeling and infant sociomoral evaluation. *British Journal of Developmental Psychology, 36,* 482–500.

Steele, H., & Steele, J. (Eds.) (2019). *Handbook of attachment-based interventions.* New York: Guilford.

Steele, J., Waters, E., Crowell, J., & Treboux, D. (1998, June). *Self-report measures of attachment: Secure bonds to other attachment measures and attachment theory.* Paper presented at the meeting of the International Society for the Study of Personal Relationships, Saratoga Springs, NY.

Stefansson, K.K., & others (2018). School engagement and intentional self-regulation: A reciprocal relation in adolescence. *Journal of Adolescence, 64,* 23–33.

Steiger, A.E., Allemand, M., Robins, R.W., & Fend, H.A. (2014). Low and decreasing self-esteem during adolescence predict adult depression two decades later. *Journal of Personality and Social Psychology, 106,* 325–338.

Stein, G.L., & others (2019). Making my family proud: The unique combination of familism pride to the psychological adjustment of Latinx emerging adults. *Cultural Diversity and Ethnic Minority Psychology, 25,* 188–198.

Steinbach, A. (2019). Children's and parents' well-being in joint physical custody: A literature review. *Family Process, 58,* 353–369.

Steinbach, A., & others (2020, in press). Stability and change in intergenerational family relations across two decades: Findings from the German Aging Survey, 1996–2014. *Journals of Gerontology B: Psychological Sciences and Social Sciences.*

Steinberg, D.B., & others (2019). Onset trajectories of sexting and other sexual behaviors across high school: A longitudinal growth mixture modeling approach. *Archives of Sexual Behavior, 48,* 2321–2331.

Steinberg, L. (2014). *Age of opportunity.* Boston: Houghton Mifflin Harcourt.

Steinberg, L. (2015a). How should the science of adolescent brain pathology inform legal policy? In J. Bhabha (Ed.), *Coming of age.* Philadelphia: University of Pennsylvania Press.

Steinberg, L. (2015b). The neural underpinnings of adolescent risk-taking: The roles of reward-seeking, impulse control, and peers. In G. Oettigen & P. Gollwitzer (Eds.), *Self-regulation in adolescence.* New York: Cambridge University Press.

Steinberg, L., & others (2019). Around the world, adolescence is a time of heightened sensation seeking and immature self-regulation. *Developmental Science, 21,* 1–13.

Steinberg, S. (2011, June 11). *New dating site helps college students find love.* CNN Living. Retrieved February 27, 2013, from www.cnn.com/2011/LIVING/06/22date.my.school/index.html

Steiner, J.E. (1979). Human facial expressions in response to taste and smell stimulation. *Advances in Child Development and Behavior, 13,* 257–295.

Stelzer, E.M., & others (2020). Prolonged grief disorder and the cultural crisis. *Frontiers in Psychology, 10,* 2982.

Stenbacka, M., Moberg, T., & Jokinen, J. (2019). Adolescent criminality: Multiple adverse health outcomes and mortality pattern in Swedish men. *BMC Public Health, 19*(1), 400.

Stenberg, G. (2017). Does contingency in adults' responding influence 12-month-old infants' social referencing? *Infant Behavior and Development, 49,* 9–20.

Stenholm, S., & others (2014). Age-related trajectories of physical functioning in work and retirement: The role of sociodemographic factors, lifestyles, and disease. *Journal of Epidemiology and Community Health, 68,* 503–509.

Stenholm, S., & others (2017). Body mass indicator as a predictor of healthy and disease-free life expectancy between ages 50 and 75: A multicohort study. *International Journal of Obesity, 41,* 769–775.

Stensvehagen, M.T., & others (2019). How women experience and cope with daily hassles after sexual abuse—A retrospective qualitative study. *Scandinavian Journal of Caring Science, 33*(2), 487–497.

Stepaniak, U., & others (2016). Antioxidant vitamin intake and mortality in three Central and Eastern European urban populations: The HAPIEE study. *European Journal of Nutrition, 55,* 547–560.

Stephan, Y., & others (2017). Personality and frailty: Evidence from four samples. *Journal of Research on Personality, 66,* 46–53.

Stephan, Y., & others (2018). Higher IQ in adolescence is related to a younger subjective age in later life: Findings from the Wisconsin Longitudinal Study. *Intelligence, 69,* 195–199.

Stepler, R. (2017). *Led by baby boomers, divorce rates climb for America's 50+ population.* Washington, DC: Pew Research Center.

Stepler, R. (2017, April 6). *Number of U.S. adults cohabiting with a partner continues to rise, especially among those 50 and older.* Washington, DC: Pew Research Center.

Steptoe, A., Deaton, A., & Stone, A.A. (2015). Subjective well being, health, and aging. *Lancet, 385,* 640–648.

Sterling, M.R., & others (2020, in press). Understanding the workflow of home health care for patients with heart failure: Challenges and opportunities. *Journal of General Internal Medicine.*

Stern, C., West, T.V., Jost, J.T., & Rule, N.Q. (2013). The politics of gaydar: Ideological differences in the use of gendered cues in categorizing sexual orientation. *Journal of Personality and Social Psychology, 104,* 520–541.

Stern, D.N. (2010). A new look at parent-infant interaction: Infant arousal dynamics. In B.M. Lester & J.D. Sparrow (Eds.), *Nurturing children and families: Building on the legacy of T. Berry Brazelton.* New York: Wiley.

Stern, D.N., Beebe, B., Jaffe, J., & Bennett, S.L. (1977). The infant's stimulus world during social interaction: A study of caregiver behaviors with particular reference to repetition and timing. In H.R. Schaffer (Ed.), *Studies in mother-infant interaction.* London: Academic Press.

Sternberg, K., Williams, W.M., & Sternberg, R.J. (2019). How parents can maximize children's cognitive abilities. In M.H. Bornstein (Ed.), *Handbook of parenting* (3rd ed.). New York: Elsevier.

Sternberg, R.J. (1986). *Intelligence applied.* San Diego: Harcourt Brace Jovanovich.

Sternberg, R.J. (1988). *The triangle of love.* New York: Basic Books.

Sternberg, R.J. (2004). Individual differences in cognitive development. In U. Goswami (Ed.), *Blackwell handbook of childhood cognitive development.* Malden, MA: Blackwell.

Sternberg, R.J. (2010). Componential models of creativity. In M. Runco & S. Spritzker (Eds.), *Encyclopedia of creativity.* New York: Elsevier.

Sternberg, R.J. (2014). Teaching about the nature of intelligence. *Intelligence, 42,* 176–179.

Sternberg, R.J. (2016). What does it mean to be intelligent? In R.J. Sternberg & others (Eds.), *Scientists making a difference.* New York: Cambridge University Press.

Sternberg, R.J. (2017). Intelligence and competence in theory and practice. In A.J. Elliot & C.S. Dweck (Eds.), *Handbook of competence and motivation* (2nd ed.). New York: Guilford.

Sternberg, R.J. (2018). Triarchic theory of intelligence. In B. Frey (Eds.), *SAGE encyclopedia of educational research, measurement, and evaluation.* Thousand Oaks, CA: Sage.

Sternberg, R.J. (2019a). Intelligence. In R.J. Sternberg & W.E. Pickren (Eds.), *Cambridge handbook of the intellectual history of psychology.* New York: Cambridge University Press.

Sternberg, R.J. (2019b). Race to Samarra: The critical importance of wisdom. In R.J. Sternberg & J. Gluck (Eds.), *Cambridge handbook of wisdom.* New York: Cambridge University Press.

Sternberg, R.J. (2019c). Enhancing people's creativity. In J.C. Kaufman, & R.J. Sternberg (Eds.), *Cambridge handbook of creativity* (2nd ed.). New York: Cambridge University Press.

Sternberg, R.J. (2020a). The concept of intelligence. In R.J. Sternberg (Ed.), *Cambridge handbook of intelligence.* New York: Cambridge University Press.

Sternberg, R.J. (2020b). Speculations on the future of intelligence research. In R.J. Sternberg (Ed.), *Cambridge handbook of intelligence.* New York: Cambridge University Press.

Sternberg, R.J. (2020c). Intelligence and creativity. In R.J. Sternberg (Ed.), *Cambridge handbook of intelligence.* New York: Cambridge University Press.

Sternberg, R.J. (2020d). The augmented theory of successful intelligence. In R.J. Sternberg (Ed.), *Cambridge handbook of intelligence.* New York: Cambridge University Press.

Sternberg, R.J. (2020e). Psychological theory and research in the twentieth century. In R.J. Sternberg (Ed.), *Cambridge handbook of intelligence.* New York: Cambridge University Press.

Sternberg, R.J., & Glueck, J. (Eds.) (2019). *Cambridge handbook of wisdom.* New York: Cambridge University Press.

Sternberg, R.J., & Halpern, D.F. (Eds.) (2020). *Critical thinking in psychology* (2nd ed.). New York: Cambridge University Press.

Sternberg, R.J., & Kaufman, J.C. (2018a). Theories and conceptions of giftedness. In S. Pfeiffer (Ed.), *Handbook of giftedness in children* (2nd ed.). New York: Springer.

Sternberg, R.J., Kaufman, J.C., & Roberts, A.M. (2019). The relation of creativity to intelligence and wisdom. In J.C. Kaufman & R.J. Sternberg (Eds.), *Cambridge handbook of creativity* (2nd ed.). New York: Cambridge University Press.

Sternberg, R.J., & Sternberg, K. (Eds.) (2019). *The new psychology of love* (2nd ed.). New York: Cambridge University Press.

Sterns, H., & Huyck, M.H. (2001). The role of work in midlife. In M. Lachman (Ed.), *Handbook of midlife development.* New York: Wiley.

Sterns, H.L., Barrett, G.V., & Alexander, R.A. (1985). Accidents and the aging individual. In J.E. Birren & K.W. Schaie (Eds.), *Handbook of the psychology of aging.* New York: Van Nostrand Reinhold.

Steur, F.B., Applefield, J.M., & Smith, R. (1971). Televised aggression and interpersonal aggression of preschool children. *Journal of Experimental Child Psychology, 11,* 442–447.

Stevanovic, J., & others (2020). Physical exercise and liver "fitness": Role of mitochondrial function and epigenetics-related mechanisms in non-alcoholic fatty liver disease. *Molecular Metabolism, 32,* 1–14.

Stevenson, H.W. (1995). Mathematics achievements of American students: First in the world by the year 2000. In C.A. Nelson (Ed.), *Basic and applied perspectives on learning, cognition, and development.* Minneapolis: University of Minnesota Press.

Stevenson, H.W. (2000). Middle childhood: Education and schooling. In A. Kazdin (Ed.), *Encyclopedia of psychology.* Washington, DC, & New York: American Psychological Association and Oxford University Press.

Stevenson, H.W., Hofer, B.K., & Randel, B. (1999). *Middle childhood: Education and schooling.* Unpublished manuscript, Department of Psychology, University of Michigan, Ann Arbor.

Stevenson, H.W., Lee, S., & Stigler, J.W. (1986). Mathematics achievement of Chinese, Japanese, and American children. *Science, 231,* 693–699.

Stevenson, H.W., & Zusho, A. (2002). Adolescence in China and Japan: Adapting to a changing environment. In B.B. Brown, R.W. Larson, & T.S. Saraswathi (Eds.), *The world's youth.* New York: Cambridge University Press.

Stevenson, H.W., & others (1990). Contexts of achievement. *Monographs of the Society for Research in Child Development, 55*(Serial No. 221).

Stewart, A.J., & Deaux, K. (2019). Personality and social contexts as sources of change and continuity across the life span. In K. Deaux & M. Snyder (Eds.), *Oxford handbook of personality and social psychology.* New York: Oxford University Press.

Stewart, A.J., Ostrove, J.M., & Helson, R. (2001). Middle aging in women: Patterns of personality change from the 30s to the 50s. *Journal of Adult Development, 8,* 23–37.

Stewart, D.E., & Vigod, S.N. (2019). Postpartum depression: Pathophysiology, treatment, and emerging therapeutics. *Annual Review of Medicine, 70,* 183–196.

Stewart, J.G., & others (2017). Cognitive control deficits differentiate adolescent suicide ideators from attempters. *Journal of Clinical Psychology, 78,* e614–e621.

Stice, E., & others (2019). Meta-analytic review of dissonance-based eating disorder prevention programs: Intervention, participant, and facilitator features that predict larger effects. *Clinical Psychology Review, 70,* 91–107.

Stillman, T.F., Maner, J.K., & Baumeister, R.F. (2010). Thin slice of violence: Distinguishing violent from nonviolent sex offenders at a glance. *Evolution of Human Behavior, 31,* 298-303.

Stipek, D. (2005, February 16). Commentary in *USA TODAY,* p. 10.

Stokes, C.E., & Raley, R.K. (2009). Cohabitation. In D. Carr (Ed.), *Encyclopedia of the life course and human development.* Boston: Gale Cengage.

Stolove, C.A., Galatzer-Levy, I.R., & Bonanno, G.A. (2017). Emergence of depression following job loss prospectively predicts lower rates of reemployment. *Psychiatry Research, 253,* 79-83.

Stolzenberg, E.B., & others (2019). *The American college freshman: National norms fall 2017.* Los Angeles: Higher Education Research Institute, UCLA.

Stone, A., & Bosworth, R.G. (2020, in press). Exploring infant sensitivity to visual language using eye tracking and the preferential looking paradigm. *Journal of Visual Experiments.*

Stoner, M.C.D., & others (2019). The relationship between school dropout and pregnancy among adolescent girls and young women in South Africa: A HPTN 068 analysis. *Health Education and Behavior, 46,* 559-568.

Stones, M., & Stones, L. (2007). Sexuality, sensuality, and intimacy. In J.E. Birren (Ed.), *Encyclopedia of gerontology* (2nd ed.). San Diego: Academic Press.

Storey, A.E., Alloway, H., & Walsh, C.J. (2020, in press). Dads: Progress in understanding the neuroendocrine basis of human fathering behavior. *Hormones and Behavior.*

Straatmann, V.S., & others (2020, in press). Disease or function? What matters most for self-rated health in older people depends on age. *Aging. Clinical and Experimental Research.*

Strada, E.A. (2019). Psychological issues and bereavement. *Primary Care, 46,* 373-386.

Strandberg, T. (2019). Preventive effects of physical activity in old people. In R. Fernandez-Ballesteros & others (Eds.), *Cambridge handbook of successful aging.* New York: Cambridge University Press.

Strenze, T. (2007). Intelligence and socioeconomic success: A meta-analytic review of longitudinal research. *Intelligence, 35,* 401-426.

Strickhouser, J.E., Zell, E., & Krizan, Z. (2017). Does personality predict health and well-being? A metasynthesis. *Health Psychology, 36,* 797-810.

Strickland, B., & Chemla, E. (2018). Cross-linguistic regularities and learner biases reflect "core" mechanics. *PLoS One, 13*(1), e0184132.

Stringa, N., & others (2020, in press). Physical activity as moderator of the association between APOE and cognitive decline in older adults: Results from three longitudinal cohort studies. *Journals of Gerontology A: Biological Sciences and Medical Sciences.*

Stroebe, M., & Schut, H. (2015). Family matters in bereavement: Toward an integrative interpersonal coping model. *Perspectives in Psychological Science, 10,* 873-879.

Stroebe, M., & Schut, H. (2017). The dual process model of coping with bereavement—Rationale and description. In M. Barkam & others (Eds.), *Clinical psychology II—Treatments and interventions.* Thousand Oaks, CA: Sage.

Stroebe, M., & others (2017a). Grief is not a disease, but bereavement merits medical awareness. *Lancet, 389*(1), 347-349.

Stroebe, M., & others (2017b). Models of coping and bereavement—An updated overview. *Journal of Studies in Psychology, 38*(3), 582-607.

Strohminger, N. (2018). Identity is essentially moral. In K. Gray & J. Graham (Eds.), *Atlas of moral psychology.* New York: Guilford.

Strom, M., & others (2019). Is breast feeding associated with offspring IQ at age 5? Findings from prospective cohort: Lifestyle during pregnancy study. *BMJ Open, 9*(5), e023134.

Stroope, S., McFarland, M.J., & Uecker, J.E. (2015). Marital characteristics and the sexual relationships of U.S. older adults: An analysis of national social life, health, and aging project data. *Archives of Sexual Behavior, 44,* 233-247.

Strough, J., Leszczynski, J.P., Neely, T.L., Flinn, J.A., & Margrett, J. (2007). From adolescence to later adulthood: Femininity, masculinity and androgyny in six age groups. *Sex Roles, 57,* 385-396.

Stubbs, B., Brefka, S., & Denkinger, M.D. (2015). What works to prevent falls in community-dwelling older adults? An umbrella review of meta-analyses of randomized controlled trials. *Physical Therapy, 95,* 1095-1110.

Stuebe, A.M., & Schwartz, E.G. (2010). The risks and benefits of infant feeding practices for women and their children. *Journal of Perinatology, 30,* 155-162.

Sturge-Apple, M.L., & others (2019). Parental maltreatment. In M.H. Bornstein (Ed.), *Handbook of parenting* (3rd ed.). New York: Routledge.

Sturman, M.C. (2003). Searching for the inverted U-shaped relationship between time and performance: Meta-analyses of the experience/performance, tenure/performance, and age/performance relationships. *Journal of Management, 29,* 609-640.

Su, Y., D'Arcy, C., & Meng, X. (2020, in press). Social support and positive coping skills act as mediators buffering the impact of childhood maltreatment on psychological distress and positive mental health in adulthood: Analysis of a national population-based sample. *American Journal of Epidemiology.*

Suarez, L., & others (2011). Maternal smoking, passive tobacco smoke, and neural tube defects. *Birth Defects Research A: Clinical and Molecular Teratology, 91,* 29-33.

Suarez-Rivera, C., Smith, L.B., & Yu, C. (2019). Multimodal parent behaviors within joint attention support sustained attention in infants. *Developmental Psychology, 55,* 96-109.

Subedi, A., & others (2020). Use of magnetic resonance imaging to identify immune checkpoint inhibitor-induced inflammatory arthritis. *JAMA Network Open, 3*(2), e200032.

Substance Abuse and Mental Health Services Administration (2003). *Aging and substance abuse.* Washington, DC: U.S. Department of Health and Human Services.

Sueur, C., & others (2019). Mechanisms of network evolution: A focus on socioecological factors, intermediary mechanism, and selection pressures. *Primates, 60,* 167-181.

Sugden, K., & others (2019). Establishing a generalized polyepigenetic biomarker for tobacco smoking. *Translational Psychiatry, 9*(1), 92.

Sugita, Y. (2004). Experience in early infancy is indispensable for color perception. *Current Biology, 14,* 1267-1271.

Sui, X., & others (2007). Cardiorespiratory fitness and adiposity as mortality predictors in older adults. *Journal of the American Medical Association, 298,* 2507-2516.

Suitor, J.J., Gilligan, M., & Pillemer, K. (2016). Stability, change, and complexity in later life families. In L.K. George & G.F. Ferraro (Eds.), *Handbook of aging and the social sciences* (8th ed.). New York: Elsevier.

Sullivan, A.R., & Fenelon, A. (2014). Patterns of widowhood mortality. *Journals of Gerontology B: Psychological Sciences and Social Sciences, 69,* 53-62.

Sullivan, H.S. (1953). *The interpersonal theory of psychiatry.* New York: W.W. Norton.

Sullivan, K., & Sullivan, A. (1980). Adolescent-parent separation. *Developmental Psychology, 16,* 93-99.

Sullivan, R., & Wilson, D. (2018). Neurobiology of infant attachment. *Annual Review of Psychology* (Vol. 69). Palo Alto, CA: Annual Reviews.

Summit, A.K., & others (2019). Integration of onsite long-acting reversible contraception services into school-based health centers. *Journal of School Health, 89,* 226-231.

Sun, K.L. (2015). *There's no limit: Mathematics teaching for a growth mindset.* Doctoral dissertation, Stanford University, Stanford, CA.

Sun, X., & others (2017). Longitudinal links between work experiences and marital satisfaction in African American dual-earner couples. *Journal of Family Psychology, 31,* 1029-1039.

Sun, Y., & others (2016). From genetic studies to precision medicine in alcohol dependence. *Behavioral Pharmacology, 27,* 87-99.

Sun, Y.Q., & others (2019). Body mass index and all-cause mortality in HUNT and UK Biobank studies: Linear and non-linear mendelian randomization analyses. *BMJ, 364,* l1042.

Sung, J.E., & others (2017). Effects of age, working memory, and word order on passive-sentence comprehension: Evidence from a verb-final language. *International Psychogeriatrics, 29,* 939-948.

Super, C., & Harkness, S. (1997). The cultural structuring of child development. In J.W. Berry, Y.H. Poortinga, & J. Pandey (Eds.), *Handbook of cross-cultural psychology: Theory and method* (Vol. 2). Boston: Allyn & Bacon.

Surti, K., & Langeslag, S.J.E. (2019). Perceived ability to regulate love. *PLoS One, 14*(5), e0216523.

Susman, E.J., & Dorn, L.D. (2013). Puberty: Its role in development. In I.B. Weiner & others (Eds.), *Handbook of psychology* (2nd ed., Vol. 6). New York: Wiley.

Sutcliffe, K., & others (2012). Comparing midwife-led and doctor-led maternity care: A systematic review of reviews. *Journal of Advanced Nursing, 68*(11), 2376-2386.

Sutin, A.R., & others (2016). Parent-reported bullying and child weight gain between ages 6 and 15. *Child Obesity, 12,* 482-487.

Sutton, T.E., Simons, L.G., & Tyler, K.A. (2020, in press). Hooking-up and sexual victimization on campus: Examining moderators of risk. *Journal of Interpersonal Violence.*

Suzman, R.M., Harris, T., Hadley, E.C., Kovar, M.G., & Weindruch, R. (1992). The robust oldest old: Optimistic perspectives for increasing healthy life expectancy. In R.M. Suzman, D.P. Willis, & K.G. Manton (Eds.), *The oldest old.* New York: Oxford University Press.

Swainson, M.G., Ingle, L., & Carroll, S. (2019). Cardiorespiratory fitness as a predictor of short-term and lifetime estimated cardiovascular disease risk. *Scandinavian Journal of Medicine and Science in Sports, 29,* 1402-1413.

Swamy, G.K., Ostbye, T., & Skjaerven, R. (2008). Association of preterm birth with long-term survival, reproduction, and next generation preterm birth. *JAMA, 299,* 1429-1436.

Sweeney, M.M. (2009). Remarriage. In D. Carr (Ed.), *Encyclopedia of the life course and human development.* Boston: Gale Cengage.

Sweeney, M.M. (2010). Remarriage and stepfamilies: Strategic sites for family scholarship in the 21st century. *Journal of Marriage and the Family, 72,* 667-684.

Swenor, B.K., & others (2019). Vision impairment and cognitive outcomes in older adults: The Health ABC Study. *Journals of Gerontology A: Biological Sciences and Medical Sciences, 74,* 1454-1460.

Swift, A. (2016, June 24). *Euthanasia still acceptable to a majority in U.S.* Washington, DC: Gallup.

Syed, M., Pasupathi, M., & McLean, K.C. (2020). Master narratives, ethics, and morality. In L.A. Jensen (Ed.), *Oxford handbook of moral development.* New York: Oxford University Press.

Sykes, C.J. (1995). *Dumbing down our kids: Why America's children feel good about themselves but can't read, write, or add.* New York: St. Martin's Press.

Syme, C., & others (2019). Sex differences in blood pressure hemodynamics in middle-aged adults with overweight and obesity. *Hypertension, 74,* 407-412.

Szinovacz, M.E. (2009). Grandparenthood. In D. Carr (Ed.), *Encyclopedia of the life course and human development.* Boston: Gale Cengage.

Szwedo, D.E., Hessel, E.T., & Allen, J.P. (2017). Supportive romantic relationships as predictors of resilience against early adolescent maternal negativity. *Journal of Youth and Adolescence, 46,* 454-465.

T

Taggart, J., Eisen, S., & Lillard, A.S. (2018). Pretense. In M.H. Bornstein (Ed.), *SAGE encyclopedia of life-span human development.* Thousand Oaks, CA: Sage.

Taggart, T., & others (2019). A person-centered approach to the study of Black adolescent religiosity, racial identity, and sexual initiation. *Journal of Research on Adolescence, 29,* 402-413.

Taige, N.M., & others (2007). Antenatal maternal stress and long-term effects on child neurodevelopment: How and why? *Journal of Child Psychology and Psychiatry, 48,* 245-261.

Takacs, Z.K., & Kassai, R. (2019). The efficacy of different interventions to foster children's executive function skills: A series of meta-analyses. *Psychological Bulletin, 145,* 653-697.

Talamas, S.N., Mavor, K.I., & Perrett, D.I. (2016). Blinded by beauty: Attractiveness bias and accurate perceptions of academic performance. *PLoS One, 11*(2), e148284.

Taliaferro, L.A., & others (2020, in press). Associations between connections to parents and friends and non-suicidal self-injury among adolescents: The mediating role of developmental assets. *Clinical Child Psychology and Psychiatry.*

Tamana, S.K., & others (2019). Screen-time is associated with inattention problems in preschoolers: Results from the CHILD birth cohort study. *PLoS, 14*(4), e0213995.

Tamis-LeMonda, C.S., & Lockman, J.J. (Eds.) (2020). *Handbook of infant development.* New York: Cambridge University Press.

Tamis-LeMonda, C.S., & others (2019). Language and play in parent-child interactions. In M.H. Bornstein (Ed.), *Handbook of parenting* (3rd ed.). New York: Elsevier.

Tamrakar, S.R., & Bastakoti, R. (2019). Determinants of infertility in couples. *Journal of Nepal Health Research Council, 17,* 85-89.

Tan, B.W., Pooley, J.A., & Speelman, C.P. (2016). A meta-analytic review of the efficacy of physical exercise interventions on cognition in individuals with autism spectrum disorders and ADHD. *Journal of Autism and Developmental Disorders, 46,* 3126-3143.

Tan, E.J., Xue, Q.L., Li, T., Carlson, M.C., & Fried, L.P. (2007). Volunteering: A physical activity intervention for older adults—The Experience Corps program in Baltimore. *Journal of Urban Health, 83,* 954-969.

Tan, M., & Grigorenko, E.L. (2019). Genetics/genomics and intelligence. In R.J. Sternberg (Ed.), *Human intelligence.* New York: Cambridge University Press.

Tan, M.E., & others (2017). Employment status among the Singapore elderly and its correlates. *Psychogeriatrics, 17,* 155-163.

Tan, P.Z., Armstrong, L.M., & Cole, P.M. (2013). Relations between temperament and anger regulation over early childhood. *Social Development, 22,* 755-772.

Tan, Q. (2020, in press). Harnessing the power of twins in epigenetic association studies: Causal inference and more. *Epigenomics, 12,* 1-3.

Tan, Q., & others (2020, in press). Cohort differences in the risk of selected candidate genes on all-cause mortality at advanced ages. *Archives of Epidemiology.*

Tanajak, P., & others (2017). Vildagliptin and caloric restriction for cardioprotection in pre-diabetic rats. *Journal of Endocrinology, 232,* 189-204.

Tang, A., & others (2017). Shyness trajectories across the first four decades predict mental health outcomes. *Journal of Abnormal Child Psychology, 45,* 1621-1633.

Tang, P.C., & others (2014). Resveratrol and cardiovascular health—Promising therapeutic or hopeless illusion? *Pharmacological Research, 90,* 88-115.

Tang, S., Davis-Kean, P.E., Chen, M., & Sexton, H.R. (2016). Adolescent pregnancy's intergenerational effects: Does an adolescent mother's education have consequences for children's achievement? *Journal of Research on Adolescence, 26,* 180-193.

Tang, X., & others (2019). Building grit: The longitudinal pathways between mindset, commitment, grit, and academic outcomes. *Journal of Youth and Adolescence, 48,* 850-863.

Tanhehco, Y.C., & Bhatia, M. (2019). Hematopoietic stem cell transplantation and cellular therapy in sickle cell disease: Where we are now? *Current Opinion in Hematology, 26,* 448-452.

Tannen, D. (1990). *You just don't understand: Women and men in conversation.* New York: Ballantine.

Tannenbaum, C., & Boyle, J. (2019, June 21). *The consequences of aging populations.* Retrieved July 12, 2019, from www.advisorperspectives.com

Tanprasertsuk, J., & others (2020). Concentrations of circulating phylloquinone, but not cerebral menaquinone-4, are positively correlated with a wide range of cognitive measures: Exploratory findings in centenarians. *Journal of Nutrition, 150,* 82-90.

Tarokh, L., & Carskadon, M.A. (2010). Developmental changes in the human sleep EEG during early adolescence. *Sleep, 33,* 801-809.

Tarraf, W., & others (2020). Cardiovascular risk and cognitive function in middle-aged and older Hispanics/Latinos: Results from the Hispanic Community Health Study/Study of Latinos (HCHS/SOL). *Journal of Alzheimer's Disease, 73,* 103-116.

Tartaglia, N.R., & others (2017). Autism spectrum disorder in males with sex chromosome aneuploidy: XXY/Klinefelter syndrome, XYY, and XXYY. *Journal of Developmental and Behavioral Pediatrics, 38,* 197-207.

Tarzia, L. (2020, in press). Toward an ecological understanding of intimate partner sexual violence. *Journal of Interpersonal Violence.*

Tas, D., & others (2020, in press). The effects of parental and peer factors on psychiatric symptoms in adolescents with obesity. *Eating and Weight Disorders.*

Tashiro, T., & Frazier, P. (2003). "I'll never be in a relationship like that again." *Personal Relationships, 10,* 113-128.

Tasker, F.L., & Golombok, S. (1997). *Growing up in a lesbian family: Effects on child development.* New York: Guilford.

Taubert, M., & others (2020, in press). Converging patterns of aging-associated brain volume loss and tissue microstructure differences. *Neurobiology of Aging.*

Taylor, C., & others (2016). Examining ways that a mindfulness-based intervention reduces stress in public school teachers: A mixed-methods study. *Mindfulness, 7,* 115–129.

Taylor, H., & others (2016). Neonatal outcomes of waterbirth: A systematic review and meta-analysis. *Archives of Disease in Childhood: Fetal and Neonatal Edition, 101,* F357–F365.

Taylor, H.O., & others (2018). Social isolation, depression, and psychological distress among older adults. *Journal of Aging and Health, 30,* 229–246.

Taylor, K., & others (2019). Prioritizing putative influential genes in cardiovascular disease susceptibility by applying tissue-specific Mendelian randomization. *Genome Medicine, 11*(1), 6.

Taylor, S.E. (2011). Tend and befriend theory. In A.M. van Lange, A.W. Kruglanski, & E.T. Higgins (Eds.), *Handbook of theories of social psychology.* Thousand Oaks, CA: Sage.

Taylor, S.E. (2018). *Health psychology* (10th ed.). New York: McGraw-Hill.

Taylor, S.E., & Stanton, A.L. (2021). *Health psychology* (11th ed.). New York: McGraw-Hill.

Taylor, Z.E., Widaman, K.F., & Robins, R.W. (2018). Longitudinal relations of economic hardship and effortful control to active coping in Latino youth. *Journal of Research on Adolescence, 28,* 396–411.

Teach for America (2020). *Teach for America.* Retrieved January 28, 2020, from www.teachforamerica.org

Teague, M., Mackenzie, S., & Rosenthal, D. (2019). *Your health today* (7th ed.). New York: McGraw-Hill.

Teater, B., & Chonody, J.M. (2020, in press). What attributes of successful aging are important to older adults? The development of a multidimensional definition of successful aging. *Social Work and Health Care.*

Telkemeyer, S., & others (2011). Acoustic processing of temporally modulated sounds in infants: Evidence from a combined near-infrared spectroscopy and EEG study. *Frontiers in Psychology, 2,* 62.

Telljohann, S., & others (2020). *Health education: Elementary and middle school applications* (9th ed.). New York: McGraw-Hill.

Tener, D., Katz, C., & Kaufmann, Y. (2020, in press). "And I let it all out": Survivors' sibling sexual abuse disclosures. *Journal of Interpersonal Violence.*

Terman, L. (1925). *Genetic studies of genius. Vol. 1: Mental and physical traits of a thousand gifted children.* Stanford, CA: Stanford University Press.

Terracciano, A., & others (2017). Personality traits and risk of cognitive impairment and dementia. *Journal of Psychiatric Research, 89,* 22–27.

Terrell, J.M., & others (2021, under review). Features of effective youth development programs: Contextual safety and the "big three" components of positive youth development programs in Rwanda. *Child and Youth Care Forum.*

Terry, D.F., Nolan, V.G., Andersen, S.L., Perls, T.T., & Cawthon, R. (2008). Association of longer telomeres with better health in centenarians. *Journals of Gerontology A: Biological Sciences and Medical Sciences, 63,* 809–812.

Teshale, S.M., & Lachman, M.E. (2016). Managing daily happiness: The relationship between selection,

optimization, and compensation strategies and well-being in adulthood. *Psychology and Aging, 31,* 687–692.

Tessler, F., & others (2019). Investigating gene-gene and gene-environment interactions in the association between overnutrition and obesity-related phenotypes. *Frontiers in Genetics, 10,* 151.

Tetering, M.A.J.V., & others (2020). Sex differences in self-regulation in early, middle, and late adolescence: A large-scale cross-sectional study. *PLoS One, 15*(1), e0227607.

Teti, D.M., & others (2016). Sleep arrangements, parent-infant sleep during the first year, and family functioning. *Developmental Psychology, 52,* 1169–1181.

Tetzlaff, A., Schmidt, R., Brauhardt, A., & Hilbert, A. (2016). Family functioning in adolescents with binge-eating disorder. *European Eating Disorders Review, 24,* 430–433.

Teufl, L., & others (2020). How fathers' attachment security and education contribute to early child language skills above and beyond mothers: Parent-child conversation under scrutiny. *Attachment and Human Development, 22,* 71–84.

Thaler, L., & others (2020). Methylation of the OXTR gene in women with anorexia nervosa: Relationship to social behavior. *European Eating Disorders Review, 28,* 79–86.

Tham, E.K., Schneider, N., & Broekman, B.F. (2017). Infant sleep and its relation to cognition and growth: A narrative review. *Nature and Science of Sleep, 9,* 135–149.

Thanh, N.X., & Jonsson, E. (2016). Life expectancy of people with fetal alcohol syndrome. *Journal of Population Therapeutics and Clinical Pharmacology, 23,* e53–e59.

Thapar, A., Collishaw, S., Pine, D.S., & Thapar, A.K. (2012). Depression in adolescence. *Lancet, 379,* 1056–1067.

Tharp, R.G. (1994). Intergroup differences among Native Americans in socialization and child cognition: An erthogenetic analysis. In P.M. Greenfield & R. Cocking (Eds.), *Cross-cultural roots of minority child development.* Mahwah, NJ: Erlbaum.

The, N.S., & others (2010). Association of adolescent obesity with risk of severe obesity in adulthood. *JAMA, 304,* 2042–2047.

Thelen, E. (2000). Perception and motor development. In A. Kazdin (Ed.), *Encyclopedia of psychology.* Washington, DC, & New York: American Psychological Association and Oxford University Press.

Thelen, E., & others (1993). The transition to reaching: Mapping intention and intrinsic dynamics. *Child Development, 64,* 1058–1098.

Thelen, E., & Smith, L.B. (1998). Dynamic systems theory. In W. Damon & R. Lerner (Eds.), *Handbook of child psychology* (5th ed., Vol. 1.). New York: Wiley.

Thelen, E., & Smith, L.B. (2006). Dynamic development of action and thought. In W. Damon & R. Lerner (Eds.), *Handbook of child psychology* (6th ed.). New York: Wiley.

Thiele, D.M., & Whelan, T.A. (2008). The relationship between grandparent satisfaction, meaning, and generativity. *International Journal of Aging and Human Development, 66,* 21–48.

Thio, A., Taylor, J.D., & Schwartz, M.D. (2019). *Deviant behavior* (12th ed.). Upper Saddle River, NJ: Pearson.

Thoma, S.J., & Bebeau, M. (2008). *Moral judgment competency is declining over time: Evidence from 20 years of defining issues test data.* Paper presented at the meeting of the American Educational Research Association, New York, NY.

Thomas, A., & Chess, S. (1991). Temperament in adolescence and its functional significance. In R.M. Lerner, A.C. Petersen, & J. Brooks-Gunn (Eds.), *Encyclopedia of adolescence* (Vol. 2). New York: Garland.

Thomas, A., & Gullich, A. (2019). Childhood practice and play as determinants of adolescent intrinsic and extrinsic motivation among elite young athletes. *European Journal of Sport Science, 19*(8), 1120–1129.

Thomas, A.K., & Gutchess, A. (2020). *Cambridge handbook of cognitive aging.* New York: Routledge.

Thomas, J.R., & Hognas, R.S. (2015). The effect of parental divorce on the health of adult children. *Longitudinal and Life Course Studies, 6,* 279–302.

Thomas, M., & Ansari, D. (2020). Why is neuroscience relevant to education? In M. Thomas, D. Mareschal, & I. Dumonthell (Eds.), *Educational neuroscience.* New York: Routledge.

Thomas, M.S.C., & Johnson, M.H. (2008). New advances in understanding sensitive periods in brain development. *Current Directions in Psychological Science, 17,* 1–5.

Thomason, M.E., & Thompson, P.M. (2011). Diffusion imaging, white matter, and psychopathology. *Annual Review of Clinical Psychology* (Vol. 7). Palo Alto, CA: Annual Reviews.

Thompson, A.E., & Voyer, D. (2014). Sex differences in the ability to recognize non-verbal displays of emotion: A meta-analysis. *Cognition and Emotion, 28,* 1164–1195.

Thompson, J.J., Manore, M., & Vaughan, L. (2020). *The science of nutrition* (5th ed.). Upper Saddle River, NJ: Pearson.

Thompson, L.W., & others (2020, in press). Incidence of nonaccidental head trauma in infants: A call to revisit prevention strategies. *Journal of Neurosurgery. Pediatrics.*

Thompson, R., & Murachver, T. (2001). Predicting gender from electronic discourse. *British Journal of Social Psychology, 40,* 193–201.

Thompson, R., & others (2017). Is the use of physical discipline associated with aggressive behaviors in children? *Academic Pediatrics, 17,* 34–44.

Thompson, R.A. (2006). The development of the person. In W. Damon & R. Lerner (Eds.), *Handbook of child psychology* (6th ed.). New York: Wiley.

Thompson, R.A. (2009). Early foundations: Conscience and the development of moral character. In D. Narváez & D. Lapsley (Eds.), *Moral self, identity and character: Prospects for a new field of study.* New York: Cambridge University Press.

Thompson, R.A. (2011). The emotionate child. In D. Cicchetti & G.I. Roisman (Eds.), *The origins and organization of adaptation and maladaptation. Minnesota Symposium on Child Psychology* (Vol. 36). New York: Wiley.

Thompson, R.A. (2012). Whither the preoperational child? Toward a life-span moral development theory. *Perspectives on Child Development, 6,* 423–429.

Thompson, R.A. (2015). Relationships, regulation, and development. In R.M. Lerner (Ed.), *Handbook of child psychology and developmental science* (7th ed.). New York: Wiley.

Thompson, R.A. (2016). Early attachment and later development: New questions. In J. Cassidy & P.R. Shaver (Eds.), *Handbook of attachment* (3rd ed.). New York: Guilford.

Thompson, R.A. (2019). Emotion dysregulation and early social relationships. In T.P. Beauchaine & S.E. Crowell (Eds.), *Oxford handbook of emotion dysregulation.* New York: Oxford University Press.

Thompson, R.A. (2019). Emotion dysregulation: A theme in search of a definition. *Development and Psychopathology, 31,* 805–815.

Thompson, R.A. (2020). Early moral development and attachment theory. In D.J. Laible & others (Eds.), *Oxford handbook of parenting and moral development.* New York: Oxford University Press.

Thompson, R.A. (2020). On what is read, shared, and felt: Parent-child conversation about stories. *Attachment and Human Development, 22,* 85–89.

Thompson, R.A., & Baumrind, D. (2019). The ethics of parenting. In M.H. Bornstein (Ed.), *Handbook of parenting* (3rd ed.). New York: Routledge.

Thompson, R.A., & Goodvin, R. (2016). Social support and developmental psychopathology. In D. Cicchetti (Ed.), *Developmental psychopathology* (3rd ed.). New York: Wiley.

Thompson, R.A., & Newton, E.K. (2013). Baby altruists? Examining the complexity of prosocial motivation in young children. *Infancy, 18,* 120–133.

Thompson, R.A., & Virmani, E.A. (2010). Self and personality. In M.H. Bornstein (Ed.), *Handbook of cultural developmental science.* New York: Psychology Press.

Thompson, R.A., Winer, A.C., & Goodvin, R. (2011). The individual child: Temperament, emotion, self, and personality. In M.H. Bornstein & M.E. Lamb (Eds.), *Developmental science: An advanced textbook* (6th ed.). New York: Psychology Press/ Taylor & Francis.

Thompson, R.A., & others (2009, April). *Parent-child relationships, conversation, and developing emotion regulation.* Paper presented at the meeting of the Society for Research in Child Development, Denver.

Thornberg, R., & others (2020). Bullying among children and adolescents. *Scandinavian Journal of Psychology, 61*(1), 1–5.

Thornton, R. (2017). Acquisition of questions. In J. Lidz, W. Snyder, & J. Pater (Eds.), *Oxford handbook of developmental linguistics.* New York: Oxford University Press.

Tian, J., & others (2019). Socioeconomic position over the life course from childhood and smoking status in mid-adulthood: Results from a 25-year follow-up study. *BMC Public Health, 19*(1), 169.

Tian, S., & Xu, Y. (2016). Association of sarcopenic obesity with the risk of all-cause mortality: A meta-analysis of prospective cohort studies. *Geriatrics and Gerontology International, 16,* 155–166.

Tichko, P., & Large, E.W. (2019). Modeling infants' perceptual narrowing to musical rhythms: Neural oscillation and Hebbian plasticity. *Annals of the New York Academy of Sciences, 1453*(1), 125–139.

Tiego, J., & others (2020, in press). Common mechanisms of executive attention underlie executive function and effortful control in children. *Developmental Science.*

Tieu, L., & others (2018). Children's comprehension of plural predicate conjunction. *Journal of Child Language, 45,* 242–259.

Tiggemann, M., & Slater, A. (2017). Facebook and body image concern in adolescent girls: A prospective study. *International Journal of Eating Disorders, 50,* 80–83.

Tikhonov, A.A., & others (2019). Bicultural identity harmony and American identity are associated with positive mental health in U.S. racial and ethnic minority adolescents. *Cultural Diversity and Ethnic Minority Psychology, 25,* 494–504.

Timmermans, S., & others (2011). Individual accumulation of heterogeneous risks explains inequalities within deprived neighborhoods. *European Journal of Epidemiology, 26*(2), 165–180.

TIMSS (2015). *TIMSS 2015 and TIMSS advanced 2015 international results.* Chestnut Hill, MA: TIMSS.

Tiso, F.V. (2019). Methodology in research on the rainbow body: Anthropological and psychological reflections on death and dying. *Journal of Religion and Health, 58,* 725–736.

Tistarelli, N., & others (2020). The nature and nurture of ADHD and its comorbidities: A narrative review of twin studies. *Neuroscience and Biobehavioral Reviews, 109,* 63–77.

Toepfer, P., & others (2019). A role of oxytocin receptor gene grain tissue expression quantitative trait locus rs237895 in the intergenerational transmission of the effects of maternal child maltreatment. *Journal of the American Academy of Child and Adolescent Psychiatry, 58,* 1207–1216.

Toh, W.X., Yang, H., & Haranto, A. (2020, in press). Executive function and subjective well-being in middle and late adulthood: Evidence from the Midlife Development in the United States Study. *Journals of Gerontology B: Psychological Sciences and Social Sciences.*

Tolani, N., & Brooks-Gunn, J. (2008). Family support, international trends. In M.M. Haith & J.B. Benson (Eds.), *Encyclopedia of infant and early childhood development.* New York: Wiley.

Tole, F., & others (2019). The role of pre-, peri-, and postnatal risk factors in bipolar disorder and adult ADHD. *Journal of Neural Transmission, 126,* 1117–1126.

Tomasello, M. (2006). Acquiring linguistic constructions. In W. Damon & R. Lerner (Eds.), *Handbook of child psychology* (6th ed.). New York: Wiley.

Tomasello, M. (2014). *A natural history of human thinking.* Cambridge, MA: Harvard University Press.

Tomasello, M., & Hamann, K. (2012). Collaboration in young children. *Quarterly Journal of Experimental Psychology, 65,* 1–12.

Tomaszewski Farias, S., & others (2018). Compensation strategies in older adults: Association with cognition and everyday function. *American Journal of Alzheimer's Disease and Other Dementias, 33,* 184–191.

Tomkinson, G.R., & Wong, S.H.S. (2019). Special issue: Global matrix 3.0—An introduction to the report cards on the physical activity of children and youth from five Asian countries and regions. *ScienceDirect, 17*(1), 1–2.

Tomlinson, M., & others (2016). Improving early childhood care and development, HIV-testing, treatment and support, and nutrition in Mokhotlong, Lesotho: Study protocol for a cluster randomized controlled trial. *Trials, 17*(1), 538.

Tompkins, G.E. (2019). *Teaching writing* (7th ed.). Upper Saddle River, NJ: Pearson.

Tompkins, G.E., & Rodgers, E. (2020). *Literacy in the early grades* (5th ed.). Upper Saddle River, NJ: Pearson.

Tompkins, V., Farrar, M.J., & Montgomery, D.E. (2019). Speaking your mind: Language and narrative in young children's theory of mind development. *Advances in Child Behavior and Development, 56,* 109–140.

Tompkins, V., & others (2017). Child language and parent discipline mediate the relation between family income and false belief understanding. *Journal of Experimental Psychology, 158,* 1–18.

Tonnies, E., & Trushina, E. (2017). Oxidative stress, synaptic dysfunction, and Alzheimer's disease. *Journal of Alzheimer's Disease, 57,* 1105–1121.

Tononi, G., & Cirelli, C. (2019). Sleep and synaptic down-selection. *European Journal of Neuroscience.* doi:10.1111/ejn.14335

Tooley, U.A., & others (2020, in press). Associations between neighborhood SES and functional brain network development. *Cerebral Cortex.*

Top, N., Liew, J., & Luo, W. (2017). Family and school influences on youths' behavioral and academic outcomes: Cross-level interactions between parental monitoring and character development curriculum. *Journal of Genetic Psychology, 178,* 108–118.

Topa, G., Depolo, M., & Alcover, C.M. (2018). Early retirement: A meta-analysis of its antecedent and subsequent correlates. *Frontiers in Psychology, 8,* 2157.

Topa, G., Lunceford, G., & Boyatzis, R.E. (2018). Financial planning for retirement: A psychosocial perspective. *Frontiers in Psychology, 8,* 2338.

Tornblom, A.W., & others (2020, in press). Who is at risk for dying young from suicide and sudden violent death? Common and specific risk factors among children, adolescents, and adults. *Suicide and Life-Threatening Behavior.*

Toro, C.A., Aylwin, C.F., & Lomniczi, A. (2018). Hypothalamic epigenetics driving female puberty. *Journal of Neuroendocrinology, 30*(7), e12589.

Torres-Ramos, S., & others (2020). A brain connectivity characterization of children with different levels of mathematical achievement based on graph metrics. *PLoS One, 15*(1), e0227613.

Torstveit, L., Sutterlin, S., & Lugo, R.G. (2016). Empathy, guilt proneness, and gender: Relative contributions to prosocial behavior. *European Journal of Psychology, 12,* 260-275.

Tosun Guleroglu, F., Mucuk, S., & Ozgurluk, I. (2020, in press). The effect of mother-infant skin-to-skin contact on the involution process and maternal postpartum fatigue during the early postpartum period. *Women and Health.*

Toubiana, S., & Selig, S. (2020). Human subelomeric DNA methylation: Regulation and roles in telomere function. *Current Opinion in Genetics and Development, 60,* 9-16.

Toupance, S., & Benetos, A. (2019). Telomere dynamics and aging related diseases. In R. Fernandez-Ballesteros & others (Eds.), *Cambridge handbook of successful aging.* New York: Cambridge University Press.

Touron, D.R. (2015). Memory avoidance by older adults: When 'old dogs' won't perform their 'new tricks.' *Current Directions in Psychological Science, 24,* 170-176.

Toy, W., Nai, Z.L., & Lee, H.W. (2016). Extraversion and agreeableness: Divergent routes to daily satisfaction with social relationships. *Journal of Personality, 84,* 121-134.

Trainor, L.J., & He, C. (2013). Auditory and musical development. In P.D. Zelazo (Ed.), *Handbook of developmental psychology.* New York: Oxford University Press.

Traisrisilp, K., & Tongsong, T. (2015). Pregnancy outcomes of mothers with very advanced age (40 years and more). *Journal of the Medical Association of Thailand, 98,* 117-122.

Tran, S.P., & Raffaelli, M. (2020, in press). Configurations of autonomy and relatedness in a multiethnic U.S. sample of parent-adolescent dyads. *Journal of Research on Adolescence.*

Trautner, H.M., & others (2005). Rigidity and flexibility of gender stereotypes in children: Developmental or differential? *Infant and Child Development, 14,* 365-381.

Travers, J.L., & others (2020, in press). Factors associated with dissatisfaction in medical care quality among older Medicare beneficiaries suffering from mental illness. *Journal of Aging and Social Policy.*

Treas, J., & Gubernskaya, Z. (2016). Immigration, aging, and the life course. In L.K. George & K.F. Ferraro (Eds.), *Handbook of aging and the social sciences* (8th ed.). New York: Elsevier.

Trehub, S.E., Schneider, B.A., Thorpe, L.A., & Judge, P. (1991). Observational measures of auditory sensitivity in early infancy. *Developmental Psychology, 27,* 40-49.

Trelle, A.N., Henson, R.N., & Simons, J.S. (2015). Identifying age-invariant and age-limited mechanisms for enhanced memory performance: Insights from self-referential processing in younger and older adults. *Psychology and Aging, 30,* 324-333.

Trickett, P.K., Negriff, S., Ji, J., & Peckins, M. (2011). Child maltreatment and adolescent development. *Journal of Research on Adolescence, 21,* 3-20.

Trimble, J.E. (1988, August). *The enculturation of contemporary psychology.* Paper presented at the meeting of the American Psychological Association, New Orleans.

Trude, A.C.B., & others (2018). A youth-leader program in Baltimore City recreation centers: Lessons learned and applications. *Health Promotion Practice, 19,* 75-85.

Truglio, R.T., & Kotler, J.A. (2014). Language, literacy, and media: What's the word on *Sesame Street?* In E.T. Gershoff, R.S. Mistry, & D.A. Crosby (Eds.), *Societal contexts of child development.* New York: Oxford University Press.

Trujillo, P., & others (2019). Dopamine effects on frontal cortical blood flow and motor inhibition in Parkinson's disease. *Cortex, 115,* 99-111.

Trzesniewski, K.H., Donnellan, M.B., & Robins, R.W. (2013). Development of self-esteem. In V. Zeigler-Hill (Ed.), *Self-esteem.* New York: Psychology Press.

Trzesniewski, K.H., & others (2006). Adolescent low self-esteem is a risk factor for adult poor health, criminal behavior, and limited economic prospects. *Developmental Psychology, 42,* 381-390.

Tsai, H.J., & Chang, F.K. (2019). Associations of exercise, nutritional status, and smoking with cognitive decline among older adults in Taiwan: Results from a longitudinal population-based study. *Archives of Gerontology and Geriatrics, 82,* 133-138.

Tsai, W.I., & others (2020, in press). Symptoms of prolonged grief and major depressive disorders: Distinctiveness and temporal relationship in the first 2 years of bereavement for family caregivers of terminally ill cancer patients. *Psychooncology.*

Tsang, A., & others (2008). Common persistent pain conditions in developed and developing countries: Gender and age differences and comorbidity with depression-anxiety disorders. *Journal of Pain, 9,* 883-891.

Tsang, L.P.M., & others (2019). Autism spectrum disorder: Early identification and management in primary care. *Singapore Medical Journal, 60,* 324-328.

Tsang, T.W., & others (2016). Prenatal alcohol exposure, FASD, and child behavior: A meta-analysis. *Pediatrics, 137,* e20152542.

Tsapanou, A., & others (2019). Brain biomarkers and cognition across adulthood. *Human Brain Mapping, 40,* 3832-3842.

Tso, W., & others (2016). Sleep duration and school readiness of Chinese preschool children. *Journal of Pediatrics, 169,* 266-271.

Tso, W., & others (2019). Early sleep deprivation and attention deficit/hyperactivity disorder. *Pediatric Research, 85,* 449-455.

Tsutsui, T.W. (2020). Dental pulp stem cells: Advances to applications. *Stem Cells Cloning, 13,* 33-42.

Tubay, A.T., & others (2019). The effects of group prenatal care on infant birthweight and maternal well-being: A randomized controlled trial. *Military Medicine, 154,* e440-e446.

Tucker-Drob, E.M., Brandmaier, A.M., & Lindenberger, U. (2019). Coupled cognitive changes in adulthood: A meta-analysis. *Psychological Bulletin, 145,* 273-301.

Turiano, N.A., Mroczek, D.K., Moynihan, J., & Chapman, B.P. (2013). Big 5 personality traits and interleukin-6: Evidence for "healthy neuroticism" in a U.S. population sample. *Brain, Behavior, and Immunity, 28,* 83-89.

Turiel, E. (2018). Reasoning at the root of morality. In K. Gray & J. Graham (Eds.), *Atlas of moral psychology.* New York: Guilford.

Turk, E., & others (2019). Functional connectome of the fetal brain. *Journal of Neuroscience, 39*(49), 9716-9724.

Turkeltaub, P.E., Gareau, L., Flowers, D.L., Zeffiro, T.A., & Eden, G.F. (2003). Development of neural mechanisms for reading. *Nature Neuroscience, 6,* 767-773.

Turnbull, A., & others (2020). *Exceptional lives* (9th ed.). Upper Saddle River, NJ: Pearson.

Turner, B.F. (1982). Sex-related differences in aging. In B.B. Wolman (Ed.), *Handbook of developmental psychology.* Englewood Cliffs, NJ: Prentice Hall.

Turner, J., Flatley, C., & Kumar, S. (2020, in press). Epidural use in labor is not associated with an increased risk of maternal or neonatal morbidity when the second stage is prolonged. *Australian and New Zealand Journal of Obstetrics and Gynecology.*

Turner, J.H. (2019). Long-acting reversible contraceptives: Addressing adolescents' barriers. *Nurse Practitioner, 44,* 23-30.

Turner, S., & others (2017). The relationship between childhood sexual abuse and mental health outcomes among males: Results from a nationally representative United States sample. *Child Abuse and Neglect, 66,* 64-72.

Twait, E., & Horowitz-Kraus, T. (2019). Functional connectivity of cognitive control and visual regions during verb generation is related to improved reading in children. *Brain Connectivity, 9,* 500-507.

Tweed, E.J., & others (2016). Five-minute Apgar scores and educational outcomes: Retrospective cohort study of 751,369 children. *Archives of Disease in Child, Fetal, and Neonatal Medicine, 101,* F121-F126.

Twenge, J., & Campbell, K. (2020). *Personality psychology* (2nd ed.). Upper Saddle River, NJ: Pearson.

Twenge, J.M., Hisler, G.C., & Krizan, Z. (2019). Associations between screen time and sleep duration are primarily driven by portable electronic devices: Evidence from a population-based study of U.S. children 0-17. *Sleep Medicine, 56,* 211-218.

Twenge, J.M., Konrath, S., Foster, J.D., Campbell, W.K., & Bushman, B.J. (2008a). Egos inflating over time: A cross-temporal meta-analysis of the Narcissistic Personality Inventory. *Journal of Personality, 76,* 875-902.

Twenge, J.M., Konrath, S., Foster, J.D., Campbell, W.K., & Bushman, B.J. (2008b). Further evidence of an increase in narcissism among college students. *Journal of Personality, 76,* 919-928.

Twenge, J.M., & Martin, G.N. (2020). Gender differences in associations between digital media use and psychological well-being: Evidence from three large data sets. *Journal of Adolescence, 79,* 91–102.

Twilhaar, E.S., & others (2019). Academic trajectories of very preterm born children at school age. *Archives of Disease in Childhood: Fetal and Neonatal Edition, 104,* F419–F423.

Tye, K.M. (2019). Neural circuit mechanisms for switching emotional tracks: From positive to negative and back again. In A.S. Fox & others (Eds.), *The nature of emotion* (2nd ed.). New York: Oxford University Press.

Tylka, T.L., Lumeng, J.C., & Eneli, I.U. (2015). Maternal intuitive eating as a moderator of the association between concern about child weight and restrictive child feeding. *Appetite, 95,* 158–165.

Tyrell, F.A., & others (2016). Family influences on Mexican American adolescents' romantic relationships: Moderation by gender and culture. *Journal of Research on Adolescence, 26,* 142–158.

U

U.S. Bureau of Labor Statistics (2013). *Volunteering in the United States: 2013.* Washington, DC:

U.S. Census Bureau (2012). *Age and sex composition in the United States: 2012.* Washington, DC: Author.

U.S. Census Bureau (2013). *Marriages, births, and deaths.* Washington, DC: U.S. Department of Labor.

U.S. Census Bureau (2015). *Population statistics.* Washington, DC: Author.

U.S. Census Bureau (2016). *Families and living arrangements: 2015.* Washington, DC: Author.

U.S. Census Bureau (2018). *Births, deaths, marriages, and divorces.* Washington, DC: Author.

U.S. Census Bureau (2018). *People.* Washington, DC: Author.

U.S. Census Bureau (2019). *Births, deaths, marriages, divorces.* Washington, DC: Author.

U.S. Census Bureau (2019). *Cohabitation.* Washington, DC: Author.

U.S. Department of Education Office of Civil Rights (2018). *School suspensions.* Retrieved 7/10/2020 from ocdata.ed.gov

U.S. Department of Energy (2001). *The human genome project.* Washington, DC: Author.

U.S. Department of Health and Human Services (2017). *Child maltreatment 2017.* Washington, DC: Author.

U.S. Department of Health and Human Services (2019). *Folic acid.* Retrieved June 1, 2019, from www.cdc.gov/ncbddd/folicacid/

U.S. Food and Drug Administration (2019). *OxyContin.* Washington, DC: Author.

Udo, T., & Grilo, C.M. (2019). Psychiatric and medical correlates of DSM-5 eating disorders in a nationally representative sample of adults in the United States. *International Journal of Eating Disorders, 52,* 42–50.

Uemura, K., & others (2018). Behavioral projective factors of increased depressive symptoms in community-dwelling older adults: A prospective cohort study. *International Journal of Geriatric Psychiatry, 33,* e234–e241.

Ulfsdottir, H., Saltvedt, S., & Georgsson, S. (2018). Waterbirth in Sweden—A comparative study. *Acta Obstetricia et Gynecologica Scandinavica, 97,* 341–348.

Ullah, M., & Sun, Z. (2019). Klotho deficiency accelerates stem cells aging by impairing telomerase activity. *Journals of Gerontology A: Biological Sciences and Medical Sciences, 74,* 1396–1407.

Umana-Taylor, A. (2018). Intervening in cultural development: The case of ethnic-racial identity. *Development and Psychopathology, 30*(5), 1907–1922.

Umana-Taylor, A., & Hill, N.E. (2020). Ethnic-racial socialization in the family. A decade's advance on precursors and outcomes. *Journal of Marriage and the Family, 82,* 244–271.

Umana-Taylor, A., & others (2014). Ethnic and racial identity revisited: An integrated conceptualization. *Child Development, 85,* 21–39.

Umana-Taylor, A., & others (2020, in press). National identity development and friendship network dynamics among immigrant and non-immigrant youth. *Journal of Youth and Adolescence.*

UNAIDS (2019). *UNAIDS fact sheet.* Retrieved February 17, 2020, from https://www.unaids.org/sites/default/files/media_asset/UNAIDS_FactSheet_en.pdf

Unalmis Erdogan, S., Yanikkerem, E., & Goker, A. (2017). Effects of low back massage on perceived birth pain and satisfaction. *Complementary Therapies in Clinical Practice, 28,* 169–175.

Uncapher, M.R., & Wagner, A.D. (2018). Minds and brains of media multitaskers: Current findings and future directions. *Proceedings of the National Academy of Sciences USA, 115*(40), 9889–9896.

UNICEF (2007). *The state of the world's children: 2007.* Geneva, Switzerland: UNICEF.

UNICEF (2015). *The state of the world's children: 2015.* Geneva, Switzerland: UNICEF.

UNICEF (2018). *The state of the world's children: 2018.* Geneva, Switzerland: UNICEF.

UNICEF (2020). *The state of the world's children: 2020.* Geneva, Switzerland: UNICEF.

United Income (2019). Older Americans in the workforce. Washington, DC: Author.

United Nations (2017). *World population aging: 2017.* New York: United Nations.

Unson, C., & Richardson, M. (2013). Insights into the experiences of older workers and change: Through the lens of selection, optimization, and compensation. *Gerontologist, 53,* 484–494.

Urbano Blackford, J., & Zald, D.H. (2019). Inhibited temperament and intrinsic versus extrinsic influences on fear circuits. In A.S. Fox & others (Eds.), *The nature of emotion* (2nd ed.). New York: Oxford University Press.

Urry, L.A., & others (2020). *Campbell biology in focus* (3rd ed.). Upper Saddle River, NJ: Pearson.

Utkin, Y.N. (2019). Aging affects nicotinic acetylcholine receptors in the brain. *Central Nervous System Agents in Medicinal Chemistry, 19,* 119–124.

Uwaezuoke, S.N., Eneh, C.I., & Ndu, I.K. (2017). Relationship between exclusive breastfeeding and lower risk of childhood obesity: A narrative review of published evidence. *Clinical Medicine Insights: Pediatrics.* doi:10.1177/1179556517690196

V

Vaca, F.E., & others (2020, in press). Longitudinal associations of 12th-grade binge drinking with risky driving and high-risk driving. *Pediatrics.*

Vaillant, G.E. (1977). *Adaptation of life.* Boston: Little, Brown.

Vaillant, G.E. (1992). Is there a natural history of addiction? In C.P. O'Brien & J.H. Jaffe (Eds.), *Addictive states.* Cambridge, MA: Harvard University Press.

Vaillant, G.E. (2002). *Aging well.* Boston: Little, Brown.

Vaish, A. (2018). The prosocial functions of early emotions: The case of guilt. *Current Opinion in Psychology, 20,* 25–29.

Vaish, A., Carpenter, M., & Tomasello, M. (2016). The early emergence of guilt-motivated prosocial behavior. *Child Development, 87,* 1772–1782.

Vaish, K., Patra, S., & Chhabra, P. (2020). Functional disability among elderly: A community-based cross-sectional study. *Journal of Family Medicine and Primary Care, 9,* 253–258.

Valech, N., & others (2018). Executive and language subjective cognitive decline complaints discriminate preclinical Alzheimer's disease from normal aging. *Journal of Alzheimer's Disease, 61,* 689–703.

Valenzuela-Araujo, D., & others (2020, in press). Leaving paper behind: Improving healthcare navigation by Latino parents through video-based education. *Journal of Immigrant and Minority Health.*

Valera, M.C., Gourdy, P., Tremollieres, F., & Arnal, J.F. (2015). From the Women's Health Initiative to the combination of estrogen and selective estrogen receptor modulators to avoid progestin addition. *Maturitas, 82,* 274–277.

Valeri, G., & others (2020, in press). Executive functions and symptom severity in an Italian sample of intellectually able preschoolers with autism spectrum disorder. *Journal of Autism and Developmental Disorders.*

Valimaki, T.H., & others (2016). Impact of Alzheimer's disease on the family caregiver's long-term quality of life: Results from the ALSOVA follow-up study. *Quality of Life Research, 25,* 687–697.

van Bussel, E.F., & others (2019). A cardiovascular prediction model for older people: Development and validation in a primary care population. *Journal of Clinical Hypertension, 21,* 1145–1152.

Van de Vondervoort, J., & Hamlin, J.K. (2016). Evidence for intuitive morality: Preverbal infants make sociomoral evaluations. *Child Development Perspectives, 10,* 143–148.

Van de Vondervoort, J., & Hamlin, J.K. (2018). The infantile roots of sociomoral evaluations. In K. Gray & J. Graham (Eds.), *The atlas of moral psychology.* New York: Guilford.

van den Boom, D.C. (1989). Neonatal irritability and the development of attachment. In G.A. Kohnstamm, J.E. Bates, & M.K. Rothbart (Eds.), *Temperament in childhood.* New York: Wiley.

van den Dries, L., Juffer, F., van IJzendoorn, M.H., & Bakermans-Kranenburg, M.J. (2010). Infants' physical and cognitive development after international adoption from foster care or institutions in China. *Journal of Developmental and Behavioral Pediatrics, 31,* 144–150.

Van den Eynde, V. (2020, in press). The facts on psychiatric euthanasia in the Netherlands. *Australas Psychiatry.*

van der Burg, D., & others (2019). Diagnosis and treatment of patients with comorbid substance use disorder and adult attention-deficit and hyperactivity disorder: A review of recent publications. *Current Opinion in Psychology, 32,* 300–306.

van der Knoop, B., & others (2020, in press). Additional value of advanced neurosonography and magnetic resonance imaging in fetuses at risk for brain damage. *Ultrasound in Obstetrics and Gynecology.*

van der Leeuw, G., & others (2018). The effect of pain on major cognitive impairment in older adults. *Journal of Pain, 19,* 1435–1444.

van der Veek, S.M.C., & others (2019). Baby's first bites: A randomized controlled trial to assess the effects of vegetable-exposure and sensitive feeding on vegetable acceptance, eating behavior, and weight gain in infants and toddlers. *BMC Pediatrics, 19*(1), 266.

van der Veer, R., & Zavershneva, E. (2018). The final chapter in Vygotsky's *Thinking and Speech:* A reader's guide. *Journal of the History of the Behavioral Sciences, 54,* 101–116.

van Deurzen, L., & Vanhoutte, B. (2019). A longitudinal study of allostatic load in later life: The role of sex, birth cohorts, and risk accumulation. *Research on Aging, 41,* 419–442.

van Doeselaar, L., & others (2020, in press). Adolescents' identity formation: Linking the narrative and the dual-cycle approach. *Journal of Youth and Adolescence.*

van Dongen, E.J.I., & others (2020, in press). Effectiveness of a diet and resistance exercise intervention on muscle health in older adults: ProMuscle in Practice. *Journal of the American Medical Directors Association.*

van Dongen, J., & others (2019). Epigenome-wide association study of attention-deficit/hyperactivity disorder symptoms in adults. *Biological Psychiatry, 86,* 599–607.

Van Doren, J., & others (2019). Sustained effects of neurofeedback in ADHD: A systematic review and meta-analysis. *European Child and Adolescent Development, 28,* 293–305.

Van Duijvenvoorde, A.C.K., & others (2019). A three-way longitudinal study of subcortical resting-state connectivity in adolescence: Testing age- and puberty-related changes. *Human Brain Mapping, 40,* 3769–3783.

van Egmond, M.C., & others (2020, in press). Self-esteem, motivation, and school attendance among sub-Saharan African girls: A self-determination theory perspective. *International Journal of Psychology.*

Van Elderen, S.S., & others (2016). Brain volume as an integrated marker for the risk of death in a community-based sample: Age gene/environment susceptibility—Reykjavik study. *Journals of Gerontology A: Biological Sciences and Medical Sciences, 71,* 131–137.

van Geel, M., Vedder, P., & Tanilon, J. (2014). Relationship between peer victimization, cyberbullying, and suicide in children and adolescents: A meta-analysis. *JAMA Pediatrics, 168,* 435–442.

van Goethem, A.A.J., & others (2012). The role of adolescents' morality and identity in volunteering: Age and gender differences in the process model. *Journal of Adolescence, 35,* 509–520.

Van Hecke, A., & others (2019). Leadership in nursing and midwifery: Activities and associated competencies of advanced practice nurses and midwives. *Journal of Nursing Management, 27,* 1261–1274.

Van Hecke, V., & others (2012). Infant responding to joint attention, executive processes, and self-regulation in preschool children. *Infant Development and Behavior, 35,* 303–311.

Van Hedel, K., & others (2015). Marital status, labor force activity, and mortality: A study in the USA and six European countries. *Scandinavian Journal of Public Health, 43,* 469–480.

Van Hulle, C.A., & others (2017). Infant stranger fear trajectories predict anxious behaviors and diurnal cortisol rhythm during childhood. *Development and Psychopathology, 29,* 1119–1130.

van IJzendoorn, M.H., & Kroonenberg, P.M. (1988). Cross-cultural patterns of attachment: A meta-analysis of the Strange Situation. *Child Development, 59,* 147–156.

Van Lieshout, R.J., & others (2020, in press). Public health nurse delivered group cognitive behavioral therapy (CBT) for postpartum depression: A pilot study. *Public Health Nursing.*

Van Malderen, E., & others (2019). The interplay of self-regulation and affectivity in binge eating among adolescents. *European Child and Adolescent Psychiatry, 28,* 1447–1460.

Van Ness, P.H., & others (2019). Chronic conditions, medically supportive care partners, and functional disability among cognitively impaired adults. *Innovations in Aging, 3*(2), igz018.

Van Norstrand, D.W., & others (2012). Connexin43 mutation causes heterogeneous gap junction loss and sudden infant death. *Circulation, 125,* 474–481.

Van Ryzin, M.J., Carlson, E.A., & Sroufe, L.A. (2011). Attachment discontinuity in a high-risk sample. *Attachment and Human Development, 13,* 381–401.

Van Scheppingen, M.A., & Leopold, T. (2020, in press). Trajectories of life satisfaction before, upon, and after divorce: Evidence from a new matching approach. *Journal of Personality and Social Psychology.*

van Wijk, I.C., & others (2019). Behavioral genetics of temperament from frontal asymmetry in early childhood. *Journal of Experimental Child Psychology, 179,* 348–361.

Vandell, D.L., & others (2010). Do effects of early childcare extend to age 15 years? From the NICHD Study of Early Child Care and Youth Development. *Child Development, 81,* 737–756.

Vandendriessche, A., & others (2019). Does sleep mediate the association between school pressure, physical activity, screen time, and psychological symptoms in early adolescents? A 12-country study. *International Journal of Environmental Research and Public Health, 16,* 6.

Vander Wyst, K.B., & others (2020, in press). Comparison and characterization of prenatal nutrition counseling among large-for-gestational-age deliveries by pre-pregnancy BMI. *Nutrients.*

Vanderlinden, J., Boen, F., & van Uffelen, J.G.Z. (2020). Effects of physical activity programs on sleep outcomes in older adults: A systematic review. *International Journal of Behavioral Nutrition and Physical Activity, 17,* 11.

Vanhaelen, Q. (2015). Aging as an optimization between cellular maintenance requirements and evolutionary constraints. *Current Aging Science, 8,* 110–119.

VanKim, N.A., & Laska, M.N. (2012). Socioeconomic disparities in emerging adult weight and weight behaviors. *American Journal of Health Behavior, 3*(4), 433–445.

VanMeter, F., Handley, E.D., & Cicchetti, D. (2020). The role of coping strategies in the pathway between child maltreatment and internalizing and externalizing behaviors. *Child Abuse and Neglect, 101,* 104323.

Vargas, S.M., Huey, S.J., & Miranda, J. (2020, in press). A critical review of current evidence on multiple types of discrimination and mental health. *American Journal of Orthopsychiatry.*

Varner, M.W., & others (2014). Association between stillbirth and illicit drug use and smoking during pregnancy. *Obstetrics and Gynecology, 123,* 113–125.

Vasa, F., & others (2020, in press). Conservative and disruptive modes of adolescent change in human brain functionality. *Proceedings of the National Academy of Sciences U.S.A.*

Vasung, L., & others (2019). Ex vivo fetal brain MRI: Recent advances, challenges, and future directions. *NeuroImage, 195,* 23–27.

Vaughn, B.E., Elmore-Staton, L., Shin, N., & el-Sheikh, M. (2015). Sleep as a support for social competence, peer relations, and cognitive functioning in preschool children. *Behavioral Sleep Medicine, 13,* 92–106.

Vaughn, C.P., & others (2019). AGS report on engagement related to the NIH Inclusion Across the Lifespan Policy. *Journal of the American Geriatrics Association, 67,* 211–217.

Vazsonyi, A.T., & Huang, L. (2010). Where self-control comes from: On the development of self-control and its relationship to deviance over time. *Developmental Psychology, 46,* 245–257.

Vedder, P., & Phinney, J. (2014). Identity formation in bicultural youth. In V. Benet-Martinez & Y. Hong (Eds.), *Oxford handbook of multicultural identity.* New York: Oxford University Press.

Veerman, J.L., & others (2012). Television viewing time and reduced life expectancy: A life table analysis. *British Journal of Sports Medicine, 46,* 927–930.

Veldhuizen, R.A.W., & others (2019). The effects of aging and exercise on lung mechanics, surfactant, and alveolar macrophages. *Experimental Lung Research, 45* (5-6), 113-122.

Veldman, S.L., Palmer, K.K., Okely, A.D., & Robinson, L.E. (2017). Promoting ball skills in preschool-age girls. *Journal of Science and Medicine in Sport, 20,* 50-54.

Velez, C.E., Wolchik, S.A., Tein, J.Y., & Sandler, I. (2011). Protecting children from the consequences of divorce: A longitudinal study of the effects of parenting on children's coping responses. *Child Development, 82,* 244-257.

Veness, C., Prior, M., Eadie, P., Bavin, E., & Reilly, S. (2014). Predicting autism diagnosis by 7 years of age using parent report of infant social communication skills. *Journal of Pediatrics and Child Health, 50,* 693-700.

Venetsanou, F., & Kambas, A. (2017). Can motor proficiency in preschool age affect physical activity in adolescence? *Pediatric Exercise Science, 49,* 254-259.

Venetsanou, F., & others (2019). Physical activity in preschool children: Trends over time and associations with body mass index and screen time. *Annals of Human Biology, 46,* 393-399.

Venkatesh, H.N., & others (2020). Molecular signature of the immune response to yoga therapy in stress-related chronic disease conditions: An insight. *International Journal of Yoga, 13,* 9-17.

Venneri, A., & others (2019). Beyond episodic memory: Semantic processing as independent predictor of hippocampal/perirhinal volume in aging and mild cognitive impairment due to Alzheimer's disease. *Neuropsychology. 33.* 523-533.

Venners, S.A., & others (2004). Paternal smoking and pregnancy loss: A prospective study using a biomarker of pregnancy. *American Journal of Epidemiology, 159,* 993-1001.

Verbeek, M., & others (2020). A warm nest or 'the talk'? Exploring and explaining relations between general and sexually-specific parenting and adolescent sexual emotions. *Journal of Adolescent Health, 66,* 210-216.

Verhaeghen, P. (2013). *The elements of cognitive aging: Meta-analyses of age-related differences in processing speed and their consequences.* New York: Oxford University Press.

Verhagen, J., & Leseman, P. (2016). How do verbal short-term memory and working memory relate to the acquisition of vocabulary and grammar? A comparison between first and second language learners. *Journal of Experimental Child Psychology, 141,* 65-82.

Verhallen, A.M., & others (2019). Romantic relationship breakup: An experimental mode to study effects of stress on depression (-like) symptoms. *PLoS One, 14*(5), e0217320.

Verhees, M.W.F.T., & others (2019). State attachment variability across distressing situations in middle childhood. *Social Development, 29,* 196-216.

Vernon, L., Modecki, K.L., & Barber, B.L. (2018). Mobile phones in the bedroom: Trajectories of sleep habits and subsequent adolescent psychological development. *Child Development, 89,* 66-77.

Vernooij, M.W., & van Buchem, M.A. (2020). Neuroimaging in dementia. In J. Hodler & others (Eds.), *Diseases of the brain, head, and neck.* New York: Springer.

Vernucci, S., & others (2020, in press). Working memory training in children: A review of basic methodological criteria. *Psychological Reports.*

Veronelli, L., & others (2020, in press). Setting the midpoint of sentences: The role of the left hemisphere. *Neuropsychologia.*

Veronneau, M.H., Racer, K.H., Fosco, G.M., & Dishion, T.J. (2014). The contribution of adolescent effortful control to early adult educational attainment. *Journal of Educational Psychology, 106,* 730-743.

Verschueren, K. (2020). Attachment, self-esteem, and socio-emotional adjustment: There is more than just the mother. *Attachment and Human Development, 22,* 105-109.

Verstaen, A., & others (2020). Age-related changes in emotional behavior: Evidence from a 13-year longitudinal study of long-term married couples. *Emotion, 20,* 149-163.

Verze, P., & others (2020, in press). Efficacy and safety of low-intensive shockwave therapy plus tadalafil 5 mg once daily in men with type 2 diabetes mellitus and erectile dysfunction: A matched-pair comparison study. *Asian Journal of Andrology.*

Vespa, J. (2017, April). The changing economics and demographics of young adulthood: 1975-2016. *Current Population Reports,* P20-579. Washington, DC: U.S. Census Bureau.

Vidal, S., & others (2017). Maltreatment, family environment, and social risk factors: Determinants of the child welfare to juvenile justice transition among maltreated children and adolescents. *Child Abuse and Neglect, 63,* 7-18.

Vieira, A.P.B., & others (2019). Infants' age and walking experience shapes perception-action coupling when crossing obstacles. *Perceptual and Motor Skills, 128,* 185-201.

Vihman, M.M. (2019). First word learning. In S-A. Rueschemeyer & M. Gareth Gaskell (Eds.), *Oxford handbook of psycholinguistics* (2nd ed.). New York: Oxford University Press.

Vihman, M.M. (2020). *Phonological templates in development.* New York: Oxford University Press.

Villa-Gonzalez, R., & others (2020). A systematic review of acute exercise as a coadjuvant treatment of ADHD in young people. *Psicothema, 32,* 67-74.

Villarreal, M., & others (2019). Four-year health trajectories of children prenatally exposed to cocaine and/or cannabis. A retrospective, cohort study in La Pampa, Argentina. *Archivos Argentinos de Pediatria, 117,* 360-367.

Vinanzi, S., & others (2019). Would a robot trust you? Developmental robotics model of trust and theory of mind. *Philosophical Transactions of the Royal Society B: Biological Sciences, 374,* 1771.

Vinik, J., Almas, A., & Grusec, J. (2011). Mothers' knowledge of what distresses and comforts their children predicts children's coping, empathy, and prosocial behavior. *Parenting: Science and Practice, 11,* 56-71.

Virnig, B., & others (2004). Does Medicare managed care provide equal treatment for mental illness across race? *Archives of General Psychiatry, 61,* 201-205.

Virta, J.J., & others (2013). Midlife cardiovascular risk factors and late cognitive impairment. *European Journal of Epidemiology, 28,* 405-416.

Visher, E., & Visher, J. (1989). Parenting coalitions after remarriage: Dynamics and therapeutic guidelines. *Family Relations, 38,* 65-70.

Visser, L., & others (2020, in press). Cesarean section at term and the risk of preterm birth in subsequent pregnancy: A longitudinal linked national cohort study. *BJOG.*

Vitaro, F., Boivin, M., & Poulin, F. (2018). The interface of aggression and peer relations in childhood and adolescence. In W.M. Bukowski & others (Eds.), *Handbook of peer interaction, relationships, and groups* (2nd ed.). New York: Guilford.

Vittrup, B., Holden, G.W., & Buck, M. (2006). Attitudes predict the use of physical punishment: A prospective study of the emergence of disciplinary practices. *Pediatrics, 117,* 2055-2064.

Vo, V.A., Li, R., Kornell, N., Pouget, A., & Cantlon, J.F. (2014). Young children bet on their numerical skills: Metacognition in the numerical domain. *Psychological Science, 25,* 1712-1721.

Voce, A., & Anderson, K.G. (2020, in press). The interaction between parental behavior and motivations to drink alcohol in high school students. *American Journal of Drug and Alcohol Abuse.*

Vockel, M., & others (2020, in press). The X chromosome and male infertility. *Human Genetics.*

Vogels-Broeke, M., de Vries, R., & Nieuwenhuijze, M. (2020, in press). Dimensions in women's experience of the perinatal period. *Midwifery.*

Vogt, B.A. (2019). Cingulate impairments in ADHD: Comorbidities, connections, and treatment. *Handbook of Clinical Neurology, 166,* 297-314.

Voigt, R.G., & others (2017). Academic achievement in adults with a history of attention-deficit/hyperactivity disorder: A population-based prospective study. *Journal of Developmental and Behavioral Pediatrics, 38,* 1-11.

Volkow, N.D., & others (2020, in press). An examination of child and adolescent neurodevelopment through National Institutes of Health studies. *Public Health Reports.*

von Bonsdorff, M.B., & others (2011). Work ability in midlife as a predictor of mortality and disability in later life: A 28-year prospective follow-up study. *Canadian Medical Association Journal, 183,* E235-E242.

von Bonsdorff, M.B., & others (2012). Work ability as a determinant of old age disability severity: Evidence from the 28-year Finnish longitudinal study on municipal employees. *Aging: Clinical and Experimental Research, 24,* 354-360.

Von Soest, T., & others (2018). Self-esteem across the second half of life: The role of socioeconomic status, physical health, social relationships, and personality factors. *Journal of Personality and Social Psychology, 114,* 945-958.

Voorpostel, M., & Blieszner, R. (2008). Intergenerational solidarity and support between adult siblings. *Journal of Marriage and the Family, 70,* 157–167.

Vorona, R.D., & others (2014). Adolescent crash rates and school start times in two Central Virginia counties, 2009–2011: A follow-up study to a Southeastern Virginia study, 2007–2008. *Journal of Clinical Sleep Medicine, 10,* 1169–1177.

Voss, U., & Klimke, A. (2018). Dreaming during REM sleep: Autobiographically meaningful or a simple reflection of a Hebbian-based memory consolidation process? *Archives of Italian Biology, 156,* 99–111.

Vosylis, R., Erentaite, R., & Crocetti, E. (2018). Global versus domain-specific identity processes. *Emerging Adulthood, 6,* 32–41.

Votruba-Drzal, E., Coley, R.L., & Chase-Lansdale, P.L. (2004). Child care and low-income children's development: Direct and moderated effects. *Child Development, 75,* 296–312.

Vranas, K.C., & others (2020). The association of Physician Orders for Life-Sustaining Treatment with intensity of treatment among patients presenting to the emergency department. *Annals of Emergency Medicine, 75,* 171–180.

Vu, J.A. (2016). The fourth 'R': Relationships, shifting from risk to resilience. In K.E. Sanders & A.W. Guerra (Eds.), *The culture of child care.* New York: Oxford University Press.

Vukelich, C., & others (2020). *Helping children learn language and literacy* (5th ed.). Upper Saddle River, NJ: Pearson.

Vuolo, M., Staff, J., & Mortimer, J.T. (2012). Weathering the great recession: Psychological and behavioral trajectories in the transition from school to work. *Developmental Psychology, 48,* 1759–1773.

Vurpillot, E. (1968). The development of scanning strategies and their relation to visual differentiation. *Journal of Experimental Child Psychology, 6,* 632–650.

Vygotsky, L.S. (1962). *Thought and language.* Cambridge, MA: MIT Press.

W

Wachs, T.D. (1994). Fit, context and the transition between temperament and personality. In C. Halverson, G. Kohnstamm, & R. Martin (Eds.), *The developing structure of personality from infancy to adulthood.* Hillsdale, NJ: Erlbaum.

Wachs, T.D. (2000). *Necessary but not sufficient.* Washington, DC: American Psychological Association.

Wade, M., & others (2019). Long-term effects of institutional rearing, foster care, and brain activity on memory and executive functioning. *PNAS, 116,* 1803–1813.

Wade, M., & others (2020). Telomere length and psychopathology: Specificity and direction of effects within the Bucharest Early Intervention Project. *Journal of the American Academy of Child and Adolescent Psychiatry, 59,* 140–148.

Wagers, K.B., & Kiel, E.J. (2019). The influence of parenting and temperament on empathy development in toddlers. *Journal of Family Psychology, 33,* 391–400.

Wagner, D.A. (2018). *Human development and international development.* New York: Routledge.

Wagner, J., Hoppmann, C., Ram, N., & Gerstorf, D. (2015). Self-esteem is relatively stable late in life: The role of resources in the health, self-regulation, and social domains. *Developmental Psychology, 51,* 136–149.

Wagner, J.B., & others (2020, in press). Attentional bias to fearful faces in infants at high risk for autism spectrum disorder. *Emotion.*

Walden, T. (1991). Infant social referencing. In J. Garber & K. Dodge (Eds.), *The development of emotional regulation and dysregulation.* New York: Cambridge University Press.

Waldenstrom, U., Cnattingius, S., Norman, M., & Schytt, E. (2015). Advanced maternal age and stillbirth risk in nulliparous and parous women. *Obstetrics and Gynecology, 126,* 355–362.

Waldinger, R.J., Vaillant, G.E., & Orav, E.J. (2007). Childhood sibling relationships as a predictor of major depression in adulthood: A 30-year prospective study. *American Journal of Psychiatry, 164,* 949–954.

Walker, A. (2019). The promise of active aging. In R. Fernandez-Ballesteros & others (Eds.), *Cambridge handbook of successful aging.* New York: Cambridge University Press.

Walker, D.A., & others (2020, in press). Leptomeningeal malignancy of childhood: Sharing learning between childhood leukemia and brain tumor trials. *Lancet Child and Adolescent Health.*

Walker, L.J. (2002). In W. Damon (Ed.), *Bringing in a new era of character education.* Stanford, CA: Hoover Press.

Walker, L.J. (2004). Progress and prospects in the psychology of moral development. *Merrill-Palmer Quarterly, 50,* 546–557.

Walker, L.J. (2016). Prosocial exemplarity in adolescence and adulthood. In L.M. Padilla-Walker & G. Carlo (Eds.), *Prosocial development.* New York: Oxford University Press.

Walker, L.J., & Frimer, J.A. (2009). Moral personality exemplified. In D. Narváez & D.K. Lapsley (Eds.), *Personality, identity and character: Explorations in moral psychology* (pp. 232–255). New York: Cambridge University Press.

Walker, S. (2006). Unpublished review of J.W. Santrock's *Topical approach to life-span development* (3rd ed.). New York: McGraw-Hill.

Wallace, L.N. (2017). Siblings and adolescent weapon carrying: Contributions of genetics, shared environment, and nonshared environment. *Youth Violence and Juvenile Justice, 15,* 264–280.

Wallenborg, K., & others (2009). Red wine triggers cell death and thiroredoxin reductase inhibition: Effects beyond resveratrol and SIRT 1. *Experimental Cell Research, 315,* 1360–1371.

Waller, E.M., & Rose, A.J. (2010). Adjustment trade-offs of co-rumination in mother-adolescent relationships. *Journal of Adolescence, 33,* 487–497.

Wallerstein, A., & others (2019). Primary topography-guided LASIK: Refractive, visual, and subjective quality of vision outcomes for astigmatism >2.00 diopters. *Journal of Refractive Surgery, 35,* 78–86.

Walsh, B.A., & Mortensen, J.A. (2020). *Transforming Early Head Start home visiting.* New York: Routledge.

Walter, I., & others (2019). The efficacy of the attachment-based SAFE prevention program: A randomized control trial including mothers and fathers. *Attachment and Human Development, 21,* 510–531.

Walters, G.D. (2020, in press). Prosocial peers as risk, protective, and promotive factors for the prevention of delinquency and drug use. *Journal of Youth and Adolescence.*

Walters, M.E., & others (2017). Effects of a training program for home health workers on the provision of preventive activities and on the health-related behavior of their clients: A quasi-experimental study. *International Journal of Nursing Studies, 74,* 61–66.

Walton, K.E., & Roberts, B.W. (2004). On the relationship between substance abuse and personality traits: Abstainers are not maladjusted. *Journal of Research in Personality, 38,* 515–535.

Wan, G.W.Y., & Leung, P.W.L. (2010). Factors accounting for youth suicide attempt in Hong Kong: A model building. *Journal of Adolescence, 33,* 575–582.

Wandell, P.E., Carlsson, A.C., & Theobald, H. (2009). The association between BMI value and long-term mortality. *International Journal of Obesity, 33,* 577–582.

Wang, B., & Guo, W. (2020). Exercise mode and attentional networks in older adults: A cross-sectional study. *PeerJ, 8,* e8364.

Wang, B., & others (2020a, in press). FOXO3a is stabilized by USP18-mediated de-ISGylation and inhibits TGF-*b*1-induced fibronectin expression. *Journal of Investigative Medicine.*

Wang, B., & others (2020b). Integrative omics approach to identifying genes associated with atrial fibrillation. *Circulation Research, 126*(3), 350–360.

Wang, C., & others (2016). Coevolution of adolescent friendship networks and smoking and drinking behaviors with consideration of parental influence. *Psychology of Addictive Behaviors, 30,* 312–324.

Wang, C., & others (2020, in press). MMP9, XCXR1, TLR6, and MPO participant in the progression of coronary artery disease. *Journal of Cellular Physiology.*

Wang, C.D., & others (2020). Grandparents as the primary care providers for their grandchildren: A cross-cultural comparison of Chinese and U.S. samples. *International Journal of Aging and Human Development, 35,* 280–289.

Wang, D.S., & others (2020). Association between child abuse exposure and the risk of psychiatric disorders: A nationwide cohort study in Taiwan. *Child Abuse and Neglect, 101,* 104362.

Wang, D.X., & others (2019). A candidate-gene approach identifies novel associations between common variants in/near syndromic obesity genes and body-mass index in pediatric and adult European populations. *Diabetes, 68,* 724–732.

Wang, H., & others (2019). Cell-autonomous and non-autonomous roles of *daf-16* in muscle function and mitochondrial capacity in aging *C. elegans*. *Aging, 11*, 2295-2311.

Wang, H., & others (2020, in press). Middle-aged children's coping strategies with tensions in the aging parent-child tie. *International Journal of Aging and Human Development*.

Wang, H., Lee, J.H., & Tian, Y. (2019). Critical genes in white adipose tissue based on gene expression profile following exercise. *International Journal of Sports Medicine, 40*, 57-61.

Wang, J., & others (2017). Breastfeeding and respiratory tract infections during the first 2 years of life. *ERJ Open Research, 3*, 2.

Wang, M., & Shi, J. (2016). Work, retirement, and aging. In K.W. Schaie & S.L. Willis (Eds.), *Handbook of the psychology of aging* (8th ed.). New York: Elsevier.

Wang, M., & others (2020, in press). Identifying autism spectrum disorder with multi-site fMRI via low-rank domain adaptation. *IEEE Transactions on Medical Imaging*.

Wang, N., Wilcox, I., & Lal, S. (2020, in press). Cholesterol lowering: To live longer, start younger? *Aging*.

Wang, P.Y., & others (2019). Relationship of sleep quality, smartphone dependence, and health-related behaviors in female junior college students. *PLoS One, 14*(4), e0214769.

Wang, R., & others (2017). Parental age and risk of pediatric cancer in the offspring: A population-based record-linkage study in California. *American Journal of Epidemiology, 186*, 843-856.

Wang, S., & others (2019). Brain functional organization with language lateralization. *Cerebral Cortex, 29*, 4312-4320.

Wang, S., & others (2019). The prevalence of depression and anxiety symptoms among overweight/obese and non-overweight/non-obese children/adolescents in China: A systematic review and meta-analysis. *International Journal of Environmental Research and Public Health, 16*, 3.

Wang, S.C., & others (2019). The experience of parents living with a child with cancer at the end of life. *European Journal of Cancer Care, 28*(4), e13061.

Wang, W., & Parker, K. (2014, September 24). *Record share of Americans have never married.* Washington, DC: Pew Research Center.

Wang, Y., & Hawk, S.T. (2020, in press). Expressive enhancement, suppression, and flexibility in childhood and adolescence: Longitudinal links with peer relations. *Emotion*.

Wang, Y., & Yip, T. (2020, in press). Parallel changes in ethnic/racial discrimination and identity in high school. *Journal of Youth and Adolescence*.

Wang, Y., & others (2019). Prenatal tobacco exposure modulated the association of genetic variants with diagnosed ADHD and its symptom domain in children: A community based case-control study. *Scientific Reports, 9*(1), 4274.

Wang, Y., & others (2020). Altered resting functional network typology assessed using graph theory in youth with attention-deficit/hyperactivity disorder. *Progress in Neuropsychopharmacology and Biological Psychiatry, 98*, 109796.

Wang, Y., & others (2020). Associations of unhealthy lifestyles with metabolic syndrome in Chinese rural aged females. *Scientific Reports, 10*(1), 2718.

Wang, Z.W., Hua, J., & Xu, Y.H. (2015). The relationship between gentle tactile stimulation on the fetus and its temperament 3 months after birth. *Behavioral Neuroscience, 2015*, 371906.

Ward, E.V. (2018). Reduced recognition and priming in older relative to young adults for incidental and intentional information. *Consciousness and Cognition, 57*, 62-73.

Ward, L.M., Moorman, J., & Grower, P. (2019). Entertainment media's role in the sexual socialization of Western youth: A review of research from 2000-2017. In S. Lamb & J. Gilbert (Eds.), *Cambridge handbook of sexual development.* New York: Cambridge University Press.

Ward, W.F., & others (2005). Effects of age and caloric restriction on lipid peroxidation: Measurement of oxidative stress by F2-isoprostane levels. *Journals of Gerontology A: Biological Sciences and Medical Sciences, 60*, 847-851.

Warr, P. (2004). Work, well-being, and mental health. In J. Baring, E.K. Kelloway, & M.R. Frone (Eds.), *Handbook of work stress.* Thousand Oaks, CA. Sage.

Warren, S.F., & others (2017). The longitudinal effects of parenting on adaptive behavior in children with fragile X syndrome. *Journal of Autism and Developmental Disorders, 47*, 768-784.

Warshak, R.A. (2017, June). Personal communication, Department of Psychology, University of Texas at Dallas, Richardson.

Wataganara, T., & others (2016). Fetal magnetic resonance imaging and ultrasound. *Journal of Perinatal Medicine, 44*, 533-542.

Watamura, S.E., Phillips, D.A., Morrissey, D.A., McCartney, T.W., & Bub, K. (2011). Double jeopardy: Poorer social-emotional outcomes for children in the NICHD SECCYD who experience home and child-care environments that convey risk. *Child Development, 82*, 48-65.

Waters, S.F., West, T.V., & Mendes, W.B. (2014). Stress contagion: Physiological covariation between mothers and infants. *Psychological Science, 25*, 934-942.

Waters, T.E., Ruiz, S.K., & Roisman, G.I. (2017). Origins of secure base script knowledge and the developmental construction of attachment representations. *Child Development, 88*, 198-209.

Watkins, L., & others (2019). An interest-based intervention package to increase peer social interaction in young children with autism spectrum disorder. *Journal of Applied Behavior Analysis, 52*, 132-149.

Watson, G.L., Arcona, A.P., Antonuccio, D.O., & Healy, D. (2014). Shooting the messenger: The case of ADHD. *Journal of Contemporary Psychotherapy, 44*, 43-52.

Watson, J.A., Randolph, S.M., & Lyons, J.L. (2005). African-American grandmothers as health educators in the family. *International Journal of Aging and Human Development, 60*, 343-356.

Watson, J.B. (1928). *Psychological care of infant and child.* New York: W.W. Norton.

Wattamwar, K., & others (2017). Increases in the rate of age-related hearing loss in the older old. *JAMA Otolaryngology—Head and Neck Surgery, 143*, 41-45.

Watts, C., & Zimmerman, C. (2002). Violence against women: Global scope and magnitude. *Lancet, 359*, 1232-1237.

Watts, T.W., & others (2018). The Chicago School Readiness Project: Examining long-term impacts of an early childhood intervention. *PLoS One, 13*(7), e0200144.

Waxman, S., & others (2013). Are nouns learned before verbs? Infants provide insight into a longstanding debate. *Child Development Perspectives, 7*, 155-159.

Weakley, A., & Schmitter-Edgecombe, M. (2014). Analysis of verbal fluency ability in Alzheimer's disease: The role of clustering, switching, and semantic proximities. *Archives of Clinical Neuropsychology, 29*, 256-268.

Weaver, J.M., & Schofield, T.J. (2015). Mediation and moderation of divorce effects on children's behavior problems. *Journal of Family Psychology, 29*, 39-48.

Webber, T.A., & others (2017). Neural outcome processing of peer-influenced risk-taking behavior in late adolescence: Preliminary evidence for gene × environment interactions. *Experimental and Clinical Psychopharmacology, 25*, 31-40.

Webster, J.D., & others (2018). Wisdom and meaning in emerging adulthood. *Emerging Adulthood, 6*, 118-136.

Webster, P.J., & others (2020, in press). Processing of real-world dynamic natural stimuli in autism is linked to corticobasal function. *Autism Research*.

Wechsler, H., & others (2002). Trends in college binge drinking during a period of increased prevention efforts: Findings from four Harvard School of Public Health college alcohol study surveys, 1993-2001. *Journal of American College Health, 50*, 203-217.

Weech-Maldonado, R., & others (2020, in press). Nursing home quality and financial performance: Is there a business case for quality? *Inquiry*.

Weersing, V.R., & others (2016). Prevention of depression in at-risk adolescents: Predictors and moderators of acute effects. *Journal of the American Academy of Child and Adolescent Psychiatry, 55*, 219-226.

Weger, H.W., Cole, M., & Akbulut, V. (2019). Relationship maintenance across platonic and non-platonic cross-sex friendships in emerging adults. *Journal of Social Psychology, 159*, 15-29.

Wei, J., & others (2019). Late-life depression and cognitive function among older adults in the U.S.: The National Health and Nutrition Examination Survey, 2011-2014. *Journal of Psychiatric Research 111*, 30-35.

Wei, W., & Ji, S. (2018). Cellular senescence: Molecular mechanisms and pathogenicity. *Journal of Cellular Physiology, 233,* 9121-9135.

Weikert, D.P. (1993). Long-term positive effects in the Perry Preschool Head Start Program. Unpublished data, High Scope Foundation, Ypsilanti, MI.

Weiler, L.M., & Taussig, H.N. (2019). The moderating effect of risk exposure on an efficacious intervention for maltreated children. *Journal of Clinical Child and Adolescent Psychology, 48*(Suppl. 1), S194-S201.

Weinraub, M., & Kaufman, R. (2019). Single parenthood. In M.H. Bornstein (Ed.), *Handbook of parenting* (3rd ed.). New York: Elsevier.

Weinraub, M., & others (2012). Patterns of developmental change in infants' nighttime sleep awakenings from 6 to 36 months of age. *Developmental Psychology, 48*(6), 1511-1528.

Weinstein, B.E., Sirow, L.W., & Moser, S. (2016). Relating hearing aid use to social and emotional loneliness in older adults. *American Journal of Audiology, 25,* 54-61.

Weinstein, N., & others (2019). Autonomous orientation predicts longevity: New findings from the Nun Study. *Journal of Personality, 87,* 181-193.

Weisman, O., Zagoory-Sharon, O., & Feldman, R. (2014). Oxytocin administration, salivary testosterone, and father-infant social behavior. *Progress in Neuro-Psychopharmacology and Biological Psychiatry, 49,* 47-52.

Weiss, K., & others (2020, in press). Management of three preterm infants with phenylketonuria. *Nutrition.*

Weissmark, M.S. (2020). *The science of diversity.* New York: Oxford University Press.

Weitkamp, K., & Seiffge-Krenke, I. (2019). The association between parental rearing dimensions and adolescent psychopathology: A cross-cultural study. *Journal of Youth and Adolescence, 48,* 469-483.

Wellman, H.M. (2011). Developing a theory of mind. In U. Goswami (Ed.), *Wiley-Blackwell handbook of childhood cognitive development* (2nd ed.). New York: Wiley.

Wellman, H.M. (2015). *Making minds.* New York: Oxford University Press.

Wellman, H.M., Cross, D., & Watson, J. (2001). Meta-analysis of theory-of-mind development: The truth about false belief. *Child Development, 72,* 655-684.

Wellman, H.M., & Woolley, J.D. (1990). From simple desires to ordinary beliefs: The early development of everyday psychology. *Cognition, 35,* 245-275.

Wellman, R.J., & others (2018). Socioeconomic status is associated with the prevalence and co-occurrence of risk factors for cigarette smoking initiation during adolescence. *International Journal of Public Health, 63,* 125-136.

Welmer, A.K., Rizzuto, D., Qiu, C., Caracciolo, B., & Laukka, E.J. (2014). Walking speed, processing speed, and dementia: A population-based longitudinal study. *Journals of Gerontology A: Biological Sciences and Medical Sciences, 69,* 1503-1510.

Wen, X., & others (2020). Detecting the information of functional connectivity networks in normal aging and using deep learning from a big data perspective. *Frontiers in Neuroscience, 13,* 1435.

Wendelken, C., & others (2017). Frontoparietal structural connectivity in childhood predicts development of functional connectivity and reasoning ability: A large-scale investigation. *Journal of Neuroscience, 37,* 8549-8558.

Wenestam, C.G., & Wass, H. (1987). Swedish and U.S. children's thinking about death: A qualitative study and cross-cultural comparison. *Death Studies, 11,* 99-121.

Wenger, N.S., & others (2003). The quality of medical care provided to vulnerable community-dwelling older patients. *Annals of Internal Medicine, 139,* 740-747.

Wennergren, G., & others (2015). Updated Swedish advice on reducing the risk of sudden infant death syndrome. *Acta Pediatrica, 104,* 444-448.

Wentzel, K.R. (1997). Student motivation in middle school: The role of perceived pedagogical caring. *Journal of Educational Psychology, 89,* 411-419.

Wentzel, K.R., & Asher, S.R. (1995). The academic lives of neglected, rejected, popular and controversial children. *Child Development. 66,* 754-763.

Wentzel, K.R., & Ramani, G. (Eds.) (2016). *Handbook of social influences in school contexts.* New York: Routledge.

Werner, N.E., & others (2014). Maternal social coaching quality interrupts the development of relational aggression during early childhood. *Social Development, 23,* 470-486.

Wesche, R., & Leftkowitz, E.S. (2020). Normative sexual development and milestones. In S. Hupp & J. Jewell (Eds.), *Encyclopedia of child and adolescent development.* New York: Wiley.

West, S.K., & others (2010). Older drivers and failure to stop at red lights. *Journals of Gerontology A: Biological Sciences and Medical Sciences, 65A,* 179-183.

Westerhof, G.J. (2009). Age identity. In D. Carr (Ed.), *Encyclopedia of the life course and human development.* Boston: Gale Cengage.

Westermann, G., Thomas, M.S.C., & Karmiloff-Smith, A. (2011). Neuroconstructivism. In U. Goswami (Ed.), *Wiley-Blackwell handbook of childhood cognitive development* (2nd ed.). New York: Wiley.

Westrate, N.M., & Gluck, J. (2017). Hard-earned wisdom: Exploratory processing of difficult life experience is positively associated with wisdom. *Developmental Psychology, 53,* 800-814.

Whaley, S.E., Jiang, L., Gomez, J., & Jenks, E. (2011). Literacy promotion for families participating in the Women, Infants, and Children program. *Pediatrics, 127,* 454-461.

Wheeler, L.A., & others (2017). Mexican-origin youth's risk behavior from adolescence to young adulthood: The role of familism values. *Developmental Psychology, 53,* 126-137.

Whitbourne, S.K., & Meeks, S. (2011). Psychopathology, bereavement, and aging. In K.W. Schaie & S.L. Willis (Eds.), *Handbook of the psychology of aging* (7th ed.). New York: Elsevier.

White, C.L., & others (2018). Advancing care for family caregivers of persons with dementia through caregiver and community partnerships. *Research Involvement and Engagement, 4,* 1.

White, E.R., & others (2017). Freshman year alcohol and marijuana use prospectively predict time to college graduation and subsequent adult roles and independence. *Journal of American College Health, 6,* 118-136.

White, L. (2019). Segmentation of speech. In S-A. Rueschemeyer & M. Gareth Gaskell (Eds.), *Oxford handbook of psycholinguistics* (2nd ed.). New York: Oxford University Press.

White, M.J., & others (2017). Calorie restriction attenuates terminal differentiation of immune cells. *Frontiers in Neuroscience, 7,* 667.

White, R.E., & Carlson, S.M. (2016). What would Batman do? Self-distancing improves executive function in young children. *Developmental Science, 19,* 419-426.

White, R.M.B., & others (2019). U.S. Mexican parents' use of harsh parenting in the context of neighborhood danger. *Journal of Family Psychology, 33,* 77-87.

White, V., & others (2018). Adolescents' alcohol use and strength of policy relating to youth access, trading hours, and driving under the influence: Findings from Australia. *Addiction, 113,* 1030-1042.

Whiteman, S.D., McHale, S.M., & Soli, A. (2011). Theoretical perspectives on sibling relationships. *Journal of Family Theory and Review, 3,* 124-139.

Whiting, W.L., & Murdock, K.K. (2016). Emerging adults' sleep patterns and attentional capture: Pivotal role of consistency. *Cognitive Processes, 17,* 155-162.

Wickramasekara, R.N., & Stessman, H.A.F. (2019). Histone 4 lysine 20 methylation: A case for neurodevelopmental disease. *Biology, 8*(1).

Wicks, S., Berger, Z., & Camic, P.M. (2019). It's how I am. . . it's what I am. . . it's a part of who I am: A narrative of the impact of adolescent-onset chronic illness on identity formation in young people. *Clinical Child Psychology and Psychiatry, 24,* 40-52.

Widiger, T.A. (2009). Neuroticism. In M.R. Leary & R.H. Hoyle (Eds.), *Handbook of individual differences in social behavior.* New York: Guilford.

Widman, L., Choukas-Bradley, S., Helms, S.W., & Prinstein, M.J. (2016). Adolescent susceptibility to peer influence in sexual situations. *Journal of Adolescent Health, 58,* 323-329.

Widman, L., & McNulty, J.K. (2010). Sexual narcissism and the perpetration of sexual aggression. *Archives of Sexual Behavior, 39,* 939-946.

Widom, C.S., Czaja, S.J., & DuMont, K.A. (2015). Intergenerational transmission of child abuse and neglect: Real or detection bias? *Science, 347,* 1480-1485.

Wiecko, F.M. (2014). Late-onset offending: Fact or fiction. *International Journal of Offender Therapy and Comparative Criminology, 58,* 107-129.

Wiesen, S.E., Watkins, R.M., & Needham, A.W. (2016). Active motor training has long-term effects on infants' object exploration. *Frontiers in Psychology, 7,* 599.

Wigfield, A., Rosenzweig, E.Q., & Eccles, J.S. (2017). Achievement values, interactions, interventions, and future directions. In A.J. Elliott, C.S. Dweck, & D.S. Yeager (Eds.), *Handbook of competence and motivation* (2nd ed.). New York: Guilford.

Wijndaele, K., & others (2017). Mortality risk reductions from substituting screen time by discretionary activities. *Medicine and Science in Sports and Exercise, 49,* 1111–1119.

Wike, R. (2014, January 14). French more accepting of infidelity than people in other countries. *Pew Research Center.*

Wild, J., & others (2019). Metabolomics for improved treatment monitoring of phenylketonuria: Urinary biomarkers for non-invasive assessment of dietary adherence and nutritional deficiencies. *The Analyst, 144*(22), 6595–6608.

Wiley, D.C., & others (2020, in press). Managing sex education controversy deep in the heart of Texas: A case study of the North East Independent School District (NEISD). *American Journal of Sexuality Education.*

Wilkinson-Lee, A.M., Russell, S.T., Lee, F.C.H., & The Latina/o Teen Pregnancy Prevention Workgroup (2006). Practitioners' perspectives on cultural sensitivity in Latina pregnancy prevention. *Family Relations, 55,* 376–389.

Willcox, B.J., & Willcox, M.D. (2014). Caloric restriction, caloric restriction mimetics, and healthy aging in Okinawa: Controversies and clinical implications. *Current Opinion in Clinical Nutrition and Metabolic Care, 17,* 51–58.

Willcox, B.J., Willcox, D.C., & Suzuki, M. (2017). Demographic, phenotypic, and genetic characteristics of centenarians in Okinawa and Japan: Part 1–Centenarians in Okinawa. *Mechanisms of Aging and Development, 165*(Pt. B), 75–79.

Willcox, B.J., Willcox, M.D., & Suzuki, M. (2002). *The Okinawa Program.* New York: Crown.

Willcox, D.C., Willcox, B.J., He, Q., Wang, N.C., & Suzuki, M. (2008). They really are that old: A validation study of centenarian prevalence in Okinawa. *Journals of Gerontology A: Biological Sciences and Medical Sciences, 63,* 338–349.

Willcox, D.C., Willcox, B.J., Sokolovsky, J., & Sakihara, S. (2007). The cultural context of "successful aging" among older women weavers in a Northern Okinawan village: The role of productive activity. *Journal of Cross Cultural Gerontology, 22,* 137–165.

Willey, J., Sandman, K., & Wood, D. (2020). *Prescott's microbiology* (11th ed.). New York: McGraw-Hill.

Williams, D.P., & others (2019). Stereotype threat, trait preservation, and vagal activity: Evidence for mechanisms underpinning health disparities in Black Americans. *Ethnicity and Health, 24,* 909–926.

Williams, G.L., Keigher, S., & Williams, A.V. (2012). Spiritual well-being among older African Americans in a Midwestern city. *Journal of Religion and Health, 51*(2), 355–370.

Williams, R.D., & others (2018). High-risk driving behaviors among 12th grade students: Differences between alcohol-only and alcohol mixed with energy drink users. *Substance Use and Misuse, 53,* 137–142.

Williamson, D. (2013). *Of years of love, and a long goodbye.* Retrieved from www.telegram.com/article/20130929/COLUMN01/309299933

Williamson, H.C., & others (2018). Premarital education and later relationship help-seeking. *Journal of Family Psychology, 32,* 276–281.

Williamson, R.A., Donohue, M.R., & Tully, E.C. (2013). Learning how to help others: Two-year-olds' social learning of a prosocial act. *Journal of Experimental Child Psychology, 114,* 543–550.

Willie, T.C., & others (2018). "Think like a man": How sexual cultural scripting and masculinity influence changes in men's use of intimate partner violence. *American Journal of Community Psychology, 61,* 240–250.

Willinger, U., & others (2019). Developmental steps in metaphorical language abilities: The influence of age, gender, cognitive flexibility, information processing speed, and analogical reasoning. *Language and Speech, 62,* 207–228.

Willink, A., Reed, N.S., & Lin, F.R. (2019). Cost-benefit analysis of hearing care services: What is it worth to Medicare? *Journal of the American Geriatrics Society, 67,* 784–789.

Willis, J., & Todorov, A. (2006). First impressions: Making up your mind after a 100-ms exposure to a face. *Psychological Science, 17,* 592–598.

Willis, S.L., & Belleville, S. (2016). Cognitive training in later adulthood. In K.W. Schaie & S.L. Willis (Eds.), *Handbook of the psychology of aging* (8th ed.). New York: Elsevier.

Willis, S.L., & Martin, M. (2005). Preface. In S.C. Willis & M. Martin (Eds.), *Middle adulthood.* Thousand Oaks, CA: Sage.

Willis, S.L., & Schaie, K.W. (2005). Cognitive trajectory in midlife and cognitive functioning in old age. In S.L. Willis & M. Martin (Eds.), *Middle adulthood.* Thousand Oaks, CA: Sage.

Willis, S.L., & Schaie, K.W. (2006). A co-constructionist view of the third age: The case of cognition. *Annual Review of Gerontology and Geriatrics* (Vol. 26). Palo Alto, CA: Annual Reviews.

Willoughby, B.J., & Belt, D. (2016). Marital orientation and relationship well-being among cohabiting couples. *Journal of Family Psychology, 30,* 181–192.

Willoughby, B.J., Hall, S.S., & Goff, S. (2015). Marriage matters but how much? Marital centrality among young adults. *Journal of Psychology, 149,* 796–817.

Willoughby, B.J., & James, S.L. (2017). *The marriage paradox.* New York: Oxford University Press.

Willoughby, M.T., Wylie, A.C., & Little, M.H. (2019). Testing longitudinal associations between executive function and academic achievement. *Developmental Psychology, 55,* 767–779.

Willoughby, M.T., & others (2017). Developmental delays in executive function from 3 to 5 years of age predict kindergarten academic readiness. *Journal of Learning Disabilities, 50,* 359–372.

Willumsen, J., & Bull, F. (2020). Development of WHO guidelines on physical activity, sedentary behavior, and sleep for children less than 5 years of age. *Journal of Physical Activity and Health, 17,* 96–100.

Wilson, A.E., Shuey, K.M., & Elder, G.H. (2003). Ambivalence in relationships of adult children to aging parents and in-laws. *Journal of Marriage and the Family, 65,* 1055–1072.

Wilson, D.M., & others (2013). The preferred place of the last days: Results of a representative population-based public survey. *Journal of Palliative Medicine, 16,* 502–508.

Wilson, L.C., & Miller, K.E. (2016). Meta-analysis of the prevalence of unacknowledged rape. *Trauma, Violence, and Abuse, 17,* 149–159.

Wilson, M.N., & others (2018). Driving under the influence behaviors among high school students who mix alcohol with energy drinks. *Preventive Medicine, 111,* 402–409.

Wilson, N., Lee, J.J., & Bei, B. (2019). Postpartum fatigue and depression: A systematic review and meta-analysis. *Journal of Affective Disorders, 246,* 224–233.

Wilson, R.S., & others (2002). Participation in cognitively stimulating activities and risk of incident Alzheimer disease. *JAMA, 287,* 742–748.

Wilson, R.S., & others (2018). Terminal decline of episodic memory and perceptual speed in a biracial population. *Neuropsychology, Development, and Cognition B: Aging, Neuropsychology, and Cognition, 25,* 378–389.

Wilson, S., & others (2020, in press). Minnesota Center for Twin and Family Research. *Twin Research and Human Genetics.*

Wilson, S.F., & others (2017). Doulas for surgical management of miscarriage and abortion: A randomized controlled trial. *American Journal of Obstetrics and Gynecology, 216,* e1–e44.

Winer, J.R., & others (2019). Sleep as a potential biomarker of tau and b-amyloid burden in the human brain. *Journal of Neuroscience, 39,* 6315–6324.

Winerman, L. (2005, January). Leading the way. *Monitor on Psychology, 36*(1), 64–67.

Wing, R., & others (2007). "STOP Regain": Are there negative effects of daily weighing? *Journal of Consulting and Clinical Psychology, 75,* 652–656.

Wingfield, A., & Lash, A. (2016). Audition and language comprehension in adult aging: Stability in the face of change. In K.W. Schaie & S.L. Willis (Eds.), *Handbook of the psychology of aging* (8th ed.). New York: Elsevier.

Wink, P., & Dillon, M. (2002). Spiritual development across the adult life course. Findings from a longitudinal study. *Journal of Adult Development, 9,* 79–94.

Winner, E. (1996). *Gifted children: Myths and realities.* New York: Basic Books.

Winner, E. (2009). Toward broadening our understanding of giftedness: The spatial domain. In F.D. Horowitz, R.F. Subotnik, & D.J. Matthews (Eds.), *The development of giftedness and talent across the life span.* Washington, DC: American Psychological Association.

Winner, E. (2014). Child prodigies and adult genius: A weak link. In D.K. Simonton (Ed.), *Wiley-Blackwell handbook of genius.* New York: Wiley.

Winner, F. (1986, August). Where pelicans kiss seals. *Psychology Today,* pp. 24–35.

Winsler, A., Carlton, M.P., & Barry, M.J. (2000). Age-related changes in preschool children's systematic use of private speech in a natural setting. *Journal of Child Language, 27,* 665–687.

Witherington, D.C., Campos, J.J., Harriger, J.A., Bryan, C., & Margett, T.E. (2010). Emotion and its development in infancy. In J.G. Bremner & T.D. Wachs (Eds.), *Wiley-Blackwell handbook of infant development* (2nd ed.). New York: Wiley.

Withers, M., Kharazmi, N., & Lim, E. (2018). Traditional beliefs and practices in pregnancy, childbirth, and postpartum: A review of the evidence from Asian countries. *Midwifery, 56,* 158–170.

Witkin, H.A., & others (1976). Criminality in XYY and XXY men. *Science, 193,* 547–555.

Witte, A.V., & others (2014). Long-chain omega-3 fatty acids improve brain function and structure in older adults. *Cerebral Cortex, 24,* 3059–3068.

Wittig, S.L., & Spatz, D.L. (2008). Induced lactation: Gaining a better understanding. *MCN, The Journal of Maternal Child Nursing, 33,* 76–81.

Wladis, C., Hachey, A., & Conway, K. (2018). No time for college? An investigation of time, poverty, and parenthood. *Journal of Higher Education, 89,* 807–831.

Wolf, S., & McCoy, D.C. (2019). The role of executive function and social-emotional skills in the development of literacy and numeracy during preschool: A cross-lagged longitudinal survey. *Developmental Science, 22*(4), e12800.

Wolf, T., & Zimprich, D. (2020, in press). What characterizes the reminiscence bump in autobiographical memory? New answers to an old question. *Memory and Cognition.*

Wolfe, K.L., & others (2019). Hopelessness as a predictor of suicide ideation in depressed male and female adolescent youth. *Suicide and Life-Threatening Behavior, 49*(1), 253–263.

Wolff, J.K., & others (2016). Translating good intentions into physical activity: Older adults with low prospective memory ability profit from planning. *Journal of Behavioral Medicine, 39,* 472–482.

Wolitzky-Taylor, K.B., & others (2011). Reporting rape in a national sample of college women. *American Journal of College Health, 59,* 582–587.

Wolke, D., Lee, K., & Guy, A. (2017). Cyberbullying: A storm in a teacup? *European Child and Adolescent Psychiatry, 26,* 899–908.

Wolke, D., & Lereya, S.T. (2015). Long-term effects of bullying. *Archives of Disease in Childhood, 100,* 879–885.

Wong, C.G., & Stevens, M.C. (2012). The effects of stimulant medication on working memory functional connectivity in attention-deficit/hyperactivity disorder. *Biological Psychiatry, 71,* 458–466.

Wong, K., & others (2019). The role of mindful parenting in individual and social decision-making in children. *Frontiers in Psychology, 10,* 550.

Wong, M., & others (2017). Use of time and adolescent health-related quality of life/wellbeing: A scoping review. *Acta Pediatrica, 106,* 1239–1245.

Wong, M.M., & Brower, K.J. (2012). The prospective relationship between sleep problems and suicidal behavior in the National Longitudinal Study of Adolescent Health. *Journal of Psychiatric Research, 46,* 953–959.

Wong, S.P.W., & others (2020, in press). Risk factors and birth outcomes associated with teenage pregnancy: A Canadian sample. *Journal of Pediatric and Adolescent Gynecology.*

Wood, D., Harms, P., & Vazire, S. (2010). Perceiver effects as projective tests: What your perceptions of others say about you. *Journal of Personality and Social Psychology, 99,* 174–190.

Woodhead, Z.V.J., & others (2019). Testing the unitary theory of language lateralization using functional transcranial Doppler sonography in adults. *Royal Society Open Science, 6*(3), 181801.

Woodhouse, S.S., & others (2019). The Circle of Security intervention. In H. Steele & M. Steele (Eds.), *Handbook of attachment-based interventions.* New York: Guilford.

Woodhouse, S.S., & others (2020). Secure base provision: A new approach to examining links between maternal caregiving and infant attachment. *Child Development, 91,* e249–e265.

Woods, S.P., & others (2014). Event-based prospective memory is independently associated with self-report of medication management in older adults. *Aging and Mental Health, 18,* 745–753.

Woodward, A.L., & Markman, E.M. (1998). Early word learning. In D. Kuhn & R.S. Siegler (Eds.), *Handbook of child psychology* (5th ed., Vol. 2). New York: Wiley.

World Health Organization (2000, February 2). *Adolescent health behavior in 28 countries.* Geneva, Switzerland: World Health Organization.

World Health Organization (2019). *Guidelines on physical activity, sedentary behavior, and sleep for children under 5 years of age.* Geneva, Switzerland: Author.

World Health Organization (2020). *Adolescent pregnancy: Fact sheet.* Geneva, Switzerland: World Health Organization.

Worthington, E.L. (1989). Religious faith across the life span: Implications for counseling and research. *Counseling Psychologist, 17,* 555–612.

Wraw, C., & others (2018). Intelligence in youth and health behaviors in middle age. *Intelligence, 69,* 71–86.

Wright, H., Jenks, R.A., & Demeyere, N. (2019). Frequent sexual activity predicts specific cognitive abilities in older adults. *Journals of Gerontology B: Psychological Sciences and Social Sciences, 74,* 47–51.

Wright, J. (2006, March 16). *Boomers in the bedroom: Sexual attitudes and behaviours in the boomer generation.* Ipsos Reid survey. Retrieved February 28, 2009, from http://www.ipsos-na.com

Wright, M.R. (2020, in press). Relationship quality among older cohabitors: A comparison to remarrieds. *Journals of Gerontology B: Psychological Sciences and Social Sciences.*

Wright, M.R., & Brown, S.L. (2017). Psychological well-being among older adults: The role of partnership status. *Journal of Marriage and the Family, 79,* 833–849.

Wrzus, C., Hanel, M., Wagner, J., & Neyer, F.J. (2013). Social network changes and life events across the life span: A meta-analysis. *Psychological Bulletin, 139*(1), 53–80.

Wu, L., & others (2020, in press). Telomerase: Key regulator of inflammation and cancer. *Pharmacology Research.*

Wu, M., & others (2019). Resveratrol alleviates chemotherapy-induced oogonial stem cell apoptosis and ovarian aging in mice. *Aging, 11,* 1030–1044.

Wu, R., & Scerif, G. (2018). Attention. In M.H. Bornstein (Ed.), *SAGE encyclopedia of lifespan human development.* Thousand Oaks, CA: Sage.

Wu, T., Gao, X., Chen, M., & van Dam, R.M. (2009). Long-term effectiveness of diet-plus-exercise interventions vs. diet-only interventions for weight loss: A meta-analysis. *Obesity Review, 10,* 313–323.

Wu, W., & others (2020). Medium-to-high late-life physical activity is associated with lower risk of incident dementia: The Shanghai Aging Study. *Journal of Alzheimer's Disease, 73,* 751–758.

Wu, Y., & Jobson, L. (2019). Maternal reminiscing and child autobiographical memory elaboration: A meta-analytic review. *Developmental Psychology, 55,* 2505–2521.

Wu, Y., & others (2019). Adverse maternal and neonatal outcomes among singleton pregnancies in women of very advanced maternal age: A retrospective cohort study. *BMC Pregnancy and Childbirth, 19*(1), 3.

X

Xiang, J., & others (2020, in press). A new method to identify fetal sex and trisomy 21 from the amniocentesis of pregnant women. *Human Cell.*

Xiao, Q., Wu, M., & Zeng, T. (2019). Social support networks in Chinese older adults: Health outcomes and health related behaviors: A path analysis. *Aging and Mental Health, 23,* 1382–1390.

Xiao, S.X., & others (2019). Characteristics of preschool gender enforcers and peers who associate with them. *Sex Roles, 81,* 671–685.

Xie, C., & others (2017). Exercise and dietary program-induced weight reduction is associated with cognitive function in obese adolescents: A longitudinal study. *PeerJ, 5,* e3286.

Xie, L., & others (2020, in press). United States prevalence of pediatric asthma by environmental smoke exposure, 2016–2017. *Journal of Asthma.*

Xie, Q., & Young, M.E. (1999). Integrated child development in rural China. *Education: The World Bank.* Washington, DC: The World Bank.

Xie, W., Mallin, B.M., & Richards, J.E. (2018). Development of infant sustained attention and its relation to EEG oscillations: An EEG and cortical course analysis study. *Developmental Science, 21*(3), e12562.

Xie, W., Mallin, B.M., & Richards, J.E. (2019). Development of brain functional connectivity and its relation to infant sustained attention in the first year of life. *Developmental Science, 22*(1), e12703.

Xie, W., & Richards, J.E. (2016). Effects of interstimulus intervals on behavioral, heart rate, and event-related potential indices of infant engagement and sustained attention. *Psychophysiology, 53,* 1128–1142.

Xie, W., & Richards, J.E. (2017). The relation between infant covert orienting, sustained attention, and brain activity. *Brain Topography, 30,* 198–219.

Xie, W., & others (2019). Neural correlates of facial emotion processing in infancy. *Developmental Science, 22*(3), e12758.

Xiu-Ying, H., & others (2012). Living arrangements and risk for late life depression: A meta-analysis of published literature. *International Journal of Psychiatry in Medicine, 43,* 19–34.

Xu, A., & others (2019). Microtubule regulators act in the nervous system to modulate fat metabolism and longevity through DAF-16 in *C. elegans. Aging Cell, 18*(2), e12884.

Xu, H., Wen, L.M., Hardy, L.L., & Rissel, C. (2016). Associations of outdoor play and screen time with nocturnal sleep duration and pattern among young children. *Acta Pediatrica, 105,* 297–303.

Xu, J. (2016). Mortality among centenarians in the United States, 2000-2014. *NCHS Data Brief, 233,* 1–8.

Xu, M.D., & others (2020). Mortality in the United States, 2018. *NCHS Data Brief, No. 355,* 1–8.

Xu, P., & others (2019). Intergenerational financial exchange and cognitive impairment among older adults in China. *Aging and Mental Health, 23,* 1209–1217.

Xu, R., & others (2019). Metabolomic analysis reveals metabolic characteristics of children with short stature caused by growth hormone deficiency. *Clinical Science, 133,* 777–788.

Xu, R., & others (2019). Parental overweight and hypertension are associated with their children's blood pressure. *Nutrition and Metabolism, 16,* 35.

Xu, W., & others (2015). Meta-analysis of modifiable risk factors for Alzheimer's disease. *Journal of Neurology, Neurosurgery, and Psychiatry, 86,* 1299–1306.

Xu, X., & others (2020). Feature selection and combination of information in the functional brain connectome for discrimination of mild cognitive impairment and analyses of altered brain patterns. *Frontiers in Aging Neuroscience, 12,* 28.

Xuan, X., & others (2019). Relationship among school socioeconomic status, teacher-student relationship, and middle school students' academic achievement in China: Using the multilevel mediation model. *PLoS One, 14,* e0213783

Xue, Y., Yang, Y., & Huang, T. (2019). Effects of chronic exercise interventions on executive function among children and adolescents: A systematic review with meta-analysis. *British Journal of Sports Medicine, 53,* 1397–1404.

Y

Yakoboski, P.J. (2011). Worries and plans as individuals approach retirement. *Benefits Quarterly, 27,* 34–37.

Yamada, K., & others (2020). MicroRNA 16-5p is upregulated in calorie-restricted mice and modulates inflammatory cytokines of macrophages. *Gene, 725,* 144191.

Yamakawa, M., & others (2015). Breast-feeding and hospitalization for asthma in early childhood: A nationwide longitudinal survey in Japan. *Public Health Nutrition, 18,* 1756–1761.

Yamaoka, Y., Fujwara, T., & Tamiya, N. (2016). Association between maternal postpartum depression and unintentional injury among 4-month-old infants in Japan. *Maternal and Child Health Journal, 20,* 326–336.

Yang, C., & others (2020, in press). Effectiveness of combined cognitive and physical interventions to enhance functioning in older adults with mild cognitive impairment: A systematic review of randomized controlled trials. *Gerontologist.*

Yang, F. (2020, in press). Widowhood and loneliness among Chinese older adults: The role of education and gender. *Aging and Mental Health.*

Yang, H.L., & others (2019). The construction and evaluation of executive attention training to improve selective attention, focused attention, and divided attention for older adults with mild cognitive impairment: A randomized controlled trial. *American Journal of Geriatric Psychiatry, 27,* 1257–1267.

Yang, J.R., & Chen, X. (2019). Dosage sensitivity of X-linked genes in human embryonic single cells. *BMC Genomics, 20*(1), 42.

Yang, L., & others (2016). Longer sleep duration and midday napping are associated with a higher risk of CHD incidence in middle-aged and older Chinese: The Dongfeng-Tongji Cohort Study. *Sleep, 39,* 645–652.

Yang, N., & Lee, S.M. (2020, in press). The development and validation of the meaning making in grief scale. *Death Studies.*

Yang, P., & others (2020). Neuronal mitochondria-targeted micelles relieving oxidative stress for delayed progression of Alzheimer's disease. *Biomaterials, 238,* 119–884.

Yang, S., & Park, S. (2017). A sociocultural approach to children's perceptions of death and loss. *Omega, 76,* 53–77.

Yang, S., & others (2020, in press). Access to fruit and vegetable markets and childhood obesity: A systematic review. *Obesity Reviews.*

Yang, X., & others (2020, in press). Combined effects of physical activity and calcium on bone health in children and adolescents: A systematic review of randomized controlled trials. *World Journal of Pediatrics.*

Yang, Y. (2008). Social inequalities in happiness in the United States, 1972-2004: An age-period-cohort analysis. *American Sociological Review, 73,* 204–226.

Yasumura, A., & others (2019). Age-related differences in frontal lobe function in children with ADHD. *Brain Development, 41,* 577–586.

Yates, L.B., Djuousse, L., Kurth, T., Buring, J.E., & Gaziano, J.M. (2008). Exceptional longevity in men: Modifiable factors associated with survival and function to age 90 years. *Archives of Internal Medicine, 168,* 284–290.

Yavorsky, J.E., Dush, C.M., & Schoppe-Sullivan, S.J. (2015). The production of inequality: The gender division of labor across the transition to parenthood. *Journal of Marriage and the Family, 77,* 662–679.

Yazigi, A., & others (2017). Fetal and neonatal abnormalities due to congenital rubella syndrome: A review of the literature. *Journal of Maternal-Fetal and Neonatal Medicine, 30,* 274–278.

Ye, Y., Yang, Z., & Lei, J. (2019). Stochastic telomere shortening and the route to limitless replicative potential. *Journal of Computational Biology, 23,* 350–363.

Yeager, D.S., Dahl, R., & Dweck, C.S. (2018). Why interventions to influence adolescent behavior often fail but could succeed. *Perspectives on Psychological Science, 13,* 101–122.

Yeh, S.T., Ng, Y.Y., & Wu, S.C. (2020). Association of psychiatric and physical illnesses with suicide in older adults in Taiwan. *Journal of Affective Disorders, 264,* 425–429.

Yen, H.Y., & Lin, L.J. (2018). A systematic review of reminiscence therapy for older adults in Taiwan. *Journal of Nursing Research, 26,* 138–150.

Yen, Y.F., & others (2018). Association of advance directives completion with the utilization of life-sustaining treatments during the end-of-life care in older patients. *Journal of Pain and Symptom Management, 55,* 265–271.

Yeo, G., & Yoshikawa, T. (2019). To the future of ethnogeriatric research and publication. *Journal of the American Geriatrics Society, 67*(6), 20–22.

Yeo, S.C., & others (2019). Associations of sleep duration on school nights with self-rated health, overweight, and depression symptoms in adolescents: Problems and possible solutions. *Sleep Medicine, 60,* 96–108.

Yeung, A.W.K., & others (2019). Antioxidants: Scientific literature landscape analysis. *Oxidative Stress and Cellular Longevity, 2019,* 8278454.

Yildiz, E., & others (2020, in press). Comparison of sleep problems among adolescents who attempted suicide and healthy adolescents. *Journal of Nervous and Mental Disease.*

Yin, R.K. (2012). Case study methods. In H. Cooper (Ed.), *APA handbook of research methods in psychology.* Washington, DC: American Psychological Association.

Yip, P.S., & others (2015). The roles of culture and gender in the relationship between divorce and suicide risk: A meta-analysis. *Social Science and Medicine, 138,* 87–94.

Yogman, M., & others (2018). The power of play: A pediatric role in enhancing skills in young children. *Pediatrics, 142,* 3.

Yong, H.H., & others (2018). Do predictors of smoking relapse change as a function of duration of abstinence? Findings from the United States, Canada, United Kingdom, and Australia. *Addiction, 113,* 1295–1304.

Yoo, J., Kim, &., Cho, E.R., & Jee, S.H. (2017). Biological age as a useful index to predict seventeen-year survival and mortality in Koreans. *BMC Geriatrics, 17*(1), 7.

Yoo, K.B., & others (2016). Association between employment status change and depression in Korean adults. *BMJ Open, 6*(3), e008570.

Yoon, D.S., & others (2019). MPK-1/ERK is required for the full activity of resveratrol in extended lifespan and reproduction. *Aging Cell, 18*(1), e12867.

Yoon, S.H., & others (2015). Correlates of self-reported sleep duration in middle-aged and elderly Koreans: From the Health Examinees Study. *PLoS One, 10*(5), e0123510.

Yopp, J.M., & others (2019). Psychological and parental functioning of widowed fathers: The first two years. *Journal of Family Psychology, 33*, 565–574.

Young, K.T. (1990). American conceptions of infant development from 1955 to 1984: What the experts are telling parents. *Child Development, 61*, 17–28.

Youniss, J., McLellan, J.A., & Yates, M. (1999). Religion, community service, and identity in American youth. *Journal of Adolescence, 22*, 243–253.

Yousefi, M., & others (2013). Relationships between age of puberty onset and height at age 18 years in girls and boys. *World Journal of Pediatrics, 9*(3), 230–238.

Yu, C., Suanda, S.H., & Smith, L.B. (2019). Infant sustained attention but not joint attention to objects at 9 months predicts vocabulary at 12 and 15 months. *Developmental Science, 22*(1), e12735.

Yu, J., & others (2020, in press). Depressive symptoms among elderly men and women who transition to widowhood: Comparisons with long term married and long term widowed over a 10-year period. *Journal of Women and Aging.*

Yu, S., & Hu, G. (2017). Can higher-proficiency L2 learners benefit from working with lower-proficiency partners in peer feedback? *Teaching in Higher Education, 22*, 178–192.

Yu, Y., & others (2019). Maternal diabetes during pregnancy and early onset of cardiovascular disease in offspring: Population cohort study with 40 years of follow-up. *BMJ, 367*, l6398.

Yuan, J., & others (2020, in press). Two conserved epigenetic regulators prevent healthy aging. *Nature.*

Yunus, R.M., & Hairi, N.N. (2020, in press). Ageism. *Asia-Pacific Journal of Public Health.*

Z

Zafarullah, M., & Tassone, F. (2019). Molecular biomarkers in fragile X syndrome. *Brain Sciences, 9*, 5.

Zai, C.C., & others (2019). An examination of genes, stress, and suicidal behavior in two First Nations communities: The role of the brain-derived neurotropic factor gene. *Psychiatry Research, 275*, 247–252.

Zammit, A.R., & others (2018). Identification of heterogeneous cognitive subgroups in community-dwelling older adults: A latent class analysis of the Einstein Aging Study. *Journal of the International Neuropsychology Society, 24*, 511–523.

Zannas, A.S., & others (2012). Stressful life events, perceived stress, and 12-month course of geriatric depression: Direct effects and moderation by the 5-HTTLPR and COMT Val158Met polymorphisms. *Stress, 15*(4), 425–434.

Zarrindast, M-R., & Khakpai, F. (2019). The modulatory role of nicotine on cognitive and non-cognitive functions. *Brain Research, 1710*, 92–101.

Zawadzki, M.J., & others (2019). Understanding stress in daily life: A coordinated analysis of the factors associated with the frequency of reporting stress. *Journal of Behavioral Medicine, 42*, 545–560.

Zayas, V., Mischel, W., & Pandey, G. (2014). Mind and brain in delay of gratification. In V.F. Reyna & V. Zayas (Eds.), *The neuroscience of risky decision making.* Washington, DC: American Psychological Association.

Zdolska-Wawrzkiewicz, A., & others (2019). The dynamics of becoming a mother during pregnancy and after childbirth. *International Journal of Environmental Research and Public Health, 17*, 1.

Zeiders, K.A., & others (2020, in press). Latina/o youths' discrimination experiences in the U.S. Southwest: Estimates from three studies. *Applied Developmental Science.*

Zeifman, D., & Hazan, C. (2008). Pair bonds as attachments: Reevaluating the evidence. In J. Cassidy & P.R. Shaver (Eds.), *Handbook of attachment* (2nd ed.). New York: Guilford.

Zeifman, D.M., & St. James-Roberts, I. (2017). Parenting the crying infant. *Current Opinion in Psychology, 15*, 149–154.

Zelazo, P.D. (2013). Developmental psychology: A new synthesis. In P.D. Zelazo (Ed.), *Handbook of developmental psychology.* New York: Wiley.

Zelazo, P.D., & Muller, U. (2011). Executive function in typical and atypical children. In U. Goswami (Ed.), *Wiley-Blackwell handbook of childhood cognitive development* (2nd ed.). New York: Wiley.

Zelazo, P.D., & others (2018). Mindfulness plus reflection training: Effects on executive function in early childhood. *Frontiers in Psychology, 9*, 208.

Zeng, Y., & Shen, K. (2010). Resilience significantly contributes to exceptional longevity. *Current Gerontology and Geriatrics Research.* doi:10.1155/2010/525693

Zeng, Y., & others (2016). Interaction between the FOXO1A-209 genotype and tea drinking is significantly associated with reduced mortality at advanced ages. *Rejuvenation Research, 19*, 195–203.

Zeskind, P.S., Klein, L., & Marshall, T.R. (1992). Adults' perceptions of experimental modifications of durations and expiratory sounds in infant crying. *Developmental Psychology, 28*, 1153–1162.

Zettel-Watson, L., & others (2017). Aging well: Processing speed inhibition and working memory related to balance and aerobic endurance. *Geriatrics and Gerontology International, 17*, 108–115.

Zhang, D., & others (2017). Is maternal smoking during pregnancy associated with an increased risk of congenital heart defects among offspring? A systematic review and meta-analysis of observational studies. *Journal of Maternal-Fetal and Neonatal Medicine, 30*, 645–657.

Zhang, F., & Roeyers, H. (2019). Exploring brain functions in autism spectrum disorder: A systematic review of functional near-infrared spectroscopy (fNIRS) studies. *International Journal of Psychophysiology, 137*, 41–53.

Zhang, H., & others (2020). Prolonged grief disorder in Chinese Shidu parents who have lost their only child. *European Journal of Psychotraumatology, 11*(1), 1726071.

Zhang, J., & others (2019). Digital media and depressive symptoms among Chinese adolescents: A cross-sectional study. *Heliyon, 5*(5), e01554.

Zhang, J., & others (2019). Prenatal diagnosis of Tay-Sachs disease. *Methods in Molecular Biology, 1885*, 233–250.

Zhang, L., & others (2019). Decreased information replacement of working memory after sleep deprivation: Evidence from an event-related potential study. *Frontiers in Neuroscience, 13*, 408.

Zhang, M., & others (2020). Parent-adolescent acculturation profiles and language brokering experiences in Mexican immigrant families. *Journal of Youth and Adolescence, 49*, 335–351.

Zhang, W., Braun, K.L., & Wu, Y.Y. (2017). The educational, racial, and gender crossovers in life satisfaction: Findings from the Longitudinal Health and Retirement Study. *Archives in Gerontology and Geriatrics, 73*, 60–68.

Zhang, W., & others (2017). Reconsidering parenting in Chinese culture: Subtypes, stability, and change of maternal parenting style during early adolescence. *Journal of Youth and Adolescence, 46*, 1117–1136.

Zhang, W., & others (2019). Education, activity engagement, and cognitive function in U.S. Chinese older adults. *Journal of the American Geriatrics Society, 67*(S3), S525–S531.

Zhang, X., & Wang, J. (2019). Massage intervention for preterm infants by their mothers: A randomized controlled trial. *Journal for Specialists in Pediatric Nursing, 24*(2), e12238.

Zhang, X., & others (2019). Association of sarcopenic obesity with the risk of all-cause mortality among adults over a broad range of different settings: An updated meta-analysis. *BMC Geriatrics, 19*(1), 183.

Zhang, Y., & Liu, H. (2020, in press). A national longitudinal study of partnered sex, relationship quality, and mental health among older adults. *Journals of Gerontology B: Psychological and Social Sciences.*

Zhang, Y., & others (2016). A cross-cultural comparison of climacteric symptoms, self-esteem, and perceived social support between Mosuo women and Han Chinese women. *Menopause, 23*, 784–791.

Zhao, H., Seibert, S.E., & Lumpkin, G.T. (2010). The relationship of personality to entrepreneurial intentions and performance: A meta-analytic review. *Journal of Management, 36*, 381–404.

Zhao, J., & others (2020, in press). LncRNAs a new target for post-stroke recovery. *Current Pharmaceutical Design.*

Zhao, X., & others (2019). The conjoint analysis of microstructural and morphological changes of gray matter during aging. *Frontiers in Neurology, 10*, 184.

Zhaoyang, R., & Martire, L.M. (2020, in press). The influence of family and friend confidants on marital quality in older couples. *Journals of Gerontology B: Psychological Sciences and Social Sciences.*

Zheng, Y., & others (2017). Capturing parenting as a multidimensional and dynamic construct with a person-oriented approach. *Prevention Science, 18,* 281–291.

Zheng, Y., & others (2020, in press). Development and preliminary investigation of a decision to support informed choice among patients with age-related cataract. *International Ophthalmology.*

Zheng, Z., & others (2019). Episodic reconstruction contributes to high-confidence false recognition memories in older adults: Evidence from event-related potentials. *Brain and Cognition, 132,* 13–21.

Zhi, L., & others (2019). Loss of PINK1 causes age-dependent decrease in dopamine release and mitochondrial dysfunction. *Neurobiology of Aging, 75,* 1–10.

Zhong, B.L., & others (2017). Loneliness and cognitive function in older adults: Findings from the Chinese Longitudinal Healthy Longevity Survey. *Journals of Gerontology B: Psychological Sciences and Social Sciences, 72,* 120–128.

Zhou, B., & others (2015). Genetic and environmental influences on obesity-related phenotypes in Chinese twins reared apart and together. *Behavior Genetics, 45,* 427–437.

Zhou, P., & others (2020, in press). Association of small dense low-density lipoprotein cholesterol with stroke risk, severity, and progress. *Journal of Atherosclerosis and Thrombosis.*

Zhou, Q. (2013). *Commentary in S. Smith, Children of "tiger parents" develop more aggression and depression, research shows.* Retrieved July 20, 2013, from www.cbsnews.com/news/children-of-tiger-parents-develop-more-aggression-and-depression-research-shows/

Zhou, Q., & others (2012). Asset and protective factors for Asian American children's mental health adjustment. *Child Development Perspectives, 6,* 312–319.

Zhou, Y., & others (2018). Weight changes since age 20 and cardiovascular risk factors in a middle-aged Chinese population. *Journal of Public Health, 40,* 253–261.

Zhou, Y., & others (2019). The restorative effect of work after unemployment: An intraindividual analysis of subjective well-being recovery through reemployment. *Journal of Applied Psychology, 104,* 1195–1206.

Zhou, Z., & others (2020). Low-density lipoprotein cholesterol and Alzheimer's disease: A systematic review and meta-analysis. *Frontiers in Aging Neuroscience, 12,* 5.

Zhu, Z., & others (2019). Association of age-related macular degeneration with risk of all-cause and specific-cause mortality in the National Health and Nutrition Examination Survey, 2005 to 2008. *JAMA Ophthalmology, 137,* 248–257.

Ziegler, D.A., Janowich, J.R., & Gazzaley, A. (2018). Differential impact of interference on internally- and externally-directed attention. *Scientific Reports, 8*(1), 2498.

Ziermans, T., & others (2017). Formal thought disorder and executive functioning in children and adolescents with autism spectrum disorder: Old leads and new avenues. *Journal of Autism and Developmental Disorders, 48,* 1756–1768.

Zigler, E.F., Gilliam, W.S., & Barnett, W.S. (Eds.) (2011). *The pre-K debates: Controversies and issues.* Baltimore: Paul H. Brookes.

Zigler, E.F., Gilliam, W.S., & Jones, S.M. (2006). *A vision for universal preschool education.* New York: Cambridge University Press.

Zigler, E.F., & Styfco, S.J. (1994). Head Start: Criticisms in a constructive context. *American Psychologist, 49,* 127–132.

Zijlmans, J., & others (2020, in press). Disentangling multiproblem behavior in male young adults: A cluster analysis. *Development and Psychopathology.*

Zimmer-Gembeck, M.J., & others (2019). Improved perceptions of emotion regulation and reflective functioning of parents: Two additional positive outcomes of parent-child interaction therapy. *Behavior Therapy, 50,* 340–352.

Zimmerman, C.A., & others (2019). Stress dynamically regulates co-expression networks of glucocorticoid receptor-dependent MDD and SCZ risk genes. *Translational Psychiatry, 9*(1), 41.

Ziol-Guest, K.M. (2009). Child custody and support. In D. Carr (Ed.), *Encyclopedia of the life course and human development.* Boston: Gale Cengage.

Zortea, T.C., Gray, C.M., & O'Connor, R.C. (2020, in press). The relationship between adult attachment and suicidal thoughts and behaviors: A systematic review. *Archives of Suicide Research.*

Zorzetti, R., & others (2019). Low affective temperament consistency during development: Results from a large retrospective study. *Journal of Affective Disorders, 248,* 180–184.

Zosh, J., & others (2017). Putting the education back in education apps: How content and context interact to promote learning. In R. Barr & D. Linebarger (Eds.), *Media exposure during infancy and early childhood.* New York: Springer.

Zucker, K.J., Lawrence, A.A., & Kreukels, B.P. (2016). Gender dysforia in adults. *Annual Review of Psychology, 12,* 217–247.

name index

Baker, J. K., 237
Baker, K. M., 355
Baker, L., 442
Baker, N. A., 456
Bakermans-Kranenburg, M. J., 69, 183, 184, 185
Bakota, L., 532
Balantekin, K. N., 386
Balasubramaniam, M., 572
Balfour, B., 199
Ball, C., 238, 255
Ball, K., 539
Ballintyn, B., 109
Balon, R., 617
Baltes, M., 536
Baltes, P. B., 5, 6, 7, 15, 19, 52, 473, 528, 529, 554, 560, 563, 586, 587
Balzer, B. W., 344, 345
Bamaca-Colbert, M., 383
Bandura, A., 26, 52, 239, 242, 287, 310, 365, 429, 493, 601
Bangen, K. J., 560
Bangsbo, J., 563
Banja, J., 619
Bank, S., 202
Banker, S. M., 275
Banks, J. A., 256, 330, 332, 392, 393
Banks, M., 131
Bannon, F., 618
Baradon, T., 185
Baran, C. N., 610
Barat, O., 532
Barati, E., 63
Barber, B., 393
Barbieri, M., 561
Barbonetti, A., 481
Barbosa, M., 93
Bardeen, J., 286
Bardid, F., 202
Bargh, J. A., 445
Barhight, L. R., 326
Barker, R., 324
Barkin, C., 400
Barlett, C., 326
Barlow, E., 351
Barnes, A., 327
Barnes, M., 445
Barnett, M. A., 173, 187
Barnett, M. D., 611
Baron, J., 285
Baron, N. S., 163
Barooah, A., 548
Barr, R., 129, 262, 394
Barragan, V., 350, 400
Barrett, A., 448
Barrett, G., 539
Barrett, T. M., 125
Barry, A. E., 381
Barry, C., 10
Barry, J., 504
Barry, L. C., 571
Barry, M., 212, 350
Bartel, A. P., 189
Bartel, K., 357
Barter, M., 55
Bartick, M. C., 114, 115, 116
Bartl, H., 621
Bartolomeo, P., 109
Bartsch, K., 219
Bashor, C. J., 57
Basile, K. C., 424
Bass, L., 219
Bassett, H., 169, 236, 320
Bastakoti, R., 63
Basu Roy, S., 524
Bates, E., 178

Bates, J. E., 173, 174, 175, 176, 177
Bateson, P., 26
Batsis, J. A., 476, 546
Batty, P., 56
Baudry, S., 559
Bauer, J., 527, 545
Bauer, K. W., 205
Bauer, P. J., 150, 151, 216, 217, 283, 286
Baum, G. L., 107
Bauman, K. E., 360
Baumeister, R. F., 309, 443, 492–493
Baumrind, D., 244–245, 247
Bauserman, R., 254
Bavishi, C., 431
Bay-Cheng, L., 349
Baydar, N., 188
Baye, K., 115
Bayik Temel, A., 173
Bayleyegn, A., 95
Bayliss, D., 308, 376
Beal, M. A., 86
Bean, D., 317
Bear, D. R., 296, 297
Beard, V. R., 624
Beardslee, M., 310
Beauchamp, G., 133
Beaver, K. M., 398
Bebeau, M., 315
Bechtold, A. G., 134
Beck, K. H., 536, 539
Beck, L., 442
Beck, S., 19, 69, 188
Becker, C., 537
Becker, M., 319
Becker, S. P., 203, 358
Bedford, V. H., 512
Bedi, R., 537
Bednar, R. L., 309
Beeghly, M., 82
Beghetto, R. A., 286, 287, 294, 295
Bei, B., 97
Bekris, L. M., 573
Beksac, M. S., 62
Belchior, P., 564
Belenguer-Varea, A., 527
Bell, M. A., 32, 107, 108, 147, 148, 153, 169, 176, 217, 218, 236
Bell, R., 592
Bell, S. M., 173
Bell, T., 588
Belleville, S., 563
Bellon, E., 286
Belon, K., 357
Belsky, D. W., 310
Belsky, J., 177, 184, 187, 192
Belt, D., 451
Beltran-Sanchez, H., 118
Belyakin, S., 56
Bem, S. L., 464
Benck, L. R., 478
Bendayan, R., 562
Benders, M., 79
Bendersky, M., 128
Bendezu, J. J., 396
Benenson, J. F., 243
Benetos, A., 527, 529, 541
Benfante, R., 532
Bengesai, A. V., 350
Bengtson, V. L., 514, 590
Benichov, J., 566
Benitez, V. L., 215
Benka, J., 252
Benner, A., 368, 396
Bennett, C., 332, 392
Bennett, K. M., 594
Bennie, J. A., 416

Benson, B., 350
Benson, J. E., 220
Benson, L., 415
Benson, R., 598, 599
Bercovitz, K. E., 590, 601
Berdugo-Vega, G., 533
Berenbaum, S. A., 240, 315, 317, 318
Berenguer, C., 221
Berenson, G. S., 273
Berge, J. M., 355
Bergen, D., 261
Berger, S. E., 122, 124
Berger, Z., 378
Bergeron, K. E., 309
Bergh, C., 85, 86
Berglind, D., 262
Bergman, A. S., 615
Bergman, L. R., 488
Bergstrom, Z., 558
Berke, D. S., 320
Berkman, B., 60
Berko, J., 222
Berko Gleason, J., 297
Berland, A., 623, 624
Berlanga-Macias, C., 116
Berlyne, D. E., 260
Berman, M. G., 215, 218
Bermudez, J. L., 6
Bernal, G., 398
Bernard, J. Y., 117
Bernard, K., 64, 182, 183, 185, 251, 322
Berndt, T. J., 327, 367
Bernier, A., 107, 218
Bernier, R., 278
Bernitz, S., 91
Bernstein, J. P. K., 534
Bernstein, R., 383
Berridge, K. C., 169
Bersamin, M. M., 420
Berscheid, E., 446
Bertenthal, B. I., 131
Bertucci, F., 60
Besnard, J., 559
Best, D. L., 9, 37, 240, 317
Bettinger, E. P., 335
Bevens, C. L., 424
Bewersdorf, J. P., 54
Beydoun, H. A., 535
Beyene, Y., 480
Beyers, E., 446
Beyers, W., 322, 382, 383, 408, 410
Bezilla, R., 577
Bezzina, C., 57
Bhatia, M., 59
Bhatt, R., 151, 152
Bhattacharya, I., 344
Bi, H., 76, 80
Bialecka-Pikul, M., 367
Bialik, K., 252
Bialystok, E., 298, 299, 567
Bian, Z., 537
Bianchi, D., 348
Bianchi, D. W., 58, 80
Bibbo, J., 535
Bibok, M. B., 218
Bick, D., 115, 116
Bick, J., 108, 110, 201
Biczo, A., 57
Biehle, S. N., 187
Bielak, A. A. M., 562
Bierman, K. L., 325, 328, 440
Biernat, E., 87
Biernat, M., 424
Bifulco, A., 595
Bigelow, J., 228
Bigler, R., 242, 317

Benson, B., 350
Bijlenga, D., 277
Bindler, R. C., 107
Binet, A., 288
Binns, C., 115
Birch, L. L., 386
Birch, R., 131
Birch, S. A., 236
Bird, A. L., 94
Birditt, K. S., 455, 515, 516, 595
Birkeland, M. S., 308
Birman, B. F., 329
Birmingham, R. S., 185
Bisbe, M., 52
Bischoff, K. E., 610
Bjarehed, M., 326
Bjorklund, D. F., 51
Black, M. M., 115, 204, 206
Blackwell, D. L., 416
Blackwell, L. S., 335
Blair, C., 217, 236, 284
Blair, S. N., 543, 546
Blake, J. S., 114, 115, 117, 203, 272, 355, 414, 415, 475
Blakemore, J. E. O., 240, 315, 317, 318
Blakey, J., 91
Blanchard-Fields, F., 597
Blanck, H., 415
Blanck-Lubarsch, M., 81
Bland, L. M., 329
Bland, R., 106
Blanken, A. E., 574
Blankenship, T. L., 145, 217
Blanner Kristiansen, C., 623
Blatny, M., 440
Blaye, A., 365
Blazer, D., 571, 572
Bleker, L. S., 68
Blendon, R., 591
Blieszner, R. A., 446, 459, 463, 464, 510, 512, 515, 593, 596
Block, J., 440
Bloom, B., 295
Bloom, L., 157
Blumberg, M., 113
Blyth, D., 346
Boardman, G., 11
Bobkova, N. V., 533
Bochart, D., 489
Bock, J., 424
Bodenschatz, C. M., 130
Bodrova, E., 213, 260, 284
Boehm, I., 361
Boele, S., 238
Boen, F., 535
Boers, E., 393
Boespflug, E. L., 563
Bogaert, A. F., 421
Bogart, L. M., 326
Bogg, T., 588
Bohlmeijer, E., 584
Boivin, M., 258, 324
Bojorquez, G. R., 11, 343
Boland, J., 614
Boldt, L., 240
Bombard, J. M., 113, 114
Bonafe, M., 529
Bonanno, G. A., 433, 619, 621
Bonazzo, C., 369
Bonura, K. B., 590
Boon, L. I., 575
Booth, A., 152, 254
Booth, M., 391
Booth-Laforce, C., 259
Booth-LeDoux, S. M., 433
Bor, W., 396
Borbon-Castro, N. A., 544, 572

Crawford, D., 272
Crede, M., 590
Creswell, K. G., 417
Crewther, S., 536
Cribbet, M. R., 535
Crichlow-Ball, C., 357
Crnic, K. A., 237
Crocetti, E., 378, 379
Crockenberg, S. B., 169, 176
Crockett, L., 351
Crombez, G., 149
Crookston, J., 189
Cropley, M., 203
Crosnoe, R., 8, 367, 368, 369, 392, 396, 450
Cross, D., 220, 327
Crossley, M., 566
Crouter, A. C., 252, 383
Crowley, J. E., 510, 511
Crowley, K., 30
Crowley, M., 321
Crowley, S., 357
Crume, T., 82
Cruz-Saez, S., 308
Csikszentmihalyi, M., 7, 428
Cubbin, C., 94, 350
Cucina, J. M., 290
Cueli, M., 277
Cuevas, K., 32, 107, 108
Cuevas, P. E. Q., 584
Cuevas-Sierra, A., 54
Cui, R., 574
Culen, C., 58
Cullen, F., 425
Culp, K. M., 368
Cummings, E. M., 253
Cummings, K., 113
Cundiff, J. M., 541
Cunha, A. B., 125
Cunha, A. I. L., 544
Cunningham, A., 68
Cunningham, C., 544
Cunningham, C. E., 327
Cunningham, M., 433
Cunningham, S. A., 204
Cunningham, S. D., 87
Cunningham, S. J., 217
Cupito, S., 90
Curl, A., 535, 597
Curran, K., 246
Curran, M., 187
Currie, E. R., 622
Currier, D., 87
Currier, J., 623
Curtindale, L. M., 32, 148, 153
Curtis, E. M., 542
Cusack, R., 559
Cutuli, J., 94
Cvencek, D., 317
Czaja, S., 249
Czekierda, K., 492

Dabholkar, A., 109
Da Costa, L., 546
da Costa Souza, A., 54
Dagenais, C., 426
Daglish, A., 362
Dahl, A., 188, 235
Dahl, R. E., 335, 348
Dahlenburg, S., 361
Dahm, C. C., 477
Daiello, L. A., 563
Daigneault, I., 426
Dale, B., 293
D'Alessandro, A., 477
Daley, C., 293
Dalle Grave, R., 346, 361

D'Amelio, M., 532
Damian, R., 507, 588
D'Amico, E. J., 343, 360
Damoiseaux, J. S., 565
Damon, W., 316, 431
D'Andrea, S., 481
Dane, M., 298
Danforth, M., 622
D'Angelo, C. M., 188, 246
Daniels, H., 23, 210, 211, 212
Danilovich, M., 535
Dankulincova Veselska, Z., 381
Danner, D., 534
Dantas, R., 115
Dantchev, S., 51
Daoulah, A., 455
Darby-Stewart, A., 87
Darcy, E., 361
D'Arcy, C., 250, 601
Dariotis, J. K., 285
Darling, E. K., 87
Darling, N., 382
Darling Rasmussen, P., 183
Darwin, C., 50, 53
Das, R., 132
D'Ascenzi, F., 87
Dash, T., 567
da Silva, G., 115
Dasinger, J. H., 54, 573
Datar, A., 273
Dauber, S., 396
Daugherty, J., 451
Daum, M., 299
Dautovich, N., 534
Dauvier, B., 365
D'Aversa, E., 62
David, J., 255
Davidov, M., 171
Davidson, A., 243
Davidson, J., 294, 538
Davie, P., 115, 116
Davies, A., 323
Davies, E., 185
Davies, G., 290
Davies, P. T., 253
Davies, R., 92
Davila, H., 613
Davis, B., 240, 241, 317
Davis, B. E., 124
Davis, D., 486, 555
Davis, E. B., 623
Davis, E. M., 540
Davis, K., 380
Davis, L., 459
Davis, M. C., 535
Davis, S. F., 20
Davis, S. W., 564
Davison, S. M., 204
Daw, J., 409
Dawson, G., 278
Dawson, S. J., 538
Day, K., 212
Day, N., 83
Day, R., 131
Dayton, C. J., 173, 319
Deans, J., 236
de Araujo, T. E., 76
Dearing, E., 331
Deary, I. J., 290, 563
Deater-Deckard, K., 176, 188
Deaton, A., 16, 17
Deaux, K., 499, 506
de Barse, L. M., 115
Debnam, K. J., 381
Debnath, R., 108, 110
de Boer, B., 159

de Bruin, E., 203
DeCasper, A., 132
Deci, E., 430
Deckert, M., 288
Dee, D. L., 353
Deeg, D. J. H., 474
De Genna, N. M., 82
De Giovanni, N., 82
de Greeff, J. W., 272
de Guzman, N., 346
de Haan, M., 109, 147, 186
Dehcheshmeh, F., 92
DeJong, G. F., 146
DeJong, W., 417
de Koning, L., 273
de la Fuente, J., 531, 536
De La Fuente, M., 19
de la Mata, M. L., 217
DeLamater, J., 52, 241, 254, 348, 349, 353, 421, 422, 539
Delaney, E. K., 599
Delello, J., 592
Delgado, M. Y., 384
Del Giudice, M., 446
Del Gobbo, L. C., 539
de Lima, D. B., 559
de Lima, L., 612
DeLisi, M., 259
Delker, B., 383
DeLoache, J., 153
DeLongis, A., 456
Del Rio-Bermudez, C., 113
Del Tredici, K., 485
de Magalhaes, J., 531
Demakakos, P., 355, 559
Demanchick, S. P., 259
de Manzano, O., 291
Demasi, M., 539, 541
de Medeiros, T. S., 81
Demeyere, N., 482, 540
Demir-Lira, E., 162
Demirtas-Zorbaz, S., 258, 324
Demnitz, N., 535
Demuth, K., 155, 223
Dempster, F. N., 216
Denard, P. J., 538
Denault, A., 370
Denervaud, S., 225
Denford, S., 354
Deng, C., 334
Deng, Y., 345
Denham, J., 544
Denham, S., 169, 236, 320
Den Heijer, A. E., 278
DeNicola, N., 83
Denier, N., 568
Denk, F., 133
Denkinger, M., 536
Denmark, F. L., 37
Denney, N. W., 486
Dennis, M., 110
Dennis, N., 564
Denton, M., 380
Deoni, S. C., 201
De Paepe, A., 149
DePasquale, C., 249, 250
DePasquale, N., 593
DePaulo, B., 449
De Pergola, G., 477
Depolo, M., 569
DeRicco, B., 417
DeRose, L., 345
Derry, K., 308, 376
DeSesso, M., 80
Desilver, D., 333
De Smedt, B., 286

Desmennu, A. T., 308
Desombre, C., 293
Deutsch, A., 360
Dev, D., 199
Devakumar, D., 352
de Villiers, T. J., 476, 480
Devine, R., 219, 220, 221, 235
DeVito, A., 534
de Vries, R., 89
Dewald-Kaufmann, J., 203
de Weerth, C., 116
de Williams, A., 149
de Wind, A. W., 488
Dewitz, P. F., 275, 297
DeZolt, D., 319
Dhindsa, D. S., 455
Diamond, A., 13, 145, 260, 284, 310
Diamond, L. M., 348, 349, 389, 422
Dias, C. C., 112
Diaz, A., 108
Diaz, E. C., 85
Diaz-Rico, L. T., 8, 38, 299
DiBennardo, R., 456
Dickinson, D., 289
Dickinson, W. J., 596
Diego, M., 96
Diekelmann, S., 111
Diekmann, R., 527, 545
Diener, E., 17, 507
Dierickx, S., 608, 611
Di Giosia, P., 477
Dillon, M., 490
Dimitropoulos, G., 361
Dimock, M., 35
Dimri, M., 530
Ding, Y., 282
Dinger, M., 413
Dion, K., 447
Dirk, J., 324
Dishion, T., 320, 325, 396
Distefano, R., 217
Dittus, P. J., 382
Dixon, R., 590, 601
Dixon, S., 246
Djelantik, A. A. M. J., 620
Dobson, C., 90
Dodge, K. A., 325, 401
Dodson, L., 323
Doenyas, C., 220
Dogan, G., 610
Doherty, M., 219
Dolbin, M. L., 514
Dolbin-MacNab, M., 514, 515
Dollar, J., 169, 173, 180, 236, 311, 439
Dols, A., 572
Dombrovski, A. Y., 572
Domenech-Abella, J., 591
Dominguez-Cruz, M. G., 57
Domiteaux, M., 507
Donaldson, G., 483
Donatelle, R. J., 118, 203, 272, 355, 356, 359, 415
Dong, B., 272
Dong, F., 416
Dong, W., 382
Dong, X. S., 569
Donnellan, B., 506, 507, 509, 510
Donnellan, M., 376, 447, 507
Donohue, M., 239
Donovan, M. K., 354
Doom, J., 312
Doom, J. R., 392
Dora, B., 188
Dorffner, G., 533
Dorling, J., 546
Dorn, L., 345, 479

Jarjat, G., 555, 557
Jaruratanasirikul, S., 85
Jasinska, K. K., 299
Jauniaux, E., 79
Jefferson, T., 539, 541
Jelalian, E., 203
Jelsma, E., 387
Jenkins, J., 220
Jenks, R., 482, 540
Jenks, S., 570
Jensen, T. M., 322
Jensen-Campbell, L., 507
Jenzer, T., 176
Jeremic, S., 546
Jessen, S., 180
Jeste, D. V., 6, 560
Jeyanthi, S., 277
Ji, B. T., 87
Ji, G., 251
Ji, H., 546
Ji, L., 536
Ji, N., 532
Ji, S., 530
Jia, P., 57
Jiang, Q., 248
Jiang, X., 342
Jiang, Y., 10, 574
Jiao, S., 251
Jimenez-Trevino, L., 399
Jin, M. M., 530
Jin, S., 76, 80, 444
Jin, Y., 298
Jindal, H. A., 538
Jing, Q., 251
Jirstrom, K., 480
Jo, J., 92
Jobson, L., 283
Jocson, R., 255, 256, 330, 392, 393
Joh, A., 125
Johansson, M., 286
John, A., 399
John, N. A., 453
John, O., 508, 512
John-Akinola, Y. O., 308
Johnson, A. A., 477
Johnson, A. E., 169
Johnson, C., 456, 595
Johnson, D., 511
Johnson, J. A., 329
Johnson, J. D., 530
Johnson, J. P., 275
Johnson, J. S., 298
Johnson, M., 107, 108, 147, 270, 298
Johnson, P., 171
Johnson, R., 33, 535
Johnson, S. P., 127, 131, 134, 145, 147, 148
Johnson, W., 591
Johnston, C., 95, 258, 450
Johnston, J., 277
Johnston, L. D., 359
Jokinen, J., 400
Jolicoeur-Martineau, A., 177
Jones, C. R. G., 221
Jones, E., 108, 624
Jones, J., 225, 226
Jones, L., 90
Jones, M. C., 346
Jones, M. M., 591
Jones, P. S., 595
Jones, S., 152
Jones, T., 481
Jongenelis, M. I., 597
Jonides, J., 215
Jonkman, C. S., 331
Jonsson, E., 81
Jordan, J. W., 388

Jordan, M., 299
Jorgensen, M. J., 351
Jose, A., 451
Joseph, J., 50
Joseph, P. V., 415
Joshanloo, M., 17
Joshi, A., 32
Joshi, H., 310
Josselson, R., 378
Jovanovic, V., 17
Joyner, K., 389, 456
Ju, H., 492
Juang, L., 176, 255, 379
Juang, L. P., 384
Judd, F., 480
Juhnke, G., 326, 327
Julian, M. M., 64, 112
Jun, J., 584
Jung, C., 472–473
Jung, H., 547
Jung, S., 118
Jung, W., 126
Junior, L., 273
Jurcau, A., 573
Jusczyk, P. W., 132
Jylhava, J., 188

Kabiri, M., 535
Kacmar, K., 433
Kadlaskar, G., 108
Kadosh, K., 398
Kaelber, D., 273
Kaewpradub, N., 346
Kagan, J., 170, 171, 172, 174, 175, 176, 184
Kahana, B., 601
Kahana, E., 601
Kahlbaugh, P., 589
Kahn, J. A., 355
Kahrs, B., 126
Kail, B., 597
Kalanithi, P., 617
Kalashnikova, M., 68
Kaldahl, J., 609
Kalish, C., 222
Kalish, R. A., 615, 616, 619
Kalish, V. B., 546
Kaloustian, G., 185
Kalvin, C., 440
Kalyango, Y., 346
Kalyvianakis, D., 481
Kambas, A., 202
Kaminski, P., 249
Kamp Dush, C. M., 450
Kamza, A., 215
Kanakogi, Y., 157
Kanazawa, S., 117
Kandler, C., 429
Kanesarajah, J., 473
Kang, J., 299
Kang, N., 376
Kann, L., 349, 351, 352, 355, 356, 399
Kanner, A. D., 502
Kansky, J., 389
Kantrowitz, B., 233
Kapitansky, O., 475
Kaplan, P., 610
Kaplan, R., 30
Kaplinski, M., 273
Kapoor, J., 432
Kar, B., 117
Karasik, L. B., 124
Karel, M., 621
Karimian, M., 63
Karmel, M., 178
Karmiloff-Smith, A., 111
Karney, B., 451

Karniol, R., 464
Karoly, L., 228
Karreman, A., 247
Kashdan, T. B., 421
Kassai, R., 284
Kassing, F., 401
Kastbom, A. A., 350
Kastenbaum, R. J., 608, 613, 616, 617
Kataoka, Y., 542
Kato, T., 448
Katsiaficas, D., 411
Katsiki, N., 546
Katz, B., 558
Katz, C., 249
Katz, L., 227
Kauchak, D., 328
Kauffman, J., 276, 279, 294
Kaufman, A., 288
Kaufman, J. C., 287, 288, 294, 295, 428
Kaufman, J. M., 480
Kaufman, R., 256
Kaufman, S. B., 429, 507
Kaufmann, Y., 249
Kaup, A., 507, 588
Kaur, S., 478, 534
Kauser, R., 245
Kaushal, N., 544
Kavanaugh, R. D., 221
Kavle, J. A., 115
Kavosi, Z., 92
Kawas, C., 546
Kayama, H., 559
Kayir, S., 610
Kaymak, D., 61
Kaywork, J., 169, 170
Kazachkova, N., 62
Kearney, P., 82
Kearsley, R., 172
Keating, D. P., 295, 365, 366, 427
Keen, R., 126, 130
Keigher, S., 577
Keisberg, G., 81
Keith, J., 380
Kelleher, K., 206
Keller, A., 234
Keller, H., 178, 183
Kelley, C., 473
Kelley, G., 489
Kelley, K., 489
Kellman, P., 127, 131
Kelly, C., 221
Kelly, D. J., 130
Kelly, D. M., 481
Kelly, E., 488
Kelly, J., 131, 323, 460, 461
Kelly, M., 95, 99
Kelly, Y., 346
Keltner, K. W., 334
Kempermann, G., 532, 533
Kendler, K. S., 66, 67, 360, 455
Kendrick, C., 251
Kennedy, J., 188
Kennedy, K. M., 532, 558
Kennedy, R. S., 326
Kennell, H., 99
Kennell, J., 99
Kenny, R., 55, 527
Kenny, S., 131
Kent, B., 577
Kenyon, C., 55
Kerig, P. K., 187
Kerns, K., 322
Kershaw, K. N., 501
Kershaw, P., 591
Kershner, J. R., 275
Kersting, A., 130

Kerstis, B., 99, 383
Kesaniemi, J., 54
Ketcham, P., 118, 203, 355, 356, 359, 415
Keunen, K., 79
Keyser, J., 459
Khairullah, A., 344
Khakpai, F., 418
Khalsa, A. S., 204
Khan, F., 383, 441
Khan, H. T. A., 350
Khan, L., 346
Khan, S. S., 475, 546
Kharazmi, N., 92
Kharitonova, M., 282
Khodaeian, M., 546
Khoury, J., 81
Khurana, A., 262, 394
Kibele, A., 555
Kiel, E., 176
Kieliszek, D., 330
Killoren, S., 513
Kim, A., 511
Kim, D. J., 201
Kim, E., 400, 508
Kim, G. J., 542
Kim, H., 250, 286, 376, 400, 442
Kim, J., 60, 356, 376, 396
Kim, J. I., 54
Kim, Kayoung, 573
Kim, K. H., 286
Kim, K. W., 356
Kim, Kyungmin, 515, 595
Kim, P., 10, 186
Kim, Sanghag, 184, 240
Kim, S. H., 543
Kim, Sujin, 346, 350, 566, 623
Kim, S. Y., 385, 393
Kimberlin, D., 84
Kimble, M., 425
Kim-Spoon, J., 148, 384
Kindermann, T., 386
King, A., 160
King, B., 421, 624
King, J., 361
King, L., 584
King, L. A., 421, 422, 464, 465
King, P., 380, 381, 490
King, R. B., 335
King, V., 594
King-Casas, B., 384
Kingdon, D., 81
Kingerlee, R., 504
Kingsbury, A., 85
Kinney, H., 113
Kinnunen, J. M., 418
Kins, E., 408, 410
Kinsler, J. J., 348
Kintzel, D., 570
Kinugawa, K., 6, 13, 31, 485, 528, 532, 533, 554, 563, 564, 565
Kinzler, K., 181
Kiran, S., 275
Kircaburun, K., 507
Kirk, E., 224
Kirk, S., 224
Kirkegaard, E., 291
Kirkham, N., 156
Kirkorian, H., 130
Kisilevsky, B. S., 132
Kit, B. K., 206
Kito, M., 447
Kivnik, H., 515
Klaus, M., 99
Klein, A. C., 330
Klein, L., 171, 426
Klein, M. R., 188, 246

Klein, S., 319
Kleinman, C., 98
Kliegel, M., 558
Kliegman, R. M., 200, 201, 270
Klil-Drori, S., 545
Klimke, A., 113
Klimstra, T. A., 378
Kline, D., 476, 536
Klinenberg, E., 449, 450
Klug, W. S., 53, 55, 56
Klumb, P., 536
Knafo-Noam, A., 238
Knifsend, C., 370
Knight, L., 421
Knofe, H., 51
Knopfli, B., 511
Knox, M., 246
Ko, A., 51, 478
Ko, E., 84
Koball, H., 10
Kobayashi, L. C., 591
Koch, S., 98
Kochanska, G., 184, 240, 253
Kochenderfer-Ladd, B., 259
Kocherginsky, M., 596
Koch-Weser, S., 613
Kocur, J., 250
Koehler, K., 414
Koenig, H. G., 491, 572, 577
Koenig, L., 380
Koenig, M., 235, 610
Koenig, W., 476–477
Koh, H., 352
Kohlberg, L., 313–316
Kohlenberg, M., 486
Kohlhoff, J., 182, 186
Kohn, J. N., 534
Kok, F. M., 276
Kok, R., 201
Kokkinos, P., 544
Koksal Akyol, A., 238
Koksvik, G. H., 612
Kolata, G., 545
Kolesnik, A., 108
Kollar, M., 10
Kolokotroni, P., 508, 589
Kolovos, S., 415, 416
Komter, A., 516, 595
Konetzka, R., 591
Kong, A., 87
Kong, L. N., 596
Konner, M., 408
Kontis, V., 523
Koo, Y. J., 85
Koopman-Verhoeff, M. E., 203
Koorevaar, A. M., 589
Kopp, F., 150
Koppelman, K. L., 332
Kopystynska, O., 187
Korat, O., 223
Korner, L. M., 237, 241
Kornhaber, W., 290
Kornienko, O., 325
Korte, J., 584
Kosar, I., 610
Kostel Bal, S., 57
Kostelny, K., 9, 343
Koster, M., 130
Kotarska, K., 530
Kothandan, S. K., 205
Kotler, J., 263
Kotre, J., 499
Kouklari, E., 363, 364
Kovach, C. R., 560
Kowal, M., 451, 453

Kowalska, M., 529
Kowalski, M., 216
Kowalski, R. M., 326
Koyanagi, A., 326, 399, 478
Koytun, A. S., 279
Kozbelt, A., 428
Kozhimmanil, K. B., 90
Kozol, J., 306, 330
Kracht, C. L., 204, 262, 356
Kraemer, J., 13
Kraen, M., 539
Kramer, A. F., 563
Kramer, A. S., 354
Kramer, H., 311
Kramer, L., 250, 251
Kramer, M., 34, 204
Krampe, R., 295, 486
Krashia, P., 532
Krause, N., 490, 491, 493, 572, 577, 590
Krauss, S., 308
Kravdal, O., 252
Kraybill, J., 148
Krell-Roesch, J., 562
Kresovich, K., 19
Kretch, K., 122, 127
Kreth, M., 113
Krettenauer, T., 316, 317
Kreukels, B., 9, 464
Kreutzer, M., 286
Kreye, M., 172
Kriemler, S., 272
Kring, A. M., 320
Krishnan, P., 612
Krishnappa, P., 481
Krisnana, I., 244, 259
Krizan, Z., 357, 507
Kroger, J., 343, 377, 379
Krogh-Jespersen, S., 181
Kroonenberg, P., 69, 183
Krous, H., 114
Krueger, J., 309
Kruger, J., 415
Kruger, T. H. C., 241
Kruk, J., 530
Krumrei, E., 491
Kruszka, P., 58
Krzepota, J., 87
Kuang, W., 526
Kubik-Huch, R., 573
Kübler-Ross, E., 616–617
Kuchay, R., 294
Kudesia, R., 352
Kuebli, J., 311
Kuersten-Hogan, R., 187
Kuhl, P. K., 107, 156, 161
Kuhn, B., 247
Kuhn, D., 147, 364, 366
Kuhn, S., 557
Kulke, L., 148
Kulu, H., 455
Kumar, K., 203
Kumar, S., 90, 99
Kunnen, E. S., 379
Kunzmann, U., 16, 560, 562
Kunzweiler, C., 66
Kuo, H. W., 273
Kuo, L., 299
Kuo, P. X., 184
Kuperberg, A., 451
Kurdek, L. A., 456
Kurita, S., 562
Kuwahara, Y., 530
Kvaavik, E., 395
Kvalo, S. E., 284
Kwak, Y., 398
Kwan, K. M. W., 243

Kwitek, A. E., 415
Kwitowski, M., 345
Kwok, C., 361
Kwon, D., 109, 201, 271
Kwon, M., 356

Laborte-Lemoyne, E., 87
Labouvie-Vief, G., 427
Lacelle, C., 250
Lachman, M. E., 257, 392, 472, 473, 474, 475, 486, 501, 503, 561, 586, 590, 601
Ladd, G., 258, 259, 324, 325
Ladhani, S. N., 84
Ladouceur, C. D., 347
Laflin, M., 350
LaFrance, M., 320
Lafreniere, D., 538
Lagana, L., 564
Lagattuta, K. H., 220, 311
Lahat, A., 174
Laheij-Rooijakkers, L. A. E., 571
Lai, A., 83, 279
Lai, M. Y., 561
Laible, D. J., 180, 238, 240, 244, 247, 315
Laisk, T., 529
Lakhdir, M. P. A., 249
Lakoski, S., 478
Lal, S., 477
Lalley, P. M., 539
Lam, C., 547
Lamb, M. E., 99, 184, 190, 216, 217, 254
Lamballais, S., 559
Lambert, C., 308
Lambez, B., 277
Lamb-Parker, F., 226
Lamela, D., 253
Lamidi, E., 450
Lamm, C., 108
Lamont, R. A., 17
Lampard, A. M., 361
Lampignano, L., 477
Lampit, A., 564
Lampl, M., 107
Lamy, S., 432
Lan, X., 218
Landale, N., 393
Landau, B., 152
Landes, S., 613
Landis, T. D., 217
Lane, A., 272
Lane, H., 153
Lang, P., 169
Langer, E. J., 285, 548, 590, 601, 617
Langer, R. D., 480
Langeslag, S., 446
Langstrom, N., 422
Lanning, R. K., 89
Lansford, J. E., 9, 247, 252, 253, 254, 315, 350, 600
Lantagne, A., 446
Lantolf, J., 211
Lany, J., 156
Lanyan, A., 542
Lanz, M., 408
Lapsley, D., 317
Laranjo, J., 221
Lardone, M. C., 345
Large, E., 147
Larkina, M., 151, 217
Laroo, N., 566
Larsen-Rife, D., 507
Larson, F. B., 574
Larson, J., 387
Larson, N., 415
Larson, R. J., 17
Larson, R. W., 256, 343, 390, 391

Larzelere, R., 247
Larzelere, R. E., 245, 247
Lash, A., 566
Laska, M., 413
Lasko, D., 96
Last, B. S., 218
La Starza, S., 57
Lathrop, A. L., 127
Latimer, C. S., 534
Latorre, J., 611
LaTourrette, A., 130
Latt, M. D., 532
Lau, J. S., 414
Lau, J. Y., 398
Lau, Y., 479
Lau-Barraco, C., 417
Laube, C., 344
Laubjerg, M., 64
Lauderdale, D. S., 533
Lauer, E. A., 118
Lauharatanahirun, N., 348
Laumann, E. O., 482
Laureiro-Martinez, D., 586
Laurent, J., 383
Laurent, J. S., 270
Lauretti, E., 573
Laurin, R., 293
Laurita, A., 185
Laursen, B., 257, 328, 330, 386, 396
Lautenbacher, S., 538
Lavalliere, M., 539
Lavender, J. M., 361
Lavner, J., 451, 458
Lawrence, A., 9, 464
Lawson, C., 152
Lawson, K. M., 376, 382, 440
Layh, M., 424
Lazris, A., 613
Lazzarotto, S., 538
Le, Y., 247
Leahey, T., 617
Leaper, C., 242, 317, 462, 464
Lear, M. K., 326, 399
Leatherdale, S., 394
Lecouvey, G., 558
Ledesma, K., 64
Lee, A., 57
Lee, C., 530
Lee, E., 6, 432
Lee, G., 574
Lee, H., 507
Lee, I., 544
Lee, J. A., 511
Lee, J. B., 9
Lee, J. E., 601
Lee, J. H., 54, 508
Lee, Jinsol, 242
Lee, J. J., 97
Lee, Joohyun, 133
Lee, Juwon, 445
Lee, Kang, 127, 153, 180, 235, 308
Lee, Kathleen, 284
Lee, K. S., 326, 327
Lee, K. Y., 54
Lee, Kyunghee, 226
Lee, M., 115
Lee, N., 475
Lee, R. Y., 611
Lee, S., 58
Lee, S. H., 127, 418, 530
Lee, S. M., 622
Lee, W. J., 601
Lee, Y. J., 92
Lee, Y. S., 577
Leerkes, E. M., 169, 170, 171, 173, 184
Lees, R., 530

Malone, J., 319
Malone, S., 133
Maloy, R. W., 261, 393, 395
Maltby, L. E., 174
Malti, T., 238, 259, 315
Mamun, A. A., 414
Manara, A., 610
Manca, T., 490
Mandara, J., 322
Mandler, J. M., 150, 151, 152, 153
Manenti, R., 564
Maner, J., 443
Manfredini, R., 454
Maniago, J., 95
Mann, N., 538
Mann, T., 415
Manning, L., 577
Manning, W., 450–451, 456
Manore, M., 204, 272, 414, 415
Mansor, N., 564
Mansour, L., 564
Mansourian, M., 477
Manton, K. I., 491
Mantri, S., 561
Manuck, S., 69
Manvellian, A., 454, 460
Manzanares, S., 62
Manzardo, A., 279
Mao, X., 536
Maoz, H., 277
Maravilla, J. C., 353
Marceau, K., 345
Marcell, J. J., 475
Marchetti, D., 82
Marchetti, F., 86
Marchman, V., 161
Marcia, J. E., 377–378, 379
Marcovitch, S., 145
Marcus, G., 455
Mares, M-L., 262
Mareschal, D., 13
Margolis, R., 409
Mariathasan, S., 537
Marien, S., 542
Marini, D., 62
Marin-Jimenez, N., 477
Mark, K. S., 82
Markham, C. M., 350
Markham, K. B., 94
Markman, E. M., 158
Markman, H. J., 453
Marks, A., 6, 8, 11, 38, 69, 345, 361
Markus, H. R., 510
Marousez, L., 54
Marques, A., 489
Marrus, N., 123
Marselle, M., 501
Marsh, H., 181, 235
Marshall, K., 547
Marshall, N. A., 201
Marshall, S. L., 309
Marshall, T., 171
Marsiglia, F. F., 359
Marsiske, M., 532, 536
Marston, K. J., 486
Marszalek, S., 544
Martin, A., 215, 271, 595
Martin, C. K., 546
Martin, C. L., 243, 317
Martin, G., 393
Martin, J. A., 89, 245
Martin, K., 171, 172
Martin, L., 18, 588
Martin, M., 253, 474
Martin, S., 426
Martinelli, M., 538

Martinez-Brockman, J. L., 118
Martinez-Ramirez, O. C., 54
Martin-Perpiña, M., 394
Martire, L., 596
Martz, M., 359
Mascalo, M., 427
Mash, C., 134
Mash, E., 276, 277, 278, 312, 395
Mason-Apps, E., 150
Masoodi, N., 574
Masson, W., 476
Masten, A. S., 7, 10, 11, 284, 285, 312, 409
Master, A., 335
Mastergeorge, A. M., 226
Masters, R. K., 545
Mastin, J., 150
Matas, L., 172
Mateen, S., 529
Matei, A., 94
Mather, M., 586
Mathews, R. A., 433
Mathey, S., 566
Mat Husin, H., 85
Matias, M., 433
Matricciani, L., 202
Matsumoto, D., 176, 255, 390
Matthews, K., 489
Matthews, K. A., 541
Mattock, K., 132
Matz-Costa, C., 598
Maurer, D., 134
Mavor, K., 443
May, M., 239
Maye, M., 278
Mayo, J. A., 86
Mayor, S., 116
Mazumder, S., 95
Mazzeo, S., 345
Mazzucato, V., 256
Mbugua Gitau, G., 85
McAbee, S., 507
McAdams, D., 378
McAdams, T., 398
McAllister, S., 92
McAuley, P., 546
McBride, K. L., 58
McCabe, F., 97
McCabe, K., 507
McCaffery, J., 69
McCann, T., 11
McCarroll, J. E., 249
McCarthy, A., 545
McCartney, K., 191, 193
McClain, C., 617
McClellan, M. D., 582
McClelland, M. M., 215, 217, 236, 284, 310
McCleskey, S., 612
McCluney, C. L., 598
McClure, E. R., 150
McConnachie, A. L., 64
McCormack, T., 125
McCourt, S., 401
McCoy, D. C., 217, 226, 237
McCoy, M. B., 118
McCrae, R., 501, 506, 507
McCright, J., 161
McCue, K., 83
McCullough, M. B., 345
McCullough, M. E., 490
McCutcheon, H., 92
McCutcheon, V. V., 418
McDaniel, M., 558
McDermott, E., 393
McDermott, J., 64, 65

McDonald, K., 324
McDonald, N., 179
McDonough, L., 152
McDougall, S., 109
McDowell, J. J., 51
McElroy, S. L., 416
McElvany, N., 319
McFarland, M., 456
McGarry, J., 97
McGee, K., 279
McGee, T. R., 396
McGillion, M., 157
McGlothen-Bell, K., 95
McGovern, G., 343, 391
McGrath, J., 81
McGrath, S., 99
McGue, M., 380
McHale, J., 187, 247
McHale, S., 247, 251, 252, 383, 512
McIsaac, C., 388, 389
McKay, A., 428
McKechanie, A. G., 58
McKee, I., 514
McKellar, S. E., 319
McKenna, K. Y. A., 445
McKenna, K., 478
McKenzie, B., 131
McKone, K., 346
McLaughlin, K., 613
McLaughlin, K. A., 312
McLean, K. C., 377, 378, 380
McLellan, J., 381
McLeod, S., 442
McLoyd, V., 255, 256, 330, 392, 393
McMahon, S., 133
McManus, R., 55, 527
McMillan, D., 413
McMillen, C., 330
McNeely, C. A., 256
McNulty, J., 424, 442
McQuillan, M. E., 173, 176
McRae, C. S., 533
McSween, M. P., 559
McWhorter, R., 592
Meacham, J., 234
Meadows, S., 454
Mechler, K., 613
Medina-Alva, P., 94
Medrano, G., 8
Meeks, L., 204, 205, 271, 355
Meeks, S., 590, 615
Meeks, T. W., 560
Meerlo, P., 97
Meert, K. L., 623
Meghelli, L., 85
Mehlhausen-Hassoen, D., 246
Mehta, V., 573
Meier, E. A., 612
Meins, E., 220
Meisel, V., 277
Mekonnen, A., 95
Meland, E., 252
Meldrum, R. C., 290
Melendez, J. C., 507, 588
Melendez-Rhodes, T., 247
Melhuish, E., 192
Mellott, J., 532
Meltzer, A., 445
Meltzoff, A. N., 149, 151, 153, 169, 317
Melzi, G., 188
Melzoff, A., 146
Memitz, S. A., 451
Memone, L., 482
Mendes, A., 620
Mendes, W., 171

Mendle, J., 346
Mendoza, L., 558
Menec, V., 576
Meng, X., 250, 601
Menn, L., 157, 222
Mennella, J. A., 133
Menon, R., 76
Menyuk, P., 157
Mepham, S., 106
Meque, I., 278
Merchant, S. J., 612
Mercurio, L. Y., 277
Mercy, J., 205
Meredith, N. V., 200
Merewood, A., 117
Merrick, J. S., 284
Merrill, D. M., 512, 516
Mervak, B. M., 61
Merz, E. C., 201
Mesiano, S. A., 94
Mesman, J., 183
Messelink, M., 375
Messiah, S. E., 83
Messinger, D. B., 171, 172
Messinger, D. S., 128
Metcalfe, J., 287
Meteyard, L., 154
Meusel, L. A., 558
Meuwissen, A., 218
Meyer, A., 566
Mezulis, A., 241
Mezzacappa, E., 310
Mi, S. J., 202
Mi, Y., 573
Michael, G., 203
Michael, R. T., 420, 421, 481
Mick, P., 538
Mickelson, K. D., 187
Micks, E., 479
Midouhas, E., 310
Miech, R. A., 358, 359
Miga, E. M., 383
Mike, A., 507
Mikkola, T. M., 538
Mikulincer, M., 442, 443
Mila, M., 58
Milberg, A., 621
Miles, A., 577
Milisav, L., 546
Miller, A., 445
Miller, A. L., 310, 320, 376
Miller, B., 350
Miller, C., 11, 456
Miller, C. F., 317
Miller, C. J., 277
Miller, H., 442
Miller, J. B., 462
Miller, J. G., 238, 314, 315, 320
Miller, K., 424
Miller, L., 592
Miller, M. D., 620
Miller, M. S., 570
Miller, N., 258
Miller, P., 109
Miller, P. H., 22, 24, 363
Miller, R., 68
Miller, S., 79
Miller-Perrin, C., 250
Milligan, K., 81
Mills, B., 366
Mills, C., 215, 235, 308
Mills, D., 215
Mills, H., 87
Mills, K., 365
Mills-Koonce, W., 173
Milne, E., 86

O'Brien, B., 544
O'Brien, J. L., 556
O'Brien, L., 358
O'Brien, M., 190
Obsuth, I., 276
O'Callaghan, F. V., 203
Ochs, E., 162
O'Connell, M., 545
O'Connor, M. F., 620
O'Connor, M. J., 81, 184
O'Connor, R., 442
O'Dell, C., 526
Odouli, R., 114
Oelke, N. D., 590
Offer, D., 342
Ogden, C. L., 204
Ogden, T., 341
Ogletree, A. M., 446, 463, 596
O'Grady, C., 159
O'Grady, S., 120
Ogunjimi, A. I., 249
Oh, S., 82
Oh, W., 399
O'Halloran, A. M., 556
Ohan, J., 308, 376
O'Hara, M., 97
O'Higgins Norman, J., 326
Ohlin, A., 94
Okada, K., 481
O'Keefe, J. H., 543
O'Keeffe, L., 82
Oktay-Gur, N., 219
Okubo, Y., 536
Okumu, M., 343, 350, 400
Okun, M. A., 597
Okun, M. S., 532
Okun-Singer, H., 169
Oldehinkel, A., 375
Olderbak, S., 320
O'Leary, A., 286
O'Leary, K., 451
Olenik-Shemesh, D., 327
Olesen, K., 568
Oleti, T., 95
Olfson, M., 576
Oliffe, J., 99
Oliver, B., 250
Olivieri, F., 529
Ollen, E., 254
Olmstead, S., 419–420
Olsavsky, A. L., 187
Olsen, J., 317
Olsen, R., 524
Olson, B. H., 118
Olweus, D., 327
O'Neel, C., 356
Onetti, W., 367
Ongley, S., 238
Onwuegbuzi, A., 293
Operto, F. F., 58
Opfer, J., 208
Oppenauer, V., 414
Orav, E., 512
Orimaye, S. O., 566
Ornstein, K. A., 593
Ornstein, P. A., 107, 201, 270, 283, 284
Orosova, O., 252
Orosz, G., 446
O'Rourke, K. M., 89
Orri, M., 399
Orson, C., 391
Ortet, G., 507
Orth, U., 308, 448
Orzabal, M. R., 82
Oshika, T., 476
Ossher, L., 557

Ossmy, O., 120, 122, 127, 134, 135, 147
Ostan, R., 524
Ostbye, T., 94
Oster, H., 133
Ostergaard, S. D., 276
Ostrove, J., 499, 508
O'Sullivan, L. F., 448
Oswald, F., 507
Ota, M., 156
Othman, E. A., 109
O'Toole, J., 32
Ou, S. R., 257, 331
Ouch, S., 456
Oudekerk, B. A., 384
Overland, G., 10
Owens, E. B., 245
Owens, J., 357
Owsley, C., 134, 146
Ozgurluk, I., 97
Ozturk Donmez, R., 173

Paasch, E., 346
Paavilainen, E., 249
Pace, A., 156
Padilla, C., 187
Padilla-Walker, L. M., 315, 410, 411, 459
Padmanabhanunni, A., 320
Pados, B., 95
Paganini-Hill, A., 546
Page, R., 204, 205, 271, 355
Pagiatakis, C., 68
Pahor, M., 534
Palacios-Barrios, E., 310
Palermo, T. M., 202
Pallini, S., 376
Palmeira, L., 416
Palmer, A., 284, 312
Palmer, R. H. C., 418
Palmore, E. B., 590
Paluck, E., 320
Pan, B. A., 161, 297
Pan, C. Y., 271, 277
Pan, H., 620
Pan, Z., 262, 524
Panagiotaki, G., 614
Papastavrou, E., 575
Papernow, P. L., 594, 595
Parade, S. H., 173, 177
Parashar, S., 54
Parasher, R., 277
Parcianello, R. R., 83
Parens, E., 277
Parent, J., 262
Parillo, V. N., 330, 332
Parish-Morris, J., 157
Parisi, J. M., 562
Park, C. B., 573
Park, C. L., 491, 577, 617, 623
Park, D. C., 486, 533, 563, 564, 565
Park, E., 400
Park, H., 481, 511
Park, M., 86
Park, M. J., 398, 413
Park, S., 614
Park, S. H., 476
Park, Y. M., 399
Parkay, F. W., 329
Parke, R. D., 6, 9, 18, 38, 69, 168, 185, 189, 190, 245, 252, 254, 322
Parker, C. B., 585
Parker, H. W., 118
Parker, J., 259, 324, 327
Parker, K., 35, 452
Parker, M., 7, 205, 271, 273, 355, 356
Parker, S. L., 502
Parkes, A., 247

Parkinson, P., 190
Parks, O., 116
Parnass, J., 243
Parra, G., 248
Parra-Cardona, J. R., 516
Parrish, D., 583
Parrott, A. C., 76
Parsons, K., 273
Parsons, T. D., 36
Parthemer, J., 188
Pascalis, O., 127, 153, 180
Paschall, K., 226
Pascual-Sagastizabal, E., 240
Pasley, K., 323
Passuth, P., 504
Pastuszak, A., 481
Pasupathi, M., 377, 380
Patchin, J., 327, 348
Pate, R. R., 271, 272
Patel, D., 481
Patel, J., 57
Patel, K. V., 535
Pathman, T., 151
Patra, S., 541
Patrick, J., 417
Patrick, M., 359
Patterson, C. J., 254, 255, 456
Patterson, G. D., 59
Patterson, G. R., 396
Pattie, A., 563
Patton, G. C., 355
Patton, L. K., 108
Paul, C., 586
Paul, S., 97
Pauletti, R. E., 464
Paulhus, D. L., 251
Paunesku, D., 335
Paus, T., 348
Paydar, M., 477
Payer, L., 480
Payne, B., 566
Payne, J. L., 54
Paysnick, A., 409
Pearce, L., 380
Pearlman, E., 66
Pearson, R. M., 86
Pechorro, P., 396
Peck, T., 262
Pedersen, E. R., 417
Pedersen, M. T., 544
Pedersen, N. L., 488, 489
Pedersen, S., 286, 386
Peek, M. K., 594
Peel, E., 8, 9
Peets, K., 326
Pei, G., 57
Pei, Y., 516
Peitzmeier, S. M., 390
Peixoto, C. E., 216
Pellegrini, A. D., 51
Pelton, S., 116
Penas, S., 256
Penazzi, L., 532
Pencina, K. M., 477
Peng, H., 536
Pennequin, V., 281, 286
Peplak, J., 315
Peplau, L., 421, 422, 456
Peralta, L. R., 257, 392
Perdue, K. L., 107, 108, 179
Pereira, C., 535
Pereira-Lancha, L., 273
Perelli-Harris, B., 455, 460
Perez, H., 95
Perez, H. C. S., 620
Perez, S., 211

Perez-Edgar, K., 174
Perez-Escamilla, R., 117
Perez-Fuentes, M. D. C., 507, 508
Perez-Sousa, M. A., 571, 572
Perkins, S., 161
Perkisas, S., 561
Perlman, L., 66
Perls, T. T., 524, 525, 528
Perozynski, L., 250
Perreira, K. M., 256
Perrett, D., 443
Perrin, P., 422
Perrin, R., 250
Perrotte, J. K., 417
Perry, N. B., 141, 169, 176, 180, 236, 311
Perry, S. E., 201, 272
Perry, T. B., 327
Perry-Jenkins, M., 459
Persky, H., 298
Pesta, B. J., 290
Peter, B., 275
Peterman, K., 125
Peters, S., 557
Petersen, I. T., 68
Petersen, J., 421
Peterson, C. C., 221
Peterson, S. R., 309
Petersson, B., 64
Petitto, L-A., 299
Petrangelo, A., 83
Petridou, A., 415
Petroni, M. L., 415
Petrova, M., 15, 409
Petrovic, A., 543
Petry, N., 205
Pettis, K., 612
Pettit, G. S., 175, 176
Peyre, H., 400
Pfeifer, C. M., 62
Pfeifer, M., 174
Phillipou, A., 361
Phinney, J., 379
Phinney, J. S., 378
Pi, Y. L., 110
Piaget, J., 22–23, 134, 140–147, 151, 153, 207–210, 214, 235, 259, 280–281, 313, 315, 362–363, 380, 427
Pianta, R., 191
Piazza, E. A., 149, 150, 160, 180
Piazza, J., 530, 596
Picherot, G., 262
Piedimonte, G., 84
Piehler, T., 320
Pieloch, K., 345
Pieperhoff, P., 485
Piercy, K., 486
Pierotti, S., 316
Pietromonaco, P., 442
Pignolo, R. J., 55
Pijl, M. K. J., 108
Pike, A., 250
Pilegaard, H., 416
Pillemer, K., 593, 594
Pinborg, A., 85, 86
Pinderhughes, E., 63, 64, 65, 251
Pinela, C., 285
Pinninti, S., 84
Pino, E. C., 392
Pinquart, M., 244, 245, 584
Pinto, N. M., 61
Pinto, T. M., 187
Piotrowski, C., 250
Pisoni, D. B., 132
Pittinsky, T. L., 7, 29
Pizza, V., 479

Rose, S., 216
Roseberry, S., 161
Rose-Clarke, K., 11
Rosen, L., 188, 189
Rosen, R. C., 481
Rosenberg, S., 501
Rosenblith, J. F., 149
Rosenfeld, A., 509
Rosenfeld, B., 617
Rosengren, K., 614
Rosenson, R., 476–477
Rosenstein, D., 133
Rosenthal, D., 7, 205, 271, 383
Rosenthal, S., 184, 441
Rosenthal, Z., 95
Rosenzweig, E., 367, 368
Rösler, F., 7
Rosmarin, D., 491
Rosmatunisah, A., 355
Ross, A. P., 108
Ross, J., 217
Ross, K., 275
Ross, L. A., 539, 555
Ross, N., 249
Ross, V., 622
Rosselli, M., 567
Rossi, A. S., 516
Rossler, W., 478
Rossom, R. C., 571
Rostamian, S., 559
Rostamzadeh, D., 530
Rosthoj, S., 274
Rote, W., 382
Rotenberg, J., 548
Roth, A., 618
Roth, B., 290
Roth, W., 203, 204, 272, 355, 377, 378, 379, 408, 416
Rothbart, M. K., 172, 174, 175, 177, 215, 281
Rothbaum, F., 387
Rothman, E., 346
Rothman, K., 424
Rotman, S. A., 204
Roudkenar, M., 530
Roushandeh, A., 530
Rovee-Collier, C., 129, 148, 150
Rowe, A., 442
Rowe, J. W., 5, 597
Rowland, B., 390
Roy, K., 591
Royer, C., 216, 217
Rozanski, A., 431
Rozycka, A., 532
Rozzini, R., 543
Ruba, A., 146
Rubeling, H., 183
Rubin, A., 583
Rubin, K. H., 258, 259, 324, 325
Rubio-Fernandez, P., 298
Rubio-Ruiz, M. E., 476
Ruble, D., 307, 317
Rudolph, K., 424
Rudolph, K. D., 346
Ruffman, T., 146
Ruisch, I. H., 83
Ruiz, J. M., 594
Ruiz, L., 357
Ruiz, S., 383
Ruiz-Casares, M., 350
Rumbaut, R., 379
Rumberger, R. W., 369
Runco, M., 285
Rupp, D., 590
Russell, A. M., 381
Russell, S., 361
Russell, V., 442

Russo, M., 561
Russo-Netzer, P., 499
Rutkowski, E., 273
Rutledge, M., 569
Ryan, A., 324, 328, 385, 386
Ryan, R., 187, 346, 430
Ryff, C. D., 499
Rypma, B., 532
Ryskina, K., 547
Ryu, E., 444

Saad, L., 432
Saadatmand, Z., 225
Saafir, A., 258, 324, 386
Saajanaho, M., 544
Saarni, C., 170, 312
Saavedra, J., 271, 528
Sabatelli, R. M., 443
Sabbagh, M. A., 218, 220
Sabbatinelli, J., 529
Sabir, M., 584
Sacco, S., 617
Saccuzzo, D., 30
Sackett, P., 293
Sadatpoor, S. O., 575
Sadeghi, B., 204
Sadeh, A., 112, 114
Sadowska, D., 87
Saeed, O., 116
Saez de Urabain, I., 108
Safa, M. D., 38
Saffran, J., 156
Safranek, S., 81
Sagi-Schwartz, A., 183
Saisanen, L., 278
Saito, Y., 561
Sakaluk, J., 421
Sakreida, K., 159, 163
Salapatek, P., 134
Saleh, L., 87
Salhi, L., 558
Saling, L., 566
Saling, M., 566
Salman-Engin, S., 247
Salminen, A., 531
Salmivalli, C., 326
Salthouse, T. A., 6, 485, 486, 487, 532, 554, 555, 558, 564, 566
Saltvedt, S., 92
Salvatore, J. E., 441
Salzberg, S. L., 54
Salzwedel, A. P., 82
Samaei, N. M., 530
Samara, M., 326
Samek, A., 316
Sampathkumar, N. K., 524
Sananpanichkul, P., 92
Sandel, M., 206
Sandercock, G., 205
Sanders, J. J., 610
Sanders, K., 190
Sanders, R., 365
Sanders, W., 262
Sandholdt, H., 597
Sandler, I., 615
Sandler, L., 615
Sandman, K., 18, 51
Sanfilippo, J. S., 344
Sanghavi, P., 591
Sanglier, T., 571, 576
Sangree, W. H., 600
Sanner, C., 253, 322
Sanson, A., 177
Santacreu, M., 475, 600, 601
Santelli, J., 349, 354
Santi, D., 63

Santiago-Ortiz, A., 370
Santrock, J., 323, 411
Sanyaolu, A., 204
Sanzenbacher, G., 569
Sapp, S., 490
Sarant, J., 538
Sarchiapone, M., 356
Sardinha, L. B., 546
Sarganas, G., 273
Sartor, C., 381
Satorres, E., 584
Sattler, F., 361
Satyanarayana, A., 530
Sauber-Schatz, E. K., 272
Savadatti, S. S., 477
Savage, J. S., 386
Savani, K., 286
Savelieva, K., 477
Savin-Williams, R. C., 348, 349, 389, 422, 465
Savvidou, M., 79
Sawyer, R. K., 287
Sayehmiri, K., 458, 507, 508
Saywitz, K. J., 217
Sbarra, D. A., 448, 454, 455, 460, 594
Scarabino, D., 529
Scarr, S., 67–68
Scerif, G., 214
Schachner, A., 134
Schacter, D. L., 282
Schaefer, R. T., 38
Schaeffer, C., 433
Schafer, M. J., 546
Schaffer, H. R., 182
Schaffer, M. A., 353
Schaie, K. W., 15, 16, 34, 35, 474, 483–485, 486, 501, 504, 529, 560, 561, 565, 566, 600
Scharbach, K., 612
Scharer, J., 620
Scheeren, R., 357
Scheibe, S., 528
Schein, S., 614
Scher, A., 172
Scherr, R., 357
Scheuer, H., 347
Schick, A., 188
Schieffelin, B., 162
Schiele, M. A., 620
Schieman, S., 571
Schiff, W. J., 115, 117, 204, 205, 272, 273, 355, 414, 415, 477, 545
Schiffman, S. S., 538
Schindler-Ruwisch, J., 118
Schlam, T. R., 218
Schlegel, P., 58
Schlosnagle, L., 596
Schmank, C., 557
Schmidt, A., 324
Schmidt, E. B., 611
Schmidt, E. L., 539, 565
Schmidt, S., 91, 537
Schmiedek, E., 308
Schmiedek, F., 324
Schmitt, D., 27
Schmitter-Edgecombe, M., 566
Schneider, A. L. C., 107, 201, 270, 283, 532
Schneider, N., 114
Schneider, S., 417
Schneider, W., 216, 288
Schnellbacher, G. J., 564
Schnitker, S., 381
Schnittker, J., 597
Schnohr, P., 489, 544
Schoen, C. N., 107
Schoen, M., 107
Schoenfeld, E. A., 458

Schoffstall, C., 326
Schofield, T., 253, 254
Schonert-Reichl, K. A., 285
Schooler, C., 568
Schoon, I., 8, 257
Schoppe-Sullivan, S. J., 184, 187, 322, 459
Schorr, I., 464
Schubert, S. A., 57
Schukle, S., 507
Schulenberg, J. E., 359, 396, 416, 417, 418
Schulkin, J., 479
Schultz, A., 219
Schultz, M., 157
Schunk, D. H., 25, 310, 430
Schupmann, W., 60
Schurz, H., 56
Schut, H., 621
Schutten, D., 394
Schwade, J. A., 157
Schwartz, D., 326
Schwartz, E., 116
Schwartz, J., 18, 68, 588
Schwartz, M., 396, 449, 454
Schwartz, S. J., 15, 379, 409
Schwartz-Mette, R., 320
Schweinhart, L. J., 227
Scialfa, C., 476, 536
Scott, B., 449, 454
Scott, M., 594
Scott, R., 146, 147, 219
Scullin, M., 558
Sebastian-Enesco, C., 324
Sebastiani, P., 525
Seccombe, K. T., 449, 451, 454
Sedgh, G., 352
Seeman, T., 530
Segerberg, O., 526
Segerstrom, S. C., 585
Seibert, A., 322
Seibert, S., 507
Seidel Malkinson, T., 109
Seiffert, D. J., 60
Seiffge-Krenke, I., 446, 513
Seiter, L., 411
Sek, A., 537
Selcuk, B., 220
Selig, S., 529
Selkie, E., 345, 346
Sellers, S., 599
Selman, R. L., 308
Semega, J., 10
Semenov, A., 364
Sen, B., 359
Sengpiel, V., 81
Senia, J., 506, 507, 509, 510
Senju, A., 108
Seo, Y., 133
Serbin, M., 537
Seror, V., 62
Serra, E., 245
Serra, M., 287
Serrano-Pozo, A., 574
Sesker, A. A., 507
Sethna, V., 189
Setterson, R., 472
Severinsson, E., 623, 624
Sewdas, R., 567
Sewell, K., 622
Sexton, B., 545
Seymour, J., 612
Sezer Efe, Y., 94
Sgoifo, A., 97
Shafto, M., 566
Shah, M., 133
Shahed, S., 590
Shan, Z. Y., 532

Shang, C., 276
Shankaran, S., 82
Shannon, F., 117
Shapiro, A., 188
Sharifian, N., 562
Sharland, M., 84
Sharma, P., 86, 573
Sharma, R., 95
Sharma, V., 573
Sharp, E. S., 507, 589
Sharp, S., 623
Shatz, M., 223
Shaver, P., 439, 440, 441, 442, 443
Shaw, P., 276
Shaw, S., 94
Shay, J., 529
Shayer, M., 292
Shaywitz, B., 275
Shaywitz, S., 275
Shear, M., 620
Shebloski, B., 250–251
Sheehan, D. K., 615
Sheehan, M., 247
Sheffler, J., 530
Sheffler, P., 335
Sheldon, S., 557
Sheldrick, R., 278
Shelton, L., 28
Shen, K., 526
Shen, L., 546
Shen, Y., 109
Shenhav, A., 315
Sheridan, M., 282
Sherman, L., 365
Sherwood, C. C., 531
Sheth, M., 95
Shi, B., 85
Shi, J., 568, 596
Shieh, J., 530
Shimony-Kanat, S., 272
Shin, H., 328, 386
Shinan-Altman, S., 472
Shiner, R. L., 439, 506
Shing, Y., 282
Shivers, E., 190, 191
Shlaer, B., 109
Shneidman, O., 181
Shoaib, A., 156
Sholma, V., 56
Shore, L., 568
Shorey, S., 479
Shors, T. J., 533
Short, D., 488
Shrout, P. E., 122
Shuey, E., 292
Shuey, K., 595
Shulman, S., 383, 388
Sica, L., 379
Sichimba, F., 183, 185
Siebelink, N. M., 277
Siedlecki, K. L., 485, 557
Siegel, A., 559
Siegel, L., 299
Siegel, R., 352
Siegler, I., 501
Siegler, R. S., 24, 214, 485
Siegrist, J., 489
Sierra, T. A., 458
Sifaki, M., 475
Sigman, M., 86
Silva, C., 374
Silva, K., 365, 366
Silver, R., 622
Silverman, M. E., 98
Sim, W. H., 278
Simcock, G., 153

Simeone, D., 529
Simha, S., 392
Simmons, D., 85
Simmons, R., 346
Simms, N., 282
Simon, A., 573
Simon, E. J., 51, 69
Simon, R., 448
Simon, T., 288
Simonetti, G. D., 206
Simoni, M., 63
Simons, J. S., 420, 558
Simons, L. G., 350, 386, 419
Simons, R., 386
Simonton, D. K., 428
Simpkins, S., 322, 370, 516
Simpson, D., 447, 453
Simpson, G., 511
Simpson, H. B., 361
Sims, R., 573
Sims, T., 16, 585, 596
Sinclair, H., 515
Sinclair-Palm, J., 464, 465
Singer, A. E., 612
Singer, D., 261
Singh, P., 56
Singh, S., 397
Singh, T., 573
Sinkovic, M., 540
Sinnott, J. D., 427
Siopi, A., 415, 477
Sirard, J. R., 355
Sirkanta, J., 203
Sirois, F., 541
Sirotkin, Y., 187, 247
Sirow, L., 538
Sirsch, U., 408
Sitterle, K., 323
Siu, P., 471
Sivam, A., 538
Sivasankaran, S., 273
Skaper, S. D., 532
Skarabela, B., 156
Skelton, A. E., 131
Skerrett, P., 544
Skinner, B. F., 25, 148
Skjaerven, R., 94
Skocajic, M., 243
Skogbrott Birkeland, M., 346
Skoglund, R., 595
Skorska, M. N., 421
Skovronek, E., 486
Skowronski, G. A., 90
Slade, A., 185
Slane, M., 32
Slater, A., 131, 146, 361
Slaughter, V., 221
Slavich, G. M., 397
Sleet, D., 205
Sliwinski, M., 484, 502
Slobin, D., 158
Sloutsky, V., 286
Slutske, W., 360
Smaldino, S. E., 258, 395
Small, B. J., 562
Small, H., 554
Smarius, L. J., 171
Smetana, J. G., 238, 255, 314, 316, 382
Smith, A., 204
Smith, A. D., 557
Smith, A. J., 620
Smith, A. R., 410, 411
Smith, C., 92, 212, 380
Smith, E., 422
Smith, G., 532
Smith, I., 221

Smith, J., 15, 84, 162, 508, 560
Smith, K., 159
Smith, L., 99, 119, 130, 149, 150, 152, 180, 540
Smith, P., 514
Smith, R., 20, 243, 262, 320, 386, 558
Smith, S. G., 596
Smith, T., 359, 462, 612
Smithson, L., 114
Smock, P., 451
Smokowski, P. R., 398
Smoreda, Z., 462
Smyth, J., 502
Snapp, C., 92
Snieder, H., 488
Snow, C., 299
Snowdon, D. A., 534
Snyder, J., 533
Soboroff, S., 473
Sobowale, K., 507
Soderstrom, M., 478
Soenens, B., 322, 382, 383
Sohail, R., 95
Soli, A., 512
Solovieva, Y., 260
Son, J., 530
Soneji, S., 118, 359
Sonenstein, F., 419
Song, A., 349
Song, Y., 345, 531
Sonnby, K., 383
Sonnenberg, J., 359
Sontag, L., 397
Sood, A. B., 615
Sophian, C., 145
Sorensen, L., 401
Sorman, D. E., 561
Sorokowska, A., 451, 453
Sorokowski, P., 451, 453
Sosa, G., 564
Soska, K. C., 121, 146
South Palomares, J., 443
Souto-Gallardo, M. C., 203
Souza, A., 555
Sowell, E. R., 270
Spangler, G., 184
Speakman, J. R., 51
Specht, J., 507
Speelman, C., 277
Spelke, E. S., 134, 145, 146
Spence, A. P., 532
Spence, C., 134
Spence, M., 132
Spence, R., 595
Spencer, C., 425
Spieker, S. J., 185, 398
Spinewine, A., 542
Spinrad, T., 238, 314, 315, 316, 320
Spira, A., 535
Sprecher, S., 421
Spreng, R., 185
Spruyt, K., 111
Squeglia, L., 359
Srivastava, S., 544
Sroufe, L. A., 172, 183, 184, 441
Ssegonia, R., 398
Stack, J., 235
Stacks, A. M., 248
Stadd, K., 95
Staff, J., 432
Stafford, E., 322
Staiano, A., 204, 262
Staley, C., 411
Stalgaitis, C. A., 388
Stancil, S. L., 81

Stanley, S. M., 451, 453
Stanley-Hagan, M., 252, 253
Stanovich, K. E., 29
Stanton, A., 503
Stark, E., 509
Starr, L. R., 390
Staudinger, U. M., 5, 7, 473, 554, 560, 563, 586, 587
Stavrinos, D., 588
Stawski, R., 17, 484, 530
Steck, N., 612
Steckler, C. M., 181
Steele, H., 184
Steele, J., 184, 441
Stefansson, K. K., 376
Steffen, V., 320
Steiger, A. E., 308
Stein, G. L., 257
Steinbach, A., 254, 515
Steinbeck, K., 345
Steinberg, D. B., 348
Steinberg, L., 245, 348, 365, 366, 384
Steinberg, S., 444
Steiner, J. E., 133
Stelzer, E. M., 620
Stenbacka, M., 400
Stenberg, G., 181
Stenholm, S., 475, 568
Stensvehagen, M. T., 502
Stepaniak, U., 546
Stephan, Y., 290, 589
Stepler, R., 511, 594
Steptoe, A., 16, 413
Sterling, M. R., 591
Stern, C., 443
Stern, D. N., 188
Stern, W., 288
Sternberg, K., 322, 445, 446
Sternberg, R. J., 24, 285, 286, 287, 288, 289, 290, 291, 292, 293, 294, 295, 322, 445, 446, 560
Sterns, H., 488, 539
Stessman, H., 54
Steur, F., 262
Stevanovic, J., 530
Stevens, M., 277
Stevenson, H. W., 245, 333, 334
Stevinson, C., 535
Stewart, A., 499, 506, 508
Stewart, D., 98
Stewart, J. B., 319
Stewart, J. G., 365
St. George, S. M., 184
Stice, E., 415
Stillman, T., 443
Stipek, D., 309
Stoel-Gammon, C., 157, 222
Stokes, C., 450
Stokes, K., 394
Stokes, L., 320
Stolberg, U., 172
Stoler, J. M., 81
Stolove, C., 433
Stolzenberg, E. B., 380, 411
Stone, A., 16, 129, 130
Stone, E., 242
Stoner, M. C. D., 352
Stones, L., 481
Stones, M., 481
Storey, A., 185
Stosic, M., 62
Stovall-McClough, K., 250
Straatmann, V. S., 591
Strada, E. A., 620
Strandberg, T., 52, 485, 543, 544, 545, 585, 601

Strathearn, L., 186
Strickhouser, J., 507
Strickland, B., 146
Strickland, C., 87
Stringa, N., 528
Stroebe, M., 621
Strohminger, N., 317
Strom, M., 117
Strong, M., 464
Stroope, S., 456
Strough, J., 596, 599
Stubbs, B., 536
Studer, J., 427
Stuebe, A., 116
Sturge-Apple, M. L., 248
Sturman, M. C., 487
Styfco, S., 226
Style, C., 454
Su, Y., 250
Suanda, S., 130, 150
Suarez, L., 79
Suarez-Rivera, C., 149, 180
Subedi, A., 541
Suchecki, D., 97
Sueur, C., 529
Sugden, K., 54
Sugita, Y., 131
Sui, X., 543
Suitor, J., 593, 594
Suk, M., 399
Sullivan, A., 384, 623
Sullivan, H. S., 386
Sullivan, K., 384
Sullivan, M. W., 128
Sullivan, R., 170, 186
Summerville, A., 488
Summit, A. K., 351
Sun, K. L., 335
Sun, X., 433
Sun, Y., 418
Sun, Y. Q., 545
Sun, Z., 529
Sung, J. E., 566
Super, C., 112, 124
Super, E., 185
Surti, K., 446
Suslow, T., 130
Susman, E., 345, 479
Sutcliffe, K., 89
Sutherland, C., 443
Sutin, A. R., 326, 507
Sutter, M., 422
Sutterlin, S., 238
Sutton, T., 419
Suzman, R. M., 528
Suzuki, M., 527
Swain, J., 161, 186
Swainson, M., 477
Swamy, G., 94
Sweeney, M. M., 456
Swenor, B. K., 536
Swift, A., 612
Sydorenko, O., 611
Syed, M., 377, 378, 379, 380, 408, 409
Sykes, C. J., 309
Syme, C., 475, 477
Szinovacz, M. E., 514
Szwedo, D., 389

Tacutu, R., 531
Taggart, J., 259, 260, 261
Taggart, T., 349, 350
Taige, N. M., 86
Takacs, Z., 284
Talamas, S., 443
Taliaferro, L. A., 28

Talib, H., 352
Tamana, S. K., 262
Tamis-LeMonda, C. S., 124, 147, 259, 260
Tamiya, N., 98
Tamrakar, S., 63
Tan, B., 277
Tan, D., 90
Tan, E. J., 597
Tan, M., 290
Tan, M. E., 568
Tan, P., 170, 175
Tan, Q., 69, 527
Tan, Y., 55
Tanajak, P., 546
Tang, A., 440
Tang, P. C., 543
Tang, S., 352, 530, 624
Tang, X., 430
Tanhehco, Y., 59
Tanilon, J., 327, 400
Tannen, D., 462, 464
Tannenbaum, C., 473
Tanprasertsuk, J., 526
Tardif, T., 257
Tariku, A., 115
Tarnopolsky, M., 535
Tarokh, L., 66, 357
Tarraf, W., 561
Tartaglia, N. R., 58
Tarzia, L., 424
Tas, D., 326
Tashiro, T., 448
Tasker, F., 254
Tassone, F., 58
Taubert, M., 531
Taussig, H., 250
Taylor, C., 285
Taylor, H., 92
Taylor, H. A., 87
Taylor, H. O., 571
Taylor, J., 396, 571
Taylor, K., 55
Taylor, M., 624
Taylor, N., 545
Taylor, S. E., 503, 504
Taylor, Z., 376
Teague, M., 7, 205, 271
Teater, B., 528
Tehrani, H. G., 92
Telkemeyer, S., 109
Teller, D., 131
Telljohann, S., 7, 205
Temple, J., 257, 331
Tenenbaum, G., 590
Tener, D., 249
Terblanche, E., 555
Terman, L., 294
Terracciano, A., 507, 508
Terrell, J. M., 343
Terrill, A., 538
Terry, D. F., 529
Tesch-Romer, C., 295
Teshale, S., 501, 586
Tessler, F., 57
Tetering, M. A. J. V., 376
Teti, D. M., 113
Tetzlaff, A., 416
Teufl, L., 184
Thaler, L., 188
Tham, E., 114
Thanh, N., 81
Thapar, A., 400
Tharp, R. G., 212
The, N. S., 355
Thelen, E., 107, 119, 120, 121, 135
Theobald, H., 546

Theun, F., 252
Thiele, D., 514
Thio, A., 396
Thoma, S., 315
Thomas, A., 18, 19, 174, 175, 430, 439
Thomas, C., 83
Thomas, J., 253
Thomas, M., 6, 111, 298
Thomason, M., 270
Thompson, A., 320
Thompson, J., 204, 272, 414, 415
Thompson, L. W., 107
Thompson, M., 433
Thompson, P., 270
Thompson, R. A., 162, 163, 170, 173, 176, 178, 179, 180, 181, 184, 185, 188, 189, 234, 235, 236, 238, 240, 244, 247, 312, 315, 462
Thorburn, D., 530
Thornberg, R., 326, 327
Thornton, R., 222
Thorsen, K., 488
Thurman, S., 125
Tian, J., 257, 485
Tian, L., 384
Tian, S., 476
Tian, Y., 54
Tiberius, V., 235
Tice, K., 370
Tichko, P., 147
Tiego, J., 215
Tieu, L., 222
Tiggemann, M., 361
Tikhonov, A. A., 257
Tilton-Weaver, L., 382
Timmermans, S., 94
Tiso, F. V., 609
Tistarelli, N., 276
Tobin, S., 585
Todorov, A., 443
Toepfer, P., 186
Toews, M., 425
Toh, W., 559
Tolani, N., 190
Tomalski, P., 108, 149
Tomasello, M., 160, 222, 235, 240
Tomassini, C., 596
Tomaszewski Farias, S., 558
Tomkinson, G., 205
Tommerdahl, M., 111
Tompkins, G. E., 160, 162, 223, 297, 298, 329
Tompkins, V., 220
Tongsong, T., 85
Tonnies, E., 546
Tononi, G., 111
Tooley, U. A., 347
Top, N., 382
Topa, G., 569, 591
Tornblom, A. W., 399
Toro, C., 345
Torres, L., 481
Torres-Ramos, S., 270
Torstveit, L., 238
Tosun Guleroglu, F., 97
Toth, S., 249, 250
Toubiana, S., 529
Toupance, S., 527, 529
Touron, D. R., 558
Towler, L., 540
Toy, W., 507
Trabucchi, M., 543
Tracey, I., 133
Trainor, L., 132
Traisrisilp, K., 85
Tran, S., 383

Traupman, E., 125
Trauten, M., 472
Trautner, H. M., 317
Travers, J. L., 576
Treas, J., 598
Treasure, J., 362
Treger, S., 421
Trehub, S. E., 132
Trelle, A., 558
Trickett, P. K., 249
Trimble, J. E., 38
Troll, L., 595
Troop, W., 325
Troxel, N., 320
Troy, M., 185
Trude, A. C. B., 401
Truglio, R., 263
Trujillo, C., 586
Trujillo, P., 575
Trushina, E., 546
Trzesniewski, K. H., 335, 375, 376
Tsai, H., 545
Tsai, W. I., 620
Tsang, A., 538
Tsang, L. P. M., 278
Tsang, T. W., 81
Tsapanou, A., 555
Tseng, H., 524
Tsermentseli, S., 363, 364
Tso, W., 203
Tsutsui, T. W., 533
Tubay, A. T., 87
Tucker-Drob, E., 485, 507
Tudella, E., 125
Tufik, S., 480
Tuleski, S., 210
Tullett, A., 464
Tully, E., 239
Turel, O., 273
Turiano, N. A., 508
Turiel, E., 316
Turk, E., 78
Turkeltaub, P. E., 271
Turnbull, A., 275, 276, 279, 294
Turner, B. F., 599
Turner, J., 90
Turner, J. H., 351
Turner, L., 33
Turner, M., 425
Turner, R., 349
Turner, S., 399
Twait, E., 271
Tweed, E. J., 93
Twenge, J. M., 308, 357, 375, 376, 393
Twilhaar, E. S., 95
Tye, K. M., 169
Tyler, K., 419
Tylka, T., 204
Tyrell, F. A., 389

Uccelli, P., 297
Udo, T., 362
Udry, J., 389
Uecker, J., 456, 577
Uemura, K., 571
Uhlenberg, P., 514
Ulfsdottir, H., 92
Ullah, M., 529
Ullen, F., 291
Umana-Taylor, A., 9, 246, 379, 385, 393
Unalmis Erdogan, S., 92
Uncapher, M., 394
Unda, J., 586
Unson, C., 568
Updegrove, A., 397
Urbano Blackford, J., 173

subject index

Ambiguous line drawing, 220, 221
American dream, 431
American Psychological Association
  (APA), code of ethics, 36
Amish culture, 624–625
Amnesia, infantile, 150–151
Amniocentesis, 62
Amnion, 76
Amniotic fluid, 62, 76, 77
Amniotic sac, 92
Amygdala, 186, 271, 347
Amyloid plaques, 573
Analgesia, 90
Anal stage (Freud), 21
Analytical intelligence, 289
Androgens, 241
Androgyny, 321, 464, 599
Anemia
  iron deficiency, 205
  sickle-cell, 59
Anencephaly, 79
Anesthesia, 90
Anger
  in adolescence, 345
  in males, 320
  of parents, 246–247
  peer rejection and, 325
  as stage of dying, 616
Anger cry, 171
Animism, 208
Anorexia nervosa, 361
A-not-B error, 145
Antibiotics, as teratogens, 81
Antibullying campaigns, 327
Antidepressants
  for adolescents, 398
  for older adults, 572
  for postpartum depression, 98
  as teratogens, 86
Antioxidants, 546
Antisocial behavior
  early maturation and, 346
  early sex and, 350
  and friendship, 387
  peer rejection and, 325
  perspective taking and, 308
  self-esteem and, 309
Anxiety
  and bullying, 326
  divorce and, 455
  in emerging adulthood, 409
  exercise and, 416
  in grief, 623
  in infants, 172
  maternal, 86
  and moral development, 238
  peer pressure and, 387
  rape and, 424
  self-esteem and, 308
  separation (*See* Separation anxiety)
  sleep and, 356
  stereotype threat and, 293
  stranger, 172
Anxious attachment style, 442, 594
Apgar Scale, 91–93
Aphasia, 159
Apolipoprotein E, 573
Arranged marriage, 453
Arteriosclerosis, 417, 477
Arthritis, 478–479, 541–542
Artificial intelligence (AI), 24
Ascend program, 11
Asian Americans
  academic achievement of, 334
  and autonomy, 383
  families, 256

in late adulthood, 541
marriage of, 451
overweight, 414
and parent-adolescent conflict, 384–385
parenting styles of, 245, 257, 334
peer relations of, 386
romantic relationships of, 389
sexual attitudes of, 421
statistics related to, 9
students, 332
Asperger syndrome, 278
Assimilation, in infants, 142
Assisted suicide, 611–612
Asthma
  breast feeding and, 115
  massage for children with, 96
  secondhand smoke and, 206, 418
Attachment
  in adolescence, 383
  adoption and, 65
  breast feeding and, 116
  caregivers and, 182, 183, 184, 185
  developmental social neuroscience
    and, 185–186
  in early adulthood, 440–443
  and effortful control, 376
  ethological theory on, 27
  explanation of, 181
  in families, 322
  individual differences in, 182–185
  in infants, 27, 181–186
  internal working model of, 182
  in late adulthood, 594–595
  and moral development, 240
  and parent-adolescent conflict, 384
  peer relations and, 259
  in postpartum period, 99
  response to crying and, 173
  in romantic relationships, 441–443
  and self-esteem, 308
Attachment-focused reminiscence
    therapy, 584
Attention
  in adults, 148
  control of, in adolescence, 365
  divided, 556
  in early childhood, 214–215
  executive, 215, 217, 556
  exercise and, 271–272
  explanation of, 148
  habituation and, 149
  in infants, 148–150, 180–181
  joint, 149–150, 180–181
  and juvenile delinquency, 396–397
  in late adulthood, 555–556
  mindfulness training for, 285
  selective, 556
  sustained, 148–149, 215, 556
Attention deficit hyperactivity disorder
    (ADHD), 276
  Apgar scores and, 93
  brain development in, 276–277
  diagnosis of, 276
  effort control in, 175
  environmental influences on, 276
  explanation of, 276
  heredity and, 276
  long-term outcomes of, 276
  massage for children with, 96
  maternal smoking and, 82, 276
  preterm birth and, 95, 276
  sleep deprivation and, 203
  statistics related to, 276
  treatment of, 277–278
Attraction, in early adulthood, 443–445
Audiologist, 46

Authoritarian parenting, 244, 245–246, 334
Authoritative parenting, 244–245, 334, 396
Autism/autism spectrum disorder, 278–279
  causes of, 279
  characteristics of, 278
  early warning signs of, 278
  explanation of, 278
  joint attention in, 150
  massage for children with, 96
  paternal age and, 87
  statistics related to, 278
  theory of mind in, 221
Autistic disorder, 278
Autobiographical memory, 217, 283, 557
Autonomous morality, 239
Autonomy, in adolescence, 383
Autonomy vs. shame and doubt stage
  (Erikson), 21, 22, 179
Average children, 324
Avoidant attachment style, 442, 595
Axon, 109
Ayacucho Mission, 118

Babbling, 156–157, 160
Babies. *See* Infants; Newborns
Baby Boomers, 36
Baltimore Experience Corps program, 562
Bandura's social cognitive theory, 26
Bargaining (stage of dying), 616, 617
Basic cry, 171
Beauty, 445
Beckwith-Wiedemann syndrome, 57
Behavior. *See also* Antisocial behavior;
    Prosocial behavior; Risky
    behaviors, in adolescence; Risky
    behaviors, in early adulthood
  adaptive, 50–51
  evolution and, 51–52
  health-compromising, 354
  health-enhancing, 354
  helping, 320–321
  of infants, managing and guiding,
    188–189
  moral, 239, 314
  sexual, 349, 481–482
Behavioral and social cognitive theories,
    25–26
Behavioral disorders. *See* Emotional and
    behavioral disorders
Behavioral inhibition (Kagan), 174–175
Behavior genetics, 66–69
Behaviorism, 25–26
Behavior management treatment
  for ADHD, 277
  for autism, 279
Beliefs, false, 220
Bem Sex Role Inventory, 464
Bereavement. *See* Grief/grieving
Berkeley Longitudinal Studies, 508
Bias
  ethnicity and, 393
  referral, 275
  in research, 37–38
  in schools, 332
Bicultural identity, 379
Bicultural orientation, 257
Big Five factors of personality, 506–508, 588
Bilingual education, 299, 300
Bilingualism, 298–299, 566–567
Binet intelligence tests, 288
Binge drinking
  in adolescence, 358–359
  divorce and, 511
  in early adulthood, 409, 417–418
  extreme, 417
  in late adulthood, 542

Binge eating disorder (BED), 415–416
Biological age, 17, 528
Biological influences
  on ADHD, 276
  on alcoholism, 418
  on Alzheimer disease, 573, 574
  on autism, 279
  on depression, 68, 398
  on eating disorders, 361, 416
  on emotions, 169
  on gender development, 240–241
  on giftedness, 295
  on intelligence, 290–291
  on language development, 159
  on longevity, 55, 525, 527
  on overweight, 272–273, 415
  on sexual orientation, 422
  on suicide, 399
  on temperament, 176
Biological processes
  connecting cognitive and socioemotional
    processes with, 13–14
  explanation of, 13
Biological sensitivity to context model, 177
Biological theories of aging, 529–531
Birth control. *See* Contraceptive use
Birth defects, 61–62. *See also* Teratogens
Birth order, 251
Birth parents, 64, 65
Birth process. *See* Childbirth
Bisexuality, 421
Blastocyst, 75, 76
Blended stepfamilies, 323
Blood pressure. *See also* Hypertension
  exercise and, 271, 355
  in late adulthood, 539, 541
  overweight and, 272, 273
Blood screening, maternal, 62
Bodily-kinesthetic intelligence, 289
Body image, 345–346
  and depression, 397
  gender differences in, 346, 375
  and self-esteem, 375
  social media and, 345, 346
Body mass index (BMI), 204, 272
Bonding
  breast feeding and, 116
  explanation of, 100
  in postpartum period, 99–100
Bone density, 476, 542
"Boomerang kids," 512, 513
Booster seats, 272
Bottle feeding, 105–106, 115–117
Boys. *See* Males
Bradley Method, 90
Brain/brain development. *See also* Neurons
  in ADHD, 276–277
  in adolescence, 347–348
  and attention, 148
  children learning about, 335
  cortical thickening in, 270
  in early childhood, 201
  early experience and, 110
  exercise and, 355
  gender differences in, 318
  hemispheres of, 108, 109
  hypertension and, 477
  and infant-mother attachment, 186
  in infants, 107–111
  and language development, 159
  in late adulthood, 531–533, 555,
    564–565
  mapping, 108–109
  and memory, 150, 151
  in middle and late childhood, 270–271
  myelination in, 109, 201, 271, 532

Brain/brain development—*Cont.*
  neuroconstructivist view of, 110–111
  plasticity of, 335, 347, 563
  prenatal, 78–79
  and self-regulation, 310
  size of, in primates, 51
  sleep and, 111
  swiss army knife theory of, 51–52
  synaptic pruning in, 271, 347
  volume of, 531–532
Brain death, 610
Brain games, 563–564
Brain imaging techniques
  in ADHD, 276
  in adolescence, 31, 347
  in Alzheimer disease, 573, 574
  for data collection, 31–32
  fetal, 61–62
  in infancy, 107
  in late adulthood, 564–565
  in learning disabilities, 275, 276
Brain networks, 347
"Brainology" (workshop), 335
Brainstorming, 287
Brazelton Neonatal Behavioral
        Assessment (NBAS), 93
Breast cancer, 116, 479
Breast feeding, 105–106, 115–117, 123
Breech position, 91
Bringing Home Baby (workshop), 188
Broca's area, 159
Bronfenbrenner's ecological theory, 27–28
Brothers. *See* Siblings
Bulimia nervosa, 361–362
Bullying
  authoritarian parenting and, 244
  peers and, 326–327, 386
  and suicide, 399

CA. *See* Chronological age
Caffeine
  adolescents using, 357
  as teratogen, 81
Calorie restriction, and aging, 546
Cancer
  free radicals and, 529
  and hospice care, 613
  in late adulthood, 541
  in middle adulthood, 479
  in middle and late childhood, 273–274
Car accidents, 358
Cardiovascular disease
  alcohol use and, 417
  and Alzheimer disease, 573–574
  divorce and, 455
  in late adulthood, 539, 541
  in middle adulthood, 475, 476–477, 479
  in middle and late childhood, 273
  overweight and, 414
  sleep deprivation and, 414
Cardiovascular fitness, breast feeding
        and, 116
Career counselor, 44, 412
Career identity, 376, 432
Career mystique, 431
Careers. *See also* Work
  developmental changes in, 430–431
  in early adulthood, 429–434
  impact of work and, 432–433
  in middle adulthood, 488
  occupational outlook and, 432
Careers in life-span development, 43–46
  audiologist, 46
  career counselor, 44, 412
  child-care director, 191
  child life specialist, 46, 274

child psychiatrist, 313
child welfare worker, 46
clinical psychologist, 8, 44, 98
college/university professor, 43,
        463, 492
community psychologist, 423
counseling psychologist, 44, 463
developmental psychologist, 37, 219
doulas, 89–90
drug counselor, 45
early childhood educator, 43–44
educational psychologist, 37, 44
elementary school teacher, 43
exceptional children (special
        education) teacher, 43
family and consumer science educator,
        44, 353
genetic counselor, 46, 60
geriatric nurse, 45, 547
geriatric physician, 45
gerontologist, 44
health psychologist, 397
home-care aides, 548
home health aide, 46
home hospice nurse, 613
marriage and family therapist, 46, 248
neonatal nurse, 45
nurse-midwife, 45, 87, 89
obstetrician/gynecologist, 45
occupational therapist, 45
parent educator, 459
pastoral counselor, 492
pediatrician, 45
pediatric nurse, 45
perinatal nurse, 91
physical therapist, 45
postpartum expert, 98
preschool/kindergarten teacher, 44
psychiatrist, 44, 313
rehabilitation counselor, 44–45
researcher, 43, 368, 517
school counselor, 44
school psychologist, 44
secondary school teacher, 43
social worker, 45
social work professor and
        administrator, 599
speech therapist, 46
teacher of English language
        learners, 299
Teach for America instructor, 331
therapeutic/recreation therapist, 45–46
toy designer, 219
Caregivers
  and attachment, 182, 183, 184, 185
  and eating behavior in early childhood,
        203–204
  and eating behavior in infants, 115
  emotional expressiveness of, 237
  and emotional regulation in children,
        237–238
  and emotions in infants, 170
  engaged in joint attention, 150
  fathers as, 168, 189
  grandparents as, 515
  impatient, 179
  of infants, 188, 189–190
  interacting with infants, 180–181
  and language development, 160,
        161–162
  and moral development, 240
  and motor development, 120, 124
  of older adults, 593, 596
  responding to crying, 173
  and separation protest, 172
  stress in, 515, 593

Care perspective, 315
Car seats, 272
CASEL. *See* Collaborative for Academic,
        Social, and Emotional Learning
Case studies, 31
Casual dating, 388
Casual sex, 419–420
Cataracts
  in infants, 134
  in older adults, 537
Categorization
  in infants, 151–153
  in middle and late childhood, 296
  perceptual, 152
C. elegans, 55–56
Cell-free DNA testing, 62
Cellular clock theory, 529
Cellular process theories of aging,
        529–530
Centenarians, 524–528
  factors involved in increased life span
        of, 525–526, 527–528
  opinions of, 526
  statistics related to, 524
  studies of, 524–526
CenteringPregnancy, 87–88
Center on Ethnic and Minority Aging
        (CEMA), 599
Central executive, 282
Centration, 209–210
Cephalocaudal pattern, 106–107
Cerebral cortex, 108, 109, 148, 150, 270
Cesarean delivery, 91
Change. *See* Stability-change issue
Chastity, 453
Chemotherapy, 274
Chernobyl nuclear power plant, 83
Childbirth, 88–96
  assessing newborn after, 91–93
  methods of, 90–91, 92
  physical adjustments after, 97
  setting and attendants of, 89–90
  stages of, 88–89
  trends in, 459–460
Child booster seats, 272
Child care, 190–193
  parental leave, 190
  quality and quantity of, 192–193
  strategies for, 193
  variations in, 190–193
Child-care director, 191
Child-care teacher, 225
Child-centered kindergarten, 225
Child-directed speech, 161–162
Childhood. *See also* Adolescents; Early
        childhood; Infants; Middle and
        late childhood
  length of, 51
  time perception in, 471
Childhood amnesia, 150–151
Child life specialist, 46, 274
Child maltreatment
  authoritarian parenting and, 244
  and brain development, 201
  contexts of, 249
  developmental consequences of,
        249–250
  discipline and, 189
  in early childhood, 248–250
  and juvenile delinquency, 396
  punishment as, 246–247
  statistics related to, 248
  and suicide, 399
  types of, 248–249
Child neglect, 249
Child-Parent Center Program, 331
Child psychiatrist, 313

Children
  adopted, 63–65, 67
  adult (*See* Adult children)
  average, 324
  bilingual, 298–299
  controversial, 324
  gifted, 294–295
  immigrant (*See* Immigrant children)
  living with grandparents, 514–515
  mindful, 285
  neglected, 324
  popular, 324–325
  in poverty, 10, 11
  rejected, 324, 325
  resilience of, 10–11
  social policy and, 9–11
  stress in, 10
Child welfare worker, 46
Chinese Longitudinal Healthy Longevity
        Survey, 526
Chlamydia, 352, 423
Cholesterol, 475, 476–477
Chorionic villus sampling (CVS), 62
Chromosomal abnormalities, 57–58
Chromosomes
  explanation of, 53
  genes and, 53–56
  and sex differences, 241
Chronic disorders. *See also specific disorders*
  in centenarians, 525
  exercise and, 544
  explanation of, 478
  and health care, 591
  in late adulthood, 525, 541
  in middle adulthood, 478–479
Chronological age (CA), 17, 288, 472, 528
Chronosystem, 28
Cigarettes. *See* Tobacco use
Circular reactions
  explanation of, 143
  primary, 143
  secondary, 143–144, 145
  tertiary, 143, 144
Circulatory system, in late adulthood, 539
Circumcision, 133
Cisgender people, 465
City Connects program, 331
Classification, 281
Climacteric, 479
Clinical psychologist, 8, 44, 98
Clique, 388
Closed adoption, 64
Cocaine, as teratogen, 82–83
Coeducation, 319
Cognitive behavioral therapy, 398
Cognitive control, 365
Cognitive development
  in adolescence, 362–366
  in adopted children, 64
  in early adulthood, 426–429
  in early childhood, 207–221
  gender differences in, 318–319
  in infants, 139–164
  in late adulthood, 554–565
  in middle adulthood, 482–487
  in middle and late childhood, 280–296
  play and, 259
  and religion, 380–381
  screen time and, 262
  sleep and, 114, 414, 534
  theories of (*See* Cognitive theories)
  "use it or lose it" concept and, 562
Cognitive flexibility, 365
Cognitive mechanics, 554
Cognitive neuroscience, 564–565
Cognitive pragmatics, 555

Effortful control, 175, 376
Egg, 54–55, 76
Egocentrism
  adolescent, 363
  in early childhood, 207–208, 235–236
  explanation of, 207
  in preoperational stage, 207–208
Eight frames of mind (Gardner), 289–290
Elaboration, 283
Electra complex, 241
Electroconvulsive treatment (ECT), 572
Electroencephalography (EEG)
  in ADHD, 277
  in determining death, 610
  explanation of, 32
  in infancy, 107
Elementary school teacher, 43
ELLs. *See* English language learners
Embryo, 75
Embryonic period, 75–77, 80–81
Emerging adulthood. *See also* Early
    adulthood
  changing landscape of, 409–410
  explanation of, 15, 408
  identity in, 378–379, 408
  key features of, 408–409
  markers of, 410–411
  sleep problems in, 357–358
Emotional abuse, 249
Emotional and behavioral disorders, 278
Emotional development
  in early childhood, 236–238
  in infants, 169–173
  in middle and late childhood, 311–313
Emotional expression
  in early childhood, 236
  gender differences in, 320
  in infants, 171–172
Emotional stability, 506, 507–508
Emotion-coaching parents, 237–238
Emotion-dismissing parents, 237–238
Emotions
  in adolescence, 348
  amygdala and, 347
  biological influences on, 169
  cognitive processes and, 169
  in early childhood, 219
  environmental influences on, 170
  explanation of, 169
  gender differences in, 319–320
  in infants, 169–173
  maternal, and prenatal development, 86
  in middle and late childhood, 311
  in moral reasoning, 315
  other-conscious, 170
  in postpartum period, 97–99
  primary, 170
  "reading," in others, 181
  regulation of, 172–173, 236–238
  in romantic love, 446
  self-conscious, 170–171, 236
  sleep and, 356
  strategies for redirecting, 311
  thinking influenced by, 427
  understanding, 236, 311
Emotion security theory, 253
Empathy, 238, 311
Empiricists, 134
Employment. *See* Careers; Work
Empty nest syndrome, 512, 513
Encoding, 150
Endoderm, 75
End-of-life care, 610–611, 612–613
English language learners (ELLs), 299, 300
Environmental hazards, and prenatal
    development, 83–84

Environmental influences
  on alcoholism, 418
  behavior genetics and, 68–69
  on brain development, 110, 111
  on depression, 68, 398
  on emotions, 170
  on genetic disorders, 58–59
  on giftedness, 295
  importance of, 18–19
  on intelligence, 291–292
  on language development, 160–163
  on motor development, 120
  on overweight, 272, 273, 415
Environmental pollutants, 84
Environmental stimulation, 287
Epidural block, 90
Epigenetic view, 68, 188
Episodic growth, 107
Episodic memory, 557, 563
Equilibration, 142
Erectile dysfunction (ED), 481
Erikson's psychosocial theory, 21–22
  explanation of, 20
  on identity, 22, 377
  on late adulthood, 583–584
  on middle adulthood, 499–500
  stages in, 21–22
Eros, 446
Eskimo infants, SIDS in, 114
ESSA, 330
Estradiol, 344
Estrogens, 241, 480
Ethical issues. *See also* Moral
    development
  bias and, 37–38
  in research, 36
Ethnic bias, 37–38
Ethnic gloss, 38
Ethnic identity, 377, 379
Ethnicity
  and adolescence, 342, 392–393
  and adolescent pregnancy, 352, 353
  and adolescent sexuality, 349, 350
  and Alzheimer disease, 573
  and autonomy, 383
  and breast feeding, 117
  and dating, 389
  and dropout rates, 369
  and effortful control, 376
  and emotional expressiveness, 237
  and exercise, 355
  explanation of, 9
  and giftedness, 295
  and grandparenting, 514, 515
  and height, 200
  and intelligence, 292–293
  and juvenile delinquency, 396
  in late adulthood, 541, 591, 598
  and life expectancy, 523–524
  and marriage, 451
  and nutrition, 118
  and overweight, 273, 414
  and parenting, 245–246, 256–257
  and peer relations, 386
  and poverty, 10, 591
  and preterm birth, 94
  and pubertal onset, 345
  and religiousness, 577
  in schools, 332–333
  and SIDS, 114
  and socioeconomic status, 393
  and suicide, 399–400
  and tobacco use, 524
Ethology, 26–27
Euthanasia, 611–612
Every Student Succeeds Act (ESSA), 330

Evocative genotype-environment
    correlations, 67
Evolution
  and culture, 52
  ethology and, 26
  and life-span development, 52
  processes of, 50–51
Evolutionary psychology
  evaluating, 52
  explanation of, 51–52
  on gender development, 241
Evolutionary theory, of aging, 529
Exceptional children (special education)
    teacher, 43
Executive attention, 215, 217, 556
Executive function
  in ADHD, 277
  in adolescence, 364–365
  in autism, 278
  cool, 364
  in early childhood, 217–218
  exercise and, 271–272
  explanation of, 217
  hot, 364
  in late adulthood, 559
  in middle and late childhood, 282,
    284–285
  and perspective taking, 307
  sleep and, 478
  and theory of mind, 220
Exercise
  in ADHD, 277
  in adolescence, 355–356
  aerobic, 416
  and depression, 355, 416, 572
  in early adulthood, 409, 415, 416
  in early childhood, 205
  importance of, 271, 355
  and information processing, 555
  in late adulthood, 522, 535, 539,
    543–545, 561
  and longevity, 528, 544
  in middle adulthood, 477, 478
  in middle and late childhood, 271–272
  for postpartum depression, 98
  during pregnancy, 87, 94
  screen time and, 272, 356, 416
Exosystem, 27
Expanding, 162
Expectations, and perceptual development,
    145–146
Experiment, 33
Experimental groups, 33–34
Experimental research, 33–34
Expertise, 282, 283, 486, 560
Explicit memory, 150, 151, 216, 556
Expressive vocabulary, 157
Extracurricular activities, 369–370
Extraversion, 506, 507, 589
Extraversion/surgency, 175
Extreme binge drinking, 417
Extremely low birth weight newborns, 93
Extremely preterm infants, 94
Extrinsic motivation, 430
Eye, diseases of, 537
Eye-tracking equipment, 32, 122, 129–130

Face-to-face play, 180
Falls, in late adulthood, 536
False beliefs, 220
Familiarity, and attraction, 443–445
Families
  in adolescence, 382–385, 391
  attachment in, 322
  in changing society, 251–257
  cultural differences in, 391

  divorced, 252–254, 255
  in early childhood, 244–258
  effects of child care on, 192–193
  immigrant, 256–257, 516, 598
  in infancy, 187–190
  jobs related to, 46
  in late adulthood, 592–595
  in middle and late childhood, 321–323
  and moral development, 315
  single-parent, 251, 252, 256
  stepfamilies, 322–323, 456, 594
  and substance abuse, 360
  and suicide, 399
  working parents, 187, 252
Familism, 393
Family and consumer science educator,
    44, 353
Family Bereavement Program, 615
Family management, 322
Family Matters program, 360
Family policy, improving, 11
Family therapist, 46, 248
Family therapy, for eating disorders, 361
FASD. *See* Fetal alcohol spectrum
    disorders
Fast mapping, 222
Fast Track, 401
Fathers
  adolescent, 352–353
  attachment to, 184
  as caregivers, 168, 189
  child maltreatment by, 249
  divorce and, 253
  and executive function, 218
  and gender development, 242
  of infants, 187–190
  involved in infant care, 168, 189
  as managers, 322
  oxytocin levels in, 186
  parenting styles of, 246
  in postpartum period, 98–99
  and prenatal development, 86–87
  and shaken baby syndrome, 107
  sibling favored by, 250–251
  working, 252
Fatuous love, 446
Fear
  in emerging adulthood, 410
  in emotional and behavioral
    disorders, 278
  in infants, 172
  rape and, 424
Feedback, to adolescents, 410
Females. *See also* Mothers
  ADHD in, 276
  aggression in, 320
  autism in, 278
  autonomy granted to, 383
  body image of, 346, 375
  as bullies, 326
  as carriers of X-linked diseases, 56
  chromosome structure of, 55
  chronic disorders in, 479
  cognitive development of, 318–319
  communication styles of, 462
  depression in, 389, 390, 397, 398,
    503, 571
  divorce and, 253, 254, 455, 511
  dropout rates for, 369
  eating disorders in, 361, 362, 416
  educational opportunities of, 9, 390
  and exercise, 355
  friendships of, 386
  gender development and, 240–243,
    462, 598–599
  gender roles of, 240, 241, 242

Growth mindset, 333–335, 429
Guilt, 21, 22, 234, 238, 240
Gusii culture, 124, 505
Gynecologist, 45

Habits
  explanation of, 143
  first, 143
Habituation, 128–129, 149, 152
Happiness, age and, 16–17
Hate crimes, 422
Hausa culture, 185
Head Start programs, 204, 226–227, 237
Health
  in adolescence, 355–358, 390
  divorce and, 511
  in early adulthood, 409, 413–414
  function of, 7
  gender differences in, 463
  in late adulthood, 541–549, 561–562
  marriage and, 454
  in middle and late childhood, 272
  religiosity and, 381, 490–491
Health care
  for older adults, 591
  rising costs of, 591
  social policy and, 11
Health-compromising behaviors, 354
Health-enhancing behaviors, 354
Health psychologist, 397
Hearing
  in infants, 132
  in late adulthood, 537–538
  in middle adulthood, 476
Hearing aid, 538
Hearing loss, 476
Heart arrhythmias, 113
Heart rate, 32
Height
  in early childhood, 200–201
  in infancy, 107
  in late adulthood, 535
  in middle adulthood, 475
  in middle and late childhood, 270
  in puberty, 344
"Helicopter parents," 513
Helping behavior, 320–321
Hemispheres, of brain, 108, 109
Hemophilia, 56, 59
Heredity-environment correlations, 67–68.
        See also Nature-nurture issue
Heroin, as teratogen, 83
Herpes, genital, 84, 423
Heteronomous morality, 239
Heterosexuality, 420–421
High-amplitude sucking, 129
High-density lipoprotein (HDL), 477
Higher Education Research Institute, 411
High-intensity drinking, 417
High school
  explanation of, 368–369
  transition to college from, 411
High/Scope Foundation, 401
Hippocampus, 150, 347, 533, 565
Hispanic Americans. See Latinos/Latinas
Historical contexts
  of death, 609
  of life expectancy, 6
  and midlife development, 504
HIV
  in adolescence, 352
  in early adulthood, 422–423
  in early childhood, 206
  in mother, and breast feeding,
        105–106, 117
  and prenatal development, 84

Home-based care, 613
Home births, 89
Home-care aides, 548
Home health aide, 46
Home hospice nurse, 613
Homicide, in adolescence, 358
Homosexuality. See Gays; Lesbians
"Hooking up," 419–420
Hormonal stress theory, 530–531
Hormone replacement therapy
        (HRT), 480
Hormones
  explanation of, 344
  and gender development, 241
  genes and, 54
  in menopause, 480
  in middle-aged men, 480–481
  puberty and, 31, 344–345
  stress and, 31, 54, 530–531
Hospice, 612, 618
Hospice nurse, 613
Hospitalization, breast feeding and, 116
Hospitals
  childbirth in, 89
  rooming-in arrangements in, 99
Hot executive function, 364
Hot flashes, 480
Human faces, perception of, 127–130
Human Genome Project, 53–54, 59
Human immunodeficiency virus. See HIV
Huntington's disease, 59
Hydroxyurea therapy, 59
Hyperactivity, 276. See also Attention
        deficit hyperactivity disorder
Hypertension
  in late adulthood, 541
  in metabolic syndrome, 477
  in middle adulthood, 475, 476, 477, 479
  overweight and, 273, 414
  parental smoking and, 206
  and preterm birth, 94
  work stress and, 432
Hypnosis, during childbirth, 92
Hypothalamus, 186
Hypotheses, 20
Hypothetical-deductive reasoning, 363

IDEA. See Individuals with Disabilities
        Education Act
Idealism, 363
Identical twins, 49, 50, 55, 66–67,
        291, 415
Identity
  in adolescence, 376–380
  cultural, 377, 379
  developmental changes in, 377–378
  digital environment and, 380
  in emerging adulthood, 378–379, 408
  Erikson's view of, 22, 377
  ethnic, 377, 379
  explanation of, 376–377
  narrative, 378
  religion and, 380
  transgender, 9, 464–465
Identity achievement, 377, 378
Identity confusion, 22, 377, 445
Identity diffusion, 377, 378
Identity foreclosure, 377, 378
Identity moratorium, 377, 378
Identity vs. identity confusion stage
        (Erikson), 22, 377, 445
"I Have a Dream" (program), 369
Illness. See also Chronic disorders
  in early childhood, 205–206
  in middle and late childhood, 272
Imaginary audience, 363–364

Imitation
  deferred, 151
  in infants, 151
  research on, 26
Immanent justice, 239
Immigrant children
  adolescent, 370, 379, 384–385, 389,
        392–393
  bilingual education for, 299
  challenges of, 392, 393
  and conflict with parents, 384–385
  and extracurricular activities, 370
  identity development in, 379
  poverty interventions for, 331
  romantic relationships of, 389
  undocumented, 393
Immigrant families, 256–257, 516, 598
Immune system
  breast feeding and, 116
  exercise and, 545
Implicit memory, 150, 151, 216, 556
Imprinting
  genetic, 56–57
  process, 26, 27
Impulsivity, 276
Inattention, 276. See also Attention
        deficit hyperactivity disorder
Inclusion, 279
Independence, in infants, 179, 180
Independent variables, 33
Individual differences, explanation
        of, 288
Individualistic cultures, 600
Individualized education plan (IEP), 279
Individuals with Disabilities Education
        Act (IDEA), 279
Inductive reasoning, 483, 484
Indulgent parenting, 245
Industry vs. inferiority stage (Erikson),
        21, 22, 310–311
Infantile amnesia, 150–151
Infants. See also Newborns
  adopted, 64, 65
  attachment in, 27, 181–186
  attention in, 148–150, 180–181
  brain development in, 107–111
  cognitive development in, 139–164
  death in, 113–114, 614
  defined, 14
  emotional development in, 169–173
  growth patterns in, 106–107
  height and weight of, 107
  language development in, 153–164
  learning in, 148–153
  massage for, 95, 96
  memory in, 150–151
  morality in, 146–147
  motor development in, 107, 114,
        119–126
  nutrition in, 105–106, 114–117, 123
  perceptual development in, 126–136
  personality development in, 177–179
  physical development in, 106–119
  playing, 260
  preterm and low birth weight, 77, 82,
        83, 86, 93–95, 352
  sensory development in, 126–136
  sleep in, 111–114
  social orientation/understanding in,
        179–181
  social relationships in, 187–193
  temperament in, 173–177
Infatuation, 446
Inferiority, 21, 22, 310–311
Infertility, 63
Information management, 382

Information processing
  in adolescence, 364–366
  in autism, 278
  in early childhood, 214–221
  in gifted children, 295
  improving, 283–284
  in late adulthood, 555, 566
  in middle adulthood, 485–486
  in middle and late childhood, 281–288
  speed of, 485, 555
Information-processing theory, 24
Informed consent, 36
Inheritance
  polygenic, 57
  X-linked, 56
Inhibition
  in ADHD, 277
  in bilingual children, 298
  in early adulthood, 439–440
  and executive function, 284
  working memory and, 282
Initiative vs. guilt stage (Erikson), 21, 22, 234
Inner speech, 211–212
Insecure avoidant babies, 182, 185, 441
Insecure disorganized babies, 183, 185
Insecure resistant babies, 183, 185
Insomnia, 203, 432, 571
Instrumental reminiscence therapy, 584
Insulin resistance, in metabolic
        syndrome, 477
Integrity vs. despair stage (Erikson), 22, 583
Intellectual disability, 293–294
Intellectual identity, 377
Intellectual risks, 287
Intelligence, 288–293
  breast feeding and, 116–117
  crystallized, 483, 484
  explanation of, 288
  extremes of, 293–295
  fluid, 483, 484
  genetics and, 290–291
  individual differences in, 288
  and juvenile delinquency, 396–397
  maternal alcohol use and, 81
  in middle adulthood, 483–485
  in middle and late childhood, 288–293
  theories of, 289–290
  types of, 289–290
Intelligence quotient (IQ), 288
Intelligence tests
  Binet tests, 288
  culture-fair, 292
  culture-reduced, 292
  increase and decrease in scores, 292
  interpretation of, 290–293
  Stanford-Binet, 30–31, 288, 290, 291,
        293, 294
  use of, 293
  Wechsler scales, 289, 290
Interactionist view of language
        development, 162–163
Interactive view of language, 160
Intergenerational relationships, 515–516
Intermodal perception, 133–134
Internalization of schemes, 143, 144
Internal working model of attachment, 182
International adoption, 64
International infant adoption, 64
Interpersonal intelligence, 290
Intervention programs, 400–401
Interviews, 30
Intimacy
  cultural differences in, 447
  explanation of, 445–446
  in friendships, 327, 386
  in triarchic theory of love, 446

emotional and behavioral disorders in, 278
and exercise, 355
friendships of, 386
gender development and, 240–243, 463, 598–599
gender roles of, 240, 241, 242
gender stereotypes of, 243, 317, 321
as grandparents, 514
growth of, 200
hearing loss in, 476
hormones of, 344–345, 480–481
infertility in, 63
in intergenerational relationships, 516
juvenile delinquent, 396
learning disabilities in, 275
marital satisfaction in, 451, 452
media use of, 393
midlife development in, 504
midlife transitions in, 500
moral reasoning in, 315
obesity in, 414, 475
pain sensitivity in, 538
peer pressure and, 387
peer-rejected, 325
physical development in, 318
pubertal onset of, 344, 345, 346
as rape victims, 424
religious, 380, 490
remarried, 456
self-esteem in, 375
self-regulation in, 376
sexual attitudes of, 419–420, 421, 481, 482
sexual harassment of, 426
sexual orientation in, 421
sleep in, 478
socioemotional development in, 319–320
stress in, 503, 504
suicide in, 399, 572
and temperament, 176
X-linked diseases in, 56
Mali tribe, 124
Malnutrition
in early childhood, 205, 206
in infancy, 117
Managed-care organizations, 547–548
Marijuana
in early adulthood, 418
as teratogen, 83
Marital satisfaction, 451, 452, 458
Marriage. See also Remarriage
before and after children, 187
arranged, 453
benefits of, 454
cultural differences in, 452, 453
in late adulthood, 593
in middle adulthood, 510–511
practices for successful, 457–458
retirement and, 488, 593
same-sex, 254–255, 456
statistics related to, 451, 452
trends in, 452
Marriage therapist, 46, 248
Married adults
dual-earner, 187, 433
overview of, 451
premarital education and, 453–454
Masculinity, 317, 424, 463, 464, 598–599
Massage
during childbirth, 92, 96
for infants, 124
for preterm infants, 95, 96
Matching hypothesis, 445
Maternal age
and prenatal development, 85–86
statistics related to, 459

Maternal blood screening, 62
Maternal diseases, and prenatal development, 84
Maternity leave, 190
Mathematical intelligence, 289
Math skills
creative thinking in, 286
cultural differences in, 333
in dyscalculia, 275
executive function and, 217
gender differences in, 318
of infants, 146
Maturation, 119
Mayo Clinic Study of Aging, 562
MCI. See Mild cognitive impairment
Meaning-making coping, 491
Meaning of life, 492–493, 577, 617
Measles, 84
Media. See also Social media
on adolescents, 342
and eating disorders, 361
Media multitasking, 394
Media time. See Screen time
Medicaid, 591
Medicare, 591, 613
Medication. See Drugs
Medicine, careers in, 45–46
MEG. See Magnetoencephalography
Meiosis, 54, 55
Melatonin, 357
Memory
autobiographical, 217, 283, 557
in early childhood, 215–217
episodic, 557, 563
explicit, 150, 151, 216, 556
fuzzy trace theory of, 284
implicit, 150, 151, 216, 556
in infants, 150–151
knowledge about, 286
in late adulthood, 532, 556–559
long-term, 216–217, 282, 283–284, 486
in middle adulthood, 485–486
in middle and late childhood, 282–284
prospective, 558
role of expertise in, 282, 283
semantic, 557
short-term, 216, 283
sleep and, 111
source, 558
strategies for improving, 283–284
verbal, 483, 484, 485–486, 568
working (See Working memory)
Memory-relevant language, 283–284
Memory-span task, 216
Men. See Males
Menarche, 344, 345, 346, 479
Menopause, 477, 479–480
Mental age (MA), 288
Mental health. See also Depression
exercise and, 545
in late adulthood, 571–576
Mental imagery, 283
Mental injury, 249
Mental vocabulary, 296
Mesoderm, 75
Mesosystem, 27
Metabolic syndrome, 477
Metacognition
explanation of, 286
in late adulthood, 559–560
in middle and late childhood, 286–288
Metalinguistic awareness, 297
Metamemory, 286
Methadone, 83
Methylation, 54, 573
Me Too Movement, 426

MFIP. See Minnesota Family Investment Program
Microcephaly, 61, 84
Microgenetic method, 24
Microsystem, 27
Middle adulthood
attitudes toward death in, 615
career challenges and changes in, 488
characteristics of, 473–474
chronic disorders in, 478–479
cognitive development in, 482–487
contexts of development in, 504–505
creativity in, 428
defined, 15, 473
divorce in, 511
empty nest syndrome in, 512, 513
exercise in, 477, 478
friendships in, 512
grandparenting in, 514–515
intergenerational relationships in, 515–516
leisure in, 488–489
life-events approach to, 501–503
longitudinal studies of, 506–510
love and marriage in, 510–511
midlife transitions in, 472–473, 500–501
mortality rates in, 479
physical changes in, 474–478
religion and spirituality in, 490–493
sexuality in, 479–482
sibling relationships in, 512
stage theories of, 499–501
stress in, 502, 503–504
time perception in, 471
work in, 487–488
Middle and late childhood
adopted children in, 65
attitudes toward death in, 614, 615
brain development in, 270–271
cognitive development in, 280–296
death in, 272, 273, 614
defined, 14–15
emotional development in, 311–313
exercise in, 271–272
families in, 321–323
gender/gender development in, 317–321
health in, 272–274
information processing in, 281–288
intelligence in, 288–293
language development in, 296–300
memory in, 282–284
moral development in, 313–317
motor development in, 271
overweight and obesity in, 269, 272–273
peer relations in, 324–328
physical development in, 270–274
self in, 307–311
thinking in, 284–286
Middle school, 367
Midlife, 472–473, 474
Midlife consciousness, 509
Midlife crises, 500–501
Midlife in the United States Study (MIDUS), 482
Midwife, 45, 87, 89
Mild cognitive impairment (MCI), 574
Millennials, 35, 36
Mills College Study, 508–509
Mindfulness, 285, 560
Mindfulness training, 277, 285
Mindset, 333–335, 429
Minnesota Family Investment Program (MFIP), 11
Minnesota Study of Twins Reared Apart, 49
Miscarriage, 74, 86
Mistrust, 21, 22, 177–178

Mitochondrial theory, 530
Mitosis, 54
Mixed mindset, 333
Modeling. See Observational learning
Monozygotic twins. See Identical twins
Montessori approach, 225
Moral behavior, 239, 314
Moral character, 317
Moral development
in adolescence, 314
domain theory of, 316
in early childhood, 238–240
explanation of, 238
Kohlberg's levels of, 313, 314–315
in middle and late childhood, 313–317
moral personality and, 317
moral thought and moral behavior and, 314
Piaget on, 238–239, 313
prosocial behavior and, 316
Moral exemplars, 317
Moral feelings, 238
Moral identity, 317
Morality
autonomous, 239
heteronomous, 239
in infants, 146–147
Moral personality, 317
Moral reasoning, 238–239, 314–315
Moral thought, 314
Morbidity, compression of, 525
Moro reflex, 120, 121
Morpheme, 154
Morphology, 154, 155, 221–222
Mortality. See Death
Mothers
and academic achievement, 334
adolescent, 352, 353
with anorexia nervosa, 361
attachment to, 183, 184, 185–186
child maltreatment by, 250
divorce and, 253
and emotions in infants, 171
and executive function, 218
and gender development, 242
goodness of fit between child and, 177
and hazards to prenatal development, 79–86
of infants, 187–190
infants reading facial expression of, 181
and language development, 160, 161
and literacy, 223
as managers, 322
parenting styles of, 246
in postpartum period, 97–100
prenatal care for, 87–88
prenatal diagnostic testing of, 61–63
and romantic relationships in adolescence, 389
sibling favored by, 250–251
stress in, 171
working, 252
Motivation
in early adulthood, 430
encouraging internal, 287
extrinsic, 430
intrinsic, 430
sleep and, 356
of toddlers, 179
Motor development
dynamic systems view of, 119–120
in early childhood, 201–202
in infants, 107, 114, 119–126
in middle and late childhood, 271
reflexes and, 121
Motor vehicle accidents, 358, 455

and emotional regulation, 238
and exercise, 355
and gender development, 242–243
in infancy, 180
and juvenile delinquency, 386, 387, 396
in middle and late childhood, 324–328
and moral reasoning, 239
parental influences on, 259
positive, 324
and sexuality, 350
social media and, 386–387
and substance abuse, 360
Peers
mindset of, 335
social cognition about, 325–326
as teachers, 212
Peer status, 324–325
People with disabilities. *See* Disabilities
Perception
and action, 119, 135
in early childhood, 219
explanation of, 126, 127
of human faces, 127–130
intermodal, 133–134
studies on, 128–130
visual (*See* Visual perception)
Perceptual categorization, 152
Perceptual constancy, 131
Perceptual development
in early childhood, 202
ecological view of, 127
expectations and, 145–146
in infants, 126–136
measures of, 32
nature-nurture issue and, 134
Perceptual-motor coupling, 125, 135,
538–539
Perceptual narrowing, 130
Perceptual speed, 483, 484
Perimenopause, 479
Perinatal nurse, 91
"Permaparenting," 513
Perry Preschool program, 226–227, 401
Personal control, 503–504
Personal fable, 364
Personality
Big Five factors of, 506–508, 588
and creativity, 429
in late adulthood, 588–589
moral, 317
Personality development
cumulative personality model of, 509
in infants, 177–179
Personal life investments, 587
Perspective taking, 307–308
Pessimism, 508
Phallic stage (Freud), 21
Phenotype, 56
Phenylalanine, 58–59, 60
Phenylketonuria (PKU), 58–59, 60
Phoneme, 154
Phonics approach, 297
Phonology, 154, 155, 221–222
Physical abuse, 248–249
Physical attractiveness, 445
Physical development
in adolescence, 343–354
careers in, 45–46
in early adulthood, 412–419
in early childhood, 200–207
gender differences in, 318
in infants, 106–119
in late adulthood, 531–540
in middle adulthood, 474–482
in middle and late childhood, 270–274
Physical identity, 377

Physical punishment, 246–247
Physical therapist, 45
Physician-assisted suicide, 611–612
Physician Orders for Life-Sustaining
Treatment (POLST), 611
Physiological measures, for data
collection, 31–32
Piaget's cognitive development theory
on adolescence, 362–363
on early adulthood, 427
on early childhood, 207–210
on egocentrism, 207–208, 235–236
explanation of, 22
on infants, 141–147
on middle and late childhood, 280–281
on moral development, 238–239, 313
on play, 259
stages of, 22–23 (*See also specific stages*)
Vygotsky's theory compared to, 212–214
Pincer grip, 125–126
PISA. *See* Program for International
Student Assessment
Pitch, of sound, 132
Pitocin, 90
PKU. *See* Phenylketonuria
Placenta, 76, 77, 89
Planfulness, of attention, 215
Planning, 430
Plasticity, 6, 111, 335, 347, 563
Play
in early childhood, 259–261
face-to-face, 180
functions of, 259–260
gender behavior and, 242
in infancy, 260
trends in, 261
types of, 260–261
Play therapy, 259
Political identity, 376
Pollutants, as teratogens, 84
Polygenic inheritance, 57
Popular children, 324–325
Postconventional reasoning, 314
Postformal thought, 427
Post-millennials, 35, 36
Postnatal maternal depression, 112
Postpartum blues, 97, 98
Postpartum depression, 97–99
Postpartum expert, 98
Postpartum period, 97–100
bonding in, 99–100
emotional and psychological
adjustments in, 97–99
explanation of, 97
physical adjustments in, 97
Post-traumatic stress disorder (PTSD)
disasters and, 312
in grief, 620, 622
rape and, 424
Posture, development of, 121–122
Poverty
in adolescence, 348, 392
and adolescent pregnancy, 352, 353
and adolescent sexuality, 350
and brain development, 201
and breast feeding, 117
and child care, 192
children in, 10, 11
and coparenting, 247–248
and dropout rates, 369
in early adulthood, 413
and eating behavior in infants, 115
and education, 226–227
ethnicity and, 10, 591
and families, 257
and illness and death, 206

and juvenile delinquency, 396
and language development, 160–161
in late adulthood, 541, 567, 591, 598
in middle adulthood, 477
and mindset, 335
and nutrition, 118, 205
and overweight, 415
and premarital education, 454
and preterm birth, 94
and safety, 206
and schools, 306, 330–331
and screen time, 204, 262
and secondhand smoke, 206
and self-regulation, 310
and SIDS, 114
and stress, 393
Practical intelligence, 289
Practice play, 260
Pragmatics, 155, 223, 297
Praise, 309
Precocity, 295
Preconventional reasoning, 314
Prefrontal cortex
in adolescence, 347, 348
aging and, 532, 533
in early childhood, 221
in infants, 110, 186
in late adulthood, 564
in middle and late childhood, 270, 276,
284, 310
Pregaming, 417
Pregnancy. *See also* Prenatal development
in adolescents, 85, 94, 349,
352–353, 354
diagnostic testing during, 61–63
exercise during, 87, 94
intimate partner violence during, 87
loss of, 74
overweight during, 115
prenatal care in, 87–88
prevention of unwanted, 351
sleep deprivation in, 97
Prejudice, 9, 393
Premarital education, 453–454
Premature retirement, 488
Prenatal care, 87–88
Prenatal development, 75–88
of brain, 78–79
embryonic period in, 75–77, 80–81
fetal period in, 77–78, 80, 81
germinal period in, 75, 76
normal, 88
of taste, 133
teratology and hazards to, 79–87
trimesters of, 78
Prenatal diagnostic tests, 61–63
Prenatal genetic testing, 60
Prenatal maternal depression, 112
Prenatal period, 14
Preoperational stage (Piaget), 207–210
centration in, 209–210
explanation of, 22–23, 207
intuitive thought substage of, 209
symbolic function substage of, 207–209
Preoperational thought, 207
Prepared childbirth, 90–91
Preschool education, universal, 228
Preschool teacher, 44
Preschool years. *See* Early childhood
Prescription drugs, as teratogens, 81
Pretense/symbolic play, 260
Preterm infants, 77, 82, 83, 86, 93–95
Prevention/intervention programs,
400–401
Pride, 170, 379
Primary circular reactions, 143

Primary emotions, 170
Primates, brain size in, 51
Private speech, 211–212
Privileges, deprivation of, 322
Problem solving, 486
Process imprinting, 26, 27
Progestin, 94
Program for International Student
Assessment (PISA), 333
Project Head Start, 204, 226–227, 237
Prolonged grief disorder, 620–621
Prone position, sleeping in, 113, 114
Prosocial behavior
authoritative parenting and, 245
and friendship, 387
gender differences in, 320
moral behavior and, 239, 315, 316
perspective taking and, 308
self-esteem and, 309
sympathy and, 238
television and, 263
Prospective memory, 558
Provisional thinking, 427
Proximodistal pattern, 107
Psychiatrist, 44, 313
Psychoactive drugs, as teratogens, 81–83
Psychoanalytic theories
Erikson and, 20, 21–22
evaluating, 22
explanation of, 20
Freud and, 20–21
of gender, 241
Psychological abuse, 249
Psychological age, 17–18, 528
Psychologist
clinical, 8, 44, 98
community, 423
counseling, 44, 463
developmental, 37, 219
educational, 37, 44
health, 397
school, 44
Psychosocial development. *See* Erikson's
psychosocial theory
Psychosocial moratorium, 377
PTSD. *See* Post-traumatic stress disorder
Puberty, 343–347
body image in, 345–346, 375
early and late maturation in, 346–347
explanation of, 344
hormonal changes in, 31, 344–345
physical growth in, 344
romantic attractions in, 388
sexual maturation in, 344
timing and variations in, 345
Pukapukan culture, 89
Punishment
for aggression, 320
deprivation of privileges as, 322
effects of, 25
immanent justice and, 239
and motivation, 430
physical, 246–247
and preconventional reasoning, 314
Purpose, 431, 493
Pyschosexual development, 21

Quality of life, 611

Racism, 379
Radioactive contamination, 83
Random assignment, in research, 33–34
Rapamycin, 530
Rape, 424–425
Rapport talk, 462
Reactivity, 173

Shape constancy, 131
Shared reading, 162
Shared sleeping, 113, 114
Sharing, 171, 250, 316
Short-term memory, 216, 283
Shyness, 19, 25, 174, 325, 440
Siblings
    birth order and, 251
    in early childhood, 250–251
    and juvenile delinquency, 396
    in middle adulthood, 512
    relationship between, 250–251
Sickle-cell anemia, 59
SIDS. See Sudden infant death syndrome
Sightlines project, 585
Silent Generation, 36
Similarity, and attraction, 443–445
Simple reflexes, 143
Single adults, 449–450
Single-parent families, 251, 252, 256
Single-sex education, 319
Sirtuin theory, 530
Sisters. See Siblings
Size constancy, 131
Skepticism, 308
Skinner's operant conditioning, 25
Sleep
    in adolescence, 356–358
    bullying and, 326
    and cognitive development, 114,
        414, 534
    divorce and, 511
    duration of, 534–535
    in early adulthood, 413, 414
    in early childhood, 202–203
    in emerging adulthood, 357–358
    and executive function, 478
    functions of, 111–112
    in infants, 111–114
    in late adulthood, 533–535, 571
    in middle adulthood, 478
    mindfulness training for, 285
    overweight and, 273, 534
    in postpartum period, 97
    in pregnancy, 97
    problems with, 203, 414, 534
    REM, 112–113
    screen time and, 203, 393
Sleep in America survey, 97
Slow-to-warm-up child, 174
Small for date infants, 93
Smell
    in infants, 133
    in late adulthood, 538
Smiling, 171–172
Smoking. See Tobacco use
Social age, 18, 528
Social clock, 504
Social cognition, 325–326
Social cognitive theory
    explanation of, 26
    of gender, 242
Social competence
    parenting styles and, 245
    and peer status, 324–325
    screen time and, 262
Social constructivist approach, 212
Social conventional reasoning, 316
Social-emotional education programs,
    311–312
Social influences, on gender development,
    241–243
Social integration, 596–597
Social interaction, and language
    development, 160–161
Social isolation, giftedness and, 295

Socialization, reciprocal, 188, 246
Social knowledge, 325–326
Social media
    and adolescent egocentrism, 364
    and body image, 345, 346
    and eating disorders, 361
    gender differences in use of, 393
    and identity development, 380
    increase in use of, 395
    older adults using, 592
    and peer relations, 386–387
Social orientation, in infants, 179–181
Social play, 260
Social policy
    and adolescents, 343
    and children, 9–11
    explanation of, 9, 343
    and older adults, 590–592
Social referencing, 181
Social relationships
    convoy model of, 596
    and emotional development, 170
    and emotional expression, 171–172
    in infancy, 187–193
    in late adulthood, 585, 592–597
    and longevity, 527–528
Social roles, expectations about, 314
Social role theory, 241
Social smile, 172
Social support, 596
Social understanding
    in early childhood, 235–236
    in infants, 179–181
    in middle and late childhood, 307–308
Social worker, 45
Social work professor and
        administrator, 599
Sociocultural cognitive theory. See
        Vygotsky's sociocultural
        cognitive theory
Sociocultural contexts, function of, 8–9
Socioeconomic status (SES). See also
        Poverty
    in adolescence, 348, 392
    and adolescent pregnancy, 352, 353
    and adolescent sexuality, 350
    and bilingual education, 299
    and child care, 192
    in early adulthood, 413
    ethnicity and, 393
    and executive function, 218
    explanation of, 9
    of families, 257
    and intelligence, 291
    and juvenile delinquency, 396
    and language development, 160–161
    in late adulthood, 541, 567, 591
    in middle adulthood, 477
    and overweight, 415
    and self-regulation, 310
Socioemotional development. See also
        Emotional development;
        Emotions; Personality;
        Personality development
    gender differences in, 319–320
    in late adulthood, 583–588
    peer relations and, 258
Socioemotional processes
    connecting biological and cognitive
        processes with, 13–14
    explanation of, 13
Socioemotional selectivity theory,
    585–586
Sonography, ultrasound, 61, 62
Sounds, recognition of, 156
Source memory, 558

Spanking, 244, 246–247
Spatial intelligence, 289
Spatial orientation, 483, 484
Spatial thinking, 51
Special education, 279
Special education teacher, 43
Speech
    child-directed, 161–162
    inner, 211–212
    private, 211–212
    telegraphic, 158
Speech therapist, 46
Sperm, 54–55, 76
Spina bifida, 59, 61, 79, 85
Spirituality
    in adolescence, 380–381
    defined, 490, 491
    in grief, 623
    in late adulthood, 577
    and longevity, 528
    in middle adulthood, 490–493
Spoken vocabulary, 157
Stability-change issue, 19
Stagnation, 22, 499
Stalking, 425
Standardized tests, 30–31, 329–330
Stanford-Binet intelligence test, 30–31,
        288, 290, 291, 293, 294
Statistical learning, 156
Stepfamilies, 322–323, 456, 594
Stereotypes
    of adolescents, 342
    gender, 242, 243, 252, 317, 320–321
    of older adults, 590
Stereotype threat, 293
"Sticky mittens" experience, 125
Stillbirth, 82, 84, 85
Stimulant medications, for ADHD, 277
STIs. See Sexually transmitted infections
Storm-and-stress view of adolescence, 342
Stranger anxiety, 172
Strange Situation, 182–183
Strength, loss of, in middle adulthood,
        475–476
Strength training, 544
Stress
    and ADHD, 276
    in adolescence, 397, 398
    age and, 503
    of birth, newborn coping with, 93
    bullying and, 326
    in caregivers, 515, 593
    in children, 10
    coping with, 312–313, 376
    in early adulthood, 411, 503
    and emotions, 169
    and gene expression, 54
    and hormones, 31, 54, 530–531
    intergenerational, 516
    leisure time and, 489
    and longevity, 525, 527
    in middle adulthood, 502, 503–504
    in mothers, 171
    oxidative, 530, 573
    poverty and, 393
    and prenatal development, 86
    religion and spirituality and, 491
    remarriage and, 456
    and suicide, 399
    unemployment and, 433
    work and, 432
Substance abuse
    in adolescence, 341, 350, 358–360
    attachment and, 383
    in early adulthood, 413, 416–418
    in late adulthood, 542–543

peers and, 386, 387
    rape and, 424
    religiosity and, 381
    romantic relationships and, 389
Successful aging, 16, 586, 600–601
Sucking, in infants
    as accommodation, 142
    and eating behavior, 114
    as habit, 143
    high-amplitude, 129
    reflexes and, 120, 121
Sucking reflex, 120, 121
Sudden infant death syndrome (SIDS),
        113–114, 614
Suicidal ideation
    bullying and, 326, 327
    "friends with benefits" and, 420
    in late adulthood, 571, 572
    rape and, 424
    sleep and, 356
    triggers of, 572
Suicide
    in adolescence, 358, 398–400
    assisted, 611–612
    divorce and, 455
    in late adulthood, 528, 572
    self-esteem and, 308
Suicide attempts, 399, 465
Supercentenarians, 524, 525
Supine position, sleeping in, 113
Surgency. See Extraversion/surgency
Surveys, 30
"Survival of the fittest," 50, 51
Susceptibility genes, 55
Susceptibility to suggestion, 216–217
Sustained attention, 148–149, 215, 556
Swaddling, 124
Swiss army knife theory, 51–52
Symbol
    Piaget on, 144, 208
    in play, 260
Symbolic function substage, 207–209
Symbolic play, 260
Sympathy, 238, 311
Synapses, 109
Synaptic pruning, 271, 347
Syntax, 154–155, 222–223
Synthetic opioids, as teratogens, 83
Syphilis, 84, 423

Taste
    in infants, 133
    in late adulthood, 538
Tau, 573
Tay-Sachs disease, 59
Teacher-centered approach, 329
Teacher of English language
        learners, 299
Teachers, 43–44. See also Education;
        Schools
    bias reduced by, 332
    with constructivist philosophy,
        328–329
    critical thinking taught by, 285
    as cultural mediators, 333
    drop in warmth of, 367
    with growth mindset, 335
    in inner city schools, 306, 330–331
    on intelligence of students, 289
    memory-relevant language used by,
        283–284
Teacher-student conflict, 368
Teach for America, 331
Teaching strategies
    based on Vygotsky's theory, 212
    and executive function, 218